The Bible for Hope

{Caring for People God's Way}

Presented To

____

Given By

____

Date and Occasion

____

The Bible for Hope

{Caring for People God's Way}

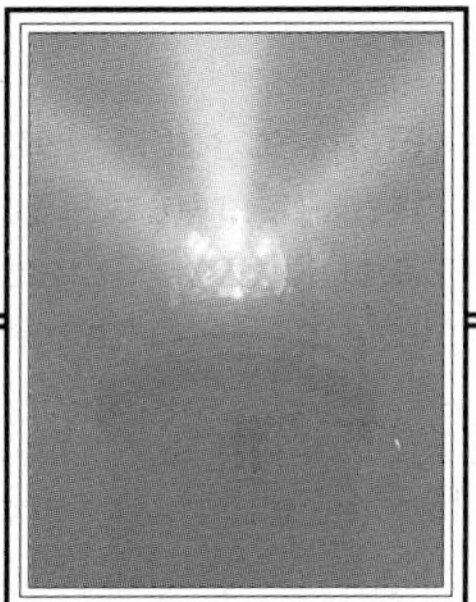

NEW KING JAMES VERSION®

Tim Clinton
President, American Association of Christian Counselors
Executive Editor

Edward Hindson
General Editor

George Ohlschlager
Consulting Editor

Thomas Nelson
Since 1798

NASHVILLE DALLAS MEXICO CITY RIO DE JANEIRO BEIJING

www.thomasnelson.com

THE BIBLE FOR HOPE:
CARING FOR PEOPLE GOD'S WAY
(FORMERLY TITLED *THE SOUL CARE BIBLE*)

Published in Nashville, TN, by Thomas Nelson.
Thomas Nelson is a trademark of Thomas Nelson, Inc.

Produced by The Livingstone Corporation
Edited by Linda Taylor, *Project Editor, Bibles*

Typeset by Red Wing Typesetting

Printed in China
1 2 3 4 5 6 7 8 9 — 09 08 07

Well-known Christian leaders endorse *The Bible for Hope* for all who need God's care:

"As I pored through the pages of *The Bible for Hope* I felt hopeful. I thought of all the people I meet along the way who look at life past, present, and future with a sense of futility and frustration. The Word of God is their answer. *The Bible for Hope* is a very practical tool, filled with 'real life' examples to encourage them along the path to victorious living."
H.B. London Jr.
Vice President, Ministry Outreach / Pastoral Ministries
Focus on the Family

"*The Bible for Hope* reminds us how deeply God knows, understands, and cares for each of us. It offers a path of healing and greater intimacy with Him."
Josh McDowell
Josh McDowell Ministries

"*The Bible for Hope* provides a greater understanding of God's guidelines for helping us to live happier, healthier lives. The applications for each passage of Scripture make it easier for us to grasp His infinite love for us and understand why caring for our souls should be a priority."
Paul Meier
Psychiatrist, Co-founder and Medical Director of New Life Clinics

"*The Bible for Hope* is written with compassion and concern. There is nothing like it. It will meet people at the point of their need and is destined to be a resource to which all of us will continually resort."
Woodrow Kroll
President and Senior Bible Teacher
Back to the Bible

"I used to live with anxiety, depression, fear, hopelessness, and emotional pain every day of my life. I don't live with any of those things anymore, because I've learned the truth about who God is, how He wants me to live, who He made me to be, and how great His love is for me. This same truth is there for you, too, and it can now be most easily found in *The Bible for Hope.*"
Stormie Omartian
Author, singer, dancer, actress

"*The Bible for Hope* will enable both trained and untrained people helpers to become Bible-based encouragers who can effectively minister to the many needy souls in our culture. I enthusiastically recommend this much needed resource."
Tim LaHaye
Author, pastor, Christian educator

"I am genuinely excited about *The Bible for Hope!* We finally have a tool both pastors and counselors can use together to help hurting people. Representing the best of biblical scholarship and counseling insight, it is written in a warm and practical style that informs the mind, encourages the heart, and moves the soul. Every Christian needs this Bible."
Jerry Falwell
Chancellor, Liberty University

Contents

The Old Testament

THE NEW TESTAMENT

Dedication

To all those who dare to be open to the heart of God
and to the suffering of others.

May you be
encouraged to reach beyond yourselves,
gifted to impart wisdom and comfort, and
blessed as you give care and nurture to another.

About the Editors

Timothy Clinton, Ed.D., LPC, LMFT

Tim is President of the 40,000-member American Association of Christian Counselors (AACC), the largest and most diverse Christian counseling association in the world. He is Professor of Counseling and Pastoral Care and Executive Director of the Center for Christian Counseling and Family Studies at Liberty University. Licensed in Virginia as both a Professional Counselor (LPC) and Marriage and Family Therapist (LMFT), he is President and maintains a part-time counseling practice with Light Counseling, Inc., in Lynchburg, Virginia, and also serves part-time as Pastor of Caring Ministries at Calvary Church in Charlotte, North Carolina. Tim holds certification from the National Board of Certified Counselors and serves on the Virginia Board of Counseling. He hosts a national radio call-in program on Christian counseling and living, and is a featured guest expert on the nationally syndicated *Al Denson Television Show.*

Tim coauthored *Competent Christian Counseling* and *Baby Boomer Blues,* and is the author of *Before a Bad Goodbye: How to Turn Your Marriage Around,* and, with his wife Julie, *The Marriage You Always Wanted.* He is a contributing editor for *Christian Counseling Today* magazine and the *National Liberty Journal,* a columnist for *Parent Life* magazine, and the "Inside Law & Ethics" co-columnist in *The Christian Counseling Connection.*

Tim is a Liberty University graduate with B.S. and M.A. degrees in pastoral ministries and counseling. He has Ed.S. and Ed.D. degrees in counselor education from the College of William and Mary in Virginia. Tim and his wife, Julie, and their two children live in Forest, Virginia.

Edward Hindson, Th.D., D.Min., D.Phil.

Ed is Professor of Religion at Liberty Baptist Theological Seminary, and serves as Dean of the Institute of Biblical Studies, and Assistant to the Chancellor at Liberty University in Lynchburg, Virginia. He serves on the Executive Committee of the Pre-Trib Research Center. He is also a faculty member of AACC's Center for Biblical Counseling and is Director of the Division of Pastoral Counseling in AACC. He is a pastor, theologian, scholar, and speaker of world renown.

Ed is coeditor of *The Knowing Jesus Study Bible,* served as Associate Editor of *The Tim LaHaye Prophecy Study Bible,* was a contributor to *The Complete Bible Commentary,* and served as a translator for the New King James Version of the Bible. He is the author of many other books on the Bible, prophecy, pastoral ministry, and counseling, including *Earth's Final Hour* and *Totally Sufficient.* He also writes an ongoing column for the *National Liberty Journal.*

An M.A. graduate of Trinity Evangelical Divinity School, Ed has a Th.D. from Trinity Graduate School, a D.Min. from Westminster Theological Seminary, and a D.Phil. from the University of South Africa. Ed and his wife, Donna, live in Forest, Virginia.

George Ohlschlager, J.D., LCSW

George is Executive Director of the American Board of Christian Counselors, the national Christian counselor credentialing, ethics management, and advocacy agency of the AACC. He is Director of Policy and Professional Affairs for the AACC, a Program Director of the Geneva Institute, and is also founding editor and primary writer of *AACC eNews & cNotes,* the monthly electronic newsletter of the AACC. George chairs the Law and Ethics Committee of the AACC, and drafted the new *AACC Christian Counseling Code of Ethics.* He is a Licensed Clinical Social Worker (LCSW) and maintains a worldwide consulting, coaching, training, and clinical-ethics development practice in conjunction with AACC and Light Counseling. He is a part-time faculty member of AACC's Center for Biblical Counseling, and in pastoral counseling at Western Seminary in Portland, Oregon.

George is coauthor of *Competent Christian Counseling, Law for the Christian Counselor, Sexual Misconduct in Counseling and Ministry,* and the *Liability Management Notebook for Pastoral Counselors.* He is the "Inside Law & Ethics" co-columnist in the *Christian Counseling Connection.*

George holds an M.A. in counseling psychology and biblical-theological studies from Trinity Evangelical Divinity School. He has M.S.W. and J.D. degrees from a dual-degree, interdisciplinary studies program in social work and law at the University of Iowa. George and his wife, Lorraine, and their three children live in Lynchburg, Virginia.

Contributors

The following contributors wrote or cowrote the two-page theme articles indicated after their names. The articles can be located by consulting the Topical Index.

Dan Allender, Ph.D. *(Healing/Recovery; Love; Suffering)*
Stephen Arterburn, M.Ed. *(Cults; Sexual Integrity)*
Sabrina D. Black, M.A. *(Prejudice)*
Ron Blue, M.B.A. *(Money)*
Dianna Booher, M.A. *(Gossip)*
Vernon Brewer, D.D. *(Self-Denial)*
Stuart Briscoe, D.D. *(Pride)*
David M. Carder, M.A. *(Adultery)*
Gary D. Chapman, Ph.D. *(Love Languages)*
John R. Cheydleur, Ph.D. *(Discouragement)*
James Clinton, B.S. *(God's Promises; Salvation)*
Julie Clinton, M.A. *(Marital Communication)*
Tim Clinton, Ed.D. *(Jealousy; Marital Communication; Marital Problems; Mental Illness; Weakness; Work)*
Henry Cloud, Ph.D. *(Boundaries)*
Rod Cooper, Ph.D. *(Men's Issues)*
Alan Corry, M.A. *(Singleness)*
Larry Crabb, Ph.D. *(Knowing God)*
Freda V. Crews, D.Min. *(Life Transitions; Truth)*
Joe Dallas, B.A. *(Homosexuality)*
Al Denson, B.S. *(Praise and Worship)*
Jesse Dillinger, M.A. *(Accountability; Eating Disorders)*
Richard Dobbins, Ph.D. *(Emotional Life)*
Howard Eyrich, D.Min. *(Communication)*
Jerry Falwell, LL.D. *(Faith)*
Marnie C. Ferree, M.A. *(Sexual Sin)*
Paris M. Finner-Williams, Ph.D. *(Prejudice)*
Gary R. Habermas, Ph.D. *(Doubt)*
Linda Carruth Hager, M.A. *(Infertility)*
W. David Hager, M.D. *(Infertility)*
Archibald D. Hart, Ph.D. *(Anxiety; Self-Esteem)*
Don Hawkins, D.Min. *(Mentoring; Responsibility)*
Ron Hawkins, Ed.D. *(Change/Maturity; Sin)*
Liz Curtis Higgs, B.A. *(Joy)*
Edward Hindson, D.Phil. *(Judgmentalism; Knowing Jesus; Presence of the Holy Spirit; Spiritual Disciplines)*
Rosemarie Scotti Hughes, Ph.D. *(Worry)*
June Hunt, B.M. *(Conflict)*
Gregory L. Jantz, Ph.D. *(Eating Disorders)*
Barbara Johnson *(Compassion)*
Jerry Johnston, D.Min. *(Occult)*
Grace Ketterman, M.D. *(Parenting)*
Woodrow Kroll, Th.D. *(Death; Responsibility)*

Carol Kuykendall, B.S. *(Motherhood)*
Mark R. Laaser, Ph.D. *(Addictions; Sexual Sin; Trauma)*
Tim LaHaye, D.Min. *(Eternal Life)*
Diane Langberg, Ph.D. *(Abuse)*
H. B. London, D.D. *(Burnout)*
Daniel Lovett, D.Min. *(Attitudes)*
Fred Lowery, D.Min. *(Marriage)*
Michael R. Lyles, M.D. *(Genetic Issues; Depression)*
Grant L. Martin, Ph.D. *(Children Problems)*
Dawson McAllister *(Adolescent Development; Obedience)*
Josh McDowell, M.Div. *(Adolescent Problems; Tolerance)*
Robert McGee, M.S. *(Insecurity)*
Paul Meier, M.D. *(Child Development; Mental Illness)*
David R. Miller, Ph.D. *(Blended Families)*
Dan Mitchell, Th.D. *(Legalism)*
Gary W. Moon, Ph.D. *(Fear/Fear of God)*
Elisa Morgan, M.Div. *(Motherhood)*
Lloyd Ogilvie, Chaplain of the U.S. Senate *(Wisdom)*
George Ohlschlager, J.D. *(Health/Spirituality; Mental Illness; Pain; Weakness; Work)*
Gary J. Oliver, Ph.D. *(Anger; Failure)*
Stormie Omartian *(Prayer)*
John Ortberg, Ph.D. *(Spiritual Growth)*
Miriam Stark Parent, Ph.D. *(Loneliness)*
Les Parrott, Ph.D. *(Guilt/Shame; Premarital Relationships; Relationships)*
Leslie Parrott, Ed.D. *(Premarital Relationships; Relationships)*
Craig Parshall, J.D. *(Abortion; Values)*
Janet Parshall, B.A. *(Abortion; Values)*
Clifford L. Penner, Ph.D. *(Sex in Marriage)*
Joyce J. Penner, M.N. *(Sex in Marriage)*
David Powlison, Ph.D. *(Spiritual Warfare)*
Barbara Rosberg, B.F.A. *(Temptation)*
Gary Rosberg, Ed.D. *(Temptation)*
Doug Rosenau, Ed.D. *(Sexuality)*
David Seamands, M.A. *(Aging/Elderly)*
Mark Shadoan, M.S.W. *(Drug Abuse)*
Gary Smalley, D.Lit. *(Honor)*
Greg Smalley, Psy.D. *(Honor)*
Patrick Springle, M.A. *(Trust)*
Gary P. Stewart, Th.D. *(Suicide)*
Nick Stinnett, Ph.D. *(Family Life)*
David Stoop, Ph.D. *(Family Problems)*
Charles R. Swindoll, D.D. *(Decision Making)*
Joni Eareckson Tada *(Bitterness)*
Siang-Yang Tan, Ph.D. *(Pain)*
Chris Thurman, Ph.D. *(Belief; Perfectionism)*
Cynthia Ulrich Tobias, M.Ed. *(Child Discipline)*
John Townsend, Ph.D. *(Boundaries)*
John Trent, Ph.D. *(Attachment/Blessing; Hope)*
Leslie Vernick, M.S.W. *(Stress; Violence)*
E. Glenn Wagner, Ph.D. *(Repentance)*
Tom Whiteman, Ph.D. *(Divorce/Separation)*
Earl Wilson, Ph.D. *(Restoration)*
Sandra Wilson, D.Min. *(Restoration)*
Sandra D. Wilson, Ph.D. *(Trials; Women's Issues)*
Robert Wolgemuth, B.A. *(Fatherhood)*
Everett L. Worthington, Jr., Ph.D. *(Forgiveness)*
H. Norman Wright, D.D. *(Crises; Grief/Loss)*

Bible references provided by Clayton Rothmann

Writers

Bruce Barton, Jeanette Dall, Jonathan Farrar, Chris Fawkes, Carol Fielding, Mary Ann Lackland, Mary Larsen, Scott Larsen, Sally Marcey, Randy Southern, Linda Taylor, Neil Wilson, Len Woods

Livingstone Staff

Bruce Barton, Katie Gieser, Ashley Taylor, Linda Taylor, Dave Veerman, Neil Wilson

INTRODUCTION TO

The Bible for Hope

Timothy Clinton, Ed Hindson, George Ohlschlager

Life is full of trouble. But you know that. No one goes through life unscathed. Maybe you've recently walked the dark road of suffering. Maybe you are doing so now, or know someone close to you suffering at this very moment.

If so, we hope that you will come to love *The Bible for Hope,* for this Bible was written for you and those you care about.

The entire Bible is a story of a "sacred love"—of God's immeasurable love toward you, a love made complete in the life, death, and resurrection of Jesus. This love is wide enough to cover every sorrow and deep enough to swallow the worst pain imaginable.

God longs to share this love with everyone on earth, and with you personally. He is eager to reveal this love to you, if you would receive it. He wants you to partake of His glory, to be enveloped with His joy, and to enjoy the sweetest intimacy with Himself.

But, as in the beginning, men and women still incline their ears to evil's deception—that man is the measure of all things and God is not needed. We have suffered the consequences of this terrible lie ever since. Now, billions of people and an abused planet groan under the weight of the accumulated sin of hundreds of generations.

We are still susceptible to evil's intent to confuse us and turn our hearts and minds away from the One who created us for Himself. The Grand Lie still attempts to deceive. Confused and divided in spirit, people often turn to false lovers. Many have idols—whether images in ancient stone or modern markets and feel-good addictions. Such betrayal grieves God deeply, yet He still pursues us relentlessly.

The Bible gives us stories of real people with real problems. It constantly shows us God's compassion and grace as He seeks to bring us back to Himself. The only true solution to life's problems begins in the pages of this book—God's holy Word to us. The awesome message of the Bible is that the God of the universe loves us, cares for us deeply, and desires to have a relationship with us. He alone is our faithful source of strength and our hope in the journey.

The Hope and Healing Ministry

God has called each of us to have a relationship with Him; He has also called us to reach out to others, whatever their needs. We are dedicated to encouraging believers in this vital ministry of caring for others' souls.

Caring for people God's way means we are compassionate and loving to someone suffering from sorrow, pain, and tribulation. Everyone has suffered life's travails. We generally suffer alone, and sometimes we call out for help, seeking hope and direction. At times, God's Word has ministered to us. At other times, however, our struggle with sin, shame, and suffering has become overwhelming.

With help from God and other believers, we can not only survive trouble, but we can learn the deeper lessons of faith. With help, we are able to move through brokenness and suffering to become wiser, humbler, stronger, and more understanding and caring toward others. The Bible says:

> *Blessed be the God and Father of our Lord Jesus Christ, the Father of mercies and God of all comfort, who comforts us in all our tribulation, that we may be able to comfort those who are in any trouble, with the comfort with which we ourselves are comforted by God.*
>
> (2 Corinthians 1:3, 4)

The Bible for Hope is meant to be a tool to help God's people survive, even thrive, in the midst of the difficulties of life. We believe that God will come alive in His Word—and then He will assist us in the call to help others. This particular edition is designed to lift up those who are suffering, those who are seeking direction, and then to guide us to walk humbly yet powerfully with those who need a friend to come alongside during the dark paths of their journey.

Hope and Healing for Souls in the Modern Age

In our developed, modern world that overflows with abundance, more and more people are searching for fulfillment by amassing fortunes, pursuing pleasure, or acquiring power. A profound spiritual discontent animates and motivates the pursuit of filling the "hole in our soul."

Christian soul care is designed to help people get from wherever they are to a place of greater intimacy with and maturity in Christ. Jesus is the Alpha and Omega of such ministry. Soul care starts with Him and asks His Spirit to transform both the helper and the one being helped. Soul care also ends with Him, revealing His Spirit and character alive in us and pouring out of us.

We can view the helping ministry of the church as a three-legged stool. The first leg is the pastor (or pastoral counselor). This is where most counseling starts and often ends. Like the family physician, the pastor is usually the first to intervene and the one responsible for oversight and referral, when needed, to the other two legs. The second leg is the lay helpers working in volunteer ministry under pastoral and church supervision. The third leg is the professional Christian counselor, to whom the more severe and difficult cases are referred. All three legs must be strong and working in unison to fulfill their ministry to hurting souls.

This Bible gives helpers throughout the body of Christ an opportunity to increase knowledge, hone skills, search the Spirit, and reflect on the moral and ethical dilemmas that they will face in the work of ministry. Helping others to grow up in Christ is a wonderful calling, but one that we must practice with all humility and grace, knowing we are responsible to God and to those helped. We need to seek each other's support, with each person trusting the other to hold them accountable for their work. We must strive to one day see Jesus smiling on us and declaring: "Well done, good and faithful servant" (Matt. 25:21).

In short, this Bible is designed to help God's people help themselves and others too.

Goals of *The Bible for Hope*

This Bible is geared to help believers grow up in Christ and to show how to be effective helpers, assisting others to become more like Christ. This Bible is designed to:

- describe 116 of life's most difficult problems and outline the divine path of healing, God's way through each one;
- help believers to more confidently know and use God's Word as they deal with, or help another person deal with, these difficulties; and
- provide practical tools, usable strategies, and clear direction as we work through our own life challenges with God's help, and assist others in doing the same.

This Bible is structured to help believers achieve these goals from a problem-to-solution format. Each of the 116 areas of life difficulty are covered in four different ways:

1. A *theme article* by an expert in that particular field defines the subject in a clear and concise way and then encourages action to overcome the problem or help someone overcome the problem.
2. A *key passage note* is located at a targeted passage for each topic. The note briefly describes God's overarching plan regarding that particular topic or difficulty.
3. There is also a *personality profile* of a Bible person who struggled with this issue. Sometimes the person is a good example; sometimes we learn from his or her bad example.
4. *Soul notes* are located throughout the Bible text where a verse or passage speaks to one of the topics. These short notes point out what God's Word says about this topic.

Other features include:

- "see" references that tie together the theme article, key passage note, and personality profile for each of the 116 topics;
- introductions to each Bible book;
- *soul quotes* that focus on encouraging Bible verses; and
- a subject index-concordance.

Elements of Hope and Healing Ministry

Modern research is confirming what the Scriptures revealed thousands of years ago: It is the person and the character of the helper, not the technique or model of counseling, that is the more crucial variable for counseling success. People who desire to have a hope and healing ministry should cultivate the following six fundamental attributes:

1. Compassion

Our best motivation for helping is rooted in a deep-seated compassion for others. Compassion is the heart of the hope and healing ministry. It allows us, beyond mere intellectual understanding, to feel the struggles of others—to mourn when they mourn and rejoice when they rejoice. People being helped respond to compassion by drawing near in a deeper trust. This simply won't happen unless a helper is filled with compassion.

2. Knowledge

Helpers need to be equipped with sufficient knowledge to attain excellence in ministry. We need to gain knowledge of the Scriptures, of personal and interpersonal dynamics, and of the issue at hand. Also, we must have a good knowledge of the person being helped. Not only is it important to have a clear grasp of the problem, but even more we have to know the strengths, hopes, and aspirations of the one being helped. We must be able to:

- help others to tell their story honestly, and then accurately define with them the problem(s) to be addressed;
- help others to set clear goals for changes that reflect godly values, are owned by them, and are doable with the resources available;
- guide others into a study of the Scriptures so that both the goals and the ways to achieve them are biblically sound; and
- help others to translate their current change into principles for lifelong learning and living, leaving them able to continue growth after counseling.

3. Skill

Helping others grow up in Christ is a practiced skill, one that usually improves as one does it more and more. We need not be professionally trained, but we should attempt to learn as much as we can. We need to learn how:

- to listen well, hearing others accurately without distorting their perceptions with our own judgments;
- to join with and accurately reflect the emotions of others;
- to understand and assess the spiritual condition of others, knowing how to help them get unstuck and move through the blockages between them and God;
- to give the right word at the right time, and to be silent at the appropriate times;
- to encourage and guide godly action, rather than merely listening and reflecting; and
- to help others dig more deeply into God and His Word for solace and direction, rather than just telling them what to do.

4. Holy Spirit's Power

True Christian counseling always has an invisible partner present—the Holy Spirit. His presence can help resolve any quandary, break through any resistance, and overcome any fear that arises in the helping process.

We helpers must tune our inner ear to hear the voice of the Spirit. A properly tuned ear will also hear the pacing instructions of the Spirit—when to slow down and linger, and when to forge ahead and confront something with boldness.

God knows the right word and the right time to use it. We will be forever changed as helpers when we learn to rely on that still, small voice inside. If we want our ministry to have eternal significance, we must remember that without Him and the Spirit He gave us, we can do nothing.

5. Ethical Integrity

If we lack ethical integrity, the word gets out and will be known by all. Eventually, no one will come to us for help. In a sense this is a logical extension of Holy Spirit reliance, because building and maintaining impeccable ethics cannot be done by our own strength. It is a continuing work of sanctification that God does in and through us.

6. Body Life

We must be members of a body of believers. In the church there is strength we don't have, wisdom we have not attained, support we cannot give to ourselves, discipline we have yet to grow into, and mercy beyond all that any one person can know or give. When we mourn, that weight is shared throughout the body, and when we rejoice, that power is multiplied throughout the body. Our undeniable interconnectedness is one big reason why we have helping ministry at all.

Helping ministry in the body of Christ will also help set and maintain clear limits—respecting the limits of our time, energy, knowledge, and skill. Sometimes helping—especially helping those in crisis—calls for intervention by many people who must learn to work together for the good of others. The body will also include other helpers who are more experienced or more easily connectable to those who are being helped, so that one person isn't overwhelmed by the problems of all.

The Helping Model of Jesus

The very best model of helping is Jesus Himself. He was *compassionate* with others. He challenged false beliefs and dark thoughts with His *knowledge* of the truth. He *skillfully* gave people life-changing hope. He promised rest and peace through the *Holy Spirit*. He was the model of *ethical integrity.* He got others (who would be part of his *body*) involved in the process. Notice how all these elements of helping were alive in the call of Nathanael, recorded in John 1:45–51.

First, Jesus relied on Philip. He used the *body* (another person) to assist in His work of calling this new disciple. Jesus knew Nathanael (with supernatural *knowledge)* and knew Nathanael's skepticism would be a barrier unless He sent a friend. Though God can bypass these steps with power beyond compare, He chooses to use us to help bring others to Him.

Philip's intervention helped get Nathanael oriented to Jesus, approaching Him instead of moving away from Him. Jesus then did something unusual, something unexpected, something very *skillful.* He proclaimed about Nathanael that he was an Israelite with no deceit. Again, He *knew* Nathanael deeply—Jesus clearly saw the depths of the man's soul. We can trust God for supernatural knowledge; at other times, He will simply give us discernment so that we can see where we need to help.

By the fullness of the *Holy Spirit*, Jesus saw all of these things in Nathanael's soul. Rather than challenging his skepticism, Jesus affirmed the best hopes and aspirations of Nathanael. In doing so, He disarmed Nathanael's resistance and drew him in deeper to that secret place of transforming faith. God has given us that same Holy Spirit to help and guide us as we help others.

Jesus then spoke to Nathanael in a *compassionate* way that was designed to keep him walking with and growing in Christ. As we get involved in the hurts of others, our compassion for them will remove many barriers.

Notice also the *ethical* respect that Jesus had for Nathanael throughout the encounter. Nathanael's best interests were always paramount, and the problems of his skepticism and resistance were respected and dealt with forthrightly. Jesus never lapsed into tricks or coercion, nor did He use His power to intimidate or overwhelm. He sought to persuade, respecting the need to bring Nathanael to a voluntary exclamation of the Truth. As we maintain our ethics, we build a level of trust with others.

Was Nathanael changed? Yes! He was transformed by the love and power of the Messiah and became a dedicated disciple.

Beginning with skepticism, moving to wariness, and then to hopefulness is a process that those who seek to help others face just about universally. Yet we can count on God:

- to give us compassion;
- to help us find the knowledge we need;
- to help us discover the skills to intervene;
- to give us His Holy Spirit to partner with us;
- to challenge us to maintain our ethical integrity; and
- to surround us with others who can give help, encourage, or act as a resource.

May God bless you as you are helped and seek to help others. We pray that this Bible will be a great help to you in your ministry of hope and healing.

PREFACE TO THE

New King James Version

The purpose of this most recent revision of the King James Version is in harmony with the purpose of the original King James scholars: "Not to make a new translation . . . but to make a good one better." The New King James Version is a continuation of the labors of the King James translators, unlocking for today's readers the spiritual treasures found especially in the Authorized Version of the Holy Bible.

While seeking to maintain the excellent *form* of the traditional English Bible, special care has also been taken to preserve the work of *precision* which is the legacy of the King James translators.

Where new translation has been necessary, the most complete representation of the original has been rendered by considering the definition and usage of the Hebrew, Aramaic, and Greek words in their contexts. This translation principle, known as *complete equivalence,* seeks to preserve accurately all of the information in the text while presenting it in good literary form.

In addition to accuracy, the translators have also sought to maintain those lyrical and devotional qualities that are so highly regarded in the King James Version. The thought flow and selection of phrases from the King James Version have been preserved wherever possible without sacrificing clarity.

The format of the New King James Version is designed to enhance the vividness, devotional quality, and usefulness of the Bible. Words or phrases in italics indicate expressions in the original language that require clarification by additional English words, as was done in the King James Version. Oblique type in the New Testament indicates a quotation from the Old Testament. Poetry is structured as verse to reflect the form and beauty of the passage in the original language. The covenant name of God was usually translated from the Hebrew as LORD or GOD, using capital letters as shown, as in the King James Version. This convention is also maintained in the New King James Version when the Old Testament is quoted in the New.

The Hebrew text used for the Old Testament is the 1967/1977 Stuttgart edition of the *Biblia Hebraica,* with frequent comparisons to the Bomberg edition of 1524-25. Ancient versions and the Dead Sea Scrolls were consulted, but the Hebrew is followed wherever possible. Significant variations, explanations, and alternate renderings are mentioned in footnotes.

The Greek text used for the New Testament is the one that was followed by the King James translators: the traditional text of the Greek-speaking churches, called the Received Text or Textus Receptus, first published in 1516. Footnotes indicate significant variants from the Textus Receptus as found in two other editions of the Greek New Testament:

(1) NU-Text: These variations generally represent the Alexandrian or Egyptian text type as found in the critical text published in the twenty-sixth edition of the Nestle-Aland Greek New Testament (N) and in the United Bible Societies' third edition (U).
(2) M-Text: These variations represent readings found in the text of the first edition of *The Greek New Testament According to the Majority Text,* which follows the consensus of the majority of surviving New Testament manuscripts.

The textual notes in the New King James Version make no evaluation, but objectively present the facts about variant readings.

Old Testament

Genesis

Everyone needs a second chance. We all make bad choices and then must face the consequences of those bad choices. Then we try to make better choices the next time around. All the while, we are painfully aware of our tendency to fail, to disappoint, to mess things up. We need hope, forgiveness, and another chance.

Genesis means "beginning." Written by Moses to the people of Israel, this book tells the story of the beginning of the world, the beginning of sin, and the beginning of God's plan for redeeming sinful people. Genesis lays bare the lives of people who are just like us—real people with real problems. They struggle with uncertainty, fear, loneliness, jealousy, despair, and anger. Yet God patiently works in these imperfect people, and their faith emerges above their imperfections. God gives them second chances, and they grow and change as He works in their lives. As they make their journey through life, these people discover that God loves them, comforts them, and guides them—no matter how painful or confusing their situation might be. He does the same for us.

God is full of compassion and grace. His work in the lives of Abraham, Sarah, Isaac, Jacob, and Joseph shows that we don't need to be perfect. Instead we need the perfect God. His divine presence and promises point us toward hope in spite of our sins, failures, and struggles. Genesis reveals that God longs to have an intimate relationship with us—and to give us second chances.

SOUL CONCERNS IN GENESIS

SEXUALITY	(1:27, 28)
INFERTILITY	(18:11, 12)
FAMILY PROBLEMS	(CH. 25)
BLENDED FAMILIES	(CH. 29)
TEMPTATION	(39:6–15)
ATTACHMENT/BLESSING	(CH. 49)

The History of Creation

1 In the beginning God created the heavens and the earth. [2]The earth was without form, and void; and darkness *was*[a] on the face of the deep. And the Spirit of God was hovering over the face of the waters.

[3]Then God said, "Let there be light"; and there was light. [4]And God saw the light, that *it was* good; and God divided the light from the darkness. [5]God called the light Day, and the darkness He called Night. So the evening and the morning were the first day.

[6]Then God said, "Let there be a firmament in the midst of the waters, and let it divide the waters from the waters." [7]Thus God made the firmament, and divided the waters which *were* under the firmament from the waters which *were* above the firmament; and it was so. [8]And God called the firmament Heaven. So the evening and the morning were the second day.

[9]Then God said, "Let the waters under the heavens be gathered together into one place, and let the dry *land* appear"; and it was so. [10]And God called the dry *land* Earth, and the gathering together of the waters He called Seas. And God saw that *it was* good.

[11]Then God said, "Let the earth bring forth grass, the herb *that* yields seed, *and* the fruit tree *that* yields fruit according to its kind, whose seed *is* in itself, on the earth"; and it was so. [12]And the earth brought forth grass, the herb *that* yields seed according to its kind, and the tree *that* yields fruit, whose seed *is* in itself according to its kind. And God saw that *it was* good. [13]So the evening and the morning were the third day.

[14]Then God said, "Let there be lights in the firmament of the heavens to divide the day from the night; and let them be for signs and seasons, and for days and years; [15]and let them be for lights in the firmament of the heavens to give light on the earth"; and it was so. [16]Then God made two great lights: the greater light to rule the day, and the lesser light to rule the night. *He made* the stars also. [17]God set them in the firmament of the heavens to give light on the earth, [18]and to rule over the day and over the night, and to divide the light from the darkness. And God saw that *it was* good. [19]So the evening and the morning were the fourth day.

[20]Then God said, "Let the waters abound with an abundance of living creatures, and let birds fly above the earth across the face of the firmament of the heavens." [21]So God created great sea creatures and every living thing that moves, with which the waters abounded, according to their kind, and every winged bird according to its kind. And God saw that *it was* good. [22]And God blessed them, saying, "Be fruitful and multiply, and fill the waters in the seas, and let birds multiply on the earth." [23]So the evening and the morning were the fifth day.

[24]Then God said, "Let the earth bring forth the living creature according to its kind: cattle and creeping thing and beast of the earth, *each* according to its kind"; and it was so. [25]And God made the beast of the earth according to its kind, cattle according to its kind, and everything that creeps on the earth according to its kind. And God saw that *it was* good.

[26]Then God said, "Let Us make man in Our image, according to Our likeness; let them have dominion over the fish of the sea, over the birds of the air, and over the cattle, over all[a] the earth and over every creeping thing that creeps on the earth." [27]So God created man in His *own* image; in the image of God He created him; male and female He created them. [28]Then God blessed them, and God said to them, "Be fruitful and multiply; fill the earth and subdue it; have dominion over the fish of the sea, over the birds of the air, and over every living thing that moves on the earth."

> So God created man in His own image; in the image of God He created him; male and female He created them.
>
> GENESIS 1:27

[29]And God said, "See, I have given you every herb *that* yields seed which *is* on the face of all the earth, and every tree whose fruit yields seed; to you it shall be for food. [30]Also, to every beast of the earth, to every bird of the air, and to everything that creeps on the earth, in which *there is* life, *I have given* every green herb for food"; and it was so. [31]Then God saw everything that He had made, and indeed *it*

1:2 [a]Words in italic type have been added for clarity. They are not found in the original Hebrew or Aramaic. **1:26** [a]Syriac reads *all the wild animals of.*

was very good. So the evening and the morning were the sixth day.

2 Thus the heavens and the earth, and
all the host of them, were finished. [2]And
on the seventh day God ended His work which
He had done, and He rested on the seventh
day from all His work which He had done.
[3]Then God blessed the seventh day and sanctified it, because in it He rested from all His
work which God had created and made.

[4]This *is* the history[a] of the heavens and the
earth when they were created, in the day that
the LORD God made the earth and the heavens,
[5]before any plant of the field was in the earth
and before any herb of the field had grown.
For the LORD God had not caused it to rain on
the earth, and *there was* no man to till the
ground; [6]but a mist went up from the earth
and watered the whole face of the ground.

[7]And the LORD God formed man *of* the dust
of the ground, and breathed into his nostrils
the breath of life; and man became a living
being.

LIFE IN GOD'S GARDEN

[8]The LORD God planted a garden eastward
in Eden, and there He put the man whom He
had formed. [9]And out of the ground the LORD
God made every tree grow that is pleasant to
the sight and good for food. The tree of life
was also in the midst of the garden, and the
tree of the knowledge of good and evil.

[10]Now a river went out of Eden to water the
garden, and from there it parted and became
four riverheads. [11]The name of the first *is* Pi-
shon; it *is* the one which skirts the whole land
of Havilah, where *there is* gold. [12]And the gold
of that land *is* good. Bdellium and the onyx
stone *are* there. [13]The name of the second
river *is* Gihon; it *is* the one which goes around
the whole land of Cush. [14]The name of the
third river *is* Hiddekel;[a] it *is* the one which
goes toward the east of Assyria. The fourth
river *is* the Euphrates.

[15]Then the LORD God took the man and put
him in the garden of Eden to tend and keep it.
[16]And the LORD God commanded the man,
saying, "Of every tree of the garden you may
freely eat; [17]but of the tree of the knowledge of
good and evil you shall not eat, for in the day
that you eat of it you shall surely die."

[18]And the LORD God said, "*It is* not good that
man should be alone; I will make him a helper

2:4 [a]Hebrew *toledoth,* literally *generations*
2:14 [a]Or *Tigris*

KEY PASSAGE

Sexuality

GOD CREATED SEX

(1:27, 28)

God created sex and declared it "good." Along with the rest of creation, however, sex has been affected by sin. Scripture teaches God's plan for human sexuality:

- Sex is for both procreation (1:28) and pleasure (Prov. 5:18, 19; Song of Solomon).
- Sex is to be enjoyed only between a man and a woman married to each other (1 Cor. 7:2–5). The intimacy of sex is designed to bond the couple in a lifelong union (Gen. 2:24; Matt. 19:5).
- Sex outside of marriage is strictly prohibited (Ex. 20:14; Prov. 5:1–11; 6:23–33; 7:5–27).
- Both heterosexual and homosexual immorality are strongly condemned in Scripture (Rom. 1:26–28; 1 Thess. 4:3) because our bodies are the "temple of the Holy Spirit" (1 Cor. 6:13–20).

God takes great joy when His children enjoy what He has given, provided they do so within His guidelines.

To Learn More: Turn to the article about sexuality on pages 6, 7. See also the personality profile of Adam and Eve on page 9.

CREATED BY A LOVING GOD

DOUG ROSENAU

(Genesis 1:27, 28)

Our world is permeated by sexual images, ideas, and behaviors. Magazine covers, television shows, and movies are filled with sexual messages. With all this emphasis on sex, it is important that we remind ourselves that God is the creator of sexuality. When we understand God's sexual blueprint and the reasons He gave us this important gift, we realize why He pronounced it "good." Sexuality and the act of sex itself were designed by the loving Creator long before sex was used to sell magazines and products. To really appreciate sexuality, however, we must view sex from God's perspective.

WHY DID GOD CREATE SEXUALITY?

God created people for relationships. He also created human beings with gender—male and female. According to the Bible, both genders were created in God's image and neither gender was valued above the other. Different cultures have stereotyped the roles of men and women in different ways. Although there is a great deal of debate about what is intrinsic to being male or female, the Bible is clear that both are image-bearers of God and find their completion in a relationship with Him. "So God created man in His own image; in the image of God He created him; male and female He created them. . . . God saw everything that He had made, and indeed it was very good" (Gen. 1:27, 31).

God gives a beautiful picture of His own nature with maleness and femaleness and their complementary interactive whole. Creating gender and opposite sexes produced the intimate concepts of marriage and family. God uses this pattern to demonstrate a very personal love relationship that He enters into with His people. He made Adam and Eve, the first lovers, incomplete without each other. "Therefore a man shall leave his father and mother and be joined to his wife, and they shall become one flesh" (Gen. 2:24).

The biblical concept of sexuality helps people understand the complexity of God Himself. It is not just a behavior (having sex) or a gender (male or female). Sexuality is a foundational part of who people are and how they learn about relating to God and one another intimately.

EXPRESSING SEXUALITY

God planned for the sexual relationship to be experienced only between a man and a woman within the covenant commitment of marriage. The sexual union is intended to help people express spiritual intimacy, emotional bonding, passionate excitement, personal fulfillment, and genuine nurturing. One of the great mysteries of life unfolds when marital partners are made complete in the "one flesh" union that God created for them with their soul mate for life. Stepping outside that plan always brings pain because God's laws about sexuality are in place for people's own good.

MAINTAINING SEXUAL INTEGRITY

It takes conscious choices and a disciplined thought life to be sexually faithful to one's spouse. Sexual integrity requires resisting sexual temptation. Each marital partner must make godly choices to avoid ungodly sexual desires that can erupt into sin (1 Thess. 4:3–7; James 1:14, 15).

Society is filled with sexual messages that can tempt people into sin. Setting healthy boundaries for one's thought life as well as for the physical expression of sexuality will help a person maintain sexual integrity. This will mean "bringing every thought into captivity to the obedience of Christ" (2 Cor. 10:5). It will mean treating each other like brothers and sisters in the family of God "with all purity" (1 Tim. 5:2) in the rich interaction of male and female relationships.

Sexuality has been distorted by the Fall and sexual experience has been perverted by sin. Sexual brokenness results in a loss of sexual integrity and hinders the genuineness of people's relationships to others. Marriage alone cannot cure sexual brokenness. Christ alone can redeem people's sexuality through repentance and forgiveness. Only in Him can they experience a redeemed sexuality that leads to disciplined maturity, healthy boundaries, and marital faithfulness.

HEALING SEXUAL SINS

Sexual sins have devastating consequences, but even these sins can be forgiven by God. Jesus invites people to come to Him with their sins. The following are five tools to use in the process of healing sexual sins.

1. *Confession*: Sexual sins thrive on secrecy. To experience complete healing, people must first confess the sin to God—He hears and forgives (Prov. 28:13; 1 John 1:9).
2. *Repentance*: This involves recognizing and accepting responsibility for sexual sin. Repentance frees people to make the changes needed for restoration (2 Cor. 7:10).
3. *Forgiveness*: People need to forgive themselves and the other people involved. Letting go of resentment and shame is crucial to the healing of sexual sins (Col. 3:13).
4. *Sorrow*: Sexuality misused can cause painful consequences and losses. This pain can move people to sorrow. Jesus promises healing to those who grieve (James 4:9, 10).
5. *Restitution*: Making restitution for harmful behaviors can bring reconciliation and restoration of intimacy. This may take different forms, depending on the situation. Each person should seek God's guidance regarding how to make restitution in matters of sexual sin (Ezek. 33:14, 15).

CELEBRATING SEXUALITY

A married couple can truly celebrate their sexuality by giving pleasure to each other. This involves more than just sex. It means living honestly, sincerely, and joyfully within the covenant relationship of marriage. It is not simply a euphemism that the Old Testament uses the word "know" for sexual intercourse (Gen. 4:1). The Hebrew word for "to know" carries a deep meaning of intimacy. This foundation of covenant commitment is the groundwork for the celebration of marital lovemaking. God's plan has been right from the beginning—and it still works today.

FURTHER MEDITATION:

Other passages to study about the issue of sexuality include:

- Deuteronomy 22:13–30
- Proverbs 5:15–23; 6:20–35
- Song of Solomon 7:1–13
- Matthew 5:27–30
- 1 Corinthians 6:12—7:16

To Learn More: Turn to the key passage note on sexuality at Genesis 1:27, 28 on page 5. See also the personality profile of Adam and Eve on page 9.

comparable to him." 19Out of the ground the
LORD God formed every beast of the field and
every bird of the air, and brought *them* to
Adam to see what he would call them. And
whatever Adam called each living creature,
that *was* its name. 20So Adam gave names to all
cattle, to the birds of the air, and to every beast
of the field. But for Adam there was not found
a helper comparable to him.
21And the LORD God caused a deep sleep to
fall on Adam, and he slept; and He took one of
his ribs, and closed up the flesh in its place.
22Then the rib which the LORD God had taken
from man He made into a woman, and He
brought her to the man.
23And Adam said:

"This *is* now bone of my bones
And flesh of my flesh;
She shall be called Woman,
Because she was taken out of Man."

24Therefore a man shall leave his father and
mother and be joined to his wife, and they
shall become one flesh.
25And they were both naked, the man and
his wife, and were not ashamed.

THE TEMPTATION AND FALL OF MAN

3 Now the serpent was more cunning than
any beast of the field which the LORD God
had made. And he said to the woman, "Has
God indeed said, 'You shall not eat of every
tree of the garden'?"
2And the woman said to the serpent, "We
may eat the fruit of the trees of the garden; 3but
of the fruit of the tree which *is* in the midst of
the garden, God has said, 'You shall not eat it,
nor shall you touch it, lest you die.' "
4Then the serpent said to the woman, "You
will not surely die. 5For God knows that in the
day you eat of it your eyes will be opened, and
you will be like God, knowing good and evil."
6So when the woman saw that the tree *was*
good for food, that it *was* pleasant to the eyes,
and a tree desirable to make *one* wise, she
took of its fruit and ate. She also gave to her
husband with her, and he ate. 7Then the eyes
of both of them were opened, and they knew
that they *were* naked; and they sewed fig
leaves together and made themselves coverings.
8And they heard the sound of the LORD God
walking in the garden in the cool of the day,
and Adam and his wife hid themselves from

SOUL NOTE

Make Your Choice *(2:16, 17)* God provided an entire garden of fruit trees to satisfy Adam's hunger as well as his taste buds. Adam, and soon Eve, were allowed to eat freely of every tree. But then God put *one* forbidden tree in the garden—just *one*—and told Adam, "You shall not eat" from that tree. In order for there to be loving obedience, there had to be the option for disobedience. Adam was given a clear boundary and a clear choice with clear consequences for disobedience. We also face choices every day. When we observe God's boundaries, we show our love for Him.
Topic: Boundaries

SOUL NOTE

Alone? *(2:18)* God's provision of a "helper" for Adam was not a condescending comment on singleness but an approval of marriage. God was concerned for Adam's loneliness, for He created people to have relationships—with Him and with others. Single adults include never-marrieds as well as separated, divorced, and widowed persons. Though issues may differ, each one faces the potential problems of aloneness, such as isolation, insecurity, and feelings of rejection. Being "unattached" can foster destructive responses, or it can encourage the development of a deeper relationship with God. There's nothing wrong with being single—just don't go it alone!
Topic: Singleness

the presence of the LORD God among the trees
of the garden.
[9]Then the LORD God called to Adam and
said to him, "Where *are* you?"
[10]So he said, "I heard Your voice in the garden, and I was afraid because I was naked;
and I hid myself."
[11]And He said, "Who told you that you *were*
naked? Have you eaten from the tree of which
I commanded you that you should not eat?"
[12]Then the man said, "The woman whom
You gave *to be* with me, she gave me of the
tree, and I ate."
[13]And the LORD God said to the woman,
"What *is* this you have done?"
The woman said, "The serpent deceived
me, and I ate."
[14]So the LORD God said to the serpent:

"Because you have done this,
You *are* cursed more than all cattle,
And more than every beast of the field;
On your belly you shall go,
And you shall eat dust
All the days of your life.
15 And I will put enmity
Between you and the woman,
And between your seed and her Seed;
He shall bruise your head,
And you shall bruise His heel."

PERSONALITY PROFILE

Sexuality

ADAM AND EVE: GOD'S DESIGN FOR SEXUALITY

(GENESIS 2:18–25)

God invented sex. He built sexuality into people's original design. When God finished His work of creation, including the creation of man and woman, God pronounced it all, "very good." Later, when Adam saw what God had created out of his own rib, he said roughly the same thing. God allowed Adam to experience what it meant to be alone; then He created someone with whom Adam could know togetherness. It was the original case of bonding at first sight. One look and Adam was smitten.

God created Adam and Eve as a relationship unit, with sex as part of the glue to hold them together. From the beginning, God designed sexuality as one aspect of a wonderful relationship between a man and woman. But, as powerful a tool against human aloneness as sex is, it cannot do its work without another vital component of the man-woman relationship. That component is called *marriage*.

When God performed Adam and Eve's wedding in the garden, He spelled out several aspects (besides sex) that make up the marriage relationship as He intended it. Genesis 2:24, 25 describes these aspects:

- leaving other significant relationships,
- joining to each other, and
- becoming one flesh.

That process results in a complete disclosure of one person to the other: They are "naked" but "not ashamed." The invasion of sin into the world, however, complicated every part of life, including sex. Only Adam and Eve experienced the original version of married life. But sex continued as a lasting blessing even after the Fall. The Bible describes three important purposes of marital sex: procreation, loving pleasure, and resistance of sexual sin.

For every married couple since Adam and Eve, keeping sex a blessed part of their marriage takes work and faithfulness. When a man and woman enter and live out their marital relationship under God's guidelines and purposes, they can still expect to discover, as Adam and Eve did so long ago, that marital sex can indeed be "very good."

To Learn More: Turn to the article about sexuality on pages 6, 7. See also the key passage note at Genesis 1:27, 28 on page 5.

[16]To the woman He said:

"I will greatly multiply your sorrow and
your conception;
In pain you shall bring forth children;
Your desire *shall be* for your husband,
And he shall rule over you."

[17]Then to Adam He said, "Because you have
heeded the voice of your wife, and have eaten
from the tree of which I commanded you, saying, 'You shall not eat of it':

"Cursed *is* the ground for your sake;
In toil you shall eat *of* it
All the days of your life.
18 Both thorns and thistles it shall bring
forth for you,
And you shall eat the herb of the field.
19 In the sweat of your face you shall eat
bread
Till you return to the ground,
For out of it you were taken;
For dust you *are*,
And to dust you shall return."

[20]And Adam called his wife's name Eve, because she was the mother of all living.
[21]Also for Adam and his wife the LORD God
made tunics of skin, and clothed them.
[22]Then the LORD God said, "Behold, the
man has become like one of Us, to know good
and evil. And now, lest he put out his hand
and take also of the tree of life, and eat, and
live forever"— [23]therefore the LORD God sent
him out of the garden of Eden to till the

PERSONALITY PROFILE

Guilt/Shame

ADAM'S GUILT; ADAM'S SHAME

(GENESIS 3)

While He had Adam's undivided attention, God gave him some very specific instructions: "Of every tree of the garden you may freely eat; but of the tree of the knowledge of good and evil you shall not eat, for in the day that you eat of it you shall surely die" (Gen. 2:16, 17). God offered to Adam an opportunity to experience the full freedom that grows out of obedience.

Shortly after that, God introduced Eve to Adam. The two of them received God's blessing and began their perfect life together. At this point there was no sin or suffering in the idyllic garden God gave them as a home.

One of Adam's duties was to help Eve understand God's instructions. He apparently gave Eve the condensed version: "See that tree over there, honey? God told us not to even touch it. Got that?" Eve was an easy prey for Satan because perhaps Adam didn't tell her the whole story. That's why God held Adam ultimately responsible for the sin that infected the human race when the couple ate of the forbidden fruit.

Even before God's confrontation, however, Adam already knew he had sinned. He felt that inner awareness of wrongdoing called *guilt*. He also realized that fear of exposure called *shame*. This powerful combination was given by God as an internal corrective. It could have brought Adam to repentance and confession. Instead, Adam tried to cope with guilt and shame by avoidance and denial. Adam found himself suddenly terrified of God's approach. He hid in shame. Gently questioned, Adam excused his behavior. Eve followed Adam's lead. The rest of us have done the same thing.

As long as we blame others and refuse to take responsibility for our wrong actions, we remain mired in sin. Guilt and shame rule our lives and cut us off from God's redemptive healing. But God invites us to own our sin and confess it to Him. When we do so, God is "faithful and just to forgive us our sins and to cleanse us from all unrighteousness" (1 John 1:9).

To Learn More: Turn to the article about guilt/shame on pages 600, 601. See also the key passage note at Romans 8:1 on page 1474.

ground from which he was taken. [24]So He
drove out the man; and He placed cherubim at
the east of the garden of Eden, and a flaming
sword which turned every way, to guard the
way to the tree of life.

Cain Murders Abel

4 Now Adam knew Eve his wife, and she
conceived and bore
Cain, and said, "I have
acquired a man from the
LORD." [2]Then she bore
again, this time his
brother Abel. Now Abel
was a keeper of sheep,
but Cain was a tiller of
the ground. [3]And in the process of time it came
to pass that Cain brought an offering of the
fruit of the ground to the LORD. [4]Abel also
brought of the firstborn of his flock and of their
fat. And the LORD respected Abel and his offering, [5]but He did not respect Cain and his offering. And Cain was very angry, and his
countenance fell.
[6]So the LORD said to Cain, "Why are you
angry? And why has your countenance fallen?
[7]If you do well, will you not be accepted? And
if you do not do well, sin lies at the door.
And its desire *is* for
you, but you should
rule over it."
[8]Now Cain talked
with Abel his brother;[a]
and it came to pass,
when they were in the
field, that Cain rose up
against Abel his brother and killed him.

> Sin lies at the door.
> And its desire is for you,
> but you should rule over it.
>
> GENESIS 4:7

4:8 [a]Samaritan Pentateuch, Septuagint, Syriac, and Vulgate add *"Let us go out to the field."*

PERSONALITY PROFILE

Anger

ANGRY AS CAIN?

(GENESIS 4)

Cain had a problem with anger. It wasn't that he got angry. God didn't warn him because he *got* angry; God warned him because he *stayed* angry.

The incident that provoked Cain's anger occurred during a worship service. The brothers met to offer sacrifices to God. Cain brought an assortment of farm goods as an offering; Abel presented an offering of special value. Cain did his duty; Abel gave his best. God was pleased with Abel's offering, but rejected Cain's. The older brother was furious.

Cain's original anger actually represented a positive response. But the anger missed its target. Cain should have been furious with himself. Instead, Cain's anger became a deadly weapon looking for a new target. At that point, God intervened. He corrected Cain's misplaced anger and offered him another opportunity: "If you do well, will you not be accepted? And if you do not do well, sin lies at the door. And its desire is for you, but you should rule over it" (Gen. 4:7).

Adam's firstborn opened the door for sin. Cain got angry at God and took it out on his younger brother Abel. Anger became murderous jealousy. Soon, Abel lay dead in a field. Killing his brother did little for Cain's anger. When God approached him, Cain denied knowing or caring where his brother might be. He resented the consequences of his sin. Cain displayed no remorse or repentance. He became stuck in his anger.

As Cain demonstrates, anger must be ruled or it will rule. Uncontrolled anger quickly becomes a destructive tyrant. When we invite God to help us identify the causes of our anger and take corrective measures, anger can become a servant rather than a master in our lives. God's Word gives powerful counsel when it notes, "Be angry, and do not sin" (Eph. 4:26).

To Learn More: Turn to the article about anger on pages 692, 693. See also the key passage note at Ephesians 4:26, 27 on page 1554.

9Then the LORD said to Cain, "Where *is* Abel
your brother?"
He said, "I do not know. *Am* I my brother's
keeper?"
10And He said, "What have you done? The
voice of your brother's blood cries out to Me
from the ground. 11So now you *are* cursed
from the earth, which has opened its mouth to
receive your brother's blood from your hand.
12When you till the ground, it shall no longer
yield its strength to you. A fugitive and a vagabond you shall be on the earth."
13And Cain said to the LORD, "My punishment *is* greater than I can bear! 14Surely You
have driven me out this day from the face of
the ground; I shall be hidden from Your face; I
shall be a fugitive and a vagabond on the
earth, and it will happen *that* anyone who
finds me will kill me."
15And the LORD said to him, "Therefore,[a]
whoever kills Cain, vengeance shall be taken
on him sevenfold." And the LORD set a mark on
Cain, lest anyone finding him should kill him.

THE FAMILY OF CAIN

16Then Cain went out from the presence of
the LORD and dwelt in the land of Nod on the
east of Eden. 17And Cain knew his wife, and
she conceived and bore Enoch. And he built a
city, and called the name of the city after the
name of his son—Enoch. 18To Enoch was born
Irad; and Irad begot Mehujael, and Mehujael
begot Methushael, and Methushael begot Lamech.
19Then Lamech took for himself two wives:
the name of one *was* Adah, and the name of
the second *was* Zillah. 20And Adah bore Jabal.
He was the father of those who dwell in tents
and have livestock. 21His brother's name *was*
Jubal. He was the father of all those who play
the harp and flute. 22And as for Zillah, she
also bore Tubal-Cain, an instructor of every
craftsman in bronze and iron. And the sister
of Tubal-Cain *was* Naamah.
23Then Lamech said to his wives:

"Adah and Zillah, hear my voice;
Wives of Lamech, listen to my speech!
For I have killed a man for wounding
me,
Even a young man for hurting me.
24 If Cain shall be avenged sevenfold,
Then Lamech seventy-sevenfold."

A NEW SON

25And Adam knew his wife again, and she
bore a son and named him Seth, "For God has
appointed another seed for me instead of
Abel, whom Cain killed." 26And as for Seth, to
him also a son was born; and he named him
Enosh.[a] Then *men* began to call on the name
of the LORD.

THE FAMILY OF ADAM

5 This is the book of the genealogy of Adam.
In the day that God created man, He made
him in the likeness of God. 2He created them
male and female, and blessed them and called
them Mankind in the day they were created.
3And Adam lived one hundred and thirty
years, and begot *a son* in his own likeness, after his image, and named him Seth. 4After he
begot Seth, the days of Adam were eight hundred years; and he had sons and daughters.
5So all the days that Adam lived were nine
hundred and thirty years; and he died.
6Seth lived one hundred and five years, and
begot Enosh. 7After he begot Enosh, Seth lived
eight hundred and seven years, and had sons
and daughters. 8So all the days of Seth were
nine hundred and twelve years; and he died.
9Enosh lived ninety years, and begot
Cainan.[a] 10After he begot Cainan, Enosh lived
eight hundred and fifteen years, and had sons
and daughters. 11So all the days of Enosh were
nine hundred and five years; and he died.
12Cainan lived seventy years, and begot
Mahalalel. 13After he begot Mahalalel, Cainan
lived eight hundred and forty years, and
had sons and daughters. 14So all the days of
Cainan were nine hundred and ten years; and
he died.
15Mahalalel lived sixty-five years, and begot
Jared. 16After he begot Jared, Mahalalel lived
eight hundred and thirty years, and had sons
and daughters. 17So all the days of Mahalalel
were eight hundred and ninety-five years; and
he died.
18Jared lived one hundred and sixty-two
years, and begot Enoch. 19After he begot
Enoch, Jared lived eight hundred years, and
had sons and daughters. 20So all the days of
Jared were nine hundred and sixty-two years;
and he died.

4:15 [a]Following Masoretic Text and Targum; Septuagint, Syriac, and Vulgate read *Not so.*
4:26 [a]Greek *Enos* **5:9** [a]Hebrew *Qenan*

21Enoch lived sixty-five years, and begot
Methuselah. 22After he begot Methuselah,
Enoch walked with God three hundred years,
and had sons and daughters. 23So all the days
of Enoch were three hundred and sixty-five
years. 24And Enoch walked with God; and he
was not, for God took him.

25Methuselah lived one hundred and eighty-
seven years, and begot Lamech. 26After he begot Lamech, Methuselah lived seven hundred
and eighty-two years, and had sons and
daughters. 27So all the days of Methuselah
were nine hundred and sixty-nine years; and
he died.

28Lamech lived one hundred and eighty-two
years, and had a son. 29And he called his
name Noah, saying, "This *one* will comfort us
concerning our work and the toil of our
hands, because of the ground which the LORD
has cursed." 30After he begot Noah, Lamech
lived five hundred and ninety-five years, and
had sons and daughters. 31So all the days of
Lamech were seven hundred and seventy-
seven years; and he died.

32And Noah was five hundred years old, and
Noah begot Shem, Ham, and Japheth.

THE WICKEDNESS AND JUDGMENT OF MAN

6 Now it came to pass, when men began
to multiply on the face of the earth, and
daughters were born to them, 2that the sons of
God saw the daughters of men, that they *were*
beautiful; and they took wives for themselves
of all whom they chose.

3And the LORD said, "My Spirit shall not
strive[a] with man forever, for he *is* indeed flesh;
yet his days shall be one hundred and twenty
years." 4There were giants on the earth in those
days, and also afterward, when the sons of God
came in to the daughters of men and they bore
children to them. Those *were* the mighty men
who *were* of old, men of renown.

5Then the LORD[a] saw that the wickedness of
man *was* great in the earth, and *that* every intent of the thoughts of his heart *was* only evil
continually. 6And the LORD was sorry that He
had made man on the earth, and He was
grieved in His heart. 7So the LORD said, "I will
destroy man whom I have created from the
face of the earth, both man and beast, creeping thing and birds of the air, for I am sorry
that I have made them." 8But Noah found
grace in the eyes of the LORD.

NOAH PLEASES GOD

9This is the genealogy of Noah. Noah was a
just man, perfect in his generations. Noah
walked with God. 10And Noah begot three
sons: Shem, Ham, and Japheth.

11The earth also was corrupt before God,
and the earth was filled with violence. 12So
God looked upon the earth, and indeed it was
corrupt; for all flesh had corrupted their way
on the earth.

THE ARK PREPARED

13And God said to Noah, "The end of all
flesh has come before Me, for the earth is
filled with violence through them; and behold, I will destroy them with the earth.
14Make yourself an ark of gopherwood; make
rooms in the ark, and cover it inside and outside with pitch. 15And this is how you shall
make it: The length of the ark *shall be* three
hundred cubits, its width fifty cubits, and its
height thirty cubits. 16You shall make a window for the ark, and you shall finish it to a cubit from above; and set the door of the ark in
its side. You shall make it *with* lower, second,
and third *decks*. 17And behold, I Myself am
bringing floodwaters on the earth, to destroy
from under heaven all flesh in which *is* the
breath of life; everything that *is* on the earth
shall die. 18But I will establish My covenant
with you; and you shall go into the ark—you,
your sons, your wife, and your sons' wives
with you. 19And of every living thing of all
flesh you shall bring two of every *sort* into the
ark, to keep *them* alive with you; they shall be
male and female. 20Of the birds after their
kind, of animals after their kind, and of every
creeping thing of the earth after its kind, two
of every *kind* will come to you to keep *them*
alive. 21And you shall take for yourself of all
food that is eaten, and you shall gather *it* to
yourself; and it shall be food for you and for
them."

22Thus Noah did; according to all that God
commanded him, so he did.

THE GREAT FLOOD

7 Then the LORD said to Noah, "Come into
the ark, you and all your household, because I have seen *that* you *are* righteous before

---

6:3 [a]Septuagint, Syriac, Targum, and Vulgate read *abide.* **6:5** [a]Following Masoretic Text and Targum; Vulgate reads *God;* Septuagint reads *LORD God.*

Me in this generation. [2]You shall take with you seven each of every clean animal, a male and his female; two each of animals that *are* unclean, a male and his female; [3]also seven each of birds of the air, male and female, to keep the species alive on the face of all the earth. [4]For after seven more days I will cause it to rain on the earth forty days and forty nights, and I will destroy from the face of the earth all living things that I have made." [5]And Noah did according to all that the LORD commanded him. [6]Noah *was* six hundred years old when the floodwaters were on the earth.

[7]So Noah, with his sons, his wife, and his sons' wives, went into the ark because of the waters of the flood. [8]Of clean animals, of animals that *are* unclean, of birds, and of everything that creeps on the earth, [9]two by two they went into the ark to Noah, male and female, as God had commanded Noah. [10]And it came to pass after seven days that the waters of the flood were on the earth. [11]In the six hundredth year of Noah's life, in the second month, the seventeenth day of the month, on that day all the fountains of the great deep were broken up, and the windows of heaven were opened. [12]And the rain was on the earth forty days and forty nights.

[13]On the very same day Noah and Noah's sons, Shem, Ham, and Japheth, and Noah's wife and the three wives of his sons with them, entered the ark— [14]they and every beast after its kind, all cattle after their kind, every creeping thing that creeps on the earth after its kind, and every bird after its kind, every bird of every sort. [15]And they went into the ark to Noah, two by two, of all flesh in which *is* the breath of life. [16]So those that entered, male and female of all flesh, went in as God had commanded him; and the LORD shut him in.

[17]Now the flood was on the earth forty days. The waters increased and lifted up the ark, and it rose high above the earth. [18]The waters prevailed and greatly increased on the earth, and the ark moved about on the surface of the waters. [19]And the waters prevailed exceedingly on the earth, and all the high hills under the whole heaven were covered. [20]The waters prevailed fifteen cubits upward, and the mountains were covered. [21]And all flesh died that moved on the earth: birds and cattle and beasts and every creeping thing that creeps on the earth, and every man. [22]All in whose nostrils *was* the breath of the spirit[a] of life, all that *was* on the dry *land,* died. [23]So He destroyed all living things which were on the face of the ground: both man and cattle, creeping thing and bird of the air. They were destroyed from the earth. Only Noah and those who *were* with him in the ark remained *alive.* [24]And the waters prevailed on the earth one hundred and fifty days.

NOAH'S DELIVERANCE

8 Then God remembered Noah, and every living thing, and all the animals that *were* with him in the ark. And God made a wind to pass over the earth, and the waters subsided. [2]The fountains of the deep and the windows of heaven were also stopped, and the rain from heaven was restrained. [3]And the waters receded continually from the earth. At the end of the hundred and fifty days the waters decreased. [4]Then the ark rested in the seventh month, the seventeenth day of the month, on the mountains of Ararat. [5]And the waters decreased continually until the tenth month. In the tenth *month,* on the first *day* of the month, the tops of the mountains were seen.

[6]So it came to pass, at the end of forty days, that Noah opened the window of the ark which he had made. [7]Then he sent out a raven, which kept going to and fro until the waters had dried up from the earth. [8]He also sent out from himself a dove, to see if the waters had receded from the face of the ground. [9]But the dove found no resting place for the sole of her foot, and she returned into the ark to him, for the waters *were* on the face of the whole earth. So he put out his hand and took her, and drew her into the ark to himself. [10]And he waited yet another seven days, and again he sent the dove out from the ark. [11]Then the dove came to him in the evening, and behold, a freshly plucked olive leaf *was* in her mouth; and Noah knew that the waters had receded from the earth. [12]So he waited yet another seven days and sent out the dove, which did not return again to him anymore.

[13]And it came to pass in the six hundred and first year, in the first *month,* the first *day* of the month, that the waters were dried up from the earth; and Noah removed the covering of the ark and looked, and indeed the surface of the ground was dry. [14]And in the second month,

---

7:22 [a]Septuagint and Vulgate omit *of the spirit.*

on the twenty-seventh day of the month, the earth was dried.

[15]Then God spoke to Noah, saying, [16]"Go out of the ark, you and your wife, and your sons and your sons' wives with you. [17]Bring out with you every living thing of all flesh that *is* with you: birds and cattle and every creeping thing that creeps on the earth, so that they may abound on the earth, and be fruitful and multiply on the earth." [18]So Noah went out, and his sons and his wife and his sons' wives with him. [19]Every animal, every creeping thing, every bird, *and* whatever creeps on the earth, according to their families, went out of the ark.

> The rainbow shall be in the cloud, and I will look on it to remember the everlasting covenant between God and every living creature of all flesh that is on the earth.
>
> GENESIS 9:16

God's Covenant with Creation

[20]Then Noah built an altar to the LORD, and took of every clean animal and of every clean bird, and offered burnt offerings on the altar. [21]And the LORD smelled a soothing aroma. Then the LORD said in His heart, "I will never again curse the ground for man's sake, although the imagination of man's heart *is* evil from his youth; nor will I again destroy every living thing as I have done.

22 "While the earth remains,
Seedtime and harvest,
Cold and heat,
Winter and summer,
And day and night
Shall not cease."

9 So God blessed Noah and his sons, and said to them: "Be fruitful and multiply, and fill the earth.[a] [2]And the fear of you and the dread of you shall be on every beast of the earth, on every bird of the air, on all that move *on* the earth, and on all the fish of the sea. They are given into your hand. [3]Every moving thing that lives shall be food for you. I have given you all things, even as the green herbs. [4]But you shall not eat flesh with its life, *that is,* its blood. [5]Surely for your lifeblood I will demand *a reckoning;* from the hand of every beast I will require it, and from the hand of man. From the hand of every man's brother I will require the life of man.

6 "Whoever sheds man's blood,
By man his blood shall be shed;
For in the image of God
He made man.
7 And as for you, be fruitful and multiply;
Bring forth abundantly in the earth
And multiply in it."

[8]Then God spoke to Noah and to his sons with him, saying: [9]"And as for Me, behold, I establish My covenant with you and with your descendants[a] after you, [10]and with every living creature that *is* with you: the birds, the cattle, and every beast of the earth with you, of all that go out of the ark, every beast of the earth. [11]Thus I establish My covenant with you: Never again shall all flesh be cut off by the waters of the flood; never again shall there be a flood to destroy the earth."

[12]And God said: "This *is* the sign of the

9:1 [a]Compare Genesis 1:28 **9:9** [a]Literally *seed*

SOUL NOTE

A Violent Society *(9:6)* To find evidence of violence in society, just open a newspaper. Violence reflects the darkness of the human soul—the sinful nature. God dealt harshly with Noah's generation because they were evil and the earth was "filled with violence" (6:11). People's violence toward one another grieves God. After the Flood, God instructed succeeding generations to hold people accountable for their violent behavior and to punish them appropriately. It's OK to desire that people receive just consequences for their violent behavior, but leave revenge to God. In the end, He will deal justly with all people. **Topic: Violence**

covenant which I make between Me and you, and every living creature that *is* with you, for perpetual generations: [13]I set My rainbow in the cloud, and it shall be for the sign of the covenant between Me and the earth. [14]It shall be, when I bring a cloud over the earth, that the rainbow shall be seen in the cloud; [15]and I will remember My covenant which *is* between Me and you and every living creature of all flesh; the waters shall never again become a flood to destroy all flesh. [16]The rainbow shall be in the cloud, and I will look on it to remember the everlasting covenant between God and every living creature of all flesh that *is* on the earth." [17]And God said to Noah, "This *is* the sign of the covenant which I have established between Me and all flesh that *is* on the earth."

NOAH AND HIS SONS

[18]Now the sons of Noah who went out of the ark were Shem, Ham, and Japheth. And Ham *was* the father of Canaan. [19]These three *were* the sons of Noah, and from these the whole earth was populated.

[20]And Noah began *to be* a farmer, and he planted a vineyard. [21]Then he drank of the wine and was drunk, and became uncovered in his tent. [22]And Ham, the father of Canaan, saw the nakedness of his father, and told his two brothers outside. [23]But Shem and Japheth took a garment, laid *it* on both their shoulders, and went backward and covered the nakedness of their father. Their faces *were* turned away, and they did not see their father's nakedness.

[24]So Noah awoke from his wine, and knew what his younger son had done to him. [25]Then he said:

"Cursed *be* Canaan;
A servant of servants
He shall be to his brethren."

[26]And he said:

PERSONALITY PROFILE

NOAH: FLOATING ON GOD'S PROMISES

(GENESIS 9)

Never underestimate the power of one person, especially one who believes God's promises. One good man can turn the tide of history. Long before the Flood, Noah learned that reliance on God would keep him afloat through life.

Noah received the divine order to build an ark because he found favor with God. In a world drowning in sin, Noah was chosen to prepare for the safety of a handful. God told Noah that because wickedness throughout the world was unrestrained, "everything that is on the earth shall die. But I will establish My covenant with you; and you shall go into the ark—you, your sons, your wife, and your sons' wives with you" (Gen. 6:17, 18).

Noah believed God and followed His instructions, building a huge ship on dry land. His neighbors could not imagine a purpose or need for such a vessel. We can only imagine the ridicule he must have endured! His ark became a monument to persistence. His faithful obedience brought about the salvation of his family. He became, like Adam, the second father of the human race.

After the Flood, God created the first rainbow as a sign of His perpetual promise to Noah and his descendants that He would never again destroy the earth by water. God's promises are trustworthy. God fulfills His promises even when we fail completely to hold up our side of the covenant. The rainbow reminds us of one part of God's commitment to us.

We may often feel surrounded by the rising tide of immorality in today's world. God's promises remain a safe vessel. In spite of overwhelming odds and the temptation to discouragement, God's faithfulness to Noah reveals that He will also keep the "great and precious promises" He has given us (2 Pet. 1:4).

To Learn More: Turn to the article about God's promises on pages 220, 221. See also the key passage note at 2 Peter 1:4 on page 1668.

"Blessed *be* the LORD,
The God of Shem,
And may Canaan be his servant.
27 May God enlarge Japheth,
And may he dwell in the tents of Shem;
And may Canaan be his servant."

28 And Noah lived after the flood three hundred and fifty years. 29 So all the days of Noah were nine hundred and fifty years; and he died.

NATIONS DESCENDED FROM NOAH

10 Now this *is* the genealogy of the sons of Noah: Shem, Ham, and Japheth. And sons were born to them after the flood.

2 The sons of Japheth *were* Gomer, Magog, Madai, Javan, Tubal, Meshech, and Tiras. 3 The sons of Gomer *were* Ashkenaz, Riphath,[a] and Togarmah. 4 The sons of Javan *were* Elishah, Tarshish, Kittim, and Dodanim.[a] 5 From these the coastland *peoples* of the Gentiles were separated into their lands, everyone according to his language, according to their families, into their nations.

6 The sons of Ham *were* Cush, Mizraim, Put,[a] and Canaan. 7 The sons of Cush *were* Seba, Havilah, Sabtah, Raamah, and Sabtechah; and the sons of Raamah *were* Sheba and Dedan.

8 Cush begot Nimrod; he began to be a mighty one on the earth. 9 He was a mighty hunter before the LORD; therefore it is said, "Like Nimrod the mighty hunter before the LORD." 10 And the beginning of his kingdom was Babel, Erech, Accad, and Calneh, in the land of Shinar. 11 From that land he went to Assyria and built Nineveh, Rehoboth Ir, Calah, 12 and Resen between Nineveh and Calah (that *is* the principal city).

13 Mizraim begot Ludim, Anamim, Lehabim, Naphtuhim, 14 Pathrusim, and Casluhim (from whom came the Philistines and Caphtorim).

15 Canaan begot Sidon his firstborn, and Heth; 16 the Jebusite, the Amorite, and the Girgashite; 17 the Hivite, the Arkite, and the Sinite; 18 the Arvadite, the Zemarite, and the Hamathite. Afterward the families of the Canaanites were dispersed. 19 And the border of the Canaanites was from Sidon as you go toward Gerar, as far as Gaza; then as you go toward Sodom, Gomorrah, Admah, and Zeboiim, as far as Lasha. 20 These *were* the sons of Ham, according to their families, according to their languages, in their lands *and* in their nations.

21 And *children* were born also to Shem, the father of all the children of Eber, the brother of Japheth the elder. 22 The sons of Shem *were* Elam, Asshur, Arphaxad, Lud, and Aram. 23 The sons of Aram *were* Uz, Hul, Gether, and Mash.[a] 24 Arphaxad begot Salah,[a] and Salah begot Eber. 25 To Eber were born two sons: the name of one *was* Peleg, for in his days the earth was divided; and his brother's name *was* Joktan. 26 Joktan begot Almodad, Sheleph, Hazarmaveth, Jerah, 27 Hadoram, Uzal, Diklah, 28 Obal,[a] Abimael, Sheba, 29 Ophir, Havilah, and Jobab. All these *were* the sons of Joktan. 30 And their dwelling place was from Mesha as you go toward Sephar, the mountain of the east. 31 These *were* the sons of Shem, according to their families, according to their languages, in their lands, according to their nations.

32 These *were* the families of the sons of Noah, according to their generations, in their nations; and from these the nations were divided on the earth after the flood.

THE TOWER OF BABEL

11 Now the whole earth had one language and one speech. 2 And it came to pass, as they journeyed from the east, that they found a plain in the land of Shinar, and they dwelt there. 3 Then they said to one another, "Come, let us make bricks and bake *them* thoroughly." They had brick for stone, and they had asphalt for mortar. 4 And they said, "Come, let us build ourselves a city, and a tower whose top *is* in the heavens; let us make a name for ourselves, lest we be scattered abroad over the face of the whole earth."

5 But the LORD came down to see the city and the tower which the sons of men had built. 6 And the LORD said, "Indeed the people *are* one and they all have one language, and this is what they begin to do; now nothing that they propose to do will be withheld from them. 7 Come, let Us go down and there confuse their language, that they may not understand one

10:3 [a]Spelled *Diphath* in 1 Chronicles 1:6
10:4 [a]Spelled *Rodanim* in Samaritan Pentateuch and 1 Chronicles 1:7 **10:6** [a]Or *Phut*
10:23 [a]Called *Meshech* in Septuagint and 1 Chronicles 1:17 **10:24** [a]Following Masoretic Text, Vulgate, and Targum; Septuagint reads *Arphaxad begot Cainan, and Cainan begot Salah* (compare Luke 3:35, 36). **10:28** [a]Spelled *Ebal* in 1 Chronicles 1:22

another's speech." 8So the LORD scattered them
abroad from there over the face of all the earth,
and they ceased building the city. 9Therefore its
name is called Babel, because there the LORD
confused the language of all the earth; and
from there the LORD scattered them abroad
over the face of all the earth.

SHEM'S DESCENDANTS

10This *is* the genealogy of Shem: Shem *was*
one hundred years old, and begot Arphaxad
two years after the flood. 11After he begot Arphaxad, Shem lived five hundred years, and
begot sons and daughters.
12Arphaxad lived thirty-five years, and begot Salah. 13After he begot Salah, Arphaxad
lived four hundred and three years, and begot
sons and daughters.
14Salah lived thirty years, and begot Eber.
15After he begot Eber, Salah lived four hundred and three years, and begot sons and
daughters.
16Eber lived thirty-four years, and begot Peleg. 17After he begot Peleg, Eber lived four
hundred and thirty years, and begot sons and
daughters.
18Peleg lived thirty years, and begot Reu.
19After he begot Reu, Peleg lived two hundred
and nine years, and begot sons and daughters.
20Reu lived thirty-two years, and begot Serug. 21After he begot Serug, Reu lived two
hundred and seven years, and begot sons and
daughters.
22Serug lived thirty years, and begot Nahor.
23After he begot Nahor, Serug lived two hundred years, and begot sons and daughters.
24Nahor lived twenty-nine years, and begot
Terah. 25After he begot Terah, Nahor lived one
hundred and nineteen years, and begot sons
and daughters.
26Now Terah lived seventy years, and begot
Abram, Nahor, and Haran.

TERAH'S DESCENDANTS

27This *is* the genealogy of Terah: Terah begot Abram, Nahor, and Haran. Haran begot
Lot. 28And Haran died before his father Terah in his native land, in Ur of the Chaldeans. 29Then Abram and Nahor took wives:
the name of Abram's wife *was* Sarai, and the
name of Nahor's wife, Milcah, the daughter
of Haran the father of Milcah and the father
of Iscah. 30But Sarai was barren; she had no
child.
31And Terah took his son Abram and his
grandson Lot, the son of Haran, and his
daughter-in-law Sarai, his son Abram's wife,
and they went out with them from Ur of the
Chaldeans to go to the land of Canaan; and
they came to Haran and dwelt there. 32So the
days of Terah were two hundred and five
years, and Terah died in Haran.

PROMISES TO ABRAM

12 Now the LORD had said to Abram:

"Get out of your country,
From your family
And from your father's house,
To a land that I will show you.
2 I will make you a great nation;
I will bless you
And make your name great;
And you shall be a blessing.
3 I will bless those who bless you,
And I will curse him who curses you;
And in you all the families of the earth
shall be blessed."

4So Abram departed as the LORD had spoken
to him, and Lot went with him. And Abram
was seventy-five years old when he departed
from Haran. 5Then Abram took Sarai his wife
and Lot his brother's son, and all their possessions that they had gathered, and the people
whom they had acquired in Haran, and they
departed to go to the land of Canaan. So they
came to the land of Canaan. 6Abram passed
through the land to the place of Shechem, as
far as the terebinth tree of Moreh.[a] And the
Canaanites *were* then in the land.
7Then the LORD appeared to Abram and
said, "To your descendants I will give this
land." And there he built an altar to the LORD,
who had appeared to him. 8And he moved
from there to the mountain east of Bethel, and
he pitched his tent *with* Bethel on the west
and Ai on the east; there he built an altar to
the LORD and called on the name of the LORD.
9So Abram journeyed, going on still toward
the South.[a]

ABRAM IN EGYPT

10Now there was a famine in the land, and
Abram went down to Egypt to dwell there, for
the famine *was* severe in the land. 11And it

12:6 [a]Hebrew *Alon Moreh* **12:9** [a]Hebrew *Negev*

came to pass, when he was close to entering Egypt, that he said to Sarai his wife, "Indeed I know that you *are* a woman of beautiful countenance. 12Therefore it will happen, when the Egyptians see you, that they will say, 'This *is* his wife'; and they will kill me, but they will let you live. 13Please say you *are* my sister, that it may be well with me for your sake, and that I[a] may live because of you."

14So it was, when Abram came into Egypt, that the Egyptians saw the woman, that she *was* very beautiful. 15The princes of Pharaoh also saw her and commended her to Pharaoh. And the woman was taken to Pharaoh's house. 16He treated Abram well for her sake. He had sheep, oxen, male donkeys, male and female servants, female donkeys, and camels.

17But the LORD plagued Pharaoh and his house with great plagues because of Sarai, Abram's wife. 18And Pharaoh called Abram and said, "What *is* this you have done to me? Why did you not tell me that she *was* your wife? 19Why did you say, 'She *is* my sister'? I might have taken her as my wife. Now therefore, here is your wife; take *her* and go your way." 20So Pharaoh commanded *his* men concerning him; and they sent him away, with his wife and all that he had.

ABRAM INHERITS CANAAN

13 Then Abram went up from Egypt, he and his wife and all that he had, and Lot with him, to the South.[a] 2Abram *was* very rich in livestock, in silver, and in gold. 3And he went on his journey from the South as far as Bethel, to the place where his tent had been at the beginning, between Bethel and Ai, 4to the place of the altar which he had made there at first. And there Abram called on the name of the LORD.

5Lot also, who went with Abram, had flocks and herds and tents. 6Now the land was not able to support them, that they might dwell together, for their possessions were so great that they could not dwell together. 7And there was strife between the herdsmen of Abram's livestock and the herdsmen of Lot's livestock. The Canaanites and the Perizzites then dwelt in the land.

8So Abram said to Lot, "Please let there be no strife between you and me, and between my herdsmen and your herdsmen; for we *are* brethren. 9*Is* not the whole land before you? Please separate from me. If *you take* the left, then I will go to the right; or, if *you go* to the right, then I will go to the left."

10And Lot lifted his eyes and saw all the plain of Jordan, that it *was* well watered everywhere (before the LORD destroyed Sodom and Gomorrah) like the garden of the LORD, like the land of Egypt as you go toward Zoar. 11Then Lot chose for himself all the plain of Jordan, and Lot journeyed east. And they separated from each other. 12Abram dwelt in the land of Canaan, and Lot dwelt in the cities of the plain and pitched *his* tent even as far as Sodom. 13But the men of Sodom *were* exceedingly wicked and sinful against the LORD.

14And the LORD said to Abram, after Lot had separated from him: "Lift your eyes now and look from the place where you are—northward, southward, eastward, and westward; 15for all the land which you see I give to you and your descendants[a] forever. 16And I will make your descendants as the dust of the earth; so that if a man could number the dust of the earth, *then* your descendants also could be numbered. 17Arise, walk in the land through its length and its width, for I give it to you."

18Then Abram moved *his* tent, and went and dwelt by the terebinth trees of Mamre,[a] which *are* in Hebron, and built an altar there to the LORD.

LOT'S CAPTIVITY AND RESCUE

14 And it came to pass in the days of Amraphel king of Shinar, Arioch king of Ellasar, Chedorlaomer king of Elam, and Tidal king of nations,[a] 2*that* they made war with Bera king of Sodom, Birsha king of Gomorrah, Shinab king of Admah, Shemeber king of Zeboiim, and the king of Bela (that is, Zoar). 3All these joined together in the Valley of Siddim (that is, the Salt Sea). 4Twelve years they served Chedorlaomer, and in the thirteenth year they rebelled.

5In the fourteenth year Chedorlaomer and the kings that *were* with him came and attacked the Rephaim in Ashteroth Karnaim, the Zuzim in Ham, the Emim in Shaveh Kiriathaim, 6and the Horites in their mountain of Seir, as far as El Paran, which *is* by the wilderness. 7Then they turned back and came to

12:13 [a]Literally *my soul* **13:1** [a]Hebrew *Negev*
13:15 [a]Literally *seed,* and so throughout the book
13:18 [a]Hebrew *Alon Mamre* **14:1** [a]Hebrew *goyim*

En Mishpat (that *is,* Kadesh), and attacked all
the country of the Amalekites, and also the
Amorites who dwelt in Hazezon Tamar.
8And the king of Sodom, the king of Gomorrah, the king of Admah, the king of Zeboiim,
and the king of Bela (that *is,* Zoar) went out
and joined together in battle in the Valley of
Siddim 9against Chedorlaomer king of Elam,
Tidal king of nations,[a] Amraphel king of Shinar, and Arioch king of Ellasar—four kings
against five. 10Now the Valley of Siddim *was*
full of asphalt pits; and the kings of Sodom and
Gomorrah fled; *some* fell there, and the remainder fled to the mountains. 11Then they took all
the goods of Sodom and Gomorrah, and all
their provisions, and went their way. 12They
also took Lot, Abram's brother's son who
dwelt in Sodom, and his goods, and departed.
13Then one who had escaped came and told
Abram the Hebrew, for he dwelt by the terebinth trees of Mamre[a] the Amorite, brother of
Eshcol and brother of Aner; and they *were* allies with Abram. 14Now when Abram heard
that his brother was
taken captive, he armed
his three hundred and
eighteen trained *ser-*
vants who were born in
his own house, and
went in pursuit as far as
Dan. 15He divided his
forces against them by
night, and he and his servants attacked them
and pursued them as far as Hobah, which *is*
north of Damascus. 16So he brought back all
the goods, and also brought back his brother
Lot and his goods, as well as the women and
the people.
17And the king of Sodom went out to meet
him at the Valley of Shaveh (that *is,* the King's
Valley), after his return from the defeat of
Chedorlaomer and the kings who *were* with
him.

> The word of the LORD came to Abram in a vision, saying, "Do not be afraid, Abram. I am your shield, your exceedingly great reward."
> GENESIS 15:1

ABRAM AND MELCHIZEDEK

18Then Melchizedek king of Salem brought
out bread and wine; he *was* the priest of God
Most High. 19And he blessed him and said:

"Blessed be Abram of God Most High,
Possessor of heaven and earth;
20 And blessed be God Most High,
Who has delivered your enemies into
your hand."

And he gave him a tithe of all.
21Now the king of Sodom said to Abram,
"Give me the persons, and take the goods for
yourself."
22But Abram said to the king of Sodom, "I
have raised my hand to the LORD, God Most
High, the Possessor of heaven and earth,
23that I *will take* nothing, from a thread to a
sandal strap, and that I will not take anything
that *is* yours, lest you should say, 'I have made
Abram rich'— 24except only what the young
men have eaten, and the portion of the men
who went with me: Aner, Eshcol, and Mamre;
let them take their portion."

GOD'S COVENANT WITH ABRAM

15 After these things the word of the
LORD came to Abram in a vision, saying, "Do not be afraid, Abram. I *am* your
shield, your exceedingly great reward."
2But Abram said, "Lord GOD, what will You
give me, seeing I go childless, and the heir of
my house *is* Eliezer of Damascus?" 3Then
Abram said, "Look, You
have given me no off-
spring; indeed one born
in my house is my heir!"
4And behold, the
word of the LORD *came*
to him, saying, "This
one shall not be your
heir, but one who will
come from your own body shall be your heir."
5Then He brought him outside and said,
"Look now toward heaven, and count the
stars if you are able to number them." And He
said to him, "So shall your descendants be."
6And he believed in the LORD, and He accounted it to him for righteousness.
7Then He said to him, "I *am* the LORD, who
brought you out of Ur of the Chaldeans, to
give you this land to inherit it."
8And he said, "Lord GOD, how shall I know
that I will inherit it?"
9So He said to him, "Bring Me a three-year-
old heifer, a three-year-old female goat, a
three-year-old ram, a turtledove, and a young
pigeon." 10Then he brought all these to Him
and cut them in two, down the middle, and
placed each piece opposite the other; but he
did not cut the birds in two. 11And when the

14:9 [a]Hebrew *goyim* **14:13** [a]Hebrew *Alon Mamre*

vultures came down on the carcasses, Abram
drove them away.
[12]Now when the sun was going down, a
deep sleep fell upon Abram; and behold, horror *and* great darkness fell upon him. [13]Then
He said to Abram: "Know certainly that your
descendants will be strangers in a land *that is*
not theirs, and will serve them, and they will
afflict them four hundred years. [14]And also the
nation whom they serve I will judge; afterward they shall come out with great possessions. [15]Now as for you, you shall go to your
fathers in peace; you shall be buried at a good
old age. [16]But in the fourth generation they
shall return here, for the iniquity of the Amorites *is* not yet complete."
[17]And it came to pass, when the sun went
down and it was dark, that behold, there appeared a smoking oven and a burning torch
that passed between those pieces. [18]On the
same day the LORD made a covenant with
Abram, saying:
"To your descendants I have given this land,
from the river of Egypt to the great river, the
River Euphrates— [19]the Kenites, the Kenez-
zites, the Kadmonites, [20]the Hittites, the
Perizzites, the Rephaim, [21]the Amorites, the
Canaanites, the Girgashites, and the Jebusites."

HAGAR AND ISHMAEL

16 Now Sarai, Abram's wife, had borne
him no *children.* And she had an
Egyptian maidservant whose name was Hagar. [2]So Sarai said to Abram, "See now, the
LORD has restrained me from bearing *children.*
Please, go in to my maid; perhaps I shall obtain children by her." And Abram heeded the
voice of Sarai. [3]Then Sarai, Abram's wife, took
Hagar her maid, the Egyptian, and gave her to
her husband Abram to be his wife, after
Abram had dwelt ten years in the land of Canaan. [4]So he went in to Hagar, and she conceived. And when she saw that she had

PERSONALITY PROFILE

Faith

ABRAHAM: STEPPING OUT ON FAITH

(GENESIS 15)

Abraham practiced an inside-out faith. What he believed in his mind and heart he put to action with his life. He turned trust into travel and experienced God's grace and power along the way.

God chose Abraham and invited him on a faith-stretching journey. Abraham had to pack up his large and wealthy clan, leave a lush river valley, and trust God's protection and guidance. God directed him to Canaan, a hardscrabble land of warring tribes. God's promise had included both a land and a legacy. God told Abraham He would give him a place and make from him a people. "Get out of your country . . . to a land that I will show you. I will make you a great nation; I will bless you. . . . And in you all the families of the earth shall be blessed" (Gen. 12:1–3).

The promise of a land came true long before the promise of a child. When Abraham and Sarah were very old, well past childbearing years, God promised them a son who would be the tangible evidence and living carrier of God's promise. As often happens during a divine waiting period, the people involved thought of possible ways to help God accomplish His plan. But their efforts only served to make their situation more complicated. Like us, Abraham wasn't always sure what faith required him to do.

Despite their all-too-real imperfections, Sarah and Abraham are listed among the heroes in the "Hall of Faith" in Hebrews 11. God eventually did bless them with their promised son Isaac. Through them the nation of Israel was born, the lineage of Jesus Christ was begun, and the plan to bless the world with a Savior continued to develop. God's plan rested on the shoulders of a man who practiced inside-out faith.

To Learn More: Turn to the article about faith on pages 1634, 1635. See also the key passage note at Hebrews 11:1–6 on page 1632.

conceived, her mistress became despised in her eyes.

5Then Sarai said to Abram, "My wrong *be* upon you! I gave my maid into your embrace; and when she saw that she had conceived, I became despised in her eyes. The LORD judge between you and me."

6So Abram said to Sarai, "Indeed your maid *is* in your hand; do to her as you please." And when Sarai dealt harshly with her, she fled from her presence.

7Now the Angel of the LORD found her by a spring of water in the wilderness, by the spring on the way to Shur. 8And He said, "Hagar, Sarai's maid, where have you come from, and where are you going?"

She said, "I am fleeing from the presence of my mistress Sarai."

9The Angel of the LORD said to her, "Return to your mistress, and submit yourself under her hand." 10Then the Angel of the LORD said to her, "I will multiply your descendants exceedingly, so that they shall not be counted for multitude." 11And the Angel of the LORD said to her:

"Behold, you *are* with child,
And you shall bear a son.
You shall call his name Ishmael,
Because the LORD has heard your
affliction.
12 He shall be a wild man;
His hand *shall be* against every man,
And every man's hand against him.
And he shall dwell in the presence of all
his brethren."

13Then she called the name of the LORD who spoke to her, You-Are-the-God-Who-Sees; for she said, "Have I also here seen Him who sees me?" 14Therefore the well was called Beer Lahai Roi;[a] observe, *it is* between Kadesh and Bered.

15So Hagar bore Abram a son; and Abram named his son, whom Hagar bore, Ishmael. 16Abram *was* eighty-six years old when Hagar bore Ishmael to Abram.

The Sign of the Covenant

17 When Abram was ninety-nine years old, the LORD appeared to Abram and said to him, "I *am* Almighty God; walk before Me and be blameless. 2And I will make My covenant between Me and you, and will multiply you exceedingly." 3Then Abram fell on his face, and God talked with him, saying: 4"As for Me, behold, My covenant is with you, and you shall be a father of many nations. 5No longer shall your name be called Abram, but your name shall be Abraham; for I have made you a father of many nations. 6I will make you exceedingly fruitful; and I will make nations of you, and kings shall come from you. 7And I will establish My covenant between Me and you and your descendants after you in their generations, for an everlasting covenant, to be God to you and your descendants after you. 8Also I give to you and your descendants after you the land in which you are a stranger, all the land of Canaan, as an everlasting possession; and I will be their God."

9And God said to Abraham: "As for you, you shall keep My covenant, you and your descendants after you throughout their generations. 10This *is* My covenant which you shall keep, between Me and you and your descendants after you: Every male child among you shall be circumcised; 11and you shall be circumcised in the flesh of your foreskins, and it shall be a sign of the covenant between Me and you. 12He who is eight days old among you shall be circumcised, every male child in your generations, he who is born in your house or bought with money from any foreigner who is not your descendant. 13He who is born in your house and he who is bought with your money must be circumcised, and My covenant shall be in your flesh for an everlasting covenant. 14And the uncircumcised male child, who is not circumcised in the flesh of his foreskin, that person shall be cut off from his people; he has broken My covenant."

15Then God said to Abraham, "As for Sarai your wife, you shall not call her name Sarai, but Sarah *shall be* her name. 16And I will bless her and also give you a son by her; then I will bless her, and she shall be *a mother of* nations; kings of peoples shall be from her."

17Then Abraham fell on his face and laughed, and said in his heart, "Shall *a child* be born to a man who is one hundred years old? And shall Sarah, who is ninety years old, bear *a child?*" 18And Abraham said to God, "Oh, that Ishmael might live before You!"

19Then God said: "No, Sarah your wife shall

16:14 [a]Literally *Well of the One Who Lives and Sees Me*

bear you a son, and you shall call his name Isaac; I will establish My covenant with him for an everlasting covenant, *and* with his descendants after him. [20]And as for Ishmael, I have heard you. Behold, I have blessed him, and will make him fruitful, and will multiply him exceedingly. He shall beget twelve princes, and I will make him a great nation. [21]But My covenant I will establish with Isaac, whom Sarah shall bear to you at this set time next year." [22]Then He finished talking with him, and God went up from Abraham.

[23]So Abraham took Ishmael his son, all who were born in his house and all who were bought with his money, every male among the men of Abraham's house, and circumcised the flesh of their foreskins that very same day, as God had said to him. [24]Abraham *was* ninety-nine years old when he was circumcised in the flesh of his foreskin. [25]And Ishmael his son *was* thirteen years old when he was circumcised in the flesh of his foreskin. [26]That very same day Abraham was circumcised, and his son Ishmael; [27]and all the men of his house, born in the house or bought with money from a foreigner, were circumcised with him.

The Son of Promise

18 Then the LORD appeared to him by the terebinth trees of Mamre,[a] as he was sitting in the tent door in the heat of the day. [2]So he lifted his eyes and looked, and behold, three men were standing by him; and when he saw *them,* he ran from the tent door to meet them, and bowed himself to the ground, [3]and said, "My Lord, if I have now found favor in Your sight, do not pass on by Your servant. [4]Please let a little water be brought, and wash your feet, and rest yourselves under the tree. [5]And I will bring a morsel of bread, that you may refresh your hearts. After that you may pass by, inasmuch as you have come to your servant."

They said, "Do as you have said."

[6]So Abraham hurried into the tent to Sarah and said, "Quickly, make ready three measures of fine meal; knead *it* and make cakes." [7]And Abraham ran to the herd, took a tender and good calf, gave *it* to a young man, and he hastened to prepare it. [8]So he took butter and milk and the calf which he had prepared, and set *it* before them; and he stood by them under the tree as they ate.

[9]Then they said to him, "Where *is* Sarah your wife?"

So he said, "Here, in the tent."

[10]And He said, "I will certainly return to you according to the time of life, and behold, Sarah your wife shall have a son."

(Sarah was listening in the tent door which *was* behind him.) [11]Now Abraham and Sarah were old, well advanced in age; *and* Sarah had passed the age of childbearing.[a] [12]Therefore Sarah laughed within herself, saying, "After I have grown old, shall I have pleasure, my lord being old also?"

[13]And the LORD said to Abraham, "Why did Sarah laugh, saying, 'Shall I surely bear *a child,* since I am old?' [14]Is anything too hard for the LORD? At the appointed time I will return to you, according to the time of life, and Sarah shall have a son."

[15]But Sarah denied *it,* saying, "I did not laugh," for she was afraid.

And He said, "No, but you did laugh!"

Is anything too hard for the LORD?

GENESIS 18:14

18:1 [a]Hebrew *Alon Mamre* **18:11** [a]Literally *the manner of women had ceased to be with Sarah*

SOUL NOTE

That's a Laugh! *(18:11, 12)* When she heard God's promise, Sarah laughed first in disbelief. Later, she laughed with joy (21:6). The desire to be a parent is powerful, and Sarah had gone to great extremes to have a child. What can a couple do as they face what the Bible calls "barrenness"? First, they should pray. They can consult with a doctor and see what measures are possible (considering their personal feelings and their budget). They can look into other options, such as adoption. But ultimately, they must trust God's plan for their lives. **Topic: Infertility**

STILLBORN DREAMS: THE HEARTBREAK OF INFERTILITY

W. DAVID HAGER AND LINDA CARRUTH HAGER

(Genesis 18:11, 12)

An estimated 15 to 18 percent of all married couples struggle with infertility. Physicians define infertility as the inability to conceive after one year of unprotected sex. Since most couples desire to procreate, the failure to do so often generates bitterness, anger, hostility, and depression. Couples may blame each other for their inability to conceive and/or begin avoiding friends who have become parents. But perhaps the most difficult emotion to own and work through is the anger we feel toward God when our prayers are not answered in the way we hoped.

KNOWING GOD CARES

Romans 11:33 says that the ways and wisdom of God are so deep and unsearchable that they are "past finding out." We must remember that God is big enough to take our confusion and to work through it with us. We must be willing to own our true emotions and bring them to Him.

Infertile couples need to know that God cares deeply about their inability to conceive. He designed the process of procreation when He created people in His own image. This intricate process whereby a brain produces hormones which stimulate ovaries to produce eggs or testicles to produce sperm was conceived by the Master Reproductive Endocrinologist.

Recognizing that this intricately designed mechanism was not functioning normally, God intervened in the lives of several biblical couples. Consider, for example, Abraham and Sarah (Gen. 17:16) and Zacharias and Elizabeth (Luke 1:13). These miraculous conceptions demonstrate God's compassion for infertile couples.

In Bible times, a woman who was unable to become pregnant was described as "barren." Modern medicine gives us a fuller understanding of this term. Some couples may be "barren" because the man does not produce enough sperm to fertilize an egg. In other cases, the woman fails to ovulate or does not produce adequate hormones to maintain a pregnancy. A woman may also be infertile when her fallopian tubes, which carry the egg from the ovary to the uterus, are blocked due to previous infection. For example, bacteria from sexually transmitted diseases denude the lining of tiny, hairlike cilia, leaving it like a barren desert.

If our own choices have caused a sexually transmitted disease to lead to the grief of infertility, it can be a crushing blow. Yet we are still not beyond the mercy and grace of God. He stands ready to forgive us if we recognize the mistakes we have made and determine to walk in a better way. But He does not always remove the consequences of bad choices. However, He is willing and able to redeem our mistakes. What is required is the willingness to die to *our* ways of fulfilling our dreams. He always gives us hope for the future. Of course, our dreams and hopes may not look the way we expected them to look. Without an adjustment of our vision, we will miss the joy and fulfillment the Father is offering to us through His redeeming gift of love.

TRUSTING GOD'S WAYS

Regardless of the cause of infertility, the couple must treat each other with love, avoiding shame and blame. Prayer is the greatest resource during these difficult times. Sometimes a "no" from God is a provision and protection that a couple refuses to receive. We must not let our self-worth be defined by our ability to have children. We lose a sense of direction and purpose when we hold our personal happiness hostage to our limited idea of what it means to be fertile and to nurture new life. Yes, the inability to conceive a child is undeniably painful and requires us to jump huge hurdles of faith in order to go on with a life that is not going as we hoped or planned. But, we can admit our pain while still clinging to the promises of God for abundant life. Though our capacity to produce life in one specific way may be altered, we can be very sure that our loving heavenly Father will fulfill those very ideas and desires in some way in every human being He has created.

Our Creator has given to the human mind the capacity to cultivate life in amazing ways. Techniques of assisted reproduction involving stimulation of ovulation or facilitating the placement of the husband's sperm to be proximate to his wife's egg for fertilization do not appear to be contrary to God's Word. But a couple must understand the risks involved. There is always the risk of conceiving a child with a congenital defect. Pursuit of assisted reproduction also can cause deep division in the marriage with feelings of inadequacy on the part of one or both partners. The process of using donor sperm from another male or donor eggs from another woman should be discouraged, for it may result in a conception contrary to God's design, with the biological parent being asked to give up the rights to his or her own offspring.

While we pray earnestly, our spirits must remain soft and pliable, willing to receive God's will in His way and time. Ecclesiastes 3:11 says, "He has made everything beautiful in its time. Also He has put eternity in their hearts, except that no one can find out the work that God does from beginning to end."

Our God is a God of love, and His ways are unfathomable, worthy of our trust and calling for our submission. This intimate love exchange will produce a rich harvest of peace and joy that will go deeper than our pain. We must pray that our hearts and minds will be opened to His unique ways of fulfilling our dreams.

FURTHER MEDITATION:

Other passages to study about the issue of infertility include:

➢ 1 Samuel 1:1—2:26
➢ Proverbs 30:15, 16
➢ Luke 1:5–80

To Learn More: Turn to the key passage note on infertility at I Samuel 2:5 on page 345. See also the personality profile of Hannah on page 345.

Abraham Intercedes for Sodom

16Then the men rose from there and looked
toward Sodom, and Abraham went with them
to send them on the way. 17And the LORD said,
"Shall I hide from Abraham what I am doing,
18since Abraham shall surely become a great
and mighty nation, and all the nations of the
earth shall be blessed in him? 19For I have
known him, in order that he may command
his children and his household after him, that
they keep the way of the LORD, to do righteousness and justice, that the LORD may bring
to Abraham what He has spoken to him."
20And the LORD said, "Because the outcry
against Sodom and Gomorrah is great, and because their sin is very grave, 21I will go down
now and see whether they have done altogether according to the outcry against it that
has come to Me; and if not, I will know."

22Then the men turned away from there and
went toward Sodom, but Abraham still stood
before the LORD. 23And Abraham came near
and said, "Would You also destroy the righteous with the wicked? 24Suppose there were
fifty righteous within the city; would You also
destroy the place and not spare *it* for the fifty
righteous that were in it? 25Far be it from You
to do such a thing as this, to slay the righteous
with the wicked, so that the righteous should
be as the wicked; far be it from You! Shall not
the Judge of all the earth do right?"

26So the LORD said, "If I find in Sodom fifty
righteous within the city, then I will spare all
the place for their sakes."

27Then Abraham answered and said, "Indeed now, I who *am but* dust and ashes have
taken it upon myself to speak to the Lord:
28Suppose there were five less than the fifty
righteous; would You destroy all of the city for
lack of five?"

So He said, "If I find there forty-five, I will
not destroy *it*."

29And he spoke to Him yet again and said,

PERSONALITY PROFILE

Parenting

ABRAHAM: A PARENT'S HEART

(GENESIS 18:19)

Abraham loved his children. In fact, the first time the Bible uses the word "love" occurs when God describes the relationship between Abraham and his son Isaac (Gen. 22:2). Abraham showered his kids with affection and hope, as any good parent will do. Better yet, he loved and obeyed God even more than he loved his children.

The birth of Isaac brought great joy to Abraham's house, for it fulfilled God's promise against impossible odds. Abraham was 100 years old and Sarah 90 at Isaac's birth. Although Isaac was the promised child, he wasn't Abraham's first. Years earlier, in a rash attempt to assist God, Sarah suggested that her husband might have a child with the much younger slave girl Hagar, a child Sarah planned to call her own. But Sarah misread her own feelings. Once Ishmael was born, Sarah rejected him and his mother. She eventually insisted that Abraham expel them from his house. This was not an easy decision for Abraham; after all, Ishmael *was* his son.

Later, Abraham had a much harder decision to make. God asked him to sacrifice his son Isaac. The deliberate manner in which Abraham obeyed speaks volumes about painful faithfulness. And surely it spoke volumes to his son, Isaac, about his father's priorities. For Abraham, nothing was more important than God.

Earlier God had said of Abraham, "I have known him, in order that he may command his children and his household after him, that they keep the way of the LORD, to do righteousness and justice" (Gen. 18:19). Abraham's parenting reflected his character, and his character was grounded in his faith in God. Whether they like it or not, parents live out their commitment to God. If that commitment is their central focus, parents will then be able to model a life of faith to their children.

To Learn More: Turn to the article about parenting on pages 826, 827. See also the key passage note at I Samuel 1:27, 28 on page 344.

"Suppose there should be forty found there?"
So He said, "I will not do *it* for the sake of
forty."
30Then he said, "Let not the Lord be angry,
and I will speak: Suppose thirty should be
found there?"
So He said, "I will not do *it* if I find thirty
there."
31And he said, "Indeed now, I have taken it
upon myself to speak to the Lord: Suppose
twenty should be found there?"
So He said, "I will not destroy *it* for the sake
of twenty."
32Then he said, "Let not the Lord be angry,
and I will speak but once more: Suppose ten
should be found there?"
And He said, "I will not destroy *it* for the
sake of ten." 33So the LORD went His way as
soon as He had finished speaking with Abraham; and Abraham returned to his place.

SODOM'S DEPRAVITY

19 Now the two angels came to Sodom in
the evening, and Lot was sitting in the
gate of Sodom. When Lot saw *them,* he rose to
meet them, and he bowed himself with his
face toward the ground. 2And he said, "Here
now, my lords, please turn in to your servant's
house and spend the night, and wash your
feet; then you may rise early and go on your
way."
And they said, "No, but we will spend the
night in the open square."
3But he insisted strongly; so they turned in

SOUL NOTE

Being There *(18:19)* God chose Abraham, desiring that he "command his children" regarding the way of the Lord, righteousness, and justice. This implies that Abraham would be involved in his children's lives in order to teach them.

A parent's caring involvement in his or her children's lives is a crucial factor in the children's development. Being a great parent starts with knowing God and is fulfilled in consistent teaching, fair discipline, and loving actions toward one's children. Clearly God expects parents to be present in their children's lives to teach them the way of the Lord.

Topic: Child Development

KEY PASSAGE

Abuse

TRAGIC CHAIN OF EVENTS

(19:4–9)

Lot's terrible actions reveal the tragic chain of events that often occurs in sexual abuse cases. When he shockingly suggested that the evil men rape his daughters instead of his guests, Lot was trying to substitute one sexual sin for another. He jeopardized his own daughters and violated his responsibility as a parent. Despite the angels' miraculous intervention (Gen. 19:11), the spiritual and psychological damage had been done. The daughters' later incestuous relationships with their father was another link in the chain reaction of sexual abuse (Gen. 19:30–38).

Sexual abuse, in any form, results in low self-esteem, conflict over sexual identity, inability to trust, isolation, and feelings of guilt and shame. It can result in long-term physical and psychological damage. As in the case of all sinful actions, the abuser usually fabricates a rationale for his or her conduct. The morbid story of Lot's daughters illustrates this all too well.

To Learn More: Turn to the article about abuse on pages 328, 329. See also the personality profile of the Levite's concubine on page 327.

to him and entered his house. Then he made them a feast, and baked unleavened bread, and they ate.

4Now before they lay down, the men of the city, the men of Sodom, both old and young, all the people from every quarter, surrounded the house. 5And they called to Lot and said to him, "Where are the men who came to you tonight? Bring them out to us that we may know them *carnally*."

6So Lot went out to them through the doorway, shut the door behind him, 7and said, "Please, my brethren, do not do so wickedly! 8See now, I have two daughters who have not known a man; please, let me bring them out to you, and you may do to them as you wish; only do nothing to these men, since this is the reason they have come under the shadow of my roof."

9And they said, "Stand back!" Then they said, "This one came in to stay *here*, and he keeps acting as a judge; now we will deal worse with you than with them." So they pressed hard against the man Lot, and came near to break down the door. 10But the men reached out their hands and pulled Lot into the house with them, and shut the door. 11And they struck the men who *were* at the doorway of the house with blindness, both small and great, so that they became weary *trying* to find the door.

Sodom and Gomorrah Destroyed

12Then the men said to Lot, "Have you anyone else here? Son-in-law, your sons, your daughters, and whomever you have in the city—take *them* out of this place! 13For we will destroy this place, because the outcry against them has grown great before the face of the LORD, and the LORD has sent us to destroy it."

14So Lot went out and spoke to his sons-in-law, who had married his daughters, and said, "Get up, get out of this place; for the LORD will

PERSONALITY PROFILE

Boundaries

LOT'S BLURRED BOUNDARIES

(GENESIS 19)

When Lot settled near Sodom (Gen. 13:12), he picked a dangerous neighborhood. Lot's life teaches us that problems inevitably follow our poor decisions—even decisions that look very good when they are made. When our choices leave our boundaries too open to the ways of the world, we place ourselves at risk. And sometimes we place others at risk, too.

Lot was Abraham's nephew. They traveled together from Mesopotamia when Abraham set out on his journey of obedience. By the time the two men were ready to settle in Canaan, both were wealthy. Their flocks were vying for the same grazing lands. Abraham suggested a parting of their households and gave Lot the first choice. Lot picked the Jordan valley near Sodom as an ideal location for his animals. What is best for livestock may not be good for people, however. Living in and around Sodom eventually corrupted Lot and his family. He later had to be dragged out of Sodom one step ahead of destruction. He lost his wife and all his earthly possessions. Lot paid a high price for blurred boundaries.

As it did for Lot, too much worldliness can have negative effects. Our boundaries are at risk when we dabble in activities and live by the world's values. What others call entertainment often turns out to be a web of gradual entrapment. Increasing numbness toward sinful behavior indicates breached boundaries.

God's Word provides dependable boundaries. Even the Ten Commandments (Ex. 20) describe important limits. We need God's wisdom in sharpening blurred boundaries. He can help us decide what it means for us to live the life that Jesus described as in the world, but not of the world (John 17). We also need God's help in rebuilding and guarding our breached boundaries. Lot's losses should provide a sobering incentive.

To Learn More: Turn to the article about boundaries on pages 106, 107. See also the key passage note at 2 Corinthians 6:14 on page 1525.

destroy this city!" But to his sons-in-law he
seemed to be joking.
[15]When the morning dawned, the angels
urged Lot to hurry, saying, "Arise, take your
wife and your two daughters who are here,
lest you be consumed in the punishment of
the city." [16]And while he lingered, the men
took hold of his hand, his wife's hand, and the
hands of his two daughters, the LORD being
merciful to him, and they brought him out and
set him outside the city. [17]So it came to pass,
when they had brought them outside, that he[a]
said, "Escape for your life! Do not look behind
you nor stay anywhere in the plain. Escape to
the mountains, lest you be destroyed."
[18]Then Lot said to them, "Please, no, my
lords! [19]Indeed now, your servant has found
favor in your sight, and you have increased
your mercy which you have shown me by saving my life; but I cannot escape to the mountains, lest some evil overtake me and I die.
[20]See now, this city *is* near *enough* to flee to,
and it *is* a little one; please let me escape there
(*is* it not a little one?) and my soul shall live."
[21]And he said to him, "See, I have favored
you concerning this thing also, in that I will
not overthrow this city for which you have
spoken. [22]Hurry, escape there. For I cannot do
anything until you arrive there."
Therefore the name of the city was called
Zoar.
[23]The sun had risen upon the earth when
Lot entered Zoar. [24]Then the LORD rained
brimstone and fire on Sodom and Gomorrah,
from the LORD out of the heavens. [25]So He
overthrew those cities, all the plain, all the inhabitants of the cities, and what grew on the
ground.

19:17 [a]Septuagint, Syriac, and Vulgate read *they.*

PERSONALITY PROFILE

Homo-sexuality

SODOM'S FEARFUL FATE

(GENESIS 19)

Few places in the world care to vie with Sodom's reputation for immorality. The city was ripe for God's judgment. Perversely empowered by a mob mentality, a gang of Sodomite men demanded that Lot hand over two guests for homosexual rape. Their identity as God's messengers mattered little to the mob, but it sealed the fate of the city.

The deep question is not whether the "sin of Sodom" was violence or sexual perversion, but how both these behaviors became the character of a city. Perversity rarely takes over a single part of life. It appears in multiple forms—poly-perversity.

By the time Abraham and Lot visited Sodom, the city had degenerated into a festering cesspool of sin and immorality. The destruction of the city after Abraham's negotiation with God indicates that there were not even ten righteous souls left within its walls. So God sent his angel messengers to warn Lot and his family and help them escape before destruction rained down on the city.

In spite of efforts by some of today's gay theologians to revise and reinterpret Sodom's story, the clear message of Genesis 19 has always referred to homosexual violence. It is generally thought that the Sodomites also practiced bestiality, sex with children and adolescents, heterosexual rape, and adultery, along with other unspeakable forms of sexual perversity and violence. The severity of their punishment ought not to conceal the horrors of their behavior.

Though both homosexuality and rape are consistently condemned in the Scriptures, they are not isolated from other sexual sins, or sin in general. Whether heterosexual sin or homosexual sin, God calls us to forsake all sexual sin and to know the transforming power of His redeeming and healing grace. To choose otherwise puts us in the company of the citizens of Sodom.

To Learn More: Turn to the article about homosexuality on pages 1466, 1467. See also the key passage note at Romans 1:18–32 on page 1465.

[26]But his wife looked back behind him, and
she became a pillar of salt.
[27]And Abraham went early in the morning
to the place where he had stood before the
LORD. [28]Then he looked toward Sodom and
Gomorrah, and toward all the land of the
plain; and he saw, and behold, the smoke of
the land which went up like the smoke of a
furnace. [29]And it came to pass, when God destroyed the cities of the plain, that God remembered Abraham, and sent Lot out of the
midst of the overthrow, when He overthrew
the cities in which Lot had dwelt.

The Descendants of Lot

[30]Then Lot went up out of Zoar and dwelt in
the mountains, and his two daughters were
with him; for he was afraid to dwell in Zoar.
And he and his two daughters dwelt in a cave.
[31]Now the firstborn said to the younger, "Our
father *is* old, and *there is* no man on the earth
to come in to us as is the custom of all the
earth. [32]Come, let us make our father drink
wine, and we will lie with him, that we may
preserve the lineage of our father." [33]So they
made their father drink wine that night. And
the firstborn went in and lay with her father,
and he did not know when she lay down or
when she arose.
[34]It happened on the next day that the firstborn said to the younger, "Indeed I lay with
my father last night; let us make him drink
wine tonight also, and you go in *and* lie with
him, that we may preserve the lineage of our
father." [35]Then they made their father drink
wine that night also. And the younger arose
and lay with him, and he did not know when
she lay down or when she arose.
[36]Thus both the daughters of Lot were with
child by their father. [37]The firstborn bore a son
and called his name Moab; he *is* the father of
the Moabites to this day. [38]And the younger,
she also bore a son and called his name Ben-
Ammi; he *is* the father of the people of Ammon to this day.

Abraham and Abimelech

20 And Abraham journeyed from there to
the South, and dwelt between Kadesh
and Shur, and stayed in Gerar. [2]Now Abraham
said of Sarah his wife, "She *is* my sister." And
Abimelech king of Gerar sent and took Sarah.
[3]But God came to Abimelech in a dream by
night, and said to him, "Indeed you *are* a dead
man because of the woman whom you have
taken, for she *is* a man's wife."
[4]But Abimelech had not come near her; and
he said, "Lord, will You slay a righteous nation also? [5]Did he not say to me, 'She *is* my sister'? And she, even she herself said, 'He *is* my
brother.' In the integrity of my heart and innocence of my hands I have done this."
[6]And God said to him in a dream, "Yes, I
know that you did this in the integrity of your
heart. For I also withheld you from sinning
against Me; therefore I did not let you touch
her. [7]Now therefore, restore the man's wife;
for he *is* a prophet, and he will pray for you
and you shall live. But if you do not restore
her, know that you shall surely die, you and all
who *are* yours."
[8]So Abimelech rose early in the morning,
called all his servants, and told all these things
in their hearing; and the men were very much
afraid. [9]And Abimelech called Abraham and
said to him, "What have you done to us? How
have I offended you, that you have brought on
me and on my kingdom a great sin? You have
done deeds to me that ought not to be done."
[10]Then Abimelech said to Abraham, "What
did you have in view, that you have done this
thing?"
[11]And Abraham said, "Because I thought,
surely the fear of God *is* not in this place; and

SOUL NOTE

When Changes Come *(19:26)* The Bible tells little about Lot's wife except that she "looked back" at Sodom. The angels had dragged Lot and his family out of the doomed city, warning them not to look behind as they fled (19:16, 17). Why did Lot's wife disobey? Did she miss the comfort of the place? Did she fear the unknown future? Change can be difficult, because it means exchanging familiarity for the unknown. But God is with us; He is the constant even as our lives keep changing. He knows what is unknown, so trust Him and don't look back. **Topic: Life Transitions**

they will kill me on account of my wife. [12]But
indeed *she is* truly my sister. She *is* the daughter of my father, but not the daughter of my
mother; and she became my wife. [13]And it
came to pass, when God caused me to wander
from my father's house, that I said to her,
'This *is* your kindness that you should do for
me: in every place, wherever we go, say of me,
"He *is* my brother." ' "
[14]Then Abimelech took sheep, oxen, and
male and female servants, and gave *them* to
Abraham; and he restored Sarah his wife to
him. [15]And Abimelech said, "See, my land *is*
before you; dwell where it pleases you."
[16]Then to Sarah he said, "Behold, I have given
your brother a thousand *pieces* of silver; indeed this vindicates you[a] before all who *are*
with you and before everybody." Thus she
was rebuked.
[17]So Abraham prayed to God; and God
healed Abimelech, his wife, and his female
servants. Then they bore *children;* [18]for the
LORD had closed up all the wombs of the
house of Abimelech because of Sarah, Abraham's wife.

ISAAC IS BORN

21 And the LORD visited Sarah as He had
said, and the LORD did for Sarah as He
had spoken. [2]For Sarah conceived and bore
Abraham a son in his old age, at the set time
of which God had spoken to him. [3]And Abraham called the name of his son who was born
to him—whom Sarah bore to him—Isaac.
[4]Then Abraham circumcised his son Isaac
when he was eight days old, as God had commanded him. [5]Now Abraham was one hundred years old when his son Isaac was born to
him. [6]And Sarah said, "God has made me
laugh, *and* all who hear will laugh with me."
[7]She also said, "Who would have said to Abraham that Sarah would nurse children? For I
have borne *him* a son in his old age."

20:16 [a]Literally *it is a covering of the eyes for you*

PERSONALITY PROFILE

Joy

ISAAC: UNEXPECTED LAUGHTER

(GENESIS 21)

When did Isaac discover he was the punch line of a joke? His parents were so old when God informed them about his arrival that they laughed out loud. Abraham and Sarah's incredulity in the face of God's promise was best contradicted by their descendant Jesus when He said, "The things which are impossible with men are possible with God" (Luke 18:27).

From a human perspective, God's plan was laughable. It flew in the face of common sense. Ninety-year-old women don't get pregnant. Sarah knew about God's long-standing promise to her husband. She had even tried to make it come true by arranging for her husband to have a child with her slave Hagar. But God had other plans.

Like the unexpected final words of a hilarious comment, Sarah turned up pregnant in her old age. When Isaac was born, she named him "laughter." What else would fit a child who had caused such mirth? Sarah voiced her mixture of delight and embarrassment when she said, "God has made me laugh, and all who hear will laugh with me" (Gen. 21:6).

The result of trust in God takes the form of joy, which instigates genuine laughter. The psalmist wrote, "Weeping may endure for a night, but joy comes in the morning" (Ps. 30:5). Sarah may have laughed in disbelief or even in frustration as the years rolled by, but when Isaac was born, she discovered what real laughter felt like. The rich laughter that rises in those who have known God's faithfulness expresses a deep satisfaction.

God will be faithful to His promises in your life. You may have to wait, but the joy God brings will be as real to you as the laughter that finally filled Sarah's life.

To Learn More: Turn to the article about joy on pages 614, 615. See also the key passage note at Proverbs 15:13–15 on page 817.

HAGAR AND ISHMAEL DEPART

8So the child grew and was weaned. And
Abraham made a great feast on the same day
that Isaac was weaned.
9And Sarah saw the son of Hagar the Egyptian, whom she had borne to Abraham, scoff-
ing. 10Therefore she said to Abraham, "Cast
out this bondwoman and her son; for the son
of this bondwoman shall not be heir with my
son, *namely* with Isaac." 11And the matter was
very displeasing in Abraham's sight because
of his son.
12But God said to Abraham, "Do not let it be
displeasing in your sight because of the lad or
because of your bondwoman. Whatever Sarah
has said to you, listen to her voice; for in Isaac
your seed shall be called. 13Yet I will also
make a nation of the son of the bondwoman,
because he *is* your seed."
14So Abraham rose early in the morning,
and took bread and a skin of water; and putting *it* on her shoulder, he gave *it* and the boy
to Hagar, and sent her away. Then she departed and wandered in the Wilderness of Beersheba. 15And the water in the skin was used
up, and she placed the boy under one of the
shrubs. 16Then she went and sat down across
from *him* at a distance of about a bowshot; for
she said to herself, "Let me not see the death
of the boy." So she sat opposite *him,* and lifted
her voice and wept.
17And God heard the voice of the lad. Then
the angel of God called to Hagar out of heav-
en, and said to her, "What ails you, Hagar?
Fear not, for God has heard the voice of the
lad where he *is.* 18Arise, lift up the lad and
hold him with your hand, for I will make him
a great nation."
19Then God opened her eyes, and she saw a
well of water. And she went and filled the skin
with water, and gave the lad a drink. 20So God
was with the lad; and he grew and dwelt in the
wilderness, and became an archer. 21He dwelt
in the Wilderness of Paran; and his mother
took a wife for him from the land of Egypt.

A COVENANT WITH ABIMELECH

22And it came to pass at that time that
Abimelech and Phichol, the commander of his
army, spoke to Abraham, saying, "God *is* with
you in all that you do. 23Now therefore, swear
to me by God that you will not deal falsely
with me, with my offspring, or with my posterity; but that according to the kindness that I
have done to you, you will do to me and to the
land in which you have dwelt."
24And Abraham said, "I will swear."
25Then Abraham rebuked Abimelech because of a well of water which Abimelech's
servants had seized. 26And Abimelech said, "I
do not know who has done this thing; you did

KEY PASSAGE

Blended Families

BLENDING TWO FAMILIES

(21:9–11)

Blended families face special challenges, as Abraham discovered. From the beginning, it had been Sarah's idea to use Hagar, the slave girl, as a surrogate mother for their heir Ishmael (Gen. 16:1–16). But once Sarah had Isaac, her attitude quickly changed. By the time Isaac was born, Ishmael was a teenager. Some time later, when little Isaac was weaned, Ishmael "scoffed" (mocked him) at the family feast, setting off Sarah's anger (Gen. 21:9). In this case, God advised Abraham to send Hagar and Ishmael away, for the covenant promise was to be accomplished through Isaac. Yet God intervened miraculously to spare Hagar and Ishmael, showing His love and grace to the rejected woman and her child (Gen. 21:14–21).

Blended families need special wisdom from God in order to bring together two separate worlds and to love each other unconditionally. And for those who feel that they have been "sent away," God promises grace and provision, saying, "Fear not" (Gen. 21:17).

To Learn More: Turn to the article about blended families on pages 46, 47. See also the personality profile of Jacob's family on page 45.

not tell me, nor had I heard *of it* until today." [27]So Abraham took sheep and oxen and gave them to Abimelech, and the two of them made a covenant. [28]And Abraham set seven ewe lambs of the flock by themselves.

[29]Then Abimelech asked Abraham, "What *is the meaning of* these seven ewe lambs which you have set by themselves?"

[30]And he said, "You will take *these* seven ewe lambs from my hand, that they may be my witness that I have dug this well." [31]Therefore he called that place Beersheba,[a] because the two of them swore an oath there.

[32]Thus they made a covenant at Beersheba. So Abimelech rose with Phichol, the commander of his army, and they returned to the land of the Philistines. [33]Then *Abraham* planted a tamarisk tree in Beersheba, and there called on the name of the LORD, the Everlasting God. [34]And Abraham stayed in the land of the Philistines many days.

ABRAHAM'S FAITH CONFIRMED

22 Now it came to pass after these things that God tested Abraham, and said to him, "Abraham!"

And he said, "Here I am."

[2]Then He said, "Take now your son, your only *son* Isaac, whom you love, and go to the land of Moriah, and offer him there as a burnt offering on one of the mountains of which I shall tell you."

[3]So Abraham rose early in the morning and saddled his donkey, and took two of his young men with him, and Isaac his son; and he split the wood for the burnt offering, and arose and went to the place of which God had told him. [4]Then on the third day Abraham lifted his eyes and saw the place afar off. [5]And Abraham said to his young men, "Stay here with the donkey; the lad[a] and I will go yonder and worship, and we will come back to you."

[6]So Abraham took the wood of the burnt offering and laid *it* on Isaac his son; and he took the fire in his hand, and a knife, and the two of them went together. [7]But Isaac spoke to Abraham his father and said, "My father!"

And he said, "Here I am, my son."

Then he said, "Look, the fire and the wood, but where *is* the lamb for a burnt offering?"

[8]And Abraham said, "My son, God will provide for Himself the lamb for a burnt offering." So the two of them went together.

[9]Then they came to the place of which God had told him. And Abraham built an altar there and placed the wood in order; and he bound Isaac his son and laid him on the altar, upon the wood. [10]And Abraham stretched out his hand and took the knife to slay his son.

[11]But the Angel of the LORD called to him from heaven and said, "Abraham, Abraham!"

So he said, "Here I am."

[12]And He said, "Do not lay your hand on the lad, or do anything to him; for now I know that you fear God, since you have not withheld your son, your only *son,* from Me."

[13]Then Abraham lifted his eyes and looked, and there behind *him was* a ram caught in a thicket by its horns. So Abraham went and took the ram, and offered it up for a burnt offering instead of his son. [14]And Abraham called the name of the place, The-LORD-Will-Provide;[a] as it is said *to* this day, "In the Mount of the LORD it shall be provided."

[15]Then the Angel of the LORD called to Abraham a second time out of heaven, [16]and said: "By Myself I have sworn, says the LORD, because you have done this thing, and have not withheld your son, your only *son*— [17]blessing I will bless you, and multiplying I will multiply your descendants as the stars of the heaven and as the sand which *is* on the seashore; and your descendants shall possess the gate of their enemies. [18]In your seed all the nations of the earth shall be blessed, because you have obeyed My voice." [19]So Abraham returned to his young men, and they rose and went together to Beersheba; and Abraham dwelt at Beersheba.

THE FAMILY OF NAHOR

[20]Now it came to pass after these things that it was told Abraham, saying, "Indeed Milcah also has borne children to your brother Nahor: [21]Huz his firstborn, Buz his brother, Kemuel the father of Aram, [22]Chesed, Hazo, Pildash, Jidlaph, and Bethuel." [23]And Bethuel begot Rebekah.[a] These eight Milcah bore to Nahor, Abraham's brother. [24]His concubine, whose name was Reumah, also bore Tebah, Gaham, Thahash, and Maachah.

21:31 [a]Literally *Well of the Oath* or *Well of the Seven* **22:5** [a]Or *young man* **22:14** [a]Hebrew *YHWH Yireh* **22:23** [a]Spelled *Rebecca* in Romans 9:10

Sarah's Death and Burial

23 Sarah lived one hundred and twenty-seven years; *these were* the years of the life of Sarah. 2So Sarah died in Kirjath Arba (that *is,* Hebron) in the land of Canaan, and Abraham came to mourn for Sarah and to weep for her.

3Then Abraham stood up from before his dead, and spoke to the sons of Heth, saying, 4"I *am* a foreigner and a visitor among you. Give me property for a burial place among you, that I may bury my dead out of my sight."

5And the sons of Heth answered Abraham, saying to him, 6"Hear us, my lord: You *are* a mighty prince among us; bury your dead in the choicest of our burial places. None of us will withhold from you his burial place, that you may bury your dead."

7Then Abraham stood up and bowed himself to the people of the land, the sons of Heth. 8And he spoke with them, saying, "If it is your wish that I bury my dead out of my sight, hear me, and meet with Ephron the son of Zohar for me, 9that he may give me the cave of Machpelah which he has, which *is* at the end of his field. Let him give it to me at the full price, as property for a burial place among you."

10Now Ephron dwelt among the sons of Heth; and Ephron the Hittite answered Abraham in the presence of the sons of Heth, all who entered at the gate of his city, saying, 11"No, my lord, hear me: I give you the field and the cave that *is* in it; I give it to you in the presence of the sons of my people. I give it to you. Bury your dead!"

12Then Abraham bowed himself down before the people of the land; 13and he spoke to Ephron in the hearing of the people of the land, saying, "If you *will give it,* please hear me. I will give you money for the field; take *it* from me and I will bury my dead there."

14And Ephron answered Abraham, saying to him, 15"My lord, listen to me; the land *is worth* four hundred shekels of silver. What *is* that between you and me? So bury your dead." 16And Abraham listened to Ephron; and Abraham weighed out the silver for Ephron which he had named in the hearing of the sons of Heth, four hundred shekels of silver, currency of the merchants.

17So the field of Ephron which *was* in Machpelah, which *was* before Mamre, the field and the cave which *was* in it, and all the trees that *were* in the field, which *were* within all the surrounding borders, were deeded 18to Abraham as a possession in the presence of the sons of Heth, before all who went in at the gate of his city.

19And after this, Abraham buried Sarah his wife in the cave of the field of Machpelah, before Mamre (that *is,* Hebron) in the land of Canaan. 20So the field and the cave that *is* in it were deeded to Abraham by the sons of Heth as property for a burial place.

A Bride for Isaac

24 Now Abraham was old, well advanced in age; and the LORD had blessed Abraham in all things. 2So Abraham said to the oldest servant of his house, who ruled over all that he had, "Please, put your hand under my thigh, 3and I will make you swear by the LORD, the God of heaven and the God of the earth, that you will not take a wife for my son from the daughters of the Canaanites, among whom I dwell; 4but you shall go to my country and to my family, and take a wife for my son Isaac."

5And the servant said to him, "Perhaps the woman will not be willing to follow me to this land. Must I take your son back to the land from which you came?"

6But Abraham said to him, "Beware that you do not take my son back there. 7The LORD God of heaven, who took me from my father's house and from the land of my family, and who spoke to me and swore to me, saying, 'To your descendants[a] I give this land,' He will send His angel before you, and you shall take a wife for my son from there. 8And if the woman is not willing to follow you, then you will be released from this oath; only do not take my son back there." 9So the servant put his hand under the thigh of Abraham his master, and swore to him concerning this matter.

10Then the servant took ten of his master's camels and departed, for all his master's goods *were in* his hand. And he arose and went to Mesopotamia, to the city of Nahor. 11And he made his camels kneel down outside the city by a well of water at evening time, the time when women go out to draw *water.* 12Then he said, "O LORD God of my master Abraham, please give me success this day,

---

24:7 [a]Literally *seed*

and show kindness to my master Abraham.
13Behold, *here* I stand by the well of water,
and the daughters of the men of the city are
coming out to draw water. 14Now let it be that
the young woman to whom I say, 'Please let
down your pitcher that I may drink,' and she
says, 'Drink, and I will also give your camels a
drink'—*let* her *be the one* You have appointed
for Your servant Isaac. And by this I will know
that You have shown kindness to my master."

15And it happened, before he had finished
speaking, that behold, Rebekah, who was
born to Bethuel, son of Milcah, the wife of Nahor, Abraham's brother, came out with her
pitcher on her shoulder. 16Now the young
woman *was* very beautiful to behold, a virgin;
no man had known her. And she went down
to the well, filled her pitcher, and came up.
17And the servant ran to meet her and said,
"Please let me drink a little water from your
pitcher."

18So she said, "Drink, my lord." Then she
quickly let her pitcher down to her hand, and
gave him a drink. 19And when she had finished giving him a drink, she said, "I will
draw *water* for your camels also, until they
have finished drinking." 20Then she quickly
emptied her pitcher into the trough, ran back
to the well to draw *water,* and drew for all his
camels. 21And the man, wondering at her, remained silent so as to know whether the LORD
had made his journey prosperous or not.

22So it was, when the camels had finished
drinking, that the man took a golden nose ring
weighing half a shekel, and two bracelets for
her wrists weighing ten *shekels* of gold, 23and
said, "Whose daughter *are* you? Tell me,
please, is there room *in* your father's house
for us to lodge?"

24So she said to him, "I *am* the daughter of
Bethuel, Milcah's son, whom she bore to Nahor." 25Moreover she said to him, "We have
both straw and feed enough, and room to
lodge."

26Then the man bowed down his head and
worshiped the LORD. 27And he said, "Blessed
be the LORD God of my master Abraham, who
has not forsaken His mercy and His truth toward my master. As for me, being on the way,
the LORD led me to the house of my master's
brethren." 28So the young woman ran and told
her mother's household these things.

29Now Rebekah had a brother whose name
was Laban, and Laban ran out to the man by
the well. 30So it came to pass, when he saw
the nose ring, and the bracelets on his sister's
wrists, and when he heard the words of his
sister Rebekah, saying, "Thus the man spoke
to me," that he went to the man. And there he
stood by the camels at the well. 31And he said,
"Come in, O blessed of the LORD! Why do you
stand outside? For I have prepared the house,
and a place for the camels."

32Then the man came to the house. And he
unloaded the camels, and provided straw and
feed for the camels, and water to wash his feet
and the feet of the men who *were* with him.
33*Food* was set before him to eat, but he said, "I
will not eat until I have told about my errand."

And he said, "Speak on."

34So he said, "I *am* Abraham's servant.
35The LORD has blessed my master greatly, and
he has become great; and He has given him
flocks and herds, silver and gold, male and
female servants, and camels and donkeys.
36And Sarah my master's wife bore a son to
my master when she was old; and to him he
has given all that he has. 37Now my master
made me swear, saying, 'You shall not take a
wife for my son from the daughters of the Canaanites, in whose land I dwell; 38but you
shall go to my father's house and to my family, and take a wife for my son.' 39And I said to
my master, 'Perhaps the woman will not follow me.' 40But he said to me, 'The LORD, before whom I walk, will send His angel with
you and prosper your way; and you shall take
a wife for my son from my family and from my
father's house. 41You will be clear from this
oath when you arrive among my family; for if
they will not give *her* to you, then you will be
released from my oath.'

42"And this day I came to the well and said,
'O LORD God of my master Abraham, if You
will now prosper the way in which I go, 43be-
hold, I stand by the well of water; and it shall
come to pass that when the virgin comes out
to draw *water,* and I say to her, "Please give
me a little water from your pitcher to drink,"
44and she says to me, "Drink, and I will draw
for your camels also,"—*let* her *be* the woman
whom the LORD has appointed for my
master's son.'

45"But before I had finished speaking in my
heart, there was Rebekah, coming out with
her pitcher on her shoulder; and she went
down to the well and drew *water.* And I said
to her, 'Please let me drink.' 46And she made

haste and let her pitcher down from her *shoul-*
der, and said, 'Drink, and I will give your camels a drink also.' So I drank, and she gave the
camels a drink also. 47Then I asked her, and
said, 'Whose daughter *are* you?' And she said,
'The daughter of Bethuel, Nahor's son, whom
Milcah bore to him.' So I put the nose ring on
her nose and the bracelets on her wrists. 48And
I bowed my head and worshiped the LORD, and
blessed the LORD God of my master Abraham,
who had led me in the way of truth to take the
daughter of my master's brother for his son.
49Now if you will deal kindly and truly with
my master, tell me. And if not, tell me, that I
may turn to the right hand or to the left."

50Then Laban and Bethuel answered and
said, "The thing comes from the LORD; we cannot speak to you either bad or good. 51Here *is*
Rebekah before you; take *her* and go, and let
her be your master's son's wife, as the LORD
has spoken."

52And it came to pass, when Abraham's servant heard their words, that he worshiped the
LORD, *bowing himself* to the earth. 53Then the
servant brought out jewelry of silver, jewelry of
gold, and clothing, and gave *them* to Rebekah.
He also gave precious things to her brother and
to her mother.

54And he and the men who *were* with him
ate and drank and stayed all night. Then they
arose in the morning, and he said, "Send me
away to my master."

55But her brother and her mother said, "Let
the young woman stay with us *a few* days, at
least ten; after that she may go."

56And he said to them, "Do not hinder me,
since the LORD has prospered my way; send
me away so that I may go to my master."

57So they said, "We will call the young
woman and ask her personally." 58Then they
called Rebekah and said to her, "Will you go
with this man?"

And she said, "I will go."

59So they sent away Rebekah their sister and
her nurse, and Abraham's servant and his men.
60And they blessed Rebekah and said to her:

"Our sister, *may* you *become*
The mother of thousands of ten
thousands;
And may your descendants possess
The gates of those who hate them."

61Then Rebekah and her maids arose, and
they rode on the camels and followed the
man. So the servant took Rebekah and departed.

62Now Isaac came from the way of Beer Lahai Roi, for he dwelt in the South. 63And Isaac
went out to meditate in the field in the evening; and he lifted his eyes and looked, and
there, the camels *were* coming. 64Then Rebekah lifted her eyes, and when she saw Isaac
she dismounted from her camel; 65for she had
said to the servant, "Who *is* this man walking
in the field to meet us?"

The servant said, "It *is* my master." So she
took a veil and covered herself.

66And the servant told Isaac all the things
that he had done. 67Then Isaac brought her
into his mother Sarah's tent; and he took Rebekah and she became his wife, and he loved
her. So Isaac was comforted after his mother's
death.

ABRAHAM AND KETURAH

25 Abraham again took a wife, and her
name *was* Keturah. 2And she bore
him Zimran, Jokshan, Medan, Midian, Ishbak, and Shuah. 3Jokshan begot Sheba and
Dedan. And the sons of Dedan were Asshu-
rim, Letushim, and Leummim. 4And the sons
of Midian *were* Ephah, Epher, Hanoch,
Abidah, and Eldaah. All these *were* the children of Keturah.

5And Abraham gave all that he had to Isaac.
6But Abraham gave gifts to the sons of the
concubines which Abraham had; and while
he was still living he sent them eastward,
away from Isaac his son, to the country of the
east.

ABRAHAM'S DEATH AND BURIAL

7This *is* the sum of the years of Abraham's
life which he lived: one hundred and seventy-
five years. 8Then Abraham breathed his last
and died in a good old age, an old man and
full *of years,* and was gathered to his people.
9And his sons Isaac and Ishmael buried him
in the cave of Machpelah, which *is* before
Mamre, in the field of Ephron the son of Zohar the Hittite, 10the field which Abraham
purchased from the sons of Heth. There Abraham was buried, and Sarah his wife. 11And it
came to pass, after the death of Abraham,
that God blessed his son Isaac. And Isaac
dwelt at Beer Lahai Roi.

The Families of Ishmael and Isaac

[12]Now this *is* the genealogy of Ishmael,
Abraham's son, whom Hagar the Egyptian,
Sarah's maidservant, bore to Abraham. [13]And
these *were* the names of the sons of Ishmael,
by their names, according to their generations: The firstborn of Ishmael, Nebajoth;
then Kedar, Adbeel, Mibsam, [14]Mishma, Dumah, Massa, [15]Hadar,[a] Tema, Jetur, Naphish,
and Kedemah. [16]These *were* the sons of Ishmael and these *were* their names, by their
towns and their settlements, twelve princes
according to their nations. [17]These *were* the
years of the life of Ishmael: one hundred and
thirty-seven years; and he breathed his last
and died, and was gathered to his people.
[18](They dwelt from Havilah as far as Shur,
which *is* east of Egypt as you go toward
Assyria.) He died in the presence of all his
brethren.

[19]This *is* the genealogy of Isaac, Abraham's
son. Abraham begot Isaac. [20]Isaac was forty
years old when he took Rebekah as wife, the
daughter of Bethuel the Syrian of Padan Aram,
the sister of Laban the Syrian. [21]Now Isaac
pleaded with the LORD for his wife, because
she *was* barren; and the LORD granted his plea,
and Rebekah his wife conceived. [22]But the
children struggled together within her; and
she said, "If *all is* well, why *am I like* this?" So
she went to inquire of the LORD.

[23]And the LORD said to her:

"Two nations *are* in your womb,

25:15 [a]Masoretic Text reads *Hadad.*

PERSONALITY PROFILE

Family Problems

ABRAHAM TO JOSEPH: A BLESSED AND DYSFUNCTIONAL FAMILY TREE

(GENESIS 25)

There are no hidden skeletons in Abraham's family closets. Their sins and failures lie bare for the world to see. These people knew God, and sometimes it didn't make much difference in their behavior. From Abraham through Isaac and Jacob to Joseph—every generation was both blessed by God and wracked with sin and deceit.

Abraham failed to wait for the son of promise and bore Ishmael by a slave girl. The resulting enmity haunts his descendants to this day. Isaac and Rebekah lived at odds with each other in their marriage. Their differences led to deceit and pain in the lives of their twin sons, Jacob and Esau. Later, Jacob's favoritism rankled most of his sons. They, in turn, deceived their father into living with years of grief because he thought his favorite son Joseph had been killed. In the pages of Genesis we read of unfair comparisons, favoritism, divided loyalties, competition, greed, and envy.

Yet the patriarchs knew and loved God. Even though they couldn't always live up to their faith, they lived by it. These men had no Bibles to read, no church to attend, no accountability groups. When God spoke, they listened, and they did their best to pass that reverence for God on to their children. They cherished and clung to the promise God made to Abraham. They believed in their bones that God would remain faithful. Did they love God? Certainly. Did they make mistakes in daily living? Who doesn't? Yet God reported their failures to offer us hope: If He kept His promises with them, He will keep them with us.

Today's families are no more perfect—except that we do have God's Word to teach us and people around us to help. The family is the most powerful influence on children's lives. Make your home a place of refuge, love, stability, provision, protection, and learning about God. Then trust God to keep His promises.

To Learn More: Turn to the article about family problems on pages 38, 39. See also the key passage note at Genesis 37:3 on page 58.

Family Problems

NO PERFECT FAMILIES

DAVID STOOP

(Genesis 25)

How difficult it is for a family that is facing difficult problems. When a family is in pain, the family members hurt deeply. Parents mourn when their older children rebel. Siblings may struggle with rivalry. There are as many types of family problems as there are families. Usually a family embroiled in a problem feels as though they are the only ones who have ever suffered in that way. But even the great families of the Bible had problems.

One of Adam and Eve's sons murdered their other son. Genesis continues to record the histories of several families that also had serious problems. God worked mightily in the lives of Abraham and Sarah and their descendants, but that did not exempt those families from having struggles.

Family problems are directly related to the reality of sin—sometimes a specific sin, sometimes sinfulness in general. All families are touched by each individual's inherent sinfulness. While all sin is the same in God's eyes, sins have varying degrees of effect on families. And different families will deal differently with different sins.

So when an ugly problem rears its head in a family, how can the family members discover its source, define it, and deal with it?

DISCOVERING AND DEFINING THE PROBLEM

When there are problems in a family, the natural tendency is to want to define the problem, place the blame, and then try to fix it. How we define the problem will determine whom we will blame, as well as the solutions we will try. For instance, in the story of Jacob and Esau in Genesis 25, the problem could be defined in different ways: the sibling rivalry between Jacob and Esau, Esau's impulsiveness, Jacob's greed, or Isaac and Rebekah's parenting.

Depending on who gets blamed, one might suggest for a solution that Esau and Jacob learn to get along, or that Esau learn more self-control, or that Jacob practice generosity, or that Rebekah and Isaac improve their parenting skills. Although these proposed solutions might produce some short-term results, the family patterns would probably change very little. A different approach is necessary.

DEALING WITH THE PROBLEM

Looking for the Patterns
Most family problems have to do with patterns that have been occurring over time. For example, the competition between Jacob and Esau was part of a larger pattern that had existed for several generations. Genesis 25:28 says that Isaac loved Esau but Rebekah loved Jacob. This shows a pattern of favoritism in this family.

In the family's previous generation, the same pattern of favoring one child over another occurred with Abraham and Sarah when they favored Isaac and rejected Ishmael (Gen. 21). The family pattern of favoritism would be repeated in Jacob's family as he would favor one of his wives, and then would favor that wife's children. Across four generations of Abraham's family, each generation had a pattern of favoring some family members and rejecting others.

Each family facing difficult problems should dig deeply and be objective in order to find a pattern that may have been in place for years, perhaps even generations. This part of the process will require honesty and careful self-evaluation, but identifying a pattern is the only way to correctly diagnose and then deal with the problem.

Facing the Truth

After discovering the patterns that have created the current problems, the next step is a willingness to face the truth. When families are not willing to acknowledge the patterns that are causing problems, those patterns will only continue. Sometimes it is necessary to find an objective, trustworthy person from outside the family who can explore the family patterns. In the family of Abraham, Isaac, and Jacob, Joseph was the one who finally spoke the truth to his brothers (Gen. 45). The pattern of favoritism and sibling rivalry had resulted in the brothers actually selling another brother into slavery to get rid of him. The brothers may have done evil, but God turned it around for good. Joseph said, "God sent me before you to preserve a posterity for you in the earth, and to save your lives by a great deliverance" (Gen. 45:7).

Changing Family Patterns Through Forgiveness

Discovering long-standing patterns in a family can be discouraging. It may seem that nothing can be done to change the pattern. But a family can do the same thing that God does with each person's past—they can forgive. That means canceling the emotional debts that are owed us (Col. 2:13, 14). Forgiveness may take some time. Family members may need to look at some difficult and painful family patterns many times to be sure that they know what they are forgiving.

Forgiveness does not mean forgetting or excusing the sin. Nor does it mean that reconciliation will follow. Even when forgiveness is one-sided, it can be very healthy for the one forgiving. Reconciliation, however, requires action on the part of both the forgiver and the offender. If Joseph's brothers had refused to accept his forgiveness and resume the relationship, then Joseph's forgiving them would not have led to reconciliation. Joseph could forgive because he understood that God had taken his brothers' evil actions and used them to further His purpose.

Forgiveness and reconciliation can break the longstanding patterns in a family. To deal with family problems, family members need to pray for guidance to see the *real* problem, face the truth of their own responsibility in the problem, and seek God's help in making needed changes. Giving and accepting forgiveness and resolving to change can begin the healing that God desires for us and our families.

FURTHER MEDITATION:

Other passages to study about the issue of family problems include:

- ➢ Genesis 37:1–11
- ➢ Deuteronomy 6:1–25
- ➢ Proverbs 22:6
- ➢ Ephesians 6:1–4

To Learn More: Turn to the key passage note on family problems at Genesis 37:3 on page 58. See also the personality profile of the families of Abraham to Joseph on page 37.

Two peoples shall be separated from
your body;
One people shall be stronger than the
other,
And the older shall serve the younger."

24 So when her days were fulfilled *for her* to give birth, indeed *there were* twins in her womb. 25 And the first came out red. *He was* like a hairy garment all over; so they called his name Esau.[a] 26 Afterward his brother came out, and his hand took hold of Esau's heel; so his name was called Jacob.[a] Isaac *was* sixty years old when she bore them.

27 So the boys grew. And Esau was a skillful hunter, a man of the field; but Jacob was a mild man, dwelling in tents. 28 And Isaac loved Esau because he ate *of his* game, but Rebekah loved Jacob.

Esau Sells His Birthright

29 Now Jacob cooked a stew; and Esau came in from the field, and he *was* weary. 30 And Esau said to Jacob, "Please feed me with that same red *stew,* for I *am* weary." Therefore his name was called Edom.[a]

31 But Jacob said, "Sell me your birthright as of this day."

32 And Esau said, "Look, I *am* about to die; so what *is* this birthright to me?"

33 Then Jacob said, "Swear to me as of this day."

So he swore to him, and sold his birthright to Jacob. 34 And Jacob gave Esau bread and stew of lentils; then he ate and drank, arose, and went his way. Thus Esau despised *his* birthright.

Isaac and Abimelech

26 There was a famine in the land, besides the first famine that was in the days of Abraham. And Isaac went to Abimelech king of the Philistines, in Gerar.

2 Then the LORD appeared to him and said: "Do not go down to Egypt; live in the land of which I shall tell you. 3 Dwell in this land, and I will be with you and bless you; for to you and your descendants I give all these lands, and I will perform the oath which I swore to Abraham your father. 4 And I will make your descendants multiply as the stars of heaven; I will give to your descendants all these lands; and in your seed all the nations of the earth shall be blessed; 5 because Abraham obeyed My voice and kept My charge, My commandments, My statutes, and My laws."

6 So Isaac dwelt in Gerar. 7 And the men of the place asked about his wife. And he said, "She *is* my sister"; for he was afraid to say, "*She is* my wife," *because he thought,* "lest the men of the place kill me for Rebekah, because she *is* beautiful to behold." 8 Now it came to pass, when he had been there a long time, that Abimelech king of the Philistines looked through a window, and saw, and there was Isaac, showing endearment to Rebekah his wife. 9 Then Abimelech called Isaac and said, "Quite obviously she *is* your wife; so how could you say, 'She *is* my sister'?"

Isaac said to him, "Because I said, 'Lest I die on account of her.' "

10 And Abimelech said, "What *is* this you have done to us? One of the people might soon have lain with your wife, and you would have brought guilt on us." 11 So Abimelech charged all *his* people, saying, "He who touches this man or his wife shall surely be put to death."

12 Then Isaac sowed in that land, and reaped in the same year a hundredfold; and the LORD blessed him. 13 The man began to prosper, and continued prospering until he became very prosperous; 14 for he had possessions of flocks and possessions of herds and a great number of servants. So the Philistines envied him. 15 Now the Philistines had stopped up all the wells which his father's servants had dug in the days of Abraham his father, and they had filled them with earth. 16 And Abimelech said to Isaac, "Go away from us, for you are much mightier than we."

17 Then Isaac departed from there and pitched his tent in the Valley of Gerar, and dwelt there. 18 And Isaac dug again the wells of water which they had dug in the days of Abraham his father, for the Philistines had stopped them up after the death of Abraham. He called them by the names which his father had called them.

19 Also Isaac's servants dug in the valley, and found a well of running water there. 20 But the herdsmen of Gerar quarreled with Isaac's herdsmen, saying, "The water *is* ours." So he called the name of the well Esek,[a] because they quarreled with him. 21 Then they dug an-

25:25 [a]Literally *Hairy* **25:26** [a]Literally *Supplanter*
25:30 [a]Literally *Red* **26:20** [a]Literally *Quarrel*

other well, and they quarreled over that *one*
also. So he called its name Sitnah.[a] 22And he
moved from there and dug another well, and
they did not quarrel over it. So he called its
name Rehoboth,[a] because he said, "For now
the LORD has made room for us, and we shall
be fruitful in the land."

23Then he went up from there to Beersheba.
24And the LORD appeared to him the same
night and said, "I *am* the God of your father
Abraham; do not fear, for I *am* with you. I will
bless you and multiply your descendants for
My servant Abraham's sake." 25So he built an
altar there and called on the name of the
LORD, and he pitched his tent there; and there
Isaac's servants dug a well.

26Then Abimelech came to him from Gerar
with Ahuzzath, one of his friends, and Phichol
the commander of his army. 27And Isaac said
to them, "Why have you come to me, since you
hate me and have sent me away from you?"

28But they said, "We have certainly seen
that the LORD is with you. So we said, 'Let
there now be an oath between us, between
you and us; and let us make a covenant with
you, 29that you will do us no harm, since we
have not touched you, and since we have
done nothing to you but good and have sent
you away in peace. You *are* now the blessed of
the LORD.' "

30So he made them a feast, and they ate and
drank. 31Then they arose early in the morning
and swore an oath with one another; and
Isaac sent them away, and they departed from
him in peace.

32It came to pass the same day that Isaac's
servants came and told him about the well
which they had dug, and said to him, "We
have found water." 33So he called it Shebah.[a]
Therefore the name of the city *is* Beersheba[b]
to this day.

34When Esau was forty years old, he took as
wives Judith the daughter of Beeri the Hittite,
and Basemath the daughter of Elon the Hittite.
35And they were a grief of mind to Isaac and
Rebekah.

Isaac Blesses Jacob

27 Now it came to pass, when Isaac was
old and his eyes were so dim that he
could not see, that he called Esau his older son
and said to him, "My son."

And he answered him, "Here I am."

2Then he said, "Behold now, I am old. I do
not know the day of my death. 3Now therefore, please take your weapons, your quiver
and your bow, and go out to the field and hunt
game for me. 4And make me savory food, such
as I love, and bring *it* to me that I may eat, that
my soul may bless you before I die."

5Now Rebekah was listening when Isaac
spoke to Esau his son. And Esau went to the
field to hunt game and to bring *it*. 6So Rebekah
spoke to Jacob her son, saying, "Indeed I
heard your father speak to Esau your brother,
saying, 7'Bring me game and make savory
food for me, that I may eat it and bless you in
the presence of the LORD before my death.'
8Now therefore, my son, obey my voice according to what I command you. 9Go now to
the flock and bring me from there two choice
kids of the goats, and I will make savory food
from them for your father, such as he loves.
10Then you shall take *it* to your father, that he
may eat *it*, and that he may bless you before
his death."

11And Jacob said to Rebekah his mother,
"Look, Esau my brother *is* a hairy man, and I
am a smooth-*skinned* man. 12Perhaps my father will feel me, and I shall seem to be a deceiver to him; and I shall bring a curse on
myself and not a blessing."

13But his mother said to him, "*Let* your curse
be on me, my son; only obey my voice, and go,
get *them* for me." 14And he went and got *them*
and brought *them* to his mother, and his
mother made savory food, such as his father
loved. 15Then Rebekah took the choice clothes
of her elder son Esau, which *were* with her in
the house, and put them on Jacob her younger
son. 16And she put the skins of the kids of the
goats on his hands and on the smooth part of
his neck. 17Then she gave the savory food and
the bread, which she had prepared, into the
hand of her son Jacob.

18So he went to his father and said, "My father."

And he said, "Here I am. Who *are* you, my
son?"

19Jacob said to his father, "I *am* Esau your
firstborn; I have done just as you told me;
please arise, sit and eat of my game, that your
soul may bless me."

26:21 [a]Literally *Enmity* **26:22** [a]Literally
Spaciousness **26:33** [a]Literally *Oath* or *Seven*
[b]Literally *Well of the Oath* or *Well of the Seven*

20 But Isaac said to his son, "How *is it* that
you have found *it* so quickly, my son?"
And he said, "Because the LORD your God
brought *it* to me."
21 Isaac said to Jacob, "Please come near,
that I may feel you, my son, whether you *are*
really my son Esau or not." 22 So Jacob went
near to Isaac his father, and he felt him and
said, "The voice *is* Jacob's voice, but the
hands *are* the hands of Esau." 23 And he did
not recognize him, because his hands were
hairy like his brother Esau's hands; so he
blessed him.
24 Then he said, "*Are* you really my son Esau?"
He said, "I *am*."
25 He said, "Bring *it* near to me, and I will eat
of my son's game, so that my soul may bless
you." So he brought *it* near to him, and he ate;
and he brought him wine, and he drank.
26 Then his father Isaac said to him, "Come
near now and kiss me, my son." 27 And he
came near and kissed him; and he smelled the
smell of his clothing, and blessed him and
said:

"Surely, the smell of my son
Is like the smell of a field
Which the LORD has blessed.
28 Therefore may God give you
Of the dew of heaven,
Of the fatness of the earth,
And plenty of grain and wine.
29 Let peoples serve you,
And nations bow down to you.

PERSONALITY PROFILE

Marital Problems

REBEKAH AND ISAAC: FOR WORSE

(GENESIS 27)

Isaac and Rebekah had a fairy-tale courtship. They were brought together by God's power and loved each other from their first encounter. But it seems that they failed to work at their relationship with the diligence that true lovers practice, for in the end, we find them invalidating each other instead of loving and honoring each other.

Granted there were some unusual stresses in the early years of their marriage. Rebekah was infertile for a long time. When she did get pregnant, twins were born. The boys (Jacob and Esau) had distinctly differing characters right from birth. Unfortunately, each parent chose a favorite. Isaac favored Esau; Rebekah doted on Jacob. The marriage seems to have grown distant. When such division begins to erupt, secrecy replaces honesty, loyalties divide, manipulation occurs.

Years later, while in a foreign country to escape a famine, Isaac introduced Rebekah as his sister because he was afraid for his own life. His lack of chivalry must have had a chilling effect on his wife.

When the boys were forty years old, Esau married two women without his parents' approval. Rebekah, ever protective of Jacob, decided to conspire with her son against her husband. They devised a plan to gain for Jacob the blessing that belonged to Esau as the oldest.

Wait a minute! Rebekah conspired with her son to lie to her husband? Clearly, over time, the love they had felt for each other had disintegrated into lack of communication and companionship. Rebekah's closest friend was no longer her husband, but her son. Rebekah no longer honored her husband, so Jacob did not honor his father.

Conflicts happen in every marriage, and can be resolved when handled in a healthy, respectful manner. But couples must guard against allowing fissures to develop into uncrossable canyons. Keep open the lines of communication. Times change, circumstances change, people change. But a marriage can grow stronger, not weaker, if both spouses are willing to repair the fissures with the putty of communication and committed love.

To Learn More: Turn to the article about marital problems on pages 1576, 1577. See also the key passage note at Colossians 3:18, 19 on page 1575.

Be master over your brethren,
And let your mother's sons bow down to
you.
Cursed *be* everyone who curses you,
And blessed *be* those who bless you!"

Esau's Lost Hope

30Now it happened, as soon as Isaac had finished blessing Jacob, and Jacob had scarcely
gone out from the presence of Isaac his father,
that Esau his brother came in from his hunting. 31He also had made savory food, and
brought it to his father, and said to his father,
"Let my father arise and eat of his son's game,
that your soul may bless me."

32And his father Isaac said to him, "Who *are*
you?"

So he said, "I *am* your son, your firstborn,
Esau."

33Then Isaac trembled exceedingly, and
said, "Who? Where *is* the one who hunted
game and brought *it* to me? I ate all *of it* before
you came, and I have blessed him—*and* indeed he shall be blessed."

34When Esau heard the words of his father,
he cried with an exceedingly great and bitter
cry, and said to his father, "Bless me—me
also, O my father!"

35But he said, "Your brother came with deceit and has taken away your blessing."

36And *Esau* said, "Is he not rightly named Jacob? For he has supplanted me these two
times. He took away my birthright, and now
look, he has taken away my blessing!" And
he said, "Have you not reserved a blessing
for me?"

37Then Isaac answered and said to Esau,
"Indeed I have made him your master, and all
his brethren I have given to him as servants;
with grain and wine I have sustained him.
What shall I do now for you, my son?"

38And Esau said to his father, "Have you
only one blessing, my father? Bless me—me
also, O my father!" And Esau lifted up his
voice and wept.

39Then Isaac his father answered and said to
him:

"Behold, your dwelling shall be of the
fatness of the earth,
And of the dew of heaven from above.
40 By your sword you shall live,
And you shall serve your brother;
And it shall come to pass, when you
become restless,
That you shall break his yoke from your
neck."

Jacob Escapes from Esau

41So Esau hated Jacob because of the blessing with which his father blessed him, and
Esau said in his heart, "The days of mourning

KEY PASSAGE

Attachment/ Blessing

BLESSING OUR CHILDREN

(27:30–36)

Everyone needs a parent's blessing to be affirmed and assured that he or she is good and has a promising future. This ancient practice served as the last will and testament of one generation to the next. The Bible reveals that usually the father would give both the birthright and the blessing to his eldest son. This "birthright" conveyed to the eldest son the position of leadership in the family and generally provided him with a double portion of the family inheritance. Esau sold his birthright willingly (Gen. 25:29–34), but Jacob stole the blessing by deceiving his father (Gen. 27:1–36). Esau at last comprehended his great loss and the Bible tells us "he cried with an exceedingly great and bitter cry" (Gen. 27:34).

Although the times and culture are different, parents still need to bless their children. All children need from their parents positive words, meaningful touch, and active commitment in their lives.

To Learn More: Turn to the article about attachment/blessing on pages 76, 77. See also the personality profile of Jacob on page 75.

for my father are at hand; then I will kill my
brother Jacob."
42And the words of Esau her older son were
told to Rebekah. So she sent and called Jacob
her younger son, and said to him, "Surely your
brother Esau comforts himself concerning you
by intending to kill you. 43Now therefore, my
son, obey my voice: arise, flee to my brother
Laban in Haran. 44And stay with him a few
days, until your brother's fury turns away,
45until your brother's anger turns away from
you, and he forgets what you have done to
him; then I will send
and bring you from
there. Why should I be
bereaved also of you
both in one day?"
46And Rebekah said
to Isaac, "I am weary of
my life because of the
daughters of Heth; if Ja-
cob takes a wife of the
daughters of Heth, like these *who are* the
daughters of the land, what good will my life
be to me?"

> Behold, I am with you and will keep you wherever you go, and will bring you back to this land; for I will not leave you until I have done what I have spoken to you.
>
> GENESIS 28:15

28 Then Isaac called Jacob and blessed
him, and charged him, and said to
him: "You shall not take a wife from the
daughters of Canaan. 2Arise, go to Padan
Aram, to the house of Bethuel your mother's
father; and take yourself a wife from there of
the daughters of Laban your mother's brother.

3 "May God Almighty bless you,
And make you fruitful and multiply you,
That you may be an assembly of
peoples;
4 And give you the blessing of Abraham,
To you and your descendants with you,
That you may inherit the land
In which you are a stranger,
Which God gave to Abraham."

5So Isaac sent Jacob away, and he went to
Padan Aram, to Laban the son of Bethuel the
Syrian, the brother of Rebekah, the mother of
Jacob and Esau.

Esau Marries Mahalath

6Esau saw that Isaac had blessed Jacob and
sent him away to Padan Aram to take himself
a wife from there, *and that* as he blessed him
he gave him a charge, saying, "You shall not
take a wife from the daughters of Canaan,"
7and that Jacob had obeyed his father and his
mother and had gone to
Padan Aram. 8Also Esau
saw that the daughters
of Canaan did not
please his father Isaac.
9So Esau went to Ishma-
el and took Mahalath
the daughter of Ishma-
el, Abraham's son, the
sister of Nebajoth, to be
his wife in addition to the wives he had.

Jacob's Vow at Bethel

10Now Jacob went out from Beersheba and
went toward Haran. 11So he came to a certain
place and stayed there all night, because the
sun had set. And he took one of the stones of
that place and put it at his head, and he lay
down in that place to sleep. 12Then he
dreamed, and behold, a ladder *was* set up on
the earth, and its top reached to heaven; and
there the angels of God were ascending and descending on it.
13And behold, the LORD stood above it and
said: "I *am* the LORD God of Abraham your father and the God of Isaac; the land on which
you lie I will give to you and your descendants. 14Also your descendants shall be as the
dust of the earth; you shall spread abroad to
the west and the east, to the north and the

SOUL NOTE

Afraid of God? *(28:16–19)* After Jacob stole Esau's blessing, Esau wanted to kill him (27:41). Jacob ran, and on his lonely journey he lay down to rest and had a strange dream. Jacob realized that God had revealed Himself, and the Bible tells us that Jacob "was afraid." Jacob later remembered this moment as a turning point in his life: "God Almighty appeared to me at Luz in the land of Canaan and blessed me" (48:3). God's awesomeness should inspire fear (reverence), but don't stop there. Let it lead you to faith. **Topic: Fear/Fear of God**

south; and in you and in your seed all the families of the earth shall be blessed. [15]Behold, I
am with you and will keep you wherever you
go, and will bring you back to this land; for I
will not leave you until I have done what I
have spoken to you."
[16]Then Jacob awoke from his sleep and
said, "Surely the LORD is in this place, and I
did not know *it*." [17]And he was afraid and
said, "How awesome *is* this place! This *is*
none other than the house of God, and this *is*
the gate of heaven!"
[18]Then Jacob rose early in the morning, and
took the stone that he had put at his head, set
it up as a pillar, and poured oil on top of it.
[19]And he called the name of that place
Bethel;[a] but the name of that city had been
Luz previously. [20]Then Jacob made a vow,
saying, "If God will be with me, and keep me
in this way that I am going, and give me bread
to eat and clothing to put on, [21]so that I come
back to my father's house in peace, then the
LORD shall be my God. [22]And this stone which
I have set as a pillar shall be God's house, and
of all that You give me I will surely give a
tenth to You."

JACOB MEETS RACHEL

29 So Jacob went on his journey and
came to the land of the people of the
East. [2]And he looked, and saw a well in the
field; and behold, there *were* three flocks of
sheep lying by it; for out of that well they watered the flocks. A large stone *was* on the
well's mouth. [3]Now all the flocks would be
gathered there; and they would roll the stone

28:19 [a]Literally *House of God*

PERSONALITY PROFILE

Blended Families

JACOB'S BLENDED FAMILY

(GENESIS 29)

Jacob didn't plan on multiple wives; his father-in-law, Laban, had helped create that complication. The sisters Jacob married were so fiercely competitive that each put another woman in her husband's bed. Jacob fathered twelve sons and at least one daughter with four women. Though the events that shaped his family were bizarre, the results have a contemporary look: Jacob became the father of a blended family.

Jacob loved his wife Rachel, who had been his first love. He apparently treated the rest of the women in his life with care and respect, but he favored Rachel. Instead of helping Rachel see her unique position and deal with her jealousy toward her older sister, Jacob allowed the vicious battles to rage under his roof. He escalated the war by accepting other women into his bed.

Jacob also contributed to the chaos by obviously favoring Rachel's son Joseph. Instead of providing leadership in his home, Jacob allowed each person to struggle alone. He received cultural, but not genuine, respect from most of his sons. He allowed his family to drift into sin, hatred, and murder. He made little or no effort to intervene in desperate situations. He held his sons responsible for their mistakes, but he certainly bore part of the responsibility for his lack of clear direction. He caused most of his own deepest sorrows.

Blended families require special attention. They need more, not less, work than single couple families because the relationships increase in complication with the number of people involved. Individual children need to experience genuine love from someone, and parents are not automatically interchangeable. The challenge to make a blended family work requires the participation of everyone, particularly the adults. Passive parenting produces deadly results.

Blended parents who persist in depending on God, who regularly ask Him for wisdom, who take an active role in all their children's welfare, are pursuing the right path. The road has unusual difficulties. Those who follow the divine Guide find their way home.

To Learn More: Turn to the article about blended families on pages 46, 47. See also the key passage note at Genesis 21:9–11 on page 32.

BRINGING THEM TOGETHER: THE CHALLENGE OF BLENDING FAMILIES

DAVID R. MILLER

(Genesis 29)

The family nest is being shaken as never before. Today, only one family in four consists of a mother and father and their biological children. If the current trend continues, more than half of all marriages occurring in a given year will end in divorce. In most developed countries, half of all births are to unmarried women. These factors and others eventually result in many remarried families with children, or blended families.

In the Scriptures we can clearly see that God considers children precious and that He is concerned about their welfare (Matt. 18:6, 7; Mark 10:14–16; Eph. 6:4; Col. 3:21). Certainly there are many single-parent homes where the children are dearly loved and well cared for, based on great sacrifice and hard work by the single parent. But we also know that children benefit from having two parents as they grow: Research clearly indicates that children living in a two-parent home, even a remarriage home, are significantly better off than children living in a single-parent home. But the blending of families brings with it a special set of challenges.

CHANGES AND LOSSES

Blended families involve children from previous marriages or relationships. They result when parents—divorced or never married—remarry or marry. Most contain children from only one of the newly married partners; however, some are comprised of children from both partners' previous relationships.

Consider the possible changes and adjustments for the new family's members: the end of (at least) one marriage, new living arrangements, new family members, a new school, the loss of friends, a new church, a new last name. The children may be cut off from formerly close grandparents and relatives. In all remarriage families, loss and change present common emotional challenges.

DIFFERENT HISTORIES

Each member of the blended family has his or her own history, perceptions, and memories and is asked to merge and compromise them with those of other family members. What was once familiar is now reworked: Christmas and other holiday traditions, birthday celebrations, vacations, daily routines, etc. Personal history is not easily surrendered by someone who already has gone through many other changes.

DIFFERENT EXPECTATIONS

Bible-based guidance is essential for remarriages resulting in blended families. Unfulfilled expectations are the major reason subsequent marriages end in divorce. There are expectations about parenting and discipline, finances, and how to express affection, respect, anger, and unhappiness. What about expectations concerning holidays and vacations? What about different rules during noncustodial visits? Assumptions are detrimental. Clarify expectations!

RELATIONAL STRUGGLES

Children in remarriages need love, attention, discipline, understanding, and acceptance. Parents in blended families often struggle with loyalty issues arising from feeling that one's children need to be defended against the stepparent or stepsiblings.

The children may not be as thrilled about the remarriage arrangement as their parents are. This phenomenon is sometimes called "the myth of instant love" and can create problems unless understood and dealt with very early in the developing relationship of the blended family. Often, children feel that by loving and accepting a stepparent they are rejecting their biological parent, which can further complicate matters.

TWO FAMILIES

Visitation is an extremely common source of stress in blended families. The children will experience two realities, one with the blended family and the other with part-time visitation. Life can get even more complicated if the noncustodial parent remarries to create another blended family! Visitation arrangements also become tricky if the noncustodial parent lives far away. The feelings and needs of the children can create quite a challenging scenario for everyone.

WHAT'S A PARENT TO DO?

1. *Deal with family losses and transitions.* Children in blended families need time to feel normal again and should be encouraged to share their feelings of loss and their memories of how things used to be. Visitation time and events with the noncustodial parent should be respected.
2. *Acknowledge different developmental needs.* Parents can help themselves and their children by taking age and maturity level into consideration and not attempting to treat all the children the same way.
3. *Establish new family traditions.* While not rejecting the traditions of the previous family life or of the noncustodial parent, the blended family should set out to create its own family traditions and events.
4. *Build a solid marital relationship.* Spouses must be intentional about taking time alone to love, support, and care for each other. A strong marriage is crucial to the entire transition and overall functioning of the family.
5. *Build a parenting coalition.* Be sure to include the non-custodial parent if at all possible. Children, especially teenagers, are greatly stabilized by seeing parents unified, having one voice. Mom and dad should try to minimize disagreement about the kids in their presence. Consistent parenting helps to alleviate children's insecurity following divorce and also builds their trust in the parental unit.
6. *Accept continual changes in family composition.* Children will come and go as visitation arrangements occur, and they may even wish to live with their other parent for a time. Perhaps a new baby or two will come along and further stir the emotional mix. The couple's commitment to each other and to their children, along with tolerance and patience in transition, will facilitate a smoother new beginning.

Those of us who work with blended families invariably find ourselves drawn back to the issue of what's best for the children. Simply stated, kids are better off with two parents than with one. Be courageous and committed. Blended families can work!

FURTHER MEDITATION:

Other passages to study about the issue of blended families:

- ➢ Ruth 3:7–14
- ➢ 2 Samuel 13:1–2
- ➢ Esther 2:15–17

To Learn More: Turn to the key passage note on blended families at Genesis 21:9–11 on page 32. See also the personality profile of Jacob's family on page 45.

from the well's mouth, water the sheep, and
put the stone back in its place on the well's
mouth.
4 And Jacob said to them, "My brethren,
where *are* you from?"
And they said, "We *are* from Haran."
5 Then he said to them, "Do you know Laban the son of Nahor?"
And they said, "We know him."
6 So he said to them, "Is he well?"
And they said, "*He is* well. And look, his
daughter Rachel is coming with the sheep."
7 Then he said, "Look, *it is* still high day; *it is*
not time for the cattle to be gathered together.
Water the sheep, and go and feed *them.*"
8 But they said, "We cannot until all the
flocks are gathered together, and they have
rolled the stone from the well's mouth; then
we water the sheep."
9 Now while he was still speaking with
them, Rachel came with her father's sheep,
for she was a shepherdess. 10 And it came to
pass, when Jacob saw Rachel the daughter of
Laban his mother's brother, and the sheep of
Laban his mother's brother, that Jacob went
near and rolled the stone from the well's
mouth, and watered the flock of Laban his
mother's brother. 11 Then Jacob kissed Rachel,
and lifted up his voice and wept. 12 And Jacob
told Rachel that he *was* her father's relative
and that he *was* Rebekah's son. So she ran and
told her father.
13 Then it came to pass, when Laban heard
the report about Jacob his sister's son, that
he ran to meet him, and embraced him and
kissed him, and brought him to his house. So
he told Laban all these things. 14 And Laban
said to him, "Surely you *are* my bone and
my flesh." And he stayed with him for a
month.

Jacob Marries Leah and Rachel

15 Then Laban said to Jacob, "Because you
are my relative, should you therefore serve me
for nothing? Tell me, what *should* your wages
be?" 16 Now Laban had two daughters: the
name of the elder *was* Leah, and the name of
the younger *was* Rachel. 17 Leah's eyes *were*
delicate, but Rachel was beautiful of form and
appearance.
18 Now Jacob loved Rachel; so he said, "I
will serve you seven years for Rachel your
younger daughter."
19 And Laban said, "*It is* better that I give her
to you than that I should give her to another
man. Stay with me." 20 So Jacob served seven
years for Rachel, and they seemed *only* a few
days to him because of the love he had for her.
21 Then Jacob said to Laban, "Give *me* my
wife, for my days are fulfilled, that I may go in
to her." 22 And Laban gathered together all the
men of the place and made a feast. 23 Now it
came to pass in the evening, that he took Leah
his daughter and brought her to Jacob; and he
went in to her. 24 And Laban gave his maid Zilpah to his daughter Leah *as* a maid. 25 So it
came to pass in the morning, that behold, it
was Leah. And he said to Laban, "What is this
you have done to me? Was it not for Rachel
that I served you? Why then have you deceived me?"
26 And Laban said, "It must not be done so
in our country, to give the younger before the
firstborn. 27 Fulfill her week, and we will give
you this one also for the service which you
will serve with me still another seven years."
28 Then Jacob did so and fulfilled her week.
So he gave him his daughter Rachel as wife
also. 29 And Laban gave his maid Bilhah to his
daughter Rachel as a maid. 30 Then *Jacob* also
went in to Rachel, and he also loved Rachel

SOUL NOTE

Trying to Earn Love *(29:32)* Although Jacob loved Rachel more than Leah (29:30), Rachel envied her sister Leah who had children while Rachel was barren (30:1). Leah thought that having children would win Jacob's love, while Rachel thought that not having children meant Jacob would love her less. Both women were wrong.

Hannah felt the same. She struggled with her barrenness, but her husband acted wisely, declaring his love for her (1 Sam. 1:8). Couples facing infertility must not let that draw them apart, but instead draw closer together as they declare their love for each other.

Topic: Infertility

more than Leah. And he served with Laban
still another seven years.

THE CHILDREN OF JACOB

31 When the LORD saw that Leah *was* unloved, He opened her womb; but Rachel *was*
barren. 32 So Leah conceived and bore a son,
and she called his name Reuben;[a] for she said,
"The LORD has surely looked on my affliction.
Now therefore, my husband will love me."
33 Then she conceived again and bore a son,
and said, "Because the LORD has heard that I
am unloved, He has therefore given me this
son also." And she called his name Simeon.[a]
34 She conceived again and bore a son, and
said, "Now this time my husband will become
attached to me, because I have borne him
three sons." Therefore his name was called
Levi.[a] 35 And she conceived again and bore a
son, and said, "Now I will praise the LORD."
Therefore she called his name Judah.[a] Then
she stopped bearing.

30 Now when Rachel saw that she bore
Jacob no children, Rachel envied her
sister, and said to Jacob, "Give me children, or
else I die!"
2 And Jacob's anger was aroused against Rachel, and he said, "*Am* I in the place of God,
who has withheld from you the fruit of the
womb?"

29:32 [a]Literally *See, a Son* **29:33** [a]Literally *Heard* **29:34** [a]Literally *Attached* **29:35** [a]Literally *Praise*

PERSONALITY PROFILE

Jealousy

RACHEL AND LEAH: JEALOUS SISTERS

(GENESIS 30:8)

Probably no situation on earth could bring out the worst sibling rivalry between sisters than for them to be married to the same man. Both Rachel and Leah were Jacob's wives. They battled for his attention and for his affection. No weapon was considered off-limits.

Rachel originally captured Jacob's heart. He labored seven years for her father Laban in exchange for Rachel's hand in marriage. Jacob didn't mind the wait because he was in love. The years "seemed only a few days to him because of the love he had for her" (Gen. 29:20). But Laban turned out to be a treacherous father-in-law. On their wedding night, he substituted Leah for Rachel; and by the time Jacob woke up to the deception, he was already married. Laban completed his plan by offering to let Jacob still marry Rachel as long as he committed to another seven years of labor. Overnight, Jacob's home became a place of conflict.

Although Rachel had Jacob's heart, she was at first unable to have his children. Leah gave Jacob four sons. Rachel became so upset that she insisted that Jacob have children with her servant Bilhah. The two sons Jacob had with Bilhah were a costly and bitter victory for Rachel. The sisters bickered constantly.

Monogamy certainly would have been a better option for this family, but it probably would not have kept Rachel and Leah from jealous battles. Jacob could have practiced greater wisdom and compassion with his wives, but his love for Rachel blinded him to many mistakes. Leah never got over being the second-place wife. Rachel allowed her insecurities and envy toward her sister to disrupt the special place she had with Jacob.

Envy and jealousy grow as by-products of comparisons with others. Favorable comparisons tend to lead to pride and arrogance. Unfavorable ones lead to dejection and anger. Comparisons with others rarely promote goodness. In contrast, God calls us to find our worth in Him. The love God expressed to us in Christ releases us from the vicious cycle of jealousy.

To Learn More: Turn to the article about jealousy on pages 1656, 1657. See also the key passage note at Numbers 5:29 on page 176.

3 So she said, "Here is my maid Bilhah; go in to her, and she will bear *a child* on my knees, that I also may have children by her." 4 Then she gave him Bilhah her maid as wife, and Jacob went in to her. 5 And Bilhah conceived and bore Jacob a son. 6 Then Rachel said, "God has judged my case; and He has also heard my voice and given me a son." Therefore she called his name Dan.[a] 7 And Rachel's maid Bilhah conceived again and bore Jacob a second son. 8 Then Rachel said, "With great wrestlings I have wrestled with my sister, *and* indeed I have prevailed." So she called his name Naphtali.[a]

9 When Leah saw that she had stopped bearing, she took Zilpah her maid and gave her to Jacob as wife. 10 And Leah's maid Zilpah bore Jacob a son. 11 Then Leah said, "A troop comes!"[a] So she called his name Gad.[b] 12 And Leah's maid Zilpah bore Jacob a second son. 13 Then Leah said, "I am happy, for the daughters will call me blessed." So she called his name Asher.[a]

14 Now Reuben went in the days of wheat harvest and found mandrakes in the field, and brought them to his mother Leah. Then Rachel said to Leah, "Please give me *some* of your son's mandrakes."

15 But she said to her, "*Is it* a small matter that you have taken away my husband? Would you take away my son's mandrakes also?"

And Rachel said, "Therefore he will lie with you tonight for your son's mandrakes."

16 When Jacob came out of the field in the evening, Leah went out to meet him and said, "You must come in to me, for I have surely hired you with my son's mandrakes." And he lay with her that night.

17 And God listened to Leah, and she conceived and bore Jacob a fifth son. 18 Leah said, "God has given me my wages, because I have given my maid to my husband." So she called his name Issachar.[a] 19 Then Leah conceived again and bore Jacob a sixth son. 20 And Leah said, "God has endowed me *with* a good endowment; now my husband will dwell with me, because I have borne him six sons." So she called his name Zebulun.[a] 21 Afterward she bore a daughter, and called her name Dinah.

22 Then God remembered Rachel, and God listened to her and opened her womb. 23 And she conceived and bore a son, and said, "God has taken away my reproach." 24 So she called his name Joseph,[a] and said, "The LORD shall add to me another son."

JACOB'S AGREEMENT WITH LABAN

25 And it came to pass, when Rachel had borne Joseph, that Jacob said to Laban, "Send me away, that I may go to my own place and to my country. 26 Give *me* my wives and my children for whom I have served you, and let me go; for you know my service which I have done for you."

27 And Laban said to him, "Please *stay,* if I have found favor in your eyes, *for* I have learned by experience that the LORD has blessed me for your sake." 28 Then he said, "Name me your wages, and I will give *it.*"

29 So *Jacob* said to him, "You know how I have served you and how your livestock has been with me. 30 For what you had before I *came was* little, and it has increased to a great amount; the LORD has blessed you since my coming. And now, when shall I also provide for my own house?"

31 So he said, "What shall I give you?"

And Jacob said, "You shall not give me anything. If you will do this thing for me, I will again feed and keep your flocks: 32 Let me pass through all your flock today, removing from there all the speckled and spotted sheep, and all the brown ones among the lambs, and the spotted and speckled among the goats; and *these* shall be my wages. 33 So my righteousness will answer for me in time to come, when the subject of my wages comes before you: every one that *is* not speckled and spotted among the goats, and brown among the lambs, will be considered stolen, if *it is* with me."

34 And Laban said, "Oh, that it were according to your word!" 35 So he removed that day the male goats that were speckled and spotted, all the female goats that were speckled and spotted, every one that had *some* white in it, and all the brown ones among the lambs, and gave *them* into the hand of his sons. 36 Then he put three days' journey between himself and Jacob, and Jacob fed the rest of Laban's flocks.

30:6 [a]Literally *Judge* **30:8** [a]Literally *My Wrestling* **30:11** [a]Following Qere, Syriac, and Targum; Kethib, Septuagint, and Vulgate read *in fortune.* [b]Literally *Troop* or *Fortune*
30:13 [a]Literally *Happy* **30:18** [a]Literally *Wages*
30:20 [a]Literally *Dwelling* **30:24** [a]Literally *He Will Add*

[37]Now Jacob took for himself rods of green
poplar and of the almond and chestnut trees,
peeled white strips in them, and exposed the
white which *was* in the rods. [38]And the rods
which he had peeled, he set before the flocks
in the gutters, in the watering troughs where
the flocks came to drink, so that they should
conceive when they came to drink. [39]So the
flocks conceived before the rods, and the
flocks brought forth streaked, speckled, and
spotted. [40]Then Jacob separated the lambs,
and made the flocks face toward the streaked
and all the brown in the flock of Laban; but he
put his own flocks by themselves and did not
put them with Laban's flock.

[41]And it came to pass, whenever the stronger livestock conceived, that Jacob placed the
rods before the eyes of the livestock in the gutters, that they might conceive among the rods.
[42]But when the flocks were feeble, he did not
put *them* in; so the feebler were Laban's and
the stronger Jacob's. [43]Thus the man became
exceedingly prosperous, and had large flocks,
female and male servants, and camels and
donkeys.

Jacob Flees from Laban

31 Now *Jacob* heard the words of Laban's sons, saying, "Jacob has taken
away all that was our father's, and from what
was our father's he has acquired all this
wealth." [2]And Jacob saw the countenance of
Laban, and indeed it *was* not *favorable* toward
him as before. [3]Then the LORD said to Jacob,
"Return to the land of your fathers and to your
family, and I will be with you."

[4]So Jacob sent and called Rachel and Leah to
the field, to his flock, [5]and said to them, "I see
your father's countenance, that it *is* not *favorable* toward me as before; but the God of my
father has been with me. [6]And you know that
with all my might I have served your father.
[7]Yet your father has deceived me and changed
my wages ten times, but God did not allow him
to hurt me. [8]If he said thus: 'The speckled shall
be your wages,' then all the flocks bore speckled. And if he said thus: 'The streaked shall be
your wages,' then all the flocks bore streaked.
[9]So God has taken away the livestock of your
father and given *them* to me.

[10]"And it happened, at the time when the
flocks conceived, that I lifted my eyes and saw
in a dream, and behold, the rams which
leaped upon the flocks *were* streaked, speckled, and gray-spotted. [11]Then the Angel of God
spoke to me in a dream, saying, 'Jacob.' And I
said, 'Here I am.' [12]And He said, 'Lift your eyes
now and see, all the rams which leap on the
flocks *are* streaked, speckled, and gray-
spotted; for I have seen all that Laban is doing
to you. [13]I *am* the God of Bethel, where you
anointed the pillar *and* where you made a vow
to Me. Now arise, get out of this land, and return to the land of your family.' "

[14]Then Rachel and Leah answered and said
to him, "Is there still any portion or inheritance for us in our father's house? [15]Are we
not considered strangers by him? For he has
sold us, and also completely consumed our
money. [16]For all these riches which God has
taken from our father are *really* ours and our
children's; now then, whatever God has said
to you, do it."

[17]Then Jacob rose and set his sons and his
wives on camels. [18]And he carried away all
his livestock and all his possessions which he
had gained, his acquired livestock which he
had gained in Padan Aram, to go to his father
Isaac in the land of Canaan. [19]Now Laban had
gone to shear his sheep, and Rachel had stolen the household idols that were her father's.
[20]And Jacob stole away, unknown to Laban

SOUL NOTE

Violated Trust *(31:7)* Jacob had been deceived several times by his father-in-law. Both in his marriages and in his employment, Jacob found Laban to be less than honest. Jacob no longer trusted Laban, so he took his family and left.

Trust involves being trustworthy and being willing to trust another. Earlier in his life, Jacob too had been a deceiver. He had experienced the hurt and separation that violated trust brings into a family. Jacob fled because he had deceived (27:43); here he fled because he had been deceived. Violated trust can destroy relationships. How much better to build a bond of trust with those closest to us. **Topic: Trust**

the Syrian, in that he did not tell him that he
intended to flee. 21So he fled with all that he
had. He arose and crossed the river, and headed toward the mountains of Gilead.

LABAN PURSUES JACOB

22And Laban was told on the third day that
Jacob had fled. 23Then he took his brethren
with him and pursued him for seven days'
journey, and he overtook him in the mountains of Gilead. 24But God had come to Laban
the Syrian in a dream by night, and said to
him, "Be careful that you speak to Jacob neither good nor bad."

25So Laban overtook Jacob. Now Jacob had
pitched his tent in the mountains, and Laban
with his brethren pitched in the mountains of
Gilead.

26And Laban said to Jacob: "What have you
done, that you have stolen away unknown to
me, and carried away my daughters like captives *taken* with the sword? 27Why did you
flee away secretly, and steal away from me,
and not tell me; for I might have sent you
away with joy and songs, with timbrel and
harp? 28And you did not allow me to kiss my
sons and my daughters. Now you have done
foolishly in *so* doing. 29It is in my power to do
you harm, but the God of your father spoke to
me last night, saying, 'Be careful that you
speak to Jacob neither good nor bad.' 30And
now you have surely gone because you greatly
long for your father's house, *but* why did you
steal my gods?"

31Then Jacob answered and said to Laban,
"Because I was afraid, for I said, 'Perhaps you
would take your daughters from me by force.'
32With whomever you find your gods, do not
let him live. In the presence of our brethren,
identify what I have of yours and take *it* with
you." For Jacob did not know that Rachel had
stolen them.

33And Laban went into Jacob's tent, into
Leah's tent, and into the two maids' tents, but
he did not find *them*. Then he went out of
Leah's tent and entered Rachel's tent. 34Now
Rachel had taken the household idols, put
them in the camel's saddle, and sat on them.
And Laban searched all about the tent but did
not find *them*. 35And she said to her father,
"Let it not displease my lord that I cannot rise
before you, for the manner of women *is* with
me." And he searched but did not find the
household idols.

36Then Jacob was angry and rebuked Laban,
and Jacob answered and said to Laban: "What
is my trespass? What *is* my sin, that you have
so hotly pursued me? 37Although you have
searched all my things, what part of your
household things have you found? Set *it* here
before my brethren and your brethren, that
they may judge between us both! 38These
twenty years I *have been* with you; your ewes
and your female goats have not miscarried
their young, and I have not eaten the rams of
your flock. 39That which was torn *by beasts* I
did not bring to you; I bore the loss of it. You
required it from my hand, *whether* stolen by
day or stolen by night. 40*There* I was! In the day
the drought consumed me, and the frost by
night, and my sleep departed from my eyes.
41Thus I have been in your house twenty years;
I served you fourteen years for your two
daughters, and six years for your flock, and
you have changed my wages ten times. 42Un-
less the God of my father, the God of Abraham
and the Fear of Isaac, had been with me, surely
now you would have sent me away empty-
handed. God has seen my affliction and the labor of my hands, and rebuked *you* last night."

LABAN'S COVENANT WITH JACOB

43And Laban answered and said to Jacob,
"*These* daughters *are* my daughters, and *these*
children *are* my children, and *this* flock *is* my
flock; all that you see *is* mine. But what can I
do this day to these my daughters or to their
children whom they have borne? 44Now therefore, come, let us make a covenant, you and I,
and let it be a witness between you and me."

45So Jacob took a stone and set it up *as* a pillar. 46Then Jacob said to his brethren, "Gather
stones." And they took stones and made a
heap, and they ate there on the heap. 47Laban
called it Jegar Sahadutha,[a] but Jacob called it
Galeed.[b] 48And Laban said, "This heap *is* a
witness between you and me this day." Therefore its name was called Galeed, 49also
Mizpah,[a] because he said, "May the LORD
watch between you and me when we are absent one from another. 50If you afflict my
daughters, or if you take *other* wives besides
my daughters, *although* no man *is* with us—
see, God *is* witness between you and me!"

31:47 [a]Literally, in Aramaic, *Heap of Witness*
[b]Literally, in Hebrew, *Heap of Witness*
31:49 [a]Literally *Watch*

[51]Then Laban said to Jacob, "Here is this heap and here is *this* pillar, which I have placed between you and me. [52]This heap *is* a witness, and *this* pillar *is* a witness, that I will not pass beyond this heap to you, and you will not pass beyond this heap and this pillar to me, for harm. [53]The God of Abraham, the God of Nahor, and the God of their father judge between us." And Jacob swore by the Fear of his father Isaac. [54]Then Jacob offered a sacrifice on the mountain, and called his brethren to eat bread. And they ate bread and stayed all night on the mountain. [55]And early in the morning Laban arose, and kissed his sons and daughters and blessed them. Then Laban departed and returned to his place.

Esau Comes to Meet Jacob

32 So Jacob went on his way, and the angels of God met him. [2]When Jacob saw them, he said, "This *is* God's camp." And he called the name of that place Mahanaim.[a]

[3]Then Jacob sent messengers before him to Esau his brother in the land of Seir, the country of Edom. [4]And he commanded them, saying, "Speak thus to my lord Esau, 'Thus your servant Jacob says: "I have dwelt with Laban and stayed there until now. [5]I have oxen, donkeys, flocks, and male and female servants; and I have sent to tell my lord, that I may find favor in your sight." ' "

[6]Then the messengers returned to Jacob, saying, "We came to your brother Esau, and he also is coming to meet you, and four hundred men *are* with him." [7]So Jacob was greatly afraid and distressed; and he divided the people that *were* with him, and the flocks and herds and camels, into two companies. [8]And he said, "If Esau comes to the one company and attacks it, then the other company which is left will escape."

[9]Then Jacob said, "O God of my father Abraham and God of my father Isaac, the LORD who said to me, 'Return to your country and to your family, and I will deal well with you': [10]I am not worthy of the least of all the mercies and of all the truth which You have shown Your servant; for I crossed over this Jordan with my staff, and now I have become two companies. [11]Deliver me, I pray, from the hand of my brother, from the hand of Esau; for I fear him, lest he come and attack me *and* the mother with the children. [12]For You said, 'I will surely treat you well, and make your descendants as the sand of the sea, which cannot be numbered for multitude.' "

[13]So he lodged there that same night, and took what came to his hand as a present for Esau his brother: [14]two hundred female goats and twenty male goats, two hundred ewes and twenty rams, [15]thirty milk camels with their colts, forty cows and ten bulls, twenty female donkeys and ten foals. [16]Then he delivered *them* to the hand of his servants, every drove by itself, and said to his servants, "Pass over before me, and put some distance between successive droves." [17]And he commanded the first one, saying, "When Esau my brother meets you and asks you, saying, 'To whom do you belong, and where are you going? Whose *are* these in front of you?' [18]then you shall say, 'They *are* your servant Jacob's. It *is* a present sent to my lord Esau; and behold, he also *is* behind us.' " [19]So he commanded the second, the third, and all who followed the droves, saying, "In this manner you shall speak to Esau when you find him; [20]and also say, 'Behold, your servant Jacob *is* behind us.' " For he said, "I will appease him with the present that goes before me, and afterward I will see his face; perhaps he will accept me." [21]So the present went on over before him, but he himself lodged that night in the camp.

Wrestling with God

[22]And he arose that night and took his two wives, his two female servants, and his eleven sons, and crossed over the ford of Jabbok. [23]He took them, sent them over the brook, and sent over what he had. [24]Then Jacob was left alone; and a Man wrestled with him until the breaking of day. [25]Now when He saw that He did not prevail against him, He touched the socket of his hip; and the socket of Jacob's hip was out of joint as He wrestled with him. [26]And He said, "Let Me go, for the day breaks."

But he said, "I will not let You go unless You bless me!"

[27]So He said to him, "What *is* your name?"

He said, "Jacob."

[28]And He said, "Your name shall no longer be called Jacob, but Israel;[a] for you have struggled with God and with men, and have prevailed."

32:2 [a]Literally *Double Camp* **32:28** [a]Literally *Prince with God*

[29]Then Jacob asked, saying, "Tell *me* Your name, I pray."

And He said, "Why *is* it *that* you ask about My name?" And He blessed him there.

[30]So Jacob called the name of the place Peniel:[a] "For I have seen God face to face, and my life is preserved." [31]Just as he crossed over Penuel[a] the sun rose on him, and he limped on his hip. [32]Therefore to this day the children of Israel do not eat the muscle that shrank, which *is* on the hip socket, because He touched the socket of Jacob's hip in the muscle that shrank.

Jacob and Esau Meet

33 Now Jacob lifted his eyes and looked, and there, Esau was coming, and with him were four hundred men. So he divided the children among Leah, Rachel, and the two maidservants. [2]And he put the maidservants and their children in front, Leah and her children behind, and Rachel and Joseph last. [3]Then he crossed over before them and bowed himself to the ground seven times, until he came near to his brother.

[4]But Esau ran to meet him, and embraced him, and fell on his neck and kissed him, and they wept. [5]And he lifted his eyes and saw the women and children, and said, "Who *are* these with you?"

So he said, "The children whom God has graciously given your servant." [6]Then the maidservants came near, they and their children, and bowed down. [7]And Leah also came near with her children, and they bowed down. Afterward Joseph and Rachel came near, and they bowed down.

[8]Then Esau said, "What *do* you *mean by* all this company which I met?"

And he said, "*These are* to find favor in the sight of my lord."

[9]But Esau said, "I have enough, my brother; keep what you have for yourself."

[10]And Jacob said, "No, please, if I have now found favor in your sight, then receive my present from my hand, inasmuch as I have seen your face as though I had seen the face of God, and you were pleased with me. [11]Please, take my blessing that is brought to you, because God has dealt graciously with me, and because I have enough." So he urged him, and he took *it*.

[12]Then Esau said, "Let us take our journey; let us go, and I will go before you."

[13]But Jacob said to him, "My lord knows that the children *are* weak, and the flocks and herds which are nursing *are* with me. And if the men should drive them hard one day, all the flock will die. [14]Please let my lord go on ahead before his servant. I will lead on slowly at a pace which the livestock that go before me, and the children, are able to endure, until I come to my lord in Seir."

[15]And Esau said, "Now let me leave with you *some* of the people who *are* with me."

But he said, "What need is there? Let me find favor in the sight of my lord." [16]So Esau returned that day on his way to Seir. [17]And Jacob journeyed to Succoth, built himself a house, and made booths for his livestock. Therefore the name of the place is called Succoth.[a]

Jacob Comes to Canaan

[18]Then Jacob came safely to the city of Shechem, which *is* in the land of Canaan, when he came from Padan Aram; and he pitched his tent before the city. [19]And he bought the parcel of land, where he had pitched his tent, from the children of Hamor, Shechem's father, for one hundred pieces of money. [20]Then he erected an altar there and called it El Elohe Israel.[a]

The Dinah Incident

34 Now Dinah the daughter of Leah, whom she had borne to Jacob, went out to see the daughters of the land. [2]And when Shechem the son of Hamor the Hivite, prince of the country, saw her, he took her and lay with her, and violated her. [3]His soul was strongly attracted to Dinah the daughter of Jacob, and he loved the young woman and spoke kindly to the young woman. [4]So Shechem spoke to his father Hamor, saying, "Get me this young woman as a wife."

[5]And Jacob heard that he had defiled Dinah his daughter. Now his sons were with his livestock in the field; so Jacob held his peace until they came. [6]Then Hamor the father of Shechem went out to Jacob to speak with him. [7]And the sons of Jacob came in from the field when they heard *it;* and the men were grieved and very angry, because he had done a dis-

---

32:30 [a]Literally *Face of God* **32:31** [a]Same as *Peniel,* verse 30 **33:17** [a]Literally *Booths* **33:20** [a]Literally *God, the God of Israel*

graceful thing in Israel by lying with Jacob's daughter, a thing which ought not to be done. 8But Hamor spoke with them, saying, "The soul of my son Shechem longs for your daughter. Please give her to him as a wife. 9And make marriages with us; give your daughters to us, and take our daughters to yourselves. 10So you shall dwell with us, and the land shall be before you. Dwell and trade in it, and acquire possessions for yourselves in it."

11Then Shechem said to her father and her brothers, "Let me find favor in your eyes, and whatever you say to me I will give. 12Ask me ever so much dowry and gift, and I will give according to what you say to me; but give me the young woman as a wife."

13But the sons of Jacob answered Shechem and Hamor his father, and spoke deceitfully, because he had defiled Dinah their sister. 14And they said to them, "We cannot do this thing, to give our sister to one who is uncircumcised, for that *would be* a reproach to us. 15But on this *condition* we will consent to you: If you will become as we *are,* if every male of you is circumcised, 16then we will give our daughters to you, and we will take your daughters to us; and we will dwell with you, and we will become one people. 17But if you will not heed us and be circumcised, then we will take our daughter and be gone."

18And their words pleased Hamor and Shechem, Hamor's son. 19So the young man did not delay to do the thing, because he delighted in Jacob's daughter. He *was* more honorable than all the household of his father.

20And Hamor and Shechem his son came to the gate of their city, and spoke with the men of their city, saying: 21"These men *are* at peace with us. Therefore let them dwell in the land and trade in it. For indeed the land *is* large enough for them. Let us take their daughters to us as wives, and let us give them our daughters. 22Only on this *condition* will the men consent to dwell with us, to be one people: if every male among us is circumcised as they *are* circumcised. 23*Will* not their livestock, their property, and every animal of theirs *be* ours? Only let us consent to them, and they will dwell with us." 24And all who went out of the gate of his city heeded Hamor and Shechem his son; every male was circumcised, all who went out of the gate of his city.

25Now it came to pass on the third day, when they were in pain, that two of the sons of Jacob, Simeon and Levi, Dinah's brothers, each took his sword and came boldly upon the city and killed all the males. 26And they killed Hamor and Shechem his son with the edge of the sword, and took Dinah from Shechem's house, and went out. 27The sons of Jacob came upon the slain, and plundered the city, because their sister had been defiled. 28They took their sheep, their oxen, and their donkeys, what *was* in the city and what *was* in the field, 29and all their wealth. All their little ones and their wives they took captive; and they plundered even all that *was* in the houses.

30Then Jacob said to Simeon and Levi, "You have troubled me by making me obnoxious among the inhabitants of the land, among the Canaanites and the Perizzites; and since I *am* few in number, they will gather themselves together against me and kill me. I shall be destroyed, my household and I."

31But they said, "Should he treat our sister like a harlot?"

Jacob's Return to Bethel

35 Then God said to Jacob, "Arise, go up to Bethel and dwell there; and make an altar there to God, who appeared to you

SOUL NOTE

An Inexcusable Act *(34:2)* Shechem first "lay with" Dinah and "violated her," then claimed to love her and to want to marry her. While his love for her may have been genuine, his actions were inexcusable. He said he wanted to marry Dinah, but he had already done evil. A young man may think he is in love, but to force a woman to have sex with him violates and abuses her. This does not show love at all. For Shechem, his act resulted in death and destruction for an entire city. The consequences of such abuse, no matter how one tries to justify it, are far-reaching and destructive.

Topic: Abuse

when you fled from the face of Esau your brother."

2And Jacob said to his household and to all who *were* with him, "Put away the foreign gods that *are* among you, purify yourselves, and change your garments. 3Then let us arise and go up to Bethel; and I will make an altar there to God, who answered me in the day of my distress and has been with me in the way which I have gone." 4So they gave Jacob all the foreign gods which *were* in their hands, and the earrings which *were* in their ears; and Jacob hid them under the terebinth tree which *was* by Shechem.

5And they journeyed, and the terror of God was upon the cities that *were* all around them, and they did not pursue the sons of Jacob. 6So Jacob came to Luz (that *is,* Bethel), which *is* in the land of Canaan, he and all the people who *were* with him. 7And he built an altar there and called the place El Bethel,[a] because there God appeared to him when he fled from the face of his brother.

8Now Deborah, Rebekah's nurse, died, and she was buried below Bethel under the terebinth tree. So the name of it was called Allon Bachuth.[a]

9Then God appeared to Jacob again, when he came from Padan Aram, and blessed him. 10And God said to him, "Your name *is* Jacob; your name shall not be called Jacob anymore, but Israel shall be your name." So He called his name Israel. 11Also God said to him: "I *am* God Almighty. Be fruitful and multiply; a nation and a company of nations shall proceed from you, and kings shall come from your body. 12The land which I gave Abraham and Isaac I give to you; and to your descendants after you I give this land." 13Then God went up from him in the place where He talked with him. 14So Jacob set up a pillar in the place where He talked with him, a pillar of stone; and he poured a drink offering on it, and he poured oil on it. 15And Jacob called the name of the place where God spoke with him, Bethel.

DEATH OF RACHEL

16Then they journeyed from Bethel. And when there was but a little distance to go to Ephrath, Rachel labored *in childbirth,* and she had hard labor. 17Now it came to pass, when she was in hard labor, that the midwife said to her, "Do not fear; you will have this son also." 18And so it was, as her soul was departing (for she died), that she called his name Ben-Oni;[a] but his father called him Benjamin.[b] 19So Rachel died and was buried on the way to Ephrath (that *is,* Bethlehem). 20And Jacob set a pillar on her grave, which *is* the pillar of Rachel's grave to this day.

21Then Israel journeyed and pitched his tent beyond the tower of Eder. 22And it happened, when Israel dwelt in that land, that Reuben went and lay with Bilhah his father's concubine; and Israel heard *about it.*

JACOB'S TWELVE SONS

Now the sons of Jacob were twelve: 23the sons of Leah *were* Reuben, Jacob's firstborn, and Simeon, Levi, Judah, Issachar, and Zebulun; 24the sons of Rachel *were* Joseph and Benjamin; 25the sons of Bilhah, Rachel's maidservant, *were* Dan and Naphtali; 26and the sons of Zilpah, Leah's maidservant, *were* Gad and Asher. These *were* the sons of Jacob who were born to him in Padan Aram.

DEATH OF ISAAC

27Then Jacob came to his father Isaac at Mamre, or Kirjath Arba[a] (that *is,* Hebron), where Abraham and Isaac had dwelt. 28Now the days of Isaac were one hundred and eighty years. 29So Isaac breathed his last and died, and was gathered to his people, *being* old and full of days. And his sons Esau and Jacob buried him.

THE FAMILY OF ESAU

36 Now this *is* the genealogy of Esau, who is Edom. 2Esau took his wives from the daughters of Canaan: Adah the daughter of Elon the Hittite; Aholibamah the daughter of Anah, the daughter of Zibeon the Hivite; 3and Basemath, Ishmael's daughter, sister of Nebajoth. 4Now Adah bore Eliphaz to Esau, and Basemath bore Reuel. 5And Aholibamah bore Jeush, Jaalam, and Korah. These *were* the sons of Esau who were born to him in the land of Canaan.

6Then Esau took his wives, his sons, his daughters, and all the persons of his household, his cattle and all his animals, and all his goods which he had gained in the land of Ca-

---

35:7 [a]Literally *God of the House of God*
35:8 [a]Literally *Terebinth of Weeping*
35:18 [a]Literally *Son of My Sorrow* [b]Literally *Son of the Right Hand* **35:27** [a]Literally *Town of Arba*

naan, and went to a country away from the presence of his brother Jacob. [7]For their possessions were too great for them to dwell together, and the land where they were strangers could not support them because of their livestock. [8]So Esau dwelt in Mount Seir. Esau *is* Edom.

[9]And this *is* the genealogy of Esau the father of the Edomites in Mount Seir. [10]These *were* the names of Esau's sons: Eliphaz the son of Adah the wife of Esau, and Reuel the son of Basemath the wife of Esau. [11]And the sons of Eliphaz were Teman, Omar, Zepho,[a] Gatam, and Kenaz.

[12]Now Timna was the concubine of Eliphaz, Esau's son, and she bore Amalek to Eliphaz. These *were* the sons of Adah, Esau's wife.

[13]These *were* the sons of Reuel: Nahath, Zerah, Shammah, and Mizzah. These were the sons of Basemath, Esau's wife.

[14]These were the sons of Aholibamah, Esau's wife, the daughter of Anah, the daughter of Zibeon. And she bore to Esau: Jeush, Jaalam, and Korah.

The Chiefs of Edom

[15]These *were* the chiefs of the sons of Esau. The sons of Eliphaz, the firstborn *son* of Esau, were Chief Teman, Chief Omar, Chief Zepho, Chief Kenaz, [16]Chief Korah,[a] Chief Gatam, *and* Chief Amalek. These *were* the chiefs of Eliphaz in the land of Edom. They *were* the sons of Adah.

[17]These *were* the sons of Reuel, Esau's son: Chief Nahath, Chief Zerah, Chief Shammah, and Chief Mizzah. These *were* the chiefs of Reuel in the land of Edom. These *were* the sons of Basemath, Esau's wife.

[18]And these *were* the sons of Aholibamah, Esau's wife: Chief Jeush, Chief Jaalam, and Chief Korah. These *were* the chiefs *who descended* from Aholibamah, Esau's wife, the daughter of Anah. [19]These *were* the sons of Esau, who is Edom, and these *were* their chiefs.

The Sons of Seir

[20]These *were* the sons of Seir the Horite who inhabited the land: Lotan, Shobal, Zibeon, Anah, [21]Dishon, Ezer, and Dishan. These *were* the chiefs of the Horites, the sons of Seir, in the land of Edom.

[22]And the sons of Lotan were Hori and Hemam.[a] Lotan's sister *was* Timna.

[23]These *were* the sons of Shobal: Alvan,[a] Manahath, Ebal, Shepho,[b] and Onam.

[24]These *were* the sons of Zibeon: both Ajah and Anah. This *was the* Anah who found the water[a] in the wilderness as he pastured the donkeys of his father Zibeon. [25]These *were* the children of Anah: Dishon and Aholibamah the daughter of Anah.

[26]These *were* the sons of Dishon:[a] Hemdan,[b] Eshban, Ithran, and Cheran. [27]These *were* the sons of Ezer: Bilhan, Zaavan, and Akan.[a] [28]These *were* the sons of Dishan: Uz and Aran.

[29]These *were* the chiefs of the Horites: Chief Lotan, Chief Shobal, Chief Zibeon, Chief Anah, [30]Chief Dishon, Chief Ezer, and Chief Dishan. These *were* the chiefs of the Horites, according to their chiefs in the land of Seir.

The Kings of Edom

[31]Now these *were* the kings who reigned in the land of Edom before any king reigned over the children of Israel: [32]Bela the son of Beor reigned in Edom, and the name of his city *was* Dinhabah. [33]And when Bela died, Jobab the son of Zerah of Bozrah reigned in his place. [34]When Jobab died, Husham of the land of the Temanites reigned in his place. [35]And when Husham died, Hadad the son of Bedad, who attacked Midian in the field of Moab, reigned in his place. And the name of his city *was* Avith. [36]When Hadad died, Samlah of Masrekah reigned in his place. [37]And when Samlah died, Saul of Rehoboth-*by*-the-River reigned in his place. [38]When Saul died, Baal-Hanan the son of Achbor reigned in his place. [39]And when Baal-Hanan the son of Achbor died, Hadar[a] reigned in his place; and the name of his city *was* Pau.[b] His wife's name *was* Mehetabel, the daughter of Matred, the daughter of Mezahab.

36:11 [a]Spelled *Zephi* in 1 Chronicles 1:36
36:16 [a]Samaritan Pentateuch omits *Chief Korah.*
36:22 [a]Spelled *Homam* in 1 Chronicles 1:39
36:23 [a]Spelled *Alian* in 1 Chronicles 1:40 [b]Spelled *Shephi* in 1 Chronicles 1:40 **36:24** [a]Following Masoretic Text and Vulgate (*hot springs*); Septuagint reads *Jamin;* Targum reads *mighty men;* Talmud interprets as *mules.* **36:26** [a]Hebrew *Dishan* [b]Spelled *Hamran* in 1 Chronicles 1:41
36:27 [a]Spelled *Jaakan* in 1 Chronicles 1:42
36:39 [a]Spelled *Hadad* in Samaritan Pentateuch, Syriac, and 1 Chronicles 1:50 [b]Spelled *Pai* in 1 Chronicles 1:50

THE CHIEFS OF ESAU

[40]And these *were* the names of the chiefs of Esau, according to their families and their places, by their names: Chief Timnah, Chief Alvah,[a] Chief Jetheth, [41]Chief Aholibamah, Chief Elah, Chief Pinon, [42]Chief Kenaz, Chief Teman, Chief Mibzar, [43]Chief Magdiel, and Chief Iram. These *were* the chiefs of Edom, according to their dwelling places in the land of their possession. Esau *was* the father of the Edomites.

JOSEPH DREAMS OF GREATNESS

37 Now Jacob dwelt in the land where his father was a stranger, in the land of Canaan. [2]This *is* the history of Jacob.

Joseph, *being* seventeen years old, was feeding the flock with his brothers. And the lad *was* with the sons of Bilhah and the sons of Zilpah, his father's wives; and Joseph brought a bad report of them to his father.

[3]Now Israel loved Joseph more than all his children, because he *was* the son of his old age. Also he made him a tunic of *many* colors. [4]But when his brothers saw that their father loved him more than all his brothers, they hated him and could not speak peaceably to him.

[5]Now Joseph had a dream, and he told *it* to his brothers; and they hated him even more. [6]So he said to them, "Please hear this dream which I have dreamed: [7]There we were, binding sheaves in the field. Then behold, my sheaf arose and also stood upright; and indeed your sheaves stood all around and bowed down to my sheaf."

[8]And his brothers said to him, "Shall you indeed reign over us? Or shall you indeed have dominion over us?" So they hated him even more for his dreams and for his words.

[9]Then he dreamed still another dream and told it to his brothers, and said, "Look, I have dreamed another dream. And this time, the sun, the moon, and the eleven stars bowed down to me."

[10]So he told *it* to his father and his brothers; and his father rebuked him and said to him, "What *is* this dream that you have dreamed? Shall your mother and I and your brothers indeed come to bow down to the earth before you?" [11]And his brothers envied him, but his father kept the matter *in mind.*

JOSEPH SOLD BY HIS BROTHERS

[12]Then his brothers went to feed their father's flock in Shechem. [13]And Israel said to Joseph, "Are not your brothers feeding *the*

36:40 [a]Spelled *Aliah* in 1 Chronicles 1:51

KEY PASSAGE

Family Problems

SIBLING RIVALRY

(37:3)

No families are exempt from problems. Perhaps the most common family problem is sibling rivalry, which is sometimes exacerbated by parental favoritism. This happened in Jacob's family. Joseph was the first son of Jacob's favorite wife Rachel (Gen. 30:22–24). As such, he quickly became his father's favorite child, leading to family conflict fueled by jealousy. Joseph's brothers despised his favored status, symbolized by his multicolored tunic (Gen. 37:3). When he revealed his dreams to his half brothers, they became even more angry at him (Gen. 37:5–11). Tragically, their jealousy resulted in Joseph being sold as a slave (Gen. 37:28), and Jacob being told that his favorite son was dead (Gen. 37:33).

Favoritism will quickly divide a family and cause problems among children for years to come. Parents must:

- understand that their children are different and appreciate those differences.
- love them equally.
- not overtly show favoritism but be careful to treat them fairly.

To Learn More: Turn to the article about family problems on pages 38, 39. See also the personality profile of the families of Abraham to Joseph on page 37.

flock in Shechem? Come, I will send you to them."

So he said to him, "Here I am."

[14]Then he said to him, "Please go and see if it is well with your brothers and well with the flocks, and bring back word to me." So he sent him out of the Valley of Hebron, and he went to Shechem.

[15]Now a certain man found him, and there he was, wandering in the field. And the man asked him, saying, "What are you seeking?"

[16]So he said, "I am seeking my brothers. Please tell me where they are feeding *their flocks.*"

[17]And the man said, "They have departed from here, for I heard them say, 'Let us go to Dothan.' " So Joseph went after his brothers and found them in Dothan.

[18]Now when they saw him afar off, even before he came near them, they conspired against him to kill him. [19]Then they said to one another, "Look, this dreamer is coming! [20]Come therefore, let us now kill him and cast him into some pit; and we shall say, 'Some wild beast has devoured him.' We shall see what will become of his dreams!"

[21]But Reuben heard *it,* and he delivered him out of their hands, and said, "Let us not kill him." [22]And Reuben said to them, "Shed no blood, *but* cast him into this pit which *is* in the wilderness, and do not lay a hand on him"—that he might deliver him out of their hands, and bring him back to his father.

[23]So it came to pass, when Joseph had come to his brothers, that they stripped Joseph *of* his tunic, the tunic of *many* colors that *was* on him. [24]Then they took him and cast him into a pit. And the pit *was* empty; *there was* no water in it.

[25]And they sat down to eat a meal. Then they lifted their eyes and looked, and there was a company of Ishmaelites, coming from Gilead with their camels, bearing spices, balm, and myrrh, on their way to carry *them* down to Egypt. [26]So Judah said to his brothers, "What profit *is there* if we kill our brother and conceal his blood? [27]Come and let us sell him to the Ishmaelites, and let not our hand be upon him, for he *is* our brother *and* our flesh." And his brothers listened. [28]Then Midianite traders passed by; so *the brothers* pulled Joseph up and lifted him out of the pit, and sold him to the Ishmaelites for twenty *shekels* of silver. And they took Joseph to Egypt.

[29]Then Reuben returned to the pit, and indeed Joseph *was* not in the pit; and he tore his clothes. [30]And he returned to his brothers and said, "The lad *is* no *more;* and I, where shall I go?"

[31]So they took Joseph's tunic, killed a kid of the goats, and dipped the tunic in the blood. [32]Then they sent the tunic of *many* colors, and they brought *it* to their father and said, "We have found this. Do you know whether it *is* your son's tunic or not?"

[33]And he recognized it and said, "*It is* my son's tunic. A wild beast has devoured him. Without doubt Joseph is torn to pieces." [34]Then Jacob tore his clothes, put sackcloth on his waist, and mourned for his son many days. [35]And all his sons and all his daughters arose to comfort him; but he refused to be comforted, and he said, "For I shall go down into the grave to my son in mourning." Thus his father wept for him.

[36]Now the Midianites[a] had sold him in Egypt to Potiphar, an officer of Pharaoh *and* captain of the guard.

JUDAH AND TAMAR

38 It came to pass at that time that Judah departed from his brothers, and visited a certain Adullamite whose name *was* Hirah. [2]And Judah saw there a daughter of a certain Canaanite whose name *was* Shua, and he married her and went in to her. [3]So she conceived and bore a son, and he called his name Er. [4]She conceived again and bore a son, and she called his name Onan. [5]And she conceived yet again and bore a son, and called his name Shelah. He was at Chezib when she bore him.

[6]Then Judah took a wife for Er his firstborn, and her name *was* Tamar. [7]But Er, Judah's firstborn, was wicked in the sight of the LORD, and the LORD killed him. [8]And Judah said to Onan, "Go in to your brother's wife and marry her, and raise up an heir to your brother." [9]But Onan knew that the heir would not be his; and it came to pass, when he went in to his brother's wife, that he emitted on the ground, lest he should give an heir to his brother. [10]And the thing which he did displeased the LORD; therefore He killed him also.

[11]Then Judah said to Tamar his daughter-in-law, "Remain a widow in your father's house till my son Shelah is grown." For he said,

37:36 [a]Masoretic Text reads *Medanites.*

"Lest he also die like his brothers." And Tamar went and dwelt in her father's house.

12Now in the process of time the daughter of Shua, Judah's wife, died; and Judah was comforted, and went up to his sheepshearers at Timnah, he and his friend Hirah the Adullamite. 13And it was told Tamar, saying, "Look, your father-in-law is going up to Timnah to shear his sheep." 14So she took off her widow's garments, covered *herself* with a veil and wrapped herself, and sat in an open place which *was* on the way to Timnah; for she saw that Shelah was grown, and she was not given to him as a wife. 15When Judah saw her, he thought she *was* a harlot, because she had covered her face. 16Then he turned to her by the way, and said, "Please let me come in to you"; for he did not know that she *was* his daughter-in-law.

So she said, "What will you give me, that you may come in to me?"

17And he said, "I will send a young goat from the flock."

So she said, "Will you give *me* a pledge till you send *it?*"

18Then he said, "What pledge shall I give you?"

So she said, "Your signet and cord, and your staff that *is* in your hand." Then he gave *them* to her, and went in to her, and she conceived by him. 19So she arose and went away, and laid aside her veil and put on the garments of her widowhood.

20And Judah sent the young goat by the hand of his friend the Adullamite, to receive *his* pledge from the woman's hand, but he did not find her. 21Then he asked the men of that place, saying, "Where is the harlot who *was* openly by the roadside?"

And they said, "There was no harlot in this *place.*"

22So he returned to Judah and said, "I cannot find her. Also, the men of the place said there was no harlot in this *place.*"

23Then Judah said, "Let her take *them* for herself, lest we be shamed; for I sent this young goat and you have not found her."

24And it came to pass, about three months after, that Judah was told, saying, "Tamar your daughter-in-law has played the harlot; furthermore she *is* with child by harlotry."

So Judah said, "Bring her out and let her be burned!"

25When she *was* brought out, she sent to her father-in-law, saying, "By the man to whom these belong, I *am* with child." And she said, "Please determine whose these *are*—the signet and cord, and staff."

26So Judah acknowledged *them* and said, "She has been more righteous than I, because I did not give her to Shelah my son." And he never knew her again.

27Now it came to pass, at the time for giving birth, that behold, twins *were* in her womb. 28And so it was, when she was giving birth, that *the one* put out *his* hand; and the midwife took a scarlet *thread* and bound it on his hand, saying, "This one came out first." 29Then it happened, as he drew back his hand, that his brother came out unexpectedly; and she said, "How did you break through? *This* breach *be* upon you!" Therefore his name was called Perez.[a] 30Afterward his brother came out who had the scarlet *thread* on his hand. And his name was called Zerah.

JOSEPH A SLAVE IN EGYPT

39 Now Joseph had been taken down to Egypt. And Potiphar, an officer of Pharaoh, captain of the guard, an Egyptian, bought him from the Ishmaelites who had taken him down there. 2The LORD was with Jo-

38:29 [a]Literally *Breach* or *Breakthrough*

SOUL NOTE

Can't Hide It *(38:16)* Sexual sin, even when supposedly occurring in secret, has consequences—some immediate, some far-reaching. Tamar had been wronged, and so sought the only way she knew how to right that wrong. Judah propositioned Tamar, thinking her merely a prostitute. This complicated story, based on ancient cultural norms, seems unfamiliar to readers today, but it does reveal the manipulation and exposure that is sure to occur with sexual sin. Some may think that they can hide the sin, but they get caught. And God sees all sin anyway. **Topic: Sexual Sin**

seph, and he was a successful man; and he
was in the house of his master the Egyptian.
3And his master saw that the LORD *was* with
him and that the LORD made all he did to prosper in his hand. 4So Joseph found favor in his
sight, and served him. Then he made him
overseer of his house, and all *that* he had he
put under his authority. 5So it was, from the
time *that* he had made him overseer of his
house and all that he had, that the LORD
blessed the Egyptian's house for Joseph's
sake; and the blessing of the LORD was on all
that he had in the house and in the field.
6Thus he left all that he had in Joseph's hand,
and he did not know what he had except for
the bread which he ate.

Now Joseph was handsome in form and appearance.

7And it came to pass after these things that
his master's wife cast longing eyes on Joseph,
and she said, "Lie with me."

8But he refused and said to his master's
wife, "Look, my master does not know what *is*
with me in the house, and he has committed
all that he has to my hand. 9*There is* no one
greater in this house than I, nor has he kept
back anything from me but you, because you
are his wife. How then can I do this great
wickedness, and sin against God?"

10So it was, as she spoke to Joseph day by
day, that he did not heed her, to lie with her *or*
to be with her.

11But it happened about this time, when Joseph went into the house to do his work, and
none of the men of the house *was* inside,
12that she caught him by his garment, saying,
"Lie with me." But he left his garment in her
hand, and fled and ran outside. 13And so it
was, when she saw that he had left his garment in her hand and fled outside, 14that she
called to the men of her house and spoke to
them, saying, "See, he has brought in to us a
Hebrew to mock us. He came in to me to lie
with me, and I cried out with a loud voice.
15And it happened, when he heard that I lifted
my voice and cried out, that he left his garment with me, and fled and went outside."

16So she kept his garment with her until his
master came home. 17Then she spoke to him
with words like these, saying, "The Hebrew
servant whom you brought to us came in to
me to mock me; 18so it happened, as I lifted
my voice and cried out, that he left his garment with me and fled outside."

19So it was, when his master heard the
words which his wife spoke to him, saying,
"Your servant did to me after this manner,"
that his anger was aroused. 20Then Joseph's
master took him and put him into the prison,
a place where the king's prisoners *were* confined. And he was there in the prison. 21But
the LORD was with Joseph and showed him
mercy, and He gave him favor in the sight of
the keeper of the prison. 22And the keeper of
the prison committed to Joseph's hand all the
prisoners who *were* in the prison; whatever
they did there, it was his doing. 23The keeper
of the prison did not look into anything *that
was* under *Joseph's* authority,[a] because the
LORD was with him; and whatever he did, the
LORD made *it* prosper.

THE PRISONERS' DREAMS

40 It came to pass after these things *that*
the butler and the baker of the king of
Egypt offended their lord, the king of Egypt.
2And Pharaoh was angry with his two officers,
the chief butler and the chief baker. 3So he put
them in custody in the house of the captain
of the guard, in the prison, the place where

39:23 [a]Literally *his hand*

SOUL NOTE

Sometimes You've Got to Run! *(39:7–12)* Lust has no logic. Sometimes you can't talk someone out of doing wrong—you just have to get out of the way. Potiphar's wife presented Joseph a difficult dilemma. Giving in to temptation would offend his master; resisting it would offend his master's wife. Joseph knew only one answer to this moral challenge: View it from God's perspective. Thus he concluded that violating his sexual integrity would be a "great wickedness" and "sin against God." Sexual sin hurts one's relationship with God and can destroy relationships with others. Joseph realized that he had no choice but to run! **Topic: Sexual Integrity**

THE WHISPERS OF TEMPTATION

GARY AND BARBARA ROSBERG

(Genesis 39:6–15)

Temptation. It whispers to us, appeals to our pleasure, arouses our interest, and can cause us to fall all too quickly. Temptation is like stepping into the quicksand of sin and sinking fast. When temptation leads to sin, people respond in many ways. Some weep bitterly with regret and shame, but most hide within the crevices of their soul—afraid, alone, hurt, and ashamed—with waves of guilt crashing in around them. These and similar feelings are common when we know we have gone too far, made the wrong choices, and led a reckless life. When we make poor decisions, we self-destruct—yet it was our choosing that got us there.

SATAN'S SUBTLETIES

Temptation seems to creep around when we least expect it. We deceive ourselves into thinking that we are strong and can handle it. Satan knows just when to push our buttons, however. At precisely the wrong time—when our vigilance is weak and our defenses are down—the Enemy presents us with his temptation. He has a way of deceiving us into thinking it is all right, making us see various shades of gray rather than the black and white of right and wrong.

Seeing our weaknesses, Satan will tempt us and offer compelling reasons to compromise. We are tempted toward greed as neighbors and coworkers assert that more is better—and then they live "the good life." We are tempted to gossip when we are genuinely concerned about someone, yet go too far by uncovering details that hurt and wound. We are tempted into wrong relationships because we fall prey to the myth that somebody is better than nobody. We are tempted to steal a few small items from the office because we feel we deserve it. Temptation to sexual gratification and lust creep into our thoughts as mass media flood our senses with sensuality.

Society says, "Live for the moment, seize the day!" We don't have to look for sin; it finds us, even chases us. By failing to walk or run from temptation, we lose. We lose strength, self-respect, health, security, and safety. We embrace a life of regret. And that is why we must guard our hearts.

TRYING TO FILL A NEED

Often people try to use things, places, and people to bandage a wound in the soul and meet a need that cannot humanly be met. The need was created by God for only God to fill. Everything else will feel incomplete. Everyone has emotional needs that they try to meet in invalid ways such as friendships, emotional affairs, ministry, church work, and obsessions with appearance, food, and money. They grab onto false ways to meet their needs.

People long to be valued as whole and complete persons, for who they are not just for what they do. Many people search for another person to meet the need; then they get frustrated when the need is still unmet. It is God who satisfies emotionally. God wants to reside in that deep place of our souls.

STANDING OR FALLING?

We must look at temptation for what it really is. Temptation, when it stands alone, is merely a withering, shrinking lure. Despite its prevalence, it has no power unless we choose to surrender to it. Remember that temptation itself is not a sin—Jesus was tempted—but yielding to temptation *is* sin.

Everyone can remember falling to temptation. The memory stirs up feelings of being dirty, empty, drained, and even exploited. Grieving the sin is natural and healthy before a righteous God. These feelings and memories can serve as reminders to guard our hearts and minds.

➢ *Confess to God* the brokenness and admit the sin to Him (Ps. 34:18).
➢ *Be willing to be broken.* God delights in a broken and contrite heart (Ps. 51:17) and will meet you at your lowest point. No friend, mate, or parent can go to the depth of this valley of isolation; only God can walk it with you.
➢ *Make a list.* Write down what you have learned through this difficult life lesson. What have you learned about God? What has been revealed about other people's characters? What have you learned about yourself?
➢ *Create a second column on your list titled "The New Me,"* signifying your transformed life. "And do not be conformed to this world, but be transformed by the renewing of your mind" (Rom. 12:2). List areas of life that need to be lived differently.
➢ *Make a third column titled, "Action Plans."* Integrating these specific plans into your daily lifestyle will support transformed living. Daily prayer, continual confession to God, accountability to a friend, daily Bible reading, journaling spiritual growth, identifying weak spots, and watching for the dangers of temptation are examples. At this point, decide what needs to be done to deal with any consequences for the sin. People to whom you must apologize? Restitution to be made? Ask God's guidance in deciding how to handle these needs for action.
➢ *Choose like-minded friends.* Identify other people who will encourage faithfulness and help you to run from temptation (Phil. 2:1–4).

Remember, we are never alone in our temptations. We have a mighty God who has the transforming power to change us, make us godly people, satisfy our deepest needs, be our greatest defense against the enemy, protect us, keep us from temptation, and deliver us from evil. Our victory has already been won through Christ.

FURTHER MEDITATION:

Other passages to study about the issue of temptation include:

➢ Genesis 3
➢ Matthew 4:1–11; 6:13; 26:41
➢ 1 Corinthians 10:1–13
➢ 2 Corinthians 7:10, 11; 11:3
➢ Ephesians 6:10–20
➢ 1 Thessalonians 5:22
➢ Titus 2:11, 12
➢ James 1:12–16; 4:7–10
➢ 1 Peter 5:8, 9
➢ 1 John 1:9

To Learn More: Turn to the key passage note on temptation at Matthew 4:1–11 on page 1233. See also the personality profile of Samson on page 320.

Joseph *was* confined. [4]And the captain of the guard charged Joseph with them, and he served them; so they were in custody for a while.

[5]Then the butler and the baker of the king of Egypt, who *were* confined in the prison, had a dream, both of them, each man's dream in one night *and* each man's dream with its *own* interpretation. [6]And Joseph came in to them in the morning and looked at them, and saw that they *were* sad. [7]So he asked Pharaoh's officers who *were* with him in the custody of his lord's house, saying, "Why do you look *so* sad today?"

[8]And they said to him, "We each have had a dream, and *there is* no interpreter of it."

So Joseph said to them, "Do not interpretations belong to God? Tell *them* to me, please."

[9]Then the chief butler told his dream to Joseph, and said to him, "Behold, in my dream a vine *was* before me, [10]and in the vine *were* three branches; it *was* as though it budded, its blossoms shot forth, and its clusters brought forth ripe grapes. [11]Then Pharaoh's cup *was* in my hand; and I took the grapes and pressed them into Pharaoh's cup, and placed the cup in Pharaoh's hand."

[12]And Joseph said to him, "This *is* the interpretation of it: The three branches *are* three days. [13]Now within three days Pharaoh will lift up your head and restore you to your place, and you will put Pharaoh's cup in his hand according to the former manner, when you were his butler. [14]But remember me when it is well with you, and please show kindness to me; make mention of me to Pharaoh, and get me out of this house. [15]For indeed I was stolen away from the land of the Hebrews; and also I have done nothing here that they should put me into the dungeon."

[16]When the chief baker saw that the interpretation was good, he said to Joseph, "I also *was* in my dream, and there *were* three white baskets on my head. [17]In the uppermost basket *were* all kinds of baked goods for Pharaoh, and the birds ate them out of the basket on my head."

[18]So Joseph answered and said, "This *is* the interpretation of it: The three baskets *are* three days. [19]Within three days Pharaoh will lift off your head from you and hang you on a tree; and the birds will eat your flesh from you."

[20]Now it came to pass on the third day, *which was* Pharaoh's birthday, that he made a feast for all his servants; and he lifted up the head of the chief butler and of the chief baker among his servants. [21]Then he restored the chief butler to his butlership again, and he placed the cup in Pharaoh's hand. [22]But he hanged the chief baker, as Joseph had interpreted to them. [23]Yet the chief butler did not remember Joseph, but forgot him.

PHARAOH'S DREAMS

41 Then it came to pass, at the end of two full years, that Pharaoh had a dream; and behold, he stood by the river. [2]Suddenly there came up out of the river seven cows, fine looking and fat; and they fed in the meadow. [3]Then behold, seven other cows came up after them out of the river, ugly and gaunt, and stood by the *other* cows on the bank of the river. [4]And the ugly and gaunt cows ate up the seven fine looking and fat cows. So Pharaoh awoke. [5]He slept and dreamed a second time; and suddenly seven heads of grain came up on one stalk, plump and good. [6]Then behold, seven thin heads, blighted by the east wind, sprang up after them. [7]And the seven thin heads devoured the seven plump and full heads. So Pharaoh awoke, and indeed, *it was* a dream. [8]Now it came to pass in the morning that his spirit was troubled, and he sent and called for all the magicians of Egypt and all its wise men. And Pharaoh told them his dreams, but *there was* no one who could interpret them for Pharaoh.

[9]Then the chief butler spoke to Pharaoh, saying: "I remember my faults this day. [10]When Pharaoh was angry with his servants, and put me in custody in the house of the captain of the guard, *both* me and the chief baker, [11]we each had a dream in one night, he and I. Each of us dreamed according to the interpretation of his *own* dream. [12]Now there *was* a young Hebrew man with us there, a servant of the captain of the guard. And we told him, and he interpreted our dreams for us; to each man he interpreted according to his *own* dream. [13]And it came to pass, just as he interpreted for us, so it happened. He restored me to my office, and he hanged him."

[14]Then Pharaoh sent and called Joseph, and they brought him quickly out of the dungeon; and he shaved, changed his clothing, and came to Pharaoh. [15]And Pharaoh said to Jo-

seph, "I have had a dream, and *there is* no one
who can interpret it. But I have heard it said of
you *that* you can understand a dream, to interpret it."
16So Joseph answered Pharaoh, saying, "*It*
is not in me; God will give Pharaoh an answer
of peace."
17Then Pharaoh said to Joseph: "Behold, in
my dream I stood on the bank of the river.
18Suddenly seven cows came up out of the
river, fine looking and fat; and they fed in the
meadow. 19Then behold, seven other cows
came up after them, poor and very ugly and
gaunt, such ugliness as I have never seen in all
the land of Egypt. 20And the gaunt and ugly
cows ate up the first seven, the fat cows.
21When they had eaten them up, no one
would have known that they had eaten them,
for they *were* just as ugly as at the beginning.
So I awoke. 22Also I saw in my dream, and
suddenly seven heads came up on one stalk,
full and good. 23Then behold, seven heads,
withered, thin, *and* blighted by the east wind,
sprang up after them. 24And the thin heads devoured the seven good heads. So I told *this* to
the magicians, but *there was* no one who
could explain *it* to me."
25Then Joseph said to Pharaoh, "The dreams
of Pharaoh *are* one; God has shown Pharaoh
what He *is* about to do: 26The seven good cows
are seven years, and the seven good heads *are*
seven years; the dreams *are* one. 27And the
seven thin and ugly cows which came up after
them *are* seven years, and the seven empty
heads blighted by the east wind are seven years
of famine. 28This *is* the thing which I have spoken to Pharaoh. God has shown Pharaoh what
He *is* about to do. 29Indeed seven years of great
plenty will come throughout all the land of
Egypt; 30but after them seven years of famine
will arise, and all the plenty will be forgotten
in the land of Egypt; and the famine will deplete the land. 31So the plenty will not be
known in the land because of the famine following, for it *will be* very severe. 32And the
dream was repeated to Pharaoh twice because
the thing *is* established by God, and God will
shortly bring it to pass.
33"Now therefore, let Pharaoh select a discerning and wise man, and set him over the
land of Egypt. 34Let Pharaoh do *this,* and let
him appoint officers over the land, to collect
one-fifth *of the produce* of the land of Egypt in
the seven plentiful years. 35And let them gather
all the food of those good years that are coming, and store up grain under the authority of
Pharaoh, and let them keep food in the cities.
36Then that food shall be as a reserve for the
land for the seven years of famine which shall
be in the land of Egypt, that the land may not
perish during the famine."

JOSEPH'S RISE TO POWER

37So the advice was good in the eyes of
Pharaoh and in the eyes of all his servants.
38And Pharaoh said to his servants, "Can we
find *such a one* as this, a man in whom *is* the
Spirit of God?"
39Then Pharaoh said to Joseph, "Inasmuch as
God has shown you all this, *there is* no one as
discerning and wise as you. 40You shall be over
my house, and all my people shall be ruled according to your word; only in regard to the
throne will I be greater than you." 41And Pharaoh said to Joseph, "See, I have set you over all
the land of Egypt."
42Then Pharaoh took his signet ring off his
hand and put it on Joseph's hand; and he
clothed him in garments of fine linen and put
a gold chain around his neck. 43And he had
him ride in the second chariot which he had;
and they cried out before him, "Bow the
knee!" So he set him over all the land of
Egypt. 44Pharaoh also said to Joseph, "I *am*
Pharaoh, and without your consent no man
may lift his hand or foot in all the land of
Egypt." 45And Pharaoh called Joseph's name
Zaphnath-Paaneah. And he gave him as a wife
Asenath, the daughter of Poti-Pherah priest of
On. So Joseph went out over *all* the land of
Egypt.
46Joseph was thirty years old when he stood
before Pharaoh king of Egypt. And Joseph
went out from the presence of Pharaoh, and
went throughout all the land of Egypt. 47Now
in the seven plentiful years the ground
brought forth abundantly. 48So he gathered up
all the food of the seven years which were in
the land of Egypt, and laid up the food in the
cities; he laid up in every city the food of the
fields which surrounded them. 49Joseph gathered very much grain, as the sand of the sea,
until he stopped counting, for *it was* immeasurable.
50And to Joseph were born two sons before
the years of famine came, whom Asenath, the
daughter of Poti-Pherah priest of On, bore to
him. 51Joseph called the name of the firstborn

Manasseh:[a] "For God has made me forget all
my toil and all my father's house." 52And the
name of the second he called Ephraim:[a] "For
God has caused me to be fruitful in the land of
my affliction."

53Then the seven years of plenty which
were in the land of Egypt ended, 54and the
seven years of famine began to come, as Joseph had said. The famine was in all lands,
but in all the land of Egypt there was bread.
55So when all the land of Egypt was famished,
the people cried to Pharaoh for bread. Then
Pharaoh said to all the Egyptians, "Go to Joseph; whatever he says to you, do." 56The
famine was over all the face of the earth, and
Joseph opened all the storehouses[a] and sold
to the Egyptians. And the famine became severe in the land of Egypt. 57So all countries
came to Joseph in Egypt to buy *grain,* because
the famine was severe in all lands.

Joseph's Brothers Go to Egypt

42 When Jacob saw that there was grain
in Egypt, Jacob said to his sons, "Why
do you look at one another?" 2And he said,
"Indeed I have heard that there is grain in
Egypt; go down to that place and buy for us
there, that we may live and not die."

3So Joseph's ten brothers went down to buy
grain in Egypt. 4But Jacob did not send
Joseph's brother Benjamin with his brothers,
for he said, "Lest some calamity befall him."
5And the sons of Israel went to buy *grain*
among those who journeyed, for the famine
was in the land of Canaan.

6Now Joseph *was* governor over the land;
and it was he who sold to all the people of the
land. And Joseph's brothers came and bowed
down before him with *their* faces to the earth.
7Joseph saw his brothers and recognized
them, but he acted as a stranger to them and
spoke roughly to them. Then he said to them,
"Where do you come from?"

And they said, "From the land of Canaan to
buy food."

8So Joseph recognized his brothers, but they
did not recognize him. 9Then Joseph remembered the dreams which he had dreamed about
them, and said to them, "You *are* spies! You
have come to see the nakedness of the land!"

10And they said to him, "No, my lord, but
your servants have come to buy food. 11We *are*
all one man's sons; we *are* honest *men;* your
servants are not spies."

12But he said to them, "No, but you have
come to see the nakedness of the land."

13And they said, "Your servants *are* twelve
brothers, the sons of one man in the land of
Canaan; and in fact, the youngest *is* with our
father today, and one *is* no more."

14But Joseph said to them, "It *is* as I spoke
to you, saying, 'You *are* spies!' 15In this *manner* you shall be tested: By the life of Pharaoh,
you shall not leave this place unless your
youngest brother comes here. 16Send one of
you, and let him bring your brother; and you
shall be kept in prison, that your words may
be tested to see whether *there is* any truth in
you; or else, by the life of Pharaoh, surely you
are spies!" 17So he put them all together in
prison three days.

18Then Joseph said to them the third day,
"Do this and live, *for* I fear God: 19If you *are*
honest *men,* let one of your brothers be confined to your prison house; but you, go and
carry grain for the famine of your houses.
20And bring your youngest brother to me;
so your words will be verified, and you shall
not die."

And they did so. 21Then they said to one another, "We *are* truly guilty concerning our
brother, for we saw the anguish of his soul
when he pleaded with us, and we would not
hear; therefore this distress has come
upon us."

22And Reuben answered them, saying, "Did
I not speak to you, saying, 'Do not sin against
the boy'; and you would not listen? Therefore
behold, his blood is now required of us." 23But
they did not know that Joseph understood
them, for he spoke to them through an interpreter. 24And he turned himself away from
them and wept. Then he returned to them
again, and talked with them. And he took Simeon from them and bound him before their
eyes.

The Brothers Return to Canaan

25Then Joseph gave a command to fill their
sacks with grain, to restore every man's
money to his sack, and to give them provisions for the journey. Thus he did for them.
26So they loaded their donkeys with the grain
and departed from there. 27But as one *of them*
opened his sack to give his donkey feed at the

41:51 [a]Literally *Making Forgetful* **41:52** [a]Literally *Fruitfulness* **41:56** [a]Literally *all that was in them*

encampment, he saw his money; and there it
was, in the mouth of his sack. 28So he said to
his brothers, "My money has been restored,
and there it is, in my sack!" Then their hearts
failed *them* and they were afraid, saying to
one another, "What *is* this *that* God has done
to us?"

29Then they went to Jacob their father in the
land of Canaan and told him all that had happened to them, saying: 30"The man *who is* lord
of the land spoke roughly to us, and took us
for spies of the country. 31But we said to him,
'We *are* honest *men;* we are not spies. 32We
are twelve brothers, sons of our father; one *is*
no *more,* and the youngest *is* with our father
this day in the land of Canaan.' 33Then the
man, the lord of the country, said to us, 'By
this I will know that you *are* honest *men:*
Leave one of your brothers *here* with me, take
food for the famine of your households, and
be gone. 34And bring your youngest brother to
me; so I shall know that you *are* not spies, but
that you *are* honest *men.* I will grant your
brother to you, and you may trade in the
land.' "

35Then it happened as they emptied their
sacks, that surprisingly each man's bundle of
money *was* in his sack; and when they and
their father saw the bundles of money, they
were afraid. 36And Jacob their father said to
them, "You have bereaved me: Joseph is no
more, Simeon is no *more,* and you want to take
Benjamin. All these things are against me."

37Then Reuben spoke to his father, saying,
"Kill my two sons if I do not bring him *back* to
you; put him in my hands, and I will bring
him back to you."

38But he said, "My son shall not go down
with you, for his brother is dead, and he is left
alone. If any calamity should befall him along
the way in which you go, then you would
bring down my gray hair with sorrow to the
grave."

Joseph's Brothers Return with Benjamin

43 Now the famine *was* severe in the
land. 2And it came to pass, when they
had eaten up the grain which they had
brought from Egypt, that their father said to
them, "Go back, buy us a little food."

3But Judah spoke to him, saying, "The man
solemnly warned us, saying, 'You shall not see
my face unless your brother *is* with you.' 4If
you send our brother with us, we will go
down and buy you food. 5But if you will not
send *him,* we will not go down; for the man
said to us, 'You shall not see my face unless
your brother *is* with you.' "

6And Israel said, "Why did you deal *so*
wrongfully with me *as* to tell the man whether
you had still *another* brother?"

7But they said, "The man asked us point-
edly about ourselves and our family, saying,
'*Is* your father still alive? Have you *another*
brother?' And we told him according to these
words. Could we possibly have known that he
would say, 'Bring your brother down'?"

8Then Judah said to Israel his father, "Send
the lad with me, and we will arise and go, that
we may live and not die, both we and you *and*
also our little ones. 9I myself will be surety for
him; from my hand you shall require him. If I
do not bring him *back* to you and set him before you, then let me bear the blame forever.
10For if we had not lingered, surely by now we
would have returned this second time."

11And their father Israel said to them, "If *it
must be* so, then do this: Take some of the best
fruits of the land in your vessels and carry
down a present for the man—a little balm and
a little honey, spices and myrrh, pistachio
nuts and almonds. 12Take double money in
your hand, and take back in your hand the
money that was returned in the mouth of your
sacks; perhaps it was an oversight. 13Take
your brother also, and arise, go back to the
man. 14And may God Almighty give you mercy before the man, that he may release your
other brother and Benjamin. If I am bereaved,
I am bereaved!"

15So the men took that present and Benjamin, and they took double money in their
hand, and arose and went down to Egypt; and
they stood before Joseph. 16When Joseph saw
Benjamin with them, he said to the steward of
his house, "Take *these* men to my home, and
slaughter an animal and make ready; for *these*
men will dine with me at noon." 17Then the
man did as Joseph ordered, and the man
brought the men into Joseph's house.

18Now the men were afraid because they
were brought into Joseph's house; and they
said, "*It is* because of the money, which was
returned in our sacks the first time, that we
are brought in, so that he may make a case
against us and seize us, to take us as slaves
with our donkeys."

19When they drew near to the steward of

Joseph's house, they talked with him at the door of the house, 20and said, "O sir, we indeed came down the first time to buy food; 21but it happened, when we came to the encampment, that we opened our sacks, and there, *each* man's money *was* in the mouth of his sack, our money in full weight; so we have brought it back in our hand. 22And we have brought down other money in our hands to buy food. We do not know who put our money in our sacks."

23But he said, "Peace *be* with you, do not be afraid. Your God and the God of your father has given you treasure in your sacks; I had your money." Then he brought Simeon out to them.

24So the man brought the men into Joseph's house and gave *them* water, and they washed their feet; and he gave their donkeys feed. 25Then they made the present ready for Joseph's coming at noon, for they heard that they would eat bread there.

26And when Joseph came home, they brought him the present which *was* in their hand into the house, and bowed down before him to the earth. 27Then he asked them about *their* well-being, and said, "*Is* your father well, the old man of whom you spoke? *Is* he still alive?"

28And they answered, "Your servant our father *is* in good health; he *is* still alive." And they bowed their heads down and prostrated themselves.

29Then he lifted his eyes and saw his brother Benjamin, his mother's son, and said, "*Is* this your younger brother of whom you spoke to me?" And he said, "God be gracious to you, my son." 30Now his heart yearned for his brother; so Joseph made haste and sought *somewhere* to weep. And he went into *his* chamber and wept there. 31Then he washed his face and came out; and he restrained himself, and said, "Serve the bread."

32So they set him a place by himself, and them by themselves, and the Egyptians who ate with him by themselves; because the Egyptians could not eat food with the Hebrews, for that *is* an abomination to the Egyptians. 33And they sat before him, the firstborn according to his birthright and the youngest according to his youth; and the men looked in astonishment at one another. 34Then he took servings to them from before him, but Benjamin's serving was five times as much as any of theirs. So they drank and were merry with him.

JOSEPH'S CUP

44 And he commanded the steward of his house, saying, "Fill the men's sacks with food, as much as they can carry, and put each man's money in the mouth of his sack. 2Also put my cup, the silver cup, in the mouth of the sack of the youngest, and his grain money." So he did according to the word that Joseph had spoken. 3As soon as the morning dawned, the men were sent away, they and their donkeys. 4When they had gone out of the city, *and* were not *yet* far off, Joseph said to his steward, "Get up, follow the men; and when you overtake them, say to them, 'Why have you repaid evil for good? 5*Is* not this *the one* from which my lord drinks, and with which he indeed practices divination? You have done evil in so doing.'"

6So he overtook them, and he spoke to them these same words. 7And they said to him, "Why does my lord say these words? Far be it from us that your servants should do such a thing. 8Look, we brought back to you from the land of Canaan the money which we found in the mouth of our sacks. How then could we steal silver or gold from your lord's house? 9With whomever of your servants it is found, let him die, and we also will be my lord's slaves."

10And he said, "Now also *let* it *be* according to your words; he with whom it is found shall be my slave, and you shall be blameless." 11Then each man speedily let down his sack to the ground, and each opened his sack. 12So he searched. He began with the oldest and left off with the youngest; and the cup was found in Benjamin's sack. 13Then they tore their clothes, and each man loaded his donkey and returned to the city.

14So Judah and his brothers came to Joseph's house, and he *was* still there; and they fell before him on the ground. 15And Joseph said to them, "What deed *is* this you have done? Did you not know that such a man as I can certainly practice divination?"

16Then Judah said, "What shall we say to my lord? What shall we speak? Or how shall we clear ourselves? God has found out the iniquity of your servants; here we are, my lord's slaves, both we and *he* also with whom the cup was found."

17But he said, "Far be it from me that I should do so; the man in whose hand the cup was found, he shall be my slave. And as for you, go up in peace to your father."

Judah Intercedes for Benjamin

18Then Judah came near to him and said: "O my lord, please let your servant speak a word in my lord's hearing, and do not let your anger burn against your servant; for you *are* even like Pharaoh. 19My lord asked his servants, saying, 'Have you a father or a brother?' 20And we said to my lord, 'We have a father, an old man, and a child of *his* old age, *who is* young; his brother is dead, and he alone is left of his mother's children, and his father loves him.' 21Then you said to your servants, 'Bring him down to me, that I may set my eyes on him.' 22And we said to my lord, 'The lad cannot leave his father, for *if* he should leave his father, *his father* would die.' 23But you said to your servants, 'Unless your youngest brother comes down with you, you shall see my face no more.'

24"So it was, when we went up to your servant my father, that we told him the words of my lord. 25And our father said, 'Go back *and* buy us a little food.' 26But we said, 'We cannot go down; if our youngest brother is with us, then we will go down; for we may not see the man's face unless our youngest brother *is* with us.' 27Then your servant my father said to us, 'You know that my wife bore me two sons; 28and the one went out from me, and I said, "Surely he is torn to pieces"; and I have not seen him since. 29But if you take this one also from me, and calamity befalls him, you shall bring down my gray hair with sorrow to the grave.'

30"Now therefore, when I come to your servant my father, and the lad *is* not with us, since his life is bound up in the lad's life, 31it will happen, when he sees that the lad *is* not *with us,* that he will die. So your servants will bring down the gray hair of your servant our father with sorrow to the grave. 32For your servant became surety for the lad to my father, saying, 'If I do not bring him *back* to you, then I shall bear the blame before my father forever.' 33Now therefore, please let your servant remain instead of the lad as a slave to my lord, and let the lad go up with his brothers. 34For how shall I go up to my father if the lad *is* not with me, lest perhaps I see the evil that would come upon my father?"

Joseph Revealed to His Brothers

45 Then Joseph could not restrain himself before all those who stood by him, and he cried out, "Make everyone go out from me!" So no one stood with him while Joseph made himself known to his brothers. 2And he wept aloud, and the Egyptians and the house of Pharaoh heard *it.*

3Then Joseph said to his brothers, "I *am* Joseph; does my father still live?" But his brothers could not answer him, for they were dismayed in his presence. 4And Joseph said to his brothers, "Please come near to me." So they came near. Then he said: "I *am* Joseph your brother, whom you sold into Egypt. 5But now, do not therefore be grieved or angry with yourselves because you sold me here; for God sent me before you to preserve life. 6For these two years the famine *has been* in the land, and *there are* still five years in which *there will be* neither plowing nor harvesting. 7And God sent me before you to preserve a posterity for you in the earth, and to save your lives by a great deliverance. 8So now *it was* not you *who* sent me here, but God; and He has made me a father to Pharaoh, and lord of all his house, and a ruler throughout all the land of Egypt.

9"Hurry and go up to my father, and say to

SOUL NOTE

God Will Take Care of Them *(44:30)* Judah interceded for Benjamin, sobbing to Joseph that his father would die if Benjamin were not returned safely, because Jacob's life was "bound up in the lad's life." While parents must love and protect their children, to be "bound up" in a child's life will lead a parent to be overprotective. A parent who has lost a child may be especially protective of other children, trying to control their lives so as to avoid any more pain. But parents need to release their children, entrusting them to God's protection. **Topic: Grief/Loss**

him, 'Thus says your son Joseph: "God has
made me lord of all Egypt; come down to me,
do not tarry. [10]You shall dwell in the land of
Goshen, and you shall be near to me, you and
your children, your children's children, your
flocks and your herds, and all that you have.
[11]There I will provide for you, lest you and your
household, and all that you have, come to poverty; for *there are* still five years of famine." '
[12]"And behold, your eyes and the eyes of my
brother Benjamin see that *it is* my mouth that
speaks to you. [13]So you shall tell my father of
all my glory in Egypt, and of all that you have
seen; and you shall hurry and bring my father
down here."
[14]Then he fell on his brother Benjamin's
neck and wept, and Benjamin wept on his
neck. [15]Moreover he kissed all his brothers
and wept over them, and after that his brothers talked with him.
[16]Now the report of it was heard in
Pharaoh's house, saying, "Joseph's brothers
have come." So it pleased Pharaoh and his servants well. [17]And Pharaoh said to Joseph, "Say
to your brothers, 'Do this: Load your animals
and depart; go to the land of Canaan. [18]Bring
your father and your households and come to
me; I will give you the best of the land of
Egypt, and you will eat the fat of the land.
[19]Now you are commanded—do this: Take

PERSONALITY PROFILE

Forgiveness

JOSEPH'S FORGIVENESS

(GENESIS 45:5)

The power to forgive comes as a divine gift. We choose to forgive, but God empowers our forgiveness. The desire for vengeance can be so overpowering that without God's intervention, genuine forgiveness rarely takes place. God enabled Joseph to choose forgiveness when his brothers deserved retribution. God used that willingness to assure the survival of the very brothers who had conspired to end Joseph's life.

Joseph's early years offer a case study of a dysfunctional family. For years, he was Rachel and Jacob's only son. Jacob had ten other sons by three other women, but Joseph received special treatment. When Rachel died giving birth to Benjamin, Joseph had already become his father's favorite. Jacob singled Joseph out with a special coat of many colors. His brothers despised him.

Intense competition between their mothers, along with Jacob's favoritism, fueled jealousy and resentment among the brothers toward Joseph. Benjamin was probably too young to be involved. Joseph didn't help matters by sharing a couple of his dreams with the rest of the family. These dreams highlighted his future role as ruler over his family. Even Jacob was shocked. The brothers decided to kill Joseph.

God's intervention led to the brothers' modifying their murderous plans. Instead, they sold Joseph into slavery. They soaked the special coat in animal blood and used it to convince Jacob that his favored son had been killed by wild beasts.

Joseph's next years were a roller coaster of experiences. Divine intervention eventually ushered him into Pharaoh's palace where he managed the food supplies in Egypt during a widespread famine.

That famine brought Joseph's brothers back into his life. They came for food and had no idea that they were at the mercy of the brother they had betrayed. When Joseph finally revealed his identity, his brothers were terrified. They knew what they deserved. But instead of revenge, Joseph offered forgiveness and mercy, thanking God who worked out everything for His glory.

Joseph demonstrated the cost of forgiveness. We forgive, not by making the offense unimportant, but by loving the offender. For that, we need God's help.

To Learn More: Turn to the article about forgiveness on pages 1520, 1521. See also the key passage note at Matthew 18:21–35 on page 1260.

carts out of the land of Egypt for your little ones and your wives; bring your father and come. [20]Also do not be concerned about your goods, for the best of all the land of Egypt *is* yours.' "

[21]Then the sons of Israel did so; and Joseph gave them carts, according to the command of Pharaoh, and he gave them provisions for the journey. [22]He gave to all of them, to each man, changes of garments; but to Benjamin he gave three hundred *pieces* of silver and five changes of garments. [23]And he sent to his father these *things:* ten donkeys loaded with the good things of Egypt, and ten female donkeys loaded with grain, bread, and food for his father for the journey. [24]So he sent his brothers away, and they departed; and he said to them, "See that you do not become troubled along the way."

[25]Then they went up out of Egypt, and came to the land of Canaan to Jacob their father. [26]And they told him, saying, "Joseph *is* still alive, and he *is* governor over all the land of Egypt." And Jacob's heart stood still, because he did not believe them. [27]But when they told him all the words which Joseph had said to them, and when he saw the carts which Joseph had sent to carry him, the spirit of Jacob their father revived. [28]Then Israel said, "*It is* enough. Joseph my son *is* still alive. I will go and see him before I die."

Jacob's Journey to Egypt

46 So Israel took his journey with all that he had, and came to Beersheba, and offered sacrifices to the God of his father Isaac. [2]Then God spoke to Israel in the visions of the night, and said, "Jacob, Jacob!"

And he said, "Here I am."

[3]So He said, "I *am* God, the God of your father; do not fear to go down to Egypt, for I will make of you a great nation there. [4]I will go down with you to Egypt, and I will also surely bring you up *again;* and Joseph will put his hand on your eyes."

[5]Then Jacob arose from Beersheba; and the sons of Israel carried their father Jacob, their little ones, and their wives, in the carts which Pharaoh had sent to carry him. [6]So they took their livestock and their goods, which they had acquired in the land of Canaan, and went to Egypt, Jacob and all his descendants with him. [7]His sons and his sons' sons, his daughters and his sons' daughters, and all his descendants he brought with him to Egypt.

[8]Now these *were* the names of the children of Israel, Jacob and his sons, who went to Egypt: Reuben *was* Jacob's firstborn. [9]The sons of Reuben *were* Hanoch, Pallu, Hezron, and Carmi. [10]The sons of Simeon *were* Jemuel,[a] Jamin, Ohad, Jachin,[b] Zohar,[c] and Shaul, the son of a Canaanite woman. [11]The sons of Levi *were* Gershon, Kohath, and Merari. [12]The sons of Judah *were* Er, Onan, Shelah, Perez, and Zerah (but Er and Onan died in the land of Canaan). The sons of Perez were Hezron and Hamul. [13]The sons of Issachar *were* Tola, Puvah,[a] Job,[b] and Shimron. [14]The sons of Zebulun *were* Sered, Elon, and Jahleel. [15]These *were* the sons of Leah, whom she bore to Jacob in Padan Aram, with his daughter Dinah. All the persons, his sons and his daughters, *were* thirty-three.

[16]The sons of Gad *were* Ziphion,[a] Haggi, Shuni, Ezbon,[b] Eri, Arodi,[c] and Areli. [17]The sons of Asher *were* Jimnah, Ishuah, Isui, Beriah, and Serah, their sister. And the sons of Beriah *were* Heber and Malchiel. [18]These *were* the sons of Zilpah, whom Laban gave to Leah his daughter; and these she bore to Jacob: sixteen persons.

[19]The sons of Rachel, Jacob's wife, *were* Joseph and Benjamin. [20]And to Joseph in the land of Egypt were born Manasseh and Ephraim, whom Asenath, the daughter of Poti-Pherah priest of On, bore to him. [21]The sons of Benjamin *were* Belah, Becher, Ashbel, Gera, Naaman, Ehi, Rosh, Muppim, Huppim,[a] and Ard. [22]These *were* the sons of Rachel, who were born to Jacob: fourteen persons in all.

[23]The son of Dan *was* Hushim.[a] [24]The sons of Naphtali *were* Jahzeel,[a] Guni, Jezer, and Shillem.[b] [25]These *were* the sons of Bilhah, whom Laban gave to Rachel his daughter, and she bore these to Jacob: seven persons in all.

[26]All the persons who went with Jacob to Egypt, who came from his body, besides

46:10 [a]Spelled *Nemuel* in 1 Chronicles 4:24 [b]Called *Jarib* in 1 Chronicles 4:24 [c]Called *Zerah* in 1 Chronicles 4:24 **46:13** [a]Spelled *Puah* in 1 Chronicles 7:1 [b]Same as *Jashub* in Numbers 26:24 and 1 Chronicles 7:1 **46:16** [a]Spelled *Zephon* in Samaritan Pentateuch, Septuagint, and Numbers 26:15 [b]Called *Ozni* in Numbers 26:16 [c]Spelled *Arod* in Numbers 26:17 **46:21** [a]Called *Hupham* in Numbers 26:39 **46:23** [a]Called *Shuham* in Numbers 26:42 **46:24** [a]Spelled *Jahziel* in 1 Chronicles 7:13 [b]Spelled *Shallum* in 1 Chronicles 7:13

Jacob's sons' wives, *were* sixty-six persons in
all. 27And the sons of Joseph who were born
to him in Egypt *were* two persons. All the
persons of the house of Jacob who went to
Egypt were seventy.

Jacob Settles in Goshen

28Then he sent Judah before him to Joseph,
to point out before him *the way* to Goshen.
And they came to the land of Goshen. 29So Joseph made ready his chariot and went up to
Goshen to meet his father Israel; and he presented himself to him, and fell on his neck
and wept on his neck a good while.
30And Israel said to Joseph, "Now let me
die, since I have seen your face, because you
are still alive."
31Then Joseph said to his brothers and to his
father's household, "I will go up and tell Pharaoh, and say to him, 'My brothers and those
of my father's house, who *were* in the land of
Canaan, have come to me. 32And the men *are*
shepherds, for their occupation has been to
feed livestock; and they have brought their
flocks, their herds, and all that they have.' 33So
it shall be, when Pharaoh calls you and says,
'What is your occupation?' 34that you shall
say, 'Your servants' occupation has been with
livestock from our youth even till now, both
we *and* also our fathers,' that you may dwell
in the land of Goshen; for every shepherd *is* an
abomination to the Egyptians."

47 Then Joseph went and told Pharaoh,
and said, "My father and my brothers,
their flocks and their herds and all that they
possess, have come from the land of Canaan;
and indeed they *are* in the land of Goshen."
2And he took five men from among his brothers and presented them to Pharaoh. 3Then
Pharaoh said to his brothers, "What *is* your
occupation?"
And they said to Pharaoh, "Your servants
are shepherds, both we *and* also our fathers."
4And they said to Pharaoh, "We have come to
dwell in the land, because your servants have
no pasture for their flocks, for the famine *is*
severe in the land of Canaan. Now therefore,
please let your servants dwell in the land of
Goshen."
5Then Pharaoh spoke to Joseph, saying,
"Your father and your brothers have come to
you. 6The land of Egypt *is* before you. Have
your father and brothers dwell in the best of
the land; let them dwell in the land of Goshen.
And if you know *any* competent men among
them, then make them chief herdsmen over
my livestock."
7Then Joseph brought in his father Jacob
and set him before Pharaoh; and Jacob blessed
Pharaoh. 8Pharaoh said to Jacob, "How old
are you?"
9And Jacob said to Pharaoh, "The days of
the years of my pilgrimage *are* one hundred
and thirty years; few and evil have been the
days of the years of my life, and they have not
attained to the days of the years of the life of
my fathers in the days of their pilgrimage."
10So Jacob blessed Pharaoh, and went out
from before Pharaoh.
11And Joseph situated his father and his
brothers, and gave them a possession in the
land of Egypt, in the best of the land, in the
land of Rameses, as Pharaoh had commanded.
12Then Joseph provided his father, his brothers, and all his father's household with bread,
according to the number in *their* families.

Joseph Deals with the Famine

13Now *there was* no bread in all the land; for
the famine *was* very severe, so that the land of
Egypt and the land of Canaan languished because of the famine. 14And Joseph gathered up

SOUL NOTE

Together Again *(46:30)* Years of pain and deception ended as Joseph and Jacob embraced and wept together. This family had survived intense jealousy, great tragedy, crises, separation, fear, and grief. Yet Joseph understood that God's hand had been on his life, so he was able to forgive his brothers. His willingness to forgive and to leave the past to God made this family reunion a joyous occasion. There is great joy when separated family members can reconcile and reunite. Sometimes it takes a willingness for the family members to forgive one another and move on, trusting God.
Topic: Family Problems

all the money that was found in the land of Egypt and in the land of Canaan, for the grain which they bought; and Joseph brought the money into Pharaoh's house.

15So when the money failed in the land of Egypt and in the land of Canaan, all the Egyptians came to Joseph and said, "Give us bread, for why should we die in your presence? For the money has failed."

16Then Joseph said, "Give your livestock, and I will give you *bread* for your livestock, if the money is gone." 17So they brought their livestock to Joseph, and Joseph gave them bread *in exchange* for the horses, the flocks, the cattle of the herds, and for the donkeys. Thus he fed them with bread *in exchange* for all their livestock that year.

18When that year had ended, they came to him the next year and said to him, "We will not hide from my lord that our money is gone; my lord also has our herds of livestock. There is nothing left in the sight of my lord but our bodies and our lands. 19Why should we die before your eyes, both we and our land? Buy us and our land for bread, and we and our land will be servants of Pharaoh; give *us* seed, that we may live and not die, that the land may not be desolate."

20Then Joseph bought all the land of Egypt for Pharaoh; for every man of the Egyptians sold his field, because the famine was severe upon them. So the land became Pharaoh's. 21And as for the people, he moved them into the cities,[a] from *one* end of the borders of Egypt to the *other* end. 22Only the land of the priests he did not buy; for the priests had rations *allotted to them* by Pharaoh, and they ate their rations which Pharaoh gave them; therefore they did not sell their lands.

23Then Joseph said to the people, "Indeed I have bought you and your land this day for Pharaoh. Look, *here is* seed for you, and you shall sow the land. 24And it shall come to pass in the harvest that you shall give one-fifth to Pharaoh. Four-fifths shall be your own, as seed for the field and for your food, for those of your households and as food for your little ones."

25So they said, "You have saved our lives; let us find favor in the sight of my lord, and we will be Pharaoh's servants." 26And Joseph made it a law over the land of Egypt to this day, *that* Pharaoh should have one-fifth, except for the land of the priests only, *which* did not become Pharaoh's.

Joseph's Vow to Jacob

27So Israel dwelt in the land of Egypt, in the country of Goshen; and they had possessions there and grew and multiplied exceedingly. 28And Jacob lived in the land of Egypt seventeen years. So the length of Jacob's life was one hundred and forty-seven years. 29When the time drew near that Israel must die, he called his son Joseph and said to him, "Now if I have found favor in your sight, please put your hand under my thigh, and deal kindly and truly with me. Please do not bury me in Egypt, 30but let me lie with my fathers; you shall carry me out of Egypt and bury me in their burial place."

And he said, "I will do as you have said."

31Then he said, "Swear to me." And he swore to him. So Israel bowed himself on the head of the bed.

Jacob Blesses Joseph's Sons

48 Now it came to pass after these things that Joseph was told, "Indeed your father *is* sick"; and he took with him his two sons, Manasseh and Ephraim. 2And Jacob was told, "Look, your son Joseph is coming to you"; and Israel strengthened himself and sat up on the bed. 3Then Jacob said to Joseph: "God Almighty appeared to me at Luz in the land of Canaan and blessed me, 4and said to me, 'Behold, I will make you fruitful and multiply you, and I will make of you a multitude of people, and give this land to your descendants after you *as* an everlasting possession.' 5And now your two sons, Ephraim and Manasseh, who were born to you in the land of Egypt before I came to you in Egypt, *are* mine; as Reuben and Simeon, they shall be mine. 6Your offspring whom you beget after them shall be yours; they will be called by the name of their brothers in their inheritance. 7But as for me, when I came from Padan, Rachel died beside me in the land of Canaan on the way, when *there was* but a little distance to go to Ephrath; and I buried her there on the way to Ephrath (that is, Bethlehem)."

8Then Israel saw Joseph's sons, and said, "Who *are* these?"

9Joseph said to his father, "They *are* my sons, whom God has given me in this *place.*"

47:21 [a]Following Masoretic Text and Targum; Samaritan Pentateuch, Septuagint, and Vulgate read *made the people virtual slaves.*

And he said, "Please bring them to me, and
I will bless them." [10]Now the eyes of Israel
were dim with age, *so that* he could not see.
Then Joseph brought them near him, and he
kissed them and embraced them. [11]And Israel
said to Joseph, "I had not thought to see your
face; but in fact, God has also shown me your
offspring!"

[12]So Joseph brought them from beside his
knees, and he bowed down with his face to
the earth. [13]And Joseph took them both,
Ephraim with his right hand toward Israel's
left hand, and Manasseh with his left hand toward Israel's right hand, and brought *them*
near him. [14]Then Israel stretched out his right
hand and laid *it* on Ephraim's head, who *was*
the younger, and his left hand on Manasseh's
head, guiding his hands knowingly, for Manasseh *was* the firstborn. [15]And he blessed Joseph, and said:

"God, before whom my fathers Abraham
and Isaac walked,
The God who has fed me all my life long
to this day,
16 The Angel who has redeemed me from
all evil,
Bless the lads;
Let my name be named upon them,
And the name of my fathers Abraham
and Isaac;
And let them grow into a multitude in
the midst of the earth."

[17]Now when Joseph saw that his father laid
his right hand on the head of Ephraim, it displeased him; so he took hold of his father's
hand to remove it from Ephraim's head to
Manasseh's head. [18]And Joseph said to his father, "Not so, my father, for this *one is* the
firstborn; put your right hand on his head."

[19]But his father refused and said, "I know,
my son, I know. He also shall become a people,
and he also shall be great; but truly his younger
brother shall be greater than he, and his
descendants shall become a multitude of nations."

[20]So he blessed them that day, saying, "By
you Israel will bless, saying, 'May God make
you as Ephraim and as Manasseh!' " And thus
he set Ephraim before Manasseh.

[21]Then Israel said to Joseph, "Behold, I am
dying, but God will be with you and bring you
back to the land of your fathers. [22]Moreover I
have given to you one portion above your
brothers, which I took from the hand of the
Amorite with my sword and my bow."

JACOB'S LAST WORDS TO HIS SONS

49 And Jacob called his sons and said,
"Gather together, that I may tell you
what shall befall you in the last days:

2 "Gather together and hear, you sons of
Jacob,
And listen to Israel your father.

3 "Reuben, you are my firstborn,
My might and the beginning of my
strength,
The excellency of dignity and the
excellency of power.
4 Unstable as water, you shall not excel,
Because you went up to your father's
bed;
Then you defiled *it*—
He went up to my couch.

5 "Simeon and Levi *are* brothers;
Instruments of cruelty *are in* their
dwelling place.
6 Let not my soul enter their council;
Let not my honor be united to their
assembly;
For in their anger they slew a man,
And in their self-will they hamstrung an
ox.
7 Cursed *be* their anger, for *it is* fierce;
And their wrath, for it is cruel!
I will divide them in Jacob
And scatter them in Israel.

8 "Judah, you *are he* whom your brothers
shall praise;
Your hand *shall be* on the neck of your
enemies;
Your father's children shall bow down
before you.
9 Judah *is* a lion's whelp;
From the prey, my son, you have gone
up.
He bows down, he lies down as a lion;
And as a lion, who shall rouse him?
10 The scepter shall not depart from Judah,
Nor a lawgiver from between his feet,
Until Shiloh comes;
And to Him *shall be* the obedience of the
people.

11 Binding his donkey to the vine,
And his donkey's colt to the choice vine,
He washed his garments in wine,
And his clothes in the blood of grapes.
12 His eyes *are* darker than wine,
And his teeth whiter than milk.

13 "Zebulun shall dwell by the haven of the sea;
He *shall become* a haven for ships,
And his border shall adjoin Sidon.

14 "Issachar is a strong donkey,
Lying down between two burdens;
15 He saw that rest *was* good,
And that the land *was* pleasant;
He bowed his shoulder to bear *a burden,*
And became a band of slaves.

16 "Dan shall judge his people
As one of the tribes of Israel.
17 Dan shall be a serpent by the way,
A viper by the path,
That bites the horse's heels
So that its rider shall fall backward.
18 I have waited for your salvation,
O LORD!

19 "Gad, a troop shall tramp upon him,
But he shall triumph at last.

20 "Bread from Asher *shall be* rich,
And he shall yield royal dainties.

21 "Naphtali *is* a deer let loose;
He uses beautiful words.

22 "Joseph *is* a fruitful bough,

PERSONALITY PROFILE

Attachment/ Blessing

JACOB AND THE ART OF BLESSING

(GENESIS 49)

One of the most sacred family events in ancient Middle Eastern cultures was the passing of the blessing from one generation to the next. As the last of the great Jewish patriarchs, Jacob's blessing marked the transition from family to nation. Jacob gathered his sons around his deathbed and spoke meaningful words to each. They were about to become the 12 tribes of Israel. God allowed Jacob to speak prophetically about his sons' futures.

Joseph received a double portion of the inheritance, although he was not the firstborn son. First Chronicles 5:1 explains that this was due to Reuben's forfeiting his birthright as the oldest by dishonoring his father. Joseph's two sons Ephraim and Manasseh each became a tribe. There was no tribe of Joseph, but Joseph's role in Egypt as the savior of the family placed him in the role of eldest and protector.

Jacob's words proved remarkably accurate for each of his sons. He described their character and foresaw those traits passed on to their descendants. He was both blunt and complimentary. His perspective allowed his sons the knowledge that their father had been thinking about them. He had been praying for them, too.

Each child wants to be known and loved by his or her parents. Blessings flow when children hear their mother or father express intimate and individualized thoughts about them. For Christian parents, the blessing involves sharing hopes and prayers for each of our children. If we question the importance of these gestures, we merely have to examine how we long to hear the same words from our own parents.

Effective parents find a way to include words of blessing in their relationship with their children. These are priceless gifts that can shape a child's life. The process begins when we look into our child's eyes and say, "I love you." After that, we fill in the details. Bless your children.

To Learn More: Turn to the article about attachment/blessing on pages 76, 77. See also the key passage note at Genesis 27:30–36 on page 43.

THE BLESSING

JOHN TRENT

(Genesis 49)

The Hebrew word for *blessing* is one of the most important words in the Bible. It is used over 640 times in the Old Testament and is pictured in God's original plan for humankind: Genesis 1:27, 28 states that after God created a man and a woman in His own image, He blessed them. What an encouraging truth to know that we were created for blessing!

While unique spiritual and prophetic aspects of the blessing lay with the patriarchs alone (as seen in Gen. 49), the basic relational elements of the blessing provide powerful tools to communicate acceptance, protection, and affirmation that still apply today. The presence or absence of these elements can help us determine whether our home is, or our parents' home was, a place of blessing. A study of the blessing always begins in the context of parental acceptance. However, in studying the blessing in the Scriptures, we find that its principles can be used in any intimate relationship.

THE BASIC ELEMENTS OF THE BLESSING

There are five basic elements to blessing others, as described below.

Meaningful Touch

When Isaac blessed his son, he said: "Come near now and kiss me, my son" (Gen. 27:26). This was not an isolated incident. Each time the blessing was given in the Scriptures, meaningful touch provided a caring background to the words that would be spoken. Kissing, hugging, and laying on of hands were all a part of bestowing the blessing.

Meaningful touch has many beneficial effects. The act of touch is a key to communicating warmth, personal acceptance, and affirmation. For Isaac, as well as for any person who wishes to see the blessing grow and develop in a child, spouse, or friend, touch is an integral part of the blessing.

A Spoken Message

Words have an immense power to build us up or tear us down emotionally. This is particularly true when it comes to giving or gaining family approval. Many people can clearly remember the words of praise that their parents spoke years ago. Others can remember just as clearly the negative words that they heard. Throughout Scripture, we find a keen recognition of the power and importance of spoken words. In the very beginning, God spoke and the world came into being (Gen. 1:3). When God sent His Son to communicate His love and complete His plan of salvation, it was His Word that "became flesh and dwelt among us" (John 1:14). God has always communicated His blessings through spoken words.

Attaching "High Value"

To value something means to attach honor to it. In Hebrew, the verb "to bless" literally means, "to bow the knee." The words of blessing should carry with them the recognition that the person being blessed is valuable and has redeeming qualities. In Scripture, recognition is based on who a person is, not simply on his or her performance. In Genesis 27:27–29, Isaac used a word picture to describe how valuable his son was to him: "The smell of my son is like the smell of a field which the LORD has blessed." Word pictures are a powerful way of communicating acceptance and high value—the third element of the family blessing.

Picturing a Special Future

Isaac said to his son Jacob, "May God give you of the dew of heaven, of the fatness of the earth. . . . Let peoples serve you, and nations bow down to you" (Gen. 27:28, 29). Parents today cannot predict another person's future with biblical accuracy. We can, however, encourage the person to set meaningful goals. We can also convey to them that the gifts and character traits they have right now are attributes that God can bless and use in the future. With this fourth element of the blessing, a child can gain a sense of security in the present and grow in confidence to serve God and others in the future.

An Active Commitment to Fulfill the Blessing

The last element of the blessing pictures the responsibility that goes with giving the blessing. For the patriarchs, not only their words, but also God Himself stood behind the blessing that they bestowed on their children. Parents today need to rely on the Lord to give them the strength and staying power to confirm their children's blessings. They too have God's Word through Scripture as a guide, plus the power of the indwelling Holy Spirit.

Why is an active commitment so important when it comes to bestowing the blessing? Words alone cannot communicate the blessing; they need to be backed with a commitment to doing everything possible to help the one being blessed to be successful. We can tell a child, "You have the talent to be a very good pianist," but if we neglect to provide a way for the child to practice piano, our lack of commitment has undermined our message. The fifth element of the blessing, an active commitment, is crucial to seeing the blessing communicated in our homes.

The blessing provides five basic elements—meaningful touch, a spoken message, attaching high value to the one being blessed, picturing a special future, and confirming the blessing by active commitment—to communicate love and acceptance. These key ingredients have the power to bring warmth, healing, and hope to our intimate relationships. They are the very relational elements God uses in blessing His children!

FURTHER MEDITATION:

Other passages to study about the issue of attachment/blessing include:

➢ Genesis 27:27–36; 35:9–15
➢ Proverbs 31:28
➢ Ezekiel 34:26
➢ Galatians 4:6, 7
➢ Ephesians 1:3–6; 6:4
➢ 1 Peter 3:8, 9

To Learn More: Turn to the key passage note on attachment/blessing at Genesis 27:30–36 on page 43. See also the personality profile of Jacob on page 75.

A fruitful bough by a well;
His branches run over the wall.
23 The archers have bitterly grieved him,
Shot *at him* and hated him.
24 But his bow remained in strength,
And the arms of his hands were made
strong
By the hands of the Mighty *God* of Jacob
(From there *is* the Shepherd, the Stone
of Israel),
25 By the God of your father who will help
you,
And by the Almighty who will bless you
With blessings of heaven above,
Blessings of the deep that lies beneath,
Blessings of the breasts and of the
womb.
26 The blessings of your father
Have excelled the blessings of my
ancestors,
Up to the utmost bound of the
everlasting hills.
They shall be on the head of Joseph,
And on the crown of the head of him
who was separate from his brothers.

27 "Benjamin is a ravenous wolf;
In the morning he shall devour the prey,
And at night he shall divide the spoil."

28All these *are* the twelve tribes of Israel,
and this *is* what their father spoke to them.
And he blessed them; he blessed each one according to his own blessing.

JACOB'S DEATH AND BURIAL

29Then he charged them and said to them: "I
am to be gathered to my people; bury me with
my fathers in the cave that *is* in the field of
Ephron the Hittite, 30in the cave that *is* in the
field of Machpelah, which *is* before Mamre in
the land of Canaan, which Abraham bought
with the field of Ephron the Hittite as a possession for a burial place. 31There they buried Abraham and Sarah his wife, there they buried Isaac
and Rebekah his wife, and there I buried Leah.
32The field and the cave that *is* there *were* purchased from the sons of Heth." 33And when Jacob had finished commanding his sons, he
drew his feet up into the bed and breathed his
last, and was gathered to his people.

50 Then Joseph fell on his father's face
and wept over him, and kissed him.
2And Joseph commanded his servants the
physicians to embalm his father. So the physicians embalmed Israel. 3Forty days were required for him, for such are the days required
for those who are embalmed; and the Egyptians mourned for him seventy days.

4Now when the days of his mourning were
past, Joseph spoke to the household of Pharaoh, saying, "If now I have found favor in
your eyes, please speak in the hearing of Pharaoh, saying, 5'My father made me swear, saying, "Behold, I am dying; in my grave which I
dug for myself in the land of Canaan, there you
shall bury me." Now therefore, please let me
go up and bury my father, and I will come
back.' "

6And Pharaoh said, "Go up and bury your
father, as he made you swear."

7So Joseph went up to bury his father; and
with him went up all the servants of Pharaoh,
the elders of his house, and all the elders of
the land of Egypt, 8as well as all the house
of Joseph, his brothers, and his father's house.
Only their little ones, their flocks, and their
herds they left in the land of Goshen. 9And
there went up with him both chariots and
horsemen, and it was a very great gathering.

10Then they came to the threshing floor of
Atad, which *is* beyond the Jordan, and they
mourned there with a great and very solemn
lamentation. He observed seven days of
mourning for his father. 11And when the inhabitants of the land, the Canaanites, saw the
mourning at the threshing floor of Atad, they
said, "This *is* a deep mourning of the Egyptians." Therefore its name was called Abel
Mizraim,[a] which *is* beyond the Jordan.

12So his sons did for him just as he had commanded them. 13For his sons carried him to the
land of Canaan, and buried him in the cave of
the field of Machpelah, before Mamre, which
Abraham bought with the field from Ephron
the Hittite as property for a burial place. 14And
after he had buried his father, Joseph returned
to Egypt, he and his brothers and all who went
up with him to bury his father.

JOSEPH REASSURES HIS BROTHERS

15When Joseph's brothers saw that their father was dead, they said, "Perhaps Joseph will
hate us, and may actually repay us for all the
evil which we did to him." 16So they sent *mes-*

50:11 [a]Literally *Mourning of Egypt*

sengers to Joseph, saying, "Before your father
died he commanded, saying, [17]'Thus you shall
say to Joseph: "I beg you, please forgive the
trespass of your brothers and their sin; for they
did evil to you." ' Now, please, forgive the trespass of the servants of the God of your father."
And Joseph wept when they spoke to him.
[18]Then his brothers also went and fell down
before his face, and they said, "Behold, we *are*
your servants."
[19]Joseph said to them, "Do not be afraid, for
am I in the place of God?
[20]But as for you, you
meant evil against me;
but God meant it for
good, in order to bring it
about as *it is* this day, to
save many people alive.
[21]Now therefore, do not
be afraid; I will provide
for you and your little ones." And he comforted
them and spoke kindly to them.

> "But as for you, you meant evil against me; but God meant it for good."
>
> GENESIS 50:20

DEATH OF JOSEPH

[22]So Joseph dwelt in Egypt, he and his
father's household. And Joseph lived one
hundred and ten years. [23]Joseph saw Ephraim's children to the third *generation.* The
children of Machir, the son of Manasseh, were
also brought up on Joseph's knees.
[24]And Joseph said to his brethren, "I am dying; but God will surely visit you, and bring
you out of this land to the land of which He
swore to Abraham, to Isaac, and to Jacob."
[25]Then Joseph took an
oath from the children
of Israel, saying, "God
will surely visit you,
and you shall carry up
my bones from here."
[26]So Joseph died, *being*
one hundred and ten
years old; and they em-
balmed him, and he was put in a coffin in
Egypt.

SOUL NOTE

Rising Above the Pain *(50:20)* If anyone had good reason for revenge, it was Joseph. His brothers' jealousy provoked them to horrible abuse—selling him as a common slave to be taken away forever (37:11–28). Before being raised to power in Egypt, Joseph had lost thirteen years of personal freedom. When Jacob died, the brothers feared that Joseph, now a powerful ruler, would exact his revenge. Instead, Joseph wisely understood that God had sovereignly overruled his brothers' abuse, making their evil turn out for good. Such a response can only come from those who trust God to rule—and overrule—in their lives. **Topic: Abuse**

Exodus

atch a talk show. Carefully observe your neighbors. The evidence is clear: Our world is filled with people in bondage to shameful passions and addictive behaviors. Is it any wonder so many feel hopeless and desperate?

The Old Testament book of Exodus (meaning "the way out") paints a vivid picture of deliverance. God hears the cries of His people who are slaves in Egypt (2:23, 24). With compassion, He calls Moses to lead Israel out of bondage (3:1—13:22). Following a dramatic rescue at the Red Sea (chapter 14), God takes His people on an extended spiritual retreat to Mount Sinai. There He reveals both His Law and His plans for the tabernacle, in effect demonstrating that ultimate freedom—freedom of the soul—comes only when we are living and worshiping as God intended.

Written by Moses, the Book of Exodus is not just about Israel's journey out of slavery. It also details the beginning of the nation's journey to the Promised Land. At the center of this drama of redemption is the writer of the book, an ordinary man who becomes a hero. At times, Moses is the epitome of great faith (14:13). At other times, he is bound by human fears (3:11—4:17) and frustrations (32:19). Like all of us, Moses must learn to trust God in both good times and bad. Again and again, God intervenes with grace and deliverance—reminding us that no one is hopelessly beyond the reach of His loving touch. He alone can set people free.

SOUL CONCERNS IN EXODUS

Israel's Suffering in Egypt

1 Now these *are* the names of the children
of Israel who came to Egypt; each man
and his household came with Jacob: [2]Reuben,
Simeon, Levi, and Judah; [3]Issachar, Zebulun,
and Benjamin; [4]Dan, Naphtali, Gad, and Asher.
[5]All those who were descendants[a] of Jacob
were seventy[b] persons (for Joseph was in
Egypt *already*). [6]And Joseph died, all his
brothers, and all that generation. [7]But the children of Israel were fruitful and increased
abundantly, multiplied and grew exceedingly
mighty; and the land was filled with them.

[8]Now there arose a new king over Egypt,
who did not know Joseph. [9]And he said to his
people, "Look, the people of the children of Israel *are* more and mightier than we; [10]come,
let us deal shrewdly with them, lest they
multiply, and it happen, in the event of war,
that they also join our enemies and fight
against us, and *so* go up out of the land."
[11]Therefore they set taskmasters over them
to afflict them with their burdens. And they
built for Pharaoh supply cities, Pithom and
Raamses. [12]But the more they afflicted them,
the more they multiplied and grew. And they
were in dread of the children of Israel. [13]So the
Egyptians made the children of Israel serve
with rigor. [14]And they made their lives bitter
with hard bondage—in mortar, in brick, and
in all manner of service in the field. All their
service in which they made them serve *was*
with rigor.

[15]Then the king of Egypt spoke to the Hebrew midwives, of whom the name of one *was*
Shiphrah and the name of the other Puah;
[16]and he said, "When you do the duties of a
midwife for the Hebrew women, and see *them*
on the birthstools, if it *is* a son, then you shall
kill him; but if it *is* a daughter, then she shall
live." [17]But the midwives feared God, and did
not do as the king of Egypt commanded them,
but saved the male children alive. [18]So the
king of Egypt called for the midwives and said
to them, "Why have you done this thing, and
saved the male children alive?"

[19]And the midwives said to Pharaoh, "Because the Hebrew women *are* not like the
Egyptian women; for they *are* lively and give
birth before the midwives come to them."

[20]Therefore God dealt well with the midwives, and the people multiplied and grew
very mighty. [21]And so it was, because the midwives feared God, that He provided households for them.

[22]So Pharaoh commanded all his people,
saying, "Every son who is born[a] you shall cast
into the river, and every daughter you shall
save alive."

Moses Is Born

2 And a man of the house of Levi went and
took *as wife* a daughter of Levi. [2]So the
woman conceived and bore a son. And when
she saw that he *was* a beautiful *child,* she hid
him three months. [3]But when she could no
longer hide him, she took an ark of bulrushes
for him, daubed it with asphalt and pitch, put
the child in it, and laid *it* in the reeds by the
river's bank. [4]And his sister stood afar off, to
know what would be done to him.

[5]Then the daughter of Pharaoh came down
to bathe at the river. And her maidens walked
along the riverside; and when she saw the ark
among the reeds, she sent her maid to get it.
[6]And when she opened *it,* she saw the child,
and behold, the baby wept. So she had compassion on him, and said, "This is one of the
Hebrews' children."

1:5 [a]Literally *who came from the loins of* [b]Dead Sea Scrolls and Septuagint read *seventy-five* (compare Acts 7:14). **1:22** [a]Samaritan Pentateuch, Septuagint, and Targum add *to the Hebrews.*

SOUL NOTE

Seeing God in Suffering *(1:11)* A thirst for God often grows from suffering. The Israelites became slaves, were forced to build great cities for Pharaoh, and were brutally afflicted by their taskmasters. God is not the author of evil. He allows it sometimes, however, to His own people—not to destroy them but to bring about a greater good. God would soon perform great miracles on behalf of Israel. The suffering they had experienced brought them to complete dependence on God, who alone could free them. **Topic: Trials**

7Then his sister said to Pharaoh's daughter, "Shall I go and call a nurse for you from the Hebrew women, that she may nurse the child for you?"

8And Pharaoh's daughter said to her, "Go." So the maiden went and called the child's mother. 9Then Pharaoh's daughter said to her, "Take this child away and nurse him for me, and I will give *you* your wages." So the woman took the child and nursed him. 10And the child grew, and she brought him to Pharaoh's daughter, and he became her son. So she called his name Moses,[a] saying, "Because I drew him out of the water."

Moses Flees to Midian

11Now it came to pass in those days, when Moses was grown, that he went out to his brethren and looked at their burdens. And he saw an Egyptian beating a Hebrew, one of his brethren. 12So he looked this way and that way, and when he saw no one, he killed the Egyptian and hid him in the sand. 13And when he went out the second day, behold, two Hebrew men were fighting, and he said to the one who did the wrong, "Why are you striking your companion?"

14Then he said, "Who made you a prince and a judge over us? Do you intend to kill me as you killed the Egyptian?"

So Moses feared and said, "Surely this thing is known!" 15When Pharaoh heard of this matter, he sought to kill Moses. But Moses fled from the face of Pharaoh and dwelt in the land of Midian; and he sat down by a well.

16Now the priest of Midian had seven daughters. And they came and drew water, and they filled the troughs to water their father's flock. 17Then the shepherds came and drove them away; but Moses stood up and helped them, and watered their flock.

18When they came to Reuel their father, he said, "How *is it that* you have come so soon today?"

19And they said, "An Egyptian delivered us from the hand of the shepherds, and he also drew enough water for us and watered the flock."

20So he said to his daughters, "And where *is* he? Why *is* it *that* you have left the man? Call him, that he may eat bread."

21Then Moses was content to live with the man, and he gave Zipporah his daughter to Moses. 22And she bore *him* a son. He called his name Gershom,[a] for he said, "I have been a stranger in a foreign land."

23Now it happened in the process of time that the king of Egypt died. Then the children of Israel groaned because of the bondage, and they cried out; and their cry came up to God because of the bondage. 24So God heard their groaning, and God remembered His covenant with Abraham, with Isaac, and with Jacob. 25And God looked upon the children of Israel, and God acknowledged *them*.

Moses at the Burning Bush

3 Now Moses was tending the flock of Jethro his father-in-law, the priest of Midian. And he led the flock to the back of the desert, and came to Horeb, the mountain of God. 2And the Angel of the LORD appeared to him in a flame of fire from the midst of a bush. So he looked, and behold, the bush was burning with fire, but the bush *was* not consumed. 3Then Moses said, "I will now turn aside and see this great sight, why the bush does not burn."

4So when the LORD saw that he turned aside to look, God called to him from the midst of the bush and said, "Moses, Moses!"

2:10 [a]Literally *Drawn Out* **2:22** [a]Literally *Stranger There*

SOUL NOTE

Leaving Justice to God *(2:11, 12)* Violence and murder have been around since Cain killed Abel. Moses' desire for justice was certainly correct, but his actions were not. Killing the Egyptian and hiding him in the sand went too far. Physical force may have been necessary, but not murder. Although this act did not thwart God's plans for him, Moses still faced the consequences of his action. To keep from being killed himself, Moses had to run far from the life he had known.

Topic: Violence

And he said, "Here I am."
5Then He said, "Do not draw near this
place. Take your sandals off your feet, for the
place where you stand *is* holy ground." 6More-
over He said, "I *am* the God of your father—
the God of Abraham, the God of Isaac, and the
God of Jacob." And Moses hid his face, for he
was afraid to look upon God.
7And the LORD said: "I have surely seen the
oppression of My people who *are* in Egypt,
and have heard their cry because of their taskmasters, for I know their sorrows. 8So I have
come down to deliver them out of the hand of
the Egyptians, and to bring them up from that
land to a good and large land, to a land flowing with milk and honey, to the place of the
Canaanites and the Hittites and the Amorites
and the Perizzites and the Hivites and the Jebusites. 9Now therefore, behold, the cry of the
children of Israel has come to Me, and I have
also seen the oppression with which the Egyptians oppress them. 10Come now, therefore,
and I will send you to Pharaoh that you may
bring My people, the children of Israel, out of
Egypt."
11But Moses said to God, "Who *am* I that I
should go to Pharaoh, and that I should bring
the children of Israel out of Egypt?"
12So He said, "I will certainly be with you.
And this *shall be* a sign to you that I have sent
you: When you have brought the people out of
Egypt, you shall serve God on this mountain."
13Then Moses said to God, "Indeed, *when* I
come to the children of Israel and say to them,
'The God of your fathers has sent me to you,'
and they say to me, 'What *is* His name?' what
shall I say to them?"
14And God said to Moses, "I AM WHO I
AM." And He said, "Thus you shall say to the
children of Israel, 'I AM has sent me to you.' "
15Moreover God said to Moses, "Thus you
shall say to the children of Israel: 'The LORD
God of your fathers, the God of Abraham, the
God of Isaac, and the God of Jacob, has sent
me to you. This *is* My name forever, and this *is*
My memorial to all generations.' 16Go and
gather the elders of Israel together, and say to
them, 'The LORD God of your fathers, the God
of Abraham, of Isaac, and of Jacob, appeared
to me, saying, "I have surely visited you and
seen what is done to you in Egypt; 17and I
have said I will bring you up out of the affliction of Egypt to the land of the Canaanites and
the Hittites and the Amorites and the Perizzites and the Hivites and the Jebusites, to a
land flowing with milk and honey." ' 18Then
they will heed your voice; and you shall come,
you and the elders of Israel, to the king of

SOUL NOTE

Listen to God *(3:1–6)* Moses had run from Egypt, but God was determined to use him for the task of bringing his people out of slavery there. God then spoke, warned of His holiness, described who He was, and gave Moses the task. When we read God's Word, we are in His presence. God speaks through His Word, shows us His holiness, tells us about Himself, and gives us tasks. Come to God's Word, and you will discover who He is and what He wants you to do. **Topic: Knowing God**

SOUL NOTE

God Is with You *(3:11)* Moses was certain God was making a mistake by choosing him to lead the Israelites. His five excuses indicated a lack of confidence in his ability to get the job done. He had: (1) a crisis of identity ("who am I?" 3:11); (2) a crisis of authority ("what is His name?" 3:13); (3) a crisis of faith ("they will not believe me," 4:1); (4) a crisis of ability ("I am not eloquent," 4:10); and (5) a crisis of obedience ("send . . . whomever else," 4:13). Yet as God was with him, Moses led the nation to freedom. With God's help and guidance, great things are possible. **Topic: Self-Esteem**

Genetic Issues

STRENGTH IN WEAKNESS

MICHAEL R. LYLES

(Exodus 4:11)

Many people have thought, "If only I could change this one thing, my life would be so different, so much more useful."

Not long ago, a man came for help after his father was admitted to the hospital for a psychosis. His problem? He feared becoming like his father and devastating his family. Depressed about the future, he believed that he had his father's genes and, therefore, the same fate. Another man came, worried about his father's Alzheimer's disease. He wondered if he should marry or have children because of his probability for contracting the disease.

Both of these patients felt despair over these genetic issues. They were ready to give up on life. A sense of stigma colored their ability to see beyond what they believed were predetermined genetic problems.

Every person can identify something that they wish could be different in their family, personality, or physical or emotional makeup. Many people wrestle with congenital or genetic problems about which they have no choice. They may have a physical disability such as cerebral palsy, paralysis, or blindness. Others may suffer with a cognitive disability such as dyslexia or a neurological problem like Huntington's disease. Still others recognize that an issue with a parent, such as alcoholism or a manic-depressive illness, may also affect them.

People commonly wish to change something in their genetic makeup or inherent abilities. Even some of the most influential Bible characters struggled with this concern. For example, Moses wished for more eloquent speech; the apostle Paul struggled with a thorn in the flesh. In both cases, God took these men in their weakness and used them to do great things.

When God chose Moses to carry His message to Pharaoh, Moses was aware of a disability. He focused on his slowness of speech and decided that his disability would eliminate him from carrying out God's plan (Ex. 4:10). God promised that He would help Moses to speak and would teach him what to say. When Moses still felt inadequate to do what God was asking, God provided more help through Moses' brother Aaron. God promised, "I will be with your mouth and with his mouth, and I will teach you what you shall do" (Ex. 4:15).

Paul's thorn in the flesh was a disability that caused him pain and distress (2 Cor. 12:7–10). He pleaded with God repeatedly to take it away, but God chose not to. Paul was certainly engaged in doing the Lord's will and could have benefited from having his thorn removed. But God chose otherwise. Paul could have been bitter. Instead, he learned that because of Christ, "when I am weak, then I am strong" (2 Cor. 12:10). Paul learned that it took faith to believe God was in control and to trust Him in spite of the infirmity. God restores and renews (2 Cor. 5:17); at times, however, He gives more grace for endurance. "My grace is sufficient for you, for My strength is made perfect in weakness" (2 Cor. 12:9). What appears to be defeat becomes victory: "We have this treasure in earthen vessels, that the excellence of the power may be of God and not of us" (2 Cor. 4:7).

God chose to use both Paul and Moses for His purposes. He also chose not to change or heal them; instead, He asked them to serve Him in their weaknesses for His glory!

Everyone has at least one major challenge to deal with in life, something that cannot be changed. We can choose to focus on the problem and our powerlessness, or we can focus on who God is and what He wants for our lives. Although we are painfully aware of our weakness, we often forget that others also struggle. One patient complained about her best friend whom she thought was perfect. This friend always looked perfect and seemed to live the perfect life. As this woman left the office, she met the next patient in the waiting room—her best friend.

PRACTICAL CONSIDERATIONS

1. We are not alone, no matter what the problem. "No temptation has overtaken you except such as is common to man" (1 Cor. 10:13).
2. God loves us and promises to be with us. He cares about our situation, even if He doesn't change it. "God resists the proud, but gives grace to the humble" (James 4:6).
3. God desires that we know Him. As we remember who He is and His love for us, we can avoid living in despair. "Hear, O LORD, when I cry with my voice! Have mercy also upon me, and answer me. When You said, 'Seek My face,' my heart said to You, 'Your face, LORD, I will seek'" (Ps. 27:7, 8).
4. When we come to the end of our own resources, God's work of grace in our lives will be more clearly evident. "I have been crucified with Christ; it is no longer I who live, but Christ lives in me; and the life which I now live in the flesh I live by faith in the Son of God, who loved me and gave Himself for me" (Gal. 2:20).
5. Instead of focusing on weaknesses, focus on what God has given us in Christ. God knows our circumstances and gives us His strength. "Be anxious for nothing, but in everything by prayer and supplication, with thanksgiving, let your requests be made known to God" (Phil. 4:6).

Remember, God is always at work. He wants to work in and through us—just as we are.

FURTHER MEDITATION:

Other passages to study about genetic issues include:

- Psalm 139
- Isaiah 35
- Matthew 11:4, 5
- 1 Corinthians 15:50–57
- James 5:13–18

To Learn More: Turn to the key passage note on genetic issues at Isaiah 35:1–6 on page 914. See also the personality profile of the blind man on page 1388.

Egypt; and you shall say to him, 'The LORD
God of the Hebrews has met with us; and now,
please, let us go three days' journey into the
wilderness, that we may sacrifice to the LORD
our God.' 19But I am sure that the king of
Egypt will not let you go, no, not even by a
mighty hand. 20So I will stretch out My hand
and strike Egypt with all My wonders which I
will do in its midst; and after that he will let
you go. 21And I will give this people favor in
the sight of the Egyptians; and it shall be,
when you go, that you shall not go empty-
handed. 22But every woman shall ask of her
neighbor, namely, of her who dwells near her
house, articles of silver, articles of gold, and
clothing; and you shall put *them* on your sons
and on your daughters. So you shall plunder
the Egyptians."

MIRACULOUS SIGNS FOR PHARAOH

4 Then Moses answered and said, "But
suppose they will not believe me or listen
to my voice; suppose they say, 'The LORD has
not appeared to you.' "

2So the LORD said to him, "What *is* that in
your hand?"

He said, "A rod."

3And He said, "Cast it on the ground." So he
cast it on the ground, and it became a serpent;
and Moses fled from it. 4Then the LORD said to
Moses, "Reach out your hand and take *it* by the
tail" (and he reached out his hand and caught
it, and it became a rod in his hand), 5"that they
may believe that the LORD God of their fathers,
the God of Abraham, the God of Isaac, and the
God of Jacob, has appeared to you."

6Furthermore the LORD said to him, "Now
put your hand in your
bosom." And he put his
hand in his bosom, and
when he took it out, be-
hold, his hand *was* lep-
rous, like snow. 7And
He said, "Put your hand
in your bosom again."
So he put his hand in
his bosom again, and
drew it out of his bo-
som, and behold, it was restored like his *other*
flesh. 8"Then it will be, if they do not believe
you, nor heed the message of the first sign,
that they may believe the message of the latter
sign. 9And it shall be, if they do not believe
even these two signs, or listen to your voice,
that you shall take water from the river[a] and
pour *it* on the dry *land.* The water which you
take from the river will become blood on the
dry *land.*"

10Then Moses said to the LORD, "O my Lord,
I *am* not eloquent, neither before nor since
You have spoken to Your servant; but I *am*
slow of speech and slow of tongue."

11So the LORD said to him, "Who has made
man's mouth? Or who makes the mute, the
deaf, the seeing, or the blind? *Have* not I, the
LORD? 12Now therefore, go, and I will be with
your mouth and teach you what you shall say."

13But he said, "O my Lord, please send by
the hand of whomever *else* You may send."

14So the anger of the LORD was kindled
against Moses, and He said: "Is not Aaron the
Levite your brother? I know that he can speak
well. And look, he is also coming out to meet
you. When he sees you, he will be glad in his
heart. 15Now you shall speak to him and put
the words in his mouth. And I will be with
your mouth and with his mouth, and I will
teach you what you shall do. 16So he shall be
your spokesman to the people. And he himself
shall be as a mouth for you, and you shall be
to him as God. 17And you shall take this rod in
your hand, with which you shall do the
signs."

MOSES GOES TO EGYPT

18So Moses went and returned to Jethro his
father-in-law, and said to him, "Please let me
go and return to my brethren who *are* in
Egypt, and see whether they are still alive."

And Jethro said to Moses, "Go in peace."

19Now the LORD said to Moses in Midian,
"Go, return to Egypt;
for all the men who
sought your life are
dead." 20Then Moses
took his wife and his
sons and set them on a
donkey, and he re-
turned to the land of
Egypt. And Moses took
the rod of God in his
hand.

21And the LORD said to Moses, "When you
go back to Egypt, see that you do all those
wonders before Pharaoh which I have put in
your hand. But I will harden his heart, so that

> So the people believed; and when they heard that the LORD had visited the children of Israel and that He had looked on their affliction, then they bowed their heads and worshiped.
>
> EXODUS 4:31

4:9 [a]That is, the Nile

he will not let the people go. [22]Then you shall
say to Pharaoh, 'Thus says the LORD: "Israel *is*
My son, My firstborn. [23]So I say to you, let My
son go that he may serve Me. But if you refuse
to let him go, indeed I will kill your son, your
firstborn." ' "
[24]And it came to pass on the way, at the encampment, that the LORD met him and sought
to kill him. [25]Then Zipporah took a sharp
stone and cut off the foreskin of her son and
cast *it* at *Moses'*[a] feet, and said, "Surely you
are a husband of blood to me!" [26]So He let him
go. Then she said, "*You are* a husband of
blood!"—because of the circumcision.
[27]And the LORD said to Aaron, "Go into the
wilderness to meet Moses." So he went and
met him on the mountain of God, and kissed
him. [28]So Moses told Aaron all the words of
the LORD who had sent him, and all the signs
which He had commanded him. [29]Then Moses
and Aaron went and gathered together all the
elders of the children of Israel. [30]And Aaron
spoke all the words which the LORD had spoken to Moses. Then he did the signs in the
sight of the people. [31]So the people believed;
and when they heard that the LORD had visited
the children of Israel and that He had looked
on their affliction, then they bowed their
heads and worshiped.

FIRST ENCOUNTER WITH PHARAOH

5 Afterward Moses and Aaron went in and
told Pharaoh, "Thus says the LORD God of
Israel: 'Let My people go, that they may hold a
feast to Me in the wilderness.' "
[2]And Pharaoh said, "Who *is* the LORD, that I
should obey His voice to let Israel go? I do not
know the LORD, nor will I let Israel go."
[3]So they said, "The God of the Hebrews
has met with us. Please, let us go three days'

4:25 [a]Literally *his*

PERSONALITY PROFILE

Work

AARON: SERVING TOGETHER

(EXODUS 4:27)

Before God called Moses to return to Egypt and lead Israel to the Promised Land, He sent for backup. Even as Moses and God debated the former's leadership qualifications, Aaron was already on the way. God had an answer for all Moses' excuses. But Moses persisted in dodging God's call. God finally silenced Moses' resistance with anger. It took God's passion to get Moses' full attention. God then agreed to assign Aaron as Moses' spokesman and assistant.

Moses and Aaron functioned as a task force. They fulfilled God's plan to free the Israelites because they worked together. Some people make their greatest contribution, not as individual stars, but as part of a team—in relationship to another or to a group. History is full of good working teams whose accomplishments are greater than the sum of their individual parts. In the Bible, we see David and Jonathan, Paul and Silas, Mary and Martha, and Peter, James, and John.

Like Aaron, some teammates always play "backup," never stepping into the starring role. During the infamous golden calf incident, Aaron learned a valuable lesson about himself—he wasn't cut out to lead alone. His most effective role was derived from his unique relationship with Moses. The mark of a successful supporting teammate is a commitment to promote and enhance the lead player, and to do so without jealousy or competition.

Aaron left an effective legacy as he labored with Moses. He accepted his secondary role, and did the work that was asked of him with courage and gusto. In our vocations, we should look for "significant others" who can share our goals and vision for the task. Sometimes we will lead; most often we will find ourselves supporting the efforts of other people. Until we know how to support, we will not be ready to lead.

To Learn More: Turn to the article about work on pages 1590, 1591. See also the key passage note at 2 Thessalonians 3:10–12 on page 1588.

journey into the desert and sacrifice to the LORD our God, lest He fall upon us with pestilence or with the sword."

[4]Then the king of Egypt said to them, "Moses and Aaron, why do you take the people from their work? Get *back* to your labor." [5]And Pharaoh said, "Look, the people of the land *are* many now, and you make them rest from their labor!"

[6]So the same day Pharaoh commanded the taskmasters of the people and their officers, saying, [7]"You shall no longer give the people straw to make brick as before. Let them go and gather straw for themselves. [8]And you shall lay on them the quota of bricks which they made before. You shall not reduce it. For they are idle; therefore they cry out, saying, 'Let us go *and* sacrifice to our God.' [9]Let more work be laid on the men, that they may labor in it, and let them not regard false words."

[10]And the taskmasters of the people and their officers went out and spoke to the people, saying, "Thus says Pharaoh: 'I will not give you straw. [11]Go, get yourselves straw where you can find it; yet none of your work will be reduced.' " [12]So the people were scattered abroad throughout all the land of Egypt to gather stubble instead of straw. [13]And the taskmasters forced *them* to hurry, saying, "Fulfill your work, *your* daily quota, as when there was straw." [14]Also the officers of the children of Israel, whom Pharaoh's taskmasters had set over them, were beaten *and* were asked, "Why have you not fulfilled your task in making brick both yesterday and today, as before?"

[15]Then the officers of the children of Israel came and cried out to Pharaoh, saying, "Why are you dealing thus with your servants? [16]There is no straw given to your servants, and they say to us, 'Make brick!' And indeed your servants *are* beaten, but the fault *is* in your *own* people."

[17]But he said, "You *are* idle! Idle! Therefore you say, 'Let us go *and* sacrifice to the LORD.' [18]Therefore go now *and* work; for no straw shall be given you, yet you shall deliver the quota of bricks." [19]And the officers of the children of Israel saw *that* they *were* in trouble after it was said, "You shall not reduce *any* bricks from your daily quota."

[20]Then, as they came out from Pharaoh, they met Moses and Aaron who stood there to meet them. [21]And they said to them, "Let the LORD look on you and judge, because you have made us abhorrent in the sight of Pharaoh and in the sight of his servants, to put a sword in their hand to kill us."

ISRAEL'S DELIVERANCE ASSURED

[22]So Moses returned to the LORD and said, "Lord, why have You brought trouble on this people? Why *is* it You have sent me? [23]For since I came to Pharaoh to speak in Your name, he has done evil to this people; neither have You delivered Your people at all."

6 Then the LORD said to Moses, "Now you shall see what I will do to Pharaoh. For with a strong hand he will let them go, and with a strong hand he will drive them out of his land."

[2]And God spoke to Moses and said to him: "I *am* the LORD. [3]I appeared to Abraham, to Isaac, and to Jacob, as God Almighty, but *by* My name LORD[a] I was not known to them. [4]I have also established My covenant with them, to give them the land of Canaan, the land of their pilgrimage, in which they were strangers. [5]And I have also heard the groaning of the children of Israel whom the Egyptians keep in bondage, and I have remembered My covenant. [6]Therefore say to the children of Israel: 'I *am* the LORD; I will bring you out from under the burdens of the Egyptians, I will rescue you from their bondage, and I will redeem you with an outstretched arm and with great judgments. [7]I will take you as My people, and I will be your God. Then you shall know that I *am* the LORD your God who brings you out from under the burdens of the Egyptians. [8]And I will bring you into the land which I swore to give to Abraham, Isaac, and Jacob; and I will give it to you *as* a heritage: I *am* the LORD.' " [9]So Moses spoke thus to the children of Israel; but they did not heed Moses, because of anguish of spirit and cruel bondage.

[10]And the LORD spoke to Moses, saying, [11]"Go in, tell Pharaoh king of Egypt to let the children of Israel go out of his land."

> "I will take you as My people, and I will be your God."
> EXODUS 6:7

6:3 [a]Hebrew *YHWH,* traditionally *Jehovah*

12 And Moses spoke before the LORD, saying,
"The children of Israel have not heeded me.
How then shall Pharaoh heed me, for I *am* of
uncircumcised lips?"
13 Then the LORD spoke to Moses and Aaron,
and gave them a command for the children of
Israel and for Pharaoh king of Egypt, to bring
the children of Israel out of the land of Egypt.

THE FAMILY OF MOSES AND AARON

14 These *are* the heads of their fathers'
houses: The sons of Reuben, the firstborn of Israel, *were* Hanoch, Pallu, Hezron, and Carmi.
These are the families of Reuben. 15 And the
sons of Simeon *were* Jemuel,[a] Jamin, Ohad,
Jachin, Zohar, and Shaul the son of a Canaanite woman. These *are* the families of Simeon.
16 These *are* the names of the sons of Levi according to their generations: Gershon, Kohath,
and Merari. And the years of the life of Levi
were one hundred and thirty-seven. 17 The sons
of Gershon *were* Libni and Shimi according to
their families. 18 And the sons of Kohath *were*
Amram, Izhar, Hebron, and Uzziel. And the
years of the life of Kohath *were* one hundred
and thirty-three. 19 The sons of Merari *were*
Mahli and Mushi. These *are* the families of
Levi according to their generations.
20 Now Amram took for himself Jochebed,
his father's sister, as wife; and she bore him
Aaron and Moses. And the years of the life of
Amram *were* one hundred and thirty-seven.
21 The sons of Izhar *were* Korah, Nepheg, and
Zichri. 22 And the sons of Uzziel *were* Mishael,
Elzaphan, and Zithri. 23 Aaron took to himself
Elisheba, daughter of Amminadab, sister of
Nahshon, as wife; and she bore him Nadab,
Abihu, Eleazar, and Ithamar. 24 And the sons of
Korah *were* Assir, Elkanah, and Abiasaph.
These are the families of the Korahites. 25 Eleazar, Aaron's son, took for himself one of the
daughters of Putiel as wife; and she bore him
Phinehas. These *are* the heads of the fathers'
houses of the Levites according to their families.
26 These *are the same* Aaron and Moses to
whom the LORD said, "Bring out the children
of Israel from the land of Egypt according to
their armies." 27 These *are* the ones who spoke
to Pharaoh king of Egypt, to bring out the children of Israel from Egypt. These *are the same*
Moses and Aaron.

AARON IS MOSES' SPOKESMAN

28 And it came to pass, on the day the LORD
spoke to Moses in the land of Egypt, 29 that the
LORD spoke to Moses, saying, "I *am* the LORD.
Speak to Pharaoh king of Egypt all that I say to
you."
30 But Moses said before the LORD, "Behold,
I *am* of uncircumcised lips, and how shall
Pharaoh heed me?"
7 So the LORD said to Moses: "See, I have
made you *as* God to Pharaoh, and Aaron
your brother shall be your prophet. 2 You shall
speak all that I command you. And Aaron
your brother shall tell Pharaoh to send the
children of Israel out of his land. 3 And I will
harden Pharaoh's heart, and multiply My
signs and My wonders in the land of Egypt.
4 But Pharaoh will not heed you, so that I may
lay My hand on Egypt and bring My armies
and My people, the children of Israel, out of
the land of Egypt by great judgments. 5 And
the Egyptians shall know that I *am* the LORD,
when I stretch out My hand on Egypt and
bring out the children of Israel from among
them."
6 Then Moses and Aaron did *so;* just as the
LORD commanded them, so they did. 7 And
Moses *was* eighty years old and Aaron eighty-
three years old when they spoke to Pharaoh.

6:15 [a]Spelled *Nemuel* in Numbers 26:12

SOUL NOTE

Catch the Vision *(7:2)* It's not enough to be *called* a leader—you must *act* like a leader if you expect people to follow you. That's the challenge Moses and Aaron faced as they prepared to meet with Pharaoh and to convince the Israelites. God had already authorized them to speak on His behalf. Now it was up to them to communicate that authority. A good leader must be able to articulate the vision, communicate the message, and express inner passion so others can envision the goal and strive for it. **Topic: Work**

AARON'S MIRACULOUS ROD

8Then the LORD spoke to Moses and Aaron, saying, 9"When Pharaoh speaks to you, saying, 'Show a miracle for yourselves,' then you shall say to Aaron, 'Take your rod and cast *it* before Pharaoh, *and* let it become a serpent.' " 10So Moses and Aaron went in to Pharaoh, and they did so, just as the LORD commanded. And Aaron cast down his rod before Pharaoh and before his servants, and it became a serpent.

11But Pharaoh also called the wise men and the sorcerers; so the magicians of Egypt, they also did in like manner with their enchantments. 12For every man threw down his rod, and they became serpents. But Aaron's rod swallowed up their rods. 13And Pharaoh's heart grew hard, and he did not heed them, as the LORD had said.

THE FIRST PLAGUE: WATERS BECOME BLOOD

14So the LORD said to Moses: "Pharaoh's heart *is* hard; he refuses to let the people go. 15Go to Pharaoh in the morning, when he goes out to the water, and you shall stand by the river's bank to meet him; and the rod which was turned to a serpent you shall take in your hand. 16And you shall say to him, 'The LORD God of the Hebrews has sent me to you, saying, "Let My people go, that they may serve Me in the wilderness"; but indeed, until now you would not hear! 17Thus says the LORD: "By this you shall know that I *am* the LORD. Behold, I will strike the waters which *are* in the river with the rod that *is* in my hand, and they shall be turned to blood. 18And the fish that *are* in the river shall die, the river shall stink, and the Egyptians will loathe to drink the water of the river." ' "

19Then the LORD spoke to Moses, "Say to Aaron, 'Take your rod and stretch out your hand over the waters of Egypt, over their streams, over their rivers, over their ponds, and over all their pools of water, that they may become blood. And there shall be blood throughout all the land of Egypt, both in *buckets of* wood and *pitchers of* stone.' " 20And Moses and Aaron did so, just as the LORD commanded. So he lifted up the rod and struck the waters that *were* in the river, in the sight of Pharaoh and in the sight of his servants. And all the waters that *were* in the river were turned to blood. 21The fish that *were* in the river died, the river stank, and the Egyptians could not drink the water of the river. So there was blood throughout all the land of Egypt.

22Then the magicians of Egypt did so with their enchantments; and Pharaoh's heart grew hard, and he did not heed them, as the LORD had said. 23And Pharaoh turned and went into his house. Neither was his heart moved by this. 24So all the Egyptians dug all around the river for water to drink, because they could not drink the water of the river. 25And seven days passed after the LORD had struck the river.

THE SECOND PLAGUE: FROGS

8 And the LORD spoke to Moses, "Go to Pharaoh and say to him, 'Thus says the LORD: "Let My people go, that they may serve Me. 2But if you refuse to let *them* go, behold, I will smite all your territory with frogs. 3So the river shall bring forth frogs abundantly, which shall go up and come into your house, into your bedroom, on your bed, into the houses of your servants, on your people, into your ovens, and into your kneading bowls. 4And the frogs shall come up on you, on your people, and on all your servants." ' "

5Then the LORD spoke to Moses, "Say to Aaron, 'Stretch out your hand with your rod over the streams, over the rivers, and over the ponds, and cause frogs to come up on the land of Egypt.' " 6So Aaron stretched out his hand over the waters of Egypt, and the frogs came up and covered the land of Egypt. 7And the magicians did so with their enchantments, and brought up frogs on the land of Egypt.

8Then Pharaoh called for Moses and Aaron, and said, "Entreat the LORD that He may take away the frogs from me and from my people; and I will let the people go, that they may sacrifice to the LORD."

9And Moses said to Pharaoh, "Accept the honor of saying when I shall intercede for you, for your servants, and for your people, to destroy the frogs from you and your houses, *that* they may remain in the river only."

10So he said, "Tomorrow." And he said, "*Let it be* according to your word, that you may know that *there is* no one like the LORD our God. 11And the frogs shall depart from you, from your houses, from your servants, and from your people. They shall remain in the river only."

12Then Moses and Aaron went out from Pharaoh. And Moses cried out to the LORD concerning the frogs which He had brought against Pharaoh. 13 So the LORD did according to the word of Moses. And the frogs died out of the houses, out of the courtyards, and out of the fields. 14 They gathered them together in heaps, and the land stank. 15 But when Pharaoh saw that there was relief, he hardened his heart and did not heed them, as the LORD had said.

THE THIRD PLAGUE: LICE

16 So the LORD said to Moses, "Say to Aaron, 'Stretch out your rod, and strike the dust of the land, so that it may become lice throughout all the land of Egypt.' " 17 And they did so. For Aaron stretched out his hand with his rod and struck the dust of the earth, and it became lice on man and beast. All the dust of the land became lice throughout all the land of Egypt.

18 Now the magicians so worked with their enchantments to bring forth lice, but they could not. So there were lice on man and beast. 19 Then the magicians said to Pharaoh, "This *is* the finger of God." But Pharaoh's heart grew hard, and he did not heed them, just as the LORD had said.

THE FOURTH PLAGUE: FLIES

20 And the LORD said to Moses, "Rise early in the morning and stand before Pharaoh as he comes out to the water. Then say to him, 'Thus says the LORD: "Let My people go, that they may serve Me. 21 Or else, if you will not let My people go, behold, I will send swarms *of flies* on you and your servants, on your people and into your houses. The houses of the Egyptians shall be full of swarms *of flies,* and also the ground on which they *stand.* 22 And in that day I will set apart the land of Goshen, in which My people dwell, that no swarms *of flies* shall be there, in order that you may know that I *am* the LORD in the midst of the land. 23 I will make a difference[a] between My people and your people. Tomorrow this sign shall be." ' " 24 And the LORD did so. Thick swarms *of flies* came into the house of Pharaoh, *into* his servants' houses, and into all the land of Egypt. The land was corrupted because of the swarms *of flies.*

25 Then Pharaoh called for Moses and Aaron, and said, "Go, sacrifice to your God in the land."

26 And Moses said, "It is not right to do so, for we would be sacrificing the abomination of the Egyptians to the LORD our God. If we sacrifice the abomination of the Egyptians before their eyes, then will they not stone us? 27 We will go three days' journey into the wilderness and sacrifice to the LORD our God as He will command us."

28 So Pharaoh said, "I will let you go, that you may sacrifice to the LORD your God in the wilderness; only you shall not go very far away. Intercede for me."

29 Then Moses said, "Indeed I am going out from you, and I will entreat the LORD, that the swarms *of flies* may depart tomorrow from Pharaoh, from his servants, and from his people. But let Pharaoh not deal deceitfully anymore in not letting the people go to sacrifice to the LORD."

30 So Moses went out from Pharaoh and entreated the LORD. 31 And the LORD did according to the word of Moses; He removed the swarms *of flies* from Pharaoh, from his servants, and from his people. Not one remained. 32 But Pharaoh hardened his heart at this time also; neither would he let the people go.

THE FIFTH PLAGUE: LIVESTOCK DISEASED

9 Then the LORD said to Moses, "Go in to Pharaoh and tell him, 'Thus says the LORD God of the Hebrews: "Let My people go, that they may serve Me. 2 For if you refuse to let *them* go, and still hold them, 3 behold, the hand of the LORD will be on your cattle in the field, on the horses, on the donkeys, on the camels, on the oxen, and on the sheep—a very severe pestilence. 4 And the LORD will make a difference between the livestock of Israel and the livestock of Egypt. So nothing shall die of all *that* belongs to the children of Israel." ' " 5 Then the LORD appointed a set time, saying, "Tomorrow the LORD will do this thing in the land."

6 So the LORD did this thing on the next day, and all the livestock of Egypt died; but of the livestock of the children of Israel, not one died. 7 Then Pharaoh sent, and indeed, not even one of the livestock of the Israelites was dead. But the heart of Pharaoh became hard, and he did not let the people go.

THE SIXTH PLAGUE: BOILS

8 So the LORD said to Moses and Aaron, "Take for yourselves handfuls of ashes from a

---

8:23 [a]Literally *set a ransom* (compare Exodus 9:4 and 11:7)

furnace, and let Moses scatter it toward the
heavens in the sight of Pharaoh. 9And it will
become fine dust in all the land of Egypt, and
it will cause boils that break out in sores on
man and beast throughout all the land of
Egypt." 10Then they took ashes from the furnace and stood before Pharaoh, and Moses
scattered *them* toward heaven. And *they*
caused boils that break out in sores on man
and beast. 11And the magicians could not
stand before Moses because of the boils, for
the boils were on the magicians and on all the
Egyptians. 12But the LORD hardened the heart
of Pharaoh; and he did not heed them, just as
the LORD had spoken to Moses.

THE SEVENTH PLAGUE: HAIL

13Then the LORD said to Moses, "Rise early
in the morning and stand before Pharaoh, and
say to him, 'Thus says the LORD God of the Hebrews: "Let My people go, that they may serve
Me, 14for at this time I will send all My plagues
to your very heart, and on your servants and
on your people, that you may know that *there
is* none like Me in all the earth. 15Now if I had
stretched out My hand and struck you and
your people with pestilence, then you would
have been cut off from the earth. 16But indeed
for this *purpose* I have raised you up, that I
may show My power *in* you, and that My
name may be declared in all the earth. 17As yet
you exalt yourself against My people in that
you will not let them go. 18Behold, tomorrow
about this time I will cause very heavy hail to
rain down, such as has not been in Egypt
since its founding until now. 19Therefore send
now *and* gather your livestock and all that you
have in the field, for the hail shall come down
on every man and every animal which is
found in the field and is not brought home;
and they shall die." ' "

20He who feared the word of the LORD
among the servants of Pharaoh made his servants and his livestock flee to the houses.
21But he who did not regard the word of the
LORD left his servants and his livestock in the
field.

22Then the LORD said to Moses, "Stretch out
your hand toward heaven, that there may be
hail in all the land of Egypt—on man, on
beast, and on every herb of the field, throughout the land of Egypt." 23And Moses stretched
out his rod toward heaven; and the LORD sent
thunder and hail, and fire darted to the
ground. And the LORD rained hail on the land
of Egypt. 24So there was hail, and fire mingled
with the hail, so very heavy that there was
none like it in all the land of Egypt since it became a nation. 25And the hail struck throughout the whole land of Egypt, all that *was* in the
field, both man and beast; and the hail struck
every herb of the field and broke every tree of
the field. 26Only in the land of Goshen, where
the children of Israel *were,* there was no hail.

27And Pharaoh sent and called for Moses
and Aaron, and said to them, "I have sinned
this time. The LORD *is* righteous, and my people and I *are* wicked. 28Entreat the LORD, that
there may be no *more* mighty thundering and
hail, for *it is* enough. I will let you go, and you
shall stay no longer."

29So Moses said to him, "As soon as I have
gone out of the city, I will spread out my
hands to the LORD; the thunder will cease, and
there will be no more hail, that you may know
that the earth *is* the LORD's. 30But as for you
and your servants, I know that you will not yet
fear the LORD God."

31Now the flax and the barley were struck,
for the barley *was* in the head and the flax *was*
in bud. 32But the wheat and the spelt were not
struck, for they *are* late crops.

SOUL NOTE

Don't Fight God *(9:12)* If God "hardened" Pharaoh's heart, was the hapless leader just a pawn in God's plan? Not at all! He was the ruler of Egypt. God did not take control of Pharaoh's will and force his decisions. This man was responsible for his own actions. As God appealed to him to release the Israelites, Pharaoh became even more determined to keep them in bondage. What resulted was a contest of wills—Pharaoh's against God's. Eventually God won, and Pharaoh's will was broken. Fighting against God is a losing proposition. It will only exhaust you, deplete your energies, and mess up your life. **Topic: Attitudes**

33So Moses went out of the city from Pharaoh and spread out his hands to the LORD; then the thunder and the hail ceased, and the rain was not poured on the earth. 34And when Pharaoh saw that the rain, the hail, and the thunder had ceased, he sinned yet more; and he hardened his heart, he and his servants. 35So the heart of Pharaoh was hard; neither would he let the children of Israel go, as the LORD had spoken by Moses.

THE EIGHTH PLAGUE: LOCUSTS

10 Now the LORD said to Moses, "Go in to Pharaoh; for I have hardened his heart and the hearts of his servants, that I may show these signs of Mine before him, 2and that you may tell in the hearing of your son and your son's son the mighty things I have done in Egypt, and My signs which I have done among them, that you may know that I *am* the LORD."

3So Moses and Aaron came in to Pharaoh and said to him, "Thus says the LORD God of the Hebrews: 'How long will you refuse to humble yourself before Me? Let My people go, that they may serve Me. 4Or else, if you refuse to let My people go, behold, tomorrow I will bring locusts into your territory. 5And they shall cover the face of the earth, so that no one will be able to see the earth; and they shall eat the residue of what is left, which remains to you from the hail, and they shall eat every tree which grows up for you out of the field. 6They shall fill your houses, the houses of all your servants, and the houses of all the Egyptians—which neither your fathers nor your fathers' fathers have seen, since the day that they were on the earth to this day.' " And he turned and went out from Pharaoh.

7Then Pharaoh's servants said to him, "How long shall this man be a snare to us? Let the men go, that they may serve the LORD their God. Do you not yet know that Egypt is destroyed?"

8So Moses and Aaron were brought again to Pharaoh, and he said to them, "Go, serve the LORD your God. Who *are* the ones that are going?"

9And Moses said, "We will go with our young and our old; with our sons and our daughters, with our flocks and our herds we will go, for we must hold a feast to the LORD."

10Then he said to them, "The LORD had better be with you when I let you and your little ones go! Beware, for evil is ahead of you. 11Not so! Go now, you *who are* men, and serve the LORD, for that is what you desired." And they were driven out from Pharaoh's presence.

12Then the LORD said to Moses, "Stretch out your hand over the land of Egypt for the locusts, that they may come upon the land of Egypt, and eat every herb of the land—all that the hail has left." 13So Moses stretched out his rod over the land of Egypt, and the LORD brought an east wind on the land all that day and all *that* night. When it was morning, the east wind brought the locusts. 14And the locusts went up over all the land of Egypt and rested on all the territory of Egypt. *They were* very severe; previously there had been no such locusts as they, nor shall there be such after them. 15For they covered the face of the whole earth, so that the land was darkened; and they ate every herb of the land and all the fruit of the trees which the hail had left. So there remained nothing green on the trees or on the plants of the field throughout all the land of Egypt.

16Then Pharaoh called for Moses and Aaron in haste, and said, "I have sinned against the LORD your God and against you. 17Now therefore, please forgive my sin only this once, and entreat the LORD your God, that He may take away from me this death only." 18So he went out from Pharaoh and entreated the LORD. 19And the LORD turned a very strong west wind, which took the locusts away and blew them into the Red Sea. There remained not one locust in all the territory of Egypt. 20But the LORD hardened Pharaoh's heart, and he did not let the children of Israel go.

THE NINTH PLAGUE: DARKNESS

21Then the LORD said to Moses, "Stretch out your hand toward heaven, that there may be darkness over the land of Egypt, darkness *which* may even be felt." 22So Moses stretched out his hand toward heaven, and there was thick darkness in all the land of Egypt three days. 23They did not see one another; nor did anyone rise from his place for three days. But all the children of Israel had light in their dwellings.

24Then Pharaoh called to Moses and said, "Go, serve the LORD; only let your flocks and your herds be kept back. Let your little ones also go with you."

25But Moses said, "You must also give us

sacrifices and burnt offerings, that we may sacrifice to the LORD our God. [26]Our livestock also shall go with us; not a hoof shall be left behind. For we must take some of them to serve the LORD our God, and even we do not know with what we must serve the LORD until we arrive there."

[27]But the LORD hardened Pharaoh's heart, and he would not let them go. [28]Then Pharaoh said to him, "Get away from me! Take heed to yourself and see my face no more! For in the day you see my face you shall die!"

[29]So Moses said, "You have spoken well. I will never see your face again."

DEATH OF THE FIRSTBORN ANNOUNCED

11 And the LORD said to Moses, "I will bring one more plague on Pharaoh and on Egypt. Afterward he will let you go from here. When he lets *you* go, he will surely drive you out of here altogether. [2]Speak now in the hearing of the people, and let every man ask from his neighbor and every woman from her neighbor, articles of silver and articles of gold." [3]And the LORD gave the people favor in the sight of the Egyptians. Moreover the man Moses *was* very great in the land of Egypt, in the sight of Pharaoh's servants and in the sight of the people.

[4]Then Moses said, "Thus says the LORD: 'About midnight I will go out into the midst of Egypt; [5]and all the firstborn in the land of Egypt shall die, from the firstborn of Pharaoh who sits on his throne, even to the firstborn of the female servant who *is* behind the handmill, and all the firstborn of the animals. [6]Then there shall be a great cry throughout all the land of Egypt, such as was not like it *before,* nor shall be like it again. [7]But against none of the children of Israel shall a dog move its tongue, against man or beast, that you may know that the LORD does make a difference between the Egyptians and Israel.' [8]And all these your servants shall come down to me and bow down to me, saying, 'Get out, and all the people who follow you!' After that I will go out." Then he went out from Pharaoh in great anger.

[9]But the LORD said to Moses, "Pharaoh will not heed you, so that My wonders may be multiplied in the land of Egypt." [10]So Moses and Aaron did all these wonders before Pharaoh; and the LORD hardened Pharaoh's heart, and he did not let the children of Israel go out of his land.

THE PASSOVER INSTITUTED

12 Now the LORD spoke to Moses and Aaron in the land of Egypt, saying, [2]"This month *shall be* your beginning of months; it *shall be* the first month of the year to you. [3]Speak to all the congregation of Israel, saying: 'On the tenth of this month every man shall take for himself a lamb, according to the house of *his* father, a lamb for a household. [4]And if the household is too small for the lamb, let him and his neighbor next to his house take *it* according to the number of the persons; according to each man's need you shall make your count for the lamb. [5]Your lamb shall be without blemish, a male of the first year. You may take *it* from the sheep or from the goats. [6]Now you shall keep it until the fourteenth day of the same month. Then the whole assembly of the congregation of Israel shall kill it at twilight. [7]And they shall take *some* of the blood and put *it* on the two doorposts and on the lintel of the houses where they eat it. [8]Then they shall eat the flesh on that night; roasted in fire, with unleavened bread *and* with bitter *herbs* they shall eat it. [9]Do not eat it raw, nor boiled at all with water, but roasted in fire—its head with its legs and its entrails. [10]You shall let none of

SOUL NOTE

Truth or Consequences? *(12:3)* In this final plague, God required the Israelites to apply the blood of a sacrificial lamb to the doorposts of their houses. "When I see the blood, I will pass over you," God promised (12:13). This placement of blood between God and man pictures the blood of Christ's sacrifice on the Cross, which pays for believers' sins and causes God's wrath to pass over them (Heb. 9:11–28). Those who do not respond to God's truth will face the tragic consequences of their unbelief. **Topic: Belief**

it remain until morning, and what remains of it until morning you shall burn with fire. [11]And thus you shall eat it: *with* a belt on your waist, your sandals on your feet, and your staff in your hand. So you shall eat it in haste. It *is* the LORD's Passover.

[12]'For I will pass through the land of Egypt on that night, and will strike all the firstborn in the land of Egypt, both man and beast; and against all the gods of Egypt I will execute judgment: I *am* the LORD. [13]Now the blood shall be a sign for you on the houses where you *are*. And when I see the blood, I will pass over you; and the plague shall not be on you to destroy *you* when I strike the land of Egypt.

[14]'So this day shall be to you a memorial; and you shall keep it as a feast to the LORD throughout your generations. You shall keep it as a feast by an everlasting ordinance. [15]Seven days you shall eat unleavened bread. On the first day you shall remove leaven from your houses. For whoever eats leavened bread from the first day until the seventh day, that person shall be cut off from Israel. [16]On the first day *there shall be* a holy convocation, and on the seventh day there shall be a holy convocation for you. No manner of work shall be done on them; but *that* which everyone must eat—that only may be prepared by you. [17]So you shall observe *the Feast of* Unleavened Bread, for on this same day I will have brought your armies out of the land of Egypt. Therefore you shall observe this day throughout your generations as an everlasting ordinance. [18]In the first *month*, on the fourteenth day of the month at evening, you shall eat unleavened bread, until the twenty-first day of the month at evening. [19]For seven days no leaven shall be found in your houses, since whoever eats what is leavened, that same person shall be cut off from the congregation of Israel, whether *he is* a stranger or a native of the land. [20]You shall eat nothing leavened; in all your dwellings you shall eat unleavened bread.' "

[21]Then Moses called for all the elders of Israel and said to them, "Pick out and take lambs for yourselves according to your families, and kill the Passover *lamb*. [22]And you shall take a bunch of hyssop, dip *it* in the blood that *is* in the basin, and strike the lintel and the two doorposts with the blood that *is* in the basin. And none of you shall go out of the door of his house until morning. [23]For the LORD will pass through to strike the Egyptians; and when He sees the blood on the lintel and on the two doorposts, the LORD will pass over the door and not allow the destroyer to come into your houses to strike *you*. [24]And you shall observe this thing as an ordinance for you and your sons forever. [25]It will come to pass when you come to the land which the LORD will give you, just as He promised, that you shall keep this service. [26]And it shall be, when your children say to you, 'What do you mean by this service?' [27]that you shall say, 'It *is* the Passover sacrifice of the LORD, who passed over the houses of the children of Israel in Egypt when He struck the Egyptians and delivered our households.' " So the people bowed their heads and worshiped. [28]Then the children of Israel went away and did *so;* just as the LORD had commanded Moses and Aaron, so they did.

The Tenth Plague: Death of the Firstborn

[29]And it came to pass at midnight that the LORD struck all the firstborn in the land of Egypt, from the firstborn of Pharaoh who sat on his throne to the firstborn of the captive who *was* in the dungeon, and all the firstborn of livestock. [30]So Pharaoh rose in the night, he, all his servants, and all the Egyptians; and there was a great cry in Egypt, for *there was* not a house where *there was* not one dead.

The Exodus

[31]Then he called for Moses and Aaron by night, and said, "Rise, go out from among my people, both you and the children of Israel. And go, serve the LORD as you have said. [32]Also take your flocks and your herds, as you have said, and be gone; and bless me also."

[33]And the Egyptians urged the people, that they might send them out of the land in haste. For they said, "We *shall* all *be* dead." [34]So the people took their dough before it was leavened, having their kneading bowls bound up in their clothes on their shoulders. [35]Now the children of Israel had done according to the word of Moses, and they had asked from the Egyptians articles of silver, articles of gold, and clothing. [36]And the LORD had given the people favor in the sight of the Egyptians, so that they granted them *what they requested*. Thus they plundered the Egyptians.

[37]Then the children of Israel journeyed from Rameses to Succoth, about six hundred thousand men on foot, besides children. [38]A mixed multitude went up with them also, and flocks

and herds—a great deal of livestock. 39And
they baked unleavened cakes of the dough
which they had brought out of Egypt; for it
was not leavened, because they were driven
out of Egypt and could not wait, nor had they
prepared provisions for themselves.
40Now the sojourn of the children of Israel
who lived in Egypt[a] *was* four hundred and
thirty years. 41And it came to pass at the end
of the four hundred and thirty years—on that
very same day—it came to pass that all the
armies of the LORD went out from the land of
Egypt. 42It *is* a night of solemn observance to
the LORD for bringing them out of the land of
Egypt. This *is* that night of the LORD, a solemn
observance for all the children of Israel
throughout their generations.

PASSOVER REGULATIONS

43And the LORD said to Moses and Aaron,
"This *is* the ordinance of the Passover: No foreigner shall eat it. 44But every man's servant
who is bought for money, when you have circumcised him, then he may eat it. 45A sojourner and a hired servant shall not eat it.
46In one house it shall be eaten; you shall not
carry any of the flesh outside the house, nor
shall you break one of its bones. 47All the congregation of Israel shall keep it. 48And when a
stranger dwells with you *and wants* to keep
the Passover to the LORD, let all his males be
circumcised, and then let him come near and
keep it; and he shall be as a native of the land.
For no uncircumcised person shall eat it.
49One law shall be for the native-born and for
the stranger who dwells among you."
50Thus all the children of Israel did; as the
LORD commanded Moses and Aaron, so they
did. 51And it came to pass, on that very same
day, that the LORD brought the children of Israel out of the land of Egypt according to their
armies.

THE FIRSTBORN CONSECRATED

13 Then the LORD spoke to Moses, saying,
2"Consecrate to Me all the firstborn,
whatever opens the womb among the children
of Israel, *both* of man and beast; it is Mine."

THE FEAST OF UNLEAVENED BREAD

3And Moses said to the people: "Remember
this day in which you went out of Egypt, out
of the house of bondage; for by strength of
hand the LORD brought you out of this *place*.
No leavened bread shall be eaten. 4On this day
you are going out, in the month Abib. 5And it
shall be, when the LORD brings you into the
land of the Canaanites and the Hittites and the
Amorites and the Hivites and the Jebusites,
which He swore to your fathers to give you, a
land flowing with milk and honey, that you
shall keep this service in this month. 6Seven
days you shall eat unleavened bread, and on
the seventh day *there shall be* a feast to the
LORD. 7Unleavened bread shall be eaten seven
days. And no leavened bread shall be seen
among you, nor shall leaven be seen among
you in all your quarters. 8And you shall tell
your son in that day, saying, '*This is done* because of what the LORD did for me when I
came up from Egypt.' 9It shall be as a sign to
you on your hand and as a memorial between
your eyes, that the LORD's law may be in your
mouth; for with a strong hand the LORD has
brought you out of Egypt. 10You shall therefore
keep this ordinance in its season from year to
year.

THE LAW OF THE FIRSTBORN

11"And it shall be, when the LORD brings you
into the land of the Canaanites, as He swore to
you and your fathers, and gives it to you,
12that you shall set apart to the LORD all that
open the womb, that is, every firstborn that
comes from an animal which you have; the
males *shall be* the LORD's. 13But every firstborn of a donkey you shall redeem with a
lamb; and if you will not redeem *it*, then you
shall break its neck. And all the firstborn of
man among your sons you shall redeem. 14So
it shall be, when your son asks you in time to
come, saying, 'What *is* this?' that you shall say
to him, 'By strength of hand the LORD brought
us out of Egypt, out of the house of bondage.
15And it came to pass, when Pharaoh was
stubborn about letting us go, that the LORD
killed all the firstborn in the land of Egypt,
both the firstborn of man and the firstborn of
beast. Therefore I sacrifice to the LORD all
males that open the womb, but all the firstborn of my sons I redeem.' 16It shall be as a
sign on your hand and as frontlets between
your eyes, for by strength of hand the LORD
brought us out of Egypt."

12:40 [a]Samaritan Pentateuch and Septuagint read *Egypt and Canaan*.

THE WILDERNESS WAY

17Then it came to pass, when Pharaoh had
let the people go, that God did not lead them
by way of the land of the Philistines, although
that *was* near; for God said, "Lest perhaps the
people change their minds when they see war,
and return to Egypt." 18So God led the people
around *by* way of the wilderness of the Red
Sea. And the children of Israel went up in orderly ranks out of the land of Egypt.
19And Moses took the bones of Joseph with
him, for he had placed the children of Israel
under solemn oath, say-
ing, "God will surely
visit you, and you shall
carry up my bones from
here with you."[a]
20So they took their
journey from Succoth
and camped in Etham
at the edge of the wilderness. 21And the LORD
went before them by day in a pillar of cloud to
lead the way, and by night in a pillar of fire to
give them light, so as to go by day and night.
22He did not take away the pillar of cloud by
day or the pillar of fire by night *from* before
the people.

> "The LORD will fight for you, and you shall hold your peace."
> EXODUS 14:14

THE RED SEA CROSSING

14 Now the LORD spoke to Moses, saying:
2"Speak to the children of Israel, that
they turn and camp before Pi Hahiroth, between Migdol and the sea, opposite Baal Zephon; you shall camp before it by the sea. 3For
Pharaoh will say of the children of Israel,
'They *are* bewildered by the land; the wilderness has closed them in.' 4Then I will harden
Pharaoh's heart, so that he will pursue them;
and I will gain honor over Pharaoh and over
all his army, that the Egyptians may know that
I *am* the LORD." And they did so.
5Now it was told the king of Egypt that the
people had fled, and the heart of Pharaoh and
his servants was turned against the people;
and they said, "Why have we done this, that
we have let Israel go from serving us?" 6So he
made ready his chariot and took his people
with him. 7Also, he took six hundred choice
chariots, and all the chariots of Egypt with captains over every one of them. 8And the LORD
hardened the heart of Pharaoh king of Egypt,
and he pursued the children of Israel; and the
children of Israel went out with boldness. 9So
the Egyptians pursued them, all the horses
and chariots of Pharaoh,
his horsemen and his
army, and overtook
them camping by the
sea beside Pi Hahiroth,
before Baal Zephon.
10And when Pharaoh
drew near, the children
of Israel lifted their eyes, and behold, the
Egyptians marched after them. So they were
very afraid, and the children of Israel cried out
to the LORD. 11Then they said to Moses, "Because *there were* no graves in Egypt, have you
taken us away to die in the wilderness? Why
have you so dealt with us, to bring us up out
of Egypt? 12*Is* this not the word that we told
you in Egypt, saying, 'Let us alone that we
may serve the Egyptians'? For *it would have
been* better for us to serve the Egyptians than
that we should die in the wilderness."
13And Moses said to the people, "Do not be
afraid. Stand still, and see the salvation of the
LORD, which He will accomplish for you today.
For the Egyptians whom you see today, you
shall see again no more forever. 14The LORD
will fight for you, and you shall hold your
peace."
15And the LORD said to Moses, "Why do

13:19 [a]Genesis 50:25

SOUL NOTE

Panic or Power *(14:10)* The Israelites found themselves trapped between Pharaoh's army and the waters of the Red Sea. In panic, they accused Moses of leading them to their deaths (14:11, 12). By this time, Moses had seen enough of the power of God to respond in confidence. He told the frightened Israelites: "Do not be afraid. Stand still, and see the salvation of the LORD" (14:13). Then God miraculously parted the waters (14:21, 22). What unyielding obstacles are you facing? Don't panic. Instead, turn to God and trust in His power to do what seems impossible. **Topic: Worry**

you cry to Me? Tell the children of Israel to go forward. [16]But lift up your rod, and stretch out your hand over the sea and divide it. And the children of Israel shall go on dry *ground* through the midst of the sea. [17]And I indeed will harden the hearts of the Egyptians, and they shall follow them. So I will gain honor over Pharaoh and over all his army, his chariots, and his horsemen. [18]Then the Egyptians shall know that I *am* the LORD, when I have gained honor for Myself over Pharaoh, his chariots, and his horsemen."

[19]And the Angel of God, who went before the camp of Israel, moved and went behind them; and the pillar of cloud went from before them and stood behind them. [20]So it came between the camp of the Egyptians and the camp of Israel. Thus it was a cloud and darkness *to the one,* and it gave light by night *to the other,* so that the one did not come near the other all that night.

[21]Then Moses stretched out his hand over the sea; and the LORD caused the sea to go *back* by a strong east wind all that night, and made the sea into dry *land,* and the waters were divided. [22]So the children of Israel went into the midst of the sea on the dry *ground,* and the waters *were* a wall to them on their right hand and on their left. [23]And the Egyptians pursued and went after them into the midst of the sea, all Pharaoh's horses, his chariots, and his horsemen.

[24]Now it came to pass, in the morning watch, that the LORD looked down upon the army of the Egyptians through the pillar of fire and cloud, and He troubled the army of the Egyptians. [25]And He took off[a] their chariot wheels, so that they drove them with difficulty; and the Egyptians said, "Let us flee from the face of Israel, for the LORD fights for them against the Egyptians."

[26]Then the LORD said to Moses, "Stretch out your hand over the sea, that the waters may come back upon the Egyptians, on their chariots, and on their horsemen." [27]And Moses stretched out his hand over the sea; and when the morning appeared, the sea returned to its full depth, while the Egyptians were fleeing into it. So the LORD overthrew the Egyptians in the midst of the sea. [28]Then the waters returned and covered the chariots, the horsemen, *and* all the army of Pharaoh that came into the sea after them. Not so much as one of them remained. [29]But the children of Israel had walked on dry *land* in the midst of the sea, and the waters *were* a wall to them on their right hand and on their left.

[30]So the LORD saved Israel that day out of the hand of the Egyptians, and Israel saw the Egyptians dead on the seashore. [31]Thus Israel saw the great work which the LORD had done in Egypt; so the people feared the LORD, and believed the LORD and His servant Moses.

"The LORD is my strength
and song . . . and
I will praise Him."
EXODUS 15:2

THE SONG OF MOSES

15 Then Moses and the children of Israel sang this song to the LORD, and spoke, saying:

"I will sing to the LORD,
For He has triumphed gloriously!
The horse and its rider
He has thrown into the sea!
2 The LORD *is* my strength and song,
And He has become my salvation;
He *is* my God, and I will praise Him;

14:25 [a]Samaritan Pentateuch, Septuagint, and Syriac read *bound.*

SOUL NOTE

A New Song *(15:1)* Moses and the Israelites took time to praise and worship God for miraculous deliverance. They sang (15:1) and danced (15:20). The focus of their praise was on God. "I will sing to the LORD, for He has triumphed gloriously! . . . The LORD is my strength and song," they sang (15:1, 2). Worship may take many expressions, but it must focus on God. Genuine praise pleases Him. In your praise and worship, focus on God. **Topic: Praise and Worship**

My father's God, and I will exalt Him.
3 The LORD *is* a man of war;
The LORD *is* His name.
4 Pharaoh's chariots and his army He has cast into the sea;
His chosen captains also are drowned in the Red Sea.
5 The depths have covered them;
They sank to the bottom like a stone.

6 "Your right hand, O LORD, has become glorious in power;
Your right hand, O LORD, has dashed the enemy in pieces.
7 And in the greatness of Your excellence
You have overthrown those who rose against You;
You sent forth Your wrath;
It consumed them like stubble.
8 And with the blast of Your nostrils
The waters were gathered together;
The floods stood upright like a heap;
The depths congealed in the heart of the sea.
9 The enemy said, 'I will pursue,
I will overtake,
I will divide the spoil;
My desire shall be satisfied on them.
I will draw my sword,
My hand shall destroy them.'
10 You blew with Your wind,
The sea covered them;
They sank like lead in the mighty waters.

11 "Who *is* like You, O LORD, among the gods?
Who *is* like You, glorious in holiness,
Fearful in praises, doing wonders?
12 You stretched out Your right hand;
The earth swallowed them.
13 You in Your mercy have led forth
The people whom You have redeemed;
You have guided *them* in Your strength
To Your holy habitation.

14 "The people will hear *and* be afraid;
Sorrow will take hold of the inhabitants of Philistia.
15 Then the chiefs of Edom will be dismayed;
The mighty men of Moab,
Trembling will take hold of them;
All the inhabitants of Canaan will melt away.
16 Fear and dread will fall on them;
By the greatness of Your arm
They will be *as* still as a stone,
Till Your people pass over, O LORD,
Till the people pass over
Whom You have purchased.
17 You will bring them in and plant them
In the mountain of Your inheritance,
In the place, O LORD, *which* You have made
For Your own dwelling,
The sanctuary, O LORD, *which* Your hands have established.

18 "The LORD shall reign forever and ever."

19 For the horses of Pharaoh went with his
chariots and his horsemen into the sea, and
the LORD brought back the waters of the sea
upon them. But the children of Israel went on
dry *land* in the midst of the sea.

THE SONG OF MIRIAM

20 Then Miriam the prophetess, the sister of
Aaron, took the timbrel in her hand; and all the
women went out after her with timbrels and
with dances. 21 And Miriam answered them:

"Sing to the LORD,
For He has triumphed gloriously!

SOUL NOTE

The Single Life *(15:20)* Is being single better than being married? Or is it the other way around? It is true that single people have freedom to serve God in any capacity, without concern over spouses or children (1 Cor. 7). Miriam, most likely a single woman, played a significant role in the spiritual life of Israel, and she is the first woman to be called a "prophetess." Singleness never denotes inferiority—God has special work for all of His people whether they are single or married. **Topic: Singleness**

The horse and its rider
He has thrown into the sea!"

Bitter Waters Made Sweet

[22]So Moses brought Israel from the Red Sea;
then they went out into the Wilderness of
Shur. And they went three days in the wilderness and found no water. [23]Now when they
came to Marah, they could not drink the waters of Marah, for they *were* bitter. Therefore
the name of it was called Marah.[a] [24]And the
people complained against Moses, saying,
"What shall we drink?" [25]So he cried out to
the LORD, and the LORD showed him a tree.
When he cast *it* into the waters, the waters
were made sweet.
There He made a statute and an ordinance
for them, and there He tested them, [26]and
said, "If you diligently heed the voice of the
LORD your God and do what is right in His
sight, give ear to His commandments and
keep all His statutes, I will put none of the diseases on you which I have brought on the
Egyptians. For I *am* the LORD who heals you."
[27]Then they came to Elim, where there *were*
twelve wells of water and seventy palm trees;
so they camped there by the waters.

Bread from Heaven

16 And they journeyed from Elim, and all
the congregation of the children of Israel came to the Wilderness of Sin, which is
between Elim and Sinai, on the fifteenth day
of the second month after they departed from
the land of Egypt. [2]Then the whole congregation of the children of Israel complained
against Moses and Aaron in the wilderness.
[3]And the children of Israel said to them, "Oh,
that we had died by the hand of the LORD in
the land of Egypt, when we sat by the pots of
meat *and* when we ate bread to the full! For
you have brought us out into this wilderness
to kill this whole assembly with hunger."
[4]Then the LORD said to Moses, "Behold, I
will rain bread from heaven for you. And the
people shall go out and gather a certain quota
every day, that I may test them, whether they
will walk in My law or not. [5]And it shall be on
the sixth day that they shall prepare what they
bring in, and it shall be twice as much as they
gather daily."
[6]Then Moses and Aaron said to all the children of Israel, "At evening you shall know that
the LORD has brought you out of the land of
Egypt. [7]And in the morning you shall see the
glory of the LORD; for He hears your complaints against the LORD. But what *are* we, that
you complain against us?" [8]Also Moses said,
"*This shall be seen* when the LORD gives you
meat to eat in the evening, and in the morning
bread to the full; for the LORD hears your complaints which you make against Him. And
what *are* we? Your complaints *are* not against
us but against the LORD."
[9]Then Moses spoke to Aaron, "Say to all the
congregation of the children of Israel, 'Come
near before the LORD, for He has heard your
complaints.' " [10]Now it came to pass, as Aaron
spoke to the whole congregation of the children of Israel, that they looked toward the wilderness, and behold, the glory of the LORD
appeared in the cloud.
[11]And the LORD spoke to Moses, saying, [12]"I
have heard the complaints of the children of
Israel. Speak to them, saying, 'At twilight you
shall eat meat, and in the morning you shall
be filled with bread. And you shall know that I
am the LORD your God.' "
[13]So it was that quails came up at evening
and covered the camp, and in the morning the

15:23 [a]Literally *Bitter*

SOUL NOTE

Lost in the Desert *(16:1–3)* Wandering in the vast Sinai wilderness, the Israelites soon forgot God's miraculous power and began to complain about their lack of food and water. Although they had witnessed God's power, they still moaned at their inconveniences. Their problem wasn't the wilderness; it was their attitude. "Your complaints are not against us but against the LORD," Moses and Aaron reminded them (16:8). "Wilderness" experiences will make or break a person. The difference is in the attitude. **Topic: Attitudes**

dew lay all around the camp. 14And when the
layer of dew lifted, there, on the surface of
the wilderness, was a small round substance,
as fine as frost on the ground. 15So when the
children of Israel saw *it,* they said to one another, "What is it?" For they did not know
what it *was.*

And Moses said to them, "This *is* the bread
which the LORD has given you to eat. 16This is
the thing which the LORD has commanded:
'Let every man gather it according to each
one's need, one omer for each person, *according to the* number of persons; let every man
take for *those* who *are* in his tent.' "

17Then the children of Israel did so and
gathered, some more, some less. 18So when
they measured *it* by omers, he who gathered
much had nothing left over, and he who gathered little had no lack. Every man had gathered according to each one's need. 19And
Moses said, "Let no one leave any of it till
morning." 20Notwithstanding they did not
heed Moses. But some of them left part of it
until morning, and it bred worms and stank.
And Moses was angry with them. 21So they
gathered it every morning, every man according to his need. And when the sun became
hot, it melted.

22And so it was, on the sixth day, *that* they
gathered twice as much bread, two omers for
each one. And all the rulers of the congregation came and told Moses. 23Then he said
to them, "This *is what* the LORD has said: 'Tomorrow *is* a Sabbath rest, a holy Sabbath to
the LORD. Bake what you will bake *today,* and
boil what you will boil; and lay up for yourselves all that remains, to be kept until morning.' " 24So they laid it up till morning, as
Moses commanded; and it did not stink, nor
were there any worms in it. 25Then Moses
said, "Eat that today, for today *is* a Sabbath
to the LORD; today you will not find it in the
field. 26Six days you shall gather it, but on
the seventh day, the Sabbath, there will be
none."

27Now it happened *that some* of the people
went out on the seventh day to gather, but
they found none. 28And the LORD said to Moses, "How long do you refuse to keep My commandments and My laws? 29See! For the LORD
has given you the Sabbath; therefore He gives
you on the sixth day bread for two days. Let
every man remain in his place; let no man go
out of his place on the seventh day." 30So the
people rested on the seventh day.

31And the house of Israel called its name
Manna.[a] And it *was* like white coriander seed,
and the taste of it *was* like wafers *made* with
honey.

32Then Moses said, "This *is* the thing which
the LORD has commanded: 'Fill an omer with
it, to be kept for your generations, that they
may see the bread with which I fed you in the
wilderness, when I brought you out of the
land of Egypt.' " 33And Moses said to Aaron,
"Take a pot and put an omer of manna in it,
and lay it up before the LORD, to be kept for
your generations." 34As the LORD commanded
Moses, so Aaron laid it up before the Testimony, to be kept. 35And the children of Israel
ate manna forty years, until they came to an
inhabited land; they ate manna until they
came to the border of the land of Canaan.
36Now an omer *is* one-tenth of an ephah.

WATER FROM THE ROCK

17 Then all the congregation of the children of Israel set out on their journey
from the Wilderness of Sin, according to the
commandment of the LORD, and camped in
Rephidim; but *there was* no water for the people to drink. 2Therefore the people contended

16:31 [a]Literally *What?* (compare Exodus 16:15)

SOUL NOTE

The Rest of the Story *(16:23)* God gave His people a day of rest, a day when they were not supposed to work. But everyone had to work hard in preparation on the day before, in order to be able to rest completely on the Sabbath. To take full advantage of our day of rest and worship, we too need to prepare ahead of time. That way, we won't need to run to the store or finish a work project. We need to be organized enough to be ready to rest and focus on God on Sundays. **Topic: Work**

with Moses, and said, "Give us water, that we may drink."

So Moses said to them, "Why do you contend with me? Why do you tempt the LORD?"

[3]And the people thirsted there for water, and the people complained against Moses, and said, "Why *is* it you have brought us up out of Egypt, to kill us and our children and our livestock with thirst?"

[4]So Moses cried out to the LORD, saying, "What shall I do with this people? They are almost ready to stone me!"

[5]And the LORD said to Moses, "Go on before the people, and take with you some of the elders of Israel. Also take in your hand your rod with which you struck the river, and go. [6]Behold, I will stand before you there on the rock in Horeb; and you shall strike the rock, and water will come out of it, that the people may drink."

And Moses did so in the sight of the elders of Israel. [7]So he called the name of the place Massah[a] and Meribah,[b] because of the contention of the children of Israel, and because they tempted the LORD, saying, "Is the LORD among us or not?"

VICTORY OVER THE AMALEKITES

[8]Now Amalek came and fought with Israel in Rephidim. [9]And Moses said to Joshua, "Choose us some men and go out, fight with Amalek. Tomorrow I will stand on the top of the hill with the rod of God in my hand." [10]So Joshua did as Moses said to him, and fought with Amalek. And Moses, Aaron, and Hur went up to the top of the hill. [11]And so it was, when Moses held up his hand, that Israel prevailed; and when he let down his hand, Amalek prevailed. [12]But Moses' hands *became* heavy; so they took a stone and put *it* under him, and he sat on it. And Aaron and Hur supported his hands, one on one side, and the other on the other side; and his hands were steady until the going down of the sun. [13]So Joshua defeated Amalek and his people with the edge of the sword.

[14]Then the LORD said to Moses, "Write this *for* a memorial in the book and recount *it* in the hearing of Joshua, that I will utterly blot out the remembrance of Amalek from under heaven." [15]And Moses built an altar and called its name, The-LORD-Is-My-Banner;[a] [16]for he said, "Because the LORD has sworn: the LORD *will have* war with Amalek from generation to generation."

JETHRO'S ADVICE

18 And Jethro, the priest of Midian, Moses' father-in-law, heard of all that God had done for Moses and for Israel His people—that the LORD had brought Israel out of Egypt. [2]Then Jethro, Moses' father-in-law, took Zipporah, Moses' wife, after he had sent her back, [3]with her two sons, of whom the name of one *was* Gershom (for he said, "I have been a stranger in a foreign land")[a] [4]and the name of the other *was* Eliezer[a] (for *he said,* "The God of my father *was* my help, and delivered me from the sword of Pharaoh"); [5]and Jethro, Moses' father-in-law, came with his sons and his wife to Moses in the wilderness, where he was encamped at the mountain of God. [6]Now he had said to Moses, "I, your father-in-law Jethro, am coming to you with your wife and her two sons with her."

[7]So Moses went out to meet his father-in-law, bowed down, and kissed him. And they asked each other about *their* well-being, and

---

17:7 [a]Literally *Tempted* [b]Literally *Contention* **17:15** [a]Hebrew *YHWH Nissi* **18:3** [a]Compare Exodus 2:22 **18:4** [a]Literally *My God Is Help*

SOUL NOTE

Look Again *(17:7)* The Israelites lived by sight and not by faith. Even though God provided daily miracles of food and water in the Sinai wilderness, the people complained and doubted His continued goodness toward them. The world says, "Show me, and I'll believe it." God says, "Believe it, and I will show you." If you are in a wilderness of testing or a valley of doubt, don't question God's love because He is not answering you the way you want. Instead, look around and recognize what God is doing for you. **Topic: Doubt**

they went into the tent. 8And Moses told his
father-in-law all that the LORD had done to
Pharaoh and to the Egyptians for Israel's sake,
all the hardship that had come upon them on
the way, and *how* the LORD had delivered
them. 9Then Jethro rejoiced for all the good
which the LORD had done for Israel, whom He
had delivered out of the hand of the Egyptians. 10And Jethro said, "Blessed *be* the LORD,
who has delivered you out of the hand of the
Egyptians and out of the hand of Pharaoh, *and*
who has delivered the people from under the
hand of the Egyptians. 11Now I know that the
LORD *is* greater than all the gods; for in the
very thing in which they behaved proudly, *He*
was above them." 12Then Jethro, Moses' father-in-law, took[a] a burnt offering and *other*
sacrifices *to offer* to God. And Aaron came
with all the elders of Israel to eat bread with
Moses' father-in-law before God.

13And so it was, on the next day, that Moses
sat to judge the people; and the people stood
before Moses from morning until evening.
14So when Moses' father-in-law saw all that he
did for the people, he said, "What *is* this thing
that you are doing for the people? Why do you
alone sit, and all the people stand before you
from morning until evening?"

15And Moses said to his father-in-law, "Because the people come to me to inquire of
God. 16When they have a difficulty, they come
to me, and I judge between one and another;
and I make known the statutes of God and His
laws."

17So Moses' father-in-law said to him, "The
thing that you do *is* not good. 18Both you and
these people who *are* with you will surely

18:12 [a]Following Masoretic Text and Septuagint; Syriac, Targum, and Vulgate read *offered.*

PERSONALITY PROFILE

Burnout

JETHRO: A FRIEND IN NEED

(EXODUS 18:17, 18)

When we are stressed, a powerful asset can be the blessing of someone a little older, a wiser voice of experience, to help us handle the pressure. In that person's wisdom is our relief.

Moses discovered a mentor when he needed one most—*after* he led the Israelites out of Egyptian captivity. Confronting Pharaoh, it seems, was easier than trying to lead the millions of Israelites to the Promised Land. To avoid being overwhelmed by this task, Moses needed wise and seasoned counsel. He received it from Jethro, his father-in-law.

Jethro joined Moses in the wilderness with Moses' wife and sons as the Israelites traveled toward the Promised Land. Jethro rejoiced in all that God had done, and the deliverance story strengthened his own faith. But Jethro also saw his son-in-law burning the candle at both ends. He saw the dysfunctional judging process that Moses attempted to shoulder alone, and he suggested a better way. He encouraged Moses to delegate the judging of some of the minor disputes to godly men who were able to know the people and deal intimately with their needs. Moses then became more like a supreme court, dealing only with the legal issues that affected the entire nation.

Jethro demonstrated that those outside a situation can bring valuable perspective to those who may be overwhelmed in it. Fresh eyes can often see the obvious way out that tired eyes have overlooked. Jethro showed Moses where he could get the help he desperately needed. God had provided plenty of wise leaders all around Moses, but Moses needed help to see them.

At different times, God sends us mentors, guides, helpers, and burden-bearers. They can assist us in performing the tasks that God sets before us. Before you burn out, look around for those helpers whom God may have sent your way.

To Learn More: Turn to the article about burnout on pages 920, 921. See also the key passage note at Matthew 11:28–30 on page 1247.

wear yourselves out. For this thing *is* too much for you; you are not able to perform it by yourself. 19Listen now to my voice; I will give you counsel, and God will be with you: Stand before God for the people, so that you may bring the difficulties to God. 20And you shall teach them the statutes and the laws, and show them the way in which they must walk and the work they must do. 21Moreover you shall select from all the people able men, such as fear God, men of truth, hating covetousness; and place *such* over them *to be* rulers of thousands, rulers of hundreds, rulers of fifties, and rulers of tens. 22And let them judge the people at all times. Then it will be *that* every great matter they shall bring to you, but every small matter they themselves shall judge. So it will be easier for you, for they will bear *the burden* with you. 23If you do this thing, and God *so* commands you, then you will be able to endure, and all this people will also go to their place in peace."

24So Moses heeded the voice of his father-in-law and did all that he had said. 25And Moses chose able men out of all Israel, and made them heads over the people: rulers of thousands, rulers of hundreds, rulers of fifties, and rulers of tens. 26So they judged the people at all times; the hard cases they brought to Moses, but they judged every small case themselves.

27Then Moses let his father-in-law depart, and he went his way to his own land.

ISRAEL AT MOUNT SINAI

19 In the third month after the children of Israel had gone out of the land of Egypt, on the same day, they came *to* the Wilderness of Sinai. 2For they had departed from Rephidim, had come *to* the Wilderness of Sinai, and camped in the wilderness. So Israel camped there before the mountain.

3And Moses went up to God, and the LORD called to him from the mountain, saying, "Thus you shall say to the house of Jacob, and tell the children of Israel: 4'You have seen what I did to the Egyptians, and *how* I bore you on eagles' wings and brought you to Myself. 5Now therefore, if you will indeed obey My voice and keep My covenant, then you shall be a special treasure to Me above all people; for all the earth *is* Mine. 6And you shall be to Me a kingdom of priests and a holy nation.' These *are* the words which you shall speak to the children of Israel."

7So Moses came and called for the elders of the people, and laid before them all these words which the LORD commanded him. 8Then all the people answered together and said, "All that the LORD has spoken we will do." So Moses brought back the words of the people to the LORD. 9And the LORD said to Moses, "Behold, I come to you in the thick cloud, that the people may hear when I speak with you, and believe you forever."

So Moses told the words of the people to the LORD.

10Then the LORD said to Moses, "Go to the people and consecrate them today and tomorrow, and let them wash their clothes. 11And let them be ready for the third day. For on the third day the LORD will come down upon Mount Sinai in the sight of all the people. 12You shall set bounds for the people all around, saying, 'Take heed to yourselves *that* you do *not* go up to the mountain or touch its base. Whoever touches the mountain shall surely be put to death. 13Not a hand shall touch him, but he shall surely be stoned or shot *with an arrow;* whether man or beast, he shall not live.' When the trumpet sounds long, they shall come near the mountain."

14So Moses went down from the mountain to the people and sanctified the people, and they washed their clothes. 15And he said to the people, "Be ready for the third day; do not come near *your* wives."

16Then it came to pass on the third day, in the morning, that there were thunderings and lightnings, and a thick cloud on the mountain; and the sound of the trumpet was very loud, so that all the people who *were* in the camp trembled. 17And Moses brought the people out of the camp to meet with God, and they stood at the foot of the mountain. 18Now Mount Sinai *was* completely in smoke, because the LORD descended upon it in fire. Its smoke ascended like the smoke of a furnace, and the whole mountain[a] quaked greatly. 19And when the blast of the trumpet sounded long and became louder and louder, Moses spoke, and God answered him by voice. 20Then the LORD came down upon Mount Sinai, on the top of the mountain. And the LORD called Moses to the top of the mountain, and Moses went up.

21And the LORD said to Moses, "Go down and warn the people, lest they break through

---

19:18 [a]Septuagint reads *all the people.*

to gaze at the LORD, and many of them perish.
22Also let the priests who come near the LORD
consecrate themselves, lest the LORD break
out against them."
23But Moses said to the LORD, "The people
cannot come up to Mount Sinai; for You
warned us, saying, 'Set bounds around the
mountain and consecrate it.' "
24Then the LORD said to him, "Away! Get
down and then come up, you and Aaron with
you. But do not let the priests and the people
break through to come up to the LORD, lest He
break out against them." 25So Moses went
down to the people and spoke to them.

THE TEN COMMANDMENTS

20 And God spoke all these words, saying:

2 "I *am* the LORD your God, who brought you out of the land of Egypt, out of the house of bondage.
3 "You shall have no other gods before Me.
4 "You shall not make for yourself a carved image—any likeness *of anything* that *is* in heaven above, or that *is* in the earth beneath, or that *is* in the water
under the earth; 5you shall not bow down to them nor serve them. For I, the LORD your God, *am* a jealous God, visiting the iniquity of the fathers upon the children to the third and fourth *generations* of those who hate
Me, 6but showing mercy to thousands, to those who love Me and keep My commandments.
7 "You shall not take the name of the LORD your God in vain, for the LORD will not hold *him* guiltless who takes His name in vain.
8 "Remember the Sabbath day, to keep it
holy. 9Six days you shall labor and do
all your work, 10but the seventh day *is*
the Sabbath of the LORD your God. *In it* you shall do no work: you, nor your son, nor your daughter, nor your male servant, nor your female servant, nor your cattle, nor your stranger who *is*
within your gates. 11For *in* six days the
LORD made the heavens and the earth, the sea, and all that *is* in them, and rested the seventh day. Therefore the LORD blessed the Sabbath day and hallowed it.
12 "Honor your father and your mother, that your days may be long upon the land which the LORD your God is giving you.
13 "You shall not murder.
14 "You shall not commit adultery.
15 "You shall not steal.
16 "You shall not bear false witness against your neighbor.
17 "You shall not covet your neighbor's house; you shall not covet your neighbor's wife, nor his male servant, nor his female servant, nor his ox, nor his donkey, nor anything that *is* your neighbor's."

THE PEOPLE AFRAID OF GOD'S PRESENCE

18Now all the people witnessed the thunderings, the lightning flashes, the sound of
the trumpet, and the mountain smoking; and
when the people saw *it,* they trembled and
stood afar off. 19Then they said to Moses, "You
speak with us, and we will hear; but let not
God speak with us, lest we die."
20And Moses said to the people, "Do not
fear; for God has come to test you, and that His
fear may be before you, so that you may not
sin." 21So the people stood afar off, but Moses
drew near the thick darkness where God *was.*

THE LAW OF THE ALTAR

22Then the LORD said to Moses, "Thus you
shall say to the children of Israel: 'You have

SOUL NOTE

His Alone *(20:5)* God gets jealous? Yes, but this is a different kind of jealousy than what we experience. God's jealousy is perfect, for He wants us to be exclusively His. When people break this commandment—when they turn to other gods—God wants them back. He doesn't want to share our affections with anyone or anything else. How fortunate for us that He is a jealous God, showing mercy to the multitudes of those who love and obey Him. **Topic: Jealousy**

SETTING HEALTHY BOUNDARIES

Boundaries

HENRY CLOUD AND JOHN TOWNSEND

(Exodus 20:1–17)

Many people struggle with relationships in which there is irresponsibility, hurt, or control. They don't know how to handle conflict or even their own responsibilities. Fortunately, God has provided people with a great deal of teaching on how to order our lives with the help of boundaries.

Boundaries are simply defined as property lines. Just as a fence shows where one yard ends and another begins, a boundary indicates what belongs to us and what belongs to others. Whenever we encounter words in the Bible like truth, righteousness, justice, honesty, integrity, and holiness, we should pay attention. They describe some aspect of boundaries for God's people.

Boundaries are a tool that God uses to serve three of His most important values: Love, Responsibility, and Freedom.

BOUNDARIES PROMOTE LOVE

God is the essence of love (1 John 4:16). God's boundaries are very clear between what He loves and what He cannot abide. For example, God loves righteousness and justice (Ps. 33:5), His people (2 Chr. 2:11), and the world (John 3:16). At the same time, He sets boundaries on His love and actually hates certain things (Prov. 6:16–19; Zech. 8:17).

God enacts boundaries with His people to promote a loving relationship. He provides structures that teach people how to love and follow Him. God gave the Ten Commandments for people's well-being (Ex. 20:1–17). He uses boundaries to make life safe enough for us to return His love.

Likewise, we are to use boundaries to promote love and connection with others. When people live within their God-ordained boundaries, they can be safe and trusting with each other. As we walk in truth and righteousness, and require that of others, love flourishes.

BOUNDARIES DEFINE RESPONSIBILITY

Boundaries help people clarify how to take responsibility for their lives before God. They also help people understand the extent and limits of their responsibilities to others.

God is clear about His purposes and tasks. He creates and maintains the universe (Gen. 1:1; Col. 1:17), seeks and saves the lost (Luke 19:10), and keeps His promises (Num. 23:19). He also knows what is *not* His responsibility. He is not responsible for evil (Job 34:10), confusion (1 Cor. 14:33), or temptation (James 1:13).

We also are to take responsibility over our lives by setting boundaries to, for example, guard our hearts (Prov. 4:23), take up our crosses (Luke 9:23), be good stewards (Matt. 25:14–30), and grow the fruit of the Spirit (Gal. 5:22, 23).

Boundaries help us to know our responsibilities to others. We are to love others, but without rescuing or enabling them (Lev. 19:15; Prov. 19:19; 2 Thess. 3:10). We are to know when to protect ourselves from the sin or immaturity of others (Prov. 22:3; Matt. 7:6) and when to turn the other cheek (Matt. 5:39). We are to confront and provide consequences for those who are hurtful or irresponsible (Matt. 18:15–17; 1 Cor.

5:1–5). Boundaries help us to become a conduit for God's truth, justice, and discipline. When clear boundaries are not kept, relationships can deteriorate in destructive ways.

BOUNDARIES PROTECT FREEDOM

Boundaries preserve the freedom to choose God's paths. We can only truly love God and others when we are free.

God uses boundaries to establish His freedom, His independence. No one instructs Him (Is. 40:13, 14). He makes choices because He knows they are the right choices. He is free to say no to our requests (2 Cor. 12:7–10).

Boundaries protect our freedom with other people. We can freely choose to submit our lives to God, no matter what others say (Josh. 24:15). We can choose our paths and have personal preferences and opinions. Freedom has consequences, however. We are free to move away from God, as well as toward Him. Boundaries give us freedom, but we need to use our freedom to look forward to the path He has for us, instead of back at the old ways.

DEVELOPING HEALTHY BOUNDARIES

Perhaps we have found that love does not flow freely from us to God or to another person. Perhaps we are taking responsibility for someone else's feelings. Or we suffer from a lack of freedom in our choices—being controlled by our own conflicts or someone else's manipulation. Following are some suggestions for developing boundaries:

➢ Become aware of areas of your life that show boundary problems and explore the roots of those conflicts.
➢ Meet regularly with caring people who will tell the truth, say no, and help you set limits.
➢ Take ownership of the problem rather than blaming others.
➢ Give and receive forgiveness.
➢ Risk telling the truth to God and to safe people in your life.
➢ Set limits and establish consequences with those who are irresponsible or controlling.
➢ Learn to give freely to those who legitimately need our help.

God knows these issues and has provided a solution through biblical boundaries. We can take Him at His word and begin to develop the ability to form our boundaries and stand firm within them.

FURTHER MEDITATION:

Other passages to study about the issue of boundaries include:

➢ Exodus 18:13–24
➢ Proverbs 10:18
➢ Matthew 5:37; 7:6; 18:15–20
➢ 2 Corinthians 9:6, 7
➢ Galatians 5:1–23; 6:1–7
➢ Ephesians 4:25

To Learn More: Turn to the key passage note on boundaries at 2 Corinthians 6:14 on page 1525. See also the personality profile of Lot on page 28.

seen that I have talked with you from heaven. 23You shall not make *anything to be* with Me—gods of silver or gods of gold you shall not make for yourselves. 24An altar of earth you shall make for Me, and you shall sacrifice on it your burnt offerings and your peace offerings, your sheep and your oxen. In every place where I record My name I will come to you, and I will bless you. 25And if you make Me an altar of stone, you shall not build it of hewn stone; for if you use your tool on it, you have profaned it. 26Nor shall you go up by steps to My altar, that your nakedness may not be exposed on it.'

THE LAW CONCERNING SERVANTS

21 "Now these *are* the judgments which you shall set before them: 2If you buy a Hebrew servant, he shall serve six years; and in the seventh he shall go out free and pay nothing. 3If he comes in by himself, he shall go out by himself; if he *comes in* married, then his wife shall go out with him. 4If his master has given him a wife, and she has borne him sons or daughters, the wife and her children shall be her master's, and he shall go out by himself. 5But if the servant plainly says, 'I love my master, my wife, and my children; I will not go out free,' 6then his master shall bring him to the judges. He shall also bring him to the door, or to the doorpost, and his master shall pierce his ear with an awl; and he shall serve him forever.

7"And if a man sells his daughter to be a female slave, she shall not go out as the male slaves do. 8If she does not please her master, who has betrothed her to himself, then he shall let her be redeemed. He shall have no right to sell her to a foreign people, since he has dealt deceitfully with her. 9And if he has betrothed her to his son, he shall deal with her according to the custom of daughters. 10If he takes another *wife,* he shall not diminish her food, her clothing, and her marriage rights. 11And if he does not do these three for her, then she shall go out free, without *paying* money.

THE LAW CONCERNING VIOLENCE

12"He who strikes a man so that he dies shall surely be put to death. 13However, if he did not lie in wait, but God delivered *him* into his hand, then I will appoint for you a place where he may flee.

14"But if a man acts with premeditation against his neighbor, to kill him by treachery, you shall take him from My altar, that he may die.

15"And he who strikes his father or his mother shall surely be put to death.

16"He who kidnaps a man and sells him, or if he is found in his hand, shall surely be put to death.

17"And he who curses his father or his mother shall surely be put to death.

18"If men contend with each other, and one strikes the other with a stone or with *his* fist, and he does not die but is confined to *his* bed, 19if he rises again and walks about outside with his staff, then he who struck *him* shall be acquitted. He shall only pay *for* the loss of his time, and shall provide *for him* to be thoroughly healed.

20"And if a man beats his male or female servant with a rod, so that he dies under his hand, he shall surely be punished. 21Notwithstanding, if he remains alive a day or two, he shall not be punished; for he *is* his property.

22"If men fight, and hurt a woman with child, so that she gives birth prematurely, yet no harm follows, he shall surely be punished accordingly as the woman's husband imposes on him; and he shall pay as the judges *determine.* 23But if *any* harm follows, then you

SOUL NOTE

Choosing Life *(21:22)* What kindness God shows! The list of laws in Exodus 21:1–32 provide an important statement of human rights. This verse shows God's protection of the most defenseless people on the planet—children in the womb. Even causing a premature but otherwise healthy birth was a punishable offense. If either the mother or the baby was harmed or killed, punishment was served by a strict proportionality: life for life, eye for eye, tooth for tooth. God is the champion of life, and has always protected women, children, and the weakest members of society. **Topic: Abortion**

shall give life for life, 24eye for eye, tooth for
tooth, hand for hand, foot for foot, 25burn for
burn, wound for wound, stripe for stripe.
26“If a man strikes the eye of his male or female servant, and destroys it, he shall let him
go free for the sake of his eye. 27And if he
knocks out the tooth of his male or female servant, he shall let him go free for the sake of his
tooth.

Animal Control Laws

28“If an ox gores a man or a woman to
death, then the ox shall surely be stoned, and
its flesh shall not be eaten; but the owner of
the ox *shall be* acquitted. 29But if the ox
tended to thrust with its horn in times past,
and it has been made known to his owner, and
he has not kept it confined, so that it has
killed a man or a woman, the ox shall be
stoned and its owner also shall be put to
death. 30If there is imposed on him a sum of
money, then he shall pay to redeem his life,
whatever is imposed on him. 31Whether it has
gored a son or gored a daughter, according to
this judgment it shall be done to him. 32If the
ox gores a male or female servant, he shall
give to their master thirty shekels of silver,
and the ox shall be stoned.
33“And if a man opens a pit, or if a man digs
a pit and does not cover it, and an ox or a donkey falls in it, 34the owner of the pit shall make
it good; he shall give money to their owner,
but the dead *animal* shall be his.
35“If one man's ox hurts another's, so that it
dies, then they shall sell the live ox and divide
the money from it; and the dead *ox* they shall
also divide. 36Or if it was known that the ox
tended to thrust in time past, and its owner
has not kept it confined, he shall surely pay ox
for ox, and the dead animal shall be his own.

Responsibility for Property

22 “If a man steals an ox or a sheep, and
slaughters it or sells it, he shall restore
five oxen for an ox and four sheep for a sheep.
2If the thief is found breaking in, and he is
struck so that he dies, *there shall be* no guilt
for his bloodshed. 3If the sun has risen on
him, *there shall be* guilt for his bloodshed. He
should make full restitution; if he has nothing,
then he shall be sold for his theft. 4If the theft
is certainly found alive in his hand, whether it
is an ox or donkey or sheep, he shall restore
double.
5“If a man causes a field or vineyard to be
grazed, and lets loose his animal, and it feeds
in another man's field, he shall make restitution from the best of his own field and the best
of his own vineyard.
6“If fire breaks out and catches in thorns, so
that stacked grain, standing grain, or the field
is consumed, he who kindled the fire shall
surely make restitution.
7“If a man delivers to his neighbor money or
articles to keep, and it is stolen out of the
man's house, if the thief is found, he shall pay
double. 8If the thief is not found, then the
master of the house shall be brought to the
judges *to see* whether he has put his hand into
his neighbor's goods.
9“For any kind of trespass, *whether it concerns* an ox, a donkey, a sheep, or clothing, *or*
for any kind of lost thing which *another*
claims to be his, the cause of both parties shall
come before the judges; *and* whomever the
judges condemn shall pay double to his neighbor. 10If a man delivers to his neighbor a donkey, an ox, a sheep, or any animal to keep,
and it dies, is hurt, or driven away, no one seeing *it,* 11*then* an oath of the LORD shall be between them both, that he has not put his hand
into his neighbor's goods; and the owner of it
shall accept *that,* and he shall not make *it*
good. 12But if, in fact, it is stolen from him, he
shall make restitution to the owner of it. 13If it
is torn to pieces *by a beast, then* he shall bring
it as evidence, *and* he shall not make good
what was torn.
14“And if a man borrows *anything* from his
neighbor, and it becomes injured or dies, the
owner of it not *being* with it, he shall surely
make *it* good. 15If its owner *was* with it, he
shall not make *it* good; if it *was* hired, it came
for its hire.

Moral and Ceremonial Principles

16“If a man entices a virgin who is not betrothed, and lies with her, he shall surely pay
the bride-price for her *to be* his wife. 17If her
father utterly refuses to give her to him, he
shall pay money according to the bride-price
of virgins.
18“You shall not permit a sorceress to live.
19“Whoever lies with an animal shall surely
be put to death.
20“He who sacrifices to *any* god, except to
the LORD only, he shall be utterly destroyed.
21“You shall neither mistreat a stranger nor

oppress him, for you were strangers in the land of Egypt.

22"You shall not afflict any widow or fatherless child. 23If you afflict them in any way, *and* they cry at all to Me, I will surely hear their cry; 24and My wrath will become hot, and I will kill you with the sword; your wives shall be widows, and your children fatherless.

25"If you lend money to *any of* My people *who are* poor among you, you shall not be like a moneylender to him; you shall not charge him interest. 26If you ever take your neighbor's garment as a pledge, you shall return it to him before the sun goes down. 27For that *is* his only covering, it *is* his garment for his skin. What will he sleep in? And it will be that when he cries to Me, I will hear, for I *am* gracious.

28"You shall not revile God, nor curse a ruler of your people.

29"You shall not delay *to offer* the first of your ripe produce and your juices. The firstborn of your sons you shall give to Me. 30Likewise you shall do with your oxen *and* your sheep. It shall be with its mother seven days; on the eighth day you shall give it to Me.

31"And you shall be holy men to Me: you shall not eat meat torn *by beasts* in the field; you shall throw it to the dogs.

Justice for All

23 "You shall not circulate a false report. Do not put your hand with the wicked to be an unrighteous witness. 2You shall not follow a crowd to do evil; nor shall you testify in a dispute so as to turn aside after many to pervert *justice.* 3You shall not show partiality to a poor man in his dispute.

4"If you meet your enemy's ox or his donkey going astray, you shall surely bring it back to him again. 5If you see the donkey of one who hates you lying under its burden, and you would refrain from helping it, you shall surely help him with it.

6"You shall not pervert the judgment of your poor in his dispute. 7Keep yourself far from a false matter; do not kill the innocent and righteous. For I will not justify the wicked. 8And you shall take no bribe, for a bribe blinds the discerning and perverts the words of the righteous.

9"Also you shall not oppress a stranger, for you know the heart of a stranger, because you were strangers in the land of Egypt.

The Law of Sabbaths

10"Six years you shall sow your land and gather in its produce, 11but the seventh *year* you shall let it rest and lie fallow, that the poor of your people may eat; and what they leave, the beasts of the field may eat. In like manner you shall do with your vineyard *and* your olive grove. 12Six days you shall do your work, and on the seventh day you shall rest, that your ox and your donkey may rest, and the son of your female servant and the stranger may be refreshed.

13"And in all that I have said to you, be circumspect and make no mention of the name of other gods, nor let it be heard from your mouth.

Three Annual Feasts

14"Three times you shall keep a feast to Me in the year: 15You shall keep the Feast of Unleavened Bread (you shall eat unleavened bread seven days, as I commanded you, at the time appointed in the month of Abib, for in it you came out of Egypt; none shall appear before Me empty); 16and the Feast of Harvest, the firstfruits of your labors which you have sown in the field; and the Feast of Ingathering at the end of the year, when you have gathered in *the fruit of* your labors from the field.

17"Three times in the year all your males shall appear before the Lord GOD.[a]

18"You shall not offer the blood of My sacrifice with leavened bread; nor shall the fat of My sacrifice remain until morning. 19The first of the firstfruits of your land you shall bring into the house of the LORD your God. You shall not boil a young goat in its mother's milk.

The Angel and the Promises

20"Behold, I send an Angel before you to keep you in the way and to bring you into the place which I have prepared. 21Beware of Him and obey His voice; do not provoke Him, for He will not pardon your transgressions; for My name *is* in Him. 22But if you indeed obey His voice and do all that I speak, then I will be an enemy to your enemies and an adversary to your adversaries. 23For My Angel will go before you and bring you in to the Amorites and the Hittites and the Perizzites and the Canaanites and the Hivites and the Jebusites; and I

23:17 [a]Hebrew *YHWH,* usually translated *LORD*

will cut them off. 24You shall not bow down to their gods, nor serve them, nor do according to their works; but you shall utterly overthrow them and completely break down their *sacred* pillars.

25"So you shall serve the LORD your God, and He will bless your bread and your water. And I will take sickness away from the midst of you. 26No one shall suffer miscarriage or be barren in your land; I will fulfill the number of your days.

> "All that the LORD has said we will do, and be obedient."
> EXODUS 24:7

27"I will send My fear before you, I will cause confusion among all the people to whom you come, and will make all your enemies turn *their* backs to you. 28And I will send hornets before you, which shall drive out the Hivite, the Canaanite, and the Hittite from before you. 29I will not drive them out from before you in one year, lest the land become desolate and the beasts of the field become too numerous for you. 30Little by little I will drive them out from before you, until you have increased, and you inherit the land. 31And I will set your bounds from the Red Sea to the sea, Philistia, and from the desert to the River.[a] For I will deliver the inhabitants of the land into your hand, and you shall drive them out before you. 32You shall make no covenant with them, nor with their gods. 33They shall not dwell in your land, lest they make you sin against Me. For *if* you serve their gods, it will surely be a snare to you."

Israel Affirms the Covenant

24 Now He said to Moses, "Come up to the LORD, you and Aaron, Nadab and Abihu, and seventy of the elders of Israel, and worship from afar. 2And Moses alone shall come near the LORD, but they shall not come near; nor shall the people go up with him."

3So Moses came and told the people all the words of the LORD and all the judgments. And all the people answered with one voice and said, "All the words which the LORD has said we will do." 4And Moses wrote all the words of the LORD. And he rose early in the morning, and built an altar at the foot of the mountain, and twelve pillars according to the twelve tribes of Israel. 5Then he sent young men of the children of Israel, who offered burnt offerings and sacrificed peace offerings of oxen to the LORD. 6And Moses took half the blood and put *it* in basins, and half the blood he sprinkled on the altar. 7Then he took the Book of the Covenant and read in the hearing of the people. And they said, "All that the LORD has said we will do, and be obedient." 8And Moses took the blood, sprinkled *it* on the people, and said, "This is the blood of the covenant which the LORD has made with you according to all these words."

On the Mountain with God

9Then Moses went up, also Aaron, Nadab, and Abihu, and seventy of the elders of Israel, 10and they saw the God of Israel. And *there was* under His feet as it were a paved work of sapphire stone, and it was like the very heavens in *its* clarity. 11But on the nobles of the children of Israel He did not lay His hand. So they saw God, and they ate and drank.

12Then the LORD said to Moses, "Come up to Me on the mountain and be there; and I will give you tablets of stone, and the law and commandments which I have written, that you may teach them."

23:31 [a]Hebrew *Nahar,* the Euphrates

SOUL NOTE

Meeting with God *(24:12)* As the leaders of Israel assembled at Mount Sinai to worship God, only Moses was permitted to "come near" the Lord (24:2). The others had to worship God "from afar" (24:1). We will not go up onto Mount Sinai as Moses did, but every day we can come near to God through worship and prayer. Because of Christ, we can "come boldly to the throne of grace" (Heb. 4:16). The closer we draw to God's presence, the more clearly we will hear His voice, and the more our lives will be transformed. **Topic: Praise and Worship**

13So Moses arose with his assistant Joshua, and Moses went up to the mountain of God. 14And he said to the elders, "Wait here for us until we come back to you. Indeed, Aaron and Hur *are* with you. If any man has a difficulty, let him go to them." 15Then Moses went up into the mountain, and a cloud covered the mountain.

16Now the glory of the LORD rested on Mount Sinai, and the cloud covered it six days. And on the seventh day He called to Moses out of the midst of the cloud. 17The sight of the glory of the LORD *was* like a consuming fire on the top of the mountain in the eyes of the children of Israel. 18So Moses went into the midst of the cloud and went up into the mountain. And Moses was on the mountain forty days and forty nights.

OFFERINGS FOR THE SANCTUARY

25 Then the LORD spoke to Moses, saying: 2"Speak to the children of Israel, that they bring Me an offering. From everyone who gives it willingly with his heart you shall take My offering. 3And this *is* the offering which you shall take from them: gold, silver, and bronze; 4blue, purple, and scarlet *thread,* fine linen, and goats' *hair;* 5ram skins dyed red, badger skins, and acacia wood; 6oil for the light, and spices for the anointing oil and for the sweet incense; 7onyx stones, and stones to be set in the ephod and in the breastplate. 8And let them make Me a sanctuary, that I may dwell among them. 9According to all that I show you, *that is,* the pattern of the tabernacle and the pattern of all its furnishings, just so you shall make *it.*

THE ARK OF THE TESTIMONY

10"And they shall make an ark of acacia wood; two and a half cubits *shall be* its length, a cubit and a half its width, and a cubit and a half its height. 11And you shall overlay it with pure gold, inside and out you shall overlay it, and shall make on it a molding of gold all around. 12You shall cast four rings of gold for it, and put *them* in its four corners; two rings *shall be* on one side, and two rings on the other side. 13And you shall make poles *of* acacia wood, and overlay them with gold. 14You shall put the poles into the rings on the sides of the ark, that the ark may be carried by them. 15The poles shall be in the rings of the ark; they shall not be taken from it. 16And you shall put into the ark the Testimony which I will give you.

17"You shall make a mercy seat of pure gold; two and a half cubits *shall be* its length and a cubit and a half its width. 18And you shall make two cherubim of gold; of hammered work you shall make them at the two ends of the mercy seat. 19Make one cherub at one end, and the other cherub at the other end; you shall make the cherubim at the two ends of it *of one piece* with the mercy seat. 20And the cherubim shall stretch out *their* wings above, covering the mercy seat with their wings, and they shall face one another; the faces of the cherubim *shall be* toward the mercy seat. 21You shall put the mercy seat on top of the ark, and in the ark you shall put the Testimony that I will give you. 22And there I will meet with you, and I will speak with you from above the mercy seat, from between the two cherubim which *are* on the ark of the Testimony, about everything which I will give you in commandment to the children of Israel.

THE TABLE FOR THE SHOWBREAD

23"You shall also make a table of acacia wood; two cubits *shall be* its length, a cubit its width, and a cubit and a half its height. 24And you shall overlay it with pure gold, and make a molding of gold all around. 25You shall make

SOUL NOTE

Together *(25:1–9)* Worship modes were not arbitrary in ancient Israel. The proper patterns and procedures of worship were clearly defined by God, as were the explicit details of the worship center called the tabernacle. The construction and financing of the tabernacle involved the entire community. As believers build a church through planning, giving, and serving, they gain a sense of ownership and participation in God's house. Worshiping together as a community of believers shows what it means to be part of the family of God. **Topic: Praise and Worship**

for it a frame of a handbreadth all around, and you shall make a gold molding for the frame all around. 26And you shall make for it four rings of gold, and put the rings on the four corners that *are* at its four legs. 27The rings shall be close to the frame, as holders for the poles to bear the table. 28And you shall make the poles of acacia wood, and overlay them with gold, that the table may be carried with them. 29You shall make its dishes, its pans, its pitchers, and its bowls for pouring. You shall make them of pure gold. 30And you shall set the showbread on the table before Me always.

The Gold Lampstand

31"You shall also make a lampstand of pure gold; the lampstand shall be of hammered work. Its shaft, its branches, its bowls, its *ornamental* knobs, and flowers shall be *of one piece.* 32And six branches shall come out of its sides: three branches of the lampstand out of one side, and three branches of the lampstand out of the other side. 33Three bowls *shall be* made like almond *blossoms* on one branch, *with* an *ornamental* knob and a flower, and three bowls made like almond *blossoms* on the other branch, *with* an *ornamental* knob and a flower—and so for the six branches that come out of the lampstand. 34On the lampstand itself four bowls *shall be* made like almond *blossoms, each with* its *ornamental* knob and flower. 35And *there shall be* a knob under the *first* two branches of the same, a knob under the *second* two branches of the same, and a knob under the *third* two branches of the same, according to the six branches that extend from the lampstand. 36Their knobs and their branches *shall be of one piece;* all of it *shall be* one hammered piece of pure gold. 37You shall make seven lamps for it, and they shall arrange its lamps so that they give light in front of it. 38And its wick-trimmers and their trays *shall be* of pure gold. 39It shall be made of a talent of pure gold, with all these utensils. 40And see to it that you make *them* according to the pattern which was shown you on the mountain.

The Tabernacle

26 "Moreover you shall make the tabernacle *with* ten curtains *of* fine woven linen and blue, purple, and scarlet *thread;* with artistic designs of cherubim you shall weave them. 2The length of each curtain *shall be* twenty-eight cubits, and the width of each curtain four cubits. And every one of the curtains shall have the same measurements. 3Five curtains shall be coupled to one another, and *the other* five curtains *shall be* coupled to one another. 4And you shall make loops of blue *yarn* on the edge of the curtain on the selvedge of *one* set, and likewise you shall do on the outer edge of *the other* curtain of the second set. 5Fifty loops you shall make in the one curtain, and fifty loops you shall make on the edge of the curtain that *is* on the end of the second set, that the loops may be clasped to one another. 6And you shall make fifty clasps of gold, and couple the curtains together with the clasps, so that it may be one tabernacle.

7"You shall also make curtains of goats' *hair,* to be a tent over the tabernacle. You shall make eleven curtains. 8The length of each curtain *shall be* thirty cubits, and the width of each curtain four cubits; and the eleven curtains shall all have the same measurements. 9And you shall couple five curtains by themselves and six curtains by themselves, and you shall double over the sixth curtain at the forefront of the tent. 10You shall make fifty loops on the edge of the curtain that is outermost in *one* set, and fifty loops on the edge of the curtain of the second set. 11And you shall make fifty bronze clasps, put the clasps into the loops, and couple the tent together, that it may be one. 12The remnant that remains of the curtains of the tent, the half curtain that remains, shall hang over the back of the tabernacle. 13And a cubit on one side and a cubit on the other side, of what remains of the length of the curtains of the tent, shall hang over the sides of the tabernacle, on this side and on that side, to cover it.

14"You shall also make a covering of ram skins dyed red for the tent, and a covering of badger skins above that.

15"And for the tabernacle you shall make the boards of acacia wood, standing upright. 16Ten cubits *shall be* the length of a board, and a cubit and a half *shall be* the width of each board. 17Two tenons *shall be* in each board for binding one to another. Thus you shall make for all the boards of the tabernacle. 18And you shall make the boards for the tabernacle, twenty boards for the south side. 19You shall make forty sockets of silver under the twenty boards: two sockets under each of the boards for its two tenons. 20And for the second side of the tabernacle, the north side, *there shall be* twenty boards 21and their forty sockets of silver: two sockets under each of the boards. 22For the far side of the tabernacle, westward, you shall make six boards. 23And you shall also make two boards for the two back corners of the tabernacle. 24They shall be coupled together at the bottom and they shall be coupled together at the top by one ring. Thus it shall be for both of them. They shall be for the two corners. 25So there shall be eight boards with their sockets of silver—sixteen sockets—two sockets under each of the boards.

26"And you shall make bars of acacia wood: five for the boards on one side of the tabernacle, 27five bars for the boards on the other side of the tabernacle, and five bars for the boards of the side of the tabernacle, for the far side westward. 28The middle bar shall pass through the midst of the boards from end to end. 29You shall overlay the boards with gold, make their rings of gold *as* holders for the bars, and overlay the bars with gold. 30And you shall raise up the tabernacle according to its pattern which you were shown on the mountain.

31"You shall make a veil woven of blue, purple, and scarlet *thread,* and fine woven linen. It shall be woven with an artistic design of cherubim. 32You shall hang it upon the four pillars of acacia *wood* overlaid with gold. Their hooks *shall be* gold, upon four sockets of silver. 33And you shall hang the veil from the clasps. Then you shall bring the ark of the Testimony in there, behind the veil. The veil shall be a divider for you between the holy *place* and the Most Holy. 34You shall put the mercy seat upon the ark of the Testimony in the Most Holy. 35You shall set the table outside the veil, and the lampstand across from the table on the side of the tabernacle toward the south; and you shall put the table on the north side.

36"You shall make a screen for the door of the tabernacle, *woven of* blue, purple, and scarlet *thread,* and fine woven linen, made by a weaver. 37And you shall make for the screen five pillars of acacia *wood,* and overlay them with gold; their hooks *shall be* gold, and you shall cast five sockets of bronze for them.

The Altar of Burnt Offering

27 "You shall make an altar of acacia wood, five cubits long and five cubits wide—the altar shall be square—and its height *shall be* three cubits. 2You shall make its horns on its four corners; its horns shall be of one piece with it. And you shall overlay it with bronze. 3Also you shall make its pans to receive its ashes, and its shovels and its basins and its forks and its firepans; you shall make all its utensils of bronze. 4You shall make a grate for it, a network of bronze; and on the network you shall make four bronze rings at its four corners. 5You shall put it under the rim of the altar beneath, that the network may be midway up the altar. 6And you shall make poles for the altar, poles of acacia wood, and overlay them with bronze. 7The poles shall be put in the rings, and the poles shall be on the two sides of the altar to bear it. 8You shall make it hollow with boards; as it was shown you on the mountain, so shall they make *it.*

The Court of the Tabernacle

9"You shall also make the court of the tabernacle. For the south side *there shall be* hangings for the court *made of* fine woven linen, one hundred cubits long for one side. 10And its twenty pillars and their twenty sockets *shall be* bronze. The hooks of the pillars and their bands *shall be* silver. 11Likewise along the length of the north side *there shall be* hangings one hundred *cubits* long, with its twenty pillars and their twenty sockets of bronze, and the hooks of the pillars and their bands of silver.

12"And along the width of the court on the west side *shall be* hangings of fifty cubits, with their ten pillars and their ten sockets. 13The width of the court on the east side *shall be* fifty cubits. 14The hangings on *one* side *of the gate shall be* fifteen cubits, *with* their three pillars and their three sockets. 15And on the other side *shall be* hangings of fifteen *cubits, with* their three pillars and their three sockets.

16"For the gate of the court *there shall be* a screen twenty cubits long, *woven of* blue, purple, and scarlet *thread,* and fine woven linen, made by a weaver. It *shall have* four pillars and four sockets. 17All the pillars around the court shall have bands of silver; their hooks *shall be* of silver and their sockets of bronze. 18The length of the court *shall be* one hundred cubits, the width fifty throughout, and the height five cubits, *made of* fine woven linen, and its sockets of bronze. 19All the utensils of the tabernacle for all its service, all its pegs, and all the pegs of the court, *shall be* of bronze.

The Care of the Lampstand

20“And you shall command the children of
Israel that they bring you pure oil of pressed
olives for the light, to cause the lamp to burn
continually. 21In the tabernacle of meeting,
outside the veil which *is* before the Testimony,
Aaron and his sons shall tend it from evening
until morning before the LORD. *It shall be* a
statute forever to their generations on behalf
of the children of Israel.

Garments for the Priesthood

28 “Now take Aaron your brother, and his
sons with him, from among the children of Israel, that he may minister to Me as
priest, Aaron *and* Aaron’s sons: Nadab, Abihu, Eleazar, and Ithamar. 2And you shall make
holy garments for Aaron your brother, for
glory and for beauty. 3So you shall speak to all
who are gifted artisans, whom I have filled
with the spirit of wisdom, that they may make
Aaron’s garments, to consecrate him, that he
may minister to Me as priest. 4And these *are*
the garments which they shall make: a breastplate, an ephod,[a] a robe, a skillfully woven tunic, a turban, and a sash. So they shall make
holy garments for Aaron your brother and his
sons, that he may minister to Me as priest.

The Ephod

5“They shall take the gold, blue, purple, and
scarlet *thread,* and the fine linen, 6and they
shall make the ephod of gold, blue, purple,
and scarlet *thread,* and fine woven linen, artistically worked. 7It shall have two shoulder
straps joined at its two edges, and *so* it shall
be joined together. 8And the intricately woven
band of the ephod, which *is* on it, shall be of
the same workmanship, *made of* gold, blue,
purple, and scarlet *thread,* and fine woven
linen.

9“Then you shall take two onyx stones and
engrave on them the names of the sons of Israel: 10six of their names on one stone and six
names on the other stone, in order of their
birth. 11With the work of an engraver in stone,
like the engravings of a signet, you shall engrave the two stones with the names of the
sons of Israel. You shall set them in settings of
gold. 12And you shall put the two stones on
the shoulders of the ephod *as* memorial stones
for the sons of Israel. So Aaron shall bear their
names before the LORD on his two shoulders
as a memorial. 13You shall also make settings
of gold, 14and you shall make two chains of
pure gold like braided cords, and fasten the
braided chains to the settings.

The Breastplate

15“You shall make the breastplate of judgment. Artistically woven according to the
workmanship of the ephod you shall make it:
of gold, blue, purple, and scarlet *thread,* and
fine woven linen, you shall make it. 16It shall
be doubled into a square: a span *shall be* its
length, and a span *shall be* its width. 17And
you shall put settings of stones in it, four rows
of stones: *The first* row *shall be* a sardius, a
topaz, and an emerald; *this shall be* the first
row; 18the second row *shall be* a turquoise, a
sapphire, and a diamond; 19the third row, a jacinth, an agate, and an amethyst; 20and the
fourth row, a beryl, an onyx, and a jasper.
They shall be set in gold settings. 21And the
stones shall have the names of the sons of Israel, twelve according to their names, *like* the
engravings of a signet, each one with its own
name; they shall be according to the twelve
tribes.

22“You shall make chains for the breastplate
at the end, like braided cords of pure gold.
23And you shall make two rings of gold for the
breastplate, and put the two rings on the two
ends of the breastplate. 24Then you shall put
the two braided *chains* of gold in the two rings
which are on the ends of the breastplate;
25and the *other* two ends of the two braided
chains you shall fasten to the two settings,
and put them on the shoulder straps of the
ephod in the front.

26“You shall make two rings of gold, and put
them on the two ends of the breastplate, on
the edge of it, which is on the inner side of the
ephod. 27And two *other* rings of gold you shall
make, and put them on the two shoulder
straps, underneath the ephod toward its front,
right at the seam above the intricately woven
band of the ephod. 28They shall bind the
breastplate by means of its rings to the rings
of the ephod, using a blue cord, so that it is
above the intricately woven band of the
ephod, and so that the breastplate does not
come loose from the ephod.

29“So Aaron shall bear the names of the
sons of Israel on the breastplate of judgment
over his heart, when he goes into the holy

28:4 [a]That is, an ornamented vest

place, as a memorial before the LORD continually. 30 And you shall put in the breastplate of judgment the Urim and the Thummim,[a] and they shall be over Aaron's heart when he goes in before the LORD. So Aaron shall bear the judgment of the children of Israel over his heart before the LORD continually.

Other Priestly Garments

31 "You shall make the robe of the ephod all of blue. 32 There shall be an opening for his head in the middle of it; it shall have a woven binding all around its opening, like the opening in a coat of mail, so that it does not tear. 33 And upon its hem you shall make pomegranates of blue, purple, and scarlet, all around its hem, and bells of gold between them all around: 34 a golden bell and a pomegranate, a golden bell and a pomegranate, upon the hem of the robe all around. 35 And it shall be upon Aaron when he ministers, and its sound will be heard when he goes into the holy *place* before the LORD and when he comes out, that he may not die.

36 "You shall also make a plate of pure gold and engrave on it, *like* the engraving of a signet:

HOLINESS TO THE LORD.

37 And you shall put it on a blue cord, that it may be on the turban; it shall be on the front of the turban. 38 So it shall be on Aaron's forehead, that Aaron may bear the iniquity of the holy things which the children of Israel hallow in all their holy gifts; and it shall always be on his forehead, that they may be accepted before the LORD.

39 "You shall skillfully weave the tunic of fine linen *thread,* you shall make the turban of fine linen, and you shall make the sash of woven work.

40 "For Aaron's sons you shall make tunics, and you shall make sashes for them. And you shall make hats for them, for glory and beauty. 41 So you shall put them on Aaron your brother and on his sons with him. You shall anoint them, consecrate them, and sanctify them, that they may minister to Me as priests. 42 And you shall make for them linen trousers to cover their nakedness; they shall reach from the waist to the thighs. 43 They shall be on Aaron and on his sons when they come into the tabernacle of meeting, or when they come near the altar to minister in the holy *place,* that they do not incur iniquity and die. *It shall be* a statute forever to him and his descendants after him.

Aaron and His Sons Consecrated

29 "And this is what you shall do to them to hallow them for ministering to Me as priests: Take one young bull and two rams without blemish, 2 and unleavened bread, unleavened cakes mixed with oil, and unleavened wafers anointed with oil (you shall make them of wheat flour). 3 You shall put them in one basket and bring them in the basket, with the bull and the two rams.

4 "And Aaron and his sons you shall bring to the door of the tabernacle of meeting, and you shall wash them with water. 5 Then you shall take the garments, put the tunic on Aaron, and the robe of the ephod, the ephod, and the breastplate, and gird him with the intricately woven band of the ephod. 6 You shall put the turban on his head, and put the holy crown on the turban. 7 And you shall take the anointing oil, pour *it* on his head, and anoint him. 8 Then you shall bring his sons and put tunics on them. 9 And you shall gird them with sashes, Aaron and his sons, and put the hats on them. The priesthood shall be theirs for a perpetual statute. So you shall consecrate Aaron and his sons.

10 "You shall also have the bull brought before the tabernacle of meeting, and Aaron and his sons shall put their hands on the head of the bull. 11 Then you shall kill the bull before the LORD, *by* the door of the tabernacle of meeting. 12 You shall take *some* of the blood of the bull and put *it* on the horns of the altar with your finger, and pour all the blood beside the base of the altar. 13 And you shall take all the fat that covers the entrails, the fatty lobe *attached* to the liver, and the two kidneys and the fat that *is* on them, and burn *them* on the altar. 14 But the flesh of the bull, with its skin and its offal, you shall burn with fire outside the camp. It *is* a sin offering.

15 "You shall also take one ram, and Aaron and his sons shall put their hands on the head of the ram; 16 and you shall kill the ram, and you shall take its blood and sprinkle *it* all around on the altar. 17 Then you shall cut the ram in pieces, wash its entrails and its legs,

28:30 [a]Literally *the Lights and the Perfections* (compare Leviticus 8:8)

and put *them* with its pieces and with its
head. [18]And you shall burn the whole ram on
the altar. It *is* a burnt offering to the LORD; it *is*
a sweet aroma, an offering made by fire to the
LORD.
[19]"You shall also take the other ram, and
Aaron and his sons shall put their hands on
the head of the ram. [20]Then you shall kill the
ram, and take some of its blood and put *it* on
the tip of the right ear of Aaron and on the tip
of the right ear of his sons, on the thumb of
their right hand and on the big toe of their
right foot, and sprinkle the blood all around
on the altar. [21]And you shall take some of the
blood that is on the altar, and some of the
anointing oil, and sprinkle *it* on Aaron and on
his garments, on his sons and on the garments
of his sons with him; and he and his garments
shall be hallowed, and his sons and his sons'
garments with him.
[22]"Also you shall take the fat of the ram, the
fat tail, the fat that covers the entrails, the
fatty lobe *attached to* the liver, the two kidneys and the fat on them, the right thigh (for it
is a ram of consecration), [23]one loaf of bread,
one cake *made with* oil, and one wafer from
the basket of the unleavened bread that *is* before the LORD; [24]and you shall put all these in
the hands of Aaron and in the hands of his
sons, and you shall wave them *as* a wave offering before the LORD. [25]You shall receive
them back from their hands and burn *them* on
the altar as a burnt offering, as a sweet aroma
before the LORD. It *is* an offering made by fire
to the LORD.
[26]"Then you shall take the breast of the ram
of Aaron's consecration and wave it *as* a wave
offering before the LORD; and it shall be your
portion. [27]And from the ram of the consecration you shall consecrate the breast of the
wave offering which is waved, and the thigh
of the heave offering which is raised, of *that*
which *is* for Aaron and of *that* which is for his
sons. [28]It shall be from the children of Israel
for Aaron and his sons by a statute forever. For
it is a heave offering; it shall be a heave offering from the children of Israel from the sacrifices of their peace offerings, *that is,* their
heave offering to the LORD.
[29]"And the holy garments of Aaron shall be
his sons' after him, to be anointed in them
and to be consecrated in them. [30]That son
who becomes priest in his place shall put
them on for seven days, when he enters the
tabernacle of meeting to minister in the holy
place.
[31]"And you shall take the ram of the consecration and boil its flesh in the holy place.
[32]Then Aaron and his sons shall eat the flesh
of the ram, and the bread that *is* in the basket,
by the door of the tabernacle of meeting.
[33]They shall eat those things with which the
atonement was made, to consecrate *and* to
sanctify them; but an outsider shall not eat
them, because they *are* holy. [34]And if any of
the flesh of the consecration offerings, or of
the bread, remains until the morning, then
you shall burn the remainder with fire. It shall
not be eaten, because it *is* holy.
[35]"Thus you shall do to Aaron and his sons,
according to all that I have commanded you.
Seven days you shall consecrate them. [36]And
you shall offer a bull every day *as* a sin offering for atonement. You shall cleanse the altar
when you make atonement for it, and you
shall anoint it to sanctify it. [37]Seven days you
shall make atonement for the altar and sanctify it. And the altar shall be most holy. Whatever touches the altar must be holy.[a]

THE DAILY OFFERINGS

[38]"Now this *is* what you shall offer on the
altar: two lambs of the first year, day by day
continually. [39]One lamb you shall offer in the
morning, and the other lamb you shall offer at
twilight. [40]With the one lamb shall be one-
tenth *of an ephah* of flour mixed with one-
fourth of a hin of pressed oil, and one-fourth of
a hin of wine *as* a drink offering. [41]And the
other lamb you shall offer at twilight; and you
shall offer with it the grain offering and the
drink offering, as in the morning, for a sweet
aroma, an offering made by fire to the LORD.
[42]*This shall be* a continual burnt offering
throughout your generations *at* the door of the
tabernacle of meeting before the LORD, where I
will meet you to speak with you. [43]And there I
will meet with the children of Israel, and *the
tabernacle* shall be sanctified by My glory. [44]So
I will consecrate the tabernacle of meeting and
the altar. I will also consecrate both Aaron and
his sons to minister to Me as priests. [45]I will
dwell among the children of Israel and will be
their God. [46]And they shall know that I *am* the
LORD their God, who brought them up out of

29:37 [a]Compare Numbers 4:15 and Haggai 2:11–13

the land of Egypt, that I may dwell among
them. I *am* the LORD their God.

THE ALTAR OF INCENSE

30 "You shall make an altar to burn incense on; you shall make it of acacia
wood. 2A cubit *shall be* its length and a cubit
its width—it shall be square—and two cubits
shall be its height. Its horns *shall be* of one
piece with it. 3And you shall overlay its top, its
sides all around, and its horns with pure gold;
and you shall make for it a molding of gold all
around. 4Two gold rings you shall make for it,
under the molding on both its sides. You shall
place *them* on its two sides, and they will be
holders for the poles with which to bear it.
5You shall make the poles of acacia wood, and
overlay them with gold. 6And you shall put it
before the veil that *is* before the ark of the Testimony, before the mercy seat that *is* over the
Testimony, where I will meet with you.

7"Aaron shall burn on it sweet incense every
morning; when he tends the lamps, he shall
burn incense on it. 8And when Aaron lights
the lamps at twilight, he shall burn incense
on it, a perpetual incense before the LORD
throughout your generations. 9You shall not
offer strange incense on it, or a burnt offering,
or a grain offering; nor shall you pour a drink
offering on it. 10And Aaron shall make atonement upon its horns once a year with the
blood of the sin offering of atonement; once a
year he shall make atonement upon it
throughout your generations. It *is* most holy to
the LORD."

THE RANSOM MONEY

11Then the LORD spoke to Moses, saying:
12"When you take the census of the children
of Israel for their number, then every man
shall give a ransom for himself to the LORD,
when you number them, that there may be no
plague among them when *you* number them.
13This is what everyone among those who are
numbered shall give: half a shekel according
to the shekel of the sanctuary (a shekel *is*
twenty gerahs). The half-shekel *shall be* an
offering to the LORD. 14Everyone included
among those who are numbered, from twenty
years old and above, shall give an offering to
the LORD. 15The rich shall not give more and
the poor shall not give less than half a shekel,
when *you* give an offering to the LORD, to
make atonement for yourselves. 16And you
shall take the atonement money of the children of Israel, and shall appoint it for the service of the tabernacle of meeting, that it may
be a memorial for the children of Israel before
the LORD, to make atonement for yourselves."

THE BRONZE LAVER

17Then the LORD spoke to Moses, saying:
18"You shall also make a laver of bronze, with
its base also of bronze, for washing. You shall
put it between the tabernacle of meeting and
the altar. And you shall put water in it, 19for
Aaron and his sons shall wash their hands and
their feet in water from it. 20When they go into
the tabernacle of meeting, or when they come
near the altar to minister, to burn an offering
made by fire to the LORD, they shall wash with
water, lest they die. 21So they shall wash their
hands and their feet, lest they die. And it shall
be a statute forever to them—to him and his
descendants throughout their generations."

THE HOLY ANOINTING OIL

22Moreover the LORD spoke to Moses, saying: 23"Also take for yourself quality spices—
five hundred *shekels* of liquid myrrh, half as
much sweet-smelling cinnamon (two hundred
and fifty *shekels*), two hundred and fifty *shek-*

SOUL NOTE

A Gentle Reminder *(30:1)* The altar of incense was a visible reminder of the importance of daily prayer. Located inside the tabernacle itself (40:26, 27), it was much smaller than the altar of burnt offering, which was inside the courtyard by the main entrance. Priests burned sweet-smelling incense on the altar of incense daily to represent the prayers of God's people. The sweet aroma of the incense wafting to heaven symbolized God's pleasure with His people's prayers. What reminds you to pray and worship daily? **Topic: Prayer**

els of sweet-smelling cane, [24]five hundred *shekels* of cassia, according to the shekel of the sanctuary, and a hin of olive oil. [25]And you shall make from these a holy anointing oil, an ointment compounded according to the art of the perfumer. It shall be a holy anointing oil. [26]With it you shall anoint the tabernacle of meeting and the ark of the Testimony; [27]the table and all its utensils, the lampstand and its utensils, and the altar of incense; [28]the altar of burnt offering with all its utensils, and the laver and its base. [29]You shall consecrate them, that they may be most holy; whatever touches them must be holy.[a] [30]And you shall anoint Aaron and his sons, and consecrate them, that *they* may minister to Me as priests.

[31]"And you shall speak to the children of Israel, saying: 'This shall be a holy anointing oil to Me throughout your generations. [32]It shall not be poured on man's flesh; nor shall you make *any other* like it, according to its composition. It *is* holy, *and* it shall be holy to you. [33]Whoever compounds *any* like it, or whoever puts *any* of it on an outsider, shall be cut off from his people.' "

The Incense

[34]And the LORD said to Moses: "Take sweet spices, stacte and onycha and galbanum, and pure frankincense with *these* sweet spices; there shall be equal amounts of each. [35]You shall make of these an incense, a compound according to the art of the perfumer, salted, pure, *and* holy. [36]And you shall beat *some* of it very fine, and put some of it before the Testimony in the tabernacle of meeting where I will meet with you. It shall be most holy to you. [37]But *as for* the incense which you shall make, you shall not make any for yourselves, according to its composition. It shall be to you holy for the LORD. [38]Whoever makes *any* like it, to smell it, he shall be cut off from his people."

Artisans for Building the Tabernacle

31 Then the LORD spoke to Moses, saying: [2]"See, I have called by name Bezalel the son of Uri, the son of Hur, of the tribe of Judah. [3]And I have filled him with the Spirit of God, in wisdom, in understanding, in knowledge, and in all *manner of* workmanship, [4]to design artistic works, to work in gold, in silver, in bronze, [5]in cutting jewels for setting, in carving wood, and to work in all *manner of* workmanship.

[6]"And I, indeed I, have appointed with him Aholiab the son of Ahisamach, of the tribe of Dan; and I have put wisdom in the hearts of all the gifted artisans, that they may make all that I have commanded you: [7]the tabernacle of meeting, the ark of the Testimony and the mercy seat that *is* on it, and all the furniture of the tabernacle— [8]the table and its utensils, the pure *gold* lampstand with all its utensils, the altar of incense, [9]the altar of burnt offering with all its utensils, and the laver and its base— [10]the garments of ministry,[a] the holy garments for Aaron the priest and the garments of his sons, to minister as priests, [11]and the anointing oil and sweet incense for the holy *place*. According to all that I have commanded you they shall do."

The Sabbath Law

[12]And the LORD spoke to Moses, saying, [13]"Speak also to the children of Israel, saying: 'Surely My Sabbaths you shall keep, for it *is* a sign between Me and you throughout your generations, that *you* may know that I *am* the LORD who sanctifies you. [14]You shall keep the Sabbath, therefore, for *it is* holy to you. Everyone who profanes it shall surely be put to death; for whoever does *any* work on it, that person shall be cut off from among his people. [15]Work shall be done for six days, but the seventh *is* the Sabbath of rest, holy to the LORD. Whoever does *any* work on the Sabbath day, he shall surely be put to death. [16]Therefore the children of Israel shall keep the Sabbath, to observe the Sabbath throughout their generations *as* a perpetual covenant. [17]It *is* a sign between Me and the children of Israel forever; for *in* six days the LORD made the heavens and the earth, and on the seventh day He rested and was refreshed.' "

> "Surely My Sabbaths you shall keep, for it is a sign between Me and you throughout your generations, that you may know that I am the LORD who sanctifies you."
> EXODUS 31:13

30:29 [a]Compare Numbers 4:15 and Haggai 2:11–13 **31:10** [a]Or *woven garments*

18And when He had made an end of speaking with him on Mount Sinai, He gave Moses
two tablets of the Testimony, tablets of stone,
written with the finger of God.

The Gold Calf

32 Now when the people saw that Moses
delayed coming down from the mountain, the people gathered together to Aaron,
and said to him, "Come, make us gods that
shall go before us; for *as for* this Moses, the
man who brought us up out of the land of
Egypt, we do not know what has become of
him."

2And Aaron said to them, "Break off the
golden earrings which *are* in the ears of your
wives, your sons, and your daughters, and
bring *them* to me." 3So all the people broke off
the golden earrings which *were* in their ears,
and brought *them* to Aaron. 4And he received
the gold from their hand, and he fashioned it
with an engraving tool, and made a molded
calf.

Then they said, "This *is* your god, O Israel,
that brought you out of the land of Egypt!"

5So when Aaron saw *it,* he built an altar before it. And Aaron made a proclamation and
said, "Tomorrow *is* a feast to the LORD." 6Then
they rose early on the next day, offered burnt
offerings, and brought peace offerings; and
the people sat down to eat and drink, and rose
up to play.

7And the LORD said to Moses, "Go, get
down! For your people whom you brought out
of the land of Egypt have corrupted *themselves.* 8They have turned aside quickly out of
the way which I commanded them. They have
made themselves a molded calf, and worshiped it and sacrificed to it, and said, 'This *is*
your god, O Israel, that brought you out of the
land of Egypt!' " 9And the LORD said to Moses,
"I have seen this people, and indeed it *is* a
stiff-necked people! 10Now therefore, let Me
alone, that My wrath may burn hot against
them and I may consume them. And I will
make of you a great nation."

11Then Moses pleaded with the LORD his
God, and said: "LORD, why does Your wrath
burn hot against Your people whom You have
brought out of the land of Egypt with great
power and with a mighty hand? 12Why should
the Egyptians speak, and say, 'He brought
them out to harm them, to kill them in the
mountains, and to consume them from the
face of the earth'? Turn from Your fierce
wrath, and relent from this harm to Your people. 13Remember Abraham, Isaac, and Israel,
Your servants, to whom You swore by Your
own self, and said to them, 'I will multiply
your descendants as the stars of heaven; and
all this land that I have spoken of I give to
your descendants, and they shall inherit
it forever.' "[a] 14So the LORD relented from
the harm which He said He would do to His
people.

15And Moses turned and went down from
the mountain, and the two tablets of the Testimony *were* in his hand. The tablets *were* written on both sides; on the one *side* and on the
other they were written. 16Now the tablets
were the work of God, and the writing *was* the
writing of God engraved on the tablets.

17And when Joshua heard the noise of the
people as they shouted, he said to Moses,
"*There is* a noise of war in the camp."

18But he said:

"*It is* not the noise of the shout of victory,
Nor the noise of the cry of defeat,
But the sound of singing I hear."

19So it was, as soon as he came near the
camp, that he saw the calf *and* the dancing. So
Moses' anger became hot, and he cast the tab-

32:13 [a]Genesis 13:15 and 22:17

SOUL NOTE

Hot Anger *(32:19)* The Israelites had thrown off all restraint and were reveling in the vilest sin while Moses was talking with God on the mountain. When Moses heard and saw what they had done, he smashed the tablets of the Ten Commandments, burned the golden calf, ground it to powder, and made the people consume it. Jesus also showed anger when He cleansed the temple (John 2:13–17). Some evil situations justify righteous, "hot anger" as a wake-up call for sinners. **Topic: Anger**

lets out of his hands and broke them at the foot of the mountain. [20]Then he took the calf which they had made, burned *it* in the fire, and ground *it* to powder; and he scattered *it* on the water and made the children of Israel drink *it*. [21]And Moses said to Aaron, "What did this people do to you that you have brought *so* great a sin upon them?"

[22]So Aaron said, "Do not let the anger of my lord become hot. You know the people, that they *are set* on evil. [23]For they said to me, 'Make us gods that shall go before us; *as for* this Moses, the man who brought us out of the land of Egypt, we do not know what has become of him.' [24]And I said to them, 'Whoever has any gold, let them break *it* off.' So they gave *it* to me, and I cast it into the fire, and this calf came out."

[25]Now when Moses saw that the people *were* unrestrained (for Aaron had not restrained them, to *their* shame among their enemies), [26]then Moses stood in the entrance of the camp, and said, "Whoever *is* on the LORD's side—*come* to me!" And all the sons of Levi gathered themselves together to him. [27]And he said to them, "Thus says the LORD God of Israel: 'Let every man put his sword on his side, and go in and out from entrance to entrance throughout the camp, and let every man kill his brother, every man his companion, and every man his neighbor.' " [28]So the sons of Levi did according to the word of Moses. And about three thousand men of the people fell that day. [29]Then Moses said, "Consecrate yourselves today to the LORD, that He may bestow on you a blessing this day, for every man has opposed his son and his brother."

[30]Now it came to pass on the next day that Moses said to the people, "You have committed a great sin. So now I will go up to the LORD; perhaps I can make atonement for your sin." [31]Then Moses returned to the LORD and said, "Oh, these people have committed a great sin, and have made for themselves a god of gold! [32]Yet now, if You will forgive their sin—but if not, I pray, blot me out of Your book which You have written."

[33]And the LORD said to Moses, "Whoever has sinned against Me, I will blot him out of My book. [34]Now therefore, go, lead the people to *the place* of which I have spoken to you. Behold, My Angel shall go before you. Nevertheless, in the day when I visit for punishment, I will visit punishment upon them for their sin."

[35]So the LORD plagued the people because of what they did with the calf which Aaron made.

THE COMMAND TO LEAVE SINAI

33 Then the LORD said to Moses, "Depart *and* go up from here, you and the people whom you have brought out of the land of Egypt, to the land of which I swore to Abraham, Isaac, and Jacob, saying, 'To your descendants I will give it.' [2]And I will send *My* Angel before you, and I will drive out the Canaanite and the Amorite and the Hittite and the Perizzite and the Hivite and the Jebusite. [3]*Go up* to a land flowing with milk and honey; for I will not go up in your midst, lest I consume you on the way, for you *are* a stiff-necked people."

[4]And when the people heard this bad news, they mourned, and no one put on his ornaments. [5]For the LORD had said to Moses, "Say to the children of Israel, 'You *are* a stiff-necked people. I could come up into your midst in one moment and consume you. Now therefore, take off your ornaments, that I may know what to do to you.' " [6]So the children of Israel stripped themselves of their ornaments by Mount Horeb.

SOUL NOTE

Forgiven *(32:32)* Forgiveness is given to those who repent. The people had sinned greatly against God, and Moses pleaded with God to forgive them. Moses was even willing to take their punishment for them. But God's loving and just response was: "Whoever has sinned against Me, I will blot him out of My book" (32:33). God would punish the guilty ones. God is always ready to forgive those who recognize their sin and come to Him in repentance. Those who are guilty and unrepentant, however, will be punished. **Topic: Forgiveness**

Moses Meets with the Lord

7Moses took his tent and pitched it outside
the camp, far from the camp, and called it the
tabernacle of meeting. And it came to pass
that everyone who sought the LORD went out
to the tabernacle of meeting which *was* outside the camp. 8So it was, whenever Moses
went out to the tabernacle, *that* all the people
rose, and each man stood *at* his tent door and
watched Moses until he had gone into the tabernacle. 9And it came to pass, when Moses
entered the tabernacle, that the pillar of cloud
descended and stood *at* the door of the tabernacle, and *the* LORD talked with Moses. 10All
the people saw the pillar of cloud standing *at*
the tabernacle door, and all the people rose
and worshiped, each man *in* his tent door. 11So
the LORD spoke to Moses face to face, as a man
speaks to his friend. And he would return to
the camp, but his servant Joshua the son of
Nun, a young man, did not depart from the
tabernacle.

The Promise of God's Presence

12Then Moses said to the LORD, "See, You
say to me, 'Bring up this people.' But You have
not let me know whom You will send with me.
Yet You have said, 'I know you by name, and
you have also found grace in My sight.' 13Now
therefore, I pray, if I have found grace in Your
sight, show me now Your way, that I may
know You and that I may find grace in Your
sight. And consider that this nation *is* Your
people."

14And He said, "My Presence will go *with
you,* and I will give you rest."

15Then he said to Him, "If Your Presence
does not go *with us,* do not bring us up from
here. 16For how then will it be known that
Your people and I have found grace in Your
sight, except You go with us? So we shall be
separate, Your people and I, from all the people who *are* upon the face of the earth."

17So the LORD said to Moses, "I will also do
this thing that you have spoken; for you have
found grace in My sight, and I know you by
name."

18And he said, "Please, show me Your glory."

19Then He said, "I will make all My goodness pass before you, and I will proclaim the
name of the LORD before you. I will be gracious to whom I will be gracious, and I will
have compassion on whom I will have compassion." 20But He said, "You cannot see My
face; for no man shall see Me, and live." 21And
the LORD said, "Here is a place by Me, and you
shall stand on the rock. 22So it shall be, while
My glory passes by, that I will put you in the
cleft of the rock, and will cover you with My
hand while I pass by. 23Then I will take away
My hand, and you shall see My back; but My
face shall not be seen."

Moses Makes New Tablets

34 And the LORD said to Moses, "Cut two
tablets of stone like the first *ones,* and
I will write on *these* tablets the words that
were on the first tablets which you broke. 2So
be ready in the morning, and come up in the
morning to Mount Sinai, and present yourself
to Me there on the top of the mountain. 3And
no man shall come up with you, and let no
man be seen throughout all the mountain; let
neither flocks nor herds feed before that
mountain."

4So he cut two tablets of stone like the first
ones. Then Moses rose early in the morning
and went up Mount Sinai, as the LORD had
commanded him; and he took in his hand the
two tablets of stone.

5Now the LORD descended in the cloud and
stood with him there, and proclaimed the
name of the LORD. 6And the LORD passed
before him and proclaimed, "The LORD, the
LORD God, merciful and gracious, longsuffering, and abounding in goodness and

SOUL NOTE

Face to Face *(33:11)* Moses enjoyed an amazing relationship with God. In fact, God spoke to Moses "face to face, as a man speaks to his friend." God wants to know His obedient servants that deeply. He wants to communicate with us as easily as we speak to our friends. Jesus said, "I have called you friends, for all things that I heard from My Father I have made known to you" (John 15:15). We can know God that deeply if we commit ourselves to love, serve, and obey Him. **Topic: Knowing God**

truth, [7]keeping mercy for thousands, forgiving iniquity and transgression and sin, by no means clearing *the guilty,* visiting the iniquity of the fathers upon the children and the children's children to the third and the fourth generation."

[8]So Moses made haste and bowed his head toward the earth, and worshiped. [9]Then he said, "If now I have found grace in Your sight, O Lord, let my Lord, I pray, go among us, even though we *are* a stiff-necked people; and pardon our iniquity and our sin, and take us as Your inheritance."

The Covenant Renewed

[10]And He said: "Behold, I make a covenant. Before all your people I will do marvels such as have not been done in all the earth, nor in any nation; and all the people among whom you *are* shall see the work of the LORD. For it *is* an awesome thing that I will do with you. [11]Observe what I command you this day. Behold, I am driving out from before you the Amorite and the Canaanite and the Hittite and the Perizzite and the Hivite and the Jebusite. [12]Take heed to yourself, lest you make a covenant with the inhabitants of the land where you are going, lest it be a snare in your midst. [13]But you shall destroy their altars, break their *sacred* pillars, and cut down their wooden images [14](for you shall worship no other god, for the LORD, whose name *is* Jealous, *is* a jealous God), [15]lest you make a covenant with the inhabitants of the land, and they play the harlot with their gods and make sacrifice to their gods, and *one of them* invites you and you eat of his sacrifice, [16]and you take of his daughters for your sons, and his daughters play the harlot with their gods and make your sons play the harlot with their gods.

> "Before all your people I will do marvels such as have not been done in all the earth, nor in any nation; and all the people among whom you are shall see the work of the LORD. For it is an awesome thing that I will do with you."
>
> EXODUS 34:10

[17]"You shall make no molded gods for yourselves.

[18]"The Feast of Unleavened Bread you shall keep. Seven days you shall eat unleavened bread, as I commanded you, in the appointed time of the month of Abib; for in the month of Abib you came out from Egypt.

[19]"All that open the womb *are* Mine, and every male firstborn among your livestock, *whether* ox or sheep. [20]But the firstborn of a donkey you shall redeem with a lamb. And if you will not redeem *him,* then you shall break his neck. All the firstborn of your sons you shall redeem.

"And none shall appear before Me empty-handed.

[21]"Six days you shall work, but on the seventh day you shall rest; in plowing time and in harvest you shall rest.

[22]"And you shall observe the Feast of Weeks, of the firstfruits of wheat harvest, and the Feast of Ingathering at the year's end.

[23]"Three times in the year all your men shall appear before the Lord, the LORD God of Israel. [24]For I will cast out the nations before you and enlarge your borders; neither will any man covet your land when you go up to appear before the LORD your God three times in the year.

[25]"You shall not offer the blood of My sacrifice with leaven, nor shall the sacrifice of the Feast of the Passover be left until morning.

[26]"The first of the firstfruits of your land you shall bring to the house of the LORD your God. You shall not boil a young goat in its mother's milk."

[27]Then the LORD said to Moses, "Write these words, for according to the tenor of these words I have made a covenant with you and with Israel." [28]So he was there with the LORD forty days and forty nights; he neither ate bread nor drank water. And He wrote on the tablets the words of the covenant, the Ten Commandments.[a]

The Shining Face of Moses

[29]Now it was so, when Moses came down from Mount Sinai (and the two tablets of the Testimony *were* in Moses' hand when he came down from the mountain), that Moses did not know that the skin of his face shone while he talked with Him. [30]So when Aaron and all the children of Israel saw Moses, behold, the skin

---

34:28 [a]Literally *Ten Words*

of his face shone, and they were afraid to come near him. [31]Then Moses called to them, and Aaron and all the rulers of the congregation returned to him; and Moses talked with them. [32]Afterward all the children of Israel came near, and he gave them as commandments all that the LORD had spoken with him on Mount Sinai. [33]And when Moses had finished speaking with them, he put a veil on his face. [34]But whenever Moses went in before the LORD to speak with Him, he would take the veil off until he came out; and he would come out and speak to the children of Israel whatever he had been commanded. [35]And whenever the children of Israel saw the face of Moses, that the skin of Moses' face shone, then Moses would put the veil on his face again, until he went in to speak with Him.

SABBATH REGULATIONS

35 Then Moses gathered all the congregation of the children of Israel together, and said to them, "These *are* the words which the LORD has commanded *you* to do: [2]Work shall be done for six days, but the seventh day shall be a holy day for you, a Sabbath of rest to the LORD. Whoever does any work on it shall be put to death. [3]You shall kindle no fire throughout your dwellings on the Sabbath day."

OFFERINGS FOR THE TABERNACLE

[4]And Moses spoke to all the congregation of the children of Israel, saying, "This *is* the thing which the LORD commanded, saying: [5]'Take from among you an offering to the LORD. Whoever *is* of a willing heart, let him bring it as an offering to the LORD: gold, silver, and bronze; [6]blue, purple, and scarlet *thread,* fine linen, and goats' *hair;* [7]ram skins dyed red, badger skins, and acacia wood; [8]oil for the light, and spices for the anointing oil and for the sweet incense; [9]onyx stones, and stones to be set in the ephod and in the breastplate.

ARTICLES OF THE TABERNACLE

[10]'All *who are* gifted artisans among you shall come and make all that the LORD has commanded: [11]the tabernacle, its tent, its covering, its clasps, its boards, its bars, its pillars, and its sockets; [12]the ark and its poles, *with* the mercy seat, and the veil of the covering; [13]the table and its poles, all its utensils, and the showbread; [14]also the lampstand for the light, its utensils, its lamps, and the oil for the light; [15]the incense altar, its poles, the anointing oil, the sweet incense, and the screen for the door at the entrance of the tabernacle; [16]the altar of burnt offering with its bronze grating, its poles, all its utensils, *and* the laver and its base; [17]the hangings of the court, its pillars, their sockets, and the screen for the gate of the court; [18]the pegs of the tabernacle, the pegs of the court, and their cords; [19]the garments of ministry,[a] for ministering in the holy *place*—the holy garments for Aaron the priest and the garments of his sons, to minister as priests.' "

THE TABERNACLE OFFERINGS PRESENTED

[20]And all the congregation of the children of Israel departed from the presence of Moses. [21]Then everyone came whose heart was stirred, and everyone whose spirit was willing, *and* they brought the LORD's offering for the work of the tabernacle of meeting, for all its service, and for the holy garments. [22]They came, both men and women, as many as had a willing heart, *and* brought earrings and nose rings, rings and necklaces, all jewelry of gold, that is, every man who *made* an offering of gold to the LORD. [23]And every man, with whom was found blue, purple, and scarlet *thread,* fine linen, goats' *hair,* red skins of rams, and badger skins, brought *them.* [24]Everyone who offered an offering of silver or bronze brought the LORD's offering. And everyone with whom was found acacia wood for any work of the service, brought *it.* [25]All the women *who were* gifted artisans spun yarn with their hands, and brought what they had spun, of blue, purple, *and* scarlet, and fine linen. [26]And all the women whose hearts stirred with wisdom spun yarn of goats' *hair.* [27]The rulers brought onyx stones, and the stones to be set in the ephod and in the breastplate, [28]and spices and oil for the light, for the anointing oil, and for the sweet incense. [29]The children of Israel brought a freewill offering to the LORD, all the men and women whose hearts were willing to bring *material* for all kinds of work which the LORD, by the hand of Moses, had commanded to be done.

THE ARTISANS CALLED BY GOD

[30]And Moses said to the children of Israel, "See, the LORD has called by name Bezalel the son of Uri, the son of Hur, of the tribe of Ju-

35:19 [a]Or *woven garments*

dah; 31and He has filled him with the Spirit of
God, in wisdom and understanding, in knowledge and all manner of workmanship, 32to design artistic works, to work in gold and silver
and bronze, 33in cutting jewels for setting, in
carving wood, and to work in all manner of
artistic workmanship.
34"And He has put in his heart the ability to
teach, *in* him and Aholiab the son of Ahisamach, of the tribe of Dan. 35He has filled them
with skill to do all manner of work of the engraver and the designer and the tapestry
maker, in blue, purple, and scarlet *thread,* and
fine linen, and of the weaver—those who do
every work and those who design artistic
works.

36 "And Bezalel and Aholiab, and every
gifted artisan in whom the LORD has
put wisdom and understanding, to know how
to do all manner of work for the service of the
sanctuary, shall do according to all that the
LORD has commanded."

The People Give More than Enough

2Then Moses called Bezalel and Aholiab,
and every gifted artisan in whose heart the
LORD had put wisdom, everyone whose heart
was stirred, to come and do the work. 3And
they received from Moses all the offering
which the children of Israel had brought for
the work of the service of making the sanctuary. So they continued bringing to him freewill
offerings every morning. 4Then all the craftsmen who were doing all the work of the sanctuary came, each from the work he was doing,
5and they spoke to Moses, saying, "The people bring much more than enough for the service of the work which the LORD commanded
us to do."
6So Moses gave a commandment, and they
caused it to be proclaimed throughout the
camp, saying, "Let neither man nor woman do
any more work for the offering of the sanctuary." And the people were restrained from
bringing, 7for the material they had was sufficient for all the work to be done—indeed too
much.

Building the Tabernacle

8Then all the gifted artisans among them
who worked on the tabernacle made ten curtains woven of fine linen, and of blue, purple,
and scarlet *thread; with* artistic designs of
cherubim they made them. 9The length of
each curtain *was* twenty-eight cubits, and the
width of each curtain four cubits; the curtains
were all the same size. 10And he coupled five
curtains to one another, and *the other* five curtains he coupled to one another. 11He made
loops of blue *yarn* on the edge of the curtain
on the selvedge of one set; likewise he did on
the outer edge of *the other* curtain of the second set. 12Fifty loops he made on one curtain,
and fifty loops he made on the edge of the curtain on the end of the second set; the loops
held one *curtain* to another. 13And he made
fifty clasps of gold, and coupled the curtains
to one another with the clasps, that it might
be one tabernacle.
14He made curtains of goats' *hair* for the
tent over the tabernacle; he made eleven curtains. 15The length of each curtain *was* thirty
cubits, and the width of each curtain four cubits; the eleven curtains *were* the same size.
16He coupled five curtains by themselves and
six curtains by themselves. 17And he made
fifty loops on the edge of the curtain that is
outermost in one set, and fifty loops he made
on the edge of the curtain of the second set.
18He also made fifty bronze clasps to couple
the tent together, that it might be one. 19Then
he made a covering for the tent of ram skins
dyed red, and a covering of badger skins
above *that.*

SOUL NOTE

On the Job *(36:1)* How can the Holy Spirit be present in your work? Whatever job you have, you can work as though God were your employer. Bezalel and Aholiab were gifted by God. The trained men and women who worked to build the tabernacle had been gifted and motivated by the Holy Spirit. Their finished product shows that excellence was their hallmark. Together, this team modeled the Spirit's presence in their work—for they worked hard and with excellence. In any work you do, let God shine through every aspect of it. **Topic: Work**

[20]For the tabernacle he made boards of acacia wood, standing upright. [21]The length of each board *was* ten cubits, and the width of each board a cubit and a half. [22]Each board had two tenons for binding one to another. Thus he made for all the boards of the tabernacle. [23]And he made boards for the tabernacle, twenty boards for the south side. [24]Forty sockets of silver he made to go under the twenty boards: two sockets under each of the boards for its two tenons. [25]And for the other side of the tabernacle, the north side, he made twenty boards [26]and their forty sockets of silver: two sockets under each of the boards. [27]For the west side of the tabernacle he made six boards. [28]He also made two boards for the two back corners of the tabernacle. [29]And they were coupled at the bottom and coupled together at the top by one ring. Thus he made both of them for the two corners. [30]So there were eight boards and their sockets—sixteen sockets of silver—two sockets under each of the boards.

[31]And he made bars of acacia wood: five for the boards on one side of the tabernacle, [32]five bars for the boards on the other side of the tabernacle, and five bars for the boards of the tabernacle on the far side westward. [33]And he made the middle bar to pass through the boards from one end to the other. [34]He overlaid the boards with gold, made their rings of gold *to be* holders for the bars, and overlaid the bars with gold.

[35]And he made a veil of blue, purple, and scarlet *thread,* and fine woven linen; it was worked *with* an artistic design of cherubim. [36]He made for it four pillars of acacia *wood,* and overlaid them with gold, with their hooks of gold; and he cast four sockets of silver for them.

[37]He also made a screen for the tabernacle door, of blue, purple, and scarlet *thread,* and fine woven linen, made by a weaver, [38]and its five pillars with their hooks. And he overlaid their capitals and their rings with gold, but their five sockets *were* bronze.

Making the Ark of the Testimony

37 Then Bezalel made the ark of acacia wood; two and a half cubits *was* its length, a cubit and a half its width, and a cubit and a half its height. [2]He overlaid it with pure gold inside and outside, and made a molding of gold all around it. [3]And he cast for it four rings of gold *to be set* in its four corners: two rings on one side, and two rings on the other side of it. [4]He made poles of acacia wood, and overlaid them with gold. [5]And he put the poles into the rings at the sides of the ark, to bear the ark. [6]He also made the mercy seat of pure gold; two and a half cubits *was* its length and a cubit and a half its width. [7]He made two cherubim of beaten gold; he made them of one piece at the two ends of the mercy seat: [8]one cherub at one end on this side, and the other cherub at the *other* end on that side. He made the cherubim at the two ends *of one piece* with the mercy seat. [9]The cherubim spread out *their* wings above, *and* covered the mercy seat with their wings. They faced one another; the faces of the cherubim were toward the mercy seat.

Making the Table for the Showbread

[10]He made the table of acacia wood; two cubits *was* its length, a cubit its width, and a cubit and a half its height. [11]And he overlaid it with pure gold, and made a molding of gold all around it. [12]Also he made a frame of a handbreadth all around it, and made a molding of gold for the frame all around it. [13]And he cast for it four rings of gold, and put the rings on the four corners that *were* at its four legs. [14]The rings were close to the frame, as holders for the poles to bear the table. [15]And he made the poles of acacia wood to bear the table, and overlaid them with gold. [16]He made of pure gold the utensils which were on the table: its dishes, its cups, its bowls, and its pitchers for pouring.

Making the Gold Lampstand

[17]He also made the lampstand of pure gold; of hammered work he made the lampstand. Its shaft, its branches, its bowls, its *ornamental* knobs, and its flowers were of the same piece. [18]And six branches came out of its sides: three branches of the lampstand out of one side, and three branches of the lampstand out of the other side. [19]There were three bowls made like almond *blossoms* on one branch, with an *ornamental* knob and a flower, and three bowls made like almond *blossoms* on the other branch, with an *ornamental* knob and a flower—and so for the six branches coming out of the lampstand. [20]And on the lampstand itself *were* four bowls made like almond *blossoms, each with* its *ornamental*

knob and flower. 21*There was* a knob under the *first* two branches of the same, a knob under the *second* two branches of the same, and a knob under the *third* two branches of the same, according to the six branches extending from it. 22Their knobs and their branches were of one piece; all of it *was* one hammered piece of pure gold. 23And he made its seven lamps, its wick-trimmers, and its trays of pure gold. 24Of a talent of pure gold he made it, with all its utensils.

Making the Altar of Incense

25He made the incense altar of acacia wood. Its length *was* a cubit and its width a cubit—*it was* square—and two cubits *was* its height. Its horns were *of one piece* with it. 26And he overlaid it with pure gold: its top, its sides all around, and its horns. He also made for it a molding of gold all around it. 27He made two rings of gold for it under its molding, by its two corners on both sides, as holders for the poles with which to bear it. 28And he made the poles of acacia wood, and overlaid them with gold.

Making the Anointing Oil and the Incense

29He also made the holy anointing oil and the pure incense of sweet spices, according to the work of the perfumer.

Making the Altar of Burnt Offering

38 He made the altar of burnt offering of acacia wood; five cubits *was* its length and five cubits its width—*it was* square—and its height *was* three cubits. 2He made its horns on its four corners; the horns were *of one piece* with it. And he overlaid it with bronze. 3He made all the utensils for the altar: the pans, the shovels, the basins, the forks, and the firepans; all its utensils he made of bronze. 4And he made a grate of bronze network for the altar, under its rim, midway from the bottom. 5He cast four rings for the four corners of the bronze grating, *as* holders for the poles. 6And he made the poles of acacia wood, and overlaid them with bronze. 7Then he put the poles into the rings on the sides of the altar, with which to bear it. He made the altar hollow with boards.

Making the Bronze Laver

8He made the laver of bronze and its base of bronze, from the bronze mirrors of the serving women who assembled at the door of the tabernacle of meeting.

Making the Court of the Tabernacle

9Then he made the court on the south side; the hangings of the court *were of* fine woven linen, one hundred cubits long. 10There *were* twenty pillars for them, with twenty bronze sockets. The hooks of the pillars and their bands *were* silver. 11On the north side *the hangings were* one hundred cubits *long,* with twenty pillars and their twenty bronze sockets. The hooks of the pillars and their bands *were* silver. 12And on the west side *there were* hangings of fifty cubits, with ten pillars and their ten sockets. The hooks of the pillars and their bands *were* silver. 13For the east side *the hangings were* fifty cubits. 14The hangings of one side *of the gate were* fifteen cubits *long, with* their three pillars and their three sockets, 15and the same for the other side of the court gate; on this side and that *were* hangings of fifteen cubits, *with* their three pillars and their three sockets. 16All the hangings of the court all around *were of* fine woven linen. 17The sockets for the pillars *were* bronze, the hooks of the pillars and their bands *were* silver, and the overlay of their capitals *was* silver; and all the pillars of the court had bands of silver. 18The screen for the gate of the court *was* woven of blue, purple, and scarlet *thread,* and of fine woven linen. The length *was* twenty cubits, and the height along its width *was* five cubits, corresponding to the hangings of the court. 19And *there were* four pillars *with* their four sockets of bronze; their hooks *were* silver, and the overlay of their capitals and their bands *was* silver. 20All the pegs of the tabernacle, and of the court all around, *were* bronze.

Materials of the Tabernacle

21This is the inventory of the tabernacle, the tabernacle of the Testimony, which was counted according to the commandment of Moses, for the service of the Levites, by the hand of Ithamar, son of Aaron the priest.

22Bezalel the son of Uri, the son of Hur, of the tribe of Judah, made all that the LORD had commanded Moses. 23And with him *was* Aholiab the son of Ahisamach, of the tribe of Dan, an engraver and designer, a weaver of blue, purple, and scarlet *thread,* and of fine linen.

24All the gold that was used in all the work

of the holy *place,* that is, the gold of the offering, was twenty-nine talents and seven hundred and thirty shekels, according to the shekel of the sanctuary. 25And the silver from those who were numbered of the congregation *was* one hundred talents and one thousand seven hundred and seventy-five shekels, according to the shekel of the sanctuary: 26a bekah for each man (*that is,* half a shekel, according to the shekel of the sanctuary), for everyone included in the numbering from twenty years old and above, for six hundred and three thousand, five hundred and fifty *men.* 27And from the hundred talents of silver were cast the sockets of the sanctuary and the bases of the veil: one hundred sockets from the hundred talents, one talent for each socket. 28Then from the one thousand seven hundred and seventy-five *shekels* he made hooks for the pillars, overlaid their capitals, and made bands for them.

29The offering of bronze *was* seventy talents and two thousand four hundred shekels. 30And with it he made the sockets for the door of the tabernacle of meeting, the bronze altar, the bronze grating for it, and all the utensils for the altar, 31the sockets for the court all around, the bases for the court gate, all the pegs for the tabernacle, and all the pegs for the court all around.

Making the Garments of the Priesthood

39 Of the blue, purple, and scarlet *thread* they made garments of ministry,[a] for ministering in the holy *place,* and made the holy garments for Aaron, as the LORD had commanded Moses.

Making the Ephod

2He made the ephod of gold, blue, purple, and scarlet *thread,* and of fine woven linen. 3And they beat the gold into thin sheets and cut *it into* threads, to work *it* in *with* the blue, purple, and scarlet *thread,* and the fine linen, *into* artistic designs. 4They made shoulder straps for it to couple *it* together; it was coupled together at its two edges. 5And the intricately woven band of his ephod that *was* on it *was* of the same workmanship, *woven of* gold, blue, purple, and scarlet *thread,* and of fine woven linen, as the LORD had commanded Moses.

6And they set onyx stones, enclosed in settings of gold; they were engraved, as signets are engraved, with the names of the sons of Israel. 7He put them on the shoulders of the ephod *as* memorial stones for the sons of Israel, as the LORD had commanded Moses.

Making the Breastplate

8And he made the breastplate, artistically woven like the workmanship of the ephod, of gold, blue, purple, and scarlet *thread,* and of fine woven linen. 9They made the breastplate square by doubling it; a span *was* its length and a span its width when doubled. 10And they set in it four rows of stones: a row with a sardius, a topaz, and an emerald was the first row; 11the second row, a turquoise, a sapphire, and a diamond; 12the third row, a jacinth, an agate, and an amethyst; 13the fourth row, a beryl, an onyx, and a jasper. *They were* enclosed in settings of gold in their mountings. 14*There were* twelve stones according to the names of the sons of Israel: according to their names, *engraved like* a signet, each one with its own name according to the twelve tribes. 15And they made chains for the breastplate at the ends, like braided cords of pure gold. 16They also made two settings of gold and two gold rings, and put the two rings on the two ends of the breastplate. 17And they put the two braided *chains* of gold in the two rings on the ends of the breastplate. 18The two ends of the two braided *chains* they fastened in the two settings, and put them on the shoulder straps of the ephod in the front. 19And they made two rings of gold and put *them* on the two ends of the breastplate, on the edge of it, which *was* on the inward side of the ephod. 20They made two *other* gold rings and put them on the two shoulder straps, underneath the ephod toward its front, right at the seam above the intricately woven band of the ephod. 21And they bound the breastplate by means of its rings to the rings of the ephod with a blue cord, so that it would be above the intricately woven band of the ephod, and that the breastplate would not come loose from the ephod, as the LORD had commanded Moses.

Making the Other Priestly Garments

22He made the robe of the ephod of woven work, all of blue. 23And *there was* an opening in the middle of the robe, like the opening in a coat of mail, *with* a woven binding all around the opening, so that it would not tear. 24They

39:1 [a]Or *woven garments*

made on the hem of the robe pomegranates of blue, purple, and scarlet, and of fine woven *linen.* 25And they made bells of pure gold, and put the bells between the pomegranates on the hem of the robe all around between the pomegranates: 26a bell and a pomegranate, a bell and a pomegranate, all around the hem of the robe to minister in, as the LORD had commanded Moses.

27They made tunics, artistically woven of fine linen, for Aaron and his sons, 28a turban of fine linen, exquisite hats of fine linen, short trousers of fine woven linen, 29and a sash of fine woven linen with blue, purple, and scarlet *thread,* made by a weaver, as the LORD had commanded Moses.

30Then they made the plate of the holy crown of pure gold, and wrote on it an inscription *like* the engraving of a signet:

HOLINESS TO THE LORD.

31And they tied to it a blue cord, to fasten *it* above on the turban, as the LORD had commanded Moses.

THE WORK COMPLETED

32Thus all the work of the tabernacle of the tent of meeting was finished. And the children of Israel did according to all that the LORD had commanded Moses; so they did. 33And they brought the tabernacle to Moses, the tent and all its furnishings: its clasps, its boards, its bars, its pillars, and its sockets; 34the covering of ram skins dyed red, the covering of badger skins, and the veil of the covering; 35the ark of the Testimony with its poles, and the mercy seat; 36the table, all its utensils, and the showbread; 37the pure *gold* lampstand with its lamps (the lamps set in order), all its utensils, and the oil for light; 38the gold altar, the anointing oil, and the sweet incense; the screen for the tabernacle door; 39the bronze altar, its grate of bronze, its poles, and all its utensils; the laver with its base; 40the hangings of the court, its pillars and its sockets, the screen for the court gate, its cords, and its pegs; all the utensils for the service of the tabernacle, for the tent of meeting; 41and the garments of ministry,[a] to minister in the holy *place:* the holy garments for Aaron the priest, and his sons' garments, to minister as priests.

42According to all that the LORD had commanded Moses, so the children of Israel did all the work. 43Then Moses looked over all the work, and indeed they had done it; as the LORD had commanded, just so they had done it. And Moses blessed them.

THE TABERNACLE ERECTED AND ARRANGED

40 Then the LORD spoke to Moses, saying: 2"On the first day of the first month you shall set up the tabernacle of the tent of meeting. 3You shall put in it the ark of the Testimony, and partition off the ark with the veil. 4You shall bring in the table and arrange the things that are to be set in order on it; and you shall bring in the lampstand and light its lamps. 5You shall also set the altar of gold for the incense before the ark of the Testimony, and put up the screen for the door of the tabernacle. 6Then you shall set the altar of the burnt offering before the door of the tabernacle of the tent of meeting. 7And you shall set the laver between the tabernacle of meeting and the altar, and put water in it. 8You shall set up the court all around, and hang up the screen at the court gate.

9"And you shall take the anointing oil, and anoint the tabernacle and all that *is* in it; and you shall hallow it and all its utensils, and it shall be holy. 10You shall anoint the altar of the burnt offering and all its utensils, and consecrate the altar. The altar shall be most holy. 11And you shall anoint the laver and its base, and consecrate it.

12"Then you shall bring Aaron and his sons to the door of the tabernacle of meeting and wash them with water. 13You shall put the holy garments on Aaron, and anoint him and consecrate him, that he may minister to Me as priest. 14And you shall bring his sons and clothe them with tunics. 15You shall anoint them, as you anointed their father, that they may minister to Me as priests; for their anointing shall surely be an everlasting priesthood throughout their generations."

16Thus Moses did; according to all that the LORD had commanded him, so he did.

17And it came to pass in the first month of the second year, on the first *day* of the month, *that* the tabernacle was raised up. 18So Moses raised up the tabernacle, fastened its sockets, set up its boards, put in its bars, and raised up its pillars. 19And he spread out the tent over the tabernacle and put the covering of the tent

---

39:41 [a]Or *woven garments*

on top of it, as the LORD had commanded Moses. [20]He took the Testimony and put *it* into
the ark, inserted the poles through the rings of
the ark, and put the mercy seat on top of the
ark. [21]And he brought the ark into the tabernacle, hung up the veil of the covering, and par-
titioned off the ark of the Testimony, as the
LORD had commanded Moses.

[22]He put the table in the tabernacle of meeting, on the north side of the tabernacle, outside the veil; [23]and he set the bread in order
upon it before the LORD, as the LORD had commanded Moses. [24]He put the lampstand in the
tabernacle of meeting, across from the table,
on the south side of the tabernacle; [25]and he
lit the lamps before the LORD, as the LORD had
commanded Moses. [26]He put the gold altar in
the tabernacle of meeting in front of the veil;
[27]and he burned sweet incense on it, as the
LORD had commanded Moses. [28]He hung up
the screen *at* the door of the tabernacle. [29]And
he put the altar of burnt offering *before* the
door of the tabernacle of the tent of meeting,
and offered upon it the burnt offering and the
grain offering, as the LORD had commanded
Moses. [30]He set the laver between the tabernacle of meeting and the altar, and put water
there for washing; [31]and Moses, Aaron, and
his sons would wash their hands and their feet
with water from it. [32]Whenever they went into
the tabernacle of meeting, and when they
came near the altar, they washed, as the LORD
had commanded Moses. [33]And he raised up
the court all around the tabernacle and the altar, and hung up the screen of the court gate.
So Moses finished the work.

THE CLOUD AND THE GLORY

[34]Then the cloud covered the tabernacle of
meeting, and the glory of the LORD filled the
tabernacle. [35]And Moses was not able to enter
the tabernacle of meeting, because the cloud
rested above it, and the glory of the LORD filled
the tabernacle. [36]Whenever the cloud was
taken up from above the tabernacle, the children of Israel would go onward in all their
journeys. [37]But if the cloud was not taken up,
then they did not journey till the day that it
was taken up. [38]For the cloud of the LORD *was*
above the tabernacle by day, and fire was over
it by night, in the sight of all the house of Israel, throughout all their journeys.

SOUL NOTE

Glory Be! *(40:34)* The cloud and the glory represented God's presence with His people. "The glory of the LORD filled the tabernacle" upon its completion, signifying His pleasure with the home that the people had built according to His instructions. Thousands of years later, God's glory again entered the temple in Jesus Christ. That glory is present in Christians' lives through the Holy Spirit. Believers are temples of the Holy Spirit filled with God's glorious presence (I Cor. 6:19). God promises to be in us and to guide us, even as He guided the Israelites across the vast wilderness to the Promised Land. **Topic: God's Promises**

Leviticus

At times we all stand before God with stained souls, uncomfortably aware of our sin. Some run away and hide from God, as Adam did. Others yield to the redemptive work of God and experience forgiveness and cleansing.

Leviticus is a book about holiness. Written by Moses, Leviticus explains how to live God's way and spells out the sacrifices for sin that the Israelites had to make. If you were a Hebrew, you had to offer a sacrifice—killing an animal by slitting its throat—knowing that your sin had caused that animal to die. This act made God's people take sin seriously. While the concept of sacrifice may seem harsh to us today, it was meant to point to the ultimate sacrifice—the atoning death of Jesus on the Cross. There, He died as the "Lamb of God who takes away the sin of the world" (John 1:29).

The book calls God's people to holiness (Lev. 11:44, 45; 19:2; see also 1 Pet. 1:15, 16). The purity of God stands in marked contrast to the sinful nature of human beings. We are created "in His image," but we are not by nature what He is. Because of Christ—His death and resurrection that atone for our sins—we can become holy by allowing God to form His perfect life in us. After we trust Christ for salvation, if we continually confess our sins and thankfully invite His redemptive work to be formed in us, we are called "holy."

SOUL CONCERNS IN LEVITICUS

The Burnt Offering

1 Now the LORD called to Moses, and spoke
to him from the tabernacle of meeting, saying, 2“Speak to the children of Israel, and say to
them: ‘When any one of you brings an offering
to the LORD, you shall bring your offering of the
livestock—of the herd and of the flock.
3‘If his offering *is* a burnt sacrifice of the
herd, let him offer a male without blemish; he
shall offer it of his own free will at the door of
the tabernacle of meeting before the LORD.
4Then he shall put his hand on the head of the
burnt offering, and it will be accepted on his
behalf to make atonement for him. 5He shall
kill the bull before the LORD; and the priests,
Aaron’s sons, shall bring the blood and sprinkle the blood all around on the altar that *is by*
the door of the tabernacle of meeting. 6And he
shall skin the burnt offering and cut it into its
pieces. 7The sons of Aaron the priest shall put
fire on the altar, and lay the wood in order on
the fire. 8Then the priests, Aaron’s sons, shall
lay the parts, the head, and the fat in order on
the wood that *is* on the fire upon the altar;
9but he shall wash its entrails and its legs with
water. And the priest shall burn all on the altar
as a burnt sacrifice, an offering made by fire, a
sweet aroma to the LORD.
10‘If his offering *is* of the flocks—of the
sheep or of the goats—as a burnt sacrifice, he
shall bring a male without blemish. 11He shall
kill it on the north side of the altar before the
LORD; and the priests, Aaron’s sons, shall
sprinkle its blood all around on the altar.
12And he shall cut it into its pieces, with its
head and its fat; and the priest shall lay them
in order on the wood that *is* on the fire upon
the altar; 13but he shall wash the entrails and
the legs with water. Then the priest shall bring
it all and burn *it* on the altar; it *is* a burnt sacrifice, an offering made by fire, a sweet aroma
to the LORD.
14‘And if the burnt sacrifice of his offering to
the LORD *is* of birds, then he shall bring his offering of turtledoves or young pigeons. 15The
priest shall bring it to the altar, wring off its
head, and burn *it* on the altar; its blood shall
be drained out at the side of the altar. 16And he
shall remove its crop with its feathers and cast
it beside the altar on the east side, into the
place for ashes. 17Then he shall split it at its
wings, *but* shall not divide *it* completely; and
the priest shall burn it on the altar, on the
wood that *is* on the fire. It *is* a burnt sacrifice,
an offering made by fire, a sweet aroma to the
LORD.

The Grain Offering

2 ‘When anyone offers a grain offering to
the LORD, his offering shall be *of* fine flour.
And he shall pour oil on it, and put frankincense on it. 2He shall bring it to Aaron’s sons,
the priests, one of whom shall take from it his
handful of fine flour and oil with all the frankincense. And the priest shall burn *it as* a memorial on the altar, an offering made by fire, a
sweet aroma to the LORD. 3The rest of the
grain offering *shall be* Aaron’s and his sons’. *It*
is most holy of the offerings to the LORD made
by fire.
4‘And if you bring as an offering a grain offering baked in the oven, *it shall be* unleavened cakes of fine flour mixed with oil, or
unleavened wafers anointed with oil. 5But if
your offering *is* a grain offering *baked* in a
pan, *it shall be of* fine flour, unleavened,
mixed with oil. 6You shall break it in pieces
and pour oil on it; it *is* a grain offering.
7‘If your offering *is* a grain offering *baked* in
a covered pan, it shall be made *of* fine flour
with oil. 8You shall bring the grain offering
that is made of these things to the LORD. And
when it is presented to the priest, he shall
bring it to the altar. 9Then the priest shall take

SOUL NOTE

Serious Business *(1:4, 5)* Many people regard sin rather casually, but that was difficult for the ancient Israelites. They had to bring a special animal, place a hand on its head, and then kill it as an atonement for their sin. Every bleeding sacrifice was an immediate reminder that sin stood between them and God. These sacrifices also pointed to the sacrificial death of one far more precious—the perfect Son of God, Jesus Christ. His death paid, once for all, the total penalty for our sin. Also, it reminds us of the seriousness of sin. Sin is costly, but Jesus paid the price. **Topic: Sin**

from the grain offering a memorial portion, and burn *it* on the altar. *It is* an offering made by fire, a sweet aroma to the LORD. 10And what is left of the grain offering *shall be* Aaron's and his sons'. *It is* most holy of the offerings to the LORD made by fire.

11'No grain offering which you bring to the LORD shall be made with leaven, for you shall burn no leaven nor any honey in any offering to the LORD made by fire. 12As for the offering of the firstfruits, you shall offer them to the LORD, but they shall not be burned on the altar for a sweet aroma. 13And every offering of your grain offering you shall season with salt; you shall not allow the salt of the covenant of your God to be lacking from your grain offering. With all your offerings you shall offer salt.

14'If you offer a grain offering of your firstfruits to the LORD, you shall offer for the grain offering of your firstfruits green heads of grain roasted on the fire, grain beaten from full heads. 15And you shall put oil on it, and lay frankincense on it. It *is* a grain offering. 16Then the priest shall burn the memorial portion: *part* of its beaten grain and *part* of its oil, with all the frankincense, as an offering made by fire to the LORD.

The Peace Offering

3 'When his offering *is* a sacrifice of a peace offering, if he offers *it* of the herd, whether male or female, he shall offer it without blemish before the LORD. 2And he shall lay his hand on the head of his offering, and kill it *at* the door of the tabernacle of meeting; and Aaron's sons, the priests, shall sprinkle the blood all around on the altar. 3Then he shall offer from the sacrifice of the peace offering an offering made by fire to the LORD. The fat that covers the entrails and all the fat that *is* on the entrails, 4the two kidneys and the fat that *is* on them by the flanks, and the fatty lobe *attached* to the liver above the kidneys, he shall remove; 5and Aaron's sons shall burn it on the altar upon the burnt sacrifice, which *is* on the wood that *is* on the fire, *as* an offering made by fire, a sweet aroma to the LORD.

6'If his offering as a sacrifice of a peace offering to the LORD *is* of the flock, *whether* male or female, he shall offer it without blemish. 7If he offers a lamb as his offering, then he shall offer it before the LORD. 8And he shall lay his hand on the head of his offering, and kill it before the tabernacle of meeting; and Aaron's sons shall sprinkle its blood all around on the altar.

9'Then he shall offer from the sacrifice of the peace offering, as an offering made by fire to the LORD, its fat *and* the whole fat tail which he shall remove close to the backbone. And the fat that covers the entrails and all the fat that *is* on the entrails, 10the two kidneys and the fat that *is* on them by the flanks, and the fatty lobe *attached* to the liver above the kidneys, he shall remove; 11and the priest shall burn *them* on the altar *as* food, an offering made by fire to the LORD.

12'And if his offering *is* a goat, then he shall offer it before the LORD. 13He shall lay his hand on its head and kill it before the tabernacle of meeting; and the sons of Aaron shall sprinkle its blood all around on the altar. 14Then he shall offer from it his offering, as an offering made by fire to the LORD. The fat that covers the entrails and all the fat that *is* on the entrails, 15the two kidneys and the fat that *is* on them by the flanks, and the fatty lobe *attached* to the liver above the kidneys, he shall remove; 16and the priest shall burn them on the altar *as* food, an offering made by fire for a sweet aroma; all the fat *is* the LORD's.

17'*This shall be* a perpetual statute throughout your generations in all your dwellings: you shall eat neither fat nor blood.' "

The Sin Offering

4 Now the LORD spoke to Moses, saying, 2"Speak to the children of Israel, saying: 'If a person sins unintentionally against any of the commandments of the LORD *in anything* which ought not to be done, and does any of them, 3if the anointed priest sins, bringing guilt on the people, then let him offer to the LORD for his sin which he has sinned a young bull without blemish as a sin offering. 4He shall bring the bull to the door of the tabernacle of meeting before the LORD, lay his hand on the bull's head, and kill the bull before the LORD. 5Then the anointed priest shall take some of the bull's blood and bring it to the tabernacle of meeting. 6The priest shall dip his finger in the blood and sprinkle some of the blood seven times before the LORD, in front of the veil of the sanctuary. 7And the priest shall put some of the blood on the horns of the altar of sweet incense before the LORD, which is in the tabernacle of meeting; and he shall pour the remaining blood of the bull at the base of the altar of the burnt offering, which is at the door of the tabernacle of meeting. 8He shall take from it all the fat of the bull as the sin offering. The fat that covers the entrails and all the fat which *is* on the entrails, 9the two kidneys and the fat that *is* on them by the flanks, and the fatty lobe *attached* to the liver above the kidneys, he shall remove, 10as it was taken from the bull of the sacrifice of the peace offering; and the priest shall burn them on the altar of the burnt offering. 11But the bull's hide and all its flesh, with its head and legs, its entrails and offal— 12the whole bull he shall carry outside the camp to a clean place, where the ashes are poured out, and burn it on wood with fire; where the ashes are poured out it shall be burned.

13'Now if the whole congregation of Israel sins unintentionally, and the thing is hidden from the eyes of the assembly, and they have done *something against* any of the commandments of the LORD *in anything* which should not be done, and are guilty; 14when the sin which they have committed becomes known, then the assembly shall offer a young bull for the sin, and bring it before the tabernacle of meeting. 15And the elders of the congregation shall lay their hands on the head of the bull before the LORD. Then the bull shall be killed before the LORD. 16The anointed priest shall bring some of the bull's blood to the tabernacle of meeting. 17Then the priest shall dip his finger in the blood and sprinkle *it* seven times before the LORD, in front of the veil. 18And he shall put *some* of the blood on the horns of the altar which *is* before the LORD, which *is* in the tabernacle of meeting; and he shall pour the remaining blood at the base of the altar of burnt offering, which is at the door of the tabernacle of meeting. 19He shall take all the fat from it and burn *it* on the altar. 20And he shall do with the bull as he did with the bull as a sin offering; thus he shall do with it. So the priest shall make atonement for them, and it shall be forgiven them. 21Then he shall carry the bull outside the camp, and burn it as he burned the first bull. It *is* a sin offering for the assembly.

22'When a ruler has sinned, and done *something* unintentionally *against* any of the commandments of the LORD his God *in anything* which should not be done, and is guilty, 23or if his sin which he has committed comes to his knowledge, he shall bring as his offering a kid of the goats, a male without blemish. 24And he shall lay his hand on the head of the goat, and kill it at the place where they kill the burnt offering before the LORD. It *is* a sin offering. 25The priest shall take some of the blood of the sin offering with his finger, put *it* on the horns of the altar of burnt offering, and pour its blood at the base of the altar of burnt offering. 26And he shall burn all its fat on the altar, like the fat of the sacrifice of the peace offering. So the priest shall make atonement for him concerning his sin, and it shall be forgiven him.

27'If anyone of the common people sins unintentionally by doing *something against* any of the commandments of the LORD *in anything* which ought not to be done, and is guilty, 28or if his sin which he has committed comes to his knowledge, then he shall bring as his offering a kid of the goats, a female without blemish, for his sin which he has committed. 29And he shall lay his hand on the head of the sin offering, and kill the sin offering at the place of the burnt offering. 30Then the priest shall take *some* of its blood with his finger, put *it* on the horns of the altar of burnt offering, and pour all *the remaining* blood at the base of the altar. 31He shall remove all its fat, as fat is removed from the sacrifice of the peace offering; and the priest shall burn it on the altar for a sweet aroma to the LORD. So the priest shall

SOUL NOTE

Always a Way *(4:3)* Biblical law assumed that leaders would fail just like everybody else. By commanding a sin offering for the anointed priests (4:3) and for the rulers (4:22–26), God made it clear that their leaders were not gods. Sooner or later, these human authorities would need atonement for their sins, just like everyone else. We should not be shocked when religious and political leaders fail. No one can live above sin without God's help, and no one is beyond God's grace. There is always a way for sinners, even sinful leaders, to be forgiven. **Topic: Sin**

make atonement for him, and it shall be forgiven him.

[32]'If he brings a lamb as his sin offering, he shall bring a female without blemish. [33]Then he shall lay his hand on the head of the sin offering, and kill it as a sin offering at the place where they kill the burnt offering. [34]The priest shall take *some* of the blood of the sin offering with his finger, put *it* on the horns of the altar of burnt offering, and pour all *the remaining* blood at the base of the altar. [35]He shall remove all its fat, as the fat of the lamb is removed from the sacrifice of the peace offering. Then the priest shall burn it on the altar, according to the offerings made by fire to the LORD. So the priest shall make atonement for his sin that he has committed, and it shall be forgiven him.

The Trespass Offering

5 'If a person sins in hearing the utterance of an oath, and *is* a witness, whether he has seen or known *of the matter*—if he does not tell *it*, he bears guilt.

[2]'Or if a person touches any unclean thing, whether *it is* the carcass of an unclean beast, or the carcass of unclean livestock, or the carcass of unclean creeping things, and he is unaware of it, he also shall be unclean and guilty. [3]Or if he touches human uncleanness—whatever uncleanness with which a man may be defiled, and he is unaware of it—when he realizes *it*, then he shall be guilty.

[4]'Or if a person swears, speaking thoughtlessly with *his* lips to do evil or to do good, whatever *it is* that a man may pronounce by an oath, and he is unaware of it—when he realizes *it*, then he shall be guilty in any of these *matters*.

[5]'And it shall be, when he is guilty in any of these *matters*, that he shall confess that he has sinned in that *thing*; [6]and he shall bring his trespass offering to the LORD for his sin which he has committed, a female from the flock, a lamb or a kid of the goats as a sin offering. So the priest shall make atonement for him concerning his sin.

[7]'If he is not able to bring a lamb, then he shall bring to the LORD, for his trespass which he has committed, two turtledoves or two young pigeons: one as a sin offering and the other as a burnt offering. [8]And he shall bring them to the priest, who shall offer *that* which *is* for the sin offering first, and wring off its head from its neck, but shall not divide *it* completely. [9]Then he shall sprinkle *some* of the blood of the sin offering on the side of the altar, and the rest of the blood shall be drained out at the base of the altar. It *is* a sin offering. [10]And he shall offer the second *as* a burnt offering according to the prescribed manner. So the priest shall make atonement on his behalf for his sin which he has committed, and it shall be forgiven him.

[11]'But if he is not able to bring two turtledoves or two young pigeons, then he who sinned shall bring for his offering one-tenth of an ephah of fine flour as a sin offering. He shall put no oil on it, nor shall he put frankincense on it, for it *is* a sin offering. [12]Then he shall bring it to the priest, and the priest shall take his handful of it as a memorial portion, and burn *it* on the altar according to the offerings made by fire to the LORD. It *is* a sin offering. [13]The priest shall make atonement for him, for his sin that he has committed in any of these matters; and it shall be forgiven him. *The rest* shall be the priest's as a grain offering.' "

Offerings with Restitution

[14]Then the LORD spoke to Moses, saying: [15]"If a person commits a trespass, and sins unintentionally in regard to the holy things of the LORD, then he shall bring to the LORD as his trespass offering a ram without blemish from

SOUL NOTE

To Tell the Truth *(5:1)* The strictest honesty was required in telling a story under oath. To witness something and not tell the truth about it caused the person who had been a witness to bear the guilt. As when an oath is spoken in court proceedings to "tell the truth, the whole truth, and nothing but the truth," a witness was bound to speak truthfully and not to hide or shade their meaning in any way. Telling the truth should be a way of life for God's people (Matt. 5:37).
Topic: Communication

the flocks, with your valuation in shekels of
silver according to the shekel of the sanctuary,
as a trespass offering. 16And he shall make
restitution for the harm that he has done in regard to the holy thing, and shall add one-fifth
to it and give it to the priest. So the priest shall
make atonement for him with the ram of the
trespass offering, and it shall be forgiven him.
17"If a person sins, and commits any of
these things which are forbidden to be done
by the commandments of the LORD, though he
does not know *it,* yet he is guilty and shall
bear his iniquity. 18And he shall bring to the
priest a ram without blemish from the flock,
with your valuation, as a trespass offering. So
the priest shall make atonement for him regarding his ignorance in which he erred and
did not know *it,* and it shall be forgiven him.
19It is a trespass offering; he has certainly trespassed against the LORD."

6 And the LORD spoke to Moses, saying: 2"If
a person sins and commits a trespass
against the LORD by lying to his neighbor
about what was delivered to him for safekeeping, or about a pledge, or about a robbery, or if
he has extorted from his neighbor, 3or if he
has found what was lost and lies concerning
it, and swears falsely—in any one of these
things that a man may do in which he sins:
4then it shall be, because he has sinned and is
guilty, that he shall restore what he has stolen,
or the thing which he has extorted, or what
was delivered to him for safekeeping, or the
lost thing which he found, 5or all that about
which he has sworn falsely. He shall restore
its full value, add one-fifth more to it, *and* give
it to whomever it belongs, on the day of his
trespass offering. 6And he shall bring his trespass offering to the LORD, a ram without blemish from the flock, with your valuation, as a
trespass offering, to the priest. 7So the priest
shall make atonement for him before the
LORD, and he shall be forgiven for any one of
these things that he may have done in which
he trespasses."

The Law of the Burnt Offering

8Then the LORD spoke to Moses, saying,
9"Command Aaron and his sons, saying, 'This
is the law of the burnt offering: The burnt offering *shall be* on the hearth upon the altar all
night until morning, and the fire of the altar
shall be kept burning on it. 10And the priest
shall put on his linen garment, and his linen
trousers he shall put on his body, and take up
the ashes of the burnt offering which the fire
has consumed on the altar, and he shall put
them beside the altar. 11Then he shall take off
his garments, put on other garments, and carry
the ashes outside the camp to a clean place.
12And the fire on the altar shall be kept burning
on it; it shall not be put out. And the priest
shall burn wood on it every morning, and lay
the burnt offering in order on it; and he shall
burn on it the fat of the peace offerings. 13A fire
shall always be burning on the altar; it shall
never go out.

The Law of the Grain Offering

14'This *is* the law of the grain offering: The
sons of Aaron shall offer it on the altar before
the LORD. 15He shall take from it his handful of
the fine flour of the grain offering, with its oil,
and all the frankincense which *is* on the grain
offering, and shall burn *it* on the altar *for* a
sweet aroma, as a memorial to the LORD. 16And
the remainder of it Aaron and his sons shall
eat; with unleavened bread it shall be eaten in
a holy place; in the court of the tabernacle of
meeting they shall eat it. 17It shall not be
baked with leaven. I have given it *as* their portion of My offerings made by fire; it *is* most

SOUL NOTE

Making Things Right *(6:1–7)* It is natural to try to escape responsibility for wrongdoing, and it's easy to rationalize mistakes. The Old Testament offerings were designed so that the offender might receive God's forgiveness. But the wrongdoer also had to take responsibility for his or her behavior by making restitution to the person who had been wronged. We, too, must take responsibility for the effects of our sins on others. We need to be reconciled not only to God, but also to those whom we have wronged. Biblical law holds us responsible for our own behavior.
Topic: Forgiveness

holy, like the sin offering and the trespass offering. 18All the males among the children of Aaron may eat it. *It shall be* a statute forever in your generations concerning the offerings made by fire to the LORD. Everyone who touches them must be holy.' "[a]

19And the LORD spoke to Moses, saying, 20"This *is* the offering of Aaron and his sons, which they shall offer to the LORD, *beginning* on the day when he is anointed: one-tenth of an ephah of fine flour as a daily grain offering, half of it in the morning and half of it at night. 21It shall be made in a pan with oil. *When it is* mixed, you shall bring it in. The baked pieces of the grain offering you shall offer *for* a sweet aroma to the LORD. 22The priest from among his sons, who is anointed in his place, shall offer it. *It is* a statute forever to the LORD. It shall be wholly burned. 23For every grain offering for the priest shall be wholly burned. It shall not be eaten."

The Law of the Sin Offering

24Also the LORD spoke to Moses, saying, 25"Speak to Aaron and to his sons, saying, 'This *is* the law of the sin offering: In the place where the burnt offering is killed, the sin offering shall be killed before the LORD. It *is* most holy. 26The priest who offers it for sin shall eat it. In a holy place it shall be eaten, in the court of the tabernacle of meeting. 27Everyone who touches its flesh must be holy.[a] And when its blood is sprinkled on any garment, you shall wash that on which it was sprinkled, in a holy place. 28But the earthen vessel in which it is boiled shall be broken. And if it is boiled in a bronze pot, it shall be both scoured and rinsed in water. 29All the males among the priests may eat it. It *is* most holy. 30But no sin offering from which *any* of the blood is brought into the tabernacle of meeting, to make atonement in the holy *place,*[a] shall be eaten. It shall be burned in the fire.

The Law of the Trespass Offering

7 'Likewise this *is* the law of the trespass offering (it *is* most holy): 2In the place where they kill the burnt offering they shall kill the trespass offering. And its blood he shall sprinkle all around on the altar. 3And he shall offer from it all its fat. The fat tail and the fat that covers the entrails, 4the two kidneys and the fat that *is* on them by the flanks, and the fatty lobe *attached* to the liver above the kidneys, he shall remove; 5and the priest shall burn them on the altar *as* an offering made by fire to the LORD. It *is* a trespass offering. 6Every male among the priests may eat it. It shall be eaten in a holy place. It *is* most holy. 7The trespass offering *is* like the sin offering; *there is* one law for them both: the priest who makes atonement with it shall have *it.* 8And the priest who offers anyone's burnt offering, that priest shall have for himself the skin of the burnt offering which he has offered. 9Also every grain offering that is baked in the oven and all that is prepared in the covered pan, or in a pan, shall be the priest's who offers it. 10Every grain offering, *whether* mixed with oil or dry, shall belong to all the sons of Aaron, to one *as much* as the other.

The Law of Peace Offerings

11'This *is* the law of the sacrifice of peace offerings which he shall offer to the LORD: 12If he offers it for a thanksgiving, then he shall offer, with the sacrifice of thanksgiving, unleavened cakes mixed with oil, unleavened wafers anointed with oil, or cakes of blended flour mixed with oil. 13Besides the cakes, *as* his offering he shall offer leavened bread with the sacrifice of thanksgiving of his peace offering. 14And from it he shall offer one cake from each offering *as* a heave offering to the LORD. It shall belong to the priest who sprinkles the blood of the peace offering.

15'The flesh of the sacrifice of his peace offering for thanksgiving shall be eaten the same day it is offered. He shall not leave any of it until morning. 16But if the sacrifice of his offering *is* a vow or a voluntary offering, it shall be eaten the same day that he offers his sacrifice; but on the next day the remainder of it also may be eaten; 17the remainder of the flesh of the sacrifice on the third day must be burned with fire. 18And if *any* of the flesh of the sacrifice of his peace offering is eaten at all on the third day, it shall not be accepted, nor shall it be imputed to him; it shall be an abomination *to* him who offers it, and the person who eats of it shall bear guilt.

19'The flesh that touches any unclean thing shall not be eaten. It shall be burned with fire. And as for the *clean* flesh, all who are clean

6:18 [a]Compare Numbers 4:15 and Haggai 2:11–13
6:27 [a]Compare Numbers 4:15 and Haggai 2:11–13
6:30 [a]The Most Holy Place when capitalized

may eat of it. [20]But the person who eats the flesh of the sacrifice of the peace offering that *belongs* to the LORD, while he is unclean, that person shall be cut off from his people. [21]Moreover the person who touches any unclean thing, *such as* human uncleanness, *an* unclean animal, or any abominable unclean thing,[a] and who eats the flesh of the sacrifice of the peace offering that *belongs* to the LORD, that person shall be cut off from his people.' "

FAT AND BLOOD MAY NOT BE EATEN

[22]And the LORD spoke to Moses, saying, [23]"Speak to the children of Israel, saying: 'You shall not eat any fat, of ox or sheep or goat. [24]And the fat of an animal that dies *naturally,* and the fat of what is torn by wild beasts, may be used in any other way; but you shall by no means eat it. [25]For whoever eats the fat of the animal of which men offer an offering made by fire to the LORD, the person who eats *it* shall be cut off from his people. [26]Moreover you shall not eat any blood in any of your dwellings, *whether* of bird or beast. [27]Whoever eats any blood, that person shall be cut off from his people.' "

THE PORTION OF AARON AND HIS SONS

[28]Then the LORD spoke to Moses, saying, [29]"Speak to the children of Israel, saying: 'He who offers the sacrifice of his peace offering to the LORD shall bring his offering to the LORD from the sacrifice of his peace offering. [30]His own hands shall bring the offerings made by fire to the LORD. The fat with the breast he shall bring, that the breast may be waved *as* a wave offering before the LORD. [31]And the priest shall burn the fat on the altar, but the breast shall be Aaron's and his sons'. [32]Also the right thigh you shall give to the priest *as* a heave offering from the sacrifices of your peace offerings. [33]He among the sons of Aaron, who offers the blood of the peace offering and the fat, shall have the right thigh for *his* part. [34]For the breast of the wave offering and the thigh of the heave offering I have taken from the children of Israel, from the sacrifices of their peace offerings, and I have given them to Aaron the priest and to his sons from the children of Israel by a statute forever.' "

[35]This *is* the consecrated portion for Aaron and his sons, from the offerings made by fire to the LORD, on the day when *Moses* presented them to minister to the LORD as priests. [36]The LORD commanded this to be given to them by the children of Israel, on the day that He anointed them, *by* a statute forever throughout their generations.

[37]This *is* the law of the burnt offering, the grain offering, the sin offering, the trespass offering, the consecrations, and the sacrifice of the peace offering, [38]which the LORD commanded Moses on Mount Sinai, on the day when He commanded the children of Israel to offer their offerings to the LORD in the Wilderness of Sinai.

AARON AND HIS SONS CONSECRATED

8 And the LORD spoke to Moses, saying: [2]"Take Aaron and his sons with him, and the garments, the anointing oil, a bull as the sin offering, two rams, and a basket of unleavened bread; [3]and gather all the congregation together at the door of the tabernacle of meeting."

[4]So Moses did as the LORD commanded him. And the congregation was gathered together at the door of the tabernacle of meeting. [5]And Moses said to the congregation, "This *is* what the LORD commanded to be done."

7:21 [a]Following Masoretic Text, Septuagint, and Vulgate; Samaritan Pentateuch, Syriac, and Targum read *swarming thing* (compare 5:2).

SOUL NOTE

Just Do It! *(7:37, 38)* Talk is cheap. Speaking a commitment is easy, but it is another thing entirely to live out that commitment. Leviticus spells out practical ways by which God's people could express their commitments to Him. The sacrifices were inconvenient and costly, but they underlined the importance of right living. The sacrifices turned words into actions. Believers today live their faith by their actions. The New Testament expresses it like this: "Let us not love in word or in tongue, but in deed and in truth" (I John 3:18). **Topic: Love**

6Then Moses brought Aaron and his sons
and washed them with water. 7And he put the
tunic on him, girded him with the sash,
clothed him with the robe, and put the ephod
on him; and he girded him with the intricately
woven band of the ephod, and with it tied *the
ephod* on him. 8Then he put the breastplate on
him, and he put the Urim and the Thummim[a]
in the breastplate. 9And he put the turban on
his head. Also on the turban, on its front, he
put the golden plate, the holy crown, as the
LORD had commanded Moses.

10Also Moses took the anointing oil, and
anointed the tabernacle and all that *was* in it,
and consecrated them. 11He sprinkled some of
it on the altar seven times, anointed the altar
and all its utensils, and the laver and its base,
to consecrate them. 12And he poured some of
the anointing oil on Aaron's head and anointed him, to consecrate him.

13Then Moses brought Aaron's sons and put
tunics on them, girded them with sashes, and
put hats on them, as the LORD had commanded Moses.

14And he brought the bull for the sin offering. Then Aaron and his sons laid their hands
on the head of the bull for the sin offering,
15and Moses killed *it*. Then he took the blood,
and put *some* on the horns of the altar all
around with his finger, and purified the altar.
And he poured the blood at the base of the altar, and consecrated it, to make atonement for
it. 16Then he took all the fat that *was* on the
entrails, the fatty lobe *attached to* the liver,
and the two kidneys with their fat, and Moses
burned *them* on the altar. 17But the bull, its
hide, its flesh, and its offal, he burned with
fire outside the camp, as the LORD had commanded Moses.

18Then he brought the ram as the burnt offering. And Aaron and his sons laid their
hands on the head of the ram, 19and Moses
killed *it*. Then he sprinkled the blood all
around on the altar. 20And he cut the ram into
pieces; and Moses burned the head, the
pieces, and the fat. 21Then he washed the entrails and the legs in water. And Moses burned
the whole ram on the altar. It *was* a burnt sacrifice for a sweet aroma, an offering made by
fire to the LORD, as the LORD had commanded
Moses.

22And he brought the second ram, the ram
of consecration. Then Aaron and his sons laid
their hands on the head of the ram, 23and Moses killed *it*. Also he took *some* of its blood
and put it on the tip of Aaron's right ear, on
the thumb of his right hand, and on the big toe
of his right foot. 24Then he brought Aaron's
sons. And Moses put *some* of the blood on the
tips of their right ears, on the thumbs of their
right hands, and on the big toes of their right
feet. And Moses sprinkled the blood all
around on the altar. 25Then he took the fat and
the fat tail, all the fat that *was* on the entrails,
the fatty lobe *attached to* the liver, the two kidneys and their fat, and the right thigh; 26and
from the basket of unleavened bread that was
before the LORD he took one unleavened cake,
a cake of bread *anointed with* oil, and one
wafer, and put *them* on the fat and on the right
thigh; 27and he put all *these* in Aaron's hands
and in his sons' hands, and waved them *as* a
wave offering before the LORD. 28Then Moses
took them from their hands and burned *them*
on the altar, on the burnt offering. They *were*
consecration offerings for a sweet aroma. That
was an offering made by fire to the LORD.
29And Moses took the breast and waved it *as* a
wave offering before the LORD. It was Moses'
part of the ram of consecration, as the LORD
had commanded Moses.

30Then Moses took some of the anointing oil
and some of the blood which *was* on the altar,
and sprinkled *it* on Aaron, on his garments,
on his sons, and on the garments of his sons
with him; and he consecrated Aaron, his garments, his sons, and the garments of his sons
with him.

31And Moses said to Aaron and his sons,
"Boil the flesh *at* the door of the tabernacle of
meeting, and eat it there with the bread that *is*
in the basket of consecration offerings, as I
commanded, saying, 'Aaron and his sons shall
eat it.' 32What remains of the flesh and of the
bread you shall burn with fire. 33And you shall
not go outside the door of the tabernacle of
meeting *for* seven days, until the days of your
consecration are ended. For seven days he
shall consecrate you. 34As he has done this
day, *so* the LORD has commanded to do, to
make atonement for you. 35Therefore you
shall stay *at* the door of the tabernacle of
meeting day and night for seven days, and
keep the charge of the LORD, so that you may
not die; for so I have been commanded." 36So

8:8 [a]Literally *the Lights and the Perfections* (compare Exodus 28:30)

Aaron and his sons did all the things that the LORD had commanded by the hand of Moses.

THE PRIESTLY MINISTRY BEGINS

9 It came to pass on the eighth day that Moses called Aaron and his sons and the elders of Israel. [2]And he said to Aaron, "Take for yourself a young bull as a sin offering and a ram as a burnt offering, without blemish, and offer *them* before the LORD. [3]And to the children of Israel you shall speak, saying, 'Take a kid of the goats as a sin offering, and a calf and a lamb, *both* of the first year, without blemish, as a burnt offering, [4]also a bull and a ram as peace offerings, to sacrifice before the LORD, and a grain offering mixed with oil; for today the LORD will appear to you.' "

[5]So they brought what Moses commanded before the tabernacle of meeting. And all the congregation drew near and stood before the LORD. [6]Then Moses said, "This *is* the thing which the LORD commanded you to do, and the glory of the LORD will appear to you." [7]And Moses said to Aaron, "Go to the altar, offer your sin offering and your burnt offering, and make atonement for yourself and for the people. Offer the offering of the people, and make atonement for them, as the LORD commanded."

[8]Aaron therefore went to the altar and killed the calf of the sin offering, which *was* for himself. [9]Then the sons of Aaron brought the blood to him. And he dipped his finger in the blood, put *it* on the horns of the altar, and poured the blood at the base of the altar. [10]But the fat, the kidneys, and the fatty lobe from the liver of the sin offering he burned on the altar, as the LORD had commanded Moses. [11]The flesh and the hide he burned with fire outside the camp.

[12]And he killed the burnt offering; and Aaron's sons presented to him the blood, which he sprinkled all around on the altar. [13]Then they presented the burnt offering to him, with its pieces and head, and he burned *them* on the altar. [14]And he washed the entrails and the legs, and burned *them* with the burnt offering on the altar.

[15]Then he brought the people's offering, and took the goat, which *was* the sin offering for the people, and killed it and offered it for sin, like the first one. [16]And he brought the burnt offering and offered it according to the prescribed manner. [17]Then he brought the grain offering, took a handful of it, and burned *it* on the altar, besides the burnt sacrifice of the morning.

[18]He also killed the bull and the ram *as* sacrifices of peace offerings, which *were* for the people. And Aaron's sons presented to him the blood, which he sprinkled all around on the altar, [19]and the fat from the bull and the ram—the fatty tail, what covers *the entrails* and the kidneys, and the fatty lobe *attached to* the liver; [20]and they put the fat on the breasts. Then he burned the fat on the altar; [21]but the breasts and the right thigh Aaron waved *as* a wave offering before the LORD, as Moses had commanded.

[22]Then Aaron lifted his hand toward the people, blessed them, and came down from offering the sin offering, the burnt offering, and peace offerings. [23]And Moses and Aaron went into the tabernacle of meeting, and came out and blessed the people. Then the glory of the LORD appeared to all the people, [24]and fire came out from before the LORD and consumed the burnt offering and the fat on the altar. When all the people saw *it,* they shouted and fell on their faces.

THE PROFANE FIRE OF NADAB AND ABIHU

10 Then Nadab and Abihu, the sons of Aaron, each took his censer and put fire in it, put incense on it, and offered profane

SOUL NOTE

Into God's Arms *(10:1–3)* Christian parents hope to see their children grow up to follow Christ. While the Bible offers practical guidance for raising children, there are no automatic assurances, no guarantees. Aaron, the high priest and leader of Israel's worship, saw his two older sons, Nadab and Abihu, die because they violated God's laws. No one can be certain how his or her children will turn out. Even the best parents will experience parenting challenges. As with all other aspects of life, parents must yield their children to the arms of God. **Topic: Parenting**

fire before the LORD, which He had not commanded them. 2So fire went out from the LORD
and devoured them, and they died before the
LORD. 3And Moses said to Aaron, "This is
what the LORD spoke, saying:

> 'By those who come near Me
> I must be regarded as holy;
> And before all the people
> I must be glorified.' "

So Aaron held his peace.

4Then Moses called Mishael and Elzaphan,
the sons of Uzziel the uncle of Aaron, and said
to them, "Come near, carry your brethren
from before the sanctuary out of the camp."
5So they went near and carried them by their
tunics out of the camp, as Moses had said.

6And Moses said to Aaron, and to Eleazar
and Ithamar, his sons, "Do not uncover your
heads nor tear your clothes, lest you die, and
wrath come upon all the people. But let your
brethren, the whole house of Israel, bewail the
burning which the LORD has kindled. 7You
shall not go out from the door of the tabernacle of meeting, lest you die, for the anointing
oil of the LORD *is* upon you." And they did according to the word of Moses.

Conduct Prescribed for Priests

8Then the LORD spoke to Aaron, saying:
9"Do not drink wine or intoxicating drink,
you, nor your sons with you, when you go
into the tabernacle of meeting, lest you die. *It
shall be* a statute forever throughout your generations, 10that you may distinguish between
holy and unholy, and between unclean and
clean, 11and that you may teach the children of
Israel all the statutes which the LORD has spoken to them by the hand of Moses."

12And Moses spoke to Aaron, and to Eleazar
and Ithamar, his sons who were left: "Take the
grain offering that remains of the offerings
made by fire to the LORD, and eat it without
leaven beside the altar; for it *is* most holy.
13You shall eat it in a holy place, because it *is*
your due and your sons' due, of the sacrifices
made by fire to the LORD; for so I have been
commanded. 14The breast of the wave offering
and the thigh of the heave offering you shall
eat in a clean place, you, your sons, and your
daughters with you; for *they are* your due and
your sons' due, *which* are given from the sacrifices of peace offerings of the children of Israel. 15The thigh of the heave offering and the
breast of the wave offering they shall bring
with the offerings of fat made by fire, to offer
as a wave offering before the LORD. And it
shall be yours and your sons' with you, by a
statute forever, as the LORD has commanded."

16Then Moses made careful inquiry about
the goat of the sin offering, and there it was—
burned up. And he was angry with Eleazar
and Ithamar, the sons of Aaron *who were* left,
saying, 17"Why have you not eaten the sin offering in a holy place, since it *is* most holy,
and *God* has given it to you to bear the guilt of
the congregation, to make atonement for them
before the LORD? 18See! Its blood was not
brought inside the holy *place;*[a] indeed you
should have eaten it in a holy *place,* as I commanded."

19And Aaron said to Moses, "Look, this day
they have offered their sin offering and their
burnt offering before the LORD, and such
things have befallen me! *If* I had eaten the sin
offering today, would it have been accepted in
the sight of the LORD?" 20So when Moses heard
that, he was content.

Foods Permitted and Forbidden

11 Now the LORD spoke to Moses and
Aaron, saying to them, 2"Speak to the
children of Israel, saying, 'These *are* the animals which you may eat among all the
animals that *are* on the earth: 3Among the animals, whatever divides the hoof, having cloven hooves *and* chewing the cud—that you
may eat. 4Nevertheless these you shall not eat
among those that chew the cud or those that
have cloven hooves: the camel, because it
chews the cud but does not have cloven
hooves, is unclean to you; 5the rock hyrax,
because it chews the cud but does not have
cloven hooves, *is* unclean to you; 6the hare,
because it chews the cud but does not have
cloven hooves, *is* unclean to you; 7and the
swine, though it divides the hoof, having cloven hooves, yet does not chew the cud, *is* unclean to you. 8Their flesh you shall not eat,
and their carcasses you shall not touch. They
are unclean to you.

9'These you may eat of all that *are* in the
water: whatever in the water has fins and
scales, whether in the seas or in the rivers—
that you may eat. 10But all in the seas or in the

10:18 [a]The Most Holy Place when capitalized

LEGALISM—FOCUSING ON THE LAW

DAN MITCHELL

(Leviticus 11)

"Do that and you're grounded." Parents "lay down the law" for various infractions so they can protect their children from danger and train them to do what is right. These rules, along with parents' reaction to behavior, form the foundation and guideposts for people's adult lives. For the Israelites, the law revealed on Mount Sinai formed the foundation for their community. The purpose of this law was to show the Israelites how to be holy, just as God is holy (Lev. 11:45).

GOD ALONE SAVES

As effective as God's law is in pointing out right and wrong, problems occur when we focus on the law alone. This leaves us frustrated and dismayed because the law cannot make us holy (Gal. 2:16; 3:10; Heb. 10:1).

The Bible is clear: Salvation is from God through faith in Christ (Rom. 5:6–8; Eph. 2:8). We cannot save ourselves by obeying the law (Gal. 3:11). Yet, for the Christian, the law continues to have some value. Our works don't save us—but they *are* a natural outgrowth of our relationship with God.

THE TEMPTATION OF LEGALISM

Some Christians are tempted toward legalism—focusing on the law. They stress conformity to rules, believing that obedience to rules is integral to salvation. Many times, the rules on which legalists focus aren't even in the Bible, but they are set up as salvation indicators. Like the Pharisees of Jesus' day, legalists set up a fence of human-made laws to keep themselves from sinning. Jesus clearly censured the Pharisees for legalism (Matt. 23:2–4). To those who believed that they would be saved by their own works, the apostle Paul wrote that their focus on the law canceled out Christ's work on their behalf (Gal. 5:1, 2).

The opposite tendency is just as dangerous, however. Some Christians claim that their behavior has nothing to do with their Christianity. Theologians call these people "antinomians" (against law). Paul admonished such people to stop sinning and to "glorify God" with their behavior (1 Cor. 6:20).

MAINTAINING THE BALANCE

The Bible encourages believers to balance the two extremes—the impulse to reject the law entirely, and the inclination to concentrate on works. John Calvin and Martin Luther thought much about the proper role of the law in a Christian's life. They identified three roles for the law:

- First, the law gives everyone—both believer and unbeliever—guidelines on how to order society. It shows everyone what is right and wrong.
- Second, the law drives people to Christ, by showing how evil they are—how short they have fallen of God's standard.
- Third, the law gives believers principles for living.

FREEDOM FOR LEGALISTS

Discussing the Rules

The first step to freedom from legalism is to discuss the rules—both the rules enforced by others and the rules of one's own conscience. There is nothing wrong with having personal convictions and abstaining from certain activities. In fact, Christians should be self-controlled (2 Pet. 1:6) and should avoid tempting situations (Prov. 4:14, 15). Moreover, Paul encourages Christians to tolerate each other's personal convictions, so that no one may be tempted to do something against their conscience (1 Cor. 8:1–13). But we run into problems when these rules become criteria by which a group determines whether someone is saved.

Although legalism can occur in various ways, there are a number of telltale signs. Often, legalism overemphasizes appearances—like hair length, clothing, or music. Typically, every rule has a well-thought-out rationale. Usually, the rule is designed to protect people from temptation; for example, "Card-playing may tempt someone to gamble, so don't do it." Often there is an authority figure providing interpretation and enforcement. Also, legalism cannot tolerate ambiguity, so nearly every facet of life has a rule. Taken to the extreme, legalism gets to be a test of salvation.

Legalism creates many victims. Sometimes a child affected by legalism grows up to be a rebel, refusing to accept rules in life. Legalism can also create a guilt-ridden person who constantly evaluates their life by certain strict standards. This type of person often has trouble accepting God's forgiveness.

The lives of legalists are defined by rules. They need to talk about the subtle effects of rules on them. Do the rules produce guilt? Does the law spark anger and rebellion? Discussing the rules will help legalists to identify the attitudes that are imprisoning them.

Focusing on God

Because legalism focuses on appearances, the antidote to legalism is focusing on God and His love. Our Lord unconditionally loves us. In fact, Christ loved us so much, He died for us when we were still His enemies (Rom. 5:6–8). Just as the prodigal son came back to his father with nothing, so we come to God with nothing—no good works, no trophies, no awards. We come to God to accept what only He can give us—salvation through His Son. Our works amount to nothing. God's grace is everything. Reminding ourselves of God's amazing gift of salvation is the best way to fight legalism.

Living as God's Child

The Holy Spirit is in our hearts as evidence of our relationship to God (Gal. 4:5–7). The Spirit frees us from the law's condemnation and gives us the power to do what is right (Rom. 8:1–5). We are no longer slaves to the law; we are God's children (Rom. 8:15; Gal. 3:26–29). We are to live in the freedom God gives. "Therefore if the Son makes you free, you shall be free indeed" (John 8:36).

FURTHER MEDITATION:

Other passages to study about the issue of legalism include:

- 1 Corinthians 10:23—11:1
- Galatians 2:11—4:7
- Ephesians 2:8, 9
- Philippians 3:1—4:1
- Colossians 2:11–23
- Titus 2:11–14
- James 2:14–26

To Learn More: Turn to the key passage note on legalism at Romans 7:6–14 on page 1473. See also the personality profile of the Pharisees on page 1269.

rivers that do not have fins and scales, all that
move in the water or any living thing which *is*
in the water, they *are* an abomination to you.
11They shall be an abomination to you; you
shall not eat their flesh, but you shall regard
their carcasses as an abomination. 12Whatever
in the water does not have fins or scales—that
shall be an abomination to you.

13'And these you shall regard as an abomination among the birds; they shall not be eaten,
they *are* an abomination: the eagle, the vulture,
the buzzard, 14the kite, and the falcon after its
kind; 15every raven after its kind, 16the ostrich,
the short-eared owl, the sea gull, and the hawk
after its kind; 17the little owl, the fisher owl,
and the screech owl; 18the white owl, the jackdaw, and the carrion vulture; 19the stork, the
heron after its kind, the hoopoe, and the bat.

20'All flying insects that creep on *all* fours
shall be an abomination to you. 21Yet these
you may eat of every flying insect that creeps
on *all* fours: those which have jointed legs
above their feet with which to leap on the
earth. 22These you may eat: the locust after its
kind, the destroying locust after its kind, the
cricket after its kind, and the grasshopper after its kind. 23But all *other* flying insects which
have four feet *shall be* an abomination to you.

Unclean Animals

24'By these you shall become unclean; whoever touches the carcass of any of them shall
be unclean until evening; 25whoever carries
part of the carcass of any of them shall wash
his clothes and be unclean until evening:
26*The carcass* of any animal which divides the
foot, but is not cloven-hoofed or does not
chew the cud, *is* unclean to you. Everyone
who touches it shall be unclean. 27And whatever goes on its paws, among all kinds of animals that go on *all* fours, those *are* unclean to
you. Whoever touches any such carcass shall
be unclean until evening. 28Whoever carries
any such carcass shall wash his clothes and be
unclean until evening. It *is* unclean to you.

29'These also *shall be* unclean to you among
the creeping things that creep on the earth:
the mole, the mouse, and the large lizard after
its kind; 30the gecko, the monitor lizard, the
sand reptile, the sand lizard, and the chame-
leon. 31These *are* unclean to you among all
that creep. Whoever touches them when they
are dead shall be unclean until evening.
32Anything on which *any* of them falls, when
they are dead shall be unclean, whether *it is*
any item of wood or clothing or skin or sack,
whatever item *it is,* in which *any* work is
done, it must be put in water. And it shall be
unclean until evening; then it shall be clean.
33Any earthen vessel into which *any* of them
falls you shall break; and whatever *is* in it
shall be unclean: 34in such a vessel, any edible
food upon which water falls becomes unclean, and any drink that may be drunk from
it becomes unclean. 35And everything on
which *a part* of *any such* carcass falls shall be
unclean; *whether it is* an oven or cooking
stove, it shall be broken down; *for* they *are* unclean, and shall be unclean to you. 36Never-
theless a spring or a cistern, *in which there is*
plenty of water, shall be clean, but whatever
touches any such carcass becomes unclean.
37And if a part of *any such* carcass falls on any
planting seed which is to be sown, it *remains*
clean. 38But if water is put on the seed, and if
a part of *any such* carcass falls on it, it *becomes* unclean to you.

39'And if any animal which you may eat
dies, he who touches its carcass shall be unclean until evening. 40He who eats of its carcass shall wash his clothes and be unclean
until evening. He also who carries its carcass

SOUL NOTE

Body and Soul *(11:44, 45)* Holiness was the basis of God's ethical requirements as well as an expression of His character. God still desires to make us "holy and without blame" (Eph. 1:4). In Old Testament times, holiness was a matter of both body and soul, and the law regulated cleanness in matters such as food and bodily discharges. The priest had a primary role in dealing with both physical and spiritual needs. Today, we generally separate the two subjects—leaving a gap between medicine and ministry, between health and religion. But God reveals the unity of the human person—both body and soul are His concern. **Topic: Health/Spirituality**

shall wash his clothes and be unclean until evening.

[41]'And every creeping thing that creeps on the earth *shall be* an abomination. It shall not be eaten. [42]Whatever crawls on its belly, whatever goes on *all* fours, or whatever has many feet among all creeping things that creep on the earth—these you shall not eat, for they *are* an abomination. [43]You shall not make yourselves abominable with any creeping thing that creeps; nor shall you make yourselves unclean with them, lest you be defiled by them. [44]For I *am* the LORD your God. You shall therefore consecrate yourselves, and you shall be holy; for I *am* holy. Neither shall you defile yourselves with any creeping thing that creeps on the earth. [45]For I *am* the LORD who brings you up out of the land of Egypt, to be your God. You shall therefore be holy, for I *am* holy.

[46]'This *is* the law of the animals and the birds and every living creature that moves in the waters, and of every creature that creeps on the earth, [47]to distinguish between the unclean and the clean, and between the animal that may be eaten and the animal that may not be eaten.' "

THE RITUAL AFTER CHILDBIRTH

12 Then the LORD spoke to Moses, saying, [2]"Speak to the children of Israel, saying: 'If a woman has conceived, and borne a male child, then she shall be unclean seven days; as in the days of her customary impurity she shall be unclean. [3]And on the eighth day the flesh of his foreskin shall be circumcised. [4]She shall then continue in the blood of *her* purification thirty-three days. She shall not touch any hallowed thing, nor come into the sanctuary until the days of her purification are fulfilled.

[5]'But if she bears a female child, then she shall be unclean two weeks, as in her customary impurity, and she shall continue in the blood of *her* purification sixty-six days.

[6]'When the days of her purification are fulfilled, whether for a son or a daughter, she shall bring to the priest a lamb of the first year as a burnt offering, and a young pigeon or a turtledove as a sin offering, to the door of the tabernacle of meeting. [7]Then he shall offer it before the LORD, and make atonement for her. And she shall be clean from the flow of her blood. This *is* the law for her who has borne a male or a female.

[8]'And if she is not able to bring a lamb, then she may bring two turtledoves or two young pigeons—one as a burnt offering and the other as a sin offering. So the priest shall make atonement for her, and she will be clean.' "

THE LAW CONCERNING LEPROSY

13 And the LORD spoke to Moses and Aaron, saying: [2]"When a man has on the skin of his body a swelling, a scab, or a bright spot, and it becomes on the skin of his body *like* a leprous[a] sore, then he shall be brought to Aaron the priest or to one of his sons the priests. [3]The priest shall examine the sore on the skin of the body; and if the hair on the sore has turned white, and the sore appears *to be* deeper than the skin of his body, it *is* a leprous sore. Then the priest shall examine him, and pronounce him unclean. [4]But if the bright spot *is* white on the skin of his body, and does not appear *to be* deeper than the skin, and its hair has not turned white, then the priest shall isolate *the one who has* the sore seven days. [5]And the priest shall examine him on the seventh day; and indeed *if* the sore appears to be as it was, *and* the sore has not spread on the skin, then the priest shall isolate him another seven days. [6]Then the priest shall examine him again on the seventh day; and indeed *if* the sore has faded, *and* the sore has not spread on the skin, then the priest shall pronounce him clean; it *is only* a scab, and he shall wash his clothes and be clean. [7]But if the scab should at all spread over the skin, after he has been seen by the priest for his cleansing, he shall be seen by the priest again. [8]And *if* the priest sees that the scab has indeed spread on the skin, then the priest shall pronounce him unclean. It *is* leprosy.

[9]"When the leprous sore is on a person, then he shall be brought to the priest. [10]And the priest shall examine *him;* and indeed *if* the swelling on the skin *is* white, and it has turned the hair white, and *there is* a spot of raw flesh in the swelling, [11]it *is* an old leprosy on the skin of his body. The priest shall pronounce him unclean, and shall not isolate him, for he *is* unclean.

[12]"And if leprosy breaks out all over the

13:2 [a]Hebrew *saraath,* disfiguring skin diseases, including leprosy, and so in verses 2–46 and 14:1–32

skin, and the leprosy covers all the skin of *the*
one who has the sore, from his head to his
foot, wherever the priest looks, 13then the
priest shall consider; and indeed *if* the leprosy
has covered all his body, he shall pronounce
him clean *who has* the sore. It has all turned
white. He *is* clean. 14But when raw flesh appears on him, he shall be unclean. 15And the
priest shall examine the raw flesh and pronounce him to be unclean; *for* the raw flesh *is*
unclean. It *is* leprosy. 16Or if the raw flesh
changes and turns white again, he shall come
to the priest. 17And the priest shall examine
him; and indeed *if* the sore has turned white,
then the priest shall pronounce *him* clean *who*
has the sore. He *is* clean.

18"If the body develops a boil in the skin,
and it is healed, 19and in the place of the boil
there comes a white swelling or a bright spot,
reddish-white, then it shall be shown to the
priest; 20and *if*, when the priest sees it, it indeed *appears* deeper than the skin, and its
hair has turned white, the priest shall pronounce him unclean. It *is* a leprous sore
which has broken out of the boil. 21But if the
priest examines it, and indeed *there are* no
white hairs in it, and it *is* not deeper than the
skin, but has faded, then the priest shall isolate him seven days; 22and if it should at all
spread over the skin, then the priest shall pronounce him unclean. It *is* a leprous sore. 23But
if the bright spot stays in one place, *and* has
not spread, it *is* the scar of the boil; and the
priest shall pronounce him clean.

24"Or if the body receives a burn on its skin
by fire, and the raw *flesh* of the burn becomes
a bright spot, reddish-white or white, 25then
the priest shall examine it; and indeed *if* the
hair of the bright spot has turned white, and it
appears deeper than the skin, it *is* leprosy broken out in the burn. Therefore the priest shall
pronounce him unclean. It *is* a leprous sore.
26But if the priest examines it, and indeed
there are no white hairs in the bright spot, and
it *is* not deeper than the skin, but has faded,
then the priest shall isolate him seven days.
27And the priest shall examine him on the seventh day. If it has at all spread over the skin,
then the priest shall pronounce him unclean.
It *is* a leprous sore. 28But if the bright spot
stays in one place, *and* has not spread on the
skin, but has faded, it *is* a swelling from the
burn. The priest shall pronounce him clean,
for it *is* the scar from the burn.

29"If a man or woman has a sore on the head
or the beard, 30then the priest shall examine
the sore; and indeed if it appears deeper than
the skin, *and there is* in it thin yellow hair, then
the priest shall pronounce him unclean. It *is* a
scaly leprosy of the head or beard. 31But if the
priest examines the scaly sore, and indeed it
does not appear deeper than the skin, and *there*
is no black hair in it, then the priest shall isolate *the one who has* the scale seven days.
32And on the seventh day the priest shall examine the sore; and indeed *if* the scale has not
spread, and there is no yellow hair in it, and
the scale does not appear deeper than the skin,
33he shall shave himself, but the scale he shall
not shave. And the priest shall isolate *the one*
who has the scale another seven days. 34On the
seventh day the priest shall examine the scale;
and indeed *if* the scale has not spread over the
skin, and does not appear deeper than the skin,
then the priest shall pronounce him clean. He
shall wash his clothes and be clean. 35But if the
scale should at all spread over the skin after his
cleansing, 36then the priest shall examine him;
and indeed *if* the scale has spread over the
skin, the priest need not seek for yellow hair.
He *is* unclean. 37But if the scale appears to be at
a standstill, and there is black hair grown up in
it, the scale has healed. He *is* clean, and the
priest shall pronounce him clean.

38"If a man or a woman has bright spots on
the skin of the body, *specifically* white bright

SOUL NOTE

Preventive Care *(ch. 13)* God wanted His people to be healthy. The detailed laws of chapter 13 deal with detecting, examining, quarantining, cleansing, and restoring people who had leprosy, a skin disease, or another physical malady. God also gave specific instructions concerning the cleanliness of clothes and houses (13:47–59). If God cares so much about our health, then so should we.

Topic: Health/Spirituality

spots, [39]then the priest shall look; and indeed *if* the bright spots on the skin of the body *are* dull white, it *is* a white spot *that* grows on the skin. He *is* clean.

[40]"As for the man whose hair has fallen from his head, he *is* bald, *but* he *is* clean. [41]He whose hair has fallen from his forehead, he *is* bald on the forehead, *but* he *is* clean. [42]And if there is on the bald head or bald forehead a reddish-white sore, it *is* leprosy breaking out on his bald head or his bald forehead. [43]Then the priest shall examine it; and indeed *if* the swelling of the sore *is* reddish-white on his bald head or on his bald forehead, as the appearance of leprosy on the skin of the body, [44]he is a leprous man. He *is* unclean. The priest shall surely pronounce him unclean; his sore *is* on his head.

[45]"Now the leper on whom the sore *is*, his clothes shall be torn and his head bare; and he shall cover his mustache, and cry, 'Unclean! Unclean!' [46]He shall be unclean. All the days he has the sore he shall be unclean. He *is* unclean, and he shall dwell alone; his dwelling *shall be* outside the camp.

The Law Concerning Leprous Garments

[47]"Also, if a garment has a leprous plague[a] in it, *whether it is* a woolen garment or a linen garment, [48]whether *it is* in the warp or woof of linen or wool, whether in leather or in anything made of leather, [49]and if the plague is greenish or reddish in the garment or in the leather, whether in the warp or in the woof, or in anything made of leather, it *is* a leprous plague and shall be shown to the priest. [50]The priest shall examine the plague and isolate *that which has* the plague seven days. [51]And he shall examine the plague on the seventh day. If the plague has spread in the garment, either in the warp or in the woof, in the leather *or* in anything made of leather, the plague *is* an active leprosy. It *is* unclean. [52]He shall therefore burn that garment in which is the plague, whether warp or woof, in wool or in linen, or anything of leather, for it *is* an active leprosy; *the garment* shall be burned in the fire.

[53]"But if the priest examines *it*, and indeed the plague has not spread in the garment, either in the warp or in the woof, or in anything made of leather, [54]then the priest shall command that they wash *the thing* in which *is* the plague; and he shall isolate it another seven days. [55]Then the priest shall examine the plague after it has been washed; and indeed *if* the plague has not changed its color, though the plague has not spread, it *is* unclean, and you shall burn it in the fire; it continues eating away, *whether* the damage *is* outside or inside. [56]If the priest examines *it*, and indeed the plague has faded after washing it, then he shall tear it out of the garment, whether out of the warp or out of the woof, or out of the leather. [57]But if it appears again in the garment, either in the warp or in the woof, or in anything made of leather, it *is* a spreading *plague;* you shall burn with fire that in which is the plague. [58]And if you wash the garment, either warp or woof, or whatever is made of leather, if the plague has disappeared from it, then it shall be washed a second time, and shall be clean.

[59]"This *is* the law of the leprous plague in a garment of wool or linen, either in the warp or woof, or in anything made of leather, to pronounce it clean or to pronounce it unclean."

The Ritual for Cleansing Healed Lepers

14 Then the LORD spoke to Moses, saying, [2]"This shall be the law of the leper for the day of his cleansing: He shall be brought to the priest. [3]And the priest shall go out of the camp, and the priest shall examine *him;* and indeed, *if* the leprosy is healed in the leper, [4]then the priest shall command to take for him who is to be cleansed two living *and* clean birds, cedar wood, scarlet, and hyssop. [5]And the priest shall command that one of the birds be killed in an earthen vessel over running water. [6]As for the living bird, he shall take it, the cedar wood and the scarlet and the hyssop, and dip them and the living bird in the blood of the bird *that was* killed over the running water. [7]And he shall sprinkle it seven times on him who is to be cleansed from the leprosy, and shall pronounce him clean, and shall let the living bird loose in the open field. [8]He who is to be cleansed shall wash his clothes, shave off all his hair, and wash himself in water, that he may be clean. After that he shall come into the camp, and shall stay outside his tent seven days. [9]But on the seventh day he shall shave all the hair off his head and his beard and his eyebrows—all his

13:47 [a]A mold, fungus, or similar infestation, and so in verses 47–59

hair he shall shave off. He shall wash his
clothes and wash his body in water, and he
shall be clean.
10“And on the eighth day he shall take two
male lambs without blemish, one ewe lamb of
the first year without blemish, three-tenths *of
an ephah* of fine flour mixed with oil as a
grain offering, and one log of oil. 11Then the
priest who makes *him* clean shall present the
man who is to be made clean, and those
things, before the LORD, *at* the door of the tabernacle of meeting. 12And the priest shall take
one male lamb and offer it as a trespass offering, and the log of oil, and wave them *as* a
wave offering before the LORD. 13Then he
shall kill the lamb in the place where he
kills the sin offering and the burnt offering,
in a holy place; for as the sin offering *is* the
priest's, so *is* the trespass offering. It *is* most
holy. 14The priest shall take *some* of the blood
of the trespass offering, and the priest shall
put *it* on the tip of the right ear of him who is
to be cleansed, on the thumb of his right
hand, and on the big toe of his right foot.
15And the priest shall take *some* of the log of
oil, and pour *it* into the palm of his own left
hand. 16Then the priest shall dip his right finger in the oil that *is* in his left hand, and shall
sprinkle some of the oil with his finger seven
times before the LORD. 17And of the rest of the
oil in his hand, the priest shall put *some* on
the tip of the right ear of him who is to be
cleansed, on the thumb of his right hand, and
on the big toe of his right foot, on the blood of
the trespass offering. 18The rest of the oil that
is in the priest's hand he shall put on the head
of him who is to be cleansed. So the priest
shall make atonement for him before the
LORD.
19“Then the priest shall offer the sin offering, and make atonement for him who is to be
cleansed from his uncleanness. Afterward he
shall kill the burnt offering. 20And the priest
shall offer the burnt offering and the grain offering on the altar. So the priest shall make
atonement for him, and he shall be clean.
21“But if he *is* poor and cannot afford it,
then he shall take one male lamb *as* a trespass
offering to be waved, to make atonement for
him, one-tenth *of an ephah* of fine flour mixed
with oil as a grain offering, a log of oil, 22and
two turtledoves or two young pigeons, such as
he is able to afford: one shall be a sin offering
and the other a burnt offering. 23He shall bring
them to the priest on the eighth day for his
cleansing, to the door of the tabernacle of
meeting, before the LORD. 24And the priest
shall take the lamb of the trespass offering
and the log of oil, and the priest shall wave
them *as* a wave offering before the LORD.
25Then he shall kill the lamb of the trespass
offering, and the priest shall take *some* of the
blood of the trespass offering and put *it* on
the tip of the right ear of him who is to be
cleansed, on the thumb of his right hand, and
on the big toe of his right foot. 26And the priest
shall pour some of the oil into the palm of his
own left hand. 27Then the priest shall sprinkle
with his right finger *some* of the oil that *is* in
his left hand seven times before the LORD.
28And the priest shall put *some* of the oil that
is in his hand on the tip of the right ear of him
who is to be cleansed, on the thumb of the
right hand, and on the big toe of his right foot,
on the place of the blood of the trespass offering. 29The rest of the oil that *is* in the priest's
hand he shall put on the head of him who is to
be cleansed, to make atonement for him before the LORD. 30And he shall offer one of the
turtledoves or young pigeons, such as he can
afford— 31such as he is able to afford, the one
as a sin offering and the other *as* a burnt offering, with the grain offering. So the priest shall
make atonement for him who is to be
cleansed before the LORD. 32This *is* the law *for
one* who had a leprous sore, who cannot afford the usual cleansing.”

THE LAW CONCERNING LEPROUS HOUSES

33And the LORD spoke to Moses and Aaron,
saying: 34“When you have come into the land
of Canaan, which I give you as a possession,
and I put the leprous plague[a] in a house in the
land of your possession, 35and he who owns
the house comes and tells the priest, saying,
'It seems to me that *there is* some plague in
the house,' 36then the priest shall command
that they empty the house, before the priest
goes *into it* to examine the plague, that all that
is in the house may not be made unclean; and
afterward the priest shall go in to examine the
house. 37And he shall examine the plague; and
indeed *if* the plague *is* on the walls of the house
with ingrained streaks, greenish or reddish,
which appear to be deep in the wall, 38then the

14:34 [a]Decomposition by mildew, mold, dry rot, etc., and so in verses 34–53

priest shall go out of the house, to the door of the house, and shut up the house seven days. 39And the priest shall come again on the seventh day and look; and indeed *if* the plague has spread on the walls of the house, 40then the priest shall command that they take away the stones in which *is* the plague, and they shall cast them into an unclean place outside the city. 41And he shall cause the house to be scraped inside, all around, and the dust that they scrape off they shall pour out in an unclean place outside the city. 42Then they shall take other stones and put *them* in the place of *those* stones, and he shall take other mortar and plaster the house.

43"Now if the plague comes back and breaks out in the house, after he has taken away the stones, after he has scraped the house, and after it is plastered, 44then the priest shall come and look; and indeed *if* the plague has spread in the house, it *is* an active leprosy in the house. It *is* unclean. 45And he shall break down the house, its stones, its timber, and all the plaster of the house, and he shall carry *them* outside the city to an unclean place. 46Moreover he who goes into the house at all while it is shut up shall be unclean until evening. 47And he who lies down in the house shall wash his clothes, and he who eats in the house shall wash his clothes.

48"But if the priest comes in and examines *it*, and indeed the plague has not spread in the house after the house was plastered, then the priest shall pronounce the house clean, because the plague is healed. 49And he shall take, to cleanse the house, two birds, cedar wood, scarlet, and hyssop. 50Then he shall kill one of the birds in an earthen vessel over running water; 51and he shall take the cedar wood, the hyssop, the scarlet, and the living bird, and dip them in the blood of the slain bird and in the running water, and sprinkle the house seven times. 52And he shall cleanse the house with the blood of the bird and the running water and the living bird, with the cedar wood, the hyssop, and the scarlet. 53Then he shall let the living bird loose outside the city in the open field, and make atonement for the house, and it shall be clean.

54"This *is* the law for any leprous sore and scale, 55for the leprosy of a garment and of a house, 56for a swelling and a scab and a bright spot, 57to teach when *it is* unclean and when *it is* clean. This *is* the law of leprosy."

The Law Concerning Bodily Discharges

15 And the LORD spoke to Moses and Aaron, saying, 2"Speak to the children of Israel, and say to them: 'When any man has a discharge from his body, his discharge *is* unclean. 3And this shall be his uncleanness in regard to his discharge—whether his body runs with his discharge, or his body is stopped up by his discharge, it *is* his uncleanness. 4Every bed is unclean on which he who has the discharge lies, and everything on which he sits shall be unclean. 5And whoever touches his bed shall wash his clothes and bathe in water, and be unclean until evening. 6He who sits on anything on which he who has the discharge sat shall wash his clothes and bathe in water, and be unclean until evening. 7And he who touches the body of him who has the discharge shall wash his clothes and bathe in water, and be unclean until evening. 8If he who has the discharge spits on him who is clean, then he shall wash his clothes and bathe in water, and be unclean until evening. 9Any saddle on which he who has the discharge rides shall be unclean. 10Whoever touches anything that was under him shall be unclean until evening. He who carries *any of* those things shall wash his clothes and bathe in water, and be unclean until evening. 11And whomever the one who has the discharge touches, and has not rinsed his hands in water, he shall wash his clothes and bathe in water, and be unclean until evening. 12The vessel of earth that he who has the discharge touches shall be broken, and every vessel of wood shall be rinsed in water.

13'And when he who has a discharge is cleansed of his discharge, then he shall count for himself seven days for his cleansing, wash his clothes, and bathe his body in running water; then he shall be clean. 14On the eighth day he shall take for himself two turtledoves or two young pigeons, and come before the LORD, to the door of the tabernacle of meeting, and give them to the priest. 15Then the priest shall offer them, the one *as* a sin offering and the other *as* a burnt offering. So the priest shall make atonement for him before the LORD because of his discharge.

16'If any man has an emission of semen, then he shall wash all his body in water, and be unclean until evening. 17And any garment and any leather on which there is semen, it shall be washed with water, and be unclean

until evening. 18Also, when a woman lies with
a man, and *there is* an emission of semen, they
shall bathe in water, and be unclean until evening.
19'If a woman has a discharge, *and* the discharge from her body is blood, she shall be set
apart seven days; and whoever touches her
shall be unclean until evening. 20Everything
that she lies on during her impurity shall be
unclean; also everything that she sits on shall
be unclean. 21Whoever touches her bed shall
wash his clothes and bathe in water, and
be unclean until evening. 22And whoever
touches anything that she sat on shall wash
his clothes and bathe in water, and be unclean
until evening. 23If *anything* is on *her* bed or on
anything on which she sits, when he touches
it, he shall be unclean until evening. 24And if
any man lies with her at all, so that her impurity is on him, he shall be unclean seven days;
and every bed on which he lies shall be unclean.
25'If a woman has a discharge of blood for
many days, other than at the time of her *customary* impurity, or if it runs beyond her *usual
time of* impurity, all the days of her unclean discharge shall be as the days of her *customary*
impurity. She *shall be* unclean. 26Every bed on
which she lies all the days of her discharge
shall be to her as the bed of her impurity; and
whatever she sits on shall be unclean, as the
uncleanness of her impurity. 27Whoever
touches those things shall be unclean; he shall
wash his clothes and bathe in water, and be
unclean until evening.
28'But if she is cleansed of her discharge,
then she shall count for herself seven days,
and after that she shall be clean. 29And on the
eighth day she shall take for herself two turtledoves or two young pigeons, and bring them
to the priest, to the door of the tabernacle of
meeting. 30Then the priest shall offer the one
as a sin offering and the other *as* a burnt offering, and the priest shall make atonement for
her before the LORD for the discharge of her
uncleanness.
31'Thus you shall separate the children of Israel from their uncleanness, lest they die in
their uncleanness when they defile My tabernacle that *is* among them. 32This *is* the law for
one who has a discharge, and *for him* who
emits semen and is unclean thereby, 33and for
her who is indisposed because of her *customary* impurity, and for one who has a discharge,
either man or woman, and for him who lies
with her who is unclean.' "

THE DAY OF ATONEMENT

16 Now the LORD spoke to Moses after the
death of the two sons of Aaron, when
they offered *profane fire* before the LORD, and
died; 2and the LORD said to Moses: "Tell Aaron
your brother not to come at *just* any time into
the Holy *Place* inside the veil, before the mercy
seat which *is* on the ark, lest he die; for I will
appear in the cloud above the mercy seat.
3"Thus Aaron shall come into the Holy *Place:*
with *the blood of* a young bull as a sin offering,
and *of* a ram as a burnt offering. 4He shall put
the holy linen tunic and the linen trousers on
his body; he shall be girded with a linen sash,
and with the linen turban he shall be attired.
These *are* holy garments. Therefore he shall
wash his body in water, and put them on. 5And
he shall take from the congregation of the children of Israel two kids of the goats as a sin offering, and one ram as a burnt offering.
6"Aaron shall offer the bull as a sin offering,
which *is* for himself, and make atonement for
himself and for his house. 7He shall take the
two goats and present them before the LORD *at*
the door of the tabernacle of meeting. 8Then
Aaron shall cast lots for the two goats: one lot
for the LORD and the other lot for the scapegoat. 9And Aaron shall bring the goat on which
the LORD's lot fell, and offer it *as* a sin offering.
10But the goat on which the lot fell to be the
scapegoat shall be presented alive before the
LORD, to make atonement upon it, *and* to let it
go as the scapegoat into the wilderness.
11"And Aaron shall bring the bull of the sin
offering, which is for himself, and make atonement for himself and for his house, and shall
kill the bull as the sin offering which *is* for himself. 12Then he shall take a censer full of burning coals of fire from the altar before the LORD,
with his hands full of sweet incense beaten
fine, and bring *it* inside the veil. 13And he shall
put the incense on the fire before the LORD, that
the cloud of incense may cover the mercy seat
that *is* on the Testimony, lest he die. 14He shall
take some of the blood of the bull and sprinkle
it with his finger on the mercy seat on the east
side; and before the mercy seat he shall sprinkle some of the blood with his finger seven
times.
15"Then he shall kill the goat of the sin offering, which *is* for the people, bring its blood

inside the veil, do with that blood as he did
with the blood of the bull, and sprinkle it on
the mercy seat and before the mercy seat. [16]So
he shall make atonement for the Holy *Place,*
because of the uncleanness of the children of
Israel, and because of their transgressions, for
all their sins; and so he shall do for the tabernacle of meeting which remains among them
in the midst of their uncleanness. [17]There
shall be no man in the tabernacle of meeting
when he goes in to make atonement in the
Holy *Place,* until he comes out, that he may
make atonement for himself, for his household, and for all the assembly of Israel. [18]And
he shall go out to the altar that *is* before the
LORD, and make atonement for it, and shall
take some of the blood of the bull and some of
the blood of the goat, and put it on the horns
of the altar all around. [19]Then he shall sprinkle some of the blood on it with his finger
seven times, cleanse it, and consecrate it from
the uncleanness of the children of Israel.

[20]"And when he has made an end of atoning
for the Holy *Place,* the tabernacle of meeting,
and the altar, he shall bring the live goat.
[21]Aaron shall lay both his hands on the head
of the live goat, confess over it all the iniquities of the children of Israel, and all their
transgressions, concerning all their sins, putting them on the head of the goat, and shall
send *it* away into the wilderness by the hand
of a suitable man. [22]The goat shall bear on itself all their iniquities to an uninhabited land;
and he shall release the goat in the wilderness.

[23]"Then Aaron shall come into the tabernacle of meeting, shall take off the linen garments which he put on when he went into the
Holy *Place,* and shall leave them there. [24]And
he shall wash his body with water in a holy
place, put on his garments, come out and offer
his burnt offering and the burnt offering of the
people, and make atonement for himself and
for the people. [25]The fat of the sin offering he
shall burn on the altar. [26]And he who released
the goat as the scapegoat shall wash his
clothes and bathe his body in water, and afterward he may come into the camp. [27]The bull
for the sin offering and the goat *for* the sin
offering, whose blood was brought in to make
atonement in the Holy *Place,* shall be carried
outside the camp. And they shall burn in the
fire their skins, their flesh, and their offal.
[28]Then he who burns them shall wash his
clothes and bathe his body in water, and afterward he may come into the camp.

[29]"*This* shall be a statute forever for you: In
the seventh month, on the tenth *day* of the
month, you shall afflict your souls, and do no
work at all, *whether* a native of your own country or a stranger who dwells among you. [30]For
on that day *the priest* shall make atonement for
you, to cleanse you, *that* you may be clean
from all your sins before the LORD. [31]It *is* a sabbath of solemn rest for you, and you shall afflict your souls. *It is* a statute forever. [32]And the
priest, who is anointed and consecrated to
minister as priest in his father's place, shall
make atonement, and put on the linen clothes,
the holy garments; [33]then he shall make atonement for the Holy Sanctuary,[a] and he shall
make atonement for the tabernacle of meeting
and for the altar, and he shall make atonement
for the priests and for all the people of the assembly. [34]This shall be an everlasting statute
for you, to make atonement for the children of
Israel, for all their sins, once a year." And he
did as the LORD commanded Moses.

THE SANCTITY OF BLOOD

17 And the LORD spoke to Moses, saying,
[2]"Speak to Aaron, to his sons, and to all
the children of Israel, and say to them, 'This *is*

16:33 [a]That is, the Most Holy Place

SOUL NOTE

A Nation Under God *(16:32, 33)* Once each year the Israelites were to humble themselves by prayer and fasting on the day of atonement. National atonement was a serious matter that involved two sacrifices: A bull would be sacrificed for the priests, and a goat for the people (16:11–19). The blood would be used to purify the holy place, and the bodies of the slaughtered animals would be taken outside the camp and burned (16:27). God promises to honor the nation that honors Him (2 Chr. 7:14). **Topic: Repentance**

the thing which the LORD has commanded, saying: [3]“Whatever man of the house of Israel who kills an ox or lamb or goat in the camp, or who kills *it* outside the camp, [4]and does not bring it to the door of the tabernacle of meeting to offer an offering to the LORD before the tabernacle of the LORD, the guilt of bloodshed shall be imputed to that man. He has shed blood; and that man shall be cut off from among his people, [5]to the end that the children of Israel may bring their sacrifices which they offer in the open field, that they may bring them to the LORD at the door of the tabernacle of meeting, to the priest, and offer them *as* peace offerings to the LORD. [6]And the priest shall sprinkle the blood on the altar of the LORD *at* the door of the tabernacle of meeting, and burn the fat for a sweet aroma to the LORD. [7]They shall no more offer their sacrifices to demons, after whom they have played the harlot. This shall be a statute forever for them throughout their generations.” ’

[8]“Also you shall say to them: ‘Whatever man of the house of Israel, or of the strangers who dwell among you, who offers a burnt offering or sacrifice, [9]and does not bring it to the door of the tabernacle of meeting, to offer it to the LORD, that man shall be cut off from among his people.

[10]‘And whatever man of the house of Israel, or of the strangers who dwell among you, who eats any blood, I will set My face against that person who eats blood, and will cut him off from among his people. [11]For the life of the flesh *is* in the blood, and I have given it to you upon the altar to make atonement for your souls; for it *is* the blood *that* makes atonement for the soul.’ [12]Therefore I said to the children of Israel, ‘No one among you shall eat blood, nor shall any stranger who dwells among you eat blood.’

> “For the life of the flesh is in the blood, and I have given it to you upon the altar to make atonement for your souls; for it is the blood that makes atonement for the soul.”
>
> LEVITICUS 17:11

[13]“Whatever man of the children of Israel, or of the strangers who dwell among you, who hunts and catches any animal or bird that may be eaten, he shall pour out its blood and cover it with dust; [14]for *it is* the life of all flesh. Its blood sustains its life. Therefore I said to the children of Israel, ‘You shall not eat the blood of any flesh, for the life of all flesh is its blood. Whoever eats it shall be cut off.’

[15]“And every person who eats what died *naturally* or what was torn *by beasts, whether he is* a native of your own country or a stranger, he shall both wash his clothes and bathe in water, and be unclean until evening. Then he shall be clean. [16]But if he does not wash *them* or bathe his body, then he shall bear his guilt.”

LAWS OF SEXUAL MORALITY

18 Then the LORD spoke to Moses, saying, [2]“Speak to the children of Israel, and say to them: ‘I am the LORD your God. [3]According to the doings of the land of Egypt, where you dwelt, you shall not do; and according to the doings of the land of Canaan, where I am bringing you, you shall not do; nor shall you walk in their ordinances. [4]You shall observe My judgments and keep My ordinances, to walk in them: I *am* the LORD your God. [5]You shall therefore keep My statutes and My judgments, which if a man does, he shall live by them: I *am* the LORD.

[6]‘None of you shall approach anyone who is near of kin to him, to uncover his nakedness: I *am* the LORD. [7]The nakedness of your father or the nakedness of your mother you shall not uncover. She *is* your mother; you shall not uncover her nakedness. [8]The nakedness of your father’s wife you shall not uncover; it *is* your father’s nakedness. [9]The nakedness of your sister, the daughter of your father, or the daughter of your mother, *whether* born at home or elsewhere, their nakedness you shall not uncover. [10]The nakedness of your son’s daughter or your daughter’s daughter, their nakedness you shall not uncover; for theirs *is* your own nakedness. [11]The nakedness of your father’s wife’s daughter, begotten by your father—she *is* your sister—you shall not uncover her nakedness. [12]You shall not uncover the nakedness of your father’s sister; she *is* near of kin to your father. [13]You shall not uncover the nakedness of your mother’s sister, for she *is* near of kin to your mother. [14]You shall not uncover the nakedness of your father’s brother. You shall not approach his wife; she *is* your aunt. [15]You shall not uncover the nakedness of your daughter-in-law—she *is* your son’s wife—you shall not uncover

her nakedness. 16You shall not uncover the
nakedness of your brother's wife; it *is* your
brother's nakedness. 17You shall not uncover
the nakedness of a woman and her daughter,
nor shall you take her son's daughter or her
daughter's daughter, to uncover her nakedness. They *are* near of kin to her. It *is* wickedness. 18Nor shall you take a woman as a rival to
her sister, to uncover her nakedness while the
other is alive.
19'Also you shall not approach a woman to
uncover her nakedness as long as she is in her
customary impurity. 20Moreover you shall not
lie carnally with your neighbor's wife, to defile yourself with her. 21And you shall not let
any of your descendants pass through *the fire*
to Molech, nor shall you profane the name of
your God: I *am* the LORD. 22You shall not lie
with a male as with a woman. It *is* an abomination. 23Nor shall you mate with any animal,
to defile yourself with it. Nor shall any woman
stand before an animal to mate with it. It *is*
perversion.
24'Do not defile your-
selves with any of these
things; for by all these
the nations are defiled,
which I am casting out
before you. 25For the
land is defiled; there-
fore I visit the punishment of its iniquity upon
it, and the land vomits out its inhabitants.
26You shall therefore keep My statutes and My
judgments, and shall not commit *any* of these
abominations, *either* any of your own nation or
any stranger who dwells among you 27(for all
these abominations the men of the land have
done, who *were* before you, and thus the land
is defiled), 28lest the land vomit you out also
when you defile it, as it vomited out the nations that *were* before you. 29For whoever commits any of these abominations, the persons
who commit *them* shall be cut off from among
their people.
30'Therefore you shall keep My ordinance,
so that *you* do not commit *any* of these abominable customs which were committed before
you, and that you do not defile yourselves by
them: I *am* the LORD your God.' "

> "You shall be holy,
> for I the LORD your
> God am holy."
> LEVITICUS 19:2

MORAL AND CEREMONIAL LAWS

19 And the LORD spoke to Moses, saying,
2"Speak to all the congregation of the
children of Israel, and say to them: 'You shall
be holy, for I the LORD
your God *am* holy.
3'Every one of you
shall revere his mother
and his father, and keep
My Sabbaths: I *am* the
LORD your God.
4'Do not turn to idols,
nor make for yourselves molded gods: I *am*
the LORD your God.

SOUL NOTE

A Sin Against God *(18:22)* This charge against homosexual relations appears in a section including rules against marital infidelity and bestiality. This is one of a number of passages in both testaments that, taken together and interpreted plainly, reveal that homosexual conduct is a great offense to God. It is called "an abomination." The Bible always regards it as a serious violation of God's plan for sexual expression. **Topic: Homosexuality**

SOUL NOTE

Honor and Respect *(19:3)* Respect for parents goes along with respect for God. Even when fully grown, children should honor and respect their parents, even if they haven't always been examples of godly parenting. When a mother and a father show respect for their parents, they set a good example for *their* children. God highly regards parenthood and its responsibilities. Parents should model their devotion to God through godly respect for their own parents. **Topic: Family Life**

5‘And if you offer a sacrifice of a peace offering to the LORD, you shall offer it of your own
free will. 6It shall be eaten the same day you
offer *it,* and on the next day. And if any remains until the third day, it shall be burned in
the fire. 7And if it is eaten at all on the third
day, it *is* an abomination. It shall not be accepted. 8Therefore *everyone* who eats it shall
bear his iniquity, because he has profaned the
hallowed *offering* of the LORD; and that person
shall be cut off from his people.

9‘When you reap the harvest of your land,
you shall not wholly reap the corners of your
field, nor shall you gather the gleanings of your
harvest. 10And you shall not glean your vineyard, nor shall you gather *every* grape of your
vineyard; you shall leave them for the poor and
the stranger: I *am* the LORD your God.

11‘You shall not steal, nor deal falsely, nor
lie to one another. 12And you shall not swear
by My name falsely, nor shall you profane the
name of your God: I *am* the LORD.

13‘You shall not cheat your neighbor, nor
rob *him.* The wages of him who is hired shall
not remain with you all night until morning.
14You shall not curse the deaf, nor put a stumbling block before the blind, but shall fear
your God: I *am* the LORD.

15‘You shall do no injustice in judgment.
You shall not be partial to the poor, nor honor
the person of the mighty. In righteousness you
shall judge your neighbor. 16You shall not go
about *as* a talebearer among your people; nor
shall you take a stand against the life of your
neighbor: I *am* the LORD.

17‘You shall not hate your brother in your
heart. You shall surely rebuke your neighbor,
and not bear sin because of him. 18You shall
not take vengeance, nor bear any grudge
against the children of your people, but you
shall love your neighbor as yourself: I *am* the
LORD.

19‘You shall keep My statutes. You shall not
let your livestock breed with another kind.
You shall not sow your field with mixed seed.
Nor shall a garment of mixed linen and wool
come upon you.

20‘Whoever lies carnally with a woman who
is betrothed to a man as a concubine, and who
has not at all been redeemed nor given her
freedom, for this there shall be scourging; *but*
they shall not be put to death, because she
was not free. 21And he shall bring his trespass
offering to the LORD, to the door of the tabernacle of meeting, a ram as a trespass offering.
22The priest shall make atonement for him
with the ram of the trespass offering before
the LORD for his sin which he has committed.
And the sin which he has committed shall be
forgiven him.

SOUL NOTE

Living Justly *(19:16)* The law was designed to help God's people live justly with one another. "You shall do no injustice," God commanded (19:15). In relation to this command, God tells them not to gossip. Gossip is a form of character assassination that reflects hatred (19:17). We should confront wrongdoing directly, not gossip with others about it. God expects us to live above our frustrations and to love our neighbors as ourselves (19:18). Jesus taught this same principle (Matt. 22:39).
Topic: Gossip

SOUL NOTE

Staying Pure *(19:29)* How can we help our children to stay pure in a world filled with sexual deviance and abuse? In an environment of sexual promiscuity, parents are responsible for protecting their children. God gave women and children great dignity and divine respect. The law in this passage warns fathers not to prostitute their daughters, a terrible form of child abuse. Parents must take seriously their duty of guarding their children's morals, teaching them about sexual purity and helping them to maintain it. **Topic: Abuse**

23‘When you come into the land, and have
planted all kinds of trees for food, then you
shall count their fruit as uncircumcised.
Three years it shall be as uncircumcised to
you. *It* shall not be eaten. 24But in the fourth
year all its fruit shall be holy, a praise to the
LORD. 25And in the fifth year you may eat its
fruit, that it may yield to you its increase: I *am*
the LORD your God.
26‘You shall not eat *anything* with the blood,
nor shall you practice divination or soothsaying. 27You shall not shave around the sides of
your head, nor shall you disfigure the edges of
your beard. 28You shall not make any cuttings
in your flesh for the dead, nor tattoo any
marks on you: I *am* the LORD.
29‘Do not prostitute your daughter, to cause
her to be a harlot, lest the land fall into harlotry, and the land become full of wickedness.
30‘You shall keep My Sabbaths and reverence My sanctuary: I *am* the LORD.
31‘Give no regard to mediums and familiar
spirits; do not seek after them, to be defiled by
them: I *am* the LORD your God.
32‘You shall rise before the gray headed and
honor the presence of an old man, and fear
your God: I *am* the LORD.
33‘And if a stranger dwells with you in your
land, you shall not mistreat him. 34The stranger who dwells among you shall be to you as
one born among you, and you shall love him
as yourself; for you were strangers in the land
of Egypt: I *am* the LORD your God.
35‘You shall do no injustice in judgment, in
measurement of length, weight, or volume.
36You shall have honest scales, honest weights,
an honest ephah, and an honest hin: I *am* the
LORD your God, who brought you out of the
land of Egypt.
37‘Therefore you shall observe all My statutes and all My judgments, and perform them:
I *am* the LORD.’ ”

PENALTIES FOR BREAKING THE LAW

20 Then the LORD spoke to Moses, saying,
2“Again, you shall say to the children
of Israel: ‘Whoever of the children of Israel, or
of the strangers who dwell in Israel, who gives
any of his descendants to Molech, he shall
surely be put to death. The people of the land
shall stone him with stones. 3I will set My face
against that man, and will cut him off from his
people, because he has given *some* of his descendants to Molech, to defile My sanctuary
and profane My holy name. 4And if the people
of the land should in any way hide their eyes
from the man, when he gives *some* of his descendants to Molech, and they do not kill him,
5then I will set My face against that man and
against his family; and I will cut him off from
his people, and all who prostitute themselves
with him to commit harlotry with Molech.

SOUL NOTE

Elder Care *(19:32)* God’s laws include prohibitions against disrespecting the elderly. The “gray headed” and the “old man” are to be treated with honor and respect. This treatment reflects a just society. The fact that laws are needed against elder abuse—physical, sexual, verbal, or financial—shows how far modern society has strayed from this basic attitude of respect. The Bible commands respect for one’s elders, who have much to teach from their vast experience. **Topic: Aging/Elderly**

SOUL NOTE

Which Craft? *(20:6–9)* Chapter 20 prohibits occult practices, including consulting mediums, practicing witchcraft, and sacrificing children. The prophet Samuel told King Saul that his rebellion was like the “sin of witchcraft” (1 Sam. 15:22, 23). In the Bible, rebellion is pictured as the work of Satan. What begins as a spirit of resistance often leads to a person’s spiritual downfall. God does not leave doubt about His moral and spiritual absolutes. His answer to the human dilemma is to keep Satan’s influence and attitudes far from us. **Topic: Occult**

6'And the person who turns to mediums and
familiar spirits, to prostitute himself with
them, I will set My face against that person
and cut him off from his people. 7Consecrate
yourselves therefore, and be holy, for I *am* the
LORD your God. 8And you shall keep My statutes, and perform them: I *am* the LORD who
sanctifies you.
9'For everyone who curses his father or his
mother shall surely be put to death. He has
cursed his father or his mother. His blood
shall be upon him.
10'The man who commits adultery with *another* man's wife, *he* who commits adultery
with his neighbor's wife, the adulterer and the
adulteress, shall surely be put to death. 11The
man who lies with his father's wife has uncovered his father's nakedness; both of them shall
surely be put to death. Their blood *shall be*
upon them. 12If a man lies with his daughter-
in-law, both of them shall surely be put to
death. They have committed perversion. Their
blood *shall be* upon them. 13If a man lies with a
male as he lies with a woman, both of them
have committed an abomination. They shall
surely be put to death. Their blood *shall be*
upon them. 14If a man marries a woman and
her mother, it *is* wickedness. They shall be
burned with fire, both he and they, that there
may be no wickedness among you. 15If a man
mates with an animal, he shall surely be put to
death, and you shall kill the animal. 16If a
woman approaches any animal and mates with
it, you shall kill the woman and the animal.
They shall surely be put to death. Their blood
is upon them.
17'If a man takes his sister, his father's
daughter or his mother's daughter, and sees
her nakedness and she sees his nakedness, it
is a wicked thing. And they shall be cut off in
the sight of their people. He has uncovered his
sister's nakedness. He shall bear his guilt. 18If
a man lies with a woman during her sickness
and uncovers her nakedness, he has exposed
her flow, and she has uncovered the flow of
her blood. Both of them shall be cut off from
their people.
19'You shall not uncover the nakedness of
your mother's sister nor of your father's sister,
for that would uncover his near of kin. They
shall bear their guilt. 20If a man lies with his
uncle's wife, he has uncovered his uncle's nakedness. They shall bear their sin; they shall
die childless. 21If a man takes his brother's
wife, it *is* an unclean thing. He has uncovered
his brother's nakedness. They shall be childless.
22'You shall therefore keep all My statutes
and all My judgments, and perform them, that
the land where I am bringing you to dwell
may not vomit you out. 23And you shall not
walk in the statutes of the nation which I am
casting out before you; for they commit all
these things, and therefore I abhor them. 24But
I have said to you, "You shall inherit their
land, and I will give it to you to possess, a land
flowing with milk and honey." I *am* the LORD
your God, who has separated you from the
peoples. 25You shall therefore distinguish between clean animals and unclean, between
unclean birds and clean, and you shall not
make yourselves abominable by beast or by
bird, or by any kind of living thing that creeps
on the ground, which I have separated from
you as unclean. 26And you shall be holy to Me,
for I the LORD *am* holy, and have separated
you from the peoples, that you should be
Mine.
27'A man or a woman who is a medium, or
who has familiar spirits, shall surely be put to
death; they shall stone them with stones.
Their blood *shall be* upon them.' "

REGULATIONS FOR CONDUCT OF PRIESTS

21 And the LORD said to Moses, "Speak to
the priests, the sons of Aaron, and say
to them: 'None shall defile himself for the
dead among his people, 2except for his relatives who are nearest to him: his mother, his
father, his son, his daughter, and his brother;
3also his virgin sister who is near to him, who
has had no husband, for her he may defile
himself. 4*Otherwise* he shall not defile himself,
being a chief man among his people, to profane himself.
5'They shall not make any bald *place* on
their heads, nor shall they shave the edges of
their beards nor make any cuttings in their
flesh. 6They shall be holy to their God and not
profane the name of their God, for they offer
the offerings of the LORD made by fire, *and* the
bread of their God; therefore they shall be
holy. 7They shall not take a wife *who is* a harlot or a defiled woman, nor shall they take a
woman divorced from her husband; for *the
priest*[a] is holy to his God. 8Therefore you shall

21:7 [a]Literally *he*

consecrate him, for he offers the bread of your
God. He shall be holy to you, for I the LORD,
who sanctify you, *am* holy. 9The daughter of
any priest, if she profanes herself by playing
the harlot, she profanes her father. She shall
be burned with fire.
10'*He who is* the high priest among his brethren, on whose head the anointing oil was
poured and who is consecrated to wear the
garments, shall not uncover his head nor tear
his clothes; 11nor shall he go near any dead
body, nor defile himself for his father or his
mother; 12nor shall he go out of the sanctuary,
nor profane the sanctuary of his God; for the
consecration of the anointing oil of his God *is*
upon him: I *am* the LORD. 13And he shall take
a wife in her virginity. 14A widow or a divorced woman or a defiled woman *or* a harlot—these he shall not marry; but he shall
take a virgin of his own people as wife. 15Nor
shall he profane his posterity among his people, for I the LORD sanctify him.' "
16And the LORD spoke to Moses, saying,
17"Speak to Aaron, saying: 'No man of your
descendants in *succeeding* generations, who
has *any* defect, may approach to offer the
bread of his God. 18For any man who has a defect shall not approach: a man blind or lame,
who has a marred *face* or any *limb* too long,
19a man who has a broken foot or broken
hand, 20or is a hunchback or a dwarf, or *a*
man who has a defect in his eye, or eczema or
scab, or is a eunuch. 21No man of the descendants of Aaron the priest, who has a defect,
shall come near to offer the offerings made by
fire to the LORD. He has a defect; he shall not
come near to offer the bread of his God. 22He
may eat the bread of his God, *both* the most
holy and the holy; 23only he shall not go near
the veil or approach the altar, because he has
a defect, lest he profane My sanctuaries; for I
the LORD sanctify them.' "
24And Moses told *it* to Aaron and his sons,
and to all the children of Israel.

22 Then the LORD spoke to Moses, saying,
2"Speak to Aaron and his sons, that
they separate themselves from the holy things
of the children of Israel, and that they do not
profane My holy name *by* what they dedicate
to Me: I *am* the LORD. 3Say to them: 'Whoever
of all your descendants throughout your generations, who goes near the holy things which
the children of Israel dedicate to the LORD,
while he has uncleanness upon him, that person shall be cut off from My presence: I *am*
the LORD.
4'Whatever man of the descendants of
Aaron, who *is* a leper or has a discharge, shall
not eat the holy offerings until he is clean.
And whoever touches anything made unclean
by a corpse, or a man who has had an emission of semen, 5or whoever touches any
creeping thing by which he would be made
unclean, or any person by whom he would
become unclean, whatever his uncleanness
may be— 6the person who has touched any
such thing shall be unclean until evening, and
shall not eat the holy *offerings* unless he
washes his body with water. 7And when the
sun goes down he shall be clean; and afterward he may eat the holy *offerings,* because it
is his food. 8Whatever dies *naturally* or is torn
by beasts he shall not eat, to defile himself
with it: I *am* the LORD.
9'They shall therefore keep My ordinance,
lest they bear sin for it and die thereby, if they
profane it: I the LORD sanctify them.
10'No outsider shall eat the holy *offering;*
one who dwells with the priest, or a hired servant, shall not eat the holy thing. 11But if the
priest buys a person with his money, he may
eat it; and one who is born in his house may
eat his food. 12If the priest's daughter is married to an outsider, she may not eat of the holy
offerings. 13But if the priest's daughter is a
widow or divorced, and has no child, and has
returned to her father's house as in her youth,
she may eat her father's food; but no outsider
shall eat it.
14'And if a man eats the holy *offering* unintentionally, then he shall restore a holy *offer-*
ing to the priest, and add one-fifth to it. 15They
shall not profane the holy *offerings* of the children of Israel, which they offer to the LORD,
16or allow them to bear the guilt of trespass
when they eat their holy *offerings;* for I the
LORD sanctify them.' "

Offerings Accepted and Not Accepted

17And the LORD spoke to Moses, saying,
18"Speak to Aaron and his sons, and to all the
children of Israel, and say to them: 'Whatever
man of the house of Israel, or of the strangers
in Israel, who offers his sacrifice for any of his
vows or for any of his freewill offerings, which
they offer to the LORD as a burnt offering—
19*you shall offer* of your own free will a male
without blemish from the cattle, from the

sheep, or from the goats. 20Whatever has a defect, you shall not offer, for it shall not be acceptable on your behalf. 21And whoever offers a sacrifice of a peace offering to the LORD, to fulfill *his* vow, or a freewill offering from the cattle or the sheep, it must be perfect to be accepted; there shall be no defect in it. 22Those *that are* blind or broken or maimed, or have an ulcer or eczema or scabs, you shall not offer to the LORD, nor make an offering by fire of them on the altar to the LORD. 23Either a bull or a lamb that has any limb too long or too short you may offer *as* a freewill offering, but for a vow it shall not be accepted.

24'You shall not offer to the LORD what is bruised or crushed, or torn or cut; nor shall you make *any offering of them* in your land. 25Nor from a foreigner's hand shall you offer any of these as the bread of your God, because their corruption *is* in them, *and* defects *are* in them. They shall not be accepted on your behalf.' "

26And the LORD spoke to Moses, saying: 27"When a bull or a sheep or a goat is born, it shall be seven days with its mother; and from the eighth day and thereafter it shall be accepted as an offering made by fire to the LORD. 28*Whether it is* a cow or ewe, do not kill both her and her young on the same day. 29And when you offer a sacrifice of thanksgiving to the LORD, offer *it* of your own free will. 30On the same day it shall be eaten; you shall leave none of it until morning: I *am* the LORD.

31"Therefore you shall keep My commandments, and perform them: I *am* the LORD. 32You shall not profane My holy name, but I will be hallowed among the children of Israel. I *am* the LORD who sanctifies you, 33who brought you out of the land of Egypt, to be your God: I *am* the LORD."

FEASTS OF THE LORD

23 And the LORD spoke to Moses, saying, 2"Speak to the children of Israel, and say to them: 'The feasts of the LORD, which you shall proclaim *to be* holy convocations, these *are* My feasts.

THE SABBATH

3'Six days shall work be done, but the seventh day *is* a Sabbath of solemn rest, a holy convocation. You shall do no work *on it;* it *is* the Sabbath of the LORD in all your dwellings.

THE PASSOVER AND UNLEAVENED BREAD

4'These *are* the feasts of the LORD, holy convocations which you shall proclaim at their appointed times. 5On the fourteenth *day* of the first month at twilight *is* the LORD's Passover. 6And on the fifteenth day of the same month *is* the Feast of Unleavened Bread to the LORD; seven days you must eat unleavened bread. 7On the first day you shall have a holy convocation; you shall do no customary work on it. 8But you shall offer an offering made by fire to the LORD for seven days. The seventh day *shall be* a holy convocation; you shall do no customary work *on it.*' "

THE FEAST OF FIRSTFRUITS

9And the LORD spoke to Moses, saying, 10"Speak to the children of Israel, and say to them: 'When you come into the land which I give to you, and reap its harvest, then you shall bring a sheaf of the firstfruits of your harvest to the priest. 11He shall wave the sheaf before the LORD, to be accepted on your behalf; on the day after the Sabbath the priest shall wave it. 12And you shall offer on that day, when you wave the sheaf, a male lamb of the first year, without blemish, as a burnt offering to the LORD. 13Its grain offering *shall be* two-tenths *of an ephah* of fine flour mixed with oil, an offering made by fire to the LORD, for a sweet aroma; and its drink offering *shall be* of wine, one-fourth of a hin. 14You shall eat neither bread nor parched grain nor fresh grain until the same day that you have brought an offering to your God; *it shall be* a statute forever throughout your generations in all your dwellings.

THE FEAST OF WEEKS

15'And you shall count for yourselves from the day after the Sabbath, from the day that you brought the sheaf of the wave offering: seven Sabbaths shall be completed. 16Count fifty days to the day after the seventh Sabbath; then you shall offer a new grain offering to the LORD. 17You shall bring from your dwellings two wave *loaves* of two-tenths *of an ephah.* They shall be of fine flour; they shall be baked with leaven. *They are* the firstfruits to the LORD. 18And you shall offer with the bread seven lambs of the first year, without blemish, one young bull, and two rams. They shall be *as* a burnt offering to the LORD, with their

grain offering and their drink offerings, an offering made by fire for a sweet aroma to the
LORD. 19Then you shall sacrifice one kid of the
goats as a sin offering, and two male lambs of
the first year as a sacrifice of a peace offering.
20The priest shall wave them with the bread of
the firstfruits *as* a wave offering before the
LORD, with the two lambs. They shall be holy
to the LORD for the priest. 21And you shall proclaim on the same day *that* it is a holy convocation to you. You shall do no customary work
on it. It shall be a statute forever in all your
dwellings throughout your generations.

22'When you reap the harvest of your land,
you shall not wholly reap the corners of your
field when you reap, nor shall you gather any
gleaning from your harvest. You shall leave
them for the poor and for the stranger: I *am*
the LORD your God.' "

THE FEAST OF TRUMPETS

23Then the LORD spoke to Moses, saying,
24"Speak to the children of Israel, saying: 'In
the seventh month, on the first *day* of the
month, you shall have a sabbath-*rest*, a memorial of blowing of trumpets, a holy convocation. 25You shall do no customary work *on
it;* and you shall offer an offering made by fire
to the LORD.' "

THE DAY OF ATONEMENT

26And the LORD spoke to Moses, saying:
27"Also the tenth *day* of this seventh month
shall be the Day of Atonement. It shall be a
holy convocation for you; you shall afflict your
souls, and offer an offering made by fire to the
LORD. 28And you shall do no work on that same
day, for it *is* the Day of Atonement, to make
atonement for you before the LORD your God.
29For any person who is not afflicted *in soul* on
that same day shall be cut off from his people.
30And any person who does any work on that
same day, that person I will destroy from
among his people. 31You shall do no manner of
work; *it shall be* a statute forever throughout
your generations in all your dwellings. 32It *shall
be* to you a sabbath of *solemn* rest, and you
shall afflict your souls; on the ninth *day* of the
month at evening, from evening to evening,
you shall celebrate your sabbath."

THE FEAST OF TABERNACLES

33Then the LORD spoke to Moses, saying,
34"Speak to the children of Israel, saying: 'The
fifteenth day of this seventh month *shall be*
the Feast of Tabernacles *for* seven days to the
LORD. 35On the first day *there shall be* a holy
convocation. You shall do no customary work
on it. 36*For* seven days you shall offer an offering made by fire to the LORD. On the eighth
day you shall have a holy convocation, and
you shall offer an offering made by fire to the
LORD. It *is* a sacred assembly, *and* you shall do
no customary work *on it.*

37'These *are* the feasts of the LORD which
you shall proclaim *to be* holy convocations, to
offer an offering made by fire to the LORD, a
burnt offering and a grain offering, a sacrifice
and drink offerings, everything on its day—
38besides the Sabbaths of the LORD, besides
your gifts, besides all your vows, and besides
all your freewill offerings which you give to
the LORD.

39'Also on the fifteenth day of the seventh
month, when you have gathered in the fruit of
the land, you shall keep the feast of the LORD
for seven days; on the first day *there shall be* a
sabbath-*rest*, and on the eighth day a sabbath-
rest. 40And you shall take for yourselves on the
first day the fruit of beautiful trees, branches
of palm trees, the boughs of leafy trees, and
willows of the brook; and you shall rejoice
before the LORD your God for seven days.
41You shall keep it as a feast to the LORD for
seven days in the year. *It shall be* a statute forever in your generations. You shall celebrate it
in the seventh month. 42You shall dwell in
booths for seven days. All who are native Israelites shall dwell in booths, 43that your generations may know that I made the children of
Israel dwell in booths when I brought them
out of the land of Egypt: I *am* the LORD your
God.' "

44So Moses declared to the children of Israel
the feasts of the LORD.

CARE OF THE TABERNACLE LAMPS

24 Then the LORD spoke to Moses, saying:
2"Command the children of Israel that
they bring to you pure oil of pressed olives for
the light, to make the lamps burn continually.
3Outside the veil of the Testimony, in the tabernacle of meeting, Aaron shall be in charge of
it from evening until morning before the LORD
continually; *it shall be* a statute forever in
your generations. 4He shall be in charge of the
lamps on the pure *gold* lampstand before the
LORD continually.

THE BREAD OF THE TABERNACLE

5"And you shall take fine flour and bake twelve cakes with it. Two-tenths *of an ephah* shall be in each cake. 6You shall set them in two rows, six in a row, on the pure *gold* table before the LORD. 7And you shall put pure frankincense on *each* row, that it may be on the bread for a memorial, an offering made by fire to the LORD. 8Every Sabbath he shall set it in order before the LORD continually, *being taken* from the children of Israel by an everlasting covenant. 9And it shall be for Aaron and his sons, and they shall eat it in a holy place; for it *is* most holy to him from the offerings of the LORD made by fire, by a perpetual statute."

THE PENALTY FOR BLASPHEMY

10Now the son of an Israelite woman, whose father *was* an Egyptian, went out among the children of Israel; and this Israelite *woman's* son and a man of Israel fought each other in the camp. 11And the Israelite woman's son blasphemed the name *of the LORD* and cursed; and so they brought him to Moses. (His mother's name *was* Shelomith the daughter of Dibri, of the tribe of Dan.) 12Then they put him in custody, that the mind of the LORD might be shown to them.

13And the LORD spoke to Moses, saying, 14"Take outside the camp him who has cursed; then let all who heard *him* lay their hands on his head, and let all the congregation stone him.

15"Then you shall speak to the children of Israel, saying: 'Whoever curses his God shall bear his sin. 16And whoever blasphemes the name of the LORD shall surely be put to death. All the congregation shall certainly stone him, the stranger as well as him who is born in the land. When he blasphemes the name *of the LORD,* he shall be put to death.

17'Whoever kills any man shall surely be put to death. 18Whoever kills an animal shall make it good, animal for animal.

19'If a man causes disfigurement of his neighbor, as he has done, so shall it be done to him— 20fracture for fracture, eye for eye, tooth for tooth; as he has caused disfigurement of a man, so shall it be done to him. 21And whoever kills an animal shall restore it; but whoever kills a man shall be put to death. 22You shall have the same law for the stranger and for one from your own country; for I *am* the LORD your God.' "

23Then Moses spoke to the children of Israel; and they took outside the camp him who had cursed, and stoned him with stones. So the children of Israel did as the LORD commanded Moses.

THE SABBATH OF THE SEVENTH YEAR

25 And the LORD spoke to Moses on Mount Sinai, saying, 2"Speak to the children of Israel, and say to them: 'When you come into the land which I give you, then the land shall keep a sabbath to the LORD. 3Six years you shall sow your field, and six years you shall prune your vineyard, and gather its fruit; 4but in the seventh year there shall be a sabbath of solemn rest for the land, a sabbath to the LORD. You shall neither sow your field nor prune your vineyard. 5What grows of its own accord of your harvest you shall not reap, nor gather the grapes of your untended vine, *for* it is a year of rest for the land. 6And the sabbath *produce* of the land shall be food for you: for you, your male and female servants, your hired man, and the stranger who dwells with you, 7for your livestock and the beasts that *are* in your land—all its produce shall be for food.

THE YEAR OF JUBILEE

8'And you shall count seven sabbaths of years for yourself, seven times seven years; and the time of the seven sabbaths of years shall be to you forty-nine years. 9Then you shall cause the trumpet of the Jubilee to sound on the tenth *day* of the seventh month; on the Day of Atonement you shall make the trumpet to sound throughout all your land. 10And you shall consecrate the fiftieth year, and proclaim liberty throughout *all* the land to all its inhabitants. It shall be a Jubilee for you; and each of you shall return to his possession, and each of you shall return to his family. 11That fiftieth year shall be a Jubilee to you; in it you shall neither sow nor reap what grows of its own accord, nor gather *the grapes* of your untended vine. 12For it *is* the Jubilee; it shall be holy to you; you shall eat its produce from the field.

13'In this Year of Jubilee, each of you shall return to his possession. 14And if you sell anything to your neighbor or buy from your neighbor's hand, you shall not oppress one another. 15According to the number of years after the Jubilee you shall buy from your neighbor, and according to the number of years of crops he shall sell to you. [16]According to the multitude of years you shall increase its price, and according to the fewer number of years you shall diminish its price; for he sells to you *according* to the number *of the years* of the crops. [17]Therefore you shall not oppress one another, but you shall fear your God; for I *am* the LORD your God.

Provisions for the Seventh Year

[18]'So you shall observe My statutes and keep My judgments, and perform them; and you will dwell in the land in safety. [19]Then the land will yield its fruit, and you will eat your fill, and dwell there in safety.

[20]'And if you say, "What shall we eat in the seventh year, since we shall not sow nor gather in our produce?" [21]Then I will command My blessing on you in the sixth year, and it will bring forth produce enough for three years. [22]And you shall sow in the eighth year, and eat old produce until the ninth year; until its produce comes in, you shall eat *of* the old *harvest*.

Redemption of Property

[23]'The land shall not be sold permanently, for the land *is* Mine; for you *are* strangers and sojourners with Me. [24]And in all the land of your possession you shall grant redemption of the land.

[25]'If one of your brethren becomes poor, and has sold *some* of his possession, and if his redeeming relative comes to redeem it, then he may redeem what his brother sold. [26]Or if the man has no one to redeem it, but he himself becomes able to redeem it, [27]then let him count the years since its sale, and restore the remainder to the man to whom he sold it, that he may return to his possession. [28]But if he is not able to have *it* restored to himself, then what was sold shall remain in the hand of him who bought it until the Year of Jubilee; and in the Jubilee it shall be released, and he shall return to his possession.

[29]'If a man sells a house in a walled city, then he may redeem it within a whole year after it is sold; *within* a full year he may redeem it. [30]But if it is not redeemed within the space of a full year, then the house in the walled city shall belong permanently to him who bought it, throughout his generations. It shall not be released in the Jubilee. [31]However the houses of villages which have no wall around them shall be counted as the fields of the country. They may be redeemed, and they shall be released in the Jubilee. [32]Nevertheless the cities of the Levites, *and* the houses in the cities of their possession, the Levites may redeem at any time. [33]And if a man purchases a house from the Levites, then the house that was sold in the city of his possession shall be released in the Jubilee; for the houses in the cities of the Levites *are* their possession among the children of Israel. [34]But the field of the common-land of their cities may not be sold, for it *is* their perpetual possession.

Lending to the Poor

[35]'If one of your brethren becomes poor, and falls into poverty among you, then you shall help him, like a stranger or a sojourner, that he may live with you. [36]Take no usury or interest from him; but fear your God, that your brother may live with you. [37]You shall not lend him your money for usury, nor lend him your food at a profit. [38]I *am* the LORD your God, who brought you out of the land of Egypt, to give you the land of Canaan *and* to be your God.

The Law Concerning Slavery

[39]'And if *one of* your brethren *who dwells* by you becomes poor, and sells himself to you, you shall not compel him to serve as a slave. [40]As a hired servant *and* a sojourner he shall be with you, *and* shall serve you until the Year of Jubilee. [41]And *then* he shall depart from you—he and his children with him—and shall return to his own family. He shall return to the possession of his fathers. [42]For they *are* My servants, whom I brought out of the land of Egypt; they shall not be sold as slaves. [43]You shall not rule over him with rigor, but you shall fear your God. [44]And as for your male and female slaves whom you may have—from the nations that are around you, from them you may buy male and female slaves. [45]Moreover you may buy the children of the strangers who dwell among you, and their families who are with you, which they beget in your land; and they shall become your property. [46]And you may take them as an inheritance for your children after you, to inherit *them as* a possession; they shall be your permanent slaves. But regarding your brethren, the children of Israel, you shall not rule over one another with rigor.

[47]'Now if a sojourner or stranger close to you becomes rich, and *one of* your brethren

who dwells by him becomes poor, and sells
himself to the stranger *or* sojourner close to
you, or to a member of the stranger's family,
48after he is sold he may be redeemed again.
One of his brothers may redeem him; 49or his
uncle or his uncle's son may redeem him; or
anyone who is near of kin to him in his family
may redeem him; or if he is able he may redeem himself. 50Thus he shall reckon with
him who bought him: The price of his release
shall be according to the number of years,
from the year that he was sold to him until the
Year of Jubilee; *it shall be* according to the
time of a hired servant for him. 51If *there are*
still many years *remaining,* according to them
he shall repay the price of his redemption
from the money with which he was bought.
52And if there remain but a few years until the
Year of Jubilee, then he shall reckon with him,
and according to his years he shall repay him
the price of his redemption. 53He shall be with
him as a yearly hired servant, and he shall not
rule with rigor over him in your sight. 54And if
he is not redeemed in these *years,* then he
shall be released in the Year of Jubilee—he
and his children with him. 55For the children
of Israel *are* servants to Me; they *are* My servants whom I brought out of the land of
Egypt: I *am* the LORD your God.

PROMISE OF BLESSING AND RETRIBUTION

26 'You shall not make idols for
yourselves;
neither a carved image nor a *sacred* pillar
shall you rear up for yourselves;
nor shall you set up an engraved stone in
your land, to bow down to it;
for I *am* the LORD your God.
2 You shall keep My Sabbaths and reverence My sanctuary:
I *am* the LORD.

3 'If you walk in My statutes and keep My
commandments, and perform them,
4 then I will give you rain in its season, the
land shall yield its produce, and the
trees of the field shall yield their fruit.
5 Your threshing shall last till the time of
vintage, and the vintage shall last till
the time of sowing;

KEY PASSAGE

Knowing God

THE GOD WHO CAN BE KNOWN

(26:9–13)

God delivered the Israelites from bondage in Egypt that they might know Him personally. His laws were designed to protect and bless them in their new land. He promised:

- to confirm His covenant with them,
- to set His tabernacle among them, and
- to walk among them and be their God (26:9, 11, 12).

God's commitments to Israel reflect His soul care for them. "My soul shall not abhor you," He assured them (26:11). God also promises that He will never turn His back on us and forsake us. As with Israel, God has

- a covenant with us (Luke 22:20),
- a temple within us (1 Cor. 6:19), and
- a presence among us (Matt. 28:20).

God's expressions of love and grace toward Israel were the responses of His heart toward them. He wanted to know them personally. God also wants to know us personally.

To Learn More: Turn to the article about knowing God on pages 164, 165. See also the personality profile of the Ethiopian eunuch on page 1430.

you shall eat your bread to the full, and
dwell in your land safely.
6 I will give peace in the land, and you shall
lie down, and none will make *you*
afraid;
I will rid the land of evil beasts,
and the sword will not go through your
land.
7 You will chase your enemies, and they
shall fall by the sword before you.
8 Five of you shall chase a hundred, and a
hundred of you shall put ten thousand
to flight;
your enemies shall fall by the sword before you.

9 'For I will look on you favorably and make
you fruitful, multiply you and confirm
My covenant with you.
10 You shall eat the old harvest, and clear
out the old because of the new.
11 I will set My tabernacle among you, and
My soul shall not abhor you.
12 I will walk among you and be your God,
and you shall be
My people.
13 I *am* the LORD
your God, who
brought you out
of the land of
Egypt, that *you*
should not be
their slaves;
I have broken the bands of your yoke and
made you walk upright.

14 'But if you do not obey Me, and do not
observe all these commandments,
15 and if you despise My statutes, or if your
soul abhors My judgments, so that
you do not perform all My commandments, *but* break My covenant,
16 I also will do this to you:
I will even appoint terror over you, wasting disease and fever which shall consume the eyes and cause sorrow of
heart.
And you shall sow your seed in vain, for
your enemies shall eat it.
17 I will set My face against you, and you
shall be defeated by your enemies.
Those who hate you shall reign over you,
and you shall flee when no one pursues you.

18 'And after all this, if you do not obey Me,
then I will punish you seven times
more for your sins.
19 I will break the pride of your power;
I will make your heavens like iron and
your earth like bronze.
20 And your strength shall be spent in vain;
for your land shall not yield its produce,
nor shall the trees of the land yield
their fruit.

21 'Then, if you walk contrary to Me, and are
not willing to obey Me, I will bring on
you seven times more plagues, according to your sins.
22 I will also send wild beasts among you,
which shall rob you of your children,
destroy your livestock, and make you
few in number;
and your highways shall be desolate.

23 'And if by these things you are not reformed by Me, but walk contrary
to Me,
24 then I also will walk
contrary to you,
and I will punish
you yet seven
times for your
sins.
25 And I will bring a
sword against you
that will execute
the vengeance of the covenant;
when you are gathered together within
your cities I will send pestilence
among you;
and you shall be delivered into the hand
of the enemy.
26 When I have cut off your supply of bread,
ten women shall bake your bread in
one oven, and they shall bring back
your bread by weight, and you shall
eat and not be satisfied.

27 'And after all this, if you do not obey Me,
but walk contrary to Me,
28 then I also will walk contrary to you in
fury;
and I, even I, will chastise you seven
times for your sins.
29 You shall eat the flesh of your sons, and
you shall eat the flesh of your daughters.

"I will set My tabernacle among you,
and My soul shall not abhor you.
I will walk among you and be your
God, and you shall be My people."
LEVITICUS 26:11, 12

KNOWING GOD

LARRY CRABB

(Leviticus 26:9–13)

Theology becomes rich only when it survives the onslaught of pain. A sound theology leads us through our pain to a fuller experience of God and, therefore, a fuller experience of faith, hope, and love. We learn to enjoy God more than anyone or anything else.

Pain that can open our hearts to search for God is deep pain. Such pain is not the peevish pain of a grumbler who mutters or mumbles in discontent. It is not the angry pain of a narcissist who finds out that being self-centered has consequences. It is not the usual psychological hurt we hear so much about today that creates a thirst for nothing more than liking ourselves better and enjoying life more. Rather, it is the pain of those who want to enjoy pleasures they cannot find and who fear that misery seems inevitable and perhaps deserved.

Pain makes people stand still and think about something outside of themselves, something more important and more interesting than their own concerns about who they are and how they are getting on. Pain compels people to ask terrifying questions about themselves, life, and God.

WHAT REALLY MATTERS?

When helping people to feel loved and worthwhile has become the central mission of the church, God is used more than worshiped—and that doesn't work. We are learning not to worship God in self-denial and costly service, but to heal our memories, overcome our addictions, lift our depressions, improve our self-images, establish self-preserving boundaries, substitute self-love for self-hatred, and replace our shame with affirming acceptance of who we are.

Recovery from pain is absorbing an increasing share of the church's energy. And that is alarming. Although the gospel does bless us with a new identity that was meant to be enjoyed, it calls us to higher values. The gospel teaches self-acceptance, values like turning the other cheek, esteeming others as greater than ourselves, going the second mile, enduring rejection and persecution, living not for the pleasures of this life but for those of the next, and clinging to the promises of God when we do not feel His goodness.

We need a way of handling our lives that combines a passionate sensitivity to our deepest struggles with a tender insistence that something matters more than how we feel. It is healthy to face the pain in our souls, to feel bad when others violate our dignity, to admit to ourselves how desperately we long to feel loved and valued and accepted as we are. But, in the middle of all this, we need to remember that the point of Christianity is not us, but the *God who cares for us*. Our hunger does not obligate God. He is not a waiter who, at the snap of our fingers, runs out of heaven's kitchen loaded down with trays of food to fill our empty stomachs. With His blood, Christ purchased a people for God and made us priests to serve Him. *We exist for Him*, not the other way around.

HOW DO WE FIND GOD?

Many people have become more committed to relieving the pain behind their problems than using that pain to wrestle more passionately with the character and purposes of God. Feeling better has become more important than finding God. As a result, many happily camp on biblical ideas that help them feel loved and accepted, and they pass over scriptures that call them to higher ground. They focus on themselves instead of on the stunning revelation of a God gracious enough to love people who hated Him, a God worthy to be honored above everyone and everything else.

God invites us to enter into a relationship with Him on His terms. He invites us to join Him in achieving His great purpose: the overthrowing of evil and the bringing together of all things in Christ. He invites us, in short, to find *Him*. And He lets us know that in the process of finding Him, we will find ourselves.

We must, however, do more than superficially agree that finding God is a higher priority than solving our problems. Somehow that purpose must reach our hearts until the reality of God crowds out every other reality. Until we are moved to know Him with a passion that we feel nowhere else, we will not use the struggles of life as an impetus to find God. Until our passion for finding God is deeper than any other passion, we will arrange our lives according to our taste, not God's.

To feel a deep, throbbing passion about our well-being in this world is as natural as breathing. And nothing is wrong with that, *unless we feel no deeper passion*. God has told us to love Him with a passion that exceeds all other passions. Until we chase after God like a thirsty deer looking for water, pursuing Him with passion, we will not find Him. We cannot talk about loving God until we come to grips with our raging passion for ourselves. We cannot and will not love anyone but ourselves until we meet God in a way that stirs us to race after Him with a single-minded intensity to get to know Him.

God knows everything about us. He is aware of our struggles and longs for us to know Him through His Son, Jesus Christ. He is the answer to our problems. To believe in Christ is *faith*. To wait for Him is *hope*. To serve Him is *love*. That is what it means to find God. It is a passion to trust a sovereign Savior who will reveal the Father in response to faith in Him.

FURTHER MEDITATION:

Other passages to study about the issue of knowing God include:

- ➢ Exodus 20:1–3
- ➢ Psalms 14; 15
- ➢ Hosea 6:1–3
- ➢ John 1:1–3; 3:16; 14:7–11
- ➢ Hebrews 12:29
- ➢ 1 John 3:20; 4:7–10

To Learn More: Turn to the key passage note on knowing God at Leviticus 26:9–13 on page 162. See also the personality profile of the Ethiopian eunuch on page 1430.

30 I will destroy your high places, cut down
your incense altars, and cast your carcasses on the lifeless forms of your
idols;
and My soul shall abhor you.
31 I will lay your cities waste and bring your
sanctuaries to desolation, and I will
not smell the fragrance of your sweet
aromas.
32 I will bring the land to desolation, and
your enemies who dwell in it shall be
astonished at it.
33 I will scatter you among the nations and
draw out a sword after you;
your land shall be desolate and your cities waste.
34 Then the land shall enjoy its sabbaths as
long as it lies desolate and you *are* in
your enemies' land;
then the land shall rest and enjoy its sabbaths.
35 As long as *it* lies desolate it shall rest—
for the time it did not rest on your sabbaths when you dwelt in it.

36 'And as for those of you who are left, I will
send faintness into their hearts in the
lands of their enemies;
the sound of a shaken leaf shall cause
them to flee;
they shall flee as though fleeing from a
sword, and they shall fall when no one
pursues.
37 They shall stumble over one another, as
it were before a sword, when no one
pursues;
and you shall have no *power* to stand before your enemies.
38 You shall perish among the nations, and
the land of your enemies shall eat you
up.
39 And those of you who are left shall waste
away in their iniquity in your enemies'
lands;
also in their fathers' iniquities, which are
with them, they shall waste away.

40 '*But* if they confess their iniquity and the
iniquity of their fathers, with their unfaithfulness in which they were unfaithful to Me, and that they also have
walked contrary to Me,
41 and *that* I also have walked contrary to
them and have brought them into the
land of their enemies;
if their uncircumcised hearts are humbled, and they accept their guilt—
42 then I will remember My covenant with
Jacob, and My covenant with Isaac
and My covenant with Abraham I will
remember;
I will remember the land.
43 The land also shall be left empty by them,
and will enjoy its sabbaths while it lies
desolate without them;
they will accept their guilt, because they
despised My judgments and because
their soul abhorred My statutes.
44 Yet for all that, when they are in the land
of their enemies, I will not cast them
away, nor shall I abhor them, to utterly destroy them and break My covenant with them;
for I *am* the LORD their God.
45 But for their sake I will remember the
covenant of their ancestors, whom I
brought out of the land of Egypt in the
sight of the nations, that I might be
their God:
I *am* the LORD.' "

46These *are* the statutes and judgments and
laws which the LORD made between Himself
and the children of Israel on Mount Sinai by
the hand of Moses.

REDEEMING PERSONS AND PROPERTY DEDICATED TO GOD

27 Now the LORD spoke to Moses, saying,
2"Speak to the children of Israel, and
say to them: 'When a man consecrates by a
vow certain persons to the LORD, according to
your valuation, 3if your valuation is of a male
from twenty years old up to sixty years old,
then your valuation shall be fifty shekels of
silver, according to the shekel of the sanctuary. 4If it *is* a female, then your valuation shall
be thirty shekels; 5and if from five years old up
to twenty years old, then your valuation for a
male shall be twenty shekels, and for a female
ten shekels; 6and if from a month old up to
five years old, then your valuation for a male
shall be five shekels of silver, and for a female
your valuation shall be three shekels of silver;
7and if from sixty years old and above, if *it is* a
male, then your valuation shall be fifteen
shekels, and for a female ten shekels.
8'But if he is too poor to pay your valuation,

then he shall present himself before the priest,
and the priest shall set a value for him; according to the ability of him who vowed, the
priest shall value him.

9'If *it is* an animal that men may bring as an
offering to the LORD, all that *anyone* gives to
the LORD shall be holy. 10He shall not substitute it or exchange it, good for bad or bad for
good; and if he at all exchanges animal for
animal, then both it and the one exchanged
for it shall be holy. 11If *it is* an unclean animal
which they do not offer as a sacrifice to the
LORD, then he shall present the animal before
the priest; 12and the priest shall set a value for
it, whether it is good or bad; as you, the priest,
value it, so it shall be. 13But if he *wants* at all
to redeem it, then he must add one-fifth to
your valuation.

14'And when a man dedicates his house *to
be* holy to the LORD, then the priest shall set a
value for it, whether it is good or bad; as the
priest values it, so it shall stand. 15If he who
dedicated it *wants to* redeem his house, then
he must add one-fifth of the money of your
valuation to it, and it shall be his.

16'If a man dedicates to the LORD *part* of a
field of his possession, then your valuation
shall be according to the seed for it. A homer
of barley seed *shall be valued* at fifty shekels
of silver. 17If he dedicates his field from the
Year of Jubilee, according to your valuation it
shall stand. 18But if he dedicates his field after
the Jubilee, then the priest shall reckon to him
the money due according to the years that
remain till the Year of Jubilee, and it shall be
deducted from your valuation. 19And if he
who dedicates the field ever wishes to redeem
it, then he must add one-fifth of the money of
your valuation to it, and it shall belong to him.
20But if he does not want to redeem the field,
or if he has sold the field to another man, it
shall not be redeemed anymore; 21but the
field, when it is released in the Jubilee, shall
be holy to the LORD, as a devoted field; it shall
be the possession of the priest.

22'And if a man dedicates to the LORD a field
which he has bought, which is not the field of
his possession, 23then the priest shall reckon
to him the worth of your valuation, up to the
Year of Jubilee, and he shall give your valuation on that day *as* a holy *offering* to the LORD.
24In the Year of Jubilee the field shall return to
him from whom it was bought, to the one who
owned the land as a possession. 25And all your
valuations shall be according to the shekel of
the sanctuary: twenty gerahs to the shekel.

26'But the firstborn of the animals, which
should be the LORD's firstborn, no man shall
dedicate; whether *it is* an ox or sheep, it *is* the
LORD's. 27And if *it is* an unclean animal, then
he shall redeem *it* according to your valuation,
and shall add one-fifth to it; or if it is not
redeemed, then it shall be sold according to
your valuation.

28'Nevertheless no devoted *offering* that a
man may devote to the LORD of all that he has,
both man and beast, or the field of his possession, shall be sold or redeemed; every devoted
offering is most holy to the LORD. 29No person
under the ban, who may become doomed to
destruction among men, shall be redeemed,
but shall surely be put to death. 30And all the
tithe of the land, *whether* of the seed of the
land *or* of the fruit of the tree, *is* the LORD's. It
is holy to the LORD. 31If a man wants at all to
redeem *any* of his tithes, he shall add one-fifth
to it. 32And concerning the tithe of the herd or
the flock, of whatever passes under the rod,
the tenth one shall be holy to the LORD. 33He
shall not inquire whether it is good or bad, nor
shall he exchange it; and if he exchanges it at
all, then both it and the one exchanged for it
shall be holy; it shall not be redeemed.' "

34These *are* the commandments which the
LORD commanded Moses for the children of Israel on Mount Sinai.

Numbers

Fear can immobilize. Fearful people often do not think straight and run off in the wrong direction to escape the source of their fear. The world can be quite scary, and at times, Christians will become afraid. On those occasions, they can either run away from God, thinking that He cannot handle their fears, or they can run to God for protection.

The Israelites were poised to enter the Promised Land, but in their fear they grumbled against God. Having heard the spies' report of giants in the land, they decided that they would have preferred to die in Egypt than to have to enter the frightful land, even though they had already been promised victory! They forqot God's promises, God's provision, and God's past miraculous intervention to free them from Egypt. Their fear led to unbelief. Suddenly the giants were too big, they thought—even for God.

God did not take their unbelief lightly. The problem was not their fear, but that they had let the fear turn them away from God. Because their fear revealed their unbelief and rebellion, God told the people they could not enter the land. He would wait for the entire older generation (with two exceptions) to die before He would lead their children into the land. In the meantime, God sent them on a forty-year ordeal of wandering around the Sinai wilderness.

Don't allow fear to immobilize you. Instead, run to God for battle instructions. No problem is too big for Him.

SOUL CONCERN IN NUMBERS

The First Census of Israel

1 Now the LORD spoke to Moses in the Wilderness of Sinai, in the tabernacle of meeting, on the first *day* of the second month, in the second year after they had come out of the land of Egypt, saying: 2“Take a census of all the congregation of the children of Israel, by their families, by their fathers' houses, according to the number of names, every male individually, 3from twenty years old and above—all who *are able to* go to war in Israel. You and Aaron shall number them by their armies. 4And with you there shall be a man from every tribe, each one the head of his father's house.

5“These are the names of the men who shall stand with you: from Reuben, Elizur the son of Shedeur; 6from Simeon, Shelumiel the son of Zurishaddai; 7from Judah, Nahshon the son of Amminadab; 8from Issachar, Nethanel the son of Zuar; 9from Zebulun, Eliab the son of Helon; 10from the sons of Joseph: from Ephraim, Elishama the son of Ammihud; from Manasseh, Gamaliel the son of Pedahzur; 11from Benjamin, Abidan the son of Gideoni; 12from Dan, Ahiezer the son of Ammishaddai; 13from Asher, Pagiel the son of Ocran; 14from Gad, Eliasaph the son of Deuel;[a] 15from Naphtali, Ahira the son of Enan.” 16These *were* chosen from the congregation, leaders of their fathers' tribes, heads of the divisions in Israel.

17Then Moses and Aaron took these men who had been mentioned by name, 18and they assembled all the congregation together on the first *day* of the second month; and they recited their ancestry by families, by their fathers' houses, according to the number of names, from twenty years old and above, each one individually. 19As the LORD commanded Moses, so he numbered them in the Wilderness of Sinai.

20Now the children of Reuben, Israel's oldest son, their genealogies by their families, by their fathers' house, according to the number of names, every male individually, from twenty years old and above, all who *were able to* go to war: 21those who were numbered of the tribe of Reuben *were* forty-six thousand five hundred.

22From the children of Simeon, their genealogies by their families, by their fathers' house, of those who were numbered, according to the number of names, every male individually, from twenty years old and above, all who *were able to* go to war: 23those who were numbered of the tribe of Simeon *were* fifty-nine thousand three hundred.

24From the children of Gad, their genealogies by their families, by their fathers' house, according to the number of names, from twenty years old and above, all who *were able to* go to war: 25those who were numbered of the tribe of Gad *were* forty-five thousand six hundred and fifty.

26From the children of Judah, their genealogies by their families, by their fathers' house, according to the number of names, from twenty years old and above, all who *were able to* go to war: 27those who were numbered of the tribe of Judah *were* seventy-four thousand six hundred.

28From the children of Issachar, their genealogies by their families, by their fathers' house, according to the number of names, from twenty years old and above, all who *were able to* go to war: 29those who were numbered of the tribe of Issachar *were* fifty-four thousand four hundred.

30From the children of Zebulun, their genealogies by their families, by their fathers' house, according to the number of names, from twenty years old and above, all who *were able to* go to war: 31those who were numbered of the tribe of Zebulun *were* fifty-seven thousand four hundred.

32From the sons of Joseph, the children of Ephraim, their genealogies by their families, by their fathers' house, according to the number of names, from twenty years old and above, all who *were able to* go to war: 33those who were numbered of the tribe of Ephraim *were* forty thousand five hundred.

34From the children of Manasseh, their genealogies by their families, by their fathers' house, according to the number of names, from twenty years old and above, all who *were able to* go to war: 35those who were numbered of the tribe of Manasseh *were* thirty-two thousand two hundred.

36From the children of Benjamin, their genealogies by their families, by their fathers' house, according to the number of names, from twenty years old and above, all who *were able to* go to war: 37those who were numbered of the tribe of Benjamin *were* thirty-five thousand four hundred.

38From the children of Dan, their genealogies

1:14 [a]Spelled *Reuel* in 2:14

by their families, by their fathers' house, according to the number of names, from twenty years old and above, all who *were able to* go to war: 39those who were numbered of the tribe of Dan *were* sixty-two thousand seven hundred.

40From the children of Asher, their genealogies by their families, by their fathers' house, according to the number of names, from twenty years old and above, all who *were able to* go to war: 41those who were numbered of the tribe of Asher *were* forty-one thousand five hundred.

42From the children of Naphtali, their genealogies by their families, by their fathers' house, according to the number of names, from twenty years old and above, all who *were able to* go to war: 43those who were numbered of the tribe of Naphtali *were* fifty-three thousand four hundred.

44These are the ones who were numbered, whom Moses and Aaron numbered, with the leaders of Israel, twelve men, each one representing his father's house. 45So all who were numbered of the children of Israel, by their fathers' houses, from twenty years old and above, all who *were able to* go to war in Israel— 46all who were numbered were six hundred and three thousand five hundred and fifty.

47But the Levites were not numbered among them by their fathers' tribe; 48for the LORD had spoken to Moses, saying: 49"Only the tribe of Levi you shall not number, nor take a census of them among the children of Israel; 50but you shall appoint the Levites over the tabernacle of the Testimony, over all its furnishings, and over all things that belong to it; they shall carry the tabernacle and all its furnishings; they shall attend to it and camp around the tabernacle. 51And when the tabernacle is to go forward, the Levites shall take it down; and when the tabernacle is to be set up, the Levites shall set it up. The outsider who comes near shall be put to death. 52The children of Israel shall pitch their tents, everyone by his own camp, everyone by his own standard, according to their armies; 53but the Levites shall camp around the tabernacle of the Testimony, that there may be no wrath on the congregation of the children of Israel; and the Levites shall keep charge of the tabernacle of the Testimony."

54Thus the children of Israel did; according to all that the LORD commanded Moses, so they did.

THE TRIBES AND LEADERS BY ARMIES

2 And the LORD spoke to Moses and Aaron, saying: 2"Everyone of the children of Israel shall camp by his own standard, beside the emblems of his father's house; they shall camp some distance from the tabernacle of meeting. 3On the east side, toward the rising of the sun, those of the standard of the forces with Judah shall camp according to their armies; and Nahshon the son of Amminadab *shall be* the leader of the children of Judah." 4And his army was numbered at seventy-four thousand six hundred.

5"Those who camp next to him *shall be* the tribe of Issachar, and Nethanel the son of Zuar *shall be* the leader of the children of Issachar." 6And his army was numbered at fifty-four thousand four hundred.

7"Then *comes* the tribe of Zebulun, and Eliab the son of Helon *shall be* the leader of the children of Zebulun." 8And his army was numbered at fifty-seven thousand four hundred. 9"All who were numbered according to their armies of the forces with Judah, one hundred and eighty-six thousand four hundred—these shall break camp first.

10"On the south side *shall be* the standard of the forces with Reuben according to their armies, and the leader of the children of Reuben *shall be* Elizur the son of Shedeur." 11And his army was numbered at forty-six thousand five hundred.

12"Those who camp next to him *shall be* the tribe of Simeon, and the leader of the children of Simeon *shall be* Shelumiel the son of Zurishaddai." 13And his army was numbered at fifty-nine thousand three hundred.

14"Then *comes* the tribe of Gad, and the leader of the children of Gad *shall be* Eliasaph the son of Reuel."[a] 15And his army was numbered at forty-five thousand six hundred and fifty. 16"All who were numbered according to their armies of the forces with Reuben, one hundred and fifty-one thousand four hundred and fifty—they shall be the second to break camp.

17"And the tabernacle of meeting shall move out with the camp of the Levites in the middle of the camps; as they camp, so they shall move out, everyone in his place, by their standards.

18"On the west side *shall be* the standard of

2:14 [a]Spelled *Deuel* in 1:14 and 7:42

the forces with Ephraim according to their armies, and the leader of the children of Ephraim *shall be* Elishama the son of Ammihud."
[19]And his army was numbered at forty thousand five hundred.

[20]"Next to him *comes* the tribe of Manasseh, and the leader of the children of Manasseh *shall be* Gamaliel the son of Pedahzur." [21]And
his army was numbered at thirty-two thousand two hundred.

[22]"Then *comes* the tribe of Benjamin, and the leader of the children of Benjamin *shall be* Abidan the son of Gideoni." [23]And his army
was numbered at thirty-five thousand four hundred. [24]"All who were numbered according to their armies of the forces with Ephraim, one hundred and eight thousand one hundred—they shall be the third to break camp.

[25]"The standard of the forces with Dan *shall be* on the north side according to their armies, and the leader of the children of Dan *shall be* Ahiezer the son of Ammishaddai." [26]And his
army was numbered at sixty-two thousand seven hundred.

[27]"Those who camp next to him *shall be* the tribe of Asher, and the leader of the children of Asher *shall be* Pagiel the son of Ocran." [28]And
his army was numbered at forty-one thousand five hundred.

[29]"Then *comes* the tribe of Naphtali, and the leader of the children of Naphtali *shall be* Ahira the son of Enan." [30]And his army was
numbered at fifty-three thousand four hundred. [31]"All who were numbered of the forces
with Dan, one hundred and fifty-seven thousand six hundred—they shall break camp last, with their standards."

[32]These *are* the ones who were numbered of
the children of Israel by their fathers' houses. All who were numbered according to their armies of the forces *were* six hundred and three thousand five hundred and fifty. [33]But the Levites were not numbered among the children of Israel, just as the LORD commanded Moses.

[34]Thus the children of Israel did according
to all that the LORD commanded Moses; so they camped by their standards and so they broke camp, each one by his family, according to their fathers' houses.

THE SONS OF AARON

3 Now these *are* the records of Aaron and Moses when the LORD spoke with Moses on Mount Sinai. [2]And these *are* the names of
the sons of Aaron: Nadab, the firstborn, and Abihu, Eleazar, and Ithamar. [3]These *are* the
names of the sons of Aaron, the anointed priests, whom he consecrated to minister as priests. [4]Nadab and Abihu had died before the
LORD when they offered profane fire before the LORD in the Wilderness of Sinai; and they had no children. So Eleazar and Ithamar ministered as priests in the presence of Aaron their father.

THE LEVITES SERVE IN THE TABERNACLE

[5]And the LORD spoke to Moses, saying:
[6]"Bring the tribe of Levi near, and present them before Aaron the priest, that they may serve him. [7]And they shall attend to his needs
and the needs of the whole congregation before the tabernacle of meeting, to do the work of the tabernacle. [8]Also they shall attend to all
the furnishings of the tabernacle of meeting, and to the needs of the children of Israel, to do the work of the tabernacle. [9]And you shall
give the Levites to Aaron and his sons; they *are* given entirely to him[a] from among the children of Israel. [10]So you shall appoint

3:9 [a]Samaritan Pentateuch and Septuagint read *Me.*

SOUL NOTE

Who's Calling? *(3:1–13)* When God gives us a calling, it's accompanied by responsibility and accountability. God chose Aaron and his descendants to be the priests of Israel, and He chose the tribe of Levi to serve under Aaron "to do the work of the tabernacle" (3:7). God greatly honored the Levites when He separated them for special service and said, "They shall be Mine" (3:13). With this honor came the responsibility of performing their duties as God commanded. When God calls us to serve Him, He both honors us and gives us great responsibility. As we serve, we must remember that we are accountable to Him (Eph. 6:7). **Topic: Accountability**

Aaron and his sons, and they shall attend to
their priesthood; but the outsider who comes
near shall be put to death."
11Then the LORD spoke to Moses, saying:
12"Now behold, I Myself have taken the Levites from among the children of Israel instead
of every firstborn who opens the womb
among the children of Israel. Therefore the
Levites shall be Mine, 13because all the firstborn *are* Mine. On the day that I struck all the
firstborn in the land of Egypt, I sanctified to
Myself all the firstborn in Israel, both man and
beast. They shall be Mine: I *am* the LORD."

Census of the Levites Commanded

14Then the LORD spoke to Moses in the Wilderness of Sinai, saying: 15"Number the children of Levi by their fathers' houses, by their
families; you shall number every male from a
month old and above."
16So Moses numbered them according to the
word of the LORD, as he was commanded.
17These were the sons of Levi by their names:
Gershon, Kohath, and Merari. 18And these *are*
the names of the sons of Gershon by their
families: Libni and Shimei. 19And the sons of
Kohath by their families: Amram, Izehar, Hebron, and Uzziel. 20And the sons of Merari by
their families: Mahli and Mushi. These *are* the
families of the Levites by their fathers' houses.
21From Gershon *came* the family of the Libnites and the family of the Shimites; these
were the families of the Gershonites. 22Those
who were numbered, according to the number
of all the males from a month old and above—
of those who were numbered *there were* seven
thousand five hundred. 23The families of the
Gershonites were to camp behind the tabernacle westward. 24And the leader of the father's
house of the Gershonites *was* Eliasaph the son
of Lael. 25The duties of the children of Gershon in the tabernacle of meeting *included* the
tabernacle, the tent with its covering, the
screen for the door of the tabernacle of meeting, 26the screen for the door of the court, the
hangings of the court which *are* around the
tabernacle and the altar, and their cords, according to all the work relating to them.
27From Kohath *came* the family of the Amramites, the family of the Izharites, the family
of the Hebronites, and the family of the Uzzielites; these *were* the families of the Kohathites. 28According to the number of all the
males, from a month old and above, *there*
were eight thousand six[a] hundred keeping
charge of the sanctuary. 29The families of the
children of Kohath were to camp on the south
side of the tabernacle. 30And the leader of the
fathers' house of the families of the Kohathites
was Elizaphan the son of Uzziel. 31Their duty
included the ark, the table, the lampstand, the
altars, the utensils of the sanctuary with
which they ministered, the screen, and all the
work relating to them.
32And Eleazar the son of Aaron the priest
was to be chief over the leaders of the Levites,
with oversight of those who kept charge of the
sanctuary.
33From Merari *came* the family of the Mahlites and the family of the Mushites; these
were the families of Merari. 34And those who
were numbered, according to the number of
all the males from a month old and above,
were six thousand two hundred. 35The leader
of the fathers' house of the families of Merari
was Zuriel the son of Abihail. These *were* to
camp on the north side of the tabernacle.
36And the appointed duty of the children of
Merari *included* the boards of the tabernacle,
its bars, its pillars, its sockets, its utensils, all
the work relating to them, 37and the pillars of
the court all around, with their sockets, their
pegs, and their cords.
38Moreover those who were to camp before
the tabernacle on the east, before the tabernacle of meeting, *were* Moses, Aaron, and his
sons, keeping charge of the sanctuary, to meet
the needs of the children of Israel; but the outsider who came near was to be put to death.
39All who were numbered of the Levites,
whom Moses and Aaron numbered at the
commandment of the LORD, by their families,
all the males from a month old and above,
were twenty-two thousand.

Levites Dedicated Instead of the Firstborn

40Then the LORD said to Moses: "Number all
the firstborn males of the children of Israel
from a month old and above, and take the
number of their names. 41And you shall take
the Levites for Me—I *am* the LORD—instead of
all the firstborn among the children of Israel,
and the livestock of the Levites instead of all
the firstborn among the livestock of the chil-

3:28 [a]Some manuscripts of the Septuagint read *three.*

dren of Israel." 42So Moses numbered all the firstborn among the children of Israel, as the LORD commanded him. 43And all the firstborn males, according to the number of names from a month old and above, of those who were numbered of them, were twenty-two thousand two hundred and seventy-three.

44Then the LORD spoke to Moses, saying: 45"Take the Levites instead of all the firstborn among the children of Israel, and the livestock of the Levites instead of their livestock. The Levites shall be Mine: I *am* the LORD. 46And for the redemption of the two hundred and seventy-three of the firstborn of the children of Israel, who are more than the number of the Levites, 47you shall take five shekels for each one individually; you shall take *them* in the currency of the shekel of the sanctuary, the shekel of twenty gerahs. 48And you shall give the money, with which the excess number of them is redeemed, to Aaron and his sons."

49So Moses took the redemption money from those who were over and above those who were redeemed by the Levites. 50From the firstborn of the children of Israel he took the money, one thousand three hundred and sixty-five *shekels,* according to the shekel of the sanctuary. 51And Moses gave their redemption money to Aaron and his sons, according to the word of the LORD, as the LORD commanded Moses.

Duties of the Sons of Kohath

4 Then the LORD spoke to Moses and Aaron, saying: 2"Take a census of the sons of Kohath from among the children of Levi, by their families, by their fathers' house, 3from thirty years old and above, even to fifty years old, all who enter the service to do the work in the tabernacle of meeting.

4"This *is* the service of the sons of Kohath in the tabernacle of meeting, *relating to* the most holy things: 5When the camp prepares to journey, Aaron and his sons shall come, and they shall take down the covering veil and cover the ark of the Testimony with it. 6Then they shall put on it a covering of badger skins, and spread over *that* a cloth entirely of blue; and they shall insert its poles.

7"On the table of showbread they shall spread a blue cloth, and put on it the dishes, the pans, the bowls, and the pitchers for pouring; and the showbread[a] shall be on it. 8They shall spread over them a scarlet cloth, and cover the same with a covering of badger skins; and they shall insert its poles. 9And they shall take a blue cloth and cover the lampstand of the light, with its lamps, its wick-trimmers, its trays, and all its oil vessels, with which they service it. 10Then they shall put it with all its utensils in a covering of badger skins, and put *it* on a carrying beam.

11"Over the golden altar they shall spread a blue cloth, and cover it with a covering of badger skins; and they shall insert its poles. 12Then they shall take all the utensils of service with which they minister in the sanctuary, put *them* in a blue cloth, cover them with a covering of badger skins, and put *them* on a carrying beam. 13Also they shall take away the ashes from the altar, and spread a purple cloth over it. 14They shall put on it all its implements with which they minister there—the firepans, the forks, the shovels, the basins, and all the utensils of the altar—and they shall spread on it a covering of badger skins, and insert its poles. 15And when Aaron and his sons have finished covering the sanctuary and all the furnishings of the sanctuary, when the camp is set to go, then the sons of Kohath shall come to carry *them;* but they shall not touch any holy thing, lest they die.

"These *are* the things in the tabernacle of meeting which the sons of Kohath are to carry.

16"The appointed duty of Eleazar the son of Aaron the priest *is* the oil for the light, the sweet incense, the daily grain offering, the anointing oil, the oversight of all the tabernacle, of all that *is* in it, with the sanctuary and its furnishings."

17Then the LORD spoke to Moses and Aaron, saying: 18"Do not cut off the tribe of the families of the Kohathites from among the Levites; 19but do this in regard to them, that they may live and not die when they approach the most holy things: Aaron and his sons shall go in and appoint each of them to his service and his task. 20But they shall not go in to watch while the holy things are being covered, lest they die."

Duties of the Sons of Gershon

21Then the LORD spoke to Moses, saying: 22"Also take a census of the sons of Gershon, by their fathers' house, by their families. 23From thirty years old and above, even to fifty

4:7 [a]Literally *the continual bread*

years old, you shall number them, all who enter to perform the service, to do the work in
the tabernacle of meeting. 24This *is* the service
of the families of the Gershonites, in serving
and carrying: 25They shall carry the curtains
of the tabernacle and the tabernacle of meeting *with* its covering, the covering of badger
skins that *is* on it, the screen for the door of
the tabernacle of meeting, 26the screen for the
door of the gate of the court, the hangings of
the court which *are* around the tabernacle and
altar, and their cords, all the furnishings for
their service and all that is made for these
things: so shall they serve.

27"Aaron and his sons shall assign all the
service of the sons of the Gershonites, all their
tasks and all their service. And you shall appoint to them all their tasks as their duty.
28This *is* the service of the families of the sons
of Gershon in the tabernacle of meeting. And
their duties *shall be* under the authority[a] of
Ithamar the son of Aaron the priest.

Duties of the Sons of Merari

29"*As for* the sons of Merari, you shall number them by their families and by their fathers'
house. 30From thirty years old and above, even
to fifty years old, you shall number them,
everyone who enters the service to do the
work of the tabernacle of meeting. 31And this
is what they must carry as all their service for
the tabernacle of meeting: the boards of the
tabernacle, its bars, its pillars, its sockets,
32and the pillars around the court with their
sockets, pegs, and cords, with all their furnishings and all their service; and you shall
assign *to each man* by name the items he must
carry. 33This *is* the service of the families of
the sons of Merari, as all their service for the
tabernacle of meeting, under the authority[a] of
Ithamar the son of Aaron the priest."

Census of the Levites

34And Moses, Aaron, and the leaders of the
congregation numbered the sons of the Kohathites by their families and by their fathers'
house, 35from thirty years old and above, even
to fifty years old, everyone who entered the
service for work in the tabernacle of meeting;
36and those who were numbered by their families were two thousand seven hundred and
fifty. 37These *were* the ones who were numbered of the families of the Kohathites, all
who might serve in the tabernacle of meeting,
whom Moses and Aaron numbered according
to the commandment of the LORD by the hand
of Moses.

38And those who were numbered of the
sons of Gershon, by their families and by their
fathers' house, 39from thirty years old and
above, even to fifty years old, everyone who
entered the service for work in the tabernacle
of meeting— 40those who were numbered by
their families, by their fathers' house, were
two thousand six hundred and thirty. 41These
are the ones who were numbered of the families of the sons of Gershon, of all who might
serve in the tabernacle of meeting, whom Moses and Aaron numbered according to the
commandment of the LORD.

42Those of the families of the sons of Merari
who were numbered, by their families, by
their fathers' house, 43from thirty years old
and above, even to fifty years old, everyone
who entered the service for work in the tabernacle of meeting— 44those who were numbered by their families were three thousand
two hundred. 45These *are* the ones who were
numbered of the families of the sons of Merari, whom Moses and Aaron numbered according to the word of the LORD by the hand of
Moses.

46All who were numbered of the Levites,
whom Moses, Aaron, and the leaders of Israel
numbered, by their families and by their fathers' houses, 47from thirty years old and
above, even to fifty years old, everyone who
came to do the work of service and the work
of bearing burdens in the tabernacle of meeting— 48those who were numbered were eight
thousand five hundred and eighty.

49According to the commandment of the
LORD they were numbered by the hand of Moses, each according to his service and according to his task; thus were they numbered by
him, as the LORD commanded Moses.

Ceremonially Unclean Persons Isolated

5 And the LORD spoke to Moses, saying:
2"Command the children of Israel that
they put out of the camp every leper, everyone
who has a discharge, and whoever becomes
defiled by a corpse. 3You shall put out both
male and female; you shall put them outside
the camp, that they may not defile their camps
in the midst of which I dwell." 4And the chil-

4:28 [a]Literally *hand* **4:33** [a]Literally *hand*

dren of Israel did so, and put them outside the
camp; as the LORD spoke to Moses, so the children of Israel did.

CONFESSION AND RESTITUTION

5Then the LORD spoke to Moses, saying,
6"Speak to the children of Israel: 'When a man
or woman commits any sin that men commit
in unfaithfulness against the LORD, and that
person is guilty, 7then he shall confess the sin
which he has committed. He shall make restitution for his trespass in full, plus one-fifth of
it, and give *it* to the one he has wronged. 8But
if the man has no relative to whom restitution
may be made for the wrong, the restitution for
the wrong *must go* to the LORD for the priest,
in addition to the ram of the atonement with
which atonement is made for him. 9Every offering of all the holy things of the children of
Israel, which they bring to the priest, shall be
his. 10And every man's holy things shall be
his; whatever any man gives the priest shall
be his.' "

CONCERNING UNFAITHFUL WIVES

11And the LORD spoke to Moses, saying,
12"Speak to the children of Israel, and say to
them: 'If any man's wife goes astray and be-
haves unfaithfully toward him, 13and a man
lies with her carnally, and it is hidden from
the eyes of her husband, and it is concealed
that she has defiled herself, and *there was* no
witness against her, nor was she caught— 14if
the spirit of jealousy comes upon him and he
becomes jealous of his wife, who has defiled
herself; or if the spirit of jealousy comes upon
him and he becomes jealous of his wife, although she has not defiled herself— 15then the
man shall bring his wife to the priest. He shall
bring the offering required for her, one-tenth
of an ephah of barley meal; he shall pour no
oil on it and put no frankincense on it, because it *is* a grain offering of jealousy, an offering for remembering, for bringing iniquity to
remembrance.

16'And the priest shall bring her near, and
set her before the LORD. 17The priest shall take
holy water in an earthen vessel, and take
some of the dust that is on the floor of the tabernacle and put *it* into the water. 18Then the
priest shall stand the woman before the LORD,
uncover the woman's head, and put the offering for remembering in her hands, which *is*
the grain offering of jealousy. And the priest
shall have in his hand the bitter water that
brings a curse. 19And the priest shall put her
under oath, and say to the woman, "If no man
has lain with you, and if you have not gone
astray to uncleanness *while* under your
husband's *authority,* be free from this bitter
water that brings a curse. 20But if you have
gone astray *while* under your husband's *authority,* and if you have defiled yourself and
some man other than your husband has lain
with you"— 21then the priest shall put the
woman under the oath of the curse, and he
shall say to the woman—"the LORD make you
a curse and an oath among your people, when
the LORD makes your thigh rot and your belly
swell; 22and may this water that causes the
curse go into your stomach, and make *your*
belly swell and *your* thigh rot."

'Then the woman shall say, "Amen, so be it."

23'Then the priest shall write these curses in
a book, and he shall scrape *them* off into the
bitter water. 24And he shall make the woman
drink the bitter water that brings a curse, and
the water that brings the curse shall enter her
to become bitter. 25Then the priest shall take
the grain offering of jealousy from the
woman's hand, shall wave the offering before
the LORD, and bring it to the altar; 26and the
priest shall take a handful of the offering, as
its memorial portion, burn *it* on the altar, and

SOUL NOTE

Owning Up *(5:6, 7)* God's Law provided the opportunity for a person to correct his or her mistakes by making restitution to the offended person. These laws of restitution held people accountable for their behavior. A person who had wronged another had to *admit* doing wrong and then *do* whatever was possible in order to make things right again. The principle is important today. People should take responsibility for their behavior and, when it's needed, make restitution to the one whom they have wronged. **Topic: Conflict**

afterward make the woman drink the water.
27When he has made her drink the water, then
it shall be, if she has defiled herself and behaved unfaithfully toward her husband, that
the water that brings a curse will enter her
and become bitter, and her belly will swell,
her thigh will rot, and the woman will become
a curse among her people. 28But if the woman
has not defiled herself, and is clean, then she
shall be free and may conceive children.
29'This *is* the law of jealousy, when a wife,
while under her husband's *authority,* goes
astray and defiles herself, 30or when the spirit
of jealousy comes upon a man, and he becomes jealous of his wife; then he shall stand
the woman before the LORD, and the priest
shall execute all this law upon her. 31Then the
man shall be free from iniquity, but that
woman shall bear her guilt.' "

THE LAW OF THE NAZIRITE

6 Then the LORD spoke to Moses, saying,
2"Speak to the children of Israel, and say
to them: 'When either a man or woman consecrates an offering to take the vow of a Nazirite, to separate himself to the LORD, 3he shall
separate himself from wine and *similar* drink;
he shall drink neither vinegar made from wine
nor vinegar made from *similar* drink; neither
shall he drink any grape juice, nor eat fresh
grapes or raisins. 4All the days of his separation he shall eat nothing that is produced by
the grapevine, from seed to skin.
5'All the days of the vow of his separation
no razor shall come upon his head; until the
days are fulfilled for which he separated himself to the LORD, he shall be holy. *Then* he
shall let the locks of the hair of his head grow.
6All the days that he separates himself to the

KEY PASSAGE

Jealousy

THE WEDGE OF JEALOUSY

(5:29)

The ancient Israelites had a complex ritual for dealing with jealousy. Their detailed process (Num. 5:11–31) recognized the destructive potential of a jealous husband or wife. The most important part was that they dealt with this issue before the Lord (Num. 5:30). Jealousy can destroy any relationship, and in a marriage, it can drive in a wedge of mistrust.

Protection from the wedge of jealousy begins with honesty. Each spouse should honestly consider his or her own tendency toward jealousy, answering the question, "What makes me jealous?" Each spouse should honestly tell his or her feelings. Then they can discuss what they could do for each other to alleviate those feelings. Complete honesty and trust will help to obliterate jealousy.

To Learn More: Turn to the article about jealousy on pages 1656, 1657. See also the personality profile of Rachel and Leah on page 49.

SOUL NOTE

Speaking the Truth *(6:2–21)* The Nazirite vow included separation from the world and consecration to the Lord. A person could take the vow for a certain amount of time in order to focus on God. Taking this vow was very serious, and the person was expected to follow all the procedures described here. How easily people "promise" to do something, but how hard it may be to keep that promise. Vows (promises) are very important—whether they are made to God or to other people. God does not take them lightly, and neither should we (Matt. 5:37). **Topic: Truth**

LORD he shall not go near a dead body. 7He
shall not make himself unclean even for his
father or his mother, for his brother or his sister, when they die, because his separation to
God *is* on his head. 8All the days of his separation he shall be holy to the LORD.
9'And if anyone dies very suddenly beside
him, and he defiles his consecrated head, then
he shall shave his head on the day of his
cleansing; on the seventh day he shall shave
it. 10Then on the eighth day he shall bring two
turtledoves or two young pigeons to the
priest, to the door of the tabernacle of meeting; 11and the priest shall offer one as a sin offering and *the* other as a burnt offering, and
make atonement for him, because he sinned
in regard to the corpse; and he shall sanctify
his head that same day. 12He shall consecrate
to the LORD the days of his separation, and
bring a male lamb in its first year as a trespass
offering; but the former days shall be lost, because his separation was
defiled.
13'Now this *is* the law
of the Nazirite: When
the days of his separa-
tion are fulfilled, he
shall be brought to the
door of the tabernacle
of meeting. 14And he
shall present his offer-
ing to the LORD: one male lamb in its first year
without blemish as a burnt offering, one ewe
lamb in its first year without blemish as a sin
offering, one ram without blemish as a peace
offering, 15a basket of unleavened bread,
cakes of fine flour mixed with oil, unleavened
wafers anointed with oil, and their grain offering with their drink offerings.
16'Then the priest shall bring *them* before the
LORD and offer his sin offering and his burnt
offering; 17and he shall offer the ram as a sacrifice of a peace offering to the LORD, with the
basket of unleavened bread; the priest shall
also offer its grain offering and its drink offering. 18Then the Nazirite shall shave his consecrated head *at* the door of the tabernacle of
meeting, and shall take the hair from his consecrated head and put *it* on the fire which is under the sacrifice of the peace offering.
19'And the priest shall take the boiled shoulder of the ram, one unleavened cake from the
basket, and one unleavened wafer, and put
them upon the hands of the Nazirite after he
has shaved his consecrated *hair,* 20and the
priest shall wave them as a wave offering before the LORD; they *are* holy for the priest, together with the breast of the wave offering
and the thigh of the heave offering. After that
the Nazirite may drink wine.'
21"This is the law of the Nazirite who vows
to the LORD the offering for his separation, and
besides that, whatever else his hand is able to provide; according to the vow which he takes, so he must do according to the law of his separation."

> "The LORD bless you and keep you;
> the LORD make His face shine upon
> you, and be gracious to you;
> the LORD lift up His countenance
> upon you, and give you peace."
> NUMBERS 6:24–26

THE PRIESTLY BLESSING

22And the LORD spoke
to Moses, saying: 23"Speak to Aaron and his
sons, saying, 'This is the way you shall bless
the children of Israel. Say to them:

24 "The LORD bless you and keep you;
25 The LORD make His face shine upon you,
And be gracious to you;
26 The LORD lift up His countenance upon
you,
And give you peace." '

SOUL NOTE

Bless You *(6:22–27)* This beautiful blessing was a way of asking for God's divine favor upon the people. To have the Lord's "face shine upon" someone pictures that person experiencing pleasure in God's presence. To have the Lord "lift up His countenance upon" someone pictures God, in turn, experiencing pleasure in the presence of the person. While the ancient form of blessing may be unfamiliar, the words of this prayer seek God's pleasure, protection, grace, favor, and peace on others. When we pray for others, we also can use these words as a blessing upon them.
Topic: Attachment/Blessing

27"So they shall put My name on the children of Israel, and I will bless them."

Offerings of the Leaders

7 Now it came to pass, when Moses had finished setting up the tabernacle, that he anointed it and consecrated it and all its furnishings, and the altar and all its utensils; so he anointed them and consecrated them. 2Then the leaders of Israel, the heads of their fathers' houses, who *were* the leaders of the tribes and over those who were numbered, made an offering. 3And they brought their offering before the LORD, six covered carts and twelve oxen, a cart for *every* two of the leaders, and for each one an ox; and they presented them before the tabernacle.

4Then the LORD spoke to Moses, saying, 5"Accept *these* from them, that they may be used in doing the work of the tabernacle of meeting; and you shall give them to the Levites, *to* every man according to his service." 6So Moses took the carts and the oxen, and gave them to the Levites. 7Two carts and four oxen he gave to the sons of Gershon, according to their service; 8and four carts and eight oxen he gave to the sons of Merari, according to their service, under the authority[a] of Ithamar the son of Aaron the priest. 9But to the sons of Kohath he gave none, because theirs *was* the service of the holy things, *which* they carried on their shoulders.

10Now the leaders offered the dedication *offering* for the altar when it was anointed; so the leaders offered their offering before the altar. 11For the LORD said to Moses, "They shall offer their offering, one leader each day, for the dedication of the altar."

12And the one who offered his offering on the first day *was* Nahshon the son of Amminadab, from the tribe of Judah. 13His offering *was* one silver platter, the weight of which *was* one hundred and thirty *shekels,* and one silver bowl of seventy shekels, according to the shekel of the sanctuary, both of them full of fine flour mixed with oil as a grain offering; 14one gold pan of ten *shekels,* full of incense; 15one young bull, one ram, and one male lamb in its first year, as a burnt offering; 16one kid of the goats as a sin offering; 17and for the sacrifice of peace offerings: two oxen, five rams, five male goats, and five male lambs in their first year. This *was* the offering of Nahshon the son of Amminadab.

18On the second day Nethanel the son of Zuar, leader of Issachar, presented *an offering.* 19*For* his offering he offered one silver platter, the weight of which *was* one hundred and thirty *shekels,* and one silver bowl of seventy shekels, according to the shekel of the sanctuary, both of them full of fine flour mixed with oil as a grain offering; 20one gold pan of ten *shekels,* full of incense; 21one young bull, one ram, and one male lamb in its first year, as a burnt offering; 22one kid of the goats as a sin offering; 23and as the sacrifice of peace offerings: two oxen, five rams, five male goats, and five male lambs in their first year. This *was* the offering of Nethanel the son of Zuar.

24On the third day Eliab the son of Helon, leader of the children of Zebulun, *presented an offering.* 25His offering *was* one silver platter, the weight of which *was* one hundred and thirty *shekels,* and one silver bowl of seventy shekels, according to the shekel of the sanctuary, both of them full of fine flour mixed with oil as a grain offering; 26one gold pan of ten *shekels,* full of incense; 27one young bull, one ram, and one male lamb in its first year, as a burnt offering; 28one kid of the goats as a sin offering; 29and for the sacrifice of peace offerings: two oxen, five rams, five male goats, and five male lambs in their first year. This *was* the offering of Eliab the son of Helon.

30On the fourth day Elizur the son of Shedeur, leader of the children of Reuben, *presented an offering.* 31His offering *was* one silver platter, the weight of which *was* one hundred and thirty *shekels,* and one silver bowl of seventy shekels, according to the shekel of the sanctuary, both of them full of fine flour mixed with oil as a grain offering; 32one gold pan of ten *shekels,* full of incense; 33one young bull, one ram, and one male lamb in its first year, as a burnt offering; 34one kid of the goats as a sin offering; 35and as the sacrifice of peace offerings: two oxen, five rams, five male goats, and five male lambs in their first year. This *was* the offering of Elizur the son of Shedeur.

36On the fifth day Shelumiel the son of Zurishaddai, leader of the children of Simeon, *presented an offering.* 37His offering *was* one silver platter, the weight of which *was* one hundred and thirty *shekels,* and one silver bowl of seventy shekels, according to the shekel of the sanctuary, both of them full of

---

7:8 [a]Literally *hand*

fine flour mixed with oil as a grain offering; 38 one gold pan of ten *shekels,* full of incense; 39 one young bull, one ram, and one male lamb in its first year, as a burnt offering; 40 one kid of the goats as a sin offering; 41 and as the sacrifice of peace offerings: two oxen, five rams, five male goats, and five male lambs in their first year. This *was* the offering of Shelumiel the son of Zurishaddai.

42 On the sixth day Eliasaph the son of Deuel,[a] leader of the children of Gad, *presented an offering.* 43 His offering *was* one silver platter, the weight of which *was* one hundred and thirty *shekels,* and one silver bowl of seventy shekels, according to the shekel of the sanctuary, both of them full of fine flour mixed with oil as a grain offering; 44 one gold pan of ten *shekels,* full of incense; 45 one young bull, one ram, and one male lamb in its first year, as a burnt offering; 46 one kid of the goats as a sin offering; 47 and as the sacrifice of peace offerings: two oxen, five rams, five male goats, and five male lambs in their first year. This *was* the offering of Eliasaph the son of Deuel.

48 On the seventh day Elishama the son of Ammihud, leader of the children of Ephraim, *presented an offering.* 49 His offering *was* one silver platter, the weight of which *was* one hundred and thirty *shekels,* and one silver bowl of seventy shekels, according to the shekel of the sanctuary, both of them full of fine flour mixed with oil as a grain offering; 50 one gold pan of ten *shekels,* full of incense; 51 one young bull, one ram, and one male lamb in its first year, as a burnt offering; 52 one kid of the goats as a sin offering; 53 and as the sacrifice of peace offerings: two oxen, five rams, five male goats, and five male lambs in their first year. This *was* the offering of Elishama the son of Ammihud.

54 On the eighth day Gamaliel the son of Pedahzur, leader of the children of Manasseh, *presented an offering.* 55 His offering *was* one silver platter, the weight of which *was* one hundred and thirty *shekels,* and one silver bowl of seventy shekels, according to the shekel of the sanctuary, both of them full of fine flour mixed with oil as a grain offering; 56 one gold pan of ten *shekels,* full of incense; 57 one young bull, one ram, and one male lamb in its first year, as a burnt offering; 58 one kid of the goats as a sin offering; 59 and as the sacrifice of peace offerings: two oxen, five rams, five male goats, and five male lambs in their first year. This *was* the offering of Gamaliel the son of Pedahzur.

60 On the ninth day Abidan the son of Gideoni, leader of the children of Benjamin, *presented an offering.* 61 His offering *was* one silver platter, the weight of which *was* one hundred and thirty *shekels,* and one silver bowl of seventy shekels, according to the shekel of the sanctuary, both of them full of fine flour mixed with oil as a grain offering; 62 one gold pan of ten *shekels,* full of incense; 63 one young bull, one ram, and one male lamb in its first year, as a burnt offering; 64 one kid of the goats as a sin offering; 65 and as the sacrifice of peace offerings: two oxen, five rams, five male goats, and five male lambs in their first year. This *was* the offering of Abidan the son of Gideoni.

66 On the tenth day Ahiezer the son of Ammishaddai, leader of the children of Dan, *presented an offering.* 67 His offering *was* one silver platter, the weight of which *was* one hundred and thirty *shekels,* and one silver bowl of seventy shekels, according to the shekel of the sanctuary, both of them full of fine flour mixed with oil as a grain offering; 68 one gold pan of ten *shekels,* full of incense; 69 one young bull, one ram, and one male lamb in its first year, as a burnt offering; 70 one kid of the goats as a sin offering; 71 and as the sacrifice of peace offerings: two oxen, five rams, five male goats, and five male lambs in their first year. This *was* the offering of Ahiezer the son of Ammishaddai.

72 On the eleventh day Pagiel the son of Ocran, leader of the children of Asher, *presented an offering.* 73 His offering *was* one silver platter, the weight of which *was* one hundred and thirty *shekels,* and one silver bowl of seventy shekels, according to the shekel of the sanctuary, both of them full of fine flour mixed with oil as a grain offering; 74 one gold pan of ten *shekels,* full of incense; 75 one young bull, one ram, and one male lamb in its first year, as a burnt offering; 76 one kid of the goats as a sin offering; 77 and as the sacrifice of peace offerings: two oxen, five rams, five male goats, and five male lambs in their first year. This *was* the offering of Pagiel the son of Ocran.

78 On the twelfth day Ahira the son of Enan, leader of the children of Naphtali, *presented an offering.* 79 His offering *was* one silver platter,

7:42 [a]Spelled *Reuel* in 2:14

the weight of which *was* one hundred and thirty *shekels,* and one silver bowl of seventy shekels, according to the shekel of the sanctuary, both of them full of fine flour mixed with oil as a grain offering; 80one gold pan of ten *shekels,* full of incense; 81one young bull, one ram, and one male lamb in its first year, as a burnt offering; 82one kid of the goats as a sin offering; 83and as the sacrifice of peace offerings: two oxen, five rams, five male goats, and five male lambs in their first year. This *was* the offering of Ahira the son of Enan.

84This *was* the dedication *offering* for the altar from the leaders of Israel, when it was anointed: twelve silver platters, twelve silver bowls, and twelve gold pans. 85Each silver platter *weighed* one hundred and thirty *shekels* and each bowl seventy *shekels.* All the silver of the vessels *weighed* two thousand four hundred *shekels,* according to the shekel of the sanctuary. 86The twelve gold pans full of incense *weighed* ten *shekels* apiece, according to the shekel of the sanctuary; all the gold of the pans *weighed* one hundred and twenty *shekels.* 87All the oxen for the burnt offering *were* twelve young bulls, the rams twelve, the male lambs in their first year twelve, with their grain offering, and the kids of the goats as a sin offering twelve. 88And all the oxen for the sacrifice of peace offerings were twenty-four bulls, the rams sixty, the male goats sixty, and the lambs in their first year sixty. This *was* the dedication *offering* for the altar after it was anointed.

89Now when Moses went into the tabernacle of meeting to speak with Him, he heard the voice of One speaking to him from above the mercy seat that *was* on the ark of the Testimony, from between the two cherubim; thus He spoke to him.

ARRANGEMENT OF THE LAMPS

8 And the LORD spoke to Moses, saying: 2"Speak to Aaron, and say to him, 'When you arrange the lamps, the seven lamps shall give light in front of the lampstand.' " 3And Aaron did so; he arranged the lamps to face toward the front of the lampstand, as the LORD commanded Moses. 4Now this workmanship of the lampstand *was* hammered gold; from its shaft to its flowers it *was* hammered work. According to the pattern which the LORD had shown Moses, so he made the lampstand.

CLEANSING AND DEDICATION OF THE LEVITES

5Then the LORD spoke to Moses, saying: 6"Take the Levites from among the children of Israel and cleanse them *ceremonially.* 7Thus you shall do to them to cleanse them: Sprinkle water of purification on them, and let them shave all their body, and let them wash their clothes, and *so* make themselves clean. 8Then let them take a young bull with its grain offering of fine flour mixed with oil, and you shall take another young bull as a sin offering. 9And you shall bring the Levites before the tabernacle of meeting, and you shall gather together the whole congregation of the children of Israel. 10So you shall bring the Levites before the LORD, and the children of Israel shall lay their hands on the Levites; 11and Aaron shall offer the Levites before the LORD *like* a wave offering from the children of Israel, that they may perform the work of the LORD. 12Then the Levites shall lay their hands on the heads of the young bulls, and you shall offer one as a sin offering and the other as a burnt offering to the LORD, to make atonement for the Levites.

13"And you shall stand the Levites before Aaron and his sons, and then offer them *like* a wave offering to the LORD. 14Thus you shall separate the Levites from among the children of Israel, and the Levites shall be Mine. 15After that the Levites shall go in to service the tabernacle of meeting. So you shall cleanse them and offer them *like* a wave offering. 16For they *are* wholly given to Me from among the children of Israel; I have taken them for Myself instead of all who open the womb, the firstborn of all the children of Israel. 17For all the firstborn among the children of Israel *are* Mine, *both* man and beast; on the day that I struck all the firstborn in the land of Egypt I sanctified them to Myself. 18I have taken the Levites instead of all the firstborn of the children of Israel. 19And I have given the Levites as a gift to Aaron and his sons from among the children of Israel, to do the work for the children of Israel in the tabernacle of meeting, and to make atonement for the children of Israel, that there be no plague among the children of Israel when the children of Israel come near the sanctuary."

20Thus Moses and Aaron and all the congregation of the children of Israel did to the Levites; according to all that the LORD commanded Moses concerning the Levites, so the children of Israel did to them. 21And the Levites purified themselves and washed their clothes; then Aaron presented them *like* a wave offering before the LORD, and Aaron made atonement for them to cleanse them. 22After that the Levites went in to do their work in the tabernacle of meeting before Aaron and his sons; as the LORD commanded Moses concerning the Levites, so they did to them.

23Then the LORD spoke to Moses, saying, 24"This *is* what *pertains* to the Levites: From twenty-five years old and above one may enter to perform service in the work of the tabernacle of meeting; 25and at the age of fifty years they must cease performing this work, and shall work no more. 26They may minister with their brethren in the tabernacle of meeting, to attend to needs, but they *themselves* shall do no work. Thus you shall do to the Levites regarding their duties."

THE SECOND PASSOVER

9 Now the LORD spoke to Moses in the Wilderness of Sinai, in the first month of the second year after they had come out of the land of Egypt, saying: 2"Let the children of Israel keep the Passover at its appointed time. 3On the fourteenth day of this month, at twilight, you shall keep it at its appointed time. According to all its rites and ceremonies you shall keep it." 4So Moses told the children of Israel that they should keep the Passover. 5And they kept the Passover on the fourteenth day of the first month, at twilight, in the Wilderness of Sinai; according to all that the LORD commanded Moses, so the children of Israel did.

6Now there were *certain* men who were defiled by a human corpse, so that they could not keep the Passover on that day; and they came before Moses and Aaron that day. 7And those men said to him, "We *became* defiled by a human corpse. Why are we kept from presenting the offering of the LORD at its appointed time among the children of Israel?"

8And Moses said to them, "Stand still, that I may hear what the LORD will command concerning you."

9Then the LORD spoke to Moses, saying, 10"Speak to the children of Israel, saying: 'If anyone of you or your posterity is unclean because of a corpse, or *is* far away on a journey, he may still keep the LORD's Passover. 11On the fourteenth day of the second month, at twilight, they may keep it. They shall eat it with unleavened bread and bitter herbs. 12They shall leave none of it until morning, nor break one of its bones. According to all the ordinances of the Passover they shall keep it. 13But the man who *is* clean and is not on a journey, and ceases to keep the Passover, that same person shall be cut off from among his people, because he did not bring the offering of the LORD at its appointed time; that man shall bear his sin.

14'And if a stranger dwells among you, and would keep the LORD's Passover, he must do so according to the rite of the Passover and according to its ceremony; you shall have one ordinance, both for the stranger and the native of the land.' "

THE CLOUD AND THE FIRE

15Now on the day that the tabernacle was raised up, the cloud covered the tabernacle, the tent of the Testimony; from evening until morning it was above the tabernacle like the appearance of fire. 16So it was always: the cloud covered it *by day,* and the appearance of fire by night. 17Whenever the cloud was taken up from above the tabernacle, after that the children of Israel would journey; and in the place where the cloud settled, there the children of Israel would pitch their tents. 18At the command of the LORD the children of Israel would journey, and at the command of the LORD they would camp; as long as the cloud stayed above the tabernacle they remained encamped. 19Even when the cloud continued long, many days above the tabernacle, the children of Israel kept the charge of the LORD and did not journey. 20So it was, when the cloud was above the tabernacle a few days: according to the command of the LORD they would remain encamped, and according to the command of the LORD they would journey. 21So it was, when the cloud remained only from evening until morning: when the cloud was taken up in the morning, then they would journey; whether by day or by night, whenever the cloud was taken up, they would journey. 22*Whether it was* two days, a month, or a year that the cloud remained above the tabernacle, the children of Israel would remain encamped and not journey; but when it was taken up, they would journey. 23At the command of the LORD they remained encamped, and at the command of the LORD they journeyed; they kept the charge of the LORD, at the command of the LORD by the hand of Moses.

Two Silver Trumpets

10 And the LORD spoke to Moses, saying: 2"Make two silver trumpets for yourself; you shall make them of hammered work; you shall use them for calling the congregation and for directing the movement of the camps. 3When they blow both of them, all the congregation shall gather before you at the door of the tabernacle of meeting. 4But if they blow *only* one, then the leaders, the heads of the divisions of Israel, shall gather to you. 5When you sound the advance, the camps that lie on the east side shall then begin their journey. 6When you sound the advance the second time, then the camps that lie on the south side shall begin their journey; they shall sound the call for them to begin their journeys. 7And when the assembly is to be gathered together, you shall blow, but not sound the advance. 8The sons of Aaron, the priests, shall blow the trumpets; and these shall be to you as an ordinance forever throughout your generations.

9"When you go to war in your land against the enemy who oppresses you, then you shall sound an alarm with the trumpets, and you will be remembered before the LORD your God, and you will be saved from your enemies. 10Also in the day of your gladness, in your appointed feasts, and at the beginning of your months, you shall blow the trumpets over your burnt offerings and over the sacrifices of your peace offerings; and they shall be a memorial for you before your God: I *am* the LORD your God."

Departure from Sinai

11Now it came to pass on the twentieth *day* of the second month, in the second year, that the cloud was taken up from above the tabernacle of the Testimony. 12And the children of Israel set out from the Wilderness of Sinai on their journeys; then the cloud settled down in the Wilderness of Paran. 13So they started out for the first time according to the command of the LORD by the hand of Moses.

14The standard of the camp of the children of Judah set out first according to their armies; over their army was Nahshon the son of Amminadab. 15Over the army of the tribe of the children of Issachar *was* Nethanel the son of Zuar. 16And over the army of the tribe of the children of Zebulun *was* Eliab the son of Helon.

17Then the tabernacle was taken down; and the sons of Gershon and the sons of Merari set out, carrying the tabernacle.

18And the standard of the camp of Reuben set out according to their armies; over their army *was* Elizur the son of Shedeur. 19Over the army of the tribe of the children of Simeon *was* Shelumiel the son of Zurishaddai. 20And over the army of the tribe of the children of Gad *was* Eliasaph the son of Deuel.

21Then the Kohathites set out, carrying the holy things. (The tabernacle would be prepared for their arrival.)

22And the standard of the camp of the children of Ephraim set out according to their armies; over their army *was* Elishama the son of Ammihud. 23Over the army of the tribe of the children of Manasseh *was* Gamaliel the son of Pedahzur. 24And over the army of the tribe of the children of Benjamin *was* Abidan the son of Gideoni.

25Then the standard of the camp of the children of Dan (the rear guard of all the camps) set out according to their armies; over their army *was* Ahiezer the son of Ammishaddai. 26Over the army of the tribe of the children of Asher *was* Pagiel the son of Ocran. 27And over the army of the tribe of the children of Naphtali *was* Ahira the son of Enan.

28Thus *was* the order of march of the chil-

SOUL NOTE

Let Others Help *(10:29–31)* When Moses led the people of Israel through the wilderness, he utilized a combination of divine and human guidance. He followed the cloud of the Lord's presence (9:15–23; 10:34), and he invited Hobab, who knew about surviving in the wilderness, to act as a guide (10:29–31). Moses realized the value of human resources to help him accomplish a divinely appointed task. In the same way today, God teaches us His truth through His Word, but He also uses significant others to help us apply that truth to our daily lives. As you serve God, make use of the resources He gives you. **Topic: Mentoring**

dren of Israel, according to their armies, when
they began their journey.
29 Now Moses said to Hobab the son of
Reuel[a] the Midianite, Moses' father-in-law,
"We are setting out for the place of which the
LORD said, 'I will give it to you.' Come with us,
and we will treat you well; for the LORD has
promised good things to Israel."
30 And he said to him, "I will not go, but I will
depart to my *own* land and to my relatives."
31 So *Moses* said, "Please do not leave, inasmuch as you know how we are to camp in the
wilderness, and you can be our eyes. 32 And it
shall be, if you go with us—indeed it shall
be—that whatever good the LORD will do to
us, the same we will do to you."
33 So they departed from the mountain of the
LORD on a journey of three days; and the ark of
the covenant of the LORD went before them for
the three days' journey, to search out a resting
place for them. 34 And the cloud of the LORD
was above them by day when they went out
from the camp.
35 So it was, whenever the ark set out, that
Moses said:

"Rise up, O LORD!
Let Your enemies be scattered,
And let those who hate You flee before
You."

36 And when it rested, he said:

"Return, O LORD,
To the many thousands of Israel."

THE PEOPLE COMPLAIN

11 Now *when* the people complained, it
displeased the LORD; for the LORD
heard *it,* and His anger was aroused. So the
fire of the LORD burned among them, and consumed *some* in the outskirts of the camp.
2 Then the people cried out to Moses, and
when Moses prayed to the LORD, the fire was
quenched. 3 So he called the name of the place
Taberah,[a] because the fire of the LORD had
burned among them.
4 Now the mixed multitude who were
among them yielded to intense craving; so the
children of Israel also wept again and said:
"Who will give us meat to eat? 5 We remember
the fish which we ate freely in Egypt, the cucumbers, the melons, the leeks, the onions,
and the garlic; 6 but now our whole being *is*
dried up; *there is* nothing at all except this
manna *before* our eyes!"
7 Now the manna *was* like coriander seed,
and its color like the color of bdellium. 8 The
people went about and gathered *it,* ground *it*
on millstones or beat *it* in the mortar, cooked
it in pans, and made cakes of it; and its taste
was like the taste of pastry prepared with oil.
9 And when the dew fell on the camp in the
night, the manna fell on it.
10 Then Moses heard the people weeping
throughout their families, everyone at the
door of his tent; and the anger of the LORD was
greatly aroused; Moses also was displeased.
11 So Moses said to the LORD, "Why have You
afflicted Your servant? And why have I not
found favor in Your sight, that You have laid
the burden of all these people on me? 12 Did I
conceive all these people? Did I beget them,
that You should say to me, 'Carry them in your
bosom, as a guardian carries a nursing child,'

10:29 [a]Septuagint reads *Raguel* (compare Exodus 2:18). **11:3** [a]Literally *Burning*

SOUL NOTE

Food Fixations *(11:4–9)* Preoccupation with food can indicate an eating disorder. When people become overly focused on food, their dependence on God suffers. The Israelites, while not having an eating disorder, *did* experience a "perspective disorder" because of their focus on food. Their preoccupation with foods they did not have caused them to lose sight of God's miraculous and loving provision of manna. So today, when people become preoccupied with anything other than God, they can lose their perspective of God's care for them. People with eating disorders need to refocus on their worth in God's eyes and be thankful for God's provision.
Topic: Eating Disorders

to the land which You swore to their fathers? 13Where am I to get meat to give to all these people? For they weep all over me, saying, 'Give us meat, that we may eat.' 14I am not able to bear all these people alone, because the burden *is* too heavy for me. 15If You treat me like this, please kill me here and now—if I have found favor in Your sight—and do not let me see my wretchedness!"

THE SEVENTY ELDERS

16So the LORD said to Moses: "Gather to Me seventy men of the elders of Israel, whom you know to be the elders of the people and officers over them; bring them to the tabernacle of meeting, that they may stand there with you. 17Then I will come down and talk with you there. I will take of the Spirit that *is* upon you and will put *the same* upon them; and they shall bear the burden of the people with you, that you may not bear *it* yourself alone. 18Then you shall say to the people, 'Consecrate yourselves for tomorrow, and you shall eat meat; for you have wept in the hearing of the LORD, saying, "Who will give us meat to eat? For *it was* well with us in Egypt." Therefore the LORD will give you meat, and you shall eat. 19You shall eat, not one day, nor two days, nor five days, nor ten days, nor twenty days, 20but *for* a whole month, until it comes out of your nostrils and becomes loathsome to you, because you have despised the LORD who is among you, and have wept before Him, saying, "Why did we ever come up out of Egypt?" ' "

21And Moses said, "The people whom I *am* among *are* six hundred thousand men on foot; yet You have said, 'I will give them meat, that they may eat *for* a whole month.' 22Shall flocks and herds be slaughtered for them, to provide enough for them? Or shall all the fish of the sea be gathered together for them, to provide enough for them?"

23And the LORD said to Moses, "Has the LORD's arm been shortened? Now you shall see whether what I say will happen to you or not." 24So Moses went out and told the people the words of the LORD, and he gathered the seventy men of the elders of the people and placed them around the tabernacle. 25Then the LORD came down in the cloud, and spoke to him, and took of the Spirit that *was* upon him, and placed *the same* upon the seventy elders; and it happened, when the Spirit rested upon them, that they prophesied, although they never did *so* again.[a]

26But two men had remained in the camp: the name of one *was* Eldad, and the name of the other Medad. And the Spirit rested upon them. Now they *were* among those listed, but who had not gone out to the tabernacle; yet they prophesied in the camp. 27And a young man ran and told Moses, and said, "Eldad and Medad are prophesying in the camp."

28So Joshua the son of Nun, Moses' assistant, *one* of his choice men, answered and said, "Moses my lord, forbid them!"

29Then Moses said to him, "Are you zealous for my sake? Oh, that all the LORD's people were prophets *and* that the LORD would put His Spirit upon them!" 30And Moses returned to the camp, he and the elders of Israel.

THE LORD SENDS QUAIL

31Now a wind went out from the LORD, and it brought quail from the sea and left *them* fluttering near the camp, about a day's journey on this side and about a day's journey on the other side, all around the camp, and about two cubits above the surface of the ground. 32And the

11:25 [a]Targum and Vulgate read *did not cease.*

SOUL NOTE

Going It Alone *(11:16, 17)* Pushing hard with many hours and demands can become counterproductive. We need to set boundaries around our time and energy to protect ourselves. God is aware of our limitations and encourages us to lighten the load by delegating responsibility to others who can help us be more productive and effective. The leader always carries greater responsibility, but he or she can alleviate the stress of going it alone by sharing the load. We should consider our responsibilities and how we can delegate to others in order to get the job done.
Topic: Burnout

people stayed up all that day, all night, and all
the next day, and gathered the quail (he who
gathered least gathered ten homers); and they
spread *them* out for themselves all around the
camp. [33]But while the meat *was* still between
their teeth, before it was chewed, the wrath of
the LORD was aroused against the people, and
the LORD struck the people with a very great
plague. [34]So he called the name of that place
Kibroth Hattaavah,[a] because there they buried
the people who had yielded to craving.
[35]From Kibroth Hattaavah the people moved
to Hazeroth, and camped at Hazeroth.

DISSENSION OF AARON AND MIRIAM

12 Then Miriam and Aaron spoke against
Moses because of the Ethiopian woman
whom he had married; for he had married an
Ethiopian woman. [2]So they said, "Has the
LORD indeed spoken only through Moses? Has
He not spoken through us also?" And the LORD
heard *it.* [3](Now the man Moses *was* very humble, more than all men who *were* on the face
of the earth.)
[4]Suddenly the LORD said to Moses, Aaron,
and Miriam, "Come out, you three, to the tabernacle of meeting!" So the three came out.
[5]Then the LORD came down in the pillar of
cloud and stood *in* the door of the tabernacle,
and called Aaron and Miriam. And they both
went forward. [6]Then He said,

"Hear now My words:
If there is a prophet among you,
I, the LORD, make Myself known to him
in a vision;

11:34 [a]Literally *Graves of Craving*

PERSONALITY PROFILE

Judgmentalism

AARON AND MIRIAM: A CASE STUDY IN JUDGMENTALISM

(NUMBERS 12)

While he was living in Midian, Moses had married Zipporah, the daughter of Reuel, a Midianite priest (Ex. 2:21). It is likely that she is the "Ethiopian woman" referred to in Numbers 12:1, of whom Aaron and Miriam disapproved. Their expression leaves it unclear whether their resentment was because Moses' wife was dark-skinned or simply not a Hebrew. In either case, their underlying problem had to do with jealousy toward Moses. They expressed it by treating his wife with disrespect. They also questioned Moses' authority as the spokesman for God, implying that Moses had grown proud. But they actually revealed their own self-centeredness.

Aaron and Miriam had been chosen for influential roles among the leaders of Israel. But they directly challenged Moses by telling the people that their word was just as godly and important as their brother's. God came directly to Moses' defense, chastising both Aaron and Miriam for their ungodly judgments and striking Miriam with leprosy. Moses did not retaliate, but "cried out to the LORD, saying, 'Please heal her, O God, I pray!' " (Num. 12:13). Miriam was indeed healed, but was sent out of the camp for seven days. When she returned, she seems to have been healed not only of leprosy, but also of her judgmental attitudes.

A "leprosy of the spirit" often infects judgmental Christians today as it did Aaron and Miriam. They cannot distinguish between right judgments and judgmental attitudes. This pattern eats away at the soul, filling it with jealousy, envy, fear, pride, and self-righteousness. Prejudice and racism flow from this same infection. Judgmental Christians are not only rejected by unbelievers, but eventually are avoided like lepers were. Fellow Christians feel betrayed by those who project such a negative image of believers before the watching world. Repentance and godly humility are the only effective treatments against the path of judgmentalism.

To Learn More: Turn to the article about judgmentalism on pages 1324, 1325. See also the key passage note at Luke 6:37 on page 1326.

Insecurity

DISCOVERING THE DECEPTIONS

ROBERT MCGEE

(Numbers 13:30–33)

Evil flourishes when we base our self-worth on what we do or what others think of us. Destined to drink the cup of failure, we'll soon learn that we can never do enough or be good enough. Many believers discover that their lives seem very similar to the lives of those who have never accepted Christ. So they try to gain value and meaning in their lives by obtaining the approval of people. They are tormented by past failures. They experience loneliness and alienation. In short, they are insecure.

Many people are seeking relief from emotional, relational, and spiritual insecurity. Their intense feeling of insecurity, along with the related thought patterns, is debilitating and painful. People who experience insecurity need to focus on the underlying reasons for the insecurity, not simply on finding ways to escape it. Feelings of insecurity reveal that something important is wrong with a person's foundational beliefs. As a fever indicates a physical illness, insecurity indicates a faith ailment that needs attention.

Insecurity is a common experience because of the effects of being born into a fallen human race. If people understand the ramifications of that liability, then they will also understand that life is a constant struggle to gain more and more freedom from this "birth defect." Scripture is replete with warnings about our natural condition. Before becoming believers, people are "dead in trespasses and sins" (Eph. 2:1). They walk "in the futility of their mind, having their understanding darkened, being alienated from the life of God, because of the ignorance that is in them, because of the blindness of their heart" (Eph. 4:17, 18). They also have "an evil conscience" from which they need to be cleansed (Heb. 10:22).

We are warned, however, that the battle for security and significance is far from over at the moment we become God's children. Believers must be on their guard about accepting deceptions. Being deceived is simply believing something to be true that is false and, conversely, believing something to be false that is true.

DOUBLE DECEPTIONS

Two prime deceptions are the cause of many people's insecurity. The first prime deception is that people don't realize that they are plagued by many deceptions. Only God can reveal the deceptions that hinder people's lives. These deceptions come in all shapes and sizes, in varying degrees, with varying sources. No amount of contemplation or reasoning can reveal every person's deceptions. Yet they constantly see the effects of those deceptions on their lives.

The second prime deception is that what people think they believe isn't what they truly believe. People often give intellectual assent to truth, but sadly, they don't entrust their lives to it. For example, if a person had a harsh, condemning father, usually their early beliefs about the heavenly Father are that He also is harsh and condemning. Later in life, they might be told that God is really a loving Father. But unless these early beliefs are confronted as deception, the person will give only intellectual assent to the belief that God is loving. They *think* that they believe that God is a loving God, yet they struggle to trust Him.

These "heart beliefs" are what actually control the person's understanding and experience of God. When people begin life as babies, they have no defense against absorbing the deceptions around them. That, combined with the natural mind that is antagonistic to the things of God, has encouraged people to entrust their lives to critical beliefs that are false. False critical or heart beliefs then influence their lives and their beliefs about God and themselves.

TIME TO ASK SOME QUESTIONS

People usually do not question the beliefs to which they entrust themselves. Most people can trace almost all of their insecurity to a deception about how they believe God responds to their failures, their sins, and their times of falling short of His standards. Every perception of God, every way a person interacts with Him, is built on what they believe is the basis of their relationship with Him.

Satan has been quite successful in distorting this aspect of a person's relationship with God. Many Christians hold a distorted view of grace and God's unconditional love. They know intellectually what these mean, but their hearts don't believe what their heads acknowledge. People fail consistently because of the sin nature; if they are not relying completely on the grace and love of God, they will feel that He has abandoned them or, even worse, that He has become their enemy.

When a person experiences insecurity, God desires that they come to Him and allow the Holy Spirit to reveal the deceptions on which they depend. They need not be frightened by experiencing insecurity, worry, anxiety, or lack of peace. God allows these experiences so that He can show His people the deceptions on which they are relying, and then remove those deceptions. He wants to set us free from insecurity so that we can be truly secure in Him. He will set us free when we seek Him, in spite of our fears and insecurity.

FURTHER MEDITATION:

Other passages to study about the issue of insecurity include:

- Psalm 23
- Psalm 34:18–22
- Isaiah 43:1–3
- Matthew 10:29–31
- Ephesians 1:3–14
- 1 John 2:1, 2

To Learn More: Turn to the key passage note on insecurity at Numbers 13:30–33 on page 189. See also the personality profile of Moses on page 219.

I speak to him in a dream.
7 Not so with My servant Moses;
He *is* faithful in all My house.
8 I speak with him face to face,
Even plainly, and not in dark sayings;
And he sees the form of the LORD.
Why then were you not afraid
To speak against My servant Moses?"

[9]So the anger of the LORD was aroused
against them, and He departed. [10]And when
the cloud departed from above the tabernacle,
suddenly Miriam *became* leprous, as *white as*
snow. Then Aaron turned toward Miriam, and
there she was, a leper. [11]So Aaron said to Moses, "Oh, my lord! Please do not lay *this* sin on
us, in which we have done foolishly and in
which we have sinned. [12]Please do not let her
be as one dead, whose flesh is half consumed
when he comes out of his mother's womb!"
[13]So Moses cried out to the LORD, saying,
"Please heal her, O God, I pray!"
[14]Then the LORD said to Moses, "If her father had but spit in her face, would she not be
shamed seven days? Let her be shut out of
the camp seven days, and afterward she may
be received *again.*" [15]So Miriam was shut out
of the camp seven days, and the people did
not journey till Miriam was brought in *again.*
[16]And afterward the people moved from Hazeroth and camped in the Wilderness of Paran.

SPIES SENT INTO CANAAN

13 And the LORD spoke to Moses, saying,
[2]"Send men to spy out the land of Canaan, which I am giving to the children of Israel; from each tribe of
their fathers you shall
send a man, every one a
leader among them."
[3]So Moses sent them
from the Wilderness of
Paran according to the
command of the LORD,
all of them men who *were* heads of the children of Israel. [4]Now these *were* their names:
from the tribe of Reuben, Shammua the son of
Zaccur; [5]from the tribe of Simeon, Shaphat the
son of Hori; [6]from the tribe of Judah, Caleb
the son of Jephunneh; [7]from the tribe of Issachar, Igal the son of Joseph; [8]from the tribe of
Ephraim, Hoshea[a] the son of Nun; [9]from the
tribe of Benjamin, Palti the son of Raphu;
[10]from the tribe of Zebulun, Gaddiel the son of
Sodi; [11]from the tribe of Joseph, *that is,* from
the tribe of Manasseh, Gaddi the son of Susi;
[12]from the tribe of Dan, Ammiel the son of Ge-
malli; [13]from the tribe of Asher, Sethur the son
of Michael; [14]from the tribe of Naphtali, Nahbi
the son of Vophsi; [15]from the tribe of Gad, Ge-
uel the son of Machi.
[16]These *are* the names of the men whom
Moses sent to spy out the land. And Moses
called Hoshea[a] the son of Nun, Joshua.
[17]Then Moses sent them to spy out the land
of Canaan, and said to them, "Go up this *way*
into the South, and go up to the mountains,
[18]and see what the land is like: whether the
people who dwell in it *are* strong or weak, few
or many; [19]whether the land they dwell in *is*
good or bad; whether the cities they inhabit
are like camps or strongholds; [20]whether the
land *is* rich or poor; and whether there are forests there or not. Be of good courage. And
bring some of the fruit of the land." Now the
time *was* the season of the first ripe grapes.
[21]So they went up and spied out the land
from the Wilderness of Zin as far as Rehob,
near the entrance of Hamath. [22]And they went
up through the South and came to Hebron;
Ahiman, Sheshai, and Talmai, the descendants of Anak, *were* there. (Now Hebron was
built seven years before Zoan in Egypt.)
[23]Then they came to the Valley of Eshcol, and
there cut down a branch with one cluster of
grapes; they carried it between two of them on
a pole. *They* also *brought* some of the pomegranates and figs. [24]The place was called the
Valley of Eshcol,[a] because of the cluster which
the men of Israel cut down there. [25]And they
returned from spying
out the land after forty
days.
[26]Now they departed
and came back to Mo-
ses and Aaron and all
the congregation of the
children of Israel in the
Wilderness of Paran, at Kadesh; they brought
back word to them and to all the congregation, and showed them the fruit of the land.
[27]Then they told him, and said: "We went to
the land where you sent us. It truly flows with
milk and honey, and this *is* its fruit. [28]Never-

> "Let us go up at once and take possession, for we are well able to overcome it."
> NUMBERS 13:30

13:8 [a]Septuagint and Vulgate read *Oshea.*
13:16 [a]Septuagint and Vulgate read *Oshea.*
13:24 [a]Literally *Cluster*

theless the people who dwell in the land *are*
strong; the cities *are* fortified *and* very large;
moreover we saw the descendants of Anak
there. 29The Amalekites dwell in the land of
the South; the Hittites, the Jebusites, and the
Amorites dwell in the mountains; and the Canaanites dwell by the sea and along the banks
of the Jordan."
30Then Caleb quieted the people before
Moses, and said, "Let us go up at once and
take possession, for we are well able to overcome it."
31But the men who had gone up with him
said, "We are not able to go up against the
people, for they *are* stronger than we." 32And
they gave the children of Israel a bad report of
the land which they had spied out, saying,
"The land through which we have gone as
spies *is* a land that devours its inhabitants,
and all the people whom we saw in it *are* men
of *great* stature. 33There we saw the giants[a]
(the descendants of Anak came from the
giants); and we were like grasshoppers in our
own sight, and so we were in their sight."

Israel Refuses to Enter Canaan

14 So all the congregation lifted up their
voices and cried, and the people wept
that night. 2And all the children of Israel complained against Moses and Aaron, and the
whole congregation said to them, "If only we
had died in the land of Egypt! Or if only we had

13:33 [a]Hebrew *nephilim*

KEY PASSAGE

WE WERE LIKE GRASSHOPPERS!

(13:30–33)

Insecurity often occurs through comparing ourselves with others. Discouraging comments, negative thinking, and unreasonable expectations can also make us feel insecure. When the ten spies compared themselves to the well-armed Canaanites and their heavily fortified cities, they concluded: "We were like grasshoppers in our own sight." The result was fear, unbelief, and rebellion against God's plan for the people to take the land.

Measuring oneself against others will lead to insecurity. We can always find someone who is better looking, wealthier, better dressed, more spiritual, or more intelligent. We'll see "giants" next to whom we feel like "grasshoppers." Instead, we are to measure ourselves "within the limits of the sphere which God appointed us" (2 Cor. 10:13). In other words, we should be asking how we are doing with the looks, wealth, appearance, brains, and special abilities that God has given us. Ultimately we are accountable only to Him.

To Learn More: Turn to the article about insecurity on pages 186, 187. See also the personality profiles of Moses on page 219.

SOUL NOTE

Lost Hope *(14:1–4)* The Israelites were camped at the edge of the Promised Land, but the negative report of the spies caused them to lose hope and perspective. They wanted to go back to Egypt, forgetting that they had been slaves there. They were afraid to enter the land, forgetting the miracles God had performed to deliver them from Egypt. Lost hope and lost perspective meant a lost land, for God refused to let them enter. When feeling hopeless, we should check our perspective, remembering where God has brought us, and allowing Him to work new miracles in our lives.
Topic: Hope

died in this wilderness! 3Why has the LORD
brought us to this land to fall by the sword,
that our wives and children should become
victims? Would it not be better for us to return
to Egypt?" 4So they said to one another, "Let
us select a leader and return to Egypt."

5Then Moses and Aaron fell on their faces
before all the assembly of the congregation of
the children of Israel.

6But Joshua the son of Nun and Caleb the
son of Jephunneh, *who were* among those
who had spied out the land, tore their clothes;
7and they spoke to all the congregation of the
children of Israel, saying: "The land we
passed through to spy out *is* an exceedingly
good land. 8If the LORD delights in us, then He
will bring us into this land and give it to us, 'a
land which flows with milk and honey.'[a] 9Only
do not rebel against the LORD, nor fear the
people of the land, for they *are* our bread;
their protection has departed from them, and
the LORD *is* with us. Do not fear them."

10And all the congregation said to stone
them with stones. Now the glory of the LORD
appeared in the tabernacle of meeting before
all the children of Israel.

Moses Intercedes for the People

11Then the LORD said to Moses: "How long
will these people reject Me? And how long will
they not believe Me, with all the signs which I
have performed among them? 12I will strike
them with the pestilence and disinherit them,
and I will make of you a nation greater and
mightier than they."

13And Moses said to the LORD: "Then the
Egyptians will hear *it,* for by Your might You
brought these people up from among them,
14and they will tell *it* to the inhabitants of this
land. They have heard that You, LORD, *are*
among these people; that You, LORD, are seen
face to face and Your cloud stands above them,
and You go before them in a pillar of cloud by
day and in a pillar of fire by night. 15Now *if* You
kill these people as one man, then the nations
which have heard of Your fame will speak, saying, 16'Because the LORD was not able to bring
this people to the land which He swore to give
them, therefore He killed them in the wilderness.' 17And now, I pray, let the power of my
Lord be great, just as You have spoken, saying,
18'The LORD is longsuffering and abundant in
mercy, forgiving iniquity and transgression;
but He by no means clears *the guilty,* visiting
the iniquity of the fathers on the children to the
third and fourth *generation.'*[a] 19Pardon the iniquity of this people, I pray, according to the
greatness of Your mercy, just as You have forgiven this people, from Egypt even until now."

20Then the LORD said: "I have pardoned, according to your word; 21but truly, as I live, all
the earth shall be filled with the glory of the
LORD— 22because all these men who have
seen My glory and the signs which I did in
Egypt and in the wilderness, and have put Me
to the test now these ten times, and have not
heeded My voice, 23they certainly shall not see
the land of which I swore to their fathers, nor
shall any of those who rejected Me see it.
24But My servant Caleb, because he has a different spirit in him and has followed Me fully, I
will bring into the land where he went, and his
descendants shall inherit it. 25Now the Amalekites and the Canaanites dwell in the valley;
tomorrow turn and move out into the wilderness by the Way of the Red Sea."

Death Sentence on the Rebels

26And the LORD spoke to Moses and Aaron,
saying, 27"How long *shall I bear with* this evil

14:8 [a]Exodus 3:8 **14:18** [a]Exodus 34:6, 7

SOUL NOTE

Won't They Ever Learn? *(14:1–4)* Chronic complainers gripe about anything and everything. The Israelites had grumbled against God and Moses ever since leaving Egypt (see, for example, Ex. 15:24; 16:3; 17:2; Num. 11:1, 4), and they would continue to complain (Num. 16:3, 41; 20:2, 3; 21:5). In every circumstance, we have a choice: We can complain, or we can trust God's ability to handle any situation. Complaining means inaction; faith means moving ahead with God. Trusting Him with our problems is the first real step in overcoming them. **Topic: Attitudes**

congregation who complain against Me? I
have heard the complaints which the children
of Israel make against Me. [28]Say to them, 'As I
live,' says the LORD, 'just as you have spoken
in My hearing, so I will do to you: [29]The carcasses of you who have complained against
Me shall fall in this wilderness, all of you who
were numbered, according to your entire
number, from twenty years old and above.
[30]Except for Caleb the son of Jephunneh and
Joshua the son of Nun, you shall by no means
enter the land which I swore I would make
you dwell in. [31]But your little ones, whom you
said would be victims, I will bring in, and they
shall know the land which you have despised.
[32]But *as for* you, your carcasses shall fall in
this wilderness. [33]And your sons shall be
shepherds in the wilderness forty years, and
bear the brunt of your infidelity, until your
carcasses are consumed in the wilderness.
[34]According to the number of the days in
which you spied out the land, forty days, for
each day you shall bear your guilt one year,
namely forty years, and you shall know My rejection. [35]I the LORD have spoken this. I will
surely do so to all this evil congregation who
are gathered together against Me. In this wilderness they shall be consumed, and there
they shall die.' "

[36]Now the men whom Moses sent to spy out
the land, who returned and made all the congregation complain against him by bringing a
bad report of the land, [37]those very men who
brought the evil report about the land, died by
the plague before the LORD. [38]But Joshua the
son of Nun and Caleb the son of Jephunneh
remained alive, of the men who went to spy
out the land.

A Futile Invasion Attempt

[39]Then Moses told these words to all the
children of Israel, and the people mourned
greatly. [40]And they rose early in the morning
and went up to the top of the mountain, saying, "Here we are, and we will go up to the
place which the LORD has promised, for we
have sinned!"

[41]And Moses said, "Now why do you transgress the command of the LORD? For this will
not succeed. [42]Do not go up, lest you be defeated by your enemies, for the LORD *is* not
among you. [43]For the Amalekites and the
Canaanites *are* there before you, and you shall
fall by the sword; because you have turned
away from the LORD, the LORD will not be with
you."

[44]But they presumed to go up to the mountaintop. Nevertheless, neither the ark of the
covenant of the LORD nor Moses departed
from the camp. [45]Then the Amalekites and the
Canaanites who dwelt in that mountain came
down and attacked them, and drove them
back as far as Hormah.

Laws of Grain and Drink Offerings

15 And the LORD spoke to Moses, saying,
[2]"Speak to the children of Israel, and
say to them: 'When you have come into the
land you are to inhabit, which I am giving to
you, [3]and you make an offering by fire to the
LORD, a burnt offering or a sacrifice, to fulfill a
vow or as a freewill offering or in your appointed feasts, to make a sweet aroma to the
LORD, from the herd or the flock, [4]then he who
presents his offering to the LORD shall bring a
grain offering of one-tenth *of an ephah* of fine
flour mixed with one-fourth of a hin of oil;
[5]and one-fourth of a hin of wine as a drink offering you shall prepare with the burnt offering or the sacrifice, for each lamb. [6]Or for a
ram you shall prepare as a grain offering two-
tenths *of an ephah* of fine flour mixed with
one-third of a hin of oil; [7]and as a drink offering you shall offer one-third of a hin of wine
as a sweet aroma to the LORD. [8]And when you
prepare a young bull as a burnt offering, or as
a sacrifice to fulfill a vow, or as a peace offering to the LORD, [9]then shall be offered with the
young bull a grain offering of three-tenths *of
an ephah* of fine flour mixed with half a hin of
oil; [10]and you shall bring as the drink offering
half a hin of wine as an offering made by fire,
a sweet aroma to the LORD.

[11]'Thus it shall be done for each young bull,
for each ram, or for each lamb or young goat.
[12]According to the number that you prepare,
so you shall do with everyone according to
their number. [13]All who are native-born shall
do these things in this manner, in presenting
an offering made by fire, a sweet aroma to the
LORD. [14]And if a stranger dwells with you, or
whoever *is* among you throughout your generations, and would present an offering made by
fire, a sweet aroma to the LORD, just as you do,
so shall he do. [15]One ordinance *shall be* for you
of the assembly and for the stranger who
dwells *with you*, an ordinance forever throughout your generations; as you are, so shall the

stranger be before the LORD. 16One law and one custom shall be for you and for the stranger who dwells with you.' "[a]

17Again the LORD spoke to Moses, saying, 18"Speak to the children of Israel, and say to them: 'When you come into the land to which I bring you, 19then it will be, when you eat of the bread of the land, that you shall offer up a heave offering to the LORD. 20You shall offer up a cake of the first of your ground meal *as* a heave offering; as a heave offering of the threshing floor, so shall you offer it up. 21Of the first of your ground meal you shall give to the LORD a heave offering throughout your generations.

Laws Concerning Unintentional Sin

22'If you sin unintentionally, and do not observe all these commandments which the LORD has spoken to Moses— 23all that the LORD has commanded you by the hand of Moses, from the day the LORD gave commandment and onward throughout your generations— 24then it will be, if it is unintentionally committed, without the knowledge of the congregation, that the whole congregation shall offer one young bull as a burnt offering, as a sweet aroma to the LORD, with its grain offering and its drink offering, according to the ordinance, and one kid of the goats as a sin offering. 25So the priest shall make atonement for the whole congregation of the children of Israel, and it shall be forgiven them, for it was unintentional; they shall bring their offering, an offering made by fire to the LORD, and their sin offering before the LORD, for their unintended sin. 26It shall be forgiven the whole congregation of the children of Israel and the stranger who dwells among them, because all the people *did it* unintentionally.

27'And if a person sins unintentionally, then he shall bring a female goat in its first year as a sin offering. 28So the priest shall make atonement for the person who sins unintentionally, when he sins unintentionally before the LORD, to make atonement for him; and it shall be forgiven him. 29You shall have one law for him who sins unintentionally, *for* him who is native-born among the children of Israel and for the stranger who dwells among them.

Law Concerning Presumptuous Sin

30'But the person who does *anything* presumptuously, *whether he is* native-born or a stranger, that one brings reproach on the LORD, and he shall be cut off from among his people. 31Because he has despised the word of the LORD, and has broken His commandment, that person shall be completely cut off; his guilt *shall be* upon him.' "

Penalty for Violating the Sabbath

32Now while the children of Israel were in the wilderness, they found a man gathering sticks on the Sabbath day. 33And those who found him gathering sticks brought him to Moses and Aaron, and to all the congregation. 34They put him under guard, because it had not been explained what should be done to him.

35Then the LORD said to Moses, "The man must surely be put to death; all the congregation shall stone him with stones outside the camp." 36So, as the LORD commanded Moses, all the congregation brought him outside the camp and stoned him with stones, and he died.

Tassels on Garments

37Again the LORD spoke to Moses, saying, 38"Speak to the children of Israel: Tell them to make tassels on the corners of their garments throughout their generations, and to put a blue thread in the tassels of the corners. 39And you shall have the tassel, that you may look upon it and remember all the commandments of the LORD and do them, and that you *may* not follow the harlotry to which your own heart and your own eyes are inclined, 40and that you may remember and do all My commandments, and be holy for your God. 41I *am* the LORD your God, who brought you out of the land of Egypt, to be your God: I *am* the LORD your God."

Rebellion Against Moses and Aaron

16 Now Korah the son of Izhar, the son of Kohath, the son of Levi, with Dathan and Abiram the sons of Eliab, and On the son of Peleth, sons of Reuben, took *men;* 2and they rose up before Moses with some of the children of Israel, two hundred and fifty leaders of the congregation, representatives of the congregation, men of renown. 3They gathered together against Moses and Aaron, and said to them, "*You take* too much upon yourselves, for all the congregation *is* holy, every one of

15:16 [a]Compare Exodus 12:49

them, and the LORD *is* among them. Why then
do you exalt yourselves above the assembly of
the LORD?"
4 So when Moses heard *it,* he fell on his face;
5 and he spoke to Korah and all his company,
saying, "Tomorrow morning the LORD will
show who *is* His and *who is* holy, and will
cause *him* to come near to Him. That one
whom He chooses He will cause to come near
to Him. 6 Do this: Take censers, Korah and all
your company; 7 put fire in them and put incense in them before the LORD tomorrow, and
it shall be *that* the man whom the LORD
chooses *is* the holy one. *You take* too much
upon yourselves, you sons of Levi!"
8 Then Moses said to Korah, "Hear now, you
sons of Levi: 9 *Is it* a small thing to you that the
God of Israel has separated you from the congregation of Israel, to bring you near to Himself, to do the work of the tabernacle of the
LORD, and to stand before the congregation to
serve them; 10 and that He has brought you
near *to Himself,* you and all your brethren, the
sons of Levi, with you? And are you seeking
the priesthood also? 11 Therefore you and all
your company *are* gathered together against
the LORD. And what *is* Aaron that you complain against him?"
12 And Moses sent to call Dathan and Abiram the sons of Eliab, but they said, "We will
not come up! 13 *Is it* a small thing that you
have brought us up out of a land flowing with
milk and honey, to kill us in the wilderness,
that you should keep acting like a prince over
us? 14 Moreover you have not brought us into a
land flowing with milk and honey, nor given
us inheritance of fields and vineyards. Will
you put out the eyes of these men? We will not
come up!"
15 Then Moses was very angry, and said to
the LORD, "Do not respect their offering. I
have not taken one donkey from them, nor
have I hurt one of them."
16 And Moses said to Korah, "Tomorrow, you
and all your company be present before the
LORD—you and they, as well as Aaron. 17 Let
each take his censer and put incense in it, and
each of you bring his censer before the LORD,
two hundred and fifty censers; both you and
Aaron, each *with* his censer." 18 So every man
took his censer, put fire in it, laid incense on
it, and stood at the door of the tabernacle of
meeting with Moses and Aaron. 19 And Korah
gathered all the congregation against them at
the door of the tabernacle of meeting. Then the
glory of the LORD appeared to all the congregation.
20 And the LORD spoke to Moses and Aaron,
saying, 21 "Separate yourselves from among
this congregation, that I may consume them in
a moment."
22 Then they fell on their faces, and said,
"O God, the God of the spirits of all flesh, shall
one man sin, and You be angry with all the
congregation?"
23 So the LORD spoke to Moses, saying,
24 "Speak to the congregation, saying, 'Get
away from the tents of Korah, Dathan, and
Abiram.' "
25 Then Moses rose and went to Dathan and
Abiram, and the elders of Israel followed him.
26 And he spoke to the congregation, saying,
"Depart now from the tents of these wicked
men! Touch nothing of theirs, lest you be consumed in all their sins." 27 So they got away
from around the tents of Korah, Dathan, and
Abiram; and Dathan and Abiram came out
and stood at the door of their tents, with their
wives, their sons, and their little children.
28 And Moses said: "By this you shall know
that the LORD has sent me to do all these
works, for *I have* not *done them* of my own

SOUL NOTE

Don't Be Stubborn! *(16:12)* Dathan and Abiram stubbornly refused to discuss their differences with Moses. How different the outcome might have been if they had been willing to listen to Moses. Instead, they let their pride get in the way and stubbornly refused to listen to Moses as God's appointed leader. A strong will can be a valuable asset if it grows out of the character strength of commitment. But stubbornness arising from a wrong attitude and selfishness is a great liability.
Topic: Attitudes

will. 29If these men die naturally like all men, or if they are visited by the common fate of all men, *then* the LORD has not sent me. 30But if the LORD creates a new thing, and the earth opens its mouth and swallows them up with all that belongs to them, and they go down alive into the pit, then you will understand that these men have rejected the LORD."

31Now it came to pass, as he finished speaking all these words, that the ground split apart under them, 32and the earth opened its mouth and swallowed them up, with their households and all the men with Korah, with all *their* goods. 33So they and all those with them went down alive into the pit; the earth closed over them, and they perished from among the assembly. 34Then all Israel who *were* around them fled at their cry, for they said, "Lest the earth swallow us up *also!*"

35And a fire came out from the LORD and consumed the two hundred and fifty men who were offering incense.

36Then the LORD spoke to Moses, saying: 37"Tell Eleazar, the son of Aaron the priest, to pick up the censers out of the blaze, for they are holy, and scatter the fire some distance away. 38The censers of these men who sinned against their own souls, let them be made into hammered plates as a covering for the altar. Because they presented them before the LORD, therefore they are holy; and they shall be a sign to the children of Israel." 39So Eleazar the priest took the bronze censers, which those who were burned up had presented, and they were hammered out as a covering on the altar, 40*to be* a memorial to the children of Israel that no outsider, who *is* not a descendant of Aaron, should come near to offer incense before the LORD, that he might not become like Korah and his companions, just as the LORD had said to him through Moses.

COMPLAINTS OF THE PEOPLE

41On the next day all the congregation of the children of Israel complained against Moses and Aaron, saying, "You have killed the people of the LORD." 42Now it happened, when the congregation had gathered against Moses and Aaron, that they turned toward the tabernacle of meeting; and suddenly the cloud covered it, and the glory of the LORD appeared. 43Then Moses and Aaron came before the tabernacle of meeting.

44And the LORD spoke to Moses, saying, 45"Get away from among this congregation, that I may consume them in a moment."

And they fell on their faces.

46So Moses said to Aaron, "Take a censer and put fire in it from the altar, put incense *on it,* and take it quickly to the congregation and make atonement for them; for wrath has gone out from the LORD. The plague has begun." 47Then Aaron took *it* as Moses commanded, and ran into the midst of the assembly; and already the plague had begun among the people. So he put in the incense and made atonement for the people. 48And he stood between the dead and the living; so the plague was stopped. 49Now those who died in the plague were fourteen thousand seven hundred, besides those who died in the Korah incident. 50So Aaron returned to Moses at the door of the tabernacle of meeting, for the plague had stopped.

THE BUDDING OF AARON'S ROD

17 And the LORD spoke to Moses, saying: 2"Speak to the children of Israel, and get from them a rod from each father's house, all their leaders according to their fathers' houses—twelve rods. Write each man's name on his rod. 3And you shall write Aaron's name on the rod of Levi. For there shall be one rod

SOUL NOTE

Go Directly to God *(17:10, 11)* When Aaron's rod miraculously "sprouted and put forth buds" (17:8), God was showing clearly that He had chosen Aaron to serve as Israel's high priest. The high priest served as the intermediary between the people and God. This important position foreshadowed Christ who is our great High Priest (Heb. 8:1–6; 9:11–22). Instead of offering sacrifices of animals, however, Christ offered Himself as the final sacrifice for sin. Because of Christ, believers can go directly to God for forgiveness and help. **Topic: Crises**

for the head of *each* father's house. [4]Then you
shall place them in the tabernacle of meeting
before the Testimony, where I meet with you.
[5]And it shall be *that* the rod of the man whom
I choose will blossom; thus I will rid Myself of
the complaints of the children of Israel, which
they make against you."

[6]So Moses spoke to the children of Israel,
and each of their leaders gave him a rod
apiece, for each leader according to their fathers' houses, twelve rods; and the rod of
Aaron *was* among their rods. [7]And Moses
placed the rods before the LORD in the tabernacle of witness.

[8]Now it came to pass on the next day that
Moses went into the tabernacle of witness,
and behold, the rod of Aaron, of the house of
Levi, had sprouted and put forth buds, had
produced blossoms and yielded ripe almonds.
[9]Then Moses brought out all the rods from
before the LORD to all the children of Israel;
and they looked, and each man took his rod.

[10]And the LORD said to Moses, "Bring
Aaron's rod back before the Testimony, to be
kept as a sign against the rebels, that you may
put their complaints away from Me, lest they
die." [11]Thus did Moses; just as the LORD had
commanded him, so he did.

[12]So the children of Israel spoke to Moses,
saying, "Surely we die, we perish, we all perish! [13]Whoever even comes near the tabernacle
of the LORD must die. Shall we all utterly die?"

DUTIES OF PRIESTS AND LEVITES

18 Then the LORD said to Aaron: "You
and your sons and your father's house
with you shall bear the iniquity *related to* the
sanctuary, and you and your sons with you
shall bear the iniquity *associated with* your
priesthood. [2]Also bring with you your brethren of the tribe of Levi, the tribe of your father,
that they may be joined with you and serve
you while you and your sons *are* with you before the tabernacle of witness. [3]They shall attend to your needs and all the needs of the
tabernacle; but they shall not come near the
articles of the sanctuary and the altar, lest they
die—they and you also. [4]They shall be joined
with you and attend to the needs of the tabernacle of meeting, for all the work of the tabernacle; but an outsider shall not come near
you. [5]And you shall attend to the duties of the
sanctuary and the duties of the altar, that
there *may* be no more wrath on the children of
Israel. [6]Behold, I Myself have taken your
brethren the Levites from among the children
of Israel; *they are* a gift to you, given by the
LORD, to do the work of the tabernacle of
meeting. [7]Therefore you and your sons with
you shall attend to your priesthood for everything at the altar and behind the veil; and you
shall serve. I give your priesthood *to you* as a
gift for service, but the outsider who comes
near shall be put to death."

OFFERINGS FOR SUPPORT OF THE PRIESTS

[8]And the LORD spoke to Aaron: "Here, I Myself have also given you charge of My heave
offerings, all the holy gifts of the children of
Israel; I have given them as a portion to you
and your sons, as an ordinance forever. [9]This
shall be yours of the most holy things *reserved*
from the fire: every offering of theirs, every
grain offering and every sin offering and every
trespass offering which they render to Me,
shall be most holy for you and your sons. [10]In
a most holy *place* you shall eat it; every male
shall eat it. It shall be holy to you.

[11]"This also *is* yours: the heave offering of
their gift, with all the wave offerings of the
children of Israel; I have given them to you,
and your sons and daughters with you, as an
ordinance forever. Everyone who is clean in
your house may eat it.

SOUL NOTE

The Gift *(18:6, 7)* Work is a gift? That's exactly what God told the Levites whom he had chosen to serve in the tabernacle: "I give your priesthood to you as a gift for service." God makes work sacred. Almost any job can be done for the glory of God. Those who see their vocations as gifts through which they can serve God gain a whole new perspective. "And whatever you do in word or deed, do all in the name of the Lord Jesus" (Col. 3:17). **Topic: Work**

12"All the best of the oil, all the best of the new wine and the grain, their firstfruits which they offer to the LORD, I have given them to you. 13Whatever first ripe fruit is in their land, which they bring to the LORD, shall be yours. Everyone who is clean in your house may eat it.

14"Every devoted thing in Israel shall be yours.

15"Everything that first opens the womb of all flesh, which they bring to the LORD, whether man or beast, shall be yours; nevertheless the firstborn of man you shall surely redeem, and the firstborn of unclean animals you shall redeem. 16And those redeemed of the devoted things you shall redeem when one month old, according to your valuation, for five shekels of silver, according to the shekel of the sanctuary, which *is* twenty gerahs. 17But the firstborn of a cow, the firstborn of a sheep, or the firstborn of a goat you shall not redeem; they *are* holy. You shall sprinkle their blood on the altar, and burn their fat *as* an offering made by fire for a sweet aroma to the LORD. 18And their flesh shall be yours, just as the wave breast and the right thigh are yours.

19"All the heave offerings of the holy things, which the children of Israel offer to the LORD, I have given to you and your sons and daughters with you as an ordinance forever; it *is* a covenant of salt forever before the LORD with you and your descendants with you."

20Then the LORD said to Aaron: "You shall have no inheritance in their land, nor shall you have any portion among them; I *am* your portion and your inheritance among the children of Israel.

TITHES FOR SUPPORT OF THE LEVITES

21"Behold, I have given the children of Levi all the tithes in Israel as an inheritance in return for the work which they perform, the work of the tabernacle of meeting. 22Hereafter the children of Israel shall not come near the tabernacle of meeting, lest they bear sin and die. 23But the Levites shall perform the work of the tabernacle of meeting, and they shall bear their iniquity; *it shall be* a statute forever, throughout your generations, that among the children of Israel they shall have no inheritance. 24For the tithes of the children of Israel, which they offer up *as* a heave offering to the LORD, I have given to the Levites as an inheritance; therefore I have said to them, 'Among the children of Israel they shall have no inheritance.' "

THE TITHE OF THE LEVITES

25Then the LORD spoke to Moses, saying, 26"Speak thus to the Levites, and say to them: 'When you take from the children of Israel the tithes which I have given you from them as your inheritance, then you shall offer up a heave offering of it to the LORD, a tenth of the tithe. 27And your heave offering shall be reckoned to you as though *it were* the grain of the threshing floor and as the fullness of the winepress. 28Thus you shall also offer a heave offering to the LORD from all your tithes which you receive from the children of Israel, and you shall give the LORD's heave offering from it to Aaron the priest. 29Of all your gifts you shall offer up every heave offering due to the LORD, from all the best of them, the consecrated part of them.' 30Therefore you shall say to them: 'When you have lifted up the best of it, then *the rest* shall be accounted to the Levites as the produce of the threshing floor and as the produce of the winepress. 31You may eat it in any place, you and your households, for it *is* your reward for your work in the tabernacle of meeting. 32And you shall bear no sin because of it, when you have lifted up the best of it. But you shall not profane the holy gifts of the children of Israel, lest you die.' "

LAWS OF PURIFICATION

19 Now the LORD spoke to Moses and Aaron, saying, 2"This *is* the ordinance of the law which the LORD has commanded, saying: 'Speak to the children of Israel, that they bring you a red heifer without blemish, in which there *is* no defect *and* on which a yoke has never come. 3You shall give it to Eleazar the priest, that he may take it outside the camp, and it shall be slaughtered before him; 4and Eleazar the priest shall take some of its blood with his finger, and sprinkle some of its blood seven times directly in front of the tabernacle of meeting. 5Then the heifer shall be burned in his sight: its hide, its flesh, its blood, and its offal shall be burned. 6And the priest shall take cedar wood and hyssop and scarlet, and cast *them* into the midst of the fire burning the heifer. 7Then the priest shall wash his clothes, he shall bathe in water, and afterward he shall come into the camp; the priest shall be unclean until evening. 8And the one

who burns it shall wash his clothes in water,
bathe in water, and shall be unclean until evening. 9Then a man *who is* clean shall gather
up the ashes of the heifer, and store *them* outside the camp in a clean place; and they shall
be kept for the congregation of the children of
Israel for the water of purification;[a] it *is* for
purifying from sin. 10And the one who gathers
the ashes of the heifer shall wash his clothes,
and be unclean until evening. It shall be a statute forever to the children of Israel and to the
stranger who dwells among them.

11'He who touches the dead body of anyone
shall be unclean seven days. 12He shall purify
himself with the water on the third day and on
the seventh day; *then* he will be clean. But if he
does not purify himself on the third day and on
the seventh day, he will not be clean. 13Who-
ever touches the body of anyone who has died,
and does not purify himself, defiles the tabernacle of the LORD. That person shall be cut off
from Israel. He shall be unclean, because the
water of purification was not sprinkled on him;
his uncleanness *is* still on him.

14'This *is* the law when a man dies in a tent:
All who come into the tent and all who *are* in
the tent shall be unclean seven days; 15and
every open vessel, which has no cover fastened on it, *is* unclean. 16Whoever in the open
field touches one who is slain by a sword or
who has died, or a bone of a man, or a grave,
shall be unclean seven days.

17'And for an unclean *person* they shall take
some of the ashes of the heifer burnt for purification from sin, and running water shall be
put on them in a vessel. 18A clean person shall
take hyssop and dip *it* in the water, sprinkle *it*
on the tent, on all the vessels, on the persons
who were there, or on the one who touched a
bone, the slain, the dead, or a grave. 19The
clean *person* shall sprinkle the unclean on the
third day and on the seventh day; and on the
seventh day he shall purify himself, wash his
clothes, and bathe in water; and at evening he
shall be clean.

20'But the man who is unclean and does not
purify himself, that person shall be cut off
from among the assembly, because he has defiled the sanctuary of the LORD. The water of
purification has not been sprinkled on him;
he *is* unclean. 21It shall be a perpetual statute
for them. He who sprinkles the water of purification shall wash his clothes; and he who
touches the water of purification shall be unclean until evening. 22Whatever the unclean
person touches shall be unclean; and the person who touches *it* shall be unclean until evening.' "

MOSES' ERROR AT KADESH

20 Then the children of Israel, the whole
congregation, came into the Wilderness of Zin in the first month, and the people
stayed in Kadesh; and Miriam died there and
was buried there.

2Now there was no water for the congregation; so they gathered together against Moses
and Aaron. 3And the people contended with
Moses and spoke, saying: "If only we had died
when our brethren died before the LORD!
4Why have you brought up the assembly of
the LORD into this wilderness, that we and our
animals should die here? 5And why have you
made us come up out of Egypt, to bring us to
this evil place? It *is* not a place of grain or figs
or vines or pomegranates; nor *is* there any water to drink." 6So Moses and Aaron went from
the presence of the assembly to the door of the
tabernacle of meeting, and they fell on their
faces. And the glory of the LORD appeared to
them.

7Then the LORD spoke to Moses, saying,

19:9 [a]Literally *impurity*

SOUL NOTE

Can't Take It Back *(20:7–13)* It was too late—Moses couldn't take it back. He had exploded in anger, so God punished him. Anger can be the most damaging of all emotions, causing people to say or do things they regret. Out-of-control anger can ruin friendships and marriages and even cause nations to go to war. Some people end up living forever with the consequences of choices made in a moment of heated anger. People who struggle with destructive anger must find help to discover alternative ways to manage it. This begins by turning it over to God. **Topic: Anger**

8“Take the rod; you and your brother Aaron gather the congregation together. Speak to the rock before their eyes, and it will yield its water; thus you shall bring water for them out of the rock, and give drink to the congregation and their animals.” 9So Moses took the rod from before the LORD as He commanded him.

10And Moses and Aaron gathered the assembly together before the rock; and he said to them, “Hear now, you rebels! Must we bring water for you out of this rock?” 11Then Moses lifted his hand and struck the rock twice with his rod; and water came out abundantly, and the congregation and their animals drank.

12Then the LORD spoke to Moses and Aaron, “Because you did not believe Me, to hallow Me in the eyes of the children of Israel, therefore you shall not bring this assembly into the land which I have given them.”

13This *was* the water of Meribah,[a] because the children of Israel contended with the LORD, and He was hallowed among them.

Passage Through Edom Refused

14Now Moses sent messengers from Kadesh to the king of Edom. “Thus says your brother Israel: ‘You know all the hardship that has befallen us, 15how our fathers went down to Egypt, and we dwelt in Egypt a long time, and the Egyptians afflicted us and our fathers. 16When we cried out to the LORD, He heard our voice and sent the Angel and brought us up out of Egypt; now here we are in Kadesh, a city on the edge of your border. 17Please let us pass through your country. We will not pass through fields or vineyards, nor will we drink water from wells; we will go along the King’s Highway; we will not turn aside to the right hand or to the left until we have passed through your territory.’ ”

18Then Edom said to him, “You shall not pass through my *land*, lest I come out against you with the sword.”

19So the children of Israel said to him, “We will go by the Highway, and if I or my livestock drink any of your water, then I will pay for it; let me only pass through on foot, nothing *more*.”

20Then he said, “You shall not pass through.” So Edom came out against them with many men and with a strong hand. 21Thus Edom refused to give Israel passage through his territory; so Israel turned away from him.

Death of Aaron

22Now the children of Israel, the whole congregation, journeyed from Kadesh and came to Mount Hor. 23And the LORD spoke to Moses and Aaron in Mount Hor by the border of the land of Edom, saying: 24“Aaron shall be gathered to his people, for he shall not enter the land which I have given to the children of Israel, because you rebelled against My word at the water of Meribah. 25Take Aaron and Eleazar his son, and bring them up to Mount Hor; 26and strip Aaron of his garments and put them on Eleazar his son; for Aaron shall be gathered *to his people* and die there.” 27So Moses did just as the LORD commanded, and they went up to Mount Hor in the sight of all the congregation. 28Moses stripped Aaron of his garments and put them on Eleazar his son; and Aaron died there on the top of the mountain. Then Moses and Eleazar came down from the mountain. 29Now when all the congregation saw that Aaron was dead, all the house of Israel mourned for Aaron thirty days.

Canaanites Defeated at Hormah

21 The king of Arad, the Canaanite, who dwelt in the South, heard that Israel was coming on the road to Atharim. Then he fought against Israel and took *some* of them prisoners. 2So Israel made a vow to the LORD, and said, “If You will indeed deliver this people into my hand, then I will utterly destroy their cities.” 3And the LORD listened to the voice of Israel and delivered up the Canaanites, and they utterly destroyed them and their cities. So the name of that place was called Hormah.[a]

The Bronze Serpent

4Then they journeyed from Mount Hor by the Way of the Red Sea, to go around the land of Edom; and the soul of the people became very discouraged on the way. 5And the people spoke against God and against Moses: “Why have you brought us up out of Egypt to die in the wilderness? For *there is* no food and no water, and our soul loathes this worthless

---

20:13 [a]Literally *Contention* **21:3** [a]Literally *Utter Destruction*

bread." [6]So the LORD sent fiery serpents among the people, and they bit the people; and many of the people of Israel died.

[7]Therefore the people came to Moses, and said, "We have sinned, for we have spoken against the LORD and against you; pray to the LORD that He take away the serpents from us." So Moses prayed for the people.

[8]Then the LORD said to Moses, "Make a fiery *serpent,* and set it on a pole; and it shall be that everyone who is bitten, when he looks at it, shall live." [9]So Moses made a bronze serpent, and put it on a pole; and so it was, if a serpent had bitten anyone, when he looked at the bronze serpent, he lived.

FROM MOUNT HOR TO MOAB

[10]Now the children of Israel moved on and camped in Oboth. [11]And they journeyed from Oboth and camped at Ije Abarim, in the wilderness which *is* east of Moab, toward the sunrise. [12]From there they moved and camped in the Valley of Zered. [13]From there they moved and camped on the other side of the Arnon, which *is* in the wilderness that extends from the border of the Amorites; for the Arnon *is* the border of Moab, between Moab and the Amorites. [14]Therefore it is said in the Book of the Wars of the LORD:

"Waheb in Suphah,[a]
The brooks of the Arnon,
15 And the slope of the brooks
That reaches to the dwelling of Ar,
And lies on the border of Moab."

[16]From there *they went* to Beer, which *is* the well where the LORD said to Moses, "Gather the people together, and I will give them water." [17]Then Israel sang this song:

"Spring up, O well!
All of you sing to it—
18 The well the leaders sank,
Dug by the nation's nobles,
By the lawgiver, with their staves."

And from the wilderness *they went* to Mattanah, [19]from Mattanah to Nahaliel, from Nahaliel to Bamoth, [20]and from Bamoth, *in* the valley that *is* in the country of Moab, to the top of Pisgah which looks down on the wasteland.[a]

KING SIHON DEFEATED

[21]Then Israel sent messengers to Sihon king of the Amorites, saying, [22]"Let me pass through your land. We will not turn aside into fields or vineyards; we will not drink water from wells. We will go by the King's Highway until we have passed through your territory." [23]But Sihon would not allow Israel to pass through his territory. So Sihon gathered all his people together and went out against Israel in the wilderness, and he came to Jahaz and fought against Israel. [24]Then Israel defeated him with the edge of the sword, and took possession of his land from the Arnon to the Jabbok, as far as the people of Ammon; for the border of the people of Ammon *was* fortified. [25]So Israel took all these cities, and Israel dwelt in all the cities of the Amorites, in Heshbon and in all its villages. [26]For Heshbon *was* the city of Sihon king of the Amorites, who had fought against the former king of Moab, and had taken all his land from his hand as far as the Arnon. [27]Therefore those who speak in proverbs say:

21:14 [a]Ancient unknown places; Vulgate reads *What He did in the Red Sea.* **21:20** [a]Hebrew *Jeshimon*

SOUL NOTE

Deliverance *(21:8, 9)* A pole with one or two snakes on it is often used as an emblem of the medical profession and a symbol of healing. It reminds us of this biblical event. God told Moses to make a bronze serpent and place it on a pole. He promised that everyone who looked at the pole by faith would be healed. In the New Testament, Jesus used this incident to illustrate His willingness to die on the Cross and be "lifted up" so that all who look to Him by faith might be saved (John 3:14, 15). That is the ultimate healing that Christ offers to all people and which all people need—healing from sin. **Topic: Health/Spirituality**

"Come to Heshbon, let it be built;
Let the city of Sihon be repaired.

28 "For fire went out from Heshbon,
A flame from the city of Sihon;
It consumed Ar of Moab,
The lords of the heights of the Arnon.
29 Woe to you, Moab!
You have perished, O people of
Chemosh!
He has given his sons as fugitives,
And his daughters into captivity,
To Sihon king of the Amorites.

30 "But we have shot at them;
Heshbon has perished as far as Dibon.
Then we laid waste as far as Nophah,
Which *reaches* to Medeba."

31 Thus Israel dwelt in the land of the Amorites. 32 Then Moses sent to spy out Jazer; and
they took its villages and drove out the Amorites who *were* there.

King Og Defeated

33 And they turned and went up by the way
to Bashan. So Og king of Bashan went out
against them, he and all his people, to battle at
Edrei. 34 Then the LORD said to Moses, "Do not
fear him, for I have delivered him into your
hand, with all his people and his land; and
you shall do to him as you did to Sihon king
of the Amorites, who dwelt at Heshbon." 35 So
they defeated him, his sons, and all his people, until there was no survivor left him; and
they took possession of his land.

Balak Sends for Balaam

22 Then the children of Israel moved,
and camped in the plains of Moab on
the side of the Jordan *across from* Jericho.
2 Now Balak the son of Zippor saw all that
Israel had done to the Amorites. 3 And Moab
was exceedingly afraid of the people because
they *were* many, and Moab was sick with
dread because of the children of Israel. 4 So
Moab said to the elders of Midian, "Now this
company will lick up everything around us, as
an ox licks up the grass of the field." And Balak the son of Zippor *was* king of the Moabites
at that time. 5 Then he sent messengers to Balaam the son of Beor at Pethor, which *is* near
the River[a] in the land of the sons of his
people,[b] to call him, saying: "Look, a people
has come from Egypt. See, they cover the face
of the earth, and are settling next to me!
6 Therefore please come at once, curse this
people for me, for they *are* too mighty for me.
Perhaps I shall be able to defeat them and
drive them out of the land, for I know that he
whom you bless *is* blessed, and he whom you
curse is cursed."
7 So the elders of Moab and the elders of
Midian departed with the diviner's fee in their
hand, and they came to Balaam and spoke to
him the words of Balak. 8 And he said to them,
"Lodge here tonight, and I will bring back
word to you, as the LORD speaks to me." So
the princes of Moab stayed with Balaam.
9 Then God came to Balaam and said, "Who
are these men with you?"
10 So Balaam said to God, "Balak the son of
Zippor, king of Moab, has sent to me, *saying,*
11 'Look, a people has come out of Egypt, and
they cover the face of the earth. Come now,
curse them for me; perhaps I shall be able to
overpower them and drive them out.' "
12 And God said to Balaam, "You shall not go
with them; you shall not curse the people, for
they *are* blessed."
13 So Balaam rose in the morning and said to
the princes of Balak, "Go back to your land,
for the LORD has refused to give me permission to go with you."
14 And the princes of Moab rose and went
to Balak, and said, "Balaam refuses to come
with us."
15 Then Balak again sent princes, more numerous and more honorable than they. 16 And
they came to Balaam and said to him, "Thus
says Balak the son of Zippor: 'Please let nothing hinder you from coming to me; 17 for I will
certainly honor you greatly, and I will do
whatever you say to me. Therefore please
come, curse this people for me.' "
18 Then Balaam answered and said to the
servants of Balak, "Though Balak were to give
me his house full of silver and gold, I could
not go beyond the word of the LORD my God,
to do less or more. 19 Now therefore, please,
you also stay here tonight, that I may know
what more the LORD will say to me."
20 And God came to Balaam at night and said
to him, "If the men come to call you, rise *and*
go with them; but only the word which I

22:5 [a]That is, the Euphrates [b]Or *the people of Amau*

speak to you—that you shall do." [21]So Balaam rose in the morning, saddled his donkey, and went with the princes of Moab.

Balaam, the Donkey, and the Angel

[22]Then God's anger was aroused because he went, and the Angel of the LORD took His stand in the way as an adversary against him. And he was riding on his donkey, and his two servants *were* with him. [23]Now the donkey saw the Angel of the LORD standing in the way with His drawn sword in His hand, and the donkey turned aside out of the way and went into the field. So Balaam struck the donkey to turn her back onto the road. [24]Then the Angel of the LORD stood in a narrow path between the vineyards, *with* a wall on this side and a wall on that side. [25]And when the donkey saw the Angel of the LORD, she pushed herself against the wall and crushed Balaam's foot against the wall; so he struck her again. [26]Then the Angel of the LORD went further, and stood in a narrow place where there *was* no way to turn either to the right hand or to the left. [27]And when the donkey saw the Angel of the LORD, she lay down under Balaam; so Balaam's anger was aroused, and he struck the donkey with his staff.

[28]Then the LORD opened the mouth of the donkey, and she said to Balaam, "What have I done to you, that you have struck me these three times?"

[29]And Balaam said to the donkey, "Because you have abused me. I wish there were a sword in my hand, for now I would kill you!"

[30]So the donkey said to Balaam, "*Am* I not your donkey on which you have ridden, ever since *I became* yours, to this day? Was I ever disposed to do this to you?"

And he said, "No."

[31]Then the LORD opened Balaam's eyes, and he saw the Angel of the LORD standing in the way with His drawn sword in His hand; and he bowed his head and fell flat on his face. [32]And the Angel of the LORD said to him, "Why have you struck your donkey these three times? Behold, I have come out to stand against you, because *your* way is perverse before Me. [33]The donkey saw Me and turned aside from Me these three times. If she had not turned aside from Me, surely I would also have killed you by now, and let her live."

[34]And Balaam said to the Angel of the LORD, "I have sinned, for I did not know You stood in the way against me. Now therefore, if it displeases You, I will turn back."

[35]Then the Angel of the LORD said to Balaam, "Go with the men, but only the word that I speak to you, that you shall speak." So Balaam went with the princes of Balak.

[36]Now when Balak heard that Balaam was coming, he went out to meet him at the city of Moab, which *is* on the border at the Arnon, the boundary of the territory. [37]Then Balak said to Balaam, "Did I not earnestly send to you, calling for you? Why did you not come to me? Am I not able to honor you?"

[38]And Balaam said to Balak, "Look, I have come to you! Now, have I any power at all to say anything? The word that God puts in my mouth, that I must speak." [39]So Balaam went with Balak, and they came to Kirjath Huzoth. [40]Then Balak offered oxen and sheep, and he sent *some* to Balaam and to the princes who *were* with him.

Balaam's First Prophecy

[41]So it was, the next day, that Balak took Balaam and brought him up to the high places of Baal, that from there he might observe the extent of the people.

23 Then Balaam said to Balak, "Build seven altars for me here, and prepare for me here seven bulls and seven rams."

[2]And Balak did just as Balaam had spoken, and Balak and Balaam offered a bull and a ram on *each* altar. [3]Then Balaam said to Balak, "Stand by your burnt offering, and I will go; perhaps the LORD will come to meet me, and whatever He shows me I will tell you." So he went to a desolate height. [4]And God met Balaam, and he said to Him, "I have prepared the seven altars, and I have offered on *each* altar a bull and a ram."

[5]Then the LORD put a word in Balaam's mouth, and said, "Return to Balak, and thus you shall speak." [6]So he returned to him, and there he was, standing by his burnt offering, he and all the princes of Moab.

[7]And he took up his oracle and said:

"Balak the king of Moab has brought me
from Aram,
From the mountains of the east.
'Come, curse Jacob for me,
And come, denounce Israel!'

8 "How shall I curse whom God has not
cursed?
And how shall I denounce *whom* the
LORD has not denounced?
9 For from the top of the rocks I see him,
And from the hills I behold him;
There! A people dwelling alone,
Not reckoning itself among the nations.

10 "Who can count the dust[a] of Jacob,
Or number one-fourth of Israel?
Let me die the death of the righteous,
And let my end be like his!"

11Then Balak said to Balaam, "What have
you done to me? I took you to curse my enemies, and look, you have blessed *them* bountifully!"
12So he answered and said, "Must I not take
heed to speak what the LORD has put in my
mouth?"

BALAAM'S SECOND PROPHECY

13Then Balak said to
him, "Please come with
me to another place
from which you may
see them; you shall see
only the outer part of
them, and shall not see
them all; curse them for
me from there." 14So he brought him to the
field of Zophim, to the top of Pisgah, and built
seven altars, and offered a bull and a ram on
each altar.
15And he said to Balak, "Stand here by your
burnt offering while I meet[a] *the LORD* over
there."
16Then the LORD met Balaam, and put a
word in his mouth, and said, "Go back to Balak, and thus you shall speak." 17So he came
to him, and there he was, standing by his
burnt offering, and the princes of Moab were
with him. And Balak said to him, "What has
the LORD spoken?"
18Then he took up his oracle and said:

"Rise up, Balak, and hear!
Listen to me, son of Zippor!

19 "God *is* not a man, that He should lie,
Nor a son of man, that He should
repent.
Has He said, and will He not do?
Or has He spoken, and will He not make
it good?
20 Behold, I have received *a command* to
bless;
He has blessed, and I cannot reverse it.

21 "He has not observed iniquity in Jacob,
Nor has He seen wickedness in Israel.
The LORD his God *is* with him,
And the shout of a King *is* among them.
22 God brings them out of Egypt;
He has strength like a wild ox.

23 "For *there is* no sorcery against Jacob,
Nor any divination against Israel.
It now must be said of Jacob
And of Israel, 'Oh, what God has done!'
24 Look, a people rises like a lioness,
And lifts itself up like a lion;
It shall not lie down until it devours the
prey,
And drinks the blood of the slain."

> "It now must be said of
> Jacob and of Israel,
> 'Oh, what God has done!' "
> NUMBERS 23:23

25Then Balak said to
Balaam, "Neither curse
them at all, nor bless
them at all!"
26So Balaam answered
and said to Balak, "Did I
not tell you, saying, 'All
that the LORD speaks,
that I must do'?"

BALAAM'S THIRD PROPHECY

27Then Balak said to Balaam, "Please come,
I will take you to another place; perhaps it will
please God that you may curse them for me
from there." 28So Balak took Balaam to the top
of Peor, that overlooks the wasteland.[a] 29Then
Balaam said to Balak, "Build for me here
seven altars, and prepare for me here seven
bulls and seven rams." 30And Balak did as Balaam had said, and offered a bull and a ram on
every altar.

24 Now when Balaam saw that it pleased
the LORD to bless Israel, he did not go
as at other times, to seek to use sorcery, but he
set his face toward the wilderness. 2And Balaam raised his eyes, and saw Israel encamped

---

23:10 [a]Or *dust cloud* **23:15** [a]Following Masoretic Text, Targum, and Vulgate; Syriac reads *call;* Septuagint reads *go and ask God.* **23:28** [a]Hebrew *Jeshimon*

according to their tribes; and the Spirit of God came upon him.

3Then he took up his oracle and said:

"The utterance of Balaam the son of Beor,
The utterance of the man whose eyes are opened,
4 The utterance of him who hears the words of God,
Who sees the vision of the Almighty,
Who falls down, with eyes wide open:

5 "How lovely are your tents, O Jacob!
Your dwellings, O Israel!
6 Like valleys that stretch out,
Like gardens by the riverside,
Like aloes planted by the LORD,
Like cedars beside the waters.
7 He shall pour water from his buckets,
And his seed *shall be* in many waters.

"His king shall be higher than Agag,
And his kingdom shall be exalted.

8 "God brings him out of Egypt;
He has strength like a wild ox;
He shall consume the nations, his enemies;
He shall break their bones
And pierce *them* with his arrows.
9 'He bows down, he lies down as a lion;
And as a lion, who shall rouse him?'[a]

"Blessed *is* he who blesses you,
And cursed *is* he who curses you."

10Then Balak's anger was aroused against Balaam, and he struck his hands together; and Balak said to Balaam, "I called you to curse my enemies, and look, you have bountifully blessed *them* these three times! 11Now therefore, flee to your place. I said I would greatly honor you, but in fact, the LORD has kept you back from honor."

12So Balaam said to Balak, "Did I not also speak to your messengers whom you sent to me, saying, 13'If Balak were to give me his house full of silver and gold, I could not go beyond the word of the LORD, to do good or bad of my own will. What the LORD says, that I must speak'? 14And now, indeed, I am going to my people. Come, I will advise you what this people will do to your people in the latter days."

Balaam's Fourth Prophecy

15So he took up his oracle and said:

"The utterance of Balaam the son of Beor,
And the utterance of the man whose eyes are opened;
16 The utterance of him who hears the words of God,
And has the knowledge of the Most High,
Who sees the vision of the Almighty,
Who falls down, with eyes wide open:

17 "I see Him, but not now;
I behold Him, but not near;
A Star shall come out of Jacob;
A Scepter shall rise out of Israel,
And batter the brow of Moab,
And destroy all the sons of tumult.[a]

18 "And Edom shall be a possession;
Seir also, his enemies, shall be a possession,
While Israel does valiantly.
19 Out of Jacob One shall have dominion,
And destroy the remains of the city."

20Then he looked on Amalek, and he took up his oracle and said:

"Amalek *was* first among the nations,
But *shall be* last until he perishes."

21Then he looked on the Kenites, and he took up his oracle and said:

"Firm is your dwelling place,
And your nest is set in the rock;
22 Nevertheless Kain shall be burned.
How long until Asshur carries you away captive?"

23Then he took up his oracle and said:

"Alas! Who shall live when God does this?
24 But ships *shall come* from the coasts of Cyprus,[a]
And they shall afflict Asshur and afflict Eber,

24:9 [a]Genesis 49:9 **24:17** [a]Hebrew *Sheth* (compare Jeremiah 48:45) **24:24** [a]Hebrew *Kittim*

And so shall *Amalek*,[b] until he
perishes."

25So Balaam rose and departed and returned
to his place; Balak also went his way.

ISRAEL'S HARLOTRY IN MOAB

25 Now Israel remained in Acacia
Grove,[a] and the people began to commit harlotry with the women of Moab. 2They
invited the people to the sacrifices of their
gods, and the people ate and bowed down to
their gods. 3So Israel was joined to Baal of
Peor, and the anger of the LORD was aroused
against Israel.
4Then the LORD said to Moses, "Take all the
leaders of the people and hang the offenders
before the LORD, out in the sun, that the fierce
anger of the LORD may turn away from Israel."
5So Moses said to the judges of Israel, "Every one of you kill his men who were joined to
Baal of Peor."
6And indeed, one of the children of Israel
came and presented to his brethren a Midianite woman in the sight of Moses and in the
sight of all the congregation of the children of
Israel, who *were* weeping at the door of the
tabernacle of meeting. 7Now when Phinehas
the son of Eleazar, the son of Aaron the priest,
saw *it*, he rose from among the congregation
and took a javelin in his hand; 8and he went
after the man of Israel into the tent and thrust
both of them through, the man of Israel, and
the woman through her body. So the plague
was stopped among the children of Israel.
9And those who died in the plague were twenty-four thousand.
10Then the LORD spoke to Moses, saying:
11"Phinehas the son of Eleazar, the son of
Aaron the priest, has turned back My wrath
from the children of Israel, because he was
zealous with My zeal among them, so that I
did not consume the children of Israel in My
zeal. 12Therefore say, 'Behold, I give to him
My covenant of peace; 13and it shall be to him
and his descendants after him a covenant of
an everlasting priesthood, because he was
zealous for his God, and made atonement for
the children of Israel.' "
14Now the name of the Israelite who was
killed, who was killed with the Midianite
woman, *was* Zimri the son of Salu, a leader
of a father's house among the Simeonites.
15And the name of the Midianite woman who
was killed *was* Cozbi the daughter of Zur; he
was head of the people of a father's house in
Midian.
16Then the LORD spoke to Moses, saying:
17"Harass the Midianites, and attack them;
18for they harassed you with their schemes by
which they seduced you in the matter of Peor
and in the matter of Cozbi, the daughter of a
leader of Midian, their sister, who was killed
in the day of the plague because of Peor."

THE SECOND CENSUS OF ISRAEL

26 And it came to pass, after the plague,
that the LORD spoke to Moses and Eleazar the son of Aaron the priest, saying:
2"Take a census of all the congregation of the
children of Israel from twenty years old and
above, by their fathers' houses, all who are
able to go to war in Israel." 3So Moses and Eleazar the priest spoke with them in the plains
of Moab by the Jordan, *across from* Jericho,
saying: 4"*Take a census of the people* from
twenty years old and above, just as the LORD
commanded Moses and the children of Israel
who came out of the land of Egypt."
5Reuben *was* the firstborn of Israel. The children of Reuben *were: of* Hanoch, the family of

24:24 [b]Literally *he* or *that one* **25:1** [a]Hebrew *Shittim*

SOUL NOTE

Sleeping with the Enemy *(25:1)* The Israelites' commitment to God was violated by their sexual indulgence with the women of Moab. The Israelite men committed sexual sin with these foreign women, and this led to the men worshiping the foreign gods as well. Sexual sin always progresses, drawing people farther and farther from God. What may start as an "innocent" flirtation with sin can lead to deadly consequences. Dabbling around the edges of sexual sin can take hold and consume a person, leading to pain and brokenness. **Topic: Sexual Sin**

the Hanochites; *of* Pallu, the family of the Palluites; 6*of* Hezron, the family of the Hezronites; *of* Carmi, the family of the Carmites. 7These *are* the families of the Reubenites: those who were numbered of them were forty-three thousand seven hundred and thirty. 8And the son of Pallu *was* Eliab. 9The sons of Eliab *were* Nemuel, Dathan, and Abiram. These *are* the Dathan and Abiram, representatives of the congregation, who contended against Moses and Aaron in the company of Korah, when they contended against the LORD; 10and the earth opened its mouth and swallowed them up together with Korah when that company died, when the fire devoured two hundred and fifty men; and they became a sign. 11Nevertheless the children of Korah did not die.

12The sons of Simeon according to their families *were: of* Nemuel,[a] the family of the Nemuelites; *of* Jamin, the family of the Jaminites; *of* Jachin,[b] the family of the Jachinites; 13*of* Zerah,[a] the family of the Zarhites; *of* Shaul, the family of the Shaulites. 14These *are* the families of the Simeonites: twenty-two thousand two hundred.

15The sons of Gad according to their families *were: of* Zephon,[a] the family of the Zephonites; *of* Haggi, the family of the Haggites; *of* Shuni, the family of the Shunites; 16*of* Ozni,[a] the family of the Oznites; *of* Eri, the family of the Erites; 17*of* Arod,[a] the family of the Arodites; *of* Areli, the family of the Arelites. 18These *are* the families of the sons of Gad according to those who were numbered of them: forty thousand five hundred.

19The sons of Judah *were* Er and Onan; and Er and Onan died in the land of Canaan. 20And the sons of Judah according to their families were: *of* Shelah, the family of the Shelanites; *of* Perez, the family of the Parzites; *of* Zerah, the family of the Zarhites. 21And the sons of Perez were: *of* Hezron, the family of the Hezronites; *of* Hamul, the family of the Hamulites. 22These *are* the families of Judah according to those who were numbered of them: seventy-six thousand five hundred.

23The sons of Issachar according to their families *were: of* Tola, the family of the Tolaites; of Puah,[a] the family of the Punites;[b] 24of Jashub, the family of the Jashubites; of Shimron, the family of the Shimronites. 25These *are* the families of Issachar according to those who were numbered of them: sixty-four thousand three hundred.

26The sons of Zebulun according to their families *were:* of Sered, the family of the Sardites; of Elon, the family of the Elonites; of Jahleel, the family of the Jahleelites. 27These *are* the families of the Zebulunites according to those who were numbered of them: sixty thousand five hundred.

28The sons of Joseph according to their families, by Manasseh and Ephraim, *were:* 29The sons of Manasseh: of Machir, the family of the Machirites; and Machir begot Gilead; of Gilead, the family of the Gileadites. 30These *are* the sons of Gilead: *of* Jeezer,[a] the family of the Jeezerites; of Helek, the family of the Helekites; 31*of* Asriel, the family of the Asrielites; *of* Shechem, the family of the Shechemites; 32*of* Shemida, the family of the Shemidaites; *of* Hepher, the family of the Hepherites. 33Now Zelophehad the son of Hepher had no sons, but daughters; and the names of the daughters of Zelophehad *were* Mahlah, Noah, Hoglah, Milcah, and Tirzah. 34These *are* the families of Manasseh; and those who were numbered of them *were* fifty-two thousand seven hundred.

35These *are* the sons of Ephraim according to their families: of Shuthelah, the family of the Shuthalhites; of Becher,[a] the family of the Bachrites; of Tahan, the family of the Tahanites. 36And these *are* the sons of Shuthelah: of Eran, the family of the Eranites. 37These *are* the families of the sons of Ephraim according to those who were numbered of them: thirty-two thousand five hundred.

These *are* the sons of Joseph according to their families.

38The sons of Benjamin according to their families were: of Bela, the family of the Belaites; of Ashbel, the family of the Ashbelites; of Ahiram, the family of the Ahiramites; 39of Shupham,[a] the family of the Shuphamites; of

26:12 [a]Spelled *Jemuel* in Genesis 46:10 and Exodus 6:15 [b]Called *Jarib* in 1 Chronicles 4:24
26:13 [a]Called *Zohar* in Genesis 46:10
26:15 [a]Called *Ziphion* in Genesis 46:16
26:16 [a]Called *Ezbon* in Genesis 46:16
26:17 [a]Spelled *Arodi* in Samaritan Pentateuch, Syriac, and Genesis 46:16 **26:23** [a]Hebrew *Puvah* (compare Genesis 46:13 and 1 Chronicles 7:1); Samaritan Pentateuch, Septuagint, Syriac, and Vulgate read *Puah.* [b]Samaritan Pentateuch, Septuagint, Syriac, and Vulgate read *Puaites.*
26:30 [a]Called *Abiezer* in Joshua 17:2
26:35 [a]Called *Bered* in 1 Chronicles 7:20
26:39 [a]Masoretic Text reads *Shephupham,* spelled *Shephuphan* in 1 Chronicles 8:5.

Hupham,[b] the family of the Huphamites. [40]And the sons of Bela were Ard[a] and Naaman: *of* *Ard,* the family of the Ardites; of Naaman, the family of the Naamites. [41]These *are* the sons of Benjamin according to their families; and those who were numbered of them *were* forty-five thousand six hundred.

[42]These *are* the sons of Dan according to their families: of Shuham,[a] the family of the Shuhamites. These *are* the families of Dan according to their families. [43]All the families of the Shuhamites, according to those who were numbered of them, *were* sixty-four thousand four hundred.

[44]The sons of Asher according to their families *were:* of Jimna, the family of the Jimnites; of Jesui, the family of the Jesuites; of Beriah, the family of the Beriites. [45]Of the sons of Beriah: of Heber, the family of the Heberites; of Malchiel, the family of the Malchielites. [46]And the name of the daughter of Asher *was* Serah. [47]These *are* the families of the sons of Asher according to those who were numbered of them: fifty-three thousand four hundred.

[48]The sons of Naphtali according to their families *were:* of Jahzeel,[a] the family of the Jahzeelites; of Guni, the family of the Gunites; [49]of Jezer, the family of the Jezerites; of Shillem, the family of the Shillemites. [50]These *are* the families of Naphtali according to their families; and those who were numbered of them *were* forty-five thousand four hundred.

[51]These *are* those who were numbered of the children of Israel: six hundred and one thousand seven hundred and thirty.

[52]Then the LORD spoke to Moses, saying: [53]"To these the land shall be divided as an inheritance, according to the number of names. [54]To a large *tribe* you shall give a larger inheritance, and to a small *tribe* you shall give a smaller inheritance. Each shall be given its inheritance according to those who were numbered of them. [55]But the land shall be divided by lot; they shall inherit according to the names of the tribes of their fathers. [56]According to the lot their inheritance shall be divided between the larger and the smaller."

[57]And these *are* those who were numbered of the Levites according to their families: of Gershon, the family of the Gershonites; of Kohath, the family of the Kohathites; of Merari, the family of the Merarites. [58]These *are* the families of the Levites: the family of the Libnites, the family of the Hebronites, the family of the Mahlites, the family of the Mushites, and the family of the Korathites. And Kohath begot Amram. [59]The name of Amram's wife *was* Jochebed the daughter of Levi, who was born to Levi in Egypt; and to Amram she bore Aaron and Moses and their sister Miriam. [60]To Aaron were born Nadab and Abihu, Eleazar and Ithamar. [61]And Nadab and Abihu died when they offered profane fire before the LORD.

[62]Now those who were numbered of them were twenty-three thousand, every male from a month old and above; for they were not numbered among the other children of Israel, because there was no inheritance given to them among the children of Israel.

[63]These *are* those who were numbered by Moses and Eleazar the priest, who numbered the children of Israel in the plains of Moab by the Jordan, *across from* Jericho. [64]But among these there was not a man of those who were numbered by Moses and Aaron the priest when they numbered the children of Israel in the Wilderness of Sinai. [65]For the LORD had said of them, "They shall surely die in the wilderness." So there was not left a man of them, except Caleb the son of Jephunneh and Joshua the son of Nun.

INHERITANCE LAWS

27 Then came the daughters of Zelophehad the son of Hepher, the son of Gilead, the son of Machir, the son of Manasseh, from the families of Manasseh the son of Joseph; and these *were* the names of his daughters: Mahlah, Noah, Hoglah, Milcah, and Tirzah. [2]And they stood before Moses, before Eleazar the priest, and before the leaders and all the congregation, *by* the doorway of the tabernacle of meeting, saying: [3]"Our father died in the wilderness; but he was not in the company of those who gathered together against the LORD, in company with Korah, but he died in his own sin; and he had no sons. [4]Why should the name of our father be removed from among his family because he had no son? Give us a possession among our father's brothers."

[5]So Moses brought their case before the LORD.

26:39 [b]Called *Huppim* in Genesis 46:21
26:40 [a]Called *Addar* in 1 Chronicles 8:3
26:42 [a]Called *Hushim* in Genesis 46:23
26:48 [a]Spelled *Jahziel* in 1 Chronicles 7:13

6And the LORD spoke to Moses, saying: 7"The daughters of Zelophehad speak *what is* right; you shall surely give them a possession of inheritance among their father's brothers, and cause the inheritance of their father to pass to them. 8And you shall speak to the children of Israel, saying: 'If a man dies and has no son, then you shall cause his inheritance to pass to his daughter. 9If he has no daughter, then you shall give his inheritance to his brothers. 10If he has no brothers, then you shall give his inheritance to his father's brothers. 11And if his father has no brothers, then you shall give his inheritance to the relative closest to him in his family, and he shall possess it.' " And it shall be to the children of Israel a statute of judgment, just as the LORD commanded Moses.

JOSHUA THE NEXT LEADER OF ISRAEL

12Now the LORD said to Moses: "Go up into this Mount Abarim, and see the land which I have given to the children of Israel. 13And when you have seen it, you also shall be gathered to your people, as Aaron your brother was gathered. 14For in the Wilderness of Zin, during the strife of the congregation, you rebelled against My command to hallow Me at the waters before their eyes." (These *are* the waters of Meribah, at Kadesh in the Wilderness of Zin.)

15Then Moses spoke to the LORD, saying: 16"Let the LORD, the God of the spirits of all flesh, set a man over the congregation, 17who may go out before them and go in before them, who may lead them out and bring them in, that the congregation of the LORD may not be like sheep which have no shepherd."

18And the LORD said to Moses: "Take Joshua the son of Nun with you, a man in whom *is* the Spirit, and lay your hand on him; 19set him before Eleazar the priest and before all the congregation, and inaugurate him in their sight. 20And you shall give *some* of your authority to him, that all the congregation of the children of Israel may be obedient. 21He shall stand before Eleazar the priest, who shall inquire before the LORD for him by the judgment of the Urim. At his word they shall go out, and at his word they shall come in, he and all the children of Israel with him—all the congregation."

22So Moses did as the LORD commanded him. He took Joshua and set him before Eleazar the priest and before all the congregation. 23And he laid his hands on him and inaugurated him, just as the LORD commanded by the hand of Moses.

DAILY OFFERINGS

28 Now the LORD spoke to Moses, saying, 2"Command the children of Israel, and say to them, 'My offering, My food for My offerings made by fire as a sweet aroma to Me, you shall be careful to offer to Me at their appointed time.'

3"And you shall say to them, 'This *is* the offering made by fire which you shall offer to the LORD: two male lambs in their first year without blemish, day by day, as a regular burnt offering. 4The one lamb you shall offer in the morning, the other lamb you shall offer in the evening, 5and one-tenth of an ephah of fine flour as a grain offering mixed with one-fourth of a hin of pressed oil. 6*It is* a regular burnt offering which was ordained at Mount Sinai for a sweet aroma, an offering made by fire to the LORD. 7And its drink offering *shall be* one-fourth of a hin for each lamb; in a holy *place* you shall pour out the drink to the LORD as an offering. 8The other lamb you shall offer in the evening; as the morning grain offering

SOUL NOTE

God Is Fair *(27:1–11)* Land was customarily inherited by the sons of a family. This would keep the land in the family generation after generation. When daughters married they went to another family and so were not included in the settlement of the estate. The daughters of Zelophehad, however, appealed to Moses to allow them to inherit the land because their father had died without leaving any sons. God allowed the women to inherit the land, showing His concern for them. God treated them fairly, even making an exception in the Law for them.

Topic: Women's Issues

and its drink offering, you shall offer *it* as an
offering made by fire, a sweet aroma to the
LORD.

SABBATH OFFERINGS

9'And on the Sabbath day two lambs in their
first year, without blemish, and two-tenths *of
an ephah* of fine flour as a grain offering,
mixed with oil, with its drink offering— 10*this
is* the burnt offering for every Sabbath, besides the regular burnt offering with its drink
offering.

MONTHLY OFFERINGS

11'At the beginnings of your months you
shall present a burnt offering to the LORD: two
young bulls, one ram, and seven lambs in
their first year, without blemish; 12three-
tenths *of an ephah* of fine flour as a grain
offering, mixed with oil, for each bull; two-
tenths *of an ephah* of fine flour as a grain offering, mixed with oil, for the one ram; 13and
one-tenth *of an ephah* of fine flour, mixed
with oil, as a grain offering for each lamb, as a
burnt offering of sweet aroma, an offering
made by fire to the LORD. 14Their drink offering shall be half a hin of wine for a bull, one-
third of a hin for a ram, and one-fourth of a
hin for a lamb; this *is* the burnt offering for
each month throughout the months of the
year. 15Also one kid of the goats as a sin offering to the LORD shall be offered, besides the
regular burnt offering and its drink offering.

OFFERINGS AT PASSOVER

16'On the fourteenth day of the first month
is the Passover of the LORD. 17And on the fifteenth day of this month *is* the feast; unleavened bread shall be eaten for seven days. 18On
the first day *you shall have* a holy convocation. You shall do no customary work. 19And
you shall present an offering made by fire as a
burnt offering to the LORD: two young bulls,
one ram, and seven lambs in their first year.
Be sure they are without blemish. 20Their
grain offering shall be of fine flour mixed with
oil: three-tenths *of an ephah* you shall offer for
a bull, and two-tenths for a ram; 21you shall
offer one-tenth *of an ephah* for each of the
seven lambs; 22also one goat *as* a sin offering,
to make atonement for you. 23You shall offer
these besides the burnt offering of the morning, which *is* for a regular burnt offering. 24In
this manner you shall offer the food of the offering made by fire daily for seven days, as a
sweet aroma to the LORD; it shall be offered
besides the regular burnt offering and its
drink offering. 25And on the seventh day you
shall have a holy convocation. You shall do no
customary work.

OFFERINGS AT THE FEAST OF WEEKS

26'Also on the day of the firstfruits, when
you bring a new grain offering to the LORD at
your *Feast of* Weeks, you shall have a holy
convocation. You shall do no customary work.
27You shall present a burnt offering as a sweet
aroma to the LORD: two young bulls, one ram,
and seven lambs in their first year, 28with their
grain offering of fine flour mixed with oil:
three-tenths *of an ephah* for each bull, two-
tenths for the one ram, 29and one-tenth for
each of the seven lambs; 30*also* one kid of the
goats, to make atonement for you. 31Be sure
they are without blemish. You shall present
them with their drink offerings, besides the
regular burnt offering with its grain offering.

OFFERINGS AT THE FEAST OF TRUMPETS

29 'And in the seventh month, on the first
day of the month, you shall have a
holy convocation. You shall do no customary

SOUL NOTE

Come to God *(28:2)* For the Hebrews, worship meant regularly bringing offerings to God at appointed times. This continually reminded them that they belonged to God, and it helped them focus on His greatness. For today's believers, worship is accomplished by daily communication with God, commitment to serve Him, and regular gatherings for worship with other believers. Regular worship, both public and private, helps us keep our focus on who God is and what He has done for us. **Topic: Praise and Worship**

work. For you it is a day of blowing the trumpets. 2You shall offer a burnt offering as a sweet aroma to the LORD: one young bull, one ram, *and* seven lambs in their first year, without blemish. 3Their grain offering *shall be* fine flour mixed with oil: three-tenths *of an ephah* for the bull, two-tenths for the ram, 4and one-tenth for each of the seven lambs; 5also one kid of the goats *as* a sin offering, to make atonement for you; 6besides the burnt offering with its grain offering for the New Moon, the regular burnt offering with its grain offering, and their drink offerings, according to their ordinance, as a sweet aroma, an offering made by fire to the LORD.

Offerings on the Day of Atonement

7'On the tenth *day* of this seventh month you shall have a holy convocation. You shall afflict your souls; you shall not do any work. 8You shall present a burnt offering to the LORD *as* a sweet aroma: one young bull, one ram, *and* seven lambs in their first year. Be sure they are without blemish. 9Their grain offering *shall be of* fine flour mixed with oil: three-tenths *of an ephah* for the bull, two-tenths for the one ram, 10and one-tenth for each of the seven lambs; 11also one kid of the goats *as* a sin offering, besides the sin offering for atonement, the regular burnt offering with its grain offering, and their drink offerings.

Offerings at the Feast of Tabernacles

12'On the fifteenth day of the seventh month you shall have a holy convocation. You shall do no customary work, and you shall keep a feast to the LORD seven days. 13You shall present a burnt offering, an offering made by fire as a sweet aroma to the LORD: thirteen young bulls, two rams, *and* fourteen lambs in their first year. They shall be without blemish. 14Their grain offering *shall be of* fine flour mixed with oil: three-tenths *of an ephah* for each of the thirteen bulls, two-tenths for each of the two rams, 15and one-tenth for each of the fourteen lambs; 16also one kid of the goats *as* a sin offering, besides the regular burnt offering, its grain offering, and its drink offering.

17'On the second day *present* twelve young bulls, two rams, fourteen lambs in their first year without blemish, 18and their grain offering and their drink offerings for the bulls, for the rams, and for the lambs, by their number, according to the ordinance; 19also one kid of the goats *as* a sin offering, besides the regular burnt offering with its grain offering, and their drink offerings.

20'On the third day *present* eleven bulls, two rams, fourteen lambs in their first year without blemish, 21and their grain offering and their drink offerings for the bulls, for the rams, and for the lambs, by their number, according to the ordinance; 22also one goat *as* a sin offering, besides the regular burnt offering, its grain offering, and its drink offering.

23'On the fourth day *present* ten bulls, two rams, *and* fourteen lambs in their first year, without blemish, 24and their grain offering and their drink offerings for the bulls, for the rams, and for the lambs, by their number, according to the ordinance; 25also one kid of the goats *as* a sin offering, besides the regular burnt offering, its grain offering, and its drink offering.

26'On the fifth day *present* nine bulls, two rams, *and* fourteen lambs in their first year without blemish, 27and their grain offering and their drink offerings for the bulls, for the rams, and for the lambs, by their number, according to the ordinance; 28also one goat *as* a sin offering, besides the regular burnt offering, its grain offering, and its drink offering.

29'On the sixth day *present* eight bulls, two rams, *and* fourteen lambs in their first year without blemish, 30and their grain offering and their drink offerings for the bulls, for the rams, and for the lambs, by their number, according to the ordinance; 31also one goat *as* a sin offering, besides the regular burnt offering, its grain offering, and its drink offering.

32'On the seventh day *present* seven bulls, two rams, *and* fourteen lambs in their first year without blemish, 33and their grain offering and their drink offerings for the bulls, for the rams, and for the lambs, by their number, according to the ordinance; 34also one goat *as* a sin offering, besides the regular burnt offering, its grain offering, and its drink offering.

35'On the eighth day you shall have a sacred assembly. You shall do no customary work. 36You shall present a burnt offering, an offering made by fire as a sweet aroma to the LORD: one bull, one ram, seven lambs in their first year without blemish, 37and their grain offering and their drink offerings for the bull, for the ram, and for the lambs, by their number, according to the ordinance; 38also one goat *as* a sin offering, besides the regular burnt offering, its grain offering, and its drink offering.

39'These you shall present to the LORD at your appointed feasts (besides your vowed offerings and your freewill offerings) as your burnt offerings and your grain offerings, as your drink offerings and your peace offerings.' "

40So Moses told the children of Israel everything, just as the LORD commanded Moses.

THE LAW CONCERNING VOWS

30 Then Moses spoke to the heads of the tribes concerning the children of Israel, saying, "This *is* the thing which the LORD has commanded: 2If a man makes a vow to the LORD, or swears an oath to bind himself by some agreement, he shall not break his word; he shall do according to all that proceeds out of his mouth.

3"Or if a woman makes a vow to the LORD, and binds *herself* by some agreement while in her father's house in her youth, 4and her father hears her vow and the agreement by which she has bound herself, and her father holds his peace, then all her vows shall stand, and every agreement with which she has bound herself shall stand. 5But if her father overrules her on the day that he hears, then none of her vows nor her agreements by which she has bound herself shall stand; and the LORD will release her, because her father overruled her.

6"If indeed she takes a husband, while bound by her vows or by a rash utterance from her lips by which she bound herself, 7and her husband hears *it,* and makes no response to her on the day that he hears, then her vows shall stand, and her agreements by which she bound herself shall stand. 8But if her husband overrules her on the day that he hears *it,* he shall make void her vow which she took and what she uttered with her lips, by which she bound herself, and the LORD will release her.

9"Also any vow of a widow or a divorced woman, by which she has bound herself, shall stand against her.

10"If she vowed in her husband's house, or bound herself by an agreement with an oath, 11and her husband heard *it,* and made no response to her *and* did not overrule her, then all her vows shall stand, and every agreement by which she bound herself shall stand. 12But if her husband truly made them void on the day he heard *them,* then whatever proceeded from her lips concerning her vows or concerning the agreement binding her, it shall not stand; her husband has made them void, and the LORD will release her. 13Every vow and every binding oath to afflict her soul, her husband may confirm it, or her husband may make it void. 14Now if her husband makes no response whatever to her from day to day, then he confirms all her vows or all the agreements that bind her; he confirms them, because he made no response to her on the day that he heard *them.* 15But if he does make them void after he has heard *them,* then he shall bear her guilt."

16These *are* the statutes which the LORD commanded Moses, between a man and his wife, and between a father and his daughter in her youth in her father's house.

VENGEANCE ON THE MIDIANITES

31 And the LORD spoke to Moses, saying: 2"Take vengeance on the Midianites for the children of Israel. Afterward you shall be gathered to your people."

3So Moses spoke to the people, saying, "Arm some of yourselves for war, and let them go against the Midianites to take vengeance for the LORD on Midian. 4A thousand from each tribe of all the tribes of Israel you shall send to the war."

5So there were recruited from the divisions of Israel one thousand from *each* tribe, twelve thousand armed for war. 6Then Moses sent them to the war, one thousand from *each* tribe; he sent them to the war with Phinehas the son of Eleazar the priest, with the holy articles and the signal trumpets in his hand. 7And they warred against the Midianites, just as the LORD commanded Moses, and they killed all the males. 8They killed the kings of Midian with *the rest of* those who were killed—Evi, Rekem, Zur, Hur, and Reba, the five kings of Midian. Balaam the son of Beor they also killed with the sword.

9And the children of Israel took the women of Midian captive, with their little ones, and took as spoil all their cattle, all their flocks, and all their goods. 10They also burned with fire all the cities where they dwelt, and all their forts. 11And they took all the spoil and all the booty—of man and beast.

RETURN FROM THE WAR

12 Then they brought the captives, the booty, and the spoil to Moses, to Eleazar the priest, and to the congregation of the children of Israel, to the camp in the plains of Moab by the Jordan, *across from* Jericho. 13 And Moses, Eleazar the priest, and all the leaders of the congregation, went to meet them outside the camp. 14 But Moses was angry with the officers of the army, *with* the captains over thousands and captains over hundreds, who had come from the battle.

15 And Moses said to them: "Have you kept all the women alive? 16 Look, these *women* caused the children of Israel, through the counsel of Balaam, to trespass against the LORD in the incident of Peor, and there was a plague among the congregation of the LORD. 17 Now therefore, kill every male among the little ones, and kill every woman who has known a man intimately. 18 But keep alive for yourselves all the young girls who have not known a man intimately. 19 And as for you, remain outside the camp seven days; whoever has killed any person, and whoever has touched any slain, purify yourselves and your captives on the third day and on the seventh day. 20 Purify every garment, everything made of leather, everything woven of goats' *hair,* and everything made of wood."

21 Then Eleazar the priest said to the men of war who had gone to the battle, "This *is* the ordinance of the law which the LORD commanded Moses: 22 Only the gold, the silver, the bronze, the iron, the tin, and the lead, 23 everything that can endure fire, you shall put through the fire, and it shall be clean; and it shall be purified with the water of purification. But all that cannot endure fire you shall put through water. 24 And you shall wash your clothes on the seventh day and be clean, and afterward you may come into the camp."

DIVISION OF THE PLUNDER

25 Now the LORD spoke to Moses, saying: 26 "Count up the plunder that was taken—of man and beast—you and Eleazar the priest and the chief fathers of the congregation; 27 and divide the plunder into two parts, between those who took part in the war, who went out to battle, and all the congregation. 28 And levy a tribute for the LORD on the men of war who went out to battle: one of every five hundred of the persons, the cattle, the donkeys, and the sheep; 29 take *it* from their half, and give *it* to Eleazar the priest as a heave offering to the LORD. 30 And from the children of Israel's half you shall take one of every fifty, drawn from the persons, the cattle, the donkeys, and the sheep, from all the livestock, and give them to the Levites who keep charge of the tabernacle of the LORD." 31 So Moses and Eleazar the priest did as the LORD commanded Moses.

32 The booty remaining from the plunder, which the men of war had taken, was six hundred and seventy-five thousand sheep, 33 seventy-two thousand cattle, 34 sixty-one thousand donkeys, 35 and thirty-two thousand persons in all, of women who had not known a man intimately. 36 And the half, the portion for those who had gone out to war, was in number three hundred and thirty-seven thousand five hundred sheep; 37 and the LORD's tribute of the sheep was six hundred and seventy-five. 38 The cattle *were* thirty-six thousand, of which the LORD's tribute *was* seventy-two. 39 The donkeys *were* thirty thousand five hundred, of which the LORD's tribute *was* sixty-one. 40 The persons *were* sixteen thousand, of which the LORD's tribute *was* thirty-two persons. 41 So Moses gave the tribute *which was* the LORD's heave offering to Eleazar the priest, as the LORD commanded Moses.

SOUL NOTE

Kill Everybody? *(31:17, 18)* The command to kill everyone was part of God's plan to cleanse the land of evil influences and prepare it for the Israelites. The violence does not sit well with modern tastes, but it was God's judgment against these pagan nations. God knew that evil influences can affect a nation like yeast affects a batch of dough. Likewise, allowing a little bit of sin to stay in our lives will eventually have a profound effect. As the Israelites were called to eradicate the evil in the land, so believers should seek out and destroy sin in their lives. **Topic: Violence**

42And from the children of Israel's half, which Moses separated from the men who fought— 43now the half belonging to the congregation was three hundred and thirty-seven thousand five hundred sheep, 44thirty-six thousand cattle, 45thirty thousand five hundred donkeys, 46and sixteen thousand persons— 47and from the children of Israel's half Moses took one of every fifty, drawn from man and beast, and gave them to the Levites, who kept charge of the tabernacle of the LORD, as the LORD commanded Moses.

48Then the officers who *were* over thousands of the army, the captains of thousands and captains of hundreds, came near to Moses; 49and they said to Moses, "Your servants have taken a count of the men of war who *are* under our command, and not a man of us is missing. 50Therefore we have brought an offering for the LORD, what every man found of ornaments of gold: armlets and bracelets and signet rings and earrings and necklaces, to make atonement for ourselves before the LORD." 51So Moses and Eleazar the priest received the gold from them, all the fashioned ornaments. 52And all the gold of the offering that they offered to the LORD, from the captains of thousands and captains of hundreds, was sixteen thousand seven hundred and fifty shekels. 53(The men of war had taken spoil, every man for himself.) 54And Moses and Eleazar the priest received the gold from the captains of thousands and of hundreds, and brought it into the tabernacle of meeting as a memorial for the children of Israel before the LORD.

The Tribes Settling East of the Jordan

32 Now the children of Reuben and the children of Gad had a very great multitude of livestock; and when they saw the land of Jazer and the land of Gilead, that indeed the region *was* a place for livestock, 2the children of Gad and the children of Reuben came and spoke to Moses, to Eleazar the priest, and to the leaders of the congregation, saying, 3"Ataroth, Dibon, Jazer, Nimrah, Heshbon, Elealeh, Shebam, Nebo, and Beon, 4the country which the LORD defeated before the congregation of Israel, *is* a land for livestock, and your servants have livestock." 5Therefore they said, "If we have found favor in your sight, let this land be given to your servants as a possession. Do not take us over the Jordan."

6And Moses said to the children of Gad and to the children of Reuben: "Shall your brethren go to war while you sit here? 7Now why will you discourage the heart of the children of Israel from going over into the land which the LORD has given them? 8Thus your fathers did when I sent them away from Kadesh Barnea to see the land. 9For when they went up to the Valley of Eshcol and saw the land, they discouraged the heart of the children of Israel, so that they did not go into the land which the LORD had given them. 10So the LORD's anger was aroused on that day, and He swore an oath, saying, 11'Surely none of the men who came up from Egypt, from twenty years old and above, shall see the land of which I swore to Abraham, Isaac, and Jacob, because they have not wholly followed Me, 12except Caleb the son of Jephunneh, the Kenizzite, and Joshua the son of Nun, for they have wholly followed the LORD.' 13So the LORD's anger was aroused against Israel, and He made them wander in the wilderness forty years, until all the generation that had done evil in the sight of the LORD was gone. 14And look! You have risen in your fathers' place, a brood of sinful men, to increase still more the fierce anger of the LORD against Israel. 15For if you turn away from following Him, He will once again leave them in the wilderness, and you will destroy all these people."

16Then they came near to him and said: "We will build sheepfolds here for our livestock, and cities for our little ones, 17but we ourselves will be armed, ready *to go* before the children of Israel until we have brought them to their place; and our little ones will dwell in the fortified cities because of the inhabitants of the land. 18We will not return to our homes until every one of the children of Israel has received his inheritance. 19For we will not inherit with them on the other side of the Jordan and beyond, because our inheritance has fallen to us on this eastern side of the Jordan."

20Then Moses said to them: "If you do this thing, if you arm yourselves before the LORD for the war, 21and all your armed men cross over the Jordan before the LORD until He has driven out His enemies from before Him, 22and the land is subdued before the LORD, then afterward you may return and be blameless before the LORD and before Israel; and this land shall be your possession before the LORD. 23But if you do not do so, then take note, you have sinned against the LORD; and be sure your sin will find you out. [24]Build cities for your little ones and folds for your sheep, and do what has proceeded out of your mouth."

[25]And the children of Gad and the children of Reuben spoke to Moses, saying: "Your servants will do as my lord commands. [26]Our little ones, our wives, our flocks, and all our livestock will be there in the cities of Gilead; [27]but your servants will cross over, every man armed for war, before the LORD to battle, just as my lord says."

[28]So Moses gave command concerning them to Eleazar the priest, to Joshua the son of Nun, and to the chief fathers of the tribes of the children of Israel. [29]And Moses said to them: "If the children of Gad and the children of Reuben cross over the Jordan with you, every man armed for battle before the LORD, and the land is subdued before you, then you shall give them the land of Gilead as a possession. [30]But if they do not cross over armed with you, they shall have possessions among you in the land of Canaan."

[31]Then the children of Gad and the children of Reuben answered, saying: "As the LORD has said to your servants, so we will do. [32]We will cross over armed before the LORD into the land of Canaan, but the possession of our inheritance *shall remain* with us on this side of the Jordan."

[33]So Moses gave to the children of Gad, to the children of Reuben, and to half the tribe of Manasseh the son of Joseph, the kingdom of Sihon king of the Amorites and the kingdom of Og king of Bashan, the land with its cities within the borders, the cities of the surrounding country. [34]And the children of Gad built Dibon and Ataroth and Aroer, [35]Atroth and Shophan and Jazer and Jogbehah, [36]Beth Nimrah and Beth Haran, fortified cities, and folds for sheep. [37]And the children of Reuben built Heshbon and Elealeh and Kirjathaim, [38]Nebo and Baal Meon (*their* names being changed) and Shibmah; and they gave *other* names to the cities which they built.

[39]And the children of Machir the son of Manasseh went to Gilead and took it, and dispossessed the Amorites who *were* in it. [40]So Moses gave Gilead to Machir the son of Manasseh, and he dwelt in it. [41]Also Jair the son of Manasseh went and took its small towns, and called them Havoth Jair.[a] [42]Then Nobah went and took Kenath and its villages, and he called it Nobah, after his own name.

ISRAEL'S JOURNEY FROM EGYPT REVIEWED

33 These *are* the journeys of the children of Israel, who went out of the land of Egypt by their armies under the hand of Moses and Aaron. [2]Now Moses wrote down the starting points of their journeys at the command of the LORD. And these *are* their journeys according to their starting points:

[3]They departed from Rameses in the first month, on the fifteenth day of the first month; on the day after the Passover the children of Israel went out with boldness in the sight of all the Egyptians. [4]For the Egyptians were burying all *their* firstborn, whom the LORD had killed among them. Also on their gods the LORD had executed judgments.

[5]Then the children of Israel moved from Rameses and camped at Succoth. [6]They departed from Succoth and camped at Etham, which *is* on the edge of the wilderness. [7]They moved from Etham and turned back to Pi Hahiroth, which *is* east of Baal Zephon; and they camped near Migdol. [8]They departed from before Hahiroth[a] and passed through the midst of the sea into the wilderness, went three days' journey in the Wilderness of Etham, and camped at Marah. [9]They moved from Marah and came to Elim. At Elim *were* twelve springs of water and seventy palm trees; so they camped there.

[10]They moved from Elim and camped by the Red Sea. [11]They moved from the Red Sea and camped in the Wilderness of Sin. [12]They journeyed from the Wilderness of Sin and camped at Dophkah. [13]They departed from Dophkah and camped at Alush. [14]They moved from Alush and camped at Rephidim, where there was no water for the people to drink.

[15]They departed from Rephidim and camped in the Wilderness of Sinai. [16]They moved from the Wilderness of Sinai and camped at Kibroth Hattaavah. [17]They departed from Kibroth Hattaavah and camped at Hazeroth. [18]They departed from Hazeroth and camped at Rithmah. [19]They departed from Rithmah and camped at Rimmon Perez. [20]They departed from Rimmon Perez and camped at Libnah. [21]They moved from Libnah and camped at Rissah. [22]They journeyed from Rissah and camped at Kehelathah. [23]They went from Kehelathah and

---

32:41 [a]Literally *Towns of Jair* **33:8** [a]Many Hebrew manuscripts, Samaritan Pentateuch, Syriac, Targum, and Vulgate read *from Pi Hahiroth* (compare verse 7).

camped at Mount Shepher. 24They moved from Mount Shepher and camped at Haradah. 25They moved from Haradah and camped at Makheloth. 26They moved from Makheloth and camped at Tahath. 27They departed from Tahath and camped at Terah. 28They moved from Terah and camped at Mithkah. 29They went from Mithkah and camped at Hashmonah. 30They departed from Hashmonah and camped at Moseroth. 31They departed from Moseroth and camped at Bene Jaakan. 32They moved from Bene Jaakan and camped at Hor Hagidgad. 33They went from Hor Hagidgad and camped at Jotbathah. 34They moved from Jotbathah and camped at Abronah. 35They departed from Abronah and camped at Ezion Geber. 36They moved from Ezion Geber and camped in the Wilderness of Zin, which *is* Kadesh. 37They moved from Kadesh and camped at Mount Hor, on the boundary of the land of Edom.

38Then Aaron the priest went up to Mount Hor at the command of the LORD, and died there in the fortieth year after the children of Israel had come out of the land of Egypt, on the first *day* of the fifth month. 39Aaron *was* one hundred and twenty-three years old when he died on Mount Hor.

40Now the king of Arad, the Canaanite, who dwelt in the South in the land of Canaan, heard of the coming of the children of Israel.

41So they departed from Mount Hor and camped at Zalmonah. 42They departed from Zalmonah and camped at Punon. 43They departed from Punon and camped at Oboth. 44They departed from Oboth and camped at Ije Abarim, at the border of Moab. 45They departed from Ijim[a] and camped at Dibon Gad. 46They moved from Dibon Gad and camped at Almon Diblathaim. 47They moved from Almon Diblathaim and camped in the mountains of Abarim, before Nebo. 48They departed from the mountains of Abarim and camped in the plains of Moab by the Jordan, *across from* Jericho. 49They camped by the Jordan, from Beth Jesimoth as far as the Abel Acacia Grove[a] in the plains of Moab.

Instructions for the Conquest of Canaan

50Now the LORD spoke to Moses in the plains of Moab by the Jordan, *across from* Jericho, saying, 51"Speak to the children of Israel, and say to them: 'When you have crossed the Jordan into the land of Canaan, 52then you shall drive out all the inhabitants of the land from before you, destroy all their engraved stones, destroy all their molded images, and demolish all their high places; 53you shall dispossess *the inhabitants of* the land and dwell in it, for I have given you the land to possess. 54And you shall divide the land by lot as an inheritance among your families; to the larger you shall give a larger inheritance, and to the smaller you shall give a smaller inheritance; there everyone's *inheritance* shall be whatever falls to him by lot. You shall inherit according to the tribes of your fathers. 55But if you do not drive out the inhabitants of the land from before you, then it shall be that those whom you let remain *shall be* irritants in your eyes and thorns in your sides, and they shall harass you in the land where you dwell. 56Moreover it shall be *that* I will do to you as I thought to do to them.' "

The Appointed Boundaries of Canaan

34 Then the LORD spoke to Moses, saying, 2"Command the children of Israel, and say to them: 'When you come into the land of Canaan, this *is* the land that shall fall to you as an inheritance—the land of Canaan to its boundaries. 3Your southern border shall be from the Wilderness of Zin along the border of Edom; then your southern border shall extend eastward to the end of the Salt Sea; 4your border shall turn from the southern side of the Ascent of Akrabbim, continue to Zin, and be on the south of Kadesh Barnea; then it shall go on to Hazar Addar, and continue to Azmon; 5the border shall turn from Azmon to the Brook of Egypt, and it shall end at the Sea.

6'As for the western border, you shall have the Great Sea for a border; this shall be your western border.

7'And this shall be your northern border: From the Great Sea you shall mark out your *border* line to Mount Hor; 8from Mount Hor you shall mark out *your border* to the entrance of Hamath; then the direction of the border shall be toward Zedad; 9the border shall proceed to Ziphron, and it shall end at Hazar Enan. This shall be your northern border.

10'You shall mark out your eastern border from Hazar Enan to Shepham; 11the border

---

33:45 [a]Same as *Ije Abarim,* verse 44
33:49 [a]Hebrew *Abel Shittim*

shall go down from Shepham to Riblah on the east side of Ain; the border shall go down and reach to the eastern side of the Sea of Chinnereth; [12]the border shall go down along the Jordan, and it shall end at the Salt Sea. This shall be your land with its surrounding boundaries.' "

[13]Then Moses commanded the children of Israel, saying: "This *is* the land which you shall inherit by lot, which the LORD has commanded to give to the nine tribes and to the half-tribe. [14]For the tribe of the children of Reuben according to the house of their fathers, and the tribe of the children of Gad according to the house of their fathers, have received *their inheritance;* and the half-tribe of Manasseh has received its inheritance. [15]The two tribes and the half-tribe have received their inheritance on this side of the Jordan, *across from* Jericho eastward, toward the sunrise."

THE LEADERS APPOINTED TO DIVIDE THE LAND

[16]And the LORD spoke to Moses, saying, [17]"These *are* the names of the men who shall divide the land among you as an inheritance: Eleazar the priest and Joshua the son of Nun. [18]And you shall take one leader of every tribe to divide the land for the inheritance. [19]These *are* the names of the men: from the tribe of Judah, Caleb the son of Jephunneh; [20]from the tribe of the children of Simeon, Shemuel the son of Ammihud; [21]from the tribe of Benjamin, Elidad the son of Chislon; [22]a leader from the tribe of the children of Dan, Bukki the son of Jogli; [23]from the sons of Joseph: a leader from the tribe of the children of Manasseh, Hanniel the son of Ephod, [24]and a leader from the tribe of the children of Ephraim, Kemuel the son of Shiphtan; [25]a leader from the tribe of the children of Zebulun, Elizaphan the son of Parnach; [26]a leader from the tribe of the children of Issachar, Paltiel the son of Azzan; [27]a leader from the tribe of the children of Asher, Ahihud the son of Shelomi; [28]and a leader from the tribe of the children of Naphtali, Pedahel the son of Ammihud."

[29]These *are* the ones the LORD commanded to divide the inheritance among the children of Israel in the land of Canaan.

CITIES FOR THE LEVITES

35 And the LORD spoke to Moses in the plains of Moab by the Jordan *across from* Jericho, saying: [2]"Command the children of Israel that they give the Levites cities to dwell in from the inheritance of their possession, and you shall *also* give the Levites common-land around the cities. [3]They shall have the cities to dwell in; and their common-land shall be for their cattle, for their herds, and for all their animals. [4]The common-land of the cities which you will give the Levites *shall extend* from the wall of the city outward a thousand cubits all around. [5]And you shall measure outside the city on the east side two thousand cubits, on the south side two thousand cubits, on the west side two thousand cubits, and on the north side two thousand cubits. The city *shall be* in the middle. This shall belong to them as common-land for the cities.

[6]"Now among the cities which you will give to the Levites *you shall appoint* six cities of refuge, to which a manslayer may flee. And to these you shall add forty-two cities. [7]So all the cities you will give to the Levites *shall be* forty-eight; these *you shall give* with their common-land. [8]And the cities which you will give *shall be* from the possession of the children of Israel; from the larger *tribe* you shall give many, from the smaller you shall give few. Each shall give some of its cities to the Levites, in proportion to the inheritance that each receives."

CITIES OF REFUGE

[9]Then the LORD spoke to Moses, saying, [10]"Speak to the children of Israel, and say to them: 'When you cross the Jordan into the land of Canaan, [11]then you shall appoint cities to be cities of refuge for you, that the manslayer who kills any person accidentally may flee there. [12]They shall be cities of refuge for you from the avenger, that the manslayer may not die until he stands before the congregation in judgment. [13]And of the cities which you give, you shall have six cities of refuge. [14]You shall appoint three cities on this side of the Jordan, and three cities you shall appoint in the land of Canaan, *which* will be cities of refuge. [15]These six cities shall be for refuge for the children of Israel, for the stranger, and for the sojourner among them, that anyone who kills a person accidentally may flee there.

[16]'But if he strikes him with an iron implement, so that he dies, he *is* a murderer; the murderer shall surely be put to death. [17]And if he strikes him with a stone in the hand, by which one could die, and he does die, he *is* a

murderer; the murderer shall surely be put to death. [18]Or *if* he strikes him with a wooden hand weapon, by which one could die, and he does die, he *is* a murderer; the murderer shall surely be put to death. [19]The avenger of blood himself shall put the murderer to death; when he meets him, he shall put him to death. [20]If he pushes him out of hatred or, while lying in wait, hurls something at him so that he dies, [21]or in enmity he strikes him with his hand so that he dies, the one who struck *him* shall surely be put to death. He *is* a murderer. The avenger of blood shall put the murderer to death when he meets him.

[22]'However, if he pushes him suddenly without enmity, or throws anything at him without lying in wait, [23]or uses a stone, by which a man could die, throwing *it* at him without seeing *him,* so that he dies, while he was not his enemy or seeking his harm, [24]then the congregation shall judge between the manslayer and the avenger of blood according to these judgments. [25]So the congregation shall deliver the manslayer from the hand of the avenger of blood, and the congregation shall return him to the city of refuge where he had fled, and he shall remain there until the death of the high priest who was anointed with the holy oil. [26]But if the manslayer at any time goes outside the limits of the city of refuge where he fled, [27]and the avenger of blood finds him outside the limits of his city of refuge, and the avenger of blood kills the manslayer, he shall not be guilty of blood, [28]because he should have remained in his city of refuge until the death of the high priest. But after the death of the high priest the manslayer may return to the land of his possession.

[29]'And these *things* shall be a statute of judgment to you throughout your generations in all your dwellings. [30]Whoever kills a person, the murderer shall be put to death on the testimony of witnesses; but one witness is not *sufficient* testimony against a person for the death *penalty.* [31]Moreover you shall take no ransom for the life of a murderer who *is* guilty of death, but he shall surely be put to death. [32]And you shall take no ransom for him who has fled to his city of refuge, that he may return to dwell in the land before the death of the priest. [33]So you shall not pollute the land where you *are;* for blood defiles the land, and no atonement can be made for the land, for the blood that is shed on it, except by the blood of him who shed it. [34]Therefore do not defile the land which you inhabit, in the midst of which I dwell; for I the LORD dwell among the children of Israel.' "

Marriage of Female Heirs

36 Now the chief fathers of the families of the children of Gilead the son of Machir, the son of Manasseh, of the families of the sons of Joseph, came near and spoke before Moses and before the leaders, the chief fathers of the children of Israel. [2]And they said: "The LORD commanded my lord *Moses* to give the land as an inheritance by lot to the children of Israel, and my lord was commanded by the LORD to give the inheritance of our brother Zelophehad to his daughters. [3]Now if they are married to any of the sons of the *other* tribes of the children of Israel, then their inheritance will be taken from the inheritance of our fathers, and it will be added to the inheritance of the tribe into which they marry; so it will be taken from the lot of our inheritance. [4]And when the Jubilee of the children of Israel comes, then their inheritance will be added to the inheritance of the tribe into which they marry; so their inheritance will be taken away from the inheritance of the tribe of our fathers."

[5]Then Moses commanded the children of Israel according to the word of the LORD, saying: "What the tribe of the sons of Joseph speaks is right. [6]This *is* what the LORD commands concerning the daughters of Zelophehad, saying, 'Let them marry whom they think best, but they may marry only within the family of their father's tribe.' [7]So the inheritance of the children of Israel shall not change hands from tribe to tribe, for every one of the children of Israel shall keep the inheritance of the tribe of his fathers. [8]And every daughter who possesses an inheritance in any tribe of the children of Israel shall be the wife of one of the family of her father's tribe, so that the children of Israel each may possess the inheritance of his fathers. [9]Thus no inheritance shall change hands from *one* tribe to another, but every tribe of the children of Israel shall keep its own inheritance."

[10]Just as the LORD commanded Moses, so did the daughters of Zelophehad; [11]for Mahlah, Tirzah, Hoglah, Milcah, and Noah, the daughters of Zelophehad, were married to the

sons of their father's brothers. [12]They were
married into the families of the children of Manasseh the son of Joseph, and their inheritance remained in the tribe of their father's family.

[13]These *are* the commandments and the judgments which the LORD commanded the children of Israel by the hand of Moses in the plains of Moab by the Jordan, *across from* Jericho.

Deuteronomy

What can people do about wasted years? What truths learned in the "wasted" years of life should be passed on to the younger generation?

These are the issues of the Book of Deuteronomy, written by Moses. On the plains of Moab, just east of the Jordan River, Moses had gathered the new generation of Israelites (those who survived the forty years of wandering detailed in Numbers). The challenge before them was great; the opportunities were even greater. The earlier generation had turned from God. Had this new generation learned from that mistake?

The great leader reiterated God's law for the twelve tribes (the title "Deuteronomy" literally means "second law"). Moses also renewed the covenant agreement between God and Israel. He then transferred leadership to Joshua, who would take the people the rest of the way.

Deuteronomy is a strong call to allegiance to God. The older generation of Israelites never reached the Promised Land because of fear and unbelief. But the younger generation had the opportunity to learn from their parents' errors and experience God's blessing in their lives.

This is a book about rebounding from failure. Though probably not for as long as the wilderness wanderings, most of us can confess to wasted years—years of wandering and confusion when we did not obey the call and commands of God. Read on for an encouraging reminder that God will lead us out of the wilderness, if and when we simply say yes to His call.

SOUL CONCERNS IN DEUTERONOMY

The Previous Command to Enter Canaan

1 These *are* the words which Moses spoke
to all Israel on this side of the Jordan in
the wilderness, in the plain[a] opposite Suph,[b]
between Paran, Tophel, Laban, Hazeroth, and
Dizahab. 2*It is* eleven days' *journey* from Horeb by way of Mount Seir to Kadesh Barnea.
3Now it came to pass in the fortieth year, in
the eleventh month, on the first *day* of the
month, *that* Moses spoke to the children of Israel according to all that the LORD had given
him as commandments to them, 4after he had
killed Sihon king of the Amorites, who dwelt
in Heshbon, and Og king of Bashan, who
dwelt at Ashtaroth in[a] Edrei.
5On this side of the Jordan in the land of
Moab, Moses began to explain this law, saying, 6"The LORD our God spoke to us in Horeb,
saying: 'You have dwelt long enough at this
mountain. 7Turn and take your journey, and
go to the mountains of the Amorites, to all the
neighboring *places* in the plain,[a] in the mountains and in the lowland, in the South and on
the seacoast, to the land of the Canaanites and
to Lebanon, as far as the great river, the River
Euphrates. 8See, I have set the land before
you; go in and possess the land which the
LORD swore to your fathers—to Abraham,
Isaac, and Jacob—to give to them and their
descendants after them.'

1:1 [a]Hebrew *arabah* [b]One manuscript of the Septuagint, also Targum and Vulgate, read *Red Sea.* **1:4** [a]Septuagint, Syriac, and Vulgate read *and* (compare Joshua 12:4). **1:7** [a]Hebrew *arabah*

PERSONALITY PROFILE

Insecurity

MOSES: HUMBLE OR INSECURE?

(DEUTERONOMY 1)

Moses had an amazing early childhood. Born in secret, lovingly abandoned, miraculously rescued, unexpectedly raised, Moses appears in the Bible as a person with an unusually varied past. The mystery that surrounds Moses' growth to adulthood offers few clues, but the man who eventually served as God's chosen leader of the chosen people was more prepared to lead than he realized.

Moses' life spanned 120 years. The first 40 were devoted to academic and leadership training—Egyptian style. The second 40 years Moses spent in the desert, where he practiced leading sheep through the wilderness. Thus he was unknowingly prepared to lead people through the same terrain. The last 40 years were spent in the stressful role of champion and leader of a nation on the move.

Each phase in Moses' life began with a crisis. By the time he was 40, his instincts to protect his people were well intentioned but poorly timed (Ex. 2:11–15). He killed an Egyptian guard and had to flee for his life into the desert. There he stayed until God called him. That call (Ex. 3:1—4:17) reveals much about Moses' character. He questioned, avoided, and resisted God's direction. He had lived with the failure and shame of his actions in Egypt for almost 40 years. He had grown accustomed to what seemed like insignificance. But God had plans for Moses' combination of ability and insecurity, a combination that made Moses a humble man.

God used Moses' experiences to hone his abilities and shape his character. Moses' training improved his gifts, his failures deepened his dependence on God, and God made the loving effort to convince Moses of His plans.

God can use our insecurities and uncertainties as effective tools in our lives. They can make us useful in God's service. God can make strengths out of weaknesses. We might allow them to come between God and us, but God transforms them into part of the living bridge that connects us with the One who loves us best of all.

To Learn More: Turn to the article about insecurity on pages 186, 187. See also the key passage note at Numbers 13:30–33 on page 189.

God's Promises

FINDING THE COURAGE TO BELIEVE

JAMES CLINTON

(Deuteronomy 1:8–11)

Rain splashing against a windowpane can evoke many emotions—comfort in the face of natural forces or restlessness during the idle rainy days of childhood. When a drizzle turns into a downpour and deafening thunder shakes the windows, people often become fearful.

Inevitably, the storm subsides and a ray of sunshine breaks through the clouds. A bright, multicolored rainbow may even appear. The rainbow stands as a reminder of God's faithfulness, that He will keep His promises. The rainbow first appeared to Noah centuries ago when God promised that He would never again destroy the earth with a flood: "This is the sign of the covenant which I make between Me and you. . . . I set My rainbow in the cloud. . . . It shall be, when I bring a cloud over the earth, that the rainbow shall be seen in the cloud; and I will remember My covenant" (Gen. 9:12–15).

THE FOUNDATION OF A PROMISE

A promise is essentially a guarantee that something will happen. A promise is only as good as the person who makes it, however. A person who has broken promise after promise cannot be trusted.

Most people try to keep their promises, but that doesn't always happen. They may forget or get distracted or change their minds. Some, of course, never intended to keep their promise in the first place. Sometimes they change their minds. In a world of broken promises, however, God's promises are certain. He never forgets; He never makes a promise He does not intend to keep; He never changes His mind.

Behind all the promises in Scripture stands our loyal, faithful God who can never lie (Num. 23:19). And He has proven Himself true to His word again and again—whether it was His promise to provide Abraham with an heir (Gen. 15:4, 5; 17:15–22; 21:1–7) or to deliver the Israelites from slavery (Gen. 15:13–16; 50:24–26; Ex. 2:23–25; 3:7–10; 12:31–42). Because the estimated nearly three thousand promises recorded in the Bible are given by God Himself, we can be absolutely certain that they will come true.

GOD'S PROMISES TO HIS PEOPLE

Scripture holds two kinds of promises: *conditional* and *unconditional. Conditional* promises are those that will be fulfilled if the recipient does something. Leviticus 26:3–13 contains conditional promises. If the Israelites remained faithful to God and kept His commands, God promised to make their land fruitful.

Unconditional promises have no conditions attached. They will happen no matter what. The conditional promise mentioned above, that God would make the land fruitful if the Israelites obeyed, is couched in God's *unconditional* promise: God's covenant with Abraham, promising that his descendants will become a great nation and that all the families of the earth will be blessed through him (Gen. 12:1–3; 15:1–18). God didn't require anything from Abraham when He made that promise. Though the Israelites sinned against God and eventually faced defeat and captivity, God always preserved a remnant of faithful people. Eventually, of course, Abraham's descendant, Jesus Christ, fulfilled the promise as He became a blessing to the entire world.

God's ultimate unconditional promise is that "whoever calls on the name of the LORD shall be saved" (Joel 2:32; Rom. 10:13). To guarantee this promise of salvation, God gave His Son, Jesus, to die for our sin. This unconditional promise of salvation to those who believe forms the basis of God's new covenant with humanity and of all His other promises (Heb. 8:7–12). God also promises His presence with His people. Jesus told His followers, "I am with you always, even to the end of the age" (Matt. 28:20).

From the beginning, God wanted to make a certain nation His own special people. He promised to make Abraham's descendants into a nation that would enjoy a special relationship with Him (Gen. 12:2, 3). At Mount Sinai, God even called the Israelites "My people" (Lev. 26:12). Through Christ's sacrifice on the Cross, God invites all people to join His family of faith (John 1:12; 1 Pet. 2:9, 10; 1 John 3:1, 2). "For all the promises of God in [Christ] are Yes" (2 Cor. 1:20). In Christ, all of God's promises to save are fulfilled (Is. 35:3, 4; Matt. 1:21; 1 Tim. 1:15). Out of every nation, God is calling people to be His children (Rom. 8:16, 17; Rev. 5:9; 7:9). Indeed, He promises us that no one can snatch us out of His Son's hand (John 10:28).

The Bible is filled with wonderful promises from God. Believers can call on God and fully expect Him to answer in marvelous ways.

STANDING ON GOD'S PROMISES

When the storms assault us, we may find it difficult to trust in what we cannot see, to believe in what God has promised. During those times, it takes courage to lean on the invisible God. I've had to do just that throughout my life—and very recently with the loss of my wife of fifty years. That's what the heroes of faith did (Heb. 11). In his lifetime, Abraham never saw the numerous descendants that God had promised (Gen. 15:4, 5), but he still believed in the God who made the promise because he knew that God was faithful.

Nothing is too hard for our all-powerful God. We need Abraham's courage to believe. We need to stand on God's promises, though the dark clouds of troubles and trials roll over our lives. God's certain promises give us hope and comfort. How many promises do we know and claim?

FURTHER MEDITATION:

Other passages to study about the issue of God's promises include:

- ➢ Genesis 18:1–15
- ➢ Mark 11:24
- ➢ Romans 4:13–25
- ➢ Hebrews 11:11–16
- ➢ 2 Peter 1:4

To Learn More: Turn to the key passage note on God's promises at 2 Peter 1:4 on page 1668. See also the personality profile of Noah on page 16.

Tribal Leaders Appointed

9"And I spoke to you at that time, saying: 'I
alone am not able to bear you. 10The LORD
your God has multiplied you, and here you *are*
today, as the stars of heaven in multitude.
11May the LORD God of your fathers make you
a thousand times more numerous than you
are, and bless you as He has promised you!
12How can I alone bear your problems and
your burdens and your complaints? 13Choose
wise, understanding, and knowledgeable men
from among your tribes, and I will make them
heads over you.' 14And you answered me and
said, 'The thing which you have told *us* to do
is good.' 15So I took the heads of your tribes,
wise and knowledgeable men, and made them
heads over you, leaders of thousands, leaders
of hundreds, leaders of fifties, leaders of tens,
and officers for your tribes.

16"Then I commanded your judges at that
time, saying, 'Hear *the cases* between your
brethren, and judge righ-
teously between a man
and his brother or the
stranger who is with him.
17You shall not show par-
tiality in judgment; you
shall hear the small as
well as the great; you
shall not be afraid in any
man's presence, for the
judgment *is* God's. The case that is too hard for
you, bring to me, and I will hear it.' 18And I
commanded you at that time all the things
which you should do.

> "You shall not show partiality in judgment; you shall hear the small as well as the great; you shall not be afraid in any man's presence, for the judgment is God's."
> DEUTERONOMY 1:17

Israel's Refusal to Enter the Land

19"So we departed from Horeb, and went
through all that great and terrible wilderness
which you saw on the way to the mountains
of the Amorites, as the LORD our God had
commanded us. Then we came to Kadesh Barnea. 20And I said to you, 'You have come to
the mountains of the Amorites, which the
LORD our God is giving us. 21Look, the LORD
your God has set the land before you; go up
and possess *it,* as the LORD God of your fathers has spoken to you; do not fear or be discouraged.'

22"And every one of you came near to me
and said, 'Let us send men before us, and let
them search out the land for us, and bring
back word to us of the way by which we
should go up, and of the cities into which we
shall come.'

23"The plan pleased me well; so I took
twelve of your men, one man from *each* tribe.
24And they departed and went up into the
mountains, and came to the Valley of Eshcol,
and spied it out. 25They also took *some* of the
fruit of the land in their hands and brought *it*
down to us; and they brought back word to us,
saying, '*It is* a good land
which the LORD our God
is giving us.'

26"Nevertheless you
would not go up, but re-
belled against the com-
mand of the LORD your
God; 27and you com-
plained in your tents,
and said, 'Because the
LORD hates us, He has brought us out of the
land of Egypt to deliver us into the hand of the
Amorites, to destroy us. 28Where can we go
up? Our brethren have discouraged our hearts,
saying, "The people *are* greater and taller than
we; the cities *are* great and fortified up to
heaven; moreover we have seen the sons of
the Anakim there." '

29"Then I said to you, 'Do not be terrified, or
afraid of them. 30The LORD your God, who

SOUL NOTE

The Promise Keeper *(1:8)* God explained to the Israelites that they were about to enter the Promised Land in fulfillment of His promises to their forefathers—Abraham, Isaac, and Jacob. The nation had multiplied "as the stars of heaven" (1:10), also fulfilling a promise (Gen. 15:5). Like Israel, people sin, rebel, turn away, and face punishment. Regardless of their actions, however, God always keeps His promises in the end. Read God's Word and claim His promises for your life.
Topic: God's Promises

goes before you, He will fight for you, according to all He did for you in Egypt before your eyes, 31and in the wilderness where you saw how the LORD your God carried you, as a man carries his son, in all the way that you went until you came to this place.' 32Yet, for all that, you did not believe the LORD your God, 33who went in the way before you to search out a place for you to pitch your tents, to show you the way you should go, in the fire by night and in the cloud by day.

The Penalty for Israel's Rebellion

34"And the LORD heard the sound of your words, and was angry, and took an oath, saying, 35'Surely not one of these men of this evil generation shall see that good land of which I swore to give to your fathers, 36except Caleb the son of Jephunneh; he shall see it, and to him and his children I am giving the land on which he walked, because he wholly followed the LORD.' 37The LORD was also angry with me for your sakes, saying, 'Even you shall not go in there. 38Joshua the son of Nun, who stands before you, he shall go in there. Encourage him, for he shall cause Israel to inherit it.

39'Moreover your little ones and your children, who you say will be victims, who today have no knowledge of good and evil, they shall go in there; to them I will give it, and they shall possess it. 40But *as for* you, turn and take your journey into the wilderness by the Way of the Red Sea.'

41"Then you answered and said to me, 'We have sinned against the LORD; we will go up and fight, just as the LORD our God commanded us.' And when everyone of you had girded on his weapons of war, you were ready to go up into the mountain.

42"And the LORD said to me, 'Tell them, "Do not go up nor fight, for I *am* not among you; lest you be defeated before your enemies." ' 43So I spoke to you; yet you would not listen, but rebelled against the command of the LORD, and presumptuously went up into the mountain. 44And the Amorites who dwelt in that mountain came out against you and chased you as bees do, and drove you back from Seir to Hormah. 45Then you returned and wept before the LORD, but the LORD would not listen to your voice nor give ear to you.

46"So you remained in Kadesh many days, according to the days that you spent *there.*

The Desert Years

2 "Then we turned and journeyed into the wilderness of the Way of the Red Sea, as the LORD spoke to me, and we skirted Mount Seir for many days.

2"And the LORD spoke to me, saying: 3'You have skirted this mountain long enough; turn northward. 4And command the people, saying, "You *are about to* pass through the territory of your brethren, the descendants of Esau, who live in Seir; and they will be afraid of you. Therefore watch yourselves carefully. 5Do not meddle with them, for I will not give you *any* of their land, no, not so much as one footstep, because I have given Mount Seir to Esau *as* a possession. 6You shall buy food from them with money, that you may eat; and you shall also buy water from them with money, that you may drink.

7"For the LORD your God has blessed you in all the work of your hand. He knows your trudging through this great wilderness. These forty years the LORD your God *has been* with you; you have lacked nothing." '

> "For the LORD your God has blessed you in all the work of your hand. He knows your trudging through this great wilderness. These forty years the LORD your God has been with you; you have lacked nothing."
> DEUTERONOMY 2:7

8"And when we passed beyond our brethren, the descendants of Esau who dwell in Seir, away from the road of the plain, away from Elath and Ezion Geber, we turned and passed by way of the Wilderness of Moab. 9Then the LORD said to me, 'Do not harass Moab, nor contend with them in battle, for I will not give you *any* of their land *as* a possession, because I have given Ar to the descendants of Lot *as* a possession.' "

10(The Emim had dwelt there in times past, a people as great and numerous and tall as the Anakim. 11They were also regarded as giants,[a] like the Anakim, but the Moabites call them Emim. 12The Horites formerly dwelt in Seir, but the descendants of Esau dispossessed

---

2:11 [a]Hebrew *rephaim*

them and destroyed them from before them,
and dwelt in their place, just as Israel did to
the land of their possession which the LORD
gave them.)
13" 'Now rise and cross over the Valley of
the Zered.' So we crossed over the Valley of
the Zered. 14And the time we took to come
from Kadesh Barnea until we crossed over the
Valley of the Zered *was* thirty-eight years, until all the generation of the men of war was
consumed from the midst of the camp, just as
the LORD had sworn to them. 15For indeed the
hand of the LORD was against them, to destroy
them from the midst of the camp until they
were consumed.
16"So it was, when all the men of war had
finally perished from among the people, 17that
the LORD spoke to me, saying: 18'This day you
are to cross over at Ar, the boundary of Moab.
19And *when* you come near the people of Ammon, do not harass them or meddle with
them, for I will not give you *any* of the land of
the people of Ammon *as* a possession, because I have given it to the descendants of Lot
as a possession.' "
20(That was also regarded as a land of
giants;[a] giants formerly dwelt there. But the
Ammonites call them Zamzummim, 21a people as great and numerous and tall as the
Anakim. But the LORD destroyed them before
them, and they dispossessed them and dwelt
in their place, 22just as He had done for the descendants of Esau, who dwelt in Seir, when
He destroyed the Horites from before them.
They dispossessed them and dwelt in their
place, even to this day. 23And the Avim, who
dwelt in villages as far as Gaza—the Caphtorim, who came from Caphtor, destroyed
them and dwelt in their place.)
24" 'Rise, take your journey, and cross over
the River Arnon. Look, I have given into your
hand Sihon the Amorite, king of Heshbon, and
his land. Begin to possess *it*, and engage him
in battle. 25This day I will begin to put the
dread and fear of you upon the nations under
the whole heaven, who shall hear the report
of you, and shall tremble and be in anguish
because of you.'

KING SIHON DEFEATED

26"And I sent messengers from the Wilderness of Kedemoth to Sihon king of Heshbon,
with words of peace, saying, 27'Let me pass
through your land; I will keep strictly to the
road, and I will turn neither to the right nor to
the left. 28You shall sell me food for money,
that I may eat, and give me water for money,
that I may drink; only let me pass through on
foot, 29just as the descendants of Esau who
dwell in Seir and the Moabites who dwell in
Ar did for me, until I cross the Jordan to the
land which the LORD our God is giving us.'
30"But Sihon king of Heshbon would not let
us pass through, for the LORD your God hardened his spirit and made his heart obstinate,
that He might deliver him into your hand, as *it*
is this day.
31"And the LORD said to me, 'See, I have begun to give Sihon and his land over to you. Begin to possess *it*, that you may inherit his
land.' 32Then Sihon and all his people came
out against us to fight at Jahaz. 33And the
LORD our God delivered him over to us; so we
defeated him, his sons, and all his people.
34We took all his cities at that time, and we
utterly destroyed the men, women, and little
ones of every city; we left none remaining.
35We took only the livestock as plunder for
ourselves, with the spoil of the cities which
we took. 36From Aroer, which *is* on the bank

2:20 [a]Hebrew *rephaim*

SOUL NOTE

Armed and Ready *(2:24, 25)* God always keeps His promises, but that doesn't mean that life will be easy or smooth. God had promised a land to Israel and had made all the nations fear them, but the Israelites would have to battle against powerful armies in order to see the promise fulfilled. God gave Israel victories, but they had to trust God and fight. We too will see God's promises fulfilled, but we may have to fight some battles along the way—perhaps against fear, temptation, or suffering. Whatever we face, we must remember that God promises victory if we depend on Him.
Topic: God's Promises

of the River Arnon, and *from* the city that *is* in the ravine, as far as Gilead, there was not one city too strong for us; the LORD our God delivered all to us. 37Only you did not go near the land of the people of Ammon—anywhere along the River Jabbok, or to the cities of the mountains, or wherever the LORD our God had forbidden us.

KING OG DEFEATED

3 “Then we turned and went up the road to Bashan; and Og king of Bashan came out against us, he and all his people, to battle at Edrei. 2And the LORD said to me, ‘Do not fear him, for I have delivered him and all his people and his land into your hand; you shall do to him as you did to Sihon king of the Amorites, who dwelt at Heshbon.’

3“So the LORD our God also delivered into our hands Og king of Bashan, with all his people, and we attacked him until he had no survivors remaining. 4And we took all his cities at that time; there was not a city which we did not take from them: sixty cities, all the region of Argob, the kingdom of Og in Bashan. 5All these cities *were* fortified with high walls, gates, and bars, besides a great many rural towns. 6And we utterly destroyed them, as we did to Sihon king of Heshbon, utterly destroying the men, women, and children of every city. 7But all the livestock and the spoil of the cities we took as booty for ourselves.

8“And at that time we took the land from the hand of the two kings of the Amorites who *were* on this side of the Jordan, from the River Arnon to Mount Hermon 9(the Sidonians call Hermon Sirion, and the Amorites call it Senir), 10all the cities of the plain, all Gilead, and all Bashan, as far as Salcah and Edrei, cities of the kingdom of Og in Bashan.

11“For only Og king of Bashan remained of the remnant of the giants.[a] Indeed his bedstead *was* an iron bedstead. (*Is* it not in Rabbah of the people of Ammon?) Nine cubits *is* its length and four cubits its width, according to the standard cubit.

THE LAND EAST OF THE JORDAN DIVIDED

12“And this land, *which* we possessed at that time, from Aroer, which *is* by the River Arnon, and half the mountains of Gilead and its cities, I gave to the Reubenites and the Gadites. 13The rest of Gilead, and all Bashan, the kingdom of Og, I gave to half the tribe of Manasseh. (All the region of Argob, with all Bashan, was called the land of the giants.[a] 14Jair the son of Manasseh took all the region of Argob, as far as the border of the Geshurites and the Maachathites, and called Bashan after his own name, Havoth Jair,[a] to this day.)

15“Also I gave Gilead to Machir. 16And to the Reubenites and the Gadites I gave from Gilead as far as the River Arnon, the middle of the river as *the* border, as far as the River Jabbok, the border of the people of Ammon; 17the plain also, with the Jordan as *the* border, from Chinnereth as far as the east side of the Sea of the Arabah (the Salt Sea), below the slopes of Pisgah.

18“Then I commanded you at that time, saying: ‘The LORD your God has given you this land to possess. All you men of valor shall cross over armed before your brethren, the children of Israel. 19But your wives, your little ones, and your livestock (I know that you have much livestock) shall stay in your cities which I have given you, 20until the LORD has given rest to your brethren as to you, and they also possess the land which the LORD your God is giving them beyond the Jordan. Then each of you may return to his possession which I have given you.’

21“And I commanded Joshua at that time, saying, ‘Your eyes have seen all that the LORD your God has done to these two kings; so will the LORD do to all the kingdoms through which you pass. 22You must not fear them, for the LORD your God Himself fights for you.’

MOSES FORBIDDEN TO ENTER THE LAND

23“Then I pleaded with the LORD at that time, saying: 24‘O Lord GOD, You have begun to show Your servant Your greatness and Your mighty hand, for what god *is there* in heaven or on earth who can do *anything* like Your works and Your mighty *deeds?* 25I pray, let me cross over and see the good land beyond the Jordan, those pleasant mountains, and Lebanon.’

26“But the LORD was angry with me on your account, and would not listen to me. So the LORD said to me: ‘Enough of that! Speak no more to Me of this matter. 27Go up to the top of Pisgah, and lift your eyes toward the west, the north, the south, and the east; behold *it*

3:11 [a]Hebrew *rephaim* **3:13** [a]Hebrew *rephaim*
3:14 [a]Literally *Towns of Jair*

with your eyes, for you shall not cross over
this Jordan. 28But command Joshua, and encourage him and strengthen him; for he shall
go over before this people, and he shall cause
them to inherit the land which you will see.'
29"So we stayed in the valley opposite Beth
Peor.

MOSES COMMANDS OBEDIENCE

4 "Now, O Israel, listen to the statutes and
the judgments which I teach you to observe, that you may live, and go in and possess the land which the LORD God of your
fathers is giving you. 2You shall not add to the
word which I command you, nor take from it,
that you may keep the commandments of the
LORD your God which I command you. 3Your
eyes have seen what the LORD did at Baal Peor;
for the LORD your God has destroyed from
among you all the men who followed Baal of
Peor. 4But you who held fast to the LORD your
God *are* alive today, every one of you.
5"Surely I have taught you statutes and
judgments, just as the LORD my God commanded me, that you should act according *to*
them in the land which you go to possess.
6Therefore be careful to observe *them;* for this
is your wisdom and your understanding in the
sight of the peoples who will hear all these
statutes, and say, 'Surely this great nation *is* a
wise and understanding people.'
7"For what great nation *is there* that has God
so near to it, as the LORD our God *is* to us, for
whatever *reason* we may call upon Him? 8And
what great nation *is there* that has *such* statutes and righteous judgments as are in all this
law which I set before you this day? 9Only take
heed to yourself, and diligently keep yourself,
lest you forget the things your eyes have seen,
and lest they depart from your heart all the
days of your life. And teach them to your children and your grandchildren, 10*especially con-*
cerning the day you stood before the LORD
your God in Horeb, when the LORD said to me,
'Gather the people to Me, and I will let them
hear My words, that they may learn to fear Me
all the days they live on the earth, and *that*
they may teach their children.'
11"Then you came near and stood at the foot
of the mountain, and the mountain burned
with fire to the midst of heaven, with darkness, cloud, and thick darkness. 12And the
LORD spoke to you out of the midst of the fire.
You heard the sound of the words, but saw no
form; *you* only *heard* a voice. 13So He declared
to you His covenant which He commanded
you to perform, the Ten Commandments; and
He wrote them on two tablets of stone. 14And

KEY PASSAGE

Child Develop-ment

TEACH YOUR CHILDREN WELL

(4:9, 10)

Parents are responsible for raising and guiding their children from infancy to adulthood. Parents influence their children in all areas of development—social, physical, emotional, mental, and spiritual. Moses advised parents to "take heed" and "diligently keep" themselves, not forgetting what God had done for them. These parents had seen God's mighty miracles on their behalf as He had rescued them, had revealed Himself to them, and had given them His Word—especially the Ten Commandments. "Teach them to your children and your grandchildren," said Moses.

That is true soul care from one generation to the next. Christian parents can help their children develop spiritually by:

- sharing the story of how God rescued them from sin,
- telling what God has done in their lives,
- modeling the Christian life, and
- teaching God's Word and how it applies in everyday life.

To Learn More: Turn to the article about child development on pages 228, 229. See also the personality profile of Jesus on page 1317.

the LORD commanded me at that time to teach you statutes and judgments, that you might observe them in the land which you cross over to possess.

BEWARE OF IDOLATRY

[15]"Take careful heed to yourselves, for you saw no form when the LORD spoke to you at Horeb out of the midst of the fire, [16]lest you act corruptly and make for yourselves a carved image in the form of any figure: the likeness of male or female, [17]the likeness of any animal that *is* on the earth or the likeness of any winged bird that flies in the air, [18]the likeness of anything that creeps on the ground or the likeness of any fish that *is* in the water beneath the earth. [19]And *take heed,* lest you lift your eyes to heaven, and *when* you see the sun, the moon, and the stars, all the host of heaven, you feel driven to worship them and serve them, which the LORD your God has given to all the peoples under the whole heaven as a heritage. [20]But the LORD has taken you and brought you out of the iron furnace, out of Egypt, to be His people, an inheritance, as you are this day. [21]Furthermore the LORD was angry with me for your sakes, and swore that I would not cross over the Jordan, and that I would not enter the good land which the LORD your God is giving you as an inheritance. [22]But I must die in this land, I must not cross over the Jordan; but you shall cross over and possess that good land. [23]Take heed to yourselves, lest you forget the covenant of the LORD your God which He made with you, and make for yourselves a carved image in the form of anything which the LORD your God has forbidden you. [24]For the LORD your God *is* a consuming fire, a jealous God.

[25]"When you beget children and grandchildren and have grown old in the land, and act corruptly and make a carved image in the form of anything, and do evil in the sight of the LORD your God to provoke Him to anger, [26]I call heaven and earth to witness against you this day, that you will soon utterly perish from the land which you cross over the Jordan to possess; you will not prolong *your* days in it, but will be utterly destroyed. [27]And the LORD will scatter you among the peoples, and you will be left few in number among the nations where the LORD will drive you. [28]And there you will serve gods, the work of men's hands, wood and stone, which neither see nor hear nor eat nor smell. [29]But from there you will seek the LORD your God, and you will find *Him* if you seek Him with all your heart and with all your soul. [30]When you are in distress, and all these things come upon you in the latter days, when you turn to the LORD your God and obey His voice [31](for the LORD your God *is* a merciful God), He will not forsake you nor destroy you, nor forget the covenant of your fathers which He swore to them.

> "But from there you will seek the LORD your God, and you will find Him if you seek Him with all your heart and with all your soul."
>
> **DEUTERONOMY 4:29**

[32]"For ask now concerning the days that are past, which were before you, since the day that God created man on the earth, and *ask* from one end of heaven to the other, whether *any* great *thing* like this has happened, or *anything* like it has been heard. [33]Did *any* people *ever* hear the voice of God speaking out of the midst of the fire, as you have heard, and live? [34]Or did God *ever* try to go *and* take for Himself a nation from the midst of *another* nation, by trials, by signs, by wonders, by war, by a mighty hand and an outstretched arm, and by great terrors, according to all that the LORD your God did for you in Egypt before your eyes? [35]To you it was shown, that you might know that the LORD Himself *is* God; *there is* none other besides Him. [36]Out of heaven He let you hear His voice, that He might instruct you; on earth He showed you His great fire, and you heard His words out of the midst of the fire. [37]And because He loved your fathers, therefore He chose their descendants after them; and He brought you out of Egypt with His Presence, with His mighty power, [38]driving out from before you nations greater and mightier than you, to bring you in, to give you their land *as* an inheritance, as *it is* this day. [39]Therefore know this day, and consider *it* in your heart, that the LORD Himself *is* God in heaven above and on the earth beneath; *there is* no other. [40]You shall therefore keep His statutes and His commandments which I command you today, that it may go well with you and with your children after you, and that you may prolong *your* days in the land which the LORD your God is giving you for all time."

Child Development

RAISING OUR CHILDREN

PAUL MEIER

(Deuteronomy 4:9, 10)

One of the most important responsibilities and privileges that the Lord entrusts to people is to love and nurture children, teaching them about Him (Deut. 4:9, 10; 11:19). In the Old Testament, children are called "a heritage" and "a reward" (Ps. 127:3). Whether or not people have children of their own, they still have a shared responsibility for the nurture and care of the children in their lives.

God cares about children. He is "the helper of the fatherless" (Ps. 10:14) and the One who takes care of those children who have been forsaken by parents (Ps. 27:10). Our own responsibility for child rearing extends beyond that of the children in our own families. There is a great need for the healthy involvement of Christian adults in the lives of our children as mentors, teachers, and coaches, as well as a need to support and encourage other parents.

THREE FACTORS IN DEVELOPMENT

As we consider the growth and development of children, there are three factors that affect the kind of adults they will become: (1) who God created them to be, (2) the environment in which they grow, and (3) the choices that they make.

God's Unique Creations

God created each child to be unique, with different personality traits, levels of intelligence, physical characteristics, and even differing energy and activity levels. Children in the same family differ remarkably from each other from the moment they're born. King David was amazed at these God-designed differences when he exclaimed, "You formed my inward parts; You covered me in my mother's womb. I will praise You, for I am fearfully and wonderfully made" (Ps. 139:13, 14).

A Nurturing Environment

The environment in which children are nurtured is as vital to their development as are their God-given genetic gifts. In Proverbs 22:6, Solomon encourages parents to "train up a child in the way he should go, and when he is old he will not depart from it." Parents are wisely instructed by Solomon to bring up their children in an environment shaped by and infused with biblical principles. God, the heavenly Father, models His love in people's lives, and they in turn have the privilege and responsibility of loving their children just as He continually loves them!

Moses told the people of Israel to remember what they had seen and known of the Lord's goodness and to pass that knowledge on to their children (Deut. 4:9). God's desire was that parents would teach their children and grandchildren to hear His word and to reverence Him. Moses' words assume that the parents themselves have a first-hand knowledge of God's love and goodness. Perhaps one of the primary tasks of child rearing is to remember what God has done and is doing in our own lives and to share that with our children. In addition, children who grow up in a relationship with parents and other adults who live their faith will have not only the knowledge of God, but also a strong example of the truth of God's word in action.

Paul provided a wonderful model when he described himself as a father to the believers at Thessalonica (1 Thess. 2:11). He loved the believers deeply, so he encouraged, comforted, and urged them to live worthy of God, who had called them into His kingdom and glory. Paul's example extends to us as we seek to encourage, comfort, and communicate the love of Christ to the children in our families and communities.

Ability to Choose

However, God has also created every person with the ability to make choices. As children grow, parents have increasingly less control over their choices. Our children make their own choices every day, and some of those choices are life-changing. Even though children can have wonderful God-given gifts and abilities, and have grown up in a loving, Christ-centered environment, they can still make poor choices. Part of child rearing is to help children learn to make good choices and to encourage them with love and forgiveness when they must work through the consequences of poor choices. As we decrease, the rules increase, and children must take on more responsibility.

Psychiatric research has shown that children who grow up with the following five factors will have a better chance of making choices that will positively affect their own lives as well as those of the generations to come:

1. Lots of unconditional love.
2. Reasonable boundaries and discipline.
3. Consistency in parenting principles and family values.
4. Expectation that the children will follow their parents' example, not just their words.
5. Bonding with healthy male and female authority figures (either Mom and Dad, or healthy grandparents, aunts, uncles, Sunday school teachers, school teachers, coaches, or other mentors).

All of these factors are consistent with what Scripture teaches and can be put into practice in our families as well as in our Christian communities.

PREPARED FOR LIFE

As parents and those concerned for the development of children, we know that God has created our children in the way that He has chosen and that our children will make their own choices. We can love them, create safe, consistent environments for them to grow in, and model Christlike lives, and we can teach them the truth of the Scriptures. As they emerge from the dependence of childhood to the interdependence of adulthood, we can continue to pray for them and to thank the Lord for the role that He has allowed us to play in their lives.

FURTHER MEDITATION:

Other passages to study about the issue of child development include:

- Genesis 18:19
- Proverbs 20:7, 11; 22:15; 23:13, 24; 29:15
- Ecclesiastes 11:9, 10
- Matthew 19:13, 14
- Mark 9:36, 37
- Ephesians 6:1–4
- 2 Timothy 3:14, 15

To Learn More: Turn to the key passage note on child development at Deuteronomy 4:9, 10 on page 226. See also the personality profile of Jesus on page 1317.

CITIES OF REFUGE EAST OF THE JORDAN

41Then Moses set apart three cities on this
side of the Jordan, toward the rising of the
sun, 42that the manslayer might flee there,
who kills his neighbor unintentionally, without having hated him in time past, and that by
fleeing to one of these cities he might live:
43Bezer in the wilderness on the plateau for
the Reubenites, Ramoth in Gilead for the Gadites, and Golan in Bashan for the Manassites.

INTRODUCTION TO GOD'S LAW

44Now this *is* the law which Moses set before the children of Israel. 45These *are* the testimonies, the statutes, and the judgments
which Moses spoke to the children of Israel
after they came out of Egypt, 46on this side of
the Jordan, in the valley opposite Beth Peor, in
the land of Sihon king of the Amorites, who
dwelt at Heshbon, whom Moses and the children of Israel defeated after they came out of
Egypt. 47And they took possession of his land
and the land of Og king of Bashan, two kings
of the Amorites, who *were* on this side of the
Jordan, toward the rising of the sun, 48from
Aroer, which *is* on the bank of the River Arnon, even to Mount Sion[a] (that is, Hermon),
49and all the plain on the east side of the Jordan as far as the Sea of the Arabah, below the
slopes of Pisgah.

THE TEN COMMANDMENTS REVIEWED

5 And Moses called all Israel, and said to
them: "Hear, O Israel, the statutes and
judgments which I speak in your hearing today, that you may learn them and be careful to
observe them. 2The LORD our God made a covenant with us in Horeb. 3The LORD did not
make this covenant with our fathers, but with
us, those who *are* here today, all of us who *are*
alive. 4The LORD talked with you face to face
on the mountain from the midst of the fire. 5I
stood between the LORD and you at that time,
to declare to you the word of the LORD; for you
were afraid because of the fire, and you did
not go up the mountain. *He* said:

6 'I *am* the LORD your God who brought you
out of the land of Egypt, out of the
house of bondage.
7 'You shall have no other gods before Me.
8 'You shall not make for yourself a carved
image—any likeness *of anything* that
is in heaven above, or that *is* in the
earth beneath, or that *is* in the water
under the earth; 9you shall not bow
down to them nor serve them. For I,
the LORD your God, *am* a jealous God,
visiting the iniquity of the fathers
upon the children to the third and
fourth *generations* of those who hate
Me, 10but showing mercy to thousands, to those who love Me and keep
My commandments.
11 'You shall not take the name of the LORD
your God in vain, for the LORD will not
hold *him* guiltless who takes His name
in vain.
12 'Observe the Sabbath day, to keep it holy,
as the LORD your God commanded
you. 13Six days you shall labor and do
all your work, 14but the seventh day *is*
the Sabbath of the LORD your God. *In it*
you shall do no work: you, nor your
son, nor your daughter, nor your male
servant, nor your female servant, nor
your ox, nor your donkey, nor any of
your cattle, nor your stranger who *is*

4:48 [a]Syriac reads *Sirion* (compare 3:9).

SOUL NOTE

Honor Your Parents *(5:16)* God stated in His Ten Commandments that He requires all people to honor their parents. Adults can honor their parents by treating them with respect and helping to meet their needs, especially as they become elderly. Doing so will be a great lesson to their children. Parents must teach their children what it means to "honor" them. This can be done as Mom and Dad honor Grandpa and Grandma, and as they honor God as their ultimate authority. Children will see and learn what it means to honor one's parents and then to honor God as one's ultimate authority as well. **Topic: Honor**

within your gates, that your male servant and your female servant may rest
as well as you. 15And remember that
you were a slave in the land of Egypt,
and the LORD your God brought you
out from there by a mighty hand and
by an outstretched arm; therefore the
LORD your God commanded you to
keep the Sabbath day.
16 'Honor your father and your mother, as
the LORD your God has commanded
you, that your days may be long, and
that it may be well with you in the
land which the LORD your God is giving you.
17 'You shall not murder.
18 'You shall not commit adultery.
19 'You shall not steal.
20 'You shall not bear false witness against
your neighbor.
21 'You shall not covet
your neighbor's
wife; and you
shall not desire
your neighbor's
house, his field,
his male ser-
vant, his female
servant, his ox,
his donkey, or
anything that *is* your neighbor's.'
22"These words the LORD spoke to all your
assembly, in the mountain from the midst of
the fire, the cloud, and the thick darkness,
with a loud voice; and He added no more. And
He wrote them on two tablets of stone and
gave them to me.

> "You shall walk in all the ways which the LORD your God has commanded you, that you may live and that it may be well with you, and that you may prolong your days in the land which you shall possess."
> DEUTERONOMY 5:33

THE PEOPLE AFRAID OF GOD'S PRESENCE

23"So it was, when you heard the voice from
the midst of the darkness, while the mountain
was burning with fire, that you came near to
me, all the heads of your tribes and your elders. 24And you said: 'Surely the LORD our God
has shown us His glory and His greatness, and
we have heard His voice from the midst of the
fire. We have seen this day that God speaks
with man; yet he *still* lives. 25Now therefore,
why should we die? For this great fire will consume us; if we hear the voice of the LORD our
God anymore, then we shall die. 26For who *is*
there of all flesh who has heard the voice of
the living God speaking from the midst of the
fire, as we *have,* and lived? 27You go near and
hear all that the LORD our God may say, and
tell us all that the LORD our God says to you,
and we will hear and do *it.*'
28"Then the LORD heard the voice of your
words when you spoke to me, and the LORD
said to me: 'I have heard the voice of the
words of this people which they have spoken
to you. They are right *in* all that they have
spoken. 29Oh, that they had such a heart in
them that they would fear Me and always
keep all My commandments, that it might be
well with them and with their children forever! 30Go and say to them, "Return to your
tents." 31But as for you, stand here by Me, and
I will speak to you all the commandments, the
statutes, and the judgments which you shall
teach them, that they may observe *them* in the
land which I am giving them to possess.'
32"Therefore you shall be careful to do as
the LORD your God has
commanded you; you
shall not turn aside to
the right hand or to the
left. 33You shall walk in
all the ways which the
LORD your God has
commanded you, that
you may live and *that it*
may be well with you,
and *that* you may pro-
long *your* days in the land which you shall
possess.

THE GREATEST COMMANDMENT

6 "Now this *is* the commandment, *and*
these are the statutes and judgments
which the LORD your God has commanded to
teach you, that you may observe *them* in the
land which you are crossing over to possess,
2that you may fear the LORD your God, to keep
all His statutes and His commandments which
I command you, you and your son and your
grandson, all the days of your life, and that
your days may be prolonged. 3Therefore hear,
O Israel, and be careful to observe *it,* that it
may be well with you, and that you may
multiply greatly as the LORD God of your fathers has promised you—'a land flowing with
milk and honey.'[a]
4"Hear, O Israel: The LORD our God, the
LORD *is* one![a] 5You shall love the LORD your

6:3 [a]Exodus 3:8 **6:4** [a]Or *The LORD is our God, the LORD alone* (that is, the only one)

God with all your heart, with all your soul,
and with all your strength.
6"And these words which I command you
today shall be in your heart. 7You shall teach
them diligently to your
children, and shall talk
of them when you sit in
your house, when you
walk by the way, when
you lie down, and when
you rise up. 8You shall
bind them as a sign on
your hand, and they shall be as frontlets between your eyes. 9You shall write them on the
doorposts of your house and on your gates.

> "You shall love the LORD your God with all your heart, with all your soul, and with all your strength."
>
> DEUTERONOMY 6:5

CAUTION AGAINST DISOBEDIENCE

10"So it shall be, when the LORD your God
brings you into the land of which He swore to
your fathers, to Abraham, Isaac, and Jacob, to
give you large and beautiful cities which you
did not build, 11houses full of all good things,
which you did not fill, hewn-out wells which
you did not dig, vineyards and olive trees
which you did not plant—when you have eat-
en and are full— 12*then* beware, lest you forget
the LORD who brought you out of the land of
Egypt, from the house of bondage. 13You shall
fear the LORD your God and serve Him, and
shall take oaths in His name. 14You shall not
go after other gods, the gods of the peoples
who *are* all around you 15(for the LORD your
God *is* a jealous God among you), lest the anger of the LORD your God be aroused against
you and destroy you from the face of the
earth.
16"You shall not tempt the LORD your God as
you tempted *Him* in Massah. 17You shall diligently keep the commandments of the LORD
your God, His testimonies, and His statutes
which He has commanded you. 18And you
shall do *what is* right and good in the sight of
the LORD, that it may be well with you, and
that you may go in and possess the good land
of which the LORD swore to your fathers, 19to
cast out all your enemies from before you, as
the LORD has spoken.
20"When your son
asks you in time to
come, saying, 'What *is
the meaning of* the tes-
timonies, the statutes,
and the judgments which
the LORD our God has
commanded you?' 21then you shall say to
your son: 'We were slaves of Pharaoh in Egypt,
and the LORD brought us out of Egypt with a
mighty hand; 22and the LORD showed signs and
wonders before our eyes, great and severe,
against Egypt, Pharaoh, and all his household.
23Then He brought us out from there, that He
might bring us in, to give us the land of which
He swore to our fathers. 24And the LORD commanded us to observe all these statutes, to
fear the LORD our God, for our good always,
that He might preserve us alive, as *it is* this
day. 25Then it will be righteousness for us, if
we are careful to observe all these commandments before the LORD our God, as He has
commanded us.'

A CHOSEN PEOPLE

7 "When the LORD your God brings you into
the land which you go to possess, and has
cast out many nations before you, the Hittites
and the Girgashites and the Amorites and the
Canaanites and the Perizzites and the Hivites
and the Jebusites, seven nations greater and
mightier than you, 2and when the LORD your
God delivers them over to you, you shall conquer them *and* utterly destroy them. You shall
make no covenant with them nor show mercy
to them. 3Nor shall you make marriages with
them. You shall not give your daughter to their

SOUL NOTE

A Godly Heritage *(6:4–9)* God wants His people to teach His commandments to their children, by words and by example. To talk about God and His commands when sitting, walking, lying down, and getting up emphasizes the importance of making God's Word a part of every aspect of daily living. Such demonstrations make it clear to children that the Word of God has authority over every area of life. Parents give children much, but the greatest gift they can give is a godly heritage.
Topic: Child Development

son, nor take their daughter for your son. 4For
they will turn your sons away from following
Me, to serve other gods; so the anger of the
LORD will be aroused against you and destroy
you suddenly. 5But thus you shall deal with
them: you shall destroy their altars, and break
down their *sacred* pillars, and cut down their
wooden images,[a] and
burn their carved im-
ages with fire.
6"For you *are* a holy
people to the LORD your
God; the LORD your God
has chosen you to be a
people for Himself, a
special treasure above
all the peoples on the
face of the earth. 7The
LORD did not set His love on you nor choose
you because you were more in number than
any other people, for you were the least of all
peoples; 8but because the LORD loves you, and
because He would keep the oath which He
swore to your fathers, the LORD has brought
you out with a mighty hand, and redeemed
you from the house of bondage, from the hand
of Pharaoh king of Egypt.
9"Therefore know that the LORD your God,
He *is* God, the faithful God who keeps covenant and mercy for a thousand generations
with those who love Him and keep His commandments; 10and He repays those who hate
Him to their face, to destroy them. He will not
be slack with him who hates Him; He will repay him to his face. 11Therefore you shall keep
the commandment, the statutes, and the judgments which I command you today, to observe them.

> "Therefore know that the LORD your God, He is God, the faithful God who keeps covenant and mercy for a thousand generations with those who love Him and keep His commandments."
>
> DEUTERONOMY 7:9

BLESSINGS OF OBEDIENCE

12"Then it shall come to pass, because you
listen to these judgments, and keep and do
them, that the LORD your God will keep with
you the covenant and the mercy which He
swore to your fathers. 13And He will love you
and bless you and multiply you; He will also
bless the fruit of your womb and the fruit of
your land, your grain and your new wine and
your oil, the increase of your cattle and the offspring of your flock, in
the land of which He
swore to your fathers to
give you. 14You shall be
blessed above all peo-
ples; there shall not be a
male or female barren
among you or among
your livestock. 15And
the LORD will take away
from you all sickness,
and will afflict you with none of the terrible
diseases of Egypt which you have known, but
will lay *them* on all those who hate you. 16Also
you shall destroy all the peoples whom the
LORD your God delivers over to you; your eye
shall have no pity on them; nor shall you serve
their gods, for that *will be* a snare to you.
17"If you should say in your heart, 'These
nations are greater than I; how can I dispossess them?'— 18you shall not be afraid of
them, *but* you shall remember well what the
LORD your God did to Pharaoh and to all
Egypt: 19the great trials which your eyes saw,
the signs and the wonders, the mighty hand
and the outstretched arm, by which the LORD
your God brought you out. So shall the LORD
your God do to all the peoples of whom you
are afraid. 20Moreover the LORD your God will
send the hornet among them until those who
are left, who hide themselves from you, are
destroyed. 21You shall not be terrified of them;
for the LORD your God, the great and awesome

7:5 [a]Hebrew *Asherim,* Canaanite deities

SOUL NOTE

Do Not Be Afraid *(7:17–21)* The Christian life is not easy. Believers face difficulties, pain, suffering, and sorrow. In situations that seem impossible they sometimes become afraid. God told Israel not to be afraid when the battle seemed too great. Instead, they should remember what He had done for them in the past and take heart. We must look at our fearful situations in the light of what God has already done for us, remembering that "the great and awesome God" will be going into battle with us. **Topic: Fear/Fear of God**

God, *is* among you. [22]And the LORD your God
will drive out those nations before you little
by little; you will be unable to destroy them at
once, lest the beasts of the field become *too*
numerous for you. [23]But the LORD your God
will deliver them over to you, and will inflict
defeat upon them until they are destroyed.
[24]And He will deliver their kings into your
hand, and you will destroy their name from
under heaven; no one shall be able to stand
against you until you have destroyed them.
[25]You shall burn the carved images of their
gods with fire; you shall not covet the silver or
gold *that is* on them, nor take *it* for yourselves,
lest you be snared by it; for it *is* an abomination to the LORD your God. [26]Nor shall you
bring an abomination into your house, lest you
be doomed to destruction like it. You shall utterly detest it and utterly abhor it, for it *is* an
accursed thing.

REMEMBER THE LORD YOUR GOD

8 "Every commandment which I command
you today you must be careful to observe,
that you may live and multiply, and go in and
possess the land of which the LORD swore to
your fathers. [2]And you shall remember that
the LORD your God led you all the way these
forty years in the wilderness, to humble you
and test you, to know what *was* in your heart,
whether you would keep His commandments
or not. [3]So He humbled you, allowed you to
hunger, and fed you with manna which you
did not know nor did your fathers know, that
He might make you know that man shall not
live by bread alone; but man lives by every
word that proceeds from the mouth of the
LORD. [4]Your garments did not wear out on
you, nor did your foot swell these forty years.
[5]You should know in your heart that as a man
chastens his son, *so* the LORD your God chastens you.

[6]"Therefore you shall keep the commandments of the LORD your God, to walk in His
ways and to fear Him. [7]For the LORD your God
is bringing you into a good land, a land of
brooks of water, of fountains and springs, that
flow out of valleys and hills; [8]a land of wheat
and barley, of vines and fig trees and pomegranates, a land of olive oil and honey; [9]a land
in which you will eat bread without scarcity,
in which you will lack nothing; a land whose
stones *are* iron and out of whose hills you can
dig copper. [10]When you have eaten and are
full, then you shall bless the LORD your God
for the good land which He has given you.

[11]"Beware that you do not forget the LORD
your God by not keeping His commandments,
His judgments, and His statutes which I command you today, [12]lest—*when* you have eaten
and are full, and have built beautiful houses
and dwell *in them;* [13]and *when* your herds and
your flocks multiply, and your silver and your
gold are multiplied, and all that you have is
multiplied; [14]when your heart is lifted up, and
you forget the LORD your God who brought
you out of the land of Egypt, from the house of
bondage; [15]who led you through that great
and terrible wilderness, *in which were* fiery
serpents and scorpions and thirsty land where
there was no water; who brought water for
you out of the flinty rock; [16]who fed you in the
wilderness with manna, which your fathers
did not know, that He might humble you and
that He might test you, to do you good in the
end— [17]then you say in your heart, 'My power
and the might of my hand have gained me this
wealth.'

[18]"And you shall remember the LORD your
God, for *it is* He who gives you power to get
wealth, that He may establish His covenant
which He swore to your fathers, as *it is* this
day. [19]Then it shall be, if you by any means
forget the LORD your God, and follow other
gods, and serve them and worship them, I testify against you this day that you shall surely
perish. [20]As the nations which the LORD destroys before you, so you shall perish, because
you would not be obedient to the voice of the
LORD your God.

ISRAEL'S REBELLIONS REVIEWED

9 "Hear, O Israel: You *are* to cross over the
Jordan today, and go in to dispossess nations greater and mightier than yourself, cities
great and fortified up to heaven, [2]a people
great and tall, the descendants of the Anakim,
whom you know, and *of whom* you heard *it
said,* 'Who can stand before the descendants
of Anak?' [3]Therefore understand today that
the LORD your God *is* He who goes over before
you *as* a consuming fire. He will destroy them
and bring them down before you; so you shall
drive them out and destroy them quickly, as
the LORD has said to you.

[4]"Do not think in your heart, after the LORD

your God has cast them out before you, saying, 'Because of my righteousness the LORD has brought me in to possess this land'; but *it is* because of the wickedness of these nations *that* the LORD is driving them out from before you. 5*It is* not because of your righteousness or the uprightness of your heart *that* you go in to possess their land, but because of the wickedness of these nations *that* the LORD your God drives them out from before you, and that He may fulfill the word which the LORD swore to your fathers, to Abraham, Isaac, and Jacob. 6Therefore understand that the LORD your God is not giving you this good land to possess because of your righteousness, for you *are* a stiff-necked people.

7"Remember! Do not forget how you provoked the LORD your God to wrath in the wilderness. From the day that you departed from the land of Egypt until you came to this place, you have been rebellious against the LORD. 8Also in Horeb you provoked the LORD to wrath, so that the LORD was angry *enough* with you to have destroyed you. 9When I went up into the mountain to receive the tablets of stone, the tablets of the covenant which the LORD made with you, then I stayed on the mountain forty days and forty nights. I neither ate bread nor drank water. 10Then the LORD delivered to me two tablets of stone written with the finger of God, and on them *were* all the words which the LORD had spoken to you on the mountain from the midst of the fire in the day of the assembly. 11And it came to pass, at the end of forty days and forty nights, *that* the LORD gave me the two tablets of stone, the tablets of the covenant.

12"Then the LORD said to me, 'Arise, go down quickly from here, for your people whom you brought out of Egypt have acted corruptly; they have quickly turned aside from the way which I commanded them; they have made themselves a molded image.'

13"Furthermore the LORD spoke to me, saying, 'I have seen this people, and indeed they are a stiff-necked people. 14Let Me alone, that I may destroy them and blot out their name from under heaven; and I will make of you a nation mightier and greater than they.'

15"So I turned and came down from the mountain, and the mountain burned with fire; and the two tablets of the covenant *were* in my two hands. 16And I looked, and behold, you had sinned against the LORD your God—had made for yourselves a molded calf! You had turned aside quickly from the way which the LORD had commanded you. 17Then I took the two tablets and threw them out of my two hands and broke them before your eyes. 18And I fell down before the LORD, as at the first, forty days and forty nights; I neither ate bread nor drank water, because of all your sin which you committed in doing wickedly in the sight of the LORD, to provoke Him to anger. 19For I was afraid of the anger and hot displeasure with which the LORD was angry with you, to destroy you. But the LORD listened to me at that time also. 20And the LORD was very angry with Aaron *and* would have destroyed him; so I prayed for Aaron also at the same time. 21Then I took your sin, the calf which you had made, and burned it with fire and crushed it *and* ground *it* very small, until it was as fine as dust; and I threw its dust into the brook that descended from the mountain.

22"Also at Taberah and Massah and Kibroth Hattaavah you provoked the LORD to wrath. 23Likewise, when the LORD sent you from Kadesh Barnea, saying, 'Go up and possess the land which I have given you,' then you rebelled against the commandment of the LORD your God, and you did not believe Him nor obey His voice. 24You have been rebellious against the LORD from the day that I knew you.

25"Thus I prostrated myself before the LORD; forty days and forty nights I kept prostrating myself, because the LORD had said He would destroy you. 26Therefore I prayed to the LORD, and said: 'O Lord GOD, do not destroy Your people and Your inheritance whom You have redeemed through Your greatness, whom You have brought out of Egypt with a mighty hand. 27Remember Your servants, Abraham, Isaac, and Jacob; do not look on the stubbornness of this people, or on their wickedness or their sin, 28lest the land from which You brought us should say, "Because the LORD was not able to bring them to the land which He promised them, and because He hated them, He has brought them out to kill them in the wilderness." 29Yet they *are* Your people and Your inheritance, whom You brought out by Your mighty power and by Your outstretched arm.'

The Second Pair of Tablets

10 "At that time the LORD said to me, 'Hew for yourself two tablets of stone like the first, and come up to Me on the mountain and make yourself an ark of wood. 2And I will write on the tablets the words that were on the first tablets, which you broke; and you shall put them in the ark.'

3"So I made an ark of acacia wood, hewed two tablets of stone like the first, and went up the mountain, having the two tablets in my hand. 4And He wrote on the tablets according to the first writing, the Ten Commandments, which the LORD had spoken to you in the mountain from the midst of the fire in the day of the assembly; and the LORD gave them to me. 5Then I turned and came down from the mountain, and put the tablets in the ark which I had made; and there they are, just as the LORD commanded me."

> "What does the LORD your God require of you, but to fear the LORD your God, to walk in all His ways and to love Him, to serve the LORD your God with all your heart and with all your soul, and to keep the commandments of the LORD and His statutes which I command you today for your good?"
>
> DEUTERONOMY 10:12, 13

6(Now the children of Israel journeyed from the wells of Bene Jaakan to Moserah, where Aaron died, and where he was buried; and Eleazar his son ministered as priest in his stead. 7From there they journeyed to Gudgodah, and from Gudgodah to Jotbathah, a land of rivers of water. 8At that time the LORD separated the tribe of Levi to bear the ark of the covenant of the LORD, to stand before the LORD to minister to Him and to bless in His name, to this day. 9Therefore Levi has no portion nor inheritance with his brethren; the LORD *is* his inheritance, just as the LORD your God promised him.)

10"As at the first time, I stayed in the mountain forty days and forty nights; the LORD also heard me at that time, *and* the LORD chose not to destroy you. 11Then the LORD said to me, 'Arise, begin *your* journey before the people, that they may go in and possess the land which I swore to their fathers to give them.'

THE ESSENCE OF THE LAW

12"And now, Israel, what does the LORD your God require of you, but to fear the LORD your God, to walk in all His ways and to love Him, to serve the LORD your God with all your heart and with all your soul, 13*and* to keep the commandments of the LORD and His statutes which I command you today for your good? 14Indeed heaven and the highest heavens belong to the LORD your God, *also* the earth with all that *is* in it. 15The LORD delighted only in your fathers, to love them; and He chose their descendants after them, you above all peoples, as *it is* this day. 16Therefore circumcise the foreskin of your heart, and be stiff-necked no longer. 17For the LORD your God *is* God of gods and Lord of lords, the great God, mighty and awesome, who shows no partiality nor takes a bribe. 18He administers justice for the fatherless and the widow, and loves the stranger, giving him food and clothing. 19Therefore love the stranger, for you were strangers in the land of Egypt. 20You shall fear the LORD your God; you shall serve Him, and to Him you shall hold fast, and take oaths in His name. 21He *is* your praise, and He *is* your God, who has done for you these great and awesome things which your eyes have seen. 22Your fathers went down to Egypt with seventy persons, and now the LORD your God has made you as the stars of heaven in multitude.

SOUL NOTE

Seriously Now *(10:12, 13)* What does it mean to "fear the LORD"? Fearing God means to reverence Him, to take Him seriously. How can we do that? By our obedience. These verses say that God's people must "walk in all His ways," loving Him, serving Him, and keeping His commandments. Why? Because these commandments are for our good. God gave His laws, not to keep people from enjoying life, but to help them find ultimate joy and purpose through a relationship with Him. Fear of God leads to true fulfillment. **Topic: Fear/Fear of God**

Love and Obedience Rewarded

11 "Therefore you shall love the LORD
your God, and keep His charge, His
statutes, His judgments, and His commandments always. 2Know today that *I do* not *speak*
with your children, who have not known and
who have not seen the chastening of the LORD
your God, His greatness and His mighty hand
and His outstretched arm— 3His signs and His
acts which He did in the midst of Egypt, to
Pharaoh king of Egypt, and to all his land;
4what He did to the
army of Egypt, to their
horses and their chari-
ots: how He made the
waters of the Red Sea
overflow them as they
pursued you, and *how*
the LORD has destroyed
them to this day; 5what
He did for you in the wilderness until you
came to this place; 6and what He did to Dathan and Abiram the sons of Eliab, the son of
Reuben: how the earth opened its mouth and
swallowed them up, their households, their
tents, and all the substance that *was* in their
possession, in the midst of all Israel— 7but
your eyes have seen every great act of the
LORD which He did.
8"Therefore you shall keep every commandment which I command you today, that you
may be strong, and go in and possess the land
which you cross over to possess, 9and that you
may prolong *your* days in the land which the
LORD swore to give your fathers, to them and
their descendants, 'a land flowing with milk
and honey.'[a] 10For the land which you go to
possess *is* not like the land of Egypt from
which you have come, where you sowed your
seed and watered *it* by foot, as a vegetable
garden; 11but the land which you cross over to
possess *is* a land of hills and valleys, which
drinks water from the rain of heaven, 12a land
for which the LORD your God cares; the eyes of
the LORD your God *are* always on it, from the
beginning of the year to the very end of the
year.
13'And it shall be that if you earnestly obey
My commandments which I command you today, to love the LORD your God and serve Him
with all your heart and with all your soul,
14then I[a] will give *you* the rain for your land in
its season, the early rain and the latter rain,
that you may gather in your grain, your new
wine, and your oil.
15And I will send grass
in your fields for your
livestock, that you may
eat and be filled.' 16Take
heed to yourselves, lest
your heart be deceived,
and you turn aside and
serve other gods and
worship them, 17lest the LORD's anger be
aroused against you, and He shut up the heavens so that there be no rain, and the land yield
no produce, and you perish quickly from the
good land which the LORD is giving you.
18"Therefore you shall lay up these words of
mine in your heart and in your soul, and bind
them as a sign on your hand, and they shall be
as frontlets between your eyes. 19You shall
teach them to your children, speaking of them
when you sit in your house, when you walk by
the way, when you lie down, and when you
rise up. 20And you shall write them on the
doorposts of your house and on your gates,
21that your days and the days of your children
may be multiplied in the land of which the
LORD swore to your fathers to give them, like
the days of the heavens above the earth.
22"For if you carefully keep all these

> "Therefore you shall lay up these words of mine in your heart and in your soul, and bind them as a sign on your hand."
> DEUTERONOMY 11:18

11:9 [a]Exodus 3:8 **11:14** [a]Following Masoretic Text and Targum; Samaritan Pentateuch, Septuagint, and Vulgate read *He*.

SOUL NOTE

Teach Them Well *(11:18, 19)* So important were the words of 4:9, 10 that they are repeated here. God commands parents to teach their children about Him and His love for them. Parental soul care involves a commitment to teach children in the ways of God. Parents should be able to sense teachable moments with their children. Then they can instruct them in God's ways. Home is the incubator where small hearts and hands are trained to serve God. **Topic: Parenting**

commandments which I command you to do—to love the LORD your God, to walk in all His ways, and to hold fast to Him— 23then the LORD will drive out all these nations from before you, and you will dispossess greater and mightier nations than yourselves. 24Every place on which the sole of your foot treads shall be yours: from the wilderness and Lebanon, from the river, the River Euphrates, even to the Western Sea,[a] shall be your territory. 25No man shall be able to stand against you; the LORD your God will put the dread of you and the fear of you upon all the land where you tread, just as He has said to you.

26"Behold, I set before you today a blessing and a curse: 27the blessing, if you obey the commandments of the LORD your God which I command you today; 28and the curse, if you do not obey the commandments of the LORD your God, but turn aside from the way which I command you today, to go after other gods which you have not known. 29Now it shall be, when the LORD your God has brought you into the land which you go to possess, that you shall put the blessing on Mount Gerizim and the curse on Mount Ebal. 30*Are* they not on the other side of the Jordan, toward the setting sun, in the land of the Canaanites who dwell in the plain opposite Gilgal, beside the terebinth trees of Moreh? 31For you will cross over the Jordan and go in to possess the land which the LORD your God is giving you, and you will possess it and dwell in it. 32And you shall be careful to observe all the statutes and judgments which I set before you today.

A Prescribed Place of Worship

12 "These *are* the statutes and judgments which you shall be careful to observe in the land which the LORD God of your fathers is giving you to possess, all the days that you live on the earth. 2You shall utterly destroy all the places where the nations which you shall dispossess served their gods, on the high mountains and on the hills and under every green tree. 3And you shall destroy their altars, break their *sacred* pillars, and burn their wooden images with fire; you shall cut down the carved images of their gods and destroy their names from that place. 4You shall not worship the LORD your God *with* such *things*.

5"But you shall seek the place where the LORD your God chooses, out of all your tribes, to put His name for His dwelling place; and there you shall go. 6There you shall take your burnt offerings, your sacrifices, your tithes, the heave offerings of your hand, your vowed offerings, your freewill offerings, and the firstborn of your herds and flocks. 7And there you shall eat before the LORD your God, and you shall rejoice in all to which you have put your hand, you and your households, in which the LORD your God has blessed you.

8"You shall not at all do as we are doing here today—every man doing whatever *is* right in his own eyes— 9for as yet you have not come to the rest and the inheritance which the LORD your God is giving you. 10But *when* you cross over the Jordan and dwell in the land which the LORD your God is giving you to inherit, and He gives you rest from all your enemies round about, so that you dwell in safety, 11then there will be the place where the LORD your God chooses to make His name abide. There you shall bring all that I command you: your burnt offerings, your sacrifices, your tithes, the heave offerings of your hand, and all your choice offerings which you vow to the LORD. 12And you shall rejoice before the LORD your God, you and your sons and your daughters, your male and female servants, and the Levite who *is* within your gates, since he has no portion nor inheritance with you. 13Take heed to yourself that you do not offer your burnt offerings in every place that you see; 14but in the place which the LORD chooses, in one of your tribes, there you shall offer your burnt offerings, and there you shall do all that I command you.

15"However, you may slaughter and eat meat within all your gates, whatever your heart desires, according to the blessing of the LORD your God which He has given you; the unclean and the clean may eat of it, of the gazelle and the deer alike. 16Only you shall not eat the blood; you shall pour it on the earth like water. 17You may not eat within your gates the tithe of your grain or your new wine or your oil, of the firstborn of your herd or your flock, of any of your offerings which you vow, of your freewill offerings, or of the heave offering of your hand. 18But you must eat them before the LORD your God in the place which the LORD your God chooses, you and your son and your daughter, your male servant and your female servant,

---

11:24 [a]That is, the Mediterranean

and the Levite who *is* within your gates; and you shall rejoice before the LORD your God in all to which you put your hands. 19Take heed to yourself that you do not forsake the Levite as long as you live in your land.

20“When the LORD your God enlarges your border as He has promised you, and you say, ‘Let me eat meat,’ because you long to eat meat, you may eat as much meat as your heart desires. 21If the place where the LORD your God chooses to put His name is too far from you, then you may slaughter from your herd and from your flock which the LORD has given you, just as I have commanded you, and you may eat within your gates as much as your heart desires. 22Just as the gazelle and the deer are eaten, so you may eat them; the unclean and the clean alike may eat them. 23Only be sure that you do not eat the blood, for the blood *is* the life; you may not eat the life with the meat. 24You shall not eat it; you shall pour it on the earth like water. 25You shall not eat it, that it may go well with you and your children after you, when you do *what is* right in the sight of the LORD. 26Only the holy things which you have, and your vowed offerings, you shall take and go to the place which the LORD chooses. 27And you shall offer your burnt offerings, the meat and the blood, on the altar of the LORD your God; and the blood of your sacrifices shall be poured out on the altar of the LORD your God, and you shall eat the meat. 28Observe and obey all these words which I command you, that it may go well with you and your children after you forever, when you do *what is* good and right in the sight of the LORD your God.

Beware of False Gods

29“When the LORD your God cuts off from before you the nations which you go to dispossess, and you displace them and dwell in their land, 30take heed to yourself that you are not ensnared to follow them, after they are destroyed from before you, and that you do not inquire after their gods, saying, ‘How did these nations serve their gods? I also will do likewise.’ 31You shall not worship the LORD your God in that way; for every abomination to the LORD which He hates they have done to their gods; for they burn even their sons and daughters in the fire to their gods.

32“Whatever I command you, be careful to observe it; you shall not add to it nor take away from it.

Punishment of Apostates

13 “If there arises among you a prophet or a dreamer of dreams, and he gives you a sign or a wonder, 2and the sign or the wonder comes to pass, of which he spoke to you, saying, ‘Let us go after other gods’—which you have not known—‘and let us serve them,’ 3you shall not listen to the words of that prophet or that dreamer of dreams, for the LORD your God is testing you to know whether you love the LORD your God with all your heart and with all your soul. 4You shall walk after the LORD your God and fear Him, and keep His commandments and obey His voice; you shall serve Him and hold fast to Him. 5But that prophet or that dreamer of dreams shall be put to death, because he has spoken in order to turn *you* away from the LORD your God, who brought you out of the land of Egypt and redeemed you from the house of bondage, to entice you from the way in which the LORD your God commanded you to walk. So you shall put away the evil from your midst.

6“If your brother, the son of your mother, your son or your daughter, the wife of your bosom, or your friend who is as your own soul, secretly entices you, saying, ‘Let us go and serve other gods,’ which you have not known,

SOUL NOTE

Sticking to the Truth *(13:1–5)* Satan always draws people away from God, and he often works through willing people. This passage warns that if someone claims to be a prophet of God but points people toward other gods, then that person is a false prophet. Under Old Testament law, a false prophet was to be put to death. Teaching that was obviously false was taken seriously and punished accordingly. God’s people must have discernment, refusing to listen to anyone who speaks anything different from the truth found in God’s Word. That truth will keep us from error. **Topic: Truth**

neither you nor your fathers, 7of the gods of the people which *are* all around you, near to you or far off from you, from *one* end of the earth to the *other* end of the earth, 8you shall not consent to him or listen to him, nor shall your eye pity him, nor shall you spare him or conceal him; 9but you shall surely kill him; your hand shall be first against him to put him to death, and afterward the hand of all the people. 10And you shall stone him with stones until he dies, because he sought to entice you away from the LORD your God, who brought you out of the land of Egypt, from the house of bondage. 11So all Israel shall hear and fear, and not again do such wickedness as this among you.

12"If you hear someone in one of your cities, which the LORD your God gives you to dwell in, saying, 13'Corrupt men have gone out from among you and enticed the inhabitants of their city, saying, "Let us go and serve other gods" '— which you have not known— 14then you shall inquire, search out, and ask diligently. And *if it is* indeed true *and* certain *that* such an abomination was committed among you, 15you shall surely strike the inhabitants of that city with the edge of the sword, utterly destroying it, all that is in it and its livestock— with the edge of the sword. 16And you shall gather all its plunder into the middle of the street, and completely burn with fire the city and all its plunder, for the LORD your God. It shall be a heap forever; it shall not be built again. 17So none of the accursed things shall remain in your hand, that the LORD may turn from the fierceness of His anger and show you mercy, have compassion on you and multiply you, just as He swore to your fathers, 18because you have listened to the voice of the LORD your God, to keep all His commandments which I command you today, to do *what is* right in the eyes of the LORD your God.

IMPROPER MOURNING

14 "You *are* the children of the LORD your God; you shall not cut yourselves nor shave the front of your head for the dead. 2For you *are* a holy people to the LORD your God, and the LORD has chosen you to be a people for Himself, a special treasure above all the peoples who *are* on the face of the earth.

CLEAN AND UNCLEAN MEAT

3"You shall not eat any detestable thing. 4These *are* the animals which you may eat: the ox, the sheep, the goat, 5the deer, the gazelle, the roe deer, the wild goat, the mountain goat,[a] the antelope, and the mountain sheep. 6And you may eat every animal with cloven hooves, having the hoof split into two parts, *and that* chews the cud, among the animals. 7Nevertheless, of those that chew the cud or have cloven hooves, you shall not eat, *such as* these: the camel, the hare, and the rock hyrax; for they chew the cud but do not have cloven hooves; they *are* unclean for you. 8Also the swine is unclean for you, because it has cloven hooves, yet *does* not *chew* the cud; you shall not eat their flesh or touch their dead carcasses.

9"These you may eat of all that *are* in the waters: you may eat all that have fins and scales. 10And whatever does not have fins and scales you shall not eat; it *is* unclean for you.

11"All clean birds you may eat. 12But these you shall not eat: the eagle, the vulture, the buzzard, 13the red kite, the falcon, and the kite after their kinds; 14every raven after its kind; 15the ostrich, the short-eared owl, the sea gull, and the hawk after their kinds; 16the little owl, the screech owl, the white owl, 17the jackdaw, the carrion vulture, the fisher owl, 18the stork, the heron after its kind, and the hoopoe and the bat.

19"Also every creeping thing that flies is unclean for you; they shall not be eaten.

20"You may eat all clean birds.

21"You shall not eat anything that dies *of itself;* you may give it to the alien who *is* within your gates, that he may eat it, or you may sell it to a foreigner; for you *are* a holy people to the LORD your God.

"You shall not boil a young goat in its mother's milk.

TITHING PRINCIPLES

22"You shall truly tithe all the increase of your grain that the field produces year by year. 23And you shall eat before the LORD your God, in the place where He chooses to make His name abide, the tithe of your grain and your new wine and your oil, of the firstborn of your herds and your flocks, that you may learn to fear the LORD your God always. 24But if the journey is too long for you, so that you are not able to carry *the tithe, or* if the place where the LORD your God chooses to put His name is too

14:5 [a]Or *addax*

far from you, when the LORD your God has blessed you, [25]then you shall exchange *it* for money, take the money in your hand, and go to the place which the LORD your God chooses. [26]And you shall spend that money for whatever your heart desires: for oxen or sheep, for wine or similar drink, for whatever your heart desires; you shall eat there before the LORD your God, and you shall rejoice, you and your household. [27]You shall not forsake the Levite who *is* within your gates, for he has no part nor inheritance with you.

[28]"At the end of *every* third year you shall bring out the tithe of your produce of that year and store *it* up within your gates. [29]And the Levite, because he has no portion nor inheritance with you, and the stranger and the fatherless and the widow who *are* within your gates, may come and eat and be satisfied, that the LORD your God may bless you in all the work of your hand which you do.

DEBTS CANCELED EVERY SEVEN YEARS

15 "At the end of *every* seven years you shall grant a release *of debts.* [2]And this *is* the form of the release: Every creditor who has lent *anything* to his neighbor shall release *it;* he shall not require *it* of his neighbor or his brother, because it is called the LORD's release. [3]Of a foreigner you may require *it;* but you shall give up your claim to what is owed by your brother, [4]except when there may be no poor among you; for the LORD will greatly bless you in the land which the LORD your God is giving you to possess *as* an inheritance— [5]only if you carefully obey the voice of the LORD your God, to observe with care all these commandments which I command you today. [6]For the LORD your God will bless you just as He promised you; you shall lend to many nations, but you shall not borrow; you shall reign over many nations, but they shall not reign over you.

GENEROSITY TO THE POOR

[7]"If there is among you a poor man of your brethren, within any of the gates in your land which the LORD your God is giving you, you shall not harden your heart nor shut your hand from your poor brother, [8]but you shall open your hand wide to him and willingly lend him sufficient for his need, whatever he needs. [9]Beware lest there be a wicked thought in your heart, saying, 'The seventh year, the year of release, is at hand,' and your eye be evil against your poor brother and you give him nothing, and he cry out to the LORD against you, and it become sin among you. [10]You shall surely give to him, and your heart should not be grieved when you give to him, because for this thing the LORD your God will bless you in all your works and in all to which you put your hand. [11]For the poor will never cease from the land; therefore I command you, saying, 'You shall open your hand wide to your brother, to your poor and your needy, in your land.'

THE LAW CONCERNING BONDSERVANTS

[12]"If your brother, a Hebrew man, or a Hebrew woman, is sold to you and serves you six years, then in the seventh year you shall let him go free from you. [13]And when you send him away free from you, you shall not let him go away empty-handed; [14]you shall supply him liberally from your flock, from your threshing floor, and from your winepress. *From what* the LORD your God has blessed you with, you shall give to him. [15]You shall remember that you were a slave in the land of Egypt, and the LORD your God redeemed you; therefore I command you this thing today. [16]And if it happens that he says to you, 'I will not go away from you,' because he loves you and your house, since he prospers with you, [17]then you shall take an awl and thrust *it* through his ear to the door, and he shall be your servant forever. Also to your female servant you shall do likewise. [18]It shall not seem hard to you when you send him away free from you; for he has been worth a double hired servant in serving you six years. Then the LORD your God will bless you in all that you do.

THE LAW CONCERNING FIRSTBORN ANIMALS

[19]"All the firstborn males that come from your herd and your flock you shall sanctify to the LORD your God; you shall do no work with the firstborn of your herd, nor shear the firstborn of your flock. [20]You and your household shall eat *it* before the LORD your God year by year in the place which the LORD chooses. [21]But if there is a defect in it, *if it is* lame or blind *or has* any serious defect, you shall not sacrifice it to the LORD your God. [22]You may eat it within your gates; the unclean and the clean *person* alike *may eat it,* as *if it were* a gazelle or a deer. [23]Only you shall not eat its

blood; you shall pour it on the ground like water.

The Passover Reviewed

16 "Observe the month of Abib, and keep the Passover to the LORD your God, for in the month of Abib the LORD your God brought you out of Egypt by night. [2]Therefore you shall sacrifice the Passover to the LORD your God, from the flock and the herd, in the place where the LORD chooses to put His name. [3]You shall eat no leavened bread with it; seven days you shall eat unleavened bread with it, *that is,* the bread of affliction (for you came out of the land of Egypt in haste), that you may remember the day in which you came out of the land of Egypt all the days of your life. [4]And no leaven shall be seen among you in all your territory for seven days, nor shall *any* of the meat which you sacrifice the first day at twilight remain overnight until morning.

[5]"You may not sacrifice the Passover within any of your gates which the LORD your God gives you; [6]but at the place where the LORD your God chooses to make His name abide, there you shall sacrifice the Passover at twilight, at the going down of the sun, at the time you came out of Egypt. [7]And you shall roast and eat *it* in the place which the LORD your God chooses, and in the morning you shall turn and go to your tents. [8]Six days you shall eat unleavened bread, and on the seventh day there *shall be* a sacred assembly to the LORD your God. You shall do no work *on it.*

The Feast of Weeks Reviewed

[9]"You shall count seven weeks for yourself; begin to count the seven weeks from *the time* you begin *to put* the sickle to the grain. [10]Then you shall keep the Feast of Weeks to the LORD your God with the tribute of a freewill offering from your hand, which you shall give as the LORD your God blesses you. [11]You shall rejoice before the LORD your God, you and your son and your daughter, your male servant and your female servant, the Levite who *is* within your gates, the stranger and the fatherless and the widow who *are* among you, at the place where the LORD your God chooses to make His name abide. [12]And you shall remember that you were a slave in Egypt, and you shall be careful to observe these statutes.

The Feast of Tabernacles Reviewed

[13]"You shall observe the Feast of Tabernacles seven days, when you have gathered from your threshing floor and from your winepress. [14]And you shall rejoice in your feast, you and your son and your daughter, your male servant and your female servant and the Levite, the stranger and the fatherless and the widow, who *are* within your gates. [15]Seven days you shall keep a sacred feast to the LORD your God in the place which the LORD chooses, because the LORD your God will bless you in all your produce and in all the work of your hands, so that you surely rejoice.

[16]"Three times a year all your males shall appear before the LORD your God in the place which He chooses: at the Feast of Unleavened Bread, at the Feast of Weeks, and at the Feast of Tabernacles; and they shall not appear before the LORD empty-handed. [17]Every man *shall give* as he is able, according to the blessing of the LORD your God which He has given you.

Justice Must Be Administered

[18]"You shall appoint judges and officers in all your gates, which the LORD your God gives you, according to your tribes, and they shall judge the people with just judgment. [19]You shall not pervert justice; you shall not show partiality, nor take a bribe, for a bribe blinds the eyes of the wise and twists the words of the righteous. [20]You shall follow what is altogether just, that you may live and inherit the land which the LORD your God is giving you.

[21]"You shall not plant for yourself any tree, as a wooden image, near the altar which you build for yourself to the LORD your God. [22]You shall not set up a *sacred* pillar, which the LORD your God hates.

17 "You shall not sacrifice to the LORD your God a bull or sheep which has any blemish *or* defect, for that *is* an abomination to the LORD your God.

[2]"If there is found among you, within any of your gates which the LORD your God gives you, a man or a woman who has been wicked in the sight of the LORD your God, in transgressing His covenant, [3]who has gone and served other gods and worshiped them, either the sun or moon or any of the host of heaven, which I have not commanded, [4]and it is told you, and you hear *of it,* then you shall inquire diligently. And if *it is* indeed true *and* certain that such an abomination has been committed

in Israel, 5then you shall bring out to your
gates that man or woman who has committed
that wicked thing, and shall stone to death
that man or woman with stones. 6Whoever is
deserving of death shall be put to death on the
testimony of two or three witnesses; he shall
not be put to death on the testimony of one
witness. 7The hands of the witnesses shall be
the first against him to put him to death, and
afterward the hands of all the people. So you
shall put away the evil from among you.
8"If a matter arises which is too hard for you
to judge, between degrees of guilt for bloodshed, between one judgment or another, or
between one punishment or another, matters
of controversy within your gates, then you
shall arise and go up to the place which the
LORD your God chooses. 9And you shall come
to the priests, the Levites, and to the judge
there in those days, and inquire *of them;* they
shall pronounce upon you the sentence of
judgment. 10You shall do according to the sentence which they pronounce upon you in that
place which the LORD chooses. And you shall
be careful to do according to all that they order you. 11According to the sentence of the law
in which they instruct you, according to the
judgment which they tell you, you shall do;
you shall not turn aside *to* the right hand or *to*
the left from the sentence which they pronounce upon you. 12Now the man who acts
presumptuously and will not heed the priest
who stands to minister there before the LORD
your God, or the judge, that man shall die. So
you shall put away the evil from Israel. 13And
all the people shall hear and fear, and no longer act presumptuously.

PRINCIPLES GOVERNING KINGS

14"When you come to the land which the
LORD your God is giving you, and possess it
and dwell in it, and say, 'I will set a king over
me like all the nations that *are* around me,'
15you shall surely set a king over you whom
the LORD your God chooses; *one* from among
your brethren you shall set as king over you;
you may not set a foreigner over you, who *is*
not your brother. 16But he shall not multiply
horses for himself, nor cause the people to return to Egypt to multiply horses, for the LORD
has said to you, 'You shall not return that way
again.' 17Neither shall he multiply wives for
himself, lest his heart turn away; nor shall he
greatly multiply silver and gold for himself.

18"Also it shall be, when he sits on the throne
of his kingdom, that he shall write for himself a
copy of this law in a book, from *the one* before
the priests, the Levites. 19And it shall be with
him, and he shall read it all the days of his life,
that he may learn to fear the LORD his God and
be careful to observe all the words of this law
and these statutes, 20that his heart may not be
lifted above his brethren, that he may not turn
aside from the commandment *to* the right hand
or *to* the left, and that he may prolong *his*
days in his kingdom, he and his children in the
midst of Israel.

THE PORTION OF THE PRIESTS AND LEVITES

18 "The priests, the Levites—all the tribe
of Levi—shall have no part nor inheritance with Israel; they shall eat the offerings
of the LORD made by fire, and His portion.
2Therefore they shall have no inheritance
among their brethren; the LORD is their inheritance, as He said to them.
3"And this shall be the priest's due from the
people, from those who offer a sacrifice,
whether *it is* bull or sheep: they shall give to
the priest the shoulder, the cheeks, and the
stomach. 4The firstfruits of your grain and
your new wine and your oil, and the first of
the fleece of your sheep, you shall give him.
5For the LORD your God has chosen him out of
all your tribes to stand to minister in the name
of the LORD, him and his sons forever.
6"So if a Levite comes from any of your
gates, from where he dwells among all Israel,
and comes with all the desire of his mind to
the place which the LORD chooses, 7then he
may serve in the name of the LORD his God as
all his brethren the Levites *do,* who stand
there before the LORD. 8They shall have equal
portions to eat, besides what comes from the
sale of his inheritance.

AVOID WICKED CUSTOMS

9"When you come into the land which the
LORD your God is giving you, you shall not
learn to follow the abominations of those nations. 10There shall not be found among you
anyone who makes his son or his daughter
pass through the fire, *or one* who practices
witchcraft, *or* a soothsayer, or one who interprets omens, or a sorcerer, 11or one who con-
jures spells, or a medium, or a spiritist, or one
who calls up the dead. 12For all who do these
things *are* an abomination to the LORD, and

because of these abominations the LORD your
God drives them out from before you. 13You
shall be blameless before the LORD your God.
14For these nations which you will dispossess
listened to soothsayers and diviners; but as for
you, the LORD your God has not appointed
such for you.

A New Prophet Like Moses

15“The LORD your God will raise up for you
a Prophet like me from your midst, from your
brethren. Him you shall hear, 16according to
all you desired of the LORD your God in Horeb
in the day of the assembly, saying, ‘Let me not
hear again the voice of the LORD my God, nor
let me see this great fire anymore, lest I die.’
17“And the LORD said to me: ‘What they
have spoken is good. 18I will raise up for them
a Prophet like you from among their brethren,
and will put My words in His mouth, and He
shall speak to them all that I command Him.
19And it shall be *that* whoever will not hear
My words, which He speaks in My name, I
will require *it* of him. 20But the prophet who
presumes to speak a word in My name, which
I have not commanded him to speak, or who
speaks in the name of other gods, that prophet
shall die.’ 21And if you say in your heart, ‘How
shall we know the word which the LORD has
not spoken?’— 22when a prophet speaks in the
name of the LORD, if the thing does not happen or come to pass, that *is* the thing which
the LORD has not spoken; the prophet has spoken it presumptuously; you shall not be afraid
of him.

Three Cities of Refuge

19 “When the LORD your God has cut off
the nations whose land the LORD your
God is giving you, and you dispossess them
and dwell in their cities and in their houses,
2you shall separate three cities for yourself in
the midst of your land which the LORD your
God is giving you to possess. 3You shall prepare roads for yourself, and divide into three
parts the territory of your land which the LORD
your God is giving you to inherit, that any
manslayer may flee there.
4“And this *is* the case of the manslayer who
flees there, that he may live: Whoever kills his
neighbor unintentionally, not having hated
him in time past— 5as when *a man* goes to the
woods with his neighbor to cut timber, and his
hand swings a stroke with the ax to cut down
the tree, and the head slips from the handle
and strikes his neighbor so that he dies—he
shall flee to one of these cities and live; 6lest
the avenger of blood, while his anger is hot,
pursue the manslayer and overtake him, because the way is long, and kill him, though he
was not deserving of death, since he had not
hated the victim in time past. 7Therefore I
command you, saying, ‘You shall separate
three cities for yourself.’
8“Now if the LORD your God enlarges your
territory, as He swore to your fathers, and
gives you the land which He promised to give
to your fathers, 9and if you keep all these commandments and do them, which I command
you today, to love the LORD your God and to
walk always in His ways, then you shall add
three more cities for yourself besides these
three, 10lest innocent blood be shed in the
midst of your land which the LORD your God is
giving you *as* an inheritance, and *thus* guilt of
bloodshed be upon you.
11“But if anyone hates his neighbor, lies in
wait for him, rises against him and strikes him
mortally, so that he dies, and he flees to one of
these cities, 12then the elders of his city shall
send and bring him from there, and deliver him
over to the hand of the avenger of blood, that

SOUL NOTE

Steer Clear! *(18:9–14)* The Bible is very clear in its condemnation of witchcraft and other occult practices. The Israelites were told to drive such people out of the land. Worshipers of Satan, such as witches and other members of satanic cults, still exist today. Forms of the occult are also found in New Age teachings, psychic hotlines, astrology and astrological charts, horoscopes, and the tricks of tarot card readers. All of these are from the realm of Satan. Believers must discern the evil inherent in these practices and steer clear of any involvement with them. **Topic: Occult**

voice; he is a glutton and a drunkard.' [21]Then
all the men of his city shall stone him to death
with stones; so you shall put away the evil
from among you, and all Israel shall hear and
fear.

MISCELLANEOUS LAWS

[22]"If a man has committed a sin deserving
of death, and he is put to death, and you hang
him on a tree, [23]his body shall not remain
overnight on the tree, but you shall surely
bury him that day, so that you do not defile
the land which the LORD your God is giving
you *as* an inheritance; for he who is hanged *is*
accursed of God.

22 "You shall not see your brother's ox or
his sheep going astray, and hide yourself from them; you shall certainly bring them
back to your brother. [2]And if your brother *is*
not near you, or if you do not know him, then
you shall bring it to your own house, and it
shall remain with you until your brother seeks
it; then you shall restore it to him. [3]You shall
do the same with his donkey, and so shall you
do with his garment; with any lost thing of
your brother's, which he has lost and you
have found, you shall do likewise; you must
not hide yourself.

[4]"You shall not see your brother's donkey or
his ox fall down along the road, and hide
yourself from them; you shall surely help him
lift *them* up again.

[5]"A woman shall not wear anything that
pertains to a man, nor shall a man put on a
woman's garment, for all who do so *are* an
abomination to the LORD your God.

[6]"If a bird's nest happens to be before you
along the way, in any tree or on the ground,
with young ones or eggs, with the mother sitting on the young or on the eggs, you shall not
take the mother with the young; [7]you shall
surely let the mother go, and take the young
for yourself, that it may be well with you and
that you may prolong *your* days.

[8]"When you build a new house, then you
shall make a parapet for your roof, that you
may not bring guilt of bloodshed on your
household if anyone falls from it.

[9]"You shall not sow your vineyard with different kinds of seed, lest the yield of the seed
which you have sown and the fruit of your
vineyard be defiled.

[10]"You shall not plow with an ox and a donkey together.

[11]"You shall not wear a garment of different
sorts, *such as* wool and linen mixed together.

[12]"You shall make tassels on the four corners of the clothing with which you cover
yourself.

LAWS OF SEXUAL MORALITY

[13]"If any man takes a wife, and goes in to
her, and detests her, [14]and charges her with
shameful conduct, and brings a bad name on
her, and says, 'I took this woman, and when I
came to her I found she *was* not a virgin,'
[15]then the father and mother of the young
woman shall take and bring out *the evidence
of* the young woman's virginity to the elders of
the city at the gate. [16]And the young woman's
father shall say to the elders, 'I gave my
daughter to this man as wife, and he detests
her. [17]Now he has charged her with shameful
conduct, saying, "I found your daughter *was*
not a virgin," and yet these *are the evidences
of* my daughter's virginity.' And they shall
spread the cloth before the elders of the city.
[18]Then the elders of that city shall take that
man and punish him; [19]and they shall fine him
one hundred *shekels* of silver and give *them* to
the father of the young woman, because he
has brought a bad name on a virgin of Israel.
And she shall be his wife; he cannot divorce
her all his days.

[20]"But if the thing is true, *and evidences of*
virginity are not found for the young woman,
[21]then they shall bring out the young woman
to the door of her father's house, and the men
of her city shall stone her to death with
stones, because she has done a disgraceful
thing in Israel, to play the harlot in her
father's house. So you shall put away the evil
from among you.

[22]"If a man is found lying with a woman
married to a husband, then both of them shall
die—the man that lay with the woman, and
the woman; so you shall put away the evil
from Israel.

[23]"If a young woman *who is* a virgin is betrothed to a husband, and a man finds her in
the city and lies with her, [24]then you shall
bring them both out to the gate of that city,
and you shall stone them to death with stones,
the young woman because she did not cry out
in the city, and the man because he humbled
his neighbor's wife; so you shall put away the
evil from among you.

[25]"But if a man finds a betrothed young

woman in the countryside, and the man forces
her and lies with her, then only the man who
lay with her shall die. 26But you shall do nothing to the young woman; *there is* in the young
woman no sin *deserving* of death, for just as
when a man rises against his neighbor and
kills him, even so *is* this matter. 27For he found
her in the countryside, *and* the betrothed
young woman cried out, but *there was* no one
to save her.

28"If a man finds a young woman *who is* a
virgin, who is not betrothed, and he seizes her
and lies with her, and they are found out,
29then the man who lay with her shall give to
the young woman's father fifty *shekels* of silver, and she shall be his wife because he has
humbled her; he shall not be permitted to divorce her all his days.

30"A man shall not take his father's wife, nor
uncover his father's bed.

THOSE EXCLUDED FROM THE CONGREGATION

23 "He who is emasculated by crushing
or mutilation shall not enter the assembly of the LORD.

2"One of illegitimate birth shall not enter
the assembly of the LORD; even to the tenth
generation none of his *descendants* shall enter
the assembly of the LORD.

3"An Ammonite or Moabite shall not enter
the assembly of the LORD; even to the tenth
generation none of his *descendants* shall enter
the assembly of the LORD forever, 4because
they did not meet you with bread and water
on the road when you came out of Egypt, and
because they hired against you Balaam the
son of Beor from Pethor of Mesopotamia,[a] to
curse you. 5Nevertheless the LORD your God
would not listen to Balaam, but the LORD your
God turned the curse into a blessing for you,
because the LORD your God loves you. 6You
shall not seek their peace nor their prosperity
all your days forever.

7"You shall not abhor an Edomite, for he *is*
your brother. You shall not abhor an Egyptian,
because you were an alien in his land. 8The
children of the third generation born to them
may enter the assembly of the LORD.

CLEANLINESS OF THE CAMPSITE

9"When the army goes out against your enemies, then keep yourself from every wicked
thing. 10If there is any man among you who
becomes unclean by some occurrence in the
night, then he shall go outside the camp; he
shall not come inside the camp. 11But it shall
be, when evening comes, that he shall wash
with water; and when the sun sets, he may
come into the camp.

12"Also you shall have a place outside the
camp, where you may go out; 13and you shall
have an implement among your equipment,
and when you sit down outside, you shall dig
with it and turn and cover your refuse. 14For
the LORD your God walks in the midst of your
camp, to deliver you and give your enemies
over to you; therefore your camp shall be holy,
that He may see no unclean thing among you,
and turn away from you.

MISCELLANEOUS LAWS

15"You shall not give back to his master the
slave who has escaped from his master to you.
16He may dwell with you in your midst, in the
place which he chooses within one of your
gates, where it seems best to him; you shall
not oppress him.

17"There shall be no *ritual* harlot[a] of the
daughters of Israel, or a perverted[b] one of the
sons of Israel. 18You shall not bring the wages
of a harlot or the price of a dog to the house of
the LORD your God for any vowed offering, for
both of these *are* an abomination to the LORD
your God.

19"You shall not charge interest to your
brother—interest on money *or* food *or* anything that is lent out at interest. 20To a foreigner you may charge interest, but to your
brother you shall not charge interest, that the
LORD your God may bless you in all to which
you set your hand in the land which you are
entering to possess.

21"When you make a vow to the LORD your
God, you shall not delay to pay it; for the LORD
your God will surely require it of you, and it
would be sin to you. 22But if you abstain from
vowing, it shall not be sin to you. 23That
which has gone from your lips you shall keep
and perform, for you voluntarily vowed to the
LORD your God what you have promised with
your mouth.

24"When you come into your neighbor's
vineyard, you may eat your fill of grapes at

23:4 [a]Hebrew *Aram Naharaim* **23:17** [a]Hebrew *qedeshah,* feminine of *qadesh* (see note *b*) [b]Hebrew *qadesh,* that is, one practicing sodomy and prostitution in religious rituals

your pleasure, but you shall not put *any* in
your container. 25When you come into your
neighbor's standing grain, you may pluck the
heads with your hand, but you shall not use a
sickle on your neighbor's standing grain.

Law Concerning Divorce

24 "When a man takes a wife and marries her, and it happens that she finds
no favor in his eyes because he has found
some uncleanness in her, and he writes her a
certificate of divorce, puts *it* in her hand, and
sends her out of his house, 2when she has departed from his house, and goes and becomes
another man's *wife*, 3*if* the latter husband detests her and writes her a certificate of divorce, puts *it* in her hand, and sends her out of
his house, or if the latter husband dies who
took her as his wife, 4*then* her former husband
who divorced her must not take her back to be
his wife after she has been defiled; for that *is*
an abomination before the LORD, and you
shall not bring sin on the land which the LORD
your God is giving you *as* an inheritance.

Miscellaneous Laws

5"When a man has taken a new wife, he
shall not go out to war or be charged with any
business; he shall be free at home one year,
and bring happiness to his wife whom he has
taken.

6"No man shall take the lower or the upper
millstone in pledge, for he takes *one's* living in
pledge.

7"If a man is found kidnapping any of his
brethren of the children of Israel, and mistreats him or sells him, then that kidnapper
shall die; and you shall put away the evil from
among you.

8"Take heed in an outbreak of leprosy, that
you carefully observe and do according to all
that the priests, the Levites, shall teach you;
just as I commanded them, *so* you shall be
careful to do. 9Remember what the LORD your
God did to Miriam on the way when you came
out of Egypt!

10"When you lend your brother anything,
you shall not go into his house to get his
pledge. 11You shall stand outside, and the man
to whom you lend shall bring the pledge out
to you. 12And if the man *is* poor, you shall not
keep his pledge overnight. 13You shall in any
case return the pledge to him again when the
sun goes down, that he may sleep in his own
garment and bless you; and it shall be righteousness to you before the LORD your God.

14"You shall not oppress a hired servant *who
is* poor and needy, *whether* one of your brethren or one of the aliens who *is* in your land
within your gates. 15Each day you shall give
him his wages, and not let the sun go down on
it, for he *is* poor and has set his heart on it;
lest he cry out against you to the LORD, and it
be sin to you.

16"Fathers shall not be put to death for *their*
children, nor shall children be put to death for
their fathers; a person shall be put to death for
his own sin.

17"You shall not pervert justice due the
stranger or the fatherless, nor take a widow's
garment as a pledge. 18But you shall remember that you were a slave in Egypt, and the
LORD your God redeemed you from there;
therefore I command you to do this thing.

19"When you reap your harvest in your field,
and forget a sheaf in the field, you shall not go
back to get it; it shall be for the stranger, the
fatherless, and the widow, that the LORD your
God may bless you in all the work of your
hands. 20When you beat your olive trees, you

SOUL NOTE

Helpless But Not Hopeless *(24:1–4)* God desires marriages to stay together. Because sin has infected all relationships, however, some marriages do not survive. Moses' commands regarding divorce were given in a culture where a man could divorce his wife verbally and leave her with no property or rights. These commandments regulating divorce in Israel protected those left most helpless—the woman and her children. The Bible does not give people an easy way out of their commitments. People are expected to honor their commitments; Jesus later made it clear that Moses's words were not to be taken as promoting easy divorce. Divorce should be the exception, not the rule. **Topic: Divorce/Separation**

Divorce/ Separation

DIVORCE RECOVERY

TOM WHITEMAN

(Deuteronomy 24:1–4)

"I'll never forget the day he told me that he was leaving," said Marcy. "I thought I would die. I just couldn't imagine that God would let this happen to me and to my children. It seems like just yesterday even though it was about eighteen months ago."

Marcy's story is similar to thousands of others. For her, divorce was not an option. She knew that whatever happened, her commitment to God, to her husband, and to her three young children dictated that she would work out the problems in her marriage. She tried to keep her part of the commitment, but unfortunately she could not influence her husband's decision.

Too many times, I meet committed Christians who are getting divorced against their will. How do these families move on? Can anything redemptive come out of such pain?

From my own experience and from having ministered to thousands of separated and divorced people for over fifteen years, let me assure you that God can take the worst events in our lives and use them for good. This transformation requires prayer, time, support from others, and wise decisions.

Here are some key elements that are required for a healthy divorce recovery.

EMOTIONAL NEEDS

During and after a divorce, most people feel as if they are on an emotional roller coaster, vacillating between desperation to get the spouse back no matter what and feelings of anger and revulsion toward the spouse. People who go through a divorce are extremely vulnerable. Many feel a deep emptiness within their soul. One recently divorced woman described it this way, "I felt like I had a huge hole in my chest, like part of me had been ripped away. I walked around feeling as if people could see right through me. I was embarrassed and ashamed."

This vulnerability can make the divorced person prone to other hurts. For example, it is common for them to feel rejected by family and friends. Others are drawn to anyone who pays attention or strokes the damaged areas of their lives. People who have been recently divorced need to be careful about forming new relationships or making any major changes. They need close accountability with a friend or counselor who will help guard and protect them from making poor choices or from moving forward too quickly into new relationships.

TIME

The grieving process takes time—realistically, at least two to five years. People typically go through stages of denial, anger, bargaining, and depression. The final stage is acceptance, when they learn to be satisfied with the changes that God has allowed them to experience and to move forward in a productive new lifestyle.

SOCIAL NEEDS

Divorce ends a primary relationship and often many social relationships as well. After a divorce, people may be very vulnerable to "rebound relationships" and may need friends to help them through the trauma. Divorced people should wait at least two years before involvement in romantic relationships. The emptiness in one's soul after a divorce requires God's healing and completeness apart from a romantic relationship. No human can substitute for the work of God in someone's life.

SPIRITUAL NEEDS

Most Christians who go through a divorce feel guilt and shame. Often they feel, "Maybe I should have, or could have, done more." These feelings may be compounded by the reactions of others, who in an effort to discourage divorce are afraid to minister to those who experience this brokenness for fear of appearing to condone divorce. Divorced people need to hear the truth that God loves, forgives, and offers full fellowship with Him. Yes, God hates divorce because He understands, through the life of His Son, the hurt and pain of betrayal, rejection, and abandonment. Divorce has negative consequences, but God can take the worst things in life and use them for good and for the good of others.

THE NEED TO FORGIVE

Another part of spiritual healing comes through divorced people forgiving themselves and those who have hurt them. Without such forgiveness, they can never be truly healed and released. Most divorced people blame themselves, so healing includes confessing those mistakes and then accepting the forgiveness that God offers (1 John 1:9). As long as they wallow in self-pity, guilt, and self-condemnation, those who have been divorced will never realize the blessings that God has in store for them.

Divorced people will also struggle with forgiving others who have wounded them so deeply. True forgiveness means that they are able to rise above the pain from those who have wronged them, pray for them, and wish them well. At some point, they make a decision to forgive—but the process of forgiveness may take a lifetime. Especially if there are children involved, new issues will continually arise. When that happens, they should take those issues to the Lord one more time and recommit themselves to a lifestyle of forgiveness.

GIVING BACK

The final step of recovery, following the teachings of Christ, is to focus on giving back to others (2 Cor. 1:3–7). Giving to others too early in the process will only lead to new pain. In the proper time, however, comforting with the comfort that has been received can give divorced people purpose, meaning, and fulfillment.

FURTHER MEDITATION:

Other passages to study about the issue of divorce/separation include:

- ➢ Malachi 2:16
- ➢ Matthew 5:31, 32; 19:1–10
- ➢ Mark 10:1–12
- ➢ Romans 7:2, 3
- ➢ 1 Corinthians 7:10–16

To Learn More: Turn to the key passage note on divorce/separation at Matthew 19:3–8 on page 1261. See also the personality profile of the woman at the well on page 1376. See also the articles on marital problems on pages 1576, 1577 and marital communication on pages 1660, 1661.

shall not go over the boughs again; it shall be for the stranger, the fatherless, and the widow. 21When you gather the grapes of your vineyard, you shall not glean *it* afterward; it shall be for the stranger, the fatherless, and the widow. 22And you shall remember that you were a slave in the land of Egypt; therefore I command you to do this thing.

25 "If there is a dispute between men, and they come to court, that *the judges* may judge them, and they justify the righteous and condemn the wicked, 2then it shall be, if the wicked man deserves to be beaten, that the judge will cause him to lie down and be beaten in his presence, according to his guilt, with a certain number of blows. 3Forty blows he may give him *and* no more, lest he should exceed this and beat him with many blows above these, and your brother be humiliated in your sight.

4"You shall not muzzle an ox while it treads out *the grain.*

Marriage Duty of the Surviving Brother

5"If brothers dwell together, and one of them dies and has no son, the widow of the dead man shall not be *married* to a stranger outside *the family;* her husband's brother shall go in to her, take her as his wife, and perform the duty of a husband's brother to her. 6And it shall be *that* the firstborn son which she bears will succeed to the name of his dead brother, that his name may not be blotted out of Israel. 7But if the man does not want to take his brother's wife, then let his brother's wife go up to the gate to the elders, and say, 'My husband's brother refuses to raise up a name to his brother in Israel; he will not perform the duty of my husband's brother.' 8Then the elders of his city shall call him and speak to him. But *if* he stands firm and says, 'I do not want to take her,' 9then his brother's wife shall come to him in the presence of the elders, remove his sandal from his foot, spit in his face, and answer and say, 'So shall it be done to the man who will not build up his brother's house.' 10And his name shall be called in Israel, 'The house of him who had his sandal removed.'

Miscellaneous Laws

11"If *two* men fight together, and the wife of one draws near to rescue her husband from the hand of the one attacking him, and puts out her hand and seizes him by the genitals, 12then you shall cut off her hand; your eye shall not pity *her.*

13"You shall not have in your bag differing weights, a heavy and a light. 14You shall not have in your house differing measures, a large and a small. 15You shall have a perfect and just weight, a perfect and just measure, that your days may be lengthened in the land which the LORD your God is giving you. 16For all who do such things, all who behave unrighteously, *are* an abomination to the LORD your God.

Destroy the Amalekites

17"Remember what Amalek did to you on the way as you were coming out of Egypt, 18how he met you on the way and attacked your rear ranks, all the stragglers at your rear, when you *were* tired and weary; and he did not fear God. 19Therefore it shall be, when the LORD your God has given you rest from your enemies all around, in the land which the LORD your God is giving you to possess *as* an inheritance, *that* you will blot out the remembrance of Amalek from under heaven. You shall not forget.

Offerings of Firstfruits and Tithes

26 "And it shall be, when you come into the land which the LORD your God is giving you *as* an inheritance, and you possess it and dwell in it, 2that you shall take some of the first of all the produce of the ground, which you shall bring from your land that the LORD your God is giving you, and put *it* in a basket and go to the place where the LORD your God chooses to make His name abide. 3And you shall go to the one who is priest in those days, and say to him, 'I declare today to the LORD your[a] God that I have come to the country which the LORD swore to our fathers to give us.'

4"Then the priest shall take the basket out of your hand and set it down before the altar of the LORD your God. 5And you shall answer and say before the LORD your God: 'My father *was* a Syrian,[a] about to perish, and he went down to Egypt and dwelt there, few in number; and there he became a nation, great, mighty, and populous. 6But the Egyptians mistreated us, afflicted us, and laid hard bondage on us. 7Then we cried out to the LORD God of

26:3 [a]Septuagint reads *my.* **26:5** [a]Or *Aramean*

our fathers, and the LORD heard our voice and looked on our affliction and our labor and our oppression. 8So the LORD brought us out of Egypt with a mighty hand and with an outstretched arm, with great terror and with signs and wonders. 9He has brought us to this place and has given us this land, "a land flowing with milk and honey";[a] 10and now, behold, I have brought the firstfruits of the land which you, O LORD, have given me.'

"Then you shall set it before the LORD your God, and worship before the LORD your God. 11So you shall rejoice in every good *thing* which the LORD your God has given to you and your house, you and the Levite and the stranger who *is* among you.

12"When you have finished laying aside all the tithe of your increase in the third year—the year of tithing—and have given *it* to the Levite, the stranger, the fatherless, and the widow, so that they may eat within your gates and be filled, 13then you shall say before the LORD your God: 'I have removed the holy *tithe* from *my* house, and also have given them to the Levite, the stranger, the fatherless, and the widow, according to all Your commandments which You have commanded me; I have not transgressed Your commandments, nor have I forgotten *them.* 14I have not eaten any of it when in mourning, nor have I removed *any* of it for an unclean *use,* nor given *any* of it for the dead. I have obeyed the voice of the LORD my God, and have done according to all that You have commanded me. 15Look down from Your holy habitation, from heaven, and bless Your people Israel and the land which You have given us, just as You swore to our fathers, "a land flowing with milk and honey." '[a]

A Special People of God

16"This day the LORD your God commands you to observe these statutes and judgments; therefore you shall be careful to observe them with all your heart and with all your soul. 17Today you have proclaimed the LORD to be your God, and that you will walk in His ways and keep His statutes, His commandments, and His judgments, and that you will obey His voice. 18Also today the LORD has proclaimed you to be His special people, just as He promised you, that *you* should keep all His commandments, 19and that He will set you high above all nations which He has made, in praise, in name, and in honor, and that you may be a holy people to the LORD your God, just as He has spoken."

The Law Inscribed on Stones

27 Now Moses, with the elders of Israel, commanded the people, saying: "Keep all the commandments which I command you today. 2And it shall be, on the day when you cross over the Jordan to the land which the LORD your God is giving you, that you shall set up for yourselves large stones, and whitewash them with lime. 3You shall write on them all the words of this law, when you have crossed over, that you may enter the land which the LORD your God is giving you, 'a land flowing with milk and honey,'[a] just as the LORD God of your fathers promised you. 4Therefore it shall be, when you have crossed over the Jordan, *that* on Mount Ebal you shall set up these stones, which I command you today, and you shall whitewash them with lime. 5And there you shall build an altar to the LORD your God, an altar of stones; you shall not use an iron *tool* on them. 6You shall build with whole stones the altar of the LORD your God, and offer burnt offerings on it to the LORD your God. 7You shall offer peace offerings, and shall eat there, and rejoice before the LORD your God. 8And you shall write very plainly on the stones all the words of this law."

9Then Moses and the priests, the Levites, spoke to all Israel, saying, "Take heed and listen, O Israel: This day you have become the people of the LORD your God. 10Therefore you shall obey the voice of the LORD your God, and observe His commandments and His statutes which I command you today."

Curses Pronounced from Mount Ebal

11And Moses commanded the people on the same day, saying, 12"These shall stand on Mount Gerizim to bless the people, when you have crossed over the Jordan: Simeon, Levi, Judah, Issachar, Joseph, and Benjamin; 13and these shall stand on Mount Ebal to curse: Reuben, Gad, Asher, Zebulun, Dan, and Naphtali.

14"And the Levites shall speak with a loud voice and say to all the men of Israel: 15'Cursed *is* the one who makes a carved or

---

26:9 [a]Exodus 3:8 **26:15** [a]Exodus 3:8
27:3 [a]Exodus 3:8

molded image, an abomination to the LORD, the work of the hands of the craftsman, and sets *it* up in secret.'

"And all the people shall answer and say, 'Amen!'

16'Cursed *is* the one who treats his father or his mother with contempt.'

"And all the people shall say, 'Amen!'

17'Cursed *is* the one who moves his neighbor's landmark.'

"And all the people shall say, 'Amen!'

18'Cursed *is* the one who makes the blind to wander off the road.'

"And all the people shall say, 'Amen!'

19'Cursed *is* the one who perverts the justice due the stranger, the fatherless, and widow.'

"And all the people shall say, 'Amen!'

20'Cursed *is* the one who lies with his father's wife, because he has uncovered his father's bed.'

"And all the people shall say, 'Amen!'

21'Cursed *is* the one who lies with any kind of animal.'

"And all the people shall say, 'Amen!'

22'Cursed *is* the one who lies with his sister, the daughter of his father or the daughter of his mother.'

"And all the people shall say, 'Amen!'

23'Cursed *is* the one who lies with his mother-in-law.'

"And all the people shall say, 'Amen!'

24'Cursed *is* the one who attacks his neighbor secretly.'

"And all the people shall say, 'Amen!'

25'Cursed *is* the one who takes a bribe to slay an innocent person.'

"And all the people shall say, 'Amen!'

26'Cursed *is* the one who does not confirm *all* the words of this law by observing them.'

"And all the people shall say, 'Amen!' "

BLESSINGS ON OBEDIENCE

28 "Now it shall come to pass, if you diligently obey the voice of the LORD your God, to observe carefully all His commandments which I command you today, that the LORD your God will set you high above all nations of the earth. 2And all these blessings shall come upon you and overtake you, because you obey the voice of the LORD your God:

3"Blessed *shall* you *be* in the city, and blessed *shall* you *be* in the country.

4"Blessed *shall be* the fruit of your body, the produce of your ground and the increase of your herds, the increase of your cattle and the offspring of your flocks.

5"Blessed *shall be* your basket and your kneading bowl.

6"Blessed *shall* you *be* when you come in, and blessed *shall* you *be* when you go out.

7"The LORD will cause your enemies who rise against you to be defeated before your face; they shall come out against you one way and flee before you seven ways.

8"The LORD will command the blessing on you in your storehouses and in all to which you set your hand, and He will bless you in the land which the LORD your God is giving you.

9"The LORD will establish you as a holy people to Himself, just as He has sworn to you, if you keep the commandments of the LORD your God and walk in His ways. 10Then all peoples of the earth shall see that you are called by the name of the LORD, and they shall be afraid of you. 11And the LORD will grant you plenty of goods, in the fruit of your body, in the increase of your livestock, and in the produce of your ground, in the land of which the LORD swore to your fathers to give you. 12The LORD will open to you His good treasure, the heavens, to give the rain to your land in its season,

SOUL NOTE

Loving Warnings *(28:2, 15)* Chapter 28 contains a list of blessings and curses. The people of Israel would experience the blessings if they kept their part of the covenant by obeying God. The curses, however, were God's certain punishment for disobedience. These curses were loving warnings about the natural consequences of sin. Wrongdoing toward God or others has tragic consequences. God's strong words are meant to help people avoid the consequences that will come from disobeying Him and hurting others. **Topic: Obedience**

and to bless all the work of your hand. You
shall lend to many nations, but you shall not
borrow. 13And the LORD will make you the
head and not the tail; you shall be above only,
and not be beneath, if you heed the commandments of the LORD your God, which I
command you today, and are careful to observe *them.* 14So you shall not turn aside from
any of the words which I command you this
day, *to* the right or the left, to go after other
gods to serve them.

Curses on Disobedience

15"But it shall come to pass, if you do not
obey the voice of the LORD your God, to observe carefully all His commandments and
His statutes which I command you today, that
all these curses will come upon you and overtake you:

16"Cursed *shall* you *be* in the city, and
cursed *shall* you *be* in the country.

17"Cursed *shall be* your basket and your
kneading bowl.

18"Cursed *shall be* the fruit of your body and
the produce of your land, the increase of your
cattle and the offspring of your flocks.

19"Cursed *shall* you *be* when you come in,
and cursed *shall* you *be* when you go out.

20"The LORD will send on you cursing, confusion, and rebuke in all that you set your
hand to do, until you are destroyed and until
you perish quickly, because of the wickedness
of your doings in which you have forsaken
Me. 21The LORD will make the plague cling
to you until He has consumed you from the
land which you are going to possess. 22The
LORD will strike you with consumption, with
fever, with inflammation, with severe burning
fever, with the sword, with scorching, and
with mildew; they shall pursue you until you
perish. 23And your heavens which *are* over
your head shall be bronze, and the earth
which is under you *shall be* iron. 24The LORD
will change the rain of your land to powder
and dust; from the heaven it shall come down
on you until you are destroyed.

25"The LORD will cause you to be defeated
before your enemies; you shall go out one way
against them and flee seven ways before them;
and you shall become troublesome to all the
kingdoms of the earth. 26Your carcasses shall
be food for all the birds of the air and the
beasts of the earth, and no one shall frighten
them away. 27The LORD will strike you with the
boils of Egypt, with tumors, with the scab, and
with the itch, from which you cannot be
healed. 28The LORD will strike you with madness
and blindness and confusion of heart. 29And you
shall grope at noonday, as a blind man gropes
in darkness; you shall not prosper in your
ways; you shall be only oppressed and plundered continually, and no one shall save *you.*

30"You shall betroth a wife, but another man
shall lie with her; you shall build a house, but
you shall not dwell in it; you shall plant a
vineyard, but shall not gather its grapes.
31Your ox *shall be* slaughtered before your
eyes, but you shall not eat of it; your donkey
shall be violently taken away from before you,
and shall not be restored to you; your sheep
shall be given to your enemies, and you shall
have no one to rescue *them.* 32Your sons and
your daughters *shall be* given to another people, and your eyes shall look and fail *with
longing* for them all day long; and *there shall
be* no strength in your hand. 33A nation whom
you have not known shall eat the fruit of your
land and the produce of your labor, and you
shall be only oppressed and crushed continually. 34So you shall be driven mad because of
the sight which your eyes see. 35The LORD will
strike you in the knees and on the legs with
severe boils which cannot be healed, and from
the sole of your foot to the top of your head.

36"The LORD will bring you and the king
whom you set over you to a nation which neither you nor your fathers have known, and
there you shall serve other gods—wood and
stone. 37And you shall become an astonishment, a proverb, and a byword among all nations where the LORD will drive you.

38"You shall carry much seed out to the field
but gather little in, for the locust shall consume it. 39You shall plant vineyards and tend
them, but you shall neither drink *of* the wine
nor gather the *grapes;* for the worms shall eat
them. 40You shall have olive trees throughout
all your territory, but you shall not anoint
yourself with the oil; for your olives shall drop
off. 41You shall beget sons and daughters, but
they shall not be yours; for they shall go into
captivity. 42Locusts shall consume all your
trees and the produce of your land.

43"The alien who *is* among you shall rise
higher and higher above you, and you shall
come down lower and lower. 44He shall lend
to you, but you shall not lend to him; he shall
be the head, and you shall be the tail.

45“Moreover all these curses shall come upon you and pursue and overtake you, until you are destroyed, because you did not obey the voice of the LORD your God, to keep His commandments and His statutes which He commanded you. 46And they shall be upon you for a sign and a wonder, and on your descendants forever.

47“Because you did not serve the LORD your God with joy and gladness of heart, for the abundance of everything, 48therefore you shall serve your enemies, whom the LORD will send against you, in hunger, in thirst, in nakedness, and in need of everything; and He will put a yoke of iron on your neck until He has destroyed you. 49The LORD will bring a nation against you from afar, from the end of the earth, *as swift* as the eagle flies, a nation whose language you will not understand, 50a nation of fierce countenance, which does not respect the elderly nor show favor to the young. 51And they shall eat the increase of your livestock and the produce of your land, until you are destroyed; they shall not leave you grain or new wine or oil, *or* the increase of your cattle or the offspring of your flocks, until they have destroyed you.

52“They shall besiege you at all your gates until your high and fortified walls, in which you trust, come down throughout all your land; and they shall besiege you at all your gates throughout all your land which the LORD your God has given you. 53You shall eat the fruit of your own body, the flesh of your sons and your daughters whom the LORD your God has given you, in the siege and desperate straits in which your enemy shall distress you. 54The sensitive and very refined man among you will be hostile toward his brother, toward the wife of his bosom, and toward the rest of his children whom he leaves behind, 55so that he will not give any of them the flesh of his children whom he will eat, because he has nothing left in the siege and desperate straits in which your enemy shall distress you at all your gates. 56The tender and delicate woman among you, who would not venture to set the sole of her foot on the ground because of her delicateness and sensitivity, will refuse[a] to the husband of her bosom, and to her son and her daughter, 57her placenta which comes out from between her feet and her children whom she bears; for she will eat them secretly for lack of everything in the siege and desperate straits in which your enemy shall distress you at all your gates.

58“If you do not carefully observe all the words of this law that are written in this book, that you may fear this glorious and awesome name, THE LORD YOUR GOD, 59then the LORD will bring upon you and your descendants extraordinary plagues—great and prolonged plagues—and serious and prolonged sicknesses. 60Moreover He will bring back on you all the diseases of Egypt, of which you were afraid, and they shall cling to you. 61Also every sickness and every plague, which *is* not written in this Book of the Law, will the LORD bring upon you until you are destroyed. 62You shall be left few in number, whereas you were as the stars of heaven in multitude, because you would not obey the voice of the LORD your God. 63And it shall be, *that* just as the LORD rejoiced over you to do you good and multiply you, so the LORD will rejoice over you to destroy you and bring you to nothing; and you shall be plucked from off the land which you go to possess.

64“Then the LORD will scatter you among all peoples, from one end of the earth to the other, and there you shall serve other gods, which neither you nor your fathers have known—wood and stone. 65And among those nations you shall find no rest, nor shall the sole of your foot have a resting place; but there the LORD will give you a trembling heart, failing eyes, and anguish of soul. 66Your life shall hang in doubt before you; you shall fear day and night, and have no assurance of life. 67In the morning you shall say, ‘Oh, that it were evening!’ And at evening you shall say, ‘Oh, that it were morning!’ because of the fear which terrifies your heart, and because of the sight which your eyes see.

68“And the LORD will take you back to Egypt in ships, by the way of which I said to you, ‘You shall never see it again.’ And there you shall be offered for sale to your enemies as male and female slaves, but no one will buy *you.*”

THE COVENANT RENEWED IN MOAB

29 These *are* the words of the covenant which the LORD commanded Moses to make with the children of Israel in the land of Moab, besides the covenant which He made with them in Horeb.

28:56 [a]Literally *her eye shall be evil toward*

[2]Now Moses called all Israel and said to them: “You have seen all that the LORD did before your eyes in the land of Egypt, to Pharaoh and to all his servants and to all his land— [3]the great trials which your eyes have seen, the signs, and those great wonders. [4]Yet the LORD has not given you a heart to perceive and eyes to see and ears to hear, to this *very* day. [5]And I have led you forty years in the wilderness. Your clothes have not worn out on you, and your sandals have not worn out on your feet. [6]You have not eaten bread, nor have you drunk wine or *similar* drink, that you may know that I *am* the LORD your God. [7]And when you came to this place, Sihon king of Heshbon and Og king of Bashan came out against us to battle, and we conquered them. [8]We took their land and gave it as an inheritance to the Reubenites, to the Gadites, and to half the tribe of Manasseh. [9]Therefore keep the words of this covenant, and do them, that you may prosper in all that you do.

[10]“All of you stand today before the LORD your God: your leaders and your tribes and your elders and your officers, all the men of Israel, [11]your little ones and your wives—also the stranger who *is* in your camp, from the one who cuts your wood to the one who draws your water— [12]that you may enter into covenant with the LORD your God, and into His oath, which the LORD your God makes with you today, [13]that He may establish you today as a people for Himself, and *that* He may be God to you, just as He has spoken to you, and just as He has sworn to your fathers, to Abraham, Isaac, and Jacob.

[14]“I make this covenant and this oath, not with you alone, [15]but with *him* who stands here with us today before the LORD our God, as well as with *him* who *is* not here with us today [16](for you know that we dwelt in the land of Egypt and that we came through the nations which you passed by, [17]and you saw their abominations and their idols which *were* among them—wood and stone and silver and gold); [18]so that there may not be among you man or woman or family or tribe, whose heart turns away today from the LORD our God, to go *and* serve the gods of these nations, and that there may not be among you a root bearing bitterness or wormwood; [19]and so it may not happen, when he hears the words of this curse, that he blesses himself in his heart, saying, ‘I shall have peace, even though I follow the dictates[a] of my heart’—as though the drunkard could be included with the sober.

[20]“The LORD would not spare him; for then the anger of the LORD and His jealousy would burn against that man, and every curse that is written in this book would settle on him, and the LORD would blot out his name from under heaven. [21]And the LORD would separate him from all the tribes of Israel for adversity, according to all the curses of the covenant that are written in this Book of the Law, [22]so that the coming generation of your children who rise up after you, and the foreigner who comes from a far land, would say, when they see the plagues of that land and the sicknesses which the LORD has laid on it:

[23]‘The whole land *is* brimstone, salt, and burning; it is not sown, nor does it bear, nor does any grass grow there, like the overthrow of Sodom and Gomorrah, Admah, and Zeboiim, which the LORD overthrew in His anger and His wrath.’ [24]All nations would say, ‘Why has the LORD done so to this land? What does the heat of this great anger mean?’ [25]Then *people* would say: ‘Because they have forsaken the covenant of the LORD God of their fathers, which He made with them when He brought them out of the land of Egypt; [26]for they went and served other gods and worshiped them, gods that they did not know and that He had not given to them. [27]Then the anger of the LORD was aroused against this land, to bring on it every curse that is written in this book. [28]And the LORD uprooted them from their land in anger, in wrath, and in great indignation, and cast them into another land, as *it is* this day.’

[29]“The secret *things belong* to the LORD our God, but those *things which are* revealed *belong* to us and to our children forever, that *we* may do all the words of this law.

The Blessing of Returning to God

30 “Now it shall come to pass, when all these things come upon you, the blessing and the curse which I have set before you, and you call *them* to mind among all the nations where the LORD your God drives you, [2]and you return to the LORD your God and obey His voice, according to all that I command you today, you and your children, with all your heart and with all your soul, [3]that the LORD your God will bring you back from captivity,

29:19 [a]Or *stubbornness*

and have compassion on you, and gather you again from all the nations where the LORD your God has scattered you. 4If *any* of you are driven out to the farthest *parts* under heaven, from there the LORD your God will gather you, and from there He will bring you. 5Then the LORD your God will bring you to the land which your fathers possessed, and you shall possess it. He will prosper you and multiply you more than your fathers. 6And the LORD your God will circumcise your heart and the heart of your descendants, to love the LORD your God with all your heart and with all your soul, that you may live.

7"Also the LORD your God will put all these curses on your enemies and on those who hate you, who persecuted you. 8And you will again obey the voice of the LORD and do all His commandments which I command you today. 9The LORD your God will make you abound in all the work of your hand, in the fruit of your body, in the increase of your livestock, and in the produce of your land for good. For the LORD will again rejoice over you for good as He rejoiced over your fathers, 10if you obey the voice of the LORD your God, to keep His commandments and His statutes which are written in this Book of the Law, *and* if you turn to the LORD your God with all your heart and with all your soul.

The Choice of Life or Death

11"For this commandment which I command you today *is* not *too* mysterious for you, nor *is* it far off. 12It *is* not in heaven, that you should say, 'Who will ascend into heaven for us and bring it to us, that we may hear it and do it?' 13Nor *is* it beyond the sea, that you should say, 'Who will go over the sea for us and bring it to us, that we may hear it and do it?' 14But the word *is* very near you, in your mouth and in your heart, that you may do it.

15"See, I have set before you today life and good, death and evil, 16in that I command you today to love the LORD your God, to walk in His ways, and to keep His commandments, His statutes, and His judgments, that you may live and multiply; and the LORD your God will bless you in the land which you go to possess. 17But if your heart turns away so that you do not hear, and are drawn away, and worship other gods and serve them, 18I announce to you today that you shall surely perish; you shall not prolong *your* days in the land which you cross over the Jordan to go in and possess. 19I call heaven and earth as witnesses today against you, *that* I have set before you life and death, blessing and cursing; therefore choose life, that both you and your descendants may live; 20that you may love the LORD your God, that you may obey His voice, and that you may cling to Him, for He *is* your life and the length of your days; and that you may dwell in the land which the LORD swore to your fathers, to Abraham, Isaac, and Jacob, to give them."

Joshua the New Leader of Israel

31 Then Moses went and spoke these words to all Israel. 2And he said to them: "I *am* one hundred and twenty years old today. I can no longer go out and come in. Also the LORD has said to me, 'You shall not cross over this Jordan.' 3The LORD your God Himself crosses over before you; He will destroy these nations from before you, and you shall dispossess them. Joshua himself crosses over before you, just as the LORD has said. 4And the LORD will do to them as He did to Sihon and Og, the kings of the Amorites and their land, when He destroyed them. 5The LORD will give them over to you, that you may do to them according to every commandment which I have commanded you. 6Be strong and of good courage, do not fear nor be afraid of them; for the LORD your God, He *is* the One who goes with you. He will not leave you nor forsake you."

7Then Moses called Joshua and said to him in the sight of all Israel, "Be strong and of good courage, for you must go with this people to the land which the LORD has sworn to their fathers to give them, and you shall cause them to inherit it. 8And the LORD, He *is* the One who goes before you. He will be with you, He will not leave you nor forsake you; do not fear nor be dismayed."

The Law to Be Read Every Seven Years

9So Moses wrote this law and delivered it to the priests, the sons of Levi, who bore the ark of the covenant of the LORD, and to all the elders of Israel. 10And Moses commanded them, saying: "At the end of *every* seven years, at the appointed time in the year of release, at the Feast of Tabernacles, 11when all Israel comes to appear before the LORD your God in the place which He chooses, you shall read this

law before all Israel in their hearing. [12]Gather
the people together, men and women and little
ones, and the stranger who *is* within your
gates, that they may hear and that they may
learn to fear the LORD your God and carefully
observe all the words of this law, [13]and *that*
their children, who have not known it, may
hear and learn to fear the LORD your God as
long as you live in the land which you cross
the Jordan to possess."

PREDICTION OF ISRAEL'S REBELLION

[14]Then the LORD said to Moses, "Behold, the
days approach when you must die; call
Joshua, and present yourselves in the tabernacle of meeting, that I may inaugurate him."

So Moses and Joshua went and presented
themselves in the tabernacle of meeting.
[15]Now the LORD appeared at the tabernacle in
a pillar of cloud, and the pillar of cloud stood
above the door of the tabernacle.

[16]And the LORD said to Moses: "Behold, you
will rest with your fathers; and this people
will rise and play the harlot with the gods of
the foreigners of the land, where they go *to be*
among them, and they will forsake Me and
break My covenant which I have made with
them. [17]Then My anger shall be aroused
against them in that day, and I will forsake
them, and I will hide My face from them, and
they shall be devoured. And many evils and
troubles shall befall them, so that they will say
in that day, 'Have not these evils come upon
us because our God *is* not among us?' [18]And I
will surely hide My face in that day because of
all the evil which they have done, in that they
have turned to other gods.

[19]"Now therefore, write down this song for
yourselves, and teach it to the children of Israel; put it in their mouths, that this song may
be a witness for Me against the children of Israel. [20]When I have brought them to the land
flowing with milk and honey, of which I swore
to their fathers, and they have eaten and filled
themselves and grown fat, then they will turn
to other gods and serve them; and they will
provoke Me and break My covenant. [21]Then it
shall be, when many evils and troubles have
come upon them, that this song will testify
against them as a witness; for it will not be
forgotten in the mouths of their descendants,
for I know the inclination of their behavior today, even before I have brought them to the
land of which I swore *to give them.*"

[22]Therefore Moses wrote this song the same
day, and taught it to the children of Israel.
[23]Then He inaugurated Joshua the son of Nun,
and said, "Be strong and of good courage; for
you shall bring the children of Israel into the
land of which I swore to them, and I will be
with you."

[24]So it was, when Moses had completed
writing the words of this law in a book, when
they were finished, [25]that Moses commanded
the Levites, who bore the ark of the covenant
of the LORD, saying: [26]"Take this Book of the
Law, and put it beside the ark of the covenant
of the LORD your God, that it may be there as a
witness against you; [27]for I know your rebellion and your stiff neck. *If* today, while I am
yet alive with you, you have been rebellious
against the LORD, then how much more after
my death? [28]Gather to me all the elders of your
tribes, and your officers, that I may speak
these words in their hearing and call heaven
and earth to witness against them. [29]For I
know that after my death you will become
utterly corrupt, and turn aside from the way
which I have commanded you. And evil will
befall you in the latter days, because you will
do evil in the sight of the LORD, to provoke Him
to anger through the work of your hands."

SOUL NOTE

Never Alone *(31:7, 8)* God encouraged Joshua through these words of Moses (later repeated in Josh. 1:6). He promised to be with Joshua in the coming task of conquering the land, so Joshua should be "strong and of good courage." God also promises to be with us in the pressures and challenges of life. The tasks ahead may be difficult, the enemy powerful, and the work immense, but God calls His people to trust Him. "He is the One who goes before you. He will be with you, He will not leave you nor forsake you." **Topic: God's Promises**

THE SONG OF MOSES

30Then Moses spoke in the hearing of all the
assembly of Israel the words of this song until
they were ended:

32 "Give ear, O heavens, and I will
speak;
And hear, O earth, the words of my
mouth.
2 Let my teaching drop as the rain,
My speech distill as the dew,
As raindrops on the tender herb,
And as showers on the grass.
3 For I proclaim the name of the LORD:
Ascribe greatness
to our God.
4 *He is* the Rock,
His work *is*
perfect;
For all His ways
are justice,
A God of truth and
without
injustice;
Righteous and
upright *is* He.

"For I proclaim the name of the LORD: Ascribe greatness to our God. He is the Rock, His work is perfect; for all His ways are justice, a God of truth and without injustice; righteous and upright is He."
DEUTERONOMY 32:3, 4

5 "They have corrupted themselves;
They are not His children,
Because of their blemish:
A perverse and crooked generation.
6 Do you thus deal with the LORD,
O foolish and unwise people?
Is He not your Father, *who* bought you?
Has He not made you and established
you?

7 "Remember the days of old,
Consider the years of many
generations.
Ask your father, and he will show you;
Your elders, and they will tell you:
8 When the Most High divided their
inheritance to the nations,
When He separated the sons of Adam,
He set the boundaries of the peoples
According to the number of the children
of Israel.
9 For the LORD's portion *is* His people;
Jacob *is* the place of His inheritance.

10 "He found him in a desert land
And in the wasteland, a howling
wilderness;
He encircled him, He instructed him,
He kept him as the apple of His eye.
11 As an eagle stirs up its nest,
Hovers over its young,
Spreading out its wings, taking them up,
Carrying them on its wings,
12 *So* the LORD alone led him,
And *there was* no foreign god with him.

13 "He made him ride in the heights of the
earth,
That he might eat the produce of the
fields;
He made him draw honey from the rock,
And oil from the
flinty rock;
14 Curds from the
cattle, and milk
of the flock,
With fat of lambs;
And rams of the
breed of Bashan,
and goats,
With the choicest
wheat;
And you drank
wine, the blood
of the grapes.

15 "But Jeshurun grew fat and kicked;
You grew fat, you grew thick,
You are obese!
Then he forsook God *who* made him,
And scornfully esteemed the Rock of his
salvation.
16 They provoked Him to jealousy with
foreign *gods;*
With abominations they provoked Him
to anger.
17 They sacrificed to demons, not to God,
To gods they did not know,
To new *gods,* new arrivals
That your fathers did not fear.
18 Of the Rock *who* begot you, you are
unmindful,
And have forgotten the God who
fathered you.

19 "And when the LORD saw *it,* He spurned
them,
Because of the provocation of His sons
and His daughters.
20 And He said: 'I will hide My face from
them,

I will see what their end *will be,*
For they *are* a perverse generation,
Children in whom *is* no faith.
21 They have provoked Me to jealousy by *what* is not God;
They have moved Me to anger by their foolish idols.
But I will provoke them to jealousy by *those who are* not a nation;
I will move them to anger by a foolish nation.
22 For a fire is kindled in My anger,
And shall burn to the lowest hell;
It shall consume the earth with her increase,
And set on fire the foundations of the mountains.

23 'I will heap disasters on them;
I will spend My arrows on them.
24 *They shall be* wasted with hunger,
Devoured by pestilence and bitter destruction;
I will also send against them the teeth of beasts,
With the poison of serpents of the dust.
25 The sword shall destroy outside;
There shall be terror within
For the young man and virgin,
The nursing child with the man of gray hairs.
26 I would have said, "I will dash them in pieces,
I will make the memory of them to cease from among men,"
27 Had I not feared the wrath of the enemy,
Lest their adversaries should misunderstand,
Lest they should say, "Our hand *is* high;
And it is not the LORD who has done all this." '

28 "For they *are* a nation void of counsel,
Nor *is there any* understanding in them.
29 Oh, that they were wise, *that* they understood this,
That they would consider their latter end!
30 How could one chase a thousand,
And two put ten thousand to flight,
Unless their Rock had sold them,
And the LORD had surrendered them?
31 For their rock *is* not like our Rock,
Even our enemies themselves *being* judges.
32 For their vine *is* of the vine of Sodom
And of the fields of Gomorrah;
Their grapes *are* grapes of gall,
Their clusters *are* bitter.
33 Their wine *is* the poison of serpents,
And the cruel venom of cobras.

34 '*Is* this not laid up in store with Me,
Sealed up among My treasures?
35 Vengeance is Mine, and recompense;
Their foot shall slip in *due* time;
For the day of their calamity *is* at hand,
And the things to come hasten upon them.'

36 "For the LORD will judge His people
And have compassion on His servants,
When He sees that *their* power is gone,
And *there is* no one *remaining,* bond or free.
37 He will say: 'Where *are* their gods,
The rock in which they sought refuge?
38 Who ate the fat of their sacrifices,
And drank the wine of their drink offering?
Let them rise and help you,
And be your refuge.

39 'Now see that I, *even* I, *am* He,
And *there is* no God besides Me;
I kill and I make alive;
I wound and I heal;
Nor *is there any* who can deliver from My hand.
40 For I raise My hand to heaven,
And say, "*As* I live forever,
41 If I whet My glittering sword,
And My hand takes hold on judgment,
I will render vengeance to My enemies,
And repay those who hate Me.
42 I will make My arrows drunk with blood,
And My sword shall devour flesh,
With the blood of the slain and the captives,
From the heads of the leaders of the enemy." '

43 "Rejoice, O Gentiles, *with* His people;[a]
For He will avenge the blood of His servants,

32:43 [a]A Dead Sea Scroll fragment adds *And let all the gods (angels) worship Him* (compare Septuagint and Hebrews 1:6).

And render vengeance to His
adversaries;
He will provide atonement for His land
and His people."

44So Moses came with Joshua[a] the son of
Nun and spoke all the words of this song in
the hearing of the people. 45Moses finished
speaking all these words to all Israel, 46and he
said to them: "Set your hearts on all the words
which I testify among you today, which you
shall command your children to be careful to
observe—all the words of this law. 47For it *is*
not a futile thing for you, because it *is* your
life, and by this word you shall prolong *your*
days in the land which you cross over the Jordan to possess."

Moses to Die on Mount Nebo

48Then the LORD spoke to Moses that very
same day, saying: 49"Go up this mountain of
the Abarim, Mount Nebo, which *is* in the land
of Moab, across from Jericho; view the land of
Canaan, which I give to the children of Israel
as a possession; 50and die on the mountain
which you ascend, and be gathered to your
people, just as Aaron your brother died on
Mount Hor and was gathered to his people;
51because you trespassed against Me among
the children of Israel at the waters of Meribah
Kadesh, in the Wilderness of Zin, because you
did not hallow Me in the midst of the children
of Israel. 52Yet you shall see the land before
you, though you shall not go there, into the
land which I am giving to the children of Israel."

Moses' Final Blessing on Israel

33 Now this *is* the blessing with which
Moses the man of God blessed the
children of Israel before his death. 2And he
said:

"The LORD came from Sinai,
And dawned on them from Seir;
He shone forth from Mount Paran,
And He came with ten thousands of
saints;
From His right hand
Came a fiery law for them.
3 Yes, He loves the people;
All His saints *are* in Your hand;
They sit down at Your feet;
Everyone receives Your words.
4 Moses commanded a law for us,
A heritage of the congregation of Jacob.
5 And He was King in Jeshurun,
When the leaders of the people were
gathered,
All the tribes of Israel together.

6 "Let Reuben live, and not die,
Nor let his men be few."

7And this he said of Judah:

"Hear, LORD, the voice of Judah,
And bring him to his people;
Let his hands be sufficient for him,
And may You be a help against his
enemies."

8And of Levi he said:

"*Let* Your Thummim and Your Urim *be*
with Your holy one,
Whom You tested at Massah,
And with whom You contended at the
waters of Meribah,
9 Who says of his father and mother,
'I have not seen them';
Nor did he acknowledge his brothers,

32:44 [a]Hebrew *Hoshea* (compare Numbers 13:8, 16)

SOUL NOTE

Faithful Generations *(33:1)* Chapter 33 contains a series of blessings that Moses pronounced on the tribes of Israel. These are similar to Jacob's blessings on his twelve sons, the ancestors to these tribes (Gen. 49). Jacob's blessings revealed each son's character and potential. A person's true character tends to be reflected in his or her children and grandchildren. What legacy will you leave?
Topic: Attachment/Blessing

Or know his own children;
For they have observed Your word
And kept Your covenant.
10 They shall teach Jacob Your judgments,
And Israel Your law.
They shall put incense before You,
And a whole burnt sacrifice on Your
altar.
11 Bless his substance, LORD,
And accept the work of his hands;
Strike the loins of those who rise against
him,
And of those who hate him, that they
rise not again."

12 Of Benjamin he said:

"The beloved of the LORD shall dwell in
safety by Him,
Who shelters him all the day long;
And he shall dwell between His
shoulders."

13 And of Joseph he said:

"Blessed of the LORD
is his land,
With the precious
things of heaven,
with the dew,
And the deep lying beneath,
14 With the precious fruits of the sun,
With the precious produce of the
months,
15 With the best things of the ancient
mountains,
With the precious things of the
everlasting hills,
16 With the precious things of the earth
and its fullness,
And the favor of Him who dwelt in the
bush.
Let *the blessing* come 'on the head of
Joseph,
And on the crown of the head of him
who was separate from his brothers.'[a]
17 His glory *is like* a firstborn bull,
And his horns *like* the horns of the wild
ox;
Together with them
He shall push the peoples
To the ends of the earth;
They *are* the ten thousands of Ephraim,
And they *are* the thousands of
Manasseh."

18 And of Zebulun he said:

"Rejoice, Zebulun, in your going out,
And Issachar in your tents!
19 They shall call the peoples *to* the
mountain;
There they shall offer sacrifices of
righteousness;
For they shall partake *of* the abundance
of the seas
And *of* treasures hidden in the sand."

20 And of Gad he said:

"Blessed *is* he who enlarges Gad;
He dwells as a lion,
And tears the arm and the crown of his
head.
21 He provided the first
part for himself,
Because a
lawgiver's
portion was
reserved there.
He came *with* the
heads of the
people;
He administered the justice of the LORD,
And His judgments with Israel."

> "The eternal God is your refuge, and underneath are the everlasting arms."
> DEUTERONOMY 33:27

22 And of Dan he said:

"Dan *is* a lion's whelp,
He shall leap from Bashan."

23 And of Naphtali he said:

"O Naphtali, satisfied with favor,
And full of the blessing of the LORD,
Possess the west and the south."

24 And of Asher he said:

"Asher *is* most blessed of sons;
Let him be favored by his brothers,
And let him dip his foot in oil.
25 Your sandals *shall be* iron and bronze;
As your days, *so shall* your strength *be*.

33:16 [a]Genesis 49:26

26 "*There is* no one like the God of
Jeshurun,
Who rides the heavens to help you,
And in His excellency on the clouds.
27 The eternal God *is your* refuge,
And underneath *are* the everlasting
arms;
He will thrust out the enemy from before
you,
And will say, 'Destroy!'
28 Then Israel shall dwell in safety,
The fountain of Jacob alone,
In a land of grain and new wine;
His heavens shall also drop dew.
29 Happy *are* you, O Israel!
Who *is* like you, a people saved by the
LORD,
The shield of your help
And the sword of your majesty!
Your enemies shall submit to you,
And you shall tread down their high
places."

MOSES DIES ON MOUNT NEBO

34 Then Moses went up from the plains
of Moab to Mount Nebo, to the top of
Pisgah, which is across from Jericho. And the
LORD showed him all the land of Gilead as far
as Dan, [2]all Naphtali and the land of Ephraim
and Manasseh, all the land of Judah as far as
the Western Sea,[a] [3]the South, and the plain of
the Valley of Jericho, the city of palm trees, as
far as Zoar. [4]Then the LORD said to him, "This
is the land of which I swore to give Abraham,
Isaac, and Jacob, saying, 'I will give it to your
descendants.' I have caused you to see *it* with
your eyes, but you shall not cross over there."
[5]So Moses the servant of the LORD died there
in the land of Moab, according to the word of
the LORD. [6]And He buried him in a valley in
the land of Moab, opposite Beth Peor; but no
one knows his grave to this day. [7]Moses *was*
one hundred and twenty years old when he
died. His eyes were not dim nor his natural
vigor diminished. [8]And the children of Israel
wept for Moses in the plains of Moab thirty
days. So the days of weeping *and* mourning for
Moses ended.
[9]Now Joshua the son of Nun was full of the
spirit of wisdom, for Moses had laid his hands
on him; so the children of Israel heeded him,
and did as the LORD had commanded Moses.
[10]But since then there has not arisen in Israel a prophet like Moses, whom the LORD
knew face to face, [11]in all the signs and wonders which the LORD sent him to do in the land
of Egypt, before Pharaoh, before all his servants, and in all his land, [12]and by all that
mighty power and all the great terror which
Moses performed in the sight of all Israel.

34:2 [a]That is, the Mediterranean

SOUL NOTE

Age Is No Object *(34:7–12)* Moses was 120 years old when he died. He had returned to Egypt to deal with Pharaoh when he was 80 and had been mightily used by God to free Israel from slavery (Ex. 7:7). Moses had spent the last forty years of his life in the wilderness leading the people of God who were being punished for their disobedience (Num. 14:32–35). Our generation tends to emphasize the importance of youth, but God uses servants of all ages. Age does not limit God's ability to work through people. As long as we have breath, we should be serving God.
Topic: Aging/Elderly

Joshua

Sometimes life is difficult. The tasks before us appear overwhelming and we wonder if we can accomplish them. We don't have to read too far in the Bible to recognize a pattern: God repeatedly asks His children to believe the incredible and attempt the impossible.

Abraham went to an unknown land that God promised to give to his descendants. Moses led Abraham's many descendants out of Egypt and back to the edge of the Promised Land. Moses passed the leadership to Joshua (Deut. 31:7, 8) who was to lead the Israelites in conquering the land.

This book written by Joshua teaches us not to be content with a timid faith. Joshua was a courageous military leader and a man of great spiritual influence. The key to his leadership, however, was not reliance on his abundant talents, but on his faith in God. Under Joshua's command, the nation learned to step out by faith against overwhelming opposition. By faith they crossed the Jordan River into the land (ch. 4). By faith they reestablished the rite of circumcision to emphasize dedication to God (ch. 5). By faith they conquered Jericho (ch. 6) and, in a relatively short time, much of the remaining land.

God had promised Abraham that his descendants would eventually possess the land of Canaan. The story of this conquest assures us that God always keeps His promises. We can have victory, even over what seems impossible, if we put our faith in God.

SOUL CONCERNS IN JOSHUA

DISCOURAGEMENT	(1:6–8)
AGING/ELDERLY	(CH. 14)
FAMILY LIFE	(24:15)

OVERCOMING DISCOURAGEMENT

JOHN R. CHEYDLEUR

(Joshua 1:6–8)

Life is filled with problems, challenges, and disappointments. The school fundraiser didn't go as well as we had hoped. The team finished the season last despite our best coaching efforts. The job presentation did not receive glowing reviews despite all our hard work and late nights of preparation. The report from the doctor was worse than we expected.

Things happen that foil our best-laid plans. Often, we find ourselves let down and discouraged. Sometimes, it's so bad that we just want to give up. Discouragement sets in and says, "Why bother? Nobody cares anyhow." Despite the circumstances, discouragement doesn't have to overwhelm us. We can learn from it, benefit from it, and overcome it.

FACING UP TO DISCOURAGEMENT

Discouragement is not the same as clinical depression. Long-term depression is often the result of unacknowledged anger turned inward upon oneself. By contrast, discouragement comes from a conscious awareness of our lack of ability to overcome a difficult situation.

When we are discouraged, our faith is often put to the test. It is time for us to reassess our goals and reevaluate our responses. In some cases, we will find that there were circumstances that were beyond our control—like the weather, unexpected company, or the emergence of a misplaced bill. While these things aggravate us, they need not overwhelm us. God is also the God of the unexpected. He sees these things before we do and chooses to use them to shape our personal and spiritual lives to our own good: "We know that all things work together for good to those who love God, to those who are the called according to His purpose" (Rom. 8:28).

Discouragement ought to be our first indication that it is time to pray. We often become discouraged because we get busy and neglect prayer. Many believers are discouraged by life's problems and have a lack of confidence that they can deal effectively with life's toughest challenges. We need to call on God to help us understand His guidance in the midst of our circumstances.

UNDERLYING CAUSES OF DISCOURAGEMENT

There are three underlying causes for discouragement: (1) lack of confidence in God; (2) lack of confidence in ourselves; or (3) lack of direction for the future. Joshua faced these same challenges when he led the children of Israel into the Promised Land. God told Joshua, "Be strong and of good courage" (Josh. 1:6). God reminded him that the key to overcoming discouragement was a vital, personal relationship with Him. The Lord told him, "This Book of the Law shall not depart from your mouth, but you shall meditate in it day and night, that you may observe to do according to all that is written in it. For then you will make your way prosperous, and then you will have good success" (Josh. 1:8).

KEYS TO OVERCOMING DISCOURAGEMENT

Once we really believe that God loves us and cares about us, we can begin to have confidence in His plan for our lives. The key is lining up our lives and our prayers with the wise and certain promises of God's Word. When we quote the promises of God back to Him in our prayers, we are agreeing with what God has already promised and reordering our lives accordingly. These key thoughts can help:

1. *Ride out the storm.* Some people never realize their potential because they are beaten down by the storms of life and give up too soon. We must not quit.
2. *Realize that God uses ordinary people.* We don't have to be spiritual giants to experience God's grace in our lives. He chooses ordinary people to accomplish extraordinary things for Him (1 Cor. 1:26, 27).
3. *Don't be defeated by the negatives.* We must keep our focus on Christ and the wonderful possibilities in our lives. Listening to the negative voices that say, "You can't . . ." or "It will never work . . ." will only discourage us.
4. *Focus on Christ.* It helps to envision what He can do for us and what we can do for Him. No life is meaningless if Christ is at the center of it.
5. *Remember that we are special.* God uniquely created us and designed us to serve Him. No one else can do what we can do for Him. We are uniquely gifted to minister to people no one else will ever meet or touch. We must not give up just because there are challenges and obstacles.
6. *Focus on behavior.* We must do what is right, no matter how we feel. We should make sure our behavior determines our feelings rather than allowing our feelings to determine our behavior. This sets us free to be creative, confident, and committed.
7. *Be persistent.* There is an interesting story in the Bible about a persistent widow who insisted that a judge give her legal protection. He finally granted her request because she wouldn't give up (Luke 18:1–8). We actualize the impossible when we honor God with our faith.

The answer to discouragement is getting our focus off ourselves and our limited resources and focusing on the unlimited power of God. He can do for us what we cannot do for ourselves. Even in the face of life's greatest challenges, His grace is sufficient. When we give our discouragement to God, He can encourage and draw us ever closer to Him.

FURTHER MEDITATION:

Other passages to study about the issue of discouragement include:

- ➢ Psalms 25:1–22; 40:1–3; 55:22; 56:1–13; 91:1–16
- ➢ Isaiah 41:10
- ➢ Jeremiah 15:16; 29:11; 33:3
- ➢ Habakkuk 3:17–19
- ➢ Zephaniah 3:14, 15
- ➢ Romans 8:35–39
- ➢ 2 Corinthians 12:9, 10
- ➢ Philippians 4:11–13, 19

To Learn More: Turn to the key passage note on discouragement at 1 Peter 5:7 on page 1665. See also the personality profile of Nehemiah on page 605.

God's Commission to Joshua

1 After the death of Moses the servant of the LORD, it came to pass that the LORD spoke to Joshua the son of Nun, Moses' assistant, saying: 2"Moses My servant is dead. Now therefore, arise, go over this Jordan, you and all this people, to the land which I am giving to them—the children of Israel. 3Every place that the sole of your foot will tread upon I have given you, as I said to Moses. 4From the wilderness and this Lebanon as far as the great river, the River Euphrates, all the land of the Hittites, and to the Great Sea toward the going down of the sun, shall be your territory. 5No man shall *be able to* stand before you all the days of your life; as I was with Moses, *so* I will be with you. I will not leave you nor forsake you. 6Be strong and of good courage, for to this people you shall divide as an inheritance the land which I swore to their fathers to give them. 7Only be strong and very courageous, that you may observe to do according to all the law which Moses My servant commanded you; do not turn from it to the right hand or to the left, that you may prosper wherever you go. 8This Book of the Law shall not depart from your mouth, but you shall meditate in it day and night, that you may observe to do according to all that is written in it. For then you will make your way prosperous, and then you will have good success. 9Have I not commanded you? Be strong and of good courage; do not be afraid, nor be dismayed, for the LORD your God *is* with you wherever you go."

> "Have I not commanded you?
> Be strong and of good courage;
> do not be afraid, nor be dismayed,
> for the LORD your God is with
> you wherever you go."
>
> JOSHUA 1:9

The Order to Cross the Jordan

10Then Joshua commanded the officers of the people, saying, 11"Pass through the camp and command the people, saying, 'Prepare provisions for yourselves, for within three days you will cross over this Jordan, to go in to possess the land which the LORD your God is giving you to possess.' "

12And to the Reubenites, the Gadites, and half the tribe of Manasseh Joshua spoke, saying, 13"Remember the word which Moses the servant of the LORD commanded you, saying, 'The LORD your God is giving you rest and is giving you this land.' 14Your wives, your little ones, and your livestock shall remain in the land which Moses gave you on this side of the Jordan. But you shall pass before your brethren armed, all your mighty men of valor, and help them, 15until the LORD has given your brethren rest, as He *gave* you, and they also have taken possession of the land which the LORD your God is giving them. Then you shall return to the land of your possession and enjoy it, which Moses the LORD's servant gave you on this side of the Jordan toward the sunrise."

16So they answered Joshua, saying, "All that you command us we will do, and wherever you send us we will go. 17Just as we heeded Moses in all things, so we will heed you. Only the LORD your God be with you, as He was with Moses. 18Whoever rebels against your command and does not heed your words, in all that you command him, shall be put to death. Only be strong and of good courage."

SOUL NOTE

The Whole Truth *(1:8, 9)* Joshua faced the challenge of leading the Israelites into the Promised Land. To encourage him, God urged him to meditate day and night on the Book of the Law (Moses' writings). God promised Joshua that doing so would make him prosperous and successful. This is not a promise of earthly prosperity—although certainly following God's rules for living will have a positive effect on our lives. But living by the truth of God's Word will make us successful in God's eyes. That kind of success is eternal. **Topic: Truth**

Rahab Hides the Spies

2 Now Joshua the son of Nun sent out two men from Acacia Grove[a] to spy secretly, saying, "Go, view the land, especially Jericho."

So they went, and came to the house of a harlot named Rahab, and lodged there. 2And it was told the king of Jericho, saying, "Behold, men have come here tonight from the children of Israel to search out the country."

3So the king of Jericho sent to Rahab, saying, "Bring out the men who have come to you, who have entered your house, for they have come to search out all the country."

4Then the woman took the two men and hid them. So she said, "Yes, the men came to me, but I did not know where they *were* from. 5And it happened as the gate was being shut, when it was dark, that the men went out. Where the men went I do not know; pursue them quickly, for you may overtake them." 6(But she had brought them up to the roof and hidden them with the stalks of flax, which she had laid in order on the roof.) 7Then the men pursued them by the road to the Jordan, to the fords. And as soon as those who pursued them had gone out, they shut the gate.

8Now before they lay down, she came up to them on the roof, 9and said to the men: "I know that the LORD has given you the land, that the terror of you has fallen on us, and that all the inhabitants of the land are fainthearted because of you. 10For we have heard how the LORD dried up the water of the Red Sea for you when you came out of Egypt, and what you did to the two kings of the Amorites who *were* on the other side of the Jordan, Sihon and Og, whom you utterly destroyed. 11And as soon as we heard *these things,* our hearts melted; neither did there remain any more courage in anyone because of you, for the LORD your God, He *is* God in heaven above and on earth beneath. 12Now therefore, I beg you, swear to me by the LORD, since I have shown you kindness, that you also will show kindness to my father's house, and give me a true token, 13and spare my father, my mother, my brothers, my sisters, and all that they have, and deliver our lives from death."

14So the men answered her, "Our lives for yours, if none of you tell this business of ours. And it shall be, when the LORD has given us the land, that we will deal kindly and truly with you."

15Then she let them down by a rope through the window, for her house *was* on the city wall; she dwelt on the wall. 16And she said to them, "Get to the mountain, lest the pursuers meet you. Hide there three days, until the pursuers have returned. Afterward you may go your way."

17So the men said to her: "We *will be* blameless of this oath of yours which you have made us swear, 18unless, *when* we come into the land, you bind this line of scarlet cord in the window through which you let us down, and unless you bring your father, your mother, your brothers, and all your father's household to your own home. 19So it shall be *that* whoever goes outside the doors of your house into the street, his blood *shall be* on his own head, and we *will be* guiltless. And whoever is with you in the house, his blood *shall be* on our head if a hand is laid on him. 20And if you tell this business of ours, then we will be free from your oath which you made us swear."

21Then she said, "According to your words, so *be* it." And she sent them away, and they departed. And she bound the scarlet cord in the window.

22They departed and went to the mountain, and stayed there three days until the pursuers returned. The pursuers sought *them* all along

2:1 [a]Hebrew *Shittim*

SOUL NOTE

Included *(2:1–16)* Courageous Rahab risked her life for the people of Israel. She was convinced that their God was "God in heaven above and on earth beneath"—the one true God (2:11). Her employment as a harlot did not place her beyond God's grace. All people are sinners and must come to God for forgiveness, regardless of their past. Rahab left her former life and joined the Israelites. She later appears in the genealogy of Jesus (Matt. 1:5). **Topic: Sin**

the way, but did not find *them.* 23So the two men returned, descended from the mountain, and crossed over; and they came to Joshua the son of Nun, and told him all that had befallen them. 24And they said to Joshua, "Truly the LORD has delivered all the land into our hands, for indeed all the inhabitants of the country are fainthearted because of us."

ISRAEL CROSSES THE JORDAN

3 Then Joshua rose early in the morning; and they set out from Acacia Grove[a] and came to the Jordan, he and all the children of Israel, and lodged there before they crossed over. 2So it was, after three days, that the officers went through the camp; 3and they commanded the people, saying, "When you see the ark of the covenant of the LORD your God, and the priests, the Levites, bearing it, then you shall set out from your place and go after it. 4Yet there shall be a space between you and it, about two thousand cubits by measure. Do not come near it, that you may know the way by which you must go, for you have not passed *this* way before."

5And Joshua said to the people, "Sanctify yourselves, for tomorrow the LORD will do wonders among you." 6Then Joshua spoke to the priests, saying, "Take up the ark of the covenant and cross over before the people."

So they took up the ark of the covenant and went before the people.

7And the LORD said to Joshua, "This day I will begin to exalt you in the sight of all Israel, that they may know that, as I was with Moses, *so* I will be with you. 8You shall command the priests who bear the ark of the covenant, saying, 'When you have come to the edge of the water of the Jordan, you shall stand in the Jordan.' "

9So Joshua said to the children of Israel, "Come here, and hear the words of the LORD your God." 10And Joshua said, "By this you shall know that the living God *is* among you, and *that* He will without fail drive out from before you the Canaanites and the Hittites and the Hivites and the Perizzites and the Girgashites and the Amorites and the Jebusites: 11Behold, the ark of the covenant of the Lord of all the earth is crossing over before you into the Jordan. 12Now therefore, take for yourselves twelve men from the tribes of Israel, one man from every tribe. 13And it shall come to pass, as soon as the soles of the feet of the priests who bear the ark of the LORD, the Lord of all the earth, shall rest in the waters of the Jordan, *that* the waters of the Jordan shall be cut off, the waters that come down from upstream, and they shall stand as a heap."

14So it was, when the people set out from their camp to cross over the Jordan, with the priests bearing the ark of the covenant before the people, 15and as those who bore the ark came to the Jordan, and the feet of the priests who bore the ark dipped in the edge of the water (for the Jordan overflows all its banks during the whole time of harvest), 16that the waters which came down from upstream stood *still, and* rose in a heap very far away at Adam, the city that *is* beside Zaretan. So the waters that went down into the Sea of the Arabah, the Salt Sea, failed, *and* were cut off; and the people crossed over opposite Jericho. 17Then the priests who bore the ark of the covenant of the LORD stood firm on dry ground in the midst of the Jordan; and all Israel crossed over on dry ground, until all the people had crossed completely over the Jordan.

THE MEMORIAL STONES

4 And it came to pass, when all the people had completely crossed over the Jordan,

3:1 [a]Hebrew *Shittim*

SOUL NOTE

Know the Way *(3:4)* It could be said of every new day that we "have not passed this way before." Every day brings new experiences and new challenges that stretch our faith in God. Without God, people are left to wonder what direction to take. With God, believers can know that every new day is in His hands and He will guide according to His eternal plan. As the Israelites followed the ark in order to "know the way," so we can look to God and His Word in order to know the way He wants us to go. **Topic: Decision Making**

that the LORD spoke to Joshua, saying: 2“Take
for yourselves twelve men from the people,
one man from every tribe, 3and command
them, saying, ‘Take for yourselves twelve
stones from here, out of the midst of the Jordan, from the place where the priests’ feet
stood firm. You shall carry them over with you
and leave them in the lodging place where you
lodge tonight.’ ”

4Then Joshua called the twelve men whom
he had appointed from the children of Israel,
one man from every tribe; 5and Joshua said to
them: “Cross over before the ark of the LORD
your God into the midst of the Jordan, and
each one of you take up a stone on his shoulder, according to the number of the tribes of
the children of Israel, 6that this may be a sign
among you when your children ask in time to
come, saying, ‘What do these stones *mean* to
you?’ 7Then you shall answer them that the
waters of the Jordan were cut off before the
ark of the covenant of the LORD; when it
crossed over the Jordan, the waters of the Jordan were cut off. And these stones shall be for
a memorial to the children of Israel forever.”

8And the children of Israel did so, just as
Joshua commanded, and took up twelve
stones from the midst of the Jordan, as the
LORD had spoken to Joshua, according to the
number of the tribes of the children of Israel,
and carried them over with them to the place
where they lodged, and laid them down there.
9Then Joshua set up twelve stones in the
midst of the Jordan, in the place where the
feet of the priests who bore the ark of the covenant stood; and they are there to this day.

10So the priests who bore the ark stood in
the midst of the Jordan until everything was
finished that the LORD had commanded
Joshua to speak to the people, according to all
that Moses had commanded Joshua; and the
people hurried and crossed over. 11Then it
came to pass, when all the people had completely crossed over, that the ark of the LORD
and the priests crossed over in the presence of
the people. 12And the men of Reuben, the men
of Gad, and half the tribe of Manasseh crossed
over armed before the children of Israel, as
Moses had spoken to them. 13About forty
thousand prepared for war crossed over before the LORD for battle, to the plains of Jericho. 14On that day the LORD exalted Joshua in
the sight of all Israel; and they feared him,
as they had feared Moses, all the days of his
life.

15Then the LORD spoke to Joshua, saying,
16“Command the priests who bear the ark of
the Testimony to come up from the Jordan.”
17Joshua therefore commanded the priests,
saying, “Come up from the Jordan.” 18And it
came to pass, when the priests who bore the
ark of the covenant of the LORD had come
from the midst of the Jordan, *and* the soles of
the priests’ feet touched the dry land, that the
waters of the Jordan returned to their place
and overflowed all its banks as before.

19Now the people came up from the Jordan
on the tenth *day* of the first month, and they
camped in Gilgal on the east border of Jericho.
20And those twelve stones which they took
out of the Jordan, Joshua set up in Gilgal.
21Then he spoke to the children of Israel, saying: “When your children ask their fathers in
time to come, saying, ‘What *are* these stones?’
22then you shall let your children know, saying, ‘Israel crossed over this Jordan on dry
land’; 23for the LORD your God dried up the
waters of the Jordan before you until you had
crossed over, as the LORD your God did to the
Red Sea, which He dried up before us until we
had crossed over, 24that all the peoples of the
earth may know the hand of the LORD, that it
is mighty, that you may fear the LORD your
God forever.”

SOUL NOTE

Pass It On *(4:19–24)* The memorial of twelve stones was to remind the people of God’s miracles on their behalf. In the future, children who saw the memorial would ask their parents what it meant. Then the parents could tell how God dried up the Jordan River just as He had dried up the Red Sea, allowing the Israelites to cross both bodies of water on dry land. It is the responsibility of parents to pass along to their children the stories of how God has worked in their lives. This will strengthen their children’s faith. **Topic: Parenting**

The Second Generation Circumcised

5 So it was, when all the kings of the Amorites who *were* on the west side of the Jordan, and all the kings of the Canaanites who *were* by the sea, heard that the LORD had dried up the waters of the Jordan from before the children of Israel until we[a] had crossed over, that their heart melted; and there was no spirit in them any longer because of the children of Israel.

2At that time the LORD said to Joshua, "Make flint knives for yourself, and circumcise the sons of Israel again the second time." 3So Joshua made flint knives for himself, and circumcised the sons of Israel at the hill of the foreskins.[a] 4And this *is* the reason why Joshua circumcised them: All the people who came out of Egypt *who were* males, all the men of war, had died in the wilderness on the way, after they had come out of Egypt. 5For all the people who came out had been circumcised, but all the people born in the wilderness, on the way as they came out of Egypt, had not been circumcised. 6For the children of Israel walked forty years in the wilderness, till all the people *who were* men of war, who came out of Egypt, were consumed, because they did not obey the voice of the LORD—to whom the LORD swore that He would not show them the land which the LORD had sworn to their fathers that He would give us, "a land flowing with milk and honey."[a] 7Then Joshua circumcised their sons *whom* He raised up in their place; for they were uncircumcised, because they had not been circumcised on the way.

8So it was, when they had finished circumcising all the people, that they stayed in their places in the camp till they were healed. 9Then the LORD said to Joshua, "This day I have rolled away the reproach of Egypt from you." Therefore the name of the place is called Gilgal[a] to this day.

10Now the children of Israel camped in Gilgal, and kept the Passover on the fourteenth day of the month at twilight on the plains of Jericho. 11And they ate of the produce of the land on the day after the Passover, unleavened bread and parched grain, on the very same day. 12Then the manna ceased on the day after they had eaten the produce of the land; and the children of Israel no longer had manna, but they ate the food of the land of Canaan that year.

The Commander of the Army of the Lord

13And it came to pass, when Joshua was by Jericho, that he lifted his eyes and looked, and behold, a Man stood opposite him with His sword drawn in His hand. And Joshua went to Him and said to Him, "*Are* You for us or for our adversaries?"

14So He said, "No, but *as* Commander of the army of the LORD I have now come."

And Joshua fell on his face to the earth and worshiped, and said to Him, "What does my Lord say to His servant?"

15Then the Commander of the LORD's army said to Joshua, "Take your sandal off your foot, for the place where you stand *is* holy." And Joshua did so.

The Destruction of Jericho

6 Now Jericho was securely shut up because of the children of Israel; none went out, and none came in. 2And the LORD said to Joshua: "See! I have given Jericho into your hand, its king, *and* the mighty men of valor. 3You shall march around the city, all *you* men of war; you shall go all around the city once. This you shall do six days. 4And seven priests shall bear seven trumpets of rams' horns before the ark. But the seventh day you shall march around the city seven times, and the priests shall blow the trumpets. 5It shall come to pass, when they make a long *blast* with the ram's horn, *and* when you hear the sound of the trumpet, that all the people shall shout with a great shout; then the wall of the city will fall down flat. And the people shall go up every man straight before him."

6Then Joshua the son of Nun called the priests and said to them, "Take up the ark of the covenant, and let seven priests bear seven trumpets of rams' horns before the ark of the LORD." 7And he said to the people, "Proceed, and march around the city, and let him who is armed advance before the ark of the LORD."

8So it was, when Joshua had spoken to the people, that the seven priests bearing the seven trumpets of rams' horns before the LORD advanced and blew the trumpets, and the ark of the covenant of the LORD followed them. 9The

---

5:1 [a]Following Kethib; Qere, some Hebrew manuscripts and editions, Septuagint, Syriac, Targum, and Vulgate read *they.* **5:3** [a]Hebrew *Gibeath Haaraloth* **5:6** [a]Exodus 3:8 **5:9** [a]Literally *Rolling*

armed men went before the priests who blew
the trumpets, and the rear guard came after the
ark, while *the priests* continued blowing the
trumpets. 10 Now Joshua had commanded the
people, saying, "You shall not shout or make
any noise with your voice, nor shall a word
proceed out of your mouth, until the day I say
to you, 'Shout!' Then you shall shout." 11 So he
had the ark of the LORD circle the city, going
around *it* once. Then they came into the camp
and lodged in the camp.

12 And Joshua rose early in the morning, and
the priests took up the ark of the LORD. 13 Then
seven priests bearing seven trumpets of rams'
horns before the ark of the LORD went on continually and blew with the trumpets. And the
armed men went before them. But the rear
guard came after the ark of the LORD, while
the priests continued blowing the trumpets.
14 And the second day they marched around
the city once and returned to the camp. So
they did six days.

15 But it came to pass on the seventh day
that they rose early, about the dawning of the
day, and marched around the city seven times
in the same manner. On that day only they
marched around the city seven times. 16 And
the seventh time it happened, when the
priests blew the trumpets, that Joshua said to
the people: "Shout, for the LORD has given you
the city! 17 Now the city shall be doomed by
the LORD to destruction, it and all who *are* in
it. Only Rahab the harlot shall live, she and all
who *are* with her in the house, because she
hid the messengers that we sent. 18 And you,
by all means abstain from the accursed things,
lest you become accursed when you take of
the accursed things, and make the camp of Israel a curse, and trouble it. 19 But all the silver
and gold, and vessels of bronze and iron, *are*
consecrated to the LORD; they shall come into
the treasury of the LORD."

20 So the people shouted when *the priests*
blew the trumpets. And it happened when the
people heard the sound of the trumpet, and
the people shouted with a great shout, that the
wall fell down flat. Then the people went up
into the city, every man straight before him,
and they took the city. 21 And they utterly destroyed all that *was* in the city, both man and
woman, young and old, ox and sheep and
donkey, with the edge of the sword.

22 But Joshua had said to the two men who
had spied out the country, "Go into the harlot's
house, and from there bring out the woman
and all that she has, as you swore to her."
23 And the young men who had been spies went
in and brought out Rahab, her father, her
mother, her brothers, and all that she had. So
they brought out all her relatives and left them
outside the camp of Israel. 24 But they burned
the city and all that *was* in it with fire. Only the
silver and gold, and the vessels of bronze and
iron, they put into the treasury of the house of
the LORD. 25 And Joshua spared Rahab the harlot, her father's household, and all that she
had. So she dwells in Israel to this day, because
she hid the messengers whom Joshua sent to
spy out Jericho.

26 Then Joshua charged *them* at that time,
saying, "Cursed *be* the man before the LORD
who rises up and builds this city Jericho; he
shall lay its foundation with his firstborn, and
with his youngest he shall set up its gates."

27 So the LORD was with Joshua, and his
fame spread throughout all the country.

DEFEAT AT AI

7 But the children of Israel committed a
trespass regarding the accursed things, for
Achan the son of Carmi, the son of Zabdi,[a] the
son of Zerah, of the tribe of Judah, took of the
accursed things; so the anger of the LORD
burned against the children of Israel.

2 Now Joshua sent men from Jericho to Ai,
which *is* beside Beth Aven, on the east side of
Bethel, and spoke to them, saying, "Go up and
spy out the country." So the men went up and
spied out Ai. 3 And they returned to Joshua
and said to him, "Do not let all the people go
up, but let about two or three thousand men
go up and attack Ai. Do not weary all the people there, for *the people of Ai are* few." 4 So
about three thousand men went up there from
the people, but they fled before the men of Ai.
5 And the men of Ai struck down about thirty-
six men, for they chased them *from* before the
gate as far as Shebarim, and struck them
down on the descent; therefore the hearts of
the people melted and became like water.

6 Then Joshua tore his clothes, and fell to the
earth on his face before the ark of the LORD
until evening, he and the elders of Israel; and
they put dust on their heads. 7 And Joshua
said, "Alas, Lord GOD, why have You brought
this people over the Jordan at all—to deliver

7:1 [a]Called *Zimri* in 1 Chronicles 2:6

us into the hand of the Amorites, to destroy
us? Oh, that we had been content, and dwelt
on the other side of the Jordan! 8O Lord, what
shall I say when Israel turns its back before its
enemies? 9For the Canaanites and all the inhabitants of the land will hear *it*, and surround us, and cut off our name from the earth.
Then what will You do for Your great name?"

THE SIN OF ACHAN

10So the LORD said to Joshua: "Get up! Why
do you lie thus on your face? 11Israel has
sinned, and they have also transgressed My
covenant which I commanded them. For they
have even taken some of the accursed things,
and have both stolen and deceived; and they
have also put *it* among their own stuff.
12Therefore the children of Israel could not
stand before their enemies, *but* turned *their*
backs before their enemies, because they have
become doomed to destruction. Neither will I
be with you anymore, unless you destroy the
accursed from among you. 13Get up, sanctify
the people, and say, 'Sanctify yourselves for
tomorrow, because thus says the LORD God of
Israel: "*There is* an accursed thing in your
midst, O Israel; you cannot stand before your
enemies until you take away the accursed
thing from among you." 14In the morning
therefore you shall be brought according to
your tribes. And it shall be *that* the tribe
which the LORD takes shall come according to
families; and the family which the LORD takes
shall come by households; and the household
which the LORD takes shall come man by man.
15Then it shall be *that* he who is taken with
the accursed thing shall be burned with fire,
he and all that he has, because he has transgressed the covenant of the LORD, and because
he has done a disgraceful thing in Israel.' "

16So Joshua rose early in the morning and
brought Israel by their tribes, and the tribe
of Judah was taken. 17He brought the clan
of Judah, and he took the family of the
Zarhites; and he brought the family of the
Zarhites man by man, and Zabdi was taken.
18Then he brought his household man by
man, and Achan the son of Carmi, the son of
Zabdi, the son of Zerah, of the tribe of Judah,
was taken.

19Now Joshua said to Achan, "My son, I beg
you, give glory to the LORD God of Israel, and
make confession to Him, and tell me now
what you have done; do not hide *it* from me."

20And Achan answered Joshua and said,
"Indeed I have sinned against the LORD God of
Israel, and this is what I have done: 21When I
saw among the spoils a beautiful Babylonian
garment, two hundred shekels of silver, and a
wedge of gold weighing fifty shekels, I coveted
them and took them. And there they are, hidden in the earth in the midst of my tent, with
the silver under it."

22So Joshua sent messengers, and they ran
to the tent; and there it was, hidden in his
tent, with the silver under it. 23And they took
them from the midst of the tent, brought them
to Joshua and to all the children of Israel, and
laid them out before the LORD. 24Then Joshua,
and all Israel with him, took Achan the son of
Zerah, the silver, the garment, the wedge of
gold, his sons, his daughters, his oxen, his
donkeys, his sheep, his tent, and all that he
had, and they brought them to the Valley of
Achor. 25And Joshua said, "Why have you
troubled us? The LORD will trouble you this
day." So all Israel stoned him with stones; and
they burned them with fire after they had
stoned them with stones.

26Then they raised over him a great heap of
stones, still there to this day. So the LORD
turned from the fierceness of His anger. There-

SOUL NOTE

It Hurts *(7:22–25)* Achan sinned by taking some of the plunder from Jericho for himself, an act that had been forbidden (6:19). As a result, the Israelites lost the next battle. When Achan's sin was discovered, he and his entire family paid the ultimate price. Sin always hurts the sinner and others. No one sins in a vacuum; sins always have consequences. Perhaps we would be more willing to turn away from sin if we could see the consequences that will affect not only us, but those dearest to us.

Topic: Sin

fore the name of that place has been called the
Valley of Achor[a] to this day.

THE FALL OF AI

8 Now the LORD said to Joshua: "Do not be
afraid, nor be dismayed; take all the
people of war with you, and arise, go up to Ai.
See, I have given into your hand the king of
Ai, his people, his city, and his land. 2And you
shall do to Ai and its king as you did to Jericho
and its king. Only its spoil and its cattle you
shall take as booty for yourselves. Lay an ambush for the city behind it."

3So Joshua arose, and all the people of war,
to go up against Ai; and Joshua chose thirty
thousand mighty men of valor and sent them
away by night. 4And he commanded them,
saying: "Behold, you shall lie in ambush
against the city, behind the city. Do not go
very far from the city, but all of you be ready.
5Then I and all the people who *are* with me
will approach the city; and it will come about,
when they come out against us as at the first,
that we shall flee before them. 6For they will
come out after us till we have drawn them
from the city, for they will say, '*They are* fleeing before us as at the first.' Therefore we will
flee before them. 7Then you shall rise from the
ambush and seize the city, for the LORD your
God will deliver it into your hand. 8And it will
be, when you have taken the city, *that* you
shall set the city on fire. According to the commandment of the LORD you shall do. See, I
have commanded you."

9Joshua therefore sent them out; and they
went to lie in ambush, and stayed between
Bethel and Ai, on the west side of Ai; but
Joshua lodged that night among the people.
10Then Joshua rose up early in the morning
and mustered the people, and went up, he and
the elders of Israel, before the people to Ai.
11And all the people of war who *were* with him
went up and drew near; and they came before
the city and camped on the north side of Ai.
Now a valley *lay* between them and Ai. 12So
he took about five thousand men and set them
in ambush between Bethel and Ai, on the west
side of the city. 13And when they had set the
people, all the army that *was* on the north of
the city, and its rear guard on the west of the
city, Joshua went that night into the midst of
the valley.

14Now it happened, when the king of Ai
saw *it,* that the men of the city hurried and rose
early and went out against Israel to battle, he
and all his people, at an appointed place before the plain. But he did not know that *there
was* an ambush against him behind the city.
15And Joshua and all Israel made as if they
were beaten before them, and fled by the way
of the wilderness. 16So all the people who
were in Ai were called together to pursue them.
And they pursued Joshua and were drawn
away from the city. 17There was not a man left
in Ai or Bethel who did not go out after Israel.
So they left the city open and pursued Israel.

18Then the LORD said to Joshua, "Stretch out
the spear that *is* in your hand toward Ai, for I
will give it into your hand." And Joshua
stretched out the spear that *was* in his hand
toward the city. 19So *those in* ambush arose
quickly out of their place; they ran as soon as
he had stretched out his hand, and they entered the city and took it, and hurried to set
the city on fire. 20And when the men of Ai
looked behind them, they saw, and behold,
the smoke of the city ascended to heaven. So
they had no power to flee this way or that
way, and the people who had fled to the wilderness turned back on the pursuers.

21Now when Joshua and all Israel saw that
the ambush had taken the city and that the
smoke of the city ascended, they turned back
and struck down the men of Ai. 22Then the
others came out of the city against them; so
they were *caught* in the midst of Israel, some
on this side and some on that side. And they
struck them down, so that they let none of
them remain or escape. 23But the king of Ai
they took alive, and brought him to Joshua.

24And it came to pass when Israel had made
an end of slaying all the inhabitants of Ai in the
field, in the wilderness where they pursued
them, and when they all had fallen by the edge
of the sword until they were consumed, that all
the Israelites returned to Ai and struck it with
the edge of the sword. 25So it was *that* all who
fell that day, both men and women, *were*
twelve thousand—all the people of Ai. 26For
Joshua did not draw back his hand, with which
he stretched out the spear, until he had utterly
destroyed all the inhabitants of Ai. 27Only the
livestock and the spoil of that city Israel took
as booty for themselves, according to the word
of the LORD which He had commanded Joshua.
28So Joshua burned Ai and made it a heap

7:26 [a]Literally *Trouble*

forever, a desolation to this day. [29]And the king of Ai he hanged on a tree until evening. And as soon as the sun was down, Joshua commanded that they should take his corpse down from the tree, cast it at the entrance of the gate of the city, and raise over it a great heap of stones *that remains* to this day.

Joshua Renews the Covenant

[30]Now Joshua built an altar to the LORD God of Israel in Mount Ebal, [31]as Moses the servant of the LORD had commanded the children of Israel, as it is written in the Book of the Law of Moses: "an altar of whole stones over which no man has wielded an iron *tool*."[a] And they offered on it burnt offerings to the LORD, and sacrificed peace offerings. [32]And there, in the presence of the children of Israel, he wrote on the stones a copy of the law of Moses, which he had written. [33]Then all Israel, with their elders and officers and judges, stood on either side of the ark before the priests, the Levites, who bore the ark of the covenant of the LORD, the stranger as well as he who was born among them. Half of them *were* in front of Mount Gerizim and half of them in front of Mount Ebal, as Moses the servant of the LORD had commanded before, that they should bless the people of Israel. [34]And afterward he read all the words of the law, the blessings and the cursings, according to all that is written in the Book of the Law. [35]There was not a word of all that Moses had commanded which Joshua did not read before all the assembly of Israel, with the women, the little ones, and the strangers who were living among them.

The Treaty with the Gibeonites

9 And it came to pass when all the kings who *were* on this side of the Jordan, in the hills and in the lowland and in all the coasts of the Great Sea toward Lebanon—the Hittite, the Amorite, the Canaanite, the Perizzite, the Hivite, and the Jebusite—heard *about it,* [2]that they gathered together to fight with Joshua and Israel with one accord.

[3]But when the inhabitants of Gibeon heard what Joshua had done to Jericho and Ai, [4]they worked craftily, and went and pretended to be ambassadors. And they took old sacks on their donkeys, old wineskins torn and mended, [5]old and patched sandals on their feet, and old garments on themselves; and all the bread of their provision was dry *and* moldy. [6]And they went to Joshua, to the camp at Gilgal, and said to him and to the men of Israel, "We have come from a far country; now therefore, make a covenant with us."

[7]Then the men of Israel said to the Hivites, "Perhaps you dwell among us; so how can we make a covenant with you?"

[8]But they said to Joshua, "We *are* your servants."

And Joshua said to them, "Who *are* you, and where do you come from?"

[9]So they said to him: "From a very far country your servants have come, because of the name of the LORD your God; for we have heard of His fame, and all that He did in Egypt, [10]and all that He did to the two kings of the Amorites who *were* beyond the Jordan—to Sihon king of Heshbon, and Og king of Bashan, who was at Ashtaroth. [11]Therefore our elders and all the inhabitants of our country spoke to us, saying, 'Take provisions with you for the journey, and go to meet them, and say to them, "We *are* your servants; now therefore, make a covenant with us." ' [12]This bread of ours we took hot *for* our provision from our houses on the day we departed to come to you. But now

8:31 [a]Deuteronomy 27:5, 6

SOUL NOTE

Don't Forget to Pray *(9:14, 15)* The leaders of Israel did not pray and "ask counsel of the LORD" before they made their agreement with the Gibeonites. If they had prayed, God would have revealed the Gibeonites' deception. Then Israel would not have been guilty of disobeying God's command (Ex. 23:32). The Israelites had been victorious over many cities, but that success may have caused them to become lax in seeking guidance from God. When life is going well and we think we have everything under control, we must not forget to pray, continually seeking God's guidance.
Topic: Prayer

look, it is dry and moldy. 13And these wineskins which we filled *were* new, and see, they are torn; and these our garments and our sandals have become old because of the very long journey."

14Then the men of Israel took some of their provisions; but they did not ask counsel of the LORD. 15So Joshua made peace with them, and made a covenant with them to let them live; and the rulers of the congregation swore to them.

16And it happened at the end of three days, after they had made a covenant with them, that they heard that they *were* their neighbors who dwelt near them. 17Then the children of Israel journeyed and came to their cities on the third day. Now their cities *were* Gibeon, Chephirah, Beeroth, and Kirjath Jearim. 18But the children of Israel did not attack them, because the rulers of the congregation had sworn to them by the LORD God of Israel. And all the congregation complained against the rulers.

19Then all the rulers said to all the congregation, "We have sworn to them by the LORD God of Israel; now therefore, we may not touch them. 20This we will do to them: We will let them live, lest wrath be upon us because of the oath which we swore to them." 21And the rulers said to them, "Let them live, but let them be woodcutters and water carriers for all the congregation, as the rulers had promised them."

22Then Joshua called for them, and he spoke to them, saying, "Why have you deceived us, saying, 'We *are* very far from you,' when you dwell near us? 23Now therefore, you *are* cursed, and none of you shall be freed from being slaves—woodcutters and water carriers for the house of my God."

24So they answered Joshua and said, "Because your servants were clearly told that the LORD your God commanded His servant Moses to give you all the land, and to destroy all the inhabitants of the land from before you; therefore we were very much afraid for our lives because of you, and have done this thing. 25And now, here we are, in your hands; do with us as it seems good and right to do to us." 26So he did to them, and delivered them out of the hand of the children of Israel, so that they did not kill them. 27And that day Joshua made them woodcutters and water carriers for the congregation and for the altar of the LORD, in the place which He would choose, even to this day.

The Sun Stands Still

10 Now it came to pass when Adoni-Zedek king of Jerusalem heard how Joshua had taken Ai and had utterly destroyed it—as he had done to Jericho and its king, so he had done to Ai and its king—and how the inhabitants of Gibeon had made peace with Israel and were among them, 2that they feared greatly, because Gibeon *was* a great city, like one of the royal cities, and because it *was* greater than Ai, and all its men *were* mighty. 3Therefore Adoni-Zedek king of Jerusalem sent to Hoham king of Hebron, Piram king of Jarmuth, Japhia king of Lachish, and Debir king of Eglon, saying, 4"Come up to me and help me, that we may attack Gibeon, for it has made peace with Joshua and with the children of Israel." 5Therefore the five kings of the Amorites, the king of Jerusalem, the king of Hebron, the king of Jarmuth, the king of Lachish, *and* the king of Eglon, gathered together and went up, they and all their armies, and camped before Gibeon and made war against it.

6And the men of Gibeon sent to Joshua at the camp at Gilgal, saying, "Do not forsake your servants; come up to us quickly, save us and help us, for all the kings of the Amorites who dwell in the mountains have gathered together against us."

7So Joshua ascended from Gilgal, he and all the people of war with him, and all the mighty men of valor. 8And the LORD said to Joshua, "Do not fear them, for I have delivered them into your hand; not a man of them shall stand before you." 9Joshua therefore came upon them suddenly, having marched all night from Gilgal. 10So the LORD routed them before Israel, killed them with a great slaughter at Gibeon, chased them along the road that goes to Beth Horon, and struck them down as far as Azekah and Makkedah. 11And it happened, as they fled before Israel *and* were on the descent of Beth Horon, that the LORD cast down large hailstones from heaven on them as far as Azekah, and they died. *There were* more who died from the hailstones than the children of Israel killed with the sword.

12Then Joshua spoke to the LORD in the day when the LORD delivered up the Amorites before the children of Israel, and he said in the sight of Israel:

"Sun, stand still over Gibeon;
And Moon, in the Valley of Aijalon."
13 So the sun stood still,
And the moon stopped,
Till the people had revenge
Upon their enemies.

Is this not written in the Book of Jasher? So
the sun stood still in the midst of heaven, and
did not hasten to go *down* for about a whole
day. 14And there has been no day like that, before it or after it, that the LORD heeded the
voice of a man; for the LORD fought for Israel.
15Then Joshua returned, and all Israel with
him, to the camp at Gilgal.

THE AMORITE KINGS EXECUTED

16But these five kings had fled and hidden
themselves in a cave at Makkedah. 17And
it was told Joshua, saying, "The five kings
have been found hidden in the cave at Makkedah."
18So Joshua said, "Roll large stones against
the mouth of the cave, and set men by it to
guard them. 19And do not stay *there* yourselves, *but* pursue your enemies, and attack
their rear *guard*. Do not allow them to enter
their cities, for the LORD your God has delivered them into your hand." 20Then it happened, while Joshua and the children of Israel
made an end of slaying them with a very great
slaughter, till they had finished, that those
who escaped entered fortified cities. 21And all
the people returned to the camp, to Joshua at
Makkedah, in peace.
No one moved his tongue against any of the
children of Israel.
22Then Joshua said, "Open the mouth of the
cave, and bring out those five kings to me from
the cave." 23And they did so, and brought out
those five kings to him from the cave: the king
of Jerusalem, the king of Hebron, the king of
Jarmuth, the king of Lachish, *and* the king of
Eglon.
24So it was, when they brought out those
kings to Joshua, that Joshua called for all the
men of Israel, and said to the captains of the
men of war who went with him, "Come near,
put your feet on the necks of these kings."
And they drew near and put their feet on their
necks. 25Then Joshua said to them, "Do not be
afraid, nor be dismayed; be strong and of good
courage, for thus the LORD will do to all your
enemies against whom you fight." 26And afterward Joshua struck them and killed them,
and hanged them on five trees; and they were
hanging on the trees until evening. 27So it was
at the time of the going down of the sun *that*
Joshua commanded, and they took them
down from the trees, cast them into the cave
where they had been hidden, and laid large
stones against the cave's mouth, *which remain* until this very day.

CONQUEST OF THE SOUTHLAND

28On that day Joshua took Makkedah, and
struck it and its king with the edge of the
sword. He utterly destroyed them[a]—all the
people who *were* in it. He let none remain. He
also did to the king of Makkedah as he had
done to the king of Jericho.
29Then Joshua passed from Makkedah, and
all Israel with him, to Libnah; and they fought
against Libnah. 30And the LORD also delivered
it and its king into the hand of Israel; he struck
it and all the people who *were* in it with the
edge of the sword. He let none remain in it,
but did to its king as he had done to the king
of Jericho.
31Then Joshua passed from Libnah, and all
Israel with him, to Lachish; and they encamped against it and fought against it. 32And
the LORD delivered Lachish into the hand of Israel, who took it on the second day, and
struck it and all the people who *were* in it with
the edge of the sword, according to all that he
had done to Libnah. 33Then Horam king of
Gezer came up to help Lachish; and Joshua
struck him and his people, until he left him
none remaining.
34From Lachish Joshua passed to Eglon, and
all Israel with him; and they encamped
against it and fought against it. 35They took it
on that day and struck it with the edge of the
sword; all the people who *were* in it he utterly
destroyed that day, according to all that he
had done to Lachish.
36So Joshua went up from Eglon, and all Israel with him, to Hebron; and they fought
against it. 37And they took it and struck it with
the edge of the sword—its king, all its cities,
and all the people who *were* in it; he left none
remaining, according to all that he had done

10:28 [a]Following Masoretic Text and most authorities; many Hebrew manuscripts, some manuscripts of the Septuagint, and some manuscripts of the Targum read *it*.

to Eglon, but utterly destroyed it and all the people who *were* in it.

[38]Then Joshua returned, and all Israel with him, to Debir; and they fought against it. [39]And he took it and its king and all its cities; they struck them with the edge of the sword and utterly destroyed all the people who *were* in it. He left none remaining; as he had done to Hebron, so he did to Debir and its king, as he had done also to Libnah and its king.

[40]So Joshua conquered all the land: the mountain country and the South[a] and the lowland and the wilderness slopes, and all their kings; he left none remaining, but utterly destroyed all that breathed, as the LORD God of Israel had commanded. [41]And Joshua conquered them from Kadesh Barnea as far as Gaza, and all the country of Goshen, even as far as Gibeon. [42]All these kings and their land Joshua took at one time, because the LORD God of Israel fought for Israel. [43]Then Joshua returned, and all Israel with him, to the camp at Gilgal.

THE NORTHERN CONQUEST

11 And it came to pass, when Jabin king of Hazor heard *these things,* that he sent to Jobab king of Madon, to the king of Shimron, to the king of Achshaph, [2]and to the kings who *were* from the north, in the mountains, in the plain south of Chinneroth, in the lowland, and in the heights of Dor on the west, [3]to the Canaanites in the east and in the west, the Amorite, the Hittite, the Perizzite, the Jebusite in the mountains, and the Hivite below Hermon in the land of Mizpah. [4]So they went out, they and all their armies with them, *as* many people *as* the sand that *is* on the seashore in multitude, with very many horses and chariots. [5]And when all these kings had met together, they came and camped together at the waters of Merom to fight against Israel.

[6]But the LORD said to Joshua, "Do not be afraid because of them, for tomorrow about this time I will deliver all of them slain before Israel. You shall hamstring their horses and burn their chariots with fire." [7]So Joshua and all the people of war with him came against them suddenly by the waters of Merom, and they attacked them. [8]And the LORD delivered them into the hand of Israel, who defeated them and chased them to Greater Sidon, to the Brook Misrephoth,[a] and to the Valley of Mizpah eastward; they attacked them until they left none of them remaining. [9]So Joshua did to them as the LORD had told him: he hamstrung their horses and burned their chariots with fire.

[10]Joshua turned back at that time and took Hazor, and struck its king with the sword; for Hazor was formerly the head of all those kingdoms. [11]And they struck all the people who *were* in it with the edge of the sword, utterly destroying *them.* There was none left breathing. Then he burned Hazor with fire.

[12]So all the cities of those kings, and all their kings, Joshua took and struck with the edge of the sword. He utterly destroyed them, as Moses the servant of the LORD had commanded. [13]But *as for* the cities that stood on their mounds,[a] Israel burned none of them, except Hazor only, *which* Joshua burned. [14]And all the spoil of these cities and the livestock, the children of Israel took as booty for themselves; but they struck every man with the edge of the sword until they had destroyed them, and they left none breathing. [15]As the LORD had commanded Moses his servant, so Moses commanded Joshua, and so Joshua did. He left nothing undone of all that the LORD had commanded Moses.

SUMMARY OF JOSHUA'S CONQUESTS

[16]Thus Joshua took all this land: the mountain country, all the South, all the land of Goshen, the lowland, and the Jordan plain[a]—the mountains of Israel and its lowlands, [17]from Mount Halak and the ascent to Seir, even as far as Baal Gad in the Valley of Lebanon below Mount Hermon. He captured all their kings, and struck them down and killed them. [18]Joshua made war a long time with all those kings. [19]There was not a city that made peace with the children of Israel, except the Hivites, the inhabitants of Gibeon. All *the others* they took in battle. [20]For it was of the LORD to harden their hearts, that they should come against Israel in battle, that He might utterly destroy them, *and* that they might receive no mercy, but that He might destroy them, as the LORD had commanded Moses.

[21]And at that time Joshua came and cut off the Anakim from the mountains: from Hebron,

---

10:40 [a]Hebrew *Negev,* and so throughout this book **11:8** [a]Hebrew *Misrephoth Maim*
11:13 [a]Hebrew *tel,* a heap of successive city ruins
11:16 [a]Hebrew *arabah*

from Debir, from Anab, from all the mountains of Judah, and from all the mountains of Israel; Joshua utterly destroyed them with their cities. 22None of the Anakim were left in the land of the children of Israel; they remained only in Gaza, in Gath, and in Ashdod.

23So Joshua took the whole land, according to all that the LORD had said to Moses; and Joshua gave it as an inheritance to Israel according to their divisions by their tribes. Then the land rested from war.

THE KINGS CONQUERED BY MOSES

12 These *are* the kings of the land whom the children of Israel defeated, and whose land they possessed on the other side of the Jordan toward the rising of the sun, from the River Arnon to Mount Hermon, and all the eastern Jordan plain: 2*One king was* Sihon king of the Amorites, who dwelt in Heshbon *and* ruled half of Gilead, from Aroer, which is on the bank of the River Arnon, from the middle of that river, even as far as the River Jabbok, *which is* the border of the Ammonites, 3and the eastern Jordan plain from the Sea of Chinneroth as far as the Sea of the Arabah (the Salt Sea), the road to Beth Jeshimoth, and southward below the slopes of Pisgah. 4*The other king was* Og king of Bashan and his territory, *who was* of the remnant of the giants, who dwelt at Ashtaroth and at Edrei, 5and reigned over Mount Hermon, over Salcah, over all Bashan, as far as the border of the Geshurites and the Maachathites, and over half of Gilead *to* the border of Sihon king of Heshbon.

6These Moses the servant of the LORD and the children of Israel had conquered; and Moses the servant of the LORD had given it *as* a possession to the Reubenites, the Gadites, and half the tribe of Manasseh.

THE KINGS CONQUERED BY JOSHUA

7And these *are* the kings of the country which Joshua and the children of Israel conquered on this side of the Jordan, on the west, from Baal Gad in the Valley of Lebanon as far as Mount Halak and the ascent to Seir, which Joshua gave to the tribes of Israel *as* a possession according to their divisions, 8in the mountain country, in the lowlands, in the *Jordan* plain, in the slopes, in the wilderness, and in the South—the Hittites, the Amorites, the Canaanites, the Perizzites, the Hivites, and the Jebusites: 9the king of Jericho, one; the king of Ai, which *is* beside Bethel, one; 10the king of Jerusalem, one; the king of Hebron, one; 11the king of Jarmuth, one; the king of Lachish, one; 12the king of Eglon, one; the king of Gezer, one; 13the king of Debir, one; the king of Geder, one; 14the king of Hormah, one; the king of Arad, one; 15the king of Libnah, one; the king of Adullam, one; 16the king of Makkedah, one; the king of Bethel, one; 17the king of Tappuah, one; the king of Hepher, one; 18the king of Aphek, one; the king of Lasharon, one; 19the king of Madon, one; the king of Hazor, one; 20the king of Shimron Meron, one; the king of Achshaph, one; 21the king of Taanach, one; the king of Megiddo, one; 22the king of Kedesh, one; the king of Jokneam in Carmel, one; 23the king of Dor in the heights of Dor, one; the king of the people of Gilgal, one; 24the king of Tirzah, one—all the kings, thirty-one.

REMAINING LAND TO BE CONQUERED

13 Now Joshua was old, advanced in years. And the LORD said to him: "You are old, advanced in years, and there remains very much land yet to be possessed. 2This is the land that yet remains: all the territory of the Philistines and all *that of* the Geshurites, 3from Sihor, which *is* east of Egypt, as far as the border of Ekron northward (*which* is counted as Canaanite); the five lords of the Philistines—the Gazites, the Ashdodites, the Ashkelonites, the Gittites, and the Ekronites; also the Avites; 4from the south, all the land of the Canaanites, and Mearah that belongs to the Sidonians as far as Aphek, to the border of the Amorites; 5the land of the Gebalites,[a] and all Lebanon, toward the sunrise, from Baal Gad below Mount Hermon as far as the entrance to Hamath; 6all the inhabitants of the mountains from Lebanon as far as the Brook Misrephoth,[a] *and* all the Sidonians—them I will drive out from before the children of Israel; only divide it by lot to Israel as an inheritance, as I have commanded you. 7Now therefore, divide this land as an inheritance to the nine tribes and half the tribe of Manasseh."

THE LAND DIVIDED EAST OF THE JORDAN

8With the other half-tribe the Reubenites and the Gadites received their inheritance,

---

13:5 [a]Or *Giblites* **13:6** [a]Hebrew *Misrephoth Maim*

which Moses had given them, beyond the Jordan eastward, as Moses the servant of the LORD had given them: [9]from Aroer which *is* on the bank of the River Arnon, and the town that *is* in the midst of the ravine, and all the plain of Medeba as far as Dibon; [10]all the cities of Sihon king of the Amorites, who reigned in Heshbon, as far as the border of the children of Ammon; [11]Gilead, and the border of the Geshurites and Maachathites, all Mount Hermon, and all Bashan as far as Salcah; [12]all the kingdom of Og in Bashan, who reigned in Ashtaroth and Edrei, who remained of the remnant of the giants; for Moses had defeated and cast out these.

[13]Nevertheless the children of Israel did not drive out the Geshurites or the Maachathites, but the Geshurites and the Maachathites dwell among the Israelites until this day.

[14]Only to the tribe of Levi he had given no inheritance; the sacrifices of the LORD God of Israel made by fire *are* their inheritance, as He said to them.

The Land of Reuben

[15]And Moses had given to the tribe of the children of Reuben *an inheritance* according to their families. [16]Their territory was from Aroer, which *is* on the bank of the River Arnon, and the city that *is* in the midst of the ravine, and all the plain by Medeba; [17]Heshbon and all its cities that *are* in the plain: Dibon, Bamoth Baal, Beth Baal Meon, [18]Jahaza, Kedemoth, Mephaath, [19]Kirjathaim, Sibmah, Zereth Shahar on the mountain of the valley, [20]Beth Peor, the slopes of Pisgah, and Beth Jeshimoth—[21]all the cities of the plain and all the kingdom of Sihon king of the Amorites, who reigned in Heshbon, whom Moses had struck with the princes of Midian: Evi, Rekem, Zur, Hur, and Reba, who *were* princes of Sihon dwelling in the country. [22]The children of Israel also killed with the sword Balaam the son of Beor, the soothsayer, among those who were killed by them. [23]And the border of the children of Reuben was the bank of the Jordan. This *was* the inheritance of the children of Reuben according to their families, the cities and their villages.

The Land of Gad

[24]Moses also had given *an inheritance* to the tribe of Gad, to the children of Gad according to their families. [25]Their territory was Jazer, and all the cities of Gilead, and half the land of the Ammonites as far as Aroer, which *is* before Rabbah, [26]and from Heshbon to Ramath Mizpah and Betonim, and from Mahanaim to the border of Debir, [27]and in the valley Beth Haram, Beth Nimrah, Succoth, and Zaphon, the rest of the kingdom of Sihon king of Heshbon, with the Jordan as *its* border, as far as the edge of the Sea of Chinnereth, on the other side of the Jordan eastward. [28]This *is* the inheritance of the children of Gad according to their families, the cities and their villages.

Half the Tribe of Manasseh (East)

[29]Moses also had given *an inheritance* to half the tribe of Manasseh; it was for half the tribe of the children of Manasseh according to their families: [30]Their territory was from Mahanaim, all Bashan, all the kingdom of Og king of Bashan, and all the towns of Jair which are in Bashan, sixty cities; [31]half of Gilead, and Ashtaroth and Edrei, cities of the kingdom of Og in Bashan, *were* for the children of Machir the son of Manasseh, for half of the children of Machir according to their families.

[32]These *are the areas* which Moses had distributed as an inheritance in the plains of Moab on the other side of the Jordan, by Jericho eastward. [33]But to the tribe of Levi Moses had given no inheritance; the LORD God of Israel *was* their inheritance, as He had said to them.

The Land Divided West of the Jordan

14 These *are the areas* which the children of Israel inherited in the land of Canaan, which Eleazar the priest, Joshua the son of Nun, and the heads of the fathers of the tribes of the children of Israel distributed as an inheritance to them. [2]Their inheritance *was* by lot, as the LORD had commanded by the hand of Moses, for the nine tribes and the half-tribe. [3]For Moses had given the inheritance of the two tribes and the half-tribe on the other side of the Jordan; but to the Levites he had given no inheritance among them. [4]For the children of Joseph were two tribes: Manasseh and Ephraim. And they gave no part to the Levites in the land, except cities to dwell *in,* with their common-lands for their livestock and their property. [5]As the LORD had commanded Moses, so the children of Israel did; and they divided the land.

Aging/ Elderly

GRACEFULLY GROWING OLDER

DAVID SEAMANDS

(Joshua 14)

Growing older is certainly no easy journey. The gray (or disappearing) hair, the new aches and pains, the need to slow down—all of these are natural, but unwanted, signs of aging. Western culture idolizes youthfulness and is constantly trying to reverse, or at least slow down, the aging process.

Life is often pictured as a bell-shaped journey. Beginning with birth, people climb through infancy and toward adulthood. It's all an uphill climb until sometime around "midlife" when the slope begins its descent, and people are "over the hill." At that point, many want to recapture those "upward" years, trying to look young, feel young, and act young. But nothing can stop the aging process and, too often, people become discontented and depressed.

With all the bad news, it is encouraging to discover that God sees aging very differently than we do. The Bible says that God is not someone we must wait to meet until after we grow old and reach the *end* of life. No, He had plans for us even before we *began* (Eph. 1:4), and will be with us at *every stage* of life (Deut. 33:25, 27). In this God's-eye view, aging is merely the final phase of an upward climb from earth to heaven.

With this encouragement, consider what the Bible teaches about how we should live as we grow older.

STAY HEALTHY

Like all people of all ages, older people should take care of the physical body (1 Cor. 3:16, 17), mind (Phil. 4:8), and spirit (Rom. 12:1, 2). Taking proper care of the body through diet and regular physical activity, maintaining social relationships, and finding continuing meaning and purpose in life are vital contributions to healthy aging. The best medical research done by The MacArthur Foundation Consortium on Successful Aging confirms what the Bible says: The habits people form and the choices they make greatly influence how they fare in old age. Someone has said, "People don't really grow old, rather they get old because they stop growing." When people maintain the central purpose of life itself—to glorify God by loving Him and others—they can maintain their health whatever their age.

KEEP SERVING

The prayer of all people should be for God to "teach us to number our days, that we may gain a heart of wisdom" (Ps. 90:12). As people age, they are a resource of wisdom and learning gained over many years. "Wisdom is with aged men, and with length of days, understanding" (Job 12:12). Younger Christians of new generations need counselors, mentors, and encouragers. When the Levites had completed their years of service in the tabernacle, their experience and devotion was not lost to retirement at the age of fifty. Instead they were called to give assistance to the younger workers (Num. 8:26).

We should be realistic and understand that the wisdom gained by age will result in less *doing* and more *being*. Despite physical limitations and lifestyle changes, we always have the opportunity for a rich prayer life. Throughout their lives, people can be "not lagging in diligence, fervent in spirit, serving the Lord; rejoicing in hope, patient in tribulation, continuing steadfastly in prayer; distributing to the needs of the saints, given to hospitality" (Rom. 12:11–13).

God promised Abraham that he would live to be "a good old age" (Gen. 15:15). The psalmist wrote, "With long life I will satisfy him, and show him My salvation" (Ps. 91:16). Solomon, in his wise proverbs, added, "The silver-haired head is a crown of glory, if it is found in the way of righteousness. . . . The splendor of old men is their gray head" (Prov. 16:31; 20:29). The elderly have a special place in God's plan. Far from being abandoned and useless, they have a lifetime of experience and wisdom to share with others.

BE HOPEFUL

The Bible is very realistic about the natural losses, special needs, and difficulties people may experience as they grow older. Psalm 90:10 sounds like the preface to a Medicare document: "The days of our lives are seventy years; and if by reason of strength they are eighty years, yet their boast is only labor and sorrow; for it is soon cut off, and we fly away." Or consider the description of old age in Ecclesiastes 12:1–7.

Well-known people in Scripture illustrate the pains, losses, and afflictions of the elderly. Isaac lost his eyesight (Gen. 27:1); David could not stay warm, and his failing strength required special care (1 Kin. 1:1–4). Paul referred to himself as "Paul, the aged" (Philem. 9). In 2 Timothy 4:9–21, Paul alludes to both the physical and emotional pains of old age—feelings of abandonment and loneliness, being let down by fellow workers, and saying goodbye to friends he might not ever see again in this world.

As difficult and challenging as the physical life becomes, sufficient strength is promised: "My grace is sufficient for you, for My strength is made perfect in weakness" (2 Cor. 12:9). With the prospect of the end of life on earth there is the promise of eternal life: "We do not lose heart. Even though our outward man is perishing, yet the inward man is being renewed day by day. . . . We do not look at the things which are seen, but at the things which are not seen. For the things which are seen are temporary, but the things which are not seen are eternal" (2 Cor. 4:16, 18).

FURTHER MEDITATION:

Other passages to study about the issue of aging/elderly include:

- ➢ Ruth 4:15
- ➢ Psalms 37:25; 71:9, 18; 91:14–16; 92:12–15
- ➢ Proverbs 17:6; 23:22
- ➢ Lamentations 3:22, 23
- ➢ Luke 2:25–38
- ➢ 2 Corinthians 4:7–18
- ➢ Titus 2:1–5

To Learn More: Turn to the key passage note on aging/elderly at Psalm 71:9 on page 737. See also the personality profile of Caleb on page 284.

CALEB INHERITS HEBRON

[6]Then the children of Judah came to Joshua
in Gilgal. And Caleb the son of Jephunneh the
Kenizzite said to him: "You know the word
which the LORD said to Moses the man of God
concerning you and me in Kadesh Barnea. [7]I
was forty years old when Moses the servant of
the LORD sent me from Kadesh Barnea to spy
out the land, and I brought back word to him
as *it was* in my heart. [8]Nevertheless my brethren who went up with me made the heart of
the people melt, but I wholly followed the
LORD my God. [9]So Moses swore on that day,
saying, 'Surely the land where your foot has
trodden shall be your inheritance and your
children's forever, because you have wholly
followed the LORD my God.' [10]And now, behold, the LORD has kept me alive, as He said,
these forty-five years, ever since the LORD
spoke this word to Moses while Israel wandered in the wilderness; and now, here I am
this day, eighty-five years old. [11]As yet I *am as*
strong this day as on the day that Moses sent
me; just as my strength *was* then, so now *is*
my strength for war, both for going out and for
coming in. [12]Now therefore, give me this
mountain of which the LORD spoke in that
day; for you heard in that day how the
Anakim *were* there, and *that* the cities *were*
great *and* fortified. It may be that the LORD
will be with me, and I shall be able to drive
them out as the LORD said."

[13]And Joshua blessed him, and gave Hebron
to Caleb the son of Jephunneh as an inheritance. [14]Hebron therefore became the inheritance of Caleb the son of Jephunneh the
Kenizzite to this day, because he wholly followed the LORD God of Israel. [15]And the name
of Hebron formerly was Kirjath Arba (*Arba*
was the greatest man among the Anakim).

Then the land had rest from war.

THE LAND OF JUDAH

15 So *this* was the lot of the tribe of the
children of Judah according to their
families:

The border of Edom at the Wilderness of
Zin southward *was* the extreme southern
boundary. [2]And their southern border began
at the shore of the Salt Sea, from the bay that

PERSONALITY PROFILE

Aging/ Elderly

THE GRACEFUL AGING OF CALEB

(JOSHUA 14:6–15)

Caleb was a faithful warrior in the mold of Moses and Joshua, his contemporaries. Caleb and Joshua outlived the generation of Jews who escaped Egypt to enter and possess the Promised Land. Robust at the age of 85, Caleb remained an active and strong leader. He participated in the conquest of the Promised Land. Caleb received the special privilege of claiming the lands he and his progeny would possess. His actions always flowed from a bold and obedient faith.

The Bible identifies a key to Caleb's lifelong health, vitality, and special favor with God. He "wholly followed the LORD" (Josh. 14:8). His career probably started with a significant role in the exodus from Egypt. Later, Caleb and Joshua gave the positive minority report among the twelve spies Moses had sent to scout the land. The other ten expressed fear and voted to turn back. Caleb and Joshua believed that God would deliver the land into their hands in spite of scary giants and fortified cities. Caleb and Joshua were outvoted, but when the rest of their generation died, because of their unbelief, in the wilderness, Caleb and Joshua were blessed by God to live in the Promised Land.

Caleb remembered the promise of God, spoken through Moses, that his inheritance would be grand and that he would be blessed. He is a wonderful model for the proposition that a faithful life—one that perseveres through every trial and hardship—is rewarded with blessings in old age.

To Learn More: Turn to the article about aging/elderly on pages 282, 283. See also the key passage note at Psalm 71:9 on page 737.

faces southward. 3 Then it went out to the southern side of the Ascent of Akrabbim, passed along to Zin, ascended on the south side of Kadesh Barnea, passed along to Hezron, went up to Adar, and went around to Karkaa. 4 *From there* it passed toward Azmon and went out to the Brook of Egypt; and the border ended at the sea. This shall be your southern border.

5 The east border *was* the Salt Sea as far as the mouth of the Jordan.

And the border on the northern quarter *began* at the bay of the sea at the mouth of the Jordan. 6 The border went up to Beth Hoglah and passed north of Beth Arabah; and the border went up to the stone of Bohan the son of Reuben. 7 Then the border went up toward Debir from the Valley of Achor, and it turned northward toward Gilgal, which *is* before the Ascent of Adummim, which *is* on the south side of the valley. The border continued toward the waters of En Shemesh and ended at En Rogel. 8 And the border went up by the Valley of the Son of Hinnom to the southern slope of the Jebusite *city* (which *is* Jerusalem). The border went up to the top of the mountain that *lies* before the Valley of Hinnom westward, which *is* at the end of the Valley of Rephaim[a] northward. 9 Then the border went around from the top of the hill to the fountain of the water of Nephtoah, and extended to the cities of Mount Ephron. And the border went around to Baalah (which *is* Kirjath Jearim). 10 Then the border turned westward from Baalah to Mount Seir, passed along to the side of Mount Jearim on the north (which *is* Chesalon), went down to Beth Shemesh, and passed on to Timnah. 11 And the border went out to the side of Ekron northward. Then the border went around to Shicron, passed along to Mount Baalah, and extended to Jabneel; and the border ended at the sea.

12 The west border *was* the coastline of the Great Sea. This *is* the boundary of the children of Judah all around according to their families.

Caleb Occupies Hebron and Debir

13 Now to Caleb the son of Jephunneh he gave a share among the children of Judah, according to the commandment of the LORD to Joshua, *namely,* Kirjath Arba, which *is* Hebron (*Arba was* the father of Anak). 14 Caleb drove out the three sons of Anak from there: Sheshai, Ahiman, and Talmai, the children of Anak. 15 Then he went up from there to the inhabitants of Debir (formerly the name of Debir *was* Kirjath Sepher).

16 And Caleb said, "He who attacks Kirjath Sepher and takes it, to him I will give Achsah my daughter as wife." 17 So Othniel the son of Kenaz, the brother of Caleb, took it; and he gave him Achsah his daughter as wife. 18 Now it was so, when she came *to him,* that she persuaded him to ask her father for a field. So she dismounted from *her* donkey, and Caleb said to her, "What do you wish?" 19 She answered, "Give me a blessing; since you have given me land in the South, give me also springs of water." So he gave her the upper springs and the lower springs.

The Cities of Judah

20 This *was* the inheritance of the tribe of the children of Judah according to their families:

21 The cities at the limits of the tribe of the children of Judah, toward the border of Edom in the South, were Kabzeel, Eder, Jagur, 22 Kinah, Dimonah, Adadah, 23 Kedesh, Hazor, Ithnan, 24 Ziph, Telem, Bealoth, 25 Hazor, Hadattah, Kerioth, Hezron (which *is* Hazor), 26 Amam, Shema, Moladah, 27 Hazar Gaddah, Heshmon, Beth Pelet, 28 Hazar Shual, Beersheba, Bizjothjah, 29 Baalah, Ijim, Ezem, 30 Eltolad, Chesil, Hormah, 31 Ziklag, Madmannah, Sansannah, 32 Lebaoth, Shilhim, Ain, and Rimmon: all the cities *are* twenty-nine, with their villages.

33 In the lowland: Eshtaol, Zorah, Ashnah, 34 Zanoah, En Gannim, Tappuah, Enam, 35 Jarmuth, Adullam, Socoh, Azekah, 36 Sharaim, Adithaim, Gederah, and Gederothaim: fourteen cities with their villages; 37 Zenan, Hadashah, Migdal Gad, 38 Dilean, Mizpah, Joktheel, 39 Lachish, Bozkath, Eglon, 40 Cabbon, Lahmas,[a] Kithlish, 41 Gederoth, Beth Dagon, Naamah, and Makkedah: sixteen cities with their villages; 42 Libnah, Ether, Ashan, 43 Jiphtah, Ashnah, Nezib, 44 Keilah, Achzib, and Mareshah: nine cities with their villages; 45 Ekron, with its towns and villages; 46 from Ekron to the sea, all that *lay* near Ashdod, with their villages; 47 Ashdod with its towns and villages, Gaza with its towns and villages—as far as the Brook of Egypt and the Great Sea with *its* coastline.

15:8 [a]Literally *Giants* **15:40** [a]Or *Lahmam*

48And in the mountain country: Shamir, Jattir, Sochoh, 49Dannah, Kirjath Sannah (which *is* Debir), 50Anab, Eshtemoh, Anim, 51Goshen, Holon, and Giloh: eleven cities with their villages; 52Arab, Dumah, Eshean, 53Janum, Beth Tappuah, Aphekah, 54Humtah, Kirjath Arba (which *is* Hebron), and Zior: nine cities with their villages; 55Maon, Carmel, Ziph, Juttah, 56Jezreel, Jokdeam, Zanoah, 57Kain, Gibeah, and Timnah: ten cities with their villages; 58Halhul, Beth Zur, Gedor, 59Maarath, Beth Anoth, and Eltekon: six cities with their villages; 60Kirjath Baal (which *is* Kirjath Jearim) and Rabbah: two cities with their villages.

61In the wilderness: Beth Arabah, Middin, Secacah, 62Nibshan, the City of Salt, and En Gedi: six cities with their villages.

63As for the Jebusites, the inhabitants of Jerusalem, the children of Judah could not drive them out; but the Jebusites dwell with the children of Judah at Jerusalem to this day.

Ephraim and West Manasseh

16 The lot fell to the children of Joseph from the Jordan, by Jericho, to the waters of Jericho on the east, to the wilderness that goes up from Jericho through the mountains to Bethel, 2then went out from Bethel to Luz,[a] passed along to the border of the Archites at Ataroth, 3and went down westward to the boundary of the Japhletites, as far as the boundary of Lower Beth Horon to Gezer; and it ended at the sea.

4So the children of Joseph, Manasseh and Ephraim, took their inheritance.

The Land of Ephraim

5The border of the children of Ephraim, according to their families, was *thus:* The border of their inheritance on the east side was Ataroth Addar as far as Upper Beth Horon.

6And the border went out toward the sea on the north side of Michmethath; then the border went around eastward to Taanath Shiloh, and passed by it on the east of Janohah. 7Then it went down from Janohah to Ataroth and Naarah,[a] reached to Jericho, and came out at the Jordan.

8The border went out from Tappuah westward to the Brook Kanah, and it ended at the sea. This *was* the inheritance of the tribe of the children of Ephraim according to their families. 9The separate cities for the children of Ephraim *were* among the inheritance of the children of Manasseh, all the cities with their villages.

10And they did not drive out the Canaanites who dwelt in Gezer; but the Canaanites dwell among the Ephraimites to this day and have become forced laborers.

The Other Half-Tribe of Manasseh (West)

17 There was also a lot for the tribe of Manasseh, for he *was* the firstborn of Joseph: *namely* for Machir the firstborn of Manasseh, the father of Gilead, because he was a man of war; therefore he was given Gilead and Bashan. 2And there was *a lot* for the rest of the children of Manasseh according to their families: for the children of Abiezer,[a] the children of Helek, the children of Asriel, the children of Shechem, the children of Hepher, and the children of Shemida; these *were* the male children of Manasseh the son of Joseph according to their families.

3But Zelophehad the son of Hepher, the son of Gilead, the son of Machir, the son of Manasseh, had no sons, but only daughters. And these *are* the names of his daughters: Mahlah, Noah, Hoglah, Milcah, and Tirzah. 4And they came near before Eleazar the priest, before Joshua the son of Nun, and before the rulers, saying, "The LORD commanded Moses to give us an inheritance among our brothers." Therefore, according to the commandment of the LORD, he gave them an inheritance among their father's brothers. 5Ten shares fell to Manasseh, besides the land of Gilead and Bashan, which *were* on the other side of the Jordan, 6because the daughters of Manasseh received an inheritance among his sons; and the rest of Manasseh's sons had the land of Gilead.

7And the territory of Manasseh was from Asher to Michmethath, that *lies* east of Shechem; and the border went along south to the inhabitants of En Tappuah. 8Manasseh had the land of Tappuah, but Tappuah on the border of Manasseh *belonged* to the children of Ephraim. 9And the border descended to the Brook Kanah, southward to the brook. These cities of Ephraim *are* among the cities of Manasseh. The border of Manasseh *was* on the north side of the brook; and it ended at the sea.

16:2 [a]Septuagint reads *Bethel* (that is, Luz).
16:7 [a]Or *Naaran* (compare 1 Chronicles 7:28)
17:2 [a]Called *Jeezer* in Numbers 26:30

10 Southward *it was* Ephraim's, northward *it was* Manasseh's, and the sea was its border. Manasseh's territory was adjoining Asher on the north and Issachar on the east. 11 And in Issachar and in Asher, Manasseh had Beth Shean and its towns, Ibleam and its towns, the inhabitants of Dor and its towns, the inhabitants of En Dor and its towns, the inhabitants of Taanach and its towns, and the inhabitants of Megiddo and its towns—three hilly regions. 12 Yet the children of Manasseh could not drive out *the inhabitants of* those cities, but the Canaanites were determined to dwell in that land. 13 And it happened, when the children of Israel grew strong, that they put the Canaanites to forced labor, but did not utterly drive them out.

More Land for Ephraim and Manasseh

14 Then the children of Joseph spoke to Joshua, saying, "Why have you given us *only* one lot and one share to inherit, since we *are* a great people, inasmuch as the LORD has blessed us until now?"

15 So Joshua answered them, "If you *are* a great people, *then* go up to the forest *country* and clear a place for yourself there in the land of the Perizzites and the giants, since the mountains of Ephraim are too confined for you."

16 But the children of Joseph said, "The mountain country is not enough for us; and all the Canaanites who dwell in the land of the valley have chariots of iron, *both those* who *are* of Beth Shean and its towns and *those* who *are* of the Valley of Jezreel."

17 And Joshua spoke to the house of Joseph—to Ephraim and Manasseh—saying, "You *are* a great people and have great power; you shall not have *only* one lot, 18 but the mountain country shall be yours. Although it *is* wooded, you shall cut it down, and its farthest extent shall be yours; for you shall drive out the Canaanites, though they have iron chariots *and* are strong."

The Remainder of the Land Divided

18 Now the whole congregation of the children of Israel assembled together at Shiloh, and set up the tabernacle of meeting there. And the land was subdued before them. 2 But there remained among the children of Israel seven tribes which had not yet received their inheritance.

3 Then Joshua said to the children of Israel: "How long will you neglect to go and possess the land which the LORD God of your fathers has given you? 4 Pick out from among you three men for *each* tribe, and I will send them; they shall rise and go through the land, survey it according to their inheritance, and come *back* to me. 5 And they shall divide it into seven parts. Judah shall remain in their territory on the south, and the house of Joseph shall remain in their territory on the north. 6 You shall therefore survey the land in seven parts and bring *the survey* here to me, that I may cast lots for you here before the LORD our God. 7 But the Levites have no part among you, for the priesthood of the LORD *is* their inheritance. And Gad, Reuben, and half the tribe of Manasseh have received their inheritance beyond the Jordan on the east, which Moses the servant of the LORD gave them."

8 Then the men arose to go away; and Joshua charged those who went to survey the land, saying, "Go, walk through the land, survey it, and come back to me, that I may cast lots for you here before the LORD in Shiloh." 9 So the men went, passed through the land, and wrote the survey in a book in seven parts by cities; and they came to Joshua at the camp in Shiloh. 10 Then Joshua cast lots for them in Shiloh before the LORD, and there Joshua divided the land to the children of Israel according to their divisions.

The Land of Benjamin

11 Now the lot of the tribe of the children of Benjamin came up according to their families, and the territory of their lot came out between the children of Judah and the children of Joseph. 12 Their border on the north side began at the Jordan, and the border went up to the side of Jericho on the north, and went up through the mountains westward; it ended at the Wilderness of Beth Aven. 13 The border went over from there toward Luz, to the side of Luz (which *is* Bethel) southward; and the border descended to Ataroth Addar, near the hill that *lies* on the south side of Lower Beth Horon.

14 Then the border extended around the west side to the south, from the hill that *lies* before Beth Horon southward; and it ended at Kirjath Baal (which *is* Kirjath Jearim), a city of the children of Judah. This *was* the west side.

15 The south side *began* at the end of Kirjath

Jearim, and the border extended on the west and went out to the spring of the waters of Nephtoah. 16Then the border came down to the end of the mountain that *lies* before the Valley of the Son of Hinnom, which *is* in the Valley of the Rephaim[a] on the north, descended to the Valley of Hinnom, to the side of the Jebusite *city* on the south, and descended to En Rogel. 17And it went around from the north, went out to En Shemesh, and extended toward Geliloth, which is before the Ascent of Adummim, and descended to the stone of Bohan the son of Reuben. 18Then it passed along toward the north side of Arabah,[a] and went down to Arabah. 19And the border passed along to the north side of Beth Hoglah; then the border ended at the north bay at the Salt Sea, at the south end of the Jordan. This *was* the southern boundary.

20The Jordan was its border on the east side. This *was* the inheritance of the children of Benjamin, according to its boundaries all around, according to their families.

21Now the cities of the tribe of the children of Benjamin, according to their families, were Jericho, Beth Hoglah, Emek Keziz, 22Beth Arabah, Zemaraim, Bethel, 23Avim, Parah, Ophrah, 24Chephar Haammoni, Ophni, and Gaba: twelve cities with their villages; 25Gibeon, Ramah, Beeroth, 26Mizpah, Chephirah, Mozah, 27Rekem, Irpeel, Taralah, 28Zelah, Eleph, Jebus (which *is* Jerusalem), Gibeath, *and* Kirjath: fourteen cities with their villages. This was the inheritance of the children of Benjamin according to their families.

Simeon's Inheritance with Judah

19 The second lot came out for Simeon, for the tribe of the children of Simeon according to their families. And their inheritance was within the inheritance of the children of Judah. 2They had in their inheritance Beersheba (Sheba), Moladah, 3Hazar Shual, Balah, Ezem, 4Eltolad, Bethul, Hormah, 5Ziklag, Beth Marcaboth, Hazar Susah, 6Beth Lebaoth, and Sharuhen: thirteen cities and their villages; 7Ain, Rimmon, Ether, and Ashan: four cities and their villages; 8and all the villages that *were* all around these cities as far as Baalath Beer, Ramah of the South. This *was* the inheritance of the tribe of the children of Simeon according to their families.

9The inheritance of the children of Simeon *was included* in the share of the children of Judah, for the share of the children of Judah was too much for them. Therefore the children of Simeon had *their* inheritance within the inheritance of that people.

The Land of Zebulun

10The third lot came out for the children of Zebulun according to their families, and the border of their inheritance was as far as Sarid. 11Their border went toward the west and to Maralah, went to Dabbasheth, and extended along the brook that is east of Jokneam. 12Then from Sarid it went eastward toward the sunrise along the border of Chisloth Tabor, and went out toward Daberath, bypassing Japhia. 13And from there it passed along on the east of Gath Hepher, toward Eth Kazin, and extended to Rimmon, which borders on Neah. 14Then the border went around it on the north side of Hannathon, and it ended in the Valley of Jiphthah El. 15Included were Kattath, Nahallal, Shimron, Idalah, and Bethlehem: twelve cities with their villages. 16This *was* the inheritance of the children of Zebulun according to their families, these cities with their villages.

The Land of Issachar

17The fourth lot came out to Issachar, for the children of Issachar according to their families. 18And their territory went to Jezreel, and *included* Chesulloth, Shunem, 19Haphraim, Shion, Anaharath, 20Rabbith, Kishion, Abez, 21Remeth, En Gannim, En Haddah, and Beth Pazzez. 22And the border reached to Tabor, Shahazimah, and Beth Shemesh; their border ended at the Jordan: sixteen cities with their villages. 23This *was* the inheritance of the tribe of the children of Issachar according to their families, the cities and their villages.

The Land of Asher

24The fifth lot came out for the tribe of the children of Asher according to their families. 25And their territory included Helkath, Hali, Beten, Achshaph, 26Alammelech, Amad, and Mishal; it reached to Mount Carmel westward, along *the Brook* Shihor Libnath. 27It turned toward the sunrise to Beth Dagon; and it reached to Zebulun and to the Valley of Jiphthah El, then northward beyond Beth Emek and Neiel, bypassing Cabul *which was* on the left,

---

18:16 [a]Literally *Giants* **18:18** [a]Or *Beth Arabah* (compare 15:6 and 18:22)

[28]including Ebron,[a] Rehob, Hammon, and Kanah, as far as Greater Sidon. [29]And the border turned to Ramah and to the fortified city of Tyre; then the border turned to Hosah, and ended at the sea by the region of Achzib. [30]Also Ummah, Aphek, and Rehob *were included:* twenty-two cities with their villages. [31]This *was* the inheritance of the tribe of the children of Asher according to their families, these cities with their villages.

The Land of Naphtali

[32]The sixth lot came out to the children of Naphtali, for the children of Naphtali according to their families. [33]And their border began at Heleph, enclosing the territory from the terebinth tree in Zaanannim, Adami Nekeb, and Jabneel, as far as Lakkum; it ended at the Jordan. [34]From Heleph the border extended westward to Aznoth Tabor, and went out from there toward Hukkok; it adjoined Zebulun on the south side and Asher on the west side, and ended at Judah by the Jordan toward the sunrise. [35]And the fortified cities *are* Ziddim, Zer, Hammath, Rakkath, Chinnereth, [36]Adamah, Ramah, Hazor, [37]Kedesh, Edrei, En Hazor, [38]Iron, Migdal El, Horem, Beth Anath, and Beth Shemesh: nineteen cities with their villages. [39]This *was* the inheritance of the tribe of the children of Naphtali according to their families, the cities and their villages.

The Land of Dan

[40]The seventh lot came out for the tribe of the children of Dan according to their families. [41]And the territory of their inheritance was Zorah, Eshtaol, Ir Shemesh, [42]Shaalabbin, Aijalon, Jethlah, [43]Elon, Timnah, Ekron, [44]Eltekeh, Gibbethon, Baalath, [45]Jehud, Bene Berak, Gath Rimmon, [46]Me Jarkon, and Rakkon, with the region near Joppa. [47]And the border of the children of Dan went beyond these, because the children of Dan went up to fight against Leshem and took it; and they struck it with the edge of the sword, took possession of it, and dwelt in it. They called Leshem, Dan, after the name of Dan their father. [48]This *is* the inheritance of the tribe of the children of Dan according to their families, these cities with their villages.

Joshua's Inheritance

[49]When they had made an end of dividing the land as an inheritance according to their borders, the children of Israel gave an inheritance among them to Joshua the son of Nun. [50]According to the word of the LORD they gave him the city which he asked for, Timnath Serah in the mountains of Ephraim; and he built the city and dwelt in it.

[51]These *were* the inheritances which Eleazar the priest, Joshua the son of Nun, and the heads of the fathers of the tribes of the children of Israel divided as an inheritance by lot in Shiloh before the LORD, at the door of the tabernacle of meeting. So they made an end of dividing the country.

The Cities of Refuge

20 The LORD also spoke to Joshua, saying, [2]"Speak to the children of Israel, saying: 'Appoint for yourselves cities of refuge, of which I spoke to you through Moses, [3]that the slayer who kills a person accidentally *or* unintentionally may flee there; and they shall be your refuge from the avenger of blood. [4]And when he flees to one of those cities, and stands at the entrance of the gate of the city, and declares his case in the hearing of the elders of that city, they shall take him into the city as one of them, and give him a place, that he may dwell among them. [5]Then if the avenger of blood pursues him, they shall not deliver the slayer into his hand, because he struck his neighbor unintentionally, but did not hate him beforehand. [6]And he shall dwell in that city until he stands before the congregation for judgment, *and* until the death of the one who is high priest in those days. Then the slayer may return and come to his own city and his own house, to the city from which he fled.' "

[7]So they appointed Kedesh in Galilee, in the mountains of Naphtali, Shechem in the mountains of Ephraim, and Kirjath Arba (which *is* Hebron) in the mountains of Judah. [8]And on the other side of the Jordan, by Jericho eastward, they assigned Bezer in the wilderness on the plain, from the tribe of Reuben, Ramoth in Gilead, from the tribe of Gad, and Golan in Bashan, from the tribe of Manasseh. [9]These were the cities appointed for all the children of Israel and for the stranger who dwelt among them, that whoever killed a

---

19:28 [a]Following Masoretic Text, Targum, and Vulgate; a few Hebrew manuscripts read *Abdon* (compare 21:30 and 1 Chronicles 6:74).

person accidentally might flee there, and not die by the hand of the avenger of blood until he stood before the congregation.

Cities of the Levites

21 Then the heads of the fathers' *houses* of the Levites came near to Eleazar the priest, to Joshua the son of Nun, and to the heads of the fathers' *houses* of the tribes of the children of Israel. [2]And they spoke to them at Shiloh in the land of Canaan, saying, "The LORD commanded through Moses to give us cities to dwell in, with their common-lands for our livestock." [3]So the children of Israel gave to the Levites from their inheritance, at the commandment of the LORD, these cities and their common-lands:

[4]Now the lot came out for the families of the Kohathites. And the children of Aaron the priest, *who were* of the Levites, had thirteen cities by lot from the tribe of Judah, from the tribe of Simeon, and from the tribe of Benjamin. [5]The rest of the children of Kohath had ten cities by lot from the families of the tribe of Ephraim, from the tribe of Dan, and from the half-tribe of Manasseh.

[6]And the children of Gershon had thirteen cities by lot from the families of the tribe of Issachar, from the tribe of Asher, from the tribe of Naphtali, and from the half-tribe of Manasseh in Bashan.

[7]The children of Merari according to their families had twelve cities from the tribe of Reuben, from the tribe of Gad, and from the tribe of Zebulun.

[8]And the children of Israel gave these cities with their common-lands by lot to the Levites, as the LORD had commanded by the hand of Moses.

[9]So they gave from the tribe of the children of Judah and from the tribe of the children of Simeon these cities which are designated by name, [10]which were for the children of Aaron, one of the families of the Kohathites, *who were* of the children of Levi; for the lot was theirs first. [11]And they gave them Kirjath Arba (*Arba was* the father of Anak), which *is* Hebron, in the mountains of Judah, with the common-land surrounding it. [12]But the fields of the city and its villages they gave to Caleb the son of Jephunneh as his possession.

[13]Thus to the children of Aaron the priest they gave Hebron with its common-land (a city of refuge for the slayer), Libnah with its common-land, [14]Jattir with its common-land, Eshtemoa with its common-land, [15]Holon with its common-land, Debir with its common-land, [16]Ain with its common-land, Juttah with its common-land, and Beth Shemesh with its common-land: nine cities from those two tribes; [17]and from the tribe of Benjamin, Gibeon with its common-land, Geba with its common-land, [18]Anathoth with its common-land, and Almon with its common-land: four cities. [19]All the cities of the children of Aaron, the priests, *were* thirteen cities with their common-lands.

[20]And the families of the children of Kohath, the Levites, the rest of the children of Kohath, even they had the cities of their lot from the tribe of Ephraim. [21]For they gave them Shechem with its common-land in the mountains of Ephraim (a city of refuge for the slayer), Gezer with its common-land, [22]Kibzaim with its common-land, and Beth Horon with its common-land: four cities; [23]and from the tribe of Dan, Eltekeh with its common-land, Gibbethon with its common-land, [24]Aijalon with its common-land, *and* Gath Rimmon with its common-land: four cities; [25]and from the half-tribe of Manasseh, Tanach with its common-land and Gath Rimmon with its common-land: two cities. [26]All the ten cities with their common-lands were for the rest of the families of the children of Kohath.

[27]Also to the children of Gershon, of the families of the Levites, from the *other* half-tribe of Manasseh, *they gave* Golan in Bashan with its common-land (a city of refuge for the slayer), and Be Eshterah with its common-land: two cities; [28]and from the tribe of Issachar, Kishion with its common-land, Daberath with its common-land, [29]Jarmuth with its common-land, *and* En Gannim with its common-land: four cities; [30]and from the tribe of Asher, Mishal with its common-land, Abdon with its common-land, [31]Helkath with its common-land, and Rehob with its common-land: four cities; [32]and from the tribe of Naphtali, Kedesh in Galilee with its common-land (a city of refuge for the slayer), Hammoth Dor with its common-land, and Kartan with its common-land: three cities. [33]All the cities of the Gershonites according to their families *were* thirteen cities with their common-lands.

[34]And to the families of the children of Merari, the rest of the Levites, from the tribe of Zebulun, Jokneam with its common-land,

Kartah with its common-land, [35]Dimnah with its common-land, *and* Nahalal with its common-land: four cities; [36]and from the tribe of Reuben, Bezer with its common-land, Jahaz with its common-land, [37]Kedemoth with its common-land, and Mephaath with its common-land: four cities;[a] [38]and from the tribe of Gad, Ramoth in Gilead with its common-land (a city of refuge for the slayer), Mahanaim with its common-land, [39]Heshbon with its common-land, *and* Jazer with its common-land: four cities in all. [40]So all the cities for the children of Merari according to their families, the rest of the families of the Levites, were *by* their lot twelve cities.

[41]All the cities of the Levites within the possession of the children of Israel *were* forty-eight cities with their common-lands. [42]Every one of these cities had its common-land surrounding it; thus *were* all these cities.

The Promise Fulfilled

[43]So the LORD gave to Israel all the land of which He had sworn to give to their fathers, and they took possession of it and dwelt in it. [44]The LORD gave them rest all around, according to all that He had sworn to their fathers. And not a man of all their enemies stood against them; the LORD delivered all their enemies into their hand. [45]Not a word failed of any good thing which the LORD had spoken to the house of Israel. All came to pass.

Eastern Tribes Return to Their Lands

22 Then Joshua called the Reubenites, the Gadites, and half the tribe of Manasseh, [2]and said to them: "You have kept all that Moses the servant of the LORD commanded you, and have obeyed my voice in all that I commanded you. [3]You have not left your brethren these many days, up to this day, but have kept the charge of the commandment of the LORD your God. [4]And now the LORD your God has given rest to your brethren, as He promised them; now therefore, return and go to your tents *and* to the land of your possession, which Moses the servant of the LORD gave you on the other side of the Jordan. [5]But take careful heed to do the commandment and the law which Moses the servant of the LORD commanded you, to love the LORD your God, to walk in all His ways, to keep His commandments, to hold fast to Him, and to serve Him with all your heart and with all your soul." [6]So Joshua blessed them and sent them away, and they went to their tents.

"But take careful heed to do the commandment and the law which Moses the servant of the LORD commanded you, to love the LORD your God, to walk in all His ways, to keep His commandments, to hold fast to Him, and to serve Him with all your heart and with all your soul."
JOSHUA 22:5

[7]Now to half the tribe of Manasseh Moses had given a possession in Bashan, but to the *other* half of it Joshua gave *a possession* among their brethren on this side of the Jordan, westward. And indeed, when Joshua sent them away to their tents, he blessed them, [8]and spoke to them, saying, "Return with much riches to your tents, with very much livestock, with silver, with gold, with bronze, with iron, and with very much clothing. Divide the spoil of your enemies with your brethren."

[9]So the children of Reuben, the children of Gad, and half the tribe of Manasseh returned, and departed from the children of Israel at Shiloh, which *is* in the land of Canaan, to go to the country of Gilead, to the land of their possession, which they had obtained according to the word of the LORD by the hand of Moses.

An Altar by the Jordan

[10]And when they came to the region of the Jordan which *is* in the land of Canaan, the children of Reuben, the children of Gad, and half the tribe of Manasseh built an altar there by the Jordan—a great, impressive altar. [11]Now the children of Israel heard *someone* say, "Behold, the children of Reuben, the children of Gad, and half the tribe of Manasseh have built an altar on the frontier of the land of Canaan, in the region of the Jordan—on the children of Israel's side." [12]And when the children of Israel heard *of it,* the whole congregation of the children of Israel gathered together at Shiloh to go to war against them.

[13]Then the children of Israel sent Phinehas

21:37 [a]Following Septuagint and Vulgate (compare 1 Chronicles 6:78,79); Masoretic Text, Bomberg, and Targum omit verses 36 and 37.

the son of Eleazar the priest to the children of Reuben, to the children of Gad, and to half the tribe of Manasseh, into the land of Gilead, 14and with him ten rulers, one ruler each from the chief house of every tribe of Israel; and each one *was* the head of the house of his father among the divisions[a] of Israel. 15Then they came to the children of Reuben, to the children of Gad, and to half the tribe of Manasseh, to the land of Gilead, and they spoke with them, saying, 16"Thus says the whole congregation of the LORD: 'What treachery *is* this that you have committed against the God of Israel, to turn away this day from following the LORD, in that you have built for yourselves an altar, that you might rebel this day against the LORD? 17*Is* the iniquity of Peor not enough for us, from which we are not cleansed till this day, although there was a plague in the congregation of the LORD, 18but that you must turn away this day from following the LORD? And it shall be, if you rebel today against the LORD, that tomorrow He will be angry with the whole congregation of Israel. 19Nevertheless, if the land of your possession *is* unclean, *then* cross over to the land of the possession of the LORD, where the LORD's tabernacle stands, and take possession among us; but do not rebel against the LORD, nor rebel against us, by building yourselves an altar besides the altar of the LORD our God. 20Did not Achan the son of Zerah commit a trespass in the accursed thing, and wrath fell on all the congregation of Israel? And that man did not perish alone in his iniquity.' "

21Then the children of Reuben, the children of Gad, and half the tribe of Manasseh answered and said to the heads of the divisions[a] of Israel: 22"The LORD God of gods, the LORD God of gods, He knows, and let Israel itself know—if *it is* in rebellion, or if in treachery against the LORD, do not save us this day. 23If we have built ourselves an altar to turn from following the LORD, or if to offer on it burnt offerings or grain offerings, or if to offer peace offerings on it, let the LORD Himself require *an account*. 24But in fact we have done it for fear, for a reason, saying, 'In time to come your descendants may speak to our descendants, saying, "What have you to do with the LORD God of Israel? 25For the LORD has made the Jordan a border between you and us, *you* children of Reuben and children of Gad. You have no part in the LORD." So your descendants would make our descendants cease fearing the LORD.' 26Therefore we said, 'Let us now prepare to build ourselves an altar, not for burnt offering nor for sacrifice, 27but *that* it *may be* a witness between you and us and our generations after us, that we may perform the service of the LORD before Him with our burnt offerings, with our sacrifices, and with our peace offerings; that your descendants may not say to our descendants in time to come, "You have no part in the LORD." ' 28Therefore we said that it will be, when they say *this* to us or to our generations in time to come, that we may say, 'Here is the replica of the altar of the LORD which our fathers made, though not for burnt offerings nor for sacrifices; but it *is* a witness between you and us.' 29Far be it from us that we should rebel against the LORD, and turn from following the LORD this day, to build an altar for burnt offerings, for grain offerings, or for sacrifices, besides the altar of the LORD our God which *is* before His tabernacle."

30Now when Phinehas the priest and the rulers of the congregation, the heads of the divisions[a] of Israel who *were* with him, heard the words that the children of Reuben, the children of Gad, and the children of Manasseh spoke, it pleased them. 31Then Phinehas the son of Eleazar the priest said to the children of Reuben, the children of Gad, and the children of Manasseh, "This day we perceive that the LORD *is* among us, because you have not committed this treachery against the LORD. Now you have delivered the children of Israel out of the hand of the LORD."

32And Phinehas the son of Eleazar the priest, and the rulers, returned from the children of Reuben and the children of Gad, from the land of Gilead to the land of Canaan, to the children of Israel, and brought back word to them. 33So the thing pleased the children of Israel, and the children of Israel blessed God; they spoke no more of going against them in battle, to destroy the land where the children of Reuben and Gad dwelt.

34The children of Reuben and the children of Gad[a] called the altar, *Witness*, "For *it is* a witness between us that the LORD *is* God."

22:14 [a]Literally *thousands* **22:21** [a]Literally *thousands* **22:30** [a]Literally *thousands*
22:34 [a]Septuagint adds *and half the tribe of Manasseh.*

Joshua's Farewell Address

23 Now it came to pass, a long time after the LORD had given rest to Israel from all their enemies round about, that Joshua was old, advanced in age. 2And Joshua called for all Israel, for their elders, for their heads, for their judges, and for their officers, and said to them:

"I am old, advanced in age. 3You have seen all that the LORD your God has done to all these nations because of you, for the LORD your God *is* He who has fought for you. 4See, I have divided to you by lot these nations that remain, to be an inheritance for your tribes, from the Jordan, with all the nations that I have cut off, as far as the Great Sea westward. 5And the LORD your God will expel them from before you and drive them out of your sight. So you shall possess their land, as the LORD your God promised you. 6Therefore be very courageous to keep and to do all that is written in the Book of the Law of Moses, lest you turn aside from it to the right hand or to the left, 7*and* lest you go among these nations, these who remain among you. You shall not make mention of the name of their gods, nor cause *anyone* to swear *by them;* you shall not serve them nor bow down to them, 8but you shall hold fast to the LORD your God, as you have done to this day. 9For the LORD has driven out from before you great and strong nations; but *as for* you, no one has been able to stand against you to this day. 10One man of you shall chase a thousand, for the LORD your God *is* He who fights for you, as He promised you. 11Therefore take careful heed to yourselves, that you love the LORD your God. 12Or else, if indeed you do go back, and cling to the remnant of these nations—these that remain among you—and make marriages with them, and go in to them and they to you, 13know for certain that the LORD your God will no longer drive out these nations from before you. But they shall be snares and traps to you, and scourges on your sides and thorns in your eyes, until you perish from this good land which the LORD your God has given you.

14"Behold, this day I *am* going the way of all the earth. And you know in all your hearts and in all your souls that not one thing has failed of all the good things which the LORD your God spoke concerning you. All have come to pass for you; not one word of them has failed. 15Therefore it shall come to pass, that as all the good things have come upon you which the LORD your God promised you, so the LORD will bring upon you all harmful things, until He has destroyed you from this good land which the LORD your God has given you. 16When you have transgressed the covenant of the LORD your God, which He commanded you, and have gone and served other gods, and bowed down to them, then the anger of the LORD will burn against you, and you shall perish quickly from the good land which He has given you."

The Covenant at Shechem

24 Then Joshua gathered all the tribes of Israel to Shechem and called for the elders of Israel, for their heads, for their judges, and for their officers; and they presented themselves before God. 2And Joshua said to all the people, "Thus says the LORD God of Israel: 'Your fathers, *including* Terah, the father of Abraham and the father of Nahor, dwelt on the other side of the River[a] in old times; and they served other gods. 3Then I took your father Abraham from the other side of the River, led him throughout all the land of Canaan, and multiplied his descendants and gave him Isaac. 4To Isaac I gave Jacob and Esau. To Esau I gave the mountains of Seir to possess, but Jacob and his children went down to Egypt. 5Also I sent Moses and Aaron, and I plagued Egypt, according to what I did among them. Afterward I brought you out.

6'Then I brought your fathers out of Egypt, and you came to the sea; and the Egyptians pursued your fathers with chariots and horsemen to the Red Sea. 7So they cried out to the LORD; and He put darkness between you and the Egyptians, brought the sea upon them, and covered them. And your eyes saw what I did in Egypt. Then you dwelt in the wilderness a long time. 8And I brought you into the land of the Amorites, who dwelt on the other side of the Jordan, and they fought with you. But I gave them into your hand, that you might possess their land, and I destroyed them from before you. 9Then Balak the son of Zippor, king of Moab, arose to make war against Israel, and sent and called Balaam the son of Beor to curse you. 10But I would not listen to Balaam;

24:2 [a]Hebrew *Nahar,* the Euphrates, and so in verses 3, 14, and 15

Family Life

STRONG FAMILIES

NICK STINNETT

(Joshua 24:15)

Think about it for a moment. If you faced a situation—a disease, a house ablaze, a tornado—that created within you the fear that you were about to die, what would be your last thoughts? Your job? Bank account? Prestige? Dirty dishes in the sink? Your upcoming vacation?

Probably not! You would be like many others in concluding that, next to your relationship with God, the bottom line of life is family. Our family is our most important responsibility, achievement, and legacy. We are confronted daily with evidence that the quality of family life is crucial to our happiness, emotional well-being, and mental health.

Healthy, happy families have six common characteristics.

COMMITMENT

Commitment creates the warm, loving environment in which family members grow. It offers a harbor that shelters family members from the destructive forces of fear, anxiety, and loneliness.

At the heart of commitment to the family unit is dedication to the marriage relationship. God sees the commitment of husband and wife to each other as so crucial to families that He robustly condemns any violation of that marital commitment (Mal. 2:13–16; Matt. 19:8, 9; Eph. 5:25, 28; Titus 2:4). Commitment means to be there and not abandon each other. But it goes further. It says, "We will do whatever it takes to love each other as we should."

APPRECIATION

Expressions of appreciation and affection permeate relationships in strong families. God has made it known that He wants to be appreciated and told of that appreciation. On one occasion, Jesus heard the pleas of ten lepers who cried out for healing. All ten were healed, but only one came back to say thank you. Jesus was clearly pleased with the one who came back to show gratitude and just as clearly disappointed in the nine who did not (Luke 17:11–19).

Members of strong families express appreciation to each other by thanking each other for everyday things (as well as the big stuff), by seeing the good qualities in each other, by encouraging each other, and by sharing gentle humor and affection. They are sincere and lavish in their affirmations of each other.

COMMUNICATION

No one wants to feel all alone in the world. Elijah became despondent when he thought he was the only one who stood up for God. Feeling all alone carries a mixture of terror and despair. But God assured Elijah that he was not alone (1 Kin. 19:10–18).

Every person needs to know that he or she is part of a whole: Communication is the process through which this sense of belonging is related. Communication helps us feel connected to other people through the exchange of information. It also helps with solving problems and resolving conflicts in constructive ways.

TIME TOGETHER

Chances are, our best memories are of simple times shared with our family and friends—times that probably did not require lots of money or elaborate preparations. Read in Ecclesiastes and hear Solomon's view that most of us waste time. Solomon tried pleasure, riches, fame, sex, and all the other pursuits common to mankind. He finally concluded that we should live simply, concentrating on those things that are truly important.

Members of strong families spend much time together playing, working, talking, having fun, and just hanging out together. They have resolved the current debate over quality time versus quantity of time. Families need both: Families need large quantities of good quality time to flourish. Many things demand our time; therefore, that time becomes a precious gift we give to our loved ones.

ABILITY TO COPE WITH STRESS AND CRISES

People in strong families still live in a real world. They encounter the same daily strains and frustrations as everyone else; they also experience the major crises of life such as serious illness, loss of a job, death, or natural disaster. They have an ability to deal with both stress and crises in ways that are effective. They manage to make it through.

People in strong families call on their commitment to each other and their good communication skills to help them work out ways to get through their difficulties. They pull together. They manage to see some good in the situation—no matter how bleak it may be. Sometimes, the only good in the situation is that they have each other to rely on. They rely heavily on their faith in God in difficult times.

SPIRITUAL WELL-BEING

The importance of a spiritual center cannot be overstated when it comes to strong families. Reliance upon a power above and beyond themselves is the glue that holds families together and makes them strong. Jesus talked about the importance of building our "house" on the right foundation (Matt. 7:24, 25). Spiritual foundations give meaning and purpose to life: freedom from anxiety, guilt, fear, and low self-esteem as well as a hopeful, confident outlook. Connections with other people who share our religious beliefs give support and encouragement during difficult times. Spiritual foundations offer many guidelines for daily living. Forgiveness, patience, kindness, honesty, and helping others are all taught as virtues. Families with strong spiritual well-being know that God is there watching, caring, loving, and guiding. They know they can turn to God at any time for guidance (James 1:5). When people believe in these basic truths and abide by them, their lives have direction and they can know what is right and what is wrong. They have learned the value of putting God's Word into practice. As James said, "Be doers of the word, and not hearers only" (James 1:22).

FURTHER MEDITATION:

Other passages to study about the issue of family life include:

- ➢ Genesis 12:3
- ➢ Exodus 20:12
- ➢ Psalms 68:6; 107:41
- ➢ Acts 16:33

To Learn More: Turn to the key passage note on family life at Psalm 127:3–5 on page 778. See also the personality profile of Timothy on page 1604.

therefore he continued to bless you. So I delivered you out of his hand. [11]Then you went
over the Jordan and came to Jericho. And the
men of Jericho fought against you—*also* the
Amorites, the Perizzites,
the Canaanites, the Hit-
tites, the Girgashites,
the Hivites, and the Jeb-
usites. But I delivered
them into your hand. [12]I
sent the hornet before
you which drove them
out from before you,
also the two kings of the Amorites, *but* not
with your sword or with your bow. [13]I have
given you a land for which you did not labor,
and cities which you did not build, and you
dwell in them; you eat of the vineyards and olive groves which you did not plant.'
[14]"Now therefore, fear the LORD, serve Him
in sincerity and in truth, and put away the
gods which your fathers served on the other
side of the River and in Egypt. Serve the LORD!
[15]And if it seems evil to you to serve the
LORD, choose for yourselves this day whom
you will serve, whether
the gods which your fa-
thers served that *were*
on the other side of the
River, or the gods of the
Amorites, in whose land
you dwell. But as for me
and my house, we will
serve the LORD."
[16]So the people answered and said: "Far be
it from us that we should forsake the LORD to
serve other gods; [17]for the LORD our God *is* He
who brought us and our fathers up out of the
land of Egypt, from the house of bondage,
who did those great signs in our sight, and
preserved us in all the way that we went and
among all the people through whom we

> "Choose for yourselves this day whom you will serve. . . . But as for me and my house, we will serve the LORD."
>
> JOSHUA 24:15

PERSONALITY PROFILE

Decision Making

THE GODLY DECISION MAKING OF JOSHUA

(JOSHUA 24:14, 15)

Joshua was the successor of Moses, training under his leadership and watching his example for many years. Born in Egypt under slavery, Joshua witnessed the miracles of deliverance. Moses and Joshua shared an unquenchable faith in God. They sojourned together in the wilderness for decades, set their sights together on the land of Canaan, and served the Israelite people with grace and justice. And, although Moses led the people out of Egypt, Joshua led them into the Promised Land.

Joshua acknowledged God in his decision making. Although God's battle plan for Jericho probably sounded unmilitary to the soldier in Joshua, he followed the instructions precisely. He sought God's direction and obeyed it even when it didn't match his own hunches. He practiced the priceless lesson that God does not offer guidance as an optional suggestion. God's ways are *the* way.

Even with extensive victories behind him, Joshua still faced constant challenges in godly decision making. Great faith was needed to live in Palestine and remain true to the God of Abraham. The Canaanites believed in numerous nature gods and worshiped many idols. The Israelites were constantly tempted to yield to the prevailing pagan rites. Joshua demonstrated a finely honed resistance to these temptations and often delivered sharp exhortations against pagan idolatry. Joshua made the decision to remain faithful. "As for me and my house, we will serve the LORD" became a powerful statement of his allegiance to God (Josh. 24:15). Today, when siren calls to pleasure, power, and riches are all around us, we need to decide to follow and honor God deliberately—and we need to repeat that decision every day.

To Learn More: Turn to the article about decision making on pages 1484, 1485. See also the key passage note at 1 John 5:14 on page 1682.

passed. [18]And the LORD drove out from before us all the people, including the Amorites who dwelt in the land. We also will serve the LORD, for He *is* our God."

[19]But Joshua said to the people, "You cannot serve the LORD, for He *is* a holy God. He *is* a jealous God; He will not forgive your transgressions nor your sins. [20]If you forsake the LORD and serve foreign gods, then He will turn and do you harm and consume you, after He has done you good."

[21]And the people said to Joshua, "No, but we will serve the LORD!"

[22]So Joshua said to the people, "You *are* witnesses against yourselves that you have chosen the LORD for yourselves, to serve Him."

And they said, "*We are* witnesses!"

[23]"Now therefore," *he said,* "put away the foreign gods which *are* among you, and incline your heart to the LORD God of Israel."

[24]And the people said to Joshua, "The LORD our God we will serve, and His voice we will obey!"

[25]So Joshua made a covenant with the people that day, and made for them a statute and an ordinance in Shechem.

[26]Then Joshua wrote these words in the Book of the Law of God. And he took a large stone, and set it up there under the oak that *was* by the sanctuary of the LORD. [27]And Joshua said to all the people, "Behold, this stone shall be a witness to us, for it has heard all the words of the LORD which He spoke to us. It shall therefore be a witness to you, lest you deny your God." [28]So Joshua let the people depart, each to his own inheritance.

DEATH OF JOSHUA AND ELEAZAR

[29]Now it came to pass after these things that Joshua the son of Nun, the servant of the LORD, died, *being* one hundred and ten years old. [30]And they buried him within the border of his inheritance at Timnath Serah, which *is* in the mountains of Ephraim, on the north side of Mount Gaash.

[31]Israel served the LORD all the days of Joshua, and all the days of the elders who outlived Joshua, who had known all the works of the LORD which He had done for Israel.

[32]The bones of Joseph, which the children of Israel had brought up out of Egypt, they buried at Shechem, in the plot of ground which Jacob had bought from the sons of Hamor the father of Shechem for one hundred pieces of silver, and which had become an inheritance of the children of Joseph.

[33]And Eleazar the son of Aaron died. They buried him in a hill *belonging to* Phinehas his son, which was given to him in the mountains of Ephraim.

SOUL NOTE

We Will Serve the Lord *(24:14, 15)* As the people began settling the Promised Land, Joshua told them that they would need to make a choice between their God and the gods of the land. His challenge to the families of Israel rings down through the centuries. All people must make this choice, beginning with parents who are responsible for their families. Joshua made his choice clear: "As for me and my house, we will serve the LORD." Effective leadership of your family begins with making that same choice and leading by example. **Topic: Family Life**

Judges

It's one of the most important, and yet most overlooked laws of life: We are most vulnerable to trouble immediately following great triumph. This is the legacy of the nation of Israel during the dismal time of the judges.

After conquering and settling the Promised Land, the Israelites let down their guard. Chronic disregard for God and His Law led to a "dark age" of spiritual decline and civil anarchy. One of the constant problems in the Book of Judges was idolatry. Israel was surrounded by pagan nations who worshiped false gods. In time, the Israelites gave in to the cultural pressure to acknowledge gods like Baal and Asherah as their own, causing religious confusion, moral depravity, and civil catastrophe.

This depressing record (written by an unknown author) documents six cycles of national rebellion, repentance, and restoration. Each time Israel plunged into sin, they were conquered by a neighboring nation. In each moment of crisis, God raised up a military leader who would judge the nation, call them to renewed faith in God, and deliver them from oppression.

The last verse in the book acts as a fitting summary for the entire period: "In those days there was no king in Israel; everyone did what was right in his own eyes" (21:25). We live in a similar era, where the operating credo is "do your own thing." How important, then, for us to heed the warning of Judges: The results of soul neglect are very ugly indeed!

Soul Concerns in Judges

Eating Disorders	(3:17)
Suicide	(16:28–30)
Abuse	(19:25)

THE CONTINUING CONQUEST OF CANAAN

1 Now after the death of Joshua it came to pass that the children of Israel asked the LORD, saying, "Who shall be first to go up for us against the Canaanites to fight against them?"

2And the LORD said, "Judah shall go up. Indeed I have delivered the land into his hand."

3So Judah said to Simeon his brother, "Come up with me to my allotted territory, that we may fight against the Canaanites; and I will likewise go with you to your allotted territory." And Simeon went with him. 4Then Judah went up, and the LORD delivered the Canaanites and the Perizzites into their hand; and they killed ten thousand men at Bezek. 5And they found Adoni-Bezek in Bezek, and fought against him; and they defeated the Canaanites and the Perizzites. 6Then Adoni-Bezek fled, and they pursued him and caught him and cut off his thumbs and big toes. 7And Adoni-Bezek said, "Seventy kings with their thumbs and big toes cut off used to gather *scraps* under my table; as I have done, so God has repaid me." Then they brought him to Jerusalem, and there he died.

8Now the children of Judah fought against Jerusalem and took it; they struck it with the edge of the sword and set the city on fire. 9And afterward the children of Judah went down to fight against the Canaanites who dwelt in the mountains, in the South,[a] and in the lowland. 10Then Judah went against the Canaanites who dwelt in Hebron. (Now the name of Hebron *was* formerly Kirjath Arba.) And they killed Sheshai, Ahiman, and Talmai.

11From there they went against the inhabitants of Debir. (The name of Debir *was* formerly Kirjath Sepher.)

12Then Caleb said, "Whoever attacks Kirjath Sepher and takes it, to him I will give my daughter Achsah as wife." 13And Othniel the son of Kenaz, Caleb's younger brother, took it; so he gave him his daughter Achsah as wife. 14Now it happened, when she came *to him,* that she urged him[a] to ask her father for a field. And she dismounted from *her* donkey, and Caleb said to her, "What do you wish?" 15So she said to him, "Give me a blessing; since you have given me land in the South, give me also springs of water."

And Caleb gave her the upper springs and the lower springs.

16Now the children of the Kenite, Moses' father-in-law, went up from the City of Palms with the children of Judah into the Wilderness of Judah, which *lies* in the South *near* Arad; and they went and dwelt among the people. 17And Judah went with his brother Simeon, and they attacked the Canaanites who inhabited Zephath, and utterly destroyed it. So the name of the city was called Hormah. 18Also Judah took Gaza with its territory, Ashkelon with its territory, and Ekron with its territory. 19So the LORD was with Judah. And they drove out the mountaineers, but they could not drive out the inhabitants of the lowland, because they had chariots of iron. 20And they gave Hebron to Caleb, as Moses had said. Then he expelled from there the three sons of Anak. 21But the children of Benjamin did not drive out the Jebusites who inhabited Jerusalem; so the Jebusites dwell with the children of Benjamin in Jerusalem to this day.

22And the house of Joseph also went up against Bethel, and the LORD *was* with them. 23So the house of Joseph sent men to spy out Bethel. (The name of the city *was* formerly Luz.) 24And when the spies saw a man coming out of the city, they said to him, "Please show us the entrance to the city, and we will show you mercy." 25So he showed them the entrance to the city, and they struck the city with the edge of the sword; but they let the man and all his family go. 26And the man went to the land of the Hittites, built a city, and called its name Luz, which *is* its name to this day.

INCOMPLETE CONQUEST OF THE LAND

27However, Manasseh did not drive out *the inhabitants of* Beth Shean and its villages, or Taanach and its villages, or the inhabitants of Dor and its villages, or the inhabitants of Ibleam and its villages, or the inhabitants of Megiddo and its villages; for the Canaanites were determined to dwell in that land. 28And it came to pass, when Israel was strong, that they put the Canaanites under tribute, but did not completely drive them out.

29Nor did Ephraim drive out the Canaanites who dwelt in Gezer; so the Canaanites dwelt in Gezer among them.

30Nor did Zebulun drive out the inhabitants of Kitron or the inhabitants of Nahalol; so the

---

1:9 [a]Hebrew *Negev,* and so throughout this book
1:14 [a]Septuagint and Vulgate read *he urged her.*

Canaanites dwelt among them, and were put
under tribute.
[31]Nor did Asher drive out the inhabitants of
Acco or the inhabitants of Sidon, or of Ahlab,
Achzib, Helbah, Aphik, or Rehob. [32]So the
Asherites dwelt among the Canaanites, the inhabitants of the land; for they did not drive
them out.
[33]Nor did Naphtali drive out the inhabitants
of Beth Shemesh or the inhabitants of Beth
Anath; but they dwelt among the Canaanites,
the inhabitants of the land. Nevertheless the
inhabitants of Beth Shemesh and Beth Anath
were put under tribute to them.
[34]And the Amorites forced the children of
Dan into the mountains, for they would not allow them to come down to the valley; [35]and
the Amorites were determined to dwell in
Mount Heres, in Aijalon, and in Shaalbim;[a]
yet when the strength of the house of Joseph
became greater, they were put under tribute.
[36]Now the boundary of the Amorites *was*
from the Ascent of Akrabbim, from Sela, and
upward.

Israel's Disobedience

2 Then the Angel of the LORD came up from
Gilgal to Bochim, and said: "I led you up
from Egypt and brought you to the land of
which I swore to your fathers; and I said, 'I
will never break My covenant with you. [2]And
you shall make no covenant with the inhabitants of this land; you shall tear down their
altars.' But you have not obeyed My voice.
Why have you done this? [3]Therefore I also
said, 'I will not drive them out before you; but
they shall be *thorns* in your side,[a] and their
gods shall be a snare to you.' " [4]So it was,
when the Angel of the LORD spoke these
words to all the children of Israel, that the
people lifted up their voices and wept.
[5]Then they called the name of that place
Bochim;[a] and they sacrificed there to the
LORD. [6]And when Joshua had dismissed the
people, the children of Israel went each to his
own inheritance to possess the land.

Death of Joshua

[7]So the people served the LORD all the days
of Joshua, and all the days of the elders who
outlived Joshua, who had seen all the great
works of the LORD which He had done for Israel. [8]Now Joshua the son of Nun, the servant
of the LORD, died *when he was* one hundred
and ten years old. [9]And they buried him within the border of his inheritance at Timnath
Heres, in the mountains of Ephraim, on the
north side of Mount Gaash. [10]When all that
generation had been gathered to their fathers,
another generation arose after them who did
not know the LORD nor the work which He
had done for Israel.

Israel's Unfaithfulness

[11]Then the children of Israel did evil in the
sight of the LORD, and served the Baals; [12]and
they forsook the LORD God of their fathers,
who had brought them out of the land of
Egypt; and they followed other gods from
among the gods of the people who *were* all
around them, and they bowed down to them;
and they provoked the LORD to anger. [13]They
forsook the LORD and served Baal and the
Ashtoreths.[a] [14]And the anger of the LORD was
hot against Israel. So He delivered them into
the hands of plunderers who despoiled them;
and He sold them into the hands of their ene-

1:35 [a]Spelled *Shaalabbin* in Joshua 19:42
2:3 [a]Septuagint, Targum, and Vulgate read *enemies to you.* **2:5** [a]Literally *Weeping* **2:13** [a]Canaanite goddesses

SOUL NOTE

Tell the Stories *(2:10)* Israel had flourished under Joshua's leadership. At some point, however, the older generation had stopped telling the stories of God and His faithfulness to their children. The sad result was that "another generation arose after them who did not know the LORD nor the work which He had done for Israel." A major part of children's development involves spiritual training—and parents are the main source of their information. Will our children know of God's mighty works throughout the Bible and in our lives? Or will they "not know the LORD nor the work" that He has done for us? **Topic: Child Development**

mies all around, so that they could no longer
stand before their enemies. [15]Wherever they
went out, the hand of the LORD was against
them for calamity, as the LORD had said, and
as the LORD had sworn to them. And they
were greatly distressed.
[16]Nevertheless, the LORD raised up judges
who delivered them out of the hand of those
who plundered them. [17]Yet they would not listen to their judges, but they played the harlot
with other gods, and bowed down to them.
They turned quickly from the way in which
their fathers walked, in obeying the commandments of the LORD; they did not do so.
[18]And when the LORD raised up judges for
them, the LORD was with the judge and delivered them out of the hand of their enemies all
the days of the judge; for the LORD was moved
to pity by their groaning because of those who
oppressed them and harassed them. [19]And it
came to pass, when the
judge was dead, that
they reverted and be-
haved more corruptly
than their fathers, by
following other gods, to
serve them and bow
down to them. They did
not cease from their own doings nor from
their stubborn way.
[20]Then the anger of the LORD was hot against
Israel; and He said, "Because this nation has
transgressed My covenant which I commanded their fathers, and has not heeded My voice,
[21]I also will no longer drive out before them
any of the nations which Joshua left when he
died, [22]so that through them I may test Israel,
whether they will keep the ways of the
LORD, to walk in them as their fathers kept
them, or not." [23]Therefore the LORD left those
nations, without driving them out immediately; nor did He deliver them into the hand of
Joshua.

> When the children of Israel cried out to the LORD, the LORD raised up a deliverer.
>
> JUDGES 3:9

THE NATIONS REMAINING IN THE LAND

3 Now these *are* the nations which the LORD
left, that He might test Israel by them,
that is, all who had not known any of the wars
in Canaan [2](*this was* only so that the generations of the children of Israel might be taught
to know war, at least those who had not formerly known it), [3]*namely,* five lords of the
Philistines, all the Canaanites, the Sidonians,
and the Hivites who dwelt in Mount Lebanon,
from Mount Baal Hermon to the entrance of
Hamath. [4]And they were *left, that He might*
test Israel by them, to know whether they
would obey the commandments of the LORD,
which He had commanded their fathers by the
hand of Moses.
[5]Thus the children of Israel dwelt among
the Canaanites, the Hit-
tites, the Amorites, the
Perizzites, the Hivites,
and the Jebusites. [6]And
they took their daugh-
ters to be their wives,
and gave their daugh-
ters to their sons; and
they served their gods.

OTHNIEL

[7]So the children of Israel did evil in the sight
of the LORD. They forgot the LORD their God,
and served the Baals and Asherahs.[a] [8]There-
fore the anger of the LORD was hot against Israel, and He sold them into the hand of
Cushan-Rishathaim king of Mesopotamia; and
the children of Israel served Cushan-Rishathaim eight years. [9]When the children of Israel

3:7 [a]Name or symbol for Canaanite goddesses

SOUL NOTE

Cycles *(3:7, 8)* The Book of Judges describes cycles of sin and judgment in Israel. When everything was going great, the nation would forget God and turn to idols. God would punish them for it, then they would cry out to Him in repentance, and He would send a deliverer (judge) to help them against their oppressors (3:7, 12; 4:1; 6:1; 8:33; 10:6; 13:1). When the people sinned, they were held accountable and were punished for breaking their covenant with God. While God is rich in mercy, He still holds people accountable for their sins and allows them to face the consequences of their behavior in their lives. **Topic: Accountability**

EATING DISORDERS: ANOREXIA AND BULIMIA NERVOSA

JESSE DILLINGER AND GREGORY L. JANTZ

(Judges 3:17)

In today's society, one can't be too beautiful or too thin. The message of the prime importance of external beauty is warped and dangerous! The pressures to look or be a certain way provide big business, though not without great cost to the consumer. The message of perfection as being thinner and better often results in women and men using harmful means to reach that perceived level of perfection.

The eating disorders called anorexia and bulimia nervosa are two life struggles that have recently emerged within our culture and have caused much suffering.

BRIEF EXPLANATIONS

Bulimia Nervosa

People who have bulimia consume large amounts of food in a short period of time (bingeing), then feel out of control and unable to stop eating. Bingeing is often followed by various methods to expel the food from the body—vomiting, diuretics, laxatives, or excessive exercise. While their bodies are usually normal in size, people with bulimia often base their self-worth on their weight and shape, feeling that they must be thinner.

The exact cause of bulimia is unknown. Culture and glamorized norms certainly contribute. Bulimia can be impacted by stress or be a response to trauma. In most cases, bulimia begins during high school or college.

Some common warning signs include: secretive behavior coupled with trips to the bathroom after eating, laxative or diuretic abuse, heart palpitations, depression, social withdrawal, restrictive dieting, frequent and obvious weight fluctuations, and a preoccupation with body weight and appearance.

There are many reasons why bulimia is serious, including the possibility of esophageal tears, gastric ruptures, and dehydration. In addition, psychological, social, and emotional damage are often experienced by those struggling with bulimia.

Anorexia

Where bulimia is a battle with excessive eating, anorexia involves a pattern of not eating enough. Those affected by it are in a battle for control. If they cannot control other parts of their lives, they will control their food intake. People with anorexia refuse to keep their body weight at a normal level because they are unable to accurately view the shape and size of their own bodies. They may be very thin, but still think they are fat. They try to continue to lose weight through a much lower level of food intake, often coupled with extreme amounts of exercise. Similar to bulimia, their body weight affects their self-esteem.

The daily grind of those who experience anorexia is exhausting. Food is meticulously prepared and calories counted. Much time is spent on the scale and in front of the mirror. On top of that, hours can be spent exercising. Essentially, people who suffer with this disease are starving themselves to death. The underlying futile attempt at perfection lurks continuously. This attempt at perfection is fueled by several fears: fear of fat, fear of failure, fear of being less than perfect, fear of rejection, or fear of losing control.

TREATMENT CONCERNS

How to Be Helpful
It is vital to understand the presence of the symptoms of bulimia and anorexia in order to help those who suffer. Seldom will the person suffering initiate the process of healing, which often begins with hospitalization. The prospects of facing the problem and getting help are extremely threatening.

Helping someone who suffers with either of these life struggles requires large amounts of love and patience. Just as these patterns are intense and severe, so also does our love need to be. First John 4:18 reminds us that "perfect love casts out fear"—even the fears described above. Healing relationships with people and with God is essential. People who desire to help must be willing to speak the truth. Self-deception often drives those with one of these disorders to downplay the seriousness of the problem and even to make promises to stop their destructive behavior. Though it may be tempting to give them some slack and time to change on their own, it is not advisable. Just as lies fuel bulimia and anorexia, lies will be used to avoid getting the proper help. Love, patience, persistence, and discernment are vital to offering help and encouragement to people in these situations.

Spiritual Encouragement
Since these struggles are both spiritual and psychological, they must be dealt with in like fashion. The behaviors that comprise these difficulties are illegitimate attempts to deal with anxiety and stress. Failing to deal with the underlying factors that are driving the discomfort will not lead to healing, but will provide only surface-level "band-aids" that will eventually fail.

People dealing with these struggles can benefit from prayer and Scripture reading to help them alter the way that they see themselves. God is powerful enough to break through their defenses and chains of bondage. From Christ, believers gain their righteousness, their perfection, before God. Perfection is found only in Christ and is a work of the Spirit, not accomplished through their own efforts. God's grace is sufficient to cover imperfection. People facing these difficulties need to see perfection not in the mirror or on the scale, but in the blood of Christ shed for them.

Psychological Treatment
The seriousness of bulimia and anorexia must not be taken lightly. Of course, God is all-powerful, but people who suffer from these diseases need to also seek professional help. Psychologists and psychiatrists who are believers and have been trained in this area know the best methods for treatment. This process can be long, but with a focus on God, the support of others, and the endurance and determination to fight, healing is attainable. Recognizing the symptoms and instilling hope are the beginning steps toward wholeness.

FURTHER MEDITATION:

Other passages to study about the issue of eating disorders include:

- ➢ Proverbs 23:21
- ➢ Romans 14:14–23
- ➢ 1 Corinthians 6:19, 20
- ➢ Colossians 3:17

To Learn More: Turn to the key passage note on eating disorders at Proverbs 23:2 on page 832. See also the personality profile of Eli on page 350.

cried out to the LORD, the LORD raised up a deliverer for the children of Israel, who delivered them: Othniel the son of Kenaz, Caleb's younger brother. [10]The Spirit of the LORD came upon him, and he judged Israel. He went out to war, and the LORD delivered Cushan-Rishathaim king of Mesopotamia into his hand; and his hand prevailed over Cushan-Rishathaim. [11]So the land had rest for forty years. Then Othniel the son of Kenaz died.

EHUD

[12]And the children of Israel again did evil in the sight of the LORD. So the LORD strengthened Eglon king of Moab against Israel, because they had done evil in the sight of the LORD. [13]Then he gathered to himself the people of Ammon and Amalek, went and defeated Israel, and took possession of the City of Palms. [14]So the children of Israel served Eglon king of Moab eighteen years.

[15]But when the children of Israel cried out to the LORD, the LORD raised up a deliverer for them: Ehud the son of Gera, the Benjamite, a left-handed man. By him the children of Israel sent tribute to Eglon king of Moab. [16]Now Ehud made himself a dagger (it was double-edged and a cubit in length) and fastened it under his clothes on his right thigh. [17]So he brought the tribute to Eglon king of Moab. (Now Eglon *was* a very fat man.) [18]And when he had finished presenting the tribute, he sent away the people who had carried the tribute. [19]But he himself turned back from the stone images that *were* at Gilgal, and said, "I have a secret message for you, O king."

He said, "Keep silence!" And all who attended him went out from him.

[20]So Ehud came to him (now he was sitting upstairs in his cool private chamber). Then Ehud said, "I have a message from God for you." So he arose from *his* seat. [21]Then Ehud reached with his left hand, took the dagger from his right thigh, and thrust it into his belly. [22]Even the hilt went in after the blade, and the fat closed over the blade, for he did not draw the dagger out of his belly; and his entrails came out. [23]Then Ehud went out through the porch and shut the doors of the upper room behind him and locked them.

[24]When he had gone out, *Eglon's*[a] servants came to look, and *to their* surprise, the doors of the upper room were locked. So they said, "He is probably attending to his needs in the cool chamber." [25]So they waited till they were embarrassed, and still he had not opened the doors of the upper room. Therefore they took the key and opened *them.* And there was their master, fallen dead on the floor.

[26]But Ehud had escaped while they delayed, and passed beyond the stone images and escaped to Seirah. [27]And it happened, when he arrived, that he blew the trumpet in the mountains of Ephraim, and the children of Israel went down with him from the mountains; and he led them. [28]Then he said to them, "Follow *me,* for the LORD has delivered your enemies the Moabites into your hand." So they went down after him, seized the fords of the Jordan leading to Moab, and did not allow anyone to cross over. [29]And at that time they killed about ten thousand men of Moab, all stout men of valor; not a man escaped. [30]So Moab was subdued that day under the hand of Israel. And the land had rest for eighty years.

SHAMGAR

[31]After him was Shamgar the son of Anath, who killed six hundred men of the Philistines with an ox goad; and he also delivered Israel.

3:24 [a]Literally *his*

SOUL NOTE

She Saved the Day *(4:4–10)* Deborah, who was a prophet, was also the only woman judge mentioned in Judges. Her spiritual influence and practical leadership saved Israel in a time of crisis. Barak hesitated to lead the nation into battle and would go only if Deborah accompanied him. Deborah predicted that the battle would be won at the "hand of a woman" (4:9). This woman turned out to be Jael, who killed the enemy's commander. These women were both rescuers for their nation. God uses anyone—man or woman—who trusts in Him. **Topic: Women's Issues**

Deborah

4 When Ehud was dead, the children of Israel again did evil in the sight of the LORD.
[2]So the LORD sold them into the hand of Jabin
king of Canaan, who reigned in Hazor. The
commander of his army *was* Sisera, who
dwelt in Harosheth Hagoyim. [3]And the children of Israel cried out to the LORD; for Jabin
had nine hundred chariots of iron, and for
twenty years he had harshly oppressed the
children of Israel.
[4]Now Deborah, a prophetess, the wife of
Lapidoth, was judging Israel at that time. [5]And
she would sit under the palm tree of Deborah
between Ramah and Bethel in the mountains
of Ephraim. And the children of Israel came
up to her for judgment. [6]Then she sent and
called for Barak the son of Abinoam from Kedesh in Naphtali, and said to him, "Has not
the LORD God of Israel commanded, 'Go and
deploy *troops* at Mount Tabor; take with you
ten thousand men of the sons of Naphtali and
of the sons of Zebulun; [7]and against you I will
deploy Sisera, the commander of Jabin's
army, with his chariots and his multitude at
the River Kishon; and I will deliver him into
your hand'?"
[8]And Barak said to her, "If you will go with
me, then I will go; but if you will not go with
me, I will not go!"
[9]So she said, "I will surely go with you; nevertheless there will be no glory for you in the
journey you are taking, for the LORD will sell
Sisera into the hand of a woman." Then Deborah arose and went with Barak to Kedesh.
[10]And Barak called Zebulun and Naphtali to
Kedesh; he went up with ten thousand men
under his command,[a] and Deborah went up
with him.
[11]Now Heber the Kenite, of the children of
Hobab the father-in-law of Moses, had separated himself from the Kenites and pitched his
tent near the terebinth tree at Zaanaim, which
is beside Kedesh.
[12]And they reported to Sisera that Barak the
son of Abinoam had gone up to Mount Tabor.
[13]So Sisera gathered together all his chariots,
nine hundred chariots of iron, and all the
people who *were* with him, from Harosheth
Hagoyim to the River Kishon.
[14]Then Deborah said to Barak, "Up! For this
is the day in which the LORD has delivered Sisera into your hand. Has not the LORD gone out
before you?" So Barak went down from Mount
Tabor with ten thousand men following him.
[15]And the LORD routed Sisera and all *his* chariots and all *his* army with the edge of the
sword before Barak; and Sisera alighted from
his chariot and fled away on foot. [16]But Barak
pursued the chariots and the army as far as
Harosheth Hagoyim, and all the army of Sisera
fell by the edge of the sword; not a man was
left.
[17]However, Sisera had fled away on foot to
the tent of Jael, the wife of Heber the Kenite;
for *there was* peace between Jabin king of Hazor and the house of Heber the Kenite. [18]And
Jael went out to meet Sisera, and said to him,
"Turn aside, my lord, turn aside to me; do not
fear." And when he had turned aside with her
into the tent, she covered him with a blanket.
[19]Then he said to her, "Please give me a little water to drink, for I am thirsty." So she
opened a jug of milk, gave him a drink, and
covered him. [20]And he said to her, "Stand at
the door of the tent, and if any man comes and
inquires of you, and says, 'Is there any man
here?' you shall say, 'No.' "
[21]Then Jael, Heber's wife, took a tent peg
and took a hammer in her hand, and went
softly to him and drove the peg into his temple, and it went down into the ground; for he
was fast asleep and weary. So he died. [22]And
then, as Barak pursued Sisera, Jael came out
to meet him, and said to him, "Come, I will
show you the man whom you seek." And
when he went into her *tent*, there lay Sisera,
dead with the peg in his temple.
[23]So on that day God subdued Jabin king of
Canaan in the presence of the children of Israel. [24]And the hand of the children of Israel
grew stronger and stronger against Jabin king
of Canaan, until they had destroyed Jabin king
of Canaan.

The Song of Deborah

5 Then Deborah and Barak the son of Abinoam sang on that day, saying:

2 "When leaders lead in Israel,
When the people willingly offer
themselves,
Bless the LORD!

3 "Hear, O kings! Give ear, O princes!
I, *even* I, will sing to the LORD;

4:10 [a]Literally *at his feet*

I will sing praise to the LORD God of
Israel.

4 "LORD, when You went out from Seir,
When You marched from the field of
Edom,
The earth trembled and the heavens
poured,
The clouds also poured water;
5 The mountains gushed before the LORD,
This Sinai, before the LORD God of Israel.

6 "In the days of Shamgar, son of Anath,
In the days of Jael,
The highways were deserted,
And the travelers walked along the
byways.
7 Village life ceased, it ceased in Israel,
Until I, Deborah, arose,
Arose a mother in Israel.
8 They chose new gods;
Then *there was* war in the gates;
Not a shield or spear was seen among
forty thousand in Israel.
9 My heart *is* with the rulers of Israel
Who offered themselves willingly with
the people.
Bless the LORD!

10 "Speak, you who ride on white donkeys,
Who sit in judges' attire,
And who walk along the road.
11 Far from the noise of the archers, among
the watering places,
There they shall recount the righteous
acts of the LORD,
The righteous acts *for* His villagers in
Israel;
Then the people of the LORD shall go
down to the gates.

12 "Awake, awake, Deborah!
Awake, awake, sing a song!
Arise, Barak, and lead your captives
away,
O son of Abinoam!

13 "Then the survivors came down, the
people against the nobles;
The LORD came down for me against the
mighty.
14 From Ephraim *were* those whose roots
were in Amalek.
After you, Benjamin, with your peoples,
From Machir rulers came down,
And from Zebulun those who bear the
recruiter's staff.
15 And the princes of Issachar[a] *were* with
Deborah;
As Issachar, so *was* Barak
Sent into the valley under his
command;[b]
Among the divisions of Reuben
There were great resolves of heart.
16 Why did you sit among the sheepfolds,
To hear the pipings for the flocks?
The divisions of Reuben have great
searchings of heart.
17 Gilead stayed beyond the Jordan,
And why did Dan remain on ships?[a]
Asher continued at the seashore,
And stayed by his inlets.
18 Zebulun *is* a people *who* jeopardized
their lives to the point of death,
Naphtali also, on the heights of the
battlefield.

19 "The kings came *and* fought,
Then the kings of Canaan fought
In Taanach, by the waters of Megiddo;
They took no spoils of silver.
20 They fought from the heavens;
The stars from their courses fought
against Sisera.
21 The torrent of Kishon swept them away,
That ancient torrent, the torrent of
Kishon.
O my soul, march on in strength!
22 Then the horses' hooves pounded,
The galloping, galloping of his steeds.
23 'Curse Meroz,' said the angel[a] of the
LORD,
'Curse its inhabitants bitterly,
Because they did not come to the help of
the LORD,
To the help of the LORD against the
mighty.'

24 "Most blessed among women is Jael,
The wife of Heber the Kenite;
Blessed is she among women in tents.
25 He asked for water, she gave milk;
She brought out cream in a lordly bowl.

5:15 [a]Following Septuagint, Syriac, Targum, and Vulgate; Masoretic Text reads *And my princes in Issachar.* [b]Literally *at his feet* **5:17** [a]Or *at ease* **5:23** [a]Or *Angel*

26 She stretched her hand to the tent peg,
Her right hand to the workmen's
hammer;
She pounded Sisera, she pierced his
head,
She split and struck through his temple.
27 At her feet he sank, he fell, he lay still;
At her feet he sank, he fell;
Where he sank, there he fell dead.

28 "The mother of Sisera looked through the
window,
And cried out through the lattice,
'Why is his chariot *so* long in coming?
Why tarries the clatter of his chariots?'
29 Her wisest ladies answered her,
Yes, she answered herself,
30 'Are they not finding and dividing the
spoil:
To every man a girl *or* two;
For Sisera, plunder of dyed garments,
Plunder of garments embroidered and
dyed,
Two pieces of dyed embroidery for the
neck of the looter?'

31 "Thus let all Your
enemies perish,
O LORD!
But *let* those who
love Him *be* like
the sun
When it comes out
in full strength."

"Thus let all Your enemies perish, O LORD! But let those who love Him be like the sun when it comes out in full strength."
JUDGES 5:31

So the land had rest for forty years.

MIDIANITES OPPRESS ISRAEL

6 Then the children of Israel did evil in the
sight of the LORD. So the LORD delivered
them into the hand of Midian for seven years,
2and the hand of Midian prevailed against Israel. Because of the Midianites, the children of
Israel made for themselves the dens, the
caves, and the strongholds which *are* in the
mountains. 3So it was, whenever Israel had
sown, Midianites would come up; also Amalekites and the people of the East would come
up against them. 4Then they would encamp
against them and destroy the produce of the
earth as far as Gaza, and leave no sustenance
for Israel, neither sheep nor ox nor donkey.
5For they would come up with their livestock
and their tents, coming in as numerous as locusts; both they and their camels were without number; and they would enter the land to
destroy it. 6So Israel was greatly impoverished
because of the Midianites, and the children of
Israel cried out to the LORD.
7And it came to pass, when the children of
Israel cried out to the LORD because of the
Midianites, 8that the LORD sent a prophet to
the children of Israel, who said to them,
"Thus says the LORD God of Israel: 'I brought
you up from Egypt and brought you out of the
house of bondage; 9and I delivered you out of
the hand of the Egyptians and out of the hand
of all who oppressed you, and drove them out
before you and gave you their land. 10Also I
said to you, "I *am* the LORD your God; do not
fear the gods of the Amorites, in whose land
you dwell." But you have not obeyed My
voice.' "

GIDEON

11Now the Angel of the LORD came and sat
under the terebinth tree which *was* in Ophrah,
which *belonged* to Joash the Abiezrite, while
his son Gideon threshed wheat in the winepress, in order to hide *it*
from the Midianites.
12And the Angel of the
LORD appeared to him,
and said to him, "The
LORD *is* with you, you
mighty man of valor!"
13Gideon said to Him,
"O my lord,[a] if the LORD
is with us, why then has all this happened to
us? And where *are* all His miracles which our
fathers told us about, saying, 'Did not the LORD
bring us up from Egypt?' But now the LORD has
forsaken us and delivered us into the hands of
the Midianites."
14Then the LORD turned to him and said,
"Go in this might of yours, and you shall save
Israel from the hand of the Midianites. Have I
not sent you?"
15So he said to Him, "O my Lord,[a] how can I
save Israel? Indeed my clan *is* the weakest in
Manasseh, and I *am* the least in my father's
house."
16And the LORD said to him, "Surely I will be
with you, and you shall defeat the Midianites
as one man."

6:13 [a]Hebrew *adoni,* used of man **6:15** [a]Hebrew *Adonai,* used of God

[17]Then he said to Him, "If now I have found
favor in Your sight, then show me a sign that it
is You who talk with me. [18]Do not depart from
here, I pray, until I come to You and bring out
my offering and set *it* before You."

And He said, "I will wait until you come
back."

[19]So Gideon went in and prepared a young
goat, and unleavened bread from an ephah of
flour. The meat he put in a basket, and he put
the broth in a pot; and he brought *them* out to
Him under the terebinth tree and presented
them. [20]The Angel of God said to him, "Take
the meat and the unleavened bread and lay
them on this rock, and pour out the broth."
And he did so.

[21]Then the Angel of the LORD put out the
end of the staff that *was* in His hand, and
touched the meat and the unleavened bread;
and fire rose out of the rock and consumed the
meat and the unleavened bread. And the Angel of the LORD departed out of his sight.

[22]Now Gideon perceived that He *was* the
Angel of the LORD. So Gideon said, "Alas,
O Lord GOD! For I have seen the Angel of the
LORD face to face."

[23]Then the LORD said to him, "Peace *be* with
you; do not fear, you shall not die." [24]So Gid-

PERSONALITY PROFILE

Fear/Fear of God

GIDEON AND THE FEAR OF GOD

(JUDGES 6)

Gideon knew fear. He wasn't cowardly, just cautious. His courage had a strong component of fear that actually made him an effective warrior. He figured the odds. He took risks but planned to survive. He demonstrated a willingness to resist a superior enemy—with caution. That is why God's messenger found Gideon in concealment. That is why Gideon tested God's guidance. And that is also why Gideon had to learn a new lesson about fear—the fear of God.

God reached Gideon during a military mission. Gideon was conducting a wheat threshing operation under the camouflage of a winepress. His act of resistance included a fair amount of desperation and danger. The people of Israel had been driven underground for almost seven years by the repeated pillaging of their Midianite oppressors. Obtaining wheat had become a dangerous enterprise. For Gideon and his men, discovery by their enemies would have meant losing the wheat and probably their lives. These factors explain Gideon's response to the stranger he noticed sitting under the tree that overlooked the winepress.

When God's messenger greeted Gideon with a compliment, he brushed it aside and expressed a complaint about God. "If the LORD is with us," asked Gideon, "why then has all this happened to us?" (Judg. 6:13). Instead of an answer, God gave Gideon a command. Gideon responded with an offering. God then replied with a miracle and specific directions. Gideon obeyed by destroying a Baal altar and starting a war. Thirty-two thousand Israelites joined Gideon to fight, but they were no match for the huge army of the Midianites. Faced with apparent annihilation, Gideon asked for further confirmation of God's blessing: He put out a fleece as a means of getting a signal from God.

God confirmed both Gideon's blessing and His own role in the outcome of the battle. He downsized Gideon's fighting force to a mere 300 warriors. They did little more than light up the scene while God insured that the Midianites slaughtered one another. In all these events, Gideon's fear affected his behavior. But fear didn't prevent him from obeying or acting courageously. Fear actually clarified the choices and pointed to God as the real source of victory. Gideon discovered a deeper courage in respecting God's commands.

To Learn More: Turn to the article about fear/fear of God on pages 800, 801. See also the key passage note at Proverbs 1:7 on page 798.

eon built an altar there to the LORD, and called it The-LORD-*Is*-Peace.[a] To this day it *is* still in Ophrah of the Abiezrites.

25Now it came to pass the same night that the LORD said to him, "Take your father's young bull, the second bull of seven years old, and tear down the altar of Baal that your father has, and cut down the wooden image[a] that *is* beside it; 26and build an altar to the LORD your God on top of this rock in the proper arrangement, and take the second bull and offer a burnt sacrifice with the wood of the image which you shall cut down." 27So Gideon took ten men from among his servants and did as the LORD had said to him. But because he feared his father's household and the men of the city too much to do *it* by day, he did *it* by night.

Gideon Destroys the Altar of Baal

28And when the men of the city arose early in the morning, there was the altar of Baal, torn down; and the wooden image that *was* beside it was cut down, and the second bull was being offered on the altar *which had been* built. 29So they said to one another, "Who has done this thing?" And when they had inquired and asked, they said, "Gideon the son of Joash has done this thing." 30Then the men of the city said to Joash, "Bring out your son, that he may die, because he has torn down the altar of Baal, and because he has cut down the wooden image that *was* beside it."

31But Joash said to all who stood against him, "Would you plead for Baal? Would you save him? Let the one who would plead for him be put to death by morning! If he *is* a god, let him plead for himself, because his altar has been torn down!" 32Therefore on that day he called him Jerubbaal,[a] saying, "Let Baal plead against him, because he has torn down his altar."

33Then all the Midianites and Amalekites, the people of the East, gathered together; and they crossed over and encamped in the Valley of Jezreel. 34But the Spirit of the LORD came upon Gideon; then he blew the trumpet, and the Abiezrites gathered behind him. 35And he sent messengers throughout all Manasseh, who also gathered behind him. He also sent messengers to Asher, Zebulun, and Naphtali; and they came up to meet them.

The Sign of the Fleece

36So Gideon said to God, "If You will save Israel by my hand as You have said— 37look, I shall put a fleece of wool on the threshing floor; if there is dew on the fleece only, and *it is* dry on all the ground, then I shall know that You will save Israel by my hand, as You have said." 38And it was so. When he rose early the next morning and squeezed the fleece together, he wrung the dew out of the fleece, a bowlful of water. 39Then Gideon said to God, "Do not be angry with me, but let me speak just once more: Let me test, I pray, just once more with the fleece; let it now be dry only on the fleece, but on all the ground let there be dew." 40And God did so that night. It was dry on the fleece only, but there was dew on all the ground.

Gideon's Valiant Three Hundred

7 Then Jerubbaal (that *is*, Gideon) and all the people who *were* with him rose early and encamped beside the well of Harod, so that the camp of the Midianites was on the north side of them by the hill of Moreh in the valley.

2And the LORD said to Gideon, "The people who *are* with you *are* too many for Me to give the Midianites into their hands, lest Israel claim glory for itself against Me, saying, 'My own hand has saved me.' 3Now therefore, proclaim in the hearing of the people, saying, 'Whoever *is* fearful and afraid, let him turn and depart at once from Mount Gilead.' " And twenty-two thousand of the people returned, and ten thousand remained.

4But the LORD said to Gideon, "The people *are* still *too* many; bring them down to the water, and I will test them for you there. Then it will be, *that* of whom I say to you, 'This one shall go with you,' the same shall go with you; and of whomever I say to you, 'This one shall not go with you,' the same shall not go." 5So he brought the people down to the water. And the LORD said to Gideon, "Everyone who laps from the water with his tongue, as a dog laps, you shall set apart by himself; likewise everyone who gets down on his knees to drink." 6And the number of those who lapped, *putting* their hand to their mouth, was three hundred men; but all the rest of the people got down on their knees to drink water. 7Then the LORD said to Gideon, "By the three hundred men

---

6:24 [a]Hebrew *YHWH Shalom* **6:25** [a]Hebrew *Asherah,* a Canaanite goddess **6:32** [a]Literally *Let Baal Plead*

who lapped I will save you, and deliver the
Midianites into your hand. Let all the *other*
people go, every man to his place." 8So the
people took provisions and their trumpets in
their hands. And he sent away all *the rest of*
Israel, every man to his tent, and retained
those three hundred men. Now the camp of
Midian was below him in the valley.

9It happened on the same night that the
LORD said to him, "Arise, go down against the
camp, for I have delivered it into your hand.
10But if you are afraid to go down, go down to
the camp with Purah your servant, 11and you
shall hear what they say; and afterward your
hands shall be strengthened to go down
against the camp." Then he went down with
Purah his servant to the outpost of the armed
men who *were* in the camp. 12Now the Midianites and Amalekites, all the people of the
East, were lying in the valley as numerous as
locusts; and their camels *were* without number, as the sand by the seashore in multitude.

13And when Gideon had come, there was a
man telling a dream to his companion. He
said, "I have had a dream: *To my* surprise, a
loaf of barley bread tumbled into the camp of
Midian; it came to a tent and struck it so that it
fell and overturned, and the tent collapsed."

14Then his companion answered and said,
"This *is* nothing else but the sword of Gideon
the son of Joash, a man of Israel! Into his
hand God has delivered Midian and the whole
camp."

15And so it was, when Gideon heard the telling of the dream and its interpretation, that he
worshiped. He returned to the camp of Israel,
and said, "Arise, for the LORD has delivered
the camp of Midian into your hand." 16Then
he divided the three hundred men *into* three
companies, and he put a trumpet into every
man's hand, with empty pitchers, and torches
inside the pitchers. 17And he said to them,
"Look at me and do likewise; watch, and
when I come to the edge of the camp you shall
do as I do: 18When I blow the trumpet, I and
all who *are* with me, then you also blow the
trumpets on every side of the whole camp,
and say, '*The sword of* the LORD and of Gideon!' "

19So Gideon and the hundred men who *were*
with him came to the outpost of the camp at
the beginning of the middle watch, just as
they had posted the watch; and they blew the
trumpets and broke the pitchers that *were* in
their hands. 20Then the three companies blew
the trumpets and broke the pitchers—they
held the torches in their left hands and the
trumpets in their right hands for blowing—
and they cried, "The sword of the LORD and of
Gideon!" 21And every man stood in his place
all around the camp; and the whole army ran
and cried out and fled. 22When the three hundred blew the trumpets, the LORD set every
man's sword against his companion throughout the whole camp; and the army fled to Beth
Acacia,[a] toward Zererah, as far as the border
of Abel Meholah, by Tabbath.

23And the men of Israel gathered together
from Naphtali, Asher, and all Manasseh, and
pursued the Midianites.

24Then Gideon sent messengers throughout
all the mountains of Ephraim, saying, "Come
down against the Midianites, and seize from
them the watering places as far as Beth Barah
and the Jordan." Then all the men of Ephraim
gathered together and seized the watering
places as far as Beth Barah and the Jordan.
25And they captured two princes of the Midianites, Oreb and Zeeb. They killed Oreb at the
rock of Oreb, and Zeeb they killed at the winepress of Zeeb. They pursued Midian and
brought the heads of Oreb and Zeeb to Gideon
on the other side of the Jordan.

GIDEON SUBDUES THE MIDIANITES

8 Now the men of Ephraim said to him,
"Why have you done this to us by not calling us when you went to fight with the Midianites?" And they reprimanded him sharply.

2So he said to them, "What have I done now
in comparison with you? *Is* not the gleaning *of*
the grapes of Ephraim better than the vintage
of Abiezer? 3God has delivered into your
hands the princes of Midian, Oreb and Zeeb.
And what was I able to do in comparison with
you?" Then their anger toward him subsided
when he said that.

4When Gideon came to the Jordan, he and
the three hundred men who *were* with him
crossed over, exhausted but still in pursuit.
5Then he said to the men of Succoth, "Please
give loaves of bread to the people who follow
me, for they are exhausted, and I am pursuing
Zebah and Zalmunna, kings of Midian."

6And the leaders of Succoth said, "*Are* the

7:22 [a]Hebrew *Beth Shittah*

hands of Zebah and Zalmunna now in your hand, that we should give bread to your army?"

7So Gideon said, "For this cause, when the LORD has delivered Zebah and Zalmunna into my hand, then I will tear your flesh with the thorns of the wilderness and with briers!" 8Then he went up from there to Penuel and spoke to them in the same way. And the men of Penuel answered him as the men of Succoth had answered. 9So he also spoke to the men of Penuel, saying, "When I come back in peace, I will tear down this tower!"

10Now Zebah and Zalmunna *were* at Karkor, and their armies with them, about fifteen thousand, all who were left of all the army of the people of the East; for one hundred and twenty thousand men who drew the sword had fallen. 11Then Gideon went up by the road of those who dwell in tents on the east of Nobah and Jogbehah; and he attacked the army while the camp felt secure. 12When Zebah and Zalmunna fled, he pursued them; and he took the two kings of Midian, Zebah and Zalmunna, and routed the whole army.

13Then Gideon the son of Joash returned from battle, from the Ascent of Heres. 14And he caught a young man of the men of Succoth and interrogated him; and he wrote down for him the leaders of Succoth and its elders, seventy-seven men. 15Then he came to the men of Succoth and said, "Here are Zebah and Zalmunna, about whom you ridiculed me, saying, '*Are* the hands of Zebah and Zalmunna now in your hand, that we should give bread to your weary men?' " 16And he took the elders of the city, and thorns of the wilderness and briers, and with them he taught the men of Succoth. 17Then he tore down the tower of Penuel and killed the men of the city.

18And he said to Zebah and Zalmunna, "What kind of men *were they* whom you killed at Tabor?"

So they answered, "As you *are,* so *were* they; each one resembled the son of a king."

19Then he said, "They *were* my brothers, the sons of my mother. *As* the LORD lives, if you had let them live, I would not kill you." 20And he said to Jether his firstborn, "Rise, kill them!" But the youth would not draw his sword; for he was afraid, because he *was* still a youth.

21So Zebah and Zalmunna said, "Rise yourself, and kill us; for as a man *is, so is* his strength." So Gideon arose and killed Zebah and Zalmunna, and took the crescent ornaments that *were* on their camels' necks.

Gideon's Ephod

22Then the men of Israel said to Gideon, "Rule over us, both you and your son, and your grandson also; for you have delivered us from the hand of Midian."

23But Gideon said to them, "I will not rule over you, nor shall my son rule over you; the LORD shall rule over you." 24Then Gideon said to them, "I would like to make a request of you, that each of you would give me the earrings from his plunder." For they had golden earrings, because they *were* Ishmaelites.

25So they answered, "We will gladly give *them.*" And they spread out a garment, and each man threw into it the earrings from his plunder. 26Now the weight of the gold earrings that he requested was one thousand seven hundred *shekels* of gold, besides the crescent ornaments, pendants, and purple robes which *were* on the kings of Midian, and besides the chains that *were* around their camels' necks. 27Then Gideon made it into an ephod and set it up in his city, Ophrah. And all Israel played the harlot with it there. It became a snare to Gideon and to his house.

28Thus Midian was subdued before the children of Israel, so that they lifted their heads no more. And the country was quiet for forty years in the days of Gideon.

Death of Gideon

29Then Jerubbaal the son of Joash went and dwelt in his own house. 30Gideon had seventy sons who were his own offspring, for he had many wives. 31And his concubine who *was* in Shechem also bore him a son, whose name he called Abimelech. 32Now Gideon the son of Joash died at a good old age, and was buried in the tomb of Joash his father, in Ophrah of the Abiezrites.

33So it was, as soon as Gideon was dead, that the children of Israel again played the harlot with the Baals, and made Baal-Berith their god. 34Thus the children of Israel did not remember the LORD their God, who had delivered them from the hands of all their enemies on every side; 35nor did they show kindness to the house of Jerubbaal (Gideon) in accordance with the good he had done for Israel.

Abimelech's Conspiracy

9 Then Abimelech the son of Jerubbaal
went to Shechem, to his mother's brothers, and spoke with them and with all the family of the house of his mother's father, saying,
2"Please speak in the hearing of all the men of
Shechem: 'Which is better for you, that all
seventy of the sons of Jerubbaal reign over
you, or that one reign over you?' Remember
that I *am* your own flesh and bone."
3And his mother's brothers spoke all these
words concerning him in the hearing of all the
men of Shechem; and their heart was inclined
to follow Abimelech, for they said, "He is our
brother." 4So they gave him seventy *shekels* of
silver from the temple of Baal-Berith, with
which Abimelech hired worthless and reckless men; and they followed him. 5Then he
went to his father's house at Ophrah and
killed his brothers, the seventy sons of
Jerubbaal, on one stone. But Jotham the youngest son of Jerubbaal was left, because he hid
himself. 6And all the men of Shechem gathered together, all of Beth Millo, and they went
and made Abimelech king beside the terebinth tree at the pillar that *was* in Shechem.

The Parable of the Trees

7Now when they told Jotham, he went and
stood on top of Mount Gerizim, and lifted his
voice and cried out. And he said to them:

"Listen to me, you men of Shechem,
That God may listen to you!

8 "The trees once went forth to anoint a
king over them.
And they said to the olive tree,
'Reign over us!'
9 But the olive tree said to them,
'Should I cease giving my oil,
With which they honor God and men,
And go to sway over trees?'

10 "Then the trees said to the fig tree,
'You come *and* reign over us!'
11 But the fig tree said to them,
'Should I cease my sweetness and my
good fruit,
And go to sway over trees?'

12 "Then the trees said to the vine,
'You come *and* reign over us!'
13 But the vine said to them,
'Should I cease my new wine,
Which cheers *both* God and men,
And go to sway over trees?'

14 "Then all the trees said to the bramble,
'You come *and* reign over us!'
15 And the bramble said to the trees,
'If in truth you anoint me as king over
you,
Then come *and* take shelter in my
shade;
But if not, let fire come out of the
bramble
And devour the cedars of Lebanon!'

16"Now therefore, if you have acted in truth
and sincerity in making Abimelech king, and
if you have dealt well with Jerubbaal and his
house, and have done to him as he deserves—
17for my father fought for you, risked his life,
and delivered you out of the hand of Midian;
18but you have risen up against my father's
house this day, and killed his seventy sons on
one stone, and made Abimelech, the son of
his female servant, king over the men of Shechem, because he is your brother— 19if then
you have acted in truth and sincerity with
Jerubbaal and with his house this day, *then*

SOUL NOTE

Self-Destruction *(9:5)* The tragic story of Abimelech pictures extreme violence used for selfish reasons. This illegitimate son of Gideon and a concubine (8:29–31) brought disaster upon the rest of Gideon's family. Conspiring to take his father's place of leadership in Israel, Abimelech "hired worthless and reckless men" (9:4) to follow him and help him kill all seventy of his half brothers. Violence and murder became his way of dealing with all threats to his power (9:22–49). In the end, however, his violent ways resulted in his own destruction (9:50–56). Violence doesn't really resolve anything, and ultimately leads to more violence. **Topic: Violence**

rejoice in Abimelech, and let him also rejoice in you. 20But if not, let fire come from Abimelech and devour the men of Shechem and Beth Millo; and let fire come from the men of Shechem and from Beth Millo and devour Abimelech!" 21And Jotham ran away and fled; and he went to Beer and dwelt there, for fear of Abimelech his brother.

Downfall of Abimelech

22After Abimelech had reigned over Israel three years, 23God sent a spirit of ill will between Abimelech and the men of Shechem; and the men of Shechem dealt treacherously with Abimelech, 24that the crime *done* to the seventy sons of Jerubbaal might be settled and their blood be laid on Abimelech their brother, who killed them, and on the men of Shechem, who aided him in the killing of his brothers. 25And the men of Shechem set men in ambush against him on the tops of the mountains, and they robbed all who passed by them along that way; and it was told Abimelech.

26Now Gaal the son of Ebed came with his brothers and went over to Shechem; and the men of Shechem put their confidence in him. 27So they went out into the fields, and gathered *grapes* from their vineyards and trod *them,* and made merry. And they went into the house of their god, and ate and drank, and cursed Abimelech. 28Then Gaal the son of Ebed said, "Who *is* Abimelech, and who *is* Shechem, that we should serve him? *Is he* not the son of Jerubbaal, and *is not* Zebul his officer? Serve the men of Hamor the father of Shechem; but why should we serve him? 29If only this people were under my authority![a] Then I would remove Abimelech." So he[b] said to Abimelech, "Increase your army and come out!"

30When Zebul, the ruler of the city, heard the words of Gaal the son of Ebed, his anger was aroused. 31And he sent messengers to Abimelech secretly, saying, "Take note! Gaal the son of Ebed and his brothers have come to Shechem; and here they are, fortifying the city against you. 32Now therefore, get up by night, you and the people who *are* with you, and lie in wait in the field. 33And it shall be, as soon as the sun is up in the morning, *that* you shall rise early and rush upon the city; and *when* he and the people who are with him come out against you, you may then do to them as you find opportunity."

34So Abimelech and all the people who *were* with him rose by night, and lay in wait against Shechem in four companies. 35When Gaal the son of Ebed went out and stood in the entrance to the city gate, Abimelech and the people who *were* with him rose from lying in wait. 36And when Gaal saw the people, he said to Zebul, "Look, people are coming down from the tops of the mountains!"

But Zebul said to him, "You see the shadows of the mountains as *if they were* men."

37So Gaal spoke again and said, "See, people are coming down from the center of the land, and another company is coming from the Diviners'[a] Terebinth Tree."

38Then Zebul said to him, "Where indeed *is* your mouth now, with which you said, 'Who is Abimelech, that we should serve him?' *Are* not these the people whom you despised? Go out, if you will, and fight with them now."

39So Gaal went out, leading the men of Shechem, and fought with Abimelech. 40And Abimelech chased him, and he fled from him; and many fell wounded, to the *very* entrance of the gate. 41Then Abimelech dwelt at Arumah, and Zebul drove out Gaal and his brothers, so that they would not dwell in Shechem.

42And it came about on the next day that the people went out into the field, and they told Abimelech. 43So he took his people, divided them into three companies, and lay in wait in the field. And he looked, and there were the people, coming out of the city; and he rose against them and attacked them. 44Then Abimelech and the company that *was* with him rushed forward and stood at the entrance of the gate of the city; and the *other* two companies rushed upon all who *were* in the fields and killed them. 45So Abimelech fought against the city all that day; he took the city and killed the people who *were* in it; and he demolished the city and sowed it with salt.

46Now when all the men of the tower of Shechem had heard *that,* they entered the stronghold of the temple of the god Berith. 47And it was told Abimelech that all the men of the tower of Shechem were gathered together. 48Then Abimelech went up to Mount Zalmon, he and all the people who *were* with him. And Abimelech took an ax in his hand and cut down a bough from the trees, and

---

9:29 [a]Literally *hand* [b]Following Masoretic Text and Targum; Dead Sea Scrolls read *they;* Septuagint reads *I.* **9:37** [a]Hebrew *Meonenim*

took it and laid *it* on his shoulder; then he said
to the people who were with him, "What you
have seen me do, make haste *and* do as I *have*
done." 49So each of the people likewise cut
down his own bough and followed Abimelech, put *them* against the stronghold, and set
the stronghold on fire above them, so that all
the people of the tower of Shechem died,
about a thousand men and women.

50Then Abimelech went to Thebez, and he
encamped against Thebez and took it. 51But
there was a strong tower in the city, and all the
men and women—all the people of the city—
fled there and shut themselves in; then they
went up to the top of the tower. 52So Abimelech came as far as the tower and fought
against it; and he drew near the door of the
tower to burn it with fire. 53But a certain
woman dropped an upper millstone on Abimelech's head and crushed his skull. 54Then he
called quickly to the young man, his armorbearer, and said to him, "Draw your sword
and kill me, lest men say of me, 'A woman
killed him.' " So his young man thrust him
through, and he died. 55And when the men of
Israel saw that Abimelech was dead, they departed, every man to his place.

56Thus God repaid the wickedness of Abimelech, which he had done to his father by killing his seventy brothers. 57And all the evil of
the men of Shechem God returned on their
own heads, and on them came the curse of Jotham the son of Jerubbaal.

Tola

10 After Abimelech there arose to save
Israel Tola the son of Puah, the son of
Dodo, a man of Issachar; and he dwelt in Sha-
mir in the mountains of Ephraim. 2He judged
Israel twenty-three years; and he died and was
buried in Shamir.

Jair

3After him arose Jair, a Gileadite; and he
judged Israel twenty-two years. 4Now he had
thirty sons who rode on thirty donkeys; they
also had thirty towns, which are called
"Havoth Jair"[a] to this day, which *are* in the
land of Gilead. 5And Jair died and was buried
in Camon.

Israel Oppressed Again

6Then the children of Israel again did evil in
the sight of the LORD, and served the Baals
and the Ashtoreths, the gods of Syria, the gods
of Sidon, the gods of Moab, the gods of the
people of Ammon, and the gods of the Philistines; and they forsook the LORD and did not
serve Him. 7So the anger of the LORD was hot
against Israel; and He sold them into the
hands of the Philistines and into the hands of
the people of Ammon. 8From that year they
harassed and oppressed the children of Israel
for eighteen years—all the children of Israel
who *were* on the other side of the Jordan in
the land of the Amorites, in Gilead. 9Moreover
the people of Ammon crossed over the Jordan
to fight against Judah also, against Benjamin,
and against the house of Ephraim, so that Israel was severely distressed.

10And the children of Israel cried out to the
LORD, saying, "We have sinned against You,
because we have both forsaken our God and
served the Baals!"

11So the LORD said to the children of Israel,
"*Did I* not *deliver you* from the Egyptians and
from the Amorites and from the people of
Ammon and from the Philistines? 12Also the
Sidonians and Amalekites and Maonites[a] oppressed you; and you cried out to Me, and I
delivered you from their hand. 13Yet you have
forsaken Me and served other gods. Therefore
I will deliver you no more. 14Go and cry out to
the gods which you have chosen; let them deliver you in your time of distress."

15And the children of Israel said to the LORD,
"We have sinned! Do to us whatever seems
best to You; only deliver us this day, we pray."
16So they put away the foreign gods from
among them and served the LORD. And His
soul could no longer endure the misery of Israel.

17Then the people of Ammon gathered together and encamped in Gilead. And the children of Israel assembled together and
encamped in Mizpah. 18And the people, the
leaders of Gilead, said to one another, "Who *is*
the man who will begin the fight against the
people of Ammon? He shall be head over all
the inhabitants of Gilead."

Jephthah

11 Now Jephthah the Gileadite was a
mighty man of valor, but he *was* the

10:4 [a]Literally *Towns of Jair* (compare Numbers 32:41 and Deuteronomy 3:14) **10:12** [a]Some Septuagint manuscripts read *Midianites.*

son of a harlot; and Gilead begot Jephthah. 2Gilead's wife bore sons; and when his wife's sons grew up, they drove Jephthah out, and said to him, "You shall have no inheritance in our father's house, for you *are* the son of another woman." 3Then Jephthah fled from his brothers and dwelt in the land of Tob; and worthless men banded together with Jephthah and went out *raiding* with him.

4It came to pass after a time that the people of Ammon made war against Israel. 5And so it was, when the people of Ammon made war against Israel, that the elders of Gilead went to get Jephthah from the land of Tob. 6Then they said to Jephthah, "Come and be our commander, that we may fight against the people of Ammon."

7So Jephthah said to the elders of Gilead, "Did you not hate me, and expel me from my father's house? Why have you come to me now when you are in distress?"

8And the elders of Gilead said to Jephthah, "That is why we have turned again to you now, that you may go with us and fight against the people of Ammon, and be our head over all the inhabitants of Gilead."

9So Jephthah said to the elders of Gilead, "If you take me back home to fight against the people of Ammon, and the LORD delivers them to me, shall I be your head?"

10And the elders of Gilead said to Jephthah, "The LORD will be a witness between us, if we do not do according to your words." 11Then Jephthah went with the elders of Gilead, and the people made him head and commander over them; and Jephthah spoke all his words before the LORD in Mizpah.

12Now Jephthah sent messengers to the king of the people of Ammon, saying, "What do you have against me, that you have come to fight against me in my land?"

13And the king of the people of Ammon answered the messengers of Jephthah, "Because Israel took away my land when they came up out of Egypt, from the Arnon as far as the Jabbok, and to the Jordan. Now therefore, restore those *lands* peaceably."

14So Jephthah again sent messengers to the king of the people of Ammon, 15and said to him, "Thus says Jephthah: 'Israel did not take away the land of Moab, nor the land of the people of Ammon; 16for when Israel came up from Egypt, they walked through the wilderness as far as the Red Sea and came to Kadesh. 17Then Israel sent messengers to the king of Edom, saying, "Please let me pass through your land." But the king of Edom would not heed. And in like manner they sent to the king of Moab, but he would not *consent.* So Israel remained in Kadesh. 18And they went along through the wilderness and bypassed the land of Edom and the land of Moab, came to the east side of the land of Moab, and encamped on the other side of the Arnon. But they did not enter the border of Moab, for the Arnon *was* the border of Moab. 19Then Israel sent messengers to Sihon king of the Amorites, king of Heshbon; and Israel said to him, "Please let us pass through your land into our place." 20But Sihon did not trust Israel to pass through his territory. So Sihon gathered all his people together, encamped in Jahaz, and fought against Israel. 21And the LORD God of Israel delivered Sihon and all his people into the hand of Israel, and they defeated them. Thus Israel gained possession of all the land of the Amorites, who inhabited that country. 22They took possession of all the territory of the Amorites, from the Arnon to the Jabbok and from the wilderness to the Jordan.

23'And now the LORD God of Israel has dispossessed the Amorites from before His people

SOUL NOTE

Rejected *(11:1–3)* Jephthah was rejected by the rest of his family because his mother was a harlot (prostitute). His half brothers' prejudice against him was so intense that they drove him out of their home. People face prejudice for all kinds of reasons, such as skin color, race, or disabilities. Prejudice can cause people to turn away from what could otherwise be a good friendship or working relationship. In fact, these people who had driven Jephthah out later realized they needed him (11:4–8). The Bible teaches that we should not be prejudiced against anyone, for all people are created by God and all are one in Christ (Gal. 3:26–28). **Topic: Prejudice**

Israel; should you then possess it? [24]Will you not possess whatever Chemosh your god gives you to possess? So whatever the LORD our God takes possession of before us, we will possess. [25]And now, *are* you any better than Balak the son of Zippor, king of Moab? Did he ever strive against Israel? Did he ever fight against them? [26]While Israel dwelt in Heshbon and its villages, in Aroer and its villages, and in all the cities along the banks of the Arnon, for three hundred years, why did you not recover *them* within that time? [27]Therefore I have not sinned against you, but you wronged me by fighting against me. May the LORD, the Judge, render judgment this day between the children of Israel and the people of Ammon.' " [28]However, the king of the people of Ammon did not heed the words which Jephthah sent him.

Jephthah's Vow and Victory

[29]Then the Spirit of the LORD came upon Jephthah, and he passed through Gilead and Manasseh, and passed through Mizpah of Gilead; and from Mizpah of Gilead he advanced *toward* the people of Ammon. [30]And Jephthah made a vow to the LORD, and said, "If You will indeed deliver the people of Ammon into my hands, [31]then it will be that whatever comes out of the doors of my house to meet me, when I return in peace from the people of Ammon, shall surely be the LORD's, and I will offer it up as a burnt offering."

[32]So Jephthah advanced toward the people of Ammon to fight against them, and the LORD delivered them into his hands. [33]And he defeated them from Aroer as far as Minnith—twenty cities—and to Abel Keramim,[a] with a very great slaughter. Thus the people of Ammon were subdued before the children of Israel.

Jephthah's Daughter

[34]When Jephthah came to his house at Mizpah, there was his daughter, coming out to meet him with timbrels and dancing; and she *was his* only child. Besides her he had neither son nor daughter. [35]And it came to pass, when he saw her, that he tore his clothes, and said, "Alas, my daughter! You have brought me very low! You are among those who trouble me! For I have given my word to the LORD, and I cannot go back on it."

[36]So she said to him, "My father, *if* you have given your word to the LORD, do to me according to what has gone out of your mouth, because the LORD has avenged you of your enemies, the people of Ammon." [37]Then she said to her father, "Let this thing be done for me: let me alone for two months, that I may go and wander on the mountains and bewail my virginity, my friends and I."

[38]So he said, "Go." And he sent her away *for* two months; and she went with her friends, and bewailed her virginity on the mountains. [39]And it was so at the end of two months that she returned to her father, and he carried out his vow with her which he had vowed. She knew no man.

And it became a custom in Israel [40]*that* the daughters of Israel went four days each year to lament the daughter of Jephthah the Gileadite.

Jephthah's Conflict with Ephraim

12 Then the men of Ephraim gathered together, crossed over toward Zaphon, and said to Jephthah, "Why did you cross over to fight against the people of Ammon, and did not call us to go with you? We will burn your house down on you with fire!"

[2]And Jephthah said to them, "My people and I were in a great struggle with the people of Ammon; and when I called you, you did not deliver me out of their hands. [3]So when I saw that you would not deliver *me,* I took my life in my hands and crossed over against the people of Ammon; and the LORD delivered them into my hand. Why then have you come up to me this day to fight against me?" [4]Now Jephthah gathered together all the men of Gilead and fought against Ephraim. And the men of Gilead defeated Ephraim, because they said, "You Gileadites *are* fugitives of Ephraim among the Ephraimites *and* among the Manassites." [5]The Gileadites seized the fords of the Jordan before the Ephraimites *arrived.* And when *any* Ephraimite who escaped said, "Let me cross over," the men of Gilead would say to him, "*Are* you an Ephraimite?" If he said, "No," [6]then they would say to him, "Then say, 'Shibboleth'!" And he would say, "Sibboleth," for he could not pronounce *it* right. Then they would take him and kill him at the fords of the Jordan. There fell at that time forty-two thousand Ephraimites.

[7]And Jephthah judged Israel six years. Then

11:33 [a]Literally *Plain of Vineyards*

Jephthah the Gileadite died and was buried
among the cities of Gilead.

IBZAN, ELON, AND ABDON

8After him, Ibzan of Bethlehem judged Israel. 9He had thirty sons. And he gave away
thirty daughters in marriage, and brought in
thirty daughters from elsewhere for his sons.
He judged Israel seven years. 10Then Ibzan
died and was buried at Bethlehem.
11After him, Elon the Zebulunite judged Israel. He judged Israel ten years. 12And Elon
the Zebulunite died and was buried at Aijalon
in the country of Zebulun.
13After him, Abdon the son of Hillel the
Pirathonite judged Israel. 14He had forty sons
and thirty grandsons, who rode on seventy
young donkeys. He judged Israel eight years.
15Then Abdon the son of Hillel the Pirathonite
died and was buried in Pirathon in the land of
Ephraim, in the mountains of the Amalekites.

THE BIRTH OF SAMSON

13 Again the children of Israel did evil in
the sight of the LORD, and the LORD delivered them into the hand of the Philistines
for forty years.
2Now there was a certain man from Zorah,
of the family of the Danites, whose name *was*
Manoah; and his wife *was* barren and had no
children. 3And the Angel of the LORD appeared
to the woman and said to her, "Indeed now,
you are barren and have borne no children,
but you shall conceive and bear a son. 4Now
therefore, please be careful not to drink wine
or *similar* drink, and not to eat anything unclean. 5For behold, you shall conceive and
bear a son. And no razor shall come upon his
head, for the child shall be a Nazirite to God
from the womb; and he shall begin to deliver
Israel out of the hand of the Philistines."
6So the woman came and told her husband,
saying, "A Man of God came to me, and His
countenance *was* like the countenance of the
Angel of God, very awesome; but I did not ask
Him where He *was* from, and He did not tell
me His name. 7And He said to me, 'Behold,
you shall conceive and bear a son. Now drink
no wine or *similar* drink, nor eat anything unclean, for the child shall be a Nazirite to God
from the womb to the day of his death.' "
8Then Manoah prayed to the LORD, and
said, "O my Lord, please let the Man of God
whom You sent come to us again and teach us
what we shall do for the child who will be
born."
9And God listened to the voice of Manoah,
and the Angel of God came to the woman
again as she was sitting in the field; but Manoah her husband *was* not with her. 10Then
the woman ran in haste and told her husband,
and said to him, "Look, the Man who came to
me the *other* day has just now appeared to
me!"
11So Manoah arose and followed his wife.
When he came to the Man, he said to Him,
"Are You the Man who spoke to this woman?"
And He said, "I *am.*"
12Manoah said, "Now let Your words come
to pass! What will be the boy's rule of life, and
his work?"
13So the Angel of the LORD said to Manoah,
"Of all that I said to the woman let her be careful. 14She may not eat anything that comes
from the vine, nor may she drink wine or *similar* drink, nor eat anything unclean. All that I
commanded her let her observe."
15Then Manoah said to the Angel of the
LORD, "Please let us detain You, and we will
prepare a young goat for You."
16And the Angel of the LORD said to Manoah, "Though you detain Me, I will not eat

SOUL NOTE

Good Insights *(13:2–24)* Manoah's wife is not named, but her faith shines through this passage. She was childless, but one day the Angel of the Lord appeared and promised a son. She and Manoah sought God's guidance, listened to God's rules for them and their son, and brought an offering in thanks. Manoah became afraid when he realized that they had "seen God," but his wife's good insight revealed her trust in God (13:22, 23). At times, one spouse may have insights that the other does not. Manoah's wife trusted God and helped Manoah do the same.
Topic: Marital Communication

your food. But if you offer a burnt offering, you must offer it to the LORD." (For Manoah did not know He *was* the Angel of the LORD.)

17Then Manoah said to the Angel of the LORD, "What *is* Your name, that when Your words come *to pass* we may honor You?"

18And the Angel of the LORD said to him, "Why do you ask My name, seeing it *is* wonderful?"

19So Manoah took the young goat with the grain offering, and offered it upon the rock to the LORD. And He did a wondrous thing while Manoah and his wife looked on— 20it happened as the flame went up toward heaven from the altar—the Angel of the LORD ascended in the flame of the altar! When Manoah and his wife saw *this,* they fell on their faces to the ground. 21When the Angel of the LORD appeared no more to Manoah and his wife, then Manoah knew that He *was* the Angel of the LORD.

22And Manoah said to his wife, "We shall surely die, because we have seen God!"

23But his wife said to him, "If the LORD had desired to kill us, He would not have accepted a burnt offering and a grain offering from our hands, nor would He have shown us all these *things,* nor would He have told us *such things* as these at this time."

24So the woman bore a son and called his name Samson; and the child grew, and the LORD blessed him. 25And the Spirit of the LORD began to move upon him at Mahaneh Dan[a] between Zorah and Eshtaol.

SAMSON'S PHILISTINE WIFE

14 Now Samson went down to Timnah, and saw a woman in Timnah of the daughters of the Philistines. 2So he went up and told his father and mother, saying, "I have seen a woman in Timnah of the daughters of the Philistines; now therefore, get her for me as a wife."

3Then his father and mother said to him, "*Is there* no woman among the daughters of your brethren, or among all my people, that you must go and get a wife from the uncircumcised Philistines?"

And Samson said to his father, "Get her for me, for she pleases me well."

4But his father and mother did not know that it was of the LORD—that He was seeking an occasion to move against the Philistines. For at that time the Philistines had dominion over Israel.

5So Samson went down to Timnah with his father and mother, and came to the vineyards of Timnah.

Now *to his* surprise, a young lion *came* roaring against him. 6And the Spirit of the LORD came mightily upon him, and he tore the lion apart as one would have torn apart a young goat, though *he had* nothing in his hand. But he did not tell his father or his mother what he had done.

7Then he went down and talked with the woman; and she pleased Samson well. 8After some time, when he returned to get her, he turned aside to see the carcass of the lion. And behold, a swarm of bees and honey *were* in the carcass of the lion. 9He took some of it in his hands and went along, eating. When he came to his father and mother, he gave *some* to them, and they also ate. But he did not tell them that he had taken the honey out of the carcass of the lion.

10So his father went down to the woman. And Samson gave a feast there, for young men used to do so. 11And it happened, when they saw him, that they brought thirty companions to be with him.

12Then Samson said to them, "Let me pose a riddle to you. If you can correctly solve and explain it to me within the seven days of the feast, then I will give you thirty linen garments and thirty changes of clothing. 13But if you cannot explain *it* to me, then you shall give me thirty linen garments and thirty changes of clothing."

And they said to him, "Pose your riddle, that we may hear it."

14So he said to them:

"Out of the eater came something to eat,
And out of the strong came something
sweet."

Now for three days they could not explain the riddle.

15But it came to pass on the seventh[a] day that they said to Samson's wife, "Entice your husband, that he may explain the riddle to us, or else we will burn you and your father's house with fire. Have you invited us in order to take what is ours? *Is that* not *so?*"

13:25 [a]Literally *Camp of Dan* (compare 18:12)
14:15 [a]Following Masoretic Text, Targum, and Vulgate; Septuagint and Syriac read *fourth.*

16Then Samson's wife wept on him, and said, "You only hate me! You do not love me! You have posed a riddle to the sons of my people, but you have not explained *it* to me."

And he said to her, "Look, I have not explained *it* to my father or my mother; so should I explain *it* to you?" 17Now she had wept on him the seven days while their feast lasted. And it happened on the seventh day that he told her, because she pressed him so much. Then she explained the riddle to the sons of her people. 18So the men of the city said to him on the seventh day before the sun went down:

"What *is* sweeter than honey?
And what *is* stronger than a lion?"

And he said to them:

"If you had not plowed with my heifer,
You would not have solved my riddle!"

19Then the Spirit of the LORD came upon him mightily, and he went down to Ashkelon and killed thirty of their men, took their apparel, and gave the changes *of clothing* to those who had explained the riddle. So his anger was aroused, and he went back up to his father's house. 20And Samson's wife was *given* to his companion, who had been his best man.

Samson Defeats the Philistines

15 After a while, in the time of wheat harvest, it happened that Samson visited his wife with a young goat. And he said, "Let me go in to my wife, into *her* room." But her father would not permit him to go in.

2Her father said, "I really thought that you thoroughly hated her; therefore I gave her to your companion. *Is* not her younger sister better than she? Please, take her instead."

3And Samson said to them, "This time I shall be blameless regarding the Philistines if I harm them!" 4Then Samson went and caught three hundred foxes; and he took torches, turned *the foxes* tail to tail, and put a torch between each pair of tails. 5When he had set the torches on fire, he let *the foxes* go into the standing grain of the Philistines, and burned up both the shocks and the standing grain, as well as the vineyards *and* olive groves.

6Then the Philistines said, "Who has done this?"

And they answered, "Samson, the son-in-law of the Timnite, because he has taken his wife and given her to his companion." So the Philistines came up and burned her and her father with fire.

7Samson said to them, "Since you would do a thing like this, I will surely take revenge on you, and after that I will cease." 8So he attacked them hip and thigh with a great slaughter; then he went down and dwelt in the cleft of the rock of Etam.

9Now the Philistines went up, encamped in Judah, and deployed themselves against Lehi. 10And the men of Judah said, "Why have you come up against us?"

So they answered, "We have come up to arrest Samson, to do to him as he has done to us."

11Then three thousand men of Judah went down to the cleft of the rock of Etam, and said to Samson, "Do you not know that the Philistines rule over us? What *is* this you have done to us?"

And he said to them, "As they did to me, so I have done to them."

12But they said to him, "We have come down to arrest you, that we may deliver you into the hand of the Philistines."

Then Samson said to them, "Swear to me that you will not kill me yourselves."

13So they spoke to him, saying, "No, but we will tie you securely and deliver you into their hand; but we will surely not kill you." And they bound him with two new ropes and brought him up from the rock.

14When he came to Lehi, the Philistines came shouting against him. Then the Spirit of the LORD came mightily upon him; and the ropes that *were* on his arms became like flax that is burned with fire, and his bonds broke loose from his hands. 15He found a fresh jawbone of a donkey, reached out his hand and took it, and killed a thousand men with it. 16Then Samson said:

"With the jawbone of a donkey,
Heaps upon heaps,
With the jawbone of a donkey
I have slain a thousand men!"

17And so it was, when he had finished speaking, that he threw the jawbone from his hand, and called that place Ramath Lehi.[a]

15:17 [a]Literally *Jawbone Height*

[18]Then he became very thirsty; so he cried out to the LORD and said, "You have given this great deliverance by the hand of Your servant; and now shall I die of thirst and fall into the hand of the uncircumcised?" [19]So God split the hollow place that *is* in Lehi,[a] and water came out, and he drank; and his spirit returned, and he revived. Therefore he called its name En Hakkore,[b] which is in Lehi to this day. [20]And he judged Israel twenty years in the days of the Philistines.

SAMSON AND DELILAH

16 Now Samson went to Gaza and saw a harlot there, and went in to her. [2]*When* the Gazites *were told,* "Samson has come here!" they surrounded *the place* and lay in wait for him all night at the gate of the city. They were quiet all night, saying, "In the morning, when it is daylight, we will kill him." [3]And Samson lay *low* till midnight; then he arose at midnight, took hold of the doors of the gate of the city and the two gateposts, pulled them up, bar and all, put *them* on his shoulders, and carried them to the top of the hill that faces Hebron.

[4]Afterward it happened that he loved a woman in the Valley of Sorek, whose name *was* Delilah. [5]And the lords of the Philistines came up to her and said to her, "Entice him, and find out where his great strength *lies,* and by what *means* we may overpower him, that we may bind him to afflict him; and every one of us will give you eleven hundred *pieces* of silver."

15:19 [a]Literally *Jawbone* (compare verse 14) [b]Literally *Spring of the Caller*

PERSONALITY PROFILE

SAMSON: YIELDING TO TEMPTATION

(JUDGES 16)

Temptation

Samson, one of history's strongest men, displayed remarkable weakness when it came to temptation. His astonishing physical abilities were unfortunately not matched by his moral qualities. He fooled himself into thinking that his great strength could save him from any predicament. Samson squandered God's gift on thoughtless actions and petty offenses. He was so busy delivering himself from trouble that achieving the temporary deliverance of his people came about almost as an accident.

Samson impulsively married a Philistine woman who was coerced into betraying him. This folly led to a series of confrontations that resulted in temporary relief for Israel from the oppression of the Philistines. Years later, he visited a prostitute in Gaza and almost fell into an ambush. Then he fell for Delilah who then was bribed to betray Samson. He failed to realize the danger behind her efforts to discover the key to his power. He toyed with her temptations. But Samson's physical strength was no match for Delilah's persistence, and he eventually betrayed himself by telling her the secret of his strength.

Samson temporarily lost his strength when his hair was shorn. His captors then destroyed his eyes. Samson was left with little else but a determination to serve God.

In Samson's life we find a gold mine of valuable lessons about temptation. Among the treasures are these:

- Strength and success in one area will not make us immune to temptation in another.
- Unbroken patterns lead us downward or upward—temptation returns wherever it has any success.
- Flirting with temptation makes our defeat almost certain.
- Temptation and failure may limit our usefulness to God, but it doesn't cut us off from His grace.
- No matter how bad things get, let the last word be a prayer!

To Learn More: Turn to the article about temptation on pages 62, 63. See also the key passage note at Matthew 4:1–11 on page 1233.

[6]So Delilah said to Samson, "Please tell me where your great strength *lies*, and with what you may be bound to afflict you."

[7]And Samson said to her, "If they bind me with seven fresh bowstrings, not yet dried, then I shall become weak, and be like any *other* man."

[8]So the lords of the Philistines brought up to her seven fresh bowstrings, not yet dried, and she bound him with them. [9]Now *men were* lying in wait, staying with her in the room. And she said to him, "The Philistines *are* upon you, Samson!" But he broke the bowstrings as a strand of yarn breaks when it touches fire. So the secret of his strength was not known.

[10]Then Delilah said to Samson, "Look, you have mocked me and told me lies. Now, please tell me what you may be bound with."

[11]So he said to her, "If they bind me securely with new ropes that have never been used, then I shall become weak, and be like any *other* man."

[12]Therefore Delilah took new ropes and bound him with them, and said to him, "The Philistines *are* upon you, Samson!" And *men were* lying in wait, staying in the room. But he broke them off his arms like a thread.

[13]Delilah said to Samson, "Until now you have mocked me and told me lies. Tell me what you may be bound with."

And he said to her, "If you weave the seven locks of my head into the web of the loom"—

[14]So she wove *it* tightly with the batten of the loom, and said to him, "The Philistines *are* upon you, Samson!" But he awoke from his sleep, and pulled out the batten and the web from the loom.

[15]Then she said to him, "How can you say, 'I love you,' when your heart *is* not with me? You have mocked me these three times, and have not told me where your great strength *lies*." [16]And it came to pass, when she pestered him daily with her words and pressed him, *so* that his soul was vexed to death, [17]that he told her all his heart, and said to her, "No razor has ever come upon my head, for I *have been* a Nazirite to God from my mother's womb. If I am shaven, then my strength will leave me, and I shall become weak, and be like any *other* man."

[18]When Delilah saw that he had told her all his heart, she sent and called for the lords of the Philistines, saying, "Come up once more, for he has told me all his heart." So the lords of the Philistines came up to her and brought the money in their hand. [19]Then she lulled him to sleep on her knees, and called for a man and had him shave off the seven locks of his head. Then she began to torment him,[a] and his strength left him. [20]And she said, "The Philistines *are* upon you, Samson!" So he awoke from his sleep, and said, "I will go out as before, at other times, and shake myself free!" But he did not know that the LORD had departed from him.

[21]Then the Philistines took him and put out his eyes, and brought him down to Gaza. They bound him with bronze fetters, and he became a grinder in the prison. [22]However, the hair of his head began to grow again after it had been shaven.

Samson Dies with the Philistines

[23]Now the lords of the Philistines gathered together to offer a great sacrifice to Dagon their god, and to rejoice. And they said:

> "Our god has delivered into our hands
> Samson our enemy!"

16:19 [a]Following Masoretic Text, Targum, and Vulgate; Septuagint reads *he began to be weak.*

SOUL NOTE

True Love? *(16:15)* Samson had lied to Delilah three times, and Delilah had shown three times that she was willing to betray him to the Philistines. "How can you say, 'I love you?' " she asked, when he would not tell her the truth about his strength. Samson lied to Delilah; Delilah lied to Samson and was willing to sell him out for eleven hundred pieces of silver (16:5). Both supposedly were in love with each other. Whatever these two had going on, it was not love. True love "does not rejoice in iniquity, but rejoices in the truth" (1 Cor. 13:6). **Topic: Love**

CHOOSE LIFE

GARY P. STEWART

(Judges 16:28–30)

Some have described suicide as a permanent solution to a temporary problem. From a Christian perspective, however, suicide is not permanent and solves nothing. Each individual is created in the image of God and is, therefore, an immortal being with responsibilities and accountability beyond the grave.

In reality, suicide is a *selfish* action taken against oneself in order to eliminate what is experienced as unrelenting pain. It is the tragic and lethal culmination of a psychological process that results from unresolved events that create depression and hopelessness. Someone who commits suicide often cannot see any hope that the future will be different than the painful past or present. People who end their lives are generally burdened by a number of unresolved events or problems that are mostly, if not always, resolvable. Without coping skills and without the help of friends, professional assistance, or loved ones, unresolved burdens grow heavier until the weight becomes unbearable and the individual is weakened to the point of despair. The problem is not that such despairing people want to die; it is that they do not know how to live.

The relatives and friends of the person who commits suicide are also victims. They must deal with loss, pain, and perhaps even guilt as a result of the suicide.

SUICIDES IN THE BIBLE

Samson's death, recorded in Judges 16:28–30, occurred in association with an act of war that both avenged his humiliation at the hands of the Philistines and was accomplished with direct permission from God. Although Samson technically caused his own death, his selfless and contrite act is similar to those who, when facing an enemy, are willing to sacrifice their own lives for a cause that is greater than themselves. Samson's choice to sacrifice his life is very different from the decision of those who choose to take their lives because of personal loss, disappointment, and despair.

There are six instances of suicide in the Bible, five in the Old Testament (excluding Samson) and one in the New Testament. The one suicide recorded in the New Testament was that of Judas Iscariot, who hanged himself after betraying Jesus (Matt. 27:5). Two of the suicides recorded in the Old Testament, those of Abimelech and Saul, occurred after each was seriously wounded in battle (Judg. 9:50–55; 1 Sam. 31:1–6). Ahithophel took his own life when Absalom did not receive his counsel (2 Sam. 17:23). Zimri, king of Israel, chose to burn his palace and kill himself rather than be captured by his enemies (1 Kin. 16:18).

It is important to note that none of these six suicides was viewed favorably or as a legitimate option, even in the most difficult of times.

THE BIBLICAL RESPONSE TO SUICIDE

A biblical understanding of God and life inspires hope while it diminishes despair. Each human being will suffer whether a child of God or not. A believer's knowledge and love for God gives hope that suffering is never without a purpose. So rather than curse or blame God for the troubles of life, we choose to live by faith in Him.

Too often in the church, believers are

unresponsive to their brothers and sisters who struggle in their faith, and sometimes too busy to involve themselves in the lives of their neighbors. It is the responsibility of mature Christians to be sensitive to the needs of those around them and to gently encourage and support those who are struggling. In so doing, they assist others in carrying their burdens (Gal. 6:1–3) and so fulfill the law of Christ which is to love God and one's neighbor (Matt. 22:37–40). The church can be a safe place where people can really talk about their problems, build trust, and learn from each other. Isolation, whether initiated by someone who is struggling or by those too busy to care, only heightens the possibility that thoughts about and attempts at suicide will occur.

When someone is struggling with despair or depression, and certainly when someone admits to having thoughts of taking his or her life, then professional help is needed. It is the responsibility of the caring friend to not carry that burden alone, but to take action to make sure that the friend gets help quickly.

IN CONCLUSION

Each of us plays a small, though vital, role in God's comprehensive plan to redeem the world. As believers, we are images (reflections) of God's will and character in a dark and depraved world. The more we understand and trust in the God of Scripture, the better we project faith, hope, and love to the world. The greater understanding each of us has of God and His will, the less despair each of us will experience in our lives.

An important element of faith is the knowledge or awareness that our understanding of God is incomplete. Knowing God intimately is a lifetime endeavor that includes both lows and highs emotionally and physically. We are spiritually, physically, and emotionally broken and wounded people living in a broken and wounded society. God is the mender no matter what the circumstances. As God told the people of Israel through His servant, Moses, "I have set before you life and death . . . therefore choose life, that both you and your descendants may live; that you may love the LORD your God, that you may obey His voice, and that you may cling to Him, for He is your life and the length of your days" (Deut. 30:19, 20).

FURTHER MEDITATION:

Other passages to study about the issue of suicide include:

- Psalm 40:1–3; 119:116
- Proverbs 13:12
- Jeremiah 29:11
- Ephesians 1:15–21

To Learn More: Turn to the key passage note on suicide at I Samuel 31:4 on page 386. See also the personality profile of Judas on page 1276.

24When the people saw him, they praised their god; for they said:

> "Our god has delivered into our hands
> our enemy,
> The destroyer of our land,
> And the one who multiplied our dead."

25So it happened, when their hearts were merry, that they said, "Call for Samson, that he may perform for us." So they called for Samson from the prison, and he performed for them. And they stationed him between the pillars. 26Then Samson said to the lad who held him by the hand, "Let me feel the pillars which support the temple, so that I can lean on them." 27Now the temple was full of men and women. All the lords of the Philistines *were* there—about three thousand men and women on the roof watching while Samson performed.

28Then Samson called to the LORD, saying, "O Lord GOD, remember me, I pray! Strengthen me, I pray, just this once, O God, that I may with one *blow* take vengeance on the Philistines for my two eyes!" 29And Samson took hold of the two middle pillars which supported the temple, and he braced himself against them, one on his right and the other on his left. 30Then Samson said, "Let me die with the Philistines!" And he pushed with *all his* might, and the temple fell on the lords and all the people who *were* in it. So the dead that he killed at his death were more than he had killed in his life.

31And his brothers and all his father's household came down and took him, and brought *him* up and buried him between Zorah and Eshtaol in the tomb of his father Manoah. He had judged Israel twenty years.

MICAH'S IDOLATRY

17 Now there was a man from the mountains of Ephraim, whose name *was* Micah. 2And he said to his mother, "The eleven hundred *shekels* of silver that were taken from you, and on which you put a curse, even saying it in my ears—here *is* the silver with me; I took it."

And his mother said, "*May you be* blessed by the LORD, my son!" 3So when he had returned the eleven hundred *shekels* of silver to his mother, his mother said, "I had wholly dedicated the silver from my hand to the LORD for my son, to make a carved image and a molded image; now therefore, I will return it to you." 4Thus he returned the silver to his mother. Then his mother took two hundred *shekels* of silver and gave them to the silversmith, and he made it into a carved image and a molded image; and they were in the house of Micah.

5The man Micah had a shrine, and made an ephod and household idols;[a] and he consecrated one of his sons, who became his priest. 6In those days *there was* no king in Israel; everyone did *what was* right in his own eyes.

7Now there was a young man from Bethlehem in Judah, of the family of Judah; he *was* a Levite, and was staying there. 8The man departed from the city of Bethlehem in Judah to stay wherever he could find *a place*. Then he came to the mountains of Ephraim, to the house of Micah, as he journeyed. 9And Micah said to him, "Where do you come from?"

So he said to him, "I *am* a Levite from Bethlehem in Judah, and I am on my way to find *a place* to stay."

10Micah said to him, "Dwell with me, and

17:5 [a]Hebrew *teraphim*

SOUL NOTE

Never Too Late *(16:28–30)* Samson once had great potential. He had been set apart by God to "begin to deliver Israel out of the hand of the Philistines" (13:5). Yet at the end of his life, he was a blinded prisoner, chained in a Philistine temple. Samson had failed God in many ways, but in the end, God still used him to accomplish His purposes. As the pagan temple crashed down, Samson killed many Philistines and began to free Israel from them. No matter how badly we have failed God, it is never too late to return to Him and let Him work through us. **Topic: Failure**

be a father and a priest to me, and I will give
you ten *shekels* of silver per year, a suit of
clothes, and your sustenance." So the Levite
went in. [11]Then the Levite was content to
dwell with the man; and the young man became like one of his sons to him. [12]So Micah
consecrated the Levite, and the young man
became his priest, and lived in the house of
Micah. [13]Then Micah said, "Now I know that
the LORD will be good to me, since I have a
Levite as priest!"

THE DANITES ADOPT MICAH'S IDOLATRY

18 In those days *there was* no king in Israel. And in those days the tribe of the
Danites was seeking an inheritance for itself
to dwell in; for until that day *their* inheritance
among the tribes of Israel had not fallen to
them. [2]So the children of Dan sent five men of
their family from their territory, men of valor
from Zorah and Eshtaol, to spy out the land
and search it. They said to them, "Go, search
the land." So they went to the mountains of
Ephraim, to the house of Micah, and lodged
there. [3]While they *were* at the house of Micah,
they recognized the voice of the young Levite.
They turned aside and said to him, "Who
brought you here? What are you doing in this
place? What do you have here?"

[4]He said to them, "Thus and so Micah did
for me. He has hired me, and I have become
his priest."

[5]So they said to him, "Please inquire of God,
that we may know whether the journey on
which we go will be prosperous."

[6]And the priest said to them, "Go in peace.
The presence of the LORD *be* with you on your
way."

[7]So the five men departed and went to Laish. They saw the people who *were* there, how
they dwelt safely, in the manner of the Sidonians, quiet and secure. *There were* no rulers in
the land who might put *them* to shame for
anything. They *were* far from the Sidonians,
and they had no ties with anyone.[a]

[8]Then *the spies* came back to their brethren
at Zorah and Eshtaol, and their brethren said
to them, "What *is* your *report?*"

[9]So they said, "Arise, let us go up against
them. For we have seen the land, and indeed it
is very good. *Would* you *do* nothing? Do not
hesitate to go, *and* enter to possess the land.
[10]When you go, you will come to a secure people and a large land. For God has given it into
your hands, a place where *there is* no lack of
anything that *is* on the earth."

[11]And six hundred men of the family of the
Danites went from there, from Zorah and Eshtaol, armed with weapons of war. [12]Then they
went up and encamped in Kirjath Jearim in
Judah. (Therefore they call that place Mahaneh Dan[a] to this day. There *it is,* west of
Kirjath Jearim.) [13]And they passed from there
to the mountains of Ephraim, and came to the
house of Micah.

[14]Then the five men who had gone to spy
out the country of Laish answered and said to
their brethren, "Do you know that there are in
these houses an ephod, household idols, a
carved image, and a molded image? Now
therefore, consider what you should do." [15]So
they turned aside there, and came to the
house of the young Levite man—to the house
of Micah—and greeted him. [16]The six hundred
men armed with their weapons of war, who
were of the children of Dan, stood by the entrance of the gate. [17]Then the five men who
had gone to spy out the land went up. Entering there, they took the carved image, the
ephod, the household idols, and the molded
image. The priest stood at the entrance of the
gate with the six hundred men *who were*
armed with weapons of war.

[18]When these went into Micah's house and
took the carved image, the ephod, the household idols, and the molded image, the priest
said to them, "What are you doing?"

[19]And they said to him, "Be quiet, put your
hand over your mouth, and come with us; be
a father and a priest to us. *Is it* better for you
to be a priest to the household of one man, or
that you be a priest to a tribe and a family in
Israel?" [20]So the priest's heart was glad; and
he took the ephod, the household idols, and
the carved image, and took his place among
the people.

[21]Then they turned and departed, and put
the little ones, the livestock, and the goods in
front of them. [22]When they were a good way
from the house of Micah, the men who *were* in
the houses near Micah's house gathered together and overtook the children of Dan.
[23]And they called out to the children of Dan.
So they turned around and said to Micah,

18:7 [a]Following Masoretic Text, Targum, and Vulgate; Septuagint reads *with Syria.*
18:12 [a]Literally *Camp of Dan*

"What ails you, that you have gathered such a company?"

24So he said, "You have taken away my gods which I made, and the priest, and you have gone away. Now what more do I have? How can you say to me, 'What ails you?' "

25And the children of Dan said to him, "Do not let your voice be heard among us, lest angry men fall upon you, and you lose your life, with the lives of your household!" 26Then the children of Dan went their way. And when Micah saw that they *were* too strong for him, he turned and went back to his house.

Danites Settle in Laish

27So they took *the things* Micah had made, and the priest who had belonged to him, and went to Laish, to a people quiet and secure; and they struck them with the edge of the sword and burned the city with fire. 28*There was* no deliverer, because it *was* far from Sidon, and they had no ties with anyone. It was in the valley that belongs to Beth Rehob. So they rebuilt the city and dwelt there. 29And they called the name of the city Dan, after the name of Dan their father, who was born to Israel. However, the name of the city formerly *was* Laish.

30Then the children of Dan set up for themselves the carved image; and Jonathan the son of Gershom, the son of Manasseh,[a] and his sons were priests to the tribe of Dan until the day of the captivity of the land. 31So they set up for themselves Micah's carved image which he made, all the time that the house of God was in Shiloh.

The Levite's Concubine

19 And it came to pass in those days, when *there was* no king in Israel, that there was a certain Levite staying in the remote mountains of Ephraim. He took for himself a concubine from Bethlehem in Judah. 2But his concubine played the harlot against him, and went away from him to her father's house at Bethlehem in Judah, and was there four whole months. 3Then her husband arose and went after her, to speak kindly to her *and* bring her back, having his servant and a couple of donkeys with him. So she brought him into her father's house; and when the father of the young woman saw him, he was glad to meet him. 4Now his father-in-law, the young woman's father, detained him; and he stayed with him three days. So they ate and drank and lodged there.

5Then it came to pass on the fourth day that they arose early in the morning, and he stood to depart; but the young woman's father said to his son-in-law, "Refresh your heart with a morsel of bread, and afterward go your way." 6So they sat down, and the two of them ate and drank together. Then the young woman's father said to the man, "Please be content to stay all night, and let your heart be merry." 7And when the man stood to depart, his father-in-law urged him; so he lodged there again. 8Then he arose early in the morning on the fifth day to depart, but the young woman's father said, "Please refresh your heart." So they delayed until afternoon; and both of them ate.

9And when the man stood to depart—he and his concubine and his servant—his father-in-law, the young woman's father, said to him, "Look, the day is now drawing toward evening; please spend the night. See, the day is coming to an end; lodge here, that your heart may be merry. Tomorrow go your way early, so that you may get home."

10However, the man was not willing to spend that night; so he rose and departed, and came opposite Jebus (that *is,* Jerusalem). With him were the two saddled donkeys; his concubine *was* also with him. 11They *were* near Jebus, and the day was far spent; and the servant said to his master, "Come, please, and let us turn aside into this city of the Jebusites and lodge in it."

12But his master said to him, "We will not turn aside here into a city of foreigners, who *are* not of the children of Israel; we will go on to Gibeah." 13So he said to his servant, "Come, let us draw near to one of these places, and spend the night in Gibeah or in Ramah." 14And they passed by and went their way; and the sun went down on them near Gibeah, which belongs to Benjamin. 15They turned aside there to go in to lodge in Gibeah. And when he went in, he sat down in the open square of the city, for no one would take them into *his* house to spend the night.

16Just then an old man came in from his work in the field at evening, who also *was* from the mountains of Ephraim; he was staying in Gibeah, whereas the men of the place

18:30 [a]Septuagint and Vulgate read *Moses.*

were Benjamites. 17And when he raised his eyes, he saw the traveler in the open square of the city; and the old man said, "Where are you going, and where do you come from?"

18So he said to him, "We *are* passing from Bethlehem in Judah toward the remote mountains of Ephraim; I *am* from there. I went to Bethlehem in Judah; *now* I am going to the house of the LORD. But there *is* no one who will take me into his house, 19although we have both straw and fodder for our donkeys, and bread and wine for myself, for your female servant, and for the young man *who is* with your servant; *there is* no lack of anything."

20And the old man said, "Peace *be* with you! However, *let* all your needs *be* my responsibility; only do not spend the night in the open square." 21So he brought him into his house, and gave fodder to the donkeys. And they washed their feet, and ate and drank.

GIBEAH'S CRIME

22As they were enjoying themselves, suddenly certain men of the city, perverted men,[a] surrounded the house *and* beat on the door. They spoke to the master of the house, the old man, saying, "Bring out the man who came to your house, that we may know him *carnally!*"

23But the man, the master of the house, went out to them and said to them, "No, my brethren! I beg you, do not act *so* wickedly! Seeing this man has come into my house, do not commit this outrage. 24Look, *here is* my virgin daughter and *the man's*[a] concubine; let me bring them out now. Humble them, and do with them as you please; but to this man do not do such a vile thing!" 25But the men would not heed him. So the man took his concubine

19:22 [a]Literally *sons of Belial* **19:24** [a]Literally *his*

PERSONALITY PROFILE

THE LEVITE'S CONCUBINE

(JUDGES 19)

Abuse

Whether abusive acts have to do with power, things, or people, the results lead to destruction. When the writer of Judges concluded this journal about a nation in disarray, he summarized the chaos with these words, "In those days there was no king in Israel; everyone did what was right in his own eyes" (Judg. 21:25). No pattern of behavior leads to horrific abuses more quickly than when each person does whatever they want to do without regard to some external standard. The account of the woman abused by her husband and by strangers demonstrates this.

When the man from Ephraim took a concubine from Bethlehem, he ignored God's rules for relationships. She wasn't allowed to be a marriage partner; she was property. Her rebellion was a cry for dignity.

The Levite's trip to Bethlehem to retrieve his concubine turned into a tragedy of errors. On the return trip, the couple found themselves under the narrow hospitality of a man from Gibeah—wide enough to guarantee the Levite's safety even at the cost of his host's daughter, but utterly excluding the concubine. She was eventually offered as a sexual diversion to a mob that surrounded the house. Their intended homosexual assault on the Levite became a vicious gang rape of the concubine, resulting in her death.

Apparently oblivious to his own cowardice and abuse, the Levite dismembered the woman's body and sent parts throughout Israel, demanding justice. Even though the nation of Israel acted to exact justice on Gibeah, they also had to suffer as a result of the pervasive atmosphere of sin among the people. Sinful abuses not only led to death; almost as many Israelites as Benjamites died during the judgment of Gibeah. The nation had to be shocked and horrified into realizing the spreading effects of the abuse of God's law and the resulting abuses of persons created in His image.

To Learn More: Turn to the article about abuse on pages 328, 329. See also the key passage note at Genesis 19:4–9 on page 27.

HOPE FOR HEALING

DIANE LANGBERG

(Judges 19:25)

No one wants to think about sexual abuse—especially abuse of children or young people. However, statistics show that one in four females and one in six males are sexually molested prior to the age of eighteen. Such numbers indicate that many people are looking at life and spiritual matters through the lens of sexual abuse. And with such numbers, it is also certain that our church congregations include many people who are aching from having been sexually abused.

SEXUAL ABUSE DEFINED

Sexual abuse occurs when an older person sexually exploits a child in order to satisfy the abuser's needs. It consists of any sexual activity—verbal, visual, or physical—engaged in with a minor. Verbal sexual abuse includes comments about a person's body, lewd remarks, and the discussion of sexual activity. Visual sexual abuse includes pornography and being forced to view sexual activity of any kind. Physical abuse includes fondling or sexual contact.

Sexual abuse is most often perpetrated by an adult who has ready access to the child by virtue of authority or kinship. It can be a one-time occurrence or span many years. The majority of abusers of both male and female victims are male. When sexual abuse begins, the average age of the child is between six and twelve. The child is considered unable to consent due to developmental immaturity and an inability to understand sexual behavior. Sexual abuse is illegal in all fifty states.

SCRIPTURE AND SEXUAL ABUSE

Scripture says much that relates to the topic of sexual abuse. Except within the context of a marriage, all sexual relationships are wrong. Scripture constantly demonstrates God's love and care for children as an example for all people to emulate.

Scripture also has direct references to sexual abuse. Tamar was raped by her half brother Amnon, and from that point on "remained desolate in her brother Absalom's house" (2 Sam. 13:20). Judges 19 describes a woman's gang-rape by a group of crazed men. That hideous abuse and the protection of the abusers by the Benjamites caused a terrible war in Israel that cost 40,000 men their lives.

HOPE FOR HEALING

To be abused is to be touched by evil. Evil, like good, has an impact. There are many things that contribute to the impact of sexual abuse in a life. No two people are alike.

It is important for people to understand how the abuse has impacted them. What has it taught them? Where has it harmed them? Healing is applied knowledgeably only when a wound is understood. It is also crucial to know that no matter what the extent of the damage, no matter how badly one has been wounded, there is hope for healing.

Abuse that is frequent and of long duration has more severe effects. The more closely related the perpetrator and the victim, and the wider the age difference, the more severe the effects. Abuse by males is often considered more harmful, as is abuse involving penetrations of any kind, or abuse that is sadistic or violent.

Chronic childhood abuse does damage

to the body, the mind, the emotions, and the ability to relate to another person. The damage is multiplied over and over again during the essential developmental time when the child is forming a foundation for adulthood. Just as a young sapling can be trained to grow straight and tall or misshapen and twisted during its formative years, so a child can be impacted by life's early experiences.

People who have been chronically abused learn that bodies are for hurting and believe they have no choice about what happens to them. Healing will mean learning how to care for their bodies—to protect them from harm and maintain their integrity. It is very healing for survivors to see that Jesus lived in a body that was also abused. He was hit, spit on, humiliated, and left naked in front of others. The Healer, who is scarred for all eternity, knows the pain of abuse.

Sexual abuse also results in damage to the emotions—fear, grief, anger, and guilt often govern abused people's lives. It will take hard work to learn to deal with these emotions. But it can be done. Nothing is outside of God's power to heal and control.

Sexual abuse also damages people's thinking. Abused people lie to themselves that the abuse was not really bad, that the abuse was their fault, or that the abuse occurred because they are worthless. God hates abuse because He hates all evil. But He does not hate the victims. Abuse is the fault of the abusers, not the victims. Abuse victims will need help to hear God's truth speak louder than the lies of abuse.

Sexual abuse also deeply damages victims' spirits and ability to relate to God. Abuse hinders their ability to hope, may make them afraid of God, or make them unable to trust Him. Victims often struggle to understand why God allowed the abuse to occur.

We can help victims of abuse by helping them to focus on the character of God. The person of Christ and the Word of God teach the truth about who God is. As they learn more about God's power and ability to heal, they can place their past *and* their future in God's hands.

FURTHER MEDITATION:

Other passages to study about the issue of abuse include:

- Genesis 50:20
- Psalms 11; 27; 119:50, 73–88
- 2 Corinthians 1:3–7
- 1 Thessalonians 5:14

To Learn More: **Turn to the key passage note on abuse at Genesis 19:4–9 on page 27. See also the personality profile of the Levite's concubine on page 327.**

and brought *her* out to them. And they knew her and abused her all night until morning; and when the day began to break, they let her go.

26Then the woman came as the day was dawning, and fell down at the door of the man's house where her master *was,* till it was light.

27When her master arose in the morning, and opened the doors of the house and went out to go his way, there was his concubine, fallen *at* the door of the house with her hands on the threshold. 28And he said to her, "Get up and let us be going." But there was no answer. So the man lifted her onto the donkey; and the man got up and went to his place.

29When he entered his house he took a knife, laid hold of his concubine, and divided her into twelve pieces, limb by limb,[a] and sent her throughout all the territory of Israel. 30And so it was that all who saw it said, "No such deed has been done or seen from the day that the children of Israel came up from the land of Egypt until this day. Consider it, confer, and speak up!"

Israel's War with the Benjamites

20 So all the children of Israel came out, from Dan to Beersheba, as well as from the land of Gilead, and the congregation gathered together as one man before the LORD at Mizpah. 2And the leaders of all the people, all the tribes of Israel, presented themselves in the assembly of the people of God, four hundred thousand foot soldiers who drew the sword. 3(Now the children of Benjamin heard that the children of Israel had gone up to Mizpah.)

Then the children of Israel said, "Tell *us,* how did this wicked deed happen?"

4So the Levite, the husband of the woman who was murdered, answered and said, "My concubine and I went into Gibeah, which belongs to Benjamin, to spend the night. 5And the men of Gibeah rose against me, and surrounded the house at night because of me. They intended to kill me, but instead they ravished my concubine so that she died. 6So I took hold of my concubine, cut her in pieces, and sent her throughout all the territory of the inheritance of Israel, because they committed lewdness and outrage in Israel. 7Look! All of you *are* children of Israel; give your advice and counsel here and now!"

8So all the people arose as one man, saying, "None *of us* will go to his tent, nor will any turn back to his house; 9but now this *is* the thing which we will do to Gibeah: *We will go up* against it by lot. 10We will take ten men out of *every* hundred throughout all the tribes of Israel, a hundred out of *every* thousand, and a thousand out of *every* ten thousand, to make provisions for the people, that when they come to Gibeah in Benjamin, they may repay all the vileness that they have done in Israel." 11So all the men of Israel were gathered against the city, united together as one man.

12Then the tribes of Israel sent men through all the tribe of Benjamin, saying, "What *is* this wickedness that has occurred among you? 13Now therefore, deliver up the men, the perverted men[a] who *are* in Gibeah, that we may put them to death and remove the evil from Israel!" But the children of Benjamin would not listen to the voice of their brethren, the children of Israel. 14Instead, the children of Benjamin gathered together from their cities to Gibeah, to go to battle against the children of Israel. 15And from their cities at that time the children of Benjamin numbered twenty-six thousand men who drew the sword, besides the inhabitants of Gibeah, who numbered seven hundred select men. 16Among all this people *were* seven hundred select men *who were* left-handed; every one could sling a stone at a hair's *breadth* and not miss. 17Now besides Benjamin, the men of Israel numbered four hundred thousand men who drew the sword; all of these *were* men of war.

18Then the children of Israel arose and went up to the house of God[a] to inquire of God. They said, "Which of us shall go up first to battle against the children of Benjamin?"

The LORD said, "Judah first!"

19So the children of Israel rose in the morning and encamped against Gibeah. 20And the men of Israel went out to battle against Benjamin, and the men of Israel put themselves in battle array to fight against them at Gibeah. 21Then the children of Benjamin came out of Gibeah, and on that day cut down to the ground twenty-two thousand men of the Israelites. 22And the people, that is, the men of Israel, encouraged themselves and again formed the battle line at the place where they

19:29 [a]Literally *with her bones* **20:13** [a]Literally *sons of Belial* **20:18** [a]Or *Bethel*

had put themselves in array on the first day. [23]Then the children of Israel went up and wept before the LORD until evening, and asked counsel of the LORD, saying, "Shall I again draw near for battle against the children of my brother Benjamin?"

And the LORD said, "Go up against him."

[24]So the children of Israel approached the children of Benjamin on the second day. [25]And Benjamin went out against them from Gibeah on the second day, and cut down to the ground eighteen thousand more of the children of Israel; all these drew the sword.

[26]Then all the children of Israel, that is, all the people, went up and came to the house of God[a] and wept. They sat there before the LORD and fasted that day until evening; and they offered burnt offerings and peace offerings before the LORD. [27]So the children of Israel inquired of the LORD (the ark of the covenant of God *was* there in those days, [28]and Phinehas the son of Eleazar, the son of Aaron, stood before it in those days), saying, "Shall I yet again go out to battle against the children of my brother Benjamin, or shall I cease?"

And the LORD said, "Go up, for tomorrow I will deliver them into your hand."

[29]Then Israel set men in ambush all around Gibeah. [30]And the children of Israel went up against the children of Benjamin on the third day, and put themselves in battle array against Gibeah as at the other times. [31]So the children of Benjamin went out against the people, *and* were drawn away from the city. They began to strike down *and* kill some of the people, as at the other times, in the highways (one of which goes up to Bethel and the other to Gibeah) and in the field, about thirty men of Israel. [32]And the children of Benjamin said, "They *are* defeated before us, as at first."

But the children of Israel said, "Let us flee and draw them away from the city to the highways." [33]So all the men of Israel rose from their place and put themselves in battle array at Baal Tamar. Then Israel's men in ambush burst forth from their position in the plain of Geba. [34]And ten thousand select men from all Israel came against Gibeah, and the battle was fierce. But *the Benjamites*[a] did not know that disaster *was* upon them. [35]The LORD defeated Benjamin before Israel. And the children of Israel destroyed that day twenty-five thousand one hundred Benjamites; all these drew the sword.

[36]So the children of Benjamin saw that they were defeated. The men of Israel had given ground to the Benjamites, because they relied on the men in ambush whom they had set against Gibeah. [37]And the men in ambush quickly rushed upon Gibeah; the men in ambush spread out and struck the whole city with the edge of the sword. [38]Now the appointed signal between the men of Israel and the men in ambush was that they would make a great cloud of smoke rise up from the city, [39]whereupon the men of Israel would turn in battle. Now Benjamin had begun to strike *and* kill about thirty of the men of Israel. For they said, "Surely they are defeated before us, as *in* the first battle." [40]But when the cloud began to rise from the city in a column of smoke, the Benjamites looked behind them, and there was the whole city going up *in smoke* to heaven. [41]And when the men of Israel turned back, the men of Benjamin panicked, for they saw that disaster had come upon them. [42]Therefore they turned *their backs* before the men of Israel in the direction of the wilderness; but the battle overtook them, and whoever *came* out of the cities they destroyed in their midst. [43]They surrounded the Benjamites, chased them, *and* easily trampled them down as far as the front of Gibeah toward the east. [44]And eighteen thousand men of Benjamin fell; all these *were* men of valor. [45]Then they[a] turned and fled toward the wilderness to the rock of Rimmon; and they cut down five thousand of them on the highways. Then they pursued them relentlessly up to Gidom, and killed two thousand of them. [46]So all who fell of Benjamin that day were twenty-five thousand men who drew the sword; all these *were* men of valor.

[47]But six hundred men turned and fled toward the wilderness to the rock of Rimmon, and they stayed at the rock of Rimmon for four months. [48]And the men of Israel turned back against the children of Benjamin, and struck them down with the edge of the sword—from *every* city, men and beasts, all who were found. They also set fire to all the cities they came to.

WIVES PROVIDED FOR THE BENJAMITES

21 Now the men of Israel had sworn an oath at Mizpah, saying, "None of us

---

20:26 [a]Or *Bethel* **20:34** [a]Literally *they*
20:45 [a]Septuagint reads *the rest.*

shall give his daughter to Benjamin as a wife."
2Then the people came to the house of God,[a]
and remained there before God till evening.
They lifted up their voices and wept bitterly,
3and said, "O LORD God of Israel, why has this
come to pass in Israel, that today there should
be one tribe *missing* in Israel?"

4So it was, on the next morning, that the
people rose early and built an altar there, and
offered burnt offerings and peace offerings.
5The children of Israel said, "Who *is there*
among all the tribes of Israel who did not
come up with the assembly to the LORD?" For
they had made a great oath concerning anyone who had not come up to the LORD at Mizpah, saying, "He shall surely be put to death."
6And the children of Israel grieved for Benjamin their brother, and said, "One tribe is cut
off from Israel today. 7What shall we do for
wives for those who remain, seeing we have
sworn by the LORD that we will not give them
our daughters as wives?"

8And they said, "What one *is there* from the
tribes of Israel who did not come up to Mizpah to the LORD?" And, in fact, no one had
come to the camp from Jabesh Gilead to the
assembly. 9For when the people were counted,
indeed, not one of the inhabitants of Jabesh
Gilead *was* there. 10So the congregation sent
out there twelve thousand of their most valiant men, and commanded them, saying, "Go
and strike the inhabitants of Jabesh Gilead
with the edge of the sword, including the
women and children. 11And this *is* the thing
that you shall do: You shall utterly destroy every male, and every woman who has known a
man intimately." 12So they found among the
inhabitants of Jabesh Gilead four hundred
young virgins who had not known a man intimately; and they brought them to the camp at
Shiloh, which is in the land of Canaan.

13Then the whole congregation sent *word* to
the children of Benjamin who *were* at the rock
of Rimmon, and announced peace to them.
14So Benjamin came back at that time, and
they gave them the women whom they had
saved alive of the women of Jabesh Gilead;
and yet they had not found enough for them.

15And the people grieved for Benjamin, because the LORD had made a void in the tribes
of Israel.

16Then the elders of the congregation said,
"What shall we do for wives for those who remain, since the women of Benjamin have
been destroyed?" 17And they said, "*There
must be* an inheritance for the survivors of
Benjamin, that a tribe may not be destroyed
from Israel. 18However, we cannot give them
wives from our daughters, for the children of
Israel have sworn an oath, saying, 'Cursed *be*
the one who gives a wife to Benjamin.' "
19Then they said, "In fact, *there is* a yearly
feast of the LORD in Shiloh, which *is* north of
Bethel, on the east side of the highway that
goes up from Bethel to Shechem, and south of
Lebonah."

20Therefore they instructed the children of
Benjamin, saying, "Go, lie in wait in the vineyards, 21and watch; and just when the daughters of Shiloh come out to perform their
dances, then come out from the vineyards,
and every man catch a wife for himself from
the daughters of Shiloh; then go to the land of
Benjamin. 22Then it shall be, when their fathers or their brothers come to us to complain,
that we will say to them, 'Be kind to them for
our sakes, because we did not take a wife for
any of them in the war; for *it is* not *as though*
you have given the *women* to them at this

21:2 [a]Or *Bethel*

SOUL NOTE

Whatever Seems Right *(21:25)* The Israelites had no king and no commitment to God. Thus they did whatever seemed right in their own eyes. When people remove God from life, they are left with no guidelines other than what *they* think is right. Our culture today says we must be tolerant of everything—even blatant sin. Israel's tolerance of sin turned them away from God. Christians should be tolerant of different viewpoints, but should not condone beliefs or practices that would lead away from God's standards. We must be completely intolerant of sin and remove it from our lives. **Topic: Tolerance**

time, making yourselves guilty of your oath.' "
[23]And the children of Benjamin did so; they
took enough wives for their number from
those who danced, whom they caught. Then
they went and returned to their inheritance,
and they rebuilt the cities and dwelt in them.

[24]So the children of Israel departed from there
at that time, every man to his tribe and family;
they went out from there, every man to his inheritance.
[25]In those days *there was* no king in Israel;
everyone did *what was* right in his own eyes.

Ruth

To the familiar short list of "death and taxes" we can add one other certainty in life: grief. When we lose what we value, we grieve. Our losses may be obvious to all—a spouse, a child, a job, our health. Or they may be more private—the loss of status, relational intimacy, a secret dream. Everyone grieves. The question is: Will we let that grief paralyze our lives?

Ruth was a young Moabite woman who had married an Israelite. When all the men in this extended family died, the women faced uncertain futures. But Ruth clung to her mother-in-law, Naomi, pledging, "Wherever you go, I will go; and wherever you lodge, I will lodge; your people shall be my people, and your God, my God" (1:16).

Although Ruth and Naomi lived on the edge of poverty, God provided amply for their needs. They returned to Israel, where Ruth met and married a wealthy farmer named Boaz. In the house of Boaz, both Ruth and Naomi found joy.

The Book of Ruth is a primer on handling grief. It shows that God's compassion and faithful friends can give us the courage to meet grief head-on. Ruth's life is a great encouragement to those whose souls are bent low by the grief of the past and the seeming hopelessness of the future. In the words of the psalm writer, "Weeping may endure for a night, but joy comes in the morning" (Ps. 30:5).

SOUL CONCERN IN RUTH

Elimelech's Family Goes to Moab

1 Now it came to pass, in the days when the judges ruled, that there was a famine in the land. And a certain man of Bethlehem, Judah, went to dwell in the country of Moab, he and his wife and his two sons. [2]The name of the man *was* Elimelech, the name of his wife *was* Naomi, and the names of his two sons *were* Mahlon and Chilion—Ephrathites of Bethlehem, Judah. And they went to the country of Moab and remained there. [3]Then Elimelech, Naomi's husband, died; and she was left, and her two sons. [4]Now they took wives of the women of Moab: the name of the one *was* Orpah, and the name of the other Ruth. And they dwelt there about ten years. [5]Then both Mahlon and Chilion also died; so the woman survived her two sons and her husband.

Naomi Returns with Ruth

[6]Then she arose with her daughters-in-law that she might return from the country of Moab, for she had heard in the country of Moab that the LORD had visited His people by giving them bread. [7]Therefore she went out from the place where she was, and her two daughters-in-law with her; and they went on the way to return to the land of Judah. [8]And Naomi said to her two daughters-in-law, "Go, return each to her mother's house. The LORD deal kindly with you, as you have dealt with the dead and with me. [9]The LORD grant that you may find rest, each in the house of her husband."

So she kissed them, and they lifted up their voices and wept. [10]And they said to her, "Surely we will return with you to your people."

[11]But Naomi said, "Turn back, my daughters; why will you go with me? *Are* there still sons in my womb, that they may be your husbands? [12]Turn back, my daughters, go—for I am too old to have a husband. If I should say I have hope, *if* I should have a husband tonight and should also bear sons, [13]would you wait for them till they were grown? Would you restrain yourselves from having husbands? No, my daughters; for it grieves me very much for your sakes that the hand of the LORD has gone out against me!"

[14]Then they lifted up their voices and wept again; and Orpah kissed her mother-in-law, but Ruth clung to her.

[15]And she said, "Look, your sister-in-law has gone back to her people and to her gods; return after your sister-in-law."

[16]But Ruth said:

"Entreat me not to leave you,
Or to turn back from following after you;
For wherever you go, I will go;
And wherever you lodge, I will lodge;
Your people *shall be* my people,
And your God, my God.
17 Where you die, I will die,
And there will I be buried.
The LORD do so to me, and more also,
If *anything but* death parts you and me."

[18]When she saw that she was determined to go with her, she stopped speaking to her.

[19]Now the two of them went until they came to Bethlehem. And it happened, when they had come to Bethlehem, that all the city was excited because of them; and the women said, "*Is* this Naomi?"

[20]But she said to them, "Do not call me Naomi;[a] call me Mara,[b] for the Almighty has

1:20 [a]Literally *Pleasant* [b]Literally *Bitter*

SOUL NOTE

The Language of Love *(1:16, 17)* People say "I love you" in many different ways. It is often said best through actions. Ruth showed her love for Naomi by staying with her and by working hard to support them both (2:6, 7). Ruth loved and trusted Naomi, so she followed Naomi's advice in going to Boaz (3:1–9). Boaz was also a man of action, immediately handling the matter of providing for Ruth and becoming the redeemer for these women (3:18). We may not always hear the words, "I love you," but, if we listen, we may hear them through another's kind actions toward us.
Topic: Love Languages

dealt very bitterly with me. [21]I went out full,
and the LORD has brought me home again
empty. Why do you call me Naomi, since the
LORD has testified against me, and the Almighty has afflicted me?"

[22]So Naomi returned, and Ruth the Moabitess her daughter-in-law with her, who returned from the country of Moab. Now they came to Bethlehem at the beginning of barley harvest.

RUTH MEETS BOAZ

2 There was a relative of Naomi's husband, a man of great wealth, of the family of
Elimelech. His name *was* Boaz. [2]So Ruth the
Moabitess said to Naomi, "Please let me go to the field, and glean heads of grain after *him* in whose sight I may find favor."

And she said to her, "Go, my daughter."

[3]Then she left, and went and gleaned in the
field after the reapers. And she happened to come to the part of the field *belonging* to Boaz, who *was* of the family of Elimelech.

[4]Now behold, Boaz came from Bethlehem,
and said to the reapers, "The LORD *be* with you!"

And they answered him, "The LORD bless you!"

[5]Then Boaz said to his servant who was in
charge of the reapers, "Whose young woman *is* this?"

[6]So the servant who was in charge of the
reapers answered and said, "It *is* the young Moabite woman who came back with Naomi
from the country of Moab. [7]And she said,
'Please let me glean and gather after the reap-

PERSONALITY PROFILE

Sexual Integrity

RUTH & BOAZ — SEXUAL INTEGRITY IN PREMARITAL RELATIONSHIPS

(RUTH 2—3)

The way in which a couple meets and the story of their courtship reveals much about their marriage prospects. Ruth and Boaz lived one of the Bible's most romantic love stories. As in every true love story, Ruth and Boaz had their share of sorrow, difficulty, adventure, and victory. Where fools rush in, Ruth and Boaz walked wisely.

Boaz met Ruth shortly after she arrived in Bethlehem with Naomi, her mother-in-law, who was returning home. Both women were widows. They were also friends. Naomi's God had become Ruth's. The lovely Moabitess graciously assumed the role of resourceful provider for the two women, never guessing what surprises God had in store.

Ruth showed up during the harvest of Boaz's fields, gleaning the leftovers to feed Naomi and herself. Boaz noticed her. A few tactful questions later, Boaz began to demonstrate special attention toward Ruth. He encouraged her to stay with his work crew. He informed her that she was under his guarantee of safety because of her special care for his relative Naomi.

During the harvest days, mutual respect and appreciation became special affection between Ruth and Boaz. Under Naomi's guidance, Ruth let Boaz know she was open to his role as kinsman-redeemer, meaning that he would marry her, care for her, and perhaps carry on the family line. Boaz praised her character and promised to take action. When it was all said and done, their marriage made them part of the ancestry of Jesus.

Sexual possibilities were undoubtedly part of Ruth and Boaz's story, but they did not use sex to determine their relationship. They are a romantic tribute to the power of sexual integrity before marriage.

To Learn More: Turn to the articles about sexual integrity on pages 1608, 1609 and premarital relationships on pages 338, 339. See also the key passage note on sexual integrity at 1 Corinthians 6:15 on page 1499, and the key passage note on premarital relationships at Amos 3:3 on page 1151.

ers among the sheaves.' So she came and has
continued from morning until now, though
she rested a little in the house."
8Then Boaz said to Ruth, "You will listen,
my daughter, will you not? Do not go to glean
in another field, nor go from here, but stay
close by my young women. 9*Let* your eyes *be*
on the field which they reap, and go after
them. Have I not commanded the young men
not to touch you? And when you are thirsty,
go to the vessels and drink from what the
young men have drawn."
10So she fell on her face, bowed down to the
ground, and said to him, "Why have I found
favor in your eyes, that you should take notice
of me, since I *am* a foreigner?"
11And Boaz answered and said to her, "It has
been fully reported to me, all that you have
done for your mother-in-law since the death of
your husband, and *how* you have left your father and your mother and the land of your
birth, and have come to a people whom you
did not know before. 12The LORD repay your
work, and a full reward be given you by the
LORD God of Israel, under whose wings you
have come for refuge."
13Then she said, "Let me find favor in your
sight, my lord; for you have comforted me,
and have spoken kindly to your maidservant,
though I am not like one of your maidservants."
14Now Boaz said to her at mealtime, "Come
here, and eat of the bread, and dip your piece
of bread in the vinegar." So she sat beside the
reapers, and he passed parched *grain* to her;
and she ate and was satisfied, and kept some
back. 15And when she rose up to glean, Boaz
commanded his young men, saying, "Let her
glean even among the sheaves, and do not reproach her. 16Also let *grain* from the bundles
fall purposely for her; leave *it* that she may
glean, and do not rebuke her."
17So she gleaned in the field until evening,
and beat out what she had gleaned, and it was
about an ephah of barley. 18Then she took *it*
up and went into the city, and her mother-in-
law saw what she had gleaned. So she
brought out and gave to her what she had kept
back after she had been satisfied.
19And her mother-in-law said to her,
"Where have you gleaned today? And where
did you work? Blessed be the one who took
notice of you."
So she told her mother-in-law with whom
she had worked, and said, "The man's name
with whom I worked today *is* Boaz."
20Then Naomi said to her daughter-in-law,
"Blessed *be* he of the LORD, who has not forsaken His kindness to the living and the
dead!" And Naomi said to her, "This man *is* a
relation of ours, one of our close relatives."
21Ruth the Moabitess said, "He also said to
me, 'You shall stay close by my young men
until they have finished all my harvest.' "
22And Naomi said to Ruth her daughter-in-
law, "*It is* good, my daughter, that you go out
with his young women, and that people do
not meet you in any other field." 23So she
stayed close by the young women of Boaz, to
glean until the end of barley harvest and
wheat harvest; and she dwelt with her mother-
in-law.

RUTH'S REDEMPTION ASSURED

3 Then Naomi her mother-in-law said to
her, "My daughter, shall I not seek security for you, that it may be well with you?
2Now Boaz, whose young women you were
with, *is he* not our relative? In fact, he is winnowing barley tonight at the threshing floor.
3Therefore wash yourself and anoint yourself,
put on your *best* garment and go down to the
threshing floor; *but* do not make yourself
known to the man until he has finished eating
and drinking. 4Then it shall be, when he lies
down, that you shall notice the place where
he lies; and you shall go in, uncover his feet,
and lie down; and he will tell you what you
should do."
5And she said to her, "All that you say to me
I will do."
6So she went down to the threshing floor
and did according to all that her mother-in-
law instructed her. 7And after Boaz had eaten
and drunk, and his heart was cheerful, he
went to lie down at the end of the heap of
grain; and she came softly, uncovered his feet,
and lay down.
8Now it happened at midnight that the man
was startled, and turned himself; and there, a
woman was lying at his feet. 9And he said,
"Who *are* you?"
So she answered, "I *am* Ruth, your maidservant. Take your maidservant under your
wing,[a] for you are a close relative."

3:9 [a]Or *Spread the corner of your garment over your maidservant*

Premarital Relationships

THE DATING GAME

LES AND LESLIE PARROTT

(Ruth 3:10–14)

Falling in love can be a dizzying experience. Once the spark of attraction catches flame, love can quickly turn into a raging fire of unreasonable passion. Engulfed by its heat, people sometimes sacrifice all sound judgment. The Song of Solomon says, "Many waters cannot quench love, nor can the floods drown it" (Song 8:7). Love can cause some people to "lose their head," and they lose their capacity to think clearly. This is why Scripture admonishes people to seek wisdom: "Get wisdom, and in all your getting, get understanding" (Prov. 4:7).

The word *wisdom* often elicits images of old men with long beards, but wisdom does not necessarily come with age. If that were so, the Bible would not tell us to be wise right now. Neither is wisdom the result of a high IQ. Being brilliant does not necessarily mean being wise. Wisdom is defined as "a common-sense understanding of what is true, right, or lasting."

Wisdom is vital throughout life, but it is particularly important in the dating process. As people date, they usually put their best foot forward and are not completely genuine; they face temptation to sexual sin; they deal with many strong emotions—all while they are attempting to decide on the person with whom they will spend the rest of life, "for better or worse." Obviously, people who are in the process of dating are better off seeking God's discernment regarding the character of the people they date.

Wisdom helps people avoid embarrassing mistakes, to not jump to conclusions or make decisions without first gathering the facts. Some who are in the process of dating think that the exhilaration of infatuation will last forever. They need wisdom to guide them into a strong relationship based on more than exciting feelings. Romance focuses mostly on emotion; true love is grounded in character; true character is discerned through wisdom.

DISCERNING A PERSON'S CHARACTER

Wisdom is not concerned with *doing* but with *being*, so it can be difficult to spot. But a wise person will have a steady demeanor and attitude over a long period of time that will reveal his or her wisdom (or the lack of it). That is why people generally date for many months. They need to see each other in a variety of situations across a span of time. Wisdom, or lack of wisdom, will emerge over time in hundreds of ways great and small. It will help, then, for people to have some idea what to look for as they date a person over a period of time.

Spiritual or Worldly?

Evangelist Billy Graham once said, "Knowledge is horizontal; wisdom is vertical—it comes down from above." Spiritual wisdom can only be given by the Holy Spirit. For this reason, Christians should only date other Christians. There cannot be a true spiritual dimension in a person who is not a believer. Even then, however, people must be discerning. Anyone can say the right words and act the right way for a time, but the genuine person will eventually be revealed. Even if the other person is a believer, each person must still carefully consider the depth of that person's faith. Does the other have a heart for God? Does he or she possess true spiritual wisdom? Of course, everyone is a pilgrim on the path and no one will be perfect, but those who are dating must ask God for discernment and guidance as they consider this other person's personal relationship with God.

Humble or Self-centered?
Humility is an important attribute in a date. Proverbs 11:2 warns, "When pride comes, then comes shame; but with the humble is wisdom." A humble person seeks the other's good. A humble person can ask for help. Only a truly humble person will be able to love his or her spouse completely, according to the kind of love described in 1 Corinthians 13: "Love suffers long and is kind; love does not envy; loves does not parade itself, is not puffed up; does not behave rudely, does not seek its own . . ." (1 Cor. 13:4, 5). Such love is fundamental to a positive and lasting relationship.

Genuine or Deceptive?
Sincerity is a valuable virtue. Going on a date, however, is often a showcase, a place to conceal shortcomings. As they are dating, many people try to disguise their flaws and defects; others attempt to exaggerate their positive qualities, or even lie. This can cause people to obsess about how to look, what to say, how to eat. The whole routine is misleading. For this reason, it is particularly important to look beyond the veneer by dating over a period of time and by doing things together in a variety of situations. The real person will eventually emerge—for better or worse. But it would be better to discover that real person *before* making the "for better or worse" vow!

SO IS IT LOVE OR INFATUATION?

Even when a person is dating a spiritual, humble, and genuine person, how can real love be distinguished from temporary infatuation? Several characteristics separate true love from infatuation. Infatuation is based on physical characteristics; love is based on the whole person. Infatuation is instant ("love at first sight"); love grows steadily over time. Infatuation can be lost in a moment, for it is based only on feelings; love is a commitment that remains as feelings come and go. Infatuation meets *my* needs; love meets *our* needs.

The decision you are making will last a lifetime. Take your time and make it wisely.

FURTHER MEDITATION:

Other passages to study about the issue of premarital relationships include:

- 1 Kings 11:1–13
- Proverbs 2; 5—9
- Ecclesiastes 4:9–12
- Amos 3:3
- 1 Corinthians 13
- 2 Corinthians 6:14–18

To Learn More: Turn to the key passage note on premarital relationships at Amos 3:3 on page 1151. See also the personality profile of Ruth and Boaz on page 336.

10Then he said, "Blessed *are* you of the
LORD, my daughter! For you have shown more
kindness at the end than at the beginning, in
that you did not go after young men, whether
poor or rich. 11And now, my daughter, do not
fear. I will do for you all that you request, for
all the people of my town know that you *are* a
virtuous woman. 12Now it is true that I *am* a
close relative; however, there is a relative closer than I. 13Stay this night, and in the morning
it shall be *that* if he will perform the duty of a
close relative for you—good; let him do it. But
if he does not want to perform the duty for
you, then I will perform the duty for you, *as*
the LORD lives! Lie down until morning."

14So she lay at his feet until morning, and
she arose before one could recognize another.
Then he said, "Do not let it be known that the
woman came to the threshing floor." 15Also he
said, "Bring the shawl that *is* on you and hold
it." And when she held it, he measured six
ephahs of barley, and laid *it* on her. Then she[a]
went into the city.

16When she came to her mother-in-law, she
said, "*Is* that you, my daughter?"

Then she told her all that the man had done
for her. 17And she said, "These six *ephahs* of
barley he gave me; for he said to me, 'Do not
go empty-handed to your mother-in-law.' "

18Then she said, "Sit still, my daughter, until you know how the matter will turn out; for
the man will not rest until he has concluded
the matter this day."

BOAZ REDEEMS RUTH

4 Now Boaz went up to the gate and sat
down there; and behold, the close relative
of whom Boaz had spoken came by. So Boaz
said, "Come aside, friend,[a] sit down here." So
he came aside and sat down. 2And he took ten
men of the elders of the city, and said, "Sit
down here." So they sat down. 3Then he said
to the close relative, "Naomi, who has come
back from the country of Moab, sold the piece
of land which *belonged* to our brother Elimelech. 4And I thought to inform you, saying,
'Buy *it* back in the presence of the inhabitants
and the elders of my people. If you will redeem *it,* redeem *it;* but if you[a] will not redeem
it, then tell me, that I may know; for *there is*
no one but you to redeem *it,* and I *am* next
after you.' "

And he said, "I will redeem *it.*"

5Then Boaz said, "On the day you buy the
field from the hand of Naomi, you must also
buy *it* from Ruth the Moabitess, the wife of the
dead, to perpetuate[a] the name of the dead
through his inheritance."

6And the close relative said, "I cannot redeem *it* for myself, lest I ruin my own inheritance. You redeem my right of redemption for
yourself, for I cannot redeem *it.*"

7Now this *was the custom* in former times in
Israel concerning redeeming and exchanging,
to confirm anything: one man took off his sandal and gave *it* to the other, and this *was* a
confirmation in Israel.

8Therefore the close relative said to Boaz,
"Buy *it* for yourself." So he took off his sandal.
9And Boaz said to the elders and all the people, "You *are* witnesses this day that I have
bought all that was Elimelech's, and all that
was Chilion's and Mahlon's, from the hand of
Naomi. 10Moreover, Ruth the Moabitess, the
widow of Mahlon, I have acquired as my wife,

3:15 [a]Many Hebrew manuscripts, Syriac, and Vulgate read *she;* Masoretic Text, Septuagint, and Targum read *he.* **4:1** [a]Hebrew *peloni almoni;* literally *so and so* **4:4** [a]Following many Hebrew manuscripts, Septuagint, Syriac, Targum, and Vulgate; Masoretic Text reads *he.* **4:5** [a]Literally *raise up*

SOUL NOTE

People of Character *(3:11)* Marriages in this culture were generally arranged by a girl's parents. In Ruth's case, Naomi did the arranging by instructing her to approach Boaz, a near kinsman, whose duty it would be to marry her. Boaz had heard about Ruth (2:11, 12) and had great respect for her because she was known as "a virtuous woman" (3:11). Ruth appreciated Boaz's kindness to her and Naomi. Although our culture is very different, people who are dating should look at the other person's character before deciding whether to marry. In the long run, character is what will matter most. **Topic: Premarital Relationships**

to perpetuate the name of the dead through
his inheritance, that the name of the dead may
not be cut off from among his brethren and
from his position at the gate.[a] You *are* witnesses this day."
11And all the people who *were* at the gate,
and the elders, said, "*We are* witnesses. The
LORD make the woman who is coming to your
house like Rachel and Leah, the two who built
the house of Israel; and may you prosper in
Ephrathah and be famous in Bethlehem.
12May your house be like the house of Perez,
whom Tamar bore to Judah, because of the
offspring which the LORD will give you from
this young woman."

Descendants of Boaz and Ruth

13So Boaz took Ruth and she became his
wife; and when he went in to her, the LORD
gave her conception, and she bore a son.
14Then the women said to Naomi, "Blessed *be*
the LORD, who has not left you this day without a close relative; and may his name be famous in Israel! 15And may he be to you a
restorer of life and a nourisher of your old age;
for your daughter-in-law, who loves you, who
is better to you than seven sons, has borne
him." 16Then Naomi took the child and laid
him on her bosom, and became a nurse to him.
17Also the neighbor women gave him a name,
saying, "There is a son born to Naomi." And
they called his name Obed. He *is* the father of
Jesse, the father of David.
18Now this *is* the genealogy of Perez: Perez
begot Hezron; 19Hezron begot Ram, and Ram
begot Amminadab; 20Amminadab begot Nahshon, and Nahshon begot Salmon;[a] 21Salmon
begot Boaz, and Boaz begot Obed; 22Obed begot Jesse, and Jesse begot David.

4:10 [a]Probably his civic office **4:20** [a]Hebrew *Salmah*

1 Samuel

Some people make a mess of their lives. Others make a difference with their lives.

Nowhere is this contrast more clear than in the Book of 1 Samuel. Following the dark period of the judges, Israel demands a king so they can be like all the pagan nations around them. The prophet Samuel, at God's insistence, anoints Saul. Though Saul's reign begins well, he soon lapses into a lifestyle of disobedience.

In the meantime, God is preparing a new king for Israel—a young shepherd named David who has a passionate heart for God (13:14). Throughout the latter half of the book, David demonstrates the kingly qualities of courage, character, and faith by boldly killing the giant Goliath, faithfully serving the increasingly paranoid Saul, and trusting God during the years he must live as a fugitive, hiding himself from Saul's murderous rage.

As Saul sinks further into depravity, David grows in faithfulness and strength, preparing to be a great leader for God. By the end of the book, the contrast between the two leaders is stark. Saul is spiritually bankrupt—mentally and emotionally disturbed, consumed with jealous hatred, and suicidal. David, on the other hand, has grown into a leader who is walking closely with God. He is faithful to God, battle-tested, and ready to lead Israel.

Let 1 Samuel remind you that every choice of the soul has consequences. Our lives can be a mess, or they can make a difference. The choice is ours.

SOUL CONCERNS IN 1 SAMUEL

MENTAL ILLNESS	(16:14–23)
OCCULT	(28:7)

The Family of Elkanah

1 Now there was a certain man of Ramathaim Zophim, of the mountains of Ephraim, and his name *was* Elkanah the son of Jeroham, the son of Elihu,[a] the son of Tohu,[b] the son of Zuph, an Ephraimite. [2]And he had two wives: the name of one *was* Hannah, and the name of the other Peninnah. Peninnah had children, but Hannah had no children. [3]This man went up from his city yearly to worship and sacrifice to the LORD of hosts in Shiloh. Also the two sons of Eli, Hophni and Phinehas, the priests of the LORD, *were* there. [4]And whenever the time came for Elkanah to make an offering, he would give portions to Peninnah his wife and to all her sons and daughters. [5]But to Hannah he would give a double portion, for he loved Hannah, although the LORD had closed her womb. [6]And her rival also provoked her severely, to make her miserable, because the LORD had closed her womb. [7]So it was, year by year, when she went up to the house of the LORD, that she provoked her; therefore she wept and did not eat.

Hannah's Vow

[8]Then Elkanah her husband said to her, "Hannah, why do you weep? Why do you not eat? And why is your heart grieved? *Am* I not better to you than ten sons?"

[9]So Hannah arose after they had finished eating and drinking in Shiloh. Now Eli the priest was sitting on the seat by the doorpost of the tabernacle[a] of the LORD. [10]And she *was* in bitterness of soul, and prayed to the LORD and wept in anguish. [11]Then she made a vow and said, "O LORD of hosts, if You will indeed look on the affliction of Your maidservant and remember me, and not forget Your maidservant, but will give Your maidservant a male child, then I will give him to the LORD all the days of his life, and no razor shall come upon his head."

[12]And it happened, as she continued praying before the LORD, that Eli watched her mouth. [13]Now Hannah spoke in her heart; only her lips moved, but her voice was not heard. Therefore Eli thought she was drunk. [14]So Eli said to her, "How long will you be drunk? Put your wine away from you!"

[15]But Hannah answered and said, "No, my lord, I *am* a woman of sorrowful spirit. I have drunk neither wine nor intoxicating drink, but have poured out my soul before the LORD. [16]Do not consider your maidservant a wicked woman,[a] for out of the abundance of my complaint and grief I have spoken until now."

[17]Then Eli answered and said, "Go in peace, and the God of Israel grant your petition which you have asked of Him."

[18]And she said, "Let your maidservant find favor in your sight." So the woman went her way and ate, and her face was no longer *sad.*

Samuel Is Born and Dedicated

[19]Then they rose early in the morning and worshiped before the LORD, and returned and came to their house at Ramah. And Elkanah knew Hannah his wife, and the LORD remembered her. [20]So it came to pass in the process of time that Hannah conceived and bore a son, and called his name Samuel,[a] *saying,* "Because I have asked for him from the LORD."

[21]Now the man Elkanah and all his house went up to offer to the LORD the yearly sacrifice and his vow. [22]But Hannah did not go up, for she said to her husband, "*Not* until the child is weaned; then I will take him, that he may appear before the LORD and remain there forever."

[23]So Elkanah her husband said to her, "Do what seems best to you; wait until you have weaned him. Only let the LORD establish His[a] word." Then the woman stayed and nursed her son until she had weaned him.

[24]Now when she had weaned him, she took him up with her, with three bulls,[a] one ephah of flour, and a skin of wine, and brought him to the house of the LORD in Shiloh. And the child *was* young. [25]Then they slaughtered a bull, and brought the child to Eli. [26]And she said, "O my lord! As your soul lives, my lord, I *am* the woman who stood by you here, praying to the LORD. [27]For this child I prayed, and the LORD has granted me my petition which I asked of Him. [28]Therefore I also have lent him to the LORD; as long as he lives he shall be lent to the LORD." So they worshiped the LORD there.

1:1 [a]Spelled *Eliel* in 1 Chronicles 6:34 [b]Spelled *Toah* in 1 Chronicles 6:34 **1:9** [a]Hebrew *heykal,* palace or temple **1:16** [a]Literally *daughter of Belial* **1:20** [a]Literally *Heard by God*
1:23 [a]Following Masoretic Text, Targum, and Vulgate; Dead Sea Scrolls, Septuagint, and Syriac read *your.* **1:24** [a]Dead Sea Scrolls, Septuagint, and Syriac read *a three-year-old bull.*

HANNAH'S PRAYER

2 And Hannah prayed and said:

"My heart rejoices in the LORD;
My horn[a] is exalted in the LORD.
I smile at my enemies,
Because I rejoice in Your salvation.

2 "No one is holy like the LORD,
For *there is* none besides You,
Nor *is there* any rock like our God.

3 "Talk no more so very proudly;
Let no arrogance come from your mouth,
For the LORD *is* the God of knowledge;
And by Him actions are weighed.

4 "The bows of the mighty men *are* broken,
And those who stumbled are girded with
strength.

5 *Those who were* full have hired
themselves out for bread,
And the hungry have ceased *to hunger.*
Even the barren has borne seven,
And she who has many children has
become feeble.

6 "The LORD kills and makes alive;
He brings down to the grave and brings
up.
7 The LORD makes poor and makes rich;
He brings low and lifts up.
8 He raises the poor from the dust
And lifts the beggar from the ash heap,
To set *them* among princes
And make them inherit the throne of
glory.

2:1 [a]That is, strength

SOUL NOTE

On Loan *(1:27, 28)* Children are gifts from God. In ancient Israelite culture, not having children was seen as a great tragedy. Samuel's birth was a blessing to Hannah. To thank God for answering her prayer, Hannah kept her promise and dedicated Samuel to serve the Lord at the tabernacle. Her words to Eli the high priest serve as a model for all parents. Even as parents care for and raise their children, they must remember that each child ultimately belongs to God. Parents give their children back to the Lord when they entrust their children to God and His guidance. **Topic: Motherhood**

KEY PASSAGE

Parenting

A MOST IMPORTANT JOB

(1:27, 28)

Parenting is demanding and rewarding. Many people prepare and study for years to enter a chosen profession, but parenting is usually on-the-job training. Moreover, it is a job with no retirement plan.

The family unit, created by God, is the basic foundation of every society. God calls children "a reward" (Ps. 127:3). He commands parents to raise their children with loving discipline (Prov. 10:1, 5; 13:1; 15:20), bringing them up "in the training and admonition of the Lord" (Eph. 6:4). The goal of parenting is to eventually let the children go. Like Hannah, parents begin that letting-go process right away as they understand that their children are God's gifts. They are lent to us for a time, and we give them back to God as we allow them to follow His guidance in their lives.

Turn to the article about parenting on pages 826, 827. See also the personality profile of Abraham on page 26.

KEY PASSAGE

Infertility

HANNAH'S HURT

(2:5)

Hannah's infertility caused great distress because children were seen as a sign of God's blessing. By extension, therefore, barrenness was seen as a curse. Children were important for the continuance of the family line and family inheritance.

Infertility still causes pain, although perhaps for different reasons. Like Hannah, women who are infertile often hear others' painful comments—even when people don't mean to be hurtful. Barrenness does not make a woman any less important in God's eyes. It is not a curse. Women facing infertility can pray, as Hannah did. God may answer the prayer miraculously, as He did for Hannah, and provide a child. He may answer the prayer in other ways. Infertile couples should pray, being open to God's different ways of answering.

To Learn More: Turn to the article about infertility on pages 24, 25. See also the personality profile of Hannah on this page.

PERSONALITY PROFILE

Infertility

HANNAH—COPING WITH INFERTILITY

(1 SAMUEL 2:5)

Hannah loved her husband. Elkanah loved her in return, though their relationship was somewhat complicated by a second wife in the house—Peninnah. Hannah struggled to accept her husband's repeated demonstrations of affection because she was unable to give him children. The "fault" was hers, for her rival Peninnah seemed to have no difficulty conceiving. Hannah's shame deepened under Peninnah's resentful attacks. Elkanah's assurances that his love for Hannah wasn't based on her fertility fell on deaf ears. Instead of love, she heard only reminders of her failure.

After years of humiliation, Hannah turned to God in a special way. We don't know how often she prayed about her infertility, but during one trip to Shiloh she gave her problem to God. She made a painful vow: If God would give her a son, she would present the child back to God for lifelong service. Hannah made no promises about her own feelings, or threats about what she would do if God chose not to accept her vow. She simply gave up her part of a long struggle. She returned to her husband, leaving her burden with God.

Within months, Hannah conceived and gave birth to Samuel, and she kept her promise. When she returned to Shiloh, Hannah brought her toddler and presented him to Eli for upbringing in the temple. He grew into a mighty man of God—a prophet, priest, and judge. Meanwhile, Hannah had other children. God demonstrated His faithfulness to Hannah. In her life, God's answer opened her womb. But the deeper, more important, healing occurred in her soul. She finally understood that God had heard her. Such a settled faith allowed her to dedicate Samuel.

Modern medicine has made great strides in overcoming infertility, and God is still there hearing prayer. Hannah's example to women remains one of hope. God knows their sorrow, and He remains faithful.

To Learn More: Turn to the article about infertility on pages 24, 25. See also the key passage note at I Samuel 2:5 on this page.

"For the pillars of the earth *are* the LORD's,
And He has set the world upon them.
9 He will guard the feet of His saints,
But the wicked shall be silent in
darkness.

"For by strength no man shall prevail.
10 The adversaries of the LORD shall be
broken in pieces;
From heaven He will thunder against
them.
The LORD will judge the ends of the earth.

"He will give strength to His king,
And exalt the horn of His anointed."

[11]Then Elkanah went to his house at Ramah.
But the child ministered to the LORD before Eli
the priest.

THE WICKED SONS OF ELI

[12]Now the sons of Eli *were* corrupt;[a] they
did not know the LORD. [13]And the priests' custom with the people *was that* when any man
offered a sacrifice, the priest's servant would
come with a three-pronged fleshhook in his
hand while the meat was boiling. [14]Then he
would thrust *it* into the pan, or kettle, or caldron, or pot; and the priest would take for
himself all that the fleshhook brought up. So
they did in Shiloh to all the Israelites who
came there. [15]Also, before they burned the fat,
the priest's servant would come and say to the
man who sacrificed, "Give meat for roasting
to the priest, for he will not take boiled meat
from you, but raw."
[16]And *if* the man said to him, "They should

2:12 [a]Literally *sons of Belial*

PERSONALITY PROFILE

Adolescent Problems

ELI'S SONS—WAYWARD CHILDREN

(1 SAMUEL 2:12)

Eli served as a priest and judge in Israel. His two sons, Hophni and Phinehas, grew up in the shadow of God's house, but they never learned to respect God.

Eli's sons had the privileges of their father's vocation, but they twisted their responsibilities into evil acts. They threatened violence and practiced sexual abuse. When Eli attempted to correct them verbally, they displayed the same disrespect for him that they had for God. Their response reveals a long-standing pattern of a lack of discipline in Eli's home. God's judgment on the entire household confirms that problem.

Hophni and Phinehas did not understand the reality of consequences. They continued blindly toward death as warnings turned into prophecies. The way in which they had learned to take advantage of their position led them to assume that they could manipulate the ark of God like a magical device. They wrongly believed that carrying the ark into battle somehow made them immune to defeat (1 Sam. 4:1–11), just as they thought pretending to be priests had kept them immune from punishment. Their mistake cost them their lives.

Although the sons suffered consequences, Eli had to bear the responsibility for the conditions that had led to God's judgment on his family. By allowing his sons to remain in their positions, Eli himself had dishonored God. Apart from his words, Eli displayed an inability to discipline his sons. He confronted, but did not follow through with consequences.

One of the hardest parental tasks involves confronting wayward children. Delay only makes the job more difficult. Fear of being rejected by that son or daughter often leads to hesitation, denial, and soft correction. A parent may call it love, but the failure to discipline and correct is actually cowardice. Bold parental love doesn't always result in positive responses from children, but responsibilities are kept clear. Children have a better opportunity to learn right and wrong when their parents give them both the tender and the tough sides of love.

To Learn More: Turn to the article about adolescent problems on pages 410, 411. See also the key passage note at Luke 15:17, 18 on page 1349.

really burn the fat first; *then* you may take *as*
much as your heart desires," he would then
answer him, "*No,* but you must give *it* now;
and if not, I will take *it* by force."
17Therefore the sin of the young men was
very great before the LORD, for men abhorred
the offering of the LORD.

Samuel's Childhood Ministry

18But Samuel ministered before the LORD,
even as a child, wearing a linen ephod.
19Moreover his mother used to make him a little robe, and bring *it* to him year by year when
she came up with her husband to offer the
yearly sacrifice. 20And Eli would bless Elkanah
and his wife, and say, "The LORD give you descendants from this woman for the loan that
was given to the LORD." Then they would go
to their own home.
21And the LORD visited Hannah, so that she
conceived and bore three sons and two daughters. Meanwhile the child Samuel grew before
the LORD.

Prophecy Against Eli's Household

22Now Eli was very old; and he heard everything his sons did to all Israel,[a] and how they
lay with the women who assembled at the
door of the tabernacle of meeting. 23So he said
to them, "Why do you do such things? For I
hear of your evil dealings from all the people.
24No, my sons! For *it is* not a good report that
I hear. You make the LORD's people transgress.
25If one man sins against another, God will
judge him. But if a man sins against the LORD,
who will intercede for him?" Nevertheless
they did not heed the voice of their father, because the LORD desired to kill them.
26And the child Samuel grew in stature, and
in favor both with the LORD and men.
27Then a man of God came to Eli and said to
him, "Thus says the LORD: 'Did I not clearly
reveal Myself to the house of your father when
they were in Egypt in Pharaoh's house? 28Did I
not choose him out of all the tribes of Israel *to*
be My priest, to offer upon My altar, to burn
incense, and to wear an ephod before Me?
And did I not give to the house of your father
all the offerings of the children of Israel made
by fire? 29Why do you kick at My sacrifice and
My offering which I have commanded *in My*
dwelling place, and honor your sons more

2:22 [a]Following Masoretic Text, Targum, and Vulgate; Dead Sea Scrolls and Septuagint omit the rest of this verse.

SOUL NOTE

What a Contrast! *(2:17, 18)* Eli, the high priest of Israel, had "corrupt" sons who "did not know the LORD" (2:12). Their hearts were so hard that God decided to kill them. In their responsible position as priests, their corruption deserved extreme punishment. In vivid contrast, Samuel "ministered before the LORD, even as a child" (2:18). When God spoke to Israel, he spoke not to Eli, but to Samuel (3:10). God's guidance and blessing come to His obedient servants. But those who reject Him are left to their own ways—and will face judgment. **Topic: Obedience**

SOUL NOTE

Growing Up *(2:21, 26)* Young Samuel was growing "in stature, and in favor both with the LORD and men." The Bible describes Jesus' growth in a similar manner: He "increased in wisdom and stature, and in favor with God and men" (Luke 2:52). Children grow physically, intellectually, emotionally, socially, and spiritually. Just as parents feed their children good food to help them grow strong physically, they should also provide guidance and opportunities in the various areas of life so that the children can grow in wisdom and favor with God and the people around them.
Topic: Child Development

than Me, to make yourselves fat with the
best of all the offerings of Israel My people?'
30Therefore the LORD God of Israel says: 'I said
indeed *that* your house and the house of your
father would walk before Me forever.' But now
the LORD says: 'Far be it from Me; for those
who honor Me I will honor, and those who
despise Me shall be lightly esteemed. 31Be-
hold, the days are coming that I will cut off
your arm and the arm of your father's house,
so that there will not be an old man in your
house. 32And you will see an enemy *in My*
dwelling place, *despite* all the good which God
does for Israel. And there shall not be an old
man in your house forever. 33But any of your
men *whom* I do not cut off from My altar shall
consume your eyes and grieve your heart. And
all the descendants of your house shall die in
the flower of their age. 34Now this *shall be* a
sign to you that will come upon your two
sons, on Hophni and Phinehas: in one day
they shall die, both of them. 35Then I will raise
up for Myself a faithful priest *who* shall do according to what *is* in My heart and in My
mind. I will build him a sure house, and he
shall walk before My anointed forever.
36And it shall come to pass that everyone
who is left in your house will come *and* bow
down to him for a piece of silver and a morsel
of bread, and say, "Please, put me in one of
the priestly positions, that I may eat a piece of
bread." ' "

SAMUEL'S FIRST PROPHECY

3 Now the boy Samuel ministered to the
LORD before Eli. And the word of the LORD
was rare in those days; *there was* no widespread revelation. 2And it came to pass at that
time, while Eli *was* lying down in his place,
and when his eyes had begun to grow so dim
that he could not see, 3and before the lamp of
God went out in the tabernacle[a] of the LORD
where the ark of God *was,* and while Samuel
was lying down, 4that the LORD called Samuel.
And he answered, "Here I am!" 5So he ran to
Eli and said, "Here I am, for you called me."

And he said, "I did not call; lie down
again." And he went and lay down.

6Then the LORD called yet again, "Samuel!"

So Samuel arose and went to Eli, and said,
"Here I am, for you called me." He answered,
"I did not call, my son; lie down again."
7(Now Samuel did not yet know the LORD, nor
was the word of the LORD yet revealed to him.)

8And the LORD called Samuel again the third
time. So he arose and went to Eli, and said,
"Here I am, for you did call me."

Then Eli perceived that the LORD had called the
boy. 9Therefore Eli said to Samuel, "Go, lie down;
and it shall be, if He calls you, that you must say,
'Speak, LORD, for Your servant hears.' " So Samuel went and lay down in his place.

10Now the LORD came and stood and called
as at other times, "Samuel! Samuel!"

And Samuel answered, "Speak, for Your
servant hears."

11Then the LORD said to Samuel: "Behold, I
will do something in Israel at which both ears
of everyone who hears it will tingle. 12In that
day I will perform against Eli all that I have
spoken concerning his house, from beginning
to end. 13For I have told him that I will judge
his house forever for the iniquity which he
knows, because his sons made themselves
vile, and he did not restrain them. 14And
therefore I have sworn to the house of Eli that
the iniquity of Eli's house shall not be atoned
for by sacrifice or offering forever."

3:3 [a]Hebrew *heykal,* palace or temple

SOUL NOTE

Intervene! *(3:13)* Eli's sons "made themselves vile, and he did not restrain them." Eli did not discipline his sons even though they were priests under his supervision. These men were treating the sacrifices of the people with contempt (2:12–17) and were committing sexual sin with women of the tabernacle. Eli, as parent and as high priest, certainly had the authority to deal with his sons, but he chose not to do anything. Eventually, God stepped in. God gives parents authority over their children. Parents should use that authority wisely to guide their children away from sin.
Topic: Parenting

[15]So Samuel lay down until morning,[a] and opened the doors of the house of the LORD. And Samuel was afraid to tell Eli the vision. [16]Then Eli called Samuel and said, "Samuel, my son!"

He answered, "Here I am."

[17]And he said, "What *is* the word that *the LORD* spoke to you? Please do not hide *it* from me. God do so to you, and more also, if you hide anything from me of all the things that He said to you." [18]Then Samuel told him everything, and hid nothing from him. And he said, "It *is* the LORD. Let Him do what seems good to Him."

[19]So Samuel grew, and the LORD was with him and let none of his words fall to the ground. [20]And all Israel from Dan to Beersheba knew that Samuel *had been* established as a prophet of the LORD. [21]Then the LORD appeared again in Shiloh. For the LORD revealed Himself to Samuel in Shiloh by the word of the LORD.

4 And the word of Samuel came to all Israel.[a]

The Ark of God Captured

Now Israel went out to battle against the Philistines, and encamped beside Ebenezer; and the Philistines encamped in Aphek. [2]Then the Philistines put themselves in battle array against Israel. And when they joined battle, Israel was defeated by the Philistines, who killed about four thousand men of the army in the field. [3]And when the people had come into the camp, the elders of Israel said, "Why has the LORD defeated us today before the Philistines? Let us bring the ark of the covenant of the LORD from Shiloh to us, that when it comes among us it may save us from the hand of our enemies." [4]So the people sent to Shiloh, that they might bring from there the ark of the covenant of the LORD of hosts, who dwells *between* the cherubim. And the two sons of Eli, Hophni and Phinehas, *were* there with the ark of the covenant of God.

[5]And when the ark of the covenant of the LORD came into the camp, all Israel shouted so loudly that the earth shook. [6]Now when the Philistines heard the noise of the shout, they said, "What *does* the sound of this great shout in the camp of the Hebrews *mean?*" Then they understood that the ark of the LORD had come into the camp. [7]So the Philistines were afraid, for they said, "God has come into the camp!" And they said, "Woe to us! For such a thing has never happened before. [8]Woe to us! Who will deliver us from the hand of these mighty gods? These *are* the gods who struck the Egyptians with all the plagues in the wilderness. [9]Be strong and conduct yourselves like men, you Philistines, that you do not become servants of the Hebrews, as they have been to you. Conduct yourselves like men, and fight!"

[10]So the Philistines fought, and Israel was defeated, and every man fled to his tent. There was a very great slaughter, and there fell of Israel thirty thousand foot soldiers. [11]Also the ark of God was captured; and the two sons of Eli, Hophni and Phinehas, died.

Death of Eli

[12]Then a man of Benjamin ran from the battle line the same day, and came to Shiloh with his clothes torn and dirt on his head. [13]Now when he came, there was Eli, sitting on a seat by the wayside watching,[a] for his heart trembled for the ark of God. And when the man came into the city and told *it,* all the city cried out. [14]When Eli heard the noise of the outcry, he said, "What *does* the sound of this tumult *mean?*" And the man came quickly and told Eli. [15]Eli was ninety-eight years old, and his eyes were so dim that he could not see.

[16]Then the man said to Eli, "I *am* he who came from the battle. And I fled today from the battle line."

And he said, "What happened, my son?"

[17]So the messenger answered and said, "Israel has fled before the Philistines, and there has been a great slaughter among the people. Also your two sons, Hophni and Phinehas, are dead; and the ark of God has been captured."

[18]Then it happened, when he made mention of the ark of God, that Eli fell off the seat backward by the side of the gate; and his neck was broken and he died, for the man was old and heavy. And he had judged Israel forty years.

Ichabod

[19]Now his daughter-in-law, Phinehas' wife, was with child, *due* to be delivered; and when

---

3:15 [a]Following Masoretic Text, Targum, and Vulgate; Septuagint adds *and he arose in the morning.* **4:1** [a]Following Masoretic Text and Targum; Septuagint and Vulgate add *And it came to pass in those days that the Philistines gathered themselves together to fight;* Septuagint adds further *against Israel.* **4:13** [a]Following Masoretic Text and Vulgate; Septuagint reads *beside the gate watching the road.*

she heard the news that the ark of God was
captured, and that her father-in-law and her
husband were dead, she bowed herself and
gave birth, for her labor pains came upon her.
20And about the time of her death the women
who stood by her said to her, "Do not fear, for
you have borne a son." But she did not answer, nor did she regard *it*. 21Then she named
the child Ichabod,[a] saying, "The glory has departed from Israel!" because the ark of God
had been captured and because of her father-
in-law and her husband. 22And she said, "The
glory has departed from Israel, for the ark of
God has been captured."

The Philistines and the Ark

5 Then the Philistines took the ark of God
and brought it from Ebenezer to Ashdod.
2When the Philistines took the ark of God,
they brought it into the house of Dagon[a] and
set it by Dagon. 3And when the people of Ashdod arose early in the morning, there was Dagon, fallen on its face to the earth before the
ark of the LORD. So they took Dagon and set it
in its place again. 4And when they arose early
the next morning, there was Dagon, fallen on
its face to the ground before the ark of the
LORD. The head of Dagon and both the palms
of its hands *were* broken off on the threshold;
only Dagon's torso[a] was left of it. 5Therefore
neither the priests of Dagon nor any who
come into Dagon's house tread on the threshold of Dagon in Ashdod to this day.
6But the hand of the LORD was heavy on the

4:21 [a]Literally *Inglorious* **5:2** [a]A Philistine idol
5:4 [a]Following Septuagint, Syriac, Targum, and Vulgate; Masoretic Text reads *Dagon*.

PERSONALITY PROFILE

Eating Disorders

ELI: UNBRIDLED APPETITES

(1 SAMUEL 4:18)

Eli died as a pathetic father, overwhelmed by the consequences of his own failures. His two sons had just died violently. The beloved ark of the covenant had fallen into enemy hands. He had been warned, but the shock of his worst fears suddenly coming true led to his death. The biblical autopsy reveals the cause of death: a broken neck resulting from a fall against a gate, compounded by the victim's age (98) and his weight.

Eli may have been a glutton; we don't know. Words spoken years before his death, when God sent a prophet to warn Eli, indicate a possible problem: "Why do you kick at My sacrifice and My offering . . . to make yourselves fat with the best of all the offerings of Israel My people?" (1 Sam. 2:29). At best, Eli's story describes a father and sons who lived undisciplined lives. They ate too much and exercised too little.

We now know that some kinds of obesity have a strong genetic influence. In Eli's life, however, weight appears as part of a pattern. Lack of self-control—even a lust for various pleasures—reveals a disturbing family dynamic in Eli's line. We see in his sons unbridled appetites for mischief and illicit sex that were never curbed. These behaviors were at least enabled, if not modeled, by the father. God's eventual judgment affected individual family members as well as Eli's entire family structure.

Overeating, lax parenting, and whatever else Eli may have struggled with are all clues to a deeper problem—a disordered character. The specifics are not as important as the traits they reveal. What traits in your life have not been surrendered to God's control? Excusing or denying the clues doesn't get rid of them. At the center lies the decision to be a person whose life belongs to ourselves or to God. If we belong to God, doesn't it make sense to let Him deal with the sins for which Jesus Christ gave His life? Only the Creator knows how to bring order to our character.

To Learn More: Turn to the article about eating disorders on pages 302, 303. See also the key passage note at Proverbs 23:2 on page 832.

people of Ashdod, and He ravaged them and struck them with tumors,[a] *both* Ashdod and its territory. [7]And when the men of Ashdod saw how *it was,* they said, "The ark of the God of Israel must not remain with us, for His hand is harsh toward us and Dagon our god." [8]Therefore they sent and gathered to themselves all the lords of the Philistines, and said, "What shall we do with the ark of the God of Israel?"

And they answered, "Let the ark of the God of Israel be carried away to Gath." So they carried the ark of the God of Israel away. [9]So it was, after they had carried it away, that the hand of the LORD was against the city with a very great destruction; and He struck the men of the city, both small and great, and tumors broke out on them.

[10]Therefore they sent the ark of God to Ekron. So it was, as the ark of God came to Ekron, that the Ekronites cried out, saying, "They have brought the ark of the God of Israel to us, to kill us and our people!" [11]So they sent and gathered together all the lords of the Philistines, and said, "Send away the ark of the God of Israel, and let it go back to its own place, so that it does not kill us and our people." For there was a deadly destruction throughout all the city; the hand of God was very heavy there. [12]And the men who did not die were stricken with the tumors, and the cry of the city went up to heaven.

THE ARK RETURNED TO ISRAEL

6 Now the ark of the LORD was in the country of the Philistines seven months. [2]And the Philistines called for the priests and the diviners, saying, "What shall we do with the ark of the LORD? Tell us how we should send it to its place."

[3]So they said, "If you send away the ark of the God of Israel, do not send it empty; but by all means return *it* to Him *with* a trespass offering. Then you will be healed, and it will be known to you why His hand is not removed from you."

[4]Then they said, "What *is* the trespass offering which we shall return to Him?"

They answered, "Five golden tumors and five golden rats, *according to* the number of the lords of the Philistines. For the same plague *was* on all of you and on your lords. [5]Therefore you shall make images of your tumors and images of your rats that ravage the land, and you shall give glory to the God of Israel; perhaps He will lighten His hand from you, from your gods, and from your land. [6]Why then do you harden your hearts as the Egyptians and Pharaoh hardened their hearts? When He did mighty things among them, did they not let the people go, that they might depart? [7]Now therefore, make a new cart, take two milk cows which have never been yoked, and hitch the cows to the cart; and take their calves home, away from them. [8]Then take the ark of the LORD and set it on the cart; and put the articles of gold which you are returning to Him *as* a trespass offering in a chest by its side. Then send it away, and let it go. [9]And watch: if it goes up the road to its own territory, to Beth Shemesh, *then* He has done us this great evil. But if not, then we shall know that *it is* not His hand *that* struck us—it happened to us by chance."

[10]Then the men did so; they took two milk cows and hitched them to the cart, and shut up their calves at home. [11]And they set the ark of the LORD on the cart, and the chest with the gold rats and the images of their tumors. [12]Then the cows headed straight for the road to Beth Shemesh, *and* went along the highway, lowing as they went, and did not turn aside to the right hand or the left. And the lords of the Philistines went after them to the border of Beth Shemesh.

[13]Now *the people of* Beth Shemesh *were* reaping their wheat harvest in the valley; and they lifted their eyes and saw the ark, and rejoiced to see *it.* [14]Then the cart came into the field of Joshua of Beth Shemesh, and stood there; a large stone *was* there. So they split the wood of the cart and offered the cows as a burnt offering to the LORD. [15]The Levites took down the ark of the LORD and the chest that *was* with it, in which *were* the articles of gold, and put *them* on the large stone. Then the men of Beth Shemesh offered burnt offerings and made sacrifices the same day to the LORD. [16]So when the five lords of the Philistines had seen *it,* they returned to Ekron the same day.

[17]These *are* the golden tumors which the Philistines returned *as* a trespass offering to the LORD: one for Ashdod, one for Gaza, one for Ashkelon, one for Gath, one for Ekron;

5:6 [a]Probably bubonic plague. Septuagint and Vulgate add here *And in the midst of their land rats sprang up, and there was a great death panic in the city.*

18and the golden rats, *according to* the number
of all the cities of the Philistines *belonging* to
the five lords, *both* fortified cities and country
villages, even as far as the large *stone of* Abel
on which they set the ark of the LORD, *which*
stone remains to this day in the field of Joshua
of Beth Shemesh.
19Then He struck the men of Beth Shemesh,
because they had looked into the ark of the
LORD. He struck fifty thousand and seventy
men[a] of the people, and the people lamented
because the LORD had struck the people with a
great slaughter.

THE ARK AT KIRJATH JEARIM

20And the men of Beth Shemesh said, "Who
is able to stand before this holy LORD God?
And to whom shall it go up from us?" 21So
they sent messengers to the inhabitants of
Kirjath Jearim, saying, "The Philistines have
brought back the ark of the LORD; come down
and take it up with you."

7 Then the men of Kirjath Jearim came and
took the ark of the LORD, and brought it
into the house of Abinadab on the hill, and
consecrated Eleazar his son to keep the ark of
the LORD.

SAMUEL JUDGES ISRAEL

2So it was that the ark remained in Kirjath
Jearim a long time; it was there twenty years.
And all the house of Israel lamented after the
LORD.
3Then Samuel spoke to all the house of Israel, saying, "If you return to the LORD with all
your hearts, *then* put away the foreign gods
and the Ashtoreths[a] from among you, and prepare your hearts for the LORD, and serve Him
only; and He will deliver you from the hand
of the Philistines." 4So the children of Israel
put away the Baals and the Ashtoreths,[a] and
served the LORD only.
5And Samuel said, "Gather all Israel to Mizpah, and I will pray to the LORD for you." 6So
they gathered together at Mizpah, drew water,
and poured *it* out before the LORD. And they
fasted that day, and said there, "We have
sinned against the LORD." And Samuel judged
the children of Israel at Mizpah.
7Now when the Philistines heard that the
children of Israel had gathered together at
Mizpah, the lords of the Philistines went up
against Israel. And when the children of Israel
heard *of it,* they were afraid of the Philistines.
8So the children of Israel said to Samuel, "Do
not cease to cry out to the LORD our God for
us, that He may save us from the hand of the
Philistines."
9And Samuel took a suckling lamb and offered *it as* a whole burnt offering to the LORD.
Then Samuel cried out to the LORD for Israel,
and the LORD answered him. 10Now as Samuel
was offering up the burnt offering, the Philistines drew near to battle against Israel. But the
LORD thundered with a loud thunder upon the
Philistines that day, and so confused them
that they were overcome before Israel. 11And
the men of Israel went out of Mizpah and pursued the Philistines, and drove them back as
far as below Beth Car. 12Then Samuel took a
stone and set *it* up between Mizpah and Shen,
and called its name Ebenezer,[a] saying, "Thus
far the LORD has helped us."
13So the Philistines were subdued, and they
did not come anymore into the territory of Israel. And the hand of the LORD was against the
Philistines all the days of Samuel. 14Then the
cities which the Philistines had taken from Israel were restored to Israel, from Ekron to
Gath; and Israel recovered its territory from
the hands of the Philistines. Also there was
peace between Israel and the Amorites.
15And Samuel judged Israel all the days of
his life. 16He went from year to year on a circuit to Bethel, Gilgal, and Mizpah, and judged
Israel in all those places. 17But he always returned to Ramah, for his home *was* there.
There he judged Israel, and there he built an
altar to the LORD.

ISRAEL DEMANDS A KING

8 Now it came to pass when Samuel was
old that he made his sons judges over Israel. 2The name of his firstborn was Joel, and
the name of his second, Abijah; *they were*
judges in Beersheba. 3But his sons did not
walk in his ways; they turned aside after dishonest gain, took bribes, and perverted justice.
4Then all the elders of Israel gathered together and came to Samuel at Ramah, 5and
said to him, "Look, you are old, and your sons

6:19 [a]Or *He struck seventy men of the people and fifty oxen of a man* **7:3** [a]Canaanite goddesses **7:4** [a]Canaanite goddesses **7:12** [a]Literally *Stone of Help*

do not walk in your ways. Now make us a king to judge us like all the nations."

6But the thing displeased Samuel when they said, "Give us a king to judge us." So Samuel prayed to the LORD. 7And the LORD said to Samuel, "Heed the voice of the people in all that they say to you; for they have not rejected you, but they have rejected Me, that I should not reign over them. 8According to all the works which they have done since the day that I brought them up out of Egypt, even to this day—with which they have forsaken Me and served other gods—so they are doing to you also. 9Now therefore, heed their voice. However, you shall solemnly forewarn them, and show them the behavior of the king who will reign over them."

10So Samuel told all the words of the LORD to the people who asked him for a king. 11And he said, "This will be the behavior of the king who will reign over you: He will take your sons and appoint *them* for his own chariots and *to be* his horsemen, and *some* will run before his chariots. 12He will appoint captains over his thousands and captains over his fifties, *will set some* to plow his ground and reap his harvest, and *some* to make his weapons of war and equipment for his chariots. 13He will take your daughters *to be* perfumers, cooks, and bakers. 14And he will take the best of your fields, your vineyards, and your olive groves, and give *them* to his servants. 15He will take a tenth of your grain and your vintage, and give it to his officers and servants. 16And he will take your male servants, your female servants, your finest young men,[a] and your donkeys, and put *them* to his work. 17He will take a tenth of your sheep. And you will be his servants. 18And you will cry out in that day because of your king whom you have chosen for yourselves, and the LORD will not hear you in that day."

19Nevertheless the people refused to obey the voice of Samuel; and they said, "No, but we will have a king over us, 20that we also may be like all the nations, and that our king may judge us and go out before us and fight our battles."

21And Samuel heard all the words of the people, and he repeated them in the hearing of the LORD. 22So the LORD said to Samuel, "Heed their voice, and make them a king."

And Samuel said to the men of Israel, "Every man go to his city."

SAUL CHOSEN TO BE KING

9 There was a man of Benjamin whose name *was* Kish the son of Abiel, the son of Zeror, the son of Bechorath, the son of Aphiah, a Benjamite, a mighty man of power. 2And he had a choice and handsome son whose name *was* Saul. *There was* not a more handsome person than he among the children of Israel. From his shoulders upward *he was* taller than any of the people.

3Now the donkeys of Kish, Saul's father, were lost. And Kish said to his son Saul, "Please take one of the servants with you, and arise, go and look for the donkeys." 4So he passed through the mountains of Ephraim and through the land of Shalisha, but they did not find *them*. Then they passed through the land of Shaalim, and *they were* not *there*. Then he passed through the land of the Benjamites, but they did not find *them*.

5When they had come to the land of Zuph, Saul said to his servant who *was* with him, "Come, let us return, lest my father cease *caring* about the donkeys and become worried about us."

6And he said to him, "Look now, *there is* in this city a man of God, and *he is* an honorable

8:16 [a]Septuagint reads *cattle*.

SOUL NOTE

Copycat *(8:22)* God had been Israel's sovereign leader, but the people wanted a human king, refusing to heed Samuel's warnings (8:10–22). So God told Samuel to do as they asked. The people desired a king because they wanted to be like other nations (8:5, 20). God had brought the Israelites into their land so they would be distinct from those nations, so this was a step in the wrong direction. To compromise our faith by desiring to be like the world is to lose our distinctness as God's people. **Topic: Attitudes**

man; all that he says surely comes to pass. So let us go there; perhaps he can show us the way that we should go."

7Then Saul said to his servant, "But look, *if* we go, what shall we bring the man? For the bread in our vessels is all gone, and *there is* no present to bring to the man of God. What do we have?"

8And the servant answered Saul again and said, "Look, I have here at hand one-fourth of a shekel of silver. I will give *that* to the man of God, to tell us our way." 9(Formerly in Israel, when a man went to inquire of God, he spoke thus: "Come, let us go to the seer"; for *he who is* now *called* a prophet was formerly called a seer.)

10Then Saul said to his servant, "Well said; come, let us go." So they went to the city where the man of God *was.*

11As they went up the hill to the city, they met some young women going out to draw water, and said to them, "Is the seer here?"

12And they answered them and said, "Yes, there he is, just ahead of you. Hurry now; for today he came to this city, because there is a sacrifice of the people today on the high place. 13As soon as you come into the city, you will surely find him before he goes up to the high place to eat. For the people will not eat until he comes, because he must bless the sacrifice; afterward those who are invited will eat. Now therefore, go up, for about this time you will find him." 14So they went up to the city. As they were coming into the city, there was Samuel, coming out toward them on his way up to the high place.

15Now the LORD had told Samuel in his ear the day before Saul came, saying, 16"Tomorrow about this time I will send you a man from the land of Benjamin, and you shall anoint him commander over My people Israel, that he may save My people from the hand of the Philistines; for I have looked upon My people, because their cry has come to Me."

17So when Samuel saw Saul, the LORD said to him, "There he is, the man of whom I spoke to you. This one shall reign over My people." 18Then Saul drew near to Samuel in the gate, and said, "Please tell me, where *is* the seer's house?"

19Samuel answered Saul and said, "I *am* the seer. Go up before me to the high place, for you shall eat with me today; and tomorrow I will let you go and will tell you all that *is* in your heart. 20But as for your donkeys that were lost three days ago, do not be anxious about them, for they have been found. And on whom *is* all the desire of Israel? *Is it* not on you and on all your father's house?"

21And Saul answered and said, "*Am* I not a Benjamite, of the smallest of the tribes of Israel, and my family the least of all the families of the tribe[a] of Benjamin? Why then do you speak like this to me?"

22Now Samuel took Saul and his servant and brought them into the hall, and had them sit in the place of honor among those who were invited; there *were* about thirty persons. 23And Samuel said to the cook, "Bring the portion which I gave you, of which I said to you, 'Set it apart.' " 24So the cook took up the thigh with its upper part and set *it* before Saul. And *Samuel* said, "Here it is, what was kept back. *It* was set apart for you. Eat; for until this time it has been kept for you, since I said I invited the people." So Saul ate with Samuel that day.

25When they had come down from the high place into the city, *Samuel* spoke with Saul on the top of the house.[a] 26They arose early; and it was about the dawning of the day that Samuel called to Saul on the top of the house, saying, "Get up, that I may send you on your way." And Saul arose, and both of them went outside, he and Samuel.

Saul Anointed King

27As they were going down to the outskirts of the city, Samuel said to Saul, "Tell the servant to go on ahead of us." And he went on. "But you stand here awhile, that I may announce to you the word of God."

10 Then Samuel took a flask of oil and poured *it* on his head, and kissed him and said: "*Is it* not because the LORD has anointed you commander over His inheritance?[a] 2When you have departed from me today, you will find two men by Rachel's tomb

---

9:21 [a]Literally *tribes* **9:25** [a]Following Masoretic Text and Targum; Septuagint omits *He spoke with Saul on the top of the house;* Septuagint and Vulgate add *And he prepared a bed for Saul on the top of the house, and he slept.* **10:1** [a]Following Masoretic Text, Targum, and Vulgate; Septuagint reads *His people Israel; and you shall rule the people of the Lord;* Septuagint and Vulgate add *And you shall deliver His people from the hands of their enemies all around them. And this shall be a sign to you, that God has anointed you to be a prince.*

in the territory of Benjamin at Zelzah; and they will say to you, 'The donkeys which you went to look for have been found. And now your father has ceased caring about the donkeys and is worrying about you, saying, "What shall I do about my son?" ' 3Then you shall go on forward from there and come to the terebinth tree of Tabor. There three men going up to God at Bethel will meet you, one carrying three young goats, another carrying three loaves of bread, and another carrying a skin of wine. 4And they will greet you and give you two *loaves* of bread, which you shall receive from their hands. 5After that you shall come to the hill of God where the Philistine garrison *is*. And it will happen, when you have come there to the city, that you will meet a group of prophets coming down from the high place with a stringed instrument, a tambourine, a flute, and a harp before them; and they will be prophesying. 6Then the Spirit of the LORD will come upon you, and you will prophesy with them and be turned into another man. 7And let it be, when these signs come to you, *that* you do as the occasion demands; for God *is* with you. 8You shall go down before me to Gilgal; and surely I will come down to you to offer burnt offerings *and* make sacrifices of peace offerings. Seven days you shall wait, till I come to you and show you what you should do."

9So it was, when he had turned his back to go from Samuel, that God gave him another heart; and all those signs came to pass that day. 10When they came there to the hill, there was a group of prophets to meet him; then the Spirit of God came upon him, and he prophesied among them. 11And it happened, when all who knew him formerly saw that he indeed prophesied among the prophets, that the people said to one another, "What *is* this *that* has come upon the son of Kish? *Is* Saul also among the prophets?" 12Then a man from there answered and said, "But who *is* their father?" Therefore it became a proverb: "*Is* Saul also among the prophets?" 13And when he had finished prophesying, he went to the high place.

14Then Saul's uncle said to him and his servant, "Where did you go?"

So he said, "To look for the donkeys. When we saw that *they were* nowhere *to be found*, we went to Samuel."

15And Saul's uncle said, "Tell me, please, what Samuel said to you."

16So Saul said to his uncle, "He told us plainly that the donkeys had been found." But about the matter of the kingdom, he did not tell him what Samuel had said.

SAUL PROCLAIMED KING

17Then Samuel called the people together to the LORD at Mizpah, 18and said to the children of Israel, "Thus says the LORD God of Israel: 'I brought up Israel out of Egypt, and delivered you from the hand of the Egyptians *and* from the hand of all kingdoms and from those who oppressed you.' 19But you have today rejected your God, who Himself saved you from all your adversities and your tribulations; and you have said to Him, 'No, set a king over us!' Now therefore, present yourselves before the LORD by your tribes and by your clans."[a]

20And when Samuel had caused all the tribes of Israel to come near, the tribe of Benjamin was chosen. 21When he had caused the tribe of Benjamin to come near by their families, the family of Matri was chosen. And Saul the son of Kish was chosen. But when they sought him, he could not be found. 22Therefore they inquired of the LORD further, "Has the man come here yet?"

And the LORD answered, "There he is, hidden among the equipment."

23So they ran and brought him from there;

10:19 [a]Literally *thousands*

SOUL NOTE

Insecure and Afraid *(10:22)* The soon-to-be-crowned king of Israel was "hidden among the equipment." God had chosen Saul, but apparently Saul was insecure and afraid. Moses too had been insecure about his calling, begging God to send someone else (Ex. 4:13). When God calls someone to a task, He promises to be with them and to accomplish His work through them. The job may be difficult, but God will be there. Be secure in God's call. **Topic: Insecurity**

and when he stood among the people, he was taller than any of the people from his shoulders upward. 24And Samuel said to all the people, "Do you see him whom the LORD has chosen, that *there is* no one like him among all the people?"

So all the people shouted and said, "Long live the king!"

25Then Samuel explained to the people the behavior of royalty, and wrote *it* in a book and laid *it* up before the LORD. And Samuel sent all the people away, every man to his house. 26And Saul also went home to Gibeah; and valiant *men* went with him, whose hearts God had touched. 27But some rebels said, "How can this man save us?" So they despised him, and brought him no presents. But he held his peace.

SAUL SAVES JABESH GILEAD

11 Then Nahash the Ammonite came up and encamped against Jabesh Gilead; and all the men of Jabesh said to Nahash, "Make a covenant with us, and we will serve you."

2And Nahash the Ammonite answered them, "On this *condition* I will make *a covenant* with you, that I may put out all your right eyes, and bring reproach on all Israel."

3Then the elders of Jabesh said to him, "Hold off for seven days, that we may send messengers to all the territory of Israel. And then, if *there is* no one to save us, we will come out to you."

4So the messengers came to Gibeah of Saul and told the news in the hearing of the people. And all the people lifted up their voices and wept. 5Now there was Saul, coming behind the herd from the field; and Saul said, "What *troubles* the people, that they weep?" And they told him the words of the men of Jabesh. 6Then the Spirit of God came upon Saul when he heard this news, and his anger was greatly aroused. 7So he took a yoke of oxen and cut them in pieces, and sent *them* throughout all the territory of Israel by the hands of messengers, saying, "Whoever does not go out with Saul and Samuel to battle, so it shall be done to his oxen."

And the fear of the LORD fell on the people, and they came out with one consent. 8When he numbered them in Bezek, the children of Israel were three hundred thousand, and the men of Judah thirty thousand. 9And they said to the messengers who came, "Thus you shall say to the men of Jabesh Gilead: 'Tomorrow, by *the time* the sun is hot, you shall have help.' " Then the messengers came and reported *it* to the men of Jabesh, and they were glad. 10Therefore the men of Jabesh said, "Tomorrow we will come out to you, and you may do with us whatever seems good to you."

11So it was, on the next day, that Saul put the people in three companies; and they came into the midst of the camp in the morning watch, and killed Ammonites until the heat of the day. And it happened that those who survived were scattered, so that no two of them were left together.

12Then the people said to Samuel, "Who *is* he who said, 'Shall Saul reign over us?' Bring the men, that we may put them to death."

13But Saul said, "Not a man shall be put to death this day, for today the LORD has accomplished salvation in Israel."

14Then Samuel said to the people, "Come, let us go to Gilgal and renew the kingdom there." 15So all the people went to Gilgal, and there they made Saul king before the LORD in Gilgal. There they made sacrifices of peace offerings before the LORD, and there Saul and all the men of Israel rejoiced greatly.

SAMUEL'S ADDRESS AT SAUL'S CORONATION

12 Now Samuel said to all Israel: "Indeed I have heeded your voice in all that you said to me, and have made a king over you. 2And now here is the king, walking before you; and I am old and grayheaded, and look, my sons *are* with you. I have walked before you from my childhood to this day. 3Here I am. Witness against me before the LORD and before His anointed: Whose ox have I taken, or whose donkey have I taken, or whom have I cheated? Whom have I oppressed, or from whose hand have I received *any* bribe with which to blind my eyes? I will restore *it* to you."

4And they said, "You have not cheated us or oppressed us, nor have you taken anything from any man's hand."

5Then he said to them, "The LORD *is* witness against you, and His anointed *is* witness this day, that you have not found anything in my hand."

And they answered, "*He is* witness."

6Then Samuel said to the people, "*It is* the LORD who raised up Moses and Aaron, and who brought your fathers up from the land of Egypt. [7]Now therefore, stand still, that I may reason with you before the LORD concerning all the righteous acts of the LORD which He did to you and your fathers: [8]When Jacob had gone into Egypt,[a] and your fathers cried out to the LORD, then the LORD sent Moses and Aaron, who brought your fathers out of Egypt and made them dwell in this place. [9]And when they forgot the LORD their God, He sold them into the hand of Sisera, commander of the army of Hazor, into the hand of the Philistines, and into the hand of the king of Moab; and they fought against them. [10]Then they cried out to the LORD, and said, 'We have sinned, because we have forsaken the LORD and served the Baals and Ashtoreths;[a] but now deliver us from the hand of our enemies, and we will serve You.' [11]And the LORD sent Jerubbaal,[a] Bedan,[b] Jephthah, and Samuel,[c] and delivered you out of the hand of your enemies on every side; and you dwelt in safety. [12]And when you saw that Nahash king of the Ammonites came against you, you said to me, 'No, but a king shall reign over us,' when the LORD your God *was* your king.

[13]"Now therefore, here is the king whom you have chosen *and* whom you have desired. And take note, the LORD has set a king over you. [14]If you fear the LORD and serve Him and obey His voice, and do not rebel against the commandment of the LORD, then both you and the king who reigns over you will continue following the LORD your God. [15]However, if you do not obey the voice of the LORD, but rebel against the commandment of the LORD, then the hand of the LORD will be against you, as *it was* against your fathers.

[16]"Now therefore, stand and see this great thing which the LORD will do before your eyes: [17]*Is* today not the wheat harvest? I will call to the LORD, and He will send thunder and rain, that you may perceive and see that your wickedness *is* great, which you have done in the sight of the LORD, in asking a king for yourselves."

[18]So Samuel called to the LORD, and the LORD sent thunder and rain that day; and all the people greatly feared the LORD and Samuel.

[19]And all the people said to Samuel, "Pray for your servants to the LORD your God, that we may not die; for we have added to all our sins the evil of asking a king for ourselves."

[20]Then Samuel said to the people, "Do not fear. You have done all this wickedness; yet do not turn aside from following the LORD, but serve the LORD with all your heart. [21]And do not turn aside; for *then you would go* after empty things which cannot profit or deliver, for they *are* nothing. [22]For the LORD will not forsake His people, for His great name's sake, because it has pleased the LORD to make you His people. [23]Moreover, as for me, far be it from me that I should sin against the LORD in ceasing to pray for you; but I will teach you the good and the right way. [24]Only fear the LORD, and serve Him in truth with all your heart; for consider what great things He has done for you. [25]But if you still do wickedly, you shall be swept away, both you and your king."

SAUL'S UNLAWFUL SACRIFICE

13 Saul reigned one year; and when he had reigned two years over Israel,[a] [2]Saul chose for himself three thousand *men* of

12:8 [a]Following Masoretic Text, Targum, and Vulgate; Septuagint adds *and the Egyptians afflicted them.* **12:10** [a]Canaanite goddesses **12:11** [a]Syriac reads *Deborah*; Targum reads *Gideon.* [b]Septuagint and Syriac read *Barak;* Targum reads *Simson.* [c]Syriac reads *Simson.* **13:1** [a]The Hebrew is difficult (compare 2 Samuel 5:4; 2 Kings 14:2; see also 2 Samuel 2:10; Acts 13:21).

SOUL NOTE

Keep on Praying *(12:23)* The prophet Samuel was heartbroken that the Israelites desired a king. But God told Samuel to do as they asked (8:6, 7). Despite his disappointment, Samuel stated that he would not "sin against the LORD in ceasing to pray" for them (12:23). Loved ones may make choices with which we disagree. Like Samuel, we should be committed to continuing to pray for them. Persevering in prayer is our responsibility and should be our commitment. **Topic: Prayer**

Israel. Two thousand were with Saul in Michmash and in the mountains of Bethel, and a thousand were with Jonathan in Gibeah of Benjamin. The rest of the people he sent away, every man to his tent.

[3]And Jonathan attacked the garrison of the Philistines that *was* in Geba, and the Philistines heard *of it.* Then Saul blew the trumpet throughout all the land, saying, "Let the Hebrews hear!" [4]Now all Israel heard it said *that* Saul had attacked a garrison of the Philistines, and *that* Israel had also become an abomination to the Philistines. And the people were called together to Saul at Gilgal.

[5]Then the Philistines gathered together to fight with Israel, thirty[a] thousand chariots and six thousand horsemen, and people as the sand which *is* on the seashore in multitude. And they came up and encamped in Michmash, to the east of Beth Aven. [6]When the men of Israel saw that they were in danger (for the people were distressed), then the people hid in caves, in thickets, in rocks, in holes, and in pits. [7]And *some of* the Hebrews crossed over the Jordan to the land of Gad and Gilead.

As for Saul, he *was* still in Gilgal, and all the people followed him trembling. [8]Then he waited seven days, according to the time set by Samuel. But Samuel did not come to Gilgal; and the people were scattered from him. [9]So Saul said, "Bring a burnt offering and peace offerings here to me." And he offered the burnt offering. [10]Now it happened, as soon as he had finished presenting the burnt offering, that Samuel came; and Saul went out to meet him, that he might greet him.

[11]And Samuel said, "What have you done?"

Saul said, "When I saw that the people were scattered from me, and *that* you did not come within the days appointed, and *that* the Philistines gathered together at Michmash, [12]then I said, 'The Philistines will now come down on me at Gilgal, and I have not made supplication to the LORD.' Therefore I felt compelled, and offered a burnt offering."

[13]And Samuel said to Saul, "You have done foolishly. You have not kept the commandment of the LORD your God, which He commanded you. For now the LORD would have established your kingdom over Israel forever. [14]But now your kingdom shall not continue. The LORD has sought for Himself a man after His own heart, and the LORD has commanded him *to be* commander over His people, because you have not kept what the LORD commanded you."

[15]Then Samuel arose and went up from Gilgal to Gibeah of Benjamin.[a] And Saul numbered the people present with him, about six hundred men.

No Weapons for the Army

[16]Saul, Jonathan his son, and the people present with them remained in Gibeah of Benjamin. But the Philistines encamped in Michmash. [17]Then raiders came out of the camp of the Philistines in three companies. One company turned onto the road to Ophrah, to the land of Shual, [18]another company turned to the road *to* Beth Horon, and another company turned *to* the road of the border that overlooks the Valley of Zeboim toward the wilderness.

[19]Now there was no blacksmith to be found throughout all the land of Israel, for the Philis-

13:5 [a]Following Masoretic Text, Septuagint, Targum, and Vulgate; Syriac and some manuscripts of the Septuagint read *three.* **13:15** [a]Following Masoretic Text and Targum; Septuagint and Vulgate add *And the rest of the people went up after Saul to meet the people who fought against them, going from Gilgal to Gibeah in the hill of Benjamin.*

SOUL NOTE

After God's Heart *(13:14)* Samuel had told Saul to wait until he arrived at Gilgal to offer the sacrifices (10:8). When Samuel did not arrive soon enough, however, Saul decided to offer the sacrifice himself. When Samuel arrived, Saul had plenty of excuses, but, in reality, this new king had "not kept the commandment of the LORD" (13:13). God rejected Saul and promised to give Israel's leadership to "a man after His own heart" (13:14). To be successful for God, we must have hearts for God—hearts that have been changed by the power of an intimate relationship with Him.
Topic: Knowing God

tines said, "Lest the Hebrews make swords or
spears." 20But all the Israelites would go down
to the Philistines to sharpen each man's plow-
share, his mattock, his ax, and his sickle;
21and the charge for a sharpening was a pim[a]
for the plowshares, the mattocks, the forks,
and the axes, and to set the points of the
goads. 22So it came about, on the day of battle,
that there was neither sword nor spear found
in the hand of any of the people who *were*
with Saul and Jonathan. But they were found
with Saul and Jonathan his son.
23And the garrison of the Philistines went
out to the pass of Michmash.

Jonathan Defeats the Philistines

14 Now it happened one day that Jonathan the son of Saul said to the young
man who bore his armor, "Come, let us go
over to the Philistines' garrison that *is* on the
other side." But he did not tell his father. 2And
Saul was sitting in the outskirts of Gibeah under a pomegranate tree which *is* in Migron.
The people who *were* with him *were* about six
hundred men. 3Ahijah the son of Ahitub,
Ichabod's brother, the son of Phinehas, the
son of Eli, the LORD's priest in Shiloh, was
wearing an ephod. But the people did not
know that Jonathan had gone.
4Between the passes, by which Jonathan
sought to go over to the Philistines' garrison,
there was a sharp rock on one side and a sharp
rock on the other side. And the name of one
was Bozez, and the name of the other Seneh.
5The front of one faced northward opposite
Michmash, and the other southward opposite
Gibeah.
6Then Jonathan said to the young man who
bore his armor, "Come, let us go over to the
garrison of these uncircumcised; it may be
that the LORD will work for us. For nothing
restrains the LORD from saving by many or
by few."
7So his armorbearer said to him, "Do all
that is in your heart. Go then; here I am with
you, according to your heart."
8Then Jonathan said, "Very well, let us
cross over to *these* men, and we will show
ourselves to them. 9If they say thus to us,
'Wait until we come to you,' then we will
stand still in our place and not go up to them.
10But if they say thus, 'Come up to us,' then we
will go up. For the LORD has delivered them
into our hand, and this *will be* a sign to us."
11So both of them showed themselves to the
garrison of the Philistines. And the Philistines
said, "Look, the Hebrews are coming out of
the holes where they have hidden." 12Then
the men of the garrison called to Jonathan and
his armorbearer, and said, "Come up to us,
and we will show you something."
Jonathan said to his armorbearer, "Come up
after me, for the LORD has delivered them into
the hand of Israel." 13And Jonathan climbed
up on his hands and knees with his
armorbearer after him; and they fell before
Jonathan. And as he came after him, his
armorbearer killed them. 14That first slaughter
which Jonathan and his armorbearer made
was about twenty men within about half an
acre of land.[a]
15And there was trembling in the camp, in
the field, and among all the people. The garrison and the raiders also trembled; and the
earth quaked, so that it was a very great trembling. 16Now the watchmen of Saul in Gibeah
of Benjamin looked, and *there* was the multitude, melting away; and they went here and
there. 17Then Saul said to the people who *were*
with him, "Now call the roll and see who has
gone from us." And when they had called the
roll, surprisingly, Jonathan and his armorbearer *were* not *there*. 18And Saul said to Ahijah, "Bring the ark[a] of God here" (for at that
time the ark[b] of God was with the children of
Israel). 19Now it happened, while Saul talked
to the priest, that the noise which *was* in the
camp of the Philistines continued to increase;
so Saul said to the priest, "Withdraw your
hand." 20Then Saul and all the people who
were with him assembled, and they went to
the battle; and indeed every man's sword was
against his neighbor, *and there was* very great
confusion. 21Moreover the Hebrews *who* were
with the Philistines before that time, who
went up with them into the camp *from the*
surrounding *country*, they also joined the Israelites who *were* with Saul and Jonathan.
22Likewise all the men of Israel who had hidden in the mountains of Ephraim, *when* they
heard that the Philistines fled, they also followed hard after them in the battle. 23So the

13:21 [a]About two-thirds shekel weight
14:14 [a]Literally *half the area plowed by a yoke* (of oxen in a day) **14:18** [a]Following Masoretic Text, Targum, and Vulgate; Septuagint reads *ephod*. [b]Following Masoretic Text, Targum, and Vulgate; Septuagint reads *ephod*.

LORD saved Israel that day, and the battle shifted to Beth Aven.

SAUL'S RASH OATH

[24]And the men of Israel were distressed that day, for Saul had placed the people under oath, saying, "Cursed *is* the man who eats *any* food until evening, before I have taken vengeance on my enemies." So none of the people tasted food. [25]Now all *the people* of the land came to a forest; and there was honey on the ground. [26]And when the people had come into the woods, there was the honey, dripping; but no one put his hand to his mouth, for the people feared the oath. [27]But Jonathan had not heard his father charge the people with the oath; therefore he stretched out the end of the rod that *was* in his hand and dipped it in a honeycomb, and put his hand to his mouth; and his countenance brightened. [28]Then one of the people said, "Your father strictly charged the people with an oath, saying, 'Cursed *is* the man who eats food this day.' " And the people were faint.

[29]But Jonathan said, "My father has troubled the land. Look now, how my countenance has brightened because I tasted a little of this honey. [30]How much better if the people had eaten freely today of the spoil of their enemies which they found! For now would there not have been a much greater slaughter among the Philistines?"

[31]Now they had driven back the Philistines that day from Michmash to Aijalon. So the people were very faint. [32]And the people rushed on the spoil, and took sheep, oxen, and calves, and slaughtered *them* on the ground; and the people ate *them* with the blood. [33]Then they told Saul, saying, "Look, the people are sinning against the LORD by eating with the blood!"

So he said, "You have dealt treacherously; roll a large stone to me this day." [34]Then Saul said, "Disperse yourselves among the people, and say to them, 'Bring me here every man's ox and every man's sheep, slaughter *them* here, and eat; and do not sin against the LORD by eating with the blood.' " So every one of the people brought his ox with him that night, and slaughtered *it* there. [35]Then Saul built an altar to the LORD. This was the first altar that he built to the LORD.

[36]Now Saul said, "Let us go down after the Philistines by night, and plunder them until the morning light; and let us not leave a man of them."

And they said, "Do whatever seems good to you."

Then the priest said, "Let us draw near to God here."

[37]So Saul asked counsel of God, "Shall I go down after the Philistines? Will You deliver them into the hand of Israel?" But He did not answer him that day. [38]And Saul said, "Come over here, all you chiefs of the people, and know and see what this sin was today. [39]For *as* the LORD lives, who saves Israel, though it be in Jonathan my son, he shall surely die." But not a man among all the people answered him. [40]Then he said to all Israel, "You be on one side, and my son Jonathan and I will be on the other side."

And the people said to Saul, "Do what seems good to you."

[41]Therefore Saul said to the LORD God of Israel, "Give a perfect *lot.*"[a] So Saul and Jonathan were taken, but the people escaped. [42]And Saul said, "Cast *lots* between my son Jonathan and me." So Jonathan was taken. [43]Then Saul said to Jonathan, "Tell me what you have done."

And Jonathan told him, and said, "I only tasted a little honey with the end of the rod that *was* in my hand. So now I must die!"

[44]Saul answered, "God do so and more also; for you shall surely die, Jonathan."

[45]But the people said to Saul, "Shall Jonathan die, who has accomplished this great deliverance in Israel? Certainly not! *As* the LORD lives, not one hair of his head shall fall to the ground, for he has worked with God this day." So the people rescued Jonathan, and he did not die.

[46]Then Saul returned from pursuing the Philistines, and the Philistines went to their own place.

SAUL'S CONTINUING WARS

[47]So Saul established his sovereignty over Israel, and fought against all his enemies on every side, against Moab, against the people

---

14:41 [a]Following Masoretic Text and Targum; Septuagint and Vulgate read *Why do You not answer Your servant today? If the injustice is with me or Jonathan my son, O Lord God of Israel, give proof; and if You say it is with Your people Israel, give holiness.*

of Ammon, against Edom, against the kings of Zobah, and against the Philistines. Wherever he turned, he harassed *them.*[a] 48And he gathered an army and attacked the Amalekites, and delivered Israel from the hands of those who plundered them.

49The sons of Saul were Jonathan, Jishui,[a] and Malchishua. And the names of his two daughters *were these:* the name of the firstborn Merab, and the name of the younger Michal. 50The name of Saul's wife *was* Ahinoam the daughter of Ahimaaz. And the name of the commander of his army *was* Abner the son of Ner, Saul's uncle. 51Kish *was* the father of Saul, and Ner the father of Abner *was* the son of Abiel.

52Now there was fierce war with the Philistines all the days of Saul. And when Saul saw any strong man or any valiant man, he took him for himself.

SAUL SPARES KING AGAG

15 Samuel also said to Saul, "The LORD sent me to anoint you king over His people, over Israel. Now therefore, heed the voice of the words of the LORD. 2Thus says the LORD of hosts: 'I will punish Amalek *for* what he did to Israel, how he ambushed him on the way when he came up from Egypt. 3Now go and attack Amalek, and utterly destroy all that they have, and do not spare them. But kill both man and woman, infant and nursing child, ox and sheep, camel and donkey.' "

4So Saul gathered the people together and numbered them in Telaim, two hundred thousand foot soldiers and ten thousand men of Judah. 5And Saul came to a city of Amalek, and lay in wait in the valley.

6Then Saul said to the Kenites, "Go, depart, get down from among the Amalekites, lest I destroy you with them. For you showed kindness to all the children of Israel when they came up out of Egypt." So the Kenites departed from among the Amalekites. 7And Saul attacked the Amalekites, from Havilah all the way to Shur, which is east of Egypt. 8He also took Agag king of the Amalekites alive, and utterly destroyed all the people with the edge of the sword. 9But Saul and the people spared Agag and the best of the sheep, the oxen, the fatlings, the lambs, and all *that was* good, and were unwilling to utterly destroy them. But everything despised and worthless, that they utterly destroyed.

SAUL REJECTED AS KING

10Now the word of the LORD came to Samuel, saying, 11"I greatly regret that I have set up Saul *as* king, for he has turned back from following Me, and has not performed My commandments." And it grieved Samuel, and he cried out to the LORD all night. 12So when Samuel rose early in the morning to meet Saul, it was told Samuel, saying, "Saul went to Carmel, and indeed, he set up a monument for himself; and he has gone on around, passed by, and gone down to Gilgal." 13Then Samuel went to Saul, and Saul said to him, "Blessed *are* you of the LORD! I have performed the commandment of the LORD."

14But Samuel said, "What then *is* this bleating of the sheep in my ears, and the lowing of the oxen which I hear?"

15And Saul said, "They have brought them from the Amalekites; for the people spared the best of the sheep and the oxen, to sacrifice to the LORD your God; and the rest we have utterly destroyed."

16Then Samuel said to Saul, "Be quiet! And I will tell you what the LORD said to me last night."

And he said to him, "Speak on."

17So Samuel said, "When you *were* little in your own eyes, *were* you not head of the tribes of Israel? And did not the LORD anoint you king over Israel? 18Now the LORD sent you on a mission, and said, 'Go, and utterly destroy the sinners, the Amalekites, and fight against them until they are consumed.' 19Why then did you not obey the voice of the LORD? Why did you swoop down on the spoil, and do evil in the sight of the LORD?"

20And Saul said to Samuel, "But I have obeyed the voice of the LORD, and gone on the mission on which the LORD sent me, and brought back Agag king of Amalek; I have utterly destroyed the Amalekites. 21But the people took of the plunder, sheep and oxen, the best of the things which should have been utterly destroyed, to sacrifice to the LORD your God in Gilgal."

22So Samuel said:

"Has the LORD *as great* delight in burnt
offerings and sacrifices,

14:47 [a]Septuagint and Vulgate read *prospered.*
14:49 [a]Called *Abinadab* in 1 Chronicles 8:33 and 9:39

As in obeying the voice of the LORD?
Behold, to obey is better than sacrifice,
And to heed than the fat of rams.
23 For rebellion *is as* the sin of witchcraft,
And stubbornness *is as* iniquity and
idolatry.
Because you have rejected the word of
the LORD,
He also has rejected you from *being* king."

24 Then Saul said to Samuel, "I have sinned,
for I have transgressed the commandment of
the LORD and your words, because I feared the
people and obeyed their voice. 25 Now therefore, please pardon my sin, and return with
me, that I may worship the LORD."
26 But Samuel said to Saul, "I will not return
with you, for you have rejected the word of
the LORD, and the LORD has rejected you from
being king over Israel."
27 And as Samuel turned around to go away,
Saul seized the edge of his robe, and it tore.
28 So Samuel said to him, "The LORD has torn
the kingdom of Israel from you today, and has
given it to a neighbor of yours, *who is* better
than you. 29 And also the Strength of Israel will
not lie nor relent. For He *is* not a man, that He
should relent."
30 Then he said, "I have sinned; *yet* honor
me now, please, before the elders of my people and before Israel, and return with me, that
I may worship the LORD your God." 31 So Samuel turned back after Saul, and Saul worshiped the LORD.
32 Then Samuel said, "Bring Agag king of the
Amalekites here to me." So Agag came to him
cautiously.
And Agag said, "Surely the bitterness of
death is past."
33 But Samuel said, "As your sword has made

PERSONALITY PROFILE

Obedience

SAUL'S DISOBEDIENCE

(1 SAMUEL 15:17–23)

"We want a king!" Years after settling in the Promised Land, the Israelites clamored for a ruler so they could be "like all the nations" (1 Sam. 8:5). They had been graciously chosen to be like no other nation, but they forgot that God was their only true king and protector. They also forgot specific warnings about the cost of kings, precautions that God had given them through Moses (Deut. 17:14–20).

The judge Samuel reluctantly anointed Saul as the first king of Israel. Saul was tall, handsome, and had the right reputation as a respected military leader. Unfortunately, Saul's admirable qualities were overshadowed by a dark side that came to dominate his life. From the start of his reign, Saul demonstrated a tendency to cut corners, tell half-truths, justify bad behavior, and blame others for his own mistakes. He was determined to reign his own way, which often meant direct disobedience to God.

Saul also suffered from terrible bouts of depression, spirit oppression, and despair. David's miraculous triumph over Goliath and the resulting praise of the people stirred in Saul feelings of fear and jealousy. He hated David as a possible rival for the throne. He overlooked his own failures and allowed murderous intentions toward David to take root in his soul. Obsessive hatred poisoned and ruled Saul's life until the time of his death.

Saul repeatedly disobeyed God's directions. He tried to cover up his willfulness before God. Samuel confronted him each time with the truth that it is always better to obey God than to offer sacrifices. Saul thought he could replace obedience with appearance. He chose his own way (even witchcraft), rather than the way of the Lord. His ways seemed right to him, but they led to death.

The lessons from Saul's life include the truth that there is no effective substitute for obedience to God. If our way isn't God's way, it's the wrong way.

To Learn More: Turn to the article about obedience on pages 1686, 1687. See also the key passage note at 1 Samuel 15:22 on page 363.

women childless, so shall your mother be
childless among women." And Samuel hacked
Agag in pieces before the LORD in Gilgal.
34Then Samuel went to Ramah, and Saul
went up to his house at Gibeah of Saul. 35And
Samuel went no more to see Saul until the day
of his death. Nevertheless Samuel mourned
for Saul, and the LORD regretted that He had
made Saul king over Israel.

DAVID ANOINTED KING

16 Now the LORD said to Samuel, "How
long will you mourn for Saul, seeing I
have rejected him from reigning over Israel?
Fill your horn with oil,
and go; I am sending
you to Jesse the Beth-
lehemite. For I have
provided Myself a king
among his sons."
2And Samuel said,
"How can I go? If Saul
hears *it,* he will kill me."
But the LORD said, "Take a heifer with you,
and say, 'I have come to sacrifice to the LORD.'
3Then invite Jesse to the sacrifice, and I will
show you what you shall do; you shall anoint
for Me the one I name to you."
4So Samuel did what the LORD said, and
went to Bethlehem. And the elders of the town
trembled at his coming, and said, "Do you
come peaceably?"
5And he said, "Peaceably; I have come to
sacrifice to the LORD. Sanctify yourselves, and
come with me to the sacrifice." Then he consecrated Jesse and his sons, and invited them
to the sacrifice.
6So it was, when they came, that he looked
at Eliab and said, "Surely the LORD's anointed
is before Him!"
7But the LORD said to Samuel, "Do not look
at his appearance or at his physical stature,
because I have refused him. For *the LORD does*
not *see* as man sees;[a] for man looks at the outward appearance, but the LORD looks at the
heart."
8So Jesse called Abinadab, and made him
pass before Samuel. And
he said, "Neither has the
LORD chosen this one."
9Then Jesse made Sham-
mah pass by. And he
said, "Neither has the
LORD chosen this one."
10Thus Jesse made
seven of his sons pass
before Samuel. And Samuel said to Jesse, "The
LORD has not chosen these." 11And Samuel said
to Jesse, "Are all the young men here?" Then
he said, "There remains yet the youngest, and
there he is, keeping the sheep."

> "The LORD does not see as man sees; for man looks at the outward appearance, but the LORD looks at the heart."
> 1 SAMUEL 16:7

16:7 [a]Septuagint reads *For God does not see as man sees;* Targum reads *It is not by the appearance of a man;* Vulgate reads *Nor do I judge according to the looks of a man.*

KEY PASSAGE

Obedience

BETTER THAN SACRIFICE

(15:22)

A form of this theme occurs in several places in the Bible: "To obey is better than sacrifice" (see also Ps. 40:6–8; 51:16, 17; Prov. 21:3; Is. 1:11–17; Jer. 7:21–23; Hos. 6:6; Mic. 6:6–8; Matt. 12:7; Mark 12:33; Heb. 10:8, 9). Clearly this is an important concept for God's people.

Saul had been told to wait for Samuel so that Samuel could offer the sacrifice. Saul, however, fearing the enemy, rushed to perform the sacrifice, thinking that it would magically provide protection. In this act, Saul disobeyed Samuel, as well as God's laws regarding the offering of sacrifices (the king was not to do it). God doesn't perform for people because of a ritual sacrifice or any other religious act; He acts on behalf of His obedient people. God wants obedience that flows out of love for Him.

To Learn More: Turn to the article about obedience on pages 1686, 1687. See also the personality profile of Saul on page 362.

MENTAL ILLNESS: REDUCING SUFFERING IN THE CHURCH

Mental Illness

PAUL MEIER, TIM CLINTON, & GEORGE OHLSCHLAGER

(1 Samuel 16:14–23)

No one escapes periods of trouble in life. Everyone struggles with problems in life, such as periods of being down, struggles with grief, or handling relationship difficulties. But what compels people to "go crazy," commit suicide, cut themselves deliberately, or hurt others mindlessly? What causes some to hear voices or have hallucinations without drugs? These unique maladies and extreme behaviors indicate deeper problems.

THE REALITY OF MENTAL ILLNESS

Human suffering is ultimately tied to sin. Sometimes it is directly influenced by demonic activity (1 Sam. 26:14-23). Mental disorders also involve suffering that is sometimes related to or rooted in biological, genetic, and physiological problems. When mental illness interacts with sin problems, relationship problems, or other kinds of illness, a person, marriage, or family can become overwhelmed.

Studies of clinical disorders in the twentieth century have revealed patterns that manifest a more serious level of disorder. We have also developed more effective interventions that promise hope and healing.

The failure to understand and treat the multiple reasons that people suffer—including understanding the distinctions between sin, mental illness, and demonic influence—has significant consequences. Some people are just confessing sins when they should also be taking medicine. Others are blaming nonexistent illnesses when they should be confessing their sins. Demons are being cast out of schizophrenics who need medical treatment. People who need exorcism and relief from demons are put into mental hospitals and drugged into complacency.

THE TREATMENT OF MENTAL ILLNESS

Misdiagnosis and improper treatment still remains all too common at the intersection of mental health and Christian ministry. Sometimes well-meaning Christians discourage those suffering mental illness from getting professional counseling or medical help. Far too many people in the church suffer needlessly because someone in a position of influence falsely believes that a "spiritual" solution alone is the answer to every problem. Instead, Christians must understand that physicians, balm, salve, and other medicines were used throughout the Scriptures. Just as a diabetic needs insulin to live, those with mental illness sometimes need medicine to correct their disordered brain chemistry.

In many cases, there is no one single cause for a problem, but the weight of multiple issues has added up to a personal or family crisis. Some cases *do* require medicine, counseling, and spiritual warfare because sin, illness, and demon oppression are all at issue. A comprehensive approach to Christian counseling treatment should use a collaborative team of specialists—doctors, psychologists, counselors, social workers, health educators, nutritionists, physical therapists, and others—to understand and treat the many dimensions of the problem.

As a Christian psychiatrist who runs a nationwide network of clinics and as a medical doctor, I (Paul Meier) deal with these issues and questions on a daily basis. My interest and specialty is in the biogenetic and physical bases of mental disorders. I treat patients who were born with high and low levels of crucial chemicals in the brain—what we call neurotransmitters—that are essential to the proper functioning of brain and body.

Low levels of serotonin, for example, cause a variety of depressive disorders or lifelong obsessive-compulsive traits. Patients with dopamine or GABA abnormalities often have high-energy manic episodes that involve paranoid delusions, feelings of grandeur and power, even hallucinations. Manic episodes are almost always controlled with GABA correcting medicines. The voices that often get attributed to demons nearly always disappear with the proper treatment of dopamine medicines. Auditory hallucinations, in other words, are rarely demonic, but are more a function of an inherited disorder that affects the auditory regions of the brain.

WORKING TOGETHER TO HELP THOSE WHO SUFFER

Mental disorders are a significant issue in society and in the church. We believe that the church and the mental health professions—which for too long have been at odds with one another—must work together. We believe that the church, in fact, is anointed by God to be specially designed for the care and comfort of the mentally ill—a "spiritual hospital" for those who suffer this way.

We all face times when the wise counsel of our pastor, friend, colleague, or doctor is essential for our safety and well-being. A small but significant percentage of the populace—including the body of Christ—will suffer from the kinds of mental disorders that require the special knowledge and treatment of a psychiatrist and other specialized caregivers.

A Christian psychiatrist should understand and respect the spiritual as well as the emotional, relational, and physical realms of life, and should incorporate God's truth about the totality of persons into their work. Christian counselors can help others deal with the thinking, feeling, and behavioral effects of mental disorders, and should be a welcome part of the entire treatment team. Any kind of helping professional should be in close consultation with the patient's pastor. Our common goal is to help all sufferers free their souls and be able to grow up and mature in Christ.

The pastor is the one who maintains an ongoing relationship with the suffering church member, so he or she has a special role as the shepherd, acting as the "case manager." The pastor is usually best suited to assist the church member in using treatment and making the transition back into life in the church and the community.

The church is critical in the care and solace of those suffering with mental disorders. These people are very often isolated, fearful, confused, and in need of the unconditional love of Christians to repair and return to vital living.

FURTHER MEDITATION:

Other passages to study about the issue of mental illness include:

- Psalm 34:18
- Proverbs 13:12
- Isaiah 40:27–31
- James 1:12–27

To Learn More: Turn to the key passage note on mental illness at Daniel 4:33 on page 1110. See also the personality profile of Nebuchadnezzar on page 1111.

And Samuel said to Jesse, "Send and bring him. For we will not sit down[a] till he comes here." [12]So he sent and brought him in. Now he *was* ruddy, with bright eyes, and good-looking. And the LORD said, "Arise, anoint him; for this *is* the one!" [13]Then Samuel took the horn of oil and anointed him in the midst of his brothers; and the Spirit of the LORD came upon David from that day forward. So Samuel arose and went to Ramah.

A Distressing Spirit Troubles Saul

[14]But the Spirit of the LORD departed from Saul, and a distressing spirit from the LORD troubled him. [15]And Saul's servants said to him, "Surely, a distressing spirit from God is troubling you. [16]Let our master now command your servants, *who are* before you, to seek out a man *who is* a skillful player on the harp. And it shall be that he will play it with his hand when the distressing spirit from God is upon you, and you shall be well."

[17]So Saul said to his servants, "Provide me now a man who can play well, and bring *him* to me."

[18]Then one of the servants answered and said, "Look, I have seen a son of Jesse the Bethlehemite, *who is* skillful in playing, a mighty man of valor, a man of war, prudent in speech, and a handsome person; and the LORD *is* with him."

[19]Therefore Saul sent messengers to Jesse, and said, "Send me your son David, who *is* with the sheep." [20]And Jesse took a donkey *loaded with* bread, a skin of wine, and a young goat, and sent *them* by his son David to Saul. [21]So David came to Saul and stood before him. And he loved him greatly, and he became his armorbearer. [22]Then Saul sent to Jesse, saying, "Please let David stand before me, for he has found favor in my sight." [23]And so it was, whenever the spirit from God was upon Saul, that David would take a harp and play *it* with his hand. Then Saul would become refreshed and well, and the distressing spirit would depart from him.

David and Goliath

17 Now the Philistines gathered their armies together to battle, and were gathered at Sochoh, which *belongs* to Judah; they encamped between Sochoh and Azekah, in Ephes Dammim. [2]And Saul and the men of Israel were gathered together, and they encamped in the Valley of Elah, and drew up in battle array against the Philistines. [3]The Philistines stood on a mountain on one side, and Israel stood on a mountain on the other side, with a valley between them.

[4]And a champion went out from the camp of the Philistines, named Goliath, from Gath, whose height *was* six cubits and a span. [5]*He had* a bronze helmet on his head, and he *was* armed with a coat of mail, and the weight of the coat *was* five thousand shekels of bronze. [6]And *he had* bronze armor on his legs and a bronze javelin between his shoulders. [7]Now the staff of his spear *was* like a weaver's beam, and his iron spearhead *weighed* six hundred shekels; and a shield-bearer went before him. [8]Then he stood and cried out to the armies of Israel, and said to them, "Why have you come out to line up for battle? *Am* I not a Philistine, and you the servants of Saul? Choose a man for yourselves, and let him come down to me. [9]If he is able to fight with me and kill me, then we will be your servants. But if I prevail against him and kill him, then

16:11 [a]Following Septuagint and Vulgate; Masoretic Text reads *turn around;* Targum and Syriac read *turn away.*

SOUL NOTE

Distressed *(16:14–23)* Saul displayed classic characteristics of mental disorder, including wide mood swings and fits of depression and anger. A person can develop such debilitating emotional symptoms for many reasons. In this case, Scripture indicates that "a distressing spirit from the LORD troubled" Saul (16:14). Saul's heart had turned from God, so God sovereignly permitted affliction by a spirit of distress—possibly a demonic influence—to occur. Not all mental disorders are a result of direct demonic influence, but like any sickness or disease, the battle for our minds is a result of the Fall and Satan's presence in this world. **Topic: Mental Illness**

you shall be our servants and serve us." 10 And the Philistine said, "I defy the armies of Israel this day; give me a man, that we may fight together." 11 When Saul and all Israel heard these words of the Philistine, they were dismayed and greatly afraid.

12 Now David *was* the son of that Ephrathite of Bethlehem Judah, whose name *was* Jesse, and who had eight sons. And the man was old, advanced *in years,* in the days of Saul. 13 The three oldest sons of Jesse had gone to follow Saul to the battle. The names of his three sons who went to the battle *were* Eliab the firstborn, next to him Abinadab, and the third Shammah. 14 David *was* the youngest. And the three oldest followed Saul. 15 But David occasionally went and returned from Saul to feed his father's sheep at Bethlehem.

16 And the Philistine drew near and presented himself forty days, morning and evening.

17 Then Jesse said to his son David, "Take now for your brothers an ephah of this dried *grain* and these ten loaves, and run to your brothers at the camp. 18 And carry these ten cheeses to the captain of *their* thousand, and see how your brothers fare, and bring back news of them." 19 Now Saul and they and all the men of Israel *were* in the Valley of Elah, fighting with the Philistines.

20 So David rose early in the morning, left the sheep with a keeper, and took *the things* and went as Jesse had commanded him. And he came to the camp as the army was going out to the fight and shouting for the battle. 21 For Israel and the Philistines had drawn up in battle array, army against army. 22 And David left his supplies in the hand of the supply keeper, ran to the army, and came and greeted his brothers. 23 Then as he talked with them, there was the champion, the Philistine of Gath, Goliath by name, coming up from the armies of the Philistines; and he spoke according to the same words. So David heard *them.* 24 And all the men of Israel, when they saw the man, fled from him and were dreadfully afraid. 25 So the men of Israel said, "Have you seen this man who has come up? Surely he has come up to defy Israel; and it shall be *that* the man who kills him the king will enrich with great riches, will give him his daughter, and give his father's house exemption *from taxes* in Israel."

26 Then David spoke to the men who stood by him, saying, "What shall be done for the man who kills this Philistine and takes away the reproach from Israel? For who *is* this uncircumcised Philistine, that he should defy the armies of the living God?"

27 And the people answered him in this manner, saying, "So shall it be done for the man who kills him."

28 Now Eliab his oldest brother heard when he spoke to the men; and Eliab's anger was aroused against David, and he said, "Why did you come down here? And with whom have you left those few sheep in the wilderness? I know your pride and the insolence of your heart, for you have come down to see the battle."

29 And David said, "What have I done now? *Is there* not a cause?" 30 Then he turned from him toward another and said the same thing; and these people answered him as the first ones *did.*

31 Now when the words which David spoke were heard, they reported *them* to Saul; and he sent for him. 32 Then David said to Saul, "Let no man's heart fail because of him; your servant will go and fight with this Philistine."

33 And Saul said to David, "You are not able to go against this Philistine to fight with him; for you *are* a youth, and he a man of war from his youth."

34 But David said to Saul, "Your servant used to keep his father's sheep, and when a lion or a bear came and took a lamb out of the flock, 35 I went out after it and struck it, and delivered *the lamb* from its mouth; and when it arose against me, I caught *it* by its beard, and struck and killed it. 36 Your servant has killed both lion and bear; and this uncircumcised Philistine will be like one of them, seeing he has defied the armies of the living God." 37 Moreover David said, "The LORD, who delivered me from the paw of the lion and from the paw of the bear, He will deliver me from the hand of this Philistine."

And Saul said to David, "Go, and the LORD be with you!"

38 So Saul clothed David with his armor, and he put a bronze helmet on his head; he also clothed him with a coat of mail. 39 David fastened his sword to his armor and tried to walk, for he had not tested *them.* And David said to Saul, "I cannot walk with these, for I have not tested *them.*" So David took them off.

40 Then he took his staff in his hand; and he

chose for himself five smooth stones from the
brook, and put them in a shepherd's bag, in a
pouch which he had, and his sling was in his
hand. And he drew near to the Philistine. 41So
the Philistine came, and began drawing near to
David, and the man who bore the shield *went*
before him. 42And when the Philistine looked
about and saw David, he disdained him; for he
was *only* a youth, ruddy and good-looking.
43So the Philistine said to David, "*Am* I a dog,
that you come to me with sticks?" And the Philistine cursed David by his gods. 44And the
Philistine said to David, "Come to me, and I
will give your flesh to the birds of the air and
the beasts of the field!"

45Then David said to the Philistine, "You
come to me with a sword, with a spear, and
with a javelin. But I come to you in the name of
the LORD of hosts, the God of the armies of Israel, whom you have de-
fied. 46This day the LORD
will deliver you into my
hand, and I will strike
you and take your head
from you. And this day I
will give the carcasses of
the camp of the Philis-
tines to the birds of the
air and the wild beasts
of the earth, that all the earth may know that
there is a God in Israel. 47Then all this assembly shall know that the LORD does not save
with sword and spear; for the battle *is* the
LORD's, and He will give you into our hands."

48So it was, when the Philistine arose and
came and drew near to meet David, that David
hurried and ran toward the army to meet the
Philistine. 49Then David put his hand in his
bag and took out a stone; and he slung *it* and
struck the Philistine in his forehead, so that
the stone sank into his forehead, and he fell
on his face to the earth. 50So David prevailed
over the Philistine with a sling and a stone,
and struck the Philistine and killed him. But
there was no sword in the hand of David.
51Therefore David ran and stood over the Philistine, took his sword and drew it out of its
sheath and killed him, and cut off his head
with it.

And when the Philistines saw that their
champion was dead, they fled. 52Now the men
of Israel and Judah arose and shouted, and
pursued the Philistines as far as the entrance
of the valley[a] and to the gates of Ekron. And
the wounded of the Philistines fell along the
road to Shaaraim, even as far as Gath and Ekron. 53Then the children of Israel returned
from chasing the Philistines, and they plundered their tents. 54And David took the head
of the Philistine and brought it to Jerusalem,
but he put his armor in his tent.

55When Saul saw David going out against the
Philistine, he said to Ab-
ner, the commander of
the army, "Abner, whose
son *is* this youth?"

And Abner said, "As
your soul lives, O king, I
do not know."

56So the king said,
"Inquire whose son this
young man *is*."

57Then, as David returned from the slaughter of the Philistine, Abner took him and
brought him before Saul with the head of the
Philistine in his hand. 58And Saul said to him,
"Whose son *are* you, young man?"

So David answered, "*I am* the son of your
servant Jesse the Bethlehemite."

"Then all this assembly shall know that the LORD does not save with sword and spear; for the battle is the LORD's, and He will give you into our hands."
1 SAMUEL 17:47

SAUL RESENTS DAVID

18 Now when he had finished speaking
to Saul, the soul of Jonathan was knit

17:52 [a]Following Masoretic Text, Syriac, Targum, and Vulgate; Septuagint reads *Gath*.

SOUL NOTE

Secret Weapon *(17:45)* Goliath of Gath was a champion, a warrior experienced at combat. Not only that, he was a giant of a man armed with giant weapons. Young David had only a sling and some small stones. But David had something that Goliath didn't—faith in the living God. When David came at Goliath "in the name of the LORD of hosts," there was no competition. With faith, we can do anything God calls us to do, even defeat the "giants" in our lives. **Topic: Faith**

to the soul of David, and Jonathan loved him as his own soul. 2Saul took him that day, and would not let him go home to his father's house anymore. 3Then Jonathan and David made a covenant, because he loved him as his own soul. 4And Jonathan took off the robe that *was* on him and gave it to David, with his armor, even to his sword and his bow and his belt.

5So David went out wherever Saul sent him, *and* behaved wisely. And Saul set him over the men of war, and he was accepted in the sight of all the people and also in the sight of Saul's servants. 6Now it had happened as they were coming *home,* when David was returning from the slaughter of the Philistine, that the women had come out of all the cities of Israel, singing and dancing, to meet King Saul, with tambourines, with joy, and with musical instruments. 7So the women sang as they danced, and said:

"Saul has slain his thousands,
And David his ten thousands."

8Then Saul was very angry, and the saying displeased him; and he said, "They have ascribed to David ten thousands, and to me they have ascribed *only* thousands. Now *what* more can he have but the kingdom?" 9So Saul eyed David from that day forward.

10And it happened on the next day that the distressing spirit from God came upon Saul, and he prophesied inside the house. So David played *music* with his hand, as at other times; but *there was* a spear in Saul's hand. 11And Saul cast the spear, for he said, "I will pin David to the wall!" But David escaped his presence twice.

12Now Saul was afraid of David, because the LORD was with him, but had departed from Saul. 13Therefore Saul removed him from his presence, and made him his captain over a thousand; and he went out and came in before the people. 14And David behaved wisely in all his ways, and the LORD *was* with him. 15Therefore, when Saul saw that he behaved very wisely, he was afraid of him. 16But all Israel and Judah loved David, because he went out and came in before them.

David Marries Michal

17Then Saul said to David, "Here is my older daughter Merab; I will give her to you as a wife. Only be valiant for me, and fight the LORD's battles." For Saul thought, "Let my hand not be against him, but let the hand of the Philistines be against him."

18So David said to Saul, "Who *am* I, and what *is* my life *or* my father's family in Israel, that I should be son-in-law to the king?" 19But it happened at the time when Merab, Saul's daughter, should have been given to David, that she was given to Adriel the Meholathite as a wife.

20Now Michal, Saul's daughter, loved David. And they told Saul, and the thing pleased him. 21So Saul said, "I will give her to him, that she may be a snare to him, and that the hand of the Philistines may be against him." Therefore Saul said to David a second time, "You shall be my son-in-law today."

22And Saul commanded his servants, "Communicate with David secretly, and say, 'Look, the king has delight in you, and all his servants love you. Now therefore, become the king's son-in-law.' "

23So Saul's servants spoke those words in the hearing of David. And David said, "Does it seem to you *a* light *thing* to be a king's son-in-law, seeing I *am* a poor and lightly esteemed man?" 24And the servants of Saul told him, saying, "In this manner David spoke."

25Then Saul said, "Thus you shall say to David: 'The king does not desire any dowry but one hundred foreskins of the Philistines, to

SOUL NOTE

Green with Envy *(18:8)* Saul became jealous of David's victory over Goliath and the national attention that it received. The young warrior had upstaged the king. Saul's jealousy led to anger, resentment, fear, and attempted murder (18:11). Like a seething cauldron ready to tip at any moment, uncontrolled jealousy can lead to destruction. We must take our jealousy to God, asking Him to help us appreciate others' talents while showing us how best to use our own. **Topic: Jealousy**

take vengeance on the king's enemies.' " But
Saul thought to make David fall by the hand of
the Philistines. [26]So when his servants told
David these words, it pleased David well to
become the king's son-in-law. Now the days
had not expired; [27]therefore David arose and
went, he and his men, and killed two hundred
men of the Philistines. And David brought
their foreskins, and they gave them in full
count to the king, that he might become the
king's son-in-law. Then Saul gave him Michal
his daughter as a wife.

[28]Thus Saul saw and knew that the LORD
was with David, and *that* Michal, Saul's
daughter, loved him; [29]and Saul was still more
afraid of David. So Saul became David's enemy continually. [30]Then the princes of the Philistines went out *to war.* And so it was,
whenever they went out, *that* David behaved
more wisely than all the servants of Saul, so
that his name became highly esteemed.

SAUL PERSECUTES DAVID

19 Now Saul spoke to Jonathan his son
and to all his servants, that they
should kill David; but Jonathan, Saul's son,
delighted greatly in David. [2]So Jonathan told
David, saying, "My father Saul seeks to kill
you. Therefore please be on your guard until
morning, and stay in a secret *place* and hide.
[3]And I will go out and stand beside my father
in the field where you *are,* and I will speak
with my father about you. Then what I observe, I will tell you."

[4]Thus Jonathan spoke well of David to
Saul his father, and said to him, "Let not the
king sin against his servant, against David,
because he has not sinned against you, and
because his works *have been* very good toward you. [5]For he took his life in his hands
and killed the Philistine, and the LORD brought
about a great deliverance for all Israel. You
saw *it* and rejoiced. Why then will you sin

PERSONALITY PROFILE

Bitterness

SAUL AND THE POISON OF BITTER FRUIT

(1 SAMUEL 19)

King Saul wasted his last years in hatred and anger. He sank deeper into darkness and tormented suffering as his battle-scarred body and soul yielded to age. Fears, jealousies, murderous thoughts, and violent rage consumed him without relief. He attempted to kill David, driving David to life as a fugitive and wasting kingdom resources trying to track down and eliminate him. Others also suffered. Saul unjustly accused the priests of Nob of conspiring with David, and he had 85 of them killed. Once the killing started in Nob, no one was spared—neither men, women, children, nor animals.

Saul's choices caused a tidal wave of evil to flood his soul. He lost all godliness or restraint. Even David's mercy in sparing Saul's life twice had no softening effect that lasted. His soul was hardened and unresponsive to any message from God. He collected a legacy of evil and bitterness.

Facing his final battle, Saul was terrified by the overwhelming might of the Philistines. Samuel was dead and God was silent. Desperate, Saul consulted a medium—an ancient psychic who practiced divination in direct violation of God's law. The message he received sealed his fate. During the battle, with defeat in sight, Saul fell on his own sword. Bitterness finally turned into self-destruction.

Saul's journey to his doom followed a well-traveled path. People continue to discover that resistance against God's Spirit gains strength with practice. Such lives even show up in the church. These people are bitter, angry, divisive, and dark in thought and deed. As David treated Saul with mercy and respect, so must we treat such people. They must be lovingly called to repentance. The church can speak truth to them while taking care not to join them on their bitter journey.

To Learn More: Turn to the article about bitterness on pages 658, 659. See also the key passage note at Hebrews 12:12–29 on page 1637.

against innocent blood, to kill David without a cause?"

6So Saul heeded the voice of Jonathan, and Saul swore, "*As* the LORD lives, he shall not be killed." 7Then Jonathan called David, and Jonathan told him all these things. So Jonathan brought David to Saul, and he was in his presence as in times past.

8And there was war again; and David went out and fought with the Philistines, and struck them with a mighty blow, and they fled from him.

9Now the distressing spirit from the LORD came upon Saul as he sat in his house with his spear in his hand. And David was playing *music* with *his* hand. 10Then Saul sought to pin David to the wall with the spear, but he slipped away from Saul's presence; and he drove the spear into the wall. So David fled and escaped that night.

11Saul also sent messengers to David's house to watch him and to kill him in the morning. And Michal, David's wife, told him, saying, "If you do not save your life tonight, tomorrow you will be killed." 12So Michal let David down through a window. And he went and fled and escaped. 13And Michal took an image and laid *it* in the bed, put a cover of goats' *hair* for his head, and covered *it* with clothes. 14So when Saul sent messengers to take David, she said, "He *is* sick."

15Then Saul sent the messengers *back* to see David, saying, "Bring him up to me in the bed, that I may kill him." 16And when the messengers had come in, there was the image in the bed, with a cover of goats' *hair* for his head. 17Then Saul said to Michal, "Why have you deceived me like this, and sent my enemy away, so that he has escaped?"

And Michal answered Saul, "He said to me, 'Let me go! Why should I kill you?' "

18So David fled and escaped, and went to Samuel at Ramah, and told him all that Saul had done to him. And he and Samuel went and stayed in Naioth. 19Now it was told Saul, saying, "Take note, David *is* at Naioth in Ramah!" 20Then Saul sent messengers to take David. And when they saw the group of prophets prophesying, and Samuel standing *as* leader over them, the Spirit of God came upon the messengers of Saul, and they also prophesied. 21And when Saul was told, he sent other messengers, and they prophesied likewise. Then Saul sent messengers again the third time, and they prophesied also. 22Then he also went to Ramah, and came to the great well that *is* at Sechu. So he asked, and said, "Where *are* Samuel and David?"

And *someone* said, "Indeed *they are* at Naioth in Ramah." 23So he went there to Naioth in Ramah. Then the Spirit of God was upon him also, and he went on and prophesied until he came to Naioth in Ramah. 24And he also stripped off his clothes and prophesied before Samuel in like manner, and lay down naked all that day and all that night. Therefore they say, "*Is* Saul also among the prophets?"[a]

JONATHAN'S LOYALTY TO DAVID

20 Then David fled from Naioth in Ramah, and went and said to Jonathan, "What have I done? What *is* my iniquity, and what *is* my sin before your father, that he seeks my life?"

2So Jonathan said to him, "By no means! You shall not die! Indeed, my father will do nothing either great or small without first telling me. And why should my father hide this thing from me? It *is* not *so!*"

3Then David took an oath again, and said, "Your father certainly knows that I have found favor in your eyes, and he has said, 'Do not let Jonathan know this, lest he be grieved.' But truly, *as* the LORD lives and *as* your soul lives, *there is* but a step between me and death."

4So Jonathan said to David, "Whatever you yourself desire, I will do *it* for you."

5And David said to Jonathan, "Indeed tomorrow *is* the New Moon, and I should not fail to sit with the king to eat. But let me go, that I may hide in the field until the third *day* at evening. 6If your father misses me at all, then say, 'David earnestly asked *permission* of me that he might run over to Bethlehem, his city, for *there is* a yearly sacrifice there for all the family.' 7If he says thus: '*It is* well,' your servant will be safe. But if he is very angry, be sure that evil is determined by him. 8Therefore you shall deal kindly with your servant, for you have brought your servant into a covenant of the LORD with you. Nevertheless, if there is iniquity in me, kill me yourself, for why should you bring me to your father?"

9But Jonathan said, "Far be it from you! For if I knew certainly that evil was determined by

---

19:24 [a]Compare 1 Samuel 10:12

my father to come upon you, then would I not
tell you?"
10 Then David said to Jonathan, "Who will
tell me, or what *if* your father answers you
roughly?"
11 And Jonathan said to David, "Come, let us
go out into the field." So both of them went
out into the field. 12 Then Jonathan said to David: "The LORD God of Israel *is witness!* When
I have sounded out my father sometime tomorrow, *or* the third *day*, and indeed *there is*
good toward David, and I do not send to you
and tell you, 13 may the LORD do so and much
more to Jonathan. But if it pleases my father
to do you evil, then I will report it to you and
send you away, that you may go in safety. And
the LORD be with you as He has been with my
father. 14 And you shall not only show me the
kindness of the LORD while I still live, that I
may not die; 15 but you shall not cut off your
kindness from my house forever, no, not when
the LORD has cut off every one of the enemies
of David from the face of the earth." 16 So Jonathan made *a covenant* with the house of David, *saying*, "Let the LORD require *it* at the
hand of David's enemies."
17 Now Jonathan again caused David to vow,
because he loved him; for he loved him as he
loved his own soul. 18 Then Jonathan said to
David, "Tomorrow *is* the New Moon; and you
will be missed, because your seat will be empty. 19 And *when* you have stayed three days, go
down quickly and come to the place where
you hid on the day of the deed; and remain by
the stone Ezel. 20 Then I will shoot three arrows to the side, as though I shot at a target;
21 and there I will send a lad, *saying*, 'Go, find
the arrows.' If I expressly say to the lad, 'Look,
the arrows *are* on this side of you; get them
and come'—then, as the LORD lives, *there is*
safety for you and no harm. 22 But if I say thus
to the young man, 'Look, the arrows *are* be-

PERSONALITY PROFILE

Relationships

DAVID AND JONATHAN—BEST OF FRIENDS

(1 SAMUEL 20)

David and Jonathan shared a rare friendship. Born out of youthful mutual admiration, their relationship stood the test of difficult decisions and conflicting loyalties. Jonathan, the king's son and future heir, befriended David, his father's champion. Both men demonstrated courage and fine leadership abilities. They came to trust one another with their lives.

Then came the conflict between Saul, the king, and David. Jonathan found himself caught between his father and his best friend. At first, he found it hard to accept his father's change of heart toward David. The temptation was to choose one over the other. Jonathan had a better plan. He chose the truth and faithfulness to God. He remained loyal to both his father and to David. He managed to keep them apart so he wouldn't have to take a side.

His wisdom earned him David's deep gratitude and Saul's resentment. To Jonathan's credit, he did not allow his father's attitude to drive him away. He died with his father in battle. Until then, it was apparent that Jonathan was never threatened by David's popularity. Whether or not he knew that Samuel had anointed David as the next king, Jonathan remained loyal. He displayed all the best character of a true friend.

Most of us desire to have a friend like Jonathan in our lives. We don't necessarily have control over that. But we can decide to be a friend to others like Jonathan. David and Jonathan were not in the same place, with the same choices. Jonathan made his relationship with David an area in which he practiced his faithfulness to God. Integrity, truth, intimacy, and loyalty characterized his side of the friendship. In what ways are you seeking to be a Jonathan in someone else's life?

To Learn More: Turn to the article about relationships on pages 856, 857. See also the key passage note at Ephesians 4:31, 32 on page 1556.

yond you'—go your way, for the LORD has sent you away. [23]And as for the matter which you and I have spoken of, indeed the LORD *be* between you and me forever."

[24]Then David hid in the field. And when the New Moon had come, the king sat down to eat the feast. [25]Now the king sat on his seat, as at other times, on a seat by the wall. And Jonathan arose,[a] and Abner sat by Saul's side, but David's place was empty. [26]Nevertheless Saul did not say anything that day, for he thought, "Something has happened to him; he *is* unclean, surely he *is* unclean." [27]And it happened the next day, the second *day* of the month, that David's place was empty. And Saul said to Jonathan his son, "Why has the son of Jesse not come to eat, either yesterday or today?"

[28]So Jonathan answered Saul, "David earnestly asked *permission* of me *to go* to Bethlehem. [29]And he said, 'Please let me go, for our family has a sacrifice in the city, and my brother has commanded me *to be there.* And now, if I have found favor in your eyes, please let me get away and see my brothers.' Therefore he has not come to the king's table."

[30]Then Saul's anger was aroused against Jonathan, and he said to him, "You son of a perverse, rebellious *woman!* Do I not know that you have chosen the son of Jesse to your own shame and to the shame of your mother's nakedness? [31]For as long as the son of Jesse lives on the earth, you shall not be established, nor your kingdom. Now therefore, send and bring him to me, for he shall surely die."

[32]And Jonathan answered Saul his father, and said to him, "Why should he be killed? What has he done?" [33]Then Saul cast a spear at him to kill him, by which Jonathan knew that it was determined by his father to kill David.

[34]So Jonathan arose from the table in fierce anger, and ate no food the second day of the month, for he was grieved for David, because his father had treated him shamefully.

[35]And so it was, in the morning, that Jonathan went out into the field at the time appointed with David, and a little lad *was* with him. [36]Then he said to his lad, "Now run, find the arrows which I shoot." As the lad ran, he shot an arrow beyond him. [37]When the lad had come to the place where the arrow was which Jonathan had shot, Jonathan cried out after the lad and said, "*Is* not the arrow beyond you?" [38]And Jonathan cried out after the lad, "Make haste, hurry, do not delay!" So Jonathan's lad gathered up the arrows and came back to his master. [39]But the lad did not know anything. Only Jonathan and David knew of the matter. [40]Then Jonathan gave his weapons to his lad, and said to him, "Go, carry *them* to the city."

[41]As soon as the lad had gone, David arose from *a place* toward the south, fell on his face to the ground, and bowed down three times. And they kissed one another; and they wept together, but David more so. [42]Then Jonathan said to David, "Go in peace, since we have both sworn in the name of the LORD, saying, 'May the LORD be between you and me, and between your descendants and my descendants, forever.' " So he arose and departed, and Jonathan went into the city.

DAVID AND THE HOLY BREAD

21 Now David came to Nob, to Ahimelech the priest. And Ahimelech was afraid when he met David, and said to him, "Why *are* you alone, and no one is with you?"

[2]So David said to Ahimelech the priest, "The king has ordered me on some business, and said to me, 'Do not let anyone know anything about the business on which I send you, or what I have commanded you.' And I have directed *my* young men to such and such a place. [3]Now therefore, what have you on hand? Give *me* five *loaves of* bread in my hand, or whatever can be found."

[4]And the priest answered David and said, "*There is* no common bread on hand; but there is holy bread, if the young men have at least kept themselves from women."

[5]Then David answered the priest, and said to him, "Truly, women *have been* kept from us about three days since I came out. And the vessels of the young men are holy, and *the bread is* in effect common, even though it was consecrated in the vessel this day."

[6]So the priest gave him holy *bread;* for there was no bread there but the showbread which had been taken from before the LORD, in order to put hot bread *in its place* on the day when it was taken away.

20:25 [a]Following Masoretic Text, Syriac, Targum, and Vulgate; Septuagint reads *he sat across from Jonathan.*

7 Now a certain man of the servants of Saul
was there that day, detained before the LORD.
And his name *was* Doeg, an Edomite, the chief
of the herdsmen who *belonged* to Saul.
8 And David said to Ahimelech, "Is there not
here on hand a spear or a sword? For I have
brought neither my sword nor my weapons
with me, because the king's business required
haste."
9 So the priest said, "The sword of Goliath
the Philistine, whom you killed in the Valley of
Elah, there it is, wrapped in a cloth behind the
ephod. If you will take that, take *it*. For *there is*
no other except that one here."
And David said, "*There is* none like it; give
it to me."

DAVID FLEES TO GATH

10 Then David arose and fled that day from
before Saul, and went to Achish the king of
Gath. 11 And the servants of Achish said to
him, "*Is* this not David the king of the land?
Did they not sing of him to one another in
dances, saying:

> 'Saul has slain his thousands,
> And David his ten thousands'?"[a]

12 Now David took these words to heart, and
was very much afraid of Achish the king of
Gath. 13 So he changed his behavior before
them, pretended madness in their hands,
scratched on the doors of the gate, and let his
saliva fall down on his beard. 14 Then Achish
said to his servants, "Look, you see the man is
insane. Why have you brought him to me?
15 Have I need of madmen, that you have
brought this *fellow* to play the madman in my
presence? Shall this *fellow* come into my
house?"

DAVID'S FOUR HUNDRED MEN

22 David therefore departed from there
and escaped to the cave of Adullam.
So when his brothers and all his father's
house heard *it*, they went down there to him.
2 And everyone *who was* in distress, everyone
who *was* in debt, and everyone *who was* discontented gathered to him. So he became captain over them. And there were about four
hundred men with him.
3 Then David went from there to Mizpah of
Moab; and he said to the king of Moab,
"Please let my father and mother come here
with you, till I know what God will do for
me." 4 So he brought them before the king of
Moab, and they dwelt with him all the time
that David was in the stronghold.
5 Now the prophet Gad said to David, "Do
not stay in the stronghold; depart, and go to
the land of Judah." So David departed and
went into the forest of Hereth.

SAUL MURDERS THE PRIESTS

6 When Saul heard that David and the men
who *were* with him had been discovered—
now Saul was staying in Gibeah under a tamarisk tree in Ramah, with his spear in his hand,
and all his servants standing about him—
7 then Saul said to his servants who stood
about him, "Hear now, you Benjamites! Will
the son of Jesse give every one of you fields
and vineyards, *and* make you all captains of
thousands and captains of hundreds? 8 All of
you have conspired against me, and *there is* no
one who reveals to me that my son has made a
covenant with the son of Jesse; and *there is*
not one of you who is sorry for me or reveals
to me that my son has stirred up my servant
against me, to lie in wait, as *it is* this day."
9 Then answered Doeg the Edomite, who
was set over the servants of Saul, and said, "I
saw the son of Jesse going to Nob, to Ahimelech the son of Ahitub. 10 And he inquired of
the LORD for him, gave him provisions, and
gave him the sword of Goliath the Philistine."
11 So the king sent to call Ahimelech the
priest, the son of Ahitub, and all his father's
house, the priests who *were* in Nob. And they
all came to the king. 12 And Saul said, "Hear
now, son of Ahitub!"
He answered, "Here I am, my lord."
13 Then Saul said to him, "Why have you
conspired against me, you and the son of
Jesse, in that you have given him bread and a
sword, and have inquired of God for him, that
he should rise against me, to lie in wait, as it is
this day?"
14 So Ahimelech answered the king and said,
"And who among all your servants *is as* faithful as David, who is the king's son-in-law,
who goes at your bidding, and is honorable in
your house? 15 Did I then begin to inquire of
God for him? Far be it from me! Let not the
king impute anything to his servant, *or* to any

21:11 [a]Compare 1 Samuel 18:7

in the house of my father. For your servant knew nothing of all this, little or much."

[16]And the king said, "You shall surely die, Ahimelech, you and all your father's house!" [17]Then the king said to the guards who stood about him, "Turn and kill the priests of the LORD, because their hand also *is* with David, and because they knew when he fled and did not tell it to me." But the servants of the king would not lift their hands to strike the priests of the LORD. [18]And the king said to Doeg, "You turn and kill the priests!" So Doeg the Edomite turned and struck the priests, and killed on that day eighty-five men who wore a linen ephod. [19]Also Nob, the city of the priests, he struck with the edge of the sword, both men and women, children and nursing infants, oxen and donkeys and sheep—with the edge of the sword.

[20]Now one of the sons of Ahimelech the son of Ahitub, named Abiathar, escaped and fled after David. [21]And Abiathar told David that Saul had killed the LORD's priests. [22]So David said to Abiathar, "I knew that day, when Doeg the Edomite *was* there, that he would surely tell Saul. I have caused *the death* of all the persons of your father's house. [23]Stay with me; do not fear. For he who seeks my life seeks your life, but with me you *shall be* safe."

DAVID SAVES THE CITY OF KEILAH

23 Then they told David, saying, "Look, the Philistines are fighting against Keilah, and they are robbing the threshing floors."

[2]Therefore David inquired of the LORD, saying, "Shall I go and attack these Philistines?"

And the LORD said to David, "Go and attack the Philistines, and save Keilah."

[3]But David's men said to him, "Look, we are afraid here in Judah. How much more then if we go to Keilah against the armies of the Philistines?" [4]Then David inquired of the LORD once again.

And the LORD answered him and said, "Arise, go down to Keilah. For I will deliver the Philistines into your hand." [5]And David and his men went to Keilah and fought with the Philistines, struck them with a mighty blow, and took away their livestock. So David saved the inhabitants of Keilah.

[6]Now it happened, when Abiathar the son of Ahimelech fled to David at Keilah, *that* he went down *with* an ephod in his hand.

[7]And Saul was told that David had gone to Keilah. So Saul said, "God has delivered him into my hand, for he has shut himself in by entering a town that has gates and bars." [8]Then Saul called all the people together for war, to go down to Keilah to besiege David and his men.

[9]When David knew that Saul plotted evil against him, he said to Abiathar the priest, "Bring the ephod here." [10]Then David said, "O LORD God of Israel, Your servant has certainly heard that Saul seeks to come to Keilah to destroy the city for my sake. [11]Will the men of Keilah deliver me into his hand? Will Saul come down, as Your servant has heard? O LORD God of Israel, I pray, tell Your servant."

And the LORD said, "He will come down."

[12]Then David said, "Will the men of Keilah deliver me and my men into the hand of Saul?"

And the LORD said, "They will deliver *you.*"

[13]So David and his men, about six hundred, arose and departed from Keilah and went wherever they could go. Then it was told Saul that David had escaped from Keilah; so he halted the expedition.

DAVID IN WILDERNESS STRONGHOLDS

[14]And David stayed in strongholds in the wilderness, and remained in the mountains in the Wilderness of Ziph. Saul sought him every day, but God did not deliver him into his hand. [15]So David saw that Saul had come out to seek his life. And David *was* in the Wilderness of Ziph in a forest.[a] [16]Then Jonathan, Saul's son, arose and went to David in the woods and strengthened his hand in God. [17]And he said to him, "Do not fear, for the hand of Saul my father shall not find you. You shall be king over Israel, and I shall be next to you. Even my father Saul knows that." [18]So the two of them made a covenant before the LORD. And David stayed in the woods, and Jonathan went to his own house.

[19]Then the Ziphites came up to Saul at Gibeah, saying, "Is David not hiding with us in strongholds in the woods, in the hill of Hachilah, which *is* on the south of Jeshimon? [20]Now therefore, O king, come down according to all the desire of your soul to come down; and our part *shall be* to deliver him into the king's hand."

23:15 [a]Or *in Horesh*

[21]And Saul said, "Blessed *are* you of the LORD, for you have compassion on me. [22]Please go and find out for sure, and see the place where his hideout is, *and* who has seen him there. For I am told he is very crafty. [23]See therefore, and take knowledge of all the lurking places where he hides; and come back to me with certainty, and I will go with you. And it shall be, if he is in the land, that I will search for him throughout all the clans[a] of Judah."

[24]So they arose and went to Ziph before Saul. But David and his men *were* in the Wilderness of Maon, in the plain on the south of Jeshimon. [25]When Saul and his men went to seek *him,* they told David. Therefore he went down to the rock, and stayed in the Wilderness of Maon. And when Saul heard *that,* he pursued David in the Wilderness of Maon. [26]Then Saul went on one side of the mountain, and David and his men on the other side of the mountain. So David made haste to get away from Saul, for Saul and his men were encircling David and his men to take them.

[27]But a messenger came to Saul, saying, "Hurry and come, for the Philistines have invaded the land!" [28]Therefore Saul returned from pursuing David, and went against the Philistines; so they called that place the Rock of Escape.[a] [29]Then David went up from there and dwelt in strongholds at En Gedi.

DAVID SPARES SAUL

24 Now it happened, when Saul had returned from following the Philistines, that it was told him, saying, "Take note! David *is* in the Wilderness of En Gedi." [2]Then Saul took three thousand chosen men from all Israel, and went to seek David and his men on the Rocks of the Wild Goats. [3]So he came to the sheepfolds by the road, where there *was* a cave; and Saul went in to attend to his needs. (David and his men were staying in the recesses of the cave.) [4]Then the men of David said to him, "This is the day of which the LORD said to you, 'Behold, I will deliver your enemy into your hand, that you may do to him as it seems good to you.' " And David arose and secretly cut off a corner of Saul's robe. [5]Now it happened afterward that David's heart troubled him because he had cut Saul's *robe.* [6]And he said to his men, "The LORD forbid that I should do this thing to my master, the LORD's anointed, to stretch out my hand against him, seeing he *is* the anointed of the LORD." [7]So David restrained his servants with *these* words, and did not allow them to rise against Saul. And Saul got up from the cave and went on *his* way.

[8]David also arose afterward, went out of the cave, and called out to Saul, saying, "My lord the king!" And when Saul looked behind him, David stooped with his face to the earth, and bowed down. [9]And David said to Saul: "Why do you listen to the words of men who say, 'Indeed David seeks your harm'? [10]Look, this day your eyes have seen that the LORD delivered you today into my hand in the cave, and *someone* urged *me* to kill you. But *my eye* spared you, and I said, 'I will not stretch out my hand against my lord, for he *is* the LORD's anointed.' [11]Moreover, my father, see! Yes, see the corner of your robe in my hand! For in that I cut off the corner of your robe, and did not kill you, know and see that *there is* neither evil nor rebellion in my hand, and I have not sinned against you. Yet you hunt my life to take it. [12]Let the LORD judge between you and me, and let the LORD avenge me on you. But my hand shall not be against you. [13]As the proverb of the ancients says, 'Wickedness proceeds from the wicked.' But my hand shall not

23:23 [a]Literally *thousands* **23:28** [a]Hebrew *Sela Hammahlekoth*

SOUL NOTE

Just Trust *(24:6)* Saul had been attempting to kill David. Surely David, who had been secretly anointed as the next king of Israel (16:13), would have been justified to kill Saul in self-defense so he could finally take over. David realized, however, that he had to respect Saul as God's anointed king and leave vengeance to God (24:12). While it would have been easier on David to get rid of his enemy, David trusted God to handle the situation. When we face difficult situations, we may not understand God's timing, but we must trust Him to lead us and do what is best. **Topic: Trust**

be against you. 14After whom has the king of Israel come out? Whom do you pursue? A dead dog? A flea? 15Therefore let the LORD be judge, and judge between you and me, and see and plead my case, and deliver me out of your hand."

16So it was, when David had finished speaking these words to Saul, that Saul said, "*Is* this your voice, my son David?" And Saul lifted up his voice and wept. 17Then he said to David: "You *are* more righteous than I; for you have rewarded me with good, whereas I have rewarded you with evil. 18And you have shown this day how you have dealt well with me; for when the LORD delivered me into your hand, you did not kill me. 19For if a man finds his enemy, will he let him get away safely? Therefore may the LORD reward you with good for what you have done to me this day. 20And now I know indeed that you shall surely be king, and that the kingdom of Israel shall be established in your hand. 21Therefore swear now to me by the LORD that you will not cut off my descendants after me, and that you will not destroy my name from my father's house."

22So David swore to Saul. And Saul went home, but David and his men went up to the stronghold.

DEATH OF SAMUEL

25 Then Samuel died; and the Israelites gathered together and lamented for him, and buried him at his home in Ramah. And David arose and went down to the Wilderness of Paran.[a]

DAVID AND THE WIFE OF NABAL

2Now *there was* a man in Maon whose business *was* in Carmel, and the man *was* very rich. He had three thousand sheep and a thousand goats. And he was shearing his sheep in Carmel. 3The name of the man *was* Nabal, and the name of his wife Abigail. And *she was* a woman of good understanding and beautiful appearance; but the man *was* harsh and evil in *his* doings. He *was of the house of* Caleb.

4When David heard in the wilderness that Nabal was shearing his sheep, 5David sent ten young men; and David said to the young men, "Go up to Carmel, go to Nabal, and greet him in my name. 6And thus you shall say to him who lives *in prosperity:* 'Peace *be* to you, peace to your house, and peace to all that you have! 7Now I have heard that you have shearers. Your shepherds were with us, and we did not hurt them, nor was there anything missing from them all the while they were in Carmel. 8Ask your young men, and they will tell you. Therefore let *my* young men find favor in your eyes, for we come on a feast day. Please give whatever comes to your hand to your servants and to your son David.' "

9So when David's young men came, they spoke to Nabal according to all these words in the name of David, and waited.

10Then Nabal answered David's servants, and said, "Who *is* David, and who *is* the son of Jesse? There are many servants nowadays who break away each one from his master. 11Shall I then take my bread and my water and my meat that I have killed for my shearers, and give *it* to men when I do not know where they *are* from?"

12So David's young men turned on their heels and went back; and they came and told him all these words. 13Then David said to his men, "Every man gird on his sword." So every man girded on his sword, and David also girded on his sword. And about four hundred men went with David, and two hundred stayed with the supplies.

25:1 [a]Following Masoretic Text, Syriac, Targum, and Vulgate; Septuagint reads *Maon*.

SOUL NOTE

In the Middle *(25:14–17)* Abigail used great courage and wisdom. Her husband, Nabal, had insulted David and his men—not a wise move. David got angry and was ready to attack—also not a wise move. In between these two stepped Abigail. She honestly explained her husband's behavior and appealed to David with wise words and the provisions that he and his men had originally requested (25:8). Abigail's wisdom saved both her household from destruction and David from shedding innocent blood. Wisdom has great power to resolve great problems. **Topic: Wisdom**

14Now one of the young men told Abigail, Nabal's wife, saying, "Look, David sent messengers from the wilderness to greet our master; and he reviled them. 15But the men *were* very good to us, and we were not hurt, nor did we miss anything as long as we accompanied them, when we were in the fields. 16They were a wall to us both by night and day, all the time we were with them keeping the sheep. 17Now therefore, know and consider what you will do, for harm is determined against our master and against all his household. For he *is such* a scoundrel[a] that *one* cannot speak to him."

18Then Abigail made haste and took two hundred *loaves* of bread, two skins of wine, five sheep already dressed, five seahs of roasted *grain,* one hundred clusters of raisins, and two hundred cakes of figs, and loaded *them* on donkeys. 19And she said to her servants, "Go on before me; see, I am coming after you." But she did not tell her husband Nabal.

20So it was, *as* she rode on the donkey, that she went down under cover of the hill; and there were David and his men, coming down toward her, and she met them. 21Now David had said, "Surely in vain I have protected all that this *fellow* has in the wilderness, so that nothing was missed of all that *belongs* to him. And he has repaid me evil for good. 22May God do so, and more also, to the enemies of David, if I leave one male of all who *belong* to him by morning light."

23Now when Abigail saw David, she dismounted quickly from the donkey, fell on her face before David, and bowed down to the ground. 24So she fell at his feet and said: "On me, my lord, *on* me *let* this iniquity *be!* And please let your maidservant speak in your ears, and hear the words of your maidservant. 25Please, let not my lord regard this scoundrel Nabal. For as his name *is,* so *is* he: Nabal[a] *is* his name, and folly *is* with him! But I, your maidservant, did not see the young men of my lord whom you sent. 26Now therefore, my lord, *as* the LORD lives and *as* your soul lives, since the LORD has held you back from coming to bloodshed and from avenging yourself with your own hand, now then, let your enemies and those who seek harm for my lord be as Nabal. 27And now this present which your maidservant has brought to my lord, let it be given to the young men who follow my lord. 28Please forgive the trespass of your maidservant. For the LORD will certainly make for my lord an enduring house, because my lord fights the battles of the LORD, and evil is not found in you throughout your days. 29Yet a man has risen to pursue you and seek your life, but the life of my lord shall be bound in the bundle of the living with the LORD your God; and the lives of your enemies He shall sling out, *as from* the pocket of a sling. 30And it shall come to pass, when the LORD has done for my lord according to all the good that He has spoken concerning you, and has appointed you ruler over Israel, 31that this will be no grief to you, nor offense of heart to my lord, either that you have shed blood without cause, or that my lord has avenged himself. But when the LORD has dealt well with my lord, then remember your maidservant."

32Then David said to Abigail: "Blessed *is* the LORD God of Israel, who sent you this day to meet me! 33And blessed *is* your advice and blessed *are* you, because you have kept me this day from coming to bloodshed and from avenging myself with my own hand. 34For indeed, *as* the LORD God of Israel lives, who has kept me back from hurting you, unless you had hurried and come to meet me, surely by morning light no males would have been left to Nabal!" 35So David received from her hand what she had brought him, and said to her, "Go up in peace to your house. See, I have heeded your voice and respected your person."

36Now Abigail went to Nabal, and there he was, holding a feast in his house, like the feast of a king. And Nabal's heart *was* merry within him, for he *was* very drunk; therefore she told him nothing, little or much, until morning light. 37So it was, in the morning, when the wine had gone from Nabal, and his wife had told him these things, that his heart died within him, and he became *like* a stone. 38Then it happened, *after* about ten days, that the LORD struck Nabal, and he died.

39So when David heard that Nabal was dead, he said, "Blessed *be* the LORD, who has pleaded the cause of my reproach from the hand of Nabal, and has kept His servant from evil! For the LORD has returned the wickedness of Nabal on his own head."

And David sent and proposed to Abigail, to take her as his wife. 40When the servants of David had come to Abigail at Carmel, they

---

25:17 [a]Literally *son of Belial* **25:25** [a]Literally *Fool*

spoke to her saying, "David sent us to you, to ask you to become his wife."

41Then she arose, bowed her face to the earth, and said, "Here is your maidservant, a servant to wash the feet of the servants of my lord." 42So Abigail rose in haste and rode on a donkey, attended by five of her maidens; and she followed the messengers of David, and became his wife. 43David also took Ahinoam of Jezreel, and so both of them were his wives.

44But Saul had given Michal his daughter, David's wife, to Palti[a] the son of Laish, who *was* from Gallim.

David Spares Saul a Second Time

26 Now the Ziphites came to Saul at Gibeah, saying, "Is David not hiding in the hill of Hachilah, opposite Jeshimon?" 2Then Saul arose and went down to the Wilderness of Ziph, having three thousand chosen men of Israel with him, to seek David in the Wilderness of Ziph. 3And Saul encamped in the hill of Hachilah, which *is* opposite Jeshimon, by the road. But David stayed in the wilderness, and he saw that Saul came after him into the wilderness. 4David therefore sent out spies, and understood that Saul had indeed come.

5So David arose and came to the place where Saul had encamped. And David saw the place where Saul lay, and Abner the son of Ner, the commander of his army. Now Saul lay within the camp, with the people encamped all around him. 6Then David answered, and said to Ahimelech the Hittite and to Abishai the son of Zeruiah, brother of Joab, saying, "Who will go down with me to Saul in the camp?"

And Abishai said, "I will go down with you."

7So David and Abishai came to the people by night; and there Saul lay sleeping within the camp, with his spear stuck in the ground by his head. And Abner and the people lay all around him. 8Then Abishai said to David, "God has delivered your enemy into your hand this day. Now therefore, please, let me strike him at once with the spear, right to the earth; and I will not *have to strike* him a second time!"

9But David said to Abishai, "Do not destroy him; for who can stretch out his hand against the LORD's anointed, and be guiltless?" 10David said furthermore, "*As* the LORD lives, the LORD shall strike him, or his day shall come to die, or he shall go out to battle and perish. 11The LORD forbid that I should stretch out my hand against the LORD's anointed. But please, take now the spear and the jug of water that *are* by his head, and let us go." 12So David took the spear and the jug of water *by* Saul's head, and they got away; and no man saw or knew *it* or awoke. For they *were* all asleep, because a deep sleep from the LORD had fallen on them.

13Now David went over to the other side, and stood on the top of a hill afar off, a great distance *being* between them. 14And David called out to the people and to Abner the son of Ner, saying, "Do you not answer, Abner?"

Then Abner answered and said, "Who *are* you, calling out to the king?"

15So David said to Abner, "*Are* you not a man? And who *is* like you in Israel? Why then have you not guarded your lord the king? For one of the people came in to destroy your lord the king. 16This thing that you have done *is* not good. *As* the LORD lives, you deserve to die, because you have not guarded your master, the LORD's anointed. And now see where the king's spear *is,* and the jug of water that *was* by his head."

17Then Saul knew David's voice, and said, "*Is* that your voice, my son David?"

David said, "*It is* my voice, my lord, O king." 18And he said, "Why does my lord thus pursue his servant? For what have I done, or what evil *is* in my hand? 19Now therefore, please, let my lord the king hear the words of his servant: If the LORD has stirred you up against me, let Him accept an offering. But if *it is* the children of men, *may* they *be* cursed before the LORD, for they have driven me out this day from sharing in the inheritance of the LORD, saying, 'Go, serve other gods.' 20So now, do not let my blood fall to the earth before the face of the LORD. For the king of Israel has come out to seek a flea, as when one hunts a partridge in the mountains."

21Then Saul said, "I have sinned. Return, my son David. For I will harm you no more, because my life was precious in your eyes this day. Indeed I have played the fool and erred exceedingly."

22And David answered and said, "Here is the king's spear. Let one of the young men

25:44 [a]Spelled *Paltiel* in 2 Samuel 3:15

come over and get it. 23May the LORD repay every man *for* his righteousness and his faithfulness; for the LORD delivered you into *my* hand today, but I would not stretch out my hand against the LORD's anointed. 24And indeed, as your life was valued much this day in my eyes, so let my life be valued much in the eyes of the LORD, and let Him deliver me out of all tribulation."

25Then Saul said to David, "*May* you *be* blessed, my son David! You shall both do great things and also still prevail."

So David went on his way, and Saul returned to his place.

DAVID ALLIED WITH THE PHILISTINES

27 And David said in his heart, "Now I shall perish someday by the hand of Saul. *There is* nothing better for me than that I should speedily escape to the land of the Philistines; and Saul will despair of me, to seek me anymore in any part of Israel. So I shall escape out of his hand." 2Then David arose and went over with the six hundred men who *were* with him to Achish the son of Maoch, king of Gath. 3So David dwelt with Achish at Gath, he and his men, each man with his household, *and* David with his two wives, Ahinoam the Jezreelitess, and Abigail the Carmelitess, Nabal's widow. 4And it was told Saul that David had fled to Gath; so he sought him no more.

5Then David said to Achish, "If I have now found favor in your eyes, let them give me a place in some town in the country, that I may dwell there. For why should your servant dwell in the royal city with you?" 6So Achish gave him Ziklag that day. Therefore Ziklag has belonged to the kings of Judah to this day. 7Now the time that David dwelt in the country of the Philistines was one full year and four months.

8And David and his men went up and raided the Geshurites, the Girzites,[a] and the Amalekites. For those nations were the inhabitants of the land from of old, as you go to Shur, even as far as the land of Egypt. 9Whenever David attacked the land, he left neither man nor woman alive, but took away the sheep, the oxen, the donkeys, the camels, and the apparel, and returned and came to Achish. 10Then Achish would say, "Where have you made a raid today?" And David would say, "Against the southern *area* of Judah, or against the southern *area* of the Jerahmeelites, or against the southern *area* of the Kenites." 11David would save neither man nor woman alive, to bring *news* to Gath, saying, "Lest they should inform on us, saying, 'Thus David did.' " And thus *was* his behavior all the time he dwelt in the country of the Philistines. 12So Achish believed David, saying, "He has made his people Israel utterly abhor him; therefore he will be my servant forever."

28 Now it happened in those days that the Philistines gathered their armies together for war, to fight with Israel. And Achish said to David, "You assuredly know that you will go out with me to battle, you and your men."

2So David said to Achish, "Surely you know what your servant can do."

And Achish said to David, "Therefore I will make you one of my chief guardians forever."

SAUL CONSULTS A MEDIUM

3Now Samuel had died, and all Israel had lamented for him and buried him in Ramah, in his own city. And Saul had put the mediums and the spiritists out of the land.

4Then the Philistines gathered together, and came and encamped at Shunem. So Saul gathered all Israel together, and they encamped at Gilboa. 5When Saul saw the army of the Philistines, he was afraid, and his heart trembled greatly. 6And when Saul inquired of the LORD, the LORD did not answer him, either by dreams or by Urim or by the prophets.

7Then Saul said to his servants, "Find me a woman who is a medium, that I may go to her and inquire of her."

And his servants said to him, "In fact, *there is* a woman who is a medium at En Dor."

8So Saul disguised himself and put on other clothes, and he went, and two men with him; and they came to the woman by night. And he said, "Please conduct a séance for me, and bring up for me the one I shall name to you."

9Then the woman said to him, "Look, you know what Saul has done, how he has cut off the mediums and the spiritists from the land. Why then do you lay a snare for my life, to cause me to die?"

10And Saul swore to her by the LORD, saying, "*As* the LORD lives, no punishment shall come upon you for this thing."

27:8 [a]Or *Gezrites*

[11]Then the woman said, "Whom shall I bring up for you?"

And he said, "Bring up Samuel for me."

[12]When the woman saw Samuel, she cried out with a loud voice. And the woman spoke to Saul, saying, "Why have you deceived me? For you *are* Saul!"

[13]And the king said to her, "Do not be afraid. What did you see?"

And the woman said to Saul, "I saw a spirit[a] ascending out of the earth."

[14]So he said to her, "What *is* his form?"

And she said, "An old man is coming up, and he *is* covered with a mantle." And Saul perceived that it *was* Samuel, and he stooped with *his* face to the ground and bowed down.

[15]Now Samuel said to Saul, "Why have you disturbed me by bringing me up?"

And Saul answered, "I am deeply distressed; for the Philistines make war against me, and God has departed from me and does not answer me anymore, neither by prophets nor by dreams. Therefore I have called you, that you may reveal to me what I should do."

[16]Then Samuel said: "So why do you ask me, seeing the LORD has departed from you and has become your enemy? [17]And the LORD has done for Himself[a] as He spoke by me. For the LORD has torn the kingdom out of your hand and given it to your neighbor, David.
[18]Because you did not obey the voice of the LORD nor execute His fierce wrath upon Amalek, therefore the LORD has done this thing to you this day. [19]Moreover the LORD will also deliver Israel with you into the hand of the

28:13 [a]Hebrew *elohim* **28:17** [a]Or *him,* that is, David

PERSONALITY PROFILE

Occult

THE WITCH OF EN DOR— THE OCCULT TEMPTATION

(1 SAMUEL 28:7)

One night the medium that lived in En Dor had an unexpected visitor. Her customer was in disguise, but she assumed he must be someone of means, since he was in the company of two men. When he asked her to conduct a séance for him, she was frightened. King Saul had recently banned all witches and mediums from the land. In addition, the ancient laws of God spoke in no uncertain terms against witchcraft (Lev. 19:31; Deut. 18:9–14). She suspected a trap. She did not yet realize the identity of her guest—King Saul himself.

Ironically, the stranger granted the witch immunity with an oath to God. He asked her to summon up Samuel from the dead. Much to her shock, Samuel actually appeared. She now knew that her customer was the king, and the matter was out of her hands. She was terrified.

Samuel had devastating news for Saul. God really had deserted him. His fate and the fate of his army were sealed. His own disobedience, including the consulting of the witch, had created a distance between the king and God that could now only be bridged by judgment.

Once Saul had ignored God's guidance, he left himself exposed. Once Samuel had died, that solitude had overwhelmed Saul. He didn't even have Samuel's bad news to keep him company. He didn't realize how much help he needed until he had cut himself off from every good source. In desperation, he reached for evil.

The more people turn away from the true things of God, the more we can expect to see a rising interest in the occult. People need answers. Once they have rejected the true source, they are exposed to the temptation to look to evil sources for guidance. The attraction of the occult may be fascinating and powerful, but it is deadly.

To Learn More: Turn to the article about the occult on pages 382, 383. See also the key passage note at Ephesians 6:10–20 on page 1559.

THE OCCULT

JERRY JOHNSTON

(1 Samuel 28:7)

Young people are turning to the satanic and the demonic at rates unparalleled since medieval times. They are experimenting with astrology, witchcraft, divination, and more. Satan has cleverly convinced the modern mind that he is not to be taken seriously until all other spiritual options are exhausted. Then when empty souls turn to him in desperation, he can take them over completely. C. S. Lewis wrote that there are two equal and opposite errors into which people can fall about demons: One is to not believe they exist; the other is to believe they exist, and to feel an excessive interest in them.

The current fad of satanism is reaching epidemic proportions in developed countries. There is compelling evidence of the existence of an international network of satanic cults. The United States harbors the fastest growing and most highly organized body of satanists in the world. Today's occult practices include a variety of activities such as witchcraft, voodoo, astrology, divination, visualization, and spiritism.

The psychological packaging of occultism has made it more acceptable to moderns. The appeal is that the occult will help the experimenter to have an experience that transcends previous spiritual emptiness. Experimentation with the occult is like experimenting with drugs. Once someone starts, it's hard to quit. Most people who become involved get in deeper than they ever intended to, and they stay in longer than they ever thought they would.

WITCHCRAFT AND SATANISM

Satanic circles, ritual dances, incantations to the devil, human and animal sacrifices, and the drinking of blood have all been part of satanic worship for centuries. These practices can be found in settings ranging from primitive tribes to modern educated circles. In every case where such arts are practiced, evil spirits (demons) or the devil himself are called upon in some manifestation of destructive power.

Witchcraft, sorcery, divination, and magic are ancient and universal. Every culture, primitive or civilized, Eastern or Western, has had its share of magicians, sorcerers, and witches. What possesses an Adolf Hitler to exterminate six million Jews? What provokes a Saddam Hussein to assassinate his own officers? What compels a Charles Manson to murder innocent people? What disturbing influence causes a Jeffrey Dahmer to rape, kill, and cannibalize his victims? What tempts people to reject the grace of God and renounce the glories of heaven? Is it not Satan and his demons?

The Bible treats occultism as a serious threat. Pharaoh's sorcerers were able to mimic some of Moses' miracles (Ex. 7:22; 8:7). Two sorcerers, Simon (Acts 8:9–11) and Elymas (Acts 13:8–10), as well as the medium at Philippi (Acts 16:16–18), seem to have had powers that went well beyond normal human ability or trickery.

Several Bible passages clearly condemn witchcraft and demonism (for example, Ex. 22:18; Lev. 19:26; 1 Sam. 15:23). The apostle Paul, in enumerating "the works of the flesh," included sorcery, and said "those who practice such things will not inherit the kingdom of God" (Gal. 5:19–21). In Revelation 21:8 and 22:15, sorcerers, murderers, and idolaters are pictured as being excluded from heaven and cast into the lake of fire.

THE DOCTRINE OF SATAN AND DEMONS

The existence of Satan is taught in several Old Testament books and by every New Testament writer. Jesus Himself referred to Satan several times (for example, Matt. 13:39; Luke 10:18; 11:18). Satan is represented both as an angel of light (2 Cor. 11:14) and as "the great dragon . . . that serpent of old" (Rev. 12:9). Satan is described as the tempter (1 Thess. 3:5), the ruler of this world (John 12:31), the god of this age (2 Cor. 4:4), the prince of the power of the air (Eph. 2:2), and the accuser of the brethren (Rev. 12:10). He deceives the nations (Rev. 20:3), blinds the minds of unbelievers (2 Cor. 4:4), and hinders the work of believers (1 Thess. 2:18).

Demons are described in the Bible as fallen angels over whom Satan rules (Matt. 12:24; Eph. 6:11, 12). They are spirit beings (Matt. 17:18) who attempt to thwart the purposes of God (Dan. 10:10–14). Demon possession refers to a demon residing in a person and exerting direct control and influence over that person. Most biblical scholars believe that Christians cannot be possessed by demons because they are indwelt by the Holy Spirit. However, believers can be the targets of demonic activity. Demon possession can result in physical disease (Matt. 9:32, 33) and in some cases, mental derangement (Matt. 17:15–18). Eventually, the Bible predicts, all demons will be cast into the lake of fire along with Satan (Matt. 25:41; Rev. 20:10).

Dabbling in occult fads, symbols, or practices is the first step toward serious trouble for curiosity seekers. Eventually it can lead to hard-core satanic cult activity, even including animal and human sacrifice. Behind the variety of witches, mediums, psychic healers, and parapsychologists looms the actual spirit power that is the source of their knowledge and strength. In our modern culture, satanism expresses itself in a variety of ways—sexual perversion, ritual abuse of children, excessive violence, the misuse of drugs, and the epidemic proportion of suicide. Satanism especially offers to fit the needs and wants of middle- and upper-class teens of high intelligence who are creative, curious, and possibly underachievers with low self-esteem.

Believers must take this aspect of spiritual warfare seriously as they attempt to minister to today's generation.

FURTHER MEDITATION:

Other passages to study about the issue of the occult include:

- ➢ Leviticus 20:27
- ➢ Deuteronomy 18:9–14
- ➢ 1 Samuel 15:23; 28:3–25
- ➢ Acts 26:18
- ➢ 2 Corinthians 11:12–15
- ➢ Ephesians 2:1–3
- ➢ 1 Peter 5:8

To Learn More: Turn to the key passage note on the occult at Ephesians 6:10–20 on page 1559. See also the personality profile of the witch of En Dor on page 381.

Philistines. And tomorrow you and your sons *will be* with me. The LORD will also deliver the army of Israel into the hand of the Philistines."

20Immediately Saul fell full length on the ground, and was dreadfully afraid because of the words of Samuel. And there was no strength in him, for he had eaten no food all day or all night.

21And the woman came to Saul and saw that he was severely troubled, and said to him, "Look, your maidservant has obeyed your voice, and I have put my life in my hands and heeded the words which you spoke to me. 22Now therefore, please, heed also the voice of your maidservant, and let me set a piece of bread before you; and eat, that you may have strength when you go on *your* way."

23But he refused and said, "I will not eat."

So his servants, together with the woman, urged him; and he heeded their voice. Then he arose from the ground and sat on the bed. 24Now the woman had a fatted calf in the house, and she hastened to kill it. And she took flour and kneaded *it,* and baked unleavened bread from it. 25So she brought *it* before Saul and his servants, and they ate. Then they rose and went away that night.

THE PHILISTINES REJECT DAVID

29 Then the Philistines gathered together all their armies at Aphek, and the Israelites encamped by a fountain which *is* in Jezreel. 2And the lords of the Philistines passed in review by hundreds and by thousands, but David and his men passed in review at the rear with Achish. 3Then the princes of the Philistines said, "What *are* these Hebrews *doing here?"*

And Achish said to the princes of the Philistines, "*Is* this not David, the servant of Saul king of Israel, who has been with me these days, or these years? And to this day I have found no fault in him since he defected *to me.*"

4But the princes of the Philistines were angry with him; so the princes of the Philistines said to him, "Make this fellow return, that he may go back to the place which you have appointed for him, and do not let him go down with us to battle, lest in the battle he become our adversary. For with what could he reconcile himself to his master, if not with the heads of these men? 5*Is* this not David, of whom they sang to one another in dances, saying:

'Saul has slain his thousands,
And David his ten thousands'?"[a]

6Then Achish called David and said to him, "Surely, *as* the LORD lives, you have been upright, and your going out and your coming in with me in the army *is* good in my sight. For to this day I have not found evil in you since the day of your coming to me. Nevertheless the lords do not favor you. 7Therefore return now, and go in peace, that you may not displease the lords of the Philistines."

8So David said to Achish, "But what have I done? And to this day what have you found in your servant as long as I have been with you, that I may not go and fight against the enemies of my lord the king?"

9Then Achish answered and said to David, "I know that you *are* as good in my sight as an angel of God; nevertheless the princes of the Philistines have said, 'He shall not go up with us to the battle.' 10Now therefore, rise early in the morning with your master's servants who have come with you.[a] And as soon as you are up early in the morning and have light, depart."

11So David and his men rose early to depart in the morning, to return to the land of the Philistines. And the Philistines went up to Jezreel.

DAVID'S CONFLICT WITH THE AMALEKITES

30 Now it happened, when David and his men came to Ziklag, on the third day, that the Amalekites had invaded the South and Ziklag, attacked Ziklag and burned it with fire, 2and had taken captive the women and those who *were* there, from small to great; they did not kill anyone, but carried *them* away and went their way. 3So David and his men came to the city, and there it was, burned with fire; and their wives, their sons, and their daughters had been taken captive. 4Then David and the people who *were* with him lifted up their voices and wept, until they had no more power to weep. 5And David's two wives, Ahinoam the Jezreelitess, and Abigail the widow of Nabal

---

29:5 [a]Compare 1 Samuel 18:7 **29:10** [a]Following Masoretic Text, Targum, and Vulgate; Septuagint adds *and go to the place which I have selected for you there; and set no bothersome word in your heart, for you are good before me. And rise on your way.*

the Carmelite, had been taken captive. 6Now
David was greatly distressed, for the people
spoke of stoning him, because the soul of all
the people was grieved, every man for his sons
and his daughters. But David strengthened
himself in the LORD his God.

7Then David said to Abiathar the priest,
Ahimelech's son, "Please bring the ephod
here to me." And Abiathar brought the ephod
to David. 8So David inquired of the LORD, saying, "Shall I pursue this troop? Shall I overtake
them?"

And He answered him, "Pursue, for you
shall surely overtake *them* and without fail recover *all.*"

9So David went, he and the six hundred
men who *were* with him, and came to the
Brook Besor, where those stayed who were
left behind. 10But David pursued, he and four
hundred men; for two hundred stayed *behind,*
who were so weary that they could not cross
the Brook Besor.

11Then they found an Egyptian in the field,
and brought him to David; and they gave him
bread and he ate, and they let him drink water. 12And they gave him a piece of a cake of
figs and two clusters of raisins. So when he
had eaten, his strength came back to him; for
he had eaten no bread nor drunk water for
three days and three nights. 13Then David said
to him, "To whom do you *belong,* and where
are you from?"

And he said, "I *am* a young man from
Egypt, servant of an Amalekite; and my master left me behind, because three days ago I
fell sick. 14We made an invasion of the southern *area* of the Cherethites, in the *territory*
which *belongs* to Judah, and of the southern
area of Caleb; and we burned Ziklag with
fire."

15And David said to him, "Can you take me
down to this troop?"

So he said, "Swear to me by God that you
will neither kill me nor deliver me into the
hands of my master, and I will take you down
to this troop."

16And when he had brought him down,
there they were, spread out over all the land,
eating and drinking and dancing, because of
all the great spoil which they had taken from
the land of the Philistines and from the land of
Judah. 17Then David attacked them from twilight until the evening of the next day. Not a
man of them escaped, except four hundred
young men who rode on camels and fled. 18So
David recovered all that the Amalekites had
carried away, and David rescued his two
wives. 19And nothing of theirs was lacking, either small or great, sons or daughters, spoil or
anything which they had taken from them;
David recovered all. 20Then David took all the
flocks and herds they had driven before those
other livestock, and said, "This *is* David's
spoil."

21Now David came to the two hundred men
who had been so weary that they could not
follow David, whom they also had made to
stay at the Brook Besor. So they went out to
meet David and to meet the people who *were*
with him. And when David came near the
people, he greeted them. 22Then all the wicked and worthless men[a] of those who went
with David answered and said, "Because they
did not go with us, we will not give them *any*
of the spoil that we have recovered, except for
every man's wife and children, that they may
lead *them* away and depart."

23But David said, "My brethren, you shall
not do so with what the LORD has given us,
who has preserved us and delivered into our
hand the troop that came against us. 24For
who will heed you in this matter? But as his

30:22 [a]Literally *men of Belial*

SOUL NOTE

No More Tears *(30:4–6)* When David and his army returned to Ziklag and found the city burned and their families gone, they "lifted up their voices and wept, until they had no more power to weep." Grief can blanket our lives until we feel completely overwhelmed. There is nothing wrong with that, for it is a natural feeling. In that darkness, however, there is a ray of hope. David found it. He "strengthened himself in the LORD his God." God will not take away the sorrow, but He will strengthen people as they bear it. **Topic: Grief/Loss**

part *is* who goes down to the battle, so *shall* his part *be* who stays by the supplies; they shall share alike." 25So it was, from that day forward; he made it a statute and an ordinance for Israel to this day.

26Now when David came to Ziklag, he sent *some* of the spoil to the elders of Judah, to his friends, saying, "Here is a present for you from the spoil of the enemies of the LORD"— 27to *those* who *were* in Bethel, *those* who *were* in Ramoth of the South, *those* who *were* in Jattir, 28*those* who *were* in Aroer, *those* who *were* in Siphmoth, *those* who *were* in Eshtemoa, 29*those* who *were* in Rachal, *those* who *were* in the cities of the Jerahmeelites, *those* who *were* in the cities of the Kenites, 30*those* who *were* in Hormah, *those* who *were* in Chorashan,[a] *those* who *were* in Athach, 31*those* who *were* in Hebron, and to all the places where David himself and his men were accustomed to rove.

The Tragic End of Saul and His Sons

31 Now the Philistines fought against Israel; and the men of Israel fled from before the Philistines, and fell slain on Mount Gilboa. 2Then the Philistines followed hard after Saul and his sons. And the Philistines killed Jonathan, Abinadab, and Malchishua, Saul's sons. 3The battle became fierce against Saul. The archers hit him, and he was severely wounded by the archers.

4Then Saul said to his armorbearer, "Draw your sword, and thrust me through with it, lest these uncircumcised men come and thrust me through and abuse me."

But his armorbearer would not, for he was greatly afraid. Therefore Saul took a sword and fell on it. 5And when his armorbearer saw that Saul was dead, he also fell on his sword, and died with him. 6So Saul, his three sons, his armorbearer, and all his men died together that same day.

7And when the men of Israel who *were* on the other side of the valley, and *those* who *were* on the other side of the Jordan, saw that the men of Israel had fled and that Saul and his sons were dead, they forsook the cities and fled; and the Philistines came and dwelt in them. 8So it happened the next day, when the Philistines came to strip the slain, that they found Saul and his three sons fallen on Mount Gilboa. 9And they cut off his head and stripped off his armor, and sent *word* throughout the land of the Philistines, to proclaim *it in* the temple of their idols and among the people. 10Then they put his armor in the temple of the Ashtoreths, and they fastened his body to the wall of Beth Shan.[a]

11Now when the inhabitants of Jabesh Gile-

30:30 [a]Or *Borashan* **31:10** [a]Spelled *Beth Shean* in Joshua 17:11 and elsewhere

KEY PASSAGE

Suicide

THE DEATH OF A KING

(31:4)

Saul's army was losing the battle against the Philistines. Ancient kings did not want to be taken prisoner, because the victorious army would treat a captured king with contempt—either humiliating him as a captive or torturing him until he died. Having been mortally wounded, Saul asked his armorbearer to finish the job so he would not be captured alive. The armorbearer refused, so Saul committed suicide by falling on his own sword.

Because Saul had turned away from God, he was left completely to his own devices. He had great potential in his position as the chosen king of Israel, but he squandered it with jealousy, anger, and disobedience. In the end, when all was lost, he believed he had nowhere to turn but to death. Suicide is attractive to a desperate person. Such people need to be shown God's gracious love and forgiveness. There is always hope with God.

To Learn More: Turn to the article about suicide on pages 322, 323. See also the personality profile of Judas on page 1276.

ad heard what the Philistines had done to Saul, [12]all the valiant men arose and traveled all night, and took the body of Saul and the bodies of his sons from the wall of Beth Shan; and they came to Jabesh and burned them there. [13]Then they took their bones and buried *them* under the tamarisk tree at Jabesh, and fasted seven days.

2 Samuel

Leaders are chosen for many reasons: their talent, skill, experience, knowledge, faithfulness, personal charisma, or political astuteness. Second Samuel is an intimate portrait of the life and reign of David, the man who was, arguably, Israel's greatest leader. Faithful but flawed, driven by both holy and impure passions, King David was brilliant in leading the people of Israel but failed to manage his own personal life.

Following Saul's death, David brought stability to Israel. With patience, honor, and kindness he consolidated the kingdom. He established Jerusalem as the capital, brought the ark of the covenant there, and envisioned the temple that Solomon would one day build. He victoriously battled Philistines, Moabites, and Syrians, uniting Palestine under his strong, benevolent hand.

Yet sin still lurked in David's heart. He yielded to the tempting beauty of Bathsheba. He indulged his son Absalom to the point where correction had no value to the young man. David became well acquainted with the awful consequences of sin.

The lesson of 2 Samuel has nothing to do with living a sinless life—none of us can do that. God loved and blessed David because he humbled himself. When confronted with his sins, David acknowledged them and turned from them. Though David suffered the wages of sin in numerous ways, God restored him to a place of favor in His divine plan. He will do the same for us when we confess and do not defend our sins.

SOUL CONCERNS IN 2 SAMUEL

The Report of Saul's Death

1 Now it came to pass after the death of
Saul, when David had returned from the
slaughter of the Amalekites, and David had
stayed two days in Ziklag, 2on the third day,
behold, it happened that a man came from
Saul's camp with his clothes torn and dust on
his head. So it was, when he came to David,
that he fell to the ground and prostrated himself.
3And David said to him, "Where have you
come from?"
So he said to him, "I have escaped from the
camp of Israel."
4Then David said to him, "How did the matter go? Please tell me."
And he answered, "The people have fled
from the battle, many of the people are fallen
and dead, and Saul and Jonathan his son are
dead also."
5So David said to the young man who told
him, "How do you know that Saul and Jonathan his son are dead?"
6Then the young man who told him said,
"As I happened by chance *to be* on Mount Gilboa, there was Saul, leaning on his spear; and
indeed the chariots and horsemen followed
hard after him. 7Now when he looked behind
him, he saw me and called to me. And I answered, 'Here I am.' 8And he said to me, 'Who
are you?' So I answered him, 'I *am* an Amalekite.' 9He said to me again, 'Please stand over
me and kill me, for anguish has come upon
me, but my life still *remains* in me.' 10So I
stood over him and killed him, because I was
sure that he could not live after he had fallen.
And I took the crown that *was* on his head and
the bracelet that *was* on his arm, and have
brought them here to my lord."
11Therefore David took hold of his own
clothes and tore them, and *so did* all the men
who *were* with him. 12And they mourned and
wept and fasted until evening for Saul and for
Jonathan his son, for the people of the LORD
and for the house of Israel, because they had
fallen by the sword.
13Then David said to the young man who
told him, "Where *are* you from?"
And he answered, "I *am* the son of an alien,
an Amalekite."
14So David said to him, "How was it you
were not afraid to put forth your hand to destroy the LORD's anointed?" 15Then David
called one of the young men and said, "Go
near, *and* execute him!" And he struck him so
that he died. 16So David said to him, "Your
blood *is* on your own head, for your own
mouth has testified against you, saying, 'I
have killed the LORD's anointed.' "

The Song of the Bow

17Then David lamented with this lamentation over Saul and over Jonathan his son,
18and he told *them* to teach the children of Judah *the Song of* the Bow; indeed *it is* written in
the Book of Jasher:

19 "The beauty of Israel is slain on your high places!
How the mighty have fallen!
20 Tell *it* not in Gath,
Proclaim *it* not in the streets of Ashkelon—
Lest the daughters of the Philistines rejoice,
Lest the daughters of the uncircumcised triumph.

21 "O mountains of Gilboa,
Let there be no dew nor rain upon you,
Nor fields of offerings.
For the shield of the mighty is cast away there!
The shield of Saul, not anointed with oil.

SOUL NOTE

Express It *(1:17)* David expressed genuine grief over the deaths of Saul and Jonathan. It seems natural that David would grieve Jonathan's death, for they had been best friends (1 Sam. 18:1). King Saul, however, had been hunting David, desiring to kill him (1 Sam. 19:1, 2). Yet David lamented the loss of Israel's king and prince. Expressing sorrow is a healthy response to grief. David poured out his sorrow in words that honored the anointed king and his son. Putting grief into words is a healthy way to handle the pain and honor those who have died. **Topic: Grief/Loss**

22 From the blood of the slain,
From the fat of the mighty,
The bow of Jonathan did not turn back,
And the sword of Saul did not return
empty.

23 "Saul and Jonathan
were beloved
and pleasant in
their lives,
And in their death
they were not
divided;
They were swifter than eagles,
They were stronger than lions.

24 "O daughters of Israel, weep over Saul,
Who clothed you in scarlet, with
luxury;
Who put ornaments of gold on your
apparel.

25 "How the mighty have fallen in the midst
of the battle!
Jonathan *was* slain in your high places.
26 I am distressed for you, my brother
Jonathan;
You have been very pleasant to me;
Your love to me was wonderful,
Surpassing the love of women.

27 "How the mighty have fallen,
And the weapons of war perished!"

DAVID ANOINTED KING OF JUDAH

2 It happened after this that David inquired
of the LORD, saying, "Shall I go up to any
of the cities of Judah?"

And the LORD said to him, "Go up."

David said, "Where shall I go up?"

And He said, "To Hebron."

2So David went up there, and his two wives
also, Ahinoam the Jezreelitess, and Abigail
the widow of Nabal the Carmelite. 3And David
brought up the men who *were* with him, every
man with his household. So they dwelt in the
cities of Hebron.

4Then the men of Judah came, and there
they anointed David king over the house of
Judah. And they told David, saying, "The men
of Jabesh Gilead *were the ones* who buried
Saul." 5So David sent messengers to the men
of Jabesh Gilead, and said to them, "You *are*
blessed of the LORD, for you have shown this
kindness to your lord, to Saul, and have buried him. 6And now may the LORD show kindness and truth to you. I also will repay you
this kindness, because you have done this
thing. 7Now therefore,
let your hands be
strengthened, and be
valiant; for your master
Saul is dead, and also
the house of Judah has
anointed me king over
them."

> "And now may the LORD show kindness and truth to you. I also will repay you this kindness, because you have done this thing."
> 2 SAMUEL 2:6

ISHBOSHETH MADE KING OF ISRAEL

8But Abner the son of Ner, commander of
Saul's army, took Ishbosheth[a] the son of Saul
and brought him over to Mahanaim; 9and he
made him king over Gilead, over the
Ashurites, over Jezreel, over Ephraim, over
Benjamin, and over all Israel. 10Ishbosheth,
Saul's son, *was* forty years old when he began
to reign over Israel, and he reigned two years.
Only the house of Judah followed David.
11And the time that David was king in Hebron
over the house of Judah was seven years and
six months.

ISRAEL AND JUDAH AT WAR

12Now Abner the son of Ner, and the servants of Ishbosheth the son of Saul, went out
from Mahanaim to Gibeon. 13And Joab the
son of Zeruiah, and the servants of David,
went out and met them by the pool of Gibeon.
So they sat down, one on one side of the pool
and the other on the other side of the pool.
14Then Abner said to Joab, "Let the young
men now arise and compete before us."

And Joab said, "Let them arise."

15So they arose and went over by number,
twelve from Benjamin, *followers* of Ishbosheth
the son of Saul, and twelve from the servants
of David. 16And each one grasped his opponent by the head and *thrust* his sword in his
opponent's side; so they fell down together.
Therefore that place was called the Field of
Sharp Swords,[a] which *is* in Gibeon. 17So there
was a very fierce battle that day, and Abner
and the men of Israel were beaten before the
servants of David.

18Now the three sons of Zeruiah were there:
Joab and Abishai and Asahel. And Asahel *was*

2:8 [a]Called *Esh-Baal* in 1 Chronicles 8:33 and 9:39
2:16 [a]Hebrew *Helkath Hazzurim*

as fleet of foot as a wild gazelle. 19So Asahel
pursued Abner, and in going he did not turn
to the right hand or to the left from following
Abner.
20Then Abner looked behind him and said,
"*Are* you Asahel?"
He answered, "I *am.*"
21And Abner said to him, "Turn aside to
your right hand or to your left, and lay hold on
one of the young men and take his armor for
yourself." But Asahel would not turn aside
from following him. 22So Abner said again to
Asahel, "Turn aside from following me. Why
should I strike you to the ground? How then
could I face your brother Joab?" 23However, he
refused to turn aside. Therefore Abner struck
him in the stomach with the blunt end of the
spear, so that the spear came out of his back;
and he fell down there and died on the spot.
So it was *that* as many as came to the place
where Asahel fell down and died, stood still.
24Joab and Abishai also pursued Abner. And
the sun was going down when they came to
the hill of Ammah, which *is* before Giah by the
road to the Wilderness of Gibeon. 25Now the
children of Benjamin gathered together behind Abner and became a unit, and took their
stand on top of a hill. 26Then Abner called to
Joab and said, "Shall the sword devour forever? Do you not know that it will be bitter in
the latter end? How long will it be then until
you tell the people to return from pursuing
their brethren?"
27And Joab said, "*As* God lives, unless you
had spoken, surely then by morning all the
people would have given up pursuing their
brethren." 28So Joab blew a trumpet; and all
the people stood still and did not pursue Israel
anymore, nor did they fight anymore. 29Then
Abner and his men went on all that night
through the plain, crossed over the Jordan,
and went through all Bithron; and they came
to Mahanaim.
30So Joab returned from pursuing Abner.
And when he had gathered all the people together, there were missing of David's servants
nineteen men and Asahel. 31But the servants
of David had struck down, of Benjamin and
Abner's men, three hundred and sixty men
who died. 32Then they took up Asahel and
buried him in his father's tomb, which *was in*
Bethlehem. And Joab and his men went all
night, and they came to Hebron at daybreak.

3 Now there was a long war between the
house of Saul and the house of David. But
David grew stronger and stronger, and the
house of Saul grew weaker and weaker.

SONS OF DAVID

2Sons were born to David in Hebron: His
firstborn was Amnon by Ahinoam the Jezreelitess; 3his second, Chileab, by Abigail the
widow of Nabal the Carmelite; the third, Absalom the son of Maacah, the daughter of Talmai, king of Geshur; 4the fourth, Adonijah the
son of Haggith; the fifth, Shephatiah the son
of Abital; 5and the sixth, Ithream, by David's
wife Eglah. These were born to David in Hebron.

ABNER JOINS FORCES WITH DAVID

6Now it was so, while there was war between the house of Saul and the house of David, that Abner was strengthening *his hold* on
the house of Saul.
7And Saul had a concubine, whose name
was Rizpah, the daughter of Aiah. So *Ishbosheth* said to Abner, "Why have you gone in to
my father's concubine?"
8Then Abner became very angry at the
words of Ishbosheth, and said, "*Am* I a dog's
head that belongs to Judah? Today I show

SOUL NOTE

Wise Up *(3:1–5)* This list of David's sons by various wives reveals the starting point of many of the family problems David would face. As the various princes would seek attention and position, they would also wreak havoc on the family. Eventually, one son would rape a half sister, that sister's brother would kill the rapist, others would commit treason against their father and set themselves up as kings. David, it seems, did not discipline his children well (1 Kin. 1:6). Although David ruled the nation wisely, he could have faced less pain if he had used the same wisdom to run his family.
Topic: Family Problems

loyalty to the house of Saul your father, to his brothers, and to his friends, and have not delivered you into the hand of David; and you charge me today with a fault concerning this woman? 9May God do so to Abner, and more also, if I do not do for David as the LORD has sworn to him—10to transfer the kingdom from the house of Saul, and set up the throne of David over Israel and over Judah, from Dan to Beersheba." 11And he could not answer Abner another word, because he feared him.

12Then Abner sent messengers on his behalf to David, saying, "Whose *is* the land?" saying *also,* "Make your covenant with me, and indeed my hand *shall be* with you to bring all Israel to you."

13And *David* said, "Good, I will make a covenant with you. But one thing I require of you: you shall not see my face unless you first bring Michal, Saul's daughter, when you come to see my face." 14So David sent messengers to Ishbosheth, Saul's son, saying, "Give *me* my wife Michal, whom I betrothed to myself for a hundred foreskins of the Philistines." 15And Ishbosheth sent and took her from *her* husband, from Paltiel[a] the son of Laish. 16Then her husband went along with her to Bahurim, weeping behind her. So Abner said to him, "Go, return!" And he returned.

17Now Abner had communicated with the elders of Israel, saying, "In time past you were seeking for David *to be* king over you. 18Now then, do *it!* For the LORD has spoken of David, saying, 'By the hand of My servant David, I[a] will save My people Israel from the hand of the Philistines and the hand of all their enemies.' " 19And Abner also spoke in the hearing of Benjamin. Then Abner also went to speak in the hearing of David in Hebron all that seemed good to Israel and the whole house of Benjamin.

20So Abner and twenty men with him came to David at Hebron. And David made a feast for Abner and the men who *were* with him. 21Then Abner said to David, "I will arise and go, and gather all Israel to my lord the king, that they may make a covenant with you, and that you may reign over all that your heart desires." So David sent Abner away, and he went in peace.

JOAB MURDERS ABNER

22At that moment the servants of David and Joab came from a raid and brought much spoil with them. But Abner *was* not with David in Hebron, for he had sent him away, and he had gone in peace. 23When Joab and all the troops that *were* with him had come, they told Joab, saying, "Abner the son of Ner came to the king, and he sent him away, and he has gone in peace." 24Then Joab came to the king and said, "What have you done? Look, Abner came to you; why *is* it *that* you sent him away, and he has already gone? 25Surely you realize that Abner the son of Ner came to deceive you, to know your going out and your coming in, and to know all that you are doing."

26And when Joab had gone from David's presence, he sent messengers after Abner, who brought him back from the well of Sirah. But David did not know *it.* 27Now when Abner had returned to Hebron, Joab took him aside in the gate to speak with him privately, and there stabbed him in the stomach, so that he died for the blood of Asahel his brother.

28Afterward, when David heard *it,* he said, "My kingdom and I *are* guiltless before the LORD forever of the blood of Abner the son of Ner. 29Let it rest on the head of Joab and on all his father's house; and let there never fail to be in the house of Joab one who has a discharge or is a leper, who leans on a staff or falls by the sword, or who lacks bread." 30So Joab and Abishai his brother killed Abner, because he had killed their brother Asahel at Gibeon in the battle.

DAVID'S MOURNING FOR ABNER

31Then David said to Joab and to all the people who were with him, "Tear your clothes, gird yourselves with sackcloth, and mourn for Abner." And King David followed the coffin. 32So they buried Abner in Hebron; and the king lifted up his voice and wept at the grave of Abner, and all the people wept. 33And the king sang *a lament* over Abner and said:

"Should Abner die as a fool dies?
34 Your hands were not bound
Nor your feet put into fetters;
As a man falls before wicked men, *so*
you fell."

3:15 [a]Spelled *Palti* in 1 Samuel 25:44
3:18 [a]Following many Hebrew manuscripts, Septuagint, Syriac, and Targum; Masoretic Text reads *he.*

Then all the people wept over him again.
35And when all the people came to persuade
David to eat food while it was still day, David
took an oath, saying, "God do so to me, and
more also, if I taste bread or anything else till
the sun goes down!" 36Now all the people
took note *of it,* and it pleased them, since
whatever the king did pleased all the people.
37For all the people and all Israel understood
that day that it had not been the king's *intent*
to kill Abner the son of Ner. 38Then the king
said to his servants, "Do you not know that a
prince and a great man has fallen this day in
Israel? 39And I *am* weak today, though anointed king; and these men, the sons of Zeruiah,
are too harsh for me. The LORD shall repay the
evildoer according to his wickedness."

Ishbosheth Is Murdered

4 When Saul's son[a] heard that Abner had
died in Hebron, he lost heart, and all Israel was troubled. 2Now Saul's son *had* two
men *who were* captains of troops. The name of
one *was* Baanah and the name of the other
Rechab, the sons of Rimmon the Beerothite, of
the children of Benjamin. (For Beeroth also
was *part* of Benjamin, 3because the Beer-
othites fled to Gittaim and have been sojourners there until this day.)
4Jonathan, Saul's son, had a son *who was*
lame in *his* feet. He was five years old when
the news about Saul and Jonathan came from
Jezreel; and his nurse took him up and fled.
And it happened, as she made haste to flee,
that he fell and became lame. His name *was*
Mephibosheth.[a]
5Then the sons of Rimmon the Beerothite,
Rechab and Baanah, set out and came at
about the heat of the day to the house of
Ishbosheth, who was lying on his bed at noon.
6And they came there, all the way into the
house, *as though* to get wheat, and they
stabbed him in the stomach. Then Rechab and
Baanah his brother escaped. 7For when they
came into the house, he was lying on his bed
in his bedroom; then they struck him and
killed him, beheaded him and took his head,
and were all night escaping through the plain.
8And they brought the head of Ishbosheth to
David at Hebron, and said to the king, "Here is
the head of Ishbosheth, the son of Saul your
enemy, who sought your life; and the LORD
has avenged my lord the king this day of Saul
and his descendants."
9But David answered Rechab and Baanah
his brother, the sons of Rimmon the Beerothite, and said to them, "*As* the LORD lives, who
has redeemed my life from all adversity,
10when someone told me, saying, 'Look, Saul
is dead,' thinking to have brought good news,
I arrested him and had him executed in Ziklag—the one who *thought* I would give him a
reward for *his* news. 11How much more, when
wicked men have killed a righteous person in
his own house on his bed? Therefore, shall I
not now require his blood at your hand and
remove you from the earth?" 12So David commanded his young men, and they executed
them, cut off their hands and feet, and hanged
them by the pool in Hebron. But they took the
head of Ishbosheth and buried *it* in the tomb
of Abner in Hebron.

David Reigns over All Israel

5 Then all the tribes of Israel came to David
at Hebron and spoke, saying, "Indeed we
are your bone and your flesh. 2Also, in time
past, when Saul was king over us, you were
the one who led Israel out and brought them
in; and the LORD said to you, 'You shall shepherd My people Israel, and be ruler over Israel.' " 3Therefore all the elders of Israel came
to the king at Hebron, and King David made a
covenant with them at Hebron before the
LORD. And they anointed David king over Israel. 4David *was* thirty years old when he began
to reign, *and* he reigned forty years. 5In Hebron he reigned over Judah seven years and
six months, and in Jerusalem he reigned
thirty-three years over all Israel and Judah.

The Conquest of Jerusalem

6And the king and his men went to Jerusalem against the Jebusites, the inhabitants of
the land, who spoke to David, saying, "You
shall not come in here; but the blind and the
lame will repel you," thinking, "David cannot
come in here." 7Nevertheless David took the
stronghold of Zion (that *is,* the City of David).
8Now David said on that day, "Whoever
climbs up by way of the water shaft and de-
feats the Jebusites (the lame and the blind,
who are hated by David's soul), *he shall be
chief and captain.*"[a] Therefore they say, "The

4:1 [a]That is, Ishbosheth **4:4** [a]Called *Merib-Baal* in 1 Chronicles 8:34 and 9:40 **5:8** [a]Compare 1 Chronicles 11:6

blind and the lame shall not come into the house."

[9]Then David dwelt in the stronghold, and called it the City of David. And David built all around from the Millo[a] and inward. [10]So David went on and became great, and the LORD God of hosts *was* with him.

[11]Then Hiram king of Tyre sent messengers to David, and cedar trees, and carpenters and masons. And they built David a house. [12]So David knew that the LORD had established him as king over Israel, and that He had exalted His kingdom for the sake of His people Israel.

[13]And David took more concubines and wives from Jerusalem, after he had come from Hebron. Also more sons and daughters were born to David. [14]Now these *are* the names of those who were born to him in Jerusalem: Shammua,[a] Shobab, Nathan, Solomon, [15]Ibhar, Elishua,[a] Nepheg, Japhia, [16]Elishama, Eliada, and Eliphelet.

The Philistines Defeated

[17]Now when the Philistines heard that they had anointed David king over Israel, all the Philistines went up to search for David. And David heard *of it* and went down to the stronghold. [18]The Philistines also went and deployed themselves in the Valley of Rephaim. [19]So David inquired of the LORD, saying, "Shall I go up against the Philistines? Will You deliver them into my hand?"

And the LORD said to David, "Go up, for I will doubtless deliver the Philistines into your hand."

[20]So David went to Baal Perazim, and David defeated them there; and he said, "The LORD has broken through my enemies before me, like a breakthrough of water." Therefore he called the name of that place Baal Perazim.[a] [21]And they left their images there, and David and his men carried them away.

[22]Then the Philistines went up once again and deployed themselves in the Valley of Rephaim. [23]Therefore David inquired of the LORD, and He said, "You shall not go up; circle around behind them, and come upon them in front of the mulberry trees. [24]And it shall be, when you hear the sound of marching in the tops of the mulberry trees, then you shall advance quickly. For then the LORD will go out before you to strike the camp of the Philistines." [25]And David did so, as the LORD commanded him; and he drove back the Philistines from Geba[a] as far as Gezer.

The Ark Brought to Jerusalem

6 Again David gathered all *the* choice *men* of Israel, thirty thousand. [2]And David arose and went with all the people who *were* with him from Baale Judah to bring up from there the ark of God, whose name is called by the Name,[a] the LORD of Hosts, who dwells *between* the cherubim. [3]So they set the ark of God on a new cart, and brought it out of the house of Abinadab, which *was* on the hill; and Uzzah and Ahio, the sons of Abinadab, drove the new cart.[a] [4]And they brought it out of the house of Abinadab, which *was* on the hill, accompanying the ark of God; and Ahio went before the ark. [5]Then David and all the house of Israel played *music* before the LORD on all kinds of *instruments of* fir wood, on harps, on stringed instruments, on tambourines, on sistrums, and on cymbals.

[6]And when they came to Nachon's threshing floor, Uzzah put out *his hand* to the ark of God and took hold of it, for the oxen stumbled. [7]Then the anger of the LORD was aroused against Uzzah, and God struck him there for *his* error; and he died there by the ark of God. [8]And David became angry because of the LORD's outbreak against Uzzah; and he called the name of the place Perez Uzzah[a] to this day.

[9]David was afraid of the LORD that day; and he said, "How can the ark of the LORD come to me?" [10]So David would not move the ark of the LORD with him into the City of David; but David took it aside into the house of Obed-Edom the Gittite. [11]The ark of the LORD remained in the house of Obed-Edom the Gittite three months. And the LORD blessed Obed-Edom and all his household.

[12]Now it was told King David, saying, "The LORD has blessed the house of Obed-Edom and all that *belongs* to him, because of the ark of God." So David went and brought up the

---

5:9 [a]Literally *The Landfill* **5:14** [a]Spelled *Shimea* in 1 Chronicles 3:5 **5:15** [a]Spelled *Elishama* in 1 Chronicles 3:6 **5:20** [a]Literally *Master of Breakthroughs* **5:25** [a]Following Masoretic Text, Targum, and Vulgate; Septuagint reads *Gibeon.* **6:2** [a]Septuagint, Targum, and Vulgate omit *by the Name;* many Hebrew manuscripts and Syriac read *there.* **6:3** [a]Septuagint adds *with the ark.* **6:8** [a]Literally *Outburst Against Uzzah*

ark of God from the house of Obed-Edom to the City of David with gladness. 13And so it was, when those bearing the ark of the LORD had gone six paces, that he sacrificed oxen and fatted sheep. 14Then David danced before the LORD with all *his* might; and David *was* wearing a linen ephod. 15So David and all the house of Israel brought up the ark of the LORD with shouting and with the sound of the trumpet.

16Now as the ark of the LORD came into the City of David, Michal, Saul's daughter, looked through a window and saw King David leaping and whirling before the LORD; and she despised him in her heart. 17So they brought the ark of the LORD, and set it in its place in the midst of the tabernacle that David had erected for it. Then David offered burnt offerings and peace offerings before the LORD. 18And when David had finished offering burnt offerings and peace offerings, he blessed the people in the name of the LORD of hosts. 19Then he distributed among all the people, among the whole multitude of Israel, both the women and the men, to everyone a loaf of bread, a piece *of meat,* and a cake of raisins. So all the people departed, everyone to his house.

20Then David returned to bless his household. And Michal the daughter of Saul came out to meet David, and said, "How glorious was the king of Israel today, uncovering himself today in the eyes of the maids of his servants, as one of the base fellows shamelessly uncovers himself!"

21So David said to Michal, "*It was* before the LORD, who chose me instead of your father and all his house, to appoint me ruler over the people of the LORD, over Israel. Therefore I

PERSONALITY PROFILE

Attitudes

MICHAL—WATCH YOUR ATTITUDE

(2 SAMUEL 6:16)

The qualities about David that first caught Michal's attention and captured her heart were the same qualities that she came to resent. David was handsome, heroic, and had a heart for God. Perhaps Michal misunderstood the kind of single-minded devotion David had toward God as nothing more than an endearing trait she hoped one day would be centered on her. If David killed the giant Goliath for God, what might he do for a lover?

When news of his daughter's love for the shepherd-hero reached the king's ears, Saul was already scheming to eliminate David. He set a trap for David using his own daughter as the prize (1 Sam. 18:17–29). David met the challenge, however, and received Michal's hand in marriage.

The young couple had few days of happiness. After all, the father of the bride kept trying to kill the groom. When Michal helped her husband escape from a deadly ambush her father arranged, Saul punished her by giving her to another man (1 Sam. 25:44). David eventually got her back (2 Sam. 3:14–16), but by then she was merely one of several wives he had collected. Michal had to accept yet another disappointment in life.

Resentment and bitterness in Michal finally erupted on the day the ark of the covenant was brought into Jerusalem (2 Sam. 6:1–23). David led the parade, leaping and dancing in his joy before God, as Michal watched him from a palace window. She considered his behavior excessive and unnecessary and confronted him with shameful derision. Her pent-up frustrations may have been understandable, but her timing and target were tragic. Instead of gaining her husband's attention, she demeaned his faith and was punished by God for it.

Injustices and hardships that come our way cannot excuse bad attitudes. We are responsible for our responses. When we entrust our lives to God, we will still face pain, but He helps us to keep the pain from giving us a bad attitude toward life.

To Learn More: Turn to the article about attitudes on pages 1174, 1175. See also the key passage note at Romans 12:1, 2 on page 1482.

will play *music* before the LORD. 22And I will be even more undignified than this, and will be humble in my own sight. But as for the maidservants of whom you have spoken, by them I will be held in honor."

23Therefore Michal the daughter of Saul had no children to the day of her death.

GOD'S COVENANT WITH DAVID

7 Now it came to pass when the king was dwelling in his house, and the LORD had given him rest from all his enemies all around, 2that the king said to Nathan the prophet, "See now, I dwell in a house of cedar, but the ark of God dwells inside tent curtains."

3Then Nathan said to the king, "Go, do all that *is* in your heart, for the LORD *is* with you."

4But it happened that night that the word of the LORD came to Nathan, saying, 5"Go and tell My servant David, 'Thus says the LORD: "Would you build a house for Me to dwell in? 6For I have not dwelt in a house since the time that I brought the children of Israel up from Egypt, even to this day, but have moved about in a tent and in a tabernacle. 7Wherever I have moved about with all the children of Israel, have I ever spoken a word to anyone from the tribes of Israel, whom I commanded to shepherd My people Israel, saying, 'Why have you not built Me a house of cedar?' " ' 8Now therefore, thus shall you say to My servant David, 'Thus says the LORD of hosts: "I took you from the sheepfold, from following the sheep, to be ruler over My people, over Israel. 9And I have been with you wherever you have gone, and have cut off all your enemies from before you, and have made you a great name, like the name of the great men who *are* on the earth. 10Moreover I will appoint a place for My people Israel, and will plant them, that they may dwell in a place of their own and move no more; nor shall the sons of wickedness oppress them anymore, as previously, 11since the time that I commanded judges *to be* over My people Israel, and have caused you to rest from all your enemies. Also the LORD tells you that He will make you a house.[a]

12"When your days are fulfilled and you rest with your fathers, I will set up your seed after you, who will come from your body, and I will establish his kingdom. 13He shall build a house for My name, and I will establish the throne of his kingdom forever. 14I will be his Father, and he shall be My son. If he commits iniquity, I will chasten him with the rod of men and with the blows of the sons of men. 15But My mercy shall not depart from him, as I took *it* from Saul, whom I removed from before you. 16And your house and your kingdom shall be established forever before you.[a] Your throne shall be established forever." ' "

17According to all these words and according to all this vision, so Nathan spoke to David.

> "Therefore You are great, O Lord GOD. For there is none like You, nor is there any God besides You, according to all that we have heard with our ears."
>
> 2 SAMUEL 7:22

DAVID'S THANKSGIVING TO GOD

18Then King David went in and sat before the LORD; and he said: "Who *am* I, O Lord GOD? And what is my house, that You have brought me this far? 19And yet this was a small thing in Your sight, O Lord GOD; and You have also spoken of Your servant's house for a great while to come. *Is* this the manner of man, O Lord GOD? 20Now what more can David say to You? For You, Lord GOD, know Your servant. 21For Your word's sake, and according to Your own heart, You have done all these great things, to make Your servant know *them*. 22Therefore You are great, O Lord GOD.[a] For *there is* none like You, nor *is there any* God besides You, according to all that we have heard with our ears. 23And who *is* like Your people, like Israel, the one nation on the earth whom God went to redeem for Himself as a people, to make for Himself a name—and to do for Yourself great and awesome deeds for Your land—before Your people whom You redeemed for Yourself from Egypt, the nations, and their gods? 24For You have made Your people Israel Your very own people forever; and You, LORD, have become their God.

25"Now, O LORD God, the word which You have spoken concerning Your servant and concerning his house, establish *it* forever and

7:11 [a]That is, a royal dynasty **7:16** [a]Septuagint reads *Me.* **7:22** [a]Targum and Syriac read *O LORD God.*

do as You have said. 26So let Your name be
magnified forever, saying, 'The LORD of hosts
is the God over Israel.' And let the house of
Your servant David be established before You.
27For You, O LORD of hosts, God of Israel, have
revealed *this* to Your servant, saying, 'I will
build you a house.' Therefore Your servant
has found it in his heart to pray this prayer
to You.
28"And now, O Lord GOD, You are God, and
Your words are true, and You have promised
this goodness to Your servant. 29Now therefore, let it please You to bless the house of
Your servant, that it may continue before You
forever; for You, O Lord GOD, have spoken *it*,
and with Your blessing let the house of Your
servant be blessed forever."

DAVID'S FURTHER CONQUESTS

8 After this it came to pass that David attacked the Philistines and subdued them.
And David took Metheg Ammah from the
hand of the Philistines.
2Then he defeated Moab. Forcing them
down to the ground, he measured them off
with a line. With two lines he measured off
those to be put to death, and with one full line
those to be kept alive. So the Moabites became David's servants, *and* brought tribute.
3David also defeated Hadadezer the son of
Rehob, king of Zobah, as he went to recover
his territory at the River Euphrates. 4David
took from him one thousand *chariots*, seven
hundred[a] horsemen, and twenty thousand
foot soldiers. Also David hamstrung all the
chariot horses, except that he spared *enough*
of them for one hundred chariots.
5When the Syrians of Damascus came to
help Hadadezer king of Zobah, David killed
twenty-two thousand of the Syrians. 6Then
David put garrisons in Syria of Damascus; and
the Syrians became David's servants, *and*
brought tribute. So the LORD preserved David
wherever he went. 7And David took the
shields of gold that had belonged to the servants of Hadadezer, and brought them to Jerusalem. 8Also from Betah[a] and from Berothai,
cities of Hadadezer, King David took a large
amount of bronze.
9When Toi[a] king of Hamath heard that David had defeated all the army of Hadadezer,
10then Toi sent Joram[a] his son to King David,
to greet him and bless him, because he had
fought against Hadadezer and defeated him
(for Hadadezer had been at war with Toi); and
Joram brought with him articles of silver, articles of gold, and articles of bronze. 11King David also dedicated these to the LORD, along
with the silver and gold that he had dedicated
from all the nations which he had subdued—
12from Syria,[a] from Moab, from the people of
Ammon, from the Philistines, from Amalek,
and from the spoil of Hadadezer the son of Rehob, king of Zobah.
13And David made *himself* a name when
he returned from killing eighteen thousand
Syrians[a] in the Valley of Salt. 14He also put
garrisons in Edom; throughout all Edom he
put garrisons, and all the Edomites became
David's servants. And the LORD preserved David wherever he went.

DAVID'S ADMINISTRATION

15So David reigned over all Israel; and David
administered judgment and justice to all his
people. 16Joab the son of Zeruiah *was* over the
army; Jehoshaphat the son of Ahilud *was* recorder; 17Zadok the son of Ahitub and Ahimelech the son of Abiathar *were* the priests;
Seraiah[a] *was* the scribe; 18Benaiah the son of
Jehoiada *was over* both the Cherethites and
the Pelethites; and David's sons were chief
ministers.

DAVID'S KINDNESS TO MEPHIBOSHETH

9 Now David said, "Is there still anyone
who is left of the house of Saul, that I may
show him kindness for Jonathan's sake?"
2And *there was* a servant of the house of
Saul whose name *was* Ziba. So when they had
called him to David, the king said to him, "*Are*
you Ziba?"
He said, "At your service!"
3Then the king said, "*Is* there not still someone of the house of Saul, to whom I may show
the kindness of God?"
And Ziba said to the king, "There is still a
son of Jonathan *who is* lame in *his* feet."
4So the king said to him, "Where *is* he?"

8:4 [a]Or *seven thousand* (compare 1 Chronicles 18:4) **8:8** [a]Spelled *Tibhath* in 1 Chronicles 18:8
8:9 [a]Spelled *Tou* in 1 Chronicles 18:9
8:10 [a]Spelled *Hadoram* in 1 Chronicles 18:10
8:12 [a]Septuagint, Syriac, and some Hebrew manuscripts read *Edom*. **8:13** [a]Septuagint, Syriac, and some Hebrew manuscripts read *Edomites* (compare 1 Chronicles 18:12). **8:17** [a]Spelled *Shavsha* in 1 Chronicles 18:16

And Ziba said to the king, "Indeed he *is* in the house of Machir the son of Ammiel, in Lo Debar."

5Then King David sent and brought him out of the house of Machir the son of Ammiel, from Lo Debar.

6Now when Mephibosheth the son of Jonathan, the son of Saul, had come to David, he fell on his face and prostrated himself. Then David said, "Mephibosheth?"

And he answered, "Here is your servant!"

7So David said to him, "Do not fear, for I will surely show you kindness for Jonathan your father's sake, and will restore to you all the land of Saul your grandfather; and you shall eat bread at my table continually."

8Then he bowed himself, and said, "What *is* your servant, that you should look upon such a dead dog as I?"

9And the king called to Ziba, Saul's servant, and said to him, "I have given to your master's son all that belonged to Saul and to all his house. 10You therefore, and your sons and your servants, shall work the land for him, and you shall bring in *the harvest,* that your master's son may have food to eat. But Mephibosheth your master's son shall eat bread at my table always." Now Ziba had fifteen sons and twenty servants.

11Then Ziba said to the king, "According to all that my lord the king has commanded his servant, so will your servant do."

"As for Mephibosheth," *said the king,* "he shall eat at my table[a] like one of the king's sons." 12Mephibosheth had a young son whose name *was* Micha. And all who dwelt in the house of Ziba *were* servants of Mephibosheth. 13So Mephibosheth dwelt in Jerusalem, for he ate continually at the king's table. And he was lame in both his feet.

THE AMMONITES AND SYRIANS DEFEATED

10 It happened after this that the king of the people of Ammon died, and Hanun his son reigned in his place. 2Then David said, "I will show kindness to Hanun the son of Nahash, as his father showed kindness to me."

So David sent by the hand of his servants to comfort him concerning his father. And David's servants came into the land of the people of Ammon. 3And the princes of the people of Ammon said to Hanun their lord, "Do you think that David really honors your father because he has sent comforters to you? Has David not *rather* sent his servants to you to search the city, to spy it out, and to overthrow it?"

4Therefore Hanun took David's servants, shaved off half of their beards, cut off their garments in the middle, at their buttocks, and sent them away. 5When they told David, he sent to meet them, because the men were greatly ashamed. And the king said, "Wait at Jericho until your beards have grown, and *then* return."

6When the people of Ammon saw that they had made themselves repulsive to David, the people of Ammon sent and hired the Syrians of Beth Rehob and the Syrians of Zoba, twenty thousand foot soldiers; and from the king of Maacah one thousand men, and from Ish-Tob twelve thousand men. 7Now when David heard *of it,* he sent Joab and all the army of the mighty men. 8Then the people of Ammon came out and put themselves in battle array at the entrance of the gate. And the Syrians of Zoba, Beth Rehob, Ish-Tob, and Maacah *were* by themselves in the field.

9:11 [a]Septuagint reads *David's table.*

SOUL NOTE

Honorable *(9:7)* Mephibosheth was the son of Jonathan, David's best friend. With Saul and Jonathan dead, Mephibosheth was technically in line for the throne. Threats to David's position were not unusual (even his own sons would try to take his throne), but David's dealing with this potential threat *was* unusual. Instead of killing the potential rival, as most kings would, he brought Mephibosheth to live in the palace with him. This act honored a promise that David had made to Jonathan (1 Sam. 20:14, 15). At risk to himself, David kept his promise. Honorable people keep their word.
Topic: Honor

9 When Joab saw that the battle line was
against him before and behind, he chose some
of Israel's best and put *them* in battle array
against the Syrians. 10 And the rest of the people he put under the command of Abishai his
brother, that he might set *them* in battle array
against the people of Ammon. 11 Then he said,
"If the Syrians are too strong for me, then you
shall help me; but if the people of Ammon are
too strong for you, then I will come and help
you. 12 Be of good courage, and let us be strong
for our people and for the cities of our God.
And may the LORD do *what is* good in His
sight."

13 So Joab and the people who *were* with
him drew near for the battle against the Syrians, and they fled before him. 14 When the
people of Ammon saw that the Syrians were
fleeing, they also fled before Abishai, and entered the city. So Joab returned from the people of Ammon and went to Jerusalem.

15 When the Syrians saw that they had been
defeated by Israel, they gathered together.
16 Then Hadadezer[a] sent and brought out the
Syrians who *were* beyond the River,[b] and they
came to Helam. And Shobach the commander
of Hadadezer's army *went* before them.
17 When it was told David, he gathered all Israel, crossed over the Jordan, and came to
Helam. And the Syrians set themselves in battle array against David and fought with him.
18 Then the Syrians fled before Israel; and David killed seven hundred charioteers and forty
thousand horsemen of the Syrians, and struck
Shobach the commander of their army, who
died there. 19 And when all the kings *who were*
servants to Hadadezer[a] saw that they were defeated by Israel, they made peace with Israel
and served them. So the Syrians were afraid to
help the people of Ammon anymore.

DAVID, BATHSHEBA, AND URIAH

11 It happened in the spring of the year,
at the time when kings go out *to battle*, that David sent Joab and his servants with
him, and all Israel; and they destroyed the
people of Ammon and besieged Rabbah. But
David remained at Jerusalem.

2 Then it happened one evening that David
arose from his bed and walked on the roof of
the king's house. And from the roof he saw a
woman bathing, and the woman *was* very
beautiful to behold. 3 So David sent and inquired about the woman. And *someone* said,
"*Is* this not Bathsheba, the daughter of Eliam,
the wife of Uriah the Hittite?" 4 Then David
sent messengers, and took her; and she came
to him, and he lay with her, for she was
cleansed from her impurity; and she returned
to her house. 5 And the woman conceived; so
she sent and told David, and said, "I *am* with
child."

6 Then David sent to Joab, *saying*, "Send me
Uriah the Hittite." And Joab sent Uriah to David. 7 When Uriah had come to him, David
asked how Joab was doing, and how the people were doing, and how the war prospered.
8 And David said to Uriah, "Go down to your
house and wash your feet." So Uriah departed
from the king's house, and a gift *of food* from
the king followed him. 9 But Uriah slept at the
door of the king's house with all the servants
of his lord, and did not go down to his house.
10 So when they told David, saying, "Uriah did
not go down to his house," David said to
Uriah, "Did you not come from a journey?
Why did you not go down to your house?"

11 And Uriah said to David, "The ark and Israel and Judah are dwelling in tents, and my
lord Joab and the servants of my lord are encamped in the open fields. Shall I then go to
my house to eat and drink, and to lie with my
wife? *As* you live, and *as* your soul lives, I will
not do this thing."

12 Then David said to Uriah, "Wait here today also, and tomorrow I will let you depart."
So Uriah remained in Jerusalem that day and
the next. 13 Now when David called him, he
ate and drank before him; and he made him
drunk. And at evening he went out to lie on
his bed with the servants of his lord, but he
did not go down to his house.

14 In the morning it happened that David
wrote a letter to Joab and sent *it* by the hand
of Uriah. 15 And he wrote in the letter, saying,
"Set Uriah in the forefront of the hottest battle,
and retreat from him, that he may be struck
down and die." 16 So it was, while Joab besieged the city, that he assigned Uriah to a
place where he knew there *were* valiant men.
17 Then the men of the city came out and
fought with Joab. And *some* of the people of
the servants of David fell; and Uriah the Hittite died also.

18 Then Joab sent and told David all the

10:16 [a]Hebrew *Hadarezer* [b]That is, the Euphrates
10:19 [a]Hebrew *Hadarezer*

things concerning the war, 19and charged the
messenger, saying, "When you have finished
telling the matters of the war to the king, 20if it
happens that the king's wrath rises, and he
says to you: 'Why did you approach so near to
the city when you fought? Did you not know
that they would shoot from the wall? 21Who
struck Abimelech the son of Jerubbesheth?[a]
Was it not a woman who cast a piece of a millstone on him from the wall, so that he died in
Thebez? Why did you go near the wall?'—
then you shall say, 'Your servant Uriah the Hittite is dead also.' "
22So the messenger went, and came and
told David all that Joab had sent by him.
23And the messenger said to David, "Surely
the men prevailed against us and came out to
us in the field; then we drove them back as far
as the entrance of the gate. 24The archers shot
from the wall at your servants; and *some* of
the king's servants are dead, and your servant
Uriah the Hittite is dead also."
25Then David said to the messenger, "Thus
you shall say to Joab: 'Do not let this thing displease you, for the sword devours one as well
as another. Strengthen your attack against the
city, and overthrow it.' So encourage him."
26When the wife of Uriah heard that Uriah
her husband was dead, she mourned for her
husband. 27And when her mourning was over,
David sent and brought her to his house, and
she became his wife and bore him a son. But

11:21 [a]Same as *Jerubbaal* (Gideon), Judges 6:32ff

PERSONALITY PROFILE

Sexual Sin

DAVID AND BATHSHEBA—COSTLY COVER-UP

(2 SAMUEL 11)

King David enjoyed the perks that come with power. His privileges included multiple wives and concubines. Although sexual satisfaction was always available, it did not insulate David from sexual temptation. Boredom and wandering attention made the king vulnerable. While casually viewing Jerusalem from his high palace porch one evening, David noticed a beautiful woman bathing.

The accidental glance became a fantasy. The fantasy evolved into fact-finding. David discovered the woman was Bathsheba, the wife of one of his military leaders. He summoned her to the palace and took sexual advantage of her. She later notified David that she was pregnant. Sinful decisions continued to escalate in damage, and they widened the group involved.

After a failed attempt to trick Uriah into sleeping with his wife so he would think he had caused Bathsheba's pregnancy, David took more desperate and deceitful actions. He ordered his general Joab to place Uriah in an exposed battle situation where he would almost surely be killed. This led to Uriah's death and David's attempt to cover up the sexual situation by a hasty marriage to Bathsheba.

Fortunately for David, God didn't give up on him, nor did the prophet Nathan. Deep in sin and denial, David needed a fearless friend with the wisdom to lance a cancerous boil of guilt. When Nathan did that (2 Sam. 12:1–15), David repented. Although the repentance was genuine, the consequences were costly. The baby David and Bathsheba conceived in sin died shortly after childbirth.

This sordid episode in David's life reveals the power of temptation and the destructiveness of sin. Sexual sin often leads to lies, cover-up, and deception that only further complicate the lives of those involved. The most destructive cover-ups are the ones that seem to work. They leave sin free to create a havoc of guilt and shame behind the scenes. Though repentance may be costly, it eventually yields better results than hidden and unconfessed sin.

To Learn More: Turn to the article about sexual sin on pages 1582, 1583. See also the key passage note at 1 Thessalonians 4:3–7 on page 1581.

the thing that David had done displeased the
LORD.

NATHAN'S PARABLE AND DAVID'S CONFESSION

12 Then the LORD sent Nathan to David.
And he came to him, and said to him:
"There were two men in one city, one rich and
the other poor. [2]The rich *man* had exceedingly
many flocks and herds. [3]But the poor *man* had
nothing, except one little ewe lamb which he
had bought and nourished; and it grew up together with him and with his children. It ate of
his own food and drank from his own cup and
lay in his bosom; and it was like a daughter to
him. [4]And a traveler came to the rich man,
who refused to take from his own flock and
from his own herd to prepare one for the way-
faring man who had come to him; but he took
the poor man's lamb and prepared it for the
man who had come to him."
[5]So David's anger was greatly aroused
against the man, and he said to Nathan, "*As*
the LORD lives, the man who has done this
shall surely die! [6]And he shall restore fourfold
for the lamb, because he did this thing and because he had no pity."
[7]Then Nathan said to David, "You *are* the
man! Thus says the LORD God of Israel: 'I
anointed you king over Israel, and I delivered
you from the hand of Saul. [8]I gave you your
master's house and your master's wives into
your keeping, and gave you the house of Israel
and Judah. And if *that had been* too little, I
also would have given you much more! [9]Why
have you despised the commandment of the
LORD, to do evil in His sight? You have killed
Uriah the Hittite with the sword; you have
taken his wife *to be* your wife, and have killed
him with the sword of the people of Ammon.
[10]Now therefore, the sword shall never depart
from your house, because you have despised
Me, and have taken the wife of Uriah the Hittite to be your wife.' [11]Thus says the LORD:
'Behold, I will raise up adversity against you
from your own house; and I will take your
wives before your eyes and give *them* to your

PERSONALITY PROFILE

NATHAN—AN HONEST FRIEND

(2 SAMUEL 12)

Everyone can use a friend like Nathan. Such a friend shows up not only when wanted, but especially when needed. In Nathan, David had the added benefit of a friend who brought God's perspective into their relationship.

Shortly after David succeeded in covering up a shocking episode of sexual sin followed by conspiracy and murder, his friend Nathan showed up one day with a story (2 Sam. 12:1–12). Nathan's vivid parable became a tool God used to shatter David's denial of sin. Nathan confronted David about his sin and called him into accountability before God. Sometimes such accountability can be done privately and personally. Other times, sins of a public nature must be dealt with in a public manner.

In David's case, the sin may have seemed private, but the cover-up and the consequences were public. Not only did the child conceived with Bathsheba die, but God also announced that the sword of violence would never depart from David's house (2 Sam. 12:10). His own family would try to betray and kill him.

Nathan remained a friend to David and Bathsheba. His confrontation of their sin was not intended to destroy them, but to help them clear their consciences and deal with their behavior properly. Although he couldn't change the consequences that followed, Nathan's faithful friendship allowed David and Bathsheba to make the best before God of a shameful event. They may not have wanted everything he offered them as a friend, but he gave it to them anyway. God showed him what they really needed.

Do you have any friends like Nathan? Could you be a friend like Nathan?

To Learn More: Turn to the article about accountability on pages 966, 967. See also the key passage note at Romans 14:12 on page 1487.

HEALTH AND SPIRITUALITY

GEORGE OHLSCHLAGER

(2 Samuel 12:1–23)

It was one of those uneasy moments in counseling. The skeptical client, chafing at my challenge, reversed roles and bore right in. "If God is so good, if knowing Him is so good for you, why are *you* so sick?"

He was challenging the onset of diabetes, depression, and heart disease in my life—a dark triad of trouble that had assaulted me in my late forties. I was caught off guard by his attack and his implied assumption that my illness was evidence that God was not so good. After an awkward silence, I suddenly realized how backward my client was viewing things, how good God truly had been.

"You know," I answered him, "considering my chaotic childhood and the way I abused my body in my youth, by all rights I should be dead by now. I am paying the wages of my past sins, and that is a sad and sobering truth. But the fact that I stand here at all, that I survived my heart attack and live today, is a testimony to God's goodness to me." And that, I told my now-disarmed client, was a truth worth celebrating.

A vital Christian faith yields good health in every way. Furthermore, as my case demonstrates, it lengthens life and gives meaning to it like nothing else can.

Yet the 20th-century world has received two sharply conflicting views about the relationship of health and Christian spirituality. The Bible has revealed a positive relationship—asserting that a strong spiritual life yields good health. Obedience to the call and commands of God yields life and peace, while disobedience brings death—the wages of sin.

In contrast, some of the leading lights of psychology and psychiatry have argued that religion is pathological, an irrational crutch that has reinforced disease and disorder rather than healing it. Furthermore, most mental health professionals are less religious and more atheistic than the general populace, and consider religion to be of little value in helping others.

The professionals should more seriously study their own research. The truth about health and spirituality is there in plain view.

RESEARCH ON HEALTH AND CHRISTIAN SPIRITUALITY

Buried among thousands of studies in health and mental health over the past half-century are a few gems that look at the relationship between religion and health.

Mental health and well-being. Increased religious commitment reduced suicidal behavior. In fact, one study showed that church attendance rates predicted suicide better than any other factor. Religious commitment also correlated with reduced drug abuse. A large survey of 14,000 youth indicated the lowest abuse rates among conservative religious groups, and the highest rates among the nonreligious and liberal religious groups. The importance of religion to the teenager was the key—religious values that were internalized in youth had more power than fear or peer pressure. Further, dynamic faith correlated with less depression. Religious commitment was shown to counteract the hopelessness and despair of depression. Seventeen different studies over four decades showed that less distress, a greater sense of well-being, and the occurrence of fewer psychiatric symptoms were all related to higher levels of religious commitment and church participation.

Health and disease. One study showed that even after allowing for the influence of smoking and socioeconomic status, the death rate for males who attended church frequently was just 60 percent of that of infrequent or nonattenders. Women who attended infrequently were twice as likely to die as those who did. Numerous studies have shown that higher levels of religious commitment produce healthier lifestyles, and are related to lower blood pressure levels and reduced hypertension.

Relationships. Every study on marriage showed greater levels of marital satisfaction, exposing the fallacy that religious people stay together in unhappy unions because their faith demands it. Further, the myth that religious people are sexually repressed and unhappy is exploded by numerous findings that indicated highly religious women were more satisfied with their sexual lives than either nonreligious or even moderately religious women. All five studies on divorce showed that divorce rates were reduced as religious commitment increased.

LIVING OUT TRUE RELIGION

Another way that religion has been studied distinguishes intrinsic and extrinsic religion. Intrinsic religion represents a dynamic faith, where people internalize their beliefs and live consistent with their moral teachings. Extrinsic religion, on the other hand, is religion for social status or personal gain. Comparing the two, the health benefits accrue to those living an intrinsic faith. Those espousing only an extrinsic faith were no more healthy than those who had no religion at all.

True believers live out their faith and walk daily in the presence of God. They pray for and seek the peace of God to surround and infuse them experientially. They live longer and stay healthy longer, show higher levels of life satisfaction, higher levels of personal contentment, have an ability to endure hardship and suffering, and show a consistently higher practice of forgiving others, thanksgiving, and laughter.

Those who refuse to forgive, who maintain a core of jealousy, envy, or bitterness, and who complain and blame are more prone to illness, psychiatric disorders, and a shorter, less contented life. Unrepented sin, ingratitude, and unforgiveness carries a weight that grows and accumulates throughout life. It does not stop on its own, but piles on until it becomes a crushing load.

Jesus' yoke is far lighter—it is freedom and renewal. Life lived daily in Christ includes the assurance of salvation and the promise of eternal life. It is also the best prescription for good health.

FURTHER MEDITATION:

Other passages to study about the issue of health/spirituality include:

- ➢ Psalm 38:3
- ➢ Proverbs 3:7, 8; 4:20–22; 12:18; 16:24
- ➢ Jeremiah 33:6
- ➢ James 5:13–16
- ➢ 3 John 2

To Learn More: Turn to the key passage note on health/spirituality at Proverbs 17:22 on page 821. See also the personality profile of Paul on page 1536.

neighbor, and he shall lie with your wives in the sight of this sun. 12For you did *it* secretly, but I will do this thing before all Israel, before the sun.' "

13So David said to Nathan, "I have sinned against the LORD."

And Nathan said to David, "The LORD also has put away your sin; you shall not die. 14However, because by this deed you have given great occasion to the enemies of the LORD to blaspheme, the child also *who is* born to you shall surely die." 15Then Nathan departed to his house.

The Death of David's Son

And the LORD struck the child that Uriah's wife bore to David, and it became ill. 16David therefore pleaded with God for the child, and David fasted and went in and lay all night on the ground. 17So the elders of his house arose *and went* to him, to raise him up from the ground. But he would not, nor did he eat food with them. 18Then on the seventh day it came to pass that the child died. And the servants of David were afraid to tell him that the child was dead. For they said, "Indeed, while the child was alive, we spoke to him, and he would not heed our voice. How can we tell him that the child is dead? He may do some harm!"

19When David saw that his servants were whispering, David perceived that the child was dead. Therefore David said to his servants, "Is the child dead?"

And they said, "He is dead."

20So David arose from the ground, washed and anointed himself, and changed his clothes; and he went into the house of the LORD and worshiped. Then he went to his own house; and when he requested, they set food before him, and he ate. 21Then his servants said to him, "What *is* this that you have done? You fasted and wept for the child *while he was* alive, but when the child died, you arose and ate food."

22And he said, "While the child was alive, I fasted and wept; for I said, 'Who can tell *whether* the LORD[a] will be gracious to me, that the child may live?' 23But now he is dead; why should I fast? Can I bring him back again? I shall go to him, but he shall not return to me."

12:22 [a]A few Hebrew manuscripts and Syriac read *God.*

SOUL NOTE

Spiritual Health *(12:1–23)* Psalm 51 records David's lament after being confronted by Nathan. Evidently David had felt no guilt until God, through Nathan, revealed his sin to him. When David felt the crushing weight of his guilt, he felt sick and tormented. "I acknowledge my transgressions, and my sin is always before me," he said (Ps. 51:3). David had withdrawn from God and failed spiritually. The result was devastating. The pain sent him back to God, for God alone could restore him. Guilt can crush people, or it can send them to God for forgiveness and spiritual restoration.
Topic: Health/Spirituality

SOUL NOTE

Me First *(12:13)* As Nathan spun his story, David flashed with anger. "The man who has done this shall surely die!" he exclaimed (12:5). David clearly saw the rich man's sin, but failed to make the connection with his own actions toward Uriah and Bathsheba until Nathan said, "You are the man!" (12:7). It is easy for us to hear a sermon or read a Bible passage and think of other people to whom it applies. Instead, we should first ask, "What can I learn that will help me grow spiritually?"
Topic: Change/Maturity

Solomon Is Born

24Then David comforted Bathsheba his
wife, and went in to her and lay with her. So
she bore a son, and he[a] called his name Solomon. Now the LORD loved him, 25and He sent
word by the hand of Nathan the prophet: So
he[a] called his name Jedidiah,[b] because of the
LORD.

Rabbah Is Captured

26Now Joab fought against Rabbah of the
people of Ammon, and took the royal city.
27And Joab sent messengers to David, and
said, "I have fought against Rabbah, and I
have taken the city's water *supply.* 28Now
therefore, gather the rest of the people together and encamp against the city and take it,
lest I take the city and it be called after my
name." 29So David gathered all the people together and went to Rabbah, fought against it,
and took it. 30Then he took their king's crown
from his head. Its weight *was* a talent of gold,
with precious stones. And it was *set* on
David's head. Also he brought out the spoil of
the city in great abundance. 31And he brought
out the people who *were* in it, and put *them to*
work with saws and iron picks and iron axes,
and made them cross over to the brick works.
So he did to all the cities of the people of Ammon. Then David and all the people returned
to Jerusalem.

Amnon and Tamar

13 After this Absalom the son of David
had a lovely sister, whose name *was*
Tamar; and Amnon the son of David loved her.
2Amnon was so distressed over his sister
Tamar that he became sick; for she *was* a
virgin. And it was improper for Amnon to do
anything to her. 3But Amnon had a friend
whose name *was* Jonadab the son of Shimeah,
David's brother. Now Jonadab *was* a very
crafty man. 4And he said to him, "Why *are*
you, the king's son, becoming thinner day after day? Will you not tell me?"

Amnon said to him, "I love Tamar, my
brother Absalom's sister."

5So Jonadab said to him, "Lie down on your
bed and pretend to be ill. And when your father comes to see you, say to him, 'Please let
my sister Tamar come and give me food, and
prepare the food in my sight, that I may see *it*
and eat it from her hand.' " 6Then Amnon lay
down and pretended to be ill; and when the
king came to see him, Amnon said to the king,
"Please let Tamar my sister come and make a
couple of cakes for me in my sight, that I may
eat from her hand."

7And David sent home to Tamar, saying,
"Now go to your brother Amnon's house, and
prepare food for him." 8So Tamar went to her
brother Amnon's house; and he was lying
down. Then she took flour and kneaded *it,*
made cakes in his sight, and baked the cakes.
9And she took the pan and placed *them* out
before him, but he refused to eat. Then Amnon said, "Have everyone go out from me."
And they all went out from him. 10Then Amnon said to Tamar, "Bring the food into the
bedroom, that I may eat from your hand."
And Tamar took the cakes which she had
made, and brought *them* to Amnon her
brother in the bedroom. 11Now when she had
brought *them* to him to eat, he took hold of
her and said to her, "Come, lie with me, my
sister."

12But she answered him, "No, my brother,
do not force me, for no such thing should be

12:24 [a]Following Kethib, Septuagint, and Vulgate; Qere, a few Hebrew manuscripts, Syriac, and Targum read *she.* **12:25** [a]Qere, some Hebrew manuscripts, Syriac, and Targum read *she.* [b]Literally *Beloved of the LORD*

SOUL NOTE

Eternal Hope *(12:23)* After the death of David and Bathsheba's first son, David's only consolation was that eventually he would "go to him." While the child was alive, David had begged God to spare his life. When the child died, however, David was confident that the boy was with God and he would see him again. Christian parents who have faced the devastation of the death of a young child can take hope in David's faith that God will bring the little ones to Himself. **Topic: Death**

done in Israel. Do not do this disgraceful thing! 13And I, where could I take my shame? And as for you, you would be like one of the fools in Israel. Now therefore, please speak to the king; for he will not withhold me from you." 14However, he would not heed her voice; and being stronger than she, he forced her and lay with her.

15Then Amnon hated her exceedingly, so that the hatred with which he hated her *was* greater than the love with which he had loved her. And Amnon said to her, "Arise, be gone!"

16So she said to him, "No, indeed! This evil of sending me away *is* worse than the other that you did to me."

But he would not listen to her. 17Then he called his servant who attended him, and said, "Here! Put this *woman* out, away from me, and bolt the door behind her." 18Now she had on a robe of many colors, for the king's virgin daughters wore such apparel. And his servant put her out and bolted the door behind her.

19Then Tamar put ashes on her head, and tore her robe of many colors that *was* on her, and laid her hand on her head and went away crying bitterly. 20And Absalom her brother said to her, "Has Amnon your brother been with you? But now hold your peace, my sister. He *is* your brother; do not take this thing to heart." So Tamar remained desolate in her brother Absalom's house.

21But when King David heard of all these things, he was very angry. 22And Absalom spoke to his brother Amnon neither good nor bad. For Absalom hated Amnon, because he had forced his sister Tamar.

PERSONALITY PROFILE

Children Problems/ Trials

TAMAR—A LEGACY OF TRIALS

(2 SAMUEL 13)

The painful legacy of turmoil that David provoked by his sin with Bathsheba soon spread to other family members. David's children, Amnon and Tamar, were snared by the curse. Amnon acted out a sexual obsession with Tamar, his half sister, by conspiring with a friend to trick her into being alone with him. The trap worked. Tamar begged for mercy and desperately suggested an honorable solution of marriage to Amnon. Since they were half siblings, the arrangement was possible. In spite of her pleading, Amnon raped her.

Once he had abused her, Amnon shamefully rejected Tamar. She lived in disgrace as a desolate woman in her brother Absalom's house. The painful loneliness of her life was a trial she faced as part of a legacy in her family. For although David was aware of the tragedy unfolding in his family and got angry, he actually did nothing. Meanwhile, Tamar's brother Absalom festered in hatred and planned vengeance on Amnon. There was more than Tamar's honor at stake. Amnon's position as the firstborn son and likely heir to the throne certainly increased Absalom's desire to see him eliminated. Years later, Absalom lured Amnon away from the palace and killed him.

These trials could have been avoided. Even though David's heart was broken by the behavior of his children, he never tried to correct the injustices. Perhaps his own guilt and shame immobilized him. His denial and delay only let matters fester and worsen. The consequences were devastating.

The trials experienced by David's children speak volumes about David's own lack of self-control and his lack of parental discipline. Parents cannot insulate their children from all trials and disappointments, nor should they. Parents must, however, provide positive examples and positive discipline to help their children avoid some kinds of trials that they shouldn't have to face.

To Learn More: Turn to the article about children problems on pages 1222, 1223. See also the key passage note on children problems at James 1:27 on page 1644. Turn to the article about trials on pages 706, 707. See also the key passage note on trials at Psalm 34:18 on page 704.

Absalom Murders Amnon

23And it came to pass, after two full years, that Absalom had sheepshearers in Baal Hazor, which *is* near Ephraim; so Absalom invited all the king's sons. 24Then Absalom came to the king and said, "Kindly note, your servant has sheepshearers; please, let the king and his servants go with your servant."

25But the king said to Absalom, "No, my son, let us not all go now, lest we be a burden to you." Then he urged him, but he would not go; and he blessed him.

26Then Absalom said, "If not, please let my brother Amnon go with us."

And the king said to him, "Why should he go with you?" 27But Absalom urged him; so he let Amnon and all the king's sons go with him.

28Now Absalom had commanded his servants, saying, "Watch now, when Amnon's heart is merry with wine, and when I say to you, 'Strike Amnon!' then kill him. Do not be afraid. Have I not commanded you? Be courageous and valiant." 29So the servants of Absalom did to Amnon as Absalom had commanded. Then all the king's sons arose, and each one got on his mule and fled.

30And it came to pass, while they were on the way, that news came to David, saying, "Absalom has killed all the king's sons, and not one of them is left!" 31So the king arose and tore his garments and lay on the ground, and all his servants stood by with their clothes torn. 32Then Jonadab the son of Shimeah, David's brother, answered and said, "Let not my lord suppose they have killed all the young men, the king's sons, for only Amnon is dead. For by the command of Absalom this has been determined from the day that he forced his sister Tamar. 33Now therefore, let not my lord the king take the thing to his heart, to think that all the king's sons are dead. For only Amnon is dead."

Absalom Flees to Geshur

34Then Absalom fled. And the young man who was keeping watch lifted his eyes and looked, and there, many people were coming from the road on the hillside behind him.[a] 35And Jonadab said to the king, "Look, the king's sons are coming; as your servant said, so it is." 36So it was, as soon as he had finished speaking, that the king's sons indeed came, and they lifted up their voice and wept. Also the king and all his servants wept very bitterly.

37But Absalom fled and went to Talmai the son of Ammihud, king of Geshur. And *David* mourned for his son every day. 38So Absalom fled and went to Geshur, and was there three years. 39And King David[a] longed to go to[b] Absalom. For he had been comforted concerning Amnon, because he was dead.

Absalom Returns to Jerusalem

14 So Joab the son of Zeruiah perceived that the king's heart *was* concerned about Absalom. 2And Joab sent to Tekoa and brought from there a wise woman, and said to her, "Please pretend to be a mourner, and put on mourning apparel; do not anoint yourself with oil, but act like a woman who has been mourning a long time for the dead. 3Go to the king and speak to him in this manner." So Joab put the words in her mouth.

4And when the woman of Tekoa spoke[a] to the king, she fell on her face to the ground and prostrated herself, and said, "Help, O king!"

5Then the king said to her, "What troubles you?"

And she answered, "Indeed I *am* a widow, my husband is dead. 6Now your maidservant had two sons; and the two fought with each other in the field, and *there was* no one to part them, but the one struck the other and killed him. 7And now the whole family has risen up against your maidservant, and they said, 'Deliver him who struck his brother, that we may execute him for the life of his brother whom he killed; and we will destroy the heir also.' So they would extinguish my ember that is left, and leave to my husband *neither* name nor remnant on the earth."

8Then the king said to the woman, "Go to your house, and I will give orders concerning you."

9And the woman of Tekoa said to the king, "My lord, O king, *let* the iniquity *be* on me and on my father's house, and the king and his throne *be* guiltless."

13:34 [a]Septuagint adds *And the watchman went and told the king, and said, "I see men from the way of Horonaim, from the regions of the mountains."* **13:39** [a]Following Masoretic Text, Syriac, and Vulgate; Septuagint reads *the spirit of the king;* Targum reads *the soul of King David.* [b]Following Masoretic Text and Targum; Septuagint and Vulgate read *ceased to pursue after.*
14:4 [a]Many Hebrew manuscripts, Septuagint, Syriac, and Vulgate read *came.*

10 So the king said, "Whoever says *anything*
to you, bring him to me, and he shall not
touch you anymore."
11 Then she said, "Please let the king remember the LORD your God, and do not permit the
avenger of blood to destroy anymore, lest they
destroy my son."
And he said, "*As* the LORD lives, not one
hair of your son shall fall to the ground."
12 Therefore the woman said, "Please, let
your maidservant speak *another* word to my
lord the king."
And he said, "Say on."
13 So the woman said: "Why then have you
schemed such a thing against the people of
God? For the king speaks this thing as one
who is guilty, *in that* the king does not bring
his banished one home again. 14 For we will
surely die and *become* like water spilled on the
ground, which cannot be gathered up again.
Yet God does not take away a life; but He devises means, so that His banished ones are not
expelled from Him. 15 Now therefore, I have
come to speak of this thing to my lord the king
because the people have made me afraid. And
your maidservant said, 'I will now speak to
the king; it may be that the king will perform
the request of his maidservant. 16 For the king
will hear and deliver his maidservant from the
hand of the man *who would* destroy me and
my son together from the inheritance of God.'
17 Your maidservant said, 'The word of my lord
the king will now be comforting; for as the
angel of God, so *is* my lord the king in discerning good and evil. And may the LORD your God
be with you.' "
18 Then the king answered and said to the
woman, "Please do not hide from me anything
that I ask you."
And the woman said, "Please, let my lord
the king speak."
19 So the king said, "*Is* the hand of Joab with
you in all this?" And the woman answered
and said, "*As* you live, my lord the king, no
one can turn to the right hand or to the left
from anything that my lord the king has spoken. For your servant Joab commanded me,
and he put all these words in the mouth of
your maidservant. 20 To bring about this
change of affairs your servant Joab has done
this thing; but my lord *is* wise, according to
the wisdom of the angel of God, to know
everything that *is* in the earth."
21 And the king said to Joab, "All right, I have
granted this thing. Go therefore, bring back
the young man Absalom."
22 Then Joab fell to the ground on his face
and bowed himself, and thanked the king.
And Joab said, "Today your servant knows
that I have found favor in your sight, my lord,
O king, in that the king has fulfilled the request of his servant." 23 So Joab arose and
went to Geshur, and brought Absalom to Jerusalem. 24 And the king said, "Let him return to
his own house, but do not let him see my
face." So Absalom returned to his own house,
but did not see the king's face.

David Forgives Absalom

25 Now in all Israel there was no one who was
praised as much as Absalom for his good looks.
From the sole of his foot to the crown of his
head there was no blemish in him. 26 And when
he cut the hair of his head—at the end of every
year he cut *it* because it was heavy on him—
when he cut it, he weighed the hair of his head
at two hundred shekels according to the king's
standard. 27 To Absalom were born three sons,
and one daughter whose name *was* Tamar. She
was a woman of beautiful appearance.
28 And Absalom dwelt two full years in Jerusalem, but did not see the king's face. 29 Therefore Absalom sent for Joab, to send him to the
king, but he would not come to him. And
when he sent again the second time, he would
not come. 30 So he said to his servants, "See,
Joab's field is near mine, and he has barley
there; go and set it on fire." And Absalom's
servants set the field on fire.
31 Then Joab arose and came to Absalom's
house, and said to him, "Why have your servants set my field on fire?"
32 And Absalom answered Joab, "Look, I
sent to you, saying, 'Come here, so that I may
send you to the king, to say, "Why have I
come from Geshur? *It would be* better for me
to be there still." ' Now therefore, let me see
the king's face; but if there is iniquity in me,
let him execute me."
33 So Joab went to the king and told him.
And when he had called for Absalom, he came
to the king and bowed himself on his face to
the ground before the king. Then the king
kissed Absalom.

Absalom's Treason

15 After this it happened that Absalom
provided himself with chariots and

horses, and fifty men to run before him. [2]Now Absalom would rise early and stand beside the way to the gate. *So* it was, whenever anyone who had a lawsuit came to the king for a decision, that Absalom would call to him and say, "What city *are* you from?" And he would say, "Your servant *is* from such and such a tribe of Israel." [3]Then Absalom would say to him, "Look, your case *is* good and right; but *there is* no deputy of the king to hear you." [4]Moreover Absalom would say, "Oh, that I were made judge in the land, and everyone who has any suit or cause would come to me; then I would give him justice." [5]And *so* it was, whenever anyone came near to bow down to him, that he would put out his hand and take him and kiss him. [6]In this manner Absalom acted toward all Israel who came to the king for judgment. So Absalom stole the hearts of the men of Israel.

[7]Now it came to pass after forty[a] years that Absalom said to the king, "Please, let me go to Hebron and pay the vow which I made to the LORD. [8]For your servant took a vow while I dwelt at Geshur in Syria, saying, 'If the LORD indeed brings me back to Jerusalem, then I will serve the LORD.' "

[9]And the king said to him, "Go in peace." So he arose and went to Hebron.

[10]Then Absalom sent spies throughout all the tribes of Israel, saying, "As soon as you hear the sound of the trumpet, then you shall say, 'Absalom reigns in Hebron!' " [11]And with Absalom went two hundred men invited from Jerusalem, and they went along innocently and did not know anything. [12]Then Absalom sent for Ahithophel the Gilonite, David's counselor, from his city—from Giloh—while he offered sacrifices. And the conspiracy grew strong, for the people with Absalom continually increased in number.

David Escapes from Jerusalem

[13]Now a messenger came to David, saying, "The hearts of the men of Israel are with Absalom."

[14]So David said to all his servants who *were* with him at Jerusalem, "Arise, and let us flee, or we shall not escape from Absalom. Make haste to depart, lest he overtake us suddenly and bring disaster upon us, and strike the city with the edge of the sword."

[15]And the king's servants said to the king, "We *are* your servants, *ready to do* whatever my lord the king commands." [16]Then the king went out with all his household after him. But the king left ten women, concubines, to keep the house. [17]And the king went out with all the people after him, and stopped at the outskirts. [18]Then all his servants passed before him; and all the Cherethites, all the Pelethites, and all the Gittites, six hundred men who had followed him from Gath, passed before the king.

[19]Then the king said to Ittai the Gittite, "Why are you also going with us? Return and remain with the king. For you *are* a foreigner and also an exile from your own place. [20]In fact, you came *only* yesterday. Should I make you wander up and down with us today, since I go I know not where? Return, and take your brethren back. Mercy and truth *be* with you."

[21]But Ittai answered the king and said, "*As* the LORD lives, and *as* my lord the king lives, surely in whatever place my lord the king shall be, whether in death or life, even there also your servant will be."

[22]So David said to Ittai, "Go, and cross over." Then Ittai the Gittite and all his men and all the little ones who *were* with him

---

15:7 [a]Septuagint manuscripts, Syriac, and Josephus read *four.*

SOUL NOTE

One Person Can Forgive *(14:33)* Despite his pain and anger, David "kissed Absalom," expressing his love and forgiveness. Despite all that Absalom had done, David allowed for the possibility of reconciliation by forgiving his son. Absalom, however, had no tears, no repentance, no change of heart. Indeed, Absalom would eventually try to take his father's throne (15:10). One person can forgive, but it takes two to reconcile. Forgiveness does not guarantee reconciliation. Forgiveness, however, does put salve on those who are willing to let go of the hurt and wrongs done by others. **Topic: Forgiveness**

THE DISCONNECTED GENERATION

JOSH MCDOWELL

(2 Samuel 15)

"I'm so lonely I can't stand it. I want to be special to somebody, but there's nobody who cares about me. I can't remember anybody ever touching me, or smiling at me, or wanting to be with me. I feel so empty inside."

"It's like I have this really heavy heart and this burden on my back, but I don't know what it is. There's something in me that makes me want to cry, and I don't even know what it is."

Hear the words of teens—the outstanding representatives of the "disconnected generation." They are part of the population group referred to as the Echo Boomers, born between 1977 and 1994. Primarily the offspring of the Baby Boomer generation, today's teenage population is over 30 million strong. They are perhaps the richest, most populous, best-educated, and most physically fit generation in history. Kids are growing up in a prosperous society with unprecedented career opportunities and access to virtually limitless information. And yet, more than any other generation before theirs, they feel disconnected. Even kids from good Christian homes feel alienated from their parents, from adults in general, and from society as a whole. Lacking a sense of personal identity, today's teens feel adrift in a hostile world.

ADOLESCENCE MEANS CHANGE

When children enter adolescence, sometimes it seems like a metamorphosis gone bad. In some ways, it appears that a beautiful butterfly is being transformed into an ugly caterpillar. Almost overnight, these cute, cherubic, charming little kids who were a delight to be around turn into erratic, moody, and often unruly teenagers. One minute they are all smiles, and the next minute they blow their stack or stomp away sullen and silent. Once-perfect kids can be forgetful, irresponsible, impulsive, contradictory, insolent, and confused—sometimes all in the same day!

A lot of young people are good kids whose priorities for school, work, money, or use of time are a little out of whack—or at least they don't match parents' priorities for them. They are no longer quick to obey and easy to control. In fact, parents wonder and worry at times if they will soon be totally beyond their control.

RESPONDING TO THE CHANGE

So, how do parents respond to their emerging teenagers? In a genuinely sincere but misguided attempt to help, many think the primary answer to teenager angst and struggle is more structure. More rules. So they lay down the law and tighten the screws. Assuming that their primary job is to fix the problem, correct the misbehavior, enforce the rules, or right the wrong, their well-meaning efforts often leave kids feeling more disconnected from their own families.

Clearly, adults must provide clear guidance and hold their children accountable for their actions even when they feel confused and disconnected. Teens need to follow certain rules even when they think they have the right to make up their own rules. But here is the critical question: How do parents provide appropriate rules and guidelines for children without prompting them to disconnect relationally?

The answer relates directly to how the rules are presented. Parents must be challenged to present rules in the context of loving relationships. Biblical principles and personal experience with youth show that young people do not respond to rules; they respond to relationships. Two formulas illustrate the contrast:

Rules – Relationships = Rebellion
Rules + Relationships = Response

The real challenge is learning to enter each young person's sometimes complex and confusing world and make a relational connection at a deep emotional level. If kids perceive that their parents are more concerned about the rules than they are about them, the kids will be tempted to disregard the rules. When kids know that they are more important to their parents than the rules—that parents love them no matter what they do or do not do—they are much more likely to follow the guidelines. The difference is a relational context for the rules that govern a family.

Notice how important "relationship" was to God. Speaking for God, Moses said, "And now, Israel, what does the LORD your God require of you, but . . . to keep the commandments of the LORD and His statutes which I command you today for your good?" (Deut. 10:12, 13). As rebellious as Israel was at times, God always treated them like a loving Father, doing everything for their good. The Ten Commandments were given as a safeguard and a blessing, not a burden. The Law was God's loving effort to protect and provide for His people.

Many adults believe that the rules and regulations they lay down for their children are "for their own good." But what is often missing is the relational factor. Telling kids, "I'm doing this for your own good," will not cut it if they seldom see or hear unconditional love through time, attention, and care. Rules without relationship lead to a relational disconnect, which prompts rebellion. But rules within a loving relationship usually lead to a positive response.

Not all children will rebel; many will rebel, but in varying degrees. Adolescence is a time of discovering one's individuality and what God is preparing for each teenager's future. It is a time of uncertainty, wonder about the future, desire to be cared for at home while at the same time wanting (and needing) to eventually be out on their own. With love, open communication, and constant prayer, parents can weather these turbulent times, preparing their children to be responsible, God-honoring adults.

FURTHER MEDITATION:

Other passages to study about the issues of adolescent problems include:

- ➢ Deuteronomy 6:1–25
- ➢ Proverbs 3:12; 29:17
- ➢ Ecclesiastes 12:1
- ➢ Matthew 7:7–12
- ➢ Luke 15:11–32
- ➢ Ephesians 6:4

To Learn More: Turn to the key passage note on adolescent problems at Luke 15:17, 18 on page 1349. See also the personality profile of Eli's sons on page 346.

crossed over. 23And all the country wept with a loud voice, and all the people crossed over. The king himself also crossed over the Brook Kidron, and all the people crossed over toward the way of the wilderness.

24There was Zadok also, and all the Levites with him, bearing the ark of the covenant of God. And they set down the ark of God, and Abiathar went up until all the people had finished crossing over from the city. 25Then the king said to Zadok, "Carry the ark of God back into the city. If I find favor in the eyes of the LORD, He will bring me back and show me *both* it and His dwelling place. 26But if He says thus: 'I have no delight in you,' here I am, let Him do to me as seems good to Him." 27The king also said to Zadok the priest, "*Are* you *not* a seer? Return to the city in peace, and your two sons with you, Ahimaaz your son, and Jonathan the son of Abiathar. 28See, I will wait in the plains of the wilderness until word comes from you to inform me." 29Therefore Zadok and Abiathar carried the ark of God back to Jerusalem. And they remained there.

30So David went up by the Ascent of the *Mount of* Olives, and wept as he went up; and he had his head covered and went barefoot. And all the people who *were* with him covered their heads and went up, weeping as they went up. 31Then *someone* told David, saying, "Ahithophel *is* among the conspirators with Absalom." And David said, "O LORD, I pray, turn the counsel of Ahithophel into foolishness!"

32Now it happened when David had come to the top *of the mountain,* where he worshiped God—there was Hushai the Archite coming to meet him with his robe torn and dust on his head. 33David said to him, "If you go on with me, then you will become a burden to me. 34But if you return to the city, and say to Absalom, 'I will be your servant, O king; *as* I *was* your father's servant previously, so I *will* now also *be* your servant,' then you may defeat the counsel of Ahithophel for me. 35And *do* you not *have* Zadok and Abiathar the priests with you there? Therefore it will be *that* whatever you hear from the king's house, you shall tell to Zadok and Abiathar the priests. 36Indeed *they have* there with them their two sons, Ahimaaz, Zadok's *son,* and Jonathan, Abiathar's *son;* and by them you shall send me everything you hear."

37So Hushai, David's friend, went into the city. And Absalom came into Jerusalem.

MEPHIBOSHETH'S SERVANT

16 When David was a little past the top *of the mountain,* there was Ziba the servant of Mephibosheth, who met him with a couple of saddled donkeys, and on them two hundred *loaves* of bread, one hundred clusters of raisins, one hundred summer fruits, and a skin of wine. 2And the king said to Ziba, "What do you mean to do with these?"

So Ziba said, "The donkeys *are* for the king's household to ride on, the bread and summer fruit for the young men to eat, and the wine for those who are faint in the wilderness to drink."

3Then the king said, "And where *is* your master's son?"

And Ziba said to the king, "Indeed he is staying in Jerusalem, for he said, 'Today the house of Israel will restore the kingdom of my father to me.' "

4So the king said to Ziba, "Here, all that *belongs* to Mephibosheth *is* yours."

And Ziba said, "I humbly bow before you, *that* I may find favor in your sight, my lord, O king!"

SOUL NOTE

Do Them a Favor *(15:14)* David had not dealt decisively with Amnon's rape of Tamar, so Absalom had taken matters into his own hands. David did not deal decisively with Absalom's murder of Amnon, nor with Absalom's treason. Absalom was used to getting his own way without facing consequences, and had seen the same pattern with the rest of his siblings. Absalom's story pictures an undisciplined child becoming an undisciplined adult. When parents discipline their children, they do so knowing that they are doing their children a favor—saving them from the tragic consequences of an undisciplined life. **Topic: Child Discipline**

Shimei Curses David

5Now when King David came to Bahurim, there was a man from the family of the house of Saul, whose name *was* Shimei the son of Gera, coming from there. He came out, cursing continuously as he came. 6And he threw stones at David and at all the servants of King David. And all the people and all the mighty men *were* on his right hand and on his left. 7Also Shimei said thus when he cursed: "Come out! Come out! You bloodthirsty man, you rogue! 8The LORD has brought upon you all the blood of the house of Saul, in whose place you have reigned; and the LORD has delivered the kingdom into the hand of Absalom your son. So now you *are caught* in your own evil, because you are a bloodthirsty man!"

9Then Abishai the son of Zeruiah said to the king, "Why should this dead dog curse my lord the king? Please, let me go over and take off his head!"

10But the king said, "What have I to do with you, you sons of Zeruiah? So let him curse, because the LORD has said to him, 'Curse David.' Who then shall say, 'Why have you done so?' "

11And David said to Abishai and all his servants, "See how my son who came from my own body seeks my life. How much more now *may this* Benjamite? Let him alone, and let him curse; for so the LORD has ordered him. 12It may be that the LORD will look on my affliction,[a] and that the LORD will repay me with good for his cursing this day." 13And as David and his men went along the road, Shimei went along the hillside opposite him and cursed as he went, threw stones at him and kicked up dust. 14Now the king and all the people who *were* with him became weary; so they refreshed themselves there.

The Advice of Ahithophel

15Meanwhile Absalom and all the people, the men of Israel, came to Jerusalem; and Ahithophel *was* with him. 16And so it was, when Hushai the Archite, David's friend, came to Absalom, that Hushai said to Absalom, "*Long* live the king! *Long* live the king!"

17So Absalom said to Hushai, "*Is* this your loyalty to your friend? Why did you not go with your friend?"

18And Hushai said to Absalom, "No, but whom the LORD and this people and all the men of Israel choose, his I will be, and with him I will remain. 19Furthermore, whom should I serve? *Should I* not *serve* in the presence of his son? As I have served in your father's presence, so will I be in your presence."

20Then Absalom said to Ahithophel, "Give advice as to what we should do."

21And Ahithophel said to Absalom, "Go in to your father's concubines, whom he has left to keep the house; and all Israel will hear that you are abhorred by your father. Then the hands of all who are with you will be strong." 22So they pitched a tent for Absalom on the top of the house, and Absalom went in to his father's concubines in the sight of all Israel.

23Now the advice of Ahithophel, which he gave in those days, *was* as if one had inquired at the oracle of God. So *was* all the advice of Ahithophel both with David and with Absalom.

17 Moreover Ahithophel said to Absalom, "Now let me choose twelve thousand men, and I will arise and pursue David tonight. 2I will come upon him while he *is* weary and weak, and make him afraid. And all the people who *are* with him will flee, and I will strike only the king. 3Then I will bring back all the people to you. When all return except the man whom you seek, all the people will be at peace." 4And the saying pleased Absalom and all the elders of Israel.

The Advice of Hushai

5Then Absalom said, "Now call Hushai the Archite also, and let us hear what he says too." 6And when Hushai came to Absalom, Absalom spoke to him, saying, "Ahithophel has spoken in this manner. Shall we do as he says? If not, speak up."

7So Hushai said to Absalom: "The advice that Ahithophel has given *is* not good at this time. 8For," said Hushai, "you know your father and his men, that they *are* mighty men, and they *are* enraged in their minds, like a bear robbed of her cubs in the field; and your father *is* a man of war, and will not camp with the people. 9Surely by now he is hidden in some pit, or in some *other* place. And it will be, when some of them are overthrown at the first, that whoever hears *it* will say, 'There is a

---

16:12 [a]Following Kethib, Septuagint, Syriac, and Vulgate; Qere reads *my eyes;* Targum reads *tears of my eyes.*

slaughter among the people who follow Absalom.' 10And even he *who is* valiant, whose heart *is* like the heart of a lion, will melt completely. For all Israel knows that your father *is* a mighty man, and *those* who *are* with him *are* valiant men. 11Therefore I advise that all Israel be fully gathered to you, from Dan to Beersheba, like the sand that *is* by the sea for multitude, and that you go to battle in person. 12So we will come upon him in some place where he may be found, and we will fall on him as the dew falls on the ground. And of him and all the men who *are* with him there shall not be left so much as one. 13Moreover, if he has withdrawn into a city, then all Israel shall bring ropes to that city; and we will pull it into the river, until there is not one small stone found there."

14So Absalom and all the men of Israel said, "The advice of Hushai the Archite *is* better than the advice of Ahithophel." For the LORD had purposed to defeat the good advice of Ahithophel, to the intent that the LORD might bring disaster on Absalom.

Hushai Warns David to Escape

15Then Hushai said to Zadok and Abiathar the priests, "Thus and so Ahithophel advised Absalom and the elders of Israel, and thus and so I have advised. 16Now therefore, send quickly and tell David, saying, 'Do not spend this night in the plains of the wilderness, but speedily cross over, lest the king and all the people who *are* with him be swallowed up.' " 17Now Jonathan and Ahimaaz stayed at En Rogel, for they dared not be seen coming into the city; so a female servant would come and tell them, and they would go and tell King David. 18Nevertheless a lad saw them, and told Absalom. But both of them went away quickly and came to a man's house in Bahurim, who had a well in his court; and they went down into it. 19Then the woman took and spread a covering over the well's mouth, and spread ground grain on it; and the thing was not known. 20And when Absalom's servants came to the woman at the house, they said, "Where *are* Ahimaaz and Jonathan?"

So the woman said to them, "They have gone over the water brook."

And when they had searched and could not find *them,* they returned to Jerusalem. 21Now it came to pass, after they had departed, that they came up out of the well and went and told King David, and said to David, "Arise and cross over the water quickly. For thus has Ahithophel advised against you." 22So David and all the people who *were* with him arose and crossed over the Jordan. By morning light not one of them was left who had not gone over the Jordan.

23Now when Ahithophel saw that his advice was not followed, he saddled a donkey, and arose and went home to his house, to his city. Then he put his household in order, and hanged himself, and died; and he was buried in his father's tomb.

24Then David went to Mahanaim. And Absalom crossed over the Jordan, he and all the men of Israel with him. 25And Absalom made Amasa captain of the army instead of Joab. This Amasa *was* the son of a man whose name *was* Jithra,[a] an Israelite,[b] who had gone in to Abigail the daughter of Nahash, sister of Zeruiah, Joab's mother. 26So Israel and Absalom encamped in the land of Gilead.

27Now it happened, when David had come to Mahanaim, that Shobi the son of Nahash from Rabbah of the people of Ammon, Machir the son of Ammiel from Lo Debar, and Barzillai the Gileadite from Rogelim, 28brought beds and basins, earthen vessels and wheat, barley and flour, parched *grain* and beans, lentils and parched *seeds,* 29honey and curds, sheep and cheese of the herd, for David and the people who *were* with him to eat. For they said, "The people are hungry and weary and thirsty in the wilderness."

Absalom's Defeat and Death

18 And David numbered the people who *were* with him, and set captains of thousands and captains of hundreds over them. 2Then David sent out one third of the people under the hand of Joab, one third under the hand of Abishai the son of Zeruiah, Joab's brother, and one third under the hand of Ittai the Gittite. And the king said to the people, "I also will surely go out with you myself."

3But the people answered, "You shall not go

17:25 [a]Spelled *Jether* in 1 Chronicles 2:17 and elsewhere [b]Following Masoretic Text, some manuscripts of the Septuagint, and Targum; some manuscripts of the Septuagint read *Ishmaelite* (compare 1 Chronicles 2:17); Vulgate reads *of Jezrael.*

out! For if we flee away, they will not care
about us; nor if half of us die, will they care
about us. But *you are* worth ten thousand of
us now. For you are now more help to us in
the city."
4Then the king said to them, "Whatever
seems best to you I will do." So the king stood
beside the gate, and all the people went out by
hundreds and by thousands. 5Now the king
had commanded Joab, Abishai, and Ittai, saying, "*Deal* gently for my sake with the young
man Absalom." And all the people heard
when the king gave all the captains orders
concerning Absalom.
6So the people went out into the field of battle against Israel. And the battle was in the
woods of Ephraim. 7The people of Israel were
overthrown there before the servants of David, and a great slaughter of twenty thousand
took place there that day. 8For the battle there
was scattered over the face of the whole countryside, and the woods devoured more people
that day than the sword devoured.
9Then Absalom met the servants of David.
Absalom rode on a mule. The mule went under the thick boughs of a great terebinth tree,
and his head caught in the terebinth; so he
was left hanging between heaven and earth.
And the mule which *was* under him went on.
10Now a certain man saw *it* and told Joab, and
said, "I just saw Absalom hanging in a terebinth tree!"

PERSONALITY PROFILE

DAVID AND ABSALOM— A CRISIS IN THE MAKING

(2 SAMUEL 18:5–19)

Before he died, David had the crushing experience of watching at least three of his sons destroy their own lives. Two of them tried to replace their own father as king by force.

The third-born son, Absalom, attempted the first coup. He paid for his temporary success with his life. David loved Absalom deeply, but failed to discipline his son or give him wise direction. He stood by helplessly after Absalom killed his half brother Amnon and then fled the country. When he finally returned, Absalom suffered no consequences for his past behavior.

David's passivity allowed Absalom to shape their relationship. He bluffed his father into forgiving him. In fact, he began to lay the groundwork for taking over the throne. He used his considerable charm and "stole the hearts of the men of Israel" (2 Sam. 15:6).

Once he had gathered key allies and the support of the people, Absalom rebelled. David did not resist his son's revolution; instead, he fled Jerusalem. Eventually, however, the superior military strategy of David and his generals defeated Absalom's forces. Even then, David's intention was to spare his son. But Joab, David's chief of staff, killed the traitor.

Although the crisis for the kingdom was over, David mourned Absalom, a son whose undisciplined life had drifted from crisis to crisis. David remained silent when he should have intervened. Fear of losing his son clouded David's ability to see that his son was already lost. David's love was so full of fear that it unintentionally brought about the very thing David feared most.

Some crises come into our lives from situations beyond our control. In those situations, we trust in God, knowing that He is "a very present help in trouble" (Ps. 46:1). Some crises come from unwise choices that we make. In those cases, God is still a "very present help," but He may not take away the natural consequences of those choices. In a crisis, turn to God. Seek what He may want to teach you through it. Change what needs to change, then trust God for the rest.

To Learn More: Turn to the article about crises on pages 1194, 1195. See also the key passage note at Psalm 46:1 on page 717.

11So Joab said to the man who told him, "You just saw *him!* And why did you not strike him there to the ground? I would have given you ten *shekels* of silver and a belt."

12But the man said to Joab, "Though I were to receive a thousand *shekels* of silver in my hand, I would not raise my hand against the king's son. For in our hearing the king commanded you and Abishai and Ittai, saying, 'Beware lest anyone *touch* the young man Absalom!'[a] 13Otherwise I would have dealt falsely against my own life. For there is nothing hidden from the king, and you yourself would have set yourself against *me.*"

14Then Joab said, "I cannot linger with you." And he took three spears in his hand and thrust them through Absalom's heart, while he was *still* alive in the midst of the terebinth tree. 15And ten young men who bore Joab's armor surrounded Absalom, and struck and killed him.

16So Joab blew the trumpet, and the people returned from pursuing Israel. For Joab held back the people. 17And they took Absalom and cast him into a large pit in the woods, and laid a very large heap of stones over him. Then all Israel fled, everyone to his tent.

18Now Absalom in his lifetime had taken and set up a pillar for himself, which *is* in the King's Valley. For he said, "I have no son to keep my name in remembrance." He called the pillar after his own name. And to this day it is called Absalom's Monument.

David Hears of Absalom's Death

19Then Ahimaaz the son of Zadok said, "Let me run now and take the news to the king, how the LORD has avenged him of his enemies."

20And Joab said to him, "You shall not take the news this day, for you shall take the news another day. But today you shall take no news, because the king's son is dead." 21Then Joab said to the Cushite, "Go, tell the king what you have seen." So the Cushite bowed himself to Joab and ran.

22And Ahimaaz the son of Zadok said again to Joab, "But whatever happens, please let me also run after the Cushite."

So Joab said, "Why will you run, my son, since you have no news ready?"

23"But whatever happens," *he said,* "let me run."

So he said to him, "Run." Then Ahimaaz ran by way of the plain, and outran the Cushite.

24Now David was sitting between the two gates. And the watchman went up to the roof over the gate, to the wall, lifted his eyes and looked, and there was a man, running alone. 25Then the watchman cried out and told the king. And the king said, "If he *is* alone, *there is* news in his mouth." And he came rapidly and drew near.

26Then the watchman saw *another* man running, and the watchman called to the gatekeeper and said, "There is *another* man, running alone!"

And the king said, "He also brings news."

27So the watchman said, "I think the running of the first is like the running of Ahimaaz the son of Zadok."

And the king said, "He *is* a good man, and comes with good news."

28So Ahimaaz called out and said to the king, "All is well!" Then he bowed down with his face to the earth before the king, and said, "Blessed *be* the LORD your God, who has delivered up the men who raised their hand against my lord the king!"

29The king said, "Is the young man Absalom safe?"

Ahimaaz answered, "When Joab sent the king's servant and *me* your servant, I saw a great tumult, but I did not know what *it was about.*"

30And the king said, "Turn aside *and* stand here." So he turned aside and stood still.

31Just then the Cushite came, and the Cushite said, "There is good news, my lord the king! For the LORD has avenged you this day of all those who rose against you."

32And the king said to the Cushite, "Is the young man Absalom safe?"

So the Cushite answered, "May the enemies of my lord the king, and all who rise against you to do harm, be like *that* young man!"

David's Mourning for Absalom

33Then the king was deeply moved, and went up to the chamber over the gate, and wept. And as he went, he said thus: "O my son Absalom—my son, my son Absalom—if only I had died in your place! O Absalom my son, my son!"

18:12 [a]The ancient versions read *'Protect the young man Absalom for me!'*

19 And Joab was told, "Behold, the king
is weeping and mourning for Absa-
lom." 2So the victory that day was *turned* into
mourning for all the people. For the people
heard it said that day, "The king is grieved for
his son." 3And the people stole back into the
city that day, as people who are ashamed steal
away when they flee in battle. 4But the king
covered his face, and the king cried out with a
loud voice, "O my son Absalom! O Absalom,
my son, my son!"
5Then Joab came into the house to the king,
and said, "Today you have disgraced all your
servants who today have saved your life, the
lives of your sons and daughters, the lives of
your wives and the lives of your concubines,
6in that you love your enemies and hate your
friends. For you have declared today that you
regard neither princes nor servants; for today I
perceive that if Absalom had lived and all of
us had died today, then it would have pleased
you well. 7Now therefore, arise, go out and
speak comfort to your servants. For I swear by
the LORD, if you do not go out, not one will
stay with you this night. And that will be
worse for you than all the evil that has befallen you from your youth until now." 8Then
the king arose and sat in the gate. And they
told all the people, saying, "There is the king,
sitting in the gate." So all the people came before the king.
For everyone of Israel had fled to his tent.

DAVID RETURNS TO JERUSALEM

9Now all the people were in a dispute
throughout all the tribes of Israel, saying,
"The king saved us from the hand of our enemies, he delivered us from the hand of the
Philistines, and now he has fled from the land
because of Absalom. 10But Absalom, whom
we anointed over us, has died in battle. Now
therefore, why do you say nothing about
bringing back the king?"
11So King David sent to Zadok and Abiathar
the priests, saying, "Speak to the elders of Judah, saying, 'Why are you the last to bring the
king back to his house, since the words of all
Israel have come to the king, to his *very*
house? 12You *are* my brethren, you *are* my
bone and my flesh. Why then are you the last
to bring back the king?' 13And say to Amasa,
'*Are* you not my bone and my flesh? God do so
to me, and more also, if you are not commander of the army before me continually in
place of Joab.' " 14So he swayed the hearts of
all the men of Judah, just as *the heart of* one
man, so that they sent *this word* to the king:
"Return, you and all your servants!"
15Then the king returned and came to the
Jordan. And Judah came to Gilgal, to go to
meet the king, to escort the king across the
Jordan. 16And Shimei the son of Gera, a Benjamite, who *was* from Bahurim, hurried and
came down with the men of Judah to meet
King David. 17*There were* a thousand men of
Benjamin with him, and Ziba the servant of
the house of Saul, and his fifteen sons and his
twenty servants with him; and they went over
the Jordan before the king. 18Then a ferryboat
went across to carry over the king's household, and to do what he thought good.

DAVID'S MERCY TO SHIMEI

Now Shimei the son of Gera fell down before the king when he had crossed the Jordan.
19Then he said to the king, "Do not let my lord
impute iniquity to me, or remember what
wrong your servant did on the day that my
lord the king left Jerusalem, that the king
should take *it* to heart. 20For I, your servant,
know that I have sinned. Therefore here I am,
the first to come today of all the house of Joseph to go down to meet my lord the king."
21But Abishai the son of Zeruiah answered
and said, "Shall not Shimei be put to death for
this, because he cursed the LORD's anointed?"
22And David said, "What have I to do with
you, you sons of Zeruiah, that you should be
adversaries to me today? Shall any man be put
to death today in Israel? For do I not know that
today I *am* king over Israel?" 23Therefore the
king said to Shimei, "You shall not die." And
the king swore to him.

DAVID AND MEPHIBOSHETH MEET

24Now Mephibosheth the son of Saul came
down to meet the king. And he had not cared
for his feet, nor trimmed his mustache, nor
washed his clothes, from the day the king departed until the day he returned in peace. 25So
it was, when he had come to Jerusalem to
meet the king, that the king said to him, "Why
did you not go with me, Mephibosheth?"
26And he answered, "My lord, O king, my
servant deceived me. For your servant said, 'I
will saddle a donkey for myself, that I may
ride on it and go to the king,' because your
servant *is* lame. 27And he has slandered your

servant to my lord the king, but my lord the
king *is* like the angel of God. Therefore do
what is good in your eyes. 28For all my father's
house were but dead men before my lord the
king. Yet you set your servant among those
who eat at your own table. Therefore what
right have I still to cry out anymore to the
king?"
29So the king said to him, "Why do you
speak anymore of your matters? I have said,
'You and Ziba divide the land.' "
30Then Mephibosheth said to the king,
"Rather, let him take it all, inasmuch as my
lord the king has come back in peace to his
own house."

DAVID'S KINDNESS TO BARZILLAI

31And Barzillai the Gileadite came down
from Rogelim and went across the Jordan with
the king, to escort him across the Jordan. 32Now
Barzillai was a very aged man, eighty years
old. And he had provided the king with supplies while he stayed at Mahanaim, for he *was*
a very rich man. 33And the king said to Barzillai, "Come across with me, and I will provide
for you while you are with me in Jerusalem."
34But Barzillai said to the king, "How long
have I to live, that I should go up with the king
to Jerusalem? 35I *am* today eighty years old.
Can I discern between the good and bad? Can
your servant taste what I eat or what I drink?
Can I hear any longer the voice of singing men
and singing women? Why then should your
servant be a further burden to my lord the
king? 36Your servant will go a little way across
the Jordan with the king. And why should the
king repay me *with* such a reward? 37Please let
your servant turn back again, that I may die in
my own city, near the grave of my father and
mother. But here is your servant Chimham; let
him cross over with my lord the king, and do
for him what seems good to you."

PERSONALITY PROFILE

Restoration

DAVID RESTORED

(2 SAMUEL 19:9–43)

When the Scriptures report that David was a man after God's own heart, the implication is not that he was perfect or without sin. David proved himself capable of shocking sinfulness.

He lied, lusted, deceived others, committed adultery, murdered someone who trusted him, neglected his family, and failed as a father. He willfully disobeyed God. He suffered deeply as a result of his transgressions.

Then why did God have such a high regard for this all-too-fallible king? David was a humble man—approachable, merciful, just in his rulings, repentant in spirit, and faithful to God. He had a deep confidence in God's grace and mercy. He was assured that God's good plans included both himself and the nation of Israel.

When confronted with his sins, David did not hesitate to repent. His sins were terrible, but he did not persist in them. Even when the way back to fellowship with God was paved with pain, David readily returned. That was the heart for God that endeared David to his Maker.

Even after losing his kingdom to his son Absalom, David's confidence remained fixed on God. He understood that much of the chaos in his life was self-inflicted. He did not cut himself off from God's grace. He also accepted the restoration of the kingdom that God accomplished on David's behalf. He understood God had a large plan, and that David's family was part of it. David's heart for God was a lasting heritage in the lineage of Jesus Christ. The term "Son of David" (Matt. 1:1) by which Jesus identified Himself, offers a timeless tribute to the depth and length of God's restoration. The Son of God was also the Son of David. No one is beyond God's reach or too lost for His grace.

To Learn More: Turn to the article about restoration on pages 1412, 1413. See also the key passage note at Galatians 6:1–5 on page 1543.

38 And the king answered, "Chimham shall cross over with me, and I will do for him what seems good to you. Now whatever you request of me, I will do for you." 39 Then all the people went over the Jordan. And when the king had crossed over, the king kissed Barzillai and blessed him, and he returned to his own place.

The Quarrel About the King

40 Now the king went on to Gilgal, and Chimham[a] went on with him. And all the people of Judah escorted the king, and also half the people of Israel. 41 Just then all the men of Israel came to the king, and said to the king, "Why have our brethren, the men of Judah, stolen you away and brought the king, his household, and all David's men with him across the Jordan?"

42 So all the men of Judah answered the men of Israel, "Because the king *is* a close relative of ours. Why then are you angry over this matter? Have we ever eaten at the king's *expense?* Or has he given us any gift?"

43 And the men of Israel answered the men of Judah, and said, "We have ten shares in the king; therefore we also have more *right* to David than you. Why then do you despise us—were we not the first to advise bringing back our king?"

Yet the words of the men of Judah were fiercer than the words of the men of Israel.

The Rebellion of Sheba

20 And there happened to be there a rebel,[a] whose name *was* Sheba the son of Bichri, a Benjamite. And he blew a trumpet, and said:

"We have no share in David,
Nor do we have inheritance in the son of Jesse;
Every man to his tents, O Israel!"

2 So every man of Israel deserted David, *and* followed Sheba the son of Bichri. But the men of Judah, from the Jordan as far as Jerusalem, remained loyal to their king.

3 Now David came to his house at Jerusalem. And the king took the ten women, his concubines whom he had left to keep the house, and put them in seclusion and supported them, but did not go in to them. So they were shut up to the day of their death, living in widowhood.

4 And the king said to Amasa, "Assemble the men of Judah for me within three days, and be present here yourself." 5 So Amasa went to assemble *the men of* Judah. But he delayed longer than the set time which David had appointed him. 6 And David said to Abishai, "Now Sheba the son of Bichri will do us more harm than Absalom. Take your lord's servants and pursue him, lest he find for himself fortified cities, and escape us." 7 So Joab's men, with the Cherethites, the Pelethites, and all the mighty men, went out after him. And they went out of Jerusalem to pursue Sheba the son of Bichri. 8 When they *were* at the large stone which *is* in Gibeon, Amasa came before them. Now Joab was dressed in battle armor; on it was a belt *with* a sword fastened in its sheath at his hips; and as he was going forward, it fell out. 9 Then Joab said to Amasa, "*Are* you in health, my brother?" And Joab took Amasa by the beard with his right hand to kiss him. 10 But Amasa did not notice the sword that *was* in Joab's hand. And he struck him with it in the stomach, and his entrails poured out on the ground; and he did not *strike* him again. Thus he died.

Then Joab and Abishai his brother pursued Sheba the son of Bichri. 11 Meanwhile one of Joab's men stood near Amasa, and said, "Whoever favors Joab and whoever *is* for David—follow Joab!" 12 But Amasa wallowed in *his* blood in the middle of the highway. And when the man saw that all the people stood still, he moved Amasa from the highway to the field and threw a garment over him, when he saw that everyone who came upon him halted. 13 When he was removed from the highway, all the people went on after Joab to pursue Sheba the son of Bichri.

14 And he went through all the tribes of Israel to Abel and Beth Maachah and all the Berites. So they were gathered together and also went after *Sheba.*[a] 15 Then they came and besieged him in Abel of Beth Maachah; and they cast up a siege mound against the city, and it stood by the rampart. And all the people who *were* with Joab battered the wall to throw it down.

16 Then a wise woman cried out from the

19:40 [a]Masoretic Text reads *Chimhan.*
20:1 [a]Literally *man of Belial* **20:14** [a]Literally *him*

city, "Hear, hear! Please say to Joab, 'Come nearby, that I may speak with you.' " 17When he had come near to her, the woman said, "*Are* you Joab?"

He answered, "I *am*."

Then she said to him, "Hear the words of your maidservant."

And he answered, "I am listening."

18So she spoke, saying, "They used to talk in former times, saying, 'They shall surely seek *guidance* at Abel,' and so they would end *disputes.* 19I *am among the* peaceable *and* faithful in Israel. You seek to destroy a city and a mother in Israel. Why would you swallow up the inheritance of the LORD?"

20And Joab answered and said, "Far be it, far be it from me, that I should swallow up or destroy! 21That *is* not so. But a man from the mountains of Ephraim, Sheba the son of Bichri by name, has raised his hand against the king, against David. Deliver him only, and I will depart from the city."

So the woman said to Joab, "Watch, his head will be thrown to you over the wall." 22Then the woman in her wisdom went to all the people. And they cut off the head of Sheba the son of Bichri, and threw *it* out to Joab. Then he blew a trumpet, and they withdrew from the city, every man to his tent. So Joab returned to the king at Jerusalem.

DAVID'S GOVERNMENT OFFICERS

23And Joab *was* over all the army of Israel; Benaiah the son of Jehoiada *was* over the Cherethites and the Pelethites; 24Adoram *was* in charge of revenue; Jehoshaphat the son of Ahilud *was* recorder; 25Sheva *was* scribe; Zadok and Abiathar *were* the priests; 26and Ira the Jairite was a chief minister under David.

DAVID AVENGES THE GIBEONITES

21 Now there was a famine in the days of David for three years, year after year; and David inquired of the LORD. And the LORD answered, "*It is* because of Saul and *his* bloodthirsty house, because he killed the Gibeonites." 2So the king called the Gibeonites and spoke to them. Now the Gibeonites *were* not of the children of Israel, but of the remnant of the Amorites; the children of Israel had sworn protection to them, but Saul had sought to kill them in his zeal for the children of Israel and Judah.

3Therefore David said to the Gibeonites, "What shall I do for you? And with what shall I make atonement, that you may bless the inheritance of the LORD?"

4And the Gibeonites said to him, "We will have no silver or gold from Saul or from his house, nor shall you kill any man in Israel for us."

So he said, "Whatever you say, I will do for you."

5Then they answered the king, "As for the man who consumed us and plotted against us, *that* we should be destroyed from remaining in any of the territories of Israel, 6let seven men of his descendants be delivered to us, and we will hang them before the LORD in Gibeah of Saul, *whom* the LORD chose."

And the king said, "I will give *them.*"

7But the king spared Mephibosheth the son of Jonathan, the son of Saul, because of the LORD's oath that *was* between them, between David and Jonathan the son of Saul. 8So the king took Armoni and Mephibosheth, the two sons of Rizpah the daughter of Aiah, whom she bore to Saul, and the five sons of Michal[a] the daughter of Saul, whom she brought up for Adriel the son of Barzillai the Meholathite; 9and he delivered them into the hands of the Gibeonites, and they hanged them on the hill before the LORD. So they fell, *all* seven together, and were put to death in the days of harvest, in the first *days,* in the beginning of barley harvest.

10Now Rizpah the daughter of Aiah took sackcloth and spread it for herself on the rock, from the beginning of harvest until the late rains poured on them from heaven. And she did not allow the birds of the air to rest on them by day nor the beasts of the field by night.

11And David was told what Rizpah the daughter of Aiah, the concubine of Saul, had done. 12Then David went and took the bones of Saul, and the bones of Jonathan his son, from the men of Jabesh Gilead who had stolen them from the street of Beth Shan,[a] where the Philistines had hung them up, after the Philistines had struck down Saul in Gilboa. 13So he brought up the bones of Saul and the bones of Jonathan his son from there; and they gath-

---

21:8 [a]Or *Merab* (compare 1 Samuel 18:19 and 25:44; 2 Samuel 3:14 and 6:23) **21:12** [a]Spelled *Beth Shean* in Joshua 17:11 and elsewhere

ered the bones of those who had been hanged.
[14]They buried the bones of Saul and Jonathan
his son in the country of Benjamin in Zelah, in
the tomb of Kish his father. So they performed
all that the king commanded. And after that
God heeded the prayer for the land.

PHILISTINE GIANTS DESTROYED

[15]When the Philistines were at war again
with Israel, David and his servants with him
went down and fought against the Philistines;
and David grew faint. [16]Then Ishbi-Benob,
who *was* one of the sons of the giant, the
weight of whose bronze spear *was* three hundred *shekels,* who was bearing a new *sword,*
thought he could kill David. [17]But Abishai the
son of Zeruiah came to his aid, and struck the
Philistine and killed him. Then the men of
David swore to him, saying, "You shall go out
no more with us to battle, lest you quench the
lamp of Israel."

[18]Now it happened afterward that there was
again a battle with the Philistines at Gob.
Then Sibbechai the Hushathite killed Saph,[a]
who *was* one of the sons of the giant. [19]Again
there was war at Gob with the Philistines,
where Elhanan the son of Jaare-Oregim[a] the
Bethlehemite killed *the brother of* Goliath the
Gittite, the shaft of whose spear *was* like a
weaver's beam.

[20]Yet again there was war at Gath, where
there was a man of *great* stature, who had six
fingers on each hand and six toes on each
foot, twenty-four in number; and he also was
born to the giant. [21]So when he defied Israel,
Jonathan the son of Shimea,[a] David's brother,
killed him.

[22]These four were born to the giant in Gath,
and fell by the hand of David and by the hand
of his servants.

PRAISE FOR GOD'S DELIVERANCE

22 Then David spoke to the LORD the
words of this song, on the day when
the LORD had delivered him from the hand of
all his enemies, and from the hand of Saul.
[2]And he said:[a]

"The LORD *is* my rock and my fortress
and my deliverer;
3 The God of my strength, in whom I will
trust;
My shield and the horn of my salvation,
My stronghold and my refuge;
My Savior, You save me from violence.
4 I will call upon the LORD, *who is worthy*
to be praised;
So shall I be saved from my enemies.

5 "When the waves of death surrounded
me,
The floods of ungodliness made me
afraid.
6 The sorrows of Sheol surrounded me;
The snares of death confronted me.
7 In my distress I called upon the LORD,
And cried out to my God;
He heard my voice from His temple,
And my cry *entered* His ears.

8 "Then the earth shook and trembled;
The foundations of heaven[a] quaked and
were shaken,
Because He was angry.

21:18 [a]Spelled *Sippai* in 1 Chronicles 20:4
21:19 [a]Spelled *Jair* in 1 Chronicles 20:5
21:21 [a]Spelled *Shammah* in 1 Samuel 16:9 and elsewhere **22:2** [a]Compare Psalm 18
22:8 [a]Following Masoretic Text, Septuagint, and Targum; Syriac and Vulgate read *hills* (compare Psalm 18:7).

SOUL NOTE

Trust in Me *(22:2, 3)* David's song praised God for deliverance from enemies. David expressed his love for "the God of my strength, in whom I will trust." David had faced many enemies, trials, and problems. He had sinned against God and had reaped the consequences. David's words reveal a heart that, though imperfect, constantly desired to seek God's way and follow Him. Thus God called him "a man after His own heart" (I Sam. 13:14). People do not need to be perfect before God can use them, but they need to be willing to put their trust in Him. **Topic: Trust**

Stress

STRESS MANAGEMENT

LESLIE VERNICK

(2 Samuel 22)

At times, we all experience physical, emotional and spiritual exhaustion. One more interruption, delay, or problem may send us tumbling over the edge. Many of us try to get more done in less time with better results. We try to juggle the demands of home, church, work, and family life. Living on the ragged edge, we become worn out, stressed out, and eventually we can burn out.

Stress not only dampens our spirits and frazzles our nerves, but the constant rush of adrenaline overstimulates the heart and can weaken the immune system, leaving us prone to more illnesses and stress-related problems.

In our time-driven culture, stress is an inevitable part of life, so we have to learn to manage it. Let's look at what God says about stress and how Christians are to handle the reality of a stress-filled life and still maintain that inner peace that God promises.

GOD'S REMEDY FOR STRESS

Consider What God Is Doing—James 1:2–4
One of the best antidotes to stress is seeing God's purposes in the difficulties He allows in our lives. James counsels that we are to consider it all joy when we face trials of various kinds, because these will produce something good in us. The "good" God wants to do is to conform us to the image of Christ. He may use certain situations to develop one of the fruits of the Spirit in us. Knowing that God uses every situation, even the petty, irritating situations of life, to teach us to become more like Jesus helps us to feel less stressed by things we cannot control.

The apostle Paul experienced many life stresses that would put most of us over the edge. Yet he did not get discouraged or overwhelmed. By focusing on God's eternal perspective, Paul was able to endure all kinds of difficulties with inner peace and joy (2 Cor. 4:16–18).

Take Time Each Day to Be Alone with God—Psalm 46:10
Planned times of quiet and solitude are a good balance to a busy life. Cultivating a heart of prayer helps us see God's perspective and to more fully experience His presence throughout the day (Ps. 16:8–11). Many of us use prayer as a way to change a stressful situation. Although this is not a bad idea, prayer often does not change the situation as much as it changes us. As we purposely quiet our hearts each day, the Holy Spirit has a chance to change the way we see our difficulties. That may be just what we need in order to better cope with our situation.

Guard Our Hearts—Proverbs 4:23
Jesus tells us not to let our hearts be troubled or afraid (John 14:27). Stress has a way of orienting us toward the things that are wrong in our lives. We need to guard our hearts and minds against negativity and pessimism. There are times when we will not understand God or His ways (Is. 55:8), but He gives us enough information about His character that even when we do not understand or are confused, we can rest in His faithfulness and His holy goodness. He delights in us when we trust Him, even when we do not understand (Hab. 3:17–19). We must take time each day to check our thinking and take every thought cap-

tive to the obedience of Christ (2 Cor. 10:5).

Number Our Days and Live Intentionally—Psalm 90:12
Sometimes we get stressed out because we are majoring in minor things. At the end of our life, many of us will realize that we have spent most of our time on what matters least, and the least time on those things that matter most. We need to decide what is really important, choose our priorities, and live for them. Life is full of choices. When we become more intentional about the way we spend our time and energy, we learn to say no to things that are just not that important.

Remember Our Limits—Psalm 103:14
Often our lives become filled with stress because we refuse to accept our limits. We are not God. We are not all-knowing or able to assume total control. We are human beings. We need to sleep, eat, and relax. Yet, at times we live our lives in a way that ignores these realities, which can result in a host of stress-related ailments. When we are feeling overwhelmed, perhaps that is a reminder that we are not living within the limits and boundaries that God has created for us. It may be time to reevaluate, cut back, say no, or slow down.

Cultivate a Thankful Heart—1 Thessalonians 5:18
We must learn to count our blessings every day. Many of us must work to see the good in life and to cultivate a grateful heart. As we do this, we will feel more positive and the little things that go wrong will cease to look so important.

FINAL TIPS

Stress can affect the body, mind, and spirit. We must pay attention to each area to reduce the effects of stress on our overall well-being. If we do not learn to control stress, it will eventually control us. To protect our bodies, we need to get adequate rest, exercise regularly, eat well, and learn to breathe deeply. To protect our minds, we should think truthfully, refuse to make mountains out of molehills, and set priorities. Finally, to protect our spirits, we need to meditate on God and His Word, learn to trust God, and pray without ceasing.

FURTHER MEDITATION:

Other passages to study about the issue of stress include:

- Psalms 46; 55:22
- Isaiah 26:3; 40:28–31
- Matthew 11:28–30
- Galatians 6:9, 10

To Learn More: Turn to the key passage note on stress at 2 Corinthians 4:9 on page 1522. See also the personality profile of James on page 1641.

9 Smoke went up from His nostrils,
And devouring fire from His mouth;
Coals were kindled by it.
10 He bowed the heavens also, and came down
With darkness under His feet.
11 He rode upon a cherub, and flew;
And He was seen[a] upon the wings of the wind.
12 He made darkness canopies around Him,
Dark waters *and* thick clouds of the skies.
13 From the brightness before Him
Coals of fire were kindled.

14 "The LORD thundered from heaven,
And the Most High uttered His voice.
15 He sent out arrows and scattered them;
Lightning bolts, and He vanquished them.
16 Then the channels of the sea were seen,
The foundations of the world were uncovered,
At the rebuke of the LORD,
At the blast of the breath of His nostrils.

17 "He sent from above, He took me,
He drew me out of many waters.
18 He delivered me from my strong enemy,
From those who hated me;
For they were too strong for me.
19 They confronted me in the day of my calamity,
But the LORD was my support.
20 He also brought me out into a broad place;
He delivered me because He delighted in me.

21 "The LORD rewarded me according to my righteousness;
According to the cleanness of my hands
He has recompensed me.
22 For I have kept the ways of the LORD,
And have not wickedly departed from my God.
23 For all His judgments *were* before me;
And *as for* His statutes, I did not depart from them.
24 I was also blameless before Him,
And I kept myself from my iniquity.
25 Therefore the LORD has recompensed me according to my righteousness,
According to my cleanness in His eyes.[a]

26 "With the merciful You will show Yourself merciful;
With a blameless man You will show Yourself blameless;
27 With the pure You will show Yourself pure;
And with the devious You will show Yourself shrewd.
28 You will save the humble people;
But Your eyes *are* on the haughty, *that* You may bring *them* down.

29 "For You *are* my lamp, O LORD;
The LORD shall enlighten my darkness.
30 For by You I can run against a troop;
By my God I can leap over a wall.
31 *As for* God, His way *is* perfect;
The word of the LORD *is* proven;
He *is* a shield to all who trust in Him.

"For You are my lamp, O LORD;
the LORD shall enlighten my darkness."
2 SAMUEL 22:29

32 "For who *is* God, except the LORD?
And who *is* a rock, except our God?
33 God *is* my strength *and* power,[a]
And He makes my[b] way perfect.
34 He makes my[a] feet like the *feet* of deer,
And sets me on my high places.
35 He teaches my hands to make war,
So that my arms can bend a bow of bronze.

22:11 [a]Following Masoretic Text and Septuagint; many Hebrew manuscripts, Syriac, and Vulgate read *He flew* (compare Psalm 18:10); Targum reads *He spoke with power.* **22:25** [a]Septuagint, Syriac, and Vulgate read *the cleanness of my hands in His sight* (compare Psalm 18:24); Targum reads *my cleanness before His word.* **22:33** [a]Dead Sea Scrolls, Septuagint, Syriac, and Vulgate read *It is God who arms me with strength* (compare Psalm 18:32); Targum reads *It is God who sustains me with strength.* [b]Following Qere, Septuagint, Syriac, Targum, and Vulgate (compare Psalm 18:32); Kethib reads *His.* **22:34** [a]Following Qere, Septuagint, Syriac, Targum, and Vulgate (compare Psalm 18:33); Kethib reads *His.*

36 "You have also given me the shield of
Your salvation;
Your gentleness has made me great.
37 You enlarged my path under me;
So my feet did not slip.

38 "I have pursued my enemies and
destroyed them;
Neither did I turn back again till they
were destroyed.
39 And I have destroyed them and
wounded them,
So that they could not rise;
They have fallen under my feet.
40 For You have armed me with strength for
the battle;
You have subdued under me those who
rose against me.
41 You have also given me the necks of my
enemies,
So that I destroyed those who hated me.
42 They looked, but *there was* none to
save;
Even to the LORD, but He did not answer
them.
43 Then I beat them as fine as the dust of
the earth;
I trod them like dirt in the streets,
And I spread them out.

44 "You have also delivered me from the
strivings of my people;
You have kept me as the head of the
nations.
A people I have not known shall serve me.
45 The foreigners submit to me;
As soon as they hear, they obey me.
46 The foreigners fade away,
And come frightened[a] from their hideouts.

47 "The LORD lives!
Blessed *be* my Rock!
Let God be exalted,
The Rock of my salvation!
48 *It is* God who avenges me,
And subdues the peoples under me;
49 He delivers me from my enemies.
You also lift me up above those who rise
against me;
You have delivered me from the violent
man.
50 Therefore I will give thanks to You,
O LORD, among the Gentiles,
And sing praises to Your name.

51 "*He is* the tower of salvation to His king,
And shows mercy to His anointed,
To David and his descendants
forevermore."

DAVID'S LAST WORDS

23 Now these *are* the last words of David.

Thus says David the son of Jesse;
Thus says the man raised up on high,
The anointed of the God of Jacob,
And the sweet psalmist of Israel:

2 "The Spirit of the LORD spoke by me,
And His word *was* on my tongue.
3 The God of Israel said,
The Rock of Israel spoke to me:
'He who rules over men *must be* just,
Ruling in the fear of God.
4 And *he shall be* like the light of the
morning *when* the sun rises,
A morning without clouds,
Like the tender grass *springing* out of the
earth,
By clear shining after rain.'

5 "Although my house *is* not so with God,
Yet He has made with me an everlasting
covenant,
Ordered in all *things* and secure.
For *this is* all my salvation and all *my*
desire;
Will He not make *it* increase?
6 But *the sons* of rebellion *shall* all *be* as
thorns thrust away,
Because they cannot be taken with
hands.
7 But the man *who* touches them
Must be armed with iron and the shaft
of a spear,
And they shall be utterly burned with
fire in *their* place."

DAVID'S MIGHTY MEN

8These *are* the names of the mighty men
whom David had: Josheb-Basshebeth[a] the
Tachmonite, chief among the captains.[b] He

22:46 [a]Following Septuagint, Targum, and Vulgate (compare Psalm 18:45); Masoretic Text reads *gird themselves*. **23:8** [a]Literally *One Who Sits in the Seat* (compare 1 Chronicles 11:11) [b]Following Masoretic Text and Targum; Septuagint and Vulgate read *the three*.

was called Adino the Eznite, because he had
killed eight hundred men at one time. 9And
after him *was* Eleazar the son of Dodo,[a] the
Ahohite, *one* of the three mighty men with
David when they defied the Philistines *who*
were gathered there for battle, and the men of
Israel had retreated. 10He arose and attacked
the Philistines until his hand was weary, and
his hand stuck to the sword. The LORD
brought about a great victory that day; and the
people returned after him only to plunder.
11And after him *was* Shammah the son of Agee
the Hararite. The Philistines had gathered together into a troop where there was a piece of
ground full of lentils. So the people fled from
the Philistines. 12But he stationed himself in
the middle of the field, defended it, and killed
the Philistines. So the LORD brought about a
great victory.

13Then three of the thirty chief men went
down at harvest time and came to David at the
cave of Adullam. And the troop of Philistines
encamped in the Valley of Rephaim. 14David
was then in the stronghold, and the garrison
of the Philistines *was* then *in* Bethlehem.
15And David said with longing, "Oh, that
someone would give me a drink of the water
from the well of Bethlehem, which *is* by the
gate!" 16So the three mighty men broke
through the camp of the Philistines, drew water from the well of Bethlehem that *was* by the
gate, and took it and brought *it* to David. Nevertheless he would not drink it, but poured it
out to the LORD. 17And he said, "Far be it from
me, O LORD, that I should do this! Is *this not*
the blood of the men who went in *jeopardy of*
their lives?" Therefore he would not drink it.

These things were done by the three mighty
men.

18Now Abishai the brother of Joab, the son
of Zeruiah, was chief of *another* three.[a] He
lifted his spear against three hundred *men,*
killed *them,* and won a name among *these*
three. 19Was he not the most honored of three?
Therefore he became their captain. However,
he did not attain to the *first* three.

20Benaiah *was* the son of Jehoiada, the son
of a valiant man from Kabzeel, who had done
many deeds. He had killed two lion-like
heroes of Moab. He also had gone down and
killed a lion in the midst of a pit on a snowy
day. 21And he killed an Egyptian, a spectacular
man. The Egyptian *had* a spear in his hand; so
he went down to him with a staff, wrested the
spear out of the Egyptian's hand, and killed
him with his own spear. 22These *things* Benaiah the son of Jehoiada did, and won a name
among three mighty men. 23He was more honored than the thirty, but he did not attain to
the *first* three. And David appointed him over
his guard.

24Asahel the brother of Joab *was* one of the
thirty; Elhanan the son of Dodo of Bethlehem,
25Shammah the Harodite, Elika the Harodite,
26Helez the Paltite, Ira the son of Ikkesh the
Tekoite, 27Abiezer the Anathothite, Mebunnai
the Hushathite, 28Zalmon the Ahohite, Maharai
the Netophathite, 29Heleb the son of Baanah
(the Netophathite), Ittai the son of Ribai from
Gibeah of the children of Benjamin, 30Benaiah
a Pirathonite, Hiddai from the brooks of Gaash,
31Abi-Albon the Arbathite, Azmaveth the Barhumite, 32Eliahba the Shaalbonite (of the sons
of Jashen), Jonathan, 33Shammah the Hararite,
Ahiam the son of Sharar the Hararite, 34Eliphe-
let the son of Ahasbai, the son of the Maachathite, Eliam the son of Ahithophel the Gilonite,
35Hezrai[a] the Carmelite, Paarai the Arbite,
36Igal the son of Nathan of Zobah, Bani the
Gadite, 37Zelek the Ammonite, Naharai the Beerothite (armorbearer of Joab the son of Zeruiah), 38Ira the Ithrite, Gareb the Ithrite, 39*and*
Uriah the Hittite: thirty-seven in all.

DAVID'S CENSUS OF ISRAEL AND JUDAH

24 Again the anger of the LORD was
aroused against Israel, and He moved
David against them to say, "Go, number Israel
and Judah."

2So the king said to Joab the commander of
the army who *was* with him, "Now go
throughout all the tribes of Israel, from Dan to
Beersheba, and count the people, that I may
know the number of the people."

3And Joab said to the king, "Now may the
LORD your God add to the people a hundred
times more than there are, and may the eyes
of my lord the king see *it.* But why does my
lord the king desire this thing?" 4Nevertheless
the king's word prevailed against Joab and
against the captains of the army. Therefore
Joab and the captains of the army went out

23:9 [a]Spelled *Dodai* in 1 Chronicles 27:4
23:18 [a]Following Masoretic Text, Septuagint, and Vulgate; some Hebrew manuscripts and Syriac read *thirty;* Targum reads *the mighty men.*
23:35 [a]Spelled *Hezro* in 1 Chronicles 11:37

from the presence of the king to count the
people of Israel.
5And they crossed over the Jordan and
camped in Aroer, on the right side of the town
which *is* in the midst of the ravine of Gad, and
toward Jazer. 6Then they came to Gilead and
to the land of Tahtim Hodshi; they came to
Dan Jaan and around to Sidon; 7and they
came to the stronghold of Tyre and to all the
cities of the Hivites and the Canaanites. Then
they went out to South Judah *as far as* Beersheba. 8So when they had gone through all the
land, they came to Jerusalem at the end of
nine months and twenty days. 9Then Joab
gave the sum of the number of the people to
the king. And there were in Israel eight hundred thousand valiant men who drew the
sword, and the men of Judah were five hundred thousand men.

THE JUDGMENT ON DAVID'S SIN

10And David's heart condemned him after
he had numbered the people. So David said to
the LORD, "I have sinned greatly in what I
have done; but now, I pray, O LORD, take away
the iniquity of Your servant, for I have done
very foolishly."
11Now when David arose in the morning,
the word of the LORD came to the prophet
Gad, David's seer, saying, 12"Go and tell David, 'Thus says the LORD: "I offer you three
things; choose one of them for yourself, that I
may do *it* to you." ' " 13So Gad came to David
and told him; and he said to him, "Shall
seven[a] years of famine come to you in your
land? Or shall you flee three months before
your enemies, while they pursue you? Or shall
there be three days' plague in your land? Now
consider and see what answer I should take
back to Him who sent me."
14And David said to Gad, "I am in great distress. Please let us fall into the hand of the
LORD, for His mercies *are* great; but do not let
me fall into the hand of man."
15So the LORD sent a plague upon Israel
from the morning till the appointed time.
From Dan to Beersheba seventy thousand men
of the people died. 16And when the angel[a]
stretched out His hand over Jerusalem to destroy it, the LORD relented from the destruction, and said to the angel who was destroying
the people, "It is enough; now restrain your
hand." And the angel of the LORD was by the
threshing floor of Araunah[b] the Jebusite.
17Then David spoke to the LORD when he
saw the angel who was striking the people,
and said, "Surely I have sinned, and I have
done wickedly; but these sheep, what have
they done? Let Your hand, I pray, be against
me and against my father's house."

THE ALTAR ON THE THRESHING FLOOR

18And Gad came that day to David and said
to him, "Go up, erect an altar to the LORD on
the threshing floor of Araunah the Jebusite."
19So David, according to the word of Gad,
went up as the LORD commanded. 20Now
Araunah looked, and saw the king and his servants coming toward him. So Araunah went
out and bowed before the king with his face to
the ground.
21Then Araunah said, "Why has my lord the
king come to his servant?"
And David said, "To buy the threshing floor
from you, to build an altar to the LORD, that
the plague may be withdrawn from the people."
22Now Araunah said to David, "Let my lord
the king take and offer up whatever *seems*
good to him. Look, *here are* oxen for burnt sacrifice, and threshing implements and the yokes
of the oxen for wood. 23All these, O king, Araunah has given to the king."
And Araunah said to the king, "May the
LORD your God accept you."
24Then the king said to Araunah, "No, but I
will surely buy *it* from you for a price; nor will
I offer burnt offerings to the LORD my God
with that which costs me nothing." So David
bought the threshing floor and the oxen for fifty shekels of silver. 25And David built there an
altar to the LORD, and offered burnt offerings
and peace offerings. So the LORD heeded the
prayers for the land, and the plague was withdrawn from Israel.

24:13 [a]Following Masoretic Text, Syriac, Targum, and Vulgate; Septuagint reads *three* (compare 1 Chronicles 21:12). **24:16** [a]Or *Angel* [b]Spelled *Ornan* in 1 Chronicles 21:15

1 Kings

How can something that starts so well end so badly? Why do loving marriages fail, promising businesses go bankrupt, churches split, and spiritually vital people drift away from God?

First Kings, possibly written by the prophet Jeremiah, provides clues to these mysteries. The first eleven chapters describe Solomon's wise and able leadership over Israel. A magnificent temple is built in Jerusalem to the glory of God. Wealth, splendor, and fame are Solomon's as he reigns over a glorious united kingdom.

But almost imperceptibly, Solomon's heart is stolen away by his foreign wives and their pagan gods. As he forsakes the Lord, he sets the nation on a path of political ruin and spiritual decadence. The final eleven chapters detail the breakup of the kingdom under Solomon's son Rehoboam in 931 B.C.

The ten northern tribes become known collectively as Israel and are ruled by a succession of wicked kings. The two southern tribes take the name of the larger tribe, Judah. Although Judah is blessed with a few God-honoring rulers, most of her leaders are evil as well.

First Kings teaches a number of sobering lessons: It is not enough merely to begin well; short-lived religious zeal is not sufficient; beware of unhealthy affections; sin is deceptive and addictive; what you do *for* God is not nearly so important as what you do *with* God. Solomon's story reminds us that the state of one's heart will ultimately determine the outcome of one's life and legacy.

SOUL CONCERNS IN 1 KINGS

MENTORING	(CH. 1—2)
WISDOM	(3:5–14)
SIN	(8:31–40)

Adonijah Presumes to Be King

1 Now King David was old, advanced in
years; and they put covers on him, but he
could not get warm. [2]Therefore his servants
said to him, "Let a young woman, a virgin, be
sought for our lord the king, and let her stand
before the king, and let her care for him; and
let her lie in your bosom, that our lord the
king may be warm." [3]So they sought for a
lovely young woman throughout all the territory of Israel, and found Abishag the Shunammite, and brought her to the king. [4]The young
woman *was* very lovely; and she cared for the
king, and served him; but the king did not
know her.

[5]Then Adonijah the son of Haggith exalted
himself, saying, "I will be king"; and he prepared for himself chariots and horsemen, and
fifty men to run before him. [6](And his father
had not rebuked him at any time by saying,
"Why have you done so?" He *was* also very
good-looking. *His mother* had borne him after
Absalom.) [7]Then he conferred with Joab the
son of Zeruiah and with Abiathar the priest,
and they followed and helped Adonijah. [8]But
Zadok the priest, Benaiah the son of Jehoiada,
Nathan the prophet, Shimei, Rei, and the
mighty men who *belonged* to David were not
with Adonijah.

[9]And Adonijah sacrificed sheep and oxen
and fattened cattle by the stone of Zoheleth,
which *is* by En Rogel; he also invited all his
brothers, the king's sons, and all the men of
Judah, the king's servants. [10]But he did not
invite Nathan the prophet, Benaiah, the
mighty men, or Solomon his brother.

[11]So Nathan spoke to Bathsheba the mother
of Solomon, saying, "Have you not heard that
Adonijah the son of Haggith has become king,
and David our lord does not know *it?* [12]Come,
please, let me now give you advice, that you
may save your own life and the life of your
son Solomon. [13]Go immediately to King David
and say to him, 'Did you not, my lord, O king,
swear to your maidservant, saying, "Assuredly
your son Solomon shall reign after me, and he
shall sit on my throne"? Why then has Adonijah become king?' [14]Then, while you are still
talking there with the king, I also will come in
after you and confirm your words."

[15]So Bathsheba went into the chamber to
the king. (Now the king was very old, and Abishag the Shunammite was serving the king.)
[16]And Bathsheba bowed and did homage to
the king. Then the king said, "What is your
wish?"

[17]Then she said to him, "My lord, you swore
by the LORD your God to your maidservant,
saying, 'Assuredly Solomon your son shall
reign after me, and he shall sit on my throne.'
[18]So now, look! Adonijah has become king;
and now, my lord the king, you do not know
about *it.* [19]He has sacrificed oxen and fattened
cattle and sheep in abundance, and has invited all the sons of the king, Abiathar the
priest, and Joab the commander of the army;
but Solomon your servant he has not invited.
[20]And as for you, my lord, O king, the eyes of
all Israel *are* on you, that you should tell them
who will sit on the throne of my lord the king
after him. [21]Otherwise it will happen, when
my lord the king rests with his fathers, that I
and my son Solomon will be counted as offenders."

[22]And just then, while she was still talking
with the king, Nathan the prophet also came
in. [23]So they told the king, saying, "Here is Nathan the prophet." And when he came in before the king, he bowed down before the king
with his face to the ground. [24]And Nathan
said, "My lord, O king, have you said, 'Adonijah shall reign after me, and he shall sit on my

SOUL NOTE

A Good Investment *(1:5, 6)* David was very ill, and one of his sons, Adonijah, set up a scheme to take over the kingdom. The Bible says of Adonijah that "his father had not rebuked him at any time." One of David's apparent weaknesses was the inability to discipline his children. Many severe conflicts had arisen within his family among the various half brothers. David's failures as a father led to a number of failures and sins in his children. Parents always influence their children—for good and bad. There is no substitute for invested, caring, loving parents who discipline when necessary.
Topic: Parenting

Mentoring

MASTER MENTORING

DON HAWKINS

(1 Kings 1—2)

Elijah had served God faithfully, and then he faithfully trained his replacement, Elisha. That training process is called "mentoring" or "discipling." Spiritual mentoring is vital to the continuation of the Christian faith. It was the discipling of new believers by older believers that allowed Christianity to continue across centuries. Many Christians owe their mature faith to the mentoring of mature Christians who helped them grow spiritually.

Perhaps the best outline for discipleship was given by the Master Himself in John 17. In this chapter, Jesus gives a framework for the process of discipleship that can be broken down into six steps.

STEP 1: EXAMPLE

Jesus said, "I have manifested Your name to the men whom You have given Me out of the world" (John 17:6). In His work with the disciples, Jesus displayed God's nature, character, and person. For example, Malachi 3:6 presents God as unchanging, "For I am the LORD, I do not change." Jesus also demonstrated a consistency in word and action that went far beyond what any human being has ever shown. Furthermore, God is all-knowing, omniscient. Job described Him as having perfect knowledge (Job 37:16), and Isaiah affirmed that the all-knowing God needs no teacher (Is. 40:13, 14). Throughout His ministry, Jesus demonstrated His knowledge of the human heart, of circumstances, and even of the future.

Paul also followed this pattern. While he was not perfect as was Jesus, he earnestly lived to serve God and urged Corinthian believers to imitate him (1 Cor. 4:16). Every successful mentor must begin at the same place: providing an example for those being discipled.

STEP 2: EVANGELISM

For the first-century followers of Christ, faith in Him became the cornerstone on which all life and ministry were based. John 17 reveals the source of the faith that Peter and others came to express. Jesus said, "For I have given to them [the apostles] the words which You have given Me; and they have received them, and have known surely that I came forth from You; and they have believed that You sent Me" (John 17:8).

Clearly the proclamation of the message of Jesus and the salvation He offered became the focal point of the ministry of these early Christians. Wherever they went, they spread the gospel of Jesus Christ.

Such sharing is the key way for the message of salvation to spread. People must first accept salvation before they can grow in the faith. Evangelism was an integral part of the process of discipling by Jesus and the first-century church. Every successful mentor is able to share the Good News of Christ.

STEP 3: INTERCESSION

In John 17:9 Jesus declared, "I pray for them." Later in this chapter, He added, "I do not pray for these alone, but also for those who will believe in Me through their word" (John 17:20). Jesus made it very clear that His ministry was, and continues to be, one of intercession for His followers (Rom. 8:34).

Jesus also prayed specifically. He prayed for His followers to be unified, protected, and sanctified (John 17:11, 15, 17). Every aspect of a believer's life—emotional, physical and spiritual—is covered in this intercessory prayer.

Every successful mentor must be committed to prayer—and particularly to intercessory prayer.

STEP 4: ENCOURAGEMENT

Working through "the lust of the flesh, the lust of the eyes, and the pride of life" (1 John 2:16), Satan seeks to trip us up daily. As our Great Shepherd, Jesus has committed Himself to protecting and encouraging us. In John 17:12, He said to the Father, "I kept them in Your name."

While mentors cannot provide the protection of an omnipresent Savior, part of their "keeping ministry" involves the role of encourager. Encouragement is one of the most essential ingredients for successful discipling. Like shepherds, mentors are called alongside the sheep to help them.

Verbal encouragement is key, but mentors can also encourage in other ways—such as taking time, sharing a meal, providing help, or even sharing a hug. Every successful mentor communicates that he or she will care for and stand by those who need help.

STEP 5: EDIFICATION

As He prepared to return to His Father in heaven, Jesus explained that He was providing a resource for the edification of His followers: "I have given to them the words which You have given Me" (John 17:8). Jesus communicated Scripture to His disciples during His teaching ministry. Approximately ten percent of what Jesus shared with His disciples was right from the Old Testament.

When it comes to discipling, there is no substitute for the Bible. It is the Word that brings change and growth to people's lives. In its most basic form, discipleship involves a relationship in which the Scripture is infused into a life to produce Christlike character. Every successful mentor continues to study God's Word to be able to teach others.

STEP 6: EXTENSION

In John 17:18, Jesus declared, "I also have sent them into the world." Jesus intended for His disciples to extend themselves by making other disciples. The goal of the mentoring process is to develop mature believers who then can mentor others. Paul wrote to Timothy, "The things that you have heard from me among many witnesses, commit these to faithful men who will be able to teach others also" (2 Tim. 2:2). Every successful mentor has students who become mentors for others.

FINAL REVIEW

Jesus intended for every believer to be plugged into a vital, growing relationship with the Savior—being discipled and eventually reaching out to mentor others in the faith. By following the steps of John 17, all believers can successfully mentor others.

FURTHER MEDITATION:

Other passages to study about the issue of mentoring include:

- Numbers 10:29–32
- Matthew 10:24
- Mark 1:16–18
- 1 Corinthians 4:15–17
- Titus 2:2–8
- Philemon 8–16

To Learn More: Turn to the key passage note on mentoring at 2 Timothy 2:2 on page 1606. See also the personality profile of Elijah and Elisha on page 465.

throne'? 25For he has gone down today, and
has sacrificed oxen and fattened cattle and
sheep in abundance, and has invited all the
king's sons, and the commanders of the army,
and Abiathar the priest; and look! They are
eating and drinking before him; and they say,
'*Long* live King Adonijah!' 26But he has not
invited me—me your servant—nor Zadok the
priest, nor Benaiah the son of Jehoiada, nor
your servant Solomon. 27Has this thing been
done by my lord the king, and you have not
told your servant who should sit on the throne
of my lord the king after him?"

David Proclaims Solomon King

28Then King David answered and said, "Call
Bathsheba to me." So she came into the king's
presence and stood before the king. 29And the
king took an oath and said, "*As* the LORD lives,
who has redeemed my life from every distress,
30just as I swore to you by the LORD God of Israel, saying, 'Assuredly Solomon your son
shall be king after me, and he shall sit on my
throne in my place,' so I certainly will do this
day."

31Then Bathsheba bowed with *her* face to
the earth, and paid homage to the king, and
said, "Let my lord King David live forever!"

32And King David said, "Call to me Zadok
the priest, Nathan the prophet, and Benaiah
the son of Jehoiada." So they came before the
king. 33The king also said to them, "Take with
you the servants of your lord, and have Solomon my son ride on my own mule, and take
him down to Gihon. 34There let Zadok the
priest and Nathan the prophet anoint him king
over Israel; and blow the horn, and say, '*Long*
live King Solomon!' 35Then you shall come up
after him, and he shall come and sit on my
throne, and he shall be king in my place. For I
have appointed him to be ruler over Israel and
Judah."

36Benaiah the son of Jehoiada answered the
king and said, "Amen! May the LORD God of
my lord the king say so *too*. 37As the LORD has
been with my lord the king, even so may He
be with Solomon, and make his throne greater
than the throne of my lord King David."

38So Zadok the priest, Nathan the prophet,
Benaiah the son of Jehoiada, the Cherethites,
and the Pelethites went down and had Solomon ride on King David's mule, and took
him to Gihon. 39Then Zadok the priest took a
horn of oil from the tabernacle and anointed
Solomon. And they blew the horn, and all the
people said, "*Long* live King Solomon!" 40And
all the people went up after him; and the people played the flutes and rejoiced with great
joy, so that the earth *seemed to* split with their
sound.

41Now Adonijah and all the guests who *were*
with him heard *it* as they finished eating. And
when Joab heard the sound of the horn, he
said, "Why *is* the city in such a noisy uproar?"
42While he was still speaking, there came Jonathan, the son of Abiathar the priest. And Adonijah said to him, "Come in, for you *are* a
prominent man, and bring good news."

43Then Jonathan answered and said to Adonijah, "No! Our lord King David has made Solomon king. 44The king has sent with him
Zadok the priest, Nathan the prophet, Benaiah
the son of Jehoiada, the Cherethites, and the
Pelethites; and they have made him ride on
the king's mule. 45So Zadok the priest and Nathan the prophet have anointed him king at
Gihon; and they have gone up from there rejoicing, so that the city is in an uproar. This *is*
the noise that you have heard. 46Also Solomon
sits on the throne of the kingdom. 47And
moreover the king's servants have gone to
bless our lord King David, saying, 'May God
make the name of Solomon better than your
name, and may He make his throne greater
than your throne.' Then the king bowed himself on the bed. 48Also the king said thus,
'Blessed *be* the LORD God of Israel, who has
given *one* to sit on my throne this day, while
my eyes see *it!*' "

49So all the guests who were with Adonijah
were afraid, and arose, and each one went his
way.

50Now Adonijah was afraid of Solomon; so
he arose, and went and took hold of the horns
of the altar. 51And it was told Solomon, saying,
"Indeed Adonijah is afraid of King Solomon;
for look, he has taken hold of the horns of the
altar, saying, 'Let King Solomon swear to me
today that he will not put his servant to death
with the sword.' "

52Then Solomon said, "If he proves himself a worthy man, not one hair of him shall
fall to the earth; but if wickedness is found
in him, he shall die." 53So King Solomon
sent them to bring him down from the altar.
And he came and fell down before King
Solomon; and Solomon said to him, "Go to
your house."

David's Instructions to Solomon

2 Now the days of David drew near that he should die, and he charged Solomon his son, saying: 2"I go the way of all the earth; be strong, therefore, and prove yourself a man. 3And keep the charge of the LORD your God: to walk in His ways, to keep His statutes, His commandments, His judgments, and His testimonies, as it is written in the Law of Moses, that you may prosper in all that you do and wherever you turn; 4that the LORD may fulfill His word which He spoke concerning me, saying, 'If your sons take heed to their way, to walk before Me in truth with all their heart and with all their soul,' He said, 'you shall not lack a man on the throne of Israel.'

5"Moreover you know also what Joab the son of Zeruiah did to me, *and* what he did to the two commanders of the armies of Israel, to Abner the son of Ner and Amasa the son of Jether, whom he killed. And he shed the blood of war in peacetime, and put the blood of war on his belt that *was* around his waist, and on his sandals that *were* on his feet. 6Therefore do according to your wisdom, and do not let his gray hair go down to the grave in peace.

7"But show kindness to the sons of Barzillai the Gileadite, and let them be among those who eat at your table, for so they came to me when I fled from Absalom your brother.

8"And see, *you have* with you Shimei the son of Gera, a Benjamite from Bahurim, who cursed me with a malicious curse in the day when I went to Mahanaim. But he came down to meet me at the Jordan, and I swore to him by the LORD, saying, 'I will not put you to death with the sword.' 9Now therefore, do not hold him guiltless, for you *are* a wise man and know what you ought to do to him; but bring his gray hair down to the grave with blood."

Death of David

10So David rested with his fathers, and was buried in the City of David. 11The period that David reigned over Israel *was* forty years; seven years he reigned in Hebron, and in Jerusalem he reigned thirty-three years. 12Then Solomon sat on the throne of his father David; and his kingdom was firmly established.

Solomon Executes Adonijah

13Now Adonijah the son of Haggith came to Bathsheba the mother of Solomon. So she said, "Do you come peaceably?"

And he said, "Peaceably." 14Moreover he said, "I have something *to say* to you."

And she said, "Say it."

15Then he said, "You know that the kingdom was mine, and all Israel had set their expectations on me, that I should reign. However, the kingdom has been turned over, and has become my brother's; for it was his from the LORD. 16Now I ask one petition of you; do not deny me."

And she said to him, "Say it."

17Then he said, "Please speak to King Solomon, for he will not refuse you, that he may give me Abishag the Shunammite as wife."

18So Bathsheba said, "Very well, I will speak for you to the king."

19Bathsheba therefore went to King Solomon, to speak to him for Adonijah. And the king rose up to meet her and bowed down to her, and sat down on his throne and had a throne set for the king's mother; so she sat at his right hand. 20Then she said, "I desire one small petition of you; do not refuse me."

And the king said to her, "Ask it, my mother, for I will not refuse you."

21So she said, "Let Abishag the Shunammite be given to Adonijah your brother as wife."

22And King Solomon answered and said to his mother, "Now why do you ask Abishag the Shunammite for Adonijah? Ask for him the kingdom also—for he *is* my older brother—for him, and for Abiathar the priest, and for Joab the son of Zeruiah." 23Then King Solomon swore by the LORD, saying, "May God do so to me, and more also, if Adonijah has not spoken this word against his own life! 24Now therefore, *as* the LORD lives, who has confirmed me and set me on the throne of David my father, and who has established a house[a] for me, as He promised, Adonijah shall be put to death today!"

25So King Solomon sent by the hand of Benaiah the son of Jehoiada; and he struck him down, and he died.

Abiathar Exiled, Joab Executed

26And to Abiathar the priest the king said, "Go to Anathoth, to your own fields, for you *are* deserving of death; but I will not put you to death at this time, because you carried the ark of the Lord GOD before my father David, and because you were afflicted every time my

---

2:24 [a]That is, a royal dynasty

father was afflicted." 27 So Solomon removed Abiathar from being priest to the LORD, that he might fulfill the word of the LORD which He spoke concerning the house of Eli at Shiloh.

28 Then news came to Joab, for Joab had defected to Adonijah, though he had not defected to Absalom. So Joab fled to the tabernacle of the LORD, and took hold of the horns of the altar. 29 And King Solomon was told, "Joab has fled to the tabernacle of the LORD; there *he is,* by the altar." Then Solomon sent Benaiah the son of Jehoiada, saying, "Go, strike him down." 30 So Benaiah went to the tabernacle of the LORD, and said to him, "Thus says the king, 'Come out!' "

And he said, "No, but I will die here." And Benaiah brought back word to the king, saying, "Thus said Joab, and thus he answered me."

31 Then the king said to him, "Do as he has said, and strike him down and bury him, that you may take away from me and from the house of my father the innocent blood which Joab shed. 32 So the LORD will return his blood on his head, because he struck down two men more righteous and better than he, and killed them with the sword—Abner the son of Ner, the commander of the army of Israel, and Amasa the son of Jether, the commander of the army of Judah—though my father David did not know *it.* 33 Their blood shall therefore return upon the head of Joab and upon the head of his descendants forever. But upon David and his descendants, upon his house and his throne, there shall be peace forever from the LORD."

34 So Benaiah the son of Jehoiada went up and struck and killed him; and he was buried in his own house in the wilderness. 35 The king put Benaiah the son of Jehoiada in his place over the army, and the king put Zadok the priest in the place of Abiathar.

SHIMEI EXECUTED

36 Then the king sent and called for Shimei, and said to him, "Build yourself a house in Jerusalem and dwell there, and do not go out from there anywhere. 37 For it shall be, on the day you go out and cross the Brook Kidron, know for certain you shall surely die; your blood shall be on your own head."

38 And Shimei said to the king, "The saying *is* good. As my lord the king has said, so your servant will do." So Shimei dwelt in Jerusalem many days.

39 Now it happened at the end of three years, that two slaves of Shimei ran away to Achish the son of Maachah, king of Gath. And they told Shimei, saying, "Look, your slaves *are* in Gath!" 40 So Shimei arose, saddled his donkey, and went to Achish at Gath to seek his slaves. And Shimei went and brought his slaves from Gath. 41 And Solomon was told that Shimei had gone from Jerusalem to Gath and had come back. 42 Then the king sent and called for Shimei, and said to him, "Did I not make you swear by the LORD, and warn you, saying, 'Know for certain that on the day you go out and travel anywhere, you shall surely die'? And you said to me, 'The word I have heard *is* good.' 43 Why then have you not kept the oath of the LORD and the commandment that I gave you?" 44 The king said moreover to Shimei, "You know, as your heart acknowledges, all the wickedness that you did to my father David; therefore the LORD will return your wickedness on your own head. 45 But King Solomon *shall be* blessed, and the throne of David shall be established before the LORD forever."

46 So the king commanded Benaiah the son of Jehoiada; and he went out and struck him down, and he died. Thus the kingdom was established in the hand of Solomon.

SOLOMON REQUESTS WISDOM

3 Now Solomon made a treaty with Pharaoh king of Egypt, and married Pharaoh's daughter; then he brought her to the City of David until he had finished building his own house, and the house of the LORD, and the wall all around Jerusalem. 2 Meanwhile the people sacrificed at the high places, because there was no house built for the name of the LORD until those days. 3 And Solomon loved the LORD, walking in the statutes of his father David, except that he sacrificed and burned incense at the high places.

4 Now the king went to Gibeon to sacrifice there, for that *was* the great high place: Solomon offered a thousand burnt offerings on that altar. 5 At Gibeon the LORD appeared to Solomon in a dream by night; and God said, "Ask! What shall I give you?"

6 And Solomon said: "You have shown great mercy to Your servant David my father, because he walked before You in truth, in righteousness, and in uprightness of heart with You; You have continued this great kindness for him, and You have given him a son to sit

on his throne, as *it is* this day. 7Now, O LORD
my God, You have made Your servant king
instead of my father David, but I *am* a little
child; I do not know *how* to go out or come
in. 8And Your servant *is* in the midst of Your
people whom You have chosen, a great
people, too numerous to be numbered or
counted. 9Therefore give to Your servant an
understanding heart to judge Your people,
that I may discern between good and evil. For
who is able to judge this great people of
Yours?"
10The speech pleased the LORD, that Solomon had asked this thing. 11Then God said to
him: "Because you have asked this thing, and
have not asked long life for yourself, nor have
asked riches for yourself, nor have asked the
life of your enemies, but have asked for yourself understanding to discern justice, 12be-
hold, I have done according to your words;
see, I have given you a wise and understanding heart, so that there has not been anyone
like you before you, nor shall any like you
arise after you. 13And I have also given you
what you have not asked: both riches and
honor, so that there shall not be anyone like
you among the kings all your days. 14So if you
walk in My ways, to keep My statutes and My
commandments, as your father David walked,
then I will lengthen your days."
15Then Solomon awoke; and indeed it had
been a dream. And he came to Jerusalem and
stood before the ark of the covenant of the
LORD, offered up burnt offerings, offered
peace offerings, and made a feast for all his
servants.

PERSONALITY PROFILE

Wisdom

SOLOMON: HAVING WISDOM VS. USING WISDOM

(1 KINGS 3)

Solomon had it all. There is no doubt that he ruled over the golden age of Israel. He had riches beyond compare, fame beyond imagination, and wisdom greater than anyone who ever lived. All of this, of course, came from God.

Solomon was one of several sons of David and Bathsheba (1 Chr. 3:5). David had promised the kingdom to Solomon (1 Kin. 1:17), whom God had chosen to succeed him (1 Chr. 28:5). God wanted to bless Israel through Solomon's reign. One night, therefore, God told Solomon to ask for anything and He would give it to him. Solomon knew what he needed most—wisdom to rule the nation.

When God answers a prayer, He doesn't go halfway. Solomon wasn't given just a little wisdom; he became the wisest man who ever lived! His wisdom became known internationally, and people came from all over the world just to meet him (1 Kin. 4:29–34). Solomon built the magnificent temple in Jerusalem as well as many other buildings. He wrote books, including the biblical books of Proverbs, Ecclesiastes, and Song of Solomon.

Solomon struggled, however, at putting his wisdom into practice at home. He "loved many foreign women" from the surrounding nations (1 Kin. 11:1), with whom the Lord had commanded Israel not to intermarry. God said, "Surely they will turn away your hearts after other gods" (1 Kin. 11:2), but Solomon did not listen. He married not one or two, but 700 women, and, as if that weren't enough, he had 300 concubines. What God predicted came true, of course: "His wives turned his heart after others gods; and his heart was not loyal to the LORD his God" (1 Kin. 11:4).

Like Solomon, someone may be wise in many areas, but not in managing their own life. Solomon did much for his nation with his wisdom, but his unwise lack of restraint caused him to lose his kingdom (1 Kin. 11:11). A truly wise person knows how to apply God-given wisdom in life.

To Learn More: Turn to the article about wisdom on pages 436, 437. See also the key passage note at James 1:5 on page 1642.

Wisdom

WISDOM

LLOYD OGILVIE

(1 Kings 3:5–14)

Wisdom is the special gift of the Lord in our quest to know His will for our lives. Wisdom goes beyond mere intellect and knowledge and encompasses a God-given ability to perceive people and situations with spiritual clarity. Wisdom is the vertical thrust of the mind of God into our minds, making discernment possible on the horizontal level of human relationships. With God's wisdom, we can know His plans and purposes.

Life is an endless succession of choices and decisions. We are called on to evaluate, analyze, and decide about what is right and best for our lives. The possibility of error is enormous. Therefore, we need God's wisdom in order to understand and do His will.

When young King Solomon succeeded his father as the king of Israel, he felt acutely the need for divine wisdom in order to administer the kingdom of Israel. In a dream, the Lord appeared to Solomon and promised to give him anything he asked for. Solomon asked for wisdom. God was pleased with the request, saying, "I have done according to your words; see, I have given you a wise and understanding heart, so that there has not been anyone like you before you, nor shall any like you arise after you" (1 Kin. 3:12). The Bible records that "Solomon's wisdom excelled the wisdom of all the men of the East and all the wisdom of Egypt. For he was wiser than all men" (1 Kin. 4:30, 31). Solomon's reign over Israel expressed his wisdom—as did his writings, sayings, and proverbs.

However, Solomon's great wisdom did not always affect his own lifestyle. Even as he received great wisdom to rule the nation, he also foolishly intermarried with many foreign women. Eventually, those women proved to be his downfall. "But King Solomon loved many foreign women. . . . Solomon clung to these in love . . . and his wives turned away his heart. For it was so, when Solomon was old, that his wives turned his heart after other gods; and his heart was not loyal to the LORD his God" (1 Kin. 11:1–4). Clearly, wisdom must be applied to one's own personal life as well.

Despite Solomon's later mistakes, we must not diminish our appreciation of his God-given gift of wisdom. Solomon is distinguished not just for his judgments or his brilliant leadership, but for the wisdom God gave him.

GIFT OF WISDOM

The same capacity of wisdom is offered to us as well, so that we can know and do the will of God. The Bible promises: "If any of you lacks wisdom, let him ask of God, who gives to all liberally and without reproach, and it will be given to him" (James 1:5). God usually follows a gift with the opportunity for us to use it. That way, we will know that the power we have been given is from Him. All God's gifts are for ministry, not just for our own private enjoyment. God allowed Solomon to use his wisdom to make wise judgments, as well as to write books in our Bible—such as Proverbs—to which we still turn for guidance.

We do not need to wander aimlessly through life, uncertain and confused. Our purpose is to know and do God's will. Whatever we discover of the nature of the universe can guide us only as we grow in

Christ. Wisdom grows in us as we grow in Christ.

Jesus referred to Himself as "greater than Solomon." Christ was Wisdom Incarnate. And yet, people resisted the splendor of Wisdom's radiance. No wonder Jesus said, "The queen of the South [the Queen of Sheba] will rise up in the judgment with the men of this generation and condemn them, for she came from the ends of the earth to hear the wisdom of Solomon; and indeed a greater than Solomon is here" (Luke 11:31). Solomon had gone as far as any human being in experiencing the precious gift of wisdom. Christ said to the people of His day that what had made King Solomon great, and what was sought after by the leaders of His own time, was present with them. All that Jesus taught about God and His ultimate purpose for our lives came out of the limitless storehouse of wisdom He had with God before the foundation of the world.

GROWING IN WISDOM

For us today, in the confusing complications of our lives, the promise of wisdom means that in Christ we can receive, experience, and communicate the depth perception of true wisdom. Christ was, and now is, the power of God utilized to accomplish His ultimate purpose to create a people whom He loves and who will love Him. When we receive Christ, we receive wisdom.

Wisdom indwelling us integrates knowledge and guides our decisions. The ultimate choice of making Christ Lord of our lives is followed by a million choices in daily life which are guided by what will further our ultimate purpose: to live in fellowship with Him forever.

We do not need to wander aimlessly through life, uncertain and confused. We know whose we are and for what we were created. Our purpose is to know and do Wisdom's will. Whatever we discover of the nature of the universe can now be guided by our ultimate destiny. Wisdom grows in us as we grow in Christ.

FURTHER MEDITATION:

Other passages to study about the issue of wisdom include:

- ➢ Deuteronomy 17:18–20
- ➢ Joshua 1:8
- ➢ Proverbs 2:1–9; 5:1–6; 16:6
- ➢ Matthew 7:24–27; 13:18–23
- ➢ 2 Timothy 3:14–17

To Learn More: Turn to the key passage note on wisdom at James 1:5 on page 1642. See also the personality profile of Solomon on page 435.

Solomon's Wise Judgment

[16]Now two women *who were* harlots came to the king, and stood before him. [17]And one woman said, "O my lord, this woman and I dwell in the same house; and I gave birth while she *was* in the house. [18]Then it happened, the third day after I had given birth, that this woman also gave birth. And we *were* together; no one *was* with us in the house, except the two of us in the house. [19]And this woman's son died in the night, because she lay on him. [20]So she arose in the middle of the night and took my son from my side, while your maidservant slept, and laid him in her bosom, and laid her dead child in my bosom. [21]And when I rose in the morning to nurse my son, there he was, dead. But when I had examined him in the morning, indeed, he was not my son whom I had borne."

[22]Then the other woman said, "No! But the living one *is* my son, and the dead one *is* your son."

And the first woman said, "No! But the dead one *is* your son, and the living one *is* my son."

Thus they spoke before the king.

[23]And the king said, "The one says, 'This *is* my son, who lives, and your son *is* the dead one'; and the other says, 'No! But your son *is* the dead one, and my son *is* the living one.' " [24]Then the king said, "Bring me a sword." So they brought a sword before the king. [25]And the king said, "Divide the living child in two, and give half to one, and half to the other."

[26]Then the woman whose son *was* living spoke to the king, for she yearned with compassion for her son; and she said, "O my lord, give her the living child, and by no means kill him!"

But the other said, "Let him be neither mine nor yours, *but* divide *him*."

[27]So the king answered and said, "Give the first woman the living child, and by no means kill him; she *is* his mother."

[28]And all Israel heard of the judgment which the king had rendered; and they feared the king, for they saw that the wisdom of God *was* in him to administer justice.

Solomon's Administration

4 So King Solomon was king over all Israel. [2]And these *were* his officials: Azariah the son of Zadok, the priest; [3]Elihoreph and Ahijah, the sons of Shisha, scribes; Jehoshaphat the son of Ahilud, the recorder; [4]Benaiah the son of Jehoiada, over the army; Zadok and

SOUL NOTE

Just Ask *(3:5–14)* Solomon could have asked for anything, but he knew what he needed most: "an understanding heart to . . . discern between good and evil." Solomon's position as king would require him to make decisions that would affect all of God's people. He wanted to rule those people well. God says that anyone can ask for wisdom: "If any of you lacks wisdom, let him ask of God, who gives to all liberally and without reproach, and it will be given to him" (James 1:5). Regardless of position in life, every believer should seek God's wisdom. **Topic: Wisdom**

SOUL NOTE

Mother's Love *(3:16–27)* This story illustrates Solomon's wisdom. Two women had borne children; one child had died and both women claimed the living child. Solomon's proposed solution was to divide the child in half with a sword. Immediately the real mother cried out, telling the king to give the living child to the other woman rather than kill him. Solomon knew that the woman who responded was the real mother, for she was willing to give up her child to someone else to save his life. Such is the depth of a mother's love—giving of herself for the best of her child.
Topic: Motherhood

Abiathar, the priests; 5Azariah the son of Nathan, over the officers; Zabud the son of Nathan, a priest *and* the king's friend; 6Ahishar, over the household; and Adoniram the son of Abda, over the labor force.

7And Solomon had twelve governors over all Israel, who provided food for the king and his household; each one made provision for one month of the year. 8These *are* their names: Ben-Hur,[a] in the mountains of Ephraim; 9Ben-Deker,[a] in Makaz, Shaalbim, Beth Shemesh, and Elon Beth Hanan; 10Ben-Hesed,[a] in Arubboth; to him *belonged* Sochoh and all the land of Hepher; 11Ben-Abinadab,[a] *in* all the regions of Dor; he had Taphath the daughter of Solomon as wife; 12Baana the son of Ahilud, *in* Taanach, Megiddo, and all Beth Shean, which *is* beside Zaretan below Jezreel, from Beth Shean to Abel Meholah, as far as the other side of Jokneam; 13Ben-Geber,[a] in Ramoth Gilead; to him *belonged* the towns of Jair the son of Manasseh, in Gilead; to him *also belonged* the region of Argob in Bashan—sixty large cities with walls and bronze gate-bars; 14Ahinadab the son of Iddo, *in* Mahanaim; 15Ahimaaz, in Naphtali; he also took Basemath the daughter of Solomon as wife; 16Baanah the son of Hushai, in Asher and Aloth; 17Jehoshaphat the son of Paruah, in Issachar; 18Shimei the son of Elah, in Benjamin; 19Geber the son of Uri, in the land of Gilead, *in* the country of Sihon king of the Amorites, and of Og king of Bashan. *He was* the only governor who *was* in the land.

Prosperity and Wisdom of Solomon's Reign

20Judah and Israel *were* as numerous as the sand by the sea in multitude, eating and drinking and rejoicing. 21So Solomon reigned over all kingdoms from the River[a] *to* the land of the Philistines, as far as the border of Egypt. *They* brought tribute and served Solomon all the days of his life.

22Now Solomon's provision for one day was thirty kors of fine flour, sixty kors of meal, 23ten fatted oxen, twenty oxen from the pastures, and one hundred sheep, besides deer, gazelles, roebucks, and fatted fowl.

24For he had dominion over all *the region* on this side of the River[a] from Tiphsah even to Gaza, namely over all the kings on this side of the River; and he had peace on every side all around him. 25And Judah and Israel dwelt safely, each man under his vine and his fig tree, from Dan as far as Beersheba, all the days of Solomon.

26Solomon had forty[a] thousand stalls of horses for his chariots, and twelve thousand horsemen. 27And these governors, each man in his month, provided food for King Solomon and for all who came to King Solomon's table. There was no lack in their supply. 28They also brought barley and straw to the proper place, for the horses and steeds, each man according to his charge.

29And God gave Solomon wisdom and exceedingly great understanding, and largeness of heart like the sand on the seashore. 30Thus Solomon's wisdom excelled the wisdom of all the men of the East and all the wisdom of Egypt. 31For he was wiser than all men—than Ethan the Ezrahite, and Heman, Chalcol, and Darda, the sons of Mahol; and his fame was in all the surrounding nations. 32He spoke three thousand proverbs, and his songs were one thousand and five. 33Also he spoke of trees, from the cedar tree of Lebanon even to the hyssop that springs out of the wall; he spoke also of animals, of birds, of creeping things, and of fish. 34And men of all nations, from all the kings of the earth who had heard of his wisdom, came to hear the wisdom of Solomon.

Solomon Prepares to Build the Temple

5 Now Hiram king of Tyre sent his servants to Solomon, because he heard that they had anointed him king in place of his father, for Hiram had always loved David. 2Then Solomon sent to Hiram, saying:

3 You know how my father David could
not build a house for the name of the
LORD his God because of the wars which
were fought against him on every side,
until the LORD put *his foes*[a] under the
soles of his feet.

4 But now the LORD my God has given me
rest on every side; *there is* neither
adversary nor evil occurrence.

4:8 [a]Literally *Son of Hur* **4:9** [a]Literally *Son of Deker* **4:10** [a]Literally *Son of Hesed*
4:11 [a]Literally *Son of Abinadab* **4:13** [a]Literally *Son of Geber* **4:21** [a]That is, the Euphrates
4:24 [a]That is, the Euphrates **4:26** [a]Following Masoretic Text and most other authorities; some manuscripts of the Septuagint read *four* (compare 2 Chronicles 9:25). **5:3** [a]Literally *them*

5 And behold, I propose to build a house
for the name of the LORD my God, as the
LORD spoke to my father David, saying,
"Your son, whom I will set on your
throne in your
place, he shall
build the house for
My name."
6 Now therefore,
command that they
cut down cedars
for me from Lebanon; and my servants
will be with your servants, and I will
pay you wages for your servants
according to whatever you say. For you
know *there is* none among us who has
skill to cut timber like the Sidonians.

7 So it was, when Hiram heard the words of
Solomon, that he rejoiced greatly and said,

Blessed *be* the LORD this day, for He has
given David a wise son over this great
people!

8 Then Hiram sent to Solomon, saying:

I have considered *the message* which
you sent me, *and* I will do all you desire
concerning the cedar and cypress logs.
9 My servants shall bring *them* down from
Lebanon to the sea; I will float them in
rafts by sea to the place you indicate to
me, and will have them broken apart
there; then you can take *them* away. And
you shall fulfill my desire by giving food
for my household.

10 Then Hiram gave Solomon cedar and cypress logs *according to* all his desire. 11 And
Solomon gave Hiram twenty thousand kors of
wheat *as* food for his household, and twenty[a]
kors of pressed oil. Thus Solomon gave to Hiram year by year.
12 So the LORD gave Solomon wisdom, as He
had promised him; and
there was peace be-
tween Hiram and Sol-
omon, and the two of
them made a treaty to-
gether.
13 Then King Solomon
raised up a labor force out of all Israel; and the
labor force was thirty thousand men. 14 And he
sent them to Lebanon, ten thousand a month
in shifts: they were one month in Lebanon
and two months at home; Adoniram *was* in
charge of the labor force. 15 Solomon had seventy thousand who carried burdens, and
eighty thousand who quarried *stone* in the
mountains, 16 besides three thousand three
hundred[a] from the chiefs of Solomon's deputies, who supervised the people who labored
in the work. 17 And the king commanded them
to quarry large stones, costly stones, *and*
hewn stones, to lay the foundation of the
temple.[a] 18 So Solomon's builders, Hiram's
builders, and the Gebalites quarried *them;* and
they prepared timber and stones to build the
temple.

> So the LORD gave Solomon wisdom,
> as He had promised him.
> **1 KINGS 5:12**

SOLOMON BUILDS THE TEMPLE

6 And it came to pass in the four hundred
and eightieth[a] year after the children of Is-

5:11 [a]Following Masoretic Text, Targum, and Vulgate; Septuagint and Syriac read *twenty thousand.* **5:16** [a]Following Masoretic Text, Targum, and Vulgate; Septuagint reads *three thousand six hundred.* **5:17** [a]Literally *house,* and so frequently throughout this book **6:1** [a]Following Masoretic Text, Targum, and Vulgate; Septuagint reads *fortieth.*

SOUL NOTE

Family First *(5:12–14)* God had given Solomon wisdom to rule the nation. There was peace in the land, so the nation could devote itself and its resources to building a glorious temple for God. Even as Solomon planned its construction, he used great wisdom. He drew upon the nation's labor force, divided it into three groups, and rotated the groups so they would be one month in Jerusalem and then two months at home. Solomon allowed for continuous work without burning out his workers or hurting their families. No matter how important the work, the workers' families must not be neglected. **Topic: Work**

rael had come out of the land of Egypt, in the fourth year of Solomon's reign over Israel, in the month of Ziv, which *is* the second month, that he began to build the house of the LORD. [2]Now the house which King Solomon built for the LORD, its length *was* sixty cubits, its width twenty, and its height thirty cubits. [3]The vestibule in front of the sanctuary[a] of the house *was* twenty cubits long across the width of the house, *and* the width of *the vestibule*[b] *extended* ten cubits from the front of the house. [4]And he made for the house windows with beveled frames.

[5]Against the wall of the temple he built chambers all around, *against* the walls of the temple, all around the sanctuary and the inner sanctuary.[a] Thus he made side chambers all around it. [6]The lowest chamber *was* five cubits wide, the middle *was* six cubits wide, and the third *was* seven cubits wide; for he made narrow ledges around the outside of the temple, so that *the support beams* would not be fastened into the walls of the temple. [7]And the temple, when it was being built, was built with stone finished at the quarry, so that no hammer or chisel *or* any iron tool was heard in the temple while it was being built. [8]The doorway for the middle story[a] *was* on the right side of the temple. They went up by stairs to the middle *story,* and from the middle to the third.

[9]So he built the temple and finished it, and he paneled the temple with beams and boards of cedar. [10]And he built side chambers against the entire temple, each five cubits high; they were attached to the temple with cedar beams.

[11]Then the word of the LORD came to Solomon, saying: [12]"*Concerning* this temple which you are building, if you walk in My statutes, execute My judgments, keep all My commandments, and walk in them, then I will perform My word with you, which I spoke to your father David. [13]And I will dwell among the children of Israel, and will not forsake My people Israel."

[14]So Solomon built the temple and finished it. [15]And he built the inside walls of the temple with cedar boards; from the floor of the temple to the ceiling he paneled the inside with wood; and he covered the floor of the temple with planks of cypress. [16]Then he built the twenty-cubit room at the rear of the temple, from floor to ceiling, with cedar boards; he built *it* inside as the inner sanctuary, as the Most Holy *Place.* [17]And in front of it the temple sanctuary was forty cubits *long.* [18]The inside of the temple was cedar, carved with ornamental buds and open flowers. All *was* cedar; there was no stone *to be* seen.

[19]And he prepared the inner sanctuary inside the temple, to set the ark of the covenant of the LORD there. [20]The inner sanctuary *was* twenty cubits long, twenty cubits wide, and twenty cubits high. He overlaid it with pure gold, and overlaid the altar of cedar. [21]So Solomon overlaid the inside of the temple with pure gold. He stretched gold chains across the front of the inner sanctuary, and overlaid it with gold. [22]The whole temple he overlaid with gold, until he had finished all the temple; also he overlaid with gold the entire altar that *was* by the inner sanctuary.

[23]Inside the inner sanctuary he made two cherubim *of* olive wood, *each* ten cubits high. [24]One wing of the cherub *was* five cubits, and the other wing of the cherub five cubits: ten cubits from the tip of one wing to the tip of the other. [25]And the other cherub *was* ten cubits; both cherubim *were* of the same size and shape. [26]The height of one cherub *was* ten cubits, and so *was* the other cherub. [27]Then he set the cherubim inside the inner room;[a] and they stretched out the wings of the cherubim so that the wing of the one touched *one* wall, and the wing of the other cherub touched the other wall. And their wings touched each other in the middle of the room. [28]Also he overlaid the cherubim with gold.

[29]Then he carved all the walls of the temple all around, both the inner and outer *sanctuaries,* with carved figures of cherubim, palm trees, and open flowers. [30]And the floor of the temple he overlaid with gold, both the inner and outer *sanctuaries.*

[31]For the entrance of the inner sanctuary he made doors *of* olive wood; the lintel *and* doorposts *were* one-fifth *of the wall.* [32]The two doors *were of* olive wood; and he carved on them figures of cherubim, palm trees, and open flowers, and overlaid *them* with gold;

6:3 [a]Hebrew *heykal;* here the main room of the temple, elsewhere called the holy place (compare Exodus 26:33 and Ezekiel 41:1) [b]Literally *it*
6:5 [a]Hebrew *debir;* here the inner room of the temple, elsewhere called the Most Holy Place (compare verse 16) **6:8** [a]Following Masoretic Text and Vulgate; Septuagint reads *upper story;* Targum reads *ground story.* **6:27** [a]Literally *house*

and he spread gold on the cherubim and on the palm trees. 33So for the door of the sanctuary he also made doorposts *of* olive wood, one-fourth *of the wall.* 34And the two doors *were of* cypress wood; two panels *comprised* one folding door, and two panels *comprised* the other folding door. 35Then he carved cherubim, palm trees, and open flowers *on them,* and overlaid *them* with gold applied evenly on the carved work.

36And he built the inner court with three rows of hewn stone and a row of cedar beams.

37In the fourth year the foundation of the house of the LORD was laid, in the month of Ziv. 38And in the eleventh year, in the month of Bul, which is the eighth month, the house was finished in all its details and according to all its plans. So he was seven years in building it.

Solomon's Other Buildings

7 But Solomon took thirteen years to build his own house; so he finished all his house.

2He also built the House of the Forest of Lebanon; its length *was* one hundred cubits, its width fifty cubits, and its height thirty cubits, with four rows of cedar pillars, and cedar beams on the pillars. 3And *it was* paneled with cedar above the beams that *were* on forty-five pillars, fifteen *to* a row. 4*There were* windows *with beveled frames in* three rows, and window *was* opposite window *in* three tiers. 5And all the doorways and doorposts *had* rectangular frames; and window *was* opposite window *in* three tiers.

6He also made the Hall of Pillars: its length *was* fifty cubits, and its width thirty cubits; and in front of them *was* a portico with pillars, and a canopy *was* in front of them.

7Then he made a hall for the throne, the Hall of Judgment, where he might judge; and *it was* paneled with cedar from floor to ceiling.[a]

8And the house where he dwelt *had* another court inside the hall, of like workmanship. Solomon also made a house like this hall for Pharaoh's daughter, whom he had taken *as wife.*

9All these *were of* costly stones cut to size, trimmed with saws, inside and out, from the foundation to the eaves, and also on the outside to the great court. 10The foundation *was of* costly stones, large stones, some ten cubits and some eight cubits. 11And above *were* costly stones, hewn to size, and cedar wood. 12The great court *was* enclosed with three rows of hewn stones and a row of cedar beams. So were the inner court of the house of the LORD and the vestibule of the temple.

Hiram the Craftsman

13Now King Solomon sent and brought Huram[a] from Tyre. 14He *was* the son of a widow from the tribe of Naphtali, and his father *was* a man of Tyre, a bronze worker; he was filled with wisdom and understanding and skill in working with all kinds of bronze work. So he came to King Solomon and did all his work.

The Bronze Pillars for the Temple

15And he cast two pillars of bronze, each one eighteen cubits high, and a line of twelve cubits measured the circumference of each. 16Then he made two capitals *of* cast bronze, to set on the tops of the pillars. The height of one capital *was* five cubits, and the height of the other capital *was* five cubits. 17*He made* a lattice network, with wreaths of chainwork, for the capitals which *were* on top of the pillars: seven chains for one capital and seven for the other capital. 18So he made the pillars, and two rows of pomegranates above the network all around to cover the capitals that *were* on top; and thus he did for the other capital.

19The capitals which *were* on top of the pillars in the hall *were* in the shape of lilies, four cubits. 20The capitals on the two pillars also *had pomegranates* above, by the convex surface which *was* next to the network; and there *were* two hundred such pomegranates in rows on each of the capitals all around.

21Then he set up the pillars by the vestibule of the temple; he set up the pillar on the right and called its name Jachin, and he set up the pillar on the left and called its name Boaz. 22The tops of the pillars were in the shape of lilies. So the work of the pillars was finished.

The Sea and the Oxen

23And he made the Sea of cast bronze, ten cubits from one brim to the other; *it was* completely round. Its height *was* five cubits, and a line of thirty cubits measured its circumference.

7:7 [a]Literally *floor,* that is, of the upper level
7:13 [a]Hebrew *Hiram* (compare 2 Chronicles 2:13, 14)

24 Below its brim *were* ornamental buds encircling it all around, ten to a cubit, all the way
around the Sea. The ornamental buds *were*
cast in two rows when it was cast. 25 It stood
on twelve oxen: three looking toward the
north, three looking toward the west, three
looking toward the south, and three looking
toward the east; the Sea *was set* upon them,
and all their back parts *pointed* inward. 26 It
was a handbreadth thick; and its brim was
shaped like the brim of a cup, *like* a lily blossom. It contained two thousand[a] baths.

The Carts and the Lavers

27 He also made ten carts of bronze; four cubits *was* the length of each cart, four cubits its
width, and three cubits its height. 28 And this
was the design of the carts: They had panels,
and the panels *were* between frames; 29 on the
panels that *were* between the frames *were*
lions, oxen, and cherubim. And on the frames
was a pedestal on top. Below the lions and
oxen *were* wreaths of plaited work. 30 Every
cart had four bronze wheels and axles of
bronze, and its four feet had supports. Under
the laver *were* supports of cast *bronze* beside
each wreath. 31 Its opening inside the crown at
the top *was* one cubit in diameter; and the
opening *was* round, shaped *like* a pedestal,
one and a half cubits in outside diameter; and
also on the opening *were* engravings, but the
panels were square, not round. 32 Under the
panels *were* the four wheels, and the axles of
the wheels *were joined* to the cart. The height
of a wheel *was* one and a half cubits. 33 The
workmanship of the wheels *was* like the
workmanship of a chariot wheel; their axle
pins, their rims, their spokes, and their hubs
were all of cast *bronze*. 34 And *there were* four
supports at the four corners of each cart; its
supports *were* part of the cart itself. 35 On the
top of the cart, at the height of half a cubit, *it*
was perfectly round. And on the top of the
cart, its flanges and its panels *were* of the
same casting. 36 On the plates of its flanges and
on its panels he engraved cherubim, lions,
and palm trees, wherever there was a clear
space on each, with wreaths all around. 37 Thus
he made the ten carts. All of them were of the
same mold, one measure, *and* one shape.
38 Then he made ten lavers of bronze; each
laver contained forty baths, *and* each laver
was four cubits. On each of the ten carts *was* a
laver. 39 And he put five carts on the right side
of the house, and five on the left side of the
house. He set the Sea on the right side of the
house, toward the southeast.

Furnishings of the Temple

40 Huram[a] made the lavers and the shovels
and the bowls. So Huram finished doing all
the work that he was to do for King Solomon
for the house of the LORD: 41 the two pillars, the
two bowl-shaped capitals that *were* on top of
the two pillars; the two networks covering the
two bowl-shaped capitals which *were* on top
of the pillars; 42 four hundred pomegranates
for the two networks (two rows of pomegranates for each network, to cover the two bowl-
shaped capitals that *were* on top of the
pillars); 43 the ten carts, and ten lavers on the
carts; 44 one Sea, and twelve oxen under the
Sea; 45 the pots, the shovels, and the bowls.
All these articles which Huram[a] made for
King Solomon *for* the house of the LORD *were*
of burnished bronze. 46 In the plain of Jordan
the king had them cast in clay molds, between
Succoth and Zaretan. 47 And Solomon did not
weigh all the articles, because *there were* so
many; the weight of the bronze was not determined.

48 Thus Solomon had all the furnishings
made for the house of the LORD: the altar of
gold, and the table of gold on which *was* the
showbread; 49 the lampstands of pure gold,
five on the right *side* and five on the left in
front of the inner sanctuary, with the flowers
and the lamps and the wick trimmers of gold;
50 the basins, the trimmers, the bowls, the
ladles, and the censers of pure gold; and the
hinges of gold, *both* for the doors of the inner
room (the Most Holy *Place*) *and* for the doors
of the main hall of the temple.

51 So all the work that King Solomon had
done for the house of the LORD was finished;
and Solomon brought in the things which his
father David had dedicated: the silver and the
gold and the furnishings. He put them in the
treasuries of the house of the LORD.

The Ark Brought into the Temple

8 Now Solomon assembled the elders of
Israel and all the heads of the tribes, the

7:26 [a]Or *three thousand* (compare 2 Chronicles 4:5) **7:40** [a]Hebrew *Hiram* (compare 2 Chronicles 2:13, 14) **7:45** [a]Hebrew *Hiram* (compare 2 Chronicles 2:13, 14)

chief fathers of the children of Israel, to King
Solomon in Jerusalem, that they might bring
up the ark of the covenant of the LORD from
the City of David, which *is* Zion. [2]Therefore all
the men of Israel assembled with King Solomon at the feast in the month of Ethanim,
which *is* the seventh month. [3]So all the elders
of Israel came, and the priests took up the ark.
[4]Then they brought up the ark of the LORD,
the tabernacle of meeting, and all the holy
furnishings that *were* in the tabernacle. The
priests and the Levites brought them up. [5]Also
King Solomon, and all the congregation of
Israel who were assembled with him, *were*
with him before the ark, sacrificing sheep and
oxen that could not be
counted or numbered
for multitude. [6]Then the
priests brought in the
ark of the covenant of
the LORD to its place,
into the inner sanctuary
of the temple, to the
Most Holy *Place,* under the wings of the
cherubim. [7]For the cherubim spread *their* two
wings over the place of the ark, and the cherubim overshadowed the ark and its poles. [8]The
poles extended so that the ends of the poles
could be seen from the holy *place,* in front of
the inner sanctuary; but they could not be
seen from outside. And they are there to this
day. [9]Nothing *was* in the ark except the two
tablets of stone which Moses put there at
Horeb, when the LORD made *a covenant* with
the children of Israel, when they came out of
the land of Egypt.
[10]And it came to pass, when the priests
came out of the holy *place,* that the cloud
filled the house of the LORD, [11]so that the
priests could not continue ministering because of the cloud; for the glory of the LORD
filled the house of the LORD.

> The glory of the LORD filled the house of the LORD.
>
> 1 KINGS 8:11

[12]Then Solomon spoke:

"The LORD said He would dwell in the
dark cloud.
13 I have surely built You an exalted house,
And a place for You to dwell in forever."

SOLOMON'S SPEECH AT COMPLETION OF THE WORK

[14]Then the king turned around and blessed
the whole assembly of Israel, while all the assembly of Israel was standing. [15]And he said:
"Blessed *be* the LORD God of Israel, who spoke
with His mouth to my father David, and with
His hand has fulfilled *it,* saying, [16]'Since the
day that I brought My
people Israel out of
Egypt, I have chosen no
city from any tribe of
Israel *in which* to build
a house, that My name
might be there; but I
chose David to be over
My people Israel.' [17]Now it was in the heart of
my father David to build a temple[a] for the
name of the LORD God of Israel. [18]But the LORD
said to my father David, 'Whereas it was in
your heart to build a temple for My name, you
did well that it was in your heart. [19]Neverthe-
less you shall not build the temple, but your
son who will come from your body, he shall
build the temple for My name.' [20]So the LORD
has fulfilled His word which He spoke; and I
have filled the position of my father David,
and sit on the throne of Israel, as the LORD
promised; and I have built a temple for the
name of the LORD God of Israel. [21]And there I
have made a place for the ark, in which *is* the
covenant of the LORD which He made with our

8:17 [a]Literally *house,* and so in verses 18–20

SOUL NOTE

God Hears *(8:22–30)* Solomon's prayer at the dedication of the temple is one of the exemplary prayers of the Old Testament. He acknowledged the Lord God of Israel, keeper of the covenant and giver of mercy. Solomon asked God to hear the prayers of His people when they came to the temple to pray (8:30). The glorious God, who is greater than the heavens, heard and answered Solomon's prayer, and He hears and answers ours. Those who humbly come to God in reverence and awe, bringing their praise and requests, will not be disappointed. **Topic: Prayer**

fathers, when He brought them out of the land
of Egypt."

Solomon's Prayer of Dedication

22 Then Solomon stood before the altar of
the LORD in the presence of all the assembly of
Israel, and spread out his hands toward
heaven; 23 and he said: "LORD God of Israel,
there is no God in heaven above or on earth
below like You, who keep *Your* covenant and
mercy with Your servants who walk before
You with all their hearts. 24 You have kept what
You promised Your servant David my father;
You have both spoken with Your mouth and
fulfilled *it* with Your hand, as *it is* this day.
25 Therefore, LORD God of Israel, now keep
what You promised Your servant David my father, saying, 'You shall not fail to have a man
sit before Me on the throne of Israel, only if
your sons take heed to their way, that they
walk before Me as you have walked before
Me.' 26 And now I pray, O God of Israel, let Your
word come true, which You have spoken to
Your servant David my father.
27 "But will God indeed dwell on the earth?
Behold, heaven and the heaven of heavens
cannot contain You. How much less this temple which I have built! 28 Yet regard the prayer
of Your servant and his supplication, O LORD
my God, and listen to the cry and the prayer
which Your servant is praying before You today: 29 that Your eyes may be open toward this
temple night and day, toward the place of
which You said, 'My name shall be there,' that
You may hear the prayer which Your servant
makes toward this place. 30 And may You hear
the supplication of Your servant and of Your
people Israel, when they pray toward this
place. Hear in heaven Your dwelling place;
and when You hear, forgive.
31 "When anyone sins against his neighbor,
and is forced to take an oath, and comes *and*
takes an oath before Your altar in this temple,
32 then hear in heaven, and act, and judge Your
servants, condemning the wicked, bringing
his way on his head, and justifying the righteous by giving him according to his righteousness.
33 "When Your people Israel are defeated before an enemy because they have sinned
against You, and when they turn back to You
and confess Your name, and pray and make
supplication to You in this temple, 34 then hear
in heaven, and forgive the sin of Your people
Israel, and bring them back to the land which
You gave to their fathers.
35 "When the heavens are shut up and there
is no rain because they have sinned against
You, when they pray toward this place and
confess Your name, and turn from their sin because You afflict them, 36 then hear in heaven,
and forgive the sin of Your servants, Your people Israel, that You may teach them the good
way in which they should walk; and send rain
on Your land which You have given to Your
people as an inheritance.
37 "When there is famine in the land, pestilence *or* blight *or* mildew, locusts *or* grasshoppers; when their enemy besieges them in the
land of their cities; whatever plague or whatever sickness *there is;* 38 whatever prayer,
whatever supplication is made by anyone, *or*
by all Your people Israel, when each one
knows the plague of his own heart, and
spreads out his hands toward this temple:
39 then hear in heaven Your dwelling place,
and forgive, and act, and give to everyone according to all his ways, whose heart You know
(for You alone know the hearts of all the sons
of men), 40 that they may fear You all the days
that they live in the land which You gave to
our fathers.
41 "Moreover, concerning a foreigner, who *is*
not of Your people Israel, but has come from a

SOUL NOTE

Just a Prayer Away *(8:33–40)* The temple was to be a house of prayer and a place of repentance. When the people of Israel sinned, Solomon prayed that God would hear their prayers of repentance and forgive them. This would happen continually, for sin is a constant reality. Solomon's prayer reveals God's compassion in dealing with His people when they have failed. God wants to forgive, and He offers it when He sees our repentance and change of heart. He wants His people to come to Him, so He can heal and forgive. **Topic: Sin**

Sin

VICTORIOUS LIVING

RON HAWKINS

(1 Kings 8:31–40)

No one likes to talk about sin. We risk being labeled old-fashioned and insensitive if we insist that sin is a central issue in the struggles people face. However, insist we must, for it is the clear teaching of Scripture that sin is: (1) a condition inherited from Adam, (2) a lifelong challenge for Christians, and (3) a series of battles that can be won through the power of the Lord Jesus Christ and the Holy Spirit.

SIN—A CONDITION INHERITED FROM ADAM

All of humanity finds its origin in the union of Adam and Eve. Tragically, this connection means that we are controlled by Adam's fallen sinful nature—hence, we are sinners who need change. In the Bible, sin is described as: lawlessness and faithlessness, falling short of the mark, rebellion against authority, and an indifference to or crossing of established boundaries. Above all, sin destroys a vital relationship with God. Failure to deal with sin results in a corruption of our being and, ultimately, spiritual and physical death (Rom. 6:23).

SIN—A LIFELONG CHALLENGE

The Bible says that God loves people, pursues sinners, and has done all that is necessary to restore us to fellowship with Himself. However, we must believe and confess Christ as Savior in order to be set free from sin (Rom. 10:9, 10). Then the indwelling Holy Spirit provides us with the power to overcome sin on a daily basis and make progress toward Christlike character. When we fail to be obedient to Christ's teachings, God insists that we acknowledge these failures as sin, repent, confess, seek forgiveness, recommit to obedience, and seek restoration to God and one another (1 John 1:9). Yet sin will continue to be a challenge as long as we live. Paul recognized this as he battled with his sin (Rom. 7:19–25).

TRAINING, NOT TRYING, TO OVERCOME SIN

Believers have been delivered from sin, but they still must work to overcome sinful habits. This is accomplished not by "trying" to overcome sin, but by engaging in a training regimen that results in the mastery of disciplines that help us make the right choices. In our everyday life and soul care ministries, we must remind ourselves and God's children that overcoming sinful thoughts and behaviors must be the goal, and that the pattern for overcoming sin transcends times and cultures. This pattern is fleshed out for the nation of Israel in 1 Kings 8:31–40. The consequences of unconfessed sin are broken fellowship with God and others, as well as the experience of God's discipline.

Sincere Christians can train for godliness by making godly choices with regard to various areas of life. For example:

The Mind—The Bible is the centerpiece in God's plan for transforming us from the old ways in Adam to the new ways in Christ. The reading and memorizing of God's Word, and the instruction received through it, are God's primary agents for helping His children in their battle against sin. Making certain that God's Word is richly dwelling in the mind is the first priority for people who desire to overcome sin.

The Will—Truth in the mind must be acted upon. We have been given by our Creator the freedom to choose and are responsible for our choices. The will is open or closed to the Spirit and others as a consequence of these choices. In our battle against sin, we must *choose* to put off old behaviors that appealed to the flesh and replace them with new behaviors like Bible study, worship, prayer, and fasting, which foster richer connections with God and others.

The Body—The body is the seat of appetites like hunger, thirst, and physical desire. God intends that we should enjoy these appetites within the guidelines provided in Scripture. We must learn these guidelines and stay within them in order to keep our bodies away from sin.

The Emotions—We must choose to pay careful attention to our emotions. The absence of positive emotions is often the first indication that someone is believing or behaving poorly. When beliefs are based in error or left unsupported by appropriate actions, people experience the loss of joy. Emotions are powerful allies in our quest to determine whether one's beliefs and behavior are supported by truth.

The Holy Spirit—Paul insists that fulfilling the will of God requires the filling of the Holy Spirit (Eph. 5:15–21). The crucial issue is the *choice* to follow the Spirit's lead. God's Word richly nestled in the mind is a prerequisite for and a companion to the Spirit-filled life. The list of behaviors and experiences that flow from the life of one whose mind is "richly" filled with the Word of God (Col. 3:12–21) is virtually identical to the list of behaviors that flow from the Spirit-filled life (Gal. 5:22–25). Choosing to be filled with the Holy Spirit moment by moment is vitally important for those who would experience God's peace and power.

Community—The believing community that we call the church is essential for soul care and the healing of hurts. We grow to maturity in Christ only when we choose to be surrounded by a group of people who love us, share with us, dream with us, exhort us regarding our shortcomings, and applaud us for our advances.

Overcoming sin is possible through good choices and the power of the resurrected Christ. Believers will not be "sinless" until heaven, but in the meantime, we can experience marvelous victories in our battle with our enemy called "sin."

FURTHER MEDITATION:

Other passages to study about the issue of sin include:

➢ John 3:1–8
➢ 1 Corinthians 6:19, 20
➢ 2 Corinthians 5:17–21
➢ Ephesians 5:1–21
➢ 2 Timothy 3:15–17
➢ Hebrews 4:12; 12:1, 2
➢ James 1:15; 4:17
➢ 1 John 2:15, 16; 3:1–9

To Learn More: Turn to the key passage note on sin at 1 John 1:9 on page 1675. See also the personality profile of Isaiah on page 883.

far country for Your name's sake 42(for they will hear of Your great name and Your strong hand and Your outstretched arm), when he comes and prays toward this temple, 43hear in heaven Your dwelling place, and do according to all for which the foreigner calls to You, that all peoples of the earth may know Your name and fear You, as *do* Your people Israel, and that they may know that this temple which I have built is called by Your name.

44"When Your people go out to battle against their enemy, wherever You send them, and when they pray to the LORD toward the city which You have chosen and the temple which I have built for Your name, 45then hear in heaven their prayer and their supplication, and maintain their cause.

46"When they sin against You (for *there is* no one who does not sin), and You become angry with them and deliver them to the enemy, and they take them captive to the land of the enemy, far or near; 47*yet* when they come to themselves in the land where they were carried captive, and repent, and make supplication to You in the land of those who took them captive, saying, 'We have sinned and done wrong, we have committed wickedness'; 48and *when* they return to You with all their heart and with all their soul in the land of their enemies who led them away captive, and pray to You toward their land which You gave to their fathers, the city which You have chosen and the temple which I have built for Your name: 49then hear in heaven Your dwelling place their prayer and their supplication, and maintain their cause, 50and forgive Your people who have sinned against You, and all their transgressions which they have transgressed against You; and grant them compassion before those who took them captive, that they may have compassion on them 51(for they *are* Your people and Your inheritance, whom You brought out of Egypt, out of the iron furnace), 52that Your eyes may be open to the supplication of Your servant and the supplication of Your people Israel, to listen to them whenever they call to You. 53For You separated them from among all the peoples of the earth *to be* Your inheritance, as You spoke by Your servant Moses, when You brought our fathers out of Egypt, O Lord GOD."

SOLOMON BLESSES THE ASSEMBLY

54And so it was, when Solomon had finished praying all this prayer and supplication to the LORD, that he arose from before the altar of the LORD, from kneeling on his knees with his hands spread up to heaven. 55Then he stood and blessed all the assembly of Israel with a loud voice, saying: 56"Blessed *be* the LORD, who has given rest to His people Israel, according to all that He promised. There has not failed one word of all His good promise, which He promised through His servant Moses. 57May the LORD our God be with us, as He was with our fathers. May He not leave us nor forsake us, 58that He may incline our hearts to Himself, to walk in all His ways, and to keep His commandments and His statutes and His judgments, which He commanded our fathers. 59And may these words of mine, with which I have made supplication before the LORD, be near the LORD our God day and night, that He may maintain the cause of His servant and the cause of His people Israel, as each day may require, 60that all the peoples of the earth may know that the LORD *is* God; *there is* no other. 61Let your heart therefore be loyal to the LORD our God, to walk in His statutes and keep His commandments, as at this day."

SOUL NOTE

God Never Changes *(8:56)* God keeps His promises. "There has not failed one word of all His good promise, which He promised through His servant Moses." God had promised to deliver Israel from Egypt, lead them through the wilderness, and guide them into the Promised Land. Hundreds of years had passed; many of the people had sinned and faced punishment. This generation of Israelites reemphasized their confidence in God's promises. God's Word contains His promises to the faithful. Believers can still claim those promises, for God will never change and will always keep His promises. **Topic: God's Promises**

Solomon Dedicates the Temple

62Then the king and all Israel with him offered sacrifices before the LORD. 63And Solomon offered a sacrifice of peace offerings,
which he offered to the LORD, twenty-two
thousand bulls and one hundred and twenty
thousand sheep. So the king and all the children of Israel dedicated the house of the
LORD. 64On the same day the king consecrated the middle of the court that *was* in front
of the house of the LORD; for there he offered burnt offerings, grain offerings, and
the fat of the peace offerings, because the
bronze altar that *was* before the LORD *was*
too small to receive the burnt offerings, the
grain offerings, and the fat of the peace offerings.

65At that time Solomon held a feast, and all
Israel with him, a great assembly from the entrance of Hamath to the Brook of Egypt, before
the LORD our God, seven days and seven *more*
days—fourteen days. 66On the eighth day he
sent the people away; and they blessed the
king, and went to their tents joyful and glad
of heart for all the good that the LORD had
done for His servant David, and for Israel His
people.

God's Second Appearance to Solomon

9 And it came to pass, when Solomon had
finished building the house of the LORD
and the king's house, and all Solomon's desire
which he wanted to do, 2that the LORD appeared to Solomon the second time, as He had
appeared to him at Gibeon. 3And the LORD
said to him: "I have heard your prayer and
your supplication that you have made before
Me; I have consecrated this house which you
have built to put My name there forever, and
My eyes and My heart will be there perpetually. 4Now if you walk before Me as your father David walked, in integrity of heart and in
uprightness, to do according to all that I have
commanded you, *and* if you keep My statutes
and My judgments, 5then I will establish the
throne of your kingdom over Israel forever, as
I promised David your father, saying, 'You
shall not fail to have a man on the throne of
Israel.' 6*But* if you or your sons at all turn from
following Me, and do not keep My commandments *and* My statutes which I have set before
you, but go and serve other gods and worship
them, 7then I will cut off Israel from the land
which I have given them; and this house which
I have consecrated for My name I will cast out
of My sight. Israel will be a proverb and a byword among all peoples. 8And *as for* this
house, *which* is exalted, everyone who passes
by it will be astonished and will hiss, and say,
'Why has the LORD done thus to this land and
to this house?' 9Then they will answer, 'Because they forsook the LORD their God, who
brought their fathers out of the land of Egypt,
and have embraced other gods, and worshiped them and served them; therefore the
LORD has brought all this calamity on them.' "

Solomon and Hiram Exchange Gifts

10Now it happened at the end of twenty
years, when Solomon had built the two
houses, the house of the LORD and the king's
house 11(Hiram the king of Tyre had supplied
Solomon with cedar and cypress and gold, as
much as he desired), *that* King Solomon then
gave Hiram twenty cities in the land of Galilee. 12Then Hiram went from Tyre to see the
cities which Solomon had given him, but they
did not please him. 13So he said, "What *kind
of* cities *are* these which you have given me,
my brother?" And he called them the land of

SOUL NOTE

Seriously *(9:5)* God told Solomon that He would establish his kingdom forever. At the same time, God warned Solomon that if he turned away from Him, He would deal severely with both Solomon and Israel. This passage contains both potential blessings and curses, based on people's responses. Believers are accountable to God. Their choices will not only affect them, but others as well, such as family and friends. The king's choices affected the entire nation. God is serious about His relationship with us; we should be just as serious in our responses to Him.

Topic: Accountability

Cabul,[a] as they are to this day. 14Then Hiram sent the king one hundred and twenty talents of gold.

SOLOMON'S ADDITIONAL ACHIEVEMENTS

15And this *is* the reason for the labor force which King Solomon raised: to build the house of the LORD, his own house, the Millo,[a] the wall of Jerusalem, Hazor, Megiddo, and Gezer. 16(Pharaoh king of Egypt had gone up and taken Gezer and burned it with fire, had killed the Canaanites who dwelt in the city, and had given it *as* a dowry to his daughter, Solomon's wife.) 17And Solomon built Gezer, Lower Beth Horon, 18Baalath, and Tadmor in the wilderness, in the land *of Judah,* 19all the storage cities that Solomon had, cities for his chariots and cities for his cavalry, and whatever Solomon desired to build in Jerusalem, in Lebanon, and in all the land of his dominion.

20All the people *who were* left of the Amorites, Hittites, Perizzites, Hivites, and Jebusites, who *were* not of the children of Israel—21that is, their descendants who were left in the land after them, whom the children of Israel had not been able to destroy completely—from these Solomon raised forced labor, as it is to this day. 22But of the children of Israel Solomon made no forced laborers, because they *were* men of war and his servants: his officers, his captains, commanders of his chariots, and his cavalry.

23Others *were* chiefs of the officials who *were* over Solomon's work: five hundred and fifty, who ruled over the people who did the work.

24But Pharaoh's daughter came up from the City of David to her house which *Solomon*[a] had built for her. Then he built the Millo.

25Now three times a year Solomon offered burnt offerings and peace offerings on the altar which he had built for the LORD, and he burned incense with them *on the altar* that *was* before the LORD. So he finished the temple.

26King Solomon also built a fleet of ships at Ezion Geber, which *is* near Elath[a] on the shore of the Red Sea, in the land of Edom. 27Then Hiram sent his servants with the fleet, seamen who knew the sea, to work with the servants of Solomon. 28And they went to Ophir, and acquired four hundred and twenty talents of gold from there, and brought *it* to King Solomon.

THE QUEEN OF SHEBA'S PRAISE OF SOLOMON

10 Now when the queen of Sheba heard of the fame of Solomon concerning the name of the LORD, she came to test him with hard questions. 2She came to Jerusalem with a very great retinue, with camels that bore spices, very much gold, and precious stones; and when she came to Solomon, she spoke with him about all that was in her heart. 3So Solomon answered all her questions; there was nothing so difficult for the king that he could not explain *it* to her. 4And when the queen of Sheba had seen all the wisdom of Solomon, the house that he had built, 5the food on his table, the seating of his servants, the service of his waiters and their apparel, his cupbearers, and his entryway by which he went up to the house of the LORD, there was no more spirit in her. 6Then she said to the king: "It was a true report which I heard in my own land about your words and your wisdom. 7However I did not believe the words until I came and saw with my own eyes; and indeed the half was not told me. Your wisdom

9:13 [a]Literally *Good for Nothing* **9:15** [a]Literally *The Landfill* **9:24** [a]Literally *he* (compare 2 Chronicles 8:11) **9:26** [a]Hebrew *Eloth* (compare 2 Kings 14:22)

SOUL NOTE

Wise Words, Wise Acts *(10:1–13)* Solomon's wisdom was divinely given and internationally acclaimed (4:29–34; 10:23, 24). The queen of Sheba traveled a long distance "to test him with hard questions" (10:1), only to discover that Solomon could answer every one. The queen was overwhelmed and could only praise the God of Israel for giving His people such a leader. Wisdom attracts others and points them to God. The wise actions and wise words that sprinkle our everyday lives will reflect to others our great God. **Topic: Wisdom**

and prosperity exceed the fame of which I
heard. 8Happy *are* your men and happy *are*
these your servants, who stand continually
before you *and* hear your wisdom! 9Blessed
be the LORD your God, who delighted in you,
setting you on the throne of Israel! Because
the LORD has loved Israel forever, therefore He
made you king, to do justice and righteousness."
10Then she gave the king one hundred and
twenty talents of gold, spices in great quantity, and precious stones. There never again
came such abundance of spices as the queen
of Sheba gave to King Solomon. 11Also, the
ships of Hiram, which brought gold from
Ophir, brought great *quantities* of almug[a]
wood and precious stones from Ophir. 12And
the king made steps of the almug wood for the
house of the LORD and for the king's house,
also harps and stringed instruments for singers. There never again came such almug
wood, nor has the like been seen to this day.
13Now King Solomon gave the queen of
Sheba all she desired, whatever she asked, besides what Solomon had given her according
to the royal generosity. So she turned and
went to her own country, she and her servants.

SOLOMON'S GREAT WEALTH

14The weight of gold that came to Solomon
yearly was six hundred and sixty-six talents of
gold, 15besides *that* from the traveling mer
chants, from the income of traders, from all
the kings of Arabia, and from the governors of
the country.
16And King Solomon made two hundred
large shields *of* hammered gold; six hundred
shekels of gold went into each shield. 17He
also *made* three hundred shields *of* hammered
gold; three minas of gold went into each
shield. The king put them in the House of the
Forest of Lebanon.
18Moreover the king made a great throne of
ivory, and overlaid it with pure gold. 19The
throne had six steps, and the top of the throne
was round at the back; *there were* armrests on
either side of the place of the seat, and two
lions stood beside the armrests. 20Twelve lions
stood there, one on each side of the six steps;
nothing like *this* had been made for any *other*
kingdom.
21All King Solomon's drinking vessels *were*
gold, and all the vessels of the House of the
Forest of Lebanon *were* pure gold. Not *one was*
silver, for this was accounted as nothing in the
days of Solomon. 22For the king had merchant
ships[a] at sea with the fleet of Hiram. Once every three years the merchant ships came
bringing gold, silver, ivory, apes, and monkeys.[b] 23So King Solomon surpassed all the
kings of the earth in riches and wisdom.
24Now all the earth sought the presence of
Solomon to hear his wisdom, which God had
put in his heart. 25Each man brought his present: articles of silver and gold, garments, armor, spices, horses, and mules, at a set rate
year by year.
26And Solomon gathered chariots and
horsemen; he had one thousand four hundred
chariots and twelve thousand horsemen,
whom he stationed[a] in the chariot cities and
with the king at Jerusalem. 27The king made
silver *as common* in Jerusalem as stones, and
he made cedar trees as abundant as the sycamores which *are* in the lowland.
28Also Solomon had horses imported from
Egypt and Keveh; the king's merchants bought
them in Keveh at the *current* price. 29Now a
chariot that was imported from Egypt cost six

10:11 [a]Or *algum* (compare 2 Chronicles 9:10, 11) **10:22** [a]Literally *ships of Tarshish,* deep-sea vessels [b]Or *peacocks* **10:26** [a]Following Septuagint, Syriac, Targum, and Vulgate (compare 2 Chronicles 9:25); Masoretic Text reads *led.*

SOUL NOTE

Heavenly Accounting *(10:14–29)* Solomon's wisdom resulted in great wealth, just as God had promised (3:13). Solomon's choices led to an incredible abundance of blessing for the nation so that they could build the nation and the glorious temple. Solomon also enriched himself, just as Samuel had warned many years before (1 Sam. 8:10–18). Money can be a great blessing and can do much for God and His people. It can also be used to enrich oneself at the expense of others. **Topic: Money**

hundred *shekels* of silver, and a horse one
hundred and fifty; and thus, through their
agents,[a] they exported *them* to all the kings of
the Hittites and the kings of Syria.

SOLOMON'S HEART TURNS FROM THE LORD

11 But King Solomon loved many foreign
women, as well as the daughter of
Pharaoh: women of the Moabites, Ammonites, Edomites, Sidonians, *and* Hittites—
2from the nations of whom the LORD had said
to the children of Israel, "You shall not intermarry with them, nor they with you. Surely
they will turn away your hearts after their
gods." Solomon clung to these in love. 3And
he had seven hundred wives, princesses, and
three hundred concubines; and his wives
turned away his heart. 4For it was so, when
Solomon was old, that his wives turned his
heart after other gods; and his heart was not
loyal to the LORD his God, as *was* the heart of
his father David. 5For Solomon went after
Ashtoreth the goddess of the Sidonians, and
after Milcom the abomination of the Ammonites. 6Solomon did evil in the sight of the
LORD, and did not fully follow the LORD, as *did*
his father David. 7Then Solomon built a high
place for Chemosh the abomination of Moab,
on the hill that *is* east of Jerusalem, and for
Molech the abomination of the people of Ammon. 8And he did likewise for all his foreign
wives, who burned incense and sacrificed to
their gods.

9So the LORD became angry with Solomon,
because his heart had turned from the LORD
God of Israel, who had appeared to him twice,
10and had commanded him concerning this
thing, that he should not go after other gods;
but he did not keep what the LORD had commanded. 11Therefore the LORD said to Solomon, "Because you have done this, and have
not kept My covenant and My statutes, which
I have commanded you, I will surely tear the
kingdom away from you and give it to your
servant. 12Nevertheless I will not do it in your
days, for the sake of your father David; I will
tear it out of the hand of your son. 13However
I will not tear away the whole kingdom; I will
give one tribe to your son for the sake of My
servant David, and for the sake of Jerusalem
which I have chosen."

ADVERSARIES OF SOLOMON

14Now the LORD raised up an adversary
against Solomon, Hadad the Edomite; he *was*
a descendant of the king in Edom. 15For it happened, when David was in Edom, and Joab
the commander of the army had gone up to
bury the slain, after he had killed every male
in Edom 16(because for six months Joab remained there with all Israel, until he had cut
down every male in Edom), 17that Hadad fled
to go to Egypt, he and certain Edomites of his
father's servants with him. Hadad *was* still a
little child. 18Then they arose from Midian and
came to Paran; and they took men with them
from Paran and came to Egypt, to Pharaoh
king of Egypt, who gave him a house, apportioned food for him, and gave him land. 19And
Hadad found great favor in the sight of Pharaoh, so that he gave him as wife the sister of
his own wife, that is, the sister of Queen Tahpenes. 20Then the sister of Tahpenes bore him
Genubath his son, whom Tahpenes weaned
in Pharaoh's house. And Genubath was in
Pharaoh's household among the sons of Pharaoh.

21So when Hadad heard in Egypt that David
rested with his fathers, and that Joab the commander of the army was dead, Hadad said to

10:29 [a]Literally *by their hands*

SOUL NOTE

Closer or Farther Away? *(11:1–13)* What a sad commentary on a great king! Solomon had been blessed with world-acclaimed wisdom and wealth, but his wisdom did not extend to his passions. God gave the nation peace, but Solomon continued the age-old tradition of marrying foreign women to obtain alliances. Solomon "loved many foreign women" and "clung to these in love" (11:1, 2). These relationships led to his downfall, for these women turned his heart to other gods. Our relationships can help us grow closer to God, or they can cause us to turn from Him. We must make careful choices in marriage and friendship. **Topic: Relationships**

Pharaoh, "Let me depart, that I may go to my
own country."
[22]Then Pharaoh said to him, "But what have
you lacked with me, that suddenly you seek to
go to your own country?"
So he answered, "Nothing, but do let me go
anyway."
[23]And God raised up *another* adversary
against him, Rezon the son of Eliadah, who
had fled from his lord, Hadadezer king of Zobah. [24]So he gathered men to him and became
captain over a band *of raiders,* when David
killed those *of Zobah.* And they went to Damascus and dwelt there, and reigned in Damascus. [25]He was an adversary of Israel all the
days of Solomon (besides the trouble that Hadad *caused*); and he abhorred Israel, and
reigned over Syria.

Jeroboam's Rebellion

[26]Then Solomon's servant, Jeroboam the
son of Nebat, an Ephraimite from Zereda,
whose mother's name *was* Zeruah, a widow,
also rebelled against the king.
[27]And this *is* what caused him to rebel
against the king: Solomon had built the Millo
and repaired the damages to the City of David
his father. [28]The man Jeroboam *was* a mighty
man of valor; and Solomon, seeing that the
young man was industrious, made him the officer over all the labor force of the house of Joseph.
[29]Now it happened at that time, when Jeroboam went out of Jerusalem, that the prophet
Ahijah the Shilonite met him on the way; and
he had clothed himself with a new garment,
and the two *were* alone in the field. [30]Then
Ahijah took hold of the new garment that *was*
on him, and tore it *into* twelve pieces. [31]And
he said to Jeroboam, "Take for yourself ten
pieces, for thus says the LORD, the God of Israel: 'Behold, I will tear the kingdom out of
the hand of Solomon and will give ten tribes
to you [32](but he shall have one tribe for the
sake of My servant David, and for the sake of
Jerusalem, the city which I have chosen out of
all the tribes of Israel), [33]because they have[a]
forsaken Me, and worshiped Ashtoreth the
goddess of the Sidonians, Chemosh the god of
the Moabites, and Milcom the god of the people of Ammon, and have not walked in My
ways to do *what is* right in My eyes and *keep*
My statutes and My judgments, as *did* his father David. [34]However I will not take the
whole kingdom out of his hand, because I
have made him ruler all the days of his life for
the sake of My servant David, whom I chose
because he kept My commandments and My
statutes. [35]But I will take the kingdom out of
his son's hand and give it to you—ten tribes.
[36]And to his son I will give one tribe, that My
servant David may always have a lamp before
Me in Jerusalem, the city which I have chosen
for Myself, to put My name there. [37]So I will
take you, and you shall reign over all your
heart desires, and you shall be king over Israel. [38]Then it shall be, if you heed all that I
command you, walk in My ways, and do *what*
is right in My sight, to keep My statutes and
My commandments, as My servant David did,
then I will be with you and build for you an
enduring house, as I built for David, and will
give Israel to you. [39]And I will afflict the descendants of David because of this, but not
forever.' "
[40]Solomon therefore sought to kill Jeroboam. But Jeroboam arose and fled to Egypt,
to Shishak king of Egypt, and was in Egypt
until the death of Solomon.

Death of Solomon

[41]Now the rest of the acts of Solomon, all
that he did, and his wisdom, *are* they not written in the book of the acts of Solomon? [42]And
the period that Solomon reigned in Jerusalem
over all Israel *was* forty years. [43]Then Solomon rested with his fathers, and was buried
in the City of David his father. And Rehoboam
his son reigned in his place.

The Revolt Against Rehoboam

12 And Rehoboam went to Shechem, for
all Israel had gone to Shechem to
make him king. [2]So it happened, when Jeroboam the son of Nebat heard *it* (he was still in
Egypt, for he had fled from the presence of
King Solomon and had been dwelling in
Egypt), [3]that they sent and called him. Then
Jeroboam and the whole assembly of Israel
came and spoke to Rehoboam, saying, [4]"Your
father made our yoke heavy; now therefore,
lighten the burdensome service of your father,
and his heavy yoke which he put on us, and
we will serve you."
[5]So he said to them, "Depart *for* three days,

11:33 [a]Following Masoretic Text and Targum; Septuagint, Syriac, and Vulgate read *he has.*

then come back to me." And the people departed.
6Then King Rehoboam consulted the elders
who stood before his father Solomon while he
still lived, and he said, "How do you advise
me to answer these people?"
7And they spoke to him, saying, "If you will
be a servant to these people today, and serve
them, and answer them, and speak good
words to them, then they will be your servants
forever."
8But he rejected the advice which the elders
had given him, and consulted the young men
who had grown up with him, who stood
before him. 9And he said to them, "What
advice do you give? How should we answer
this people who have spoken to me, saying,
'Lighten the yoke which your father put
on us'?"
10Then the young men who had grown up
with him spoke to him, saying, "Thus you
should speak to this people who have spoken
to you, saying, 'Your father made our yoke
heavy, but you make *it* lighter on us'—thus
you shall say to them: 'My little *finger* shall be
thicker than my father's waist! 11And now,
whereas my father put a heavy yoke on you, I
will add to your yoke; my father chastised you
with whips, but I will chastise you with
scourges!' "[a]
12So Jeroboam and all the people came to
Rehoboam the third day, as the king had directed, saying, "Come back to me the third
day." 13Then the king answered the people
roughly, and rejected the advice which the elders had given him; 14and he spoke to them
according to the advice of the young men, saying, "My father made your yoke heavy, but I
will add to your yoke; my father chastised you
with whips, but I will chastise you with
scourges!"[a] 15So the king did not listen to the
people; for the turn *of events* was from the
LORD, that He might fulfill His word, which
the LORD had spoken by Ahijah the Shilonite
to Jeroboam the son of Nebat.
16Now when all Israel saw that the king did
not listen to them, the people answered the
king, saying:

> "What share have we in David?
> *We have* no inheritance in the son of
> Jesse.
> To your tents, O Israel!
> Now, see to your own house, O David!"

So Israel departed to their tents. 17But Rehoboam reigned over the children of Israel who
dwelt in the cities of Judah.
18Then King Rehoboam sent Adoram, who
was in charge of the revenue; but all Israel
stoned him with stones, and he died. Therefore King Rehoboam mounted his chariot
in haste to flee to Jerusalem. 19So Israel has
been in rebellion against the house of David to
this day.
20Now it came to pass when all Israel heard
that Jeroboam had come back, they sent for
him and called him to the congregation, and
made him king over all Israel. There was none
who followed the house of David, but the tribe
of Judah only.
21And when Rehoboam came to Jerusalem,
he assembled all the house of Judah with the
tribe of Benjamin, one hundred and eighty
thousand chosen *men* who were warriors, to
fight against the house of Israel, that he might
restore the kingdom to Rehoboam the son of
Solomon. 22But the word of God came to Shemaiah the man of God, saying, 23"Speak to Rehoboam the son of Solomon, king of Judah, to
all the house of Judah and Benjamin, and to
the rest of the people, saying, 24'Thus says the
LORD: "You shall not go up nor fight against

12:11 [a]Literally *scorpions* **12:14** [a]Literally *scorpions*

SOUL NOTE

Wise Counsel *(12:8–11)* Solomon had been a wise king with wise advisors, but he did not have a wise son. Rehoboam failed to heed the counsel of the older men who had served his father, listening instead to his peers. Rehoboam's unwillingness to listen to the older and wiser men ultimately led to the division of his kingdom. It is wise to seek counsel, but then we must compare that advice to God's Word. God knows the way we should go. **Topic: Decision Making**

your brethren the children of Israel. Let every
man return to his house, for this thing is from
Me." ' " Therefore they obeyed the word of the
LORD, and turned back, according to the word
of the LORD.

JEROBOAM'S GOLD CALVES

[25]Then Jeroboam built Shechem in the
mountains of Ephraim, and dwelt there. Also
he went out from there and built Penuel.
[26]And Jeroboam said in his heart, "Now the
kingdom may return to the house of David:
[27]If these people go up to offer sacrifices in
the house of the LORD at Jerusalem, then the
heart of this people will turn back to their
lord, Rehoboam king of Judah, and they will
kill me and go back to Rehoboam king of
Judah."

[28]Therefore the king asked advice, made
two calves of gold, and said to the people, "It
is too much for you to go up to Jerusalem.
Here are your gods, O Israel, which brought
you up from the land of Egypt!" [29]And he set
up one in Bethel, and the other he put in Dan.
[30]Now this thing became a sin, for the people
went *to worship* before the one as far as Dan.
[31]He made shrines[a] on the high places, and
made priests from every class of people, who
were not of the sons of Levi.

[32]Jeroboam ordained a feast on the fifteenth
day of the eighth month, like the feast that
was in Judah, and offered sacrifices on the altar. So he did at Bethel, sacrificing to the
calves that he had made. And at Bethel he in-
stalled the priests of the high places which he
had made. [33]So he made offerings on the altar
which he had made at Bethel on the fifteenth
day of the eighth month, in the month which
he had devised in his own heart. And he ordained a feast for the children of Israel, and
offered sacrifices on the altar and burned incense.

THE MESSAGE OF THE MAN OF GOD

13 And behold, a man of God went from
Judah to Bethel by the word of the
LORD, and Jeroboam stood by the altar to burn
incense. [2]Then he cried out against the altar
by the word of the LORD, and said, "O altar,
altar! Thus says the LORD: 'Behold, a child, Josiah by name, shall be born to the house of
David; and on you he shall sacrifice the priests
of the high places who burn incense on you,
and men's bones shall be burned on you.' "
[3]And he gave a sign the same day, saying,
"This *is* the sign which the LORD has spoken:
Surely the altar shall split apart, and the ashes
on it shall be poured out."

[4]So it came to pass when King Jeroboam
heard the saying of the man of God, who cried
out against the altar in Bethel, that he stretched
out his hand from the altar, saying, "Arrest
him!" Then his hand, which he stretched out
toward him, withered, so that he could not pull
it back to himself. [5]The altar also was split
apart, and the ashes poured out from the altar,
according to the sign which the man of God
had given by the word of the LORD. [6]Then the
king answered and said to the man of God,
"Please entreat the favor of the LORD your God,
and pray for me, that my hand may be restored
to me."

So the man of God entreated the LORD, and
the king's hand was restored to him, and became as before. [7]Then the king said to the
man of God, "Come home with me and refresh yourself, and I will give you a reward."

[8]But the man of God said to the king, "If you
were to give me half your house, I would not
go in with you; nor would I eat bread nor
drink water in this place. [9]For so it was commanded me by the word of the LORD, saying,

---

12:31 [a]Literally *a house*

SOUL NOTE

Convenient Religion *(12:25–33)* After Israel divided into northern and southern kingdoms, the new king in the north, Jeroboam, did not want his people traveling into the southern kingdom to Jerusalem to worship at the temple. So he made convenient worship places for them, two shrines in the northern kingdom where his people could worship golden calves. The people took advantage of this convenient religion. Today, a smorgasbord of religions is available and close at hand. But anything other than Christianity is false. Seek after God alone. **Topic: Cults**

'You shall not eat bread, nor drink water, nor return by the same way you came.' " 10So he went another way and did not return by the way he came to Bethel.

Death of the Man of God

11Now an old prophet dwelt in Bethel, and his sons came and told him all the works that the man of God had done that day in Bethel; they also told their father the words which he had spoken to the king. 12And their father said to them, "Which way did he go?" For his sons had seen[a] which way the man of God went who came from Judah. 13Then he said to his sons, "Saddle the donkey for me." So they saddled the donkey for him; and he rode on it, 14and went after the man of God, and found him sitting under an oak. Then he said to him, "*Are* you the man of God who came from Judah?"

And he said, "I *am.*"

15Then he said to him, "Come home with me and eat bread."

16And he said, "I cannot return with you nor go in with you; neither can I eat bread nor drink water with you in this place. 17For I have been told by the word of the LORD, 'You shall not eat bread nor drink water there, nor return by going the way you came.' "

18He said to him, "I too *am* a prophet as you *are,* and an angel spoke to me by the word of the LORD, saying, 'Bring him back with you to your house, that he may eat bread and drink water.' " (He was lying to him.)

19So he went back with him, and ate bread in his house, and drank water.

20Now it happened, as they sat at the table, that the word of the LORD came to the prophet who had brought him back; 21and he cried out to the man of God who came from Judah, saying, "Thus says the LORD: 'Because you have disobeyed the word of the LORD, and have not kept the commandment which the LORD your God commanded you, 22but you came back, ate bread, and drank water in the place of which *the LORD* said to you, "Eat no bread and drink no water," your corpse shall not come to the tomb of your fathers.' "

23So it was, after he had eaten bread and after he had drunk, that he saddled the donkey for him, the prophet whom he had brought back. 24When he was gone, a lion met him on the road and killed him. And his corpse was thrown on the road, and the donkey stood by it. The lion also stood by the corpse. 25And there, men passed by and saw the corpse thrown on the road, and the lion standing by the corpse. Then they went and told *it* in the city where the old prophet dwelt.

26Now when the prophet who had brought him back from the way heard *it,* he said, "It *is* the man of God who was disobedient to the word of the LORD. Therefore the LORD has delivered him to the lion, which has torn him and killed him, according to the word of the LORD which He spoke to him." 27And he spoke to his sons, saying, "Saddle the donkey for me." So they saddled *it.* 28Then he went and found his corpse thrown on the road, and the donkey and the lion standing by the corpse. The lion had not eaten the corpse nor torn the donkey. 29And the prophet took up the corpse of the man of God, laid it on the donkey, and brought it back. So the old prophet came to the city to mourn, and to bury him. 30Then he laid the corpse in his own tomb; and they mourned over him, *saying,* "Alas, my brother!" 31So it was, after he had buried him, that he spoke to his sons, saying, "When I am dead, then bury me in the tomb where the man of God *is* buried; lay my bones beside his bones. 32For the saying which he cried out by the word of the LORD against the altar in Bethel, and against all the shrines[a] on the high places which *are* in the cities of Samaria, will surely come to pass."

33After this event Jeroboam did not turn from his evil way, but again he made priests from every class of people for the high places; whoever wished, he consecrated him, and he became *one* of the priests of the high places. 34And this thing was the sin of the house of Jeroboam, so as to exterminate and destroy *it* from the face of the earth.

Judgment on the House of Jeroboam

14 At that time Abijah the son of Jeroboam became sick. 2And Jeroboam said to his wife, "Please arise, and disguise yourself, that they may not recognize you as the wife of Jeroboam, and go to Shiloh. Indeed, Ahijah the prophet *is* there, who told me that *I would be* king over this people. 3Also take with you ten loaves, *some* cakes, and a jar of honey, and go to him; he will tell you what

13:12 [a]Septuagint, Syriac, Targum, and Vulgate read *showed him.* **13:32** [a]Literally *houses*

will become of the child." [4]And Jeroboam's wife did so; she arose and went to Shiloh, and came to the house of Ahijah. But Ahijah could not see, for his eyes were glazed by reason of his age.

[5]Now the LORD had said to Ahijah, "Here is the wife of Jeroboam, coming to ask you something about her son, for he *is* sick. Thus and thus you shall say to her; for it will be, when she comes in, that she will pretend *to be* another *woman.*"

[6]And so it was, when Ahijah heard the sound of her footsteps as she came through the door, he said, "Come in, wife of Jeroboam. Why do you pretend *to be* another *person?* For I *have been* sent to you *with* bad *news.* [7]Go, tell Jeroboam, 'Thus says the LORD God of Israel: "Because I exalted you from among the people, and made you ruler over My people Israel, [8]and tore the kingdom away from the house of David, and gave it to you; and *yet* you have not been as My servant David, who kept My commandments and who followed Me with all his heart, to do only *what was* right in My eyes; [9]but you have done more evil than all who were before you, for you have gone and made for yourself other gods and molded images to provoke Me to anger, and have cast Me behind your back—[10]therefore behold! I will bring disaster on the house of Jeroboam, and will cut off from Jeroboam every male in Israel, bond and free; I will take away the remnant of the house of Jeroboam, as one takes away refuse until it is all gone. [11]The dogs shall eat whoever belongs to Jeroboam and dies in the city, and the birds of the air shall eat whoever dies in the field; for the LORD has spoken!" ' [12]Arise therefore, go to your own house. When your feet enter the city, the child shall die. [13]And all Israel shall mourn for him and bury him, for he is the only one of Jeroboam who shall come to the grave, because in him there is found something good toward the LORD God of Israel in the house of Jeroboam.

[14]"Moreover the LORD will raise up for Himself a king over Israel who shall cut off the house of Jeroboam; this is the day. What? Even now! [15]For the LORD will strike Israel, as a reed is shaken in the water. He will uproot Israel from this good land which He gave to their fathers, and will scatter them beyond the River,[a] because they have made their wooden images,[b] provoking the LORD to anger. [16]And He will give Israel up because of the sins of Jeroboam, who sinned and who made Israel sin."

[17]Then Jeroboam's wife arose and departed, and came to Tirzah. When she came to the threshold of the house, the child died. [18]And they buried him; and all Israel mourned for him, according to the word of the LORD which He spoke through His servant Ahijah the prophet.

DEATH OF JEROBOAM

[19]Now the rest of the acts of Jeroboam, how he made war and how he reigned, indeed they *are* written in the book of the chronicles of the kings of Israel. [20]The period that Jeroboam reigned *was* twenty-two years. So he rested with his fathers. Then Nadab his son reigned in his place.

REHOBOAM REIGNS IN JUDAH

[21]And Rehoboam the son of Solomon reigned in Judah. Rehoboam *was* forty-one years old when he became king. He reigned seventeen years in Jerusalem, the city which the LORD had chosen out of all the tribes of Israel, to put His name there. His mother's name *was* Naamah, an Ammonitess. [22]Now Judah did evil in the sight of the LORD, and they provoked Him to jealousy with their sins which they committed, more than all that their fathers had done. [23]For they also built for themselves high places, *sacred* pillars, and wooden images on every high hill and under every green tree. [24]And there were also perverted persons[a] in the land. They did according to all the abominations of the nations which the LORD had cast out before the children of Israel.

[25]It happened in the fifth year of King Rehoboam *that* Shishak king of Egypt came up against Jerusalem. [26]And he took away the treasures of the house of the LORD and the treasures of the king's house; he took away everything. He also took away all the gold shields which Solomon had made. [27]Then King Rehoboam made bronze shields in their place, and committed *them* to the hands of the captains of the guard, who guarded the

---

14:15 [a]That is, the Euphrates [b]Hebrew *Asherim,* Canaanite deities **14:24** [a]Hebrew *qadesh,* that is, one practicing sodomy and prostitution in religious rituals

doorway of the king's house. 28And whenever the king entered the house of the LORD, the guards carried them, then brought them back into the guardroom.

29Now the rest of the acts of Rehoboam, and all that he did, *are* they not written in the book of the chronicles of the kings of Judah? 30And there was war between Rehoboam and Jeroboam all *their* days. 31So Rehoboam rested with his fathers, and was buried with his fathers in the City of David. His mother's name *was* Naamah, an Ammonitess. Then Abijam[a] his son reigned in his place.

Abijam Reigns in Judah

15 In the eighteenth year of King Jeroboam the son of Nebat, Abijam became king over Judah. 2He reigned three years in Jerusalem. His mother's name *was* Maachah the granddaughter of Abishalom. 3And he walked in all the sins of his father, which he had done before him; his heart was not loyal to the LORD his God, as was the heart of his father David. 4Nevertheless for David's sake the LORD his God gave him a lamp in Jerusalem, by setting up his son after him and by establishing Jerusalem; 5because David did *what was* right in the eyes of the LORD, and had not turned aside from anything that He commanded him all the days of his life, except in the matter of Uriah the Hittite. 6And there was war between Rehoboam[a] and Jeroboam all the days of his life. 7Now the rest of the acts of Abijam, and all that he did, *are* they not written in the book of the chronicles of the kings of Judah? And there was war between Abijam and Jeroboam.

8So Abijam rested with his fathers, and they buried him in the City of David. Then Asa his son reigned in his place.

Asa Reigns in Judah

9In the twentieth year of Jeroboam king of Israel, Asa became king over Judah. 10And he reigned forty-one years in Jerusalem. His grandmother's name *was* Maachah the granddaughter of Abishalom. 11Asa did *what was* right in the eyes of the LORD, as *did* his father David. 12And he banished the perverted persons[a] from the land, and removed all the idols that his fathers had made. 13Also he removed Maachah his grandmother from *being* queen mother, because she had made an obscene image of Asherah.[a] And Asa cut down her obscene image and burned *it* by the Brook Kidron. 14But the high places were not removed. Nevertheless Asa's heart was loyal to the LORD all his days. 15He also brought into the house of the LORD the things which his father had dedicated, and the things which he himself had dedicated: silver and gold and utensils.

16Now there was war between Asa and Baasha king of Israel all their days. 17And Baasha king of Israel came up against Judah, and built Ramah, that he might let none go out or come in to Asa king of Judah. 18Then Asa took all the silver and gold *that was* left in the treasuries of the house of the LORD and the treasuries of the king's house, and delivered them into the hand of his servants. And King Asa sent them to Ben-Hadad the son of Tabrimmon, the son of Hezion, king of Syria, who dwelt in Damascus, saying, 19"*Let there be* a treaty between you and me, as there was between my father and your father. See, I have sent you a present of silver and gold. Come and break your treaty with Baasha king of Israel, so that he will withdraw from me."

20So Ben-Hadad heeded King Asa, and sent the captains of his armies against the cities of Israel. He attacked Ijon, Dan, Abel Beth Maachah, and all Chinneroth, with all the land of Naphtali. 21Now it happened, when Baasha heard *it,* that he stopped building Ramah, and remained in Tirzah.

22Then King Asa made a proclamation throughout all Judah; none *was* exempted. And they took away the stones and timber of Ramah, which Baasha had used for building; and with them King Asa built Geba of Benjamin, and Mizpah.

23The rest of all the acts of Asa, all his might, all that he did, and the cities which he built, *are* they not written in the book of the chronicles of the kings of Judah? But in the time of his old age he was diseased in his feet. 24So Asa rested with his fathers, and was buried with his fathers in the City of David his father. Then Jehoshaphat his son reigned in his place.

14:31 [a]Spelled *Abijah* in 2 Chronicles 12:16ff **15:6** [a]Following Masoretic Text, Septuagint, Targum, and Vulgate; some Hebrew manuscripts and Syriac read *Abijam.* **15:12** [a]Hebrew *qedeshim,* that is, those practicing sodomy and prostitution in religious rituals **15:13** [a]A Canaanite goddess

NADAB REIGNS IN ISRAEL

25 Now Nadab the son of Jeroboam became
king over Israel in the second year of Asa king
of Judah, and he reigned over Israel two years.
26 And he did evil in the sight of the LORD, and
walked in the way of his father, and in his sin
by which he had made Israel sin.

27 Then Baasha the son of Ahijah, of the
house of Issachar, conspired against him. And
Baasha killed him at Gibbethon, which *be-*
longed to the Philistines, while Nadab and all
Israel laid siege to Gibbethon. 28 Baasha killed
him in the third year of Asa king of Judah, and
reigned in his place. 29 And it was so, when he
became king, *that* he killed all the house of
Jeroboam. He did not leave to Jeroboam anyone that breathed, until he had destroyed him,
according to the word of the LORD which He
had spoken by His servant Ahijah the Shilonite, 30 because of the sins of Jeroboam, which
he had sinned and by which he had made Israel sin, because of his provocation with
which he had provoked the LORD God of Israel
to anger.

31 Now the rest of the acts of Nadab, and all
that he did, *are* they not written in the book of
the chronicles of the kings of Israel? 32 And
there was war between Asa and Baasha king
of Israel all their days.

BAASHA REIGNS IN ISRAEL

33 In the third year of Asa king of Judah, Baasha the son of Ahijah became king over all Israel in Tirzah, and *reigned* twenty-four years.
34 He did evil in the sight of the LORD, and
walked in the way of Jeroboam, and in his sin
by which he had made Israel sin.

16 Then the word of the LORD came to
Jehu the son of Hanani, against Baasha, saying: 2 "Inasmuch as I lifted you out of
the dust and made you ruler over My people
Israel, and you have walked in the way of Jeroboam, and have made My people Israel sin,
to provoke Me to anger with their sins, 3 surely
I will take away the posterity of Baasha and
the posterity of his house, and I will make
your house like the house of Jeroboam the son
of Nebat. 4 The dogs shall eat whoever belongs
to Baasha and dies in the city, and the birds of
the air shall eat whoever dies in the fields."

5 Now the rest of the acts of Baasha, what he
did, and his might, *are* they not written in the
book of the chronicles of the kings of Israel?
6 So Baasha rested with his fathers and was
buried in Tirzah. Then Elah his son reigned in
his place.

7 And also the word of the LORD came by the
prophet Jehu the son of Hanani against Baasha and his house, because of all the evil that
he did in the sight of the LORD in provoking
Him to anger with the work of his hands, in
being like the house of Jeroboam, and because he killed them.

ELAH REIGNS IN ISRAEL

8 In the twenty-sixth year of Asa king of Judah, Elah the son of Baasha became king over
Israel, *and reigned* two years in Tirzah. 9 Now
his servant Zimri, commander of half *his* chariots, conspired against him as he was in Tirzah drinking himself drunk in the house of
Arza, steward of *his* house in Tirzah. 10 And
Zimri went in and struck him and killed him
in the twenty-seventh year of Asa king of Judah, and reigned in his place.

11 Then it came to pass, when he began to
reign, as soon as he was seated on his throne,
that he killed all the household of Baasha; he
did not leave him one male, neither of his relatives nor of his friends. 12 Thus Zimri destroyed all the household of Baasha, according
to the word of the LORD, which He spoke
against Baasha by Jehu the prophet, 13 for all
the sins of Baasha and the sins of Elah his son,
by which they had sinned and by which they
had made Israel sin, in provoking the LORD
God of Israel to anger with their idols.

14 Now the rest of the acts of Elah, and all
that he did, *are* they not written in the book of
the chronicles of the kings of Israel?

ZIMRI REIGNS IN ISRAEL

15 In the twenty-seventh year of Asa king of
Judah, Zimri had reigned in Tirzah seven
days. And the people *were* encamped against
Gibbethon, which *belonged* to the Philistines.
16 Now the people *who were* encamped heard it
said, "Zimri has conspired and also has killed
the king." So all Israel made Omri, the commander of the army, king over Israel that day
in the camp. 17 Then Omri and all Israel with
him went up from Gibbethon, and they besieged Tirzah. 18 And it happened, when Zimri
saw that the city was taken, that he went into
the citadel of the king's house and burned the
king's house down upon himself with fire, and
died, 19 because of the sins which he had committed in doing evil in the sight of the LORD, in

walking in the way of Jeroboam, and in his sin which he had committed to make Israel sin.

20 Now the rest of the acts of Zimri, and the treason he committed, *are* they not written in the book of the chronicles of the kings of Israel?

Omri Reigns in Israel

21 Then the people of Israel were divided into two parts: half of the people followed Tibni the son of Ginath, to make him king, and half followed Omri. 22 But the people who followed Omri prevailed over the people who followed Tibni the son of Ginath. So Tibni died and Omri reigned. 23 In the thirty-first year of Asa king of Judah, Omri became king over Israel, *and reigned* twelve years. Six years he reigned in Tirzah. 24 And he bought the hill of Samaria from Shemer for two talents of silver; then he built on the hill, and called the name of the city which he built, Samaria, after the name of Shemer, owner of the hill. 25 Omri did evil in the eyes of the LORD, and did worse than all who *were* before him. 26 For he walked in all the ways of Jeroboam the son of Nebat, and in his sin by which he had made Israel sin, provoking the LORD God of Israel to anger with their idols.

27 Now the rest of the acts of Omri which he did, and the might that he showed, *are* they not written in the book of the chronicles of the kings of Israel?

28 So Omri rested with his fathers and was buried in Samaria. Then Ahab his son reigned in his place.

Ahab Reigns in Israel

29 In the thirty-eighth year of Asa king of Judah, Ahab the son of Omri became king over Israel; and Ahab the son of Omri reigned over Israel in Samaria twenty-two years. 30 Now Ahab the son of Omri did evil in the sight of the LORD, more than all who *were* before him. 31 And it came to pass, as though it had been a trivial thing for him to walk in the sins of Jeroboam the son of Nebat, that he took as wife Jezebel the daughter of Ethbaal, king of the Sidonians; and he went and served Baal and worshiped him. 32 Then he set up an altar for Baal in the temple of Baal, which he had built in Samaria. 33 And Ahab made a wooden image.[a] Ahab did more to provoke the LORD God of Israel to anger than all the kings of Israel who were before him. 34 In his days Hiel of Bethel built Jericho. He laid its foundation with Abiram his firstborn, and with his youngest *son* Segub he set up its gates, according to the word of the LORD, which He had spoken through Joshua the son of Nun.[a]

Elijah Proclaims a Drought

17 And Elijah the Tishbite, of the inhabitants of Gilead, said to Ahab, "*As* the LORD God of Israel lives, before whom I stand, there shall not be dew nor rain these years, except at my word."

2 Then the word of the LORD came to him, saying, 3 "Get away from here and turn eastward, and hide by the Brook Cherith, which flows into the Jordan. 4 And it will be *that* you shall drink from the brook, and I have commanded the ravens to feed you there."

5 So he went and did according to the word of the LORD, for he went and stayed by the Brook Cherith, which flows into the Jordan. 6 The ravens brought him bread and meat in the morning, and bread and meat in the evening; and he drank from the brook. 7 And it happened after a while that the brook dried up, because there had been no rain in the land.

Elijah and the Widow

8 Then the word of the LORD came to him, saying, 9 "Arise, go to Zarephath, which *belongs* to Sidon, and dwell there. See, I have commanded a widow there to provide for you." 10 So he arose and went to Zarephath. And when he came to the gate of the city, indeed a widow *was* there gathering sticks. And he called to her and said, "Please bring me a little water in a cup, that I may drink." 11 And as she was going to get *it*, he called to her and said, "Please bring me a morsel of bread in your hand."

12 So she said, "As the LORD your God lives, I do not have bread, only a handful of flour in a bin, and a little oil in a jar; and see, I *am* gathering a couple of sticks that I may go in and prepare it for myself and my son, that we may eat it, and die."

13 And Elijah said to her, "Do not fear; go *and* do as you have said, but make me a small cake from it first, and bring *it* to me; and afterward make *some* for yourself and your son.

16:33 [a]Hebrew *Asherah,* a Canaanite goddess **16:34** [a]Compare Joshua 6:26

14For thus says the LORD God of Israel: 'The bin of flour shall not be used up, nor shall the jar of oil run dry, until the day the LORD sends rain on the earth.' "

15So she went away and did according to the word of Elijah; and she and he and her household ate for *many* days. 16The bin of flour was not used up, nor did the jar of oil run dry, according to the word of the LORD which He spoke by Elijah.

Elijah Revives the Widow's Son

17Now it happened after these things *that* the son of the woman who owned the house became sick. And his sickness was so serious that there was no breath left in him. 18So she said to Elijah, "What have I to do with you, O man of God? Have you come to me to bring my sin to remembrance, and to kill my son?"

19And he said to her, "Give me your son." So he took him out of her arms and carried him to the upper room where he was staying, and laid him on his own bed. 20Then he cried out to the LORD and said, "O LORD my God, have You also brought tragedy on the widow with whom I lodge, by killing her son?" 21And he stretched himself out on the child three times, and cried out to the LORD and said, "O LORD my God, I pray, let this child's soul come back to him." 22Then the LORD heard the voice of Elijah; and the soul of the child came back to him, and he revived.

23And Elijah took the child and brought him down from the upper room into the house, and gave him to his mother. And Elijah said, "See, your son lives!"

24Then the woman said to Elijah, "Now by this I know that you *are* a man of God, *and* that the word of the LORD in your mouth *is* the truth."

Elijah's Message to Ahab

18 And it came to pass *after* many days that the word of the LORD came to Elijah, in the third year, saying, "Go, present yourself to Ahab, and I will send rain on the earth."

2So Elijah went to present himself to Ahab; and *there was* a severe famine in Samaria. 3And Ahab had called Obadiah, who *was* in charge of *his* house. (Now Obadiah feared the LORD greatly. 4For so it was, while Jezebel massacred the prophets of the LORD, that Obadiah had taken one hundred prophets and hidden them, fifty to a cave, and had fed them with bread and water.) 5And Ahab had said to Obadiah, "Go into the land to all the springs of water and to all the brooks; perhaps we may find grass to keep the horses and mules alive, so that we will not have to kill any livestock." 6So they divided the land between them to explore it; Ahab went one way by himself, and Obadiah went another way by himself.

7Now as Obadiah was on his way, suddenly Elijah met him; and he recognized him, and fell on his face, and said, "*Is* that you, my lord Elijah?"

8And he answered him, "*It is* I. Go, tell your master, 'Elijah *is here.*' "

9So he said, "How have I sinned, that you are delivering your servant into the hand of Ahab, to kill me? 10*As* the LORD your God lives, there is no nation or kingdom where my master has not sent someone to hunt for you; and when they said, '*He is* not *here,*' he took an oath from the kingdom or nation that they could not find you. 11And now you say, 'Go, tell your master, "Elijah *is here*" '! 12And it shall come to pass, *as soon as* I am gone from you, that the Spirit of the LORD will carry you to a place I do not know; so when I go and tell Ahab, and he cannot find you, he will kill me. But I your servant have feared the LORD from my youth. 13Was it not reported to my lord what I did when Jezebel killed the prophets of the LORD, how I hid one hundred men of the LORD's prophets, fifty to a cave, and fed them with bread and water? 14And now you say, 'Go, tell your master, "Elijah *is here.*" ' He will kill me!"

15Then Elijah said, "*As* the LORD of hosts lives, before whom I stand, I will surely present myself to him today."

16So Obadiah went to meet Ahab, and told him; and Ahab went to meet Elijah.

17Then it happened, when Ahab saw Elijah, that Ahab said to him, "*Is that* you, O troubler of Israel?"

18And he answered, "I have not troubled Israel, but you and your father's house *have,* in that you have forsaken the commandments of the LORD and have followed the Baals. 19Now therefore, send *and* gather all Israel to me on Mount Carmel, the four hundred and fifty prophets of Baal, and the four hundred prophets of Asherah,[a] who eat at Jezebel's table."

18:19 [a]A Canaanite goddess

Elijah's Mount Carmel Victory

20So Ahab sent for all the children of Israel, and gathered the prophets together on Mount Carmel. 21And Elijah came to all the people, and said, "How long will you falter between two opinions? If the LORD *is* God, follow Him; but if Baal, follow him." But the people answered him not a word. 22Then Elijah said to the people, "I alone am left a prophet of the LORD; but Baal's prophets *are* four hundred and fifty men. 23Therefore let them give us two bulls; and let them choose one bull for themselves, cut it in pieces, and lay *it* on the wood, but put no fire *under it;* and I will prepare the other bull, and lay *it* on the wood, but put no fire *under it.* 24Then you call on the name of your gods, and I will call on the name of the LORD; and the God who answers by fire, He is God."

So all the people answered and said, "It is well spoken."

25Now Elijah said to the prophets of Baal, "Choose one bull for yourselves and prepare *it* first, for you *are* many; and call on the name of your god, but put no fire *under it.*"

26So they took the bull which was given them, and they prepared *it,* and called on the name of Baal from morning even till noon, saying, "O Baal, hear us!" But *there was* no voice; no one answered. Then they leaped about the altar which they had made.

27And so it was, at noon, that Elijah mocked them and said, "Cry aloud, for he *is* a god; either he is meditating, or he is busy, or he is on a journey, *or* perhaps he is sleeping and must be awakened." 28So they cried aloud, and cut themselves, as was their custom, with knives and lances, until the blood gushed out on them. 29And when midday was past, they prophesied until the *time* of the offering of the *evening* sacrifice. But *there was* no voice; no one answered, no one paid attention.

30Then Elijah said to all the people, "Come near to me." So all the people came near to him. And he repaired the altar of the LORD *that was* broken down. 31And Elijah took twelve stones, according to the number of the tribes of the sons of Jacob, to whom the word of the LORD had come, saying, "Israel shall be your name."[a] 32Then with the stones he built an altar in the name of the LORD; and he made a trench around the altar large enough to hold two seahs of seed. 33And he put the wood in order, cut the bull in pieces, and laid *it* on the wood, and said, "Fill four waterpots with water, and pour *it* on the burnt sacrifice and on the wood." 34Then he said, "Do *it* a second time," and they did *it* a second time; and he said, "Do *it* a third time," and they did *it* a third time. 35So the water ran all around the altar; and he also filled the trench with water.

36And it came to pass, at *the time of* the offering of the *evening* sacrifice, that Elijah the prophet came near and said, "LORD God of Abraham, Isaac, and Israel, let it be known this day that You *are* God in Israel and I *am* Your servant, and *that* I have done all these things at Your word. 37Hear me, O LORD, hear me, that this people may know that You *are* the LORD God, and *that* You have turned their hearts back *to You* again."

38Then the fire of the LORD fell and consumed the burnt sacrifice, and the wood and the stones and the dust, and it licked up the water that *was* in the trench. 39Now when all the people saw *it,* they fell on their faces; and they said, "The LORD, He *is* God! The LORD, He *is* God!"

40And Elijah said to them, "Seize the prophets of Baal! Do not let one of them escape!" So they seized them; and Elijah brought them

18:31 [a]Genesis 32:28

SOUL NOTE

No Other God *(18:26)* One of the great religious confrontations of all time occurred between Elijah and the prophets of Baal. Elijah had challenged the prophets of Baal to build an altar, lay a sacrifice on it, and call on their god to send fire from the sky to consume the sacrifice. No answer came. When Elijah called on the one true God, however, "the fire of the LORD fell" (18:38). There is no other God. No matter how dominant evil appears to be, no matter what foothold it is gaining, God rules supreme. **Topic: Cults**

down to the Brook Kishon and executed them there.

The Drought Ends

41Then Elijah said to Ahab, "Go up, eat and drink; for *there is* the sound of abundance of rain." 42So Ahab went up to eat and drink. And Elijah went up to the top of Carmel; then he bowed down on the ground, and put his face between his knees, 43and said to his servant, "Go up now, look toward the sea."

So he went up and looked, and said, "*There is* nothing." And seven times he said, "Go again."

44Then it came to pass the seventh *time,* that he said, "There is a cloud, as small as a man's hand, rising out of the sea!" So he said, "Go up, say to Ahab, 'Prepare *your chariot,* and go down before the rain stops you.' "

45Now it happened in the meantime that the sky became black with clouds and wind, and there was a heavy rain. So Ahab rode away and went to Jezreel. 46Then the hand of the LORD came upon Elijah; and he girded up his loins and ran ahead of Ahab to the entrance of Jezreel.

Elijah Escapes from Jezebel

19 And Ahab told Jezebel all that Elijah had done, also how he had executed all the prophets with the sword. 2Then Jezebel sent a messenger to Elijah, saying, "So let the gods do *to me,* and more also, if I do not make your life as the life of one of them by tomorrow about this time." 3And when he saw *that,* he arose and ran for his life, and went to Beersheba, which *belongs* to Judah, and left his servant there.

4But he himself went a day's journey into the wilderness, and came and sat down under a broom tree. And he prayed that he might die, and said, "It is enough! Now, LORD, take my life, for I *am* no better than my fathers!"

5Then as he lay and slept under a broom tree, suddenly an angel[a] touched him, and said to him, "Arise *and* eat." 6Then he looked, and there by his head *was* a cake baked on coals, and a jar of water. So he ate and drank, and lay down again. 7And the angel[a] of the LORD came back the second time, and touched him, and said, "Arise *and* eat, because the journey *is* too great for you." 8So he arose, and ate and drank; and he went in the strength of that food forty days and forty nights as far as Horeb, the mountain of God.

9And there he went into a cave, and spent the night in that place; and behold, the word of the LORD *came* to him, and He said to him, "What are you doing here, Elijah?"

10So he said, "I have been very zealous for the LORD God of hosts; for the children of Israel have forsaken Your covenant, torn down Your altars, and killed Your prophets with the

19:5 [a]Or *Angel* **19:7** [a]Or *Angel*

KEY PASSAGE

Depression

FINDING A WAY THROUGH THE DARKNESS

(19:1–18)

Exhausted by his confrontation with the prophets of Baal and fearing for his own life, Elijah fled into the wilderness. There, all alone, he prayed that he might die (19:4). Elijah had just seen God accomplish a great miracle at his hand and spark a revival among the people. Yet, alone and afraid, Elijah couldn't take it anymore.

Life has highs and lows, and as in a mountain range, the lows often come right after the highs. We may scale the heights of spiritual victory only to soon find ourselves in the dark valley of depression. While certain forms of clinical depression should be professionally treated, many depressed feelings are part of life's ups and downs. It helps to keep our perspective so as not to be surprised by the down times. Like Elijah, we should listen for God's "still small voice" (19:12) to comfort us.

To Learn More: Turn to the article about depression on pages 780, 781. See also the personality profile of Elijah on page 464.

sword. I alone am left; and they seek to take
my life."

GOD'S REVELATION TO ELIJAH

11Then He said, "Go out, and stand on the
mountain before the LORD." And behold, the
LORD passed by, and a great and strong wind
tore into the mountains and broke the rocks in
pieces before the LORD, *but* the LORD *was* not
in the wind; and after the wind an earthquake,
but the LORD *was* not in the earthquake; 12and
after the earthquake a fire, *but* the LORD *was*
not in the fire; and after the fire a still small
voice.

13So it was, when Elijah heard *it*, that he
wrapped his face in his mantle and went out
and stood in the entrance of the cave. Suddenly a voice *came* to him, and said, "What
are you doing here, Elijah?"

14And he said, "I have been very zealous for
the LORD God of hosts; because the children of
Israel have forsaken Your covenant, torn down
Your altars, and killed Your prophets with the
sword. I alone am left; and they seek to take
my life."

15Then the LORD said to him: "Go, return on
your way to the Wilderness of Damascus; and
when you arrive, anoint Hazael *as* king over

PERSONALITY PROFILE

ELIJAH AND THE DARKNESS OF DEPRESSION

(1 KINGS 19:1–18)

Depression has an insidious way of draining energy, twisting values, and assaulting faith. And depression can affect anyone, even a great prophet of God. Elijah stands out as one of Israel's greatest prophets. He exuded great courage in the face of evil, fearlessly confronting King Ahab and the false prophets of Baal (1 Kin. 18:17–40). Yet when Queen Jezebel threatened to kill him, Elijah ran for his life and lapsed into a deep depression.

Elijah prayed to God to let him die. He lost his appetite; his thinking was disturbed; he withdrew from everyone. During this dark period, he curled up under a tree, wanting to die. Elijah's painful experience teaches that even the most courageous and spiritually mature believer can struggle with depression.

Elijah acted courageously, but when Jezebel threatened him, he reacted in fear. Fear is prevalent in many kinds of depression—anxiety and depression coexist in 70 percent of those diagnosed with depression. As Proverbs 12:25 reveals: "Anxiety in the heart of man causes depression, but a good word makes it glad."

God responded mercifully. He did not castigate or condemn Elijah for his condition—something that many depressed Christians expect from God. Instead, God provided rest and food and then encouraged Elijah to "go" and continue his ministry. This reveals the best principles for helping a person who is depressed:

- encourage the person to take care of himself or herself physically;
- encourage action but keep it simple;
- encourage the person to be goal-directed and then support every accomplishment.

God also addressed Elijah's distorted thinking. In his isolation, Elijah missed the fact that he was not the only faithful one left in Israel—God told him that 7,000 others had not bowed to Baal. Next, God sent Elijah to train Elisha for his future work in Israel (1 Kin. 19:19–21). The call to help others is a common antidote to the disabling self-absorption and social withdrawal of depression.

Through all of this, Elijah learned that God would never forsake him. Even in the depths of depression God shows loving concern and a way out.

To Learn More: Turn to the article about depression on pages 780, 781. See also the key passage note at 1 Kings 19:1–18 on page 463.

Syria. 16Also you shall anoint Jehu the son of
Nimshi *as* king over Israel. And Elisha the son
of Shaphat of Abel Meholah you shall anoint
as prophet in your place. 17It shall be *that*
whoever escapes the sword of Hazael, Jehu
will kill; and whoever escapes the sword of
Jehu, Elisha will kill. 18Yet I have reserved
seven thousand in Israel, all whose knees
have not bowed to Baal, and every mouth that
has not kissed him."

SOUL NOTE

A Still Small Voice *(19:12)* Elijah had just gained a great spiritual victory for Israel against the prophets of Baal (18:16–40). Elijah knew God intimately and served Him faithfully. After his great victory, however, Elijah felt alone and depressed, so God lovingly reached out to His servant. God had miraculously delivered fire from heaven; now God could speak in "a still small voice." God had worked national revival; He was also at work in individual lives, like Elijah's. God may perform great miracles; more often, however, He is quietly at work in the souls of His people.
Topic: Knowing God

PERSONALITY PROFILE

ELIJAH AND ELISHA: A TOUGH ACT TO FOLLOW

(1 KINGS 19:19)

The mantle (or cloak) that Elijah tossed over Elisha's shoulders carried heavy responsibility. Elijah had served God faithfully for many years as a prophet with an unpopular message. He had served God and the nation well, but in order for such service to continue, he needed to train a successor. God provided one in Elisha.

God told Elijah to anoint Elisha "as prophet in your place" (1 Kin. 19:16). Elijah lost no time finding Elisha, throwing his mantle on him, and then taking him along as prophet-in-training. Leaving home, Elisha literally burned his bridges behind him—slaughtering his twelve yoke of oxen and burning his farming equipment. Elisha took up the mantle and didn't look back. He followed Elijah and learned from him, realizing that he would one day replace the great prophet. Elijah became a faithful teacher and beloved mentor; Elisha became a willing and capable student.

The day of reckoning finally came. Even though Elisha had been well-trained, he did not look forward to losing his master and mentor. Elisha knew something big was about to happen, so he refused to leave his mentor's side. In fact, it seems that everyone knew that Elijah would soon be taken away, even the prophets at Jericho (2 Kin. 2:5). Before he was to go to heaven, Elijah asked what last act he could do for Elisha. The student wisely answered, "Please let a double portion of your spirit be upon me" (2 Kin. 2:9). Elisha did not want more fame or more miracle-working power; he merely wanted to be able to serve well and to follow faithfully in his mentor's footsteps.

The mentoring relationship is not just for replacements—it also applies to all believers who share and teach the faith. New believers need to be trained in the basics of God's Word and in how to live for Him. Older and wiser believers can help them by taking seriously the role of mentor. Younger believers should find someone who can train them in the faith.

To Learn More: Turn to the article about mentoring on pages 430, 431. See also the key passage note at 2 Timothy 2:2 on page 1606.

Elisha Follows Elijah

19So he departed from there, and found Elisha the son of Shaphat, who *was* plowing *with* twelve yoke *of oxen* before him, and he was with the twelfth. Then Elijah passed by him and threw his mantle on him. 20And he left the oxen and ran after Elijah, and said, "Please let me kiss my father and my mother, and *then* I will follow you."

And he said to him, "Go back again, for what have I done to you?"

21So *Elisha* turned back from him, and took a yoke of oxen and slaughtered them and boiled their flesh, using the oxen's equipment, and gave it to the people, and they ate. Then he arose and followed Elijah, and became his servant.

Ahab Defeats the Syrians

20 Now Ben-Hadad the king of Syria gathered all his forces together; thirty-two kings *were* with him, with horses and chariots. And he went up and besieged Samaria, and made war against it. 2Then he sent messengers into the city to Ahab king of Israel, and said to him, "Thus says Ben-Hadad: 3'Your silver and your gold *are* mine; your loveliest wives and children are mine.' "

4And the king of Israel answered and said, "My lord, O king, just as you say, I and all that I have *are* yours."

5Then the messengers came back and said, "Thus speaks Ben-Hadad, saying, 'Indeed I have sent to you, saying, "You shall deliver to me your silver and your gold, your wives and your children"; 6but I will send my servants to you tomorrow about this time, and they shall search your house and the houses of your servants. And it shall be, *that* whatever is pleasant in your eyes, they will put *it* in their hands and take *it*.' "

7So the king of Israel called all the elders of the land, and said, "Notice, please, and see how this *man* seeks trouble, for he sent to me for my wives, my children, my silver, and my gold; and I did not deny him."

8And all the elders and all the people said to him, "Do not listen or consent."

9Therefore he said to the messengers of Ben-Hadad, "Tell my lord the king, 'All that you sent for to your servant the first time I will do, but this thing I cannot do.' "

And the messengers departed and brought back word to him.

10Then Ben-Hadad sent to him and said, "The gods do so to me, and more also, if enough dust is left of Samaria for a handful for each of the people who follow me."

11So the king of Israel answered and said, "Tell *him*, 'Let not the one who puts on *his armor* boast like the one who takes *it off*.' "

12And it happened when *Ben-Hadad* heard this message, as he and the kings *were* drinking at the command post, that he said to his servants, "Get ready." And they got ready to attack the city.

13Suddenly a prophet approached Ahab king of Israel, saying, "Thus says the LORD: 'Have you seen all this great multitude? Behold, I will deliver it into your hand today, and you shall know that I *am* the LORD.' "

14So Ahab said, "By whom?"

And he said, "Thus says the LORD: 'By the young leaders of the provinces.' "

Then he said, "Who will set the battle in order?"

And he answered, "You."

15Then he mustered the young leaders of the provinces, and there were two hundred and thirty-two; and after them he mustered all the people, all the children of Israel—seven thousand.

16So they went out at noon. Meanwhile Ben-Hadad and the thirty-two kings helping him were getting drunk at the command post. 17The young leaders of the provinces went out first. And Ben-Hadad sent out *a patrol*, and they told him, saying, "Men are coming out of Samaria!" 18So he said, "If they have come out for peace, take them alive; and if they have come out for war, take them alive."

19Then these young leaders of the provinces went out of the city with the army which followed them. 20And each one killed his man; so the Syrians fled, and Israel pursued them; and Ben-Hadad the king of Syria escaped on a horse with the cavalry. 21Then the king of Israel went out and attacked the horses and chariots, and killed the Syrians with a great slaughter.

22And the prophet came to the king of Israel and said to him, "Go, strengthen yourself; take note, and see what you should do, for in the spring of the year the king of Syria will come up against you."

The Syrians Again Defeated

23Then the servants of the king of Syria said to him, "Their gods *are* gods of the hills.

Therefore they were stronger than we; but if
we fight against them in the plain, surely we
will be stronger than they. 24So do this
thing: Dismiss the kings, each from his position, and put captains in their places; 25and
you shall muster an army like the army that
you have lost, horse for horse and chariot
for chariot. Then we will fight against them
in the plain; surely we will be stronger than
they."

And he listened to their voice and did so.

26So it was, in the spring of the year, that
Ben-Hadad mustered the Syrians and went up
to Aphek to fight against Israel. 27And the children of Israel were mustered and given provisions, and they went against them. Now the
children of Israel encamped before them like
two little flocks of goats, while the Syrians
filled the countryside.

28Then a man of God came and spoke to the
king of Israel, and said, "Thus says the LORD:
'Because the Syrians have said, "The LORD *is*
God of the hills, but He *is* not God of the valleys," therefore I will deliver all this great multitude into your hand, and you shall know that
I *am* the LORD.' " 29And they encamped opposite each other for seven days. So it was that
on the seventh day the battle was joined; and
the children of Israel killed one hundred thousand foot soldiers *of* the Syrians in one day.
30But the rest fled to Aphek, into the city; then
a wall fell on twenty-seven thousand of the
men *who were* left.

And Ben-Hadad fled and went into the city,
into an inner chamber.

Ahab's Treaty with Ben-Hadad

31Then his servants said to him, "Look now,
we have heard that the kings of the house of
Israel *are* merciful kings. Please, let us put
sackcloth around our waists and ropes around
our heads, and go out to the king of Israel;
perhaps he will spare your life." 32So they
wore sackcloth around their waists and *put*
ropes around their heads, and came to the
king of Israel and said, "Your servant Ben-
Hadad says, 'Please let me live.' "

And he said, "*Is* he still alive? He *is* my
brother."

33Now the men were watching closely to see
whether *any sign of mercy would come* from
him; and they quickly grasped *at this word*
and said, "Your brother Ben-Hadad."

So he said, "Go, bring him." Then Ben-
Hadad came out to him; and he had him come
up into the chariot.

34So *Ben-Hadad* said to him, "The cities
which my father took from your father I will
restore; and you may set up marketplaces for
yourself in Damascus, as my father did in Samaria."

Then *Ahab said,* "I will send you away with
this treaty." So he made a treaty with him and
sent him away.

Ahab Condemned

35Now a certain man of the sons of the
prophets said to his neighbor by the word of
the LORD, "Strike me, please." And the man refused to strike him. 36Then he said to him,
"Because you have not obeyed the voice of the
LORD, surely, as soon as you depart from me, a
lion shall kill you." And as soon as he left him,
a lion found him and killed him.

37And he found another man, and said,
"Strike me, please." So the man struck him,
inflicting a wound. 38Then the prophet departed and waited for the king by the road,
and disguised himself with a bandage over his
eyes. 39Now as the king passed by, he cried
out to the king and said, "Your servant went
out into the midst of the battle; and there, a
man came over and brought a man to me, and
said, 'Guard this man; if by any means he is
missing, your life shall be for his life, or else
you shall pay a talent of silver.' 40While your
servant was busy here and there, he was
gone."

Then the king of Israel said to him, "So
shall your judgment *be;* you yourself have decided *it.*"

41And he hastened to take the bandage
away from his eyes; and the king of Israel recognized him as one of the prophets. 42Then he
said to him, "Thus says the LORD: 'Because
you have let slip out of *your* hand a man
whom I appointed to utter destruction, therefore your life shall go for his life, and your
people for his people.' "

43So the king of Israel went to his house sullen and displeased, and came to Samaria.

Naboth Is Murdered for His Vineyard

21 And it came to pass after these things
that Naboth the Jezreelite had a vineyard which *was* in Jezreel, next to the palace
of Ahab king of Samaria. 2So Ahab spoke to
Naboth, saying, "Give me your vineyard, that

I may have it for a vegetable garden, because
it *is* near, next to my house; and for it I will
give you a vineyard better than it. *Or,* if it
seems good to you, I will give you its worth in
money."

3But Naboth said to Ahab, "The LORD forbid
that I should give the inheritance of my fathers to you!"

4So Ahab went into his house sullen and
displeased because of the word which Naboth
the Jezreelite had spoken to him; for he had
said, "I will not give you the inheritance of my
fathers." And he lay down on his bed, and
turned away his face, and would eat no food.
5But Jezebel his wife came to him, and said to
him, "Why is your spirit so sullen that you eat
no food?"

6He said to her, "Because I spoke to Naboth
the Jezreelite, and said to him, 'Give me your
vineyard for money; or else, if it pleases you, I
will give you *another* vineyard for it.' And he
answered, 'I will not give you my vineyard.' "

7Then Jezebel his wife said to him, "You
now exercise authority over Israel! Arise, eat
food, and let your heart be cheerful; I will give
you the vineyard of Naboth the Jezreelite."

8And she wrote letters in Ahab's name,
sealed *them* with his seal, and sent the letters
to the elders and the nobles who *were* dwelling in the city with Naboth. 9She wrote in the
letters, saying,

> Proclaim a fast, and seat Naboth with
> high honor among the people; 10and seat
> two men, scoundrels, before him to bear
> witness against him, saying, "You have
> blasphemed God and the king." *Then*
> take him out, and stone him, that he
> may die.

11So the men of his city, the elders and nobles who were inhabitants of his city, did as
Jezebel had sent to them, as it *was* written in
the letters which she had sent to them. 12They
proclaimed a fast, and seated Naboth with
high honor among the people. 13And two men,
scoundrels, came in and sat before him; and
the scoundrels witnessed against him, against
Naboth, in the presence of the people, saying,
"Naboth has blasphemed God and the king!"
Then they took him outside the city and
stoned him with stones, so that he died.
14Then they sent to Jezebel, saying, "Naboth
has been stoned and is dead."

15And it came to pass, when Jezebel heard
that Naboth had been stoned and was dead,
that Jezebel said to Ahab, "Arise, take possession of the vineyard of Naboth the Jezreelite, which he refused to give you for money;
for Naboth is not alive, but dead." 16So it
was, when Ahab heard that Naboth was dead,
that Ahab got up and went down to take
possession of the vineyard of Naboth the Jezreelite.

THE LORD CONDEMNS AHAB

17Then the word of the LORD came to Elijah
the Tishbite, saying, 18"Arise, go down to meet
Ahab king of Israel, who *lives* in Samaria.
There *he is,* in the vineyard of Naboth, where
he has gone down to take possession of it.
19You shall speak to him, saying, 'Thus says
the LORD: "Have you murdered and also taken
possession?" ' And you shall speak to him,
saying, 'Thus says the LORD: "In the place
where dogs licked the blood of Naboth, dogs
shall lick your blood, even yours." ' "

20So Ahab said to Elijah, "Have you found
me, O my enemy?"

And he answered, "I have found *you,* because you have sold yourself to do evil in the
sight of the LORD: 21'Behold, I will bring calamity on you. I will take away your posterity,
and will cut off from Ahab every male in Is-

SOUL NOTE

Catch Up *(21:1–16)* It is difficult to read the tragic story of innocent Naboth being killed so a pouting king could have another vineyard. Naboth had been correct in refusing to sell the land, for it was a part of his family inheritance. But Ahab and Jezebel, the most evil twosome to reign in Israel, got their way. Jezebel schemed to have Naboth killed. Eventually, Jezebel died a horrible death, experiencing the violence she had used against others (2 Kin. 9:30–37). Violence has a way of catching up with people. **Topic: Violence**

rael, both bond and free. [22]I will make your
house like the house of Jeroboam the son of
Nebat, and like the house of Baasha the son
of Ahijah, because of the provocation with
which you have provoked *Me* to anger, and
made Israel sin.' [23]And concerning Jezebel the
LORD also spoke, saying, 'The dogs shall eat
Jezebel by the wall[a] of Jezreel.' [24]The dogs
shall eat whoever belongs to Ahab and dies in
the city, and the birds of the air shall eat whoever dies in the field."
[25]But there was no one like Ahab who sold
himself to do wickedness in the sight of the
LORD, because Jezebel his wife stirred him up.
[26]And he behaved very abominably in following idols, according to all *that* the Amorites
had done, whom the LORD had cast out before
the children of Israel.
[27]So it was, when Ahab heard those words,
that he tore his clothes and put sackcloth on
his body, and fasted and lay in sackcloth, and
went about mourning.
[28]And the word of the LORD came to Elijah
the Tishbite, saying, [29]"See how Ahab has
humbled himself before Me? Because he has
humbled himself before Me, I will not bring
the calamity in his days. In the days of his son
I will bring the calamity on his house."

MICAIAH WARNS AHAB

22 Now three years passed without war
between Syria and Israel. [2]Then it
came to pass, in the third year, that Jehoshaphat the king of Judah went down to *visit* the
king of Israel.

21:23 [a]Following Masoretic Text and Septuagint; some Hebrew manuscripts, Syriac, Targum, and Vulgate read *plot of ground* (compare 2 Kings 9:36).

PERSONALITY PROFILE

Violence

NABOTH: IN THE PATH OF AN EVIL KING

(1 KINGS 21)

King Ahab ruled Samaria with an iron fist. He and his wife Jezebel have become synonymous with evil. "There was no one like Ahab who sold himself to do wickedness in the sight of the LORD, because Jezebel his wife stirred him up" (1 Kin. 21:25). These two made a truly gruesome twosome, as the story of Naboth's vineyard reveals.

Naboth was in the wrong place at the wrong time. His beautiful vineyard, a part of his family inheritance, sat within yearning distance of the king's palace in Samaria. Ahab decided that he wanted to own that lovely vineyard, and so he offered to buy it. But Naboth refused. He did not want to sell off a piece of property that had been in his family for generations. So he was well within his rights to refuse.

Ahab went home and pouted. Like a child who didn't get his way, Ahab lay on his bed and refused to eat.

Enter Jezebel, the scheming wife who would stop at nothing to get *her* way. She heard Ahab's complaint and took matters into her own hands. If Ahab wouldn't exercise his authority as king to take the vineyard, then Jezebel would get it for him another way. She devised a plan whereby Naboth would be both defamed and murdered. After the plan was carried out, Ahab simply "went down to take possession of the vineyard of Naboth" (1 Kin. 21:16). He thought he had gotten away with it until the prophet Elijah knocked on his door with some bad news.

History is filled with evil people who stopped at nothing to get their way, and violence against godly people is a reality of life. Believers cannot assume that they will be exempt from violence. God is still in charge, however. Jezebel had bloody hands, and her awful death would be a fitting end to her horrible life (1 Kin. 21:23; 2 Kin. 9:30–37). Violence only breeds violence. In the end, God will have the final say. He promises to one day destroy evil forever.

To Learn More: Turn to the article about violence on pages 526, 527. See also the key passage note at Psalm 11:5 on page 685.

3 And the king of Israel said to his servants,
"Do you know that Ramoth in Gilead *is* ours, but
we hesitate to take it out of the hand of the king
of Syria?" 4 So he said to Jehoshaphat, "Will
you go with me to fight at Ramoth Gilead?"
Jehoshaphat said to the king of Israel, "I *am*
as you *are,* my people as your people, my
horses as your horses." 5 Also Jehoshaphat
said to the king of Israel, "Please inquire for
the word of the LORD today."
6 Then the king of Israel gathered the prophets together, about four hundred men, and
said to them, "Shall I go against Ramoth Gilead to fight, or shall I refrain?"
So they said, "Go up, for the Lord will deliver *it* into the hand of the king."
7 And Jehoshaphat said, "*Is there* not still a
prophet of the LORD here, that we may inquire
of Him?"[a]
8 So the king of Israel said to Jehoshaphat,
"*There is* still one man, Micaiah the son of Imlah, by whom we may inquire of the LORD; but
I hate him, because he does not prophesy
good concerning me, but evil."
And Jehoshaphat said, "Let not the king say
such things!"
9 Then the king of Israel called an officer
and said, "Bring Micaiah the son of Imlah
quickly!"
10 The king of Israel and Jehoshaphat the
king of Judah, having put on *their* robes, sat
each on his throne, at a threshing floor at the
entrance of the gate of Samaria; and all the
prophets prophesied before them. 11 Now Zedekiah the son of Chenaanah had made horns
of iron for himself; and he said, "Thus says

22:7 [a]Or *him*

PERSONALITY PROFILE

MICAIAH: WHEN THE TRUTH IS NOT TOLERATED

(1 KINGS 22:8)

How valuable is the lone voice of truth amongst the clamor of lies! How brave is the one who speaks the truth when no one wants to hear it! Micaiah was a prophet who would not tolerate anything but the truth. Ahab was a king who could not tolerate the truth. When these two met, sparks flew.

Ahab, king of Israel, and Jehoshaphat, king of Judah, were forming an alliance to go to war against Syria. This was a bad idea in the first place—Ahab was an evil king who worshiped idols and surrounded himself with false prophets; Jehoshaphat had been a good king who led his nation back to God. So at their summit meeting, Jehoshaphat requested guidance from the Lord as to whether they should go to war. Ahab marched in 400 prophets who, not surprisingly, prophesied great success. Jehoshaphat felt a bit uneasy and asked for a true prophet of the Lord. Ahab knew of such a prophet, but hated him because "he does not prophesy good concerning me, but evil."

Micaiah was brought to the summit meeting. He played along at first, just to reveal the silliness of kings who seek prophecies to confirm what they want to hear. When pressed for the truth, however, Micaiah came through with a flourish, predicting defeat for the kings and death for Ahab should they go to war. Micaiah was outvoted 400 to 1, so the kings went to war, only to be defeated. Thinking he could outwit the prophecy, Ahab disguised himself. But God's word could not be thwarted, and Ahab was killed.

The mantra in today's culture is tolerance. People must tolerate anything and everything, except those who don't do the same. People love to hear what they want to hear, but find it hard to tolerate those who speak truth when it doesn't agree with them. Their refusal to listen doesn't make the truth any less true. In a world clamoring with lies, God needs people who are unafraid to speak the truth.

To Learn More: Turn to the article about tolerance on pages 1694, 1695. See also the key passage note at 2 Peter 2:12–22 on page 1672.

the LORD: 'With these you shall gore the Syrians until they are destroyed.' " [12]And all the
prophets prophesied so, saying, "Go up to Ramoth Gilead and prosper, for the LORD will
deliver *it* into the king's hand."
[13]Then the messenger who had gone to call
Micaiah spoke to him, saying, "Now listen,
the words of the prophets with one accord encourage the king. Please, let your word be like
the word of one of them, and speak encouragement."
[14]And Micaiah said, "*As* the LORD lives,
whatever the LORD says to me, that I will
speak."
[15]Then he came to the king; and the king
said to him, "Micaiah, shall we go to war
against Ramoth Gilead, or shall we refrain?"
And he answered him, "Go and prosper, for
the LORD will deliver *it* into the hand of the
king!"
[16]So the king said to him, "How many times
shall I make you swear that you tell me nothing but the truth in the name of the LORD?"
[17]Then he said, "I saw all Israel scattered on
the mountains, as sheep that have no shepherd. And the LORD said, 'These have no master. Let each return to his house in peace.' "
[18]And the king of Israel said to Jehoshaphat,
"Did I not tell you he would not prophesy
good concerning me, but evil?"
[19]Then *Micaiah* said, "Therefore hear the
word of the LORD: I saw the LORD sitting on
His throne, and all the host of heaven standing
by, on His right hand and on His left. [20]And
the LORD said, 'Who will persuade Ahab to go
up, that he may fall at Ramoth Gilead?' So one
spoke in this manner, and another spoke in
that manner. [21]Then a spirit came forward and
stood before the LORD, and said, 'I will persuade him.' [22]The LORD said to him, 'In what
way?' So he said, 'I will go out and be a lying
spirit in the mouth of all his prophets.' And the
LORD said, 'You shall persuade *him*, and also
prevail. Go out and do so.' [23]Therefore look!
The LORD has put a lying spirit in the mouth of
all these prophets of yours, and the LORD has
declared disaster against you."
[24]Now Zedekiah the son of Chenaanah went
near and struck Micaiah on the cheek, and
said, "Which way did the spirit from the LORD
go from me to speak to you?"
[25]And Micaiah said, "Indeed, you shall see
on that day when you go into an inner chamber to hide!"
[26]So the king of Israel said, "Take Micaiah,
and return him to Amon the governor of the
city and to Joash the king's son; [27]and say,
'Thus says the king: "Put this *fellow* in prison,
and feed him with bread of affliction and water of affliction, until I come in peace." ' "
[28]But Micaiah said, "If you ever return in
peace, the LORD has not spoken by me." And
he said, "Take heed, all you people!"

AHAB DIES IN BATTLE

[29]So the king of Israel and Jehoshaphat the
king of Judah went up to Ramoth Gilead.
[30]And the king of Israel said to Jehoshaphat, "I
will disguise myself and go into battle; but
you put on your robes." So the king of Israel
disguised himself and went into battle.
[31]Now the king of Syria had commanded the
thirty-two captains of his chariots, saying,
"Fight with no one small or great, but only
with the king of Israel." [32]So it was, when the
captains of the chariots saw Jehoshaphat, that
they said, "Surely it *is* the king of Israel!"
Therefore they turned aside to fight against
him, and Jehoshaphat cried out. [33]And it happened, when the captains of the chariots saw
that it *was* not the king of Israel, that they
turned back from pursuing him. [34]Now a *certain* man drew a bow at random, and struck
the king of Israel between the joints of his armor. So he said to the driver of his chariot,
"Turn around and take me out of the battle,
for I am wounded."
[35]The battle increased that day; and the king
was propped up in his chariot, facing the Syrians, and died at evening. The blood ran out
from the wound onto the floor of the chariot.
[36]Then, as the sun was going down, a shout
went throughout the army, saying, "Every
man to his city, and every man to his own
country!"
[37]So the king died, and was brought to Samaria. And they buried the king in Samaria.
[38]Then *someone* washed the chariot at a pool
in Samaria, and the dogs licked up his blood
while the harlots bathed,[a] according to the
word of the LORD which He had spoken.
[39]Now the rest of the acts of Ahab, and all
that he did, the ivory house which he built
and all the cities that he built, *are* they not
written in the book of the chronicles of the

22:38 [a]Syriac and Targum read *they washed his armor.*

kings of Israel? 40 So Ahab rested with his fathers. Then Ahaziah his son reigned in his place.

Jehoshaphat Reigns in Judah

41 Jehoshaphat the son of Asa had become king over Judah in the fourth year of Ahab king of Israel. 42 Jehoshaphat *was* thirty-five years old when he became king, and he reigned twenty-five years in Jerusalem. His mother's name *was* Azubah the daughter of Shilhi. 43 And he walked in all the ways of his father Asa. He did not turn aside from them, doing *what was* right in the eyes of the LORD. Nevertheless the high places were not taken away, *for* the people offered sacrifices and burned incense on the high places. 44 Also Jehoshaphat made peace with the king of Israel.

45 Now the rest of the acts of Jehoshaphat, the might that he showed, and how he made war, *are* they not written in the book of the chronicles of the kings of Judah? 46 And the rest of the perverted persons,[a] who remained in the days of his father Asa, he banished from the land. 47 *There was* then no king in Edom, only a deputy of the king.

48 Jehoshaphat made merchant ships[a] to go to Ophir for gold; but they never sailed, for the ships were wrecked at Ezion Geber. 49 Then Ahaziah the son of Ahab said to Jehoshaphat, "Let my servants go with your servants in the ships." But Jehoshaphat would not.

50 And Jehoshaphat rested with his fathers, and was buried with his fathers in the City of David his father. Then Jehoram his son reigned in his place.

Ahaziah Reigns in Israel

51 Ahaziah the son of Ahab became king over Israel in Samaria in the seventeenth year of Jehoshaphat king of Judah, and reigned two years over Israel. 52 He did evil in the sight of the LORD, and walked in the way of his father and in the way of his mother and in the way of Jeroboam the son of Nebat, who had made Israel sin; 53 for he served Baal and worshiped him, and provoked the LORD God of Israel to anger, according to all that his father had done.

22:46 [a]Hebrew *qadesh,* that is, one practicing sodomy and prostitution in religious rituals **22:48** [a]Or *ships of Tarshish*

2 Kings

Nobody really gets away with anything. Sin always has a price tag—consequences—and has an effect on someone else. "Do not be deceived, God is not mocked; for whatever a man sows, that he will also reap" (Gal. 6:7).

The theme of the terrible results of sin, so prominent in 1 Kings, is also dominant in 2 Kings. Possibly written by Jeremiah, this book reveals how idolatry and pagan worship infected the Israelites. Chapters 1—17 focus on the steady spiritual decline of both nations and conclude with the Assyrian captivity of the northern kingdom of Israel in 722 B.C. Chapters 18—25 document the demise of the southern kingdom of Judah at the hands of the Babylonians in 586 B.C.

Against the dark backdrop of the Hebrews' degradation and decline, the faithfulness and mercy of God is clearly seen. He sends a steady stream of prophets—Elijah, Elisha, and Isaiah—to call His people back to righteousness, but to no avail. He raises up a handful of godly kings in Judah, but each of their attempts at reform is eventually overshadowed by godless living. In the end, Jerusalem is sacked by the Babylonians, the temple is destroyed, and the people are taken away in captivity.

Many of the applications of 2 Kings are intensely personal: Are we living in sin? Are we ignoring God's attempts to draw us back to Himself? Do we really believe we can escape the terrible consequences of disobedience? Ask God to speak to you as you read this eye-opening book.

SOUL CONCERNS IN 2 KINGS

MONEY	(5:20–27)
DEATH	(20:1–3)

God Judges Ahaziah

1 Moab rebelled against Israel after the death of Ahab.

2Now Ahaziah fell through the lattice of his upper room in Samaria, and was injured; so he sent messengers and said to them, "Go, inquire of Baal-Zebub, the god of Ekron, whether I shall recover from this injury." 3But the angel[a] of the LORD said to Elijah the Tishbite, "Arise, go up to meet the messengers of the king of Samaria, and say to them, '*Is it* because *there is* no God in Israel *that* you are going to inquire of Baal-Zebub, the god of Ekron?' 4Now therefore, thus says the LORD: 'You shall not come down from the bed to which you have gone up, but you shall surely die.' " So Elijah departed.

5And when the messengers returned to him, he said to them, "Why have you come back?"

6So they said to him, "A man came up to meet us, and said to us, 'Go, return to the king who sent you, and say to him, "Thus says the LORD: '*Is it* because *there is* no God in Israel *that* you are sending to inquire of Baal-Zebub, the god of Ekron? Therefore you shall not come down from the bed to which you have gone up, but you shall surely die.' " ' "

7Then he said to them, "What kind of man *was it* who came up to meet you and told you these words?"

8So they answered him, "A hairy man wearing a leather belt around his waist."

And he said, "It *is* Elijah the Tishbite."

9Then the king sent to him a captain of fifty with his fifty men. So he went up to him; and there he was, sitting on the top of a hill. And he spoke to him: "Man of God, the king has said, 'Come down!' "

10So Elijah answered and said to the captain of fifty, "If I *am* a man of God, then let fire come down from heaven and consume you and your fifty men." And fire came down from heaven and consumed him and his fifty. 11Then he sent to him another captain of fifty with his fifty men.

And he answered and said to him: "Man of God, thus has the king said, 'Come down quickly!' "

12So Elijah answered and said to them, "If I *am* a man of God, let fire come down from heaven and consume you and your fifty men." And the fire of God came down from heaven and consumed him and his fifty.

13Again, he sent a third captain of fifty with his fifty men. And the third captain of fifty went up, and came and fell on his knees before Elijah, and pleaded with him, and said to him: "Man of God, please let my life and the life of these fifty servants of yours be precious in your sight. 14Look, fire has come down from heaven and burned up the first two captains of fifties with their fifties. But let my life now be precious in your sight."

15And the angel[a] of the LORD said to Elijah, "Go down with him; do not be afraid of him." So he arose and went down with him to the king. 16Then he said to him, "Thus says the LORD: 'Because you have sent messengers to inquire of Baal-Zebub, the god of Ekron, *is it* because *there is* no God in Israel to inquire of His word? Therefore you shall not come down from the bed to which you have gone up, but you shall surely die.' "

17So *Ahaziah* died according to the word of the LORD which Elijah had spoken. Because he had no son, Jehoram[a] became king in his place, in the second year of Jehoram the son of Jehoshaphat, king of Judah.

18Now the rest of the acts of Ahaziah which he did, *are* they not written in the book of the chronicles of the kings of Israel?

1:3 [a]Or *Angel* **1:15** [a]Or *Angel* **1:17** [a]The son of Ahab king of Israel (compare 3:1)

SOUL NOTE

Facing Mortality *(1:6)* King Ahaziah feared that he might not recover from a serious injury. He sent messengers to "inquire of Baal-Zebub, the god of Ekron" whether he would live or die. People most often do not want to face their own mortality. In Ahaziah's case, he sought help from a false god instead of turning to the Lord. People facing death often come to grips with the reality of their need for a relationship with God. Be ready to share your faith with those who are looking for answers in a time of great need. **Topic: Death**

Elijah Ascends to Heaven

2 And it came to pass, when the LORD was
about to take up Elijah into heaven by a
whirlwind, that Elijah went with Elisha from
Gilgal. 2Then Elijah said to Elisha, "Stay here,
please, for the LORD has sent me on to Bethel."
But Elisha said, "*As* the LORD lives, and *as*
your soul lives, I will not leave you!" So they
went down to Bethel.
3Now the sons of the prophets who *were* at
Bethel came out to Elisha, and said to him,
"Do you know that the LORD will take away
your master from over you today?"
And he said, "Yes, I know; keep silent!"
4Then Elijah said to him, "Elisha, stay here,
please, for the LORD has sent me on to Jericho."
But he said, "*As* the LORD lives, and *as* your
soul lives, I will not leave you!" So they came
to Jericho.
5Now the sons of the prophets who *were* at
Jericho came to Elisha and said to him, "Do
you know that the LORD will take away your
master from over you today?"
So he answered, "Yes, I know; keep silent!"
6Then Elijah said to him, "Stay here, please,
for the LORD has sent me on to the Jordan."
But he said, "*As* the LORD lives, and *as* your
soul lives, I will not leave you!" So the two of
them went on. 7And fifty men of the sons of
the prophets went and stood facing *them* at a
distance, while the two of them stood by the
Jordan. 8Now Elijah took his mantle, rolled *it*
up, and struck the water; and it was divided
this way and that, so that the two of them
crossed over on dry ground.
9And so it was, when they had crossed over,
that Elijah said to Elisha, "Ask! What may I do
for you, before I am taken away from you?"
Elisha said, "Please let a double portion of
your spirit be upon me."
10So he said, "You have asked a hard thing.
Nevertheless, if you see me *when I am* taken
from you, it shall be so for you; but if not, it
shall not be *so.*" 11Then it happened, as they
continued on and talked, that suddenly a
chariot of fire *appeared* with horses of fire,
and separated the two of them; and Elijah
went up by a whirlwind into heaven.
12And Elisha saw *it,* and he cried out, "My
father, my father, the chariot of Israel and its
horsemen!" So he saw him no more. And he
took hold of his own clothes and tore them
into two pieces. 13He also took up the mantle
of Elijah that had fallen from him, and went
back and stood by the bank of the Jordan.
14Then he took the mantle of Elijah that had
fallen from him, and struck the water, and said,
"Where *is* the LORD God of Elijah?" And when
he also had struck the water, it was divided
this way and that; and Elisha crossed over.
15Now when the sons of the prophets who
were from Jericho saw him, they said, "The
spirit of Elijah rests on Elisha." And they came
to meet him, and bowed to the ground before
him. 16Then they said to him, "Look now,
there are fifty strong men with your servants.
Please let them go and search for your master,
lest perhaps the Spirit of the LORD has taken
him up and cast him upon some mountain or
into some valley."
And he said, "You shall not send anyone."
17But when they urged him till he was
ashamed, he said, "Send *them!*" Therefore
they sent fifty men, and they searched for
three days but did not find him. 18And when
they came back to him, for he had stayed in
Jericho, he said to them, "Did I not say to you,
'Do not go'?"

Elisha Performs Miracles

19Then the men of the city said to Elisha,
"Please notice, the situation of this city *is*
pleasant, as my lord sees; but the water *is*
bad, and the ground barren."

SOUL NOTE

Sell Out *(2:6)* The relationship between Elijah, the elder prophet, and Elisha, the prophet-in-training, exemplifies the influence of a strong mentor. When Elijah asked Elisha, "What may I do for you, before I am taken away from you?" (2:9), Elisha knew what he wanted. He had seen what God had done through Elijah, and Elisha wanted God to use him even more. A life lived for God will inspire others to be sold out for God as well. Invest in someone else what God has entrusted to you.
Topic: Mentoring

20And he said, "Bring me a new bowl, and
put salt in it." So they brought *it* to him.
21Then he went out to the source of the water,
and cast in the salt there, and said, "Thus says
the LORD: 'I have healed this water; from it
there shall be no more death or barrenness.' "
22So the water remains healed to this day, according to the word of Elisha which he spoke.

23Then he went up from there to Bethel; and
as he was going up the road, some youths
came from the city and mocked him, and said
to him, "Go up, you baldhead! Go up, you
baldhead!"

24So he turned around and looked at them,
and pronounced a curse on them in the name
of the LORD. And two female bears came out
of the woods and mauled forty-two of the
youths.

25Then he went from there to Mount Carmel, and from there he returned to Samaria.

Moab Rebels Against Israel

3 Now Jehoram the son of Ahab became
king over Israel at Samaria in the eighteenth year of Jehoshaphat king of Judah, and
reigned twelve years. 2And he did evil in the
sight of the LORD, but not like his father and
mother; for he put away the *sacred* pillar of
Baal that his father had made. 3Nevertheless
he persisted in the sins of Jeroboam the son of
Nebat, who had made Israel sin; he did not
depart from them.

4Now Mesha king of Moab was a sheepbreeder, and he regularly paid the king of Israel one hundred thousand lambs and the
wool of one hundred thousand rams. 5But it
happened, when Ahab died, that the king of
Moab rebelled against the king of Israel.

6So King Jehoram went out of Samaria at
that time and mustered all Israel. 7Then he
went and sent to Jehoshaphat king of Judah,
saying, "The king of Moab has rebelled
against me. Will you go with me to fight
against Moab?"

And he said, "I will go up; I *am* as you *are,*
my people as your people, my horses as your
horses." 8Then he said, "Which way shall we
go up?"

And he answered, "By way of the Wilderness of Edom."

9So the king of Israel went with the king
of Judah and the king of Edom, and they
marched on that roundabout route seven
days; and there was no water for the army, nor
for the animals that followed them. 10And the
king of Israel said, "Alas! For the LORD has
called these three kings together to deliver
them into the hand of Moab."

11But Jehoshaphat said, "*Is there* no prophet
of the LORD here, that we may inquire of the
LORD by him?"

So one of the servants of the king of Israel
answered and said, "Elisha the son of Shaphat
is here, who poured water on the hands of
Elijah."

12And Jehoshaphat said, "The word of the
LORD is with him." So the king of Israel and Jehoshaphat and the king of Edom went down
to him.

13Then Elisha said to the king of Israel,
"What have I to do with you? Go to the prophets of your father and the prophets of your
mother."

But the king of Israel said to him, "No, for
the LORD has called these three kings *together*
to deliver them into the hand of Moab."

14And Elisha said, "*As* the LORD of hosts
lives, before whom I stand, surely were it not
that I regard the presence of Jehoshaphat king
of Judah, I would not look at you, nor see you.
15But now bring me a musician."

Then it happened, when the musician
played, that the hand of the LORD came upon
him. 16And he said, "Thus says the LORD:
'Make this valley full of ditches.' 17For thus
says the LORD: 'You shall not see wind, nor
shall you see rain; yet that valley shall be
filled with water, so that you, your cattle, and
your animals may drink.' 18And this is a simple matter in the sight of the LORD; He will
also deliver the Moabites into your hand.
19Also you shall attack every fortified city and
every choice city, and shall cut down every
good tree, and stop up every spring of water,
and ruin every good piece of land with stones."

20Now it happened in the morning, when
the grain offering was offered, that suddenly
water came by way of Edom, and the land was
filled with water.

21And when all the Moabites heard that the
kings had come up to fight against them, all
who were able to bear arms and older were
gathered; and they stood at the border. 22Then
they rose up early in the morning, and the sun
was shining on the water; and the Moabites
saw the water on the other side *as* red as
blood. 23And they said, "This is blood; the
kings have surely struck swords and have

killed one another; now therefore, Moab, to
the spoil!"
24 So when they came to the camp of Israel,
Israel rose up and attacked the Moabites, so
that they fled before them; and they entered
their land, killing the Moabites. 25 Then they
destroyed the cities, and each man threw a
stone on every good piece of land and filled it;
and they stopped up all the springs of water
and cut down all the good trees. But they left
the stones of Kir Haraseth *intact.* However the
slingers surrounded and attacked it.
26 And when the king of Moab saw that the
battle was too fierce for him, he took with him
seven hundred men who drew swords, to
break through to the king of Edom, but they
could not. 27 Then he took his eldest son who
would have reigned in his place, and offered
him *as* a burnt offering upon the wall; and
there was great indignation against Israel. So
they departed from him and returned to *their
own* land.

Elisha and the Widow's Oil

4 A certain woman of the wives of the sons
of the prophets cried out to Elisha, saying,
"Your servant my husband is dead, and you
know that your servant feared the LORD. And
the creditor is coming to take my two sons to
be his slaves."
2 So Elisha said to her, "What shall I do for
you? Tell me, what do you have in the house?"
And she said, "Your maidservant has nothing
in the house but a jar of oil."
3 Then he said, "Go, borrow vessels from everywhere, from all your neighbors—empty
vessels; do not gather just a few. 4 And when
you have come in, you shall shut the door behind you and your sons; then pour it into all
those vessels, and set aside the full ones."
5 So she went from him and shut the door
behind her and her sons, who brought *the vessels* to her; and she poured *it* out. 6 Now it came
to pass, when the vessels were full, that she
said to her son, "Bring me another vessel."
And he said to her, "*There is* not another
vessel." So the oil ceased. 7 Then she came and
told the man of God. And he said, "Go, sell the
oil and pay your debt; and you *and* your sons
live on the rest."

Elisha Raises the Shunammite's Son

8 Now it happened one day that Elisha went
to Shunem, where there *was* a notable woman,
and she persuaded him to eat some food. So it
was, as often as he passed by, he would turn in
there to eat some food. 9 And she said to her
husband, "Look now, I know that this *is* a holy
man of God, who passes by us regularly.
10 Please, let us make a small upper room on the
wall; and let us put a bed for him there, and a
table and a chair and a lampstand; so it will be,
whenever he comes to us, he can turn in
there."
11 And it happened one day that he came
there, and he turned in to the upper room and
lay down there. 12 Then he said to Gehazi his
servant, "Call this Shunammite woman."
When he had called her, she stood before him.
13 And he said to him, "Say now to her, 'Look,
you have been concerned for us with all this
care. What *can I* do for you? Do you want me
to speak on your behalf to the king or to the
commander of the army?' "
She answered, "I dwell among my own
people."
14 So he said, "What then *is* to be done for
her?"
And Gehazi answered, "Actually, she has no
son, and her husband is old."
15 So he said, "Call her." When he had called
her, she stood in the doorway. 16 Then he said,
"About this time next year you shall embrace
a son."
And she said, "No, my lord. Man of God, do
not lie to your maidservant!"
17 But the woman conceived, and bore a son
when the appointed time had come, of which
Elisha had told her.
18 And the child grew. Now it happened one
day that he went out to his father, to the reapers. 19 And he said to his father, "My head, my
head!"
So he said to a servant, "Carry him to his
mother." 20 When he had taken him and
brought him to his mother, he sat on her knees
till noon, and *then* died. 21 And she went up
and laid him on the bed of the man of God,
shut *the door* upon him, and went out. 22 Then
she called to her husband, and said, "Please
send me one of the young men and one of the
donkeys, that I may run to the man of God and
come back."
23 So he said, "Why are you going to him today? *It is* neither the New Moon nor the Sabbath."
And she said, "*It is* well." 24 Then she saddled a donkey, and said to her servant, "Drive,

and go forward; do not slacken the pace for me unless I tell you." [25]And so she departed, and went to the man of God at Mount Carmel.

So it was, when the man of God saw her afar off, that he said to his servant Gehazi, "Look, the Shunammite woman! [26]Please run now to meet her, and say to her, '*Is it* well with you? *Is it* well with your husband? *Is it* well with the child?' "

And she answered, "*It is* well." [27]Now when she came to the man of God at the hill, she caught him by the feet, but Gehazi came near to push her away. But the man of God said, "Let her alone; for her soul *is* in deep distress, and the LORD has hidden *it* from me, and has not told me."

[28]So she said, "Did I ask a son of my lord? Did I not say, 'Do not deceive me'?"

[29]Then he said to Gehazi, "Get yourself ready, and take my staff in your hand, and be on your way. If you meet anyone, do not greet him; and if anyone greets you, do not answer him; but lay my staff on the face of the child."

[30]And the mother of the child said, "*As* the LORD lives, and *as* your soul lives, I will not leave you." So he arose and followed her. [31]Now Gehazi went on ahead of them, and laid the staff on the face of the child; but *there was* neither voice nor hearing. Therefore he went back to meet him, and told him, saying, "The child has not awakened."

[32]When Elisha came into the house, there was the child, lying dead on his bed. [33]He went in therefore, shut the door behind the two of them, and prayed to the LORD. [34]And he went up and lay on the child, and put his mouth on his mouth, his eyes on his eyes, and his hands on his hands; and he stretched himself out on the child, and the flesh of the child became warm. [35]He returned and walked back and forth in the house, and again went up and stretched himself out on him; then the child sneezed seven times, and the child opened his eyes. [36]And he called Gehazi and said, "Call this Shunammite woman." So he called her. And when she came in to him, he said, "Pick up your son." [37]So she went in, fell at his feet, and bowed to the ground; then she picked up her son and went out.

ELISHA PURIFIES THE POT OF STEW

[38]And Elisha returned to Gilgal, and *there was* a famine in the land. Now the sons of the prophets *were* sitting before him; and he said to his servant, "Put on the large pot, and boil stew for the sons of the prophets." [39]So one went out into the field to gather herbs, and found a wild vine, and gathered from it a lapful of wild gourds, and came and sliced *them* into the pot of stew, though they did not know *what they were.* [40]Then they served it to the men to eat. Now it happened, as they were eating the stew, that they cried out and said, "Man of God, *there is* death in the pot!" And they could not eat *it.*

[41]So he said, "Then bring some flour." And he put *it* into the pot, and said, "Serve *it* to the people, that they may eat." And there was nothing harmful in the pot.

ELISHA FEEDS ONE HUNDRED MEN

[42]Then a man came from Baal Shalisha, and brought the man of God bread of the firstfruits, twenty loaves of barley bread, and newly ripened grain in his knapsack. And he said, "Give *it* to the people, that they may eat."

[43]But his servant said, "What? Shall I set this before one hundred men?"

He said again, "Give it to the people, that they may eat; for thus says the LORD: 'They shall eat and have *some* left over.' " [44]So he set *it* before them; and they ate and had *some* left over, according to the word of the LORD.

NAAMAN'S LEPROSY HEALED

5 Now Naaman, commander of the army of the king of Syria, was a great and honorable man in the eyes of his master, because by him the LORD had given victory to Syria. He was also a mighty man of valor, *but* a leper. [2]And the Syrians had gone out on raids, and had brought back captive a young girl from the land of Israel. She waited on Naaman's wife. [3]Then she said to her mistress, "If only my master *were* with the prophet who *is* in Samaria! For he would heal him of his leprosy." [4]And *Naaman* went in and told his master, saying, "Thus and thus said the girl who *is* from the land of Israel."

[5]Then the king of Syria said, "Go now, and I will send a letter to the king of Israel."

So he departed and took with him ten talents of silver, six thousand *shekels* of gold, and ten changes of clothing. [6]Then he brought the letter to the king of Israel, which said,

> Now be advised, when this letter comes to you, that I have sent Naaman my

servant to you, that you may heal him of
his leprosy.

7And it happened, when the king of Israel read
the letter, that he tore his clothes and said,
"*Am* I God, to kill and make alive, that this
man sends a man to me to heal him of his leprosy? Therefore please consider, and see how
he seeks a quarrel with me."
8So it was, when Elisha the man of God
heard that the king of Israel had torn his
clothes, that he sent to the king, saying, "Why
have you torn your clothes? Please let him
come to me, and he shall know that there is a
prophet in Israel."
9Then Naaman went with his horses and
chariot, and he stood at the door of Elisha's
house. 10And Elisha sent a messenger to him,
saying, "Go and wash in the Jordan seven
times, and your flesh shall be restored to you,
and *you shall* be clean." 11But Naaman became furious, and went away and said, "Indeed, I said to myself, 'He will surely come
out *to me,* and stand and call on the name of
the LORD his God, and wave his hand over the
place, and heal the leprosy.' 12*Are* not the
Abanah[a] and the Pharpar, the rivers of Damascus, better than all the waters of Israel? Could
I not wash in them and be clean?" So he
turned and went away in a rage. 13And his servants came near and spoke to him, and said,
"My father, *if* the prophet had told you *to do*
something great, would you not have done *it?*
How much more then, when he says to you,
'Wash, and be clean'?" 14So he went down and
dipped seven times in the Jordan, according to
the saying of the man of God; and his flesh
was restored like the flesh of a little child, and
he was clean.
15And he returned to the man of God, he
and all his aides, and came and stood before
him; and he said, "Indeed, now I know that
there is no God in all the earth, except in Israel; now therefore, please take a gift from
your servant."
16But he said, "*As* the LORD lives, before
whom I stand, I will receive nothing." And he
urged him to take *it,* but he refused.
17So Naaman said, "Then, if not, please let
your servant be given two mule-loads of
earth; for your servant will no longer offer
either burnt offering or sacrifice to other gods,
but to the LORD. 18Yet in this thing may the
LORD pardon your servant: when my master
goes into the temple of Rimmon to worship
there, and he leans on my hand, and I bow
down in the temple of Rimmon—when I bow
down in the temple of Rimmon, may the LORD
please pardon your servant in this thing."
19Then he said to him, "Go in peace." So he
departed from him a short distance.

Gehazi's Greed

20But Gehazi, the servant of Elisha the man
of God, said, "Look, my master has spared Naaman this Syrian, while not receiving from his
hands what he brought; but *as* the LORD lives,
I will run after him and take something from
him." 21So Gehazi pursued Naaman. When
Naaman saw *him* running after him, he got
down from the chariot to meet him, and said,
"*Is* all well?"
22And he said, "All *is* well. My master has
sent me, saying, 'Indeed, just now two young
men of the sons of the prophets have come to
me from the mountains of Ephraim. Please
give them a talent of silver and two changes of
garments.' "
23So Naaman said, "Please, take two talents." And he urged him, and bound two talents of silver in two bags, with two changes of
garments, and handed *them* to two of his servants; and they carried *them* on ahead of him.
24When he came to the citadel, he took *them*
from their hand, and stored *them* away in the
house; then he let the men go, and they departed. 25Now he went in and stood before his
master. Elisha said to him, "Where *did you go,*
Gehazi?"
And he said, "Your servant did not go anywhere."
26Then he said to him, "Did not my heart go
with you when the man turned back from his
chariot to meet you? *Is it* time to receive
money and to receive clothing, olive groves
and vineyards, sheep and oxen, male and female servants? 27Therefore the leprosy of Naaman shall cling to you and your descendants
forever." And he went out from his presence
leprous, *as white* as snow.

The Floating Ax Head

6 And the sons of the prophets said to Elisha, "See now, the place where we dwell
with you is too small for us. 2Please, let us go

5:12 [a]Following Kethib, Septuagint, and Vulgate; Qere, Syriac, and Targum read *Amanah*.

Money

MASTERING YOUR MONEY

RON BLUE

(2 Kings 5:20–27)

According to a financial analyst for a major television network, financial and emotional security are inextricably linked. From a secular perspective, financial security is often synonymous with affluence and success. The world thinks that the person who has enough money will feel safe and satisfied.

From a Christian perspective, financial and emotional security run much deeper. Paul advised Timothy to pursue godliness along with contentment, pointing out that "the love of money is a root of all kinds of evil" (1 Tim. 6:10). Paul recognized what countless others have discovered: Either we will master our money, or it will master us. Furthermore, it is the financial freedom that comes with mastering our money—rather than the actual amount of money that we have—that serves as the link between financial security and emotional well-being.

WHAT TO KNOW ABOUT MASTERING YOUR MONEY

Mastering our money begins with discovering what the Bible says about financial management. Jesus Christ talked about money—and how to handle it—more than any other single issue. Why? Because "where your treasure is, there your heart will be also" (Matt. 6:21).

Our treasure is what is most important to us, where the heart is. God knows that our hearts cannot be devoted both to Him and to wealth or material pursuits. "You cannot serve God and mammon [money]" (Matt. 6:24). Jesus didn't say it would be *difficult* to serve both; He said it would be *impossible*. We *cannot*; therefore, we must choose.

When it comes to choosing our treasure, we really have only two options. Either we can store up treasures on earth, or we can store up treasure in heaven (Matt. 6:19, 20). Jesus recommends the latter—and if we want to follow His advice, we must start by acknowledging God's ownership of everything that we have.

The bottom line is this: *God owns it all.* What does that mean in practical terms? First, it means that God has the right to take or use whatever He wants whenever He wants. We are simply managers of the resources He entrusts to us.

Second, if we acknowledge God's position as the ultimate owner, then every spending decision we make becomes a spiritual decision. Instead of asking whether or not we can afford to buy something, our questions should revolve around whether or not God would want us to use His resources in that way.

Finally, the proof, as they say, is in the pudding. If we really believe that God owns it all, our convictions will show up in our checkbook. What does our checkbook say about our goals and priorities? What does it say about who is in charge?

Have we mastered our money—or is it mastering us?

WHAT TO DO TO MASTER YOUR MONEY

Four biblically based principles for mastering our money have stood the tests of time and experience:

1. *Spend less than you earn.* No matter how much money people have, there will always be unlimited ways to spend it. Spending less than we earn is the number

one key to achieving financial freedom and security—regardless of what happens in the overall economy.

2. *Avoid the use of debt.* The average American family devotes 25 percent of its spendable income—the amount left after taxes—to paying off outstanding debts! Not only does going into debt presume upon the future, but it precommits our resources, limits our financial flexibility, and dictates what we can (and cannot) afford to do down the road.

3. *Maintain liquidity.* We must build liquidity—that is, cash or assets that can be readily converted to cash—before we embark on more sophisticated investment strategies. By keeping at least three- to six-months worth of living expenses in a bank account or money market fund, we can ride out minor emergencies and unexpected expenses that might otherwise derail our budget and cause us to take on unwanted debt.

4. *Set long-term goals.* Any financial advisor will say that setting goals is the cornerstone of sound financial planning. Goals provide direction in life—and the longer-term our perspective is, the better our current financial decisions will be.

GENEROSITY: THE KEY TO CONTENTMENT

These four principles—spend less than we earn, avoid debt, maintain liquidity, and set goals—provide a framework for gaining control of our finances. But finding true peace, contentment, and security goes beyond wise investing, careful budgeting, and debt-free living. These are all valuable, but the real secret to financial freedom and emotional health comes when we learn to hold our resources with an open hand. In order to experience genuine joy, we must be willing to give.

The Bible commands believers to be generous. Why is God so interested in our generosity? It's not because He needs the money. Rather, God asks us to give because of what giving does for us: It breaks the power of money. The world's perspective—that accumulation equals success—creates a bondage to money. Under this philosophy, any thought of giving money away comes as a threat to our security. Consumed by the need to stockpile funds, we become slaves to our finances.

When we give, on the other hand, we acknowledge our dependence on God and our willingness to love and serve Him. We stand on the promise of Matthew 6:8, that our heavenly Father knows what we need before we ask Him. Money no longer has a hold on us—and we become free to give God that which He wants most of all: our hearts. Where our treasure is, our hearts will be also.

FURTHER MEDITATION:

Other passages to study about the issue of money include:

- Proverbs 3:9, 10; 11:24–26; 17:18, 23; 19:17; 21:13, 20; 22:7, 9, 26, 27
- Haggai 1:3–11
- Matthew 19:16–30
- Luke 6:38; 12:16–21; 14:16–24; 16:1–9; 21:1–4

To Learn More: Turn to the key passage note on money at 1 Timothy 6:6–10 on page 1599. See also the personality profile of the rich young ruler on page 1295.

to the Jordan, and let every man take a beam from there, and let us make there a place where we may dwell."

So he answered, "Go."

[3]Then one said, "Please consent to go with your servants."

And he answered, "I will go." [4]So he went with them. And when they came to the Jordan, they cut down trees. [5]But as one was cutting down a tree, the iron *ax head* fell into the water; and he cried out and said, "Alas, master! For it was borrowed."

[6]So the man of God said, "Where did it fall?" And he showed him the place. So he cut off a stick, and threw *it* in there; and he made the iron float. [7]Therefore he said, "Pick *it* up for yourself." So he reached out his hand and took it.

The Blinded Syrians Captured

[8]Now the king of Syria was making war against Israel; and he consulted with his servants, saying, "My camp *will be* in such and such a place." [9]And the man of God sent to the king of Israel, saying, "Beware that you do not pass this place, for the Syrians are coming down there." [10]Then the king of Israel sent *someone* to the place of which the man of God had told him. Thus he warned him, and he was watchful there, not just once or twice.

[11]Therefore the heart of the king of Syria was greatly troubled by this thing; and he called his servants and said to them, "Will you not show me which of us *is* for the king of Israel?"

[12]And one of his servants said, "None, my lord, O king; but Elisha, the prophet who *is* in Israel, tells the king of Israel the words that you speak in your bedroom."

[13]So he said, "Go and see where he *is,* that I may send and get him."

And it was told him, saying, "Surely *he is* in Dothan."

[14]Therefore he sent horses and chariots and a great army there, and they came by night and surrounded the city. [15]And when the servant of the man of God arose early and went out, there was an army, surrounding the city with horses and chariots. And his servant said to him, "Alas, my master! What shall we do?"

[16]So he answered, "Do not fear, for those who *are* with us *are* more than those who *are* with them." [17]And Elisha prayed, and said, "LORD, I pray, open his eyes that he may see." Then the LORD opened the eyes of the young man, and he saw. And behold, the mountain *was* full of horses and chariots of fire all around Elisha. [18]So when *the Syrians* came down to him, Elisha prayed to the LORD, and said, "Strike this people, I pray, with blindness." And He struck them with blindness according to the word of Elisha.

[19]Now Elisha said to them, "This *is* not the way, nor *is* this the city. Follow me, and I will bring you to the man whom you seek." But he led them to Samaria.

[20]So it was, when they had come to Samaria, that Elisha said, "LORD, open the eyes of these *men,* that they may see." And the LORD opened their eyes, and they saw; and there *they were,* inside Samaria!

[21]Now when the king of Israel saw them, he said to Elisha, "My father, shall I kill *them?* Shall I kill *them?*"

[22]But he answered, "You shall not kill *them.* Would you kill those whom you have taken captive with your sword and your bow? Set food and water before them, that they may eat and drink and go to their master." [23]Then he prepared a great feast for them; and after they ate and drank, he sent them away and they went to their master. So the bands of Syrian *raiders* came no more into the land of Israel.

Syria Besieges Samaria in Famine

[24]And it happened after this that Ben-Hadad king of Syria gathered all his army, and went up and besieged Samaria. [25]And there was a great famine in Samaria; and indeed they besieged it until a donkey's head was *sold* for eighty *shekels* of silver, and one-fourth of a kab of dove droppings for five *shekels* of silver.

[26]Then, as the king of Israel was passing by on the wall, a woman cried out to him, saying, "Help, my lord, O king!"

[27]And he said, "If the LORD does not help you, where can I find help for you? From the threshing floor or from the winepress?" [28]Then the king said to her, "What is troubling you?"

And she answered, "This woman said to me, 'Give your son, that we may eat him today, and we will eat my son tomorrow.' [29]So we boiled my son, and ate him. And I said to her on the next day, 'Give your son, that we may eat him'; but she has hidden her son."

[30]Now it happened, when the king heard

the words of the woman, that he tore his
clothes; and as he passed by on the wall, the
people looked, and there underneath *he had*
sackcloth on his body. 31Then he said, "God do
so to me and more also, if the head of Elisha
the son of Shaphat remains on him today!"
32But Elisha was sitting in his house, and
the elders were sitting with him. And *the king*
sent a man ahead of him, but before the messenger came to him, he said to the elders, "Do
you see how this son of a murderer has sent
someone to take away my head? Look, when
the messenger comes, shut the door, and hold
him fast at the door. *Is* not the sound of his
master's feet behind him?" 33And while he was
still talking with them, there was the messenger, coming down to him; and then *the king*
said, "Surely this calamity *is* from the LORD;
why should I wait for the LORD any longer?"

7 Then Elisha said, "Hear the word of the
LORD. Thus says the LORD: 'Tomorrow
about this time a seah of fine flour *shall be*
sold for a shekel, and two seahs of barley for a
shekel, at the gate of Samaria.' "
2So an officer on whose hand the king
leaned answered the man of God and said,
"Look, *if* the LORD would make windows in
heaven, could this thing be?"

And he said, "In fact, you shall see *it* with
your eyes, but you shall not eat of it."

THE SYRIANS FLEE

3Now there were four leprous men at the
entrance of the gate; and they said to one another, "Why are we sitting here until we die?
4If we say, 'We will enter the city,' the famine
is in the city, and we shall die there. And if we
sit here, we die also. Now therefore, come, let
us surrender to the army of the Syrians. If they
keep us alive, we shall live; and if they kill us,
we shall only die." 5And they rose at twilight
to go to the camp of the Syrians; and when
they had come to the outskirts of the Syrian
camp, to their surprise no one *was* there. 6For
the LORD had caused the army of the Syrians
to hear the noise of chariots and the noise of
horses—the noise of a great army; so they said
to one another, "Look, the king of Israel has
hired against us the kings of the Hittites and
the kings of the Egyptians to attack us!"
7Therefore they arose and fled at twilight, and
left the camp intact—their tents, their horses,
and their donkeys—and they fled for their
lives. 8And when these lepers came to the outskirts of the camp, they went into one tent and
ate and drank, and carried from it silver and
gold and clothing, and went and hid *them;*
then they came back and entered another tent,
and carried *some* from there *also,* and went
and hid *it.*
9Then they said to one another, "We are not
doing right. This day *is* a day of good news,
and we remain silent. If we wait until morning
light, some punishment will come upon us.
Now therefore, come, let us go and tell the
king's household." 10So they went and called
to the gatekeepers of the city, and told them,
saying, "We went to the Syrian camp, and surprisingly no one *was* there, not a human
sound—only horses and donkeys tied, and the
tents intact." 11And the gatekeepers called out,
and they told *it* to the king's household inside.
12So the king arose in the night and said to
his servants, "Let me now tell you what the
Syrians have done to us. They know that we
are hungry; therefore they have gone out of
the camp to hide themselves in the field, saying, 'When they come out of the city, we shall
catch them alive, and get into the city.' "
13And one of his servants answered and
said, "Please, let several *men* take five of the
remaining horses which are left in the city.
Look, they *may either become* like all the multitude of Israel that are left in it; or indeed, *I*
say, they *may become* like all the multitude of
Israel left from those who are consumed; so
let us send them and see." 14Therefore they
took two chariots with horses; and the king
sent them in the direction of the Syrian army,
saying, "Go and see." 15And they went after
them to the Jordan; and indeed all the road
was full of garments and weapons which the
Syrians had thrown away in their haste. So the
messengers returned and told the king. 16Then
the people went out and plundered the tents
of the Syrians. So a seah of fine flour was *sold*
for a shekel, and two seahs of barley for a
shekel, according to the word of the LORD.
17Now the king had appointed the officer on
whose hand he leaned to have charge of the
gate. But the people trampled him in the gate,
and he died, just as the man of God had said,
who spoke when the king came down to him.
18So it happened just as the man of God had
spoken to the king, saying, "Two seahs of barley for a shekel, and a seah of fine flour for a
shekel, shall be *sold* tomorrow about this time
in the gate of Samaria."

19Then that officer had answered the man
of God, and said, "Now look, *if* the LORD
would make windows in heaven, could such a
thing be?"
And he had said, "In fact, you shall see *it*
with your eyes, but you shall not eat of it."
20And so it happened to him, for the people
trampled him in the gate, and he died.

THE KING RESTORES THE SHUNAMMITE'S LAND

8 Then Elisha spoke to the woman whose
son he had restored to life, saying, "Arise
and go, you and your household, and stay
wherever you can; for the LORD has called for a
famine, and furthermore, it will come upon the
land for seven years." 2So the woman arose
and did according to the saying of the man of
God, and she went with her household and
dwelt in the land of the Philistines seven years.
3It came to pass, at the end of seven years,
that the woman returned from the land of the
Philistines; and she went to make an appeal to
the king for her house and for her land. 4Then
the king talked with Gehazi, the servant of the
man of God, saying, "Tell me, please, all the
great things Elisha has done." 5Now it happened, as he was telling the king how he had
restored the dead to life, that there was the
woman whose son he had restored to life, appealing to the king for her house and for her
land. And Gehazi said, "My lord, O king, this
is the woman, and this *is* her son whom Elisha
restored to life." 6And when the king asked
the woman, she told him.
So the king appointed a certain officer for
her, saying, "Restore all that *was* hers, and all
the proceeds of the field from the day that she
left the land until now."

DEATH OF BEN-HADAD

7Then Elisha went to Damascus, and Ben-
Hadad king of Syria was sick; and it was told
him, saying, "The man of God has come
here." 8And the king said to Hazael, "Take a
present in your hand, and go to meet the man
of God, and inquire of the LORD by him, saying, 'Shall I recover from this disease?' " 9So
Hazael went to meet him and took a present
with him, of every good thing of Damascus,
forty camel-loads; and he came and stood before him, and said, "Your son Ben-Hadad king
of Syria has sent me to you, saying, 'Shall I
recover from this disease?' "
10And Elisha said to him, "Go, say to him,
'You shall certainly recover.' However the
LORD has shown me that he will really
die." 11Then he set his countenance in a stare
until he was ashamed; and the man of God
wept. 12And Hazael said, "Why is my lord
weeping?"
He answered, "Because I know the evil that
you will do to the children of Israel: Their
strongholds you will set on fire, and their
young men you will kill with the sword; and
you will dash their children, and rip open
their women with child."
13So Hazael said, "But what *is* your servant—a dog, that he should do this gross
thing?"
And Elisha answered, "The LORD has
shown me that you *will become* king over
Syria."
14Then he departed from Elisha, and came
to his master, who said to him, "What did Elisha say to you?" And he answered, "He told
me you would surely recover." 15But it happened on the next day that he took a thick
cloth and dipped *it* in water, and spread *it* over
his face so that he died; and Hazael reigned in
his place.

JEHORAM REIGNS IN JUDAH

16Now in the fifth year of Joram the son of
Ahab, king of Israel, Jehoshaphat *having been*

SOUL NOTE

The Wrong Path *(8:15)* Ben-Hadad, king of Syria, had sent Hazael to ask Elisha if he would recover from his disease. Elisha responded that Ben-Hadad would die and that Hazael would take his place as king. The prophet's words came true the next day, for God had revealed to Elijah the treachery in Hazael's heart. Instead of waiting for God's timing, Hazael assassinated the king. Taking matters into our own hands never accomplishes God's purposes. A life of violence brings its own path of destruction.
Topic: Violence

king of Judah, Jehoram the son of Jehoshaphat began to reign as king of Judah. 17He was
thirty-two years old when he became king,
and he reigned eight years in Jerusalem. 18And
he walked in the way of the kings of Israel,
just as the house of Ahab had done, for the
daughter of Ahab was his wife; and he did evil
in the sight of the LORD. 19Yet the LORD would
not destroy Judah, for the sake of his servant
David, as He promised him to give a lamp to
him *and* his sons forever.

20In his days Edom revolted against Judah's
authority, and made a king over themselves.
21So Joram[a] went to Zair, and all his chariots
with him. Then he rose by night and attacked
the Edomites who had surrounded him and
the captains of the chariots; and the troops
fled to their tents. 22Thus Edom has been in
revolt against Judah's authority to this day.
And Libnah revolted at that time.

23Now the rest of the acts of Joram, and all
that he did, *are* they not written in the book of
the chronicles of the kings of Judah? 24So Joram rested with his fathers, and was buried
with his fathers in the City of David. Then
Ahaziah his son reigned in his place.

Ahaziah Reigns in Judah

25In the twelfth year of Joram the son of
Ahab, king of Israel, Ahaziah the son of Jehoram, king of Judah, began to reign. 26Ahaziah
was twenty-two years old when he became
king, and he reigned one year in Jerusalem.
His mother's name *was* Athaliah the granddaughter of Omri, king of Israel. 27And he
walked in the way of the house of Ahab, and
did evil in the sight of the LORD, like the house
of Ahab, for he *was* the son-in-law of the
house of Ahab.

28Now he went with Joram the son of Ahab
to war against Hazael king of Syria at Ramoth
Gilead; and the Syrians wounded Joram.
29Then King Joram went back to Jezreel to recover from the wounds which the Syrians had
inflicted on him at Ramah, when he fought
against Hazael king of Syria. And Ahaziah the
son of Jehoram, king of Judah, went down to
see Joram the son of Ahab in Jezreel, because
he was sick.

Jehu Anointed King of Israel

9 And Elisha the prophet called one of the
sons of the prophets, and said to him,
"Get yourself ready, take this flask of oil in
your hand, and go to Ramoth Gilead. 2Now
when you arrive at that place, look there for
Jehu the son of Jehoshaphat, the son of Nimshi, and go in and make him rise up from
among his associates, and take him to an inner room. 3Then take the flask of oil, and pour
it on his head, and say, 'Thus says the LORD:
"I have anointed you king over Israel." ' Then
open the door and flee, and do not delay."

4So the young man, the servant of the
prophet, went to Ramoth Gilead. 5And when
he arrived, there *were* the captains of the army
sitting; and he said, "I have a message for you,
Commander."

Jehu said, "For which *one* of us?"

And he said, "For you, Commander." 6Then
he arose and went into the house. And he
poured the oil on his head, and said to him,
"Thus says the LORD God of Israel: 'I have
anointed you king over the people of the
LORD, over Israel. 7You shall strike down the
house of Ahab your master, that I may avenge
the blood of My servants the prophets, and the
blood of all the servants of the LORD, at the
hand of Jezebel. 8For the whole house of Ahab
shall perish; and I will cut off from Ahab all
the males in Israel, both bond and free. 9So I
will make the house of Ahab like the house of
Jeroboam the son of Nebat, and like the house
of Baasha the son of Ahijah. 10The dogs shall
eat Jezebel on the plot *of ground* at Jezreel,
and *there shall be* none to bury *her.*' " And he
opened the door and fled.

11Then Jehu came out to the servants of his
master, and *one* said to him, "*Is* all well? Why
did this madman come to you?"

And he said to them, "You know the man
and his babble."

12And they said, "A lie! Tell us now."

So he said, "Thus and thus he spoke to me,
saying, 'Thus says the LORD: "I have anointed
you king over Israel." ' "

13Then each man hastened to take his garment and put *it* under him on the top of the
steps; and they blew trumpets, saying, "Jehu
is king!"

Joram of Israel Killed

14So Jehu the son of Jehoshaphat, the son of
Nimshi, conspired against Joram. (Now Joram
had been defending Ramoth Gilead, he and all
Israel, against Hazael king of Syria. 15But King

8:21 [a]Spelled *Jehoram* in verse 16

Joram had returned to Jezreel to recover from the wounds which the Syrians had inflicted on him when he fought with Hazael king of Syria.) And Jehu said, "If you are so minded, let no one leave *or* escape from the city to go and tell *it* in Jezreel." 16So Jehu rode in a chariot and went to Jezreel, for Joram was laid up there; and Ahaziah king of Judah had come down to see Joram.

17Now a watchman stood on the tower in Jezreel, and he saw the company of Jehu as he came, and said, "I see a company of men."

And Joram said, "Get a horseman and send him to meet them, and let him say, *'Is it* peace?' "

18So the horseman went to meet him, and said, "Thus says the king: *'Is it* peace?' "

And Jehu said, "What have you to do with peace? Turn around and follow me."

So the watchman reported, saying, "The messenger went to them, but is not coming back."

19Then he sent out a second horseman who came to them, and said, "Thus says the king: '*Is it* peace?' "

And Jehu answered, "What have you to do with peace? Turn around and follow me."

20So the watchman reported, saying, "He went up to them and is not coming back; and the driving *is* like the driving of Jehu the son of Nimshi, for he drives furiously!"

21Then Joram said, "Make ready." And his chariot was made ready. Then Joram king of Israel and Ahaziah king of Judah went out, each in his chariot; and they went out to meet Jehu, and met him on the property of Naboth the Jezreelite. 22Now it happened, when Joram saw Jehu, that he said, *"Is it* peace, Jehu?"

So he answered, "What peace, as long as the harlotries of your mother Jezebel and her witchcraft *are so* many?"

23Then Joram turned around and fled, and said to Ahaziah, "Treachery, Ahaziah!" 24Now Jehu drew his bow with full strength and shot Jehoram between his arms; and the arrow came out at his heart, and he sank down in his chariot. 25Then *Jehu* said to Bidkar his captain, "Pick *him* up, *and* throw him into the tract of the field of Naboth the Jezreelite; for remember, when you and I were riding together behind Ahab his father, that the LORD laid this burden upon him: 26'Surely I saw yesterday the blood of Naboth and the blood of his sons,' says the LORD, 'and I will repay you in this plot,' says the LORD. Now therefore, take *and* throw him on the plot *of ground,* according to the word of the LORD."

AHAZIAH OF JUDAH KILLED

27But when Ahaziah king of Judah saw *this,* he fled by the road to Beth Haggan.[a] So Jehu pursued him, and said, "Shoot him also in the chariot." *And they shot him* at the Ascent of Gur, which is by Ibleam. Then he fled to Megiddo, and died there. 28And his servants carried him in the chariot to Jerusalem, and buried him in his tomb with his fathers in the City of David. 29In the eleventh year of Joram the son of Ahab, Ahaziah had become king over Judah.

JEZEBEL'S VIOLENT DEATH

30Now when Jehu had come to Jezreel, Jezebel heard *of it;* and she put paint on her eyes and adorned her head, and looked through a window. 31Then, as Jehu entered at the gate, she said, *"Is it* peace, Zimri, murderer of your master?"

32And he looked up at the window, and said, "Who *is* on my side? Who?" So two *or* three eunuchs looked out at him. 33Then he said, "Throw her down." So they threw her down, and *some* of her blood spattered on the wall and on the horses; and he trampled her underfoot. 34And when he had gone in, he ate and drank. Then he said, "Go now, see to this accursed *woman,* and bury her, for she was a king's daughter." 35So they went to bury her, but they found no more of her than the skull and the feet and the palms of *her* hands. 36Therefore they came back and told him. And he said, "This *is* the word of the LORD, which He spoke by His servant Elijah the Tishbite, saying, 'On the plot *of ground* at Jezreel dogs shall eat the flesh of Jezebel;[a] 37and the corpse of Jezebel shall be as refuse on the surface of the field, in the plot at Jezreel, so that they shall not say, "Here *lies* Jezebel." ' "

AHAB'S SEVENTY SONS KILLED

10 Now Ahab had seventy sons in Samaria. And Jehu wrote and sent letters to Samaria, to the rulers of Jezreel,[a] to the

---

9:27 [a]Literally *The Garden House* **9:36** [a]1 Kings 21:23 **10:1** [a]Following Masoretic Text, Syriac, and Targum; Septuagint reads *Samaria;* Vulgate reads *city.*

elders, and to those who reared Ahab's *sons,* saying:

> 2 Now as soon as this letter comes to you, since your master's sons *are* with you, and you have chariots and horses, a fortified city also, and weapons, 3choose the best qualified of your master's sons, set *him* on his father's throne, and fight for your master's house.

4But they were exceedingly afraid, and said, "Look, two kings could not stand up to him; how then can we stand?" 5And he who *was* in charge of the house, and he who *was* in charge of the city, the elders also, and those who reared *the sons,* sent to Jehu, saying, "We *are* your servants, we will do all you tell us; but we will not make anyone king. Do *what is* good in your sight." 6Then he wrote a second letter to them, saying:

> If you *are* for me and will obey my voice, take the heads of the men, your master's sons, and come to me at Jezreel by this time tomorrow.

Now the king's sons, seventy persons, *were* with the great men of the city, *who* were rearing them. 7So it was, when the letter came to them, that they took the king's sons and slaughtered seventy persons, put their heads in baskets and sent *them* to him at Jezreel.

8Then a messenger came and told him, saying, "They have brought the heads of the king's sons."

And he said, "Lay them in two heaps at the entrance of the gate until morning."

9So it was, in the morning, that he went out and stood, and said to all the people, "You *are* righteous. Indeed I conspired against my master and killed him; but who killed all these? 10Know now that nothing shall fall to the earth of the word of the LORD which the LORD spoke concerning the house of Ahab; for the LORD has done what He spoke by His servant Elijah." 11So Jehu killed all who remained of the house of Ahab in Jezreel, and all his great men and his close acquaintances and his priests, until he left him none remaining.

Ahaziah's Forty-two Brothers Killed

12And he arose and departed and went to Samaria. On the way, at Beth Eked[a] of the Shepherds, 13Jehu met with the brothers of Ahaziah king of Judah, and said, "Who *are* you?"

So they answered, "We *are* the brothers of Ahaziah; we have come down to greet the sons of the king and the sons of the queen mother."

14And he said, "Take them alive!" So they took them alive, and killed them at the well of Beth Eked, forty-two men; and he left none of them.

The Rest of Ahab's Family Killed

15Now when he departed from there, he met Jehonadab the son of Rechab, *coming* to meet him; and he greeted him and said to him, "Is your heart right, as my heart *is* toward your heart?"

And Jehonadab answered, "It is."

Jehu said, "If it is, give *me* your hand." So he gave *him* his hand, and he took him up to him into the chariot. 16Then he said, "Come with me, and see my zeal for the LORD." So they had him ride in his chariot. 17And when he came to Samaria, he killed all who remained to Ahab in Samaria, till he had destroyed them, according to the word of the LORD which He spoke to Elijah.

Worshipers of Baal Killed

18Then Jehu gathered all the people together, and said to them, "Ahab served Baal a little, Jehu will serve him much. 19Now therefore, call to me all the prophets of Baal, all his servants, and all his priests. Let no one be missing, for I have a great sacrifice for Baal. Whoever is missing shall not live." But Jehu acted deceptively, with the intent of destroying the worshipers of Baal. 20And Jehu said, "Proclaim a solemn assembly for Baal." So they proclaimed *it.* 21Then Jehu sent throughout all Israel; and all the worshipers of Baal came, so that there was not a man left who did not come. So they came into the temple[a] of Baal, and the temple of Baal was full from one end to the other. 22And he said to the one in charge of the wardrobe, "Bring out vestments for all the worshipers of Baal." So he brought out vestments for them. 23Then Jehu and Jehonadab the son of Rechab went into the temple of Baal, and said to the worshipers of Baal,

10:12 [a]Or *The Shearing House* **10:21** [a]Literally *house,* and so elsewhere in this chapter

"Search and see that no servants of the LORD are here with you, but only the worshipers of Baal." [24]So they went in to offer sacrifices and burnt offerings. Now Jehu had appointed for himself eighty men on the outside, and had said, "*If* any of the men whom I have brought into your hands escapes, *whoever lets him escape, it shall be* his life for the life of the other."

[25]Now it happened, as soon as he had made an end of offering the burnt offering, that Jehu said to the guard and to the captains, "Go in *and* kill them; let no one come out!" And they killed them with the edge of the sword; then the guards and the officers threw *them* out, and went into the inner room of the temple of Baal. [26]And they brought the *sacred* pillars out of the temple of Baal and burned them. [27]Then they broke down the *sacred* pillar of Baal, and tore down the temple of Baal and made it a refuse dump to this day. [28]Thus Jehu destroyed Baal from Israel.

[29]However Jehu did not turn away from the sins of Jeroboam the son of Nebat, who had made Israel sin, *that is,* from the golden calves that *were* at Bethel and Dan. [30]And the LORD said to Jehu, "Because you have done well in doing *what is* right in My sight, *and* have done to the house of Ahab all that *was* in My heart, your sons shall sit on the throne of Israel to the fourth *generation.*" [31]But Jehu took no heed to walk in the law of the LORD God of Israel with all his heart; for he did not depart from the sins of Jeroboam, who had made Israel sin.

DEATH OF JEHU

[32]In those days the LORD began to cut off *parts* of Israel; and Hazael conquered them in all the territory of Israel [33]from the Jordan eastward: all the land of Gilead—Gad, Reuben, and Manasseh—from Aroer, which *is* by the River Arnon, including Gilead and Bashan.

[34]Now the rest of the acts of Jehu, all that he did, and all his might, *are* they not written in the book of the chronicles of the kings of Israel? [35]So Jehu rested with his fathers, and they buried him in Samaria. Then Jehoahaz his son reigned in his place. [36]And the period that Jehu reigned over Israel in Samaria *was* twenty-eight years.

ATHALIAH REIGNS IN JUDAH

11 When Athaliah the mother of Ahaziah saw that her son was dead, she arose and destroyed all the royal heirs. [2]But Jehosheba, the daughter of King Joram, sister of Ahaziah, took Joash the son of Ahaziah, and stole him away from among the king's sons *who were* being murdered; and they hid him and his nurse in the bedroom, from Athaliah, so that he was not killed. [3]So he was hidden with her in the house of the LORD for six years, while Athaliah reigned over the land.

JOASH CROWNED KING OF JUDAH

[4]In the seventh year Jehoiada sent and brought the captains of hundreds—of the bodyguards and the escorts—and brought them into the house of the LORD to him. And he made a covenant with them and took an oath from them in the house of the LORD, and showed them the king's son. [5]Then he commanded them, saying, "This *is* what you shall do: One-third of you who come on duty on the Sabbath shall be keeping watch over the king's house, [6]one-third *shall be* at the gate of Sur, and one-third at the gate behind the escorts. You shall keep the watch of the house, lest it be broken down. [7]The two contingents of you who go off duty on the Sabbath shall keep the watch of the house of the LORD for the king. [8]But you shall surround the king on all sides, every man with his weapons in his hand; and whoever comes within range, let him be put to death. You are to be with the king as he goes out and as he comes in."

[9]So the captains of the hundreds did according to all that Jehoiada the priest commanded. Each of them took his men who were to be on duty on the Sabbath, with those who were going off duty on the Sabbath, and came to Jehoiada the priest. [10]And the priest gave the captains of hundreds the spears and shields which *had belonged* to King David, that were in the temple of the LORD. [11]Then the escorts stood, every man with his weapons in his hand, all around the king, from the right side of the temple to the left side of the temple, by the altar and the house. [12]And he brought out the king's son, put the crown on him, and *gave him* the Testimony;[a] they made him king and anointed him, and they clapped their hands and said, "Long live the king!"

11:12 [a]That is, the Law (compare Exodus 25:16, 21 and Deuteronomy 31:9)

Death of Athaliah

[13]Now when Athaliah heard the noise of the escorts *and* the people, she came to the people *in* the temple of the LORD. [14]When she looked, there was the king standing by a pillar according to custom; and the leaders and the trumpeters were by the king. All the people of the land were rejoicing and blowing trumpets. So Athaliah tore her clothes and cried out, "Treason! Treason!"

[15]And Jehoiada the priest commanded the captains of the hundreds, the officers of the army, and said to them, "Take her outside under guard, and slay with the sword whoever follows her." For the priest had said, "Do not let her be killed in the house of the LORD." [16]So they seized her; and she went by way of the horses' entrance *into* the king's house, and there she was killed.

[17]Then Jehoiada made a covenant between the LORD, the king, and the people, that they should be the LORD's people, and *also* between the king and the people. [18]And all the people of the land went to the temple of Baal, and tore it down. They thoroughly broke in pieces its altars and images, and killed Mattan the priest of Baal before the altars. And the priest appointed officers over the house of the LORD. [19]Then he took the captains of hundreds, the bodyguards, the escorts, and all the people of the land; and they brought the king down from the house of the LORD, and went by way of the gate of the escorts to the king's house. Then he sat on the throne of the kings. [20]So all the people of the land rejoiced; and the city was quiet, for they had slain Athaliah with the sword *in* the king's house. [21]Jehoash *was* seven years old when he became king.

Jehoash Repairs the Temple

12 In the seventh year of Jehu, Jehoash[a] became king, and he reigned forty years in Jerusalem. His mother's name *was* Zibiah of Beersheba. [2]Jehoash did *what was* right in the sight of the LORD all the days in which Jehoiada the priest instructed him. [3]But the high places were not taken away; the people still sacrificed and burned incense on the high places.

[4]And Jehoash said to the priests, "All the money of the dedicated gifts that are brought into the house of the LORD—each man's census money, each man's assessment money[a]—*and* all the money that a man purposes in his heart to bring into the house of the LORD, [5]let the priests take *it* themselves, each from his constituency; and let them repair the damages of the temple, wherever any dilapidation is found."

[6]Now it was so, by the twenty-third year of King Jehoash, *that* the priests had not repaired the damages of the temple. [7]So King Jehoash called Jehoiada the priest and the *other* priests, and said to them, "Why have you not repaired the damages of the temple? Now therefore, do not take *more* money from your constituency, but deliver it for repairing the damages of the temple." [8]And the priests agreed that they would neither receive *more* money from the people, nor repair the damages of the temple.

[9]Then Jehoiada the priest took a chest, bored a hole in its lid, and set it beside the altar, on the right side as one comes into the house of the LORD; and the priests who kept the door put there all the money brought into the house of the LORD. [10]So it was, whenever they saw that *there was* much money in the chest, that the king's scribe and the high priest came up and put it in bags, and counted the money that was found in the house of the LORD. [11]Then they gave the money, which had been apportioned, into the hands of those

12:1 [a]Spelled *Joash* in 11:2ff **12:4** [a]Compare Leviticus 27:2ff

SOUL NOTE

Childcare *(12:1, 2)* Jehoash was a godly king who "did what was right in the sight of the LORD all the days in which Jehoiada the priest instructed him." He was only seven years old when he became king (11:21), so he needed instruction. Children do not have natural wisdom, so they must be taught and guided by those who love them. Patient instruction and consistent mentoring will prepare children to take on the tasks God has for them. **Topic: Child Development**

who did the work, who had the oversight of the house of the LORD; and they paid it out to the carpenters and builders who worked on the house of the LORD, [12]and to masons and stonecutters, and for buying timber and hewn stone, to repair the damage of the house of the LORD, and for all that was paid out to repair the temple. [13]However there were not made for the house of the LORD basins of silver, trimmers, sprinkling-bowls, trumpets, any articles of gold or articles of silver, from the money brought into the house of the LORD. [14]But they gave that to the workmen, and they repaired the house of the LORD with it. [15]Moreover they did not require an account from the men into whose hand they delivered the money to be paid to workmen, for they dealt faithfully. [16]The money from the trespass offerings and the money from the sin offerings was not brought into the house of the LORD. It belonged to the priests.

Hazael Threatens Jerusalem

[17]Hazael king of Syria went up and fought against Gath, and took it; then Hazael set his face to go up to Jerusalem. [18]And Jehoash king of Judah took all the sacred things that his fathers, Jehoshaphat and Jehoram and Ahaziah, kings of Judah, had dedicated, and his own sacred things, and all the gold found in the treasuries of the house of the LORD and in the king's house, and sent *them* to Hazael king of Syria. Then he went away from Jerusalem.

Death of Joash

[19]Now the rest of the acts of Joash,[a] and all that he did, *are* they not written in the book of the chronicles of the kings of Judah?

[20]And his servants arose and formed a conspiracy, and killed Joash in the house of the Millo,[a] which goes down to Silla. [21]For Jozachar[a] the son of Shimeath and Jehozabad the son of Shomer,[b] his servants, struck him. So he died, and they buried him with his fathers in the City of David. Then Amaziah his son reigned in his place.

Jehoahaz Reigns in Israel

13 In the twenty-third year of Joash[a] the son of Ahaziah, king of Judah, Jehoahaz the son of Jehu became king over Israel in Samaria, *and reigned* seventeen years. [2]And he did evil in the sight of the LORD, and followed the sins of Jeroboam the son of Nebat, who had made Israel sin. He did not depart from them.

[3]Then the anger of the LORD was aroused against Israel, and He delivered them into the hand of Hazael king of Syria, and into the hand of Ben-Hadad the son of Hazael, all *their* days. [4]So Jehoahaz pleaded with the LORD, and the LORD listened to him; for He saw the oppression of Israel, because the king of Syria oppressed them. [5]Then the LORD gave Israel a deliverer, so that they escaped from under the hand of the Syrians; and the children of Israel dwelt in their tents as before. [6]Nevertheless they did not depart from the sins of the house of Jeroboam, who had made Israel sin, *but* walked in them; and the wooden image[a] also remained in Samaria. [7]For He left of the army of Jehoahaz only fifty horsemen, ten chariots, and ten thousand foot soldiers; for the king of Syria had destroyed them and made them like the dust at threshing.

[8]Now the rest of the acts of Jehoahaz, all that he did, and his might, *are* they not written in the book of the chronicles of the kings of Israel? [9]So Jehoahaz rested with his fathers, and they buried him in Samaria. Then Joash his son reigned in his place.

Jehoash Reigns in Israel

[10]In the thirty-seventh year of Joash king of Judah, Jehoash[a] the son of Jehoahaz became king over Israel in Samaria, *and reigned* sixteen years. [11]And he did evil in the sight of the LORD. He did not depart from all the sins of Jeroboam the son of Nebat, who made Israel sin, *but* walked in them.

[12]Now the rest of the acts of Joash, all that he did, and his might with which he fought against Amaziah king of Judah, *are* they not written in the book of the chronicles of the kings of Israel? [13]So Joash rested with his fathers. Then Jeroboam sat on his throne. And Joash was buried in Samaria with the kings of Israel.

Death of Elisha

[14]Elisha had become sick with the illness of which he would die. Then Joash the king of Is-

---

12:19 [a]Spelled *Jehoash* in 12:1ff **12:20** [a]Literally *The Landfill* **12:21** [a]Called *Zabad* in 2 Chronicles 24:26 [b]Called *Shimrith* in 2 Chronicles 24:26 **13:1** [a]Spelled *Jehoash* in 12:1ff **13:6** [a]Hebrew *Asherah,* a Canaanite goddess **13:10** [a]Spelled *Joash* in verse 9

rael came down to him, and wept over his
face, and said, "O my father, my father, the
chariots of Israel and their horsemen!"
15And Elisha said to him, "Take a bow and
some arrows." So he took himself a bow and
some arrows. 16Then he said to the king of Israel, "Put your hand on the bow." So he put
his hand *on it,* and Elisha put his hands on the
king's hands. 17And he said, "Open the east
window"; and he opened *it.* Then Elisha said,
"Shoot"; and he shot. And he said, "The arrow of the LORD's deliverance and the arrow
of deliverance from Syria; for you must strike
the Syrians at Aphek till you have destroyed
them." 18Then he said, "Take the arrows"; so
he took *them.* And he said to the king of Israel, "Strike the ground"; so he struck three
times, and stopped. 19And the man of God was
angry with him, and said, "You should have
struck five or six times; then you would have
struck Syria till you had destroyed *it!* But now
you will strike Syria *only* three times."
20Then Elisha died, and they buried him.
And the *raiding* bands from Moab invaded the
land in the spring of the year. 21So it was, as
they were burying a man, that suddenly they
spied a band *of raiders;* and they put the man
in the tomb of Elisha; and when the man was
let down and touched the bones of Elisha, he
revived and stood on his feet.

Israel Recaptures Cities from Syria

22And Hazael king of Syria oppressed Israel
all the days of Jehoahaz. 23But the LORD was
gracious to them, had compassion on them,
and regarded them, because of His covenant
with Abraham, Isaac, and Jacob, and would
not yet destroy them or cast them from His
presence.
24Now Hazael king of Syria died. Then Ben-
Hadad his son reigned in his place. 25And
Jehoash[a] the son of Jehoahaz recaptured from
the hand of Ben-Hadad, the son of Hazael, the
cities which he had taken out of the hand of
Jehoahaz his father by war. Three times Joash
defeated him and recaptured the cities of Israel.

Amaziah Reigns in Judah

14 In the second year of Joash the son of
Jehoahaz, king of Israel, Amaziah the
son of Joash, king of Judah, became king. 2He
was twenty-five years old when he became
king, and he reigned twenty-nine years in Jerusalem. His mother's name was Jehoaddan
of Jerusalem. 3And he did *what was* right in
the sight of the LORD, yet not like his father
David; he did everything as his father Joash
had done. 4However the high places were not
taken away, and the people still sacrificed and
burned incense on the high places.
5Now it happened, as soon as the kingdom
was established in his hand, that he executed
his servants who had murdered his father the
king. 6But the children of the murderers he did
not execute, according to what is written in
the Book of the Law of Moses, in which the
LORD commanded, saying, "Fathers shall not
be put to death for their children, nor shall
children be put to death for their fathers; but a
person shall be put to death for his own sin."[a]
7He killed ten thousand Edomites in the Valley of Salt, and took Sela by war, and called its
name Joktheel to this day.
8Then Amaziah sent messengers to Jehoash[a] the son of Jehoahaz, the son of Jehu,
king of Israel, saying, "Come, let us face one
another *in battle.*" 9And Jehoash king of Israel
sent to Amaziah king of Judah, saying, "The
thistle that *was* in Lebanon sent to the cedar
that *was* in Lebanon, saying, 'Give your
daughter to my son as wife'; and a wild beast
that *was* in Lebanon passed by and trampled
the thistle. 10You have indeed defeated Edom,
and your heart has lifted you up. Glory *in that,*
and stay at home; for why should you meddle
with trouble so that you fall—you and Judah
with you?"
11But Amaziah would not heed. Therefore
Jehoash king of Israel went out; so he and
Amaziah king of Judah faced one another at
Beth Shemesh, which *belongs* to Judah. 12And
Judah was defeated by Israel, and every man
fled to his tent. 13Then Jehoash king of Israel
captured Amaziah king of Judah, the son of
Jehoash, the son of Ahaziah, at Beth Shemesh; and he went to Jerusalem, and broke
down the wall of Jerusalem from the Gate of
Ephraim to the Corner Gate—four hundred
cubits. 14And he took all the gold and silver,
all the articles that were found in the house of
the LORD and in the treasuries of the king's
house, and hostages, and returned to Samaria.
15Now the rest of the acts of Jehoash which

13:25 [a]Spelled *Joash* in verses 12–14, 25
14:6 [a]Deuteronomy 24:16 **14:8** [a]Spelled *Joash* in 13:12ff and 2 Chronicles 25:17ff

he did—his might, and how he fought with Amaziah king of Judah—*are* they not written in the book of the chronicles of the kings of Israel? [16]So Jehoash rested with his fathers, and was buried in Samaria with the kings of Israel. Then Jeroboam his son reigned in his place.

[17]Amaziah the son of Joash, king of Judah, lived fifteen years after the death of Jehoash the son of Jehoahaz, king of Israel. [18]Now the rest of the acts of Amaziah, *are* they not written in the book of the chronicles of the kings of Judah? [19]And they formed a conspiracy against him in Jerusalem, and he fled to Lachish; but they sent after him to Lachish and killed him there. [20]Then they brought him on horses, and he was buried at Jerusalem with his fathers in the City of David.

[21]And all the people of Judah took Azariah,[a] who *was* sixteen years old, and made him king instead of his father Amaziah. [22]He built Elath and restored it to Judah, after the king rested with his fathers.

Jeroboam II Reigns in Israel

[23]In the fifteenth year of Amaziah the son of Joash, king of Judah, Jeroboam the son of Joash, king of Israel, became king in Samaria, *and reigned* forty-one years. [24]And he did evil in the sight of the LORD; he did not depart from all the sins of Jeroboam the son of Nebat, who had made Israel sin. [25]He restored the territory of Israel from the entrance of Hamath to the Sea of the Arabah, according to the word of the LORD God of Israel, which He had spoken through His servant Jonah the son of Amittai, the prophet who *was* from Gath Hepher. [26]For the LORD saw *that* the affliction of Israel *was* very bitter; and whether bond or free, there was no helper for Israel. [27]And the LORD did not say that He would blot out the name of Israel from under heaven; but He saved them by the hand of Jeroboam the son of Joash.

[28]Now the rest of the acts of Jeroboam, and all that he did—his might, how he made war, and how he recaptured for Israel, from Damascus and Hamath, *what had belonged* to Judah—*are* they not written in the book of the chronicles of the kings of Israel? [29]So Jeroboam rested with his fathers, the kings of Israel. Then Zechariah his son reigned in his place.

Azariah Reigns in Judah

15 In the twenty-seventh year of Jeroboam king of Israel, Azariah the son of Amaziah, king of Judah, became king. [2]He was sixteen years old when he became king, and he reigned fifty-two years in Jerusalem. His mother's name *was* Jecholiah of Jerusalem. [3]And he did *what was* right in the sight of the LORD, according to all that his father Amaziah had done, [4]except that the high places were not removed; the people still sacrificed and burned incense on the high places. [5]Then the LORD struck the king, so that he was a leper until the day of his death; so he dwelt in an isolated house. And Jotham the king's son *was* over the *royal* house, judging the people of the land.

[6]Now the rest of the acts of Azariah, and all that he did, *are* they not written in the book of the chronicles of the kings of Judah? [7]So Azariah rested with his fathers, and they buried him with his fathers in the City of David. Then Jotham his son reigned in his place.

Zechariah Reigns in Israel

[8]In the thirty-eighth year of Azariah king of Judah, Zechariah the son of Jeroboam reigned over Israel in Samaria six months. [9]And he did evil in the sight of the LORD, as his fathers had done; he did not depart from the sins of Jeroboam the son of Nebat, who had made Israel sin. [10]Then Shallum the son of Jabesh conspired against him, and struck and killed him in front of the people; and he reigned in his place.

[11]Now the rest of the acts of Zechariah, indeed they *are* written in the book of the chronicles of the kings of Israel.

[12]This *was* the word of the LORD which He spoke to Jehu, saying, "Your sons shall sit on the throne of Israel to the fourth *generation*."[a] And so it was.

Shallum Reigns in Israel

[13]Shallum the son of Jabesh became king in the thirty-ninth year of Uzziah[a] king of Judah; and he reigned a full month in Samaria. [14]For Menahem the son of Gadi went up from Tirzah, came to Samaria, and struck Shallum the son of Jabesh in Samaria and killed him; and he reigned in his place.

[15]Now the rest of the acts of Shallum, and

14:21 [a]Called *Uzziah* in 2 Chronicles 26:1ff, Isaiah 6:1, and elsewhere **15:12** [a]2 Kings 10:30 **15:13** [a]Called *Azariah* in 14:21ff and 15:1ff

the conspiracy which he led, indeed they *are* written in the book of the chronicles of the kings of Israel. 16 Then from Tirzah, Menahem attacked Tiphsah, all who *were* there, and its territory. Because they did not surrender, therefore he attacked *it*. All the women there who were with child he ripped open.

Menahem Reigns in Israel

17 In the thirty-ninth year of Azariah king of Judah, Menahem the son of Gadi became king over Israel, *and reigned* ten years in Samaria. 18 And he did evil in the sight of the LORD; he did not depart all his days from the sins of Jeroboam the son of Nebat, who had made Israel sin. 19 Pul[a] king of Assyria came against the land; and Menahem gave Pul a thousand talents of silver, that his hand might be with him to strengthen the kingdom under his control. 20 And Menahem exacted the money from Israel, from all the very wealthy, from each man fifty shekels of silver, to give to the king of Assyria. So the king of Assyria turned back, and did not stay there in the land.

21 Now the rest of the acts of Menahem, and all that he did, *are* they not written in the book of the chronicles of the kings of Israel? 22 So Menahem rested with his fathers. Then Pekahiah his son reigned in his place.

Pekahiah Reigns in Israel

23 In the fiftieth year of Azariah king of Judah, Pekahiah the son of Menahem became king over Israel in Samaria, *and reigned* two years. 24 And he did evil in the sight of the LORD; he did not depart from the sins of Jeroboam the son of Nebat, who had made Israel sin. 25 Then Pekah the son of Remaliah, an officer of his, conspired against him and killed him in Samaria, in the citadel of the king's house, along with Argob and Arieh; and with him were fifty men of Gilead. He killed him and reigned in his place.

26 Now the rest of the acts of Pekahiah, and all that he did, indeed they *are* written in the book of the chronicles of the kings of Israel.

Pekah Reigns in Israel

27 In the fifty-second year of Azariah king of Judah, Pekah the son of Remaliah became king over Israel in Samaria, *and reigned* twenty years. 28 And he did evil in the sight of the LORD; he did not depart from the sins of Jeroboam the son of Nebat, who had made Israel sin. 29 In the days of Pekah king of Israel, Tiglath-Pileser king of Assyria came and took Ijon, Abel Beth Maachah, Janoah, Kedesh, Hazor, Gilead, and Galilee, all the land of Naphtali; and he carried them captive to Assyria. 30 Then Hoshea the son of Elah led a conspiracy against Pekah the son of Remaliah, and struck and killed him; so he reigned in his place in the twentieth year of Jotham the son of Uzziah.

31 Now the rest of the acts of Pekah, and all that he did, indeed they *are* written in the book of the chronicles of the kings of Israel.

Jotham Reigns in Judah

32 In the second year of Pekah the son of Remaliah, king of Israel, Jotham the son of Uzziah, king of Judah, began to reign. 33 He was twenty-five years old when he became king, and he reigned sixteen years in Jerusalem. His mother's name *was* Jerusha[a] the daughter of Zadok. 34 And he did *what was* right in the sight of the LORD; he did according to all that his father Uzziah had done. 35 However the high places were not removed; the people still sacrificed and burned incense on the high places. He built the Upper Gate of the house of the LORD.

36 Now the rest of the acts of Jotham, and all that he did, *are* they not written in the book of the chronicles of the kings of Judah? 37 In those days the LORD began to send Rezin king of Syria and Pekah the son of Remaliah against Judah. 38 So Jotham rested with his fathers, and was buried with his fathers in the City of David his father. Then Ahaz his son reigned in his place.

Ahaz Reigns in Judah

16 In the seventeenth year of Pekah the son of Remaliah, Ahaz the son of Jotham, king of Judah, began to reign. 2 Ahaz *was* twenty years old when he became king, and he reigned sixteen years in Jerusalem; and he did not do *what was* right in the sight of the LORD his God, as his father David *had done*. 3 But he walked in the way of the kings of Israel; indeed he made his son pass through the fire, according to the abominations of the nations whom the LORD had cast out from before the children of Israel. 4 And he sacrificed

---

15:19 [a]That is, Tiglath-Pileser III (compare verse 29)
15:33 [a]Spelled *Jerushah* in 2 Chronicles 27:1

and burned incense on the high places, on the
hills, and under every green tree.
[5]Then Rezin king of Syria and Pekah the son
of Remaliah, king of Israel, came up to Jerusalem to *make* war; and they besieged Ahaz but
could not overcome *him*. [6]At that time Rezin
king of Syria captured Elath for Syria, and
drove the men of Judah from Elath. Then the
Edomites[a] went to Elath, and dwell there to
this day.
[7]So Ahaz sent messengers to Tiglath-Pileser
king of Assyria, saying, "I *am* your servant
and your son. Come up and save me from the
hand of the king of Syria and from the hand of
the king of Israel, who rise up against me."
[8]And Ahaz took the silver and gold that was
found in the house of the LORD, and in the
treasuries of the king's house, and sent *it as* a
present to the king of Assyria. [9]So the king of
Assyria heeded him; for the king of Assyria
went up against Damascus and took it, carried
its people captive to Kir, and killed Rezin.
[10]Now King Ahaz went to Damascus to meet
Tiglath-Pileser king of Assyria, and saw an altar that *was* at Damascus; and King Ahaz sent
to Urijah the priest the design of the altar and
its pattern, according to all its workmanship.
[11]Then Urijah the priest built an altar according to all that King Ahaz had sent from Damascus. So Urijah the priest made *it* before
King Ahaz came back from Damascus. [12]And
when the king came back from Damascus, the
king saw the altar; and the king approached
the altar and made offerings on it. [13]So he
burned his burnt offering and his grain offering; and he poured his drink offering and
sprinkled the blood of his peace offerings on
the altar. [14]He also brought the bronze altar
which *was* before the LORD, from the front of
the temple—from between the *new* altar and
the house of the LORD—and put it on the north
side of the *new* altar. [15]Then King Ahaz commanded Urijah the priest, saying, "On the
great *new* altar burn the morning burnt offering, the evening grain offering, the king's
burnt sacrifice, and his grain offering, with the
burnt offering of all the people of the land,
their grain offering, and their drink offerings;
and sprinkle on it all the blood of the burnt
offering and all the blood of the sacrifice. And
the bronze altar shall be for me to inquire *by*."
[16]Thus did Urijah the priest, according to all
that King Ahaz commanded.
[17]And King Ahaz cut off the panels of the
carts, and removed the lavers from them; and
he took down the Sea from the bronze oxen
that *were* under it, and put it on a pavement of
stones. [18]Also he removed the Sabbath pavilion which they had built in the temple, and he
removed the king's outer entrance from the
house of the LORD, on account of the king of
Assyria.
[19]Now the rest of the acts of Ahaz which he
did, *are* they not written in the book of the
chronicles of the kings of Judah? [20]So Ahaz
rested with his fathers, and was buried with
his fathers in the City of David. Then Hezekiah his son reigned in his place.

Hoshea Reigns in Israel

17 In the twelfth year of Ahaz king of Judah, Hoshea the son of Elah became
king of Israel in Samaria, *and he reigned* nine
years. [2]And he did evil in the sight of the
LORD, but not as the kings of Israel who were
before him. [3]Shalmaneser king of Assyria
came up against him; and Hoshea became his
vassal, and paid him tribute money. [4]And the
king of Assyria uncovered a conspiracy by Hoshea; for he had sent messengers to So, king
of Egypt, and brought no tribute to the king of
Assyria, as *he had done* year by year. There-

16:6 [a]Some ancient authorities read *Syrians*.

SOUL NOTE

Through the Fire *(16:3)* Ahaz was an evil king who worshiped idols. Instead of following the example of his ancestor David, Ahaz chose to follow the other evil kings of Israel. The statement, "He made his son pass through the fire," refers to child sacrifice to the god Molech. Such disregard for human life and abuse of children created an atmosphere of political chaos and spiritual degradation throughout his kingdom. When the most innocent are not protected, there is little safety for anyone.
Topic: Abuse

fore the king of Assyria shut him up, and bound him in prison.

Israel Carried Captive to Assyria

[5]Now the king of Assyria went throughout all the land, and went up to Samaria and besieged it for three years. [6]In the ninth year of Hoshea, the king of Assyria took Samaria and carried Israel away to Assyria, and placed them in Halah and by the Habor, the River of Gozan, and in the cities of the Medes.

[7]For so it was that the children of Israel had sinned against the LORD their God, who had brought them up out of the land of Egypt, from under the hand of Pharaoh king of Egypt; and they had feared other gods, [8]and had walked in the statutes of the nations whom the LORD had cast out from before the children of Israel, and of the kings of Israel, which they had made. [9]Also the children of Israel secretly did against the LORD their God things that *were* not right, and they built for themselves high places in all their cities, from watchtower to fortified city. [10]They set up for themselves *sacred* pillars and wooden images[a] on every high hill and under every green tree. [11]There they burned incense on all the high places, like the nations whom the LORD had carried away before them; and they did wicked things to provoke the LORD to anger, [12]for they served idols, of which the LORD had said to them, "You shall not do this thing."

[13]Yet the LORD testified against Israel and against Judah, by all of His prophets, every seer, saying, "Turn from your evil ways, and keep My commandments *and* My statutes, according to all the law which I commanded your fathers, and which I sent to you by My servants the prophets." [14]Nevertheless they would not hear, but stiffened their necks, like the necks of their fathers, who did not believe in the LORD their God. [15]And they rejected His statutes and His covenant that He had made with their fathers, and His testimonies which He had testified against them; they followed idols, became idolaters, and *went* after the nations who *were* all around them, *concerning* whom the LORD had charged them that they should not do like them. [16]So they left all the commandments of the LORD their God, made for themselves a molded image *and* two calves, made a wooden image and worshiped all the host of heaven, and served Baal. [17]And they caused their sons and daughters to pass through the fire, practiced witchcraft and soothsaying, and sold themselves to do evil in the sight of the LORD, to provoke Him to anger. [18]Therefore the LORD was very angry with Israel, and removed them from His sight; there was none left but the tribe of Judah alone.

[19]Also Judah did not keep the commandments of the LORD their God, but walked in the statutes of Israel which they made. [20]And the LORD rejected all the descendants of Israel, afflicted them, and delivered them into the hand of plunderers, until He had cast them from His sight. [21]For He tore Israel from the house of David, and they made Jeroboam the son of Nebat king. Then Jeroboam drove Israel from following the LORD, and made them commit a great sin. [22]For the children of Israel walked in all the sins of Jeroboam which he did; they did not depart from them, [23]until the LORD removed Israel out of His sight, as He had said by all His servants the prophets. So Israel was carried away from their own land to Assyria, *as it is* to this day.

Assyria Resettles Samaria

[24]Then the king of Assyria brought *people* from Babylon, Cuthah, Ava, Hamath, and from Sepharvaim, and placed *them* in the cities

17:10 [a]Hebrew *Asherim,* Canaanite deities

SOUL NOTE

The End *(17:22, 23)* The sins of the people of the northern kingdom of Israel were so serious that God allowed Assyria to conquer and deport them. Beginning with Jeroboam, an unbroken chain of evil kings had led the nation far from God. God had sent prophets to warn them, but finally He sent punishment. Israel's downfall resulted from their flagrant disobedience. They had been given opportunities to repent, but had refused. Their failure as a nation under God followed the spiritual failure as a nation devoted to God. **Topic: Failure**

of Samaria instead of the children of Israel; and they took possession of Samaria and dwelt in its cities. [25]And it was so, at the beginning of their dwelling there, *that* they did not fear the LORD; therefore the LORD sent lions among them, which killed *some* of them. [26]So they spoke to the king of Assyria, saying, "The nations whom you have removed and placed in the cities of Samaria do not know the rituals of the God of the land; therefore He has sent lions among them, and indeed, they are killing them because they do not know the rituals of the God of the land." [27]Then the king of Assyria commanded, saying, "Send there one of the priests whom you brought from there; let him go and dwell there, and let him teach them the rituals of the God of the land." [28]Then one of the priests whom they had carried away from Samaria came and dwelt in Bethel, and taught them how they should fear the LORD.

[29]However every nation continued to make gods of its own, and put *them* in the shrines on the high places which the Samaritans had made, *every* nation in the cities where they dwelt. [30]The men of Babylon made Succoth Benoth, the men of Cuth made Nergal, the men of Hamath made Ashima, [31]and the Avites made Nibhaz and Tartak; and the Sepharvites burned their children in fire to Adrammelech and Anammelech, the gods of Sepharvaim. [32]So they feared the LORD, and from every class they appointed for themselves priests of the high places, who sacrificed for them in the shrines of the high places. [33]They feared the LORD, yet served their own gods—according to the rituals of the nations from among whom they were carried away.

[34]To this day they continue practicing the former rituals; they do not fear the LORD, nor do they follow their statutes or their ordinances, or the law and commandment which the LORD had commanded the children of Jacob, whom He named Israel, [35]with whom the LORD had made a covenant and charged them, saying: "You shall not fear other gods, nor bow down to them nor serve them nor sacrifice to them; [36]but the LORD, who brought you up from the land of Egypt with great power and an outstretched arm, Him you shall fear, Him you shall worship, and to Him you shall offer sacrifice. [37]And the statutes, the ordinances, the law, and the commandment which He wrote for you, you shall be careful to observe forever; you shall not fear other gods. [38]And the covenant that I have made with you, you shall not forget, nor shall you fear other gods. [39]But the LORD your God you shall fear; and He will deliver you from the hand of all your enemies." [40]However they did not obey, but they followed their former rituals. [41]So these nations feared the LORD, yet served their carved images; also their children and their children's children have continued doing as their fathers did, even to this day.

Hezekiah Reigns in Judah

18 Now it came to pass in the third year of Hoshea the son of Elah, king of Israel, *that* Hezekiah the son of Ahaz, king of Judah, began to reign. [2]He was twenty-five years old when he became king, and he reigned twenty-nine years in Jerusalem. His mother's name *was* Abi[a] the daughter of Zechariah. [3]And he did *what was* right in the sight of the LORD, according to all that his father David had done.

[4]He removed the high places and broke the *sacred* pillars, cut down the wooden image[a] and broke in pieces the bronze serpent that Moses had made; for until those days the children of Israel burned incense to it, and called it Nehushtan.[b] [5]He trusted in the LORD God of Israel, so that after him was none like him among all the kings of Judah, nor who were before him. [6]For he held fast to the LORD; he did not depart from following Him, but kept His commandments, which the LORD had commanded Moses. [7]The LORD was with him; he prospered wherever he went. And he rebelled against the king of Assyria and did not serve him. [8]He subdued the Philistines, as far as Gaza and its territory, from watchtower to fortified city.

[9]Now it came to pass in the fourth year of King Hezekiah, which *was* the seventh year of Hoshea the son of Elah, king of Israel, *that* Shalmaneser king of Assyria came up against Samaria and besieged it. [10]And at the end of three years they took it. In the sixth year of Hezekiah, that *is,* the ninth year of Hoshea king of Israel, Samaria was taken. [11]Then the king of Assyria carried Israel away captive to

---

18:2 [a]Called *Abijah* in 2 Chronicles 29:1ff
18:4 [a]Hebrew *Asherah,* a Canaanite goddess [b]Literally *Bronze Thing*

Assyria, and put them in Halah and by the Habor, the River of Gozan, and in the cities of the Medes, [12]because they did not obey the voice of the LORD their God, but transgressed His covenant *and* all that Moses the servant of the LORD had commanded; and they would neither hear nor do *them.*

[13]And in the fourteenth year of King Hezekiah, Sennacherib king of Assyria came up against all the fortified cities of Judah and took them. [14]Then Hezekiah king of Judah sent to the king of Assyria at Lachish, saying, "I have done wrong; turn away from me; whatever you impose on me I will pay." And the king of Assyria assessed Hezekiah king of Judah three hundred talents of silver and thirty talents of gold. [15]So Hezekiah gave *him* all the silver that was found in the house of the LORD and in the treasuries of the king's house. [16]At that time Hezekiah stripped *the gold from* the doors of the temple of the LORD, and *from* the pillars which Hezekiah king of Judah had overlaid, and gave it to the king of Assyria.

SENNACHERIB BOASTS AGAINST THE LORD

[17]Then the king of Assyria sent *the* Tartan,[a] *the* Rabsaris,[b] *and the* Rabshakeh[c] from Lachish, with a great army against Jerusalem, to King Hezekiah. And they went up and came to Jerusalem. When they had come up, they went and stood by the aqueduct from the upper pool, which *was* on the highway to the Fuller's Field. [18]And when they had called to the king, Eliakim the son of Hilkiah, who *was* over the household, Shebna the scribe, and Joah the son of Asaph, the recorder, came out to them. [19]Then *the* Rabshakeh said to them, "Say now to Hezekiah, 'Thus says the great king, the king of Assyria: "What confidence *is* this in which you trust? [20]You speak of *having* plans and power for war; but *they are* mere words. And in whom do you trust, that you rebel against me? [21]Now look! You are trusting in the staff of this broken reed, Egypt, on which if a man leans, it will go into his hand and pierce it. So *is* Pharaoh king of Egypt to all who trust in him. [22]But if you say to me, 'We trust in the LORD our God,' *is* it not He whose high places and whose altars Hezekiah has taken away, and said to Judah and Jerusalem, 'You shall worship before this altar in Jerusalem'?" ' [23]Now therefore, I urge you, give a pledge to my master the king of Assyria, and I will give you two thousand horses—if you are able on your part to put riders on them! [24]How then will you repel one captain of the least of my master's servants, and put your trust in Egypt for chariots and horsemen? [25]Have I now come up without the LORD against this place to destroy it? The LORD said to me, 'Go up against this land, and destroy it.' "

[26]Then Eliakim the son of Hilkiah, Shebna, and Joah said to *the* Rabshakeh, "Please speak to your servants in Aramaic, for we understand *it;* and do not speak to us in Hebrew[a] in the hearing of the people who *are* on the wall."

[27]But *the* Rabshakeh said to them, "Has my master sent me to your master and to you to speak these words, and not to the men who sit on the wall, who will eat and drink their own waste with you?"

[28]Then *the* Rabshakeh stood and called out with a loud voice in Hebrew, and spoke, saying, "Hear the word of the great king, the king of Assyria! [29]Thus says the king: 'Do not let Hezekiah deceive you, for he shall not be able to deliver you from his hand; [30]nor let Hezekiah make you trust in the LORD, saying, "The LORD will surely deliver us; this city shall not be given into the hand of the king of Assyria." ' [31]Do not listen to Hezekiah; for thus says the king of Assyria: 'Make *peace* with me by a present and come out to me; and every one of you eat from his own vine and every one from his own fig tree, and every one of you drink the waters of his own cistern; [32]until I come and take you away to a land like your own land, a land of grain and new wine, a land of bread and vineyards, a land of olive groves and honey, that you may live and not die. But do not listen to Hezekiah, lest he persuade you, saying, "The LORD will deliver us." [33]Has any of the gods of the nations at all delivered its land from the hand of the king of Assyria? [34]Where *are* the gods of Hamath and Arpad? Where *are* the gods of Sepharvaim and Hena and Ivah? Indeed, have they delivered Samaria from my hand? [35]Who among all the gods of the lands have delivered their countries from my hand, that the LORD should deliver Jerusalem from my hand?' "

[36]But the people held their peace and answered him not a word; for the king's

---

18:17 [a]A title, probably *Commander in Chief* [b]A title, probably *Chief Officer* [c]A title, probably *Chief of Staff* or *Governor* **18:26** [a]Literally *Judean*

commandment was, "Do not answer him."
37Then Eliakim the son of Hilkiah, who *was*
over the household, Shebna the scribe, and
Joah the son of Asaph, the recorder, came to
Hezekiah with *their* clothes torn, and told him
the words of *the* Rabshakeh.

ISAIAH ASSURES DELIVERANCE

19 And so it was, when King Hezekiah
heard *it,* that he tore his clothes, covered himself with sackcloth, and went into the
house of the LORD. 2Then he sent Eliakim,
who *was* over the household, Shebna the
scribe, and the elders of the priests, covered
with sackcloth, to Isaiah the prophet, the son
of Amoz. 3And they said to him, "Thus says
Hezekiah: 'This day *is* a day of trouble, and rebuke, and blasphemy;
for the children have
come to birth, but *there*
is no strength to bring
them forth. 4It may be
that the LORD your God
will hear all the words
of *the* Rabshakeh, whom
his master the king of
Assyria has sent to re-
proach the living God, and will rebuke the
words which the LORD your God has heard.
Therefore lift up *your* prayer for the remnant
that is left.' "
5So the servants of King Hezekiah came to
Isaiah. 6And Isaiah said to them, "Thus you
shall say to your master, 'Thus says the LORD:
"Do not be afraid of the words which you have
heard, with which the servants of the king of
Assyria have blasphemed Me. 7Surely I will
send a spirit upon him, and he shall hear a rumor and return to his own land; and I will
cause him to fall by the sword in his own
land." ' "

SENNACHERIB'S THREAT AND HEZEKIAH'S PRAYER

8Then *the* Rabshakeh returned and found
the king of Assyria warring against Libnah, for
he heard that he had departed from Lachish.
9And the king heard concerning Tirhakah king
of Ethiopia, "Look, he has come out to make
war with you." So he again sent messengers to
Hezekiah, saying, 10"Thus you shall speak to
Hezekiah king of Judah, saying: 'Do not let
your God in whom you trust deceive you, saying, "Jerusalem shall not be given into the
hand of the king of Assyria." 11Look! You have
heard what the kings of Assyria have done to
all lands by utterly destroying them; and shall
you be delivered? 12Have the gods of the nations delivered those whom my fathers have
destroyed, Gozan and Haran and Rezeph, and
the people of Eden who *were* in Telassar?
13Where *is* the king of Hamath, the king of Arpad, and the king of the city of Sepharvaim,
Hena, and Ivah?' "
14And Hezekiah received the letter from the
hand of the messengers, and read it; and Hezekiah went up to the house of the LORD, and
spread it before the LORD. 15Then Hezekiah
prayed before the LORD, and said: "O LORD
God of Israel, *the One* who dwells *between* the
cherubim, You are God, You alone, of all the
kingdoms of the earth.
You have made heaven
and earth. 16Incline Your
ear, O LORD, and hear;
open Your eyes, O LORD,
and see; and hear the
words of Sennacherib,
which he has sent to re-
proach the living God.
17Truly, LORD, the kings
of Assyria have laid waste the nations and
their lands, 18and have cast their gods into the
fire; for they *were* not gods, but the work of
men's hands—wood and stone. Therefore
they destroyed them. 19Now therefore, O LORD
our God, I pray, save us from his hand, that all
the kingdoms of the earth may know that You
are the LORD God, You alone."

"Incline Your ear, O LORD, and hear;
open Your eyes, O LORD,
and see; and hear the words of
Sennacherib, which he has sent
to reproach the living God."
2 KINGS 19:16

THE WORD OF THE LORD CONCERNING SENNACHERIB

20Then Isaiah the son of Amoz sent to Hezekiah, saying, "Thus says the LORD God of Israel: 'Because you have prayed to Me against
Sennacherib king of Assyria, I have heard.'
21This *is* the word which the LORD has spoken
concerning him:

'The virgin, the daughter of Zion,
Has despised you, laughed you to scorn;
The daughter of Jerusalem
Has shaken *her* head behind your back!

22 'Whom have you reproached and
blasphemed?
Against whom have you raised *your*
voice,

And lifted up your eyes on high?
Against the Holy *One* of Israel.
23 By your messengers you have reproached the Lord,
And said: "By the multitude of my chariots
I have come up to the height of the mountains,
To the limits of Lebanon;
I will cut down its tall cedars
And its choice cypress trees;
I will enter the extremity of its borders,
To its fruitful forest.
24 I have dug and drunk strange water,
And with the soles of my feet I have dried up
All the brooks of defense."

25 'Did you not hear long ago
How I made it,
From ancient times that I formed it?
Now I have brought it to pass,
That you should be
For crushing fortified cities *into* heaps of ruins.
26 Therefore their inhabitants had little power;
They were dismayed and confounded;
They were *as* the grass of the field
And the green herb,
As the grass on the housetops
And *grain* blighted before it is grown.

27 'But I know your dwelling place,
Your going out and your coming in,
And your rage against Me.
28 Because your rage against Me and your tumult
Have come up to My ears,
Therefore I will put My hook in your nose
And My bridle in your lips,
And I will turn you back
By the way which you came.

29'This *shall be* a sign to you:

You shall eat this year such as grows of itself,
And in the second year what springs from the same;
Also in the third year sow and reap,
Plant vineyards and eat the fruit of them.
30 And the remnant who have escaped of the house of Judah
Shall again take root downward,
And bear fruit upward.
31 For out of Jerusalem shall go a remnant,
And those who escape from Mount Zion.
The zeal of the LORD of hosts[a] will do this.'

32"Therefore thus says the LORD concerning the king of Assyria:

'He shall not come into this city,
Nor shoot an arrow there,
Nor come before it with shield,
Nor build a siege mound against it.
33 By the way that he came,
By the same shall he return;
And he shall not come into this city,'
Says the LORD.
34 'For I will defend this city, to save it
For My own sake and for My servant David's sake.' "

SENNACHERIB'S DEFEAT AND DEATH

35And it came to pass on a certain night that
the angel[a] of the LORD went out, and killed in
the camp of the Assyrians one hundred and
eighty-five thousand; and when *people* arose
early in the morning, there were the corpses—
all dead. 36So Sennacherib king of Assyria departed and went away, returned *home*, and
remained at Nineveh. 37Now it came to pass,
as he was worshiping in the temple of Nisroch
his god, that his sons Adrammelech and Sharezer struck him down with the sword; and
they escaped into the land of Ararat. Then
Esarhaddon his son reigned in his place.

HEZEKIAH'S LIFE EXTENDED

20 In those days Hezekiah was sick and
near death. And Isaiah the prophet,
the son of Amoz, went to him and said to him,
"Thus says the LORD: 'Set your house in order,
for you shall die, and not live.' "
2Then he turned his face toward the wall,
and prayed to the LORD, saying, 3"Remember
now, O LORD, I pray, how I have walked before
You in truth and with a loyal heart, and have

19:31 [a]Following many Hebrew manuscripts and ancient versions (compare Isaiah 37:32); Masoretic Text omits *of hosts*. **19:35** [a]Or *Angel*

Death

FINALLY HOME

WOODROW KROLL

(2 Kings 20:1–3)

Tears, sorrow, anguish, dread, fear: All of these words apply to death. Joy, freedom, healing, newness, eternity: For believers, these words as well apply to death. Loss hurts. Even Jesus wept at the death of a loved one (John 11:35). While we sorrow, however, we sorrow not as those who have no hope. Along with the tears and sorrow, believers know that death is only the end of life on earth and the beginning of life in heaven.

Death was not God's original desire for humanity. God created human beings for life, not death. Adam had received the breath of life (Gen. 2:7). It was not until Adam and Eve sinned that death arrived. God said that Adam's punishment for his sin would be as follows: "In the sweat of your face you shall eat bread till you return to the ground, for out of it you were taken; for dust you are, and to dust you shall return" (Gen. 3:19). Genesis 5:5 says, "So all the days that Adam lived were nine hundred and thirty years; and *he died*" (italics mine). So began the cycle of birth and death that will continue until Christ returns. The apostle Paul explained it this way: "Therefore, just as through one man sin entered the world, and death through sin, and thus death spread to all men, because all sinned" (Rom. 5:12).

Death is difficult because it is loss—real and painful because loved ones are gone; symbolic because it reminds us of lost innocence, sin, and punishment. Death is a painful reality faced by every person. We lose people we love; we will one day die ourselves. How should believers view this dreaded event called death?

HOW SHOULD I VIEW DEATH?

Death is distasteful and dreaded; few would say they look forward to it. Death is viewed very differently from God's perspective, however. Humans see death as something to be avoided as long as possible; God views it as something to be anticipated. Humans see death as a gloomy, dark night; God describes it as a glorious new day. Humans see death as the end of the journey; God sees it as the beginning of the best journey of all. Your perspective on death will dramatically affect your ability to handle it.

For Christians, the approach of death can be a time of positive anticipation because we enjoy God and long to be with Him forever. Like Abraham, we are looking for a city "whose builder and maker is God" (Heb. 11:10). Death is not a time to be feared or shunned; it is a time to anticipate hearing our Master say, "Well done, good and faithful servant. . . . Enter into the joy of your lord" (Matt. 25:21). Who would not anticipate that reception?

Death is not a dark, gloomy night, nor is it the end of everything. Instead, death is a door to a bright new future. It brings closure to one phase of life, but opens up an eternal phase that will be far better than humans can even imagine.

AM I PREPARED TO DIE?

Death is a reality. No one has found a cure for it. Sooner or later, therefore, all people have to face death. Each person must eventually ask the question, "Am I prepared to die?" The Bible is clear about how to prepare for our eternal future. In fact, it is as simple as ABC. All people need to:

Admit that they are not ready to go to heaven when they die because they are sinners. The Bible says, "For all have sinned and fall short of the glory of God" (Rom. 3:23). All people have sinned; therefore, no one deserves to be in heaven with God for eternity. "The wages of sin is death" (Rom. 6:23). Fortunately, God made a provision so that people can join Him in heaven. They must . . .

Believe that although they are sinners, Jesus Christ died to pay the penalty for sin and save them from its punishment. Salvation is not a matter of turning over a new leaf or trying to live so that good works outweigh bad works. Salvation is the loving act of God whereby He sent His Son, Jesus, to die on Calvary's cross to pay sin's death penalty. "For God so loved the world that He gave His only begotten Son, that whoever believes in Him should not perish but have everlasting life" (John 3:16). Those who believe this must then . . .

Confess to God that they believe what God's Word says, that they are sinners, and that they believe Jesus died to save them from sin and its penalty. The apostle Paul wrote, "If you confess with your mouth the Lord Jesus and believe in your heart that God raised Him from the dead, you will be saved" (Rom. 10:9).

HOW WILL IT ALL END?

For Christians, physical pain and suffering may not be alleviated on earth, but it is only temporary. God has a glorious future for us because we have trusted Jesus Christ as our Savior, our Healer, our coming King. For the Christian, death is not the end. "O Death, where is your sting?" exulted Paul. "Thanks be to God, who gives us the victory through our Lord Jesus Christ" (1 Cor. 15:55, 57). Death is the doorway to our final destination—eternal life with God in heaven. Then we will finally be home.

FURTHER MEDITATION:

Other passages to study about the issue of death include:

- Psalm 116:15
- John 11:1–44
- Romans 6:23
- 1 Corinthians 15:12–58
- 2 Corinthians 5:8
- 1 Thessalonians 4:13–18
- Revelation 21; 22

To Learn More: Turn to the key passage note on death at 1 Corinthians 15:20–22 on page 1514. See also the personality profile of Hezekiah on page 503.

done *what was* good in Your sight." And Hezekiah wept bitterly.
[4]And it happened, before Isaiah had gone
out into the middle court, that the word of the
LORD came to him, saying, [5]"Return and tell
Hezekiah the leader of My people, 'Thus says
the LORD, the God of David your father: "I
have heard your prayer, I have seen your
tears; surely I will heal you. On the third day
you shall go up to the house of the LORD. [6]And
I will add to your days fifteen years. I will deliver you and this city from the hand of the
king of Assyria; and I will defend this city for
My own sake, and for the sake of My servant
David." ' "
[7]Then Isaiah said, "Take a lump of figs." So
they took and laid *it* on the boil, and he recovered.
[8]And Hezekiah said to Isaiah, "What *is* the
sign that the LORD will heal me, and that I
shall go up to the house of the LORD the third
day?"
[9]Then Isaiah said, "This is the sign to you
from the LORD, that the LORD will do the thing
which He has spoken: *shall* the shadow go forward ten degrees or go backward ten degrees?"
[10]And Hezekiah answered, "It is an easy
thing for the shadow to go down ten degrees;
no, but let the shadow go backward ten degrees."
[11]So Isaiah the prophet cried out to the
LORD, and He brought the shadow ten degrees
backward, by which it had gone down on the
sundial of Ahaz.

The Babylonian Envoys

[12]At that time Berodach-Baladan[a] the son of
Baladan, king of Babylon, sent letters and a
present to Hezekiah, for he heard that Hezekiah had been sick. [13]And Hezekiah was attentive to them, and showed them all the
house of his treasures—the silver and gold,
the spices and precious ointment, and all[a] his
armory—all that was found among his treasures. There was nothing in his house or in all
his dominion that Hezekiah did not show
them.
[14]Then Isaiah the prophet went to King Hezekiah, and said to him, "What did these men
say, and from where did they come to you?"
So Hezekiah said, "They came from a far
country, from Babylon."
[15]And he said, "What have they seen in
your house?"
So Hezekiah answered, "They have seen all
that *is* in my house; there is nothing among
my treasures that I have not shown them."
[16]Then Isaiah said to Hezekiah, "Hear the
word of the LORD: [17]'Behold, the days are coming when all that *is* in your house, and what
your fathers have accumulated until this day,
shall be carried to Babylon; nothing shall be
left,' says the LORD. [18]'And they shall take away
some of your sons who will descend from you,
whom you will beget; and they shall be eunuchs in the palace of the king of Babylon.' "
[19]So Hezekiah said to Isaiah, "The word of
the LORD which you have spoken *is* good!" For
he said, "Will there not be peace and truth at
least in my days?"

Death of Hezekiah

[20]Now the rest of the acts of Hezekiah—all
his might, and how he made a pool and a tunnel and brought water into the city—*are* they
not written in the book of the chronicles of the
kings of Judah? [21]So Hezekiah rested with his
fathers. Then Manasseh his son reigned in his
place.

20:12 [a]Spelled *Merodach-Baladan* in Isaiah 39:1
20:13 [a]Following many Hebrew manuscripts, Syriac, and Targum; Masoretic Text omits *all*.

SOUL NOTE

Ultimate Healing *(20:1–11)* God does not heal every person who prays for healing. He does, however, heal many who ask. Hezekiah's experience teaches the importance of throwing ourselves on God's mercy. God can and does still heal. He has the power to do so. At times healing a person is within His plan; at other times it is not. We must always remember, however, that total and permanent healing will come when we see Him face to face. God will work in our brokenness to show His deep love and give His abiding peace. **Topic: Healing/Recovery**

Manasseh Reigns in Judah

21 Manasseh *was* twelve years old when
he became king, and he reigned fifty-
five years in Jerusalem. His mother's name
was Hephzibah. [2]And he did evil in the sight
of the LORD, according to the abominations of
the nations whom the LORD had cast out before the children of Israel. [3]For he rebuilt the
high places which Hezekiah his father had destroyed; he raised up altars for Baal, and made
a wooden image,[a] as Ahab king of Israel had
done; and he worshiped all the host of
heaven[b] and served them. [4]He also built altars

21:3 [a]Hebrew *Asherah,* a Canaanite goddess [b]The gods of the Assryians

PERSONALITY PROFILE

Death

THE UNWELCOME VISITOR

(2 KINGS 20:1–3)

Death happens to everyone, and no one escapes it this side of the Lord's return. The Bible records just two men, Enoch and Elijah, who were allowed to arrive in heaven without passing through this dreadful portal. Everyone else eventually meets that unwelcome visitor, even as the Son of God Himself did.

One day death knocked on King Hezekiah's door. He was a good and godly king who ruled over the southern kingdom of Judah. After the evil reign of Ahaz, the new king Hezekiah cleaned house—literally. He tore down pagan altars and "trusted in the LORD God of Israel" (2 Kin. 18:5). When the Assyrians attacked the nation, Hezekiah went to the temple and prayed for God's deliverance. God miraculously intervened, killing most of the enemy army and sending their king scurrying home, where he was assassinated. Judah was safe for a while.

But then Hezekiah became very ill, and Isaiah arrived to tell him to set his house in order because he would soon die. Hezekiah reacted predictably—he "wept bitterly" (20:3) and pleaded with God for his life. And God answered, giving Hezekiah fifteen more years.

Believers know that the joys of heaven are on the other side of death's door, but we still cling to this life. What person has not, upon receiving news of impending death, wept bitterly to God? Many have stories of God's mercy and healing. But even those who have died could tell us stories of healing—ultimate healing upon seeing the face of their Lord!

The greatest fear is the unknown. We know of heaven, but we don't understand it. We prepare for death by faith, knowing we must go through the door alone. But believers have the truth that God who knows and loves them is on the other side, waiting with open arms. For believers, death is not the end—it is the beginning of eternity with God.

To Learn More: Turn to the article about death on pages 500, 501. See also the key passage note at 1 Corinthians 15:20–22 on page 1514.

SOUL NOTE

Doctor's Orders *(20:7)* God promised to heal Hezekiah. He could have intervened miraculously; He could have sent Isaiah to touch and heal him. Instead, God sent Isaiah with a prescription. The phrase, "Take a lump of figs," probably referred to a poultice that would relieve the boil. When we are ill, we should seek healing. God may intervene miraculously, or He may send doctors and medicines. In either case, He is ultimately in control to heal His people or to bring them home to Him.

Topic: Health/Spirituality

in the house of the LORD, of which the LORD
had said, "In Jerusalem I will put My name."
5And he built altars for all the host of heaven
in the two courts of the house of the LORD.
6Also he made his son pass through the fire,
practiced soothsaying, used witchcraft, and
consulted spiritists and mediums. He did
much evil in the sight of the LORD, to provoke
Him to anger. 7He even set a carved image of
Asherah[a] that he had made, in the house of
which the LORD had said to David and to Solomon his son, "In this house and in Jerusalem, which I have chosen out of all the tribes
of Israel, I will put My name forever; 8and I
will not make the feet of Israel wander anymore from the land which I gave their fathers—only if they are careful to do according
to all that I have commanded them, and according to all the law that My servant Moses
commanded them." 9But they paid no attention, and Manasseh seduced them to do more
evil than the nations whom the LORD had destroyed before the children of Israel.
10And the LORD spoke by His servants the
prophets, saying, 11"Because Manasseh king
of Judah has done these abominations (he has
acted more wickedly than all the Amorites
who *were* before him, and has also made Judah sin with his idols), 12therefore thus says
the LORD God of Israel: 'Behold, *I* am bringing
such calamity upon Jerusalem and Judah, that
whoever hears of it, both his ears will tingle.
13And I will stretch over Jerusalem the measuring line of Samaria and the plummet of the
house of Ahab; I will wipe Jerusalem as *one*
wipes a dish, wiping *it* and turning *it* upside
down. 14So I will forsake the remnant of My
inheritance and deliver them into the hand of
their enemies; and they shall become victims
of plunder to all their enemies, 15because they
have done evil in My sight, and have provoked
Me to anger since the day their fathers came
out of Egypt, even to this day.' "
16Moreover Manasseh shed very much innocent blood, till he had filled Jerusalem from
one end to another, besides his sin by which
he made Judah sin, in doing evil in the sight of
the LORD.
17Now the rest of the acts of Manasseh—all
that he did, and the sin that he committed—
are they not written in the book of the chronicles of the kings of Judah? 18So Manasseh
rested with his fathers, and was buried in the
garden of his own house, in the garden of
Uzza. Then his son Amon reigned in his place.

AMON'S REIGN AND DEATH

19Amon *was* twenty-two years old when he
became king, and he reigned two years in Jerusalem. His mother's name *was* Meshulle-
meth the daughter of Haruz of Jotbah. 20And
he did evil in the sight of the LORD, as his father Manasseh had done. 21So he walked in all
the ways that his father had walked; and he
served the idols that his father had served,
and worshiped them. 22He forsook the LORD
God of his fathers, and did not walk in the way
of the LORD.
23Then the servants of Amon conspired
against him, and killed the king in his own
house. 24But the people of the land executed
all those who had conspired against King
Amon. Then the people of the land made his
son Josiah king in his place.
25Now the rest of the acts of Amon which he
did, *are* they not written in the book of the
chronicles of the kings of Judah? 26And he was
buried in his tomb in the garden of Uzza.
Then Josiah his son reigned in his place.

21:7 [a]A Canaanite goddess

SOUL NOTE

A Dangerous World *(21:6)* Manasseh was one of many evil kings who reigned in Judah. He encouraged idolatry and occult practices. Like Ahaz (16:3), he sacrificed his son in the fire, practiced soothsaying, used witchcraft, and consulted spiritists and mediums. Extensive witchcraft and satanic worship even culminated in Manasseh's setting up an idol in God's temple (21:7). The occult is a dangerous trap—a world of darkness, horror, and death. While some may be fascinated by its power, they must understand that it is power that seeks only to destroy them eventually. **Topic: Occult**

Josiah Reigns in Judah

22 Josiah *was* eight years old when he
became king, and he reigned thirty-
one years in Jerusalem. His mother's name
was Jedidah the daughter of Adaiah of Bozkath. [2]And he did *what was* right in the sight
of the LORD, and walked in all the ways of his
father David; he did not turn aside to the right
hand or to the left.

Hilkiah Finds the Book of the Law

[3]Now it came to pass, in the eighteenth year
of King Josiah, *that* the king sent Shaphan the
scribe, the son of Azaliah, the son of Meshullam, to the house of the LORD, saying: [4]"Go up
to Hilkiah the high priest, that he may count
the money which has been brought into the
house of the LORD, which the doorkeepers
have gathered from the people. [5]And let them
deliver it into the hand of those doing the
work, who are the overseers in the house of
the LORD; let them give it to those who *are* in
the house of the LORD doing the work, to repair the damages of the house—[6]to carpenters
and builders and masons—and to buy timber
and hewn stone to repair the house. [7]However
there need be no accounting made with them
of the money delivered into their hand, because they deal faithfully."
[8]Then Hilkiah the high priest said to Shaphan the scribe, "I have found the Book of the
Law in the house of the LORD." And Hilkiah
gave the book to Shaphan, and he read it. [9]So
Shaphan the scribe went to the king, bringing
the king word, saying, "Your servants have
gathered the money that was found in the
house, and have delivered it into the hand of
those who do the work, who oversee the house
of the LORD." [10]Then Shaphan the scribe
showed the king, saying, "Hilkiah the priest
has given me a book." And Shaphan read it
before the king.
[11]Now it happened, when the king heard the
words of the Book of the Law, that he tore his
clothes. [12]Then the king commanded Hilkiah
the priest, Ahikam the son of Shaphan, Achbor[a] the son of Michaiah, Shaphan the scribe,
and Asaiah a servant of the king, saying,
[13]"Go, inquire of the LORD for me, for the people and for all Judah, concerning the words of
this book that has been found; for great *is* the

22:12 [a]*Abdon the son of Michah* in 2 Chronicles 34:20

SOUL NOTE

Just One Child *(22:1, 2)* After the evil reigns of Manasseh and Amon, Josiah became king. Josiah saw the evil legacy left by his grandfather and father, and apparently wanted to rule differently. Somehow Josiah learned about God and chose to serve Him. Perhaps he had learned about God from the godly people in the land. Maybe it was his mother, Jedidah, mentioned here. Someone told this young boy the truth about God, and during his years as king he turned the nation around. We never know how our lives might affect one child who may grow up to serve the Lord.
Topic: Mentoring

SOUL NOTE

Back in Line *(22:11)* When the Book of the Law was rediscovered in the temple and read to King Josiah, the king "tore his clothes," showing his extreme sorrow over how far the nation had strayed from God's commands. He also realized how angry God must have been at the nation (22:13). Josiah repented for himself and on behalf of the nation, and then acted immediately to bring them back to God. When we are made aware of sin, we should act immediately—repenting and turning our lives around in order to get back in line with God's will. **Topic: Repentance**

wrath of the LORD that is aroused against us, because our fathers have not obeyed the words of this book, to do according to all that is written concerning us."

14So Hilkiah the priest, Ahikam, Achbor, Shaphan, and Asaiah went to Huldah the prophetess, the wife of Shallum the son of Tikvah, the son of Harhas, keeper of the wardrobe. (She dwelt in Jerusalem in the Second Quarter.) And they spoke with her. 15Then she said to them, "Thus says the LORD God of Israel, 'Tell the man who sent you to Me, 16"Thus says the LORD: 'Behold, I will bring calamity on this place and on its inhabitants—all the words of the book which the king of Judah has read—17because they have forsaken Me and burned incense to other gods, that they might provoke Me to anger with all the works of their hands. Therefore My wrath shall be aroused against this place and shall not be quenched.' " ' 18But as for the king of Judah, who sent you to inquire of the LORD, in this manner you shall speak to him, 'Thus says the LORD God of Israel: "*Concerning* the words which you have heard—19because your heart was tender, and you humbled yourself before the LORD when you heard what I spoke against this place and against its inhabitants, that they would become a desolation and a curse, and you tore your clothes and wept before Me, I also have heard *you,"* says the LORD. 20"Surely, therefore, I will gather you to your fathers, and you shall be gathered to your grave in peace; and your eyes shall not see all the calamity which I will bring on this place." ' " So they brought back word to the king.

JOSIAH RESTORES TRUE WORSHIP

23 Now the king sent them to gather all the elders of Judah and Jerusalem to him. 2The king went up to the house of the LORD with all the men of Judah, and with him all the inhabitants of Jerusalem—the priests and the prophets and all the people, both small and great. And he read in their hearing all the words of the Book of the Covenant which had been found in the house of the LORD.

3Then the king stood by a pillar and made a covenant before the LORD, to follow the LORD and to keep His commandments and His testimonies and His statutes, with all *his* heart and all *his* soul, to perform the words of this covenant that were written in this book. And all the people took a stand for the covenant. 4And the king commanded Hilkiah the high priest, the priests of the second order, and the doorkeepers, to bring out of the temple of the LORD all the articles that were made for Baal, for Asherah,[a] and for all the host of heaven;[b] and he burned them outside Jerusalem in the fields of Kidron, and carried their ashes to Bethel. 5Then he removed the idolatrous priests whom the kings of Judah had ordained to burn incense on the high places in the cities of Judah and in the places all around Jerusalem, and those who burned incense to Baal, to the sun, to the moon, to the constellations, and to all the host of heaven. 6And he brought out the wooden image[a] from the house of the LORD, to the Brook Kidron outside Jerusalem, burned it at the Brook Kidron and ground *it* to ashes, and threw its ashes on the graves of the common people. 7Then he tore down the *ritual* booths of the perverted persons[a] that *were* in the house of the LORD, where the women wove hangings for the wooden image. 8And he brought all the priests from the cities of Judah, and defiled the high places where the priests had burned incense, from Geba to Beersheba; also he broke down the high places at the gates which *were* at the entrance of the Gate of Joshua the governor of the city, which *were* to the left of the city gate. 9Nevertheless the priests of the high places did not come up to the altar of the LORD in Jerusalem, but they ate unleavened bread among their brethren.

10And he defiled Topheth, which *is* in the Valley of the Son[a] of Hinnom, that no man might make his son or his daughter pass through the fire to Molech. 11Then he removed the horses that the kings of Judah had dedicated to the sun, at the entrance to the house of the LORD, by the chamber of Nathan-Melech, the officer who *was* in the court; and he burned the chariots of the sun with fire. 12The altars that *were* on the roof, the upper chamber of Ahaz, which the kings of Judah had made, and the altars which Manasseh had made in the two courts of the house of the

---

23:4 [a]A Canaanite goddess [b]The gods of the Assyrians **23:6** [a]Hebrew *Asherah,* a Canaanite goddess **23:7** [a]Hebrew *qedeshim,* that is, those practicing sodomy and prostitution in religious rituals **23:10** [a]Kethib reads *Sons.*

LORD, the king broke down and pulverized there, and threw their dust into the Brook Kidron. 13 Then the king defiled the high places that *were* east of Jerusalem, which *were* on the south of the Mount of Corruption, which Solomon king of Israel had built for Ashtoreth the abomination of the Sidonians, for Chemosh the abomination of the Moabites, and for Milcom the abomination of the people of Ammon. 14 And he broke in pieces the *sacred* pillars and cut down the wooden images, and filled their places with the bones of men.

15 Moreover the altar that *was* at Bethel, *and* the high place which Jeroboam the son of Nebat, who made Israel sin, had made, both that altar and the high place he broke down; and he burned the high place *and* crushed *it* to powder, and burned the wooden image. 16 As Josiah turned, he saw the tombs that *were* there on the mountain. And he sent and took the bones out of the tombs and burned *them* on the altar, and defiled it according to the word of the LORD which the man of God proclaimed, who proclaimed these words. 17 Then he said, "What gravestone *is* this that I see?"

So the men of the city told him, "*It is* the tomb of the man of God who came from Judah and proclaimed these things which you have done against the altar of Bethel."

18 And he said, "Let him alone; let no one move his bones." So they let his bones alone, with the bones of the prophet who came from Samaria.

19 Now Josiah also took away all the shrines of the high places that *were* in the cities of Samaria, which the kings of Israel had made to provoke the LORD[a] to anger; and he did to them according to all the deeds he had done in Bethel. 20 He executed all the priests of the high places who *were* there, on the altars, and burned men's bones on them; and he returned to Jerusalem.

21 Then the king commanded all the people, saying, "Keep the Passover to the LORD your God, as *it is* written in this Book of the Covenant." 22 Such a Passover surely had never been held since the days of the judges who judged Israel, nor in all the days of the kings of Israel and the kings of Judah. 23 But in the eighteenth year of King Josiah this Passover was held before the LORD in Jerusalem. 24 Moreover Josiah put away those who consulted mediums and spiritists, the household gods and idols, all the abominations that were seen in the land of Judah and in Jerusalem, that he might perform the words of the law which were written in the book that Hilkiah the priest found in the house of the LORD. 25 Now before him there was no king like him, who turned to the LORD with all his heart, with all his soul, and with all his might, according to all the Law of Moses; nor after him did *any* arise like him.

Impending Judgment on Judah

26 Nevertheless the LORD did not turn from the fierceness of His great wrath, with which His anger was aroused against Judah, because of all the provocations with which Manasseh had provoked Him. 27 And the LORD said, "I will also remove Judah from My sight, as I have removed Israel, and will cast off this city Jerusalem which I have chosen, and the house of which I said, 'My name shall be there.' "[a]

Josiah Dies in Battle

28 Now the rest of the acts of Josiah, and all that he did, *are* they not written in the book of the chronicles of the kings of Judah? 29 In his days Pharaoh Necho king of Egypt went to the aid of the king of Assyria, to the River Euphrates; and King Josiah went against him. And *Pharaoh Necho* killed him at Megiddo when he confronted him. 30 Then his servants moved his body in a chariot from Megiddo, brought him to Jerusalem, and buried him in his own tomb. And the people of the land took Jehoahaz the son of Josiah, anointed him, and made him king in his father's place.

The Reign and Captivity of Jehoahaz

31 Jehoahaz *was* twenty-three years old when he became king, and he reigned three months in Jerusalem. His mother's name *was* Hamutal the daughter of Jeremiah of Libnah. 32 And he did evil in the sight of the LORD, according to all that his fathers had done. 33 Now Pharaoh Necho put him in prison at Riblah in the land of Hamath, that he might not reign in Jerusalem; and he imposed on the land a tribute of one hundred talents of silver and a talent of gold. 34 Then Pharaoh Necho made Eliakim the son of Josiah king in place of his father Josiah, and changed his name to

---

23:19 [a]Following Septuagint, Syriac, and Vulgate; Masoretic Text and Targum omit *the LORD.*
23:27 [a]1 Kings 8:29

Jehoiakim. And *Pharaoh* took Jehoahaz and went to Egypt, and he[a] died there.

Jehoiakim Reigns in Judah

35So Jehoiakim gave the silver and gold to Pharaoh; but he taxed the land to give money according to the command of Pharaoh; he exacted the silver and gold from the people of the land, from every one according to his assessment, to give *it* to Pharaoh Necho. 36Jehoiakim *was* twenty-five years old when he became king, and he reigned eleven years in Jerusalem. His mother's name *was* Zebudah the daughter of Pedaiah of Rumah. 37And he did evil in the sight of the LORD, according to all that his fathers had done.

Judah Overrun by Enemies

24 In his days Nebuchadnezzar king of Babylon came up, and Jehoiakim became his vassal *for* three years. Then he turned and rebelled against him. 2And the LORD sent against him *raiding* bands of Chaldeans, bands of Syrians, bands of Moabites, and bands of the people of Ammon; He sent them against Judah to destroy it, according to the word of the LORD which He had spoken by His servants the prophets. 3Surely at the commandment of the LORD *this* came upon Judah, to remove *them* from His sight because of the sins of Manasseh, according to all that he had done, 4and also because of the innocent blood that he had shed; for he had filled Jerusalem with innocent blood, which the LORD would not pardon.

5Now the rest of the acts of Jehoiakim, and all that he did, *are* they not written in the book of the chronicles of the kings of Judah? 6So Jehoiakim rested with his fathers. Then Jehoiachin his son reigned in his place.

7And the king of Egypt did not come out of his land anymore, for the king of Babylon had taken all that belonged to the king of Egypt from the Brook of Egypt to the River Euphrates.

The Reign and Captivity of Jehoiachin

8Jehoiachin *was* eighteen years old when he became king, and he reigned in Jerusalem three months. His mother's name *was* Nehushta the daughter of Elnathan of Jerusalem. 9And he did evil in the sight of the LORD, according to all that his father had done.

10At that time the servants of Nebuchadnezzar king of Babylon came up against Jerusalem, and the city was besieged. 11And Nebuchadnezzar king of Babylon came against the city, as his servants were besieging it. 12Then Jehoiachin king of Judah, his mother, his servants, his princes, and his officers went out to the king of Babylon; and the king of Babylon, in the eighth year of his reign, took him prisoner.

The Captivity of Jerusalem

13And he carried out from there all the treasures of the house of the LORD and the treasures of the king's house, and he cut in pieces all the articles of gold which Solomon king of Israel had made in the temple of the LORD, as the LORD had said. 14Also he carried into captivity all Jerusalem: all the captains and all the mighty men of valor, ten thousand captives, and all the craftsmen and smiths. None remained except the poorest people of the land. 15And he carried Jehoiachin captive to Babylon. The king's mother, the king's wives, his officers, and the mighty of the land he carried into captivity from Jerusalem to Babylon. 16All the valiant men, seven thousand, and craftsmen and smiths, one thousand, all *who were* strong *and* fit for war, these the king of Babylon brought captive to Babylon.

Zedekiah Reigns in Judah

17Then the king of Babylon made Mattaniah, *Jehoiachin's*[a] uncle, king in his place, and changed his name to Zedekiah.

18Zedekiah *was* twenty-one years old when he became king, and he reigned eleven years in Jerusalem. His mother's name *was* Hamutal the daughter of Jeremiah of Libnah. 19He also did evil in the sight of the LORD, according to all that Jehoiakim had done. 20For because of the anger of the LORD *this* happened in Jerusalem and Judah, that He finally cast them out from His presence. Then Zedekiah rebelled against the king of Babylon.

The Fall and Captivity of Judah

25 Now it came to pass in the ninth year of his reign, in the tenth month, on the tenth *day* of the month, *that* Nebuchadnezzar king of Babylon and all his army came against Jerusalem and encamped against it; and they built a siege wall against it all around. 2So the city was besieged until the

---

23:34 [a]That is, Jehoahaz **24:17** [a]Literally *his*

eleventh year of King Zedekiah. [3]By the ninth *day* of the *fourth* month the famine had become so severe in the city that there was no food for the people of the land.

[4]Then the city wall was broken through, and all the men of war *fled* at night by way of the gate between two walls, which was by the king's garden, even though the Chaldeans *were* still encamped all around against the city. And *the king*[a] went by way of the plain.[b] [5]But the army of the Chaldeans pursued the king, and they overtook him in the plains of Jericho. All his army was scattered from him. [6]So they took the king and brought him up to the king of Babylon at Riblah, and they pronounced judgment on him. [7]Then they killed the sons of Zedekiah before his eyes, put out the eyes of Zedekiah, bound him with bronze fetters, and took him to Babylon.

[8]And in the fifth month, on the seventh *day* of the month (which *was* the nineteenth year of King Nebuchadnezzar king of Babylon), Nebuzaradan the captain of the guard, a servant of the king of Babylon, came to Jerusalem. [9]He burned the house of the LORD and the king's house; all the houses of Jerusalem, that is, all the houses of the great, he burned with fire. [10]And all the army of the Chaldeans who *were with* the captain of the guard broke down the walls of Jerusalem all around.

[11]Then Nebuzaradan the captain of the guard carried away captive the rest of the people *who* remained in the city and the defectors who had deserted to the king of Babylon, with the rest of the multitude. [12]But the captain of the guard left *some* of the poor of the land as vinedressers and farmers. [13]The bronze pillars that *were* in the house of the LORD, and the carts and the bronze Sea that *were* in the house of the LORD, the Chaldeans broke in pieces, and carried their bronze to Babylon. [14]They also took away the pots, the shovels, the trimmers, the spoons, and all the bronze utensils with which the priests ministered. [15]The firepans and the basins, the things of solid gold and solid silver, the captain of the guard took away. [16]The two pillars, one Sea, and the carts, which Solomon had made for the house of the LORD, the bronze of all these articles was beyond measure. [17]The height of one pillar *was* eighteen cubits, and the capital on it *was* of bronze. The height of the capital was three cubits, and the network and pomegranates all around the capital were all of bronze. The second pillar was the same, with a network.

[18]And the captain of the guard took Seraiah the chief priest, Zephaniah the second priest, and the three doorkeepers. [19]He also took out of the city an officer who had charge of the men of war, five men of the king's close associates who were found in the city, the chief recruiting officer of the army, who mustered the people of the land, and sixty men of the people of the land *who were* found in the city. [20]So Nebuzaradan, captain of the guard, took these and brought them to the king of Babylon at Riblah. [21]Then the king of Babylon struck them and put them to death at Riblah in the land of Hamath. Thus Judah was carried away captive from its own land.

Gedaliah Made Governor of Judah

[22]Then he made Gedaliah the son of Ahikam, the son of Shaphan, governor over the people who remained in the land of Judah, whom Nebuchadnezzar king of Babylon had left. [23]Now when all the captains of the armies, they and *their* men, heard that the king of Babylon had made Gedaliah governor, they came to Gedaliah at Mizpah—Ishmael the son of Nethaniah, Johanan the son of Careah, Seraiah the son of Tanhumeth the Netophathite, and Jaazaniah[a] the son of a Maachathite, they and their men. [24]And Gedaliah took an oath before them and their men, and said to them, "Do not be afraid of the servants of the Chaldeans. Dwell in the land and serve the king of Babylon, and it shall be well with you."

[25]But it happened in the seventh month that Ishmael the son of Nethaniah, the son of Elishama, of the royal family, came with ten men and struck and killed Gedaliah, the Jews, as well as the Chaldeans who were with him at Mizpah. [26]And all the people, small and great, and the captains of the armies, arose and went to Egypt; for they were afraid of the Chaldeans.

Jehoiachin Released from Prison

[27]Now it came to pass in the thirty-seventh year of the captivity of Jehoiachin king of Judah, in the twelfth month, on the twenty-seventh *day* of the month, *that* Evil-Merodach[a]

25:4 [a]Literally *he* [b]Or *Arabah,* that is, the Jordan Valley **25:23** [a]Spelled *Jezaniah* in Jeremiah 40:8 **25:27** [a]Literally *Man of Marduk*

king of Babylon, in the year that he began to
reign, released Jehoiachin king of Judah from
prison. 28He spoke kindly to him, and gave him
a more prominent seat than those of the kings
who *were* with him in Babylon. 29So Jehoiachin
changed from his prison garments, and he ate
bread regularly before the king all the days of
his life. 30And as for his provisions, *there was* a
regular ration given him by the king, a portion
for each day, all the days of his life.

1 Chronicles

It's been said that it is possible for humans to live several weeks without food, and a few days without water; however, it is impossible for us to live for any length of time without hope. Can you think of anything defeated, discouraged, and weary people need more than the comforting assurance that God is in control?

First and Second Chronicles are a short history of Israel written to the Hebrews returning from Israel's 70-year exile in Babylon. These Jews faced the immense task of rebuilding their city Jerusalem, their temple—in fact, their whole nation. This is why the author, thought to be Ezra, emphasized the best of Israel's history in order to provide much-needed encouragement. The books rely heavily on 1 and 2 Samuel and 1 and 2 Kings, and are intended to show that God's promises will be fulfilled regardless of the faithfulness of the people and the nation.

The first nine chapters of 1 Chronicles focus on the royal line of David—the line from which Messiah would come. What a comfort this reminder must have been! Interestingly, the author focused only on the most positive aspects of David's reign, skipping his sin with Bathsheba and its consequences. By highlighting David's triumphs, he gave the exiles a blueprint of sorts for how to rebuild their nation.

The Israelites needed a renewal of hope at this daunting time in their history. Perhaps similar encouragement is your biggest need right now. Let the promises of God's faithfulness minister to your soul as you read.

SOUL CONCERNS IN 1 CHRONICLES

FATHERHOOD	(3:1)
VIOLENCE	(11:23)
LIFE TRANSITIONS	(CH. 23)

The Family of Adam—Seth to Abraham

1 Adam, Seth, Enosh, 2Cainan,[a] Mahalalel, Jared, 3Enoch, Methuselah, Lamech, 4Noah,[a] Shem, Ham, and Japheth.

5The sons of Japheth *were* Gomer, Magog, Madai, Javan, Tubal, Meshech, and Tiras. 6The sons of Gomer *were* Ashkenaz, Diphath,[a] and Togarmah. 7The sons of Javan *were* Elishah, Tarshishah,[a] Kittim, and Rodanim.[b]

8The sons of Ham *were* Cush, Mizraim, Put, and Canaan. 9The sons of Cush *were* Seba, Havilah, Sabta,[a] Raama,[b] and Sabtecha. The sons of Raama *were* Sheba and Dedan. 10Cush begot Nimrod; he began to be a mighty one on the earth. 11Mizraim begot Ludim, Anamim, Lehabim, Naphtuhim, 12Pathrusim, Casluhim (from whom came the Philistines and the Caphtorim). 13Canaan begot Sidon, his firstborn, and Heth; 14the Jebusite, the Amorite, and the Girgashite; 15the Hivite, the Arkite, and the Sinite; 16the Arvadite, the Zemarite, and the Hamathite.

17The sons of Shem *were* Elam, Asshur, Arphaxad, Lud, Aram, Uz, Hul, Gether, and Meshech.[a] 18Arphaxad begot Shelah, and Shelah begot Eber. 19To Eber were born two sons: the name of one *was* Peleg,[a] for in his days the earth was divided; and his brother's name *was* Joktan. 20Joktan begot Almodad, Sheleph, Hazarmaveth, Jerah, 21Hadoram, Uzal, Diklah, 22Ebal,[a] Abimael, Sheba, 23Ophir, Havilah, and Jobab. All these *were* the sons of Joktan.

24Shem, Arphaxad, Shelah, 25Eber, Peleg, Reu, 26Serug, Nahor, Terah, 27and Abram, who *is* Abraham. 28The sons of Abraham *were* Isaac and Ishmael.

The Family of Ishmael

29These *are* their genealogies: The firstborn of Ishmael *was* Nebajoth; then Kedar, Adbeel, Mibsam, 30Mishma, Dumah, Massa, Hadad,[a] Tema, 31Jetur, Naphish, and Kedemah. These *were* the sons of Ishmael.

The Family of Keturah

32Now the sons born to Keturah, Abraham's concubine, *were* Zimran, Jokshan, Medan, Midian, Ishbak, and Shuah. The sons of Jokshan *were* Sheba and Dedan. 33The sons of Midian *were* Ephah, Epher, Hanoch, Abida, and Eldaah. All these were the children of Keturah.

The Family of Isaac

34And Abraham begot Isaac. The sons of Isaac *were* Esau and Israel. 35The sons of Esau *were* Eliphaz, Reuel, Jeush, Jaalam, and Korah. 36And the sons of Eliphaz *were* Teman, Omar, Zephi,[a] Gatam, *and* Kenaz; and *by* Timna,[b] Amalek. 37The sons of Reuel *were* Nahath, Zerah, Shammah, and Mizzah.

The Family of Seir

38The sons of Seir *were* Lotan, Shobal, Zibeon, Anah, Dishon, Ezer, and Dishan. 39And the sons of Lotan *were* Hori and Homam; Lotan's sister *was* Timna. 40The sons of Shobal *were* Alian,[a] Manahath, Ebal, Shephi,[b] and Onam. The sons of Zibeon *were* Ajah and Anah. 41The son of Anah *was* Dishon. The sons of Dishon *were* Hamran,[a] Eshban, Ithran, and Cheran. 42The sons of Ezer *were* Bilhan,

---

1:2 [a]Hebrew *Qenan* **1:4** [a]Following Masoretic Text and Vulgate; Septuagint adds *the sons of Noah.* **1:6** [a]Spelled *Riphath* in Genesis 10:3 **1:7** [a]Spelled *Tarshish* in Genesis 10:4 [b]Spelled *Dodanim* in Genesis 10:4 **1:9** [a]Spelled *Sabtah* in Genesis 10:7 [b]Spelled *Raamah* in Genesis 10:7 **1:17** [a]Spelled *Mash* in Genesis 10:23 **1:19** [a]Literally *Division* **1:22** [a]Spelled *Obal* in Genesis 10:28 **1:30** [a]Spelled *Hadar* in Genesis 25:15 **1:36** [a]Spelled *Zepho* in Genesis 36:11 [b]Compare Genesis 36:12 **1:40** [a]Spelled *Alvan* in Genesis 36:23 [b]Spelled *Shepho* in Genesis 36:23 **1:41** [a]Spelled *Hemdan* in Genesis 36:26

SOUL NOTE

You Matter *(ch. 1)* The genealogies in I Chronicles were compiled after the people of Judah had been taken into captivity in Babylon. The people did not want the records of their heritage to be lost. Although the Bible tells nothing about most of these people, each name listed represents a life—a person created in God's image and valuable to Him. Our lives may never be recorded for history, but we have a moment in eternity to serve God and make a difference in others' lives. God knows the name, face, and life of each person—and He knows you. **Topic: Self-Esteem**

Zaavan, *and* Jaakan.[a] The sons of Dishan *were*
Uz and Aran.

The Kings of Edom

43Now these *were* the kings who reigned in
the land of Edom before a king reigned over
the children of Israel: Bela the son of Beor, and
the name of his city was Dinhabah. 44And
when Bela died, Jobab the son of Zerah of
Bozrah reigned in his place. 45When Jobab
died, Husham of the land of the Temanites
reigned in his place. 46And when Husham
died, Hadad the son of Bedad, who attacked
Midian in the field of Moab, reigned in his
place. The name of his city *was* Avith. 47When
Hadad died, Samlah of Masrekah reigned in
his place. 48And when Samlah died, Saul of
Rehoboth-by-the-River reigned in his place.
49When Saul died, Baal-Hanan the son of
Achbor reigned in his place. 50And when Baal-
Hanan died, Hadad[a] reigned in his place; and
the name of his city was Pai.[b] His wife's name
was Mehetabel the daughter of Matred, the
daughter of Mezahab. 51Hadad died also. And
the chiefs of Edom were Chief Timnah, Chief
Aliah,[a] Chief Jetheth, 52Chief Aholibamah,
Chief Elah, Chief Pinon, 53Chief Kenaz, Chief
Teman, Chief Mibzar, 54Chief Magdiel, and
Chief Iram. These *were* the chiefs of Edom.

The Family of Israel

2 These *were* the sons of Israel: Reuben, Simeon, Levi, Judah, Issachar, Zebulun, 2Dan,
Joseph, Benjamin, Naphtali, Gad, and Asher.

From Judah to David

3The sons of Judah *were* Er, Onan, and Shelah. *These* three were born to him by the
daughter of Shua, the Canaanitess. Er, the
firstborn of Judah, was wicked in the sight of
the LORD; so He killed him. 4And Tamar, his
daughter-in-law, bore him Perez and Zerah.
All the sons of Judah *were* five.

5The sons of Perez *were* Hezron and Hamul.
6The sons of Zerah *were* Zimri, Ethan, Heman,
Calcol, and Dara—five of them in all.

7The son of Carmi *was* Achar,[a] the troubler
of Israel, who transgressed in the accursed
thing.

8The son of Ethan *was* Azariah.

9Also the sons of Hezron who were born to
him *were* Jerahmeel, Ram, and Chelubai.[a]
10Ram begot Amminadab, and Amminadab
begot Nahshon, leader of the children of Judah; 11Nahshon begot Salma,[a] and Salma begot Boaz; 12Boaz begot Obed, and Obed begot
Jesse; 13Jesse begot Eliab his firstborn, Abinadab the second, Shimea[a] the third, 14Nethanel
the fourth, Raddai the fifth, 15Ozem the sixth,
and David the seventh.

16Now their sisters *were* Zeruiah and Abigail. And the sons of Zeruiah *were* Abishai,
Joab, and Asahel—three. 17Abigail bore Amasa; and the father of Amasa *was* Jether the
Ishmaelite.[a]

The Family of Hezron

18Caleb the son of Hezron had children by
Azubah, *his* wife, and by Jerioth. Now these
were her sons: Jesher, Shobab, and Ardon.
19When Azubah died, Caleb took Ephrath[a] as
his wife, who bore him Hur. 20And Hur begot
Uri, and Uri begot Bezalel.

21Now afterward Hezron went in to the
daughter of Machir the father of Gilead,
whom he married when he *was* sixty years
old; and she bore him Segub. 22Segub begot
Jair, who had twenty-three cities in the land of
Gilead. 23(Geshur and Syria took from them
the towns of Jair, with Kenath and its towns—
sixty towns.) All these *belonged to* the sons of
Machir the father of Gilead. 24After Hezron
died in Caleb Ephrathah, Hezron's wife Abijah
bore him Ashhur the father of Tekoa.

The Family of Jerahmeel

25The sons of Jerahmeel, the firstborn of
Hezron, *were* Ram, the firstborn, and Bunah,
Oren, Ozem, *and* Ahijah. 26Jerahmeel had another wife, whose name was Atarah; she was
the mother of Onam. 27The sons of Ram, the
firstborn of Jerahmeel, were Maaz, Jamin, and
Eker. 28The sons of Onam were Shammai
and Jada. The sons of Shammai *were* Nadab
and Abishur.

29And the name of the wife of Abishur *was*
Abihail, and she bore him Ahban and Molid.
30The sons of Nadab *were* Seled and Appaim;
Seled died without children. 31The son of

1:42 [a]Spelled *Akan* in Genesis 36:27
1:50 [a]Spelled *Hadar* in Genesis 36:39 [b]Spelled *Pau* in Genesis 36:39 **1:51** [a]Spelled *Alvah* in Genesis 36:40 **2:7** [a]Spelled *Achan* in Joshua 7:1 and elsewhere **2:9** [a]Spelled *Caleb* in 2:18, 42
2:11 [a]Spelled *Salmon* in Ruth 4:21 and Luke 3:32
2:13 [a]Spelled *Shammah* in 1 Samuel 16:9 and elsewhere **2:17** [a]Compare 2 Samuel 17:25
2:19 [a]Spelled *Ephrathah* elsewhere

Appaim *was* Ishi, the son of Ishi *was* Sheshan, and Sheshan's son *was* Ahlai. 32The sons of Jada, the brother of Shammai, *were* Jether and Jonathan; Jether died without children. 33The sons of Jonathan *were* Peleth and Zaza. These were the sons of Jerahmeel.

34Now Sheshan had no sons, only daughters. And Sheshan had an Egyptian servant whose name *was* Jarha. 35Sheshan gave his daughter to Jarha his servant as wife, and she bore him Attai. 36Attai begot Nathan, and Nathan begot Zabad; 37Zabad begot Ephlal, and Ephlal begot Obed; 38Obed begot Jehu, and Jehu begot Azariah; 39Azariah begot Helez, and Helez begot Eleasah; 40Eleasah begot Sismai, and Sismai begot Shallum; 41Shallum begot Jekamiah, and Jekamiah begot Elishama.

The Family of Caleb

42The descendants of Caleb the brother of Jerahmeel *were* Mesha, his firstborn, who was the father of Ziph, and the sons of Mareshah the father of Hebron. 43The sons of Hebron *were* Korah, Tappuah, Rekem, and Shema. 44Shema begot Raham the father of Jorkoam, and Rekem begot Shammai. 45And the son of Shammai *was* Maon, and Maon *was* the father of Beth Zur.

46Ephah, Caleb's concubine, bore Haran, Moza, and Gazez; and Haran begot Gazez. 47And the sons of Jahdai *were* Regem, Jotham, Geshan, Pelet, Ephah, and Shaaph.

48Maachah, Caleb's concubine, bore Sheber and Tirhanah. 49She also bore Shaaph the father of Madmannah, Sheva the father of Machbenah and the father of Gibea. And the daughter of Caleb *was* Achsah.

50These were the descendants of Caleb: The sons of Hur, the firstborn of Ephrathah, *were* Shobal the father of Kirjath Jearim, 51Salma the father of Bethlehem, *and* Hareph the father of Beth Gader.

52And Shobal the father of Kirjath Jearim had descendants: Haroeh, *and* half of the *families of* Manuhoth.[a] 53The families of Kirjath Jearim *were* the Ithrites, the Puthites, the Shumathites, and the Mishraites. From these came the Zorathites and the Eshtaolites.

54The sons of Salma *were* Bethlehem, the Netophathites, Atroth Beth Joab, half of the Manahethites, and the Zorites.

55And the families of the scribes who dwelt at Jabez *were* the Tirathites, the Shimeathites, *and* the Suchathites. These *were* the Kenites who came from Hammath, the father of the house of Rechab.

The Family of David

3 Now these were the sons of David who were born to him in Hebron: The firstborn *was* Amnon, by Ahinoam the Jezreelitess; the second, Daniel,[a] by Abigail the Carmelitess; 2the third, Absalom the son of Maacah, the daughter of Talmai, king of Geshur; the fourth, Adonijah the son of Haggith; 3the fifth, Shephatiah, by Abital; the sixth, Ithream, by his wife Eglah.

4*These* six were born to him in Hebron. There he reigned seven years and six months, and in Jerusalem he reigned thirty-three years. 5And these were born to him in Jerusalem: Shimea,[a] Shobab, Nathan, and Solomon—four by Bathshua[b] the daughter of Ammiel.[c] 6Also *there* were Ibhar, Elishama,[a] Eliphelet,[b] 7Nogah, Nepheg, Japhia, 8Elishama, Eliada,[a] and Eliphelet—nine *in all.* 9*These were* all the sons of David, besides the sons of the concubines, and Tamar their sister.

The Family of Solomon

10Solomon's son *was* Rehoboam; Abijah[a] *was* his son, Asa his son, Jehoshaphat his son, 11Joram[a] his son, Ahaziah his son, Joash[b] his son, 12Amaziah his son, Azariah[a] his son, Jotham his son, 13Ahaz his son, Hezekiah his son, Manasseh his son, 14Amon his son, *and* Josiah his son. 15The sons of Josiah *were* Johanan the firstborn, the second Jehoiakim, the third Zedekiah, and the fourth Shallum.[a] 16The sons of Jehoiakim *were* Jeconiah his son *and* Zedekiah[a] his son.

The Family of Jeconiah

17And the sons of Jeconiah[a] *were* Assir,[b] Shealtiel his son, 18*and* Malchiram, Pedaiah,

---

2:52 [a]Same as *the Manahethites,* verse 54
3:1 [a]Called *Chileab* in 2 Samuel 3:3 **3:5** [a]Spelled *Shammua* in 14:4 and 2 Samuel 5:14 [b]Spelled *Bathsheba* in 2 Samuel 11:3 [c]Called *Eliam* in 2 Samuel 11:3 **3:6** [a]Spelled *Elishua* in 14:5 and 2 Samuel 5:15 [b]Spelled *Elpelet* in 14:5
3:8 [a]Spelled *Beeliada* in 14:7 **3:10** [a]Spelled *Abijam* in 1 Kings 15:1 **3:11** [a]Spelled *Jehoram* in 2 Kings 1:17 and 8:16 [b]Spelled *Jehoash* in 2 Kings 12:1
3:12 [a]Called *Uzziah* in Isaiah 6:1 **3:15** [a]Called *Jehoahaz* in 2 Kings 23:31 **3:16** [a]Compare 2 Kings 24:17 **3:17** [a]Also called *Coniah* in Jeremiah 22:24 and *Jehoiachin* in 2 Kings 24:8 [b]Or *Jeconiah the captive were*

Shenazzar, Jecamiah, Hoshama, and Nedabiah. 19The sons of Pedaiah *were* Zerubbabel and Shimei. The sons of Zerubbabel *were* Meshullam, Hananiah, Shelomith their sister, 20and Hashubah, Ohel, Berechiah, Hasadiah, and Jushab-Hesed—five *in all.*

21The sons of Hananiah *were* Pelatiah and Jeshaiah, the sons of Rephaiah, the sons of Arnan, the sons of Obadiah, and the sons of Shechaniah. 22The son of Shechaniah was Shemaiah. The sons of Shemaiah *were* Hattush, Igal, Bariah, Neariah, and Shaphat—six *in all.* 23The sons of Neariah *were* Elioenai, Hezekiah, and Azrikam—three *in all.* 24The sons of Elioenai *were* Hodaviah, Eliashib, Pelaiah, Akkub, Johanan, Delaiah, and Anani—seven *in all.*

THE FAMILY OF JUDAH

4 The sons of Judah *were* Perez, Hezron, Carmi, Hur, and Shobal. 2And Reaiah the son of Shobal begot Jahath, and Jahath begot Ahumai and Lahad. These *were* the families of the Zorathites. 3These *were* the sons *of the father* of Etam: Jezreel, Ishma, and Idbash; and the name of their sister *was* Hazelelponi; 4and Penuel *was* the father of Gedor, and Ezer *was the* father of Hushah.

These *were* the sons of Hur, the firstborn of Ephrathah the father of Bethlehem.

5And Ashhur the father of Tekoa had two wives, Helah and Naarah. 6Naarah bore him Ahuzzam, Hepher, Temeni, and Haahashtari. These *were* the sons of Naarah. 7The sons of Helah *were* Zereth, Zohar, and Ethnan; 8and Koz begot Anub, Zobebah, and the families of Aharhel the son of Harum.

9Now Jabez was more honorable than his brothers, and his mother called his name Jabez,[a] saying, "Because I bore *him* in pain." 10And Jabez called on the God of Israel saying, "Oh, that You would bless me indeed, and enlarge my territory, that Your hand would be with me, and that You would keep *me* from evil, that I may not cause pain!" So God granted him what he requested.

11Chelub the brother of Shuhah begot Mehir, who *was* the father of Eshton. 12And Eshton begot Beth-Rapha, Paseah, and Tehinnah the father of Ir-Nahash. These *were* the men of Rechah.

13The sons of Kenaz *were* Othniel and Seraiah. The sons of Othniel *were* Hathath,[a] 14and Meonothai *who* begot Ophrah. Seraiah begot Joab the father of Ge Harashim,[a] for they were craftsmen. 15The sons of Caleb the son of Jephunneh *were* Iru, Elah, and Naam. The son of Elah *was* Kenaz. 16The sons of Jehallelel *were* Ziph, Ziphah, Tiria, and Asarel. 17The sons of Ezrah *were* Jether, Mered, Epher, and Jalon. And *Mered's wife*[a] *bore* Miriam, Shammai, and Ishbah the father of Eshtemoa. 18(His wife Jehudijah[a] bore Jered the father of Gedor, Heber the father of Sochoh, and Jekuthiel the father of Zanoah.) And these were the sons of Bithiah the daughter of Pharaoh, whom Mered took.

19The sons of Hodiah's wife, the sister of Naham, *were* the fathers of Keilah the Garmite and of Eshtemoa the Maachathite. 20And the sons of Shimon *were* Amnon, Rinnah, Ben-Hanan, and Tilon. And the sons of Ishi *were* Zoheth and Ben-Zoheth.

21The sons of Shelah the son of Judah *were* Er the father of Lecah, Laadah the father of Mareshah, and the families of the house of the linen workers of the house of Ashbea; 22also Jokim, the men of Chozeba, and Joash;

4:9 [a]Literally *He Will Cause Pain* **4:13** [a]Septuagint and Vulgate add *and Meonothai.* **4:14** [a]Literally *Valley of Craftsmen* **4:17** [a]Literally *she* **4:18** [a]Or *His Judean wife*

SOUL NOTE

Bless Me *(4:9, 10)* Little is written about most of the people in these lists beyond their names, but Jabez is described as a man "more honorable than his brothers," who "called on the God of Israel." Jabez prayed that God would bless him and keep him from evil so he would not cause anyone pain. Because God honored his prayer, we see that we too can pray for God's blessing on our lives. Our motivation should be so that we can use God's blessing to be a blessing to others.

Topic: Prayer

Fatherhood

SOMEONE SPECIAL

ROBERT WOLGEMUTH

(1 Chronicles 3:1)

"Any man can become a father, but it takes a special man to be a dad."

In September of 1971, just a few hours after our first baby was born, a close friend handed me a greeting card with the above inscription printed on the front. Earlier that morning I had become "any man." *I'm a father!* I whispered to myself. *Now what am I going to do?*

My primary training for this day came from my own parents. From the time I was small, I had watched them negotiate conflict among themselves. They loved and honored each other and this mutual respect gave my siblings and me a great sense of security. We knew our dad and mother had always consulted one another first.

From their example, I learned the most important thing any father can learn. It's the secret to successfully making the transition from father to dad and, amazingly, it has nothing to do with parenting skills. The secret to being a great dad is for a man to always love and serve his wife—his children's mother—first.

Missing this truth is as dangerous as a coach preparing his team for the game next week rather than the one this week. It's as treacherous as a sailor studying the weather maps for tomorrow's forecast instead of preparing for the storm today.

Proverbs 17:6 tantalizes a man with the possibility of being the "glory" of his children. However, being a great dad isn't achieved by pursuing fathering greatness; it's the byproduct—the investment dividend—of a selfless commitment to a successful marriage.

SEVEN TACTICAL STEPS TO BECOMING A GREAT DAD

Once a man has determined that his love for his wife is his priority, he then needs to build a game plan for success as a dad.

1. *Protection: Love Stands Guard*
"I will instruct you and teach you in the way you should go" (Ps. 32:8). One of the most amazing things that God has built into parents is the need to protect their young. A dad's job is to guard his children physically when they're young and defenseless, and emotionally as they grow and mature. This protection spans every conceivable dimension, from teaching his son to respect power tools to interviewing the boys who intend on taking his daughter out for a date.

2. *Conversation: Just Keep Talking*
"[Joseph] kissed all his brothers and . . . [they] talked with him" (Gen. 45:15). Giving his children the things they need is the job of every dad. The most precious gift, however, isn't a *thing*, it's a *skill*. That skill is the art of conversation. When his children are young, learning to ask good questions and listening carefully to their answers builds a bridge that connects their hearts for a lifetime. And, by the way, a dad needs to learn to listen with his eyes as well as his ears!

3. *Affection: The Power of Touch*
"[Jesus] took [the children] up in His arms" (Mark 10:16). There may be nothing more

important for a dad to learn than to understand the power of holding his children. A dad's touch communicates security and worth to a little person's heart. Not being satisfied with simply greeting the children with a smile and a nod, Jesus also touched them.

4. *Discipline: Love Must Be Painful*
"For whom the LORD loves He corrects" (Prov. 3:12). Discipline is both a verb and a noun. A dad's goal is to be able to say, "My children have discipline." That's the noun—and guess where it comes from. That's right—discipline, the verb. When children learn the rigors of discipline—modeled by a father with *self*-discipline—their lives are filled with the confidence of having discipline.

5. *Laughter: Fun to Live With*
"A merry heart makes a cheerful countenance" (Prov. 15:13). Admit it. Most men are . . . well, they're *boring*. We're too task-oriented, too focused, and too preoccupied to be any fun. And what can we do about this? Years ago, I went to a bookstore and found some help. I bought riddle books, cartoon books, and humor books. We watched a little less television, read those books, and played a few more games that didn't plug into a wall or need batteries. It worked.

6. *Faith: Jesus Loves Me*
"For God did not send His Son into the world to condemn the world, but that the world through Him might be saved" (John 3:17). There may be no more horrible word in the English language than the word "lost." And there may be no more wonderful word than the word "found." Every dad begins his life as a lost man. Only Jesus Christ has the power to truly find—save—that man. When a dad discovers this, then lives it before his family, nothing is ever the same again.

7. *Conduct: Loving Well, Living Right*
"For sin shall not have dominion over you, for you are not under law but under grace. What then? Shall we sin because we are not under law but under grace? Certainly not!" (Rom. 6:14, 15). My uncle Allon Dourte was a master fruit grower. His apples and peaches were the envy of farmers from nearly every surrounding zip code. Ironically, Uncle Allon spent very little time working on his fruit. Instead, most of his effort was spent on the health of the trees—pruning, spraying, and fertilizing. Good conduct is good fruit. Protection, conversation, affection, discipline, laughter, and faith make for good kids.

FURTHER MEDITATION:

Other passages to study about the issue of fatherhood include:

➢ Deuteronomy 6:6–9
➢ Proverbs 17:6
➢ Ephesians 6:4
➢ Colossians 3:21

To Learn More: Turn to the key passage note on fatherhood at Ephesians 6:4 on page 1558. See also the personality profile of the prodigal son's father on page 1348.

Saraph, who ruled in Moab, and Jashubi-Lehem. Now the records are ancient. 23These *were* the potters and those who dwell at Netaim[a] and Gederah;[b] there they dwelt with the king for his work.

THE FAMILY OF SIMEON

24The sons of Simeon *were* Nemuel, Jamin, Jarib,[a] Zerah,[b] *and* Shaul, 25Shallum his son, Mibsam his son, and Mishma his son. 26And the sons of Mishma *were* Hamuel his son, Zacchur his son, and Shimei his son. 27Shimei had sixteen sons and six daughters; but his brothers did not have many children, nor did any of their families multiply as much as the children of Judah.

28They dwelt at Beersheba, Moladah, Hazar Shual, 29Bilhah, Ezem, Tolad, 30Bethuel, Hormah, Ziklag, 31Beth Marcaboth, Hazar Susim, Beth Biri, and at Shaaraim. These *were* their cities until the reign of David. 32And their villages *were* Etam, Ain, Rimmon, Tochen, and Ashan—five cities— 33and all the villages that *were* around these cities as far as Baal.[a] These *were* their dwelling places, and they maintained their genealogy: 34Meshobab, Jamlech, and Joshah the son of Amaziah; 35Joel, and Jehu the son of Joshibiah, the son of Seraiah, the son of Asiel; 36Elioenai, Jaakobah, Jeshohaiah, Asaiah, Adiel, Jesimiel, and Benaiah; 37Ziza the son of Shiphi, the son of Allon, the son of Jedaiah, the son of Shimri, the son of Shemaiah— 38these mentioned by name *were* leaders in their families, and their father's house increased greatly.

39So they went to the entrance of Gedor, as far as the east side of the valley, to seek pasture for their flocks. 40And they found rich, good pasture, and the land *was* broad, quiet, and peaceful; for some Hamites formerly lived there.

41These recorded by name came in the days of Hezekiah king of Judah; and they attacked their tents and the Meunites who were found there, and utterly destroyed them, as it is to this day. So they dwelt in their place, because *there was* pasture for their flocks there. 42Now *some* of them, five hundred men of the sons of Simeon, went to Mount Seir, having as their captains Pelatiah, Neariah, Rephaiah, and Uzziel, the sons of Ishi. 43And they defeated the rest of the Amalekites who had escaped. They have dwelt there to this day.

THE FAMILY OF REUBEN

5 Now the sons of Reuben the firstborn of Israel—he *was* indeed the firstborn, but because he defiled his father's bed, his birthright was given to the sons of Joseph, the son of Israel, so that the genealogy is not listed according to the birthright; 2yet Judah prevailed over his brothers, and from him *came* a ruler, although the birthright was Joseph's— 3the sons of Reuben the firstborn of Israel were Hanoch, Pallu, Hezron, and Carmi.

4The sons of Joel *were* Shemaiah his son, Gog his son, Shimei his son, 5Micah his son, Reaiah his son, Baal his son, 6and Beerah his son, whom Tiglath-Pileser[a] king of Assyria carried into captivity. He *was* leader of the Reubenites. 7And his brethren by their families, when the genealogy of their generations was registered: the chief, Jeiel, and Zechariah, 8and Bela the son of Azaz, the son of Shema, the son of Joel, who dwelt in Aroer, as far as Nebo and Baal Meon. 9Eastward they settled as far as the entrance of the wilderness this side of the River Euphrates, because their cattle had multiplied in the land of Gilead.

10Now in the days of Saul they made war with the Hagrites, who fell by their hand; and they dwelt in their tents throughout the entire *area* east of Gilead.

THE FAMILY OF GAD

11And the children of Gad dwelt next to them in the land of Bashan as far as Salcah: 12Joel *was* the chief, Shapham the next, then Jaanai and Shaphat in Bashan, 13and their brethren of their father's house: Michael, Meshullam, Sheba, Jorai, Jachan, Zia, and Eber—seven *in all.* 14These *were* the children of Abihail the son of Huri, the son of Jaroah, the son of Gilead, the son of Michael, the son of Jeshishai, the son of Jahdo, the son of Buz; 15Ahi the son of Abdiel, the son of Guni, *was* chief of their father's house. 16And *the Gadites* dwelt in Gilead, in Bashan and in its villages, and in all the common-lands of Sharon within their borders. 17All these were registered by genealogies in the days of Jotham king of Judah, and in the days of Jeroboam king of Israel.

18The sons of Reuben, the Gadites, and half

4:23 [a]Literally *Plants* [b]Literally *Hedges*
4:24 [a]Called *Jachin* in Genesis 46:10 [b]Called *Zohar* in Genesis 46:10 **4:33** [a]Or *Baalath Beer* (compare Joshua 19:8) **5:6** [a]Hebrew *Tilgath-Pilneser*

the tribe of Manasseh *had* forty-four thousand seven hundred and sixty valiant men, men able to bear shield and sword, to shoot with the bow, and skillful in war, who went to war. [19]They made war with the Hagrites, Jetur, Naphish, and Nodab. [20]And they were helped against them, and the Hagrites were delivered into their hand, and all who *were* with them, for they cried out to God in the battle. He heeded their prayer, because they put their trust in Him. [21]Then they took away their livestock—fifty thousand of their camels, two hundred and fifty thousand of their sheep, and two thousand of their donkeys—also one hundred thousand of their men; [22]for many fell dead, because the war *was* God's. And they dwelt in their place until the captivity.

The Family of Manasseh (East)

[23]So the children of the half-tribe of Manasseh dwelt in the land. Their *numbers* increased from Bashan to Baal Hermon, that is, to Senir, or Mount Hermon. [24]These *were* the heads of their fathers' houses: Epher, Ishi, Eliel, Azriel, Jeremiah, Hodaviah, and Jahdiel. They were mighty men of valor, famous men, *and* heads of their fathers' houses.

[25]And they were unfaithful to the God of their fathers, and played the harlot after the gods of the peoples of the land, whom God had destroyed before them. [26]So the God of Israel stirred up the spirit of Pul king of Assyria, that is, Tiglath-Pileser[a] king of Assyria. He carried the Reubenites, the Gadites, and the half-tribe of Manasseh into captivity. He took them to Halah, Habor, Hara, and the river of Gozan to this day.

The Family of Levi

6 The sons of Levi *were* Gershon, Kohath, and Merari. [2]The sons of Kohath *were* Amram, Izhar, Hebron, and Uzziel. [3]The children of Amram *were* Aaron, Moses, and Miriam. And the sons of Aaron *were* Nadab, Abihu, Eleazar, and Ithamar. [4]Eleazar begot Phinehas, *and* Phinehas begot Abishua; [5]Abishua begot Bukki, and Bukki begot Uzzi; [6]Uzzi begot Zerahiah, and Zerahiah begot Meraioth; [7]Meraioth begot Amariah, and Amariah begot Ahitub; [8]Ahitub begot Zadok, and Zadok begot Ahimaaz; [9]Ahimaaz begot Azariah, and Azariah begot Johanan; [10]Johanan begot Azariah (it was he who ministered as priest in the temple that Solomon built in Jerusalem); [11]Azariah begot Amariah, and Amariah begot Ahitub; [12]Ahitub begot Zadok, and Zadok begot Shallum; [13]Shallum begot Hilkiah, and Hilkiah begot Azariah; [14]Azariah begot Seraiah, and Seraiah begot Jehozadak. [15]Jehozadak went *into captivity* when the LORD carried Judah and Jerusalem into captivity by the hand of Nebuchadnezzar.

[16]The sons of Levi *were* Gershon,[a] Kohath, and Merari. [17]These are the names of the sons of Gershon: Libni and Shimei. [18]The sons of Kohath *were* Amram, Izhar, Hebron, and Uzziel. [19]The sons of Merari *were* Mahli and Mushi. Now these *are* the families of the Levites according to their fathers: [20]Of Gershon *were* Libni his son, Jahath his son, Zimmah his son, [21]Joah his son, Iddo his son, Zerah his son, *and* Jeatherai his son. [22]The sons of Kohath *were* Amminadab his son, Korah his son, Assir his son, [23]Elkanah his son, Ebiasaph his son, Assir his son, [24]Tahath his son, Uriel his son, Uzziah his son, and Shaul his son. [25]The sons of Elkanah *were* Amasai and Ahimoth. [26]*As for* Elkanah,[a] the sons of Elkanah *were* Zophai[b] his son, Nahath[c] his son, [27]Eliab[a] his son, Jeroham his son, *and* Elkanah his son. [28]The sons of Samuel *were Joel*[a] the firstborn, and Abijah the second.[b] [29]The sons of Merari *were* Mahli, Libni his son, Shimei his son, Uzzah his son, [30]Shimea his son, Haggiah his son, *and* Asaiah his son.

Musicians in the House of the Lord

[31]Now these are the men whom David appointed over the service of song in the house of the LORD, after the ark came to rest. [32]They were ministering with music before the dwelling place of the tabernacle of meeting, until Solomon had built the house of the LORD in Jerusalem, and they served in their office according to their order.

[33]And these *are* the ones who ministered with their sons: Of the sons of the Kohathites *were* Heman the singer, the son of Joel, the son of Samuel, [34]the son of Elkanah, the son of Jeroham, the son of Eliel,[a] the son of Toah,[b]

5:26 [a]Hebrew *Tilgath-Pilneser* **6:16** [a]Hebrew *Gershom* (alternate spelling of *Gershon,* as in verses 1, 17, 20, 43, 62, and 71) **6:26** [a]Compare verse 35 [b]Spelled *Zuph* in verse 35 and 1 Samuel 1:1 [c]Compare verse 34 **6:27** [a]Compare verse 34 **6:28** [a]Following Septuagint, Syriac, and Arabic (compare verse 33 and 1 Samuel 8:2) [b]Hebrew *Vasheni* **6:34** [a]Spelled *Elihu* in 1 Samuel 1:1 [b]Spelled *Tohu* in 1 Samuel 1:1

35 the son of Zuph, the son of Elkanah, the son of Mahath, the son of Amasai, 36 the son of Elkanah, the son of Joel, the son of Azariah, the son of Zephaniah, 37 the son of Tahath, the son of Assir, the son of Ebiasaph, the son of Korah, 38 the son of Izhar, the son of Kohath, the son of Levi, the son of Israel. 39 And his brother Asaph, who stood at his right hand, *was* Asaph the son of Berachiah, the son of Shimea, 40 the son of Michael, the son of Baaseiah, the son of Malchijah, 41 the son of Ethni, the son of Zerah, the son of Adaiah, 42 the son of Ethan, the son of Zimmah, the son of Shimei, 43 the son of Jahath, the son of Gershon, the son of Levi.

44 Their brethren, the sons of Merari, on the left hand, *were* Ethan the son of Kishi, the son of Abdi, the son of Malluch, 45 the son of Hashabiah, the son of Amaziah, the son of Hilkiah, 46 the son of Amzi, the son of Bani, the son of Shamer, 47 the son of Mahli, the son of Mushi, the son of Merari, the son of Levi.

48 And their brethren, the Levites, *were* appointed to every kind of service of the tabernacle of the house of God.

The Family of Aaron

49 But Aaron and his sons offered sacrifices on the altar of burnt offering and on the altar of incense, for all the work of the Most Holy *Place,* and to make atonement for Israel, according to all that Moses the servant of God had commanded. 50 Now these *are* the sons of Aaron: Eleazar his son, Phinehas his son, Abishua his son, 51 Bukki his son, Uzzi his son, Zerahiah his son, 52 Meraioth his son, Amariah his son, Ahitub his son, 53 Zadok his son, *and* Ahimaaz his son.

Dwelling Places of the Levites

54 Now these *are* their dwelling places throughout their settlements in their territory, for they were *given* by lot to the sons of Aaron, of the family of the Kohathites: 55 They gave them Hebron in the land of Judah, with its surrounding common-lands. 56 But the fields of the city and its villages they gave to Caleb the son of Jephunneh. 57 And to the sons of Aaron they gave *one of* the cities of refuge, Hebron; also Libnah with its common-lands, Jattir, Eshtemoa with its common-lands, 58 Hilen[a] with its common-lands, Debir with its common-lands, 59 Ashan[a] with its common-lands, and Beth Shemesh with its common-lands. 60 And from the tribe of Benjamin: Geba with its common-lands, Alemeth[a] with its common-lands, and Anathoth with its common-lands. All their cities among their families *were* thirteen.

61 To the rest of the family of the tribe of the Kohathites *they gave* by lot ten cities from half the tribe of Manasseh. 62 And to the sons of Gershon, throughout their families, *they gave* thirteen cities from the tribe of Issachar, from the tribe of Asher, from the tribe of Naphtali, and from the tribe of Manasseh in Bashan. 63 To the sons of Merari, throughout their families, *they gave* twelve cities from the tribe of Reuben, from the tribe of Gad, and from the tribe of Zebulun. 64 So the children of Israel gave *these* cities with their common-lands to the Levites. 65 And they gave by lot from the tribe of the children of Judah, from the tribe of the children of Simeon, and from the tribe of the children of Benjamin these cities which are called by *their* names.

66 Now some of the families of the sons of Kohath *were given* cities as their territory from the tribe of Ephraim. 67 And they gave them *one of* the cities of refuge, Shechem with its

6:58 [a]Spelled *Holon* in Joshua 21:15
6:59 [a]Spelled *Ain* in Joshua 21:16 **6:60** [a]Spelled *Almon* in Joshua 21:18

SOUL NOTE

Sing Along *(6:31)* David selected a number of people to minister at the tabernacle with music and singing. Their job was to lead the people in worship. David was a writer of many of the psalms and a singer of songs of praise to the Lord. It is only fitting that he would institute music as a major part of worship. Today, the ministry of praise and worship in our churches owes much of its origin to David. As we sing hymns and choruses in church, we join a choir across the centuries that has praised God in song. **Topic: Praise and Worship**

common-lands, in the mountains of Ephraim, also Gezer with its common-lands, 68Jokmeam with its common-lands, Beth Horon with its common-lands, 69Aijalon with its common-lands, and Gath Rimmon with its common-lands. 70And from the half-tribe of Manasseh: Aner with its common-lands and Bileam with its common-lands, for the rest of the family of the sons of Kohath.

71From the family of the half-tribe of Manasseh the sons of Gershon *were given* Golan in Bashan with its common-lands and Ashtaroth with its common-lands. 72And from the tribe of Issachar: Kedesh with its common-lands, Daberath with its common-lands, 73Ramoth with its common-lands, and Anem with its common-lands. 74And from the tribe of Asher: Mashal with its common-lands, Abdon with its common-lands, 75Hukok with its common-lands, and Rehob with its common-lands. 76And from the tribe of Naphtali: Kedesh in Galilee with its common-lands, Hammon with its common-lands, and Kirjathaim with its common-lands.

77From the tribe of Zebulun the rest of the children of Merari *were given* Rimmon[a] with its common-lands and Tabor with its common-lands. 78And on the other side of the Jordan, across from Jericho, on the east side of the Jordan, *they were given* from the tribe of Reuben: Bezer in the wilderness with its common-lands, Jahzah with its common-lands, 79Kedemoth with its common-lands, and Mephaath with its common-lands. 80And from the tribe of Gad: Ramoth in Gilead with its common-lands, Mahanaim with its common-lands, 81Heshbon with its common-lands, and Jazer with its common-lands.

The Family of Issachar

7 The sons of Issachar *were* Tola, Puah,[a] Jashub, and Shimron—four *in all.* 2The sons of Tola *were* Uzzi, Rephaiah, Jeriel, Jahmai, Jibsam, and Shemuel, heads of their father's house. *The sons* of Tola *were* mighty men of valor in their generations; their number in the days of David *was* twenty-two thousand six hundred. 3The son of Uzzi *was* Izrahiah, and the sons of Izrahiah *were* Michael, Obadiah, Joel, and Ishiah. All five of them *were* chief men. 4And with them, by their generations, according to their fathers' houses, *were* thirty-six thousand troops ready for war; for they had many wives and sons.

5Now their brethren among all the families of Issachar *were* mighty men of valor, listed by their genealogies, eighty-seven thousand in all.

The Family of Benjamin

6*The sons* of Benjamin *were* Bela, Becher, and Jediael—three *in all.* 7The sons of Bela were Ezbon, Uzzi, Uzziel, Jerimoth, and Iri—five *in all.* They *were* heads of *their* fathers' houses, and they were listed by their genealogies, twenty-two thousand and thirty-four mighty men of valor.

8The sons of Becher *were* Zemirah, Joash, Eliezer, Elioenai, Omri, Jerimoth, Abijah, Anathoth, and Alemeth. All these *are* the sons of Becher. 9And they were recorded by genealogy according to their generations, heads of their fathers' houses, twenty thousand two hundred mighty men of valor. 10The son of Jediael *was* Bilhan, and the sons of Bilhan *were* Jeush, Benjamin, Ehud, Chenaanah, Zethan, Tharshish, and Ahishahar.

11All these sons of Jediael *were* heads of their fathers' houses; *there were* seventeen thousand two hundred mighty men of valor fit to go out for war *and* battle. 12Shuppim and Huppim[a] *were* the sons of Ir, *and* Hushim *was* the son of Aher.

The Family of Naphtali

13The sons of Naphtali *were* Jahziel,[a] Guni, Jezer, and Shallum,[b] the sons of Bilhah.

The Family of Manasseh (West)

14The descendants of Manasseh: his Syrian concubine bore him Machir the father of Gilead, the father of Asriel.[a] 15Machir took as his wife *the sister* of Huppim and Shuppim,[a] whose name *was* Maachah. The name of *Gilead's* grandson[b] *was* Zelophehad,[c] but Zelophehad begot only daughters. 16(Maachah the wife of Machir bore a son, and she called his name Peresh. The name of his brother *was* Sheresh, and his sons *were* Ulam and Rakem. 17The son of Ulam *was* Bedan.) These *were* the

---

6:77 [a]Hebrew *Rimmono,* alternate spelling of *Rimmon;* see 4:32 **7:1** [a]Spelled *Puvah* in Genesis 46:13 **7:12** [a]Called *Hupham* in Numbers 26:39 **7:13** [a]Spelled *Jahzeel* in Genesis 46:24 [b]Spelled *Shillem* in Genesis 46:24 **7:14** [a]The son of Gilead (compare Numbers 6:30, 31)
7:15 [a]Compare verse 12 [b]Literally *the second* [c]Compare Numbers 26:30–33

descendants of Gilead the son of Machir, the son of Manasseh.

18His sister Hammoleketh bore Ishhod, Abiezer, and Mahlah.

19And the sons of Shemida were Ahian, Shechem, Likhi, and Aniam.

The Family of Ephraim

20The sons of Ephraim *were* Shuthelah, Bered his son, Tahath his son, Eladah his son, Tahath his son, 21Zabad his son, Shuthelah his son, and Ezer and Elead. The men of Gath who were born in *that* land killed *them* because they came down to take away their cattle. 22Then Ephraim their father mourned many days, and his brethren came to comfort him.

23And when he went in to his wife, she conceived and bore a son; and he called his name Beriah,[a] because tragedy had come upon his house. 24Now his daughter *was* Sheerah, who built Lower and Upper Beth Horon and Uzzen Sheerah; 25and Rephah *was* his son, *as well* as Resheph, and Telah his son, Tahan his son, 26Laadan his son, Ammihud his son, Elishama his son, 27Nun[a] his son, and Joshua his son.

28Now their possessions and dwelling places *were* Bethel and its towns: to the east Naaran, to the west Gezer and its towns, and Shechem and its towns, as far as Ayyah[a] and its towns; 29and by the borders of the children of Manasseh *were* Beth Shean and its towns, Taanach and its towns, Megiddo and its towns, Dor and its towns. In these dwelt the children of Joseph, the son of Israel.

The Family of Asher

30The sons of Asher *were* Imnah, Ishvah, Ishvi, Beriah, and their sister Serah. 31The sons of Beriah *were* Heber and Malchiel, who was the father of Birzaith.[a] 32And Heber begot Japhlet, Shomer,[a] Hotham,[b] and their sister Shua. 33The sons of Japhlet *were* Pasach, Bimhal, and Ashvath. These *were* the children of Japhlet. 34The sons of Shemer *were* Ahi, Rohgah, Jehubbah, and Aram. 35And the sons of his brother Helem *were* Zophah, Imna, Shelesh, and Amal. 36The sons of Zophah *were* Suah, Harnepher, Shual, Beri, Imrah, 37Bezer, Hod, Shamma, Shilshah, Jithran,[a] and Beera. 38The sons of Jether *were* Jephunneh, Pispah, and Ara. 39The sons of Ulla *were* Arah, Haniel, and Rizia.

40All these *were* the children of Asher, heads of *their* fathers' houses, choice men, mighty men of valor, chief leaders. And they were recorded by genealogies among the army fit for battle; their number *was* twenty-six thousand.

The Family Tree of King Saul of Benjamin

8 Now Benjamin begot Bela his firstborn, Ashbel the second, Aharah[a] the third, 2Nohah the fourth, and Rapha the fifth. 3The sons of Bela *were* Addar,[a] Gera, Abihud, 4Abishua, Naaman, Ahoah, 5Gera, Shephuphan, and Huram.

6These *are* the sons of Ehud, who were the heads of the fathers' *houses* of the inhabitants of Geba, and who forced them to move to Manahath: 7Naaman, Ahijah, and Gera who forced them to move. He begot Uzza and Ahihud.

8Also Shaharaim had children in the country of Moab, after he had sent away Hushim and Baara his wives. 9By Hodesh his wife he begot Jobab, Zibia, Mesha, Malcam, 10Jeuz, Sachiah, and Mirmah. These *were* his sons, heads of their fathers' *houses*.

11And by Hushim he begot Abitub and Elpaal. 12The sons of Elpaal *were* Eber, Misham, and Shemed, who built Ono and Lod with its towns; 13and Beriah and Shema, who *were* heads of their fathers' *houses* of the inhabitants of Aijalon, who drove out the inhabitants of Gath. 14Ahio, Shashak, Jeremoth, 15Zebadiah, Arad, Eder, 16Michael, Ispah, and Joha *were* the sons of Beriah. 17Zebadiah, Meshullam, Hizki, Heber, 18Ishmerai, Jizliah, and Jobab *were* the sons of Elpaal. 19Jakim, Zichri, Zabdi, 20Elienai, Zillethai, Eliel, 21Adaiah, Beraiah, and Shimrath *were* the sons of Shimei. 22Ishpan, Eber, Eliel, 23Abdon, Zichri, Hanan, 24Hananiah, Elam, Antothijah, 25Iphdeiah, and Penuel *were* the sons of Shashak. 26Shamsherai, Shehariah, Athaliah, 27Jaareshiah, Elijah, and Zichri *were* the sons of Jeroham.

28These *were* heads of the fathers' *houses* by their generations, chief men. These dwelt in Jerusalem.

29Now the father of Gibeon, whose wife's name *was* Maacah, dwelt at Gibeon. 30And his firstborn son *was* Abdon, then Zur, Kish, Baal,

---

7:23 [a]Literally *In Tragedy* **7:27** [a]Hebrew *Non* **7:28** [a]Many Hebrew manuscripts, Bomberg, Septuagint, Targum, and Vulgate read *Gazza.* **7:31** [a]Or *Birzavith* or *Birzoth* **7:32** [a]Spelled *Shemer* in verse 34 [b]Spelled *Helem* in verse 35 **7:37** [a]Spelled *Jether* in verse 38 **8:1** [a]Spelled *Ahiram* in Numbers 26:38 **8:3** [a]Called *Ard* in Numbers 26:40

Nadab, [31]Gedor, Ahio, Zecher, [32]and Mikloth, *who* begot Shimeah.[a] They also dwelt alongside their relatives in Jerusalem, with their brethren. [33]Ner[a] begot Kish, Kish begot Saul, and Saul begot Jonathan, Malchishua, Abinadab,[b] and Esh-Baal.[c] [34]The son of Jonathan *was* Merib-Baal,[a] and Merib-Baal begot Micah. [35]The sons of Micah *were* Pithon, Melech, Tarea, and Ahaz. [36]And Ahaz begot Jehoaddah;[a] Jehoaddah begot Alemeth, Azmaveth, and Zimri; and Zimri begot Moza. [37]Moza begot Binea, Raphah[a] his son, Eleasah his son, *and* Azel his son.

[38]Azel had six sons whose names *were* these: Azrikam, Bocheru, Ishmael, Sheariah, Obadiah, and Hanan. All these *were* the sons of Azel. [39]And the sons of Eshek his brother *were* Ulam his firstborn, Jeush the second, and Eliphelet the third.

[40]The sons of Ulam were mighty men of valor—archers. *They* had many sons and grandsons, one hundred and fifty *in all.* These *were* all sons of Benjamin.

9 So all Israel was recorded by genealogies, and indeed, they *were* inscribed in the book of the kings of Israel. But Judah was carried away captive to Babylon because of their unfaithfulness. [2]And the first inhabitants who *dwelt* in their possessions in their cities *were* Israelites, priests, Levites, and the Nethinim.

Dwellers in Jerusalem

[3]Now in Jerusalem the children of Judah dwelt, and some of the children of Benjamin, and of the children of Ephraim and Manasseh: [4]Uthai the son of Ammihud, the son of Omri, the son of Imri, the son of Bani, of the descendants of Perez, the son of Judah. [5]Of the Shilonites: Asaiah the firstborn and his sons. [6]Of the sons of Zerah: Jeuel, and their brethren—six hundred and ninety. [7]Of the sons of Benjamin: Sallu the son of Meshullam, the son of Hodaviah, the son of Hassenuah; [8]Ibneiah the son of Jeroham; Elah the son of Uzzi, the son of Michri; Meshullam the son of Shephatiah, the son of Reuel, the son of Ibnijah; [9]and their brethren, according to their generations—nine hundred and fifty-six. All these men *were* heads of a father's *house* in their fathers' houses.

The Priests at Jerusalem

[10]Of the priests: Jedaiah, Jehoiarib, and Jachin; [11]Azariah the son of Hilkiah, the son of Meshullam, the son of Zadok, the son of Meraioth, the son of Ahitub, the officer over the house of God; [12]Adaiah the son of Jeroham, the son of Pashur, the son of Malchijah; Maasai the son of Adiel, the son of Jahzerah, the son of Meshullam, the son of Meshillemith, the son of Immer; [13]and their brethren, heads of their fathers' *houses*—one thousand seven hundred and sixty. *They were* very able men for the work of the service of the house of God.

The Levites at Jerusalem

[14]Of the Levites: Shemaiah the son of Hasshub, the son of Azrikam, the son of Hashabiah, of the sons of Merari; [15]Bakbakkar, Heresh, Galal, and Mattaniah the son of Micah, the son of Zichri, the son of Asaph; [16]Obadiah the son of Shemaiah, the son of Galal, the son of Jeduthun; and Berechiah the son of Asa, the son of Elkanah, who lived in the villages of the Netophathites.

The Levite Gatekeepers

[17]And the gatekeepers *were* Shallum, Akkub, Talmon, Ahiman, and their brethren. Shallum *was* the chief. [18]Until then *they had been* gatekeepers for the camps of the children of Levi at the King's Gate on the east.

[19]Shallum the son of Kore, the son of Ebiasaph, the son of Korah, and his brethren, from his father's house, the Korahites, *were* in charge of the work of the service, gatekeepers of the tabernacle. Their fathers had been keepers of the entrance to the camp of the LORD. [20]And Phinehas the son of Eleazar had been the officer over them in time past; the LORD *was* with him. [21]Zechariah the son of Meshelemiah *was* keeper of the door of the tabernacle of meeting.

[22]All those chosen as gatekeepers *were* two hundred and twelve. They were recorded by their genealogy, in their villages. David and Samuel the seer had appointed them to their trusted office. [23]So they and their children *were* in charge of the gates of the house of the LORD, the house of the tabernacle, by assignment.

8:32 [a]Spelled *Shimeam* in 9:38 **8:33** [a]Also the son of Gibeon (compare 9:36, 39) [b]Called *Jishui* in 1 Samuel 14:49 [c]Called *Ishbosheth* in 2 Samuel 2:8 and elsewhere **8:34** [a]Called *Mephibosheth* in 2 Samuel 4:4 **8:36** [a]Spelled *Jarah* in 9:42 **8:37** [a]Spelled *Rephaiah* in 9:43

24 The gatekeepers were assigned to the four directions: the east, west, north, and south. 25 And their brethren in their villages *had* to come with them from time to time for seven days. 26 For in this trusted office *were* four chief gatekeepers; they were Levites. And they had charge over the chambers and treasuries of the house of God. 27 And they lodged *all* around the house of God because they *had* the responsibility, and they *were* in charge of opening *it* every morning.

Other Levite Responsibilities

28 Now *some* of them were in charge of the serving vessels, for they brought them in and took them out by count. 29 *Some* of them *were* appointed over the furnishings and over all the implements of the sanctuary, and over the fine flour and the wine and the oil and the incense and the spices. 30 And *some* of the sons of the priests made the ointment of the spices.

31 Mattithiah of the Levites, the firstborn of Shallum the Korahite, had the trusted office over the things that were baked in the pans. 32 And some of their brethren of the sons of the Kohathites *were* in charge of preparing the showbread for every Sabbath.

33 These are the singers, heads of the fathers' *houses* of the Levites, *who lodged* in the chambers, *and were* free *from other duties;* for they were employed in *that* work day and night. 34 These heads of the fathers' *houses* of the Levites *were* heads throughout their generations. They dwelt at Jerusalem.

The Family of King Saul

35 Jeiel the father of Gibeon, whose wife's name *was* Maacah, dwelt at Gibeon. 36 His firstborn son *was* Abdon, then Zur, Kish, Baal, Ner, Nadab, 37 Gedor, Ahio, Zechariah,[a] and Mikloth. 38 And Mikloth begot Shimeam.[a] They also dwelt alongside their relatives in Jerusalem, with their brethren. 39 Ner begot Kish, Kish begot Saul, and Saul begot Jonathan, Malchishua, Abinadab, and Esh-Baal. 40 The son of Jonathan *was* Merib-Baal, and Merib-Baal begot Micah. 41 The sons of Micah *were* Pithon, Melech, Tahrea,[a] and Ahaz.[b] 42 And Ahaz begot Jarah;[a] Jarah begot Alemeth, Azmaveth, and Zimri; and Zimri begot Moza; 43 Moza begot Binea, Rephaiah[a] his son, Eleasah his son, and Azel his son.

44 And Azel had six sons whose names *were* these: Azrikam, Bocheru, Ishmael, Sheariah, Obadiah, and Hanan; these *were* the sons of Azel.

Tragic End of Saul and His Sons

10 Now the Philistines fought against Israel; and the men of Israel fled from before the Philistines, and fell slain on Mount Gilboa. 2 Then the Philistines followed hard after Saul and his sons. And the Philistines killed Jonathan, Abinadab, and Malchishua, Saul's sons. 3 The battle became fierce against Saul. The archers hit him, and he was wounded by the archers. 4 Then Saul said to his armorbearer, "Draw your sword, and thrust me through with it, lest these uncircumcised men come and abuse me." But his armorbearer would not, for he was greatly afraid. Therefore Saul took a sword and fell on it. 5 And when his armorbearer saw that Saul was dead, he also fell on his sword and died. 6 So Saul and his three sons died, and all his house died together. 7 And when all the men of Israel who *were* in the valley saw that they had fled and that Saul and his sons were dead, they

9:37 [a]Called *Zecher* in 8:31 **9:38** [a]Spelled *Shimeah* in 8:32 **9:41** [a]Spelled *Tarea* in 8:35 [b]Following Arabic, Syriac, Targum, and Vulgate (compare 8:35); Masoretic Text and Septuagint omit *and Ahaz.* **9:42** [a]Spelled *Jehoaddah* in 8:36 **9:43** [a]Spelled *Raphah* in 8:37

SOUL NOTE

Unwilling to Trust *(10:4)* Saul had been defeated in his battle against the Philistines. Having been wounded by the archers, he asked his armorbearer to kill him so that his enemies would not be able to capture him alive. When the armorbearer refused, Saul took his own life. The choice to end one's life is always a desperate one and reflects an unwillingness to trust God with life today and in the future. Saul had spent years failing to obey God. His self-destructive end came as a result of a series of self-destructive choices that he had made throughout his life. **Topic: Suicide**

forsook their cities and fled; then the Philistines came and dwelt in them.
[8]So it happened the next day, when the Philistines came to strip the slain, that they found
Saul and his sons fallen on Mount Gilboa.
[9]And they stripped him and took his head and
his armor, and sent word *throughout* the land
of the Philistines to proclaim the news *in the
temple* of their idols and among the people.
[10]Then they put his armor in the temple of
their gods, and fastened his head in the temple of Dagon.
[11]And when all Jabesh Gilead heard all that
the Philistines had done to Saul, [12]all the valiant men arose and took the body of Saul and
the bodies of his sons; and they brought them
to Jabesh, and buried their bones under the
tamarisk tree at Jabesh, and fasted seven
days.
[13]So Saul died for his unfaithfulness which
he had committed against the LORD, because
he did not keep the word of the LORD, and also
because he consulted a medium for guidance.
[14]But *he* did not inquire of the LORD; therefore
He killed him, and turned the kingdom over to
David the son of Jesse.

DAVID MADE KING OVER ALL ISRAEL

11 Then all Israel came together to David
at Hebron, saying, "Indeed we *are*
your bone and your flesh. [2]Also, in time past,
even when Saul was king, you *were* the one
who led Israel out and brought them in; and
the LORD your God said to you, 'You shall
shepherd My people Israel, and be ruler over
My people Israel.' " [3]Therefore all the elders of
Israel came to the king at Hebron, and David
made a covenant with them at Hebron before
the LORD. And they anointed David king over
Israel, according to the word of the LORD by
Samuel.

THE CITY OF DAVID

[4]And David and all Israel went to Jerusalem, which is Jebus, where the Jebusites *were*,
the inhabitants of the land. [5]But the inhabitants of Jebus said to David, "You shall not
come in here!" Nevertheless David took the
stronghold of Zion (that is, the City of David).
[6]Now David said, "Whoever attacks the Jebusites first shall be chief and captain." And
Joab the son of Zeruiah went up first, and became chief. [7]Then David dwelt in the stronghold; therefore they called it the City of David.
[8]And he built the city around it, from the
Millo[a] to the surrounding area. Joab repaired
the rest of the city. [9]So David went on and
became great, and the LORD of hosts *was*
with him.

THE MIGHTY MEN OF DAVID

[10]Now these *were* the heads of the mighty
men whom David had, who strengthened
themselves with him in his kingdom, with all
Israel, to make him king, according to the
word of the LORD concerning Israel.
[11]And this *is* the number of the mighty men
whom David had: Jashobeam the son of a
Hachmonite, chief of the captains;[a] he had
lifted up his spear against three hundred,
killed *by him* at one time.
[12]After him *was* Eleazar the son of Dodo, the
Ahohite, who *was one* of the three mighty men.
[13]He was with David at Pasdammim. Now
there the Philistines were gathered for battle,
and there was a piece of ground full of barley.
So the people fled from the Philistines. [14]But
they stationed themselves in the middle of *that*
field, defended it, and killed the Philistines. So
the LORD brought about a great victory.
[15]Now three of the thirty chief men went
down to the rock to David, into the cave of
Adullam; and the army of the Philistines encamped in the Valley of Rephaim. [16]David *was*
then in the stronghold, and the garrison of the
Philistines *was* then in Bethlehem. [17]And David said with longing, "Oh, that someone
would give me a drink of water from the well
of Bethlehem, which is by the gate!" [18]So the
three broke through the camp of the Philistines, drew water from the well of Bethlehem
that *was* by the gate, and took *it* and brought *it*
to David. Nevertheless David would not drink
it, but poured it out to the LORD. [19]And he
said, "Far be it from me, O my God, that I
should do this! Shall I drink the blood of these
men *who have put* their lives *in jeopardy?* For
at the risk of their lives they brought it."
Therefore he would not drink it. These things
were done by the three mighty men.
[20]Abishai the brother of Joab was chief of
another three.[a] He had lifted up his spear

11:8 [a]Literally *The Landfill* **11:11** [a]Following Qere; Kethib, Septuagint, and Vulgate read *the thirty* (compare 2 Samuel 23:8). **11:20** [a]Following Masoretic Text, Septuagint, and Vulgate; Syriac reads *thirty*.

Violence

VIOLENCE

LESLIE VERNICK

(1 Chronicles 11:23)

Murders, muggings, rapes, riots—daily we are assaulted with reports of hideous crimes perpetrated upon innocent victims. But violence isn't new. As early as Genesis, the Bible tells us that the "earth was filled with violence" (Gen. 6:11). The Old Testament reveals humankind's tendency to resort to violence as a means of gaining control, taking revenge, fighting back, or asserting authority. The reasons for violence in the Bible are the same reasons people use it today.

Violence is evil and God hates those who love it (Ps. 11:5). He warns believers not to envy people of violence or choose any of their behaviors (Prov. 3:31). A Christian's life is to be characterized by love, kindness, humility, gentleness, and forgiveness—not selfishness, anger and violence (Col. 3:1–17).

Christians are not immune to the devastating effects of violence or the temptation to use it, however. Many have been victims, not only perpetrated by strangers, but by the very people they live with and love. Behind the closed doors of many homes a secret kind of violence lurks, leaving tragic scars on its victims and causing lifelong consequences. People in such cases have suffered silently from relentless verbal cruelty, or physical and sometimes sexual abuse.

God cares deeply for the victims of violence. Throughout the psalms, David cries out for deliverance from the hand of the oppressor. God has a tender heart toward those who have been victimized by cruelty and violence (Ps. 5; 7; 10; 140). They can take comfort in the fact that a decisive judgment awaits those who oppress and hurt others (Rom. 12:19).

How are Christians to respond to violence when they face it? Should they resist when someone is violent toward them? The apostle Paul wrote that in his own life, he *did* fight back against violence. Instead of fists, guns, knives, or ugly words however, he used the weapons of righteousness (2 Cor. 6:3–10). Believers are in a war —a war of good versus evil, but they are not to fight a war like the world does (2 Cor. 10:3, 4). They can win this war against evil by overcoming evil with good. *Overcome* is a fighting word. How do they win over evil with good? And what does this kind of good look like?

1. *It is good to protect ourselves from violent people.*
Proverbs 27:12 says "a prudent man foresees evil and hides himself." The angel of the Lord warned Joseph to take the baby Jesus and escape to Egypt because Herod was plotting to kill Him. The apostle Paul escaped from those who sought to stone him. Believers should do what they can to remove themselves from violent or potentially violent situations.

2. *It is good to expose deeds done in darkness.*
Ephesians 5:11 says that believers are to "have no fellowship with the unfruitful works of darkness, but rather expose them." A woman was sexually assaulted by a male nurse after her surgery. Eventually she mustered up the courage to tell someone and expose the violence done to her. Her speaking up brought about changes in the way patients were handled after surgery, and hospital employees were more

rigorously screened. Evil attacked this woman, but she exposed it to keep it from harming others, and thus overcame it.

3. *It is good to speak the truth in love (Eph. 4:25).*
One woman's husband attacked her with violent, ugly words. She was afraid to confront him. Although her fears were legitimate, the only pathway to overcome this evil in her marriage was to speak the truth that his behavior was sinful, hurtful, and not a legitimate form of headship in the home. By speaking the truth from a loving heart, she demonstrated to her husband that she wasn't attacking him but, instead, was genuinely concerned for their relationship and his own spiritual well-being. She overcame evil with good.

4. *It is good to allow violent people to experience the consequences of their actions (Prov. 19:19).*
One of life's great teachers is consequences. When someone is sinned against by a violent person, it is not wrong to use the legal means of protection and justice that God provides. It is entirely legitimate to call the police, press charges, and separate oneself so that the violent person learns that this kind of behavior is unacceptable.

5. *It is good to be gracious to an enemy (Rom. 12:20).*
The last thing that people feel like doing is to be gracious to someone who has hurt them. Yet God speaks of kindness as a means of shaming an enemy. Joseph was kind and gracious to his brothers in spite of their cruelty toward him. Being kind and gracious doesn't mean to ignore the wrong or pretend it didn't happen. It means that the sin doesn't define the one sinned against. It doesn't shape them or make them into something evil. It was by Joseph's response to violence, injustice, deceit, and treachery that good won out. He reminded his brothers, "You meant evil against me; but God meant it for good" (Gen. 50:20).

God gives His people the weapons of righteousness to fight against evil and violence. These weapons may seem feeble to a spiritually untrained eye, but Paul says that they are "mighty in God" (2 Cor. 10:4). So let's "take up the whole armor of God" (Eph. 6:13) so that we can stand firm and fight the fight against evil and violence in our homes and communities.

FURTHER MEDITATION:

Other passages to study about the issue of violence include:

- Proverbs 13:2
- Isaiah 53:5
- Matthew 5:38–48
- Ephesians 4:26–32
- 1 Peter 4:15

To Learn More: Turn to the key passage note on violence at Psalm 11:5 on page 685. See also the personality profile of Naboth and Ahab on page 469.

against three hundred *men*, killed *them*, and won a name among *these* three. [21]Of the three he was more honored than the other two men. Therefore he became their captain. However he did not attain to the *first* three.

[22]Benaiah was the son of Jehoiada, the son of a valiant man from Kabzeel, who had done many deeds. He had killed two lion-like heroes of Moab. He also had gone down and killed a lion in the midst of a pit on a snowy day. [23]And he killed an Egyptian, a man of *great* height, five cubits tall. In the Egyptian's hand *there was* a spear like a weaver's beam; and he went down to him with a staff, wrested the spear out of the Egyptian's hand, and killed him with his own spear. [24]These *things* Benaiah the son of Jehoiada did, and won a name among three mighty men. [25]Indeed he was more honored than the thirty, but he did not attain to the *first* three. And David appointed him over his guard.

[26]Also the mighty warriors *were* Asahel the brother of Joab, Elhanan the son of Dodo of Bethlehem, [27]Shammoth the Harorite,[a] Helez the Pelonite,[b] [28]Ira the son of Ikkesh the Tekoite, Abiezer the Anathothite, [29]Sibbechai the Hushathite, Ilai the Ahohite, [30]Maharai the Netophathite, Heled[a] the son of Baanah the Netophathite, [31]Ithai[a] the son of Ribai of Gibeah, of the sons of Benjamin, Benaiah the Pirathonite, [32]Hurai[a] of the brooks of Gaash, Abiel[b] the Arbathite, [33]Azmaveth the Baharumite,[a] Eliahba the Shaalbonite, [34]the sons of Hashem the Gizonite, Jonathan the son of Shageh the Hararite, [35]Ahiam the son of Sacar the Hararite, Eliphal the son of Ur, [36]Hepher the Mecherathite, Ahijah the Pelonite, [37]Hezro the Carmelite, Naarai the son of Ezbai, [38]Joel the brother of Nathan, Mibhar the son of Hagri, [39]Zelek the Ammonite, Naharai the Berothite[a] (the armorbearer of Joab the son of Zeruiah), [40]Ira the Ithrite, Gareb the Ithrite, [41]Uriah the Hittite, Zabad the son of Ahlai, [42]Adina the son of Shiza the Reubenite (a chief of the Reubenites) and thirty with him, [43]Hanan the son of Maachah, Joshaphat the Mithnite, [44]Uzzia the Ashterathite, Shama and Jeiel the sons of Hotham the Aroerite, [45]Jediael the son of Shimri, and Joha his brother, the Tizite, [46]Eliel the Mahavite, Jeribai and Joshaviah the sons of Elnaam, Ithmah the Moabite, [47]Eliel, Obed, and Jaasiel the Mezobaite.

The Growth of David's Army

12 Now these *were* the men who came to David at Ziklag while he was still a fugitive from Saul the son of Kish; and they *were* among the mighty men, helpers in the war, [2]armed with bows, using both the right hand and the left in *hurling* stones and *shooting* arrows with the bow. *They were* of Benjamin, Saul's brethren.

[3]The chief *was* Ahiezer, then Joash, the sons of Shemaah the Gibeathite; Jeziel and Pelet the sons of Azmaveth; Berachah, and Jehu the Anathothite; [4]Ishmaiah the Gibeonite, a mighty man among the thirty, and over the thirty; Jeremiah, Jahaziel, Johanan, and Jozabad the Gederathite; [5]Eluzai, Jerimoth, Bealiah, Shemariah, and Shephatiah the Haruphite; [6]Elkanah, Jisshiah, Azarel, Joezer, and Jashobeam, the Korahites; [7]and Joelah and Zebadiah the sons of Jeroham of Gedor.

[8]*Some* Gadites joined David at the stronghold in the wilderness, mighty men of valor, men trained for battle, who could handle shield and spear, whose faces *were like* the faces of lions, and *were* as swift as gazelles on the mountains: [9]Ezer the first, Obadiah the second, Eliab the third, [10]Mishmannah the fourth, Jeremiah the fifth, [11]Attai the sixth, Eliel the seventh, [12]Johanan the eighth, Elzabad the ninth, [13]Jeremiah the tenth, and Machbanai the eleventh. [14]These *were* from the sons of Gad, captains of the army; the least was over a hundred, and the greatest was over a thousand. [15]These *are* the ones who crossed the Jordan in the first month, when it had overflowed all its banks; and they put to flight all *those* in the valleys, to the east and to the west.

[16]Then some of the sons of Benjamin and Judah came to David at the stronghold. [17]And David went out to meet them, and answered and said to them, "If you have come peaceably to me to help me, my heart will be united with you; but if to betray me to my enemies, since *there is* no wrong in my hands, may the God of our fathers look and bring judgment."

11:27 [a]Spelled *Harodite* in 2 Samuel 23:25 [b]Called *Paltite* in 2 Samuel 23:26 **11:30** [a]Spelled *Heleb* in 2 Samuel 23:29 and *Heldai* in 1 Chronicles 27:15 **11:31** [a]Spelled *Ittai* in 2 Samuel 23:29 **11:32** [a]Spelled *Hiddai* in 2 Samuel 23:30 [b]Spelled *Abi-Albon* in 2 Samuel 23:31 **11:33** [a]Spelled *Barhumite* in 2 Samuel 23:31 **11:39** [a]Spelled *Beerothite* in 2 Samuel 23:37

18Then the Spirit came upon Amasai, chief of the captains, *and he said:*

> "*We are* yours, O David;
> We *are* on your side, O son of Jesse!
> Peace, peace to you,
> And peace to your helpers!
> For your God helps you."

So David received them, and made them captains of the troop.

19And *some* from Manasseh defected to David when he was going with the Philistines to battle against Saul; but they did not help them, for the lords of the Philistines sent him away by agreement, saying, "He may defect to his master Saul *and endanger* our heads." 20When he went to Ziklag, those of Manasseh who defected to him were Adnah, Jozabad, Jediael, Michael, Jozabad, Elihu, and Zillethai, captains of the thousands who *were* from Manasseh. 21And they helped David against the bands *of raiders,* for they *were* all mighty men of valor, and they were captains in the army. 22For at *that* time they came to David day by day to help him, until *it was* a great army, like the army of God.

David's Army at Hebron

23Now these *were* the numbers of the divisions *that were* equipped for war, *and* came to David at Hebron to turn *over* the kingdom of Saul to him, according to the word of the LORD: 24of the sons of Judah bearing shield and spear, six thousand eight hundred armed for war; 25of the sons of Simeon, mighty men of valor fit for war, seven thousand one hundred; 26of the sons of Levi four thousand six hundred; 27Jehoiada, the leader of the Aaronites, and with him three thousand seven hundred; 28Zadok, a young man, a valiant warrior, and from his father's house twenty-two captains; 29of the sons of Benjamin, relatives of Saul, three thousand (until then the greatest part of them had remained loyal to the house of Saul); 30of the sons of Ephraim twenty thousand eight hundred, mighty men of valor, famous men throughout their father's house; 31of the half-tribe of Manasseh eighteen thousand, who were designated by name to come and make David king; 32of the sons of Issachar who had understanding of the times, to know what Israel ought to do, their chiefs were two hundred; and all their brethren were at their command; 33of Zebulun there were fifty thousand who went out to battle, expert in war with all weapons of war, stouthearted men who could keep ranks; 34of Naphtali one thousand captains, and with them thirty-seven thousand with shield and spear; 35of the Danites who could keep battle formation, twenty-eight thousand six hundred; 36of Asher, those who could go out to war, able to keep battle formation, forty thousand; 37of the Reubenites and the Gadites and the half-tribe of Manasseh, from the other side of the Jordan, one hundred and twenty thousand armed for battle with every *kind* of weapon of war.

38All these men of war, who could keep ranks, came to Hebron with a loyal heart, to make David king over all Israel; and all the rest of Israel *were* of one mind to make David king. 39And they were there with David three days, eating and drinking, for their brethren had prepared for them. 40Moreover those who were near to them, from as far away as Issachar and Zebulun and Naphtali, were bringing food on donkeys and camels, on mules and oxen—provisions of flour and cakes of figs and cakes of raisins, wine and oil and oxen and sheep abundantly, for *there was* joy in Israel.

The Ark Brought from Kirjath Jearim

13 Then David consulted with the captains of thousands and hundreds, *and* with every leader. 2And David said to all the assembly of Israel, "If *it seems* good to you, and if it is of the LORD our God, let us send out to our brethren everywhere *who are* left in all the land of Israel, and with them to the priests and Levites *who are* in their cities *and* their common-lands, that they may gather together to us; 3and let us bring the ark of our God back to us, for we have not inquired at it since the days of Saul." 4Then all the assembly said that they would do so, for the thing was right in the eyes of all the people.

5So David gathered all Israel together, from Shihor in Egypt to as far as the entrance of Hamath, to bring the ark of God from Kirjath Jearim. 6And David and all Israel went up to Baalah,[a] to Kirjath Jearim, which belonged to Judah, to bring up from there the ark of God the LORD, who dwells *between* the cherubim, where *His* name is proclaimed. 7So they

---

13:6 [a]Called *Baale Judah* in 2 Samuel 6:2

carried the ark of God on a new cart from the house of Abinadab, and Uzza and Ahio drove the cart. 8Then David and all Israel played *music* before God with all *their* might, with singing, on harps, on stringed instruments, on tambourines, on cymbals, and with trumpets.

9And when they came to Chidon's[a] threshing floor, Uzza put out his hand to hold the ark, for the oxen stumbled. 10Then the anger of the LORD was aroused against Uzza, and He struck him because he put his hand to the ark; and he died there before God. 11And David became angry because of the LORD's outbreak against Uzza; therefore that place is called Perez Uzza[a] to this day. 12David was afraid of God that day, saying, "How can I bring the ark of God to me?"

13So David would not move the ark with him into the City of David, but took it aside into the house of Obed-Edom the Gittite. 14The ark of God remained with the family of Obed-Edom in his house three months. And the LORD blessed the house of Obed-Edom and all that he had.

DAVID ESTABLISHED AT JERUSALEM

14 Now Hiram king of Tyre sent messengers to David, and cedar trees, with masons and carpenters, to build him a house. 2So David knew that the LORD had established him as king over Israel, for his kingdom was highly exalted for the sake of His people Israel.

3Then David took more wives in Jerusalem, and David begot more sons and daughters. 4And these are the names of his children whom he had in Jerusalem: Shammua,[a] Shobab, Nathan, Solomon, 5Ibhar, Elishua,[a] Elpelet,[b] 6Nogah, Nepheg, Japhia, 7Elishama, Beeliada,[a] and Eliphelet.

THE PHILISTINES DEFEATED

8Now when the Philistines heard that David had been anointed king over all Israel, all the Philistines went up to search for David. And David heard *of it* and went out against them. 9Then the Philistines went and made a raid on the Valley of Rephaim. 10And David inquired of God, saying, "Shall I go up against the Philistines? Will You deliver them into my hand?"

The LORD said to him, "Go up, for I will deliver them into your hand."

11So they went up to Baal Perazim, and David defeated them there. Then David said, "God has broken through my enemies by my hand like a breakthrough of water." Therefore they called the name of that place Baal Perazim.[a] 12And when they left their gods there, David gave a commandment, and they were burned with fire.

13Then the Philistines once again made a raid on the valley. 14Therefore David inquired again of God, and God said to him, "You shall not go up after them; circle around them, and come upon them in front of the mulberry trees. 15And it shall be, when you hear a sound of marching in the tops of the mulberry trees, then you shall go out to battle, for God has gone out before you to strike the camp of the Philistines." 16So David did as God commanded him, and they drove back the army of the Philistines from Gibeon as far as Gezer. 17Then the fame of David went out into all lands, and the LORD brought the fear of him upon all nations.

13:9 [a]Called *Nachon* in 2 Samuel 6:6
13:11 [a]Literally *Outburst Against Uzza*
14:4 [a]Spelled *Shimea* in 3:5 **14:5** [a]Spelled *Elishama* in 3:6 [b]Spelled *Eliphelet* in 3:6
14:7 [a]Spelled *Eliada* in 3:8 **14:11** [a]Literally *Master of Breakthroughs*

SOUL NOTE

Seek God's Plans First *(13:9–12)* Moses had instructed that the ark of the covenant was to be carried only with poles and only by priests (Num. 4:1–16). Uzza's intentions may have been noble, but this casual mistreatment of the ark led to his death. The entire incident shook David deeply. David stopped, stowed the ark safely, and went back to find out the correct manner for transporting it. God's people must take His commands seriously. To treat them casually is to face severe consequences. **Topic: Knowing God**

The Ark Brought to Jerusalem

15 *David* built houses for himself in the City of David; and he prepared a place for the ark of God, and pitched a tent for it. [2]Then David said, "No one may carry the ark of God but the Levites, for the LORD has chosen them to carry the ark of God and to minister before Him forever." [3]And David gathered all Israel together at Jerusalem, to bring up the ark of the LORD to its place, which he had prepared for it. [4]Then David assembled the children of Aaron and the Levites: [5]of the sons of Kohath, Uriel the chief, and one hundred and twenty of his brethren; [6]of the sons of Merari, Asaiah the chief, and two hundred and twenty of his brethren; [7]of the sons of Gershom, Joel the chief, and one hundred and thirty of his brethren; [8]of the sons of Elizaphan, Shemaiah the chief, and two hundred of his brethren; [9]of the sons of Hebron, Eliel the chief, and eighty of his brethren; [10]of the sons of Uzziel, Amminadab the chief, and one hundred and twelve of his brethren.

[11]And David called for Zadok and Abiathar the priests, and for the Levites: for Uriel, Asaiah, Joel, Shemaiah, Eliel, and Amminadab. [12]He said to them, "You *are* the heads of the fathers' *houses* of the Levites; sanctify yourselves, you and your brethren, that you may bring up the ark of the LORD God of Israel to *the place* I have prepared for it. [13]For because you *did* not *do it* the first *time,* the LORD our God broke out against us, because we did not consult Him about the proper order."

[14]So the priests and the Levites sanctified themselves to bring up the ark of the LORD God of Israel. [15]And the children of the Levites bore the ark of God on their shoulders, by its poles, as Moses had commanded according to the word of the LORD.

[16]Then David spoke to the leaders of the Levites to appoint their brethren *to be* the singers accompanied by instruments of music, stringed instruments, harps, and cymbals, by raising the voice with resounding joy. [17]So the Levites appointed Heman the son of Joel; and of his brethren, Asaph the son of Berechiah; and of their brethren, the sons of Merari, Ethan the son of Kushaiah; [18]and with them their brethren of the second *rank:* Zechariah, Ben,[a] Jaaziel, Shemiramoth, Jehiel, Unni, Eliab, Benaiah, Maaseiah, Mattithiah, Elipheleh, Mikneiah, Obed-Edom, and Jeiel, the gatekeepers; [19]the singers, Heman, Asaph, and Ethan, *were* to sound the cymbals of bronze; [20]Zechariah, Aziel, Shemiramoth, Jehiel, Unni, Eliab, Maaseiah, and Benaiah, with strings according to Alamoth; [21]Mattithiah, Elipheleh, Mikneiah, Obed-Edom, Jeiel, and Azaziah, to direct with harps on the Sheminith; [22]Chenaniah, leader of the Levites, was instructor *in charge of* the music, because he *was* skillful; [23]Berechiah and Elkanah *were* doorkeepers for the ark; [24]Shebaniah, Joshaphat, Nethanel, Amasai, Zechariah, Benaiah, and Eliezer, the priests, were to blow the trumpets before the ark of God; and Obed-Edom and Jehiah, doorkeepers for the ark.

[25]So David, the elders of Israel, and the captains over thousands went to bring up the ark of the covenant of the LORD from the house of Obed-Edom with joy. [26]And so it was, when God helped the Levites who bore the ark of the covenant of the LORD, that they offered seven bulls and seven rams. [27]David was clothed with a robe of fine linen, as were all the Levites who bore the ark, the singers, and Chenaniah the music master *with* the singers. David also wore a linen ephod. [28]Thus all Israel brought up the ark of the covenant of the LORD with shouting and with the sound of the horn, with trumpets and with cymbals, making music with stringed instruments and harps.

[29]And it happened, *as* the ark of the covenant of the LORD came to the City of David, that Michal, Saul's daughter, looked through a window and saw King David whirling and playing music; and she despised him in her heart.

The Ark Placed in the Tabernacle

16 So they brought the ark of God, and set it in the midst of the tabernacle that David had erected for it. Then they offered burnt offerings and peace offerings before God. [2]And when David had finished offering the burnt offerings and the peace offerings, he blessed the people in the name of the LORD. [3]Then he distributed to everyone of Israel, both man and woman, to everyone a loaf of bread, a piece *of meat,* and a cake of raisins.

[4]And he appointed some of the Levites to minister before the ark of the LORD, to

15:18 [a]Following Masoretic Text and Vulgate; Septuagint omits *Ben.*

commemorate, to thank, and to praise the
LORD God of Israel: [5]Asaph the chief, and next
to him Zechariah, *then* Jeiel, Shemiramoth,
Jehiel, Mattithiah, Eliab, Benaiah, and Obed-
Edom: Jeiel with stringed instruments and
harps, but Asaph made music with cymbals;
[6]Benaiah and Jahaziel the priests regularly
blew the trumpets before the ark of the covenant of God.

DAVID'S SONG OF THANKSGIVING

[7]On that day David first delivered *this psalm*
into the hand of Asaph and his brethren, to
thank the LORD:

8 Oh, give thanks to the LORD!
Call upon His name;
Make known His deeds among the
peoples!
9 Sing to Him, sing psalms to Him;
Talk of all His wondrous works!
10 Glory in His holy name;
Let the hearts of those rejoice who seek
the LORD!
11 Seek the LORD and His strength;
Seek His face evermore!
12 Remember His marvelous works which
He has done,
His wonders, and the judgments of His
mouth,
13 O seed of Israel His servant,
You children of Jacob, His chosen ones!

14 He *is* the LORD our God;
His judgments *are* in all the earth.
15 Remember His covenant forever,
The word which He commanded, for a
thousand generations,
16 *The covenant which* He made with
Abraham,
And His oath to Isaac,
17 And confirmed it to Jacob for a statute,
To Israel *for* an everlasting covenant,
18 Saying, "To you I will give the land of
Canaan
As the allotment of your inheritance,"
19 When you were few in number,
Indeed very few, and strangers in it.

20 When they went from one nation to
another,
And from *one* kingdom to another
people,
21 He permitted no man to do them wrong;
Yes, He rebuked kings for their sakes,
22 *Saying,* "Do not touch My anointed
ones,
And do My prophets no harm."[a]

23 Sing to the LORD, all the earth;
Proclaim the good news of His salvation
from day to day.
24 Declare His glory among the nations,
His wonders among all peoples.

25 For the LORD *is* great and greatly to be
praised;
He *is* also to be feared above all gods.
26 For all the gods of the peoples *are* idols,
But the LORD made the heavens.
27 Honor and majesty *are* before Him;
Strength and gladness are in His place.

28 Give to the LORD, O families of the
peoples,
Give to the LORD glory and strength.
29 Give to the LORD the glory *due* His
name;
Bring an offering, and come before Him.
Oh, worship the LORD in the beauty of
holiness!
30 Tremble before Him, all the earth.
The world also is firmly established,
It shall not be moved.

31 Let the heavens rejoice, and let the earth
be glad;
And let them say among the nations,
"The LORD reigns."
32 Let the sea roar, and all its fullness;
Let the field rejoice, and all that *is* in it.
33 Then the trees of the woods shall rejoice
before the LORD,
For He is coming to judge the earth.[a]

34 Oh, give thanks to the LORD, for *He is*
good!
For His mercy *endures* forever.[a]
35 And say, "Save us, O God of our
salvation;
Gather us together, and deliver us from
the Gentiles,
To give thanks to Your holy name,
To triumph in Your praise."

16:22 [a]Compare verses 8–22 with Psalm 105:1–15
16:33 [a]Compare verses 23–33 with Psalm 96:1–13
16:34 [a]Compare verse 34 with Psalm 106:1

36 Blessed *be* the LORD God of Israel
From everlasting to everlasting![a]

And all the people said, "Amen!" and praised the LORD.

REGULAR WORSHIP MAINTAINED

37So he left Asaph and his brothers there before the ark of the covenant of the LORD to minister before the ark regularly, as every day's work required; 38and Obed-Edom with his sixty-eight brethren, including Obed-Edom the son of Jeduthun, and Hosah, *to be* gatekeepers; 39and Zadok the priest and his brethren the priests, before the tabernacle of the LORD at the high place that *was* at Gibeon, 40to offer burnt offerings to the LORD on the altar of burnt offering regularly morning and evening, and *to do* according to all that is written in the Law of the LORD which He commanded Israel; 41and with them Heman and Jeduthun and the rest who were chosen, who were designated by name, to give thanks to the LORD, because His mercy *endures* forever; 42and with them Heman and Jeduthun, to sound aloud with trumpets and cymbals and the musical instruments of God. Now the sons of Jeduthun *were* gatekeepers.

43Then all the people departed, every man to his house; and David returned to bless his house.

GOD'S COVENANT WITH DAVID

17 Now it came to pass, when David was dwelling in his house, that David said to Nathan the prophet, "See now, I dwell in a house of cedar, but the ark of the covenant of the LORD *is* under tent curtains."

2Then Nathan said to David, "Do all that *is* in your heart, for God *is* with you."

3But it happened that night that the word of God came to Nathan, saying, 4"Go and tell My servant David, 'Thus says the LORD: "You shall not build Me a house to dwell in. 5For I have not dwelt in a house since the time that I brought up Israel, even to this day, but have gone from tent to tent, and from *one* tabernacle *to another.* 6Wherever I have moved about with all Israel, have I ever spoken a word to any of the judges of Israel, whom I commanded to shepherd My people, saying, 'Why have you not built Me a house of cedar?' " ' 7Now therefore, thus shall you say to My servant David, 'Thus says the LORD of hosts: "I took you from the sheepfold, from following the sheep, to be ruler over My people Israel. 8And I have been with you wherever you have gone, and have cut off all your enemies from before you, and have made you a name like the name of the great men who *are* on the earth. 9Moreover I will appoint a place for My people Israel, and will plant them, that they may dwell in a place of their own and move no more; nor shall the sons of wickedness oppress them anymore, as previously, 10since the time that I commanded judges *to be* over My people Israel. Also I will subdue all your enemies. Furthermore I tell you that the LORD will build you a house.[a] 11And it shall be, when your days are fulfilled, when you must go *to be* with your fathers, that I will set up your seed after you, who will be of your sons; and I will establish his kingdom. 12He shall build Me a house, and I will establish his throne forever. 13I will be his Father, and he shall be My son; and I will not take My mercy away from him, as I took *it* from *him* who was before you. 14And I will establish him in My house and in My kingdom forever; and his throne shall be established forever." ' "

16:36 [a]Compare verses 35, 36 with Psalm 106:47, 48 **17:10** [a]That is, a royal dynasty

SOUL NOTE

His Kingdom Forever *(17:12)* David told the prophet Nathan that he wanted to build a temple to house the ark of the covenant. But the Lord told Nathan that David was not to build that temple; rather, his son Solomon would do so. God promised of Solomon, "He shall build Me a house, and I will establish his throne forever." Solomon *did* build a beautiful temple for God in Jerusalem. And a King from David's line—Jesus Christ—still sits on the throne and will do so forever. God always keeps His promises. **Topic: God's Promises**

15According to all these words and according
to all this vision, so Nathan spoke to David.
16Then King David went in and sat before
the LORD; and he said: "Who *am* I, O LORD
God? And what is my house, that You have
brought me this far? 17And *yet* this was a small
thing in Your sight, O God; and You have *also*
spoken of Your servant's house for a great
while to come, and have regarded me according to the rank of a man of high degree,
O LORD God. 18What more can David *say* to
You for the honor of Your servant? For You
know Your servant. 19O LORD, for Your
servant's sake, and according to Your own
heart, You have done all this greatness, in making known all these great things. 20O LORD,
there is none like You, nor *is there any* God besides You, according to all that we have heard
with our ears. 21And who *is* like Your people
Israel, the one nation on the earth whom God
went to redeem for Himself *as* a people—to
make for Yourself a name by great and awesome deeds, by driving out nations from before
Your people whom You redeemed from Egypt?
22For You have made Your people Israel Your
very own people forever; and You, LORD, have
become their God.
23"And now, O LORD, the word which You
have spoken concerning Your servant and
concerning his house, *let it* be established forever, and do as You have said. 24So let it be established, that Your name may be magnified
forever, saying, 'The LORD of hosts, the God of
Israel, *is* Israel's God.' And let the house of
Your servant David be established before You.
25For You, O my God, have revealed to Your
servant that You will build him a house.
Therefore Your servant has found it *in his
heart* to pray before You. 26And now, LORD,
You are God, and have promised this goodness
to Your servant. 27Now You have been pleased
to bless the house of Your servant, that it may
continue before You forever; for You have
blessed it, O LORD, and *it shall be* blessed forever."

DAVID'S FURTHER CONQUESTS

18 After this it came to pass that David
attacked the Philistines, subdued them,
and took Gath and its towns from the hand of
the Philistines. 2Then he defeated Moab, and
the Moabites became David's servants, *and*
brought tribute.
3And David defeated Hadadezer[a] king of
Zobah *as far as* Hamath, as he went to establish his power by the River Euphrates. 4David
took from him one thousand chariots, seven
thousand[a] horsemen, and twenty thousand
foot soldiers. Also David hamstrung all the
chariot *horses,* except that he spared enough
of them for one hundred chariots.
5When the Syrians of Damascus came to
help Hadadezer king of Zobah, David killed
twenty-two thousand of the Syrians. 6Then
David put *garrisons* in Syria of Damascus; and
the Syrians became David's servants, *and*
brought tribute. So the LORD preserved David
wherever he went. 7And David took the
shields of gold that were on the servants of
Hadadezer, and brought them to Jerusalem.
8Also from Tibhath[a] and from Chun, cities of
Hadadezer, David brought a large amount of
bronze, with which Solomon made the bronze
Sea, the pillars, and the articles of bronze.
9Now when Tou[a] king of Hamath heard that
David had defeated all the army of Hadadezer
king of Zobah, 10he sent Hadoram[a] his son to
King David, to greet him and bless him, because he had fought against Hadadezer and
defeated him (for Hadadezer had been at war
with Tou); and *Hadoram brought with him* all
kinds of articles of gold, silver, and bronze.
11King David also dedicated these to the LORD,
along with the silver and gold that he had
brought from all *these* nations—from Edom,
from Moab, from the people of Ammon, from
the Philistines, and from Amalek.
12Moreover Abishai the son of Zeruiah
killed eighteen thousand Edomites[a] in the Valley of Salt. 13He also put garrisons in Edom,
and all the Edomites became David's servants.
And the LORD preserved David wherever he
went.

DAVID'S ADMINISTRATION

14So David reigned over all Israel, and administered judgment and justice to all his people. 15Joab the son of Zeruiah *was* over the
army; Jehoshaphat the son of Ahilud *was* recorder; 16Zadok the son of Ahitub and Abimelech the son of Abiathar *were* the priests;

18:3 [a]Hebrew *Hadarezer,* and so throughout chapters 18 and 19 **18:4** [a]Or *seven hundred* (compare 2 Samuel 8:4) **18:8** [a]Spelled *Betah* in 2 Samuel 8:8 **18:9** [a]Spelled *Toi* in 2 Samuel 8:9, 10 **18:10** [a]Spelled *Joram* in 2 Samuel 8:10 **18:12** [a]Or *Syrians* (compare 2 Samuel 8:13)

Shavsha[a] *was* the scribe; [17]Benaiah the son of Jehoiada *was* over the Cherethites and the Pelethites; and David's sons *were* chief ministers at the king's side.

THE AMMONITES AND SYRIANS DEFEATED

19 It happened after this that Nahash the king of the people of Ammon died, and his son reigned in his place. [2]Then David said, "I will show kindness to Hanun the son of Nahash, because his father showed kindness to me." So David sent messengers to comfort him concerning his father. And David's servants came to Hanun in the land of the people of Ammon to comfort him.

[3]And the princes of the people of Ammon said to Hanun, "Do you think that David really honors your father because he has sent comforters to you? Did his servants not come to you to search and to overthrow and to spy out the land?"

[4]Therefore Hanun took David's servants, shaved them, and cut off their garments in the middle, at their buttocks, and sent them away. [5]Then *some* went and told David about the men; and he sent to meet them, because the men were greatly ashamed. And the king said, "Wait at Jericho until your beards have grown, and *then* return."

[6]When the people of Ammon saw that they had made themselves repulsive to David, Hanun and the people of Ammon sent a thousand talents of silver to hire for themselves chariots and horsemen from Mesopotamia,[a] from Syrian Maacah, and from Zobah.[b] [7]So they hired for themselves thirty-two thousand chariots, with the king of Maacah and his people, who came and encamped before Medeba. Also the people of Ammon gathered together from their cities, and came to battle.

[8]Now when David heard *of it,* he sent Joab and all the army of the mighty men. [9]Then the people of Ammon came out and put themselves in battle array before the gate of the city, and the kings who had come *were* by themselves in the field.

[10]When Joab saw that the battle line was against him before and behind, he chose some of Israel's best, and put *them* in battle array against the Syrians. [11]And the rest of the people he put under the command of Abishai his brother, and they set *themselves* in battle array against the people of Ammon. [12]Then he said, "If the Syrians are too strong for me, then you shall help me; but if the people of Ammon are too strong for you, then I will help you. [13]Be of good courage, and let us be strong for our people and for the cities of our God. And may the LORD do *what is* good in His sight."

[14]So Joab and the people who *were* with him drew near for the battle against the Syrians, and they fled before him. [15]When the people of Ammon saw that the Syrians were fleeing, they also fled before Abishai his brother, and entered the city. So Joab went to Jerusalem.

[16]Now when the Syrians saw that they had been defeated by Israel, they sent messengers and brought the Syrians who were beyond the River,[a] and Shophach[b] the commander of Hadadezer's army *went* before them. [17]When it was told David, he gathered all Israel, crossed over the Jordan and came upon them, and set up in battle array against them. So when David had set up in *battle* array against the Syrians, they fought with him. [18]Then the Syrians fled before Israel; and David killed seven thousand[a] charioteers and forty thousand foot soldiers[b] of the Syrians, and killed Shophach the commander of the army. [19]And when the servants of Hadadezer saw that they were defeated by Israel, they made peace with David and became his servants. So the Syrians were not willing to help the people of Ammon anymore.

RABBAH IS CONQUERED

20 It happened in the spring of the year, at the time kings go out *to battle,* that Joab led out the armed forces and ravaged the country of the people of Ammon, and came and besieged Rabbah. But David stayed at Jerusalem. And Joab defeated Rabbah and overthrew it. [2]Then David took their king's crown from his head, and found it to weigh a talent of gold, and *there were* precious stones in it. And it was set on David's head. Also he brought out the spoil of the city in great abundance. [3]And he brought out the people who *were* in it, and put *them* to work[a] with saws, with iron picks, and with axes. So David did to

---

18:16 [a]Spelled *Seraiah* in 2 Samuel 8:17
19:6 [a]Hebrew *Aram Naharaim* [b]Spelled *Zoba* in 2 Samuel 10:6 **19:16** [a]That is, the Euphrates [b]Spelled *Shobach* in 2 Samuel 10:16 **19:18** [a]Or *seven hundred* (compare 2 Samuel 10:18) [b]Or *horsemen* (compare 2 Samuel 10:18)
20:3 [a]Septuagint reads *cut them.*

all the cities of the people of Ammon. Then
David and all the people returned *to* Jerusalem.

Philistine Giants Destroyed

4Now it happened afterward that war broke
out at Gezer with the Philistines, at which
time Sibbechai the Hushathite killed Sippai,[a]
who was one of the sons of the giant. And they
were subdued.
5Again there was war with the Philistines,
and Elhanan the son of Jair[a] killed Lahmi the
brother of Goliath the Gittite, the shaft of
whose spear *was* like a weaver's beam.
6Yet again there was war at Gath, where
there was a man of *great* stature, with twenty-
four fingers and toes, six *on each hand* and
six *on each foot;* and he also was born to the
giant. 7So when he defied Israel, Jonathan the
son of Shimea,[a] David's brother, killed him.
8These were born to the giant in Gath, and
they fell by the hand of David and by the hand
of his servants.

The Census of Israel and Judah

21 Now Satan stood up against Israel,
and moved David to number Israel.
2So David said to Joab and to the leaders of
the people, "Go, number Israel from Beersheba to Dan, and bring the number of them
to me that I may know *it.*"
3And Joab answered, "May the LORD make
His people a hundred times more than they
are. But, my lord the king, *are* they not all my
lord's servants? Why then does my lord require this thing? Why should he be a cause of
guilt in Israel?"
4Nevertheless the king's word prevailed
against Joab. Therefore Joab departed and
went throughout all Israel and came to Jerusalem. 5Then Joab gave the sum of the number
of the people to David. All Israel *had* one million one hundred thousand men who drew the
sword, and Judah *had* four hundred and seventy thousand men who drew the sword. 6But
he did not count Levi and Benjamin among
them, for the king's word was abominable to
Joab.
7And God was displeased with this thing;
therefore He struck Israel. 8So David said to
God, "I have sinned greatly, because I have
done this thing; but now, I pray, take away the
iniquity of Your servant, for I have done very
foolishly."
9Then the LORD spoke to Gad, David's seer,
saying, 10"Go and tell David, saying, 'Thus
says the LORD: "I offer you three *things;*
choose one of them for yourself, that I may do
it to you."'"
11So Gad came to David and said to him,
"Thus says the LORD: 'Choose for yourself,
12either three[a] years of famine, or three
months to be defeated by your foes with the
sword of your enemies overtaking *you,* or else
for three days the sword of the LORD—the
plague in the land, with the angel[b] of the LORD
destroying throughout all the territory of Israel.' Now consider what answer I should take
back to Him who sent me."
13And David said to Gad, "I am in great distress. Please let me fall into the hand of the
LORD, for His mercies *are* very great; but do
not let me fall into the hand of man."
14So the LORD sent a plague upon Israel, and
seventy thousand men of Israel fell. 15And
God sent an angel to Jerusalem to destroy it.
As he[a] was destroying, the LORD looked and
relented of the disaster, and said to the angel
who was destroying, "It is enough; now re-

20:4 [a]Spelled *Saph* in 2 Samuel 21:18
20:5 [a]Spelled *Jaare-Oregim* in 2 Samuel 21:19
20:7 [a]Spelled *Shimeah* in 2 Samuel 21:21 and *Shammah* in 1 Samuel 16:9 **21:12** [a]Or *seven* (compare 2 Samuel 24:13) [b]Or *Angel,* and so elsewhere in this chapter **21:15** [a]Or *He*

SOUL NOTE

In His Hands *(21:13)* God dealt severely with David for his sin of numbering the people, and He gave him three choices of punishment. David's response was that he would rather "fall into the hand of the LORD" than into the hands of his enemies. Yet David still agonized because, either way, many people would pay for his sin. Even in the anguish of the moment, however, David realized, as we all must, that our lives are ultimately in God's hands. **Topic: Crises**

strain your[b] hand." And the angel of the LORD stood by the threshing floor of Ornan[c] the Jebusite.

16Then David lifted his eyes and saw the angel of the LORD standing between earth and heaven, having in his hand a drawn sword stretched out over Jerusalem. So David and the elders, clothed in sackcloth, fell on their faces. 17And David said to God, "Was it not I who commanded the people to be numbered? I am the one who has sinned and done evil indeed; but these sheep, what have they done? Let Your hand, I pray, O LORD my God, be against me and my father's house, but not against Your people that they should be plagued."

18Therefore, the angel of the LORD commanded Gad to say to David that David should go and erect an altar to the LORD on the threshing floor of Ornan the Jebusite. 19So David went up at the word of Gad, which he had spoken in the name of the LORD. 20Now Ornan turned and saw the angel; and his four sons *who were* with him hid themselves, but Ornan continued threshing wheat. 21So David came to Ornan, and Ornan looked and saw David. And he went out from the threshing floor, and bowed before David with *his* face to the ground. 22Then David said to Ornan, "Grant me the place of *this* threshing floor, that I may build an altar on it to the LORD. You shall grant it to me at the full price, that the plague may be withdrawn from the people."

23But Ornan said to David, "Take *it* to yourself, and let my lord the king do *what is* good in his eyes. Look, I *also* give *you* the oxen for burnt offerings, the threshing implements for wood, and the wheat for the grain offering; I give *it* all."

24Then King David said to Ornan, "No, but I will surely buy *it* for the full price, for I will not take what is yours for the LORD, nor offer burnt offerings with *that which* costs *me* nothing." 25So David gave Ornan six hundred shekels of gold by weight for the place. 26And David built there an altar to the LORD, and offered burnt offerings and peace offerings, and called on the LORD; and He answered him from heaven by fire on the altar of burnt offering.

27So the LORD commanded the angel, and he returned his sword to its sheath.

28At that time, when David saw that the LORD had answered him on the threshing floor of Ornan the Jebusite, he sacrificed there. 29For the tabernacle of the LORD and the altar of the burnt offering, which Moses had made in the wilderness, *were* at that time at the high place in Gibeon. 30But David could not go before it to inquire of God, for he was afraid of the sword of the angel of the LORD.

DAVID PREPARES TO BUILD THE TEMPLE

22 Then David said, "This *is* the house of the LORD God, and this *is* the altar of burnt offering for Israel." 2So David commanded to gather the aliens who *were* in the land of Israel; and he appointed masons to cut hewn stones to build the house of God. 3And David prepared iron in abundance for the nails of the doors of the gates and for the joints, and bronze in abundance beyond measure, 4and cedar trees in abundance; for the Sidonians and those from Tyre brought much cedar wood to David.

5Now David said, "Solomon my son *is* young and inexperienced, and the house to be built for the LORD *must be* exceedingly magnificent, famous and glorious throughout all countries. I will now make preparation for it." So David made abundant preparations before his death.

6Then he called for his son Solomon, and charged him to build a house for the LORD God of Israel. 7And David said to Solomon: "My son, as for me, it was in my mind to build a house to the name of the LORD my God; 8but the word of the LORD came to me, saying, 'You have shed much blood and have made great wars; you shall not build a house for My name, because you have shed much blood on the earth in My sight. 9Behold, a son shall be born to you, who shall be a man of rest; and I will give him rest from all his enemies all around. His name shall be Solomon,[a] for I will give peace and quietness to Israel in his days. 10He shall build a house for My name, and he shall be My son, and I *will be* his Father; and I will establish the throne of his kingdom over Israel forever.' 11Now, my son, may the LORD be with you; and may you prosper, and build the house of the LORD your God, as He has said to you. 12Only may the LORD give you wisdom and understanding, and give you charge concerning Israel, that you may keep the law

21:15 [b]Or *Your* [c]Spelled *Araunah* in 2 Samuel 24:16 **22:9** [a]Literally *Peaceful*

of the LORD your God. [13]Then you will prosper, if you take care to fulfill the statutes and judgments with which the LORD charged Moses concerning Israel. Be strong and of good courage; do not fear nor be dismayed. [14]Indeed I have taken much trouble to prepare for the house of the LORD one hundred thousand talents of gold and one million talents of silver, and bronze and iron beyond measure, for it is so abundant. I have prepared timber and stone also, and you may add to them. [15]Moreover *there are* workmen with you in abundance: woodsmen and stonecutters, and all types of skillful men for every kind of work. [16]Of gold and silver and bronze and iron *there is* no limit. Arise and begin working, and the LORD be with you."

[17]David also commanded all the leaders of Israel to help Solomon his son, *saying,* [18]"*Is* not the LORD your God with you? And has He *not* given you rest on every side? For He has given the inhabitants of the land into my hand, and the land is subdued before the LORD and before His people. [19]Now set your heart and your soul to seek the LORD your God. Therefore arise and build the sanctuary of the LORD God, to bring the ark of the covenant of the LORD and the holy articles of God into the house that is to be built for the name of the LORD."

THE DIVISIONS OF THE LEVITES

23 So when David was old and full of days, he made his son Solomon king over Israel.

[2]And he gathered together all the leaders of Israel, with the priests and the Levites. [3]Now the Levites were numbered from the age of thirty years and above; and the number of individual males was thirty-eight thousand. [4]Of these, twenty-four thousand *were* to look after the work of the house of the LORD, six thousand *were* officers and judges, [5]four thousand *were* gatekeepers, and four thousand praised the LORD with *musical* instruments, "which I made," *said David,* "for giving praise."

[6]Also David separated them into divisions among the sons of Levi: Gershon, Kohath, and Merari.

[7]Of the Gershonites: Laadan[a] and Shimei. [8]The sons of Laadan: the first Jehiel, then Zetham and Joel—three *in all.* [9]The sons of Shimei: Shelomith, Haziel, and Haran—three *in all.* These were the heads of the fathers' *houses* of Laadan. [10]And the sons of Shimei: Jahath, Zina,[a] Jeush, and Beriah. These *were* the four sons of Shimei. [11]Jahath was the first and Zizah the second. But Jeush and Beriah did not have many sons; therefore they were assigned as one father's house.

[12]The sons of Kohath: Amram, Izhar, Hebron, and Uzziel—four *in all.* [13]The sons of Amram: Aaron and Moses; and Aaron was set apart, he and his sons forever, that he should sanctify the most holy things, to burn incense before the LORD, to minister to Him, and to give the blessing in His name forever. [14]Now the sons of Moses the man of God were reckoned to the tribe of Levi. [15]The sons of Moses *were* Gershon[a] and Eliezer. [16]Of the sons of Gershon, Shebuel[a] *was* the first. [17]Of the descendants of Eliezer, Rehabiah was the first. And Eliezer had no other sons, but the sons of Rehabiah were very many. [18]Of the sons of Izhar, Shelomith *was* the first. [19]Of the sons of Hebron, Jeriah *was* the first, Amariah the second, Jahaziel the third, and Jekameam the fourth. [20]Of the sons of Uzziel, Michah *was* the first and Jesshiah the second.

[21]The sons of Merari *were* Mahli and Mushi. The sons of Mahli *were* Eleazar and Kish. [22]And Eleazar died, and had no sons, but only daughters; and their brethren, the sons of Kish, took them *as wives.* [23]The sons of Mushi *were* Mahli, Eder, and Jeremoth—three *in all.*

[24]These *were* the sons of Levi by their fathers' houses—the heads of the fathers' *houses* as they were counted individually by the number of their names, who did the work for the service of the house of the LORD, from the age of twenty years and above.

[25]For David said, "The LORD God of Israel has given rest to His people, that they may dwell in Jerusalem forever"; [26]and also to the Levites, "They shall no longer carry the tabernacle, or any of the articles for its service." [27]For by the last words of David the Levites *were* numbered from twenty years old and above; [28]because their duty *was* to help the sons of Aaron in the service of the house of the LORD, in the courts and in the chambers, in the purifying of all holy things and the work of the service of the house of God, [29]both with

---

23:7 [a]Spelled *Libni* in Exodus 6:17
23:10 [a]Septuagint and Vulgate read *Zizah* (compare verse 11). **23:15** [a]Hebrew *Gershom* (compare 6:16) **23:16** [a]Spelled *Shubael* in 24:20

the showbread and the fine flour for the grain offering, with the unleavened cakes and *what is baked in* the pan, with what is mixed and with all kinds of measures and sizes; [30]to stand every morning to thank and praise the LORD, and likewise at evening; [31]and at every presentation of a burnt offering to the LORD on the Sabbaths and on the New Moons and on the set feasts, by number according to the ordinance governing them, regularly before the LORD; [32]and that they should attend to the needs of the tabernacle of meeting, the needs of the holy *place,* and the needs of the sons of Aaron their brethren in the work of the house of the LORD.

THE DIVISIONS OF THE PRIESTS

24 Now *these are* the divisions of the sons of Aaron. The sons of Aaron *were* Nadab, Abihu, Eleazar, and Ithamar. [2]And Nadab and Abihu died before their father, and had no children; therefore Eleazar and Ithamar ministered as priests. [3]Then David with Zadok of the sons of Eleazar, and Ahimelech of the sons of Ithamar, divided them according to the schedule of their service.

[4]There were more leaders found of the sons of Eleazar than of the sons of Ithamar, and *thus* they were divided. Among the sons of Eleazar *were* sixteen heads of *their* fathers' houses, and eight heads of their fathers' houses among the sons of Ithamar. [5]Thus they were divided by lot, one group as another, for there were officials of the sanctuary and officials *of the house* of God, from the sons of Eleazar and from the sons of Ithamar. [6]And the scribe, Shemaiah the son of Nethanel, *one of* the Levites, wrote them down before the king, the leaders, Zadok the priest, Ahimelech the son of Abiathar, and the heads of the fathers' *houses* of the priests and Levites, one father's house taken for Eleazar and *one* for Ithamar.

[7]Now the first lot fell to Jehoiarib, the second to Jedaiah, [8]the third to Harim, the fourth to Seorim, [9]the fifth to Malchijah, the sixth to Mijamin, [10]the seventh to Hakkoz, the eighth to Abijah, [11]the ninth to Jeshua, the tenth to Shecaniah, [12]the eleventh to Eliashib, the twelfth to Jakim, [13]the thirteenth to Huppah, the fourteenth to Jeshebeab, [14]the fifteenth to Bilgah, the sixteenth to Immer, [15]the seventeenth to Hezir, the eighteenth to Happizzez,[a] [16]the nineteenth to Pethahiah, the twentieth to Jehezekel,[a] [17]the twenty-first to Jachin, the twenty-second to Gamul, [18]the twenty-third to Delaiah, the twenty-fourth to Maaziah.

[19]This *was* the schedule of their service for coming into the house of the LORD according to their ordinance by the hand of Aaron their father, as the LORD God of Israel had commanded him.

OTHER LEVITES

[20]And the rest of the sons of Levi: of the sons of Amram, Shubael;[a] of the sons of Shubael, Jehdeiah. [21]Concerning Rehabiah, of the sons of Rehabiah, the first *was* Isshiah. [22]Of the Izharites, Shelomoth;[a] of the sons of Shelomoth, Jahath. [23]Of the sons *of Hebron,*[a] Jeriah *was the first,*[b] Amariah the second, Jahaziel the third, *and* Jekameam the fourth. [24]*Of* the sons of Uzziel, Michah; of the sons of Michah, Shamir. [25]The brother of Michah, Isshiah; of the sons of Isshiah, Zechariah. [26]The sons of Merari *were* Mahli and Mushi; the son of Jaaziah, Beno. [27]The sons of Merari by Jaaziah *were* Beno, Shoham, Zaccur, and Ibri. [28]Of Mahli: Eleazar, who had no sons. [29]Of Kish: the son of Kish, Jerahmeel.

[30]Also the sons of Mushi *were* Mahli, Eder, and Jerimoth. These *were* the sons of the Levites according to their fathers' houses.

[31]These also cast lots just as their brothers the sons of Aaron did, in the presence of King David, Zadok, Ahimelech, and the heads of the fathers' *houses* of the priests and Levites. The chief fathers *did* just as their younger brethren.

THE MUSICIANS

25 Moreover David and the captains of the army separated for the service *some* of the sons of Asaph, of Heman, and of Jeduthun, who *should* prophesy with harps, stringed instruments, and cymbals. And the number of the skilled men performing their service was: [2]Of the sons of Asaph: Zaccur, Joseph, Nethaniah, and Asharelah;[a] the sons of Asaph *were* under the direction of Asaph, who

---

24:15 [a]Septuagint and Vulgate read *Aphses.*
24:16 [a]Masoretic Text reads *Jehezkel.*
24:20 [a]Spelled *Shebuel* in 23:16 **24:22** [a]Spelled *Shelomith* in 23:18 **24:23** [a]Supplied from 23:19 (following some Hebrew manuscripts and Septuagint manuscripts) [b]Supplied from 23:19 (following some Hebrew manuscripts and Septuagint manuscripts) **25:2** [a]Spelled *Jesharelah* in verse 14

SEASONS OF LIFE

FREDA V. CREWS

(1 Chronicles 23)

Change can challenge and grow us. Life transitions are important changes that occur throughout the life cycle from the cradle to the grave. Although some transitions come easy, others roll in like angry tidal waves, leaving total devastation in their path. Transitions can be as simple as leaving a comfortable bed to begin a new day; they can be as painful as having to learn to go on alone after losing a lifetime mate.

We can allow the seasons of change to transform us, or we can resist them. To resist these changes will complicate the process, since resistance will inevitably retard and restrict the transforming power of life transitions.

LIFE IS A PERPETUAL TRANSITION

In the earliest stages of life, we are not consciously aware of the changes that are occurring and the transitions we are making. As we continue our development, we become more conscious of the changes that are taking place in our lives. At this point, it becomes healthy and necessary to recognize the inevitable role changes and transitions play in our personal development. Passively sitting by while "nature takes its course" will prove to be a self-defeating decision. Rather, we can decide to be aggressively engaged in becoming the people God intended us to be by learning to navigate the passages and transitions of life.

PARADOXES OF LIFE TRANSITIONS

There is a rhythm of opposite seasons recorded in Ecclesiastes 3:1–8. Without opposites, how do we know the reality of any experience? For example, how would we know darkness without light? How do people know they are well if they have never been sick? We read, "To everything there is a season . . . a time to weep, and a time to laugh" (Eccl. 3:1, 4). Life transitions are both predictable and unpredictable. Like the four seasons, certain seasons of life are predictable, but many of them are not. None of us can predict our seasons of weeping and laughter or our season of death. A personal crisis, such as divorce or loss of a job, can suddenly thrust any one of us into unexpected change.

Life transitions can be both sad and joyful, as there is "a time to mourn, and a time to dance" (Eccl. 3:4). A wedding is usually a time of rejoicing for everyone. But it can also bring sadness with the realization that a season of life is left behind. At the same time, a transition can be full of hope and hopelessness. A newly married couple, full of hope for their union, can soon experience the hopelessness that comes with the inability to resolve their unexpected conflicts.

Life transitions signal an ending and a beginning. The end of a stage of development, such as adolescence, signals the beginning of both the freedom and responsibility of young adulthood. Sometimes it is difficult to envision a beginning while experiencing the loss that comes from an ending. We must give ourselves permission to grieve our endings, and be encouraged by the hope of new beginnings.

HANDLING LIFE TRANSITIONS

Life transitions are inevitable. Accepting this reality is the first step necessary to effectively handling life's passages. We can avoid, or even prevent, some painful changes, but transitions are ultimately a way of life for everyone. Accepting this truth enables us to embrace life with its seasons of growth and development. For example, when we suffer grief through a death, divorce, or other significant loss, we can choose to remain angry, depressed, and hopeless, or we can choose to allow the pain to forge a passage into a new, hopeful, and meaningful life.

The second step is to allow change to work. Transitions help us become who we were meant to be. "And we know that all things work together for good to those who love God, to those who are the called according to His purpose" (Rom. 8:28). When struggling with change, it is comforting to know that God is manipulating the situation for good. Because this is true, it makes sense to stop the resistance and go with the flow! Our faith has really kicked in when we are able to submit ourselves and our life transitions to God (1 Pet. 5:6).

The third step is perseverance—the ability to hang in there during difficult circumstances. "And not only that, but we also glory in tribulations, knowing that tribulation produces perseverance; and perseverance, character; and character, hope" (Rom. 5:3, 4). God wants His children to grow strong spiritual muscles. He actually forces them to grow deep spiritual roots so they will be able to endure the storms of life (1 Pet. 1:6, 7). Character can be cultivated as we persevere through the pain of change. When we're passing through a painful transition, God's promises give hope. Hope when we are hopeless can come only through a relationship with the God who gives us such promises as: "For I know the thoughts that I think toward you, says the LORD, thoughts of peace and not of evil, to give you a future and a hope" (Jer. 29:11).

The final step is to wait for the purposes of God to unfold. When a change is painful, we can trust that God has a purpose in it. We, like nature, require the winter seasons for renewal and growth. For Christians, death is the last life transition—a passage from winter into an eternal spring. Awaiting us at the end of our final passage, Jesus will say: "Rise up, my love, my fair one, and come away. For lo, the winter is past" (Song 2:10, 11).

FURTHER MEDITATION:

Other passages to study about the issue of life transitions include:

- Psalm 16:7
- Proverbs 20:29; 23:22
- Malachi 3:6
- 1 Corinthians 13:11
- Galatians 6:9

To Learn More: Turn to the key passage note on life transitions at Ecclesiastes 3:1–11 on page 854. See also the personality profile of Timothy on page 1597.

prophesied according to the order of the king. 3Of Jeduthun, the sons of Jeduthun: Gedaliah, Zeri,[a] Jeshaiah, Shimei, Hashabiah, and Mattithiah, six,[b] under the direction of their father Jeduthun, who prophesied with a harp to give thanks and to praise the LORD. 4Of Heman, the sons of Heman: Bukkiah, Mattaniah, Uzziel,[a] Shebuel,[b] Jerimoth,[c] Hananiah, Hanani, Eliathah, Giddalti, Romamti-Ezer, Joshbekashah, Mallothi, Hothir, *and* Mahazioth. 5All these *were* the sons of Heman the king's seer in the words of God, to exalt his horn.[a] For God gave Heman fourteen sons and three daughters.

6All these *were* under the direction of their father for the music *in* the house of the LORD, with cymbals, stringed instruments, and harps, for the service of the house of God. Asaph, Jeduthun, and Heman *were* under the authority of the king. 7So the number of them, with their brethren who were instructed in the songs of the LORD, all who were skillful, *was* two hundred and eighty-eight.

8And they cast lots for their duty, the small as well as the great, the teacher with the student.

9Now the first lot for Asaph came out for Joseph; the second for Gedaliah, him with his brethren and sons, twelve; 10the third for Zaccur, his sons and his brethren, twelve; 11the fourth for Jizri,[a] his sons and his brethren, twelve; 12the fifth for Nethaniah, his sons and his brethren, twelve; 13the sixth for Bukkiah, his sons and his brethren, twelve; 14the seventh for Jesharelah,[a] his sons and his brethren, twelve; 15the eighth for Jeshaiah, his sons and his brethren, twelve; 16the ninth for Mattaniah, his sons and his brethren, twelve; 17the tenth for Shimei, his sons and his brethren, twelve; 18the eleventh for Azarel,[a] his sons and his brethren, twelve; 19the twelfth for Hashabiah, his sons and his brethren, twelve; 20the thirteenth for Shubael,[a] his sons and his brethren, twelve; 21the fourteenth for Mattithiah, his sons and his brethren, twelve; 22the fifteenth for Jeremoth,[a] his sons and his brethren, twelve; 23the sixteenth for Hananiah, his sons and his brethren, twelve; 24the seventeenth for Joshbekashah, his sons and his brethren, twelve; 25the eighteenth for Hanani, his sons and his brethren, twelve; 26the nineteenth for Mallothi, his sons and his brethren, twelve; 27the twentieth for Eliathah, his sons and his brethren, twelve; 28the twenty-first for Hothir, his sons and his brethren, twelve; 29the twenty-second for Giddalti, his sons and his brethren, twelve; 30the twenty-third for Mahazioth, his sons and his brethren, twelve; 31the twenty-fourth for Romamti-Ezer, his sons and his brethren, twelve.

THE GATEKEEPERS

26 Concerning the divisions of the gatekeepers: of the Korahites, Meshelemiah the son of Kore, of the sons of Asaph. 2And the sons of Meshelemiah *were* Zechariah the firstborn, Jediael the second, Zebadiah the third, Jathniel the fourth, 3Elam the fifth, Jehohanan the sixth, Eliehoenai the seventh.

4Moreover the sons of Obed-Edom *were* Shemaiah the firstborn, Jehozabad the second, Joah the third, Sacar the fourth, Nethanel the fifth, 5Ammiel the sixth, Issachar the seventh, Peulthai the eighth; for God blessed him.

6Also to Shemaiah his son were sons born who governed their fathers' houses, because they *were* men of great ability. 7The sons of Shemaiah *were* Othni, Rephael, Obed, and Elzabad, whose brothers Elihu and Semachiah *were* able men.

8All these *were* of the sons of Obed-Edom, they and their sons and their brethren, able men with strength for the work: sixty-two of Obed-Edom.

9And Meshelemiah had sons and brethren, eighteen able men.

10Also Hosah, of the children of Merari, had sons: Shimri the first (for *though* he was not the firstborn, his father made him the first), 11Hilkiah the second, Tebaliah the third, Zechariah the fourth; all the sons and brethren of Hosah *were* thirteen.

12Among these *were* the divisions of the gatekeepers, among the chief men, *having* duties just like their brethren, to serve in the house of the LORD. 13And they cast lots for each gate, the small as well as the great, according to their father's house. 14The lot for the East *Gate* fell to Shelemiah. Then they cast

---

25:3 [a]Spelled *Jizri* in verse 11 [b]*Shimei,* appearing in one Hebrew and several Septuagint manuscripts, completes the total of six sons (compare verse 17). **25:4** [a]Spelled *Azarel* in verse 18 [b]Spelled *Shubael* in verse 20 [c]Spelled *Jeremoth* in verse 22 **25:5** [a]That is, to increase his power or influence **25:11** [a]Spelled *Zeri* in verse 3 **25:14** [a]Spelled *Asharelah* in verse 2 **25:18** [a]Spelled *Uzziel* in verse 4 **25:20** [a]Spelled *Shebuel* in verse 4 **25:22** [a]Spelled *Jerimoth* in verse 4

lots *for* his son Zechariah, a wise counselor, and his lot came out for the North Gate; [15]to Obed-Edom the South Gate, and to his sons the storehouse.[a] [16]To Shuppim and Hosah *the lot came out* for the West Gate, with the Shallecheth Gate on the ascending highway—watchman opposite watchman. [17]On the east were *six* Levites, on the north four each day, on the south four each day, and for the storehouse[a] two by two. [18]As for the Parbar[a] on the west, *there were* four on the highway *and* two at the Parbar. [19]These were the divisions of the gatekeepers among the sons of Korah and among the sons of Merari.

The Treasuries and Other Duties

[20]Of the Levites, Ahijah *was* over the treasuries of the house of God and over the treasuries of the dedicated things. [21]The sons of Laadan, the descendants of the Gershonites of Laadan, heads of their fathers' *houses,* of Laadan the Gershonite: Jehieli. [22]The sons of Jehieli, Zetham and Joel his brother, *were* over the treasuries of the house of the LORD. [23]Of the Amramites, the Izharites, the Hebronites, and the Uzzielites: [24]Shebuel the son of Gershom, the son of Moses, *was* overseer of the treasuries. [25]And his brethren by Eliezer *were* Rehabiah his son, Jeshaiah his son, Joram his son, Zichri his son, and Shelomith his son.

[26]This Shelomith and his brethren *were* over all the treasuries of the dedicated things which King David and the heads of fathers' *houses,* the captains over thousands and hundreds, and the captains of the army, had dedicated. [27]Some of the spoils won in battles they dedicated to maintain the house of the LORD. [28]And all that Samuel the seer, Saul the son of Kish, Abner the son of Ner, and Joab the son of Zeruiah had dedicated, every dedicated *thing,* was under the hand of Shelomith and his brethren.

[29]Of the Izharites, Chenaniah and his sons *performed* duties as officials and judges over Israel outside Jerusalem.

[30]Of the Hebronites, Hashabiah and his brethren, one thousand seven hundred able men, had the oversight of Israel on the west side of the Jordan for all the business of the LORD, and in the service of the king. [31]Among the Hebronites, Jerijah *was* head of the Hebronites according to his genealogy of the fathers. In the fortieth year of the reign of David they were sought, and there were found among them capable men at Jazer of Gilead. [32]And his brethren *were* two thousand seven hundred able men, heads of fathers' *houses,* whom King David made officials over the Reubenites, the Gadites, and the half-tribe of Manasseh, for every matter pertaining to God and the affairs of the king.

The Military Divisions

27 And the children of Israel, according to their number, the heads of fathers' *houses,* the captains of thousands and hundreds and their officers, served the king in every matter of the *military* divisions. *These divisions* came in and went out month by month throughout all the months of the year, each division *having* twenty-four thousand.

[2]Over the first division for the first month *was* Jashobeam the son of Zabdiel, and in his division *were* twenty-four thousand; [3]*he was* of the children of Perez, and the chief of all the captains of the army for the first month. [4]Over the division of the second month *was* Dodai[a] an Ahohite, and of his division Mikloth also *was* the leader; in his division *were* twenty-four thousand. [5]The third captain of the army for the third month *was* Benaiah, the son of Jehoiada the priest, who was chief; in his division *were* twenty-four thousand. [6]This was the Benaiah *who was* mighty *among* the thirty, and was over the thirty; in his division *was* Ammizabad his son. [7]The fourth *captain* for the fourth month *was* Asahel the brother of Joab, and Zebadiah his son after him; in his division *were* twenty-four thousand. [8]The fifth *captain* for the fifth month *was* Shamhuth[a] the Izrahite; in his division were twenty-four thousand. [9]The sixth *captain* for the sixth month *was* Ira the son of Ikkesh the Tekoite; in his division *were* twenty-four thousand. [10]The seventh *captain* for the seventh month *was* Helez the Pelonite, of the children of Ephraim; in his division *were* twenty-four thousand. [11]The eighth *captain* for the eighth month *was* Sibbechai the Hushathite, of the Zarhites; in his division *were* twenty-four thousand. [12]The ninth *captain* for the ninth month *was* Abiezer the Anathothite, of the

26:15 [a]Hebrew *asuppim* **26:17** [a]Hebrew *asuppim* **26:18** [a]Probably a court or colonnade extending west of the temple **27:4** [a]Hebrew *Dodai,* usually spelled *Dodo* (compare 2 Samuel 23:9) **27:8** [a]Spelled *Shammoth* in 11:27 and *Shammah* in 2 Samuel 23:11

Benjamites; in his division *were* twenty-four
thousand. 13The tenth *captain* for the tenth
month *was* Maharai the Netophathite, of the
Zarhites; in his division *were* twenty-four
thousand. 14The eleventh *captain* for the eleventh month *was* Benaiah the Pirathonite, of
the children of Ephraim; in his division *were*
twenty-four thousand. 15The twelfth *captain*
for the twelfth month *was* Heldai[a] the Netophathite, of Othniel; in his division *were* twenty-
four thousand.

Leaders of Tribes

16Furthermore, over the tribes of Israel: the
officer over the Reubenites *was* Eliezer the son
of Zichri; over the Simeonites, Shephatiah the
son of Maachah; 17*over* the Levites, Hashabiah
the son of Kemuel; over the Aaronites, Zadok;
18*over* Judah, Elihu, *one* of David's brothers;
over Issachar, Omri the son of Michael; 19*over*
Zebulun, Ishmaiah the son of Obadiah; *over*
Naphtali, Jerimoth the son of Azriel; 20*over*
the children of Ephraim, Hoshea the son of
Azaziah; *over* the half-tribe of Manasseh, Joel
the son of Pedaiah; 21*over* the half-*tribe* of Manasseh in Gilead, Iddo the son of Zechariah;
over Benjamin, Jaasiel the son of Abner; 22*over*
Dan, Azarel the son of Jeroham. These *were*
the leaders of the tribes of Israel.

23But David did not take the number of
those twenty years old and under, because the
LORD had said He would multiply Israel like
the stars of the heavens. 24Joab the son of Zeruiah began a census, but he did not finish, for
wrath came upon Israel because of this census; nor was the number recorded in the account of the chronicles of King David.

Other State Officials

25And Azmaveth the son of Adiel *was* over
the king's treasuries; and Jehonathan the son
of Uzziah was over the storehouses in the
field, in the cities, in the villages, and in the
fortresses. 26Ezri the son of Chelub was over
those who did the work of the field for tilling
the ground. 27And Shimei the Ramathite *was*
over the vineyards, and Zabdi the Shiphmite
was over the produce of the vineyards for the
supply of wine. 28Baal-Hanan the Gederite
was over the olive trees and the sycamore
trees that *were* in the lowlands, and Joash *was*
over the store of oil. 29And Shitrai the Sharon-
ite *was* over the herds that fed in Sharon, and
Shaphat the son of Adlai was over the herds
that were in the valleys. 30Obil the Ishmaelite
was over the camels, Jehdeiah the Meronothite *was* over the donkeys, 31and Jaziz the
Hagrite *was* over the flocks. All these *were* the
officials over King David's property.

32Also Jehonathan, David's uncle, *was* a
counselor, a wise man, and a scribe; and Jehiel the son of Hachmoni *was* with the king's
sons. 33Ahithophel *was* the king's counselor,
and Hushai the Archite *was* the king's companion. 34After Ahithophel *was* Jehoiada the
son of Benaiah, then Abiathar. And the general of the king's army *was* Joab.

Solomon Instructed to Build the Temple

28 Now David assembled at Jerusalem all
the leaders of Israel: the officers of the
tribes and the captains of the divisions who
served the king, the captains over thousands
and captains over hundreds, and the stewards
over all the substance and possessions of the
king and of his sons, with the officials, the valiant men, and all the mighty men of valor.

2Then King David rose to his feet and said,
"Hear me, my brethren and my people: I *had* it
in my heart to build a house of rest for the ark
of the covenant of the LORD, and for the footstool of our God, and had made preparations
to build it. 3But God said to me, 'You shall not
build a house for My name, because you *have
been* a man of war and have shed blood.'
4However the LORD God of Israel chose me
above all the house of my father to be king
over Israel forever, for He has chosen Judah *to
be* the ruler. And of the house of Judah, the
house of my father, and among the sons of my
father, He was pleased with me to make *me*
king over all Israel. 5And of all my sons (for
the LORD has given me many sons) He has
chosen my son Solomon to sit on the throne of
the kingdom of the LORD over Israel. 6Now He
said to me, 'It is your son Solomon *who* shall
build My house and My courts; for I have chosen him *to be* My son, and I will be his Father.
7Moreover I will establish his kingdom forever, if he is steadfast to observe My commandments and My judgments, as it is this
day.' 8Now therefore, in the sight of all Israel,
the assembly of the LORD, and in the hearing
of our God, be careful to seek out all the commandments of the LORD your God, that you

27:15 [a]Spelled *Heled* in 11:30 and *Heleb* in 2 Samuel 23:29

may possess this good land, and leave *it* as an
inheritance for your children after you forever.
9“As for you, my son Solomon, know the
God of your father, and
serve Him with a loyal
heart and with a will-
ing mind; for the LORD
searches all hearts and
understands all the in-
tent of the thoughts. If
you seek Him, He will
be found by you; but if
you forsake Him, He
will cast you off forever.
10Consider now, for the
LORD has chosen you to
build a house for the
sanctuary; be strong, and do it.”
11Then David gave his son Solomon the
plans for the vestibule, its houses, its treasuries, its upper chambers, its inner chambers,
and the place of the mercy seat; 12and the plans
for all that he had by the Spirit, of the courts of
the house of the LORD, of all the chambers all
around, of the treasuries of the house of God,
and of the treasuries for the dedicated things;
13also for the division of the priests and the Levites, for all the work of the service of the
house of the LORD, and for all the articles of
service in the house of the LORD. 14*He gave*
gold by weight for *things* of gold, for all articles used in every kind of service; also *silver*
for all articles of silver by weight, for all articles used in every kind of service, 15the weight
for the lampstands of gold, and their lamps of
gold, by weight for each lampstand and its
lamps; for the lampstands of silver by weight,
for the lampstand and its lamps, according to
the use of each lampstand. 16And by weight *he*
gave gold for the tables of the showbread, for
each table, and silver for the tables of silver;
17also pure gold for the forks, the basins, the
pitchers of pure gold, and the golden bowls—
he gave gold by weight
for every bowl; and for
the silver bowls, *silver*
by weight for every
bowl; 18and refined gold
by weight for the altar of
incense, and for the con-
struction of the chariot,
that is, the gold cheru-
bim that spread *their*
wings and overshad-
owed the ark of the cov-
enant of the LORD. 19“All
this,” said David, “the
LORD made me understand in writing, by *His*
hand upon me, all the works of these plans.”
20And David said to his son Solomon, “Be
strong and of good courage, and do *it;* do not
fear nor be dismayed, for the LORD God—my
God—*will be* with you. He will not leave you
nor forsake you, until you have finished all the
work for the service of the house of the LORD.
21*Here are* the divisions of the priests and the
Levites for all the service of the house of God;
and every willing craftsman *will be* with you
for all manner of workmanship, for every kind
of service; also the leaders and all the people
will be completely at your command.”

> “As for you, my son Solomon, know the God of your father, and serve Him with a loyal heart and with a willing mind; for the LORD searches all hearts and understands all the intent of the thoughts. If you seek Him, He will be found by you; but if you forsake Him, He will cast you off forever.”
>
> 1 CHRONICLES 28:9

OFFERINGS FOR BUILDING THE TEMPLE

29 Furthermore King David said to all the
assembly: “My son Solomon, whom
alone God has chosen, *is* young and inexperienced; and the work *is* great, because the
temple[a] *is* not for man but for the LORD God.

29:1 [a]Literally *palace*

SOUL NOTE

Omnipresent *(28:9, 10)* David instructed Solomon to serve God “with a loyal heart and with a willing mind.” He reminded him that God “searches all hearts and understands all the intent of the thoughts.” Nothing is hidden from God. People can attempt to run from Him or hide from Him. People can pretend to be loyal to Him, but God cannot be fooled. “Man looks at the outward appearance, but the LORD looks at the heart” (1 Sam. 16:7). As believers grow spiritually, they will be sensitive to God’s presence in their lives at every moment. This will affect their every word, every action, and every thought. Remember, we always have an audience of One.

Topic: Spiritual Growth

[2]Now for the house of my God I have prepared
with all my might: gold for *things to be made*
of gold, silver for *things of* silver, bronze for
things of bronze, iron for *things of* iron, wood
for *things of* wood, onyx stones, *stones* to be
set, glistening stones of various colors, all
kinds of precious stones, and marble slabs in
abundance. [3]Moreover, because I have set my
affection on the house of my God, I have given
to the house of my God, over and above all
that I have prepared for the holy house, my
own special treasure of gold and silver:
[4]three thousand talents of gold, of the gold of
Ophir, and seven thousand talents of refined
silver, to overlay the walls of the houses; [5]the
gold for *things of* gold and the silver for *things*
of silver, and for all kinds of work *to be done*
by the hands of craftsmen. Who *then* is willing to consecrate himself this day to the
LORD?"

[6]Then the leaders of the fathers' *houses,*
leaders of the tribes of Israel, the captains of
thousands and of hundreds, with the officers
over the king's work, offered willingly. [7]They
gave for the work of the house of God five
thousand talents and ten thousand darics of
gold, ten thousand talents of silver, eighteen
thousand talents of bronze, and one hundred thousand talents of iron. [8]And whoever
had *precious* stones gave *them* to the treasury of the house of the LORD, into the hand of
Jehiel[a] the Gershonite. [9]Then the people rejoiced, for they had offered willingly, because
with a loyal heart they had offered willingly
to the LORD; and King David also rejoiced
greatly.

DAVID'S PRAISE TO GOD

[10]Therefore David blessed the LORD before
all the assembly; and David said:

"Blessed are You, LORD God of Israel, our
Father, forever and ever.

11 Yours, O LORD, *is* the greatness,
The power and the glory,
The victory and the majesty;
For all *that is* in heaven and in earth *is*
Yours;
Yours *is* the kingdom, O LORD,
And You are exalted as head over all.
12 Both riches and honor *come* from You,
And You reign over all.
In Your hand *is* power and might;
In Your hand *it is* to make great
And to give strength to all.

13 "Now therefore, our God,
We thank You
And praise Your glorious name.
14 But who *am* I, and who *are* my people,
That we should be able to offer so
willingly as this?
For all things *come* from You,
And of Your own we have given You.
15 For we *are* aliens and pilgrims before
You,
As *were* all our fathers;
Our days on earth *are* as a shadow,
And without hope.

[16]"O LORD our God, all this abundance that
we have prepared to build You a house for
Your holy name is from Your hand, and *is* all
Your own. [17]I know also, my God, that You
test the heart and have pleasure in uprightness. As for me, in the uprightness of my heart
I have willingly offered all these *things;* and
now with joy I have seen Your people, who are
present here to offer willingly to You. [18]O LORD
God of Abraham, Isaac, and Israel, our fathers, keep this forever in the intent of the
thoughts of the heart of Your people, and fix
their heart toward You. [19]And give my son

29:8 [a]Possibly the same as *Jehieli* (compare 26:21, 22)

SOUL NOTE

God Has It All *(29:10–12)* Riches and honor come from the Lord, who reigns supreme. As David "blessed the LORD before all the assembly," he reminded the people of Israel, as well as his son Solomon, that riches and blessing are not just the result of human work and effort, but are an expression of God's blessing in our lives. God gives people wealth, health, wisdom, and strength so they can serve Him and build His Kingdom. **Topic: Money**

Solomon a loyal heart to keep Your commandments and Your testimonies and Your statutes,
to do all *these things,* and to build the temple[a]
for which I have made provision."
[20]Then David said to all the assembly, "Now
bless the LORD your God." So all the assembly
blessed the LORD God of their fathers, and
bowed their heads and prostrated themselves
before the LORD and the king.

SOLOMON ANOINTED KING

[21]And they made sacrifices to the LORD and
offered burnt offerings to the LORD on the next
day: a thousand bulls, a thousand rams, a
thousand lambs, with their drink offerings,
and sacrifices in abundance for all Israel. [22]So
they ate and drank before the LORD with great
gladness on that day. And they made Solomon
the son of David king the second time, and
anointed *him* before the LORD *to be* the leader,
and Zadok *to be* priest. [23]Then Solomon sat on
the throne of the LORD as king instead of David his father, and prospered; and all Israel
obeyed him. [24]All the leaders and the mighty
men, and also all the sons of King David, submitted themselves to King Solomon. [25]So the
LORD exalted Solomon exceedingly in the sight
of all Israel, and bestowed on him *such* royal
majesty as had not been on any king before
him in Israel.

THE CLOSE OF DAVID'S REIGN

[26]Thus David the son of Jesse reigned over
all Israel. [27]And the period that he reigned
over Israel *was* forty years; seven years he
reigned in Hebron, and thirty-three *years* he
reigned in Jerusalem. [28]So he died in a good
old age, full of days and riches and honor; and
Solomon his son reigned in his place. [29]Now
the acts of King David, first and last, indeed
they *are* written in the book of Samuel the
seer, in the book of Nathan the prophet, and in
the book of Gad the seer, [30]with all his reign
and his might, and the events that happened
to him, to Israel, and to all the kingdoms of
the lands.

29:19 [a]Literally *palace*

2 Chronicles

Often things get worse before they get better. That's a theme of 2 Chronicles, "the second half" of the book written to give hope to the Hebrews following their return from exile in Babylon.

The author (likely Ezra) begins with Solomon and recounts (as he had done with David in 1 Chronicles) the highlights of his reign so as to encourage and inspire the postexilic survivors. The building of the glorious temple is a central theme, since rebuilding the temple was a primary reason the remnant had returned to Jerusalem.

Second Chronicles does document the nation's slide into idolatry and spiritual bondage. However, this bleak presentation of human depravity is seen side by side with God's redeeming love and sure promises. Though we witness the destruction of Jerusalem in the final chapter, the book ends with the divine promise that an exiled remnant would return after 70 years and rebuild Jerusalem and the temple, and that God would dwell among them.

In 2 Chronicles the contrast between good and evil kings is used to instruct and challenge the people. We see Hezekiah trusting God (and not his own resources) for military defense and victory, and we see Josiah hearing the word of the Lord and pledging to obey it, even calling the nation to follow his example. On the other hand, we see utterly evil kings like Manasseh, who made a career out of encouraging evil, constructing idols, and consulting sorcerers in the temple itself!

Second Chronicles reminds us that circumstances change and people fail, but God's promises are forever.

SOUL CONCERNS IN 2 CHRONICLES

Pride	**(26:16–19)**
Failure	**(ch. 36)**

Solomon Requests Wisdom

1 Now Solomon the son of David was
strengthened in his kingdom, and the
LORD his God *was* with him and exalted him
exceedingly.
2And Solomon spoke to all Israel, to the captains of thousands and of hundreds, to the
judges, and to every leader in all Israel, the
heads of the fathers' *houses.* 3Then Solomon,
and all the assembly with him, went to the
high place that *was* at Gibeon; for the tabernacle of meeting with God was there, which Moses the servant of the LORD had made in the
wilderness. 4But David had brought up the ark
of God from Kirjath Jearim to *the place* David
had prepared for it, for he had pitched a tent
for it at Jerusalem. 5Now the bronze altar that
Bezalel the son of Uri, the son of Hur, had
made, he put[a] before the tabernacle of the
LORD; Solomon and the assembly sought Him
there. 6And Solomon went up there to the
bronze altar before the LORD, which *was* at the
tabernacle of meeting, and offered a thousand
burnt offerings on it.
7On that night God appeared to Solomon,
and said to him, "Ask! What shall I give you?"
8And Solomon said to God: "You have
shown great mercy to David my father, and
have made me king in his place. 9Now, O LORD
God, let Your promise to David my father be
established, for You have made me king over a
people like the dust of the earth in multitude.
10Now give me wisdom and knowledge, that I
may go out and come in before this people; for
who can judge this great people of Yours?"
11Then God said to Solomon: "Because this
was in your heart, and you have not asked
riches or wealth or honor or the life of your
enemies, nor have you asked long life—but
have asked wisdom and knowledge for yourself, that you may judge My people over
whom I have made you king—12wisdom and
knowledge *are* granted to you; and I will give
you riches and wealth and honor, such as
none of the kings have had who *were* before
you, nor shall any after you have the like."

Solomon's Military and Economic Power

13So Solomon came to Jerusalem from the
high place that *was* at Gibeon, from before the
tabernacle of meeting, and reigned over Israel.
14And Solomon gathered chariots and horsemen; he had one thousand four hundred chariots and twelve thousand horsemen, whom he
stationed in the chariot cities and with the
king in Jerusalem. 15Also the king made silver
and gold as common in Jerusalem as stones,
and he made cedars as abundant as the sycamores which *are* in the lowland. 16And Solomon had horses imported from Egypt and
Keveh; the king's merchants bought them in
Keveh at the *current* price. 17They also acquired and imported from Egypt a chariot for
six hundred *shekels* of silver, and a horse for
one hundred and fifty; thus, through their
agents,[a] they exported them to all the kings of
the Hittites and the kings of Syria.

Solomon Prepares to Build the Temple

2 Then Solomon determined to build a temple for the name of the LORD, and a royal
house for himself. 2Solomon selected seventy
thousand men to bear burdens, eighty thousand to quarry *stone* in the mountains, and
three thousand six hundred to oversee them.
3Then Solomon sent to Hiram[a] king of Tyre,
saying:

1:5 [a]Some authorities read *it was there.*
1:17 [a]Literally *by their hands* **2:3** [a]Hebrew *Huram* (compare 1 Kings 5:1)

SOUL NOTE

Choose Wisely *(1:11, 12)* When God asked Solomon what he wanted, Solomon chose wisdom in order to rule the nation. God was pleased that Solomon had asked for wisdom and not riches; then He gave him riches as well. Solomon could have asked for anything he wanted, but he wisely asked for the one thing every human being needs most—divine wisdom. Solomon's actions remind us of the importance of making wise choices in our lives. Wise choices may not always lead to wealth, but they will please God. Selfish choices, however, will only lead to disappointment. **Topic: Wisdom**

As you have dealt with David my father,
and sent him cedars to build himself a
house to dwell in, *so deal with me.*
4Behold, I am building a temple for the
name of the LORD my God, to dedicate *it*
to Him, to burn before Him sweet
incense, for the continual showbread,
for the burnt offerings morning and
evening, on the Sabbaths, on the New
Moons, and on the set feasts of the LORD
our God. This *is an ordinance* forever to
Israel.

5 And the temple which I build *will be*
great, for our God is greater than all
gods. 6But who is able to build Him a
temple, since heaven and the heaven of
heavens cannot contain Him? Who *am* I
then, that I should build Him a temple,
except to burn sacrifice before Him?

7 Therefore send me at once a man skillful
to work in gold and silver, in bronze and
iron, in purple and crimson and blue,
who has skill to engrave with the skillful
men who are with me in Judah and
Jerusalem, whom David my father
provided. 8Also send me cedar and
cypress and algum logs from Lebanon,
for I know that your servants have skill
to cut timber in Lebanon; and indeed my
servants *will be* with your servants, 9to
prepare timber for me in abundance, for
the temple which I am about to build
shall be great and wonderful.

10 And indeed I will give to your servants,
the woodsmen who cut timber, twenty
thousand kors of ground wheat, twenty
thousand kors of barley, twenty
thousand baths of wine, and twenty
thousand baths of oil.

11Then Hiram king of Tyre answered in writing, which he sent to Solomon:

Because the LORD loves His people, He
has made you king over them.

12Hiram[a] also said:

Blessed *be* the LORD God of Israel, who
made heaven and earth, for He has
given King David a wise son, endowed
with prudence and understanding, who
will build a temple for the LORD and a
royal house for himself!

13 And now I have sent a skillful man,
endowed with understanding, Huram[a]
my master[b] *craftsman* 14(the son of a
woman of the daughters of Dan, and his
father was a man of Tyre), skilled to
work in gold and silver, bronze and iron,
stone and wood, purple and blue, fine
linen and crimson, and to make any
engraving and to accomplish any plan
which may be given to him, with your
skillful men and with the skillful men of
my lord David your father.

15 Now therefore, the wheat, the barley,
the oil, and the wine which my lord has
spoken of, let him send to his servants.
16And we will cut wood from Lebanon,
as much as you need; we will bring it to
you in rafts by sea to Joppa, and you
will carry it up to Jerusalem.

17Then Solomon numbered all the aliens
who *were* in the land of Israel, after the census
in which David his father had numbered
them; and there were found to be one hundred
and fifty-three thousand six hundred. 18And
he made seventy thousand of them bearers of
burdens, eighty thousand stonecutters in the
mountain, and three thousand six hundred
overseers to make the people work.

SOLOMON BUILDS THE TEMPLE

3 Now Solomon began to build the house of
the LORD at Jerusalem on Mount Moriah,
where *the LORD*[a] had appeared to his father
David, at the place that David had prepared on
the threshing floor of Ornan[b] the Jebusite.
2And he began to build on the second *day* of
the second month in the fourth year of his
reign.

3This is the foundation which Solomon laid
for building the house of God: The length *was*
sixty cubits (by cubits according to the former
measure) and the width twenty cubits. 4And

2:12 [a]Hebrew *Huram* (compare 1 Kings 5:1)
2:13 [a]Spelled *Hiram* in 1 Kings 7:13 [b]Literally *father* (compare 1 Kings 7:13,14) **3:1** [a]Literally *He,* following Masoretic Text and Vulgate; Septuagint reads *the LORD;* Targum reads *the Angel of the LORD.* [b]Spelled *Araunah* in 2 Samuel 24:16ff

the vestibule that *was* in front *of the sanctuary*[a] was twenty cubits long across the width of the house, and the height *was* one hundred and[b] twenty. He overlaid the inside with pure gold. [5]The larger room[a] he paneled with cypress which he overlaid with fine gold, and he carved palm trees and chainwork on it. [6]And he decorated the house with precious stones for beauty, and the gold *was* gold from Parvaim. [7]He also overlaid the house—the beams and doorposts, its walls and doors—with gold; and he carved cherubim on the walls.

[8]And he made the Most Holy Place. Its length was according to the width of the house, twenty cubits, and its width twenty cubits. He overlaid it with six hundred talents of fine gold. [9]The weight of the nails *was* fifty shekels of gold; and he overlaid the upper area with gold. [10]In the Most Holy Place he made two cherubim, fashioned by carving, and overlaid them with gold. [11]The wings of the cherubim *were* twenty cubits in *overall* length: one wing *of the one cherub was* five cubits, touching the wall of the room, and the other wing *was* five cubits, touching the wing of the other cherub; [12]*one* wing of the other cherub *was* five cubits, touching the wall of the room, and the other wing *also was* five cubits, touching the wing of the other cherub. [13]The wings of these cherubim spanned twenty cubits overall. They stood on their feet, and they faced inward. [14]And he made the veil of blue, purple, crimson, and fine linen, and wove cherubim into it.

[15]Also he made in front of the temple[a] two pillars thirty-five[b] cubits high, and the capital that *was* on the top of each of *them* was five cubits. [16]He made wreaths of chainwork, as in the inner sanctuary, and put *them* on top of the pillars; and he made one hundred pomegranates, and put *them* on the wreaths of chainwork. [17]Then he set up the pillars before the temple, one on the right hand and the other on the left; he called the name of the one on the right hand Jachin, and the name of the one on the left Boaz.

Furnishings of the Temple

4 Moreover he made a bronze altar: twenty cubits was its length, twenty cubits its width, and ten cubits its height.

[2]Then he made the Sea of cast *bronze,* ten cubits from one brim to the other; *it was* completely round. Its height *was* five cubits, and a line of thirty cubits measured its circumference. [3]And under it *was* the likeness of oxen encircling it all around, ten to a cubit, all the way around the Sea. The oxen *were* cast in two rows, when it was cast. [4]It stood on twelve oxen: three looking toward the north, three looking toward the west, three looking toward the south, and three looking toward the east; the Sea *was set* upon them, and all their back parts *pointed* inward. [5]It *was* a handbreadth thick; and its brim was shaped like the brim of a cup, *like* a lily blossom. It contained three thousand[a] baths.

[6]He also made ten lavers, and put five on the right side and five on the left, to wash in them; such things as they offered for the burnt offering they would wash in them, but the Sea *was* for the priests to wash in. [7]And he made ten lampstands of gold according to their design, and set *them* in the temple, five on the right side and five on the left. [8]He also made ten tables, and placed *them* in the temple, five on the right side and five on the left. And he made one hundred bowls of gold.

3:4 [a]The main room of the temple; elsewhere called the holy place (compare 1 Kings 6:3) [b]Following Masoretic Text, Septuagint, and Vulgate; Arabic, some manuscripts of the Septuagint, and Syriac omit *one hundred and.* **3:5** [a]Literally *house* **3:15** [a]Literally *house* [b]Or *eighteen* (compare 1 Kings 7:15; 2 Kings 25:17; and Jeremiah 52:21) **4:5** [a]Or *two thousand* (compare 1 Kings 7:26)

SOUL NOTE

Well Done *(3:1–17)* Chapters 3 and 4 describe the intricate details of the construction of the temple. The effort, the care, and the attention to detail with which the temple was constructed show that work done for God should be done well. There should be no room for shoddiness or halfhearted measures in our work for God. The quality of our service for Him reflects our attitude toward Him.

Topic: Work

9Furthermore he made the court of the priests, and the great court and doors for the court; and he overlaid these doors with bronze. 10He set the Sea on the right side, toward the southeast.

11Then Huram made the pots and the shovels and the bowls. So Huram finished doing the work that he was to do for King Solomon for the house of God: 12the two pillars and the bowl-shaped capitals *that were* on top of the two pillars; the two networks covering the two bowl-shaped capitals which *were* on top of the pillars; 13four hundred pomegranates for the two networks (two rows of pomegranates for each network, to cover the two bowl-shaped capitals that *were* on the pillars); 14he also made carts and the lavers on the carts; 15one Sea and twelve oxen under it; 16also the pots, the shovels, the forks—and all their articles Huram his master[a] *craftsman* made of burnished bronze for King Solomon for the house of the LORD.

17In the plain of Jordan the king had them cast in clay molds, between Succoth and Zeredah.[a] 18And Solomon had all these articles made in such great abundance that the weight of the bronze was not determined.

19Thus Solomon had all the furnishings made for the house of God: the altar of gold and the tables on which *was* the showbread; 20the lampstands with their lamps of pure gold, to burn in the prescribed manner in front of the inner sanctuary, 21with the flowers and the lamps and the wick-trimmers of gold, of purest gold; 22the trimmers, the bowls, the ladles, and the censers of pure gold. As for the entry of the sanctuary, its inner doors to the Most Holy *Place,* and the doors of the main hall of the temple, *were* gold.

> The priests could not continue ministering because of the cloud; for the glory of the LORD filled the house of God.
>
> 2 CHRONICLES 5:14

5 So all the work that Solomon had done for the house of the LORD was finished; and Solomon brought in the things which his father David had dedicated: the silver and the gold and all the furnishings. And he put *them* in the treasuries of the house of God.

THE ARK BROUGHT INTO THE TEMPLE

2Now Solomon assembled the elders of Israel and all the heads of the tribes, the chief fathers of the children of Israel, in Jerusalem, that they might bring the ark of the covenant of the LORD up from the City of David, which *is* Zion. 3Therefore all the men of Israel assembled with the king at the feast, which *was* in the seventh month. 4So all the elders of Israel came, and the Levites took up the ark. 5Then they brought up the ark, the tabernacle of meeting, and all the holy furnishings that *were* in the tabernacle. The priests and the Levites brought them up. 6Also King Solomon, and all the congregation of Israel who were assembled with him before the ark, were sacrificing sheep and oxen that could not be counted or numbered for multitude. 7Then the priests brought in the ark of the covenant of the LORD to its place, into the inner sanctuary of the temple,[a] to the Most Holy *Place,* under the wings of the cherubim. 8For the cherubim spread *their* wings over the place of the ark, and the cherubim overshadowed the ark and its poles. 9The poles extended so that the ends of the poles of the ark could be seen from *the holy place,* in front of the inner sanctuary; but they could not be seen from outside. And they are there to this day. 10Nothing was in the ark except the two tablets which Moses put *there* at Horeb, when the LORD made *a covenant* with the children of Israel, when they had come out of Egypt.

11And it came to pass when the priests came out of the *Most* Holy *Place* (for all the priests who *were* present had sanctified themselves, without keeping to their divisions), 12and the Levites *who were* the singers, all those of Asaph and Heman and Jeduthun, with their sons and their brethren, stood at the east end of the altar, clothed in white linen, having cymbals, stringed instruments and harps, and with them one hundred and twenty priests sounding with trumpets— 13indeed it came to pass, when the trumpeters and singers *were* as one, to make one sound to be heard in praising and thanking the LORD, and when they lifted up their voice with the trumpets and cymbals and instruments of music, and praised the LORD, *saying:*

4:16 [a]Literally *father* **4:17** [a]Spelled *Zaretan* in 1 Kings 7:46 **5:7** [a]Literally *house*

"*For He is* good,
For His mercy *endures* forever,"[a]

that the house, the house of the LORD, was filled with a cloud, 14so that the priests could not continue ministering because of the cloud; for the glory of the LORD filled the house of God.

6 Then Solomon spoke:

"The LORD said He would dwell in the
dark cloud.
2 I have surely built You an exalted house,
And a place for You to dwell in forever."

SOLOMON'S SPEECH UPON COMPLETION OF THE WORK

3Then the king turned around and blessed the whole assembly of Israel, while all the assembly of Israel was standing. 4And he said: "Blessed *be* the LORD God of Israel, who has fulfilled with His hands *what* He spoke with His mouth to my father David, saying, 5'Since the day that I brought My people out of the land of Egypt, I have chosen no city from any tribe of Israel *in which* to build a house, that My name might be there, nor did I choose any man to be a ruler over My people Israel. 6Yet I have chosen Jerusalem, that My name may be there, and I have chosen David to be over My people Israel.' 7Now it was in the heart of my father David to build a temple[a] for the name of the LORD God of Israel. 8But the LORD said to my father David, 'Whereas it was in your heart to build a temple for My name, you did well in that it was in your heart. 9Nevertheless you shall not build the temple, but your son who will come from your body, he shall build the temple for My name.' 10So the LORD has fulfilled His word which He spoke, and I have filled the position of my father David, and sit on the throne of Israel, as the LORD promised; and I have built the temple for the name of the LORD God of Israel. 11And there I have put the ark, in which *is* the covenant of the LORD which He made with the children of Israel."

SOLOMON'S PRAYER OF DEDICATION

12Then *Solomon*[a] stood before the altar of the LORD in the presence of all the assembly of Israel, and spread out his hands 13(for Solomon had made a bronze platform five cubits long, five cubits wide, and three cubits high, and had set it in the midst of the court; and he stood on it, knelt down on his knees before all the assembly of Israel, and spread out his hands toward heaven); 14and he said: "LORD God of Israel, *there is* no God in heaven or on earth like You, who keep *Your* covenant and mercy with Your servants who walk before You with all their hearts. 15You have kept what You promised Your servant David my father; You have both spoken with Your mouth and fulfilled *it* with Your hand, as *it is* this day. 16Therefore, LORD God of Israel, now keep what You promised Your servant David my father, saying, 'You shall not fail to have a man sit before Me on the throne of Israel, only if your sons take heed to their way, that they walk in My law as you have walked before Me.' 17And now, O LORD God of Israel, let Your word come true, which You have spoken to Your servant David.

18"But will God indeed dwell with men on the earth? Behold, heaven and the heaven of heavens cannot contain You. How much less this temple[a] which I have built! 19Yet regard the prayer of Your servant and his supplication, O LORD my God, and listen to the cry and the prayer which Your servant is praying

5:13 [a]Compare Psalm 106:1 **6:7** [a]Literally *house,* and so in verses 8–10 **6:12** [a]Literally *he* (compare 1 Kings 8:22) **6:18** [a]Literally *house*

SOUL NOTE

God Never Fails *(6:14–17)* Solomon had become king over Israel because of God's covenant with David, his father. God had promised David, "You shall not fail to have a man sit before Me on the throne of Israel, only if your sons take heed to their way." Even though the nation eventually went into captivity, God kept His promise, as He always does. Many of the sons (descendants) of David did not "take heed to their way," but one descendant of David does sit on the throne forever. Jesus Christ is the final fulfillment of God's promise to David, and He reigns forever. **Topic: God's Promises**

before You: 20that Your eyes may be open toward this temple day and night, toward the place where *You* said *You would* put Your name, that You may hear the prayer which Your servant makes toward this place. 21And may You hear the supplications of Your servant and of Your people Israel, when they pray toward this place. Hear from heaven Your dwelling place, and when You hear, forgive.

22"If anyone sins against his neighbor, and is forced to take an oath, and comes *and* takes an oath before Your altar in this temple, 23then hear from heaven, and act, and judge Your servants, bringing retribution on the wicked by bringing his way on his own head, and justifying the righteous by giving him according to his righteousness.

24"Or if Your people Israel are defeated before an enemy because they have sinned against You, and return and confess Your name, and pray and make supplication before You in this temple, 25then hear from heaven and forgive the sin of Your people Israel, and bring them back to the land which You gave to them and their fathers.

26"When the heavens are shut up and there is no rain because they have sinned against You, when they pray toward this place and confess Your name, and turn from their sin because You afflict them, 27then hear *in* heaven, and forgive the sin of Your servants, Your people Israel, that You may teach them the good way in which they should walk; and send rain on Your land which You have given to Your people as an inheritance.

28"When there is famine in the land, pestilence or blight or mildew, locusts or grasshoppers; when their enemies besiege them in the land of their cities; whatever plague or whatever sickness *there is;* 29whatever prayer, whatever supplication is *made* by anyone, or by all Your people Israel, when each one knows his own burden and his own grief, and spreads out his hands to this temple: 30then hear from heaven Your dwelling place, and forgive, and give to everyone according to all his ways, whose heart You know (for You alone know the hearts of the sons of men), 31that they may fear You, to walk in Your ways as long as they live in the land which You gave to our fathers.

32"Moreover, concerning a foreigner, who is not of Your people Israel, but has come from a far country for the sake of Your great name and Your mighty hand and Your outstretched arm, when they come and pray in this temple; 33then hear from heaven Your dwelling place, and do according to all for which the foreigner calls to You, that all peoples of the earth may know Your name and fear You, as *do* Your people Israel, and that they may know that this temple which I have built is called by Your name.

34"When Your people go out to battle against their enemies, wherever You send them, and when they pray to You toward this city which You have chosen and the temple which I have built for Your name, 35then hear from heaven their prayer and their supplication, and maintain their cause.

36"When they sin against You (for *there is* no one who does not sin), and You become angry with them and deliver them to the enemy, and they take them captive to a land far or near; 37*yet* when they come to themselves in the land where they were carried captive, and repent, and make supplication to You in the land of their captivity, saying, 'We have sinned, we have done wrong, and have committed wickedness'; 38and *when* they return to You with all their heart and with all their soul in the land of their captivity, where they have been carried captive, and pray toward their land which You gave to their fathers, the city which You have chosen, and toward the temple which I have built for Your name: 39then hear from heaven Your dwelling place their prayer and their supplications, and maintain their cause, and forgive Your people who have sinned against You. 40Now, my God, I pray, let Your eyes be open and *let* Your ears *be* attentive to the prayer *made* in this place.

41 "Now therefore,
Arise, O LORD God, to Your resting
place,
You and the ark of Your strength.
Let Your priests, O LORD God, be clothed
with salvation,
And let Your saints rejoice in goodness.

42 "O LORD God, do not turn away the face
of Your Anointed;
Remember the mercies of Your servant
David."[a]

6:42 [a]Compare Psalm 132:8–10

Solomon Dedicates the Temple

7 When Solomon had finished praying, fire came down from heaven and consumed the burnt offering and the sacrifices; and the glory of the LORD filled the temple.[a] 2And the priests could not enter the house of the LORD, because the glory of the LORD had filled the LORD's house. 3When all the children of Israel saw how the fire came down, and the glory of the LORD on the temple, they bowed their faces to the ground on the pavement, and worshiped and praised the LORD, *saying:*

> "For *He is* good,
> For His mercy *endures* forever."[a]

4Then the king and all the people offered sacrifices before the LORD. 5King Solomon offered a sacrifice of twenty-two thousand bulls and one hundred and twenty thousand sheep. So the king and all the people dedicated the house of God. 6And the priests attended to their services; the Levites also with instruments of the music of the LORD, which King David had made to praise the LORD, saying, "For His mercy *endures* forever,"[a] whenever David offered praise by their ministry. The priests sounded trumpets opposite them, while all Israel stood.

7Furthermore Solomon consecrated the middle of the court that *was* in front of the house of the LORD; for there he offered burnt offerings and the fat of the peace offerings, because the bronze altar which Solomon had made was not able to receive the burnt offerings, the grain offerings, and the fat.

8At that time Solomon kept the feast seven days, and all Israel with him, a very great assembly from the entrance of Hamath to the Brook of Egypt.[a] 9And on the eighth day they held a sacred assembly, for they observed the dedication of the altar seven days, and the feast seven days. 10On the twenty-third day of the seventh month he sent the people away to their tents, joyful and glad of heart for the good that the LORD had done for David, for Solomon, and for His people Israel. 11Thus Solomon finished the house of the LORD and the king's house; and Solomon successfully accomplished all that came into his heart to make in the house of the LORD and in his own house.

God's Second Appearance to Solomon

12Then the LORD appeared to Solomon by night, and said to him: "I have heard your prayer, and have chosen this place for Myself as a house of sacrifice. 13When I shut up heaven and there is no rain, or command the locusts to devour the land, or send pestilence among My people, 14if My people who are called by My name will humble themselves, and pray and seek My face, and turn from their wicked ways, then I will hear from heaven, and will forgive their sin and heal their land. 15Now My eyes will be open and My ears attentive to prayer *made* in this place. 16For now I have chosen and sanctified this house, that My name may be there forever; and My eyes and My heart will be there perpetually. 17As for you, if you walk before Me as your father David walked, and do according to all that I have commanded you, and if you keep My statutes and My judgments, 18then I will establish the throne of your kingdom, as I covenanted with David your father, saying, 'You shall not fail *to have* a man as ruler in Israel.'

> "If My people who are called by My name will humble themselves, and pray and seek My face, and turn from their wicked ways, then I will hear from heaven, and will forgive their sin and heal their land."
>
> 2 CHRONICLES 7:14

19"But if you turn away and forsake My statutes and My commandments which I have set before you, and go and serve other gods, and worship them, 20then I will uproot them from My land which I have given them; and this house which I have sanctified for My name I will cast out of My sight, and will make it a proverb and a byword among all peoples.

21"And *as for* this house, which is exalted, everyone who passes by it will be astonished and say, 'Why has the LORD done thus to this land and this house?' 22Then they will answer, 'Because they forsook the LORD God of their fathers, who brought them out of the land of Egypt, and embraced other gods, and worshiped them and served them; therefore He has brought all this calamity on them.' "

7:1 [a]Literally *house* **7:3** [a]Compare Psalm 106:1 **7:6** [a]Compare Psalm 106:1 **7:8** [a]That is, the Shihor (compare 1 Chronicles 13:5)

SOLOMON'S ADDITIONAL ACHIEVEMENTS

8 It came to pass at the end of twenty years, when Solomon had built the house of the LORD and his own house, [2]that the cities which Hiram[a] had given to Solomon, Solomon built them; and he settled the children of Israel there. [3]And Solomon went to Hamath Zobah and seized it. [4]He also built Tadmor in the wilderness, and all the storage cities which he built in Hamath. [5]He built Upper Beth Horon and Lower Beth Horon, fortified cities *with* walls, gates, and bars, [6]also Baalath and all the storage cities that Solomon had, and all the chariot cities and the cities of the cavalry, and all that Solomon desired to build in Jerusalem, in Lebanon, and in all the land of his dominion.

[7]All the people *who were* left of the Hittites, Amorites, Perizzites, Hivites, and Jebusites, who *were* not of Israel— [8]that is, their descendants who were left in the land after them, whom the children of Israel did not destroy—from these Solomon raised forced labor, as it is to this day. [9]But Solomon did not make the children of Israel servants for his work. Some *were* men of war, captains of his officers, captains of his chariots, and his cavalry. [10]And others *were* chiefs of the officials of King Solomon: two hundred and fifty, who ruled over the people.

[11]Now Solomon brought the daughter of Pharaoh up from the City of David to the house he had built for her, for he said, "My wife shall not dwell in the house of David king of Israel, because *the places* to which the ark of the LORD has come are holy."

[12]Then Solomon offered burnt offerings to the LORD on the altar of the LORD which he had built before the vestibule, [13]according to the daily rate, offering according to the commandment of Moses, for the Sabbaths, the New Moons, and the three appointed yearly feasts—the Feast of Unleavened Bread, the Feast of Weeks, and the Feast of Tabernacles. [14]And, according to the order of David his father, he appointed the divisions of the priests for their service, the Levites for their duties (to praise and serve before the priests) as the duty of each day required, and the gatekeepers by their divisions at each gate; for so David the man of God had commanded. [15]They did not depart from the command of the king to the priests and Levites concerning any matter or concerning the treasuries.

[16]Now all the work of Solomon was well-ordered from[a] the day of the foundation of the house of the LORD until it was finished. So the house of the LORD was completed.

[17]Then Solomon went to Ezion Geber and Elath[a] on the seacoast, in the land of Edom. [18]And Hiram sent him ships by the hand of his servants, and servants who knew the sea. They went with the servants of Solomon to Ophir, and acquired four hundred and fifty talents of gold from there, and brought it to King Solomon.

THE QUEEN OF SHEBA'S PRAISE OF SOLOMON

9 Now when the queen of Sheba heard of the fame of Solomon, she came to Jerusalem to test Solomon with hard questions, *having* a very great retinue, camels that bore spices, gold in abundance, and precious stones; and when she came to Solomon, she spoke with him about all that was in her heart. [2]So Solomon answered all her questions; there was nothing so difficult for Solomon that he could not explain it to her. [3]And when the queen of Sheba had seen the wisdom of Solomon, the house that he had built, [4]the food on his table, the seating of his servants, the service of his waiters and their apparel, his cupbearers and their apparel, and his entryway by which he went up to the house of the LORD, there was no more spirit in her.

[5]Then she said to the king: "*It was* a true report which I heard in my own land about your words and your wisdom. [6]However I did not believe their words until I came and saw with my own eyes; and indeed the half of the greatness of your wisdom was not told me. You exceed the fame of which I heard. [7]Happy *are* your men and happy *are* these your servants, who stand continually before you and hear your wisdom! [8]Blessed be the LORD your God, who delighted in you, setting you on His throne *to be* king for the LORD your God! Because your God has loved Israel, to establish them forever, therefore He made you king over them, to do justice and righteousness."

[9]And she gave the king one hundred and twenty talents of gold, spices in great abun-

8:2 [a]Hebrew *Huram* (compare 2 Chronicles 2:3) **8:16** [a]Following Septuagint, Syriac, and Vulgate; Masoretic Text reads *as far as*. **8:17** [a]Hebrew *Eloth* (compare 2 Kings 14:22)

dance, and precious stones; there never were any spices such as those the queen of Sheba gave to King Solomon.

[10]Also, the servants of Hiram and the servants of Solomon, who brought gold from Ophir, brought algum[a] wood and precious stones. [11]And the king made walkways *of* the algum[a] wood for the house of the LORD and for the king's house, also harps and stringed instruments for singers; and there were none such *as these* seen before in the land of Judah.

[12]Now King Solomon gave to the queen of Sheba all she desired, whatever she asked, *much more* than she had brought to the king. So she turned and went to her own country, she and her servants.

Solomon's Great Wealth

[13]The weight of gold that came to Solomon yearly was six hundred and sixty-six talents of gold, [14]besides *what* the traveling merchants and traders brought. And all the kings of Arabia and governors of the country brought gold and silver to Solomon. [15]And King Solomon made two hundred large shields of hammered gold; six hundred *shekels* of hammered gold went into each shield. [16]*He* also *made* three hundred shields of hammered gold; three hundred *shekels*[a] of gold went into each shield. The king put them in the House of the Forest of Lebanon.

[17]Moreover the king made a great throne of ivory, and overlaid it with pure gold. [18]The throne *had* six steps, with a footstool of gold, *which were* fastened to the throne; there were armrests on either side of the place of the seat, and two lions stood beside the armrests. [19]Twelve lions stood there, one on each side of the six steps; nothing like *this* had been made for any *other* kingdom.

[20]All King Solomon's drinking vessels *were* gold, and all the vessels of the House of the Forest of Lebanon *were* pure gold. Not *one was* silver, for this was accounted as nothing in the days of Solomon. [21]For the king's ships went to Tarshish with the servants of Hiram.[a] Once every three years the merchant ships[b] came, bringing gold, silver, ivory, apes, and monkeys.[c]

[22]So King Solomon surpassed all the kings of the earth in riches and wisdom. [23]And all the kings of the earth sought the presence of Solomon to hear his wisdom, which God had put in his heart. [24]Each man brought his present: articles of silver and gold, garments, armor, spices, horses, and mules, at a set rate year by year.

[25]Solomon had four thousand stalls for horses and chariots, and twelve thousand horsemen whom he stationed in the chariot cities and with the king at Jerusalem.

[26]So he reigned over all the kings from the River[a] to the land of the Philistines, as far as the border of Egypt. [27]The king made silver *as common* in Jerusalem as stones, and he made cedar trees as abundant as the sycamores which *are* in the lowland. [28]And they brought horses to Solomon from Egypt and from all lands.

Death of Solomon

[29]Now the rest of the acts of Solomon, first and last, *are* they not written in the book of Nathan the prophet, in the prophecy of Ahijah the Shilonite, and in the visions of Iddo the seer concerning Jeroboam the son of Nebat? [30]Solomon reigned in Jerusalem over all Israel forty years. [31]Then Solomon rested with his fathers, and was buried in the City of David his father. And Rehoboam his son reigned in his place.

The Revolt Against Rehoboam

10 And Rehoboam went to Shechem, for all Israel had gone to Shechem to make him king. [2]So it happened, when Jeroboam the son of Nebat heard *it* (he was in Egypt, where he had fled from the presence of King Solomon), that Jeroboam returned from Egypt. [3]Then they sent for him and called him. And Jeroboam and all Israel came and spoke to Rehoboam, saying, [4]"Your father made our yoke heavy; now therefore, lighten the burdensome service of your father and his heavy yoke which he put on us, and we will serve you."

[5]So he said to them, "Come back to me after three days." And the people departed.

[6]Then King Rehoboam consulted the elders who stood before his father Solomon while he still lived, saying, "How do you advise *me* to answer these people?"

9:10 [a]Or *almug* (compare 1 Kings 10:11, 12)
9:11 [a]Or *almug* (compare 1 Kings 10:11, 12)
9:16 [a]Or *three minas* (compare 1 Kings 10:17)
9:21 [a]Hebrew *Huram* (compare 1 Kings 10:22) [b]Literally *ships of Tarshish,* deep-sea vessels [c]Or *peacocks* **9:26** [a]That is, the Euphrates

[7]And they spoke to him, saying, "If you are kind to these people, and please them, and speak good words to them, they will be your servants forever."

[8]But he rejected the advice which the elders had given him, and consulted the young men who had grown up with him, who stood before him. [9]And he said to them, "What advice do you give? How should we answer this people who have spoken to me, saying, 'Lighten the yoke which your father put on us'?"

[10]Then the young men who had grown up with him spoke to him, saying, "Thus you should speak to the people who have spoken to you, saying, 'Your father made our yoke heavy, but you make *it* lighter on us'—thus you shall say to them: 'My little *finger* shall be thicker than my father's waist! [11]And now, whereas my father put a heavy yoke on you, I will add to your yoke; my father chastised you with whips, but I *will chastise you* with scourges!' "[a]

[12]So Jeroboam and all the people came to Rehoboam on the third day, as the king had directed, saying, "Come back to me the third day." [13]Then the king answered them roughly. King Rehoboam rejected the advice of the elders, [14]and he spoke to them according to the advice of the young men, saying, "My father[a] made your yoke heavy, but I will add to it; my father chastised you with whips, but I *will chastise you* with scourges!"[b] [15]So the king did not listen to the people; for the turn *of events* was from God, that the LORD might fulfill His word, which He had spoken by the hand of Ahijah the Shilonite to Jeroboam the son of Nebat.

[16]Now when all Israel *saw* that the king did not listen to them, the people answered the king, saying:

"What share have we in David?
We have no inheritance in the son of
Jesse.
Every man to your tents, O Israel!
Now see to your own house, O David!"

So all Israel departed to their tents. [17]But Rehoboam reigned over the children of Israel who dwelt in the cities of Judah.

[18]Then King Rehoboam sent Hadoram, who *was* in charge of revenue; but the children of Israel stoned him with stones, and he died. Therefore King Rehoboam mounted *his* chariot in haste to flee to Jerusalem. [19]So Israel has been in rebellion against the house of David to this day.

11 Now when Rehoboam came to Jerusalem, he assembled from the house of Judah and Benjamin one hundred and eighty thousand chosen *men* who were warriors, to fight against Israel, that he might restore the kingdom to Rehoboam.

[2]But the word of the LORD came to Shemaiah the man of God, saying, [3]"Speak to Rehoboam the son of Solomon, king of Judah, and to all Israel in Judah and Benjamin, saying, [4]'Thus says the LORD: "You shall not go up or fight against your brethren! Let every man return to his house, for this thing is from Me." ' " Therefore they obeyed the words of the LORD, and turned back from attacking Jeroboam.

REHOBOAM FORTIFIES THE CITIES

[5]So Rehoboam dwelt in Jerusalem, and built cities for defense in Judah. [6]And he built Bethlehem, Etam, Tekoa, [7]Beth Zur, Sochoh, Adullam, [8]Gath, Mareshah, Ziph, [9]Adoraim, Lachish, Azekah, [10]Zorah, Aijalon, and Hebron, which are in Judah and Benjamin, fortified cities. [11]And he fortified the strongholds, and put captains in them, and stores of food, oil, and wine. [12]Also in every city *he put* shields and spears, and made them very strong, having Judah and Benjamin on his side.

PRIESTS AND LEVITES MOVE TO JUDAH

[13]And from all their territories the priests and the Levites who *were* in all Israel took their stand with him. [14]For the Levites left their common-lands and their possessions and came to Judah and Jerusalem, for Jeroboam and his sons had rejected them from serving as priests to the LORD. [15]Then he appointed for himself priests for the high places, for the demons, and the calf idols which he had made. [16]And after *the Levites left,*[a] those from all the tribes of Israel, such as set their heart to seek the LORD God of Israel, came to Jerusalem to sacrifice to the LORD God of their

---

10:11 [a]Literally *scorpions* **10:14** [a]Following many Hebrew manuscripts, Septuagint, Syriac, and Vulgate (compare verse 10 and 1 Kings 12:14); Masoretic Text reads *I*. [b]Literally *scorpions*
11:16 [a]Literally *after them*

fathers. [17]So they strengthened the kingdom of Judah, and made Rehoboam the son of Solomon strong for three years, because they walked in the way of David and Solomon for three years.

THE FAMILY OF REHOBOAM

[18]Then Rehoboam took for himself as wife Mahalath the daughter of Jerimoth the son of David, *and of* Abihail the daughter of Eliah the son of Jesse. [19]And she bore him children: Jeush, Shamariah, and Zaham. [20]After her he took Maachah the granddaughter[a] of Absalom; and she bore him Abijah, Attai, Ziza, and Shelomith. [21]Now Rehoboam loved Maachah the granddaughter of Absalom more than all his wives and his concubines; for he took eighteen wives and sixty concubines, and begot twenty-eight sons and sixty daughters. [22]And Rehoboam appointed Abijah the son of Maachah as chief, *to be* leader among his brothers; for he *intended* to make him king. [23]He dealt wisely, and dispersed some of his sons throughout all the territories of Judah and Benjamin, to every fortified city; and he gave them provisions in abundance. He also sought many wives *for them.*

EGYPT ATTACKS JUDAH

12 Now it came to pass, when Rehoboam had established the kingdom and had strengthened himself, that he forsook the law of the LORD, and all Israel along with him. [2]And it happened in the fifth year of King Rehoboam *that* Shishak king of Egypt came up against Jerusalem, because they had transgressed against the LORD, [3]with twelve hundred chariots, sixty thousand horsemen, and people without number who came with him out of Egypt—the Lubim and the Sukkiim and the Ethiopians. [4]And he took the fortified cities of Judah and came to Jerusalem.

[5]Then Shemaiah the prophet came to Rehoboam and the leaders of Judah, who were gathered together in Jerusalem because of Shishak, and said to them, "Thus says the LORD: 'You have forsaken Me, and therefore I also have left you in the hand of Shishak.' "

[6]So the leaders of Israel and the king humbled themselves; and they said, "The LORD *is* righteous."

[7]Now when the LORD saw that they humbled themselves, the word of the LORD came to Shemaiah, saying, "They have humbled themselves; *therefore* I will not destroy them, but I will grant them some deliverance. My wrath shall not be poured out on Jerusalem by the hand of Shishak. [8]Nevertheless they will be his servants, that they may distinguish My service from the service of the kingdoms of the nations."

[9]So Shishak king of Egypt came up against Jerusalem, and took away the treasures of the house of the LORD and the treasures of the king's house; he took everything. He also carried away the gold shields which Solomon had made. [10]Then King Rehoboam made bronze shields in their place, and committed *them* to the hands of the captains of the guard, who guarded the doorway of the king's house. [11]And whenever the king entered the house of the LORD, the guard would go and bring them out; then they would take them back into the guardroom. [12]When he humbled himself, the wrath of the LORD turned from him, so as not to destroy *him* completely; and things also went well in Judah.

THE END OF REHOBOAM'S REIGN

[13]Thus King Rehoboam strengthened himself in Jerusalem and reigned. Now Rehoboam *was* forty-one years old when he became king; and he reigned seventeen years in Jerusalem, the city which the LORD had chosen out of all the tribes of Israel, to put His name there. His mother's name *was* Naamah, an Ammonitess. [14]And he did evil, because he did not prepare his heart to seek the LORD.

[15]The acts of Rehoboam, first and last, *are* they not written in the book of Shemaiah the prophet, and of Iddo the seer concerning genealogies? And *there were* wars between Rehoboam and Jeroboam all their days. [16]So Rehoboam rested with his fathers, and was buried in the City of David. Then Abijah[a] his son reigned in his place.

ABIJAH REIGNS IN JUDAH

13 In the eighteenth year of King Jeroboam, Abijah became king over Judah. [2]He reigned three years in Jerusalem. His mother's name *was* Michaiah[a] the daughter of Uriel of Gibeah.

11:20 [a]Literally *daughter,* but in the broader sense of granddaughter (compare 2 Chronicles 13:2)
12:16 [a]Spelled *Abijam* in 1 Kings 14:31
13:2 [a]Spelled *Maachah* in 11:20, 21 and 1 Kings 15:2

And there was war between Abijah and Jeroboam. 3Abijah set the battle in order with an
army of valiant warriors, four hundred thousand choice men. Jeroboam also drew up in
battle formation against him with eight hundred thousand choice men, mighty men of
valor.
4Then Abijah stood on Mount Zemaraim,
which *is* in the mountains of Ephraim, and
said, "Hear me, Jeroboam and all Israel:
5Should you not know that the LORD God of
Israel gave the dominion over Israel to David
forever, to him and his sons, by a covenant of
salt? 6Yet Jeroboam the son of Nebat, the servant of Solomon the son of David, rose up and
rebelled against his lord. 7Then worthless
rogues gathered to him, and strengthened
themselves against Rehoboam the son of Solomon, when Rehoboam was young and inexperienced and could not withstand them.
8And now you think to withstand the kingdom
of the LORD, which is in the hand of the sons
of David; and you *are* a great multitude, and
with you are the gold calves which Jeroboam
made for you as gods. 9Have you not cast out
the priests of the LORD, the sons of Aaron, and
the Levites, and made for yourselves priests,
like the peoples of *other* lands, so that whoever comes to consecrate himself with a
young bull and seven rams may be a priest of
things that are not gods? 10But as for us, the
LORD *is* our God, and we have not forsaken
Him; and the priests who minister to the LORD
are the sons of Aaron, and the Levites *attend*
to *their* duties. 11And they burn to the LORD
every morning and every evening burnt sacrifices and sweet incense; *they* also *set* the
showbread *in order on* the pure *gold* table, and
the lampstand of gold with its lamps to burn
every evening; for we keep the command of
the LORD our God, but you have forsaken Him.
12Now look, God Himself is with us as *our*
head, and His priests with sounding trumpets
to sound the alarm against you. O children of
Israel, do not fight against the LORD God of
your fathers, for you shall not prosper!"
13But Jeroboam caused an ambush to go
around behind them; so they were in front of
Judah, and the ambush *was* behind them.
14And when Judah looked around, to their
surprise the battle line *was* at both front and
rear; and they cried out to the LORD, and the
priests sounded the trumpets. 15Then the men
of Judah gave a shout; and as the men of Judah shouted, it happened that God struck Jeroboam and all Israel before Abijah and Judah.
16And the children of Israel fled before Judah,
and God delivered them into their hand.
17Then Abijah and his people struck them
with a great slaughter; so five hundred thousand choice men of Israel fell slain. 18Thus the
children of Israel were subdued at that time;
and the children of Judah prevailed, because
they relied on the LORD God of their fathers.
19And Abijah pursued Jeroboam and took
cities from him: Bethel with its villages, Jesha-
nah with its villages, and Ephrain[a] with its villages. 20So Jeroboam did not recover strength
again in the days of Abijah; and the LORD
struck him, and he died.
21But Abijah grew mighty, married fourteen
wives, and begot twenty-two sons and sixteen
daughters. 22Now the rest of the acts of Abijah, his ways, and his sayings *are* written in
the annals of the prophet Iddo.

14 So Abijah rested with his fathers, and
they buried him in the City of David.
Then Asa his son reigned in his place. In his
days the land was quiet for ten years.

ASA REIGNS IN JUDAH

2Asa did *what was* good and right in the
eyes of the LORD his God, 3for he removed the
altars of the foreign *gods* and the high places,
and broke down the *sacred* pillars and cut
down the wooden images. 4He commanded
Judah to seek the LORD God of their fathers,
and to observe the law and the commandment. 5He also removed the high places and
the incense altars from all the cities of Judah,
and the kingdom was quiet under him. 6And
he built fortified cities in Judah, for the land
had rest; he had no war in those years, because the LORD had given him rest. 7Therefore
he said to Judah, "Let us build these cities and
make walls around *them*, and towers, gates,
and bars, *while* the land *is* yet before us, because we have sought the LORD our God; we
have sought *Him*, and He has given us rest on
every side." So they built and prospered. 8And
Asa had an army of three hundred thousand
from Judah who carried shields and spears,
and from Benjamin two hundred and eighty
thousand men who carried shields and drew
bows; all these *were* mighty men of valor.
9Then Zerah the Ethiopian came out against

13:19 [a]Or *Ephron*

them with an army of a million men and three hundred chariots, and he came to Mareshah. [10]So Asa went out against him, and they set the troops in battle array in the Valley of Zephathah at Mareshah. [11]And Asa cried out to the LORD his God, and said, "LORD, *it is* nothing for You to help, whether with many or with those who have no power; help us, O LORD our God, for we rest on You, and in Your name we go against this multitude. O LORD, You *are* our God; do not let man prevail against You!"

[12]So the LORD struck the Ethiopians before Asa and Judah, and the Ethiopians fled. [13]And Asa and the people who *were* with him pursued them to Gerar. So the Ethiopians were overthrown, and they could not recover, for they were broken before the LORD and His army. And they carried away very much spoil. [14]Then they defeated all the cities around Gerar, for the fear of the LORD came upon them; and they plundered all the cities, for there was exceedingly much spoil in them. [15]They also attacked the livestock enclosures, and carried off sheep and camels in abundance, and returned to Jerusalem.

The Reforms of Asa

15 Now the Spirit of God came upon Azariah the son of Oded. [2]And he went out to meet Asa, and said to him: "Hear me, Asa, and all Judah and Benjamin. The LORD *is* with you while you are with Him. If you seek Him, He will be found by you; but if you forsake Him, He will forsake you. [3]For a long time Israel *has been* without the true God, without a teaching priest, and without law; [4]but when in their trouble they turned to the LORD God of Israel, and sought Him, He was found by them. [5]And in those times *there was* no peace to the one who went out, nor to the one who came in, but great turmoil *was* on all the inhabitants of the lands. [6]So nation was destroyed by nation, and city by city, for God troubled them with every adversity. [7]But you, be strong and do not let your hands be weak, for your work shall be rewarded!"

[8]And when Asa heard these words and the prophecy of Oded[a] the prophet, he took courage, and removed the abominable idols from all the land of Judah and Benjamin and from the cities which he had taken in the mountains of Ephraim; and he restored the altar of the LORD that *was* before the vestibule of the LORD. [9]Then he gathered all Judah and Benjamin, and those who dwelt with them from Ephraim, Manasseh, and Simeon, for they came over to him in great numbers from Israel when they saw that the LORD his God was with him.

[10]So they gathered together at Jerusalem in the third month, in the fifteenth year of the reign of Asa. [11]And they offered to the LORD at that time seven hundred bulls and seven thousand sheep from the spoil they had brought. [12]Then they entered into a covenant to seek the LORD God of their fathers with all their heart and with all their soul; [13]and whoever would not seek the LORD God of Israel was to be put to death, whether small or great, whether man or woman. [14]Then they took an oath before the LORD with a loud voice, with shouting and trumpets and rams' horns. [15]And all Judah rejoiced at the oath, for they had sworn with all their heart and sought Him with all their soul; and He was found by them, and the LORD gave them rest all around.

[16]Also he removed Maachah, the mother of Asa the king, from *being* queen mother, because she had made an obscene image of Asherah;[a] and Asa cut down her obscene image, then crushed and burned *it* by the Brook Kidron. [17]But the high places were not removed from Israel. Nevertheless the heart of Asa was loyal all his days.

[18]He also brought into the house of God the things that his father had dedicated and that he himself had dedicated: silver and gold and utensils. [19]And there was no war until the thirty-fifth year of the reign of Asa.

Asa's Treaty with Syria

16 In the thirty-sixth year of the reign of Asa, Baasha king of Israel came up against Judah and built Ramah, that he might let none go out or come in to Asa king of Judah. [2]Then Asa brought silver and gold from the treasuries of the house of the LORD and of the king's house, and sent to Ben-Hadad king of Syria, who dwelt in Damascus, saying, [3]"*Let there be* a treaty between you and me, as there was between my father and your father. See, I have sent you silver and gold; come, break your treaty with Baasha king of Israel, so that he will withdraw from me."

15:8 [a]Following Masoretic Text and Septuagint; Syriac and Vulgate read *Azariah the son of Oded* (compare verse 1). **15:16** [a]A Canaanite deity

4So Ben-Hadad heeded King Asa, and sent
the captains of his armies against the cities of
Israel. They attacked Ijon, Dan, Abel Maim,
and all the storage cities of Naphtali. 5Now it
happened, when Baasha heard *it,* that he
stopped building Ramah and ceased his work.
6Then King Asa took all Judah, and they carried away the stones and timber of Ramah,
which Baasha had used for building; and with
them he built Geba and Mizpah.

Hanani's Message to Asa

7And at that time Hanani the seer came to
Asa king of Judah, and said to him: "Because
you have relied on the king of Syria, and have
not relied on the LORD your God, therefore the
army of the king of Syria has escaped from
your hand. 8Were the Ethiopians and the
Lubim not a huge army with very many chariots and horsemen? Yet, because you relied on
the LORD, He delivered them into your hand.
9For the eyes of the LORD run to and fro
throughout the whole earth, to show Himself
strong on behalf of *those* whose heart *is* loyal
to Him. In this you have done foolishly; therefore from now on you shall have wars."
10Then Asa was angry with the seer, and put
him in prison, for *he was* enraged at him because of this. And Asa oppressed *some* of the
people at that time.

Illness and Death of Asa

11Note that the acts of Asa, first and last, are
indeed written in the book of the kings of Judah and Israel. 12And in the thirty-ninth year
of his reign, Asa became diseased in his feet,
and his malady was severe; yet in his disease
he did not seek the LORD, but the physicians.

13So Asa rested with his fathers; he died in
the forty-first year of his reign. 14They buried
him in his own tomb, which he had made for
himself in the City of David; and they laid
him in the bed which was filled with spices
and various ingredients prepared in a mixture
of ointments. They made a very great burning
for him.

Jehoshaphat Reigns in Judah

17 Then Jehoshaphat his son reigned in
his place, and strengthened himself
against Israel. 2And he placed troops in all the
fortified cities of Judah, and set garrisons in
the land of Judah and in the cities of Ephraim
which Asa his father had taken. 3Now the
LORD was with Jehoshaphat, because he
walked in the former ways of his father David;
he did not seek the Baals, 4but sought the
God[a] of his father, and walked in His commandments and not according to the acts of
Israel. 5Therefore the LORD established the
kingdom in his hand; and all Judah gave presents to Jehoshaphat, and he had riches and
honor in abundance. 6And his heart took delight in the ways of the LORD; moreover he removed the high places and wooden images
from Judah.

7Also in the third year of his reign he sent
his leaders, Ben-Hail, Obadiah, Zechariah,
Nethanel, and Michaiah, to teach in the cities
of Judah. 8And with them *he sent* Levites:
Shemaiah, Nethaniah, Zebadiah, Asahel,
Shemiramoth, Jehonathan, Adonijah, Tobijah, and Tobadonijah—the Levites; and with
them Elishama and Jehoram, the priests. 9So
they taught in Judah, and *had* the Book of the
Law of the LORD with them; they went
throughout all the cities of Judah and taught
the people.

10And the fear of the LORD fell on all the
kingdoms of the lands that *were* around Judah, so that they did not make war against
Jehoshaphat. 11Also *some* of the Philistines
brought Jehoshaphat presents and silver as
tribute; and the Arabians brought him flocks,
seven thousand seven hundred rams and
seven thousand seven hundred male goats.

12So Jehoshaphat became increasingly powerful, and he built fortresses and storage cities
in Judah. 13He had much property in the cities
of Judah; and the men of war, mighty men of
valor, *were* in Jerusalem.

14These *are* their numbers, according to
their fathers' houses. Of Judah, the captains of
thousands: Adnah the captain, and with him
three hundred thousand mighty men of valor;
15and next to him *was* Jehohanan the captain,
and with him two hundred and eighty thousand; 16and next to him *was* Amasiah the son
of Zichri, who willingly offered himself to the
LORD, and with him two hundred thousand
mighty men of valor. 17Of Benjamin: Eliada
a mighty man of valor, and with him two
hundred thousand men armed with bow and
shield; 18and next to him *was* Jehozabad,
and with him one hundred and eighty thousand prepared for war. 19These served the

17:4 [a]Septuagint reads *LORD God.*

king, besides those the king put in the fortified
cities throughout all Judah.

Micaiah Warns Ahab

18 Jehoshaphat had riches and honor in
abundance; and by marriage he allied
himself with Ahab. 2After some years he went
down to *visit* Ahab in Samaria; and Ahab
killed sheep and oxen in abundance for him
and the people who were with him, and persuaded him to go up *with him* to Ramoth
Gilead. 3So Ahab king of Israel said to Jehoshaphat king of Judah, "Will you go with me
against Ramoth Gilead?"

And he answered him, "I *am* as you *are*,
and my people as your people; *we will be* with
you in the war."

4Also Jehoshaphat said to the king of Israel,
"Please inquire for the word of the LORD
today."

5Then the king of Israel gathered the prophets together, four hundred men, and said to
them, "Shall we go to war against Ramoth Gilead, or shall I refrain?"

So they said, "Go up, for God will deliver it
into the king's hand."

6But Jehoshaphat said, "*Is there* not still a
prophet of the LORD here, that we may inquire
of Him?"[a]

7So the king of Israel said to Jehoshaphat,
"*There is* still one man by whom we may inquire of the LORD; but I hate him, because he
never prophesies good concerning me, but always evil. He *is* Micaiah the son of Imla."

And Jehoshaphat said, "Let not the king say
such things!"

8Then the king of Israel called one *of his* officers and said, "Bring Micaiah the son of Imla
quickly!"

9The king of Israel and Jehoshaphat king of
Judah, clothed in *their* robes, sat each on his
throne; and they sat at a threshing floor at the
entrance of the gate of Samaria; and all the
prophets prophesied before them. 10Now Zedekiah the son of Chenaanah had made horns
of iron for himself; and he said, "Thus says
the LORD: 'With these you shall gore the Syrians until they are destroyed.' "

11And all the prophets prophesied so, saying, "Go up to Ramoth Gilead and prosper,
for the LORD will deliver *it* into the king's
hand."

12Then the messenger who had gone to call
Micaiah spoke to him, saying, "Now listen,
the words of the prophets with one accord encourage the king. Therefore please let your
word be like *the word of* one of them, and
speak encouragement."

13And Micaiah said, "*As* the LORD lives,
whatever my God says, that I will speak."

14Then he came to the king; and the king
said to him, "Micaiah, shall we go to war
against Ramoth Gilead, or shall I refrain?"

And he said, "Go and prosper, and they
shall be delivered into your hand!"

15So the king said to him, "How many times
shall I make you swear that you tell me nothing but the truth in the name of the LORD?"

16Then he said, "I saw all Israel scattered on
the mountains, as sheep that have no shepherd. And the LORD said, 'These have no master. Let each return to his house in peace.' "

17And the king of Israel said to Jehoshaphat,
"Did I not tell you he would not prophesy
good concerning me, but evil?"

18Then *Micaiah* said, "Therefore hear the
word of the LORD: I saw the LORD sitting on
His throne, and all the host of heaven standing
on His right hand and His left. 19And the LORD
said, 'Who will persuade Ahab king of Israel
to go up, that he may fall at Ramoth Gilead?'
So one spoke in this manner, and another
spoke in that manner. 20Then a spirit came forward and stood before the LORD, and said, 'I
will persuade him.' The LORD said to him, 'In
what way?' 21So he said, 'I will go out and be a
lying spirit in the mouth of all his prophets.'
And *the LORD* said, 'You shall persuade *him*
and also prevail; go out and do so.' 22Therefore
look! The LORD has put a lying spirit in the
mouth of these prophets of yours, and the
LORD has declared disaster against you."

23Then Zedekiah the son of Chenaanah
went near and struck Micaiah on the cheek,
and said, "Which way did the spirit from the
LORD go from me to speak to you?"

24And Micaiah said, "Indeed you shall see
on that day when you go into an inner chamber to hide!"

25Then the king of Israel said, "Take Micaiah, and return him to Amon the governor of
the city and to Joash the king's son; 26and say,
'Thus says the king: "Put this *fellow* in prison,
and feed him with bread of affliction and water of affliction, until I return in peace." ' "

27But Micaiah said, "If you ever return in

18:6 [a]Or *him*

peace, the LORD has not spoken by me." And he said, "Take heed, all you people!"

AHAB DIES IN BATTLE

28So the king of Israel and Jehoshaphat the king of Judah went up to Ramoth Gilead. 29And the king of Israel said to Jehoshaphat, "I will disguise myself and go into battle; but you put on your robes." So the king of Israel disguised himself, and they went into battle.

30Now the king of Syria had commanded the captains of the chariots who *were* with him, saying, "Fight with no one small or great, but only with the king of Israel."

31So it was, when the captains of the chariots saw Jehoshaphat, that they said, "It *is* the king of Israel!" Therefore they surrounded him to attack; but Jehoshaphat cried out, and the LORD helped him, and God diverted them from him. 32For so it was, when the captains of the chariots saw that it was not the king of Israel, that they turned back from pursuing him. 33Now a certain man drew a bow at random, and struck the king of Israel between the joints of his armor. So he said to the driver of his chariot, "Turn around and take me out of the battle, for I am wounded." 34The battle increased that day, and the king of Israel propped *himself* up in *his* chariot facing the Syrians until evening; and about the time of sunset he died.

19 Then Jehoshaphat the king of Judah returned safely to his house in Jerusalem. 2And Jehu the son of Hanani the seer went out to meet him, and said to King Jehoshaphat, "Should you help the wicked and love those who hate the LORD? Therefore the wrath of the LORD *is* upon you. 3Nevertheless good things are found in you, in that you have removed the wooden images from the land, and have prepared your heart to seek God."

THE REFORMS OF JEHOSHAPHAT

4So Jehoshaphat dwelt at Jerusalem; and he went out again among the people from Beersheba to the mountains of Ephraim, and brought them back to the LORD God of their fathers. 5Then he set judges in the land throughout all the fortified cities of Judah, city by city, 6and said to the judges, "Take heed to what you are doing, for you do not judge for man but for the LORD, who *is* with you in the judgment. 7Now therefore, let the fear of the LORD be upon you; take care and do *it*, for *there is* no iniquity with the LORD our God, no partiality, nor taking of bribes."

8Moreover in Jerusalem, for the judgment of the LORD and for controversies, Jehoshaphat appointed some of the Levites and priests, and some of the chief fathers of Israel, when they returned to Jerusalem.[a] 9And he commanded them, saying, "Thus you shall act in the fear of the LORD, faithfully and with a loyal heart: 10Whatever case comes to you from your brethren who dwell in their cities, whether of bloodshed or offenses against law or commandment, against statutes or ordinances, you shall warn them, lest they trespass against the LORD and wrath come upon you and your brethren. Do this, and you will not be guilty. 11And take notice: Amariah the chief priest *is* over you in all matters of the LORD; and Zebadiah the son of Ishmael, the ruler of the house of Judah, for all the king's matters; also the Levites *will be* officials before you. Behave courageously, and the LORD will be with the good."

AMMON, MOAB, AND MOUNT SEIR DEFEATED

20 It happened after this *that* the people of Moab with the people of Ammon, and *others* with them besides the Ammonites,[a] came to battle against Jehoshaphat. 2Then some came and told Jehoshaphat, saying, "A great multitude is coming against you from beyond the sea, from Syria;[a] and they are in Hazazon Tamar" (which *is* En Gedi). 3And Jehoshaphat feared, and set himself to seek the LORD, and proclaimed a fast throughout all Judah. 4So Judah gathered together to ask *help* from the LORD; and from all the cities of Judah they came to seek the LORD.

5Then Jehoshaphat stood in the assembly of Judah and Jerusalem, in the house of the LORD, before the new court, 6and said: "O LORD God of our fathers, *are* You not God in heaven, and do You *not* rule over all the kingdoms of the nations, and in Your hand *is there not* power and might, so that no one is able to withstand You? 7*Are* You not our God, *who* drove out the inhabitants of this land before Your people Israel, and gave it to the descen-

---

19:8 [a]Septuagint and Vulgate read *for the inhabitants of Jerusalem*. **20:1** [a]Following Masoretic Text and Vulgate; Septuagint reads *Meunites* (compare 26:7). **20:2** [a]Following Masoretic Text, Septuagint, and Vulgate; some Hebrew manuscripts and Old Latin read *Edom*.

dants of Abraham Your friend forever? [8]And they dwell in it, and have built You a sanctuary in it for Your name, saying, [9]'If disaster comes upon us—sword, judgment, pestilence, or famine—we will stand before this temple and in Your presence (for Your name *is* in this temple), and cry out to You in our affliction, and You will hear and save.' [10]And now, here are the people of Ammon, Moab, and Mount Seir—whom You would not let Israel invade when they came out of the land of Egypt, but they turned from them and did not destroy them— [11]here they are, rewarding us by coming to throw us out of Your possession which You have given us to inherit. [12]O our God, will You not judge them? For we have no power against this great multitude that is coming against us; nor do we know what to do, but our eyes *are* upon You."

[13]Now all Judah, with their little ones, their wives, and their children, stood before the LORD.

[14]Then the Spirit of the LORD came upon Jahaziel the son of Zechariah, the son of Benaiah, the son of Jeiel, the son of Mattaniah, a Levite of the sons of Asaph, in the midst of the assembly. [15]And he said, "Listen, all you of Judah and you inhabitants of Jerusalem, and you, King Jehoshaphat! Thus says the LORD to you: 'Do not be afraid nor dismayed because of this great multitude, for the battle *is* not yours, but God's. [16]Tomorrow go down against them. They will surely come up by the Ascent of Ziz, and you will find them at the end of the brook before the Wilderness of Jeruel. [17]You will not *need* to fight in this *battle*. Position yourselves, stand still and see the salvation of the LORD, who is with you, O Judah and Jerusalem!' Do not fear or be dismayed; tomorrow go out against them, for the LORD *is* with you."

[18]And Jehoshaphat bowed his head with *his* face to the ground, and all Judah and the inhabitants of Jerusalem bowed before the LORD, worshiping the LORD. [19]Then the Levites of the children of the Kohathites and of the children of the Korahites stood up to praise the LORD God of Israel with voices loud and high.

[20]So they rose early in the morning and went out into the Wilderness of Tekoa; and as they went out, Jehoshaphat stood and said, "Hear me, O Judah and you inhabitants of Jerusalem: Believe in the LORD your God, and you shall be established; believe His prophets, and you shall prosper." [21]And when he had consulted with the people, he appointed those who should sing to the LORD, and who should praise the beauty of holiness, as they went out before the army and were saying:

"Praise the LORD,
For His mercy *endures* forever."[a]

[22]Now when they began to sing and to praise, the LORD set ambushes against the people of Ammon, Moab, and Mount Seir, who had come against Judah; and they were defeated. [23]For the people of Ammon and Moab stood up against the inhabitants of Mount Seir to utterly kill and destroy *them*. And when they had made an end of the inhabitants of Seir, they helped to destroy one another.

[24]So when Judah came to a place overlooking the wilderness, they looked toward the multitude; and there *were* their dead bodies, fallen on the earth. No one had escaped.

[25]When Jehoshaphat and his people came to take away their spoil, they found among them an abundance of valuables on the dead bodies,[a] and precious jewelry, which they

---

20:21 [a]Compare Psalm 106:1 **20:25** [a]A few Hebrew manuscripts, Old Latin, and Vulgate read *garments;* Septuagint reads *armor.*

SOUL NOTE

A Desperate Call *(20:20)* Jehoshaphat faced a serious crisis when he was attacked by his enemies on all sides. In his greatest moment of desperation, he ordered the nation of Israel to worship the Lord and call upon Him for deliverance. He said, "Believe in the LORD your God, and you shall be established." We can call on God even in the greatest crises and challenges of life. Jehoshaphat knew that he was inadequate to win this battle without God's help, so he focused the nation's attention on the only One who really could deliver them, the Lord Himself. **Topic: Crises**

stripped off for themselves, more than they could carry away; and they were three days gathering the spoil because there was so much. 26And on the fourth day they assembled in the Valley of Berachah, for there they blessed the LORD; therefore the name of that place was called The Valley of Berachah[a] until this day. 27Then they returned, every man of Judah and Jerusalem, with Jehoshaphat in front of them, to go back to Jerusalem with joy, for the LORD had made them rejoice over their enemies. 28So they came to Jerusalem, with stringed instruments and harps and trumpets, to the house of the LORD. 29And the fear of God was on all the kingdoms of *those* countries when they heard that the LORD had fought against the enemies of Israel. 30Then the realm of Jehoshaphat was quiet, for his God gave him rest all around.

The End of Jehoshaphat's Reign

31So Jehoshaphat was king over Judah. *He was* thirty-five years old when he became king, and he reigned twenty-five years in Jerusalem. His mother's name *was* Azubah the daughter of Shilhi. 32And he walked in the way of his father Asa, and did not turn aside from it, doing *what was* right in the sight of the LORD. 33Nevertheless the high places were not taken away, for as yet the people had not directed their hearts to the God of their fathers.

34Now the rest of the acts of Jehoshaphat, first and last, indeed they *are* written in the book of Jehu the son of Hanani, which *is* mentioned in the book of the kings of Israel.

35After this Jehoshaphat king of Judah allied himself with Ahaziah king of Israel, who acted very wickedly. 36And he allied himself with him to make ships to go to Tarshish, and they made the ships in Ezion Geber. 37But Eliezer the son of Dodavah of Mareshah prophesied against Jehoshaphat, saying, "Because you have allied yourself with Ahaziah, the LORD has destroyed your works." Then the ships were wrecked, so that they were not able to go to Tarshish.

Jehoram Reigns in Judah

21 And Jehoshaphat rested with his fathers, and was buried with his fathers in the City of David. Then Jehoram his son reigned in his place. 2He had brothers, the sons of Jehoshaphat: Azariah, Jehiel, Zechariah, Azaryahu, Michael, and Shephatiah; all these *were* the sons of Jehoshaphat king of Israel. 3Their father gave them great gifts of silver and gold and precious things, with fortified cities in Judah; but he gave the kingdom to Jehoram, because he *was* the firstborn.

4Now when Jehoram was established over the kingdom of his father, he strengthened himself and killed all his brothers with the sword, and also *others* of the princes of Israel.

5Jehoram *was* thirty-two years old when he became king, and he reigned eight years in Jerusalem. 6And he walked in the way of the kings of Israel, just as the house of Ahab had done, for he had the daughter of Ahab as a wife; and he did evil in the sight of the LORD. 7Yet the LORD would not destroy the house of David, because of the covenant that He had made with David, and since He had promised to give a lamp to him and to his sons forever.

8In his days Edom revolted against Judah's authority, and made a king over themselves. 9So Jehoram went out with his officers, and all his chariots with him. And he rose by night and attacked the Edomites who had surrounded him and the captains of the chariots. 10Thus Edom has been in revolt against Judah's authority to this day. At that time Libnah revolted against his rule, because he had forsaken the LORD God of his fathers. 11Moreover he made high places in the mountains of Judah, and caused the inhabitants of Jerusalem to commit harlotry, and led Judah astray.

12And a letter came to him from Elijah the prophet, saying,

> Thus says the LORD God of your father
> David:
> Because you have not walked in the
> ways of Jehoshaphat your father, or in
> the ways of Asa king of Judah, 13but
> have walked in the way of the kings of
> Israel, and have made Judah and the
> inhabitants of Jerusalem to play the
> harlot like the harlotry of the house of
> Ahab, and also have killed your
> brothers, those of your father's
> household, *who were* better than
> yourself, 14behold, the LORD will strike
> your people with a serious affliction—
> your children, your wives, and all your

20:26 [a]Literally *Blessing*

possessions; [15]and you *will become* very sick with a disease of your intestines, until your intestines come out by reason of the sickness, day by day.

[16]Moreover the LORD stirred up against Jehoram the spirit of the Philistines and the Arabians who *were* near the Ethiopians. [17]And they came up into Judah and invaded it, and carried away all the possessions that were found in the king's house, and also his sons and his wives, so that there was not a son left to him except Jehoahaz,[a] the youngest of his sons.

[18]After all this the LORD struck him in his intestines with an incurable disease. [19]Then it happened in the course of time, after the end of two years, that his intestines came out because of his sickness; so he died in severe pain. And his people made no burning for him, like the burning for his fathers.

[20]He was thirty-two years old when he became king. He reigned in Jerusalem eight years and, to no one's sorrow, departed. However they buried him in the City of David, but not in the tombs of the kings.

AHAZIAH REIGNS IN JUDAH

22 Then the inhabitants of Jerusalem made Ahaziah his youngest son king in his place, for the raiders who came with the Arabians into the camp had killed all the older *sons*. So Ahaziah the son of Jehoram, king of Judah, reigned. [2]Ahaziah *was* forty-two[a] years old when he became king, and he reigned one year in Jerusalem. His mother's name *was* Athaliah the granddaughter of Omri. [3]He also walked in the ways of the house of Ahab, for his mother advised him to do wickedly. [4]Therefore he did evil in the sight of the LORD, like the house of Ahab; for they were his counselors after the death of his father, to his destruction. [5]He also followed their advice, and went with Jehoram[a] the son of Ahab king of Israel to war against Hazael king of Syria at Ramoth Gilead; and the Syrians wounded Joram. [6]Then he returned to Jezreel to recover from the wounds which he had received at Ramah, when he fought against Hazael king of Syria. And Azariah[a] the son of Jehoram, king of Judah, went down to see Jehoram the son of Ahab in Jezreel, because he was sick.

[7]His going to Joram was God's occasion for Ahaziah's downfall; for when he arrived, he went out with Jehoram against Jehu the son of Nimshi, whom the LORD had anointed to cut off the house of Ahab. [8]And it happened, when Jehu was executing judgment on the house of Ahab, and found the princes of Judah and the sons of Ahaziah's brothers who served Ahaziah, that he killed them. [9]Then he searched for Ahaziah; and they caught him (he was hiding in Samaria), and brought him to Jehu. When they had killed him, they buried him, "because," they said, "he is the son of Jehoshaphat, who sought the LORD with all his heart."

So the house of Ahaziah had no one to assume power over the kingdom.

ATHALIAH REIGNS IN JUDAH

[10]Now when Athaliah the mother of Ahaziah saw that her son was dead, she arose and destroyed all the royal heirs of the house of Judah. [11]But Jehoshabeath,[a] the daughter of the king, took Joash the son of Ahaziah, and stole him away from among the king's sons who were being murdered, and put him and his nurse in a bedroom. So Jehoshabeath, the daughter of King Jehoram, the wife of Jehoiada the priest (for she was the sister of Ahaziah), hid him from Athaliah so that she did not kill him. [12]And he was hidden with them in the house of God for six years, while Athaliah reigned over the land.

JOASH CROWNED KING OF JUDAH

23 In the seventh year Jehoiada strengthened himself, *and made a* covenant with the captains of hundreds: Azariah the son of Jeroham, Ishmael the son of Jehohanan, Azariah the son of Obed, Maaseiah the son of Adaiah, and Elishaphat the son of Zichri. [2]And they went throughout Judah and gathered the Levites from all the cities of Judah, and the chief fathers of Israel, and they came to Jerusalem.

[3]Then all the assembly made a covenant with the king in the house of God. And he said to them, "Behold, the king's son shall reign, as the LORD has said of the sons of David.

21:17 [a]Elsewhere called *Ahaziah* (compare 2 Chronicles 22:1) **22:2** [a]Or *twenty-two* (compare 2 Kings 8:26) **22:5** [a]Also spelled *Joram* (compare verses 5 and 7; 2 Kings 8:28; and elsewhere) **22:6** [a]Some Hebrew manuscripts, Septuagint, Syriac, Vulgate, and 2 Kings 8:29 read *Ahaziah.* **22:11** [a]Spelled *Jehosheba* in 2 Kings 11:2

4This *is* what you shall do: One-third of you entering on the Sabbath, of the priests and the Levites, *shall be* keeping watch over the doors; 5one-third *shall be* at the king's house; and one-third at the Gate of the Foundation. All the people *shall be* in the courts of the house of the LORD. 6But let no one come into the house of the LORD except the priests and those of the Levites who serve. They may go in, for they *are* holy; but all the people shall keep the watch of the LORD. 7And the Levites shall surround the king on all sides, every man with his weapons in his hand; and whoever comes into the house, let him be put to death. You are to be with the king when he comes in and when he goes out."

8So the Levites and all Judah did according to all that Jehoiada the priest commanded. And each man took his men who were to be on duty on the Sabbath, with those who were going *off duty* on the Sabbath; for Jehoiada the priest had not dismissed the divisions. 9And Jehoiada the priest gave to the captains of hundreds the spears and the large and small shields which *had belonged* to King David, that *were* in the temple of God. 10Then he set all the people, every man with his weapon in his hand, from the right side of the temple to the left side of the temple, along by the altar and by the temple, all around the king. 11And they brought out the king's son, put the crown on him, *gave him* the Testimony,[a] and made him king. Then Jehoiada and his sons anointed him, and said, "*Long* live the king!"

Death of Athaliah

12Now when Athaliah heard the noise of the people running and praising the king, she came to the people *in* the temple of the LORD. 13*When* she looked, there was the king standing by his pillar at the entrance; and the leaders and the trumpeters *were* by the king. All the people of the land were rejoicing and blowing trumpets, also the singers with musical instruments, and those who led in praise. So Athaliah tore her clothes and said, "Treason! Treason!"

14And Jehoiada the priest brought out the captains of hundreds who were set over the army, and said to them, "Take her outside under guard, and slay with the sword whoever follows her." For the priest had said, "Do not kill her in the house of the LORD."

15So they seized her; and she went by way of the entrance of the Horse Gate *into* the king's house, and they killed her there.

16Then Jehoiada made a covenant between himself, the people, and the king, that they should be the LORD's people. 17And all the people went to the temple[a] of Baal, and tore it down. They broke in pieces its altars and images, and killed Mattan the priest of Baal before the altars. 18Also Jehoiada appointed the oversight of the house of the LORD to the hand of the priests, the Levites, whom David had assigned in the house of the LORD, to offer the burnt offerings of the LORD, as *it is* written in the Law of Moses, with rejoicing and with singing, *as it was established* by David. 19And he set the gatekeepers at the gates of the house of the LORD, so that no one *who was* in any way unclean should enter.

20Then he took the captains of hundreds, the nobles, the governors of the people, and all the people of the land, and brought the king down from the house of the LORD; and they went through the Upper Gate to the king's house, and set the king on the throne of the kingdom. 21So all the people of the land rejoiced; and the city was quiet, for they had slain Athaliah with the sword.

Joash Repairs the Temple

24 Joash *was* seven years old when he became king, and he reigned forty years in Jerusalem. His mother's name *was* Zibiah of Beersheba. 2Joash did *what was* right in the sight of the LORD all the days of Jehoiada the priest. 3And Jehoiada took two wives for him, and he had sons and daughters.

4Now it happened after this *that* Joash set his heart on repairing the house of the LORD. 5Then he gathered the priests and the Levites, and said to them, "Go out to the cities of Judah, and gather from all Israel money to repair the house of your God from year to year, and see that you do it quickly."

However the Levites did not do it quickly. 6So the king called Jehoiada the chief *priest*, and said to him, "Why have you not required the Levites to bring in from Judah and from Jerusalem the collection, *according to the commandment* of Moses the servant of the LORD and of the assembly of Israel, for the tabernacle of witness?" 7For the sons of Athaliah, that

---

23:11 [a]That is, the Law (compare Exodus 25:16, 21; 31:18) **23:17** [a]Literally *house*

wicked woman, had broken into the house of God, and had also presented all the dedicated things of the house of the LORD to the Baals.

8 Then at the king's command they made a chest, and set it outside at the gate of the house of the LORD. 9 And they made a proclamation throughout Judah and Jerusalem to bring to the LORD the collection *that* Moses the servant of God *had imposed* on Israel in the wilderness. 10 Then all the leaders and all the people rejoiced, brought their contributions, and put *them* into the chest until all had given. 11 So it was, at that time, when the chest was brought to the king's official by the hand of the Levites, and when they saw that *there was* much money, that the king's scribe and the high priest's officer came and emptied the chest, and took it and returned it to its place. Thus they did day by day, and gathered money in abundance.

12 The king and Jehoiada gave it to those who did the work of the service of the house of the LORD; and they hired masons and carpenters to repair the house of the LORD, and also those who worked in iron and bronze to restore the house of the LORD. 13 So the workmen labored, and the work was completed by them; they restored the house of God to its original condition and reinforced it. 14 When they had finished, they brought the rest of the money before the king and Jehoiada; they made from it articles for the house of the LORD, articles for serving and offering, spoons and vessels of gold and silver. And they offered burnt offerings in the house of the LORD continually all the days of Jehoiada.

Apostasy of Joash

15 But Jehoiada grew old and was full of days, and he died; *he was* one hundred and thirty years old when he died. 16 And they buried him in the City of David among the kings, because he had done good in Israel, both toward God and His house.

17 Now after the death of Jehoiada the leaders of Judah came and bowed down to the king. And the king listened to them. 18 Therefore they left the house of the LORD God of their fathers, and served wooden images and idols; and wrath came upon Judah and Jerusalem because of their trespass. 19 Yet He sent prophets to them, to bring them back to the LORD; and they testified against them, but they would not listen.

20 Then the Spirit of God came upon Zechariah the son of Jehoiada the priest, who stood above the people, and said to them, "Thus says God: 'Why do you transgress the commandments of the LORD, so that you cannot prosper? Because you have forsaken the LORD, He also has forsaken you.' " 21 So they conspired against him, and at the command of the king they stoned him with stones in the court of the house of the LORD. 22 Thus Joash the king did not remember the kindness which Jehoiada his father had done to him, but killed his son; and as he died, he said, "The LORD look on *it,* and repay!"

Death of Joash

23 So it happened in the spring of the year *that* the army of Syria came up against him; and they came to Judah and Jerusalem, and destroyed all the leaders of the people from among the people, and sent all their spoil to the king of Damascus. 24 For the army of the Syrians came with a small company of men; but the LORD delivered a very great army into their hand, because they had forsaken the LORD God of their fathers. So they executed judgment against Joash. 25 And when they had withdrawn from him (for they left him severely wounded), his own servants conspired against him because of the blood of the sons[a] of Jehoiada the priest, and killed him on his bed. So he died. And they buried him in the City of David, but they did not bury him in the tombs of the kings.

26 These are the ones who conspired against him: Zabad[a] the son of Shimeath the Ammonitess, and Jehozabad the son of Shimrith[b] the Moabitess. 27 Now *concerning* his sons, and the many oracles about him, and the repairing of the house of God, indeed they *are* written in the annals of the book of the kings. Then Amaziah his son reigned in his place.

Amaziah Reigns in Judah

25 Amaziah *was* twenty-five years old *when* he became king, and he reigned twenty-nine years in Jerusalem. His mother's name *was* Jehoaddan of Jerusalem. 2 And he did *what was* right in the sight of the LORD, but not with a loyal heart.

24:25 [a]Septuagint and Vulgate read *son* (compare verses 20–22). **24:26** [a]Or *Jozachar* (compare 2 Kings 12:21) [b]Or *Shomer* (compare 2 Kings 12:21)

[3]Now it happened, as soon as the kingdom was established for him, that he executed his servants who had murdered his father the king. [4]However he did not execute their children, but *did* as *it is* written in the Law in the Book of Moses, where the LORD commanded, saying, "The fathers shall not be put to death for their children, nor shall the children be put to death for their fathers; but a person shall die for his own sin."[a]

The War Against Edom

[5]Moreover Amaziah gathered Judah together and set over them captains of thousands and captains of hundreds, according to *their* fathers' houses, throughout all Judah and Benjamin; and he numbered them from twenty years old and above, and found them to be three hundred thousand choice *men, able* to go to war, who could handle spear and shield. [6]He also hired one hundred thousand mighty men of valor from Israel for one hundred talents of silver. [7]But a man of God came to him, saying, "O king, do not let the army of Israel go with you, for the LORD *is* not with Israel—*not with* any of the children of Ephraim. [8]But if you go, be gone! Be strong in battle! *Even so,* God shall make you fall before the enemy; for God has power to help and to overthrow."

[9]Then Amaziah said to the man of God, "But what *shall we* do about the hundred talents which I have given to the troops of Israel?"

And the man of God answered, "The LORD is able to give you much more than this." [10]So Amaziah discharged the troops that had come to him from Ephraim, to go back home. Therefore their anger was greatly aroused against Judah, and they returned home in great anger.

[11]Then Amaziah strengthened himself, and leading his people, he went to the Valley of Salt and killed ten thousand of the people of Seir. [12]Also the children of Judah took captive ten thousand alive, brought them to the top of the rock, and cast them down from the top of the rock, so that they all were dashed in pieces.

[13]But as for the soldiers of the army which Amaziah had discharged, so that they would not go with him to battle, they raided the cities of Judah from Samaria to Beth Horon, killed three thousand in them, and took much spoil.

[14]Now it was so, after Amaziah came from the slaughter of the Edomites, that he brought the gods of the people of Seir, set them up *to be* his gods, and bowed down before them and burned incense to them. [15]Therefore the anger of the LORD was aroused against Amaziah, and He sent him a prophet who said to him, "Why have you sought the gods of the people, which could not rescue their own people from your hand?"

[16]So it was, as he talked with him, that *the king* said to him, "Have we made you the king's counselor? Cease! Why should you be killed?"

Then the prophet ceased, and said, "I know that God has determined to destroy you, because you have done this and have not heeded my advice."

Israel Defeats Judah

[17]Now Amaziah king of Judah asked advice and sent to Joash[a] the son of Jehoahaz, the son of Jehu, king of Israel, saying, "Come, let us face one another *in battle.*"

[18]And Joash king of Israel sent to Amaziah king of Judah, saying, "The thistle that *was* in Lebanon sent to the cedar that was in Lebanon, saying, 'Give your daughter to my son as wife'; and a wild beast that *was* in Lebanon passed by and trampled the thistle. [19]Indeed you say that you have defeated the Edomites, and your heart is lifted up to boast. Stay at home now; why should you meddle with trouble, that you should fall—you and Judah with you?"

[20]But Amaziah would not heed, for it *came* from God, that He might give them into the hand *of their enemies,* because they sought the gods of Edom. [21]So Joash king of Israel went out; and he and Amaziah king of Judah faced one another at Beth Shemesh, which *belongs* to Judah. [22]And Judah was defeated by Israel, and every man fled to his tent. [23]Then Joash the king of Israel captured Amaziah king of Judah, the son of Joash, the son of Jehoahaz, at Beth Shemesh; and he brought him to Jerusalem, and broke down the wall of Jerusalem from the Gate of Ephraim to the Corner Gate—four hundred cubits. [24]And *he took* all the gold and silver, all the articles that were found in the house of God with Obed-Edom, the treasures of the king's house, and hostages, and returned to Samaria.

25:4 [a]Deuteronomy 24:16 **25:17** [a]Spelled *Jehoash* in 2 Kings 14:8ff

Death of Amaziah

25 Amaziah the son of Joash, king of Judah,
lived fifteen years after the death of Joash the
son of Jehoahaz, king of Israel. 26 Now the rest
of the acts of Amaziah, from first to last, indeed *are* they not written in the book of the
kings of Judah and Israel? 27 After the time that
Amaziah turned away from following the
LORD, they made a conspiracy against him in
Jerusalem, and he fled to Lachish; but they
sent after him to Lachish and killed him there.
28 Then they brought him on horses and buried
him with his fathers in the City of Judah.

Uzziah Reigns in Judah

26 Now all the people of Judah took
Uzziah,[a] who *was* sixteen years old,
and made him king instead of his father Amaziah. 2 He built Elath[a] and restored it to Judah,
after the king rested with his fathers.

3 Uzziah *was* sixteen years old when he became king, and he reigned fifty-two years in
Jerusalem. His mother's name was Jecholiah
of Jerusalem. 4 And he did *what was* right in
the sight of the LORD, according to all that
his father Amaziah had done. 5 He sought
God in the days of Zechariah, who had understanding in the visions[a] of God; and as
long as he sought the LORD, God made him
prosper.

6 Now he went out and made war against the
Philistines, and broke down the wall of Gath,
the wall of Jabneh, and the wall of Ashdod;
and he built cities *around* Ashdod and among
the Philistines. 7 God helped him against the
Philistines, against the Arabians who lived in
Gur Baal, and against the Meunites. 8 Also the
Ammonites brought tribute to Uzziah. His
fame spread as far as the entrance of Egypt,
for he became exceedingly strong.

9 And Uzziah built towers in Jerusalem at
the Corner Gate, at the Valley Gate, and at the
corner buttress of the wall; then he fortified
them. 10 Also he built towers in the desert. He
dug many wells, for he had much livestock,
both in the lowlands and in the plains; *he also
had* farmers and vinedressers in the mountains and in Carmel, for he loved the soil.

11 Moreover Uzziah had an army of fighting
men who went out to war by companies, according to the number on their roll as prepared
by Jeiel the scribe and Maaseiah the officer, under the hand of Hananiah, *one* of the king's
captains. 12 The total number of chief officers[a]
of the mighty men of valor *was* two thousand
six hundred. 13 And under their authority *was*
an army of three hundred and seven thousand
five hundred, that made war with mighty
power, to help the king against the enemy.
14 Then Uzziah prepared for them, for the entire army, shields, spears, helmets, body armor, bows, and slings *to cast* stones. 15 And he
made devices in Jerusalem, invented by skillful men, to be on the towers and the corners,
to shoot arrows and large stones. So his fame
spread far and wide, for he was marvelously
helped till he became strong.

The Penalty for Uzziah's Pride

16 But when he was strong his heart was lifted up, to *his* destruction, for he transgressed
against the LORD his God by entering the temple of the LORD to burn incense on the altar of
incense. 17 So Azariah the priest went in after
him, and with him were eighty priests of the
LORD—valiant men. 18 And they withstood
King Uzziah, and said to him, "*It* is not for
you, Uzziah, to burn incense to the LORD, but
for the priests, the sons of Aaron, who are
consecrated to burn incense. Get out of the
sanctuary, for you have trespassed! You *shall
have* no honor from the LORD God."

19 Then Uzziah became furious; and he *had*
a censer in his hand to burn incense. And
while he was angry with the priests, leprosy
broke out on his forehead, before the priests
in the house of the LORD, beside the incense
altar. 20 And Azariah the chief priest and all the
priests looked at him, and there, on his forehead, he *was* leprous; so they thrust him out
of that place. Indeed he also hurried to get
out, because the LORD had struck him.

21 King Uzziah was a leper until the day of
his death. He dwelt in an isolated house, because he was a leper; for he was cut off from
the house of the LORD. Then Jotham his son
was over the king's house, judging the people
of the land.

22 Now the rest of the acts of Uzziah, from
first to last, the prophet Isaiah the son of
Amoz wrote. 23 So Uzziah rested with his fathers, and they buried him with his fathers in
the field of burial which *belonged* to the kings,

26:1 [a]Called *Azariah* in 2 Kings 14:21ff
26:2 [a]Hebrew *Eloth* **26:5** [a]Several Hebrew manuscripts, Septuagint, Syriac, Targum, and Arabic read *fear.* **26:12** [a]Literally *chief fathers*

Pride

PRIDE PROBLEMS

STUART BRISCOE

(2 Chronicles 26:16–19)

There is a fine balance between pride and confidence. On the positive side, confidence is necessary for success. On the negative side, however, pride often leads to self-destruction. We want to be confident in what God has given us to do and what God thinks of us. Yet we don't want to have a big head and an inflated opinion about ourselves. God wants us to have a good self-image, but not to be proud.

THE PITFALLS OF PRIDE

We all need the faith to develop confidence in God, being careful not to place our confidence in ourselves. Pride motivates people to do what is best for themselves—even at the expense of others. Pride tells people that they deserve to be rewarded, promoted, and applauded. Pride won't allow people to admit their weaknesses and reach out for help. In fact, pride is the greatest factor in keeping people from seeking counseling because they don't think that they need anyone's help in dealing with their problems. Some people are so proud and self-confident that they won't even consult the Lord. They can't trust God with their lives because they prefer to trust their own instincts and abilities.

When some people begin to experience a degree of success, they become overly confident of their own abilities. They behave as if no one else in the world can do what they can do. That is to say, they get an exaggerated sense of their own importance and are puffed up with pride, making it difficult for most people to work with them. They may become boastful, arrogant, and rude. Boasting is their way of trying to look good when they suspect that they are not good. It is a private advertising business, a little campaign to publicize an image of themselves. Arrogance is an anxious grasp for power when they fear that they are weak. Rudeness is putting people down in order to hold themselves up.

GOD'S WORD AND PRIDE

Pride is the root expression of our sinful nature. Pride is so puffed up with its own importance that it can't listen to another voice with a contrary opinion to its own. Both the Old and New Testaments use "pride" in the negative sense. Pride caused Adam and Eve to violate God's Word (Gen. 3:4–6). Pride motivated Satan to rebel against God, which led to his fall. Isaiah 14:13, 14 and Ezekiel 28:11–19 are often taken as descriptions of Satan's fall. Pride, which motivated this powerful angel to set his will against God's, is portrayed as the culprit.

In the New Testament, Paul warns against several expressions of pride. Pride is particularly dangerous in the non-Christian who seeks to earn salvation. Because salvation is and must be a work of God for human beings rather than a work of human beings for God, reliance on one's own efforts distorts the gospel message. Salvation is a gift of God. It is through faith in Jesus Christ, not because of any self-achievement in which a person could take pride. Paul wrote, "For by grace you have been saved through faith, and that not of yourselves; it is the gift of God, not of works, lest anyone should boast" (Eph. 2:8, 9).

The Bible says that God resists the proud and gives grace to the humble (Prov. 3:34). Jesus exemplified the virtues of meekness, kindness, and humility (Matt. 5:3–10).

HUMILITY CONQUERS PRIDE

Humility, on the other hand, is always looking for someone to listen to, not for someone to talk to. Humility bends near those who are hurting, focusing attention on the need. Pride tells people they don't need anyone else. Humility tells them that they can't do anything without God. Humility reminds people that God is the source of their gifts and abilities. He alone can empower people to serve Him. Pride is the arrogant refusal to let God be God. Pride is saying, "I'm something apart from God." Humility says, "I am something because of God."

Love, by its very nature, is humble. Love is primarily concerned with the other's well-being, irrespective of the cost to itself. Love isn't puffed up with its own importance. Love empties itself in self-sacrifice, making the other person feel good. Love is shed abroad in our hearts by the Holy Spirit.

So how do we grow humility? First, we need a healthy view of God. When Isaiah looked through the door of heaven in prayer, he said, "I saw the Lord" (Is. 6:1). He saw the Lord in all His majesty and glory and worship, and then he saw himself and realized his own great sinfulness (Is. 6:5).

Second, we spend a lot of time in worship. We use the Word of God as a mirror. Every time we read the Bible, we look for the Lord and then we look at ourselves. When we look into God's Word, we have to see not only Him, but a reflection of who we are.

Finally, we can also do a lot of praising. Gratitude helps us cope with pride and keeps us where we should be—humbly thanking God for who He is and what He is doing through us.

FURTHER MEDITATION:

Other passages to study about the issue of pride include:

- ➢ Deuteronomy 8:11–20
- ➢ Psalm 10:2–11
- ➢ Proverbs 8:13; 13:10; 28:25; 29:23
- ➢ Obadiah 3, 4
- ➢ Acts 12:22, 23
- ➢ Romans 12:3
- ➢ 2 Timothy 3:2–5

To Learn More: Turn to the key passage note on pride at James 4:6–10 on page 1649. See also the personality profile of the king of Tyre on page 1076.

for they said, "He is a leper." Then Jotham his son reigned in his place.

Jotham Reigns in Judah

27 Jotham *was* twenty-five years old when he became king, and he reigned sixteen years in Jerusalem. His mother's name *was* Jerushah[a] the daughter of Zadok. [2]And he did *what was* right in the sight of the LORD, according to all that his father Uzziah had done (although he did not enter the temple of the LORD). But still the people acted corruptly.

[3]He built the Upper Gate of the house of the LORD, and he built extensively on the wall of Ophel. [4]Moreover he built cities in the mountains of Judah, and in the forests he built fortresses and towers. [5]He also fought with the king of the Ammonites and defeated them. And the people of Ammon gave him in that year one hundred talents of silver, ten thousand kors of wheat, and ten thousand of barley. The people of Ammon paid this to him in the second and third years also. [6]So Jotham became mighty, because he prepared his ways before the LORD his God.

[7]Now the rest of the acts of Jotham, and all his wars and his ways, indeed they *are* written in the book of the kings of Israel and Judah. [8]He was twenty-five years old when he became king, and he reigned sixteen years in Jerusalem. [9]So Jotham rested with his fathers, and they buried him in the City of David. Then Ahaz his son reigned in his place.

Ahaz Reigns in Judah

28 Ahaz *was* twenty years old when he became king, and he reigned sixteen years in Jerusalem; and he did not do *what was* right in the sight of the LORD, as his father David *had done.* [2]For he walked in the ways of the kings of Israel, and made molded images for the Baals. [3]He burned incense in the Valley of the Son of Hinnom, and burned his children in the fire, according to the abominations of the nations whom the LORD had cast out before the children of Israel. [4]And he sacrificed and burned incense on the high places, on the hills, and under every green tree.

Syria and Israel Defeat Judah

[5]Therefore the LORD his God delivered him into the hand of the king of Syria. They defeated him, and carried away a great multitude of them as captives, and brought *them* to Damascus. Then he was also delivered into the hand of the king of Israel, who defeated him with a great slaughter. [6]For Pekah the son of Remaliah killed one hundred and twenty thousand in Judah in one day, all valiant men, because they had forsaken the LORD God of their fathers. [7]Zichri, a mighty man of Ephraim, killed Maaseiah the king's son, Azrikam the officer over the house, and Elkanah *who was* second to the king. [8]And the children of Israel carried away captive of their brethren two hundred thousand women, sons, and daughters; and they also took away much spoil from them, and brought the spoil to Samaria.

Israel Returns the Captives

[9]But a prophet of the LORD was there, whose name *was* Oded; and he went out before the army that came to Samaria, and said to them: "Look, because the LORD God of your fathers was angry with Judah, He has delivered them into your hand; but you have killed them in a rage *that* reaches up to heaven. [10]And now you propose to force the children of Judah and Jerusalem to be your male and female slaves; *but are* you not also guilty before the LORD your God? [11]Now hear me, therefore, and return the captives, whom you have taken captive from your brethren, for the fierce wrath of the LORD *is* upon you."

[12]Then some of the heads of the children of Ephraim, Azariah the son of Johanan, Berechiah the son of Meshillemoth, Jehizkiah the son of Shallum, and Amasa the son of Hadlai, stood up against those who came from the war, [13]and said to them, "You shall not bring the captives here, for we *already* have offended the LORD. You intend to add to our sins and to our guilt; for our guilt is great, and *there is* fierce wrath against Israel." [14]So the armed men left the captives and the spoil before the leaders and all the assembly. [15]Then the men who were designated by name rose up and took the captives, and from the spoil they clothed all who were naked among them, dressed them and gave them sandals, gave them food and drink, and anointed them; and they let all the feeble ones ride on donkeys. So they brought them to their brethren at Jericho, the city of palm trees. Then they returned to Samaria.

27:1 [a]Spelled *Jerusha* in 2 Kings 15:33

Assyria Refuses to Help Judah

16At the same time King Ahaz sent to the kings[a] of Assyria to help him. 17For again the Edomites had come, attacked Judah, and carried away captives. 18The Philistines also had invaded the cities of the lowland and of the South of Judah, and had taken Beth Shemesh, Aijalon, Gederoth, Sochoh with its villages, Timnah with its villages, and Gimzo with its villages; and they dwelt there. 19For the LORD brought Judah low because of Ahaz king of Israel, for he had encouraged moral decline in Judah and had been continually unfaithful to the LORD. 20Also Tiglath-Pileser[a] king of Assyria came to him and distressed him, and did not assist him. 21For Ahaz took part *of the treasures* from the house of the LORD, from the house of the king, and from the leaders, and he gave *it* to the king of Assyria; but he did not help him.

Apostasy and Death of Ahaz

22Now in the time of his distress King Ahaz became increasingly unfaithful to the LORD. This *is that* King Ahaz. 23For he sacrificed to the gods of Damascus which had defeated him, saying, "Because the gods of the kings of Syria help them, I will sacrifice to them that they may help me." But they were the ruin of him and of all Israel. 24So Ahaz gathered the articles of the house of God, cut in pieces the articles of the house of God, shut up the doors of the house of the LORD, and made for himself altars in every corner of Jerusalem. 25And in every single city of Judah he made high places to burn incense to other gods, and provoked to anger the LORD God of his fathers.

26Now the rest of his acts and all his ways, from first to last, indeed they *are* written in the book of the kings of Judah and Israel. 27So Ahaz rested with his fathers, and they buried him in the city, in Jerusalem; but they did not bring him into the tombs of the kings of Israel. Then Hezekiah his son reigned in his place.

Hezekiah Reigns in Judah

29 Hezekiah became king *when he was* twenty-five years old, and he reigned twenty-nine years in Jerusalem. His mother's name *was* Abijah[a] the daughter of Zechariah. 2And he did *what was* right in the sight of the LORD, according to all that his father David had done.

Hezekiah Cleanses the Temple

3In the first year of his reign, in the first month, he opened the doors of the house of the LORD and repaired them. 4Then he brought in the priests and the Levites, and gathered them in the East Square, 5and said to them: "Hear me, Levites! Now sanctify yourselves, sanctify the house of the LORD God of your fathers, and carry out the rubbish from the holy *place.* 6For our fathers have trespassed and done evil in the eyes of the LORD our God; they have forsaken Him, have turned their faces away from the dwelling place of the LORD, and turned *their* backs *on Him.* 7They have also shut up the doors of the vestibule, put out the lamps, and have not burned incense or offered burnt offerings in the holy *place* to the God of Israel. 8Therefore the wrath of the LORD fell upon Judah and Jerusalem, and He has given them up to trouble, to desolation, and to jeering, as you see with your eyes. 9For indeed, because of this our fathers have fallen by the sword; and our sons, our daughters, and our wives *are* in captivity.

28:16 [a]Septuagint, Syriac, and Vulgate read *king* (compare verse 20). **28:20** [a]Hebrew *Tilgath-Pilneser* **29:1** [a]Spelled *Abi* in 2 Kings 18:2

SOUL NOTE

Sudden and Decisive *(29:1, 2)* Hezekiah was determined to restore the nation to spiritual greatness. "He did what was right in the sight of the LORD," and challenged the priests (29:4) and the rulers (29:20) to renew their commitments to God. He cleansed the temple and restored proper worship, bringing about a dramatic spiritual revival. So dramatic were his actions that the changes seemed to have taken place suddenly (29:36). Spiritual revival may result from a long process of growth and commitment. It also may come suddenly as a result of a deliberate and decisive response to God's calling in our lives. **Topic: Restoration**

10“Now *it is* in my heart to make a covenant with the LORD God of Israel, that His fierce wrath may turn away from us. 11My sons, do not be negligent now, for the LORD has chosen you to stand before Him, to serve Him, and that you should minister to Him and burn incense.”

12Then these Levites arose: Mahath the son of Amasai and Joel the son of Azariah, of the sons of the Kohathites; of the sons of Merari, Kish the son of Abdi and Azariah the son of Jehallelel; of the Gershonites, Joah the son of Zimmah and Eden the son of Joah; 13of the sons of Elizaphan, Shimri and Jeiel; of the sons of Asaph, Zechariah and Mattaniah; 14of the sons of Heman, Jehiel and Shimei; and of the sons of Jeduthun, Shemaiah and Uzziel.

15And they gathered their brethren, sanctified themselves, and went according to the commandment of the king, at the words of the LORD, to cleanse the house of the LORD. 16Then the priests went into the inner part of the house of the LORD to cleanse *it,* and brought out all the debris that they found in the temple of the LORD to the court of the house of the LORD. And the Levites took *it* out and carried *it* to the Brook Kidron.

17Now they began to sanctify on the first *day* of the first month, and on the eighth day of the month they came to the vestibule of the LORD. So they sanctified the house of the LORD in eight days, and on the sixteenth day of the first month they finished.

18Then they went in to King Hezekiah and said, “We have cleansed all the house of the LORD, the altar of burnt offerings with all its articles, and the table of the showbread with all its articles. 19Moreover all the articles which King Ahaz in his reign had cast aside in his transgression we have prepared and sanctified; and there they *are,* before the altar of the LORD.”

HEZEKIAH RESTORES TEMPLE WORSHIP

20Then King Hezekiah rose early, gathered the rulers of the city, and went up to the house of the LORD. 21And they brought seven bulls, seven rams, seven lambs, and seven male goats for a sin offering for the kingdom, for the sanctuary, and for Judah. Then he commanded the priests, the sons of Aaron, to offer *them* on the altar of the LORD. 22So they killed the bulls, and the priests received the blood and sprinkled *it* on the altar. Likewise they killed the rams and sprinkled the blood on the altar. They also killed the lambs and sprinkled the blood on the altar. 23Then they brought out the male goats *for* the sin offering before the king and the assembly, and they laid their hands on them. 24And the priests killed them; and they presented their blood on the altar as a sin offering to make an atonement for all Israel, for the king commanded *that* the burnt offering and the sin offering *be made* for all Israel.

25And he stationed the Levites in the house of the LORD with cymbals, with stringed instruments, and with harps, according to the commandment of David, of Gad the king’s seer, and of Nathan the prophet; for thus *was* the commandment of the LORD by His prophets. 26The Levites stood with the instruments of David, and the priests with the trumpets. 27Then Hezekiah commanded *them* to offer the burnt offering on the altar. And when the burnt offering began, the song of the LORD *also* began, with the trumpets and with the instruments of David king of Israel. 28So all the assembly worshiped, the singers sang, and the trumpeters sounded; all *this continued* until the burnt offering was finished. 29And when they had finished offering, the king and all who were present with him bowed and worshiped. 30Moreover King Hezekiah and the leaders commanded the Levites to sing praise to the LORD with the words of David and of Asaph the seer. So they sang praises with gladness, and they bowed their heads and worshiped.

31Then Hezekiah answered and said, “Now *that* you have consecrated yourselves to the LORD, come near, and bring sacrifices and thank offerings into the house of the LORD.” So the assembly brought in sacrifices and thank offerings, and as many as were of a willing heart *brought* burnt offerings. 32And the number of the burnt offerings which the assembly brought was seventy bulls, one hundred rams, *and* two hundred lambs; all these *were* for a burnt offering to the LORD. 33The consecrated things *were* six hundred bulls and three thousand sheep. 34But the priests were too few, so that they could not skin all the burnt offerings; therefore their brethren the Levites helped them until the work was ended and until the *other* priests had sanctified themselves, for the Levites were more diligent in sanctifying themselves than the priests.

35Also the burnt offerings *were* in abundance, with the fat of the peace offerings and *with* the drink offerings for *every* burnt offering.

So the service of the house of the LORD was set in order. 36Then Hezekiah and all the people rejoiced that God had prepared the people, since the events took place so suddenly.

HEZEKIAH KEEPS THE PASSOVER

30 And Hezekiah sent to all Israel and Judah, and also wrote letters to Ephraim and Manasseh, that they should come to the house of the LORD at Jerusalem, to keep the Passover to the LORD God of Israel. 2For the king and his leaders and all the assembly in Jerusalem had agreed to keep the Passover in the second month. 3For they could not keep it at the regular time,[a] because a sufficient number of priests had not consecrated themselves, nor had the people gathered together at Jerusalem. 4And the matter pleased the king and all the assembly. 5So they resolved to make a proclamation throughout all Israel, from Beersheba to Dan, that they should come to keep the Passover to the LORD God of Israel at Jerusalem, since they had not done *it* for a long *time* in the *prescribed* manner.

6Then the runners went throughout all Israel and Judah with the letters from the king and his leaders, and spoke according to the command of the king: "Children of Israel, return to the LORD God of Abraham, Isaac, and Israel; then He will return to the remnant of you who have escaped from the hand of the kings of Assyria. 7And do not be like your fathers and your brethren, who trespassed against the LORD God of their fathers, so that He gave them up to desolation, as you see. 8Now do not be stiff-necked, as your fathers *were, but* yield yourselves to the LORD; and enter His sanctuary, which He has sanctified forever, and serve the LORD your God, that the fierceness of His wrath may turn away from you. 9For if you return to the LORD, your brethren and your children *will be treated* with compassion by those who lead them captive, so that they may come back to this land; for the LORD your God *is* gracious and merciful, and will not turn *His* face from you if you return to Him."

10So the runners passed from city to city through the country of Ephraim and Manasseh, as far as Zebulun; but they laughed at them and mocked them. 11Nevertheless some from Asher, Manasseh, and Zebulun humbled themselves and came to Jerusalem. 12Also the hand of God was on Judah to give them singleness of heart to obey the command of the king and the leaders, at the word of the LORD.

13Now many people, a very great assembly, gathered at Jerusalem to keep the Feast of Unleavened Bread in the second month. 14They arose and took away the altars that *were* in Jerusalem, and they took away all the incense altars and cast *them* into the Brook Kidron. 15Then they slaughtered the Passover *lambs* on the fourteenth *day* of the second month. The priests and the Levites were ashamed, and sanctified themselves, and brought the burnt offerings to the house of the LORD. 16They stood in their place according to their custom, according to the Law of Moses the man of God; the priests sprinkled the blood *received* from the hand of the Levites. 17For *there were* many in the assembly who had not sanctified themselves; therefore the Levites had charge of the slaughter of the Passover *lambs* for everyone *who was* not clean, to sanctify *them* to the LORD. 18For a multitude of the people, many from Ephraim, Manasseh, Issachar, and Zebulun, had not cleansed

30:3 [a]That is, the first month (compare Leviticus 23:5); literally *at that time*

SOUL NOTE

Return *(30:6–12)* The northern tribes had broken away from Judah and the line of Davidic kings, setting up a system of idolatry. When Hezekiah led the southern kingdom into a spiritual revival, he wrote to the northern tribes and appealed to them to return to the temple in Jerusalem to worship the Lord. He reminded them that God is gracious and merciful to all who will return to Him. In response, some mocked God, but many humbled themselves and came to Jerusalem. God promises restoration for those who will return to Him. **Topic: Restoration**

themselves, yet they ate the Passover contrary to what was written. But Hezekiah prayed for them, saying, "May the good LORD provide atonement for everyone [19]*who* prepares his heart to seek God, the LORD God of his fathers, though *he is* not *cleansed* according to the purification of the sanctuary." [20]And the LORD listened to Hezekiah and healed the people.

[21]So the children of Israel who were present at Jerusalem kept the Feast of Unleavened Bread seven days with great gladness; and the Levites and the priests praised the LORD day by day, *singing* to the LORD, accompanied by loud instruments. [22]And Hezekiah gave encouragement to all the Levites who taught the good knowledge of the LORD; and they ate throughout the feast seven days, offering peace offerings and making confession to the LORD God of their fathers.

[23]Then the whole assembly agreed to keep *the feast* another seven days, and they kept it *another* seven days with gladness. [24]For Hezekiah king of Judah gave to the assembly a thousand bulls and seven thousand sheep, and the leaders gave to the assembly a thousand bulls and ten thousand sheep; and a great number of priests sanctified themselves. [25]The whole assembly of Judah rejoiced, also the priests and Levites, all the assembly that came from Israel, the sojourners who came from the land of Israel, and those who dwelt in Judah. [26]So there was great joy in Jerusalem, for since the time of Solomon the son of David, king of Israel, *there had* been nothing like this in Jerusalem. [27]Then the priests, the Levites, arose and blessed the people, and their voice was heard; and their prayer came *up* to His holy dwelling place, to heaven.

THE REFORMS OF HEZEKIAH

31 Now when all this was finished, all Israel who were present went out to the cities of Judah and broke the *sacred* pillars in pieces, cut down the wooden images, and threw down the high places and the altars—from all Judah, Benjamin, Ephraim, and Manasseh—until they had utterly destroyed them all. Then all the children of Israel returned to their own cities, every man to his possession.

[2]And Hezekiah appointed the divisions of the priests and the Levites according to their divisions, each man according to his service, the priests and Levites for burnt offerings and peace offerings, to serve, to give thanks, and to praise in the gates of the camp[a] of the LORD. [3]The king also *appointed* a portion of his possessions for the burnt offerings: for the morning and evening burnt offerings, the burnt offerings for the Sabbaths and the New Moons and the set feasts, as *it is* written in the Law of the LORD.

[4]Moreover he commanded the people who dwelt in Jerusalem to contribute support for the priests and the Levites, that they might devote themselves to the Law of the LORD.

[5]As soon as the commandment was circulated, the children of Israel brought in abundance the firstfruits of grain and wine, oil and honey, and of all the produce of the field; and they brought in abundantly the tithe of everything. [6]And the children of Israel and Judah, who dwelt in the cities of Judah, brought the tithe of oxen and sheep; also the tithe of holy things which were consecrated to the LORD their God they laid in heaps.

[7]In the third month they began laying them in heaps, and they finished in the seventh month. [8]And when Hezekiah and the leaders came and saw the heaps, they blessed the LORD and His people Israel. [9]Then Hezekiah questioned the priests and the Levites concerning the heaps. [10]And Azariah the chief priest, from the house of Zadok, answered him and said, "Since *the people* began to bring the offerings into the house of the LORD, we have had enough to eat and have plenty left, for the LORD has blessed His people; and what is left *is* this great abundance."

[11]Now Hezekiah commanded *them* to prepare rooms in the house of the LORD, and they prepared them. [12]Then they faithfully brought in the offerings, the tithes, and the dedicated things; Cononiah the Levite had charge of them, and Shimei his brother *was* the next. [13]Jehiel, Azaziah, Nahath, Asahel, Jerimoth, Jozabad, Eliel, Ismachiah, Mahath, and Benaiah *were* overseers under the hand of Cononiah and Shimei his brother, at the commandment of Hezekiah the king and Azariah the ruler of the house of God. [14]Kore the son of Imnah the Levite, the keeper of the East Gate, *was* over the freewill offerings to God, to distribute the offerings of the LORD and the most holy things. [15]And under him *were* Eden, Miniamin, Jeshua, Shemaiah, Amariah, and Shecaniah, *his* faithful assistants in the cities of the priests, to

---

31:2 [a]That is, the temple

distribute allotments to their brethren by divisions, to the great as well as the small.

16Besides those males from three years old and up who were written in the genealogy, they distributed to everyone who entered the house of the LORD his daily portion for the work of his service, by his division, 17and to the priests who were written in the genealogy according to their father's house, and to the Levites from twenty years old and up according to their work, by their divisions, 18and to all who were written in the genealogy—their little ones and their wives, their sons and daughters, the whole company of them—for in their faithfulness they sanctified themselves in holiness.

19Also for the sons of Aaron the priests, *who were* in the fields of the common-lands of their cities, in every single city, *there were* men who were designated by name to distribute portions to all the males among the priests and to all who were listed by genealogies among the Levites.

20Thus Hezekiah did throughout all Judah, and he did what *was* good and right and true before the LORD his God. 21And in every work that he began in the service of the house of God, in the law and in the commandment, to seek his God, he did *it* with all his heart. So he prospered.

SENNACHERIB BOASTS AGAINST THE LORD

32 After these deeds of faithfulness, Sennacherib king of Assyria came and entered Judah; he encamped against the fortified cities, thinking to win them over to himself. 2And when Hezekiah saw that Sennacherib had come, and that his purpose was to make war against Jerusalem, 3he consulted with his leaders and commanders[a] to stop the water from the springs which *were* outside the city; and they helped him. 4Thus many people gathered together who stopped all the springs and the brook that ran through the land, saying, "Why should the kings[a] of Assyria come and find much water?" 5And he strengthened himself, built up all the wall that was broken, raised *it* up to the towers, and *built* another wall outside; also he repaired the Millo[a] *in* the City of David, and made weapons and shields in abundance. 6Then he set military captains over the people, gathered them together to him in the open square of the city gate, and gave them encouragement, saying, 7"Be strong and courageous; do not be afraid nor dismayed before the king of Assyria, nor before all the multitude that *is* with him; for *there are* more with us than with him. 8With him *is* an arm of flesh; but with us *is* the LORD our God, to help us and to fight our battles." And the people were strengthened by the words of Hezekiah king of Judah.

9After this Sennacherib king of Assyria sent his servants to Jerusalem (but he and all the forces with him *laid siege* against Lachish), to Hezekiah king of Judah, and to all Judah who *were* in Jerusalem, saying, 10"Thus says Sennacherib king of Assyria: 'In what do you trust, that you remain under siege in Jerusalem? 11Does not Hezekiah persuade you to give yourselves over to die by famine and by thirst, saying, "The LORD our God will deliver us from the hand of the king of Assyria"? 12Has not the same Hezekiah taken away His high places and His altars, and commanded Judah and Jerusalem, saying, "You shall worship before one altar and burn incense on it"? 13Do you not know what I and my fathers have done to all the peoples of *other* lands? Were the gods of the nations of those lands in any way able to deliver their lands out of my hand? 14Who *was there* among all the gods of those nations that my fathers utterly destroyed that could deliver his people from my hand, that your God should be able to deliver you from my hand? 15Now therefore, do not let Hezekiah deceive you or persuade you like this, and do not believe him; for no god of any nation or kingdom was able to deliver his people from my hand or the hand of my fathers. How much less will your God deliver you from my hand?' "

16Furthermore, his servants spoke against the LORD God and against His servant Hezekiah.

17He also wrote letters to revile the LORD God of Israel, and to speak against Him, saying, "As the gods of the nations of *other* lands have not delivered their people from my hand, so the God of Hezekiah will not deliver His people from my hand." 18Then they called out with a loud voice in Hebrew[a] to the people of Jerusalem who *were* on the wall, to frighten

---

32:3 [a]Literally *mighty men* **32:4** [a]Following Masoretic Text and Vulgate; Arabic, Septuagint, and Syriac read *king*. **32:5** [a]Literally *The Landfill* **32:18** [a]Literally *Judean*

them and trouble them, that they might take
the city. [19]And they spoke against the God of
Jerusalem, as against the gods of the people of
the earth—the work of men's hands.

SENNACHERIB'S DEFEAT AND DEATH

[20]Now because of this King Hezekiah and
the prophet Isaiah, the son of Amoz, prayed
and cried out to heaven. [21]Then the LORD sent
an angel who cut down every mighty man of
valor, leader, and captain in the camp of the
king of Assyria. So he returned shamefaced to
his own land. And when he had gone into the
temple of his god, some of his own offspring
struck him down with the sword there.
[22]Thus the LORD saved Hezekiah and the inhabitants of Jerusalem from the hand of Sennacherib the king of Assyria, and from the
hand of all *others,* and guided them[a] on every
side. [23]And many brought gifts to the LORD at
Jerusalem, and presents to Hezekiah king of
Judah, so that he was exalted in the sight of all
nations thereafter.

HEZEKIAH HUMBLES HIMSELF

[24]In those days Hezekiah was sick and near
death, and he prayed to the LORD; and He
spoke to him and gave him a sign. [25]But Hezekiah did not repay according to the favor
shown him, for his heart was lifted up; therefore wrath was looming over him and over
Judah and Jerusalem. [26]Then Hezekiah humbled himself for the pride of his heart, he and
the inhabitants of Jerusalem, so that the wrath
of the LORD did not come upon them in the
days of Hezekiah.

HEZEKIAH'S WEALTH AND HONOR

[27]Hezekiah had very great riches and honor.
And he made himself treasuries for silver, for
gold, for precious stones, for spices, for
shields, and for all kinds of desirable items;
[28]storehouses for the harvest of grain, wine,
and oil; and stalls for all kinds of livestock,
and folds for flocks.[a] [29]Moreover he provided
cities for himself, and possessions of flocks
and herds in abundance; for God had given
him very much property. [30]This same Hezekiah also stopped the water outlet of Upper
Gihon, and brought the water by tunnel[a] to
the west side of the City of David. Hezekiah
prospered in all his works.
[31]However, *regarding* the ambassadors of
the princes of Babylon, whom they sent to
him to inquire about the wonder that was
done in the land, God withdrew from him, in
order to test him, that He might know all *that*
was in his heart.

DEATH OF HEZEKIAH

[32]Now the rest of the acts of Hezekiah, and
his goodness, indeed they *are* written in the
vision of Isaiah the prophet, the son of Amoz,
and in the book of the kings of Judah and Israel. [33]So Hezekiah rested with his fathers,
and they buried him in the upper tombs of the
sons of David; and all Judah and the inhabitants of Jerusalem honored him at his death.
Then Manasseh his son reigned in his place.

MANASSEH REIGNS IN JUDAH

33 Manasseh *was* twelve years old when
he became king, and he reigned fifty-
five years in Jerusalem. [2]But he did evil in the
sight of the LORD, according to the abominations of the nations whom the LORD had cast
out before the children of Israel. [3]For he rebuilt the high places which Hezekiah his father had broken down; he raised up altars for
the Baals, and made wooden images; and he
worshiped all the host of heaven[a] and served
them. [4]He also built altars in the house of the
LORD, of which the LORD had said, "In Jerusalem shall My name be forever." [5]And he built
altars for all the host of heaven in the two
courts of the house of the LORD. [6]Also he
caused his sons to pass through the fire in the
Valley of the Son of Hinnom; he practiced
soothsaying, used witchcraft and sorcery, and
consulted mediums and spiritists. He did
much evil in the sight of the LORD, to provoke
Him to anger. [7]He even set a carved image, the
idol which he had made, in the house of God,
of which God had said to David and to Solomon his son, "In this house and in Jerusalem, which I have chosen out of all the
tribes of Israel, I will put My name forever;
[8]and I will not again remove the foot of Israel
from the land which I have appointed for your
fathers—only if they are careful to do all that
I have commanded them, according to the

32:22 [a]Septuagint reads *gave them rest;* Vulgate reads *gave them treasures.* **32:28** [a]Following Septuagint and Vulgate; Arabic and Syriac omit *folds for flocks;* Masoretic Text reads *flocks for sheepfolds.* **32:30** [a]Literally *brought it straight* (compare 2 Kings 20:20) **33:3** [a]The gods of the Assyrians

whole law and the statutes and the ordinances by the hand of Moses." [9]So Manasseh seduced Judah and the inhabitants of Jerusalem to do more evil than the nations whom the LORD had destroyed before the children of Israel.

MANASSEH RESTORED AFTER REPENTANCE

[10]And the LORD spoke to Manasseh and his people, but they would not listen. [11]Therefore the LORD brought upon them the captains of the army of the king of Assyria, who took Manasseh with hooks,[a] bound him with bronze *fetters,* and carried him off to Babylon. [12]Now when he was in affliction, he implored the LORD his God, and humbled himself greatly before the God of his fathers, [13]and prayed to Him; and He received his entreaty, heard his supplication, and brought him back to Jerusalem into his kingdom. Then Manasseh knew that the LORD *was* God.

[14]After this he built a wall outside the City of David on the west side of Gihon, in the valley, as far as the entrance of the Fish Gate; and *it* enclosed Ophel, and he raised it to a very great height. Then he put military captains in all the fortified cities of Judah. [15]He took away the foreign gods and the idol from the house of the LORD, and all the altars that he had built in the mount of the house of the LORD and in Jerusalem; and he cast *them* out of the city. [16]He also repaired the altar of the LORD, sacrificed peace offerings and thank offerings on it, and commanded Judah to serve the LORD God of Israel. [17]Nevertheless the people still sacrificed on the high places, *but* only to the LORD their God.

DEATH OF MANASSEH

[18]Now the rest of the acts of Manasseh, his prayer to his God, and the words of the seers who spoke to him in the name of the LORD God of Israel, indeed they *are written* in the book[a] of the kings of Israel. [19]Also his prayer and *how God* received his entreaty, and all his sin and trespass, and the sites where he built high places and set up wooden images and carved images, before he was humbled, indeed they *are* written among the sayings of Hozai.[a] [20]So Manasseh rested with his fathers, and they buried him in his own house. Then his son Amon reigned in his place.

AMON'S REIGN AND DEATH

[21]Amon *was* twenty-two years old when he became king, and he reigned two years in Jerusalem. [22]But he did evil in the sight of the LORD, as his father Manasseh had done; for Amon sacrificed to all the carved images which his father Manasseh had made, and served them. [23]And he did not humble himself before the LORD, as his father Manasseh had humbled himself; but Amon trespassed more and more.

[24]Then his servants conspired against him, and killed him in his own house. [25]But the people of the land executed all those who had conspired against King Amon. Then the people of the land made his son Josiah king in his place.

JOSIAH REIGNS IN JUDAH

34 Josiah *was* eight years old when he became king, and he reigned thirty-one years in Jerusalem. [2]And he did *what was* right in the sight of the LORD, and walked in the ways of his father David; *he* did *not* turn aside to the right hand or to the left.

[3]For in the eighth year of his reign, while he was still young, he began to seek the God of his father David; and in the twelfth year he began to purge Judah and Jerusalem of the high places, the wooden images, the carved images, and the molded images. [4]They broke down the altars of the Baals in his presence, and the incense altars which *were* above them he cut down; and the wooden images, the carved images, and the molded images he broke in pieces, and made dust of them and scattered *it* on the graves of those who had sacrificed to them. [5]He also burned the bones of the priests on their altars, and cleansed Judah and Jerusalem. [6]And *so he did* in the cities of Manasseh, Ephraim, and Simeon, as far as Naphtali and all around, with axes.[a] [7]When he had broken down the altars and the wooden images, had beaten the carved images into powder, and cut down all the incense altars throughout all the land of Israel, he returned to Jerusalem.

HILKIAH FINDS THE BOOK OF THE LAW

[8]In the eighteenth year of his reign, when he had purged the land and the temple,[a] he sent Shaphan the son of Azaliah, Maaseiah the

---

33:11 [a]That is, nose hooks (compare 2 Kings 19:28) **33:18** [a]Literally *words* **33:19** [a]Septuagint reads *the seers.* **34:6** [a]Literally *swords* **34:8** [a]Literally *house*

governor of the city, and Joah the son of Joahaz the recorder, to repair the house of the
LORD his God. [9]When they came to Hilkiah the
high priest, they delivered the money that was
brought into the house of God, which the Levites who kept the doors had gathered from
the hand of Manasseh and Ephraim, from all
the remnant of Israel, from all Judah and Benjamin, and *which* they had brought back to Jerusalem. [10]Then they put *it* in the hand of the
foremen who had the oversight of the house of
the LORD; and they gave it to the workmen
who worked in the house of the LORD, to repair and restore the house. [11]They gave *it* to
the craftsmen and builders to buy hewn stone
and timber for beams, and to floor the houses
which the kings of Judah had destroyed.
[12]And the men did the work faithfully. Their
overseers *were* Jahath and Obadiah the Levites, of the sons of Merari, and Zechariah and
Meshullam, of the sons of the Kohathites, to
supervise. *Others of* the Levites, all of whom
were skillful with instruments of music, [13]*were*
over the burden bearers and *were* overseers of
all who did work in any kind of service. And
some of the Levites *were* scribes, officers, and
gatekeepers.
[14]Now when they brought out the money
that was brought into the house of the LORD,
Hilkiah the priest found the Book of the Law
of the LORD *given* by Moses. [15]Then Hilkiah
answered and said to Shaphan the scribe, "I
have found the Book of the Law in the house
of the LORD." And Hilkiah gave the book to
Shaphan. [16]So Shaphan carried the book to
the king, bringing the king word, saying, "All
that was committed to your servants they are
doing. [17]And they have gathered the money
that was found in the house of the LORD, and
have delivered it into the hand of the over-

PERSONALITY PROFILE

Self-Esteem

THE DIFFERENCE ONE PERSON CAN MAKE

(2 CHRONICLES 34:26–28)

What a difference one person can make. And when that person is a king, what a difference he can make for his country!

Josiah began to reign at age 8. In the eighth year of his reign, at age 16, he "began to seek the God of his father David." Through that seeking, God showed Josiah that he needed to "purge Judah and Jerusalem of the high places, the wooden images, the carved images, and the molded images" (2 Chr. 34:3). So Josiah faithfully purged the entire nation of idol worship. Then he began to repair God's temple. God rewarded Josiah's faithfulness by allowing Hilkiah the high priest to discover the Book of the Law. When the book was dusted off and read, Josiah realized with horror how far the nation had strayed from God's expectations. Josiah asked God what he should do next.

God explained through a prophet that Judah was suffering because of a long series of sinful choices that the leaders and people of the nation had made over a long period. God stated that the nation would indeed pay for its sins. But because Josiah's heart was tender, God promised his eyes would not see all the calamity which He would bring on Judah and its inhabitants (34:27, 28). The final demise of the kingdom would not occur during Josiah's lifetime, because Josiah had tried to turn the nation around.

God often works through His people to accomplish His will. One believer can help another person turn around a life; one believer can help an entire nation reverse its course. In each case, God works through one person whose life is surrendered to Him. Every believer has an important role to play in building God's Kingdom. Whether God uses us to bring one or millions to Him, we must seek and follow His will. The believer who is yielded to God will have an impact for Him.

To Learn More: Turn to the article about self-esteem on pages 960, 961. See also the key passage note at Matthew 10:29–31 on page 1245.

seers and the workmen." 18Then Shaphan the
scribe told the king, saying, "Hilkiah the priest
has given me a book." And Shaphan read it
before the king.

19Thus it happened, when the king heard
the words of the Law, that he tore his clothes.
20Then the king commanded Hilkiah, Ahikam
the son of Shaphan, Abdon[a] the son of Micah,
Shaphan the scribe, and Asaiah a servant of
the king, saying, 21"Go, inquire of the LORD for
me, and for those who are left in Israel and
Judah, concerning the words of the book that
is found; for great *is* the wrath of the LORD that
is poured out on us, because our fathers have
not kept the word of the LORD, to do according
to all that is written in this book."

22So Hilkiah and those the king *had appointed* went to Huldah the prophetess, the
wife of Shallum the son of Tokhath,[a] the son
of Hasrah,[b] keeper of the wardrobe. (She
dwelt in Jerusalem in the Second Quarter.)
And they spoke to her to that *effect*.

23Then she answered them, "Thus says the
LORD God of Israel, 'Tell the man who sent
you to Me, 24"Thus says the LORD: 'Behold, I
will bring calamity on this place and on its inhabitants, all the curses that are written in the
book which they have read before the king of
Judah, 25because they have forsaken Me and
burned incense to other gods, that they might
provoke Me to anger with all the works of their
hands. Therefore My wrath will be poured out
on this place, and not be quenched.' " ' 26But as
for the king of Judah, who sent you to inquire
of the LORD, in this manner you shall speak to
him, 'Thus says the LORD God of Israel: "*Concerning* the words which you have heard—
27because your heart was tender, and you humbled yourself before God when you heard His
words against this place and against its inhabitants, and you humbled yourself before Me,
and you tore your clothes and wept before Me,
I also have heard *you*," says the LORD. 28"Surely I will gather you to your fathers, and you
shall be gathered to your grave in peace; and
your eyes shall not see all the calamity which
I will bring on this place and its inhabitants." ' " So they brought back word to the
king.

JOSIAH RESTORES TRUE WORSHIP

29Then the king sent and gathered all the elders of Judah and Jerusalem. 30The king went
up to the house of the LORD, with all the men
of Judah and the inhabitants of Jerusalem—
the priests and the Levites, and all the people,
great and small. And he read in their hearing
all the words of the Book of the Covenant
which had been found in the house of the
LORD. 31Then the king stood in his place and
made a covenant before the LORD, to follow
the LORD, and to keep His commandments
and His testimonies and His statutes with all
his heart and all his soul, to perform the
words of the covenant that were written in
this book. 32And he made all who were present in Jerusalem and Benjamin take a stand.
So the inhabitants of Jerusalem did according
to the covenant of God, the God of their fathers. 33Thus Josiah removed all the abominations from all the country that *belonged* to the
children of Israel, and made all who were
present in Israel diligently serve the LORD their
God. All his days they did not depart from following the LORD God of their fathers.

JOSIAH KEEPS THE PASSOVER

35 Now Josiah kept a Passover to the
LORD in Jerusalem, and they slaughtered the Passover *lambs* on the fourteenth
day of the first month. 2And he set the priests
in their duties and encouraged them for the
service of the house of the LORD. 3Then he
said to the Levites who taught all Israel, who
were holy to the LORD: "Put the holy ark in the
house which Solomon the son of David, king
of Israel, built. *It shall* no longer *be* a burden
on *your* shoulders. Now serve the LORD your
God and His people Israel. 4Prepare *yourselves*
according to your fathers' houses, according
to your divisions, following the written instruction of David king of Israel and the written instruction of Solomon his son. 5And
stand in the holy *place* according to the divisions of the fathers' houses of your brethren
the *lay* people, and *according to* the division of
the father's house of the Levites. 6So slaughter
the Passover *offerings*, consecrate yourselves,
and prepare *them* for your brethren, that *they*
may do according to the word of the LORD by
the hand of Moses."

7Then Josiah gave the *lay* people lambs and
young goats from the flock, all for Passover
offerings for all who were present, to the

34:20 [a]*Achbor the son of Michaiah* in 2 Kings 22:12 **34:22** [a]Spelled *Tikvah* in 2 Kings 22:14 [b]Spelled *Harhas* in 2 Kings 22:14

number of thirty thousand, as well as three thousand cattle; these *were* from the king's possessions. [8]And his leaders gave willingly to the people, to the priests, and to the Levites. Hilkiah, Zechariah, and Jehiel, rulers of the house of God, gave to the priests for the Passover *offerings* two thousand six hundred *from the flock,* and three hundred cattle. [9]Also Conaniah, his brothers Shemaiah and Nethanel, and Hashabiah and Jeiel and Jozabad, chief of the Levites, gave to the Levites for Passover *offerings* five thousand *from the flock* and five hundred cattle.

[10]So the service was prepared, and the priests stood in their places, and the Levites in their divisions, according to the king's command. [11]And they slaughtered the Passover *offerings;* and the priests sprinkled *the blood* with their hands, while the Levites skinned *the animals.* [12]Then they removed the burnt offerings that *they* might give them to the divisions of the fathers' houses of the *lay* people, to offer to the LORD, as *it is* written in the Book of Moses. And so *they did* with the cattle. [13]Also they roasted the Passover *offerings* with fire according to the ordinance; but the *other* holy *offerings* they boiled in pots, in caldrons, and in pans, and divided *them* quickly among all the *lay* people. [14]Then afterward they prepared portions for themselves and for the priests, because the priests, the sons of Aaron, *were busy* in offering burnt offerings and fat until night; therefore the Levites prepared portions for themselves and for the priests, the sons of Aaron. [15]And the singers, the sons of Asaph, *were* in their places, according to the command of David, Asaph, Heman, and Jeduthun the king's seer. Also the gatekeepers were at each gate; they did not have to leave their position, because their brethren the Levites prepared portions for them.

[16]So all the service of the LORD was prepared the same day, to keep the Passover and to offer burnt offerings on the altar of the LORD, according to the command of King Josiah. [17]And the children of Israel who were present kept the Passover at that time, and the Feast of Unleavened Bread for seven days. [18]There had been no Passover kept in Israel like that since the days of Samuel the prophet; and none of the kings of Israel had kept such a Passover as Josiah kept, with the priests and the Levites, all Judah and Israel who were present, and the inhabitants of Jerusalem. [19]In the eighteenth year of the reign of Josiah this Passover was kept.

Josiah Dies in Battle

[20]After all this, when Josiah had prepared the temple, Necho king of Egypt came up to fight against Carchemish by the Euphrates; and Josiah went out against him. [21]But he sent messengers to him, saying, "What have I to do with you, king of Judah? *I have* not *come* against you this day, but against the house with which I have war; for God commanded me to make haste. Refrain *from meddling with* God, who *is* with me, lest He destroy you." [22]Nevertheless Josiah would not turn his face from him, but disguised himself so that he might fight with him, and did not heed the words of Necho from the mouth of God. So he came to fight in the Valley of Megiddo.

[23]And the archers shot King Josiah; and the king said to his servants, "Take me away, for I am severely wounded." [24]His servants therefore took him out of that chariot and put him in the second chariot that he had, and they brought him to Jerusalem. So he died, and was buried in *one of* the tombs of his fathers. And all Judah and Jerusalem mourned for Josiah.

[25]Jeremiah also lamented for Josiah. And to this day all the singing men and the singing women speak of Josiah in their lamentations. They made it a custom in Israel; and indeed they *are* written in the Laments.

[26]Now the rest of the acts of Josiah and his goodness, according to *what was* written in the Law of the LORD, [27]and his deeds from first to last, indeed they *are* written in the book of the kings of Israel and Judah.

The Reign and Captivity of Jehoahaz

36 Then the people of the land took Jehoahaz the son of Josiah, and made him king in his father's place in Jerusalem. [2]Jehoahaz[a] *was* twenty-three years old when he became king, and he reigned three months in Jerusalem. [3]Now the king of Egypt deposed him at Jerusalem; and he imposed on the land a tribute of one hundred talents of silver and a talent of gold. [4]Then the king of Egypt made *Jehoahaz's*[a] brother Eliakim king over Judah and Jerusalem, and changed his name to Je-

---

36:2 [a]Masoretic Text reads *Joahaz.* **36:4** [a]Literally *his*

hoiakim. And Necho took Jehoahaz[b] his brother and carried him off to Egypt.

The Reign and Captivity of Jehoiakim

5Jehoiakim *was* twenty-five years old when he became king, and he reigned eleven years in Jerusalem. And he did evil in the sight of the LORD his God. 6Nebuchadnezzar king of Babylon came up against him, and bound him in bronze *fetters* to carry him off to Babylon. 7Nebuchadnezzar also carried off *some* of the articles from the house of the LORD to Babylon, and put them in his temple at Babylon. 8Now the rest of the acts of Jehoiakim, the abominations which he did, and what was found against him, indeed they *are* written in the book of the kings of Israel and Judah. Then Jehoiachin his son reigned in his place.

The Reign and Captivity of Jehoiachin

9Jehoiachin *was* eight[a] years old when he became king, and he reigned in Jerusalem three months and ten days. And he did evil in the sight of the LORD. 10At the turn of the year King Nebuchadnezzar summoned *him* and took him to Babylon, with the costly articles from the house of the LORD, and made Zedekiah, *Jehoiakim's*[a] brother, king over Judah and Jerusalem.

Zedekiah Reigns in Judah

11Zedekiah *was* twenty-one years old when he became king, and he reigned eleven years in Jerusalem. 12He did evil in the sight of the LORD his God, *and* did not humble himself before Jeremiah the prophet, *who spoke* from the mouth of the LORD. 13And he also rebelled against King Nebuchadnezzar, who had made him swear *an oath* by God; but he stiffened his neck and hardened his heart against turning to the LORD God of Israel. 14Moreover all the leaders of the priests and the people transgressed more and more, *according* to all the abominations of the nations, and defiled the house of the LORD which He had consecrated in Jerusalem.

The Fall of Jerusalem

15And the LORD God of their fathers sent *warnings* to them by His messengers, rising up early and sending *them,* because He had compassion on His people and on His dwelling place. 16But they mocked the messengers of God, despised His words, and scoffed at His prophets, until the wrath of the LORD arose against His people, till *there was* no remedy.

17Therefore He brought against them the king of the Chaldeans, who killed their young men with the sword in the house of their sanctuary, and had no compassion on young man or virgin, on the aged or the weak; He gave *them* all into his hand. 18And all the articles from the house of God, great and small, the treasures of the house of the LORD, and the treasures of the king and of his leaders, all *these* he took to Babylon. 19Then they burned the house of God, broke down the wall of Jerusalem, burned all its palaces with fire, and destroyed all its precious possessions. 20And those who escaped from the sword he carried away to Babylon, where they became servants to him and his sons until the rule of the kingdom of Persia, 21to fulfill the word of the LORD by the mouth of Jeremiah, until the land had enjoyed her Sabbaths. As long as she lay desolate she kept Sabbath, to fulfill seventy years.

The Proclamation of Cyrus

22Now in the first year of Cyrus king of Persia, that the word of the LORD by the mouth of Jeremiah might be fulfilled, the LORD stirred

36:4 [b]Masoretic Text reads *Joahaz.* **36:9** [a]Some Hebrew manuscripts, Septuagint, Syriac, and 2 Kings 24:8 read *eighteen.* **36:10** [a]Literally *his* (compare 2 Kings 24:17)

SOUL NOTE

No Remedy *(36:5–8)* Jehoiakim got the dubious honor of being the king when Nebuchadnezzar overcame the nation and took them into captivity. He had failed his nation, but the final collapse of Judah was the result of the kings' and people's long series of wrong choices. Despite temporary reprieves during the reigns of a few good kings, Judah was at a final point of spiritual and moral decay. Judah had set a course of disobedience against God until "there was no remedy" (36:16). The nation's failure came as a result of its disobedience to God. **Topic: Failure**

Failure

GOD'S VIEW OF FAILURE

GARY J. OLIVER

(2 Chronicles 36)

The marriage that was supposed to be forever turns into a short-lived disaster. The presentation at work that should have earned a promotion completely bombs. Everyone has setbacks; everyone fails. From Genesis to Revelation, the Bible talks about the failure of people and the faithfulness of God. A careful study of Scripture reveals key principles for understanding the role of failure in spiritual growth.

THE VALUE OF FAILURE

God "is able to keep you from stumbling, and to present you faultless before the presence of His glory with exceeding joy" (Jude 24). Jude makes it clear that God is able to keep His people from slipping, tripping, and stumbling. However, He also knows that every failure has seeds of growth. He knows that apart from failure, people would have no need for His forgiveness, His communion, or His help. In His hands, failure can be one of life's greatest teachers.

Since most people tend to avoid pain, it takes the Holy Spirit working through their circumstances to lead them into a deeper identification with the Lord. God knows that the kinds of growth experiences that are the most painful are the ones people are most likely to avoid—failure and defeat.

In God's hands, failure can refine and teach in ways that success cannot. God can use failure to draw people closer to Him. Failure reaches down into the depths of people's souls and exposes deep-seated pockets of selfishness and pride. It makes them aware of their limitations. It increases their sensitivity to others. It humbles them. It helps them understand the high calling of being a servant. It reminds people how important it is to set their minds on things above (Col. 3:2). It increases their confidence that God will complete the work He began in their lives (Phil. 1:6).

FORGIVENESS OF FAILURE

Since He understands the effects of sin, God is not surprised by failure. He knows that people are frail. He also understands that we are in a battle. "For we do not wrestle against flesh and blood, but against principalities, against powers, against the rulers of the darkness of this age, against spiritual hosts of wickedness in the heavenly places" (Eph. 6:12).

When life is going well, it is easy for people to proclaim belief in a merciful, gracious, forgiving, and loving God. But when mistakes and failures dump them in the trenches of spiritual warfare, they find a new perspective of God as powerful, almighty, and in control. "The steps of a good man are ordered by the LORD, and He delights in his way. Though he fall, he shall not be utterly cast down; for the LORD upholds him with His hand. I have been young, and now am old; yet I have not seen the righteous forsaken, nor his descendents begging bread" (Ps. 37:23–25).

Consider some of the better known biblical people who were broken by failure. God did not abandon them, however. They faced the consequences of their sin (sometimes severe consequences), but God forgave and continued to use them in His service:

➢ Adam and Eve sinned and were cast out of the Garden of Eden.
➢ Moses murdered an Egyptian and it cost him forty years in the wilderness.
➢ Moses struck the rock and it cost him entrance into the Promised Land.
➢ Abraham started strong, but got caught in a series of lies.
➢ David's sin of adultery and murder cost him his integrity and the life of his son.
➢ Elijah allowed his depression to get so far out of control that he begged God to take his life.
➢ Jonah initially rejected God's plan for him.
➢ Peter proclaimed loyalty to Jesus and then denied ever knowing Him.

Sin and failure are a part of being human. First John 2:1 says, "My little children, these things I write to you, so that you may not sin." God's will for people is that they don't sin. We should do all that we can to avoid sin. If the text stopped there, however, it would be rather discouraging. However, John continues, "And if anyone sins, we have an Advocate with the Father, Jesus Christ the righteous. And He Himself is the propitiation for our sins, and not for ours only but also for the whole world" (1 John 2:1, 2). God abhors sin, but He can use what He hates to drive us to the Cross where we find forgiveness, renewed perspective, and grace to move forward.

IN GOD'S HANDS, FAILURE ISN'T FINAL

Our first response to failure is often to focus on the failure and to panic. "My ministry is over." "God will never be able to use me again." "My kids will be damaged for life." Although we must be concerned with the present, it is dangerous to develop myopic blinders for the here and now. We need to think and pray about how to cope for today, but we must also ask God to help us put the failure in the proper perspective and to help us learn what we need to from it.

Our failures can be used as stepping-stones to a deeper relationship with God. Having failed, we can still be successful in God's sight because of the incredible generosity of God's forgiveness and acceptance—for His grace not only covers our failures, it is actually able to transform them.

FURTHER MEDITATION:

Other passages to study about the issue of failure include:

➢ Deuteronomy 31:6
➢ Psalms 56; 69:5; 73:26
➢ Isaiah 43:16–19
➢ Luke 22:32
➢ 2 Corinthians 12:9
➢ Hebrews 12:1, 2
➢ 1 Peter 1:6–9

To Learn More: **Turn to the key passage note on failure at Proverbs 24:16 on page 834. See also the personality profile of Peter on page 1359.**

up the spirit of Cyrus king of Persia, so that he made a proclamation throughout all his kingdom, and also *put it* in writing, saying,

23 Thus says Cyrus king of Persia:
All the kingdoms of the earth the LORD
God of heaven has given me. And He
has commanded me to build Him a
house at Jerusalem which is in Judah.
Who *is* among you of all His people?
May the LORD his God *be* with him, and
let him go up!

SOUL NOTE

Ray of Hope *(36:23)* The people of Judah were taken captive and deported into Babylon for the next 70 years. They suffered the consequences of their own spiritual neglect. Even in this desperate moment, however, the chronicler ends his record by pointing ahead to the coming of Cyrus, the king of Persia, who would eventually allow the people of Judah to return to Jerusalem. Even in their darkest hour, there was a ray of hope for the future. God would take care of His faithful people. **Topic: Hope**

Ezra

*F*aithful has to be one of the greatest words in the English language. It means trustworthy or reliable. A faithful person is utterly dependable. To say that God is faithful means that He always keeps His promises.

The Old Testament book of Ezra (likely written by Ezra) is about God's faithfulness. It picks up the history of the Jewish people at the end of their 70-year exile. When the Babylonians were overthrown by the Persians in 539 B.C., King Cyrus issued a decree allowing the Jews to return to Jerusalem to rebuild the temple and to renew their hope in the future. This return occurred in phases. The first, involving almost 50,000 Jews, was led by Zerubbabel (chapters 1—6). The second occurred some 60 years later under Ezra the priest. Documented in chapters 7—10, the goal of this smaller return was to rebuild the spiritual condition of the people.

Despite the difficulties and discouragement faced by the returning exiles, this book is filled with hope. The people of God had been brought back to the Promised Land. Despite a long history of failure, the Hebrew people had not been abandoned by God. The Lord's ancient promises for their future benefit would be kept.

Read of God's faithfulness to His Old Testament people. As you do, keep in mind this New Testament promise: "If we are faithless, He remains faithful; He cannot deny Himself" (2 Tim. 2:13).

SOUL CONCERN IN EZRA

End of the Babylonian Captivity

1 Now in the first year of Cyrus king of Persia, that the word of the LORD by the mouth of Jeremiah might be fulfilled, the LORD stirred up the spirit of Cyrus king of Persia, so that he made a proclamation throughout all his kingdom, and also *put it* in writing, saying,

2 Thus says Cyrus king of Persia:
All the kingdoms of the earth the LORD
God of heaven has given me. And He
has commanded me to build Him a
house at Jerusalem which *is* in Judah.
3 Who *is* among you of all His people?
May his God be with him, and let him
go up to Jerusalem which *is* in Judah,
and build the house of the LORD God
of Israel (He *is* God), which *is* in
Jerusalem. 4 And whoever is left in any
place where he dwells, let the men of his
place help him with silver and gold,
with goods and livestock, besides the
freewill offerings for the house of God
which *is* in Jerusalem.

5 Then the heads of the fathers' *houses* of Judah and Benjamin, and the priests and the Levites, with all whose spirits God had moved, arose to go up and build the house of the LORD which *is* in Jerusalem. 6 And all those who *were* around them encouraged them with articles of silver and gold, with goods and livestock, and with precious things, besides all *that* was willingly offered.

7 King Cyrus also brought out the articles of the house of the LORD, which Nebuchadnezzar had taken from Jerusalem and put in the temple of his gods; 8 and Cyrus king of Persia brought them out by the hand of Mithredath the treasurer, and counted them out to Sheshbazzar the prince of Judah. 9 This *is* the number of them: thirty gold platters, one thousand silver platters, twenty-nine knives, 10 thirty gold basins, four hundred and ten silver basins of a similar *kind, and* one thousand other articles. 11 All the articles of gold and silver *were* five thousand four hundred. All *these* Sheshbazzar took with the captives who were brought from Babylon to Jerusalem.

The Captives Who Returned to Jerusalem

2 Now[a] these *are* the people of the province who came back from the captivity, of those who had been carried away, whom Nebuchadnezzar the king of Babylon had carried away to Babylon, and who returned to Jerusalem and Judah, everyone to his *own* city.

2 *Those* who came with Zerubbabel *were* Jeshua, Nehemiah, Seraiah, Reelaiah, Mordecai, Bilshan, Mispar,[a] Bigvai, Rehum,[b] *and* Baanah. The number of the men of the people of Israel: 3 the people of Parosh, two thousand one hundred and seventy-two; 4 the people of Shephatiah, three hundred and seventy-two; 5 the people of Arah, seven hundred and seventy-five; 6 the people of Pahath-Moab, of the people of Jeshua *and* Joab, two thousand eight hundred and twelve; 7 the people of Elam, one thousand two hundred and fifty-four; 8 the people of Zattu, nine hundred and forty-five; 9 the people of Zaccai, seven hundred and sixty; 10 the people of Bani,[a] six hundred and forty-two; 11 the people of Bebai, six hundred and twenty-three; 12 the people of Azgad, one thousand two hundred and twenty-two; 13 the people of Adonikam, six hundred and sixty-six; 14 the people of Bigvai, two thousand and fifty-six; 15 the people of Adin, four hundred and fifty-four; 16 the people of Ater of Hezekiah, ninety-eight; 17 the people of Bezai, three hundred and twenty-three; 18 the people of Jorah,[a] one hundred and twelve; 19 the people of Hashum, two hundred and twenty-three; 20 the people of Gibbar,[a] ninety-five; 21 the people of Bethlehem, one hundred and twenty-three; 22 the men of Netophah, fifty-six; 23 the men of Anathoth, one hundred and twenty-eight; 24 the people of Azmaveth,[a] forty-two; 25 the people of Kirjath Arim,[a] Chephirah, and Beeroth, seven hundred and forty-three; 26 the people of Ramah and Geba, six hundred and twenty-one; 27 the men of Michmas, one hundred and twenty-two; 28 the men of Bethel and Ai, two hundred and twenty-three; 29 the people of Nebo, fifty-two; 30 the people of Magbish, one hundred and fifty-six; 31 the people of the other Elam, one thousand two hundred and fifty-four; 32 the people of Harim, three hundred and twenty; 33 the people of Lod, Hadid, and Ono, seven hundred and twenty-five;

2:1 [a]Compare this chapter with Nehemiah 7:6–73.
2:2 [a]Spelled *Mispereth* in Nehemiah 7:7 [b]Spelled *Nehum* in Nehemiah 7:7 **2:10** [a]Spelled *Binnui* in Nehemiah 7:15 **2:18** [a]Called *Hariph* in Nehemiah 7:24 **2:20** [a]Called *Gibeon* in Nehemiah 7:25
2:24 [a]Called *Beth Azmaveth* in Nehemiah 7:28
2:25 [a]Called *Kirjath Jearim* in Nehemiah 7:29

34 the people of Jericho, three hundred and forty-five; 35 the people of Senaah, three thousand six hundred and thirty.

36 The priests: the sons of Jedaiah, of the house of Jeshua, nine hundred and seventy-three; 37 the sons of Immer, one thousand and fifty-two; 38 the sons of Pashhur, one thousand two hundred and forty-seven; 39 the sons of Harim, one thousand and seventeen.

40 The Levites: the sons of Jeshua and Kadmiel, of the sons of Hodaviah,[a] seventy-four.

41 The singers: the sons of Asaph, one hundred and twenty-eight.

42 The sons of the gatekeepers: the sons of Shallum, the sons of Ater, the sons of Talmon, the sons of Akkub, the sons of Hatita, and the sons of Shobai, one hundred and thirty-nine *in* all.

43 The Nethinim: the sons of Ziha, the sons of Hasupha, the sons of Tabbaoth, 44 the sons of Keros, the sons of Siaha,[a] the sons of Padon, 45 the sons of Lebanah, the sons of Hagabah, the sons of Akkub, 46 the sons of Hagab, the sons of Shalmai, the sons of Hanan, 47 the sons of Giddel, the sons of Gahar, the sons of Reaiah, 48 the sons of Rezin, the sons of Nekoda, the sons of Gazzam, 49 the sons of Uzza, the sons of Paseah, the sons of Besai, 50 the sons of Asnah, the sons of Meunim, the sons of Nephusim,[a] 51 the sons of Bakbuk, the sons of Hakupha, the sons of Harhur, 52 the sons of Bazluth,[a] the sons of Mehida, the sons of Harsha, 53 the sons of Barkos, the sons of Sisera, the sons of Tamah, 54 the sons of Neziah, and the sons of Hatipha.

55 The sons of Solomon's servants: the sons of Sotai, the sons of Sophereth, the sons of Peruda,[a] 56 the sons of Jaala, the sons of Darkon, the sons of Giddel, 57 the sons of Shephatiah, the sons of Hattil, the sons of Pochereth of Zebaim, and the sons of Ami.[a] 58 All the Nethinim and the children of Solomon's servants were three hundred and ninety-two.

59 And these *were* the ones who came up from Tel Melah, Tel Harsha, Cherub, Addan,[a] and Immer; but they could not identify their father's house or their genealogy,[b] whether they *were* of Israel: 60 the sons of Delaiah, the sons of Tobiah, and the sons of Nekoda, six hundred and fifty-two; 61 and of the sons of the priests: the sons of Habaiah, the sons of Koz,[a] and the sons of Barzillai, who took a wife of the daughters of Barzillai the Gileadite, and was called by their name. 62 These sought their listing *among* those who were registered by genealogy, but they were not found; therefore they *were excluded* from the priesthood as defiled. 63 And the governor[a] said to them that they should not eat of the most holy things till a priest could consult with the Urim and Thummim.

64 The whole assembly together *was* forty-two thousand three hundred *and* sixty, 65 besides their male and female servants, of whom *there were* seven thousand three hundred and thirty-seven; and they had two hundred men and women singers. 66 Their horses *were* seven hundred and thirty-six, their mules two hundred and forty-five, 67 their camels four hundred and thirty-five, and *their* donkeys six thousand seven hundred and twenty.

68 *Some* of the heads of the fathers' *houses,* when they came to the house of the LORD which *is* in Jerusalem, offered freely for the

2:40 [a]Spelled *Hodevah* in Nehemiah 7:43 **2:44** [a]Spelled *Sia* in Nehemiah 7:47 **2:50** [a]Spelled *Nephishesim* in Nehemiah 7:52 **2:52** [a]Spelled *Bazlith* in Nehemiah 7:54 **2:55** [a]Spelled *Perida* in Nehemiah 7:57 **2:57** [a]Spelled *Amon* in Nehemiah 7:59 **2:59** [a]Spelled *Addon* in Nehemiah 7:61 [b]Literally *seed* **2:61** [a]Or *Hakkoz* **2:63** [a]Hebrew *Tirshatha*

SOUL NOTE

Joyful Giving *(2:68, 69)* The Jews had been living in captivity for over 70 years, but they had become financially prosperous. Ezra recorded that each person willingly contributed, according to his or her ability, into the treasury of the temple so that the worship of God could be reestablished in their homeland. God never calls us to do a job without providing the resources to get it done. In response, we should gladly give back to God a portion of those resources to further His work.

Topic: Money

house of God, to erect it in its place: 69According to their ability, they gave to the treasury for the work sixty-one thousand gold drachmas, five thousand minas of silver, and one hundred priestly garments.

70So the priests and the Levites, *some* of the people, the singers, the gatekeepers, and the Nethinim, dwelt in their cities, and all Israel in their cities.

Worship Restored at Jerusalem

3 And when the seventh month had come, and the children of Israel *were* in the cities, the people gathered together as one man to Jerusalem. 2Then Jeshua the son of Jozadak[a] and his brethren the priests, and Zerubbabel the son of Shealtiel and his brethren, arose and built the altar of the God of Israel, to offer burnt offerings on it, as *it is* written in the Law of Moses the man of God. 3Though fear *had come* upon them because of the people of those countries, they set the altar on its bases; and they offered burnt offerings on it to the LORD, *both* the morning and evening burnt offerings. 4They also kept the Feast of Tabernacles, as *it is* written, and *offered* the daily burnt offerings in the number required by ordinance for each day. 5Afterwards *they offered* the regular burnt offering, and *those* for New Moons and for all the appointed feasts of the LORD that were consecrated, and *those* of everyone who willingly offered a freewill offering to the LORD. 6From the first day of the seventh month they began to offer burnt offerings to the LORD, although the foundation of the temple of the LORD had not been laid. 7They also gave money to the masons and the carpenters, and food, drink, and oil to the people of Sidon and Tyre to bring cedar logs from Lebanon to the sea, to Joppa, according to the permission which they had from Cyrus king of Persia.

Restoration of the Temple Begins

8Now in the second month of the second year of their coming to the house of God at Jerusalem, Zerubbabel the son of Shealtiel, Jeshua the son of Jozadak,[a] and the rest of their brethren the priests and the Levites, and all those who had come out of the captivity to Jerusalem, began *work* and appointed the Levites from twenty years old and above to oversee the work of the house of the LORD. 9Then Jeshua *with* his sons and brothers, Kadmiel *with* his sons, and the sons of Judah,[a] arose as one to oversee those working on the house of God: the sons of Henadad *with* their sons and their brethren the Levites.

10When the builders laid the foundation of the temple of the LORD, the priests stood[a] in their apparel with trumpets, and the Levites, the sons of Asaph, with cymbals, to praise the LORD, according to the ordinance of David king of Israel. 11And they sang responsively, praising and giving thanks to the LORD:

"For *He is* good,
For His mercy *endures* forever toward
Israel."[a]

Then all the people shouted with a great shout, when they praised the LORD, because the foundation of the house of the LORD was laid.

12But many of the priests and Levites and heads of the fathers' *houses,* old men who had seen the first temple, wept with a loud voice when the foundation of this temple was laid

3:2 [a]Spelled *Jehozadak* in 1 Chronicles 6:14
3:8 [a]Spelled *Jehozadak* in 1 Chronicles 6:14
3:9 [a]Or *Hodaviah* (compare 2:40) **3:10** [a]Following Septuagint, Syriac, and Vulgate; Masoretic Text reads *they stationed the priests.* **3:11** [a]Compare Psalm 136:1

SOUL NOTE

When Change Comes *(3:12, 13)* In grieving, it is sometimes difficult to see what good can come out of loss. When the foundation of the temple was laid by the returning exiles, the people both wept and rejoiced. They wept because the previous glorious temple built by King Solomon had been destroyed, and the new temple would not be as huge or as beautiful. Yet others rejoiced that the process of rebuilding their temple had begun. Sorrow and joy can be appropriate as God's people grieve for the past but face the future with hope. **Topic: Grief/Loss**

before their eyes. Yet many shouted aloud for joy, 13so that the people could not discern the noise of the shout of joy from the noise of the weeping of the people, for the people shouted with a loud shout, and the sound was heard afar off.

Resistance to Rebuilding the Temple

4 Now when the adversaries of Judah and Benjamin heard that the descendants of the captivity were building the temple of the LORD God of Israel, 2they came to Zerubbabel and the heads of the fathers' *houses,* and said to them, "Let us build with you, for we seek your God as you *do;* and we have sacrificed to Him since the days of Esarhaddon king of Assyria, who brought us here." 3But Zerubbabel and Jeshua and the rest of the heads of the fathers' *houses* of Israel said to them, "You may do nothing with us to build a house for our God; but we alone will build to the LORD God of Israel, as King Cyrus the king of Persia has commanded us." 4Then the people of the land tried to discourage the people of Judah. They troubled them in building, 5and hired counselors against them to frustrate their purpose all the days of Cyrus king of Persia, even until the reign of Darius king of Persia.

Rebuilding of Jerusalem Opposed

6In the reign of Ahasuerus, in the beginning of his reign, they wrote an accusation against the inhabitants of Judah and Jerusalem.

7In the days of Artaxerxes also, Bishlam, Mithredath, Tabel, and the rest of their companions wrote to Artaxerxes king of Persia; and the letter *was* written in Aramaic script, and translated into the Aramaic language. 8Rehum[a] the commander and Shimshai the scribe wrote a letter against Jerusalem to King Artaxerxes in this fashion:

9 From[a] Rehum the commander, Shimshai
the scribe, and the rest of their
companions—*representatives* of the
Dinaites, the Apharsathchites, the
Tarpelites, the people of Persia and
Erech and Babylon and Shushan,[b] the
Dehavites, the Elamites, 10and the rest of
the nations whom the great and noble
Osnapper took captive and settled in the
cities of Samaria and the remainder
beyond the River[a]—and so forth.[b]

11(This *is* a copy of the letter that they sent him)

To King Artaxerxes from your servants,
the men *of the region* beyond the River,
and so forth:[a]

12 Let it be known to the king that the Jews
who came up from you have come to us
at Jerusalem, and are building the
rebellious and evil city, and are finishing
its walls and repairing the foundations.
13Let it now be known to the king that,
if this city is built and the walls
completed, they will not pay tax, tribute,
or custom, and the king's treasury will
be diminished. 14Now because we
receive support from the palace, it was
not proper for us to see the king's
dishonor; therefore we have sent and
informed the king, 15that search may be
made in the book of the records of your
fathers. And you will find in the book of
the records and know that this city *is* a

4:8 [a]The original language of Ezra 4:8 through 6:18 is Aramaic. **4:9** [a]Literally *Then* [b]Or *Susa*
4:10 [a]That is, the Euphrates [b]Literally *and now*
4:11 [a]Literally *and now*

SOUL NOTE

Overcomers *(4:4, 5)* Believers can expect opposition when doing the work of God. In this case, the people of Judah simply wanted to rebuild their house of worship. Their neighbors were opposed to this and responded by discouraging and intimidating them. Rather than allow this opposition to paralyze them, God's people asserted their legal rights to allow the building process to continue. Believers have faced opposition in every age. With God's help and the support of other believers, we can overcome fear and discouragement and complete the work to which God has called us.
Topic: Discouragement

rebellious city, harmful to kings and provinces, and that they have incited sedition within the city in former times, for which cause this city was destroyed.

16 We inform the king that if this city is rebuilt and its walls are completed, the result will be that you will have no dominion beyond the River.

17The king sent an answer:

To Rehum the commander, *to* Shimshai the scribe, *to* the rest of their companions who dwell in Samaria, and *to* the remainder beyond the River:

Peace, and so forth.[a]

18 The letter which you sent to us has been clearly read before me. 19And I gave the command, and a search has been made, and it was found that this city in former times has revolted against kings, and rebellion and sedition have been fostered in it. 20There have also been mighty kings over Jerusalem, who have ruled over all *the region* beyond the River; and tax, tribute, and custom were paid to them. 21Now give the command to make these men cease, that this city may not be built until the command is given by me.

22 Take heed now that you do not fail to do this. Why should damage increase to the hurt of the kings?

23Now when the copy of King Artaxerxes' letter *was* read before Rehum, Shimshai the scribe, and their companions, they went up in haste to Jerusalem against the Jews, and by force of arms made them cease. 24Thus the work of the house of God which *is* at Jerusalem ceased, and it was discontinued until the second year of the reign of Darius king of Persia.

RESTORATION OF THE TEMPLE RESUMED

5 Then the prophet Haggai and Zechariah
the son of Iddo, prophets, prophesied to
the Jews who *were* in Judah and Jerusalem, in
the name of the God of Israel, *who was* over
them. 2So Zerubbabel the son of Shealtiel and
Jeshua the son of Jozadak[a] rose up and began
to build the house of God which *is* in Jerusalem; and the prophets of God *were* with them,
helping them.
3At the same time Tattenai the governor of
the region beyond the River[a] and Shethar-
Boznai and their companions came to them
and spoke thus to them: "Who has commanded you to build this temple and finish this
wall?" 4Then, accordingly, we told them the
names of the men who were constructing this
building. 5But the eye of their God was upon
the elders of the Jews, so that they could not
make them cease till a report could go to Darius. Then a written answer was returned concerning this *matter.* 6This is a copy of the letter
that Tattenai sent:

The governor of *the region* beyond the River, and Shethar-Boznai, and his companions, the Persians who *were in the region* beyond the River, to Darius the king.

7(They sent a letter to him, in which was written thus)

4:17 [a]Literally *and now* **5:2** [a]Spelled *Jehozadak* in 1 Chronicles 6:14 **5:3** [a]That is, the Euphrates

SOUL NOTE

Never Give Up *(5:1, 2)* The prophets Haggai and Zechariah not only encouraged the people of Jerusalem to rebuild the temple, but they also got involved in the labor themselves. Even before they rebuilt the city's walls, the Jews rebuilt the temple as an act of devotion to God. Living so many years without a temple and experiencing the temporary setbacks during the reconstruction only served to strengthen God's people in their resolve to complete the task at hand. Setbacks aren't always detrimental—they give time to reflect and revise plans if the need arises, allowing us to press on toward our goals. **Topic: Work**

To Darius the king:

All peace.

8 Let it be known to the king that we went into the province of Judea, to the temple of the great God, which is being built with heavy stones, and timber is being laid in the walls; and this work goes on diligently and prospers in their hands.

9 Then we asked those elders, *and* spoke thus to them: "Who commanded you to build this temple and to finish these walls?" 10We also asked them their names to inform you, that we might write the names of the men who *were* chief among them.

11 And thus they returned us an answer, saying: "We are the servants of the God of heaven and earth, and we are rebuilding the temple that was built many years ago, which a great king of Israel built and completed. 12But because our fathers provoked the God of heaven to wrath, He gave them into the hand of Nebuchadnezzar king of Babylon, the Chaldean, *who* destroyed this temple and carried the people away to Babylon. 13However, in the first year of Cyrus king of Babylon, King Cyrus issued a decree to build this house of God. 14Also, the gold and silver articles of the house of God, which Nebuchadnezzar had taken from the temple that *was* in Jerusalem and carried into the temple of Babylon—those King Cyrus took from the temple of Babylon, and they were given to one named Sheshbazzar, whom he had made governor. 15And he said to him, 'Take these articles; go, carry them to the temple *site* that *is* in Jerusalem, and let the house of God be rebuilt on its former site.' 16Then the same Sheshbazzar came *and* laid the foundation of the house of God which *is* in Jerusalem; but from that time even until now it has been under construction, and it is not finished."

17 Now therefore, if *it seems* good to the king, let a search be made in the king's treasure house, which *is* there in Babylon, whether it is *so* that a decree was issued by King Cyrus to build this house of God at Jerusalem, and let the king send us his pleasure concerning this *matter.*

The Decree of Darius

6 Then King Darius issued a decree, and a search was made in the archives,[a] where the treasures were stored in Babylon. 2And at Achmetha,[a] in the palace that *is* in the province of Media, a scroll was found, and in it a record *was* written thus:

3 In the first year of King Cyrus, King Cyrus issued a decree *concerning* the house of God at Jerusalem: "Let the house be rebuilt, the place where they offered sacrifices; and let the foundations of it be firmly laid, its height sixty cubits *and* its width sixty cubits, 4*with* three rows of heavy stones and one row of new timber. Let the expenses be paid from the king's treasury. 5Also let the gold and silver articles of the house of God, which Nebuchadnezzar took from the temple which *is* in Jerusalem and brought to Babylon, be restored and taken back to the temple which *is* in Jerusalem, *each* to its place; and deposit *them* in the house of God"—

6 Now *therefore,* Tattenai, governor of *the region* beyond the River, and Shethar-Boznai, and your companions the Persians who *are* beyond the River, keep yourselves far from there. 7Let the work of this house of God alone; let the governor of the Jews and the elders of the Jews build this house of God on its site.

8 Moreover I issue a decree *as to* what you shall do for the elders of these Jews, for the building of this house of God: Let the cost be paid at the king's expense from taxes *on the region* beyond the River; this is to be given immediately to these men, so that they are not hindered. 9And whatever they need—young bulls, rams, and lambs for the

---

6:1 [a]Literally *house of the scrolls* **6:2** [a]Probably *Ecbatana,* the ancient capital of Media

burnt offerings of the God of heaven,
wheat, salt, wine, and oil, according to
the request of the priests who *are* in
Jerusalem—let it be given them day by
day without fail, 10that they may offer
sacrifices of sweet aroma to the God of
heaven, and pray for the life of the king
and his sons.

11 Also I issue a decree that whoever alters
this edict, let a timber be pulled from his
house and erected, and let him be
hanged on it; and let his house be made
a refuse heap because of this. 12And may
the God who causes His name to dwell
there destroy any king or people who
put their hand to alter it, or to destroy
this house of God which is in Jerusalem.
I Darius issue a decree; let it be done
diligently.

The Temple Completed and Dedicated

13Then Tattenai, governor of *the region* beyond the River, Shethar-Boznai, and their
companions diligently did according to what
King Darius had sent. 14So the elders of the
Jews built, and they prospered through the
prophesying of Haggai the prophet and Zechariah the son of Iddo. And they built and finished *it,* according to the commandment of
the God of Israel, and according to the command of Cyrus, Darius, and Artaxerxes king of
Persia. 15Now the temple was finished on the
third day of the month of Adar, which was in
the sixth year of the reign of King Darius.
16Then the children of Israel, the priests and
the Levites and the rest of the descendants of
the captivity, celebrated the dedication of this
house of God with joy. 17And they offered sacrifices at the dedication of this house of God,
one hundred bulls, two hundred rams, four
hundred lambs, and as a sin offering for all
Israel twelve male goats, according to the
number of the tribes of Israel. 18They assigned
the priests to their divisions and the Levites to
their divisions, over the service of God in Jerusalem, as it is written in the Book of Moses.

The Passover Celebrated

19And the descendants of the captivity kept
the Passover on the fourteenth *day* of the first
month. 20For the priests and the Levites had
purified themselves; all of them *were ritually*
clean. And they slaughtered the Passover
lambs for all the descendants of the captivity,
for their brethren the priests, and for themselves. 21Then the children of Israel who had
returned from the captivity ate together with
all who had separated themselves from the
filth of the nations of the land in order to seek
the LORD God of Israel. 22And they kept the
Feast of Unleavened Bread seven days with
joy; for the LORD made them joyful, and
turned the heart of the king of Assyria toward
them, to strengthen their hands in the work of
the house of God, the God of Israel.

The Arrival of Ezra

7 Now after these things, in the reign of Artaxerxes king of Persia, Ezra the son of Seraiah, the son of Azariah, the son of Hilkiah,
2the son of Shallum, the son of Zadok, the son
of Ahitub, 3the son of Amariah, the son of Azariah, the son of Meraioth, 4the son of Zerahiah, the son of Uzzi, the son of Bukki, 5the
son of Abishua, the son of Phinehas, the son
of Eleazar, the son of Aaron the chief priest—
6this Ezra came up from Babylon; and he *was*
a skilled scribe in the Law of Moses, which
the LORD God of Israel had given. The king
granted him all his request, according to the
hand of the LORD his God upon him. 7*Some* of
the children of Israel, the priests, the Levites,
the singers, the gatekeepers, and the Nethinim

SOUL NOTE

God's Will, God's Way *(6:22)* God used many different people at different levels of society in different lands to accomplish the work of restoring His people to their land and of rebuilding the temple. He even "turned the heart of the king of Assyria toward them, to strengthen their hands in the work of the house of God." God brought together kings, governors, elders, prophets, and people to do His will His way. God will always accomplish His purpose, often in ways and through people we do not expect. **Topic: Knowing God**

came up to Jerusalem in the seventh year of
King Artaxerxes. [8]And Ezra came to Jerusalem
in the fifth month, which *was* in the seventh
year of the king. [9]On the first *day* of the first
month he began *his* journey from Babylon,
and on the first *day* of
the fifth month he came
to Jerusalem, according
to the good hand of his
God upon him. [10]For
Ezra had prepared his
heart to seek the Law of
the LORD, and to do *it*,
and to teach statutes
and ordinances in Israel.

> For Ezra had prepared his heart to seek the Law of the LORD, and to do it, and to teach statutes and ordinances in Israel.
>
> EZRA 7:10

THE LETTER OF ARTAXERXES TO EZRA

[11]This *is* a copy of the letter that King Artaxerxes gave Ezra the priest, the scribe, expert in
the words of the commandments of the LORD,
and of His statutes to Israel:

12 Artaxerxes,[a] king of kings,

To Ezra the priest, a scribe of the Law of
the God of heaven:

Perfect *peace*, and so forth.[b]

13 I issue a decree that all those of the
people of Israel and the priests and
Levites in my realm, who volunteer to
go up to Jerusalem, may go with you.
[14]And whereas you are being sent by the
king and his seven counselors to inquire
concerning Judah and Jerusalem, with
regard to the Law of your God which *is*
in your hand; [15]and *whereas you are* to
carry the silver and gold which the king
and his counselors have freely offered to
the God of Israel, whose dwelling *is* in
Jerusalem; [16]and *whereas* all the silver
and gold that you may find in all the
province of Babylon, along with the
freewill offering of the people and the
priests, *are to be* freely offered for the
house of their God in Jerusalem—[17]now
therefore, be careful to buy with this
money bulls, rams, and lambs, with
their grain offerings and their drink
offerings, and offer them on the altar of
the house of your God in Jerusalem.

18 And whatever seems good to you and
your brethren to do with the rest of the
silver and the gold, do it according to
the will of your God. [19]Also the articles
that are given to you for the service of
the house of your God, deliver in full
before the God of
Jerusalem. [20]And
whatever more may be
needed for the house of
your God, which you
may have occasion to
provide, pay *for it* from
the king's treasury.

21 And I, *even* I, Artaxerxes the king, issue
a decree to all the treasurers who *are
in the region* beyond the River, that
whatever Ezra the priest, the scribe of
the Law of the God of heaven, may
require of you, let it be done diligently,
[22]up to one hundred talents of silver, one
hundred kors of wheat, one hundred
baths of wine, one hundred baths of oil,
and salt without prescribed limit.
[23]Whatever is commanded by the God of
heaven, let it diligently be done for the
house of the God of heaven. For why
should there be wrath against the realm
of the king and his sons?

24 Also we inform you that it shall not be
lawful to impose tax, tribute, or custom
on any of the priests, Levites, singers,
gatekeepers, Nethinim, or servants of
this house of God. [25]And you, Ezra,
according to your God-given wisdom, set
magistrates and judges who may judge
all the people who *are in the region*
beyond the River, all such as know the
laws of your God; and teach those who
do not know *them*. [26]Whoever will not
observe the law of your God and the law
of the king, let judgment be executed
speedily on him, whether *it be* death, or
banishment, or confiscation of goods, or
imprisonment.

[27]Blessed *be* the LORD God of our fathers,
who has put *such a thing* as this in the king's
heart, to beautify the house of the LORD which
is in Jerusalem, [28]and has extended mercy to

7:12 [a]The original language of Ezra 7:12–26 is Aramaic. [b]Literally *and now*

me before the king and his counselors, and before all the king's mighty princes.

So I was encouraged, as the hand of the LORD my God *was* upon me; and I gathered leading men of Israel to go up with me.

HEADS OF FAMILIES WHO RETURNED WITH EZRA

8 These *are* the heads of their fathers' *houses,* and *this is* the genealogy of those who went up with me from Babylon, in the reign of King Artaxerxes: 2of the sons of Phinehas, Gershom; of the sons of Ithamar, Daniel; of the sons of David, Hattush; 3of the sons of Shecaniah, of the sons of Parosh, Zechariah; and registered with him *were* one hundred and fifty males; 4of the sons of Pahath-Moab, Eliehoenai the son of Zerahiah, and with him two hundred males; 5of the sons of Shechaniah,[a] Ben-Jahaziel, and with him three hundred males; 6of the sons of Adin, Ebed the son of Jonathan, and with him fifty males; 7of the sons of Elam, Jeshaiah the son of Athaliah, and with him seventy males; 8of the sons of Shephatiah, Zebadiah the son of Michael, and with him eighty males; 9of the sons of Joab, Obadiah the son of Jehiel, and with him two hundred and eighteen males; 10of the sons of Shelomith,[a] Ben-Josiphiah, and with him one hundred and sixty males; 11of the sons of Bebai, Zechariah the son of Bebai, and with him twenty-eight males; 12of the sons of Azgad, Johanan the son of Hakkatan, and with him one hundred and ten males; 13of the last sons of Adonikam, whose names *are* these—Eliphelet, Jeiel, and Shemaiah—and with them sixty males; 14also of the sons of Bigvai, Uthai and Zabbud, and with them seventy males.

> "The hand of our God is upon all those for good who seek Him, but His power and His wrath are against all those who forsake Him."
>
> EZRA 8:22

SERVANTS FOR THE TEMPLE

15Now I gathered them by the river that flows to Ahava, and we camped there three days. And I looked among the people and the priests, and found none of the sons of Levi there. 16Then I sent for Eliezer, Ariel, Shemaiah, Elnathan, Jarib, Elnathan, Nathan, Zechariah, and Meshullam, leaders; also for Joiarib and Elnathan, men of understanding. 17And I gave them a command for Iddo the chief man at the place Casiphia, and I told them what they should say to Iddo *and* his brethren[a] the Nethinim at the place Casiphia—that they should bring us servants for the house of our God. 18Then, by the good hand of our God upon us, they brought us a man of understanding, of the sons of Mahli the son of Levi, the son of Israel, namely Sherebiah, with his sons and brothers, eighteen men; 19and Hashabiah, and with him Jeshaiah of the sons of Merari, his brothers and their sons, twenty men; 20also of the Nethinim, whom David and the leaders had appointed for the service of the Levites, two hundred and twenty Nethinim. All of them were designated by name.

FASTING AND PRAYER FOR PROTECTION

21Then I proclaimed a fast there at the river of Ahava, that we might humble ourselves before our God, to seek from Him the right way for us and our little ones and all our possessions. 22For I was ashamed to request of the king an escort of soldiers and horsemen to help us against the enemy on the road, because we had spoken to the king, saying, "The hand of our God *is* upon all those for good who seek Him, but His power and His wrath *are* against all those who forsake Him." 23So we fasted and entreated our God for this, and He answered our prayer.

GIFTS FOR THE TEMPLE

24And I separated twelve of the leaders of the priests—Sherebiah, Hashabiah, and ten of their brethren with them— 25and weighed out to them the silver, the gold, and the articles, the offering for the house of our God which the king and his counselors and his princes, and all Israel *who were* present, had offered. 26I weighed into their hand six hundred and fifty talents of silver, silver articles *weighing* one hundred talents, one hundred talents of gold, 27twenty gold basins *worth* a thousand

---

8:5 [a]Following Masoretic Text and Vulgate; Septuagint reads *the sons of Zatho, Shechaniah.* **8:10** [a]Following Masoretic Text and Vulgate; Septuagint reads *the sons of Banni, Shelomith.* **8:17** [a]Following Vulgate; Masoretic Text reads *to Iddo his brother;* Septuagint reads *to their brethren.*

drachmas, and two vessels of fine polished bronze, precious as gold. 28And I said to them, "You *are* holy to the LORD; the articles *are* holy also; and the silver and the gold *are* a freewill offering to the LORD God of your fathers. 29Watch and keep *them* until you weigh *them* before the leaders of the priests and the Levites and heads of the fathers' *houses* of Israel in Jerusalem, *in* the chambers of the house of the LORD." 30So the priests and the Levites received the silver and the gold and the articles by weight, to bring *them* to Jerusalem to the house of our God.

The Return to Jerusalem

31Then we departed from the river of Ahava on the twelfth *day* of the first month, to go to Jerusalem. And the hand of our God was upon us, and He delivered us from the hand of the enemy and from ambush along the road. 32So we came to Jerusalem, and stayed there three days.

33Now on the fourth day the silver and the gold and the articles were weighed in the house of our God by the hand of Meremoth the son of Uriah the priest, and with him *was* Eleazar the son of Phinehas; with them *were* the Levites, Jozabad the son of Jeshua and Noadiah the son of Binnui, 34with the number *and* weight of everything. All the weight was written down at that time.

35The children of those who had been carried away captive, who had come from the captivity, offered burnt offerings to the God of Israel: twelve bulls for all Israel, ninety-six rams, seventy-seven lambs, and twelve male goats *as* a sin offering. All *this was* a burnt offering to the LORD.

36And they delivered the king's orders to the king's satraps and the governors *in the region* beyond the River. So they gave support to the people and the house of God.

Intermarriage with Pagans

9 When these things were done, the leaders came to me, saying, "The people of Israel and the priests and the Levites have not separated themselves from the peoples of the lands, with respect to the abominations of the Canaanites, the Hittites, the Perizzites, the Jebusites, the Ammonites, the Moabites, the Egyptians, and the Amorites. 2For they have taken some of their daughters *as wives* for themselves and their sons, so that the holy seed is mixed with the peoples of *those* lands. Indeed, the hand of the leaders and rulers has been foremost in this trespass." 3So when I heard this thing, I tore my garment and my robe, and plucked out some of the hair of my head and beard, and sat down astonished. 4Then everyone who trembled at the words of the God of Israel assembled to me, because of the transgression of those who had been carried away captive, and I sat astonished until the evening sacrifice.

5At the evening sacrifice I arose from my fasting; and having torn my garment and my robe, I fell on my knees and spread out my hands to the LORD my God. 6And I said: "O my God, I am too ashamed and humiliated to lift up my face to You, my God; for our iniquities have risen higher than *our* heads, and our guilt has grown up to the heavens. 7Since the days of our fathers to this day we *have been* very guilty, and for our iniquities we, our kings, *and* our priests have been delivered into the hand of the kings of the lands, to the sword, to captivity, to plunder, and to humiliation, as *it is* this day. 8And now for a little while grace has been *shown* from the LORD our God, to leave us a remnant to escape, and to give us a peg in His holy place, that our God may enlighten our eyes and give us a measure of revival in our bondage. 9For we *were* slaves. Yet our God did not forsake us in our bondage;

SOUL NOTE

Owning Up *(9:2–8)* Ezra's prayer confessed the sins of the nation of Israel. He was so upset over their defiance of God's law that he fell on his face before the Lord, acknowledging the people's sin as well as God's grace toward them.

Despite our mistakes and failures, God is always willing to meet us at our point of need. Sometimes we can make amends by specific actions; at other times we must suffer the consequences of our sin. But through repentance, we can experience God's grace and love.

Topic: Guilt/Shame

DEALING WITH GUILT

LES PARROTT

(Ezra 9:5–8)

A letter addressed to "Uncle Sam" said, "My conscience has been working on me, so to quiet it, I'm sending you this money order for $200." It was signed, "One of your conscience-stricken nephews." A postscript was added, saying, "P. S. If I still feel guilty, I'll send in the other $200."

It all began in the 1800's when someone sent a few cents to the United States Treasury Department. The enclosed note read: "This is payment for a reused postage stamp. It wasn't canceled so I peeled it off and used it again. The money is to ease my conscience." The government, not knowing what to do with those few pennies, created the Conscience Fund. To date, that fund has received over five million dollars.

Everyone experiences guilt now and then. And nearly everyone reacts to guilt in a predictable manner. If people fall short of a goal (such as raising the "perfect" child), they are filled with shame. "If only I had been a better parent, my child wouldn't have turned out this way." If students don't make a desired grade, they berate themselves: "No wonder I didn't pass. I'm so dumb." The merciless mental tape player replays its destructive messages, creating waves of guilt and shame. How should a person cope with these guilt-ridden feelings?

FEELING GUILTY VS. BEING GUILTY

There is a difference between *feeling* guilty and actually *being* guilty. For example, if someone were to steal a loaf of bread from the local grocer, that person would be guilty of the crime. The laws of society and the words of the Bible make this clear: Stealing is against the law and is morally wrong. This type of guilt is the result of a violation of a moral law. The person *is* guilty regardless of whether or not the person actually *feels* guilty.

On the other hand, just *feeling* guilty doesn't mean that someone has violated a moral law. Many times, failing to meet a person's expectations imposes guilt feelings that are not associated with a moral wrong. Because of the strength of their emotions, many people carry guilt they have neither earned nor deserve. They feel guilty and they don't know why.

It is possible to be guilty of an offense without necessarily feeling the emotion of guilt. For example, a person may hurt a friend's feelings without even realizing it. Unfortunately, many people also become desensitized to a sense of conviction by repeated offenses.

On the other hand, the fact that the believer is unconditionally loved by God seems to indicate that guilt feelings which are not based on the fact of guilt have absolutely no place in the sanctified life. The Bible says: "There is therefore now no condemnation to those who are in Christ Jesus" (Rom. 8:1).

Satan, not the Holy Spirit, is "the accuser" (Rev. 12:10). Satan's work is to create feelings of condemnation for the believer, resulting in overwhelming hopelessness or unnecessary guilt. The work of the Holy Spirit, however, results in conviction, forgiveness, and restoration.

DEALING WITH GUILTY FEELINGS

Most people do not have trouble knowing when they are guilty. The following tips will help those who struggle with nagging feelings of guilt:

1. Pay attention to uncomfortable feelings. Guilt, like physical pain, is a signal that something is wrong.
2. Determine whether the guilt feelings are realistic or the result of unreasonable expectations. Ask: "Why do I feel guilty?" and "Should I feel guilty?" Once a person has determined the nature and cause of feelings, it is easier to be more objective in handling them.
3. Remember that everyone is human. Punishing oneself for human errors is useless. If you forget a friend's birthday, for example, you can make it up to that person as soon as possible. However, don't follow the tendency to "replay" the mistake over and over again. Correct mistakes and move on.
4. If guilt feelings are a result of sin, ask God for forgiveness, accept His cleansing love, correct the misdeed if appropriate, and forget it. This is not a way of getting God off your back. It serves as a springboard to help jump over a guilty past into the present love of God.
5. Recognize that "telling all" can be a way of inflicting more punishment on oneself. This only eases the sense of guilt for the moment and may put unfair stress on those who are listening. Permanent relief from moral guilt comes from God's forgiveness, not public confession. In most cases, the scope of our confession should not exceed the scope of our sin.
6. If guilt feelings are unrealistic, turn off the mental tape player. Ask God for strength to do this. Ask a minister or other professional for help if necessary.

CHRIST SETS US FREE

We can deal with guilt and be sorry without self-condemnation. The apostle Paul says, "For godly sorrow produces repentance leading to salvation, not to be regretted; but the sorrow of the world produces death" (2 Cor. 7:10).

Christ did not come to condemn us and make us feel guilty. While donations to the government's Conscience Fund may ease our minds temporarily, Christ offers to remove the guilt entirely and for eternity. He came to set us free from sin and the uncomfortable emotion of guilt.

FURTHER MEDITATION:

Other passages to study about the issue of guilt/shame include:

- 2 Chronicles 30:9
- Psalms 19; 32; 38; 51; 89
- Isaiah 43:25; 54:4, 9; 55:7
- Jeremiah 33:8
- Romans 3:23
- Hebrews 10:2, 22
- 1 John 1:7–9

To Learn More: Turn to the key passage note on guilt/shame at Romans 8:1 on page 1474. See also the personality profile of Adam on page 10.

but He extended mercy to us in the sight of the kings of Persia, to revive us, to repair the house of our God, to rebuild its ruins, and to give us a wall in Judah and Jerusalem. [10]And now, O our God, what shall we say after this? For we have forsaken Your commandments, [11]which You commanded by Your servants the prophets, saying, 'The land which you are entering to possess is an unclean land, with the uncleanness of the peoples of the lands, with their abominations which have filled it from one end to another with their impurity. [12]Now therefore, do not give your daughters as wives for their sons, nor take their daughters to your sons; and never seek their peace or prosperity, that you may be strong and eat the good of the land, and leave *it* as an inheritance to your children forever.' [13]And after all that has come upon us for our evil deeds and for our great guilt, since You our God have punished us less than our iniquities *deserve,* and have given us *such* deliverance as this, [14]should we again break Your commandments, and join in marriage with the people *committing* these abominations? Would You not be angry with us until You had consumed *us,* so that *there would be* no remnant or survivor? [15]O LORD God of Israel, You *are* righteous, for we are left as a remnant, as *it is* this day. Here we *are* before You, in our guilt, though no one can stand before You because of this!"

CONFESSION OF IMPROPER MARRIAGES

10 Now while Ezra was praying, and while he was confessing, weeping, and bowing down before the house of God, a very large assembly of men, women, and children gathered to him from Israel; for the people wept very bitterly. [2]And Shechaniah the son of Jehiel, *one* of the sons of Elam, spoke up and said to Ezra, "We have trespassed against our God, and have taken pagan wives from the peoples of the land; yet now there is hope in Israel in spite of this. [3]Now therefore, let us make a covenant with our God to put away all these wives and those who have been born to them, according to the advice of my master and of those who tremble at the commandment of our God; and let it be done according to the law. [4]Arise, for *this* matter *is* your *responsibility.* We also *are* with you. Be of good courage, and do *it.*"

> "Arise, for this matter is your responsibility. We also are with you. Be of good courage, and do it."
> EZRA 10:4

[5]Then Ezra arose, and made the leaders of the priests, the Levites, and all Israel swear an oath that they would do according to this word. So they swore an oath. [6]Then Ezra rose up from before the house of God, and went into the chamber of Jehohanan the son of Eliashib; and *when* he came there, he ate no bread and drank no water, for he mourned because of the guilt of those from the captivity.

[7]And they issued a proclamation throughout Judah and Jerusalem to all the descendants of the captivity, that they must gather at Jerusalem, [8]and that whoever would not come within three days, according to the instructions of the leaders and elders, all his property would be confiscated, and he himself would be separated from the assembly of those from the captivity.

[9]So all the men of Judah and Benjamin gathered at Jerusalem within three days. It *was* the ninth month, on the twentieth of the month; and all the people sat in the open square of the house of God, trembling because of *this* matter and because of heavy rain. [10]Then Ezra the priest stood up and said to them, "You have transgressed and have taken pagan wives, adding to the guilt of Israel. [11]Now therefore, make confession to the LORD God of your fathers, and do His will; separate yourselves from the peoples of the land, and from the pagan wives."

[12]Then all the assembly answered and said with a loud voice, "Yes! As you have said, so we must do. [13]But *there are* many people; *it is* the season for heavy rain, and we are not able to stand outside. Nor *is this* the work of one or two days, for *there are* many of us who have transgressed in this matter. [14]Please, let the leaders of our entire assembly stand; and let all those in our cities who have taken pagan wives come at appointed times, together with the elders and judges of their cities, until the fierce wrath of our God is turned away from us in this matter." [15]Only Jonathan the son of Asahel and Jahaziah the son of Tikvah opposed this, and Meshullam and Shabbethai the Levite gave them support.

[16]Then the descendants of the captivity did

so. And Ezra the priest, *with* certain heads of
the fathers' *households,* were set apart by the
fathers' *households,* each of them by name;
and they sat down on the first day of the tenth
month to examine the matter. 17By the first
day of the first month they finished *questioning* all the men who had taken pagan wives.

Pagan Wives Put Away

18And among the sons of the priests who
had taken pagan wives *the following* were
found of the sons of Jeshua the son of Jozadak,[a] and his brothers: Maaseiah, Eliezer,
Jarib, and Gedaliah. 19And they gave their
promise that they would put away their wives;
and *being* guilty, *they presented* a ram of the
flock as their trespass offering.
20Also of the sons of Immer: Hanani and
Zebadiah; 21of the sons of Harim: Maaseiah,
Elijah, Shemaiah, Jehiel, and Uzziah; 22of the
sons of Pashhur: Elioenai, Maaseiah, Ishmael,
Nethanel, Jozabad, and Elasah.
23Also of the Levites: Jozabad, Shimei, Kela-
iah (the same *is* Kelita), Pethahiah, Judah,
and Eliezer.
24Also of the singers: Eliashib; and of the
gatekeepers: Shallum, Telem, and Uri.
25And others of Israel: of the sons of Parosh:
Ramiah, Jeziah, Malchiah, Mijamin, Eleazar,
Malchijah, and Benaiah; 26of the sons of Elam:
Mattaniah, Zechariah, Jehiel, Abdi, Jeremoth,
and Eliah; 27of the sons of Zattu: Elioenai,
Eliashib, Mattaniah, Jeremoth, Zabad, and
Aziza; 28of the sons of Bebai: Jehohanan, Han-
aniah, Zabbai, *and* Athlai; 29of the sons of
Bani: Meshullam, Malluch, Adaiah, Jashub,
Sheal, *and* Ramoth;[a] 30of the sons of Pahath-
Moab: Adna, Chelal, Benaiah, Maaseiah, Mat-
taniah, Bezalel, Binnui, and Manasseh; 31*of*
the sons of Harim: Eliezer, Ishijah, Malchijah,
Shemaiah, Shimeon, 32Benjamin, Malluch,
and Shemariah; 33of the sons of Hashum: Mattenai, Mattattah, Zabad, Eliphelet, Jeremai,
Manasseh, *and* Shimei; 34of the sons of Bani:
Maadai, Amram, Uel, 35Benaiah, Bedeiah,
Cheluh,[a] 36Vaniah, Meremoth, Eliashib, 37Mat-
taniah, Mattenai, Jaasai,[a] 38Bani, Binnui,
Shimei, 39Shelemiah, Nathan, Adaiah, 40Mach-
nadebai, Shashai, Sharai, 41Azarel, Shelemiah,
Shemariah, 42Shallum, Amariah, *and* Joseph;
43of the sons of Nebo: Jeiel, Mattithiah, Zabad, Zebina, Jaddai,[a] Joel, *and* Benaiah.
44All these had taken pagan wives, and
some of them had wives *by whom* they had
children.

10:18 [a]Spelled *Jehozadak* in 1 Chronicles 6:14 **10:29** [a]Or *Jeremoth* **10:35** [a]Or *Cheluhi,* or *Cheluhu* **10:37** [a]Or *Jaasu* **10:43** [a]Or *Jaddu*

SOUL NOTE

Tough Decisions *(10:10, 11)* Ezra told the men of Judah to separate from their pagan wives. Ezra's concern was to protect the spiritual integrity of the nation. He knew that if they did not put God first in every area of their lives, eventually they would repeat the errors of their forefathers. While God would not call for divorce today (1 Cor. 7:10–16), the principle is clear that at times we must separate ourselves from things that draw us away from God. **Topic: Divorce/Separation**

Nehemiah

There are many books and tapes that discuss leadership principles, and a variety of seminars that offer training in leadership techniques. Unfortunately, it seems that there are few truly great leaders.

Nehemiah was one such leader—a man who demonstrated moral courage in the face of tremendous opposition. Ezra and Nehemiah comprise one book in the Hebrew Bible, so Nehemiah was probably written by Ezra, perhaps using Nehemiah's memoirs. The Book of Nehemiah tells the remarkable story of how Nehemiah motivated a disorganized, disillusioned people to complete the difficult task of rebuilding the walls of Jerusalem—in only 52 days! Beyond mere walls, Nehemiah—together with his contemporary Ezra—also played a major role in leading the nation into spiritual renewal.

A trusted advisor to the Persian potentate, Nehemiah was heartbroken to learn of Jerusalem's broken-down walls. Armed with a compelling vision and the blessing of Artaxerxes, he led a third group of exiles home.

Nehemiah's task was not without obstacles. He had to deal with continual threats from without—at one point putting half of his workforce on military alert. He also confronted the internal problem of the wealthy taking advantage of their less fortunate brethren. In each and every situation, Nehemiah demonstrated remarkable wisdom, courage, and godliness.

No matter who or what you're trying to lead—a marriage, a family, a business, a classroom—the Book of Nehemiah offers valuable insight. Study Nehemiah's life, emulate his practices, and watch what God does in and through you!

SOUL CONCERN IN NEHEMIAH

NEHEMIAH PRAYS FOR HIS PEOPLE

1 The words of Nehemiah the son of Hachaliah.

It came to pass in the month of Chislev, *in* the twentieth year, as I was in Shushan[a] the citadel, 2that Hanani one of my brethren came with men from Judah; and I asked them concerning the Jews who had escaped, who had survived the captivity, and concerning Jerusalem. 3And they said to me, "The survivors who are left from the captivity in the province *are* there in great distress and reproach. The wall of Jerusalem *is* also broken down, and its gates *are* burned with fire."

4So it was, when I heard these words, that I sat down and wept, and mourned *for many* days; I was fasting and praying before the God of heaven.

5And I said: "I pray, LORD God of heaven, O great and awesome God, *You* who keep *Your* covenant and mercy with those who love You[a] and observe Your[b] commandments, 6please let Your ear be attentive and Your eyes open, that You may hear the prayer of Your servant which I pray before You now, day and night, for the children of Israel Your servants, and confess the sins of the children of Israel which we have sinned against You. Both my father's house and I have sinned. 7We have acted very corruptly against You, and have not kept the

1:1 [a]Or *Susa* **1:5** [a]Literally *Him* [b]Literally *His*

PERSONALITY PROFILE

Discouragement

NEHEMIAH—RISING ABOVE DISCOURAGEMENT

(NEHEMIAH 2)

What happens when people are discouraged? Some decide to give up. Others look to place blame. Still others use their discouragement as a slingshot to propel them to new heights. Nehemiah was a member of the last-named group.

Nehemiah was a Jewish exile living in Persia and serving as the cupbearer to King Artaxerxes. A cupbearer was a trusted servant with constant access to the king—tasting all food and drink before giving it to the king. Jewish exiles had already been allowed to return and rebuild, so many had gone with Ezra back to Jerusalem. Nehemiah longed for news from his homeland. Eventually he learned that, although those who had returned had rebuilt the temple, they had not yet completed the city wall. Nehemiah was heartbroken when he learned that the wall of Jerusalem was still in disrepair years after the Jewish people had returned to the city.

His discouragement was understandable. In ancient times, a city without walls was vulnerable to attack—it was a weak city. Jerusalem would not be able to stand proud or even begin to reach its former stature without a wall. Instead of allowing his discouragement to lead to despair, Nehemiah set about on a course of action to correct the problem.

After praying and planning, Nehemiah took advantage of his trusted position with the king. When the king asked why Nehemiah seemed disturbed, Nehemiah explained the situation, said a quick prayer, and boldly asked for everything he would need to take a trip to Jerusalem. Obviously, Nehemiah was ready with his request so that, when the opportunity arose, he knew exactly what to ask. The king granted the request of his trusted servant, and Nehemiah was on his way.

Discouragement can cause depression and inability to act. It can also motivate a person, giving renewed determination. Like Nehemiah, we can let discouragement cause us to find a way to solve the problem. We can pray, plan, and then move ahead, knowing that God goes with us.

To Learn More: Turn to the article about discouragement on pages 266, 267. See also the key passage note at I Peter 5:7 on page 1665.

commandments, the statutes, nor the ordinances which You commanded Your servant Moses. 8Remember, I pray, the word that You commanded Your servant Moses, saying, '*If* you are unfaithful, I will scatter you among the nations;[a] 9but *if* you return to Me, and keep My commandments and do them, though some of you were cast out to the farthest part of the heavens, *yet* I will gather them from there, and bring them to the place which I have chosen as a dwelling for My name.'[a] 10Now these *are* Your servants and Your people, whom You have redeemed by Your great power, and by Your strong hand. 11O Lord, I pray, please let Your ear be attentive to the prayer of Your servant, and to the prayer of Your servants who desire to fear Your name; and let Your servant prosper this day, I pray, and grant him mercy in the sight of this man."

For I was the king's cupbearer.

Nehemiah Sent to Judah

2 And it came to pass in the month of Nisan, in the twentieth year of King Artaxerxes, *when* wine *was* before him, that I took the wine and gave it to the king. Now I had never been sad in his presence before. 2Therefore the king said to me, "Why *is* your face sad, since you *are* not sick? This *is* nothing but sorrow of heart."

So I became dreadfully afraid, 3and said to the king, "May the king live forever! Why should my face not be sad, when the city, the place of my fathers' tombs, *lies* waste, and its gates are burned with fire?"

4Then the king said to me, "What do you request?"

So I prayed to the God of heaven. 5And I said to the king, "If it pleases the king, and if your servant has found favor in your sight, I ask that you send me to Judah, to the city of my fathers' tombs, that I may rebuild it."

6Then the king said to me (the queen also sitting beside him), "How long will your journey be? And when will you return?" So it pleased the king to send me; and I set him a time.

7Furthermore I said to the king, "If it pleases the king, let letters be given to me for the governors *of the region* beyond the River,[a] that they must permit me to pass through till I come to Judah, 8and a letter to Asaph the keeper of the king's forest, that he must give me timber to make beams for the gates of the citadel which *pertains* to the temple,[a] for the city wall, and for the house that I will occupy." And the king granted *them* to me according to the good hand of my God upon me.

9Then I went to the governors *in the region* beyond the River, and gave them the king's letters. Now the king had sent captains of the army and horsemen with me. 10When Sanballat the Horonite and Tobiah the Ammonite official[a] heard *of it,* they were deeply disturbed that a man had come to seek the well-being of the children of Israel.

Nehemiah Views the Wall of Jerusalem

11So I came to Jerusalem and was there three days. 12Then I arose in the night, I and a few men with me; I told no one what my God had put in my heart to do at Jerusalem; nor was there any animal with me, except the one on which I rode. 13And I went out by night through the Valley Gate to the Serpent Well and the Refuse Gate, and viewed the walls of Jerusalem which were broken down and its gates which were burned with fire. 14Then I went on to the Fountain Gate and to the King's Pool, but *there was* no room for the animal under me to pass. 15So I went up in the night by the valley, and viewed the wall; then I turned back and entered by the Valley Gate, and so returned. 16And the officials did not know where I had gone or what I had done; I had not yet told the Jews, the priests, the nobles, the officials, or the others who did the work.

17Then I said to them, "You see the distress that we *are* in, how Jerusalem *lies* waste, and its gates are burned with fire. Come and let us build the wall of Jerusalem, that we may no longer be a reproach." 18And I told them of the hand of my God which had been good upon me, and also of the king's words that he had spoken to me.

So they said, "Let us rise up and build." Then they set their hands to *this* good *work.*

19But when Sanballat the Horonite, Tobiah the Ammonite official, and Geshem the Arab heard *of it,* they laughed at us and despised us, and said, "What *is* this thing that you are doing? Will you rebel against the king?"

1:8 [a]Leviticus 26:33 **1:9** [a]Deuteronomy 30:2–5 **2:7** [a]That is, the Euphrates, and so elsewhere in this book **2:8** [a]Literally *house* **2:10** [a]Literally *servant,* and so elsewhere in this book

20So I answered them, and said to them, "The God of heaven Himself will prosper us; therefore we His servants will arise and build, but you have no heritage or right or memorial in Jerusalem."

Rebuilding the Wall

3 Then Eliashib the high priest rose up with his brethren the priests and built the Sheep Gate; they consecrated it and hung its doors. They built as far as the Tower of the Hundred,[a] *and* consecrated it, then as far as the Tower of Hananel. 2Next to *Eliashib*[a] the men of Jericho built. And next to them Zaccur the son of Imri built.

> "The God of heaven Himself will prosper us; therefore we His servants will arise and build."
>
> NEHEMIAH 2:20

3Also the sons of Hassenaah built the Fish Gate; they laid its beams and hung its doors with its bolts and bars. 4And next to them Meremoth the son of Urijah, the son of Koz,[a] made repairs. Next to them Meshullam the son of Berechiah, the son of Meshezabel, made repairs. Next to them Zadok the son of Baana made repairs. 5Next to them the Tekoites made repairs; but their nobles did not put their shoulders[a] to the work of their Lord.

6Moreover Jehoiada the son of Paseah and Meshullam the son of Besodeiah repaired the Old Gate; they laid its beams and hung its doors, with its bolts and bars. 7And next to them Melatiah the Gibeonite, Jadon the Meronothite, the men of Gibeon and Mizpah, repaired the residence[a] of the governor *of the region* beyond the River. 8Next to him Uzziel the son of Harhaiah, one of the goldsmiths, made repairs. Also next to him Hananiah, one[a] of the perfumers, made repairs; and they fortified Jerusalem as far as the Broad Wall. 9And next to them Rephaiah the son of Hur, leader of half the district of Jerusalem, made repairs. 10Next to them Jedaiah the son of Harumaph made repairs in front of his house. And next to him Hattush the son of Hashabniah made repairs.

11Malchijah the son of Harim and Hashub the son of Pahath-Moab repaired another section, as well as the Tower of the Ovens. 12And next to him was Shallum the son of Hallohesh, leader of half the district of Jerusalem; he and his daughters made repairs.

13Hanun and the inhabitants of Zanoah repaired the Valley Gate. They built it, hung its doors with its bolts and bars, and *repaired* a thousand cubits of the wall as far as the Refuse Gate.

14Malchijah the son of Rechab, leader of the district of Beth Haccerem, repaired the Refuse Gate; he built it and hung its doors with its bolts and bars.

15Shallun the son of Col-Hozeh, leader of the district of Mizpah, repaired the Fountain Gate; he built it, covered it, hung its doors with its bolts and bars, and repaired the wall of the Pool of Shelah by the King's Garden, as far as the stairs that go down from the City of David. 16After him Nehemiah the son of Azbuk, leader of half the district of Beth Zur, made repairs as far as *the place* in front of the tombs[a] of David, to the man-made pool, and as far as the House of the Mighty.

17After him the Levites, *under* Rehum the son of Bani, made repairs. Next to him Hashabiah, leader of half the district of Keilah, made repairs for his district. 18After him their brethren, *under* Bavai[a] the son of Henadad, leader of the *other* half of the district of Keilah, made repairs. 19And next to him Ezer the son of Jeshua, the leader of Mizpah, repaired another section in front of the Ascent to the Armory at the buttress. 20After him Baruch the son of Zabbai[a] carefully repaired the other section, from the buttress to the door of the house of Eliashib the high priest. 21After him Meremoth the son of Urijah, the son of Koz,[a] repaired another section, from the door of the house of Eliashib to the end of the house of Eliashib.

22And after him the priests, the men of the plain, made repairs. 23After him Benjamin and Hasshub made repairs opposite their house. After them Azariah the son of Maaseiah, the

---

3:1 [a]Hebrew *Hammeah,* also at 12:39 **3:2** [a]Literally *On his hand* **3:4** [a]Or *Hakkoz* **3:5** [a]Literally *necks* **3:7** [a]Literally *throne* **3:8** [a]Literally *the son* **3:16** [a]Septuagint, Syriac, and Vulgate read *tomb.* **3:18** [a]Following Masoretic Text and Vulgate; some Hebrew manuscripts, Septuagint, and Syriac read *Binnui* (compare verse 24). **3:20** [a]A few Hebrew manuscripts, Syriac, and Vulgate read *Zaccai.* **3:21** [a]Or *Hakkoz*

son of Ananiah, made repairs by his house.
24After him Binnui the son of Henadad repaired another section, from the house of Azariah to the buttress, even as far as the corner.
25Palal the son of Uzai *made repairs* opposite
the buttress, and on the tower which projects
from the king's upper house that *was* by the
court of the prison. After him Pedaiah the son
of Parosh *made repairs.*

26Moreover the Nethinim who dwelt in
Ophel *made repairs* as far as *the place* in front
of the Water Gate toward the east, and on the
projecting tower. 27After them the Tekoites repaired another section, next to the great projecting tower, and as far as the wall of Ophel.

28Beyond the Horse Gate the priests made
repairs, each in front of his *own* house. 29After
them Zadok the son of Immer made repairs in
front of his *own* house. After him Shemaiah
the son of Shechaniah, the keeper of the East
Gate, made repairs. 30After him Hananiah the
son of Shelemiah, and Hanun, the sixth son of
Zalaph, repaired another section. After him
Meshullam the son of Berechiah made repairs
in front of his dwelling. 31After him Malchijah,
one of the goldsmiths, made repairs as far as
the house of the Nethinim and of the merchants, in front of the Miphkad[a] Gate, and as
far as the upper room at the corner. 32And between the upper room at the corner, as far as
the Sheep Gate, the goldsmiths and the merchants made repairs.

THE WALL DEFENDED AGAINST ENEMIES

4 But it so happened, when Sanballat heard
that we were rebuilding the wall, that he
was furious and very
indignant, and mocked
the Jews. 2And he spoke
before his brethren and
the army of Samaria,
and said, "What are
these feeble Jews doing?
Will they fortify them-
selves? Will they offer
sacrifices? Will they
complete it in a day? Will they revive the
stones from the heaps of rubbish—*stones* that
are burned?"

3Now Tobiah the Ammonite *was* beside
him, and he said, "Whatever they build, if
even a fox goes up *on it,* he will break down
their stone wall."

4Hear, O our God, for we are despised; turn
their reproach on their own heads, and give
them as plunder to a land of captivity! 5Do not
cover their iniquity, and do not let their sin be
blotted out from before You; for they have provoked *You* to anger before the builders.

6So we built the wall, and the entire wall
was joined together up to half its *height,* for
the people had a mind to work.

7Now it happened, when Sanballat, Tobiah,
the Arabs, the Ammonites, and the Ashdodites heard that the walls of Jerusalem were
being restored and the gaps were beginning to
be closed, that they became very angry, 8and
all of them conspired together to come *and* attack Jerusalem and create confusion. 9Never-
theless we made our prayer to our God, and
because of them we set a watch against them
day and night.

10Then Judah said, "The strength of the laborers is failing, and *there is* so much rubbish
that we are not able to build the wall."

11And our adversaries said, "They will neither know nor see anything, till we come into
their midst and kill them and cause the work
to cease."

12So it was, when the Jews who dwelt
near them came, that they told us ten times,
"From whatever place you turn, *they will be*
upon us."

13Therefore I positioned *men* behind the
lower parts of the wall, at the openings; and I
set the people according to their families, with
their swords, their spears, and their bows.
14And I looked, and arose and said to the
nobles, to the leaders, and to the rest of the
people, "Do not be afraid of them. Remember
the Lord, great and awe-
some, and fight for your
brethren, your sons, your
daughters, your wives,
and your houses."

15And it happened,
when our enemies heard
that it was known to
us, and *that* God had
brought their plot to
nothing, that all of us returned to the wall,
everyone to his work. 16So it was, from that
time on, *that* half of my servants worked at
construction, while the other half held the
spears, the shields, the bows, and *wore* armor;
and the leaders *were* behind all the house of

> "Do not be afraid of them. Remember the Lord, great and awesome, and fight for your brethren, your sons, your daughters, your wives, and your houses."
> NEHEMIAH 4:14

3:31 [a]Literally *Inspection* or *Recruiting*

Judah. [17]Those who built on the wall, and those who carried burdens, loaded themselves so that with one hand they worked at construction, and with the other held a weapon. [18]Every one of the builders had his sword girded at his side as he built. And the one who sounded the trumpet *was* beside me.

[19]Then I said to the nobles, the rulers, and the rest of the people, "The work *is* great and extensive, and we are separated far from one another on the wall. [20]Wherever you hear the sound of the trumpet, rally to us there. Our God will fight for us."

[21]So we labored in the work, and half of *the men*[a] held the spears from daybreak until the stars appeared. [22]At the same time I also said to the people, "Let each man and his servant stay at night in Jerusalem, that they may be our guard by night and a working party by day." [23]So neither I, my brethren, my servants, nor the men of the guard who followed me took off our clothes, *except* that everyone took them off for washing.

Nehemiah Deals with Oppression

5 And there was a great outcry of the people and their wives against their Jewish brethren. [2]For there were those who said, "We, our sons, and our daughters *are* many; therefore let us get grain, that we may eat and live."

[3]There were also *some* who said, "We have mortgaged our lands and vineyards and houses, that we might buy grain because of the famine."

[4]There were also those who said, "We have borrowed money for the king's tax *on* our lands and vineyards. [5]Yet now our flesh *is* as the flesh of our brethren, our children as their children; and indeed we are forcing our sons and our daughters to be slaves, and *some* of our daughters have been brought into slavery. *It is* not in our power *to redeem them,* for other men have our lands and vineyards."

[6]And I became very angry when I heard their outcry and these words. [7]After serious thought, I rebuked the nobles and rulers, and said to them, "Each of you is exacting usury from his brother." So I called a great assembly against them. [8]And I said to them, "According to our ability we have redeemed our Jewish brethren who were sold to the nations. Now indeed, will you even sell your brethren? Or should they be sold to us?"

Then they were silenced and found nothing *to say.* [9]Then I said, "What you are doing *is* not good. Should you not walk in the fear of our God because of the reproach of the nations, our enemies? [10]I also, *with* my brethren and my servants, am lending them money and grain. Please, let us stop this usury! [11]Restore now to them, even this day, their lands, their vineyards, their olive groves, and their houses, also a hundredth of the money and the grain, the new wine and the oil, that you have charged them."

[12]So they said, "We will restore *it,* and will require nothing from them; we will do as you say."

Then I called the priests, and required an oath from them that they would do according to this promise. [13]Then I shook out the fold of my garment[a] and said, "So may God shake out each man from his house, and from his property, who does not perform this promise. Even thus may he be shaken out and emptied."

And all the assembly said, "Amen!" and praised the LORD. Then the people did according to this promise.

4:21 [a]Literally *them* **5:13** [a]Literally *my lap*

SOUL NOTE

A Positive Solution *(5:6)* Nehemiah's anger was righteous indignation. Many of the Jews were suffering—not at the hands of enemies, but at the hands of their rich countrymen who had lent them money. When a payment was missed, the lender would seize the debtor's land. Nehemiah was determined not to allow this to continue. He put his anger to work by calling a meeting of the moneylenders and condemning their methods. They then agreed to return the seized lands (5:12). When you feel anger burning beneath the surface, ask God to guide you toward a productive way to resolve the conflict. **Topic: Anger**

The Generosity of Nehemiah

14 Moreover, from the time that I was appointed to be their governor in the land of Judah, from the twentieth year until the thirty-second year of King Artaxerxes, twelve years, neither I nor my brothers ate the governor's provisions. 15 But the former governors who *were* before me laid burdens on the people, and took from them bread and wine, besides forty shekels of silver. Yes, even their servants bore rule over the people, but I did not do so, because of the fear of God. 16 Indeed, I also continued the work on this wall, and we[a] did not buy any land. All my servants *were* gathered there for the work.

17 And at my table *were* one hundred and fifty Jews and rulers, besides those who came to us from the nations around us. 18 Now *that* which was prepared daily *was* one ox *and* six choice sheep. Also fowl were prepared for me, and once every ten days an abundance of all kinds of wine. Yet in spite of this I did not demand the governor's provisions, because the bondage was heavy on this people.

> Remember me, my God, for good, according to all that I have done for this people.
>
> NEHEMIAH 5:19

19 Remember me, my God, for good, *according to* all that I have done for this people.

Conspiracy Against Nehemiah

6 Now it happened when Sanballat, Tobiah, Geshem the Arab, and the rest of our enemies heard that I had rebuilt the wall, and *that* there were no breaks left in it (though at that time I had not hung the doors in the gates), 2 that Sanballat and Geshem sent to me, saying, "Come, let us meet together among the villages in the plain of Ono." But they thought to do me harm.

3 So I sent messengers to them, saying, "I *am* doing a great work, so that I cannot come down. Why should the work cease while I leave it and go down to you?"

4 But they sent me this message four times, and I answered them in the same manner.

5 Then Sanballat sent his servant to me as before, the fifth time, with an open letter in his hand. 6 In it *was* written:

> It is reported among the nations, and Geshem[a] says, *that* you and the Jews plan to rebel; therefore, according to these rumors, you are rebuilding the wall, that you may be their king. 7 And you have also appointed prophets to proclaim concerning you at Jerusalem, saying, "*There is* a king in Judah!" Now these matters will be reported to the king. So come, therefore, and let us consult together.

8 Then I sent to him, saying, "No such things as you say are being done, but you invent them in your own heart."

9 For they all *were trying to* make us afraid, saying, "Their hands will be weakened in the work, and it will not be done."

Now therefore, *O God,* strengthen my hands.

10 Afterward I came to the house of Shemaiah the son of Delaiah, the son of Mehetabel, who *was* a secret informer; and he said, "Let us meet together in the house of God, within the temple, and let us close the doors of the temple, for they are coming to kill you; indeed, at night they will come to kill you."

11 And I said, "Should such a man as I flee? And who *is there* such as I who would go into the temple to save his life? I will not go in!" 12 Then I perceived that God had not sent him at all, but that he pronounced *this* prophecy against me because Tobiah and Sanballat had hired him. 13 For this reason he *was* hired, that I should be afraid and act that way and sin, so *that* they might have *cause* for an evil report, that they might reproach me.

14 My God, remember Tobiah and Sanballat, according to these their works, and the prophetess Noadiah and the rest of the prophets who would have made me afraid.

The Wall Completed

15 So the wall was finished on the twenty-fifth *day* of Elul, in fifty-two days. 16 And it happened, when all our enemies heard *of it,* and all the nations around us saw *these things,* that they were very disheartened in their own eyes; for they perceived that this work was done by our God.

5:16 [a]Following Masoretic Text; Septuagint, Syriac, and Vulgate read *I.* **6:6** [a]Hebrew *Gashmu*

17Also in those days the nobles of Judah
sent many letters to Tobiah, and *the letters of*
Tobiah came to them. 18For many in Judah
were pledged to him, because he was the son-
in-law of Shechaniah the son of Arah, and his
son Jehohanan had married the daughter of
Meshullam the son of Berechiah. 19Also they
reported his good deeds before me, and reported my words to him. Tobiah sent letters to
frighten me.

7 Then it was, when the wall was built and
I had hung the doors, when the gatekeepers, the singers, and the Levites had been appointed, 2that I gave the charge of Jerusalem
to my brother Hanani, and Hananiah the leader of the citadel, for he *was* a faithful man and
feared God more than many.

3And I said to them, "Do not let the gates of
Jerusalem be opened un-
til the sun is hot; and
while they stand *guard,*
let them shut and bar the
doors; and appoint guards
from among the inhab-
itants of Jerusalem, one
at his watch station and
another in front of his
own house."

> For they all were trying to make us afraid, saying, "Their hands will be weakened in the work, and it will not be done." Now therefore, O God, strengthen my hands.
>
> NEHEMIAH 6:9

The Captives Who Returned to Jerusalem

4Now the city *was* large and spacious, but
the people in it *were* few, and the houses *were*
not rebuilt. 5Then my God put it into my heart
to gather the nobles, the rulers, and the people, that they might be registered by genealogy. And I found a register of the genealogy of
those who had come up in the first *return,* and
found written in it:

6 These[a] *are* the people of the province
who came back from the captivity, of
those who had been carried away, whom
Nebuchadnezzar the king of Babylon
had carried away, and who returned to
Jerusalem and Judah, everyone to his
city.

7 Those who came with Zerubbabel *were*
Jeshua, Nehemiah, Azariah, Raamiah,
Nahamani, Mordecai, Bilshan,
Mispereth,[a] Bigvai, Nehum, and Baanah.

The number of the men of the people of
Israel: 8the sons of Parosh, two thousand
one hundred and seventy-two;
9the sons of Shephatiah, three hundred
and seventy-two;
10the sons of Arah, six hundred and fifty-
two;
11the sons of Pahath-Moab, of the sons of
Jeshua and Joab, two thousand eight
hundred and eighteen;
12the sons of Elam, one thousand two
hundred and fifty-four;
13the sons of Zattu, eight hundred and
forty-five;
14the sons of Zaccai, seven hundred and
sixty;
15the sons of Binnui,[a] six hundred and
forty-eight;
16the sons of Bebai, six hundred and
twenty-eight;
17the sons of Azgad,
two thousand three
hundred and twenty-
two;
18the sons of
Adonikam, six
hundred and sixty-
seven;
19the sons of Bigvai,
two thousand and
sixty-seven;
20the sons of Adin, six hundred and fifty-
five;
21the sons of Ater of Hezekiah, ninety-
eight;
22the sons of Hashum, three hundred
and twenty-eight;
23the sons of Bezai, three hundred and
twenty-four;
24the sons of Hariph,[a] one hundred and
twelve;
25the sons of Gibeon,[a] ninety-five;
26the men of Bethlehem and Netophah,
one hundred and eighty-eight;
27the men of Anathoth, one hundred and
twenty-eight;
28the men of Beth Azmaveth,[a] forty-two;
29the men of Kirjath Jearim, Chephirah,
and Beeroth, seven hundred and forty-
three;
30the men of Ramah and Geba, six

7:6 [a]Compare verses 6–72 with Ezra 2:1–70
7:7 [a]Spelled *Mispar* in Ezra 2:2 **7:15** [a]Spelled *Bani* in Ezra 2:10 **7:24** [a]Called *Jorah* in Ezra 2:18
7:25 [a]Called *Gibbar* in Ezra 2:20 **7:28** [a]Called *Azmaveth* in Ezra 2:24

hundred and twenty-one;
31the men of Michmas, one hundred and twenty-two;
32the men of Bethel and Ai, one hundred and twenty-three;
33the men of the other Nebo, fifty-two;
34the sons of the other Elam, one thousand two hundred and fifty-four;
35the sons of Harim, three hundred and twenty;
36the sons of Jericho, three hundred and forty-five;
37the sons of Lod, Hadid, and Ono, seven hundred and twenty-one;
38the sons of Senaah, three thousand nine hundred and thirty.

39 The priests: the sons of Jedaiah, of the house of Jeshua, nine hundred and seventy-three;
40the sons of Immer, one thousand and fifty-two;
41the sons of Pashhur, one thousand two hundred and forty-seven;
42the sons of Harim, one thousand and seventeen.

43 The Levites: the sons of Jeshua, of Kadmiel, *and* of the sons of Hodevah,[a] seventy-four.

44 The singers: the sons of Asaph, one hundred and forty-eight.

45 The gatekeepers: the sons of Shallum,
the sons of Ater,
the sons of Talmon,
the sons of Akkub,
the sons of Hatita,
the sons of Shobai, one hundred and thirty-eight.

46 The Nethinim: the sons of Ziha,
the sons of Hasupha,
the sons of Tabbaoth,
47the sons of Keros,
the sons of Sia,[a]
the sons of Padon,
48the sons of Lebana,[a]
the sons of Hagaba,[b]
the sons of Salmai,[c]
49the sons of Hanan,
the sons of Giddel,
the sons of Gahar,
50the sons of Reaiah,
the sons of Rezin,
the sons of Nekoda,
51the sons of Gazzam,
the sons of Uzza,
the sons of Paseah,
52the sons of Besai,
the sons of Meunim,
the sons of Nephishesim,[a]
53the sons of Bakbuk,
the sons of Hakupha,
the sons of Harhur,
54the sons of Bazlith,[a]
the sons of Mehida,
the sons of Harsha,
55the sons of Barkos,
the sons of Sisera,
the sons of Tamah,
56the sons of Neziah,
and the sons of Hatipha.

57 The sons of Solomon's servants: the sons of Sotai,
the sons of Sophereth,
the sons of Perida,[a]
58the sons of Jaala,
the sons of Darkon,
the sons of Giddel,
59the sons of Shephatiah,
the sons of Hattil,
the sons of Pochereth of Zebaim,
and the children of Amon.[a]
60All the Nethinim, and the sons of Solomon's servants, *were* three hundred and ninety-two.

61 And these *were* the ones who came up from Tel Melah, Tel Harsha, Cherub, Addon,[a] and Immer, but they could not identify their father's house nor their lineage, whether they *were* of Israel:
62the sons of Delaiah,
the sons of Tobiah,
the sons of Nekoda, six hundred and forty-two;
63and of the priests: the sons of Habaiah,

7:43 [a]Spelled *Hodaviah* in Ezra 2:40
7:47 [a]Spelled *Siaha* in Ezra 2:44 **7:48** [a]Masoretic Text reads *Lebanah.* [b]Masoretic Text reads *Hogabah.* [c]Or *Shalmai,* or *Shamlai* **7:52** [a]Spelled *Nephusim* in Ezra 2:50 **7:54** [a]Spelled *Bazluth* in Ezra 2:52 **7:57** [a]Spelled *Peruda* in Ezra 2:55 **7:59** [a]Spelled *Ami* in Ezra 2:57 **7:61** [a]Spelled *Addan* in Ezra 2:59

the sons of Koz,[a]
the sons of Barzillai, who took a wife of
the daughters of Barzillai the Gileadite,
and was called by their name.
64These sought their listing *among* those
who were registered by genealogy, but
it was not found; therefore they were
excluded from the priesthood as defiled.
65And the governor[a] said to them that
they should not eat of the most holy
things till a priest could consult with the
Urim and Thummim.

66 Altogether the whole assembly *was*
forty-two thousand three hundred and
sixty, 67besides their male and female
servants, of whom *there were* seven
thousand three hundred and thirty-
seven; and they had two hundred and
forty-five men and women singers.
68Their horses were seven hundred and
thirty-six, their mules two hundred and
forty-five, 69*their* camels four hundred
and thirty-five, *and* donkeys six
thousand seven hundred and twenty.

70 And some of the heads of the fathers'
houses gave to the work. The governor[a]
gave to the treasury one thousand gold
drachmas, fifty basins, and five hundred
and thirty priestly garments. 71Some of
the heads of the fathers' *houses* gave
to the treasury of the work twenty
thousand gold drachmas, and two
thousand two hundred silver minas.
72And that which the rest of the people
gave *was* twenty thousand gold
drachmas, two thousand silver minas,
and sixty-seven priestly garments.

73So the priests, the Levites, the gatekeepers, the singers, *some* of the people, the Nethinim, and all Israel dwelt in their cities.

Ezra Reads the Law

When the seventh month came, the children of Israel *were* in their cities.

8 Now all the people gathered together as one man in the open square that *was* in front of the Water Gate; and they told Ezra the scribe to bring the Book of the Law of Moses, which the LORD had commanded Israel. 2So Ezra the priest brought the Law before the assembly of men and women and all who *could* hear with understanding on the first day of the seventh month. 3Then he read from it in the open square that *was* in front of the Water Gate from morning until midday, before the men and women and those who could understand; and the ears of all the people *were attentive* to the Book of the Law.

4So Ezra the scribe stood on a platform of wood which they had made for the purpose; and beside him, at his right hand, stood Mattithiah, Shema, Anaiah, Urijah, Hilkiah, and Maaseiah; and at his left hand Pedaiah, Mishael, Malchijah, Hashum, Hashbadana, Zechariah, *and* Meshullam. 5And Ezra opened the book in the sight of all the people, for he was *standing* above all the people; and when he opened it, all the people stood up. 6And Ezra blessed the LORD, the great God.

Then all the people answered, "Amen, Amen!" while lifting up their hands. And they bowed their heads and worshiped the LORD with *their* faces to the ground.

7Also Jeshua, Bani, Sherebiah, Jamin, Akkub, Shabbethai, Hodijah, Maaseiah, Kelita, Azariah, Jozabad, Hanan, Pelaiah, and the Levites, helped the people to understand the Law; and the people *stood* in their place. 8So they read distinctly from the book, in the Law of God; and they gave the sense, and helped *them* to understand the reading.

9And Nehemiah, who *was* the governor,[a] Ezra the priest *and* scribe, and the Levites who taught the people said to all the people, "This day *is* holy to the LORD your God; do not mourn nor weep." For all the people wept, when they heard the words of the Law.

10Then he said to them, "Go your way, eat the fat, drink the sweet, and send portions to those for whom nothing is prepared; for *this* day *is* holy to our Lord. Do not sorrow, for the joy of the LORD is your strength."

11So the Levites quieted all the people, saying, "Be still, for the day *is* holy; do not be grieved." 12And all the people went their way to eat and drink, to send portions and rejoice greatly, because they understood the words that were declared to them.

The Feast of Tabernacles

13Now on the second day the heads of the fathers' *houses* of all the people, with the

7:63 [a]Or *Hakkoz* **7:65** [a]Hebrew *Tirshatha*
7:70 [a]Hebrew *Tirshatha* **8:9** [a]Hebrew *Tirshatha*

Joy

LAUGHING WITH JOY

LIZ CURTIS HIGGS

(Nehemiah 8:10)

What makes God laugh? We do, of course! Has it ever occurred to you that He does laugh? Or does God seem much too serious and stern to ever join us in laughter? As much as we laugh at our children, knowing so well their personalities, strengths, and weaknesses, why would God not be amused at our antics, even knowing in advance what we are going to say and do? I think that God thoroughly enjoys good humor, enjoys a good laugh, and loves to see us enjoying it as well.

Joy and laughter are part of God's plan for us. Consider these verses from God's Word:

➢ "You will show me the path of life; in Your presence is fullness of joy; at Your right hand are pleasures forevermore" (Ps. 16:11).
➢ "Be glad in the LORD and rejoice, you righteous; and shout for joy, all you upright in heart!" (Ps. 32:11).
➢ "His lord said to him, 'Well done, good and faithful servant. . . . Enter into the joy of your lord'" (Matt. 25:23).
➢ "Likewise, I say to you, there is joy in the presence of the angels of God over one sinner who repents" (Luke 15:10).
➢ "These things I have spoken to you, that My joy may remain in you, and that your joy may be full" (John 15:11).

LAUGHING WITH GOD

How one laughs with the Lord is as individual and private a decision as how one prays. Laughing is an expression of joy that comes from the heart of God Himself. Humor is encouraging and edifying to the body of Christ. The Bible says, "Whatever you do, do it heartily, as to the Lord and not to men" (Col. 3:23). Laughter comes under the category of *whatever!* Humor exhibits the joy, the passion, and the adventure of the Christian life.

The key is that the humor of one who knows God is decidedly different from the humor of this world:

Worldly Humor:
➢ Glorifies sin
➢ Puts down others
➢ Ridicules righteousness
➢ Hurts the spirit

Godly Humor:
➢ Avoids offense
➢ Builds up others
➢ Honors the Lord
➢ Heals the spirit

Laughter and music are two of God's finest gifts. They give us the ability to express our inner feelings about God with a sense of joy, anticipation, and participation. The Bible reminds us, "The joy of the LORD is your strength" (Neh. 8:10).

The best source of humor is right at the end of your nose. Especially if you're looking in the mirror. The ability to laugh at ourselves is a sign of maturity, of healthy self-esteem, and of having our priorities straight. Remember, God is on the throne, we are on the ground. *Humble, humus,* and *human* are words well-suited to our earthly imperfection compared to God's heavenly perfection. Our richest resource for laughter can be found in our merry hearts and lives.

EMOTIONAL HEALING

Even more emotionally healing than laughing at ourselves the moment something happens is to be able to continue to laugh about it as the story is repeated. A few years ago, a woman told me just such a story. Someone had given her a plant as a gift. She watered it, fed it plant food, and even set it outdoors in good weather—only to discover two years later that she had been watering a silk plant! Her family still gets a laugh out of that story today.

Laughter can be very healing. People in the medical field tell us what the Bible has declared all along: "A merry heart does good, like medicine, but a broken spirit dries the bones" (Prov. 17:22). We can make a choice to be upset, or talk about sour grapes, or be embarrassed to the point of being downright angry about a situation—or we can choose to laugh at ourselves. When we laugh, we heal.

PHYSICAL HEALING

Laughter puts the body in a state of relaxation. In a physically relaxed state, we take our foot off the pain accelerator and put on the brakes. I think our bodies were made for laughter. Our bodies were created by an amazing God who knew that we would get broken and bruised and would need all the natural painkillers we could get. Consider these key facts about laughter:

1. Laughter is a natural pain reducer.
2. Laughter increases our ability to cope with life.
3. Laughter massages our internal organs.
4. Laughter exercises our facial muscles.
5. Laughter increases the heart rate and improves circulation.
6. Laughter oxygenates the body.
7. Laughter stimulates the immune system.

We've all been in high-stress, low-strength situations where we turn to the next person and sigh, "Someday we'll laugh about this." I say, why wait? If we can see the humor potential, let's dive right in! The time and distance between the difficulty and our ability to laugh about it is what I call the "stress zone." We can't hurry the time, but we can decrease the distance between the first and the last moment we spend in the zone.

Sometimes we have to stand back to see the big picture. We have to put things in perspective. The one who knows God can even laugh in the face of death because to die with Christ in our heart is to live—and laugh—with Him, forever.

FURTHER MEDITATION:

Other passages to study about the issue of joy include:

- ➢ Psalms 30:5; 126:5
- ➢ Ecclesiastes 3:4
- ➢ Luke 2:10
- ➢ John 16:24

To Learn More: Turn to the key passage note on joy at Proverbs 15:13–15 on page 817. See also the personality profile of Isaac on page 31.

priests and Levites, were gathered to Ezra the
scribe, in order to understand the words of the
Law. [14]And they found written in the Law,
which the LORD had commanded by Moses,
that the children of Israel should dwell in
booths during the feast of the seventh month,
[15]and that they should
announce and proclaim
in all their cities and in
Jerusalem, saying, "Go
out to the mountain, and
bring olive branches,
branches of oil trees,
myrtle branches, palm
branches, and branches
of leafy trees, to make
booths, as *it is* written."
[16]Then the people went out and brought
them and made themselves booths, each one
on the roof of his house, or in their courtyards
or the courts of the house of God, and in the
open square of the Water Gate and in the open
square of the Gate of Ephraim. [17]So the whole
assembly of those who had returned from the
captivity made booths and sat under the
booths; for since the days of Joshua the son of
Nun until that day the children of Israel had
not done so. And there was very great gladness. [18]Also day by day, from the first day until the last day, he read from the Book of the
Law of God. And they kept the feast seven
days; and on the eighth day *there was* a sacred
assembly, according to the *prescribed* manner.

The People Confess Their Sins

9 Now on the twenty-fourth day of this
month the children of Israel were assembled with fasting, in sackcloth, and with dust
on their heads.[a] [2]Then those of Israelite lineage separated themselves from all foreigners;
and they stood and confessed their sins and
the iniquities of their fathers. [3]And they stood
up in their place and read from the Book of the
Law of the LORD their God *for one*-fourth of
the day; and *for another* fourth they confessed
and worshiped the LORD their God.
[4]Then Jeshua, Bani, Kadmiel, Shebaniah,
Bunni, Sherebiah, Bani, *and* Chenani stood on
the stairs of the Levites
and cried out with a
loud voice to the LORD
their God. [5]And the Le-
vites, Jeshua, Kadmiel,
Bani, Hashabniah, Sher-
ebiah, Hodijah, Sheba-
niah, *and* Pethahiah,
said:

> "Stand up and bless the LORD your God forever and ever! Blessed be Your glorious name, which is exalted above all blessing and praise!"
>
> NEHEMIAH 9:5

"Stand up *and* bless the LORD your God
Forever and ever!

"Blessed be Your glorious name,
Which is exalted above all blessing and
praise!
6 You alone *are* the LORD;
You have made heaven,
The heaven of heavens, with all their
host,
The earth and everything on it,
The seas and all that is in them,
And You preserve them all.
The host of heaven worships You.

7 "You *are* the LORD God,
Who chose Abram,
And brought him out of Ur of the
Chaldeans,
And gave him the name Abraham;
8 You found his heart faithful before You,
And made a covenant with him
To give the land of the Canaanites,
The Hittites, the Amorites,

9:1 [a]Literally *earth on them*

SOUL NOTE

Joyous Revival *(8:10)* When the Book of the Law was read to the people of Israel, they were convicted of their sins. A great revival took place as the nation recommitted itself to God. Nehemiah told them to move from sorrow over their sins to joy in hearing God's Word. "Do not sorrow, for the joy of the LORD is your strength," he said. When we face up to the seriousness of our sin, our hearts will naturally be broken. When we realize the wonderful grace of the forgiveness of sins, however, the joy of the Lord will be our strength as well. **Topic: Joy**

The Perizzites, the Jebusites,
And the Girgashites—
To give *it* to his descendants.
You have performed Your words,
For You *are* righteous.

9 "You saw the affliction of our fathers in Egypt,
And heard their cry by the Red Sea.
10 You showed signs and wonders against Pharaoh,
Against all his servants,
And against all the people of his land.
For You knew that they acted proudly against them.
So You made a name for Yourself, as *it is* this day.
11 And You divided the sea before them,
So that they went through the midst of the sea on the dry land;
And their persecutors You threw into the deep,
As a stone into the mighty waters.
12 Moreover You led them by day with a cloudy pillar,
And by night with a pillar of fire,
To give them light on the road
Which they should travel.

13 "You came down also on Mount Sinai,
And spoke with them from heaven,
And gave them just ordinances and true laws,
Good statutes and commandments.
14 You made known to them Your holy Sabbath,
And commanded them precepts, statutes and laws,
By the hand of Moses Your servant.
15 You gave them bread from heaven for their hunger,
And brought them water out of the rock for their thirst,
And told them to go in to possess the land
Which You had sworn to give them.

16 "But they and our fathers acted proudly,
Hardened their necks,
And did not heed Your commandments.
17 They refused to obey,
And they were not mindful of Your wonders
That You did among them.
But they hardened their necks,
And in their rebellion[a]
They appointed a leader
To return to their bondage.
But You *are* God,
Ready to pardon,
Gracious and merciful,
Slow to anger,
Abundant in kindness,
And did not forsake them.

18 "Even when they made a molded calf for themselves,
And said, 'This *is* your god
That brought you up out of Egypt,'
And worked great provocations,
19 Yet in Your manifold mercies
You did not forsake them in the wilderness.
The pillar of the cloud did not depart from them by day,
To lead them on the road;
Nor the pillar of fire by night,
To show them light,
And the way they should go.
20 You also gave Your good Spirit to instruct them,
And did not withhold Your manna from their mouth,
And gave them water for their thirst.
21 Forty years You sustained them in the wilderness;
They lacked nothing;
Their clothes did not wear out[a]
And their feet did not swell.

22 "Moreover You gave them kingdoms and nations,
And divided them into districts.[a]
So they took possession of the land of Sihon,
The land of[b] the king of Heshbon,
And the land of Og king of Bashan.
23 You also multiplied their children as the stars of heaven,
And brought them into the land
Which You had told their fathers
To go in and possess.

9:17 [a]Following Masoretic Text and Vulgate; Septuagint reads *in Egypt*. **9:21** [a]Compare Deuteronomy 29:5 **9:22** [a]Literally *corners* [b]Following Masoretic Text and Vulgate; Septuagint omits *The land of*.

24 So the people went in
And possessed the land;
You subdued before them the
inhabitants of the land,
The Canaanites,
And gave them into their hands,
With their kings
And the people of the land,
That they might do with them as they
wished.
25 And they took strong cities and a rich
land,
And possessed houses full of all goods,
Cisterns *already* dug, vineyards, olive
groves,
And fruit trees in abundance.
So they ate and were filled and grew fat,
And delighted themselves in Your great
goodness.

26 "Nevertheless they were disobedient
And rebelled against You,
Cast Your law behind their backs
And killed Your prophets, who testified
against them
To turn them to Yourself;
And they worked great provocations.
27 Therefore You delivered them into the
hand of their enemies,
Who oppressed them;
And in the time of their trouble,
When they cried to You,
You heard from heaven;
And according to Your abundant mercies
You gave them deliverers who saved
them
From the hand of their enemies.

28 "But after they had rest,
They again did evil before You.
Therefore You left them in the hand of
their enemies,
So that they had dominion over them;
Yet when they returned and cried out to
You,
You heard from heaven;
And many times You delivered them
according to Your mercies,
29 And testified against them,
That You might bring them back to Your
law.
Yet they acted proudly,
And did not heed Your commandments,
But sinned against Your judgments,
'Which if a man does, he shall live by
them.'[a]
And they shrugged their shoulders,
Stiffened their necks,
And would not hear.
30 Yet for many years You had patience
with them,
And testified against them by Your Spirit
in Your prophets.
Yet they would not listen;
Therefore You gave them into the hand
of the peoples of the lands.
31 Nevertheless in Your great mercy
You did not utterly consume them nor
forsake them;
For You *are* God, gracious and merciful.

32 "Now therefore, our God,
The great, the mighty, and awesome God,
Who keeps covenant and mercy:
Do not let all the trouble seem small
before You
That has come upon us,
Our kings and our princes,
Our priests and our prophets,
Our fathers and on all Your people,
From the days of the kings of Assyria
until this day.

9:29 [a]Leviticus 18:5

SOUL NOTE

Goodness Gracious *(9:26)* God's mercy is beyond measure. His people had turned away from Him many times. "They were disobedient and rebelled . . . cast Your law behind their backs and killed Your prophets, who testified against them." During the reigns of the kings, the Jews had constantly returned to idols. Finally, God punished them by sending them into captivity. Yet God "did not utterly consume them nor forsake them," because He is "gracious and merciful" (9:31). God never changes; He always shows grace and mercy to those who seek Him (Heb. 4:16). **Topic: Knowing God**

33 However You *are* just in all that has
befallen us;
For You have dealt faithfully,
But we have done wickedly.
34 Neither our kings nor our princes,
Our priests nor our fathers,
Have kept Your law,
Nor heeded Your commandments and
Your testimonies,
With which You testified against them.
35 For they have not served You in their
kingdom,
Or in the many good *things* that You
gave them,
Or in the large and rich land which You
set before them;
Nor did they turn from their wicked
works.

36 "Here we *are,* servants today!
And the land that You gave to our
fathers,
To eat its fruit and its bounty,
Here we *are,* servants in it!
37 And it yields much increase to the
kings
You have set over us,
Because of our sins;
Also they have dominion over our
bodies and our cattle
At their pleasure;
And we *are* in great distress.

38 "And because of all this,
We make a sure *covenant* and write *it;*
Our leaders, our Levites, *and* our priests
seal *it.*"

The People Who Sealed the Covenant

10 Now those who placed *their* seal on
the document were:

Nehemiah the governor, the son of
Hacaliah, and Zedekiah, 2 Seraiah,
Azariah, Jeremiah, 3 Pashhur, Amariah,
Malchijah, 4 Hattush, Shebaniah,
Malluch, 5 Harim, Meremoth, Obadiah,
6 Daniel, Ginnethon, Baruch,
7 Meshullam, Abijah, Mijamin, 8 Maaziah,
Bilgai, *and* Shemaiah. These *were* the
priests.

9 The Levites: Jeshua the son of
Azaniah, Binnui of the sons of Henadad,
and Kadmiel.

10 Their brethren: Shebaniah, Hodijah,
Kelita, Pelaiah, Hanan, 11 Micha, Rehob,
Hashabiah, 12 Zaccur, Sherebiah,
Shebaniah, 13 Hodijah, Bani, *and* Beninu.

14 The leaders of the people: Parosh,
Pahath-Moab, Elam, Zattu, Bani,
15 Bunni, Azgad, Bebai, 16 Adonijah,
Bigvai, Adin, 17 Ater, Hezekiah, Azzur,
18 Hodijah, Hashum, Bezai, 19 Hariph,
Anathoth, Nebai, 20 Magpiash,
Meshullam, Hezir, 21 Meshezabel, Zadok,
Jaddua, 22 Pelatiah, Hanan, Anaiah,
23 Hoshea, Hananiah, Hasshub,
24 Hallohesh, Pilha, Shobek, 25 Rehum,
Hashabnah, Maaseiah, 26 Ahijah, Hanan,
Anan, 27 Malluch, Harim, *and* Baanah.

The Covenant That Was Sealed

28 Now the rest of the people—the priests,
the Levites, the gatekeepers, the singers, the
Nethinim, and all those who had separated
themselves from the peoples of the lands to
the Law of God, their wives, their sons, and
their daughters, everyone who had knowledge
and understanding—29 these joined with their
brethren, their nobles, and entered into a
curse and an oath to walk in God's Law,
which was given by Moses the servant of God,
and to observe and do all the commandments
of the LORD our Lord, and His ordinances and
His statutes: 30 We would not give our daughters as wives to the peoples of the land, nor
take their daughters for our sons; 31 *if* the peoples of the land brought wares or any grain to
sell on the Sabbath day, we would not buy it
from them on the Sabbath, or on a holy day;
and we would forego the seventh year's *produce* and the exacting of every debt.

32 Also we made ordinances for ourselves, to
exact from ourselves yearly one-third of a
shekel for the service of the house of our God:
33 for the showbread, for the regular grain offering, for the regular burnt offering of the
Sabbaths, the New Moons, and the set feasts;
for the holy things, for the sin offerings to
make atonement for Israel, and all the work of
the house of our God. 34 We cast lots among the
priests, the Levites, and the people, for *bringing* the wood offering into the house of our
God, according to our fathers' houses, at the
appointed times year by year, to burn on the
altar of the LORD our God as *it is* written in
the Law.

35 And *we made ordinances* to bring the

firstfruits of our ground and the firstfruits of all fruit of all trees, year by year, to the house of the LORD; [36]to bring the firstborn of our sons and our cattle, as *it is* written in the Law, and the firstborn of our herds and our flocks, to the house of our God, to the priests who minister in the house of our God; [37]to bring the firstfruits of our dough, our offerings, the fruit from all kinds of trees, *the* new wine and oil, to the priests, to the storerooms of the house of our God; and to bring the tithes of our land to the Levites, for the Levites should receive the tithes in all our farming communities. [38]And the priest, the descendant of Aaron, shall be with the Levites when the Levites receive tithes; and the Levites shall bring up a tenth of the tithes to the house of our God, to the rooms of the storehouse.

[39]For the children of Israel and the children of Levi shall bring the offering of the grain, of the new wine and the oil, to the storerooms where the articles of the sanctuary *are, where* the priests who minister and the gatekeepers and the singers *are;* and we will not neglect the house of our God.

The People Dwelling in Jerusalem

11 Now the leaders of the people dwelt at Jerusalem; the rest of the people cast lots to bring one out of ten to dwell in Jerusalem, the holy city, and nine-tenths *were to dwell* in *other* cities. [2]And the people blessed all the men who willingly offered themselves to dwell at Jerusalem.

[3]These *are* the heads of the province who dwelt in Jerusalem. (But in the cities of Judah everyone dwelt in his own possession in their cities—Israelites, priests, Levites, Nethinim, and descendants of Solomon's servants.) [4]Also in Jerusalem dwelt *some* of the children of Judah and of the children of Benjamin.

The children of Judah: Athaiah the son of Uzziah, the son of Zechariah, the son of Amariah, the son of Shephatiah, the son of Mahalalel, of the children of Perez; [5]and Maaseiah the son of Baruch, the son of Col-Hozeh, the son of Hazaiah, the son of Adaiah, the son of Joiarib, the son of Zechariah, the son of Shiloni. [6]All the sons of Perez who dwelt at Jerusalem *were* four hundred and sixty-eight valiant men.

[7]And these are the sons of Benjamin: Sallu the son of Meshullam, the son of Joed, the son of Pedaiah, the son of Kolaiah, the son of Maaseiah, the son of Ithiel, the son of Jeshaiah; [8]and after him Gabbai *and* Sallai, nine hundred and twenty-eight. [9]Joel the son of Zichri *was* their overseer, and Judah the son of Senuah[a] *was* second over the city.

[10]Of the priests: Jedaiah the son of Joiarib, and Jachin; [11]Seraiah the son of Hilkiah, the son of Meshullam, the son of Zadok, the son of Meraioth, the son of Ahitub, *was* the leader of the house of God. [12]Their brethren who did the work of the house *were* eight hundred and twenty-two; and Adaiah the son of Jeroham, the son of Pelaliah, the son of Amzi, the son of Zechariah, the son of Pashhur, the son of Malchijah, [13]and his brethren, heads of the fathers' *houses, were* two hundred and forty-two; and Amashai the son of Azarel, the son of Ahzai, the son of Meshillemoth, the son of Immer, [14]and their brethren, mighty men of valor, *were* one hundred and twenty-eight. Their overseer *was* Zabdiel the son of *one of* the great men.[a]

[15]Also of the Levites: Shemaiah the son of Hasshub, the son of Azrikam, the son of Hashabiah, the son of Bunni; [16]Shabbethai and Jozabad, of the heads of the Levites, *had* the oversight of the business outside of the house of God; [17]Mattaniah the son of Micha,[a] the son of Zabdi, the son of Asaph, the leader *who* began the thanksgiving with prayer; Bakbukiah, the second among his brethren; and Abda the son of Shammua, the son of Galal, the son of Jeduthun. [18]All the Levites in the holy city *were* two hundred and eighty-four.

[19]Moreover the gatekeepers, Akkub, Talmon, and their brethren who kept the gates, *were* one hundred and seventy-two.

[20]And the rest of Israel, of the priests *and* Levites, *were* in all the cities of Judah, everyone in his inheritance. [21]But the Nethinim dwelt in Ophel. And Ziha and Gishpa *were* over the Nethinim.

[22]Also the overseer of the Levites at Jerusalem *was* Uzzi the son of Bani, the son of Hashabiah, the son of Mattaniah, the son of Micha, of the sons of Asaph, the singers in charge of the service of the house of God. [23]For *it was* the king's command concerning them that a certain portion should be for the singers, a quota day by day. [24]Pethahiah the son of Meshezabel, of the children of Zerah the son of

---

11:9 [a]Or *Hassenuah* **11:14** [a]Or *the son of Haggedolim* **11:17** [a]Or *Michah*

Judah, *was* the king's deputy[a] in all matters
concerning the people.

The People Dwelling Outside Jerusalem

25And as for the villages with their fields,
some of the children of Judah dwelt in Kirjath
Arba and its villages, Dibon and its villages,
Jekabzeel and its villages; 26in Jeshua, Moladah, Beth Pelet, 27Hazar Shual, and Beersheba
and its villages; 28in Ziklag and Meconah and
its villages; 29in En Rimmon, Zorah, Jarmuth,
30Zanoah, Adullam, and their villages; in Lachish and its fields; in Azekah and its villages.
They dwelt from Beersheba to the Valley of
Hinnom.

31Also the children of Benjamin from Geba
dwelt in Michmash, Aija, and Bethel, and their
villages; 32in Anathoth, Nob, Ananiah; 33in
Hazor, Ramah, Gittaim; 34in Hadid, Zeboim,
Neballat; 35in Lod, Ono, *and* the Valley of
Craftsmen. 36Some of the Judean divisions of
Levites *were* in Benjamin.

The Priests and Levites

12 Now these *are* the priests and the Levites who came up with Zerubbabel
the son of Shealtiel, and Jeshua: Seraiah, Jeremiah, Ezra, 2Amariah, Malluch, Hattush,
3Shechaniah, Rehum, Meremoth, 4Iddo, Gin-
nethoi,[a] Abijah, 5Mijamin, Maadiah, Bilgah,
6Shemaiah, Joiarib, Jedaiah, 7Sallu, Amok,
Hilkiah, *and* Jedaiah.

These *were* the heads of the priests and
their brethren in the days of Jeshua.

8Moreover the Levites *were* Jeshua, Binnui,
Kadmiel, Sherebiah, Judah, *and* Mattaniah
who led the thanksgiving *psalms,* he and his
brethren. 9Also Bakbukiah and Unni, their
brethren, *stood* across from them in *their*
duties.

10Jeshua begot Joiakim, Joiakim begot Eliashib, Eliashib begot Joiada, 11Joiada begot
Jonathan, and Jonathan begot Jaddua.

12Now in the days of Joiakim, the priests,
the heads of the fathers' *houses were:* of Sera-
iah, Meraiah; of Jeremiah, Hananiah; 13of
Ezra, Meshullam; of Amariah, Jehohanan; 14of
Melichu,[a] Jonathan; of Shebaniah,[b] Joseph;
15of Harim,[a] Adna; of Meraioth,[b] Helkai; 16of
Iddo, Zechariah; of Ginnethon, Meshullam;
17of Abijah, Zichri; *the son* of Minjamin;[a] of
Moadiah,[b] Piltai; 18of Bilgah, Shammua; of
Shemaiah, Jehonathan; 19of Joiarib, Mattenai;
of Jedaiah, Uzzi; 20of Sallai,[a] Kallai; of Amok,
Eber; 21of Hilkiah, Hashabiah; *and* of Jedaiah,
Nethanel.

22During the reign of Darius the Persian, a
record *was also kept* of the Levites and priests
who had been heads of their fathers' *houses* in
the days of Eliashib, Joiada, Johanan, and Jaddua. 23The sons of Levi, the heads of the fathers' *houses* until the days of Johanan the son
of Eliashib, *were* written in the book of the
chronicles.

24And the heads of the Levites *were* Hashabiah, Sherebiah, and Jeshua the son of Kadmiel, with their brothers across from them, to
praise *and* give thanks, group alternating with
group, according to the command of David the
man of God. 25Mattaniah, Bakbukiah, Obadiah, Meshullam, Talmon, and Akkub *were*
gatekeepers keeping the watch at the storerooms of the gates. 26These *lived* in the days of
Joiakim the son of Jeshua, the son of Jozadak,[a] and in the days of Nehemiah the governor, and of Ezra the priest, the scribe.

Nehemiah Dedicates the Wall

27Now at the dedication of the wall of Jerusalem they sought out the Levites in all their
places, to bring them to Jerusalem to celebrate
the dedication with gladness, both with
thanksgivings and singing, *with* cymbals and
stringed instruments and harps. 28And the
sons of the singers gathered together from the
countryside around Jerusalem, from the villages of the Netophathites, 29from the house
of Gilgal, and from the fields of Geba and Azmaveth; for the singers had built themselves
villages all around Jerusalem. 30Then the
priests and Levites purified themselves, and
purified the people, the gates, and the wall.

31So I brought the leaders of Judah up on
the wall, and appointed two large thanksgiving choirs. *One* went to the right hand on
the wall toward the Refuse Gate. 32After them
went Hoshaiah and half of the leaders of Judah, 33and Azariah, Ezra, Meshullam, 34Ju-
dah, Benjamin, Shemaiah, Jeremiah, 35and
some of the priests' sons with trumpets—

11:24 [a]Literally *at the king's hand* **12:4** [a]Or *Ginnethon* (compare verse 16) **12:14** [a]Or *Malluch* (compare verse 2) [b]Or *Shechaniah* (compare verse 3) **12:15** [a]Or *Rehum* (compare verse 3) [b]Or *Meremoth* (compare verse 3) **12:17** [a]Or *Mijamin* (compare verse 5) [b]Or *Maadiah* (compare verse 5) **12:20** [a]Or *Sallu* (compare verse 7) **12:26** [a]Spelled *Jehozadak* in 1 Chronicles 6:14

Zechariah the son of Jonathan, the son of Shemaiah, the son of Mattaniah, the son of Michaiah, the son of Zaccur, the son of Asaph,
36and his brethren, Shemaiah, Azarel, Milalai, Gilalai, Maai, Nethanel, Judah, *and* Hanani, with the musical instruments of David the man of God. And Ezra the scribe *went* before
them. 37By the Fountain Gate, in front of them, they went up the stairs of the City of David, on the stairway of the wall, beyond the house of David, as far as the Water Gate eastward.

38The other thanksgiving choir went the opposite *way,* and I *was* behind them with half of the people on the wall, going past the Tower
of the Ovens as far as the Broad Wall, 39and above the Gate of Ephraim, above the Old Gate, above the Fish Gate, the Tower of Hananel, the Tower of the Hundred, as far as the Sheep Gate; and they stopped by the Gate of the Prison.

40So the two thanksgiving choirs stood in the house of God, likewise I and the half of the
rulers with me; 41and the priests, Eliakim, Maaseiah, Minjamin,[a] Michaiah, Elioenai, Zechariah, *and* Hananiah, with trumpets;
42also Maaseiah, Shemaiah, Eleazar, Uzzi, Jehohanan, Malchijah, Elam, and Ezer. The singers sang loudly with Jezrahiah the director.

43Also that day they offered great sacrifices, and rejoiced, for God had made them rejoice with great joy; the women and the children also rejoiced, so that the joy of Jerusalem was heard afar off.

Temple Responsibilities

44And at the same time some were appointed over the rooms of the storehouse for the offerings, the firstfruits, and the tithes, to gather into them from the fields of the cities the portions specified by the Law for the priests and Levites; for Judah rejoiced over the priests and Levites who ministered.
45Both the singers and the gatekeepers kept the charge of their God and the charge of the purification, according to the command of David *and* Solomon his son.
46For in the days of David and Asaph of old *there were* chiefs of the singers, and songs of praise and thanksgiving to God.
47In the days of Zerubbabel and in the days of Nehemiah all Israel gave the portions for the singers and the gatekeepers, a portion for each day. They also consecrated *holy things* for the Levites, and the Levites consecrated *them* for the children of Aaron.

Principles of Separation

13 On that day they read from the Book of Moses in the hearing of the people, and in it was found written that no Ammonite or Moabite should ever come into the assembly of God,
2because they had not met the children of Israel with bread and water, but hired Balaam against them to curse them. However, our God turned the curse into a
blessing. 3So it was, when they had heard the Law, that they separated all the mixed multitude from Israel.

The Reforms of Nehemiah

4Now before this, Eliashib the priest, having authority over the storerooms of the house of our God, *was* allied with Tobiah.
5And he had prepared for him a large room, where previously they had stored the grain offerings, the frankincense, the articles, the tithes of grain, the new wine and oil, which were commanded *to be given* to the Levites and singers and gatekeepers, and the offerings for the priests.
6But during all this I was not in Jerusalem, for in the thirty-second year of Artaxerxes king of Bab-

12:41 [a]Or *Mijamin* (compare verse 5)

SOUL NOTE

Celebrate! *(12:43)* The people of Israel experienced a radical spiritual revival and national transformation as a result of the ministries of Ezra and Nehemiah. Against impossible odds, the wall of Jerusalem had been rebuilt, the temple put back into business, and the sacrifices and celebrations reinstituted. The people rejoiced with such fervor that their joy was heard in surrounding towns. When we give our lives to God to let Him work through us, we may be astounded at what He will do. God's work in and through us will be a cause for celebration, a time to "rejoice with great joy."
Topic: Joy

ylon I had returned to the king. Then after certain days I obtained leave from the king, [7]and I came to Jerusalem and discovered the evil that Eliashib had done for Tobiah, in preparing a room for him in the courts of the house of God. [8]And it grieved me bitterly; therefore I threw all the household goods of Tobiah out of the room. [9]Then I commanded them to cleanse the rooms; and I brought back into them the articles of the house of God, with the grain offering and the frankincense.

[10]I also realized that the portions for the Levites had not been given *them;* for each of the Levites and the singers who did the work had gone back to his field. [11]So I contended with the rulers, and said, "Why is the house of God forsaken?" And I gathered them together and set them in their place. [12]Then all Judah brought the tithe of the grain and the new wine and the oil to the storehouse. [13]And I appointed as treasurers over the storehouse Shelemiah the priest and Zadok the scribe, and of the Levites, Pedaiah; and next to them *was* Hanan the son of Zaccur, the son of Mattaniah; for they were considered faithful, and their task *was* to distribute to their brethren.

[14]Remember me, O my God, concerning this, and do not wipe out my good deeds that I have done for the house of my God, and for its services!

[15]In those days I saw *people* in Judah treading wine presses on the Sabbath, and bringing in sheaves, and loading donkeys with wine, grapes, figs, and all *kinds of* burdens, which they brought into Jerusalem on the Sabbath day. And I warned *them* about the day on which they were selling provisions. [16]Men of Tyre dwelt there also, who brought in fish and all kinds of goods, and sold *them* on the Sabbath to the children of Judah, and in Jerusalem.

[17]Then I contended with the nobles of Judah, and said to them, "What evil thing *is* this that you do, by which you profane the Sabbath day? [18]Did not your fathers do thus, and did not our God bring all this disaster on us and on this city? Yet you bring added wrath on Israel by profaning the Sabbath."

[19]So it was, at the gates of Jerusalem, as it began to be dark before the Sabbath, that I commanded the gates to be shut, and charged that they must not be opened till after the Sabbath. Then I posted *some* of my servants at the gates, *so that* no burdens would be brought in on the Sabbath day. [20]Now the merchants and sellers of all kinds of wares lodged outside Jerusalem once or twice.

[21]Then I warned them, and said to them, "Why do you spend the night around the wall? If you do *so* again, I will lay hands on you!" From that time on they came no *more* on the Sabbath. [22]And I commanded the Levites that they should cleanse themselves, and that they should go and guard the gates, to sanctify the Sabbath day.

Remember me, O my God, *concerning* this also, and spare me according to the greatness of Your mercy!

[23]In those days I also saw Jews *who* had married women of Ashdod, Ammon, *and* Moab. [24]And half of their children spoke the language of Ashdod, and could not speak the language of Judah, but spoke according to the language of one or the other people.

[25]So I contended with them and cursed them, struck some of them and pulled out their hair, and made them swear by God, *saying,* "You shall not give your daughters as wives to their sons, nor take their daughters for your sons or yourselves. [26]Did not Solomon king of Israel sin by these things? Yet among many nations there was no king like him, who was beloved of his God; and God made him king over all Israel. Nevertheless pagan women caused even him to sin. [27]Should we then hear of your doing all this great evil, transgressing against our God by marrying pagan women?"

[28]And *one* of the sons of Joiada, the son of Eliashib the high priest, *was* a son-in-law of Sanballat the Horonite; therefore I drove him from me.

[29]Remember them, O my God, because they have defiled the priesthood and the covenant of the priesthood and the Levites.

[30]Thus I cleansed them of everything pagan. I also assigned duties to the priests and the Levites, each to his service, [31]and *to bringing* the wood offering and the firstfruits at appointed times.

Remember me, O my God, for good!

Remember me,
O my God, for good!
NEHEMIAH 13:31

Esther

A nation at war . . . a beautiful orphan girl with a secret past who unexpectedly becomes the wife of a powerful and impulsive king . . . an aggressive villain with a secret plot for exterminating an entire race.

Is all this (a) the latest Hollywood blockbuster? (b) a new action/adventure TV miniseries? or (c) a best-selling romance novel?

The correct answer is (d) none of the above. Rather, this is the plot of the Old Testament book of Esther!

The story of Esther is a classic struggle between good and evil. It's a book about God's sovereignty and His deliverance. And it's a book about using whatever one has to do all that one can.

Written by an unknown author, Esther is unique in the Scriptures in that it never mentions God by name. Nevertheless, His presence is unmistakable. The providence and rule of God shine through for a people under bondage, exiled in a foreign land. God remembers His covenant promises to Israel and orchestrates events to protect His people. Haman, the madman who conspires to kill the Jews, serves as a sobering reminder of God's promise to Abraham that anyone who curses Israel will himself be cursed. We also learn here in Esther how and why the Feast of Purim became for the Jews an annual reminder of God's great faithfulness.

If you like mystery, suspense, romance, and intrigue, you'll love Esther. Enjoy reading this nail-biter of a book . . . and look for God's fingerprints at every turn!

SOUL CONCERN IN

ESTHER

HONOR (6:6)

The King Dethrones Queen Vashti

1 Now it came to pass in the days of Ahasuerus[a] (this *was* the Ahasuerus who reigned over one hundred and twenty-seven provinces, from India to Ethiopia), 2in those days when King Ahasuerus sat on the throne of his kingdom, which *was* in Shushan[a] the citadel, 3*that* in the third year of his reign he made a feast for all his officials and servants—the powers of Persia and Media, the nobles, and the princes of the provinces *being* before him—4when he showed the riches of his glorious kingdom and the splendor of his excellent majesty for many days, one hundred and eighty days *in all.*

5And when these days were completed, the king made a feast lasting seven days for all the people who were present in Shushan the citadel, from great to small, in the court of the garden of the king's palace. 6*There were* white and blue linen *curtains* fastened with cords of fine linen and purple on silver rods and marble pillars; *and the* couches *were* of gold and silver on a *mosaic* pavement of alabaster, turquoise, and white and black marble. 7And they served drinks in golden vessels, each vessel being different from the other, with royal wine in abundance, according to the generosity of the king. 8In accordance with the law, the drinking was not compulsory; for so the king had ordered all the officers of his household, that they should do according to each man's pleasure.

9Queen Vashti also made a feast for the women *in* the royal palace which *belonged* to King Ahasuerus.

10On the seventh day, when the heart of the king was merry with wine, he commanded Mehuman, Biztha, Harbona, Bigtha, Abagtha, Zethar, and Carcas, seven eunuchs who served in the presence of King Ahasuerus, 11to bring Queen Vashti before the king, *wearing* her royal crown, in order to show her beauty to the people and the officials, for she *was* beautiful to behold. 12But Queen Vashti refused to come at the king's command *brought* by *his* eunuchs; therefore the king was furious, and his anger burned within him.

13Then the king said to the wise men who understood the times (for this *was* the king's manner toward all who knew law and justice, 14those closest to him *being* Carshena, Shethar, Admatha, Tarshish, Meres, Marsena, and Memucan, the seven princes of Persia and Media, who had access to the king's presence, *and* who ranked highest in the kingdom): 15"What *shall we* do to Queen Vashti, according to law, because she did not obey the command of King Ahasuerus *brought to her* by the eunuchs?"

16And Memucan answered before the king and the princes: "Queen Vashti has not only wronged the king, but also all the princes, and all the people who *are* in all the provinces of King Ahasuerus. 17For the queen's behavior will become known to all women, so that they will despise their husbands in their eyes, when they report, 'King Ahasuerus commanded Queen Vashti to be brought in before him, but she did not come.' 18This very day the *noble* ladies of Persia and Media will say to all the king's officials that they have heard of the behavior of the queen. Thus *there will be* excessive contempt and wrath. 19If it pleases the king, let a royal decree go out from him, and let it be recorded in the laws of the Persians and the Medes, so that it will not be altered, that Vashti shall come no more before King Ahasuerus; and let the king give her royal position to another who is better than she. 20When the king's decree which he will make is proclaimed throughout all his empire (for it is great), all wives will honor their husbands, both great and small."

21And the reply pleased the king and the princes, and the king did according to the word of Memucan. 22Then he sent letters to all the king's provinces, to each province in its own script, and to every people in their own language, that each man should be master in his own house, and speak in the language of his own people.

Esther Becomes Queen

2 After these things, when the wrath of King Ahasuerus subsided, he remembered Vashti, what she had done, and what had been decreed against her. 2Then the king's servants who attended him said: "Let beautiful young virgins be sought for the king; 3and let the king appoint officers in all the provinces of his kingdom, that they may gather all the beautiful young virgins to Shushan the citadel, into the women's quarters, under the custody of

---

1:1 [a]Generally identified with Xerxes I (485–464 B.C.) **1:2** [a]Or *Susa,* and so throughout this book

Hegai[a] the king's eunuch, custodian of the women. And let beauty preparations be given *them.* [4]Then let the young woman who pleases the king be queen instead of Vashti."

This thing pleased the king, and he did so.

[5]In Shushan the citadel there was a certain Jew whose name *was* Mordecai the son of Jair, the son of Shimei, the son of Kish, a Benjamite. [6]*Kish*[a] had been carried away from Jerusalem with the captives who had been captured with Jeconiah[b] king of Judah, whom Nebuchadnezzar the king of Babylon had carried away. [7]And *Mordecai* had brought up Hadassah, that *is,* Esther, his uncle's daughter, for she had neither father nor mother. The young woman *was* lovely and beautiful. When her father and mother died, Mordecai took her as his own daughter.

[8]So it was, when the king's command and decree were heard, and when many young women were gathered at Shushan the citadel, *under* the custody of Hegai, that Esther also was taken to the king's palace, into the care of Hegai the custodian of the women. [9]Now the young woman pleased him, and she obtained his favor; so he readily gave beauty preparations to her, besides her allowance. Then seven choice maidservants were provided for her from the king's palace, and he moved her and her maidservants to the best *place* in the house of the women.

[10]Esther had not revealed her people or family, for Mordecai had charged her not to reveal *it.* [11]And every day Mordecai paced in front of the court of the women's quarters, to learn of Esther's welfare and what was happening to her.

[12]Each young woman's turn came to go in to King Ahasuerus after she had completed twelve months' preparation, according to the regulations for the women, for thus were the days of their preparation apportioned: six months with oil of myrrh, and six months with perfumes and preparations for beautifying women. [13]Thus *prepared, each* young woman went to the king, and she was given whatever she desired to take with her from the women's quarters to the king's palace. [14]In the evening she went, and in the morning she returned to the second house of the women, to the custody of Shaashgaz, the king's eunuch who kept the concubines. She would not go in to the king again unless the king delighted in her and called for her by name.

[15]Now when the turn came for Esther the daughter of Abihail the uncle of Mordecai, who had taken her as his daughter, to go in to the king, she requested nothing but what Hegai the king's eunuch, the custodian of the women, advised. And Esther obtained favor in the sight of all who saw her. [16]So Esther was taken to King Ahasuerus, into his royal palace, in the tenth month, which *is* the month of Tebeth, in the seventh year of his reign. [17]The king loved Esther more than all the *other* women, and she obtained grace and favor in his sight more than all the virgins; so he set the royal crown upon her head and made her queen instead of Vashti. [18]Then the king made a great feast, the Feast of Esther, for all his officials and servants; and he proclaimed a holiday in the provinces and gave gifts according to the generosity of a king.

Mordecai Discovers a Plot

[19]When virgins were gathered together a second time, Mordecai sat within the king's gate. [20]*Now* Esther had not revealed her family and her people, just as Mordecai had charged her, for Esther obeyed the command of Mordecai as when she was brought up by him.

[21]In those days, while Mordecai sat within the king's gate, two of the king's eunuchs, Bigthan and Teresh, doorkeepers, became furious and sought to lay hands on King Ahasuerus. [22]So the matter became known to Mordecai, who told Queen Esther, and Esther informed the king in Mordecai's name. [23]And when an inquiry was made into the matter, it was confirmed, and both were hanged on a gallows; and it was written in the book of the chronicles in the presence of the king.

Haman's Conspiracy Against the Jews

3 After these things King Ahasuerus promoted Haman, the son of Hammedatha the Agagite, and advanced him and set his seat above all the princes who *were* with him. [2]And all the king's servants who *were* within the king's gate bowed and paid homage to Haman, for so the king had commanded concerning him. But Mordecai would not bow or pay homage. [3]Then the king's servants who *were* within the king's gate said to Mordecai, "Why do you transgress the king's com-

2:3 [a]Hebrew *Hege* **2:6** [a]Literally *Who* [b]Same as *Jehoiachin,* 2 Kings 24:6 and elsewhere

mand?" 4Now it happened, when they spoke to him daily and he would not listen to them, that they told *it* to Haman, to see whether Mordecai's words would stand; for *Mordecai* had told them that he *was* a Jew. 5When Haman saw that Mordecai did not bow or pay him homage, Haman was filled with wrath. 6But he disdained to lay hands on Mordecai alone, for they had told him of the people of Mordecai. Instead, Haman sought to destroy all the Jews who *were* throughout the whole kingdom of Ahasuerus—the people of Mordecai.

7In the first month, which is the month of Nisan, in the twelfth year of King Ahasuerus, they cast Pur (that *is,* the lot), before Haman to determine the day and the month,[a] until *it fell on the* twelfth *month,*[b] which *is* the month of Adar.

8Then Haman said to King Ahasuerus, "There is a certain people scattered and dispersed among the people in all the provinces of your kingdom; their laws *are* different from all *other* people's, and they do not keep the king's laws. Therefore it *is* not fitting for the king to let them remain. 9If it pleases the king, let *a decree* be written that they be destroyed, and I will pay ten thousand talents of silver into the hands of those who do the work, to bring *it* into the king's treasuries."

10So the king took his signet ring from his hand and gave it to Haman, the son of Hammedatha the Agagite, the enemy of the Jews. 11And the king said to Haman, "The money and the people *are* given to you, to do with them as seems good to you."

12Then the king's scribes were called on the thirteenth day of the first month, and *a decree* was written according to all that Haman commanded—to the king's satraps, to the governors who *were* over each province, to the officials of all people, to every province according to its script, and to every people in their language. In the name of King Ahasuerus it was written, and sealed with the king's signet ring. 13And the letters were sent by couriers into all the king's provinces, to destroy, to kill, and to annihilate all the Jews, both young and old, little children and women, in one day, on the thirteenth *day* of the twelfth *month,* which *is* the month of Adar, and to plunder their possessions.[a] 14A copy of the document was to be issued as law in every province, being published for all people, that they should be ready for that day. 15The couriers went out, hastened by the king's command; and the decree was proclaimed in Shushan the citadel. So the king and Haman sat down to drink, but the city of Shushan was perplexed.

3:7 [a]Septuagint adds *to destroy the people of Mordecai in one day;* Vulgate adds *the nation of the Jews should be destroyed.* [b]Following Masoretic Text and Vulgate; Septuagint reads *and the lot fell on the fourteenth of the month.* **3:13** [a]Septuagint adds the text of the letter here.

KEY PASSAGE

Prejudice

CREATED IN GOD'S IMAGE

(3:6)

Haman hated Mordecai so intensely that he was determined to destroy all the Jews in the Persian Empire. His prejudice was focused against one Jewish man and then was extended to the Jewish race and religion. Then Haman used his powerful position with the king to try to exterminate all Jews.

Prejudice is a powerful tool of Satan. Varying degrees of prejudice can focus on physical characteristics, mental capabilities, or intellectual or religious beliefs. Prejudice always puts one person in a superior position to another. That should never be the attitude of the followers of Christ. Instead, believers ought to see all people as created in the image of God and should accept all other believers as part of God's family. In love, they should also readily share Christ with lost people of all races and nations.

To Learn More: Turn to the article about prejudice on pages 1646, 1647. See also the personality profile of Haman on page 628.

ESTHER AGREES TO HELP THE JEWS

4 When Mordecai learned all that had happened, he tore his clothes and put on sackcloth and ashes, and went out into the midst of the city. He cried out with a loud and bitter cry. 2He went as far as the front of the king's gate, for no one *might* enter the king's gate clothed with sackcloth. 3And in every province where the king's command and decree arrived, *there was* great mourning among the Jews, with fasting, weeping, and wailing; and many lay in sackcloth and ashes.

4So Esther's maids and eunuchs came and told her, and the queen was deeply distressed. Then she sent garments to clothe Mordecai and take his sackcloth away from him, but he would not accept *them.* 5Then Esther called Hathach, *one* of the king's eunuchs whom he had appointed to attend her, and she gave him a command concerning Mordecai, to learn what and why this *was.* 6So Hathach went out to Mordecai in the city square that *was* in front of the king's gate. 7And Mordecai told him all that had happened to him, and the sum of money that Haman had promised to pay into the king's treasuries to destroy the Jews. 8He also gave him a copy of the written decree for their destruction, which was given at Shushan, that he might show it to Esther and explain it to her, and that he might command her to go in to the king to make supplication to him and plead before him for her people. 9So Hathach returned and told Esther the words of Mordecai.

10Then Esther spoke to Hathach, and gave him a command for Mordecai: 11"All the king's servants and the people of the king's provinces know that any man or woman who goes into the inner court to the king, who has not been called, *he has* but one law: put *all* to death, except the one to whom the king holds out the golden scepter, that he may live. Yet I myself have not been called to go in to the king these thirty days." 12So they told Mordecai Esther's words.

13And Mordecai told *them* to answer Esther: "Do not think in your heart that you will escape in the king's palace any more than all the other Jews. 14For if you remain completely silent at this time, relief and deliverance will arise for the Jews from another place, but you and your father's house will perish. Yet who knows whether you have come to the kingdom for *such* a time as this?"

PERSONALITY PROFILE

HAMAN'S PREJUDICE: PLAYING WITH FIRE

(ESTHER 3)

Prejudice

Satan's ultimate goal is to destroy people's hearts. He especially delights in the destruction of people by other people. One of Satan's most effective means is through prejudice. How many crimes of hatred have been perpetrated by racism? How many battles have been fought between groups because of prejudice? Satan has been able to use the differences between people—from skin color to race and religious practices—as fuel for hatred's fires.

Haman was arrogant and angry. He hated the Jews in general, but he hated one Jew in particular, Mordecai, because Mordecai had refused to bow to him. Haman knew that Mordecai's resistance came from his religious convictions, so Haman hated Mordecai, his faith in God, and, therefore, all Jews. His anger at one man ignited a fire that was fueled by his pride and ambition. The harm he intended for others eventually returned to him, however, when he was hanged on the gallows he had built for Mordecai.

Prejudice continues because Satan knows it is an effective tool in his hands. Christians, however, should have no room for prejudice. If Christians are to spread God's message of salvation and "make disciples of all the nations" (Matt. 28:19), then they cannot allow a spark of prejudice to glow anywhere in their attitudes toward others.

To Learn More: Turn to the article about prejudice on pages 1646, 1647. See also the key passage note at Esther 3:6 on page 627.

15 Then Esther told *them* to reply to Mordecai: 16 "Go, gather all the Jews who are present in Shushan, and fast for me; neither eat nor drink for three days, night or day. My maids and I will fast likewise. And so I will go to the king, which *is* against the law; and if I perish, I perish!"

17 So Mordecai went his way and did according to all that Esther commanded him.[a]

Esther's Banquet

5 Now it happened on the third day that Esther put on *her* royal *robes* and stood in the inner court of the king's palace, across from the king's house, while the king sat on his royal throne in the royal house, facing the entrance of the house.[a] 2 So it was, when the king saw Queen Esther standing in the court, *that* she found favor in his sight, and the king held out to Esther the golden scepter that *was* in his hand. Then Esther went near and touched the top of the scepter.

3 And the king said to her, "What do you wish, Queen Esther? What *is* your request? It shall be given to you—up to half the kingdom!"

4 So Esther answered, "If it pleases the king, let the king and Haman come today to the banquet that I have prepared for him."

5 Then the king said, "Bring Haman quickly, that he may do as Esther has said." So the king and Haman went to the banquet that Esther had prepared.

6 At the banquet of wine the king said to Esther, "What *is* your petition? It shall be granted you. What *is* your request, up to half the kingdom? It shall be done!"

7 Then Esther answered and said, "My petition and request *is this:* 8 If I have found favor in the sight of the king, and if it pleases the king to grant my petition and fulfill my request, then let the king and Haman come to the banquet which I will prepare for them, and tomorrow I will do as the king has said."

Haman's Plot Against Mordecai

9 So Haman went out that day joyful and with a glad heart; but when Haman saw Mordecai in the king's gate, and that he did not stand or tremble before him, he was filled with indignation against Mordecai. 10 Nevertheless Haman restrained himself and went home, and he sent and called for his friends and his wife Zeresh. 11 Then Haman told them of his great riches, the multitude of his children, everything in which the king had promoted him, and how he had advanced him above the officials and servants of the king.

12 Moreover Haman said, "Besides, Queen Esther invited no one but me to come in with the king to the banquet that she prepared; and tomorrow I am again invited by her, along with the king. 13 Yet all this avails me nothing, so long as I see Mordecai the Jew sitting at the king's gate."

14 Then his wife Zeresh and all his friends said to him, "Let a gallows be made, fifty cubits high, and in the morning suggest to the king that Mordecai be hanged on it; then go merrily with the king to the banquet."

And the thing pleased Haman; so he had the gallows made.

The King Honors Mordecai

6 That night the king could not sleep. So one was commanded to bring the book of the records of the chronicles; and they were read before the king. 2 And it was found written that Mordecai had told of Bigthana and Teresh, two of the king's eunuchs, the

4:17 [a]Septuagint adds a prayer of Mordecai here.
5:1 [a]Septuagint adds many extra details in verses 1 and 2.

SOUL NOTE

Seek His Face *(4:16)* Esther fasted and prayed, and asked her people to do the same as she prepared to risk her life by approaching King Ahasuerus. In a communal act of faith, the Jewish people fasted and petitioned God. Esther knew that her strength would come from God and that He alone could turn the heart of the king. She wisely prepared herself, however, through the disciplines of prayer and fasting. God is honored when we seek His face before we embark on service for Him.
Topic: Spiritual Disciplines

LIGHTHOUSE OF HONOR

GARY SMALLEY AND GREG SMALLEY

(Esther 6:6)

Imagine you are on a small boat caught in a fierce ocean storm. As the towering waves crash all around you, your boat is barely able to stay afloat. With each passing second, you are driven closer to the deadly rocks standing guard offshore. Suddenly, you catch sight of a tiny, blinking light. Searching through the dark surf, you realize the light is your lifeline—a lighthouse.

Very few images reflect such security and hope as a lighthouse. In the same way that a lighthouse provides safety to a wayward vessel, honor builds safety in a relationship. To "honor" simply means to place high value, worth, and importance on other people by viewing them as priceless gifts—granting them a position in our lives worthy of great respect. Honor is a gift we give to others. It isn't purchased by others' actions or contingent on our emotions. We give others distinction whether or not they like it, want it, or deserve it. In marriage, honoring our mates gives legs to the words, "I love you." It puts that statement into action.

Honor is not only the first step of love, it's also the single most important principle for building an intimate relationship. Our favorite illustration of the unlimited power of treating someone as a priceless treasure is a story called *Johnny Lingo's Eight-Cow Wife,* written by Patricia McGerr. The story tells of a young islander named Johnny Lingo who paid the unheard-of price of eight cows for a wife. Most wives cost two or three cows; four or five buys a highly satisfactory wife. What made this most unusual was that the woman Johnny was buying, Sarita, was unattractive—plain, skinny, and very shy. When the teller of this story met Johnny and Sarita, she was amazed, for Sarita had become a truly beautiful woman.

Because Johnny Lingo had considered Sarita to be worth eight cows, she began to feel and present herself as an eight-cow woman. Before Johnny entered her life, Sarita was a plain island girl. After he placed incredible value upon her, she was transformed into a confident, attractive woman with a lift to her shoulders, a tilt to her chin, and a sparkle in her eyes that no one could take away.

How many "cows" do our loved ones feel they are worth? The answer will give us an idea of how much we honor them.

HONORING THOSE WE LOVE

The apostle Paul encouraged the early Christians to honor each other when he wrote, "Be kindly affectionate to one another with brotherly love, in honor giving preference to one another" (Rom. 12:10). A good literal definition of honor is, "To give preference to someone by attaching high value to them." Honor isn't just important to relationships—it is absolutely critical. Without honor, people cannot even create a functional relationship, to say nothing of attaining intimacy.

Take the Pledge

Honor has to be the center of the marriage relationship, and it is not a difficult strength to master and practice. First, take the pledge. Spouses must consciously pledge themselves to put honor at the heart of their relationship. They must commit themselves to consider each other worthy of reverence, praise, and honor without restriction. They must treat each other as treasures, and that attitude should govern all their actions and words. Why is it so important to look at our loved ones as special treasures? Because "where your treasure is, there your heart will be also" (Matt. 6:21). Whatever we highly treasure, that's where our affections, desires, and enthusiasm lie.

When people learn to treasure their mates, their positive feelings for them increase as well. This is called "confirmation bias." Confirmation bias means that whatever people believe about others, positive or negative, they will find evidence to support the belief. This can have a major impact on relationships with loved ones.

If we do not see our loved ones as priceless treasures, then we will tend to focus on their negative actions. On the other hand, if we see them as wonderful treasures, then we will focus more on their positive behavior.

Take Action

Second, take action. One mate must not only pledge to honor the other, but they must also be able to convey that honor through their words, actions, and deeds. One way for a mate to take action is to list all the things they admire about the other mate. They should post the list in a highly visible place where they and, more importantly, their mate, can see it every day. They should consider their mate's personality, appearance, thinking patterns, faith patterns, shared values, parenting skills, concerns, opinions, and life goals. The longer the list, the bigger the lighthouse and the brighter the light.

Another way to take action is to keep track of the mate's positive behavior. In other words, one mate should try to notice methodically what the other mate already does that pleases them. In order to do this, the couple must really look at each other and break through the barriers that obstruct their vision of each other's good deeds.

Whether it's marriage or friendship or whatever else, we can commit ourselves to building lighthouses of honor in our relationships that will protect us from the storms that will come. The higher the honor, the safer will be the relationship. Once we build a lighthouse, we will begin to come closer to the other person in very positive ways.

FURTHER MEDITATION:

Other passages to study about the issue of honor include:

- Exodus 20:12
- 1 Samuel 2:30
- Proverbs 15:33; 20:3
- John 5:19–23; 8:54
- Romans 13:7

To Learn More: Turn to the key passage note on honor at 1 Peter 2:17 on page 1659. See also the personality profile of the wise men on page 1230.

doorkeepers who had sought to lay hands on King Ahasuerus. 3Then the king said, "What honor or dignity has been bestowed on Mordecai for this?"

And the king's servants who attended him said, "Nothing has been done for him."

4So the king said, "Who *is* in the court?" Now Haman had *just* entered the outer court of the king's palace to suggest that the king hang Mordecai on the gallows that he had prepared for him.

5The king's servants said to him, "Haman is there, standing in the court."

And the king said, "Let him come in."

6So Haman came in, and the king asked him, "What shall be done for the man whom the king delights to honor?"

Now Haman thought in his heart, "Whom would the king delight to honor more than me?" 7And Haman answered the king, "*For* the man whom the king delights to honor, 8let a royal robe be brought which the king has worn, and a horse on which the king has ridden, which has a royal crest placed on its head. 9Then let this robe and horse be delivered to the hand of one of the king's most noble princes, that he may array the man whom the king delights to honor. Then parade him on horseback through the city square, and proclaim before him: 'Thus shall it be done to the man whom the king delights to honor!' "

10Then the king said to Haman, "Hurry, take the robe and the horse, as you have suggested, and do so for Mordecai the Jew who sits within the king's gate! Leave nothing undone of all that you have spoken."

11So Haman took the robe and the horse, arrayed Mordecai and led him on horseback through the city square, and proclaimed before him, "Thus shall it be done to the man whom the king delights to honor!"

12Afterward Mordecai went back to the king's gate. But Haman hurried to his house, mourning and with his head covered. 13When Haman told his wife Zeresh and all his friends everything that had happened to him, his wise men and his wife Zeresh said to him, "If Mordecai, before whom you have begun to fall, is of Jewish descent, you will not prevail against him but will surely fall before him."

14While they *were* still talking with him, the king's eunuchs came, and hastened to bring Haman to the banquet which Esther had prepared.

Haman Hanged Instead of Mordecai

7 So the king and Haman went to dine with Queen Esther. 2And on the second day, at the banquet of wine, the king again said to Esther, "What *is* your petition, Queen Esther? It shall be granted you. And what *is* your request, up to half the kingdom? It shall be done!"

3Then Queen Esther answered and said, "If I have found favor in your sight, O king, and if it pleases the king, let my life be given me at my petition, and my people at my request. 4For we have been sold, my people and I, to be destroyed, to be killed, and to be annihilated. Had we been sold as male and female slaves, I would have held my tongue, although the enemy could never compensate for the king's loss."

5So King Ahasuerus answered and said to Queen Esther, "Who is he, and where is he, who would dare presume in his heart to do such a thing?"

6And Esther said, "The adversary and enemy *is* this wicked Haman!"

So Haman was terrified before the king and queen.

7Then the king arose in his wrath from the banquet of wine *and went* into the palace garden; but Haman stood before Queen Esther,

SOUL NOTE

Let Others See God *(6:6)* When King Ahasuerus couldn't sleep, he read a history book. That's when he discovered that Mordecai had at one time saved the king's life. The king wanted to show due honor to Mordecai. Like King Ahasuerus, we ought to honor those who have been a blessing in our lives, no matter how small the deed or the sacrifice. Like Mordecai, we ought to help others, not out of selfish motivation or from seeking praise. Rather, we need to remember that our motive is that others may see God working in our lives. **Topic: Attitudes**

pleading for his life, for he saw that evil was determined against him by the king. 8When the king returned from the palace garden to the place of the banquet of wine, Haman had fallen across the couch where Esther *was*. Then the king said, "Will he also assault the queen while I *am* in the house?"

As the word left the king's mouth, they covered Haman's face. 9Now Harbonah, one of the eunuchs, said to the king, "Look! The gallows, fifty cubits high, which Haman made for Mordecai, who spoke good on the king's behalf, is standing at the house of Haman."

Then the king said, "Hang him on it!"

10So they hanged Haman on the gallows that he had prepared for Mordecai. Then the king's wrath subsided.

Esther Saves the Jews

8 On that day King Ahasuerus gave Queen Esther the house of Haman, the enemy of the Jews. And Mordecai came before the king, for Esther had told how he *was related* to her. 2So the king took off his signet ring, which he had taken from Haman, and gave it to Mordecai; and Esther appointed Mordecai over the house of Haman.

3Now Esther spoke again to the king, fell down at his feet, and implored him with tears to counteract the evil of Haman the Agagite, and the scheme which he had devised against the Jews. 4And the king held out the golden scepter toward Esther. So Esther arose and stood before the king, 5and said, "If it pleases the king, and if I have found favor in his sight and the thing *seems* right to the king and I am pleasing in his eyes, let it be written to revoke the letters devised by Haman, the son of Hammedatha the Agagite, which he wrote to annihilate the Jews who *are* in all the king's provinces. 6For how can I endure to see the evil that will come to my people? Or how can I endure to see the destruction of my countrymen?"

7Then King Ahasuerus said to Queen Esther and Mordecai the Jew, "Indeed, I have given Esther the house of Haman, and they have hanged him on the gallows because he *tried to* lay his hand on the Jews. 8You yourselves write *a decree* concerning the Jews, as you please, in the king's name, and seal *it* with the king's signet ring; for whatever is written in the king's name and sealed with the king's signet ring no one can revoke."

PERSONALITY PROFILE

Respon-sibility

ESTHER: THE BUCK STOPS HERE

(ESTHER 8:1–3)

Responsibility is a weighty word. To take responsibility for something involves work, commitment, problem solving, and taking the heat if something goes wrong. The phrase, "The buck stops here," means that a person must bear the weight of decisions made and take responsibility for them. The responsible person must not "pass the buck" to someone else.

Esther found herself in a position to handle a great responsibility. Her people, the Jews, were to be exterminated at the command of the king—her husband. The king did not know that Esther was a Jew, nor did he know the intrigue behind Haman's suggestion to kill all the Jews. Queen Esther knew that she was the one who should take on the responsibility of saving her people. Her cousin Mordecai perceived that God had chosen this brave young woman and placed her in that position "for such a time as this" (Esth. 4:14). And Esther rose to the occasion.

Some people run from responsibility, not wanting to take the risks or the blame. They don't want to have the buck stop with them. But when believers are doing God's work and trusting Him with the process and the outcome, they can bear that responsibility, knowing that God will see them through.

To Learn More: Turn to the article about responsibility on pages 962, 963. See also the key passage note at Matthew 25:14–30 on page 1272.

9So the king's scribes were called at that
time, in the third month, which *is* the month
of Sivan, on the twenty-third *day;* and it was
written, according to all that Mordecai commanded, to the Jews, the satraps, the governors, and the princes of the provinces from
India to Ethiopia, one hundred and twenty-
seven provinces *in all,* to every province in its
own script, to every people in their own language, and to the Jews in their own script and
language. 10And he wrote in the name of King
Ahasuerus, sealed *it* with the king's signet
ring, and sent letters by couriers on horseback, riding on royal horses bred from swift
steeds.[a]

11By these letters the king permitted the
Jews who *were* in every city to gather together
and protect their lives—to destroy, kill, and
annihilate all the forces of any people or province that would assault them, *both* little children and women, and to plunder their
possessions, 12on one day in all the provinces
of King Ahasuerus, on the thirteenth *day* of
the twelfth month, which *is* the month of
Adar.[a] 13A copy of the document was to be issued as a decree in every province and published for all people, so that the Jews would be
ready on that day to avenge themselves on
their enemies. 14The couriers who rode on
royal horses went out, hastened and pressed
on by the king's command. And the decree
was issued in Shushan the citadel.

15So Mordecai went out from the presence
of the king in royal apparel of blue and white,
with a great crown of gold and a garment of
fine linen and purple; and the city of Shushan
rejoiced and was glad. 16The Jews had light
and gladness, joy and honor. 17And in every
province and city, wherever the king's command and decree came, the Jews had joy and
gladness, a feast and a holiday. Then many of
the people of the land became Jews, because
fear of the Jews fell upon them.

THE JEWS DESTROY THEIR TORMENTORS

9 Now in the twelfth month, that *is,* the
month of Adar, on the thirteenth day, *the
time* came for the king's command and his decree to be executed. On the day that the enemies of the Jews had hoped to overpower
them, the opposite occurred, in that the Jews

8:10 [a]Literally *sons of the swift horses*
8:12 [a]Septuagint adds the text of the letter here.

SOUL NOTE

Communication Is Key *(8:3–8)* Esther pled with her husband, the king, on behalf of the Jewish people, all the while knowing she had very little status even though she was the king's wife. Their marriage was very different from marriages today, but Esther's attitude provides an excellent example of marital communication. She never presumed upon the king; she approached him with respect and courtesy. We can show the same courtesy toward a spouse by listening intently and speaking with respect and courtesy. Respectful, honest communication is important to a happy marriage.
Topic: Marital Communication

SOUL NOTE

Crisis Intervention *(8:11)* At times we must take responsibility for our own protection and the protection of others. Esther prayed for God's guidance, and then risked her life on behalf of her people. The king's agreement still needed to have a new law to put it into practice. So Ahasuerus granted Mordecai the use of his signet ring to issue a new edict. Crisis was averted through the intervention of individuals who cared enough to get involved. We must trust in God's guidance and protection, but then we may have to work and take risks in order to intervene in a difficult situation.
Topic: Crises

themselves overpowered those who hated them. 2The Jews gathered together in their cities throughout all the provinces of King Ahasuerus to lay hands on those who sought their harm. And no one could withstand them, because fear of them fell upon all people. 3And all the officials of the provinces, the satraps, the governors, and all those doing the king's work, helped the Jews, because the fear of Mordecai fell upon them. 4For Mordecai *was* great in the king's palace, and his fame spread throughout all the provinces; for this man Mordecai became increasingly prominent. 5Thus the Jews defeated all their enemies with the stroke of the sword, with slaughter and destruction, and did what they pleased with those who hated them.

6And in Shushan the citadel the Jews killed and destroyed five hundred men. 7Also Parshandatha, Dalphon, Aspatha, 8Poratha, Adalia, Aridatha, 9Parmashta, Arisai, Aridai, and Vajezatha—10the ten sons of Haman the son of Hammedatha, the enemy of the Jews—they killed; but they did not lay a hand on the plunder.

11On that day the number of those who were killed in Shushan the citadel was brought to the king. 12And the king said to Queen Esther, "The Jews have killed and destroyed five hundred men in Shushan the citadel, and the ten sons of Haman. What have they done in the rest of the king's provinces? Now what *is* your petition? It shall be granted to you. Or what *is* your further request? It shall be done."

13Then Esther said, "If it pleases the king, let it be granted to the Jews who *are* in Shushan to do again tomorrow according to today's decree, and let Haman's ten sons be hanged on the gallows."

14So the king commanded this to be done; the decree was issued in Shushan, and they hanged Haman's ten sons.

15And the Jews who *were* in Shushan gathered together again on the fourteenth day of the month of Adar and killed three hundred men at Shushan; but they did not lay a hand on the plunder.

16The remainder of the Jews in the king's provinces gathered together and protected their lives, had rest from their enemies, and killed seventy-five thousand of their enemies; but they did not lay a hand on the plunder. 17*This was* on the thirteenth day of the month of Adar. And on the fourteenth of *the month*[a] they rested and made it a day of feasting and gladness.

The Feast of Purim

18But the Jews who *were* at Shushan assembled together on the thirteenth *day,* as well as on the fourteenth; and on the fifteenth of *the month*[a] they rested, and made it a day of feasting and gladness. 19Therefore the Jews of the villages who dwelt in the unwalled towns celebrated the fourteenth day of the month of Adar *with* gladness and feasting, as a holiday, and for sending presents to one another.

20And Mordecai wrote these things and sent letters to all the Jews, near and far, who *were* in all the provinces of King Ahasuerus, 21to establish among them that they should celebrate yearly the fourteenth and fifteenth days of the month of Adar, 22as the days on which the Jews had rest from their enemies, as the month which was turned from sorrow to joy for them, and from mourning to a holiday; that they should make them days of feasting and joy, of sending presents to one another and gifts to the poor. 23So the Jews accepted the custom which they had begun, as Mordecai had written to them, 24because Haman, the

9:17 [a]Literally *it* **9:18** [a]Literally *it*

SOUL NOTE

Keep a Record *(9:26–28)* The Jews assembled to celebrate their victory on the very day on which Haman had decreed their destruction (9:1). Haman had chosen that date by casting *purim* (lots). In an ironic twist, the Jews declared that their celebration would be called *Purim.* Mordecai recorded these events so the Jewish people could celebrate their deliverance for generations to come. When exciting, happy events occur in our lives, we should keep a record, reviewing it every now and then, and thank God for giving us reasons to celebrate. **Topic: Joy**

son of Hammedatha the Agagite, the enemy of all the Jews, had plotted against the Jews to annihilate them, and had cast Pur (that *is,* the lot), to consume them and destroy them; [25]but when *Esther*[a] came before the king, he commanded by letter that this[b] wicked plot which *Haman* had devised against the Jews should return on his own head, and that he and his sons should be hanged on the gallows.

[26]So they called these days Purim, after the name Pur. Therefore, because of all the words of this letter, what they had seen concerning this matter, and what had happened to them, [27]the Jews established and imposed it upon themselves and their descendants and all who would join them, that without fail they should celebrate these two days every year, according to the written *instructions* and according to the *prescribed* time, [28]*that* these days *should be* remembered and kept throughout every generation, every family, every province, and every city, that these days of Purim should not fail *to be observed* among the Jews, and *that* the memory of them should not perish among their descendants.

[29]Then Queen Esther, the daughter of Abihail, with Mordecai the Jew, wrote with full authority to confirm this second letter about Purim. [30]And *Mordecai* sent letters to all the Jews, to the one hundred and twenty-seven provinces of the kingdom of Ahasuerus, *with* words of peace and truth, [31]to confirm these days of Purim at their *appointed* time, as Mordecai the Jew and Queen Esther had prescribed for them, and as they had decreed for themselves and their descendants concerning matters of their fasting and lamenting. [32]So the decree of Esther confirmed these matters of Purim, and it was written in the book.

Mordecai's Advancement

10 And King Ahasuerus imposed tribute on the land and *on* the islands of the sea. [2]Now all the acts of his power and his might, and the account of the greatness of Mordecai, to which the king advanced him, *are* they not written in the book of the chronicles of the kings of Media and Persia? [3]For Mordecai the Jew *was* second to King Ahasuerus, and was great among the Jews and well received by the multitude of his brethren, seeking the good of his people and speaking peace to all his countrymen.[a]

9:25 [a]Literally *she* or *it* [b]Literally *his*
10:3 [a]Literally *seed.* Septuagint and Vulgate add a dream of Mordecai here; Vulgate adds six more chapters.

Job

"Why?" we cry to God as we struggle with overwhelming grief. "How could You do this to me?" If God is good and possesses all power, how do we account for human suffering? This is one of the great dilemmas in life, and it is the focus of the Book of Job. Although the author of this book is unknown, its profound lessons touch everyone.

At the height of a happy life, Job lost just about everything, including his children and his health. Soon thereafter, a handful of friends arrived. After mourning quietly with him for a week or so, they began to offer possible explanations for his calamity—primarily the idea that bad things happen to people only as punishment for their sins.

Such simple notions, however, are neither correct nor helpful. The Book (and experience) of Job reveals the uncomfortable truth that many times there are no satisfactory answers to the "why" of suffering. Rational explanations may make intellectual sense, but they seldom provide emotional relief. Finite human beings will never fully understand life's misfortunes. We don't have all the facts, nor can we clearly see God's higher purposes.

All people face suffering. In such hard times we don't need answers as much as we need God and the faithful presence of good friends. A primary lesson of Job is that God is always there for us—even when life doesn't make sense.

SOUL CONCERNS IN JOB

JOB AND HIS FAMILY IN UZ

1 There was a man in the land of Uz, whose
name *was* Job; and that man was blameless and upright, and one who feared God and
shunned evil. 2And seven sons and three
daughters were born to him. 3Also, his possessions were seven thousand sheep, three thousand camels, five hundred yoke of oxen, five
hundred female donkeys, and a very large
household, so that this man was the greatest
of all the people of the East.
4And his sons would go and feast *in their*
houses, each on his *appointed* day, and would
send and invite their three sisters to eat and
drink with them. 5So it was, when the days of
feasting had run their course, that Job would
send and sanctify them, and he would rise
early in the morning and offer burnt offerings
according to the number of them all. For Job
said, "It may be that my sons have sinned and
cursed[a] God in their hearts." Thus Job did regularly.

SATAN ATTACKS JOB'S CHARACTER

6Now there was a day when the sons of God
came to present themselves before the LORD,
and Satan[a] also came among them. 7And the
LORD said to Satan, "From where do you
come?"
So Satan answered the LORD and said,
"From going to and fro on the earth, and from
walking back and forth on it."
8Then the LORD said to Satan, "Have you
considered My servant Job, that *there is* none
like him on the earth, a blameless and upright
man, one who fears God and shuns evil?"
9So Satan answered the LORD and said,
"Does Job fear God for nothing? 10Have You
not made a hedge around him, around his
household, and around all that he has on
every side? You have blessed the work of his

1:5 [a]Literally *blessed,* but used here in the evil sense, and so in verse 11 and 2:5, 9 **1:6** [a]Literally *the Adversary,* and so throughout this book

PERSONALITY PROFILE

Suffering

JOB'S SUFFERING

(JOB 1)

Suffering is unavoidable and inescapable. Everyone suffers—it's part of being human. The story of Job reveals a source of suffering, people's powerlessness in it, and, ultimately, God's power through it.

Job was a godly man. The beginning of the book reveals a conversation between Satan and God. Satan was convinced that Job loved God because God had blessed him. Take away his wealth, Satan argued, and Job would curse God. When that didn't work, however, Satan asked for permission to inflict more suffering—taking Job's family and then his health. Job was shattered, broken, and diseased. But through it all, Job "did not sin with his lips" (Job 2:10).

Eventually, God entered the discussion. He did not explain Job's suffering or help him make sense of his loss. Instead, God underlined the reality of His sovereignty, and the fact that He acts on His own without human advice or explanation. He expects people to trust Him and His goodness regardless of what happens.

Although Job's health and wealth were eventually restored, that is not the central message of the story. The Book of Job shows us that our love for God must not be conditioned upon how we think He is treating us. Great suffering well borne is an indication of unshakable trust in God. Faith in God must be maintained through times of trial as well as times of blessing. Such faith reflects God's nature in us, His redeeming power in Christ, and His unconditional love toward us. No matter what we face in life, we can trust that God is in control. We must rely on Him and His goodness.

To Learn More: Turn to the article about suffering on pages 646, 647. See also the key passage note at I Peter 4:12–16 on page 1664.

hands, and his possessions have increased in the land. 11But now, stretch out Your hand and touch all that he has, and he will surely curse You to Your face!"

12And the LORD said to Satan, "Behold, all that he has *is* in your power; only do not lay a hand on his *person*."

So Satan went out from the presence of the LORD.

Job Loses His Property and Children

13Now there was a day when his sons and daughters *were* eating and drinking wine in their oldest brother's house; 14and a messenger came to Job and said, "The oxen were plowing and the donkeys feeding beside them, 15when the Sabeans[a] raided *them* and took them away—indeed they have killed the servants with the edge of the sword; and I alone have escaped to tell you!"

16While he *was* still speaking, another also came and said, "The fire of God fell from heaven and burned up the sheep and the servants, and consumed them; and I alone have escaped to tell you!"

17While he *was* still speaking, another also came and said, "The Chaldeans formed three bands, raided the camels and took them away, yes, and killed the servants with the edge of the sword; and I alone have escaped to tell you!"

18While he *was* still speaking, another also came and said, "Your sons and daughters *were* eating and drinking wine in their oldest brother's house, 19and suddenly a great wind came from across[a] the wilderness and struck the four corners of the house, and it fell on the young people, and they are dead; and I alone have escaped to tell you!"

20Then Job arose, tore his robe, and shaved his head; and he fell to the ground and worshiped. 21And he said:

"Naked I came from my mother's womb,
And naked shall I return there.
The LORD gave, and the LORD has taken
away;
Blessed be the name of the LORD."

22In all this Job did not sin nor charge God with wrong.

Satan Attacks Job's Health

2 Again there was a day when the sons of God came to present themselves before the LORD, and Satan came also among them to present himself before the LORD. 2And the LORD said to Satan, "From where do you come?"

Satan answered the LORD and said, "From going to and fro on the earth, and from walking back and forth on it."

3Then the LORD said to Satan, "Have you considered My servant Job, that *there is* none like him on the earth, a blameless and upright man, one who fears God and shuns evil? And still he holds fast to his integrity, although you incited Me against him, to destroy him without cause."

4So Satan answered the LORD and said, "Skin for skin! Yes, all that a man has he will give for his life. 5But stretch out Your hand now, and touch his bone and his flesh, and he will surely curse You to Your face!"

6And the LORD said to Satan, "Behold, he *is* in your hand, but spare his life."

7So Satan went out from the presence of the LORD, and struck Job with painful boils from the sole of his foot to the crown of his head. 8And he took for himself a potsherd with which to scrape himself while he sat in the midst of the ashes.

9Then his wife said to him, "Do you still hold fast to your integrity? Curse God and die!"

10But he said to her, "You speak as one of the foolish women speaks. Shall we indeed accept good from God, and shall we not accept adversity?" In all this Job did not sin with his lips.

Job's Three Friends

11Now when Job's three friends heard of all this adversity that had come upon him, each one came from his own place—Eliphaz the Temanite, Bildad the Shuhite, and Zophar the Naamathite. For they had made an appointment together to come and mourn with him, and to comfort him. 12And when they raised their eyes from afar, and did not recognize him, they lifted their voices and wept; and each one tore his robe and sprinkled dust on his head toward heaven. 13So they sat down with him on the ground seven days and seven nights, and no one spoke a word to him, for they saw that *his* grief was very great.

1:15 [a]Literally *Sheba* (compare 6:19)
1:19 [a]Septuagint omits *across*.

JOB DEPLORES HIS BIRTH

3 After this Job opened his mouth and
cursed the day of his *birth.* 2And Job
spoke, and said:

3 "May the day perish on which I was born,
And the night *in which* it was said,
'A male child is conceived.'
4 May that day be darkness;
May God above not seek it,
Nor the light shine upon it.
5 May darkness and the shadow of death claim it;
May a cloud settle on it;
May the blackness of the day terrify it.
6 *As for* that night, may darkness seize it;
May it not rejoice[a] among the days of the year,
May it not come into the number of the months.
7 Oh, may that night be barren!
May no joyful shout come into it!
8 May those curse it who curse the day,
Those who are ready to arouse Leviathan.
9 May the stars of its morning be dark;
May it look for light, but *have* none,
And not see the dawning of the day;
10 Because it did not shut up the doors of my *mother's* womb,
Nor hide sorrow from my eyes.

11 "Why did I not die at birth?
Why did I *not* perish when I came from the womb?
12 Why did the knees receive me?
Or why the breasts, that I should nurse?
13 For now I would have lain still and been quiet,
I would have been asleep;
Then I would have been at rest
14 With kings and counselors of the earth,
Who built ruins for themselves,
15 Or with princes who had gold,
Who filled their houses *with* silver;
16 Or *why* was I not hidden like a stillborn child,

3:6 [a]Septuagint, Syriac, Targum, and Vulgate read *be joined.*

PERSONALITY PROFILE

Grief/Loss

JOB'S WIFE: LEARNING OF GOD AND GRIEF

(JOB 2)

Shattered by the loss of her children and her wealth, Job's wife was overwhelmed with grief and anger. As her husband agonized with the additional pain of boils all over his body, she lashed out at Job and his God. In essence, she said, "Still hanging on to that God of yours? Lots of good that is doing! Ending your life would be better than living in this misery." The Bible records her words, "Do you still hold fast to your integrity? Curse God and die!" (Job 2:9).

Such is the common reaction to suffering of those with no faith or awareness of God's higher purposes. While intense suffering can blind even the strongest believer to God's love and faithfulness, that blindness should only be temporary. Anger directed at God over the long term displays an unwillingness to trust His higher purposes. Anger denies both the sovereignty and the mercy of God.

Satan, the author of suffering, pain, grief, and loss, hopes to use these weapons to turn people away from God. With Job, Satan's plan didn't work. With Job's wife, however, it did. With people who understand that their lives are in God's hands, the suffering is no less intense, but the outcome is different. Instead of saying, "Curse God," they can say, "The LORD gave, and the LORD has taken away; blessed be the name of the LORD" (Job 1:21). In the midst of brokenness, God is there, joins in our pain and sorrow, and shows that His heart is for each one of us.

To Learn More: Turn to the article about grief/loss on pages 940, 941. See also the key passage note at John 11:35–44 on page 1391.

Like infants who never saw light?
17 There the wicked cease *from* troubling,
And there the weary are at rest.
18 *There* the prisoners rest together;
They do not hear the voice of the oppressor.
19 The small and great are there,
And the servant *is* free from his master.

20 "Why is light given to him who is in misery,
And life to the bitter of soul,
21 Who long for death, but it does not *come,*
And search for it more than hidden treasures;
22 Who rejoice exceedingly,
And are glad when they can find the grave?
23 *Why is light given* to a man whose way is hidden,
And whom God has hedged in?
24 For my sighing comes before I eat,[a]
And my groanings pour out like water.
25 For the thing I greatly feared has come upon me,
And what I dreaded has happened to me.
26 I am not at ease, nor am I quiet;
I have no rest, for trouble comes."

ELIPHAZ: JOB HAS SINNED

4 Then Eliphaz the Temanite answered and said:

2 "*If* one attempts a word with you, will you become weary?
But who can withhold himself from speaking?
3 Surely you have instructed many,
And you have strengthened weak hands.
4 Your words have upheld him who was stumbling,
And you have strengthened the feeble knees;
5 But now it comes upon you, and you are weary;
It touches you, and you are troubled.
6 *Is* not your reverence your confidence?
And the integrity of your ways your hope?

7 "Remember now, who *ever* perished being innocent?
Or where were the upright *ever* cut off?
8 Even as I have seen,
Those who plow iniquity
And sow trouble reap the same.
9 By the blast of God they perish,
And by the breath of His anger they are consumed.
10 The roaring of the lion,
The voice of the fierce lion,
And the teeth of the young lions are broken.
11 The old lion perishes for lack of prey,
And the cubs of the lioness are scattered.

12 "Now a word was secretly brought to me,
And my ear received a whisper of it.
13 In disquieting thoughts from the visions of the night,
When deep sleep falls on men,
14 Fear came upon me, and trembling,
Which made all my bones shake.
15 Then a spirit passed before my face;
The hair on my body stood up.
16 It stood still,
But I could not discern its appearance.
A form *was* before my eyes;
There was silence;
Then I heard a voice *saying:*
17 'Can a mortal be more righteous than God?
Can a man be more pure than his Maker?
18 If He puts no trust in His servants,
If He charges His angels with error,
19 How much more those who dwell in houses of clay,
Whose foundation is in the dust,
Who are crushed before a moth?
20 They are broken in pieces from morning till evening;
They perish forever, with no one regarding.
21 Does not their own excellence go away?
They die, even without wisdom.'

ELIPHAZ: JOB IS CHASTENED BY GOD

5 "Call out now;
Is there anyone who will answer you?
And to which of the holy ones will you turn?
2 For wrath kills a foolish man,

3:24 [a]Literally *my bread*

And envy slays a simple one.
3 I have seen the foolish taking root,
But suddenly I cursed his dwelling place.
4 His sons are far from safety,
They are crushed in the gate,
And *there is* no deliverer.
5 Because the hungry eat up his harvest,
Taking it even from the thorns,[a]
And a snare snatches their substance.[b]
6 For affliction does not come from the dust,
Nor does trouble spring from the ground;
7 Yet man is born to trouble,
As the sparks fly upward.

8 "But as for me, I would seek God,
And to God I would commit my cause—
9 Who does great things, and unsearchable,
Marvelous things without number.
10 He gives rain on the earth,
And sends waters on the fields.
11 He sets on high those who are lowly,
And those who mourn are lifted to safety.
12 He frustrates the devices of the crafty,
So that their hands cannot carry out their plans.
13 He catches the wise in their own craftiness,
And the counsel of the cunning comes quickly upon them.
14 They meet with darkness in the daytime,
And grope at noontime as in the night.
15 But He saves the needy from the sword,
From the mouth of the mighty,
And from their hand.
16 So the poor have hope,
And injustice shuts her mouth.

17 "Behold, happy *is* the man whom God corrects;
Therefore do not despise the chastening of the Almighty.
18 For He bruises, but He binds up;
He wounds, but His hands make whole.
19 He shall deliver you in six troubles,
Yes, in seven no evil shall touch you.
20 In famine He shall redeem you from death,
And in war from the power of the sword.
21 You shall be hidden from the scourge of the tongue,
And you shall not be afraid of destruction when it comes.
22 You shall laugh at destruction and famine,
And you shall not be afraid of the beasts of the earth.
23 For you shall have a covenant with the stones of the field,
And the beasts of the field shall be at peace with you.
24 You shall know that your tent *is* in peace;
You shall visit your dwelling and find nothing amiss.
25 You shall also know that your descendants *shall be* many,
And your offspring like the grass of the earth.
26 You shall come to the grave at a full age,
As a sheaf of grain ripens in its season.
27 Behold, this we have searched out;
It *is* true.
Hear it, and know for yourself."

5:5 [a]Septuagint reads *They shall not be taken from evil men;* Vulgate reads *And the armed man shall take him by violence.* [b]Septuagint reads *The might shall draw them off;* Vulgate reads *And the thirsty shall drink up their riches.*

SOUL NOTE

Give It Up *(5:8)* In times of trouble, we should turn to God. Job had more than his share of trouble, and none of it was his fault. Eliphaz had the right idea when he said that, in trouble such as Job's, he would seek God. Sometimes we think we can handle everything by ourselves. Or we may be too self-centered to give our problems to God. A crisis may be just what we need to drive us back to Him. When we trust God in our crises, He proves Himself faithful and able to see us through. **Topic: Crises**

JOB: MY COMPLAINT IS JUST

6 Then Job answered and said:

2 "Oh, that my grief were fully weighed,
And my calamity laid with it on the scales!
3 For then it would be heavier than the sand of the sea—
Therefore my words have been rash.
4 For the arrows of the Almighty *are* within me;
My spirit drinks in their poison;
The terrors of God are arrayed against me.
5 Does the wild donkey bray when it has grass,
Or does the ox low over its fodder?
6 Can flavorless food be eaten without salt?
Or is there *any* taste in the white of an egg?
7 My soul refuses to touch them;
They *are* as loathsome food to me.

8 "Oh, that I might have my request,
That God would grant *me* the thing that I long for!
9 That it would please God to crush me,
That He would loose His hand and cut me off!
10 Then I would still have comfort;
Though in anguish I would exult,
He will not spare;
For I have not concealed the words of the Holy One.

"Oh, that I might have my request, that God would grant me the thing that I long for!"
JOB 6:8

11 "What strength do I have, that I should hope?
And what *is* my end, that I should prolong my life?
12 *Is* my strength the strength of stones?
Or is my flesh bronze?
13 *Is* my help not within me?
And is success driven from me?

14 "To him who is afflicted, kindness *should be shown* by his friend,
Even though he forsakes the fear of the Almighty.
15 My brothers have dealt deceitfully like a brook,
Like the streams of the brooks that pass away,
16 Which are dark because of the ice,
And into which the snow vanishes.
17 When it is warm, they cease to flow;
When it is hot, they vanish from their place.
18 The paths of their way turn aside,
They go nowhere and perish.
19 The caravans of Tema look,
The travelers of Sheba hope for them.
20 They are disappointed because they were confident;
They come there and are confused.
21 For now you are nothing,
You see terror and are afraid.
22 Did I ever say, 'Bring *something* to me'?
Or, 'Offer a bribe for me from your wealth'?
23 Or, 'Deliver me from the enemy's hand'?
Or, 'Redeem me from the hand of oppressors'?

24 "Teach me, and I will hold my tongue;
Cause me to understand wherein I have erred.
25 How forceful are right words!
But what does your arguing prove?
26 Do you intend to rebuke *my* words,
And the speeches of a desperate one, *which are* as wind?
27 Yes, you overwhelm the fatherless,
And you undermine your friend.
28 Now therefore, be pleased to look at me;
For I would never lie to your face.
29 Yield now, let there be no injustice!
Yes, concede, my righteousness still stands!
30 Is there injustice on my tongue?
Cannot my taste discern the unsavory?

JOB: MY SUFFERING IS COMFORTLESS

7 "*Is there* not a time of hard service for man on earth?
Are not his days also like the days of a hired man?
2 Like a servant who earnestly desires the shade,

And like a hired man who eagerly looks
for his wages,
3 So I have been allotted months of
futility,
And wearisome nights have been
appointed to me.
4 When I lie down, I say, 'When shall I
arise,
And the night be ended?'
For I have had my fill of tossing till
dawn.
5 My flesh is caked with worms and dust,
My skin is cracked and breaks out
afresh.

6 "My days are swifter than a weaver's
shuttle,
And are spent without hope.
7 Oh, remember that my life *is* a breath!
My eye will never again see good.
8 The eye of him who sees me will see me
no *more;*
While your *eyes* are upon me, I shall no
longer *be.*
9 *As* the cloud disappears and vanishes
away,
So he who goes down to the grave does
not come up.
10 He shall never return to his house,
Nor shall his place know him anymore.

11 "Therefore I will not restrain my mouth;
I will speak in the anguish of my spirit;
I will complain in the bitterness of my
soul.
12 *Am* I a sea, or a sea serpent,
That You set a guard over me?
13 When I say, 'My bed will comfort me,
My couch will ease my complaint,'
14 Then You scare me with dreams
And terrify me with visions,
15 So that my soul chooses strangling
And death rather than my body.[a]
16 I loathe *my life;*
I would not live forever.
Let me alone,
For my days *are but* a breath.

17 "What *is* man, that You should exalt him,
That You should set Your heart on him,
18 That You should visit him every
morning,
And test him every moment?
19 How long?
Will You not look away from me,
And let me alone till I swallow my
saliva?
20 Have I sinned?
What have I done to You, O watcher of
men?
Why have You set me as Your target,
So that I am a burden to myself?[a]
21 Why then do You not pardon my
transgression,
And take away my iniquity?
For now I will lie down in the dust,
And You will seek me diligently,
But I *will* no longer *be.*"

BILDAD: JOB SHOULD REPENT

8 Then Bildad the Shuhite answered and said:

2 "How long will you speak these *things,*
And the words of your mouth *be like* a
strong wind?
3 Does God subvert judgment?
Or does the Almighty pervert justice?
4 If your sons have sinned against Him,
He has cast them away for their
transgression.
5 If you would earnestly seek God
And make your supplication to the
Almighty,
6 If you *were* pure and upright,
Surely now He would awake for you,
And prosper your rightful dwelling
place.
7 Though your beginning was small,
Yet your latter end would increase
abundantly.

8 "For inquire, please, of the former age,
And consider the things discovered by
their fathers;
9 For we *were born* yesterday, and know
nothing,
Because our days on earth *are* a shadow.
10 Will they not teach you and tell you,
And utter words from their heart?

11 "Can the papyrus grow up without a
marsh?
Can the reeds flourish without water?

7:15 [a]Literally *my bones* **7:20** [a]Following Masoretic Text, Targum, and Vulgate; Septuagint and Jewish tradition read *to You.*

12 While it *is* yet green *and* not cut down,
It withers before any *other* plant.
13 So *are* the paths of all who forget God;
And the hope of the hypocrite shall perish,
14 Whose confidence shall be cut off,
And whose trust *is* a spider's web.
15 He leans on his house, but it does not stand.
He holds it fast, but it does not endure.
16 He grows green in the sun,
And his branches spread out in his garden.
17 His roots wrap around the rock heap,
And look for a place in the stones.
18 If he is destroyed from his place,
Then *it* will deny him, *saying,* 'I have not seen you.'

19 "Behold, this is the joy of His way,
And out of the earth others will grow.
20 Behold, God will not cast away the blameless,
Nor will He uphold the evildoers.
21 He will yet fill your mouth with laughing,
And your lips with rejoicing.
22 Those who hate you will be clothed with shame,
And the dwelling place of the wicked will come to nothing."[a]

JOB: THERE IS NO MEDIATOR

9 Then Job answered and said:

2 "Truly I know *it is* so,
But how can a man be righteous before God?
3 If one wished to contend with Him,
He could not answer Him one time out of a thousand.
4 *God is* wise in heart and mighty in strength.
Who has hardened *himself* against Him and prospered?
5 He removes the mountains, and they do not know
When He overturns them in His anger;
6 He shakes the earth out of its place,
And its pillars tremble;
7 He commands the sun, and it does not rise;
He seals off the stars;
8 He alone spreads out the heavens,
And treads on the waves of the sea;
9 He made the Bear, Orion, and the Pleiades,
And the chambers of the south;
10 He does great things past finding out,
Yes, wonders without number.
11 If He goes by me, I do not see *Him;*
If He moves past, I do not perceive Him;
12 If He takes away, who can hinder Him?
Who can say to Him, 'What are You doing?'
13 God will not withdraw His anger,
The allies of the proud[a] lie prostrate beneath Him.

14 "How then can I answer Him,
And choose my words *to reason* with Him?
15 For though I were righteous, I could not answer Him;
I would beg mercy of my Judge.
16 If I called and He answered me,
I would not believe that He was listening to my voice.
17 For He crushes me with a tempest,
And multiplies my wounds without cause.
18 He will not allow me to catch my breath,
But fills me with bitterness.
19 If *it is a matter* of strength, indeed *He is* strong;
And if of justice, who will appoint my day *in court?*
20 Though I were righteous, my own mouth would condemn me;
Though I *were* blameless, it would prove me perverse.

21 "I am blameless, yet I do not know myself;
I despise my life.
22 It *is* all one *thing;*
Therefore I say, 'He destroys the blameless and the wicked.'
23 If the scourge slays suddenly,
He laughs at the plight of the innocent.
24 The earth is given into the hand of the wicked.
He covers the faces of its judges.
If it is not *He,* who else could it be?

25 "Now my days are swifter than a runner;
They flee away, they see no good.

8:22 [a]Literally *will not be* **9:13** [a]Hebrew *rahab*

SUFFERING AND GLORY

DAN ALLENDER

(Job 9:28)

The Bible does not hesitate to describe the human condition and the reality of living in a sinful world. Suffering is an inescapable part of that reality. The Book of Ecclesiastes teaches, "For in much wisdom is much grief, and he who increases knowledge increases sorrow" (Eccl. 1:18).

No one is immune to suffering. Suffering may come as a result of personal sin and failure. For example, some people may suffer financially by not carefully budgeting their money or being wasteful. Some people may suffer the loss of friendship through their hurtful words or gossip. However, suffering may also arise due to other people's sin and failure, or other forces outside of our control. For example, a drunk driver who causes an accident creates suffering for others. A tornado or hurricane can create great suffering for many people.

But suffering doesn't happen just to people. The Bible teaches that creation itself is suffering until a day when it will be redeemed. God Himself suffers, and looks forward to the day when He will bring His people to be with Him.

THE GROANING OF THE EARTH

The earth itself is suffering: "For the creation was subjected to futility, not willingly, but because of Him who subjected it in hope; because the creation itself also will be delivered from the bondage of corruption into the glorious liberty of the children of God" (Rom. 8:20, 21). The whole earth, inanimate and animate, suffers because of the inevitability of death and decay. Animals grow old and sick; crops and trees suffer disease, die, and decay. Suffering is not merely human; it is also earthly. Creation waits in eager anticipation of its day of redemption.

THE GROANING OF HUMANITY

We already know that people suffer—we see it or experience it every day. "We also who have the firstfruits of the Spirit, even we ourselves groan within ourselves, eagerly waiting for the adoption, the redemption of our body" (Rom. 8:23). Suffering is common to all people and is not removed by the presence of the Spirit. Being a Christian is not a "get out of suffering free" card. Christians experience suffering like everyone else. No better illustration of this principle can be found in the Bible than the Book of Job.

Satan complained to God that Job, a righteous man, served God only because his life was relatively free of suffering. A wager was made and the course of Job's suffering increased. With the increased suffering came Job's increased questions and struggles with God. His demand for a hearing concerning his questions grew to such a tempo that God deepened Job's suffering by bringing his soul low with humility. In that suffering, Job found that his deepest desire was not for relief, restitution of his losses, or a return of his reputation. He found what he wanted more than anything in the midst of his suffering was the presence of God. Suffering awakened him to a deeper desire for God.

THE GROANING OF GOD

Suffering is not merely earthly and human; it is also divine. God groans. Paul described it this way: "The Spirit also helps in our weaknesses. For we do not know what we should pray for as we ought, but the Spirit Himself makes intercession for us with groanings which cannot be uttered" (Rom. 8:26). Other religions cannot fathom the concept of an all-powerful God suffering on behalf of His people—suffering when they suffer, feeling their pain. God came to earth in the person of Christ in order to understand humanity and, ultimately, to die an agonizing death for us.

God's suffering reveals the path to glory. Jesus bore the full and complete penalty of sin and suffered judgment so God's children would never be separated from His love. Jesus' suffering became the blood offering for sin that cleanses and heals. It is the redemptive power of suffering that allows us to glimpse an incredibly small taste of what Jesus suffered on the Cross while bearing our sin. It also strips us of the illusion of autonomy and the deceit of self-righteousness. "The Spirit Himself bears witness with our spirit that we are children of God, and if children, then heirs—heirs of God and joint heirs with Christ, if indeed we suffer with Him, that we may also be glorified together" (Rom. 8:16, 17).

SUFFERING AND GLORY

Despite its painfulness, suffering can be very valuable. Suffering clarifies what the heart truly worships, especially when the pain is unexplained and unabated. Do we worship the idea of deliverance, or the Deliverer? Suffering also purifies the heart by deepening the desire for the day when all tears will be wiped away. Our growing discontent with the sin and evil in this world increases our hopefulness for heaven. Suffering not only clarifies and purifies, but it also motivates the heart to action. If we see a child cry, we offer tenderness. If we see the wounds of a victim, we offer solace. Human suffering arouses anger, invigorates action and, as a result, enables us to push back some of the darkness of the Fall. Suffering humanizes the heart and increases our hunger for God.

FURTHER MEDITATION:

Other passages to study about the issue of suffering include:

- ➢ Psalm 119:67, 71, 75
- ➢ Lamentations 3:20–25
- ➢ Acts 5:41
- ➢ Romans 8:18, 28, 29
- ➢ 1 Corinthians 12:26
- ➢ 2 Corinthians 1:3–5; 4:7–10; 12:7–10
- ➢ Philippians 1:29; 4:19
- ➢ 2 Timothy 2:8–13; 3:10–12
- ➢ Hebrews 4:15, 16
- ➢ James 1:2–4; 5:13
- ➢ 1 Peter 1:6–9; 2:19–25; 3:14, 17, 18; 4:16; 5:10

To Learn More: **Turn to the key passage note on suffering at 1 Peter 4:12–16 on page 1664. See also the personality profile of Job on page 638.**

26 They pass by like swift ships,
Like an eagle swooping on its prey.
27 If I say, 'I will forget my complaint,
I will put off my sad face and wear a smile,'
28 I am afraid of all my sufferings;
I know that You will not hold me innocent.
29 *If* I am condemned,
Why then do I labor in vain?
30 If I wash myself with snow water,
And cleanse my hands with soap,
31 Yet You will plunge me into the pit,
And my own clothes will abhor me.

32 "For *He is* not a man, as I *am,*
That I may answer Him,
And that we should go to court together.
33 Nor is there any mediator between us,
Who may lay his hand on us both.
34 Let Him take His rod away from me,
And do not let dread of Him terrify me.
35 *Then* I would speak and not fear Him,
But it is not so with me.

Job: I Would Plead with God

10 "My soul loathes my life;
I will give free course to my complaint,
I will speak in the bitterness of my soul.
2 I will say to God, 'Do not condemn me;
Show me why You contend with me.
3 *Does it* seem good to You that You should oppress,
That You should despise the work of Your hands,
And smile on the counsel of the wicked?
4 Do You have eyes of flesh?
Or do You see as man sees?
5 *Are* Your days like the days of a mortal man?
Are Your years like the days of a mighty man,
6 That You should seek for my iniquity
And search out my sin,
7 Although You know that I am not wicked,
And *there is* no one who can deliver from Your hand?

8 'Your hands have made me and fashioned me,
An intricate unity;
Yet You would destroy me.
9 Remember, I pray, that You have made me like clay.
And will You turn me into dust again?
10 Did You not pour me out like milk,
And curdle me like cheese,
11 Clothe me with skin and flesh,
And knit me together with bones and sinews?
12 You have granted me life and favor,
And Your care has preserved my spirit.

13 'And these *things* You have hidden in Your heart;
I know that this *was* with You:
14 If I sin, then You mark me,
And will not acquit me of my iniquity.
15 If I am wicked, woe to me;
Even *if* I am righteous, I cannot lift up my head.
I am full of disgrace;
See my misery!
16 If *my head* is exalted,
You hunt me like a fierce lion,
And again You show Yourself awesome against me.
17 You renew Your witnesses against me,
And increase Your indignation toward me;
Changes and war are *ever* with me.

18 'Why then have You brought me out of the womb?
Oh, that I had perished and no eye had seen me!
19 I would have been as though I had not been.
I would have been carried from the womb to the grave.
20 Are not my days few?
Cease! Leave me alone, that I may take a little comfort,
21 Before I go *to the place from which* I shall not return,
To the land of darkness and the shadow of death,
22 A land as dark as darkness *itself,*
As the shadow of death, without any order,
Where even the light *is* like darkness.' "

Zophar Urges Job to Repent

11 Then Zophar the Naamathite answered and said:

2 "Should not the multitude of words be
answered?
And should a man full of talk be
vindicated?
3 Should your empty talk make men hold
their peace?
And when you mock, should no one
rebuke you?
4 For you have said,
'My doctrine *is* pure,
And I am clean in your eyes.'
5 But oh, that God would speak,
And open His lips against you,
6 That He would show you the secrets of
wisdom!
For *they would* double *your* prudence.
Know therefore that God exacts from
you
Less than your iniquity *deserves.*

7 "Can you search out the deep things of
God?
Can you find out the limits of the
Almighty?
8 *They are* higher than heaven— what can
you do?
Deeper than Sheol— what can you
know?
9 Their measure *is* longer than the earth
And broader than the sea.

10 "If He passes by, imprisons, and gathers
to judgment,
Then who can hinder Him?
11 For He knows deceitful men;
He sees wickedness also.
Will He not then consider *it?*
12 For an empty-headed man will be wise,
When a wild donkey's colt is born a
man.

13 "If you would prepare your heart,
And stretch out your hands toward Him;
14 If iniquity *were* in your hand, *and you*
put it far away,
And would not let wickedness dwell in
your tents;
15 Then surely you could lift up your face
without spot;
Yes, you could be steadfast, and not
fear;
16 Because you would forget *your* misery,
And remember *it* as waters *that have*
passed away,
17 And *your* life would be brighter than
noonday.
Though you were dark, you would be
like the morning.
18 And you would be secure, because there
is hope;
Yes, you would dig *around you, and* take
your rest in safety.
19 You would also lie down, and no one
would make *you* afraid;
Yes, many would court your favor.
20 But the eyes of the wicked will fail,
And they shall not escape,
And their hope—loss of life!"

Job Answers His Critics

12 Then Job answered and said:

2 "No doubt you *are* the people,
And wisdom will die with you!
3 But I have understanding as well as you;
I *am* not inferior to you.
Indeed, who does not *know* such things
as these?

4 "I am one mocked by his friends,
Who called on God, and He answered
him,
The just and blameless *who is* ridiculed.
5 A lamp[a] is despised in the thought of
one who is at ease;
It is made ready for those whose feet
slip.
6 The tents of robbers prosper,
And those who provoke God are
secure—
In what God provides by His hand.

7 "But now ask the beasts, and they will
teach you;
And the birds of the air, and they will
tell you;
8 Or speak to the earth, and it will teach
you;
And the fish of the sea will explain to
you.
9 Who among all these does not know
That the hand of the LORD has done this,
10 In whose hand *is* the life of every living
thing,
And the breath of all mankind?
11 Does not the ear test words

12:5 [a]Or *disaster*

And the mouth taste its food?
12 Wisdom *is* with aged men,
And with length of days, understanding.

13 "With Him *are* wisdom and strength,
He has counsel and understanding.
14 If He breaks *a thing* down, it cannot be rebuilt;
If He imprisons a man, there can be no release.
15 If He withholds the waters, they dry up;
If He sends them out, they overwhelm the earth.
16 With Him *are* strength and prudence.
The deceived and the deceiver *are* His.
17 He leads counselors away plundered,
And makes fools of the judges.
18 He loosens the bonds of kings,
And binds their waist with a belt.
19 He leads princes[a] away plundered,
And overthrows the mighty.
20 He deprives the trusted ones of speech,
And takes away the discernment of the elders.
21 He pours contempt on princes,
And disarms the mighty.
22 He uncovers deep things out of darkness,
And brings the shadow of death to light.
23 He makes nations great, and destroys them;
He enlarges nations, and guides them.
24 He takes away the understanding[a] of the chiefs of the people of the earth,
And makes them wander in a pathless wilderness.
25 They grope in the dark without light,
And He makes them stagger like a drunken *man*.

13 "Behold, my eye has seen all *this*,
My ear has heard and understood it.
2 What you know, I also know;
I *am* not inferior to you.
3 But I would speak to the Almighty,
And I desire to reason with God.
4 But you forgers of lies,
You *are* all worthless physicians.
5 Oh, that you would be silent,
And it would be your wisdom!
6 Now hear my reasoning,
And heed the pleadings of my lips.
7 Will you speak wickedly for God,
And talk deceitfully for Him?
8 Will you show partiality for Him?
Will you contend for God?
9 Will it be well when He searches you out?
Or can you mock Him as one mocks a man?
10 He will surely rebuke you
If you secretly show partiality.
11 Will not His excellence make you afraid,
And the dread of Him fall upon you?
12 Your platitudes *are* proverbs of ashes,
Your defenses are defenses of clay.

13 "Hold your peace with me, and let me speak,
Then let come on me what *may!*
14 Why do I take my flesh in my teeth,
And put my life in my hands?
15 Though He slay me, yet will I trust Him.
Even so, I will defend my own ways before Him.
16 He also *shall* be my salvation,
For a hypocrite could not come before Him.
17 Listen carefully to my speech,
And to my declaration with your ears.
18 See now, I have prepared *my* case,
I know that I shall be vindicated.
19 Who *is* he *who* will contend with me?
If now I hold my tongue, I perish.

Job's Despondent Prayer

20 "Only two *things* do not do to me,
Then I will not hide myself from You:
21 Withdraw Your hand far from me,
And let not the dread of You make me afraid.
22 Then call, and I will answer;
Or let me speak, then You respond to me.
23 How many *are* my iniquities and sins?
Make me know my transgression and my sin.
24 Why do You hide Your face,
And regard me as Your enemy?
25 Will You frighten a leaf driven to and fro?
And will You pursue dry stubble?
26 For You write bitter things against me,
And make me inherit the iniquities of my youth.

12:19 [a]Literally *priests,* but not in a technical sense **12:24** [a]Literally *heart*

27 You put my feet in the stocks,
And watch closely all my paths.
You set a limit[a] for the soles of my feet.

28 "*Man*[a] decays like a rotten thing,
Like a garment that is moth-eaten.

14 "Man *who is* born of woman
Is of few days and full of trouble.
2 He comes forth like a flower and fades away;
He flees like a shadow and does not continue.
3 And do You open Your eyes on such a one,
And bring me[a] to judgment with Yourself?
4 Who can bring a clean *thing* out of an unclean?
No one!
5 Since his days *are* determined,
The number of his months *is* with You;
You have appointed his limits, so that he cannot pass.
6 Look away from him that he may rest,
Till like a hired man he finishes his day.

7 "For there is hope for a tree,
If it is cut down, that it will sprout again,
And that its tender shoots will not cease.
8 Though its root may grow old in the earth,
And its stump may die in the ground,
9 *Yet* at the scent of water it will bud
And bring forth branches like a plant.
10 But man dies and is laid away;
Indeed he breathes his last
And where *is* he?
11 *As* water disappears from the sea,
And a river becomes parched and dries up,
12 So man lies down and does not rise.
Till the heavens *are* no more,
They will not awake
Nor be roused from their sleep.

13 "Oh, that You would hide me in the grave,
That You would conceal me until Your wrath is past,
That You would appoint me a set time, and remember me!
14 If a man dies, shall he live *again?*
All the days of my hard service I will wait,
Till my change comes.
15 You shall call, and I will answer You;
You shall desire the work of Your hands.
16 For now You number my steps,
But do not watch over my sin.
17 My transgression *is* sealed up in a bag,
And You cover[a] my iniquity.

18 "But *as* a mountain falls *and* crumbles away,
And *as* a rock is moved from its place;
19 *As* water wears away stones,
And as torrents wash away the soil of the earth;
So You destroy the hope of man.
20 You prevail forever against him, and he passes on;
You change his countenance and send him away.
21 His sons come to honor, and he does not know *it;*
They are brought low, and he does not perceive *it.*
22 But his flesh will be in pain over it,
And his soul will mourn over it."

Eliphaz Accuses Job of Folly

15 Then Eliphaz the Temanite answered and said:

2 "Should a wise man answer with empty knowledge,
And fill himself with the east wind?
3 Should he reason with unprofitable talk,
Or by speeches with which he can do no good?
4 Yes, you cast off fear,
And restrain prayer before God.
5 For your iniquity teaches your mouth,
And you choose the tongue of the crafty.
6 Your own mouth condemns you, and not I;
Yes, your own lips testify against you.

7 "*Are* you the first man *who* was born?
Or were you made before the hills?
8 Have you heard the counsel of God?
Do you limit wisdom to yourself?

13:27 [a]Literally *inscribe a print* **13:28** [a]Literally *He*
14:3 [a]Septuagint, Syriac, and Vulgate read *him.*
14:17 [a]Literally *plaster over*

9 What do you know that we do not
know?
What do you understand that *is* not in us?
10 Both the gray-haired and the aged *are*
among us,
Much older than your father.
11 *Are* the consolations of God too small for
you,
And the word *spoken* gently[a] with you?
12 Why does your heart carry you away,
And what do your eyes wink at,
13 That you turn your spirit against God,
And let *such* words go out of your
mouth?

14 "What *is* man, that he could be pure?
And *he who is* born of a woman, that he
could be righteous?
15 If *God* puts no trust in His saints,
And the heavens are not pure in His
sight,
16 How much less man, *who is* abominable
and filthy,
Who drinks iniquity like water!

17 "I will tell you, hear me;
What I have seen I will declare,
18 What wise men have told,
Not hiding *anything received* from their
fathers,
19 To whom alone the land was given,
And no alien passed among them:
20 The wicked man writhes with pain all
his days,
And the number of years is hidden from
the oppressor.
21 Dreadful sounds *are* in his ears;
In prosperity the destroyer comes upon
him.
22 He does not believe that he will return
from darkness,
For a sword is waiting for him.
23 He wanders about for bread, *saying,*
'Where *is it?*'
He knows that a day of darkness is
ready at his hand.
24 Trouble and anguish make him afraid;
They overpower him, like a king ready
for battle.
25 For he stretches out his hand against
God,
And acts defiantly against the Almighty,
26 Running stubbornly against Him
With his strong, embossed shield.

27 "Though he has covered his face with his
fatness,
And made *his* waist heavy with fat,
28 He dwells in desolate cities,
In houses which no one inhabits,
Which are destined to become ruins.
29 He will not be rich,
Nor will his wealth continue,
Nor will his possessions overspread the
earth.
30 He will not depart from darkness;
The flame will dry out his branches,
And by the breath of His mouth he will
go away.
31 Let him not trust in futile *things,*
deceiving himself,
For futility will be his reward.
32 It will be accomplished before his time,
And his branch will not be green.
33 He will shake off his unripe grape like a
vine,
And cast off his blossom like an olive
tree.
34 For the company of hypocrites *will be*
barren,

15:11 [a]Septuagint reads *a secret thing.*

SOUL NOTE

Sincerely Wrong *(15:17–26)* Job's friends attempted to help him with their advice. Had they listened more and talked less, however, they would have been more helpful. Eliphaz was convinced that Job was being disciplined by God for his sins. He thought Job was wicked because "the wicked man writhes with pain all his days" (15:20). Eliphaz was sincere, but he was wrong. People must be very careful about making assumptions regarding others' circumstances. Things are not always what they seem. It is often more helpful to empathize with a suffering friend than to try and rush in to explain his or her suffering. **Topic: Suffering**

And fire will consume the tents of
bribery.
35 They conceive trouble and bring forth
futility;
Their womb prepares deceit."

Job Reproaches His Pitiless Friends

16 Then Job answered and said:

2 "I have heard many such things;
Miserable comforters *are* you all!
3 Shall words of wind have an end?
Or what provokes you that you answer?
4 I also could speak as you *do,*
If your soul were in my soul's place.
I could heap up words against you,
And shake my head at you;
5 *But* I would strengthen you with my
mouth,
And the comfort of my lips would relieve
your grief.

6 "Though I speak, my grief is not relieved;
And *if* I remain silent, how am I eased?
7 But now He has worn me out;
You have made desolate all my
company.
8 You have shriveled me up,
And it is a witness *against me;*
My leanness rises up against me
And bears witness to my face.
9 He tears *me* in His wrath, and hates me;
He gnashes at me with His teeth;
My adversary sharpens His gaze on me.
10 They gape at me with their mouth,
They strike me reproachfully on the
cheek,
They gather together against me.
11 God has delivered me to the ungodly,
And turned me over to the hands of the
wicked.
12 I was at ease, but He has shattered me;
He also has taken *me* by my neck, and
shaken me to pieces;
He has set me up for His target,
13 His archers surround me.
He pierces my heart[a] and does not pity;
He pours out my gall on the ground.
14 He breaks me with wound upon
wound;
He runs at me like a warrior.[a]

15 "I have sewn sackcloth over my skin,
And laid my head[a] in the dust.
16 My face is flushed from weeping,
And on my eyelids *is* the shadow of
death;
17 Although no violence *is* in my hands,
And my prayer *is* pure.

18 "O earth, do not cover my blood,
And let my cry have no *resting* place!
19 Surely even now my witness *is* in
heaven,
And my evidence *is* on high.
20 My friends scorn me;
My eyes pour out *tears* to God.
21 Oh, that one might plead for a man with
God,
As a man *pleads* for his neighbor!
22 For when a few years are finished,
I shall go the way of no return.

Job Prays for Relief

17 "My spirit is broken,
My days are extinguished,
The grave *is ready* for me.
2 *Are* not mockers with me?
And does not my eye dwell on their
provocation?

3 "Now put down a pledge for me with
Yourself.
Who *is* he *who* will shake hands with
me?
4 For You have hidden their heart from
understanding;
Therefore You will not exalt *them.*
5 He who speaks flattery to *his*
friends,
Even the eyes of his children will fail.

6 "But He has made me a byword of the
people,
And I have become one in whose face
men spit.
7 My eye has also grown dim because of
sorrow,
And all my members *are* like shadows.
8 Upright *men* are astonished at this,
And the innocent stirs himself up against
the hypocrite.
9 Yet the righteous will hold to his way,
And he who has clean hands will be
stronger and stronger.

16:13 [a]Literally *kidneys* **16:14** [a]Vulgate reads *giant.* **16:15** [a]Literally *horn*

10 "But please, come back again, all of you,[a]
For I shall not find *one* wise *man* among you.
11 My days are past,
My purposes are broken off,
Even the thoughts of my heart.
12 They change the night into day;
'The light *is* near,' *they say,* in the face of darkness.
13 If I wait *for* the grave *as* my house,
If I make my bed in the darkness,
14 If I say to corruption, 'You *are* my father,'
And to the worm, 'You *are* my mother and my sister,'
15 Where then *is* my hope?
As for my hope, who can see it?
16 *Will* they go down to the gates of Sheol?
Shall *we have* rest together in the dust?"

Bildad: The Wicked Are Punished

18 Then Bildad the Shuhite answered and said:

2 "How long *till* you put an end to words?
Gain understanding, and afterward we will speak.
3 Why are we counted as beasts,
And regarded as stupid in your sight?
4 You who tear yourself in anger,
Shall the earth be forsaken for you?
Or shall the rock be removed from its place?

5 "The light of the wicked indeed goes out,
And the flame of his fire does not shine.
6 The light is dark in his tent,
And his lamp beside him is put out.
7 The steps of his strength are shortened,
And his own counsel casts him down.
8 For he is cast into a net by his own feet,
And he walks into a snare.
9 The net takes *him* by the heel,
And a snare lays hold of him.
10 A noose *is* hidden for him on the ground,
And a trap for him in the road.
11 Terrors frighten him on every side,
And drive him to his feet.
12 His strength is starved,
And destruction *is* ready at his side.
13 It devours patches of his skin;
The firstborn of death devours his limbs.
14 He is uprooted from the shelter of his tent,
And they parade him before the king of terrors.
15 They dwell in his tent *who are* none of his;
Brimstone is scattered on his dwelling.
16 His roots are dried out below,
And his branch withers above.
17 The memory of him perishes from the earth,
And he has no name among the renowned.[a]
18 He is driven from light into darkness,
And chased out of the world.
19 He has neither son nor posterity among his people,
Nor any remaining in his dwellings.
20 Those in the west are astonished at his day,
As those in the east are frightened.
21 Surely such *are* the dwellings of the wicked,
And this *is* the place *of him who* does not know God."

Job Trusts in His Redeemer

19 Then Job answered and said:

2 "How long will you torment my soul,
And break me in pieces with words?
3 These ten times you have reproached me;
You are not ashamed *that* you have wronged me.[a]
4 And if indeed I have erred,
My error remains with me.
5 If indeed you exalt *yourselves* against me,
And plead my disgrace against me,
6 Know then that God has wronged me,
And has surrounded me with His net.

7 "If I cry out concerning wrong, I am not heard.
If I cry aloud, *there is* no justice.
8 He has fenced up my way, so that I cannot pass;
And He has set darkness in my paths.
9 He has stripped me of my glory,

17:10 [a]Following some Hebrew manuscripts, Septuagint, Syriac, and Vulgate; Masoretic Text and Targum read *all of them.* **18:17** [a]Literally *before the outside,* meaning distinguished, famous **19:3** [a]A Jewish tradition reads *make yourselves strange to me.*

And taken the crown *from* my head.
10 He breaks me down on every side,
And I am gone;
My hope He has uprooted like a tree.
11 He has also kindled His wrath against me,
And He counts me as *one of* His enemies.
12 His troops come together
And build up their road against me;
They encamp all around my tent.

13 "He has removed my brothers far from me,
And my acquaintances are completely estranged from me.
14 My relatives have failed,
And my close friends have forgotten me.
15 Those who dwell in my house, and my maidservants,
Count me as a stranger;
I am an alien in their sight.
16 I call my servant, but he gives no answer;
I beg him with my mouth.
17 My breath is offensive to my wife,
And I am repulsive to the children of my own body.
18 Even young children despise me;
I arise, and they speak against me.
19 All my close friends abhor me,
And those whom I love have turned against me.
20 My bone clings to my skin and to my flesh,
And I have escaped by the skin of my teeth.

21 "Have pity on me, have pity on me, O you my friends,
For the hand of God has struck me!
22 Why do you persecute me as God *does*,
And are not satisfied with my flesh?

23 "Oh, that my words were written!
Oh, that they were inscribed in a book!
24 That they were engraved on a rock
With an iron pen and lead, forever!
25 For I know *that* my Redeemer lives,
And He shall stand at last on the earth;
26 And after my skin is destroyed, this *I know*,
That in my flesh I shall see God,
27 Whom I shall see for myself,
And my eyes shall behold, and not another.
How my heart yearns within me!
28 If you should say, 'How shall we persecute him?'—
Since the root of the matter is found in me,
29 Be afraid of the sword for yourselves;
For wrath *brings* the punishment of the sword,
That you may know *there is* a judgment."

Zophar's Sermon on the Wicked Man

20 Then Zophar the Naamathite answered and said:

2 "Therefore my anxious thoughts make me answer,
Because of the turmoil within me.
3 I have heard the rebuke that reproaches me,
And the spirit of my understanding causes me to answer.

4 "Do you *not* know this of old,
Since man was placed on earth,
5 That the triumphing of the wicked is short,
And the joy of the hypocrite is *but* for a moment?
6 Though his haughtiness mounts up to the heavens,
And his head reaches to the clouds,
7 *Yet* he will perish forever like his own refuse;
Those who have seen him will say, 'Where is he?'
8 He will fly away like a dream, and not be found;
Yes, he will be chased away like a vision of the night.
9 The eye *that* saw him will *see him* no more,
Nor will his place behold him anymore.
10 His children will seek the favor of the poor,
And his hands will restore his wealth.
11 His bones are full of his youthful vigor,
But it will lie down with him in the dust.

12 "Though evil is sweet in his mouth,
And he hides it under his tongue,

13 *Though* he spares it and does not forsake it,
But still keeps it in his mouth,
14 *Yet* his food in his stomach turns sour;
It becomes cobra venom within him.
15 He swallows down riches
And vomits them up again;
God casts them out of his belly.
16 He will suck the poison of cobras;
The viper's tongue will slay him.
17 He will not see the streams,
The rivers flowing with honey and cream.
18 He will restore that for which he labored,
And will not swallow *it* down;
From the proceeds of business
He will get no enjoyment.
19 For he has oppressed *and* forsaken the poor,
He has violently seized a house which he did not build.

20 "Because he knows no quietness in his heart,[a]
He will not save anything he desires.
21 Nothing is left for him to eat;
Therefore his well-being will not last.
22 In his self-sufficiency he will be in distress;
Every hand of misery will come against him.
23 *When* he is about to fill his stomach,
God will cast on him the fury of His wrath,
And will rain *it* on him while he is eating.
24 He will flee from the iron weapon;
A bronze bow will pierce him through.
25 It is drawn, and comes out of the body;
Yes, the glittering *point comes* out of his gall.
Terrors *come* upon him;
26 Total darkness *is* reserved for his treasures.
An unfanned fire will consume him;
It shall go ill with him who is left in his tent.
27 The heavens will reveal his iniquity,
And the earth will rise up against him.
28 The increase of his house will depart,
And his goods will flow away in the day of His wrath.
29 This *is* the portion from God for a wicked man,
The heritage appointed to him by God."

Job's Discourse on the Wicked

21 Then Job answered and said:

2 "Listen carefully to my speech,
And let this be your consolation.
3 Bear with me that I may speak,
And after I have spoken, keep mocking.

4 "As for me, *is* my complaint against man?
And if *it were,* why should I not be impatient?
5 Look at me and be astonished;
Put *your* hand over *your* mouth.
6 Even when I remember I am terrified,
And trembling takes hold of my flesh.
7 Why do the wicked live *and* become old,
Yes, become mighty in power?
8 Their descendants are established with them in their sight,
And their offspring before their eyes.
9 Their houses *are* safe from fear,
Neither *is* the rod of God upon them.
10 Their bull breeds without failure;
Their cow calves without miscarriage.
11 They send forth their little ones like a flock,
And their children dance.
12 They sing to the tambourine and harp,
And rejoice to the sound of the flute.
13 They spend their days in wealth,
And in a moment go down to the grave.[a]
14 Yet they say to God, 'Depart from us,
For we do not desire the knowledge of Your ways.
15 Who *is* the Almighty, that we should serve Him?
And what profit do we have if we pray to Him?'
16 Indeed their prosperity *is* not in their hand;
The counsel of the wicked is far from me.

17 "How often is the lamp of the wicked put out?
How often does their destruction come upon them,
The sorrows *God* distributes in His anger?

20:20 [a]Literally *belly* **21:13** [a]Or *Sheol*

18 They are like straw before the wind,
And like chaff that a storm carries away.
19 *They say,* 'God lays up one's[a] iniquity for his children';
Let Him recompense him, that he may know *it.*
20 Let his eyes see his destruction,
And let him drink of the wrath of the Almighty.
21 For what does he care about his household after him,
When the number of his months is cut in half?

22 "Can *anyone* teach God knowledge,
Since He judges those on high?
23 One dies in his full strength,
Being wholly at ease and secure;
24 His pails[a] are full of milk,
And the marrow of his bones is moist.
25 Another man dies in the bitterness of his soul,
Never having eaten with pleasure.
26 They lie down alike in the dust,
And worms cover them.

27 "Look, I know your thoughts,
And the schemes *with which* you would wrong me.
28 For you say,
'Where *is* the house of the prince?
And where *is* the tent,[a]
The dwelling place of the wicked?'
29 Have you not asked those who travel the road?
And do you not know their signs?
30 For the wicked are reserved for the day of doom;
They shall be brought out on the day of wrath.
31 Who condemns his way to his face?
And who repays him *for what* he has done?
32 Yet he shall be brought to the grave,
And a vigil kept over the tomb.
33 The clods of the valley shall be sweet to him;
Everyone shall follow him,
As countless *have gone* before him.
34 How then can you comfort me with empty words,
Since falsehood remains in your answers?"

Eliphaz Accuses Job of Wickedness

22 Then Eliphaz the Temanite answered and said:

2 "Can a man be profitable to God,
Though he who is wise may be profitable to himself?
3 *Is it* any pleasure to the Almighty that you are righteous?
Or *is it* gain *to Him* that you make your ways blameless?

4 "Is it because of your fear of Him that He corrects you,
And enters into judgment with you?
5 *Is* not your wickedness great,
And your iniquity without end?
6 For you have taken pledges from your brother for no reason,
And stripped the naked of their clothing.
7 You have not given the weary water to drink,
And you have withheld bread from the hungry.

21:19 [a]Literally *his* **21:24** [a]Septuagint and Vulgate read *bowels;* Syriac reads *sides;* Targum reads *breasts.* **21:28** [a]Vulgate omits *the tent.*

SOUL NOTE

Difficult Times *(21:22–26)* Job did not understand why he was suffering so terribly. He had been "blameless and upright, and one who feared God and shunned evil" (1:1). His words here reveal the depth of his pain and the bitterness rising in his heart. Fortunately, Job maintained his trust in God. How we respond to struggles defines our attitude toward God. We can become bitter, or we can press on in faith, knowing that God will not subject us to more than we can handle. We should continue to trust God, no matter what. He is faithful and will see us through any crisis. **Topic: Bitterness**

BITTERNESS

Bitterness

JONI EARECKSON TADA

(Job 21:22–26)

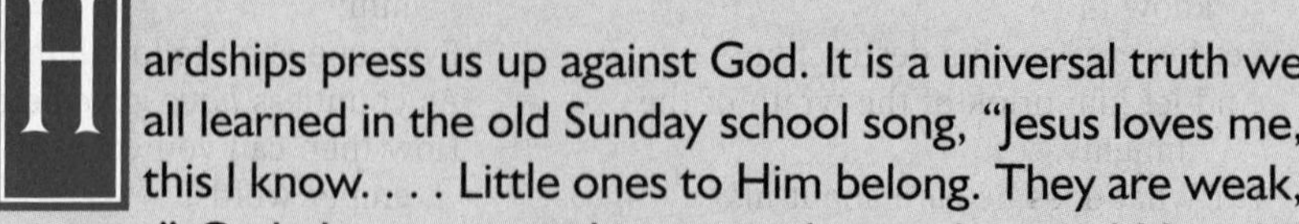

Hardships press us up against God. It is a universal truth we all learned in the old Sunday school song, "Jesus loves me, this I know. . . . Little ones to Him belong. They are weak, but He is strong." God always seems bigger to those who need Him the most; God always seems stronger to those who feel weakest; God is always most needed by those most in need. And suffering is the tool God often uses to help us need Him more.

Read Job's story. The story of his suffering, recorded in the Old Testament book of Job, is not a story about the suffering caused by torn ligaments on a football field. It is not a story of the suffering caused by a polite refusal letter for financial aid to Princeton. It is not even about the suffering of the heartache over a returned engagement ring. Instead, Job's is a story of suffering stalking a person, tearing him down, and ripping into his sanity. This is affliction spinning out of control. "Suffering like Job's would never draw me to God," we think. "It would only push me away from Him."

God Himself suffered too, however. The Son of God Himself crossed the chasm between divinity and humanity and walked onto earth. His goal was to endure the thrashing due His creatures for their rebellion against His Father, Jehovah. To this day, He requires suffering of all His followers, some of it intense—but only for their good, and never equaling what He Himself passed through.

CALLED TO SUFFER

Despite Christ's compassionate death for our sins, God's plan calls for all Christians to suffer. To encourage us, He may write some light moments into the script of our lives, but without fail, some scenes are going to break our hearts. Some of our favorite characters will die. And the movie may end earlier than we wish.

God screens the trials that come into our lives, allowing only those that accomplish His good plan. He takes no joy in human agony. These trials are not evenly distributed from person to person. This can discourage us, for we are not privy to His reasons. But in God's wisdom and love, every trial in a Christian's life is ordained from eternity past, custom-made for that believer's eternal good— even when it does not seem like it.

The core of His plan is to rescue us from our sin. Our pain, poverty, and broken hearts are not His ultimate focus. He cares about them, but they are merely symptoms of the real problem. God cares most, not about making us comfortable, but about teaching us to hate our sins, grow up spiritually, and love Him. To do this, He gives us salvation's benefits only gradually and sometimes painfully (Acts 9:16; 2 Cor. 1:5; Phil. 1:29).

FINDING CONTENTMENT

Overcoming bitterness happens when we gain contentment. This does not mean losing sorrow or saying good-bye to discomfort. Contentment means sacrificing itchy cravings to gain a settled soul. We give up one thing for another. It is hard. Hard, but sweet. We are "sorrowful, yet always rejoicing" (2 Cor. 6:10).

When it comes to contentment, God must be our aim. Whether it is wayward thought, bad-mouthing our circumstances, or comparing ourselves with others whose lives are easier, the battle involves more than eschewing evil; it involves pursuing God. Overcoming bitterness only happens when we are overcome with God.

I was driving at night recently in my handicap-equipped van when everything went dead: the engine, the lights, the brakes, and the steering. It was a very close call! My vulnerability shook me for a moment. I've always leaned hard on God's protection for the "helpless," but in my most helpless moment, my confidence was shaken.

I learned that fear and disappointment are real. They turn our focus away from God and onto ourselves. We question His love and concern for us and quickly plunge into bitterness and despair. The beginning of our Christian life may have been exhilarating. Spiritual adrenaline was pumped up. But now, we feel bitter, confused, and even angry. God has not failed us, however. We have just missed the lesson He has for us. Our life is a straight line to heaven. We need not be sidetracked by a few bumps in the road.

WHEN GOD SAYS "NO"

I remember those first terrible nights—paralyzed on a Stryker frame in the geriatric ward of a state institution. Scared, bitter, confused. A friend read the story of Jesus healing the lame man at the pool of Bethesda in John 5. "Oh, God, will you please heal me?" I whispered, crying in the night.

It was more than thirty years later when I visited the Pool of Bethesda for the first time. I looked at the ruins of the five colonnades and the steps leading down to the water. I look around in my mind's eye and see hundreds of paralyzed people. Tears well up in my eyes. Jesus answered my prayer—He said, "No."

And I'm glad. A "no" answer has driven a lot of sin from my life, strengthened my commitment to Christ, and forced me to depend on His grace. It has stretched my hope, increased my faith, and strengthened my character. Now, I can thank Him—for the wiser choice, the better answer, the richer path. That's how we overcome bitterness. We focus on Him and let healing happen on the inside.

FURTHER MEDITATION:

Other passages to study about the issue of bitterness include:

- Genesis 27:41
- Esther 5:9
- Proverbs 14:10
- Ecclesiastes 7:9
- Matthew 6:14, 15
- Acts 8:23
- Ephesians 4:26, 31, 32
- James 3:14

To Learn More: Turn to the key passage note about bitterness at Hebrews 12:12–29 on page 1637. See also the personality profile of Saul on page 370.

8 But the mighty man possessed the land,
And the honorable man dwelt in it.
9 You have sent widows away empty,
And the strength of the fatherless was crushed.
10 Therefore snares *are* all around you,
And sudden fear troubles you,
11 Or darkness *so that* you cannot see;
And an abundance of water covers you.

12 "Is not God in the height of heaven?
And see the highest stars, how lofty they are!
13 And you say, 'What does God know?
Can He judge through the deep darkness?
14 Thick clouds cover Him, so that He cannot see,
And He walks above the circle of heaven.'
15 Will you keep to the old way
Which wicked men have trod,
16 Who were cut down before their time,
Whose foundations were swept away by a flood?
17 They said to God, 'Depart from us!
What can the Almighty do to them?'[a]
18 Yet He filled their houses with good *things;*
But the counsel of the wicked is far from me.

19 "The righteous see *it* and are glad,
And the innocent laugh at them:
20 'Surely our adversaries[a] are cut down,
And the fire consumes their remnant.'

21 "Now acquaint yourself with Him, and be at peace;
Thereby good will come to you.
22 Receive, please, instruction from His mouth,
And lay up His words in your heart.
23 If you return to the Almighty, you will be built up;
You will remove iniquity far from your tents.
24 Then you will lay your gold in the dust,
And the *gold* of Ophir among the stones of the brooks.
25 Yes, the Almighty will be your gold[a]
And your precious silver;
26 For then you will have your delight in the Almighty,
And lift up your face to God.
27 You will make your prayer to Him,
He will hear you,
And you will pay your vows.
28 You will also declare a thing,
And it will be established for you;
So light will shine on your ways.
29 When they cast *you* down, and you say,
'Exaltation *will come!*'
Then He will save the humble *person.*
30 He will *even* deliver one who is not innocent;
Yes, he will be delivered by the purity of your hands."

> "Now acquaint yourself with Him, and be at peace; thereby good will come to you."
> JOB 22:21

JOB PROCLAIMS GOD'S RIGHTEOUS JUDGMENTS

23 Then Job answered and said:

2 "Even today my complaint is bitter;
My[a] hand is listless because of my groaning.
3 Oh, that I knew where I might find Him,
That I might come to His seat!
4 I would present *my* case before Him,
And fill my mouth with arguments.
5 I would know the words *which* He would answer me,
And understand what He would say to me.
6 Would He contend with me in His great power?
No! But He would take *note* of me.
7 There the upright could reason with Him,
And I would be delivered forever from my Judge.

22:17 [a]Septuagint and Syriac read *us.* **22:20** [a]Septuagint reads *substance.* **22:25** [a]The ancient versions suggest *defense;* Hebrew reads *gold* as in verse 24. **23:2** [a]Following Masoretic Text, Targum, and Vulgate; Septuagint and Syriac read *His.*

8 "Look, I go forward, but He is not *there,*
And backward, but I cannot perceive
Him;
9 When He works on the left hand, I
cannot behold *Him;*
When He turns to the right hand, I
cannot see *Him.*
10 But He knows the way that I take;
When He has tested me, I shall come
forth as gold.
11 My foot has held fast to His steps;
I have kept His way and not turned aside.
12 I have not departed from the
commandment of His lips;
I have treasured the words of His mouth
More than my necessary *food.*

13 "But He *is* unique, and who can make
Him change?
And *whatever* His soul desires, *that* He
does.
14 For He performs *what is* appointed for
me,
And many such *things are* with Him.
15 Therefore I am terrified at His presence;
When I consider *this,* I am afraid of Him.
16 For God made my heart weak,
And the Almighty terrifies me;
17 Because I was not cut off from the
presence of darkness,
And He did *not* hide deep darkness from
my face.

Job Complains of Violence on the Earth

24 "*Since* times are not hidden from the
Almighty,
Why do those who know Him see not
His days?

2 "*Some* remove landmarks;
They seize flocks violently and feed *on
them;*
3 They drive away the donkey of the
fatherless;
They take the widow's ox as a pledge.
4 They push the needy off the road;
All the poor of the land are forced to
hide.
5 Indeed, *like* wild donkeys in the desert,
They go out to their work, searching for
food.
The wilderness *yields* food for them *and*
for *their* children.
6 They gather their fodder in the field
And glean in the vineyard of the wicked.
7 They spend the night naked, without
clothing,
And have no covering in the cold.
8 They are wet with the showers of the
mountains,
And huddle around the rock for want of
shelter.

9 "*Some* snatch the fatherless from the
breast,
And take a pledge from the poor.
10 They cause *the poor* to go naked,
without clothing;
And they take away the sheaves from
the hungry.
11 They press out oil within their walls,
And tread winepresses, yet suffer
thirst.
12 The dying groan in the city,
And the souls of the wounded cry out;
Yet God does not charge *them* with
wrong.

13 "There are those who rebel against the
light;
They do not know its ways
Nor abide in its paths.
14 The murderer rises with the light;
He kills the poor and needy;

SOUL NOTE

Gaining Understanding *(23:13–17)* Job admitted that he was afraid of God because God had allowed such darkness into his life (23:16). God is not the author of evil, but He may, at times, allow the press of evil into our lives. God is sovereign, so nothing happens without His consent. In times of suffering, our emotions roll and we struggle with God. But that's when we can begin to understand God's power, sovereignty, and love. Faith forged in the crucible of suffering comes through refined and strengthened. **Topic: Emotional Life**

And in the night he is like a thief.
15 The eye of the adulterer waits for the twilight,
Saying, 'No eye will see me';
And he disguises *his* face.
16 In the dark they break into houses
Which they marked for themselves in the daytime;
They do not know the light.
17 For the morning is the same to them as the shadow of death;
If *someone* recognizes *them,*
They are in the terrors of the shadow of death.

18 "They *should be* swift on the face of the waters,
Their portion *should be* cursed in the earth,
So that no *one would* turn into the way of their vineyards.
19 As drought and heat consume the snow waters,
So the grave[a] *consumes those who* have sinned.
20 The womb *should* forget him,
The worm *should* feed sweetly on him;
He *should* be remembered no more,
And wickedness *should* be broken like a tree.
21 For he preys on the barren *who* do not bear,
And does no good for the widow.

22 "But *God* draws the mighty away with His power;
He rises up, but no *man* is sure of life.
23 He gives them security, and they rely *on it;*
Yet His eyes *are* on their ways.
24 They are exalted for a little while,
Then they are gone.
They are brought low;
They are taken out of the way like all *others;*
They dry out like the heads of grain.

25 "Now if *it is* not *so,* who will prove me a liar,
And make my speech worth nothing?"

Bildad: How Can Man Be Righteous?

25 Then Bildad the Shuhite answered and said:

2 "Dominion and fear *belong* to Him;
He makes peace in His high places.
3 Is there any number to His armies?
Upon whom does His light not rise?
4 How then can man be righteous before God?
Or how can he be pure *who is* born of a woman?
5 If even the moon does not shine,
And the stars are not pure in His sight,
6 How much less man, *who is* a maggot,
And a son of man, *who is* a worm?"

Job: Man's Frailty and God's Majesty

26 But Job answered and said:

2 "How have you helped *him who is* without power?
How have you saved the arm *that has* no strength?
3 How have you counseled *one who has* no wisdom?
And *how* have you declared sound advice to many?
4 To whom have you uttered words?
And whose spirit came from you?

5 "The dead tremble,
Those under the waters and those inhabiting them.
6 Sheol *is* naked before Him,
And Destruction has no covering.
7 He stretches out the north over empty space;
He hangs the earth on nothing.
8 He binds up the water in His thick clouds,
Yet the clouds are not broken under it.
9 He covers the face of *His* throne,
And spreads His cloud over it.
10 He drew a circular horizon on the face of the waters,
At the boundary of light and darkness.
11 The pillars of heaven tremble,
And are astonished at His rebuke.
12 He stirs up the sea with His power,
And by His understanding He breaks up the storm.
13 By His Spirit He adorned the heavens;
His hand pierced the fleeing serpent.
14 Indeed these *are* the mere edges of His ways,

24:19 [a]Or *Sheol*

And how small a whisper we hear of
Him!
But the thunder of His power who can
understand?"

Job Maintains His Integrity

27 Moreover Job continued his discourse,
and said:

2 "*As* God lives, *who* has taken away my
justice,
And the Almighty, *who* has made my
soul bitter,
3 As long as my breath *is* in me,
And the breath of God in my nostrils,
4 My lips will not speak wickedness,
Nor my tongue utter deceit.
5 Far be it from me
That I should say you are right;
Till I die I will not put away my integrity
from me.
6 My righteousness I hold fast, and will
not let it go;
My heart shall not reproach *me* as long
as I live.

7 "May my enemy be like the wicked,
And he who rises up against me like the
unrighteous.
8 For what is the hope of the hypocrite,
Though he may gain *much,*
If God takes away his life?
9 Will God hear his cry
When trouble comes upon him?
10 Will he delight himself in the Almighty?
Will he always call on God?

11 "I will teach you about the hand of God;
What *is* with the Almighty I will not
conceal.
12 Surely all of you have seen *it;*
Why then do you behave with complete
nonsense?

13 "This is the portion of a wicked man with
God,
And the heritage of oppressors, received
from the Almighty:
14 If his children are multiplied, *it is* for the
sword;
And his offspring shall not be satisfied
with bread.
15 Those who survive him shall be buried
in death,
And their[a] widows shall not weep,
16 Though he heaps up silver like dust,
And piles up clothing like clay—
17 He may pile *it* up, but the just will wear
it,
And the innocent will divide the silver.
18 He builds his house like a moth,[a]
Like a booth *which* a watchman makes.
19 The rich man will lie down,
But not be gathered *up;*[a]
He opens his eyes,
And he *is* no more.
20 Terrors overtake him like a flood;
A tempest steals him away in the night.
21 The east wind carries him away, and he
is gone;
It sweeps him out of his place.
22 It hurls against him and does not spare;
He flees desperately from its power.
23 *Men* shall clap their hands at him,
And shall hiss him out of his place.

Job's Discourse on Wisdom

28 "Surely there is a mine for silver,
And a place *where* gold is refined.
2 Iron is taken from the earth,
And copper *is* smelted *from* ore.
3 *Man* puts an end to darkness,
And searches every recess
For ore in the darkness and the shadow
of death.
4 He breaks open a shaft away from
people;
In places forgotten by feet
They hang far away from men;
They swing to and fro.
5 *As for* the earth, from it comes bread,
But underneath it is turned up as by fire;
6 Its stones *are* the source of sapphires,
And it contains gold dust.
7 *That* path no bird knows,
Nor has the falcon's eye seen it.
8 The proud lions[a] have not trodden it,
Nor has the fierce lion passed over it.
9 He puts his hand on the flint;
He overturns the mountains at the roots.

27:15 [a]Literally *his* **27:18** [a]Following Masoretic Text and Vulgate; Septuagint and Syriac read *spider* (compare 8:14); Targum reads *decay.*
27:19 [a]Following Masoretic Text and Targum; Septuagint and Syriac read *But shall not add* (that is, do it again); Vulgate reads *But take away nothing.*
28:8 [a]Literally *sons of pride,* figurative of the great lions

10 He cuts out channels in the rocks,
And his eye sees every precious thing.
11 He dams up the streams from trickling;
What is hidden he brings forth to light.

12 "But where can wisdom be found?
And where *is* the place of understanding?
13 Man does not know its value,
Nor is it found in the land of the living.
14 The deep says, '*It is* not in me';
And the sea says, '*It is* not with me.'
15 It cannot be purchased for gold,
Nor can silver be weighed *for* its price.
16 It cannot be valued in the gold of Ophir,
In precious onyx or sapphire.
17 Neither gold nor crystal can equal it,
Nor can it be exchanged for jewelry of fine gold.
18 No mention shall be made of coral or quartz,
For the price of wisdom *is* above rubies.
19 The topaz of Ethiopia cannot equal it,
Nor can it be valued in pure gold.

20 "From where then does wisdom come?
And where *is* the place of understanding?
21 It is hidden from the eyes of all living,
And concealed from the birds of the air.
22 Destruction and Death say,
'We have heard a report about it with our ears.'
23 God understands its way,
And He knows its place.
24 For He looks to the ends of the earth,
And sees under the whole heavens,
25 To establish a weight for the wind,
And apportion the waters by measure.
26 When He made a law for the rain,
And a path for the thunderbolt,
27 Then He saw *wisdom*[a] and declared it;
He prepared it, indeed, He searched it out.
28 And to man He said,
'Behold, the fear of the Lord, that *is* wisdom,
And to depart from evil *is* understanding.' "

JOB'S SUMMARY DEFENSE

29 Job further continued his discourse, and said:

2 "Oh, that I were as *in* months past,
As *in* the days *when* God watched over me;
3 When His lamp shone upon my head,
And when by His light I walked *through* darkness;
4 Just as I was in the days of my prime,
When the friendly counsel of God *was* over my tent;
5 When the Almighty *was* yet with me,
When my children *were* around me;
6 When my steps were bathed with cream,[a]
And the rock poured out rivers of oil for me!

7 "When I went out to the gate by the city,
When I took my seat in the open square,
8 The young men saw me and hid,
And the aged arose *and* stood;
9 The princes refrained from talking,
And put *their* hand on their mouth;
10 The voice of nobles was hushed,
And their tongue stuck to the roof of their mouth.
11 When the ear heard, then it blessed me,
And when the eye saw, then it approved me;
12 Because I delivered the poor who cried out,
The fatherless and *the one who* had no helper.
13 The blessing of a perishing *man* came upon me,
And I caused the widow's heart to sing for joy.
14 I put on righteousness, and it clothed me;
My justice *was* like a robe and a turban.
15 I *was* eyes to the blind,
And I *was* feet to the lame.
16 I *was* a father to the poor,
And I searched out the case *that* I did not know.
17 I broke the fangs of the wicked,
And plucked the victim from his teeth.

18 "Then I said, 'I shall die in my nest,
And multiply *my* days as the sand.
19 My root *is* spread out to the waters,

28:27 [a]Literally *it* **29:6** [a]Masoretic Text reads *wrath;* ancient versions and some Hebrew manuscripts read *cream* (compare 20:17).

And the dew lies all night on my branch.
20 My glory *is* fresh within me,
And my bow is renewed in my hand.'

21 "*Men* listened to me and waited,
And kept silence for my counsel.
22 After my words they did not speak again,
And my speech settled on them *as dew.*
23 They waited for me *as* for the rain,
And they opened their mouth wide *as* for the spring rain.
24 *If* I mocked at them, they did not believe *it,*
And the light of my countenance they did not cast down.
25 I chose the way for them, and sat as chief;
So I dwelt as a king in the army,
As one *who* comforts mourners.

30 "But now they mock at me, *men* younger than I,
Whose fathers I disdained to put with the dogs of my flock.
2 Indeed, what *profit* is the strength of their hands to me?
Their vigor has perished.
3 *They are* gaunt from want and famine,
Fleeing late to the wilderness, desolate and waste,
4 Who pluck mallow by the bushes,
And broom tree roots *for* their food.
5 They were driven out from among *men,*
They shouted at them as *at* a thief.
6 *They had* to live in the clefts of the valleys,
In caves of the earth and the rocks.
7 Among the bushes they brayed,
Under the nettles they nestled.
8 *They were* sons of fools,
Yes, sons of vile men;
They were scourged from the land.

9 "And now I am their taunting song;
Yes, I am their byword.
10 They abhor me, they keep far from me;
They do not hesitate to spit in my face.
11 Because He has loosed my[a] bowstring and afflicted me,
They have cast off restraint before me.
12 At *my* right *hand* the rabble arises;
They push away my feet,
And they raise against me their ways of destruction.
13 They break up my path,
They promote my calamity;
They have no helper.
14 They come as broad breakers;
Under the ruinous storm they roll along.
15 Terrors are turned upon me;
They pursue my honor as the wind,
And my prosperity has passed like a cloud.

16 "And now my soul is poured out because of my *plight;*
The days of affliction take hold of me.
17 My bones are pierced in me at night,
And my gnawing pains take no rest.
18 By great force my garment is disfigured;
It binds me about as the collar of my coat.
19 He has cast me into the mire,
And I have become like dust and ashes.

20 "I cry out to You, but You do not answer me;
I stand up, and You regard me.
21 *But* You have become cruel to me;
With the strength of Your hand You oppose me.
22 You lift me up to the wind and cause me to ride *on it;*
You spoil my success.
23 For I know *that* You will bring me *to* death,
And *to* the house appointed for all living.

24 "Surely He would not stretch out *His* hand against a heap of ruins,
If they cry out when He destroys *it.*
25 Have I not wept for him who was in trouble?
Has *not* my soul grieved for the poor?
26 But when I looked for good, evil came *to me;*
And when I waited for light, then came darkness.
27 My heart is in turmoil and cannot rest;
Days of affliction confront me.
28 I go about mourning, but not in the sun;
I stand up in the assembly *and* cry out for help.
29 I am a brother of jackals,

30:11 [a]Following Masoretic Text, Syriac, and Targum; Septuagint and Vulgate read *His.*

And a companion of ostriches.
30 My skin grows black and falls from me;
My bones burn with fever.
31 My harp is *turned* to mourning,
And my flute to the voice of those who weep.

31 "I have made a covenant with my eyes;
Why then should I look upon a young woman?
2 For what *is* the allotment of God from above,
And the inheritance of the Almighty from on high?
3 *Is* it not destruction for the wicked,
And disaster for the workers of iniquity?
4 Does He not see my ways,
And count all my steps?

5 "If I have walked with falsehood,
Or if my foot has hastened to deceit,
6 Let me be weighed on honest scales,
That God may know my integrity.
7 If my step has turned from the way,
Or my heart walked after my eyes,
Or if any spot adheres to my hands,
8 *Then* let me sow, and another eat;
Yes, let my harvest be rooted out.

9 "If my heart has been enticed by a woman,
Or *if* I have lurked at my neighbor's door,
10 *Then* let my wife grind for another,
And let others bow down over her.
11 For that *would be* wickedness;
Yes, it *would be* iniquity *deserving of* judgment.
12 For that *would be* a fire *that* consumes to destruction,
And would root out all my increase.

13 "If I have despised the cause of my male or female servant
When they complained against me,
14 What then shall I do when God rises up?
When He punishes, how shall I answer Him?
15 Did not He who made me in the womb make them?
Did not the same One fashion us in the womb?

16 "If I have kept the poor from *their* desire,
Or caused the eyes of the widow to fail,
17 Or eaten my morsel by myself,
So that the fatherless could not eat of it
18 (But from my youth I reared him as a father,
And from my mother's womb I guided *the widow*[a]);
19 If I have seen anyone perish for lack of clothing,
Or any poor *man* without covering;
20 If his heart[a] has not blessed me,
And *if* he was *not* warmed with the fleece of my sheep;
21 If I have raised my hand against the fatherless,
When I saw I had help in the gate;
22 *Then* let my arm fall from my shoulder,
Let my arm be torn from the socket.
23 For destruction *from* God *is* a terror to me,
And because of His magnificence I cannot endure.

24 "If I have made gold my hope,
Or said to fine gold, '*You are* my confidence';
25 If I have rejoiced because my wealth *was* great,
And because my hand had gained much;
26 If I have observed the sun[a] when it shines,
Or the moon moving *in* brightness,
27 So that my heart has been secretly enticed,
And my mouth has kissed my hand;
28 This also *would be* an iniquity *deserving of* judgment,
For I would have denied God *who is* above.

29 "If I have rejoiced at the destruction of him who hated me,
Or lifted myself up when evil found him
30 (Indeed I have not allowed my mouth to sin
By asking for a curse on his soul);
31 If the men of my tent have not said,
'Who is there that has not been satisfied with his meat?'

31:18 [a]Literally *her* (compare verse 16)
31:20 [a]Literally *loins* **31:26** [a]Literally *light*

32 (*But* no sojourner had to lodge in the
street,
For I have opened my doors to the
traveler[a]);
33 If I have covered my transgressions as
Adam,
By hiding my iniquity in my bosom,
34 Because I feared the great multitude,
And dreaded the contempt of families,
So that I kept silence
And did not go out of the door—
35 Oh, that I had one to hear me!
Here is my mark.
Oh, that the Almighty would answer me,
That my Prosecutor had written a
book!
36 Surely I would carry it on my shoulder,
And bind it on me *like* a crown;
37 I would declare to Him the number of
my steps;
Like a prince I would approach Him.

38 "If my land cries out against me,
And its furrows weep together;
39 If I have eaten its fruit[a] without money,
Or caused its owners to lose their lives;
40 *Then* let thistles grow instead of wheat,
And weeds instead of barley."

The words of Job are ended.

Elihu Contradicts Job's Friends

32 So these three men ceased answering
Job, because he *was* righteous in his
own eyes. 2Then the wrath of Elihu, the son of
Barachel the Buzite, of the family of Ram, was
aroused against Job; his wrath was aroused
because he justified himself rather than God.
3Also against his three friends his wrath was
aroused, because they had found no answer,
and *yet* had condemned Job.
4Now because they *were* years older than
he, Elihu had waited to speak to Job.[a] 5When
Elihu saw that *there was* no answer in the
mouth of these three men, his wrath was
aroused.
6So Elihu, the son of Barachel the Buzite,
answered and said:

"I *am* young in years, and you *are* very
old;
Therefore I was afraid,
And dared not declare my opinion to
you.
7 I said, 'Age[a] should speak,
And multitude of years should teach
wisdom.'
8 But *there is* a spirit in man,
And the breath of the Almighty gives
him understanding.
9 Great men[a] are not *always* wise,
Nor do the aged *always* understand
justice.

10 "Therefore I say, 'Listen to me,
I also will declare my opinion.'
11 Indeed I waited for your words,
I listened to your reasonings, while you
searched out what to say.
12 I paid close attention to you;
And surely not one of you convinced
Job,
Or answered his words—
13 Lest you say,
'We have found wisdom';
God will vanquish him, not man.
14 Now he has not directed *his* words
against me;
So I will not answer him with your
words.

15 "They are dismayed and answer no more;
Words escape them.
16 And I have waited, because they did not
speak,
Because they stood still *and* answered
no more.
17 I also will answer my part,
I too will declare my opinion.
18 For I am full of words;
The spirit within me compels me.
19 Indeed my belly *is* like wine *that* has no
vent;
It is ready to burst like new wineskins.
20 I will speak, that I may find relief;
I must open my lips and answer.
21 Let me not, I pray, show partiality to
anyone;
Nor let me flatter any man.
22 For I do not know how to flatter,
Else my Maker would soon take me
away.

31:32 [a]Following Septuagint, Syriac, Targum, and Vulgate; Masoretic Text reads *road.*
31:39 [a]Literally *its strength* **32:4** [a]Vulgate reads *till Job had spoken.* **32:7** [a]Literally *Days,* that is, years **32:9** [a]Or *Men of many years*

ELIHU CONTRADICTS JOB

33 "But please, Job, hear my speech,
And listen to all my words.
2 Now, I open my mouth;
My tongue speaks in my mouth.
3 My words *come* from my upright heart;
My lips utter pure knowledge.
4 The Spirit of God has made me,
And the breath of the Almighty gives me life.
5 If you can answer me,
Set *your words* in order before me;
Take your stand.
6 Truly I *am* as your spokesman[a] before God;
I also have been formed out of clay.
7 Surely no fear of me will terrify you,
Nor will my hand be heavy on you.

8 "Surely you have spoken in my hearing,
And I have heard the sound of *your* words, *saying,*
9 'I *am* pure, without transgression;
I *am* innocent, and *there is* no iniquity in me.
10 Yet He finds occasions against me,
He counts me as His enemy;
11 He puts my feet in the stocks,
He watches all my paths.'

12 "Look, *in* this you are not righteous.
I will answer you,
For God is greater than man.
13 Why do you contend with Him?
For He does not give an accounting of any of His words.
14 For God may speak in one way, or in another,
Yet man does not perceive it.
15 In a dream, in a vision of the night,
When deep sleep falls upon men,
While slumbering on their beds,
16 Then He opens the ears of men,
And seals their instruction.
17 In order to turn man *from his* deed,
And conceal pride from man,
18 He keeps back his soul from the Pit,
And his life from perishing by the sword.

"The Spirit of God has made me, and the breath of the Almighty gives me life."
JOB 33:4

19 "*Man* is also chastened with pain on his bed,
And with strong *pain* in many of his bones,
20 So that his life abhors bread,
And his soul succulent food.
21 His flesh wastes away from sight,
And his bones stick out *which once* were not seen.
22 Yes, his soul draws near the Pit,
And his life to the executioners.

23 "If there is a messenger for him,
A mediator, one among a thousand,
To show man His uprightness,
24 Then He is gracious to him, and says,
'Deliver him from going down to the Pit;
I have found a ransom';
25 His flesh shall be young like a child's,
He shall return to the days of his youth.
26 He shall pray to God, and He will delight in him,
He shall see His face with joy,
For He restores to man His righteousness.
27 Then he looks at men and says,
'I have sinned, and perverted *what was* right,
And it did not profit me.'
28 He will redeem his[a] soul from going down to the Pit,
And his[b] life shall see the light.

29 "Behold, God works all these *things,*
Twice, *in fact,* three *times* with a man,
30 To bring back his soul from the Pit,
That he may be enlightened with the light of life.

31 "Give ear, Job, listen to me;
Hold your peace, and I will speak.
32 If you have anything to say, answer me;
Speak, for I desire to justify you.
33 If not, listen to me;
Hold your peace, and I will teach you wisdom."

33:6 [a]Literally *as your mouth* **33:28** [a]Or *my* (Kethib) [b]Or *my* (Kethib)

Elihu Proclaims God's Justice

34 Elihu further answered and said:

2 "Hear my words, you wise *men;*
Give ear to me, you who have
knowledge.
3 For the ear tests words
As the palate tastes food.
4 Let us choose justice for ourselves;
Let us know among ourselves what *is*
good.

5 "For Job has said, 'I am righteous,
But God has taken away my justice;
6 Should I lie concerning my right?
My wound *is* incurable, *though I am*
without transgression.'
7 What man *is* like Job,
Who drinks scorn like water,
8 Who goes in company with the workers
of iniquity,
And walks with wicked men?
9 For he has said, 'It profits a man nothing
That he should delight in God.'

10 "Therefore listen to me, you men of
understanding:
Far be it from God *to do* wickedness,
And *from* the Almighty to *commit*
iniquity.
11 For He repays man
according to his
work,
And makes man to
find a reward
according to *his*
way.
12 Surely God will
never do wickedly,
Nor will the Almighty pervert justice.
13 Who gave Him charge over the earth?
Or who appointed *Him over* the whole
world?
14 If He should set His heart on it,
If He should gather to Himself His Spirit
and His breath,
15 All flesh would perish together,
And man would return to dust.

16 "If *you have* understanding, hear this;
Listen to the sound of my words:
17 Should one who hates justice govern?
Will you condemn *Him who is* most
just?
18 *Is it fitting* to say to a king, '*You are*
worthless,'
And to nobles, '*You are* wicked'?
19 Yet He is not partial to princes,
Nor does He regard the rich more than
the poor;
For they *are* all the work of His hands.
20 In a moment they die, in the middle of
the night;
The people are shaken and pass away;
The mighty are taken away without a
hand.

21 "For His eyes *are* on the ways of man,
And He sees all his steps.
22 There is no darkness nor shadow of
death
Where the workers of iniquity may hide
themselves.
23 For He need not further consider a man,
That he should go before God in
judgment.
24 He breaks in pieces mighty men without
inquiry,
And sets others in their place.
25 Therefore He knows their works;
He overthrows *them* in the night,
And they are crushed.
26 He strikes them as wicked *men*
In the open sight of others,
27 Because they
turned back
from Him,
And would not
consider any of
His ways,
28 So that they
caused the cry
of the poor to
come to Him;
For He hears the cry of the afflicted.
29 When He gives quietness, who then can
make trouble?
And when He hides *His* face, who then
can see Him,
Whether *it is* against a nation or a man
alone?—
30 That the hypocrite should not reign,
Lest the people be ensnared.

31 "For has *anyone* said to God,
'I have borne *chastening;*
I will offend no more;
32 Teach me *what* I do not see;

> "For He repays man according to his work, and makes man to find a reward according to his way."
> JOB 34:11

If I have done iniquity, I will do no more'?
33 Should He repay *it* according to your *terms*,
Just because you disavow it?
You must choose, and not I;
Therefore speak what you know.

34 "Men of understanding say to me,
Wise men who listen to me:
35 'Job speaks without knowledge,
His words *are* without wisdom.'
36 Oh, that Job were tried to the utmost,
Because *his* answers *are like* those of wicked men!
37 For he adds rebellion to his sin;
He claps *his hands* among us,
And multiplies his words against God."

Elihu Condemns Self-Righteousness

35 Moreover Elihu answered and said:

2 "Do you think this is right?
Do you say,
'My righteousness is more than God's'?
3 For you say,
'What advantage will it be to You?
What profit shall I have, more than *if* I had sinned?'

4 "I will answer you,
And your companions with you.
5 Look to the heavens and see;
And behold the clouds—
They are higher than you.
6 If you sin, what do you accomplish against Him?
Or, *if* your transgressions are multiplied, what do you do to Him?
7 If you are righteous, what do you give Him?
Or what does He receive from your hand?
8 Your wickedness affects a man such as you,
And your righteousness a son of man.

9 "Because of the multitude of oppressions they cry out;
They cry out for help because of the arm of the mighty.
10 But no one says, 'Where *is* God my Maker,
Who gives songs in the night,
11 Who teaches us more than the beasts of the earth,
And makes us wiser than the birds of heaven?'
12 There they cry out, but He does not answer,
Because of the pride of evil men.
13 Surely God will not listen to empty *talk*,
Nor will the Almighty regard it.
14 Although you say you do not see Him,
Yet justice *is* before Him, and you must wait for Him.
15 And now, because He has not punished in His anger,
Nor taken much notice of folly,
16 Therefore Job opens his mouth in vain;
He multiplies words without knowledge."

Elihu Proclaims God's Goodness

36 Elihu also proceeded and said:

2 "Bear with me a little, and I will show you
That *there are* yet words to speak on God's behalf.
3 I will fetch my knowledge from afar;
I will ascribe righteousness to my Maker.
4 For truly my words *are* not false;
One who is perfect in knowledge *is* with you.

5 "Behold, God *is* mighty, but despises *no one;*
He is mighty in strength of understanding.
6 He does not preserve the life of the wicked,
But gives justice to the oppressed.
7 He does not withdraw His eyes from the righteous;
But *they are* on the throne with kings,
For He has seated them forever,
And they are exalted.
8 And if *they are* bound in fetters,
Held in the cords of affliction,
9 Then He tells them their work and their transgressions—
That they have acted defiantly.
10 He also opens their ear to instruction,
And commands that they turn from iniquity.
11 If they obey and serve *Him*,
They shall spend their days in prosperity,

And their years in pleasures.
12 But if they do not obey,
They shall perish by the sword,
And they shall die without knowledge.[a]

13 "But the hypocrites in heart store up
wrath;
They do not cry for help when He binds
them.
14 They die in youth,
And their life *ends*
among the
perverted
persons.[a]
15 He delivers the
poor in their
affliction,
And opens their
ears in oppression.

16 "Indeed He would have brought you out
of dire distress,
Into a broad place where *there is* no
restraint;
And what is set on your table *would be*
full of richness.
17 But you are filled with the judgment due
the wicked;
Judgment and justice take hold *of*
you.
18 Because *there is* wrath, *beware* lest He
take you away with *one* blow;
For a large ransom would not help you
avoid *it.*
19 Will your riches,
Or all the mighty forces,
Keep you from distress?
20 Do not desire the night,
When people are cut off in their place.
21 Take heed, do not turn to iniquity,
For you have chosen this rather than
affliction.

22 "Behold, God is exalted by His power;
Who teaches like Him?
23 Who has assigned Him His way,
Or who has said, 'You have done
wrong'?

Elihu Proclaims God's Majesty

24 "Remember to magnify His work,
Of which men have sung.
25 Everyone has seen it;
Man looks on *it* from afar.

26 "Behold, God *is* great, and we do not
know *Him;*
Nor can the number of His years *be*
discovered.
27 For He draws up drops of water,
Which distill as rain from the mist,
28 Which the clouds drop down
And pour abundantly on man.
29 Indeed, can *anyone* understand the
spreading of clouds,
The thunder from
His canopy?
30 Look, He scatters
His light upon
it,
And covers the
depths of the
sea.
31 For by these He judges the peoples;
He gives food in abundance.
32 He covers *His* hands with lightning,
And commands it to strike.
33 His thunder declares it,
The cattle also, concerning the rising
storm.

> "Behold, God is great, and we do not know Him; nor can the number of His years be discovered."
>
> JOB 36:26

37 "At this also my heart trembles,
And leaps from its place.
2 Hear attentively the thunder of His
voice,
And the rumbling *that* comes from His
mouth.
3 He sends it forth under the whole
heaven,
His lightning to the ends of the earth.
4 After it a voice roars;
He thunders with His majestic voice,
And He does not restrain them when His
voice is heard.
5 God thunders marvelously with His
voice;
He does great things which we cannot
comprehend.
6 For He says to the snow, 'Fall *on* the
earth';
Likewise to the gentle rain and the
heavy rain of His strength.
7 He seals the hand of every man,
That all men may know His work.

36:12 [a]Masoretic Text reads *as one without knowledge.* **36:14** [a]Hebrew *qedeshim,* that is, those practicing sodomy and prostitution in religious rituals

8 The beasts go into dens,
And remain in their lairs.
9 From the chamber *of the south* comes
the whirlwind,
And cold from the scattering winds *of*
the north.
10 By the breath of God ice is given,
And the broad waters are frozen.
11 Also with moisture He saturates the
thick clouds;
He scatters His bright clouds.
12 And they swirl about, being turned by
His guidance,
That they may do whatever He
commands them
On the face of the whole earth.[a]
13 He causes it to come,
Whether for correction,
Or for His land,
Or for mercy.

14 "Listen to this, O Job;
Stand still and consider the wondrous
works of God.
15 Do you know
when God
dispatches
them,
And causes the
light of His
cloud to shine?
16 Do you know how the clouds are
balanced,
Those wondrous works of Him who is
perfect in knowledge?
17 Why *are* your garments hot,
When He quiets the earth by the south
wind?
18 With Him, have you spread out the
skies,
Strong as a cast metal mirror?

19 "Teach us what we should say to Him,
For we can prepare nothing because of
the darkness.
20 Should He be told that I *wish to* speak?
If a man were to speak, surely he would
be swallowed up.
21 Even now *men* cannot look at the light
when it is bright in the skies,
When the wind has passed and cleared
them.
22 He comes from the north *as* golden
splendor;
With God *is* awesome majesty.
23 *As for* the Almighty, we cannot find
Him;
He is excellent in power,
In judgment and abundant justice;
He does not oppress.
24 Therefore men fear Him;
He shows no partiality to any *who are*
wise of heart."

"Listen to this, O Job; stand still and consider the wondrous works of God."
JOB 37:14

THE LORD REVEALS HIS OMNIPOTENCE TO JOB

38 Then the LORD answered Job out of
the whirlwind, and said:

2 "Who *is* this who darkens counsel
By words without knowledge?
3 Now prepare yourself like a man;
I will question you, and you shall
answer Me.

4 "Where were you when I laid the
foundations of the earth?
Tell *Me,* if you have understanding.
5 Who determined
its measure-
ments?
Surely you know!
Or who stretched
the line upon it?
6 To what were its
foundations
fastened?
Or who laid its cornerstone,
7 When the morning stars sang together,
And all the sons of God shouted for joy?

8 "Or *who* shut in the sea with doors,
When it burst forth *and* issued from the
womb;
9 When I made the clouds its garment,
And thick darkness its swaddling band;
10 When I fixed My limit for it,
And set bars and doors;
11 When I said,
'This far you may come, but no farther,
And here your proud waves must stop!'

12 "Have you commanded the morning
since your days *began,*
And caused the dawn to know its place,
13 That it might take hold of the ends of
the earth,

37:12 [a]Literally *the world of the earth*

And the wicked be shaken out of it?
14 It takes on form like clay *under* a seal,
And stands out like a garment.
15 From the wicked their light is withheld,
And the upraised arm is broken.

16 "Have you entered the springs of the sea?
Or have you walked in search of the depths?
17 Have the gates of death been revealed to you?
Or have you seen the doors of the shadow of death?
18 Have you comprehended the breadth of the earth?
Tell *Me,* if you know all this.

19 "Where *is* the way *to* the dwelling of light?
And darkness, where *is* its place,
20 That you may take it to its territory,
That you may know the paths *to* its home?
21 Do you know *it,* because you were born then,
Or *because* the number of your days *is* great?

22 "Have you entered the treasury of snow,
Or have you seen the treasury of hail,
23 Which I have reserved for the time of trouble,
For the day of battle and war?
24 By what way is light diffused,
Or the east wind scattered over the earth?

25 "Who has divided a channel for the overflowing *water,*
Or a path for the thunderbolt,
26 To cause it to rain on a land *where there is* no one,
A wilderness in which *there is* no man;
27 To satisfy the desolate waste,
And cause to spring forth the growth of tender grass?
28 Has the rain a father?
Or who has begotten the drops of dew?
29 From whose womb comes the ice?
And the frost of heaven, who gives it birth?
30 The waters harden like stone,
And the surface of the deep is frozen.

31 "Can you bind the cluster of the Pleiades,
Or loose the belt of Orion?
32 Can you bring out Mazzaroth[a] in its season?
Or can you guide the Great Bear with its cubs?
33 Do you know the ordinances of the heavens?
Can you set their dominion over the earth?

34 "Can you lift up your voice to the clouds,
That an abundance of water may cover you?
35 Can you send out lightnings, that they may go,
And say to you, 'Here we *are!*'?
36 Who has put wisdom in the mind?[a]
Or who has given understanding to the heart?
37 Who can number the clouds by wisdom?
Or who can pour out the bottles of heaven,
38 When the dust hardens in clumps,
And the clods cling together?

39 "Can you hunt the prey for the lion,
Or satisfy the appetite of the young lions,
40 When they crouch in *their* dens,
Or lurk in their lairs to lie in wait?
41 Who provides food for the raven,
When its young ones cry to God,
And wander about for lack of food?

39

"Do you know the time when the wild mountain goats bear young?
Or can you mark when the deer gives birth?
2 Can you number the months *that* they fulfill?
Or do you know the time when they bear young?
3 They bow down,
They bring forth their young,
They deliver their offspring.[a]
4 Their young ones are healthy,
They grow strong with grain;
They depart and do not return to them.

38:32 [a]Literally *Constellations* **38:36** [a]Literally *inward parts* **39:3** [a]Literally *pangs,* figurative of offspring

5 "Who set the wild donkey free?
Who loosed the bonds of the onager,
6 Whose home I have made the wilderness,
And the barren land his dwelling?
7 He scorns the tumult of the city;
He does not heed the shouts of the driver.
8 The range of the mountains *is* his pasture,
And he searches after every green thing.

9 "Will the wild ox be willing to serve you?
Will he bed by your manger?
10 Can you bind the wild ox in the furrow with ropes?
Or will he plow the valleys behind you?
11 Will you trust him because his strength *is* great?
Or will you leave your labor to him?
12 Will you trust him to bring home your grain,
And gather it to your threshing floor?

13 "The wings of the ostrich wave proudly,
But are her wings and pinions *like the* kindly stork's?
14 For she leaves her eggs on the ground,
And warms them in the dust;
15 She forgets that a foot may crush them,
Or that a wild beast may break them.
16 She treats her young harshly, as though *they were* not hers;
Her labor is in vain, without concern,
17 Because God deprived her of wisdom,
And did not endow her with understanding.
18 When she lifts herself on high,
She scorns the horse and its rider.

19 "Have you given the horse strength?
Have you clothed his neck with thunder?[a]
20 Can you frighten him like a locust?
His majestic snorting strikes terror.
21 He paws in the valley, and rejoices in *his* strength;
He gallops into the clash of arms.
22 He mocks at fear, and is not frightened;
Nor does he turn back from the sword.
23 The quiver rattles against him,
The glittering spear and javelin.
24 He devours the distance with fierceness and rage;
Nor does he come to a halt because the trumpet *has* sounded.
25 At *the blast of* the trumpet he says, 'Aha!'
He smells the battle from afar,
The thunder of captains and shouting.

26 "Does the hawk fly by your wisdom,
And spread its wings toward the south?
27 Does the eagle mount up at your command,
And make its nest on high?
28 On the rock it dwells and resides,
On the crag of the rock and the stronghold.
29 From there it spies out the prey;
Its eyes observe from afar.
30 Its young ones suck up blood;
And where the slain *are*, there it *is*."

40 Moreover the LORD answered Job, and said:

2 "Shall the one who contends with the Almighty correct *Him?*
He who rebukes God, let him answer it."

JOB'S RESPONSE TO GOD

3Then Job answered the LORD and said:

4 "Behold, I am vile;
What shall I answer You?
I lay my hand over my mouth.
5 Once I have spoken, but I will not answer;
Yes, twice, but I will proceed no further."

GOD'S CHALLENGE TO JOB

6Then the LORD answered Job out of the whirlwind, and said:

7 "Now prepare yourself like a man;
I will question you, and you shall answer Me:

8 "Would you indeed annul My judgment?
Would you condemn Me that you may be justified?
9 Have you an arm like God?
Or can you thunder with a voice like His?

39:19 [a]Or *a mane*

10 Then adorn yourself *with* majesty and
splendor,
And array yourself with glory and
beauty.
11 Disperse the rage of your wrath;
Look on everyone *who is* proud, and
humble him.
12 Look on everyone *who is* proud, *and*
bring him low;
Tread down the wicked in their place.
13 Hide them in the dust together,
Bind their faces in hidden *darkness.*
14 Then I will also confess to you
That your own right hand can save you.

15 "Look now at the behemoth,[a] which I
made *along* with you;
He eats grass like an ox.
16 See now, his strength *is* in his hips,
And his power *is* in his stomach
muscles.
17 He moves his tail like a cedar;
The sinews of his thighs are tightly knit.
18 His bones *are like* beams of bronze,
His ribs like bars of iron.
19 He *is* the first of the ways of God;
Only He who made him can bring near
His sword.
20 Surely the mountains yield food for him,
And all the beasts of the field play
there.
21 He lies under the lotus trees,
In a covert of reeds and marsh.
22 The lotus trees cover him *with* their
shade;
The willows by the brook surround him.
23 Indeed the river may rage,
Yet he is not disturbed;
He is confident, though the Jordan
gushes into his mouth,
24 *Though* he takes it in his eyes,
Or one pierces *his* nose with a snare.

41

"Can you draw out Leviathan[a] with a
hook,
Or *snare* his tongue with a line *which*
you lower?
2 Can you put a reed through his nose,
Or pierce his jaw with a hook?
3 Will he make many supplications to
you?
Will he speak softly to you?
4 Will he make a covenant with you?
Will you take him as a servant forever?
5 Will you play with him as *with* a bird,
Or will you leash him for your maidens?
6 Will *your* companions make a banquet[a]
of him?
Will they apportion him among the
merchants?
7 Can you fill his skin with harpoons,
Or his head with fishing spears?
8 Lay your hand on him;
Remember the battle—
Never do it again!
9 Indeed, *any* hope of *overcoming* him is
false;
Shall *one not* be overwhelmed at the
sight of him?
10 No one *is so* fierce that he would dare
stir him up.
Who then is able to stand against Me?
11 Who has preceded Me, that I should pay
him?
Everything under heaven is Mine.

12 "I will not conceal[a] his limbs,
His mighty power, or his graceful
proportions.
13 Who can remove his outer coat?

40:15 [a]A large animal, exact identity unknown
41:1 [a]A large sea creature, exact identity unknown **41:6** [a]Or *bargain over him*
41:12 [a]Literally *keep silent about*

SOUL NOTE

The Answer *(40:1–5)* During suffering, a natural response is to question God. In distress, people either cry out *to* God, or *at* Him. Fortunately, God is not put off by questions, weak faith, or anger. Job had cried out, but God did not answer Job's questions. Instead, God revealed His sovereignty over all creation, including Job's life. God did not explain Job's suffering, nor will He necessarily explain ours. Very simply, God *is* the answer. When we have nothing else but Him, we have all that we will ever need, now and forever. His presence is enough. **Topic: Weakness**

Who can approach *him* with a double
bridle?
14 Who can open the doors of his face,
With his terrible teeth all around?
15 *His* rows of scales are *his* pride,
Shut up tightly *as with* a seal;
16 One is so near another
That no air can come between them;
17 They are joined one to another,
They stick together and cannot be
parted.
18 His sneezings flash forth light,
And his eyes *are* like the eyelids of the morning.
19 Out of his mouth go burning lights;
Sparks of fire shoot out.
20 Smoke goes out of his nostrils,
As *from* a boiling pot and burning
rushes.
21 His breath kindles coals,
And a flame goes out of his mouth.
22 Strength dwells in his neck,
And sorrow dances before him.
23 The folds of his flesh are joined
together;
They are firm on him and cannot be
moved.
24 His heart is as hard as stone,
Even as hard as the lower *millstone.*
25 When he raises himself up, the mighty
are afraid;
Because of his crashings they are beside[a]
themselves.
26 *Though* the sword reaches him, it cannot
avail;
Nor does spear, dart, or javelin.
27 He regards iron as straw,
And bronze as rotten wood.
28 The arrow cannot make him flee;
Slingstones become like stubble to him.
29 Darts are regarded as straw;
He laughs at the threat of javelins.
30 His undersides *are* like sharp potsherds;
He spreads pointed *marks* in the mire.
31 He makes the deep boil like a pot;
He makes the sea like a pot of
ointment.
32 He leaves a shining wake behind him;
One would think the deep had white
hair.
33 On earth there is nothing like him,
Which is made without fear.
34 He beholds every high *thing;*
He *is* king over all the children of pride."

JOB'S REPENTANCE AND RESTORATION

42 Then Job answered the LORD and said:

2 "I know that You can do everything,
And that no purpose *of Yours* can be
withheld from You.
3 *You asked,* 'Who *is* this who hides counsel without knowledge?'
Therefore I have uttered what I did not understand,
Things too wonderful for me, which I
did not know.
4 Listen, please, and let me speak;
You said, 'I will question you, and you
shall answer Me.'

5 "I have heard of You by the hearing of the
ear,
But now my eye sees You.
6 Therefore I abhor *myself,*
And repent in dust and ashes."

"I know that You can do everything,
and that no purpose of Yours can
be withheld from You."
JOB 42:2

7 And so it was, after the LORD had spoken
these words to Job, that the LORD said to Eliphaz the Temanite, "My wrath is aroused
against you and your two friends, for you have
not spoken of Me *what is* right, as My servant
Job *has.* 8 Now therefore, take for yourselves
seven bulls and seven rams, go to My servant
Job, and offer up for yourselves a burnt offering; and My servant Job shall pray for you. For
I will accept him, lest I deal with you *according to your* folly; because you have not spoken
of Me *what is* right, as My servant Job *has.*"
9 So Eliphaz the Temanite and Bildad the
Shuhite *and* Zophar the Naamathite went and
did as the LORD commanded them; for the
LORD had accepted Job. 10 And the LORD restored Job's losses[a] when he prayed for his
friends. Indeed the LORD gave Job twice as
much as he had before. 11 Then all his brothers,
all his sisters, and all those who had been his

41:25 [a]Or *purify themselves* **42:10** [a]Literally *Job's captivity,* that is, what was captured from Job

acquaintances before, came to him and ate
food with him in his house; and they consoled
him and comforted him for all the adversity
that the LORD had brought upon him. Each
one gave him a piece of silver and each a ring
of gold.

12Now the LORD blessed the latter *days* of
Job more than his beginning; for he had fourteen thousand sheep, six thousand camels,
one thousand yoke of oxen, and one thousand
female donkeys. 13He also had seven sons and
three daughters. 14And he called the name of
the first Jemimah, the name of the second
Keziah, and the name of the third Keren-
Happuch. 15In all the land were found no
women *so* beautiful as the daughters of Job;
and their father gave them an inheritance
among their brothers.

16After this Job lived one hundred and forty
years, and saw his children and grandchildren
for four generations. 17So Job died, old and
full of days.

SOUL NOTE

A Refuge *(42:12)* At the end of the book, God reverses the circumstances of Job's life, doubling his possessions and granting him more children. This did not erase the pain of Job's previous losses—these were never forgotten. God chose to liberally apply the salve of restoration to Job's grief. During his great pain, Job could have cursed God (2:9); instead, he chose to trust in God's faithfulness and justice. We can see our trials as opportunities to experience God's faithfulness, trusting Him completely. Complete restoration may not occur in this life, but God is faithful and will give us more than we can imagine. **Topic: Restoration**

Psalms

Fear, anger, wonder, hatred, anxiety, love, doubt, joy—the full range of emotions is experienced by everyone. However, Christians who feel depressed or angry or hateful often deny those feelings because of the mistaken conviction that believers should never feel that way, and that God wouldn't understand if they did. A reading of Psalms will quickly disprove that. The psalmists felt many emotions and freely expressed them to God. Often set to music, the Book of Psalms is the songbook of the soul.

Comprised of 150 distinct pieces (half of which were written by David), these psalms were originally set to music and used for individual and corporate worship in Israel. The great reformer John Calvin said that the Book of Psalms is "an anatomy of all parts of the soul; for there is not an emotion of which anyone can be conscious that is not here represented as in a mirror." There are lament psalms, thanksgiving psalms, pilgrimage songs, wisdom psalms, imprecatory (or judgment) psalms, praise psalms, and royal psalms.

Regardless of how they are classified, the Psalms have ministered to countless generations of God's people. They invite us to draw near to God by expressing the deepest thoughts and emotions of the human spirit—from dark depression to fearful anxiety to exuberant joy.

The psalm writers provide a model for genuine worship and real communication with God. Let these songs help you love God with all your heart and soul by teaching you to open yourself to Him.

Soul Concerns in Psalms

Trauma	(18:2–6, 25–30)
Anger	(19:14)
Trials	(34:18)
Repentance	(ch. 51)
Loneliness	(69:1–8)
Depression	(ch. 130)
Abortion	(139:16)
Praise and Worship	(ch. 149)

Book One: Psalms 1–41

PSALM 1

The Way of the Righteous and the End of the Ungodly

1 Blessed *is* the man
Who walks not in the counsel of the ungodly,
Nor stands in the path of sinners,
Nor sits in the seat of the scornful;
2 But his delight *is* in the law of the LORD,
And in His law he meditates day and night.
3 He shall be like a tree
Planted by the rivers of water,
That brings forth its fruit in its season,
Whose leaf also shall not wither;
And whatever he does shall prosper.

4 The ungodly *are* not so,
But *are* like the chaff which the wind drives away.
5 Therefore the ungodly shall not stand in the judgment,
Nor sinners in the congregation of the righteous.

6 For the LORD knows the way of the righteous,
But the way of the ungodly shall perish.

PSALM 2

The Messiah's Triumph and Kingdom

1 Why do the nations rage,
And the people plot a vain thing?
2 The kings of the earth set themselves,
And the rulers take counsel together,
Against the LORD and against His Anointed, *saying,*
3 "Let us break Their bonds in pieces
And cast away Their cords from us."

4 He who sits in the heavens shall laugh;
The LORD shall hold them in derision.
5 Then He shall speak to them in His wrath,
And distress them in His deep displeasure:
6 "Yet I have set My King
On My holy hill of Zion."

7 "I will declare the decree:
The LORD has said to Me,
'You *are* My Son,
Today I have begotten You.
8 Ask of Me, and I will give *You*
The nations *for* Your inheritance,

KEY PASSAGE

Spiritual Growth

STRONG, FRUITFUL TREES

(CH. 1)

This psalm contrasts the ways of the righteous and of the ungodly. An ungodly person is "like the chaff which the wind drives away" (1:4). That person has no substance and no roots. On the other hand, the one who is righteous is "like a tree planted by the rivers of water" (1:3). Believers are to be deeply rooted; they should continue to grow strong and bring forth good fruit. Such lives express their joy in God. These believers have grown strong in the Lord and can be used by Him to make a difference in the world.

Believers who want to grow spiritually and be rooted in their faith like strong oaks can follow the advice of this psalm:

- Steer clear of advice from the ungodly.
- Do not follow the paths of sinners.
- Delight in God's law.
- Meditate on God's law day and night.

To Learn More: Turn to the article about spiritual growth on pages 1670, 1671. See also the personality profile of Matthew on page 1243.

And the ends of the earth *for* Your
possession.
9 You shall break[a] them with a rod of
iron;
You shall dash them to pieces like a
potter's vessel.' "

10 Now therefore, be wise, O kings;
Be instructed, you judges of the earth.
11 Serve the LORD with fear,
And rejoice with trembling.
12 Kiss the Son,[a] lest He[b] be angry,
And you perish *in* the way,
When His wrath is kindled but a little.
Blessed *are* all those who put their trust
in Him.

PSALM 3

THE LORD HELPS HIS TROUBLED PEOPLE

A Psalm of David when he fled from Absalom his son.

1 LORD, how they have increased who
trouble me!
Many *are* they who rise up against me.
2 Many *are* they who say of me,
"*There is* no help for him in God." Selah

3 But You, O LORD, *are* a shield for me,
My glory and the One who lifts up my
head.
4 I cried to the LORD with my voice,
And He heard me from His holy hill.
Selah

5 I lay down and
slept;
I awoke, for the
LORD sustained
me.
6 I will not be afraid
of ten
thousands of
people
Who have set *themselves* against me all
around.

7 Arise, O LORD;
Save me, O my God!
For You have struck all my enemies on
the cheekbone;
You have broken the teeth of the
ungodly.

8 Salvation *belongs* to the LORD.
Your blessing *is* upon Your people.
Selah

PSALM 4

THE SAFETY OF THE FAITHFUL

To the Chief Musician. With stringed instruments. A Psalm of David.

1 Hear me when I call, O God of my
righteousness!
You have relieved me in *my* distress;
Have mercy on me, and hear my prayer.

2 How long, O you sons of men,
Will you turn my glory to shame?
How long will you love
worthlessness
And seek falsehood? Selah
3 But know that the LORD has set apart[a]
for Himself him who is godly;
The LORD will hear when I call to Him.

4 Be angry, and do not sin.
Meditate within your heart on your bed,
and be still. Selah
5 Offer the sacrifices of righteousness,
And put your trust in the LORD.

6 *There are* many who say,
"Who will show us *any* good?"
LORD, lift up the light of Your
countenance upon us.
7 You have put gladness in my heart,
More than in the
season that
their grain and
wine increased.
8 I will both lie
down in peace,
and sleep;
For You alone,
O LORD, make
me dwell in
safety.

I will both lie down in peace, and sleep; for You alone, O LORD, make me dwell in safety.
PSALM 4:8

2:9 [a]Following Masoretic Text and Targum; Septuagint, Syriac, and Vulgate read *rule* (compare Revelation 2:27). **2:12** [a]Septuagint and Vulgate read *Embrace discipline;* Targum reads *Receive instruction*. [b]Septuagint reads *the LORD*.
4:3 [a]Many Hebrew manuscripts, Septuagint, Targum, and Vulgate read *made wonderful*.

PSALM 5

A Prayer for Guidance

To the Chief Musician. With flutes.[a]
A Psalm of David.

1 Give ear to my words, O LORD,
Consider my meditation.
2 Give heed to the voice of my cry,
My King and my God,
For to You I will pray.
3 My voice You shall hear in the morning, O LORD;
In the morning I will direct *it* to You,
And I will look up.

4 For You *are* not a God who takes pleasure in wickedness,
Nor shall evil dwell with You.
5 The boastful shall not stand in Your sight;
You hate all workers of iniquity.
6 You shall destroy those who speak falsehood;
The LORD abhors the bloodthirsty and deceitful man.

7 But as for me, I will come into Your house in the multitude of Your mercy;
In fear of You I will worship toward Your holy temple.
8 Lead me, O LORD, in Your righteousness because of my enemies;
Make Your way straight before my face.

9 For *there is* no faithfulness in their mouth;
Their inward part *is* destruction;
Their throat *is* an open tomb;
They flatter with their tongue.
10 Pronounce them guilty, O God!
Let them fall by their own counsels;
Cast them out in the multitude of their transgressions,
For they have rebelled against You.

11 But let all those rejoice who put their trust in You;
Let them ever shout for joy, because You defend them;
Let those also who love Your name
Be joyful in You.
12 For You, O LORD, will bless the righteous;
With favor You will surround him as *with* a shield.

PSALM 6

A Prayer of Faith in Time of Distress

To the Chief Musician. With stringed instruments. On an eight-stringed harp.[a] *A Psalm of David.*

1 O LORD, do not rebuke me in Your anger,
Nor chasten me in Your hot displeasure.
2 Have mercy on me, O LORD, for I *am* weak;
O LORD, heal me, for my bones are troubled.
3 My soul also is greatly troubled;
But You, O LORD—how long?

4 Return, O LORD, deliver me!
Oh, save me for Your mercies' sake!
5 For in death *there is* no remembrance of You;
In the grave who will give You thanks?

6 I am weary with my groaning;
All night I make my bed swim;
I drench my couch with my tears.
7 My eye wastes away because of grief;
It grows old because of all my enemies.

8 Depart from me, all you workers of iniquity;
For the LORD has heard the voice of my weeping.
9 The LORD has heard my supplication;
The LORD will receive my prayer.
10 Let all my enemies be ashamed and greatly troubled;
Let them turn back *and* be ashamed suddenly.

PSALM 7

Prayer and Praise for Deliverance from Enemies

A Meditation[a] *of David, which he sang to the LORD concerning the words of Cush, a Benjamite.*

1 O LORD my God, in You I put my trust;
Save me from all those who persecute me;

5:title [a]Hebrew *nehiloth* **6:title** [a]Hebrew *sheminith* **7:title** [a]Hebrew *Shiggaion*

And deliver me,
2 Lest they tear me like a lion,
Rending *me* in pieces, while *there is* none to deliver.

3 O LORD my God, if I have done this:
If there is iniquity in my hands,
4 If I have repaid evil to him who was at peace with me,
Or have plundered my enemy without cause,
5 Let the enemy pursue me and overtake *me;*
Yes, let him trample my life to the earth,
And lay my honor in the dust. Selah

6 Arise, O LORD, in Your anger;
Lift Yourself up because of the rage of my enemies;
Rise up for me[a] *to* the judgment You have commanded!
7 So the congregation of the peoples shall surround You;
For their sakes, therefore, return on high.
8 The LORD shall judge the peoples;
Judge me, O LORD, according to my righteousness,
And according to my integrity within me.

9 Oh, let the wickedness of the wicked come to an end,
But establish the just;
For the righteous God tests the hearts and minds.
10 My defense *is* of God,
Who saves the upright in heart.

11 God *is* a just judge,
And God is angry *with the wicked* every day.

12 If he does not turn back,
He will sharpen His sword;
He bends His bow and makes it ready.
13 He also prepares for Himself instruments of death;
He makes His arrows into fiery shafts.

14 Behold, *the wicked* brings forth iniquity;
Yes, he conceives trouble and brings forth falsehood.
15 He made a pit and dug it out,
And has fallen into the ditch *which* he made.
16 His trouble shall return upon his own head,
And his violent dealing shall come down on his own crown.

17 I will praise the LORD according to His righteousness,
And will sing praise to the name of the LORD Most High.

PSALM 8

THE GLORY OF THE LORD IN CREATION

To the Chief Musician. On the instrument of Gath.[a] A Psalm of David.

1 O LORD, our Lord,
How excellent *is* Your name in all the earth,
Who have set Your glory above the heavens!

7:6 [a]Following Masoretic Text, Targum, and Vulgate; Septuagint reads *O LORD my God.*
8:title [a]Hebrew *Al Gittith*

SOUL NOTE

Special and Important *(8:3–5)* Human beings often feel small compared to the rest of creation. The psalmist asked God, "What is man that You are mindful of him, and the son of man that You visit him?" (8:4). Insignificant, sinful human beings don't seem worthy of God's care. Yet God does care, for He created people "a little lower than the angels" and crowned them "with glory and honor" (8:5). He loves us so much that He sent His Son to die for us so that we could one day have the glory and honor for which He created us. We are important to God. **Topic: Self-Esteem**

2 Out of the mouth of babes and nursing infants
You have ordained strength,
Because of Your enemies,
That You may silence the enemy and the avenger.

3 When I consider Your heavens, the work of Your fingers,
The moon and the stars, which You have ordained,
4 What is man that You are mindful of him,
And the son of man that You visit him?
5 For You have made him a little lower than the angels,[a]
And You have crowned him with glory and honor.

6 You have made him to have dominion over the works of Your hands;
You have put all *things* under his feet,
7 All sheep and oxen—
Even the beasts of the field,
8 The birds of the air,
And the fish of the sea
That pass through the paths of the seas.

9 O LORD, our Lord,
How excellent *is* Your name in all the earth!

PSALM 9

PRAYER AND THANKSGIVING FOR THE LORD'S RIGHTEOUS JUDGMENTS

To the Chief Musician. To the tune of "Death of the Son."[a] *A Psalm of David.*

1 I will praise *You,* O LORD, with my whole heart;
I will tell of all Your marvelous works.
2 I will be glad and rejoice in You;
I will sing praise to Your name, O Most High.

3 When my enemies turn back,
They shall fall and perish at Your presence.
4 For You have maintained my right and my cause;
You sat on the throne judging in righteousness.
5 You have rebuked the nations,
You have destroyed the wicked;
You have blotted out their name forever and ever.

6 O enemy, destructions are finished forever!
And you have destroyed cities;
Even their memory has perished.
7 But the LORD shall endure forever;
He has prepared His throne for judgment.
8 He shall judge the world in righteousness,
And He shall administer judgment for the peoples in uprightness.

9 The LORD also will be a refuge for the oppressed,
A refuge in times of trouble.
10 And those who know Your name will put their trust in You;
For You, LORD, have not forsaken those who seek You.

> And those who know Your name will put their trust in You; for You, LORD, have not forsaken those who seek You.
> PSALM 9:10

11 Sing praises to the LORD, who dwells in Zion!
Declare His deeds among the people.
12 When He avenges blood, He remembers them;
He does not forget the cry of the humble.

13 Have mercy on me, O LORD!
Consider my trouble from those who hate me,
You who lift me up from the gates of death,
14 That I may tell of all Your praise

8:5 [a]Hebrew *Elohim, God;* Septuagint, Syriac, Targum, and Jewish tradition translate as *angels.*
9:title [a]Hebrew *Muth Labben*

In the gates of the daughter of Zion.
I will rejoice in Your salvation.

15 The nations have sunk down in the pit
which they made;
In the net which they hid, their own foot
is caught.
16 The LORD is known *by* the judgment He
executes;
The wicked is snared in the work of his
own hands.
Meditation.[a] Selah

17 The wicked shall be turned into hell,
And all the nations that forget God.
18 For the needy shall not always be
forgotten;
The expectation of the poor shall *not*
perish forever.

19 Arise, O LORD,
Do not let man prevail;
Let the nations be judged in Your sight.
20 Put them in fear, O LORD,
That the nations may know themselves
to be but men. Selah

PSALM 10

A SONG OF CONFIDENCE IN GOD'S TRIUMPH OVER EVIL

1 Why do You stand afar off, O LORD?
Why do You hide in times of trouble?
2 The wicked in *his* pride persecutes the
poor;
Let them be caught in the plots which
they have devised.

3 For the wicked boasts of his heart's
desire;
He blesses the greedy *and* renounces the
LORD.
4 The wicked in his proud countenance
does not seek *God;*
God *is* in none of his thoughts.

5 His ways are always prospering;
Your judgments *are* far above, out of his
sight;
As for all his enemies, he sneers at them.
6 He has said in his heart, "I shall not be
moved;
I shall never be in adversity."
7 His mouth is full of cursing and deceit
and oppression;
Under his tongue *is* trouble and
iniquity.

8 He sits in the lurking places of the
villages;
In the secret places he murders the
innocent;
His eyes are secretly fixed on the
helpless.
9 He lies in wait secretly, as a lion in his
den;
He lies in wait to catch the poor;
He catches the poor when he draws him
into his net.
10 So he crouches, he lies low,
That the helpless may fall by his
strength.
11 He has said in his heart,
"God has forgotten;
He hides His face;
He will never see."

12 Arise, O LORD!
O God, lift up Your hand!
Do not forget the humble.
13 Why do the wicked renounce God?
He has said in his heart,
"You will not require *an account.*"

14 But You have seen, for You observe
trouble and grief,
To repay *it* by Your hand.
The helpless commits himself to You;
You are the helper of the fatherless.
15 Break the arm of the wicked and the evil
man;
Seek out his wickedness *until* You find
none.

16 The LORD *is* King forever and ever;
The nations have perished out of His
land.
17 LORD, You have heard the desire of the
humble;
You will prepare their heart;
You will cause Your ear to hear,
18 To do justice to the fatherless and the
oppressed,
That the man of the earth may oppress
no more.

9:16 [a]Hebrew *Higgaion*

PSALM 11

FAITH IN THE LORD'S RIGHTEOUSNESS

To the Chief Musician. A Psalm of David.

1 In the LORD I put my trust;
How can you say to my soul,
"Flee *as* a bird to your mountain"?
2 For look! The wicked bend *their* bow,
They make ready their arrow on the string,
That they may shoot secretly at the upright in heart.
3 If the foundations are destroyed,
What can the righteous do?

4 The LORD *is* in His holy temple,
The LORD's throne *is* in heaven;
His eyes behold,
His eyelids test the sons of men.
5 The LORD tests the righteous,
But the wicked and the one who loves violence His soul hates.
6 Upon the wicked He will rain coals;
Fire and brimstone and a burning wind
Shall be the portion of their cup.

7 For the LORD *is* righteous,
He loves righteousness;
His countenance beholds the upright.[a]

PSALM 12

MAN'S TREACHERY AND GOD'S CONSTANCY

To the Chief Musician. On an eight-stringed harp.[a] A Psalm of David.

1 Help, LORD, for the godly man ceases!
For the faithful disappear from among the sons of men.
2 They speak idly everyone with his neighbor;
With flattering lips *and* a double heart they speak.

3 May the LORD cut off all flattering lips,
And the tongue that speaks proud things,
4 Who have said,
"With our tongue we will prevail;
Our lips *are* our own;
Who *is* lord over us?"

5 "For the oppression of the poor, for the sighing of the needy,
Now I will arise," says the LORD;
"I will set *him* in the safety for which he yearns."

11:7 [a]Or *The upright beholds His countenance*
12:title [a]Hebrew *sheminith*

KEY PASSAGE

Violence

A VIOLENT END

(11:5)

Violence seems to be everywhere in society. From the time Cain committed the first murder (Gen. 4:8), humanity has been subject to violence. Indeed, God flooded the earth because it was filled with violence (Gen. 6:11–13). Violent people will often come to a violent end—as predicted in many proverbs (Prov. 4:16–19; 21:7) and by Jesus (Matt. 26:51). Murder, the ultimate form of violence, is forbidden in the Ten Commandments (Ex. 20:13). Jesus said that murder begins in the heart with angry and vengeful thoughts (Matt. 5:21, 22).

God's people are warned against allowing the natural emotion of anger to erupt into violence, for that harms others. Believers must also be discerning regarding television, movies, and video games, for these can desensitize a person to violence and sometimes even glorify it. With the filling of the Spirit, the believer will instead produce the fruit of love, peace, longsuffering, gentleness, and self-control (Gal. 5:22, 23).

To Learn More: Turn to the article about violence on pages 526, 527. See also the personality profile of Naboth and Ahab on page 469.

6 The words of the LORD *are* pure words,
Like silver tried in a furnace of earth,
Purified seven times.
7 You shall keep them, O LORD,
You shall preserve them from this generation forever.

8 The wicked prowl on every side,
When vileness is exalted among the sons of men.

PSALM 13

TRUST IN THE SALVATION OF THE LORD

To the Chief Musician. A Psalm of David.

1 How long, O LORD? Will You forget me forever?
How long will You hide Your face from me?
2 How long shall I take counsel in my soul,
Having sorrow in my heart daily?
How long will my enemy be exalted over me?

3 Consider *and* hear me, O LORD my God;
Enlighten my eyes,
Lest I sleep the *sleep of* death;
4 Lest my enemy say,
"I have prevailed against him";
Lest those who trouble me rejoice when I am moved.

5 But I have trusted in Your mercy;
My heart shall rejoice in Your salvation.
6 I will sing to the LORD,
Because He has dealt bountifully with me.

PSALM 14

FOLLY OF THE GODLESS, AND GOD'S FINAL TRIUMPH

To the Chief Musician. A Psalm of David.

1 The fool has said in his heart,
"*There is* no God."
They are corrupt,
They have done abominable works,
There is none who does good.

2 The LORD looks down from heaven upon the children of men,
To see if there are any who understand, who seek God.
3 They have all turned aside,
They have together become corrupt;
There is none who does good,
No, not one.

4 Have all the workers of iniquity no knowledge,
Who eat up my people *as* they eat bread,
And do not call on the LORD?
5 There they are in great fear,
For God *is* with the generation of the righteous.
6 You shame the counsel of the poor,
But the LORD *is* his refuge.

7 Oh, that the salvation of Israel *would come* out of Zion!
When the LORD brings back the captivity of His people,
Let Jacob rejoice *and* Israel be glad.

PSALM 15

THE CHARACTER OF THOSE WHO MAY DWELL WITH THE LORD

A Psalm of David.

1 LORD, who may abide in Your tabernacle?
Who may dwell in Your holy hill?

2 He who walks uprightly,
And works righteousness,
And speaks the truth in his heart;
3 He *who* does not backbite with his tongue,
Nor does evil to his neighbor,
Nor does he take up a reproach against his friend;
4 In whose eyes a vile person is despised,
But he honors those who fear the LORD;
He *who* swears to his own hurt and does not change;
5 He *who* does not put out his money at usury,
Nor does he take a bribe against the innocent.

He who does these *things* shall never be moved.

PSALM 16

THE HOPE OF THE FAITHFUL, AND THE MESSIAH'S VICTORY

A Michtam of David.

1 Preserve me,
O God, for in
You I put my
trust.

2 *O my soul,* you
have said to the
LORD,
"You *are* my Lord,
My goodness is nothing apart from You."
3 As for the saints who *are* on the earth,
"They are the excellent ones, in whom is
all my delight."

4 Their sorrows shall be multiplied who
hasten *after* another *god;*
Their drink offerings of blood I will not
offer,
Nor take up their names on my lips.

5 O LORD, *You are* the portion of my
inheritance and my cup;
You maintain my lot.
6 The lines have fallen to me in pleasant
places;
Yes, I have a good inheritance.

7 I will bless the LORD who has given me
counsel;
My heart also instructs me in the night
seasons.
8 I have set the LORD always before
me;
Because *He is* at my right hand I shall
not be moved.

9 Therefore my heart is glad, and my glory
rejoices;
My flesh also will rest in hope.
10 For You will not leave my soul in Sheol,
Nor will You allow Your Holy One to see
corruption.
11 You will show me
the path of life;
In Your presence *is*
fullness of joy;
At Your right hand
are pleasures
forevermore.

You will show me the path of life;
in Your presence is fullness of joy;
at Your right hand
are pleasures forevermore.
PSALM 16:11

PSALM 17

PRAYER WITH CONFIDENCE IN FINAL SALVATION

A Prayer of David.

1 Hear a just cause, O LORD,
Attend to my cry;
Give ear to my prayer *which is* not from
deceitful lips.
2 Let my vindication come from Your
presence;
Let Your eyes look on the things that are
upright.

3 You have tested my heart;
You have visited *me* in the night;
You have tried me and have found
nothing;
I have purposed that my mouth shall not
transgress.
4 Concerning the works of men,
By the word of Your lips,
I have kept away from the paths of the
destroyer.
5 Uphold my steps in Your paths,
That my footsteps may not slip.

SOUL NOTE

The Path of Life *(16:11)* David trusted in God and sought Him in times of need and fear. David often faced murderous enemies, yet God always preserved his life. In this psalm, David praised God for caring for, protecting, and guiding him. He foresaw a coming Holy One whom God would raise from the dead (16:9, 10), and he understood that he would have eternal life too, through that Savior. One day all believers will be in God's presence and at His right hand where there are "fullness of joy" and "pleasures forevermore." That is something worth waiting for! **Topic: Eternal Life**

6 I have called upon You, for You will hear
me, O God;
Incline Your ear to me, *and* hear my
speech.
7 Show Your marvelous lovingkindness by
Your right hand,
O You who save those who trust *in You*
From those who rise up *against them.*
8 Keep me as the apple of Your eye;
Hide me under the shadow of Your wings,
9 From the wicked who oppress me,
From my deadly enemies who surround
me.

10 They have closed up their fat *hearts;*
With their mouths they speak proudly.
11 They have now surrounded us in our
steps;
They have set their eyes, crouching
down to the earth,
12 As a lion is eager to tear his prey,
And like a young lion lurking in secret
places.

13 Arise, O LORD,
Confront him, cast him down;
Deliver my life from the wicked with
Your sword,
14 With Your hand from men, O LORD,
From men of the world *who have* their
portion in *this* life,
And whose belly You fill with Your
hidden treasure.
They are satisfied with children,
And leave the rest of their *possession* for
their babes.

15 As for me, I will see Your face in
righteousness;
I shall be satisfied when I awake in Your
likeness.

PSALM 18

God the Sovereign Savior

To the Chief Musician. A Psalm of David the servant of the LORD, who spoke to the LORD the words of this song on the day that the LORD delivered him from the hand of all his enemies and from the hand of Saul. And he said:

1 I will love You, O LORD, my strength.
2 The LORD is my rock and my fortress
and my deliverer;
My God, my strength, in whom I will
trust;
My shield and the horn of my salvation,
my stronghold.
3 I will call upon the LORD, *who is worthy*
to be praised;
So shall I be saved from my enemies.

4 The pangs of death surrounded me,
And the floods of ungodliness made me
afraid.
5 The sorrows of Sheol surrounded me;
The snares of death confronted me.
6 In my distress I called upon the LORD,
And cried out to my God;
He heard my voice from His temple,
And my cry came before Him, *even* to
His ears.

7 Then the earth shook and trembled;
The foundations of the hills also quaked
and were shaken,
Because He was angry.
8 Smoke went up from His nostrils,
And devouring fire from His mouth;
Coals were kindled by it.
9 He bowed the heavens also, and came
down
With darkness under His feet.
10 And He rode upon a cherub, and flew;
He flew upon the wings of the wind.
11 He made darkness His secret place;
His canopy around Him *was* dark
waters
And thick clouds of the skies.
12 From the brightness before Him,
His thick clouds passed with hailstones
and coals of fire.

13 The LORD thundered from heaven,
And the Most High uttered His voice,
Hailstones and coals of fire.[a]
14 He sent out His arrows and scattered the
foe,
Lightnings in abundance, and He
vanquished them.
15 Then the channels of the sea were seen,
The foundations of the world were
uncovered
At Your rebuke, O LORD,

18:13 [a]Following Masoretic Text, Targum, and Vulgate; a few Hebrew manuscripts and Septuagint omit *Hailstones and coals of fire.*

At the blast of the breath of Your
nostrils.

16 He sent from above, He took me;
He drew me out of many waters.
17 He delivered me from my strong enemy,
From those who hated me,
For they were too strong for me.
18 They confronted me in the day of my
calamity,
But the LORD was my support.
19 He also brought me out into a broad
place;
He delivered me because He delighted in
me.

20 The LORD rewarded me according to my
righteousness;
According to the cleanness of my hands
He has recompensed me.
21 For I have kept the ways of the LORD,
And have not wickedly departed from
my God.
22 For all His judgments *were* before me,
And I did not put away His statutes from
me.
23 I was also blameless before Him,
And I kept myself from my iniquity.
24 Therefore the LORD has recompensed me
according to my righteousness,
According to the cleanness of my hands
in His sight.

25 With the merciful You will show Yourself
merciful;
With a blameless man You will show
Yourself blameless;
26 With the pure You will show Yourself
pure;
And with the devious You will show
Yourself shrewd.
27 For You will save the humble people,
But will bring down haughty looks.

28 For You will light my lamp;
The LORD my God will enlighten my
darkness.
29 For by You I can run against a troop,
By my God I can leap over a wall.
30 *As for* God, His way *is* perfect;
The word of the LORD is proven;
He *is* a shield to all who trust in Him.

31 For who *is* God, except the LORD?
And who *is* a rock, except our God?
32 *It is* God who arms me with strength,
And makes my way perfect.
33 He makes my feet like the *feet of* deer,
And sets me on my high places.
34 He teaches my hands to make war,
So that my arms can bend a bow of
bronze.

35 You have also given me the shield of
Your salvation;
Your right hand has held me up,
Your gentleness has made me great.
36 You enlarged my path under me,
So my feet did not slip.

37 I have pursued my enemies and
overtaken them;
Neither did I turn back again till they
were destroyed.
38 I have wounded them,
So that they could not rise;
They have fallen under my feet.
39 For You have armed me with strength for
the battle;
You have subdued under me those who
rose up against me.
40 You have also given me the necks of my
enemies,
So that I destroyed those who hated me.
41 They cried out, but *there was* none to
save;
Even to the LORD, but He did not answer
them.
42 Then I beat them as fine as the dust
before the wind;
I cast them out like dirt in the streets.

43 You have delivered me from the strivings
of the people;
You have made me the head of the
nations;
A people I have not known shall serve
me.
44 As soon as they hear of me they obey
me;
The foreigners submit to me.
45 The foreigners fade away,
And come frightened from their
hideouts.

46 The LORD lives!
Blessed *be* my Rock!
Let the God of my salvation be exalted.

HEALING THE WOUNDS THAT BIND YOU

MARK R. LAASER

(Psalm 18:2–6, 25–30)

Some events in life cause pain that goes deeper and lasts longer. We all have met people who have experienced a horrible loss or survived a great difficulty. Counselors call such an experience "trauma." As these people go through life, they may not be aware of or remember the original damage. But at times, trauma can influence their reactions in certain unhealthy ways or cause them to make unhealthy decisions. Those whose traumas don't get healed may grow up to damage others, even their own families.

WHAT CAUSES TRAUMA?

Most experts divide trauma into two major categories. The first is *invasion* trauma. Something happens to a person that creates damage. The second is *abandonment* trauma. Something did *not* happen to a person (such as not feeling loved, protected, or nurtured) that creates damage. This second kind of trauma can be harder to recognize because the person doesn't know what they are missing, never having had it.

These two kinds of trauma affect the four aspects of people's lives: emotional, physical, sexual, spiritual.

ASPECTS OF INVASION TRAUMA

Emotional invasion occurs when people feel criticized, shamed, or blamed, either verbally or nonverbally. For example, sighs that express anger or displeasure can be taken as criticism. It occurs when people are talked out of their feelings with statements such as "Big girls don't cry," or "Christians don't feel that way." It also occurs when an adult or authority figure reverses roles and expects a child to be the caregiver—giving emotional care instead of receiving it.

Physical invasion occurs when a person is physically abused. This form of trauma may create permanent physical damage. The emotional effect of this can also be experienced if a person lives in a home in which someone else is being physically harmed.

Sexual invasion happens when a person is penetrated or touched in sexual areas outside the mutual relationship of marriage. This is a very broad definition because even consenting sexual relationships between people who are not married *can* have a traumatizing effect because it is outside of God's plan. This type of invasion can also happen when people are teased or criticized about their bodies.

Spiritual invasion takes place when people are led to believe that they are unworthy of God's love and grace. Often rigid, fear-based religious teaching, even if it is well intended, can have this effect. This results in shame that people can't seem to shake.

ASPECTS OF ABANDONMENT TRAUMA

Emotional abandonment occurs when love, attention, care, nurture, and affirmation are not given. This results in profound loneliness.

Physical abandonment happens when people's basic needs for food, shelter, and clothing aren't met. People who aren't touched enough—with hugs or cuddles—will experience a form of this called "touch deprivation." Another form occurs when people aren't getting enough information or modeling on physical self-care.

Sexual abandonment occurs when parents and other responsible adults don't educate children about and model healthy sexuality. Lack of correct information can have devastating results.

Spiritual abandonment happens when healthy spiritual teaching and modeling is not available.

The above categories can overlap. Damage in one aspect of a person's life can have an effect in another. For example, any form of trauma that happens at the hands of a religious authority figure can create profound spiritual damage.

THE EFFECTS OF TRAUMA

Symptoms of unhealed trauma can include anxiety and panic disorders, depression, anger, loneliness, attachment disorders, and addictions of all kinds. Panic, anxiety, flashbacks, and anger sometimes are labeled under the diagnosis of Post Traumatic Stress Disorder (PTSD).

Trauma survivors may cope with the remembered or not remembered trauma in a variety of ways. Some, almost unconsciously, may seek to repeat the trauma in their adult lives, hoping for a different result or trying to be in control by becoming the perpetrator of the trauma on someone else. This is called "trauma repetition." Trauma survivors may create relationships with people who treat them poorly, or they go the other direction entirely by avoiding any person or event that triggers memories of the trauma.

HEALING TRAUMA

The path to recovery includes a number of steps. Trauma survivors need:

- to be educated about the nature of trauma. Any denial may need to be confronted. Sometimes it is helpful to do this in groups of other survivors.
- comforting, accepting, and nonjudgmental listeners who believe them and offer them hope.
- help in expressing their anger about their trauma. This includes anger at the perpetrators, but may not necessarily mean confronting them. There are symbolic ways, such as writing letters to perpetrators that won't necessarily be sent, which can be just as powerful. Opportunities to be angry with God may also be needed. Discussions about how a loving God would allow trauma to happen may be helpful.
- instruction in the process of grieving the losses that the trauma has caused in their lives.
- to know that they didn't deserve their hurts and didn't cause them.
- help in structuring boundaries so that they will not be harmed again by old, current, or new relationships.
- to see the positive strengths that can result from the healing of their trauma.
- to be able, eventually, to forgive. This is the ultimate spiritual victory.

Caregivers should be aware that working with trauma survivors can bring up one's own issues of trauma. If this interferes with working with them, it will be necessary to refer them to someone else. This possible dynamic points to the fact that we all need to be in the journey. Getting our own hurts healed can make us effective in healing.

FURTHER MEDITATION:

Other passages to study about the issue of trauma include:

- Psalms 27:10; 34:18; 46:1–11; 107:20; 147:2, 3
- Proverbs 3:5–8
- Isaiah 53:1–12; 61:1–3
- 2 Corinthians 1:8–11

To Learn More: Turn to the key passage note on trauma at Lamentations 1:10–21 on page 1035. See also the personality profile of Jonah on page 1163.

CULTIVATING HEALTHY ANGER

GARY J. OLIVER

(Psalm 19:14)

Some call it: "blowing your stack," "letting off steam," "letting someone have it," "being totally ticked." Anger is often described with these negative phrases. But is all anger bad? Is it always a sin to be angry? Many Christians go through life stymied in their effort to grow and live effectively, because of their failure to acknowledge, accept, and understand the God-given emotion of anger. They are unaware of its dynamics and potential benefits.

ANGER IS A FACT OF LIFE

What is anger? While "rage," "fury," "wrath," "resentment," and "hostility" are often used to describe the emotion, anger is simply a strong feeling of irritation or displeasure. Actually, anger is experienced much more frequently than most people would like to admit. When people begrudge or disdain others, when they are annoyed, repulsed, irritated, frustrated, offended, or cross, they are probably experiencing some form of anger. Studies show that most people experience this emotion at least eight to ten times a day.

Depression, anxiety, fear, and grief drain the human body of emotional and physical energy. Anger, on the other hand, releases energy into the nervous system and makes a person ready for action. It is a personal choice whether to use that burst of energy in constructive or abusive ways.

HEALTHY VS. UNHEALTHY ANGER

When people allow anger to control them, it becomes unhealthy anger. Unhealthy anger expresses itself in a desire for revenge and can easily distort one's perspective, block the ability to love, and limit one's capacity to think clearly. At that point, people are more likely to spend their anger energy in destructive actions such as emotional, verbal, or physical abuse and violence.

The opposite of that unhealthy anger is healthy anger, which could also be called "quality anger." The Bible says, "Be angry, and do not sin" (Eph. 4:26). This type of anger depends on the help and guidance of the Holy Spirit. Healthy anger allows people to invest their emotional energy in confronting evil, righting wrongs, and changing things for the good. The energy of anger, when wisely invested, can provide greater focus and intensity and can lead to greater productivity. Martin Luther said: "When I am angry, I can write, pray, and preach well, for then my whole temperament is quickened, my understanding is sharpened, and all mundane vexations and temptations are gone."

AN ANGER MANAGEMENT PLAN

In order to confront and control unhealthy anger, a person must decide a plan of counterattack in advance. When unhealthy anger is not under control, it blocks the ability to think clearly and be objective. However, taking the time to think and pray through the following issues prepares people for an objective, reasoned investment of their anger energy, so they can respond with healthy anger.

Step 1—Be Aware of Anger

One of the many myths regarding anger is that a person with an anger problem shows it through his or her appearance and actions. However, a battle may rage inside a seemingly calm demeanor. People need to identify what makes them vulnerable to anger, how their body responds to anger, and what physical manifestations of anger they adopt when enraged.

Step 2—Accept Responsibility for Anger
Many people blame others for their problems. When God confronted Eve in the garden, she blamed the serpent for her mistake. When God confronted Adam, he first blamed Eve and, eventually, blamed God. It is easy for an angry person to say, "So and so made me angry." Other people may speak or act to cause hurt or frustration, but blaming a personal reaction on someone else is not accurate. People don't "lose" their temper. They "choose" their own temper.

Step 3—Identify the Source of Anger
Anger is a secondary emotion that is experienced in response to a primary emotion such as hurt, frustration, or fear. People who are hurt feel vulnerable to more hurt. This is especially true of very sensitive people. For many, anger is a defense mechanism against being hurt.

Frustration occurs when expectations are not met or people cannot meet their personal goals. The things that frustrate people the most usually have one characteristic in common—they really aren't very important. Identifying frustrating personalities or situations will prepare a person for handling similar encounters in the future.

Step 4—Choose How to Invest Anger Energy
This is a critical step. While we cannot always control when we will experience anger, we can choose how we will express it. With God's help, we can find creative and constructive ways to deal with anger. We can allow anger to dominate us, or we can harness anger's energy into healthy and quality responses. Quality anger involves open, honest, and direct communication. It involves speaking the truth in love. It involves declaring truth and righting wrongs. It involves being open to an apology or explanation and seeks to work toward an agreement.

For many Christians, both the experience and expression of anger have become a habit. Habits can take some time to change. The good news is that with God's help, we can change and grow. As we allow the Holy Spirit to fill us and we apply promises from God's Word, we can replace the old, unhealthy ways of responding with new, healthy and God-honoring emotional responses. As we learn creative ways to invest the God-given anger energy, and as we approach anger from a biblical perspective, we will find one of the most powerful sources of personal motivation available.

FURTHER MEDITATION:

Other passages to study about the issue of anger include:

- ➢ Psalm 37:8
- ➢ Proverbs 14:16; 15:1, 18; 16:32; 19:19; 22:24; 29:11
- ➢ Ecclesiastes 7:9
- ➢ Mark 3:5
- ➢ Ephesians 4:26–32
- ➢ Colossians 3:8, 21

To Learn More: **Turn to the key passage note on anger at Ephesians 4:26, 27 on page 1554. See also the personality profile of Cain on page 11.**

47 *It is* God who avenges me,
And subdues the peoples under me;
48 He delivers me from my enemies.
You also lift me up above those who rise against me;
You have delivered me from the violent man.
49 Therefore I will give thanks to You,
O LORD, among the Gentiles,
And sing praises to Your name.

50 Great deliverance He gives to His king,
And shows mercy to His anointed,
To David and his descendants forevermore.

PSALM 19

THE PERFECT REVELATION OF THE LORD

To the Chief Musician. A Psalm of David.

1 The heavens declare the glory of God;
And the firmament shows His handiwork.
2 Day unto day utters speech,
And night unto night reveals knowledge.
3 *There is* no speech nor language
Where their voice is not heard.
4 Their line[a] has gone out through all the earth,
And their words to the end of the world.

In them He has set a tabernacle for the sun,
5 Which *is* like a bridegroom coming out of his chamber,
And rejoices like a strong man to run its race.
6 Its rising *is* from one end of heaven,
And its circuit to the other end;
And there is nothing hidden from its heat.

7 The law of the LORD *is* perfect, converting the soul;
The testimony of the LORD *is* sure, making wise the simple;
8 The statutes of the LORD *are* right, rejoicing the heart;
The commandment of the LORD *is* pure, enlightening the eyes;
9 The fear of the LORD *is* clean, enduring forever;
The judgments of the LORD *are* true *and* righteous altogether.
10 More to be desired *are they* than gold,
Yea, than much fine gold;
Sweeter also than honey and the honeycomb.
11 Moreover by them Your servant is warned,
And in keeping them *there is* great reward.

12 Who can understand *his* errors?
Cleanse me from secret *faults.*
13 Keep back Your servant also from presumptuous *sins;*
Let them not have dominion over me.
Then I shall be blameless,
And I shall be innocent of great transgression.

> Let the words of my mouth and the meditation of my heart be acceptable in Your sight, O LORD, my strength and my Redeemer.
> PSALM 19:14

14 Let the words of my mouth and the meditation of my heart
Be acceptable in Your sight,
O LORD, my strength and my Redeemer.

PSALM 20

THE ASSURANCE OF GOD'S SAVING WORK

To the Chief Musician. A Psalm of David.

1 May the LORD answer you in the day of trouble;
May the name of the God of Jacob defend you;
2 May He send you help from the sanctuary,
And strengthen you out of Zion;
3 May He remember all your offerings,
And accept your burnt sacrifice. Selah

4 May He grant you according to your heart's *desire,*

19:4 [a]Septuagint, Syriac, and Vulgate read *sound;* Targum reads *business.*

And fulfill all your purpose.
5 We will rejoice in your salvation,
And in the name of our God we will set up *our* banners!
May the LORD fulfill all your petitions.

6 Now I know that the LORD saves His anointed;
He will answer him from His holy heaven
With the saving strength of His right hand.

7 Some *trust* in chariots, and some in horses;
But we will remember the name of the LORD our God.
8 They have bowed down and fallen;
But we have risen and stand upright.

9 Save, LORD!
May the King answer us when we call.

PSALM 21

JOY IN THE SALVATION OF THE LORD

To the Chief Musician. A Psalm of David.

1 The king shall have joy in Your strength, O LORD;
And in Your salvation how greatly shall he rejoice!
2 You have given him his heart's desire,
And have not withheld the request of his lips. Selah

3 For You meet him with the blessings of goodness;
You set a crown of pure gold upon his head.
4 He asked life from You, *and* You gave *it* to him—
Length of days forever and ever.
5 His glory *is* great in Your salvation;
Honor and majesty You have placed upon him.
6 For You have made him most blessed forever;
You have made him exceedingly glad with Your presence.
7 For the king trusts in the LORD,
And through the mercy of the Most High he shall not be moved.

8 Your hand will find all Your enemies;
Your right hand will find those who hate You.
9 You shall make them as a fiery oven in the time of Your anger;
The LORD shall swallow them up in His wrath,
And the fire shall devour them.
10 Their offspring You shall destroy from the earth,
And their descendants from among the sons of men.
11 For they intended evil against You;
They devised a plot *which* they are not able *to perform.*
12 Therefore You will make them turn their back;
You will make ready *Your arrows* on Your string toward their faces.

13 Be exalted, O LORD, in Your own strength!
We will sing and praise Your power.

PSALM 22

THE SUFFERING, PRAISE, AND POSTERITY OF THE MESSIAH

To the Chief Musician. Set to "The Deer of the Dawn."[a] *A Psalm of David.*

1 My God, My God, why have You forsaken Me?
Why are You so far from helping Me,
And from the words of My groaning?
2 O My God, I cry in the daytime, but You do not hear;
And in the night season, and am not silent.

3 But You *are* holy,
Enthroned in the praises of Israel.
4 Our fathers trusted in You;
They trusted, and You delivered them.
5 They cried to You, and were delivered;
They trusted in You, and were not ashamed.

6 But I *am* a worm, and no man;
A reproach of men, and despised by the people.
7 All those who see Me ridicule Me;

22:title [a]Hebrew *Aijeleth Hashahar*

They shoot out the lip, they shake the head, *saying,*
8 "He trusted[a] in the LORD, let Him rescue Him;
Let Him deliver Him, since He delights in Him!"

9 But You *are* He who took Me out of the womb;
You made Me trust *while* on My mother's breasts.
10 I was cast upon You from birth.
From My mother's womb
You *have been* My God.
11 Be not far from Me,
For trouble *is* near;
For *there is* none to help.

12 Many bulls have surrounded Me;
Strong *bulls* of Bashan have encircled Me.
13 They gape at Me *with* their mouths,
Like a raging and roaring lion.

14 I am poured out like water,
And all My bones are out of joint;
My heart is like wax;
It has melted within Me.
15 My strength is dried up like a potsherd,
And My tongue clings to My jaws;
You have brought Me to the dust of death.

16 For dogs have surrounded Me;
The congregation of the wicked has enclosed Me.
They pierced[a] My hands and My feet;
17 I can count all My bones.
They look *and* stare at Me.
18 They divide My garments among them,
And for My clothing they cast lots.

19 But You, O LORD, do not be far from Me;
O My Strength, hasten to help Me!
20 Deliver Me from the sword,
My precious *life* from the power of the dog.
21 Save Me from the lion's mouth
And from the horns of the wild oxen!

You have answered Me.

22 I will declare Your name to My brethren;
In the midst of the assembly I will praise You.
23 You who fear the LORD, praise Him!
All you descendants of Jacob, glorify Him,
And fear Him, all you offspring of Israel!
24 For He has not despised nor abhorred the affliction of the afflicted;
Nor has He hidden His face from Him;
But when He cried to Him, He heard.

25 My praise *shall be* of You in the great assembly;
I will pay My vows before those who fear Him.
26 The poor shall eat and be satisfied;
Those who seek Him will praise the LORD.
Let your heart live forever!

27 All the ends of the world
Shall remember and turn to the LORD,
And all the families of the nations
Shall worship before You.[a]

22:8 [a]Septuagint, Syriac, and Vulgate read *hoped;* Targum reads *praised.* **22:16** [a]Following some Hebrew manuscripts, Septuagint, Syriac, Vulgate; Masoretic Text reads *Like a lion.* **22:27** [a]Following Masoretic Text, Septuagint, and Targum; Arabic, Syriac, and Vulgate read *Him.*

SOUL NOTE

The Old Rugged Cross *(ch. 22)* This psalm written by David prophesies the crucifixion of Jesus: the ridicule He faced (22:6–8), the gruesome death on the Cross (22:14–17), and the gambling for His garments (22:18). Jesus Christ experienced agony for all of humanity. His horrible death on the Cross became the final sacrifice for sin, providing for humanity's freedom from sin. We need only accept what Jesus did on the Cross on our behalf, thank Him, and resolve to follow Him. The benefits are eternal. **Topic: Knowing Jesus**

28 For the kingdom *is* the LORD's,
And He rules over the nations.

29 All the prosperous of the earth
Shall eat and worship;
All those who go down to the dust
Shall bow before Him,
Even he who cannot keep himself alive.

30 A posterity shall serve Him.
It will be recounted of the Lord to the *next* generation,
31 They will come and declare His righteousness to a people who will be born,
That He has done *this*.

PSALM 23

THE LORD THE SHEPHERD OF HIS PEOPLE

A Psalm of David.

1 The LORD *is* my shepherd;
I shall not want.
2 He makes me to lie down in green pastures;
He leads me beside the still waters.
3 He restores my soul;
He leads me in the paths of righteousness
For His name's sake.

4 Yea, though I walk through the valley of the shadow of death,
I will fear no evil;
For You *are* with me;
Your rod and Your staff, they comfort me.
5 You prepare a table before me in the presence of my enemies;
You anoint my head with oil;
My cup runs over.
6 Surely goodness and mercy shall follow me
All the days of my life;
And I will dwell[a] in the house of the LORD
Forever.

> The LORD is my shepherd;
> I shall not want.
> PSALM 23:1

PSALM 24

THE KING OF GLORY AND HIS KINGDOM

A Psalm of David.

1 The earth *is* the LORD's, and all its fullness,
The world and those who dwell therein.
2 For He has founded it upon the seas,
And established it upon the waters.

3 Who may ascend into the hill of the LORD?
Or who may stand in His holy place?
4 He who has clean hands and a pure heart,
Who has not lifted up his soul to an idol,
Nor sworn deceitfully.
5 He shall receive blessing from the LORD,
And righteousness from the God of his salvation.
6 This *is* Jacob, the generation of those who seek Him,
Who seek Your face. Selah

23:6 [a]Following Septuagint, Syriac, Targum, and Vulgate; Masoretic Text reads *return*.

SOUL NOTE

The Gateway *(ch. 23)* This chapter expresses confidence in God in the face of death. Even death cannot separate believers from God, for in Him death is not the end, but a gateway to eternal life. Even though we may be walking through "the valley of the shadow of death" (23:4), we need not fear. God's goodness and mercy embrace us every step of the way. The threshold of death brings sorrow, but sorrow transforms to hope. Believers can face death without fear because God is there to greet them. **Topic: Death**

7 Lift up your heads, O you gates!
And be lifted up, you everlasting doors!
And the King of glory shall come in.
8 Who *is* this King of glory?
The LORD strong and mighty,
The LORD mighty in battle.
9 Lift up your heads, O you gates!
Lift up, you everlasting doors!
And the King of glory shall come in.
10 Who is this King of glory?
The LORD of hosts,
He *is* the King of glory. Selah

PSALM 25

A PLEA FOR DELIVERANCE AND FORGIVENESS

A Psalm of David.

1 To You, O LORD, I lift up my soul.
2 O my God, I trust in You;
Let me not be ashamed;
Let not my enemies triumph over me.
3 Indeed, let no one who waits on You be ashamed;
Let those be ashamed who deal treacherously without cause.

4 Show me Your ways, O LORD;
Teach me Your paths.
5 Lead me in Your truth and teach me,
For You *are* the God of my salvation;
On You I wait all the day.

6 Remember, O LORD, Your tender mercies and Your lovingkindnesses,
For they *are* from of old.
7 Do not remember the sins of my youth, nor my transgressions;
According to Your mercy remember me,
For Your goodness' sake, O LORD.

8 Good and upright *is* the LORD;
Therefore He teaches sinners in the way.
9 The humble He guides in justice,
And the humble He teaches His way.
10 All the paths of the LORD *are* mercy and truth,
To such as keep His covenant and His testimonies.
11 For Your name's sake, O LORD,
Pardon my iniquity, for it *is* great.

12 Who *is* the man that fears the LORD?
Him shall He[a] teach in the way He[b] chooses.
13 He himself shall dwell in prosperity,
And his descendants shall inherit the earth.
14 The secret of the LORD *is* with those who fear Him,
And He will show them His covenant.
15 My eyes *are* ever toward the LORD,
For He shall pluck my feet out of the net.

16 Turn Yourself to me, and have mercy on me,
For I *am* desolate and afflicted.
17 The troubles of my heart have enlarged;
Bring me out of my distresses!
18 Look on my affliction and my pain,
And forgive all my sins.
19 Consider my enemies, for they are many;
And they hate me with cruel hatred.
20 Keep my soul, and deliver me;
Let me not be ashamed, for I put my trust in You.
21 Let integrity and uprightness preserve me,
For I wait for You.

22 Redeem Israel, O God,
Out of all their troubles!

PSALM 26

A PRAYER FOR DIVINE SCRUTINY AND REDEMPTION

A Psalm of David.

1 Vindicate me, O LORD,
For I have walked in my integrity.
I have also trusted in the LORD;
I shall not slip.
2 Examine me, O LORD, and prove me;
Try my mind and my heart.
3 For Your lovingkindness *is* before my eyes,
And I have walked in Your truth.
4 I have not sat with idolatrous mortals,
Nor will I go in with hypocrites.
5 I have hated the assembly of evildoers,
And will not sit with the wicked.

6 I will wash my hands in innocence;

25:12 [a]Or *he* [b]Or *he*

So I will go about Your altar, O LORD,
7 That I may proclaim with the voice of thanksgiving,
And tell of all Your wondrous works.
8 LORD, I have loved the habitation of Your house,
And the place where Your glory dwells.

9 Do not gather my soul with sinners,
Nor my life with bloodthirsty men,
10 In whose hands *is* a sinister scheme,
And whose right hand is full of bribes.

11 But as for me, I will walk in my integrity;
Redeem me and be merciful to me.
12 My foot stands in an even place;
In the congregations I will bless the LORD.

PSALM 27

AN EXUBERANT DECLARATION OF FAITH

A Psalm of David.

1 The LORD *is* my light and my salvation;
Whom shall I fear?
The LORD *is* the strength of my life;
Of whom shall I be afraid?
2 When the wicked came against me
To eat up my flesh,
My enemies and foes,
They stumbled and fell.
3 Though an army may encamp against me,
My heart shall not fear;
Though war may rise against me,
In this I *will be* confident.

4 One *thing* I have desired of the LORD,
That will I seek:
That I may dwell in the house of the LORD
All the days of my life,
To behold the beauty of the LORD,
And to inquire in His temple.
5 For in the time of trouble
He shall hide me in His pavilion;
In the secret place of His tabernacle
He shall hide me;
He shall set me high upon a rock.

6 And now my head shall be lifted up above my enemies all around me;
Therefore I will offer sacrifices of joy in His tabernacle;
I will sing, yes, I will sing praises to the LORD.

7 Hear, O LORD, *when* I cry with my voice!
Have mercy also upon me, and answer me.
8 *When You said,* "Seek My face,"
My heart said to You, "Your face, LORD, I will seek."
9 Do not hide Your face from me;
Do not turn Your servant away in anger;
You have been my help;
Do not leave me nor forsake me,
O God of my salvation.
10 When my father and my mother forsake me,
Then the LORD will take care of me.

11 Teach me Your way, O LORD,
And lead me in a smooth path, because of my enemies.
12 Do not deliver me to the will of my adversaries;
For false witnesses have risen against me,
And such as breathe out violence.
13 *I would have lost heart,* unless I had believed
That I would see the goodness of the LORD
In the land of the living.

14 Wait on the LORD;
Be of good courage,
And He shall strengthen your heart;
Wait, I say, on the LORD!

> Wait on the LORD; be of good courage, and He shall strengthen your heart; wait, I say, on the LORD!
>
> PSALM 27:14

PSALM 28

REJOICING IN ANSWERED PRAYER

A Psalm of David.

1 To You I will cry, O LORD my Rock:
Do not be silent to me,

Lest, if You *are* silent to me,
I become like those who go down to the pit.
2 Hear the voice of my supplications
When I cry to You,
When I lift up my hands toward Your holy sanctuary.
3 Do not take me away with the wicked
And with the workers of iniquity,
Who speak peace to their neighbors,
But evil *is* in their hearts.
4 Give them according to their deeds,
And according to the wickedness of their endeavors;
Give them according to the work of their hands;
Render to them what they deserve.
5 Because they do not regard the works of the LORD,
Nor the operation of His hands,
He shall destroy them
And not build them up.

6 Blessed *be* the LORD,
Because He has heard the voice of my supplications!
7 The LORD *is* my strength and my shield;
My heart trusted in Him, and I am helped;
Therefore my heart greatly rejoices,
And with my song I will praise Him.

8 The LORD *is* their strength,[a]
And He *is* the saving refuge of His anointed.
9 Save Your people,
And bless Your inheritance;
Shepherd them also,
And bear them up forever.

PSALM 29

PRAISE TO GOD IN HIS HOLINESS AND MAJESTY

A Psalm of David.

1 Give unto the LORD, O you mighty ones,
Give unto the LORD glory and strength.
2 Give unto the LORD the glory due to His name;
Worship the LORD in the beauty of holiness.

3 The voice of the LORD *is* over the waters;
The God of glory thunders;
The LORD *is* over many waters.
4 The voice of the LORD *is* powerful;
The voice of the LORD *is* full of majesty.

5 The voice of the LORD breaks the cedars,
Yes, the LORD splinters the cedars of Lebanon.
6 He makes them also skip like a calf,
Lebanon and Sirion like a young wild ox.
7 The voice of the LORD divides the flames of fire.

8 The voice of the LORD shakes the wilderness;
The LORD shakes the Wilderness of Kadesh.
9 The voice of the LORD makes the deer give birth,
And strips the forests bare;
And in His temple everyone says, "Glory!"

10 The LORD sat *enthroned* at the Flood,
And the LORD sits as King forever.
11 The LORD will give strength to His people;
The LORD will bless His people with peace.

PSALM 30

THE BLESSEDNESS OF ANSWERED PRAYER

A Psalm. A Song at the dedication of the house of David.

1 I will extol You, O LORD, for You have lifted me up,
And have not let my foes rejoice over me.
2 O LORD my God, I cried out to You,
And You healed me.
3 O LORD, You brought my soul up from the grave;
You have kept me alive, that I should not go down to the pit.[a]

28:8 [a]Following Masoretic Text and Targum; Septuagint, Syriac, and Vulgate read *the strength of His people.* **30:3** [a]Following Qere and Targum; Kethib, Septuagint, Syriac, and Vulgate read *from those who descend to the pit.*

4 Sing praise to the LORD, you saints of His,
And give thanks at the remembrance of His holy name.[a]
5 For His anger *is but for* a moment,
His favor *is for* life;
Weeping may endure for a night,
But joy *comes* in the morning.

6 Now in my prosperity I said,
"I shall never be moved."
7 LORD, by Your favor You have made my mountain stand strong;
You hid Your face, *and* I was troubled.

8 I cried out to You, O LORD;
And to the LORD I made supplication:
9 "What profit *is there* in my blood,
When I go down to the pit?
Will the dust praise You?
Will it declare Your truth?
10 Hear, O LORD, and have mercy on me;
LORD, be my helper!"

11 You have turned for me my mourning into dancing;
You have put off my sackcloth and clothed me with gladness,
12 To the end that *my* glory may sing praise to You and not be silent.
O LORD my God, I will give thanks to You forever.

PSALM 31

THE LORD A FORTRESS IN ADVERSITY

To the Chief Musician. A Psalm of David.

1 In You, O LORD, I put my trust;
Let me never be ashamed;
Deliver me in Your righteousness.
2 Bow down Your ear to me,
Deliver me speedily;
Be my rock of refuge,
A fortress of defense to save me.

3 For You *are* my rock and my fortress;
Therefore, for Your name's sake,
Lead me and guide me.
4 Pull me out of the net which they have secretly laid for me,
For You *are* my strength.
5 Into Your hand I commit my spirit;
You have redeemed me, O LORD God of truth.

6 I have hated those who regard useless idols;
But I trust in the LORD.
7 I will be glad and rejoice in Your mercy,
For You have considered my trouble;
You have known my soul in adversities,
8 And have not shut me up into the hand of the enemy;
You have set my feet in a wide place.

9 Have mercy on me, O LORD, for I am in trouble;
My eye wastes away with grief,
Yes, my soul and my body!
10 For my life is spent with grief,
And my years with sighing;
My strength fails because of my iniquity,
And my bones waste away.
11 I am a reproach among all my enemies,
But especially among my neighbors,
And *am* repulsive to my acquaintances;
Those who see me outside flee from me.
12 I am forgotten like a dead man, out of mind;
I am like a broken vessel.
13 For I hear the slander of many;
Fear *is* on every side;
While they take counsel together against me,
They scheme to take away my life.

14 But as for me, I trust in You, O LORD;
I say, "You *are* my God."
15 My times *are* in Your hand;
Deliver me from the hand of my enemies,
And from those who persecute me.
16 Make Your face shine upon Your servant;
Save me for Your mercies' sake.
17 Do not let me be ashamed, O LORD, for I have called upon You;
Let the wicked be ashamed;
Let them be silent in the grave.
18 Let the lying lips be put to silence,
Which speak insolent things proudly and contemptuously against the righteous.

19 Oh, how great *is* Your goodness,

30:4 [a]Or *His holiness*

Which You have laid up for those who
fear You,
Which You have prepared for those who
trust in You
In the presence of the sons of men!
20 You shall hide them in the secret place
of Your presence
From the plots of man;
You shall keep them secretly in a
pavilion
From the strife of tongues.

21 Blessed *be* the LORD,
For He has shown me His marvelous
kindness in a strong city!
22 For I said in my haste,
"I am cut off from before Your eyes";
Nevertheless You heard the voice of my
supplications
When I cried out to You.

23 Oh, love the LORD, all you His saints!
For the LORD preserves the faithful,
And fully repays the proud person.
24 Be of good courage,
And He shall strengthen your heart,
All you who hope in the LORD.

PSALM 32

THE JOY OF FORGIVENESS

A Psalm of David. A Contemplation.[a]

1 Blessed *is he whose* transgression *is*
forgiven,
Whose sin *is* covered.
2 Blessed *is* the man to whom the LORD
does not impute iniquity,
And in whose spirit *there is* no deceit.

3 When I kept silent, my bones grew old
Through my groaning all the day
long.
4 For day and night Your hand was heavy
upon me;
My vitality was turned into the drought
of summer. Selah
5 I acknowledged my sin to You,
And my iniquity I have not hidden.
I said, "I will confess my transgressions
to the LORD,"
And You forgave the iniquity of my sin.
Selah

6 For this cause everyone who is godly
shall pray to You
In a time when You may be found;
Surely in a flood of great waters
They shall not come near him.
7 You *are* my hiding place;
You shall preserve me from trouble;
You shall surround me with songs of
deliverance. Selah

8 I will instruct you and teach you in the
way you should go;
I will guide you with My eye.
9 Do not be like the horse *or* like the
mule,
Which have no understanding,
Which must be harnessed with bit and
bridle,
Else they will not come near you.

10 Many sorrows *shall be* to the wicked;
But he who trusts in the LORD, mercy
shall surround him.
11 Be glad in the LORD and rejoice, you
righteous;
And shout for joy, all *you* upright in
heart!

PSALM 33

THE SOVEREIGNTY OF THE LORD IN CREATION AND HISTORY

1 Rejoice in the LORD, O you righteous!
For praise from the upright is beautiful.
2 Praise the LORD with the harp;
Make melody to Him with an instrument
of ten strings.
3 Sing to Him a new song;
Play skillfully with a shout of joy.

4 For the word of the LORD *is* right,
And all His work *is done* in truth.
5 He loves righteousness and justice;
The earth is full of the goodness of the
LORD.

6 By the word of the LORD the heavens
were made,
And all the host of them by the breath of
His mouth.

32:title [a]Hebrew *Maschil*

7 He gathers the waters of the sea together
as a heap;[a]
He lays up the deep in storehouses.

8 Let all the earth fear the LORD;
Let all the inhabitants of the world stand
in awe of Him.
9 For He spoke, and it was *done;*
He commanded, and it stood fast.

10 The LORD brings the counsel of the
nations to nothing;
He makes the plans of the peoples of no
effect.
11 The counsel of the LORD stands forever,
The plans of His heart to all generations.
12 Blessed *is* the nation whose God *is* the
LORD,
The people He has chosen as His own
inheritance.

13 The LORD looks from heaven;
He sees all the sons of men.
14 From the place of His dwelling He
looks
On all the inhabitants of the earth;
15 He fashions their hearts individually;
He considers all their works.

16 No king *is* saved by the multitude of an
army;
A mighty man is not delivered by great
strength.
17 A horse *is* a vain hope for safety;
Neither shall it deliver *any* by its great
strength.

18 Behold, the eye of the LORD *is* on those
who fear Him,
On those who hope in His mercy,
19 To deliver their soul from death,
And to keep them alive in famine.

20 Our soul waits for the LORD;
He *is* our help and our shield.
21 For our heart shall rejoice in Him,
Because we have trusted in His holy
name.
22 Let Your mercy, O LORD, be upon us,
Just as we hope in You.

PSALM 34

THE HAPPINESS OF THOSE WHO TRUST IN GOD

*A Psalm of David when he pretended
madness before Abimelech, who
drove him away, and he departed.*

1 I will bless the LORD at all times;
His praise *shall* continually *be* in my
mouth.
2 My soul shall make its boast in the
LORD;
The humble shall hear *of it* and be glad.
3 Oh, magnify the LORD with me,
And let us exalt His name together.

4 I sought the LORD, and He heard me,
And delivered me from all my fears.
5 They looked to Him and were
radiant,
And their faces were not ashamed.
6 This poor man cried out, and the LORD
heard *him,*
And saved him out of all his troubles.
7 The angel[a] of the LORD encamps all
around those who fear Him,
And delivers them.

8 Oh, taste and see that the LORD *is* good;
Blessed *is* the man *who* trusts in Him!

33:7 [a]Septuagint, Targum, and Vulgate read *in a vessel.* **34:7** [a]Or *Angel*

SOUL NOTE

Our Strength *(34:17–22)* No one wants troubles, whether they are from loss, disappointment, physical ailments, or just everyday frustrations. Like the psalmist, God's people can "cry out, and the LORD hears, and delivers them out of all their troubles." David knew from experience that "the LORD is near to those who have a broken heart." Believers can turn to God in their times of difficulty, knowing that He hears, cares, and will help them. When we are weak, He is strong. **Topic: Trials**

9 Oh, fear the LORD, you His saints!
There is no want to those who fear
Him.
10 The young lions lack and suffer hunger;
But those who seek the LORD shall not
lack any good *thing.*

11 Come, you children, listen to me;
I will teach you the fear of the LORD.
12 Who *is* the man *who* desires life,
And loves *many* days, that he may see
good?
13 Keep your tongue from evil,
And your lips from speaking deceit.
14 Depart from evil and do good;
Seek peace and pursue it.

15 The eyes of the LORD *are* on the
righteous,
And His ears *are open* to their cry.
16 The face of the LORD *is* against those
who do evil,
To cut off the remembrance of them
from the earth.

17 *The righteous* cry out, and the LORD
hears,
And delivers them out of all their
troubles.
18 The LORD *is* near to those who have a
broken heart,
And saves such as have a contrite spirit.

19 Many *are* the afflictions of the
righteous,
But the LORD delivers him out of them
all.
20 He guards all his bones;
Not one of them is broken.
21 Evil shall slay the wicked,
And those who hate the righteous shall
be condemned.
22 The LORD redeems the soul of His
servants,
And none of those who trust in Him
shall be condemned.

PSALM 35

THE LORD THE AVENGER OF HIS PEOPLE

A Psalm of David.

1 Plead *my cause,* O LORD, with those who
strive with me;
Fight against those who fight against
me.
2 Take hold of shield and buckler,
And stand up for my help.
3 Also draw out the spear,
And stop those who pursue me.

KEY PASSAGE

Trials

TESTED FAITH

(34:18)

Trials are inevitable. Everyone experiences problems and pain. The Bible figuratively describes it as rain falling "on the just and on the unjust" (Matt. 5:45). Believers can look at their trials in a different light, however. They know, as this psalm says, that "the LORD is near to those who have a broken heart." Even more, however, believers can rejoice in their trials:

- "Count it all joy when you fall into various trials, knowing that the testing of your faith produces patience" (James 1:2, 3).
- "You have been grieved by various trials, that the genuineness of your faith, being much more precious than gold that perishes, though it is tested by fire, may be found to praise, honor, and glory at the revelation of Jesus Christ" (1 Pet. 1:6, 7).

Through trials, God can work in our lives to make us more like Christ.

To Learn More: Turn to the article about trials on pages 706, 707. See also the personality profile of Tamar on page 406.

Say to my soul,
"I *am* your salvation."

4 Let those be put to shame and brought to dishonor
Who seek after my life;
Let those be turned back and brought to confusion
Who plot my hurt.
5 Let them be like chaff before the wind,
And let the angel[a] of the LORD chase *them.*
6 Let their way be dark and slippery,
And let the angel of the LORD pursue them.
7 For without cause they have hidden their net for me *in* a pit,
Which they have dug without cause for my life.
8 Let destruction come upon him unexpectedly,
And let his net that he has hidden catch himself;
Into that very destruction let him fall.

9 And my soul shall be joyful in the LORD;
It shall rejoice in His salvation.
10 All my bones shall say,
"LORD, who *is* like You,
Delivering the poor from him who is too strong for him,
Yes, the poor and the needy from him who plunders him?"

11 Fierce witnesses rise up;
They ask me *things* that I do not know.
12 They reward me evil for good,
To the sorrow of my soul.
13 But as for me, when they were sick,
My clothing *was* sackcloth;
I humbled myself with fasting;
And my prayer would return to my own heart.
14 I paced about as though *he were* my friend *or* brother;
I bowed down heavily, as one who mourns *for his* mother.

15 But in my adversity they rejoiced
And gathered together;
Attackers gathered against me,
And I did not know *it;*
They tore *at me* and did not cease;
16 With ungodly mockers at feasts
They gnashed at me with their teeth.

17 Lord, how long will You look on?
Rescue me from their destructions,
My precious *life* from the lions.
18 I will give You thanks in the great assembly;
I will praise You among many people.

19 Let them not rejoice over me who are wrongfully my enemies;
Nor let them wink with the eye who hate me without a cause.
20 For they do not speak peace,
But they devise deceitful matters
Against *the* quiet ones in the land.
21 They also opened their mouth wide against me,
And said, "Aha, aha!
Our eyes have seen *it.*"

22 *This* You have seen, O LORD;
Do not keep silence.
O Lord, do not be far from me.
23 Stir up Yourself, and awake to my vindication,
To my cause, my God and my Lord.
24 Vindicate me, O LORD my God, according to Your righteousness;
And let them not rejoice over me.
25 Let them not say in their hearts, "Ah, so we would have it!"
Let them not say, "We have swallowed him up."

26 Let them be ashamed and brought to mutual confusion
Who rejoice at my hurt;
Let them be clothed with shame and dishonor
Who exalt themselves against me.

27 Let them shout for joy and be glad,
Who favor my righteous cause;
And let them say continually,
"Let the LORD be magnified,
Who has pleasure in the prosperity of His servant."
28 And my tongue shall speak of Your righteousness
And of Your praise all the day long.

35:5 [a]Or *Angel*

THE TRIAL OF REJECTION

SANDRA D. WILSON

(Psalm 34:18)

Living in a sin-broken world is painful. Not one person will get through life without facing trials of various types, in varying degrees. Some people face trials in their physical lives; others face trials in their family relationships or friendships; others face financial difficulties. Still others face trials and persecutions simply for being Christians.

The Bible offers God's great promises for us as we face trials. James wrote, "Count it all joy when you fall into various trials, knowing that the testing of your faith produces patience" (James 1:2, 3). Peter wrote that believers who are "grieved by various trials" can trust that God is working through those difficulties to perfect their faith (1 Pet. 1:3–9).

One of the most painful trials human beings can experience is the feeling of being rejected, forsaken, or abandoned. The pain associated with this feeling affects many other areas of life.

RECOGNIZING THE TRIAL OF REJECTION

Some people attempt to protect themselves from rejection by adopting an underdependent approach to relationships. They refuse to trust anyone or to invest themselves emotionally. Others become overdependent. They cling tenaciously to relationships to avoid feeling rejected, yet they simultaneously live in fear of it. Most people use some combination of these extremes to cope with rejection.

Following are some traits identified in people who have been wounded by rejection:

- Difficulty trusting people.
- Hypersensitivity to rejection.
- Fear of criticism and anger.
- Habitually trying to rescue needy people because they doubt that "healthy" people would choose to relate to them.
- Toleration of disrespect and even abuse.
- Difficulty trusting God and His Word.

HEALING THE HURT OF REJECTION

Principle 1: Cultivate Increasing Intimacy with God

Despite his obvious failures, David was called "a man after [God's] own heart" (1 Sam. 13:14). David expressed this longing in Psalm 27:4: "One thing I have desired of the LORD . . . that I may dwell in the house of the LORD all the days of my life, to behold the beauty of the LORD." It's no coincidence that this verse comes before verse 10: "When my father and my mother forsake me, then the LORD will take care of me."

When we intentionally cultivate a spiritual environment that fosters intimacy with God, we learn to really know God, not just to know about Him. God's loyal love and eternal presence become more than just theological certainties. They become *experienced realities* in a way that anchors us when trials assail us.

Principle 2: Cultivate Increasingly Balanced Relationships with Others

God's Word contains many relational principles that promote balanced, mutually respectful relationships. Jesus exemplified guidelines for respectful interactions with people. He didn't let people tell Him what to do (Matt. 19:14). He modeled the truth that we don't have to hide our views or values to be congenial or kind. The thought of not doing that may sound terrifying—especially if stating a different opinion exposes us to the risk of rejection by people whose approval we value. Again, Jesus models the solution to that painful problem.

Principle 3: Cultivate Increasingly Realistic Expectations of Ourselves, Others, and God

Jesus clarifies this principle in John 16:32, "You . . . will leave Me alone. And yet I am not alone, because the Father is with Me." Jesus' words summarize two truths that guided His relationships and that hold the key to overcoming the hurt of rejection.

The first truth is that we can't trust people completely. Jesus never put unreserved trust in people because He knew what was in their sinful hearts (John 2:24). All people deserve respect because they bear the image of God, but that respect needs to be realistic enough to know that all people are sinners. People will always disappoint us. Jesus knew that the disciples, who had just declared that they believed He came from God, would soon abandon Him.

The second truth is that dependence on God helps us handle the hurt of rejection. Jesus' confidence in His Father's love created a sense of being "alone but not alone." It's true that Jesus knew God's faithfulness within a uniquely intimate relationship. But as we follow Jesus' God-dependent way of relating, we too will be able to better handle experiences of rejection.

If we've been deeply hurt by rejection, we may face a long process of relearning how to relate to people. We'll know that our relationships are becoming healthier and more God-dependent as we increasingly:

- reach out to others from a deepening sense of fullness in Christ,
- accept the truth that others can never meet all our needs,
- recognize that we can't do that for others either,
- choose to forgive others for their inevitable failings, and
- determine to acknowledge our inevitable failings and to request forgiveness.

There is but one Source of deep healing from rejection. Only when we find ultimate acceptance and security in God can we experience personal peace, relational rest, and healing from the pain of rejection.

IN CONCLUSION

No matter what trials we face, God cares deeply for His children, promising, "The LORD is near to all who call upon Him, to all who call upon Him in truth" (Ps. 145:18). Whatever difficulties come into our lives, God is near to us. He is stronger than rejection, stronger than any other trial we can experience. He is able to meet our every need.

FURTHER MEDITATION:

Other passages to study about the issue of trials include:

- Psalm 118:22
- Isaiah 53:3
- James 1:2
- 1 Peter 1:6–9; 2:4–7

To Learn More: Turn to the key passage note on trials at Psalm 34:18 on page 704. See also the personality profile of Tamar on page 406.

PSALM 36

MAN'S WICKEDNESS AND GOD'S PERFECTIONS

To the Chief Musician. A Psalm of David the servant of the LORD.

1 An oracle within my heart concerning
the transgression of the wicked:
There is no fear of God before his eyes.
2 For he flatters himself in his own eyes,
When he finds out his iniquity *and* when he hates.
3 The words of his mouth *are* wickedness and deceit;
He has ceased to be wise *and* to do good.
4 He devises wickedness on his bed;
He sets himself in a way *that is* not good;
He does not abhor evil.

5 Your mercy, O LORD, *is* in the heavens;
Your faithfulness *reaches* to the clouds.
6 Your righteousness *is* like the great mountains;
Your judgments *are* a great deep;
O LORD, You preserve man and beast.

7 How precious *is* Your lovingkindness, O God!
Therefore the children of men put their trust under the shadow of Your wings.
8 They are abundantly satisfied with the fullness of Your house,
And You give them drink from the river of Your pleasures.
9 For with You *is* the fountain of life;
In Your light we see light.

10 Oh, continue Your lovingkindness to those who know You,
And Your righteousness to the upright in heart.
11 Let not the foot of pride come against me,
And let not the hand of the wicked drive me away.
12 There the workers of iniquity have fallen;
They have been cast down and are not able to rise.

PSALM 37

THE HERITAGE OF THE RIGHTEOUS AND THE CALAMITY OF THE WICKED

A Psalm of David.

1 Do not fret because of evildoers,
Nor be envious of the workers of iniquity.
2 For they shall soon be cut down like the grass,
And wither as the green herb.

3 Trust in the LORD, and do good;
Dwell in the land, and feed on His faithfulness.
4 Delight yourself also in the LORD,
And He shall give you the desires of your heart.

5 Commit your way to the LORD,
Trust also in Him,
And He shall bring *it* to pass.
6 He shall bring forth your righteousness as the light,
And your justice as the noonday.

7 Rest in the LORD, and wait patiently for Him;

SOUL NOTE

Willing to Trust *(37:3–8)* God's people need not worry about evildoers, for God promises to punish them and redeem His people. David encouraged God's people to trust in the Lord (37:3), delight themselves in Him (37:4), commit their way to Him (37:5), and wait patiently for Him to act (37:7). Trusting focuses our faith and deepens our commitment. Delighting means to experience pleasure in His presence. Committing our way to God means entrusting everything in our lives to His guidance and control. Waiting patiently is sometimes difficult, but it often is the ultimate test of our trust in God. **Topic: Trust**

Do not fret because of him who prospers in his way,
Because of the man who brings wicked schemes to pass.
8 Cease from anger, and forsake wrath;
Do not fret—*it* only *causes* harm.

9 For evildoers shall be cut off;
But those who wait on the LORD,
They shall inherit the earth.
10 For yet a little while and the wicked *shall be* no *more;*
Indeed, you will look carefully for his place,
But it *shall be* no *more.*
11 But the meek shall inherit the earth,
And shall delight themselves in the abundance of peace.

12 The wicked plots against the just,
And gnashes at him with his teeth.
13 The Lord laughs at him,
For He sees that his day is coming.
14 The wicked have drawn the sword
And have bent their bow,
To cast down the poor and needy,
To slay those who are of upright conduct.
15 Their sword shall enter their own heart,
And their bows shall be broken.

16 A little that a righteous man has
Is better than the riches of many wicked.
17 For the arms of the wicked shall be broken,
But the LORD upholds the righteous.

18 The LORD knows the days of the upright,
And their inheritance shall be forever.
19 They shall not be ashamed in the evil time,
And in the days of famine they shall be satisfied.
20 But the wicked shall perish;
And the enemies of the LORD,
Like the splendor of the meadows, shall vanish.
Into smoke they shall vanish away.

21 The wicked borrows and does not repay,
But the righteous shows mercy and gives.
22 For *those* blessed by Him shall inherit the earth,
But *those* cursed by Him shall be cut off.

23 The steps of a *good* man are ordered by the LORD,
And He delights in his way.
24 Though he fall, he shall not be utterly cast down;
For the LORD upholds *him with* His hand.

25 I have been young, and *now* am old;
Yet I have not seen the righteous forsaken,
Nor his descendants begging bread.
26 *He is* ever merciful, and lends;
And his descendants *are* blessed.

27 Depart from evil, and do good;
And dwell forevermore.
28 For the LORD loves justice,
And does not forsake His saints;
They are preserved forever,
But the descendants of the wicked shall be cut off.
29 The righteous shall inherit the land,
And dwell in it forever.

30 The mouth of the righteous speaks wisdom,

SOUL NOTE

Don't Give Up *(37:23, 24)* Following God, having our steps "ordered by the LORD," does not guarantee success in every endeavor. In fact, some lessons that God wants to teach can only come through failure. When God's people fall, however, He does not allow them to be "utterly cast down." Instead, He helps them back up so that they can learn what He wants to teach them and move on toward success. The only real failures are those who give up on God and refuse to get up and go on.
Topic: Failure

And his tongue talks of justice.
31 The law of his God *is* in his heart;
None of his steps shall slide.

32 The wicked watches the righteous,
And seeks to slay him.
33 The LORD will not leave him in his hand,
Nor condemn him when he is judged.

34 Wait on the LORD,
And keep His way,
And He shall exalt you to inherit the land;
When the wicked are cut off, you shall see *it*.
35 I have seen the wicked in great power,
And spreading himself like a native green tree.
36 Yet he passed away,[a] and behold, he *was* no *more;*
Indeed I sought him, but he could not be found.

37 Mark the blameless *man,* and observe the upright;
For the future of *that* man *is* peace.
38 But the transgressors shall be destroyed together;
The future of the wicked shall be cut off.

39 But the salvation of the righteous *is* from the LORD;
He is their strength in the time of trouble.
40 And the LORD shall help them and deliver them;
He shall deliver them from the wicked,
And save them,
Because they trust in Him.

PSALM 38

PRAYER IN TIME OF CHASTENING

A Psalm of David. To bring to remembrance.

1 O LORD, do not rebuke me in Your wrath,
Nor chasten me in Your hot displeasure!
2 For Your arrows pierce me deeply,
And Your hand presses me down.

3 *There is* no soundness in my flesh
Because of Your anger,
Nor *any* health in my bones
Because of my sin.
4 For my iniquities have gone over my head;
Like a heavy burden they are too heavy for me.
5 My wounds are foul *and* festering
Because of my foolishness.

6 I am troubled, I am bowed down greatly;
I go mourning all the day long.
7 For my loins are full of inflammation,
And *there is* no soundness in my flesh.
8 I am feeble and severely broken;
I groan because of the turmoil of my heart.

9 Lord, all my desire *is* before You;
And my sighing is not hidden from You.
10 My heart pants, my strength fails me;
As for the light of my eyes, it also has gone from me.

11 My loved ones and my friends stand aloof from my plague,
And my relatives stand afar off.
12 Those also who seek my life lay snares *for me;*
Those who seek my hurt speak of destruction,
And plan deception all the day long.

13 But I, like a deaf *man,* do not hear;
And *I am* like a mute *who* does not open his mouth.
14 Thus I am like a man who does not hear,
And in whose mouth *is* no response.

15 For in You, O LORD, I hope;
You will hear, O Lord my God.
16 For I said, "*Hear me,* lest they rejoice over me,
Lest, when my foot slips, they exalt *themselves* against me."

17 For I *am* ready to fall,
And my sorrow *is* continually before me.
18 For I will declare my iniquity;
I will be in anguish over my sin.
19 But my enemies *are* vigorous, *and* they are strong;

37:36 [a]Following Masoretic Text, Septuagint, and Targum; Syriac and Vulgate read *I passed by.*

And those who hate me wrongfully have multiplied.
20 Those also who render evil for good,
They are my adversaries, because I follow *what is* good.

21 Do not forsake me, O LORD;
O my God, be not far from me!
22 Make haste to help me,
O Lord, my salvation!

PSALM 39

PRAYER FOR WISDOM AND FORGIVENESS

To the Chief Musician. To Jeduthun. A Psalm of David.

1 I said, "I will guard my ways,
Lest I sin with my tongue;
I will restrain my mouth with a muzzle,
While the wicked are before me."
2 I was mute with silence,
I held my peace *even* from good;
And my sorrow was stirred up.
3 My heart was hot within me;
While I was musing, the fire burned.
Then I spoke with my tongue:

4 "LORD, make me to know my end,
And what *is* the measure of my days,
That I may know how frail I *am*.
5 Indeed, You have made my days *as* handbreadths,
And my age *is* as nothing before You;
Certainly every man at his best state *is* but vapor. Selah
6 Surely every man walks about like a shadow;
Surely they busy themselves in vain;
He heaps up *riches*,
And does not know who will gather them.

7 "And now, Lord, what do I wait for?
My hope *is* in You.
8 Deliver me from all my transgressions;
Do not make me the reproach of the foolish.
9 I was mute, I did not open my mouth,
Because it was You who did *it*.
10 Remove Your plague from me;
I am consumed by the blow of Your hand.
11 When with rebukes You correct man for iniquity,
You make his beauty melt away like a moth;
Surely every man *is* vapor. Selah

12 "Hear my prayer, O LORD,
And give ear to my cry;
Do not be silent at my tears;
For I *am* a stranger with You,
A sojourner, as all my fathers *were*.
13 Remove Your gaze from me, that I may regain strength,
Before I go away and am no more."

PSALM 40

FAITH PERSEVERING IN TRIAL

To the Chief Musician. A Psalm of David.

1 I waited patiently for the LORD;
And He inclined to me,
And heard my cry.
2 He also brought me up out of a horrible pit,
Out of the miry clay,
And set my feet upon a rock,
And established my steps.
3 He has put a new song in my mouth—
Praise to our God;
Many will see *it* and fear,
And will trust in the LORD.

SOUL NOTE

A Raindrop in the Ocean *(39:4, 5)* People's lifetimes are but a small measure in the hand of God; it is "as nothing" to Him, like a raindrop in the ocean. Yet our life span is all the time that God has given us here. One of the great challenges of aging is to understand that, while time is passing, God is working through us to make a difference in the world. No matter what our age, we must use our time wisely, fully, actively, and selflessly, giving thanks for each new day and seeking how God would have us serve Him. **Topic: Aging/Elderly**

4 Blessed *is* that man who makes the LORD his trust,
And does not respect the proud, nor such as turn aside to lies.
5 Many, O LORD my God, *are* Your wonderful works
Which You have done;
And Your thoughts toward us
Cannot be recounted to You in order;
If I would declare and speak *of them,*
They are more than can be numbered.

6 Sacrifice and offering You did not desire;
My ears You have opened.
Burnt offering and sin offering You did not require.
7 Then I said, "Behold, I come;
In the scroll of the book *it is* written of me.
8 I delight to do Your will, O my God,
And Your law *is* within my heart."

9 I have proclaimed the good news of righteousness
In the great assembly;
Indeed, I do not restrain my lips,
O LORD, You Yourself know.
10 I have not hidden Your righteousness within my heart;
I have declared Your faithfulness and Your salvation;
I have not concealed Your lovingkindness and Your truth
From the great assembly.

11 Do not withhold Your tender mercies from me, O LORD;
Let Your lovingkindness and Your truth continually preserve me.
12 For innumerable evils have surrounded me;
My iniquities have overtaken me, so that I am not able to look up;
They are more than the hairs of my head;
Therefore my heart fails me.

13 Be pleased, O LORD, to deliver me;
O LORD, make haste to help me!
14 Let them be ashamed and brought to mutual confusion
Who seek to destroy my life;
Let them be driven backward and brought to dishonor
Who wish me evil.
15 Let them be confounded because of their shame,
Who say to me, "Aha, aha!"

16 Let all those who seek You rejoice and be glad in You;
Let such as love Your salvation say continually,
"The LORD be magnified!"
17 But I *am* poor and needy;
Yet the LORD thinks upon me.
You *are* my help and my deliverer;
Do not delay, O my God.

PSALM 41

THE BLESSING AND SUFFERING OF THE GODLY

To the Chief Musician. A Psalm of David.

1 Blessed *is* he who considers the poor;
The LORD will deliver him in time of trouble.
2 The LORD will preserve him and keep him alive,
And he will be blessed on the earth;
You will not deliver him to the will of his enemies.
3 The LORD will strengthen him on his bed of illness;
You will sustain him on his sickbed.

4 I said, "LORD, be merciful to me;
Heal my soul, for I have sinned against You."
5 My enemies speak evil of me:
"When will he die, and his name perish?"
6 And if he comes to see *me,* he speaks lies;
His heart gathers iniquity to itself;
When he goes out, he tells *it.*

7 All who hate me whisper together against me;
Against me they devise my hurt.
8 "An evil disease," *they say,* "clings to him.
And *now* that he lies down, he will rise up no more."
9 Even my own familiar friend in whom I trusted,

Who ate my bread,
Has lifted up *his* heel against me.

10 But You, O LORD, be merciful to me, and raise me up,
That I may repay them.
11 By this I know that You are well pleased with me,
Because my enemy does not triumph over me.
12 As for me, You uphold me in my integrity,
And set me before Your face forever.

13 Blessed *be* the LORD God of Israel
From everlasting to everlasting!
Amen and Amen.

BOOK TWO: PSALMS 42–72

PSALM 42

YEARNING FOR GOD IN THE MIDST OF DISTRESSES

To the Chief Musician. A Contemplation[a] *of the sons of Korah.*

1 As the deer pants for the water brooks,
So pants my soul for You, O God.
2 My soul thirsts for God, for the living God.
When shall I come and appear before God?[a]

42:title [a]Hebrew *Maschil* **42:2** [a]Following Masoretic Text and Vulgate; some Hebrew manuscripts, Septuagint, Syriac, and Targum read *I see the face of God.*

PERSONALITY PROFILE

Anxiety

DAVID: THE ANXIETIES OF A KING

(PSALM 42)

"Tears." "Cast down." "Disquieted." David, the great king of Israel, conquering hero, and slayer of Goliath, uttered these unsettling words. Evidently this man, who as a boy equipped with just a sling and his faith had conquered a giant, also faced times of anxiety and fear. Possibly the years of running from Saul's murderous jealousy traumatized David and set him up for a lifelong struggle with anxiety. He seems obsessive in his focus on his enemies. Throughout the psalms, he laments people's wickedness and violence and entreats God to deliver him and his nation from such evil. He wrote of feeling alone and forgotten by God: "I will say to God my Rock, 'Why have You forgotten me? Why do I go mourning because of the oppression of the enemy?' " (Ps. 42:9). Anxiety responds, "No one can help me—not even God." There is no peace when the mind is filled with such toxic thinking.

One of David's great contributions is the record in the Psalms of his response to his fears and anxieties. Instead of turning away from God, he grabbed more tightly onto Him. Psalm 94:19 states, "In the multitude of my anxieties within me, Your comforts delight my soul." And Psalm 34:4 exclaims: "I sought the LORD, and He heard me, and delivered me from all my fears."

David described his fears—he didn't dismiss or deny them—and then he turned them over to God. He replaced those thoughts by recalling God's goodness, power, and faithful intervention in his life. This moved him to break out in praise and thankfulness, celebrating life and worshiping the God who had never forsaken him. Because of this faithful practice over many years, David was able to proclaim his victory over anxiety:

- "The LORD is my light and my salvation; whom shall I fear? The LORD is the strength of my life; of whom shall I be afraid?" (Ps. 27:1)
- "Hope in God; for I shall yet praise Him, the help of my countenance and my God" (Ps. 42:11).

To Learn More: Turn to the article about anxiety on pages 1568, 1569. See also the key passage note at Philippians 4:6–13 on page 1567.

3 My tears have been my food day and
night,
While they continually say to me,
"Where *is* your God?"

4 When I remember these *things,*
I pour out my soul within me.
For I used to go with the multitude;
I went with them to the house of God,
With the voice of joy and praise,
With a multitude that kept a pilgrim
feast.

5 Why are you cast down, O my soul?
And *why* are you disquieted within me?
Hope in God, for I shall yet praise Him
For the help of His countenance.[a]

6 O my God,[a] my soul is cast down within
me;
Therefore I will remember You from the
land of the Jordan,
And from the heights of Hermon,
From the Hill Mizar.
7 Deep calls unto deep at the noise of Your
waterfalls;
All Your waves and billows have gone
over me.
8 The LORD will command His
lovingkindness in the daytime,
And in the night His song *shall be* with
me—
A prayer to the God of my life.

9 I will say to God my Rock,
"Why have You forgotten me?
Why do I go mourning because of the
oppression of the enemy?"
10 *As* with a breaking of my bones,
My enemies reproach me,
While they say to me all day long,
"Where *is* your God?"

11 Why are you cast down, O my soul?
And why are you disquieted within me?
Hope in God;
For I shall yet praise Him,
The help of my countenance and my God.

PSALM 43

PRAYER TO GOD IN TIME OF TROUBLE

1 Vindicate me, O God,
And plead my cause against an ungodly
nation;
Oh, deliver me from the deceitful and
unjust man!
2 For You *are* the God of my strength;
Why do You cast me off?
Why do I go mourning because of the
oppression of the enemy?

3 Oh, send out Your light and Your truth!
Let them lead me;
Let them bring me to Your holy hill
And to Your tabernacle.
4 Then I will go to the altar of God,
To God my exceeding joy;
And on the harp I will praise You,
O God, my God.

5 Why are you cast down, O my soul?
And why are you disquieted within me?

42:5 [a]Following Masoretic Text and Targum; a few Hebrew manuscripts, Septuagint, Syriac, and Vulgate read *The help of my countenance, my God.*
42:6 [a]Following Masoretic Text and Targum; a few Hebrew manuscripts, Septuagint, Syriac, and Vulgate put *my God* at the end of verse 5.

SOUL NOTE

Hope in God *(42:5–11)* David was discouraged because he had been exiled by a jealous king and so was unable to worship in the tabernacle. His soul was "cast down" and "disquieted." Such depressed feelings cause some people to turn away from God. Others like David, however, allow those disquieted, depressed feelings to make them "hope in God," remembering His goodness. During such times, living by faith takes on new meaning. Depressed people must learn to trust what they cannot feel or see, knowing that "the LORD will command His lovingkindness in the daytime, and in the night His song shall be with" them (42:8). **Topic: Depression**

Hope in God;
For I shall yet praise Him,
The help of my countenance and my God.

PSALM 44

Redemption Remembered in Present Dishonor

To the Chief Musician. A Contemplation[a] *of the sons of Korah.*

1 We have heard with our ears, O God,
Our fathers have told us,
The deeds You did in their days,
In days of old:
2 You drove out the nations with Your hand,
But them You planted;
You afflicted the peoples, and cast them out.
3 For they did not gain possession of the land by their own sword,
Nor did their own arm save them;
But it was Your right hand, Your arm, and the light of Your countenance,
Because You favored them.

4 You are my King, O God;[a]
Command[b] victories for Jacob.
5 Through You we will push down our enemies;
Through Your name we will trample those who rise up against us.
6 For I will not trust in my bow,
Nor shall my sword save me.
7 But You have saved us from our enemies,
And have put to shame those who hated us.
8 In God we boast all day long,
And praise Your name forever. Selah

9 But You have cast *us* off and put us to shame,
And You do not go out with our armies.
10 You make us turn back from the enemy,
And those who hate us have taken spoil for themselves.
11 You have given us up like sheep *intended* for food,
And have scattered us among the nations.
12 You sell Your people for *next to* nothing,
And are not enriched by selling them.

13 You make us a reproach to our neighbors,
A scorn and a derision to those all around us.
14 You make us a byword among the nations,
A shaking of the head among the peoples.
15 My dishonor *is* continually before me,
And the shame of my face has covered me,
16 Because of the voice of him who reproaches and reviles,
Because of the enemy and the avenger.

17 All this has come upon us;
But we have not forgotten You,
Nor have we dealt falsely with Your covenant.
18 Our heart has not turned back,
Nor have our steps departed from Your way;
19 But You have severely broken us in the place of jackals,
And covered us with the shadow of death.

20 If we had forgotten the name of our God,

44:title [a]Hebrew *Maschil* **44:4** [a]Following Masoretic Text and Targum; Septuagint and Vulgate read *and my God.* [b]Following Masoretic Text and Targum; Septuagint, Syriac, and Vulgate read *Who commands.*

SOUL NOTE

Antidepressant *(43:5)* David repeated his words from Psalm 42:5 and 11, for this truth truly helped him during times of great difficulty. In the final analysis, when life is difficult and trials are overwhelming, believers must "hope in God." Such hope is the confident expectation that God will bring whatever is necessary to meet our needs. Such hope trusts that God will do what is best, no matter what we might feel. Such hope praises God for who He is and what He has done. **Topic: Hope**

Or stretched out our hands to a foreign god,
21 Would not God search this out?
For He knows the secrets of the heart.
22 Yet for Your sake we are killed all day long;
We are accounted as sheep for the slaughter.

23 Awake! Why do You sleep, O Lord?
Arise! Do not cast *us* off forever.
24 Why do You hide Your face,
And forget our affliction and our oppression?
25 For our soul is bowed down to the dust;
Our body clings to the ground.
26 Arise for our help,
And redeem us for Your mercies' sake.

PSALM 45

The Glories of the Messiah and His Bride

To the Chief Musician. Set to "The Lilies."[a]
A Contemplation[b] *of the sons of Korah.*
A Song of Love.

1 My heart is overflowing with a good theme;
I recite my composition concerning the King;
My tongue *is* the pen of a ready writer.

2 You are fairer than the sons of men;
Grace is poured upon Your lips;
Therefore God has blessed You forever.
3 Gird Your sword upon *Your* thigh,
O Mighty One,
With Your glory and Your majesty.
4 And in Your majesty ride prosperously because of truth, humility, *and* righteousness;
And Your right hand shall teach You awesome things.
5 Your arrows *are* sharp in the heart of the King's enemies;
The peoples fall under You.

6 Your throne, O God, *is* forever and ever;
A scepter of righteousness *is* the scepter of Your kingdom.
7 You love righteousness and hate wickedness;
Therefore God, Your God, has anointed You
With the oil of gladness more than Your companions.
8 All Your garments are scented with myrrh and aloes *and* cassia,
Out of the ivory palaces, by which they have made You glad.
9 Kings' daughters *are* among Your honorable women;
At Your right hand stands the queen in gold from Ophir.

10 Listen, O daughter,
Consider and incline your ear;
Forget your own people also, and your father's house;
11 So the King will greatly desire your beauty;
Because He *is* your Lord, worship Him.
12 And the daughter of Tyre *will come* with a gift;
The rich among the people will seek your favor.

13 The royal daughter *is* all glorious within *the palace;*
Her clothing *is* woven with gold.
14 She shall be brought to the King in robes of many colors;
The virgins, her companions who follow her, shall be brought to You.
15 With gladness and rejoicing they shall be brought;
They shall enter the King's palace.

16 Instead of Your fathers shall be Your sons,
Whom You shall make princes in all the earth.
17 I will make Your name to be remembered in all generations;
Therefore the people shall praise You forever and ever.

PSALM 46

God the Refuge of His People and Conqueror of the Nations

To the Chief Musician. A Psalm of the sons of Korah. A Song for Alamoth.

1 God *is* our refuge and strength,
A very present help in trouble.

45:title [a]Hebrew *Shoshannim* [b]Hebrew *Maschil*

2 Therefore we will not fear,
Even though the earth be removed,
And though the mountains be carried
into the midst of the sea;
3 *Though* its waters roar *and* be troubled,
Though the mountains shake with its
swelling. Selah

4 *There is* a river whose streams shall
make glad the city of God,
The holy *place* of the tabernacle of the
Most High.
5 God *is* in the midst of her, she shall not
be moved;
God shall help her, just at the break of
dawn.
6 The nations raged, the kingdoms were
moved;
He uttered His voice, the earth melted.

7 The LORD of hosts *is* with us;
The God of Jacob *is* our refuge. Selah

8 Come, behold the works of the LORD,
Who has made desolations in the earth.
9 He makes wars cease to the end of the
earth;
He breaks the bow and cuts the spear in
two;
He burns the chariot in the fire.

10 Be still, and know that I *am* God;
I will be exalted among the nations,
I will be exalted in the earth!

11 The LORD of hosts *is* with us;
The God of Jacob *is* our refuge.
Selah

PSALM 47

PRAISE TO GOD, THE RULER OF THE EARTH

To the Chief Musician. A Psalm of the sons of Korah.

1 Oh, clap your hands, all you peoples!
Shout to God with the voice of triumph!
2 For the LORD Most High *is* awesome;
He is a great King over all the earth.
3 He will subdue the peoples under us,
And the nations under our feet.
4 He will choose our inheritance for us,
The excellence of Jacob whom He loves.
Selah

5 God has gone up with a shout,
The LORD with the sound of a trumpet.
6 Sing praises to God, sing praises!
Sing praises to our King, sing praises!
7 For God *is* the King of all the earth;
Sing praises with understanding.

8 God reigns over the nations;
God sits on His holy throne.
9 The princes of the people have gathered
together,
The people of the God of Abraham.
For the shields of the earth *belong* to God;
He is greatly exalted.

KEY PASSAGE

Crises

A MIGHTY FORTRESS

(46:1)

In ancient Israel, God told the people to set aside six cities of refuge to whom a person could run for safety in a crisis (see Num. 35:9–15). This psalm pictures God as a "refuge and strength, a very present help in trouble." During any crisis, God is our refuge. Even when it seems as though the world is coming apart like mountains crumbling (Ps. 46:3), God's people need not be afraid. Like the protective walls of a city, God is our refuge, surrounding and protecting us. David faced many crises, and he knew to run to God for safety. To "be still" and know that He is God (Ps. 46:10) means to rest in Him, even as the crisis swirls around us. Knowing who God is helps us to remember that He is ultimately in control.

To Learn More: Turn to the article about crises on pages 1194, 1195. See also the personality profile of David and Absalom on page 415.

PSALM 48

THE GLORY OF GOD IN ZION

A Song. A Psalm of the sons of Korah.

1 Great *is* the LORD, and greatly to be praised
In the city of our God,
In His holy mountain.
2 Beautiful in elevation,
The joy of the whole earth,
Is Mount Zion *on* the sides of the north,
The city of the great King.
3 God *is* in her palaces;
He is known as her refuge.

4 For behold, the kings assembled,
They passed by together.
5 They saw *it, and* so they marveled;
They were troubled, they hastened away.
6 Fear took hold of them there,
And pain, as of a woman in birth pangs,
7 *As when* You break the ships of Tarshish
With an east wind.

8 As we have heard,
So we have seen
In the city of the LORD of hosts,
In the city of our God:
God will establish it forever. Selah

9 We have thought, O God, on Your lovingkindness,
In the midst of Your temple.
10 According to Your name, O God,
So *is* Your praise to the ends of the earth;
Your right hand is full of righteousness.
11 Let Mount Zion rejoice,
Let the daughters of Judah be glad,
Because of Your judgments.

12 Walk about Zion,
And go all around her.
Count her towers;
13 Mark well her bulwarks;
Consider her palaces;
That you may tell *it* to the generation following.
14 For this *is* God,
Our God forever and ever;
He will be our guide
Even to death.[a]

PSALM 49

THE CONFIDENCE OF THE FOOLISH

To the Chief Musician. A Psalm of the sons of Korah.

1 Hear this, all peoples;
Give ear, all inhabitants of the world,
2 Both low and high,
Rich and poor together.
3 My mouth shall speak wisdom,
And the meditation of my heart *shall give* understanding.
4 I will incline my ear to a proverb;
I will disclose my dark saying on the harp.

5 Why should I fear in the days of evil,
When the iniquity at my heels surrounds me?
6 Those who trust in their wealth
And boast in the multitude of their riches,
7 None *of them* can by any means redeem *his* brother,
Nor give to God a ransom for him—

48:14 [a]Following Masoretic Text and Syriac; Septuagint and Vulgate read *Forever.*

SOUL NOTE

Secure *(49:1–10)* People can become insecure when they focus on the differences between themselves and others. There will always be someone more wealthy, more good-looking, more intelligent. But eventually life in this world will be over, and those differences will be meaningless. The only difference that ultimately matters is whether people have trusted Christ for salvation. When we feel like we don't measure up, we must look at ourselves as God sees us. If we have trusted Christ for salvation, we are eternally secure. **Topic: Insecurity**

8 For the redemption of their souls *is*
costly,
And it shall cease forever—
9 That he should continue to live
eternally,
And not see the Pit.

10 For he sees wise men die;
Likewise the fool and the senseless
person perish,
And leave their wealth to others.
11 Their inner thought *is that* their houses
will last forever,[a]
Their dwelling places to all generations;
They call *their* lands after their own
names.
12 Nevertheless man, *though* in honor, does
not remain;[a]
He is like the beasts *that* perish.

13 This is the way of those who *are* foolish,
And of their posterity who approve their
sayings. Selah
14 Like sheep they are laid in the grave;
Death shall feed on them;
The upright shall have dominion over
them in the morning;
And their beauty shall be consumed in
the grave, far from their dwelling.
15 But God will redeem my soul from the
power of the grave,
For He shall receive me. Selah

16 Do not be afraid when one becomes
rich,
When the glory of
his house is
increased;
17 For when he dies
he shall carry
nothing away;
His glory shall not
descend after
him.
18 Though while he lives he blesses
himself
(For *men* will praise you when you do
well for yourself),
19 He shall go to the generation of his
fathers;
They shall never see light.
20 A man *who is* in honor, yet does not
understand,
Is like the beasts *that* perish.

PSALM 50

God the Righteous Judge

A Psalm of Asaph.

1 The Mighty One, God the LORD,
Has spoken and called the earth
From the rising of the sun to its going
down.
2 Out of Zion, the perfection of beauty,
God will shine forth.
3 Our God shall come, and shall not keep
silent;
A fire shall devour before Him,
And it shall be very tempestuous all
around Him.

4 He shall call to the heavens from above,
And to the earth, that He may judge His
people:
5 "Gather My saints together to Me,
Those who have made a covenant with
Me by sacrifice."
6 Let the heavens declare His
righteousness,
For God Himself *is* Judge. Selah

7 "Hear, O My people, and I will speak,
O Israel, and I will testify against you;
I *am* God, your God!
8 I will not rebuke you for your sacrifices
Or your burnt offerings,
Which are continually before Me.
9 I will not take a bull from your house,
Nor goats out of your folds.
10 For every beast of the forest *is* Mine,
And the cattle on a
thousand hills.
11 I know all the
birds of the
mountains,
And the wild
beasts of the
field *are* Mine.

"Call upon Me in the day of trouble;
I will deliver you, and you
shall glorify Me."
PSALM 50:15

12 "If I were hungry, I would not tell you;
For the world *is* Mine, and all its fullness.
13 Will I eat the flesh of bulls,
Or drink the blood of goats?

49:11 [a]Septuagint, Syriac, Targum, and Vulgate read *Their graves shall be their houses forever.*
49:12 [a]Following Masoretic Text and Targum; Septuagint, Syriac, and Vulgate read *understand* (compare verse 20).

14 Offer to God thanksgiving,
And pay your vows to the Most High.
15 Call upon Me in the day of trouble;
I will deliver you, and you shall glorify
Me."

16 But to the wicked God says:
"What *right* have you to declare My
statutes,
Or take My covenant in your mouth,
17 Seeing you hate instruction
And cast My words behind you?
18 When you saw a thief, you consented[a]
with him,
And have been a partaker with
adulterers.
19 You give your mouth to evil,
And your tongue frames deceit.
20 You sit *and* speak against your brother;
You slander your own mother's son.
21 These *things* you have done, and I kept
silent;
You thought that I was altogether like
you;
But I will rebuke you,
And set *them* in order before your eyes.

22 "Now consider this, you who forget God,
Lest I tear *you* in pieces,
And *there be* none to deliver:
23 Whoever offers praise glorifies Me;
And to him who orders *his* conduct
aright
I will show the salvation of God."

PSALM 51

A Prayer of Repentance

To the Chief Musician. A Psalm of David when Nathan the prophet went to him, after he had gone in to Bathsheba.

1 Have mercy upon me, O God,
According to Your lovingkindness;
According to the multitude of Your
tender mercies,
Blot out my transgressions.
2 Wash me thoroughly from my iniquity,
And cleanse me from my sin.

3 For I acknowledge my transgressions,
And my sin *is* always before me.
4 Against You, You only, have I sinned,
And done *this* evil in Your sight—
That You may be found just when You
speak,[a]
And blameless when You judge.

5 Behold, I was brought forth in iniquity,
And in sin my mother conceived me.
6 Behold, You desire truth in the inward
parts,
And in the hidden *part* You will make
me to know wisdom.

7 Purge me with hyssop, and I shall be
clean;
Wash me, and I shall be whiter than
snow.
8 Make me hear joy and gladness,
That the bones You have broken may
rejoice.
9 Hide Your face from my sins,
And blot out all my iniquities.

10 Create in me a clean heart, O God,
And renew a steadfast spirit within me.
11 Do not cast me away from Your
presence,
And do not take Your Holy Spirit from
me.

12 Restore to me the joy of Your salvation,
And uphold me *by Your* generous Spirit.
13 *Then* I will teach transgressors Your
ways,
And sinners shall be converted to You.

14 Deliver me from the guilt of bloodshed,
O God,
The God of my salvation,
And my tongue shall sing aloud of Your
righteousness.
15 O Lord, open my lips,
And my mouth shall show forth Your
praise.
16 For You do not desire sacrifice, or else I
would give *it;*
You do not delight in burnt offering.
17 The sacrifices of God *are* a broken spirit,
A broken and a contrite heart—
These, O God, You will not despise.

18 Do good in Your good pleasure to Zion;
Build the walls of Jerusalem.

50:18 [a]Septuagint, Syriac, Targum, and Vulgate read *ran.* **51:4** [a]Septuagint, Targum, and Vulgate read *in Your words.*

19 Then You shall be pleased with the
sacrifices of righteousness,
With burnt offering and whole burnt
offering;
Then they shall offer bulls on Your altar.

PSALM 52

THE END OF THE WICKED AND THE PEACE OF THE GODLY

To the Chief Musician. A Contemplation[a] of David when Doeg the Edomite went and told Saul, and said to him, "David has gone to the house of Ahimelech."

1 Why do you boast in evil, O mighty man?
The goodness of God *endures*
continually.
2 Your tongue devises destruction,
Like a sharp razor, working deceitfully.
3 You love evil more than good,
Lying rather than speaking
righteousness. Selah
4 You love all devouring words,
You deceitful tongue.

5 God shall likewise destroy you forever;
He shall take you away, and pluck you
out of *your* dwelling place,
And uproot you from the land of the
living. Selah
6 The righteous also shall see and fear,
And shall laugh at him, *saying,*
7 "Here is the man *who* did not make God
his strength,
But trusted in the abundance of his
riches,
And strengthened himself in his
wickedness."

8 But I *am* like a green olive tree in the
house of God;
I trust in the mercy of God forever and
ever.
9 I will praise You forever,
Because You have done *it;*
And in the presence of Your saints
I will wait on Your name, for *it is* good.

PSALM 53

FOLLY OF THE GODLESS, AND THE RESTORATION OF ISRAEL

To the Chief Musician. Set to "Mahalath." A Contemplation[a] of David.

1 The fool has said in his heart,
"*There is* no God."
They are corrupt, and have done
abominable iniquity;
There is none who does good.

2 God looks down from heaven upon the
children of men,
To see if there are *any* who understand,
who seek God.
3 Every one of them has turned aside;
They have together become corrupt;
There is none who does good,
No, not one.

4 Have the workers of iniquity no
knowledge,
Who eat up my people *as* they eat bread,
And do not call upon God?
5 There they are in great fear
Where no fear was,
For God has scattered the bones of him
who encamps against you;
You have put *them* to shame,
Because God has despised them.

52:title [a]Hebrew *Maschil* **53:title** [a]Hebrew *Maschil*

SOUL NOTE

Cleansed *(ch. 51)* David wrote this psalm after he had been confronted about his sin with Bathsheba. Though sins may differ in kind, they do not differ much in degree when we consider that any sin ruins a person's relationship with God and must be confessed. David confessed his sin and cried out to God to cleanse him. He had a "broken spirit, a broken and a contrite heart" (51:17). Genuine repentance begins with the broken spirit and results in changed behavior. Repentant people confess the sin, ask for God's forgiveness, and then remove the sin from their lives. **Topic: Repentance**

THE BLESSING OF A REPENTANT HEART

E. GLENN WAGNER

(Psalm 51)

From naughty children to sneaky politicians, nobody likes to get caught. When people deny sin, hide it, or blame someone or something outside of themselves, their sin will eventually consume and drain them. David wrote, "When I kept silent, my bones grew old through my groaning all the day long. . . . My vitality was turned into the drought of summer" (Ps. 32:3, 4).

A STORY OF SIN AND REPENTANCE

After King David committed adultery with Bathsheba and she became pregnant, he tried to cover his mistake by summoning her husband, Uriah, from the battlefield. However, the plan didn't work because of Uriah's integrity. Uriah refused to take comfort with his wife while his fellow soldiers were suffering the hardships of battle. So David sent Uriah to the front lines in order to make sure that he would be killed in combat (2 Sam. 11). David's secret was safe, but only for the moment. God later sent Nathan the prophet to confront the king about his sin. Nathan's stinging rebuke exposed the king's sin. Faced with the truth, David acknowledged his sin and repented immediately. In time, David discovered the blessing of repentance.

In Psalm 51, written after his encounter with Nathan, David acknowledged that his sin was an offense against God's standard of righteousness and that he needed to repent. David begged for God's mercy on the basis of God's own lovingkindness, and because of the history of mercies God had shown so many times before. David asked God to wash him and make him clean. His plea was that he knew he had sinned, and he knew the sin was ultimately against God Himself. He knew full well that God is perfect and blameless, and therefore the perfect source of mercy for a blameworthy sinner.

RECOGNIZING SIN

Repentance begins with recognizing sin. That occurs through the process of people's conscience moving them to understand that they have done wrong. It can also occur through the words of another person (such as Nathan to King David), or through reading God's Word. When sin is revealed, sorrow is a common response. But sorrow alone cannot bring forgiveness and set people free. Confession may be good for the soul, but only confession that leads to genuine repentance has lasting results. Paul wrote in 2 Corinthians 7:10, "For godly sorrow produces repentance leading to salvation." Godly sorrow results in conviction. Because sin separates people from God, He wants to help them deal with sin when it occurs. Believers who are sensitive to God's guidance will become sensitive to their own sins, for God will reveal their sins to them.

Christians are set free from the power of sin through repentance. They still struggle with sin (Rom. 7:15–20), but they are able to recognize their sin, repent, and restore their relationship with God.

REPENTING FROM SIN

Repentance releases people from the power of sin in their lives. Repentance strengthens people's relationships with God and with others. Repentance brings healing and sets people free. Genuine repentance occurs only when people accept responsibility for their wrong choices and actions and confess their sin to God. In this way, nothing is hidden, nothing is held back. In the process of repentance, sin is abandoned and righteousness is embraced. David knew that true repentance would have to go beyond formalities like sacrifices and burnt offerings. "The sacrifices of God," said David, "are a broken spirit, a broken and a contrite heart—these, O God, You will not despise" (Ps. 51:16, 17).

When repentance is genuine, God can use our humility to reach and teach others. Out of personal brokenness, we, as repentant sinners who have been restored, are able to instruct others on the path to repentance. "Then I will teach transgressors Your ways," said David, "and sinners shall be converted to You." If God would deliver him from the guilt of bloodshed, David promised that his tongue would sing aloud of God's righteousness (Ps. 51:13, 14).

At times people refuse to repent because their hearts are hard. But who are they trying to fool? "Or do you despise the riches of His goodness, forbearance, and longsuffering, not knowing that the goodness of God leads you to repentance?" (Rom. 2:4). Out of His kindness, God calls people to repent and turn from sin. In His patience, He waits for them to respond. It is not God's plan for anyone to perish apart from Him, and He patiently waits for people to respond to His grace (2 Pet. 3:9).

GOD'S REMEDY FOR SIN

Sin is a self-inflicted wound to the soul. God's remedy for sin is to bring it into the open—through confession and repentance—so that it can be cleansed and healed. Repentance brings life to the soul by removing every impediment from a person's relationship to God. The key is not that we must keep tabs on every sin and be sure to confess each one by name in order to "be clean." The key is that we have an understanding of our basic sinfulness and an attitude of openness to God whereby, when we sin and He reveals it to us, we are quick to repent and change our ways.

We can succumb to the deceptions of sin and reap death as a result, or we can confess our sin in godly repentance and be purified by our heavenly Father. When we allow God to purify our hearts, the result is joy, gladness, and an unhindered relationship with Him.

FURTHER MEDITATION:

Other passages to study about the issue of repentance include:

- Ezekiel 33:10–16
- Matthew 9:13
- Luke 3:8; 13:1–8; 15:7, 10; 17:3, 4; 24:44–49
- Acts 3:19; 11:18; 26:20
- 1 John 1:9

To Learn More: Turn to the key passage note on repentance at 2 Corinthians 7:7–10 on page 1528. See also the personality profile of the thief on the cross on page 1361.

6 Oh, that the salvation of Israel would
come out of Zion!
When God brings back the captivity of
His people,
Let Jacob rejoice *and* Israel be glad.

PSALM 54

ANSWERED PRAYER FOR DELIVERANCE FROM ADVERSARIES

To the Chief Musician. With stringed instruments.[a] *A Contemplation*[b] *of David when the Ziphites went and said to Saul, "Is David not hiding with us?"*

1 Save me, O God, by Your name,
And vindicate me by Your strength.
2 Hear my prayer, O God;
Give ear to the words of my mouth.
3 For strangers have risen up against me,
And oppressors have sought after my
life;
They have not set God before them.
Selah

4 Behold, God *is* my helper;
The Lord *is* with those who uphold my
life.
5 He will repay my enemies for their evil.
Cut them off in Your truth.

6 I will freely sacrifice to You;
I will praise Your name, O LORD, for *it is*
good.
7 For He has delivered me out of all
trouble;
And my eye has seen *its desire* upon my
enemies.

PSALM 55

TRUST IN GOD CONCERNING THE TREACHERY OF FRIENDS

To the Chief Musician. With stringed instruments.[a] *A Contemplation*[b] *of David.*

1 Give ear to my prayer, O God,
And do not hide Yourself from my
supplication.
2 Attend to me, and hear me;
I am restless in my complaint, and moan
noisily,
3 Because of the voice of the enemy,
Because of the oppression of the wicked;
For they bring down trouble upon me,
And in wrath they hate me.

4 My heart is severely pained within me,
And the terrors of death have fallen
upon me.
5 Fearfulness and trembling have come
upon me,
And horror has overwhelmed me.
6 So I said, "Oh, that I had wings like a
dove!
I would fly away and be at rest.
7 Indeed, I would wander far off,
And remain in the wilderness. Selah
8 I would hasten my escape
From the windy storm *and* tempest."

9 Destroy, O Lord, *and* divide their
tongues,
For I have seen violence and strife in the
city.
10 Day and night they go around it on its
walls;
Iniquity and trouble *are* also in the midst
of it.
11 Destruction *is* in its midst;
Oppression and deceit do not depart
from its streets.

12 For *it is* not an enemy *who* reproaches
me;
Then I could bear *it*.
Nor *is it* one *who* hates me who has
exalted *himself* against me;
Then I could hide from him.
13 But *it was* you, a man my equal,
My companion and my acquaintance.
14 We took sweet counsel together,
And walked to the house of God in the
throng.

15 Let death seize them;
Let them go down alive into hell,
For wickedness *is* in their dwellings *and*
among them.

16 As for me, I will call upon God,
And the LORD shall save me.
17 Evening and morning and at noon
I will pray, and cry aloud,
And He shall hear my voice.

54:title [a]Hebrew *neginoth* [b]Hebrew *Maschil*
55:title [a]Hebrew *neginoth* [b]Hebrew *Maschil*

18 He has redeemed my soul in peace from
the battle *that was* against me,
For there were many against me.
19 God will hear, and afflict them,
Even He who abides from of old.
Selah
Because they do not change,
Therefore they do not fear God.

20 He has put forth his hands against those
who were at peace with him;
He has broken his covenant.
21 *The words* of his mouth were smoother
than butter,
But war *was* in his heart;
His words were softer than oil,
Yet they *were* drawn swords.

22 Cast your burden on the LORD,
And He shall sustain you;
He shall never permit the righteous to be
moved.

23 But You, O God,
shall bring them
down to the pit
of destruction;
Bloodthirsty and
deceitful men
shall not live out half their days;
But I will trust in You.

PSALM 56

PRAYER FOR RELIEF FROM TORMENTORS

To the Chief Musician. Set to "The Silent Dove in Distant Lands."[a] A Michtam of David when the Philistines captured him in Gath.

1 Be merciful to me, O God, for man
would swallow me up;
Fighting all day he oppresses me.
2 My enemies would hound *me* all day,
For *there are* many who fight against me,
O Most High.

3 Whenever I am afraid,
I will trust in You.
4 In God (I will praise His word),
In God I have put my trust;
I will not fear.
What can flesh do to me?

5 All day they twist my words;
All their thoughts *are* against me for
evil.
6 They gather together,
They hide, they mark my steps,
When they lie in wait for my life.
7 Shall they escape by iniquity?
In anger cast down the peoples,
O God!

8 You number my
wanderings;
Put my tears into
Your bottle;
Are they not in
Your book?
9 When I cry out *to
You,*
Then my enemies will turn back;
This I know, because God *is* for me.
10 In God (I will praise *His* word),
In the LORD (I will praise *His* word),
11 In God I have put my trust;
I will not be afraid.
What can man do to me?

12 Vows *made* to You *are binding* upon me,
O God;

Cast your burden on the LORD, and He shall sustain you; He shall never permit the righteous to be moved.
PSALM 55:22

56:title [a]Hebrew *Jonath Elem Rechokim*

SOUL NOTE

Heard *(55:17, 22)* God always hears our cries. Prayer is to be a constant expression of the human soul—seeking God "evening and morning and at noon." In prayer, we can cast our burdens on the Lord, knowing that He will sustain us. Prayer opens heaven's doors. There are many kinds of prayers—thanksgiving, confession, intercession, supplication, adoration. There are many ways to pray—alone, with a few others, in a large group, silently, aloud, even in song. God promises that however we pray, He will hear and sustain us. **Topic: Prayer**

I will render praises to You,
13 For You have delivered my soul from death,
Have You not *kept* my feet from falling,
That I may walk before God
In the light of the living?

PSALM 57

PRAYER FOR SAFETY FROM ENEMIES

To the Chief Musician. Set to "Do Not Destroy."[a] A Michtam of David when he fled from Saul into the cave.

1 Be merciful to me, O God, be merciful to me!
For my soul trusts in You;
And in the shadow of Your wings I will make my refuge,
Until *these* calamities have passed by.

2 I will cry out to God Most High,
To God who performs *all things* for me.
3 He shall send from heaven and save me;
He reproaches the one who would swallow me up. Selah
God shall send forth His mercy and His truth.

4 My soul *is* among lions;
I lie *among* the sons of men
Who are set on fire,
Whose teeth *are* spears and arrows,
And their tongue a sharp sword.
5 Be exalted, O God, above the heavens;
Let Your glory *be* above all the earth.

6 They have prepared a net for my steps;
My soul is bowed down;
They have dug a pit before me;
Into the midst of it they *themselves* have fallen. Selah

7 My heart is steadfast, O God, my heart is steadfast;
I will sing and give praise.
8 Awake, my glory!
Awake, lute and harp!
I will awaken the dawn.

9 I will praise You, O Lord, among the peoples;
I will sing to You among the nations.
10 For Your mercy reaches unto the heavens,
And Your truth unto the clouds.

11 Be exalted, O God, above the heavens;
Let Your glory *be* above all the earth.

PSALM 58

THE JUST JUDGMENT OF THE WICKED

To the Chief Musician. Set to "Do Not Destroy."[a] A Michtam of David.

1 Do you indeed speak righteousness, you silent ones?
Do you judge uprightly, you sons of men?
2 No, in heart you work wickedness;
You weigh out the violence of your hands in the earth.

3 The wicked are estranged from the womb;
They go astray as soon as they are born, speaking lies.
4 Their poison *is* like the poison of a serpent;
They are like the deaf cobra *that* stops its ear,
5 Which will not heed the voice of charmers,
Charming ever so skillfully.

6 Break their teeth in their mouth, O God!
Break out the fangs of the young lions, O LORD!
7 Let them flow away as waters *which* run continually;
When he bends *his bow,*
Let his arrows be as if cut in pieces.
8 *Let them be* like a snail which melts away as it goes,
Like a stillborn child of a woman, that they may not see the sun.

9 Before your pots can feel *the burning* thorns,
He shall take them away as with a whirlwind,

57:title [a]Hebrew *Al Tashcheth* **58:title** [a]Hebrew *Al Tashcheth*

As in His living and burning wrath.
10 The righteous shall rejoice when he sees
the vengeance;
He shall wash his feet in the blood of
the wicked,
11 So that men will say,
"Surely *there is* a reward for the
righteous;
Surely He is God who judges in the
earth."

PSALM 59

THE ASSURED JUDGMENT OF THE WICKED

To the Chief Musician. Set to "Do Not Destroy."[a] A Michtam of David when Saul sent men, and they watched the house in order to kill him.

1 Deliver me from my enemies,
O my God;
Defend me from those who rise up
against me.
2 Deliver me from the workers of iniquity,
And save me from bloodthirsty men.

3 For look, they lie in wait for my life;
The mighty gather against me,
Not *for* my transgression nor *for* my sin,
O LORD.
4 They run and prepare themselves
through no fault *of mine.*

Awake to help me, and behold!
5 You therefore, O LORD God of hosts, the
God of Israel,
Awake to punish all the nations;
Do not be merciful to any wicked
transgressors. Selah

6 At evening they return,
They growl like a dog,
And go all around the city.
7 Indeed, they belch with their mouth;
Swords *are* in their lips;
For *they say,* "Who hears?"

8 But You, O LORD, shall laugh at them;
You shall have all the nations in derision.
9 I will wait for You, O You his Strength;[a]
For God *is* my defense.
10 My God of mercy[a] shall come to meet
me;
God shall let me see *my desire* on my
enemies.

11 Do not slay them, lest my people forget;
Scatter them by Your power,
And bring them down,
O Lord our shield.
12 *For* the sin of their mouth *and* the words
of their lips,
Let them even be taken in their pride,
And for the cursing and lying *which* they
speak.
13 Consume *them* in wrath, consume *them,*
That they *may* not *be;*
And let them know that God rules in
Jacob
To the ends of the earth. Selah

14 And at evening they return,
They growl like a dog,
And go all around the city.
15 They wander up and down for food,
And howl[a] if they are not satisfied.

16 But I will sing of Your power;
Yes, I will sing aloud of Your mercy in
the morning;
For You have been my defense
And refuge in the day of my trouble.
17 To You, O my Strength, I will sing
praises;
For God *is* my defense,
My God of mercy.

PSALM 60

URGENT PRAYER FOR THE RESTORED FAVOR OF GOD

To the Chief Musician. Set to "Lily of the Testimony."[a] A Michtam of David. For teaching. When he fought against Mesopotamia and Syria of Zobah, and Joab returned and killed twelve thousand Edomites in the Valley of Salt.

1 O God, You have cast us off;
You have broken us down;
You have been displeased;

59:title [a]Hebrew *Al Tashcheth* **59:9** [a]Following Masoretic Text and Syriac; some Hebrew manuscripts, Septuagint, Targum, and Vulgate read *my Strength.* **59:10** [a]Following Qere; some Hebrew manuscripts, Septuagint, and Vulgate read *My God, His mercy;* Kethib, some Hebrew manuscripts and Targum read *O God, my mercy;* Syriac reads *O God, Your mercy.* **59:15** [a]Following Septuagint and Vulgate; Masoretic Text, Syriac, and Targum read *spend the night.* **60:title** [a]Hebrew *Shushan Eduth*

Oh, restore us again!
2 You have made the earth tremble;
You have broken it;
Heal its breaches, for it is shaking.
3 You have shown Your people hard things;
You have made us drink the wine of confusion.

4 You have given a banner to those who fear You,
That it may be displayed because of the truth. Selah
5 That Your beloved may be delivered,
Save *with* Your right hand, and hear me.

6 God has spoken in His holiness:
"I will rejoice;
I will divide Shechem
And measure out the Valley of Succoth.
7 Gilead *is* Mine, and Manasseh *is* Mine;
Ephraim also *is* the helmet for My head;
Judah *is* My lawgiver.
8 Moab *is* My washpot;
Over Edom I will cast My shoe;
Philistia, shout in triumph because of Me."

9 Who will bring me *to* the strong city?
Who will lead me to Edom?
10 *Is it* not You, O God, *who* cast us off?
And You, O God, *who* did not go out with our armies?
11 Give us help from trouble,
For the help of man *is* useless.
12 Through God we will do valiantly,
For *it is* He *who* shall tread down our enemies.[a]

PSALM 61

Assurance of God's Eternal Protection

To the Chief Musician. On a stringed instrument.[a] A Psalm of David.

1 Hear my cry, O God;
Attend to my prayer.
2 From the end of the earth I will cry to You,
When my heart is overwhelmed;
Lead me to the rock that is higher than I.

3 For You have been a shelter for me,
A strong tower from the enemy.
4 I will abide in Your tabernacle forever;
I will trust in the shelter of Your wings. Selah

5 For You, O God, have heard my vows;
You have given *me* the heritage of those who fear Your name.
6 You will prolong the king's life,
His years as many generations.
7 He shall abide before God forever.
Oh, prepare mercy and truth, *which* may preserve him!

8 So I will sing praise to Your name forever,
That I may daily perform my vows.

PSALM 62

A Calm Resolve to Wait for the Salvation of God

To the Chief Musician. To Jeduthun. A Psalm of David.

1 Truly my soul silently *waits* for God;
From Him *comes* my salvation.
2 He only *is* my rock and my salvation;
He is my defense;
I shall not be greatly moved.

3 How long will you attack a man?
You shall be slain, all of you,
Like a leaning wall and a tottering fence.
4 They only consult to cast *him* down from his high position;
They delight in lies;
They bless with their mouth,
But they curse inwardly. Selah

5 My soul, wait silently for God alone,
For my expectation *is* from Him.
6 He only *is* my rock and my salvation;
He is my defense;
I shall not be moved.
7 In God *is* my salvation and my glory;
The rock of my strength,
And my refuge, *is* in God.

8 Trust in Him at all times, you people;
Pour out your heart before Him;
God *is* a refuge for us. Selah

60:12 [a]Compare verses 5–12 with 108:6–13
61:title [a]Hebrew *neginah*

9 Surely men of low degree *are* a vapor,
Men of high degree *are* a lie;
If they are weighed on the scales,
They *are* altogether *lighter* than vapor.
10 Do not trust in oppression,
Nor vainly hope in robbery;
If riches increase,
Do not set *your* heart *on them.*

11 God has spoken once,
Twice I have heard this:
That power *belongs* to God.
12 Also to You, O Lord, *belongs* mercy;
For You render to each one according to
his work.

PSALM 63

Joy in the Fellowship of God

A Psalm of David when he was in the wilderness of Judah.

1 O God, You *are* my God;
Early will I seek You;
My soul thirsts for You;
My flesh longs for You
In a dry and thirsty land
Where there is no water.
2 So I have looked for You in the
sanctuary,
To see Your power and Your glory.

3 Because Your lovingkindness *is* better
than life,
My lips shall praise You.
4 Thus I will bless You while I live;
I will lift up my hands in Your name.
5 My soul shall be satisfied as with
marrow and fatness,
And my mouth shall praise *You* with
joyful lips.

6 When I remember You on my bed,
I meditate on You in the *night* watches.
7 Because You have been my help,
Therefore in the shadow of Your wings I
will rejoice.
8 My soul follows close behind You;
Your right hand upholds me.

9 But those *who* seek my life, to destroy *it,*
Shall go into the lower parts of the
earth.
10 They shall fall by the sword;
They shall be a portion for jackals.

11 But the king shall rejoice in God;
Everyone who swears by Him shall
glory;
But the mouth of those who speak lies
shall be stopped.

PSALM 64

Oppressed by the Wicked but Rejoicing in the Lord

To the Chief Musician. A Psalm of David.

1 Hear my voice, O God, in my
meditation;
Preserve my life from fear of the enemy.
2 Hide me from the secret plots of the
wicked,
From the rebellion of the workers of
iniquity,
3 Who sharpen their tongue like a sword,
And bend *their bows to shoot* their
arrows—bitter words,
4 That they may shoot in secret at the
blameless;
Suddenly they shoot at him and do not
fear.

5 They encourage themselves *in* an evil
matter;
They talk of laying snares secretly;
They say, "Who will see them?"
6 They devise iniquities:
"We have perfected a shrewd scheme."
Both the inward thought and the heart of
man are deep.

7 But God shall shoot at them *with* an
arrow;
Suddenly they shall be wounded.
8 So He will make them stumble over their
own tongue;
All who see them shall flee away.
9 All men shall fear,
And shall declare the work of God;
For they shall wisely consider His
doing.

10 The righteous shall be glad in the LORD,
and trust in Him.
And all the upright in heart shall glory.

PSALM 65

Praise to God for His Salvation and Providence

To the Chief Musician. A Psalm of David. A Song.

1 Praise is awaiting You, O God, in Zion;
And to You the vow shall be performed.
2 O You who hear prayer,
To You all flesh will come.
3 Iniquities prevail against me;
As for our transgressions,
You will provide atonement for them.

4 Blessed *is the man* You choose,
And cause to approach *You,*
That he may dwell in Your courts.
We shall be satisfied with the goodness of Your house,
Of Your holy temple.

5 *By* awesome deeds in righteousness You will answer us,
O God of our salvation,
You who are the confidence of all the ends of the earth,
And of the far-off seas;
6 Who established the mountains by His strength,
Being clothed with power;
7 You who still the noise of the seas,
The noise of their waves,
And the tumult of the peoples.
8 They also who dwell in the farthest parts are afraid of Your signs;
You make the outgoings of the morning and evening rejoice.

9 You visit the earth and water it,
You greatly enrich it;
The river of God is full of water;
You provide their grain,
For so You have prepared it.
10 You water its ridges abundantly,
You settle its furrows;
You make it soft with showers,
You bless its growth.

11 You crown the year with Your goodness,
And Your paths drip *with* abundance.
12 They drop *on* the pastures of the wilderness,
And the little hills rejoice on every side.
13 The pastures are clothed with flocks;
The valleys also are covered with grain;
They shout for joy, they also sing.

PSALM 66

Praise to God for His Awesome Works

To the Chief Musician. A Song. A Psalm.

1 Make a joyful shout to God, all the earth!
2 Sing out the honor of His name;
Make His praise glorious.
3 Say to God,
"How awesome are Your works!
Through the greatness of Your power
Your enemies shall submit themselves to You.
4 All the earth shall worship You
And sing praises to You;
They shall sing praises *to* Your name."
Selah

5 Come and see the works of God;
He is awesome *in His* doing toward the sons of men.
6 He turned the sea into dry *land;*
They went through the river on foot.

SOUL NOTE

Refining Fire *(66:10)* Silver ore must be refined by fire in order to remove its impurities. Every time the silver is heated and the dross is removed, the metal becomes more and more purified. In like manner, the fire of trials purges sin, burning away the lusts and impurities that pollute people's lives. Although unpleasant, suffering often removes the impurities from our lives and helps us grow toward perfection. God refines us "as silver is refined" so that we can reflect His glory.
Topic: Suffering

There we will rejoice in Him.
7 He rules by His power forever;
His eyes observe the nations;
Do not let the rebellious exalt
themselves. Selah

8 Oh, bless our God, you peoples!
And make the voice of His praise to be
heard,
9 Who keeps our soul among the
living,
And does not
allow our feet
to be moved.
10 For You, O God,
have tested us;
You have refined
us as silver is refined.
11 You brought us into the net;
You laid affliction on our backs.
12 You have caused men to ride over our
heads;
We went through fire and through
water;
But You brought us out to rich
fulfillment.

13 I will go into Your house with burnt
offerings;
I will pay You my vows,
14 Which my lips have uttered
And my mouth has spoken when I was
in trouble.
15 I will offer You burnt sacrifices of fat
animals,
With the sweet aroma of rams;
I will offer bulls with goats. Selah

16 Come *and* hear, all you who fear
God,
And I will declare what He has done for
my soul.
17 I cried to Him with my mouth,
And He was extolled with my
tongue.
18 If I regard iniquity in my heart,
The Lord will not hear.
19 *But* certainly God has heard *me;*
He has attended to the voice of my
prayer.

20 Blessed *be* God,
Who has not turned away my prayer,
Nor His mercy from me!

God be merciful to us and bless us,
and cause His face to shine upon us.
PSALM 67:1

PSALM 67

AN INVOCATION AND A DOXOLOGY

To the Chief Musician. On stringed instruments.[a] *A Psalm. A Song.*

1 God be merciful to us and bless us,
And cause His face to shine upon us,
Selah
2 That Your way may be known on earth,
Your salvation among all nations.

3 Let the peoples
praise You,
O God;
Let all the peoples
praise You.
4 Oh, let the nations
be glad and sing
for joy!
For You shall judge the people
righteously,
And govern the nations on earth.
Selah

5 Let the peoples praise You, O God;
Let all the peoples praise You.
6 *Then* the earth shall yield her
increase;
God, our own God, shall bless us.
7 God shall bless us,
And all the ends of the earth shall fear
Him.

PSALM 68

THE GLORY OF GOD IN HIS GOODNESS TO ISRAEL

To the Chief Musician. A Psalm of David. A Song.

1 Let God arise,
Let His enemies be scattered;
Let those also who hate Him flee before
Him.
2 As smoke is driven away,
So drive *them* away;
As wax melts before the fire,
So let the wicked perish at the presence
of God.
3 But let the righteous be glad;
Let them rejoice before God;
Yes, let them rejoice exceedingly.

67:title [a]Hebrew *neginoth*

4 Sing to God, sing praises to His name;
Extol Him who rides on the clouds,[a]
By His name YAH,
And rejoice before Him.

5 A father of the fatherless, a defender of widows,
Is God in His holy habitation.
6 God sets the solitary in families;
He brings out those who are bound into prosperity;
But the rebellious dwell in a dry *land.*

7 O God, when You went out before Your people,
When You marched through the wilderness,
Selah
8 The earth shook;
The heavens also dropped *rain* at the presence of God;
Sinai itself *was moved* at the presence of God, the God of Israel.
9 You, O God, sent a plentiful rain,
Whereby You confirmed Your inheritance,
When it was weary.
10 Your congregation dwelt in it;
You, O God, provided from Your goodness for the poor.

11 The Lord gave the word;
Great *was* the company of those who proclaimed *it:*
12 "Kings of armies flee, they flee,
And she who remains at home divides the spoil.
13 Though you lie down among the sheepfolds,
You will be like the wings of a dove covered with silver,
And her feathers with yellow gold."
14 When the Almighty scattered kings in it,
It was *white* as snow in Zalmon.

15 A mountain of God *is* the mountain of Bashan;
A mountain *of many* peaks *is* the mountain of Bashan.
16 Why do you fume with envy, you mountains of *many* peaks?
This is the mountain *which* God desires to dwell in;
Yes, the LORD will dwell *in it* forever.
17 The chariots of God *are* twenty thousand,
Even thousands of thousands;
The Lord is among them *as in* Sinai, in the Holy *Place.*
18 You have ascended on high,
You have led captivity captive;
You have received gifts among men,
Even *from* the rebellious,
That the LORD God might dwell *there.*

19 Blessed *be* the Lord,
Who daily loads us *with benefits,*
The God of our salvation! Selah
20 Our God *is* the God of salvation;
And to GOD the Lord *belong* escapes from death.

21 But God will wound the head of His enemies,
The hairy scalp of the one who still goes on in his trespasses.
22 The Lord said, "I will bring back from Bashan,
I will bring *them* back from the depths of the sea,
23 That your foot may crush *them*[a] in blood,
And the tongues of your dogs *may have* their portion from *your* enemies."

24 They have seen Your procession, O God,
The procession of my God, my King, into the sanctuary.
25 The singers went before, the players on instruments *followed* after;
Among *them were* the maidens playing timbrels.
26 Bless God in the congregations,
The Lord, from the fountain of Israel.
27 There *is* little Benjamin, their leader,
The princes of Judah *and* their company,
The princes of Zebulun *and* the princes of Naphtali.

28 Your God has commanded[a] your strength;

68:4 [a]Masoretic Text reads *deserts;* Targum reads *heavens* (compare verse 34 and Isaiah 19:1). **68:23** [a]Septuagint, Syriac, Targum, and Vulgate read *you may dip your foot.* **68:28** [a]Septuagint, Syriac, Targum, and Vulgate read *Command, O God.*

Strengthen, O God, what You have done
for us.
29 Because of Your temple at Jerusalem,
Kings will bring presents to You.
30 Rebuke the beasts of the reeds,
The herd of bulls with the calves of the
peoples,
Till everyone submits himself with
pieces of silver.
Scatter the peoples *who* delight in war.
31 Envoys will come out of Egypt;
Ethiopia will quickly stretch out her
hands to God.

32 Sing to God, you kingdoms of the earth;
Oh, sing praises to the Lord, Selah
33 To Him who rides on the heaven of
heavens, *which were* of old!
Indeed, He sends out His voice, a mighty
voice.
34 Ascribe strength to God;
His excellence *is* over Israel,
And His strength *is* in the clouds.
35 O God, *You are* more awesome than Your
holy places.
The God of Israel *is* He who gives
strength and power to *His* people.

Blessed *be* God!

PSALM 69

An Urgent Plea for Help in Trouble

To the Chief Musician. Set to "The Lilies."[a]
A Psalm of David.

1 Save me, O God!
For the waters have come up to *my*
neck.
2 I sink in deep mire,
Where *there is* no standing;
I have come into deep waters,
Where the floods overflow me.
3 I am weary with my crying;
My throat is dry;
My eyes fail while I wait for my God.

4 Those who hate me without a cause
Are more than the hairs of my head;
They are mighty who would destroy me,
Being my enemies wrongfully;
Though I have stolen nothing,
I *still* must restore *it.*

5 O God, You know my foolishness;
And my sins are not hidden from You.
6 Let not those who wait for You,
O Lord GOD of hosts, be ashamed
because of me;
Let not those who seek You be
confounded because of me, O God of
Israel.
7 Because for Your sake I have borne
reproach;
Shame has covered my face.
8 I have become a stranger to my brothers,
And an alien to my mother's children;
9 Because zeal for Your house has eaten
me up,
And the reproaches of those who
reproach You have fallen on me.
10 When I wept *and chastened* my soul
with fasting,
That became my reproach.
11 I also made sackcloth my garment;
I became a byword to them.
12 Those who sit in the gate speak against
me,
And I *am* the song of the drunkards.

13 But as for me, my prayer *is* to You,
O LORD, *in* the acceptable time;
O God, in the multitude of Your mercy,
Hear me in the truth of Your salvation.

69:title [a]Hebrew *Shoshannim*

SOUL NOTE

Never Alone *(69:1–12)* Loneliness is a heavy burden; people can feel alone even when surrounded by people. David's loneliness was so great that he felt like a stranger in his family (69:8). Even in his loneliness, however, David found himself alone with God; therefore, he was not alone at all. When our courage and strength fails, when people seem to have abandoned us, we can take comfort in knowing that God is always with us. When we know Him, we are never alone. **Topic: Loneliness**

LONELINESS AND PERSONAL GROWTH

MIRIAM STARK PARENT

(Psalm 69:1–8)

In a world of E-mail, videoconferencing, voicemail, and other inventions that keep people instantaneously connected, many people still succumb to the age-old problem of loneliness. From the Garden of Eden to the present day, people have struggled with a sense of loneliness and separateness.

THE NEED FOR CONNECTEDNESS

From the moment of birth, humans seek attachment and connection. Without attachment or relationship, infants will fail to thrive. Without a feeling of connectedness, adults may yield to depression. Because God created people in His image, He made them relational. When God saw Adam alone in the Garden of Eden, He said being alone was "not good" (Gen. 2:18). Despite His own presence and relationship with Adam, God knew people also need human relationships. Human beings need both vertical intimacy (with God) and horizontal intimacy (with people) in order to be fulfilled. Without those relationships, they are vulnerable to the complex set of emotions described as "loneliness."

When sin entered the Garden, genuine intimacy disappeared. Adam and Eve blamed each other, lied, and excused themselves. From that moment, genuine intimacy with God and with other human beings was lost. In Christ, people can rediscover the pathway to genuine intimate connection and catch glimpses of it in a relationship with God and other Christians. Yet Christians are not yet able to fully appreciate the spiritual connection this side of heaven. Therefore, loneliness continues to be the constant companion of the human race.

THE PROBLEM OF LONELINESS

Loneliness is a normal response to the perception of being alone when one desires intimacy. It is different from solitude, which is a state of being alone. Solitude may be desirable at certain times. Everyone needs moments of personal quietness and reflection when they are alone and free of distraction. Loneliness, on the other hand, comes when people don't desire to be alone or disconnected, yet perceive themselves to be either emotionally or physically isolated. It is painful and distressing to the core human need for intimacy.

People experience loneliness according to varying personalities, cultures, backgrounds, and other dynamics. Loneliness is an emotional response that is linked to a perceived cause. For example, situational loneliness is a frequent response to physical or emotional separation. It is that feeling of isolation or loss that people experience as sadness, anxiety, or a sense of deprivation in connection with a loss of some kind. It may be brief and contained, or deep and overwhelming.

Physical separation is often a cause of situational loneliness. People may find themselves swept away by a sense of loneliness in response to being separated from friends and family. They know there are those who care, whose support is, perhaps, only a phone call away, but their situation (a job or school) demands separation. The intense longing that accompanies the separation is compelling and sometimes overwhelming. Where the separation is brief, loneliness increases the joy of the reunion. When the separation is extensive (such as through death), the loneliness is harder to handle. Death, divorce, life transitions, and personal mobility are the most common causes of situational loneliness. Intimate relationships are severed, changed and forever disrupted in some way.

Emotional separation can also lead to loneliness. The loneliest people are often those in crowds. People can feel lonely when they are surrounded by those with whom they perceive little or no intimate connection. This sense of disconnectedness seems to accentuate the loneliness and often leads to greater despair. This kind of loneliness is often felt as a form of anxiety, driving some to frantic efforts at superficial connection. Singles bars, clubs, and other gathering places thrive on those who are struggling to hold this deep loneliness at bay. When physical separation is coupled with emotional separation, the loneliness can seem unbearable.

Chronic loneliness can result from underlying feelings of not belonging or not being understood. Many desperately desire intimacy, but are unable to connect due to deeply held personal beliefs or social deficits. The person feels chronically alone and isolated, unable to have any hope of "connecting" again in the future. Such chronic feelings of loneliness can lead to deep personal isolation and despair, often ending in suicide or angry, violent alienation.

WHAT TO DO ABOUT LONELINESS

People need to understand the source of loneliness. Perhaps someone's loneliness is based on a perception, not an unchangeable circumstance. Perceptions can be changed once the person sees the cause of the loneliness. Is the person feeling lonely due to a mistaken perception of the situation? Can the situation be changed?

If the loneliness is based on a real circumstance, not just perception, the person needs to accept the situation and learn to handle it in the best way possible. The best remedy for loneliness is to focus one's energies on serving others who are in need. Doing so will distract a person from his or her problems and help others in the process.

A person's loneliness may be a healthy part of the grief process as he or she deals with loss. That is natural and can pass if the person does not let the loneliness cause complete isolation from others.

The experience of loneliness can cause people to draw closer to God and to others. If we are dealing with loneliness, we need to reach out to God and to others. If we know people who are experiencing loneliness, we can help them keep from becoming isolated by being true friends to them and by reminding them that, in Christ, they are never alone.

FURTHER MEDITATION:

Other passages to study about the issue of loneliness include:

- Deuteronomy 31:6
- Psalms 23; 27
- Ecclesiastes 4:9–12
- Isaiah 49:15, 16; 54:10
- Matthew 28:20
- John 14:15–18, 23
- Romans 8:35–39
- Hebrews 10:24, 25

To Learn More: Turn to the key passage note on loneliness at Isaiah 41:10 on page 923. See also the personality profile of Jeremiah on page 989.

14 Deliver me out of the mire,
And let me not sink;
Let me be delivered from those who hate me,
And out of the deep waters.
15 Let not the floodwater overflow me,
Nor let the deep swallow me up;
And let not the pit shut its mouth on me.

16 Hear me, O LORD, for Your lovingkindness *is* good;
Turn to me according to the multitude of Your tender mercies.
17 And do not hide Your face from Your servant,
For I am in trouble;
Hear me speedily.
18 Draw near to my soul, *and* redeem it;
Deliver me because of my enemies.

19 You know my reproach, my shame, and my dishonor;
My adversaries *are* all before You.
20 Reproach has broken my heart,
And I am full of heaviness;
I looked *for someone* to take pity, but *there was* none;
And for comforters, but I found none.
21 They also gave me gall for my food,
And for my thirst they gave me vinegar to drink.

22 Let their table become a snare before them,
And their well-being a trap.
23 Let their eyes be darkened, so that they do not see;
And make their loins shake continually.
24 Pour out Your indignation upon them,
And let Your wrathful anger take hold of them.
25 Let their dwelling place be desolate;
Let no one live in their tents.
26 For they persecute the *ones* You have struck,
And talk of the grief of those You have wounded.
27 Add iniquity to their iniquity,
And let them not come into Your righteousness.
28 Let them be blotted out of the book of the living,
And not be written with the righteous.

29 But I *am* poor and sorrowful;
Let Your salvation, O God, set me up on high.
30 I will praise the name of God with a song,
And will magnify Him with thanksgiving.
31 *This* also shall please the LORD better than an ox *or* bull,
Which has horns and hooves.
32 The humble shall see *this and* be glad;
And you who seek God, your hearts shall live.
33 For the LORD hears the poor,
And does not despise His prisoners.

34 Let heaven and earth praise Him,
The seas and everything that moves in them.
35 For God will save Zion
And build the cities of Judah,
That they may dwell there and possess it.
36 Also, the descendants of His servants shall inherit it,
And those who love His name shall dwell in it.

PSALM 70

PRAYER FOR RELIEF FROM ADVERSARIES

To the Chief Musician. A Psalm of David. To bring to remembrance.

1 *Make haste,* O God, to deliver me!
Make haste to help me, O LORD!

2 Let them be ashamed and confounded
Who seek my life;
Let them be turned back[a] and confused
Who desire my hurt.
3 Let them be turned back because of their shame,
Who say, "Aha, aha!"

4 Let all those who seek You rejoice and be glad in You;
And let those who love Your salvation say continually,
"Let God be magnified!"

70:2 [a]Following Masoretic Text, Septuagint, Targum, and Vulgate; some Hebrew manuscripts and Syriac read *be appalled* (compare 40:15).

5 But I *am* poor and needy;
Make haste to me, O God!
You *are* my help and my deliverer;
O LORD, do not delay.

PSALM 71

GOD THE ROCK OF SALVATION

1 In You, O LORD, I put my trust;
Let me never be put to shame.
2 Deliver me in Your righteousness, and cause me to escape;
Incline Your ear to me, and save me.
3 Be my strong refuge,
To which I may resort continually;
You have given the commandment to save me,
For You *are* my rock and my fortress.

4 Deliver me, O my God, out of the hand of the wicked,
Out of the hand of the unrighteous and cruel man.
5 For You are my hope, O Lord GOD;
You are my trust from my youth.
6 By You I have been upheld from birth;
You are He who took me out of my mother's womb.
My praise *shall be* continually of You.

7 I have become as a wonder to many,
But You *are* my strong refuge.
8 Let my mouth be filled *with* Your praise
And with Your glory all the day.

9 Do not cast me off in the time of old age;
Do not forsake me when my strength fails.
10 For my enemies speak against me;
And those who lie in wait for my life take counsel together,
11 Saying, "God has forsaken him;
Pursue and take him, for *there is* none to deliver *him.*"

12 O God, do not be far from me;
O my God, make haste to help me!
13 Let them be confounded *and* consumed
Who are adversaries of my life;
Let them be covered *with* reproach and dishonor
Who seek my hurt.

14 But I will hope continually,
And will praise You yet more and more.
15 My mouth shall tell of Your righteousness
And Your salvation all the day,
For I do not know *their* limits.
16 I will go in the strength of the Lord GOD;
I will make mention of Your righteousness, of Yours only.

17 O God, You have taught me from my youth;

KEY PASSAGE

Aging/ Elderly

IN THE TWILIGHT

(71:9)

Growing older is inevitable, but it doesn't have to tie people to their rocking chairs. Many older people can identify with the psalmist's plea, "Do not cast me off in the time of old age; do not forsake me when my strength fails." Older people often feel that because they lack their youthful vigor, they cannot effectively serve God and will be cast aside. God says, however, that His people "shall still bear fruit in old age" (Ps. 92:14). Older believers have a lifetime of wisdom and experience that is valuable to younger people. Even in their advanced years, devoted believers can produce abundant spiritual fruit. Also, believers can and should continue to grow spiritually even in their twilight time. They can continue on and make a difference for God, helping build His kingdom. Young people must not dismiss older people; instead, they should look to their elders for the godly wisdom they have from years of knowing Christ.

To Learn More: Turn to the article about aging/elderly on pages 282, 283. See also the personality profile of Caleb on page 284.

And to this *day* I declare Your wondrous
works.
18 Now also when *I am* old and
grayheaded,
O God, do not forsake me,
Until I declare Your strength to *this*
generation,
Your power to everyone *who* is to come.

19 Also Your righteousness, O God, *is* very
high,
You who have done great things;
O God, who *is* like You?
20 *You,* who have shown me great and
severe troubles,
Shall revive me again,
And bring me up again from the depths
of the earth.
21 You shall increase my greatness,
And comfort me on every side.

22 Also with the lute I will praise You—
And Your faithfulness, O my God!
To You I will sing with the harp,
O Holy One of Israel.
23 My lips shall greatly rejoice when I sing
to You,
And my soul, which You have redeemed.
24 My tongue also shall talk of Your
righteousness all the day long;
For they are confounded,
For they are brought to shame
Who seek my hurt.

PSALM 72

Glory and Universality of the Messiah's Reign

A Psalm of Solomon.

1 Give the king Your judgments,
O God,
And Your righteousness to the king's
Son.
2 He will judge Your people with
righteousness,
And Your poor with justice.
3 The mountains will bring peace to the
people,
And the little hills, by righteousness.
4 He will bring justice to the poor of the
people;
He will save the children of the needy,
And will break in pieces the oppressor.

5 They shall fear You[a]
As long as the sun and moon endure,
Throughout all generations.
6 He shall come down like rain upon the
grass before mowing,
Like showers *that* water the earth.
7 In His days the righteous shall
flourish,
And abundance of peace,
Until the moon is no more.

8 He shall have dominion also from sea to
sea,
And from the River to the ends of the
earth.
9 Those who dwell in the wilderness will
bow before Him,
And His enemies will lick the dust.
10 The kings of Tarshish and of the isles
Will bring presents;
The kings of Sheba and Seba
Will offer gifts.
11 Yes, all kings shall fall down before
Him;
All nations shall serve Him.

12 For He will deliver the needy when he
cries,
The poor also, and *him* who has no
helper.
13 He will spare the poor and needy,
And will save the souls of the needy.
14 He will redeem their life from
oppression and violence;
And precious shall be their blood in His
sight.

15 And He shall live;
And the gold of Sheba will be given to
Him;
Prayer also will be made for Him
continually,
And daily He shall be praised.

16 There will be an abundance of grain in
the earth,
On the top of the mountains;
Its fruit shall wave like Lebanon;
And *those* of the city shall flourish like
grass of the earth.

72:5 [a]Following Masoretic Text and Targum; Septuagint and Vulgate read *They shall continue.*

17 His name shall endure forever;
His name shall continue as long as the sun.
And *men* shall be blessed in Him;
All nations shall call Him blessed.

18 Blessed *be* the LORD God, the God of Israel,
Who only does wondrous things!
19 And blessed *be* His glorious name forever!
And let the whole earth be filled *with* His glory.
Amen and Amen.

20 The prayers of David the son of Jesse are ended.

BOOK THREE: PSALMS 73–89

PSALM 73

THE TRAGEDY OF THE WICKED, AND THE BLESSEDNESS OF TRUST IN GOD

A Psalm of Asaph.

1 Truly God *is* good to Israel,
To such as are pure in heart.
2 But as for me, my feet had almost stumbled;
My steps had nearly slipped.
3 For I *was* envious of the boastful,
When I saw the prosperity of the wicked.

4 For *there are* no pangs in their death,
But their strength *is* firm.
5 They *are* not in trouble *as other* men,
Nor are they plagued like *other* men.
6 Therefore pride serves as their necklace;
Violence covers them *like* a garment.
7 Their eyes bulge[a] with abundance;
They have more than heart could wish.
8 They scoff and speak wickedly *concerning* oppression;
They speak loftily.
9 They set their mouth against the heavens,
And their tongue walks through the earth.

10 Therefore his people return here,
And waters of a full *cup* are drained by them.
11 And they say, "How does God know?
And is there knowledge in the Most High?"
12 Behold, these *are* the ungodly,
Who are always at ease;
They increase *in* riches.
13 Surely I have cleansed my heart *in* vain,
And washed my hands in innocence.
14 For all day long I have been plagued,
And chastened every morning.

15 If I had said, "I will speak thus,"
Behold, I would have been untrue to the generation of Your children.
16 When I thought *how* to understand this,
It *was* too painful for me—
17 Until I went into the sanctuary of God;
Then I understood their end.

18 Surely You set them in slippery places;
You cast them down to destruction.
19 Oh, how they are *brought* to desolation, as in a moment!
They are utterly consumed with terrors.
20 As a dream when *one* awakes,
So, Lord, when You awake,
You shall despise their image.

21 Thus my heart was grieved,
And I was vexed in my mind.
22 I *was* so foolish and ignorant;
I was *like* a beast before You.
23 Nevertheless I *am* continually with You;
You hold *me* by my right hand.
24 You will guide me with Your counsel,
And afterward receive me *to* glory.

25 Whom have I in heaven *but You?*
And *there is* none upon earth *that* I desire besides You.
26 My flesh and my heart fail;
But God *is* the strength of my heart and my portion forever.

27 For indeed, those who are far from You shall perish;
You have destroyed all those who desert You for harlotry.
28 But *it is* good for me to draw near to God;
I have put my trust in the Lord GOD,
That I may declare all Your works.

73:7 [a]Targum reads *face bulges;* Septuagint, Syriac, and Vulgate read *iniquity bulges.*

PSALM 74

A Plea for Relief from Oppressors

A Contemplation[a] *of Asaph.*

1 O God, why have You cast *us* off
forever?
Why does Your anger smoke against the
sheep of Your pasture?
2 Remember Your congregation, *which* You
have purchased of old,
The tribe of Your inheritance, *which* You
have redeemed—
This Mount Zion where You have dwelt.
3 Lift up Your feet to the perpetual
desolations.
The enemy has damaged everything in
the sanctuary.
4 Your enemies roar in the midst of Your
meeting place;
They set up their banners *for* signs.
5 They seem like men who lift up
Axes among the thick trees.
6 And now they break down its carved
work, all at once,
With axes and hammers.
7 They have set fire to Your sanctuary;
They have defiled the dwelling place of
Your name to the ground.
8 They said in their hearts,
"Let us destroy them altogether."
They have burned up all the meeting
places of God in the land.

9 We do not see our signs;
There is no longer any prophet;
Nor *is there* any among us who knows
how long.
10 O God, how long will the adversary
reproach?
Will the enemy blaspheme Your name
forever?
11 Why do You withdraw Your hand, even
Your right hand?
Take it out of Your bosom and destroy
them.
12 For God *is* my King from of old,
Working salvation in the midst of the
earth.
13 You divided the sea by Your strength;
You broke the heads of the sea serpents
in the waters.
14 You broke the heads of Leviathan in
pieces,
And gave him *as* food to the people
inhabiting the wilderness.
15 You broke open the fountain and the
flood;
You dried up mighty rivers.
16 The day *is* Yours, the night also *is*
Yours;
You have prepared the light and the sun.
17 You have set all the borders of the
earth;
You have made summer and winter.

18 Remember this, *that* the enemy has
reproached, O LORD,
And *that* a foolish people has
blasphemed Your name.
19 Oh, do not deliver the life of Your
turtledove to the wild beast!
Do not forget the life of Your poor
forever.
20 Have respect to the covenant;
For the dark places of the earth are full
of the haunts of cruelty.
21 Oh, do not let the oppressed return
ashamed!
Let the poor and needy praise Your
name.

74:title [a]Hebrew *Maschil*

SOUL NOTE

The Best Counselor *(73:23–26)* God is the ultimate counselor who is constantly with His people. The psalmist declared, "You will guide me with Your counsel, and afterward receive me to glory" (73:24). Though friends, counselors, and advisors can be helpful, we ultimately must depend on and be accountable to God. We have no one in heaven but God, no one upon earth whom we should desire more than Him. We can take comfort in knowing that God hears our deepest cries, counsels us, and promises eternity with Him. **Topic: Accountability**

22 Arise, O God, plead Your own cause;
Remember how the foolish man
reproaches You daily.
23 Do not forget the voice of Your
enemies;
The tumult of those who rise up against
You increases continually.

PSALM 75

Thanksgiving for God's Righteous Judgment

To the Chief Musician. Set to "Do Not Destroy."[a] A Psalm of Asaph. A Song.

1 We give thanks to You, O God, we give
thanks!
For Your wondrous works declare *that*
Your name is near.

2 "When I choose the proper time,
I will judge uprightly.
3 The earth and all its inhabitants are
dissolved;
I set up its pillars firmly. Selah

4 "I said to the boastful, 'Do not deal
boastfully,'
And to the wicked, 'Do not lift up the
horn.
5 Do not lift up your horn on high;
Do *not* speak with a stiff neck.' "

6 For exaltation *comes* neither from the
east
Nor from the west nor from the south.
7 But God *is* the Judge:
He puts down one,
And exalts another.
8 For in the hand of the LORD *there is* a
cup,
And the wine is red;
It is fully mixed, and He pours it out;
Surely its dregs shall all the wicked of
the earth
Drain *and* drink down.

9 But I will declare forever,
I will sing praises to the God of
Jacob.

10 "All the horns of the wicked I will also
cut off,
But the horns of the righteous shall be
exalted."

PSALM 76

The Majesty of God in Judgment

To the Chief Musician. On stringed instruments.[a] A Psalm of Asaph. A Song.

1 In Judah God *is* known;
His name *is* great in Israel.
2 In Salem[a] also is His tabernacle,
And His dwelling place in Zion.
3 There He broke the arrows of the
bow,
The shield and sword of battle. Selah

4 You *are* more glorious and excellent
Than the mountains of prey.
5 The stouthearted were plundered;
They have sunk into their sleep;
And none of the mighty men have found
the use of their hands.
6 At Your rebuke, O God of Jacob,
Both the chariot and horse were cast
into a dead sleep.

7 You, Yourself, *are* to be feared;
And who may stand in Your presence
When once You are angry?
8 You caused judgment to be heard from
heaven;
The earth feared and was still,
9 When God arose to judgment,
To deliver all the oppressed of the
earth. Selah

10 Surely the wrath of man shall praise
You;
With the remainder of wrath You shall
gird Yourself.

11 Make vows to the LORD your God, and
pay *them;*
Let all who are around Him bring
presents to Him who ought to be
feared.
12 He shall cut off the spirit of princes;
He is awesome to the kings of the
earth.

75:title [a]Hebrew *Al Tashcheth* **76:title** [a]Hebrew *neginoth* **76:2** [a]That is, Jerusalem

PSALM 77

THE CONSOLING MEMORY OF GOD'S REDEMPTIVE WORKS

To the Chief Musician. To Jeduthun. A Psalm of Asaph.

1 I cried out to God with my voice—
To God with my voice;
And He gave ear to me.
2 In the day of my trouble I sought the Lord;
My hand was stretched out in the night without ceasing;
My soul refused to be comforted.
3 I remembered God, and was troubled;
I complained, and my spirit was overwhelmed. Selah

4 You hold my eyelids *open;*
I am so troubled that I cannot speak.
5 I have considered the days of old,
The years of ancient times.
6 I call to remembrance my song in the night;
I meditate within my heart,
And my spirit makes diligent search.

7 Will the Lord cast off forever?
And will He be favorable no more?
8 Has His mercy ceased forever?
Has *His* promise failed forevermore?
9 Has God forgotten to be gracious?
Has He in anger shut up His tender mercies? Selah

10 And I said, "This *is* my anguish;
But I will remember the years of the right hand of the Most High."
11 I will remember the works of the LORD;
Surely I will remember Your wonders of old.
12 I will also meditate on all Your work,
And talk of Your deeds.
13 Your way, O God, *is* in the sanctuary;
Who *is* so great a God as *our* God?
14 You *are* the God who does wonders;
You have declared Your strength among the peoples.
15 You have with *Your* arm redeemed Your people,
The sons of Jacob and Joseph. Selah

16 The waters saw You, O God;
The waters saw You, they were afraid;
The depths also trembled.
17 The clouds poured out water;
The skies sent out a sound;
Your arrows also flashed about.
18 The voice of Your thunder *was* in the whirlwind;
The lightnings lit up the world;
The earth trembled and shook.
19 Your way *was* in the sea,
Your path in the great waters,
And Your footsteps were not known.
20 You led Your people like a flock
By the hand of Moses and Aaron.

PSALM 78

GOD'S KINDNESS TO REBELLIOUS ISRAEL

A Contemplation[a] *of Asaph.*

1 Give ear, O my people, *to* my law;
Incline your ears to the words of my mouth.
2 I will open my mouth in a parable;
I will utter dark sayings of old,
3 Which we have heard and known,
And our fathers have told us.
4 We will not hide *them* from their children,
Telling to the generation to come the praises of the LORD,
And His strength and His wonderful works that He has done.

5 For He established a testimony in Jacob,
And appointed a law in Israel,
Which He commanded our fathers,
That they should make them known to their children;
6 That the generation to come might know *them,*
The children *who* would be born,
That they may arise and declare *them* to their children,
7 That they may set their hope in God,
And not forget the works of God,
But keep His commandments;
8 And may not be like their fathers,
A stubborn and rebellious generation,
A generation *that* did not set its heart aright,
And whose spirit was not faithful to God.

78:title [a]Hebrew *Maschil*

9 The children of Ephraim, *being* armed
and carrying bows,
Turned back in the day of battle.
10 They did not keep the covenant of God;
They refused to walk in His law,
11 And forgot His works
And His wonders that He had shown
them.

12 Marvelous things He did in the sight of
their fathers,
In the land of Egypt, *in* the field of
Zoan.
13 He divided the sea and caused them to
pass through;
And He made the waters stand up like a
heap.
14 In the daytime also He led them with the
cloud,
And all the night with a light of fire.
15 He split the rocks in the wilderness,
And gave *them* drink in abundance like
the depths.
16 He also brought streams out of the rock,
And caused waters to run down like
rivers.

17 But they sinned even more against Him
By rebelling against the Most High in the
wilderness.
18 And they tested God in their heart
By asking for the food of their fancy.
19 Yes, they spoke against God:
They said, "Can God prepare a table in
the wilderness?
20 Behold, He struck the rock,
So that the waters gushed out,
And the streams overflowed.
Can He give bread also?
Can He provide meat for His people? "

21 Therefore the LORD heard *this* and was
furious;
So a fire was kindled against Jacob,
And anger also came up against Israel,
22 Because they did not believe in God,
And did not trust in His salvation.
23 Yet He had commanded the clouds
above,
And opened the doors of heaven,
24 Had rained down manna on them to eat,
And given them of the bread of heaven.
25 Men ate angels' food;
He sent them food to the full.
26 He caused an east wind to blow in the
heavens;
And by His power He brought in the
south wind.
27 He also rained meat on them like the
dust,
Feathered fowl like the sand of the seas;
28 And He let *them* fall in the midst of their
camp,
All around their dwellings.
29 So they ate and were well filled,
For He gave them their own desire.
30 They were not deprived of their craving;
But while their food *was* still in their
mouths,
31 The wrath of God came against
them,
And slew the stoutest of them,
And struck down the choice *men* of
Israel.

32 In spite of this they still sinned,
And did not believe in His wondrous
works.
33 Therefore their days He consumed in
futility,
And their years in fear.

34 When He slew them, then they sought
Him;
And they returned and sought earnestly
for God.
35 Then they remembered that God *was*
their rock,
And the Most High God their Redeemer.
36 Nevertheless they flattered Him with
their mouth,
And they lied to Him with their tongue;
37 For their heart was not steadfast with
Him,
Nor were they faithful in His covenant.
38 But He, *being* full of compassion,
forgave *their* iniquity,
And did not destroy *them*.
Yes, many a time He turned His anger
away,
And did not stir up all His wrath;
39 For He remembered that they *were but*
flesh,
A breath that passes away and does not
come again.

40 How often they provoked Him in the
wilderness,

And grieved Him in the desert!
41 Yes, again and again they tempted God,
And limited the Holy One of Israel.
42 They did not remember His power:
The day when He redeemed them from the enemy,
43 When He worked His signs in Egypt,
And His wonders in the field of Zoan;
44 Turned their rivers into blood,
And their streams, that they could not drink.
45 He sent swarms of flies among them, which devoured them,
And frogs, which destroyed them.
46 He also gave their crops to the caterpillar,
And their labor to the locust.
47 He destroyed their vines with hail,
And their sycamore trees with frost.
48 He also gave up their cattle to the hail,
And their flocks to fiery lightning.
49 He cast on them the fierceness of His anger,
Wrath, indignation, and trouble,
By sending angels of destruction *among them.*
50 He made a path for His anger;
He did not spare their soul from death,
But gave their life over to the plague,
51 And destroyed all the firstborn in Egypt,
The first of *their* strength in the tents of Ham.
52 But He made His own people go forth like sheep,
And guided them in the wilderness like a flock;
53 And He led them on safely, so that they did not fear;
But the sea overwhelmed their enemies.
54 And He brought them to His holy border,
This mountain *which* His right hand had acquired.
55 He also drove out the nations before them,
Allotted them an inheritance by survey,
And made the tribes of Israel dwell in their tents.

56 Yet they tested and provoked the Most High God,
And did not keep His testimonies,
57 But turned back and acted unfaithfully like their fathers;
They were turned aside like a deceitful bow.
58 For they provoked Him to anger with their high places,
And moved Him to jealousy with their carved images.
59 When God heard *this,* He was furious,
And greatly abhorred Israel,
60 So that He forsook the tabernacle of Shiloh,
The tent He had placed among men,
61 And delivered His strength into captivity,
And His glory into the enemy's hand.
62 He also gave His people over to the sword,
And was furious with His inheritance.
63 The fire consumed their young men,
And their maidens were not given in marriage.
64 Their priests fell by the sword,
And their widows made no lamentation.

65 Then the Lord awoke as *from* sleep,
Like a mighty man who shouts because of wine.
66 And He beat back His enemies;
He put them to a perpetual reproach.

67 Moreover He rejected the tent of Joseph,
And did not choose the tribe of Ephraim,
68 But chose the tribe of Judah,
Mount Zion which He loved.
69 And He built His sanctuary like the heights,
Like the earth which He has established forever.
70 He also chose David His servant,
And took him from the sheepfolds;
71 From following the ewes that had young He brought him,
To shepherd Jacob His people,
And Israel His inheritance.
72 So he shepherded them according to the integrity of his heart,
And guided them by the skillfulness of his hands.

PSALM 79

A Dirge and a Prayer for Israel, Destroyed by Enemies

A Psalm of Asaph.

1 O God, the nations have come into Your inheritance;
Your holy temple they have defiled;

They have laid Jerusalem in heaps.
2 The dead bodies of Your servants
They have given *as* food for the birds of the heavens,
The flesh of Your saints to the beasts of the earth.
3 Their blood they have shed like water all around Jerusalem,
And *there was* no one to bury *them.*
4 We have become a reproach to our neighbors,
A scorn and derision to those who are around us.

5 How long, LORD?
Will You be angry forever?
Will Your jealousy burn like fire?
6 Pour out Your wrath on the nations that do not know You,
And on the kingdoms that do not call on Your name.
7 For they have devoured Jacob,
And laid waste his dwelling place.

8 Oh, do not remember former iniquities against us!
Let Your tender mercies come speedily to meet us,
For we have been brought very low.
9 Help us, O God of our salvation,
For the glory of Your name;
And deliver us, and provide atonement for our sins,
For Your name's sake!
10 Why should the nations say,
"Where *is* their God?"
Let there be known among the nations in our sight
The avenging of the blood of Your servants *which has been* shed.

11 Let the groaning of the prisoner come before You;
According to the greatness of Your power
Preserve those who are appointed to die;
12 And return to our neighbors sevenfold into their bosom
Their reproach with which they have reproached You, O Lord.

13 So we, Your people and sheep of Your pasture,
Will give You thanks forever;
We will show forth Your praise to all generations.

PSALM 80

Prayer for Israel's Restoration

To the Chief Musician. Set to "The Lilies."[a]
A Testimony[b] *of Asaph. A Psalm.*

1 Give ear, O Shepherd of Israel,
You who lead Joseph like a flock;
You who dwell *between* the cherubim, shine forth!
2 Before Ephraim, Benjamin, and Manasseh,
Stir up Your strength,
And come *and* save us!

3 Restore us, O God;
Cause Your face to shine,
And we shall be saved!

4 O LORD God of hosts,
How long will You be angry
Against the prayer of Your people?
5 You have fed them with the bread of tears,
And given them tears to drink in great measure.
6 You have made us a strife to our neighbors,
And our enemies laugh among themselves.

7 Restore us, O God of hosts;
Cause Your face to shine,
And we shall be saved!

8 You have brought a vine out of Egypt;
You have cast out the nations, and planted it.
9 You prepared *room* for it,
And caused it to take deep root,
And it filled the land.
10 The hills were covered with its shadow,
And the mighty cedars with its boughs.
11 She sent out her boughs to the Sea,[a]
And her branches to the River.[b]

80:title [a]Hebrew *Shoshannim* [b]Hebrew *Eduth*
80:11 [a]That is, the Mediterranean [b]That is, the Euphrates

12 Why have You broken down her hedges,
So that all who pass by the way pluck
her *fruit?*
13 The boar out of the woods uproots it,
And the wild beast of the field devours
it.

14 Return, we beseech You, O God of hosts;
Look down from heaven and see,
And visit this vine
15 And the vineyard which Your right hand
has planted,
And the branch *that* You made strong for
Yourself.
16 *It is* burned with fire, *it is* cut down;
They perish at the rebuke of Your
countenance.
17 Let Your hand be upon the man of Your
right hand,
Upon the son of man *whom* You made
strong for Yourself.
18 Then we will not turn back from You;
Revive us, and we will call upon Your
name.

19 Restore us, O LORD God of hosts;
Cause Your face to shine,
And we shall be saved!

PSALM 81

AN APPEAL FOR ISRAEL'S REPENTANCE

To the Chief Musician. On an instrument of Gath.[a] *A Psalm of Asaph.*

1 Sing aloud to God our strength;

81:title [a]Hebrew *Al Gittith*

PERSONALITY PROFILE

Praise and Worship

PRAISING THE LORD WITH ASAPH

(PSALM 81)

Praise and worship are important to God's people and pleasing to God. People were created to bring glory to God, and God enjoys it when His people, alone or gathered with other believers, praise and worship Him.

Asaph was the leader of Israel's worship (1 Chr. 15:17) and the author of several psalms. When King David brought the ark of the covenant to the tabernacle in Jerusalem, Asaph was one of the Levites chosen "to minister before the ark of the LORD, to commemorate, to thank, and to praise the LORD God of Israel" (1 Chr. 16:4). When David wrote a song to commemorate this event, he "delivered this psalm into the hand of Asaph and his brethren, to thank the LORD" (1 Chr. 16:7).

After the joyous celebration, regular worship in the tabernacle was begun, for David "left Asaph and his brothers there before the ark of the covenant of the LORD to minister before the ark regularly, as every day's work required" (1 Chr. 16:37). Most of Asaph's job in the tabernacle was to make music. King David saw to it that praise and worship included music, for Asaph was of the group separated out to "prophesy with harps, stringed instruments, and cymbals" (1 Chr. 25:1). According to 1 Chronicles 25:6, 7, Asaph and other music leaders were under the authority of the king himself. Also, 288 singers took part in the tabernacle worship services. Clearly, times of praise and worship were well planned and accomplished, with great glory to God.

Asaph encourages Christians everywhere to express joyful praise with the exuberance of the soul set free. We can praise God with our voices (trained or untrained) and with the accompaniment of many musical instruments. When we praise God, we focus on Him and give Him glory. All believers will one day join a vast choir of angels, "ten thousand times ten thousand, and thousands of thousands" singing to Christ in heaven (Rev. 5:11–13). *That* will certainly be a time of praise and worship!

To Learn More: Turn to the article about praise and worship on pages 794, 795. See also the key passage note at John 4:23, 24 on page 1377.

Make a joyful shout to the God of Jacob.
2 Raise a song and strike the timbrel,
The pleasant harp with the lute.

3 Blow the trumpet at the time of the New Moon,
At the full moon, on our solemn feast day.
4 For this *is* a statute for Israel,
A law of the God of Jacob.
5 This He established in Joseph *as* a testimony,
When He went throughout the land of Egypt,
Where I heard a language I did not understand.

6 "I removed his shoulder from the burden;
His hands were freed from the baskets.
7 You called in trouble, and I delivered you;
I answered you in the secret place of thunder;
I tested you at the waters of Meribah. Selah

8 "Hear, O My people, and I will admonish you!
O Israel, if you will listen to Me!
9 There shall be no foreign god among you;
Nor shall you worship any foreign god.
10 I *am* the LORD your God,
Who brought you out of the land of Egypt;
Open your mouth wide, and I will fill it.

11 "But My people would not heed My voice,
And Israel would *have* none of Me.
12 So I gave them over to their own stubborn heart,
To walk in their own counsels.

13 "Oh, that My people would listen to Me,
That Israel would walk in My ways!
14 I would soon subdue their enemies,
And turn My hand against their adversaries.
15 The haters of the LORD would pretend submission to Him,
But their fate would endure forever.
16 He would have fed them also with the finest of wheat;
And with honey from the rock I would have satisfied you."

PSALM 82

A Plea for Justice

A Psalm of Asaph.

1 God stands in the congregation of the mighty;
He judges among the gods.[a]
2 How long will you judge unjustly,
And show partiality to the wicked? Selah
3 Defend the poor and fatherless;
Do justice to the afflicted and needy.
4 Deliver the poor and needy;
Free *them* from the hand of the wicked.

5 They do not know, nor do they understand;
They walk about in darkness;
All the foundations of the earth are unstable.

6 I said, "You *are* gods,[a]
And all of you *are* children of the Most High.
7 But you shall die like men,
And fall like one of the princes."

8 Arise, O God, judge the earth;
For You shall inherit all nations.

PSALM 83

Prayer to Frustrate Conspiracy Against Israel

A Song. A Psalm of Asaph.

1 Do not keep silent, O God!
Do not hold Your peace,
And do not be still, O God!
2 For behold, Your enemies make a tumult;
And those who hate You have lifted up their head.
3 They have taken crafty counsel against Your people,

82:1 [a]Hebrew *elohim, mighty ones;* that is, the judges **82:6** [a]Hebrew *elohim, mighty ones;* that is, the judges

And consulted together against Your
sheltered ones.
4 They have said, "Come, and let us cut
them off from *being* a nation,
That the name of Israel may be
remembered no more."

5 For they have consulted together with
one consent;
They form a confederacy against You:
6 The tents of Edom and the Ishmaelites;
Moab and the Hagrites;
7 Gebal, Ammon, and Amalek;
Philistia with the inhabitants of Tyre;
8 Assyria also has joined with them;
They have helped the children of Lot.
Selah

9 Deal with them as *with* Midian,
As *with* Sisera,
As *with* Jabin at the Brook Kishon,
10 Who perished at En Dor,
Who became *as* refuse on the earth.
11 Make their nobles like Oreb and like
Zeeb,
Yes, all their princes like Zebah and
Zalmunna,
12 Who said, "Let us take for ourselves
The pastures of God for a possession."

13 O my God, make them like the whirling
dust,
Like the chaff before the wind!
14 As the fire burns the woods,
And as the flame sets the mountains on
fire,
15 So pursue them with Your tempest,
And frighten them with Your storm.
16 Fill their faces with shame,
That they may seek Your name, O LORD.
17 Let them be confounded and dismayed
forever;
Yes, let them be put to shame and
perish,
18 That they may know that You, whose
name alone *is* the LORD,
Are the Most High over all the earth.

PSALM 84

The Blessedness of Dwelling in the House of God

To the Chief Musician. On an instrument of Gath.[a] *A Psalm of the sons of Korah.*

1 How lovely *is* Your tabernacle,
O LORD of hosts!
2 My soul longs, yes, even faints
For the courts of the LORD;
My heart and my flesh cry out for the
living God.

3 Even the sparrow has found a home,
And the swallow a nest for herself,
Where she may lay her young—
Even Your altars, O LORD of hosts,
My King and my God.
4 Blessed *are* those who dwell in Your
house;
They will still be praising You. Selah

5 Blessed *is* the man whose strength *is* in
You,
Whose heart *is* set on pilgrimage.
6 *As they* pass through the Valley of
Baca,
They make it a spring;
The rain also covers it with pools.
7 They go from strength to strength;
Each one appears before God in Zion.[a]

84:title [a]Hebrew *Al Gittith* **84:7** [a]Septuagint, Syriac, and Vulgate read *The God of gods shall be seen*.

SOUL NOTE

Nothing Less *(84:1, 2)* People can meet God anywhere, but going into a church provides a quiet place away from daily pressures. The psalmist longed for the "courts of the LORD" and he exclaimed, "My heart and my flesh cry out for the living God." Worship is more than just going to church and singing songs—worship is the cry of the soul to God, the desire to be with Him, praise Him, and hear His voice. We need God. Without Him, our soul experiences spiritual turbulence.

Topic: Praise and Worship

8 O LORD God of hosts, hear my prayer;
Give ear, O God of Jacob! Selah
9 O God, behold our shield,
And look upon the face of Your anointed.

10 For a day in Your courts *is* better than a thousand.
I would rather be a doorkeeper in the house of my God
Than dwell in the tents of wickedness.
11 For the LORD God *is* a sun and shield;
The LORD will give grace and glory;
No good *thing* will He withhold
From those who walk uprightly.

12 O LORD of hosts,
Blessed *is* the man who trusts in You!

PSALM 85

Prayer that the Lord Will Restore Favor to the Land

To the Chief Musician. A Psalm of the sons of Korah.

1 LORD, You have been favorable to Your land;
You have brought back the captivity of Jacob.
2 You have forgiven the iniquity of Your people;
You have covered all their sin. Selah
3 You have taken away all Your wrath;
You have turned from the fierceness of Your anger.

4 Restore us, O God of our salvation,
And cause Your anger toward us to cease.
5 Will You be angry with us forever?
Will You prolong Your anger to all generations?
6 Will You not revive us again,
That Your people may rejoice in You?
7 Show us Your mercy, LORD,
And grant us Your salvation.

8 I will hear what God the LORD will speak,
For He will speak peace
To His people and to His saints;
But let them not turn back to folly.
9 Surely His salvation *is* near to those who fear Him,
That glory may dwell in our land.

10 Mercy and truth have met together;
Righteousness and peace have kissed.
11 Truth shall spring out of the earth,
And righteousness shall look down from heaven.
12 Yes, the LORD will give *what is* good;
And our land will yield its increase.
13 Righteousness will go before Him,
And shall make His footsteps *our* pathway.

> Will You not revive us again, that Your people may rejoice in You?
> PSALM 85:6

PSALM 86

Prayer for Mercy, with Meditation on the Excellencies of the Lord

A Prayer of David.

1 Bow down Your ear, O LORD, hear me;
For I *am* poor and needy.
2 Preserve my life, for I *am* holy;
You are my God;
Save Your servant who trusts in You!
3 Be merciful to me, O Lord,
For I cry to You all day long.
4 Rejoice the soul of Your servant,
For to You, O Lord, I lift up my soul.
5 For You, Lord, *are* good, and ready to forgive,
And abundant in mercy to all those who call upon You.

6 Give ear, O LORD, to my prayer;
And attend to the voice of my supplications.
7 In the day of my trouble I will call upon You,
For You will answer me.

8 Among the gods *there is* none like You, O Lord;
Nor *are there any works* like Your works.
9 All nations whom You have made
Shall come and worship before You, O Lord,

And shall glorify Your name.
10 For You *are* great, and do wondrous things;
You alone *are* God.

11 Teach me Your way, O LORD;
I will walk in Your truth;
Unite my heart to fear Your name.
12 I will praise You, O Lord my God, with all my heart,
And I will glorify Your name forevermore.
13 For great *is* Your mercy toward me,
And You have delivered my soul from the depths of Sheol.

14 O God, the proud have risen against me,
And a mob of violent *men* have sought my life,
And have not set You before them.
15 But You, O Lord, *are* a God full of compassion, and gracious,
Longsuffering and abundant in mercy and truth.

16 Oh, turn to me, and have mercy on me!
Give Your strength to Your servant,
And save the son of Your maidservant.
17 Show me a sign for good,
That those who hate me may see *it* and be ashamed,
Because You, LORD, have helped me and comforted me.

PSALM 87

THE GLORIES OF THE CITY OF GOD

A Psalm of the sons of Korah. A Song.

1 His foundation *is* in the holy mountains.
2 The LORD loves the gates of Zion
More than all the dwellings of Jacob.
3 Glorious things are spoken of you,
O city of God! Selah

4 "I will make mention of Rahab and Babylon to those who know Me;
Behold, O Philistia and Tyre, with Ethiopia:
'This *one* was born there.' "

5 And of Zion it will be said,
"This *one* and that *one* were born in her;
And the Most High Himself shall establish her."
6 The LORD will record,
When He registers the peoples:
"This *one* was born there." Selah

7 Both the singers and the players on instruments *say,*
"All my springs *are* in you."

PSALM 88

A PRAYER FOR HELP IN DESPONDENCY

A Song. A Psalm of the sons of Korah. To the Chief Musician. Set to "Mahalath Leannoth." A Contemplation[a] of Heman the Ezrahite.

1 O LORD, God of my salvation,
I have cried out day and night before You.
2 Let my prayer come before You;
Incline Your ear to my cry.

3 For my soul is full of troubles,
And my life draws near to the grave.
4 I am counted with those who go down to the pit;
I am like a man *who has* no strength,
5 Adrift among the dead,
Like the slain who lie in the grave,
Whom You remember no more,
And who are cut off from Your hand.
6 You have laid me in the lowest pit,
In darkness, in the depths.
7 Your wrath lies heavy upon me,
And You have afflicted *me* with all Your waves. Selah
8 You have put away my acquaintances far from me;
You have made me an abomination to them;
I am shut up, and I cannot get out;
9 My eye wastes away because of affliction.

LORD, I have called daily upon You;
I have stretched out my hands to You.
10 Will You work wonders for the dead?
Shall the dead arise *and* praise You? Selah
11 Shall Your lovingkindness be declared in the grave?
Or Your faithfulness in the place of destruction?

88:title [a]Hebrew *Maschil*

12 Shall Your wonders be known in the dark?
And Your righteousness in the land of forgetfulness?

13 But to You I have cried out, O LORD,
And in the morning my prayer comes before You.
14 LORD, why do You cast off my soul?
Why do You hide Your face from me?
15 I *have been* afflicted and ready to die from *my* youth;
I suffer Your terrors;
I am distraught.
16 Your fierce wrath has gone over me;
Your terrors have cut me off.
17 They came around me all day long like water;
They engulfed me altogether.
18 Loved one and friend You have put far from me,
And my acquaintances into darkness.

PSALM 89

REMEMBERING THE COVENANT WITH DAVID, AND SORROW FOR LOST BLESSINGS

A Contemplation[a] *of Ethan the Ezrahite.*

1 I will sing of the mercies of the LORD forever;
With my mouth will I make known Your faithfulness to all generations.
2 For I have said, "Mercy shall be built up forever;
Your faithfulness You shall establish in the very heavens."

3 "I have made a covenant with My chosen,
I have sworn to My servant David:
4 'Your seed I will establish forever,
And build up your throne to all generations.' " Selah

5 And the heavens will praise Your wonders, O LORD;
Your faithfulness also in the assembly of the saints.
6 For who in the heavens can be compared to the LORD?
Who among the sons of the mighty can be likened to the LORD?
7 God is greatly to be feared in the assembly of the saints,
And to be held in reverence by all *those* around Him.
8 O LORD God of hosts,
Who *is* mighty like You, O LORD?
Your faithfulness also surrounds You.
9 You rule the raging of the sea;
When its waves rise, You still them.
10 You have broken Rahab in pieces, as one who is slain;
You have scattered Your enemies with Your mighty arm.

11 The heavens *are* Yours, the earth also *is* Yours;
The world and all its fullness, You have founded them.
12 The north and the south, You have created them;
Tabor and Hermon rejoice in Your name.
13 You have a mighty arm;
Strong is Your hand, *and* high is Your right hand.
14 Righteousness and justice *are* the foundation of Your throne;
Mercy and truth go before Your face.
15 Blessed *are* the people who know the joyful sound!
They walk, O LORD, in the light of Your countenance.
16 In Your name they rejoice all day long,
And in Your righteousness they are exalted.
17 For You *are* the glory of their strength,
And in Your favor our horn is exalted.
18 For our shield *belongs* to the LORD,
And our king to the Holy One of Israel.

19 Then You spoke in a vision to Your holy one,[a]

I will sing of the mercies of the LORD forever; with my mouth will I make known Your faithfulness to all generations.
PSALM 89:1

89:title [a]Hebrew *Maschil* **89:19** [a]Following many Hebrew manuscripts; Masoretic Text, Septuagint, Targum, and Vulgate read *holy ones*.

And said: "I have given help to *one who*
is mighty;
I have exalted one chosen from the
people.
20 I have found My servant David;
With My holy oil I have anointed him,
21 With whom My hand shall be
established;
Also My arm shall strengthen him.
22 The enemy shall not outwit him,
Nor the son of wickedness afflict him.
23 I will beat down his foes before his
face,
And plague those who hate him.

24 "But My faithfulness and My mercy *shall*
be with him,
And in My name his horn shall be
exalted.
25 Also I will set his hand over the sea,
And his right hand over the rivers.
26 He shall cry to Me, 'You *are* my
Father,
My God, and the rock of my salvation.'
27 Also I will make him *My* firstborn,
The highest of the kings of the earth.
28 My mercy I will keep for him forever,
And My covenant shall stand firm with
him.
29 His seed also I will make *to endure*
forever,
And his throne as the days of heaven.

30 "If his sons forsake My law
And do not walk in My judgments,
31 If they break My statutes
And do not keep My commandments,
32 Then I will punish their transgression
with the rod,
And their iniquity with stripes.
33 Nevertheless My lovingkindness I will
not utterly take from him,
Nor allow My faithfulness to fail.
34 My covenant I will not break,
Nor alter the word that has gone out of
My lips.
35 Once I have sworn by My holiness;
I will not lie to David:
36 His seed shall endure forever,
And his throne as the sun before Me;
37 It shall be established forever like the
moon,
Even *like* the faithful witness in the
sky." Selah

38 But You have cast off and abhorred,
You have been furious with Your
anointed.
39 You have renounced the covenant of
Your servant;
You have profaned his crown *by casting*
it to the ground.
40 You have broken down all his hedges;
You have brought his strongholds to
ruin.
41 All who pass by the way plunder
him;
He is a reproach to his neighbors.
42 You have exalted the right hand of his
adversaries;
You have made all his enemies
rejoice.
43 You have also turned back the edge of
his sword,
And have not sustained him in the
battle.
44 You have made his glory cease,
And cast his throne down to the
ground.
45 The days of his youth You have
shortened;
You have covered him with shame.
Selah

46 How long, LORD?
Will You hide Yourself forever?
Will Your wrath burn like fire?
47 Remember how short my time is;
For what futility have You created all the
children of men?
48 What man can live and not see death?
Can he deliver his life from the power of
the grave? Selah

49 Lord, where *are* Your former
lovingkindnesses,
Which You swore to David in Your
truth?
50 Remember, Lord, the reproach of Your
servants—
How I bear in my bosom *the reproach of*
all the many peoples,
51 With which Your enemies have
reproached, O LORD,
With which they have reproached the
footsteps of Your anointed.

52 Blessed *be* the LORD forevermore!
Amen and Amen.

Book Four: Psalms 90–106

PSALM 90

The Eternity of God, and Man's Frailty

A Prayer of Moses the man of God.

1 Lord, You have been our dwelling place[a]
in all generations.
2 Before the mountains were brought
forth,
Or ever You had formed the earth and
the world,
Even from everlasting to everlasting, You
are God.

3 You turn man to destruction,
And say, "Return, O children of men."
4 For a thousand years in Your sight
Are like yesterday when it is past,
And *like* a watch in the night.
5 You carry them away *like* a flood;
They are like a sleep.
In the morning they are like grass *which*
grows up:
6 In the morning it flourishes and grows
up;
In the evening it is cut down and
withers.

7 For we have been consumed by Your
anger,
And by Your wrath we are terrified.
8 You have set our iniquities before You,
Our secret *sins* in the light of Your
countenance.
9 For all our days have passed away in
Your wrath;
We finish our years like a sigh.
10 The days of our lives *are* seventy years;
And if by reason of strength *they are*
eighty years,
Yet their boast *is* only labor and sorrow;
For it is soon cut off, and we fly away.
11 Who knows the power of Your anger?
For as the fear of You, *so is* Your wrath.
12 So teach *us* to number our days,
That we may gain a heart of wisdom.

13 Return, O LORD!
How long?
And have compassion on Your servants.
14 Oh, satisfy us early with Your mercy,
That we may rejoice and be glad all our
days!
15 Make us glad according to the days *in
which* You have afflicted us,
The years *in which* we have seen evil.
16 Let Your work appear to Your servants,
And Your glory to their children.
17 And let the beauty of the LORD our God
be upon us,
And establish the work of our hands for
us;
Yes, establish the work of our hands.

PSALM 91

Safety of Abiding in the Presence of God

1 He who dwells in the secret place of the
Most High
Shall abide under the shadow of the
Almighty.
2 I will say of the LORD, "*He is* my refuge
and my fortress;
My God, in Him I will trust."

3 Surely He shall deliver you from the
snare of the fowler[a]
And from the perilous pestilence.
4 He shall cover you with His feathers,

90:1 [a]Septuagint, Targum, and Vulgate read *refuge*. **91:3** [a]That is, one who catches birds in a trap or snare

SOUL NOTE

The Shadow of the Almighty *(91:1–13)* When believers are afraid, they can run to a "refuge" and "fortress"—God Himself. God's people dwell "in the secret place of the Most High" and "abide under the shadow of the Almighty" (91:1). No place could be more safe than there! Believers can trust that God will protect them in their times of fear. This does not imply that God's people will never suffer or face difficulty; but it does promise that they need not be afraid, for they are in God's hands.
Topic: Fear/Fear of God

And under His wings you shall take refuge;
His truth *shall be your* shield and buckler.
5 You shall not be afraid of the terror by night,
Nor of the arrow *that* flies by day,
6 *Nor* of the pestilence *that* walks in darkness,
Nor of the destruction *that* lays waste at noonday.

7 A thousand may fall at your side,
And ten thousand at your right hand;
But it shall not come near you.
8 Only with your eyes shall you look,
And see the reward of the wicked.

9 Because you have made the LORD, *who is* my refuge,
Even the Most High, your dwelling place,
10 No evil shall befall you,
Nor shall any plague come near your dwelling;
11 For He shall give His angels charge over you,
To keep you in all your ways.
12 In *their* hands they shall bear you up,
Lest you dash your foot against a stone.
13 You shall tread upon the lion and the cobra,
The young lion and the serpent you shall trample underfoot.

14 "Because he has set his love upon Me, therefore I will deliver him;
I will set him on high, because he has known My name.
15 He shall call upon Me, and I will answer him;
I *will be* with him in trouble;
I will deliver him and honor him.
16 With long life I will satisfy him,
And show him My salvation."

PSALM 92

Praise to the Lord for His Love and Faithfulness

A Psalm. A Song for the Sabbath day.

1 *It is* good to give thanks to the LORD,
And to sing praises to Your name, O Most High;
2 To declare Your lovingkindness in the morning,
And Your faithfulness every night,
3 On an instrument of ten strings,
On the lute,
And on the harp,
With harmonious sound.
4 For You, LORD, have made me glad through Your work;
I will triumph in the works of Your hands.

5 O LORD, how great are Your works!
Your thoughts are very deep.
6 A senseless man does not know,
Nor does a fool understand this.
7 When the wicked spring up like grass,
And when all the workers of iniquity flourish,
It is that they may be destroyed forever.

8 But You, LORD, *are* on high forevermore.
9 For behold, Your enemies, O LORD,
For behold, Your enemies shall perish;
All the workers of iniquity shall be scattered.

10 But my horn You have exalted like a wild ox;
I have been anointed with fresh oil.
11 My eye also has seen *my desire* on my enemies;
My ears hear *my desire* on the wicked
Who rise up against me.

12 The righteous shall flourish like a palm tree,
He shall grow like a cedar in Lebanon.
13 Those who are planted in the house of the LORD
Shall flourish in the courts of our God.
14 They shall still bear fruit in old age;
They shall be fresh and flourishing,
15 To declare that the LORD is upright;
He is my rock, and *there is* no unrighteousness in Him.

PSALM 93

The Eternal Reign of the Lord

1 The LORD reigns, He is clothed with majesty;
The LORD is clothed,

He has girded Himself with strength.
Surely the world is established, so that it cannot be moved.
2 Your throne *is* established from of old;
You *are* from everlasting.

3 The floods have lifted up, O LORD,
The floods have lifted up their voice;
The floods lift up their waves.
4 The LORD on high *is* mightier
Than the noise of many waters,
Than the mighty waves of the sea.

5 Your testimonies are very sure;
Holiness adorns Your house,
O LORD, forever.

PSALM 94

GOD THE REFUGE OF THE RIGHTEOUS

1 O LORD God, to whom vengeance belongs—
O God, to whom vengeance belongs, shine forth!
2 Rise up, O Judge of the earth;
Render punishment to the proud.
3 LORD, how long will the wicked,
How long will the wicked triumph?

4 They utter speech, *and* speak insolent things;
All the workers of iniquity boast in themselves.
5 They break in pieces Your people, O LORD,
And afflict Your heritage.
6 They slay the widow and the stranger,
And murder the fatherless.
7 Yet they say, "The LORD does not see,
Nor does the God of Jacob understand."

8 Understand, you senseless among the people;
And *you* fools, when will you be wise?
9 He who planted the ear, shall He not hear?
He who formed the eye, shall He not see?
10 He who instructs the nations, shall He not correct,
He who teaches man knowledge?
11 The LORD knows the thoughts of man,
That they *are* futile.

12 Blessed *is* the man whom You instruct, O LORD,
And teach out of Your law,
13 That You may give him rest from the days of adversity,
Until the pit is dug for the wicked.
14 For the LORD will not cast off His people,
Nor will He forsake His inheritance.
15 But judgment will return to righteousness,
And all the upright in heart will follow it.

16 Who will rise up for me against the evildoers?
Who will stand up for me against the workers of iniquity?
17 Unless the LORD *had been* my help,
My soul would soon have settled in silence.
18 If I say, "My foot slips,"
Your mercy, O LORD, will hold me up.
19 In the multitude of my anxieties within me,
Your comforts delight my soul.

20 Shall the throne of iniquity, which devises evil by law,
Have fellowship with You?
21 They gather together against the life of the righteous,
And condemn innocent blood.
22 But the LORD has been my defense,
And my God the rock of my refuge.
23 He has brought on them their own iniquity,
And shall cut them off in their own wickedness;
The LORD our God shall cut them off.

PSALM 95

A CALL TO WORSHIP AND OBEDIENCE

1 Oh come, let us sing to the LORD!
Let us shout joyfully to the Rock of our salvation.
2 Let us come before His presence with thanksgiving;
Let us shout joyfully to Him with psalms.
3 For the LORD *is* the great God,
And the great King above all gods.
4 In His hand *are* the deep places of the earth;

The heights of the hills *are* His also.
5 The sea *is* His, for He made it;
And His hands formed the dry *land*.

6 Oh come, let us worship and bow down;
Let us kneel before the LORD our Maker.
7 For He *is* our God,
And we *are* the people of His pasture,
And the sheep of His hand.

Today, if you will hear His voice:
8 "Do not harden your hearts, as in the rebellion,[a]
As *in* the day of trial[b] in the wilderness,
9 When your fathers tested Me;
They tried Me, though they saw My work.
10 For forty years I was grieved with *that* generation,
And said, 'It *is* a people who go astray in their hearts,
And they do not know My ways.'
11 So I swore in My wrath,
'They shall not enter My rest.' "

Oh come, let us worship and bow down; let us kneel before the LORD our Maker.
For He is our God, and we are the people of His pasture, and the sheep of His hand.
PSALM 95:6,7

PSALM 96

A Song of Praise to God Coming in Judgment

1 Oh, sing to the LORD a new song!
Sing to the LORD, all the earth.
2 Sing to the LORD, bless His name;
Proclaim the good news of His salvation from day to day.
3 Declare His glory among the nations,
His wonders among all peoples.

4 For the LORD *is* great and greatly to be praised;
He *is* to be feared above all gods.
5 For all the gods of the peoples *are* idols,
But the LORD made the heavens.
6 Honor and majesty *are* before Him;
Strength and beauty *are* in His sanctuary.

7 Give to the LORD, O families of the peoples,
Give to the LORD glory and strength.
8 Give to the LORD the glory *due* His name;
Bring an offering, and come into His courts.
9 Oh, worship the LORD in the beauty of holiness!
Tremble before Him, all the earth.

10 Say among the nations, "The LORD reigns;
The world also is firmly established,
It shall not be moved;
He shall judge the peoples righteously."

11 Let the heavens rejoice, and let the earth be glad;
Let the sea roar, and all its fullness;
12 Let the field be joyful, and all that *is* in it.
Then all the trees of the woods will rejoice before the LORD.
13 For He is coming, for He is coming to judge the earth.
He shall judge the world with righteousness,
And the peoples with His truth.

PSALM 97

A Song of Praise to the Sovereign Lord

1 The LORD reigns;
Let the earth rejoice;
Let the multitude of isles be glad!

2 Clouds and darkness surround Him;
Righteousness and justice *are* the foundation of His throne.
3 A fire goes before Him,
And burns up His enemies round about.
4 His lightnings light the world;
The earth sees and trembles.
5 The mountains melt like wax at the presence of the LORD,

95:8 [a]Or *Meribah* [b]Or *Massah*

At the presence of the Lord of the whole
earth.
6 The heavens declare His
righteousness,
And all the peoples see His glory.

7 Let all be put to shame who serve
carved images,
Who boast of idols.
Worship Him, all *you* gods.
8 Zion hears and is glad,
And the daughters of Judah rejoice
Because of Your judgments, O LORD.
9 For You, LORD, *are* most high above all
the earth;
You are exalted far above all gods.

10 You who love the LORD, hate evil!
He preserves the souls of His saints;
He delivers them out of the hand of the
wicked.
11 Light is sown for the righteous,
And gladness for the upright in heart.
12 Rejoice in the LORD, you righteous,
And give thanks at the remembrance of
His holy name.[a]

PSALM 98

A Song of Praise to the Lord for His Salvation and Judgment

A Psalm.

1 Oh, sing to the LORD a new song!
For He has done marvelous things;
His right hand and His holy arm have
gained Him the victory.
2 The LORD has made known His
salvation;
His righteousness He has revealed in the
sight of the nations.
3 He has remembered His mercy and His
faithfulness to the house of Israel;
All the ends of the earth have seen the
salvation of our God.

4 Shout joyfully to the LORD, all the earth;
Break forth in song, rejoice, and sing
praises.
5 Sing to the LORD with the harp,
With the harp and the sound of a psalm,
6 With trumpets and the sound of a horn;
Shout joyfully before the LORD, the
King.

7 Let the sea roar, and all its fullness,
The world and those who dwell in it;
8 Let the rivers clap *their* hands;
Let the hills be joyful together before the
LORD,
9 For He is coming to judge the earth.
With righteousness He shall judge the
world,
And the peoples with equity.

PSALM 99

Praise to the Lord for His Holiness

1 The LORD reigns;
Let the peoples tremble!
He dwells *between* the cherubim;
Let the earth be moved!
2 The LORD *is* great in Zion,
And He *is* high above all the
peoples.
3 Let them praise Your great and awesome
name—
He *is* holy.

4 The King's strength also loves
justice;
You have established equity;
You have executed justice and
righteousness in Jacob.
5 Exalt the LORD our God,
And worship at His footstool—
He *is* holy.

6 Moses and Aaron were among His
priests,
And Samuel was among those who
called upon His name;
They called upon the LORD, and He
answered them.
7 He spoke to them in the cloudy
pillar;
They kept His testimonies and the
ordinance He gave them.

8 You answered them, O LORD our God;
You were to them God-Who-Forgives,
Though You took vengeance on their
deeds.
9 Exalt the LORD our God,
And worship at His holy hill;
For the LORD our God *is* holy.

97:12 [a]Or *His holiness*

PSALM 100

A Song of Praise for the Lord's Faithfulness to His People

A Psalm of Thanksgiving.

1 Make a joyful shout to the LORD, all you
lands!
2 Serve the LORD with gladness;
Come before His presence with singing.
3 Know that the LORD, He *is* God;
It is He *who* has made us, and not we
ourselves;[a]
We are His people and the sheep of His
pasture.

4 Enter into His gates with thanksgiving,
And into His courts with praise.
Be thankful to Him, *and* bless His
name.
5 For the LORD *is* good;
His mercy *is* everlasting,
And His truth *endures* to all generations.

PSALM 101

Promised Faithfulness to the Lord

A Psalm of David.

1 I will sing of mercy and justice;
To You, O LORD, I will sing praises.

2 I will behave wisely in a perfect way.
Oh, when will You come to me?
I will walk within my house with a
perfect heart.

3 I will set nothing wicked before my eyes;
I hate the work of those who fall away;
It shall not cling to me.
4 A perverse heart shall depart from me;
I will not know wickedness.

5 Whoever secretly slanders his neighbor,
Him I will destroy;
The one who has a haughty look and a
proud heart,
Him I will not endure.

6 My eyes *shall be* on the faithful of the
land,
That they may dwell with me;
He who walks in a perfect way,
He shall serve me.
7 He who works deceit shall not dwell
within my house;
He who tells lies shall not continue in
my presence.
8 Early I will destroy all the wicked of the
land,
That I may cut off all the evildoers from
the city of the LORD.

PSALM 102

The Lord's Eternal Love

A Prayer of the afflicted, when he is overwhelmed and pours out his complaint before the LORD.

1 Hear my prayer, O LORD,
And let my cry come to You.
2 Do not hide Your face from me in the
day of my trouble;
Incline Your ear to me;
In the day that I call, answer me
speedily.

3 For my days are consumed like smoke,
And my bones are burned like a hearth.

100:3 [a]Following Kethib, Septuagint, and Vulgate; Qere, many Hebrew manuscripts, and Targum read *we are His.*

SOUL NOTE

We Are His People *(100:1–3)* Psalm 100 is an expression of confidence in God. We know who we are because we know who He is: "Know that the LORD, He is God; it is He who has made us . . . we are His people" (100:3). Thus, God's people can enter His presence with thanksgiving, having confidence that His mercy and truth are available at all times. Secure in our relationship with God, we can be confident of our value in this world as we "serve the LORD with gladness" (100:2).

Topic: Self-Esteem

4 My heart is stricken and withered like grass,
So that I forget to eat my bread.
5 Because of the sound of my groaning
My bones cling to my skin.
6 I am like a pelican of the wilderness;
I am like an owl of the desert.
7 I lie awake,
And am like a sparrow alone on the housetop.

8 My enemies reproach me all day long;
Those who deride me swear an oath against me.
9 For I have eaten ashes like bread,
And mingled my drink with weeping,
10 Because of Your indignation and Your wrath;
For You have lifted me up and cast me away.
11 My days *are* like a shadow that lengthens,
And I wither away like grass.

12 But You, O LORD, shall endure forever,
And the remembrance of Your name to all generations.
13 You will arise *and* have mercy on Zion;
For the time to favor her,
Yes, the set time, has come.
14 For Your servants take pleasure in her stones,
And show favor to her dust.
15 So the nations shall fear the name of the LORD,
And all the kings of the earth Your glory.
16 For the LORD shall build up Zion;
He shall appear in His glory.
17 He shall regard the prayer of the destitute,
And shall not despise their prayer.

18 This will be written for the generation to come,
That a people yet to be created may praise the LORD.
19 For He looked down from the height of His sanctuary;
From heaven the LORD viewed the earth,
20 To hear the groaning of the prisoner,
To release those appointed to death,
21 To declare the name of the LORD in Zion,
And His praise in Jerusalem,
22 When the peoples are gathered together,
And the kingdoms, to serve the LORD.

23 He weakened my strength in the way;
He shortened my days.
24 I said, "O my God,
Do not take me away in the midst of my days;
Your years *are* throughout all generations.
25 Of old You laid the foundation of the earth,
And the heavens *are* the work of Your hands.
26 They will perish, but You will endure;
Yes, they will all grow old like a garment;
Like a cloak You will change them,
And they will be changed.
27 But You *are* the same,
And Your years will have no end.
28 The children of Your servants will continue,
And their descendants will be established before You."

PSALM 103

PRAISE FOR THE LORD'S MERCIES

A Psalm of David.

1 Bless the LORD, O my soul;
And all that is within me, *bless* His holy name!
2 Bless the LORD, O my soul,
And forget not all His benefits:
3 Who forgives all your iniquities,
Who heals all your diseases,
4 Who redeems your life from destruction,
Who crowns you with lovingkindness and tender mercies,
5 Who satisfies your mouth with good *things*,
So that your youth is renewed like the eagle's.

6 The LORD executes righteousness
And justice for all who are oppressed.
7 He made known His ways to Moses,
His acts to the children of Israel.
8 The LORD *is* merciful and gracious,
Slow to anger, and abounding in mercy.
9 He will not always strive *with us,*
Nor will He keep *His anger* forever.
10 He has not dealt with us according to our sins,

Nor punished us according to our
iniquities.

11 For as the heavens are high above the
earth,
So great is His mercy toward those who
fear Him;
12 As far as the east is from the west,
So far has He removed our
transgressions from us.
13 As a father pities *his* children,
So the LORD pities those who fear Him.
14 For He knows our frame;
He remembers that we *are* dust.

15 *As for* man, his days *are* like grass;
As a flower of the field, so he flourishes.
16 For the wind passes over it, and it is
gone,
And its place remembers it no more.[a]
17 But the mercy of the LORD *is* from
everlasting to everlasting
On those who fear Him,
And His righteousness to children's
children,
18 To such as keep His covenant,
And to those who remember His
commandments to do them.

19 The LORD has established His throne in
heaven,
And His kingdom rules over all.

20 Bless the LORD, you His angels,
Who excel in strength, who do His word,
Heeding the voice of His word.
21 Bless the LORD, all *you* His hosts,
You ministers of His, who do His
pleasure.
22 Bless the LORD, all His works,
In all places of His dominion.

Bless the LORD, O my soul!

PSALM 104

PRAISE TO THE SOVEREIGN LORD FOR HIS CREATION AND PROVIDENCE

1 Bless the LORD, O my soul!

O LORD my God, You are very great:
You are clothed with honor and majesty,
2 Who cover *Yourself* with light as *with* a
garment,
Who stretch out the heavens like a
curtain.

3 He lays the beams of His upper
chambers in the waters,
Who makes the clouds His chariot,
Who walks on the wings of the wind,
4 Who makes His angels spirits,
His ministers a flame of fire.

5 *You who* laid the foundations of the
earth,
So *that* it should not be moved forever,
6 You covered it with the deep as *with* a
garment;
The waters stood above the mountains.
7 At Your rebuke they fled;
At the voice of Your thunder they
hastened away.
8 They went up over the mountains;
They went down into the valleys,
To the place which You founded for
them.
9 You have set a boundary that they may
not pass over,
That they may not return to cover the
earth.

10 He sends the springs into the valleys;
They flow among the hills.

103:16 [a]Compare Job 7:10

SOUL NOTE

Children's Children *(103:17, 18)* One of the great promises of the Bible is that the mercy of the Lord continues from one generation to the next, even to our children's children. This does not mean that the children of believers will automatically believe in God, but that God's mercy and goodness are available to each generation that follows the good example set by the previous generation. Parents must set the right example for their children. They are living not merely for themselves; they are setting a precedent that will affect generations to come. **Topic: Parenting**

11 They give drink to every beast of the field;
The wild donkeys quench their thirst.
12 By them the birds of the heavens have their home;
They sing among the branches.
13 He waters the hills from His upper chambers;
The earth is satisfied with the fruit of Your works.

14 He causes the grass to grow for the cattle,
And vegetation for the service of man,
That he may bring forth food from the earth,
15 And wine *that* makes glad the heart of man,
Oil to make *his* face shine,
And bread *which* strengthens man's heart.
16 The trees of the LORD are full *of sap,*
The cedars of Lebanon which He planted,
17 Where the birds make their nests;
The stork has her home in the fir trees.
18 The high hills *are* for the wild goats;
The cliffs are a refuge for the rock badgers.[a]

19 He appointed the moon for seasons;
The sun knows its going down.
20 You make darkness, and it is night,
In which all the beasts of the forest creep about.
21 The young lions roar after their prey,
And seek their food from God.
22 *When* the sun rises, they gather together
And lie down in their dens.
23 Man goes out to his work
And to his labor until the evening.

24 O LORD, how manifold are Your works!
In wisdom You have made them all.
The earth is full of Your possessions—
25 This great and wide sea,
In which *are* innumerable teeming things,
Living things both small and great.
26 There the ships sail about;
There is that Leviathan
Which You have made to play there.

27 These all wait for You,
That You may give *them* their food in due season.
28 *What* You give them they gather in;
You open Your hand, they are filled with good.
29 You hide Your face, they are troubled;
You take away their breath, they die and return to their dust.
30 You send forth Your Spirit, they are created;
And You renew the face of the earth.

31 May the glory of the LORD endure forever;
May the LORD rejoice in His works.
32 He looks on the earth, and it trembles;
He touches the hills, and they smoke.

33 I will sing to the LORD as long as I live;
I will sing praise to my God while I have my being.
34 May my meditation be sweet to Him;
I will be glad in the LORD.
35 May sinners be consumed from the earth,
And the wicked be no more.

Bless the LORD, O my soul!
Praise the LORD!

PSALM 105

THE ETERNAL FAITHFULNESS OF THE LORD

1 Oh, give thanks to the LORD!
Call upon His name;
Make known His deeds among the peoples!
2 Sing to Him, sing psalms to Him;
Talk of all His wondrous works!
3 Glory in His holy name;

> Glory in His holy name;
> let the hearts of those rejoice
> who seek the LORD!
> PSALM 105:3

104:18 [a]Or *rock hyrax* (compare Leviticus 11:5)

Let the hearts of those rejoice who seek
the LORD!
4 Seek the LORD and His strength;
Seek His face evermore!
5 Remember His marvelous works which
He has done,
His wonders, and the judgments of His
mouth,
6 O seed of Abraham His servant,
You children of Jacob, His chosen ones!

7 He *is* the LORD our God;
His judgments *are* in all the earth.
8 He remembers His covenant forever,
The word *which* He commanded, for a
thousand generations,
9 *The covenant* which He made with
Abraham,
And His oath to Isaac,
10 And confirmed it to Jacob for a statute,
To Israel *as* an everlasting covenant,
11 Saying, "To you I will give the land of
Canaan
As the allotment of your inheritance,"
12 When they were few in number,
Indeed very few, and strangers in it.

13 When they went from one nation to
another,
From *one* kingdom to another people,
14 He permitted no one to do them wrong;
Yes, He rebuked kings for their sakes,
15 *Saying,* "Do not touch My anointed
ones,
And do My prophets no harm."

16 Moreover He called for a famine in the
land;
He destroyed all the provision of bread.
17 He sent a man before them—
Joseph—*who* was sold as a slave.
18 They hurt his feet with fetters,
He was laid in irons.
19 Until the time that his word came to pass,
The word of the LORD tested him.
20 The king sent and released him,
The ruler of the people let him go free.
21 He made him lord of his house,
And ruler of all his possessions,
22 To bind his princes at his pleasure,
And teach his elders wisdom.

23 Israel also came into Egypt,
And Jacob dwelt in the land of Ham.
24 He increased His people greatly,
And made them stronger than their
enemies.
25 He turned their heart to hate His people,
To deal craftily with His servants.

26 He sent Moses His servant,
And Aaron whom He had chosen.
27 They performed His signs among them,
And wonders in the land of Ham.
28 He sent darkness, and made *it* dark;
And they did not rebel against His word.
29 He turned their waters into blood,
And killed their fish.
30 Their land abounded with frogs,
Even in the chambers of their kings.
31 He spoke, and there came swarms of
flies,
And lice in all their territory.
32 He gave them hail for rain,
And flaming fire in their land.
33 He struck their vines also, and their fig
trees,
And splintered the trees of their
territory.
34 He spoke, and locusts came,
Young locusts without number,
35 And ate up all the vegetation in their
land,
And devoured the fruit of their ground.
36 He also destroyed all the firstborn in
their land,
The first of all their strength.

37 He also brought them out with silver
and gold,
And *there was* none feeble among His
tribes.
38 Egypt was glad when they departed,
For the fear of them had fallen upon
them.
39 He spread a cloud for a covering,
And fire to give light in the night.
40 *The people* asked, and He brought quail,
And satisfied them with the bread of
heaven.
41 He opened the rock, and water gushed
out;
It ran in the dry places *like* a river.

42 For He remembered His holy promise,
And Abraham His servant.
43 He brought out His people with joy,
His chosen ones with gladness.

44 He gave them the lands of the Gentiles,
And they inherited the labor of the nations,
45 That they might observe His statutes
And keep His laws.

Praise the LORD!

PSALM 106

JOY IN FORGIVENESS OF ISRAEL'S SINS

1 Praise the LORD!

Oh, give thanks to the LORD, for *He is* good!
For His mercy *endures* forever.

2 Who can utter the mighty acts of the LORD?
Who can declare all His praise?
3 Blessed *are* those who keep justice,
And he who does[a] righteousness at all times!

4 Remember me, O LORD, with the favor *You have toward* Your people.
Oh, visit me with Your salvation,
5 That I may see the benefit of Your chosen ones,
That I may rejoice in the gladness of Your nation,
That I may glory with Your inheritance.

6 We have sinned with our fathers,
We have committed iniquity,
We have done wickedly.
7 Our fathers in Egypt did not understand Your wonders;
They did not remember the multitude of Your mercies,
But rebelled by the sea—the Red Sea.

8 Nevertheless He saved them for His name's sake,
That He might make His mighty power known.
9 He rebuked the Red Sea also, and it dried up;
So He led them through the depths,
As through the wilderness.
10 He saved them from the hand of him who hated *them*,
And redeemed them from the hand of the enemy.
11 The waters covered their enemies;
There was not one of them left.
12 Then they believed His words;
They sang His praise.

13 They soon forgot His works;
They did not wait for His counsel,
14 But lusted exceedingly in the wilderness,
And tested God in the desert.
15 And He gave them their request,
But sent leanness into their soul.

16 When they envied Moses in the camp,
And Aaron the saint of the LORD,
17 The earth opened up and swallowed Dathan,
And covered the faction of Abiram.
18 A fire was kindled in their company;
The flame burned up the wicked.

19 They made a calf in Horeb,
And worshiped the molded image.
20 Thus they changed their glory
Into the image of an ox that eats grass.
21 They forgot God their Savior,
Who had done great things in Egypt,
22 Wondrous works in the land of Ham,
Awesome things by the Red Sea.
23 Therefore He said that He would destroy them,
Had not Moses His chosen one stood before Him in the breach,
To turn away His wrath, lest He destroy *them*.

24 Then they despised the pleasant land;
They did not believe His word,
25 But complained in their tents,
And did not heed the voice of the LORD.
26 Therefore He raised His hand *in an oath* against them,
To overthrow them in the wilderness,
27 To overthrow their descendants among the nations,
And to scatter them in the lands.

28 They joined themselves also to Baal of Peor,
And ate sacrifices made to the dead.

106:3 [a]Septuagint, Syriac, Targum, and Vulgate read *those who do*.

29 Thus they provoked *Him* to anger with
their deeds,
And the plague broke out among them.
30 Then Phinehas stood up and intervened,
And the plague was stopped.
31 And that was accounted to him for
righteousness
To all generations forevermore.

32 They angered *Him* also at the waters of
strife,[a]
So that it went ill with Moses on account
of them;
33 Because they rebelled against His Spirit,
So that he spoke rashly with his lips.

34 They did not destroy the peoples,
Concerning whom the LORD had
commanded them,
35 But they mingled with the Gentiles
And learned their works;
36 They served their idols,
Which became a snare to them.
37 They even sacrificed their sons
And their daughters to demons,
38 And shed innocent blood,
The blood of their sons and daughters,
Whom they sacrificed to the idols of
Canaan;
And the land was polluted with blood.
39 Thus they were defiled by their own
works,
And played the harlot by their own
deeds.

40 Therefore the wrath of the LORD was
kindled against His people,
So that He abhorred His own
inheritance.
41 And He gave them into the hand of the
Gentiles,
And those who hated them ruled over
them.
42 Their enemies also oppressed them,
And they were brought into subjection
under their hand.
43 Many times He delivered them;
But they rebelled in their counsel,
And were brought low for their iniquity.

44 Nevertheless He regarded their affliction,
When He heard their cry;
45 And for their sake He remembered His
covenant,
And relented according to the multitude
of His mercies.
46 He also made them to be pitied
By all those who carried them away
captive.

47 Save us, O LORD our God,
And gather us from among the Gentiles,
To give thanks to Your holy name,
To triumph in Your praise.

48 Blessed *be* the LORD God of Israel
From everlasting to everlasting!
And let all the people say, "Amen!"

Praise the LORD!

BOOK FIVE: PSALMS 107–150

PSALM 107

THANKSGIVING TO THE LORD FOR HIS GREAT WORKS OF DELIVERANCE

1 Oh, give thanks to the LORD, for *He is*
good!
For His mercy *endures* forever.
2 Let the redeemed of the LORD say *so,*
Whom He has redeemed from the hand
of the enemy,
3 And gathered out of the lands,
From the east and from the west,
From the north and from the south.

4 They wandered in the wilderness in a
desolate way;
They found no city to dwell in.
5 Hungry and thirsty,
Their soul fainted in them.
6 Then they cried out to the LORD in their
trouble,
And He delivered them out of their
distresses.
7 And He led them forth by the right way,
That they might go to a city for a
dwelling place.
8 Oh, that *men* would give thanks to the
LORD *for* His goodness,
And *for* His wonderful works to the
children of men!
9 For He satisfies the longing soul,
And fills the hungry soul with goodness.

106:32 [a]Or *Meribah*

10 Those who sat in darkness and in the shadow of death,
Bound in affliction and irons—
11 Because they rebelled against the words of God,
And despised the counsel of the Most High,
12 Therefore He brought down their heart with labor;
They fell down, and *there was* none to help.
13 Then they cried out to the LORD in their trouble,
And He saved them out of their distresses.
14 He brought them out of darkness and the shadow of death,
And broke their chains in pieces.
15 Oh, that *men* would give thanks to the LORD *for* His goodness,
And *for* His wonderful works to the children of men!
16 For He has broken the gates of bronze,
And cut the bars of iron in two.

17 Fools, because of their transgression,
And because of their iniquities, were afflicted.
18 Their soul abhorred all manner of food,
And they drew near to the gates of death.
19 Then they cried out to the LORD in their trouble,
And He saved them out of their distresses.
20 He sent His word and healed them,
And delivered *them* from their destructions.
21 Oh, that *men* would give thanks to the LORD *for* His goodness,
And *for* His wonderful works to the children of men!
22 Let them sacrifice the sacrifices of thanksgiving,
And declare His works with rejoicing.

23 Those who go down to the sea in ships,
Who do business on great waters,
24 They see the works of the LORD,
And His wonders in the deep.
25 For He commands and raises the stormy wind,
Which lifts up the waves of the sea.
26 They mount up to the heavens,
They go down again to the depths;
Their soul melts because of trouble.
27 They reel to and fro, and stagger like a drunken man,
And are at their wits' end.
28 Then they cry out to the LORD in their trouble,
And He brings them out of their distresses.
29 He calms the storm,
So that its waves are still.
30 Then they are glad because they are quiet;
So He guides them to their desired haven.
31 Oh, that *men* would give thanks to the LORD *for* His goodness,
And *for* His wonderful works to the children of men!
32 Let them exalt Him also in the assembly of the people,
And praise Him in the company of the elders.

33 He turns rivers into a wilderness,
And the watersprings into dry ground;
34 A fruitful land into barrenness,
For the wickedness of those who dwell in it.
35 He turns a wilderness into pools of water,
And dry land into watersprings.
36 There He makes the hungry dwell,
That they may establish a city for a dwelling place,
37 And sow fields and plant vineyards,
That they may yield a fruitful harvest.
38 He also blesses them, and they multiply greatly;
And He does not let their cattle decrease.

39 When they are diminished and brought low
Through oppression, affliction and sorrow,
40 He pours contempt on princes,
And causes them to wander in the wilderness *where there is* no way;
41 Yet He sets the poor on high, far from affliction,
And makes *their* families like a flock.
42 The righteous see *it* and rejoice,
And all iniquity stops its mouth.

43 Whoever *is* wise will observe these *things,*

And they will understand the
lovingkindness of the LORD.

PSALM 108

ASSURANCE OF GOD'S VICTORY OVER ENEMIES

A Song. A Psalm of David.

1 O God, my heart is steadfast;
I will sing and give praise, even with my glory.
2 Awake, lute and harp!
I will awaken the dawn.
3 I will praise You, O LORD, among the peoples,
And I will sing praises to You among the nations.
4 For Your mercy *is* great above the heavens,
And Your truth *reaches* to the clouds.

5 Be exalted, O God, above the heavens,
And Your glory above all the earth;
6 That Your beloved may be delivered,
Save *with* Your right hand, and hear me.

7 God has spoken in His holiness:
"I will rejoice;
I will divide Shechem
And measure out the Valley of Succoth.
8 Gilead *is* Mine; Manasseh *is* Mine;
Ephraim also *is* the helmet for My head;
Judah *is* My lawgiver.
9 Moab *is* My washpot;
Over Edom I will cast My shoe;
Over Philistia I will triumph."

10 Who will bring me *into* the strong city?
Who will lead me to Edom?
11 *Is it* not *You,* O God, *who* cast us off?
And *You,* O God, *who* did not go out with our armies?
12 Give us help from trouble,
For the help of man is useless.
13 Through God we will do valiantly,
For *it is* He *who* shall tread down our enemies.[a]

PSALM 109

PLEA FOR JUDGMENT OF FALSE ACCUSERS

To the Chief Musician. A Psalm of David.

1 Do not keep silent,
O God of my praise!
2 For the mouth of the wicked and the mouth of the deceitful
Have opened against me;
They have spoken against me with a lying tongue.
3 They have also surrounded me with words of hatred,
And fought against me without a cause.
4 In return for my love they are my accusers,
But I *give myself to* prayer.
5 Thus they have rewarded me evil for good,
And hatred for my love.

6 Set a wicked man over him,
And let an accuser[a] stand at his right hand.
7 When he is judged, let him be found guilty,
And let his prayer become sin.
8 Let his days be few,
And let another take his office.
9 Let his children be fatherless,
And his wife a widow.
10 Let his children continually be vagabonds, and beg;
Let them seek *their bread*[a] also from their desolate places.
11 Let the creditor seize all that he has,
And let strangers plunder his labor.
12 Let there be none to extend mercy to him,
Nor let there be any to favor his fatherless children.
13 Let his posterity be cut off,
And in the generation following let their name be blotted out.

14 Let the iniquity of his fathers be remembered before the LORD,
And let not the sin of his mother be blotted out.
15 Let them be continually before the LORD,
That He may cut off the memory of them from the earth;
16 Because he did not remember to show mercy,
But persecuted the poor and needy man,

108:13 [a]Compare verses 6–13 with 60:5–12 **109:6** [a]Hebrew *satan* **109:10** [a]Following Masoretic Text and Targum; Septuagint and Vulgate read *be cast out.*

That he might even slay the broken in heart.
17 As he loved cursing, so let it come to him;
As he did not delight in blessing, so let it be far from him.
18 As he clothed himself with cursing as with his garment,
So let it enter his body like water,
And like oil into his bones.
19 Let it be to him like the garment which covers him,
And for a belt with which he girds himself continually.
20 *Let* this *be* the LORD's reward to my accusers,
And to those who speak evil against my person.

21 But You, O GOD the Lord,
Deal with me for Your name's sake;
Because Your mercy *is* good, deliver me.
22 For I *am* poor and needy,
And my heart is wounded within me.
23 I am gone like a shadow when it lengthens;
I am shaken off like a locust.
24 My knees are weak through fasting,
And my flesh is feeble from lack of fatness.
25 I also have become a reproach to them;
When they look at me, they shake their heads.

26 Help me, O LORD my God!
Oh, save me according to Your mercy,
27 That they may know that this *is* Your hand—
That You, LORD, have done it!
28 Let them curse, but You bless;
When they arise, let them be ashamed,
But let Your servant rejoice.
29 Let my accusers be clothed with shame,
And let them cover themselves with their own disgrace as with a mantle.

30 I will greatly praise the LORD with my mouth;
Yes, I will praise Him among the multitude.
31 For He shall stand at the right hand of the poor,
To save *him* from those who condemn him.

PSALM 110

Announcement of the Messiah's Reign

A Psalm of David.

1 The LORD said to my Lord,
"Sit at My right hand,
Till I make Your enemies Your footstool."
2 The LORD shall send the rod of Your strength out of Zion.
Rule in the midst of Your enemies!

3 Your people *shall be* volunteers
In the day of Your power;
In the beauties of holiness, from the womb of the morning,
You have the dew of Your youth.
4 The LORD has sworn
And will not relent,
"You *are* a priest forever
According to the order of Melchizedek."

5 The Lord *is* at Your right hand;
He shall execute kings in the day of His wrath.
6 He shall judge among the nations,
He shall fill *the places* with dead bodies,
He shall execute the heads of many countries.
7 He shall drink of the brook by the wayside;
Therefore He shall lift up the head.

PSALM 111

Praise to God for His Faithfulness and Justice

1 Praise the LORD!

I will praise the LORD with *my* whole heart,
In the assembly of the upright and *in* the congregation.

2 The works of the LORD *are* great,
Studied by all who have pleasure in them.
3 His work *is* honorable and glorious,
And His righteousness endures forever.
4 He has made His wonderful works to be remembered;
The LORD *is* gracious and full of compassion.

5 He has given food to those who fear
Him;
He will ever be mindful of His covenant.
6 He has declared to His people the power
of His works,
In giving them the heritage of the
nations.

7 The works of His hands *are* verity and
justice;
All His precepts *are* sure.
8 They stand fast forever and ever,
And are done in truth and uprightness.
9 He has sent redemption to His people;
He has commanded His covenant
forever:
Holy and awesome *is* His name.

10 The fear of the LORD *is* the beginning of
wisdom;
A good understanding have all those
who do *His commandments.*
His praise endures forever.

PSALM 112

The Blessed State of the Righteous

1 Praise the LORD!

Blessed *is* the man *who* fears the LORD,
Who delights greatly in His
commandments.

2 His descendants will be mighty on
earth;
The generation of the upright will be
blessed.
3 Wealth and riches *will be* in his house,
And his righteousness endures forever.
4 Unto the upright there arises light in the
darkness;
He is gracious, and full of compassion,
and righteous.
5 A good man deals graciously and lends;
He will guide his affairs with
discretion.
6 Surely he will never be shaken;
The righteous will be in everlasting
remembrance.
7 He will not be afraid of evil tidings;
His heart is steadfast, trusting in the
LORD.
8 His heart *is* established;
He will not be afraid,
Until he sees *his desire* upon his
enemies.

9 He has dispersed abroad,
He has given to the poor;
His righteousness endures forever;
His horn will be exalted with honor.
10 The wicked will see *it* and be grieved;
He will gnash his teeth and melt away;
The desire of the wicked shall perish.

PSALM 113

The Majesty and Condescension of God

1 Praise the LORD!

Praise, O servants of the LORD,
Praise the name of the LORD!
2 Blessed be the name of the LORD
From this time forth and forevermore!
3 From the rising of the sun to its going
down
The LORD's name *is* to be praised.

4 The LORD *is* high above all nations,
His glory above the heavens.
5 Who *is* like the LORD our God,
Who dwells on high,
6 Who humbles Himself to behold
The things that are in the heavens and in
the earth?

7 He raises the poor out of the dust,
And lifts the needy out of the ash
heap,
8 That He may seat *him* with princes—
With the princes of His people.
9 He grants the barren woman a home,
Like a joyful mother of children.

Praise the LORD!

PSALM 114

The Power of God in His Deliverance of Israel

1 When Israel went out of Egypt,
The house of Jacob from a people of
strange language,
2 Judah became His sanctuary,
And Israel His dominion.

3 The sea saw *it* and fled;
Jordan turned back.
4 The mountains skipped like rams,
The little hills like lambs.
5 What ails you, O sea, that you fled?
O Jordan, *that* you turned back?
6 O mountains, *that* you skipped like rams?
O little hills, like lambs?

7 Tremble, O earth, at the presence of the Lord,
At the presence of the God of Jacob,
8 Who turned the rock *into* a pool of water,
The flint into a fountain of waters.

PSALM 115

The Futility of Idols and the Trustworthiness of God

1 Not unto us, O LORD, not unto us,
But to Your name give glory,
Because of Your mercy,
Because of Your truth.
2 Why should the Gentiles say,
"So where *is* their God?"

3 But our God *is* in heaven;
He does whatever He pleases.
4 Their idols *are* silver and gold,
The work of men's hands.
5 They have mouths, but they do not speak;
Eyes they have, but they do not see;
6 They have ears, but they do not hear;
Noses they have, but they do not smell;
7 They have hands, but they do not handle;
Feet they have, but they do not walk;
Nor do they mutter through their throat.
8 Those who make them are like them;
So is everyone who trusts in them.

9 O Israel, trust in the LORD;
He *is* their help and their shield.
10 O house of Aaron, trust in the LORD;
He *is* their help and their shield.
11 You who fear the LORD, trust in the LORD;
He *is* their help and their shield.

12 The LORD has been mindful of *us;*
He will bless us;
He will bless the house of Israel;
He will bless the house of Aaron.
13 He will bless those who fear the LORD,
Both small and great.

14 May the LORD give you increase more and more,
You and your children.
15 *May* you *be* blessed by the LORD,
Who made heaven and earth.

16 The heaven, *even* the heavens, *are* the LORD's;
But the earth He has given to the children of men.
17 The dead do not praise the LORD,
Nor any who go down into silence.
18 But we will bless the LORD
From this time forth and forevermore.

Praise the LORD!

PSALM 116

Thanksgiving for Deliverance from Death

1 I love the LORD, because He has heard
My voice *and* my supplications.
2 Because He has inclined His ear to me,
Therefore I will call *upon Him* as long as I live.

3 The pains of death surrounded me,
And the pangs of Sheol laid hold of me;
I found trouble and sorrow.
4 Then I called upon the name of the LORD:
"O LORD, I implore You, deliver my soul!"

5 Gracious *is* the LORD, and righteous;
Yes, our God *is* merciful.
6 The LORD preserves the simple;
I was brought low, and He saved me.
7 Return to your rest, O my soul,
For the LORD has dealt bountifully with you.

8 For You have delivered my soul from death,
My eyes from tears,
And my feet from falling.
9 I will walk before the LORD
In the land of the living.

10 I believed, therefore I spoke,
"I am greatly afflicted."
11 I said in my haste,
"All men *are* liars."

12 What shall I render to the LORD
For all His benefits toward me?
13 I will take up the cup of salvation,
And call upon the name of the LORD.
14 I will pay my vows to the LORD
Now in the presence of all His people.

15 Precious in the sight of the LORD
Is the death of His saints.

16 O LORD, truly I *am* Your servant;
I *am* Your servant, the son of Your maidservant;
You have loosed my bonds.
17 I will offer to You the sacrifice of thanksgiving,
And will call upon the name of the LORD.

18 I will pay my vows to the LORD
Now in the presence of all His people,
19 In the courts of the LORD's house,
In the midst of you, O Jerusalem.

Praise the LORD!

PSALM 117

LET ALL PEOPLES PRAISE THE LORD

1 Praise the LORD, all you Gentiles!
Laud Him, all you peoples!
2 For His merciful kindness is great toward us,
And the truth of the LORD *endures* forever.

Praise the LORD!

PSALM 118

PRAISE TO GOD FOR HIS EVERLASTING MERCY

1 Oh, give thanks to the LORD, for *He is* good!
For His mercy *endures* forever.

2 Let Israel now say,
"His mercy *endures* forever."
3 Let the house of Aaron now say,
"His mercy *endures* forever."
4 Let those who fear the LORD now say,
"His mercy *endures* forever."

5 I called on the LORD in distress;
The LORD answered me *and set me* in a broad place.
6 The LORD *is* on my side;
I will not fear.
What can man do to me?
7 The LORD is for me among those who help me;
Therefore I shall see *my desire* on those who hate me.
8 *It is* better to trust in the LORD
Than to put confidence in man.
9 *It is* better to trust in the LORD
Than to put confidence in princes.

10 All nations surrounded me,
But in the name of the LORD I will destroy them.
11 They surrounded me,
Yes, they surrounded me;
But in the name of the LORD I will destroy them.
12 They surrounded me like bees;
They were quenched like a fire of thorns;
For in the name of the LORD I will destroy them.
13 You pushed me violently, that I might fall,
But the LORD helped me.

SOUL NOTE

True Home *(116:15)* Death is real—everyone must die. For most, death is a great tragedy. It is sad when loved ones die, and it is natural to grieve. But God says that the death of a believer is "precious in the sight of the LORD." For believers, death is merely a gateway into the home in heaven where they ultimately belong. The time on this earth is a pilgrimage through a strange land. Through death, believers enter their true eternal home—heaven. **Topic: Death**

14 The LORD *is* my strength and song,
And He has become my salvation.[a]

15 The voice of rejoicing and salvation
Is in the tents of the righteous;
The right hand of the LORD does
valiantly.
16 The right hand of the LORD is exalted;
The right hand of the LORD does
valiantly.
17 I shall not die, but live,
And declare the works of the LORD.
18 The LORD has chastened me severely,
But He has not given me over to death.

19 Open to me the gates of righteousness;
I will go through them,
And I will praise the LORD.
20 This is the gate of the LORD,
Through which the righteous shall enter.

21 I will praise You,
For You have answered me,
And have become my salvation.

22 The stone *which* the builders rejected
Has become the chief cornerstone.
23 This was the LORD's doing;
It *is* marvelous in our eyes.
24 This *is* the day the LORD has made;
We will rejoice and be glad in it.

25 Save now, I pray, O LORD;
O LORD, I pray, send now prosperity.
26 Blessed *is* he who comes in the name of
the LORD!
We have blessed you from the house of
the LORD.
27 God *is* the LORD,
And He has given us light;
Bind the sacrifice with cords to the
horns of the altar.
28 You *are* my God, and I will praise You;
You are my God, I will exalt You.

29 Oh, give thanks to the LORD, for *He is*
good!
For His mercy *endures* forever.

PSALM 119

MEDITATIONS ON THE EXCELLENCIES OF THE WORD OF GOD

א ALEPH
1 Blessed *are* the undefiled in the way,
Who walk in the law of the LORD!
2 Blessed *are* those who keep His
testimonies,
Who seek Him with the whole heart!
3 They also do no iniquity;
They walk in His ways.
4 You have commanded *us*
To keep Your precepts diligently.
5 Oh, that my ways were directed
To keep Your statutes!
6 Then I would not be ashamed,
When I look into all Your
commandments.
7 I will praise You with uprightness of
heart,
When I learn Your righteous judgments.
8 I will keep Your statutes;
Oh, do not forsake me utterly!

ב BETH
9 How can a young man cleanse his way?
By taking heed according to Your word.
10 With my whole heart I have sought You;
Oh, let me not wander from Your
commandments!
11 Your word I have hidden in my heart,

118:14 [a]Compare Exodus 15:2

SOUL NOTE

Hide and Seek *(119:11)* So powerful is the Word of God that it can actually keep people from sinning. When believers hide Scripture in their hearts by reading, memorizing, meditating, and applying it to their lives, they are insulating themselves against the pressure of temptation. Often, people give in to the lure of temptation because their hearts and minds are not focused on God and His revelation of Himself. Believers should know in their hearts what the Bible says so that they can stand up to temptation and not sin against God. **Topic: Temptation**

That I might not sin against You.
12 Blessed *are* You, O LORD!
Teach me Your statutes.
13 With my lips I have declared
All the judgments of Your mouth.
14 I have rejoiced in the way of Your
testimonies,
As *much as* in all riches.
15 I will meditate on Your precepts,
And contemplate
Your ways.
16 I will delight
myself in Your
statutes;
I will not forget
Your word.

Your word I have hidden in my heart, that I might not sin against You.
PSALM 119:11

ג GIMEL
17 Deal bountifully with Your servant,
That I may live and keep Your word.
18 Open my eyes, that I may see
Wondrous things from Your law.
19 I *am* a stranger in the earth;
Do not hide Your commandments from
me.
20 My soul breaks with longing
For Your judgments at all times.
21 You rebuke the proud—the cursed,
Who stray from Your commandments.
22 Remove from me reproach and
contempt,
For I have kept Your testimonies.
23 Princes also sit *and* speak against me,
But Your servant meditates on Your
statutes.
24 Your testimonies also *are* my delight
And my counselors.

ד DALETH
25 My soul clings to the dust;
Revive me according to Your word.
26 I have declared my ways, and You
answered me;
Teach me Your statutes.
27 Make me understand the way of Your
precepts;
So shall I meditate on Your wonderful
works.
28 My soul melts from heaviness;
Strengthen me according to Your word.
29 Remove from me the way of lying,
And grant me Your law graciously.
30 I have chosen the way of truth;
Your judgments I have laid *before me.*
31 I cling to Your testimonies;
O LORD, do not put me to shame!
32 I will run the course of Your
commandments,
For You shall enlarge my heart.

ה HE
33 Teach me, O LORD, the way of Your
statutes,
And I shall keep it
to the end.
34 Give me
understanding,
and I shall keep
Your law;
Indeed, I shall
observe it with
my whole heart.
35 Make me walk in the path of Your
commandments,
For I delight in it.
36 Incline my heart to Your testimonies,
And not to covetousness.
37 Turn away my eyes from looking at
worthless things,
And revive me in Your way.[a]
38 Establish Your word to Your servant,
Who *is devoted* to fearing You.
39 Turn away my reproach which I dread,
For Your judgments *are* good.
40 Behold, I long for Your precepts;
Revive me in Your righteousness.

ו WAW
41 Let Your mercies come also to me,
O LORD—
Your salvation according to Your
word.
42 So shall I have an answer for him who
reproaches me,
For I trust in Your word.
43 And take not the word of truth utterly
out of my mouth,
For I have hoped in Your ordinances.
44 So shall I keep Your law continually,
Forever and ever.
45 And I will walk at liberty,
For I seek Your precepts.
46 I will speak of Your testimonies also
before kings,
And will not be ashamed.

119:37 [a]Following Masoretic Text, Septuagint, and Vulgate; Targum reads *Your words*.

47 And I will delight myself in Your
commandments,
Which I love.
48 My hands also I will lift up to Your
commandments,
Which I love,
And I will meditate on Your statutes.

ז ZAYIN

49 Remember the word to Your servant,
Upon which You have caused me to
hope.
50 This *is* my comfort in my affliction,
For Your word has given me life.
51 The proud have me in great derision,
Yet I do not turn aside from Your law.
52 I remembered Your judgments of old,
O LORD,
And have comforted myself.
53 Indignation has taken hold of me
Because of the wicked, who forsake Your
law.
54 Your statutes have been my songs
In the house of my pilgrimage.
55 I remember Your name in the night,
O LORD,
And I keep Your law.
56 This has become mine,
Because I kept Your precepts.

ח HETH

57 *You are* my portion, O LORD;
I have said that I would keep Your words.
58 I entreated Your favor with *my* whole
heart;
Be merciful to me according to Your
word.
59 I thought about my ways,
And turned my feet to Your testimonies.
60 I made haste, and did not delay
To keep Your commandments.
61 The cords of the wicked have bound me,
But I have not forgotten Your law.
62 At midnight I will rise to give thanks to
You,
Because of Your righteous judgments.
63 I *am* a companion of all who fear You,
And of those who keep Your precepts.
64 The earth, O LORD, is full of Your mercy;
Teach me Your statutes.

ט TETH

65 You have dealt well with Your servant,
O LORD, according to Your word.
66 Teach me good judgment and
knowledge,
For I believe Your commandments.
67 Before I was afflicted I went astray,
But now I keep Your word.
68 You *are* good, and do good;
Teach me Your statutes.
69 The proud have forged a lie against me,
But I will keep Your precepts with *my*
whole heart.
70 Their heart is as fat as grease,
But I delight in Your law.
71 *It is* good for me that I have been
afflicted,
That I may learn Your statutes.
72 The law of Your mouth *is* better to me
Than thousands of *coins of* gold and
silver.

י YOD

73 Your hands have made me and
fashioned me;
Give me understanding, that I may learn
Your commandments.
74 Those who fear You will be glad when
they see me,
Because I have hoped in Your word.
75 I know, O LORD, that Your judgments *are*
right,
And *that* in faithfulness You have
afflicted me.
76 Let, I pray, Your merciful kindness be for
my comfort,
According to Your word to Your servant.
77 Let Your tender mercies come to me,
that I may live;
For Your law *is* my delight.
78 Let the proud be ashamed,
For they treated me wrongfully with
falsehood;
But I will meditate on Your precepts.
79 Let those who fear You turn to me,
Those who know Your testimonies.
80 Let my heart be blameless regarding
Your statutes,
That I may not be ashamed.

כ KAPH

81 My soul faints for Your salvation,
But I hope in Your word.
82 My eyes fail *from searching* Your word,
Saying, "When will You comfort me?"
83 For I have become like a wineskin in
smoke,

Yet I do not forget Your statutes.
84 How many *are* the days of Your servant?
When will You execute judgment on those who persecute me?
85 The proud have dug pits for me,
Which *is* not according to Your law.
86 All Your commandments *are* faithful;
They persecute me wrongfully;
Help me!
87 They almost made an end of me on earth,
But I did not forsake Your precepts.
88 Revive me according to Your lovingkindness,
So that I may keep the testimony of Your mouth.

ל LAMED
89 Forever, O LORD,
Your word is settled in heaven.
90 Your faithfulness *endures* to all generations;
You established the earth, and it abides.
91 They continue this day according to Your ordinances,
For all *are* Your servants.
92 Unless Your law *had been* my delight,
I would then have perished in my affliction.
93 I will never forget Your precepts,
For by them You have given me life.
94 I *am* Yours, save me;
For I have sought Your precepts.
95 The wicked wait for me to destroy me,
But I will consider Your testimonies.
96 I have seen the consummation of all perfection,
But Your commandment *is* exceedingly broad.

מ MEM
97 Oh, how I love Your law!
It *is* my meditation all the day.
98 You, through Your commandments, make me wiser than my enemies;
For they *are* ever with me.
99 I have more understanding than all my teachers,
For Your testimonies *are* my meditation.
100 I understand more than the ancients,
Because I keep Your precepts.
101 I have restrained my feet from every evil way,
That I may keep Your word.
102 I have not departed from Your judgments,
For You Yourself have taught me.
103 How sweet are Your words to my taste,
Sweeter than honey to my mouth!
104 Through Your precepts I get understanding;
Therefore I hate every false way.

נ NUN
105 Your word *is* a lamp to my feet
And a light to my path.
106 I have sworn and confirmed
That I will keep Your righteous judgments.
107 I am afflicted very much;
Revive me, O LORD, according to Your word.
108 Accept, I pray, the freewill offerings of my mouth, O LORD,
And teach me Your judgments.
109 My life *is* continually in my hand,
Yet I do not forget Your law.
110 The wicked have laid a snare for me,
Yet I have not strayed from Your precepts.
111 Your testimonies I have taken as a heritage forever,
For they *are* the rejoicing of my heart.
112 I have inclined my heart to perform Your statutes
Forever, to the very end.

Your word is a lamp to my feet
and a light to my path.
PSALM 119:105

ס SAMEK
113 I hate the double-minded,
But I love Your law.
114 You *are* my hiding place and my shield;
I hope in Your word.
115 Depart from me, you evildoers,
For I will keep the commandments of my God!
116 Uphold me according to Your word, that I may live;
And do not let me be ashamed of my hope.
117 Hold me up, and I shall be safe,

And I shall observe Your statutes
continually.
118 You reject all those who stray from Your
statutes,
For their deceit *is* falsehood.
119 You put away all the wicked of the earth
like dross;
Therefore I love Your testimonies.
120 My flesh trembles for fear of You,
And I am afraid of Your judgments.

ע AYIN
121 I have done justice and righteousness;
Do not leave me to my oppressors.
122 Be surety for Your servant for good;
Do not let the proud oppress me.
123 My eyes fail *from seeking* Your
salvation
And Your righteous word.
124 Deal with Your servant according to Your
mercy,
And teach me Your statutes.
125 I *am* Your servant;
Give me understanding,
That I may know Your testimonies.
126 *It is* time for *You* to act, O LORD,
For they have regarded Your law as void.
127 Therefore I love Your commandments
More than gold, yes, than fine gold!
128 Therefore all *Your* precepts *concerning*
all *things*
I consider *to be* right;
I hate every false way.

פ PE
129 Your testimonies are wonderful;
Therefore my soul keeps them.
130 The entrance of Your words gives light;
It gives understanding to the simple.
131 I opened my mouth and panted,
For I longed for Your commandments.
132 Look upon me and be merciful to me,
As Your custom *is* toward those who
love Your name.
133 Direct my steps by Your word,
And let no iniquity have dominion over
me.
134 Redeem me from the oppression of man,
That I may keep Your precepts.
135 Make Your face shine upon Your
servant,
And teach me Your statutes.
136 Rivers of water run down from my eyes,
Because *men* do not keep Your law.

צ TSADDE
137 Righteous *are* You, O LORD,
And upright *are* Your judgments.
138 Your testimonies, *which* You have
commanded,
Are righteous and very faithful.
139 My zeal has consumed me,
Because my enemies have forgotten Your
words.
140 Your word *is* very pure;
Therefore Your servant loves it.
141 I *am* small and despised,
Yet I do not forget Your precepts.
142 Your righteousness *is* an everlasting
righteousness,
And Your law *is* truth.
143 Trouble and anguish have overtaken me,
Yet Your commandments *are* my
delights.
144 The righteousness of Your testimonies *is*
everlasting;
Give me understanding, and I shall live.

ק QOPH
145 I cry out with *my* whole heart;
Hear me, O LORD!
I will keep Your statutes.
146 I cry out to You;
Save me, and I will keep Your
testimonies.
147 I rise before the dawning of the
morning,
And cry for help;
I hope in Your word.
148 My eyes are awake through the *night*
watches,
That I may meditate on Your word.
149 Hear my voice according to Your
lovingkindness;
O LORD, revive me according to Your
justice.
150 They draw near who follow after
wickedness;
They are far from Your law.
151 You *are* near, O LORD,
And all Your commandments *are* truth.
152 Concerning Your testimonies,
I have known of old that You have
founded them forever.

ר RESH
153 Consider my affliction and deliver me,
For I do not forget Your law.
154 Plead my cause and redeem me;

Revive me according to Your word.
155 Salvation *is* far from the wicked,
For they do not seek Your statutes.
156 Great *are* Your tender mercies, O LORD;
Revive me according to Your judgments.
157 Many *are* my persecutors and my enemies,
Yet I do not turn from Your testimonies.
158 I see the treacherous, and am disgusted,
Because they do not keep Your word.
159 Consider how I love Your precepts;
Revive me, O LORD, according to Your lovingkindness.
160 The entirety of Your word *is* truth,
And every one of Your righteous judgments *endures* forever.

ש SHIN
161 Princes persecute me without a cause,
But my heart stands in awe of Your word.
162 I rejoice at Your word
As one who finds great treasure.
163 I hate and abhor lying,
But I love Your law.
164 Seven times a day I praise You,
Because of Your righteous judgments.
165 Great peace have those who love Your law,
And nothing causes them to stumble.
166 LORD, I hope for Your salvation,
And I do Your commandments.
167 My soul keeps Your testimonies,
And I love them exceedingly.
168 I keep Your precepts and Your testimonies,
For all my ways *are* before You.

ת TAU
169 Let my cry come before You, O LORD;
Give me understanding according to Your word.
170 Let my supplication come before You;
Deliver me according to Your word.
171 My lips shall utter praise,
For You teach me Your statutes.
172 My tongue shall speak of Your word,
For all Your commandments *are* righteousness.
173 Let Your hand become my help,
For I have chosen Your precepts.
174 I long for Your salvation, O LORD,
And Your law *is* my delight.
175 Let my soul live, and it shall praise You;
And let Your judgments help me.
176 I have gone astray like a lost sheep;
Seek Your servant,
For I do not forget Your commandments.

PSALM 120

Plea for Relief from Bitter Foes

A Song of Ascents.

1 In my distress I cried to the LORD,
And He heard me.
2 Deliver my soul, O LORD, from lying lips
And from a deceitful tongue.

3 What shall be given to you,
Or what shall be done to you,
You false tongue?
4 Sharp arrows of the warrior,
With coals of the broom tree!

5 Woe is me, that I dwell in Meshech,
That I dwell among the tents of Kedar!
6 My soul has dwelt too long
With one who hates peace.
7 I *am for* peace;
But when I speak, they *are* for war.

PSALM 121

God the Help of Those Who Seek Him

A Song of Ascents.

1 I will lift up my eyes to the hills—
From whence comes my help?
2 My help *comes* from the LORD,
Who made heaven and earth.

3 He will not allow your foot to be moved;
He who keeps you will not slumber.
4 Behold, He who keeps Israel
Shall neither slumber nor sleep.

> I will lift up my eyes to the hills—from whence comes my help? My help comes from the LORD, who made heaven and earth.
>
> PSALM 121:1, 2

5 The LORD *is* your keeper;
The LORD *is* your shade at your right hand.
6 The sun shall not strike you by day,
Nor the moon by night.

7 The LORD shall preserve you from all evil;
He shall preserve your soul.
8 The LORD shall preserve your going out and your coming in
From this time forth, and even forevermore.

PSALM 122

THE JOY OF GOING TO THE HOUSE OF THE LORD

A Song of Ascents. Of David.

1 I was glad when they said to me,
"Let us go into the house of the LORD."
2 Our feet have been standing
Within your gates, O Jerusalem!

3 Jerusalem is built
As a city that is compact together,
4 Where the tribes go up,
The tribes of the LORD,
To the Testimony of Israel,
To give thanks to the name of the LORD.
5 For thrones are set there for judgment,
The thrones of the house of David.

6 Pray for the peace of Jerusalem:
"May they prosper who love you.
7 Peace be within your walls,
Prosperity within your palaces."
8 For the sake of my brethren and companions,
I will now say, "Peace *be* within you."
9 Because of the house of the LORD our God
I will seek your good.

PSALM 123

PRAYER FOR RELIEF FROM CONTEMPT

A Song of Ascents.

1 Unto You I lift up my eyes,
O You who dwell in the heavens.
2 Behold, as the eyes of servants *look* to the hand of their masters,
As the eyes of a maid to the hand of her mistress,
So our eyes *look* to the LORD our God,
Until He has mercy on us.

3 Have mercy on us, O LORD, have mercy on us!
For we are exceedingly filled with contempt.
4 Our soul is exceedingly filled
With the scorn of those who are at ease,
With the contempt of the proud.

PSALM 124

THE LORD THE DEFENSE OF HIS PEOPLE

A Song of Ascents. Of David.

1 "If it had not been the LORD who was on our side,"
Let Israel now say—
2 "If it had not been the LORD who was on our side,
When men rose up against us,
3 Then they would have swallowed us alive,
When their wrath was kindled against us;
4 Then the waters would have overwhelmed us,
The stream would have gone over our soul;
5 Then the swollen waters
Would have gone over our soul."

6 Blessed *be* the LORD,
Who has not given us *as* prey to their teeth.
7 Our soul has escaped as a bird from the snare of the fowlers;[a]
The snare is broken, and we have escaped.
8 Our help *is* in the name of the LORD,
Who made heaven and earth.

PSALM 125

THE LORD THE STRENGTH OF HIS PEOPLE

A Song of Ascents.

1 Those who trust in the LORD
Are like Mount Zion,

124:7 [a]That is, persons who catch birds in a trap or snare

Which cannot be moved, *but* abides
forever.
2 As the mountains surround Jerusalem,
So the LORD surrounds His people
From this time forth and forever.

3 For the scepter of wickedness shall not
rest
On the land allotted to the righteous,
Lest the righteous reach out their hands
to iniquity.

4 Do good, O LORD, to *those who are*
good,
And to *those who are* upright in their
hearts.

5 As for such as turn aside to their
crooked ways,
The LORD shall lead them away
With the workers of iniquity.

Peace *be* upon Israel!

PSALM 126

A JOYFUL RETURN TO ZION

A Song of Ascents.

1 When the LORD brought back the
captivity of Zion,
We were like those who dream.
2 Then our mouth was filled with
laughter,
And our tongue with singing.
Then they said among the nations,
"The LORD has done great things for
them."
3 The LORD has done great things for us,
And we are glad.

4 Bring back our captivity, O LORD,
As the streams in the South.

5 Those who sow in tears
Shall reap in joy.
6 He who continually goes forth
weeping,
Bearing seed for sowing,
Shall doubtless come again with
rejoicing,
Bringing his sheaves *with him.*

PSALM 127

LABORING AND PROSPERING WITH THE LORD

A Song of Ascents. Of Solomon.

1 Unless the LORD builds the house,
They labor in vain who build it;
Unless the LORD guards the city,
The watchman stays awake in vain.
2 *It is* vain for you to rise up early,
To sit up late,

KEY PASSAGE

Family Life

A SOLID FOUNDATION

(127:3–5)

God values families, calling children "a heritage from the LORD." Families are the foundation of society, the place where children are taught about faith in God and given love, nurture, and guidance. So why are there so many sad and separated families? Many families have ignored God in their family life, so He is not sought when the family faces troubles and difficulty. "Unless the LORD builds the house, they labor in vain who build it," wrote Solomon (Ps. 127:1). Putting the Lord at the base does not guarantee a perfect family; it does, however, provide a foundation upon which to build and guidelines by which to make decisions and handle difficulties. The family with God as its foundation will offer a solid, stable, and loving home. And it's never too late. This kind of foundation can always be laid, even under an existing house. The structure can then be remodeled on the firmest possible footing.

To Learn More: Turn to the article about family life on pages 294, 295. See also the personality profile of Timothy on page 1604.

To eat the bread of sorrows;
For so He gives His beloved sleep.

3 Behold, children *are* a heritage from the LORD,
The fruit of the womb *is* a reward.
4 Like arrows in the hand of a warrior,
So *are* the children of one's youth.
5 Happy *is* the man who has his quiver full of them;
They shall not be ashamed,
But shall speak with their enemies in the gate.

PSALM 128

BLESSINGS OF THOSE WHO FEAR THE LORD

A Song of Ascents.

1 Blessed *is* every one who fears the LORD,
Who walks in His ways.

2 When you eat the labor of your hands,
You *shall be* happy, and *it shall be* well with you.
3 Your wife *shall be* like a fruitful vine
In the very heart of your house,
Your children like olive plants
All around your table.
4 Behold, thus shall the man be blessed
Who fears the LORD.

5 The LORD bless you out of Zion,
And may you see the good of Jerusalem
All the days of your life.
6 Yes, may you see your children's children.

Peace *be* upon Israel!

PSALM 129

SONG OF VICTORY OVER ZION'S ENEMIES

A Song of Ascents.

1 "Many a time they have afflicted me from my youth,"
Let Israel now say—
2 "Many a time they have afflicted me from my youth;
Yet they have not prevailed against me.
3 The plowers plowed on my back;
They made their furrows long."
4 The LORD *is* righteous;
He has cut in pieces the cords of the wicked.

5 Let all those who hate Zion
Be put to shame and turned back.
6 Let them be as the grass *on* the housetops,
Which withers before it grows up,
7 With which the reaper does not fill his hand,
Nor he who binds sheaves, his arms.
8 Neither let those who pass by them say,
"The blessing of the LORD *be* upon you;
We bless you in the name of the LORD!"

PSALM 130

WAITING FOR THE REDEMPTION OF THE LORD

A Song of Ascents.

1 Out of the depths I have cried to You, O LORD;
2 Lord, hear my voice!
Let Your ears be attentive
To the voice of my supplications.

3 If You, LORD, should mark iniquities,
O Lord, who could stand?

SOUL NOTE

Light in the Darkness *(ch. 130)* From the depths, the psalmist cried out to God. The writer recognized that people need God most when they are most depressed. Feelings of sadness can overwhelm a person, like impenetrable darkness. The psalmist called out to God, remembering His care (130:2), forgiveness (130:4), and redemption (130:7). Then, like a light shining in the darkness, he was willing to wait for the Lord and hope in Him (130:5–7). When life seems to be nothing but darkness, we must call out to God, trust Him, and never lose hope. **Topic: Depression**

THE VALLEY OF DEPRESSION

MICHAEL R. LYLES

(Psalm 130)

At times, everybody feels sad, down, and blue. Solomon wrote of "a time to weep" and "a time to mourn" (Eccl. 3:4). The writer of Hebrews assured believers they would have times of need in their lives (Heb. 4:16).

Depression, however, is a deeper level of emotional turmoil and can affect many people in many ways. According to research, nearly one person in five will experience significant and persistent levels of depression. Significant and persistent depression causes people to miss more work than diabetes and heart disease, as well as being a major risk factor after heart attacks and strokes. Depression affects individuals, families, coworkers, and others who are in regular contact with the depressed person. Clearly, depression is a serious concern for many people.

CAUSES OF DEPRESSION

Depression can be caused by a variety of factors, including stress, fear, loneliness, guilt, and anger. David wrote of his depression caused by unconfessed sin, leading to a groaning in his soul and a loss of strength (Ps. 38). God used depression as a signal to get Nehemiah's attention to do His work (Neh. 1; 2). Job experienced financial, personal, and relational losses that led him to curse the day he was born (Job 1—3). Elijah was so depressed after a great victory that he wanted to die (1 Kin. 19:4). Many other Bible characters shared the lonely path of depression.

Although environmental issues such as work, stress, family, and other relationships can add to depression, actually a number of medical factors are involved, including thyroid abnormalities, female hormone fluctuations, and diabetes. Nutritional shortages leading to B-12 or iron deficiencies can cause sadness. Patients with a recent history of stroke or heart attack are at high risk for depression. Common prescription drugs such as antihypertensives or oral contraceptives, and recreational drugs such as alcohol and cocaine, can cause significant levels of depression. Abnormalities in the brain's management of hormones such as serotonin and norepinephrine can also bring on overwhelming feelings of doom and gloom. Understanding the physical components that can cause depression can help to put this disorder in context and give an idea of how widespread it is.

SYMPTOMS OF DEPRESSION

Psalm 102 provides a virtual checklist of symptoms that King David experienced during a particularly stressful period in his life. "Let my cry come to You. Do not hide Your face from me in the day of my trouble" (102:1, 2). He wrote of feeling stricken physically and described losing meaning and purpose in his life: "My days are consumed like smoke, and my bones are burned like a hearth. My heart is stricken and withered like grass" (102:3, 4). He lost his appetite: "I forget to eat my bread" (102:4). He felt isolated and rejected: "I am like a pelican of the wilderness; I am like an owl of the desert" (102:6). He couldn't sleep: "I lie awake" (102:7). He had frequent crying spells: "I have eaten ashes like bread, and mingled my drink with weeping" (102:9).

Serious depression can present itself in a number of ways. When the above symptoms are experienced in a dramatic, disabling fashion for weeks or months at a time, it is called "major depression." When these symptoms are low-grade and chronic, it is called "dysthymic disorder." Depression can also alternate in a pattern of mood swings—with a person feeling irritable and then euphoric, having insomnia, or being agitated. This is called "bipolar disorder" or "manic depressive illness."

RESPONDING TO DEPRESSION

Elijah demonstrated both healthy and unhealthy responses to depression (1 Kin. 19). After the great victory on Mount Carmel, his life was threatened and he became afraid. He focused on the situation instead of on God. During a sequence of events, he sank deeper and deeper into a depressed state. His fear became so intense that he eventually ran away, isolated himself, and prayed that he would die (1 Kin. 19:4).

A summary of his behavior can be described as the HALT syndrome—a very vulnerable place for a person to be. At his most depressed state he was:

Hungry—He stopped eating.
Angry—He was mad at God for not caring about him.
Lonely—He left his servant and traveled alone.
Tired—He collapsed into sleep.

Any time a person experiences an intense combination of these characteristics, he or she is becoming vulnerable to developing some form of depression.

RECOVERING HOPE

God counteracted the HALT syndrome in Elijah's life at every level. He responded by providing food for Elijah. An angel touched Elijah, reminding him that he was not alone. Two times God encouraged Elijah to regain his strength by eating, drinking, and resting. God brought him out of the HALT syndrome, which enabled Elijah to listen and obey (1 Kin. 19:5–18).

The story of Elijah reminds us of the importance of having a real and personal relationship with God. When we are depressed, we may often feel like running away from our problems like Elijah. We must avoid isolating ourselves, as tempting as that might be. We may need to be accountable to a friend, pastor, family member, or Christian therapist who can help us through the difficult times. Depressed people must be careful to stay clear of addictive behaviors, unhealthy relationships, or socially avoidant behaviors, for these will only deepen a depressed state.

Though he felt hopeless, Elijah accepted God's help. He recognized God's voice and was strengthened and encouraged. He was then able to return to his life with a new ability to cope and a new hope for the future.

FURTHER MEDITATION:

Other passages to study about the issue of depression include:

- ➢ Psalms 27; 34; 40:1–3; 42; 43; 88; 143; 147:3
- ➢ Isaiah 41:10; 43:2
- ➢ Romans 8:18–39
- ➢ 2 Corinthians 1:8–11

To Learn More: Turn to the key passage note on depression at I Kings 19:1–18 on page 463. See also the personality profile of Elijah on page 464.

4 But *there is* forgiveness with You,
That You may be feared.

5 I wait for the LORD, my soul waits,
And in His word I do hope.
6 My soul *waits* for the Lord
More than those who watch for the morning—
Yes, more than those who watch for the morning.

7 O Israel, hope in the LORD;
For with the LORD *there is* mercy,
And with Him *is* abundant redemption.
8 And He shall redeem Israel
From all his iniquities.

PSALM 131

SIMPLE TRUST IN THE LORD

A Song of Ascents. Of David.

1 LORD, my heart is not haughty,
Nor my eyes lofty.
Neither do I concern myself with great matters,
Nor with things too profound for me.

2 Surely I have calmed and quieted my soul,
Like a weaned child with his mother;
Like a weaned child *is* my soul within me.

3 O Israel, hope in the LORD
From this time forth and forever.

PSALM 132

THE ETERNAL DWELLING OF GOD IN ZION

A Song of Ascents.

1 LORD, remember David
And all his afflictions;
2 How he swore to the LORD,
And vowed to the Mighty One of Jacob:
3 "Surely I will not go into the chamber of my house,
Or go up to the comfort of my bed;
4 I will not give sleep to my eyes
Or slumber to my eyelids,
5 Until I find a place for the LORD,
A dwelling place for the Mighty One of Jacob."

6 Behold, we heard of it in Ephrathah;
We found it in the fields of the woods.[a]
7 Let us go into His tabernacle;
Let us worship at His footstool.
8 Arise, O LORD, to Your resting place,
You and the ark of Your strength.
9 Let Your priests be clothed with righteousness,
And let Your saints shout for joy.

10 For Your servant David's sake,
Do not turn away the face of Your Anointed.

11 The LORD has sworn *in* truth to David;
He will not turn from it:
"I will set upon your throne the fruit of your body.
12 If your sons will keep My covenant
And My testimony which I shall teach them,
Their sons also shall sit upon your throne forevermore."

13 For the LORD has chosen Zion;
He has desired *it* for His dwelling place:
14 "This *is* My resting place forever;
Here I will dwell, for I have desired it.
15 I will abundantly bless her provision;
I will satisfy her poor with bread.
16 I will also clothe her priests with salvation,
And her saints shall shout aloud for joy.
17 There I will make the horn of David grow;
I will prepare a lamp for My Anointed.
18 His enemies I will clothe with shame,
But upon Himself His crown shall flourish."

PSALM 133

BLESSED UNITY OF THE PEOPLE OF GOD

A Song of Ascents. Of David.

1 Behold, how good and how pleasant *it is*
For brethren to dwell together in unity!

2 *It is* like the precious oil upon the head,
Running down on the beard,
The beard of Aaron,

132:6 [a]Hebrew *Jaar*

Running down on the edge of his
garments.
3 *It is* like the dew of Hermon,
Descending upon the mountains of Zion;
For there the LORD commanded the
blessing—
Life forevermore.

PSALM 134

PRAISING THE LORD IN HIS HOUSE AT NIGHT

A Song of Ascents.

1 Behold, bless the LORD,
All *you* servants of the LORD,
Who by night stand in the house of the
LORD!
2 Lift up your hands *in* the sanctuary,
And bless the LORD.

3 The LORD who made heaven and earth
Bless you from Zion!

PSALM 135

PRAISE TO GOD IN CREATION AND REDEMPTION

1 Praise the LORD!

Praise the name of the LORD;
Praise *Him,* O you servants of the LORD!
2 You who stand in the house of the LORD,
In the courts of the house of our God,
3 Praise the LORD, for the LORD *is* good;
Sing praises to His name, for *it is* pleasant.
4 For the LORD has chosen Jacob for Himself,
Israel for His special treasure.

5 For I know that the LORD *is* great,
And our Lord *is* above all gods.
6 Whatever the LORD pleases He does,
In heaven and in earth,
In the seas and in all deep places.
7 He causes the vapors to ascend from the
ends of the earth;
He makes lightning for the rain;
He brings the wind out of His treasuries.

8 He destroyed the firstborn of Egypt,
Both of man and beast.
9 He sent signs and wonders into the
midst of you, O Egypt,
Upon Pharaoh and all his servants.
10 He defeated many nations
And slew mighty kings—
11 Sihon king of the Amorites,
Og king of Bashan,
And all the kingdoms of Canaan—
12 And gave their land *as* a heritage,
A heritage to Israel His people.

13 Your name, O LORD, *endures* forever,
Your fame, O LORD, throughout all
generations.
14 For the LORD will judge His people,
And He will have compassion on His
servants.

15 The idols of the nations *are* silver and
gold,
The work of men's hands.
16 They have mouths, but they do not
speak;
Eyes they have, but they do not see;
17 They have ears, but they do not hear;
Nor is there *any* breath in their mouths.
18 Those who make them are like them;
So is everyone who trusts in them.

19 Bless the LORD, O house of Israel!
Bless the LORD, O house of Aaron!
20 Bless the LORD, O house of Levi!
You who fear the LORD, bless the LORD!
21 Blessed be the LORD out of Zion,
Who dwells in Jerusalem!

Praise the LORD!

> Oh, give thanks to the LORD, for He is good! For His mercy endures forever.
> PSALM 136:1

PSALM 136

THANKSGIVING TO GOD FOR HIS ENDURING MERCY

1 Oh, give thanks to the LORD, for *He is*
good!
For His mercy *endures* forever.
2 Oh, give thanks to the God of gods!

For His mercy *endures* forever.
3 Oh, give thanks to the Lord of lords!
For His mercy *endures* forever:

4 To Him who alone does great wonders,
For His mercy *endures* forever;
5 To Him who by wisdom made the heavens,
For His mercy *endures* forever;
6 To Him who laid out the earth above the waters,
For His mercy *endures* forever;
7 To Him who made great lights,
For His mercy *endures* forever—
8 The sun to rule by day,
For His mercy *endures* forever;
9 The moon and stars to rule by night,
For His mercy *endures* forever.

10 To Him who struck Egypt in their firstborn,
For His mercy *endures* forever;
11 And brought out Israel from among them,
For His mercy *endures* forever;
12 With a strong hand, and with an outstretched arm,
For His mercy *endures* forever;
13 To Him who divided the Red Sea in two,
For His mercy *endures* forever;
14 And made Israel pass through the midst of it,
For His mercy *endures* forever;
15 But overthrew Pharaoh and his army in the Red Sea,
For His mercy *endures* forever;
16 To Him who led His people through the wilderness,
For His mercy *endures* forever;
17 To Him who struck down great kings,
For His mercy *endures* forever;
18 And slew famous kings,
For His mercy *endures* forever—
19 Sihon king of the Amorites,
For His mercy *endures* forever;
20 And Og king of Bashan,
For His mercy *endures* forever—
21 And gave their land as a heritage,
For His mercy *endures* forever;
22 A heritage to Israel His servant,
For His mercy *endures* forever.
23 Who remembered us in our lowly state,
For His mercy *endures* forever;
24 And rescued us from our enemies,
For His mercy *endures* forever;
25 Who gives food to all flesh,
For His mercy *endures* forever.

26 Oh, give thanks to the God of heaven!
For His mercy *endures* forever.

PSALM 137

Longing for Zion in a Foreign Land

1 By the rivers of Babylon,
There we sat down, yea, we wept
When we remembered Zion.
2 We hung our harps
Upon the willows in the midst of it.
3 For there those who carried us away captive asked of us a song,
And those who plundered us *requested* mirth,
Saying, "Sing us *one* of the songs of Zion!"

4 How shall we sing the LORD's song
In a foreign land?
5 If I forget you, O Jerusalem,
Let my right hand forget *its skill!*
6 If I do not remember you,
Let my tongue cling to the roof of my mouth—
If I do not exalt Jerusalem
Above my chief joy.

7 Remember, O LORD, against the sons of Edom
The day of Jerusalem,
Who said, "Raze *it,* raze *it,*
To its very foundation!"

8 O daughter of Babylon, who are to be destroyed,
Happy the one who repays you as you have served us!
9 Happy the one who takes and dashes
Your little ones against the rock!

PSALM 138

The Lord's Goodness to the Faithful

A Psalm of David.

1 I will praise You with my whole heart;
Before the gods I will sing praises to You.

2 I will worship toward Your holy temple,
And praise Your name
For Your lovingkindness and Your truth;
For You have magnified Your word above all Your name.
3 In the day when I cried out, You answered me,
And made me bold *with* strength in my soul.

4 All the kings of the earth shall praise You, O LORD,
When they hear the words of Your mouth.
5 Yes, they shall sing of the ways of the LORD,
For great *is* the glory of the LORD.
6 Though the LORD *is* on high,
Yet He regards the lowly;
But the proud He knows from afar.

7 Though I walk in the midst of trouble, You will revive me;
You will stretch out Your hand
Against the wrath of my enemies,
And Your right hand will save me.
8 The LORD will perfect *that which* concerns me;
Your mercy, O LORD, *endures* forever;
Do not forsake the works of Your hands.

PSALM 139

God's Perfect Knowledge of Man

For the Chief Musician. A Psalm of David.

1 O LORD, You have searched me and known *me.*
2 You know my sitting down and my rising up;
You understand my thought afar off.
3 You comprehend my path and my lying down,
And are acquainted with all my ways.
4 For *there is* not a word on my tongue,
But behold, O LORD, You know it altogether.
5 You have hedged me behind and before,
And laid Your hand upon me.
6 *Such* knowledge *is* too wonderful for me;
It is high, I cannot *attain* it.

7 Where can I go from Your Spirit?
Or where can I flee from Your presence?
8 If I ascend into heaven, You *are* there;
If I make my bed in hell, behold, You *are there.*
9 *If* I take the wings of the morning,
And dwell in the uttermost parts of the sea,
10 Even there Your hand shall lead me,
And Your right hand shall hold me.
11 If I say, "Surely the darkness shall fall[a] on me,"
Even the night shall be light about me;
12 Indeed, the darkness shall not hide from You,
But the night shines as the day;
The darkness and the light *are* both alike *to You.*

13 For You formed my inward parts;
You covered me in my mother's womb.
14 I will praise You, for I am fearfully *and* wonderfully made;[a]
Marvelous are Your works,
And *that* my soul knows very well.
15 My frame was not hidden from You,

139:11 [a]Vulgate and Symmachus read *cover.*
139:14 [a]Following Masoretic Text and Targum; Septuagint, Syriac, and Vulgate read *You are fearfully wonderful.*

SOUL NOTE

In God's Image *(139:14)* The Bible clearly states that all people are "fearfully and wonderfully made" by God from the moment of conception. God determines each person's physical being. His people should accept any genetic limitations as part of His sovereignty over their lives. We are made in the image of God, and we know that He does not make mistakes. When we face physical or emotional difficulties because of our genetics, we must remember that we are no less important or perfect in God's eyes than someone else. God works through all kinds of people to accomplish His will. **Topic: Genetic Issues**

Abortion

THE DEBATE OF LIFE: ABORTION

CRAIG AND JANET PARSHALL

(Psalm 139:16)

Perhaps no issue in our culture has elicited such emotion as abortion. It has alienated friends, divided churches, and devastated individuals. That's because abortion is about people. It's about those who have perished and those who were responsible. It's about those who have stood fast for God's truth in the midst of an opposing culture and those who were silent. It's also about those who have sinned and yet still have the promise of redemption, forgiveness, and healing through Jesus Christ. They are our neighbors, our church members, the strangers we have never met, and our friends. The debate is about lives.

WHY SANCTIFY LIFE?

Christians who oppose abortion do so because of the sanctity of human life. It's not merely speculation or personal philosophy; the sanctity of life stands as a fundamental biblical principle. How people approach the matter of life and God's sovereign hand in its creation affects every other aspect of their relationship with God and with each other.

Psalm 139:13–16 gives a powerful, poetic look inside the wondrous world of the pregnant womb: "For You formed my inward parts; You covered me in my mother's womb. I will praise You, for I am fearfully and wonderfully made; marvelous are Your works, and that my soul knows very well. My frame was not hidden from You, when I was made in secret. . . . Your eyes saw my substance, being yet unformed, and in Your book they all were written, the days fashioned for me, when as yet there were none of them." Obviously, human life is no accident of biology. God, the grand Designer of the universe, forms the "inward parts" and works to "weave" together a masterful conception. Genesis demonstrates God as the Creator of life. "So God created man in His own image; in the image of God He created him; male and female He created them" (Gen. 1:27). A personal God personally created life so that people could have a personal family relationship with Him. God brings life into the world purposefully and deliberately. He has the compassion of a Father who yearns for His children.

God not only creates life, but He also blesses it. His creations are "fearfully and wonderfully made." The lives He creates are not inconveniences or problems—they are the highest expression of His moral goodness. In the Garden of Eden, immediately after the creation of human life, the Bible explains that God "blessed them" (Gen. 1:28). God creates and blesses life itself and, therefore, deems it sanctified.

HOW IS SANCTITY OF LIFE COMMUNICATED?

In ancient Egypt, Pharaoh gave a terrifying edict to the Jewish midwives. During the delivery of every Jewish baby, the midwives were to immediately kill the boys. They refused to comply, and God blessed their obedience (Ex. 1:17–21).

In the same manner, many Christians not only refuse to participate in or support abortion, they also exercise their right to lawfully denounce this practice. Yet in what way should Christians let their voice be heard? Scripture provides the principle of speaking the truth in love (Eph. 4:15). This same precept also describes God's nature as having both mercy and truth (Ps. 89:14). To speak the truth in love means to speak gently with Christ's confidence behind one's words.

The truth is that abortion is a corrupt practice that is protected by the courts. The Bible denounces corruption "which devises evil by law" and seeks to "condemn innocent blood" (Ps. 94:20, 21). We should communicate this hard truth, however, with the kind of gentle love that reflects the compassionate essence of God. The point is not to win the debate. The point is to win people over to the truth and to the Lord Jesus Christ. When love is our motivation for communicating truth, we can be more effective in gaining people's attention.

WHO CAN WE BLESS BY THE SANCTITY OF LIFE?

One of the most remarkable facts about the current crisis of our nation is the way that God has brought people who were deeply involved in the practice of abortion to understand the truth of God's Word. Abortionists, abortion clinic owners, and others who have had abortions have been transformed through the power of Jesus Christ.

Women who have had abortions need the healing touch of the great soul physician, Jesus Christ. An angry crowd once brought to Jesus a woman who had been caught in flagrant sin. Certainly she was morally guilty. Yet Jesus focused on her restoration, not her moral consequence. As the Son of God, He was able to forgive her and give her healing and wholeness (John 8:11).

The abortion issue is not just about death, it is about life. It is about the divine source of life, God Himself. Jesus said, "The thief does not come except to steal, and to kill, and to destroy. I have come that they may have life, and that they may have it more abundantly" (John 10:10). God's tender mercies are awesome and available for all our needs. No one is beyond hope. No one is beyond the reach of the gospel. No person is exempt from Christ's ability to lovingly communicate the truth about the sanctity of all life.

FURTHER MEDITATION:

Other passages to study about the issue of abortion include:

- Exodus 20:13; 21:22, 23
- Proverbs 28:13
- Isaiah 44:2; 46:3
- Jeremiah 1:5
- Matthew 18:1–6
- Luke 1:44
- 1 John 1:9

To Learn More: Turn to the key passage note on abortion at Psalm 139:16 on page 788. See also the personality profile of Herod on page 1231.

When I was made in secret,
And skillfully wrought in the lowest
parts of the earth.
16 Your eyes saw my substance, being yet
unformed.
And in Your book they all were written,
The days fashioned for me,
When *as yet there were* none of them.

17 How precious also are Your thoughts to
me, O God!
How great is the sum of them!
18 *If* I should count them, they would be
more in number than the sand;
When I awake, I am still with You.

19 Oh, that You would slay the wicked,
O God!
Depart from me, therefore, you
bloodthirsty men.
20 For they speak against You wickedly;
Your enemies take *Your name* in
vain.[a]
21 Do I not hate them, O LORD, who hate
You?
And do I not loathe those who rise up
against You?
22 I hate them with perfect hatred;
I count them my enemies.

23 Search me, O God, and know my heart;
Try me, and know my anxieties;
24 And see if *there is any* wicked way in
me,
And lead me in the way everlasting.

PSALM 140

PRAYER FOR DELIVERANCE FROM EVIL MEN

To the Chief Musician. A Psalm of David.

1 Deliver me, O LORD, from evil men;
Preserve me from violent men,
2 Who plan evil things in *their* hearts;
They continually gather together *for*
war.
3 They sharpen their tongues like a
serpent;
The poison of asps *is* under their lips.
Selah

4 Keep me, O LORD, from the hands of the
wicked;
Preserve me from violent men,
Who have purposed to make my steps
stumble.
5 The proud have hidden a snare for me,
and cords;
They have spread a net by the wayside;
They have set traps for me. Selah

6 I said to the LORD: "You *are* my God;
Hear the voice of my supplications,
O LORD.
7 O GOD the Lord, the strength of my
salvation,
You have covered my head in the day of
battle.

139:20 [a]Septuagint and Vulgate read *They take your cities in vain.*

KEY PASSAGE

Abortion

A NEW LIFE

(139:16)

God knows each person from the moment of conception. His eyes see the unformed body in the mother's womb, and all of the child's days are already written in His book. The prophet Jeremiah wrote these words from God, "Before I formed you in the womb I knew you" (Jer. 1:5). Many claim that a child in the womb is no more than a mass of tissue, but the Bible makes it clear that God sees the tiny embryo as a new life with a future already prepared. How sad that many children will not live beyond the womb because of abortion. To abort a child is to end a human life unjustly—in short, to commit murder. Every child conceived is a child of God.

To Learn More: Turn to the article about abortion on pages 786, 787. See also the personality profile of Herod on page 1231.

8 Do not grant, O LORD, the desires of the wicked;
Do not further his *wicked* scheme,
Lest they be exalted. Selah

9 "*As for* the head of those who surround me,
Let the evil of their lips cover them;
10 Let burning coals fall upon them;
Let them be cast into the fire,
Into deep pits, that they rise not up again.
11 Let not a slanderer be established in the earth;
Let evil hunt the violent man to overthrow *him*."

12 I know that the LORD will maintain
The cause of the afflicted,
And justice for the poor.
13 Surely the righteous shall give thanks to Your name;
The upright shall dwell in Your presence.

PSALM 141

Prayer for Safekeeping from Wickedness

A Psalm of David.

1 LORD, I cry out to You;
Make haste to me!
Give ear to my voice when I cry out to You.
2 Let my prayer be set before You *as* incense,
The lifting up of my hands *as* the evening sacrifice.

3 Set a guard, O LORD, over my mouth;
Keep watch over the door of my lips.
4 Do not incline my heart to any evil thing,
To practice wicked works
With men who work iniquity;
And do not let me eat of their delicacies.

5 Let the righteous strike me;
It shall be a kindness.
And let him rebuke me;
It shall be as excellent oil;
Let my head not refuse it.

For still my prayer *is* against the deeds of the wicked.
6 Their judges are overthrown by the sides of the cliff,
And they hear my words, for they are sweet.
7 Our bones are scattered at the mouth of the grave,
As when one plows and breaks up the earth.

8 But my eyes *are* upon You, O GOD the Lord;
In You I take refuge;
Do not leave my soul destitute.
9 Keep me from the snares they have laid for me,
And from the traps of the workers of iniquity.
10 Let the wicked fall into their own nets,
While I escape safely.

PSALM 142

A Plea for Relief from Persecutors

A Contemplation[a] *of David. A Prayer when he was in the cave.*

1 I cry out to the LORD with my voice;
With my voice to the LORD I make my supplication.
2 I pour out my complaint before Him;
I declare before Him my trouble.

3 When my spirit was overwhelmed within me,
Then You knew my path.
In the way in which I walk
They have secretly set a snare for me.
4 Look on *my* right hand and see,
For *there is* no one who acknowledges me;
Refuge has failed me;
No one cares for my soul.

5 I cried out to You, O LORD:
I said, "You *are* my refuge,
My portion in the land of the living.
6 Attend to my cry,
For I am brought very low;
Deliver me from my persecutors,
For they are stronger than I.
7 Bring my soul out of prison,
That I may praise Your name;

142:title [a]Hebrew *Maschil*

The righteous shall surround me,
For You shall deal bountifully with me."

PSALM 143

AN EARNEST APPEAL FOR GUIDANCE AND DELIVERANCE

A Psalm of David.

1 Hear my prayer, O LORD,
Give ear to my supplications!
In Your faithfulness answer me,
And in Your righteousness.
2 Do not enter into judgment with Your servant,
For in Your sight no one living is righteous.

3 For the enemy has persecuted my soul;
He has crushed my life to the ground;
He has made me dwell in darkness,
Like those who have long been dead.
4 Therefore my spirit is overwhelmed within me;
My heart within me is distressed.

5 I remember the days of old;
I meditate on all Your works;
I muse on the work of Your hands.
6 I spread out my hands to You;
My soul *longs* for You like a thirsty land.
Selah

7 Answer me speedily, O LORD;
My spirit fails!
Do not hide Your face from me,
Lest I be like those who go down into the pit.
8 Cause me to hear Your lovingkindness in the morning,
For in You do I trust;
Cause me to know the way in which I should walk,
For I lift up my soul to You.

9 Deliver me, O LORD, from my enemies;
In You I take shelter.[a]
10 Teach me to do Your will,
For You *are* my God;
Your Spirit *is* good.
Lead me in the land of uprightness.

11 Revive me, O LORD, for Your name's sake!
For Your righteousness' sake bring my soul out of trouble.
12 In Your mercy cut off my enemies,
And destroy all those who afflict my soul;
For I *am* Your servant.

PSALM 144

A SONG TO THE LORD WHO PRESERVES AND PROSPERS HIS PEOPLE

A Psalm of David.

1 Blessed *be* the LORD my Rock,
Who trains my hands for war,
And my fingers for battle—
2 My lovingkindness and my fortress,
My high tower and my deliverer,
My shield and *the One* in whom I take refuge,
Who subdues my people[a] under me.

3 LORD, what *is* man, that You take knowledge of him?
Or the son of man, that You are mindful of him?
4 Man is like a breath;
His days *are* like a passing shadow.

5 Bow down Your heavens, O LORD, and come down;
Touch the mountains, and they shall smoke.
6 Flash forth lightning and scatter them;
Shoot out Your arrows and destroy them.
7 Stretch out Your hand from above;
Rescue me and deliver me out of great waters,
From the hand of foreigners,
8 Whose mouth speaks lying words,
And whose right hand *is* a right hand of falsehood.

9 I will sing a new song to You, O God;
On a harp of ten strings I will sing praises to You,
10 *The One* who gives salvation to kings,
Who delivers David His servant
From the deadly sword.

143:9 [a]Septuagint and Vulgate read *To You I flee.* **144:2** [a]Following Masoretic Text, Septuagint, and Vulgate; Syriac and Targum read *the peoples* (compare 18:47).

11 Rescue me and deliver me from the hand
of foreigners,
Whose mouth speaks lying words,
And whose right hand *is* a right hand of
falsehood—
12 That our sons *may be* as plants grown
up in their youth;
That our daughters *may be* as
pillars,
Sculptured in palace style;
13 *That* our barns *may be* full,
Supplying all kinds of produce;
That our sheep may bring forth
thousands
And ten thousands in our fields;
14 *That* our oxen *may be* well laden;
That there be no breaking in or going
out;
That there be no outcry in our streets.
15 Happy *are* the
people who are
in such a state;
Happy *are* the
people whose
God *is* the
LORD!

> Happy are the people who are in such a state; happy are the people whose God is the LORD!
> PSALM 144:15

PSALM 145

A SONG OF GOD'S MAJESTY AND LOVE

A Praise of David.

1 I will extol You, my God, O King;
And I will bless Your name forever and
ever.
2 Every day I will bless You,
And I will praise Your name forever and
ever.
3 Great *is* the LORD, and greatly to be
praised;
And His greatness *is* unsearchable.

4 One generation shall praise Your works
to another,
And shall declare Your mighty acts.
5 I[a] will meditate on the glorious splendor
of Your majesty,
And on Your wondrous works.[b]
6 *Men* shall speak of the might of Your
awesome acts,
And I will declare Your greatness.
7 They shall utter the memory of Your
great goodness,
And shall sing of Your righteousness.
8 The LORD *is* gracious and full of
compassion,
Slow to anger and great in mercy.
9 The LORD *is* good to all,
And His tender mercies *are* over all His
works.

10 All Your works shall praise You,
O LORD,
And Your saints shall bless You.
11 They shall speak of the glory of Your
kingdom,
And talk of Your power,
12 To make known to the sons of men His
mighty acts,
And the glorious majesty of His
kingdom.
13 Your kingdom *is* an everlasting kingdom,
And Your dominion *endures* throughout
all generations.[a]

14 The LORD upholds
all who fall,
And raises up all
who are bowed
down.
15 The eyes of all
look expectantly
to You,
And You give them their food in due
season.
16 You open Your hand
And satisfy the desire of every living
thing.

17 The LORD *is* righteous in all His ways,
Gracious in all His works.
18 The LORD *is* near to all who call upon
Him,
To all who call upon Him in truth.
19 He will fulfill the desire of those who
fear Him;
He also will hear their cry and save
them.
20 The LORD preserves all who love Him,
But all the wicked He will destroy.
21 My mouth shall speak the praise of the
LORD,

145:5 [a]Following Masoretic Text and Targum; Dead Sea Scrolls, Septuagint, Syriac, and Vulgate read *They.* [b]Literally *on the words of Your wondrous works* **145:13** [a]Following Masoretic Text and Targum; Dead Sea Scrolls, Septuagint, Syriac, and Vulgate add *The LORD is faithful in all His words, And holy in all His works.*

And all flesh shall bless His holy name
Forever and ever.

PSALM 146

The Happiness of Those Whose Help Is the Lord

1 Praise the LORD!

Praise the LORD, O my soul!
2 While I live I will praise the LORD;
I will sing praises
to my God
while I have my
being.

> The LORD is gracious and full of compassion, slow to anger and great in mercy.
> PSALM 145:8

3 Do not put your
trust in princes,
Nor in a son of
man, in whom *there is* no help.
4 His spirit departs, he returns to his
earth;
In that very day his plans perish.

5 Happy *is he* who *has* the God of Jacob
for his help,
Whose hope *is* in the LORD his God,
6 Who made heaven and earth,
The sea, and all that *is* in them;
Who keeps truth forever,
7 Who executes justice for the oppressed,
Who gives food to the hungry.
The LORD gives freedom to the prisoners.

8 The LORD opens *the eyes of* the blind;
The LORD raises those who are bowed
down;
The LORD loves the righteous.
9 The LORD watches over the strangers;
He relieves the fatherless and widow;
But the way of the wicked He turns
upside down.

10 The LORD shall reign forever—
Your God, O Zion, to all generations.

Praise the LORD!

PSALM 147

Praise to God for His Word and Providence

1 Praise the LORD!
For *it is* good to sing praises to our God;
For *it is* pleasant, *and* praise is beautiful.

2 The LORD builds up Jerusalem;
He gathers together the outcasts of
Israel.
3 He heals the brokenhearted
And binds up their wounds.
4 He counts the number of the stars;
He calls them all by name.
5 Great *is* our Lord, and mighty in power;
His understanding
is infinite.
6 The LORD lifts up
the humble;
He casts the
wicked down to
the ground.

7 Sing to the
LORD with
thanksgiving;
Sing praises on the harp to our God,
8 Who covers the heavens with clouds,
Who prepares rain for the earth,
Who makes grass to grow on the
mountains.
9 He gives to the beast its food,
And to the young ravens that cry.

10 He does not delight in the strength of the
horse;
He takes no pleasure in the legs of a
man.
11 The LORD takes pleasure in those who
fear Him,
In those who hope in His mercy.

12 Praise the LORD, O Jerusalem!
Praise your God, O Zion!
13 For He has strengthened the bars of your
gates;
He has blessed your children within
you.
14 He makes peace *in* your borders,
And fills you with the finest wheat.

15 He sends out His command *to the* earth;
His word runs very swiftly.
16 He gives snow like wool;
He scatters the frost like ashes;
17 He casts out His hail like morsels;
Who can stand before His cold?
18 He sends out His word and melts them;

He causes His wind to blow, *and* the
waters flow.

19 He declares His word to Jacob,
His statutes and His judgments to Israel.
20 He has not dealt thus with any nation;
And *as for His* judgments, they have not
known them.

Praise the LORD!

PSALM 148

PRAISE TO THE LORD FROM CREATION

1 Praise the LORD!

Praise the LORD from the heavens;
Praise Him in the heights!
2 Praise Him, all His angels;
Praise Him, all His hosts!
3 Praise Him, sun and moon;
Praise Him, all you stars of light!
4 Praise Him, you heavens of heavens,
And you waters above the heavens!

5 Let them praise the name of the LORD,
For He commanded and they were
created.
6 He also established them forever and
ever;
He made a decree which shall not pass
away.

7 Praise the LORD from the earth,
You great sea creatures and all the
depths;
8 Fire and hail, snow and clouds;
Stormy wind, fulfilling His word;
9 Mountains and all hills;
Fruitful trees and all cedars;
10 Beasts and all cattle;
Creeping things and flying fowl;
11 Kings of the earth and all peoples;
Princes and all judges of the earth;
12 Both young men and maidens;
Old men and children.

13 Let them praise the name of the LORD,
For His name alone is exalted;
His glory *is* above the earth and heaven.
14 And He has exalted the horn of His
people,
The praise of all His saints—
Of the children of Israel,
A people near to Him.

Praise the LORD!

PSALM 149

PRAISE TO GOD FOR HIS SALVATION AND JUDGMENT

1 Praise the LORD!

Sing to the LORD a new song,
And His praise in the assembly of
saints.

2 Let Israel rejoice in their Maker;
Let the children of Zion be joyful in their
King.
3 Let them praise His name with the
dance;
Let them sing praises to Him with the
timbrel and harp.
4 For the LORD takes pleasure in His
people;
He will beautify the humble with
salvation.

5 Let the saints be joyful in glory;
Let them sing aloud on their beds.
6 *Let* the high praises of God *be* in their
mouth,
And a two-edged sword in their hand,
7 To execute vengeance on the nations,
And punishments on the peoples;
8 To bind their kings with chains,
And their nobles with fetters of iron;
9 To execute on them the written
judgment—
This honor have all His saints.

Praise the LORD!

PSALM 150

LET ALL THINGS PRAISE THE LORD

1 Praise the LORD!

Praise God in His sanctuary;
Praise Him in His mighty firmament!

2 Praise Him for His mighty acts;
Praise Him according to His excellent
greatness!

THE IMPORTANCE OF PRAISE AND WORSHIP

AL DENSON

(Psalm 149)

Psalms was the national hymnbook of Israel. It contains 150 poems, or psalms, to be set to music, and worship is the central theme of all of them. The psalms magnify the Lord, exalt His attributes, praise His names, His Word, and His goodness. If we want to learn how to praise and worship our Father, then let Psalms be our textbook. The Hebrew title of the Book of Psalms is "Praise" or "the Book of Praises." If we hold our Bible in our hands and turn to the middle of it, we will be in the Book of Psalms. Likewise, praise of God should be at the center of our lives.

THE PURPOSE OF PRAISE AND WORSHIP

God delights in praise because He knows it is a special way that we can relate to Him and draw closer to Him. C. S. Lewis said that just as a car is made to run on gas, God made us to run on Himself. God is powerful, sovereign, and holy, and we receive all that we are and have from Him. Apart from God, we have no energy, no power, and no fulfillment in life. Praise releases that energy and power in our lives. God wants us to praise and worship Him not because *He* needs it, but because *we* need it. Praise is a gift to us from God that helps us function more effectively. Praise can change our attitudes.

THE POWER OF PRAISE AND WORSHIP

Praise expresses and strengthens our faith. True praise is not an attempt to manipulate God into producing the results we desire; rather, true praise expresses acceptance of what God has brought into our lives. Praise helps us accept the situation whether it changes or not. Praise also makes us aware that difficult circumstances are God's blessings in disguise. When we trust God completely, He is free to work and bring victory to every situation. The victory may come in the form of having our circumstances change, or the circumstances may remain the same while the change comes in us. Either way, our faith is strengthened. Every time we are reminded how much larger God is than our problem, we will be able to trust Him more when the next test of faith comes along.

God's presence is always in us, like electricity in a lamp, but praise is the switch that turns on the power, making us more aware of His presence in our lives. When we focus our attention on God through praise, we acknowledge Him as our power source and we begin to see our problems in the light of His great power. Praise invites the Holy Spirit to make us confident that God is in control.

THE PURIFYING OF PRAISE AND WORSHIP

As fire brings the impurities in gold to the surface so they can be skimmed off, when the "heat" is turned up in our lives, the impurities come to the surface as well. If we resist the purification process, however, those impurities settle back into our lives. God wants us to be free, so He allows us to go through the "Refiner's fire" that will cause the impurities in our lives to rise to the surface. As these impurities are dealt with, the hurtful things that bind us are burned away. When we respond to the fire with praise and worship, we will experience a new purification and freedom.

THE PEACE OF PRAISE AND WORSHIP

When we give God our praise and worship, we are offering ourselves to Him completely, bowing before Him, yielding to Him fully. Often our praise will be joyful and enthusiastic, but not always. It is important to understand that God's enjoyment of our praise is not based on how we are feeling. We will bring a special kind of joy to the Lord when we praise Him even if we are depressed or exhausted. Praise causes us to enter the influence of His perspective. When that happens, the hurt, fear, frustration, or resentment we are feeling can be replaced with a peace that we never dreamed possible.

The Bible does not command us to *feel* thankful, but to *be* thankful. To give thanks when we do not feel like it is not hypocrisy; it is obedience. This does not mean that we should deny our negative thoughts and feelings. The psalmists were always honest about their feelings and told God about them. But they always combined the pouring out of their feelings with sincere praise. When, with an act of our will, we choose to keep praising in spite of our pain or confusion, God brings peace, freedom, and joy.

When we praise and worship God, we give Him something that nothing else in creation can give—love and adoration. Psalm 22:3 says that God is holy, that He is "enthroned in the praises of Israel." Psalm 84:1, 2, 4 expresses the joy of worship, "How lovely is Your tabernacle, O LORD of hosts! My soul longs, yes, even faints for the courts of the LORD; my heart and my flesh cry out for the living God. . . . Blessed are those who dwell in Your house; they will still be praising You."

We were created to be worshipers of God. He made us for Himself and He wants to have an intimate relationship with us that will last throughout eternity. Praise and worship bring to our lives purpose, power, unity, and peace. Praise and worship will bless our Father and make Him glad.

FURTHER MEDITATION:

Other passages to study about the issue of praise and worship include:

- 2 Samuel 22:2–51
- Psalms 8; 19; 27; 29; 47; 150
- Ephesians 1:3–14
- Revelation 4:4–11; 5:9–14; 7:9–17; 11:15–18; 15:3, 4

To Learn More: Turn to the key passage note on praise and worship at John 4:23, 24 on page 1377. See also the personality profile of Asaph on page 746.

3 Praise Him with the sound of the trumpet;
Praise Him with the lute and harp!
4 Praise Him with the timbrel and dance;
Praise Him with stringed instruments and flutes!
5 Praise Him with loud cymbals;
Praise Him with clashing cymbals!

6 Let everything that has breath praise the LORD.

Praise the LORD!

SOUL NOTE

Joyous Praise *(ch. 150)* Worship can be expressed to God at any time and in any place. The psalmist called for praise in the sanctuary and in the firmament. The music of praise can be loud and joyous, accompanied by trumpets, lutes, harps, timbrel, dance, stringed instruments, flutes, and cymbals. The focus of praise is God Himself—His "mighty acts" and His "excellent greatness." In short, "let everything that has breath praise the LORD" (150:6). When believers gather to worship or when they worship in solitude, they must worship joyfully! They are praising the God of the universe who loves them. He deserves our joyous praise. **Topic: Praise and Worship**

Proverbs

People often turn to the Proverbs when confused or in crisis, for this book is a collection of wise sayings based on God's perspective on life. Compiled by "Solomon the son of David, king of Israel" (1:1), the Proverbs' purpose is to help people live wisely and productively. The sayings included in this book are meant to influence people's thinking, emotions, and behavior. Obedience to these truths brings God's blessings. Disobedience leads to foolish choices and disastrous consequences.

Much of the work of soul care comes from the wisdom and instruction of these proverbs. To read them is to discover nitty-gritty truths that work as well today as they did when they were first penned. As we apply this inspired advice to our daily lives, we will find that the advice makes sense of often difficult choices. The truths contained in this book are not meant to be exhaustive or automatic, but they are potent. The Proverbs are meant to make us stop, think, and then act differently.

Proverbs is the first of three volumes of "wisdom literature" in the Bible. These proverbs are not just clever sayings to be engraved on a plaque; they are practical truths to be lived out in our lives. The Proverbs are short poems containing everything from spirit wisdom to practical advice and timely warnings. They cover a wide range of topics including marriage, family, child-rearing, work, relationships, morality, and personal responsibility. A daily dose of Proverbs is like taking spiritual vitamins to help nourish our souls.

SOUL CONCERNS IN PROVERBS

THE BEGINNING OF KNOWLEDGE

1 The proverbs of Solomon the son of David, king of Israel:

2 To know wisdom and instruction,
To perceive the words of understanding,
3 To receive the instruction of wisdom,
Justice, judgment, and equity;
4 To give prudence to the simple,
To the young man knowledge and discretion—
5 A wise *man* will hear and increase learning,
And a man of understanding will attain wise counsel,
6 To understand a proverb and an enigma,
The words of the wise and their riddles.
7 The fear of the LORD *is* the beginning of knowledge,
But fools despise wisdom and instruction.

SHUN EVIL COUNSEL

8 My son, hear the instruction of your father,
And do not forsake the law of your mother;
9 For they *will be* a graceful ornament on your head,
And chains about your neck.

10 My son, if sinners entice you,
Do not consent.
11 If they say, "Come with us,
Let us lie in wait to *shed* blood;
Let us lurk secretly for the innocent without cause;

SOUL NOTE

Find the Way *(1:4)* King Solomon compiled these proverbs to "give prudence to the simple, to the young man knowledge and discretion." Solomon wanted to help his readers to navigate the challenges and difficulties of life with greater wisdom, and ultimately with success. Through these ancient words of life experience collected by Solomon, God speaks to His people as a wise and loving Father guiding them through life's difficulties, temptations, and dilemmas. When we listen to His voice and seek His wisdom, He will show us the right way to go in every situation.
Topic: Wisdom

KEY PASSAGE

Fear/ Fear of God

AWESOME

(1:7)

The Book of Proverbs emphasizes that "the fear of the LORD is the beginning of knowledge." Fear of God means reverential awe of the Supreme Being, the Creator, the final Judge. While knowledge is possible without knowing God, it misses the point, since God is the Source of everything. It's ridiculous for humans to claim great knowledge and wisdom without having any respect for God. All human knowledge is a tiny portion of all that there is to be known, a speck of all that God has created.

Human beings then, as they seek wisdom and knowledge, should do so in the context of a proper fear of God. Then they will be able to use that wisdom and knowledge for whatever purposes God desires in order to build His kingdom. When God's people fear Him, they understand His power over their lives and willingly allow His hand to guide them.

To Learn More: Turn to the article about fear/fear of God on pages 800, 801. See also the personality profile of Gideon on page 308.

12 Let us swallow them alive like Sheol,[a]
And whole, like those who go down to the Pit;
13 We shall find all *kinds* of precious possessions,
We shall fill our houses with spoil;
14 Cast in your lot among us,
Let us all have one purse"—
15 My son, do not walk in the way with them,
Keep your foot from their path;
16 For their feet run to evil,
And they make haste to shed blood.
17 Surely, in vain the net is spread
In the sight of any bird;
18 But they lie in wait for their *own* blood,
They lurk secretly for their *own* lives.
19 So *are* the ways of everyone who is greedy for gain;
It takes away the life of its owners.

The Call of Wisdom

20 Wisdom calls aloud outside;
She raises her voice in the open squares.
21 She cries out in the chief concourses,[a]
At the openings of the gates in the city
She speaks her words:
22 "How long, you simple ones, will you love simplicity?
For scorners delight in their scorning,
And fools hate knowledge.
23 Turn at my rebuke;
Surely I will pour out my spirit on you;
I will make my words known to you.
24 Because I have called and you refused,
I have stretched out my hand and no one regarded,
25 Because you disdained all my counsel,
And would have none of my rebuke,
26 I also will laugh at your calamity;
I will mock when your terror comes,
27 When your terror comes like a storm,
And your destruction comes like a whirlwind,
When distress and anguish come upon you.

28 "Then they will call on me, but I will not answer;
They will seek me diligently, but they will not find me.
29 Because they hated knowledge
And did not choose the fear of the LORD,
30 They would have none of my counsel
And despised my every rebuke.
31 Therefore they shall eat the fruit of their own way,
And be filled to the full with their own fancies.
32 For the turning away of the simple will slay them,
And the complacency of fools will destroy them;
33 But whoever listens to me will dwell safely,
And will be secure, without fear of evil."

The Value of Wisdom

2 My son, if you receive my words,
And treasure my commands within you,
2 So that you incline your ear to wisdom,
And apply your heart to understanding;
3 Yes, if you cry out for discernment,
And lift up your voice for understanding,
4 If you seek her as silver,
And search for her as *for* hidden treasures;
5 Then you will understand the fear of the LORD,
And find the knowledge of God.

1:12 [a]Or *the grave* **1:21** [a]Septuagint, Syriac, and Targum read *top of the walls;* Vulgate reads *the head of multitudes.*

SOUL NOTE

Right Stand *(1:8–19)* Solomon often addressed his readers as "my son," teaching as a parent would instruct a beloved child. Solomon advised young people to choose their peers carefully. If friends try to entice them to sin, wise young people will choose to "not walk in the way with them" (1:15). Parents must consistently guide their children in the path of wisdom by their teaching and their example so that their children will stand for what's right. **Topic: Adolescent Problems**

ON FEARING GOD

GARY W. MOON

(Proverbs 1:7)

"No Fear." This slogan appears on the T-shirts of sports enthusiasts on the court or on the field. In response to its popularity, some Christian T-shirts began popping up with the answering slogan, "Fear God." But what is meant by the instruction, "Fear God"?

In the first few words of Proverbs 1:7, the theological foundation of this book of wisdom is established. "The fear of the LORD is the beginning of knowledge." The fear of God, as the foundation for wise living, is a recurring theme throughout Scripture.

The Book of Deuteronomy contains the great summary of God's total claim on humanity and an expected response to His requirements. It is a summary of how God's children are to live each day of life. "And now, Israel, what does the LORD your God require of you, but to fear the LORD your God . . . and to love Him" (Deut. 10:12).

There is a great riddle wrapped inside this passage. Israel was given directions that were foreign to their neighbors—to stand before God in both fear and love. Even today, living with fear and love seems to be a perplexing paradox.

THE PARADOX OF FEAR AND LOVE

Since fear is the most primitive of all human emotions, all forms of anxiety disorder are rooted in fear. Fear is also the body's natural alarm system. Any perceived threat will switch on the sympathetic nervous system's "fight or flight" response. The heart begins to race. Breathing becomes shallow and rapid. Blood flows away from the extremities and digestive organs and into the large muscles. Hands and feet become cold. Sweating increases to cool down the body which has gone into hyperdrive. In short, the person is ready to fight the object of fear or to run and hide.

When that same person experiences love (or laughter or relaxation), the body's response is very different. In this instance, it is the parasympathetic nervous system which dominates. The preparation is to approach and enjoy, not flee or fight. Fear and love are physiological opposites. So again, how can it be that people are to both fear and love God?

FEARING GOD

The word "fear" has many synonyms such as reverence, awe, dismay, dread, distress, trouble, terror, horror, and respect. However, most of these synonyms for "fear" have not survived the journey from Bible times and culture to present day. For most people, to fear means to dread instead of to hold in awe or reverence.

Some would argue that little is lost and much gained if we retranslate Proverbs 1:7 as, "The reverence of God is the beginning of wisdom." However, the fear of God does not totally equate with reverence and awe. The Hebrew concept of God was filled with wonder, awesomeness, majesty, and yes, terror and fear—a lineup that moderns may struggle to comprehend. So while substituting other words for "fear" may be helpful in certain situations or with some individuals, one must continue to pursue a deeper appreciation for God that preserves the idea of fearing Him. He is much more complex and awe-inspiring than a "big buddy in the sky." God is the ultimate Friend and Father, but He is also holy and completely "other." To see Him in all His glory might very well be enough to stop an earthly human heart.

LOVING GOD

People's love for God should create a sense of heart-pounding anguish at the very thought of moral evil, revolt, rebellion, or compromise. With this in mind, a person ought to be terrified at the possibility of living life apart from His presence or on any other terms but His own. The new person in Christ should mature into a sense of being delivered from worldly fear, since the presence of Christ's love pushes out fear: "Love has been perfected among us in this: that we may have boldness in the day of judgment; because as He is, so are we in this world. There is no fear in love; but perfect love casts out fear. . . . But he who fears has not been made perfect in love. We love Him because He first loved us" (1 John 4:17–19). The maturing disciple, however, should likewise experience a sense of terror at the possibility of being alienated from God or incurring His displeasure.

On one hand, Christ impressed upon His disciples the necessity to fear God who can destroy both the body and the soul (Matt. 10:28; Luke 12:5). He did not downplay the reality of the prospect of judgment. On the other hand, Jesus presented a radical means for overcoming fear—being led by the Spirit of God to receive a sense of adoption by which one cries, "Abba, Father" (Rom. 8:15). God's gift to His children is not a "spirit of fear, but of power and of love and of a sound mind" (2 Tim. 1:7). Through the mystery of Christ, it is possible to move from the fear of being punished in His presence, to the joy of being drawn by and into His love.

We ought to fear God, yes. But we should not run from Him. We ought to run *to* Him. We can come out of hiding and flee back into His presence and His standards for living. Then we can let fear keep us from leaving again as bonds of love grow and keep us tied to His presence.

FURTHER MEDITATION:

Other passages to study about the issue of fear/fear of God include:

- Joshua 24:14
- 1 Samuel 12:14
- Job 28:28
- Psalms 19:9; 27:1–3; 31:19; 33:18; 111:10
- Proverbs 14:26; 15:16
- Ecclesiastes 12:13
- Matthew 10:28
- 2 Corinthians 7:1

To Learn More: **Turn to the key passage note on fear/fear of God at Proverbs 1:7 on page 798. See also the personality profile of Gideon on page 308.**

6 For the LORD gives wisdom;
From His mouth *come* knowledge and understanding;
7 He stores up sound wisdom for the upright;
He is a shield to those who walk uprightly;
8 He guards the paths of justice,
And preserves the way of His saints.
9 Then you will understand righteousness and justice,
Equity *and* every good path.

10 When wisdom enters your heart,
And knowledge is pleasant to your soul,
11 Discretion will preserve you;
Understanding will keep you,
12 To deliver you from the way of evil,
From the man who speaks perverse things,
13 From those who leave the paths of uprightness
To walk in the ways of darkness;
14 Who rejoice in doing evil,
And delight in the perversity of the wicked;
15 Whose ways *are* crooked,
And *who are* devious in their paths;
16 To deliver you from the immoral woman,
From the seductress *who* flatters with her words,
17 Who forsakes the companion of her youth,
And forgets the covenant of her God.
18 For her house leads down to death,
And her paths to the dead;

PERSONALITY PROFILE

Child Discipline

THE WISE SON

(PROVERBS 2—3)

Christian parents hope to raise their children to be wise—to fear the Lord and serve Him. Wise Christian parents understand that just as God disciplines His children in order to teach them to do right, so parents must discipline their children for the same reason (Prov. 3:12). God has given parents this responsibility, and they must take it seriously.

Children need discipline—indeed, they desire it. They need to know the boundaries and the rules; they need to know that their parents will consistently discipline them should they try to cross those boundaries or break those rules. Parents who commit themselves to teaching their children to be wise will find their children's hearts open like a treasure chest, waiting to be filled. That treasure chest, filled with wisdom learned from listening to and watching their parents, can be drawn from for the rest of their lives. So how can parents teach wisdom?

First, the parents must live wisely by fearing the Lord (Prov. 1:7), trusting Him, seeking His guidance, and following His commands. When children see wisdom lived out in their homes, they will learn what it means to follow God.

Second, parents must encourage their children to build that personal relationship with God: "Trust in the LORD with all your heart" (Prov. 3:5). The Book of Proverbs advises children to learn to discern between wisdom and folly, to not despise the discipline given by parents or by God, and to continue to seek wisdom all the days of their lives.

Children need to know that their parents have placed boundaries around them because of love for them. They learn about God's love and discipline as they experience parental love and discipline. Parents who teach their children wisdom are giving them a lasting gift, for "length of days is in her right hand. . . . Her ways are ways of pleasantness, and all her paths are peace" (Prov. 3:16, 17).

To Learn More: Turn to the article about child discipline on pages 830, 831. See also the key passage note at Proverbs 22:15 on page 829.

19 None who go to her return,
Nor do they regain the paths of life—
20 So you may walk in the way of goodness,
And keep *to* the paths of righteousness.
21 For the upright will dwell in the land,
And the blameless will remain in it;
22 But the wicked will be cut off from the earth,
And the unfaithful will be uprooted from it.

GUIDANCE FOR THE YOUNG

3 My son, do not forget my law,
But let your heart keep my commands;
2 For length of days and long life
And peace they will add to you.

3 Let not mercy and truth forsake you;
Bind them around your neck,
Write them on the tablet of your heart,
4 *And* so find favor and high esteem
In the sight of God and man.

5 Trust in the LORD with all your heart,
And lean not on your own understanding;
6 In all your ways acknowledge Him,
And He shall direct[a] your paths.

7 Do not be wise in your own eyes;
Fear the LORD and depart from evil.
8 It will be health to your flesh,[a]
And strength[b] to your bones.

9 Honor the LORD with your possessions,
And with the firstfruits of all your increase;

3:6 [a]Or *make smooth* or *straight* **3:8** [a]Literally *navel,* figurative of the body [b]Literally *drink* or *refreshment*

KEY PASSAGE

Trust

TRUST IN HIM

(3:5, 6)

It's one thing for people to trust God with their eternal destiny; it is quite another for them to trust God to handle the challenges and difficulties of daily life. These verses encourage God's people to trust in God with all their hearts and acknowledge Him in all their ways. When we do so, He promises to direct, or straighten, our paths. We need to trust God to help us handle the difficult situations we face, even in cases where we can't begin to see how He could. Also, trusting the Lord means to trust Him in all areas. If we really want to know God's will for our lives, or even for our actions in a particular situation, we must begin by trusting that God cares about every aspect of living, and that He will provide what we need.

To Learn More: Turn to the article about trust on pages 1180, 1181. See also the personality profile of Habakkuk on page 1185.

SOUL NOTE

Health and Strength *(3:7, 8)* Modern medical research is proving the positive relationship between health and godliness, a fact that believers have understood for a long time. Living a godly lifestyle brings physical, emotional, and spiritual health and blessing. Being a believer will not exempt a person from physical problems, but at times it may keep a person from some kinds of diseases. And knowing that one belongs to God brings spiritual contentment that will have a positive effect on the body as well. **Topic: Health/Spirituality**

10 So your barns will be filled with plenty,
And your vats will overflow with new wine.

11 My son, do not despise the chastening of the LORD,
Nor detest His correction;
12 For whom the LORD loves He corrects,
Just as a father the son *in whom* he delights.

13 Happy *is* the man *who* finds wisdom,
And the man *who* gains understanding;
14 For her proceeds *are* better than the profits of silver,
And her gain than fine gold.
15 She *is* more precious than rubies,
And all the things you may desire cannot compare with her.
16 Length of days *is* in her right hand,
In her left hand riches and honor.
17 Her ways *are* ways of pleasantness,
And all her paths *are* peace.
18 She *is* a tree of life to those who take hold of her,
And happy *are all* who retain her.

19 The LORD by wisdom founded the earth;
By understanding He established the heavens;
20 By His knowledge the depths were broken up,
And clouds drop down the dew.

21 My son, let them not depart from your eyes—
Keep sound wisdom and discretion;
22 So they will be life to your soul
And grace to your neck.
23 Then you will walk safely in your way,
And your foot will not stumble.
24 When you lie down, you will not be afraid;
Yes, you will lie down and your sleep will be sweet.
25 Do not be afraid of sudden terror,
Nor of trouble from the wicked when it comes;
26 For the LORD will be your confidence,
And will keep your foot from being caught.

27 Do not withhold good from those to whom it is due,
When it is in the power of your hand to do *so.*
28 Do not say to your neighbor,
"Go, and come back,
And tomorrow I will give *it,*"
When *you have* it with you.
29 Do not devise evil against your neighbor,
For he dwells by you for safety's sake.
30 Do not strive with a man without cause,
If he has done you no harm.

31 Do not envy the oppressor,
And choose none of his ways;
32 For the perverse *person is* an abomination to the LORD,
But His secret counsel *is* with the upright.
33 The curse of the LORD *is* on the house of the wicked,
But He blesses the home of the just.
34 Surely He scorns the scornful,
But gives grace to the humble.
35 The wise shall inherit glory,
But shame shall be the legacy of fools.

SECURITY IN WISDOM

4 Hear, *my* children, the instruction of a father,
And give attention to know understanding;
2 For I give you good doctrine:
Do not forsake my law.
3 When I was my father's son,
Tender and the only one in the sight of my mother,
4 He also taught me, and said to me:
"Let your heart retain my words;
Keep my commands, and live.
5 Get wisdom! Get understanding!
Do not forget, nor turn away from the words of my mouth.
6 Do not forsake her, and she will preserve you;

> Wisdom is the principal thing; therefore get wisdom. And in all your getting, get understanding.
> PROVERBS 4:7

Love her, and she will keep you.
7 Wisdom *is* the principal thing;
Therefore get wisdom.
And in all your getting, get
understanding.
8 Exalt her, and she will promote you;
She will bring you honor, when you
embrace her.
9 She will place on your head an
ornament of grace;
A crown of glory she will deliver to
you."

10 Hear, my son, and receive my sayings,
And the years of your life will be many.
11 I have taught you in the way of wisdom;
I have led you in right paths.
12 When you walk, your steps will not be
hindered,
And when you run, you will not
stumble.
13 Take firm hold of instruction, do not let
go;
Keep her, for she *is* your life.

14 Do not enter the path of the wicked,
And do not walk in the way of evil.
15 Avoid it, do not travel on it;
Turn away from it and pass on.
16 For they do not sleep unless they have
done evil;
And their sleep is taken away unless
they make *someone* fall.
17 For they eat the bread of wickedness,
And drink the wine of violence.

18 But the path of the just *is* like the
shining sun,[a]
That shines ever brighter unto the
perfect day.
19 The way of the wicked *is* like darkness;
They do not know what makes them
stumble.

20 My son, give attention to my words;
Incline your ear to my sayings.
21 Do not let them depart from your eyes;
Keep them in the midst of your heart;
22 For they *are* life to those who find them,
And health to all their flesh.
23 Keep your heart with all diligence,
For out of it *spring* the issues of life.
24 Put away from you a deceitful mouth,
And put perverse lips far from you.
25 Let your eyes look straight ahead,
And your eyelids look right before you.
26 Ponder the path of your feet,
And let all your ways be established.
27 Do not turn to the right or the left;
Remove your foot from evil.

The Peril of Adultery

5 My son, pay attention to my wisdom;
Lend your ear to my understanding,
2 That you may preserve discretion,
And your lips may keep knowledge.
3 For the lips of an immoral woman drip
honey,
And her mouth *is* smoother than oil;
4 But in the end she is bitter as wormwood,
Sharp as a two-edged sword.
5 Her feet go down to death,
Her steps lay hold of hell.[a]
6 Lest you ponder *her* path of life—
Her ways are unstable;
You do not know *them.*

7 Therefore hear me now, *my* children,
And do not depart from the words of my
mouth.

4:18 [a]Literally *light* **5:5** [a]Or *Sheol*

SOUL NOTE

Beautiful Wisdom *(4:1–13)* Wisdom is "the principal thing," (4:7), and is called "good doctrine" (4:2). Wisdom refers to the core truths about life that are passed on from godly parents to their children, from generation to generation. Solomon challenges people to seek out and obtain wisdom, to never forget it or forsake it (4:5, 6). Wisdom is pictured as a woman, a beauty that a good son will pursue and court as he would a wife: Love her, exalt her, embrace her, "keep her, for she is your life" (4:13). Wisdom is of permanent importance. It should be sought ardently and treasured dearly.
Topic: Wisdom

8 Remove your way far from her,
And do not go near the door of her house,
9 Lest you give your honor to others,
And your years to the cruel *one;*
10 Lest aliens be filled with your wealth,
And your labors *go* to the house of a foreigner;
11 And you mourn at last,
When your flesh and your body are consumed,
12 And say:
"How I have hated instruction,
And my heart despised correction!
13 I have not obeyed the voice of my teachers,
Nor inclined my ear to those who instructed me!
14 I was on the verge of total ruin,
In the midst of the assembly and congregation."

15 Drink water from your own cistern,
And running water from your own well.
16 Should your fountains be dispersed abroad,
Streams of water in the streets?
17 Let them be only your own,
And not for strangers with you.
18 Let your fountain be blessed,
And rejoice with the wife of your youth.
19 *As a* loving deer and a graceful doe,
Let her breasts satisfy you at all times;
And always be enraptured with her love.
20 For why should you, my son, be enraptured by an immoral woman,
And be embraced in the arms of a seductress?

21 For the ways of man *are* before the eyes of the LORD,
And He ponders all his paths.
22 His own iniquities entrap the wicked *man,*
And he is caught in the cords of his sin.
23 He shall die for lack of instruction,
And in the greatness of his folly he shall go astray.

DANGEROUS PROMISES

6 My son, if you become surety for your friend,
If you have shaken hands in pledge for a stranger,
2 You are snared by the words of your mouth;
You are taken by the words of your mouth.
3 So do this, my son, and deliver yourself;
For you have come into the hand of your friend:
Go and humble yourself;
Plead with your friend.
4 Give no sleep to your eyes,
Nor slumber to your eyelids.

KEY PASSAGE

Adultery

ILLICIT ATTRACTION

(5:1–23)

The Bible does not speak against sexual fulfillment—in fact, sexual delight and marital love are exalted in the Song of Solomon. The Bible does, however, speak against sexual sin. One of the warnings that runs through Proverbs is to avoid the immoral woman. The warning implicitly acknowledges the power and attractiveness of illicit sex at certain times in life. Adultery is a great tragedy, for it has severe consequences. People risk all that they have built over a lifetime—marriage, family, ministry, respect, honor—when they commit adultery. Sexual sin can be very appealing, almost an overwhelming temptation.

The way out is to rejoice in one's marriage and to be satisfied with one's spouse's love (5:18, 19). Sexual fulfillment is always depicted in the Bible as within the boundaries of marriage. To violate that commitment will lead to pain, grief, and self-destruction.

To Learn More: Turn to the article about adultery on pages 1128, 1129. See also the personality profile of the woman caught in adultery on page 1384.

5 Deliver yourself like a gazelle from the hand *of the hunter*,
And like a bird from the hand of the fowler.[a]

The Folly of Indolence

6 Go to the ant, you sluggard!
Consider her ways and be wise,
7 Which, having no captain,
Overseer or ruler,
8 Provides her supplies in the summer,
And gathers her food in the harvest.
9 How long will you slumber, O sluggard?
When will you rise from your sleep?
10 A little sleep, a little slumber,
A little folding of the hands to sleep—
11 So shall your poverty come on you like a prowler,
And your need like an armed man.

The Wicked Man

12 A worthless person, a wicked man,
Walks with a perverse mouth;
13 He winks with his eyes,
He shuffles his feet,
He points with his fingers;
14 Perversity *is* in his heart,
He devises evil continually,
He sows discord.
15 Therefore his calamity shall come suddenly;
Suddenly he shall be broken without remedy.

16 These six *things* the LORD hates,
Yes, seven *are* an abomination to Him:
17 A proud look,
A lying tongue,
Hands that shed innocent blood,
18 A heart that devises wicked plans,
Feet that are swift in running to evil,
19 A false witness *who* speaks lies,
And one who sows discord among brethren.

Beware of Adultery

20 My son, keep your father's command,
And do not forsake the law of your mother.
21 Bind them continually upon your heart;
Tie them around your neck.
22 When you roam, they[a] will lead you;
When you sleep, they will keep you;
And *when* you awake, they will speak with you.
23 For the commandment *is* a lamp,
And the law a light;
Reproofs of instruction *are* the way of life,
24 To keep you from the evil woman,
From the flattering tongue of a seductress.
25 Do not lust after her beauty in your heart,
Nor let her allure you with her eyelids.
26 For by means of a harlot
A man is reduced to a crust of bread;
And an adulteress[a] will prey upon his precious life.
27 Can a man take fire to his bosom,
And his clothes not be burned?
28 Can one walk on hot coals,
And his feet not be seared?
29 So *is* he who goes in to his neighbor's wife;
Whoever touches her shall not be innocent.

30 *People* do not despise a thief
If he steals to satisfy himself when he is starving.

6:5 [a]That is, one who catches birds in a trap or snare **6:22** [a]Literally *it* **6:26** [a]Literally *a man's wife,* that is, of another

SOUL NOTE

Fresh Water *(5:15–23)* This beautiful metaphor describes the joy of marital fidelity. To "drink water from your own cistern" pictures the marriage partners belonging only to each other, "enraptured with" each other's love. By contrast, to become enraptured by another, to turn to adultery, may feel exciting at first, but will end up being "bitter as wormwood, sharp as a two-edged sword" (5:4). God's Word clearly teaches that married people should keep their vows and remain committed to each other. Adultery is embracing a false love—it will hurt everyone involved. **Topic: Adultery**

31 Yet *when* he is found, he must restore
sevenfold;
He may have to give up all the substance
of his house.
32 Whoever commits adultery with a
woman lacks understanding;
He *who* does so destroys his own soul.
33 Wounds and dishonor he will get,
And his reproach will not be wiped
away.
34 For jealousy *is* a husband's fury;
Therefore he will not spare in the day of
vengeance.
35 He will accept no recompense,
Nor will he be appeased though you give
many gifts.

7 My son, keep my words,
And treasure my commands within you.
2 Keep my commands and live,
And my law as the apple of your eye.
3 Bind them on your fingers;
Write them on the tablet of your heart.
4 Say to wisdom, "You *are* my sister,"
And call understanding *your* nearest kin,
5 That they may keep you from the
immoral woman,
From the seductress *who* flatters with
her words.

The Crafty Harlot

6 For at the window of my house
I looked through my lattice,
7 And saw among the simple,
I perceived among the youths,
A young man devoid of understanding,
8 Passing along the street near her corner;
And he took the path to her house
9 In the twilight, in the evening,
In the black and dark night.

10 And there a woman met him,
With the attire of a harlot, and a crafty
heart.
11 She *was* loud and rebellious,
Her feet would not stay at home.
12 At times *she was* outside, at times in the
open square,
Lurking at every corner.
13 So she caught him and kissed him;
With an impudent face she said to him:
14 "*I have* peace offerings with me;
Today I have paid my vows.
15 So I came out to meet you,
Diligently to seek your face,
And I have found you.
16 I have spread my bed with tapestry,
Colored coverings of Egyptian linen.
17 I have perfumed my bed
With myrrh, aloes, and cinnamon.
18 Come, let us take our fill of love until
morning;
Let us delight ourselves with love.
19 For my husband *is* not at home;
He has gone on a long journey;
20 He has taken a bag of money with him,
And will come home on the appointed
day."

21 With her enticing speech she caused him
to yield,
With her flattering lips she seduced him.
22 Immediately he went after her, as an ox
goes to the slaughter,
Or as a fool to the correction of the
stocks,[a]
23 Till an arrow struck his liver.
As a bird hastens to the snare,
He did not know it *would cost* his life.

24 Now therefore, listen to me, *my*
children;
Pay attention to the words of my
mouth:
25 Do not let your heart turn aside to her
ways,
Do not stray into her paths;
26 For she has cast down many wounded,
And all who were slain by her were
strong *men*.
27 Her house *is* the way to hell,[a]
Descending to the chambers of death.

The Excellence of Wisdom

8 Does not wisdom cry out,
And understanding lift up her voice?
2 She takes her stand on the top of the
high hill,
Beside the way, where the paths meet.
3 She cries out by the gates, at the entry of
the city,
At the entrance of the doors:
4 "To you, O men, I call,
And my voice *is* to the sons of men.

7:22 [a]Septuagint, Syriac, and Targum read *as a dog to bonds;* Vulgate reads *as a lamb . . . to bonds.*
7:27 [a]Or *Sheol*

5 O you simple ones, understand
prudence,
And you fools, be of an understanding
heart.
6 Listen, for I will speak of excellent
things,
And from the opening of my lips *will
come* right things;
7 For my mouth will speak truth;
Wickedness *is* an abomination to my
lips.
8 All the words of my mouth *are* with
righteousness;
Nothing crooked or perverse *is* in them.
9 They *are* all plain to him who
understands,
And right to those who find knowledge.
10 Receive my instruction, and not silver,
And knowledge rather than choice gold;
11 For wisdom *is* better than rubies,
And all the things one may desire cannot
be compared with her.

12 "I, wisdom, dwell with prudence,
And find out knowledge *and* discretion.
13 The fear of the LORD *is* to hate evil;
Pride and arrogance and the evil way
And the perverse mouth I hate.
14 Counsel *is* mine, and sound wisdom;
I *am* understanding, I have strength.
15 By me kings reign,
And rulers decree justice.
16 By me princes rule, and nobles,
All the judges of the earth.[a]
17 I love those who love me,
And those who seek me diligently will
find me.
18 Riches and honor *are* with me,
Enduring riches and righteousness.
19 My fruit *is* better than gold, yes, than
fine gold,
And my revenue than choice silver.
20 I traverse the way of righteousness,
In the midst of the paths of justice,
21 That I may cause those who love me to
inherit wealth,
That I may fill their treasuries.

22 "The LORD possessed me at the beginning
of His way,
Before His works of old.
23 I have been established from everlasting,
From the beginning, before there was
ever an earth.
24 When *there were* no depths I was
brought forth,
When *there were* no fountains
abounding with water.
25 Before the mountains were settled,
Before the hills, I was brought forth;
26 While as yet He had not made the earth
or the fields,
Or the primal dust of the world.
27 When He prepared the heavens, I *was*
there,
When He drew a circle on the face of the
deep,
28 When He established the clouds above,
When He strengthened the fountains of
the deep,
29 When He assigned to the sea its limit,
So that the waters would not transgress
His command,
When He marked out the foundations of
the earth,
30 Then I was beside Him *as* a master
craftsman;[a]
And I was daily *His* delight,
Rejoicing always before Him,
31 Rejoicing in His inhabited world,
And my delight *was* with the sons of
men.

32 "Now therefore, listen to me, *my*
children,
For blessed *are those who* keep my ways.
33 Hear instruction and be wise,
And do not disdain *it*.
34 Blessed is the man who listens to me,
Watching daily at my gates,
Waiting at the posts of my doors.
35 For whoever finds me finds life,
And obtains favor from the LORD;
36 But he who sins against me wrongs his
own soul;
All those who hate me love death."

THE WAY OF WISDOM

9 Wisdom has built her house,
She has hewn out her seven pillars;
2 She has slaughtered her meat,
She has mixed her wine,
She has also furnished her table.

8:16 [a]Masoretic Text, Syriac, Targum, and Vulgate read *righteousness;* Septuagint, Bomberg, and some manuscripts and editions read *earth.*
8:30 [a]A Jewish tradition reads *one brought up.*

3 She has sent out her maidens,
She cries out from the highest places of the city,
4 "Whoever *is* simple, let him turn in here!"
As for him who lacks understanding, she says to him,
5 "Come, eat of my bread
And drink of the wine I have mixed.
6 Forsake foolishness and live,
And go in the way of understanding.

7 "He who corrects a scoffer gets shame for himself,
And he who rebukes a wicked *man only* harms himself.
8 Do not correct a scoffer, lest he hate you;
Rebuke a wise *man,* and he will love you.
9 Give *instruction* to a wise *man,* and he will be still wiser;
Teach a just *man,* and he will increase in learning.

10 "The fear of the LORD *is* the beginning of wisdom,
And the knowledge of the Holy One *is* understanding.
11 For by me your days will be multiplied,
And years of life will be added to you.
12 If you are wise, you are wise for yourself,
And *if* you scoff, you will bear *it* alone."

THE WAY OF FOLLY

13 A foolish woman is clamorous;
She is simple, and knows nothing.
14 For she sits at the door of her house,
On a seat *by* the highest places of the city,
15 To call to those who pass by,
Who go straight on their way:
16 "Whoever *is* simple, let him turn in here";
And *as for* him who lacks understanding, she says to him,
17 "Stolen water is sweet,
And bread *eaten* in secret is pleasant."
18 But he does not know that the dead *are* there,
That her guests *are* in the depths of hell.[a]

WISE SAYINGS OF SOLOMON

10 The proverbs of Solomon:

A wise son makes a glad father,
But a foolish son *is* the grief of his mother.

2 Treasures of wickedness profit nothing,
But righteousness delivers from death.
3 The LORD will not allow the righteous soul to famish,
But He casts away the desire of the wicked.

4 He who has a slack hand becomes poor,
But the hand of the diligent makes rich.
5 He who gathers in summer *is* a wise son;
He who sleeps in harvest *is* a son who causes shame.

6 Blessings *are* on the head of the righteous,
But violence covers the mouth of the wicked.
7 The memory of the righteous *is* blessed,
But the name of the wicked will rot.

8 The wise in heart will receive commands,
But a prating fool will fall.

9:18 [a]Or *Sheol*

SOUL NOTE

Wisdom's House *(9:1–18)* This chapter describes wisdom and foolishness as two women. The first invites people to a feast where they can learn "the fear of the LORD" (9:6, 10). The other has not prepared a feast; what she has is only stolen water and bread. Those who accept wisdom's invitation will gain God's blessings; those who pick folly will face a life of self-indulgence leading to the depths of hell. There is a choice: We can prefer the path of wisdom or the path of foolishness. That will affect every other choice we ever make. **Topic: Wisdom**

9 He who walks with integrity walks
securely,
But he who perverts his ways will
become known.

10 He who winks with the eye causes
trouble,
But a prating fool will fall.

11 The mouth of the righteous *is* a well of
life,
But violence covers the mouth of the
wicked.

12 Hatred stirs up strife,
But love covers all sins.

13 Wisdom is found on the lips of him who
has understanding,
But a rod *is* for the back of him who is
devoid of understanding.

14 Wise *people* store up knowledge,
But the mouth of the foolish *is* near
destruction.

15 The rich man's wealth *is* his strong city;
The destruction of the poor *is* their
poverty.

16 The labor of the righteous *leads* to
life,
The wages of the wicked to sin.

17 He who keeps instruction *is in* the way
of life,
But he who refuses correction goes
astray.

18 Whoever hides hatred *has* lying lips,
And whoever spreads slander *is* a fool.

19 In the multitude of words sin is not
lacking,
But he who restrains his lips *is* wise.
20 The tongue of the righteous *is* choice
silver;
The heart of the wicked *is worth* little.
21 The lips of the righteous feed many,
But fools die for lack of wisdom.[a]

22 The blessing of the LORD makes *one*
rich,
And He adds no sorrow with it.

23 To do evil *is* like sport to a fool,
But a man of understanding has
wisdom.
24 The fear of the wicked will come upon
him,
And the desire of the righteous will be
granted.
25 When the whirlwind passes by, the
wicked *is* no *more,*
But the righteous *has* an everlasting
foundation.

26 As vinegar to the teeth and smoke to the
eyes,
So *is* the lazy *man* to those who send
him.

27 The fear of the LORD prolongs days,
But the years of the wicked will be
shortened.
28 The hope of the righteous *will be*
gladness,
But the expectation of the wicked will
perish.
29 The way of the LORD *is* strength for the
upright,
But destruction *will come* to the workers
of iniquity.

30 The righteous will never be removed,
But the wicked will not inhabit the
earth.
31 The mouth of the righteous brings forth
wisdom,
But the perverse tongue will be cut out.
32 The lips of the righteous know what is
acceptable,
But the mouth of the wicked *what is*
perverse.

11 Dishonest scales *are* an abomination
to the LORD,
But a just weight *is* His delight.

2 When pride comes, then comes shame;
But with the humble *is* wisdom.

3 The integrity of the upright will guide
them,
But the perversity of the unfaithful will
destroy them.
4 Riches do not profit in the day of wrath,

10:21 [a]Literally *heart*

But righteousness delivers from death.
5 The righteousness of the blameless will direct[a] his way aright,
But the wicked will fall by his own wickedness.
6 The righteousness of the upright will deliver them,
But the unfaithful will be caught by *their* lust.

7 When a wicked man dies, *his* expectation will perish,
And the hope of the unjust perishes.
8 The righteous is delivered from trouble,
And it comes to the wicked instead.
9 The hypocrite with *his* mouth destroys his neighbor,
But through knowledge the righteous will be delivered.
10 When it goes well with the righteous, the city rejoices;
And when the wicked perish, *there is* jubilation.
11 By the blessing of the upright the city is exalted,
But it is overthrown by the mouth of the wicked.

12 He who is devoid of wisdom despises his neighbor,
But a man of understanding holds his peace.

13 A talebearer reveals secrets,
But he who is of a faithful spirit conceals a matter.

Where there is no counsel, the people fall; but in the multitude of counselors there is safety.
PROVERBS 11:14

14 Where *there is* no counsel, the people fall;
But in the multitude of counselors *there is* safety.

15 He who is surety for a stranger will suffer,
But one who hates being surety is secure.

16 A gracious woman retains honor,
But ruthless *men* retain riches.
17 The merciful man does good for his own soul,
But *he who is* cruel troubles his own flesh.
18 The wicked *man* does deceptive work,
But he who sows righteousness *will have* a sure reward.
19 As righteousness *leads* to life,
So he who pursues evil *pursues it* to his own death.
20 Those who are of a perverse heart *are* an abomination to the LORD,
But *the* blameless in their ways *are* His delight.
21 *Though they* join forces,[a] the wicked will not go unpunished;
But the posterity of the righteous will be delivered.

22 *As* a ring of gold in a swine's snout,
So is a lovely woman who lacks discretion.

23 The desire of the righteous *is* only good,
But the expectation of the wicked *is* wrath.

24 There is *one* who scatters, yet increases more;
And there is *one* who withholds more than is right,
But it *leads* to poverty.
25 The generous soul will be made rich,
And he who waters will also be watered himself.
26 The people will curse him who withholds grain,
But blessing *will be* on the head of him who sells *it*.

27 He who earnestly seeks good finds favor,
But trouble will come to him who seeks *evil*.

28 He who trusts in his riches will fall,
But the righteous will flourish like foliage.

11:5 [a]Or *make smooth* or *straight* **11:21** [a]Literally *hand to hand*

29 He who troubles his own house will
inherit the wind,
And the fool *will be* servant to the wise
of heart.

30 The fruit of the righteous *is a* tree of life,
And he who wins souls *is* wise.

31 If the righteous will be recompensed on
the earth,
How much more the ungodly and the
sinner.

12 Whoever loves instruction loves
knowledge,
But he who hates correction *is* stupid.

2 A good *man* obtains favor from the
LORD,
But a man of wicked intentions He will
condemn.

3 A man is not established by
wickedness,
But the root of the righteous cannot be
moved.

4 An excellent[a] wife *is* the crown of her
husband,
But she who causes shame *is* like
rottenness in his bones.

5 The thoughts of the righteous *are* right,
But the counsels of the wicked *are*
deceitful.
6 The words of the wicked *are,* "Lie in
wait for blood,"
But the mouth of the upright will deliver
them.

7 The wicked are overthrown and *are* no
more,
But the house of the righteous will
stand.

8 A man will be commended according to
his wisdom,
But he who is of a perverse heart will be
despised.

9 Better *is the one* who is slighted but has
a servant,
Than he who honors himself but lacks
bread.

10 A righteous *man* regards the life of his
animal,
But the tender mercies of the wicked *are*
cruel.

11 He who tills his land will be satisfied
with bread,
But he who follows frivolity *is* devoid of
understanding.[a]

12 The wicked covet the catch of evil *men,*
But the root of the righteous yields *fruit.*
13 The wicked is ensnared by the
transgression of *his* lips,
But the righteous will come through
trouble.
14 A man will be satisfied with good by the
fruit of *his* mouth,
And the recompense of a man's hands
will be rendered to him.

15 The way of a fool *is* right in his own
eyes,
But he who heeds counsel *is* wise.
16 A fool's wrath is known at once,
But a prudent *man* covers shame.

17 He *who* speaks truth declares
righteousness,
But a false witness, deceit.
18 There is one who speaks like the
piercings of a sword,
But the tongue of the wise *promotes*
health.
19 The truthful lip shall be established
forever,
But a lying tongue *is* but for a moment.
20 Deceit is in the heart of those who
devise evil,
But counselors of peace have joy.
21 No grave trouble will overtake the
righteous,
But the wicked shall be filled with evil.
22 Lying lips *are* an abomination to the
LORD,
But those who deal truthfully *are* His
delight.

23 A prudent man conceals knowledge,
But the heart of fools proclaims
foolishness.

12:4 [a]Literally *A wife of valor* **12:11** [a]Literally *heart*

24 The hand of the diligent will rule,
But the lazy *man* will be put to forced labor.

25 Anxiety in the heart of man causes depression,
But a good word makes it glad.

26 The righteous should choose his friends carefully,
For the way of the wicked leads them astray.

27 The lazy *man* does not roast what he took in hunting,
But diligence *is* man's precious possession.

28 In the way of righteousness *is* life,
And in *its* pathway *there is* no death.

13

A wise son *heeds* his father's instruction,
But a scoffer does not listen to rebuke.

2 A man shall eat well by the fruit of *his* mouth,
But the soul of the unfaithful feeds on violence.

3 He who guards his mouth preserves his life,
But he who opens wide his lips shall have destruction.

4 The soul of a lazy *man* desires, and *has* nothing;
But the soul of the diligent shall be made rich.

5 A righteous *man* hates lying,
But a wicked *man* is loathsome and comes to shame.

6 Righteousness guards *him whose* way is blameless,
But wickedness overthrows the sinner.

7 There is one who makes himself rich, yet *has* nothing;
And one who makes himself poor, yet *has* great riches.

8 The ransom of a man's life *is* his riches,
But the poor does not hear rebuke.

9 The light of the righteous rejoices,
But the lamp of the wicked will be put out.

10 By pride comes nothing but strife,
But with the well-advised *is* wisdom.

11 Wealth *gained by* dishonesty will be diminished,
But he who gathers by labor will increase.

12 Hope deferred makes the heart sick,
But *when* the desire comes, *it is* a tree of life.

13 He who despises the word will be destroyed,
But he who fears the commandment will be rewarded.

14 The law of the wise *is* a fountain of life,
To turn *one* away from the snares of death.

15 Good understanding gains favor,
But the way of the unfaithful *is* hard.

16 Every prudent *man* acts with knowledge,
But a fool lays open *his* folly.

17 A wicked messenger falls into trouble,
But a faithful ambassador *brings* health.

18 Poverty and shame *will come* to him who disdains correction,
But he who regards a rebuke will be honored.

19 A desire accomplished is sweet to the soul,
But *it is* an abomination to fools to depart from evil.

20 He who walks with wise *men* will be wise,
But the companion of fools will be destroyed.

21 Evil pursues sinners,
But to the righteous, good shall be repaid.

22 A good *man* leaves an inheritance to his children's children,

But the wealth of the sinner is stored up
for the righteous.

23 Much food *is in* the fallow *ground* of the
poor,
And for lack of justice there is waste.[a]

24 He who spares his rod hates his son,
But he who loves him disciplines him
promptly.

25 The righteous eats to the satisfying of
his soul,
But the stomach of the wicked shall be
in want.

14 The wise woman builds her house,
But the foolish pulls it down with her
hands.

2 He who walks in his uprightness fears
the LORD,
But *he who is* perverse in his ways
despises Him.

3 In the mouth of a fool *is* a rod of pride,
But the lips of the wise will preserve
them.

4 Where no oxen *are,* the trough *is*
clean;
But much increase *comes* by the strength
of an ox.

5 A faithful witness does not lie,
But a false witness will utter lies.

6 A scoffer seeks wisdom and does not
find it,
But knowledge *is* easy to him who
understands.
7 Go from the presence of a foolish man,
When you do not perceive *in him* the
lips of knowledge.
8 The wisdom of the prudent *is* to
understand his way,
But the folly of fools *is* deceit.

9 Fools mock at sin,
But among the upright *there is* favor.

10 The heart knows its own bitterness,
And a stranger does not share its joy.

11 The house of the wicked will be
overthrown,
But the tent of the upright will flourish.

12 There is a way *that seems* right to a
man,
But its end *is* the way of death.

13 Even in laughter the heart may sorrow,
And the end of mirth *may be* grief.

14 The backslider in heart will be filled
with his own ways,
But a good man *will be satisfied* from
above.[a]

15 The simple believes every word,
But the prudent considers well his steps.
16 A wise *man* fears and departs from evil,
But a fool rages and is self-confident.
17 A quick-tempered *man* acts foolishly,
And a man of wicked intentions is
hated.
18 The simple inherit folly,
But the prudent are crowned with
knowledge.
19 The evil will bow before the good,

13:23 [a]Literally *what is swept away*
14:14 [a]Literally *from above himself*

SOUL NOTE

Balancing Act *(13:24)* When it comes to raising children, Scripture condemns the two extremes of permissiveness and child abuse. Proverbs emphasizes that parental discipline is an expression of love. Discipline and correction are a parent's way of showing love and concern. Undisciplined children often develop insecurity and a poor self-image. Moreover, they don't know how to act properly in many situations. Proper and consistent discipline, done with a balance of love and concern, communicates to a child that he or she is genuinely loved. **Topic: Child Discipline**

And the wicked at the gates of the
righteous.

20 The poor *man* is hated even by his own
neighbor,
But the rich *has* many friends.
21 He who despises his neighbor sins;
But he who has mercy on the poor,
happy *is* he.

22 Do they not go astray who devise evil?
But mercy and truth *belong* to those who
devise good.

23 In all labor there is profit,
But idle chatter[a] *leads* only to poverty.

24 The crown of the wise is their riches,
But the foolishness of fools *is* folly.

25 A true witness delivers souls,
But a deceitful *witness* speaks lies.

26 In the fear of the LORD *there is* strong
confidence,
And His children
will have a
place of refuge.
27 The fear of the
LORD *is* a
fountain of life,
To turn *one* away
from the snares
of death.

28 In a multitude of people *is* a king's
honor,
But in the lack of people *is* the downfall
of a prince.

29 *He who is* slow to wrath has great
understanding,
But *he who is* impulsive[a] exalts folly.

30 A sound heart *is* life to the body,
But envy *is* rottenness to the bones.

31 He who oppresses the poor reproaches
his Maker,
But he who honors Him has mercy on
the needy.

32 The wicked is banished in his
wickedness,
But the righteous has a refuge in his
death.

33 Wisdom rests in the heart of him who
has understanding,
But *what is* in the heart of fools is made
known.

34 Righteousness exalts a nation,
But sin *is* a reproach to *any* people.

35 The king's favor *is* toward a wise
servant,
But his wrath *is against* him who causes
shame.

15 A soft answer turns away wrath,
But a harsh word stirs up anger.
2 The tongue of the wise uses knowledge
rightly,
But the mouth of fools pours forth
foolishness.

3 The eyes of the LORD *are* in every place,
Keeping watch on the evil and the good.

4 A wholesome
tongue *is* a tree
of life,
But perverseness
in it breaks the
spirit.

A soft answer turns away wrath, but
a harsh word stirs up anger.
PROVERBS 15:1

5 A fool despises his father's instruction,
But he who receives correction is
prudent.

6 *In* the house of the righteous *there is*
much treasure,
But in the revenue of the wicked is
trouble.

7 The lips of the wise disperse knowledge,
But the heart of the fool *does* not *do* so.

8 The sacrifice of the wicked *is* an
abomination to the LORD,
But the prayer of the upright *is* His
delight.
9 The way of the wicked *is* an
abomination to the LORD,

14:23 [a]Literally *talk of the lips* **14:29** [a]Literally *short of spirit*

But He loves him who follows
righteousness.

10 Harsh discipline *is* for him who forsakes
the way,
And he who hates correction will die.

11 Hell[a] and Destruction[b] *are* before the
LORD;
So how much more the hearts of the
sons of men.

12 A scoffer does not love one who corrects
him,
Nor will he go to the wise.

13 A merry heart makes a cheerful
countenance,
But by sorrow of the heart the spirit is
broken.

14 The heart of him who has understanding
seeks knowledge,
But the mouth of fools feeds on
foolishness.

15 All the days of the afflicted *are*
evil,
But he who is of a merry heart *has* a
continual feast.

16 Better *is* a little with the fear of the
LORD,
Than great treasure with trouble.

17 Better *is* a dinner of herbs[a] where love
is,
Than a fatted calf with hatred.

18 A wrathful man stirs up strife,
But *he who is* slow to anger allays
contention.

19 The way of the lazy *man is* like a hedge
of thorns,
But the way of the upright *is* a
highway.

20 A wise son makes a father glad,
But a foolish man despises his mother.

21 Folly *is* joy *to him who is* destitute of
discernment,
But a man of understanding walks
uprightly.

22 Without counsel, plans go awry,
But in the multitude of counselors they
are established.

15:11 [a]Or *Sheol* [b]Hebrew *Abaddon* **15:17** [a]Or *vegetables*

KEY PASSAGE

Joy

REJOICE!

(15:13–15)

The Bible is a book of joy. God wants His people to be in right relationship with Him, and He promises that He will give them joy.

- Jesus prayed for His followers to have His joy (John 15:11; 17:13).
- Belief in Christ gives "joy inexpressible" (1 Pet. 1:8).
- In a time of trial, God's people can "count it all joy" (James 1:2).
- A fruit of the Spirit is joy (Gal. 5:22).
- Believers look forward to God's kingdom, described as "righteousness and peace and joy in the Holy Spirit" (Rom. 14:17).

The joy given by God should give us "a cheerful countenance" and "a merry heart" (Prov. 15:13, 15). God's people should be the most joyful people there are, because they know God, His love and salvation, and their eternal destiny. "Rejoice in the Lord always. Again I will say, rejoice!" (Phil. 4:4).

To Learn More: Turn to the article about joy on pages 614, 615. See also the personality profile of Isaac on page 31.

23 A man has joy by the answer of his mouth,
And a word *spoken* in due season, how good *it is!*

24 The way of life *winds* upward for the wise,
That he may turn away from hell[a] below.

25 The LORD will destroy the house of the proud,
But He will establish the boundary of the widow.

26 The thoughts of the wicked *are* an abomination to the LORD,
But *the words* of the pure *are* pleasant.

27 He who is greedy for gain troubles his own house,
But he who hates bribes will live.

28 The heart of the righteous studies how to answer,
But the mouth of the wicked pours forth evil.

29 The LORD *is* far from the wicked,
But He hears the prayer of the righteous.

30 The light of the eyes rejoices the heart,
And a good report makes the bones healthy.[a]

31 The ear that hears the rebukes of life
Will abide among the wise.
32 He who disdains instruction despises his own soul,
But he who heeds rebuke gets understanding.
33 The fear of the LORD *is* the instruction of wisdom,
And before honor *is* humility.

16 The preparations of the heart *belong* to man,
But the answer of the tongue *is* from the LORD.

2 All the ways of a man *are* pure in his own eyes,
But the LORD weighs the spirits.

3 Commit your works to the LORD,
And your thoughts will be established.

4 The LORD has made all for Himself,
Yes, even the wicked for the day of doom.

5 Everyone proud in heart *is* an abomination to the LORD;
Though they join forces,[a] none will go unpunished.

When a man's ways please the LORD, he makes even his enemies to be at peace with him.
PROVERBS 16:7

6 In mercy and truth
Atonement is provided for iniquity;
And by the fear of the LORD *one* departs from evil.

7 When a man's ways please the LORD,
He makes even his enemies to be at peace with him.

8 Better *is* a little with righteousness,
Than vast revenues without justice.

9 A man's heart plans his way,
But the LORD directs his steps.

10 Divination *is* on the lips of the king;
His mouth must not transgress in judgment.
11 Honest weights and scales *are* the LORD's;
All the weights in the bag *are* His work.
12 *It is* an abomination for kings to commit wickedness,
For a throne is established by righteousness.
13 Righteous lips *are* the delight of kings,
And they love him who speaks *what is* right.
14 As messengers of death *is* the king's wrath,
But a wise man will appease it.

15:24 [a]Or *Sheol* **15:30** [a]Literally *fat*
16:5 [a]Literally *hand to hand*

15 In the light of the king's face *is* life,
And his favor *is* like a cloud of the latter rain.

16 How much better to get wisdom than gold!
And to get understanding is to be chosen rather than silver.

17 The highway of the upright *is* to depart from evil;
He who keeps his way preserves his soul.

18 Pride *goes* before destruction,
And a haughty spirit before a fall.
19 Better *to be* of a humble spirit with the lowly,
Than to divide the spoil with the proud.

20 He who heeds the word wisely will find good,
And whoever trusts in the LORD, happy *is* he.

21 The wise in heart will be called prudent,
And sweetness of the lips increases learning.

22 Understanding *is* a wellspring of life to him who has it.
But the correction of fools *is* folly.

23 The heart of the wise teaches his mouth,
And adds learning to his lips.

24 Pleasant words *are like* a honeycomb,
Sweetness to the soul and health to the bones.

25 There is a way *that seems* right to a man,
But its end *is* the way of death.

26 The person who labors, labors for himself,
For his *hungry* mouth drives him *on*.

27 An ungodly man digs up evil,
And *it is* on his lips like a burning fire.
28 A perverse man sows strife,
And a whisperer separates the best of friends.
29 A violent man entices his neighbor,
And leads him in a way *that is* not good.
30 He winks his eye to devise perverse things;
He purses his lips *and* brings about evil.

31 The silver-haired head *is* a crown of glory,
If it is found in the way of righteousness.

32 *He who is* slow to anger *is* better than the mighty,
And he who rules his spirit than he who takes a city.

33 The lot is cast into the lap,
But its every decision *is* from the LORD.

17 Better *is* a dry morsel with quietness,
Than a house full of feasting[a] *with* strife.

2 A wise servant will rule over a son who causes shame,
And will share an inheritance among the brothers.

3 The refining pot *is* for silver and the furnace for gold,
But the LORD tests the hearts.

17:1 [a]Or *sacrificial meals*

SOUL NOTE

Look Down, Look Out *(16:18)* The Bible warns about the dangers of pride. At its root, pride is really the idolatry of self—worshiping oneself instead of God. A proud attitude says, "I don't need God, I can handle this myself." It is a "haughty spirit" by which people think they can look down on everyone and everything else. Such an attitude, says the Bible, goes "before a fall." Whenever people let pride control their thoughts and actions, they may succeed temporarily, but ultimately they are headed for disaster. **Topic: Pride**

4 An evildoer gives heed to false lips;
A liar listens eagerly to a spiteful tongue.

5 He who mocks the poor reproaches his Maker;
He who is glad at calamity will not go unpunished.

6 Children's children *are* the crown of old men,
And the glory of children *is* their father.

7 Excellent speech is not becoming to a fool,
Much less lying lips to a prince.

8 A present *is* a precious stone in the eyes of its possessor;
Wherever he turns, he prospers.

9 He who covers a transgression seeks love,
But he who repeats a matter separates friends.

10 Rebuke is more effective for a wise *man*
Than a hundred blows on a fool.

11 An evil *man* seeks only rebellion;
Therefore a cruel messenger will be sent against him.

12 Let a man meet a bear robbed of her cubs,
Rather than a fool in his folly.

13 Whoever rewards evil for good,
Evil will not depart from his house.

14 The beginning of strife *is like* releasing water;
Therefore stop contention before a quarrel starts.

15 He who justifies the wicked, and he who condemns the just,
Both of them alike *are* an abomination to the LORD.

16 Why *is there* in the hand of a fool the purchase price of wisdom,
Since *he has* no heart *for it?*

17 A friend loves at all times,
And a brother is born for adversity.

18 A man devoid of understanding shakes hands in a pledge,
And becomes surety for his friend.

19 He who loves transgression loves strife,
And he who exalts his gate seeks destruction.

20 He who has a deceitful heart finds no good,
And he who has a perverse tongue falls into evil.

21 He who begets a scoffer *does so* to his sorrow,
And the father of a fool has no joy.

22 A merry heart does good, *like* medicine,[a]
But a broken spirit dries the bones.

23 A wicked *man* accepts a bribe behind the back[a]
To pervert the ways of justice.

17:22 [a]Or *makes medicine even better*
17:23 [a]Literally *from the bosom*

SOUL NOTE

Children's Glory *(17:6)* The Bible takes a high view of children and of parenting. The picture that "children's children are the crown of old men" makes many grandfathers nod in agreement. The statement that "the glory of children is their father" makes many fathers feel the weight of their responsibility. Children do indeed look up to their fathers with great respect, and wise fathers do well to take that respect seriously by how they raise their children, how they live, and how they love. Fathers are always having an effect for good and bad on their kids. **Topic: Fatherhood**

24 Wisdom *is* in the sight of him who has
understanding,
But the eyes of a fool *are* on the ends of
the earth.

25 A foolish son *is* a grief to his father,
And bitterness to her who bore him.

26 Also, to punish the righteous *is* not
good,
Nor to strike princes for *their*
uprightness.

27 He who has knowledge spares his words,
And a man of understanding is of a calm
spirit.
28 Even a fool is counted wise when he
holds his peace;
When he shuts his lips, *he is considered*
perceptive.

18 A man who isolates himself seeks his
own desire;
He rages against all wise judgment.

2 A fool has no delight in understanding,
But in expressing his own heart.

3 When the wicked comes, contempt
comes also;
And with dishonor *comes* reproach.

4 The words of a man's mouth *are* deep
waters;
The wellspring of wisdom *is* a flowing
brook.

5 *It is* not good to show partiality to the
wicked,
Or to overthrow the righteous in
judgment.

6 A fool's lips enter into contention,
And his mouth calls for blows.
7 A fool's mouth *is* his destruction,
And his lips *are* the snare of his soul.
8 The words of a talebearer *are* like tasty
trifles,[a]
And they go down into the inmost body.

9 He who is slothful in his work
Is a brother to him who is a great
destroyer.

10 The name of the LORD *is* a strong tower;
The righteous run to it and are safe.
11 The rich man's wealth *is* his strong city,
And like a high wall in his own esteem.

12 Before destruction the heart of a man is
haughty,
And before honor *is* humility.

13 He who answers a matter before he
hears *it*,
It *is* folly and shame to him.

18:8 [a]A Jewish tradition reads *wounds.*

KEY PASSAGE

GOOD MEDICINE

(17:22)

A right relationship with God gives people joy (1 Pet. 1:8). That joy gives a merry heart (Prov. 15:15). That merry heart, in turn, "does good, like medicine." There is a definite relationship between godliness, joy, and good health. When people's consciences are clear and their hearts are right with God, they can experience good emotional health no matter what their circumstances. In turn, that affects their physical health. Modern science has shown the correlation between emotional and physical health; King Solomon already knew that, stating, "a broken spirit dries the bones." The bottom line: God's people should be joyful, allowing that joy to permeate every area of their lives. This will have a positive effect on both their emotional and physical health.

To Learn More: Turn to the article about health/spirituality on pages 402, 403. See also the personality profile of Paul on page 1536.

14 The spirit of a man will sustain him in sickness,
But who can bear a broken spirit?

15 The heart of the prudent acquires knowledge,
And the ear of the wise seeks knowledge.

16 A man's gift makes room for him,
And brings him before great men.

17 The first *one* to plead his cause *seems* right,
Until his neighbor comes and examines him.

18 Casting lots causes contentions to cease,
And keeps the mighty apart.

19 A brother offended *is harder to win* than a strong city,
And contentions *are* like the bars of a castle.

20 A man's stomach shall be satisfied from the fruit of his mouth;
From the produce of his lips he shall be filled.

21 Death and life *are* in the power of the tongue,
And those who love it will eat its fruit.

22 *He who* finds a wife finds a good *thing*,
And obtains favor from the LORD.

23 The poor *man* uses entreaties,
But the rich answers roughly.

24 A man *who has* friends must himself be friendly,[a]
But there is a friend *who* sticks closer than a brother.

19

Better *is* the poor who walks in his integrity
Than *one who is* perverse in his lips, and is a fool.

2 Also it is not good *for* a soul *to be* without knowledge,
And he sins who hastens with *his* feet.

3 The foolishness of a man twists his way,
And his heart frets against the LORD.

4 Wealth makes many friends,
But the poor is separated from his friend.

5 A false witness will not go unpunished,
And *he who* speaks lies will not escape.

6 Many entreat the favor of the nobility,
And every man *is* a friend to one who gives gifts.

7 All the brothers of the poor hate him;
How much more do his friends go far from him!
He may pursue *them with* words, *yet* they abandon *him*.

8 He who gets wisdom loves his own soul;
He who keeps understanding will find good.

9 A false witness will not go unpunished,
And *he who* speaks lies shall perish.

18:24 [a]Following Greek manuscripts, Syriac, Targum, and Vulgate; Masoretic Text reads *may come to ruin.*

SOUL NOTE

Just Between Us *(18:8)* Gossip wounds people. It can deeply hurt families, communities, and churches. Gossips love to take their pieces of information, their "tasty trifles," and pass them along. They have so little to occupy their minds that they feed on others' problems. Often their motive is attention, or maybe they wish to put someone down to raise themselves up. Gossip can take place when sharing prayer requests, or in blatantly divulging harmful pieces of information "just between us." Don't pass along "tasty trifles." Refuse to take part in gossip. **Topic: Gossip**

10 Luxury is not fitting for a fool,
Much less for a servant to rule over princes.

11 The discretion of a man makes him slow to anger,
And his glory *is* to overlook a transgression.

12 The king's wrath *is* like the roaring of a lion,
But his favor *is* like dew on the grass.

13 A foolish son *is* the ruin of his father,
And the contentions of a wife *are* a continual dripping.

14 Houses and riches *are* an inheritance from fathers,
But a prudent wife *is* from the LORD.

15 Laziness casts *one* into a deep sleep,
And an idle person will suffer hunger.

16 He who keeps the commandment keeps his soul,
But he who is careless[a] of his ways will die.

17 He who has pity on the poor lends to the LORD,
And He will pay back what he has given.

18 Chasten your son while there is hope,
And do not set your heart on his destruction.[a]

19 *A man of* great wrath will suffer punishment;
For if you rescue *him,* you will have to do it again.

20 Listen to counsel and receive instruction,
That you may be wise in your latter days.

21 There are many plans in a man's heart,
Nevertheless the LORD's counsel—that will stand.

22 What is desired in a man is kindness,
And a poor man is better than a liar.

23 The fear of the LORD *leads* to life,
And *he who has it* will abide in satisfaction;
He will not be visited with evil.

24 A lazy *man* buries his hand in the bowl,[a]
And will not so much as bring it to his mouth again.

25 Strike a scoffer, and the simple will become wary;
Rebuke one who has understanding, *and* he will discern knowledge.

26 He who mistreats *his* father *and* chases away *his* mother
Is a son who causes shame and brings reproach.

27 Cease listening to instruction, my son,
And you will stray from the words of knowledge.

28 A disreputable witness scorns justice,
And the mouth of the wicked devours iniquity.

19:16 [a]Literally *despises,* figurative of recklessness or carelessness **19:18** [a]Literally *to put him to death;* a Jewish tradition reads *on his crying.* **19:24** [a]Septuagint and Syriac read *bosom;* Targum and Vulgate read *armpit.*

SOUL NOTE

Fix the Faucet *(19:13, 14)* In our families we reveal our real selves. At times, actions and attitudes are at their worst at home. There is nothing worse than living in a family filled with turmoil, where a foolish child has broken a parent's heart or where grouchy spouses nag at each other like dripping faucets. The practical truths expressed in Proverbs are reminders of the importance of healthy family living. Family members should learn to treat one another with love and respect so that home is not a place of turmoil, but of blessing. **Topic: Family Life**

29 Judgments are prepared for scoffers,
And beatings for the backs of fools.

20

Wine *is* a mocker,
Strong drink *is* a brawler,
And whoever is led astray by it is not wise.

2 The wrath[a] of a king *is* like the roaring of a lion;
Whoever provokes him to anger sins *against* his own life.

3 *It is* honorable for a man to stop striving,
Since any fool can start a quarrel.

4 The lazy *man* will not plow because of winter;
He will beg during harvest and *have* nothing.

5 Counsel in the heart of man *is like* deep water,
But a man of understanding will draw it out.

6 Most men will proclaim each his own goodness,
But who can find a faithful man?

7 The righteous *man* walks in his integrity;
His children *are* blessed after him.

8 A king who sits on the throne of judgment
Scatters all evil with his eyes.

9 Who can say, "I have made my heart clean,
I am pure from my sin"?

10 Diverse weights *and* diverse measures,
They *are* both alike, an abomination to the LORD.

11 Even a child is known by his deeds,
Whether what he does *is* pure and right.

12 The hearing ear and the seeing eye,
The LORD has made them both.

13 Do not love sleep, lest you come to poverty;
Open your eyes, *and* you will be satisfied with bread.

14 "*It is* good for nothing,"[a] cries the buyer;
But when he has gone his way, then he boasts.

15 There is gold and a multitude of rubies,
But the lips of knowledge *are* a precious jewel.

16 Take the garment of one who is surety *for* a stranger,
And hold it as a pledge *when it* is for a seductress.

17 Bread gained by deceit *is* sweet to a man,
But afterward his mouth will be filled with gravel.

18 Plans are established by counsel;
By wise counsel wage war.

19 He who goes about *as* a talebearer reveals secrets;
Therefore do not associate with one who flatters with his lips.

20 Whoever curses his father or his mother,
His lamp will be put out in deep darkness.

21 An inheritance gained hastily at the beginning
Will not be blessed at the end.

22 Do not say, "I will recompense evil";
Wait for the LORD, and He will save you.

23 Diverse weights *are* an abomination to the LORD,
And dishonest scales *are* not good.

24 A man's steps *are* of the LORD;
How then can a man understand his own way?

25 *It is* a snare for a man to devote rashly *something as* holy,
And afterward to reconsider *his* vows.

20:2 [a]Literally *fear* or *terror* which is produced by the king's wrath **20:14** [a]Literally *evil, evil*

26 A wise king sifts out the wicked,
And brings the threshing wheel over
them.

27 The spirit of a man *is* the lamp of the
LORD,
Searching all the inner depths of his
heart.[a]

28 Mercy and truth preserve the king,
And by lovingkindness he upholds his
throne.

29 The glory of young men *is* their
strength,
And the splendor of old men *is* their
gray head.

30 Blows that hurt cleanse away evil,
As *do* stripes the inner depths of the
heart.[a]

21 The king's heart *is* in the hand of the
LORD,
Like the rivers of water; He turns it
wherever He wishes.

2 Every way of a man *is* right in his own
eyes,
But the LORD weighs the hearts.

3 To do righteousness and justice
Is more acceptable to the LORD than
sacrifice.

4 A haughty look, a proud heart,
And the plowing[a] of the wicked *are*
sin.

5 The plans of the diligent *lead* surely to
plenty,
But *those of* everyone *who is* hasty,
surely to poverty.

6 Getting treasures by a lying tongue
Is the fleeting fantasy of those who seek
death.[a]

7 The violence of the wicked will destroy
them,[a]
Because they refuse to do justice.

8 The way of a guilty man *is* perverse;[a]
But *as for* the pure, his work *is* right.

9 Better to dwell in a corner of a housetop,
Than in a house shared with a
contentious woman.

10 The soul of the wicked desires evil;
His neighbor finds no favor in his eyes.

11 When the scoffer is punished, the simple
is made wise;
But when the wise is instructed, he
receives knowledge.

12 The righteous *God* wisely considers the
house of the wicked,
Overthrowing the wicked for *their*
wickedness.

13 Whoever shuts his ears to the cry of the
poor
Will also cry himself and not be heard.

14 A gift in secret pacifies anger,
And a bribe behind the back,[a] strong
wrath.

15 *It is* a joy for the just to do justice,
But destruction *will come* to the workers
of iniquity.

16 A man who wanders from the way of
understanding
Will rest in the assembly of the dead.

17 He who loves pleasure *will be* a poor
man;
He who loves wine and oil will not be
rich.

18 The wicked *shall be* a ransom for the
righteous,
And the unfaithful for the upright.

19 Better to dwell in the wilderness,
Than with a contentious and angry
woman.

20:27 [a]Literally *the rooms of the belly*
20:30 [a]Literally *the rooms of the belly* **21:4** [a]Or *lamp* **21:6** [a]Septuagint reads *Pursue vanity on the snares of death;* Vulgate reads *Is vain and foolish, and shall stumble on the snares of death;* Targum reads *They shall be destroyed, and they shall fall who seek death.* **21:7** [a]Literally *drag them away* **21:8** [a]Or *The way of a man is perverse and strange* **21:14** [a]Literally *in the bosom*

Parenting

GODLY PARENTING

GRACE KETTERMAN

(Proverbs 22:6)

Parents today are grossly confused by lovely-sounding misinformation about how to raise children. An example is the rose theory. It alleges that children are like rosebuds. If no one bothers or interferes with them, they will naturally unfold into gorgeous roses. Sounds lovely! Trouble is, of course, children are not born into the plant kingdom! Children need strong and loving parents. Following are seven functions of great parenting.

NURTURING

Beyond the obvious nurturing found in healthy food, parents must feed children spiritually, mentally, emotionally, and socially. They are to teach them to play and to pray, to laugh and to cry, to handle anger correctly, to express sadness, and to recover from loss and grief. They can teach them to think, to listen, to learn, and to communicate. Above all, they must teach them about God.

PROTECTION

No infant could survive long without the protection of a loving parent. Good parents must find the proper balance of protection without overprotection. In an increasingly violent world, physical protection demands constant vigilance.

But in the eternal sense, parents must protect their children's minds. By example and teaching, parents can and must protect children from agnosticism, prejudice, and hatred. They must counter cultural trends toward superficiality and materialism, and children must be trained in the way to live so as to guard against these things. Even though they may temporarily rebel, they are likely to return to those good early teachings (Prov. 22:6).

CREATIVITY

God has given scientists knowledge that can enable most couples who have difficulty conceiving and bearing children to do so. But those who cannot conceive and carry to term might yet become parents by adoption. A friend adopted a year-old foster child. While waiting to receive the child, she learned about the foster mom—what perfume she wore, how she held, fed and changed the baby. This wise adoptive mother made the baby's transition to a new home easier.

Good parents are creative in the ways they live—how they correct their children, spend their money, plan for the future, and teach the truth of God to their families (Deut. 6:4–9).

EDUCATION

Many parents of toddlers these days seek the preschool that offers the best academic program, but preschoolers need something much more basic than knowledge. They must have the foundation of trust. Trust comes from parents' consistent response to the child's needs. The response may be in tender love or tough, but the certainty that Mom and Dad are there, they care, and they will take charge provides healthy, growing trust.

Preschoolers who learn to respect boundaries and obey rules become far safer teens. Proverbs 29:15, 17 makes it clear that children respond to the rod of correction. I like to think of this rod as that of the ever-present shepherd's rod, used to prod the wayward sheep away from danger. At times, the crook must rescue the lamb that evaded the prods and fell into real danger.

Children can learn to know right from wrong. They must learn the qualities that later become the fruits of the Holy Spirit—love, joy, peace, longsuffering, kindness, goodness, faithfulness, gentleness, and self-control (Gal. 5:22, 23). By demonstrating these superb values, parents are preparing their children for eternity.

MOTIVATION

My father would regularly ask me, "Grace, do you think you'll ever amount to anything?" His face showed me he knew I would, but he set me thinking. His further teaching was that my life was not an accident, that God had His best plan for my life. My job was to find and follow it.

Motivation to make one's life count for God is imparted by parents who bless their children with this truth and help them discover God's best. Sadly, some parents try to motivate success by pronouncing negative predictions. Done in anger, these statements become a curse, causing some children to fail because they come to believe these curses are true. God prompted Paul to write, "Children, obey your parents in all things. . . . Fathers, do not provoke your children, lest they become discouraged" (Col. 3:20, 21). When parents bless their children, it is easier for children to be obedient.

RELINQUISHMENT

The main goal of godly parenting is to turn out useful, God-fearing adults whose lives will matter. Teaching responsibility by assigning tasks, instructing as to how to do them well, and then expressing approval and appreciation will prepare children to become healthy, independent adults.

However, releasing young people into today's world is a panicky process. This process can be made more reassuring when parents remember that they are transferring them from the shelter of their parental wings to the perfect care of the heavenly Father.

A PLACE FOR RETURNING

My mom and dad are gone now, and so is the warm old home. I now visit the nearby cemetery. There I smile and remember. I weep and miss the old love. But I go from there a stronger woman because I know I'm a composite of the nurturing, protection, creativity, education, motivation, and relinquishment they put together. Above all and surrounding all is the certainty they gave me that I am a child of God, relying on Him.

FURTHER MEDITATION:

Other passages to study about the issue of parenting include:

➢ Deuteronomy 6:4–9; 11:18, 19
➢ 1 Samuel 1:19–28
➢ Psalms 34:11; 127:3–5
➢ Proverbs 23:15–26
➢ Matthew 19:14
➢ 1 Timothy 5:4
➢ 2 Timothy 1:5

To Learn More: Turn to the key passage note on parenting at I Samuel 1:27, 28 on page 344. See also the personality profile of Abraham on page 26.

20 *There is* desirable treasure,
And oil in the dwelling of the wise,
But a foolish man squanders it.

21 He who follows righteousness and mercy
Finds life, righteousness and honor.

22 A wise *man* scales the city of the mighty,
And brings down the trusted stronghold.

23 Whoever guards his mouth and tongue
Keeps his soul from troubles.

24 A proud *and* haughty *man*—
"Scoffer" *is* his name;
He acts with arrogant pride.

Whoever guards his mouth and tongue keeps his soul from troubles.
PROVERBS 21:23

25 The desire of the lazy *man* kills him,
For his hands refuse to labor.
26 He covets greedily all day long,
But the righteous gives and does not spare.

27 The sacrifice of the wicked *is* an abomination;
How much more *when* he brings it with wicked intent!

28 A false witness shall perish,
But the man who hears *him* will speak endlessly.

29 A wicked man hardens his face,
But *as for* the upright, he establishes[a] his way.

30 *There is* no wisdom or understanding
Or counsel against the LORD.

31 The horse *is* prepared for the day of battle,
But deliverance *is* of the LORD.

22 A *good* name is to be chosen rather than great riches,
Loving favor rather than silver and gold.

2 The rich and the poor have this in common,
The LORD *is* the maker of them all.

3 A prudent *man* foresees evil and hides himself,
But the simple pass on and are punished.

4 By humility *and* the fear of the LORD
Are riches and honor and life.

5 Thorns *and* snares *are* in the way of the perverse;
He who guards his soul will be far from them.

6 Train up a child in the way he should go,
And when he is old he will not depart from it.

7 The rich rules over the poor,
And the borrower *is* servant to the lender.

8 He who sows iniquity will reap sorrow,
And the rod of his anger will fail.

9 He who has a generous eye will be blessed,
For he gives of his bread to the poor.

10 Cast out the scoffer, and contention will leave;
Yes, strife and reproach will cease.

11 He who loves purity of heart
And has grace on his lips,
The king *will be* his friend.

12 The eyes of the LORD preserve knowledge,
But He overthrows the words of the faithless.

13 The lazy *man* says, "*There is* a lion outside!
I shall be slain in the streets!"

14 The mouth of an immoral woman *is* a deep pit;
He who is abhorred by the LORD will fall there.

21:29 [a]Qere and Septuagint read *understands.*

15 Foolishness *is* bound up in the heart of a
child;
The rod of correction will drive it far
from him.

16 He who oppresses the poor to increase
his *riches,*
And he who gives to the rich, *will*
surely *come* to poverty.

Sayings of the Wise

17 Incline your ear and hear the words of
the wise,
And apply your heart to my
knowledge;
18 For *it is* a pleasant thing if you keep
them within you;
Let them all be fixed upon your lips,
19 So that your trust may be in the LORD;
I have instructed you today, even you.
20 Have I not written to you excellent
things
Of counsels and knowledge,
21 That I may make you know the certainty
of the words of truth,
That you may answer words of truth
To those who send to you?

22 Do not rob the poor because he *is*
poor,
Nor oppress the afflicted at the gate;
23 For the LORD will plead their cause,
And plunder the soul of those who
plunder them.

KEY PASSAGE

SPARE AND SPOIL

(22:15)

The Bible emphasizes the importance of parental instruction and correction in raising children. God has given parents the responsibility to train their children in the way they should go (Prov. 22:6). Parents must deal with misbehavior by using corrective discipline. The "rod of correction" has gotten bad press because of the problem of child abuse. Good parents, however, understand the need for the "rod of correction," such as a spanking, but not in anger and *never* abusive. This "rod," used sparingly for only blatant misbehavior (and not childish irresponsibility), is guaranteed to drive foolishness from the heart of a child. "Do not withhold correction from a child," continued Solomon, for it will "deliver his soul from hell" (Prov. 23:13, 14). Parents show great love for their children when they lovingly and consistently discipline them. When parents train their children in the way they should go, the parents have sown seeds of hope that when their children are old they "will not depart from it" (Prov. 22:6).

To Learn More: Turn to the article about child discipline on pages 830, 831. See also the personality profile of the wise son on page 802.

SOUL NOTE

Ready to Explode *(22:24, 25)* Anger can be a dangerous emotion if it energizes destructive behavior. This proverb encourages people to "make no friendship with an angry man." People may not be able to avoid the anger expressed by others, but they can avoid close ties with "furious" people. Such people are ready to explode, and those around them will either catch the brunt of that fury or become guilty by association. The advice to stay away from people who cannot control their anger should be taken seriously. People must choose carefully those who will be their closest friends, spouses, and business partners. **Topic: Anger**

Child Discipline

BRINGING OUT THE BEST IN A STRONG-WILLED CHILD

CYNTHIA ULRICH TOBIAS

(Proverbs 22:15)

"Michael Tobias, you need to pick those toys up and put them in the basket now!" Even as I heard myself issue the order to my four-year-old, I realized I was in trouble. I sometimes forget that I am dealing with a child who is just as strong-willed as I am, and barking out orders has never been an effective means of communicating with me. But I had already climbed out on my limb, and I was not about to come back.

Noting that Mike was making no move to clean up, I moved a little further out on the limb. "Mike, if I have to pick up those toys, I am going to give them to some other kids." He shrugged. "Give them to some other kids," he said. I could not hide my surprise. Some of those toys were among his favorites. But he had just climbed out on his limb, too. Without another word, I scooped up the toys and took them to the garage. Later in the week, I gave the toys to a ministry at our church. Six months later, he had never once asked for any of those toys. He knew that he had called my bluff, and he was fully prepared to accept the consequences.

Anyone with a strong-willed child already realizes that the discipline strategies that work for other kids simply do not have the same effect. From the cradle to the grave, strong-willed children will present challenges to their parents unlike other children. Although people have often been led to believe that strong will denotes defiance, rebellion, and disobedience, that steely determination does not have to be a negative trait! When parents know how to bring out the best in a strong-willed child, they find incredible strength and possibilities without sacrificing any bottom-line accountability.

STRONG-WILLED CHILDREN AND AUTHORITY

Strong-willed children do not have trouble with authority itself—only with how it is communicated. Strong-willed children know they should not get by with bad behavior. When they push, they want their parents to push back. They just don't want the parent to simply issue orders. These children want to be treated with respect and courtesy. Instead of saying, "Get downstairs right now and get in that car!" a parent will get better cooperation with "The car is leaving in two minutes—let's go!" Instead of, "You're not watching television until that homework gets done!" try "Feel free to turn on your favorite show as soon as your homework is done." A friendly, respectful tone does not indicate weakness on a parent's part if the bottom line stays intact.

STRONG-WILLED CHILDREN AND CONTROL

Strong-willed children do not need to control their parents—they just cannot let parents take all the control away from them. These children realize the bottom line early on when it comes to the issue of control. Children always have the choice to obey or disobey. If parents use words like, "You will . . ." or "This is how it's going to be . . ." strong-willed children may end up exercising the only control they have left—disobedience—even if the consequences are unpleasant or harmful. Parents can and should enforce the rules, but they need to realize that they cannot force a child to obey them. Inspire, motivate, hold the child accountable, and the parent will find that the child's obedience becomes less and less of a battleground.

STRONG-WILLED CHILDREN AND RELATIONSHIPS

The quality of the relationship between a child and parent determines the effectiveness of discipline strategies. If parents have cultivated a relationship with their strong-willed child, the child will try much harder to cooperate and keep parents happy. On the other hand, if a child senses that the parental relationship is hostile, he or she thinks, "Why bother? They don't like me anyway!" If a child perceives that parents spend the majority of their time yelling, the relationship seems hostile.

Strong-willed children who respect the relationship with their parents do not want to shame or embarrass them. These children must be convinced of the strength of a parent's love in order to be motivated not to disappoint or jeopardize the relationship. When strong-willed children surrender their strong will to Christ, they may do so not because of the threat of eternal punishment, but because of the promise of the wonderful relationship with Jesus Christ.

STRONG-WILLED CHILDREN AND SCRIPTURE

Some parents get a little defensive about seeking the cooperation of their children. After all, the Bible mandates that children should obey their parents, right? The often-quoted "Children, obey your parents" (Eph. 6:1) is followed by "Fathers, do not provoke your children to wrath" (Eph. 6:4). Also, Proverbs 22:6 teaches, "Train up a child in the way he should go, and when he is old he will not depart from it." For "in the way he should go," the Amplified Bible has "according to his individual gifts or bents." This means that parents must consider the ways of God and each child's uniqueness. No two children are the same, and no one method of discipline and correction will work for everyone. Understanding our children's unique gifts and bents helps us to be better parents. What should stay consistent is the love and respect we communicate to each unique creation God entrusts to our care.

FURTHER MEDITATION:

Other passages to study about the issue of child discipline include:

- ➢ Deuteronomy 6:5–9; 8:5
- ➢ Proverbs 3:11, 12; 19:18; 22:6, 15; 29:15, 17
- ➢ Ephesians 6:1–4

To Learn More: **Turn to the key passage note on child discipline at Proverbs 22:15 on page 829. See also the personality profile of the wise son on page 802.**

24 Make no friendship with an angry man,
And with a furious man do not go,
25 Lest you learn his ways
And set a snare for your soul.

26 Do not be one of those who shakes hands in a pledge,
One of those who is surety for debts;
27 If you have nothing *with which* to pay,
Why should he take away your bed from under you?

28 Do not remove the ancient landmark
Which your fathers have set.

29 Do you see a man *who* excels in his work?
He will stand before kings;
He will not stand before unknown *men.*

23 When you sit down to eat with a ruler,
Consider carefully what *is* before you;
2 And put a knife to your throat
If you *are* a man given to appetite.
3 Do not desire his delicacies,
For they *are* deceptive food.

4 Do not overwork to be rich;
Because of your own understanding, cease!
5 Will you set your eyes on that which is not?
For *riches* certainly make themselves wings;
They fly away like an eagle *toward* heaven.

6 Do not eat the bread of a miser,[a]
Nor desire his delicacies;
7 For as he thinks in his heart, so *is* he.
"Eat and drink!" he says to you,
But his heart is not with you.
8 The morsel you have eaten, you will vomit up,
And waste your pleasant words.

9 Do not speak in the hearing of a fool,
For he will despise the wisdom of your words.

10 Do not remove the ancient landmark,
Nor enter the fields of the fatherless;
11 For their Redeemer *is* mighty;
He will plead their cause against you.

12 Apply your heart to instruction,
And your ears to words of knowledge.

13 Do not withhold correction from a child,
For *if* you beat him with a rod, he will not die.
14 You shall beat him with a rod,
And deliver his soul from hell.[a]

23:6 [a]Literally *one who has an evil eye*
23:14 [a]Or *Sheol*

KEY PASSAGE

Eating Disorders

EATING TOO MUCH

(23:2)

Some people attempt to fill the emptiness in their lives with drugs, alcohol, sex, money, or even hard work. Others use food, and such people find themselves trapped in emotional eating—leading to such problems as obesity and bulimia. The Bible says, "Put a knife to your throat if you are a man given to appetite." The instruction graphically pictures cutting out anything that might lead to addictions in order to feed an appetite of some kind. There is nothing wrong with food. There must be a balance, however, between enjoying what God has provided, and using food to meet emotional needs and thus allowing it to control one's life. The fruit of the Spirit called self-control applies to many areas of life, including eating. God desires to fill any emptiness, helping us to lead balanced, healthy lives.

To Learn More: Turn to the article about eating disorders on pages 302, 303. See also the personality profile of Eli on page 350.

15 My son, if your heart is wise,
My heart will rejoice—indeed, I
myself;
16 Yes, my inmost being will rejoice
When your lips speak right things.

17 Do not let your heart envy sinners,
But *be zealous* for the fear of the LORD
all the day;
18 For surely there is a hereafter,
And your hope will not be cut off.

19 Hear, my son, and be wise;
And guide your heart in the way.
20 Do not mix with winebibbers,
Or with gluttonous eaters of meat;
21 For the drunkard and the glutton will
come to poverty,
And drowsiness will clothe *a man* with
rags.

22 Listen to your father who begot you,
And do not despise your mother when
she is old.

23 Buy the truth, and do not sell *it,*
Also wisdom and instruction and
understanding.

24 The father of the righteous will greatly
rejoice,
And he who begets a wise *child* will
delight in him.
25 Let your father and your mother be
glad,
And let her who bore you rejoice.

26 My son, give me your heart,
And let your eyes observe my ways.
27 For a harlot *is* a deep pit,
And a seductress *is* a narrow well.
28 She also lies in wait as *for* a victim,
And increases the unfaithful among men.

29 Who has woe?
Who has sorrow?
Who has contentions?
Who has complaints?
Who has wounds without cause?
Who has redness of eyes?
30 Those who linger long at the wine,
Those who go in search of mixed wine.
31 Do not look on the wine when it is red,
When it sparkles in the cup,
When it swirls around smoothly;
32 At the last it bites like a serpent,
And stings like a viper.
33 Your eyes will see strange things,
And your heart will utter perverse
things.
34 Yes, you will be like one who lies down
in the midst of the sea,

KEY PASSAGE

Drug Abuse

TOXIC WASTE

(23:19–21)

Like any loving father, Solomon advises his son to be wise and to stay away from drunkards. All those addicted to alcohol can tell you about the "drowsiness" it causes, but most probably won't admit to the possibility that their drinking could clothe them with rags. Yet alcohol often leads to loss—of reputation, money, marriage, family, or employment.

Alcohol, like most drugs, is a toxic poison to which the body reacts. People first must condition themselves to the taste of alcohol. Then they often indulge in excess and get drunk—a pattern that all too often becomes a way of life. Not only does that lead to often embarrassing situations, it also leads to sickness. People addicted to alcohol can't stop drinking—they feel that they must drink in order to get moving, get through the day, or get to sleep. Alcohol becomes more important for life than God. God's people must steer clear of such indulgences.

To Learn More: Turn to the article about drug abuse on pages 852, 853. See also the personality profile of Belshazzar on page 1113.

Or like one who lies at the top of the
mast, *saying:*
35 "They have struck me, *but* I was not hurt;
They have beaten me, but I did not feel
it.
When shall I awake, that I may seek
another *drink?"*

24 Do not be envious of evil men,
Nor desire to be with them;
2 For their heart devises violence,
And their lips talk of troublemaking.

3 Through wisdom a house is built,
And by understanding it is established;
4 By knowledge the rooms are filled
With all precious and pleasant riches.

5 A wise man *is* strong,
Yes, a man of knowledge increases
strength;
6 For by wise counsel you will wage your
own war,
And in a multitude of counselors *there is*
safety.

7 Wisdom *is* too lofty for a fool;
He does not open his mouth in the
gate.

8 He who plots to do evil
Will be called a schemer.
9 The devising of foolishness *is* sin,
And the scoffer *is* an abomination to
men.

10 *If* you faint in the day of adversity,
Your strength *is* small.

11 Deliver *those who* are drawn toward
death,
And hold back *those* stumbling to the
slaughter.
12 If you say, "Surely we did not know this,"
Does not He who weighs the hearts
consider *it?*
He who keeps your soul, does He *not*
know *it?*
And will He *not* render to *each* man
according to his deeds?

13 My son, eat honey because *it is* good,
And the honeycomb *which is* sweet to
your taste;
14 So *shall* the knowledge of wisdom *be* to
your soul;
If you have found *it,* there is a prospect,
And your hope will not be cut off.

15 Do not lie in wait, O wicked *man,*
against the dwelling of the righteous;
Do not plunder his resting place;
16 For a righteous *man* may fall seven
times
And rise again,
But the wicked shall fall by calamity.

KEY PASSAGE

Failure

TRY AGAIN

(24:16)

Failure is never final until a person quits trying. As the person continues to try, failure is really no more than a setback, a possibility to learn from mistakes and try again. This verse contrasts the righteous person and the wicked person. The righteous person may fail time and time again, but they continue to "rise again," to get up and keep trying. When the wicked person fails, however, they are led into a downward spiral that causes "calamity." There is no recovery, no learning, no more trying.

Failure is a part of the human experience. It can be painful and embarrassing, but it can also be a great teacher. God's definition of success does not preclude failure, but it includes a willingness to refuse to quit, to learn from one's mistakes, and to try again. Failure can be our greatest teacher.

To Learn More: Turn to the article about failure on pages 586, 587. See also the personality profile of Peter on page 1359.

17 Do not rejoice when your enemy falls,
And do not let your heart be glad when he stumbles;
18 Lest the LORD see *it,* and it displease Him,
And He turn away His wrath from him.

19 Do not fret because of evildoers,
Nor be envious of the wicked;
20 For there will be no prospect for the evil *man;*
The lamp of the wicked will be put out.

21 My son, fear the LORD and the king;
Do not associate with those given to change;
22 For their calamity will rise suddenly,
And who knows the ruin those two can bring?

FURTHER SAYINGS OF THE WISE

23 These *things* also *belong* to the wise:

It is not good to show partiality in judgment.
24 He who says to the wicked, "You *are* righteous,"
Him the people will curse;
Nations will abhor him.
25 But those who rebuke *the wicked* will have delight,
And a good blessing will come upon them.

26 He who gives a right answer kisses the lips.

27 Prepare your outside work,
Make it fit for yourself in the field;
And afterward build your house.

28 Do not be a witness against your neighbor without cause,
For would you deceive[a] with your lips?
29 Do not say, "I will do to him just as he has done to me;
I will render to the man according to his work."

30 I went by the field of the lazy *man,*
And by the vineyard of the man devoid of understanding;
31 And there it was, all overgrown with thorns;
Its surface was covered with nettles;
Its stone wall was broken down.
32 When I saw *it,* I considered *it* well;
I looked on *it and* received instruction:
33 A little sleep, a little slumber,
A little folding of the hands to rest;
34 So shall your poverty come *like* a prowler,
And your need like an armed man.

FURTHER WISE SAYINGS OF SOLOMON

25 These also *are* proverbs of Solomon
which the men of Hezekiah king of Judah copied:

2 *It is* the glory of God to conceal a matter,
But the glory of kings *is* to search out a matter.

3 *As* the heavens for height and the earth for depth,
So the heart of kings *is* unsearchable.

4 Take away the dross from silver,
And it will go to the silversmith *for* jewelry.
5 Take away the wicked from before the king,
And his throne will be established in righteousness.

6 Do not exalt yourself in the presence of the king,
And do not stand in the place of the great;
7 For *it is* better that he say to you,
"Come up here,"
Than that you should be put lower in the presence of the prince,
Whom your eyes have seen.

8 Do not go hastily to court;
For what will you do in the end,
When your neighbor has put you to shame?
9 Debate your case with your neighbor,
And do not disclose the secret to another;
10 Lest he who hears *it* expose your shame,
And your reputation be ruined.

24:28 [a]Septuagint and Vulgate read *Do not deceive.*

11 A word fitly spoken *is like* apples of gold
In settings of silver.
12 *Like* an earring of gold and an ornament
of fine gold
Is a wise rebuker
to an obedient
ear.

A word fitly spoken is like apples of gold in settings of silver.
PROVERBS 25:11

13 Like the cold of
snow in time of
harvest
Is a faithful messenger to those who
send him,
For he refreshes the soul of his
masters.

14 Whoever falsely boasts of giving
Is like clouds and wind without rain.

15 By long forbearance a ruler is
persuaded,
And a gentle tongue breaks a bone.

16 Have you found honey?
Eat only as much as you need,
Lest you be filled with it and vomit.

17 Seldom set foot in your neighbor's
house,
Lest he become weary of you and hate
you.

18 A man who bears false witness against
his neighbor
Is like a club, a sword, and a sharp
arrow.

19 Confidence in an unfaithful *man* in time
of trouble
Is like a bad tooth and a foot out of
joint.

20 *Like* one who takes away a garment in
cold weather,
And like vinegar on soda,
Is one who sings songs to a heavy heart.

21 If your enemy is hungry, give him bread
to eat;
And if he is thirsty, give him water to
drink;
22 For *so* you will heap coals of fire on his
head,
And the LORD will reward you.

23 The north wind brings forth rain,
And a backbiting tongue an angry
countenance.

24 *It is* better to dwell
in a corner of a
housetop,
Than in a house
shared with a
contentious
woman.

25 *As* cold water to a weary soul,
So *is* good news from a far country.

26 A righteous *man* who falters before the
wicked
Is like a murky spring and a polluted
well.

27 *It is* not good to eat much honey;
So to seek one's own glory *is not* glory.

28 Whoever *has* no rule over his own spirit
Is like a city broken down, without
walls.

26 As snow in summer and rain in
harvest,
So honor is not fitting for a fool.

2 Like a flitting sparrow, like a flying
swallow,
So a curse without cause shall not alight.

3 A whip for the horse,
A bridle for the donkey,
And a rod for the fool's back.
4 Do not answer a fool according to his
folly,
Lest you also be like him.
5 Answer a fool according to his folly,
Lest he be wise in his own eyes.
6 He who sends a message by the hand of
a fool
Cuts off *his own* feet *and* drinks
violence.
7 *Like* the legs of the lame that hang limp
Is a proverb in the mouth of fools.
8 Like one who binds a stone in a sling
Is he who gives honor to a fool.
9 *Like* a thorn *that* goes into the hand of a
drunkard
Is a proverb in the mouth of fools.

10 The great *God* who formed everything
Gives the fool *his* hire and the
transgressor *his* wages.[a]
11 As a dog returns to his own vomit,
So a fool repeats his folly.
12 Do you see a man wise in his own eyes?
There is more hope for a fool than for
him.

13 The lazy *man* says, "*There is* a lion in
the road!
A fierce lion *is* in the streets!"
14 *As* a door turns on its hinges,
So *does* the lazy *man* on his bed.
15 The lazy *man* buries his hand in the
bowl;[a]
It wearies him to bring it back to his
mouth.
16 The lazy *man is* wiser in his own eyes
Than seven men who can answer
sensibly.

17 He who passes by *and* meddles in a
quarrel not his own
Is like one who takes a dog by the ears.

18 Like a madman who throws firebrands,
arrows, and death,
19 *Is* the man *who* deceives his neighbor,
And says, "I was only joking!"

20 Where *there is* no wood, the fire goes
out;
And where *there is* no talebearer, strife
ceases.
21 *As* charcoal *is* to burning coals, and
wood to fire,
So *is* a contentious man to kindle strife.
22 The words of a talebearer *are* like tasty
trifles,
And they go down into the inmost body.
23 Fervent lips with a wicked heart
Are like earthenware covered with silver
dross.

24 He who hates, disguises *it* with his
lips,
And lays up deceit within himself;
25 When he speaks kindly, do not believe
him,
For *there are* seven abominations in his
heart;
26 *Though his* hatred is covered by deceit,
His wickedness will be revealed before
the assembly.

27 Whoever digs a pit will fall into it,
And he who rolls a stone will have it roll
back on him.

28 A lying tongue hates *those who are*
crushed by it,
And a flattering mouth works ruin.

27 Do not boast about tomorrow,
For you do not know what a day may
bring forth.

2 Let another man praise you, and not
your own mouth;
A stranger, and not your own lips.

3 A stone *is* heavy and sand *is* weighty,
But a fool's wrath *is* heavier than both
of them.

4 Wrath *is* cruel and anger a torrent,
But who *is* able to stand before
jealousy?

26:10 [a]The Hebrew is difficult; ancient and modern translators differ greatly. **26:15** [a]Compare 19:24

SOUL NOTE

Burn It Out *(26:20–26)* Repeating Proverbs 18:8, gossip is once again described as "tasty." Talebearers love to pass along information, but such people are no more than "fervent lips with a wicked heart" (26:23). Gossips cannot be trusted: When they speak kindly, they should not be believed (26:25). A gossip who willingly passes along information *to* us will also be glad to pass along information *about* us. Believers ought to avoid gossips. Listening to a gossip adds fuel to the fire; to refuse to listen will force the fire to burn itself out. **Topic: Gossip**

Gossip

THE POWER OF GOSSIP

DIANNA BOOHER

(Proverbs 26:20–26)

"Have you heard about what happened to her?" "If they didn't want people to know, they shouldn't have done it." "I'm just concerned about her marriage. I wanted others to know what I heard was happening so we could all pray about it."

Gossip embroils at least three people in a harmful activity: the speaker, the listener, and the person who is the topic of conversation. Gossip sneaks into conversations under the guise of innocent information, truthful facts, or even as a misguided matter of prayer. Gossip is not an innocent pastime. It is sin.

THE MATTER OF GOSSIP

Gossip, as opposed to innocent conversation, typically involves rumors, opinions, or "inside" information. The matter of gossip may even be truthful facts. However, the subject of the facts must be examined. Is it personal and private? Would the subject of the gossip consider the information intimate? Oftentimes, the very allure of gossip is its sensational subject matter that exploits another person's personal issues.

THE MANNER OF GOSSIP

Listeners can recognize the warning signs that a conversation is about to go downhill. Usually, gossip is shared in lowered tones among a select few people. In fact, Proverbs refers to a gossip as a "whisperer" (Prov. 16:28). Often, gossips feel inclined to add a caveat to their conversation with a demand for secrecy. "Don't tell anyone I said this but . . ." or a similar introduction should be a signal that the information should not be shared. Listening to the information will encourage the gossip to keep talking—to the next person and the next and the next.

THE MOTIVE OF GOSSIP

There are several common reasons why people succumb to the urge either to gossip or listen to gossip. Gossips often feel important that they have the inside story; it is their way of getting much-desired attention. Listeners may listen to the scoop for the same reason. They feel flattered to be included as part of the "in-the-know" group. Some people enjoy contention, and gossip becomes a means of fanning the flame. Some try to make up for their own sense of inadequacy by cutting down others. Discrediting another person offers a quick, although not permanent, fix for envious feelings. Boredom can also tempt the gossip into destructive conversation.

LISTENING TO GOSSIP

A nod or even silence is often taken as agreement to the rumor at hand. It's easy to get one's name passed along as a conspirator in the gossip: "Susan and I were talking about that yesterday. Frankly, we think . . ." Merely listening can embroil a person in the harmful effects of gossip. Another danger in listening to gossip is that it takes time away from important activities like family or a job. Gossip also becomes dangerous when we, as the listeners, become the targets to be influenced. One may be tempted to believe something untrue, thereby coloring one's judgment without all the facts.

RESPONDING TO GOSSIP

"I don't believe what you've heard is true." "I don't know about you, but I really don't pay much attention to the grapevine—things get so twisted." "Have you checked that out? Things like that have a way of being misinterpreted." Responses like these can discourage a gossip from continuing. Body language can also indicate one's disinterest.

When people discover themselves to be the object of gossip, they probably will want to set the record straight. The first inclination may be revenge. Instead, if the hurt is minor, they should ignore what they can. However, if personal integrity, credibility, job, or Christian witness may be in jeopardy, they must take action by going to the source of the gossip and setting the record straight with the appropriate truthful information. It should be clear to the gossips that they should discontinue saying anything more about the situation in light of the true facts. Many gossips will deny that they said what was heard, but most of them will stop once they know they have been identified as the source.

If Christians think their reputation may be damaged with others (a boss, spouse, neighbor) because of the rumor, they also may want to talk to those people to set the record straight. Without tattling on the gossip, they can explain the full situation and circumstances. Then they can take comfort in God's promise that He will take care of the situation in the big picture (Rom. 12:19). Graciousness is the best response to gossip.

QUITTING THE HABIT

A gossip must enlist the help of others in order to break the habit. Letting family and close friends know that one sincerely wants to stop gossiping helps stop gossip before it starts. Their gentle reminders (either verbally or with a subtle cue) will help curb the conversation when it gets dangerously close to gossip. Over time, they can learn to change the subject and go on to something else. Philippians 4:8 gives foolproof advice for getting over the habit of gossip: "Finally, brethren, whatever things are true, whatever things are noble, whatever things are just, whatever things are pure, whatever things are lovely, whatever things are of good report, if there is any virtue and if there is anything praiseworthy—meditate on these things."

FURTHER MEDITATION:

Other passages to study about the issue of gossip include:

- Leviticus 19:16
- Proverbs 11:9, 13; 16:28
- Ecclesiastes 7:21
- 2 Corinthians 12:20
- 1 Timothy 5:13
- 1 Peter 4:15

To Learn More: Turn to the key passage note on gossip at James 3:5–18 on page 1648. See also the personality profile of Diotrephes on page 1691.

5 Open rebuke *is* better
Than love carefully concealed.

6 Faithful *are* the wounds of a friend,
But the kisses of an enemy *are* deceitful.

7 A satisfied soul loathes the honeycomb,
But to a hungry soul every bitter thing *is* sweet.

8 Like a bird that wanders from its nest
Is a man who wanders from his place.

9 Ointment and perfume delight the heart,
And the sweetness of a man's friend *gives delight* by hearty counsel.

10 Do not forsake your own friend or your father's friend,
Nor go to your brother's house in the day of your calamity;
Better *is* a neighbor nearby than a brother far away.

11 My son, be wise, and make my heart glad,
That I may answer him who reproaches me.

12 A prudent *man* foresees evil *and* hides himself;
The simple pass on *and* are punished.

13 Take the garment of him who is surety for a stranger,
And hold it in pledge *when* he is surety for a seductress.

14 He who blesses his friend with a loud voice, rising early in the morning,
It will be counted a curse to him.

15 A continual dripping on a very rainy day
And a contentious woman are alike;
16 Whoever restrains her restrains the wind,
And grasps oil with his right hand.

17 *As* iron sharpens iron,
So a man sharpens the countenance of his friend.

18 Whoever keeps the fig tree will eat its fruit;
So he who waits on his master will be honored.

19 As in water face *reflects* face,
So a man's heart *reveals* the man.

20 Hell[a] and Destruction[b] are never full;
So the eyes of man are never satisfied.

21 The refining pot *is* for silver and the furnace for gold,
And a man *is valued* by what others say of him.

22 Though you grind a fool in a mortar with a pestle along with crushed grain,
Yet his foolishness will not depart from him.

23 Be diligent to know the state of your flocks,
And attend to your herds;
24 For riches *are* not forever,
Nor does a crown *endure* to all generations.

27:20 [a]Or *Sheol* [b]Hebrew *Abaddon*

SOUL NOTE

Sharpener *(27:17)* Believers' interaction with other believers is one of the most important aspects of Christian friendship and fellowship. Because they love us, Christian friends can hold us accountable, help us see our blind spots, and show us better ways to live. "As iron sharpens iron," one Christian can sharpen the other Christian's character by holding them accountable for words and actions. When we allow Christian friends to sharpen us, we can learn and grow in areas that we might never have noticed on our own. God can work through our believing friends to teach us and guide us. **Topic: Accountability**

25 *When* the hay is removed, and the tender grass shows itself,
And the herbs of the mountains are gathered in,
26 The lambs *will provide* your clothing,
And the goats the price of a field;
27 *You shall have* enough goats' milk for your food,
For the food of your household,
And the nourishment of your maidservants.

28

The wicked flee when no one pursues,
But the righteous are bold as a lion.

2 Because of the transgression of a land, many *are* its princes;
But by a man of understanding *and* knowledge
Right will be prolonged.

3 A poor man who oppresses the poor
Is like a driving rain which leaves no food.

4 Those who forsake the law praise the wicked,
But such as keep the law contend with them.

5 Evil men do not understand justice,
But those who seek the LORD understand all.

6 Better *is* the poor who walks in his integrity
Than one perverse *in his* ways, though he *be* rich.

7 Whoever keeps the law *is* a discerning son,
But a companion of gluttons shames his father.

8 One who increases his possessions by usury and extortion
Gathers it for him who will pity the poor.

9 One who turns away his ear from hearing the law,
Even his prayer *is* an abomination.

10 Whoever causes the upright to go astray in an evil way,
He himself will fall into his own pit;
But the blameless will inherit good.

11 The rich man *is* wise in his own eyes,
But the poor who has understanding searches him out.

12 When the righteous rejoice, *there is* great glory;
But when the wicked arise, men hide themselves.

13 He who covers his sins will not prosper,
But whoever confesses and forsakes *them* will have mercy.

14 Happy *is* the man who is always reverent,
But he who hardens his heart will fall into calamity.

15 *Like* a roaring lion and a charging bear
Is a wicked ruler over poor people.

16 A ruler who lacks understanding *is* a great oppressor,
But he who hates covetousness will prolong *his* days.

17 A man burdened with bloodshed will flee into a pit;
Let no one help him.

18 Whoever walks blamelessly will be saved,
But *he who is* perverse *in his* ways will suddenly fall.

19 He who tills his land will have plenty of bread,
But he who follows frivolity will have poverty enough!

20 A faithful man will abound with blessings,
But he who hastens to be rich will not go unpunished.

21 To show partiality *is* not good,
Because for a piece of bread a man will transgress.

22 A man with an evil eye hastens after
riches,
And does not consider that poverty will
come upon him.

23 He who rebukes a man will find more
favor afterward
Than he who flatters with the tongue.

24 Whoever robs his father or his mother,
And says, "*It is* no transgression,"
The same *is* companion to a destroyer.

25 He who is of a proud heart stirs up strife,
But he who trusts in the LORD will be
prospered.

26 He who trusts in his own heart is a fool,
But whoever walks wisely will be
delivered.

27 He who gives to the poor will not lack,
But he who hides his eyes will have
many curses.

28 When the wicked arise, men hide
themselves;
But when they perish, the righteous
increase.

29 He who is often rebuked, *and*
hardens *his* neck,
Will suddenly be destroyed, and that
without remedy.

2 When the righteous are in authority, the
people rejoice;
But when a wicked *man* rules, the
people groan.

3 Whoever loves wisdom makes his father
rejoice,
But a companion of harlots wastes *his*
wealth.

4 The king establishes the land by justice,
But he who receives bribes overthrows
it.

5 A man who flatters his neighbor
Spreads a net for his feet.

6 By transgression an evil man is snared,
But the righteous sings and rejoices.

7 The righteous considers the cause of the
poor,
But the wicked does not understand *such*
knowledge.

8 Scoffers set a city aflame,
But wise *men* turn away wrath.

9 *If* a wise man contends with a foolish
man,
Whether *the fool* rages or laughs, *there is*
no peace.

10 The bloodthirsty hate the blameless,
But the upright seek his well-being.[a]

11 A fool vents all his feelings,[a]
But a wise *man* holds them back.

12 If a ruler pays attention to lies,
All his servants *become* wicked.

13 The poor *man* and the oppressor have
this in common:
The LORD gives light to the eyes of
both.

14 The king who judges the poor with
truth,
His throne will be established forever.

15 The rod and rebuke give wisdom,
But a child left *to himself* brings shame
to his mother.

16 When the wicked are multiplied,
transgression increases;
But the righteous will see their fall.

17 Correct your son, and he will give you
rest;
Yes, he will give delight to your soul.

18 Where *there is* no revelation,[a] the people
cast off restraint;
But happy *is* he who keeps the law.

19 A servant will not be corrected by mere
words;
For though he understands, he will not
respond.

29:10 [a]Literally *soul* **29:11** [a]Literally *spirit*
29:18 [a]Or *prophetic vision*

20 Do you see a man hasty in his words?
There is more hope for a fool than for him.

21 He who pampers his servant from childhood
Will have him as a son in the end.

22 An angry man stirs up strife,
And a furious man abounds in transgression.

23 A man's pride will bring him low,
But the humble in spirit will retain honor.

24 Whoever is a partner with a thief hates his own life;
He swears to tell the truth,[a] but reveals nothing.

25 The fear of man brings a snare,
But whoever trusts in the LORD shall be safe.

26 Many seek the ruler's favor,
But justice for man *comes* from the LORD.

27 An unjust man *is* an abomination to the righteous,
And *he who is* upright in the way *is* an abomination to the wicked.

THE WISDOM OF AGUR

30 The words of Agur the son of Jakeh, *his* utterance. This man declared to Ithiel—to Ithiel and Ucal:

2 Surely I *am* more stupid than *any* man,
And do not have the understanding of a man.
3 I neither learned wisdom
Nor have knowledge of the Holy One.

4 Who has ascended into heaven, or descended?
Who has gathered the wind in His fists?
Who has bound the waters in a garment?
Who has established all the ends of the earth?
What *is* His name, and what *is* His Son's name,
If you know?

> Every word of God is pure;
> He is a shield to those who put their trust in Him.
> PROVERBS 30:5

5 Every word of God *is* pure;
He *is* a shield to those who put their trust in Him.
6 Do not add to His words,
Lest He rebuke you, and you be found a liar.

7 Two *things* I request of You
(Deprive me not before I die):
8 Remove falsehood and lies far from me;
Give me neither poverty nor riches—
Feed me with the food allotted to me;
9 Lest I be full and deny *You*,
And say, "Who *is* the LORD?"
Or lest I be poor and steal,
And profane the name of my God.

29:24 [a]Literally *hears the adjuration*

SOUL NOTE

God-given Responsibility *(29:15, 17)* Discipline teaches wisdom. Children who are lovingly disciplined learn right from wrong. Parents have the God-given responsibility to raise their children with correction and discipline so that those children grow into responsible adults. Proper, loving, and consistent discipline builds character and stability in children. Parents must take their responsibility seriously, preparing their children to become responsible adults who understand the love and discipline of God. **Topic: Child Discipline**

10 Do not malign a servant to his master,
Lest he curse you, and you be found
guilty.

11 *There is* a generation *that* curses its
father,
And does not bless its mother.
12 *There is* a generation *that is* pure in its
own eyes,
Yet is not washed from its filthiness.
13 *There is* a generation—oh, how lofty are
their eyes!
And their eyelids are lifted up.
14 *There is* a generation whose teeth *are*
like swords,
And whose fangs *are like* knives,
To devour the poor from off the earth,
And the needy from *among* men.

15 The leech has two daughters—
Give *and* Give!

There are three *things that* are never
satisfied,
Four never say, "Enough!":
16 The grave,[a]
The barren womb,
The earth *that* is not satisfied with
water—
And the fire never says, "Enough!"

17 The eye *that* mocks *his* father,
And scorns obedience to *his* mother,
The ravens of the valley will pick it out,
And the young eagles will eat it.

18 There are three *things which* are too
wonderful for me,
Yes, four *which* I do not understand:
19 The way of an eagle in the air,
The way of a serpent on a rock,
The way of a ship in the midst of the sea,
And the way of a man with a virgin.

20 This *is* the way of an adulterous woman:
She eats and wipes her mouth,
And says, "I have done no
wickedness."

21 For three *things* the earth is perturbed,
Yes, for four it cannot bear up:
22 For a servant when he reigns,
A fool when he is filled with food,
23 A hateful *woman* when she is married,
And a maidservant who succeeds her
mistress.

24 There are four *things which* are little on
the earth,
But they *are* exceedingly wise:
25 The ants *are* a people not strong,
Yet they prepare their food in the
summer;
26 The rock badgers[a] are a feeble folk,
Yet they make their homes in the crags;
27 The locusts have no king,
Yet they all advance in ranks;
28 The spider[a] skillfully grasps with its
hands,
And it is in kings' palaces.

29 There are three *things which* are majestic
in pace,
Yes, four *which* are stately in walk:
30 A lion, *which is* mighty among beasts
And does not turn away from any;
31 A greyhound,[a]
A male goat also,
And a king *whose* troops *are* with him.[b]

32 If you have been foolish in exalting
yourself,
Or if you have devised evil, *put your*
hand on *your* mouth.
33 For *as* the churning of milk produces
butter,
And wringing the nose produces blood,
So the forcing of wrath produces strife.

THE WORDS OF KING LEMUEL'S MOTHER

31 The words of King Lemuel, the utterance which his mother taught him:

2 What, my son?
And what, son of my womb?
And what, son of my vows?
3 Do not give your strength to women,
Nor your ways to that which destroys
kings.

4 *It is* not for kings, O Lemuel,
It is not for kings to drink wine,
Nor for princes intoxicating drink;

30:16 [a]Or *Sheol* **30:26** [a]Or *hyraxes* **30:28** [a]Or *lizard* **30:31** [a]Exact identity unknown [b]A Jewish tradition reads *a king against whom there is no uprising.*

5 Lest they drink and forget the law,
And pervert the justice of all the afflicted.
6 Give strong drink to him who is perishing,
And wine to those who are bitter of heart.
7 Let him drink and forget his poverty,
And remember his misery no more.

8 Open your mouth for the speechless,
In the cause of all *who are* appointed to die.[a]
9 Open your mouth, judge righteously,
And plead the cause of the poor and needy.

The Virtuous Wife

10 Who[a] can find a virtuous[b] wife?
For her worth *is* far above rubies.
11 The heart of her husband safely trusts her;
So he will have no lack of gain.
12 She does him good and not evil
All the days of her life.
13 She seeks wool and flax,
And willingly works with her hands.
14 She is like the merchant ships,
She brings her food from afar.
15 She also rises while it is yet night,
And provides food for her household,
And a portion for her maidservants.
16 She considers a field and buys it;
From her profits she plants a vineyard.
17 She girds herself with strength,
And strengthens her arms.
18 She perceives that her merchandise *is* good,
And her lamp does not go out by night.
19 She stretches out her hands to the distaff,
And her hand holds the spindle.

31:8 [a]Literally *sons of passing away*
31:10 [a]Verses 10 through 31 are an alphabetic acrostic in Hebrew (compare Psalm 119). [b]Literally *a wife of valor,* in the sense of all forms of excellence

PERSONALITY PROFILE

Women's Issues

THE VIRTUOUS WOMAN

(PROVERBS 31:10–31)

For years, women have read this portrait of the virtuous woman and sighed at the seeming impossibility of doing all that she does. If this woman represents perfection, then it's an unattainable perfection, as impossible as the touched-up perfection of the model on the magazine cover. Many women feel that they simply can never meet the ideal.

Throughout the Book of Proverbs, wisdom has been portrayed as a woman, with the pronoun "she." In this final chapter, wisdom is once again embodied—this time as a virtuous wife. These verses form an acrostic poem, meaning that each verse begins with a successive letter of the Hebrew alphabet. The description of this woman, then, includes many characteristics—all noble, but not all necessary in the same woman in order for her to be considered wise, virtuous, or ideal. However, her life should challenge our steps daily. This woman is a good and devoted wife, a hard worker, a manager of wealth and of servants, a discerning consumer, and a caring mother. She reaches out to help the poor. She runs her own business. She is praised by her family.

It would be incorrect to hold up these verses as the ideal which any woman who wants to be virtuous must achieve. Instead, the picture is meant to inspire women to be faithful wives and mothers, to run their households well, to have strength of character, and to use their gifts for God's glory. This woman is virtuous because her life is ordered by her reverence for God. All Christian women can aspire to that.

To Learn More: Turn to the article about women's issues on pages 846, 847. See also the key passage note at Titus 2:3–5 on page 1615.

Women's Issues

WOMEN OF GOD

SANDRA D. WILSON

(Proverbs 31)

She's a mystery to most. She's mind-boggling to many. She's the virtuous woman described in Proverbs 31:10–31. The word translated "virtuous" is the same Hebrew word translated "able" in Exodus 18:21. This word describes someone who is capable, strong, and valiant. The end of the Proverbs passage contains the secret to this remarkable woman's success: She feared the Lord (Prov. 31:30). Her reverential awe of God motivated and guided who she was and what she did. Consequently, this beloved wife and mother represents an ideal for women of God through the ages. But she is not the only virtuous example in Scripture. There are many inspiring women who should be admired.

BIBLICAL WOMEN OF GOD

Several virtuous Old Testament women can be noted. There is Moses' sister, Miriam, a patriot and prophetess who proclaimed in song God's goodness to Israel (Ex. 15:20, 21). In Exodus 35:20–29, unnamed women worshiped God and ministered to the believing assembly with their generosity and their creative skills. Ruth learned to trust God through her relationship with a godly mother-in-law (Ruth 1:16, 17). Hannah trusted God for a child, and kept her promise to God when the boy was born (1 Sam. 1:8–28). Esther bravely did her part to save her people (Esth. 4:13–17).

In the New Testament, Mary the mother of Jesus responded with astonishing faith to the angel's declaration (Luke 1:38). The prophetess Anna spoke of Israel's Messiah to all who came to the temple (Luke 2:36–38).

Jesus Himself repeatedly shattered cultural and ceremonial expectations by His interactions with women. For example, in John 4:7–42, Jesus revealed His identity to an unnamed woman, many times married, who subsequently became the first Samaritan evangelist. Both Mary and Martha were women of God. In settling the conflict between them, Jesus must have shocked bystanders by explicitly affirming Mary's better choice to be a disciple (Luke 10:38–42).

In the early church, women of God ministered wherever they were. Lydia, a successful businesswoman, became the first Christian convert in Europe (Acts 16:14). Priscilla and her husband, Aquila, ministered to Paul and many other believers (Acts 18:2, 24–28; Rom. 16:3–5).

BEING WOMEN OF GOD

In a culture where values and expectations appear to shift constantly, women of God need to anchor their lives in timeless truths of Scripture and the examples of the godly women (and men) of the Bible. The following are some guidelines to successful living:

Make Knowing God the Top Priority
This is not easy when a woman is busy with family and/or career as well as church and community service. Nevertheless, cultivating ever-increasing intimacy with God needs to be a lifelong priority. To really know God, as opposed to merely knowing about God, Christians must intentionally create a spiritual environment. This means God is given one's undivided attention in ways that foster an intimate and interac-

tive relationship. It requires times of solitude and stillness to develop inner quietness in order to hear God speak His thoughts from His Word and by His Spirit.

Commit to Knowing and Living in Truth
This means sifting through one's belief systems to retain and strengthen biblically based thinking and to discard unbiblical misbeliefs. The idea of committing to truth often seems most frightening to those who were most wounded in the past by abuse and neglect. A Christian counselor will help untangle childhood perceptions from reality. A Christ-centered support group can provide encouragement and accountability for the journey.

Seek Healthy Christian Relationships
An unbiblical overdependence on human relationships can lead to an "approval-addiction" that has the power to elevate the praise of people above the approval of God. Sometimes women draw a sense of personal worth from the quality of their relationships. If so, they are apt to believe they can "fix" every relationship with every person if they try hard enough. Romans 12:18 outlines the limits of a Christian's responsibility to live in harmony with others.

Find or Become a Godly Mentor
Titus 2:3–5 refers to a healthy model of mentoring between older and younger women. A mentor models Christ-centered living and encourages others during their struggles. For the mentor and the one being mentored, the experience is both edifying and humbling. Learning and blessing flow in both directions when people experience a purposeful and honest relationship with one another. Connection between godly older and younger women is sorely needed in churches today to offset the cultural assault upon biblical values.

Maintain Realistic Expectations
Reality-based expectations benefit women in their approach to themselves, to others, and to God. With regard to themselves, it means that they seek increasing maturity in Christlikeness rather than perfection. This is not an apologetic for sloppy or sinful living; it is an acceptance of reality and of realistic expectations. Women do well to maintain an attitude of humility, never assuming that they have completely mastered any lesson. They must stay teachable by walking very close to the Teacher.

Having realistic expectations for others means that women can freely cultivate friendships and pour themselves into their families while remembering that even the best of people cannot meet their deepest longings. Others will disappoint them. Only God can do all things perfectly.

WOMEN OF GOD IN THE TWENTY-FIRST CENTURY

Women of God were the last to leave the cross of Christ and the first to arrive at the tomb. Since that time, rules and roles for women have changed dramatically. Yet as the twenty-first century unfolds, one constant remains amid personal transitions and cultural upheavals: Like their biblical ancestors, women of God still worship, serve, and proclaim His goodness with their words and with their deeds.

FURTHER MEDITATION:

Other passages to study about the issue of women's issues include:

- ➢ Genesis 2:18–25
- ➢ Proverbs 9:1–18; 11:16; 14:1
- ➢ 1 Peter 3:1–6

To Learn More: Turn to the key passage note on women's issues at Titus 2:3–5 on page 1615. See also the personality profile of the virtuous woman on page 845.

20 She extends her hand to the poor,
Yes, she reaches out her hands to the
needy.
21 She is not afraid of snow for her
household,
For all her household *is* clothed with
scarlet.
22 She makes tapestry for herself;
Her clothing *is* fine linen and purple.
23 Her husband is known in the gates,
When he sits among the elders of the
land.
24 She makes linen garments and sells
them,
And supplies sashes for the merchants.
25 Strength and honor *are* her clothing;
She shall rejoice in time to come.
26 She opens her mouth with wisdom,
And on her tongue *is* the law of
kindness.
27 She watches over the ways of her
household,
And does not eat the bread of idleness.
28 Her children rise up and call her blessed;
Her husband *also,* and he praises her:
29 "Many daughters have done well,
But you excel them all."
30 Charm *is* deceitful and beauty *is*
passing,
But a woman *who* fears the LORD, she
shall be praised.
31 Give her of the fruit of her hands,
And let her own works praise her in the
gates.

SOUL NOTE

The Ideal Woman *(31:10–31)* Who was this "virtuous wife," and why all these characteristics of perfection? This picture of the ideal is meant to be a guideline, not a list of demands. While many of the characteristics focus on this woman's household duties and responsibilities, she also works outside the home and has servants and wealth to manage. Obviously, not every woman has everything in common with this one—individual lives are different. But women can learn from this woman's wise use of her blessings and abilities, her love for and helpfulness to her husband, and her positive guidance and example to her children. **Topic: Women's Issues**

Ecclesiastes

A 16-ounce container has eight ounces of water in it. "The glass is half empty!" the pessimist grumbles. "I bet the water is tainted!" the cynic charges. "Water?" the skeptic scoffs. "I think the whole thing's an illusion!"

Ecclesiastes is the ideal book for the rampant pessimism, cynicism, and skepticism of our times. It wrestles with the deepest struggles of the human soul in its attempt to find meaning and purpose in life. The author—widely thought to be Solomon—provides us with an honest view of human life in a fallen world.

Some view the author as a disillusioned pessimist who has lapsed into despair. Others see him as an astute realist who recognizes the limitations of human wisdom. This much is clear: The author demonstrates that a mere earthly, human perspective on life's greatest issues leaves us bewildered and unsatisfied.

This book reminds us that short-term pleasure often leads to long-term despair. Attempts to acquire more money, indulge in pleasure, and become famous leave the soul empty. Escape, denial, and withdrawal provide no more relief than indulgence, indifference, or excess. Learning can result in cynicism (1:7, 8), pleasure leads to disappointment (2:1, 2); wealth often brings trouble (5:12), and human wisdom may very well end in despair (11:1–8).

In the end, the weary writer turns his perspective toward God. His hopeful conclusion? It's through a relationship with the Creator that a person is able to find ultimate meaning and purpose. If your soul is marred by pessimism, cynicism, or skepticism, you've come to the right place!

SOUL CONCERNS IN ECCLESIASTES

The Vanity of Life

1 The words of the Preacher, the son of David, king in Jerusalem.

2 "Vanity[a] of vanities," says the Preacher;
"Vanity of vanities, all *is* vanity."

3 What profit has a man from all his labor
In which he toils under the sun?
4 *One* generation passes away, and *another* generation comes;
But the earth abides forever.
5 The sun also rises, and the sun goes down,
And hastens to the place where it arose.
6 The wind goes toward the south,
And turns around to the north;
The wind whirls about continually,
And comes again on its circuit.
7 All the rivers run into the sea,
Yet the sea *is* not full;
To the place from which the rivers come,
There they return again.
8 All things *are* full of labor;
Man cannot express *it*.
The eye is not satisfied with seeing,
Nor the ear filled with hearing.
9 That which has been *is* what will be,
That which *is* done is what will be done,
And *there is* nothing new under the sun.
10 Is there anything of which it may be said,
"See, this *is* new"?
It has already been in ancient times before us.
11 *There is* no remembrance of former *things*,
Nor will there be any remembrance of *things* that are to come
By *those* who will come after.

The Grief of Wisdom

12 I, the Preacher, was king over Israel in Jerusalem. 13 And I set my heart to seek and
search out by wisdom concerning all that is
done under heaven; this burdensome task
God has given to the sons of man, by which
they may be exercised. 14 I have seen all the
works that are done under the sun; and indeed, all *is* vanity and grasping for the wind.

1:2 [a]Or *Absurdity, Frustration, Futility, Nonsense;* and so throughout this book

SOUL NOTE

Life's Secret *(1:1, 2)* "Vanity of vanities, all is vanity." The words of Solomon describe the attitude of one who "has it all," but realizes that there is still a feeling of emptiness. The word "vanity" means "vapor" and pictures how quickly life passes. Like Solomon, many feel that their lives are meaningless, too. But in the final chapter, Solomon gives the solution to humanity's dilemma: "Fear God and keep His commandments" (12:13). Because life is fleeting, God's people should accept every day as a gift from God, reverencing Him and living to please Him. That is the secret to a successful life. **Topic: Emotional Life**

SOUL NOTE

Looking for Meaning *(1:16–18)* Wisdom is much to be desired, yet it can lead to great frustration. "In much wisdom is much grief, and he who increases knowledge increases sorrow." The more people know, the more they feel responsible for that knowledge, and the more they realize the extent of their ignorance. Having great wisdom did not guarantee that Solomon would live wisely. Wisdom and knowledge for their own sakes do not give meaning to life; in fact, the wisest and most brilliant may face the most aching realization that something is missing. Without God, wisdom and knowledge are ultimately meaningless. **Topic: Wisdom**

15 *What is* crooked cannot be made straight,
And what is lacking cannot be numbered.

[16]I communed with my heart, saying,
"Look, I have attained greatness, and have
gained more wisdom than all who were before
me in Jerusalem. My heart has understood
great wisdom and knowledge." [17]And I set my
heart to know wisdom and to know madness
and folly. I perceived that this also is grasping
for the wind.

18 For in much wisdom *is* much grief,
And he who increases knowledge increases sorrow.

The Vanity of Pleasure

2 I said in my heart, "Come now, I will test
you with mirth; therefore enjoy pleasure";
but surely, this also *was* vanity. [2]I said of
laughter—"Madness!"; and of mirth, "What
does it accomplish?" [3]I searched in my heart
how to gratify my flesh with wine, while guiding my heart with wisdom, and how to lay
hold on folly, till I might see what *was* good
for the sons of men to do under heaven all the
days of their lives.

[4]I made my works great, I built myself
houses, and planted myself vineyards. [5]I made
myself gardens and orchards, and I planted all
kinds of fruit trees in them. [6]I made myself
water pools from which to water the growing
trees of the grove. [7]I acquired male and female
servants, and had servants born in my house.
Yes, I had greater possessions of herds and
flocks than all who were in Jerusalem before
me. [8]I also gathered for myself silver and gold
and the special treasures of kings and of the
provinces. I acquired male and female singers,
the delights of the sons of men, *and* musical
instruments[a] of all kinds.

[9]So I became great and excelled more than
all who were before me in Jerusalem. Also my
wisdom remained with me.

10 Whatever my eyes desired I did not keep from them.
I did not withhold my heart from any pleasure,
For my heart rejoiced in all my labor;
And this was my reward from all my labor.
11 Then I looked on all the works that my hands had done
And on the labor in which I had toiled;
And indeed all *was* vanity and grasping for the wind.
There was no profit under the sun.

The End of the Wise and the Fool

12 Then I turned myself to consider wisdom and madness and folly;
For what *can* the man *do* who succeeds the king?—
Only what he has already done.
13 Then I saw that wisdom excels folly
As light excels darkness.
14 The wise man's eyes *are* in his head,
But the fool walks in darkness.
Yet I myself perceived
That the same event happens to them all.

15 So I said in my heart,
"As it happens to the fool,
It also happens to me,
And why was I then more wise?"
Then I said in my heart,
"This also *is* vanity."
16 For *there is* no more remembrance of the wise than of the fool forever,

2:8 [a]Exact meaning unknown

SOUL NOTE

Out of Control *(2:1–3)* King Solomon had the money, the time, and the power to indulge himself in any pleasure he desired. He sought to gratify himself with wine, only to find that he still struggled to find meaning and purpose in life.

Thousands of years ago, this king discovered what many still don't seem to know—alcohol will not solve any problems, nor will it fill the emptiness within that drives people to such excess in the first place. Alcohol is a temporary salve, ultimately leaving drinkers empty in their search for peace and significance. **Topic: Drug Abuse**

Drug Abuse

THE TRAP OF SUBSTANCE ABUSE

MARK SHADOAN

(Ecclesiastes 2:1–3)

Craig helps coach his son's softball team, helps the kids with their homework and rarely misses a game or recital. He's devoted to his job, works long hours, and often brings projects home on weekends. People know him as a great neighbor and good friend. What they don't know is that he is a substance abuser on his way to an engulfing addiction.

WHO SUFFERS FROM SUBSTANCE DISORDERS?

The prevalence of substance-induced disorders is high. In the United States, about 13 million people have some form of alcohol-related disorder. In addition, it is estimated that a minimum of 10 percent of any given community has some form of substance disorder diagnosis. Most substance abusers go undetected, however. For example, because women tend to drink covertly and are unlikely to act out socially, men represent a greater proportion of the statistics.

Substance disorders affect all strata of society. Women tend to have higher abuses with prescriptive drugs. Young adults between the ages of 18 and 29 tend to abuse alcohol more than any age group. Senior citizens seem to have the lowest statistics regarding abuse. Contrary to stereotypes, typical substance abusers are difficult to pick out of a crowd. They work, raise families, even go to church, and appear to have normal lives.

TYPES OF DISORDERS

Two kinds of problems are identified as substance disorders—one is called *abuse*, the other is called *addiction*.

Substance abuse refers to the excessive, problematic use of a substance as a mechanism for coping with stress. Abuse does not mean addiction, although it may result in addiction. Substance addiction refers to dependency on that substance in order to function. It spills over into one's personal life, family, friends, and even one's relationship with God. Addiction has a strong psychological and physical component where a pattern of use covers four stages: (1) experimentation, (2) heavy social or recreational use, (3) learning to use a substance for a mood altering effect, and (4) a clear addictive stage that is marked by physical and/or psychological dependence regardless of the consequences. At this last stage, the path to sobriety usually necessitates some form of intensive intervention.

REASONS FOR DISORDERS

Substance disorders are rooted in an individual's attempt to avoid or ease pain. Drugs or alcohol, with their ability to shut out the world and give a false "high," ease the person's pain—for a while. Persistent triggers such as learned behavior, poor coping skills, avoidance of responsibility, stressful events, and mood disorders can bring on abusive drinking; in addition, addictive family patterns appear as a factor in alcoholism. With substance addiction, the person's relationship to the substance is idolatrous. The person lives for the substance and is dependent on it just to "feel normal."

Substance abusers typically vacillate

between denial, anger, guilt, frustration, and fear when dealing with their own addictions. They often express annoyance when questioned or criticized. Many will use anger in an attempt to control others' responses to their behavior. Some will attempt to reduce their usage in an attempt to help themselves deal with their addiction. One way or another, each of these behaviors is the addict's way of avoiding responsibility for getting the help they really need.

RESOURCES FOR RECOVERY

Substance disorder is often a family problem; therefore, treatment should include individual and family therapy that focuses on changing faulty belief systems and patterns that enable substance disorders. Someone suffering from substance disorders must learn to identify needs and communicate feelings within the family structure in healthy ways. Even if substance abusers refuse help, their families should seek help in order to be able to cope with the abusers and find out how to help them deal with their addiction more effectively.

Ecclesiastes 2:1–3 discusses the misuse of drunken pleasure to deal with life. The writer gratified himself with wine in order to find mirth and pleasure, only to discover that this was "vanity." Recovering alcoholics and drug addicts will attest to the vanity, the futility, of trying to find pleasure or to dull pain through alcohol or drugs.

The Bible has a different approach to dealing with pain and life's difficulties. It encourages Christians to endure and persevere so God can work in their lives: "Count it all joy when you fall into various trials, knowing that the testing of your faith produces patience" (James 1:2, 3). People who have stood the test will receive a crown of life (James 1:12, 13). God promises to help people work through whatever personal problems they may face. To focus on avoiding pain leads to an exclusive focus on self and a refusal to trust God and learn the lessons He wants to teach through the pain or trial.

Recovery from substance abuse is a process of renewal: "I beseech you therefore, brethren, by the mercies of God, that you present your bodies a living sacrifice, holy, acceptable to God, which is your reasonable service. And do not be conformed to this world, but be transformed by the renewing of your mind, that you may prove what is that good and acceptable and perfect will of God" (Rom. 12:1, 2). "Therefore put to death your members which are on the earth: fornication, uncleanness, passion, evil desire, and covetousness, which is idolatry" (Col. 3:5). The choice is between using substances to avoid pain or developing the mind of Christ to access spiritual resources for recovery.

FURTHER MEDITATION:

Other passages to study about the issue of drug abuse include:

- ➢ Proverbs 20:1; 21:17; 23:21
- ➢ Romans 8:28; 13:13
- ➢ 1 Corinthians 6:19, 20; 10:13
- ➢ Ephesians 5:18
- ➢ 1 Thessalonians 5:4–10
- ➢ 1 John 1:9

To Learn More: Turn to the key passage note on drug abuse at Proverbs 23:19–21 on page 833. See also the personality profile of Belshazzar on page 1113.

Since all that now *is* will be forgotten in
the days to come.
And how does a wise *man* die?
As the fool!

17 Therefore I hated life because the work that
was done under the sun *was* distressing to me,
for all *is* vanity and grasping for the wind.
18 Then I hated all my labor in which I had
toiled under the sun, because I must leave it to
the man who will come after me. 19 And who
knows whether he will be wise or a fool? Yet
he will rule over all my labor in which I toiled
and in which I have shown myself wise under
the sun. This also *is* vanity. 20 Therefore I
turned my heart and despaired of all the labor
in which I had toiled under the sun. 21 For
there is a man whose labor *is* with wisdom,
knowledge, and skill; yet he must leave his
heritage to a man who has not labored for it.
This also *is* vanity and a great evil. 22 For what
has man for all his labor, and for the striving
of his heart with which he has toiled under
the sun? 23 For all his days *are* sorrowful, and
his work burdensome; even in the night his
heart takes no rest. This also is vanity.
24 Nothing *is* better for a man *than* that he
should eat and drink, and *that* his soul should
enjoy good in his labor. This also, I saw, was
from the hand of God. 25 For who can eat, or
who can have enjoyment, more than I?[a] 26 For
God gives wisdom and knowledge and joy to a
man who *is* good in His sight; but to the sinner He gives the work of gathering and collecting, that he may give to *him who is* good
before God. This also *is* vanity and grasping
for the wind.

Everything Has Its Time

3 To everything *there is* a season,
A time for every purpose under heaven:

2 A time to be born,
And a time to die;
A time to plant,
And a time to pluck *what is* planted;
3 A time to kill,
And a time to heal;
A time to break down,
And a time to build up;
4 A time to weep,
And a time to laugh;
A time to mourn,
And a time to dance;
5 A time to cast away stones,
And a time to gather stones;
A time to embrace,
And a time to refrain from embracing;
6 A time to gain,
And a time to lose;

2:25 [a]Following Masoretic Text, Targum, and Vulgate; some Hebrew manuscripts, Septuagint, and Syriac read *without Him.*

KEY PASSAGE

Life Transitions

A TIME FOR EVERYTHING

(3:1–11)

In beautiful poetry, Solomon reminds his readers that life continues to march on through a series of inevitable transitions. There are times for birth, death, weeping, laughing, mourning, dancing, silence, speaking, and even war and peace. People cannot control these situations, and their reactions to them are natural. Sometimes laughter is the only response, sometimes tears. Without God, powerful contrasts cause people pain and indicate meaninglessness in life.

As joyous or painful as they may be, these are natural transitions. If people have God in their lives, they can trust Him through the changes, knowing that every day that passes brings them closer to their eternal destiny in the presence of God Himself. Solomon observed that God "has put eternity in their hearts" (3:11). Nothing short of the promise of eternity can give true meaning to the changes and transitions of this life.

To Learn More: Turn to the article about life transitions on pages 540, 541. See also the personality profile of Timothy on page 1597.

A time to keep,
And a time to throw away;
7 A time to tear,
And a time to sew;
A time to keep silence,
And a time to speak;
8 A time to love,
And a time to hate;
A time of war,
And a time of peace.

THE GOD-GIVEN TASK

[9]What profit has the worker from that in which he labors? [10]I have seen the God-given task with which the sons of men are to be occupied. [11]He has made everything beautiful in its time. Also He has put eternity in their hearts, except that no one can find out the work that God does from beginning to end.

[12]I know that nothing *is* better for them than to rejoice, and to do good in their lives, [13]and also that every man should eat and drink and enjoy the good of all his labor—it *is* the gift of God.

14 I know that whatever God does,
It shall be forever.
Nothing can be added to it,
And nothing taken from it.
God does *it,* that men should fear before Him.
15 That which is has already been,
And what is to be has already been;
And God requires an account of what is past.

INJUSTICE SEEMS TO PREVAIL

[16]Moreover I saw under the sun:

In the place of judgment,
Wickedness *was* there;
And *in* the place of righteousness,
Iniquity *was* there.

[17]I said in my heart,

"God shall judge the righteous and the wicked,
For *there is* a time there for every purpose and for every work."

[18]I said in my heart, "Concerning the condition of the sons of men, God tests them, that they may see that they themselves are *like* animals." [19]For what happens to the sons of men also happens to animals; one thing befalls them: as one dies, so dies the other. Surely, they all have one breath; man has no advantage over animals, for all *is* vanity. [20]All go to one place: all are from the dust, and all return to dust. [21]Who knows the spirit of the sons of men, which goes upward, and the spirit of the animal, which goes down to the earth?[a] [22]So I perceived that nothing *is* better than that a man should rejoice in his own works, for that *is* his heritage. For who can bring him to see what will happen after him?

4 Then I returned and considered all the oppression that is done under the sun:

And look! The tears of the oppressed,
But they have no comforter—
On the side of their oppressors *there is* power,
But they have no comforter.
2 Therefore I praised the dead who were already dead,
More than the living who are still alive.
3 Yet, better than both *is he* who has never existed,
Who has not seen the evil work that is done under the sun.

THE VANITY OF SELFISH TOIL

[4]Again, I saw that for all toil and every skillful work a man is envied by his neighbor. This also *is* vanity and grasping for the wind.

5 The fool folds his hands
And consumes his own flesh.
6 Better a handful *with* quietness
Than both hands full, *together with* toil and grasping for the wind.

[7]Then I returned, and I saw vanity under the sun:

8 There is one alone, without companion:
He has neither son nor brother.
Yet *there is* no end to all his labors,
Nor is his eye satisfied with riches.
But he never asks,
"For whom do I toil and deprive myself of good?"

3:21 [a]Septuagint, Syriac, Targum, and Vulgate read *Who knows whether the spirit . . . goes upward, and whether . . . goes downward to the earth?*

Relationships

BUILDING GOOD RELATIONSHIPS

LES AND LESLIE PARROTT

(Ecclesiastes 4:9)

A pioneering band of researchers has recently studied the age-old mystery of what makes people happy, and their answer is not what might be expected. What comes up consistently at the top of the charts is not success, good looks, or any of those enviable assets. The clear winner is relationships—close relationships.

What can be done to build good relationships? To be honest, the answer is "not much." We cannot *do* a whole lot to cultivate healthy relationships. Techniques do not work. Real relationships evolve out of *being* a certain kind of person. We must focus on *who* we are in relationships rather than what we *do*. Following are a few of the most important ways of "being" in order to build good relationships:

BE SOMEONE WHO LISTENS

At the heart of every good relationship is the ability to listen and understand what another person is saying. Without accurate listening, a good relationship can never be built. People who have good relationships take the time to hear what the other person is saying. They don't have a habit of interrupting or jumping to conclusions. They listen to the feelings the person is expressing, and they know how to respond appropriately. Like a mirror reflects an image, we can reflect the person's message by saying something like, "What I hear you saying is . . . " This kind of a reflection lets the person know we are really interested in accurately understanding. It also does wonders for building good relationships.

BE SOMEONE WHO IS SAFE

A close relationship is built on feelings of security. If people do not feel safe, there is no hope of them ever opening up and being authentic. People who keep their word create a sense of security for people in a relationship. They follow through on the promises they make. If we promise to keep a secret, we must keep it. We must keep our word. Once we have earned a person's trust, our relationship will flourish.

BE SOMEONE WHO LENDS A HAND

In rewarding relationships, people not only have feelings of security, they also help each other out. Sometimes that help may be seen in tangible ways—a ride to a ball game, for example. And sometimes it may be through giving reassurance before they take a big test or have that big interview. The point is that we should help them because we *want* to, not because we *have* to. As the saying goes, "That's what friends are for."

BE SOMEONE WHO WALKS IN ANOTHER'S SHOES

To build good relationships, people have to learn to see the world from another person's perspective. The fancy word for this is "empathy," which can unlock mysteries by helping them understand the other person better. Once we put ourselves in other people's shoes, we begin to understand why they might react, feel, and think the way they do. Of course, empathy does not come naturally; it takes work. It takes a decision to see life as another person sees it. But the relational dividends of empathy are well worth the effort.

BE SOMEONE WHO CAN RECEIVE

When the scales of a relationship are unbalanced—when one is always receiving and one is always giving—both people will eventually feel cheated. In healthy relationships, people meet each other's needs. There is a give and take that keeps both people in balance. We can allow people to care for us as much as we care for them. We must not fall into the trap of thinking that in order to be a good friend we have to do all the giving.

BE SOMEONE WHO WEATHERS TURBULENCE

Almost every good relationship eventually encounters a rough spot, a time when both people feel like giving up. It is a scary phase in relationships, usually indicating that both parties are going beneath the surface to talk about their true feelings, their likes and dislikes, the good and the bad. But if we are mature enough, and if we persevere, the time of relational turbulence can lead to a deeper, more genuine, and more authentic relationship than before. Conflict is often the temporary price we pay for deepening intimacy in relationships.

BE SOMEONE WHO KNOWS WHEN TO CALL IT QUITS

There are some relationships that are not worth the work. Of course, every relationship needs nurturing, but some relationships, no matter how hard people try to make them work, are doomed to disaster. If we are in a relationship that leads us to do things that we do not want to do, the relationship is not healthy and should be stopped. If we are in a relationship where we are constantly trying to win the person's approval or never feel accepted, the relationship is probably not a good one. When that is the case, we need to call it quits before the other person's rejection damages us and limits our usefulness to God.

In summary, relationships are complex and require some fundamental elements and time. In building relationships, it is more profitable to examine ourselves to determine the type of person we are, rather than focusing only on the things we do.

FURTHER MEDITATION:

Other passages to study about the issue of relationships include:

- ➢ Proverbs 13:20; 17:17; 22:24; 27:6–9
- ➢ Luke 6:28
- ➢ John 13:34, 35
- ➢ Romans 12:9–21
- ➢ Philippians 2:3, 4
- ➢ Colossians 3:13
- ➢ 1 John 4:7, 8

To Learn More: Turn to the key passage note on relationships at Ephesians 4:31, 32 on page 1556. See also the personality profile of David and Jonathan on page 372.

This also *is* vanity and a grave misfortune.

The Value of a Friend

9 Two *are* better than one,
Because they have a good reward for their labor.
10 For if they fall, one will lift up his companion.
But woe to him *who is* alone when he falls,
For *he has* no one to help him up.
11 Again, if two lie down together, they will keep warm;
But how can one be warm *alone?*
12 Though one may be overpowered by another, two can withstand him.
And a threefold cord is not quickly broken.

Popularity Passes Away

13 Better a poor and wise youth
Than an old and foolish king who will be admonished no more.
14 For he comes out of prison to be king,
Although he was born poor in his kingdom.
15 I saw all the living who walk under the sun;
They were with the second youth who stands in his place.
16 *There was* no end of all the people over whom he was made king;
Yet those who come afterward will not rejoice in him.
Surely this also *is* vanity and grasping for the wind.

Fear God, Keep Your Vows

5 Walk prudently when you go to the house of God; and draw near to hear rather than to give the sacrifice of fools, for they do not know that they do evil.

2 Do not be rash with your mouth,
And let not your heart utter anything hastily before God.
For God *is* in heaven, and you on earth;
Therefore let your words be few.
3 For a dream comes through much activity,
And a fool's voice *is known* by *his* many words.

4 When you make a vow to God, do not delay to pay it;
For *He has* no pleasure in fools.
Pay what you have vowed—
5 Better not to vow than to vow and not pay.

6Do not let your mouth cause your flesh to sin,
nor say before the messenger *of God* that it
was an error. Why should God be angry at
your excuse[a] and destroy the work of your
hands? 7For in the multitude of dreams and
many words *there is* also vanity. But fear God.

The Vanity of Gain and Honor

8If you see the oppression of the poor, and
the violent perversion of justice and righteousness in a province, do not marvel at the matter; for high official watches over high official, and higher officials are over them.
9Moreover the profit of the land is for all;
even the king is served from the field.

10 He who loves silver will not be satisfied with silver;

5:6 [a]Literally *voice*

SOUL NOTE

Eternal Friendships *(4:9–12)* The Preacher observed the importance of friendships. God created people to be in relationship with Him and in relationships with one another. Friends who work on a task can rejoice together in its accomplishment. Friends can help each other—if one should fall, the other is there to "help him up." Those who have both a strong relationship with God and strong friendships with other believers will have bonds that strengthen life's joys and limit life's sorrows. Friendships among believers are precious, for they have the bond of Christ and of eternity. We should both find good friends and be good friends. **Topic: Relationships**

Nor he who loves abundance, with
increase.
This also *is* vanity.

11 When goods increase,
They increase who eat them;
So what profit have the owners
Except to see *them* with their eyes?

12 The sleep of a laboring man *is* sweet,
Whether he eats little or much;
But the abundance of the rich will not
permit him to sleep.

13 There is a severe evil *which* I have seen
under the sun:
Riches kept for their owner to his hurt.
14 But those riches perish through
misfortune;
When he begets a son, *there is* nothing
in his hand.
15 As he came from his mother's womb,
naked shall he return,
To go as he came;
And he shall take nothing from his labor
Which he may carry away in his hand.

16 And this also *is* a severe evil—
Just exactly as he came, so shall he go.
And what profit has he who has labored
for the wind?
17 All his days he also eats in darkness,
And *he has* much sorrow and sickness
and anger.

18Here is what I have seen: *It is* good and fitting *for one* to eat and drink, and to enjoy the
good of all his labor in which he toils under
the sun all the days of his life which God gives
him; for it *is* his heritage. 19As for every man
to whom God has given riches and wealth,
and given him power to eat of it, to receive his
heritage and rejoice in his labor—this *is* the
gift of God. 20For he will not dwell unduly on
the days of his life, because God keeps *him*
busy with the joy of his heart.

6 There is an evil which I have seen under
the sun, and it *is* common among men: 2A
man to whom God has given riches and
wealth and honor, so that he lacks nothing for
himself of all he desires; yet God does not give
him power to eat of it, but a foreigner consumes it. This *is* vanity, and it *is* an evil affliction.

3If a man begets a hundred *children* and
lives many years, so that the days of his years
are many, but his soul is not satisfied with
goodness, or indeed he has no burial, I say

SOUL NOTE

Money Chains *(5:12)* Many people desire to be rich, thinking that they will have no more worries. That is a paradox, however. A wealthy person may appear to live well, but "the abundance of the rich will not permit him to sleep." The rich lie awake worrying about losing their money, while poor laborers sleep soundly. Riches give freedom to do many things, but the chains of worry often ruin any true enjoyment. The moral is that God would have us be content whatever our financial status, for all wealth ultimately belongs to Him. **Topic: Money**

SOUL NOTE

Fruits of Our Labors *(5:18, 19)* Work is a double-edged sword in Scripture. Transformed into "sweat" as part of the Curse after the Fall (Gen. 3:19), work is also an honored activity through which God delivers many blessings. The Bible emphasizes the importance of work as a God-given activity in life, and it says that the ability to enjoy the fruits of one's labor is also something that God provides us. The ability to work, enjoy that work, make money, and enjoy and share that income with others—"this is the gift of God." **Topic: Work**

that a stillborn child *is* better than he—4for it
comes in vanity and departs in darkness, and
its name is covered with darkness. 5Though it
has not seen the sun or known *anything*, this
has more rest than that man, 6even if he lives
a thousand years twice—but has not seen
goodness. Do not all go to one place?

7 All the labor of man *is* for his mouth,
And yet the soul is not satisfied.
8 For what more has the wise *man* than
the fool?
What does the poor man have,
Who knows *how* to walk before the
living?
9 Better *is* the sight of the eyes than the
wandering of desire.
This also *is* vanity and grasping for the
wind.

10 Whatever one is, he has been named
already,
For it is known that he *is* man;
And he cannot contend with Him who is
mightier than he.
11 Since there are many things that
increase vanity,
How *is* man the better?

12For who knows what *is* good for man in
life, all the days of his vain life which he
passes like a shadow? Who can tell a man
what will happen after him under the sun?

The Value of Practical Wisdom

7 A good name *is* better than precious
ointment,
And the day of death than the day of
one's birth;
2 Better to go to the
house of
mourning
Than to go to the
house of
feasting,
For that *is* the end of all men;
And the living will take *it* to heart.
3 Sorrow *is* better than laughter,
For by a sad countenance the heart is
made better.
4 The heart of the wise *is* in the house of
mourning,
But the heart of fools *is* in the house of
mirth.

> A good name is better than precious ointment.
> ECCLESIASTES 7:1

5 *It is* better to hear the rebuke of the wise
Than for a man to hear the song of
fools.
6 For like the crackling of thorns under a
pot,
So *is* the laughter of the fool.
This also is vanity.
7 Surely oppression destroys a wise *man's*
reason,
And a bribe debases the heart.

8 The end of a thing *is* better than its
beginning;
The patient in spirit *is* better than the
proud in spirit.
9 Do not hasten in your spirit to be angry,
For anger rests in the bosom of fools.
10 Do not say,
"Why were the former days better than
these?"
For you do not inquire wisely concerning
this.

11 Wisdom *is* good with an inheritance,
And profitable to those who see the
sun.
12 For wisdom *is* a defense *as* money *is* a
defense,
But the excellence of knowledge *is that*
wisdom gives life to those who have
it.

13 Consider the work of God;
For who can make straight what He has
made crooked?
14 In the day of prosperity be joyful,
But in the day of adversity
consider:
Surely God has
appointed the
one as well as
the other,
So that man can
find out nothing
that will come
after him.

15I have seen everything in my days of vanity:

There is a just *man* who perishes in his
righteousness,
And there is a wicked *man* who
prolongs *life* in his wickedness.

16 Do not be overly righteous,
Nor be overly wise:
Why should you destroy yourself?
17 Do not be overly wicked,
Nor be foolish:
Why should you die before your time?
18 *It is* good that you grasp this,
And also not remove your hand from the other;
For he who fears God will escape them all.

19 Wisdom strengthens the wise
More than ten rulers of the city.

20 For *there is* not a just man on earth who does good
And does not sin.

21 Also do not take to heart everything people say,
Lest you hear your servant cursing you.
22 For many times, also, your own heart has known
That even you have cursed others.

23 All this I have proved by wisdom.
I said, "I will be wise";
But it *was* far from me.
24 As for that which is far off and exceedingly deep,
Who can find it out?
25 I applied my heart to know,
To search and seek out wisdom and the reason *of things,*
To know the wickedness of folly,
Even of foolishness *and* madness.
26 And I find more bitter than death
The woman whose heart *is* snares and nets,
Whose hands *are* fetters.
He who pleases God shall escape from her,
But the sinner shall be trapped by her.

27 "Here is what I have found," says the Preacher,
"*Adding* one thing to the other to find out the reason,
28 Which my soul still seeks but I cannot find:
One man among a thousand I have found,
But a woman among all these I have not found.
29 Truly, this only I have found:
That God made man upright,
But they have sought out many schemes."

8 Who *is* like a wise *man?*
And who knows the interpretation of a thing?
A man's wisdom makes his face shine,
And the sternness of his face is changed.

Obey Authorities for God's Sake

2I *say,* "Keep the king's commandment for
the sake of your oath to God. 3Do not be hasty
to go from his presence. Do not take your
stand for an evil thing, for he does whatever
pleases him."

4 Where the word of a king *is, there is* power;
And who may say to him, "What are you doing?"
5 He who keeps his command will experience nothing harmful;
And a wise man's heart discerns both time and judgment,

SOUL NOTE

No More Tears *(7:13, 14)* Some things cannot be fixed this side of heaven. Solomon observed that there are times when the crooked cannot be made straight: Some people stricken with cancer will die; some disabilities will never be healed. Solomon advises people to expect both good and bad in life—to enjoy the days of prosperity and be prepared for the days of adversity. No one goes through life without facing difficulties and problems. God never allows our journey here on earth to become so easy that we lose sight of heaven, where God promises to wipe every tear from our eyes (Rev. 21:4). **Topic: Trials**

6 Because for every matter there is a time
and judgment,
Though the misery of man increases
greatly.
7 For he does not know what will happen;
So who can tell him when it will occur?
8 No one has power over the spirit to
retain the spirit,
And no one has power in the day of
death.
There is no release from that war,
And wickedness will not deliver those
who are given to it.

9All this I have seen, and applied my heart
to every work that is done under the sun:
There is a time in which one man rules over
another to his own hurt.

Death Comes to All

10Then I saw the wicked buried, who had
come and gone from the place of holiness, and
they were forgotten[a] in the city where they
had so done. This also *is* vanity. 11Because the
sentence against an evil work is not executed
speedily, therefore the heart of the sons of
men is fully set in them to do evil. 12Though a
sinner does evil a hundred *times,* and his *days*
are prolonged, yet I surely know that it will be
well with those who fear God, who fear before
Him. 13But it will not be well with the wicked;
nor will he prolong *his* days, *which are* as a
shadow, because he does not fear before God.
14There is a vanity which occurs on earth,
that there are just *men* to whom it happens according to the work of the wicked; again,
there are wicked *men* to whom it happens according to the work of the righteous. I said
that this also *is* vanity.
15So I commended enjoyment, because a
man has nothing better under the sun than to
eat, drink, and be merry; for this will remain
with him in his labor *all* the days of his life
which God gives him under the sun.
16When I applied my heart to know wisdom
and to see the business that is done on earth,
even though one sees no sleep day or night,
17then I saw all the work of God, that a man
cannot find out the work that is done under
the sun. For though a man labors to discover
it, yet he will not find *it;* moreover, though a
wise *man* attempts to know *it,* he will not be
able to find *it.*

9 For I considered all this in my heart, so
that I could declare it all: that the righteous and the wise and their works *are* in the
hand of God. People know neither love nor
hatred *by* anything *they see* before them. 2All
things *come* alike to all:

One event *happens* to the righteous and
the wicked;
To the good,[a] the clean, and the
unclean;
To him who sacrifices and him who does
not sacrifice.
As is the good, so *is* the sinner;
He who takes an oath as *he* who fears
an oath.

3This *is* an evil in all that is done under the
sun: that one thing *happens* to all. Truly the
hearts of the sons of men are full of evil; madness *is* in their hearts while they live, and after
that *they go* to the dead. 4But for him who is
joined to all the living there is hope, for a living dog is better than a dead lion.

8:10 [a]Some Hebrew manuscripts, Septuagint, and Vulgate read *praised.* **9:2** [a]Septuagint, Syriac, and Vulgate read *good and bad.*

SOUL NOTE

Get Together *(9:9)* People get married because they want to be with one another. It is tragic, then, when married people spend very little time together. Caught up in the busy routines of each day, some spouses quickly go their separate ways and spend their time and energy in other matters. If this persists long enough, usually the joy of that marriage relationship begins to wane. Therefore, the Bible speaks to married people very practically when it encourages them to "live joyfully" with the one they love, to spend time with one another, and to enjoy one another's company. **Topic: Marriage**

5 For the living know that they will die;
But the dead know nothing,
And they have no more reward,
For the memory of them is forgotten.
6 Also their love, their hatred, and their envy have now perished;
Nevermore will they have a share
In anything done under the sun.

7 Go, eat your bread with joy,
And drink your wine with a merry heart;
For God has already accepted your works.
8 Let your garments always be white,
And let your head lack no oil.

9Live joyfully with the wife whom you love
all the days of your vain life which He has
given you under the sun, all your days of vanity; for that *is* your portion in life, and in the
labor which you perform under the sun.
10Whatever your hand finds to do, do *it* with
your might; for *there is* no work or device or
knowledge or wisdom in the grave where you
are going.
11I returned and saw under the sun that—

The race *is* not to the swift,
Nor the battle to the strong,
Nor bread to the wise,
Nor riches to men of understanding,
Nor favor to men of skill;
But time and chance happen to them all.
12 For man also does not know his time:
Like fish taken in a cruel net,
Like birds caught in a snare,
So the sons of men *are* snared in an evil time,
When it falls suddenly upon them.

Wisdom Superior to Folly

13This wisdom I have also seen under the
sun, and it *seemed* great to me: 14*There was* a
little city with few men in it; and a great king
came against it, besieged it, and built great
snares[a] around it. 15Now there was found in it
a poor wise man, and he by his wisdom delivered the city. Yet no one remembered that
same poor man.
16Then I said:

"Wisdom *is* better than strength.
Nevertheless the poor man's wisdom *is* despised,
And his words are not heard.
17 Words of the wise, *spoken* quietly, *should be* heard
Rather than the shout of a ruler of fools.
18 Wisdom *is* better than weapons of war;
But one sinner destroys much good."

10 Dead flies putrefy[a] the perfumer's ointment,
And cause it to give off a foul odor;
So does a little folly to one respected for wisdom *and* honor.
2 A wise man's heart *is* at his right hand,
But a fool's heart at his left.
3 Even when a fool walks along the way,
He lacks wisdom,
And he shows everyone *that* he *is* a fool.
4 If the spirit of the ruler rises against you,
Do not leave your post;
For conciliation pacifies great offenses.

5 There is an evil I have seen under the sun,
As an error proceeding from the ruler:
6 Folly is set in great dignity,
While the rich sit in a lowly place.
7 I have seen servants on horses,
While princes walk on the ground like servants.

8 He who digs a pit will fall into it,
And whoever breaks through a wall will be bitten by a serpent.
9 He who quarries stones may be hurt by them,
And he who splits wood may be endangered by it.
10 If the ax is dull,
And one does not sharpen the edge,
Then he must use more strength;
But wisdom brings success.

11 A serpent may bite when *it is* not charmed;
The babbler is no different.
12 The words of a wise man's mouth *are* gracious,
But the lips of a fool shall swallow him up;
13 The words of his mouth begin with foolishness,

9:14 [a]Septuagint, Syriac, and Vulgate read *bulwarks.* **10:1** [a]Targum and Vulgate omit *putrefy.*

And the end of his talk *is* raving
madness.
14 A fool also multiplies words.
No man knows what is to be;
Who can tell him what will be after
him?
15 The labor of fools wearies them,
For they do not even know how to go to
the city!

16 Woe to you, O land, when your king *is* a
child,
And your princes feast in the morning!
17 Blessed *are* you, O land, when your king
is the son of nobles,
And your princes feast at the proper
time—
For strength and not for drunkenness!
18 Because of laziness the building
decays,
And through idleness of hands the house
leaks.
19 A feast is made for laughter,
And wine makes merry;
But money answers everything.

20 Do not curse the king, even in your
thought;
Do not curse the rich, even in your
bedroom;
For a bird of the air may carry your
voice,
And a bird in flight may tell the matter.

The Value of Diligence

11 Cast your bread upon the waters,
For you will find it after many days.
2 Give a serving to seven, and also to
eight,
For you do not know what evil will be
on the earth.

3 If the clouds are full of rain,
They empty *themselves* upon the earth;
And if a tree falls to the south or the
north,
In the place where the tree falls, there it
shall lie.
4 He who observes the wind will not sow,
And he who regards the clouds will not
reap.

5 As you do not know what *is* the way of
the wind,[a]
Or how the bones *grow* in the womb of
her who is with child,
So you do not know the works of God
who makes everything.
6 In the morning sow your seed,
And in the evening do not withhold your
hand;
For you do not know which will
prosper,
Either this or that,
Or whether both alike *will be* good.

7 Truly the light is sweet,
And *it is* pleasant for the eyes to behold
the sun;
8 But if a man lives many years
And rejoices in them all,
Yet let him remember the days of
darkness,
For they will be many.
All that is coming *is* vanity.

11:5 [a]Or *spirit*

SOUL NOTE

Youthful Exuberance *(11:9, 10)* How young people live and what they do will lay the groundwork for the rest of their lives. Solomon observed that there is something wonderful and exuberant about adolescence. He challenged his young readers to rejoice in their youth, but he also told them to set boundaries on that youthful excitement so that they do not destroy their lives. Many people spend their lives facing the consequences of bad choices made during adolescence. Young people must develop a personal relationship with God that will positively affect their actions and attitudes, allowing them to enjoy their youth without making devastating mistakes.
Topic: Boundaries

Seek God in Early Life

9 Rejoice, O young man, in your youth,
And let your heart cheer you in the days of your youth;
Walk in the ways of your heart,
And in the sight of your eyes;
But know that for all these
God will bring you into judgment.
10 Therefore remove sorrow from your heart,
And put away evil from your flesh,
For childhood and youth *are* vanity.

12 Remember now your Creator in the days of your youth,
Before the difficult days come,
And the years draw near when you say,
"I have no pleasure in them":
2 While the sun and the light,
The moon and the stars,
Are not darkened,
And the clouds do not return after the rain;
3 In the day when the keepers of the house tremble,
And the strong men bow down;
When the grinders cease because they are few,
And those that look through the windows grow dim;
4 When the doors are shut in the streets,
And the sound of grinding is low;
When one rises up at the sound of a bird,
And all the daughters of music are brought low.
5 Also they are afraid of height,
And of terrors in the way;
When the almond tree blossoms,
The grasshopper is a burden,
And desire fails.
For man goes to his eternal home,
And the mourners go about the streets.

6 *Remember your Creator* before the silver cord is loosed,[a]
Or the golden bowl is broken,
Or the pitcher shattered at the fountain,
Or the wheel broken at the well.
7 Then the dust will return to the earth as it was,
And the spirit will return to God who gave it.

8 "Vanity of vanities," says the Preacher,
"All *is* vanity."

The Whole Duty of Man

9And moreover, because the Preacher was wise, he still taught the people knowledge; yes, he pondered and sought out *and* set in order many proverbs. 10The Preacher sought to find acceptable words; and *what was* written *was* upright—words of truth. 11The words of the wise are like goads, and the words of scholars[a] are like well-driven nails,

> Let us hear the conclusion of the whole matter: Fear God and keep His commandments, for this is man's all.
>
> ECCLESIASTES 12:13

12:6 [a]Following Qere and Targum; Kethib reads *removed;* Septuagint and Vulgate read *broken.*
12:11 [a]Literally *masters of the assemblies*

SOUL NOTE

This Old House *(12:1–7)* The day will come when people will have to face the challenges of old age. Solomon described the human body as an old house whose windows are darkened and doors are shut—when the physical body can no longer keep up, or when the mind is no longer alert. What may appear to be a tragic loss from a human standpoint is viewed very differently from God's perspective. In the end, the body will return to the dust, but "the spirit will return to God who gave it" (12:7). The search for significance finds what it's looking for in a relationship with the eternal God. **Topic: Aging/Elderly**

given by one Shepherd. [12]And further, my son,
be admonished by these. Of making many
books *there is* no end, and much study *is* wearisome to the flesh.

[13]Let us hear the conclusion of the whole
matter:

Fear God and keep His commandments,
For this is man's all.
14 For God will bring every work into
judgment,
Including every secret thing,
Whether good or evil.

Song of Solomon

Among the many false charges leveled at Christianity is the idea that it is "prudish" about sex. Nothing could be further from the truth. Consider the Old Testament book known as the Song of Solomon that unabashedly celebrates the joy and intimacy of sexual love in marriage.

Attributed to Solomon, this is the song of a couple who have eyes only for each other. Solomon appears as a young shepherd who falls in love with a lowly Shulamite girl. He promises to marry her upon his return. When he returns, much to her surprise, he appears as king. Accompanied by his entire entourage, he takes her back to Jerusalem in his royal coach to become his bride.

Among the poem's many beautiful expressions is the delicate exhortation: "Do not stir up nor awaken love until it pleases" (2:7; 3:5; 8:4). This phrase expresses the importance of sexual abstinence before marriage. It recognizes that the passions of youth can be aroused before a relationship of true commitment has been established. Sex, then, is a jewel that must await the right setting.

The beauty and honesty of this love song serve as an important corrective to the sexual perversions of our age. Here is a balanced portrait of married love that is neither obscene nor ashamed; it shows neither erotic excess nor sexual denial. The Song of Solomon reminds us that sexual love is truly a celebration of two souls united in marriage!

1 The song of songs, which *is* Solomon's.

THE BANQUET

The Shulamite[a]

2 Let him kiss me with the kisses of his mouth—
For your[b] love *is* better than wine.
3 Because of the fragrance of your good ointments,
Your name *is* ointment poured forth;
Therefore the virgins love you.
4 Draw me away!

The Daughters of Jerusalem

We will run after you.[a]

The Shulamite

The king has brought me into his chambers.

The Daughters of Jerusalem

We will be glad and rejoice in you.[b]

We will remember your[c] love more than wine.

The Shulamite

Rightly do they love you.[d]

5 I *am* dark, but lovely,
O daughters of Jerusalem,
Like the tents of Kedar,
Like the curtains of Solomon.
6 Do not look upon me, because I *am* dark,
Because the sun has tanned me.
My mother's sons were angry with me;
They made me the keeper of the vineyards,
But my own vineyard I have not kept.

(To Her Beloved)

7 Tell me, O you whom I love,
Where you feed *your flock,*
Where you make *it* rest at noon.
For why should I be as one who veils herself[a]
By the flocks of your companions?

The Beloved

8 If you do not know, O fairest among women,
Follow in the footsteps of the flock,
And feed your little goats
Beside the shepherds' tents.
9 I have compared you, my love,
To my filly among Pharaoh's chariots.
10 Your cheeks are lovely with ornaments,
Your neck with chains *of gold.*

The Daughters of Jerusalem

11 We will make you[a] ornaments of gold
With studs of silver.

The Shulamite

12 While the king *is* at his table,
My spikenard sends forth its fragrance.
13 A bundle of myrrh *is* my beloved to me,
That lies all night between my breasts.
14 My beloved *is* to me a cluster of henna *blooms*
In the vineyards of En Gedi.

1:2 [a]A Palestinian young woman (compare 6:13). The speaker and audience are identified according to the number, gender, and person of the Hebrew words. Occasionally the identity is not certain. [b]Masculine singular, that is, the Beloved
1:4 [a]Masculine singular, that is, the Beloved [b]Feminine singular, that is, the Shulamite [c]Masculine singular, that is, the Beloved [d]Masculine singular, that is, the Beloved
1:7 [a]Septuagint, Syriac, and Vulgate read *wanders.*
1:11 [a]Feminine singular, that is, the Shulamite

SOUL NOTE

Wedding Celebration *(1:2–4)* The Song of Solomon is a beautiful poem filled with words of love between a bride and groom. Solomon, disguised as a shepherd, meets the maiden and promises to return and take her as his bride. This book celebrates the sanctity and dignity of marriage as part of God's divine plan. Those who marry can enjoy each other as God's gift. They should seek each other's best and care for each other. Marriages need deep love, commitment, and loyalty between husband and wife in order for them to be able to give to each other sexually with enjoyment and fulfillment. **Topic: Marriage**

The Beloved

15 Behold, you *are* fair, my love!
Behold, you *are* fair!
You *have* dove's eyes.

The Shulamite

16 Behold, you *are* handsome, my beloved!
Yes, pleasant!
Also our bed *is* green.
17 The beams of our houses *are* cedar,
And our rafters of fir.

2 I *am* the rose of Sharon,
And the lily of the valleys.

The Beloved

2 Like a lily among thorns,
So is my love among the daughters.

The Shulamite

3 Like an apple tree among the trees of the woods,
So *is* my beloved among the sons.
I sat down in his shade with great delight,
And his fruit *was* sweet to my taste.

The Shulamite to the Daughters of Jerusalem

4 He brought me to the banqueting house,
And his banner over me *was* love.
5 Sustain me with cakes of raisins,
Refresh me with apples,
For I *am* lovesick.

6 His left hand *is* under my head,
And his right hand embraces me.
7 I charge you, O daughters of Jerusalem,
By the gazelles or by the does of the field,
Do not stir up nor awaken love
Until it pleases.

My beloved is mine, and I am his.
SONG OF SOLOMON 2:16

The Beloved's Request

The Shulamite

8 The voice of my beloved!
Behold, he comes
Leaping upon the mountains,
Skipping upon the hills.
9 My beloved is like a gazelle or a young stag.
Behold, he stands behind our wall;
He is looking through the windows,
Gazing through the lattice.

10 My beloved spoke, and said to me:
"Rise up, my love, my fair one,
And come away.
11 For lo, the winter is past,
The rain is over *and* gone.
12 The flowers appear on the earth;
The time of singing has come,
And the voice of the turtledove
Is heard in our land.
13 The fig tree puts forth her green figs,
And the vines *with* the tender grapes
Give a good smell.
Rise up, my love, my fair one,
And come away!

14 "O my dove, in the clefts of the rock,
In the secret *places* of the cliff,
Let me see your face,
Let me hear your voice;
For your voice *is* sweet,
And your face *is* lovely."

Her Brothers

15 Catch us the foxes,
The little foxes that spoil the vines,
For our vines *have* tender grapes.

The Shulamite

16 My beloved *is* mine, and I *am* his.
He feeds *his flock* among the lilies.

(To Her Beloved)

17 Until the day breaks
And the shadows flee away,
Turn, my beloved,
And be like a gazelle
Or a young stag
Upon the mountains of Bether.[a]

A Troubled Night

The Shulamite

3 By night on my bed I sought the one I love;

2:17 [a]Literally *Separation*

I sought him, but I did not find him.
2 "I will rise now," *I said,*
"And go about the city;
In the streets and in the squares
I will seek the one I love."
I sought him, but I did not find him.
3 The watchmen who go about the city
found me;
I said,
"Have you seen the one I love?"

4 Scarcely had I passed by them,
When I found the one I love.
I held him and would not let him go,
Until I had brought him to the house of
my mother,
And into the chamber of her who
conceived me.

5 I charge you, O daughters of Jerusalem,
By the gazelles or by the does of the
field,
Do not stir up nor awaken love
Until it pleases.

THE COMING OF SOLOMON

The Shulamite

6 Who *is* this coming out of the wilderness
Like pillars of smoke,
Perfumed with myrrh and frankincense,
With all the merchant's fragrant
powders?
7 Behold, it *is* Solomon's couch,
With sixty valiant men around it,
Of the valiant of Israel.
8 They all hold swords,
Being expert in war.
Every man *has* his sword on his thigh
Because of fear in the night.

9 Of the wood of Lebanon
Solomon the King
Made himself a palanquin:[a]
10 He made its pillars *of* silver,
Its support *of* gold,
Its seat *of* purple,
Its interior paved *with* love
By the daughters of Jerusalem.
11 Go forth, O daughters of Zion,
And see King Solomon with the crown
With which his mother crowned him
On the day of his wedding,
The day of the gladness of his heart.

THE BRIDEGROOM PRAISES THE BRIDE

The Beloved

4 Behold, you *are* fair, my love!
Behold, you *are* fair!
You *have* dove's eyes behind your veil.
Your hair *is* like a flock of goats,
Going down from Mount Gilead.
2 Your teeth *are* like a flock of shorn *sheep*
Which have come up from the washing,
Every one of which bears twins,
And none *is* barren among them.
3 Your lips *are* like a strand of scarlet,
And your mouth is lovely.
Your temples behind your veil
Are like a piece of pomegranate.
4 Your neck *is* like the tower of David,
Built for an armory,
On which hang a thousand bucklers,
All shields of mighty men.
5 Your two breasts *are* like two fawns,
Twins of a gazelle,
Which feed among the lilies.

6 Until the day breaks
And the shadows flee away,
I will go my way to the mountain of
myrrh
And to the hill of frankincense.

7 You *are* all fair, my love,
And *there is* no spot in you.
8 Come with me from Lebanon, *my*
spouse,
With me from Lebanon.
Look from the top of Amana,
From the top of Senir and Hermon,
From the lions' dens,
From the mountains of the leopards.

9 You have ravished my heart,
My sister, *my* spouse;
You have ravished my heart
With one *look* of your eyes,
With one link of your necklace.
10 How fair is your love,
My sister, *my* spouse!
How much better than wine is your love,
And the scent of your perfumes
Than all spices!
11 Your lips, O *my* spouse,
Drip as the honeycomb;

3:9 [a]A portable enclosed chair

Honey and milk *are* under your tongue;
And the fragrance of your garments
Is like the fragrance of Lebanon.

12 A garden enclosed
Is my sister, *my* spouse,
A spring shut up,
A fountain sealed.
13 Your plants *are* an orchard of
pomegranates
With pleasant fruits,
Fragrant henna with spikenard,
14 Spikenard and saffron,
Calamus and cinnamon,
With all trees of frankincense,
Myrrh and aloes,
With all the chief spices—
15 A fountain of gardens,
A well of living waters,
And streams from Lebanon.

The Shulamite

16 Awake, O north *wind,*
And come, O south!
Blow upon my garden,
Th*at* its spices may flow out.
Let my beloved come to his garden
And eat its pleasant fruits.

The Beloved

5 I have come to my garden, my sister, *my*
spouse;
I have gathered my myrrh with my spice;
I have eaten my honeycomb with my
honey;
I have drunk my wine with my milk.

PERSONALITY PROFILE

Sex in Marriage

SOLOMON AND THE SHULAMITE: THE LANGUAGE OF TRUE LOVE

(SONG OF SOLOMON 4)

When God designed marital love, he included as part of its character an intimate shamelessness. Genesis reveals that Adam and Eve were "both naked, the man and his wife, and were not ashamed" (Gen. 2:25). No fear, embarrassment, or shame complicated the early days of the original marriage. Later, echoes of that love were part of Jacob's love for Rachel (Gen. 29:18–20). That kind of innocent passion returns to the Bible pages in the Song of Solomon. In the privacy of love during the hours of anticipation before the wedding and the moments of delight in marriage, we overhear the whispered exchanges between the couple. We are slightly embarrassed at least in part because we are an eavesdropping audience. The couple has eyes and ears only for each other.

The Song of Solomon celebrates the blessing of God on the sexual relationship within marriage. The book enjoys, rather than explains, sexual intimacy. We witness how God's blessing touches the way husbands and wives see each other. It shapes their intimate conversation. What would be lust outside of marriage becomes appropriate desire when protected by genuine commitment.

In the Song of Solomon 4, the couple develop a mental picture of each other as they describe the details of each other's physical body in the most beautiful and extravagant poetic terms. Love creates its own language. The lovers' words may seem awkward unless we have been in love ourselves. Their expressions remind us, however, that sexual love within marriage is part of God's plan and purpose for our lives. God finds no shame in marital sexuality. His rules lead to the most deeply satisfying enjoyment.

The Song of Solomon powerfully illustrates the value of appreciating both the spiritual and physical qualities of our partner. When we seek to meet our spouse's needs with delight, we help to deepen sexual intimacy within marriage. Enjoy your spouse as a great gift from God to you!

To Learn More: Turn to the article about sex in marriage on pages 1500, 1501. See also the key passage note at Hebrews 13:4 on page 1638.

(To His Friends)
Eat, O friends!
Drink, yes, drink deeply,
O beloved ones!

THE SHULAMITE'S TROUBLED EVENING

The Shulamite
2 I sleep, but my heart is awake;
It is the voice of my beloved!
He knocks, *saying,*
"Open for me, my sister, my love,
My dove, my perfect one;
For my head is covered with dew,
My locks with the drops of the night."

3 I have taken off my robe;
How can I put it on *again?*
I have washed my feet;
How can I defile them?
4 My beloved put his hand
By the latch *of the door,*
And my heart yearned for him.
5 I arose to open for my beloved,
And my hands dripped *with* myrrh,
My fingers with liquid myrrh,
On the handles of the lock.

6 I opened for my beloved,
But my beloved had turned away *and*
was gone.
My heart leaped up when he spoke.
I sought him, but I could not find him;
I called him, but he gave me no answer.
7 The watchmen who went about the city
found me.
They struck me, they wounded me;
The keepers of the walls
Took my veil away from me.
8 I charge you, O daughters of Jerusalem,
If you find my beloved,
That you tell him I *am* lovesick!

The Daughters of Jerusalem
9 What *is* your beloved
More than *another* beloved,
O fairest among women?
What *is* your beloved
More than *another* beloved,
That you so charge us?

The Shulamite
10 My beloved *is* white and ruddy,
Chief among ten thousand.
11 His head *is like* the finest gold;
His locks *are* wavy,
And black as a raven.
12 His eyes *are* like doves
By the rivers of waters,
Washed with milk,
And fitly set.
13 His cheeks *are* like a bed of spices,
Banks of scented herbs.
His lips *are* lilies,
Dripping liquid myrrh.

14 His hands *are* rods of gold
Set with beryl.
His body *is* carved ivory
Inlaid *with* sapphires.
15 His legs *are* pillars of marble
Set on bases of fine gold.
His countenance *is* like Lebanon,
Excellent as the cedars.
16 His mouth *is* most sweet,
Yes, he *is* altogether lovely.
This *is* my beloved,
And this *is* my friend,
O daughters of Jerusalem!

The Daughters of Jerusalem
6 Where has your beloved gone,
O fairest among women?
Where has your beloved turned aside,
That we may seek him with you?

The Shulamite
2 My beloved has gone to his garden,
To the beds of spices,
To feed *his flock* in the gardens,
And to gather lilies.
3 I *am* my beloved's,
And my beloved *is* mine.
He feeds *his flock* among the lilies.

PRAISE OF THE SHULAMITE'S BEAUTY

The Beloved
4 O my love, you *are as* beautiful as
Tirzah,
Lovely as Jerusalem,
Awesome as *an army* with banners!
5 Turn your eyes away from me,
For they have overcome me.
Your hair *is* like a flock of goats
Going down from Gilead.
6 Your teeth *are* like a flock of sheep
Which have come up from the washing;

Every one bears twins,
And none *is* barren among them.
7 Like a piece of pomegranate
Are your temples behind your veil.

8 There are sixty queens
And eighty concubines,
And virgins without number.
9 My dove, my perfect one,
Is the only one,
The only one of her mother,
The favorite of the one who bore her.
The daughters saw her
And called her blessed,
The queens and the concubines,
And they praised her.

10 Who is she who looks forth as the morning,
Fair as the moon,
Clear as the sun,
Awesome as *an army* with banners?

The Shulamite

11 I went down to the garden of nuts
To see the verdure of the valley,
To see whether the vine had budded
And the pomegranates had bloomed.
12 Before I was even aware,
My soul had made me
As the chariots of my noble people.[a]

The Beloved and His Friends

13 Return, return, O Shulamite;
Return, return, that we may look upon you!

The Shulamite

What would you see in the Shulamite—
As it were, the dance of the two camps?[a]

EXPRESSIONS OF PRAISE

The Beloved

7 How beautiful are your feet in sandals,
O prince's daughter!
The curves of your thighs *are* like jewels,
The work of the hands of a skillful workman.
2 Your navel *is* a rounded goblet;
It lacks no blended beverage.
Your waist *is* a heap of wheat
Set about with lilies.
3 Your two breasts *are* like two fawns,
Twins of a gazelle.
4 Your neck *is* like an ivory tower,
Your eyes *like* the pools in Heshbon
By the gate of Bath Rabbim.
Your nose *is* like the tower of Lebanon
Which looks toward Damascus.
5 Your head *crowns* you like *Mount* Carmel,
And the hair of your head *is* like purple;
A king *is* held captive by *your* tresses.

6 How fair and how pleasant you are,
O love, with your delights!
7 This stature of yours is like a palm tree,
And your breasts *like* its clusters.
8 I said, "I will go up to the palm tree,
I will take hold of its branches."
Let now your breasts be like clusters of the vine,
The fragrance of your breath like apples,
9 And the roof of your mouth like the best wine.

The Shulamite

The wine goes *down* smoothly for my beloved,

6:12 [a]Hebrew *Ammi Nadib* **6:13** [a]Hebrew *Mahanaim*

SOUL NOTE

Oneness *(7:6–12)* Throughout the Song of Solomon, the husband and wife exult in each other's physical attractiveness. These explicit descriptions of their love underscore the importance of the soul relationship and deep commitment of the couple to one another. Three times a form of the refrain is repeated: "My beloved is mine, and I am his" (2:16; 6:3; 7:10). When a man and a woman become one in marriage, the bond of intimacy will strengthen their relationship. Within the bonds of marriage, God approves of and encourages sexual pleasure. **Topic: Sex in Marriage**

Moving gently the lips of sleepers.[a]
10 I *am* my beloved's,
And his desire *is* toward me.

11 Come, my beloved,
Let us go forth to the field;
Let us lodge in the villages.
12 Let us get up early to the vineyards;
Let us see if the vine has budded,
Whether the grape blossoms are open,
And the pomegranates are in bloom.
There I will give you my love.
13 The mandrakes give off a fragrance,
And at our gates *are* pleasant *fruits,*
All manner, new and old,
Which I have laid up for you, my beloved.

Set me as a seal upon your heart, as a seal upon your arm; for love is as strong as death, jealousy as cruel as the grave; its flames are flames of fire, a most vehement flame.

SONG OF SOLOMON 8:6

8 Oh, that you were like my brother,
Who nursed at my mother's breasts!
If I should find you outside,
I would kiss you;
I would not be despised.
2 I would lead you *and* bring you
Into the house of my mother,
She *who* used to instruct me.
I would cause you to drink of spiced wine,
Of the juice of my pomegranate.

(To the Daughters of Jerusalem)

3 His left hand *is* under my head,
And his right hand embraces me.
4 I charge you, O daughters of Jerusalem,
Do not stir up nor awaken love
Until it pleases.

LOVE RENEWED IN LEBANON

A Relative

5 Who *is* this coming up from the wilderness,
Leaning upon her beloved?

I awakened you under the apple tree.
There your mother brought you forth;
There she *who* bore you brought *you* forth.

The Shulamite to Her Beloved

6 Set me as a seal upon your heart,
As a seal upon your arm;
For love *is as* strong as death,
Jealousy *as* cruel as the grave;[a]
Its flames *are* flames of fire,
A most vehement[b] flame.
7 Many waters cannot quench love,
Nor can the floods drown it.
If a man would give for love
All the wealth of his house,
It would be utterly despised.

The Shulamite's Brothers

8 We have a little sister,
And she has no breasts.
What shall we do for our sister
In the day when she is spoken for?
9 If she *is* a wall,
We will build upon her
A battlement of silver;
And if she *is* a door,
We will enclose her
With boards of cedar.

The Shulamite

10 I *am* a wall,
And my breasts like towers;
Then I became in his eyes
As one who found peace.
11 Solomon had a vineyard at Baal Hamon;
He leased the vineyard to keepers;
Everyone was to bring for its fruit
A thousand silver coins.

(To Solomon)

12 My own vineyard *is* before me.
You, O Solomon, *may have* a thousand,
And those who tend its fruit two hundred.

7:9 [a]Septuagint, Syriac, and Vulgate read *lips and teeth.* **8:6** [a]Or *Sheol* [b]Literally *A flame of YAH* (a poetic form of *YHWH, the LORD*)

The Beloved

13 You who dwell in the gardens,
The companions listen for your voice—
Let me hear it!

The Shulamite

14 Make haste, my beloved,
And be like a gazelle
Or a young stag
On the mountains of spices.

Isaiah

We see them often in cartoons, and occasionally in real life—stern preacher-prophet types calling people to "Repent!" A few onlookers smile. Most shake their heads. Does anyone listen? Should anyone listen?

This book, written by the prophet Isaiah, is the first of seventeen Old Testament prophetic books. Isaiah was a prophet to the southern kingdom of Judah. He was one of Jerusalem's most prominent citizens, having access to both the royal family and the priestly leadership. His life and prophetic ministry spanned the rule of several kings.

Isaiah has sometimes been called the Old Testament "gospel" because of its messianic emphasis. The visions and language are lofty and majestic. Because God's people were deep in sin and civic confusion, they faced judgment (described in chapters 1 through 39). However, God promised to deliver His people by sending a Messiah to reign in peace and righteousness (as described in chapters 40 through 66). The picture of Christ in Isaiah 53—the Innocent Lamb and Suffering Servant—is stunning, especially since the passage describes Him in such rich detail hundreds of years before His birth.

Like the other prophets, Isaiah reminds us that our actions have consequences. We cannot turn our hearts away from God and expect His blessings. The book also assures us that comfort and peace come when we repent—turn back to God. Ultimately, Isaiah foresaw a coming day of social justice, racial harmony, and astonishing prosperity in a world where the Messiah reigns in righteousness. That's a message worth hearing!

SOUL CONCERNS IN ISAIAH

Burnout	(40:31)
Grief/Loss	(53:3, 4)
Compassion	(61:2)

1 The vision of Isaiah the son of Amoz, which he saw concerning Judah and Jerusalem in the days of Uzziah, Jotham, Ahaz, *and* Hezekiah, kings of Judah.

THE WICKEDNESS OF JUDAH

2 Hear, O heavens, and give ear, O earth!
For the LORD has spoken:
"I have nourished and brought up children,
And they have rebelled against Me;
3 The ox knows its owner
And the donkey its master's crib;
But Israel does not know,
My people do not consider."

4 Alas, sinful nation,
A people laden with iniquity,
A brood of evildoers,
Children who are corrupters!
They have forsaken the LORD,
They have provoked to anger
The Holy One of Israel,
They have turned away backward.

5 Why should you be stricken again?
You will revolt more and more.
The whole head is sick,
And the whole heart faints.
6 From the sole of the foot even to the head,
There is no soundness in it,
But wounds and bruises and putrefying sores;
They have not been closed or bound up,
Or soothed with ointment.

7 Your country *is* desolate,
Your cities *are* burned with fire;
Strangers devour your land in your presence;
And *it is* desolate, as overthrown by strangers.
8 So the daughter of Zion is left as a booth in a vineyard,
As a hut in a garden of cucumbers,
As a besieged city.
9 Unless the LORD of hosts
Had left to us a very small remnant,
We would have become like Sodom,
We would have been made like Gomorrah.

10 Hear the word of the LORD,
You rulers of Sodom;
Give ear to the law of our God,
You people of Gomorrah:
11 "To what purpose *is* the multitude of your sacrifices to Me?"
Says the LORD.
"I have had enough of burnt offerings of rams
And the fat of fed cattle.
I do not delight in the blood of bulls,
Or of lambs or goats.

12 "When you come to appear before Me,
Who has required this from your hand,
To trample My courts?
13 Bring no more futile sacrifices;
Incense is an abomination to Me.
The New Moons, the Sabbaths, and the calling of assemblies—
I cannot endure iniquity and the sacred meeting.
14 Your New Moons and your appointed feasts
My soul hates;
They are a trouble to Me,
I am weary of bearing *them.*
15 When you spread out your hands,
I will hide My eyes from you;
Even though you make many prayers,
I will not hear.
Your hands are full of blood.

"Come now, and let us reason together," says the LORD, "Though your sins are like scarlet, they shall be as white as snow; though they are red like crimson, they shall be as wool."
ISAIAH 1:18

16 "Wash yourselves, make yourselves clean;
Put away the evil of your doings from before My eyes.
Cease to do evil,
17 Learn to do good;
Seek justice,
Rebuke the oppressor;[a]
Defend the fatherless,
Plead for the widow.

1:17 [a]Some ancient versions read *the oppressed.*

18 "Come now, and let us reason together,"
Says the LORD,
"Though your sins are like scarlet,
They shall be as white as snow;
Though they are red like crimson,
They shall be as wool.
19 If you are willing and obedient,
You shall eat the good of the land;
20 But if you refuse and rebel,
You shall be devoured by the sword";
For the mouth of the LORD has spoken.

THE DEGENERATE CITY

21 How the faithful city has become a harlot!
It was full of justice;
Righteousness lodged in it,
But now murderers.
22 Your silver has become dross,
Your wine mixed with water.
23 Your princes *are* rebellious,
And companions of thieves;
Everyone loves bribes,
And follows after rewards.
They do not defend the fatherless,
Nor does the cause of the widow come before them.

24 Therefore the Lord says,
The LORD of hosts, the Mighty One of Israel,
"Ah, I will rid Myself of My adversaries,
And take vengeance on My enemies.
25 I will turn My hand against you,
And thoroughly purge away your dross,
And take away all your alloy.
26 I will restore your judges as at the first,
And your counselors as at the beginning.
Afterward you shall be called the city of righteousness, the faithful city."
27 Zion shall be redeemed with justice,
And her penitents with righteousness.
28 The destruction of transgressors and of sinners *shall be* together,
And those who forsake the LORD shall be consumed.
29 For they[a] shall be ashamed of the terebinth trees
Which you have desired;
And you shall be embarrassed because of the gardens
Which you have chosen.
30 For you shall be as a terebinth whose leaf fades,
And as a garden that has no water.
31 The strong shall be as tinder,
And the work of it as a spark;
Both will burn together,
And no one shall quench *them.*

THE FUTURE HOUSE OF GOD

2 The word that Isaiah the son of Amoz saw concerning Judah and Jerusalem.

2 Now it shall come to pass in the latter days
That the mountain of the LORD's house
Shall be established on the top of the mountains,
And shall be exalted above the hills;
And all nations shall flow to it.
3 Many people shall come and say,
"Come, and let us go up to the mountain of the LORD,
To the house of the God of Jacob;
He will teach us His ways,
And we shall walk in His paths."

1:29 [a]Following Masoretic Text, Septuagint, and Vulgate; some Hebrew manuscripts and Targum read *you.*

SOUL NOTE

Peace Plan *(2:4, 5)* How we long for peace in the world and in our homes! The Bible promises that one day all nations will live in peace when the Messiah reigns. The nations will turn their implements of war into implements of commerce: "Nation shall not lift up sword against nation, neither shall they learn war anymore" (2:4). This wonderful offer of God's peace is our promise of hope in a broken world. Until that day, God encourages us to "walk in the light of the LORD" (2:5). We walk in light when we follow God's plan for righteous living and seek guidance from His Word.
Topic: God's Promises

For out of Zion shall go forth the law,
And the word of the LORD from
Jerusalem.
4 He shall judge between the nations,
And rebuke many people;
They shall beat their swords into
plowshares,
And their spears into pruning hooks;
Nation shall not lift up sword against
nation,
Neither shall they learn war anymore.

The Day of the Lord

5 O house of Jacob, come and let us walk
In the light of the LORD.

6 For You have forsaken Your people, the
house of Jacob,
Because they are filled with eastern
ways;
They *are* soothsayers like the Philistines,
And they are pleased with the children
of foreigners.
7 Their land is also full of silver and gold,
And there is no end to their treasures;
Their land is also full of horses,
And there is no end to their chariots.
8 Their land is also full of idols;
They worship the work of their own
hands,
That which their own fingers have made.
9 People bow down,
And each man humbles himself;
Therefore do not forgive them.

10 Enter into the rock, and hide in the dust,
From the terror of the LORD
And the glory of His majesty.
11 The lofty looks of man shall be
humbled,
The haughtiness of men shall be bowed
down,
And the LORD alone shall be exalted in
that day.

12 For the day of the LORD of hosts
Shall come upon everything proud and
lofty,
Upon everything lifted up—
And it shall be brought low—
13 Upon all the cedars of Lebanon *that are*
high and lifted up,
And upon all the oaks of Bashan;
14 Upon all the high mountains,
And upon all the hills *that are* lifted up;
15 Upon every high tower,
And upon every fortified wall;
16 Upon all the ships of Tarshish,
And upon all the beautiful sloops.
17 The loftiness of man shall be bowed
down,
And the haughtiness of men shall be
brought low;
The LORD alone will be exalted in that
day,
18 But the idols He shall utterly abolish.

19 They shall go into the holes of the rocks,
And into the caves of the earth,
From the terror of the LORD
And the glory of His majesty,
When He arises to shake the earth
mightily.

20 In that day a man will cast away his
idols of silver
And his idols of gold,
Which they made, *each* for himself to
worship,
To the moles and bats,
21 To go into the clefts of the rocks,
And into the crags of the rugged rocks,
From the terror of the LORD
And the glory of His majesty,
When He arises to shake the earth
mightily.

22 Sever yourselves from such a man,
Whose breath *is* in his nostrils;
For of what account is he?

Judgment on Judah and Jerusalem

3 For behold, the Lord, the LORD of hosts,
Takes away from Jerusalem and from
Judah
The stock and the store,
The whole supply of bread and the
whole supply of water;
2 The mighty man and the man of war,
The judge and the prophet,
And the diviner and the elder;
3 The captain of fifty and the honorable
man,
The counselor and the skillful artisan,
And the expert enchanter.

4 "I will give children *to be* their princes,
And babes shall rule over them.

5 The people will be oppressed,
Every one by another and every one by
his neighbor;
The child will be insolent toward the
elder,
And the base toward the honorable."

6 When a man takes hold of his
brother
In the house of his father, *saying,*
"You have clothing;
You be our ruler,
And *let* these ruins *be* under your
power,"[a]
7 In that day he will protest, saying,
"I cannot cure *your* ills,
For in my house *is* neither food nor
clothing;
Do not make me a ruler of the people."

8 For Jerusalem stumbled,
And Judah is fallen,
Because their tongue and their doings
Are against the LORD,
To provoke the eyes of His glory.
9 The look on their countenance witnesses
against them,
And they declare their sin as Sodom;
They do not hide *it.*
Woe to their soul!
For they have brought evil upon
themselves.

10 "Say to the righteous that *it shall be* well
with them,
For they shall eat the fruit of their
doings.
11 Woe to the wicked! *It shall be* ill *with
him,*
For the reward of his hands shall be
given him.
12 *As for* My people, children *are* their
oppressors,
And women rule over them.
O My people! Those who lead you cause
you to err,
And destroy the way of your paths."

Oppression and Luxury Condemned

13 The LORD stands up to plead,
And stands to judge the people.
14 The LORD will enter into judgment
With the elders of His people
And His princes:
"For you have eaten up the vineyard;
The plunder of the poor *is* in your
houses.
15 What do you mean by crushing My
people
And grinding the faces of the poor?"
Says the Lord GOD of hosts.

16 Moreover the LORD says:

"Because the daughters of Zion are
haughty,
And walk with outstretched necks
And wanton eyes,
Walking and mincing *as* they go,
Making a jingling with their feet,
17 Therefore the Lord will strike with a
scab
The crown of the head of the daughters
of Zion,
And the LORD will uncover their secret
parts."

18 In that day the Lord will take away the
finery:
The jingling anklets, the scarves, and the
crescents;
19 The pendants, the bracelets, and the
veils;
20 The headdresses, the leg ornaments, and
the headbands;
The perfume boxes, the charms,
21 and the rings;
The nose jewels,
22 the festal apparel, and the mantles;
The outer garments, the purses,
23 and the mirrors;
The fine linen, the turbans, and the
robes.

24 And so it shall be:

Instead of a sweet smell there will be a
stench;
Instead of a sash, a rope;
Instead of well-set hair, baldness;
Instead of a rich robe, a girding of
sackcloth;
And branding instead of beauty.
25 Your men shall fall by the sword,
And your mighty in the war.

3:6 [a]Literally *hand*

26 Her gates shall lament and mourn,
And she *being* desolate shall sit on the ground.

4 And in that day seven women shall take hold of one man, saying,
"We will eat our own food and wear our own apparel;
Only let us be called by your name,
To take away our reproach."

The Renewal of Zion

2 In that day the Branch of the LORD shall be beautiful and glorious;
And the fruit of the earth *shall be* excellent and appealing
For those of Israel who have escaped.

3And it shall come to pass that *he who is* left
in Zion and remains in Jerusalem will be
called holy—everyone who is recorded among
the living in Jerusalem. 4When the Lord has
washed away the filth of the daughters of
Zion, and purged the blood of Jerusalem from
her midst, by the spirit of judgment and by the
spirit of burning, 5then the LORD will create
above every dwelling place of Mount Zion,
and above her assemblies, a cloud and smoke
by day and the shining of a flaming fire by
night. For over all the glory there *will be* a covering. 6And there will be a tabernacle for
shade in the daytime from the heat, for a place
of refuge, and for a shelter from storm and
rain.

God's Disappointing Vineyard

5 Now let me sing to my Well-beloved
A song of my Beloved regarding His vineyard:

My Well-beloved has a vineyard
On a very fruitful hill.
2 He dug it up and cleared out its stones,
And planted it with the choicest vine.
He built a tower in its midst,
And also made a winepress in it;
So He expected *it* to bring forth *good* grapes,
But it brought forth wild grapes.

3 "And now, O inhabitants of Jerusalem and men of Judah,
Judge, please, between Me and My vineyard.
4 What more could have been done to My vineyard
That I have not done in it?
Why then, when I expected *it* to bring forth *good* grapes,
Did it bring forth wild grapes?
5 And now, please let Me tell you what I will do to My vineyard:
I will take away its hedge, and it shall be burned;
And break down its wall, and it shall be trampled down.
6 I will lay it waste;
It shall not be pruned or dug,
But there shall come up briers and thorns.
I will also command the clouds
That they rain no rain on it."

7 For the vineyard of the LORD of hosts *is* the house of Israel,
And the men of Judah are His pleasant plant.
He looked for justice, but behold, oppression;
For righteousness, but behold, a cry *for help.*

Impending Judgment on Excesses

8 Woe to those who join house to house;
They add field to field,
Till *there is* no place
Where they may dwell alone in the midst of the land!
9 In my hearing the LORD of hosts *said,*
"Truly, many houses shall be desolate,
Great and beautiful ones, without inhabitant.
10 For ten acres of vineyard shall yield one bath,
And a homer of seed shall yield one ephah."

11 Woe to those who rise early in the morning,
That they may follow intoxicating drink;
Who continue until night, *till* wine inflames them!
12 The harp and the strings,
The tambourine and flute,
And wine are in their feasts;
But they do not regard the work of the LORD,
Nor consider the operation of His hands.

13 Therefore my people have gone into
captivity,
Because *they have* no knowledge;
Their honorable men *are* famished,
And their multitude dried up with
thirst.
14 Therefore Sheol has enlarged itself
And opened its mouth beyond measure;
Their glory and their multitude and their
pomp,
And he who is jubilant, shall descend
into it.
15 People shall be brought down,
Each man shall be humbled,
And the eyes of the lofty shall be
humbled.
16 But the LORD of hosts shall be exalted in
judgment,
And God who is holy shall be hallowed
in righteousness.
17 Then the lambs shall feed in their
pasture,
And in the waste places of the fat ones
strangers shall eat.

18 Woe to those who draw iniquity with
cords of vanity,
And sin as if with a cart rope;
19 That say, "Let Him make speed *and*
hasten His work,
That we may see *it;*
And let the counsel of the Holy One of
Israel draw near and come,
That we may know *it.*"

20 Woe to those who call evil good, and
good evil;
Who put darkness for light, and light for
darkness;
Who put bitter for sweet, and sweet for
bitter!

21 Woe to *those who are* wise in their own
eyes,
And prudent in their own sight!

22 Woe to men mighty at drinking wine,
Woe to men valiant for mixing
intoxicating drink,
23 Who justify the wicked for a bribe,
And take away justice from the righteous
man!

24 Therefore, as the fire devours the
stubble,
And the flame consumes the chaff,
So their root will be as rottenness,
And their blossom will ascend like dust;
Because they have rejected the law of
the LORD of hosts,
And despised the word of the Holy One
of Israel.
25 Therefore the anger of the LORD is
aroused against His people;
He has stretched out His hand against
them
And stricken them,
And the hills trembled.
Their carcasses *were* as refuse in the
midst of the streets.

For all this His anger is not turned away,
But His hand *is* stretched out still.

26 He will lift up a banner to the nations
from afar,
And will whistle to them from the end of
the earth;
Surely they shall come with speed,
swiftly.
27 No one will be weary or stumble among
them,
No one will slumber or sleep;

SOUL NOTE

Hooked *(5:11)* The prophet Isaiah warned of judgment ("woe") on those addicted to alcohol. He said that they are so dependent on it that they begin early in the morning and continue drinking until late at night. The tragedy of addiction is that it controls and dominates the desires and choices of the addicted. The even greater tragedy is the rejection by the addicted of the Lord's work in their lives: "They do not regard the work of the LORD, nor consider the operation of His hands" (5:12). God alone can provide the lasting comfort, joy, and relief that people mistakenly seek in alcohol.
Topic: Addictions

Nor will the belt on their loins be
loosed,
Nor the strap of their sandals be broken;
28 Whose arrows *are* sharp,
And all their bows bent;
Their horses' hooves will seem like
flint,
And their wheels like a whirlwind.
29 Their roaring *will be* like a lion,
They will roar like young lions;
Yes, they will roar
And lay hold of the prey;
They will carry *it* away safely,
And no one will deliver.
30 In that day they will roar against them
Like the roaring of the sea.
And if *one* looks to the land,
Behold, darkness *and* sorrow;
And the light is darkened by the clouds.

Isaiah Called to Be a Prophet

6 In the year that King Uzziah died, I saw
the Lord sitting on a throne, high and lifted up, and the train of His *robe* filled the temple. 2Above it stood seraphim; each one had
six wings: with two he covered his face, with
two he covered his feet, and with two he flew.
3And one cried to another and said:

"Holy, holy, holy *is* the LORD of hosts;
The whole earth *is* full of His glory!"

4And the posts of the door were shaken by the
voice of him who cried out, and the house was
filled with smoke.
5So I said:

"Woe *is* me, for I am undone!
Because I *am* a man of unclean lips,

PERSONALITY PROFILE

Sin

ISAIAH—SET FREE FROM SIN

(ISAIAH 6)

God is the master of the unexpected invasion, and He will use any tool at hand when He breaks through a person's defenses. The walls of arguments, excuses, and ignorance that often stand between people and God crumble under God's persistent grace. His purpose is neither to defeat nor to conquer. He wants to set us free. He knows that everything we use to try to keep God out actually only keeps us imprisoned within.

Sometimes God uses a personal crisis or someone else's troubles to get our attention. Occasionally, God uses a national crisis to prepare us for change. Such was the case with Isaiah.

The death of godly king Uzziah marked the end of an era for the nation of Judah. In that moment of crisis, the prophet Isaiah saw a new vision of God sitting on the throne of heaven. He was vividly reminded that God was still on the throne in spite of the nation's uncertain future.

Isaiah's ministry eventually spanned the reigns of several kings. But his personal preparation for ministry occurred when he faced God in all His holiness and himself in all his sinfulness. His pronouncement of "woe" (Is. 6:5) upon himself was a confession of sin. Because of his repentant heart, Isaiah received a beautiful sign of forgiveness from the Lord. In his vision of God's holiness, Isaiah saw one of the angels take a burning coal off the altar of heaven and place it upon his, Isaiah's, lips and announce that his sin had been purged.

Isaiah's acute awareness of sin was replaced by a grateful willingness to serve the God who had cleansed him. The Lord asked: "Whom shall I send, and who will go for Us?" Isaiah responded, "Here am I! Send me" (Is. 6:8). Our willingness to serve God and others will be deeply influenced by the degree to which we have received God's gracious work in our lives. If our defenses have fallen and we have been set free, we will want to be put to work just like Isaiah. Forgiveness liberates us to be useful to the Lord.

To Learn More: Turn to the article about sin on pages 446, 447. See also the key passage note at I John 1:9 on page 1675.

And I dwell in the midst of a people of
unclean lips;
For my eyes have seen the King,
The LORD of hosts."

6Then one of the seraphim flew to me, having in his hand a live coal *which* he had taken
with the tongs from the altar. 7And he touched
my mouth *with it,* and said:

"Behold, this has touched your lips;
Your iniquity is taken away,
And your sin purged."

8Also I heard the voice of the Lord, saying:

"Whom shall I send,
And who will go for Us?"

Then I said, "Here *am* I! Send me."
9And He said, "Go, and tell this people:

'Keep on hearing, but do not understand;
Keep on seeing, but do not perceive.'

10 "Make the heart of this people dull,
And their ears heavy,
And shut their eyes;
Lest they see with their eyes,
And hear with their ears,
And understand with their heart,
And return and be healed."

11Then I said, "Lord, how long?"
And He answered:

"Until the cities are laid waste and
without inhabitant,
The houses are without a man,
The land is utterly desolate,
12 The LORD has removed men far away,
And the forsaken places *are* many in the
midst of the land.
13 But yet a tenth *will be* in it,
And will return and be for consuming,
As a terebinth tree or as an oak,
Whose stump *remains* when it is cut
down.
So the holy seed *shall be* its stump."

ISAIAH SENT TO KING AHAZ

7 Now it came to pass in the days of Ahaz
the son of Jotham, the son of Uzziah, king
of Judah, *that* Rezin king of Syria and Pekah
the son of Remaliah, king of Israel, went up to
Jerusalem to *make* war against it, but could
not prevail against it. 2And it was told to the
house of David, saying, "Syria's forces are deployed in Ephraim." So his heart and the heart
of his people were moved as the trees of the
woods are moved with the wind.

3Then the LORD said to Isaiah, "Go out now
to meet Ahaz, you and Shear-Jashub[a] your
son, at the end of the aqueduct from the upper
pool, on the highway to the Fuller's Field,
4and say to him: 'Take heed, and be quiet; do
not fear or be fainthearted for these two stubs
of smoking firebrands, for the fierce anger of
Rezin and Syria, and the son of Remaliah. 5Be-
cause Syria, Ephraim, and the son of Remaliah
have plotted evil against you, saying, 6"Let us
go up against Judah and trouble it, and let us
make a gap in its wall for ourselves, and set a
king over them, the son of Tabel"— 7thus says
the Lord GOD:

"It shall not stand,
Nor shall it come to pass.
8 For the head of Syria *is* Damascus,
And the head of Damascus *is* Rezin.
Within sixty-five years Ephraim will be
broken,
So that it will not *be* a people.
9 The head of Ephraim *is* Samaria,
And the head of Samaria *is* Remaliah's
son.
If you will not believe,
Surely you shall not be established." ' "

THE IMMANUEL PROPHECY

10Moreover the LORD spoke again to Ahaz,
saying, 11"Ask a sign for yourself from the
LORD your God; ask it either in the depth or in
the height above."

12But Ahaz said, "I will not ask, nor will I
test the LORD!"

13Then he said, "Hear now, O house of David! *Is it* a small thing for you to weary men,
but will you weary my God also? 14Therefore
the Lord Himself will give you a sign: Behold,
the virgin shall conceive and bear a Son, and
shall call His name Immanuel.[a] 15Curds and
honey He shall eat, that He may know to refuse the evil and choose the good. 16For before
the Child shall know to refuse the evil and

7:3 [a]Literally *A Remnant Shall Return*
7:14 [a]Literally *God-With-Us*

choose the good, the land that you dread will
be forsaken by both her kings. [17]The LORD will
bring the king of Assyria upon you and your
people and your father's house—days that
have not come since the day that Ephraim departed from Judah."

18 And it shall come to pass in that day
That the LORD will whistle for the fly
That *is* in the farthest part of the rivers
of Egypt,
And for the bee that *is* in the land of
Assyria.
19 They will come, and all of them will
rest
In the desolate valleys and in the clefts
of the rocks,
And on all thorns and in all pastures.

20 In the same day the Lord will shave with
a hired razor,
With those from beyond the River,[a] with
the king of Assyria,
The head and the hair of the legs,
And will also remove the beard.

21 It shall be in that day
That a man will keep alive a young cow
and two sheep;
22 So it shall be, from the abundance of
milk they give,
That he will eat curds;
For curds and honey everyone will eat
who is left in the land.

23 It shall happen in that day,
That wherever there could be a
thousand vines
Worth a thousand *shekels* of silver,
It will be for briers and thorns.
24 With arrows and bows men will come
there,
Because all the land will become briers
and thorns.

25 And to any hill which could be dug with
the hoe,
You will not go there for fear of briers
and thorns;
But it will become a range for oxen
And a place for sheep to roam.

ASSYRIA WILL INVADE THE LAND

8 Moreover the LORD said to me, "Take a
large scroll, and write on it with a man's
pen concerning Maher-Shalal-Hash-Baz.[a] [2]And
I will take for Myself faithful witnesses to
record, Uriah the priest and Zechariah the son
of Jeberechiah."

[3]Then I went to the prophetess, and she
conceived and bore a son. Then the LORD said
to me, "Call his name Maher-Shalal-Hash-Baz;
[4]for before the child shall have knowledge to
cry 'My father' and 'My mother,' the riches of
Damascus and the spoil of Samaria will be
taken away before the king of Assyria."
[5]The LORD also spoke to me again, saying:

6 "Inasmuch as these people refused
The waters of Shiloah that flow softly,
And rejoice in Rezin and in Remaliah's
son;
7 Now therefore, behold, the Lord brings
up over them
The waters of the River,[a] strong and
mighty—
The king of Assyria and all his glory;
He will go up over all his channels
And go over all his banks.
8 He will pass through Judah,

7:20 [a]That is, the Euphrates **8:1** [a]Literally *Speed the Spoil, Hasten the Booty* **8:7** [a]That is, the Euphrates

SOUL NOTE

With Us *(7:14)* When King Ahaz refused to ask God for a sign of His promises, the prophet Isaiah announced that God would give His own sign to the "house of David" (the messianic line, 7:13). God promised that a virgin would bear a Son whose name, Immanuel, means "God with us." Matthew quoted this passage as being fulfilled in the miraculous virgin birth of Jesus Christ (Matt. 1:23). The coming of Christ shows that God keeps His promises to be with us personally and permanently.
Topic: God's Promises

He will overflow and pass over,
He will reach up to the neck;
And the stretching out of his wings
Will fill the breadth of Your land,
O Immanuel.[a]

9 "Be shattered, O you peoples, and be broken in pieces!
Give ear, all you from far countries.
Gird yourselves, but be broken in pieces;
Gird yourselves, but be broken in pieces.
10 Take counsel together, but it will come to nothing;
Speak the word, but it will not stand,
For God *is* with us."[a]

Fear God, Heed His Word

11 For the LORD spoke thus to me with a strong hand, and instructed me that I should not walk in the way of this people, saying:

12 "Do not say, 'A conspiracy,'
Concerning all that this people call a conspiracy,
Nor be afraid of their threats, nor be troubled.
13 The LORD of hosts, Him you shall hallow;
Let Him *be* your fear,
And *let* Him *be* your dread.
14 He will be as a sanctuary,
But a stone of stumbling and a rock of offense
To both the houses of Israel,
As a trap and a snare to the inhabitants of Jerusalem.
15 And many among them shall stumble;
They shall fall and be broken,
Be snared and taken."

> For unto us a Child is born, unto us a Son is given; and the government will be upon His shoulder. And His name will be called Wonderful, Counselor, Mighty God, Everlasting Father, Prince of Peace.
>
> ISAIAH 9:6

16 Bind up the testimony,
Seal the law among my disciples.
17 And I will wait on the LORD,
Who hides His face from the house of Jacob;
And I will hope in Him.
18 Here am I and the children whom the LORD has given me!
We are for signs and wonders in Israel
From the LORD of hosts,
Who dwells in Mount Zion.

19 And when they say to you, "Seek those
who are mediums and wizards, who whisper
and mutter," should not a people seek their
God? *Should they seek* the dead on behalf of
the living? 20 To the law and to the testimony!
If they do not speak according to this word, *it*
is because *there is* no light in them.

21 They will pass through it hard-pressed and
hungry; and it shall happen, when they are
hungry, that they will be enraged and curse
their king and their God, and look upward.
22 Then they will look to the earth, and see
trouble and darkness, gloom of anguish; and
they will be driven into darkness.

The Government of the Promised Son

9 Nevertheless the gloom *will* not *be* upon her who *is* distressed,
As when at first He lightly esteemed
The land of Zebulun and the land of Naphtali,
And afterward more heavily oppressed *her*,
By the way of the sea, beyond the Jordan,
In Galilee of the Gentiles.
2 The people who walked in darkness
Have seen a great light;
Those who dwelt in the land of the shadow of death,
Upon them a light has shined.

3 You have multiplied the nation
And increased its joy;[a]
They rejoice before You
According to the joy of harvest,
As *men* rejoice when they divide the spoil.

8:8 [a]Literally *God-With-Us* **8:10** [a]Hebrew *Immanuel* **9:3** [a]Following Qere and Targum; Kethib and Vulgate read *not increased joy;* Septuagint reads *Most of the people You brought down in Your joy.*

4 For You have broken the yoke of his burden
And the staff of his shoulder,
The rod of his oppressor,
As in the day of Midian.
5 For every warrior's sandal from the noisy battle,
And garments rolled in blood,
Will be used for burning *and* fuel of fire.

6 For unto us a Child is born,
Unto us a Son is given;
And the government will be upon His shoulder.
And His name will be called
Wonderful, Counselor, Mighty God,
Everlasting Father, Prince of Peace.
7 Of the increase of *His* government and peace
There will be no end,
Upon the throne of David and over His kingdom,
To order it and establish it with judgment and justice
From that time forward, even forever.
The zeal of the Lord of hosts will perform this.

The Punishment of Samaria

8 The Lord sent a word against Jacob,
And it has fallen on Israel.
9 All the people will know—
Ephraim and the inhabitant of Samaria—
Who say in pride and arrogance of heart:
10 "The bricks have fallen down,
But we will rebuild with hewn stones;
The sycamores are cut down,
But we will replace *them* with cedars."
11 Therefore the LORD shall set up
The adversaries of Rezin against him,
And spur his enemies on,
12 The Syrians before and the Philistines behind;
And they shall devour Israel with an open mouth.

For all this His anger is not turned away,
But His hand *is* stretched out still.

13 For the people do not turn to Him who strikes them,
Nor do they seek the LORD of hosts.
14 Therefore the LORD will cut off head and tail from Israel,
Palm branch and bulrush in one day.
15 The elder and honorable, he *is* the head;
The prophet who teaches lies, he *is* the tail.
16 For the leaders of this people cause *them* to err,
And *those who are* led by them are destroyed.
17 Therefore the Lord will have no joy in their young men,
Nor have mercy on their fatherless and widows;
For everyone *is* a hypocrite and an evildoer,
And every mouth speaks folly.

For all this His anger is not turned away,
But His hand *is* stretched out still.

18 For wickedness burns as the fire;
It shall devour the briers and thorns,
And kindle in the thickets of the forest;
They shall mount up *like* rising smoke.
19 Through the wrath of the LORD of hosts
The land is burned up,
And the people shall be as fuel for the fire;
No man shall spare his brother.
20 And he shall snatch on the right hand
And be hungry;
He shall devour on the left hand
And not be satisfied;
Every man shall eat the flesh of his own arm.
21 Manasseh *shall devour* Ephraim, and Ephraim Manasseh;
Together they *shall be* against Judah.

For all this His anger is not turned away,
But His hand *is* stretched out still.

10 "Woe to those who decree unrighteous decrees,
Who write misfortune,
Which they have prescribed
2 To rob the needy of justice,
And to take what is right from the poor of My people,
That widows may be their prey,
And *that* they may rob the fatherless.
3 What will you do in the day of punishment,

And in the desolation *which* will come
from afar?
To whom will you flee for help?
And where will you leave your glory?
4 Without Me they shall bow down among
the prisoners,
And they shall fall among the slain."

For all this His anger is not turned away,
But His hand *is* stretched out still.

Arrogant Assyria Also Judged

5 "Woe to Assyria, the rod of My anger
And the staff in whose hand is My
indignation.
6 I will send him against an ungodly
nation,
And against the people of My wrath
I will give him charge,
To seize the spoil, to take the prey,
And to tread them down like the mire of
the streets.
7 Yet he does not mean so,
Nor does his heart think so;
But *it is* in his heart to destroy,
And cut off not a few nations.
8 For he says,
'*Are* not my princes altogether kings?
9 *Is* not Calno like Carchemish?
Is not Hamath like Arpad?
Is not Samaria like Damascus?
10 As my hand has found the kingdoms of
the idols,
Whose carved images excelled those of
Jerusalem and Samaria,
11 As I have done to Samaria and her
idols,
Shall I not do also to Jerusalem and her
idols?' "

12 Therefore it shall come to pass, when the
Lord has performed all His work on Mount
Zion and on Jerusalem, *that He will say,* "I
will punish the fruit of the arrogant heart of
the king of Assyria, and the glory of his
haughty looks."
13 For he says:

"By the strength of my hand I have done
it,
And by my wisdom, for I am prudent;
Also I have removed the boundaries of
the people,
And have robbed their treasuries;
So I have put down the inhabitants like
a valiant *man.*
14 My hand has found like a nest the riches
of the people,
And as one gathers eggs *that are* left,
I have gathered all the earth;
And there was no one who moved *his*
wing,
Nor opened *his* mouth with even a
peep."

15 Shall the ax boast itself against him who
chops with it?
Or shall the saw exalt itself against him
who saws with it?
As if a rod could wield *itself* against
those who lift it up,
Or as if a staff could lift up, *as if it were*
not wood!
16 Therefore the Lord, the Lord[a] of hosts,
Will send leanness among his fat ones;
And under his glory
He will kindle a burning
Like the burning of a fire.
17 So the Light of Israel will be for a fire,
And his Holy One for a flame;
It will burn and devour
His thorns and his briers in one day.
18 And it will consume the glory of his
forest and of his fruitful field,
Both soul and body;
And they will be as when a sick man
wastes away.
19 Then the rest of the trees of his forest
Will be so few in number
That a child may write them.

The Returning Remnant of Israel

20 And it shall come to pass in that day
That the remnant of Israel,
And such as have escaped of the house
of Jacob,
Will never again depend on him who
defeated them,
But will depend on the LORD, the Holy
One of Israel, in truth.
21 The remnant will return, the remnant of
Jacob,
To the Mighty God.
22 For though your people, O Israel, be as
the sand of the sea,

10:16 [a]Following Bomberg; Masoretic Text and Dead Sea Scrolls read *YHWH* (*the* LORD).

A remnant of them will return;
The destruction decreed shall overflow
with righteousness.
23 For the Lord GOD of hosts
Will make a determined end
In the midst of all the land.

24Therefore thus says the Lord GOD of hosts:
"O My people, who dwell in Zion, do not be
afraid of the Assyrian. He shall strike you with
a rod and lift up his staff against you, in the
manner of Egypt. 25For yet a very little while
and the indignation will cease, as will My anger in their destruction." 26And the LORD of
hosts will stir up a scourge for him like the
slaughter of Midian at the rock of Oreb; *as* His
rod was on the sea, so will He lift it up in the
manner of Egypt.

27 It shall come to pass in that day
That his burden will be taken away from
your shoulder,
And his yoke from your neck,
And the yoke will be destroyed because
of the anointing oil.

28 He has come to Aiath,
He has passed Migron;
At Michmash he has attended to his
equipment.
29 They have gone along the ridge,
They have taken up lodging at Geba.
Ramah is afraid,
Gibeah of Saul has fled.
30 Lift up your voice,
O daughter of Gallim!
Cause it to be heard as far as Laish—
O poor Anathoth![a]
31 Madmenah has fled,
The inhabitants of Gebim seek refuge.
32 As yet he will remain at Nob that
day;
He will shake his fist at the mount of the
daughter of Zion,
The hill of Jerusalem.

33 Behold, the Lord,
The LORD of hosts,
Will lop off the bough with terror;
Those of high stature *will be* hewn
down,
And the haughty will be humbled.
34 He will cut down the thickets of the
forest with iron,
And Lebanon will fall by the Mighty
One.

THE REIGN OF JESSE'S OFFSPRING

11 There shall come forth a Rod from
the stem of Jesse,
And a Branch shall grow out of his roots.
2 The Spirit of the LORD shall rest upon
Him,
The Spirit of wisdom and understanding,
The Spirit of counsel and might,
The Spirit of knowledge and of the fear
of the LORD.

3 His delight *is* in the fear of the LORD,
And He shall not judge by the sight of
His eyes,
Nor decide by the hearing of His ears;
4 But with righteousness He shall judge
the poor,
And decide with equity for the meek of
the earth;
He shall strike the earth with the rod of
His mouth,
And with the breath of His lips He shall
slay the wicked.

10:30 [a]Following Masoretic Text, Targum, and Vulgate; Septuagint and Syriac read *Listen to her, O Anathoth.*

SOUL NOTE

Branching Out *(11:1, 2)* Isaiah referred to the Messiah as the Branch (see also 4:2) that would grow from the family line of King David. While David's line was still on the throne, it was cut down like a tree. God never left His people without hope, however. God promised a day when David's family line would sprout and blossom in a new way. When Jesus was born, the angel announced, "The Lord God will give Him the throne of His father David" (Luke 1:32). God's promises provide a ray of light even when life seems darkest. **Topic: God's Promises**

5 Righteousness shall be the belt of His
loins,
And faithfulness the belt of His waist.

6 "The wolf also shall dwell with the lamb,
The leopard shall lie down with the
young goat,
The calf and the young lion and the
fatling together;
And a little child shall lead them.
7 The cow and the bear shall graze;
Their young ones shall lie down
together;
And the lion shall eat straw like the ox.
8 The nursing child shall play by the
cobra's hole,
And the weaned child shall put his hand
in the viper's den.
9 They shall not hurt nor destroy in all My
holy mountain,
For the earth shall be full of the
knowledge of the LORD
As the waters cover the sea.

10 "And in that day there shall be a Root of
Jesse,
Who shall stand as a banner to the
people;
For the Gentiles shall seek Him,
And His resting place shall be glorious."

11 It shall come to pass in that day
That the Lord shall set His hand again
the second time
To recover the remnant of His people
who are left,
From Assyria and
Egypt,
From Pathros and
Cush,
From Elam and
Shinar,
From Hamath and
the islands of
the sea.

12 He will set up a banner for the nations,
And will assemble the outcasts of Israel,
And gather together the dispersed of
Judah
From the four corners of the earth.
13 Also the envy of Ephraim shall depart,
And the adversaries of Judah shall be
cut off;
Ephraim shall not envy Judah,
And Judah shall not harass Ephraim.
14 But they shall fly down upon the
shoulder of the Philistines toward the
west;
Together they shall plunder the people of
the East;
They shall lay their hand on Edom and
Moab;
And the people of Ammon shall obey
them.
15 The LORD will utterly destroy[a] the
tongue of the Sea of Egypt;
With His mighty wind He will shake His
fist over the River,[b]
And strike it in the seven streams,
And make *men* cross over dryshod.
16 There will be a highway for the remnant
of His people
Who will be left from Assyria,
As it was for Israel
In the day that he came up from the
land of Egypt.

A Hymn of Praise

12 And in that day you will say:

"O LORD, I will praise You;
Though You were angry with me,
Your anger is turned away, and You
comfort me.
2 Behold, God *is* my salvation,
I will trust and not be afraid;
'For YAH, the LORD, *is* my strength and
song;
He also has
become my
salvation.'"[a]

"Behold, God is my salvation, I will trust and not be afraid; 'For YAH, the LORD, is my strength and song; He also has become my salvation.'"
ISAIAH 12:2

3 Therefore with joy
you will draw
water
From the wells of
salvation.

4 And in that day you will say:

"Praise the LORD, call upon His name;
Declare His deeds among the peoples,
Make mention that His name is exalted.

11:15 [a]Following Masoretic Text and Vulgate; Septuagint, Syriac, and Targum read *dry up*. [b]That is, the Euphrates **12:2** [a]Exodus 15:2

5 Sing to the LORD,
For He has done excellent things;
This *is* known in all the earth.
6 Cry out and shout, O inhabitant of Zion,
For great *is* the Holy One of Israel in your midst!"

PROCLAMATION AGAINST BABYLON

13 The burden against Babylon which Isaiah the son of Amoz saw.

2 "Lift up a banner on the high mountain,
Raise your voice to them;
Wave your hand, that they may enter the gates of the nobles.
3 I have commanded My sanctified ones;
I have also called My mighty ones for My anger—
Those who rejoice in My exaltation."

4 The noise of a multitude in the mountains,
Like that of many people!
A tumultuous noise of the kingdoms of nations gathered together!
The LORD of hosts musters
The army for battle.
5 They come from a far country,
From the end of heaven—
The LORD and His weapons of indignation,
To destroy the whole land.

6 Wail, for the day of the LORD *is* at hand!
It will come as destruction from the Almighty.
7 Therefore all hands will be limp,
Every man's heart will melt,
8 And they will be afraid.
Pangs and sorrows will take hold of *them;*
They will be in pain as a woman in childbirth;
They will be amazed at one another;
Their faces *will be like* flames.

9 Behold, the day of the LORD comes,
Cruel, with both wrath and fierce anger,
To lay the land desolate;
And He will destroy its sinners from it.
10 For the stars of heaven and their constellations
Will not give their light;
The sun will be darkened in its going forth,
And the moon will not cause its light to shine.

11 "I will punish the world for *its* evil,
And the wicked for their iniquity;
I will halt the arrogance of the proud,
And will lay low the haughtiness of the terrible.
12 I will make a mortal more rare than fine gold,
A man more than the golden wedge of Ophir.
13 Therefore I will shake the heavens,
And the earth will move out of her place,
In the wrath of the LORD of hosts
And in the day of His fierce anger.
14 It shall be as the hunted gazelle,
And as a sheep that no man takes up;
Every man will turn to his own people,
And everyone will flee to his own land.
15 Everyone who is found will be thrust through,
And everyone who is captured will fall by the sword.
16 Their children also will be dashed to pieces before their eyes;
Their houses will be plundered
And their wives ravished.

17 "Behold, I will stir up the Medes against them,
Who will not regard silver;
And *as for* gold, they will not delight in it.
18 Also *their* bows will dash the young men to pieces,
And they will have no pity on the fruit of the womb;
Their eye will not spare children.
19 And Babylon, the glory of kingdoms,
The beauty of the Chaldeans' pride,
Will be as when God overthrew Sodom and Gomorrah.
20 It will never be inhabited,
Nor will it be settled from generation to generation;
Nor will the Arabian pitch tents there,
Nor will the shepherds make their sheepfolds there.
21 But wild beasts of the desert will lie there,

And their houses will be full of owls;
Ostriches will dwell there,
And wild goats will caper there.
22 The hyenas will howl in their citadels,
And jackals in their pleasant palaces.
Her time *is* near to come,
And her days will not be prolonged."

MERCY ON JACOB

14 For the LORD will have mercy on Jacob, and will still choose Israel, and
settle them in their own land. The strangers
will be joined with them, and they will cling
to the house of Jacob. 2Then people will take
them and bring them to their place, and the
house of Israel will possess them for servants
and maids in the land of the LORD; they will
take them captive whose captives they were,
and rule over their oppressors.

FALL OF THE KING OF BABYLON

3It shall come to pass in the day the LORD
gives you rest from your sorrow, and from
your fear and the hard bondage in which you
were made to serve, 4that you will take up this
proverb against the king of Babylon, and say:

"How the oppressor has ceased,
The golden[a] city ceased!
5 The LORD has broken the staff of the wicked,
The scepter of the rulers;
6 He who struck the people in wrath with a continual stroke,
He who ruled the nations in anger,
Is persecuted *and* no one hinders.
7 The whole earth is at rest *and* quiet;
They break forth into singing.
8 Indeed the cypress trees rejoice over you,
And the cedars of Lebanon,
Saying, 'Since you were cut down,
No woodsman has come up against us.'

9 "Hell from beneath is excited about you,
To meet *you* at your coming;
It stirs up the dead for you,
All the chief ones of the earth;
It has raised up from their thrones
All the kings of the nations.
10 They all shall speak and say to you:
'Have you also become as weak as we?
Have you become like us?
11 Your pomp is brought down to Sheol,
And the sound of your stringed instruments;
The maggot is spread under you,
And worms cover you.'

THE FALL OF LUCIFER

12 "How you are fallen from heaven,
O Lucifer,[a] son of the morning!
How you are cut down to the ground,
You who weakened the nations!
13 For you have said in your heart:
'I will ascend into heaven,
I will exalt my throne above the stars of God;
I will also sit on the mount of the congregation
On the farthest sides of the north;
14 I will ascend above the heights of the clouds,
I will be like the Most High.'
15 Yet you shall be brought down to Sheol,
To the lowest depths of the Pit.

16 "Those who see you will gaze at you,
And consider you, *saying:*

14:4 [a]Or *insolent* **14:12** [a]Literally *Day Star*

SOUL NOTE

The Winning Team *(14:12–15)* Although Isaiah's message was directed against the king of Babylon, many believe the imagery parallels the fall of Satan. The Evil One may have power on earth for a brief time, but God's judgment upon him has already been determined. Satan started as a great angel, and fell from his lofty position in heaven because of his pride. He sought to "be like the Most High," but God said he "shall be brought down to Sheol, to the lowest depths of the Pit" (14:14, 15). As we fight battles against evil, we must remember that the war has already been won.
Topic: Spiritual Warfare

'*Is* this the man who made the earth
tremble,
Who shook kingdoms,
17 Who made the world as a wilderness
And destroyed its cities,
Who did not open the house of his
prisoners?'

18 "All the kings of the nations,
All of them, sleep in glory,
Everyone in his own house;
19 But you are cast out of your grave
Like an abominable branch,
Like the garment of those who are slain,
Thrust through with a sword,
Who go down to the stones of the pit,
Like a corpse trodden underfoot.
20 You will not be joined with them in
burial,
Because you have destroyed your land
And slain your people.
The brood of evildoers shall never be
named.
21 Prepare slaughter for his children
Because of the iniquity of their fathers,
Lest they rise up and possess the land,
And fill the face of the world with
cities."

Babylon Destroyed

22 "For I will rise up against them," says the
LORD of hosts,
"And cut off from Babylon the name and
remnant,
And offspring and posterity," says the
LORD.
23 "I will also make it a possession for the
porcupine,
And marshes of muddy water;
I will sweep it with the broom of
destruction," says the LORD of hosts.

Assyria Destroyed

24 The LORD of hosts has sworn, saying,
"Surely, as I have thought, so it shall
come to pass,
And as I have purposed, *so* it shall
stand:
25 That I will break the Assyrian in My
land,
And on My mountains tread him
underfoot.
Then his yoke shall be removed from
them,
And his burden removed from their
shoulders.
26 This *is* the purpose that is purposed
against the whole earth,
And this *is* the hand that is stretched out
over all the nations.
27 For the LORD of hosts has purposed,
And who will annul *it?*
His hand *is* stretched out,
And who will turn it back?"

Philistia Destroyed

28 This is the burden which came in the year
that King Ahaz died.

29 "Do not rejoice, all you of Philistia,
Because the rod that struck you is
broken;
For out of the serpent's roots will come
forth a viper,
And its offspring *will be* a fiery flying
serpent.
30 The firstborn of the poor will feed,
And the needy will lie down in safety;
I will kill your roots with famine,
And it will slay your remnant.
31 Wail, O gate! Cry, O city!
All you of Philistia *are* dissolved;
For smoke will come from the north,
And no one *will be* alone in his
appointed times."

32 What will they answer the messengers
of the nation?
That the LORD has founded Zion,
And the poor of His people shall take
refuge in it.

Proclamation Against Moab

15 The burden against Moab.

Because in the night Ar of Moab is laid
waste
And destroyed,
Because in the night Kir of Moab is laid
waste
And destroyed,
2 He has gone up to the temple[a] and
Dibon,
To the high places to weep.
Moab will wail over Nebo and over
Medeba;

15:2 [a]Hebrew *bayith,* literally *house*

On all their heads *will be* baldness,
And every beard cut off.
3 In their streets they will clothe
themselves with sackcloth;
On the tops of their houses
And in their streets
Everyone will wail, weeping bitterly.
4 Heshbon and Elealeh will cry out,
Their voice shall be heard as far as
Jahaz;
Therefore the armed soldiers[a] of Moab
will cry out;
His life will be burdensome to him.

5 "My heart will cry out for Moab;
His fugitives *shall flee* to Zoar,
Like a three-year-old heifer.[a]
For by the Ascent of Luhith
They will go up with weeping;
For in the way of Horonaim
They will raise up a cry of destruction,
6 For the waters of Nimrim will be
desolate,
For the green grass has withered away;
The grass fails, there is nothing green.
7 Therefore the abundance they have
gained,
And what they have laid up,
They will carry away to the Brook of the
Willows.
8 For the cry has gone all around the
borders of Moab,
Its wailing to Eglaim
And its wailing to Beer Elim.
9 For the waters of Dimon[a] will be full of
blood;
Because I will bring more upon Dimon,[b]
Lions upon him who escapes from Moab,
And on the remnant of the land."

Moab Destroyed

16 Send the lamb to the ruler of the
land,
From Sela to the wilderness,
To the mount of the daughter of Zion.
2 For it shall be as a wandering bird
thrown out of the nest;
So shall be the daughters of Moab at the
fords of the Arnon.

3 "Take counsel, execute judgment;
Make your shadow like the night in the
middle of the day;
Hide the outcasts,
Do not betray him who escapes.
4 Let My outcasts dwell with you,
O Moab;
Be a shelter to them from the face of the
spoiler.
For the extortioner is at an end,
Devastation ceases,
The oppressors are consumed out of the
land.
5 In mercy the throne will be established;
And One will sit on it in truth, in the
tabernacle of David,
Judging and seeking justice and
hastening righteousness."

6 We have heard of the pride of Moab—
He is very proud—
Of his haughtiness and his pride and his
wrath;
But his lies *shall* not *be* so.
7 Therefore Moab shall wail for Moab;
Everyone shall wail.
For the foundations of Kir Hareseth you
shall mourn;
Surely *they are* stricken.

8 For the fields of Heshbon languish,
And the vine of Sibmah;
The lords of the nations have broken
down its choice plants,
Which have reached to Jazer
And wandered through the wilderness.
Her branches are stretched out,
They are gone over the sea.
9 Therefore I will bewail the vine of
Sibmah,
With the weeping of Jazer;
I will drench you with my tears,
O Heshbon and Elealeh;
For battle cries have fallen
Over your summer fruits and your
harvest.

10 Gladness is taken away,
And joy from the plentiful field;

15:4 [a]Following Masoretic Text, Targum, and Vulgate; Septuagint and Syriac read *loins.* **15:5** [a]Or *The Third Eglath,* an unknown city (compare Jeremiah 48:34) **15:9** [a]Following Masoretic Text and Targum; Dead Sea Scrolls and Vulgate read *Dibon;* Septuagint reads *Rimon.* [b]Following Masoretic Text and Targum; Dead Sea Scrolls and Vulgate read *Dibon;* Septuagint reads *Rimon.*

In the vineyards there will be no
singing,
Nor will there be shouting;
No treaders will tread out wine in the
presses;
I have made their shouting cease.
11 Therefore my heart shall resound like a
harp for Moab,
And my inner being for Kir Heres.

12 And it shall come to pass,
When it is seen that Moab is weary on
the high place,
That he will come to his sanctuary to
pray;
But he will not prevail.

13This *is* the word which the LORD has spoken concerning Moab since that time. 14But
now the LORD has spoken, saying, "Within
three years, as the years of a hired man, the
glory of Moab will be despised with all that
great multitude, and the remnant *will be* very
small *and* feeble."

Proclamation Against Syria and Israel

17 The burden against Damascus.

"Behold, Damascus will cease from *being*
a city,
And it will be a ruinous heap.
2 The cities of Aroer *are* forsaken;[a]
They will be for flocks
Which lie down, and no one will make
them afraid.
3 The fortress also will cease from
Ephraim,
The kingdom from Damascus,
And the remnant of Syria;
They will be as the glory of the children
of Israel,"
Says the LORD of hosts.

4 "In that day it shall come to pass
That the glory of Jacob will wane,
And the fatness of his flesh grow lean.
5 It shall be as when the harvester gathers
the grain,
And reaps the heads with his arm;
It shall be as he who gathers heads of
grain
In the Valley of Rephaim.
6 Yet gleaning grapes will be left in it,
Like the shaking of an olive tree,
Two *or* three olives at the top of the
uppermost bough,
Four *or* five in its most fruitful
branches,"
Says the LORD God of Israel.

7 In that day a man will look to his Maker,
And his eyes will have respect for the
Holy One of Israel.
8 He will not look to the altars,
The work of his hands;
He will not respect what his fingers have
made,
Nor the wooden images[a] nor the incense
altars.

9 In that day his strong cities will be as a
forsaken bough[a]
And an uppermost branch,[b]
Which they left because of the children
of Israel;
And there will be desolation.

10 Because you have forgotten the God of
your salvation,
And have not been mindful of the Rock
of your stronghold,
Therefore you will plant pleasant plants
And set out foreign seedlings;
11 In the day you will make your plant to
grow,
And in the morning you will make your
seed to flourish;
But the harvest *will be* a heap of ruins
In the day of grief and desperate sorrow.

12 Woe to the multitude of many people
Who make a noise like the roar of the
seas,
And to the rushing of nations
That make a rushing like the rushing of
mighty waters!
13 The nations will rush like the rushing of
many waters;
But *God* will rebuke them and they will
flee far away,

17:2 [a]Following Masoretic Text and Vulgate; Septuagint reads *It shall be forsaken forever;* Targum reads *Its cities shall be forsaken and desolate.* **17:8** [a]Hebrew *Asherim,* Canaanite deities **17:9** [a]Septuagint reads *Hivites;* Targum reads *laid waste;* Vulgate reads *as the plows.* [b]Septuagint reads *Amorites;* Targum reads *in ruins;* Vulgate reads *corn.*

And be chased like the chaff of the
mountains before the wind,
Like a rolling thing before the
whirlwind.
14 Then behold, at eventide, trouble!
And before the morning, he *is* no more.
This *is* the portion of those who plunder
us,
And the lot of those who rob us.

Proclamation Against Ethiopia

18 Woe to the land shadowed with
buzzing wings,
Which *is* beyond the rivers of Ethiopia,
2 Which sends ambassadors by sea,
Even in vessels of reed on the waters,
saying,
"Go, swift messengers, to a nation tall
and smooth *of skin,*
To a people terrible from their beginning
onward,
A nation powerful and treading down,
Whose land the rivers divide."

3 All inhabitants of the world and dwellers
on the earth:
When he lifts up a banner on the
mountains, you see *it;*
And when he blows a trumpet, you hear
it.
4 For so the LORD said to me,
"I will take My rest,
And I will look from My dwelling place
Like clear heat in sunshine,
Like a cloud of dew in the heat of
harvest."
5 For before the harvest, when the bud is
perfect
And the sour grape is ripening in the
flower,
He will both cut off the sprigs with
pruning hooks
And take away *and* cut down the
branches.
6 They will be left together for the
mountain birds of prey
And for the beasts of the earth;
The birds of prey will summer on them,
And all the beasts of the earth will
winter on them.

7 In that time a present will be brought to
the LORD of hosts
From[a] a people tall and smooth *of skin,*
And from a people terrible from their
beginning onward,
A nation powerful and treading down,
Whose land the rivers divide—
To the place of the name of the LORD of
hosts,
To Mount Zion.

Proclamation Against Egypt

19 The burden against Egypt.

Behold, the LORD rides on a swift cloud,
And will come into Egypt;
The idols of Egypt will totter at His
presence,
And the heart of Egypt will melt in its
midst.

2 "I will set Egyptians against Egyptians;
Everyone will fight against his brother,
And everyone against his neighbor,
City against city, kingdom against
kingdom.
3 The spirit of Egypt will fail in its midst;
I will destroy their counsel,
And they will consult the idols and the
charmers,
The mediums and the sorcerers.
4 And the Egyptians I will give
Into the hand of a cruel master,
And a fierce king will rule over them,"
Says the Lord, the LORD of hosts.

5 The waters will fail from the sea,
And the river will be wasted and dried
up.
6 The rivers will turn foul;
The brooks of defense will be emptied
and dried up;
The reeds and rushes will wither.
7 The papyrus reeds by the River,[a] by the
mouth of the River,
And everything sown by the River,
Will wither, be driven away, and be no
more.
8 The fishermen also will mourn;
All those will lament who cast hooks
into the River,
And they will languish who spread nets
on the waters.

18:7 [a]Following Dead Sea Scrolls, Septuagint, and Vulgate; Masoretic Text omits *From;* Targum reads *To.* **19:7** [a]That is, the Nile

9 Moreover those who work in fine flax
And those who weave fine fabric will be
ashamed;
10 And its foundations will be broken.
All who make wages *will be* troubled of
soul.

11 Surely the princes of Zoan *are* fools;
Pharaoh's wise counselors give foolish
counsel.
How do you say to Pharaoh, "I *am* the
son of the wise,
The son of ancient kings?"
12 Where *are* they?
Where are your wise men?
Let them tell you now,
And let them know what the LORD of
hosts has purposed against Egypt.
13 The princes of Zoan have become fools;
The princes of Noph[a] are deceived;
They have also deluded Egypt,
Those who are the mainstay of its tribes.
14 The LORD has mingled a perverse spirit
in her midst;
And they have caused Egypt to err in all
her work,
As a drunken man staggers in his vomit.
15 Neither will there be *any* work for
Egypt,
Which the head or tail,
Palm branch or bulrush, may do.[a]

16 In that day Egypt will be like women, and
will be afraid and fear because of the waving
of the hand of the LORD of hosts, which He
waves over it. 17 And the land of Judah will be
a terror to Egypt; everyone who makes mention of it will be afraid in himself, because of
the counsel of the LORD of hosts which He has
determined against it.

EGYPT, ASSYRIA, AND ISRAEL BLESSED

18 In that day five cities in the land of Egypt
will speak the language of Canaan and swear
by the LORD of hosts; one will be called the
City of Destruction.[a]
19 In that day there will be an altar to the
LORD in the midst of the land of Egypt, and a
pillar to the LORD at its border. 20 And it will be
for a sign and for a witness to the LORD of
hosts in the land of Egypt; for they will cry to
the LORD because of the oppressors, and He
will send them a Savior and a Mighty One, and
He will deliver them. 21 Then the LORD will be
known to Egypt, and the Egyptians will know
the LORD in that day, and will make sacrifice
and offering; yes, they will make a vow to the
LORD and perform *it.* 22 And the LORD will
strike Egypt, He will strike and heal *it;* they
will return to the LORD, and He will be entreated by them and heal them.
23 In that day there will be a highway from
Egypt to Assyria, and the Assyrian will come
into Egypt and the Egyptian into Assyria, and
the Egyptians will serve with the Assyrians.
24 In that day Israel will be one of three with
Egypt and Assyria—a blessing in the midst of
the land, 25 whom the LORD of hosts shall
bless, saying, "Blessed *is* Egypt My people,
and Assyria the work of My hands, and Israel
My inheritance."

THE SIGN AGAINST EGYPT AND ETHIOPIA

20 In the year that Tartan[a] came to Ashdod, when Sargon the king of Assyria
sent him, and he fought against Ashdod and
took it, 2 at the same time the LORD spoke by
Isaiah the son of Amoz, saying, "Go, and remove the sackcloth from your body, and take
your sandals off your feet." And he did so,
walking naked and barefoot.
3 Then the LORD said, "Just as My servant
Isaiah has walked naked and barefoot three
years *for* a sign and a wonder against Egypt
and Ethiopia, 4 so shall the king of Assyria lead
away the Egyptians as prisoners and the Ethiopians as captives, young and old, naked and
barefoot, with their buttocks uncovered, to
the shame of Egypt. 5 Then they shall be afraid
and ashamed of Ethiopia their expectation
and Egypt their glory. 6 And the inhabitant of
this territory will say in that day, 'Surely such
is our expectation, wherever we flee for help
to be delivered from the king of Assyria; and
how shall we escape?' "

THE FALL OF BABYLON PROCLAIMED

21 The burden against the Wilderness of
the Sea.

As whirlwinds in the South pass
through,

19:13 [a]That is, ancient Memphis
19:15 [a]Compare Isaiah 9:14–16
19:18 [a]Some Hebrew manuscripts, Arabic, Dead Sea Scrolls, Targum, and Vulgate read *Sun;* Septuagint reads *Asedek* (literally *Righteousness*).
20:1 [a]Or *the Commander in Chief*

So it comes from the desert, from a
terrible land.
2 A distressing vision is declared to me;
The treacherous dealer deals
treacherously,
And the plunderer plunders.
Go up, O Elam!
Besiege, O Media!
All its sighing I have made to cease.

3 Therefore my loins are filled with pain;
Pangs have taken hold of me, like the
pangs of a woman in labor.
I was distressed when *I* heard *it;*
I was dismayed when *I* saw *it.*
4 My heart wavered, fearfulness frightened
me;
The night for which I longed He turned
into fear for me.
5 Prepare the table,
Set a watchman in the tower,
Eat and drink.
Arise, you princes,
Anoint the shield!

6 For thus has the Lord said to me:
"Go, set a watchman,
Let him declare what he sees."
7 And he saw a chariot *with* a pair of
horsemen,
A chariot of donkeys, *and* a chariot of
camels,
And he listened earnestly with great
care.
8 Then he cried, "A lion,[a] my Lord!
I stand continually on the watchtower in
the daytime;
I have sat at my post every night.
9 And look, here comes a chariot of men
with a pair of horsemen!"
Then he answered and said,
"Babylon is fallen, is fallen!
And all the carved images of her gods
He has broken to the ground."

10 Oh, my threshing and the grain of my
floor!
That which I have heard from the LORD
of hosts,
The God of Israel,
I have declared to you.

PROCLAMATION AGAINST EDOM

11The burden against Dumah.

He calls to me out of Seir,
"Watchman, what of the night?
Watchman, what of the night?"
12 The watchman said,
"The morning comes, and also the night.
If you will inquire, inquire;
Return! Come back!"

PROCLAMATION AGAINST ARABIA

13The burden against Arabia.

In the forest in Arabia you will lodge,
O you traveling companies of Dedanites.
14 O inhabitants of the land of Tema,
Bring water to him who is thirsty;
With their bread they met him who
fled.
15 For they fled from the swords, from the
drawn sword,
From the bent bow, and from the
distress of war.

16For thus the LORD has said to me: "Within
a year, according to the year of a hired man,
all the glory of Kedar will fail; 17and the remainder of the number of archers, the mighty
men of the people of Kedar, will be diminished; for the LORD God of Israel has spoken
it."

PROCLAMATION AGAINST JERUSALEM

22 The burden against the Valley of Vision.

What ails you now, that you have all
gone up to the housetops,
2 You who are full of noise,
A tumultuous city, a joyous city?
Your slain *men are* not slain with the
sword,
Nor dead in battle.
3 All your rulers have fled together;
They are captured by the archers.
All who are found in you are bound
together;
They have fled from afar.
4 Therefore I said, "Look away from me,
I will weep bitterly;
Do not labor to comfort me
Because of the plundering of the
daughter of my people."

21:8 [a]Dead Sea Scrolls read *Then the observer cried.*

5 For *it is* a day of trouble and treading
down and perplexity
By the Lord GOD of hosts
In the Valley of Vision—
Breaking down the walls
And of crying to the mountain.
6 Elam bore the quiver
With chariots of men *and* horsemen,
And Kir uncovered the shield.
7 It shall come to pass *that* your choicest
valleys
Shall be full of chariots,
And the horsemen shall set themselves
in array at the gate.

8 He removed the protection of Judah.
You looked in that day to the armor of
the House of the Forest;
9 You also saw the damage to the city of
David,
That it was great;
And you gathered together the waters of
the lower pool.
10 You numbered the houses of
Jerusalem,
And the houses you broke down
To fortify the wall.
11 You also made a reservoir between the
two walls
For the water of the old pool.
But you did not look to its Maker,
Nor did you have respect for Him who
fashioned it long ago.

12 And in that day the Lord GOD of
hosts
Called for weeping and for mourning,
For baldness and for girding with
sackcloth.
13 But instead, joy and gladness,
Slaying oxen and killing sheep,
Eating meat and drinking wine:
"Let us eat and drink, for tomorrow we
die!"

14 Then it was revealed in my hearing by
the LORD of hosts,
"Surely for this iniquity there will be no
atonement for you,
Even to your death," says the Lord GOD
of hosts.

THE JUDGMENT ON SHEBNA

15 Thus says the Lord GOD of hosts:
"Go, proceed to this steward,
To Shebna, who *is* over the house, *and*
say:
16 'What have you here, and whom have
you here,
That you have hewn a sepulcher here,
As he who hews himself a sepulcher on
high,
Who carves a tomb for himself in a
rock?
17 Indeed, the LORD will throw you away
violently,
O mighty man,
And will surely seize you.
18 He will surely turn violently and toss
you like a ball
Into a large country;
There you shall die, and there your
glorious chariots
Shall be the shame of your master's
house.
19 So I will drive you out of your office,
And from your position he will pull you
down.[a]

20 'Then it shall be in that day,
That I will call My servant Eliakim the
son of Hilkiah;
21 I will clothe him with your robe
And strengthen him with your belt;
I will commit your responsibility into his
hand.
He shall be a father to the inhabitants of
Jerusalem
And to the house of Judah.
22 The key of the house of David
I will lay on his shoulder;
So he shall open, and no one shall shut;
And he shall shut, and no one shall
open.
23 I will fasten him *as* a peg in a secure
place,
And he will become a glorious throne to
his father's house.

24 'They will hang on him all the glory of his
father's house, the offspring and the posterity,
all vessels of small quantity, from the cups to
all the pitchers. 25 In that day,' says the LORD of
hosts, 'the peg that is fastened in the secure

22:19 [a]Septuagint omits *he will pull you down;* Syriac, Targum, and Vulgate read *I will pull you down.*

place will be removed and be cut down and
fall, and the burden that *was* on it will be cut
off; for the LORD has spoken.' "

PROCLAMATION AGAINST TYRE

23 The burden against Tyre.

Wail, you ships of Tarshish!
For it is laid waste,
So that there is no house, no harbor;
From the land of Cyprus[a] it is revealed
to them.

2 Be still, you inhabitants of the
coastland,
You merchants of Sidon,
Whom those who cross the sea have
filled.[a]
3 And on great waters the grain of Shihor,
The harvest of the River,[a] *is* her revenue;
And she is a marketplace for the nations.

4 Be ashamed, O Sidon;
For the sea has spoken,
The strength of the sea, saying,
"I do not labor, nor bring forth children;
Neither do I rear young men,
Nor bring up virgins."
5 When the report *reaches* Egypt,
They also will be in agony at the report
of Tyre.

6 Cross over to Tarshish;
Wail, you inhabitants of the coastland!
7 *Is* this your joyous *city,*
Whose antiquity *is* from ancient days,
Whose feet carried her far off to dwell?
8 Who has taken this counsel against Tyre,
the crowning *city,*
Whose merchants *are* princes,
Whose traders *are* the honorable of the
earth?
9 The LORD of hosts has purposed it,
To bring to dishonor the pride of all
glory,
To bring into contempt all the honorable
of the earth.

10 Overflow through your land like the
River,[a]
O daughter of Tarshish;
There is no more strength.
11 He stretched out His hand over the sea,
He shook the kingdoms;
The LORD has given a commandment
against Canaan
To destroy its strongholds.
12 And He said, "You will rejoice no more,
O you oppressed virgin daughter of
Sidon.
Arise, cross over to Cyprus;
There also you will have no rest."

13 Behold, the land of the Chaldeans,
This people *which* was not;
Assyria founded it for wild beasts of the
desert.
They set up its towers,
They raised up its palaces,
And brought it to ruin.

14 Wail, you ships of Tarshish!
For your strength is laid waste.

15 Now it shall come to pass in that day that
Tyre will be forgotten seventy years, according
to the days of one king. At the end of seventy
years it will happen to Tyre as *in* the song of
the harlot:

16 "Take a harp, go about the city,
You forgotten harlot;
Make sweet melody, sing many songs,
That you may be remembered."

17 And it shall be, at the end of seventy
years, that the LORD will deal with Tyre. She
will return to her hire, and commit fornication
with all the kingdoms of the world on the face
of the earth. 18 Her gain and her pay will be set
apart for the LORD; it will not be treasured nor
laid up, for her gain will be for those who
dwell before the LORD, to eat sufficiently, and
for fine clothing.

IMPENDING JUDGMENT ON THE EARTH

24 Behold, the LORD makes the earth
empty and makes it waste,
Distorts its surface
And scatters abroad its inhabitants.
2 And it shall be:
As with the people, so with the priest;

23:1 [a]Hebrew *Kittim,* western lands, especially Cyprus **23:2** [a]Following Masoretic Text and Vulgate; Septuagint and Targum read *Passing over the water;* Dead Sea Scrolls read *Your messengers passing over the sea.* **23:3** [a]That is, the Nile **23:10** [a]That is, the Nile

As with the servant, so with his master;
As with the maid, so with her mistress;
As with the buyer, so with the seller;
As with the lender, so with the borrower;
As with the creditor, so with the debtor.
3 The land shall be entirely emptied and utterly plundered,
For the LORD has spoken this word.

4 The earth mourns *and* fades away,
The world languishes *and* fades away;
The haughty people of the earth languish.
5 The earth is also defiled under its inhabitants,
Because they have transgressed the laws,
Changed the ordinance,
Broken the everlasting covenant.
6 Therefore the curse has devoured the earth,
And those who dwell in it are desolate.
Therefore the inhabitants of the earth are burned,
And few men *are* left.

7 The new wine fails, the vine languishes,
All the merry-hearted sigh.
8 The mirth of the tambourine ceases,
The noise of the jubilant ends,
The joy of the harp ceases.
9 They shall not drink wine with a song;
Strong drink is bitter to those who drink it.
10 The city of confusion is broken down;
Every house is shut up, so that none may go in.
11 *There is* a cry for wine in the streets,
All joy is darkened,
The mirth of the land is gone.
12 In the city desolation is left,
And the gate is stricken with destruction.
13 When it shall be thus in the midst of the land among the people,
It shall be like the shaking of an olive tree,
Like the gleaning of grapes when the vintage is done.

14 They shall lift up their voice, they shall sing;
For the majesty of the LORD
They shall cry aloud from the sea.
15 Therefore glorify the LORD in the dawning light,
The name of the LORD God of Israel in the coastlands of the sea.
16 From the ends of the earth we have heard songs:
"Glory to the righteous!"
But I said, "I am ruined, ruined!
Woe to me!
The treacherous dealers have dealt treacherously,
Indeed, the treacherous dealers have dealt very treacherously."

17 Fear and the pit and the snare
Are upon you, O inhabitant of the earth.
18 And it shall be
That he who flees from the noise of the fear
Shall fall into the pit,
And he who comes up from the midst of the pit
Shall be caught in the snare;
For the windows from on high are open,
And the foundations of the earth are shaken.

19 The earth is violently broken,
The earth is split open,
The earth is shaken exceedingly.
20 The earth shall reel to and fro like a drunkard,
And shall totter like a hut;
Its transgression shall be heavy upon it,
And it will fall, and not rise again.

21 It shall come to pass in that day
That the LORD will punish on high the host of exalted ones,
And on the earth the kings of the earth.
22 They will be gathered together,
As prisoners are gathered in the pit,
And will be shut up in the prison;
After many days they will be punished.
23 Then the moon will be disgraced
And the sun ashamed;
For the LORD of hosts will reign
On Mount Zion and in Jerusalem
And before His elders, gloriously.

PRAISE TO GOD

25 O LORD, You *are* my God.
I will exalt You,
I will praise Your name,

For You have done wonderful *things;*
Your counsels of old *are* faithfulness *and* truth.
2 For You have made a city a ruin,
A fortified city a ruin,
A palace of foreigners to be a city no more;
It will never be rebuilt.
3 Therefore the strong people will glorify You;
The city of the terrible nations will fear You.
4 For You have been a strength to the poor,
A strength to the needy in his distress,
A refuge from the storm,
A shade from the heat;
For the blast of the terrible ones *is* as a storm *against* the wall.
5 You will reduce the noise of aliens,
As heat in a dry place;
As heat in the shadow of a cloud,
The song of the terrible ones will be diminished.

6 And in this mountain
The LORD of hosts will make for all people
A feast of choice pieces,
A feast of wines on the lees,
Of fat things full of marrow,
Of well-refined wines on the lees.
7 And He will destroy on this mountain
The surface of the covering cast over all people,
And the veil that is spread over all nations.
8 He will swallow up death forever,
And the Lord GOD will wipe away tears from all faces;
The rebuke of His people
He will take away from all the earth;
For the LORD has spoken.

9 And it will be said in that day:
"Behold, this *is* our God;
We have waited for Him, and He will save us.
This *is* the LORD;
We have waited for Him;
We will be glad and rejoice in His salvation."

10 For on this mountain the hand of the LORD will rest,
And Moab shall be trampled down under Him,
As straw is trampled down for the refuse heap.
11 And He will spread out His hands in their midst
As a swimmer reaches out to swim,
And He will bring down their pride
Together with the trickery of their hands.
12 The fortress of the high fort of your walls
He will bring down, lay low,
And bring to the ground, down to the dust.

A SONG OF SALVATION

26 In that day this song will be sung in the land of Judah:

"We have a strong city;
God will appoint salvation *for* walls and bulwarks.
2 Open the gates,
That the righteous nation which keeps the truth may enter in.
3 You will keep *him* in perfect peace,
Whose mind *is* stayed *on You,*
Because he trusts in You.

SOUL NOTE

Final Victory *(25:8)* Death is humanity's enemy. People fear death and the sorrow it brings. This is the first prophecy of the destruction of death and grief. In Christ's death, the curse and power of death were destroyed forever. Believers have the promise of new life now and eternal life with God. Isaiah writes that "the Lord GOD will wipe away tears from all faces." In Revelation, John describes the same picture: "God will wipe away every tear from their eyes. . . . There shall be no more pain" (Rev. 21:4). For believers, death is the gateway to eternal life. **Topic: Death**

4 Trust in the LORD forever,
For in YAH, the LORD, *is* everlasting
strength.[a]
5 For He brings down those who dwell on
high,
The lofty city;
He lays it low,
He lays it low to the ground,
He brings it down to the dust.
6 The foot shall tread it down—
The feet of the poor
And the steps of the needy."

7 The way of the just *is* uprightness;
O Most Upright,
You weigh the path of the just.
8 Yes, in the way of Your judgments,
O LORD, we have waited for You;
The desire of *our* soul *is* for Your
name
And for the remembrance of You.
9 With my soul I have desired You in the
night,
Yes, by my spirit within me I will seek
You early;
For when Your judgments *are* in the
earth,
The inhabitants of the world will learn
righteousness.
10 Let grace be shown to the wicked,
Yet he will not learn righteousness;
In the land of uprightness he will deal
unjustly,
And will not behold the majesty of the
LORD.
11 LORD, *when* Your hand is lifted up, they
will not see.
But they will see and be ashamed
For *their* envy of people;
Yes, the fire of Your enemies shall
devour them.

12 LORD, You will establish peace for us,
For You have also done all our works in
us.
13 O LORD our God, masters besides You
Have had dominion over us;
But by You only we make mention of
Your name.
14 *They are* dead, they will not live;
They are deceased, they will not rise.
Therefore You have punished and
destroyed them,
And made all their memory to perish.
15 You have increased the nation, O LORD,
You have increased the nation;

26:4 [a]Or *Rock of Ages*

SOUL NOTE

Perfect Peace *(26:3)* Occasions for anxiety happen. Jesus reminded His followers that "in the world you will have tribulation" (John 16:33). The prophet Isaiah wrote that God gives peace in spite of conflict and turmoil. Peace is so basic to God's nature that it is part of His name. God the Father is the "God of peace" (Phil. 4:9; Heb. 13:20). God the Son is the Prince of Peace (Is. 9:6). And God the Holy Spirit produces peace in our lives (Gal. 5:22). To have "perfect peace," wrote Isaiah, we must focus our minds on God and trust in Him. **Topic: Anxiety**

SOUL NOTE

Secure in Him *(26:4, 5)* The answer to human insecurities is to "trust in the LORD forever." In Him we should find our security, peace, and confidence. We are surrounded by plenty of problems that fill our thoughts. Beset by fear and insecurity, we feel shaky, unstable, and unsafe. Jesus told His followers, on this eve of His death, "Peace I leave with you, My peace I give to you. . . . Let not your heart be troubled, neither let it be afraid" (John 14:27). With Christ's peace in our hearts we can be secure, knowing that He is in control. **Topic: Insecurity**

You are glorified;
You have expanded all the borders of the
land.

16 LORD, in trouble they have visited You,
They poured out a prayer *when* Your
chastening *was* upon them.
17 As a woman with child
Is in pain and cries out in her pangs,
When she draws near the time of her
delivery,
So have we been in Your sight, O LORD.
18 We have been with child, we have been
in pain;
We have, as it were, brought forth wind;
We have not accomplished any
deliverance in the earth,
Nor have the inhabitants of the world
fallen.

19 Your dead shall live;
Together with my dead body[a] they shall
arise.
Awake and sing, you who dwell in dust;
For your dew *is like* the dew of herbs,
And the earth shall cast out the dead.

Take Refuge from the Coming Judgment

20 Come, my people, enter your chambers,
And shut your doors behind you;
Hide yourself, as it were, for a little
moment,
Until the indignation is past.
21 For behold, the LORD comes out of His
place
To punish the inhabitants of the earth
for their iniquity;
The earth will also disclose her blood,
And will no more cover her slain.

27 In that day the LORD with His severe
sword, great and strong,
Will punish Leviathan the fleeing
serpent,
Leviathan that twisted serpent;
And He will slay the reptile that *is* in the
sea.

The Restoration of Israel

2 In that day sing to her,
"A vineyard of red wine![a]
3 I, the LORD, keep it,
I water it every moment;
Lest any hurt it,
I keep it night and day.
4 Fury *is* not in Me.
Who would set briers *and* thorns
Against Me in battle?
I would go through them,
I would burn them together.
5 Or let him take hold of My strength,
That he may make peace with Me;
And he shall make peace with Me."

6 Those who come He shall cause to take
root in Jacob;
Israel shall blossom and bud,
And fill the face of the world with fruit.

7 Has He struck Israel as He struck those
who struck him?
Or has He been slain according to the
slaughter of those who were slain by
Him?
8 In measure, by sending it away,
You contended with it.
He removes *it* by His rough wind
In the day of the east wind.
9 Therefore by this the iniquity of Jacob
will be covered;
And this *is* all the fruit of taking away
his sin:
When he makes all the stones of the altar
Like chalkstones that are beaten to dust,
Wooden images[a] and incense altars shall
not stand.

10 Yet the fortified city *will be* desolate,
The habitation forsaken and left like a
wilderness;
There the calf will feed, and there it will
lie down
And consume its branches.
11 When its boughs are withered, they will
be broken off;
The women come *and* set them on fire.
For it *is* a people of no understanding;
Therefore He who made them will not
have mercy on them,

26:19 [a]Following Masoretic Text and Vulgate; Syriac and Targum read *their dead bodies;* Septuagint reads *those in the tombs.* **27:2** [a]Following Masoretic Text (Kittel's *Biblia Hebraica*), Bomberg, and Vulgate; Masoretic Text (*Biblia Hebraica Stuttgartensia*), some Hebrew manuscripts, and Septuagint read *delight;* Targum reads *choice vineyard.* **27:9** [a]Hebrew *Asherim,* Canaanite deities

And He who formed them will show
them no favor.

12 And it shall come to pass in that day
That the LORD will thresh,
From the channel of the River[a] to the
Brook of Egypt;
And you will be gathered one by one,
O you children of Israel.

13 So it shall be in that day:
The great trumpet will be blown;
They will come, who are about to perish
in the land of Assyria,
And they who are outcasts in the land of
Egypt,
And shall worship the LORD in the holy
mount at Jerusalem.

Woe to Ephraim and Jerusalem

28 Woe to the crown of pride, to the
drunkards of Ephraim,
Whose glorious beauty *is* a fading
flower
Which *is* at the head of the verdant
valleys,
To those who are overcome with wine!
2 Behold, the Lord has a mighty and
strong one,
Like a tempest of hail and a destroying
storm,
Like a flood of mighty waters
overflowing,
Who will bring *them* down to the earth
with *His* hand.
3 The crown of pride, the drunkards of
Ephraim,
Will be trampled underfoot;
4 And the glorious beauty is a fading
flower
Which *is* at the head of the verdant
valley,
Like the first fruit before the summer,
Which an observer sees;
He eats it up while it is still in his hand.

5 In that day the LORD of hosts will be
For a crown of glory and a diadem of
beauty
To the remnant of His people,
6 For a spirit of justice to him who sits in
judgment,
And for strength to those who turn back
the battle at the gate.

7 But they also have erred through wine,
And through intoxicating drink are out
of the way;
The priest and the prophet have erred
through intoxicating drink,
They are swallowed up by wine,
They are out of the way through
intoxicating drink;
They err in vision, they stumble *in*
judgment.
8 For all tables are full of vomit *and*
filth;
No place *is clean.*

9 "Whom will he teach knowledge?
And whom will he make to understand
the message?
Those *just* weaned from milk?
Those *just* drawn from the breasts?
10 For precept *must be* upon precept,
precept upon precept,
Line upon line, line upon line,
Here a little, there a little."

11 For with stammering lips and another
tongue
He will speak to this people,
12 To whom He said, "This *is* the rest *with
which*
You may cause the weary to rest,"
And, "This *is* the refreshing";
Yet they would not hear.
13 But the word of the LORD was to them,
"Precept upon precept, precept upon
precept,
Line upon line, line upon line,
Here a little, there a little,"
That they might go and fall backward,
and be broken
And snared and caught.

14 Therefore hear the word of the LORD,
you scornful men,
Who rule this people who *are* in
Jerusalem,
15 Because you have said, "We have made
a covenant with death,
And with Sheol we are in agreement.
When the overflowing scourge passes
through,
It will not come to us,
For we have made lies our refuge,

27:12 [a]That is, the Euphrates

And under falsehood we have hidden
ourselves."

A Cornerstone in Zion

16Therefore thus says the Lord GOD:

"Behold, I lay in Zion a stone for a foundation,
A tried stone, a precious cornerstone, a sure foundation;
Whoever believes will not act hastily.
17 Also I will make justice the measuring line,
And righteousness the plummet;
The hail will sweep away the refuge of lies,
And the waters will overflow the hiding place.
18 Your covenant with death will be annulled,
And your agreement with Sheol will not stand;
When the overflowing scourge passes through,
Then you will be trampled down by it.
19 As often as it goes out it will take you;
For morning by morning it will pass over,
And by day and by night;
It will be a terror just to understand the report."

20 For the bed is too short to stretch out *on*,
And the covering so narrow that one cannot wrap himself *in it.*
21 For the LORD will rise up as *at* Mount Perazim,
He will be angry as in the Valley of Gibeon—
That He may do His work, His awesome work,
And bring to pass His act, His unusual act.
22 Now therefore, do not be mockers,
Lest your bonds be made strong;
For I have heard from the Lord GOD of hosts,
A destruction determined even upon the whole earth.

Listen to the Teaching of God

23 Give ear and hear my voice,
Listen and hear my speech.
24 Does the plowman keep plowing all day to sow?
Does he keep turning his soil and breaking the clods?
25 When he has leveled its surface,
Does he not sow the black cummin
And scatter the cummin,
Plant the wheat in rows,
The barley in the appointed place,
And the spelt in its place?
26 For He instructs him in right judgment,
His God teaches him.

27 For the black cummin is not threshed with a threshing sledge,
Nor is a cartwheel rolled over the cummin;
But the black cummin is beaten out with a stick,
And the cummin with a rod.
28 Bread *flour* must be ground;
Therefore he does not thresh it forever,
Break *it with* his cartwheel,
Or crush it *with* his horsemen.
29 This also comes from the LORD of hosts,
Who is wonderful in counsel *and* excellent in guidance.

Woe to Jerusalem

29 "Woe to Ariel,[a] to Ariel, the city *where* David dwelt!
Add year to year;
Let feasts come around.
2 Yet I will distress Ariel;
There shall be heaviness and sorrow,
And it shall be to Me as Ariel.
3 I will encamp against you all around,
I will lay siege against you with a mound,
And I will raise siegeworks against you.
4 You shall be brought down,
You shall speak out of the ground;
Your speech shall be low, out of the dust;
Your voice shall be like a medium's, out of the ground;
And your speech shall whisper out of the dust.

5 "Moreover the multitude of your foes
Shall be like fine dust,
And the multitude of the terrible ones

29:1 [a]That is, Jerusalem

Like chaff that passes away;
Yes, it shall be in an instant, suddenly.
6 You will be punished by the LORD of hosts
With thunder and earthquake and great noise,
With storm and tempest
And the flame of devouring fire.
7 The multitude of all the nations who fight against Ariel,
Even all who fight against her and her fortress,
And distress her,
Shall be as a dream of a night vision.
8 It shall even be as when a hungry man dreams,
And look—he eats;
But he awakes, and his soul is still empty;
Or as when a thirsty man dreams,
And look—he drinks;
But he awakes, and indeed *he is* faint,
And his soul still craves:
So the multitude of all the nations shall be,
Who fight against Mount Zion."

The Blindness of Disobedience

9 Pause and wonder!
Blind yourselves and be blind!
They are drunk, but not with wine;
They stagger, but not with intoxicating drink.
10 For the LORD has poured out on you
The spirit of deep sleep,
And has closed your eyes, namely, the prophets;
And He has covered your heads, *namely,* the seers.

11The whole vision has become to you like
the words of a book that is sealed, which *men*
deliver to one who is literate, saying, "Read
this, please."
And he says, "I cannot, for it *is* sealed."
12Then the book is delivered to one who is
illiterate, saying, "Read this, please."
And he says, "I am not literate."
13Therefore the Lord said:

"Inasmuch as these people draw near with their mouths
And honor Me with their lips,
But have removed their hearts far from Me,
And their fear toward Me is taught by the commandment of men,
14 Therefore, behold, I will again do a marvelous work
Among this people,
A marvelous work and a wonder;
For the wisdom of their wise *men* shall perish,
And the understanding of their prudent *men* shall be hidden."

15 Woe to those who seek deep to hide their counsel far from the LORD,
And their works are in the dark;
They say, "Who sees us?" and, "Who knows us?"
16 Surely you have things turned around!
Shall the potter be esteemed as the clay;
For shall the thing made say of him who made it,
"He did not make me"?
Or shall the thing formed say of him who formed it,
"He has no understanding"?

SOUL NOTE

Completely Healed *(29:18, 19)* Isaiah promised that a day would come when the deaf would hear, the blind would see, and the humble and the poor would "rejoice in the Holy One of Israel." These promises were initially fulfilled in the healings performed by Jesus, for through Him many were healed from various diseases, and the poor heard the Good News of the kingdom of heaven (Matt. 11:5). Jesus' ministry and His healings were a sign that He was the promised Messiah. The promises will be fulfilled in heaven when God's people will be completely healed.
Topic: Healing/Recovery

Future Recovery of Wisdom

17 *Is* it not yet a very little while
Till Lebanon shall be turned into a fruitful field,
And the fruitful field be esteemed as a forest?
18 In that day the deaf shall hear the words of the book,
And the eyes of the blind shall see out of obscurity and out of darkness.
19 The humble also shall increase *their* joy in the LORD,
And the poor among men shall rejoice
In the Holy One of Israel.
20 For the terrible one is brought to nothing,
The scornful one is consumed,
And all who watch for iniquity are cut off—
21 Who make a man an offender by a word,
And lay a snare for him who reproves in the gate,
And turn aside the just by empty words.

22Therefore thus says the LORD, who redeemed Abraham, concerning the house of
Jacob:

"Jacob shall not now be ashamed,
Nor shall his face now grow pale;
23 But when he sees his children,
The work of My hands, in his midst,
They will hallow My name,
And hallow the Holy One of Jacob,
And fear the God of Israel.
24 These also who erred in spirit will come to understanding,
And those who complained will learn doctrine."

Futile Confidence in Egypt

30 "Woe to the rebellious children," says the LORD,
"Who take counsel, but not of Me,
And who devise plans, but not of My Spirit,
That they may add sin to sin;
2 Who walk to go down to Egypt,
And have not asked My advice,
To strengthen themselves in the strength of Pharaoh,
And to trust in the shadow of Egypt!
3 Therefore the strength of Pharaoh
Shall be your shame,
And trust in the shadow of Egypt
Shall be *your* humiliation.
4 For his princes were at Zoan,
And his ambassadors came to Hanes.
5 They were all ashamed of a people *who* could not benefit them,
Or be help or benefit,
But a shame and also a reproach."

6The burden against the beasts of the South.

Through a land of trouble and anguish,
From which *came* the lioness and lion,
The viper and fiery flying serpent,
They will carry their riches on the backs of young donkeys,
And their treasures on the humps of camels,
To a people *who* shall not profit;
7 For the Egyptians shall help in vain and to no purpose.
Therefore I have called her
Rahab-Hem-Shebeth.[a]

A Rebellious People

8 Now go, write it before them on a tablet,
And note it on a scroll,
That it may be for time to come,
Forever and ever:
9 That this *is* a rebellious people,
Lying children,
Children *who* will not hear the law of the LORD;
10 Who say to the seers, "Do not see,"
And to the prophets, "Do not prophesy to us right things;
Speak to us smooth things, prophesy deceits.
11 Get out of the way,
Turn aside from the path,
Cause the Holy One of Israel
To cease from before us."

12Therefore thus says the Holy One of Israel:

"Because you despise this word,
And trust in oppression and perversity,
And rely on them,
13 Therefore this iniquity shall be to you
Like a breach ready to fall,

30:7 [a]Literally *Rahab Sits Idle*

A bulge in a high wall,
Whose breaking comes suddenly, in an instant.
14 And He shall break it like the breaking of the potter's vessel,
Which is broken in pieces;
He shall not spare.
So there shall not be found among its fragments
A shard to take fire from the hearth,
Or to take water from the cistern."

15For thus says the Lord GOD, the Holy One
of Israel:

"In returning and rest you shall be saved;
In quietness and confidence shall be your strength."
But you would not,
16 And you said, "No, for we will flee on horses"—
Therefore you shall flee!
And, "We will ride on swift *horses*"—
Therefore those who pursue you shall be swift!

17 One thousand *shall flee* at the threat of one,
At the threat of five you shall flee,
Till you are left as a pole on top of a mountain
And as a banner on a hill.

GOD WILL BE GRACIOUS

18 Therefore the LORD will wait, that He may be gracious to you;
And therefore He will be exalted, that He may have mercy on you.
For the LORD *is* a God of justice;
Blessed *are* all those who wait for Him.

19 For the people shall dwell in Zion at Jerusalem;
You shall weep no more.
He will be very gracious to you at the sound of your cry;
When He hears it, He will answer you.
20 And *though* the Lord gives you
The bread of adversity and the water of affliction,
Yet your teachers will not be moved into a corner anymore,
But your eyes shall see your teachers.
21 Your ears shall hear a word behind you, saying,
"This *is* the way, walk in it,"
Whenever you turn to the right hand
Or whenever you turn to the left.
22 You will also defile the covering of your images of silver,
And the ornament of your molded images of gold.
You will throw them away as an unclean thing;
You will say to them, "Get away!"

23 Then He will give the rain for your seed
With which you sow the ground,
And bread of the increase of the earth;
It will be fat and plentiful.
In that day your cattle will feed
In large pastures.
24 Likewise the oxen and the young donkeys that work the ground
Will eat cured fodder,
Which has been winnowed with the shovel and fan.
25 There will be on every high mountain
And on every high hill
Rivers *and* streams of waters,
In the day of the great slaughter,
When the towers fall.
26 Moreover the light of the moon will be as the light of the sun,
And the light of the sun will be sevenfold,
As the light of seven days,
In the day that the LORD binds up the bruise of His people
And heals the stroke of their wound.

JUDGMENT ON ASSYRIA

27 Behold, the name of the LORD comes from afar,
Burning *with* His anger,
And *His* burden *is* heavy;
His lips are full of indignation,
And His tongue like a devouring fire.
28 His breath is like an overflowing stream,
Which reaches up to the neck,
To sift the nations with the sieve of futility;
And *there shall be* a bridle in the jaws of the people,
Causing *them* to err.

29 You shall have a song
As in the night *when* a holy festival is kept,
And gladness of heart as when one goes with a flute,
To come into the mountain of the LORD,
To the Mighty One of Israel.
30 The LORD will cause His glorious voice to be heard,
And show the descent of His arm,
With the indignation of *His* anger
And the flame of a devouring fire,
With scattering, tempest, and hailstones.
31 For through the voice of the LORD
Assyria will be beaten down,
As He strikes with the rod.
32 And *in* every place where the staff of punishment passes,
Which the LORD lays on him,
It will be with tambourines and harps;
And in battles of brandishing He will fight with it.
33 For Tophet *was* established of old,
Yes, for the king it is prepared.
He has made *it* deep and large;
Its pyre *is* fire with much wood;
The breath of the LORD, like a stream of brimstone,
Kindles it.

THE FOLLY OF NOT TRUSTING GOD

31 Woe to those who go down to Egypt for help,
And rely on horses,
Who trust in chariots because *they are* many,
And in horsemen because they are very strong,
But who do not look to the Holy One of Israel,
Nor seek the LORD!
2 Yet He also *is* wise and will bring disaster,
And will not call back His words,
But will arise against the house of evildoers,
And against the help of those who work iniquity.
3 Now the Egyptians *are* men, and not God;
And their horses are flesh, and not spirit.
When the LORD stretches out His hand,
Both he who helps will fall,
And he who is helped will fall down;
They all will perish together.

GOD WILL DELIVER JERUSALEM

4 For thus the LORD has spoken to me:

"As a lion roars,
And a young lion over his prey
(When a multitude of shepherds is summoned against him,
He will not be afraid of their voice
Nor be disturbed by their noise),
So the LORD of hosts will come down
To fight for Mount Zion and for its hill.
5 Like birds flying about,
So will the LORD of hosts defend Jerusalem.
Defending, He will also deliver *it;*
Passing over, He will preserve *it.*"

6 Return *to Him* against whom the children of Israel have deeply revolted. 7 For in that day every man shall throw away his idols of silver and his idols of gold—sin, which your own hands have made for yourselves.

8 "Then Assyria shall fall by a sword not of man,
And a sword not of mankind shall devour him.
But he shall flee from the sword,
And his young men shall become forced labor.
9 He shall cross over to his stronghold for fear,
And his princes shall be afraid of the banner,"
Says the LORD,
Whose fire *is* in Zion
And whose furnace *is* in Jerusalem.

A REIGN OF RIGHTEOUSNESS

32 Behold, a king will reign in righteousness,
And princes will rule with justice.
2 A man will be as a hiding place from the wind,
And a cover from the tempest,
As rivers of water in a dry place,
As the shadow of a great rock in a weary land.
3 The eyes of those who see will not be dim,

And the ears of those who hear will
listen.
4 Also the heart of the rash will
understand knowledge,
And the tongue of the stammerers will
be ready to speak plainly.

5 The foolish person will no longer be
called generous,
Nor the miser said *to be* bountiful;
6 For the foolish person will speak
foolishness,
And his heart will work iniquity:
To practice ungodliness,
To utter error against the LORD,
To keep the hungry unsatisfied,
And he will cause the drink of the
thirsty to fail.
7 Also the schemes of the schemer *are* evil;
He devises wicked plans
To destroy the poor with lying words,
Even when the needy speaks justice.
8 But a generous man devises generous
things,
And by generosity he shall stand.

Consequences of Complacency

9 Rise up, you women who are at ease,
Hear my voice;
You complacent daughters,
Give ear to my speech.
10 In a year and *some* days
You will be troubled, you complacent
women;
For the vintage will fail,
The gathering will not come.
11 Tremble, you *women* who are at ease;
Be troubled, you complacent ones;
Strip yourselves, make yourselves bare,
And gird *sackcloth* on *your* waists.

12 People shall mourn upon their breasts
For the pleasant fields, for the fruitful
vine.
13 On the land of my people will come up
thorns *and* briers,
Yes, on all the happy homes *in* the
joyous city;
14 Because the palaces will be forsaken,
The bustling city will be deserted.
The forts and towers will become lairs
forever,
A joy of wild donkeys, a pasture of
flocks—
15 Until the Spirit is poured upon us from
on high,
And the wilderness becomes a fruitful
field,
And the fruitful field is counted as a
forest.

The Peace of God's Reign

16 Then justice will dwell in the wilderness,
And righteousness remain in the fruitful
field.
17 The work of righteousness will be peace,
And the effect of righteousness,
quietness and assurance forever.
18 My people will dwell in a peaceful
habitation,
In secure dwellings, and in quiet resting
places,
19 Though hail comes down on the forest,
And the city is brought low in
humiliation.

20 Blessed *are* you who sow beside all
waters,
Who send out freely the feet of the ox
and the donkey.

A Prayer in Deep Distress

33 Woe to you who plunder, though you
have not *been* plundered;
And you who deal treacherously, though
they have not dealt treacherously
with you!
When you cease plundering,
You will be plundered;
When you make an end of dealing
treacherously,
They will deal treacherously with you.

2 O LORD, be gracious to us;
We have waited for You.
Be their[a] arm every morning,
Our salvation also in the time of trouble.
3 At the noise of the tumult the people
shall flee;
When You lift Yourself up, the nations
shall be scattered;
4 And Your plunder shall be gathered
Like the gathering of the caterpillar;
As the running to and fro of locusts,
He shall run upon them.

33:2 [a]Septuagint omits *their;* Syriac, Targum, and Vulgate read *our.*

5 The LORD is exalted, for He dwells on
high;
He has filled Zion with justice and
righteousness.
6 Wisdom and knowledge will be the
stability of your times,
And the strength of salvation;
The fear of the LORD *is* His treasure.

7 Surely their valiant ones shall cry
outside,
The ambassadors of peace shall weep
bitterly.
8 The highways lie waste,
The traveling man ceases.
He has broken the covenant,
He has despised the cities,[a]
He regards no man.
9 The earth mourns *and* languishes,
Lebanon is shamed *and* shriveled;
Sharon is like a wilderness,
And Bashan and Carmel shake off *their*
fruits.

IMPENDING JUDGMENT ON ZION

10 "Now I will rise," says the LORD;
"Now I will be exalted,
Now I will lift Myself up.
11 You shall conceive chaff,
You shall bring forth stubble;
Your breath, *as* fire, shall devour you.
12 And the people shall be *like* the
burnings of lime;
Like thorns cut up they shall be burned
in the fire.
13 Hear, you *who are* afar off, what I have
done;
And you *who are* near, acknowledge My
might."

14 The sinners in Zion are afraid;
Fearfulness has seized the hypocrites:
"Who among us shall dwell with the
devouring fire?
Who among us shall dwell with
everlasting burnings?"
15 He who walks righteously and speaks
uprightly,
He who despises the gain of
oppressions,
Who gestures with his hands, refusing
bribes,
Who stops his ears from hearing of
bloodshed,
And shuts his eyes from seeing evil:
16 He will dwell on high;
His place of defense *will be* the fortress
of rocks;
Bread will be given him,
His water *will be* sure.

THE LAND OF THE MAJESTIC KING

17 Your eyes will see the King in His
beauty;
They will see the land that is very far
off.
18 Your heart will meditate on terror:
"Where *is* the scribe?
Where *is* he who weighs?
Where *is* he who counts the towers?"
19 You will not see a fierce people,
A people of obscure speech, beyond
perception,
Of a stammering tongue *that you* cannot
understand.

20 Look upon Zion, the city of our
appointed feasts;
Your eyes will see Jerusalem, a quiet
home,
A tabernacle *that* will not be taken
down;
Not one of its stakes will ever be
removed,
Nor will any of its cords be broken.
21 But there the majestic LORD *will be* for
us
A place of broad rivers *and* streams,
In which no galley with oars will sail,
Nor majestic ships pass by
22 (For the LORD *is* our Judge,
The LORD *is* our Lawgiver,
The LORD *is* our King;
He will save us);
23 Your tackle is loosed,
They could not strengthen their mast,
They could not spread the sail.

Then the prey of great plunder is
divided;
The lame take the prey.
24 And the inhabitant will not say, "I am
sick";

33:8 [a]Following Masoretic Text and Vulgate; Dead Sea Scrolls read *witnesses;* Septuagint omits *cities;* Targum reads *They have been removed from their cities.*

The people who dwell in it *will be*
forgiven *their* iniquity.

Judgment on the Nations

34 Come near, you nations, to hear;
And heed, you people!
Let the earth hear, and all that is in it,
The world and all things that come forth
from it.
2 For the indignation of the LORD *is*
against all nations,
And *His* fury against all their armies;
He has utterly destroyed them,
He has given them over to the slaughter.
3 Also their slain shall be thrown out;
Their stench shall rise from their corpses,
And the mountains shall be melted with
their blood.
4 All the host of heaven shall be dissolved,
And the heavens shall be rolled up like a
scroll;
All their host shall fall down
As the leaf falls from the vine,
And as *fruit* falling from a fig tree.

5 "For My sword shall be bathed in heaven;
Indeed it shall come down on Edom,
And on the people of My curse, for
judgment.
6 The sword of the LORD is filled with
blood,
It is made overflowing with fatness,
With the blood of lambs and goats,
With the fat of the kidneys of rams.
For the LORD has a sacrifice in Bozrah,
And a great slaughter in the land of
Edom.
7 The wild oxen shall come down with
them,
And the young bulls with the mighty
bulls;
Their land shall be soaked with blood,
And their dust saturated with fatness."

8 For *it is* the day of the LORD's vengeance,
The year of recompense for the cause of
Zion.
9 Its streams shall be turned into pitch,
And its dust into brimstone;
Its land shall become burning pitch.
10 It shall not be quenched night or day;
Its smoke shall ascend forever.
From generation to generation it shall lie
waste;
No one shall pass through it forever and
ever.
11 But the pelican and the porcupine shall
possess it,
Also the owl and the raven shall dwell in
it.
And He shall stretch out over it
The line of confusion and the stones of
emptiness.
12 They shall call its nobles to the
kingdom,
But none *shall be* there, and all its
princes shall be nothing.

13 And thorns shall come up in its palaces,
Nettles and brambles in its fortresses;
It shall be a habitation of jackals,
A courtyard for ostriches.
14 The wild beasts of the desert shall also
meet with the jackals,
And the wild goat shall bleat to its
companion;
Also the night creature shall rest there,
And find for herself a place of rest.
15 There the arrow snake shall make her
nest and lay *eggs*
And hatch, and gather *them* under her
shadow;
There also shall the hawks be gathered,
Every one with her mate.

16 "Search from the book of the LORD, and
read:
Not one of these shall fail;
Not one shall lack her mate.
For My mouth has commanded it, and
His Spirit has gathered them.
17 He has cast the lot for them,
And His hand has divided it among
them with a measuring line.
They shall possess it forever;
From generation to generation they shall
dwell in it."

The Future Glory of Zion

35 The wilderness and the wasteland
shall be glad for them,
And the desert shall rejoice and blossom
as the rose;
2 It shall blossom abundantly and rejoice,
Even with joy and singing.
The glory of Lebanon shall be given to
it,
The excellence of Carmel and Sharon.

They shall see the glory of the LORD,
The excellency of our God.

3 Strengthen the weak hands,
And make firm the feeble knees.
4 Say to those *who are* fearful-hearted,
"Be strong, do not fear!
Behold, your God will come *with* vengeance,
With the recompense of God;
He will come and save you."

5 Then the eyes of the blind shall be opened,
And the ears of the deaf shall be unstopped.
6 Then the lame shall leap like a deer,
And the tongue of the dumb sing.
For waters shall burst forth in the wilderness,
And streams in the desert.
7 The parched ground shall become a pool,
And the thirsty land springs of water;
In the habitation of jackals, where each lay,
There shall be grass with reeds and rushes.

8 A highway shall be there, and a road,
And it shall be called the Highway of Holiness.
The unclean shall not pass over it,
But it *shall be* for others.
Whoever walks the road, although a fool,
Shall not go astray.
9 No lion shall be there,
Nor shall *any* ravenous beast go up on it;
It shall not be found there.
But the redeemed shall walk *there,*
10 And the ransomed of the LORD shall return,
And come to Zion with singing,
With everlasting joy on their heads.
They shall obtain joy and gladness,
And sorrow and sighing shall flee away.

SENNACHERIB BOASTS AGAINST THE LORD

36 Now it came to pass in the fourteenth
year of King Hezekiah *that* Sennacherib king of Assyria came up against all the fortified cities of Judah and took them. 2Then the
king of Assyria sent *the* Rabshakeh[a] with a
great army from Lachish to King Hezekiah at
Jerusalem. And he stood by the aqueduct
from the upper pool, on the highway to the
Fuller's Field. 3And Eliakim the son of Hilkiah,
who was over the household, Shebna the
scribe, and Joah the son of Asaph, the recorder, came out to him.
4Then *the* Rabshakeh said to them, "Say
now to Hezekiah, 'Thus says the great king,
the king of Assyria: "What confidence is this
in which you trust? 5I say you speak of having

36:2 [a]A title, probably *Chief of Staff* or *Governor*

KEY PASSAGE

Genetic Issues

PROMISES OF HEALING

(35:1–6)

Isaiah 35 contrasts the world that exists with the one that God's people will inherit in the future. The prophet promised that the desert would blossom like a rose, that feeble hands, knees, and hearts would be strengthened, and that the sick would be healed. Further, Isaiah promised that God's compassion would touch the blind, the deaf, the mute, and the lame. These promises were fulfilled both physically and spiritually in Jesus Christ and His earthly ministry. In the age to come, God will bring healing to His people's bodies, and refreshment to their souls. Instead of being discouraged by the physical and genetic limitations of life, we can learn to rejoice in His certain promises of complete healing when we see Him: "For this corruptible must put on incorruption, and this mortal must put on immortality" (1 Cor. 15:53).

To Learn More: Turn to the article about genetic issues on pages 84, 85. See also the personality profile of the blind man on page 1388.

plans and power for war; but *they are* mere
words. Now in whom do you trust, that you
rebel against me? 6Look! You are trusting in
the staff of this broken reed, Egypt, on which
if a man leans, it will go into his hand and
pierce it. So *is* Pharaoh king of Egypt to all
who trust in him.
7"But if you say to me, 'We trust in the LORD
our God,' *is it* not He whose high places and
whose altars Hezekiah has taken away, and
said to Judah and Jerusalem, 'You shall worship before this altar'?" ' 8Now therefore, I
urge you, give a pledge to my master the king
of Assyria, and I will give you two thousand
horses—if you are able on your part to put riders on them! 9How then will you repel one
captain of the least of my master's servants,
and put your trust in Egypt for chariots and
horsemen? 10Have I now come up without the
LORD against this land to destroy it? The LORD
said to me, 'Go up against this land, and destroy it.' "
11Then Eliakim, Shebna, and Joah said to
the Rabshakeh, "Please speak to your servants
in Aramaic, for we understand *it;* and do not
speak to us in Hebrew[a] in the hearing of the
people who *are* on the wall."
12But *the* Rabshakeh said, "Has my master
sent me to your master and to you to speak
these words, and not to the men who sit on
the wall, who will eat and drink their own
waste with you?"
13Then *the* Rabshakeh stood and called out
with a loud voice in Hebrew, and said, "Hear
the words of the great king, the king of Assyria! 14Thus says the king: 'Do not let Hezekiah
deceive you, for he will not be able to deliver
you; 15nor let Hezekiah make you trust in the
LORD, saying, "The LORD will surely deliver
us; this city will not be given into the hand of
the king of Assyria." ' 16Do not listen to Hezekiah; for thus says the king of Assyria: 'Make
peace with me *by a* present and come out to
me; and every one of you eat from his own
vine and every one from his own fig tree, and
every one of you drink the waters of his own
cistern; 17until I come and take you away to a
land like your own land, a land of grain and
new wine, a land of bread and vineyards. 18*Beware* lest Hezekiah persuade you, saying,
"The LORD will deliver us." Has any one of the
gods of the nations delivered its land from the
hand of the king of Assyria? 19Where *are* the
gods of Hamath and Arpad? Where *are* the
gods of Sepharvaim? Indeed, have they delivered Samaria from my hand? 20Who among all
the gods of these lands have delivered their
countries from my hand, that the LORD should
deliver Jerusalem from my hand?' "
21But they held their peace and answered
him not a word; for the king's commandment
was, "Do not answer him." 22Then Eliakim the
son of Hilkiah, who *was* over the household,
Shebna the scribe, and Joah the son of Asaph,
the recorder, came to Hezekiah with *their*
clothes torn, and told him the words of *the*
Rabshakeh.

ISAIAH ASSURES DELIVERANCE

37 And so it was, when King Hezekiah
heard *it,* that he tore his clothes, covered himself with sackcloth, and went into the
house of the LORD. 2Then he sent Eliakim,
who *was* over the household, Shebna the
scribe, and the elders of the priests, covered
with sackcloth, to Isaiah the prophet, the son
of Amoz. 3And they said to him, "Thus says
Hezekiah: 'This day *is* a day of trouble and
rebuke and blasphemy; for the children have
come to birth, but *there is* no strength to bring
them forth. 4It may be that the LORD your God
will hear the words of *the* Rabshakeh, whom
his master the king of Assyria has sent to reproach the living God, and will rebuke the
words which the LORD your God has heard.
Therefore lift up *your* prayer for the remnant
that is left.' "
5So the servants of King Hezekiah came to
Isaiah. 6And Isaiah said to them, "Thus you
shall say to your master, 'Thus says the LORD:
"Do not be afraid of the words which you have
heard, with which the servants of the king of
Assyria have blasphemed Me. 7Surely I will
send a spirit upon him, and he shall hear a rumor and return to his own land; and I will
cause him to fall by the sword in his own
land." ' "

SENNACHERIB'S THREAT AND HEZEKIAH'S PRAYER

8Then *the* Rabshakeh returned, and found
the king of Assyria warring against Libnah, for
he heard that he had departed from Lachish.
9And the king heard concerning Tirhakah
king of Ethiopia, "He has come out to make
war with you." So when he heard *it,* he sent

36:11 [a]Literally *Judean*

messengers to Hezekiah, saying, 10“Thus you
shall speak to Hezekiah king of Judah, saying:
‘Do not let your God in whom you trust deceive you, saying, “Jerusalem shall not be
given into the hand of the king of Assyria.”
11Look! You have heard what the kings of Assyria have done to all lands by utterly destroying them; and shall you be delivered? 12Have
the gods of the nations delivered those whom
my fathers have destroyed, Gozan and Haran
and Rezeph, and the people of Eden who *were*
in Telassar? 13Where *is* the king of Hamath,
the king of Arpad, and the king of the city of
Sepharvaim, Hena, and Ivah?’ ”

14And Hezekiah received the letter from the
hand of the messengers, and read it; and Hezekiah went up to the house of the LORD, and
spread it before the LORD. 15Then Hezekiah
prayed to the LORD, saying: 16“O LORD of
hosts, God of Israel, *the One* who dwells *between* the cherubim, You *are* God, You alone,
of all the kingdoms of the earth. You have
made heaven and earth. 17Incline Your ear, O
LORD, and hear; open Your eyes, O LORD, and
see; and hear all the words of Sennacherib,
which he has sent to reproach the living God.
18Truly, LORD, the kings of Assyria have laid
waste all the nations and their lands, 19and
have cast their gods into the fire; for they *were*
not gods, but the work of men’s hands—wood
and stone. Therefore they destroyed them.
20Now therefore, O LORD our God, save us
from his hand, that all the kingdoms of the
earth may know that You *are* the LORD, You
alone.”

The Word of the Lord Concerning Sennacherib

21Then Isaiah the son of Amoz sent to Hezekiah, saying, “Thus says the LORD God of Israel, ‘Because you have prayed to Me against
Sennacherib king of Assyria, 22this *is* the word
which the LORD has spoken concerning him:

“The virgin, the daughter of Zion,
Has despised you, laughed you to scorn;
The daughter of Jerusalem
Has shaken *her* head behind your back!

23 “Whom have you reproached and blasphemed?
Against whom have you raised *your* voice,
And lifted up your eyes on high?
Against the Holy One of Israel.
24 By your servants you have reproached the Lord,
And said, ‘By the multitude of my chariots
I have come up to the height of the mountains,
To the limits of Lebanon;
I will cut down its tall cedars
And its choice cypress trees;
I will enter its farthest height,
To its fruitful forest.
25 I have dug and drunk water,
And with the soles of my feet I have dried up
All the brooks of defense.’

26 “Did you not hear long ago
How I made it,
From ancient times that I formed it?
Now I have brought it to pass,
That you should be
For crushing fortified cities *into* heaps of ruins.
27 Therefore their inhabitants *had* little power;
They were dismayed and confounded;
They were *as* the grass of the field
And the green herb,
As the grass on the housetops
And grain blighted before it is grown.

28 “But I know your dwelling place,
Your going out and your coming in,
And your rage against Me.
29 Because your rage against Me and your tumult
Have come up to My ears,
Therefore I will put My hook in your nose
And My bridle in your lips,
And I will turn you back
By the way which you came.” ’

30“This *shall be* a sign to you:

You shall eat this year such as grows of itself,
And the second year what springs from the same;
Also in the third year sow and reap,
Plant vineyards and eat the fruit of them.
31 And the remnant who have escaped of the house of Judah

Shall again take root downward,
And bear fruit upward.
32 For out of Jerusalem shall go a remnant,
And those who escape from Mount Zion.
The zeal of the LORD of hosts will do
this.

33"Therefore thus says the LORD concerning the king of Assyria:

'He shall not come into this city,
Nor shoot an arrow there,
Nor come before it with shield,
Nor build a siege mound against it.
34 By the way that he came,
By the same shall he return;
And he shall not come into this city,'
Says the LORD.
35 'For I will defend this city, to save it
For My own sake and for My servant
David's sake.' "

SENNACHERIB'S DEFEAT AND DEATH

36Then the angel[a] of the LORD went out, and killed in the camp of the Assyrians one hundred and eighty-five thousand; and when *people* arose early in the morning, there were the corpses—all dead. 37So Sennacherib king of Assyria departed and went away, returned *home,* and remained at Nineveh. 38Now it came to pass, as he was worshiping in the house of Nisroch his god, that his sons Adrammelech and Sharezer struck him down with the sword; and they escaped into the land of Ararat. Then Esarhaddon his son reigned in his place.

HEZEKIAH'S LIFE EXTENDED

38 In those days Hezekiah was sick and near death. And Isaiah the prophet, the son of Amoz, went to him and said to him, "Thus says the LORD: 'Set your house in order, for you shall die and not live.' "

2Then Hezekiah turned his face toward the wall, and prayed to the LORD, 3and said, "Remember now, O LORD, I pray, how I have walked before You in truth and with a loyal heart, and have done *what is* good in Your sight." And Hezekiah wept bitterly.

4And the word of the LORD came to Isaiah, saying, 5"Go and tell Hezekiah, 'Thus says the LORD, the God of David your father: "I have heard your prayer, I have seen your tears; surely I will add to your days fifteen years. 6I will deliver you and this city from the hand of the king of Assyria, and I will defend this city." ' 7And this *is* the sign to you from the LORD, that the LORD will do this thing which He has spoken: 8Behold, I will bring the shadow on the sundial, which has gone down with the sun on the sundial of Ahaz, ten degrees backward." So the sun returned ten degrees on the dial by which it had gone down.

9This is the writing of Hezekiah king of Judah, when he had been sick and had recovered from his sickness:

10 I said,
"In the prime of my life
I shall go to the gates of Sheol;
I am deprived of the remainder of my
years."
11 I said,
"I shall not see YAH,
The LORD[a] in the land of the living;
I shall observe man no more among the
inhabitants of the world.[b]
12 My life span is gone,
Taken from me like a shepherd's tent;
I have cut off my life like a weaver.
He cuts me off from the loom;
From day until night You make an end of
me.
13 I have considered until morning—
Like a lion,
So He breaks all my bones;
From day until night You make an end of
me.
14 Like a crane *or* a swallow, so I chattered;
I mourned like a dove;
My eyes fail *from looking* upward.
O LORD,[a] I am oppressed;
Undertake for me!

15 "What shall I say?
He has both spoken to me,[a]
And He Himself has done *it.*
I shall walk carefully all my years
In the bitterness of my soul.

37:36 [a]Or *Angel* **38:11** [a]Hebrew *YAH, YAH* [b]Following some Hebrew manuscripts; Masoretic Text and Vulgate read *rest;* Septuagint omits *among the inhabitants of the world;* Targum reads *land.* **38:14** [a]Following Bomberg; Masoretic Text and Dead Sea Scrolls read *Lord.* **38:15** [a]Following Masoretic Text and Vulgate; Dead Sea Scrolls and Targum read *And shall I say to Him;* Septuagint omits first half of this verse.

16 O Lord, by these *things men* live;
And in all these *things is* the life of my spirit;
So You will restore me and make me live.
17 Indeed *it was* for *my own* peace
That I had great bitterness;
But You have lovingly *delivered* my soul from the pit of corruption,
For You have cast all my sins behind Your back.
18 For Sheol cannot thank You,
Death cannot praise You;
Those who go down to the pit cannot hope for Your truth.
19 The living, the living man, he shall praise You,
As I *do* this day;
The father shall make known Your truth to the children.

20 "The LORD *was ready* to save me;
Therefore we will sing my songs with stringed instruments
All the days of our life, in the house of the LORD."

21Now Isaiah had said, "Let them take a
lump of figs, and apply *it* as a poultice on the
boil, and he shall recover."
22And Hezekiah had said, "What *is* the sign
that I shall go up to the house of the LORD?"

THE BABYLONIAN ENVOYS

39 At that time Merodach-Baladan[a] the
son of Baladan, king of Babylon, sent
letters and a present to Hezekiah, for he heard
that he had been sick and had recovered. 2And
Hezekiah was pleased with them, and showed
them the house of his treasures—the silver
and gold, the spices and precious ointment,
and all his armory—all that was found among
his treasures. There was nothing in his house
or in all his dominion that Hezekiah did not
show them.
3Then Isaiah the prophet went to King Hezekiah, and said to him, "What did these men
say, and from where did they come to you?"
So Hezekiah said, "They came to me from a
far country, from Babylon."
4And he said, "What have they seen in your
house?"
So Hezekiah answered, "They have seen all
that *is* in my house; there is nothing among
my treasures that I have not shown them."
5Then Isaiah said to Hezekiah, "Hear the
word of the LORD of hosts: 6'Behold, the days
are coming when all that *is* in your house, and
what your fathers have accumulated until this
day, shall be carried to Babylon; nothing shall
be left,' says the LORD. 7'And they shall take
away *some* of your sons who will descend from
you, whom you will beget; and they shall be
eunuchs in the palace of the king of Babylon.' "
8So Hezekiah said to Isaiah, "The word of
the LORD which you have spoken *is* good!" For
he said, "At least there will be peace and truth
in my days."

GOD'S PEOPLE ARE COMFORTED

40 "Comfort, yes, comfort My people!"
Says your God.
2 "Speak comfort to Jerusalem, and cry out to her,
That her warfare is ended,
That her iniquity is pardoned;
For she has received from the LORD's hand
Double for all her sins."

3 The voice of one crying in the wilderness:

39:1 [a]Spelled *Berodach-Baladan* in 2 Kings 20:12

SOUL NOTE

Homemade Remedies *(38:21)* As he faced death, King Hezekiah cried out to the Lord (38:2, 3). The prophet Isaiah told the king to have his servants take a "lump of figs, and apply it as a poultice on the boil," promising that Hezekiah would recover. While God can heal miraculously, He also will work through medicines to heal people. When we pray for God to heal us, we can trust Him to use all the means available. It shows no lack of faith to utilize the benefit of doctors and hospitals.
Topic: Healing/Recovery

"Prepare the way of the LORD;
Make straight in the desert[a]
A highway for our God.
4 Every valley shall be exalted
And every mountain and hill brought low;
The crooked places shall be made straight
And the rough places smooth;
5 The glory of the LORD shall be revealed,
And all flesh shall see *it* together;
For the mouth of the LORD has spoken."

6 The voice said, "Cry out!"
And he[a] said, "What shall I cry?"

"All flesh *is* grass,
And all its loveliness *is* like the flower of the field.
7 The grass withers, the flower fades,
Because the breath of the LORD blows upon it;
Surely the people *are* grass.
8 The grass withers, the flower fades,
But the word of our God stands forever."

"The grass withers, the flower fades, but the word of our God stands forever."
ISAIAH 40:8

9 O Zion,
You who bring good tidings,
Get up into the high mountain;
O Jerusalem,
You who bring good tidings,
Lift up your voice with strength,
Lift *it* up, be not afraid;
Say to the cities of Judah, "Behold your God!"

10 Behold, the Lord GOD shall come with a strong *hand,*
And His arm shall rule for Him;
Behold, His reward *is* with Him,
And His work before Him.
11 He will feed His flock like a shepherd;
He will gather the lambs with His arm,
And carry *them* in His bosom,
And gently lead those who are with young.

12 Who has measured the waters[a] in the hollow of His hand,
Measured heaven with a span
And calculated the dust of the earth in a measure?
Weighed the mountains in scales
And the hills in a balance?
13 Who has directed the Spirit of the LORD,
Or *as* His counselor has taught Him?
14 With whom did He take counsel, and *who* instructed Him,
And taught Him in the path of justice?
Who taught Him knowledge,
And showed Him the way of understanding?

15 Behold, the nations *are* as a drop in a bucket,
And are counted as the small dust on the scales;
Look, He lifts up the isles as a very little thing.
16 And Lebanon *is* not sufficient to burn,
Nor its beasts sufficient for a burnt offering.
17 All nations before Him *are* as nothing,
And they are counted by Him less than nothing and worthless.

18 To whom then will you liken God?
Or what likeness will you compare to Him?
19 The workman molds an image,
The goldsmith overspreads it with gold,
And the silversmith casts silver chains.
20 Whoever *is* too impoverished for *such* a contribution
Chooses a tree *that* will not rot;
He seeks for himself a skillful workman
To prepare a carved image *that* will not totter.

21 Have you not known?
Have you not heard?
Has it not been told you from the beginning?

40:3 [a]Following Masoretic Text, Targum, and Vulgate; Septuagint omits *in the desert.*
40:6 [a]Following Masoretic Text and Targum; Dead Sea Scrolls, Septuagint, and Vulgate read *I.*
40:12 [a]Following Masoretic Text, Septuagint, and Vulgate; Dead Sea Scrolls read *waters of the sea;* Targum reads *waters of the world.*

Burnout

OVERCOMING BURNOUT

H. B. LONDON

(Isaiah 40:31)

Will a human being ever swim across the ocean? Run a one-minute mile? Go six months without sleeping? Of course not, because of the established fact of human limits. Yet because of the rapidly changing conditions of modern living—largely due to progress always giving us more and more of everything faster and faster—we are attempting to exceed our limits in scores of areas all at the same time. The pain is palpable. People everywhere are collapsing in exhaustion, wondering what hit them.

What hit them was overload. This can be defined as the point at which our limits are exceeded. "Load" is not the problem. "Over" is the problem. We have all heard about the straw that broke the camel's back. Once a camel is maximally loaded, a mere straw will cause the break. The problem is not the load—camels love to carry loads. The problem is *over*load.

Stress is such an accepted part of our modern culture that most of us accept it as normal. In reality, stress distorts our physical, mental, and emotional health, and affects our attitudes, marriages, work, and even ministry. We can overload ourselves to the point that we burn out and are no longer effective in God's work.

PUSHING OUR LIMITS

Maximizing everything has, of course, become the American way. We push the limits as far as possible. We spend more than we have—whether it be money, time, or energy. Jesus, however, never seemed to be in a hurry. There is no indication that He worked 24-hour days. He went to sleep each night without having healed every disease in Israel. He followed God's agenda, and so He was perfectly effective.

Jesus understood what it means to be human—and what it means to have limits. Jesus knew what it meant to prioritize and balance in light of these limits and how to focus on the truly important. Our Lord realized that busyness is not necessarily godliness. He is more concerned with the quality of our lives. He calls us to be fruitful, but He also insists that our fruit should "remain," not burn out.

By contrast, we are in a hurry. Nearly everyone I know has a full plate, but most of us haven't completely thought through the performance implications of our saturated states. We continue to say "Yes," even when "Yes" is no longer an option. Once we cross the threshold of our limits, however, we reach saturation. We can't factor anything more into our lives until we take something away. As basic as this principle seems, it remains largely disregarded.

How do we know when we have reached these limits? If a car overheats, an indicator light goes on alerting us to the danger. Unfortunately, we don't have such a visible system in most cases. Therefore, we have to be more honest with ourselves about our limits.

AVOIDING BURNOUT

From the very beginning, rest has had a special significance for God (Gen. 2:3). This rest is not always easy, however. Even Moses had difficulty obeying the call to rest. He experienced unrelieved stress trying to keep two million Israelites happy as they wandered in the wilderness. God called Moses to rest and to delegate some responsibilities. Soon others helped carry Moses' burden and his stress became more manageable (Num. 11:11–17).

God's calling in our lives does not eliminate stress and burnout automatically. Nowhere does the Bible promise to ease all the stress in our lives. It does promise God's peace when we allow Him to control our lives and shape our decisions. He gives us practical ways to limit stress and avoid burnout in the framework of His design for our lives.

➢ *Accept responsibility.* We must never relinquish control of our schedules to the unpredictable and sometimes ruthless whims of the world or the demands of others. We should be active in self-examination. Nobody is locked into anything. Each of us can accomplish the needed changes if we want them badly enough.

➢ *Acknowledge limits.* We can schedule our days more sanely, more humanly, and more relationally. We need not apologize for wanting a good night's sleep; we need not believe the lie that "well-rested" is a synonym for "sluggardly."

➢ *Understand God's will.* God never guides us into an intolerable scramble of overworked feverishness. We will gain more time by properly understanding God's will for us than by all the time-saving suggestions put together.

➢ *Consciously slow the pace of life.* The pace of life has become deadly. We simply cannot permit each year to bring an increase in speed and not get caught in the exhausting consequences of such a frenzy.

➢ *Define and defend boundaries.* Jesus did not minister to everybody in Israel, even though He could have. Remember that it is not necessary to have more compassion than the Almighty.

➢ *Learn to say no.* It is easy to say no to a root canal or a colonoscopy. It is far more difficult to say no to things that are interesting and enjoyable. Yet even if everything we are doing is enjoyable, if we do not learn to say no, overload will overwhelm us.

➢ *Get less done, but do the right things.* We would do well to consider doing less, but radically prioritizing. Remember, the multiplying coefficient for our labor is the power of the Holy Spirit. The same God who spoke the universe into existence sees our faithful efforts and instructs the Holy Spirit to expand the benefit to whatever level best glorifies Him.

FURTHER MEDITATION:

Other passages to study about the issue of burnout include:

➢ Exodus 23:12
➢ Psalm 37:7
➢ Isaiah 41:10
➢ John 16:33
➢ Colossians 3:15

To Learn More: Turn to the key passage note on burnout at Matthew 11:28–30 on page 1247. See also the personality profile of Moses and Jethro on page 103.

Have you not understood from the foundations of the earth?
22 *It is* He who sits above the circle of the earth,
And its inhabitants *are* like grasshoppers,
Who stretches out the heavens like a curtain,
And spreads them out like a tent to dwell in.
23 He brings the princes to nothing;
He makes the judges of the earth useless.

24 Scarcely shall they be planted,
Scarcely shall they be sown,
Scarcely shall their stock take root in the earth,
When He will also blow on them,
And they will wither,
And the whirlwind will take them away like stubble.

25 "To whom then will you liken Me,
Or *to whom* shall I be equal?" says the Holy One.
26 Lift up your eyes on high,
And see who has created these *things,*
Who brings out their host by number;
He calls them all by name,
By the greatness of His might
And the strength of *His* power;
Not one is missing.

27 Why do you say, O Jacob,
And speak, O Israel:
"My way is hidden from the LORD,
And my just claim is passed over by my God"?
28 Have you not known?
Have you not heard?
The everlasting God, the LORD,
The Creator of the ends of the earth,
Neither faints nor is weary.
His understanding is unsearchable.
29 He gives power to the weak,
And to *those who have* no might He increases strength.
30 Even the youths shall faint and be weary,
And the young men shall utterly fall,
31 But those who wait on the LORD
Shall renew *their* strength;
They shall mount up with wings like eagles,
They shall run and not be weary,
They shall walk and not faint.

Israel Assured of God's Help

41 "Keep silence before Me, O coastlands,
And let the people renew *their* strength!
Let them come near, then let them speak;
Let us come near together for judgment.

2 "Who raised up one from the east?
Who in righteousness called him to His feet?
Who gave the nations before him,
And made *him* rule over kings?
Who gave *them* as the dust *to* his sword,
As driven stubble to his bow?
3 Who pursued them, *and* passed safely
By the way *that* he had not gone with his feet?
4 Who has performed and done *it,*
Calling the generations from the beginning?
'I, the LORD, am the first;
And with the last I *am* He.' "

SOUL NOTE

Renewed Strength *(40:31)* One of the great challenges of the Christian life is dealing with the problem of spiritual burnout. Isaiah reminded God's people of the value of waiting upon the Lord. "Waiting" does not mean inactivity; rather, it is patient service that is not overcommitted and overextended. Many desire to "mount up with wings like eagles," but they assume that the harder they run the more likely they will fly. The prophet says, however, that the harder people run the more likely they will fall. Instead, "those who wait on the LORD shall renew their strength." Such "waiting" is the antidote for spiritual burnout. **Topic: Burnout**

5 The coastlands saw *it* and feared,
The ends of the earth were afraid;
They drew near and came.
6 Everyone helped his neighbor,
And said to his brother,
"Be of good courage!"
7 So the craftsman encouraged the goldsmith;
He who smooths *with* the hammer *inspired* him who strikes the anvil,
Saying, "It *is* ready for the soldering";
Then he fastened it with pegs,
That it might not totter.

8 "But you, Israel, *are* My servant,
Jacob whom I have chosen,
The descendants of Abraham My friend.
9 *You* whom I have taken from the ends of the earth,
And called from its farthest regions,
And said to you,
'You *are* My servant,
I have chosen you and have not cast you away:
10 Fear not, for I *am* with you;
Be not dismayed, for I *am* your God.
I will strengthen you,
Yes, I will help you,
I will uphold you with My righteous right hand.'
11 "Behold, all those who were incensed against you
Shall be ashamed and disgraced;
They shall be as nothing,
And those who strive with you shall perish.
12 You shall seek them and not find them—
Those who contended with you.
Those who war against you
Shall be as nothing,
As a nonexistent thing.
13 For I, the LORD your God, will hold your right hand,
Saying to you, 'Fear not, I will help you.'

14 "Fear not, you worm Jacob,
You men of Israel!
I will help you," says the LORD
And your Redeemer, the Holy One of Israel.
15 "Behold, I will make you into a new threshing sledge with sharp teeth;
You shall thresh the mountains and beat *them* small,
And make the hills like chaff.
16 You shall winnow them, the wind shall carry them away,
And the whirlwind shall scatter them;
You shall rejoice in the LORD,
And glory in the Holy One of Israel.

KEY PASSAGE

Loneliness

HELD IN HIS ARMS

(41:10)

God reminds His people that in their loneliness and inadequacy they need not fear or be dismayed. Why? Because He is their God and because He is with them, holding them in His "righteous right hand." Everyone feels lonely at times. Sometimes, however, loneliness can become so desperate that it causes fearfulness. That fear, then, can draw the lonely person's attention away from God. God promises, however, that He will always hold His people close to Him. He says, "I will never leave you nor forsake you" (Heb. 13:5).

Lonely people must remember that Jesus has called them His friends (John 15:15), and that with Jesus they are never alone (John 14:26). Feelings of loneliness can be helped. Lonely people can attend church (Heb. 10:25), be a friend to someone else (Prov. 18:24), listen to Christian music, and pray for God to work in and through them to take away the lonely feelings.

To Learn More: Turn to the article about loneliness on pages 734, 735. See also the personality profile of Jeremiah on page 989.

17 "The poor and needy seek water, but
there is none,
Their tongues fail for thirst.
I, the LORD, will hear them;
I, the God of Israel, will not forsake
them.
18 I will open rivers in desolate heights,
And fountains in the midst of the
valleys;
I will make the wilderness a pool of
water,
And the dry land springs of water.
19 I will plant in the wilderness the cedar
and the acacia tree,
The myrtle and the oil tree;
I will set in the desert the cypress tree
and the pine
And the box tree together,
20 That they may see and know,
And consider and understand together,
That the hand of the LORD has done this,
And the Holy One of Israel has created
it.

THE FUTILITY OF IDOLS

21 "Present your case," says the LORD.
"Bring forth your strong *reasons*," says
the King of Jacob.
22 "Let them bring forth and show us what
will happen;
Let them show the former things, what
they *were*,
That we may consider them,
And know the latter end of them;
Or declare to us things to come.
23 Show the things that are to come
hereafter,
That we may know that you *are* gods;
Yes, do good or do evil,
That we may be dismayed and see *it*
together.
24 Indeed you *are* nothing,
And your work *is* nothing;
He who chooses you *is* an abomination.

25 "I have raised up one from the north,
And he shall come;
From the rising of the sun he shall call
on My name;
And he shall come against princes as
though mortar,
As the potter treads clay.
26 Who has declared from the beginning,
that we may know?
And former times, that we may say, '*He
is* righteous'?
Surely *there is* no one who shows,
Surely *there is* no one who declares,
Surely *there is* no one who hears your
words.
27 The first time *I said* to Zion,
'Look, there they are!'
And I will give to Jerusalem one who
brings good tidings.
28 For I looked, and *there was* no man;
I looked among them, but *there was* no
counselor,
Who, when I asked of them, could
answer a word.
29 Indeed they *are* all worthless;[a]
Their works *are* nothing;
Their molded images *are* wind and
confusion.

THE SERVANT OF THE LORD

42 "Behold! My Servant whom I uphold,
My Elect One *in whom* My soul
delights!
I have put My Spirit upon Him;
He will bring forth justice to the
Gentiles.
2 He will not cry out, nor raise *His
voice*,
Nor cause His voice to be heard in the
street.
3 A bruised reed He will not break,
And smoking flax He will not quench;
He will bring forth justice for truth.
4 He will not fail nor be discouraged,
Till He has established justice in the
earth;
And the coastlands shall wait for His
law."

5 Thus says God the LORD,
Who created the heavens and stretched
them out,
Who spread forth the earth and that
which comes from it,
Who gives breath to the people on it,
And spirit to those who walk on it:
6 "I, the LORD, have called You in
righteousness,
And will hold Your hand;

41:29 [a]Following Masoretic Text and Vulgate; Dead Sea Scrolls, Syriac, and Targum read *nothing;* Septuagint omits the first line.

I will keep You and give You as a covenant to the people,
As a light to the Gentiles,
7 To open blind eyes,
To bring out prisoners from the prison,
Those who sit in darkness from the prison house.
8 I *am* the LORD, that *is* My name;
And My glory I will not give to another,
Nor My praise to carved images.
9 Behold, the former things have come to pass,
And new things I declare;
Before they spring forth I tell you of them."

PRAISE TO THE LORD

10 Sing to the LORD a new song,
And His praise from the ends of the earth,
You who go down to the sea, and all that is in it,
You coastlands and you inhabitants of them!
11 Let the wilderness and its cities lift up *their voice,*
The villages *that* Kedar inhabits.
Let the inhabitants of Sela sing,
Let them shout from the top of the mountains.
12 Let them give glory to the LORD,
And declare His praise in the coastlands.
13 The LORD shall go forth like a mighty man;
He shall stir up *His* zeal like a man of war.
He shall cry out, yes, shout aloud;
He shall prevail against His enemies.

PROMISE OF THE LORD'S HELP

14 "I have held My peace a long time,
I have been still and restrained Myself.
Now I will cry like a woman in labor,
I will pant and gasp at once.
15 I will lay waste the mountains and hills,
And dry up all their vegetation;
I will make the rivers coastlands,
And I will dry up the pools.
16 I will bring the blind by a way they did not know;
I will lead them in paths they have not known.
I will make darkness light before them,
And crooked places straight.
These things I will do for them,
And not forsake them.
17 They shall be turned back,
They shall be greatly ashamed,
Who trust in carved images,
Who say to the molded images,
'You *are* our gods.'

18 "Hear, you deaf;
And look, you blind, that you may see.
19 Who *is* blind but My servant,
Or deaf as My messenger *whom* I send?
Who *is* blind as *he who is* perfect,
And blind as the LORD's servant?
20 Seeing many things, but you do not observe;
Opening the ears, but he does not hear."

ISRAEL'S OBSTINATE DISOBEDIENCE

21 The LORD is well pleased for His righteousness' sake;
He will exalt the law and make *it* honorable.
22 But this *is* a people robbed and plundered;
All of them are snared in holes,
And they are hidden in prison houses;
They are for prey, and no one delivers;
For plunder, and no one says, "Restore!"

23 Who among you will give ear to this?
Who will listen and hear for the time to come?
24 Who gave Jacob for plunder, and Israel to the robbers?
Was it not the LORD,
He against whom we have sinned?
For they would not walk in His ways,
Nor were they obedient to His law.
25 Therefore He has poured on him the fury of His anger
And the strength of battle;
It has set him on fire all around,
Yet he did not know;
And it burned him,
Yet he did not take *it* to heart.

THE REDEEMER OF ISRAEL

43 But now, thus says the LORD, who created you, O Jacob,
And He who formed you, O Israel:
"Fear not, for I have redeemed you;
I have called *you* by your name;
You *are* Mine.

2 When you pass through the waters, I
will be with you;
And through the rivers, they shall not
overflow you.
When you walk through the fire, you
shall not be burned,
Nor shall the flame scorch you.
3 For I *am* the LORD your God,
The Holy One of Israel, your Savior;
I gave Egypt for your ransom,
Ethiopia and Seba in your place.
4 Since you were precious in My sight,
You have been honored,
And I have loved you;
Therefore I will give men for you,
And people for your life.
5 Fear not, for I *am* with you;
I will bring your descendants from the
east,
And gather you from the west;
6 I will say to the north, 'Give them up!'
And to the south, 'Do not keep them
back!'
Bring My sons from afar,
And My daughters from the ends of the
earth—
7 Everyone who is called by My name,
Whom I have created for My glory;
I have formed him, yes, I have made
him."

8 Bring out the blind people who have
eyes,
And the deaf who have ears.
9 Let all the nations be gathered together,
And let the people be assembled.
Who among them can declare this,
And show us former things?
Let them bring out their witnesses, that
they may be justified;
Or let them hear and say, "*It is* truth."
10 "You *are* My witnesses," says the LORD,
"And My servant whom I have chosen,
That you may know and believe Me,
And understand that I *am* He.
Before Me there was no God formed,
Nor shall there be after Me.
11 I, *even* I, *am* the LORD,
And besides Me *there is* no savior.
12 I have declared and saved,
I have proclaimed,
And *there was* no foreign *god* among you;
Therefore you *are* My witnesses,"
Says the LORD, "that I *am* God.
13 Indeed before the day *was,* I *am* He;
And *there is* no one who can deliver out
of My hand;
I work, and who will reverse it?"

14 Thus says the LORD, your Redeemer,
The Holy One of Israel:
"For your sake I will send to Babylon,
And bring them all down as fugitives—
The Chaldeans, who rejoice in their
ships.
15 I *am* the LORD, your Holy One,
The Creator of Israel, your King."

16 Thus says the LORD, who makes a way
in the sea
And a path through the mighty waters,
17 Who brings forth the chariot and horse,
The army and the power
(They shall lie down together, they shall
not rise;
They are extinguished, they are
quenched like a wick):
18 "Do not remember the former things,
Nor consider the things of old.
19 Behold, I will do a new thing,
Now it shall spring forth;
Shall you not know it?
I will even make a road in the
wilderness

SOUL NOTE

Who We Are *(43:1)* Society determines people's importance based on what they do or what they know. God chose Israel to be His covenant people and to display His glory to the nations. God promised: "I have redeemed you; I have called you by your name; you are Mine." As a nation, Israel failed to recognize their Messiah, and God established His new covenant with all who would trust Jesus Christ as Savior. God's people know that Christ is their God, Savior, and King. Our self-esteem is not based on what we do, but on who we are in Christ. **Topic: Self-Esteem**

And rivers in the desert.
20 The beast of the field will honor Me,
The jackals and the ostriches,
Because I give waters in the wilderness
And rivers in the desert,
To give drink to My people, My
chosen.
21 This people I have formed for Myself;
They shall declare My praise.

Pleading with Unfaithful Israel

22 "But you have not called upon Me,
O Jacob;
And you have been weary of Me,
O Israel.
23 You have not brought Me the sheep for
your burnt offerings,
Nor have you honored Me with your
sacrifices.
I have not caused you to serve with
grain offerings,
Nor wearied you with incense.
24 You have bought Me no sweet cane with
money,
Nor have you satisfied Me with the fat of
your sacrifices;
But you have burdened Me with your
sins,
You have wearied Me with your
iniquities.

25 "I, *even* I, *am* He who blots out your
transgressions for My own sake;
And I will not remember your sins.
26 Put Me in remembrance;
Let us contend together;
State your *case,* that you may be
acquitted.
27 Your first father sinned,
And your mediators have transgressed
against Me.
28 Therefore I will profane the princes of
the sanctuary;
I will give Jacob to the curse,
And Israel to reproaches.

God's Blessing on Israel

44 "Yet hear me now, O Jacob My
servant,
And Israel whom I have chosen.
2 Thus says the LORD who made you
And formed you from the womb, *who*
will help you:
'Fear not, O Jacob My servant;
And you, Jeshurun, whom I have
chosen.
3 For I will pour water on him who is
thirsty,
And floods on the dry ground;
I will pour My Spirit on your
descendants,
And My blessing on your offspring;
4 They will spring up among the grass
Like willows by the watercourses.'
5 One will say, 'I *am* the LORD's';
Another will call *himself* by the name of
Jacob;
Another will write *with* his hand, 'The
LORD's,'
And name *himself* by the name of Israel.

There Is No Other God

6 "Thus says the LORD, the King of Israel,
And his Redeemer, the LORD of hosts:
'I *am* the First and I *am* the Last;
Besides Me *there is* no God.
7 And who can proclaim as I do?
Then let him declare it and set it in
order for Me,
Since I appointed the ancient people.
And the things that are coming and shall
come,

SOUL NOTE

Cleansed *(43:25)* When the guilt of past sins weighs us down, we must remember that when we seek forgiveness, God "blots out" our transgressions and forgets our sins. David prayed that God would "blot out" all of his iniquities (Ps. 51:9); Peter called the people to repent so that their "sins may be blotted out" (Acts 3:19). "Blotting out" sins pictures wiping the slate clean. Whatever sins we have committed, God promises to erase them. He knows what we have done, but He treats us as though we have never sinned. Because God has forgiven us, we must forgive ourselves.
Topic: Forgiveness

Let them show these to them.
8 Do not fear, nor be afraid;
Have I not told you from that time, and declared *it?*
You *are* My witnesses.
Is there a God besides Me?
Indeed *there is* no other Rock;
I know not *one.*' "

Idolatry Is Foolishness

9 Those who make an image, all of them *are* useless,
And their precious things shall not profit;
They *are* their own witnesses;
They neither see nor know, that they may be ashamed.
10 Who would form a god or mold an image
That profits him nothing?
11 Surely all his companions would be ashamed;
And the workmen, they *are* mere men.
Let them all be gathered together,
Let them stand up;
Yet they shall fear,
They shall be ashamed together.

12 The blacksmith with the tongs works one in the coals,
Fashions it with hammers,
And works it with the strength of his arms.
Even so, he is hungry, and his strength fails;
He drinks no water and is faint.

13 The craftsman stretches out *his* rule,
He marks one out with chalk;
He fashions it with a plane,
He marks it out with the compass,
And makes it like the figure of a man,
According to the beauty of a man, that it may remain in the house.
14 He cuts down cedars for himself,
And takes the cypress and the oak;
He secures *it* for himself among the trees of the forest.
He plants a pine, and the rain nourishes *it.*

15 Then it shall be for a man to burn,
For he will take some of it and warm himself;
Yes, he kindles *it* and bakes bread;
Indeed he makes a god and worships *it;*
He makes it a carved image, and falls down to it.
16 He burns half of it in the fire;
With this half he eats meat;
He roasts a roast, and is satisfied.
He even warms *himself* and says,
"Ah! I am warm,
I have seen the fire."
17 And the rest of it he makes into a god,
His carved image.
He falls down before it and worships *it,*
Prays to it and says,
"Deliver me, for you *are* my god!"

18 They do not know nor understand;
For He has shut their eyes, so that they cannot see,
And their hearts, so that they cannot understand.
19 And no one considers in his heart,
Nor *is there* knowledge nor understanding to say,
"I have burned half of it in the fire,
Yes, I have also baked bread on its coals;
I have roasted meat and eaten *it;*
And shall I make the rest of it an abomination?
Shall I fall down before a block of wood?"
20 He feeds on ashes;
A deceived heart has turned him aside;
And he cannot deliver his soul,
Nor say, "*Is there* not a lie in my right hand?"

Israel Is Not Forgotten

21 "Remember these, O Jacob,
And Israel, for you *are* My servant;
I have formed you, you *are* My servant;
O Israel, you will not be forgotten by Me!
22 I have blotted out, like a thick cloud, your transgressions,
And like a cloud, your sins.
Return to Me, for I have redeemed you."

23 Sing, O heavens, for the LORD has done *it!*
Shout, you lower parts of the earth;
Break forth into singing, you mountains,
O forest, and every tree in it!

For the LORD has redeemed Jacob,
And glorified Himself in Israel.

JUDAH WILL BE RESTORED

24 Thus says the LORD, your Redeemer,
And He who formed you from the womb:
"I *am* the LORD, who makes all *things*,
Who stretches out the heavens all alone,
Who spreads abroad the earth by Myself;
25 Who frustrates the signs of the babblers,
And drives diviners mad;
Who turns wise men backward,
And makes their knowledge foolishness;
26 Who confirms the word of His servant,
And performs the counsel of His messengers;
Who says to Jerusalem, 'You shall be inhabited,'
To the cities of Judah, 'You shall be built,'
And I will raise up her waste places;
27 Who says to the deep, 'Be dry!
And I will dry up your rivers';
28 Who says of Cyrus, '*He is* My shepherd,
And he shall perform all My pleasure,
Saying to Jerusalem, "You shall be built,"
And to the temple, "Your foundation shall be laid." '

CYRUS, GOD'S INSTRUMENT

45 "Thus says the LORD to His anointed,
To Cyrus, whose right hand I have held—
To subdue nations before him
And loose the armor of kings,
To open before him the double doors,
So that the gates will not be shut:
2 'I will go before you
And make the crooked places[a] straight;
I will break in pieces the gates of bronze
And cut the bars of iron.
3 I will give you the treasures of darkness
And hidden riches of secret places,
That you may know that I, the LORD,
Who call *you* by your name,
Am the God of Israel.
4 For Jacob My servant's sake,
And Israel My elect,
I have even called you by your name;
I have named you, though you have not known Me.
5 I *am* the LORD, and *there is* no other;
There is no God besides Me.
I will gird you, though you have not known Me,
6 That they may know from the rising of the sun to its setting
That *there is* none besides Me.
I *am* the LORD, and *there is* no other;
7 I form the light and create darkness,
I make peace and create calamity;
I, the LORD, do all these *things*.'

8 "Rain down, you heavens, from above,
And let the skies pour down righteousness;
Let the earth open, let them bring forth salvation,
And let righteousness spring up together.
I, the LORD, have created it.

9 "Woe to him who strives with his Maker!
Let the potsherd *strive* with the potsherds of the earth!
Shall the clay say to him who forms it,
'What are you making?'
Or shall your handiwork *say*, 'He has no hands'?
10 Woe to him who says to *his* father,
'What are you begetting?'
Or to the woman, 'What have you brought forth?' "

11 Thus says the LORD,
The Holy One of Israel, and his Maker:
"Ask Me of things to come concerning My sons;
And concerning the work of My hands, you command Me.
12 I have made the earth,
And created man on it.
I—My hands—stretched out the heavens,
And all their host I have commanded.
13 I have raised him up in righteousness,
And I will direct all his ways;
He shall build My city
And let My exiles go free,
Not for price nor reward,"
Says the LORD of hosts.

45:2 [a]Dead Sea Scrolls and Septuagint read *mountains;* Targum reads *I will trample down the walls;* Vulgate reads *I will humble the great ones of the earth.*

The Lord, the Only Savior

14 Thus says the LORD:

"The labor of Egypt and merchandise of
Cush
And of the Sabeans, men of stature,
Shall come over to you, and they shall
be yours;
They shall walk behind you,
They shall come over in chains;
And they shall bow down to you.
They will make supplication to you,
saying, 'Surely God *is* in you,
And *there is* no other;
There is no other God.' "

15 Truly You *are* God, who hide Yourself,
O God of Israel, the Savior!
16 They shall be ashamed
And also disgraced, all of them;
They shall go in confusion together,
Who are makers of idols.
17 *But* Israel shall be saved by the LORD
With an everlasting salvation;
You shall not be ashamed or disgraced
Forever and ever.

18 For thus says the LORD,
Who created the heavens,
Who is God,
Who formed the earth and made it,
Who has established it,
Who did not create it in vain,
Who formed it to be inhabited:
"I *am* the LORD, and *there is* no other.
19 I have not spoken in secret,
In a dark place of the earth;
I did not say to the seed of Jacob,
'Seek Me in vain';
I, the LORD, speak righteousness,
I declare things that are right.

20 "Assemble yourselves and come;
Draw near together,
You *who have* escaped from the nations.
They have no knowledge,
Who carry the wood of their carved
image,
And pray to a god *that* cannot save.
21 Tell and bring forth *your case;*
Yes, let them take counsel together.
Who has declared this from ancient
time?
Who has told it from that time?
Have not I, the LORD?
And *there is* no other God besides Me,
A just God and a Savior;
There is none besides Me.

22 "Look to Me, and be saved,
All you ends of the earth!
For I *am* God, and *there is* no other.
23 I have sworn by Myself;
The word has gone out of My mouth *in*
righteousness,
And shall not return,
That to Me every knee shall bow,
Every tongue shall take an oath.
24 He shall say,
'Surely in the LORD I have righteousness
and strength.
To Him *men* shall come,
And all shall be ashamed
Who are incensed against Him.
25 In the LORD all the descendants of Israel
Shall be justified, and shall glory.' "

Dead Idols and the Living God

46 Bel bows down, Nebo stoops;
Their idols were on the beasts and on
the cattle.
Your carriages *were* heavily loaded,
A burden to the weary *beast.*
2 They stoop, they bow down together;
They could not deliver the burden,
But have themselves gone into captivity.

3 "Listen to Me, O house of Jacob,
And all the remnant of the house of
Israel,
Who have been upheld *by Me* from
birth,
Who have been carried from the womb:
4 Even to *your* old age, I *am* He,
And *even* to gray hairs I will carry *you!*
I have made, and I will bear;
Even I will carry, and will deliver *you.*

5 "To whom will you liken Me, and make
Me equal
And compare Me, that we should be
alike?
6 They lavish gold out of the bag,
And weigh silver on the scales;
They hire a goldsmith, and he makes it a
god;
They prostrate themselves, yes, they
worship.

7 They bear it on the shoulder, they carry it
And set it in its place, and it stands;
From its place it shall not move.
Though *one* cries out to it, yet it cannot answer
Nor save him out of his trouble.

8 "Remember this, and show yourselves men;
Recall to mind, O you transgressors.
9 Remember the former things of old,
For I *am* God, and *there is* no other;
I am God, and *there is* none like Me,
10 Declaring the end from the beginning,
And from ancient times *things* that are not *yet* done,
Saying, 'My counsel shall stand,
And I will do all My pleasure,'
11 Calling a bird of prey from the east,
The man who executes My counsel, from a far country.
Indeed I have spoken *it;*
I will also bring it to pass.
I have purposed *it;*
I will also do it.

12 "Listen to Me, you stubborn-hearted,
Who *are* far from righteousness:
13 I bring My righteousness near, it shall not be far off;
My salvation shall not linger.
And I will place salvation in Zion,
For Israel My glory.

The Humiliation of Babylon

47 "Come down and sit in the dust,
O virgin daughter of Babylon;
Sit on the ground without a throne,
O daughter of the Chaldeans!
For you shall no more be called
Tender and delicate.
2 Take the millstones and grind meal.
Remove your veil,
Take off the skirt,
Uncover the thigh,
Pass through the rivers.
3 Your nakedness shall be uncovered,
Yes, your shame will be seen;
I will take vengeance,
And I will not arbitrate with a man."

4 *As for* our Redeemer, the LORD of hosts *is* His name,
The Holy One of Israel.

5 "Sit in silence, and go into darkness,
O daughter of the Chaldeans;
For you shall no longer be called
The Lady of Kingdoms.
6 I was angry with My people;
I have profaned My inheritance,
And given them into your hand.
You showed them no mercy;
On the elderly you laid your yoke very heavily.
7 And you said, 'I shall be a lady forever,'
So that you did not take these *things* to heart,
Nor remember the latter end of them.

8 "Therefore hear this now, *you who are* given to pleasures,
Who dwell securely,
Who say in your heart, 'I *am,* and *there is* no one else besides me;
I shall not sit *as* a widow,
Nor shall I know the loss of children';
9 But these two *things* shall come to you
In a moment, in one day:
The loss of children, and widowhood.
They shall come upon you in their fullness
Because of the multitude of your sorceries,
For the great abundance of your enchantments.

10 "For you have trusted in your wickedness;
You have said, 'No one sees me';
Your wisdom and your knowledge have warped you;
And you have said in your heart,
'I *am,* and *there is* no one else besides me.'
11 Therefore evil shall come upon you;
You shall not know from where it arises.
And trouble shall fall upon you;
You will not be able to put it off.
And desolation shall come upon you suddenly,
Which you shall not know.

12 "Stand now with your enchantments
And the multitude of your sorceries,
In which you have labored from your youth—
Perhaps you will be able to profit,
Perhaps you will prevail.

13 You are wearied in the multitude of your counsels;
Let now the astrologers, the stargazers,
And the monthly prognosticators
Stand up and save you
From what shall come upon you.
14 Behold, they shall be as stubble,
The fire shall burn them;
They shall not deliver themselves
From the power of the flame;
It shall not *be* a coal to be warmed by,
Nor a fire to sit before!
15 Thus shall they be to you
With whom you have labored,
Your merchants from your youth;
They shall wander each one to his quarter.
No one shall save you.

ISRAEL REFINED FOR GOD'S GLORY

48 "Hear this, O house of Jacob,
Who are called by the name of Israel,
And have come forth from the wellsprings of Judah;
Who swear by the name of the LORD,
And make mention of the God of Israel,
But not in truth or in righteousness;
2 For they call themselves after the holy city,
And lean on the God of Israel;
The LORD of hosts *is* His name:

3 "I have declared the former things from the beginning;
They went forth from My mouth, and I caused them to hear it.
Suddenly I did *them,* and they came to pass.
4 Because I knew that you *were* obstinate,
And your neck *was* an iron sinew,
And your brow bronze,
5 Even from the beginning I have declared *it* to you;
Before it came to pass I proclaimed *it* to you,
Lest you should say, 'My idol has done them,
And my carved image and my molded image
Have commanded them.'

6 "You have heard;
See all this.
And will you not declare *it?*
I have made you hear new things from this time,
Even hidden things, and you did not know them.
7 They are created now and not from the beginning;
And before this day you have not heard them,
Lest you should say, 'Of course I knew them.'
8 Surely you did not hear,
Surely you did not know;
Surely from long ago your ear was not opened.
For I knew that you would deal very treacherously,
And were called a transgressor from the womb.

9 "For My name's sake I will defer My anger,
And *for* My praise I will restrain it from you,
So that I do not cut you off.
10 Behold, I have refined you, but not as silver;
I have tested you in the furnace of affliction.
11 For My own sake, for My own sake, I will do *it;*
For how should *My name* be profaned?
And I will not give My glory to another.

GOD'S ANCIENT PLAN TO REDEEM ISRAEL

12 "Listen to Me, O Jacob,
And Israel, My called:
I *am* He, I *am* the First,
I *am* also the Last.
13 Indeed My hand has laid the foundation of the earth,
And My right hand has stretched out the heavens;
When I call to them,
They stand up together.

14 "All of you, assemble yourselves, and hear!
Who among them has declared these *things?*
The LORD loves him;
He shall do His pleasure on Babylon,
And His arm *shall be against* the Chaldeans.

15 I, *even* I, have spoken;
Yes, I have called him,
I have brought him, and his way will prosper.

16 "Come near to Me, hear this:
I have not spoken in secret from the beginning;
From the time that it was, I *was* there.
And now the Lord GOD and His Spirit
Have[a] sent Me."

17 Thus says the LORD, your Redeemer,
The Holy One of Israel:
"I *am* the LORD your God,
Who teaches you to profit,
Who leads you by the way you should go.
18 Oh, that you had heeded My commandments!
Then your peace would have been like a river,
And your righteousness like the waves of the sea.
19 Your descendants also would have been like the sand,
And the offspring of your body like the grains of sand;
His name would not have been cut off
Nor destroyed from before Me."

20 Go forth from Babylon!
Flee from the Chaldeans!
With a voice of singing,
Declare, proclaim this,
Utter it to the end of the earth;
Say, "The LORD has redeemed
His servant Jacob!"
21 And they did not thirst
When He led them through the deserts;
He caused the waters to flow from the rock for them;
He also split the rock, and the waters gushed out.

22 "*There is* no peace," says the LORD, "for the wicked."

THE SERVANT, THE LIGHT TO THE GENTILES

49 "Listen, O coastlands, to Me,
And take heed, you peoples from afar!
The LORD has called Me from the womb;
From the matrix of My mother He has made mention of My name.
2 And He has made My mouth like a sharp sword;
In the shadow of His hand He has hidden Me,
And made Me a polished shaft;
In His quiver He has hidden Me."

3 "And He said to me,
'You *are* My servant, O Israel,
In whom I will be glorified.'
4 Then I said, 'I have labored in vain,
I have spent my strength for nothing and in vain;
Yet surely my just reward *is* with the LORD,
And my work with my God.' "

5 "And now the LORD says,
Who formed Me from the womb *to be* His Servant,
To bring Jacob back to Him,
So that Israel is gathered to Him[a]
(For I shall be glorious in the eyes of the LORD,
And My God shall be My strength),
6 Indeed He says,
'It is too small a thing that You should be My Servant
To raise up the tribes of Jacob,
And to restore the preserved ones of Israel;
I will also give You as a light to the Gentiles,
That You should be My salvation to the ends of the earth.' "

7 Thus says the LORD,
The Redeemer of Israel, their Holy One,
To Him whom man despises,
To Him whom the nation abhors,
To the Servant of rulers:
"Kings shall see and arise,
Princes also shall worship,
Because of the LORD who is faithful,
The Holy One of Israel;
And He has chosen You."

8 Thus says the LORD:

48:16 [a]The Hebrew verb is singular. **49:5** [a]Qere, Dead Sea Scrolls, and Septuagint read *is gathered to Him;* Kethib reads *is not gathered.*

"In an acceptable time I have heard You,
And in the day of salvation I have helped You;
I will preserve You and give You
As a covenant to the people,
To restore the earth,
To cause them to inherit the desolate heritages;
9 That You may say to the prisoners, 'Go forth,'
To those who *are* in darkness, 'Show yourselves.'

"They shall feed along the roads,
And their pastures *shall be* on all desolate heights.
10 They shall neither hunger nor thirst,
Neither heat nor sun shall strike them;
For He who has mercy on them will lead them,
Even by the springs of water He will guide them.
11 I will make each of My mountains a road,
And My highways shall be elevated.
12 Surely these shall come from afar;
Look! Those from the north and the west,
And these from the land of Sinim."

13 Sing, O heavens!
Be joyful, O earth!
And break out in singing, O mountains!
For the LORD has comforted His people,
And will have mercy on His afflicted.

GOD WILL REMEMBER ZION

14 But Zion said,
"The LORD has forsaken me,
And my Lord has forgotten me."

15 "Can a woman forget her nursing child,
And not have compassion on the son of her womb?
Surely they may forget,
Yet I will not forget you.
16 See, I have inscribed you on the palms *of My hands;*
Your walls *are* continually before Me.
17 Your sons[a] shall make haste;
Your destroyers and those who laid you waste
Shall go away from you.
18 Lift up your eyes, look around and see;
All these gather together *and* come to you.
As I live," says the LORD,
"You shall surely clothe yourselves with them all as an ornament,
And bind them *on you* as a bride *does.*

19 "For your waste and desolate places,
And the land of your destruction,
Will even now be too small for the inhabitants;
And those who swallowed you up will be far away.
20 The children you will have,
After you have lost the others,
Will say again in your ears,
'The place *is* too small for me;
Give me a place where I may dwell.'
21 Then you will say in your heart,
'Who has begotten these for me,
Since I have lost my children and am desolate,
A captive, and wandering to and fro?
And who has brought these up?
There I was, left alone;
But these, where *were* they?' "

22 Thus says the Lord GOD:

"Behold, I will lift My hand in an oath to the nations,
And set up My standard for the peoples;
They shall bring your sons in *their* arms,
And your daughters shall be carried on *their* shoulders;
23 Kings shall be your foster fathers,
And their queens your nursing mothers;
They shall bow down to you with *their* faces to the earth,
And lick up the dust of your feet.

"See, I have inscribed you on the palms of My hands; your walls are continually before Me."
ISAIAH 49:16

49:17 [a]Dead Sea Scrolls, Septuagint, Targum, and Vulgate read *builders.*

Then you will know that I *am* the LORD,
For they shall not be ashamed who wait for Me."

24 Shall the prey be taken from the mighty,
Or the captives of the righteous[a] be delivered?

25But thus says the LORD:

"Even the captives of the mighty shall be taken away,
And the prey of the terrible be delivered;
For I will contend with him who contends with you,
And I will save your children.
26 I will feed those who oppress you with their own flesh,
And they shall be drunk with their own blood as with sweet wine.
All flesh shall know
That I, the LORD, *am* your Savior,
And your Redeemer, the Mighty One of Jacob."

THE SERVANT, ISRAEL'S HOPE

50 Thus says the LORD:

"Where *is* the certificate of your mother's divorce,
Whom I have put away?
Or which of My creditors *is it* to whom I have sold you?
For your iniquities you have sold yourselves,
And for your transgressions your mother has been put away.
2 Why, when I came, *was there* no man?
Why, when I called, *was there* none to answer?
Is My hand shortened at all that it cannot redeem?
Or have I no power to deliver?
Indeed with My rebuke I dry up the sea,
I make the rivers a wilderness;
Their fish stink because *there is* no water,
And die of thirst.
3 I clothe the heavens with blackness,
And I make sackcloth their covering."

4 "The Lord GOD has given Me
The tongue of the learned,
That I should know how to speak
A word in season to *him who is* weary.
He awakens Me morning by morning,
He awakens My ear
To hear as the learned.
5 The Lord GOD has opened My ear;
And I was not rebellious,
Nor did I turn away.
6 I gave My back to those who struck *Me,*
And My cheeks to those who plucked out the beard;
I did not hide My face from shame and spitting.

7 "For the Lord GOD will help Me;
Therefore I will not be disgraced;
Therefore I have set My face like a flint,
And I know that I will not be ashamed.
8 *He is* near who justifies Me;
Who will contend with Me?
Let us stand together.
Who *is* My adversary?
Let him come near Me.
9 Surely the Lord GOD will help Me;
Who *is* he *who* will condemn Me?
Indeed they will all grow old like a garment;
The moth will eat them up.

10 "Who among you fears the LORD?
Who obeys the voice of His Servant?
Who walks in darkness
And has no light?
Let him trust in the name of the LORD
And rely upon his God.
11 Look, all you who kindle a fire,
Who encircle *yourselves* with sparks:
Walk in the light of your fire and in the sparks you have kindled—
This you shall have from My hand:
You shall lie down in torment.

THE LORD COMFORTS ZION

51 "Listen to Me, you who follow after righteousness,
You who seek the LORD:
Look to the rock *from which* you were hewn,
And to the hole of the pit *from which* you were dug.
2 Look to Abraham your father,

49:24 [a]Following Masoretic Text and Targum; Dead Sea Scrolls, Syriac, and Vulgate read *the mighty;* Septuagint reads *unjustly.*

And to Sarah *who* bore you;
For I called him alone,
And blessed him and increased him."

3 For the LORD will comfort Zion,
He will comfort all her waste places;
He will make her wilderness like Eden,
And her desert like the garden of the LORD;
Joy and gladness will be found in it,
Thanksgiving and the voice of melody.

4 "Listen to Me, My people;
And give ear to Me, O My nation:
For law will proceed from Me,
And I will make My justice rest
As a light of the peoples.
5 My righteousness *is* near,
My salvation has gone forth,
And My arms will judge the peoples;
The coastlands will wait upon Me,
And on My arm they will trust.
6 Lift up your eyes to the heavens,
And look on the earth beneath.
For the heavens will vanish away like smoke,
The earth will grow old like a garment,
And those who dwell in it will die in like manner;
But My salvation will be forever,
And My righteousness will not be abolished.

7 "Listen to Me, you who know righteousness,
You people in whose heart *is* My law:
Do not fear the reproach of men,
Nor be afraid of their insults.
8 For the moth will eat them up like a garment,
And the worm will eat them like wool;
But My righteousness will be forever,
And My salvation from generation to generation."

9 Awake, awake, put on strength,
O arm of the LORD!
Awake as in the ancient days,
In the generations of old.
Are You not *the arm* that cut Rahab apart,
And wounded the serpent?

10 *Are* You not *the One* who dried up the sea,
The waters of the great deep;
That made the depths of the sea a road
For the redeemed to cross over?
11 So the ransomed of the LORD shall return,
And come to Zion with singing,
With everlasting joy on their heads.
They shall obtain joy and gladness;
Sorrow and sighing shall flee away.

12 "I, *even* I, *am* He who comforts you.
Who *are* you that you should be afraid
Of a man *who* will die,
And of the son of a man *who* will be made like grass?
13 And you forget the LORD your Maker,
Who stretched out the heavens
And laid the foundations of the earth;
You have feared continually every day
Because of the fury of the oppressor,
When *he has* prepared to destroy.
And where *is* the fury of the oppressor?
14 The captive exile hastens, that he may be loosed,
That he should not die in the pit,
And that his bread should not fail.
15 But I *am* the LORD your God,
Who divided the sea whose waves roared—
The LORD of hosts *is* His name.
16 And I have put My words in your mouth;
I have covered you with the shadow of My hand,
That I may plant the heavens,
Lay the foundations of the earth,
And say to Zion, 'You *are* My people.' "

GOD'S FURY REMOVED

17 Awake, awake!
Stand up, O Jerusalem,
You who have drunk at the hand of the LORD
The cup of His fury;
You have drunk the dregs of the cup of trembling,
And drained *it* out.
18 *There is* no one to guide her
Among all the sons she has brought forth;
Nor *is there any* who takes her by the hand
Among all the sons she has brought up.
19 These two *things* have come to you;

Who will be sorry for you?—
Desolation and destruction, famine and sword—
By whom will I comfort you?
20 Your sons have fainted,
They lie at the head of all the streets,
Like an antelope in a net;
They are full of the fury of the LORD,
The rebuke of your God.

21 Therefore please hear this, you afflicted,
And drunk but not with wine.
22 Thus says your Lord,
The LORD and your God,
Who pleads the cause of His people:
"See, I have taken out of your hand
The cup of trembling,
The dregs of the cup of My fury;
You shall no longer drink it.
23 But I will put it into the hand of those who afflict you,
Who have said to you,[a]
'Lie down, that we may walk over you.'
And you have laid your body like the ground,
And as the street, for those who walk over."

God Redeems Jerusalem

52 Awake, awake!
Put on your strength, O Zion;
Put on your beautiful garments,
O Jerusalem, the holy city!
For the uncircumcised and the unclean
Shall no longer come to you.
2 Shake yourself from the dust, arise;
Sit down, O Jerusalem!
Loose yourself from the bonds of your neck,
O captive daughter of Zion!

3For thus says the LORD:

"You have sold yourselves for nothing,
And you shall be redeemed without money."

4For thus says the Lord GOD:

"My people went down at first
Into Egypt to dwell there;
Then the Assyrian oppressed them without cause.
5 Now therefore, what have I here," says the LORD,
"That My people are taken away for nothing?
Those who rule over them
Make them wail,"[a] says the LORD,
"And My name *is* blasphemed continually every day.
6 Therefore My people shall know My name;
Therefore *they shall know* in that day
That I *am* He who speaks:
'Behold, *it is* I.' "

7 How beautiful upon the mountains
Are the feet of him who brings good news,
Who proclaims peace,
Who brings glad tidings of good *things,*
Who proclaims salvation,
Who says to Zion,
"Your God reigns!"
8 Your watchmen shall lift up *their* voices,
With their voices they shall sing together;
For they shall see eye to eye
When the LORD brings back Zion.
9 Break forth into joy, sing together,
You waste places of Jerusalem!
For the LORD has comforted His people,
He has redeemed Jerusalem.
10 The LORD has made bare His holy arm
In the eyes of all the nations;
And all the ends of the earth shall see
The salvation of our God.

11 Depart! Depart! Go out from there,
Touch no unclean *thing;*
Go out from the midst of her,
Be clean,
You who bear the vessels of the LORD.
12 For you shall not go out with haste,
Nor go by flight;
For the LORD will go before you,
And the God of Israel *will be* your rear guard.

51:23 [a]Literally *your soul* **52:5** [a]Dead Sea Scrolls read *Mock;* Septuagint reads *Marvel and wail;* Targum reads *Boast themselves;* Vulgate reads *Treat them unjustly.*

The Sin-Bearing Servant

13 Behold, My Servant shall deal prudently;
He shall be exalted and extolled and be very high.
14 Just as many were astonished at you,
So His visage was marred more than any man,
And His form more than the sons of men;
15 So shall He sprinkle[a] many nations.
Kings shall shut their mouths at Him;
For what had not been told them they shall see,
And what they had not heard they shall consider.

53 Who has believed our report?
And to whom has the arm of the LORD been revealed?
2 For He shall grow up before Him as a tender plant,
And as a root out of dry ground.
He has no form or comeliness;
And when we see Him,
There is no beauty that we should desire Him.
3 He is despised and rejected by men,
A Man of sorrows and acquainted with grief.
And we hid, as it were, *our* faces from Him;
He was despised, and we did not esteem Him.

4 Surely He has borne our griefs
And carried our sorrows;
Yet we esteemed Him stricken,
Smitten by God, and afflicted.
5 But He *was* wounded for our transgressions,
He was bruised for our iniquities;
The chastisement for our peace *was* upon Him,
And by His stripes we are healed.
6 All we like sheep have gone astray;
We have turned, every one, to his own way;
And the LORD has laid on Him the iniquity of us all.

7 He was oppressed and He was afflicted,
Yet He opened not His mouth;
He was led as a lamb to the slaughter,
And as a sheep before its shearers is silent,
So He opened not His mouth.
8 He was taken from prison and from judgment,
And who will declare His generation?
For He was cut off from the land of the living;
For the transgressions of My people He was stricken.
9 And they[a] made His grave with the wicked—
But with the rich at His death,
Because He had done no violence,
Nor *was any* deceit in His mouth.

10 Yet it pleased the LORD to bruise Him;
He has put *Him* to grief.
When You make His soul an offering for sin,
He shall see *His* seed, He shall prolong *His* days,
And the pleasure of the LORD shall prosper in His hand.
11 He shall see the labor of His soul,[a] *and* be satisfied.

52:15 [a]Or *startle* **53:9** [a]Literally *he* or *He*
53:11 [a]Following Masoretic Text, Targum, and Vulgate; Dead Sea Scrolls and Septuagint read *From the labor of His soul He shall see light.*

SOUL NOTE

Borne Our Griefs *(53:3, 4)* Isaiah's words communicate the suffering of the One who loved us and died for us. Jesus received God's punishment for our sin so that we could have peace with God (Rom. 5:1). We are healed because Jesus was wounded. He carried our sorrows so that we could find hope. No one will ever love us like Christ loves us, because no one has ever done for us what He has done. In our deepest moments of grief and loss, we need only look to Him on the Cross and realize that He understands. He alone can heal the wounded heart. **Topic: Grief/Loss**

By His knowledge My righteous Servant shall justify many,
For He shall bear their iniquities.
12 Therefore I will divide Him a portion with the great,
And He shall divide the spoil with the strong,
Because He poured out His soul unto death,
And He was numbered with the transgressors,
And He bore the sin of many,
And made intercession for the transgressors.

A Perpetual Covenant of Peace

54 "Sing, O barren,
You *who* have not borne!
Break forth into singing, and cry aloud,
You *who* have not labored with child!
For more *are* the children of the desolate
Than the children of the married woman," says the LORD.
2 "Enlarge the place of your tent,
And let them stretch out the curtains of your dwellings;
Do not spare;
Lengthen your cords,
And strengthen your stakes.
3 For you shall expand to the right and to the left,
And your descendants will inherit the nations,
And make the desolate cities inhabited.

4 "Do not fear, for you will not be ashamed;
Neither be disgraced, for you will not be put to shame;
For you will forget the shame of your youth,
And will not remember the reproach of your widowhood anymore.
5 For your Maker *is* your husband,
The LORD of hosts *is* His name;
And your Redeemer *is* the Holy One of Israel;
He is called the God of the whole earth.
6 For the LORD has called you
Like a woman forsaken and grieved in spirit,
Like a youthful wife when you were refused,"
Says your God.
7 "For a mere moment I have forsaken you,
But with great mercies I will gather you.
8 With a little wrath I hid My face from you for a moment;
But with everlasting kindness I will have mercy on you,"
Says the LORD, your Redeemer.

9 "For this *is* like the waters of Noah to Me;
For as I have sworn
That the waters of Noah would no longer cover the earth,
So have I sworn
That I would not be angry with you, nor rebuke you.
10 For the mountains shall depart
And the hills be removed,
But My kindness shall not depart from you,
Nor shall My covenant of peace be removed,"
Says the LORD, who has mercy on you.

11 "O you afflicted one,
Tossed with tempest, *and* not comforted,
Behold, I will lay your stones with colorful gems,
And lay your foundations with sapphires.
12 I will make your pinnacles of rubies,
Your gates of crystal,
And all your walls of precious stones.
13 All your children *shall be* taught by the LORD,
And great *shall be* the peace of your children.
14 In righteousness you shall be established;
You shall be far from oppression, for you shall not fear;
And from terror, for it shall not come near you.
15 Indeed they shall surely assemble, *but* not because of Me.
Whoever assembles against you shall fall for your sake.

16 "Behold, I have created the blacksmith
Who blows the coals in the fire,
Who brings forth an instrument for his work;
And I have created the spoiler to destroy.
17 No weapon formed against you shall prosper,

DEALING WITH LOSS AND GRIEF

H. NORMAN WRIGHT

(Isaiah 53: 3, 4)

EXPERIENCING LOSS

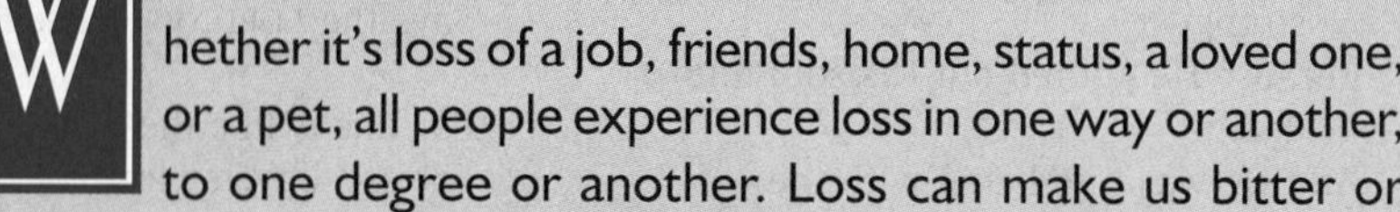

Whether it's loss of a job, friends, home, status, a loved one, or a pet, all people experience loss in one way or another, to one degree or another. Loss can make us bitter or better. Unfortunately, no one likes to talk about it very much. People seem to have an unspoken agreement with others not to talk about their losses. At times, they are not even aware of some of their losses, for the effect of the loss is very minor. Other losses, however, are felt very deeply and affect them for a lifetime. How people respond to their losses and how they allow those losses to affect them can make a difference for the rest of their lives.

Whenever loss occurs, it is important to see it in the correct perspective so they can understand the full impact of what has happened. They must identify how the current loss impacts their present lives, as well as its effect on their thoughts about the future. Loss is not the enemy, but avoiding or ignoring a loss is. Trying to avoid a loss by hiding the feelings will only cause problems in other areas—emotionally, spiritually, or physically. Dealing with loss in a healthy manner can be a major avenue to growth and life-transforming change. With each loss comes the potential for growth, insight, and understanding. Since these results are not immediate, people often fail to see these future blessings. But they must move forward. And the way to move on is to grieve.

EXPERIENCING GRIEF

Grief is defined as "intense emotional suffering caused by loss, disaster, misfortune, etc.; deep sadness." The word is derived from a Latin verb meaning "to burden." *Mourn* is defined as "to feel and express sorrow." Mourning is the expression of grief.

Grieving is like entering the valley of shadows. Grief is not fun. It is painful. It is work. It is a lingering process, often taking one to three years for significant losses. It is necessary, however, in order to deal with all kinds of loss in a healthy manner. A multitude of emotions are involved in the grief process. Many of these emotions seem to conflict with one another. With loss can come bitterness, emptiness, numbness, apathy, love, guilt, sadness, fear, disorientation, self-pity, and helplessness. When people grieve, they experience their loss psychologically through feelings, thoughts, and attitudes, socially as they interact with others, and physically as it affects their health.

Grief encompasses a number of changes. It appears differently at various times, and it comes and goes in people's lives. It is a normal, predictable, expected, and healthy reaction to a loss. Grief is each individual's personal experience and manner of dealing with any kind of loss—no matter how minor or severe it may appear to others.

Grief is not just an event; it is a process. Grief has several stages, although they are not necessarily experienced in exact order, nor does one stage have to be completed before a person moves on to the next stage. The first stage is *denial* or shock.

Intellectually, the bereaved may comprehend what has happened, but their emotions may not experience the pain yet; they may feel numb. The second stage is when they can *release* their emotions, often in the form of anger toward others. They may even get angry with God. Grieving people become preoccupied with memories of what has been lost and they may withdraw for a time. The third stage involves wrestling with feelings of *guilt and anger*. They beat themselves up emotionally as they blame themselves for not somehow preventing the loss. They feel disorganized and don't know how to move on with life. Often some level of depression may set in as they become more apathetic toward life in light of the loss. The fourth stage is *acceptance* of the loss. Reorganizing their lives, filling new roles, and reconnecting with those around them are all healthy and important facets of the healing process. A key part of this process is the ability to learn how to feel and express the pain more truly without denial and avoidance.

It helps for grieving people to have true friends who will stay with them and support them emotionally. It is important for these friends to allow the grieving person to experience all of the different intense emotions of the grieving process. Such friendships will ultimately help the person who has experienced the loss to reorganize and reconnect with the world.

BIBLICAL PRINCIPLES

The Bible has much to say about both loss and grief. People who experience loss, as well as those who come alongside them, can gain wisdom to help them through the grieving process.

Psalm 23 tells of God comforting those who walk through the "valley of the shadow of death." During the darkest hours of mourning, God never abandons His people. Isaiah 53 describes the suffering of our Savior. He experienced loss and grief so that He could understand our humanity and die in our place. He was despised and rejected, "a Man of sorrows and acquainted with grief. . . . He was wounded for our transgressions, He was bruised for our iniquities; the chastisement for our peace was upon Him, and by His stripes we are healed" (Is. 53:3, 5).

Although loss and grief are common, no amount of technology or experience can make the grieving process any easier. The hard news is that the only road to true healing is through the grief process. The good news is that God travels that road with us.

FURTHER MEDITATION:

Other passages to study about the issue of grief/loss include:

- ➢ Ruth 1:5–22
- ➢ Ecclesiastes 3:4
- ➢ Isaiah 61:1–3
- ➢ Jeremiah 31:12, 13
- ➢ John 14:1; 16:16–22
- ➢ 2 Corinthians 1:3–7
- ➢ 1 Thessalonians 4:13, 14

To Learn More: Turn to the key passage note on grief/loss at John 11:35–44 on page 1391. See also the personality profile of Job's wife on page 640.

And every tongue *which* rises against
you in judgment
You shall condemn.
This *is* the heritage of the servants of the
LORD,
And their righteousness *is* from Me,"
Says the LORD.

AN INVITATION TO ABUNDANT LIFE

55 "Ho! Everyone who thirsts,
Come to the waters;
And you who have no money,
Come, buy and eat.
Yes, come, buy wine and milk
Without money and without price.
2 Why do you spend money for *what is*
not bread,
And your wages for *what* does not
satisfy?
Listen carefully to Me, and eat *what is*
good,
And let your soul delight itself in
abundance.
3 Incline your ear, and come to Me.
Hear, and your soul shall live;
And I will make an everlasting covenant
with you—
The sure mercies of David.
4 Indeed I have given him *as* a witness to
the people,
A leader and commander for the
people.
5 Surely you shall call a nation you do not
know,
And nations *who* do not know you shall
run to you,
Because of the LORD your God,
And the Holy One of Israel;
For He has glorified you."

6 Seek the LORD while He may be found,
Call upon Him
while He is
near.
7 Let the wicked
forsake his way,
And the
unrighteous
man his
thoughts;
Let him return to the LORD,
And He will have mercy on him;
And to our God,
For He will abundantly pardon.

Seek the LORD while He may be found, call upon Him while He is near.
ISAIAH 55:6

8 "For My thoughts *are* not your thoughts,
Nor *are* your ways My ways," says the
LORD.
9 "For *as* the heavens are higher than the
earth,
So are My ways higher than your ways,
And My thoughts than your thoughts.

10 "For as the rain comes down, and the
snow from heaven,
And do not return there,
But water the earth,
And make it bring forth and bud,
That it may give seed to the sower
And bread to the eater,
11 So shall My word be that goes forth from
My mouth;
It shall not return to Me void,
But it shall accomplish what I please,
And it shall prosper *in the thing* for
which I sent it.

12 "For you shall go out with joy,
And be led out with peace;
The mountains and the hills
Shall break forth into singing before
you,
And all the trees of the field shall clap
their hands.
13 Instead of the thorn shall come up the
cypress tree,
And instead of the brier shall come up
the myrtle tree;
And it shall be to the LORD for a name,
For an everlasting sign *that* shall not be
cut off."

SALVATION FOR THE GENTILES

56 Thus says the LORD:

"Keep justice, and do righteousness,
For My salvation *is*
about to come,
And My righ-
teousness to
be revealed.
2 Blessed *is* the man
who does this,
And the son of
man *who* lays
hold on it;
Who keeps from defiling the Sabbath,
And keeps his hand from doing any
evil."

3 Do not let the son of the foreigner
Who has joined himself to the LORD
Speak, saying,
"The LORD has utterly separated me from
His people";
Nor let the eunuch say,
"Here I am, a dry tree."
4 For thus says the LORD:
"To the eunuchs who keep My Sabbaths,
And choose what pleases Me,
And hold fast My covenant,
5 Even to them I will give in My house
And within My walls a place and a name
Better than that of sons and daughters;
I will give them[a] an everlasting name
That shall not be cut off.

6 "Also the sons of the foreigner
Who join themselves to the LORD, to
serve Him,
And to love the name of the LORD, to be
His servants—
Everyone who keeps from defiling the
Sabbath,
And holds fast My covenant—
7 Even them I will bring to My holy
mountain,
And make them joyful in My house of
prayer.
Their burnt offerings and their sacrifices
Will be accepted on My altar;
For My house shall be called a house of
prayer for all nations."
8 The Lord GOD, who gathers the outcasts
of Israel, says,
"Yet I will gather to him
Others besides those who are gathered to
him."

ISRAEL'S IRRESPONSIBLE LEADERS

9 All you beasts of the field, come to
devour,
All you beasts in the forest.
10 His watchmen *are* blind,
They are all ignorant;
They *are* all dumb dogs,
They cannot bark;
Sleeping, lying down, loving to slumber.
11 Yes, *they are* greedy dogs
Which never have enough.
And they *are* shepherds
Who cannot understand;
They all look to their own way,
Every one for his own gain,
From his *own* territory.
12 "Come," *one says,* "I will bring wine,
And we will fill ourselves with
intoxicating drink;
Tomorrow will be as today,
And much more abundant."

ISRAEL'S FUTILE IDOLATRY

57 The righteous perishes,
And no man takes *it* to heart;
Merciful men *are* taken away,
While no one considers
That the righteous is taken away from
evil.
2 He shall enter into peace;
They shall rest in their beds,
Each one walking *in* his uprightness.

3 "But come here,
You sons of the sorceress,
You offspring of the adulterer and the
harlot!
4 Whom do you ridicule?
Against whom do you make a wide
mouth
And stick out the tongue?
Are you not children of transgression,
Offspring of falsehood,
5 Inflaming yourselves with gods under
every green tree,
Slaying the children in the valleys,
Under the clefts of the rocks?
6 Among the smooth *stones* of the stream
Is your portion;
They, they, *are* your lot!
Even to them you have poured a drink
offering,
You have offered a grain offering.
Should I receive comfort in these?

7 "On a lofty and high mountain
You have set your bed;
Even there you went up
To offer sacrifice.
8 Also behind the doors and their posts
You have set up your remembrance;
For you have uncovered yourself *to those
other* than Me,
And have gone up to them;
You have enlarged your bed
And made *a covenant* with them;
You have loved their bed,

56:5 [a]Literally *him*

Where you saw *their* nudity.[a]
9 You went to the king with ointment,
And increased your perfumes;
You sent your messengers far off,
And *even* descended to Sheol.
10 You are wearied in the length of your
way;
Yet you did not say, 'There is no hope.'
You have found the life of your hand;
Therefore you were not grieved.

11 "And of whom have you been afraid, or
feared,
That you have lied
And not remembered Me,
Nor taken *it* to your heart?
Is it not because I have held My peace
from of old
That you do not fear Me?
12 I will declare your righteousness
And your works,
For they will not profit you.
13 When you cry out,
Let your collection *of idols* deliver you.
But the wind will carry them all
away,
A breath will take *them*.
But he who puts his trust in Me shall
possess the land,
And shall inherit My holy mountain."

Healing for the Backslider

14 And one shall say,
"Heap it up! Heap it up!
Prepare the way,
Take the stumbling block out of the way
of My people."

15 For thus says the High and Lofty One
Who inhabits eternity, whose name *is*
Holy:
"I dwell in the high and holy *place*,
With him *who* has a contrite and humble
spirit,
To revive the spirit of the humble,
And to revive the heart of the contrite
ones.
16 For I will not contend forever,
Nor will I always be angry;
For the spirit would fail before Me,
And the souls *which* I have made.
17 For the iniquity of his covetousness
I was angry and struck him;
I hid and was angry,
And he went on backsliding in the way
of his heart.
18 I have seen his ways, and will heal him;
I will also lead him,
And restore comforts to him
And to his mourners.

19 "I create the fruit of the lips:
Peace, peace to *him who is* far off and to
him who is near,"
Says the LORD,
"And I will heal him."
20 But the wicked *are* like the troubled sea,
When it cannot rest,
Whose waters cast up mire and dirt.

21 "*There is* no peace,"
Says my God, "for the wicked."

Fasting that Pleases God

58 "Cry aloud, spare not;
Lift up your voice like a trumpet;
Tell My people their transgression,
And the house of Jacob their sins.
2 Yet they seek Me daily,
And delight to know My ways,
As a nation that did righteousness,
And did not forsake the ordinance of
their God.
They ask of Me the ordinances of
justice;
They take delight in approaching God.
3 'Why have we fasted,' *they say*, 'and You
have not seen?
Why have we afflicted our souls, and
You take no notice?'

"In fact, in the day of your fast you find
pleasure,
And exploit all your laborers.
4 Indeed you fast for strife and debate,
And to strike with the fist of
wickedness.
You will not fast as *you do* this day,
To make your voice heard on high.
5 Is it a fast that I have chosen,
A day for a man to afflict his soul?
Is it to bow down his head like a
bulrush,
And to spread out sackcloth and ashes?
Would you call this a fast,
And an acceptable day to the LORD?

57:8 [a]Literally *hand*, a euphemism

6 "*Is* this not the fast that I have chosen:
To loose the bonds of wickedness,
To undo the heavy burdens,
To let the oppressed go free,
And that you break every yoke?
7 *Is it* not to share your bread with the hungry,
And that you bring to your house the poor who are cast out;
When you see the naked, that you cover him,
And not hide yourself from your own flesh?
8 Then your light shall break forth like the morning,
Your healing shall spring forth speedily,
And your righteousness shall go before you;
The glory of the LORD shall be your rear guard.
9 Then you shall call, and the LORD will answer;
You shall cry, and He will say, 'Here I *am.*'

"If you take away the yoke from your midst,
The pointing of the finger, and speaking wickedness,
10 *If* you extend your soul to the hungry
And satisfy the afflicted soul,
Then your light shall dawn in the darkness,
And your darkness shall *be* as the noonday.
11 The LORD will guide you continually,
And satisfy your soul in drought,
And strengthen your bones;
You shall be like a watered garden,
And like a spring of water, whose waters do not fail.
12 Those from among you
Shall build the old waste places;
You shall raise up the foundations of many generations;
And you shall be called the Repairer of the Breach,
The Restorer of Streets to Dwell In.

13 "If you turn away your foot from the Sabbath,
From doing your pleasure on My holy day,
And call the Sabbath a delight,
The holy *day* of the LORD honorable,
And shall honor Him, not doing your own ways,
Nor finding your own pleasure,
Nor speaking *your own* words,
14 Then you shall delight yourself in the LORD;
And I will cause you to ride on the high hills of the earth,
And feed you with the heritage of Jacob your father.
The mouth of the LORD has spoken."

SEPARATED FROM GOD

59 Behold, the LORD's hand is not shortened,
That it cannot save;
Nor His ear heavy,
That it cannot hear.
2 But your iniquities have separated you from your God;
And your sins have hidden *His* face from you,
So that He will not hear.
3 For your hands are defiled with blood,
And your fingers with iniquity;
Your lips have spoken lies,
Your tongue has muttered perversity.

4 No one calls for justice,
Nor does *any* plead for truth.
They trust in empty words and speak lies;
They conceive evil and bring forth iniquity.
5 They hatch vipers' eggs and weave the spider's web;
He who eats of their eggs dies,
And *from* that which is crushed a viper breaks out.

6 Their webs will not become garments,
Nor will they cover themselves with their works;
Their works *are* works of iniquity,
And the act of violence *is* in their hands.
7 Their feet run to evil,

Behold, the LORD'S hand is not shortened, that it cannot save; nor His ear heavy, that it cannot hear.
ISAIAH 59:1

And they make haste to shed innocent blood;
Their thoughts *are* thoughts of iniquity;
Wasting and destruction *are* in their paths.
8 The way of peace they have not known,
And *there is* no justice in their ways;
They have made themselves crooked paths;
Whoever takes that way shall not know peace.

Sin Confessed

9 Therefore justice is far from us,
Nor does righteousness overtake us;
We look for light, but there is darkness!
For brightness, *but* we walk in blackness!
10 We grope for the wall like the blind,
And we grope as if *we had* no eyes;
We stumble at noonday as at twilight;
We are as dead *men* in desolate places.
11 We all growl like bears,
And moan sadly like doves;
We look for justice, but *there is* none;
For salvation, *but* it is far from us.
12 For our transgressions are multiplied before You,
And our sins testify against us;
For our transgressions *are* with us,
And *as for* our iniquities, we know them:
13 In transgressing and lying against the LORD,
And departing from our God,
Speaking oppression and revolt,
Conceiving and uttering from the heart words of falsehood.
14 Justice is turned back,
And righteousness stands afar off;
For truth is fallen in the street,
And equity cannot enter.
15 So truth fails,
And he *who* departs from evil makes himself a prey.

The Redeemer of Zion

Then the LORD saw *it,* and it displeased Him
That *there was* no justice.
16 He saw that *there was* no man,
And wondered that *there was* no intercessor;
Therefore His own arm brought salvation for Him;
And His own righteousness, it sustained Him.
17 For He put on righteousness as a breastplate,
And a helmet of salvation on His head;
He put on the garments of vengeance for clothing,
And was clad with zeal as a cloak.
18 According to *their* deeds, accordingly He will repay,
Fury to His adversaries,
Recompense to His enemies;
The coastlands He will fully repay.
19 So shall they fear
The name of the LORD from the west,
And His glory from the rising of the sun;
When the enemy comes in like a flood,
The Spirit of the LORD will lift up a standard against him.

20 "The Redeemer will come to Zion,
And to those who turn from transgression in Jacob,"
Says the LORD.

21 "As for Me," says the LORD, "this *is* My
covenant with them: My Spirit who *is* upon
you, and My words which I have put in your
mouth, shall not depart from your mouth, nor
from the mouth of your descendants, nor from
the mouth of your descendants' descendants,"
says the LORD, "from this time and forevermore."

The Gentiles Bless Zion

60 Arise, shine;
For your light has come!
And the glory of the LORD is risen upon you.
2 For behold, the darkness shall cover the earth,
And deep darkness the people;
But the LORD will arise over you,
And His glory will be seen upon you.
3 The Gentiles shall come to your light,
And kings to the brightness of your rising.

4 "Lift up your eyes all around, and see:
They all gather together, they come to you;
Your sons shall come from afar,
And your daughters shall be nursed at *your* side.

5 Then you shall see and become radiant,
And your heart shall swell with joy;
Because the abundance of the sea shall be turned to you,
The wealth of the Gentiles shall come to you.
6 The multitude of camels shall cover your *land,*
The dromedaries of Midian and Ephah;
All those from Sheba shall come;
They shall bring gold and incense,
And they shall proclaim the praises of the LORD.
7 All the flocks of Kedar shall be gathered together to you,
The rams of Nebaioth shall minister to you;
They shall ascend with acceptance on My altar,
And I will glorify the house of My glory.

8 "Who *are* these *who* fly like a cloud,
And like doves to their roosts?
9 Surely the coastlands shall wait for Me;
And the ships of Tarshish *will come* first,
To bring your sons from afar,
Their silver and their gold with them,
To the name of the LORD your God,
And to the Holy One of Israel,
Because He has glorified you.

10 "The sons of foreigners shall build up your walls,
And their kings shall minister to you;
For in My wrath I struck you,
But in My favor I have had mercy on you.
11 Therefore your gates shall be open continually;
They shall not be shut day or night,
That *men* may bring to you the wealth of the Gentiles,
And their kings in procession.
12 For the nation and kingdom which will not serve you shall perish,
And *those* nations shall be utterly ruined.

13 "The glory of Lebanon shall come to you,
The cypress, the pine, and the box tree together,
To beautify the place of My sanctuary;
And I will make the place of My feet glorious.
14 Also the sons of those who afflicted you
Shall come bowing to you,
And all those who despised you shall fall prostrate at the soles of your feet;
And they shall call you The City of the LORD,
Zion of the Holy One of Israel.

15 "Whereas you have been forsaken and hated,
So that no one went through *you,*
I will make you an eternal excellence,
A joy of many generations.
16 You shall drink the milk of the Gentiles,
And milk the breast of kings;
You shall know that I, the LORD, *am* your Savior
And your Redeemer, the Mighty One of Jacob.

17 "Instead of bronze I will bring gold,
Instead of iron I will bring silver,
Instead of wood, bronze,
And instead of stones, iron.
I will also make your officers peace,
And your magistrates righteousness.
18 Violence shall no longer be heard in your land,
Neither wasting nor destruction within your borders;
But you shall call your walls Salvation,
And your gates Praise.

God the Glory of His People

19 "The sun shall no longer be your light by day,
Nor for brightness shall the moon give light to you;
But the LORD will be to you an everlasting light,
And your God your glory.
20 Your sun shall no longer go down,
Nor shall your moon withdraw itself;
For the LORD will be your everlasting light,
And the days of your mourning shall be ended.
21 Also your people *shall* all *be* righteous;
They shall inherit the land forever,
The branch of My planting,
The work of My hands,
That I may be glorified.
22 A little one shall become a thousand,

And a small one a strong nation.
I, the LORD, will hasten it in its time."

THE GOOD NEWS OF SALVATION

61 "The Spirit of the Lord GOD *is* upon Me,
Because the LORD has anointed Me
To preach good tidings to the poor;
He has sent Me to heal the brokenhearted,
To proclaim liberty to the captives,
And the opening of the prison to *those who are* bound;
2 To proclaim the acceptable year of the LORD,
And the day of vengeance of our God;
To comfort all who mourn,
3 To console those who mourn in Zion,
To give them beauty for ashes,
The oil of joy for mourning,
The garment of praise for the spirit of heaviness;
That they may be called trees of righteousness,
The planting of the LORD, that He may be glorified."

4 And they shall rebuild the old ruins,
They shall raise up the former desolations,
And they shall repair the ruined cities,
The desolations of many generations.
5 Strangers shall stand and feed your flocks,
And the sons of the foreigner
Shall be your plowmen and your vinedressers.
6 But you shall be named the priests of the LORD,
They shall call you the servants of our God.
You shall eat the riches of the Gentiles,
And in their glory you shall boast.
7 Instead of your shame *you shall have* double *honor,*
And *instead of* confusion they shall rejoice in their portion.
Therefore in their land they shall possess double;
Everlasting joy shall be theirs.

8 "For I, the LORD, love justice;
I hate robbery for burnt offering;
I will direct their work in truth,

SOUL NOTE

Compassion *(61:1, 2)* Isaiah predicted that the Messiah would heal those with broken hearts and liberate spiritual captives and prisoners. God's chosen One would announce His grace to a desperate humanity as an expression of His compassion. From the beginning of His ministry, Jesus said that His purpose was to seek out lost sinners and restore them to a relationship with the Father (Luke 4:16–21). Jesus quoted Isaiah 61 to substantiate His claim to being the Messiah and to restate the purpose of His life and ministry. Jesus came to heal, teach, minister, and serve. His compassion reveals the character of God. **Topic: Compassion**

SOUL NOTE

Oil of Joy *(61:3)* God's love and understanding reach out to those who are depressed and discouraged. He promises to give consolation, beauty in place of ashes, oil of joy in place of mourning, and a garment of praise instead of a spirit of heaviness. The Bible recognizes the heaviness of depression. God's Word brings hope and encouragement to those who are weighed down, and God's people stand with those who struggle, to bring relief and restoration. God promises that He will bring restoration "that He may be glorified." **Topic: Depression**

And will make with them an everlasting
covenant.
9 Their descendants shall be known
among the Gentiles,
And their offspring among the people.
All who see them shall acknowledge
them,
That they *are* the posterity *whom* the
LORD has blessed."

10 I will greatly rejoice in the LORD,
My soul shall be joyful in my God;
For He has clothed me with the
garments of salvation,
He has covered me with the robe of
righteousness,
As a bridegroom decks *himself* with
ornaments,
And as a bride adorns *herself* with her
jewels.
11 For as the earth brings forth its bud,
As the garden causes the things that are
sown in it to spring forth,
So the Lord GOD will cause
righteousness and praise to spring
forth before all the nations.

ASSURANCE OF ZION'S SALVATION

62 For Zion's sake I will not hold My
peace,
And for Jerusalem's sake I will not rest,
Until her righteousness goes forth as
brightness,
And her salvation as a lamp *that* burns.
2 The Gentiles shall see your
righteousness,
And all kings your glory.
You shall be called by a new name,
Which the mouth of the LORD will name.
3 You shall also be a crown of glory
In the hand of the LORD,
And a royal diadem
In the hand of your God.
4 You shall no longer be termed Forsaken,
Nor shall your land any more be termed
Desolate;
But you shall be called Hephzibah,[a] and
your land Beulah;[b]
For the LORD delights in you,
And your land shall be married.
5 For *as* a young man marries a virgin,
So shall your sons marry you;
And *as* the bridegroom rejoices over the
bride,
So shall your God rejoice over you.

6 I have set watchmen on your walls,
O Jerusalem;
They shall never hold their peace day or
night.
You who make mention of the LORD, do
not keep silent,
7 And give Him no rest till He establishes
And till He makes Jerusalem a praise in
the earth.

8 The LORD has sworn by His right hand
And by the arm of His strength:
"Surely I will no longer give your grain
As food for your enemies;
And the sons of the foreigner shall not
drink your new wine,
For which you have labored.
9 But those who have gathered it shall eat
it,
And praise the LORD;
Those who have brought it together
shall drink it in My holy courts."

10 Go through,
Go through the gates!
Prepare the way for the people;
Build up,
Build up the highway!
Take out the stones,
Lift up a banner for the peoples!

11 Indeed the LORD has proclaimed
To the end of the world:
"Say to the daughter of Zion,
'Surely your salvation is coming;
Behold, His reward *is* with Him,
And His work before Him.' "
12 And they shall call them The Holy
People,
The Redeemed of the LORD;
And you shall be called Sought Out,
A City Not Forsaken.

THE LORD IN JUDGMENT AND SALVATION

63 Who *is* this who comes from Edom,
With dyed garments from Bozrah,
This *One who is* glorious in His apparel,
Traveling in the greatness of His
strength?—

62:4 [a]Literally *My Delight Is in Her* [b]Literally *Married*

COMFORT AND COMPASSION

BARBARA JOHNSON

(Isaiah 61:2)

"Why me . . . why did this happen to me?"

Has anyone gotten all the way through life without asking that question at least once or twice? (For some of us, maybe it's twice a day!)

"Why me? Why us? Why did two young boys get taken from our family?" I asked all those questions quietly in my heart for two years. I even continued to go out to speak and share comfort and hope with other parents. I wanted to believe that life would get better.

Looking back, I can see how Romans 8:28 and other verses that were quoted to me *are* all true. Romans 8:28 says, "And we know that all things work together for good to those who love God, to those who are the called according to His purpose." Yes, it's true. God *is* faithful. God does work all things together for good. Unfortunately, the timing of these reminders was all wrong. Nice little plastic, spiritual phrases do not help people unlock their grief. It is better just to put your arm around a grieving person and say, "I love you. . . . God loves you." Beyond that, it might be best just to shove a sock in your mouth and keep quiet. When grief is the freshest, words should be the fewest.

HELPING OURSELVES

There comes a time in each of our lives when trouble and difficulties seem to gang up on us. When this happens—when life gets hard—what is the creative way to handle things?

1. We must not try to do it all ourselves. We must not struggle and fret. Instead, we should do all we can about the situation and then put everything into God's hands, trusting Him. We can depend on God. He will not fail us. We need to "let go and let God."
2. We need to pray for guidance and believe that direction is being given to us. We must believe that this guidance can be trusted. We need to depend on it, because it will not fail us.
3. We need to pray for and practice a calm attitude. Disturbing situations will remain disturbing as long as we are disturbed. But when we become peaceful, conditions will begin to iron themselves out.
4. We need to saturate our lives with faith that the situation will turn out right. We should say aloud, every day, several times, "You will keep him in perfect peace, whose mind is stayed on You" (Is. 26:3), and "In quietness and confidence shall be your strength" (Is. 30:15).
5. We need to remind ourselves of one great truth: Hard experiences will pass away. They will yield. They can be changed with God's help.
6. We must always look for the light in the darkness. That light is the love of God. "Your word is a lamp to my feet and a light to my path" (Ps. 119:105).
7. We must ask the Lord to release our own creativity, ingenuity, strength, and wisdom, so we can handle the problem successfully.
8. We must never forget that God loves us. He wants to help us. We must turn to Him and gratefully accept His help.
9. We need to remember that all human beings experience troubles similar to our own. We are not alone in our struggles.
10. We must hold on to this great promise: "God is our refuge and strength, a very present help in trouble" (Ps. 46:1). God will

see us through, and a brighter day will dawn for us.

HELPING OTHERS

As Christians, we are Christ's bride, His church. When we show compassion in His name, we demonstrate His love to others. These kindnesses that we show to others don't have to be daring or costly. An encouraging word—or simply an attitude of joy—can often make all the difference to people who have given up hope. A little smile can brighten their day. And while we are smiling, we might as well go one step further and share a chuckle or two.

C. S. Lewis said that the best argument for Christianity is Christians: their joy, their certainty, and their completeness. Lewis also warned, however, that Christians can also be the strongest argument against Christianity when they are somber and joyless, or self-righteous and smug, or narrow and repressive. Then, said Lewis, Christianity "dies a thousand deaths." Let's resolve to be happy people, angels of joy and missionaries of mercy wherever we go today—and every day!

OUR GIFT TO OTHERS

One day, we will approach heaven empty-handed, with all our earthly goals littering the roadway behind us. We'll have nothing to show for our toil on earth except the life we have lived for God and the investment we have made in others by our compassion. While we can take nothing with us to heaven, we can leave a lot of important things behind that will encourage and comfort our friends and loved ones. What we really take with us to heaven is the lives we touched for God. Above all, we can pass on the gift of eternal life in Jesus Christ. It's something we don't deserve and can't buy at any price. It's God's gift to us by faith. And we can share it with others if we have the love and compassion it takes to do so.

FURTHER MEDITATION:

Other passages to study about the issue of compassion include:

- Psalms 23:4; 145:8
- Isaiah 40:1, 2, 27–31
- Lamentations 3:22, 23
- Micah 6:8
- Matthew 9:36
- 2 Timothy 1:12; 4:18
- Jude 24, 25

To Learn More: Turn to the key passage note on compassion at 2 Corinthians 1:3–5 on page 1518. See also the personality profile of the Good Samaritan on page 1334.

"I who speak in righteousness, mighty to save."

2 Why *is* Your apparel red,
And Your garments like one who treads in the winepress?

3 "I have trodden the winepress alone,
And from the peoples no one *was* with Me.
For I have trodden them in My anger,
And trampled them in My fury;
Their blood is sprinkled upon My garments,
And I have stained all My robes.
4 For the day of vengeance *is* in My heart,
And the year of My redeemed has come.
5 I looked, but *there was* no one to help,
And I wondered
That *there was* no one to uphold;
Therefore My own arm brought salvation for Me;
And My own fury, it sustained Me.
6 I have trodden down the peoples in My anger,
Made them drunk in My fury,
And brought down their strength to the earth."

God's Mercy Remembered

7 I will mention the lovingkindnesses of the LORD
And the praises of the LORD,
According to all that the LORD has bestowed on us,
And the great goodness toward the house of Israel,
Which He has bestowed on them according to His mercies,
According to the multitude of His lovingkindnesses.
8 For He said, "Surely they *are* My people,
Children *who* will not lie."
So He became their Savior.
9 In all their affliction He was afflicted,
And the Angel of His Presence saved them;
In His love and in His pity He redeemed them;
And He bore them and carried them
All the days of old.
10 But they rebelled and grieved His Holy Spirit;
So He turned Himself against them as an enemy,
And He fought against them.

11 Then he remembered the days of old,
Moses *and* his people, *saying:*
"Where *is* He who brought them up out of the sea
With the shepherd of His flock?
Where *is* He who put His Holy Spirit within them,
12 Who led *them* by the right hand of Moses,
With His glorious arm,
Dividing the water before them
To make for Himself an everlasting name,
13 Who led them through the deep,
As a horse in the wilderness,
That they might not stumble?"

14 As a beast goes down into the valley,
And the Spirit of the LORD causes him to rest,
So You lead Your people,
To make Yourself a glorious name.

A Prayer of Penitence

15 Look down from heaven,
And see from Your habitation, holy and glorious.
Where *are* Your zeal and Your strength,

SOUL NOTE

Source of Help *(63:10)* Isaiah realized that God's people had suffered greatly because they had "rebelled and grieved His Holy Spirit." Therefore, "He turned Himself against them as an enemy." The people refused to repent, and had turned away from the only One who could help them. When people rebel against God, they grieve the Holy Spirit. The New Testament says, "Do not grieve the Holy Spirit of God" (Eph. 4:30). To grieve the Holy Spirit by sin and rebellion is to turn away from our only source of hope. **Topic: Presence of the Holy Spirit**

The yearning of Your heart and Your
mercies toward me?
Are they restrained?
16 Doubtless You *are* our Father,
Though Abraham was ignorant of us,
And Israel does not acknowledge us.
You, O LORD, *are* our Father;
Our Redeemer from Everlasting *is* Your
name.
17 O LORD, why have You made us stray
from Your ways,
And hardened our heart from Your fear?
Return for Your servants' sake,
The tribes of Your inheritance.
18 Your holy people have possessed *it* but a
little while;
Our adversaries have trodden down Your
sanctuary.
19 We have become *like* those of old, over
whom You never ruled,
Those who were never called by Your
name.

64 Oh, that You would rend the heavens!
That You would come down!
That the mountains might shake at Your
presence—
2 As fire burns brushwood,
As fire causes water to boil—
To make Your name known to Your
adversaries,
That the nations may tremble at Your
presence!
3 When You did awesome things *for which*
we did not look,
You came down,
The mountains shook at Your presence.
4 For since the beginning of the world
Men have not heard nor perceived by the
ear,
Nor has the eye seen any God besides
You,
Who acts for the one who waits for Him.
5 You meet him who rejoices and does
righteousness,
Who remembers You in Your ways.
You are indeed angry, for we have
sinned—
In these ways we continue;
And we need to be saved.

6 But we are all like an unclean *thing*,
And all our righteousnesses *are* like
filthy rags;
We all fade as a leaf,
And our iniquities, like the wind,
Have taken us away.
7 And *there is* no one who calls on Your
name,
Who stirs himself up to take hold of You;
For You have hidden Your face from us,
And have consumed us because of our
iniquities.

8 But now, O LORD,
You *are* our Father;
We *are* the clay, and You our potter;
And all we *are* the work of Your hand.
9 Do not be furious, O LORD,
Nor remember iniquity forever;
Indeed, please look—we all *are* Your
people!
10 Your holy cities are a wilderness,
Zion is a wilderness,
Jerusalem a desolation.
11 Our holy and beautiful temple,
Where our fathers praised You,
Is burned up with fire;
And all our pleasant things are laid
waste.
12 Will You restrain Yourself because of
these *things*, O LORD?
Will You hold Your peace, and afflict us
very severely?

THE RIGHTEOUSNESS OF GOD'S JUDGMENT

65 "I was sought by *those who* did not
ask *for Me;*
I was found by *those who* did not seek
Me.
I said, 'Here I am, here I am,'
To a nation *that* was not called by My
name.
2 I have stretched out My hands all day
long to a rebellious people,
Who walk in a way *that is* not good,
According to their own thoughts;
3 A people who provoke Me to anger
continually to My face;
Who sacrifice in gardens,
And burn incense on altars of brick;
4 Who sit among the graves,
And spend the night in the tombs;
Who eat swine's flesh,
And the broth of abominable things is *in*
their vessels;
5 Who say, 'Keep to yourself,
Do not come near me,

For I am holier than you!'
These *are* smoke in My nostrils,
A fire that burns all the day.

6 "Behold, *it is* written before Me:
I will not keep silence, but will repay—
Even repay into their bosom—
7 Your iniquities and the iniquities of your
fathers together,"
Says the LORD,
"Who have burned incense on the
mountains
And blasphemed Me on the hills;
Therefore I will measure their former
work into their bosom."

8 Thus says the LORD:

"As the new wine is found in the cluster,
And *one* says, 'Do not destroy it,
For a blessing *is* in it,'
So will I do for My servants' sake,
That I may not destroy them all.
9 I will bring forth descendants from
Jacob,
And from Judah an heir of My
mountains;
My elect shall inherit it,
And My servants shall dwell there.
10 Sharon shall be a fold of flocks,
And the Valley of Achor a place for herds
to lie down,
For My people who have sought Me.

11 "But you *are* those who forsake the LORD,
Who forget My holy mountain,
Who prepare a table for Gad,[a]
And who furnish a drink offering for
Meni.[b]
12 Therefore I will number you for the
sword,
And you shall all bow down to the
slaughter;
Because, when I called, you did not
answer;
When I spoke, you did not hear,
But did evil before My eyes,
And chose *that* in which I do not
delight."

13 Therefore thus says the Lord GOD:

"Behold, My servants shall eat,
But you shall be hungry;
Behold, My servants shall drink,
But you shall be thirsty;
Behold, My servants shall rejoice,
But you shall be ashamed;
14 Behold, My servants shall sing for joy of
heart,
But you shall cry for sorrow of heart,
And wail for grief of spirit.
15 You shall leave your name as a curse to
My chosen;
For the Lord GOD will slay you,
And call His servants by another name;
16 So that he who blesses himself in the
earth
Shall bless himself in the God of truth;
And he who swears in the earth
Shall swear by the God of truth;
Because the former troubles are
forgotten,
And because they are hidden from My
eyes.

THE GLORIOUS NEW CREATION

17 "For behold, I create new heavens and a
new earth;

65:11 [a]Literally *Troop* or *Fortune,* a pagan deity
[b]Literally *Number* or *Destiny,* a pagan deity

SOUL NOTE

Brand New World *(65:17–20)* Isaiah is the only prophet in the Old Testament who saw all the way to the new heavens and new earth. Like the apostle John, the prophet saw a time when tears would be wiped away and God's people would live with Him in a continual state of eternal bliss (Rev. 21:4). Even the best of God's promises for this life cannot compare to His wonderful promises for the life to come. The God who loves us enough to redeem this fallen world will one day express the greatness of His love by creating a brand-new world for His children.
Topic: God's Promises

And the former shall not be remembered or come to mind.
18 But be glad and rejoice forever in what I create;
For behold, I create Jerusalem *as* a rejoicing,
And her people a joy.
19 I will rejoice in Jerusalem,
And joy in My people;
The voice of weeping shall no longer be heard in her,
Nor the voice of crying.

20 "No more shall an infant from there *live but a few* days,
Nor an old man who has not fulfilled his days;
For the child shall die one hundred years old,
But the sinner *being* one hundred years old shall be accursed.
21 They shall build houses and inhabit *them;*
They shall plant vineyards and eat their fruit.
22 They shall not build and another inhabit;
They shall not plant and another eat;
For as the days of a tree, *so shall be* the days of My people,
And My elect shall long enjoy the work of their hands.
23 They shall not labor in vain,
Nor bring forth children for trouble;
For they *shall be* the descendants of the blessed of the LORD,
And their offspring with them.

24 "It shall come to pass
That before they call, I will answer;
And while they are still speaking, I will hear.
25 The wolf and the lamb shall feed together,
The lion shall eat straw like the ox,
And dust *shall be* the serpent's food.
They shall not hurt nor destroy in all My holy mountain,"
Says the LORD.

TRUE WORSHIP AND FALSE

66 Thus says the LORD:

"Heaven *is* My throne,
And earth *is* My footstool.
Where *is* the house that you will build Me?
And where *is* the place of My rest?
2 For all those *things* My hand has made,
And all those *things* exist,"
Says the LORD.
"But on this *one* will I look:
On *him who is* poor and of a contrite spirit,
And who trembles at My word.

3 "He who kills a bull *is as if* he slays a man;
He who sacrifices a lamb, *as if* he breaks a dog's neck;
He who offers a grain offering, *as if he offers* swine's blood;
He who burns incense, *as if* he blesses an idol.
Just as they have chosen their own ways,
And their soul delights in their abominations,
4 So will I choose their delusions,
And bring their fears on them;
Because, when I called, no one answered,
When I spoke they did not hear;
But they did evil before My eyes,
And chose *that* in which I do not delight."

THE LORD VINDICATES ZION

5 Hear the word of the LORD,
You who tremble at His word:
"Your brethren who hated you,
Who cast you out for My name's sake, said,
'Let the LORD be glorified,
That we may see your joy.'
But they shall be ashamed."

6 The sound of noise from the city!
A voice from the temple!
The voice of the LORD,
Who fully repays His enemies!

7 "Before she was in labor, she gave birth;
Before her pain came,
She delivered a male child.
8 Who has heard such a thing?
Who has seen such things?
Shall the earth be made to give birth in one day?

Or shall a nation be born at once?
For as soon as Zion was in labor,
She gave birth to her children.
9 Shall I bring to the time of birth, and not
cause delivery?" says the LORD.
"Shall I who cause delivery shut up *the*
womb?" says your God.
10 "Rejoice with Jerusalem,
And be glad with her, all you who love
her;
Rejoice for joy with her, all you who
mourn for her;
11 That you may feed and be satisfied
With the consolation of her bosom,
That you may drink deeply and be
delighted
With the abundance of her glory."

12 For thus says the LORD:

"Behold, I will extend peace to her like a
river,
And the glory of the Gentiles like a
flowing stream.
Then you shall feed;
On *her* sides shall you be carried,
And be dandled on *her* knees.
13 As one whom his mother comforts,
So I will comfort you;
And you shall be comforted in
Jerusalem."

The Reign and Indignation of God

14 When you see *this,* your heart shall
rejoice,
And your bones shall flourish like grass;
The hand of the LORD shall be known to
His servants,
And *His* indignation to His enemies.
15 For behold, the LORD will come with fire
And with His chariots, like a whirlwind,
To render His anger with fury,
And His rebuke with flames of fire.
16 For by fire and by His sword
The LORD will judge all flesh;
And the slain of the LORD shall be many.

17 "Those who sanctify themselves and
purify themselves,
To go to the gardens
After an *idol* in the midst,
Eating swine's flesh and the
abomination and the mouse,
Shall be consumed together," says the
LORD.

18 "For I *know* their works and their
thoughts. It shall be that I will gather all nations and tongues; and they shall come and
see My glory. 19 I will set a sign among them;
and those among them who escape I will send
to the nations: *to* Tarshish and Pul[a] and Lud,
who draw the bow, and Tubal and Javan, *to*
the coastlands afar off who have not heard My
fame nor seen My glory. And they shall declare My glory among the Gentiles. 20 Then
they shall bring all your brethren for an offering to the LORD out of all nations, on horses
and in chariots and in litters, on mules and on
camels, to My holy mountain Jerusalem,"
says the LORD, "as the children of Israel bring
an offering in a clean vessel into the house of
the LORD. 21 And I will also take some of them
for priests *and* Levites," says the LORD.

22 "For as the new heavens and the new
earth
Which I will make shall remain before
Me," says the LORD,
"So shall your descendants and your
name remain.
23 And it shall come to pass
That from one New Moon to another,
And from one Sabbath to another,
All flesh shall come to worship before
Me," says the LORD.

24 "And they shall go forth and look
Upon the corpses of the men
Who have transgressed against Me.
For their worm does not die,
And their fire is not quenched.
They shall be an abhorrence to all
flesh."

66:19 [a]Following Masoretic Text and Targum; Septuagint reads *Put* (compare Jeremiah 46:9).

Jeremiah

It hurts when people don't listen to us. We warn a person against a certain activity, and when he or she refuses to listen, we watch in bewilderment as our warnings become reality. But then, of course, it is too late.

The prophet Jeremiah had warned the people of Judah. His book depicts a man appalled at the sins of injustice, idolatry, and immorality that were rampant in his nation. When God announced judgment, Jeremiah was devastated. With supreme compassion he pleaded with his cold and calloused countrymen to turn back to God. Faithfully, he continued to serve as God's spokesman for forty years, but the people of Judah refused to listen. Thus, because of the hardness of their hearts, God allowed Jerusalem to be ransacked and the people of Judah deported to Babylon.

Despite this bleak turn of events, Jeremiah foresaw a day when God would initiate a new covenant (ch. 31). This promise of hope was grounded in the ministry of a coming Messiah. Indeed, it is Christ's death on the Cross that makes possible this new arrangement of unconditional grace. In place of the old covenant of law written on stone tablets, the new covenant of grace is written on the hearts of all who believe.

Jeremiah had done all that he could do, but no one listened. We must speak the truth to our families, our friends, our culture, even if it seems no one listens. We must do as God says and leave the results to Him.

SOUL CONCERNS IN JEREMIAH

SELF-ESTEEM	(1:5)
RESPONSIBILITY	(1:8–10)
ACCOUNTABILITY	(3:11)
HOPE	(CH. 29)

1 The words of Jeremiah the son of Hilkiah, of the priests who *were* in Anathoth in the
land of Benjamin, 2to whom the word of the
LORD came in the days of Josiah the son of
Amon, king of Judah, in the thirteenth year of
his reign. 3It came also in the days of Jehoiakim the son of Josiah, king of Judah, until the
end of the eleventh year of Zedekiah the son
of Josiah, king of Judah, until the carrying
away of Jerusalem captive in the fifth month.

THE PROPHET IS CALLED

4Then the word of the LORD came to me,
saying:

5 "Before I formed you in the womb I knew you;
Before you were born I sanctified you;
I ordained you a prophet to the nations."

6Then said I:

"Ah, Lord GOD!
Behold, I cannot speak, for I *am* a youth."

7But the LORD said to me:

"Do not say, 'I *am* a youth,'
For you shall go to all to whom I send you,
And whatever I command you, you shall speak.
8 Do not be afraid of their faces,
For I *am* with you to deliver you," says the LORD.

9Then the LORD put forth His hand and
touched my mouth, and the LORD said to me:

"Behold, I have put My words in your mouth.
10 See, I have this day set you over the nations and over the kingdoms,
To root out and to pull down,
To destroy and to throw down,
To build and to plant."

11Moreover the word of the LORD came to
me, saying, "Jeremiah, what do you see?"
And I said, "I see a branch of an almond
tree."
12Then the LORD said to me, "You have seen
well, for I am ready to perform My word."
13And the word of the LORD came to me the
second time, saying, "What do you see?"
And I said, "I see a boiling pot, and it is facing away from the north."
14Then the LORD said to me:

"Out of the north calamity shall break forth
On all the inhabitants of the land.
15 For behold, I am calling
All the families of the kingdoms of the north," says the LORD;
"They shall come and each one set his throne
At the entrance of the gates of Jerusalem,
Against all its walls all around,
And against all the cities of Judah.
16 I will utter My judgments
Against them concerning all their wickedness,
Because they have forsaken Me,
Burned incense to other gods,
And worshiped the works of their own hands.

17 "Therefore prepare yourself and arise,
And speak to them all that I command you.

SOUL NOTE

What Might Have Been *(1:5)* One of the tragic, unanswered questions in cases of abortion is "What might have been?"—not only in the lives of the parents or even the baby, but in the world. God makes it clear that He is well-acquainted with every individual from the time each person is conceived and that He has plans for each one. God knew Jeremiah before he had been formed in his mother's womb, and He planned for Jeremiah to be a prophet. God knows everything, so He knows that some young lives will end all too soon. But how sad that so much potential will never be realized. **Topic: Abortion**

Do not be dismayed before their faces,
Lest I dismay you before them.
18 For behold, I have made you this day
A fortified city and an iron pillar,
And bronze walls against the whole land—
Against the kings of Judah,
Against its princes,
Against its priests,
And against the people of the land.
19 They will fight against you,
But they shall not prevail against you.
For I *am* with you," says the LORD, "to deliver you."

GOD'S CASE AGAINST ISRAEL

2 Moreover the word of the LORD came to
me, saying, 2"Go and cry in the hearing of
Jerusalem, saying, 'Thus says the LORD:

"I remember you,
The kindness of your youth,
The love of your betrothal,
When you went after Me in the wilderness,
In a land not sown.
3 Israel *was* holiness to the LORD,
The firstfruits of His increase.
All that devour him will offend;
Disaster will come upon them," says the LORD.' "

4Hear the word of the LORD, O house of Jacob and all the families of the house of Israel.
5Thus says the LORD:

"What injustice have your fathers found in Me,
That they have gone far from Me,
Have followed idols,
And have become idolaters?
6 Neither did they say, 'Where *is* the LORD,
Who brought us up out of the land of Egypt,
Who led us through the wilderness,
Through a land of deserts and pits,
Through a land of drought and the shadow of death,
Through a land that no one crossed
And where no one dwelt?'
7 I brought you into a bountiful country,
To eat its fruit and its goodness.
But when you entered, you defiled My land
And made My heritage an abomination.
8 The priests did not say, 'Where *is* the LORD?'
And those who handle the law did not know Me;
The rulers also transgressed against Me;
The prophets prophesied by Baal,
And walked after *things that* do not profit.

9 "Therefore I will yet bring charges against you," says the LORD,
"And against your children's children I will bring charges.
10 For pass beyond the coasts of Cyprus[a] and see,
Send to Kedar[b] and consider diligently,
And see if there has been such *a thing.*
11 Has a nation changed *its* gods,
Which *are* not gods?
But My people have changed their Glory
For *what* does not profit.
12 Be astonished, O heavens, at this,
And be horribly afraid;
Be very desolate," says the LORD.
13 "For My people have committed two evils:
They have forsaken Me, the fountain of living waters,
And hewn themselves cisterns—broken cisterns that can hold no water.

14 "*Is* Israel a servant?
Is he a homeborn *slave?*
Why is he plundered?
15 The young lions roared at him, *and* growled;
They made his land waste;
His cities are burned, without inhabitant.
16 Also the people of Noph[a] and Tahpanhes
Have broken the crown of your head.
17 Have you not brought this on yourself,
In that you have forsaken the LORD your God
When He led you in the way?
18 And now why take the road to Egypt,
To drink the waters of Sihor?
Or why take the road to Assyria,

2:10 [a]Hebrew *Kittim,* western lands, especially Cyprus [b]In the northern Arabian desert, representative of the eastern cultures **2:16** [a]That is, Memphis in ancient Egypt

SCRIPTURE'S VIEW OF SELF-ESTEEM

ARCHIBALD D. HART

(Jeremiah 1:5)

Jeremiah had a difficult life, but he had high self-esteem, for Jeremiah 1:5 says, "Before I formed you in the womb I knew you; before you were born I sanctified you; I ordained you a prophet to the nations." Clearly God had marked Jeremiah's life for great service, and Jeremiah saw himself in relation to God's plan for his life.

God has done the same for each individual (Ps. 139:16). God has each person's life in His hand; He created each person for a purpose. Every believer should stand tall with high self-esteem by understanding who he or she is in Christ.

THE MYSTERY OF SELF-ESTEEM

Self-esteem has important implications for psychological and spiritual health because it determines how people feel about themselves and what they believe they are capable of becoming. Perhaps one could call it, "the attitude of the self to the self." Unfortunately, most people feel they do not measure up. These feelings prevent people from becoming what God has in mind for them. The result is what is now labeled "low self-esteem." Low self-esteem generally describes feelings of self-hate, rejection, and an inability to accept oneself as special and unique. It not only involves self-rejection, but rejection of what God intended the person to be in Him.

HOW SELF-ESTEEM IS DERIVED

Self-esteem begins with an image or concept of oneself. It is an attitude people develop toward themselves. Therefore, if a person's self-image is distorted, that person's self-esteem will be as well. When people grow up seeing themselves as unattractive or incompetent, their self-esteem will be shaped accordingly.

Paul, however, encourages Christians to "think soberly" when it comes to evaluating themselves (Rom. 12:3). This means to think "with absolute honesty." Why is this important? Because if people cannot be honest about who they are as persons, they cannot relate to others in a healthy way. Honesty includes realizing that most people's self-image is the opposite of their true worth. Their self-concept does not reflect the indescribable value God places on their lives.

The Bible clearly identifies the problem of our sinful nature and its self-centeredness (Jer. 17:9). It also reminds us of the confusion that results from sinful thinking (Rom. 1:18–32). The human mind is not very reliable when it comes to self-concept because of our sinful nature. It easily rearranges facts and feelings to produce the wrong effect. Despite its wonderful complexity, the mind can do bizarre things. It reacts to the feedback it receives from its earliest years in such an unrealistic way that very few people reach adulthood with a clear and accurate picture of themselves. In fact, one of the reasons why personal success often cannot fix longstanding feelings of inferiority or low self-esteem is the human filtering system that downplays successes and exaggerates personal failures. Many people either distort their self-image in a negative way ("I am a terrible person") or in an exaggerated positive manner ("I am better than others"). Culture is no help in this matter because it, too, distorts realistic views of success. Is it any wonder that many people end up not liking who they are and wishing they were someone else?

HEALING PEOPLE'S SELF-ESTEEM

Romans 12:3 contains some wise advice for dealing with the consequences of a distorted self-image. The solution is no different whether one has an inflated or deflated image of oneself—both are distortions of reality. The challenge is for people to become more honest regarding how they feel about themselves. This is important not only to their emotional health, but also to their spiritual health. They need to be willing to admit their strengths as well as their weaknesses. People can learn to do this if they follow these guidelines:

Stop Degrading Oneself
Many people learn to criticize themselves in childhood, especially if their parents labeled them as inferior. Self-degradation undermines confidence and self-acceptance. They need a clear understanding of humility. Humility is not putting oneself down or denying one's God-given gifts. People really have no right to degrade themselves. When they do, they are criticizing God's handiwork. They must renew their mind by being "sober" with their thoughts.

Use Positive Reinforcement
Christians need to be able to value their positive points and appreciate the gifts God has given them in order to minister in His name. They shouldn't think that their gifts make them better than other people, but gifts are meant to be used. Believers should affirm their gifts and praise God for His work. In that way, they are praising God for making them who He wanted them to be. Positive self-statements are honest and will help reverse years of negative self-esteem.

Learn to Value True Worth
In Romans 12:3, Paul encouraged his readers to "think soberly, as God has dealt to each one a measure of faith." This means God gives His people the power to fulfill His ministries. No one is superior or inferior. Everyone has good and bad points. Believers are to celebrate the good points and ask for God's help in working on their own bad points. True value comes from God, and believers should celebrate it as part of their understanding of God's work in their lives.

Learn to Value Others
The more they work at valuing others, the greater freedom people feel to value themselves for who they are in God's sight. Romans 14:13 says, "Therefore let us not judge one another anymore. . . . " Low self-esteem is caused by self-hate. Self-hate leads to hating others. When people conquer their self-rejection, they open the door to be more accepting of both themselves and others.

FURTHER MEDITATION:

Other passages to study about the issue of self-esteem include:

- Genesis 1:26, 27
- Psalms 8:3–6; 139:1–18
- Galatians 2:20; 3:26—4:7
- Ephesians 2:4–10
- Philippians 2:1–18
- 1 Peter 2:9, 10

To Learn More: Turn to the key passage note on self-esteem at Matthew 10:29–31 on page 1245. See also the personality profile of Josiah on page 582.

RESPONSIBILITY: EQUIPPED AND WILLING

WOODROW KROLL AND DON HAWKINS

(Jeremiah 1:8–10)

The British naval hero Lord Nelson took his responsibilities very seriously. His last words were, "Thank God, I have done my duty." While that is an admirable goal, fulfilling our responsibilities is not always easy. Sometimes the tasks ahead of us seem so overwhelming that we look for excuses rather than face the possibility of failure. Jeremiah's excuse was his youthfulness (Jer. 1:6); Moses' excuse was his lack of eloquence (Ex. 4:10); Isaiah's excuse was a sense of unworthiness (Is. 6:5).

God does not call people to tasks that they can accomplish on their own, however. His ultimate purpose behind every responsibility is to teach people to find in Him the resources to fulfill their duty. When God calls people to a work, He also equips them to perform their responsibility adequately (2 Tim. 3:17). Accepting a responsibility does not guarantee someone that they will become famous; most of God's servants faithfully minister in the background. Yet with His help, people are able to do all things sufficiently. As God gave Jeremiah the duty to proclaim His message, He also equipped Jeremiah to fulfill that responsibility. In the same way, God equips believers today.

GOD'S PRESENCE

First, God equips people with His presence (Jer. 1:8). During his ministry, Jeremiah found himself in many difficult circumstances. But through it all, God's presence sustained and preserved the prophet. That same presence is with us today as we face our own responsibilities. God says, "I will never leave you nor forsake you" (Heb. 13:5). There is no place or situation to which God calls us that His presence will not follow to equip us for responsibility.

In 1858, Scottish missionary John G. Paton and his wife sailed for the New Hebrides (now called Vanuatu). Three months after they arrived on the island of Tanna, his wife died. One week later his infant son also died. Paton was plunged into sorrow. Feeling terribly alone, and surrounded by savage people who showed him no sympathy, he wrote, "Let those who have ever passed through any similar darkness as of midnight feel for me. As for all others, it would be more than vain to try to paint my sorrows. But for Jesus, and [His] fellowship—I [would] have gone mad and died." Any responsibility can be achieved when it is undergirded with the comfort of divine presence.

God's presence, as well, gives people the strength and courage to accomplish their responsibilities in spite of obstacles. A French sergeant in World War I found one of his raw recruits huddled in a foxhole paralyzed with fear. "Come, son," he said, "let's go out together and do great things for France"—and they went. God says to you and me, "Come, let us go together and meet your responsibilities."

GOD'S WORD

Second, God equips people with His Word (Jer. 1:9). Before Jeremiah accepted his responsibility, God placed His words in the young man's mouth. So, as this prophet fulfilled those responsibilities, he continually spoke forth God's Word. Jeremiah knew that only God-given words were sufficient to empower him to meet God-given responsibilities.

Nothing we have to say carries the power that God's Word does. Though we may speak with great human wisdom, it is the "wisdom that is from above" (James 3:17) that changes people's lives and turns "the world upside down" (Acts 17:6). While we may master persuasive techniques to accomplish our responsibilities, the Bible says that it is God's words that will make a difference (Is. 55:11).

Dwight L. Moody was right when he said, "The Bible wasn't given for our information but for our transformation." It is a book we need to read, study, meditate on, and apply to meet our responsibilities. When we need to know how to accomplish the tasks at hand, it is God's Word that becomes a lamp (Ps. 119:105).

GOD'S PROMISES

Finally, God equips people with His promises (Jer. 1:10). Before Jeremiah even went to work, God promised that *He* would accomplish great things through Jeremiah. Follow Jeremiah's ministry though his first warnings of imminent danger to the final downfall of Jerusalem and it is evident that God kept His promise. God's faithfulness was key to Jeremiah's ability to fulfill his responsibility.

God is equally faithful to His promises today. Someone has determined that there are 7,487 promises in the Bible. Many of these apply to us. When we are faced with monumental responsibilities, we must draw strength and courage from such precious promises as "Fear not, for I am with you; be not dismayed, for I am your God. I will strengthen you, yes, I will help you, I will uphold you with My righteous right hand" (Is. 41:10), or "Behold, I am the LORD, the God of all flesh. Is there anything too hard for Me?" (Jer. 32:27).

It is little wonder that the great missionary and founder of the China Inland Mission, Hudson Taylor, said, "The future is as bright as the promises of God." We can accept the most challenging responsibilities because we know that God will never fail to bring to pass every word He has spoken.

When tempted to hide behind excuses, step out in faith instead. Be assured that God has equipped us with His presence, His Word, and His promises so that we can adequately meet every responsibility He gives us.

FURTHER MEDITATION:

Other passages to study about the issue of responsibility include:

- ➢ Ezekiel 3:16–21
- ➢ Matthew 28:18–20
- ➢ John 20:21
- ➢ Galatians 6:1–10
- ➢ Ephesians 4:1–6
- ➢ Hebrews 3:7–15
- ➢ 1 Peter 3:15

To Learn More: Turn to the key passage note on responsibility at Matthew 25:14–30 on page 1272. See also the personality profile of Esther on page 633.

To drink the waters of the River?[a]
19 Your own wickedness will correct you,
And your backslidings will rebuke you.
Know therefore and see that *it is* an evil and bitter *thing*
That you have forsaken the LORD your God,
And the fear of Me *is* not in you,"
Says the Lord GOD of hosts.

20 "For of old I have broken your yoke *and* burst your bonds;
And you said, 'I will not transgress,'
When on every high hill and under every green tree
You lay down, playing the harlot.
21 Yet I had planted you a noble vine, a seed of highest quality.
How then have you turned before Me
Into the degenerate plant of an alien vine?
22 For though you wash yourself with lye, and use much soap,
Yet your iniquity is marked before Me,"
says the Lord GOD.

23 "How can you say, 'I am not polluted,
I have not gone after the Baals'?
See your way in the valley;
Know what you have done:
You are a swift dromedary breaking loose in her ways,
24 A wild donkey used to the wilderness,
That sniffs at the wind in her desire;
In her time of mating, who can turn her away?
All those who seek her will not weary themselves;
In her month they will find her.
25 Withhold your foot from being unshod, and your throat from thirst.
But you said, 'There is no hope.
No! For I have loved aliens, and after them I will go.'

26 "As the thief is ashamed when he is found out,
So is the house of Israel ashamed;
They and their kings and their princes, and their priests and their prophets,
27 Saying to a tree, 'You *are* my father,'
And to a stone, 'You gave birth to me.'
For they have turned *their* back to Me, and not *their* face.
But in the time of their trouble
They will say, 'Arise and save us.'
28 But where *are* your gods that you have made for yourselves?
Let them arise,
If they can save you in the time of your trouble;
For *according to* the number of your cities
Are your gods, O Judah.

29 "Why will you plead with Me?
You all have transgressed against Me,"
says the LORD.
30 "In vain I have chastened your children;
They received no correction.
Your sword has devoured your prophets
Like a destroying lion.

31 "O generation, see the word of the LORD!
Have I been a wilderness to Israel,
Or a land of darkness?
Why do My people say, 'We are lords;
We will come no more to You'?
32 Can a virgin forget her ornaments,
Or a bride her attire?
Yet My people have forgotten Me days without number.

33 "Why do you beautify your way to seek love?
Therefore you have also taught
The wicked women your ways.
34 Also on your skirts is found
The blood of the lives of the poor innocents.
I have not found it by secret search,
But plainly on all these things.
35 Yet you say, 'Because I am innocent,
Surely His anger shall turn from me.'
Behold, I will plead My case against you,
Because you say, 'I have not sinned.'
36 Why do you gad about so much to change your way?
Also you shall be ashamed of Egypt as you were ashamed of Assyria.
37 Indeed you will go forth from him
With your hands on your head;
For the LORD has rejected your trusted allies,
And you will not prosper by them.

2:18 [a]That is, the Euphrates

Israel Is Shameless

3 "They say, 'If a man divorces his wife,
And she goes from him
And becomes another man's,
May he return to her again?'
Would not that land be greatly
polluted?
But you have played the harlot with
many lovers;
Yet return to Me," says the LORD.

2 "Lift up your eyes to the desolate heights
and see:
Where have you not lain *with men?*
By the road you have sat for them
Like an Arabian in the wilderness;
And you have polluted the land
With your harlotries and your
wickedness.
3 Therefore the showers have been
withheld,
And there has been no latter rain.
You have had a harlot's forehead;
You refuse to be ashamed.
4 Will you not from this time cry to Me,
'My Father, You *are* the guide of my
youth?
5 Will He remain angry forever?
Will He keep it to the end?'
Behold, you have spoken and done evil
things,
As you were able."

A Call to Repentance

6The LORD said also to me in the days of Josiah the king: "Have you seen what backsliding Israel has done? She has gone up on every
high mountain and under every green tree,
and there played the harlot. 7And I said, after
she had done all these *things,* 'Return to Me.'
But she did not return. And her treacherous
sister Judah saw it. 8Then I saw that for all the
causes for which backsliding Israel had committed adultery, I had put her away and given
her a certificate of divorce; yet her treacherous
sister Judah did not fear, but went and played
the harlot also. 9So it came to pass, through
her casual harlotry, that she defiled the land
and committed adultery with stones and trees.
10And yet for all this her treacherous sister Judah has not turned to Me with her whole
heart, but in pretense," says the LORD.
11Then the LORD said to me, "Backsliding Israel has shown herself more righteous than
treacherous Judah. 12Go and proclaim these
words toward the north, and say:

'Return, backsliding Israel,' says the
LORD;
'I will not cause My anger to fall on
you.
For I *am* merciful,' says the LORD;
'I will not remain angry forever.
13 Only acknowledge your iniquity,
That you have transgressed against the
LORD your God,
And have scattered your charms
To alien deities under every green tree,
And you have not obeyed My voice,' says
the LORD.

14"Return, O backsliding children," says the
LORD; "for I am married to you. I will take
you, one from a city and two from a family,
and I will bring you to Zion. 15And I will give
you shepherds according to My heart, who
will feed you with knowledge and understanding.
16"Then it shall come to pass, when you are
multiplied and increased in the land in those
days," says the LORD, "that they will say no
more, 'The ark of the covenant of the LORD.' It
shall not come to mind, nor shall they remember it, nor shall they visit *it,* nor shall it be
made anymore.
17"At that time Jerusalem shall be called
The Throne of the LORD, and all the nations
shall be gathered to it, to the name of the
LORD, to Jerusalem. No more shall they follow
the dictates of their evil hearts.
18"In those days the house of Judah shall
walk with the house of Israel, and they shall
come together out of the land of the north to
the land that I have given as an inheritance to
your fathers.
19"But I said:

'How can I put you among the children
And give you a pleasant land,
A beautiful heritage of the hosts of
nations?'

"And I said:

'You shall call Me, "My Father,"
And not turn away from Me.'
20 Surely, *as* a wife treacherously departs
from her husband,

PERSONAL GROWTH THROUGH PERSONAL ACCOUNTABILITY

JESSE DILLINGER

(Jeremiah 3:11)

People need someone with whom they can be totally honest, someone with whom they can share their deep feelings and thoughts, someone with whom they can discuss their walk with God. People who have such a friend have learned a powerful secret to success in Christian growth—personal accountability.

Accountability means accounting for personal thoughts and behaviors, which are held up to a standard and evaluated. Another person or a group will hold someone accountable and offer encouragement and support as he or she tries to meet that standard. With voluntary accountability, people choose to place themselves in a relationship where someone else will ask them to account for their thoughts and behaviors.

Everyone, Christian and non-Christian, is accountable to one ultimate standard: the Word of God (Phil. 2:9–11). For Christians, the Bible remains the standard for daily decisions. Personal accountability builds a bridge between the Bible and the practice of its principles. While Christians remain on the earth, their objective is to grow spiritually into Christ's image (Phil. 3:13, 14). Accountability helps one to progress in the spiritual process of maturing.

PARTNERS IN ACCOUNTABILITY

Accountability requires self-evaluation, pure motives, and the absence of hypocritical judgment. People must not hold someone else accountable to a standard they are not willing to meet themselves. Accountability partners should be maturing Christians who have the desire and the time to invest in relationships with others. They must be able to keep reasonable confidences and be concerned enough with others' personal growth that they can be tough when it is needed.

TYPES OF ACCOUNTABILITY

Virtually any area of life can be placed in an accountability arrangement. A person may seek accountability to assist in following through with a specific task, like developing a regular pattern of family time. Someone may ask another to help in dealing honestly at work or remaining financially sound. A married couple may wish to meet with another married couple concerning healthy communication and loving treatment of each other. Changing one's attitude at work, developing a pattern of reading the Bible, telling the truth instead of "white lies," or maintaining purity in one's thought life may also represent areas in need of accountability.

Personal accountability is every Christian's privilege and responsibility (2 Cor. 5:10). People may ask God in prayer to show them what needs to be addressed in their lives. Not only will God reveal what they can't see, but He will also use others to reveal their personal weaknesses. At that point, they may desire to take advantage of other types of accountability with an individual or a group. In the individual arrangement, another person enters in to help a person. In a group setting, two or more individuals hold each other accountable. With a group devoted to living according to Scripture, there will be more praying, more encouraging, and more investment among more people.

CATEGORIES OF ACCOUNTABILITY

Restorative accountability can restore others to a relationship or church membership after they have been involved in sin substantial enough to sever the original tie (Gal. 6:1). Prior to an agreement to accountability, there must be genuine repentance on the part of the offender. Thorough forgiveness must precede accountability (2 Cor. 2:7).

Preventative accountability is sought to guard against weakness or sin (Mark 14:38; James 5:16). Examples include sexual thoughts and actions (lust and pornography), sins of indulgence (greed and gluttony), sins of the tongue (lying, gossip, slander) and sins of omission (failure to show compassion, etc.). The length of this type of accountability varies depending on the situation. For example, people traveling on business may set up a system of accountability specifically for the times they are away from their family to guard against temptation.

Constructive accountability aims at encouragement and the development of believers' spiritual growth (Heb. 10:23). These groups may meet for six months or more and may be guided by a specific Bible study.

Task-oriented accountability includes being held accountable for important activities such as keeping specific promises or meeting specific goals. This accountability ends with the completion of the task.

ENEMIES OF ACCOUNTABILITY

Enemies of accountability include denial (2 Sam. 12:1–7) and lies (Col. 3:9). If a person is not willing to admit mistakes or failures, there can be no accountability. Although one may be tempted to stretch the truth when meeting with an accountability partner, lying about one's success does not help the process.

Other obstacles to accountability include blame (Gen. 3:11–13) and pride (Rom. 12:16). Humility is a cornerstone of accountability. It is not easy to make oneself vulnerable to another person's scrutiny. However, a partner who reacts with a prideful, haughty attitude toward one's admission of disobedience is not a suitable partner for accountability. Encouragement should be used instead of insult.

However, no accountability relationship can tolerate continued sin on the part of one or both parties (Matt. 5:29, 30). There is no purpose in a group that makes a continuous litany of excuses for undisciplined behavior.

RESULTS OF ACCOUNTABILITY

When a group meets for accountability, questions are asked that encourage honesty and revelation. "Have you lied to anyone since we last met?" is an example of the type of questions that can provide structure for the meeting. Participants should also request information to monitor the development of desired thoughts and behaviors. "What specific truths have you told while being tempted to lie?"

Accountability brings the body of Christ together in a supportive way to encourage us to grow in Christ. It allows the development and use of our gifts and promotes unity within the body. We grow by doing what is right. Through accountability, our faith is strengthened by the example of others' obedience.

FURTHER MEDITATION:

Other passages to study about the issue of accountability include:

- Proverbs 12:15; 13:20; 27:6
- Galatians 6:1–5

To Learn More: Turn to the key passage note on accountability at Romans 14:12 on page 1487. See also the personality profile of David and Nathan on page 401.

So have you dealt treacherously with Me,
O house of Israel," says the LORD.

21 A voice was heard on the desolate heights,
Weeping *and* supplications of the children of Israel.
For they have perverted their way;
They have forgotten the LORD their God.

22 "Return, you backsliding children,
And I will heal your backslidings."

"Indeed we do come to You,
For You are the LORD our God.
23 Truly, in vain *is salvation hoped for* from the hills,
And from the multitude of mountains;
Truly, in the LORD our God
Is the salvation of Israel.
24 For shame has devoured
The labor of our fathers from our youth—
Their flocks and their herds,
Their sons and their daughters.
25 We lie down in our shame,
And our reproach covers us.
For we have sinned against the LORD our God,
We and our fathers,
From our youth even to this day,
And have not obeyed the voice of the LORD our God."

4 "If you will return, O Israel," says the LORD,
"Return to Me;
And if you will put away your abominations out of My sight,
Then you shall not be moved.
2 And you shall swear, 'The LORD lives,'
In truth, in judgment, and in righteousness;
The nations shall bless themselves in Him,
And in Him they shall glory."

3For thus says the LORD to the men of Judah and Jerusalem:

"Break up your fallow ground,
And do not sow among thorns.
4 Circumcise yourselves to the LORD,
And take away the foreskins of your hearts,
You men of Judah and inhabitants of Jerusalem,
Lest My fury come forth like fire,
And burn so that no one can quench *it*,
Because of the evil of your doings."

AN IMMINENT INVASION

5Declare in Judah and proclaim in Jerusalem, and say:

"Blow the trumpet in the land;
Cry, 'Gather together,'
And say, 'Assemble yourselves,
And let us go into the fortified cities.'
6 Set up the standard toward Zion.
Take refuge! Do not delay!
For I will bring disaster from the north,
And great destruction."

7 The lion has come up from his thicket,
And the destroyer of nations is on his way.
He has gone forth from his place
To make your land desolate.
Your cities will be laid waste,
Without inhabitant.
8 For this, clothe yourself with sackcloth,
Lament and wail.
For the fierce anger of the LORD
Has not turned back from us.

9 "And it shall come to pass in that day," says the LORD,
"*That* the heart of the king shall perish,
And the heart of the princes;
The priests shall be astonished,
And the prophets shall wonder."

10 Then I said, "Ah, Lord GOD!
Surely You have greatly deceived this people and Jerusalem,
Saying, 'You shall have peace,'
Whereas the sword reaches to the heart."

11 At that time it will be said
To this people and to Jerusalem,
"A dry wind of the desolate heights *blows* in the wilderness
Toward the daughter of My people—
Not to fan or to cleanse—
12 A wind too strong for these will come for Me;

Now I will also speak judgment against
them."

13 "Behold, he shall come up like clouds,
And his chariots like a whirlwind.
His horses are swifter than eagles.
Woe to us, for we are plundered!"

14 O Jerusalem, wash your heart from
wickedness,
That you may be saved.
How long shall your evil thoughts lodge
within you?
15 For a voice declares from Dan
And proclaims affliction from Mount
Ephraim:
16 "Make mention to the nations,
Yes, proclaim against Jerusalem,
That watchers come from a far
country
And raise their voice against the cities of
Judah.
17 Like keepers of a field they are against
her all around,
Because she has been rebellious against
Me," says the LORD.
18 "Your ways and your doings
Have procured these *things* for you.
This *is* your wickedness,
Because it is bitter,
Because it reaches to your heart."

SORROW FOR THE DOOMED NATION

19 O my soul, my soul!
I am pained in my very heart!
My heart makes a noise in me;
I cannot hold my peace,
Because you have heard, O my soul,
The sound of the trumpet,
The alarm of war.
20 Destruction upon destruction is cried,
For the whole land is plundered.
Suddenly my tents are plundered,
And my curtains in a moment.
21 How long will I see the standard,
And hear the sound of the trumpet?

22 "For My people *are* foolish,
They have not known Me.
They *are* silly children,
And they have no understanding.
They *are* wise to do evil,
But to do good they have no
knowledge."

23 I beheld the earth, and indeed *it was*
without form, and void;
And the heavens, they *had* no light.
24 I beheld the mountains, and indeed they
trembled,
And all the hills moved back and
forth.
25 I beheld, and indeed *there was* no
man,
And all the birds of the heavens had
fled.
26 I beheld, and indeed the fruitful land
was a wilderness,
And all its cities were broken down
At the presence of the LORD,
By His fierce anger.

27 For thus says the LORD:

"The whole land shall be desolate;
Yet I will not make a full end.
28 For this shall the earth mourn,
And the heavens above be black,
Because I have spoken.
I have purposed and will not relent,
Nor will I turn back from it.
29 The whole city shall flee from the noise
of the horsemen and bowmen.
They shall go into thickets and climb up
on the rocks.
Every city *shall be* forsaken,
And not a man shall dwell in it.

30 "And *when* you *are* plundered,
What will you do?
Though you clothe yourself with
crimson,
Though you adorn *yourself* with
ornaments of gold,
Though you enlarge your eyes with
paint,
In vain you will make yourself fair;
Your lovers will despise you;
They will seek your life.

31 "For I have heard a voice as of a woman
in labor,
The anguish as of her who brings forth
her first child,
The voice of the daughter of Zion
bewailing herself;
She spreads her hands, *saying,*
'Woe *is* me now, for my soul is weary
Because of murderers!'

THE JUSTICE OF GOD'S JUDGMENT

5 "Run to and fro through the streets of
Jerusalem;
See now and know;
And seek in her open places
If you can find a man,
If there is *anyone* who executes
judgment,
Who seeks the truth,
And I will pardon her.
2 Though they say, '*As* the LORD lives,'
Surely they swear falsely."

3 O LORD, *are* not Your eyes on the truth?
You have stricken them,
But they have not grieved;
You have consumed them,
But they have refused to receive
correction.
They have made their faces harder than
rock;
They have refused to return.

4 Therefore I said, "Surely these *are* poor.
They are foolish;
For they do not know the way of the
LORD,
The judgment of their God.
5 I will go to the great men and speak to
them,
For they have known the way of the
LORD,
The judgment of their God."

But these have altogether broken the
yoke
And burst the bonds.
6 Therefore a lion from the forest shall
slay them,
A wolf of the deserts shall destroy
them;
A leopard will watch over their cities.
Everyone who goes out from there shall
be torn in pieces,
Because their transgressions are many;
Their backslidings have increased.

7 "How shall I pardon you for this?
Your children have forsaken Me
And sworn by *those that are* not gods.
When I had fed them to the full,
Then they committed adultery
And assembled themselves by troops in
the harlots' houses.
8 They were *like* well-fed lusty stallions;
Every one neighed after his neighbor's
wife.
9 Shall I not punish *them* for these
things?" says the LORD.
"And shall I not avenge Myself on such a
nation as this?

10 "Go up on her walls and destroy,
But do not make a complete end.
Take away her branches,
For they *are* not the LORD's.
11 For the house of Israel and the house of
Judah
Have dealt very treacherously with Me,"
says the LORD.

12 They have lied about the LORD,
And said, "*It is* not He.
Neither will evil come upon us,
Nor shall we see sword or famine.
13 And the prophets become wind,
For the word *is* not in them.
Thus shall it be done to them."

14 Therefore thus says the LORD God of
hosts:

"Because you speak this word,
Behold, I will make My words in your
mouth fire,
And this people wood,
And it shall devour them.
15 Behold, I will bring a nation against you
from afar,
O house of Israel," says the LORD.
"It *is* a mighty nation,
It *is* an ancient nation,
A nation whose language you do not
know,
Nor can you understand what they say.
16 Their quiver *is* like an open tomb;
They *are* all mighty men.
17 And they shall eat up your harvest and
your bread,
Which your sons and daughters should
eat.
They shall eat up your flocks and your
herds;
They shall eat up your vines and your
fig trees;
They shall destroy your fortified
cities,
In which you trust, with the sword.

18"Nevertheless in those days," says the
LORD, "I will not make a complete end of you.
19And it will be when you say, 'Why does the
LORD our God do all these *things* to us?' then
you shall answer them, 'Just as you have forsaken Me and served foreign gods in your
land, so you shall serve aliens in a land *that is*
not yours.'

20 "Declare this in the house of Jacob
And proclaim it in Judah, saying,
21 'Hear this now, O foolish people,
Without understanding,
Who have eyes and see not,
And who have ears and hear not:
22 Do you not fear Me?' says the LORD.
'Will you not tremble at My presence,
Who have placed the sand as the bound of the sea,
By a perpetual decree, that it cannot pass beyond it?
And though its waves toss to and fro,
Yet they cannot prevail;
Though they roar, yet they cannot pass over it.
23 But this people has a defiant and rebellious heart;
They have revolted and departed.
24 They do not say in their heart,
"Let us now fear the LORD our God,
Who gives rain, both the former and the latter, in its season.
He reserves for us the appointed weeks of the harvest."
25 Your iniquities have turned these *things* away,
And your sins have withheld good from you.

26 'For among My people are found wicked *men;*
They lie in wait as one who sets snares;
They set a trap;
They catch men.
27 As a cage is full of birds,
So their houses *are* full of deceit.
Therefore they have become great and grown rich.
28 They have grown fat, they are sleek;
Yes, they surpass the deeds of the wicked;
They do not plead the cause,
The cause of the fatherless;
Yet they prosper,
And the right of the needy they do not defend.
29 Shall I not punish *them* for these *things?*'
says the LORD.
'Shall I not avenge Myself on such a nation as this?'

30 "An astonishing and horrible thing
Has been committed in the land:
31 The prophets prophesy falsely,
And the priests rule by their *own* power;
And My people love *to have it* so.
But what will you do in the end?

IMPENDING DESTRUCTION FROM THE NORTH

6 "O you children of Benjamin,
Gather yourselves to flee from the midst of Jerusalem!
Blow the trumpet in Tekoa,
And set up a signal-fire in Beth Haccerem;
For disaster appears out of the north,
And great destruction.
2 I have likened the daughter of Zion
To a lovely and delicate woman.
3 The shepherds with their flocks shall come to her.
They shall pitch *their* tents against her all around.
Each one shall pasture in his own place."

4 "Prepare war against her;
Arise, and let us go up at noon.
Woe to us, for the day goes away,
For the shadows of the evening are lengthening.
5 Arise, and let us go by night,
And let us destroy her palaces."

6For thus has the LORD of hosts said:

"Cut down trees,
And build a mound against Jerusalem.
This *is* the city to be punished.
She *is* full of oppression in her midst.
7 As a fountain wells up with water,
So she wells up with her wickedness.
Violence and plundering are heard in her.
Before Me continually *are* grief and wounds.
8 Be instructed, O Jerusalem,
Lest My soul depart from you;

Lest I make you desolate,
A land not inhabited."

9 Thus says the LORD of hosts:

"They shall thoroughly glean as a vine
the remnant of Israel;
As a grape-gatherer, put your hand back
into the branches."

10 To whom shall I speak and give
warning,
That they may hear?
Indeed their ear *is* uncircumcised,
And they cannot give heed.
Behold, the word of the LORD is a
reproach to them;
They have no delight in it.
11 Therefore I am full of the fury of the
LORD.
I am weary of holding *it* in.
"I will pour it out on the children
outside,
And on the assembly of young men
together;
For even the husband shall be taken
with the wife,
The aged with *him who is* full of days.
12 And their houses shall be turned over to
others,
Fields and wives together;
For I will stretch out My hand
Against the inhabitants of the land,"
says the LORD.
13 "Because from the least of them even to
the greatest of them,
Everyone *is* given to covetousness;
And from the prophet even to the
priest,
Everyone deals falsely.
14 They have also healed the hurt of My
people slightly,
Saying, 'Peace, peace!'
When *there is* no peace.
15 Were they ashamed when they had
committed abomination?
No! They were not at all ashamed;
Nor did they know how to blush.
Therefore they shall fall among those
who fall;
At the time I punish them,
They shall be cast down," says the LORD.

16 Thus says the LORD:

"Stand in the ways and see,
And ask for the old paths, where the
good way *is*,
And walk in it;
Then you will find rest for your souls.
But they said, 'We will not walk *in it*.'
17 Also, I set watchmen over you, *saying*,
'Listen to the sound of the trumpet!'
But they said, 'We will not listen.'
18 Therefore hear, you nations,
And know, O congregation, what *is*
among them.
19 Hear, O earth!
Behold, I will certainly bring calamity on
this people—
The fruit of their thoughts,
Because they have not heeded My words
Nor My law, but rejected it.
20 For what purpose to Me
Comes frankincense from Sheba,
And sweet cane from a far country?
Your burnt offerings *are* not acceptable,
Nor your sacrifices sweet to Me."

21 Therefore thus says the LORD:

"Behold, I will lay stumbling blocks
before this people,
And the fathers and the sons together
shall fall on them.
The neighbor and his friend shall perish."

22 Thus says the LORD:

"Behold, a people comes from the north
country,
And a great nation will be raised from
the farthest parts of the earth.
23 They will lay hold on bow and spear;
They *are* cruel and have no mercy;
Their voice roars like the sea;
And they ride on horses,
As men of war set in array against you,
O daughter of Zion."

24 We have heard the report of it;
Our hands grow feeble.
Anguish has taken hold of us,
Pain as of a woman in labor.
25 Do not go out into the field,
Nor walk by the way.
Because of the sword of the enemy,
Fear *is* on every side.
26 O daughter of my people,

Dress in sackcloth
And roll about in ashes!
Make mourning *as for* an only son, most bitter lamentation;
For the plunderer will suddenly come upon us.

27 "I have set you *as* an assayer *and* a fortress among My people,
That you may know and test their way.
28 They *are* all stubborn rebels, walking as slanderers.
They are bronze and iron,
They *are* all corrupters;
29 The bellows blow fiercely,
The lead is consumed by the fire;
The smelter refines in vain,
For the wicked are not drawn off.
30 *People* will call them rejected silver,
Because the LORD has rejected them."

TRUSTING IN LYING WORDS

7 The word that came to Jeremiah from the
LORD, saying, 2"Stand in the gate of the
LORD's house, and proclaim there this word,
and say, 'Hear the word of the LORD, all *you of*
Judah who enter in at these gates to worship
the LORD!' " 3Thus says the LORD of hosts, the
God of Israel: "Amend your ways and your doings, and I will cause you to dwell in this
place. 4Do not trust in these lying words, saying, 'The temple of the LORD, the temple of the
LORD, the temple of the LORD *are* these.'
5"For if you thoroughly amend your ways
and your doings, if you thoroughly execute
judgment between a man and his neighbor, 6*if*
you do not oppress the stranger, the fatherless, and the widow, and do not shed innocent
blood in this place, or walk after other gods to
your hurt, 7then I will cause you to dwell in
this place, in the land that I gave to your fathers forever and ever.
8"Behold, you trust in lying words that cannot profit. 9Will you steal, murder, commit
adultery, swear falsely, burn incense to Baal,
and walk after other gods whom you do not
know, 10and *then* come and stand before Me in
this house which is called by My name, and
say, 'We are delivered to do all these abominations'? 11Has this house, which is called by My
name, become a den of thieves in your eyes?
Behold, I, even I, have seen *it*," says the LORD.
12"But go now to My place which *was* in
Shiloh, where I set My name at the first, and
see what I did to it because of the wickedness
of My people Israel. 13And now, because you
have done all these works," says the LORD,
"and I spoke to you, rising up early and speaking, but you did not hear, and I called you, but
you did not answer, 14therefore I will do to the
house which is called by My name, in which
you trust, and to this place which I gave to
you and your fathers, as I have done to Shiloh.
15And I will cast you out of My sight, as I have
cast out all your brethren—the whole posterity of Ephraim.
16"Therefore do not pray for this people, nor
lift up a cry or prayer for them, nor make intercession to Me; for I will not hear you. 17Do
you not see what they do in the cities of Judah
and in the streets of Jerusalem? 18The children
gather wood, the fathers kindle the fire, and
the women knead dough, to make cakes for
the queen of heaven; and *they* pour out drink
offerings to other gods, that they may provoke
Me to anger. 19Do they provoke Me to anger?"
says the LORD. "*Do they* not *provoke* themselves, to the shame of their own faces?"
20Therefore thus says the Lord GOD: "Behold, My anger and My fury will be poured
out on this place—on man and on beast, on
the trees of the field and on the fruit of the
ground. And it will burn and not be
quenched."
21Thus says the LORD of hosts, the God of Israel: "Add your burnt offerings to your sacrifices and eat meat. 22For I did not speak to
your fathers, or command them in the day
that I brought them out of the land of Egypt,
concerning burnt offerings or sacrifices. 23But
this is what I commanded them, saying, 'Obey
My voice, and I will be your God, and you
shall be My people. And walk in all the ways
that I have commanded you, that it may be
well with you.' 24Yet they did not obey or incline their ear, but followed the counsels *and*
the dictates of their evil hearts, and went
backward and not forward. 25Since the day
that your fathers came out of the land of Egypt
until this day, I have even sent to you all My
servants the prophets, daily rising up early
and sending *them*. 26Yet they did not obey Me
or incline their ear, but stiffened their neck.
They did worse than their fathers.
27"Therefore you shall speak all these
words to them, but they will not obey you.
You shall also call to them, but they will not
answer you.

Judgment on Obscene Religion

28“So you shall say to them, ‘This *is* a nation
that does not obey the voice of the LORD their
God nor receive correction. Truth has perished
and has been cut off from their mouth. 29Cut
off your hair and cast *it* away, and take up a
lamentation on the desolate heights; for the
LORD has rejected and forsaken the generation
of His wrath.’ 30For the children of Judah have
done evil in My sight,” says the LORD. “They
have set their abominations in the house
which is called by My name, to pollute it.
31And they have built the high places of
Tophet, which *is* in the Valley of the Son of
Hinnom, to burn their sons and their daughters in the fire, which I did not command, nor
did it come into My heart.

32“Therefore behold, the days are coming,”
says the LORD, “when it will no more be called
Tophet, or the Valley of the Son of Hinnom,
but the Valley of Slaughter; for they will bury
in Tophet until there is no room. 33The corpses
of this people will be food for the birds of the
heaven and for the beasts of the earth. And no
one will frighten *them away.* 34Then I will
cause to cease from the cities of Judah and
from the streets of Jerusalem the voice of
mirth and the voice of gladness, the voice of
the bridegroom and the voice of the bride. For
the land shall be desolate.

8 “At that time,” says the LORD, “they shall
bring out the bones of the kings of Judah,
and the bones of its princes, and the bones of
the priests, and the bones of the prophets, and
the bones of the inhabitants of Jerusalem, out
of their graves. 2They shall spread them before
the sun and the moon and all the host of heav-
en, which they have loved and which they
have served and after which they have
walked, which they have sought and which
they have worshiped. They shall not be gathered nor buried; they shall be like refuse on
the face of the earth. 3Then death shall be chosen rather than life by all the residue of those
who remain of this evil family, who remain in
all the places where I have driven them,” says
the LORD of hosts.

The Peril of False Teaching

4“Moreover you shall say to them, ‘Thus
says the LORD:

“Will they fall and not rise?
Will one turn away and not return?

5 Why has this people slidden back,
Jerusalem, in a perpetual backsliding?
They hold fast to deceit,
They refuse to return.
6 I listened and heard,
But they do not speak aright.
No man repented of his wickedness,
Saying, ‘What have I done?’
Everyone turned to his own course,
As the horse rushes into the battle.

7 “Even the stork in the heavens
Knows her appointed times;
And the turtledove, the swift, and the
swallow
Observe the time of their coming.
But My people do not know the
judgment of the LORD.

8 “How can you say, ‘We *are* wise,
And the law of the LORD *is* with us’?
Look, the false pen of the scribe
certainly works falsehood.
9 The wise men are ashamed,
They are dismayed and taken.
Behold, they have rejected the word of
the LORD;
So what wisdom do they have?
10 Therefore I will give their wives to
others,
And their fields to those who will inherit
them;
Because from the least even to the
greatest
Everyone is given to covetousness;
From the prophet even to the priest
Everyone deals falsely.
11 For they have healed the hurt of the
daughter of My people slightly,
Saying, ‘Peace, peace!’
When *there is* no peace.
12 Were they ashamed when they had
committed abomination?
No! They were not at all ashamed,
Nor did they know how to blush.
Therefore they shall fall among those
who fall;
In the time of their punishment
They shall be cast down,” says the
LORD.

13 “I will surely consume them,” says the
LORD.
“No grapes *shall be* on the vine,

Nor figs on the fig tree,
And the leaf shall fade;
And *the things* I have given them shall pass away from them." ' "

14 "Why do we sit still?
Assemble yourselves,
And let us enter the fortified cities,
And let us be silent there.
For the LORD our God has put us to silence
And given us water of gall to drink,
Because we have sinned against the LORD.

15 "*We* looked for peace, but no good *came;*
And for a time of health, and there was trouble!
16 The snorting of His horses was heard from Dan.
The whole land trembled at the sound of the neighing of His strong ones;
For they have come and devoured the land and all that is in it,
The city and those who dwell in it."

17 "For behold, I will send serpents among you,
Vipers which cannot be charmed,
And they shall bite you," says the LORD.

The Prophet Mourns for the People

18 I would comfort myself in sorrow;
My heart *is* faint in me.
19 Listen! The voice,
The cry of the daughter of my people
From a far country:
"*Is* not the LORD in Zion?
Is not her King in her?"

"Why have they provoked Me to anger
With their carved images—
With foreign idols?"

20 "The harvest is past,
The summer is ended,
And we are not saved!"

21 For the hurt of the daughter of my people I am hurt.
I am mourning;
Astonishment has taken hold of me.
22 *Is there* no balm in Gilead,
Is there no physician there?
Why then is there no recovery
For the health of the daughter of my people?

9 Oh, that my head were waters,
And my eyes a fountain of tears,
That I might weep day and night
For the slain of the daughter of my people!
2 Oh, that I had in the wilderness
A lodging place for travelers;
That I might leave my people,
And go from them!
For they *are* all adulterers,
An assembly of treacherous men.

> Oh, that my head were waters, and my eyes a fountain of tears, that I might weep day and night for the slain of the daughter of my people!
> JEREMIAH 9:1

3 "And *like* their bow they have bent their tongues *for* lies.
They are not valiant for the truth on the earth.
For they proceed from evil to evil,
And they do not know Me," says the LORD.
4 "Everyone take heed to his neighbor,
And do not trust any brother;
For every brother will utterly supplant,
And every neighbor will walk with slanderers.
5 Everyone will deceive his neighbor,
And will not speak the truth;
They have taught their tongue to speak lies;
They weary themselves to commit iniquity.
6 Your dwelling place *is* in the midst of deceit;
Through deceit they refuse to know Me," says the LORD.

7 Therefore thus says the LORD of hosts:

"Behold, I will refine them and try them;
For how shall I deal with the daughter of My people?

8 Their tongue *is* an arrow shot out;
It speaks deceit;
One speaks peaceably to his neighbor
with his mouth,
But in his heart he lies in wait.
9 Shall I not punish them for these
things?" says the LORD.
"Shall I not avenge Myself on such a
nation as this?"

10 I will take up a weeping and wailing for
the mountains,
And for the dwelling places of the
wilderness a lamentation,
Because they are burned up,
So that no one can pass through;
Nor can *men* hear the voice of the
cattle.
Both the birds of the heavens and the
beasts have fled;
They are gone.

11 "I will make Jerusalem a heap of ruins, a
den of jackals.
I will make the cities of Judah desolate,
without an inhabitant."

12Who *is* the wise man who may understand this? And *who is he* to whom the mouth
of the LORD has spoken, that he may declare
it? Why does the land perish *and* burn up like
a wilderness, so that no one can pass through?
13And the LORD said, "Because they have
forsaken My law which I set before them, and
have not obeyed My voice, nor walked according to it, 14but they have walked according to
the dictates of their own hearts and after the
Baals, which their fathers taught them,"
15therefore thus says the LORD of hosts, the
God of Israel: "Behold, I will feed them, this
people, with wormwood, and give them water
of gall to drink. 16I will scatter them also
among the Gentiles, whom neither they nor

PERSONALITY PROFILE

Emotional Life

JEREMIAH SHOWS IT'S OK TO CRY

(JEREMIAH 9)

In our culture, sons are often told, "Big boys don't cry." Such well-intended advice to toughen boys to face the challenges of life often trains them to perceive their emotions as a sign of weakness and to repress them. The prophet Jeremiah, however, was not afraid to cry. He expressed his feelings loudly and clearly. His words of anger and grief teach us lessons about emotions as well as lessons about the ways in which we can communicate with God. Jeremiah was a big boy who knew when to cry.

Known as the "weeping prophet," Jeremiah cried and mourned for the people of God. He preached a message of judgment through tears that flowed from a heart of compassion. Even God's severest truth is never void of His love. God has not merely directed us to condemn sin, but also to love the sinner. Jeremiah's message offers us a wonderful example about balancing the character of God with the compassion of God.

Jeremiah also offers us an intimate view of his own relationship with God. His prayers were never edited. He did not leave out the raw anger or doubt. The prophet was not afraid that God might somehow be offended by his honest feelings. Jeremiah's awareness of his own feelings made him particularly sensitive to God's deep expressions of disappointment and sadness. He was open to the heart of God because his own heart was open to God.

Like Jeremiah, we can make it a point to pray when we feel least like praying. We can ask ourselves before we pray, "Does God just expect me to tell Him what He wants to hear; or can I really tell Him what is on my mind and heart?" Such openness allows for a healthy emotional life. The more we learn to communicate fully with God, the more we will find ourselves open to His Spirit, sensitive to His corrections, and growing in compassion for the world.

To Learn More: Turn to the article about emotional life on pages 1040, 1041. See also the key passage note at Lamentations 3:22–25 on page 1039.

their fathers have known. And I will send a
sword after them until I have consumed
them."

The People Mourn in Judgment

17Thus says the LORD of hosts:

"Consider and call for the mourning
women,
That they may come;
And send for skillful wailing women,
That they may come.
18 Let them make haste
And take up a wailing for us,
That our eyes may run with tears,
And our eyelids gush with water.
19 For a voice of wailing is heard from Zion:
'How we are plundered!
We are greatly ashamed,
Because we have forsaken the land,
Because we have been cast out of our
dwellings.' "

20 Yet hear the word of the LORD,
O women,
And let your ear receive the word of His
mouth;
Teach your daughters wailing,
And everyone her neighbor a
lamentation.
21 For death has come through our
windows,
Has entered our palaces,
To kill off the children—*no longer to be*
outside!
And the young men—*no longer* on the
streets!

22 Speak, "Thus says the LORD:

'Even the carcasses of men shall fall as
refuse on the open field,
Like cuttings after the harvester,
And no one shall gather *them*.' "

23Thus says the LORD:

"Let not the wise *man* glory in his
wisdom,
Let not the mighty *man* glory in his
might,
Nor let the rich *man* glory in his riches;
24 But let him who glories glory in this,
That he understands and knows Me,
That I *am* the LORD, exercising
lovingkindness, judgment, and
righteousness in the earth.
For in these I delight," says the LORD.

25"Behold, the days are coming," says the
LORD, "that I will punish all *who are* circumcised with the uncircumcised—26Egypt, Judah, Edom, the people of Ammon, Moab, and
all *who are* in the farthest corners, who dwell
in the wilderness. For all *these* nations *are* uncircumcised, and all the house of Israel *are* uncircumcised in the heart."

Idols and the True God

10 Hear the word which the LORD speaks
to you, O house of Israel.
2Thus says the LORD:

"Do not learn the way of the Gentiles;
Do not be dismayed at the signs of
heaven,
For the Gentiles are dismayed at them.
3 For the customs of the peoples *are* futile;
For *one* cuts a tree from the forest,
The work of the hands of the workman,
with the ax.
4 They decorate it with silver and gold;
They fasten it with nails and hammers
So that it will not topple.

SOUL NOTE

The Physical and the Spiritual *(9:25, 26)* Without inward devotion to God, the act of circumcision is about as spiritually meaningful as a haircut. Using outward symbols as evidence of spiritual superiority goes against everything God says in His Word. Anything to which people point with pride to symbolize their spirituality or to set them apart from others is, in reality, a stumbling block to their growth. People may look at the outward appearance, "but the LORD looks at the heart" (1 Sam. 16:7). **Topic: Cults**

5 They *are* upright, like a palm tree,
And they cannot speak;
They must be carried,
Because they cannot go *by themselves.*
Do not be afraid of them,
For they cannot do evil,
Nor can they do any good."

6 Inasmuch as *there is* none like You,
O LORD
(You *are* great, and Your name *is* great in might),
7 Who would not fear You, O King of the nations?
For this is Your rightful due.
For among all the wise *men* of the nations,
And in all their kingdoms,
There is none like You.
8 But they are altogether dull-hearted and foolish;
A wooden idol *is* a worthless doctrine.
9 Silver is beaten into plates;
It is brought from Tarshish,
And gold from Uphaz,
The work of the craftsman
And of the hands of the metalsmith;
Blue and purple *are* their clothing;
They *are* all the work of skillful *men.*
10 But the LORD *is* the true God;
He *is* the living God and the everlasting King.
At His wrath the earth will tremble,
And the nations will not be able to endure His indignation.

There is none like You, O LORD
(You are great, and Your name
is great in might).
JEREMIAH 10:6

11 Thus you shall say to them: "The gods
that have not made the heavens and the earth
shall perish from the earth and from under
these heavens."

12 He has made the earth by His power,
He has established the world by His wisdom,
And has stretched out the heavens at His discretion.
13 When He utters His voice,
There is a multitude of waters in the heavens:
"And He causes the vapors to ascend from the ends of the earth.
He makes lightning for the rain,
He brings the wind out of His treasuries."[a]

14 Everyone is dull-hearted, without knowledge;
Every metalsmith is put to shame by an image;
For his molded image *is* falsehood,
And *there is* no breath in them.
15 They *are* futile, a work of errors;
In the time of their punishment they shall perish.
16 The Portion of Jacob *is* not like them,
For He *is* the Maker of all *things,*
And Israel *is* the tribe of His inheritance;
The LORD of hosts *is* His name.

THE COMING CAPTIVITY OF JUDAH

17 Gather up your wares from the land,
O inhabitant of the fortress!

18 For thus says the LORD:

"Behold, I will throw out at this time
The inhabitants of the land,
And will distress them,
That they may find *it so.*"

19 Woe is me for my hurt!
My wound is severe.
But I say, "Truly this *is* an infirmity,
And I must bear it."
20 My tent is plundered,
And all my cords are broken;
My children have gone from me,
And they *are* no more.
There is no one to pitch my tent anymore,
Or set up my curtains.

21 For the shepherds have become dull-hearted,
And have not sought the LORD;
Therefore they shall not prosper,

10:13 [a]Psalm 135:7

And all their flocks shall be scattered.
22 Behold, the noise of the report has come,
And a great commotion out of the north country,
To make the cities of Judah desolate, a den of jackals.

23 O LORD, I know the way of man *is* not in himself;
It is not in man who walks to direct his own steps.
24 O LORD, correct me, but with justice;
Not in Your anger, lest You bring me to nothing.
25 Pour out Your fury on the Gentiles, who do not know You,
And on the families who do not call on Your name;
For they have eaten up Jacob,
Devoured him and consumed him,
And made his dwelling place desolate.

THE BROKEN COVENANT

11 The word that came to Jeremiah from the LORD, saying, 2"Hear the words of this covenant, and speak to the men of Judah and to the inhabitants of Jerusalem; 3and say to them, 'Thus says the LORD God of Israel: "Cursed *is* the man who does not obey the words of this covenant 4which I commanded your fathers in the day I brought them out of the land of Egypt, from the iron furnace, saying, 'Obey My voice, and do according to all that I command you; so shall you be My people, and I will be your God,' 5that I may establish the oath which I have sworn to your fathers, to give them 'a land flowing with milk and honey,'[a] as *it is* this day." ' "

And I answered and said, "So be it, LORD."

6Then the LORD said to me, "Proclaim all these words in the cities of Judah and in the streets of Jerusalem, saying: 'Hear the words of this covenant and do them. 7For I earnestly exhorted your fathers in the day I brought them up out of the land of Egypt, until this day, rising early and exhorting, saying, "Obey My voice." 8Yet they did not obey or incline their ear, but everyone followed the dictates of his evil heart; therefore I will bring upon them all the words of this covenant, which I commanded *them* to do, but *which* they have not done.' "

9And the LORD said to me, "A conspiracy has been found among the men of Judah and among the inhabitants of Jerusalem. 10They have turned back to the iniquities of their forefathers who refused to hear My words, and they have gone after other gods to serve them; the house of Israel and the house of Judah have broken My covenant which I made with their fathers."

11Therefore thus says the LORD: "Behold, I will surely bring calamity on them which they will not be able to escape; and though they cry out to Me, I will not listen to them. 12Then the cities of Judah and the inhabitants of Jerusalem will go and cry out to the gods to whom they offer incense, but they will not save them at all in the time of their trouble. 13For *according to* the number of your cities were your gods, O Judah; and *according to* the number of the streets of Jerusalem you have set up altars to *that* shameful thing, altars to burn incense to Baal.

14"So do not pray for this people, or lift up a cry or prayer for them; for I will not hear *them* in the time that they cry out to Me because of their trouble.

15 "What has My beloved to do in My house,
Having done lewd deeds with many?
And the holy flesh has passed from you.
When you do evil, then you rejoice.
16 The LORD called your name,
Green Olive Tree, Lovely *and* of Good Fruit.
With the noise of a great tumult
He has kindled fire on it,
And its branches are broken.

17"For the LORD of hosts, who planted you, has pronounced doom against you for the evil of the house of Israel and of the house of Judah, which they have done against themselves to provoke Me to anger in offering incense to Baal."

JEREMIAH'S LIFE THREATENED

18Now the LORD gave me knowledge *of it,* and I know *it;* for You showed me their doings. 19But I *was* like a docile lamb brought to the slaughter; and I did not know that they had devised schemes against me, *saying,* "Let us destroy the tree with its fruit, and let us cut

11:5 [a]Exodus 3:8

him off from the land of the living, that his name may be remembered no more."

20 But, O LORD of hosts,
You who judge righteously,
Testing the mind and the heart,
Let me see Your vengeance on them,
For to You I have revealed my cause.

21"Therefore thus says the LORD concerning
the men of Anathoth who seek your life, saying, 'Do not prophesy in the name of the LORD,
lest you die by our hand'— 22therefore thus
says the LORD of hosts: 'Behold, I will punish
them. The young men shall die by the sword,
their sons and their daughters shall die by
famine; 23and there shall be no remnant of
them, for I will bring catastrophe on the men
of Anathoth, *even* the year of their punishment.' "

JEREMIAH'S QUESTION

12 Righteous *are* You, O LORD, when I
plead with You;
Yet let me talk with You about *Your*
judgments.
Why does the way of the wicked
prosper?
Why are those happy who deal so
treacherously?
2 You have planted them, yes, they have
taken root;
They grow, yes, they bear fruit.
You *are* near in their mouth
But far from their mind.

3 But You, O LORD, know me;
You have seen me,
And You have tested my heart toward
You.
Pull them out like sheep for the
slaughter,
And prepare them for the day of slaughter.
4 How long will the land mourn,
And the herbs of every field wither?
The beasts and birds are consumed,
For the wickedness of those who dwell
there,
Because they said, "He will not see our
final end."

THE LORD ANSWERS JEREMIAH

5 "If you have run with the footmen, and
they have wearied you,
Then how can you contend with horses?
And *if* in the land of peace,
In which you trusted, *they wearied you,*
Then how will you do in the floodplain[a]
of the Jordan?
6 For even your brothers, the house of
your father,
Even they have dealt treacherously with
you;
Yes, they have called a multitude after
you.
Do not believe them,
Even though they speak smooth words
to you.

7 "I have forsaken My house, I have left My
heritage;
I have given the dearly beloved of My
soul into the hand of her enemies.
8 My heritage is to Me like a lion in the
forest;
It cries out against Me;
Therefore I have hated it.
9 My heritage *is* to Me *like* a speckled
vulture;
The vultures all around *are* against her.
Come, assemble all the beasts of the
field,
Bring them to devour!

10 "Many rulers[a] have destroyed My
vineyard,
They have trodden My portion
underfoot;
They have made My pleasant portion a
desolate wilderness.
11 They have made it desolate;
Desolate, it mourns to Me;
The whole land is made desolate,
Because no one takes *it* to heart.
12 The plunderers have come
On all the desolate heights in the
wilderness,
For the sword of the LORD shall devour
From *one* end of the land to the *other*
end of the land;
No flesh shall have peace.
13 They have sown wheat but reaped
thorns;
They have put themselves to pain *but* do
not profit.

12:5 [a]Or *thicket* **12:10** [a]Literally *shepherds* or *pastors*

But be ashamed of your harvest
Because of the fierce anger of the LORD."

14Thus says the LORD: "Against all My evil
neighbors who touch the inheritance which I
have caused My people Israel to inherit—behold, I will pluck them out of their land and
pluck out the house of Judah from among
them. 15Then it shall be, after I have plucked
them out, that I will return and have compassion on them and bring them back, everyone
to his heritage and everyone to his land. 16And
it shall be, if they will learn carefully the ways
of My people, to swear by My name, 'As the
LORD lives,' as they taught My people to swear
by Baal, then they shall be established in the
midst of My people. 17But if they do not obey,
I will utterly pluck up and destroy that nation," says the LORD.

Symbol of the Linen Sash

13 Thus the LORD said to me: "Go and get
yourself a linen sash, and put it
around your waist, but do not put it in water."
2So I got a sash according to the word of the
LORD, and put *it* around my waist.
3And the word of the LORD came to me the
second time, saying, 4"Take the sash that you
acquired, which *is* around your waist, and
arise, go to the Euphrates,[a] and hide it there in
a hole in the rock." 5So I went and hid it by the
Euphrates, as the LORD commanded me.
6Now it came to pass after many days that
the LORD said to me, "Arise, go to the Euphrates, and take from there the sash which I commanded you to hide there." 7Then I went to
the Euphrates and dug, and I took the sash
from the place where I had hidden it; and
there was the sash, ruined. It was profitable
for nothing.
8Then the word of the LORD came to me,
saying, 9"Thus says the LORD: 'In this manner
I will ruin the pride of Judah and the great
pride of Jerusalem. 10This evil people, who refuse to hear My words, who follow the dictates of their hearts, and walk after other gods
to serve them and worship them, shall be just
like this sash which is profitable for nothing.
11For as the sash clings to the waist of a man,
so I have caused the whole house of Israel and
the whole house of Judah to cling to Me,' says
the LORD, 'that they may become My people,
for renown, for praise, and for glory; but they
would not hear.'

Symbol of the Wine Bottles

12"Therefore you shall speak to them this
word: 'Thus says the LORD God of Israel: "Every bottle shall be filled with wine." '
"And they will say to you, 'Do we not certainly know that every bottle will be filled
with wine?'
13"Then you shall say to them, 'Thus says
the LORD: "Behold, I will fill all the inhabitants
of this land—even the kings who sit on
David's throne, the priests, the prophets, and
all the inhabitants of Jerusalem—with drunkenness! 14And I will dash them one against another, even the fathers and the sons together,"
says the LORD. "I will not pity nor spare nor
have mercy, but will destroy them." ' "

Pride Precedes Captivity

15 Hear and give ear:
Do not be proud,
For the LORD has spoken.
16 Give glory to the LORD your God
Before He causes darkness,
And before your feet stumble
On the dark mountains,
And while you are looking for light,
He turns it into the shadow of death

13:4 [a]Hebrew *Perath*

SOUL NOTE

The Perfect Resource *(13:15)* Some people think that God's Word is dated and somewhat limited—fine for establishing broad principles but ineffectual in providing specific daily guidance. As a result, when faced with everyday challenges and temptations, they tend to trust their own instincts and hope for the best. Only after they mess things up on their own do they turn to the Lord and His Word for help. This pride prevents them from fully experiencing God's hand in their lives. God says, "Do not be proud, for the LORD has spoken." **Topic: Pride**

And makes *it* dense darkness.
17 But if you will not hear it,
My soul will weep in secret for *your* pride;
My eyes will weep bitterly
And run down with tears,
Because the LORD's flock has been taken captive.

18 Say to the king and to the queen mother,
"Humble yourselves;
Sit down,
For your rule shall collapse, the crown of your glory."
19 The cities of the South shall be shut up,
And no one shall open *them;*
Judah shall be carried away captive, all of it;
It shall be wholly carried away captive.

20 Lift up your eyes and see
Those who come from the north.
Where *is* the flock *that* was given to you,
Your beautiful sheep?
21 What will you say when He punishes you?
For you have taught them
To be chieftains, to be head over you.
Will not pangs seize you,
Like a woman in labor?
22 And if you say in your heart,
"Why have these things come upon me?"
For the greatness of your iniquity
Your skirts have been uncovered,
Your heels made bare.
23 Can the Ethiopian change his skin or the leopard its spots?
Then may you also do good who are accustomed to do evil.

24 "Therefore I will scatter them like stubble
That passes away by the wind of the wilderness.
25 This is your lot,
The portion of your measures from Me,"
says the LORD,
"Because you have forgotten Me
And trusted in falsehood.
26 Therefore I will uncover your skirts over your face,
That your shame may appear.
27 I have seen your adulteries
And your *lustful* neighings,
The lewdness of your harlotry,
Your abominations on the hills in the fields.
Woe to you, O Jerusalem!
Will you still not be made clean?"

SWORD, FAMINE, AND PESTILENCE

14 The word of the LORD that came to Jeremiah concerning the droughts.

2 "Judah mourns,
And her gates languish;
They mourn for the land,
And the cry of Jerusalem has gone up.
3 Their nobles have sent their lads for water;
They went to the cisterns *and* found no water.
They returned with their vessels empty;
They were ashamed and confounded
And covered their heads.
4 Because the ground is parched,
For there was no rain in the land,
The plowmen were ashamed;
They covered their heads.
5 Yes, the deer also gave birth in the field,
But left because there was no grass.
6 And the wild donkeys stood in the desolate heights;
They sniffed at the wind like jackals;
Their eyes failed because *there was* no grass."

7 O LORD, though our iniquities testify against us,
Do it for Your name's sake;
For our backslidings are many,
We have sinned against You.
8 O the Hope of Israel, his Savior in time of trouble,
Why should You be like a stranger in the land,
And like a traveler *who* turns aside to tarry for a night?
9 Why should You be like a man astonished,
Like a mighty one *who* cannot save?
Yet You, O LORD, *are* in our midst,
And we are called by Your name;
Do not leave us!

10 Thus says the LORD to this people:

"Thus they have loved to wander;
They have not restrained their feet.

Therefore the LORD does not accept
them;
He will remember their iniquity now,
And punish their sins."

11Then the LORD said to me, "Do not pray for
this people, for *their* good. 12When they fast, I
will not hear their cry; and when they offer
burnt offering and grain offering, I will not accept them. But I will consume them by the
sword, by the famine, and by the pestilence."
13Then I said, "Ah, Lord GOD! Behold, the
prophets say to them, 'You shall not see the
sword, nor shall you have famine, but I will
give you assured peace in this place.' "
14And the LORD said to me, "The prophets
prophesy lies in My name. I have not sent
them, commanded them, nor spoken to them;
they prophesy to you a false vision, divination, a worthless thing, and the deceit of their
heart. 15Therefore thus says the LORD concerning the prophets who prophesy in My name,
whom I did not send, and who say, 'Sword
and famine shall not be in this land'—'By
sword and famine those prophets shall be
consumed! 16And the people to whom they
prophesy shall be cast out in the streets of Jerusalem because of the famine and the sword;
they will have no one to bury them—them nor
their wives, their sons nor their daughters—
for I will pour their wickedness on them.'
17"Therefore you shall say this word to
them:

'Let my eyes flow with tears night and
day,
And let them not cease;
For the virgin daughter of my people
Has been broken with a mighty stroke,
with a very severe blow.
18 If I go out to the field,
Then behold, those slain with the sword!
And if I enter the city,
Then behold, those sick from famine!
Yes, both prophet and priest go about in
a land they do not know.' "

THE PEOPLE PLEAD FOR MERCY

19 Have You utterly rejected Judah?
Has Your soul loathed Zion?
Why have You stricken us so that *there
is* no healing for us?
We looked for peace, but *there was* no
good;
And for the time of healing, and there
was trouble.
20 We acknowledge, O LORD, our
wickedness
And the iniquity of our fathers,
For we have sinned against You.
21 Do not abhor *us,* for Your name's sake;
Do not disgrace the throne of Your
glory.
Remember, do not break Your covenant
with us.
22 Are there any among the idols of the
nations that can cause rain?
Or can the heavens give showers?
Are You not He, O LORD our God?
Therefore we will wait for You,
Since You have made all these.

THE LORD WILL NOT RELENT

15 Then the LORD said to me, "*Even* if
Moses and Samuel stood before Me,
My mind *would* not *be* favorable toward this
people. Cast *them* out of My sight, and let
them go forth. 2And it shall be, if they say to
you, 'Where should we go?' then you shall tell
them, 'Thus says the LORD:

"Such as *are* for death, to death;
And such as *are* for the sword, to the
sword;
And such as *are* for the famine, to the
famine;
And such as *are* for the captivity, to the
captivity." '

3"And I will appoint over them four forms *of
destruction,*" says the LORD: "the sword to
slay, the dogs to drag, the birds of the heavens
and the beasts of the earth to devour and destroy. 4I will hand them over to trouble, to all
kingdoms of the earth, because of Manasseh
the son of Hezekiah, king of Judah, for what
he did in Jerusalem.

5 "For who will have pity on you,
O Jerusalem?
Or who will bemoan you?
Or who will turn aside to ask how you
are doing?
6 You have forsaken Me," says the LORD,
"You have gone backward.
Therefore I will stretch out My hand
against you and destroy you;
I am weary of relenting!

7 And I will winnow them with a
winnowing fan in the gates of the
land;
I will bereave *them* of children;
I will destroy My people,
Since they do not return from their
ways.
8 Their widows will be increased to Me
more than the sand of the seas;
I will bring against them,
Against the mother of the young men,
A plunderer at noonday;
I will cause anguish and terror to fall on
them suddenly.

9 "She languishes who has borne seven;
She has breathed her last;
Her sun has gone down
While *it was* yet day;
She has been ashamed and confounded.
And the remnant of them I will deliver
to the sword
Before their enemies," says the LORD.

JEREMIAH'S DEJECTION

10 Woe is me, my mother,
That you have borne me,
A man of strife and a man of contention
to the whole earth!
I have neither lent for interest,
Nor have men lent to me for interest.
Every one of them curses me.

11 The LORD said:

"Surely it will be well with your remnant;
Surely I will cause the enemy to
intercede with you
In the time of adversity and in the time
of affliction.
12 Can anyone break iron,
The northern iron and the bronze?
13 Your wealth and your treasures
I will give as plunder without price,
Because of all your sins,
Throughout your territories.
14 And I will make *you* cross over with[a]
your enemies
Into a land *which* you do not know;
For a fire is kindled in My anger,
Which shall burn upon you."

15 O LORD, You know;
Remember me and visit me,
And take vengeance for me on my
persecutors.
In Your enduring patience, do not take
me away.
Know that for Your sake I have suffered
rebuke.
16 Your words were found, and I ate them,
And Your word was to me the joy and
rejoicing of my heart;
For I am called by Your name,
O LORD God of hosts.
17 I did not sit in the assembly of the
mockers,
Nor did I rejoice;
I sat alone because of Your hand,
For You have filled me with indignation.
18 Why is my pain perpetual
And my wound incurable,
Which refuses to be healed?
Will You surely be to me like an
unreliable stream,
As waters *that* fail?

THE LORD REASSURES JEREMIAH

19 Therefore thus says the LORD:

"If you return,
Then I will bring you back;
You shall stand before Me;
If you take out the precious from the
vile,
You shall be as My mouth.
Let them return to you,
But you must not return to them.
20 And I will make you to this people a
fortified bronze wall;
And they will fight against you,
But they shall not prevail against you;
For I *am* with you to save you
And deliver you," says the LORD.
21 "I will deliver you from the hand of the
wicked,
And I will redeem you from the grip of
the terrible."

JEREMIAH'S LIFESTYLE AND MESSAGE

16 The word of the LORD also came to me,
saying, 2"You shall not take a wife, nor
shall you have sons or daughters in this
place." 3For thus says the LORD concerning the

15:14 [a]Following Masoretic Text and Vulgate; Septuagint, Syriac, and Targum read *cause you to serve* (compare 17:4).

sons and daughters who are born in this place,
and concerning their mothers who bore them
and their fathers who begot them in this land:
4“They shall die gruesome deaths; they shall
not be lamented nor shall they be buried, *but*
they shall be like refuse on the face of the
earth. They shall be consumed by the sword
and by famine, and their corpses shall be meat
for the birds of heaven and for the beasts of
the earth.”

5For thus says the LORD: “Do not enter the
house of mourning, nor go to lament or bemoan them; for I have taken away My peace
from this people,” says the LORD, “lovingkindness and mercies. 6Both the great and the
small shall die in this land. They shall not be
buried; neither shall men lament for them, cut
themselves, nor make themselves bald for
them. 7Nor shall *men* break *bread* in mourning for them, to comfort them for the dead;
nor shall *men* give them the cup of consolation to drink for their father or their mother.
8Also you shall not go into the house of feasting to sit with them, to eat and drink.”

9For thus says the LORD of hosts, the God of
Israel: “Behold, I will cause to cease from this
place, before your eyes and in your days, the
voice of mirth and the voice of gladness, the
voice of the bridegroom and the voice of the
bride.

10“And it shall be, when you show this people all these words, and they say to you, ‘Why
has the LORD pronounced all this great disaster against us? Or what *is* our iniquity? Or
what *is* our sin that we have committed
against the LORD our God?’ 11then you shall
say to them, ‘Because your fathers have forsaken Me,’ says the LORD; ‘they have walked
after other gods and have served them and
worshiped them, and have forsaken Me and
not kept My law. 12And you have done worse
than your fathers, for behold, each one follows the dictates of his own evil heart, so that
no one listens to Me. 13Therefore I will cast
you out of this land into a land that you do not
know, neither you nor your fathers; and there
you shall serve other gods day and night,
where I will not show you favor.’

GOD WILL RESTORE ISRAEL

14“Therefore behold, the days are coming,”
says the LORD, “that it shall no more be said,
‘The LORD lives who brought up the children
of Israel from the land of Egypt,’ 15but, ‘The
LORD lives who brought up the children of Israel from the land of the north and from all the
lands where He had driven them.’ For I will
bring them back into their land which I gave
to their fathers.

16“Behold, I will send for many fishermen,”
says the LORD, “and they shall fish them; and
afterward I will send for many hunters, and
they shall hunt them from every mountain
and every hill, and out of the holes of the
rocks. 17For My eyes *are* on all their ways; they
are not hidden from My face, nor is their iniquity hidden from My eyes. 18And first I will repay double for their iniquity and their sin,
because they have defiled My land; they have
filled My inheritance with the carcasses of
their detestable and abominable idols.”

19 O LORD, my strength and my fortress,
My refuge in the day of affliction,
The Gentiles shall come to You
From the ends of the earth and say,
“Surely our fathers have inherited lies,
Worthlessness and unprofitable *things*.”
20 Will a man make gods for himself,
Which *are* not gods?

21 “Therefore behold, I will this once cause
them to know,
I will cause them to know
My hand and My might;
And they shall know that My name *is*
the LORD.

JUDAH'S SIN AND PUNISHMENT

17 “The sin of Judah *is* written with a
pen of iron;
With the point of a diamond *it is*
engraved
On the tablet of their heart,
And on the horns of your altars,
2 While their children remember
Their altars and their wooden images[a]
By the green trees on the high hills.
3 O My mountain in the field,
I will give as plunder your wealth, all
your treasures,
And your high places of sin within all
your borders.
4 And you, even yourself,
Shall let go of your heritage which I gave
you;

17:2 [a]Hebrew *Asherim,* Canaanite deities

And I will cause you to serve your
enemies
In the land which you do not know;
For you have kindled a fire in My anger
which shall burn forever."

5 Thus says the LORD:

"Cursed *is* the man who trusts in man
And makes flesh his strength,
Whose heart departs from the LORD.
6 For he shall be like a shrub in the
desert,
And shall not see when good comes,
But shall inhabit the parched places in
the wilderness,
In a salt land
which is not
inhabited.

"Blessed is the man who trusts in the LORD, and whose hope is the LORD."
JEREMIAH 17:7

7 "Blessed *is* the man
who trusts in
the LORD,
And whose hope is
the LORD.
8 For he shall be like a tree planted by the
waters,
Which spreads out its roots by the river,
And will not fear[a] when heat comes;
But its leaf will be green,
And will not be anxious in the year of
drought,
Nor will cease from yielding fruit.

9 "The heart *is* deceitful above all *things*,
And desperately wicked;
Who can know it?
10 I, the LORD, search the heart,
I test the mind,
Even to give every man according to his
ways,
According to the fruit of his doings.

11 "*As* a partridge that broods but does not
hatch,
So is he who gets riches, but not by
right;
It will leave him in the midst of his days,
And at his end he will be a fool."

12 A glorious high throne from the
beginning
Is the place of our sanctuary.
13 O LORD, the hope of Israel,
All who forsake You shall be ashamed.

"Those who depart from Me
Shall be written in the
earth,
Because they have
forsaken the
LORD,
The fountain of living
waters."

Jeremiah Prays for Deliverance

14 Heal me, O LORD, and I shall be healed;
Save me, and I shall be saved,
For You *are* my praise.
15 Indeed they say to me,
"Where *is* the word of the LORD?
Let it come now!"
16 As for me, I have not hurried away from
being a shepherd *who* follows You,
Nor have I desired the woeful day;
You know what came out of my lips;
It was right there before You.
17 Do not be a terror to me;
You *are* my hope in the day of doom.
18 Let them be ashamed who persecute me,

17:8 [a]Qere and Targum read *see*.

SOUL NOTE

Heart Condition *(17:9, 10)* The masks and false fronts people wear to disguise their real feelings, intentions, or selves may fool the people around them but are useless against God. With a gaze more powerful than any X ray, the Lord peers beyond all facades, straight into the heart, the core of our being. What is there cannot be masked. All of our jealousies, deceitfulness, rage, and ugliness are on display for Him and subject to His judgment. The Lord does more than just *look* at the heart, however; He can transform hearts and renew people from the inside out. **Topic: Accountability**

But do not let me be put to shame;
Let them be dismayed,
But do not let me be dismayed.
Bring on them the day of doom,
And destroy them with double
destruction!

Hallow the Sabbath Day

[19]Thus the LORD said to me: "Go and stand
in the gate of the children of the people, by
which the kings of Judah come in and by
which they go out, and in all the gates of Jerusalem; [20]and say to them, 'Hear the word of
the LORD, you kings of Judah, and all Judah,
and all the inhabitants of Jerusalem, who enter by these gates. [21]Thus says the LORD: "Take
heed to yourselves, and bear no burden on the
Sabbath day, nor bring *it* in by the gates of Jerusalem; [22]nor carry a burden out of your
houses on the Sabbath day, nor do any work,
but hallow the Sabbath day, as I commanded
your fathers. [23]But they did not obey nor incline their ear, but made their neck stiff, that
they might not hear nor receive instruction.
[24]"And it shall be, if you heed Me carefully,"
says the LORD, "to bring no burden through
the gates of this city on the Sabbath day, but
hallow the Sabbath day, to do no work in it,
[25]then shall enter the gates of this city kings
and princes sitting on the throne of David, riding in chariots and on horses, they and their
princes, accompanied by the men of Judah
and the inhabitants of Jerusalem; and this city
shall remain forever. [26]And they shall come
from the cities of Judah and from the places
around Jerusalem, from the land of Benjamin
and from the lowland, from the mountains
and from the South, bringing burnt offerings
and sacrifices, grain offerings and incense,
bringing sacrifices of praise to the house of the
LORD.
[27]"But if you will not heed Me to hallow the
Sabbath day, such as not carrying a burden
when entering the gates of Jerusalem on the
Sabbath day, then I will kindle a fire in its
gates, and it shall devour the palaces of Jerusalem, and it shall not be quenched." ' "

The Potter and the Clay

18 The word which came to Jeremiah
from the LORD, saying: [2]"Arise and go
down to the potter's house, and there I will
cause you to hear My words." [3]Then I went
down to the potter's house, and there he was,
making something at the wheel. [4]And the vessel that he made of clay was marred in the
hand of the potter; so he made it again into
another vessel, as it seemed good to the potter
to make.
[5]Then the word of the LORD came to me,
saying: [6]"O house of Israel, can I not do with
you as this potter?" says the LORD. "Look, as
the clay *is* in the potter's hand, so *are* you in
My hand, O house of Israel! [7]The instant I
speak concerning a nation and concerning a
kingdom, to pluck up, to pull down, and to
destroy *it*, [8]if that nation against whom I have
spoken turns from its evil, I will relent of the
disaster that I thought to bring upon it. [9]And
the instant I speak concerning a nation and
concerning a kingdom, to build and to plant *it*,
[10]if it does evil in My sight so that it does not
obey My voice, then I will relent concerning
the good with which I said I would benefit it.
[11]"Now therefore, speak to the men of Judah and to the inhabitants of Jerusalem, saying, 'Thus says the LORD: "Behold, I am
fashioning a disaster and devising a plan
against you. Return now every one from his
evil way, and make your ways and your doings good." ' "

God's Warning Rejected

[12]And they said, "That is hopeless! So we
will walk according to our own plans, and we
will every one obey the dictates of his evil
heart."
[13]Therefore thus says the LORD:

"Ask now among the Gentiles,
Who has heard such things?
The virgin of Israel has done a very
horrible thing.
14 Will *a man* leave the snow water of
Lebanon,
Which comes from the rock of the
field?
Will the cold flowing waters be forsaken
for strange waters?

15 "Because My people have forgotten Me,
They have burned incense to worthless
idols.
And they have caused themselves to
stumble in their ways,
From the ancient paths,
To walk in pathways and not on a
highway,

16 To make their land desolate *and* a
perpetual hissing;
Everyone who passes by it will be
astonished
And shake his head.
17 I will scatter them as with an east wind
before the enemy;
I will show them[a] the back and not the
face
In the day of their calamity."

Jeremiah Persecuted

18 Then they said, "Come and let us devise
plans against Jeremiah; for the law shall not
perish from the priest, nor counsel from the
wise, nor the word from the prophet. Come
and let us attack him with the tongue, and let
us not give heed to any of his words."

19 Give heed to me, O LORD,
And listen to the voice of those who
contend with me!
20 Shall evil be repaid for good?
For they have dug a pit for my life.
Remember that I stood before You
To speak good for them,
To turn away Your wrath from them.
21 Therefore deliver up their children to the
famine,
And pour out their *blood*
By the force of the sword;
Let their wives *become* widows
And bereaved of their children.
Let their men be put to death,
Their young men *be* slain
By the sword in battle.
22 Let a cry be heard from their houses,
When You bring a troop suddenly upon
them;
For they have dug a pit to take me,
And hidden snares for my feet.
23 Yet, LORD, You know all their counsel
Which is against me, to slay *me*.
Provide no atonement for their iniquity,
Nor blot out their sin from Your sight;
But let them be overthrown before You.
Deal *thus* with them
In the time of Your anger.

The Sign of the Broken Flask

19 Thus says the LORD: "Go and get a
potter's earthen flask, and *take* some
of the elders of the people and some of the elders of the priests. 2 And go out to the Valley of
the Son of Hinnom, which *is* by the entry of
the Potsherd Gate; and proclaim there the
words that I will tell you, 3 and say, 'Hear the
word of the LORD, O kings of Judah and inhabitants of Jerusalem. Thus says the LORD of
hosts, the God of Israel: "Behold, I will bring
such a catastrophe on this place, that whoever
hears of it, his ears will tingle.

4 "Because they have forsaken Me and made
this an alien place, because they have burned
incense in it to other gods whom neither they,
their fathers, nor the kings of Judah have
known, and have filled this place with the
blood of the innocents 5 (they have also built
the high places of Baal, to burn their sons with
fire *for* burnt offerings to Baal, which I did not
command or speak, nor did it come into My
mind), 6 therefore behold, the days are coming," says the LORD, "that this place shall no
more be called Tophet or the Valley of the Son
of Hinnom, but the Valley of Slaughter. 7 And I
will make void the counsel of Judah and Jerusalem in this place, and I will cause them to
fall by the sword before their enemies and by
the hands of those who seek their lives; their
corpses I will give as meat for the birds of the
heaven and for the beasts of the earth. 8 I will
make this city desolate and a hissing; everyone who passes by it will be astonished and
hiss because of all its plagues. 9 And I will
cause them to eat the flesh of their sons and
the flesh of their daughters, and everyone
shall eat the flesh of his friend in the siege and
in the desperation with which their enemies
and those who seek their lives shall drive
them to despair." '

10 "Then you shall break the flask in the
sight of the men who go with you, 11 and say to
them, 'Thus says the LORD of hosts: "Even so I
will break this people and this city, as *one*
breaks a potter's vessel, which cannot be
made whole again; and they shall bury *them*
in Tophet till *there is* no place to bury. 12 Thus I
will do to this place," says the LORD, "and to
its inhabitants, and make this city like Tophet.
13 And the houses of Jerusalem and the houses
of the kings of Judah shall be defiled like the
place of Tophet, because of all the houses on
whose roofs they have burned incense to all
the host of heaven, and poured out drink offerings to other gods." ' "

18:17 [a]Following Septuagint, Syriac, Targum, and Vulgate; Masoretic Text reads *look them in*.

14Then Jeremiah came from Tophet, where the LORD had sent him to prophesy; and he stood in the court of the Lord's house and said to all the people, 15"Thus says the LORD of hosts, the God of Israel: 'Behold, I will bring on this city and on all her towns all the doom that I have pronounced against it, because they have stiffened their necks that they might not hear My words.' "

THE WORD OF GOD TO PASHHUR

20 Now Pashhur the son of Immer, the priest who *was* also chief governor in the house of the LORD, heard that Jeremiah prophesied these things. 2Then Pashhur struck Jeremiah the prophet, and put him in the stocks that *were* in the high gate of Benjamin, which *was* by the house of the LORD.

3And it happened on the next day that Pashhur brought Jeremiah out of the stocks. Then Jeremiah said to him, "The LORD has not called your name Pashhur, but Magor-Missabib.[a] 4For thus says the LORD: 'Behold, I will make you a terror to yourself and to all your friends; and they shall fall by the sword of their enemies, and your eyes shall see *it.* I will give all Judah into the hand of the king of Babylon, and he shall carry them captive to Babylon and slay them with the sword. 5Moreover I will deliver all the wealth of this city, all its produce, and all its precious things; all the treasures of the kings of Judah I will give into the hand of their enemies, who will plunder them, seize them, and carry them to Babylon. 6And you, Pashhur, and all who dwell in your house, shall go into captivity. You shall go to Babylon, and there you shall die, and be

20:3 [a]Literally *Fear on Every Side*

PERSONALITY PROFILE

Loneliness

JEREMIAH THE LONE PROPHET

(JEREMIAH 20)

Jeremiah didn't get a ticket to an easy life when God called him to be a prophet. In fact, Jeremiah complained that his life was too difficult. The more he was faithful to speak God's Word to the people of Israel, the more rejection he experienced. At one point Jeremiah was beaten and humiliated by the priest Pashhur and incarcerated in the stocks near the temple (Jer. 20:1, 2). The disappointed prophet found it hard to take comfort in God's earlier promise, "I am with you to deliver you" (Jer. 1:8).

Even though Jeremiah knew that Pashhur and his entire family would die in captivity in Babylon, the prophet cried out that God had deceived him. Jeremiah bemoaned the fact that he was mocked and derided daily because he had taken a stand for God. He felt that he was a solitary voice speaking the truth to a nation that did not want to hear it. He acknowledged, however, that God's Word was like a fire burning within him and it could not be held back (Jer. 20:9).

As we read Jeremiah's prayer journal, we see into the life of an intensely lonely man. His feelings spilled over each other as the prophet prayed. On the pages, anger, resentment, and self-loathing jostle with praise and confidence. But the fact that he continued to communicate with God meant that he knew he wasn't completely alone. The intensity of his feelings did not obliterate the deeper reality of God's presence. As overwhelming as his gripes and challenges were, he still found comfort in having Someone to whom he could gripe.

One of Jeremiah's most memorable messages from God can be found in Jeremiah 29:11. It provides an encouraging perspective about life: "For I know the thoughts that I think toward you, says the LORD, thoughts of peace and not of evil, to give you a future and a hope." When we think that we are alone facing the greatest challenges of our lives, the Spirit of God within us will continue to shape us and draw us out to live for God.

To Learn More: Turn to the article about loneliness on pages 734, 735. See also the key passage note at Isaiah 41:10 on page 923.

buried there, you and all your friends, to whom you have prophesied lies.' "

JEREMIAH'S UNPOPULAR MINISTRY

7 O LORD, You induced me, and I was
persuaded;
You are stronger than I, and have
prevailed.
I am in derision daily;
Everyone mocks me.
8 For when I spoke, I cried out;
I shouted, "Violence and plunder!"
Because the word of the LORD was made
to me
A reproach and a derision daily.
9 Then I said, "I will not make mention of
Him,
Nor speak anymore in His name."
But *His word* was in my heart like a
burning fire
Shut up in my bones;
I was weary of holding *it* back,
And I could not.
10 For I heard many mocking:
"Fear on every side!"
"Report," *they say,* "and we will report
it!"
All my acquaintances watched for my
stumbling, *saying,*
"Perhaps he can be induced;
Then we will prevail against him,
And we will take our revenge on him."

11 But the LORD *is* with me as a mighty,
awesome One.
Therefore my persecutors will stumble,
and will not prevail.
They will be greatly ashamed, for they
will not prosper.
Their everlasting confusion will never be
forgotten.
12 But, O LORD of hosts,
You who test the righteous,
And see the mind and heart,
Let me see Your vengeance on them;
For I have pleaded my cause before You.

13 Sing to the LORD! Praise the LORD!
For He has delivered the life of the poor
From the hand of evildoers.

14 Cursed *be* the day in which I was born!
Let the day not be blessed in which my
mother bore me!
15 Let the man *be* cursed
Who brought news to my father, saying,
"A male child has been born to you!"
Making him very glad.
16 And let that man be like the cities
Which the LORD overthrew, and did not
relent;
Let him hear the cry in the morning
And the shouting at noon,
17 Because he did not kill me from the
womb,
That my mother might have been my
grave,
And her womb always enlarged *with me.*
18 Why did I come forth from the womb to
see labor and sorrow,
That my days should be consumed with
shame?

JERUSALEM'S DOOM IS SEALED

21 The word which came to Jeremiah
from the LORD when King Zedekiah
sent to him Pashhur the son of Melchiah, and
Zephaniah the son of Maaseiah, the priest,
saying, 2"Please inquire of the LORD for us, for
Nebuchadnezzar[a] king of Babylon makes war
against us. Perhaps the LORD will deal with us
according to all His wonderful works, that *the*
king may go away from us."
3Then Jeremiah said to them, "Thus you
shall say to Zedekiah, 4'Thus says the LORD
God of Israel: "Behold, I will turn back the
weapons of war that *are* in your hands, with
which you fight against the king of Babylon
and the Chaldeans[a] who besiege you outside
the walls; and I will assemble them in the
midst of this city. 5I Myself will fight against
you with an outstretched hand and with a
strong arm, even in anger and fury and great
wrath. 6I will strike the inhabitants of this city,
both man and beast; they shall die of a great
pestilence. 7And afterward," says the LORD, "I
will deliver Zedekiah king of Judah, his servants and the people, and such as are left in
this city from the pestilence and the sword
and the famine, into the hand of Nebuchadnezzar king of Babylon, into the hand of their
enemies, and into the hand of those who seek
their life; and he shall strike them with the
edge of the sword. He shall not spare them, or
have pity or mercy." '

21:2 [a]Hebrew *Nebuchadrezzar,* and so elsewhere
21:4 [a]Or *Babylonians*

8“Now you shall say to this people, ‘Thus
says the LORD: “Behold, I set before you the
way of life and the way of death. 9He who remains in this city shall die by the sword, by
famine, and by pestilence; but he who goes out
and defects to the Chaldeans who besiege you,
he shall live, and his life shall be as a prize to
him. 10For I have set My face against this city
for adversity and not for good,” says the LORD.
“It shall be given into the hand of the king of
Babylon, and he shall burn it with fire.” ’

MESSAGE TO THE HOUSE OF DAVID

11“And concerning the house of the king of
Judah, *say,* ‘Hear the word of the LORD,
12O house of David! Thus says the LORD:

“Execute judgment in the morning;
And deliver *him who is* plundered
Out of the hand of the oppressor,
Lest My fury go forth like fire
And burn so that no one can quench *it,*
Because of the evil of your doings.

13 “Behold, I *am* against you, O inhabitant of the valley,
And rock of the plain,” says the LORD,
“Who say, ‘Who shall come down against us?
Or who shall enter our dwellings?’
14 But I will punish you according to the fruit of your doings,” says the LORD;
“I will kindle a fire in its forest,
And it shall devour all things around it.” ’ ”

22 Thus says the LORD: “Go down to the
house of the king of Judah, and there
speak this word, 2and say, ‘Hear the word of
the LORD, O king of Judah, you who sit on the
throne of David, you and your servants and
your people who enter these gates! 3Thus says
the LORD: “Execute judgment and righteousness, and deliver the plundered out of the
hand of the oppressor. Do no wrong and do no
violence to the stranger, the fatherless, or the
widow, nor shed innocent blood in this place.
4For if you indeed do this thing, then shall enter the gates of this house, riding on horses
and in chariots, accompanied by servants and
people, kings who sit on the throne of David.
5But if you will not hear these words, I swear
by Myself,” says the LORD, “that this house
shall become a desolation.” ’ ”

6For thus says the LORD to the house of the
king of Judah:

“You *are* Gilead to Me,
The head of Lebanon;
Yet I surely will make you a wilderness,
Cities *which* are not inhabited.
7 I will prepare destroyers against you,
Everyone with his weapons;
They shall cut down your choice cedars
And cast *them* into the fire.

8And many nations will pass by this city; and
everyone will say to his neighbor, ‘Why has
the LORD done so to this great city?’ 9Then
they will answer, ‘Because they have forsaken
the covenant of the LORD their God, and worshiped other gods and served them.’ ”

10 Weep not for the dead, nor bemoan him;
Weep bitterly for him who goes away,
For he shall return no more,
Nor see his native country.

MESSAGE TO THE SONS OF JOSIAH

11For thus says the LORD concerning Shallum[a] the son of Josiah, king of Judah, who
reigned instead of Josiah his father, who went
from this place: “He shall not return here anymore, 12but he shall die in the place where
they have led him captive, and shall see this
land no more.

13 “Woe to him who builds his house by unrighteousness
And his chambers by injustice,
Who uses his neighbor’s service without wages
And gives him nothing for his work,
14 Who says, ‘I will build myself a wide house with spacious chambers,
And cut out windows for it,
Paneling *it* with cedar
And painting *it* with vermilion.’

15 “Shall you reign because you enclose *yourself* in cedar?
Did not your father eat and drink,
And do justice and righteousness?
Then *it was* well with him.
16 He judged the cause of the poor and needy;

22:11 [a]Also called *Jehoahaz*

Then *it was* well.
Was not this knowing Me?" says the LORD.
17 "Yet your eyes and your heart *are* for nothing but your covetousness,
For shedding innocent blood,
And practicing oppression and violence."

18Therefore thus says the LORD concerning Jehoiakim the son of Josiah, king of Judah:

"They shall not lament for him,
Saying, 'Alas, my brother!' or 'Alas, my sister!'
They shall not lament for him,
Saying, 'Alas, master!' or 'Alas, his glory!'
19 He shall be buried with the burial of a donkey,
Dragged and cast out beyond the gates of Jerusalem.

20 "Go up to Lebanon, and cry out,
And lift up your voice in Bashan;
Cry from Abarim,
For all your lovers are destroyed.
21 I spoke to you in your prosperity,
But you said, 'I will not hear.'
This *has been* your manner from your youth,
That you did not obey My voice.
22 The wind shall eat up all your rulers,
And your lovers shall go into captivity;
Surely then you will be ashamed and humiliated
For all your wickedness.
23 O inhabitant of Lebanon,
Making your nest in the cedars,
How gracious will you be when pangs come upon you,
Like the pain of a woman in labor?

MESSAGE TO CONIAH

24"*As* I live," says the LORD, "though
Coniah[a] the son of Jehoiakim, king of Judah,
were the signet on My right hand, yet I would
pluck you off; 25and I will give you into the
hand of those who seek your life, and into the
hand *of those* whose face you fear—the hand
of Nebuchadnezzar king of Babylon and the
hand of the Chaldeans. 26So I will cast you
out, and your mother who bore you, into another country where you were not born; and
there you shall die. 27But to the land to which
they desire to return, there they shall not return.

28 "Is this man Coniah a despised, broken idol—
A vessel in which *is* no pleasure?
Why are they cast out, he and his descendants,
And cast into a land which they do not know?
29 O earth, earth, earth,
Hear the word of the LORD!
30 Thus says the LORD:
'Write this man down as childless,
A man *who* shall not prosper in his days;
For none of his descendants shall prosper,
Sitting on the throne of David,
And ruling anymore in Judah.' "

THE BRANCH OF RIGHTEOUSNESS

23 "Woe to the shepherds who destroy
and scatter the sheep of My pasture!"
says the LORD. 2Therefore thus says the LORD
God of Israel against the shepherds who feed
My people: "You have scattered My flock,
driven them away, and not attended to them.
Behold, I will attend to you for the evil of your
doings," says the LORD. 3"But I will gather the
remnant of My flock out of all countries where
I have driven them, and bring them back to
their folds; and they shall be fruitful and increase. 4I will set up shepherds over them who
will feed them; and they shall fear no more,
nor be dismayed, nor shall they be lacking,"
says the LORD.

5 "Behold, *the* days are coming," says the LORD,
"That I will raise to David a Branch of righteousness;
A King shall reign and prosper,
And execute judgment and righteousness in the earth.
6 In His days Judah will be saved,
And Israel will dwell safely;
Now this *is* His name by which He will be called:

THE LORD OUR RIGHTEOUSNESS.[a]

22:24 [a]Also called *Jeconiah* and *Jehoiachin*
23:6 [a]Hebrew *YHWH Tsidkenu*

[7]"Therefore, behold, *the* days are coming,"
says the LORD, "that they shall no longer say,
'As the LORD lives who brought up the children of Israel from the land of Egypt,' [8]but, 'As
the LORD lives who brought up and led the
descendants of the house of Israel from the
north country and from all the countries
where I had driven them.' And they shall
dwell in their own land."

False Prophets and Empty Oracles

9 My heart within me is broken
Because of the prophets;
All my bones shake.
I am like a drunken man,
And like a man whom wine has overcome,
Because of the LORD,
And because of His holy words.
10 For the land is full of adulterers;
For because of a curse the land mourns.
The pleasant places of the wilderness
are dried up.
Their course of life is evil,
And their might *is* not right.

11 "For both prophet and priest are profane;
Yes, in My house I have found their
wickedness," says the LORD.
12 "Therefore their way shall be to them
Like slippery *ways;*
In the darkness they shall be driven on
And fall in them;
For I will bring disaster on them,
The year of their punishment," says the
LORD.
13 "And I have seen folly in the prophets of
Samaria:
They prophesied by Baal
And caused My people Israel to err.
14 Also I have seen a horrible thing in the
prophets of Jerusalem:
They commit adultery and walk in lies;
They also strengthen the hands of
evildoers,
So that no one turns back from his
wickedness.
All of them are like Sodom to Me,
And her inhabitants like Gomorrah.

[15]"Therefore thus says the LORD of hosts
concerning the prophets:

'Behold, I will feed them with
wormwood,
And make them drink the water of gall;
For from the prophets of Jerusalem
Profaneness has gone out into all the
land.' "

[16]Thus says the LORD of hosts:

"Do not listen to the words of the
prophets who prophesy to you.
They make you worthless;
They speak a vision of their own heart,
Not from the mouth of the LORD.
17 They continually say to those who
despise Me,
'The LORD has said, "You shall have
peace" ';
And *to* everyone who walks according to
the dictates of his own heart, they
say,
'No evil shall come upon you.' "

18 For who has stood in the counsel of the
LORD,
And has perceived and heard His word?
Who has marked His word and heard *it?*
19 Behold, a whirlwind of the LORD has
gone forth in fury—
A violent whirlwind!
It will fall violently on the head of the
wicked.
20 The anger of the LORD will not turn
back
Until He has executed and performed the
thoughts of His heart.
In the latter days you will understand it
perfectly.

21 "I have not sent these prophets, yet they
ran.
I have not spoken to them, yet they
prophesied.
22 But if they had stood in My counsel,
And had caused My people to hear My
words,
Then they would have turned them from
their evil way
And from the evil of their doings.

23 "*Am* I a God near at hand," says the
LORD,
"And not a God afar off?
24 Can anyone hide himself in secret
places,
So I shall not see him?" says the LORD;

“Do I not fill heaven and earth?” says the
LORD.

25“I have heard what the prophets have said
who prophesy lies in My name, saying, ‘I have
dreamed, I have dreamed!’ 26How long will
this be in the heart of the prophets who prophesy lies? Indeed *they are* prophets of the deceit
of their own heart, 27who try to make My people forget My name by their dreams which
everyone tells his neighbor, as their fathers
forgot My name for Baal.

28 “The prophet who has a dream, let him
tell a dream;
And he who has My word, let him speak
My word faithfully.
What *is* the chaff to the wheat?” says the
LORD.
29 “*Is* not My word like a fire?” says the
LORD,
“And like a hammer *that* breaks the rock
in pieces?

30“Therefore behold, I *am* against the
prophets,” says the LORD, “who steal My
words every one from his neighbor. 31Behold, I
am against the prophets,” says the LORD,
“who use their tongues and say, ‘He says.’
32Behold, I *am* against those who prophesy
false dreams,” says the LORD, “and tell them,
and cause My people to err by their lies and by
their recklessness. Yet I did not send them or
command them; there-
fore they shall not profit
this people at all,” says
the LORD.
33“So when these
people or the prophet or
the priest ask you, say-
ing, ‘What is the oracle
of the LORD?’ you shall
then say to them, ‘What
oracle?’[a] I will even forsake you,” says the
LORD. 34“And *as for* the prophet and the priest
and the people who say, ‘The oracle of the
LORD!’ I will even punish that man and his
house. 35Thus every one of you shall say to his
neighbor, and every one to his brother, ‘What
has the LORD answered?’ and, ‘What has the
LORD spoken?’ 36And the oracle of the LORD
you shall mention no more. For every man’s
word will be his oracle, for you have perverted
the words of the living God, the LORD of hosts,
our God. 37Thus you shall say to the prophet,
‘What has the LORD answered you?’ and,
‘What has the LORD spoken?’ 38But since you
say, ‘The oracle of the LORD!’ therefore thus
says the LORD: ‘Because you say this word,
“The oracle of the LORD!” and I have sent to
you, saying, “Do not say, ‘The oracle of the
LORD!’ ” 39therefore behold, I, even I, will utterly forget you and forsake you, and the city
that I gave you and your fathers, and *will cast
you* out of My presence. 40And I will bring an
everlasting reproach upon you, and a perpetual shame, which shall not be forgotten.’ ”

The Sign of Two Baskets of Figs

24 The LORD showed me, and there were
two baskets of figs set before the temple of the LORD, after Nebuchadnezzar king of
Babylon had carried away captive Jeconiah
the son of Jehoiakim, king of Judah, and the
princes of Judah with the craftsmen and
smiths, from Jerusalem, and had brought
them to Babylon. 2One basket *had* very good
figs, like the figs *that are* first ripe; and the
other basket *had* very bad figs which could
not be eaten, they were so bad. 3Then the
LORD said to me, “What do you see, Jeremiah?”

And I said, “Figs, the good figs, very good;
and the bad, very bad, which cannot be eaten,
they are so bad.”

4Again the word of the LORD came to me,
saying, 5“Thus says the LORD, the God of Israel: ‘Like these good
figs, so will I acknowl-
edge those who are car-
ried away captive from
Judah, whom I have
sent out of this place for
their own good, into the
land of the Chaldeans.
6For I will set My eyes
on them for good, and I
will bring them back to this land; I will build
them and not pull *them* down, and I will plant
them and not pluck *them* up. 7Then I will give
them a heart to know Me, that I *am* the LORD;
and they shall be My people, and I will be
their God, for they shall return to Me with
their whole heart.

8‘And as the bad figs which cannot be eaten,

“Then I will give them a heart to know Me, that I am the LORD; and they shall be My people, and I will be their God, for they shall return to Me with their whole heart.”
JEREMIAH 24:7

23:33 [a]Septuagint, Targum, and Vulgate read *‘You are the burden.’*

they are so bad'—surely thus says the LORD—
'so will I give up Zedekiah the king of Judah,
his princes, the residue of Jerusalem who remain in this land, and those who dwell in the
land of Egypt. 9I will deliver them to trouble
into all the kingdoms of the earth, for *their*
harm, *to be* a reproach and a byword, a taunt
and a curse, in all places where I shall drive
them. 10And I will send the sword, the famine,
and the pestilence among them, till they are
consumed from the land that I gave to them
and their fathers.' "

Seventy Years of Desolation

25 The word that came to Jeremiah concerning all the people of Judah, in the
fourth year of Jehoiakim the son of Josiah,
king of Judah (which *was* the first year of
Nebuchadnezzar king of Babylon), 2which
Jeremiah the prophet spoke to all the people
of Judah and to all the inhabitants of Jerusalem, saying: 3"From the thirteenth year of Josiah the son of Amon, king of Judah, even to
this day, this *is* the twenty-third year in which
the word of the LORD has come to me; and I
have spoken to you, rising early and speaking,
but you have not listened. 4And the LORD has
sent to you all His servants the prophets, rising early and sending *them,* but you have not
listened nor inclined your ear to hear. 5They
said, 'Repent now everyone of his evil way
and his evil doings, and dwell in the land that
the LORD has given to you and your fathers
forever and ever. 6Do not go after other gods
to serve them and worship them, and do not
provoke Me to anger with the works of your
hands; and I will not harm you.' 7Yet you have
not listened to Me," says the LORD, "that you
might provoke Me to anger with the works of
your hands to your own hurt.
8"Therefore thus says the LORD of hosts:
'Because you have not heard My words, 9be-
hold, I will send and take all the families of
the north,' says the LORD, 'and Nebuchadnezzar the king of Babylon, My servant, and will
bring them against this land, against its inhabitants, and against these nations all around,
and will utterly destroy them, and make them
an astonishment, a hissing, and perpetual desolations. 10Moreover I will take from them the
voice of mirth and the voice of gladness, the
voice of the bridegroom and the voice of the
bride, the sound of the millstones and the
light of the lamp. 11And this whole land shall
be a desolation *and* an astonishment, and
these nations shall serve the king of Babylon
seventy years.
12'Then it will come to pass, when seventy
years are completed, *that* I will punish the
king of Babylon and that nation, the land of
the Chaldeans, for their iniquity,' says the
LORD; 'and I will make it a perpetual desolation. 13So I will bring on that land all My
words which I have pronounced against it, all
that is written in this book, which Jeremiah
has prophesied concerning all the nations.
14(For many nations and great kings shall be
served by them also; and I will repay them
according to their deeds and according to the
works of their own hands.)' "

Judgment on the Nations

15For thus says the LORD God of Israel to me:
"Take this wine cup of fury from My hand,
and cause all the nations, to whom I send you,
to drink it. 16And they will drink and stagger
and go mad because of the sword that I will
send among them."
17Then I took the cup from the LORD's hand,
and made all the nations drink, to whom the
LORD had sent me: 18Jerusalem and the cities
of Judah, its kings and its princes, to make
them a desolation, an astonishment, a hissing,
and a curse, as *it is* this day; 19Pharaoh king of
Egypt, his servants, his princes, and all his
people; 20all the mixed multitude, all the kings
of the land of Uz, all the kings of the land of
the Philistines (namely, Ashkelon, Gaza, Ekron, and the remnant of Ashdod); 21Edom,
Moab, and the people of Ammon; 22all the
kings of Tyre, all the kings of Sidon, and the
kings of the coastlands which *are* across the
sea; 23Dedan, Tema, Buz, and all *who are* in
the farthest corners; 24all the kings of Arabia
and all the kings of the mixed multitude who
dwell in the desert; 25all the kings of Zimri, all
the kings of Elam, and all the kings of the
Medes; 26all the kings of the north, far and
near, one with another; and all the kingdoms
of the world which *are* on the face of the
earth. Also the king of Sheshach[a] shall drink
after them.
27"Therefore you shall say to them, 'Thus
says the LORD of hosts, the God of Israel:
"Drink, be drunk, and vomit! Fall and rise no
more, because of the sword which I will send

25:26 [a]A code word for Babylon (compare 51:41)

among you." ' [28]And it shall be, if they refuse
to take the cup from your hand to drink, then
you shall say to them, 'Thus says the LORD of
hosts: "You shall certainly drink! [29]For behold,
I begin to bring calamity on the city which is
called by My name, and should you be utterly
unpunished? You shall not be unpunished, for
I will call for a sword on all the inhabitants of
the earth," says the LORD of hosts.'
[30]"Therefore prophesy against them all
these words, and say to them:

'The LORD will roar from on high,
And utter His voice from His holy
habitation;
He will roar mightily against His fold.
He will give a shout, as those who tread
the grapes,
Against all the inhabitants of the earth.
31 A noise will come to the ends of the
earth—
For the LORD has a controversy with the
nations;
He will plead His case with all flesh.
He will give those *who are* wicked to the
sword,' says the LORD."

[32]Thus says the LORD of hosts:

"Behold, disaster shall go forth
From nation to nation,
And a great whirlwind shall be raised up
From the farthest parts of the earth.

[33]"And at that day the slain of the LORD shall
be from *one* end of the earth even to the *other*
end of the earth. They shall not be lamented,
or gathered, or buried; they shall become refuse on the ground.

34 "Wail, shepherds, and cry!
Roll about *in the ashes,*
You leaders of the flock!
For the days of your slaughter and your
dispersions are fulfilled;
You shall fall like a precious vessel.
35 And the shepherds will have no way to
flee,
Nor the leaders of the flock to escape.
36 A voice of the cry of the shepherds,
And a wailing of the leaders to the flock
will be heard.
For the LORD has plundered their
pasture,
37 And the peaceful dwellings are cut down
Because of the fierce anger of the LORD.
38 He has left His lair like the lion;
For their land is desolate
Because of the fierceness of the
Oppressor,
And because of His fierce anger."

JEREMIAH SAVED FROM DEATH

26 In the beginning of the reign of Jehoiakim the son of Josiah, king of Judah,
this word came from the LORD, saying, [2]"Thus
says the LORD: 'Stand in the court of the
LORD's house, and speak to all the cities of Judah, which come to worship *in* the LORD's
house, all the words that I command you to
speak to them. Do not diminish a word. [3]Per-
haps everyone will listen and turn from his
evil way, that I may relent concerning the calamity which I purpose to bring on them because of the evil of their doings.' [4]And you
shall say to them, 'Thus says the LORD: "If you
will not listen to Me, to walk in My law which
I have set before you, [5]to heed the words of
My servants the prophets whom I sent to you,
both rising up early and sending *them* (but
you have not heeded), [6]then I will make this
house like Shiloh, and will make this city a
curse to all the nations of the earth." ' "
[7]So the priests and the prophets and all the
people heard Jeremiah speaking these words
in the house of the LORD. [8]Now it happened,
when Jeremiah had made an end of speaking
all that the LORD had commanded *him* to
speak to all the people, that the priests and the
prophets and all the people seized him, saying, "You will surely die! [9]Why have you
prophesied in the name of the LORD, saying,
'This house shall be like Shiloh, and this city
shall be desolate, without an inhabitant'?"
And all the people were gathered against Jeremiah in the house of the LORD.
[10]When the princes of Judah heard these
things, they came up from the king's house to
the house of the LORD and sat down in the
entry of the New Gate of the LORD's *house.*
[11]And the priests and the prophets spoke to
the princes and all the people, saying, "This
man deserves to die! For he has prophesied
against this city, as you have heard with your
ears."
[12]Then Jeremiah spoke to all the princes
and all the people, saying: "The LORD sent me
to prophesy against this house and against

this city with all the words that you have heard. 13Now therefore, amend your ways and your doings, and obey the voice of the LORD your God; then the LORD will relent concerning the doom that He has pronounced against you. 14As for me, here I am, in your hand; do with me as seems good and proper to you. 15But know for certain that if you put me to death, you will surely bring innocent blood on yourselves, on this city, and on its inhabitants; for truly the LORD has sent me to you to speak all these words in your hearing."

16So the princes and all the people said to the priests and the prophets, "This man does not deserve to die. For he has spoken to us in the name of the LORD our God."

17Then certain of the elders of the land rose up and spoke to all the assembly of the people, saying: 18"Micah of Moresheth prophesied in the days of Hezekiah king of Judah, and spoke to all the people of Judah, saying, 'Thus says the LORD of hosts:

"Zion shall be plowed *like* a field,
Jerusalem shall become heaps of ruins,
And the mountain of the temple[a]
Like the bare hills of the forest." '[b]

19Did Hezekiah king of Judah and all Judah ever put him to death? Did he not fear the LORD and seek the LORD's favor? And the LORD relented concerning the doom which He had pronounced against them. But we are doing great evil against ourselves."

20Now there was also a man who prophesied in the name of the LORD, Urijah the son of Shemaiah of Kirjath Jearim, who prophesied against this city and against this land according to all the words of Jeremiah. 21And when Jehoiakim the king, with all his mighty men and all the princes, heard his words, the king sought to put him to death; but when Urijah heard *it*, he was afraid and fled, and went to Egypt. 22Then Jehoiakim the king sent men to Egypt: Elnathan the son of Achbor, and *other* men *who went* with him to Egypt. 23And they brought Urijah from Egypt and brought him to Jehoiakim the king, who killed him with the sword and cast his dead body into the graves of the common people.

24Nevertheless the hand of Ahikam the son of Shaphan was with Jeremiah, so that they should not give him into the hand of the people to put him to death.

SYMBOL OF THE BONDS AND YOKES

27 In the beginning of the reign of Jehoiakim[a] the son of Josiah, king of Judah, this word came to Jeremiah from the LORD, saying,[b] 2"Thus says the LORD to me: 'Make for yourselves bonds and yokes, and put them on your neck, 3and send them to the king of Edom, the king of Moab, the king of the Ammonites, the king of Tyre, and the king of Sidon, by the hand of the messengers who come to Jerusalem to Zedekiah king of Judah. 4And command them to say to their masters, "Thus says the LORD of hosts, the God of Israel—thus you shall say to your masters: 5'I have made the earth, the man and the beast that *are* on the ground, by My great power and by My outstretched arm, and have given it to whom it seemed proper to Me. 6And now I have given all these lands into the hand of Nebuchadnezzar the king of Babylon, My servant; and the beasts of the field I have also given him to serve him. 7So all nations shall serve him and his son and his son's son, until the time of his land comes; and then many nations and great kings shall make him serve them. 8And it shall be, *that* the nation and kingdom which will not serve Nebuchadnezzar the king of Babylon, and which will not put its neck under the yoke of the king of Babylon, that nation I will punish,' says the LORD, 'with the sword, the famine, and the pestilence, until I have consumed them by his hand. 9Therefore do not listen to your prophets, your diviners, your dreamers, your soothsayers, or your sorcerers, who speak to you, saying, "You shall not serve the king of Babylon." 10For they prophesy a lie to you, to remove you far from your land; and I will drive you out, and you will perish. 11But the nations that bring their necks under the yoke of the king of Babylon and serve him, I will let them remain in their own land,' says the LORD, 'and they shall till it and dwell in it.' " ' "

12I also spoke to Zedekiah king of Judah according to all these words, saying, "Bring your necks under the yoke of the king of Babylon, and serve him and his people, and live! 13Why will you die, you and your people, by the

---

26:18 [a]Literally *house* [b]Compare Micah 3:12
27:1 [a]Following Masoretic Text, Targum, and Vulgate; some Hebrew manuscripts, Arabic, and Syriac read *Zedekiah* (compare 27:3, 12; 28:1). [b]Septuagint omits verse 1.

sword, by the famine, and by the pestilence, as the LORD has spoken against the nation that will not serve the king of Babylon? 14Therefore do not listen to the words of the prophets who speak to you, saying, 'You shall not serve the king of Babylon,' for they prophesy a lie to you; 15for I have not sent them," says the LORD, "yet they prophesy a lie in My name, that I may drive you out, and that you may perish, you and the prophets who prophesy to you."

16Also I spoke to the priests and to all this people, saying, "Thus says the LORD: 'Do not listen to the words of your prophets who prophesy to you, saying, "Behold, the vessels of the LORD's house will now shortly be brought back from Babylon"; for they prophesy a lie to you. 17Do not listen to them; serve the king of Babylon, and live! Why should this city be laid waste? 18But if they *are* prophets, and if the word of the LORD is with them, let them now make intercession to the LORD of hosts, that the vessels which are left in the house of the LORD, *in* the house of the king of Judah, and at Jerusalem, do not go to Babylon.'

19"For thus says the LORD of hosts concerning the pillars, concerning the Sea, concerning the carts, and concerning the remainder of the vessels that remain in this city, 20which Nebuchadnezzar king of Babylon did not take, when he carried away captive Jeconiah the son of Jehoiakim, king of Judah, from Jerusalem to Babylon, and all the nobles of Judah and Jerusalem— 21yes, thus says the LORD of hosts, the God of Israel, concerning the vessels that remain in the house of the LORD, and in the house of the king of Judah and of Jerusalem: 22'They shall be carried to Babylon, and there they shall be until the day that I visit them,' says the LORD. 'Then I will bring them up and restore them to this place.' "

HANANIAH'S FALSEHOOD AND DOOM

28 And it happened in the same year, at the beginning of the reign of Zedekiah king of Judah, in the fourth year *and* in the fifth month, *that* Hananiah the son of Azur the prophet, who *was* from Gibeon, spoke to me in the house of the LORD in the presence of the priests and of all the people, saying, 2"Thus speaks the LORD of hosts, the God of Israel, saying: 'I have broken the yoke of the king of Babylon. 3Within two full years I will bring back to this place all the vessels of the LORD's house, that Nebuchadnezzar king of Babylon took away from this place and carried to Babylon. 4And I will bring back to this place Jeconiah the son of Jehoiakim, king of Judah, with all the captives of Judah who went to Babylon,' says the LORD, 'for I will break the yoke of the king of Babylon.' "

5Then the prophet Jeremiah spoke to the prophet Hananiah in the presence of the priests and in the presence of all the people who stood in the house of the LORD, 6and the prophet Jeremiah said, "Amen! The LORD do so; the LORD perform your words which you have prophesied, to bring back the vessels of the LORD's house and all who were carried away captive, from Babylon to this place. 7Nevertheless hear now this word that I speak in your hearing and in the hearing of all the people: 8The prophets who have been before me and before you of old prophesied against many countries and great kingdoms—of war and disaster and pestilence. 9As for the prophet who prophesies of peace, when the word of the prophet comes to pass, the prophet will be known *as* one whom the LORD has truly sent."

10Then Hananiah the prophet took the yoke off the prophet Jeremiah's neck and broke it. 11And Hananiah spoke in the presence of all the people, saying, "Thus says the LORD: 'Even so I will break the yoke of Nebuchadnezzar king of Babylon from the neck of all nations within the space of two full years.' " And the prophet Jeremiah went his way.

12Now the word of the LORD came to Jeremiah, after Hananiah the prophet had broken the yoke from the neck of the prophet Jeremiah, saying, 13"Go and tell Hananiah, saying, 'Thus says the LORD: "You have broken the yokes of wood, but you have made in their place yokes of iron." 14For thus says the LORD of hosts, the God of Israel: "I have put a yoke of iron on the neck of all these nations, that they may serve Nebuchadnezzar king of Babylon; and they shall serve him. I have given him the beasts of the field also." ' "

15Then the prophet Jeremiah said to Hananiah the prophet, "Hear now, Hananiah, the LORD has not sent you, but you make this people trust in a lie. 16Therefore thus says the LORD: 'Behold, I will cast you from the face of the earth. This year you shall die, because you have taught rebellion against the LORD.' "

[17]So Hananiah the prophet died the same
year in the seventh month.

JEREMIAH'S LETTER TO THE CAPTIVES

29 Now these *are* the words of the letter
that Jeremiah the prophet sent from
Jerusalem to the remainder of the elders who
were carried away captive—to the priests, the
prophets, and all the people whom Nebuchadnezzar had carried away captive from Jerusalem to Babylon. [2](This happened after Jeconiah the king, the queen mother, the eunuchs,
the princes of Judah and Jerusalem, the craftsmen, and the smiths had departed from Jerusalem.) [3]*The letter was sent* by the hand of
Elasah the son of Shaphan, and Gemariah the
son of Hilkiah, whom Zedekiah king of Judah
sent to Babylon, to Nebuchadnezzar king of
Babylon, saying,

4 Thus says the LORD of hosts, the God of
Israel, to all who were carried away
captive, whom I have caused to be
carried away from Jerusalem to Babylon:

5 Build houses and dwell *in them;* plant
gardens and eat their fruit. [6]Take wives
and beget sons and daughters; and take
wives for your sons and give your
daughters to husbands, so that they may
bear sons and daughters—that you may
be increased there, and not diminished.
[7]And seek the peace of the city where I
have caused you to be carried away
captive, and pray to the LORD for it; for
in its peace you will have peace. [8]For
thus says the LORD of hosts, the God of
Israel: Do not let your prophets and your
diviners who are in your midst deceive
you, nor listen to your dreams which
you cause to be dreamed. [9]For they
prophesy falsely to you in My name; I
have not sent them, says the LORD.

10 For thus says the LORD: After seventy
years are completed at Babylon, I will
visit you and perform My good word
toward you, and cause you to return to
this place. [11]For I know the thoughts that
I think toward you, says the LORD,
thoughts of peace and not of evil, to give
you a future and a hope. [12]Then you will
call upon Me and go and pray to Me,
and I will listen to you. [13]And you will
seek Me and find *Me,* when you search
for Me with all your heart. [14]I will be
found by you, says the LORD, and I will
bring you back from your captivity; I

KEY PASSAGE

Hope

THE OTHER SIDE OF DESPAIR

(29:11-13)

The word *hopeless* has no place in a believer's vocabulary. If the Lord is present, so is hope. God's Word offers hope:

- Regardless of how dark or desperate a situation seems, hope abides (1 Cor. 13:13). This means that we should hold tightly to our hope.
- Our hope is anchored in Jesus Christ (1 Pet. 3:15, 16); thus it is able to withstand any attack.
- Nothing can separate us from the love of God (Rom. 8:38, 39) and the hope He brings. Any problem, situation, or affliction we face pales in comparison with the power of the Lord who can help us overcome it.

We must learn to look beyond our immediate circumstances, beyond the worry and despair that so easily grip us, and toward the proverbial light at the end of the tunnel. That light is the hope that God gives in His Word. That hope, that confident expectation, can carry us through.

To Learn More: Turn to the article about hope on pages 1000, 1001. See also the personality profile of the healed woman on page 1287.

HOPE

JOHN TRENT

(Jeremiah 29)

We are never without hope—no matter how we may feel. We are never beyond the reach of God's grace and the touch of His love—no matter how distant these may seem. Even when we are struggling, God brings people into our lives, in divine encounters of His grace. Then God uses us to pass this blessing on to others by tender touches, encouraging words, and expressions of value. We have been given the privilege of passing hope along to others. We pass hope to our children by telling them how much we love them and how special they are to us. We have the ability to project a positive future, giving them hope and encouragement for life's journey.

God gives hope to His children as well.

HOPE FOR THE FUTURE

Most of Jeremiah's prophecies were warnings of impending judgment, messages of doom for a nation that had turned its back on God. But Jeremiah also could see beyond the immediate crisis to a day when God would deliver the captives of Judah. He told the people that God would limit their captivity in Babylon to seventy years (Jer. 29:10). He told them God's plans for them after that: They would indeed return to Jerusalem. Despite their present distress, God assured them that He had "thoughts of peace . . . to give [them] a future and a hope" (Jer. 29:11).

Flash forward a few hundred years. Picture the scene. The Lord Jesus has been up all night. He has been shoved through dark alleys and paraded through rocky streets on His way from unjust trials to a hill of crucifixion. If anyone should have been "helpless" in that circumstance, it would have been Him. But read again the crucifixion passages and look at the incredible power and hope that is there: No one *took* Jesus' life. He voluntarily, purposefully, *laid it down*.

Instead of hating, He prayed "Father, forgive them" for the soldiers who nailed Him to the tree (Luke 23:34).

When He could have been concerned only about the terrible agony He was suffering, He looked down at His mother and took care of her well-being (John 19:25–27).

He cried out, "I thirst," not just because of His parched throat, but also in fulfillment of a well-known prophecy in the Psalms of what the suffering-servant Messiah would do (Ps. 69:21; John 19:28).

And finally, He completed His work with the words "It is finished" (John 19:30)—not "I am finished."

Where would such confidence come from on this deadly Friday? From the assurance of a hope-filled Sunday three days hence—a day when the Father had promised to raise Him from the dead.

Jesus knew that there was no avoiding the Cross, no covering it up or hanging anything less on it than a sinless offering. But that knowledge did not make Him helpless or hopeless. Rather, He so loved us and was so certain of God's power to raise Him that He could face Gethsemane and not flinch from completing His purpose.

The Lord Jesus' hope lay beyond the pain in His immediate future; it was in His place in heaven. Therefore, He could face the crown of thorns, the scorn, the horrible execution, and three days in a borrowed tomb—all because he had "a future and a hope." And because of Him, so do we.

HELP FOR TODAY

The next time something happens that makes us feel hopeless, we need to remember Jesus' response. His appearance before an unjust court was unfair. His being turned over for execution made escape impossible. His burial in a tomb left His disciples hopeless. But no matter what happens outside us, from defamation of character to an unfair death, we can carry hope inside because we are under the loving care and guidance of the God of Easter morning.

While Jesus was born fully man, He was also fully God, which is a mystery unfathomable this side of heaven, but a reflection of the untold strength He carried within Him to build up and bless others.

And just think—the God of unsurpassed strength finds and invests tremendous value in us. He saved us with His blood, sealed us with His Holy Spirit, and will stand next to us one day when we approach the Father's throne!

No one can know the full measure of God's family blessing unless they have a personal relationship with Jesus Christ. Without the blessing that comes directly from our heavenly Father to His children, even an earthly parental blessing can't quite fill our cup. Those who didn't receive the blessing of hope from their parents can get all they need from God—by becoming His children.

Contrary to popular belief, not every person created by God is a member of God's family. The blessing of God is given only to those who believe in His Son. Jesus said, "Most assuredly, I say to you, he who hears My word and believes in Him who sent Me has everlasting life, and shall not come into judgment, but has passed from death into life" (John 5:24).

In addition to His own blessing, God provides us with a spiritual family—other believers who become like brothers and sisters, fathers and mothers. He uses these people to help meet our needs and give us hope. Let Him use us today to touch someone else for God, bringing hope to an all-too-often hopeless world!

FURTHER MEDITATION:

Other passages to study about the issue of hope include:

- ➢ Psalms 27:1, 14; 42:5; 71:5; 146:5
- ➢ Isaiah 58:11
- ➢ John 16:33
- ➢ Romans 5:3–5
- ➢ Colossians 1:27
- ➢ 1 Thessalonians 1:3; 4:13–18
- ➢ Hebrews 13:5
- ➢ 1 Peter 4:12–19; 5:7
- ➢ 1 John 4:4

To Learn More: Turn to the key passage note on hope at Jeremiah 29:11–13 on page 999. See also the personality profile of the healed woman on page 1287.

will gather you from all the nations and
from all the places where I have driven
you, says the LORD, and I will bring you
to the place from which I cause you to
be carried away captive.

15 Because you have said, "The LORD has
raised up prophets for us in Babylon"—
[16]therefore thus says the LORD
concerning the king who sits on the
throne of David, concerning all the
people who dwell in this city, and
concerning your brethren who have not
gone out with you into captivity— [17]thus
says the LORD of hosts: Behold, I will
send on them the sword, the famine,
and the pestilence, and will make them
like rotten figs that cannot be eaten, they
are so bad. [18]And I will pursue them
with the sword, with famine, and with
pestilence; and I will deliver them to
trouble among all the kingdoms of the
earth—to be a curse, an astonishment, a
hissing, and a reproach among all the
nations where I have driven them,
[19]because they have not heeded My
words, says the LORD, which I sent to
them by My servants the prophets, rising
up early and sending *them;* neither
would you heed, says the LORD.
[20]Therefore hear the word of the LORD,
all you of the captivity, whom I have
sent from Jerusalem to Babylon.

21 Thus says the LORD of hosts, the God of
Israel, concerning Ahab the son of
Kolaiah, and Zedekiah the son of
Maaseiah, who prophesy a lie to you in
My name: Behold, I will deliver them
into the hand of Nebuchadnezzar king
of Babylon, and he shall slay them
before your eyes. [22]And because of them
a curse shall be taken up by all the
captivity of Judah who *are* in Babylon,
saying, "The LORD make you like
Zedekiah and Ahab, whom the king of
Babylon roasted in the fire"; [23]because
they have done disgraceful things in
Israel, have committed adultery with
their neighbors' wives, and have
spoken lying words in My name, which
I have not commanded them. Indeed I
know, and *am* a witness, says the
LORD.

24 You shall also speak to Shemaiah the
Nehelamite, saying, [25]Thus speaks the
LORD of hosts, the God of Israel, saying:
You have sent letters in your name to all
the people who *are* at Jerusalem, to
Zephaniah the son of Maaseiah the
priest, and to all the priests, saying,
[26]"The LORD has made you priest instead
of Jehoiada the priest, so that there
should be officers *in* the house of the
LORD over every man *who* is demented
and considers himself a prophet, that
you should put him in prison and in the
stocks. [27]Now therefore, why have you
not rebuked Jeremiah of Anathoth who
makes himself a prophet to you? [28]For he
has sent to us *in* Babylon, saying, 'This
captivity is long; build houses and dwell
in them, and plant gardens and eat their
fruit.' "

29 Now Zephaniah the priest read this
letter in the hearing of Jeremiah the
prophet. [30]Then the word of the LORD
came to Jeremiah, saying: [31]Send to all
those in captivity, saying, Thus says the
LORD concerning Shemaiah the
Nehelamite: Because Shemaiah has
prophesied to you, and I have not sent
him, and he has caused you to trust in a
lie— [32]therefore thus says the LORD:
Behold, I will punish Shemaiah the
Nehelamite and his family: he shall
not have anyone to dwell among this
people, nor shall he see the good that I
will do for My people, says the LORD,
because he has taught rebellion against
the LORD.

RESTORATION OF ISRAEL AND JUDAH

30 The word that came to Jeremiah from the LORD, saying, [2]"Thus speaks the LORD God of Israel, saying: 'Write in a book for yourself all the words that I have spoken to you. [3]For behold, the days are coming,' says the LORD, 'that I will bring back from captivity My people Israel and Judah,' says the LORD. 'And I will cause them to return to the land that I gave to their fathers, and they shall possess it.' "

[4]Now these *are* the words that the LORD spoke concerning Israel and Judah.

[5]"For thus says the LORD:

'We have heard a voice of trembling,
Of fear, and not of peace.
6 Ask now, and see,
Whether a man is ever in labor with child?
So why do I see every man *with* his hands on his loins
Like a woman in labor,
And all faces turned pale?
7 Alas! For that day *is* great,
So that none *is* like it;
And it *is* the time of Jacob's trouble,
But he shall be saved out of it.

8 'For it shall come to pass in that day,'
Says the LORD of hosts,
'*That* I will break his yoke from your neck,
And will burst your bonds;
Foreigners shall no more enslave them.
9 But they shall serve the LORD their God,
And David their king,
Whom I will raise up for them.

10 "Therefore do not fear, O My servant Jacob,' says the LORD,
'Nor be dismayed, O Israel;
For behold, I will save you from afar,
And your seed from the land of their captivity.
Jacob shall return, have rest and be quiet,
And no one shall make *him* afraid.
11 For I *am* with you,' says the LORD, 'to save you;
Though I make a full end of all nations where I have scattered you,
Yet I will not make a complete end of you.
But I will correct you in justice,
And will not let you go altogether unpunished.'

12 "For thus says the LORD:

'Your affliction *is* incurable,
Your wound *is* severe.
13 *There is* no one to plead your cause,
That you may be bound up;
You have no healing medicines.
14 All your lovers have forgotten you;
They do not seek you;
For I have wounded you with the wound of an enemy,
With the chastisement of a cruel one,
For the multitude of your iniquities,
Because your sins have increased.
15 Why do you cry about your affliction?
Your sorrow *is* incurable.
Because of the multitude of your iniquities,
Because your sins have increased,
I have done these things to you.

16 'Therefore all those who devour you shall be devoured;
And all your adversaries, every one of them, shall go into captivity;
Those who plunder you shall become plunder,
And all who prey upon you I will make a prey.
17 For I will restore health to you
And heal you of your wounds,' says the LORD,
'Because they called you an outcast *saying:*
"This *is* Zion;
No one seeks her." '

18 "Thus says the LORD:

'Behold, I will bring back the captivity of Jacob's tents,
And have mercy on his dwelling places;
The city shall be built upon its own mound,
And the palace shall remain according to its own plan.
19 Then out of them shall proceed thanksgiving
And the voice of those who make merry;
I will multiply them, and they shall not diminish;
I will also glorify them, and they shall not be small.
20 Their children also shall be as before,
And their congregation shall be established before Me;
And I will punish all who oppress them.
21 Their nobles shall be from among them,
And their governor shall come from their midst;
Then I will cause him to draw near,
And he shall approach Me;
For who *is* this who pledged his heart to approach Me?' says the LORD.
22 'You shall be My people,
And I will be your God.' "

23 Behold, the whirlwind of the LORD
Goes forth with fury,
A continuing whirlwind;
It will fall violently on the head of the
wicked.
24 The fierce anger of the LORD will not
return until He has done it,
And until He has performed the intents
of His heart.

In the latter days you will consider it.

THE REMNANT OF ISRAEL SAVED

31 "At the same time," says the LORD,
"I will be the God of all the families of
Israel, and they shall be My people."
2Thus says the LORD:

"The people who survived the sword
Found grace in the wilderness—
Israel, when I went to give him rest."

3 The LORD has appeared of old to me,
saying:
"Yes, I have loved you with an everlasting
love;
Therefore with lovingkindness I have
drawn you.
4 Again I will build you, and you shall be
rebuilt,
O virgin of Israel!
You shall again be adorned with your
tambourines,
And shall go forth in the dances of those
who rejoice.
5 You shall yet plant vines on the
mountains of Samaria;
The planters shall plant and eat *them* as
ordinary food.
6 For there shall be a day
When the watchmen will cry on Mount
Ephraim,
'Arise, and let us go up *to* Zion,
To the LORD our God.' "

7For thus says the LORD:

"Sing with gladness for Jacob,
And shout among the chief of the nations;
Proclaim, give praise, and say,
'O LORD, save Your people,
The remnant of Israel!'
8 Behold, I will bring them from the north
country,
And gather them from the ends of the
earth,
Among them the blind and the lame,
The woman with child
And the one who labors with child,
together;
A great throng shall return there.
9 They shall come with weeping,
And with supplications I will lead
them.
I will cause them to walk by the rivers of
waters,
In a straight way in which they shall not
stumble;
For I am a Father to Israel,
And Ephraim *is* My firstborn.

10 "Hear the word of the LORD, O nations,
And declare *it* in the isles afar off, and
say,
'He who scattered Israel will gather him,
And keep him as a shepherd *does* his
flock.'
11 For the LORD has redeemed Jacob,
And ransomed him from the hand of one
stronger than he.
12 Therefore they shall come and sing in
the height of Zion,
Streaming to the goodness of the LORD—
For wheat and new wine and oil,
For the young of the flock and the herd;
Their souls shall be like a well-watered
garden,
And they shall sorrow no more at all.

13 "Then shall the virgin rejoice in the
dance,
And the young men and the old,
together;
For I will turn their mourning to joy,
Will comfort them,
And make them rejoice rather than
sorrow.
14 I will satiate the soul of the priests with
abundance,
And My people shall be satisfied with
My goodness, says the LORD."

MERCY ON EPHRAIM

15Thus says the LORD:

"A voice was heard in Ramah,
Lamentation *and* bitter weeping,
Rachel weeping for her children,

Refusing to be comforted for her children,
Because they *are* no more."

16Thus says the LORD:

"Refrain your voice from weeping,
And your eyes from tears;
For your work shall be rewarded, says the LORD,
And they shall come back from the land of the enemy.
17 There is hope in your future, says the LORD,
That *your* children shall come back to their own border.

18 "I have surely heard Ephraim bemoaning himself:
'You have chastised me, and I was chastised,
Like an untrained bull;
Restore me, and I will return,
For You *are* the LORD my God.
19 Surely, after my turning, I repented;
And after I was instructed, I struck myself on the thigh;
I was ashamed, yes, even humiliated,
Because I bore the reproach of my youth.'
20 *Is* Ephraim My dear son?
Is he a pleasant child?
For though I spoke against him,
I earnestly remember him still;
Therefore My heart yearns for him;
I will surely have mercy on him, says the LORD.

21 "Set up signposts,
Make landmarks;
Set your heart toward the highway,
The way in *which* you went.
Turn back, O virgin of Israel,
Turn back to these your cities.
22 How long will you gad about,
O you backsliding daughter?
For the LORD has created a new thing in the earth—
A woman shall encompass a man."

FUTURE PROSPERITY OF JUDAH

23Thus says the LORD of hosts, the God of
Israel: "They shall again use this speech in the
land of Judah and in its cities, when I bring
back their captivity: 'The LORD bless you, O
home of justice, *and* mountain of holiness!'
24And there shall dwell in Judah itself, and in
all its cities together, farmers and those going
out with flocks. 25For I have satiated the weary
soul, and I have replenished every sorrowful
soul."

26After this I awoke and looked around, and
my sleep was sweet to me.

27"Behold, the days are coming, says the
LORD, that I will sow the house of Israel and
the house of Judah with the seed of man and
the seed of beast. 28And it shall come to pass,
that as I have watched over them to pluck up,
to break down, to throw down, to destroy, and
to afflict, so I will watch over them to build
and to plant, says the LORD. 29In those days
they shall say no more:

'The fathers have eaten sour grapes,
And the children's teeth are set on edge.'

30But every one shall die for his own iniquity;
every man who eats the sour grapes, his teeth
shall be set on edge.

A NEW COVENANT

31"Behold, the days are coming, says the
LORD, when I will make a new covenant with
the house of Israel and with the house of Judah— 32not according to the covenant that I
made with their fathers in the day *that* I took
them by the hand to lead them out of the land
of Egypt, My covenant which they broke,
though I was a husband to them,[a] says the
LORD. 33But this *is* the covenant that I will
make with the house of Israel after those days,
says the LORD: I will put My law in their
minds, and write it on their hearts; and I will
be their God, and they shall be My people.
34No more shall every man teach his neighbor,
and every man his brother, saying, 'Know the
LORD,' for they all shall know Me, from the
least of them to the greatest of them, says the
LORD. For I will forgive their iniquity, and their
sin I will remember no more."

35 Thus says the LORD,
Who gives the sun for a light by day,
The ordinances of the moon and the stars for a light by night,

31:32 [a]Following Masoretic Text, Targum, and Vulgate; Septuagint and Syriac read *and I turned away from them.*

Who disturbs the sea,
And its waves roar
(The LORD of hosts *is* His name):

36 "If those ordinances depart
From before Me, says the LORD,
Then the seed of Israel shall also cease
From being a nation before Me forever."

37Thus says the LORD:

"If heaven above can be measured,
And the foundations of the earth
searched out beneath,
I will also cast off all the seed of Israel
For all that they have done, says the
LORD.

38"Behold, the days are coming, says the LORD, that the city shall be built for the LORD from the Tower of Hananel to the Corner Gate. 39The surveyor's line shall again extend straight forward over the hill Gareb; then it shall turn toward Goath. 40And the whole valley of the dead bodies and of the ashes, and all the fields as far as the Brook Kidron, to the corner of the Horse Gate toward the east, *shall be* holy to the LORD. It shall not be plucked up or thrown down anymore forever."

JEREMIAH BUYS A FIELD

32 The word that came to Jeremiah from the LORD in the tenth year of Zedekiah king of Judah, which was the eighteenth year of Nebuchadnezzar. 2For then the king of Babylon's army besieged Jerusalem, and Jeremiah the prophet was shut up in the court of the prison, which *was in* the king of Judah's house. 3For Zedekiah king of Judah had shut him up, saying, "Why do you prophesy and say, 'Thus says the LORD: "Behold, I will give this city into the hand of the king of Babylon, and he shall take it; 4and Zedekiah king of Judah shall not escape from the hand of the Chaldeans, but shall surely be delivered into the hand of the king of Babylon, and shall speak with him face to face,[a] and see him eye to eye; 5then he shall lead Zedekiah to Babylon, and there he shall be until I visit him," says the LORD; "though you fight with the Chaldeans, you shall not succeed" '?"

6And Jeremiah said, "The word of the LORD came to me, saying, 7'Behold, Hanamel the son of Shallum your uncle will come to you, saying, "Buy my field which *is* in Anathoth, for the right of redemption *is* yours to buy *it.*" ' 8Then Hanamel my uncle's son came to me in the court of the prison according to the word of the LORD, and said to me, 'Please buy my field that *is* in Anathoth, which *is* in the country of Benjamin; for the right of inheritance *is* yours, and the redemption yours; buy *it* for yourself.' Then I knew that this was the word of the LORD. 9So I bought the field from Hanamel, the son of my uncle who *was* in Anathoth, and weighed *out to* him the money—seventeen shekels of silver. 10And I signed the deed and sealed *it,* took witnesses, and weighed the money on the scales. 11So I took the purchase deed, *both* that which was sealed *according* to the law and custom, and that which was open; 12and I gave the purchase deed to Baruch the son of Neriah, son of Mahseiah, in the presence of Hanamel my uncle's *son,* and in the presence of the witnesses who signed the purchase deed, before all the Jews who sat in the court of the prison.

13"Then I charged Baruch before them, saying, 14'Thus says the LORD of hosts, the God of Israel: "Take these deeds, both this purchase deed which is sealed and this deed which is open, and put them in an earthen vessel, that they may last many days." 15For thus says the LORD of hosts, the God of Israel: "Houses and fields and vineyards shall be possessed again in this land." '

JEREMIAH PRAYS FOR UNDERSTANDING

16"Now when I had delivered the purchase deed to Baruch the son of Neriah, I prayed to the LORD, saying: 17'Ah, Lord GOD! Behold, You have made the heavens and the earth by Your great power and outstretched arm. There is nothing too hard for You. 18*You* show lovingkindness to thousands, and repay the iniquity of the fathers into the bosom of their children after them—the Great, the Mighty God, whose name *is* the LORD of hosts. 19*You are* great in counsel and mighty in work, for Your eyes *are* open to all the ways of the sons of men, to give everyone according to his ways and according to the fruit of his doings. 20You have set signs and wonders in the land of Egypt, to this day, and in Israel and among *other* men; and You have made Yourself a name, as it is this day. 21You have brought

32:4 [a]Literally *mouth to mouth*

Your people Israel out of the land of Egypt with signs and wonders, with a strong hand and an outstretched arm, and with great terror; [22]You have given them this land, of which You swore to their fathers to give them—"a land flowing with milk and honey."[a] [23]And they came in and took possession of it, but they have not obeyed Your voice or walked in Your law. They have done nothing of all that You commanded them to do; therefore You have caused all this calamity to come upon them.

[24]'Look, the siege mounds! They have come to the city to take it; and the city has been given into the hand of the Chaldeans who fight against it, because of the sword and famine and pestilence. What You have spoken has happened; there You see *it!* [25]And You have said to me, O Lord GOD, "Buy the field for money, and take witnesses"!—yet the city has been given into the hand of the Chaldeans.' "

God's Assurance of the People's Return

[26]Then the word of the LORD came to Jeremiah, saying, [27]"Behold, I *am* the LORD, the God of all flesh. Is there anything too hard for Me? [28]Therefore thus says the LORD: 'Behold, I will give this city into the hand of the Chaldeans, into the hand of Nebuchadnezzar king of Babylon, and he shall take it. [29]And the Chaldeans who fight against this city shall come and set fire to this city and burn it, with the houses on whose roofs they have offered incense to Baal and poured out drink offerings to other gods, to provoke Me to anger; [30]because the children of Israel and the children of Judah have done only evil before Me from their youth. For the children of Israel have provoked Me only to anger with the work of their hands,' says the LORD. [31]'For this city has been to Me *a provocation of* My anger and My fury from the day that they built it, even to this day; so I will remove it from before My face [32]because of all the evil of the children of Israel and the children of Judah, which they have done to provoke Me to anger—they, their kings, their princes, their priests, their prophets, the men of Judah, and the inhabitants of Jerusalem. [33]And they have turned to Me the back, and not the face; though I taught them, rising up early and teaching *them,* yet they have not listened to receive instruction. [34]But they set their abominations in the house which is called by My name, to defile it. [35]And they built the high places of Baal which *are* in the Valley of the Son of Hinnom, to cause their sons and their daughters to pass through *the fire* to Molech, which I did not command them, nor did it come into My mind that they should do this abomination, to cause Judah to sin.'

> "Behold, I am the LORD, the God of all flesh. Is there anything too hard for Me?"
>
> JEREMIAH 32:27

[36]"Now therefore, thus says the LORD, the God of Israel, concerning this city of which you say, 'It shall be delivered into the hand of the king of Babylon by the sword, by the famine, and by the pestilence: [37]Behold, I will gather them out of all countries where I have driven them in My anger, in My fury, and in great wrath; I will bring them back to this place, and I will cause them to dwell safely. [38]They shall be My people, and I will be their God; [39]then I will give them one heart and one way, that they may fear Me forever, for the good of them and their children after them. [40]And I will make an everlasting covenant with them, that I will not turn away from doing them good; but I will put My fear in their hearts so that they will not depart from Me. [41]Yes, I will rejoice over them to do them good, and I will assuredly plant them in this land, with all My heart and with all My soul.'

[42]"For thus says the LORD: 'Just as I have brought all this great calamity on this people, so I will bring on them all the good that I have promised them. [43]And fields will be bought in this land of which you say, "*It is* desolate, without man or beast; it has been given into the hand of the Chaldeans." [44]Men will buy fields for money, sign deeds and seal *them,* and take witnesses, in the land of Benjamin, in the places around Jerusalem, in the cities of Judah, in the cities of the mountains, in the cities of the lowland, and in the cities of the South; for I will cause their captives to return,' says the LORD."

Excellence of the Restored Nation

33 Moreover the word of the LORD came to Jeremiah a second time, while he

---

32:22 [a]Exodus 3:8

was still shut up in the court of the prison,
saying, 2"Thus says the LORD who made it, the
LORD who formed it to establish it (the LORD *is*
His name): 3'Call to Me, and I will answer
you, and show you great and mighty things,
which you do not know.'

> "Call to Me, and I will answer you, and show you great and mighty things, which you do not know."
> JEREMIAH 33:3

4"For thus says the LORD, the God of Israel,
concerning the houses
of this city and the
houses of the kings of
Judah, which have been
pulled down *to fortify*[a]
against the siege mounds
and the sword: 5'They
come to fight with the
Chaldeans, but *only* to fill their places[a] with
the dead bodies of men whom I will slay in My
anger and My fury, all for whose wickedness I
have hidden My face from this city. 6Behold, I
will bring it health and healing; I will heal
them and reveal to them the abundance of
peace and truth. 7And I will cause the captives
of Judah and the captives of Israel to return,
and will rebuild those places as at the first. 8I
will cleanse them from all their iniquity by
which they have sinned against Me, and I will
pardon all their iniquities by which they have
sinned and by which they have transgressed
against Me. 9Then it shall be to Me a name of
joy, a praise, and an honor before all nations
of the earth, who shall hear all the good that I
do to them; they shall fear and tremble for all
the goodness and all the prosperity that I provide for it.'

10"Thus says the LORD: 'Again there shall be
heard in this place—of which you say, "It *is*
desolate, without man and without beast"—in
the cities of Judah, in the streets of Jerusalem
that are desolate, without man and without
inhabitant and without beast, 11the voice of
joy and the voice of gladness, the voice of the
bridegroom and the voice of the bride, the
voice of those who will say:

"Praise the LORD of hosts,
For the LORD *is* good,
For His mercy *endures* forever"—

and of those *who will* bring the sacrifice of
praise into the house of the LORD. For I will
cause the captives of the land to return as at
the first,' says the LORD.

12"Thus says the LORD of hosts: 'In this
place which is desolate, without man and
without beast, and in all its cities, there shall
again be a dwelling place of shepherds causing *their* flocks to lie down. 13In the cities of
the mountains, in the cities of the lowland, in
the cities of the South, in the land of Benjamin, in the places around Jerusalem, and in
the cities of Judah, the flocks shall again pass
under the hands of him
who counts *them*,' says
the LORD.

14'Behold, the days
are coming,' says the
LORD, 'that I will per-
form that good thing
which I have promised
to the house of Israel and to the house of
Judah:

15 'In those days and at that time
I will cause to grow up to David
A Branch of righteousness;
He shall execute judgment and
righteousness in the earth.
16 In those days Judah will be saved,
And Jerusalem will dwell safely.
And this *is the name* by which she will
be called:

THE LORD OUR RIGHTEOUSNESS.'[a]

17"For thus says the LORD: 'David shall
never lack a man to sit on the throne of the
house of Israel; 18nor shall the priests, the Levites, lack a man to offer burnt offerings before Me, to kindle grain offerings, and to
sacrifice continually.' "

THE PERMANENCE OF GOD'S COVENANT

19And the word of the LORD came to Jeremiah, saying, 20"Thus says the LORD: 'If you can
break My covenant with the day and My covenant with the night, so that there will not be
day and night in their season, 21then My covenant may also be broken with David My servant, so that he shall not have a son to reign
on his throne, and with the Levites, the
priests, My ministers. 22As the host of heaven
cannot be numbered, nor the sand of the sea
measured, so will I multiply the descendants
of David My servant and the Levites who minister to Me.' "

33:4 [a]Compare Isaiah 22:10 **33:5** [a]Compare 2 Kings 23:14 **33:16** [a]Compare 23:5, 6

23 Moreover the word of the LORD came to Jeremiah, saying, 24 "Have you not considered what these people have spoken, saying, 'The two families which the LORD has chosen, He has also cast them off'? Thus they have despised My people, as if they should no more be a nation before them.

25 "Thus says the LORD: 'If My covenant *is* not with day and night, *and if* I have not appointed the ordinances of heaven and earth, 26 then I will cast away the descendants of Jacob and David My servant, *so* that I will not take *any* of his descendants *to be* rulers over the descendants of Abraham, Isaac, and Jacob. For I will cause their captives to return, and will have mercy on them.' "

Zedekiah Warned by God

34 The word which came to Jeremiah from the LORD, when Nebuchadnezzar king of Babylon and all his army, all the kingdoms of the earth under his dominion, and all the people, fought against Jerusalem and all its cities, saying, 2 "Thus says the LORD, the God of Israel: 'Go and speak to Zedekiah king of Judah and tell him, "Thus says the LORD: 'Behold, I will give this city into the hand of the king of Babylon, and he shall burn it with fire. 3 And you shall not escape from his hand, but shall surely be taken and delivered into his hand; your eyes shall see the eyes of the king of Babylon, he shall speak with you face to face,[a] and you shall go to Babylon.' " ' 4 Yet hear the word of the LORD, O Zedekiah king of Judah! Thus says the LORD concerning you: 'You shall not die by the sword. 5 You shall die in peace; as in the ceremonies of your fathers, the former kings who were before you, so they shall burn incense for you and lament for you, *saying,* "Alas, lord!" For I have pronounced the word, says the LORD.' "

6 Then Jeremiah the prophet spoke all these words to Zedekiah king of Judah in Jerusalem, 7 when the king of Babylon's army fought against Jerusalem and all the cities of Judah that were left, against Lachish and Azekah; for *only* these fortified cities remained of the cities of Judah.

Treacherous Treatment of Slaves

8 *This is* the word that came to Jeremiah from the LORD, after King Zedekiah had made a covenant with all the people who *were* at Jerusalem to proclaim liberty to them: 9 that every man should set free his male and female slave—a Hebrew man or woman—that no one should keep a Jewish brother in bondage. 10 Now when all the princes and all the people, who had entered into the covenant, heard that everyone should set free his male and female slaves, that no one should keep them in bondage anymore, they obeyed and let *them* go. 11 But afterward they changed their minds and made the male and female slaves return, whom they had set free, and brought them into subjection as male and female slaves.

12 Therefore the word of the LORD came to Jeremiah from the LORD, saying, 13 "Thus says the LORD, the God of Israel: 'I made a covenant with your fathers in the day that I brought them out of the land of Egypt, out of the house of bondage, saying, 14 "At the end of seven years let every man set free his Hebrew brother, who has been sold to him; and when he has served you six years, you shall let him go free from you." But your fathers did not obey Me nor incline their ear. 15 Then you recently turned and did what was right in My sight—every man proclaiming liberty to his neighbor; and you made a covenant before Me in the house which is called by My name. 16 Then you turned around and profaned My name, and every one of you brought back his male and female slaves, whom you had set at liberty, at their pleasure, and brought them back into subjection, to be your male and female slaves.'

17 "Therefore thus says the LORD: 'You have not obeyed Me in proclaiming liberty, every one to his brother and every one to his neighbor. Behold, I proclaim liberty to you,' says the LORD—'to the sword, to pestilence, and to famine! And I will deliver you to trouble among all the kingdoms of the earth. 18 And I will give the men who have transgressed My covenant, who have not performed the words of the covenant which they made before Me, when they cut the calf in two and passed between the parts of it— 19 the princes of Judah, the princes of Jerusalem, the eunuchs, the priests, and all the people of the land who passed between the parts of the calf— 20 I will give them into the hand of their enemies and into the hand of those who seek their life. Their dead bodies shall be for meat for the birds of the heaven and the beasts of the

34:3 [a]Literally *mouth to mouth*

earth. 21And I will give Zedekiah king of Judah and his princes into the hand of their enemies, into the hand of those who seek their life, and into the hand of the king of Babylon's army which has gone back from you. 22Behold, I will command,' says the LORD, 'and cause them to return to this city. They will fight against it and take it and burn it with fire; and I will make the cities of Judah a desolation without inhabitant.' "

THE OBEDIENT RECHABITES

35 The word which came to Jeremiah from the LORD in the days of Jehoiakim the son of Josiah, king of Judah, saying, 2"Go to the house of the Rechabites, speak to them, and bring them into the house of the LORD, into one of the chambers, and give them wine to drink."

3Then I took Jaazaniah the son of Jeremiah, the son of Habazziniah, his brothers and all his sons, and the whole house of the Rechabites, 4and I brought them into the house of the LORD, into the chamber of the sons of Hanan the son of Igdaliah, a man of God, which *was* by the chamber of the princes, above the chamber of Maaseiah the son of Shallum, the keeper of the door. 5Then I set before the sons of the house of the Rechabites bowls full of wine, and cups; and I said to them, "Drink wine."

6But they said, "We will drink no wine, for Jonadab the son of Rechab, our father, commanded us, saying, 'You shall drink no wine, you nor your sons, forever. 7You shall not build a house, sow seed, plant a vineyard, nor have *any of these;* but all your days you shall dwell in tents, that you may live many days in the land where you are sojourners.' 8Thus we have obeyed the voice of Jonadab the son of Rechab, our father, in all that he charged us, to drink no wine all our days, we, our wives, our sons, or our daughters, 9nor to build ourselves houses to dwell in; nor do we have vineyard, field, or seed. 10But we have dwelt in tents, and have obeyed and done according to all that Jonadab our father commanded us. 11But it came to pass, when Nebuchadnezzar king of Babylon came up into the land, that we said, 'Come, let us go to Jerusalem for fear of the army of the Chaldeans and for fear of the army of the Syrians.' So we dwell at Jerusalem."

12Then came the word of the LORD to Jeremiah, saying, 13"Thus says the LORD of hosts, the God of Israel: 'Go and tell the men of Judah and the inhabitants of Jerusalem, "Will you not receive instruction to obey My words?" says the LORD. 14"The words of Jonadab the son of Rechab, which he commanded his sons, not to drink wine, are performed; for to this day they drink none, and obey their father's commandment. But although I have spoken to you, rising early and speaking, you did not obey Me. 15I have also sent to you all My servants the prophets, rising up early and sending *them,* saying, 'Turn now everyone from his evil way, amend your doings, and do not go after other gods to serve them; then you will dwell in the land which I have given you and your fathers.' But you have not inclined your ear, nor obeyed Me. 16Surely the sons of Jonadab the son of Rechab have performed the commandment of their father, which he commanded them, but this people has not obeyed Me." '

17"Therefore thus says the LORD God of hosts, the God of Israel: 'Behold, I will bring on Judah and on all the inhabitants of Jerusalem all the doom that I have pronounced against them; because I have spoken to them but they have not heard, and I have called to them but they have not answered.' "

18And Jeremiah said to the house of the Rechabites, "Thus says the LORD of hosts, the God of Israel: 'Because you have obeyed the commandment of Jonadab your father, and kept all his precepts and done according to all that he commanded you, 19therefore thus says the LORD of hosts, the God of Israel: "Jonadab the son of Rechab shall not lack a man to stand before Me forever." ' "

THE SCROLL READ IN THE TEMPLE

36 Now it came to pass in the fourth year of Jehoiakim the son of Josiah, king of Judah, *that* this word came to Jeremiah from the LORD, saying: 2"Take a scroll of a book and write on it all the words that I have spoken to you against Israel, against Judah, and against all the nations, from the day I spoke to you, from the days of Josiah even to this day. 3It may be that the house of Judah will hear all the adversities which I purpose to bring upon them, that everyone may turn from his evil way, that I may forgive their iniquity and their sin."

4Then Jeremiah called Baruch the son of

Neriah; and Baruch wrote on a scroll of a book, at the instruction of Jeremiah,[a] all the words of the LORD which He had spoken to him. 5And Jeremiah commanded Baruch, saying, "I *am* confined, I cannot go into the house of the LORD. 6You go, therefore, and read from the scroll which you have written at my instruction,[a] the words of the LORD, in the hearing of the people in the LORD's house on the day of fasting. And you shall also read them in the hearing of all Judah who come from their cities. 7It may be that they will present their supplication before the LORD, and everyone will turn from his evil way. For great *is* the anger and the fury that the LORD has pronounced against this people." 8And Baruch the son of Neriah did according to all that Jeremiah the prophet commanded him, reading from the book the words of the LORD in the LORD's house.

9Now it came to pass in the fifth year of Jehoiakim the son of Josiah, king of Judah, in the ninth month, *that* they proclaimed a fast before the LORD to all the people in Jerusalem, and to all the people who came from the cities of Judah to Jerusalem. 10Then Baruch read from the book the words of Jeremiah in the house of the LORD, in the chamber of Gemariah the son of Shaphan the scribe, in the upper court at the entry of the New Gate of the LORD's house, in the hearing of all the people.

The Scroll Read in the Palace

11When Michaiah the son of Gemariah, the son of Shaphan, heard all the words of the LORD from the book, 12he then went down to the king's house, into the scribe's chamber; and there all the princes were sitting—Elishama the scribe, Delaiah the son of Shemaiah, Elnathan the son of Achbor, Gemariah the son of Shaphan, Zedekiah the son of Hananiah, and all the princes. 13Then Michaiah declared to them all the words that he had heard when Baruch read the book in the hearing of the people. 14Therefore all the princes sent Jehudi the son of Nethaniah, the son of Shelemiah, the son of Cushi, to Baruch, saying, "Take in your hand the scroll from which you have read in the hearing of the people, and come." So Baruch the son of Neriah took the scroll in his hand and came to them. 15And they said to him, "Sit down now, and read it in our hearing." So Baruch read *it* in their hearing.

16Now it happened, when they had heard all the words, that they looked in fear from one to another, and said to Baruch, "We will surely tell the king of all these words." 17And they asked Baruch, saying, "Tell us now, how did you write all these words—at his instruction?"[a]

18So Baruch answered them, "He proclaimed with his mouth all these words to me, and I wrote *them* with ink in the book."

19Then the princes said to Baruch, "Go and hide, you and Jeremiah; and let no one know where you are."

The King Destroys Jeremiah's Scroll

20And they went to the king, into the court; but they stored the scroll in the chamber of Elishama the scribe, and told all the words in the hearing of the king. 21So the king sent Jehudi to bring the scroll, and he took it from Elishama the scribe's chamber. And Jehudi read it in the hearing of the king and in the hearing of all the princes who stood beside the king. 22Now the king was sitting in the winter house in the ninth month, with *a fire* burning on the hearth before him. 23And it happened, when Jehudi had read three or four columns, *that the king* cut it with the scribe's knife and cast *it* into the fire that *was* on the hearth, until all the scroll was consumed in the fire that *was* on the hearth. 24Yet they were not afraid, nor did they tear their garments, the king nor any of his servants who heard all these words. 25Nevertheless Elnathan, Delaiah, and Gemariah implored the king not to burn the scroll; but he would not listen to them. 26And the king commanded Jerahmeel the king's[a] son, Seraiah the son of Azriel, and Shelemiah the son of Abdeel, to seize Baruch the scribe and Jeremiah the prophet, but the LORD hid them.

Jeremiah Rewrites the Scroll

27Now after the king had burned the scroll with the words which Baruch had written at the instruction of Jeremiah,[a] the word of the LORD came to Jeremiah, saying: 28"Take yet another scroll, and write on it all the former words that were in the first scroll which Jehoiakim the king of Judah has burned. 29And you shall say to Jehoiakim king of Judah, 'Thus

36:4 [a]Literally *from Jeremiah's mouth*
36:6 [a]Literally *from my mouth* **36:17** [a]Literally *with his mouth* **36:26** [a]Hebrew *Hammelech*
36:27 [a]Literally *from Jeremiah's mouth*

says the LORD: "You have burned this scroll,
saying, 'Why have you written in it that the
king of Babylon will certainly come and destroy this land, and cause man and beast to
cease from here?' " [30]Therefore thus says the
LORD concerning Jehoiakim king of Judah:
"He shall have no one to sit on the throne of
David, and his dead body shall be cast out to
the heat of the day and the frost of the night.
[31]I will punish him, his family, and his servants for their iniquity; and I will bring on
them, on the inhabitants of Jerusalem, and on
the men of Judah all the doom that I have pronounced against them; but they did not
heed." ' "

[32]Then Jeremiah took another scroll and
gave it to Baruch the scribe, the son of Neriah,
who wrote on it at the instruction of Jeremiah[a] all the words of the book which Jehoiakim king of Judah had burned in the fire. And
besides, there were added to them many similar words.

ZEDEKIAH'S VAIN HOPE

37 Now King Zedekiah the son of Josiah
reigned instead of Coniah the son of
Jehoiakim, whom Nebuchadnezzar king of
Babylon made king in the land of Judah. [2]But
neither he nor his servants nor the people of
the land gave heed to the words of the LORD
which He spoke by the prophet Jeremiah.

[3]And Zedekiah the king sent Jehucal the
son of Shelemiah, and Zephaniah the son of
Maaseiah, the priest, to the prophet Jeremiah,
saying, "Pray now to the LORD our God for
us." [4]Now Jeremiah was coming and going
among the people, for they had not *yet* put
him in prison. [5]Then Pharaoh's army came up
from Egypt; and when the Chaldeans who
were besieging Jerusalem heard news of
them, they departed from Jerusalem.

[6]Then the word of the LORD came to the
prophet Jeremiah, saying, [7]"Thus says the
LORD, the God of Israel, 'Thus you shall say to
the king of Judah, who sent you to Me to inquire of Me: "Behold, Pharaoh's army which
has come up to help you will return to Egypt,
to their own land. [8]And the Chaldeans shall
come back and fight against this city, and take
it and burn it with fire." ' [9]Thus says the LORD:
'Do not deceive yourselves, saying, "The
Chaldeans will surely depart from us," for
they will not depart. [10]For though you had defeated the whole army of the Chaldeans who
fight against you, and there remained *only*
wounded men among them, they would rise
up, every man in his tent, and burn the city
with fire.' "

JEREMIAH IMPRISONED

[11]And it happened, when the army of the
Chaldeans left *the siege* of Jerusalem for fear
of Pharaoh's army, [12]that Jeremiah went out
of Jerusalem to go into the land of Benjamin
to claim his property there among the people.
[13]And when he was in the Gate of Benjamin, a
captain of the guard *was* there whose name
was Irijah the son of Shelemiah, the son of
Hananiah; and he seized Jeremiah the prophet, saying, "You are defecting to the Chaldeans!"

[14]Then Jeremiah said, "False! I am not defecting to the Chaldeans." But he did not listen to him.

So Irijah seized Jeremiah and brought him
to the princes. [15]Therefore the princes were
angry with Jeremiah, and they struck him and
put him in prison in the house of Jonathan the
scribe. For they had made that the prison.

[16]When Jeremiah entered the dungeon and
the cells, and Jeremiah had remained there
many days, [17]then Zedekiah the king sent and

36:32 [a]Literally *from Jeremiah's mouth*

SOUL NOTE

Wherever and Whatever *(37:15)* Jeremiah teaches that circumstances are irrelevant where the Lord's work is concerned. After being thrown into prison, Jeremiah continued to minister (37:16, 17), to fulfill God's role for him. Our responsibilities as the Lord's followers do not change with our circumstances. God does not call us to serve Him only when the conditions are right. The apostle Paul said, "I know how to be abased, and I know how to abound," but he concluded, "I can do all things through Christ who strengthens me" (Phil. 4:13). **Topic: Trials**

took him *out*. The king asked him secretly in his house, and said, "Is there *any* word from the LORD?"

And Jeremiah said, "There is." Then he said, "You shall be delivered into the hand of the king of Babylon!"

[18]Moreover Jeremiah said to King Zedekiah, "What offense have I committed against you, against your servants, or against this people, that you have put me in prison? [19]Where now *are* your prophets who prophesied to you, saying, 'The king of Babylon will not come against you or against this land?' [20]Therefore please hear now, O my lord the king. Please, let my petition be accepted before you, and do not make me return to the house of Jonathan the scribe, lest I die there."

[21]Then Zedekiah the king commanded that they should commit Jeremiah to the court of the prison, and that they should give him daily a piece of bread from the bakers' street, until all the bread in the city was gone. Thus Jeremiah remained in the court of the prison.

Jeremiah in the Dungeon

38 Now Shephatiah the son of Mattan, Gedaliah the son of Pashhur, Jucal[a] the son of Shelemiah, and Pashhur the son of Malchiah heard the words that Jeremiah had spoken to all the people, saying, [2]"Thus says the LORD: 'He who remains in this city shall die by the sword, by famine, and by pestilence; but he who goes over to the Chaldeans shall live; his life shall be as a prize to him, and he shall live.'[a] [3]Thus says the LORD: 'This city shall surely be given into the hand of the king of Babylon's army, which shall take it.' "

[4]Therefore the princes said to the king, "Please, let this man be put to death, for thus he weakens the hands of the men of war who remain in this city, and the hands of all the people, by speaking such words to them. For this man does not seek the welfare of this people, but their harm."

[5]Then Zedekiah the king said, "Look, he *is* in your hand. For the king can *do* nothing against you." [6]So they took Jeremiah and cast him into the dungeon of Malchiah the king's[a] son, which *was* in the court of the prison, and they let Jeremiah down with ropes. And in the dungeon *there was* no water, but mire. So Jeremiah sank in the mire.

[7]Now Ebed-Melech the Ethiopian, one of the eunuchs, who was in the king's house, heard that they had put Jeremiah in the dungeon. When the king was sitting at the Gate of Benjamin, [8]Ebed-Melech went out of the king's house and spoke to the king, saying: [9]"My lord the king, these men have done evil in all that they have done to Jeremiah the prophet, whom they have cast into the dungeon, and he is likely to die from hunger in the place where he is. For *there is* no more bread in the city." [10]Then the king commanded Ebed-Melech the Ethiopian, saying, "Take from here thirty men with you, and lift Jeremiah the prophet out of the dungeon before he dies." [11]So Ebed-Melech took the men with him and went into the house of the king under the treasury, and took from there old clothes and old rags, and let them down by ropes into the dungeon to Jeremiah. [12]Then Ebed-Melech the Ethiopian said to Jeremiah, "Please put these old clothes and rags under your armpits, under the ropes." And Jeremiah did so. [13]So they pulled Jeremiah up with ropes and lifted him out of the dungeon. And Jeremiah remained in the court of the prison.

Zedekiah's Fears and Jeremiah's Advice

[14]Then Zedekiah the king sent and had Jeremiah the prophet brought to him at the third entrance of the house of the LORD. And the king said to Jeremiah, "I will ask you something. Hide nothing from me."

[15]Jeremiah said to Zedekiah, "If I declare *it* to you, will you not surely put me to death? And if I give you advice, you will not listen to me."

[16]So Zedekiah the king swore secretly to Jeremiah, saying, "*As* the LORD lives, who made our very souls, I will not put you to death, nor will I give you into the hand of these men who seek your life."

[17]Then Jeremiah said to Zedekiah, "Thus says the LORD, the God of hosts, the God of Israel: 'If you surely surrender to the king of Babylon's princes, then your soul shall live; this city shall not be burned with fire, and you and your house shall live. [18]But if you do not surrender to the king of Babylon's princes, then this city shall be given into the hand of the Chaldeans; they shall burn it with fire, and you shall not escape from their hand.' "

[19]And Zedekiah the king said to Jeremiah,

38:1 [a]Same as *Jehucal* (compare 37:3)
38:2 [a]Compare 21:9 **38:6** [a]Hebrew *Hammelech*

"I am afraid of the Jews who have defected to
the Chaldeans, lest they deliver me into their
hand, and they abuse me."
20 But Jeremiah said, "They shall not deliver
you. Please, obey the voice of the LORD which
I speak to you. So it shall be well with you,
and your soul shall live. 21 But if you refuse to
surrender, this *is* the word that the LORD has
shown me: 22 'Now behold, all the women
who are left in the king of Judah's house *shall
be* surrendered to the king of Babylon's
princes, and those *women* shall say:

"Your close friends have set upon you
And prevailed against you;
Your feet have sunk in the mire,
And they have turned away again."

23 'So they shall surrender all your wives and
children to the Chaldeans. You shall not escape from their hand, but shall be taken by
the hand of the king of Babylon. And you shall
cause this city to be burned with fire.' "
24 Then Zedekiah said to Jeremiah, "Let no
one know of these words, and you shall not
die. 25 But if the princes hear that I have talked
with you, and they come to you and say to
you, 'Declare to us now what you have said to
the king, and also what the king said to you;
do not hide *it* from us, and we will not put you
to death,' 26 then you shall say to them, 'I presented my request before the king, that he
would not make me return to Jonathan's
house to die there.' "
27 Then all the princes came to Jeremiah and
asked him. And he told them according to all
these words that the king had commanded. So
they stopped speaking with him, for the conversation had not been heard. 28 Now Jeremiah
remained in the court of the prison until the
day that Jerusalem was taken. And he was
there when Jerusalem was taken.

The Fall of Jerusalem

39 In the ninth year of Zedekiah king of
Judah, in the tenth month, Nebuchadnezzar king of Babylon and all his army came
against Jerusalem, and besieged it. 2 In the
eleventh year of Zedekiah, in the fourth
month, on the ninth *day* of the month, the city
was penetrated.
3 Then all the princes of the king of Babylon
came in and sat in the Middle Gate: Nergal-
Sharezer, Samgar-Nebo, Sarsechim, Rabsaris,[a]
Nergal-Sarezer, Rabmag,[b] with the rest of the
princes of the king of Babylon.
4 So it was, when Zedekiah the king of Judah
and all the men of war saw them, that they
fled and went out of the city by night, by way
of the king's garden, by the gate between the
two walls. And he went out by way of the
plain.[a] 5 But the Chaldean army pursued them
and overtook Zedekiah in the plains of Jericho. And when they had captured him, they
brought him up to Nebuchadnezzar king of
Babylon, to Riblah in the land of Hamath,
where he pronounced judgment on him.
6 Then the king of Babylon killed the sons of
Zedekiah before his eyes in Riblah; the king of
Babylon also killed all the nobles of Judah.
7 Moreover he put out Zedekiah's eyes, and
bound him with bronze fetters to carry him off
to Babylon. 8 And the Chaldeans burned the
king's house and the houses of the people
with fire, and broke down the walls of Jerusalem. 9 Then Nebuzaradan the captain of the
guard carried away captive to Babylon the
remnant of the people who remained in the
city and those who defected to him, with the
rest of the people who remained. 10 But Nebuzaradan the captain of the guard left in the
land of Judah the poor people, who had nothing, and gave them vineyards and fields at the
same time.

Jeremiah Goes Free

11 Now Nebuchadnezzar king of Babylon
gave charge concerning Jeremiah to Nebuzaradan the captain of the guard, saying, 12 "Take
him and look after him, and do him no harm;
but do to him just as he says to you." 13 So Nebuzaradan the captain of the guard sent Nebushas-
ban, Rabsaris, Nergal-Sharezer, Rabmag, and all
the king of Babylon's chief officers; 14 then
they sent *someone* to take Jeremiah from the
court of the prison, and committed him to
Gedaliah the son of Ahikam, the son of Shaphan, that he should take him home. So he
dwelt among the people.
15 Meanwhile the word of the LORD had
come to Jeremiah while he was shut up in the
court of the prison, saying, 16 "Go and speak to
Ebed-Melech the Ethiopian, saying, 'Thus

39:3 [a]A title, probably *Chief Officer;* also verse 13 [b]A title, probably *Troop Commander;* also verse 13 **39:4** [a]Or *the Arabah,* that is, the Jordan Valley

says the LORD of hosts, the God of Israel: "Behold, I will bring My words upon this city for adversity and not for good, and they shall be *performed* in that day before you. 17But I will deliver you in that day," says the LORD, "and you shall not be given into the hand of the men of whom you *are* afraid. 18For I will surely deliver you, and you shall not fall by the sword; but your life shall be as a prize to you, because you have put your trust in Me," says the LORD.' "

JEREMIAH WITH GEDALIAH THE GOVERNOR

40 The word that came to Jeremiah from the LORD after Nebuzaradan the captain of the guard had let him go from Ramah, when he had taken him bound in chains among all who were carried away captive from Jerusalem and Judah, who were carried away captive to Babylon.

2And the captain of the guard took Jeremiah and said to him: "The LORD your God has pronounced this doom on this place. 3Now the LORD has brought *it*, and has done just as He said. Because you *people* have sinned against the LORD, and not obeyed His voice, therefore this thing has come upon you. 4And now look, I free you this day from the chains that *were* on your hand. If it seems good to you to come with me to Babylon, come, and I will look after you. But if it seems wrong for you to come with me to Babylon, remain here. See, all the land *is* before you; wherever it seems good and convenient for you to go, go there."

5Now while Jeremiah had not yet gone back, *Nebuzaradan said,* "Go back to Gedaliah the son of Ahikam, the son of Shaphan, whom the king of Babylon has made governor over the cities of Judah, and dwell with him among the people. Or go wherever it seems convenient for you to go." So the captain of the guard gave him rations and a gift and let him go. 6Then Jeremiah went to Gedaliah the son of Ahikam, to Mizpah, and dwelt with him among the people who were left in the land.

7And when all the captains of the armies who *were* in the fields, they and their men, heard that the king of Babylon had made Gedaliah the son of Ahikam governor in the land, and had committed to him men, women, children, and the poorest of the land who had not been carried away captive to Babylon, 8then they came to Gedaliah at Mizpah—Ishmael the son of Nethaniah, Johanan and Jonathan the sons of Kareah, Seraiah the son of Tanhumeth, the sons of Ephai the Netophathite, and Jezaniah[a] the son of a Maachathite, they and their men. 9And Gedaliah the son of Ahikam, the son of Shaphan, took an oath before them and their men, saying, "Do not be afraid to serve the Chaldeans. Dwell in the land and serve the king of Babylon, and it shall be well with you. 10As for me, I will indeed dwell at Mizpah and serve the Chaldeans who come to us. But you, gather wine and summer fruit and oil, put *them* in your vessels, and dwell in your cities that you have taken." 11Likewise, when all the Jews who *were* in Moab, among the Ammonites, in Edom, and who *were* in all the countries, heard that the king of Babylon had left a remnant of Judah, and that he had set over them Gedaliah the son of Ahikam, the son of Shaphan, 12then all the Jews returned out of all places where they had been driven, and came to the land of Judah, to Gedaliah at Mizpah, and gathered wine and summer fruit in abundance.

13Moreover Johanan the son of Kareah and all the captains of the forces that *were* in the fields came to Gedaliah at Mizpah, 14and said to him, "Do you certainly know that Baalis the king of the Ammonites has sent Ishmael the son of Nethaniah to murder you?" But Gedaliah the son of Ahikam did not believe them.

15Then Johanan the son of Kareah spoke secretly to Gedaliah in Mizpah, saying, "Let me go, please, and I will kill Ishmael the son of Nethaniah, and no one will know *it*. Why should he murder you, so that all the Jews who are gathered to you would be scattered, and the remnant in Judah perish?"

16But Gedaliah the son of Ahikam said to Johanan the son of Kareah, "You shall not do this thing, for you speak falsely concerning Ishmael."

INSURRECTION AGAINST GEDALIAH

41 Now it came to pass in the seventh month *that* Ishmael the son of Nethaniah, the son of Elishama, of the royal family and of the officers of the king, came with ten men to Gedaliah the son of Ahikam, at Mizpah. And there they ate bread together in Mizpah. 2Then Ishmael the son of Nethaniah, and the ten men who were with him, arose and

40:8 [a]Spelled *Jaazaniah* in 2 Kings 25:23

struck Gedaliah the son of Ahikam, the son of
Shaphan, with the sword, and killed him
whom the king of Babylon had made governor
over the land. 3Ishmael also struck down all
the Jews who were with him, *that is,* with
Gedaliah at Mizpah, and the Chaldeans who
were found there, the men of war.

4And it happened, on the second day after
he had killed Gedaliah, when as yet no one
knew *it,* 5that certain men came from Shechem, from Shiloh, and from Samaria, eighty
men with their beards shaved and their
clothes torn, having cut themselves, with offerings and incense in their hand, to bring
them to the house of the LORD. 6Now Ishmael
the son of Nethaniah went out from Mizpah to
meet them, weeping as he went along; and it
happened as he met them that he said to
them, "Come to Gedaliah the son of Ahikam!"
7So it was, when they came into the midst of
the city, that Ishmael the son of Nethaniah
killed them *and cast them* into the midst of a
pit, he and the men who were with him. 8But
ten men were found among them who said to
Ishmael, "Do not kill us, for we have treasures
of wheat, barley, oil, and honey in the field."
So he desisted and did not kill them among
their brethren. 9Now the pit into which Ishmael had cast all the dead bodies of the men
whom he had slain, because of Gedaliah, *was*
the same one Asa the king had made for fear
of Baasha king of Israel. Ishmael the son of
Nethaniah filled it with *the* slain. 10Then Ishmael carried away captive all the rest of the
people who *were* in Mizpah, the king's daughters and all the people who remained in Mizpah, whom Nebuzaradan the captain of the
guard had committed to Gedaliah the son of
Ahikam. And Ishmael the son of Nethaniah
carried them away captive and departed to go
over to the Ammonites.

11But when Johanan the son of Kareah and
all the captains of the forces that *were* with
him heard of all the evil that Ishmael the son
of Nethaniah had done, 12they took all the
men and went to fight with Ishmael the son of
Nethaniah; and they found him by the great
pool that *is* in Gibeon. 13So it was, when all
the people who *were* with Ishmael saw Johanan the son of Kareah, and all the captains of
the forces who *were* with him, that they were
glad. 14Then all the people whom Ishmael had
carried away captive from Mizpah turned
around and came back, and went to Johanan
the son of Kareah. 15But Ishmael the son of
Nethaniah escaped from Johanan with eight
men and went to the Ammonites.

16Then Johanan the son of Kareah, and all
the captains of the forces that were with him,
took from Mizpah all the rest of the people
whom he had recovered from Ishmael the son
of Nethaniah after he had murdered Gedaliah
the son of Ahikam—the mighty men of war
and the women and the children and the eunuchs, whom he had brought back from Gibeon. 17And they departed and dwelt in the
habitation of Chimham, which is near Bethlehem, as they went on their way to Egypt, 18be-
cause of the Chaldeans; for they were afraid of
them, because Ishmael the son of Nethaniah
had murdered Gedaliah the son of Ahikam,
whom the king of Babylon had made governor
in the land.

THE FLIGHT TO EGYPT FORBIDDEN

42 Now all the captains of the forces, Johanan the son of Kareah, Jezaniah the
son of Hoshaiah, and all the people, from the
least to the greatest, came near 2and said to
Jeremiah the prophet, "Please, let our petition
be acceptable to you, and pray for us to the
LORD your God, for all this remnant (since we
are left *but* a few of many, as you can see),
3that the LORD your God may show us the way
in which we should walk and the thing we
should do."

4Then Jeremiah the prophet said to them, "I
have heard. Indeed, I will pray to the LORD
your God according to your words, and it shall
be, *that* whatever the LORD answers you, I will
declare *it* to you. I will keep nothing back
from you."

5So they said to Jeremiah, "Let the LORD be
a true and faithful witness between us, if we
do not do according to everything which the
LORD your God sends us by you. 6Whether *it is*
pleasing or displeasing, we will obey the voice
of the LORD our God to whom we send you,
that it may be well with us when we obey the
voice of the LORD our God."

7And it happened after ten days that the
word of the LORD came to Jeremiah. 8Then he
called Johanan the son of Kareah, all the captains of the forces which *were* with him, and
all the people from the least even to the greatest, 9and said to them, "Thus says the LORD,
the God of Israel, to whom you sent me to present your petition before Him: 10'If you will

still remain in this land, then I will build you
and not pull *you* down, and I will plant you
and not pluck *you* up. For I relent concerning
the disaster that I have brought upon you.
11Do not be afraid of the king of Babylon, of
whom you are afraid; do not be afraid of him,'
says the LORD, 'for I *am* with you, to save you
and deliver you from his hand. 12And I will
show you mercy, that he may have mercy on
you and cause you to return to your own land.'
13"But if you say, 'We will not dwell in this
land,' disobeying the voice of the LORD your
God, 14saying, 'No, but we will go to the land
of Egypt where we shall see no war, nor hear
the sound of the trumpet, nor be hungry for
bread, and there we will dwell'— 15Then hear
now the word of the LORD, O remnant of Judah! Thus says the LORD of hosts, the God of
Israel: 'If you wholly set your faces to enter
Egypt, and go to dwell there, 16then it shall be
that the sword which you feared shall overtake you there in the land of Egypt; the famine
of which you were afraid shall follow close after you there *in* Egypt; and there you shall die.
17So shall it be with all the men who set their
faces to go to Egypt to dwell there. They shall
die by the sword, by famine, and by pestilence.
And none of them shall remain or escape from
the disaster that I will bring upon them.'
18"For thus says the LORD of hosts, the God
of Israel: 'As My anger and My fury have been
poured out on the inhabitants of Jerusalem, so
will My fury be poured out on you when you
enter Egypt. And you shall be an oath, an astonishment, a curse, and a reproach; and you
shall see this place no more.'
19"The LORD has said concerning you, O
remnant of Judah, 'Do not go to Egypt!' Know
certainly that I have admonished you this day.
20For you were hypocrites in your hearts when
you sent me to the LORD your God, saying,
'Pray for us to the LORD our God, and according to all that the LORD your God says, so declare to us and we will do *it.*' 21And I have this
day declared *it* to you, but you have not
obeyed the voice of the LORD your God, or
anything which He has sent you by me. 22Now
therefore, know certainly that you shall die by
the sword, by famine, and by pestilence in the
place where you desire to go to dwell."

JEREMIAH TAKEN TO EGYPT

43 Now it happened, when Jeremiah had
stopped speaking to all the people all
the words of the LORD their God, for which the
LORD their God had sent him to them, all these
words, 2that Azariah the son of Hoshaiah, Johanan the son of Kareah, and all the proud
men spoke, saying to Jeremiah, "You speak
falsely! The LORD our God has not sent you to
say, 'Do not go to Egypt to dwell there.' 3But
Baruch the son of Neriah has set you against
us, to deliver us into the hand of the Chaldeans, that they may put us to death or carry us
away captive to Babylon." 4So Johanan the
son of Kareah, all the captains of the forces,
and all the people would not obey the voice of
the LORD, to remain in the land of Judah. 5But
Johanan the son of Kareah and all the captains
of the forces took all the remnant of Judah
who had returned to dwell in the land of Judah, from all nations where they had been
driven— 6men, women, children, the king's
daughters, and every person whom Nebuzaradan the captain of the guard had left with Gedaliah the son of Ahikam, the son of Shaphan,
and Jeremiah the prophet and Baruch the son
of Neriah. 7So they went to the land of Egypt,
for they did not obey the voice of the LORD.
And they went as far as Tahpanhes.
8Then the word of the LORD came to Jeremiah in Tahpanhes, saying, 9"Take large stones
in your hand, and hide them in the sight of the
men of Judah, in the clay in the brick courtyard which *is* at the entrance to Pharaoh's
house in Tahpanhes; 10and say to them, 'Thus
says the LORD of hosts, the God of Israel: "Behold, I will send and bring Nebuchadnezzar
the king of Babylon, My servant, and will set
his throne above these stones that I have hidden. And he will spread his royal pavilion over
them. 11When he comes, he shall strike the
land of Egypt *and deliver* to death *those appointed* for death, and to captivity *those appointed* for captivity, and to the sword *those
appointed* for the sword. 12I[a] will kindle a fire
in the houses of the gods of Egypt, and he
shall burn them and carry them away captive.
And he shall array himself with the land of
Egypt, as a shepherd puts on his garment, and
he shall go out from there in peace. 13He shall
also break the *sacred* pillars of Beth Shemesh[a]
that *are* in the land of Egypt; and the houses of

43:12 [a]Following Masoretic Text and Targum; Septuagint, Syriac, and Vulgate read *He.*
43:13 [a]Literally *House of the Sun,* ancient On; later called Heliopolis

the gods of the Egyptians he shall burn with fire." ' "

ISRAELITES WILL BE PUNISHED IN EGYPT

44 The word that came to Jeremiah concerning all the Jews who dwell in the land of Egypt, who dwell at Migdol, at Tahpanhes, at Noph,[a] and in the country of Pathros, saying, 2"Thus says the LORD of hosts, the God of Israel: 'You have seen all the calamity that I have brought on Jerusalem and on all the cities of Judah; and behold, this day they *are* a desolation, and no one dwells in them, 3because of their wickedness which they have committed to provoke Me to anger, in that they went to burn incense *and* to serve other gods whom they did not know, they nor you nor your fathers. 4However I have sent to you all My servants the prophets, rising early and sending *them,* saying, "Oh, do not do this abominable thing that I hate!" 5But they did not listen or incline their ear to turn from their wickedness, to burn no incense to other gods. 6So My fury and My anger were poured out and kindled in the cities of Judah and in the streets of Jerusalem; and they are wasted *and* desolate, as it is this day.'

7"Now therefore, thus says the LORD, the God of hosts, the God of Israel: 'Why do you commit *this* great evil against yourselves, to cut off from you man and woman, child and infant, out of Judah, leaving none to remain, 8in that you provoke Me to wrath with the works of your hands, burning incense to other gods in the land of Egypt where you have gone to dwell, that you may cut yourselves off and be a curse and a reproach among all the nations of the earth? 9Have you forgotten the wickedness of your fathers, the wickedness of the kings of Judah, the wickedness of their wives, your own wickedness, and the wickedness of your wives, which they committed in the land of Judah and in the streets of Jerusalem? 10They have not been humbled, to this day, nor have they feared; they have not walked in My law or in My statutes that I set before you and your fathers.'

11"Therefore thus says the LORD of hosts, the God of Israel: 'Behold, I will set My face against you for catastrophe and for cutting off all Judah. 12And I will take the remnant of Judah who have set their faces to go into the land of Egypt to dwell there, and they shall all be consumed *and* fall in the land of Egypt. They shall be consumed by the sword *and* by famine. They shall die, from the least to the greatest, by the sword and by famine; and they shall be an oath, an astonishment, a curse and a reproach! 13For I will punish those who dwell in the land of Egypt, as I have punished Jerusalem, by the sword, by famine, and by pestilence, 14so that none of the remnant of Judah who have gone into the land of Egypt to dwell there shall escape or survive, lest they return to the land of Judah, to which they desire to return and dwell. For none shall return except those who escape.' "

15Then all the men who knew that their wives had burned incense to other gods, with all the women who stood by, a great multitude, and all the people who dwelt in the land of Egypt, in Pathros, answered Jeremiah, saying: 16"*As for* the word that you have spoken to us in the name of the LORD, we will not listen to you! 17But we will certainly do whatever has gone out of our own mouth, to burn incense to the queen of heaven and pour out drink offerings to her, as we have done, we and our fathers, our kings and our princes, in the cities of Judah and in the streets of Jerusalem. For *then* we had plenty of food, were well-off, and saw no trouble. 18But since we stopped burning incense to the queen of heaven and pouring out drink offerings to her, we have lacked everything and have been consumed by the sword and by famine."

19*The women also said,* "And when we burned incense to the queen of heaven and poured out drink offerings to her, did we make cakes for her, to worship her, and pour out drink offerings to her without our husbands' *permission?*"

20Then Jeremiah spoke to all the people—the men, the women, and all the people who had given him *that* answer—saying: 21"The incense that you burned in the cities of Judah and in the streets of Jerusalem, you and your fathers, your kings and your princes, and the people of the land, did not the LORD remember them, and did it *not* come into His mind? 22So the LORD could no longer bear *it,* because of the evil of your doings *and* because of the abominations which you committed. Therefore your land is a desolation, an astonishment, a curse, and without an inhabitant, as *it is* this day. 23Because you have burned incense

44:1 [a]That is, ancient Memphis

and because you have sinned against the
LORD, and have not obeyed the voice of the
LORD or walked in His law, in His statutes or in
His testimonies, therefore this calamity has
happened to you, as *at* this day."
24Moreover Jeremiah said to all the people
and to all the women, "Hear the word of the
LORD, all Judah who *are* in the land of Egypt!
25Thus says the LORD of hosts, the God of Israel, saying: 'You and your wives have spoken
with your mouths and fulfilled with your
hands, saying, "We will surely keep our vows
that we have made, to burn incense to the
queen of heaven and pour out drink offerings
to her." You will surely keep your vows and
perform your vows!' 26Therefore hear the
word of the LORD, all Judah who dwell in the
land of Egypt: 'Behold, I have sworn by My
great name,' says the LORD, 'that My name
shall no more be named in the mouth of any
man of Judah in all the land of Egypt, saying,
"The Lord GOD lives." 27Behold, I will watch
over them for adversity and not for good. And
all the men of Judah who *are* in the land of
Egypt shall be consumed by the sword and by
famine, until there is an end to them. 28Yet a
small number who escape the sword shall return from the land of Egypt to the land of Judah; and all the remnant of Judah, who have
gone to the land of Egypt to dwell there, shall
know whose words will stand, Mine or theirs.
29And this *shall be* a sign to you,' says the
LORD, 'that I will punish you in this place, that
you may know that My words will surely
stand against you for adversity.'
30"Thus says the LORD: 'Behold, I will give
Pharaoh Hophra king of Egypt into the hand
of his enemies and into the hand of those who
seek his life, as I gave Zedekiah king of Judah
into the hand of Nebuchadnezzar king of Babylon, his enemy who sought his life.' "

ASSURANCE TO BARUCH

45 The word that Jeremiah the prophet
spoke to Baruch the son of Neriah,
when he had written these words in a book at
the instruction of Jeremiah,[a] in the fourth year
of Jehoiakim the son of Josiah, king of Judah,
saying, 2"Thus says the LORD, the God of Israel, to you, O Baruch: 3'You said, "Woe is me
now! For the LORD has added grief to my sorrow. I fainted in my sighing, and I find no
rest." '
4"Thus you shall say to him, 'Thus says the
LORD: "Behold, what I have built I will break
down, and what I have planted I will pluck
up, that is, this whole land. 5And do you seek
great things for yourself? Do not seek *them;*
for behold, I will bring adversity on all flesh,"
says the LORD. "But I will give your life to you
as a prize in all places, wherever you go." ' "

JUDGMENT ON EGYPT

46 The word of the LORD which came to
Jeremiah the prophet against the nations. 2Against Egypt.
Concerning the army of Pharaoh Necho,
king of Egypt, which was by the River Euphrates in Carchemish, and which Nebuchadnezzar king of Babylon defeated in the fourth year
of Jehoiakim the son of Josiah, king of Judah:

3 "Order the buckler and shield,
And draw near to battle!
4 Harness the horses,
And mount up, you horsemen!
Stand forth with *your* helmets,
Polish the spears,
Put on the armor!
5 Why have I seen them dismayed *and*
turned back?
Their mighty ones are beaten down;
They have speedily fled,
And did not look back,
For fear *was* all around," says the LORD.
6 "Do not let the swift flee away,
Nor the mighty man escape;
They will stumble and fall
Toward the north, by the River
Euphrates.

7 "Who *is* this coming up like a flood,
Whose waters move like the rivers?
8 Egypt rises up like a flood,
And *its* waters move like the rivers;
And he says, 'I will go up *and* cover the
earth,
I will destroy the city and its
inhabitants.'
9 Come up, O horses, and rage,
O chariots!
And let the mighty men come forth:
The Ethiopians and the Libyans who
handle the shield,
And the Lydians who handle *and* bend
the bow.

45:1 [a]Literally *from Jeremiah's mouth*

10 For this *is* the day of the Lord GOD of hosts,
A day of vengeance,
That He may avenge Himself on His adversaries.
The sword shall devour;
It shall be satiated and made drunk with their blood;
For the Lord GOD of hosts has a sacrifice
In the north country by the River Euphrates.

11 "Go up to Gilead and take balm,
O virgin, the daughter of Egypt;
In vain you will use many medicines;
You shall not be cured.
12 The nations have heard of your shame,
And your cry has filled the land;
For the mighty man has stumbled against the mighty;
They both have fallen together."

BABYLONIA WILL STRIKE EGYPT

13The word that the LORD spoke to Jeremiah
the prophet, how Nebuchadnezzar king of
Babylon would come *and* strike the land of
Egypt.

14 "Declare in Egypt, and proclaim in Migdol;
Proclaim in Noph[a] and in Tahpanhes;
Say, 'Stand fast and prepare yourselves,
For the sword devours all around you.'
15 Why are your valiant *men* swept away?
They did not stand
Because the LORD drove them away.
16 He made many fall;
Yes, one fell upon another.
And they said, 'Arise!
Let us go back to our own people
And to the land of our nativity
From the oppressing sword.'
17 They cried there,
'Pharaoh, king of Egypt, *is but* a noise.
He has passed by the appointed time!'

18 "*As* I live," says the King,
Whose name *is* the LORD of hosts,
"Surely as Tabor *is* among the mountains
And as Carmel by the sea, *so* he shall come.
19 O you daughter dwelling in Egypt,
Prepare yourself to go into captivity!
For Noph[a] shall be waste and desolate, without inhabitant.

20 "Egypt *is* a very pretty heifer,
But destruction comes, it comes from the north.
21 Also her mercenaries are in her midst like fat bulls,
For they also are turned back,
They have fled away together.
They did not stand,
For the day of their calamity had come upon them,
The time of their punishment.
22 Her noise shall go like a serpent,
For they shall march with an army
And come against her with axes,
Like those who chop wood.

23 "They shall cut down her forest," says the LORD,
"Though it cannot be searched,
Because they *are* innumerable,
And more numerous than grasshoppers.
24 The daughter of Egypt shall be ashamed;
She shall be delivered into the hand
Of the people of the north."

25The LORD of hosts, the God of Israel, says:
"Behold, I will bring punishment on Amon[a] of
No,[b] and Pharaoh and Egypt, with their gods
and their kings—Pharaoh and those who trust
in him. 26And I will deliver them into the hand
of those who seek their lives, into the hand of
Nebuchadnezzar king of Babylon and the
hand of his servants. Afterward it shall be inhabited as in the days of old," says the LORD.

GOD WILL PRESERVE ISRAEL

27 "But do not fear, O My servant Jacob,
And do not be dismayed, O Israel!
For behold, I will save you from afar,
And your offspring from the land of their captivity;
Jacob shall return, have rest and be at ease;
No one shall make *him* afraid.
28 Do not fear, O Jacob My servant," says the LORD,
"For I *am* with you;

46:14 [a]That is, ancient Memphis **46:19** [a]That is, ancient Memphis **46:25** [a]A sun god [b]That is, ancient Thebes

For I will make a complete end of all the nations
To which I have driven you,
But I will not make a complete end of you.
I will rightly correct you,
For I will not leave you wholly unpunished."

JUDGMENT ON PHILISTIA

47 The word of the LORD that came to Jeremiah the prophet against the Philistines, before Pharaoh attacked Gaza.
2Thus says the LORD:

"Behold, waters rise out of the north,
And shall be an overflowing flood;
They shall overflow the land and all that is in it,
The city and those who dwell within;
Then the men shall cry,
And all the inhabitants of the land shall wail.
3 At the noise of the stamping hooves of his strong horses,
At the rushing of his chariots,
At the rumbling of his wheels,
The fathers will not look back for *their* children,
Lacking courage,
4 Because of the day that comes to plunder all the Philistines,
To cut off from Tyre and Sidon every helper who remains;
For the LORD shall plunder the Philistines,
The remnant of the country of Caphtor.
5 Baldness has come upon Gaza,
Ashkelon is cut off
With the remnant of their valley.
How long will you cut yourself?

6 "O you sword of the LORD,
How long until you are quiet?
Put yourself up into your scabbard,
Rest and be still!
7 How can it be quiet,
Seeing the LORD has given it a charge
Against Ashkelon and against the seashore?
There He has appointed it."

JUDGMENT ON MOAB

48 Against Moab.
Thus says the LORD of hosts, the God
of Israel:

"Woe to Nebo!
For it is plundered,
Kirjathaim is shamed *and* taken;
The high stronghold[a] is shamed and dismayed—
2 No more praise of Moab.
In Heshbon they have devised evil against her:
'Come, and let us cut her off as a nation.'
You also shall be cut down,
O Madmen![a]
The sword shall pursue you;
3 A voice of crying *shall be* from Horonaim:
'Plundering and great destruction!'

4 "Moab is destroyed;
Her little ones have caused a cry to be heard;[a]
5 For in the Ascent of Luhith they ascend with continual weeping;
For in the descent of Horonaim the enemies have heard a cry of destruction.

6 "Flee, save your lives!
And be like the juniper[a] in the wilderness.
7 For because you have trusted in your works and your treasures,
You also shall be taken.
And Chemosh shall go forth into captivity,
His priests and his princes together.
8 And the plunderer shall come against every city;
No one shall escape.
The valley also shall perish,
And the plain shall be destroyed,
As the LORD has spoken.

9 "Give wings to Moab,
That she may flee and get away;
For her cities shall be desolate,
Without any to dwell in them.
10 Cursed *is* he who does the work of the LORD deceitfully,
And cursed *is* he who keeps back his sword from blood.

48:1 [a]Hebrew *Misgab* **48:2** [a]A city of Moab **48:4** [a]Following Masoretic Text, Targum, and Vulgate; Septuagint reads *Proclaim it in Zoar.* **48:6** [a]Or *Aroer,* a city of Moab

11 "Moab has been at ease from his[a] youth;
He has settled on his dregs,
And has not been emptied from vessel to vessel,
Nor has he gone into captivity.
Therefore his taste remained in him,
And his scent has not changed.

12 "Therefore behold, the days are coming," says the LORD,
"That I shall send him wine-workers
Who will tip him over
And empty his vessels
And break the bottles.
13 Moab shall be ashamed of Chemosh,
As the house of Israel was ashamed of Bethel, their confidence.

14 "How can you say, 'We *are* mighty
And strong men for the war'?
15 Moab is plundered and gone up *from* her cities;
Her chosen young men have gone down to the slaughter," says the King,
Whose name *is* the LORD of hosts.

16 "The calamity of Moab *is* near at hand,
And his affliction comes quickly.
17 Bemoan him, all you who are around him;
And all you who know his name,
Say, 'How the strong staff is broken,
The beautiful rod!'

18 "O daughter inhabiting Dibon,
Come down from *your* glory,
And sit in thirst;
For the plunderer of Moab has come against you,
He has destroyed your strongholds.
19 O inhabitant of Aroer,
Stand by the way and watch;
Ask him who flees
And her who escapes;
Say, 'What has happened?'
20 Moab is shamed, for he is broken down.
Wail and cry!
Tell it in Arnon, that Moab is plundered.

21 "And judgment has come on the plain country:
On Holon and Jahzah and Mephaath,
22 On Dibon and Nebo and Beth Diblathaim,
23 On Kirjathaim and Beth Gamul and Beth Meon,
24 On Kerioth and Bozrah,
On all the cities of the land of Moab,
Far or near.
25 The horn of Moab is cut off,
And his arm is broken," says the LORD.

26 "Make him drunk,
Because he exalted *himself* against the LORD.
Moab shall wallow in his vomit,
And he shall also be in derision.
27 For was not Israel a derision to you?
Was he found among thieves?
For whenever you speak of him,
You shake *your head in scorn.*
28 You who dwell in Moab,
Leave the cities and dwell in the rock,
And be like the dove *which* makes her nest
In the sides of the cave's mouth.

29 "We have heard the pride of Moab
(He *is* exceedingly proud),
Of his loftiness and arrogance and pride,
And of the haughtiness of his heart."

30 "I know his wrath," says the LORD,
"But it *is* not right;
His lies have made nothing right.
31 Therefore I will wail for Moab,
And I will cry out for all Moab;
I[a] will mourn for the men of Kir Heres.
32 O vine of Sibmah! I will weep for you with the weeping of Jazer.
Your plants have gone over the sea,
They reach to the sea of Jazer.
The plunderer has fallen on your summer fruit and your vintage.
33 Joy and gladness are taken
From the plentiful field
And from the land of Moab;
I have caused wine to fail from the winepresses;
No one will tread with joyous shouting—
Not joyous shouting!

48:11 [a]The Hebrew uses masculine and feminine pronouns interchangeably in this chapter.
48:31 [a]Following Dead Sea Scrolls, Septuagint, and Vulgate; Masoretic Text reads *He*.

34 "From the cry of Heshbon to Elealeh and
to Jahaz
They have uttered their voice,
From Zoar to Horonaim,
Like a three-year-old heifer;[a]
For the waters of Nimrim also shall be
desolate.

35 "Moreover," says the LORD,
"I will cause to cease in Moab
The one who offers *sacrifices* in the high
places
And burns incense to his gods.
36 Therefore My heart shall wail like flutes
for Moab,
And like flutes My heart shall wail
For the men of Kir Heres.
Therefore the riches they have acquired
have perished.

37 "For every head *shall be* bald, and every
beard clipped;
On all the hands *shall be* cuts, and on
the loins sackcloth—
38 A general lamentation
On all the housetops of Moab,
And in its streets;
For I have broken Moab like a vessel in
which *is* no pleasure," says the LORD.
39 "They shall wail:
'How she is broken down!
How Moab has turned her back with
shame!'
So Moab shall be a derision
And a dismay to all those about her."

40 For thus says the LORD:

"Behold, one shall fly like an eagle,
And spread his wings over Moab.
41 Kerioth is taken,
And the strongholds are surprised;
The mighty men's hearts in Moab on
that day shall be
Like the heart of a woman in birth
pangs.
42 And Moab shall be destroyed as a
people,
Because he exalted *himself* against the
LORD.
43 Fear and the pit and the snare *shall be*
upon you,
O inhabitant of Moab," says the
LORD.
44 "He who flees from the fear shall fall into
the pit,
And he who gets out of the pit shall be
caught in the snare.
For upon Moab, upon it I will bring
The year of their punishment," says the
LORD.

45 "Those who fled stood under the shadow
of Heshbon
Because of exhaustion.
But a fire shall come out of Heshbon,
A flame from the midst of Sihon,
And shall devour the brow of Moab,
The crown of the head of the sons of
tumult.
46 Woe to you, O Moab!
The people of Chemosh perish;
For your sons have been taken captive,
And your daughters captive.

47 "Yet I will bring back the captives of
Moab
In the latter days," says the LORD.

Thus far *is* the judgment of Moab.

Judgment on Ammon

49 Against the Ammonites.
Thus says the LORD:

"Has Israel no sons?
Has he no heir?
Why *then* does Milcom[a] inherit Gad,
And his people dwell in its cities?
2 Therefore behold, the days are coming,"
says the LORD,
"That I will cause to be heard an alarm of
war
In Rabbah of the Ammonites;
It shall be a desolate mound,
And her villages shall be burned with
fire.
Then Israel shall take possession of his
inheritance," says the LORD.

3 "Wail, O Heshbon, for Ai is plundered!
Cry, you daughters of Rabbah,
Gird yourselves with sackcloth!

48:34 [a]Or *The Third Eglath,* an unknown city (compare Isaiah 15:5) **49:1** [a]Hebrew *Malcam,* literally *their king,* a god of the Ammonites; also called *Molech* (compare verse 3)

Lament and run to and fro by the walls;
For Milcom shall go into captivity
With his priests and his princes together.
4 Why do you boast in the valleys,
Your flowing valley, O backsliding daughter?
Who trusted in her treasures, *saying,*
'Who will come against me?'
5 Behold, I will bring fear upon you,"
Says the Lord GOD of hosts,
"From all those who are around you;
You shall be driven out, everyone headlong,
And no one will gather those who wander off.
6 But afterward I will bring back
The captives of the people of Ammon,"
says the LORD.

JUDGMENT ON EDOM

7Against Edom.
Thus says the LORD of hosts:

"*Is* wisdom no more in Teman?
Has counsel perished from the prudent?
Has their wisdom vanished?
8 Flee, turn back, dwell in the depths,
O inhabitants of Dedan!
For I will bring the calamity of Esau upon him,
The time *that* I will punish him.
9 If grape-gatherers came to you,
Would they not leave *some* gleaning grapes?
If thieves by night,
Would they not destroy until they have enough?
10 But I have made Esau bare;
I have uncovered his secret places,[a]
And he shall not be able to hide himself.
His descendants are plundered,
His brethren and his neighbors,
And he *is* no more.
11 Leave your fatherless children,
I will preserve *them* alive;
And let your widows trust in Me."

12For thus says the LORD: "Behold, those
whose judgment *was* not to drink of the cup
have assuredly drunk. And *are* you the one
who will altogether go unpunished? You shall
not go unpunished, but you shall surely drink
of it. 13For I have sworn by Myself," says the
LORD, "that Bozrah shall become a desolation,
a reproach, a waste, and a curse. And all its
cities shall be perpetual wastes."

14 I have heard a message from the LORD,
And an ambassador has been sent to the nations:
"Gather together, come against her,
And rise up to battle!

15 "For indeed, I will make you small among nations,
Despised among men.
16 Your fierceness has deceived you,
The pride of your heart,
O you who dwell in the clefts of the rock,
Who hold the height of the hill!
Though you make your nest as high as the eagle,
I will bring you down from there," says the LORD.[a]

17 "Edom also shall be an astonishment;
Everyone who goes by it will be astonished
And will hiss at all its plagues.
18 As in the overthrow of Sodom and Gomorrah
And their neighbors," says the LORD,
"No one shall remain there,
Nor shall a son of man dwell in it.

19 "Behold, he shall come up like a lion from the floodplain[a] of the Jordan
Against the dwelling place of the strong;
But I will suddenly make him run away from her.
And who *is* a chosen *man that* I may appoint over her?
For who *is* like Me?
Who will arraign Me?
And who *is* that shepherd
Who will withstand Me?"

20 Therefore hear the counsel of the LORD that He has taken against Edom,
And His purposes that He has proposed against the inhabitants of Teman:
Surely the least of the flock shall draw them out;
Surely He shall make their dwelling places desolate with them.

49:10 [a]Compare Obadiah 5, 6 **49:16** [a]Compare Obadiah 3, 4 **49:19** [a]Or *thicket*

21 The earth shakes at the noise of their
fall;
At the cry its noise is heard at the Red
Sea.
22 Behold, He shall come up and fly like
the eagle,
And spread His wings over Bozrah;
The heart of the mighty men of Edom in
that day shall be
Like the heart of a woman in birth
pangs.

Judgment on Damascus

[23]Against Damascus.

"Hamath and Arpad are shamed,
For they have heard bad news.
They are fainthearted;
There is trouble on the sea;
It cannot be quiet.
24 Damascus has grown feeble;
She turns to flee,
And fear has seized *her*.
Anguish and sorrows have taken her like
a woman in labor.
25 Why is the city of praise not deserted,
the city of My joy?
26 Therefore her young men shall fall in
her streets,
And all the men of war shall be cut off
in that day," says the LORD of hosts.
27 "I will kindle a fire in the wall of
Damascus,
And it shall consume the palaces of
Ben Hadad."[a]

Judgment on Kedar and Hazor

[28]Against Kedar and against the kingdoms
of Hazor, which Nebuchadnezzar king of Babylon shall strike.
Thus says the LORD:

"Arise, go up to Kedar,
And devastate the men of the East!
29 Their tents and their flocks they shall
take away.
They shall take for themselves their
curtains,
All their vessels and their camels;
And they shall cry out to them,
'Fear *is* on every side!'

30 "Flee, get far away! Dwell in the depths,
O inhabitants of Hazor!" says the LORD.
"For Nebuchadnezzar king of Babylon
has taken counsel against you,
And has conceived a plan against you.

31 "Arise, go up to the wealthy nation that
dwells securely," says the LORD,
"Which has neither gates nor bars,
Dwelling alone.
32 Their camels shall be for booty,
And the multitude of their cattle for
plunder.
I will scatter to all winds those in the
farthest corners,
And I will bring their calamity from all
its sides," says the LORD.
33 "Hazor shall be a dwelling for jackals, a
desolation forever;
No one shall reside there,
Nor son of man dwell in it."

Judgment on Elam

[34]The word of the LORD that came to Jeremiah the prophet against Elam, in the beginning
of the reign of Zedekiah king of Judah, saying,
[35]"Thus says the LORD of hosts:

'Behold, I will break the bow of Elam,
The foremost of their might.
36 Against Elam I will bring the four
winds
From the four quarters of heaven,
And scatter them toward all those
winds;
There shall be no nations where the
outcasts of Elam will not go.
37 For I will cause Elam to be dismayed
before their enemies
And before those who seek their
life.
I will bring disaster upon them,
My fierce anger,' says the LORD;
'And I will send the sword after them
Until I have consumed them.
38 I will set My throne in Elam,
And will destroy from there the king and
the princes,' says the LORD.

39 "But it shall come to pass in the latter
days:
I will bring back the captives of Elam,'
says the LORD."

49:27 [a]Compare Amos 1:4

JUDGMENT ON BABYLON AND BABYLONIA

50 The word that the LORD spoke against Babylon *and* against the land of the Chaldeans by Jeremiah the prophet.

2 "Declare among the nations,
Proclaim, and set up a standard;
Proclaim—do not conceal *it*—
Say, 'Babylon is taken, Bel is shamed.
Merodach[a] is broken in pieces;
Her idols are humiliated,
Her images are broken in pieces.'
3 For out of the north a nation comes up against her,
Which shall make her land desolate,
And no one shall dwell therein.
They shall move, they shall depart,
Both man and beast.

4 "In those days and in that time," says the LORD,
"The children of Israel shall come,
They and the children of Judah together;
With continual weeping they shall come,
And seek the LORD their God.
5 They shall ask the way to Zion,
With their faces toward it, *saying,*
'Come and let us join ourselves to the LORD
In a perpetual covenant
That will not be forgotten.'

6 "My people have been lost sheep.
Their shepherds have led them astray;
They have turned them away *on* the mountains.
They have gone from mountain to hill;
They have forgotten their resting place.
7 All who found them have devoured them;
And their adversaries said, 'We have not offended,
Because they have sinned against the LORD, the habitation of justice,
The LORD, the hope of their fathers.'

8 "Move from the midst of Babylon,
Go out of the land of the Chaldeans;
And be like the rams before the flocks.
9 For behold, I will raise and cause to come up against Babylon
An assembly of great nations from the north country,
And they shall array themselves against her;
From there she shall be captured.
Their arrows *shall be* like *those* of an expert warrior;[a]
None shall return in vain.
10 And Chaldea shall become plunder;
All who plunder her shall be satisfied," says the LORD.

11 "Because you were glad, because you rejoiced,
You destroyers of My heritage,
Because you have grown fat like a heifer threshing grain,
And you bellow like bulls,
12 Your mother shall be deeply ashamed;
She who bore you shall be ashamed.
Behold, the least of the nations *shall be* a wilderness,
A dry land and a desert.
13 Because of the wrath of the LORD
She shall not be inhabited,
But she shall be wholly desolate.
Everyone who goes by Babylon shall be horrified
And hiss at all her plagues.

14 "Put yourselves in array against Babylon all around,
All you who bend the bow;
Shoot at her, spare no arrows,
For she has sinned against the LORD.
15 Shout against her all around;
She has given her hand,
Her foundations have fallen,
Her walls are thrown down;
For it *is* the vengeance of the LORD.
Take vengeance on her.
As she has done, so do to her.
16 Cut off the sower from Babylon,
And him who handles the sickle at harvest time.
For fear of the oppressing sword
Everyone shall turn to his own people,
And everyone shall flee to his own land.

17 "Israel *is* like scattered sheep;
The lions have driven *him* away.

50:2 [a]A Babylonian god; sometimes spelled *Marduk* **50:9** [a]Following some Hebrew manuscripts, Septuagint, and Syriac; Masoretic Text, Targum, and Vulgate read *a warrior who makes childless.*

First the king of Assyria devoured him;
Now at last this Nebuchadnezzar king of
Babylon has broken his bones."

18Therefore thus says the LORD of hosts, the God of Israel:

"Behold, I will punish the king of
Babylon and his land,
As I have punished the king of Assyria.
19 But I will bring back Israel to his home,
And he shall feed on Carmel and
Bashan;
His soul shall be satisfied on Mount
Ephraim and Gilead.
20 In those days and in that time," says the
LORD,
"The iniquity of Israel shall be sought,
but *there shall be* none;
And the sins of Judah, but they shall not
be found;
For I will pardon those whom I preserve.

21 "Go up against the land of Merathaim,
against it,
And against the inhabitants of Pekod.
Waste and utterly destroy them," says
the LORD,
"And do according to all that I have
commanded you.
22 A sound of battle *is* in the land,
And of great destruction.
23 How the hammer of the whole earth has
been cut apart and broken!
How Babylon has become a desolation
among the nations!
I have laid a snare for you;
24 You have indeed been trapped,
O Babylon,
And you were not aware;
You have been found and also caught,
Because you have contended against the
LORD.
25 The LORD has opened His armory,
And has brought out the weapons of His
indignation;
For this *is* the work of the Lord GOD of
hosts
In the land of the Chaldeans.
26 Come against her from the farthest
border;
Open her storehouses;
Cast her up as heaps of ruins,
And destroy her utterly;
Let nothing of her be left.
27 Slay all her bulls,
Let them go down to the slaughter.
Woe to them!
For their day has come, the time of their
punishment.
28 The voice of those who flee and escape
from the land of Babylon
Declares in Zion the vengeance of the
LORD our God,
The vengeance of His temple.

29 "Call together the archers against
Babylon.
All you who bend the bow, encamp
against it all around;
Let none of them escape.[a]
Repay her according to her work;
According to all she has done, do to her;
For she has been proud against the
LORD,
Against the Holy One of Israel.
30 Therefore her young men shall fall in the
streets,
And all her men of war shall be cut off
in that day," says the LORD.
31 "Behold, I *am* against you,
O most haughty one!" says the Lord GOD
of hosts;
"For your day has come,
The time *that* I will punish you.[a]
32 The most proud shall stumble and fall,
And no one will raise him up;
I will kindle a fire in his cities,
And it will devour all around him."

33Thus says the LORD of hosts:

"The children of Israel *were* oppressed,
Along with the children of Judah;
All who took them captive have held
them fast;
They have refused to let them go.
34 Their Redeemer *is* strong;
The LORD of hosts *is* His name.
He will thoroughly plead their case,
That He may give rest to the land,
And disquiet the inhabitants of Babylon.

50:29 [a]Qere, some Hebrew manuscripts, Septuagint, and Targum add *to her*.
50:31 [a]Following Masoretic Text and Targum; Septuagint and Vulgate read *The time of your punishment*.

35 "A sword *is* against the Chaldeans," says
the LORD,
"Against the inhabitants of Babylon,
And against her princes and her wise
men.
36 A sword *is* against the soothsayers, and
they will be fools.
A sword *is* against her mighty men, and
they will be dismayed.
37 A sword *is* against their horses,
Against their chariots,
And against all the mixed peoples who
are in her midst;
And they will become like women.
A sword *is* against her treasures, and
they will be robbed.
38 A drought[a] *is* against her waters, and
they will be dried up.
For it *is* the land of carved images,
And they are insane with *their* idols.

39 "Therefore the wild desert beasts shall
dwell *there* with the jackals,
And the ostriches shall dwell in it.
It shall be inhabited no more forever,
Nor shall it be dwelt in from generation
to generation.
40 As God overthrew Sodom and Gomorrah
And their neighbors," says the LORD,
"*So* no one shall reside there,
Nor son of man dwell in it.

41 "Behold, a people shall come from the
north,
And a great nation and many kings
Shall be raised up from the ends of the
earth.
42 They shall hold the bow and the lance;
They *are* cruel and shall not show
mercy.
Their voice shall roar like the sea;
They shall ride on horses,
Set in array, like a man for the battle,
Against you, O daughter of Babylon.

43 "The king of Babylon has heard the report
about them,
And his hands grow feeble;
Anguish has taken hold of him,
Pangs as of a woman in childbirth.

44 "Behold, he shall come up like a lion
from the floodplain[a] of the Jordan
Against the dwelling place of the strong;
But I will make them suddenly run away
from her.
And who *is* a chosen *man that* I may
appoint over her?
For who *is* like Me?
Who will arraign Me?
And who *is* that shepherd
Who will withstand Me?"

45 Therefore hear the counsel of the LORD
that He has taken against Babylon,
And His purposes that He has proposed
against the land of the Chaldeans:
Surely the least of the flock shall draw
them out;
Surely He will make their dwelling place
desolate with them.
46 At the noise of the taking of Babylon
The earth trembles,
And the cry is heard among the nations.

THE UTTER DESTRUCTION OF BABYLON

51 Thus says the LORD:

"Behold, I will raise up against Babylon,
Against those who dwell in Leb Kamai,[a]
A destroying wind.
2 And I will send winnowers to Babylon,
Who shall winnow her and empty her
land.
For in the day of doom
They shall be against her all around.
3 Against *her* let the archer bend his bow,
And lift himself up against *her* in his
armor.
Do not spare her young men;
Utterly destroy all her army.
4 Thus the slain shall fall in the land of
the Chaldeans,
And *those* thrust through in her streets.
5 For Israel is not forsaken, nor Judah,
By his God, the LORD of hosts,
Though their land was filled with sin
against the Holy One of Israel."

6 Flee from the midst of Babylon,
And every one save his life!
Do not be cut off in her iniquity,

50:38 [a]Following Masoretic Text, Targum, and Vulgate; Syriac reads *sword;* Septuagint omits *A drought is.* **50:44** [a]Or *thicket* **51:1** [a]A code word for Chaldea (Babylonia); may be translated *The Midst of Those Who Rise Up Against Me*

For this *is* the time of the LORD's
vengeance;
He shall recompense her.
7 Babylon *was* a golden cup in the LORD's
hand,
That made all the earth drunk.
The nations drank her wine;
Therefore the nations are deranged.
8 Babylon has suddenly fallen and been
destroyed.
Wail for her!
Take balm for her pain;
Perhaps she may be healed.

9 We would have healed Babylon,
But she is not healed.
Forsake her, and let us go everyone to
his own country;
For her judgment reaches to heaven and
is lifted up to the skies.
10 The LORD has revealed our
righteousness.
Come and let us declare in Zion the
work of the LORD our God.

11 Make the arrows bright!
Gather the shields!
The LORD has raised up the spirit of the
kings of the Medes.
For His plan *is* against Babylon to
destroy it,
Because it *is* the vengeance of the LORD,
The vengeance for His temple.
12 Set up the standard on the walls of
Babylon;
Make the guard strong,
Set up the watchmen,
Prepare the ambushes.
For the LORD has both devised and done
What He spoke against the inhabitants
of Babylon.
13 O you who dwell by many waters,
Abundant in treasures,
Your end has come,
The measure of your covetousness.
14 The LORD of hosts has sworn by Himself:
"Surely I will fill you with men, as with
locusts,
And they shall lift up a shout against
you."

15 He has made the earth by His power;
He has established the world by His
wisdom,
And stretched out the heaven by His
understanding.
16 When He utters *His* voice—
There is a multitude of waters in the
heavens:
"He causes the vapors to ascend from the
ends of the earth;
He makes lightnings for the rain;
He brings the wind out of His
treasuries."[a]

17 Everyone is dull-hearted, without
knowledge;
Every metalsmith is put to shame by the
carved image;
For his molded image *is* falsehood,
And *there is* no breath in them.
18 They *are* futile, a work of errors;
In the time of their punishment they
shall perish.
19 The Portion of Jacob *is* not like them,
For He *is* the Maker of all things;
And *Israel is* the tribe of His
inheritance.
The LORD of hosts *is* His name.

20 "You *are* My battle-ax *and* weapons of
war:
For with you I will break the nation in
pieces;
With you I will destroy kingdoms;
21 With you I will break in pieces the horse
and its rider;
With you I will break in pieces the
chariot and its rider;
22 With you also I will break in pieces man
and woman;
With you I will break in pieces old and
young;
With you I will break in pieces the
young man and the maiden;
23 With you also I will break in pieces the
shepherd and his flock;
With you I will break in pieces the
farmer and his yoke of oxen;
And with you I will break in pieces
governors and rulers.

24 "And I will repay Babylon
And all the inhabitants of Chaldea
For all the evil they have done
In Zion in your sight," says the LORD.

51:16 [a]Psalm 135:7

25 "Behold, I *am* against you, O destroying mountain,
Who destroys all the earth," says the LORD.
"And I will stretch out My hand against you,
Roll you down from the rocks,
And make you a burnt mountain.
26 They shall not take from you a stone for a corner
Nor a stone for a foundation,
But you shall be desolate forever," says the LORD.

27 Set up a banner in the land,
Blow the trumpet among the nations!
Prepare the nations against her,
Call the kingdoms together against her:
Ararat, Minni, and Ashkenaz.
Appoint a general against her;
Cause the horses to come up like the bristling locusts.
28 Prepare against her the nations,
With the kings of the Medes,
Its governors and all its rulers,
All the land of his dominion.
29 And the land will tremble and sorrow;
For every purpose of the LORD shall be performed against Babylon,
To make the land of Babylon a desolation without inhabitant.
30 The mighty men of Babylon have ceased fighting,
They have remained in their strongholds;
Their might has failed,
They became *like* women;
They have burned her dwelling places,
The bars of her *gate* are broken.
31 One runner will run to meet another,
And one messenger to meet another,
To show the king of Babylon that his city is taken on *all* sides;
32 The passages are blocked,
The reeds they have burned with fire,
And the men of war are terrified.

33For thus says the LORD of hosts, the God of Israel:

"The daughter of Babylon *is* like a threshing floor
When it is time to thresh her;
Yet a little while
And the time of her harvest will come."

34 "Nebuchadnezzar the king of Babylon
Has devoured me, he has crushed me;
He has made me an empty vessel,
He has swallowed me up like a monster;
He has filled his stomach with my delicacies,
He has spit me out.
35 Let the violence *done* to me and my flesh *be* upon Babylon,"
The inhabitant of Zion will say;
"And my blood be upon the inhabitants of Chaldea!"
Jerusalem will say.

36Therefore thus says the LORD:

"Behold, I will plead your case and take vengeance for you.
I will dry up her sea and make her springs dry.
37 Babylon shall become a heap,
A dwelling place for jackals,
An astonishment and a hissing,
Without an inhabitant.
38 They shall roar together like lions,
They shall growl like lions' whelps.
39 In their excitement I will prepare their feasts;
I will make them drunk,
That they may rejoice,
And sleep a perpetual sleep
And not awake," says the LORD.
40 "I will bring them down
Like lambs to the slaughter,
Like rams with male goats.

41 "Oh, how Sheshach[a] is taken!
Oh, how the praise of the whole earth is seized!
How Babylon has become desolate among the nations!
42 The sea has come up over Babylon;
She is covered with the multitude of its waves.
43 Her cities are a desolation,
A dry land and a wilderness,
A land where no one dwells,
Through which no son of man passes.

51:41 [a]A code word for Babylon (compare Jeremiah 25:26)

44 I will punish Bel in Babylon,
And I will bring out of his mouth what he has swallowed;
And the nations shall not stream to him anymore.
Yes, the wall of Babylon shall fall.

45 "My people, go out of the midst of her!
And let everyone deliver himself from the fierce anger of the LORD.
46 And lest your heart faint,
And you fear for the rumor that *will be* heard in the land
(A rumor will come *one* year,
And after that, in *another* year
A rumor *will come,*
And violence in the land,
Ruler against ruler),
47 Therefore behold, the days are coming
That I will bring judgment on the carved images of Babylon;
Her whole land shall be ashamed,
And all her slain shall fall in her midst.
48 Then the heavens and the earth and all that *is* in them
Shall sing joyously over Babylon;
For the plunderers shall come to her from the north," says the LORD.

49 As Babylon *has caused* the slain of Israel to fall,
So at Babylon the slain of all the earth shall fall.
50 You who have escaped the sword,
Get away! Do not stand still!
Remember the LORD afar off,
And let Jerusalem come to your mind.

51 We are ashamed because we have heard reproach.
Shame has covered our faces,
For strangers have come into the sanctuaries of the LORD's house.

52 "Therefore behold, the days are coming," says the LORD,
"That I will bring judgment on her carved images,
And throughout all her land the wounded shall groan.
53 Though Babylon were to mount up to heaven,
And though she were to fortify the height of her strength,
Yet from Me plunderers would come to her," says the LORD.

54 The sound of a cry *comes* from Babylon,
And great destruction from the land of the Chaldeans,
55 Because the LORD is plundering Babylon
And silencing her loud voice,
Though her waves roar like great waters,
And the noise of their voice is uttered,
56 Because the plunderer comes against her, against Babylon,
And her mighty men are taken.
Every one of their bows is broken;
For the LORD *is* the God of recompense,
He will surely repay.

57 "And I will make drunk
Her princes and wise men,
Her governors, her deputies, and her mighty men.
And they shall sleep a perpetual sleep
And not awake," says the King,
Whose name *is* the LORD of hosts.

58 Thus says the LORD of hosts:

"The broad walls of Babylon shall be utterly broken,
And her high gates shall be burned with fire;
The people will labor in vain,
And the nations, because of the fire;
And they shall be weary."

JEREMIAH'S COMMAND TO SERAIAH

59 The word which Jeremiah the prophet
commanded Seraiah the son of Neriah, the
son of Mahseiah, when he went with Zedekiah the king of Judah to Babylon in the fourth
year of his reign. And Seraiah *was* the quarter-
master. 60 So Jeremiah wrote in a book all the
evil that would come upon Babylon, all these
words that are written against Babylon. 61 And
Jeremiah said to Seraiah, "When you arrive in
Babylon and see it, and read all these words,
62 then you shall say, 'O LORD, You have spoken against this place to cut it off, so that none
shall remain in it, neither man nor beast, but
it shall be desolate forever.' 63 Now it shall be,
when you have finished reading this book,
that you shall tie a stone to it and throw it out

into the Euphrates. 64Then you shall say, 'Thus Babylon shall sink and not rise from the catastrophe that I will bring upon her. And they shall be weary.' "

Thus far *are* the words of Jeremiah.

The Fall of Jerusalem Reviewed

52 Zedekiah *was* twenty-one years old when he became king, and he reigned eleven years in Jerusalem. His mother's name *was* Hamutal the daughter of Jeremiah of Libnah. 2He also did evil in the sight of the LORD, according to all that Jehoiakim had done. 3For because of the anger of the LORD *this* happened in Jerusalem and Judah, till He finally cast them out from His presence. Then Zedekiah rebelled against the king of Babylon.

4Now it came to pass in the ninth year of his reign, in the tenth month, on the tenth *day* of the month, *that* Nebuchadnezzar king of Babylon and all his army came against Jerusalem and encamped against it; and *they* built a siege wall against it all around. 5So the city was besieged until the eleventh year of King Zedekiah. 6By the fourth month, on the ninth day of the month, the famine had become so severe in the city that there was no food for the people of the land. 7Then the city wall was broken through, and all the men of war fled and went out of the city at night by way of the gate between the two walls, which *was* by the king's garden, even though the Chaldeans *were* near the city all around. And they went by way of the plain.[a]

8But the army of the Chaldeans pursued the king, and they overtook Zedekiah in the plains of Jericho. All his army was scattered from him. 9So they took the king and brought him up to the king of Babylon at Riblah in the land of Hamath, and he pronounced judgment on him. 10Then the king of Babylon killed the sons of Zedekiah before his eyes. And he killed all the princes of Judah in Riblah. 11He also put out the eyes of Zedekiah; and the king of Babylon bound him in bronze fetters, took him to Babylon, and put him in prison till the day of his death.

The Temple and City Plundered and Burned

12Now in the fifth month, on the tenth *day* of the month (which *was* the nineteenth year of King Nebuchadnezzar king of Babylon), Nebuzaradan, the captain of the guard, *who* served the king of Babylon, came to Jerusalem. 13He burned the house of the LORD and the king's house; all the houses of Jerusalem, that is, all the houses of the great, he burned with fire. 14And all the army of the Chaldeans who *were* with the captain of the guard broke down all the walls of Jerusalem all around. 15Then Nebuzaradan the captain of the guard carried away captive *some* of the poor people, the rest of the people who remained in the city, the defectors who had deserted to the king of Babylon, and the rest of the craftsmen. 16But Nebuzaradan the captain of the guard left *some* of the poor of the land as vinedressers and farmers.

17The bronze pillars that *were* in the house of the LORD, and the carts and the bronze Sea that *were* in the house of the LORD, the Chaldeans broke in pieces, and carried all their bronze to Babylon. 18They also took away the pots, the shovels, the trimmers, the bowls, the spoons, and all the bronze utensils with which the priests ministered. 19The basins, the firepans, the bowls, the pots, the lampstands, the spoons, and the cups, whatever *was* solid gold and whatever *was* solid silver, the captain of the guard took away. 20The two pillars, one Sea, the twelve bronze bulls which *were* under *it, and* the carts, which King Solomon had made for the house of the LORD—the bronze of all these articles was beyond measure. 21Now *concerning* the pillars: the height of one pillar *was* eighteen cubits, a measuring line of twelve cubits could measure its circumference, and its thickness *was* four fingers; *it was* hollow. 22A capital of bronze *was* on it; and the height of one capital *was* five cubits, with a network and pomegranates all around the capital, all of bronze. The second pillar, with pomegranates was the same. 23There were ninety-six pomegranates on the sides; all the pomegranates, all around on the network, *were* one hundred.

The People Taken Captive to Babylonia

24The captain of the guard took Seraiah the chief priest, Zephaniah the second priest, and the three doorkeepers. 25He also took out of the city an officer who had charge of the men of war, seven men of the king's close associates who were found in the city, the principal scribe of the army who mustered the people of

---

52:7 [a]Or *the Arabah,* that is, the Jordan Valley

the land, and sixty men of the people of the land who were found in the midst of the city. [26]And Nebuzaradan the captain of the guard took these and brought them to the king of Babylon at Riblah. [27]Then the king of Babylon struck them and put them to death at Riblah in the land of Hamath. Thus Judah was carried away captive from its own land.

[28]These *are* the people whom Nebuchadnezzar carried away captive: in the seventh year, three thousand and twenty-three Jews; [29]in the eighteenth year of Nebuchadnezzar he carried away captive from Jerusalem eight hundred and thirty-two persons; [30]in the twenty-third year of Nebuchadnezzar, Nebuzaradan the captain of the guard carried away captive of the Jews seven hundred and forty-five persons. All the persons *were* four thousand six hundred.

Jehoiachin Released from Prison

[31]Now it came to pass in the thirty-seventh year of the captivity of Jehoiachin king of Judah, in the twelfth month, on the twenty-fifth *day* of the month, *that* Evil-Merodach[a] king of Babylon, in the first *year* of his reign, lifted up the head of Jehoiachin king of Judah and brought him out of prison. [32]And he spoke kindly to him and gave him a more prominent seat than those of the kings who *were* with him in Babylon. [33]So Jehoiachin changed from his prison garments, and he ate bread regularly before the king all the days of his life. [34]And as for his provisions, there was a regular ration given him by the king of Babylon, a portion for each day until the day of his death, all the days of his life.

52:31 [a]Or *Awil-Marduk*

SOUL NOTE

A Ray of Hope *(52:32)* If the Book of Jeremiah were a movie, the last four verses would be the scene that leaves the door open for a sequel—one with a happy ending. The compassion that Evil-Merodach, king of Babylon, showed to Jehoiachin (52:31, 32) symbolizes God's compassion for His people. Just as Jehoiachin was restored to a position of power and cared for, the nations of Israel and Judah would be restored to their homeland and cared for by the Lord. God's holiness and justice should never be underestimated, but thankfully, neither should His compassion. God's compassion never fails. **Topic: Compassion**

Lamentations

What causes us to weep, to cry, to shed great tears of sadness? We do well to pay attention whenever we find our eyes filling with tears, for those emotional moments reveal much about what we value, what's important to us.

Lamentations is one such case in point. Written by the prophet Jeremiah, this book is essentially a funeral dirge mourning the fall of Jerusalem. Its five, short, tear-stained chapters depict the regrettable demise of God's rebellious people.

As a prophet, Jeremiah had predicted the fall of Jerusalem, but he wept at the fulfillment of his own prophecy. After witnessing the devastation, darkness, and despair all around him (3:1–18), Jeremiah turned his eyes heavenward. He found comfort in remembering that God keeps His covenants; He is filled with mercy, love, and goodness (3:22–24).

God's modern-day children can also find hope in God's unfailing mercy. No matter what, we are the recipients of perfect love and grace. Even divine discipline is nothing more than God's merciful attempt to draw us back to Himself! His compassion is continually extended to us and nothing can ever separate us from His love (Rom. 8:31–39).

If your heart is heavy today, listen to the tender voice of God speaking through the ancient book of Lamentations. Know that "the Lord will not cast off forever. Though He causes grief, yet He will show compassion according to the multitude of His mercies" (Lam. 3:31, 32). Through your tears, look to God.

SOUL CONCERN IN LAMENTATIONS

Jerusalem in Affliction

1 How lonely sits the city
That was full of people!
How like a widow is she,
Who *was* great among the nations!
The princess among the provinces
Has become a slave!

2 She weeps bitterly in the night,
Her tears *are* on her cheeks;
Among all her lovers
She has none to comfort *her.*
All her friends have dealt treacherously
with her;
They have become her enemies.

3 Judah has gone into captivity,
Under affliction and hard servitude;
She dwells among the nations,
She finds no rest;
All her persecutors overtake her in dire
straits.

4 The roads to Zion mourn
Because no one comes to the set
feasts.
All her gates are desolate;
Her priests sigh,
Her virgins are afflicted,
And she *is* in bitterness.

5 Her adversaries have become the master,
Her enemies prosper;
For the LORD has afflicted her
Because of the multitude of her
transgressions.
Her children have gone into captivity
before the enemy.

6 And from the daughter of Zion
All her splendor has departed.
Her princes have become like deer
That find no pasture,
That flee without strength
Before the pursuer.

7 In the days of her affliction and roaming,
Jerusalem remembers all her pleasant
things
That she had in the days of old.
When her people fell into the hand of
the enemy,
With no one to help her,
The adversaries saw her
And mocked at her downfall.[a]

8 Jerusalem has sinned gravely,
Therefore she has become vile.[a]

1:7 [a]Vulgate reads *her Sabbaths.* **1:8** [a]Septuagint and Vulgate read *moved* or *removed.*

KEY PASSAGE

Trauma

INTO THE VALLEY

(1:10–21)

Being a Christian does not guarantee a pain-free existence. In fact, our faith exposes us to difficulties and struggles that we may not otherwise have experienced. Here's what believers need to know about life's traumas:

- Suffering is not always punishment. God does allow people to face the miserable consequences of their sinful choices, but it doesn't mean that every suffering person in the world is being punished. Sometimes God allows people to suffer in order to strengthen their resolve, to shake them out of their complacency, or to help them empathize with other suffering people.
- God does not leave our side when we suffer (Ps. 23:4–6).
- God will reward us for the suffering we endure for His sake (Matt. 5:10).

When we trust in God, we can change our perspective on life's traumas from "Why me?" to "How can I grow from this?"

To Learn More: Turn to the article about trauma on pages 690, 691. See also the personality profile of Jonah on page 1163.

All who honored her despise her
Because they have seen her nakedness;
Yes, she sighs and turns away.

9 Her uncleanness *is* in her skirts;
She did not consider her destiny;
Therefore her collapse was awesome;
She had no comforter.
"O LORD, behold my affliction,
For *the* enemy is exalted!"

10 The adversary has spread his hand
Over all her pleasant things;
For she has seen the nations enter her
sanctuary,
Those whom You commanded
Not to enter Your assembly.

11 All her people sigh,
They seek bread;
They have given their valuables for food
to restore life.
"See, O LORD, and consider,
For I am scorned."

12 "*Is it* nothing to you, all you who pass
by?
Behold and see
If there is any sorrow like my sorrow,
Which has been brought on me,
Which the LORD has inflicted
In the day of His fierce anger.

13 "From above He has sent fire into my
bones,
And it overpowered them;
He has spread a net for my feet
And turned me back;
He has made me desolate
And faint all the day.

14 "The yoke of my transgressions was
bound;[a]
They were woven together by His
hands,
And thrust upon my neck.
He made my strength fail;
The Lord delivered me into the hands of
those whom I am not able to
withstand.

15 "The Lord has trampled underfoot all my
mighty *men* in my midst;
He has called an assembly against me
To crush my young men;
The Lord trampled *as* in a winepress
The virgin daughter of Judah.

16 "For these *things* I weep;
My eye, my eye overflows with water;
Because the comforter, who should
restore my life,
Is far from me.
My children are desolate
Because the enemy prevailed."

17 Zion spreads out her hands,
But no one comforts her;
The LORD has commanded concerning
Jacob
That those around him *become* his
adversaries;
Jerusalem has become an unclean thing
among them.

18 "The LORD is righteous,
For I rebelled against His
commandment.
Hear now, all peoples,
And behold my sorrow;
My virgins and my young men
Have gone into captivity.

19 "I called for my lovers,
But they deceived me;
My priests and my elders
Breathed their last in the city,
While they sought food
To restore their life.

20 "See, O LORD, that I *am* in distress;
My soul is troubled;
My heart is overturned within me,
For I have been very rebellious.
Outside the sword bereaves,
At home *it is* like death.

21 "They have heard that I sigh,
But no one comforts me.
All my enemies have heard of my
trouble;
They are glad that You have done *it*.
Bring on the day You have announced,
That they may become like me.

1:14 [a]Following Masoretic Text and Targum; Septuagint, Syriac, and Vulgate read *watched over.*

22 "Let all their wickedness come before You,
And do to them as You have done to me
For all my transgressions;
For my sighs *are* many,
And my heart *is* faint."

God's Anger with Jerusalem

2 How the Lord has covered the daughter of Zion
With a cloud in His anger!
He cast down from heaven to the earth
The beauty of Israel,
And did not remember His footstool
In the day of His anger.

2 The Lord has swallowed up and has not pitied
All the dwelling places of Jacob.
He has thrown down in His wrath
The strongholds of the daughter of Judah;
He has brought *them* down to the ground;
He has profaned the kingdom and its princes.

3 He has cut off in fierce anger
Every horn of Israel;
He has drawn back His right hand
From before the enemy.
He has blazed against Jacob like a flaming fire
Devouring all around.

4 Standing like an enemy, He has bent His bow;
With His right hand, like an adversary,
He has slain all *who were* pleasing to His eye;
On the tent of the daughter of Zion,
He has poured out His fury like fire.

5 The Lord was like an enemy.
He has swallowed up Israel,
He has swallowed up all her palaces;
He has destroyed her strongholds,
And has increased mourning and lamentation
In the daughter of Judah.

6 He has done violence to His tabernacle,
As if it were a garden;
He has destroyed His place of assembly;
The LORD has caused
The appointed feasts and Sabbaths to be forgotten in Zion.
In His burning indignation He has spurned the king and the priest.

7 The Lord has spurned His altar,
He has abandoned His sanctuary;
He has given up the walls of her palaces
Into the hand of the enemy.
They have made a noise in the house of the LORD
As on the day of a set feast.

8 The LORD has purposed to destroy
The wall of the daughter of Zion.
He has stretched out a line;
He has not withdrawn His hand from destroying;
Therefore He has caused the rampart and wall to lament;
They languished together.

9 Her gates have sunk into the ground;
He has destroyed and broken her bars.
Her king and her princes *are* among the nations;
The Law *is* no *more*,
And her prophets find no vision from the LORD.

SOUL NOTE

A Perfect Anger *(2:1)* Jerusalem was Israel's capital city. Israel was God's chosen nation. But when the people of Jerusalem turned their backs on God to pursue idols, their favored status did nothing to protect them from being punished. They had to endure God's anger, just like anyone who disobeys His commands. Unlike human anger, which is often the product of insecurity or a deficient temperament, God's anger flows from His perfect justice and holiness. But after this judgment occurred, Jeremiah wrote, "The Lord will not cast off forever. Though He causes grief, yet He will show compassion" (3:31, 32). **Topic: Anger**

10 The elders of the daughter of Zion
Sit on the ground *and* keep silence;
They throw dust on their heads
And gird themselves with sackcloth.
The virgins of Jerusalem
Bow their heads to the ground.

11 My eyes fail with tears,
My heart is troubled;
My bile is poured on the ground
Because of the destruction of the daughter of my people,
Because the children and the infants
Faint in the streets of the city.

12 They say to their mothers,
"Where *is* grain and wine?"
As they swoon like the wounded
In the streets of the city,
As their life is poured out
In their mothers' bosom.

13 How shall I console you?
To what shall I liken you,
O daughter of Jerusalem?
What shall I compare with you, that I may comfort you,
O virgin daughter of Zion?
For your ruin *is* spread wide as the sea;
Who can heal you?

14 Your prophets have seen for you
False and deceptive visions;
They have not uncovered your iniquity,
To bring back your captives,
But have envisioned for you false prophecies and delusions.

15 All who pass by clap *their* hands at you;
They hiss and shake their heads
At the daughter of Jerusalem:
"*Is* this the city that is called
'The perfection of beauty,
The joy of the whole earth'?"

16 All your enemies have opened their mouth against you;
They hiss and gnash *their* teeth.
They say, "We have swallowed *her* up!
Surely this *is* the day we have waited for;
We have found *it*, we have seen *it!*"

17 The LORD has done what He purposed;
He has fulfilled His word
Which He commanded in days of old.
He has thrown down and has not pitied,
And He has caused an enemy to rejoice over you;
He has exalted the horn of your adversaries.

18 Their heart cried out to the Lord,
"O wall of the daughter of Zion,
Let tears run down like a river day and night;
Give yourself no relief;
Give your eyes no rest.

19 "Arise, cry out in the night,
At the beginning of the watches;
Pour out your heart like water before the face of the Lord.
Lift your hands toward Him
For the life of your young children,
Who faint from hunger at the head of every street."

20 "See, O LORD, and consider!
To whom have You done this?
Should the women eat their offspring,
The children they have cuddled?[a]
Should the priest and prophet be slain
In the sanctuary of the Lord?

21 "Young and old lie
On the ground in the streets;
My virgins and my young men
Have fallen by the sword;
You have slain *them* in the day of Your anger,
You have slaughtered *and* not pitied.

22 "You have invited as to a feast day
The terrors that surround me.
In the day of the LORD's anger
There was no refugee or survivor.
Those whom I have borne and brought up
My enemies have destroyed."

THE PROPHET'S ANGUISH AND HOPE

3 I *am* the man *who* has seen affliction by the rod of His wrath.
2 He has led me and made *me* walk
In darkness and not *in* light.
3 Surely He has turned His hand against me
Time and time again throughout the day.

2:20 [a]Vulgate reads *a span long.*

4 He has aged my flesh and my skin,
And broken my bones.
5 He has besieged me
And surrounded *me* with bitterness and woe.
6 He has set me in dark places
Like the dead of long ago.

7 He has hedged me in so that I cannot get out;
He has made my chain heavy.
8 Even when I cry and shout,
He shuts out my prayer.
9 He has blocked my ways with hewn stone;
He has made my paths crooked.

10 He *has been* to me a bear lying in wait,
Like a lion in ambush.
11 He has turned aside my ways and torn me in pieces;
He has made me desolate.
12 He has bent His bow
And set me up as a target for the arrow.

13 He has caused the arrows of His quiver
To pierce my loins.[a]
14 I have become the ridicule of all my people—
Their taunting song all the day.
15 He has filled me with bitterness,
He has made me drink wormwood.

16 He has also broken my teeth with gravel,
And covered me with ashes.
17 You have moved my soul far from peace;
I have forgotten prosperity.
18 And I said, "My strength and my hope
Have perished from the LORD."

19 Remember my affliction and roaming,
The wormwood and the gall.
20 My soul still remembers
And sinks within me.
21 This I recall to my mind,
Therefore I have hope.

22 *Through* the LORD's mercies we are not consumed,
Because His compassions fail not.
23 *They are* new every morning;
Great *is* Your faithfulness.
24 "The LORD *is* my portion," says my soul,
"Therefore I hope in Him!"

3:13 [a]Literally *kidneys*

KEY PASSAGE

Emotional Life

NEW EVERY MORNING

(3:22–25)

Emotions are strange: Feelings come and go. At times, we feel as though we can conquer the world; at other times, we feel as though the world has conquered us. How can we deal with these surging emotions? How can we maintain our faith in God despite these ups and downs? God's people can trust in Him for every part of their lives—even their emotions.

- God knows our limits. He never gives us more than we—with His help—can handle (1 Cor. 10:13).
- No matter what happens today, tomorrow will be new. A fresh batch of God's mercies awaits us (Lam. 3:22, 23).
- The best response when circumstances threaten to overwhelm is to wait quietly for the Lord's help (3:25, 26).

One of the keys to maintaining a healthy emotional outlook is to leave the circumstances and challenges of everyday life in God's hands and to trust Him to do what's best.

To Learn More: Turn to the article about emotional life on pages 1040, 1041. See also the personality profile of Jeremiah on page 976.

Emotional Life

EMOTIONAL WELL-BEING

RICHARD DOBBINS

(Lamentations 3)

Columbine. Road rage. Workplace shootings. Parental advisory warnings. Abortion rights. Gay rights. The mere mention of a word or phrase can conjure up universal images of a rapidly changing culture. The unsettling issues of modern culture impact people. As they filter all of their life experiences through their thoughts and feelings, they arrive at personal interpretations of those experiences. These interpretations of life events may be positive or negative—healthy or unhealthy—and will affect their emotional life. A healthy emotional life is essential—but how can people maintain it in this evil world?

GAINING EMOTIONAL HEALTH

God's Word promises that His children can have peace, joy, and a "sound mind" (2 Tim. 1:7). The foundation of such healthy emotions, however, must be a healthy faith. Consider the following suggestions for gaining and maintaining emotional well-being in today's trying culture.

Healthy Faith Fosters Self-Worth
Even after confessing their sins and receiving God's forgiveness, many believers still have trouble finding peace and joy. Christ paid the price of human redemption. Each person is valuable, lovable, forgivable, and changeable in His sight. Emotionally healthy people see themselves as God sees them.

Healthy Faith Meets Reality
There is no earthly life without storms. *What* happens to people in life, however, is not nearly as important as *how* they choose to react to it. Emotionally healthy people can keep a correct perspective on their difficulties and react appropriately.

Healthy Faith Resists Future Shock
Healthy faith lessens one's fear of the inevitable: change. To live is to grow. To grow is to change. To resist change in life is to resist growth. Emotionally healthy people are not afraid to grow and change.

Healthy Faith Moderates Stress and Tension
A certain amount of stress and tension are essential for excitement, motivation, and growth in life. When people have healthy faith, they can trust more and worry less. Material possessions will perish with the passing of time, so people ought not spend much time or energy worrying about them. Emotionally healthy people spend time on endeavors of eternal significance that are also stress-relievers—such as enjoying close relationships.

Healthy Faith Finds Joy in Giving
Giving is contrary to human nature, but it is an essential element in Christianity. In fact, giving generously should be second nature to the developing disciple. When people give generously from the heart, they discover blessings from God (Mal. 3:10). Emotionally healthy people recognize the joy in generosity.

Healthy Faith Is Affirmed in Fellowship
Isolating oneself from other believers or adopting religious beliefs or practices that are without biblical support are harmful to healthy faith. Peter warns that, "no prophecy of Scripture is of any private interpretation" (2 Pet. 1:20). Paul advised believers to discern what is true by using sound bib-

lical interpretation (2 Tim. 3:14, 15). Emotionally healthy people identify not only with Christ but also with at least one established group of Christians.

Healthy Faith Sees God as Love
Sometimes people are limited in their understanding of God. For example, those with an overly strict earthly father may attribute an imbalanced strictness to God's character. To see Him only as the God who presided over the flood and the destruction of wickedness in Sodom and Gomorrah is to see only an angry God. While God is strict and angry at times, the Bible also says that God is love (1 John 4:16). Emotionally healthy people understand and experience God as love.

Healthy Faith Manages Anger Constructively
Properly directed, the energy anger creates can be very constructive. Anger makes a poor master, but an excellent servant. Emotionally healthy people direct the energy created by anger into constructive activities. They go for a walk and cool down instead of saying what can never be retracted or doing things that can never be undone. They put anger to work *for* them.

Healthy Faith Balances Work and Play
God gave people work in Genesis 2:15. He also gave them play, for He designated one day in seven for rest and worship (Gen. 2:2; Ex. 20:8–11). By keeping this balance, emotionally healthy people learn to work hard and rest well.

RESTORING EMOTIONAL HEALTH

People who feel emotionally unhealthy may be internalizing the pain of past or present situations. It is possible to help heal these unhealthy thoughts and feelings. There are four steps for them to follow to help "pray through" the process.

1. They need to talk honestly with God about what hurts them.
2. As they talk to God, they can let the feelings associated with the hurts come to the surface—fear, tears, anger, pain. Then they can give those feelings to God in prayer.
3. They can ask God for a new, constructive way to feel and think about the hurtful situations.
4. They can praise God for the new meaning He gives to life as they learn to see their hurts in a less painful way.

Of course, these suggestions are a process. Repeating the steps over a period of weeks or months helps bring healing and assurance. People will not find overnight relief from emotional hurts that may have lasted a lifetime. However, starting the process is a healthy beginning to gaining emotional well-being.

Even in our emotionally taxing world, Christians can enjoy the best of emotional health. A healthy faith is a helpful support in the unavoidable storms of life. It helps to remember Jeremiah's words about God: "His compassions fail not. They are new every morning; great is Your faithfulness" (Lam. 3:22, 23).

FURTHER MEDITATION:

Other passages to study about the issue of emotional life include:

- Joshua 1:5–9
- Psalms 4:7; 23
- Proverbs 3:31–33; 14:30
- John 16:20
- 2 Corinthians 7:10
- Philippians 4:9
- Colossians 3:12–17

To Learn More: Turn to the key passage note on emotional life at Lamentations 3:22–25 on page 1039. See also the personality profile of Jeremiah on page 976.

25 The LORD *is* good to those who wait for Him,
To the soul *who* seeks Him.
26 *It is* good that *one* should hope and wait quietly
For the salvation of the LORD.
27 *It is* good for a man to bear
The yoke in his youth.

28 Let him sit alone and keep silent,
Because *God* has laid *it* on him;
29 Let him put his mouth in the dust—
There may yet be hope.
30 Let him give *his* cheek to the one who strikes him,
And be full of reproach.

31 For the Lord will not cast off forever.
32 Though He causes grief,
Yet He will show compassion
According to the multitude of His mercies.
33 For He does not afflict willingly,
Nor grieve the children of men.

34 To crush under one's feet
All the prisoners of the earth,
35 To turn aside the justice *due* a man
Before the face of the Most High,
36 Or subvert a man in his cause—
The Lord does not approve.

37 Who *is* he *who* speaks and it comes to pass,
When the Lord has not commanded *it?*
38 *Is it* not from the mouth of the Most High
That woe and well-being proceed?
39 Why should a living man complain,
A man for the punishment of his sins?

40 Let us search out and examine our ways,
And turn back to the LORD;
41 Let us lift our hearts and hands
To God in heaven.
42 We have transgressed and rebelled;
You have not pardoned.

43 You have covered *Yourself* with anger
And pursued us;
You have slain *and* not pitied.
44 You have covered Yourself with a cloud,
That prayer should not pass through.
45 You have made us an offscouring and refuse
In the midst of the peoples.

46 All our enemies
Have opened their mouths against us.
47 Fear and a snare have come upon us,
Desolation and destruction.
48 My eyes overflow with rivers of water
For the destruction of the daughter of my people.

49 My eyes flow and do not cease,
Without interruption,
50 Till the LORD from heaven
Looks down and sees.
51 My eyes bring suffering to my soul
Because of all the daughters of my city.

52 My enemies without cause
Hunted me down like a bird.
53 They silenced[a] my life in the pit
And threw stones at me.
54 The waters flowed over my head;
I said, "I am cut off!"

55 I called on Your name, O LORD,
From the lowest pit.
56 You have heard my voice:
"Do not hide Your ear

3:53 [a]Septuagint reads *put to death.*

SOUL NOTE

Wait Watcher *(3:26)* "The LORD is good to those who wait for Him," wrote Jeremiah (3:25). In this world of direct access, instant credit, and immediate gratification, the idea of waiting for something seems quaint, almost outdated. Yet waiting quietly for God's blessings is a discipline that yields tremendous rewards. One can see God work in his or her life and be recharged. "Those who wait on the LORD shall renew their strength" (Is. 40:31). A time of waiting can be a time of renewal.
Topic: Hope

From my sighing, from my cry for help."
57 You drew near on the day I called on
You,
And said, "Do not fear!"

58 O Lord, You have pleaded the case for
my soul;
You have redeemed my life.
59 O LORD, You have seen *how* I am
wronged;
Judge my case.
60 You have seen all their vengeance,
All their schemes against me.

61 You have heard their reproach, O LORD,
All their schemes against me,
62 The lips of my enemies
And their whispering against me all the
day.
63 Look at their sitting down and their
rising up;
I *am* their taunting song.

64 Repay them, O LORD,
According to the work of their hands.
65 Give them a veiled[a] heart;
Your curse *be* upon them!
66 In Your anger,
Pursue and destroy them
From under the heavens of the LORD.

THE DEGRADATION OF ZION

4 How the gold has become dim!
How changed the fine gold!
The stones of the sanctuary are
scattered
At the head of every street.

2 The precious sons of Zion,
Valuable as fine gold,
How they are regarded as clay pots,
The work of the hands of the potter!

3 Even the jackals present their breasts
To nurse their young;
But the daughter of my people *is* cruel,
Like ostriches in the wilderness.

4 The tongue of the infant clings
To the roof of its mouth for thirst;
The young children ask for bread,
But no one breaks *it* for them.

5 Those who ate delicacies
Are desolate in the streets;
Those who were brought up in scarlet
Embrace ash heaps.

6 The punishment of the iniquity of the
daughter of my people
Is greater than the punishment of the sin
of Sodom,
Which was overthrown in a moment,
With no hand to help her!

7 Her Nazirites[a] were brighter than snow
And whiter than milk;
They were more ruddy in body than
rubies,
Like sapphire in their appearance.

8 *Now* their appearance is blacker than
soot;
They go unrecognized in the streets;
Their skin clings to their bones,
It has become as dry as wood.

9 *Those* slain by the sword are better off
Than *those* who die of hunger;
For these pine away,
Stricken *for lack* of the fruits of the
field.

3:65 [a]A Jewish tradition reads *sorrow of.*
4:7 [a]Or *nobles*

SOUL NOTE

In the Trenches *(3:55–57)* Soldiers speak reverently of the relationships that are forged in the heat of battle. People who struggle together through dire circumstances form a lifelong bond deeper and more intense than that of other relationships. This same kind of bond is created when we turn to God during the battles of our lives. The next time you find yourself "in the trenches," don't lose sight of the One standing right beside you. Jeremiah didn't: "I called on Your name, O LORD, from the lowest pit. . . . You drew near . . . and said, 'Do not fear!'" **Topic: Trauma**

10 The hands of the compassionate women
Have cooked their own children;
They became food for them
In the destruction of the daughter of my people.

11 The LORD has fulfilled His fury,
He has poured out His fierce anger.
He kindled a fire in Zion,
And it has devoured its foundations.

12 The kings of the earth,
And all inhabitants of the world,
Would not have believed
That the adversary and the enemy
Could enter the gates of Jerusalem—

13 Because of the sins of her prophets
And the iniquities of her priests,
Who shed in her midst
The blood of the just.

14 They wandered blind in the streets;
They have defiled themselves with blood,
So that no one would touch their garments.

15 They cried out to them,
"Go away, unclean!
Go away, go away,
Do not touch us!"
When they fled and wandered,
Those among the nations said,
"They shall no longer dwell *here.*"

16 The face[a] of the LORD scattered them;
He no longer regards them.
The people do not respect the priests
Nor show favor to the elders.

17 Still our eyes failed us,
Watching vainly for our help;
In our watching we watched
For a nation *that* could not save *us.*

18 They tracked our steps
So that we could not walk in our streets.
Our end was near;
Our days were over,
For our end had come.

19 Our pursuers were swifter
Than the eagles of the heavens.
They pursued us on the mountains
And lay in wait for us in the wilderness.

20 The breath of our nostrils, the anointed of the LORD,
Was caught in their pits,
Of whom we said, "Under his shadow
We shall live among the nations."

21 Rejoice and be glad, O daughter of Edom,
You who dwell in the land of Uz!
The cup shall also pass over to you
And you shall become drunk and make yourself naked.

22 *The punishment of* your iniquity is accomplished,
O daughter of Zion;
He will no longer send you into captivity.
He will punish your iniquity,
O daughter of Edom;
He will uncover your sins!

A Prayer for Restoration

5 Remember, O LORD, what has come upon us;
Look, and behold our reproach!
2 Our inheritance has been turned over to aliens,
And our houses to foreigners.
3 We have become orphans and waifs,
Our mothers *are* like widows.

4 We pay for the water we drink,
And our wood comes at a price.
5 *They* pursue at our heels;[a]
We labor *and* have no rest.
6 We have given our hand *to* the Egyptians
And the Assyrians, to be satisfied with bread.

7 Our fathers sinned *and are* no more,
But we bear their iniquities.
8 Servants rule over us;
There is none to deliver *us* from their hand.
9 We get our bread *at the risk* of our lives,
Because of the sword in the wilderness.

10 Our skin is hot as an oven,
Because of the fever of famine.

4:16 [a]Targum reads *anger.* **5:5** [a]Literally *necks*

11 They ravished the women in Zion,
The maidens in the cities of Judah.
12 Princes were hung up by their hands,
And elders were not respected.
13 Young men ground at the millstones;
Boys staggered under *loads of* wood.
14 The elders have ceased *gathering at* the gate,
And the young men from their music.

You, O LORD, remain forever;
Your throne from generation to generation.
LAMENTATIONS 5:19

15 The joy of our heart has ceased;
Our dance has turned into mourning.
16 The crown has fallen *from* our head.
Woe to us, for we have sinned!
17 Because of this our heart is faint;
Because of these *things* our eyes grow dim;
18 Because of Mount Zion which is desolate,
With foxes walking about on it.

19 You, O LORD, remain forever;
Your throne from generation to generation.
20 Why do You forget us forever,
And forsake us for so long a time?
21 Turn us back to You, O LORD, and we will be restored;
Renew our days as of old,
22 Unless You have utterly rejected us,
And are very angry with us!

Ezekiel

Disillusioned, demoralized. Bright hopes and dreams shattered. Great ideas ripped to shreds. Potential wasted. These feelings cause us to step back in defeat, immobilized. Such was the case for the disillusioned and demoralized Jewish people who had been deported to Babylon.

Ezekiel was the priest-in-training called to reveal God's Word to this exile community. In this book, Ezekiel describes how God revealed His glory to him (1:28; 3:12, 23). Ezekiel recorded God's messages condemning the terrible idolatry of the Jews and predicted the desecration of the temple which would cause His glory to depart (ch. 8—11). Ezekiel told the exiles that God's judgment was far from over and that Jerusalem would be totally destroyed.

Ezekiel also faced disillusionment. He found little reception for his sobering message. The same spiritual hardness that led to Judah's captivity continued afterwards as well. Steeped in tradition and resolute in their cynicism, the exiles resented Ezekiel's message and rejected both it and him.

Like most of the prophetic books, the promise of redemption follows judgment. Ezekiel predicted the restoration of the Jewish people and the rebuilding of the temple. The glory would return in a future messianic age (ch. 40—48).

The people had sinned and been punished. In their demoralized state, Ezekiel brought them God's message of hope. It was time to reassess, to learn from their mistakes, and to move on. God can do the same for us. He is with us always—even when we feel defeated. If we look, we will find the light in the darkness.

Ezekiel's Vision of God

1 Now it came to pass in the thirtieth year, in the fourth *month,* on the fifth *day* of the month, as I *was* among the captives by the River Chebar, *that* the heavens were opened and I saw visions[a] of God. 2On the fifth *day* of the month, which *was* in the fifth year of King Jehoiachin's captivity, 3the word of the LORD came expressly to Ezekiel the priest, the son of Buzi, in the land of the Chaldeans[a] by the River Chebar; and the hand of the LORD was upon him there.

4Then I looked, and behold, a whirlwind was coming out of the north, a great cloud with raging fire engulfing itself; and brightness *was* all around it and radiating out of its midst like the color of amber, out of the midst of the fire. 5Also from within it *came* the likeness of four living creatures. And this *was* their appearance: they had the likeness of a man. 6Each one had four faces, and each one had four wings. 7Their legs *were* straight, and the soles of their feet *were* like the soles of calves' feet. They sparkled like the color of burnished bronze. 8The hands of a man *were* under their wings on their four sides; and each of the four had faces and wings. 9Their wings touched one another. *The creatures* did not turn when they went, but each one went straight forward.

10As for the likeness of their faces, *each* had the face of a man; each of the four had the face of a lion on the right side, each of the four had the face of an ox on the left side, and each of the four had the face of an eagle. 11Thus *were* their faces. Their wings stretched upward; two *wings* of each one touched one another, and two covered their bodies. 12And each one went straight forward; they went wherever the spirit wanted to go, and they did not turn when they went.

13As for the likeness of the living creatures, their appearance *was* like burning coals of fire, like the appearance of torches going back and forth among the living creatures. The fire was bright, and out of the fire went lightning. 14And the living creatures ran back and forth, in appearance like a flash of lightning.

15Now as I looked at the living creatures, behold, a wheel *was* on the earth beside each living creature with its four faces. 16The appearance of the wheels and their workings *was* like the color of beryl, and all four had the same likeness. The appearance of their workings *was,* as it were, a wheel in the middle of a wheel. 17When they moved, they went toward any one of four directions; they did not turn aside when they went. 18As for their rims, they were so high they were awesome; and their rims *were* full of eyes, all around the four of them. 19When the living creatures went, the wheels went beside them; and when the living creatures were lifted up from the earth, the wheels were lifted up. 20Wherever the spirit wanted to go, they went, *because* there the spirit went; and the wheels were lifted together with them, for the spirit of the living creatures[a] *was* in the wheels. 21When those went, *these* went; when those stood, *these* stood; and when those were lifted up from the earth, the wheels were lifted up together with them, for the spirit of the living creatures[a] *was* in the wheels.

22The likeness of the firmament above the heads of the living creatures[a] *was* like the color of an awesome crystal, stretched out over their heads. 23And under the firmament their wings *spread out* straight, one toward another. Each one had two which covered one side, and each one had two which covered the other side of the body. 24When they went, I heard the noise of their wings, like the noise of many waters, like the voice of the Almighty, a tumult like the noise of an army; and when they stood still, they let down their wings. 25A voice came from above the firmament that *was* over their heads; whenever they stood, they let down their wings.

26And above the firmament over their heads *was* the likeness of a throne, in appearance like a sapphire stone; on the likeness of the throne *was* a likeness with the appearance of a man high above it. 27Also from the appearance of His waist and upward I saw, as it were, the color of amber with the appearance of fire all around within it; and from the appearance of His waist and downward I saw, as it were, the appearance of fire with brightness all around. 28Like the appearance of a rainbow in a cloud

---

1:1 [a]Following Masoretic Text, Septuagint, and Vulgate; Syriac and Targum read *a vision.* **1:3** [a]Or *Babylonians,* and so elsewhere in this book
1:20 [a]Literally *living creature;* Septuagint and Vulgate read *spirit of life;* Targum reads *creatures.*
1:21 [a]Literally *living creature;* Septuagint and Vulgate read *spirit of life;* Targum reads *creatures.*
1:22 [a]Following Septuagint, Targum, and Vulgate; Masoretic Text reads *living creature.*

on a rainy day, so *was* the appearance of the
brightness all around it. This *was* the appearance of the likeness of the glory of the LORD.

EZEKIEL SENT TO REBELLIOUS ISRAEL

So when I saw *it,* I fell on my face, and I
heard a voice of One speaking.

2 And He said to me, "Son of man, stand on
your feet, and I will speak to you." 2Then
the Spirit entered me when He spoke to me,
and set me on my feet; and I heard Him who
spoke to me. 3And He said to me: "Son of
man, I am sending you to the children of Israel, to a rebellious nation that has rebelled
against Me; they and their fathers have transgressed against Me to this very day. 4For *they*
are impudent and stubborn children. I am
sending you to them, and you shall say to
them, 'Thus says the Lord GOD.' 5As for them,
whether they hear or whether they refuse—
for they *are* a rebellious house—yet they will
know that a prophet has been among them.

6"And you, son of man, do not be afraid of
them nor be afraid of their words, though briers and thorns *are* with you and you dwell
among scorpions; do not be afraid of their
words or dismayed by their looks, though they
are a rebellious house. 7You shall speak My
words to them, whether they hear or whether
they refuse, for they *are* rebellious. 8But you,
son of man, hear what I say to you. Do not be
rebellious like that rebellious house; open
your mouth and eat what I give you."

9Now when I looked, there was a hand
stretched out to me; and behold, a scroll of a
book *was* in it. 10Then He spread it before me;
and *there was* writing on the inside and on the
outside, and written on it *were* lamentations
and mourning and woe.

3 Moreover He said to me, "Son of man, eat
what you find; eat this scroll, and go,
speak to the house of Israel." 2So I opened my
mouth, and He caused me to eat that scroll.

3And He said to me, "Son of man, feed your
belly, and fill your stomach with this scroll
that I give you." So I ate, and it was in my
mouth like honey in sweetness.

4Then He said to me: "Son of man, go to the
house of Israel and speak with My words to
them. 5For you *are* not sent to a people of unfamiliar speech and of hard language, *but* to
the house of Israel, 6not to many people of unfamiliar speech and of hard language, whose
words you cannot understand. Surely, had I
sent you to them, they would have listened to
you. 7But the house of Israel will not listen to
you, because they will not listen to Me; for all
the house of Israel *are* impudent and hard-
hearted. 8Behold, I have made your face
strong against their faces, and your forehead
strong against their foreheads. 9Like adamant
stone, harder than flint, I have made your
forehead; do not be afraid of them, nor be dismayed at their looks, though they *are* a rebellious house."

10Moreover He said to me: "Son of man, receive into your heart all My words that I speak
to you, and hear with your ears. 11And go, get
to the captives, to the children of your people,
and speak to them and tell them, 'Thus says
the Lord GOD,' whether they hear, or whether
they refuse."

12Then the Spirit lifted me up, and I heard
behind me a great thunderous voice: "Blessed
is the glory of the LORD from His place!" 13*I*
also *heard* the noise of the wings of the living
creatures that touched one another, and the
noise of the wheels beside them, and a great
thunderous noise. 14So the Spirit lifted me up
and took me away, and I went in bitterness, in
the heat of my spirit; but the hand of the LORD
was strong upon me. 15Then I came to the captives at Tel Abib, who dwelt by the River
Chebar; and I sat where they sat, and remained there astonished among them seven
days.

EZEKIEL IS A WATCHMAN

16Now it came to pass at the end of seven
days that the word of the LORD came to me,
saying, 17"Son of man, I have made you a
watchman for the house of Israel; therefore
hear a word from My mouth, and give them
warning from Me: 18When I say to the wicked,
'You shall surely die,' and you give him no
warning, nor speak to warn the wicked from
his wicked way, to save his life, that same
wicked *man* shall die in his iniquity; but his
blood I will require at your hand. 19Yet, if you
warn the wicked, and he does not turn from
his wickedness, nor from his wicked way, he
shall die in his iniquity; but you have delivered your soul.

20"Again, when a righteous *man* turns from
his righteousness and commits iniquity, and I
lay a stumbling block before him, he shall die;
because you did not give him warning, he
shall die in his sin, and his righteousness

which he has done shall not be remembered; but his blood I will require at your hand. 21Nevertheless if you warn the righteous *man* that the righteous should not sin, and he does not sin, he shall surely live because he took warning; also you will have delivered your soul."

22Then the hand of the LORD was upon me there, and He said to me, "Arise, go out into the plain, and there I shall talk with you."

23So I arose and went out into the plain, and behold, the glory of the LORD stood there, like the glory which I saw by the River Chebar; and I fell on my face. 24Then the Spirit entered me and set me on my feet, and spoke with me and said to me: "Go, shut yourself inside your house. 25And you, O son of man, surely they will put ropes on you and bind you with them, so that you cannot go out among them. 26I will make your tongue cling to the roof of your mouth, so that you shall be mute and not be one to rebuke them, for they *are* a rebellious house. 27But when I speak with you, I will open your mouth, and you shall say to them, 'Thus says the Lord GOD.' He who hears, let him hear; and he who refuses, let him refuse; for they *are* a rebellious house.

THE SIEGE OF JERUSALEM PORTRAYED

4 "You also, son of man, take a clay tablet and lay it before you, and portray on it a city, Jerusalem. 2Lay siege against it, build a siege wall against it, and heap up a mound against it; set camps against it also, and place battering rams against it all around. 3Moreover take for yourself an iron plate, and set it *as* an iron wall between you and the city. Set your face against it, and it shall be besieged, and you shall lay siege against it. This *will be* a sign to the house of Israel.

4"Lie also on your left side, and lay the iniquity of the house of Israel upon it. *According* to the number of the days that you lie on it, you shall bear their iniquity. 5For I have laid on you the years of their iniquity, according to the number of the days, three hundred and ninety days; so you shall bear the iniquity of the house of Israel. 6And when you have completed them, lie again on your right side; then you shall bear the iniquity of the house of Judah forty days. I have laid on you a day for each year.

7"Therefore you shall set your face toward the siege of Jerusalem; your arm *shall be* uncovered, and you shall prophesy against it. 8And surely I will restrain you so that you cannot turn from one side to another till you have ended the days of your siege.

9"Also take for yourself wheat, barley, beans, lentils, millet, and spelt; put them into one vessel, and make bread of them for yourself. *During* the number of days that you lie on your side, three hundred and ninety days, you shall eat it. 10And your food which you eat *shall be* by weight, twenty shekels a day; from time to time you shall eat it. 11You shall also drink water by measure, one-sixth of a hin; from time to time you shall drink. 12And you shall eat it *as* barley cakes; and bake it using fuel of human waste in their sight."

13Then the LORD said, "So shall the children of Israel eat their defiled bread among the Gentiles, where I will drive them."

14So I said, "Ah, Lord GOD! Indeed I have never defiled myself from my youth till now; I have never eaten what died of itself or was torn by beasts, nor has abominable flesh ever come into my mouth."

15Then He said to me, "See, I am giving you cow dung instead of human waste, and you shall prepare your bread over it."

16Moreover He said to me, "Son of man, surely I will cut off the supply of bread in Jerusalem; they shall eat bread by weight and with anxiety, and shall drink water by measure and with dread, 17that they may lack bread and water, and be dismayed with one another, and waste away because of their iniquity.

A SWORD AGAINST JERUSALEM

5 "And you, son of man, take a sharp sword, take it as a barber's razor, and pass *it* over your head and your beard; then take scales to weigh and divide the hair. 2You shall burn with fire one-third in the midst of the city, when the days of the siege are finished; then you shall take one-third and strike around *it* with the sword, and one-third you shall scatter in the wind: I will draw out a sword after them. 3You shall also take a small number of them and bind them in the edge of your *garment*. 4Then take some of them again and throw them into the midst of the fire, and burn them in the fire. From there a fire will go out into all the house of Israel.

5"Thus says the Lord GOD: 'This *is* Jerusalem; I have set her in the midst of the nations and the countries all around her. 6She has rebelled against My judgments by doing wickedness more than the nations, and against My statutes more than the countries that *are* all around her; for they have refused My judgments, and they have not walked in My statutes.' 7Therefore thus says the Lord GOD: 'Because you have multiplied *disobedience* more than the nations that *are* all around you, have not walked in My statutes nor kept My judgments, nor even done[a] according to the judgments of the nations that *are* all around you'—8therefore thus says the Lord GOD: 'Indeed I, even I, *am* against you and will execute judgments in your midst in the sight of the nations. 9And I will do among you what I have never done, and the like of which I will never do again, because of all your abominations. 10Therefore fathers shall eat *their* sons in your midst, and sons shall eat their fathers; and I will execute judgments among you, and all of you who remain I will scatter to all the winds.

11'Therefore, *as* I live,' says the Lord GOD, 'surely, because you have defiled My sanctuary with all your detestable things and with all your abominations, therefore I will also diminish *you;* My eye will not spare, nor will I have any pity. 12One-third of you shall die of the pestilence, and be consumed with famine in your midst; and one-third shall fall by the sword all around you; and I will scatter another third to all the winds, and I will draw out a sword after them.

13'Thus shall My anger be spent, and I will cause My fury to rest upon them, and I will be avenged; and they shall know that I, the LORD, have spoken *it* in My zeal, when I have spent My fury upon them. 14Moreover I will make you a waste and a reproach among the nations that *are* all around you, in the sight of all who pass by.

15'So it[a] shall be a reproach, a taunt, a lesson, and an astonishment to the nations that *are* all around you, when I execute judgments among you in anger and in fury and in furious rebukes. I, the LORD, have spoken. 16When I send against them the terrible arrows of famine which shall be for destruction, which I will send to destroy you, I will increase the famine upon you and cut off your supply of bread. 17So I will send against you famine and wild beasts, and they will bereave you. Pestilence and blood shall pass through you, and I will bring the sword against you. I, the LORD, have spoken.' "

JUDGMENT ON IDOLATROUS ISRAEL

6 Now the word of the LORD came to me, saying: 2"Son of man, set your face toward the mountains of Israel, and prophesy against them, 3and say, 'O mountains of Israel, hear the word of the Lord GOD! Thus says the Lord GOD to the mountains, to the hills, to the ravines, and to the valleys: "Indeed I, *even* I, will bring a sword against you, and I will destroy your high places. 4Then your altars shall be desolate, your incense altars shall be broken, and I will cast down your slain *men* before your idols. 5And I will lay the corpses of the children of Israel before their idols, and I will scatter your bones all around your altars. 6In all your dwelling places the cities shall be laid waste, and the high places shall be desolate, so that your altars may be laid waste and made desolate, your idols may be broken and made to cease, your incense altars may be cut down, and your works may be abolished. 7The slain shall fall in your midst, and you shall know that I *am* the LORD.

8"Yet I will leave a remnant, so that you may have *some* who escape the sword among the nations, when you are scattered through the countries. 9Then those of you who escape will remember Me among the nations where they are carried captive, because I was crushed by their adulterous heart which has departed from Me, and by their eyes which play the harlot after their idols; they will loathe themselves for the evils which they committed in all their abominations. 10And they shall know that I *am* the LORD; I have not said in vain that I would bring this calamity upon them."

11'Thus says the Lord GOD: "Pound your fists and stamp your feet, and say, 'Alas, for all the evil abominations of the house of Israel! For they shall fall by the sword, by famine, and by pestilence. 12He who is far off shall die by the pestilence, he who is near shall fall by the sword, and he who remains and is besieged shall die by the famine. Thus will I spend My fury upon them. 13Then you shall know that I *am* the LORD, when their slain are among their idols all around their altars, on every high hill, on all the mountaintops, un-

---

5:7 [a]Following Masoretic Text, Septuagint, Targum, and Vulgate; many Hebrew manuscripts and Syriac read *but have done* (compare 11:12).

5:15 [a]Septuagint, Syriac, Targum, and Vulgate read *you*.

der every green tree, and under every thick oak, wherever they offered sweet incense to all their idols. [14]So I will stretch out My hand against them and make the land desolate, yes, more desolate than the wilderness toward Diblah, in all their dwelling places. Then they shall know that I *am* the LORD.' " ' "

JUDGMENT ON ISRAEL IS NEAR

7 Moreover the word of the LORD came to me, saying, [2]"And you, son of man, thus says the Lord GOD to the land of Israel:

'An end! The end has come upon the
four corners of the land.
3 Now the end *has come* upon you,
And I will send My anger against you;
I will judge you according to your ways,
And I will repay you for all your
abominations.
4 My eye will not spare you,
Nor will I have pity;
But I will repay your ways,
And your abominations will be in your
midst;
Then you shall know that I *am* the
LORD!'

[5]"Thus says the Lord GOD:

'A disaster, a singular disaster;
Behold, it has come!
6 An end has come,
The end has come;
It has dawned for you;
Behold, it has come!
7 Doom has come to you, you who dwell
in the land;
The time has come,
A day of trouble *is* near,
And not of rejoicing in the mountains.
8 Now upon you I will soon pour out My
fury,
And spend My anger upon you;
I will judge you according to your
ways,
And I will repay you for all your
abominations.

9 'My eye will not spare,
Nor will I have pity;
I will repay you according to your ways,
And your abominations will be in your
midst.
Then you shall know that I *am* the LORD
who strikes.

10 'Behold, the day!
Behold, it has come!
Doom has gone out;
The rod has blossomed,
Pride has budded.
11 Violence has risen up into a rod of
wickedness;
None of them *shall remain,*
None of their multitude,
None of them;
Nor *shall there be* wailing for them.
12 The time has come,
The day draws near.

'Let not the buyer rejoice,
Nor the seller mourn,
For wrath *is* on their whole multitude.
13 For the seller shall not return to what
has been sold,
Though he may still be alive;
For the vision concerns the whole
multitude,
And it shall not turn back;
No one will strengthen himself
Who lives in iniquity.

14 'They have blown the trumpet and made
everyone ready,
But no one goes to battle;
For My wrath *is* on all their multitude.
15 The sword *is* outside,
And the pestilence and famine within.
Whoever *is* in the field
Will die by the sword;
And whoever *is* in the city,
Famine and pestilence will devour him.

16 'Those who survive will escape and be
on the mountains
Like doves of the valleys,
All of them mourning,
Each for his iniquity.
17 Every hand will be feeble,
And every knee will be *as* weak *as* water.
18 They will also be girded with sackcloth;
Horror will cover them;
Shame *will be* on every face,
Baldness on all their heads.

19 'They will throw their silver into the
streets,

And their gold will be like refuse;
Their silver and their gold will not be
able to deliver them
In the day of the wrath of the LORD;
They will not satisfy their souls,
Nor fill their stomachs,
Because it became their stumbling block
of iniquity.

20 'As for the beauty of his ornaments,
He set it in majesty;
But they made from it
The images of their abominations—
Their detestable things;
Therefore I have made it
Like refuse to them.
21 I will give it as plunder
Into the hands of strangers,
And to the wicked of the earth as spoil;
And they shall defile it.
22 I will turn My face from them,
And they will defile My secret place;
For robbers shall enter it and defile it.

23 'Make a chain,
For the land is filled with crimes of
blood,
And the city is full of violence.
24 Therefore I will bring the worst of the
Gentiles,
And they will possess their houses;
I will cause the pomp of the strong to
cease,
And their holy places shall be defiled.
25 Destruction comes;
They will seek peace, but *there shall be*
none.
26 Disaster will come upon disaster,
And rumor will be upon rumor.
Then they will seek a vision from a
prophet;
But the law will perish from the priest,
And counsel from the elders.

27 'The king will mourn,
The prince will be clothed with
desolation,
And the hands of the common people
will tremble.
I will do to them according to their way,
And according to what they deserve I
will judge them;
Then they shall know that I *am* the
LORD!' "

ABOMINATIONS IN THE TEMPLE

8 And it came to pass in the sixth year, in
the sixth *month,* on the fifth *day* of the
month, as I sat in my house with the elders of
Judah sitting before me, that the hand of the
Lord GOD fell upon me there. [2]Then I looked,
and there was a likeness, like the appearance
of fire—from the appearance of His waist and
downward, fire; and from His waist and upward, like the appearance of brightness, like
the color of amber. [3]He stretched out the form
of a hand, and took me by a lock of my hair;
and the Spirit lifted me up between earth and
heaven, and brought me in visions of God to
Jerusalem, to the door of the north gate of the
inner *court,* where the seat of the image of
jealousy *was,* which provokes to jealousy.
[4]And behold, the glory of the God of Israel *was*
there, like the vision that I saw in the plain.
[5]Then He said to me, "Son of man, lift your
eyes now toward the north." So I lifted my
eyes toward the north, and there, north of the
altar gate, was this image of jealousy in the
entrance.
[6]Furthermore He said to me, "Son of man,
do you see what they are doing, the great
abominations that the house of Israel commits
here, to make Me go far away from My sanctuary? Now turn again, you will see greater
abominations." [7]So He brought me to the door
of the court; and when I looked, there was a
hole in the wall. [8]Then He said to me, "Son of
man, dig into the wall"; and when I dug into
the wall, there was a door.
[9]And He said to me, "Go in, and see the
wicked abominations which they are doing
there." [10]So I went in and saw, and there—
every sort of creeping thing, abominable
beasts, and all the idols of the house of Israel,
portrayed all around on the walls. [11]And there
stood before them seventy men of the elders
of the house of Israel, and in their midst stood
Jaazaniah the son of Shaphan. Each man had
a censer in his hand, and a thick cloud of incense went up. [12]Then He said to me, "Son of
man, have you seen what the elders of the
house of Israel do in the dark, every man in
the room of his idols? For they say, 'The LORD
does not see us, the LORD has forsaken the
land.' "
[13]And He said to me, "Turn again, *and* you
will see greater abominations that they are doing." [14]So He brought me to the door of the
north gate of the LORD's house; and to my dis-

may, women were sitting there weeping for Tammuz.

[15]Then He said to me, "Have you seen *this,* O son of man? Turn again, you will see greater abominations than these." [16]So He brought me into the inner court of the LORD's house; and there, at the door of the temple of the LORD, between the porch and the altar, *were* about twenty-five men with their backs toward the temple of the LORD and their faces toward the east, and they were worshiping the sun toward the east.

[17]And He said to me, "Have you seen *this,* O son of man? Is it a trivial thing to the house of Judah to commit the abominations which they commit here? For they have filled the land with violence; then they have returned to provoke Me to anger. Indeed they put the branch to their nose. [18]Therefore I also will act in fury. My eye will not spare nor will I have pity; and though they cry in My ears with a loud voice, I will not hear them."

The Wicked Are Slain

9 Then He called out in my hearing with a loud voice, saying, "Let those who have charge over the city draw near, each *with* a deadly weapon in his hand." [2]And suddenly six men came from the direction of the upper gate, which faces north, each with his battle-ax in his hand. One man among them *was* clothed with linen and had a writer's inkhorn at his side. They went in and stood beside the bronze altar.

[3]Now the glory of the God of Israel had gone up from the cherub, where it had been, to the threshold of the temple.[a] And He called to the man clothed with linen, who *had* the writer's inkhorn at his side; [4]and the LORD said to him, "Go through the midst of the city, through the midst of Jerusalem, and put a mark on the foreheads of the men who sigh and cry over all the abominations that are done within it."

[5]To the others He said in my hearing, "Go after him through the city and kill; do not let your eye spare, nor have any pity. [6]Utterly slay old *and* young men, maidens and little children and women; but do not come near anyone on whom *is* the mark; and begin at My sanctuary." So they began with the elders who *were* before the temple. [7]Then He said to them, "Defile the temple, and fill the courts with the slain. Go out!" And they went out and killed in the city.

[8]So it was, that while they were killing them, I was left *alone;* and I fell on my face and cried out, and said, "Ah, Lord GOD! Will You destroy all the remnant of Israel in pouring out Your fury on Jerusalem?"

[9]Then He said to me, "The iniquity of the house of Israel and Judah *is* exceedingly great, and the land is full of bloodshed, and the city full of perversity; for they say, 'The LORD has forsaken the land, and the LORD does not see!' [10]And as for Me also, My eye will neither spare, nor will I have pity, *but* I will recompense their deeds on their own head."

[11]Just then, the man clothed with linen, who *had* the inkhorn at his side, reported back and said, "I have done as You commanded me."

The Glory Departs from the Temple

10 And I looked, and there in the firmament that was above the head of the cherubim, there appeared something like a sapphire stone, having the appearance of the likeness of a throne. [2]Then He spoke to the man clothed with linen, and said, "Go in among the wheels, under the cherub, fill your hands with coals of fire from among the

9:3 [a]Literally *house*

SOUL NOTE

Healthy Fear *(8:17)* By filling God's sanctuary with idols and other abominations, the Israelites demonstrated a dangerous lack of fear of the Lord. Evidently they felt that they could get away with it. This false security is often caused by an errant view of the Almighty. Many people claim that God is love and then stop there, as though that were His only attribute. They forget that He is also holy and just, and demands punishment for sin. Until people learn to respect God's holiness, they are as vulnerable as the ancient Israelites. **Topic: Fear/Fear of God**

cherubim, and scatter *them* over the city."
And he went in as I watched.
3Now the cherubim were standing on the
south side of the temple[a] when the man went
in, and the cloud filled the inner court. 4Then
the glory of the LORD went up from the cherub, *and paused* over the threshold of the temple; and the house was filled with the cloud,
and the court was full of the brightness of the
LORD's glory. 5And the sound of the wings of
the cherubim was heard *even* in the outer
court, like the voice of Almighty God when He
speaks.
6Then it happened, when He commanded
the man clothed in linen, saying, "Take fire
from among the wheels, from among the cherubim," that he went in and stood beside the
wheels. 7And the cherub stretched out his
hand from among the cherubim to the fire that
was among the cherubim, and took *some of it*
and put *it* into the hands of the *man* clothed
with linen, who took *it* and went out. 8The
cherubim appeared to have the form of a
man's hand under their wings.
9And when I looked, there were four wheels
by the cherubim, one wheel by one cherub
and another wheel by each other cherub; the
wheels appeared *to have* the color of a beryl
stone. 10*As for* their appearance, all four
looked alike—as it were, a wheel in the middle of a wheel. 11When they went, they went
toward *any of* their four directions; they did
not turn aside when they went, but followed
in the direction the head was facing. They did
not turn aside when they went. 12And their
whole body, with their back, their hands, their
wings, and the wheels that the four had, *were*
full of eyes all around. 13As for the wheels,
they were called in my hearing, "Wheel."
14Each one had four faces: the first face *was*
the face of a cherub, the second face the face
of a man, the third the face of a lion, and the
fourth the face of an eagle. 15And the cherubim were lifted up. This *was* the living creature I saw by the River Chebar. 16When the
cherubim went, the wheels went beside them;
and when the cherubim lifted their wings to
mount up from the earth, the same wheels
also did not turn from beside them. 17When
the cherubim[a] stood still, *the wheels* stood
still, and when *one*[b] was lifted up, *the other*[c]
lifted itself up, for the spirit of the living creature *was* in them.
18Then the glory of the LORD departed from
the threshold of the temple and stood over the
cherubim. 19And the cherubim lifted their
wings and mounted up from the earth in my
sight. When they went out, the wheels *were*
beside them; and they stood at the door of the
east gate of the LORD's house, and the glory of
the God of Israel *was* above them.
20This *is* the living creature I saw under the
God of Israel by the River Chebar, and I knew
they *were* cherubim. 21Each one had four faces
and each one four wings, and the likeness of
the hands of a man *was* under their wings.
22And the likeness of their faces *was* the same
as the faces which I had seen by the River
Chebar, their appearance and their persons.
They each went straight forward.

JUDGMENT ON WICKED COUNSELORS

11 Then the Spirit lifted me up and
brought me to the East Gate of the
LORD's house, which faces eastward; and
there at the door of the gate were twenty-five
men, among whom I saw Jaazaniah the son of
Azzur, and Pelatiah the son of Benaiah,
princes of the people. 2And He said to me:
"Son of man, these *are* the men who devise
iniquity and give wicked counsel in this city,
3who say, '*The time is* not near to build
houses; this *city is* the caldron, and we *are* the
meat.' 4Therefore prophesy against them,
prophesy, O son of man!"
5Then the Spirit of the LORD fell upon me,
and said to me, "Speak! 'Thus says the LORD:
"Thus you have said, O house of Israel; for I
know the things that come into your mind.
6You have multiplied your slain in this city,
and you have filled its streets with the slain."
7Therefore thus says the Lord GOD: "Your slain
whom you have laid in its midst, they *are* the
meat, and this *city is* the caldron; but I shall
bring you out of the midst of it. 8You have
feared the sword; and I will bring a sword
upon you," says the Lord GOD. 9"And I will
bring you out of its midst, and deliver you into
the hands of strangers, and execute judgments
on you. 10You shall fall by the sword. I will
judge you at the border of Israel. Then you
shall know that I *am* the LORD. 11This *city* shall
not be your caldron, nor shall you be the meat
in its midst. I will judge you at the border of

10:3 [a]Literally *house,* also in verses 4 and 18
10:17 [a]Literally *they* [b]Literally *they* [c]Literally *they*

Israel. 12And you shall know that I *am* the LORD; for you have not walked in My statutes nor executed My judgments, but have done according to the customs of the Gentiles which *are* all around you." ' "

13Now it happened, while I was prophesying, that Pelatiah the son of Benaiah died. Then I fell on my face and cried with a loud voice, and said, "Ah, Lord GOD! Will You make a complete end of the remnant of Israel?"

God Will Restore Israel

14Again the word of the LORD came to me, saying, 15"Son of man, your brethren, your relatives, your countrymen, and all the house of Israel in its entirety, *are* those about whom the inhabitants of Jerusalem have said, 'Get far away from the LORD; this land has been given to us as a possession.' 16Therefore say, 'Thus says the Lord GOD: "Although I have cast them far off among the Gentiles, and although I have scattered them among the countries, yet I shall be a little sanctuary for them in the countries where they have gone." ' 17Therefore say, 'Thus says the Lord GOD: "I will gather you from the peoples, assemble you from the countries where you have been scattered, and I will give you the land of Israel." ' 18And they will go there, and they will take away all its detestable things and all its abominations from there. 19Then I will give them one heart, and I will put a new spirit within them,[a] and take the stony heart out of their flesh, and give them a heart of flesh, 20that they may walk in My statutes and keep My judgments and do them; and they shall be My people, and I will be their God. 21But *as for those* whose hearts follow the desire for their detestable things and their abominations, I will recompense their deeds on their own heads," says the Lord GOD.

22So the cherubim lifted up their wings, with the wheels beside them, and the glory of the God of Israel *was* high above them. 23And the glory of the LORD went up from the midst of the city and stood on the mountain, which *is* on the east side of the city.

24Then the Spirit took me up and brought me in a vision by the Spirit of God into Chaldea,[a] to those in captivity. And the vision that I had seen went up from me. 25So I spoke to those in captivity of all the things the LORD had shown me.

Judah's Captivity Portrayed

12 Now the word of the LORD came to me, saying: 2"Son of man, you dwell in the midst of a rebellious house, which has eyes to see but does not see, and ears to hear but does not hear; for they *are* a rebellious house.

3"Therefore, son of man, prepare your belongings for captivity, and go into captivity by day in their sight. You shall go from your place into captivity to another place in their sight. It may be that they will consider, though they *are* a rebellious house. 4By day you shall bring out your belongings in their sight, as though going into captivity; and at evening you shall go in their sight, like those who go into captivity. 5Dig through the wall in their sight, and carry your belongings out through it. 6In their sight you shall bear *them* on *your* shoulders *and* carry *them* out at twilight; you shall cover your face, so that you cannot see the ground, for I have made you a sign to the house of Israel."

7So I did as I was commanded. I brought out my belongings by day, as though going into captivity, and at evening I dug through the wall with my hand. I brought *them* out at twilight, *and* I bore *them* on *my* shoulder in their sight.

8And in the morning the word of the LORD came to me, saying, 9"Son of man, has not the house of Israel, the rebellious house, said to you, 'What are you doing?' 10Say to them, 'Thus says the Lord GOD: "This burden *concerns* the prince in Jerusalem and all the house of Israel who are among them." ' 11Say, 'I *am* a sign to you. As I have done, so shall it be done to them; they shall be carried away into captivity.' 12And the prince who *is* among them shall bear *his belongings* on *his* shoulder

> "Then I will give them one heart, and I will put a new spirit within them, and take the stony heart out of their flesh, and give them a heart of flesh, that they may walk in My statutes and keep My judgments and do them; and they shall be My people, and I will be their God."
>
> EZEKIEL 11:19, 20

11:19 [a]Literally *you* **11:24** [a]Or *Babylon,* and so elsewhere in this book

at twilight and go out. They shall dig through the wall to carry *them* out through it. He shall cover his face, so that he cannot see the ground with *his* eyes. [13]I will also spread My net over him, and he shall be caught in My snare. I will bring him to Babylon, *to* the land of the Chaldeans; yet he shall not see it, though he shall die there. [14]I will scatter to every wind all who *are* around him to help him, and all his troops; and I will draw out the sword after them.

[15]"Then they shall know that I *am* the LORD, when I scatter them among the nations and disperse them throughout the countries. [16]But I will spare a few of their men from the sword, from famine, and from pestilence, that they may declare all their abominations among the Gentiles wherever they go. Then they shall know that I *am* the LORD."

Judgment Not Postponed

[17]Moreover the word of the LORD came to me, saying, [18]"Son of man, eat your bread with quaking, and drink your water with trembling and anxiety. [19]And say to the people of the land, 'Thus says the Lord GOD to the inhabitants of Jerusalem *and* to the land of Israel: "They shall eat their bread with anxiety, and drink their water with dread, so that her land may be emptied of all who are in it, because of the violence of all those who dwell in it. [20]Then the cities that are inhabited shall be laid waste, and the land shall become desolate; and you shall know that I *am* the LORD." ' "

[21]And the word of the LORD came to me, saying, [22]"Son of man, what *is* this proverb *that* you *people* have about the land of Israel, which says, 'The days are prolonged, and every vision fails'? [23]Tell them therefore, 'Thus says the Lord GOD: "I will lay this proverb to rest, and they shall no more use it as a proverb in Israel." But say to them, "The days are at hand, and the fulfillment of every vision. [24]For no more shall there be any false vision or flattering divination within the house of Israel. [25]For I *am* the LORD. I speak, and the word which I speak will come to pass; it will no more be postponed; for in your days, O rebellious house, I will say the word and perform it," says the Lord GOD.' "

[26]Again the word of the LORD came to me, saying, [27]"Son of man, look, the house of Israel is saying, 'The vision that he sees *is* for many days *from now,* and he prophesies of times far off.' [28]Therefore say to them, 'Thus says the Lord GOD: "None of My words will be postponed any more, but the word which I speak will be done," says the Lord GOD.' "

Woe to Foolish Prophets

13 And the word of the LORD came to me, saying, [2]"Son of man, prophesy against the prophets of Israel who prophesy, and say to those who prophesy out of their own heart, 'Hear the word of the LORD!' "

[3]Thus says the Lord GOD: "Woe to the foolish prophets, who follow their own spirit and have seen nothing! [4]O Israel, your prophets are like foxes in the deserts. [5]You have not gone up into the gaps to build a wall for the house of Israel to stand in battle on the day of the LORD. [6]They have envisioned futility and false divination, saying, 'Thus says the LORD!' But the LORD has not sent them; yet they hope that the word may be confirmed. [7]Have you not seen a futile vision, and have you not spoken false divination? You say, 'The LORD says,' but I have not spoken."

[8]Therefore thus says the Lord GOD: "Because you have spoken nonsense and envisioned lies, therefore I *am* indeed against you," says the Lord GOD. [9]"My hand will be against the prophets who envision futility and who divine lies; they shall not be in the assembly of My people, nor be written in the record of the house of Israel, nor shall they enter into the land of Israel. Then you shall know that I *am* the Lord GOD.

[10]"Because, indeed, because they have seduced My people, saying, 'Peace!' when *there is* no peace—and one builds a wall, and they plaster it with untempered *mortar*— [11]say to those who plaster *it* with untempered *mortar,* that it will fall. There will be flooding rain, and you, O great hailstones, shall fall; and a stormy wind shall tear *it* down. [12]Surely, when the wall has fallen, will it not be said to you, 'Where *is* the mortar with which you plastered *it?*' "

[13]Therefore thus says the Lord GOD: "I will cause a stormy wind to break forth in My fury; and there shall be a flooding rain in My anger, and great hailstones in fury to consume *it.* [14]So I will break down the wall you have plastered with untempered *mortar,* and bring it down to the ground, so that its foundation will be uncovered; it will fall, and you shall be

consumed in the midst of it. Then you shall
know that I *am* the LORD.

[15]"Thus will I accomplish My wrath on the
wall and on those who have plastered it with
untempered *mortar;* and I will say to you,
'The wall *is* no *more,* nor those who plastered
it, [16]*that is,* the prophets of Israel who prophesy concerning Jerusalem, and who see visions
of peace for her when *there is* no peace,' " says
the Lord GOD.

[17]"Likewise, son of man, set your face
against the daughters of your people, who
prophesy out of their own heart; prophesy
against them, [18]and say, 'Thus says the Lord
GOD: "Woe to the *women* who sew *magic*
charms on their sleeves[a] and make veils for
the heads of people of every height to hunt
souls! Will you hunt the souls of My people,
and keep yourselves alive? [19]And will you profane Me among My people for handfuls of barley and for pieces of bread, killing people who
should not die, and keeping people alive who
should not live, by your lying to My people
who listen to lies?"

[20]'Therefore thus says the Lord GOD: "Behold, I *am* against your *magic* charms by
which you hunt souls there like birds. I will
tear them from your arms, and let the souls
go, the souls you hunt like birds. [21]I will also
tear off your veils and deliver My people out
of your hand, and they shall no longer be as
prey in your hand. Then you shall know that I
am the LORD.

[22]"Because with lies you have made the
heart of the righteous sad, whom I have not
made sad; and you have strengthened the
hands of the wicked, so that he does not turn
from his wicked way to save his life. [23]There-
fore you shall no longer envision futility nor
practice divination; for I will deliver My people out of your hand, and you shall know that
I *am* the LORD." ' "

IDOLATRY WILL BE PUNISHED

14 Now some of the elders of Israel came
to me and sat before me. [2]And the
word of the LORD came to me, saying, [3]"Son of
man, these men have set up their idols in their
hearts, and put before them that which causes
them to stumble into iniquity. Should I let
Myself be inquired of at all by them?

[4]"Therefore speak to them, and say to
them, 'Thus says the Lord GOD: "Everyone of
the house of Israel who sets up his idols in his
heart, and puts before him what causes him to
stumble into iniquity, and then comes to the
prophet, I the LORD will answer him who
comes, according to the multitude of his idols,
[5]that I may seize the house of Israel by their
heart, because they are all estranged from Me
by their idols." '

[6]"Therefore say to the house of Israel, 'Thus
says the Lord GOD: "Repent, turn away from
your idols, and turn your faces away from all
your abominations. [7]For anyone of the house
of Israel, or of the strangers who dwell in Israel, who separates himself from Me and sets
up his idols in his heart and puts before him
what causes him to stumble into iniquity, then
comes to a prophet to inquire of him concerning Me, I the LORD will answer him by Myself.
[8]I will set My face against that man and make
him a sign and a proverb, and I will cut him
off from the midst of My people. Then you
shall know that I *am* the LORD.

[9]"And if the prophet is induced to speak
anything, I the LORD have induced that prophet, and I will stretch out My hand against him
and destroy him from among My people Israel. [10]And they shall bear their iniquity; the
punishment of the prophet shall be the same

13:18 [a]Literally *over all the joints of My hands;* Vulgate reads *under every elbow;* Septuagint and Targum read *on all elbows of the hands.*

SOUL NOTE

Beyond Sorry *(14:6)* God told the Israelites to repent of their idolatry. Repentance is more than saying, "I'm sorry"; it's a complete change of direction in one's life. The first step of true repentance is to recognize that we are moving away from God, pursuing an activity or lifestyle that opposes what He desires. The second step is to admit the sin to Him and ask for His forgiveness. The third step is to "turn away" from the sin and back to God. There is no true repentance without a change in behavior. **Topic: Repentance**

as the punishment of the one who inquired, [11]that the house of Israel may no longer stray from Me, nor be profaned anymore with all their transgressions, but that they may be My people and I may be their God," says the Lord GOD.' "

JUDGMENT ON PERSISTENT UNFAITHFULNESS

[12]The word of the LORD came again to me, saying: [13]"Son of man, when a land sins against Me by persistent unfaithfulness, I will stretch out My hand against it; I will cut off its supply of bread, send famine on it, and cut off man and beast from it. [14]Even *if* these three men, Noah, Daniel, and Job, were in it, they would deliver *only* themselves by their righteousness," says the Lord GOD.

[15]"If I cause wild beasts to pass through the land, and they empty it, and make it so desolate that no man may pass through because of the beasts, [16]*even though* these three men *were* in it, *as* I live," says the Lord GOD, "they would deliver neither sons nor daughters; only they would be delivered, and the land would be desolate.

[17]"Or *if* I bring a sword on that land, and say, 'Sword, go through the land,' and I cut off man and beast from it, [18]even *though* these three men *were* in it, *as* I live," says the Lord GOD, "they would deliver neither sons nor daughters, but only they themselves would be delivered.

[19]"Or *if* I send a pestilence into that land and pour out My fury on it in blood, and cut off from it man and beast, [20]even *though* Noah, Daniel, and Job *were* in it, *as* I live," says the Lord GOD, "they would deliver neither son nor daughter; they would deliver *only* themselves by their righteousness."

[21]For thus says the Lord GOD: "How much more it shall be when I send My four severe judgments on Jerusalem—the sword and famine and wild beasts and pestilence—to cut off man and beast from it? [22]Yet behold, there shall be left in it a remnant who will be brought out, *both* sons and daughters; surely they will come out to you, and you will see their ways and their doings. Then you will be comforted concerning the disaster that I have brought upon Jerusalem, all that I have brought upon it. [23]And they will comfort you, when you see their ways and their doings; and you shall know that I have done nothing without cause that I have done in it," says the Lord GOD.

THE OUTCAST VINE

15 Then the word of the LORD came to me, saying: [2]"Son of man, how is the wood of the vine *better* than any other wood, the vine branch which is among the trees of the forest? [3]Is wood taken from it to make any object? Or can *men* make a peg from it to hang any vessel on? [4]Instead, it is thrown into the fire for fuel; the fire devours both ends of it, and its middle is burned. Is it useful for *any* work? [5]Indeed, when it was whole, no object could be made from it. How much less will it be useful for *any* work when the fire has devoured it, and it is burned?

[6]"Therefore thus says the Lord GOD: 'Like the wood of the vine among the trees of the forest, which I have given to the fire for fuel, so I will give up the inhabitants of Jerusalem; [7]and I will set My face against them. They will go out from *one* fire, but *another* fire shall devour them. Then you shall know that I *am* the LORD, when I set My face against them. [8]Thus I will make the land desolate, because they have persisted in unfaithfulness,' says the Lord GOD."

GOD'S LOVE FOR JERUSALEM

16 Again the word of the LORD came to me, saying, [2]"Son of man, cause Jerusalem to know her abominations, [3]and say, 'Thus says the Lord GOD to Jerusalem: "Your birth and your nativity *are* from the land of Canaan; your father *was* an Amorite and your mother a Hittite. [4]*As for* your nativity, on the day you were born your navel cord was not cut, nor were you washed in water to cleanse *you;* you were not rubbed with salt nor wrapped in swaddling cloths. [5]No eye pitied you, to do any of these things for you, to have compassion on you; but you were thrown out into the open field, when you yourself were loathed on the day you were born.

[6]"And when I passed by you and saw you struggling in your own blood, I said to you in your blood, 'Live!' Yes, I said to you in your blood, 'Live!' [7]I made you thrive like a plant in the field; and you grew, matured, and became very beautiful. *Your* breasts were formed, your hair grew, but you *were* naked and bare.

[8]"When I passed by you again and looked upon you, indeed your time *was* the time of love; so I spread My wing over you and covered your nakedness. Yes, I swore an oath to you and entered into a covenant with you,

and you became Mine," says the Lord GOD.
9"Then I washed you in water; yes, I thoroughly washed off your blood, and I anointed
you with oil. 10I clothed you in embroidered
cloth and gave you sandals of badger skin; I
clothed you with fine linen and covered you
with silk. 11I adorned you with ornaments, put
bracelets on your wrists, and a chain on your
neck. 12And I put a jewel in your nose, earrings in your ears, and a beautiful crown on
your head. 13Thus you were adorned with
gold and silver, and your clothing *was of* fine
linen, silk, and embroidered cloth. You ate
pastry of fine flour, honey, and oil. You were
exceedingly beautiful, and succeeded to royalty. 14Your fame went out among the nations
because of your beauty, for it *was* perfect
through My splendor which I had bestowed
on you," says the Lord GOD.

JERUSALEM'S HARLOTRY

15"But you trusted in your own beauty,
played the harlot because of your fame, and
poured out your harlotry on everyone passing
by who *would have* it. 16You took some of your
garments and adorned multicolored high
places for yourself, and played the harlot on
them. *Such* things should not happen, nor be.
17You have also taken your beautiful jewelry
from My gold and My silver, which I had given
you, and made for yourself male images and
played the harlot with them. 18You took your
embroidered garments and covered them, and
you set My oil and My incense before them.
19Also My food which I gave you—the pastry
of fine flour, oil, and honey *which* I fed you—
you set it before them as sweet incense; and *so*
it was," says the Lord GOD.
20"Moreover you took your sons and your
daughters, whom you bore to Me, and these
you sacrificed to them to be devoured. *Were*
your *acts* of harlotry a small matter, 21that you
have slain My children and offered them up to
them by causing them to pass through *the fire?*
22And in all your abominations and acts of
harlotry you did not remember the days of
your youth, when you were naked and bare,
struggling in your blood.
23"Then it was so, after all your wickedness—'Woe, woe to you!' says the Lord GOD—
24*that* you also built for yourself a shrine, and
made a high place for yourself in every street.
25You built your high places at the head of
every road, and made your beauty to be

SOUL NOTE

God the Jilted Groom *(16:8–14)* This passage about God's love for Jerusalem despite the nation's idolatry pictures God as a jilted groom reminding His bride of all that He has done. If it seems strange to think of God as a scorned lover, it shouldn't. How often do we reject Him to follow our own desires and impulses, only to return later begging for forgiveness? We can find great comfort in the fact that our heavenly Father can empathize with the pain of someone who has been betrayed by a loved one. Knowing that He understands can help us trust Him in our own hurt and pain.
Topic: Adultery

SOUL NOTE

The Beauty Myth *(16:15)* Though "harlot" refers to Jerusalem, and the "harlotry" to spiritual idolatry, the passage also teaches about trusting in the wrong things. The city trusted in its beauty and fame; so do many people. Trusting in one's own beauty or sex appeal can lead to all kinds of problems, including sexual sin. Devastated relationships, poor self-image, and life-altering diseases are just a few of the lingering effects of sexual sin. God did not give us rules regarding our sexuality to spoil our fun; He did it to *enhance* our pleasure, to provide a guilt-free, worry-free way to express physical love. **Topic: Sexual Sin**

abhorred. You offered yourself to everyone
who passed by, and multiplied your acts of
harlotry. 26You also committed harlotry with
the Egyptians, your very fleshly neighbors,
and increased your acts of harlotry to provoke
Me to anger.

27"Behold, therefore, I stretched out My
hand against you, diminished your allotment,
and gave you up to the will of those who hate
you, the daughters of the Philistines, who
were ashamed of your lewd behavior. 28You
also played the harlot with the Assyrians, because you were insatiable; indeed you played
the harlot with them and still were not satisfied. 29Moreover you multiplied your acts of
harlotry as far as the land of the trader, Chaldea; and even then you were not satisfied.

30"How degenerate is your heart!" says the
Lord GOD, "seeing you do all these *things,* the
deeds of a brazen harlot.

JERUSALEM'S ADULTERY

31"You erected your shrine at the head of
every road, and built your high place in every
street. Yet you were not like a harlot, because
you scorned payment. 32*You are* an adulterous
wife, *who* takes strangers instead of her husband. 33Men make payment to all harlots, but
you made your payments to all your lovers,
and hired them to come to you from all
around for your harlotry. 34You are the opposite of *other* women in your harlotry, because
no one solicited you to be a harlot. In that you
gave payment but no payment was given you,
therefore you are the opposite."

JERUSALEM'S LOVERS WILL ABUSE HER

35'Now then, O harlot, hear the word of the
LORD! 36Thus says the Lord GOD: "Because
your filthiness was poured out and your nakedness uncovered in your harlotry with your
lovers, and with all your abominable idols,
and because of the blood of your children
which you gave to them, 37surely, therefore, I
will gather all your lovers with whom you
took pleasure, all those you loved, *and* all
those you hated; I will gather them from all
around against you and will uncover your nakedness to them, that they may see all your
nakedness. 38And I will judge you as women
who break wedlock or shed blood are judged;
I will bring blood upon you in fury and jealousy. 39I will also give you into their hand, and
they shall throw down your shrines and break
down your high places. They shall also strip
you of your clothes, take your beautiful jewelry, and leave you naked and bare.

40"They shall also bring up an assembly
against you, and they shall stone you with
stones and thrust you through with their
swords. 41They shall burn your houses with
fire, and execute judgments on you in the
sight of many women; and I will make you
cease playing the harlot, and you shall no
longer hire lovers. 42So I will lay to rest My
fury toward you, and My jealousy shall depart
from you. I will be quiet, and be angry no
more. 43Because you did not remember the
days of your youth, but agitated Me[a] with all
these *things,* surely I will also recompense
your deeds on *your own* head," says the Lord
GOD. "And you shall not commit lewdness in
addition to all your abominations.

MORE WICKED THAN SAMARIA AND SODOM

44"Indeed everyone who quotes proverbs
will use *this* proverb against you: 'Like mother, like daughter!' 45You *are* your mother's
daughter, loathing husband and children; and
you *are* the sister of your sisters, who loathed
their husbands and children; your mother *was*
a Hittite and your father an Amorite.

46"Your elder sister *is* Samaria, who dwells
with her daughters to the north of you; and
your younger sister, who dwells to the south
of you, *is* Sodom and her daughters. 47You did
not walk in their ways nor act according to
their abominations; but, as *if that were* too little, you became more corrupt than they in all
your ways.

48"*As* I live," says the Lord GOD, "neither
your sister Sodom nor her daughters have
done as you and your daughters have done.
49Look, this was the iniquity of your sister
Sodom: She and her daughter had pride, fullness of food, and abundance of idleness; neither did she strengthen the hand of the poor
and needy. 50And they were haughty and committed abomination before Me; therefore I
took them away as I saw *fit.*[a]

51"Samaria did not commit half of your sins;
but you have multiplied your abominations
more than they, and have justified your sisters

16:43 [a]Following Septuagint, Syriac, Targum, and Vulgate; Masoretic Text reads *were agitated with Me.*
16:50 [a]Vulgate reads *you saw;* Septuagint reads *he saw;* Targum reads *as was revealed to Me.*

by all the abominations which you have done.
52You who judged your sisters, bear your own
shame also, because the sins which you committed were more abominable than theirs;
they are more righteous than you. Yes, be disgraced also, and bear your own shame, because you justified your sisters.

53"When I bring back their captives, the
captives of Sodom and her daughters, and the
captives of Samaria and her daughters, then *I
will also bring back* the captives of your captivity among them, 54that you may bear your
own shame and be disgraced by all that you
did when you comforted them. 55When your
sisters, Sodom and her daughters, return to
their former state, and Samaria and her
daughters return to their former state, then
you and your daughters will return to your
former state. 56For your sister Sodom was not
a byword in your mouth in the days of your
pride, 57before your wickedness was uncovered. It was like the time of the reproach of the
daughters of Syria[a] and all *those* around her,
and of the daughters of the Philistines, who
despise you everywhere. 58You have paid for
your lewdness and your abominations," says
the LORD. 59For thus says the Lord GOD: "I will
deal with you as you have done, who despised
the oath by breaking the covenant.

AN EVERLASTING COVENANT

60"Nevertheless I will remember My covenant with you in the days of your youth, and
I will establish an everlasting covenant with
you. 61Then you will remember your ways and
be ashamed, when you receive your older and
your younger sisters; for I will give them to
you for daughters, but not because of My covenant with you. 62And I will establish My covenant with you. Then you shall know that I
am the LORD, 63that you may remember and
be ashamed, and never open your mouth anymore because of your shame, when I provide
you an atonement for all you have done," says
the Lord GOD.' "

THE EAGLES AND THE VINE

17 And the word of the LORD came to me,
saying, 2"Son of man, pose a riddle,
and speak a parable to the house of Israel,
3and say, 'Thus says the Lord GOD:

"A great eagle with large wings and long
pinions,
Full of feathers of various colors,
Came to Lebanon
And took from the cedar the highest
branch.
4 He cropped off its topmost young twig
And carried it to a land of trade;
He set it in a city of merchants.
5 Then he took some of the seed of the
land
And planted it in a fertile field;
He placed *it* by abundant waters
And set it like a willow tree.
6 And it grew and became a spreading
vine of low stature;
Its branches turned toward him,
But its roots were under it.
So it became a vine,
Brought forth branches,
And put forth shoots.

7 "But there was another[a] great eagle with
large wings and many feathers;
And behold, this vine bent its roots
toward him,
And stretched its branches toward him,
From the garden terrace where it had
been planted,
That he might water it.
8 It was planted in good soil by many
waters,
To bring forth branches, bear fruit,
And become a majestic vine." '

9"Say, 'Thus says the Lord GOD:

"Will it thrive?
Will he not pull up its roots,
Cut off its fruit,
And leave it to wither?
All of its spring leaves will wither,
And no great power or many people
Will be needed to pluck it up by its
roots.
10 Behold, *it is* planted,
Will it thrive?
Will it not utterly wither when the east
wind touches it?
It will wither in the garden terrace
where it grew." ' "

16:57 [a]Following Masoretic Text, Septuagint, Targum, and Vulgate; many Hebrew manuscripts and Syriac read *Edom.* **17:7** [a]Following Septuagint, Syriac, and Vulgate; Masoretic Text and Targum read *one.*

11 Moreover the word of the LORD came to me, saying, 12 "Say now to the rebellious house: 'Do you not know what these *things mean?*' Tell *them,* 'Indeed the king of Babylon went to Jerusalem and took its king and princes, and led them with him to Babylon. 13 And he took the king's offspring, made a covenant with him, and put him under oath. He also took away the mighty of the land, 14 that the kingdom might be brought low and not lift itself up, *but* that by keeping his covenant it might stand. 15 But he rebelled against him by sending his ambassadors to Egypt, that they might give him horses and many people. Will he prosper? Will he who does such *things* escape? Can he break a covenant and still be delivered?

16 '*As* I live,' says the Lord GOD, 'surely in the place *where* the king *dwells* who made him king, whose oath he despised and whose covenant he broke—with him in the midst of Babylon he shall die. 17 Nor will Pharaoh with *his* mighty army and great company do anything in the war, when they heap up a siege mound and build a wall to cut off many persons. 18 Since he despised the oath by breaking the covenant, and in fact gave his hand and still did all these *things,* he shall not escape.' "

19 Therefore thus says the Lord GOD: "*As* I live, surely My oath which he despised, and My covenant which he broke, I will recompense on his own head. 20 I will spread My net over him, and he shall be taken in My snare. I will bring him to Babylon and try him there for the treason which he committed against Me. 21 All his fugitives[a] with all his troops shall fall by the sword, and those who remain shall be scattered to every wind; and you shall know that I, the LORD, have spoken."

ISRAEL EXALTED AT LAST

22 Thus says the Lord GOD: "I will take also *one* of the highest branches of the high cedar and set *it* out. I will crop off from the topmost of its young twigs a tender one, and will plant *it* on a high and prominent mountain. 23 On the mountain height of Israel I will plant it; and it will bring forth boughs, and bear fruit, and be a majestic cedar. Under it will dwell birds of every sort; in the shadow of its branches they will dwell. 24 And all the trees of the field shall know that I, the LORD, have brought down the high tree and exalted the low tree, dried up the green tree and made the dry tree flourish; I, the LORD, have spoken and have done *it.*"

A FALSE PROVERB REFUTED

18 The word of the LORD came to me again, saying, 2 "What do you mean when you use this proverb concerning the land of Israel, saying:

'The fathers have eaten sour grapes,
And the children's teeth are set on
edge'?

3 "*As* I live," says the Lord GOD, "you shall no longer use this proverb in Israel.

4 "Behold, all souls are Mine;
The soul of the father
As well as the soul of the son is Mine;
The soul who sins shall die.
5 But if a man is just
And does what is lawful and right;
6 If he has not eaten on the mountains,
Nor lifted up his eyes to the idols of the
house of Israel,
Nor defiled his neighbor's wife,
Nor approached a woman during her
impurity;
7 If he has not oppressed anyone,
But has restored to the debtor his
pledge;
Has robbed no one by violence,
But has given his bread to the hungry
And covered the naked with clothing;
8 If he has not exacted usury
Nor taken any increase,
But has withdrawn his hand from
iniquity
And executed true judgment between
man and man;
9 *If* he has walked in My statutes
And kept My judgments faithfully—
He *is* just;
He shall surely live!"
Says the Lord GOD.

10 "If he begets a son *who is* a robber
Or a shedder of blood,
Who does any of these *things*
11 And does none of those *duties,*
But has eaten on the mountains
Or defiled his neighbor's wife;

17:21 [a]Following Masoretic Text and Vulgate; many Hebrew manuscripts and Syriac read *choice men;* Targum reads *mighty men;* Septuagint omits *All his fugitives.*

12 If he has oppressed the poor and needy,
Robbed by violence,
Not restored the pledge,
Lifted his eyes to the idols,
Or committed abomination;
13 If he has exacted usury
Or taken increase—
Shall he then live?
He shall not live!
If he has done any of these abominations,
He shall surely die;
His blood shall be upon him.

14 "*If,* however, he begets a son
Who sees all the sins which his father
has done,
And considers but does not do likewise;
15 *Who* has not eaten on the mountains,
Nor lifted his eyes to the idols of the
house of Israel,
Nor defiled his neighbor's wife;
16 Has not oppressed anyone,
Nor withheld a pledge,
Nor robbed by violence,
But has given his bread to the hungry
And covered the naked with clothing;
17 *Who* has withdrawn his hand from the
poor[a]
And not received usury or increase,
But has executed My judgments
And walked in My statutes—
He shall not die for the iniquity of his
father;
He shall surely live!

18 "*As for* his father,
Because he cruelly oppressed,
Robbed his brother by violence,
And did what *is* not good among his
people,
Behold, he shall die for his iniquity.

Turn and Live

19"Yet you say, 'Why should the son not
bear the guilt of the father?' Because the son
has done what is lawful and right, and has
kept all My statutes and observed them, he
shall surely live. 20The soul who sins shall die.
The son shall not bear the guilt of the father,
nor the father bear the guilt of the son. The
righteousness of the righteous shall be upon
himself, and the wickedness of the wicked
shall be upon himself.

21"But if a wicked man turns from all his
sins which he has committed, keeps all My
statutes, and does what is lawful and right, he
shall surely live; he shall not die. 22None of
the transgressions which he has committed
shall be remembered against him; because of
the righteousness which he has done, he shall
live. 23Do I have any pleasure at all that the
wicked should die?" says the Lord GOD, "*and*
not that he should turn from his ways and
live?

24"But when a righteous man turns away
from his righteousness and commits iniquity,
and does according to all the abominations
that the wicked *man* does, shall he live? All
the righteousness which he has done shall not
be remembered; because of the unfaithfulness
of which he is guilty and the sin which he has
committed, because of them he shall die.

25"Yet you say, 'The way of the Lord is not
fair.' Hear now, O house of Israel, is it not My
way which is fair, and your ways which are
not fair? 26When a righteous *man* turns away
from his righteousness, commits iniquity, and
dies in it, it is because of the iniquity which he
has done that he dies. 27Again, when a wicked
man turns away from the wickedness which

18:17 [a]Following Masoretic Text, Targum, and Vulgate; Septuagint reads *iniquity* (compare verse 8).

SOUL NOTE

The Verdict *(18:1–22)* This passage describes how God would not punish children for their parents' sins, but instead would hold individuals responsible for their own sins. He promised to punish the wicked, but those who turn away from all their sins and obey God will be forgiven. In fact, "none of the transgressions which he has committed shall be remembered against him," says God (18:22). God does not judge according to the extenuating circumstances of our lives. He asks but one question: "Did you turn from sin and obey Me?" Being able to answer "Yes" is the life's work of every believer. **Topic: Accountability**

he committed, and does what is lawful and
right, he preserves himself alive. 28Because he
considers and turns away from all the transgressions which he committed, he shall surely
live; he shall not die. 29Yet the house of Israel
says, 'The way of the Lord is not fair.' O house
of Israel, is it not My ways which are fair, and
your ways which are not fair?

30"Therefore I will judge you, O house of Israel, every one according to his ways," says
the Lord GOD. "Repent, and turn from all your
transgressions, so that iniquity will not be
your ruin. 31Cast away from you all the transgressions which you have committed, and get
yourselves a new heart and a new spirit. For
why should you die, O house of Israel? 32For I
have no pleasure in the death of one who
dies," says the Lord GOD. "Therefore turn and
live!"

ISRAEL DEGRADED

19 "Moreover take up a lamentation for the princes of Israel, 2and say:

'What *is* your mother? A lioness:
She lay down among the lions;
Among the young lions she nourished her cubs.
3 She brought up one of her cubs,
And he became a young lion;
He learned to catch prey,
And he devoured men.
4 The nations also heard of him;
He was trapped in their pit,
And they brought him with chains to the land of Egypt.

5 'When she saw that she waited, *that* her hope was lost,
She took another of her cubs *and* made him a young lion.
6 He roved among the lions,
And became a young lion;
He learned to catch prey;
He devoured men.
7 He knew their desolate places,[a]
And laid waste their cities;
The land with its fullness was desolated
By the noise of his roaring.
8 Then the nations set against him from the provinces on every side,
And spread their net over him;
He was trapped in their pit.
9 They put him in a cage with chains,
And brought him to the king of Babylon;
They brought him in nets,
That his voice should no longer be heard on the mountains of Israel.

10 'Your mother *was* like a vine in your bloodline,[a]
Planted by the waters,
Fruitful and full of branches
Because of many waters.
11 She had strong branches for scepters of rulers.
She towered in stature above the thick branches,
And was seen in her height amid the dense foliage.
12 But she was plucked up in fury,
She was cast down to the ground,
And the east wind dried her fruit.
Her strong branches were broken and withered;
The fire consumed them.
13 And now she *is* planted in the wilderness,
In a dry and thirsty land.
14 Fire has come out from a rod of her branches
And devoured her fruit,
So that she has no strong branch—a scepter for ruling.' "

This *is* a lamentation, and has become a lamentation.

THE REBELLIONS OF ISRAEL

20 It came to pass in the seventh year, in
the fifth *month,* on the tenth *day* of the
month, *that* certain of the elders of Israel
came to inquire of the LORD, and sat before
me. 2Then the word of the LORD came to me,
saying, 3"Son of man, speak to the elders of Israel, and say to them, 'Thus says the Lord
GOD: "Have you come to inquire of Me? *As* I
live," says the Lord GOD, "I will not be inquired
of by you." ' 4Will you judge them, son of man,
will you judge *them?* Then make known to
them the abominations of their fathers.

5"Say to them, 'Thus says the Lord GOD:

19:7 [a]Septuagint reads *He stood in insolence;* Targum reads *He destroyed its palaces;* Vulgate reads *He learned to make widows.*

19:10 [a]Literally *blood,* following Masoretic Text, Syriac, and Vulgate; Septuagint reads *like a flower on a pomegranate tree;* Targum reads *in your likeness.*

"On the day when I chose Israel and raised My hand in an oath to the descendants of the house of Jacob, and made Myself known to them in the land of Egypt, I raised My hand in an oath to them, saying, 'I *am* the LORD your God.' [6]On that day I raised My hand in an oath to them, to bring them out of the land of Egypt into a land that I had searched out for them, 'flowing with milk and honey,'[a] the glory of all lands. [7]Then I said to them, 'Each of you, throw away the abominations which are before his eyes, and do not defile yourselves with the idols of Egypt. I *am* the LORD your God.' [8]But they rebelled against Me and would not obey Me. They did not all cast away the abominations which were before their eyes, nor did they forsake the idols of Egypt. Then I said, 'I will pour out My fury on them and fulfill My anger against them in the midst of the land of Egypt.' [9]But I acted for My name's sake, that it should not be profaned before the Gentiles among whom they *were,* in whose sight I had made Myself known to them, to bring them out of the land of Egypt.

[10]"Therefore I made them go out of the land of Egypt and brought them into the wilderness. [11]And I gave them My statutes and showed them My judgments, 'which, *if* a man does, he shall live by them.'[a] [12]Moreover I also gave them My Sabbaths, to be a sign between them and Me, that they might know that I *am* the LORD who sanctifies them. [13]Yet the house of Israel rebelled against Me in the wilderness; they did not walk in My statutes; they despised My judgments, 'which, *if* a man does, he shall live by them';[a] and they greatly defiled My Sabbaths. Then I said I would pour out My fury on them in the wilderness, to consume them. [14]But I acted for My name's sake, that it should not be profaned before the Gentiles, in whose sight I had brought them out. [15]So I also raised My hand in an oath to them in the wilderness, that I would not bring them into the land which I had given *them,* 'flowing with milk and honey,'[a] the glory of all lands, [16]because they despised My judgments and did not walk in My statutes, but profaned My Sabbaths; for their heart went after their idols. [17]Nevertheless My eye spared them from destruction. I did not make an end of them in the wilderness.

[18]"But I said to their children in the wilderness, 'Do not walk in the statutes of your fathers, nor observe their judgments, nor defile yourselves with their idols. [19]I *am* the LORD your God: Walk in My statutes, keep My judgments, and do them; [20]hallow My Sabbaths, and they will be a sign between Me and you, that you may know that I *am* the LORD your God.'

[21]"Notwithstanding, the children rebelled against Me; they did not walk in My statutes, and were not careful to observe My judgments, 'which, *if* a man does, he shall live by them';[a] but they profaned My Sabbaths. Then I said I would pour out My fury on them and fulfill My anger against them in the wilderness. [22]Nevertheless I withdrew My hand and acted for My name's sake, that it should not be profaned in the sight of the Gentiles, in whose sight I had brought them out. [23]Also I raised My hand in an oath to those in the wilderness, that I would scatter them among the Gentiles and disperse them throughout the countries, [24]because they had not executed My judgments, but had despised My statutes, profaned My Sabbaths, and their eyes were fixed on their fathers' idols.

[25]"Therefore I also gave them up to statutes *that were* not good, and judgments by which they could not live; [26]and I pronounced them unclean because of their ritual gifts, in that they caused all their firstborn to pass through *the fire,* that I might make them desolate and that they might know that I am the LORD." '

[27]"Therefore, son of man, speak to the house of Israel, and say to them, 'Thus says the Lord GOD: "In this too your fathers have blasphemed Me, by being unfaithful to Me. [28]When I brought them into the land *concerning* which I had raised My hand in an oath to give them, and they saw all the high hills and all the thick trees, there they offered their sacrifices and provoked Me with their offerings. There they also sent up their sweet aroma and poured out their drink offerings. [29]Then I said to them, 'What *is* this high place to which you go?' So its name is called Bamah[a] to this day." ' [30]Therefore say to the house of Israel, 'Thus says the Lord GOD: "Are you defiling yourselves in the manner of your fathers, and committing harlotry according to their abominations? [31]For when you offer your gifts and make your sons pass through the fire, you de-

20:6 [a]Exodus 3:8 **20:11** [a]Leviticus 18:5
20:13 [a]Leviticus 18:5 **20:15** [a]Exodus 3:8
20:21 [a]Leviticus 18:5 **20:29** [a]Literally *High Place*

file yourselves with all your idols, even to this
day. So shall I be inquired of by you, O house
of Israel? *As* I live," says the Lord GOD, "I will
not be inquired of by you. 32What you have in
your mind shall never be, when you say, 'We
will be like the Gentiles, like the families in
other countries, serving wood and stone.'

GOD WILL RESTORE ISRAEL

33"*As* I live," says the Lord GOD, "surely
with a mighty hand, with an outstretched
arm, and with fury poured out, I will rule over
you. 34I will bring you out from the peoples
and gather you out of the countries where you
are scattered, with a mighty hand, with an
outstretched arm, and with fury poured out.
35And I will bring you into the wilderness of
the peoples, and there I will plead My case
with you face to face. 36Just as I pleaded My
case with your fathers in the wilderness of the
land of Egypt, so I will plead My case with
you," says the Lord GOD.

37"I will make you pass under the rod, and I
will bring you into the bond of the covenant;
38I will purge the rebels from among you, and
those who transgress against Me; I will bring
them out of the country where they dwell, but
they shall not enter the land of Israel. Then
you will know that I *am* the LORD.

39"As for you, O house of Israel," thus says
the Lord GOD: "Go, serve every one of you his
idols—and hereafter—if you will not obey Me;
but profane My holy name no more with your
gifts and your idols. 40For on My holy mountain, on the mountain height of Israel," says
the Lord GOD, "there all the house of Israel, all
of them in the land, shall serve Me; there I will
accept them, and there I will require your offerings and the firstfruits of your sacrifices, together with all your holy things. 41I will accept
you as a sweet aroma when I bring you out
from the peoples and gather you out of the
countries where you have been scattered; and
I will be hallowed in you before the Gentiles.
42Then you shall know that I *am* the LORD,
when I bring you into the land of Israel, into
the country *for* which I raised My hand in an
oath to give to your fathers. 43And there you
shall remember your ways and all your doings
with which you were defiled; and you shall
loathe yourselves in your own sight because
of all the evils that you have committed.
44Then you shall know that I *am* the LORD,
when I have dealt with you for My name's
sake, not according to your wicked ways nor
according to your corrupt doings, O house of
Israel," says the Lord GOD.' "

FIRE IN THE FOREST

45Furthermore the word of the LORD came to
me, saying, 46"Son of man, set your face toward the south; preach against the south and
prophesy against the forest land, the South,[a]
47and say to the forest of the South, 'Hear the
word of the LORD! Thus says the Lord GOD:
"Behold, I will kindle a fire in you, and it shall
devour every green tree and every dry tree in
you; the blazing flame shall not be quenched,
and all faces from the south to the north shall
be scorched by it. 48All flesh shall see that I,
the LORD, have kindled it; it shall not be
quenched." ' "

49Then I said, "Ah, Lord GOD! They say of
me, 'Does he not speak parables?' "

BABYLON, THE SWORD OF GOD

21 And the word of the LORD came to me,
saying, 2"Son of man, set your face toward Jerusalem, preach against the holy
places, and prophesy against the land of Israel; 3and say to the land of Israel, 'Thus says
the LORD: "Behold, I *am* against you, and I
will draw My sword out of its sheath and cut
off both righteous and wicked from you. 4Be-
cause I will cut off both righteous and wicked
from you, therefore My sword shall go out of
its sheath against all flesh from south *to* north,
5that all flesh may know that I, the LORD, have
drawn My sword out of its sheath; it shall not
return anymore." ' 6Sigh therefore, son of
man, with a breaking heart, and sigh with bitterness before their eyes. 7And it shall be
when they say to you, 'Why are you sighing?'
that you shall answer, 'Because of the news;
when it comes, every heart will melt, all
hands will be feeble, every spirit will faint,
and all knees will be weak *as* water. Behold, it
is coming and shall be brought to pass,' says
the Lord GOD."

8Again the word of the LORD came to me,
saying, 9"Son of man, prophesy and say,
'Thus says the LORD!' Say:

'A sword, a sword is sharpened
And also polished!
10 Sharpened to make a dreadful slaughter,

20:46 [a]Hebrew *Negev*

Polished to flash like lightning!
Should we then make mirth?
It despises the scepter of My son,
As it does all wood.
11 And He has given it to be polished,
That it may be handled;
This sword is sharpened, and it is
polished
To be given into the hand of the slayer.'

12 "Cry and wail, son of man;
For it will be against My people,
Against all the princes of Israel.
Terrors including the sword will be
against My people;
Therefore strike *your* thigh.

13 "Because *it is* a testing,
And what if *the sword* despises even the
scepter?
The scepter shall be no *more,*"

says the Lord GOD.

14 "You therefore, son of man, prophesy,
And strike *your* hands together.
The third time let the sword do double
damage.
It *is* the sword *that* slays,
The sword that slays the great *men,*
That enters their private chambers.
15 I have set the point of the sword against
all their gates,
That the heart may melt and many may
stumble.
Ah! *It is* made bright;
It is grasped for slaughter:

16 "Swords at the ready!
Thrust right!
Set your blade!
Thrust left—
Wherever your edge is ordered!

17 "I also will beat My fists together,
And I will cause My fury to rest;
I, the LORD, have spoken."

18The word of the LORD came to me again,
saying: 19"And son of man, appoint for yourself two ways for the sword of the king of Babylon to go; both of them shall go from the
same land. Make a sign; put *it* at the head of
the road to the city. 20Appoint a road for the
sword to go to Rabbah of the Ammonites, and
to Judah, into fortified Jerusalem. 21For the
king of Babylon stands at the parting of the
road, at the fork of the two roads, to use divination: he shakes the arrows, he consults the
images, he looks at the liver. 22In his right
hand is the divination for Jerusalem: to set up
battering rams, to call for a slaughter, to lift
the voice with shouting, to set battering rams
against the gates, to heap up a *siege* mound,
and to build a wall. 23And it will be to them
like a false divination in the eyes of those who
have sworn oaths with them; but he will bring
their iniquity to remembrance, that they may
be taken.

24"Therefore thus says the Lord GOD: 'Because you have made your iniquity to be remembered, in that your transgressions are
uncovered, so that in all your doings your sins
appear—because you have come to remembrance, you shall be taken in hand.

25'Now to you, O profane, wicked prince of
Israel, whose day has come, whose iniquity
shall end, 26thus says the Lord GOD:

"Remove the turban, and take off the
crown;
Nothing *shall remain* the same.
Exalt the humble, and humble the
exalted.
27 Overthrown, overthrown,
I will make it overthrown!
It shall be no *longer,*
Until He comes whose right it is,
And I will give It *to Him.*" '

A Sword Against the Ammonites

28"And you, son of man, prophesy and say,
'Thus says the Lord GOD concerning the Ammonites and concerning their reproach,' and
say:

'A sword, a sword *is* drawn,
Polished for slaughter,
For consuming, for flashing—
29 While they see false visions for you,
While they divine a lie to you,
To bring you on the necks of the wicked,
the slain
Whose day has come,
Whose iniquity *shall* end.

30 'Return *it* to its sheath.
I will judge you

In the place where you were created,
In the land of your nativity.
31 I will pour out My indignation on you;
I will blow against you with the fire of
My wrath,
And deliver you into the hands of brutal
men *who are* skillful to destroy.
32 You shall be fuel for the fire;
Your blood shall be in the midst of the
land.
You shall not be remembered,
For I the LORD have spoken.' "

SINS OF JERUSALEM

22 Moreover the word of the LORD came
to me, saying, 2"Now, son of man, will
you judge, will you judge the bloody city? Yes,
show her all her abominations! 3Then say,
'Thus says the Lord GOD: "The city sheds
blood in her own midst, that her time may
come; and she makes idols within herself to
defile herself. 4You have become guilty by the
blood which you have shed, and have defiled
yourself with the idols which you have made.
You have caused your days to draw near, and
have come to *the end of* your years; therefore I
have made you a reproach to the nations, and
a mockery to all countries. 5*Those* near and
those far from you will mock you as infamous
and full of tumult.

6"Look, the princes of Israel: each one has
used his power to shed blood in you. 7In you
they have made light of father and mother; in
your midst they have oppressed the stranger;
in you they have mistreated the fatherless and
the widow. 8You have despised My holy things
and profaned My Sabbaths. 9In you are men
who slander to cause bloodshed; in you are
those who eat on the mountains; in your
midst they commit lewdness. 10In you men
uncover their fathers' nakedness; in you they
violate women who are set apart during their
impurity. 11One commits abomination with his
neighbor's wife; another lewdly defiles his
daughter-in-law; and another in you violates
his sister, his father's daughter. 12In you they
take bribes to shed blood; you take usury and
increase; you have made profit from your
neighbors by extortion, and have forgotten
Me," says the Lord GOD.

13"Behold, therefore, I beat My fists at the
dishonest profit which you have made, and at
the bloodshed which has been in your midst.
14Can your heart endure, or can your hands remain strong, in the days when I shall deal
with you? I, the LORD, have spoken, and will
do *it*. 15I will scatter you among the nations,
disperse you throughout the countries, and remove your filthiness completely from you.
16You shall defile yourself in the sight of the
nations; then you shall know that I *am* the
LORD." ' "

ISRAEL IN THE FURNACE

17The word of the LORD came to me, saying,
18"Son of man, the house of Israel has become
dross to Me; they *are* all bronze, tin, iron, and
lead, in the midst of a furnace; they have become dross from silver. 19Therefore thus says
the Lord GOD: 'Because you have all become
dross, therefore behold, I will gather you into
the midst of Jerusalem. 20*As men* gather silver,
bronze, iron, lead, and tin into the midst of a
furnace, to blow fire on it, to melt *it;* so I will
gather *you* in My anger and in My fury, and I
will leave *you there* and melt you. 21Yes, I will
gather you and blow on you with the fire of
My wrath, and you shall be melted in its
midst. 22As silver is melted in the midst of a
furnace, so shall you be melted in its midst;
then you shall know that I, the LORD, have
poured out My fury on you.' "

ISRAEL'S WICKED LEADERS

23And the word of the LORD came to me,
saying, 24"Son of man, say to her: 'You *are* a
land that is not cleansed[a] or rained on in the
day of indignation.' 25The conspiracy of her
prophets[a] in her midst is like a roaring lion
tearing the prey; they have devoured people;
they have taken treasure and precious things;
they have made many widows in her midst.
26Her priests have violated My law and profaned My holy things; they have not distinguished between the holy and unholy, nor
have they made known *the difference* between
the unclean and the clean; and they have hidden their eyes from My Sabbaths, so that I am
profaned among them. 27Her princes in her
midst *are* like wolves tearing the prey, to shed
blood, to destroy people, and to get dishonest
gain. 28Her prophets plastered them with
untempered *mortar,* seeing false visions, and

22:24 [a]Following Masoretic Text, Syriac, and Vulgate; Septuagint reads *showered upon.*
22:25 [a]Following Masoretic Text and Vulgate; Septuagint reads *princes;* Targum reads *scribes.*

divining lies for them, saying, 'Thus says the
Lord GOD,' when the LORD had not spoken.
29The people of the land have used oppressions, committed robbery, and mistreated the
poor and needy; and they wrongfully oppress
the stranger. 30So I sought for a man among
them who would make a wall, and stand in
the gap before Me on behalf of the land, that I
should not destroy it; but I found no one.
31Therefore I have poured out My indignation
on them; I have consumed them with the fire
of My wrath; and I have recompensed their
deeds on their own heads," says the Lord GOD.

Two Harlot Sisters

23 The word of the LORD came again to me, saying:

2 "Son of man, there were two women,
The daughters of one mother.
3 They committed harlotry in Egypt,
They committed harlotry in their youth;
Their breasts were there embraced,
Their virgin bosom was there pressed.
4 Their names: Oholah[a] the elder and Oholibah[b] her sister;
They were Mine,
And they bore sons and daughters.
As for their names,
Samaria *is* Oholah, and Jerusalem *is* Oholibah.

The Older Sister, Samaria

5 "Oholah played the harlot even though she was Mine;
And she lusted for her lovers, the neighboring Assyrians,
6 *Who were* clothed in purple,
Captains and rulers,
All of them desirable young men,
Horsemen riding on horses.
7 Thus she committed her harlotry with them,
All of them choice men of Assyria;
And with all for whom she lusted,
With all their idols, she defiled herself.
8 She has never given up her harlotry *brought* from Egypt,
For in her youth they had lain with her,
Pressed her virgin bosom,
And poured out their immorality upon her.

9 "Therefore I have delivered her
Into the hand of her lovers,
Into the hand of the Assyrians,
For whom she lusted.
10 They uncovered her nakedness,
Took away her sons and daughters,
And slew her with the sword;
She became a byword among women,
For they had executed judgment on her.

The Younger Sister, Jerusalem

11"Now although her sister Oholibah saw
this, she became more corrupt in her lust than
she, and in her harlotry more corrupt than her
sister's harlotry.

12 "She lusted for the neighboring Assyrians,
Captains and rulers,
Clothed most gorgeously,
Horsemen riding on horses,
All of them desirable young men.
13 Then I saw that she was defiled;
Both *took* the same way.
14 But she increased her harlotry;
She looked at men portrayed on the wall,
Images of Chaldeans portrayed in vermilion,

23:4 [a]Literally *Her Own Tabernacle* [b]Literally *My Tabernacle Is in Her*

SOUL NOTE

Standing in the Gap *(22:30)* Israel's leaders had become completely corrupt. Jeremiah spoke of how God had "sought for a man among them who would . . . stand in the gap . . . on behalf of the land" so that God would not have to destroy it for its sins. But God "found no one." One man with great faith in God could have saved the nation, but no one could be found. God needs men to be spiritual leaders—in their homes, families, churches, and nations. To be an effective spiritual leader, a man must trust in God and be willing to be used by Him. **Topic: Men's Issues**

15 Girded with belts around their waists,
Flowing turbans on their heads,
All of them looking like captains,
In the manner of the Babylonians of
Chaldea,
The land of their nativity.
16 As soon as her eyes saw them,
She lusted for them
And sent messengers to them in
Chaldea.

17 "Then the Babylonians came to her, into
the bed of love,
And they defiled her with their
immorality;
So she was defiled by them, and
alienated herself from them.
18 She revealed her harlotry and uncovered
her nakedness.
Then I alienated Myself from her,
As I had alienated Myself from her sister.

19 "Yet she multiplied her harlotry
In calling to remembrance the days of
her youth,
When she had played the harlot in the
land of Egypt.
20 For she lusted for her paramours,
Whose flesh *is like* the flesh of donkeys,
And whose issue *is like* the issue of
horses.
21 Thus you called to remembrance the
lewdness of your youth,
When the Egyptians pressed your bosom
Because of your youthful breasts.

JUDGMENT ON JERUSALEM

22"Therefore, Oholibah, thus says the Lord
GOD:

'Behold, I will stir up your lovers against
you,
From whom you have alienated
yourself,
And I will bring them against you from
every side:
23 The Babylonians,
All the Chaldeans,
Pekod, Shoa, Koa,
All the Assyrians with them,
All of them desirable young men,
Governors and rulers,
Captains and men of renown,
All of them riding on horses.
24 And they shall come against you
With chariots, wagons, and war-horses,
With a horde of people.
They shall array against you
Buckler, shield, and helmet all around.

'I will delegate judgment to them,
And they shall judge you according to
their judgments.
25 I will set My jealousy against you,
And they shall deal furiously with you;
They shall remove your nose and your
ears,
And your remnant shall fall by the
sword;
They shall take your sons and your
daughters,
And your remnant shall be devoured by
fire.
26 They shall also strip you of your
clothes
And take away your beautiful jewelry.

27 'Thus I will make you cease your
lewdness and your harlotry
Brought from the land of Egypt,
So that you will not lift your eyes to
them,
Nor remember Egypt anymore.'

28"For thus says the Lord GOD: 'Surely I will
deliver you into the hand of those you hate,
into the hand *of those* from whom you alienated yourself. 29They will deal hatefully with
you, take away all you have worked for, and
leave you naked and bare. The nakedness of
your harlotry shall be uncovered, both your
lewdness and your harlotry. 30I will do these
things to you because you have gone as a harlot after the Gentiles, because you have become defiled by their idols. 31You have walked
in the way of your sister; therefore I will put
her cup in your hand.'
32"Thus says the Lord GOD:

'You shall drink of your sister's cup,
The deep and wide one;
You shall be laughed to scorn
And held in derision;
It contains much.
33 You will be filled with drunkenness and
sorrow,
The cup of horror and desolation,
The cup of your sister Samaria.

34 You shall drink and drain it,
You shall break its shards,
And tear at your own breasts;
For I have spoken,'
Says the Lord GOD.

35"Therefore thus says the Lord GOD:

'Because you have forgotten Me and cast
Me behind your back,
Therefore you shall bear the *penalty*
Of your lewdness and your harlotry.' "

BOTH SISTERS JUDGED

36The LORD also said to me: "Son of man,
will you judge Oholah and Oholibah? Then
declare to them their abominations. 37For they
have committed adultery, and blood *is* on
their hands. They have committed adultery
with their idols, and even sacrificed their sons
whom they bore to Me, passing them through
the fire, to devour *them.* 38Moreover they have
done this to Me: They have defiled My sanctuary on the same day and profaned My Sabbaths. 39For after they had slain their children
for their idols, on the same day they came into
My sanctuary to profane it; and indeed thus
they have done in the midst of My house.
40"Furthermore you sent for men to come
from afar, to whom a messenger *was* sent; and
there they came. And you washed yourself for
them, painted your eyes, and adorned yourself
with ornaments. 41You sat on a stately couch,
with a table prepared before it, on which you
had set My incense and My oil. 42The sound of
a carefree multitude *was* with her, and Sabeans *were* brought from the wilderness with
men of the common sort, who put bracelets
on their wrists and beautiful crowns on their
heads. 43Then I said concerning *her who had*
grown old in adulteries, 'Will they commit
harlotry with her now, and she *with them?*'
44Yet they went in to her, as men go in to a
woman who plays the harlot; thus they went
in to Oholah and Oholibah, the lewd women.
45But righteous men will judge them after the
manner of adulteresses, and after the manner
of women who shed blood, because they *are*
adulteresses, and blood *is* on their hands.
46"For thus says the Lord GOD: 'Bring up an
assembly against them, give them up to trouble and plunder. 47The assembly shall stone
them with stones and execute them with their
swords; they shall slay their sons and their
daughters, and burn their houses with fire.
48Thus I will cause lewdness to cease from the
land, that all women may be taught not to
practice your lewdness. 49They shall repay you
for your lewdness, and you shall pay for your
idolatrous sins. Then you shall know that I *am*
the Lord GOD.' "

SYMBOL OF THE COOKING POT

24 Again, in the ninth year, in the tenth
month, on the tenth *day* of the month,
the word of the LORD came to me, saying,
2"Son of man, write down the name of the
day, this very day—the king of Babylon started his siege against Jerusalem this very day.
3And utter a parable to the rebellious house,
and say to them, 'Thus says the Lord GOD:

"Put on a pot, set *it* on,
And also pour water into it.
4 Gather pieces *of meat* in it,
Every good piece,
The thigh and the shoulder.
Fill *it* with choice cuts;
5 Take the choice of the flock.
Also pile *fuel* bones under it,
Make it boil well,
And let the cuts simmer in it."

6'Therefore thus says the Lord GOD:

"Woe to the bloody city,
To the pot whose scum *is* in it,
And whose scum is not gone from it!
Bring it out piece by piece,
On which no lot has fallen.
7 For her blood is in her midst;
She set it on top of a rock;
She did not pour it on the ground,
To cover it with dust.
8 That it may raise up fury and take
vengeance,
I have set her blood on top of a rock,
That it may not be covered."

9'Therefore thus says the Lord GOD:

"Woe to the bloody city!
I too will make the pyre great.
10 Heap on the wood,
Kindle the fire;
Cook the meat well,
Mix in the spices,
And let the cuts be burned up.

11 "Then set the pot empty on the coals,
That it may become hot and its bronze
may burn,
That its filthiness may be melted in it,
That its scum may be consumed.
12 She has grown weary with lies,
And her great scum has not gone from
her.
Let her scum *be* in the fire!
13 In your filthiness *is* lewdness.
Because I have cleansed you, and you
were not cleansed,
You will not be cleansed of your
filthiness anymore,
Till I have caused My fury to rest upon
you.
14 I, the LORD, have spoken *it;*
It shall come to pass, and I will do *it;*
I will not hold back,
Nor will I spare,
Nor will I relent;
According to your ways
And according to your deeds
They[a] will judge you,"
Says the Lord GOD.' "

THE PROPHET'S WIFE DIES

15Also the word of the LORD came to me,
saying, 16"Son of man, behold, I take away
from you the desire of your eyes with one
stroke; yet you shall neither mourn nor weep,
nor shall your tears run down. 17Sigh in silence, make no mourning for the dead; bind
your turban on your head, and put your sandals on your feet; do not cover *your* lips, and
do not eat man's bread *of sorrow.*"

18So I spoke to the people in the morning,
and at evening my wife died; and the next
morning I did as I was commanded.

19And the people said to me, "Will you not
tell us what these *things signify* to us, that you
behave so?"

20Then I answered them, "The word of the
LORD came to me, saying, 21'Speak to the house
of Israel, "Thus says the Lord GOD: 'Behold, I
will profane My sanctuary, your arrogant
boast, the desire of your eyes, the delight of
your soul; and your sons and daughters whom
you left behind shall fall by the sword. 22And
you shall do as I have done; you shall not cover
your lips nor eat man's bread *of sorrow.* 23Your
turbans shall be on your heads and your sandals on your feet; you shall neither mourn nor
weep, but you shall pine away in your iniquities and mourn with one another. 24Thus
Ezekiel is a sign to you; according to all that he
has done you shall do; and when this comes,
you shall know that I *am* the Lord GOD.' "

25'And you, son of man—*will it* not *be* in the
day when I take from them their stronghold,
their joy and their glory, the desire of their
eyes, and that on which they set their minds,
their sons and their daughters: 26*that* on that
day one who escapes will come to you to let
you hear *it* with *your* ears? 27On that day your
mouth will be opened to him who has escaped; you shall speak and no longer be mute.
Thus you will be a sign to them, and they shall
know that I *am* the LORD.' "

PROCLAMATION AGAINST AMMON

25 The word of the LORD came to me, saying, 2"Son of man, set your face
against the Ammonites, and prophesy against
them. 3Say to the Ammonites, 'Hear the word
of the Lord GOD! Thus says the Lord GOD: "Because you said, 'Aha!' against My sanctuary

24:14 [a]Septuagint, Syriac, Targum, and Vulgate read *I.*

SOUL NOTE

That Which Lasts *(24:16)* God chose to tell His message to Israel through Ezekiel by causing Ezekiel's wife ("the desire of your eyes") to die suddenly. This would show the people how suddenly they would lose their temple, the desire of *their* eyes (24:21). As Ezekiel's heart was broken, so would the hearts of the people be broken. God told Ezekiel not to mourn publicly, also as a sign to the people of what was to come. Ezekiel obeyed (24:18). Such radical obedience can come only from a heart that trusts completely in God and His ultimate goodness in the face of heartbreak.
Topic: Obedience

when it was profaned, and against the land of Israel when it was desolate, and against the house of Judah when they went into captivity, 4indeed, therefore, I will deliver you as a possession to the men of the East, and they shall set their encampments among you and make their dwellings among you; they shall eat your fruit, and they shall drink your milk. 5And I will make Rabbah a stable for camels and Ammon a resting place for flocks. Then you shall know that I *am* the LORD."

6'For thus says the Lord GOD: "Because you clapped *your* hands, stamped your feet, and rejoiced in heart with all your disdain for the land of Israel, 7indeed, therefore, I will stretch out My hand against you, and give you as plunder to the nations; I will cut you off from the peoples, and I will cause you to perish from the countries; I will destroy you, and you shall know that I *am* the LORD."

Proclamation Against Moab

8'Thus says the Lord GOD: "Because Moab and Seir say, 'Look! The house of Judah *is* like all the nations,' 9therefore, behold, I will clear the territory of Moab of cities, of the cities on its frontier, the glory of the country, Beth Jeshimoth, Baal Meon, and Kirjathaim. 10To the men of the East I will give it as a possession, together with the Ammonites, that the Ammonites may not be remembered among the nations. 11And I will execute judgments upon Moab, and they shall know that I *am* the LORD."

Proclamation Against Edom

12'Thus says the Lord GOD: "Because of what Edom did against the house of Judah by taking vengeance, and has greatly offended by avenging itself on them," 13therefore thus says the Lord GOD: "I will also stretch out My hand against Edom, cut off man and beast from it, and make it desolate from Teman; Dedan shall fall by the sword. 14I will lay My vengeance on Edom by the hand of My people Israel, that they may do in Edom according to My anger and according to My fury; and they shall know My vengeance," says the Lord GOD.

Proclamation Against Philistia

15'Thus says the Lord GOD: "Because the Philistines dealt vengefully and took vengeance with a spiteful heart, to destroy because of the old hatred," 16therefore thus says the Lord GOD: "I will stretch out My hand against the Philistines, and I will cut off the Cherethites and destroy the remnant of the seacoast. 17I will execute great vengeance on them with furious rebukes; and they shall know that I *am* the LORD, when I lay My vengeance upon them." ' "

Proclamation Against Tyre

26 And it came to pass in the eleventh year, on the first *day* of the month, *that* the word of the LORD came to me, saying, 2"Son of man, because Tyre has said against Jerusalem, 'Aha! She is broken who *was* the gateway of the peoples; now she is turned over to me; I shall be filled; she is laid waste.'

3"Therefore thus says the Lord GOD: 'Behold, I *am* against you, O Tyre, and will cause many nations to come up against you, as the sea causes its waves to come up. 4And they shall destroy the walls of Tyre and break down her towers; I will also scrape her dust from her, and make her like the top of a rock. 5It shall be *a place for* spreading nets in the midst of the sea, for I have spoken,' says the Lord GOD; 'it shall become plunder for the nations. 6Also her daughter *villages* which *are* in the fields shall be slain by the sword. Then they shall know that I am the LORD.'

7"For thus says the Lord GOD: 'Behold, I will bring against Tyre from the north Nebuchadnezzar[a] king of Babylon, king of kings, with horses, with chariots, and with horsemen, and an army with many people. 8He will slay with the sword your daughter *villages* in the fields; he will heap up a siege mound against you, build a wall against you, and raise a defense against you. 9He will direct his battering rams against your walls, and with his axes he will break down your towers. 10Because of the abundance of his horses, their dust will cover you; your walls will shake at the noise of the horsemen, the wagons, and the chariots, when he enters your gates, as men enter a city that has been breached. 11With the hooves of his horses he will trample all your streets; he will slay your people by the sword, and your strong pillars will fall to the ground. 12They will plunder your riches and pillage your merchandise; they will break down your walls and destroy your pleasant houses; they will

26:7 [a]Hebrew *Nebuchadrezzar,* and so elsewhere in this book

lay your stones, your timber, and your soil in
the midst of the water. [13]I will put an end to
the sound of your songs, and the sound of
your harps shall be heard no more. [14]I will
make you like the top of a rock; you shall be *a*
place for spreading nets, and you shall never
be rebuilt, for I the LORD have spoken,' says
the Lord GOD.

[15]"Thus says the Lord GOD to Tyre: 'Will the
coastlands not shake at the sound of your fall,
when the wounded cry, when slaughter is
made in the midst of you? [16]Then all the
princes of the sea will come down from their
thrones, lay aside their robes, and take off
their embroidered garments; they will clothe
themselves with trembling; they will sit on the
ground, tremble *every* moment, and be astonished at you. [17]And they will take up a lamentation for you, and say to you:

"How you have perished,
O one inhabited by seafaring men,
O renowned city,
Who was strong at sea,
She and her inhabitants,
Who caused their terror *to be* on all her
inhabitants!
18 Now the coastlands tremble on the day
of your fall;
Yes, the coastlands by the sea are
troubled at your departure." '

[19]"For thus says the Lord GOD: 'When I
make you a desolate city, like cities that are
not inhabited, when I bring the deep upon
you, and great waters cover you, [20]then I will
bring you down with those who descend into
the Pit, to the people of old, and I will make
you dwell in the lowest part of the earth, in
places desolate from antiquity, with those
who go down to the Pit, so that you may never
be inhabited; and I shall establish glory in the
land of the living. [21]I will make you a terror,
and you *shall be* no *more;* though you are
sought for, you will never be found again,'
says the Lord GOD."

LAMENTATION FOR TYRE

27 The word of the LORD came again to
me, saying, [2]"Now, son of man, take
up a lamentation for Tyre, [3]and say to Tyre,
'You who are situated at the entrance of the
sea, merchant of the peoples on many coastlands, thus says the Lord GOD:

"O Tyre, you have said,
'I *am* perfect in beauty.'
4 Your borders *are* in the midst of the seas.
Your builders have perfected your
beauty.
5 They made all *your* planks of fir trees
from Senir;
They took a cedar from Lebanon to
make you a mast.
6 *Of* oaks from Bashan they made your
oars;
The company of Ashurites have inlaid
your planks
With ivory from the coasts of Cyprus.[a]
7 Fine embroidered linen from Egypt was
what you spread for your sail;
Blue and purple from the coasts of
Elishah was what covered you.

8 "Inhabitants of Sidon and Arvad were
your oarsmen;
Your wise men, O Tyre, were in you;
They became your pilots.
9 Elders of Gebal and its wise men
Were in you to caulk your seams;
All the ships of the sea
And their oarsmen were in you
To market your merchandise.

10 "Those from Persia, Lydia,[a] and Libya[b]
Were in your army as men of war;
They hung shield and helmet in you;
They gave splendor to you.
11 Men of Arvad with your army *were* on
your walls *all* around,
And the men of Gammad were in your
towers;
They hung their shields on your walls *all*
around;
They made your beauty perfect.

[12]"Tarshish *was* your merchant because of
your many luxury goods. They gave you silver, iron, tin, and lead for your goods. [13]Javan,
Tubal, and Meshech *were* your traders. They
bartered human lives and vessels of bronze
for your merchandise. [14]Those from the house
of Togarmah traded for your wares with
horses, steeds, and mules. [15]The men of Dedan *were* your traders; many isles *were* the
market of your hand. They brought you ivory

27:6 [a]Hebrew *Kittim,* western lands, especially Cyprus **27:10** [a]Hebrew *Lud* [b]Hebrew *Put*

tusks and ebony as payment. [16]Syria *was* your
merchant because of the abundance of goods
you made. They gave you for your wares em-
eralds, purple, embroidery, fine linen, corals,
and rubies. [17]Judah and the land of Israel *were*
your traders. They traded for your merchandise wheat of Minnith, millet, honey, oil, and
balm. [18]Damascus *was* your merchant because of the abundance of goods you made,
because of your many luxury items, with the
wine of Helbon and with white wool. [19]Dan
and Javan paid for your wares, traversing back
and forth. Wrought iron, cassia, and cane
were among your merchandise. [20]Dedan *was*
your merchant in saddlecloths for riding.
[21]Arabia and all the princes of Kedar *were* your
regular merchants. They traded with you in
lambs, rams, and goats. [22]The merchants of
Sheba and Raamah *were* your merchants.
They traded for your wares the choicest
spices, all kinds of precious stones, and gold.
[23]Haran, Canneh, Eden, the merchants of Sheba, Assyria, *and* Chilmad *were* your merchants. [24]These *were* your merchants in choice
items—in purple clothes, in embroidered garments, in chests of multicolored apparel, in
sturdy woven cords, which were in your marketplace.

25 "The ships of Tarshish were carriers of
your merchandise.
You were filled and very glorious in the
midst of the seas.
26 Your oarsmen brought you into many
waters,
But the east wind broke you in the midst
of the seas.

27 "Your riches, wares, and merchandise,
Your mariners and pilots,
Your caulkers and merchandisers,
All your men of war who *are* in you,
And the entire company which *is* in your
midst,
Will fall into the midst of the seas on the
day of your ruin.
28 The common-land will shake at the
sound of the cry of your pilots.

29 "All who handle the oar,
The mariners,
All the pilots of the sea
Will come down from their ships *and*
stand on the shore.
30 They will make their voice heard
because of you;
They will cry bitterly and cast dust on
their heads;
They will roll about in ashes;
31 They will shave themselves completely
bald because of you,
Gird themselves with sackcloth,
And weep for you
With bitterness of heart *and* bitter
wailing.
32 In their wailing for you
They will take up a lamentation,
And lament for you:
'What *city is* like Tyre,
Destroyed in the midst of the sea?

33 'When your wares went out by sea,
You satisfied many people;
You enriched the kings of the earth
With your many luxury goods and your
merchandise.
34 But you are broken by the seas in the
depths of the waters;
Your merchandise and the entire
company will fall in your midst.
35 All the inhabitants of the isles will be
astonished at you;
Their kings will be greatly afraid,
And *their* countenance will be
troubled.
36 The merchants among the peoples will
hiss at you;
You will become a horror, and *be* no
more forever.' " ' "

Proclamation Against the King of Tyre

28 The word of the LORD came to me again, saying, [2]"Son of man, say to the prince of Tyre, 'Thus says the Lord GOD:

"Because your heart *is* lifted up,
And you say, 'I *am* a god,
I sit *in* the seat of gods,
In the midst of the seas,'
Yet you *are* a man, and not a god,
Though you set your heart as the heart
of a god
3 (Behold, you *are* wiser than Daniel!
There is no secret that can be hidden
from you!
4 With your wisdom and your
understanding
You have gained riches for yourself,

And gathered gold and silver into your
treasuries;
5 By your great wisdom in trade you have
increased your riches,
And your heart is lifted up because of
your riches),"

6'Therefore thus says the Lord GOD:

"Because you have set your heart as the
heart of a god,
7 Behold, therefore, I will bring strangers
against you,
The most terrible of the nations;
And they shall draw their swords against
the beauty of your wisdom,
And defile your splendor.
8 They shall throw you down into the Pit,
And you shall die the death of the
slain
In the midst of the seas.

9 "Will you still say before him who slays
you,
'I *am* a god'?
But you *shall be* a man, and not a god,
In the hand of him who slays you.
10 You shall die the death of the
uncircumcised
By the hand of aliens;
For I have spoken," says the Lord GOD.' "

LAMENTATION FOR THE KING OF TYRE

11Moreover the word of the LORD came to
me, saying, 12"Son of man, take up a lamentation for the king of Tyre, and say to him, 'Thus
says the Lord GOD:

"You *were* the seal of perfection,
Full of wisdom and perfect in beauty.
13 You were in Eden, the garden of God;
Every precious stone *was* your covering:
The sardius, topaz, and diamond,
Beryl, onyx, and jasper,
Sapphire, turquoise, and emerald with
gold.
The workmanship of your timbrels and
pipes
Was prepared for you on the day you
were created.

14 "You *were* the anointed cherub who
covers;
I established you;

PERSONALITY PROFILE

Pride

THE PRIDE OF THE KING OF TYRE

(EZEKIEL 28:11–19)

Tyre was one of the great cities of the ancient world and the capital of the Phoenician Empire. God instructed the prophet Ezekiel to issue a "lamentation for the king of Tyre" (28:11). The language and imagery of the prophecy indicate that both the king and his great city were simply contemporary examples of the great struggle between God and a rebellion led by Satan. The pride of the king of Tyre illustrates the pride of Satan himself. In spite of being the "anointed cherub" (28:14) who served in the very presence of God, Satan fell because his pride caused him to be lifted up against God Himself. The king's fall and the destruction of the city provide a shocking picture of the results of God's judgment on that location as well as on Satan.

The reputation of the city serves as a reminder that greatness and "wisdom" come from God, and can be taken by Him. The "iniquity" (28:15) that leads to destruction refers to the pride that caused Tyre and her king, like Satan long ago, to forget their Maker. Ezekiel described the results as a "horror" (28:19). The city would be "no more forever" (28:19). Ezekiel's prophecy came true in the humiliation and displacement of Tyre as a great city. The words of Proverbs apply equally to Tyre and Satan, "Pride goes before destruction, and a haughty spirit before a fall" (Prov. 16:18).

To Learn More: Turn to the article about pride on pages 572, 573. See also the key passage note at James 4:6–10 on page 1649.

You were on the holy mountain of God;
You walked back and forth in the midst
of fiery stones.
15 You *were* perfect in your ways from the
day you were created,
Till iniquity was found in you.

16 "By the abundance of your trading
You became filled with violence within,
And you sinned;
Therefore I cast you as a profane thing
Out of the mountain of God;
And I destroyed you, O covering cherub,
From the midst of the fiery stones.

17 "Your heart was lifted up because of your
beauty;
You corrupted your wisdom for the sake
of your splendor;
I cast you to the ground,
I laid you before kings,
That they might gaze at you.

18 "You defiled your sanctuaries
By the multitude of your iniquities,
By the iniquity of your trading;
Therefore I brought fire from your midst;
It devoured you,
And I turned you to ashes upon the
earth
In the sight of all who saw you.
19 All who knew you among the peoples
are astonished at you;
You have become a horror,
And *shall be* no more forever." ' "

Proclamation Against Sidon

20Then the word of the LORD came to me,
saying, 21"Son of man, set your face toward Sidon, and prophesy against her, 22and say,
'Thus says the Lord GOD:

"Behold, I *am* against you, O Sidon;
I will be glorified in your midst;
And they shall know that I *am* the LORD,
When I execute judgments in her and
am hallowed in her.
23 For I will send pestilence upon her,
And blood in her streets;
The wounded shall be judged in her
midst
By the sword against her on every side;
Then they shall know that I *am* the
LORD.

24"And there shall no longer be a pricking
brier or a painful thorn for the house of Israel
from among all *who are* around them, who despise them. Then they shall know that I *am*
the Lord GOD."

Israel's Future Blessing

25'Thus says the Lord GOD: "When I have
gathered the house of Israel from the peoples
among whom they are scattered, and am hallowed in them in the sight of the Gentiles,
then they will dwell in their own land which I
gave to My servant Jacob. 26And they will
dwell safely there, build houses, and plant
vineyards; yes, they will dwell securely, when
I execute judgments on all those around them
who despise them. Then they shall know that
I *am* the LORD their God." ' "

Proclamation Against Egypt

29 In the tenth year, in the tenth *month,*
on the twelfth *day* of the month, the
word of the LORD came to me, saying, 2"Son of
man, set your face against Pharaoh king of
Egypt, and prophesy against him, and against
all Egypt. 3Speak, and say, 'Thus says the Lord
GOD:

"Behold, I *am* against you,
O Pharaoh king of Egypt,
O great monster who lies in the midst of
his rivers,
Who has said, 'My River[a] *is* my own;
I have made *it* for myself.'
4 But I will put hooks in your jaws,
And cause the fish of your rivers to stick
to your scales;
I will bring you up out of the midst of
your rivers,
And all the fish in your rivers will stick
to your scales.
5 I will leave you in the wilderness,
You and all the fish of your rivers;
You shall fall on the open field;
You shall not be picked up or
gathered.[a]
I have given you as food
To the beasts of the field
And to the birds of the heavens.

29:3 [a]That is, the Nile **29:5** [a]Following Masoretic Text, Septuagint, and Vulgate; some Hebrew manuscripts and Targum read *buried.*

6 "Then all the inhabitants of Egypt
Shall know that I *am* the LORD,
Because they have been a staff of reed to
the house of Israel.
7 When they took hold of you with the
hand,
You broke and tore all their shoulders;[a]
When they leaned on you,
You broke and made all their backs
quiver."

8'Therefore thus says the Lord GOD: "Surely
I will bring a sword upon you and cut off from
you man and beast. 9And the land of Egypt
shall become desolate and waste; then they
will know that I *am* the LORD, because he said,
'The River *is* mine, and I have made *it*.' 10In-
deed, therefore, I *am* against you and against
your rivers, and I will make the land of Egypt
utterly waste and desolate, from Migdol[a] *to*
Syene, as far as the border of Ethiopia. 11Nei-
ther foot of man shall pass through it nor foot
of beast pass through it, and it shall be uninhabited forty years. 12I will make the land of
Egypt desolate in the midst of the countries
that are desolate; and among the cities *that
are* laid waste, her cities shall be desolate forty
years; and I will scatter the Egyptians among
the nations and disperse them throughout the
countries."

13'Yet, thus says the Lord GOD: "At the end
of forty years I will gather the Egyptians from
the peoples among whom they were scattered.
14I will bring back the captives of Egypt and
cause them to return to the land of Pathros, to
the land of their origin, and there they shall be
a lowly kingdom. 15It shall be the lowliest of
kingdoms; it shall never again exalt itself
above the nations, for I will diminish them so
that they will not rule over the nations anymore. 16No longer shall it be the confidence of
the house of Israel, but will remind them of
their iniquity when they turned to follow
them. Then they shall know that I *am* the Lord
GOD." ' "

BABYLONIA WILL PLUNDER EGYPT

17And it came to pass in the twenty-seventh
year, in the first *month*, on the first *day* of the
month, *that* the word of the LORD came to me,
saying, 18"Son of man, Nebuchadnezzar king
of Babylon caused his army to labor strenu-
ously against Tyre; every head *was* made bald,
and every shoulder rubbed raw; yet neither he
nor his army received wages from Tyre, for the
labor which they expended on it. 19Therefore
thus says the Lord GOD: 'Surely I will give the
land of Egypt to Nebuchadnezzar king of Babylon; he shall take away her wealth, carry off
her spoil, and remove her pillage; and that
will be the wages for his army. 20I have given
him the land of Egypt *for* his labor, because
they worked for Me,' says the Lord GOD.

21'In that day I will cause the horn of the
house of Israel to spring forth, and I will open
your mouth to speak in their midst. Then they
shall know that I *am* the LORD.' "

EGYPT AND HER ALLIES WILL FALL

30 The word of the LORD came to me
again, saying, 2"Son of man, prophesy
and say, 'Thus says the Lord GOD:

"Wail, 'Woe to the day!'
3 For the day *is* near,
Even the day of the LORD *is* near;
It will be a day of clouds, the time of the
Gentiles.
4 The sword shall come upon Egypt,
And great anguish shall be in Ethiopia,
When the slain fall in Egypt,
And they take away her wealth,
And her foundations are broken down.

5"Ethiopia, Libya,[a] Lydia,[b] all the mingled
people, Chub, and the men of the lands who
are allied, shall fall with them by the sword."
6'Thus says the LORD:

"Those who uphold Egypt shall fall,
And the pride of her power shall come
down.
From Migdol *to* Syene
Those within her shall fall by the
sword,"
Says the Lord GOD.

7 "They shall be desolate in the midst of
the desolate countries,
And her cities shall be in the midst of
the cities *that are* laid waste.
8 Then they will know that I *am* the LORD,
When I have set a fire in Egypt
And all her helpers are destroyed.

29:7 [a]Following Masoretic Text and Vulgate; Septuagint and Syriac read *hand*. **29:10** [a]Or *tower* **30:5** [a]Hebrew *Put* [b]Hebrew *Lud*

9 On that day messengers shall go forth
from Me in ships
To make the careless Ethiopians afraid,
And great anguish shall come upon
them,
As on the day of Egypt;
For indeed it is coming!"

10'Thus says the Lord GOD:

"I will also make a multitude of Egypt to
cease
By the hand of Nebuchadnezzar king of
Babylon.
11 He and his people with him, the most
terrible of the nations,
Shall be brought to destroy the land;
They shall draw their swords against
Egypt,
And fill the land with the slain.
12 I will make the rivers dry,
And sell the land into the hand of the
wicked;
I will make the land waste, and all that
is in it,
By the hand of aliens.
I, the LORD, have spoken."

13'Thus says the Lord GOD:

"I will also destroy the idols,
And cause the images to cease from
Noph;[a]
There shall no longer be princes from
the land of Egypt;
I will put fear in the land of Egypt.
14 I will make Pathros desolate,
Set fire to Zoan,
And execute judgments in No.[a]
15 I will pour My fury on Sin,[a] the strength
of Egypt;
I will cut off the multitude of No,
16 And set a fire in Egypt;
Sin shall have great pain,
No shall be split open,
And Noph *shall be in* distress daily.
17 The young men of Aven[a] and Pi Beseth
shall fall by the sword,
And these *cities* shall go into captivity.
18 At Tehaphnehes[a] the day shall also be
darkened,[b]
When I break the yokes of Egypt there.
And her arrogant strength shall cease in
her;
As for her, a cloud shall cover her,
And her daughters shall go into
captivity.
19 Thus I will execute judgments on Egypt,
Then they shall know that I *am* the
LORD." ' "

PROCLAMATION AGAINST PHARAOH

20And it came to pass in the eleventh year,
in the first *month,* on the seventh *day* of the
month, *that* the word of the LORD came to me,
saying, 21"Son of man, I have broken the arm
of Pharaoh king of Egypt; and see, it has not
been bandaged for healing, nor a splint put on
to bind it, to make it strong enough to hold a
sword. 22Therefore thus says the Lord GOD:
'Surely I *am* against Pharaoh king of Egypt,
and will break his arms, both the strong one
and the one that was broken; and I will make
the sword fall out of his hand. 23I will scatter
the Egyptians among the nations, and disperse them throughout the countries. 24I will
strengthen the arms of the king of Babylon
and put My sword in his hand; but I will break
Pharaoh's arms, and he will groan before him
with the groanings of a mortally wounded
man. 25Thus I will strengthen the arms of the
king of Babylon, but the arms of Pharaoh shall
fall down; they shall know that I *am* the LORD,
when I put My sword into the hand of the king
of Babylon and he stretches it out against the
land of Egypt. 26I will scatter the Egyptians
among the nations and disperse them
throughout the countries. Then they shall
know that I *am* the LORD.' "

EGYPT CUT DOWN LIKE A GREAT TREE

31 Now it came to pass in the eleventh
year, in the third *month,* on the first
day of the month, *that* the word of the LORD
came to me, saying, 2"Son of man, say to Pharaoh king of Egypt and to his multitude:

'Whom are you like in your greatness?
3 Indeed Assyria *was* a cedar in Lebanon,
With fine branches that shaded the
forest,

30:13 [a]That is, ancient Memphis **30:14** [a]That is, ancient Thebes **30:15** [a]That is, ancient Pelusium **30:17** [a]That is, ancient On (Heliopolis)
30:18 [a]Spelled *Tahpanhes* in Jeremiah 43:7 and elsewhere [b]Following many Hebrew manuscripts, Bomberg, Septuagint, Syriac, Targum, and Vulgate; Masoretic Text reads *refrained.*

And of high stature;
And its top was among the thick boughs.
4 The waters made it grow;
Underground waters gave it height,
With their rivers running around the place where it was planted,
And sent out rivulets to all the trees of the field.

5 'Therefore its height was exalted above all the trees of the field;
Its boughs were multiplied,
And its branches became long because of the abundance of water,
As it sent them out.
6 All the birds of the heavens made their nests in its boughs;
Under its branches all the beasts of the field brought forth their young;
And in its shadow all great nations made their home.

7 'Thus it was beautiful in greatness and in the length of its branches,
Because its roots reached to abundant waters.
8 The cedars in the garden of God could not hide it;
The fir trees were not like its boughs,
And the chestnut[a] trees were not like its branches;
No tree in the garden of God was like it in beauty.
9 I made it beautiful with a multitude of branches,
So that all the trees of Eden envied it,
That *were* in the garden of God.'

10"Therefore thus says the Lord GOD: 'Because you have increased in height, and it set
its top among the thick boughs, and its heart
was lifted up in its height, 11therefore I will
deliver it into the hand of the mighty one of
the nations, and he shall surely deal with it; I
have driven it out for its wickedness. 12And
aliens, the most terrible of the nations, have
cut it down and left it; its branches have fallen
on the mountains and in all the valleys; its
boughs lie broken by all the rivers of the land;
and all the peoples of the earth have gone
from under its shadow and left it.

13 'On its ruin will remain all the birds of the heavens,
And all the beasts of the field will come to its branches—

14'So that no trees by the waters may ever
again exalt themselves for their height, nor set
their tops among the thick boughs, that no
tree which drinks water may ever be high
enough to reach up to them.

'For they have all been delivered to death,
To the depths of the earth,
Among the children of men who go down to the Pit.'

15"Thus says the Lord GOD: 'In the day
when it went down to hell, I caused mourning. I covered the deep because of it. I restrained its rivers, and the great waters were
held back. I caused Lebanon to mourn for it,
and all the trees of the field wilted because of
it. 16I made the nations shake at the sound of
its fall, when I cast it down to hell together
with those who descend into the Pit; and all
the trees of Eden, the choice and best of Lebanon, all that drink water, were comforted in
the depths of the earth. 17They also went
down to hell with it, with those *slain* by the
sword; and *those who were* its *strong* arm
dwelt in its shadows among the nations.
18'To which of the trees in Eden will you
then be likened in glory and greatness? Yet
you shall be brought down with the trees of
Eden to the depths of the earth; you shall lie in
the midst of the uncircumcised, with *those*
slain by the sword. This *is* Pharaoh and all his
multitude,' says the Lord GOD."

LAMENTATION FOR PHARAOH AND EGYPT

32 And it came to pass in the twelfth year,
in the twelfth *month,* on the first *day*
of the month, *that* the word of the LORD came
to me, saying, 2"Son of man, take up a lamentation for Pharaoh king of Egypt, and say to
him:

'You are like a young lion among the nations,
And you *are* like a monster in the seas,
Bursting forth in your rivers,
Troubling the waters with your feet,
And fouling their rivers.'

31:8 [a]Hebrew *armon*

3"Thus says the Lord GOD:

'I will therefore spread My net over you
with a company of many people,
And they will draw you up in My net.
4 Then I will leave you on the land;
I will cast you out on the open fields,
And cause to settle on you all the birds
of the heavens.
And with you I will fill the beasts of the
whole earth.
5 I will lay your flesh on the mountains,
And fill the valleys with your carcass.

6 'I will also water the land with the flow
of your blood,
Even to the mountains;
And the riverbeds will be full of you.
7 When *I* put out your light,
I will cover the heavens, and make its
stars dark;
I will cover the sun with a cloud,
And the moon shall not give her light.
8 All the bright lights of the heavens I will
make dark over you,
And bring darkness upon your land,'
Says the Lord GOD.

9'I will also trouble the hearts of many peoples, when I bring your destruction among the
nations, into the countries which you have not
known. 10Yes, I will make many peoples astonished at you, and their kings shall be horribly
afraid of you when I brandish My sword before them; and they shall tremble *every* moment, every man for his own life, in the day of
your fall.'

11"For thus says the Lord GOD: 'The sword
of the king of Babylon shall come upon you.
12By the swords of the mighty warriors, all of
them the most terrible of the nations, I will
cause your multitude to fall.

'They shall plunder the pomp of Egypt,
And all its multitude shall be destroyed.
13 Also I will destroy all its animals
From beside its great waters;
The foot of man shall muddy them no
more,
Nor shall the hooves of animals muddy
them.
14 Then I will make their waters clear,
And make their rivers run like oil,'
Says the Lord GOD.

15 'When I make the land of Egypt
desolate,
And the country is destitute of all that
once filled it,
When I strike all who dwell in it,
Then they shall know that I *am* the
LORD.

16 'This *is* the lamentation
With which they shall lament her;
The daughters of the nations shall
lament her;
They shall lament for her, for Egypt,
And for all her multitude,'
Says the Lord GOD."

EGYPT AND OTHERS CONSIGNED TO THE PIT

17It came to pass also in the twelfth year, on
the fifteenth *day* of the month, *that* the word
of the LORD came to me, saying:

18 "Son of man, wail over the multitude of
Egypt,
And cast them down to the depths of the
earth,
Her and the daughters of the famous
nations,
With those who go down to the Pit:
19 'Whom do you surpass in beauty?
Go down, be placed with the
uncircumcised.'

20 "They shall fall in the midst of *those* slain
by the sword;
She is delivered to the sword,
Drawing her and all her multitudes.
21 The strong among the mighty
Shall speak to him out of the midst of
hell
With those who help him:
'They have gone down,
They lie with the uncircumcised, slain
by the sword.'

22 "Assyria *is* there, and all her company,
With their graves all around her,
All of them slain, fallen by the sword.
23 Her graves are set in the recesses of the
Pit,
And her company is all around her
grave,
All of them slain, fallen by the sword,
Who caused terror in the land of the
living.

24 "There *is* Elam and all her multitude,
All around her grave,
All of them slain, fallen by the sword,
Who have gone down uncircumcised to
the lower parts of the earth,
Who caused their terror in the land of
the living;
Now they bear their shame with those
who go down to the Pit.
25 They have set her bed in the midst of
the slain,
With all her multitude,
With her graves all around it,
All of them uncircumcised, slain by the
sword;
Though their terror was caused
In the land of the living,
Yet they bear their shame
With those who go down to the Pit;
It was put in the midst of the slain.

26 "There *are* Meshech and Tubal and all
their multitudes,
With all their graves around it,
All of them uncircumcised, slain by the
sword,
Though they caused their terror in the
land of the living.
27 They do not lie with the mighty
Who are fallen of the uncircumcised,
Who have gone down to hell with their
weapons of war;
They have laid their swords under their
heads,
But their iniquities will be on their bones,
Because of the terror of the mighty in
the land of the living.
28 Yes, you shall be broken in the midst of
the uncircumcised,
And lie with *those* slain by the sword.

29 "There *is* Edom,
Her kings and all her princes,
Who despite their might
Are laid beside *those* slain by the sword;
They shall lie with the uncircumcised,
And with those who go down to the Pit.
30 There *are* the princes of the north,
All of them, and all the Sidonians,
Who have gone down with the slain
In shame at the terror which they caused
by their might;
They lie uncircumcised with *those* slain
by the sword,
And bear their shame with those who go
down to the Pit.

31 "Pharaoh will see them
And be comforted over all his multitude,
Pharaoh and all his army,
Slain by the sword,"
Says the Lord GOD.

32 "For I have caused My terror in the land
of the living;
And he shall be placed in the midst of
the uncircumcised
With *those* slain by the sword,
Pharaoh and all his multitude,"
Says the Lord GOD.

THE WATCHMAN AND HIS MESSAGE

33 Again the word of the LORD came to
me, saying, [2]"Son of man, speak to the
children of your people, and say to them:
'When I bring the sword upon a land, and the
people of the land take a man from their territory and make him their watchman, [3]when he
sees the sword coming upon the land, if he
blows the trumpet and warns the people,
[4]then whoever hears the sound of the trumpet
and does not take warning, if the sword comes
and takes him away, his blood shall be on his
own head. [5]He heard the sound of the trumpet, but did not take warning; his blood shall
be upon himself. But he who takes warning
will save his life. [6]But if the watchman sees
the sword coming and does not blow the
trumpet, and the people are not warned, and
the sword comes and takes *any* person from
among them, he is taken away in his iniquity;
but his blood I will require at the watchman's
hand.'

[7]"So you, son of man: I have made you a
watchman for the house of Israel; therefore
you shall hear a word from My mouth and
warn them for Me. [8]When I say to the wicked,
'O wicked *man*, you shall surely die!' and you
do not speak to warn the wicked from his way,
that wicked *man* shall die in his iniquity; but
his blood I will require at your hand. [9]Never-
theless if you warn the wicked to turn from his
way, and he does not turn from his way, he
shall die in his iniquity; but you have delivered your soul.

[10]"Therefore you, O son of man, say to the
house of Israel: 'Thus you say, "If our transgressions and our sins *lie* upon us, and we

pine away in them, how can we then live?" ' [11]Say to them: '*As* I live,' says the Lord GOD, 'I have no pleasure in the death of the wicked, but that the wicked turn from his way and live. Turn, turn from your evil ways! For why should you die, O house of Israel?'

THE FAIRNESS OF GOD'S JUDGMENT

[12]"Therefore you, O son of man, say to the children of your people: 'The righteousness of the righteous man shall not deliver him in the day of his transgression; as for the wickedness of the wicked, he shall not fall because of it in the day that he turns from his wickedness; nor shall the righteous be able to live because of *his righteousness* in the day that he sins.' [13]When I say to the righteous *that* he shall surely live, but he trusts in his own righteousness and commits iniquity, none of his righteous works shall be remembered; but because of the iniquity that he has committed, he shall die. [14]Again, when I say to the wicked, 'You shall surely die,' if he turns from his sin and does what is lawful and right, [15]*if* the wicked restores the pledge, gives back what he has stolen, and walks in the statutes of life without committing iniquity, he shall surely live; he shall not die. [16]None of his sins which he has committed shall be remembered against him; he has done what is lawful and right; he shall surely live.

> "None of his sins which he has committed shall be remembered against him; he has done what is lawful and right; he shall surely live."
>
> EZEKIEL 33:16

[17]"Yet the children of your people say, 'The way of the LORD is not fair.' But it is their way which is not fair! [18]When the righteous turns from his righteousness and commits iniquity, he shall die because of it. [19]But when the wicked turns from his wickedness and does what is lawful and right, he shall live because of it. [20]Yet you say, 'The way of the LORD is not fair.' O house of Israel, I will judge every one of you according to his own ways."

THE FALL OF JERUSALEM

[21]And it came to pass in the twelfth year of our captivity, in the tenth *month,* on the fifth *day* of the month, *that* one who had escaped from Jerusalem came to me and said, "The city has been captured!"

[22]Now the hand of the LORD had been upon me the evening before the man came who had escaped. And He had opened my mouth; so when he came to me in the morning, my mouth was opened, and I was no longer mute.

THE CAUSE OF JUDAH'S RUIN

[23]Then the word of the LORD came to me, saying: [24]"Son of man, they who inhabit those ruins in the land of Israel are saying, 'Abraham was only one, and he inherited the land. But we *are* many; the land has been given to us as a possession.'

[25]"Therefore say to them, 'Thus says the Lord GOD: "You eat *meat* with blood, you lift up your eyes toward your idols, and shed blood. Should you then possess the land? [26]You rely on your sword, you commit abominations, and you defile one another's wives. Should you then possess the land?" '

[27]"Say thus to them, 'Thus says the Lord GOD: "*As* I live, surely those who *are* in the ruins shall fall by the sword, and the one who *is* in the open field I will give to the beasts to be devoured, and those who *are* in the strongholds and caves shall die of the pestilence. [28]For I will make the land most desolate, her arrogant strength shall cease, and the mountains of Israel shall be so desolate that no one will pass through. [29]Then they shall know that I *am* the LORD, when I have made the land most desolate because of all their abominations which they have committed." '

HEARING AND NOT DOING

[30]"As for you, son of man, the children of your people are talking about you beside the walls and in the doors of the houses; and they speak to one another, everyone saying to his brother, 'Please come and hear what the word is that comes from the LORD.' [31]So they come to you as people do, they sit before you *as* My people, and they hear your words, but they do not do them; for with their mouth they show much love, *but* their hearts pursue their *own* gain. [32]Indeed you *are* to them as a very lovely song of one who has a pleasant voice and can play well on an instrument; for they hear your words, but they do not do them. [33]And when this comes to pass—surely it will come—then

they will know that a prophet has been among them.”

Irresponsible Shepherds

34 And the word of the LORD came to me, saying, 2“Son of man, prophesy against the shepherds of Israel, prophesy and say to them, ‘Thus says the Lord GOD to the shepherds: “Woe to the shepherds of Israel who feed themselves! Should not the shepherds feed the flocks? 3You eat the fat and clothe yourselves with the wool; you slaughter the fatlings, *but* you do not feed the flock. 4The weak you have not strengthened, nor have you healed those who were sick, nor bound up the broken, nor brought back what was driven away, nor sought what was lost; but with force and cruelty you have ruled them. 5So they were scattered because *there was* no shepherd; and they became food for all the beasts of the field when they were scattered. 6My sheep wandered through all the mountains, and on every high hill; yes, My flock was scattered over the whole face of the earth, and no one was seeking or searching *for them.*”

> “I will seek what was lost and bring back what was driven away, bind up the broken and strengthen what was sick.”
>
> EZEKIEL 34:16

7‘Therefore, you shepherds, hear the word of the LORD: 8“*As* I live,” says the Lord GOD, “surely because My flock became a prey, and My flock became food for every beast of the field, because *there was* no shepherd, nor did My shepherds search for My flock, but the shepherds fed themselves and did not feed My flock”— 9therefore, O shepherds, hear the word of the LORD! 10Thus says the Lord GOD: “Behold, I *am* against the shepherds, and I will require My flock at their hand; I will cause them to cease feeding the sheep, and the shepherds shall feed themselves no more; for I will deliver My flock from their mouths, that they may no longer be food for them.”

God, the True Shepherd

11‘For thus says the Lord GOD: “Indeed I Myself will search for My sheep and seek them out. 12As a shepherd seeks out his flock on the day he is among his scattered sheep, so will I seek out My sheep and deliver them from all the places where they were scattered on a cloudy and dark day. 13And I will bring them out from the peoples and gather them from the countries, and will bring them to their own land; I will feed them on the mountains of Israel, in the valleys and in all the inhabited places of the country. 14I will feed them in good pasture, and their fold shall be on the high mountains of Israel. There they shall lie down in a good fold and feed in rich pasture on the mountains of Israel. 15I will feed My flock, and I will make them lie down,” says the Lord GOD. 16“I will seek what was lost and bring back what was driven away, bind up the broken and strengthen what was sick; but I will destroy the fat and the strong, and feed them in judgment.”

17‘And *as for* you, O My flock, thus says the Lord GOD: “Behold, I shall judge between sheep and sheep, between rams and goats. 18*Is it* too little for you to have eaten up the good pasture, that you must tread down with your feet the residue of your pasture—and to have drunk of the clear waters, that you must foul the residue with your feet? 19And *as for* My flock, they eat what you have trampled with your feet, and they drink what you have fouled with your feet.”

20‘Therefore thus says the Lord GOD to them: “Behold, I Myself will judge between the fat and the lean sheep. 21Because you have pushed with side and shoulder, butted all the weak ones with your horns, and scattered them abroad, 22therefore I will save My flock, and they shall no longer be a prey; and I will judge between sheep and sheep. 23I will establish one shepherd over them, and he shall feed them—My servant David. He shall feed them and be their shepherd. 24And I, the LORD, will be their God, and My servant David a prince among them; I, the LORD, have spoken.

25“I will make a covenant of peace with them, and cause wild beasts to cease from the land; and they will dwell safely in the wilderness and sleep in the woods. 26I will make them and the places all around My hill a blessing; and I will cause showers to come down in their season; there shall be showers of blessing. 27Then the trees of the field shall yield their fruit, and the earth shall yield her increase. They shall be safe in their land; and they shall know that I *am* the LORD, when I have broken the bands of their yoke and delivered them from the hand of those who enslaved them. 28And they shall no longer be a prey for the nations, nor shall beasts of the land devour them; but they shall dwell safely, and no one shall make *them* afraid. 29I will raise up for them a garden of renown, and they shall no longer be consumed with hunger in the land, nor bear the shame of the Gentiles anymore. 30Thus they shall know that I, the LORD their God, *am* with them, and they, the house of Israel, *are* My people," says the Lord GOD.' "

31"You are My flock, the flock of My pasture; you *are* men, *and* I *am* your God," says the Lord GOD.

JUDGMENT ON MOUNT SEIR

35 Moreover the word of the LORD came to me, saying, 2"Son of man, set your face against Mount Seir and prophesy against it, 3and say to it, 'Thus says the Lord GOD:

"Behold, O Mount Seir, I *am* against you;
I will stretch out My hand against you,
And make you most desolate;
4 I shall lay your cities waste,
And you shall be desolate.
Then you shall know that I *am* the LORD.

5"Because you have had an ancient hatred, and have shed *the blood of* the children of Israel by the power of the sword at the time of their calamity, *when* their iniquity *came to an* end, 6therefore, *as* I live," says the Lord GOD, "I will prepare you for blood, and blood shall pursue you; since you have not hated blood, therefore blood shall pursue you. 7Thus I will make Mount Seir most desolate, and cut off from it the one who leaves and the one who returns. 8And I will fill its mountains with the slain; on your hills and in your valleys and in all your ravines those who are slain by the sword shall fall. 9I will make you perpetually desolate, and your cities shall be uninhabited; then you shall know that I *am* the LORD.

10"Because you have said, 'These two nations and these two countries shall be mine, and we will possess them,' although the LORD was there, 11therefore, *as* I live," says the Lord GOD, "I will do according to your anger and according to the envy which you showed in your hatred against them; and I will make Myself known among them when I judge you. 12Then you shall know that I *am* the LORD. I have heard all your blasphemies which you have spoken against the mountains of Israel, saying, 'They are desolate; they are given to us to consume.' 13Thus with your mouth you have boasted against Me and multiplied your words against Me; I have heard *them*."

14'Thus says the Lord GOD: "The whole earth will rejoice when I make you desolate. 15As you rejoiced because the inheritance of the house of Israel was desolate, so I will do to you; you shall be desolate, O Mount Seir, as well as all of Edom—all of it! Then they shall know that I *am* the LORD." '

BLESSING ON ISRAEL

36 "And you, son of man, prophesy to the mountains of Israel, and say, 'O mountains of Israel, hear the word of the LORD! 2Thus says the Lord GOD: "Because the enemy has said of you, 'Aha! The ancient heights have become our possession,' " ' 3therefore prophesy, and say, 'Thus says the Lord GOD: "Because they made *you* desolate and swallowed you up on every side, so that you became the possession of the rest of the nations, and you are taken up by the lips of talkers and slandered by the people"— 4therefore, O mountains of Israel, hear the word of the Lord GOD! Thus says the Lord GOD to the mountains, the hills, the rivers, the valleys, the desolate wastes, and the cities that have been forsaken, which became plunder and mockery to the rest of the nations all around— 5therefore thus says the Lord GOD: "Surely I have spoken in My burning jealousy against the rest of the nations and against all Edom, who gave My land to themselves as a possession, with wholehearted joy *and* spiteful minds, in order to plunder its open country." '

6"Therefore prophesy concerning the land of Israel, and say to the mountains, the hills, the rivers, and the valleys, 'Thus says the Lord GOD: "Behold, I have spoken in My jealousy and My fury, because you have borne the shame of the nations." 7Therefore thus says the Lord GOD: "I have raised My hand in an oath that surely the nations that *are* around you shall bear their own shame. 8But you, O mountains of Israel, you shall shoot forth your branches and yield your fruit to My people Israel, for they are about to come. 9For indeed I *am* for you, and I will turn to you, and you shall be tilled and sown. 10I will multiply men

upon you, all the house of Israel, all of it; and
the cities shall be inhabited and the ruins rebuilt. 11I will multiply upon you man and
beast; and they shall increase and bear young;
I will make you inhabited as in former times,
and do better *for you* than at your beginnings.
Then you shall know that I *am* the LORD.
12Yes, I will cause men to walk on you, My
people Israel; they shall take possession of
you, and you shall be their inheritance; no
more shall you bereave them *of children."*
13'Thus says the Lord GOD: "Because they
say to you, 'You devour men and bereave your
nation *of children,'* 14therefore you shall devour men no more, nor bereave your nation
anymore," says the Lord GOD. 15Nor will I let
you hear the taunts of the nations anymore,
nor bear the reproach of the peoples anymore,
nor shall you cause your nation to stumble
anymore," says the Lord GOD.' "

THE RENEWAL OF ISRAEL

16Moreover the word of the LORD came to
me, saying: 17"Son of man, when the house of
Israel dwelt in their own land, they defiled it
by their own ways and deeds; to Me their way
was like the uncleanness of a woman in her
customary impurity. 18Therefore I poured out
My fury on them for the blood they had shed
on the land, and for their idols *with which*
they had defiled it. 19So I scattered them
among the nations, and they were dispersed
throughout the countries; I judged them according to their ways and their deeds. 20When
they came to the nations, wherever they went,
they profaned My holy name—when they said
of them, 'These *are* the people of the LORD,
and yet they have gone out of His land.' 21But I
had concern for My holy name, which the
house of Israel had profaned among the nations wherever they went.
22"Therefore say to the house of Israel,
'Thus says the Lord GOD: "I do not do *this* for
your sake, O house of Israel, but for My holy
name's sake, which you have profaned among
the nations wherever you went. 23And I will
sanctify My great name, which has been profaned among the nations, which you have profaned in their midst; and the nations shall
know that I *am* the LORD," says the Lord GOD,
"when I am hallowed in you before their eyes.
24For I will take you from among the nations,
gather you out of all countries, and bring you
into your own land. 25Then I will sprinkle
clean water on you, and you shall be clean; I
will cleanse you from all your filthiness and
from all your idols. 26I will give you a new
heart and put a new spirit within you; I will
take the heart of stone out of your flesh and
give you a heart of flesh. 27I will put My Spirit
within you and cause you to walk in My statutes, and you will keep My judgments and do
them. 28Then you shall dwell in the land that I
gave to your fathers; you shall be My people,
and I will be your God. 29I will deliver you
from all your uncleannesses. I will call for the
grain and multiply it, and bring no famine
upon you. 30And I will multiply the fruit of
your trees and the increase of your fields, so
that you need never again bear the reproach of
famine among the nations. 31Then you will remember your evil ways and your deeds that
were not good; and you will loathe yourselves
in your own sight, for your iniquities and your
abominations. 32Not for your sake do I do
this," says the Lord GOD, "let it be known to
you. Be ashamed and confounded for your
own ways, O house of Israel!"
33'Thus says the Lord GOD: "On the day that
I cleanse you from all your iniquities, I will
also enable *you* to dwell in the cities, and the
ruins shall be rebuilt. 34The desolate land
shall be tilled instead of lying desolate in the
sight of all who pass by. 35So they will say,
'This land that was desolate has become like
the garden of Eden; and the wasted, desolate,
and ruined cities *are now* fortified *and* inhabited.' 36Then the nations which are left all
around you shall know that I, the LORD, have
rebuilt the ruined places *and* planted what
was desolate. I, the LORD, have spoken *it,* and
I will do *it."*
37'Thus says the Lord GOD: "I will also let
the house of Israel inquire of Me to do this for
them: I will increase their men like a flock.
38Like a flock *offered as* holy *sacrifices,* like
the flock at Jerusalem on its feast days, so
shall the ruined cities be filled with flocks of
men. Then they shall know that I *am* the
LORD." ' "

THE DRY BONES LIVE

37 The hand of the LORD came upon me
and brought me out in the Spirit of the
LORD, and set me down in the midst of the valley; and it *was* full of bones. 2Then He caused
me to pass by them all around, and behold,
there were very many in the open valley; and

indeed *they were* very dry. [3]And He said to me, "Son of man, can these bones live?"

So I answered, "O Lord GOD, You know."

[4]Again He said to me, "Prophesy to these bones, and say to them, 'O dry bones, hear the word of the LORD! [5]Thus says the Lord GOD to these bones: "Surely I will cause breath to enter into you, and you shall live. [6]I will put sinews on you and bring flesh upon you, cover you with skin and put breath in you; and you shall live. Then you shall know that I *am* the LORD." ' "

[7]So I prophesied as I was commanded; and as I prophesied, there was a noise, and suddenly a rattling; and the bones came together, bone to bone. [8]Indeed, as I looked, the sinews and the flesh came upon them, and the skin covered them over; but *there was* no breath in them.

[9]Also He said to me, "Prophesy to the breath, prophesy, son of man, and say to the breath, 'Thus says the Lord GOD: "Come from the four winds, O breath, and breathe on these slain, that they may live." ' " [10]So I prophesied as He commanded me, and breath came into them, and they lived, and stood upon their feet, an exceedingly great army.

[11]Then He said to me, "Son of man, these bones are the whole house of Israel. They indeed say, 'Our bones are dry, our hope is lost, and we ourselves are cut off!' [12]Therefore prophesy and say to them, 'Thus says the Lord GOD: "Behold, O My people, I will open your graves and cause you to come up from your graves, and bring you into the land of Israel. [13]Then you shall know that I *am* the LORD, when I have opened your graves, O My people, and brought you up from your graves. [14]I will put My Spirit in you, and you shall live, and I will place you in your own land. Then you shall know that I, the LORD, have spoken *it* and performed *it*," says the LORD.' "

> "I will put My Spirit in you, and you shall live, and I will place you in your own land. Then you shall know that I, the LORD, have spoken it and performed it," says the LORD.
>
> EZEKIEL 37:14

ONE KINGDOM, ONE KING

[15]Again the word of the LORD came to me, saying, [16]"As for you, son of man, take a stick for yourself and write on it: 'For Judah and for the children of Israel, his companions.' Then take another stick and write on it, 'For Joseph, the stick of Ephraim, and *for* all the house of Israel, his companions.' [17]Then join them one to another for yourself into one stick, and they will become one in your hand.

[18]"And when the children of your people speak to you, saying, 'Will you not show us what you *mean* by these?'— [19]say to them, 'Thus says the Lord GOD: "Surely I will take the stick of Joseph, which *is* in the hand of Ephraim, and the tribes of Israel, his companions; and I will join them with it, with the stick of Judah, and make them one stick, and they will be one in My hand." ' [20]And the sticks on which you write will be in your hand before their eyes.

[21]"Then say to them, 'Thus says the Lord GOD: "Surely I will take the children of Israel from among the nations, wherever they have gone, and will gather them from every side and bring them into their own land; [22]and I will make them one nation in the land, on the mountains of Israel; and one king shall be king over them all; they shall no longer be two nations, nor shall they ever be divided into two kingdoms again. [23]They shall not defile themselves anymore with their idols, nor with their detestable things, nor with any of their transgressions; but I will deliver them from all their dwelling places in which they have sinned, and will cleanse them. Then they shall be My people, and I will be their God.

[24]"David My servant *shall be* king over them, and they shall all have one shepherd; they shall also walk in My judgments and observe My statutes, and do them. [25]Then they shall dwell in the land that I have given to Jacob My servant, where your fathers dwelt; and they shall dwell there, they, their children, and their children's children, forever; and My servant David *shall be* their prince forever. [26]Moreover I will make a covenant of peace with them, and it shall be an everlasting covenant with them; I will establish them and multiply them, and I will set My sanctuary in their midst forevermore. [27]My tabernacle also shall be with them; indeed I will be their God, and they shall be My people. [28]The nations also will know that I, the LORD, sanctify Israel, when My sanctuary is in their midst forevermore." ' "

GOG AND ALLIES ATTACK ISRAEL

38 Now the word of the LORD came to me, saying, 2“Son of man, set your face against Gog, of the land of Magog, the prince of Rosh,[a] Meshech, and Tubal, and prophesy against him, 3and say, ‘Thus says the Lord GOD: “Behold, I *am* against you, O Gog, the prince of Rosh, Meshech, and Tubal. 4I will turn you around, put hooks into your jaws, and lead you out, with all your army, horses, and horsemen, all splendidly clothed, a great company *with* bucklers and shields, all of them handling swords. 5Persia, Ethiopia,[a] and Libya[b] are with them, all of them *with* shield and helmet; 6Gomer and all its troops; the house of Togarmah *from* the far north and all its troops—many people *are* with you.

7“Prepare yourself and be ready, you and all your companies that are gathered about you; and be a guard for them. 8After many days you will be visited. In the latter years you will come into the land of those brought back from the sword *and* gathered from many people on the mountains of Israel, which had long been desolate; they were brought out of the nations, and now all of them dwell safely. 9You will ascend, coming like a storm, covering the land like a cloud, you and all your troops and many peoples with you.”

10‘Thus says the Lord GOD: “On that day it shall come to pass *that* thoughts will arise in your mind, and you will make an evil plan: 11You will say, ‘I will go up against a land of unwalled villages; I will go to a peaceful people, who dwell safely, all of them dwelling without walls, and having neither bars nor gates’— 12to take plunder and to take booty, to stretch out your hand against the waste places *that are again* inhabited, and against a people gathered from the nations, who have acquired livestock and goods, who dwell in the midst of the land. 13Sheba, Dedan, the merchants of Tarshish, and all their young lions will say to you, ‘Have you come to take plunder? Have you gathered your army to take booty, to carry away silver and gold, to take away livestock and goods, to take great plunder?’ ” ’

14“Therefore, son of man, prophesy and say to Gog, ‘Thus says the Lord GOD: “On that day when My people Israel dwell safely, will you not know *it?* 15Then you will come from your place out of the far north, you and many peoples with you, all of them riding on horses, a great company and a mighty army. 16You will come up against My people Israel like a cloud, to cover the land. It will be in the latter days that I will bring you against My land, so that the nations may know Me, when I am hallowed in you, O Gog, before their eyes.” 17Thus says the Lord GOD: “Are *you* he of whom I have spoken in former days by My servants the prophets of Israel, who prophesied for years in those days that I would bring you against them?

JUDGMENT ON GOG

18“And it will come to pass at the same time, when Gog comes against the land of Israel,” says the Lord GOD, “*that* My fury will show in My face. 19For in My jealousy *and* in the fire of My wrath I have spoken: ‘Surely in that day there shall be a great earthquake in the land of Israel, 20so that the fish of the sea, the birds of the heavens, the beasts of the field, all creeping things that creep on the earth, and all men who *are* on the face of the earth shall shake at My presence. The mountains shall be thrown down, the steep places shall fall, and every wall shall fall to the ground.’ 21I will call for a sword against Gog throughout all My mountains,” says the Lord GOD. “Every man’s sword will be against his brother. 22And I will bring him to judgment with pestilence and bloodshed; I will rain down on him, on his troops, and on the many peoples who *are* with him, flooding rain, great hailstones, fire, and brimstone. 23Thus I will magnify Myself and sanctify Myself, and I will be known in the eyes of many nations. Then they shall know that I *am* the LORD.” ’

GOG’S ARMIES DESTROYED

39 “And you, son of man, prophesy against Gog, and say, ‘Thus says the Lord GOD: “Behold, I *am* against you, O Gog, the prince of Rosh,[a] Meshech, and Tubal; 2and I will turn you around and lead you on, bringing you up from the far north, and bring you against the mountains of Israel. 3Then I will knock the bow out of your left hand, and cause the arrows to fall out of your right hand. 4You shall fall upon the mountains of Israel, you and all your troops and the peoples who

38:2 [a]Targum, Vulgate, and Aquila read *chief prince of* (also verse 3). **38:5** [a]Hebrew *Cush* [b]Hebrew *Put* **39:1** [a]Targum, Vulgate and Aquila read *chief prince of.*

are with you; I will give you to birds of prey of
every sort and *to* the beasts of the field to be
devoured. 5You shall fall on the open field; for
I have spoken," says the Lord GOD. 6"And I
will send fire on Magog and on those who live
in security in the coastlands. Then they shall
know that I *am* the LORD. 7So I will make My
holy name known in the midst of My people
Israel, and I will not *let them* profane My holy
name anymore. Then the nations shall know
that *I am* the LORD, the Holy One in Israel.
8Surely it is coming, and it shall be done,"
says the Lord GOD. "This *is* the day of which I
have spoken.

9"Then those who dwell in the cities of Israel will go out and set on fire and burn the
weapons, both the shields and bucklers, the
bows and arrows, the javelins and spears; and
they will make fires with them for seven
years. 10They will not take wood from the field
nor cut down *any* from the forests, because
they will make fires with the weapons; and
they will plunder those who plundered them,
and pillage those who pillaged them," says
the Lord GOD.

THE BURIAL OF GOG

11"It will come to pass in that day *that* I will
give Gog a burial place there in Israel, the valley of those who pass by east of the sea; and it
will obstruct travelers, because there they will
bury Gog and all his multitude. Therefore they
will call *it* the Valley of Hamon Gog.[a] 12For
seven months the house of Israel will be burying them, in order to cleanse the land. 13In-
deed all the people of the land will be burying,
and they will gain renown for it on the day
that I am glorified," says the Lord GOD.
14"They will set apart men regularly employed, with the help of a search party,[a] to
pass through the land and bury those bodies
remaining on the ground, in order to cleanse
it. At the end of seven months they will make
a search. 15The search party will pass through
the land; and *when anyone* sees a man's bone,
he shall set up a marker by it, till the buriers
have buried it in the Valley of Hamon Gog.
16*The* name of *the* city *will* also *be* Hamonah.
Thus they shall cleanse the land." '

A TRIUMPHANT FESTIVAL

17"And as for you, son of man, thus says the
Lord GOD, 'Speak to every sort of bird and to
every beast of the field:

"Assemble yourselves and come;
Gather together from all sides to My
sacrificial meal
Which I am sacrificing for you,
A great sacrificial meal on the
mountains of Israel,
That you may eat flesh and drink blood.
18 You shall eat the flesh of the mighty,
Drink the blood of the princes of the
earth,
Of rams and lambs,
Of goats and bulls,
All of them fatlings of Bashan.
19 You shall eat fat till you are full,
And drink blood till you are drunk,
At My sacrificial meal
Which I am sacrificing for you.
20 You shall be filled at My table
With horses and riders,
With mighty men
And with all the men of war," says the
Lord GOD.

ISRAEL RESTORED TO THE LAND

21"I will set My glory among the nations; all
the nations shall see My judgment which I

39:11 [a]Literally *The Multitude of Gog* **39:14** [a]Literally *those who pass through*

SOUL NOTE

No Fooling *(39:7, 8)* Jeremiah predicted God's judgment on Gog's armies, saying, "Surely it is coming, and it shall be done." God sees and knows everything; He is completely in control of all that happens on this earth. God's power is beyond our comprehension; He will accomplish what He says He will accomplish. Nothing is left to chance with God. If we believe that, then we know that He is also in control of our lives. Nothing can happen to us that takes Him by surprise. With our lives entrusted to Him, we know that we can never be shaken. **Topic: Knowing God**

have executed, and My hand which I have laid on them. 22 So the house of Israel shall know that I *am* the LORD their God from that day forward. 23 The Gentiles shall know that the house of Israel went into captivity for their iniquity; because they were unfaithful to Me, therefore I hid My face from them. I gave them into the hand of their enemies, and they all fell by the sword. 24 According to their uncleanness and according to their transgressions I have dealt with them, and hidden My face from them." '

25 "Therefore thus says the Lord GOD: 'Now I will bring back the captives of Jacob, and have mercy on the whole house of Israel; and I will be jealous for My holy name— 26 after they have borne their shame, and all their unfaithfulness in which they were unfaithful to Me, when they dwelt safely in their *own* land and no one made *them* afraid. 27 When I have brought them back from the peoples and gathered them out of their enemies' lands, and I am hallowed in them in the sight of many nations, 28 then they shall know that I *am* the LORD their God, who sent them into captivity among the nations, but also brought them back to their land, and left none of them captive any longer. 29 And I will not hide My face from them anymore; for I shall have poured out My Spirit on the house of Israel,' says the Lord GOD."

A New City, a New Temple

40 In the twenty-fifth year of our captivity, at the beginning of the year, on the tenth *day* of the month, in the fourteenth year after the city was captured, on the very same day the hand of the LORD was upon me; and He took me there. 2 In the visions of God He took me into the land of Israel and set me on a very high mountain; on it toward the south *was* something like the structure of a city. 3 He took me there, and behold, *there was* a man whose appearance *was* like the appearance of bronze. He had a line of flax and a measuring rod in his hand, and he stood in the gateway.

4 And the man said to me, "Son of man, look with your eyes and hear with your ears, and fix your mind on everything I show you; for you *were* brought here so that I might show *them* to you. Declare to the house of Israel everything you see." 5 Now there was a wall all around the outside of the temple.[a] In the man's hand was a measuring rod six cubits long, *each being a* cubit and a handbreadth; and he measured the width of the wall structure, one rod; and the height, one rod.

The Eastern Gateway of the Temple

6 Then he went to the gateway which faced east; and he went up its stairs and measured the threshold of the gateway, *which was* one rod wide, and the other threshold *was* one rod wide. 7 Each gate chamber *was* one rod long and one rod wide; between the gate chambers *was a space of* five cubits; and the threshold of the gateway by the vestibule of the inside gate *was* one rod. 8 He also measured the vestibule of the inside gate, one rod. 9 Then he measured the vestibule of the gateway, eight cubits; and the gateposts, two cubits. The vestibule of the gate *was* on the inside. 10 In the eastern gateway *were* three gate chambers on one side and three on the other; the three *were* all the same size; also the gateposts were of the same size on this side and that side.

11 He measured the width of the entrance to the gateway, ten cubits; *and* the length of the gate, thirteen cubits. 12 *There was* a space in front of the gate chambers, one cubit *on this side* and one cubit on that side; the gate chambers *were* six cubits on this side and six cubits on that side. 13 Then he measured the gateway from the roof of *one* gate chamber to the roof of the other; the width *was* twenty-five cubits, as door faces door. 14 He measured the gateposts, sixty cubits high, and the court all around the gateway *extended* to the gatepost. 15 *From* the front of the entrance gate to the front of the vestibule of the inner gate *was* fifty cubits. 16 *There were* beveled window *frames* in the gate chambers and in their intervening archways on the inside of the gateway all around, and likewise in the vestibules. *There were* windows all around on the inside. And on each gatepost *were* palm trees.

The Outer Court

17 Then he brought me into the outer court; and *there were* chambers and a pavement made all around the court; thirty chambers faced the pavement. 18 The pavement was by the side of the gateways, corresponding to the length of the gateways; *this was* the lower pavement. 19 Then he measured the width

40:5 [a]Literally *house,* and so elsewhere in this book

from the front of the lower gateway to the front of the inner court exterior, one hundred cubits toward the east and the north.

The Northern Gateway

[20]On the outer court was also a gateway facing north, and he measured its length and its width. [21]Its gate chambers, three on this side and three on that side, its gateposts and its archways, had the same measurements as the first gate; its length *was* fifty cubits and its width twenty-five cubits. [22]Its windows and those of its archways, and also its palm trees, *had* the same measurements as the gateway facing east; it was ascended by seven steps, and its archway *was* in front of it. [23]A gate of the inner court was opposite the northern gateway, just as the eastern *gateway;* and he measured from gateway to gateway, one hundred cubits.

The Southern Gateway

[24]After that he brought me toward the south, and there a gateway was facing south; and he measured its gateposts and archways according to these same measurements. [25]*There were* windows in it and in its archways all around like those windows; its length *was* fifty cubits and its width twenty-five cubits. [26]Seven steps led up to it, and its archway *was* in front of them; and it had palm trees on its gateposts, one on this side and one on that side. [27]*There was* also a gateway on the inner court, facing south; and he measured from gateway to gateway toward the south, one hundred cubits.

Gateways of the Inner Court

[28]Then he brought me to the inner court through the southern gateway; he measured the southern gateway according to these same measurements. [29]Also its gate chambers, its gateposts, and its archways *were* according to these same measurements; *there were* windows in it and in its archways all around; *it was* fifty cubits long and twenty-five cubits wide. [30]*There were* archways all around, twenty-five cubits long and five cubits wide. [31]Its archways faced the outer court, palm trees *were* on its gateposts, and going up to it *were* eight steps.

[32]And he brought me into the inner court facing east; he measured the gateway according to these same measurements. [33]Also its gate chambers, its gateposts, and its archways *were* according to these same measurements; and *there were* windows in it and in its archways all around; *it was* fifty cubits long and twenty-five cubits wide. [34]Its archways faced the outer court, and palm trees *were* on its gateposts on this side and on that side; and going up to it *were* eight steps.

[35]Then he brought me to the north gateway and measured *it* according to these same measurements—[36]also its gate chambers, its gateposts, and its archways. It had windows all around; its length *was* fifty cubits and its width twenty-five cubits. [37]Its gateposts faced the outer court, palm trees *were* on its gateposts on this side and on that side, and going up to it *were* eight steps.

Where Sacrifices Were Prepared

[38]*There was* a chamber and its entrance by the gateposts of the gateway, where they washed the burnt offering. [39]In the vestibule of the gateway *were* two tables on this side and two tables on that side, on which to slay the burnt offering, the sin offering, and the trespass offering. [40]At the outer side of the vestibule, as one goes up to the entrance of the northern gateway, *were* two tables; and on the other side of the vestibule of the gateway *were* two tables. [41]Four tables *were* on this side and four tables on that side, by the side of the gateway, eight tables on which they slaughtered *the sacrifices.* [42]*There were* also four tables of hewn stone for the burnt offering, one cubit and a half long, one cubit and a half wide, and one cubit high; on these they laid the instruments with which they slaughtered the burnt offering and the sacrifice. [43]Inside *were* hooks, a handbreadth wide, fastened all around; and the flesh of the sacrifices *was* on the tables.

Chambers for Singers and Priests

[44]Outside the inner gate *were* the chambers for the singers in the inner court, one facing south at the side of the northern gateway, and the other facing north at the side of the southern gateway. [45]Then he said to me, "This chamber which faces south *is* for the priests who have charge of the temple. [46]The chamber which faces north *is* for the priests who have charge of the altar; these *are* the sons of Zadok, from the sons of Levi, who come near the LORD to minister to Him."

Dimensions of the Inner Court and Vestibule

47And he measured the court, one hundred cubits long and one hundred cubits wide, foursquare. The altar *was* in front of the temple. 48Then he brought me to the vestibule of the temple and measured the doorposts of the vestibule, five cubits on this side and five cubits on that side; and the width of the gateway was three cubits on this side and three cubits on that side. 49The length of the vestibule *was* twenty cubits, and the width eleven cubits; and by the steps which led up to it *there were* pillars by the doorposts, one on this side and another on that side.

Dimensions of the Sanctuary

41 Then he brought me into the sanctuary[a] and measured the doorposts, six cubits wide on one side and six cubits wide on the other side—the width of the tabernacle. 2The width of the entryway *was* ten cubits, and the side walls of the entrance *were* five cubits on this side and five cubits on the other side; and he measured its length, forty cubits, and its width, twenty cubits.

3Also he went inside and measured the doorposts, two cubits; and the entrance, six cubits *high;* and the width of the entrance, seven cubits. 4He measured the length, twenty cubits; and the width, twenty cubits, beyond the sanctuary; and he said to me, "This *is* the Most Holy *Place.*"

The Side Chambers on the Wall

5Next, he measured the wall of the temple, six cubits. The width of each side chamber all around the temple *was* four cubits on every side. 6The side chambers *were* in three stories, one above the other, thirty chambers in each story; they rested on ledges which *were* for the side chambers all around, that they might be supported, but not fastened to the wall of the temple. 7As one went up from story to story, the side chambers became wider all around, because their supporting ledges in the wall of the temple ascended like steps; therefore the width of the structure increased as one went up *from* the lowest *story* to the highest by way of the middle one. 8I also saw an elevation all around the temple; it was the foundation of the side chambers, a full rod, *that is,* six cubits *high.* 9The thickness of the outer wall of the side chambers *was* five cubits, and so also the remaining terrace by the place of the side chambers of the temple. 10And between *it and* the *wall* chambers was a width of twenty cubits all around the temple on every side. 11The doors of the side chambers opened on the terrace, one door toward the north and another toward the south; and the width of the terrace *was* five cubits all around.

The Building at the Western End

12The building that faced the separating courtyard at its western end *was* seventy cubits wide; the wall of the building *was* five cubits thick all around, and its length ninety cubits.

Dimensions and Design of the Temple Area

13So he measured the temple, one hundred cubits long; and the separating courtyard with the building and its walls *was* one hundred cubits long; 14also the width of the eastern face of the temple, including the separating courtyard, *was* one hundred cubits. 15He measured the length of the building behind it, facing the separating courtyard, with its galleries on the one side and on the other side, one hundred cubits, as well as the inner temple and the porches of the court, 16their doorposts and the beveled window frames. And the galleries all around their three stories opposite the threshold were paneled with wood from the ground to the windows—the windows were covered— 17from the space above the door, even to the inner room,[a] as well as outside, and on every wall all around, inside and outside, by measure.

18And *it was* made with cherubim and palm trees, a palm tree between cherub and cherub. *Each* cherub had two faces, 19so that the face of a man *was* toward a palm tree on one side, and the face of a young lion toward a palm tree on the other side; thus *it was* made throughout the temple all around. 20From the floor to the space above the door, and on the wall of the sanctuary, cherubim and palm trees *were* carved.

21The doorposts of the temple *were* square, *as was* the front of the sanctuary; their ap-

---

41:1 [a]Hebrew *heykal,* here the main room of the temple, sometimes called the *holy place* (compare Exodus 26:33) **41:17** [a]Literally *house,* here *the Most Holy Place*

pearance was similar. 22The altar *was* of wood, three cubits high, and its length two cubits. Its corners, its length, and its sides *were* of wood; and he said to me, "This *is* the table that *is* before the LORD."

23The temple and the sanctuary had two doors. 24The doors had two panels *apiece,* two folding panels: two *panels* for one door and two panels for the other *door.* 25Cherubim and palm trees *were* carved on the doors of the temple just as they *were* carved on the walls. A wooden canopy *was* on the front of the vestibule outside. 26*There were* beveled window *frames* and palm trees on one side and on the other, on the sides of the vestibule—also on the side chambers of the temple and on the canopies.

The Chambers for the Priests

42 Then he brought me out into the outer court, by the way toward the north; and he brought me into the chamber which *was* opposite the separating courtyard, and which *was* opposite the building toward the north. 2Facing the length, *which was* one hundred cubits (the width was fifty cubits), was the north door. 3Opposite the inner court of twenty *cubits,* and opposite the pavement of the outer court, *was* gallery against gallery in three *stories.* 4In front of the chambers, toward the inside, *was* a walk ten cubits wide, at a distance of one cubit; and their doors faced north. 5Now the upper chambers *were* shorter, because the galleries took away *space* from them more than from the lower and middle stories of the building. 6For they *were* in three *stories* and did not have pillars like the pillars of the courts; therefore *the upper level* was shortened more than the lower and middle levels from the ground up. 7And a wall which *was* outside ran parallel to the chambers, at the front of the chambers, toward the outer court; its length *was* fifty cubits. 8The length of the chambers toward the outer court *was* fifty cubits, whereas that facing the temple *was* one hundred cubits. 9At the lower chambers *was* the entrance on the east side, as one goes into them from the outer court.

10Also *there were* chambers in the thickness of the wall of the court toward the east, opposite the separating courtyard and opposite the building. 11*There was* a walk in front of them also, and their appearance *was* like the chambers which *were* toward the north; they *were* as long and as wide as the others, and all their exits and entrances *were* according to plan. 12And corresponding to the doors of the chambers that *were* facing south, as one enters them, *there was* a door in front of the walk, the way directly in front of the wall toward the east.

13Then he said to me, "The north chambers *and* the south chambers, which *are* opposite the separating courtyard, *are* the holy chambers where the priests who approach the LORD shall eat the most holy offerings. There they shall lay the most holy offerings—the grain offering, the sin offering, and the trespass offering—for the place *is* holy. 14When the priests enter them, they shall not go out of the holy *chamber* into the outer court; but there they shall leave their garments in which they minister, for they *are* holy. They shall put on other garments; then they may approach *that* which *is* for the people."

Outer Dimensions of the Temple

15Now when he had finished measuring the inner temple, he brought me out through the gateway that faces toward the east, and measured it all around. 16He measured the east side with the measuring rod,[a] five hundred rods by the measuring rod all around. 17He measured the north side, five hundred rods by the measuring rod all around. 18He measured the south side, five hundred rods by the measuring rod. 19He came around to the west side *and* measured five hundred rods by the measuring rod. 20He measured it on the four sides; it had a wall all around, five hundred *cubits* long and five hundred wide, to separate the holy areas from the common.

The Temple, the Lord's Dwelling Place

43 Afterward he brought me to the gate, the gate that faces toward the east. 2And behold, the glory of the God of Israel came from the way of the east. His voice *was* like the sound of many waters; and the earth shone with His glory. 3*It was* like the appearance of the vision which I saw—like the vision which I saw when I[a] came to destroy the city. The visions *were* like the vision which I saw by the River Chebar; and I fell on my face. 4And the glory of the LORD came into the

42:16 [a]Compare 40:5 **43:3** [a]Some Hebrew manuscripts and Vulgate read *He.*

temple by way of the gate which faces toward the east. 5The Spirit lifted me up and brought me into the inner court; and behold, the glory of the LORD filled the temple.

6Then I heard *Him* speaking to me from the temple, while a man stood beside me. 7And He said to me, "Son of man, *this is* the place of My throne and the place of the soles of My feet, where I will dwell in the midst of the children of Israel forever. No more shall the house of Israel defile My holy name, they nor their kings, by their harlotry or with the carcasses of their kings on their high places. 8When they set their threshold by My threshold, and their doorpost by My doorpost, with a wall between them and Me, they defiled My holy name by the abominations which they committed; therefore I have consumed them in My anger. 9Now let them put their harlotry and the carcasses of their kings far away from Me, and I will dwell in their midst forever.

> The Spirit lifted me up and brought me into the inner court; and behold, the glory of the LORD filled the temple.
>
> EZEKIEL 43:5

10"Son of man, describe the temple to the house of Israel, that they may be ashamed of their iniquities; and let them measure the pattern. 11And if they are ashamed of all that they have done, make known to them the design of the temple and its arrangement, its exits and its entrances, its entire design and all its ordinances, all its forms and all its laws. Write *it* down in their sight, so that they may keep its whole design and all its ordinances, and perform them. 12This *is* the law of the temple: The whole area surrounding the mountaintop *is* most holy. Behold, this *is* the law of the temple.

Dimensions of the Altar

13"These are the measurements of the altar in cubits (the *cubit is* one cubit and a handbreadth): the base one cubit high and one cubit wide, with a rim all around its edge of one span. This *is* the height of the altar: 14from the base on the ground to the lower ledge, two cubits; the width of the ledge, one cubit; from the smaller ledge to the larger ledge, four cubits; and the width of the ledge, *one* cubit. 15The altar hearth *is* four cubits high, with four horns extending upward from the hearth. 16The altar hearth *is* twelve cubits long, twelve wide, square at its four corners; 17the ledge, fourteen *cubits* long and fourteen wide on its four sides, with a rim of half a cubit around it; its base, one cubit all around; and its steps face toward the east."

Consecrating the Altar

18And He said to me, "Son of man, thus says the Lord GOD: 'These *are* the ordinances for the altar on the day when it is made, for sacrificing burnt offerings on it, and for sprinkling blood on it. 19You shall give a young bull for a sin offering to the priests, the Levites, who are of the seed of Zadok, who approach Me to minister to Me,' says the Lord GOD. 20'You shall take some of its blood and put *it* on the four horns of the altar, on the four corners of the ledge, and on the rim around it; thus you shall cleanse it and make atonement for it. 21Then you shall also take the bull of the sin offering, and burn it in the appointed place of the temple, outside the sanctuary. 22On the second day you shall offer a kid of the goats without blemish for a sin offering; and they shall cleanse the altar, as they cleansed *it* with the bull. 23When you have finished cleansing *it,* you shall offer a young bull without blemish, and a ram from the flock without blemish. 24When you offer them before the LORD, the priests shall throw salt on them, and they will offer them up *as* a burnt offering to the LORD. 25Every day for seven days you shall prepare a goat *for* a sin offering; they shall also prepare a young bull and a ram from the flock, both without blemish. 26Seven days they shall make atonement for the altar and purify it, and so consecrate *it.* 27When these days are over it shall be, on the eighth day and thereafter, that the priests shall offer your burnt offerings and your peace offerings on the altar; and I will accept you,' says the Lord GOD."

The East Gate and the Prince

44 Then He brought me back to the outer gate of the sanctuary which faces toward the east, but it *was* shut. 2And the LORD said to me, "This gate shall be shut; it shall not be opened, and no man shall enter by it, because the LORD God of Israel has entered by

it; therefore it shall be shut. 3*As for* the prince,
because he *is* the prince, he may sit in it to eat
bread before the LORD; he shall enter by way
of the vestibule of the gateway, and go out the
same way."

THOSE ADMITTED TO THE TEMPLE

4Also He brought me by way of the north
gate to the front of the temple; so I looked,
and behold, the glory of the LORD filled the
house of the LORD; and I fell on my face. 5And
the LORD said to me, "Son of man, mark well,
see with your eyes and hear with your ears, all
that I say to you concerning all the ordinances
of the house of the LORD and all its laws. Mark
well who may enter the house and all who go
out from the sanctuary.

6"Now say to the rebellious, to the house of
Israel, 'Thus says the Lord GOD: "O house of
Israel, let Us have no more of all your abominations. 7When you brought in foreigners, uncircumcised in heart and uncircumcised in
flesh, to be in My sanctuary to defile it—My
house—and when you offered My food, the
fat and the blood, then they broke My covenant because of all your abominations. 8And
you have not kept charge of My holy things,
but you have set *others* to keep charge of My
sanctuary for you." 9Thus says the Lord GOD:
"No foreigner, uncircumcised in heart or uncircumcised in flesh, shall enter My sanctuary,
including any foreigner who *is* among the
children of Israel.

LAWS GOVERNING PRIESTS

10"And the Levites who went far from Me,
when Israel went astray, who strayed away
from Me after their idols, they shall bear their
iniquity. 11Yet they shall be ministers in My
sanctuary, *as* gatekeepers of the house and
ministers of the house; they shall slay the
burnt offering and the sacrifice for the people,
and they shall stand before them to minister
to them. 12Because they ministered to them
before their idols and caused the house of Israel to fall into iniquity, therefore I have raised
My hand in an oath against them," says the
Lord GOD, "that they shall bear their iniquity.
13And they shall not come near Me to minister
to Me as priest, nor come near any of My holy
things, nor into the Most Holy *Place;* but they
shall bear their shame and their abominations
which they have committed. 14Nevertheless I
will make them keep charge of the temple, for
all its work, and for all that has to be done
in it.

15"But the priests, the Levites, the sons of
Zadok, who kept charge of My sanctuary
when the children of Israel went astray from
Me, they shall come near Me to minister to
Me; and they shall stand before Me to offer
to Me the fat and the blood," says the Lord
GOD. 16"They shall enter My sanctuary, and
they shall come near My table to minister to
Me, and they shall keep My charge. 17And it
shall be, whenever they enter the gates of the
inner court, that they shall put on linen garments; no wool shall come upon them while
they minister within the gates of the inner
court or within the house. 18They shall have
linen turbans on their heads and linen trousers on their bodies; they shall not clothe
themselves with *anything that causes* sweat.
19When they go out to the outer court, to the
outer court to the people, they shall take off
their garments in which they have ministered,
leave them in the holy chambers, and put on
other garments; and in their holy garments
they shall not sanctify the people.

20"They shall neither shave their heads, nor
let their hair grow long, but they shall keep
their hair well trimmed. 21No priest shall drink
wine when he enters the inner court. 22They
shall not take as wife a widow or a divorced
woman, but take virgins of the descendants of
the house of Israel, or widows of priests.

23"And they shall teach My people *the difference* between the holy and the unholy, and
cause them to discern between the unclean
and the clean. 24In controversy they shall
stand as judges, *and* judge it according to My
judgments. They shall keep My laws and My
statutes in all My appointed meetings, and
they shall hallow My Sabbaths.

25"They shall not defile *themselves* by coming near a dead person. Only for father or
mother, for son or daughter, for brother or unmarried sister may they defile themselves.
26After he is cleansed, they shall count seven
days for him. 27And on the day that he goes to
the sanctuary to minister in the sanctuary, he
must offer his sin offering in the inner court,"
says the Lord GOD.

28"It shall be, in regard to their inheritance,
that I *am* their inheritance. You shall give
them no possession in Israel, for I *am* their
possession. 29They shall eat the grain offering,
the sin offering, and the trespass offering;

every dedicated thing in Israel shall be theirs. 30The best of all firstfruits of any kind, and every sacrifice of any kind from all your sacrifices, shall be the priest's; also you shall give to the priest the first of your ground meal, to cause a blessing to rest on your house. 31The priests shall not eat anything, bird or beast, that died naturally or was torn *by wild beasts.*

The Holy District

45 "Moreover, when you divide the land by lot into inheritance, you shall set apart a district for the LORD, a holy section of the land; its length *shall be* twenty-five thousand *cubits,* and the width ten thousand. It *shall be* holy throughout its territory all around. 2Of this there shall be a square plot for the sanctuary, five hundred by five hundred *rods,* with fifty cubits around it for an open space. 3So this is the district you shall measure: twenty-five thousand *cubits* long and ten thousand wide; in it shall be the sanctuary, the Most Holy *Place.* 4It shall be a holy *section* of the land, belonging to the priests, the ministers of the sanctuary, who come near to minister to the LORD; it shall be a place for their houses and a holy place for the sanctuary. 5*An area* twenty-five thousand *cubits* long and ten thousand wide shall belong to the Levites, the ministers of the temple; they shall have twenty chambers as a possession.[a]

Properties of the City and the Prince

6"You shall appoint as the property of the city *an area* five thousand *cubits* wide and twenty-five thousand long, adjacent to the district of the holy *section;* it shall belong to the whole house of Israel.

7"The prince shall have *a section* on one side and the other of the holy district and the city's property; and bordering on the holy district and the city's property, extending westward on the west side and eastward on the east side, the length *shall be* side by side with one of the *tribal* portions, from the west border to the east border. 8The land shall be his possession in Israel; and My princes shall no more oppress My people, but they shall give *the rest of* the land to the house of Israel, according to their tribes."

Laws Governing the Prince

9'Thus says the Lord GOD: "Enough, O princes of Israel! Remove violence and plundering, execute justice and righteousness, and stop dispossessing My people," says the Lord GOD. 10"You shall have honest scales, an honest ephah, and an honest bath. 11The ephah and the bath shall be of the same measure, so that the bath contains one-tenth of a homer, and the ephah one-tenth of a homer; their measure shall be according to the homer. 12The shekel *shall be* twenty gerahs; twenty shekels, twenty-five shekels, *and* fifteen shekels shall be your mina.

13"This *is* the offering which you shall offer: you shall give one-sixth of an ephah from a homer of wheat, and one-sixth of an ephah from a homer of barley. 14The ordinance concerning oil, the bath of oil, *is* one-tenth of a bath from a kor. A kor *is* a homer or ten baths, for ten baths *are* a homer. 15And one lamb shall be given from a flock of two hundred, from the rich pastures of Israel. These shall be for grain offerings, burnt offerings, and peace offerings, to make atonement for them," says the Lord GOD. 16"All the people of the land shall give this offering for the prince in Israel. 17Then it shall be the prince's part *to give* burnt offerings, grain offerings, and drink offerings, at the feasts, the New Moons, the Sabbaths, and at all the appointed seasons of the house of Israel. He shall prepare the sin offering, the grain offering, the burnt offering, and the peace offerings to make atonement for the house of Israel."

Keeping the Feasts

18'Thus says the Lord GOD: "In the first *month,* on the first *day* of the month, you shall take a young bull without blemish and cleanse the sanctuary. 19The priest shall take some of the blood of the sin offering and put *it* on the doorposts of the temple, on the four corners of the ledge of the altar, and on the gateposts of the gate of the inner court. 20And so you shall do on the seventh *day* of the month for everyone who has sinned unintentionally or in ignorance. Thus you shall make atonement for the temple.

21"In the first *month,* on the fourteenth day of the month, you shall observe the Passover, a feast of seven days; unleavened bread shall be eaten. 22And on that day the prince shall

45:5 [a]Following Masoretic Text, Targum, and Vulgate; Septuagint reads *a possession, cities of dwelling.*

prepare for himself and for all the people of the land a bull *for* a sin offering. 23On the seven days of the feast he shall prepare a burnt offering to the LORD, seven bulls and seven rams without blemish, daily for seven days, and a kid of the goats daily *for* a sin offering. 24And he shall prepare a grain offering of one ephah for each bull and one ephah for each ram, together with a hin of oil for each ephah.

25"In the seventh *month,* on the fifteenth day of the month, at the feast, he shall do likewise for seven days, according to the sin offering, the burnt offering, the grain offering, and the oil."

The Manner of Worship

46 'Thus says the Lord GOD: "The gate way of the inner court that faces toward the east shall be shut the six working days; but on the Sabbath it shall be opened, and on the day of the New Moon it shall be opened. 2The prince shall enter by way of the vestibule of the gateway from the outside, and stand by the gatepost. The priests shall prepare his burnt offering and his peace offerings. He shall worship at the threshold of the gate. Then he shall go out, but the gate shall not be shut until evening. 3Likewise the people of the land shall worship at the entrance to this gateway before the LORD on the Sabbaths and the New Moons. 4The burnt offering that the prince offers to the LORD on the Sabbath day *shall be* six lambs without blemish, and a ram without blemish; 5and the grain offering *shall be one* ephah for a ram, and the grain offering for the lambs, as much as he wants to give, as well as a hin of oil with every ephah. 6On the day of the New Moon *it shall be* a young bull without blemish, six lambs, and a ram; they shall be without blemish. 7He shall prepare a grain offering of an ephah for a bull, an ephah for a ram, as much as he wants to give for the lambs, and a hin of oil with every ephah. 8When the prince enters, he shall go in by way of the vestibule of the gateway, and go out the same way.

9"But when the people of the land come before the LORD on the appointed feast days, whoever enters by way of the north gate to worship shall go out by way of the south gate; and whoever enters by way of the south gate shall go out by way of the north gate. He shall not return by way of the gate through which he came, but shall go out through the opposite gate. 10The prince shall then be in their midst. When they go in, he shall go in; and when they go out, he shall go out. 11At the festivals and the appointed feast days the grain offering shall be an ephah for a bull, an ephah for a ram, as much as he wants to give for the lambs, and a hin of oil with every ephah.

12"Now when the prince makes a voluntary burnt offering or voluntary peace offering to the LORD, the gate that faces toward the east shall then be opened for him; and he shall prepare his burnt offering and his peace offerings as he did on the Sabbath day. Then he shall go out, and after he goes out the gate shall be shut.

13"You shall daily make a burnt offering to the LORD *of* a lamb of the first year without blemish; you shall prepare it every morning. 14And you shall prepare a grain offering with it every morning, a sixth of an ephah, and a third of a hin of oil to moisten the fine flour. This grain offering is a perpetual ordinance, to be made regularly to the LORD. 15Thus they shall prepare the lamb, the grain offering, and the oil, *as* a regular burnt offering every morning."

The Prince and Inheritance Laws

16'Thus says the Lord GOD: "If the prince gives a gift *of some* of his inheritance to any of his sons, it shall belong to his sons; it is their possession by inheritance. 17But if he gives a gift of some of his inheritance to one of his servants, it shall be his until the year of liberty, after which it shall return to the prince. But his inheritance shall belong to his sons; it shall become theirs. 18Moreover the prince shall not take any of the people's inheritance by evicting them from their property; he shall provide an inheritance for his sons from his own property, so that none of My people may be scattered from his property." ' "

How the Offerings Were Prepared

19Now he brought me through the entrance, which *was* at the side of the gate, into the holy chambers of the priests which face toward the north; and there a place *was* situated at their extreme western end. 20And he said to me, "This *is* the place where the priests shall boil the trespass offering and the sin offering, *and* where they shall bake the grain offering, so that they do not bring *them* out into the outer court to sanctify the people."

[21]Then he brought me out into the outer court and caused me to pass by the four corners of the court; and in fact, in every corner of the court *there was another* court. [22]In the four corners of the court *were* enclosed courts, forty *cubits* long and thirty wide; all four corners *were* the same size. [23]*There was* a row *of building stones* all around in them, all around the four of them; and cooking hearths were made under the rows of stones all around. [24]And he said to me, "These *are* the kitchens where the ministers of the temple shall boil the sacrifices of the people."

The Healing Waters and Trees

47 Then he brought me back to the door of the temple; and there was water, flowing from under the threshold of the temple toward the east, for the front of the temple faced east; the water was flowing from under the right side of the temple, south of the altar. [2]He brought me out by way of the north gate, and led me around on the outside to the outer gateway that faces east; and there was water, running out on the right side.

[3]And when the man went out to the east with the line in his hand, he measured one thousand cubits, and he brought me through the waters; the water *came up to my* ankles. [4]Again he measured one thousand and brought me through the waters; the water *came up to my* knees. Again he measured one thousand and brought me through; the water *came up to my* waist. [5]Again he measured one thousand, *and it was* a river that I could not cross; for the water was too deep, water in which one must swim, a river that could not be crossed. [6]He said to me, "Son of man, have you seen *this?*" Then he brought me and returned me to the bank of the river.

[7]When I returned, there, along the bank of the river, *were* very many trees on one side and the other. [8]Then he said to me: "This water flows toward the eastern region, goes down into the valley, and enters the sea. *When it* reaches the sea, *its* waters are healed. [9]And it shall be *that* every living thing that moves, wherever the rivers go, will live. There will be a very great multitude of fish, because these waters go there; for they will be healed, and everything will live wherever the river goes. [10]It shall be *that* fishermen will stand by it from En Gedi to En Eglaim; they will be *places* for spreading their nets. Their fish will be of the same kinds as the fish of the Great Sea, exceedingly many. [11]But its swamps and marshes will not be healed; they will be given over to salt. [12]Along the bank of the river, on this side and that, will grow all *kinds of* trees used for food; their leaves will not wither, and their fruit will not fail. They will bear fruit every month, because their water flows from the sanctuary. Their fruit will be for food, and their leaves for medicine."

Borders of the Land

[13]Thus says the Lord GOD: "These *are* the borders by which you shall divide the land as an inheritance among the twelve tribes of Israel. Joseph *shall have two* portions. [14]You shall inherit it equally with one another; for I raised My hand in an oath to give it to your fathers, and this land shall fall to you as your inheritance.

[15]"This *shall be* the border of the land on the north: from the Great Sea, *by* the road to Hethlon, as one goes to Zedad, [16]Hamath, Berothah, Sibraim (which *is* between the border of Damascus and the border of Hamath), to Hazar Hatticon (which *is* on the border of Hauran). [17]Thus the boundary shall be from the Sea to Hazar Enan, the border of Damascus; and as for the north, northward, it is the border of Hamath. *This is* the north side.

[18]"On the east side you shall mark out the border from between Hauran and Damascus, and between Gilead and the land of Israel, along the Jordan, and along the eastern side of the sea. *This is* the east side.

[19]"The south side, toward the South,[a] *shall be* from Tamar to the waters of Meribah by Kadesh, along the brook to the Great Sea. *This is* the south side, toward the South.

[20]"The west side *shall be* the Great Sea, from the *southern* boundary until one comes to a point opposite Hamath. This *is* the west side.

[21]"Thus you shall divide this land among yourselves according to the tribes of Israel. [22]It shall be that you will divide it by lot as an inheritance for yourselves, and for the strangers who dwell among you and who bear children among you. They shall be to you as native-born among the children of Israel; they shall have an inheritance with you among the tribes of Israel. [23]And it shall be *that* in whatever

47:19 [a]Hebrew *Negev*

tribe the stranger dwells, there you shall give *him* his inheritance," says the Lord GOD.

DIVISION OF THE LAND

48 "Now these *are* the names of the tribes: From the northern border along the road to Hethlon at the entrance of Hamath, to Hazar Enan, the border of Damascus northward, in the direction of Hamath, *there shall be* one *section for* Dan from its east to its west side; [2]by the border of Dan, from the east side to the west, one *section for* Asher; [3]by the border of Asher, from the east side to the west, one *section for* Naphtali; [4]by the border of Naphtali, from the east side to the west, one *section for* Manasseh; [5]by the border of Manasseh, from the east side to the west, one *section for* Ephraim; [6]by the border of Ephraim, from the east side to the west, one *section for* Reuben; [7]by the border of Reuben, from the east side to the west, one *section for* Judah; [8]by the border of Judah, from the east side to the west, shall be the district which you shall set apart, twenty-five thousand *cubits* in width, and *in* length the same as one of the *other* portions, from the east side to the west, with the sanctuary in the center.

[9]"The district that you shall set apart for the LORD *shall be* twenty-five thousand *cubits* in length and ten thousand in width. [10]To these—to the priests—the holy district shall belong: on the north twenty-five thousand *cubits in length,* on the west ten thousand in width, on the east ten thousand in width, and on the south twenty-five thousand in length. The sanctuary of the LORD shall be in the center. [11]*It shall be* for the priests of the sons of Zadok, who are sanctified, who have kept My charge, who did not go astray when the children of Israel went astray, as the Levites went astray. [12]And *this* district of land that is set apart shall be to them a thing most holy by the border of the Levites.

[13]"Opposite the border of the priests, the Levites *shall have an area* twenty-five thousand *cubits* in length and ten thousand in width; its entire length *shall be* twenty-five thousand and its width ten thousand. [14]And they shall not sell or exchange any of it; they may not alienate this best *part* of the land, for *it is* holy to the LORD.

[15]"The five thousand *cubits* in width that remain, along the edge of the twenty-five thousand, shall be for general use by the city, for dwellings and common-land; and the city shall be in the center. [16]These *shall be* its measurements: the north side four thousand five hundred *cubits,* the south side four thousand five hundred, the east side four thousand five hundred, and the west side four thousand five hundred. [17]The common-land of the city shall be: to the north two hundred and fifty *cubits,* to the south two hundred and fifty, to the east two hundred and fifty, and to the west two hundred and fifty. [18]The rest of the length, alongside the district of the holy *section, shall be* ten thousand *cubits* to the east and ten thousand to the west. It shall be adjacent to the district of the holy *section,* and its produce shall be food for the workers of the city. [19]The workers of the city, from all the tribes of Israel, shall cultivate it. [20]The entire district *shall be* twenty-five thousand *cubits* by twenty-five thousand *cubits,* foursquare. You shall set apart the holy district with the property of the city.

[21]"The rest *shall belong* to the prince, on one side and on the other of the holy district and of the city's property, next to the twenty-five thousand *cubits* of the *holy* district as far as the eastern border, and westward next to the twenty-five thousand as far as the western border, adjacent to the *tribal* portions; *it shall belong* to the prince. It shall be the holy district, and the sanctuary of the temple *shall be* in the center. [22]Moreover, apart from the possession of the Levites and the possession of the city *which are* in the midst of what *belongs* to the prince, *the area* between the border of Judah and the border of Benjamin shall belong to the prince.

[23]"As for the rest of the tribes, from the east side to the west, Benjamin *shall have* one *section;* [24]by the border of Benjamin, from the east side to the west, Simeon *shall have* one *section;* [25]by the border of Simeon, from the east side to the west, Issachar *shall have* one *section;* [26]by the border of Issachar, from the east side to the west, Zebulun *shall have* one *section;* [27]by the border of Zebulun, from the east side to the west, Gad *shall have* one *section;* [28]by the border of Gad, on the south side, toward the South,[a] the border shall be from Tamar *to* the waters of Meribah *by* Kadesh, along the brook to the Great Sea. [29]This *is* the land which you shall divide by lot as an

48:28 [a]Hebrew *Negev*

inheritance among the tribes of Israel, and these *are* their portions," says the Lord GOD.

THE GATES OF THE CITY AND ITS NAME

[30]"These *are* the exits of the city. On the
north side, measuring four thousand five hundred *cubits* [31](the gates of the city *shall be*
named after the tribes of Israel), the three gates northward: one gate for Reuben, one gate for Judah, and one gate for Levi; [32]on the
east side, four thousand five hundred *cubits,* three gates: one gate for Joseph, one gate for Benjamin, and one gate for Dan; [33]on the
south side, measuring four thousand five hundred *cubits,* three gates: one gate for Simeon, one gate for Issachar, and one gate for Zebulun; [34]on the west side, four thousand five
hundred *cubits* with their three gates: one gate for Gad, one gate for Asher, and one gate for Naphtali. [35]All the way around *shall be* eighteen thousand *cubits;* and the name of the city from *that* day *shall be:* THE LORD *IS* THERE."[a]

48:35 [a]Hebrew *YHWH Shammah*

Daniel

"Does God *really* have my life in His hands—much less the whole world? Does He really care?"

Everyone, at one time or another, has asked this question or some form of it, raising the issue of God's sovereignty. Perhaps Daniel, more than any other Bible book, provides a clear answer. Containing the record of the Jews' seventy-year captivity in Babylon and the life experiences of an extraordinary man named Daniel, this book shows God at work in history and in individual lives.

The first half of Daniel (through chapter 6) depicts events from the prophet's personal life. It documents how the Babylonians conquered Jerusalem and deported Judah's most talented young men. These youths were immersed in Babylonian culture and pressed into royal service. Most gave in to their new lifestyle—except for Daniel and his Hebrew friends, Hananiah, Mishael, and Azariah. Because these four steadfastly followed God, they experienced His blessing and rose to influential positions within the Babylonian government. The second half of the book (starting in chapter 7) contains Daniel's visions of the future.

Daniel's integrity, courage, and wisdom provide a wonderful example for anyone who is trying to live faithfully in a faithless world. More than this, Daniel's life and the revelations given him by God remind us that God *is* in control. He *does* have our lives in His hands. As the song says, "He's got the whole world in His hands." Our souls do not have to panic or fear. History really is "His story!"

SOUL CONCERN IN DANIEL

DANIEL AND HIS FRIENDS OBEY GOD

1 In the third year of the reign of Jehoiakim
king of Judah, Nebuchadnezzar king of
Babylon came to Jerusalem and besieged it.
2And the Lord gave Jehoiakim king of Judah
into his hand, with some of the articles of the
house of God, which he carried into the land
of Shinar to the house of his god; and he
brought the articles into the treasure house of
his god.
3Then the king instructed Ashpenaz, the
master of his eunuchs, to bring some of the
children of Israel and some of the king's descendants and some of the nobles, 4young
men in whom *there was* no blemish, but good-
looking, gifted in all wisdom, possessing
knowledge and quick to understand, who *had*
ability to serve in the king's palace, and whom
they might teach the language and literature
of the Chaldeans. 5And the king appointed for
them a daily provision of the king's delicacies
and of the wine which he drank, and three
years of training for them, so that at the end of
that time they might serve before the king.
6Now from among those of the sons of Judah
were Daniel, Hananiah, Mishael, and Azariah.
7To them the chief of the eunuchs gave names:
he gave Daniel *the name* Belteshazzar; to
Hananiah, Shadrach; to Mishael, Meshach;
and to Azariah, Abed-Nego.
8But Daniel purposed in his heart that he
would not defile himself with the portion of
the king's delicacies, nor with the wine which
he drank; therefore he requested of the chief
of the eunuchs that he might not defile himself. 9Now God had brought Daniel into the
favor and goodwill of the chief of the eunuchs.
10And the chief of the eunuchs said to Daniel,
"I fear my lord the king, who has appointed
your food and drink. For why should he see

PERSONALITY PROFILE

Adolescent Development

DANIEL SERVED GOD FIRST

(DANIEL 1)

Daniel was taken captive to Babylon from his native Jerusalem when he was about 15 years old. He and his Jewish friends were thrust into a hostile environment where much pressure was put on them to accept pagan beliefs and lifestyles. The fact that Daniel "purposed in his heart" (Dan. 1:8) not to defile himself under this pressure is a great testimony to the ability of an adolescent to develop the kind of spiritual maturity that will enable them to reject peer pressure.

When Jerusalem fell to the Babylonians in the summer of 605 B.C., Daniel was only a teenager. He and several others were taken captive by the Babylonians and placed in a three-year training program in which they were expected to learn the Babylonian view of life and religion. They were even forced to learn the Babylonian language and given Babylonian names. Daniel in Hebrew means "God is my judge"; his name was changed to Belteshazzar, which in the Babylonian language means "the god Bel is my judge." It may have been as close as the Babylonians could come to translating the meaning of his name.

The verse that summarizes Jesus' adolescence serves to describe Daniel's: "And Jesus increased in wisdom and stature, and in favor with God and men" (Luke 2:52). Daniel built upon the good start he received as a child. He exercised great wisdom in discerning between acceptable Babylonian habits and those that would compromise his faith. He accepted the king's training but not the king's diet. He served the king loyally, but stopped at acknowledging the divine claim of the king. Daniel learned the new language, but he kept an old habit of daily prayer. Because he continually made God the focus of his life, Daniel made a deep impression on all he met. He grew into one of the clearest biblical examples of a godly person. Young people seeking to grow to serve God can learn much from Daniel's example.

To Learn More: Turn to the article about adolescent development on pages 1104, 1105. See also the key passage note at 1 Timothy 4:7 on page 1595.

your faces looking worse than the young men
who *are* your age? Then you would endanger
my head before the king."
11So Daniel said to the steward[a] whom the
chief of the eunuchs had set over Daniel, Hananiah, Mishael, and Azariah, 12"Please test
your servants for ten days, and let them give
us vegetables to eat and water to drink.
13Then let our appearance be examined before
you, and the appearance of the young men
who eat the portion of the king's delicacies;
and as you see fit, *so* deal with your servants."
14So he consented with them in this matter,
and tested them ten days.
15And at the end of ten days their features
appeared better and fatter in flesh than all the
young men who ate the portion of the king's
delicacies. 16Thus the steward took away their
portion of delicacies and the wine that they
were to drink, and gave them vegetables.
17As for these four young men, God gave
them knowledge and skill in all literature and
wisdom; and Daniel had understanding in all
visions and dreams.
18Now at the end of the days, when the king
had said that they should be brought in, the
chief of the eunuchs brought them in before
Nebuchadnezzar. 19Then the king interviewed
them,[a] and among them all none was found
like Daniel, Hananiah, Mishael, and Azariah;
therefore they served before the king. 20And in
all matters of wisdom *and* understanding
about which the king examined them, he
found them ten times better than all the magicians *and* astrologers who *were* in all his
realm. 21Thus Daniel continued until the first
year of King Cyrus.

Nebuchadnezzar's Dream

2 Now in the second year of Nebuchadnezzar's reign, Nebuchadnezzar had dreams;
and his spirit was *so* troubled that his sleep
left him. 2Then the king gave the command to
call the magicians, the astrologers, the sorcerers, and the Chaldeans to tell the king his
dreams. So they came and stood before the
king. 3And the king said to them, "I have had
a dream, and my spirit is anxious to know the
dream."
4Then the Chaldeans spoke to the king in
Aramaic,[a] "O king, live forever! Tell your servants the dream, and we will give the interpretation."
5The king answered and said to the Chaldeans, "My decision is firm: if you do not make
known the dream to me, and its interpretation, you shall be cut in pieces, and your
houses shall be made an ash heap. 6However,
if you tell the dream and its interpretation,
you shall receive from me gifts, rewards, and
great honor. Therefore tell me the dream and
its interpretation."
7They answered again and said, "Let the
king tell his servants the dream, and we will
give its interpretation."
8The king answered and said, "I know for
certain that you would gain time, because you
see that my decision is firm: 9if you do not
make known the dream to me, *there is only*
one decree for you! For you have agreed to
speak lying and corrupt words before me till
the time has changed. Therefore tell me the
dream, and I shall know that you can give me
its interpretation."
10The Chaldeans answered the king, and
said, "There is not a man on earth who can
tell the king's matter; therefore no king, lord,
or ruler has *ever* asked such things of any ma-
gician, astrologer, or Chaldean. 11*It is* a difficult thing that the king requests, and there is
no other who can tell it to the king except the
gods, whose dwelling is not with flesh."
12For this reason the king was angry and
very furious, and gave the command to destroy all the wise *men* of Babylon. 13So the decree went out, and they began killing the wise
men; and they sought Daniel and his companions, to kill *them.*

God Reveals Nebuchadnezzar's Dream

14Then with counsel and wisdom Daniel answered Arioch, the captain of the king's
guard, who had gone out to kill the wise *men*
of Babylon; 15he answered and said to Arioch
the king's captain, "Why is the decree from
the king so urgent?" Then Arioch made the decision known to Daniel.
16So Daniel went in and asked the king to
give him time, that he might tell the king the
interpretation. 17Then Daniel went to his
house, and made the decision known to Hananiah, Mishael, and Azariah, his companions,
18that they might seek mercies from the God of
heaven concerning this secret, so that Daniel

1:11 [a]Hebrew *Melzar,* also in verse 16
1:19 [a]Literally *talked with them* **2:4** [a]The original language of Daniel 2:4b through 7:28 is Aramaic.

HELPING TEENS GROW WITH GOD

DAWSON MCALLISTER

(Daniel 1:8)

Pimples, proms, and puberty—talk about a memorable time in life! Adults may recall those days through rose-colored glasses as a whimsical, carefree time filled with lots of fun and few responsibilities. Many think, "If I could just relive those high school days." But would they really want to do it again? Uncertainty, insecurity, relationships, rejection, curfews, cliques, homework—these are but a few of the "fun" experiences of adolescence. These sometimes painful, often confusing, years provide unique challenges even for Christian teenagers. Though there are volumes one could write about adolescent development, four issues stand out as being crucial during this time: fear, feelings, friends, and faith.

FEAR

Many men remember the first time they, as growing boys, tripped over their own feet because those feet were growing faster than any other parts of their bodies. Many women remember the experience of insecurity as they watched their bodies mature and change—never as beautifully as someone else's, and certainly never like those teen idols in their favorite magazines. The fear of not measuring up; the fear of not being acceptable and therefore accepted—these are just some of the fears of adolescence.

Being an adolescent is like being in the Army. It's not a job, it's an adventure. Helping teenagers to understand what is happening to them during this part of their life is crucial to successful navigation of the adolescent stage. Like Daniel in Babylon, many teenagers today feel out of place, besieged by temptation, and confused about what they should be doing at this point in their lives.

The challenge for parents, pastors, teachers, and counselors is to help adolescents live above their fear. Because of the power of Christ, adolescents can live a life of peace. Jesus promised, "Peace I leave with you, My peace I give to you. . . . Let not your heart be troubled, neither let it be afraid" (John 14:27).

FEELINGS

It has been said that teenagers are "walking hormones." Often, they are tossed about like the waves in the sea because of their emotions. Two teenage girls can be best friends one day and mortal enemies the next. A snide glance or a sarcastic remark can mean devastation for an adolescent.

So much of people's identity is formed during the adolescent years that it is hard not to exaggerate the role their feelings play during this time. Loneliness, depression, anxiousness, low self-worth—these feelings bubble to the surface amidst all the other issues facing the typical teenager. Increasing sensitivity causes them to feel persecuted, misunderstood, rejected, or smothered.

Adults need to teach and to be an example of Paul's instruction to the Corinthians about "bringing every thought into captivity to the obedience of Christ" (2 Cor. 10:5). Young people need to learn how to "take captive" thoughts and feelings that contradict the reality of God's Word.

FRIENDS

Relationships with friends during the adolescent years take on a whole new dimension. The term "peer pressure" describes the immense tension that exists between a teenager's knowledge of the right action to take and the temptation to follow a friend's enticement to do wrong. Acceptance by one's friends becomes the most important thing in life during the adolescent period. Longing for a place to fit in and feel accepted becomes a driving force in their everyday lives. Unfortunately for many, even many Christian teenagers, little thought is given to their spiritual life.

As enticing as it may be to fit in and feel accepted, often it comes at a high moral price. It is vital to help adolescents to understand and grasp the words of Paul, "Do not be conformed to this world, but be transformed by the renewing of your mind, that you may prove what is that good and acceptable and perfect will of God" (Rom. 12:2).

FAITH

Although many teenagers are caught up in the fads of the day, adolescence is a time when many want to discover faith in something beyond themselves. When given the opportunity, teenagers want to grapple with the deep issues of personal faith. Some hear it for the first time and question it; others are grappling with the faith handed down from their parents. Some rebel against their family's Christian faith. That rebellion may occur because they observe hypocrisy or desire attention. For many, however, it is merely a healthy exploration to discover that Jesus Christ is the only answer to the problems they are experiencing.

Adolescents may question the authenticity of the Bible, an earlier decision to follow Christ, the meaning of salvation, and the reality of eternal life. For some, the spiritual walk is more like a roller coaster than a joyous ride. They experience fluctuating highs and lows from intense spiritual mountaintops to lonely spiritual isolation.

It is during this period that adults need to assure them of God's unconditional love and acceptance. Adolescents need this period of testing and questioning in order to fully understand the faith that they profess. Many adults try to squelch this exploratory time in an adolescent's life. However, a more fruitful way of dealing with this period is to encourage teenagers to give God a chance at making a difference in their lives. As Psalm 34:8 says: "Taste and see that the LORD is good; blessed is the man who trusts in Him!"

FURTHER MEDITATION:

Other passages to study about the issue of adolescent development include:

- ➢ 1 Samuel 17
- ➢ Ecclesiastes 11:9—12:1
- ➢ Acts 2:17
- ➢ 1 Corinthians 13:11
- ➢ 2 Timothy 2:22; 3:14, 15

To Learn More: Turn to the key passage note on adolescent development at 1 Timothy 4:7 on page 1595. See also the personality profile of Daniel on page 1102.

and his companions might not perish with the rest of the wise *men* of Babylon. 19 Then the secret was revealed to Daniel in a night vision. So Daniel blessed the God of heaven.

20 Daniel answered and said:

"Blessed be the name of God forever and ever,
For wisdom and might are His.
21 And He changes the times and the seasons;
He removes kings and raises up kings;
He gives wisdom to the wise
And knowledge to those who have understanding.
22 He reveals deep and secret things;
He knows what *is* in the darkness,
And light dwells with Him.

23 "I thank You and praise You,
O God of my fathers;
You have given me wisdom and might,
And have now made known to me what we asked of You,
For You have made known to us the king's demand."

> "Blessed be the name of God forever and ever, for wisdom and might are His."
>
> DANIEL 2:20

Daniel Explains the Dream

24 Therefore Daniel went to Arioch, whom the king had appointed to destroy the wise *men* of Babylon. He went and said thus to him: "Do not destroy the wise *men* of Babylon; take me before the king, and I will tell the king the interpretation."

25 Then Arioch quickly brought Daniel before the king, and said thus to him, "I have found a man of the captives[a] of Judah, who will make known to the king the interpretation."

26 The king answered and said to Daniel, whose name *was* Belteshazzar, "Are you able to make known to me the dream which I have seen, and its interpretation?"

27 Daniel answered in the presence of the king, and said, "The secret which the king has demanded, the wise *men,* the astrologers, the magicians, and the soothsayers cannot declare to the king. 28 But there is a God in heaven who reveals secrets, and He has made known to King Nebuchadnezzar what will be in the latter days. Your dream, and the visions of your head upon your bed, were these: 29 As for you, O king, thoughts came *to* your *mind while* on your bed, *about* what would come to pass after this; and He who reveals secrets has made known to you what will be. 30 But as for me, this secret has not been revealed to me because I have more wisdom than anyone living, but for *our* sakes who make known the interpretation to the king, and that you may know the thoughts of your heart.

31 "You, O king, were watching; and behold, a great image! This great image, whose splendor *was* excellent, stood before you; and its form *was* awesome. 32 This image's head *was* of fine gold, its chest and arms of silver, its belly and thighs[a] of bronze, 33 its legs of iron, its feet partly of iron and partly of clay.[a] 34 You watched while a stone was cut out without hands, which struck the image on its feet of iron and clay, and broke them in pieces. 35 Then the iron, the clay, the bronze, the silver, and the gold were crushed together, and

2:25 [a]Literally *of the sons of the captivity*
2:32 [a]Or *sides* **2:33** [a]Or *baked clay,* and so in verses 34, 35, and 42

SOUL NOTE

Wise Move *(2:20–22)* When a car makes a noise, we call a mechanic. When a sink backs up, we call a plumber. Why is it, then, that when we experience problems in our personal lives, we insist on taking care of the situation ourselves? Daniel knew just where to go when he needed wisdom: "Blessed be the name of God forever and ever, for wisdom and might are His." God is the source of all wisdom. If we believe His ways are higher than ours, we can give up control to Him, resting in the assurance that He will give us perfect guidance. **Topic: Wisdom**

became like chaff from the summer threshing
floors; the wind carried them away so that no
trace of them was found. And the stone that
struck the image became a great mountain
and filled the whole earth.
36“This *is* the dream. Now we will tell the
interpretation of it before the king. 37You, O
king, *are* a king of kings. For the God of heav-
en has given you a kingdom, power, strength,
and glory; 38and wherever the children of men
dwell, or the beasts of the field and the birds
of the heaven, He has given *them* into your
hand, and has made you ruler over them all—
you *are* this head of gold. 39But after you shall
arise another kingdom inferior to yours; then
another, a third kingdom of bronze, which
shall rule over all the earth. 40And the fourth
kingdom shall be as strong as iron, inasmuch
as iron breaks in pieces and shatters everything; and like iron that crushes, *that kingdom*
will break in pieces and crush all the others.
41Whereas you saw the feet and toes, partly of
potter's clay and partly of iron, the kingdom
shall be divided; yet the strength of the iron
shall be in it, just as you saw the iron mixed
with ceramic clay. 42And *as* the toes of the feet
were partly of iron and partly of clay, *so* the
kingdom shall be partly strong and partly frag-
ile. 43As you saw iron mixed with ceramic
clay, they will mingle with the seed of men;
but they will not adhere to one another, just as
iron does not mix with clay. 44And in the days
of these kings the God of heaven will set up a
kingdom which shall never be destroyed; and
the kingdom shall not be left to other people;
it shall break in pieces and consume all these
kingdoms, and it shall stand forever. 45Inas-
much as you saw that the stone was cut out of
the mountain without hands, and that it broke
in pieces the iron, the bronze, the clay, the silver, and the gold—the great God has made
known to the king what will come to pass after this. The dream is certain, and its interpretation is sure.”

Daniel and His Friends Promoted

46Then King Nebuchadnezzar fell on his
face, prostrate before Daniel, and commanded
that they should present an offering and incense to him. 47The king answered Daniel,
and said, “Truly your God *is* the God of gods,
the Lord of kings, and a revealer of secrets,
since you could reveal this secret.” 48Then the
king promoted Daniel and gave him many
great gifts; and he made him ruler over the
whole province of Babylon, and chief admin-
istrator over all the wise *men* of Babylon.
49Also Daniel petitioned the king, and he set
Shadrach, Meshach, and Abed-Nego over the
affairs of the province of Babylon; but Daniel
sat in the gate[a] of the king.

The Image of Gold

3 Nebuchadnezzar the king made an image
of gold, whose height *was* sixty cubits *and*
its width six cubits. He set it up in the plain of
Dura, in the province of Babylon. 2And King
Nebuchadnezzar sent *word* to gather together
the satraps, the administrators, the governors,
the counselors, the treasurers, the judges, the
magistrates, and all the officials of the provinces, to come to the dedication of the image
which King Nebuchadnezzar had set up. 3So
the satraps, the administrators, the governors,
the counselors, the treasurers, the judges, the
magistrates, and all the officials of the provinces gathered together for the dedication of
the image that King Nebuchadnezzar had set
up; and they stood before the image that Nebuchadnezzar had set up. 4Then a herald cried
aloud: “To you it is commanded, O peoples,
nations, and languages, 5*that* at the time you
hear the sound of the horn, flute, harp, lyre,
and psaltery, in symphony with all kinds of
music, you shall fall down and worship the
gold image that King Nebuchadnezzar has set
up; 6and whoever does not fall down and worship shall be cast immediately into the midst
of a burning fiery furnace.”
7So at that time, when all the people heard
the sound of the horn, flute, harp, *and* lyre, in
symphony with all kinds of music, all the people, nations, and languages fell down *and*
worshiped the gold image which King Nebuchadnezzar had set up.

Daniel's Friends Disobey the King

8Therefore at that time certain Chaldeans
came forward and accused the Jews. 9They
spoke and said to King Nebuchadnezzar, “O
king, live forever! 10You, O king, have made a
decree that everyone who hears the sound of
the horn, flute, harp, lyre, *and* psaltery, in
symphony with all kinds of music, shall fall
down and worship the gold image; 11and whoever does not fall down and worship shall be

2:49 [a]That is, the king's court

cast into the midst of a burning fiery furnace.
12There are certain Jews whom you have set
over the affairs of the province of Babylon:
Shadrach, Meshach, and Abed-Nego; these
men, O king, have not paid due regard to you.
They do not serve your gods or worship the
gold image which you have set up."
13Then Nebuchadnezzar, in rage and fury,
gave the command to bring Shadrach, Meshach, and Abed-Nego. So they brought these
men before the king. 14Nebuchadnezzar
spoke, saying to them, "*Is it* true, Shadrach,
Meshach, and Abed-Nego, *that* you do not
serve my gods or worship the gold image
which I have set up? 15Now if you are ready at
the time you hear the sound of the horn, flute,
harp, lyre, *and* psaltery, in symphony with all
kinds of music, and you fall down and worship the image which I have made, *good!* But
if you do not worship, you shall be cast immediately into the midst of a burning fiery furnace. And who *is* the god who will deliver you
from my hands?"
16Shadrach, Meshach, and Abed-Nego answered and said to the king, "O Nebuchadnezzar, we have no need to answer you in this
matter. 17If that *is the case,* our God whom we
serve is able to deliver us from the burning fiery furnace, and He will deliver *us* from your
hand, O king. 18But if not, let it be known to
you, O king, that we do not serve your gods,
nor will we worship the gold image which you
have set up."

SAVED IN FIERY TRIAL

19Then Nebuchadnezzar was full of fury, and
the expression on his face changed toward Shadrach, Meshach, and Abed-Nego. He spoke

PERSONALITY PROFILE

Values

THREE MEN AND A POWERFUL GOD

(DANIEL 3)

Most of the Book of Daniel centers on his personal life and leadership. The story of his three Hebrew friends, however, provides a fascinating added example of young men holding to their beliefs and values in the face of pressure. Daniel's friends, whose Hebrew names were Hananiah, Mishael, and Azariah, are better known to us by their Babylonian names—Shadrach, Meshach, and Abed-Nego. Despite being taken captive to Babylon and forced to serve the king, these young men remained faithful to God.

Although their lives were threatened on several occasions, Shadrach, Meshach, and Abed-Nego faced their greatest test when they were ordered to bow and worship a huge statue of the king. The friends recognized that obedience in this case meant more than simply giving honor to the king as their leader. Because it included the requirement of worship, it actually involved a choice between ultimate loyalty to God or the king. For them, the choice was clear: They would serve the king, but they would not worship him.

When the three men were confronted and threatened, they offered a marvelous and courageous statement of faith: "O Nebuchadnezzar, we have no need to answer you in this matter. If that is the case, our God whom we serve is able to deliver us from the burning fiery furnace, and He will deliver us from your hand, O king. But if not, let it be known to you, O king, that we do not serve your gods, nor will we worship the gold image which you have set up" (3:16–18). Their tone was respectful, confident, and uncompromising. They only assumed God's unlimited ability, not what might happen to them. They were clearly ready to die rather than deny God.

The depth of our faith and our loyalty to God can only be measured against resistance. Threats of harm or whispers of compromise have this equal possible benefit in common: They provide an opportunity to test our faith. Sometimes, as in Shadrach, Meshach and Abed-Nego's lives, the test becomes a miracle!

To Learn More: Turn to the article about values on pages 1544, 1545. See also the key passage note at 2 Peter 1:5–9 on page 1669.

and commanded that they heat the furnace
seven times more than it was usually heated.
20And he commanded certain mighty men of
valor who *were* in his army to bind Shadrach,
Meshach, and Abed-Nego, *and* cast *them* into
the burning fiery furnace. 21Then these men
were bound in their coats, their trousers, their
turbans, and their *other* garments, and were
cast into the midst of the burning fiery furnace.
22Therefore, because the king's command was
urgent, and the furnace exceedingly hot, the
flame of the fire killed those men who took up
Shadrach, Meshach, and Abed-Nego. 23And
these three men, Shadrach, Meshach, and
Abed-Nego, fell down bound into the midst of
the burning fiery furnace.

24Then King Nebuchadnezzar was astonished; and he rose in haste *and* spoke, saying
to his counselors, "Did we not cast three men
bound into the midst of the fire?"

They answered and said to the king, "True,
O king."

25"Look!" he answered, "I see four men
loose, walking in the midst of the fire; and
they are not hurt, and the form of the fourth is
like the Son of God."[a]

Nebuchadnezzar Praises God

26Then Nebuchadnezzar went near the
mouth of the burning fiery furnace *and* spoke,
saying, "Shadrach, Meshach, and Abed-Nego,
servants of the Most High God, come out, and
come *here*." Then Shadrach, Meshach, and
Abed-Nego came from the midst of the fire.
27And the satraps, administrators, governors,
and the king's counselors gathered together,
and they saw these men on whose bodies the
fire had no power; the hair of their head was
not singed nor were their garments affected,
and the smell of fire was not on them.

28Nebuchadnezzar spoke, saying, "Blessed
be the God of Shadrach, Meshach, and Abed-
Nego, who sent His Angel[a] and delivered His
servants who trusted in Him, and they have
frustrated the king's word, and yielded their
bodies, that they should not serve nor worship
any god except their own God! 29Therefore I
make a decree that any people, nation, or language which speaks anything amiss against
the God of Shadrach, Meshach, and Abed-
Nego shall be cut in pieces, and their houses
shall be made an ash heap; because there is
no other God who can deliver like this."

30Then the king promoted Shadrach, Meshach, and Abed-Nego in the province of Babylon.

Nebuchadnezzar's Second Dream

4 Nebuchadnezzar the king,

To all peoples, nations, and languages
that dwell in all the earth:

Peace be multiplied to you.

2 I thought it good to declare the signs and
wonders that the Most High God has
worked for me.

3 How great *are* His signs,
And how mighty His wonders!
His kingdom *is* an everlasting kingdom,
And His dominion *is* from generation to
generation.

4 I, Nebuchadnezzar, was at rest in my
house, and flourishing in my palace. 5I
saw a dream which made me afraid, and
the thoughts on my bed and the visions
of my head troubled me. 6Therefore I

3:25 [a]Or *a son of the gods* **3:28** [a]Or *angel*

SOUL NOTE

Unflinching Faith *(3:16–18)* "But if not." With these three words (3:18), Shadrach, Meshach, and Abed-Nego offered King Nebuchadnezzar a remarkable display of faith toward God. It's one thing to walk into a fiery furnace with the knowledge that God will protect us. It's quite another thing to walk into that same furnace knowing that God may choose to let us die for reasons we don't even understand! Faith is not simply a matter of believing that God will do what we think is best for us. Faith is believing that *whatever* God does is best, regardless of how it seems to affect us. **Topic: Faith**

issued a decree to bring in all the wise
men of Babylon before me, that they
might make known to me the
interpretation of the dream. [7]Then the
magicians, the astrologers, the
Chaldeans, and the soothsayers came in,
and I told them the dream; but they did
not make known to me its interpretation.
[8]But at last Daniel came before me (his
name *is* Belteshazzar, according to the
name of my god; in him *is* the Spirit of
the Holy God), and I told the dream
before him, *saying:* [9]"Belteshazzar, chief
of the magicians, because I know that
the Spirit of the Holy God *is* in you, and
no secret troubles you, explain to me the
visions of my dream that I have seen,
and its interpretation.

10 "These *were* the visions of my head
while on my bed:

I was looking, and behold,
A tree in the midst of the earth,
And its height was great.
11 The tree grew and became strong;
Its height reached to the heavens,
And it could be seen to the ends of all
the earth.
12 Its leaves *were* lovely,
Its fruit abundant,
And in it *was* food for all.
The beasts of the field found shade
under it,
The birds of the heavens dwelt in its
branches,
And all flesh was fed from it.

13 "I saw in the visions of my head *while*
on my bed, and there was a watcher, a
holy one, coming down from heaven.
[14]He cried aloud and said thus:

'Chop down the tree and cut off its
branches,
Strip off its leaves and scatter its fruit.
Let the beasts get out from under it,
And the birds from its branches.
15 Nevertheless leave the stump and roots
in the earth,
Bound with a band of iron and bronze,
In the tender grass of the field.
Let it be wet with the dew of heaven,
And *let* him graze with the beasts
On the grass of the earth.
16 Let his heart be changed from *that of* a
man,
Let him be given the heart of a beast,
And let seven times[a] pass over him.

4:16 [a]Possibly *seven years,* and so in verses 23, 25, and 32

KEY PASSAGE

Mental Illness

WHOLENESS

(4:33)

Perhaps one of the most difficult situations for Christians to face is the problem of mental illness. For Christians to face such difficulty somehow seems sinful. It is important to remember, however, that people are whole beings. First, we are spiritual beings, created by God and incomplete without Him. Also, we are physical beings, and a physical disease can lead to psychological or spiritual problems, and vice versa. And then too, we are psychological beings, meaning that each person has a mind, emotions, and a will. The interrelationships among these three realms in our humanity mean that specific problems may have many symptoms and causes behind them. If believers face some form of an emotional problem, they should seek counsel from wise, qualified Christians who can treat them with a comprehensive approach. During such a time, other believers must surround the hurting brother or sister in prayer. God promises to help His people through even the most difficult times.

To Learn More: Turn to the article about mental illness on pages 364, 365. See also the personality profile of Nebuchadnezzar on page 1111.

17 'This decision *is* by the decree of the
watchers,
And the sentence by the word of the
holy ones,
In order that the living may know
That the Most High rules in the kingdom
of men,
Gives it to whomever He will,
And sets over it the lowest of men.'

18 "This dream I, King Nebuchadnezzar,
have seen. Now you, Belteshazzar,
declare its interpretation, since all the
wise *men* of my kingdom are not able to
make known to me the interpretation;
but you *are* able, for the Spirit of the
Holy God *is* in you."

Daniel Explains the Second Dream

19 Then Daniel, whose name was
Belteshazzar, was astonished for a time,
and his thoughts troubled him. *So* the
king spoke, and said, "Belteshazzar, do
not let the dream or its interpretation
trouble you."
Belteshazzar answered and said, "My
lord, *may* the dream concern those who
hate you, and its interpretation concern
your enemies!

20 "The tree that you saw, which grew and
became strong, whose height reached to
the heavens and which *could be seen* by
all the earth, 21whose leaves *were* lovely
and its fruit abundant, in which *was*

PERSONALITY PROFILE

Mental Illness

NEBUCHADNEZZAR'S ILLNESS

(DANIEL 4:33)

Mental and emotional instability ran rampant in Nebuchadnezzar's family. Such is the legacy and heritage of those who set themselves up as gods. Daniel tells the shocking story of the king's emotional breakdown after years of success ruling the Babylonian Empire. In spite of his great victories as a warrior and achievements as a builder, Nebuchadnezzar suffered from a form of insanity similar to what we now call lycanthropy: He believed he was a wild animal. In the king's case, the condition arose as a direct result of his pride and arrogance. Nebuchadnezzar was warned of pride's danger by Daniel, but this king chose to ignore his own insignificance before God. No sooner did the words of pride cross his lips than God removed the kingdom from his power. "He was driven from men and ate grass like oxen; his body was wet with the dew of heaven till his hair had grown like eagles' feathers and his nails like birds' claws" (Dan. 4:33).

Daniel tells us that this condition lasted for seven years, until the king's reason returned to him when he acknowledged God (Dan. 4:25, 35, 36). Presumably, Daniel and others continued to run the affairs of state while Nebuchadnezzar was in this condition. He resumed his reign as a deeply humbled man.

Nebuchadnezzar was eventually succeeded by Nabonidus, who later abdicated the throne and lived in self-imposed exile in Arabia. During this time, Belshazzar, Nebuchadnezzar's grandson, ruled Babylon as a co-regent with his father, Nabonidus. While Belshazzar was in power, the Babylonian Empire fell to the Medes and the Persians.

Modern times have witnessed similar instances where national leaders suffered from times of depression or mental breakdown but were able to continue to exercise their responsibilities. The causes are not always the same as Nebuchadnezzar's, but cases of mental disorders require compassionate treatment. For the king, time and humility provided a pathway of recovery. Those who cared for him, like Daniel, had to practice patience. The healing of mental illness is rarely an instant cure.

To Learn More: Turn to the article about mental illness on pages 364, 365. See also the key passage note at Daniel 4:33 on page 1110.

food for all, under which the beasts of
the field dwelt, and in whose branches
the birds of the heaven had their
home—[22]it *is* you, O king, who have
grown and become strong; for your
greatness has grown and reaches to the
heavens, and your dominion to the end
of the earth.

23 "And inasmuch as the king saw a
watcher, a holy one, coming down from
heaven and saying, 'Chop down the tree
and destroy it, but leave its stump and
roots in the earth, *bound* with a band of
iron and bronze in the tender grass of
the field; let it be wet with the dew of
heaven, and let him graze with the
beasts of the field, till seven times pass
over him'; [24]this is the interpretation, O
king, and this is the decree of the Most
High, which has come upon my lord the
king: [25]They shall drive you from men,
your dwelling shall be with the beasts of
the field, and they shall make you eat
grass like oxen. They shall wet you with
the dew of heaven, and seven times
shall pass over you, till you know that
the Most High rules in the kingdom of
men, and gives it to whomever He
chooses.

26 "And inasmuch as they gave the
command to leave the stump *and* roots
of the tree, your kingdom shall be
assured to you, after you come to know
that Heaven rules. [27]Therefore, O king,
let my advice be acceptable to you;
break off your sins by *being* righteous,
and your iniquities by showing mercy to
the poor. Perhaps there may be a
lengthening of your prosperity."

NEBUCHADNEZZAR'S HUMILIATION

28 All *this* came upon King
Nebuchadnezzar. [29]At the end of the
twelve months he was walking about the
royal palace of Babylon. [30]The king
spoke, saying, "Is not this great Babylon,
that I have built for a royal dwelling by
my mighty power and for the honor of
my majesty?"

31 While the word *was still* in the king's
mouth, a voice fell from heaven: "King
Nebuchadnezzar, to you it is spoken: the
kingdom has departed from you! [32]And
they shall drive you from men, and your
dwelling *shall be* with the beasts of the
field. They shall make you eat grass like
oxen; and seven times shall pass over
you, until you know that the Most High
rules in the kingdom of men, and gives
it to whomever He chooses."

33 That very hour the word was fulfilled
concerning Nebuchadnezzar; he was
driven from men and ate grass like oxen;
his body was wet with the dew of heaven
till his hair had grown like eagles'
feathers and his nails like birds' *claws.*

NEBUCHADNEZZAR PRAISES GOD

34 And at the end of the time[a] I,
Nebuchadnezzar, lifted my eyes to
heaven, and my understanding returned
to me; and I blessed the Most High and
praised and honored Him who lives
forever:

For His dominion *is* an everlasting
dominion,
And His kingdom *is* from generation to
generation.
35 All the inhabitants of the earth *are*
reputed as nothing;
He does according to His will in the
army of heaven
And *among* the inhabitants of the earth.
No one can restrain His hand
Or say to Him, "What have You done?"

36 At the same time my reason returned to
me, and for the glory of my kingdom,
my honor and splendor returned to me.
My counselors and nobles resorted to
me, I was restored to my kingdom, and
excellent majesty was added to me.
[37]Now I, Nebuchadnezzar, praise and
extol and honor the King of heaven, all
of whose works *are* truth, and His ways
justice. And those who walk in pride He
is able to put down.

BELSHAZZAR'S FEAST

5 Belshazzar the king made a great feast for
a thousand of his lords, and drank wine in

4:34 [a]Literally *days*

the presence of the thousand. 2While he tasted the wine, Belshazzar gave the command to bring the gold and silver vessels which his father Nebuchadnezzar had taken from the temple which *had been* in Jerusalem, that the king and his lords, his wives, and his concubines might drink from them. 3Then they brought the gold vessels that had been taken from the temple of the house of God which *had been* in Jerusalem; and the king and his lords, his wives, and his concubines drank from them. 4They drank wine, and praised the gods of gold and silver, bronze and iron, wood and stone.

5In the same hour the fingers of a man's hand appeared and wrote opposite the lampstand on the plaster of the wall of the king's palace; and the king saw the part of the hand that wrote. 6Then the king's countenance changed, and his thoughts troubled him, so that the joints of his hips were loosened and his knees knocked against each other. 7The king cried aloud to bring in the astrologers, the Chaldeans, and the soothsayers. The king spoke, saying to the wise *men* of Babylon, "Whoever reads this writing, and tells me its interpretation, shall be clothed with purple and *have* a chain of gold around his neck; and he shall be the third ruler in the kingdom." 8Now all the king's wise *men* came, but they could not read the writing, or make known to the king its interpretation. 9Then King Belshazzar was greatly troubled, his countenance was changed, and his lords were astonished.

10The queen, because of the words of the king and his lords, came to the banquet hall. The queen spoke, saying, "O king, live forever! Do not let your thoughts trouble you, nor let your countenance change. 11There is a man in your kingdom in whom *is* the Spirit of the

PERSONALITY PROFILE

BELSHAZZAR'S SUBSTANCE ABUSE

(DANIEL 5)

Drug Abuse

Belshazzar's drunken party has a notorious place in history. A royal celebration of a conquering dynasty became a final gasp before defeat. Belshazzar set his tables that night with the precious items taken by his father's victorious armies. Among those silver and golden bowls and cups were many taken from God's temple in Jerusalem. Those dedicated utensils were filled with party wine. God's property was dishonored.

While the king and a thousand of his officials engaged in a drunken bash at the royal palace, the invading army of Medes and Persians surrounded the city. At the high point of the festivities, the fingers of God wrote a message of judgment on the wall of the palace (Dan. 5:5). The message indicated that the Babylonian Empire would fall to the Medes and Persians that very night. History records the fact that the invading army diverted the course of the Euphrates River, tunneled under the walls of Babylon, and took the city without resistance. In their drunken state, Belshazzar and his officials were incapable of resisting the invaders.

Most drug or alcohol abusers discover sooner or later that their surrender to those controlling substances renders them defenseless. Their decision-making abilities suffer badly. Choices that appear wise through a drunken haze or drug-induced high often prove tragic. Temporary sobriety usually provides more of an opportunity to survey the disaster than to repair what has been damaged or lost. Right in the middle of enjoying everything he thought he had, Belshazzar awoke to discover he had nothing. His life went from unmanageable to unlivable in one night. He lost both the kingdom and his life.

Countless others have followed Belshazzar's way of life. They may not have had as much to lose, but they lost it all anyway. Self-abusive lives like Belshazzar's always end sadly. But those who surrender to God and live for Him receive a gift of eternal life that they can never lose. They never have to face the handwriting on the wall.

To Learn More: Turn to the article about drug abuse on pages 852, 853. See also the key passage note at Proverbs 23:19–21 on page 833.

Holy God. And in the days of your father, light and understanding and wisdom, like the wisdom of the gods, were found in him; and King Nebuchadnezzar your father—your father the king—made him chief of the magicians, astrologers, Chaldeans, *and* soothsayers. 12Inasmuch as an excellent spirit, knowledge, understanding, interpreting dreams, solving riddles, and explaining enigmas[a] were found in this Daniel, whom the king named Belteshazzar, now let Daniel be called, and he will give the interpretation."

The Writing on the Wall Explained

13Then Daniel was brought in before the king. The king spoke, and said to Daniel, "*Are* you that Daniel who is one of the captives[a] from Judah, whom my father the king brought from Judah? 14I have heard of you, that the Spirit of God *is* in you, and *that* light and understanding and excellent wisdom are found in you. 15Now the wise *men,* the astrologers, have been brought in before me, that they should read this writing and make known to me its interpretation, but they could not give the interpretation of the thing. 16And I have heard of you, that you can give interpretations and explain enigmas. Now if you can read the writing and make known to me its interpretation, you shall be clothed with purple and *have* a chain of gold around your neck, and shall be the third ruler in the kingdom."

17Then Daniel answered, and said before the king, "Let your gifts be for yourself, and give your rewards to another; yet I will read the writing to the king, and make known to him the interpretation. 18O king, the Most High God gave Nebuchadnezzar your father a kingdom and majesty, glory and honor. 19And because of the majesty that He gave him, all peoples, nations, and languages trembled and feared before him. Whomever he wished, he executed; whomever he wished, he kept alive; whomever he wished, he set up; and whomever he wished, he put down. 20But when his heart was lifted up, and his spirit was hardened in pride, he was deposed from his kingly throne, and they took his glory from him. 21Then he was driven from the sons of men, his heart was made like the beasts, and his dwelling *was* with the wild donkeys. They fed him with grass like oxen, and his body was wet with the dew of heaven, till he knew that the Most High God rules in the kingdom of men, and appoints over it whomever He chooses.

22"But you his son, Belshazzar, have not humbled your heart, although you knew all this. 23And you have lifted yourself up against the Lord of heaven. They have brought the vessels of His house before you, and you and your lords, your wives and your concubines, have drunk wine from them. And you have praised the gods of silver and gold, bronze and iron, wood and stone, which do not see or hear or know; and the God who *holds* your breath in His hand and owns all your ways, you have not glorified. 24Then the fingers[a] of the hand were sent from Him, and this writing was written.

25"And this is the inscription that was written:

MENE,[a] MENE, TEKEL,[b] UPHARSIN.[c]

26This *is* the interpretation of *each* word. MENE: God has numbered your kingdom, and finished it; 27TEKEL: You have been weighed in the balances, and found wanting; 28PERES: Your kingdom has been divided, and given to the Medes and Persians."[a] 29Then Belshazzar gave the command, and they clothed Daniel with purple and *put* a chain of gold around his neck, and made a proclamation concerning him that he should be the third ruler in the kingdom.

Belshazzar's Fall

30That very night Belshazzar, king of the Chaldeans, was slain. 31And Darius the Mede received the kingdom, *being* about sixty-two years old.

The Plot Against Daniel

6 It pleased Darius to set over the kingdom one hundred and twenty satraps, to be over the whole kingdom; 2and over these, three governors, of whom Daniel *was* one, that the satraps might give account to them, so that the king would suffer no loss. 3Then this Daniel distinguished himself above the

---

5:12 [a]Literally *untying knots,* and so in verse 16
5:13 [a]Literally *of the sons of the captivity*
5:24 [a]Literally *palm* **5:25** [a]Literally *a mina* (50 shekels) from the verb "to number" [b]Literally *a shekel* from the verb "to weigh" [c]Literally *and half-shekels* from the verb "to divide"
5:28 [a]Aramaic *Paras,* consonant with *Peres*

governors and satraps, because an excellent
spirit *was* in him; and the king gave thought to
setting him over the whole realm. 4So the governors and satraps sought to find *some* charge
against Daniel concerning the kingdom; but
they could find no charge or fault, because he
was faithful; nor was there any error or fault
found in him. 5Then these men said, "We shall
not find any charge against this Daniel unless
we find *it* against him concerning the law of
his God."
6So these governors and satraps thronged
before the king, and said thus to him: "King
Darius, live forever! 7All the governors of the
kingdom, the administrators and satraps, the
counselors and advisors, have consulted together to establish a royal statute and to make
a firm decree, that whoever petitions any god
or man for thirty days, except you, O king,
shall be cast into the den of lions. 8Now, O
king, establish the decree and sign the writing, so that it cannot be changed, according to
the law of the Medes and Persians, which does
not alter." 9Therefore King Darius signed the
written decree.

Daniel in the Lions' Den

10Now when Daniel knew that the writing
was signed, he went home. And in his upper
room, with his windows open toward Jerusalem, he knelt down on his knees three times
that day, and prayed and gave thanks before
his God, as was his custom since early days.
11Then these men assembled and found
Daniel praying and making supplication before his God. 12And they went before the king,
and spoke concerning the king's decree:
"Have you not signed a decree that every man
who petitions any god or man within thirty
days, except you, O king, shall be cast into the
den of lions?"
The king answered and said, "The thing *is*
true, according to the law of the Medes and
Persians, which does not alter."
13So they answered and said before the
king, "That Daniel, who is one of the captives[a] from Judah, does not show due regard
for you, O king, or for the decree that you
have signed, but makes his petition three
times a day."
14And the king, when he heard *these* words,
was greatly displeased with himself, and set
his heart on Daniel to deliver him; and he labored till the going down of the sun to deliver
him. 15Then these men approached the king,
and said to the king, "Know, O king, that *it is*
the law of the Medes and Persians that no decree or statute which the king establishes may
be changed."
16So the king gave the command, and they
brought Daniel and cast *him* into the den of lions. *But* the king spoke, saying to Daniel,
"Your God, whom you serve continually, He
will deliver you." 17Then a stone was brought
and laid on the mouth of the den, and the king
sealed it with his own signet ring and with the
signets of his lords, that the purpose concerning Daniel might not be changed.

Daniel Saved from the Lions

18Now the king went to his palace and spent
the night fasting; and no musicians[a] were
brought before him. Also his sleep went from
him. 19Then the king arose very early in the
morning and went in haste to the den of lions.
20And when he came to the den, he cried out
with a lamenting voice to Daniel. The king
spoke, saying to Daniel, "Daniel, servant of
the living God, has your God, whom you serve

6:13 [a]Literally *of the sons of the captivity*
6:18 [a]Exact meaning unknown

SOUL NOTE

Weigh the Options *(6:10)* Daniel was a savvy political consultant. He knew that his enemies were lying in wait for him, and he knew the penalty for praying to God. After weighing these concerns, Daniel concluded that they were nothing compared with the prospect of disrupting his relationship with God. So "with his windows open . . . he knelt down on his knees three times that day, and prayed." Daniel was unwilling to change his prayer habits, even at the risk of his own safety. He knew that where spiritual calling and everyday concerns clash, spiritual calling always takes precedence, no matter what. **Topic: Prayer**

continually, been able to deliver you from the
lions?"
[21]Then Daniel said to the king, "O king, live
forever! [22]My God sent His angel and shut the
lions' mouths, so that they have not hurt me,
because I was found innocent before Him; and
also, O king, I have done no wrong before
you."
[23]Now the king was exceedingly glad for
him, and commanded that they should take
Daniel up out of the den. So Daniel was taken
up out of the den, and no injury whatever was
found on him, because he believed in his God.

Darius Honors God

[24]And the king gave the command, and they
brought those men who had accused Daniel,
and they cast *them* into the den of lions—
them, their children, and their wives; and the
lions overpowered them, and broke all their
bones in pieces before they ever came to the
bottom of the den.
[25]Then King Darius wrote:

> To all peoples, nations, and languages
> that dwell in all the earth:
>
> Peace be multiplied to you.

26 I make a decree that in every dominion
of my kingdom *men must* tremble and
fear before the God of Daniel.

For He *is* the living God,
And steadfast forever;
His kingdom *is the one* which shall not
be destroyed,
And His dominion *shall endure* to the
end.
27 He delivers and rescues,
And He works signs and wonders
In heaven and on earth,
Who has delivered Daniel from the
power of the lions.

[28]So this Daniel prospered in the reign of
Darius and in the reign of Cyrus the Persian.

Vision of the Four Beasts

7 In the first year of Belshazzar king of Babylon, Daniel had a dream and visions of
his head *while* on his bed. Then he wrote
down the dream, telling the main facts.[a]
[2]Daniel spoke, saying, "I saw in my vision
by night, and behold, the four winds of heav-
en were stirring up the Great Sea. [3]And four
great beasts came up from the sea, each different from the other. [4]The first *was* like a lion,
and had eagle's wings. I watched till its wings
were plucked off; and it was lifted up from the
earth and made to stand on two feet like a
man, and a man's heart was given to it.
[5]"And suddenly another beast, a second,
like a bear. It was raised up on one side, and
had three ribs in its mouth between its teeth.
And they said thus to it: 'Arise, devour much
flesh!'
[6]"After this I looked, and there was another,
like a leopard, which had on its back four
wings of a bird. The beast also had four heads,
and dominion was given to it.
[7]"After this I saw in the night visions, and
behold, a fourth beast, dreadful and terrible,
exceedingly strong. It had huge iron teeth; it
was devouring, breaking in pieces, and tram-
pling the residue with its feet. It *was* different
from all the beasts that *were* before it, and it
had ten horns. [8]I was considering the horns,

7:1 [a]Literally *the head* (or *chief*) *of the words*

SOUL NOTE

A Glimpse of the Miraculous *(6:23)* King Darius and Daniel experienced the miracle of the lions' den from significantly different perspectives. The king mouthed faithful-sounding encouragement when Daniel was thrown into the pit (6:16), but his sleepless night (6:18) didn't show faith in God. Daniel, on the other hand, approached his sentence with complete confidence in God's will. As a result, Darius was only able to witness the event as a spectator, only able to appreciate it from afar. In contrast, Daniel experienced the miracle firsthand and felt the loving, protective hand of God "because he believed." When we trust in God, we will recognize His touch on our lives.
Topic: Belief

and there was another horn, a little one, coming up among them, before whom three of the first horns were plucked out by the roots. And there, in this horn, *were* eyes like the eyes of a man, and a mouth speaking pompous words.

Vision of the Ancient of Days

9 "I watched till thrones were put in place,
And the Ancient of Days was seated;
His garment *was* white as snow,
And the hair of His head *was* like pure wool.
His throne *was* a fiery flame,
Its wheels a burning fire;
10 A fiery stream issued
And came forth from before Him.
A thousand thousands ministered to Him;
Ten thousand times ten thousand stood before Him.
The court[a] was seated,
And the books were opened.

11"I watched then because of the sound of
the pompous words which the horn was
speaking; I watched till the beast was slain,
and its body destroyed and given to the burning flame. 12As for the rest of the beasts, they
had their dominion taken away, yet their lives
were prolonged for a season and a time.

13 "I was watching in the night visions,
And behold, *One* like the Son of Man,
Coming with the clouds of heaven!
He came to the Ancient of Days,
And they brought Him near before Him.
14 Then to Him was given dominion and glory and a kingdom,
That all peoples, nations, and languages should serve Him.
His dominion *is* an everlasting dominion,
Which shall not pass away,
And His kingdom *the one*
Which shall not be destroyed.

Daniel's Visions Interpreted

15"I, Daniel, was grieved in my spirit within
my body, and the visions of my head troubled
me. 16I came near to one of those who stood
by, and asked him the truth of all this. So he
told me and made known to me the interpretation of these things: 17'Those great beasts,
which are four, *are* four kings[a] *which* arise out
of the earth. 18But the saints of the Most High
shall receive the kingdom, and possess the
kingdom forever, even forever and ever.'
19"Then I wished to know the truth about
the fourth beast, which was different from all
the others, exceedingly dreadful, *with* its teeth
of iron and its nails of bronze, *which* devoured, broke in pieces, and trampled the residue with its feet; 20and the ten horns that *were*
on its head, and the other *horn* which came
up, before which three fell, namely, that horn
which had eyes and a mouth which spoke
pompous words, whose appearance *was*
greater than his fellows.
21"I was watching; and the same horn was
making war against the saints, and prevailing
against them, 22until the Ancient of Days
came, and a judgment was made *in favor* of
the saints of the Most High, and the time came
for the saints to possess the kingdom.
23"Thus he said:

'The fourth beast shall be
A fourth kingdom on earth,
Which shall be different from all *other* kingdoms,
And shall devour the whole earth,
Trample it and break it in pieces.
24 The ten horns *are* ten kings
Who shall arise from this kingdom.
And another shall rise after them;
He shall be different from the first *ones,*
And shall subdue three kings.
25 He shall speak *pompous* words against the Most High,
Shall persecute[a] the saints of the Most High,
And shall intend to change times and law.
Then *the saints* shall be given into his hand
For a time and times and half a time.

26 'But the court shall be seated,
And they shall take away his dominion,
To consume and destroy *it* forever.
27 Then the kingdom and dominion,
And the greatness of the kingdoms under the whole heaven,
Shall be given to the people, the saints of the Most High.

7:10 [a]Or *judgment* **7:17** [a]Representing their kingdoms (compare verse 23) **7:25** [a]Literally *wear out*

His kingdom *is* an everlasting kingdom,
And all dominions shall serve and obey
Him.'

28"This *is* the end of the account.[a] As for
me, Daniel, my thoughts greatly troubled me,
and my countenance changed; but I kept the
matter in my heart."

Vision of a Ram and a Goat

8 In the third year of the reign of King Belshazzar a vision appeared *to* me—to me,
Daniel—after the one that appeared to me the
first time. 2I saw in the vision, and it so happened while I was looking, that I *was* in
Shushan, the citadel, which *is* in the province
of Elam; and I saw in the vision that I was by
the River Ulai. 3Then I lifted my eyes and saw,
and there, standing beside the river, was a ram
which had two horns, and the two horns *were*
high; but one *was* higher than the other, and
the higher *one* came up last. 4I saw the ram
pushing westward, northward, and southward, so that no animal could withstand him;
nor *was there any* that could deliver from his
hand, but he did according to his will and became great.

5And as I was considering, suddenly a male
goat came from the west, across the surface of
the whole earth, without touching the ground;
and the goat *had* a notable horn between his
eyes. 6Then he came to the ram that had two
horns, which I had seen standing beside the
river, and ran at him with furious power. 7And
I saw him confronting the ram; he was moved
with rage against him, attacked the ram, and
broke his two horns. There was no power in
the ram to withstand him, but he cast him
down to the ground and trampled him; and
there was no one that could deliver the ram
from his hand.

8Therefore the male goat grew very great;
but when he became strong, the large horn
was broken, and in place of it four notable
ones came up toward the four winds of heav-
en. 9And out of one of them came a little horn
which grew exceedingly great toward the
south, toward the east, and toward the Glorious *Land.* 10And it grew up to the host of
heaven; and it cast down *some* of the host and
some of the stars to the ground, and trampled
them. 11He even exalted *himself* as high as the
Prince of the host; and by him the daily *sacrifices* were taken away, and the place of His
sanctuary was cast down. 12Because of transgression, an army was given over *to the horn*
to oppose the daily *sacrifices;* and he cast
truth down to the ground. He did *all this* and
prospered.

13Then I heard a holy one speaking; and *another* holy one said to that certain *one* who
was speaking, "How long *will* the vision *be,
concerning* the daily *sacrifices* and the transgression of desolation, the giving of both the
sanctuary and the host to be trampled underfoot?"

14And he said to me, "For two thousand
three hundred days;[a] then the sanctuary shall
be cleansed."

Gabriel Interprets the Vision

15Then it happened, when I, Daniel, had
seen the vision and was seeking the meaning,
that suddenly there stood before me one having the appearance of a man. 16And I heard a
man's voice between *the banks of* the Ulai,
who called, and said, "Gabriel, make this *man*
understand the vision." 17So he came near
where I stood, and when he came I was afraid
and fell on my face; but he said to me, "Understand, son of man, that the vision *refers* to the
time of the end."

18Now, as he was speaking with me, I was
in a deep sleep with my face to the ground;
but he touched me, and stood me upright.
19And he said, "Look, I am making known to
you what shall happen in the latter time of the
indignation; for at the appointed time the end
shall be. 20The ram which you saw, having the
two horns—*they are* the kings of Media and
Persia. 21And the male goat *is* the kingdom[a] of
Greece. The large horn that *is* between its eyes
is the first king. 22As for the broken *horn* and
the four that stood up in its place, four kingdoms shall arise out of that nation, but not
with its power.

23 "And in the latter time of their
kingdom,
When the transgressors have reached
their fullness,
A king shall arise,
Having fierce features,
Who understands sinister schemes.

7:28 [a]Literally *the word* **8:14** [a]Literally *evening-mornings* **8:21** [a]Literally *king,* representing his kingdom (compare 7:17, 23)

24 His power shall be mighty, but not by his own power;
He shall destroy fearfully,
And shall prosper and thrive;
He shall destroy the mighty, and *also* the holy people.

25 "Through his cunning
He shall cause deceit to prosper under his rule;[a]
And he shall exalt *himself* in his heart.
He shall destroy many in *their* prosperity.
He shall even rise against the Prince of princes;
But he shall be broken without *human* means.[b]

26 "And the vision of the evenings and mornings
Which was told is true;
Therefore seal up the vision,
For *it refers* to many days *in the future.*"

27 And I, Daniel, fainted and was sick for days; afterward I arose and went about the king's business. I was astonished by the vision, but no one understood it.

Daniel's Prayer for the People

9 In the first year of Darius the son of Ahasuerus, of the lineage of the Medes, who was made king over the realm of the Chaldeans— 2 in the first year of his reign I, Daniel, understood by the books the number of the years *specified* by the word of the LORD through Jeremiah the prophet, that He would accomplish seventy years in the desolations of Jerusalem.

3 Then I set my face toward the Lord God to make request by prayer and supplications, with fasting, sackcloth, and ashes. 4 And I prayed to the LORD my God, and made confession, and said, "O Lord, great and awesome God, who keeps His covenant and mercy with those who love Him, and with those who keep His commandments, 5 we have sinned and committed iniquity, we have done wickedly and rebelled, even by departing from Your precepts and Your judgments. 6 Neither have we heeded Your servants the prophets, who spoke in Your name to our kings and our princes, to our fathers and all the people of the land. 7 O Lord, righteousness *belongs* to You, but to us shame of face, as *it is* this day—to the men of Judah, to the inhabitants of Jerusalem and all Israel, those near and those far off in all the countries to which You have driven them, because of the unfaithfulness which they have committed against You.

8 "O Lord, to us *belongs* shame of face, to our kings, our princes, and our fathers, because we have sinned against You. 9 To the Lord our God *belong* mercy and forgiveness, though we have rebelled against Him. 10 We have not obeyed the voice of the LORD our God, to walk in His laws, which He set before us by His servants the prophets. 11 Yes, all Israel has transgressed Your law, and has departed so as not to obey Your voice; therefore the curse and the oath written in the Law of Moses the servant of God have been poured out on us, because we have sinned against Him. 12 And He has confirmed His words, which He spoke against us and against our judges who judged us, by bringing upon us a great disaster; for under the whole heaven such has never been done as what has been done to Jerusalem.

13 "As *it is* written in the Law of Moses, all this disaster has come upon us; yet we have not made our prayer before the LORD our God, that we might turn from our iniquities and understand Your truth. 14 Therefore the LORD has kept the disaster in mind, and brought it upon us; for the LORD our God *is* righteous in all the works which He does, though we have not obeyed His voice. 15 And now, O Lord our God, who brought Your people out of the land of Egypt with a mighty hand, and made Yourself a name, as *it is* this day—we have sinned, we have done wickedly!

16 "O Lord, according to all Your righteousness, I pray, let Your anger and Your fury be turned away from Your city Jerusalem, Your holy mountain; because for our sins, and for the iniquities of our fathers, Jerusalem and Your people *are* a reproach to all *those* around us. 17 Now therefore, our God, hear the prayer of Your servant, and his supplications, and for the Lord's sake cause Your face to shine on Your sanctuary, which is desolate. 18 O my God, incline Your ear and hear; open Your eyes and see our desolations, and the city which is called by Your name; for we do not present our supplications before You because

8:25 [a]Literally *hand* [b]Literally *hand*

of our righteous deeds, but because of Your great mercies. 19O Lord, hear! O Lord, forgive! O Lord, listen and act! Do not delay for Your own sake, my God, for Your city and Your people are called by Your name."

The Seventy-Weeks Prophecy

20Now while I *was* speaking, praying, and confessing my sin and the sin of my people Israel, and presenting my supplication before the LORD my God for the holy mountain of my God, 21yes, while I *was* speaking in prayer, the man Gabriel, whom I had seen in the vision at the beginning, being caused to fly swiftly, reached me about the time of the evening offering. 22And he informed *me,* and talked with me, and said, "O Daniel, I have now come forth to give you skill to understand. 23At the beginning of your supplications the command went out, and I have come to tell *you,* for you *are* greatly beloved; therefore consider the matter, and understand the vision:

24 "Seventy weeks[a] are determined
For your people and for your holy city,
To finish the transgression,
To make an end of[b] sins,
To make reconciliation for iniquity,
To bring in everlasting righteousness,
To seal up vision and prophecy,
And to anoint the Most Holy.

25 "Know therefore and understand,
That from the going forth of the command
To restore and build Jerusalem
Until Messiah the Prince,
There shall be seven weeks and sixty-two weeks;
The street[a] shall be built again, and the wall,[b]
Even in troublesome times.

26 "And after the sixty-two weeks
Messiah shall be cut off, but not for Himself;
And the people of the prince who is to come
Shall destroy the city and the sanctuary.
The end of it *shall be* with a flood,
And till the end of the war desolations are determined.
27 Then he shall confirm a covenant with many for one week;
But in the middle of the week
He shall bring an end to sacrifice and offering.
And on the wing of abominations shall be one who makes desolate,
Even until the consummation, which is determined,
Is poured out on the desolate."

Vision of the Glorious Man

10 In the third year of Cyrus king of Persia a message was revealed to Daniel, whose name was called Belteshazzar. The message *was* true, but the appointed time *was* long;[a] and he understood the message, and had understanding of the vision. 2In those days I, Daniel, was mourning three full weeks. 3I ate no pleasant food, no meat or wine came into my mouth, nor did I anoint myself at all, till three whole weeks were fulfilled.

4Now on the twenty-fourth day of the first month, as I was by the side of the great river, that *is,* the Tigris,[a] 5I lifted my eyes and looked, and behold, a certain man clothed in linen, whose waist *was* girded with gold of Uphaz! 6His body *was* like beryl, his face like the appearance of lightning, his eyes like torches of fire, his arms and feet like burnished bronze in color, and the sound of his words like the voice of a multitude.

7And I, Daniel, alone saw the vision, for the men who were with me did not see the vision; but a great terror fell upon them, so that they fled to hide themselves. 8Therefore I was left alone when I saw this great vision, and no strength remained in me; for my vigor was turned to frailty in me, and I retained no strength. 9Yet I heard the sound of his words; and while I heard the sound of his words I was in a deep sleep on my face, with my face to the ground.

Prophecies Concerning Persia and Greece

10Suddenly, a hand touched me, which made me tremble on my knees and *on* the palms of my hands. 11And he said to me, "O Daniel, man greatly beloved, understand the

9:24 [a]Literally *sevens,* and so throughout the chapter [b]Following Qere, Septuagint, Syriac, and Vulgate; Kethib and Theodotion read *To seal up.* **9:25** [a]Or *open square* [b]Or *moat* **10:1** [a]Or *and of great conflict* **10:4** [a]Hebrew *Hiddekel*

words that I speak to you, and stand upright,
for I have now been sent to you." While he
was speaking this word to me, I stood trembling.
12Then he said to me, "Do not fear, Daniel,
for from the first day that you set your heart to
understand, and to humble yourself before
your God, your words were heard; and I have
come because of your words. 13But the prince
of the kingdom of Persia withstood me twenty-one days; and behold, Michael, one of the
chief princes, came to help me, for I had been
left alone there with the kings of Persia. 14Now
I have come to make you understand what
will happen to your people in the latter days,
for the vision *refers* to *many* days yet *to
come.*"
15When he had spoken such words to me, I
turned my face toward the ground and became speechless. 16And suddenly, *one* having
the likeness of the sons[a] of men touched my
lips; then I opened my mouth and spoke, saying to him who stood before me, "My lord,
because of the vision my sorrows have
overwhelmed me, and I have retained no
strength. 17For how can this servant of my lord
talk with you, my lord? As for me, no strength
remains in me now, nor is any breath left in
me."
18Then again, *the one* having the likeness of
a man touched me and strengthened me.
19And he said, "O man greatly beloved, fear
not! Peace *be* to you; be strong, yes, be
strong!"
So when he spoke to me I was strengthened, and said, "Let my lord speak, for you
have strengthened me."
20Then he said, "Do you know why I have
come to you? And now I must return to fight
with the prince of Persia; and when I have
gone forth, indeed the prince of Greece will
come. 21But I will tell you what is noted in the
Scripture of Truth. (No one upholds me
against these, except Michael your prince.

11 "Also in the first year of Darius the
Mede, I, *even* I, stood up to confirm
and strengthen him.) 2And now I will tell you
the truth: Behold, three more kings will arise
in Persia, and the fourth shall be far richer
than *them* all; by his strength, through his
riches, he shall stir up all against the realm of
Greece. 3Then a mighty king shall arise, who
shall rule with great dominion, and do according to his will. 4And when he has arisen, his
kingdom shall be broken up and divided toward the four winds of heaven, but not among
his posterity nor according to his dominion
with which he ruled; for his kingdom shall be
uprooted, even for others besides these.

10:16 [a]Theodotion and Vulgate read *the son;* Septuagint reads *a hand.*

KEY PASSAGE

Spiritual Disciplines

SECOND NATURE

(10:12)

Is a spiritual discipline—such as prayer—worth the effort? The vision the Lord gave Daniel by the Tigris River answers that question. The man in the vision told Daniel, "Your words were heard; and I have come because of your words."

Spiritual disciplines are personal habits that create a focus on God. These habits help believers in their spiritual walk and spiritual growth. Disciplines such as prayer, Bible study, fasting, worship, and meditation on Scripture aid believers to deepen their relationship with God. Believers discipline themselves to strengthen their faith much as athletes discipline themselves to strengthen their muscles. These disciplines are done not to gain salvation, but out of love for Christ and a desire to be like Him. Athletes stretch various muscles and practice key skills over and over until they become second nature. Believers' spiritual lives should be enmeshed with every other part of life so that Christlikeness becomes second nature as well.

To Learn More: Turn to the article about spiritual disciplines on pages 1420, 1421. See also the personality profile of the early Christians on page 1419.

Warring Kings of North and South

5“Also the king of the South shall become
strong, as well as *one* of his princes; and he
shall gain power over him and have dominion.
His dominion *shall be* a great dominion. 6And
at the end of *some* years they shall join forces,
for the daughter of the king of the South shall
go to the king of the North to make an agreement; but she shall not retain the power of her
authority,[a] and neither he nor his authority[b]
shall stand; but she shall be given up, with
those who brought her, and with him who
begot her, and with him who strengthened
her in *those* times. 7But from a branch of her
roots *one* shall arise in his place, who shall
come with an army, enter the fortress of the
king of the North, and deal with them and prevail. 8And he shall also carry their gods captive to Egypt, with their princes[a] *and* their
precious articles of silver and gold; and he
shall continue *more* years than the king of the
North.

9“Also *the king of the North* shall come to
the kingdom of the king of the South, but shall
return to his own land. 10However his sons
shall stir up strife, and assemble a multitude
of great forces; and *one* shall certainly come
and overwhelm and pass through; then he
shall return to his fortress and stir up strife.

11“And the king of the South shall be moved
with rage, and go out and fight with him, with
the king of the North, who shall muster a
great multitude; but the multitude shall be
given into the hand of his *enemy.* 12When he
has taken away the multitude, his heart will
be lifted up; and he will cast down tens of
thousands, but he will not prevail. 13For the
king of the North will return and muster a
multitude greater than the former, and shall
certainly come at the end of some years with a
great army and much equipment.

14“Now in those times many shall rise up
against the king of the South. Also, violent
men[a] of your people shall exalt themselves in
fulfillment of the vision, but they shall fall.
15So the king of the North shall come and
build a siege mound, and take a fortified city;
and the forces[a] of the South shall not withstand *him.* Even his choice troops *shall have*
no strength to resist. 16But he who comes
against him shall do according to his own will,
and no one shall stand against him. He shall
stand in the Glorious Land with destruction in
his power.[a]

17“He shall also set his face to enter with the
strength of his whole kingdom, and upright
ones[a] with him; thus shall he do. And he shall
give him the daughter of women to destroy it;
but she shall not stand *with him,* or be for
him. 18After this he shall turn his face to the
coastlands, and shall take many. But a ruler
shall bring the reproach against them to an
end; and with the reproach removed, he shall
turn back on him. 19Then he shall turn his face
toward the fortress of his own land; but he
shall stumble and fall, and not be found.

20“There shall arise in his place one who
imposes taxes *on* the glorious kingdom; but
within a few days he shall be destroyed, but
not in anger or in battle. 21And in his place
shall arise a vile person, to whom they will
not give the honor of royalty; but he shall
come in peaceably, and seize the kingdom by
intrigue. 22With the force[a] of a flood they shall
be swept away from before him and be broken, and also the prince of the covenant.
23And after the league *is made* with him he
shall act deceitfully, for he shall come up and
become strong with a small *number of* people.
24He shall enter peaceably, even into the richest places of the province; and he shall do
what his fathers have not done, nor his forefathers: he shall disperse among them the plunder, spoil, and riches; and he shall devise his
plans against the strongholds, but *only* for a
time.

25“He shall stir up his power and his courage against the king of the South with a great
army. And the king of the South shall be
stirred up to battle with a very great and
mighty army; but he shall not stand, for they
shall devise plans against him. 26Yes, those
who eat of the portion of his delicacies shall
destroy him; his army shall be swept away,
and many shall fall down slain. 27Both these
kings’ hearts *shall be* bent on evil, and they
shall speak lies at the same table; but it shall
not prosper, for the end *will* still *be* at the appointed time. 28While returning to his land
with great riches, his heart shall be *moved*
against the holy covenant; so he shall do *damage* and return to his own land.

11:6 [a]Literally *arm* [b]Literally *arm* **11:8** [a]Or *molded images* **11:14** [a]Or *robbers,* literally *sons of breakage* **11:15** [a]Literally *arms* **11:16** [a]Literally *hand* **11:17** [a]Or *bring equitable terms* **11:22** [a]Literally *arms*

The Northern King's Blasphemies

29“At the appointed time he shall return and go toward the south; but it shall not be like the former or the latter. 30For ships from Cyprus[a] shall come against him; therefore he shall be grieved, and return in rage against the holy covenant, and do *damage.*

“So he shall return and show regard for those who forsake the holy covenant. 31And forces[a] shall be mustered by him, and they shall defile the sanctuary fortress; then they shall take away the daily *sacrifices,* and place *there* the abomination of desolation. 32Those who do wickedly against the covenant he shall corrupt with flattery; but the people who know their God shall be strong, and carry out *great exploits.* 33And those of the people who understand shall instruct many; yet *for many* days they shall fall by sword and flame, by captivity and plundering. 34Now when they fall, they shall be aided with a little help; but many shall join with them by intrigue. 35And *some* of those of understanding shall fall, to refine them, purify *them,* and make *them* white, *until* the time of the end; because *it is* still for the appointed time.

36“Then the king shall do according to his own will: he shall exalt and magnify himself above every god, shall speak blasphemies against the God of gods, and shall prosper till the wrath has been accomplished; for what has been determined shall be done. 37He shall regard neither the God[a] of his fathers nor the desire of women, nor regard any god; for he shall exalt himself above *them* all. 38But in their place he shall honor a god of fortresses; and a god which his fathers did not know he shall honor with gold and silver, with precious stones and pleasant things. 39Thus he shall act against the strongest fortresses with a foreign god, which he shall acknowledge, *and* advance *its* glory; and he shall cause them to rule over many, and divide the land for gain.

The Northern King's Conquests

40“At the time of the end the king of the South shall attack him; and the king of the North shall come against him like a whirlwind, with chariots, horsemen, and with many ships; and he shall enter the countries, overwhelm *them,* and pass through. 41He shall also enter the Glorious Land, and many *countries* shall be overthrown; but these shall escape from his hand: Edom, Moab, and the prominent people of Ammon. 42He shall stretch out his hand against the countries, and the land of Egypt shall not escape. 43He shall have power over the treasures of gold and silver, and over all the precious things of Egypt; also the Libyans and Ethiopians *shall follow* at his heels. 44But news from the east and the north shall trouble him; therefore he shall go out with great fury to destroy and annihilate many. 45And he shall plant the tents of his palace between the seas and the glorious holy mountain; yet he shall come to his end, and no one will help him.

Prophecy of the End Time

12 “At that time Michael shall stand up,
The great prince who stands *watch*
over the sons of your people;
And there shall be a time of trouble,
Such as never was since there was a
nation,
Even to that time.
And at that time your people shall be
delivered,
Every one who is found written in the
book.
2 And many of those who sleep in the
dust of the earth shall awake,
Some to everlasting life,
Some to shame *and* everlasting
contempt.
3 Those who are wise shall shine
Like the brightness
of the
firmament,
And those who
turn many to
righteousness
Like the stars
forever and ever.

> “Those who are wise shall shine like the brightness of the firmament, and those who turn many to righteousness like the stars forever and ever.”
>
> DANIEL 12:3

4“But you, Daniel, shut up the words, and seal the book until the time of the end; many shall run to and fro, and knowledge shall increase.”

5Then I, Daniel, looked; and there stood two others, one on this riverbank and the other on

---

11:30 [a]Hebrew *Kittim,* western lands, especially Cyprus **11:31** [a]Literally *arms* **11:37** [a]Or *gods*

that riverbank. 6And *one* said to the man
clothed in linen, who *was* above the waters of
the river, "How long shall the fulfillment of
these wonders *be?*"

7Then I heard the man clothed in linen, who
was above the waters of the river, when he
held up his right hand and his left hand to
heaven, and swore by Him who lives forever,
that *it shall be* for a time, times, and half *a
time;* and when the power of the holy people
has been completely shattered, all these
things shall be finished.

8Although I heard, I did not understand.
Then I said, "My lord, what *shall be* the end of
these *things?*"

9And he said, "Go *your way,* Daniel, for the
words *are* closed up and sealed till the time of
the end. 10Many shall be purified, made white,
and refined, but the wicked shall do wickedly;
and none of the wicked shall understand, but
the wise shall understand.

11"And from the time *that* the daily *sacrifice*
is taken away, and the abomination of desolation is set up, *there shall be* one thousand two
hundred and ninety days. 12Blessed *is* he who
waits, and comes to the one thousand three
hundred and thirty-five days.

13"But you, go *your way* till the end; for you
shall rest, and will arise to your inheritance at
the end of the days."

Hosea

Adultery breaks hearts, it breaks homes, and it destroys marriages and families. The sorrow caused by a spouse seeking intimacy with someone else is unspeakable. This is the story experienced by Hosea, a prophet to the northern kingdom of Israel.

Hosea is a strange love story. At the most obvious level, it details a husband's unrequited love for his wayward wife, Gomer. Despite her gross unfaithfulness, the prophet went to great lengths to find Gomer and bring her home. At a deeper level, Hosea's experience became a living object lesson for the people of Israel. Their spiritual infidelity had wounded the very heart of God; yet, amazingly, He loved them and wanted them back.

Through the prophet, we sense God's exasperation and anguish: "O Ephraim, what shall I do to you? O Judah, what shall I do to you? For your faithfulness is like a morning cloud, and like the early dew it goes away" (6:4). But we also sense God's determined love: "How can I hand you over, Israel? . . . My heart churns within Me; My sympathy is stirred. I will not execute the fierceness of My anger" (11:8, 9).

The Book of Hosea reveals both the degradation of sin and the tender side of God. One cannot read this tragic, yet triumphal, story of tough love and not be moved by the overwhelming love of God for sinners. He loves us despite our mistakes, failures, and self-centered obsessions. Only this kind of unconditional love can transform our souls.

SOUL CONCERN IN HOSEA

ADULTERY (CH. 1)

1

The word of the LORD that came to Hosea the son of Beeri, in the days of Uzziah, Jotham, Ahaz, *and* Hezekiah, kings of Judah, and in the days of Jeroboam the son of Joash, king of Israel.

THE FAMILY OF HOSEA

2When the LORD began to speak by Hosea, the LORD said to Hosea:

"Go, take yourself a wife of harlotry
And children of harlotry,
For the land has committed great harlotry
By departing from the LORD."

3So he went and took Gomer the daughter of
Diblaim, and she conceived and bore him a
son. 4Then the LORD said to him:

"Call his name Jezreel,
For in a little *while*
I will avenge the bloodshed of Jezreel on the house of Jehu,
And bring an end to the kingdom of the house of Israel.
5 It shall come to pass in that day
That I will break the bow of Israel in the Valley of Jezreel."

6And she conceived again and bore a daughter. Then *God* said to him:

"Call her name Lo-Ruhamah,[a]
For I will no longer have mercy on the house of Israel,
But I will utterly take them away.[b]
7 Yet I will have mercy on the house of Judah,
Will save them by the LORD their God,
And will not save them by bow,
Nor by sword or battle,
By horses or horsemen."

8Now when she had weaned Lo-Ruhamah,
she conceived and bore a son. 9Then *God* said:

"Call his name Lo-Ammi,[a]
For you *are* not My people,
And I will not be your *God*.

THE RESTORATION OF ISRAEL

10 "Yet the number of the children of Israel
Shall be as the sand of the sea,
Which cannot be measured or numbered.
And it shall come to pass
In the place where it was said to them,
'You *are* not My people,'[a]
There it shall be said to them,
'*You are* sons of the living God.'
11 Then the children of Judah and the children of Israel
Shall be gathered together,
And appoint for themselves one head;
And they shall come up out of the land,
For great *will be* the day of Jezreel!

2

Say to your brethren, 'My people,'[a]
And to your sisters, 'Mercy[b] *is shown.*'

GOD'S UNFAITHFUL PEOPLE

2 "Bring charges against your mother, bring charges;
For she *is* not My wife, nor *am* I her Husband!

1:6 [a]Literally *No-Mercy* [b]Or *That I may forgive them at all* **1:9** [a]Literally *Not-My-People* **1:10** [a]Hebrew *lo-ammi* (compare verse 9) **2:1** [a]Hebrew *Ammi* (compare 1:9, 10) [b]Hebrew *Ruhamah* (compare 1:6)

SOUL NOTE

The Power of Love *(1:2)* This was a strange couple—the prophet Hosea and the harlot Gomer. One person pointed others to God; the other illustrated the depths of sin. Through this marriage, God painted a picture of His relationship with Israel. Hosea showered his wife Gomer with love despite her chasing other men. In the same way, God had unconditionally loved Israel despite their pursuing other gods. God loves His people so much that despite their sins, He constantly seeks to bring them to Himself: "God demonstrates His own love toward us, in that while we were still sinners, Christ died for us" (Rom. 5:8). **Topic: Knowing God**

Let her put away her harlotries from her sight,
And her adulteries from between her breasts;
3 Lest I strip her naked
And expose her, as in the day she was born,
And make her like a wilderness,
And set her like a dry land,
And slay her with thirst.

4 "I will not have mercy on her children,
For they *are* the children of harlotry.
5 For their mother has played the harlot;
She who conceived them has behaved shamefully.
For she said, 'I will go after my lovers,
Who give *me* my bread and my water,
My wool and my linen,
My oil and my drink.'

6 "Therefore, behold,
I will hedge up your way with thorns,
And wall her in,
So that she cannot find her paths.
7 She will chase her lovers,
But not overtake them;
Yes, she will seek them, but not find *them.*
Then she will say,
'I will go and return to my first husband,
For then *it was* better for me than now.'
8 For she did not know
That I gave her grain, new wine, and oil,
And multiplied her silver and gold—
Which they prepared for Baal.

9 "Therefore I will return and take away
My grain in its time
And My new wine in its season,

PERSONALITY PROFILE

Love

HOSEA: A LESSON IN LOVE

(HOSEA 1:2–9)

"And they lived happily ever after"—so ends the typical fairy tale. We enjoy stories with fairy tale endings, but in real life "happily ever after" can be an elusive dream.

Hosea's marriage was hardly a "happily ever after" story. God told Hosea, the prophet, to live his prophecies by taking "a wife of harlotry," Gomer (Hos. 1:2). Hosea obeyed, knowing that his heart would be broken through Gomer's unfaithfulness. Eventually, Gomer left Hosea. Next, as another living lesson, God told Hosea to pursue her and buy her back. Again Hosea obeyed and did so, for "fifteen shekels of silver" (Hos. 3.2)—a very cheap price. Hosea not only brought Gomer home, but he continued to love her.

Hosea did all this to illustrate God's incredible love for His people who had committed spiritual adultery by running after other "lovers"—false gods. Despite the people's unfaithfulness, God continued to love them and pursue them in order to bring them home to Him. As He told Hosea, "Go again, love a woman who is loved by a lover and is committing adultery, just like the love of the LORD for the children of Israel, who look to other gods" (Hos. 3:1). Hosea's actions illustrated true love, God's love.

Far beyond mere sexual titillation or tingling feelings of excitement, true love is bold, and it lasts through pain and difficulty. It involves commitment and never gives up. The apostle Paul wrote, "Love suffers long . . . does not seek its own, is not provoked, thinks no evil . . . bears all things, believes all things, hopes all things, endures all things. Love never fails" (1 Cor. 13:4–8). And that's how God loves us. Just as Hosea bought Gomer back and loved her, so God has bought us and loves us.

In the same way, our love must be committed, bold, and trustworthy. Otherwise, it is not really love at all.

To Learn More: Turn to the article about love on pages 1512, 1513. See also the key passage note at 1 Corinthians 13:1–7 on page 1509.

ADULTERY

DAVID M. CARDER

(Hosea 1)

People faced with adultery struggle with some of the most painful of human emotions: abandonment and betrayal, as well as anger and despair. Although adultery strikes at the heart of the marriage covenant, forgiveness and healing are possible, and broken marriages can be and are being restored.

RISING FREQUENCY

General estimates of human behavior suggest that as many as one man in two and one woman in four have had extramarital affairs. There have been several major changes in our culture which have impacted marital faithfulness. Many individuals did not have their own emotional needs met as they were growing up, and they approach marriage with painful emotional deficits that they subconsciously hope will be filled by their spouses. These individuals may enter marriage needing, and then demanding, more affection, attention, and affirmation than any one person can give.

In the changing work environment, men and women frequently work and minister in close contact with each other, which can lead to emotional and physical intimacy. Marriages are often stressed with the pressures of the careers of each spouse. Excessive and unrealistic work demands can cause burnout, anxiety, and depression for the individuals involved. And finally, an increasing number of Christians are falling victim to individuals with a history of sexual infidelities.

Other factors such as a family history of physical and sexual abuse, an early exposure to pornography, as well as a family history of alcoholism can contribute to marital infidelity. Certain marital styles seem to increase the risk for marital unfaithfulness. *Intimacy avoidant* is a marital pattern where the spouses pick on each other and criticize each other in order to keep emotional distance in the relationship. *Conflict avoidant* is a pattern, in which emotional distance is created because neither spouse wants to discuss marital disappointments and unhappiness. As a result, both spouses settle for a less than fulfilling marital relationship. Both marital styles fail to nurture the individual spouses and leave the partners vulnerable to looking outside the marriage for their emotional needs to be met.

Stressful circumstances like the death of a loved one or a serious accident or illness can also cause a marriage to be vulnerable to infidelity. Other stressors that can create vulnerability are family transitions, such as a pregnancy or the last child leaving home, and life changes such as relocation or a change in employment.

HEALING PROCESS

Healing is possible after infidelity. Increasing numbers of couples are braving the path of healing and restoration of their marriages. To begin the healing process, both spouses will need to understand what caused the infidelity in the marriage. This will require a long, thoughtful look at the marital pattern that has developed, as well as what each person has contributed to the marital breakdown. Difficult though it is, each spouse should focus on his or her own issues as opposed to criticizing and blaming the other person for the problem of infidelity.

Like rebuilding a wall brick by brick,

a couple can begin to rebuild trust in each other by telling each other the truth and by being accountable to each other. It is vital for each person to keep his or her word. If one spouse promises to do something, he or she needs to follow through and do it. Finally, trust can be rebuilt by using gestures of affection and nonsexual touch to express caring and affirmation.

Later in the healing process, both spouses will need to take time for restoring and enriching the marriage. The restoration process involves identifying and reestablishing what was good about the marriage before the adultery. The enriching process involves learning and implementing new skills and behaviors to strengthen the relationship.

HELPING FRIENDS

At some point, you may also need to support a friend going through recovery from adultery. First of all, two of the best gifts that you can give your friend are to pray and to listen. Resist the impulse to "fix" your friend's marriage or to prejudge whether or not your friend should get divorced. He or she must make that decision.

Don't take a role in your friend's relationship where you are the go-between. Encourage both people in the relationship to talk with each other. Don't work harder at making this marriage work than your friend is working at it. This is your friend's marriage and your friend needs to work at saving it.

Be aware that being close to someone who has experienced infidelity can "rattle" your own marriage. The other person's experience can make you painfully aware of issues you are failing to deal with in your own marriage. This can be a great opportunity to work on "affair proofing" your relationship by beginning to spend time, energy, and even money on it. Most of us marry because we want to be more connected to our spouse. We want to spend more time together, to give and receive more affection. The demands of daily living can often drain energy out of these responses. Here's a chance to renew them.

Most of all, pray daily for each other and for your relationship, and don't give up working on your own marriage.

CONCLUSION

Remember that if your spouse has been unfaithful, or if you are helping a friend who is struggling with infidelity, you are not alone. Many Christians have experienced restoration in their marriages after adultery has taken place. Although the process can often take a long time, healing and recovery are possible through the Holy Spirit's work in our lives, healing, supporting, and helping spouses forgive one another and rebuild their marriage on a solid biblical foundation.

FURTHER MEDITATION:

Other passages to study about the issue of adultery include:

- Exodus 20:14, 17
- Proverbs 6:32; 28:13
- Matthew 5:27–32; 19:3–10
- Romans 13:14
- 1 Corinthians 6:9–20

To Learn More: Turn to the key passage note on adultery at Proverbs 5:1–23 on page 806. See also the personality profile of the woman caught in adultery on page 1384.

And will take back My wool and My linen,
Given to cover her nakedness.
10 Now I will uncover her lewdness in the sight of her lovers,
And no one shall deliver her from My hand.
11 I will also cause all her mirth to cease,
Her feast days,
Her New Moons,
Her Sabbaths—
All her appointed feasts.

12 "And I will destroy her vines and her fig trees,
Of which she has said,
'These *are* my wages that my lovers have given me.'
So I will make them a forest,
And the beasts of the field shall eat them.
13 I will punish her
For the days of the Baals to which she burned incense.
She decked herself with her earrings and jewelry,
And went after her lovers;
But Me she forgot," says the LORD.

GOD'S MERCY ON HIS PEOPLE

14 "Therefore, behold, I will allure her,
Will bring her into the wilderness,
And speak comfort to her.
15 I will give her her vineyards from there,

PERSONALITY PROFILE

Addictions

GOMER: ADDICTED TO ADULTERY

(HOSEA 3)

Addictions are powerful enemies to our relationship with God. Whether the addiction is to alcohol, drugs, sex, gambling, web-surfing, shopping, or whatever, addicted people can attest to their seeming inability to control their desires.

Gomer had an addiction. As a "harlot," she sold sexual favors for money. The Bible is unclear whether she had been a prostitute before Hosea married her, or if God was telling Hosea that she would become adulterous. In either case, Hosea knew what he was getting in Gomer. She married Hosea, lived with him, and had children, but the children were not Hosea's, but "children of harlotry" (Hos. 1:2).

Despite Gomer's actions, Hosea loved her. She sought comfort not in his love, however, but in her addiction. She ran to others who made love but did not love her. They used her and left her alone and empty. Then Hosea bought her back.

The story illustrates the power of love, and the faithfulness of God toward His sinful people. It also tragically illustrates the results of an addiction. For Gomer, her sexual addiction pulled her away from her family and then left her alone and empty, needing to have Hosea pay a paltry amount of money to redeem her. No one else wanted her.

Addictions usually begin very subtly—an experience, substance, or individual that brings pleasure begins to become an obsession. Eventually, the obsession takes control. Rarely can a person escape the addiction without some form of intervention. Addicts must determine to change, replace the addictive substance with something more wholesome, and then finally find a way to meet their need differently.

Addictions destroy individuals, families, friendships, reputations, and careers. Addictions make people victims of their own desires. Despite all this, God offers hope to the addict. God wants to free His people from anything that takes His rightful place in their lives. He wants to show them that He can meet all their needs. With God's help and the compassionate accountability of other believers, addicts can be set free—bought back. Jesus has already paid the price.

To Learn More: Turn to the article about addictions on pages 1186, 1187. See also the key passage note at 1 Corinthians 6:9–12 on page 1498.

And the Valley of Achor as a door of hope;
She shall sing there,
As in the days of her youth,
As in the day when she came up from the land of Egypt.

16 "And it shall be, in that day,"
Says the LORD,
"*That* you will call Me 'My Husband,'[a]
And no longer call Me 'My Master,'[b]
17 For I will take from her mouth the names of the Baals,
And they shall be remembered by their name no more.
18 In that day I will make a covenant for them
With the beasts of the field,
With the birds of the air,
And *with* the creeping things of the ground.
Bow and sword of battle I will shatter from the earth,
To make them lie down safely.

19 "I will betroth you to Me forever;
Yes, I will betroth you to Me
In righteousness and justice,
In lovingkindness and mercy;
20 I will betroth you to Me in faithfulness,
And you shall know the LORD.

21 "It shall come to pass in that day
That I will answer," says the LORD;
"I will answer the heavens,
And they shall answer the earth.
22 The earth shall answer
With grain,
With new wine,
And with oil;
They shall answer Jezreel.[a]
23 Then I will sow her for Myself in the earth,
And I will have mercy on *her who had* not obtained mercy;[a]
Then I will say to *those who were* not My people,[b]
'You *are* My people!'
And they shall say, '*You are* my God!' "

Israel Will Return to God

3 Then the LORD said to me, "Go again, love
a woman *who is* loved by a lover[a] and is
committing adultery, just like the love of the
LORD for the children of Israel, who look to
other gods and love *the* raisin cakes *of the pa-*
gans."
2So I bought her for myself for fifteen *shek-*
els of silver, and one and one-half homers of
barley. 3And I said to her, "You shall stay with
me many days; you shall not play the harlot,
nor shall you have a man—so, too, *will* I *be*
toward you."
4For the children of Israel shall abide many
days without king or prince, without sacrifice
or *sacred* pillar, without ephod or teraphim.
5Afterward the children of Israel shall return
and seek the LORD their God and David their
king. They shall fear the LORD and His goodness in the latter days.

God's Charge Against Israel

4 Hear the word of the LORD,
You children of Israel,
For the LORD *brings* a charge against the inhabitants of the land:

2:16 [a]Hebrew *Ishi* [b]Hebrew *Baali* **2:22** [a]Literally *God Will Sow* **2:23** [a]Hebrew *lo-ruhamah* [b]Hebrew *lo-ammi* **3:1** [a]Literally *friend* or *husband*

SOUL NOTE

Extraordinary Love *(3:1–5)* When Gomer was committing adultery, God told Hosea to bring her back and love her. Hosea could have refused; he could have asked the authorities to put Gomer to death instead (Deut. 22:22). Or he simply could have tried to ignore the problem. In obedience to God, however, Hosea went to Gomer and used his own money to buy her back. Reaching out after being rejected, being faithful to the unfaithful, is difficult. Yet that is the kind of love God has shown us (Rom. 3:23–26; 5:1). God reaches out every day, calling us back to Him.
Topic: Marital Problems

"There is no truth or mercy
Or knowledge of God in the land.
2 *By* swearing and lying,
Killing and stealing and committing adultery,
They break all restraint,
With bloodshed upon bloodshed.
3 Therefore the land will mourn;
And everyone who dwells there will waste away
With the beasts of the field
And the birds of the air;
Even the fish of the sea will be taken away.

4 "Now let no man contend, or rebuke another;
For your people *are* like those who contend with the priest.
5 Therefore you shall stumble in the day;
The prophet also shall stumble with you in the night;
And I will destroy your mother.
6 My people are destroyed for lack of knowledge.
Because you have rejected knowledge,
I also will reject you from being priest for Me;
Because you have forgotten the law of your God,
I also will forget your children.

7 "The more they increased,
The more they sinned against Me;
I will change[a] their glory[b] into shame.
8 They eat up the sin of My people;
They set their heart on their iniquity.
9 And it shall be: like people, like priest.
So I will punish them for their ways,
And reward them for their deeds.
10 For they shall eat, but not have enough;
They shall commit harlotry, but not increase;
Because they have ceased obeying the LORD.

THE IDOLATRY OF ISRAEL

11 "Harlotry, wine, and new wine enslave the heart.
12 My people ask counsel from their wooden *idols,*
And their staff informs them.
For the spirit of harlotry has caused *them* to stray,
And they have played the harlot against their God.
13 They offer sacrifices on the mountaintops,
And burn incense on the hills,
Under oaks, poplars, and terebinths,
Because their shade *is* good.
Therefore your daughters commit harlotry,
And your brides commit adultery.

14 "I will not punish your daughters when they commit harlotry,
Nor your brides when they commit adultery;
For *the men* themselves go apart with harlots,
And offer sacrifices with a ritual harlot.[a]
Therefore people *who* do not understand will be trampled.

15 "Though you, Israel, play the harlot,
Let not Judah offend.
Do not come up to Gilgal,
Nor go up to Beth Aven,
Nor swear an oath, *saying,* 'As the LORD lives'—

16 "For Israel is stubborn
Like a stubborn calf;
Now the LORD will let them forage
Like a lamb in open country.

17 "Ephraim *is* joined to idols,
Let him alone.
18 Their drink is rebellion,
They commit harlotry continually.
Her rulers dearly love dishonor.[a]
19 The wind has wrapped her up in its wings,
And they shall be ashamed because of their sacrifices.

IMPENDING JUDGMENT ON ISRAEL AND JUDAH

5 "Hear this, O priests!
Take heed, O house of Israel!

4:7 [a]Following Masoretic Text, Septuagint, and Vulgate; scribal tradition, Syriac, and Targum read *They will change.* [b]Following Masoretic Text, Septuagint, Syriac, Targum, and Vulgate; scribal tradition reads *My glory.* **4:14** [a]Compare Deuteronomy 23:18 **4:18** [a]Hebrew is difficult; a Jewish tradition reads *Her rulers shamefully love, 'Give!'*

Give ear, O house of the king!
For yours *is* the judgment,
Because you have been a snare to Mizpah
And a net spread on Tabor.
2 The revolters are deeply involved in slaughter,
Though I rebuke them all.
3 I know Ephraim,
And Israel is not hidden from Me;
For now, O Ephraim, you commit harlotry;
Israel is defiled.

4 "They do not direct their deeds
Toward turning to their God,
For the spirit of harlotry is in their midst,
And they do not know the LORD.
5 The pride of Israel testifies to his face;
Therefore Israel and Ephraim stumble in their iniquity;
Judah also stumbles with them.

6 "With their flocks and herds
They shall go to seek the LORD,
But they will not find *Him;*
He has withdrawn Himself from them.
7 They have dealt treacherously with the LORD,
For they have begotten pagan children.
Now a New Moon shall devour them and their heritage.

8 "Blow the ram's horn in Gibeah,
The trumpet in Ramah!
Cry aloud *at* Beth Aven,
'*Look* behind you, O Benjamin!'
9 Ephraim shall be desolate in the day of rebuke;
Among the tribes of Israel I make known what is sure.

10 "The princes of Judah are like those who remove a landmark;
I will pour out My wrath on them like water.
11 Ephraim is oppressed *and* broken in judgment,
Because he willingly walked by *human* precept.
12 Therefore I *will be* to Ephraim like a moth,
And to the house of Judah like rottenness.

13 "When Ephraim saw his sickness,
And Judah *saw* his wound,
Then Ephraim went to Assyria
And sent to King Jareb;
Yet he cannot cure you,
Nor heal you of your wound.
14 For I *will be* like a lion to Ephraim,
And like a young lion to the house of Judah.
I, *even* I, will tear *them* and go away;
I will take *them* away, and no one shall rescue.
15 I will return again to My place
Till they acknowledge their offense.
Then they will seek My face;
In their affliction they will earnestly seek Me."

A Call to Repentance

6 Come, and let us return to the LORD;
For He has torn, but He will heal us;
He has stricken, but He will bind us up.
2 After two days He will revive us;
On the third day He will raise us up,
That we may live in His sight.
3 Let us know,
Let us pursue the knowledge of the LORD.

SOUL NOTE

Turning Point *(6:1–3)* In the middle of his prophecies of impending judgment, Hosea called out to the Israelites to repent: "Return to the LORD." With this warning, Hosea was, in effect, saying there was still hope. Despite God's punishment, God would restore those who turned back to Him. He would heal, bind up, and revive—if only they would "pursue the knowledge of the LORD." Sometimes we may feel that we have gone too far—that we have sinned too many times or too seriously to ever be forgiven. Hosea's call to the wicked Israelites demonstrates that if we return to God, He will forgive us. **Topic: Repentance**

His going forth is established as the morning;
He will come to us like the rain,
Like the latter *and* former rain to the earth.

IMPENITENCE OF ISRAEL AND JUDAH

4 "O Ephraim, what shall I do to you?
O Judah, what shall I do to you?
For your faithfulness is like a morning cloud,
And like the early dew it goes away.
5 Therefore I have hewn *them* by the prophets,
I have slain them by the words of My mouth;
And your judgments *are like* light *that* goes forth.
6 For I desire mercy and not sacrifice,
And the knowledge of God more than burnt offerings.

7 "But like men[a] they transgressed the covenant;
There they dealt treacherously with Me.
8 Gilead *is* a city of evildoers
And defiled with blood.
9 As bands of robbers lie in wait for a man,
So the company of priests murder on the way to Shechem;
Surely they commit lewdness.
10 I have seen a horrible thing in the house of Israel:
There *is* the harlotry of Ephraim;
Israel is defiled.
11 Also, O Judah, a harvest is appointed for you,
When I return the captives of My people.

7 "When I would have healed Israel,
Then the iniquity of Ephraim was uncovered,
And the wickedness of Samaria.
For they have committed fraud;
A thief comes in;
A band of robbers takes spoil outside.
2 They do not consider in their hearts
That I remember all their wickedness;
Now their own deeds have surrounded them;
They are before My face.
3 They make a king glad with their wickedness,
And princes with their lies.

4 "They *are* all adulterers.
Like an oven heated by a baker—
He ceases stirring *the fire* after kneading the dough,
Until it is leavened.
5 In the day of our king
Princes have made *him* sick, inflamed with wine;
He stretched out his hand with scoffers.
6 They prepare their heart like an oven,
While they lie in wait;
Their baker[a] sleeps all night;
In the morning it burns like a flaming fire.
7 They are all hot, like an oven,
And have devoured their judges;
All their kings have fallen.
None among them calls upon Me.

8 "Ephraim has mixed himself among the peoples;
Ephraim is a cake unturned.
9 Aliens have devoured his strength,
But he does not know *it;*
Yes, gray hairs are here and there on him,
Yet he does not know *it.*
10 And the pride of Israel testifies to his face,
But they do not return to the LORD their God,
Nor seek Him for all this.

FUTILE RELIANCE ON THE NATIONS

11 "Ephraim also is like a silly dove, without sense—
They call to Egypt,
They go to Assyria.
12 Wherever they go, I will spread My net on them;
I will bring them down like birds of the air;
I will chastise them
According to what their congregation has heard.

13 "Woe to them, for they have fled from Me!
Destruction to them,
Because they have transgressed against Me!

6:7 [a]Or *like Adam* **7:6** [a]Following Masoretic Text and Vulgate; Syriac and Targum read *Their anger;* Septuagint reads *Ephraim.*

Though I redeemed them,
Yet they have spoken lies against Me.
14 They did not cry out to Me with their heart
When they wailed upon their beds.

"They assemble together for[a] grain and new wine,
They rebel against Me;[b]
15 Though I disciplined *and* strengthened their arms,
Yet they devise evil against Me;
16 They return, *but* not to the Most High;[a]
They are like a treacherous bow.
Their princes shall fall by the sword
For the cursings of their tongue.
This *shall be* their derision in the land of Egypt.

THE APOSTASY OF ISRAEL

8 "*Set* the trumpet[a] to your mouth!
He shall come like an eagle against the house of the LORD,
Because they have transgressed My covenant
And rebelled against My law.
2 Israel will cry to Me,
'My God, we know You!'
3 Israel has rejected the good;
The enemy will pursue him.

4 "They set up kings, but not by Me;
They made princes, but I did not acknowledge *them.*
From their silver and gold
They made idols for themselves—
That they might be cut off.
5 Your calf is rejected, O Samaria!
My anger is aroused against them—
How long until they attain to innocence?
6 For from Israel *is* even this:
A workman made it, and it *is* not God;
But the calf of Samaria shall be broken to pieces.

7 "They sow the wind,
And reap the whirlwind.
The stalk has no bud;
It shall never produce meal.
If it should produce,
Aliens would swallow it up.
8 Israel is swallowed up;
Now they are among the Gentiles
Like a vessel in which *is* no pleasure.
9 For they have gone up to Assyria,
Like a wild donkey alone by itself;
Ephraim has hired lovers.
10 Yes, though they have hired among the nations,
Now I will gather them;
And they shall sorrow a little,[a]
Because of the burden[b] of the king of princes.

11 "Because Ephraim has made many altars for sin,
They have become for him altars for sinning.
12 I have written for him the great things of My law,
But they were considered a strange thing.
13 *For* the sacrifices of My offerings they sacrifice flesh and eat *it,*
But the LORD does not accept them.
Now He will remember their iniquity and punish their sins.
They shall return to Egypt.

14 "For Israel has forgotten his Maker,
And has built temples;[a]
Judah also has multiplied fortified cities;
But I will send fire upon his cities,
And it shall devour his palaces."

JUDGMENT OF ISRAEL'S SIN

9 Do not rejoice, O Israel, with joy like *other* peoples,
For you have played the harlot against your God.
You have made love *for* hire on every threshing floor.
2 The threshing floor and the winepress
Shall not feed them,
And the new wine shall fail in her.

3 They shall not dwell in the LORD's land,
But Ephraim shall return to Egypt,
And shall eat unclean *things* in Assyria.

7:14 [a]Following Masoretic Text and Targum; Vulgate reads *thought upon;* Septuagint reads *slashed themselves for* (compare 1 Kings 18:28). [b]Following Masoretic Text, Syriac, and Targum; Septuagint omits *They rebel against Me;* Vulgate reads *They departed from Me.* **7:16** [a]Or *upward* **8:1** [a]Hebrew *shophar,* ram's horn **8:10** [a]Or *begin to diminish* [b]Or *oracle* **8:14** [a]Or *palaces*

4 They shall not offer wine *offerings* to the
LORD,
Nor shall their sacrifices be pleasing to
Him.
It shall be like bread of mourners to
them;
All who eat it shall be defiled.
For their bread *shall be* for their *own*
life;
It shall not come into the house of the
LORD.

5 What will you do in the appointed day,
And in the day of the feast of the LORD?
6 For indeed they are gone because of
destruction.
Egypt shall gather them up;
Memphis shall bury them.
Nettles shall possess their valuables of
silver;
Thorns *shall be* in their tents.

7 The days of punishment have come;
The days of recompense have come.
Israel knows!
The prophet *is* a fool,
The spiritual man *is* insane,
Because of the greatness of your iniquity
and great enmity.
8 The watchman of Ephraim *is* with my
God;
But the prophet *is* a fowler's[a] snare in all
his ways—
Enmity in the house of his God.
9 They are deeply corrupted,
As in the days of Gibeah.
He will remember their iniquity;
He will punish their sins.

10 "I found Israel
Like grapes in the wilderness;
I saw your fathers
As the firstfruits on the fig tree in its first
season.
But they went to Baal Peor,
And separated themselves *to that* shame;
They became an abomination like the
thing they loved.
11 *As for* Ephraim, their glory shall fly
away like a bird—
No birth, no pregnancy, and no
conception!
12 Though they bring up their children,
Yet I will bereave them to the last man.
Yes, woe to them when I depart from
them!
13 Just as I saw Ephraim like Tyre, planted
in a pleasant place,
So Ephraim will bring out his children to
the murderer."

14 Give them, O LORD—
What will You give?
Give them a miscarrying womb
And dry breasts!

15 "All their wickedness *is* in Gilgal,
For there I hated them.
Because of the evil of their deeds
I will drive them from My house;
I will love them no more.
All their princes *are* rebellious.
16 Ephraim is stricken,
Their root is dried up;
They shall bear no fruit.
Yes, were they to bear children,
I would kill the darlings of their
womb."

17 My God will cast them away,
Because they did not obey Him;
And they shall be wanderers among the
nations.

ISRAEL'S SIN AND CAPTIVITY

10 Israel empties *his* vine;
He brings forth fruit for himself.
According to the multitude of his fruit
He has increased the altars;
According to the bounty of his land
They have embellished *his sacred* pillars.
2 Their heart is divided;
Now they are held guilty.
He will break down their altars;
He will ruin their *sacred* pillars.

3 For now they say,
"We have no king,
Because we did not fear the LORD.
And as for a king, what would he do for
us?"
4 They have spoken words,
Swearing falsely in making a covenant.
Thus judgment springs up like hemlock
in the furrows of the field.

9:8 [a]That is, one who catches birds in a trap or snare

5 The inhabitants of Samaria fear
Because of the calf[a] of Beth Aven.
For its people mourn for it,
And its priests shriek for it—
Because its glory has departed from it.
6 *The idol* also shall be carried to Assyria
As a present for King Jareb.
Ephraim shall receive shame,
And Israel shall be ashamed of his own counsel.

7 *As for* Samaria, her king is cut off
Like a twig on the water.
8 Also the high places of Aven, the sin of Israel,
Shall be destroyed.
The thorn and thistle shall grow on their altars;
They shall say to the mountains, "Cover us!"
And to the hills, "Fall on us!"

9 "O Israel, you have sinned from the days of Gibeah;
There they stood.
The battle in Gibeah against the children of iniquity[a]
Did not overtake them.
10 When *it is* My desire, I will chasten them.
Peoples shall be gathered against them
When I bind them for their two transgressions.[a]
11 Ephraim *is* a trained heifer
That loves to thresh *grain;*
But I harnessed her fair neck,
I will make Ephraim pull *a plow.*
Judah shall plow;
Jacob shall break his clods."

12 Sow for yourselves righteousness;
Reap in mercy;
Break up your fallow ground,
For *it is* time to seek the LORD,
Till He comes and rains righteousness on you.

13 You have plowed wickedness;
You have reaped iniquity.
You have eaten the fruit of lies,
Because you trusted in your own way,
In the multitude of your mighty men.
14 Therefore tumult shall arise among your people,
And all your fortresses shall be plundered
As Shalman plundered Beth Arbel in the day of battle—
A mother dashed in pieces upon *her* children.
15 Thus it shall be done to you, O Bethel,
Because of your great wickedness.
At dawn the king of Israel
Shall be cut off utterly.

Sow for yourselves righteousness; reap in mercy; break up your fallow ground, for it is time to seek the LORD, till He comes and rains righteousness on you.
HOSEA 10:12

God's Continuing Love for Israel

11 "When Israel *was* a child, I loved him,
And out of Egypt I called My son.
2 *As* they called them,[a]
So they went from them;[b]
They sacrificed to the Baals,
And burned incense to carved images.

3 "I taught Ephraim to walk,
Taking them by their arms;[a]
But they did not know that I healed them.
4 I drew them with gentle cords,[a]
With bands of love,
And I was to them as those who take the yoke from their neck.[b]
I stooped *and* fed them.

5 "He shall not return to the land of Egypt;
But the Assyrian shall be his king,

10:5 [a]Literally *calves* **10:9** [a]So read many Hebrew manuscripts, Septuagint, and Vulgate; Masoretic Text reads *unruliness.* **10:10** [a]Or *in their two habitations* **11:2** [a]Following Masoretic Text and Vulgate; Septuagint reads *Just as I called them;* Targum interprets as *I sent prophets to a thousand of them.* [b]Following Masoretic Text, Targum, and Vulgate; Septuagint reads *from My face.*
11:3 [a]Some Hebrew manuscripts, Septuagint, Syriac, and Vulgate read *My arms.* **11:4** [a]Literally *cords of a man* [b]Literally *jaws*

Because they refused to repent.
6 And the sword shall slash in his cities,
Devour his districts,
And consume *them*,
Because of their own counsels.
7 My people are bent on backsliding from Me.
Though they call to the Most High,[a]
None at all exalt *Him*.

8 "How can I give you up, Ephraim?
How can I hand you over, Israel?
How can I make you like Admah?
How can I set you like Zeboiim?
My heart churns within Me;
My sympathy is stirred.
9 I will not execute the fierceness of My anger;
I will not again destroy Ephraim.
For I *am* God, and not man,
The Holy One in your midst;
And I will not come with terror.[a]

10 "They shall walk after the LORD.
He will roar like a lion.
When He roars,
Then *His* sons shall come trembling from the west;
11 They shall come trembling like a bird from Egypt,
Like a dove from the land of Assyria.
And I will let them dwell in their houses,"
Says the LORD.

GOD'S CHARGE AGAINST EPHRAIM

12 "Ephraim has encircled Me with lies,
And the house of Israel with deceit;
But Judah still walks with God,
Even with the Holy One[a] *who is* faithful.

12 "Ephraim feeds on the wind,
And pursues the east wind;
He daily increases lies and desolation.
Also they make a covenant with the Assyrians,
And oil is carried to Egypt.

2 "The LORD also *brings* a charge against Judah,
And will punish Jacob according to his ways;
According to his deeds He will recompense him.
3 He took his brother by the heel in the womb,
And in his strength he struggled with God.[a]
4 Yes, he struggled with the Angel and prevailed;
He wept, and sought favor from Him.
He found Him *in* Bethel,
And there He spoke to us—
5 That is, the LORD God of hosts.
The LORD *is* His memorable name.
6 So you, by *the help of* your God, return;
Observe mercy and justice,
And wait on your God continually.

7 "A cunning Canaanite!
Deceitful scales *are* in his hand;
He loves to oppress.
8 And Ephraim said,
'Surely I have become rich,
I have found wealth for myself;
In all my labors
They shall find in me no iniquity that *is* sin.'

9 "But I *am* the LORD your God,
Ever since the land of Egypt;
I will again make you dwell in tents,
As in the days of the appointed feast.
10 I have also spoken by the prophets,
And have multiplied visions;
I have given symbols through the witness of the prophets."

11 Though Gilead *has* idols—
Surely they are vanity—
Though they sacrifice bulls in Gilgal,
Indeed their altars *shall be* heaps in the furrows of the field.
12 Jacob fled to the country of Syria;
Israel served for a spouse,
And for a wife he tended *sheep*.
13 By a prophet the LORD brought Israel out of Egypt,
And by a prophet he was preserved.
14 Ephraim provoked *Him* to anger most bitterly;

11:7 [a]Or *upward* **11:9** [a]Or *I will not enter a city* **11:12** [a]Or *holy ones* **12:3** [a]Compare Genesis 32:28

Therefore his Lord will leave the guilt of
his bloodshed upon him,
And return his reproach upon him.

Relentless Judgment on Israel

13 When Ephraim spoke, trembling,
He exalted *himself* in Israel;
But when he offended through Baal
worship, he died.
2 Now they sin more and more,
And have made for themselves molded
images,
Idols of their silver, according to their
skill;
All of it *is* the work of craftsmen.
They say of them,
"Let the men who sacrifice[a] kiss the
calves!"
3 Therefore they shall be like the morning
cloud
And like the early dew that passes away,
Like chaff blown off from a threshing
floor
And like smoke from a chimney.

4 "Yet I *am* the LORD your God
Ever since the land of Egypt,
And you shall know no God but Me;
For *there is* no savior besides Me.
5 I knew you in the wilderness,
In the land of great drought.
6 When they had pasture, they were
filled;
They were filled and their heart was
exalted;
Therefore they forgot Me.

7 "So I will be to them like a lion;
Like a leopard by the road I will lurk;
8 I will meet them like a bear deprived *of
her cubs;*
I will tear open their rib cage,
And there I will devour them like a lion.
The wild beast shall tear them.

9 "O Israel, you are destroyed,[a]
But your help[b] *is* from Me.
10 I will be your King;[a]
Where *is any other,*
That he may save you in all your cities?
And your judges to whom you said,
'Give me a king and princes'?
11 I gave you a king in My anger,
And took *him* away in My wrath.

12 "The iniquity of Ephraim *is* bound up;
His sin *is* stored up.
13 The sorrows of a woman in childbirth
shall come upon him.
He *is* an unwise son,
For he should not stay long where
children are born.

14 "I will ransom them from the power of
the grave;[a]
I will redeem them from death.
O Death, I will be your plagues![b]
O Grave,[c] I will be your destruction![d]
Pity is hidden from My eyes."

15 Though he is fruitful among *his*
brethren,
An east wind shall come;
The wind of the LORD shall come up
from the wilderness.
Then his spring shall become dry,
And his fountain shall be dried up.
He shall plunder the treasury of every
desirable prize.
16 Samaria is held guilty,[a]
For she has rebelled against her God.
They shall fall by the sword,
Their infants shall be dashed in pieces,
And their women with child ripped
open.

Israel Restored at Last

14 O Israel, return to the LORD your
God,
For you have stumbled because of your
iniquity;
2 Take words with you,
And return to the LORD.
Say to Him,
"Take away all iniquity;
Receive *us* graciously,
For we will offer the sacrifices[a] of our
lips.
3 Assyria shall not save us,
We will not ride on horses,

13:2 [a]Or *those who offer human sacrifice* **13:9** [a]Literally *it* or *he destroyed you* [b]Literally *in your help* **13:10** [a]Septuagint, Syriac, Targum, and Vulgate read *Where is your king?* **13:14** [a]Or *Sheol* [b]Septuagint reads *where is your punishment?* [c]Or *Sheol* [d]Septuagint reads *where is your sting?* **13:16** [a]Septuagint reads *shall be disfigured* **14:2** [a]Literally *bull calves;* Septuagint reads *fruit.*

Nor will we say anymore to the work of
our hands, '*You are* our gods.'
For in You the fatherless finds mercy."

4 "I will heal their backsliding,
I will love them freely,
For My anger has turned away from
him.
5 I will be like the dew to Israel;
He shall grow like the lily,
And lengthen his roots like Lebanon.
6 His branches shall spread;
His beauty shall be like an olive tree,
And his fragrance like Lebanon.
7 Those who dwell under his shadow shall
return;
They shall be revived *like* grain,
And grow like a vine.
Their scent[a] *shall be* like the wine of
Lebanon.

8 "Ephraim *shall say,* 'What have I to do
anymore with idols?'
I have heard and observed him.
I *am* like a green cypress tree;
Your fruit is found in Me."

9 Who *is* wise?
Let him understand these things.
Who is prudent?
Let him know them.
For the ways of the LORD *are* right;
The righteous walk in them,
But transgressors stumble in them.

14:7 [a]Literally *remembrance*

SOUL NOTE

The Beauty of Forgiveness *(14:4–8)* The beauty of a lily, the sweet smell of cedars, the strength of an olive tree—God used these images to describe the results of His gracious love. Although Israel had rejected Him, God promised to restore their strength, vitality, and beauty. His love would be like sweet, refreshing dew to them. The Israelites' own sins had destroyed them, but God would rebuild them. This pictures God's forgiveness. He doesn't merely erase our sins; He restores and recreates our broken lives: "Old things have passed away; behold, all things have become new" (2 Cor. 5:17). **Topic: Forgiveness**

Joel

Everyone looks forward to special days—birthdays, anniversaries, holidays. But these seem like nothing compared to a very special day that all believers anticipate—Joel calls it "the day of the LORD."

This book was written by the prophet Joel, who may also have been a priest. In this prophecy, he speaks of the recent disasters of a devastating locust plague and a drought (around 800 B.C.) to warn Israel of an even greater judgment to come. He speaks at length of a future "day of the LORD" during which God will vindicate His righteousness by holding Israel and the nations accountable for their long history of rebellion. Joel calls that day "great and very terrible" (2:11).

Even in the midst of this grim prophecy, there are frequent glimmers of hope. That terrible day of the Lord need not be terrible for God's people. Joel goes on, saying that the "day of the LORD is near in the valley of decision," and in that day "the LORD will be a shelter for His people" (3:14, 16). God promised to restore Judah and bring about a time of unparalleled material and spiritual blessing (2:18–32; 3:18–21). "So you shall know that I am the LORD your God, dwelling in Zion My holy mountain. Then Jerusalem shall be holy" (3:17).

God always wants to bring us to a deep repentance that will lead to the renewal and restoration of our souls. A day of the Lord is still to come when He returns for His people. If we belong to Christ, we can look forward to that day of the Lord with great anticipation.

1 The word of the LORD that came to Joel the son of Pethuel.

THE LAND LAID WASTE

2 Hear this, you elders,
And give ear, all you inhabitants of the land!
Has *anything like* this happened in your days,
Or even in the days of your fathers?
3 Tell your children about it,
Let your children *tell* their children,
And their children another generation.

4 What the chewing locust[a] left, the swarming locust has eaten;
What the swarming locust left, the crawling locust has eaten;
And what the crawling locust left, the consuming locust has eaten.

5 Awake, you drunkards, and weep;
And wail, all you drinkers of wine,
Because of the new wine,
For it has been cut off from your mouth.
6 For a nation has come up against My land,
Strong, and without number;
His teeth *are* the teeth of a lion,
And he has the fangs of a fierce lion.
7 He has laid waste My vine,
And ruined My fig tree;
He has stripped it bare and thrown *it* away;
Its branches are made white.

8 Lament like a virgin girded with sackcloth
For the husband of her youth.
9 The grain offering and the drink offering
Have been cut off from the house of the LORD;
The priests mourn, who minister to the LORD.
10 The field is wasted,
The land mourns;
For the grain is ruined,
The new wine is dried up,
The oil fails.

11 Be ashamed, you farmers,
Wail, you vinedressers,
For the wheat and the barley;
Because the harvest of the field has perished.
12 The vine has dried up,
And the fig tree has withered;
The pomegranate tree,
The palm tree also,
And the apple tree—
All the trees of the field are withered;
Surely joy has withered away from the sons of men.

MOURNING FOR THE LAND

13 Gird yourselves and lament, you priests;
Wail, you who minister before the altar;
Come, lie all night in sackcloth,
You who minister to my God;
For the grain offering and the drink offering
Are withheld from the house of your God.
14 Consecrate a fast,
Call a sacred assembly;
Gather the elders
And all the inhabitants of the land
Into the house of the LORD your God,
And cry out to the LORD.

15 Alas for the day!
For the day of the LORD *is* at hand;

1:4 [a]Exact identity of these locusts is unknown.

SOUL NOTE

Teach Them Well *(1:3)* The Bible tells parents to teach their children about sin and about salvation in God (1:3; Ex. 10:2; Deut. 4:9; Ps. 22:30, 31). Joel exhorted the Israelites to remind their children of the locusts that God had sent on their land, so the children would learn the lesson God was teaching Israel. Even when it's difficult, parents should tell their children the truth about sin and what God has done for them. This will give children the opportunity to learn from their parents' mistakes.
Topic: Parenting

It shall come as destruction from the Almighty.
16 Is not the food cut off before our eyes,
Joy and gladness from the house of our God?
17 The seed shrivels under the clods,
Storehouses are in shambles;
Barns are broken down,
For the grain has withered.
18 How the animals groan!
The herds of cattle are restless,
Because they have no pasture;
Even the flocks of sheep suffer punishment.[a]

19 O LORD, to You I cry out;
For fire has devoured the open pastures,
And a flame has burned all the trees of the field.
20 The beasts of the field also cry out to You,
For the water brooks are dried up,
And fire has devoured the open pastures.

THE DAY OF THE LORD

2 Blow the trumpet in Zion,
And sound an alarm in My holy mountain!
Let all the inhabitants of the land tremble;
For the day of the LORD is coming,
For it is at hand:
2 A day of darkness and gloominess,
A day of clouds and thick darkness,
Like the morning *clouds* spread over the mountains.
A people *come,* great and strong,
The like of whom has never been;
Nor will there ever be any *such* after them,
Even for many successive generations.

3 A fire devours before them,
And behind them a flame burns;
The land *is* like the Garden of Eden before them,
And behind them a desolate wilderness;
Surely nothing shall escape them.
4 Their appearance is like the appearance of horses;
And like swift steeds, so they run.
5 With a noise like chariots
Over mountaintops they leap,
Like the noise of a flaming fire that devours the stubble,
Like a strong people set in battle array.

6 Before them the people writhe in pain;
All faces are drained of color.[a]
7 They run like mighty men,
They climb the wall like men of war;
Every one marches in formation,
And they do not break ranks.
8 They do not push one another;
Every one marches in his own column.[a]
Though they lunge between the weapons,
They are not cut down.[b]
9 They run to and fro in the city,
They run on the wall;
They climb into the houses,
They enter at the windows like a thief.

10 The earth quakes before them,
The heavens tremble;
The sun and moon grow dark,
And the stars diminish their brightness.
11 The LORD gives voice before His army,
For His camp is very great;

1:18 [a]Septuagint and Vulgate read *are made desolate.* **2:6** [a]Septuagint, Targum, and Vulgate read *gather blackness.* **2:8** [a]Literally *his own highway* [b]That is, they are not halted by losses

SOUL NOTE

Wake-Up Call *(1:15–20)* The prophet Joel lived during a time of prosperity in Judah. The more wealthy and prosperous the people became, however, the more complacent they became toward God until they had forgotten Him completely. So God sent locusts to devour the land. Joel declared that this plague was a wake-up call. We dare not forget the source of our prosperity. God owns everything, and we are responsible to Him for how we use His resources. **Topic: Money**

For strong *is the One* who executes His
word.
For the day of the LORD *is* great and very
terrible;
Who can endure it?

A Call to Repentance

12 "Now, therefore," says the LORD,
"Turn to Me with all your heart,
With fasting, with weeping, and with
mourning."
13 So rend your heart, and not your
garments;
Return to the LORD your God,
For He *is* gracious and merciful,
Slow to anger, and of great kindness;
And He relents from doing harm.
14 Who knows *if* He will turn and relent,
And leave a blessing behind Him—
A grain offering and a drink offering
For the LORD your God?

15 Blow the trumpet in Zion,
Consecrate a fast,
Call a sacred assembly;
16 Gather the people,
Sanctify the congregation,
Assemble the elders,
Gather the children and nursing babes;
Let the bridegroom go out from his
chamber,
And the bride from her dressing room.
17 Let the priests, who minister to the
LORD,
Weep between the porch and the altar;
Let them say, "Spare Your people,
O LORD,
And do not give Your heritage to
reproach,
That the nations should rule over them.
Why should they say among the peoples,
'Where *is* their God?' "

The Land Refreshed

18 Then the LORD will be zealous for His
land,
And pity His people.
19 The LORD will answer and say to His
people,
"Behold, I will send you grain and new
wine and oil,
And you will be satisfied by them;
I will no longer make you a reproach
among the nations.

20 "But I will remove far from you the
northern *army,*
And will drive him away into a barren
and desolate land,
With his face toward the eastern sea
And his back toward the western sea;
His stench will come up,
And his foul odor will rise,
Because he has done monstrous things."

21 Fear not, O land;
Be glad and rejoice,
For the LORD has done marvelous
things!
22 Do not be afraid, you beasts of the field;
For the open pastures are springing up,
And the tree bears its fruit;
The fig tree and the vine yield their
strength.
23 Be glad then, you children of Zion,
And rejoice in the LORD your God;
For He has given you the former rain
faithfully,[a]
And He will cause the rain to come
down for you—
The former rain,
And the latter rain in the first *month.*

2:23 [a]Or *the teacher of righteousness*

SOUL NOTE

The Invitation *(2:12, 13)* In the middle of this book filled with warnings and judgment stands a profound picture of God's mercy. Over the clamor of invading armies and devouring locusts, God issues a clear invitation: "Turn to Me with all your heart." In the midst of judgment, God offers mercy to those who repent. "He is gracious and merciful, slow to anger, and of great kindness." Regardless of the circumstances, God says, "Turn to Me." When we call out to our gracious and merciful God, He hears and answers. **Topic: Repentance**

24 The threshing floors shall be full of
wheat,
And the vats shall overflow with new
wine and oil.

25 "So I will restore to you the years that the
swarming locust has eaten,
The crawling locust,
The consuming locust,
And the chewing locust,[a]
My great army which I sent among you.
26 You shall eat in plenty and be satisfied,
And praise the name of the LORD your
God,
Who has dealt wondrously with you;
And My people shall never be put to
shame.
27 Then you shall know that I *am* in the
midst of Israel:
I *am* the LORD your God
And there is no other.
My people shall never be put to shame.

God's Spirit Poured Out

28 "And it shall come to pass afterward
That I will pour out My Spirit on all flesh;
Your sons and your daughters shall
prophesy,
Your old men shall dream dreams,
Your young men shall see visions.
29 And also on *My* menservants and on *My*
maidservants
I will pour out My Spirit in those days.

30 "And I will show wonders in the heavens
and in the earth:
Blood and fire and pillars of smoke.
31 The sun shall be turned into darkness,
And the moon into blood,
Before the coming of the great and
awesome day of the LORD.
32 And it shall come to pass
That whoever calls on the name of the
LORD
Shall be saved.
For in Mount Zion and in Jerusalem
there shall be deliverance,
As the LORD has said,
Among the remnant whom the LORD
calls.

God Judges the Nations

3 "For behold, in those days and at that
time,
When I bring back the captives of Judah
and Jerusalem,

2:25 [a]Compare 1:4

SOUL NOTE

Marvelous *(2:19–27)* God delights in doing miracles. He loves turning hopeless situations into delightful possibilities. Joel warned his people that a terrible army would invade their land and destroy their hope. Even the very heavens and earth would tremble at the devastation (2:10). In the face of such disaster, however, Joel spoke of a day when God would do "marvelous things" (2:21). God's works are truly marvelous. In response, we should "praise the name of the LORD" (2:26). **Topic: Joy**

SOUL NOTE

Outpouring *(2:28–32)* Joel predicted that God's grand invitation to turn to Him (2:12) would be extended to all people: "Whoever calls on the name of the LORD shall be saved." Christians are the beneficiaries of God's outpouring. The world hasn't been the same since the day a small band of apostles were energized by God's Spirit on the Day of Pentecost. On that day, Peter quoted this passage from Joel and encouraged people to repent and believe in Christ (Acts 2:16–21, 38). All who have accepted this call and received God's Spirit fulfill this prophecy of God's grace.
Topic: Presence of the Holy Spirit

2 I will also gather all nations,
And bring them down to the Valley of Jehoshaphat;
And I will enter into judgment with them there
On account of My people, My heritage Israel,
Whom they have scattered among the nations;
They have also divided up My land.
3 They have cast lots for My people,
Have given a boy *as payment* for a harlot,
And sold a girl for wine, that they may drink.

4 "Indeed, what have you to do with Me,
O Tyre and Sidon, and all the coasts of Philistia?
Will you retaliate against Me?
But if you retaliate against Me,
Swiftly and speedily I will return your retaliation upon your own head;
5 Because you have taken My silver and My gold,
And have carried into your temples My prized possessions.
6 Also the people of Judah and the people of Jerusalem
You have sold to the Greeks,
That you may remove them far from their borders.

7 "Behold, I will raise them
Out of the place to which you have sold them,
And will return your retaliation upon your own head.
8 I will sell your sons and your daughters
Into the hand of the people of Judah,
And they will sell them to the Sabeans,[a]
To a people far off;
For the LORD has spoken."

9 Proclaim this among the nations:
"Prepare for war!
Wake up the mighty men,
Let all the men of war draw near,
Let them come up.
10 Beat your plowshares into swords
And your pruning hooks into spears;
Let the weak say, 'I *am* strong.' "
11 Assemble and come, all you nations,
And gather together all around.
Cause Your mighty ones to go down there, O LORD.

12 "Let the nations be wakened, and come up to the Valley of Jehoshaphat;
For there I will sit to judge all the surrounding nations.
13 Put in the sickle, for the harvest is ripe.
Come, go down;
For the winepress is full,
The vats overflow—
For their wickedness *is* great."

14 Multitudes, multitudes in the valley of decision!
For the day of the LORD *is* near in the valley of decision.
15 The sun and moon will grow dark,
And the stars will diminish their brightness.
16 The LORD also will roar from Zion,
And utter His voice from Jerusalem;
The heavens and earth will shake;
But the LORD will be a shelter for His people,
And the strength of the children of Israel.

17 "So you shall know that I *am* the LORD your God,
Dwelling in Zion My holy mountain.
Then Jerusalem shall be holy,
And no aliens shall ever pass through her again."

Multitudes, multitudes in the valley of decision! For the day of the LORD is near in the valley of decision.
JOEL 3:14

GOD BLESSES HIS PEOPLE

18 And it will come to pass in that day
That the mountains shall drip with new wine,
The hills shall flow with milk,
And all the brooks of Judah shall be flooded with water;

3:8 [a]Literally *Shebaites* (compare Isaiah 60:6 and Ezekiel 27:22)

A fountain shall flow from the house of
the LORD
And water the Valley of Acacias.

19 "Egypt shall be a desolation,
And Edom a desolate wilderness,
Because of violence *against* the people
of Judah,
For they have shed innocent blood in
their land.
20 But Judah shall abide forever,
And Jerusalem from generation to
generation.
21 For I will acquit them of the guilt of
bloodshed, whom I had not acquitted;
For the LORD dwells in Zion."

Amos

The lure of millions of dollars draws many to spend their hard-earned money on lottery tickets. Just match a few numbers and be set for life! Many think that with so much money, they will be able to help others. Sadly, money has an uncanny ability to corrupt, to intensify greed, and to skew perspective. That hasn't changed for thousands of years. Around 760 B.C., the nation of Israel was enjoying great wealth. Unfortunately, they were also on the verge of spiritual bankruptcy.

Enter Amos—a shepherd and fig-picker abruptly called by God to deliver a series of blunt warnings to his wayward kinsmen. Amos lived near Jerusalem in Judah, but his prophecy focused on Samaria, the capital of Israel. Name a sin and the populace was guilty of it: hypocrisy, callousness, arrogance, gross idolatry, empty ritualism, injustice, immorality, self-righteousness, materialism, corruption, and greed. Worst of all was the people's shocking sense of indifference toward God.

The stern message of Amos was similar to that of most of the prophets: Turn from your sin while you still have a chance. God is slow to anger and willing to forgive, but continued sin will eventually unleash His judgment. (Tragically, the warning went unheeded.)

The Book of Amos contains a dire warning for us about materialism and greed. There's no question that wealth can be a tremendous blessing, and a resource for blessing others. Unfortunately, wealth can also poison our souls by blinding us to the deepest realities of life—the truths of God. Amos reminds us that wealth or no wealth, spiritual neglect will result in devastation and loss.

1 The words of Amos, who was among the
sheepbreeders[a] of Tekoa, which he saw
concerning Israel in the days of Uzziah king of
Judah, and in the days of Jeroboam the son of
Joash, king of Israel, two years before the
earthquake.
2And he said:

"The LORD roars from Zion,
And utters His voice from Jerusalem;
The pastures of the shepherds mourn,
And the top of Carmel withers."

JUDGMENT ON THE NATIONS

3Thus says the LORD:

"For three transgressions of Damascus,
and for four,
I will not turn away its *punishment*,
Because they have threshed Gilead with
implements of iron.
4 But I will send a fire into the house of
Hazael,
Which shall devour the palaces of Ben-
Hadad.
5 I will also break the *gate* bar of
Damascus,
And cut off the inhabitant from the
Valley of Aven,
And the one who holds the scepter from
Beth Eden.
The people of Syria shall go captive to
Kir,"
Says the LORD.

6Thus says the LORD:

"For three transgressions of Gaza, and for
four,
I will not turn away its *punishment*,
Because they took captive the whole
captivity
To deliver *them* up to Edom.
7 But I will send a fire upon the wall of
Gaza,
Which shall devour its palaces.
8 I will cut off the inhabitant from
Ashdod,
And the one who holds the scepter from
Ashkelon;
I will turn My hand against Ekron,
And the remnant of the Philistines shall
perish,"
Says the Lord GOD.

9Thus says the LORD:

"For three transgressions of Tyre, and for
four,
I will not turn away its *punishment*,
Because they delivered up the whole
captivity to Edom,
And did not remember the covenant of
brotherhood.
10 But I will send a fire upon the wall of
Tyre,
Which shall devour its palaces."

11Thus says the LORD:

"For three transgressions of Edom, and
for four,
I will not turn away its *punishment*,
Because he pursued his brother with the
sword,
And cast off all pity;
His anger tore perpetually,
And he kept his wrath forever.
12 But I will send a fire upon Teman,
Which shall devour the palaces of
Bozrah."

13Thus says the LORD:

"For three transgressions of the people of
Ammon, and for four,
I will not turn away its *punishment*,
Because they ripped open the women
with child in Gilead,
That they might enlarge their territory.
14 But I will kindle a fire in the wall of
Rabbah,
And it shall devour its palaces,
Amid shouting in the day of battle,
And a tempest in the day of the
whirlwind.
15 Their king shall go into captivity,
He and his princes together,"
Says the LORD.

2 Thus says the LORD:

"For three transgressions of Moab, and
for four,
I will not turn away its *punishment*,
Because he burned the bones of the king
of Edom to lime.

1:1 [a]Compare 2 Kings 3:4

2 But I will send a fire upon Moab,
And it shall devour the palaces of Kerioth;
Moab shall die with tumult,
With shouting *and* trumpet sound.
3 And I will cut off the judge from its midst,
And slay all its princes with him,"
Says the LORD.

JUDGMENT ON JUDAH

4Thus says the LORD:

"For three transgressions of Judah, and for four,
I will not turn away its *punishment,*
Because they have despised the law of the LORD,
And have not kept His commandments.
Their lies lead them astray,
Lies which their fathers followed.
5 But I will send a fire upon Judah,
And it shall devour the palaces of Jerusalem."

JUDGMENT ON ISRAEL

6Thus says the LORD:

"For three transgressions of Israel, and for four,
I will not turn away its *punishment,*
Because they sell the righteous for silver,
And the poor for a pair of sandals.
7 They pant after[a] the dust of the earth *which is* on the head of the poor,
And pervert the way of the humble.
A man and his father go in to the *same* girl,
To defile My holy name.
8 They lie down by every altar on clothes taken in pledge,
And drink the wine of the condemned *in* the house of their god.
9 "Yet *it was* I *who* destroyed the Amorite before them,
Whose height *was* like the height of the cedars,
And he *was as* strong as the oaks;
Yet I destroyed his fruit above
And his roots beneath.
10 Also *it was* I *who* brought you up from the land of Egypt,
And led you forty years through the wilderness,
To possess the land of the Amorite.
11 I raised up some of your sons as prophets,
And some of your young men as Nazirites.
Is it not so, O you children of Israel?"
Says the LORD.
12 "But you gave the Nazirites wine to drink,
And commanded the prophets saying,
'Do not prophesy!'

13 "Behold, I am weighed down by you,
As a cart full of sheaves is weighed down.
14 Therefore flight shall perish from the swift,
The strong shall not strengthen his power,
Nor shall the mighty deliver himself;
15 He shall not stand who handles the bow,
The swift of foot shall not escape,
Nor shall he who rides a horse deliver himself.
16 The most courageous men of might
Shall flee naked in that day,"
Says the LORD.

2:7 [a]Or *trample on*

SOUL NOTE

Justice for All *(2:6)* Amos pronounced judgment on the surrounding nations, and even on Judah, Israel's brothers and sisters to the south. Perhaps the people in Israel enjoyed hearing that these nations faced God's judgment—until Amos added Israel to his list. They, too, had sinned greatly against God, and they would be punished. There is no getting around it: God punishes sin. Just as God provided the opportunity for repentance and restoration to ancient Israel, He also offers it today through His Son, Jesus Christ. **Topic: Accountability**

AUTHORITY OF THE PROPHET'S MESSAGE

3 Hear this word that the LORD has spoken
against you, O children of Israel, against
the whole family which I brought up from the
land of Egypt, saying:

2 "You only have I known of all the families of the earth;
Therefore I will punish you for all your iniquities."

3 Can two walk together, unless they are agreed?
4 Will a lion roar in the forest, when he has no prey?
Will a young lion cry out of his den, if he has caught nothing?
5 Will a bird fall into a snare on the earth, where there is no trap for it?
Will a snare spring up from the earth, if it has caught nothing at all?
6 If a trumpet is blown in a city, will not the people be afraid?
If there is calamity in a city, will not the LORD have done *it?*

7 Surely the Lord GOD does nothing,
Unless He reveals His secret to His servants the prophets.

8 A lion has roared!
Who will not fear?
The Lord GOD has spoken!
Who can but prophesy?

PUNISHMENT OF ISRAEL'S SINS

9 "Proclaim in the palaces at Ashdod,[a]
And in the palaces in the land of Egypt, and say:
'Assemble on the mountains of Samaria;
See great tumults in her midst,
And the oppressed within her.
10 For they do not know to do right,'
Says the LORD,
'Who store up violence and robbery in their palaces.' "

11 Therefore thus says the Lord GOD:

"An adversary *shall be* all around the land;
He shall sap your strength from you,
And your palaces shall be plundered."

12 Thus says the LORD:

3:9 [a]Following Masoretic Text; Septuagint reads *Assyria*.

KEY PASSAGE

Premarital Relationships

WALKING IN AGREEMENT

(3:3)

Amos had received a prophecy from God; this meant that the predicted event would soon take place. Amos used some questions regarding interrelated events to prove that point. For example, Amos wrote, "Can two walk together, unless they are agreed?" When two people are walking together, we figure they have agreed about some things, like where and when to meet and where to go. The verse describes a general truth about relationships between people.

During a dating relationship, a couple should evaluate their agreements in various areas of life. They shouldn't "walk together" into a marriage covenant if they are not agreed in the most important issues of life—beliefs, values, and lifestyle. Paul gave the same advice when he said, "Do not be unequally yoked together with unbelievers. For what fellowship has righteousness with lawlessness?" (2 Cor. 6:14).

As Christians date, they should seek the company of other Christians. Then they should agree on the practical implications of their Christian faith. Such agreement will help them to walk through many years together.

To Learn More: Turn to the article about premarital relationships on pages 338, 339. See also the personality profile of Ruth and Boaz on page 336.

"As a shepherd takes from the mouth of a lion
Two legs or a piece of an ear,
So shall the children of Israel be taken out
Who dwell in Samaria—
In the corner of a bed and on the edge[a] of a couch!
13 Hear and testify against the house of Jacob,"
Says the Lord GOD, the God of hosts,
14 "That in the day I punish Israel for their transgressions,
I will also visit *destruction* on the altars of Bethel;
And the horns of the altar shall be cut off
And fall to the ground.
15 I will destroy the winter house along with the summer house;
The houses of ivory shall perish,
And the great houses shall have an end,"
Says the LORD.

4 Hear this word, you cows of Bashan, who *are* on the mountain of Samaria,
Who oppress the poor,
Who crush the needy,
Who say to your husbands,[a] "Bring *wine,* let us drink!"
2 The Lord GOD has sworn by His holiness:
"Behold, the days shall come upon you
When He will take you away with fishhooks,
And your posterity with fishhooks.
3 You will go out *through* broken *walls,*
Each one straight ahead of her,
And you will be cast into Harmon,"
Says the LORD.

4 "Come to Bethel and transgress,
At Gilgal multiply transgression;
Bring your sacrifices every morning,
Your tithes every three days.[a]
5 Offer a sacrifice of thanksgiving with leaven,
Proclaim *and* announce the freewill offerings;
For this you love,
You children of Israel!"
Says the Lord GOD.

ISRAEL DID NOT ACCEPT CORRECTION

6 "Also I gave you cleanness of teeth in all your cities.
And lack of bread in all your places;
Yet you have not returned to Me,"
Says the LORD.

7 "I also withheld rain from you,
When *there were* still three months to the harvest.
I made it rain on one city,
I withheld rain from another city.
One part was rained upon,
And where it did not rain the part withered.
8 So two *or* three cities wandered to another city to drink water,
But they were not satisfied;
Yet you have not returned to Me,"
Says the LORD.

9 "I blasted you with blight and mildew.
When your gardens increased,
Your vineyards,
Your fig trees,
And your olive trees,
The locust devoured *them;*
Yet you have not returned to Me,"
Says the LORD.

10 "I sent among you a plague after the manner of Egypt;
Your young men I killed with a sword,
Along with your captive horses;
I made the stench of your camps come up into your nostrils;
Yet you have not returned to Me,"
Says the LORD.

11 "I overthrew *some* of you,
As God overthrew Sodom and Gomorrah,
And you were like a firebrand plucked from the burning;
Yet you have not returned to Me,"
Says the LORD.

12 "Therefore thus will I do to you, O Israel;
Because I will do this to you,
Prepare to meet your God, O Israel!"

3:12 [a]The Hebrew is uncertain. **4:1** [a]Literally *their lords* or *their masters* **4:4** [a]Or *years* (compare Deuteronomy 14:28)

13 For behold,
He who forms mountains,
And creates the wind,
Who declares to man what his[a] thought
is,
And makes the morning darkness,
Who treads the high places of the
earth—
The LORD God of hosts *is* His name.

A LAMENT FOR ISRAEL

5 Hear this word which I take up against
you, a lamentation, O house of Israel:

2 The virgin of Israel has fallen;
She will rise no more.
She lies forsaken on her land;
There is no one to raise her up.

3For thus says the Lord GOD:

"The city that goes out by a thousand
Shall have a hundred left,
And that which goes out by a hundred
Shall have ten left to the house of
Israel."

A CALL TO REPENTANCE

4For thus says the LORD to the house of Israel:

"Seek Me and live;
5 But do not seek Bethel,
Nor enter Gilgal,
Nor pass over to Beersheba;
For Gilgal shall surely go into captivity,
And Bethel shall come to nothing.
6 Seek the LORD and live,
Lest He break out like fire *in* the house
of Joseph,
And devour *it,*
With no one to quench *it* in Bethel—
7 You who turn justice to wormwood,
And lay righteousness to rest in the
earth!"

8 He made the Pleiades and Orion;
He turns the shadow of death into
morning
And makes the day dark as night;
He calls for the waters of the sea
And pours them out on the face of the
earth;
The LORD *is* His name.
9 He rains ruin upon the strong,
So that fury comes upon the fortress.

10 They hate the one who rebukes in the
gate,
And they abhor the one who speaks
uprightly.
11 Therefore, because you tread down the
poor
And take grain taxes from him,
Though you have built houses of hewn
stone,
Yet you shall not dwell in them;
You have planted pleasant vineyards,
But you shall not drink wine from them.
12 For I know your manifold transgressions
And your mighty sins:
Afflicting the just *and* taking bribes;
Diverting the poor *from justice* at the
gate.
13 Therefore the prudent keep silent at that
time,
For it *is* an evil time.

14 Seek good and not evil,
That you may live;
So the LORD God of hosts will be with
you,

4:13 [a]Or *His*

SOUL NOTE

Bold Love *(5:14, 15)* God didn't ignore the Israelites' evil ways or deny what they were doing. Instead, He confronted them through prophets who spoke truth, and with trials designed to encourage the people to return to Him (4:6, 9–11). In all of this, God was showing His love for His own. At times, love must be bold, tough, and willing to speak the truth. People dealing with sin need the light of God's truth. Then, through repentance, they can bask in the warmth of His forgiving love.
Topic: Love

As you have spoken.
15 Hate evil, love good;
Establish justice in the gate.
It may be that the LORD God of hosts
Will be gracious to the remnant of Joseph.

THE DAY OF THE LORD

16Therefore the LORD God of hosts, the Lord, says this:

"*There shall be* wailing in all streets,
And they shall say in all the highways,
'Alas! Alas!'
They shall call the farmer to mourning,
And skillful lamenters to wailing.
17 In all vineyards *there shall be* wailing,
For I will pass through you,"
Says the LORD.

18 Woe to you who desire the day of the LORD!
For what good *is* the day of the LORD to you?
It *will be* darkness, and not light.
19 It *will be* as though a man fled from a lion,
And a bear met him!
Or *as though* he went into the house,
Leaned his hand on the wall,
And a serpent bit him!
20 *Is* not the day of the LORD darkness, and not light?
Is it not very dark, with no brightness in it?

21 "I hate, I despise your feast days,
And I do not savor your sacred assemblies.
22 Though you offer Me burnt offerings and your grain offerings,
I will not accept *them*,
Nor will I regard your fattened peace offerings.
23 Take away from Me the noise of your songs,
For I will not hear the melody of your stringed instruments.
24 But let justice run down like water,
And righteousness like a mighty stream.

"But let justice run down like water, and righteousness like a mighty stream."
AMOS 5:24

25 "Did you offer Me sacrifices and offerings
In the wilderness forty years, O house of Israel?
26 You also carried Sikkuth[a] your king[b]
And Chiun,[c] your idols,
The star of your gods,
Which you made for yourselves.
27 Therefore I will send you into captivity beyond Damascus,"
Says the LORD, whose name *is* the God of hosts.

WARNINGS TO ZION AND SAMARIA

6 Woe to you *who are* at ease in Zion,
And trust in Mount Samaria,
Notable persons in the chief nation,
To whom the house of Israel comes!
2 Go over to Calneh and see;
And from there go to Hamath the great;
Then go down to Gath of the Philistines.
Are you better than these kingdoms?
Or is their territory greater than your territory?
3 *Woe to* you who put far off the day of doom,
Who cause the seat of violence to come near;
4 Who lie on beds of ivory,
Stretch out on your couches,
Eat lambs from the flock
And calves from the midst of the stall;
5 Who sing idly to the sound of stringed instruments,
And invent for yourselves musical instruments like David;
6 Who drink wine from bowls,
And anoint yourselves with the best ointments,
But are not grieved for the affliction of Joseph.
7 Therefore they shall now go captive as the first of the captives,
And those who recline at banquets shall be removed.

5:26 [a]A pagan deity [b]Septuagint and Vulgate read *tabernacle of Moloch.* [c]A pagan deity

8 The Lord GOD has sworn by Himself,
The LORD God of hosts says:
"I abhor the pride of Jacob,
And hate his palaces;
Therefore I will deliver up *the* city
And all that is in it."

9Then it shall come to pass, that if ten men
remain in one house, they shall die. 10And
when a relative *of the dead,* with one who will
burn *the bodies,* picks up the bodies[a] to take
them out of the house, he will say to one inside the house, "*Are there* any more with
you?"

Then someone will say, "None."

And he will say, "Hold your tongue! For we dare not mention the name of the LORD."

11 For behold, the LORD gives a
command:
He will break the great house into bits,
And the little house into pieces.

12 Do horses run on rocks?
Does *one* plow *there* with oxen?
Yet you have turned justice into gall,
And the fruit of righteousness into
wormwood,
13 You who rejoice over Lo Debar,[a]
Who say, "Have we not taken Karnaim[b]
for ourselves
By our own strength?"

14 "But, behold, I will raise up a nation
against you,
O house of Israel,"
Says the LORD God of hosts;
"And they will afflict you from the
entrance of Hamath
To the Valley of the Arabah."

Vision of the Locusts

7 Thus the Lord GOD showed me: Behold,
He formed locust swarms at the beginning
of the late crop; indeed *it was* the late crop after the king's mowings. 2And so it was, when
they had finished eating the grass of the land,
that I said:

"O Lord GOD, forgive, I pray!
Oh, that Jacob may stand,
For he *is* small!"
3 *So* the LORD relented concerning this.
"It shall not be," said the LORD.

Vision of the Fire

4Thus the Lord GOD showed me: Behold, the
Lord GOD called for conflict by fire, and it consumed the great deep and devoured the territory. 5Then I said:

"O Lord GOD, cease, I pray!
Oh, that Jacob may stand,
For he *is* small!"
6 *So* the LORD relented concerning this.
"This also shall not be," said the Lord GOD.

Vision of the Plumb Line

7Thus He showed me: Behold, the Lord
stood on a wall *made* with a plumb line, with
a plumb line in His hand. 8And the LORD said
to me, "Amos, what do you see?"

And I said, "A plumb line."

Then the Lord said:

"Behold, I am setting a plumb line
In the midst of My people Israel;
I will not pass by them anymore.
9 The high places of Isaac shall be
desolate,
And the sanctuaries of Israel shall be
laid waste.
I will rise with the sword against the
house of Jeroboam."

Amaziah's Complaint

10Then Amaziah the priest of Bethel sent to
Jeroboam king of Israel, saying, "Amos has
conspired against you in the midst of the
house of Israel. The land is not able to bear all
his words. 11For thus Amos has said:

'Jeroboam shall die by the sword,
And Israel shall surely be led away
captive
From their own land.' "

12Then Amaziah said to Amos:

"Go, you seer!
Flee to the land of Judah.
There eat bread,
And there prophesy.
13 But never again prophesy at Bethel,
For it *is* the king's sanctuary,
And it *is* the royal residence."

6:10 [a]Literally *bones* **6:13** [a]Literally *Nothing* [b]Literally *Horns,* symbol of strength

[14]Then Amos answered, and said to Amaziah:

"I *was* no prophet,
Nor *was* I a son of a prophet,
But I *was* a sheepbreeder[a]
And a tender of sycamore fruit.
15 Then the LORD took me as I followed the flock,
And the LORD said to me,
'Go, prophesy to My people Israel.'
16 Now therefore, hear the word of the LORD:
You say, 'Do not prophesy against Israel,
And do not spout against the house of Isaac.'

[17]"Therefore thus says the LORD:

'Your wife shall be a harlot in the city;
Your sons and daughters shall fall by the sword;
Your land shall be divided by *survey* line;
You shall die in a defiled land;
And Israel shall surely be led away captive
From his own land.' "

VISION OF THE SUMMER FRUIT

8 Thus the Lord GOD showed me: Behold, a basket of summer fruit. [2]And He said, "Amos, what do you see?"

So I said, "A basket of summer fruit."
Then the LORD said to me:

"The end has come upon My people Israel;
I will not pass by them anymore.
3 And the songs of the temple
Shall be wailing in that day,"
Says the Lord GOD—
"Many dead bodies everywhere,
They shall be thrown out in silence."

4 Hear this, you who swallow up[a] the needy,
And make the poor of the land fail,

[5]Saying:

"When will the New Moon be past,
That we may sell grain?
And the Sabbath,
That we may trade wheat?
Making the ephah small and the shekel large,
Falsifying the scales by deceit,
6 That we may buy the poor for silver,
And the needy for a pair of sandals—
Even sell the bad wheat?"

7 The LORD has sworn by the pride of Jacob:
"Surely I will never forget any of their works.
8 Shall the land not tremble for this,
And everyone mourn who dwells in it?
All of it shall swell like the River,[a]
Heave and subside
Like the River of Egypt.

9 "And it shall come to pass in that day,"
says the Lord GOD,
"That I will make the sun go down at noon,
And I will darken the earth in broad daylight;
10 I will turn your feasts into mourning,
And all your songs into lamentation;
I will bring sackcloth on every waist,
And baldness on every head;
I will make it like mourning for an only *son,*
And its end like a bitter day.

11 "Behold, the days are coming," says the Lord GOD,
"That I will send a famine on the land,
Not a famine of bread,
Nor a thirst for water,
But of hearing the words of the LORD.
12 They shall wander from sea to sea,
And from north to east;
They shall run to and fro, seeking the word of the LORD,
But shall not find *it.*

13 "In that day the fair virgins
And strong young men
Shall faint from thirst.

7:14 [a]Compare 2 Kings 3:4 **8:4** [a]Or *trample on* (compare 2:7) **8:8** [a]That is, the Nile; some Hebrew manuscripts, Septuagint, Syriac, Targum, and Vulgate read *River;* Masoretic Text reads *the light.*

14 Those who swear by the sin[a] of Samaria,
Who say,
'As your god lives, O Dan!'
And, 'As the way of Beersheba lives!'
They shall fall and never rise again."

The Destruction of Israel

9 I saw the Lord standing by the altar, and
He said:

"Strike the doorposts, that the thresholds
may shake,
And break them on the heads of them
all.
I will slay the last of them with the
sword.
He who flees from them shall not get
away,
And he who escapes from them shall not
be delivered.

2 "Though they dig into hell,[a]
From there My hand shall take them;
Though they climb up to heaven,
From there I will bring them down;
3 And though they hide themselves on top
of Carmel,
From there I will search and take them;
Though they hide from My sight at the
bottom of the sea,
From there I will command the serpent,
and it shall bite them;
4 Though they go into captivity before
their enemies,
From there I will command the sword,
And it shall slay them.
I will set My eyes on them for harm and
not for good."

5 The Lord GOD of hosts,
He who touches the earth and it melts,
And all who dwell there mourn;
All of it shall swell like the River,[a]
And subside like the River of Egypt.
6 He who builds His layers in the sky,
And has founded His strata in the earth;
Who calls for the waters of the sea,
And pours them out on the face of the
earth—
The LORD *is* His name.

7 "*Are* you not like the people of Ethiopia
to Me,
O children of Israel?" says the LORD.
"Did I not bring up Israel from the land of
Egypt,
The Philistines from Caphtor,
And the Syrians from Kir?

8 "Behold, the eyes of the Lord GOD *are* on
the sinful kingdom,
And I will destroy it from the face of the
earth;
Yet I will not utterly destroy the house of
Jacob,"
Says the LORD.

9 "For surely I will command,
And will sift the house of Israel among
all nations,
As *grain* is sifted in a sieve;
Yet not the smallest grain shall fall to the
ground.
10 All the sinners of My people shall die by
the sword,
Who say, 'The calamity shall not
overtake nor confront us.'

Israel Will Be Restored

11 "On that day I will raise up
The tabernacle[a] of David, which has
fallen down,
And repair its damages;
I will raise up its ruins,
And rebuild it as in the days of old;
12 That they may possess the remnant of
Edom,[a]
And all the Gentiles who are called by
My name,"
Says the LORD who does this thing.

13 "Behold, the days are coming," says the
LORD,
"When the plowman shall overtake the
reaper,
And the treader of grapes him who sows
seed;
The mountains shall drip with sweet
wine,
And all the hills shall flow *with it.*
14 I will bring back the captives of My
people Israel;
They shall build the waste cities and
inhabit *them;*

8:14 [a]Or *Ashima,* a Syrian goddess **9:2** [a]Or *Sheol* **9:5** [a]That is, the Nile **9:11** [a]Literally *booth,* figure of a deposed dynasty
9:12 [a]Septuagint reads *mankind.*

They shall plant vineyards and drink
wine from them;
They shall also make gardens and eat
fruit from them.

15 I will plant them in their land,
And no longer shall they be pulled up
From the land I have given them,"
Says the LORD your God.

Obadiah

Nothing hurts more than betrayal. It cuts painfully deep and leaves a scar. And with the pain and anger usually comes an obsession for revenge.

Obadiah, the shortest book in the Old Testament, is rooted in Edom's betrayal of Israel. To really understand this prophecy, we first need to know a bit of history. Both nations, Edom and Israel, descended from Isaac and Rebekah: Edom from Esau and Israel from Jacob (Gen. 25—27). These fraternal twins had been involved in a heated rivalry literally from birth—emerging from the womb, Jacob was grasping Esau's heel (Gen. 25:24–26). Jacob continued his grasping, scheming ways until he eventually wrested the family birthright and blessing from his older brother. This betrayal resulted in Esau settling in Edom and Jacob in nearby Canaan.

What began as an ugly case of sibling rivalry accelerated into a fierce feud between two nations. When the Babylonians sacked Jerusalem in 586 B.C., the Edomites not only stood by, but they cheered the enemy! Worse, they plundered Jerusalem further, killing some Jews and turning others over to their Babylonian captors. This, combined with their smugness and godless reliance on their fortress city of Sela (Petra), was a great offense to God. He used Obadiah to warn Edom that judgment was coming, that they would be wiped off the earth, and that Israel would be restored.

Obadiah's prophecy reminds us that there can be long-term societal aftereffects from our personal and corporate actions. Unbridled pride can cause long-term consequences. Forgiveness and reconciliation become more difficult with each succeeding generation. Since hurtful actions can live on for generations, the sooner we reconcile our differences, the better.

THE COMING JUDGMENT ON EDOM

1The vision of Obadiah.

Thus says the Lord GOD concerning Edom
(We have heard a report from the LORD,
And a messenger has been sent among the nations, *saying,*
"Arise, and let us rise up against her for battle"):

2 "Behold, I will make you small among the nations;
You shall be greatly despised.
3 The pride of your heart has deceived you,
You who dwell in the clefts of the rock,
Whose habitation is high;
You who say in your heart, 'Who will bring me down to the ground?'
4 Though you ascend *as* high as the eagle,
And though you set your nest among the stars,
From there I will bring you down," says the LORD.

5 "If thieves had come to you,
If robbers by night—
Oh, how you will be cut off!—
Would they not have stolen till they had enough?
If grape-gatherers had come to you,
Would they not have left *some* gleanings?

6 "Oh, how Esau shall be searched out!
How his hidden treasures shall be sought after!
7 All the men in your confederacy
Shall force you to the border;
The men at peace with you
Shall deceive you *and* prevail against you.
Th*ose who eat* your bread shall lay a trap[a] for you.
No one is aware of it.

8 "Will I not in that day," says the LORD,
"Even destroy the wise *men* from Edom,
And understanding from the mountains of Esau?
9 Then your mighty men, O Teman, shall be dismayed,
To the end that everyone from the mountains of Esau
May be cut off by slaughter.

EDOM MISTREATED HIS BROTHER

10 "For violence against your brother Jacob,
Shame shall cover you,
And you shall be cut off forever.
11 In the day that you stood on the other side—
In the day that strangers carried captive his forces,
When foreigners entered his gates
And cast lots for Jerusalem—
Even you *were* as one of them.

12 "But you should not have gazed on the day of your brother
In the day of his captivity;[a]
Nor should you have rejoiced over the children of Judah
In the day of their destruction;
Nor should you have spoken proudly
In the day of distress.
13 You should not have entered the gate of My people

7 [a]Or *wound,* or *plot* **12** [a]Literally *on the day he became a foreigner*

SOUL NOTE

Gloating *(1–3)* The Edomites were Israel's relatives, descendants of Jacob's brother, Esau. When the Israelites faced invasion, however, Edom refused to come to their aid, even gloating over Israel's troubles behind their protective mountain peaks. The prophet Obadiah condemned them for their pride and complete indifference to the Israelites' predicament. Their mountain fortress couldn't protect them from God, however. He would judge them for their pride. "As you have done, it shall be done to you," He said (15). Indeed, "pride goes before destruction, and a haughty spirit before a fall" (Prov. 16:18). **Topic: Pride**

In the day of their calamity.
Indeed, you should not have gazed on
their affliction
In the day of their calamity,
Nor laid *hands* on their substance
In the day of their calamity.
14 You should not have stood at the
crossroads
To cut off those among them who
escaped;
Nor should you have delivered up those
among them who remained
In the day of distress.

15 "For the day of the LORD upon all the
nations *is* near;
As you have done, it shall be done to
you;
Your reprisal shall return upon your own
head.
16 For as you drank on My holy mountain,
So shall all the nations drink continually;
Yes, they shall drink, and swallow,
And they shall be as though they had
never been.

Israel's Final Triumph

17 "But on Mount Zion there shall be
deliverance,
And there shall be holiness;
The house of Jacob shall possess their
possessions.
18 The house of Jacob shall be a fire,
And the house of Joseph a flame;
But the house of Esau *shall be* stubble;
They shall kindle them and devour
them,
And no survivor shall *remain* of the
house of Esau,"
For the LORD has spoken.

19 The South[a] shall possess the mountains
of Esau,
And the Lowland shall possess Philistia.
They shall possess the fields of Ephraim
And the fields of Samaria.
Benjamin *shall possess* Gilead.
20 And the captives of this host of the
children of Israel
Shall possess the land of the Canaanites
As far as Zarephath.
The captives of Jerusalem who are in
Sepharad
Shall possess the cities of the South.[a]
21 Then saviors[a] shall come to Mount Zion
To judge the mountains of Esau,
And the kingdom shall be the LORD's.

---

19 [a]Hebrew *Negev* **20** [a]Hebrew *Negev* **21** [a]Or *deliverers*

Jonah

Visit a news site on the Internet or pick up a newspaper, and it won't take long to find a story about a nation with evil leaders that is acting cruelly against another nation, through war, invasions, or bomb threats. People hope that some kind of punishment awaits those who perpetrate evil on others. Jonah felt that way against Assyria, a powerful and cruel empire.

God longed to show mercy to the pagan Assyrians, however, and He called Jonah to preach a message of repentance in the capital city of Nineveh (ch. 1). But Jonah didn't want to go to these enemies of Israel. Jonah knew that if he obeyed God, these hated Gentiles might heed his warnings, turn to God, and find blessing! Since the self-righteous Jonah wanted the Assyrians to experience God's judgment, he ran away from his divine assignment.

Through the great fish (1:17—2:10), God eventually got Jonah to Nineveh. Confirming the prophet's worst fears, the Assyrians repented (ch. 3). Their acceptance of the grace of God is only part of the story, however. The balance of Jonah's book has to do with his personal experience in the school of God's grace (ch. 4). Using a plant, the Lord surfaced Jonah's distorted values and alarming lack of love.

As we read Jonah, we realize that our Creator is a global God who longs to pour out His love on both sinful nations and hard-hearted believers. He is "not willing that any should perish but that all should come to repentance" (2 Pet. 3:9). Rejoice! God's grace is for everyone!

Jonah's Disobedience

1 Now the word of the LORD came to Jonah the son of Amittai, saying, [2]"Arise, go to Nineveh, that great city, and cry out against it; for their wickedness has come up before Me." [3]But Jonah arose to flee to Tarshish from the presence of the LORD. He went down to Joppa, and found a ship going to Tarshish; so he paid the fare, and went down into it, to go with them to Tarshish from the presence of the LORD.

The Storm at Sea

[4]But the LORD sent out a great wind on the sea, and there was a mighty tempest on the sea, so that the ship was about to be broken up.

[5]Then the mariners were afraid; and every man cried out to his god, and threw the cargo that *was* in the ship into the sea, to lighten the load.[a] But Jonah had gone down into the lowest parts of the ship, had lain down, and was fast asleep.

[6]So the captain came to him, and said to him, "What do you mean, sleeper? Arise, call on your God; perhaps your God will consider us, so that we may not perish."

[7]And they said to one another, "Come, let us cast lots, that we may know for whose cause this trouble *has come* upon us." So they cast lots, and the lot fell on Jonah. [8]Then they said to him, "Please tell us! For whose cause *is* this trouble upon us? What is your occupation? And where do you come from? What is your country? And of what people are you?"

[9]So he said to them, "I *am* a Hebrew; and I fear the LORD, the God of heaven, who made the sea and the dry *land*."

1:5 [a]Literally *from upon them*

PERSONALITY PROFILE

Trauma

JONAH: RUNNING FROM GOD

(JONAH 1:12)

Difficult experiences come in many degrees. A trauma would be considered a situation far beyond control, one that shakes a person to the core. A trauma can lead to mental disorders or to suicide. Recovery is often slow; flashbacks are common. As difficult as traumatic experiences are, however, they can also lead a person to God.

Jonah had been called to go east to Nineveh; instead, he jumped on a ship and went west. Although he was acting in direct disobedience to God, he fell sound asleep on the ship. His conscience may not have bothered him, but God soon did. God knew that His reluctant prophet would need a traumatic experience or two to turn him around—literally. When a fierce storm tossed the ship and threatened to kill all on board, Jonah knew the reason for the storm and the solution: "Pick me up and throw me into the sea; then the sea will become calm for you. For I know that this great tempest is because of me" (1:12), he told the crew . . . and reluctantly they complied.

Immediately, a great fish swallowed Jonah. God spared his life because He still had work for Jonah to do. Trauma upon trauma eventually caused Jonah to pray: "I cried out to the LORD because of my affliction, and He answered me" (Jon. 2:2). And this conversation with God led Jonah to a promise to obey, "I will pay what I have vowed" (Jon. 2:9). Then God rescued Jonah and gave him the opportunity to fulfill his promise.

Traumatic experiences can drive people away from God or to Him. In both cases, a person may ask, "Why would God do this to me?" Those who turn *from* God ask the question in anger and accusation. Those who turn *toward* God ask the question in order to learn His lesson for their lives. When traumatic experiences come, turn to God, not away. As Jonah learned: "When my soul fainted within me, I remembered the LORD; and my prayer went up to You, into Your holy temple" (Jon. 2:7).

To Learn More: Turn to the article about trauma on pages 690, 691. See also the key passage note at Lamentations 1:10–21 on page 1035.

JONAH THROWN INTO THE SEA

10Then the men were exceedingly afraid,
and said to him, "Why have you done this?"
For the men knew that he fled from the presence of the LORD, because he had told them.
11Then they said to him, "What shall we do to
you that the sea may be calm for us?"—for the
sea was growing more tempestuous.
12And he said to them, "Pick me up and
throw me into the sea; then the sea will become calm for you. For I know that this great
tempest *is* because of me."
13Nevertheless the men rowed hard to return to land, but they could not, for the sea
continued to grow more tempestuous against
them. 14Therefore they cried out to the LORD
and said, "We pray, O LORD, please do not let
us perish for this man's life, and do not charge
us with innocent blood; for You, O LORD, have
done as it pleased You." 15So they picked up
Jonah and threw him into the sea, and the sea
ceased from its raging. 16Then the men feared
the LORD exceedingly, and offered a sacrifice
to the LORD and took vows.

JONAH'S PRAYER AND DELIVERANCE

17Now the LORD had prepared a great fish to
swallow Jonah. And Jonah was in the belly of
the fish three days and three nights.
2 Then Jonah prayed to the LORD his God
from the fish's belly. 2And he said:

"I cried out to the LORD because of my
affliction,
And He answered me.

"Out of the belly of Sheol I cried,
And You heard my voice.
3 For You cast me into the deep,
Into the heart of the seas,
And the floods surrounded me;
All Your billows and Your waves passed
over me.
4 Then I said, 'I have been cast out of
Your sight;
Yet I will look again toward Your holy
temple.'
5 The waters surrounded me, *even* to my
soul;
The deep closed around me;
Weeds were wrapped around my head.
6 I went down to the moorings of the
mountains;
The earth with its bars *closed* behind me
forever;
Yet You have brought up my life from
the pit,
O LORD, my God.

7 "When my soul fainted within me,
I remembered the LORD;
And my prayer went *up* to You,
Into Your holy temple.

8 "Those who regard worthless idols
Forsake their own Mercy.
9 But I will sacrifice to You
With the voice of thanksgiving;
I will pay what I have vowed.
Salvation *is* of the LORD."

10So the LORD spoke to the fish, and it vomited Jonah onto dry *land*.

JONAH PREACHES AT NINEVEH

3 Now the word of the LORD came to Jonah
the second time, saying, 2"Arise, go to
Nineveh, that great city, and preach to it the
message that I tell you." 3So Jonah arose and
went to Nineveh, according to the word of the
LORD. Now Nineveh was an exceedingly great

SOUL NOTE

Undeserving *(2:1–7)* Jonah didn't deserve God's forgiveness. God had said, "Go," and Jonah had run away (1:2, 3). His conscience hadn't even seemed to bother him, for during his flight from God he slept soundly (1:5). During the storm, the pagan sailors had to remind Jonah to pray (1:6). Jonah had persistently disobeyed God. Not until Jonah sank to the gloomy depths and faced certain death did he cry out to God. Mercifully and miraculously, God answered. The story of Jonah teaches that God saves the undeserving—whether a pagan nation or a wayward individual.
Topic: Salvation

city, a three-day journey[a] *in extent.* 4And Jonah began to enter the city on the first day's
walk. Then he cried out and said, "Yet forty
days, and Nineveh shall be overthrown!"

The People of Nineveh Believe

5So the people of Nineveh believed God,
proclaimed a fast, and put on sackcloth, from
the greatest to the least of them. 6Then word
came to the king of Nineveh; and he arose
from his throne and laid aside his robe, covered *himself* with sackcloth and sat in ashes.
7And he caused *it* to be proclaimed and published throughout Nineveh by the decree of
the king and his nobles, saying,

> Let neither man nor beast, herd nor
> flock, taste anything; do not let them eat,
> or drink water. 8But let man and beast be
> covered with sackcloth, and cry mightily
> to God; yes, let every one turn from his
> evil way and from the violence that is in
> his hands. 9Who can tell *if* God will turn
> and relent, and turn away from His fierce
> anger, so that we may not perish?

10Then God saw their works, that they
turned from their evil way; and God relented
from the disaster that He had said He would
bring upon them, and He did not do it.

Jonah's Anger and God's Kindness

4 But it displeased Jonah exceedingly, and
he became angry. 2So he prayed to the
LORD, and said, "Ah, LORD, was not this what I
said when I was still in my country? Therefore
I fled previously to Tarshish; for I know that
You *are* a gracious and merciful God, slow to
anger and abundant in lovingkindness, One
who relents from doing harm. 3Therefore now,
O LORD, please take my life from me, for *it is*
better for me to die than to live!"

4Then the LORD said, "*Is it* right for you to
be angry?"

5So Jonah went out of the city and sat on
the east side of the city. There he made himself a shelter and sat under it in the shade, till
he might see what would become of the city.
6And the LORD God prepared a plant[a] and
made it come up over Jonah, that it might be
shade for his head to deliver him from his misery. So Jonah was very grateful for the plant.

3:3 [a]Exact meaning unknown **4:6** [a]Hebrew *kikayon,* exact identity unknown

SOUL NOTE

Traumatic Change *(3:1–3)* Trauma changes people. Jonah had nearly died in the ocean—he couldn't help but be changed. While in the belly of a huge fish, Jonah recognized the hand of God in his circumstances. And when all hope was lost, God was there (2:7). When Jonah found himself alive on a beach, he praised God who had given him another chance. This time when God called, Jonah obeyed. Trauma changes us—whether the change is good or bad often depends on how we respond. God uses our troubles as tools to shape our souls. **Topic: Trauma**

SOUL NOTE

Pouting Prophet *(4:9)* When Jonah learned that God would spare the Ninevites, he became angry. Perhaps he was concerned that his reputation was at stake if his prediction of the city's destruction didn't come true. Perhaps he wanted a front-row seat for Nineveh's destruction—after all, Assyria was Israel's enemy. Instead of rejoicing in the repentance of wicked people, Jonah became angry. His anger at Nineveh's sinfulness was correct; his selfish anger at God's mercy on them was wrong. When we feel angry, we must honestly consider why we are angry. Anger for God's causes can be helpful; selfish anger is not. **Topic: Anger**

[7]But as morning dawned the next day God
prepared a worm, and it *so* damaged the plant
that it withered. [8]And it happened, when the
sun arose, that God prepared a vehement east
wind; and the sun beat on Jonah's head, so
that he grew faint. Then he wished death for
himself, and said, "*It is* better for me to die
than to live."

[9]Then God said to Jonah, "*Is it* right for you
to be angry about the plant?"

And he said, "*It is* right for me to be angry,
even to death!"

[10]But the LORD said, "You have had pity on
the plant for which you have not labored, nor
made it grow, which came up in a night and
perished in a night. [11]And should I not pity
Nineveh, that great city, in which are more
than one hundred and twenty thousand persons who cannot discern between their right
hand and their left—and much livestock?"

Micah

Children don't like getting caught in lies. They may say something very sweetly, but as the evidence mounts against them, they suddenly realize that they have no excuses. No matter what they say in their defense, the evidence reveals the truth.

That's the story of Micah. Israel thought they believed in God, but the evidence was against them. Micah pointed out God's charges against the people—greed, abuse of power, injustice, persecuting the prophets, and, worst of all, forsaking God Himself!

Micah was a contemporary of Isaiah, and he prophesied against Samaria and Jerusalem, the respective capitals of Israel's northern and southern kingdoms. Through him, God denounced both cities for abusing their positions of power and privilege. Then, in a surprise announcement, he predicted that the Messiah would come from neither city but would be born in the little village of Bethlehem (5:2).

In Micah's day, the population was awash in material prosperity but utterly devoid of integrity. Even the judges and priests were selling their services to the highest bidders. Shockingly, the Jews believed that God would continue to bless them. Through Micah, God put His people on trial. As the evidence mounted, it became clear that they had no excuses. They were guilty.

Micah makes clear that God's requirement for His people is "to do justly, to love mercy, and to walk humbly with your God" (6:8). Only this kind of lifestyle pays honor to the righteous judge of all the earth.

SOUL CONCERN IN MICAH

ATTITUDES (6:8)

1 The word of the LORD that came to Micah of Moresheth in the days of Jotham, Ahaz, *and* Hezekiah, kings of Judah, which he saw concerning Samaria and Jerusalem.

THE COMING JUDGMENT ON ISRAEL

2 Hear, all you peoples!
Listen, O earth, and all that is in it!
Let the Lord GOD be a witness against you,
The Lord from His holy temple.

3 For behold, the LORD is coming out of His place;
He will come down
And tread on the high places of the earth.
4 The mountains will melt under Him,
And the valleys will split
Like wax before the fire,
Like waters poured down a steep place.
5 All this is for the transgression of Jacob
And for the sins of the house of Israel.
What *is* the transgression of Jacob?
Is it not Samaria?
And what *are* the high places of Judah?
Are they not Jerusalem?

6 "Therefore I will make Samaria a heap of ruins in the field,
Places for planting a vineyard;
I will pour down her stones into the valley,
And I will uncover her foundations.
7 All her carved images shall be beaten to pieces,
And all her pay as a harlot shall be burned with the fire;
All her idols I will lay desolate,
For she gathered *it* from the pay of a harlot,
And they shall return to the pay of a harlot."

MOURNING FOR ISRAEL AND JUDAH

8 Therefore I will wail and howl,
I will go stripped and naked;
I will make a wailing like the jackals
And a mourning like the ostriches,
9 For her wounds *are* incurable.
For it has come to Judah;
It has come to the gate of My people—
To Jerusalem.

10 Tell *it* not in Gath,
Weep not at all;
In Beth Aphrah[a]
Roll yourself in the dust.
11 Pass by in naked shame, you inhabitant of Shaphir;
The inhabitant of Zaanan[a] does not go out.
Beth Ezel mourns;
Its place to stand is taken away from you.

12 For the inhabitant of Maroth pined[a] for good,
But disaster came down from the LORD
To the gate of Jerusalem.
13 O inhabitant of Lachish,
Harness the chariot to the swift steeds
(She *was* the beginning of sin to the daughter of Zion),
For the transgressions of Israel were found in you.

14 Therefore you shall give presents to Moresheth Gath;[a]
The houses of Achzib[b] *shall be* a lie to the kings of Israel.
15 I will yet bring an heir to you,
O inhabitant of Mareshah;[a]
The glory of Israel shall come to Adullam.
16 Make yourself bald and cut off your hair,
Because of your precious children;
Enlarge your baldness like an eagle,
For they shall go from you into captivity.

WOE TO EVILDOERS

2 Woe to those who devise iniquity,
And work out evil on their beds!
At morning light they practice it,
Because it is in the power of their hand.
2 They covet fields and take *them* by violence,
Also houses, and seize *them.*
So they oppress a man and his house,
A man and his inheritance.

3Therefore thus says the LORD:

1:10 [a]Literally *House of Dust* **1:11** [a]Literally *Going Out* **1:12** [a]Literally *was sick*
1:14 [a]Literally *Possession of Gath* [b]Literally *Lie*
1:15 [a]Literally *Inheritance*

"Behold, against this family I am devising
disaster,
From which you cannot remove your
necks;
Nor shall you walk haughtily,
For this *is* an evil time.
4 In that day *one* shall take up a proverb
against you,
And lament with a bitter lamentation,
saying:
'We are utterly destroyed!
He has changed the heritage of my
people;
How He has removed *it* from me!
To a turncoat He has divided our
fields.' "

5 Therefore you will have no one to
determine boundaries[a] by lot
In the assembly of the LORD.

Lying Prophets

6 "Do not prattle," *you say to those* who
prophesy.
So they shall not prophesy to you;[a]
They shall not return insult for insult.[b]
7 *You who are* named the house of
Jacob:
"Is the Spirit of the LORD restricted?
Are these His doings?
Do not My words do good
To him who walks uprightly?

8 "Lately My people have risen up as an
enemy—
You pull off the robe with the garment
From those who trust *you,* as they pass
by,
Like men returned from war.
9 The women of My people you cast out
From their pleasant houses;
From their children
You have taken away My glory forever.

10 "Arise and depart,
For this *is* not *your* rest;
Because it is defiled, it shall destroy,
Yes, with utter destruction.
11 If a man should walk in a false spirit
And speak a lie, *saying,*
'I will prophesy to you of wine and
drink,'
Even he would be the prattler of this
people.

Israel Restored

12 "I will surely assemble all of you,
O Jacob,
I will surely gather the remnant of Israel;
I will put them together like sheep of the
fold,[a]
Like a flock in the midst of their pasture;
They shall make a loud noise because of
so many people.
13 The one who breaks open will come up
before them;
They will break out,
Pass through the gate,
And go out by it;
Their king will pass before them,
With the LORD at their head."

Wicked Rulers and Prophets

3 And I said:

"Hear now, O heads of Jacob,
And you rulers of the house of Israel:
Is it not for you to know justice?
2 You who hate good and love evil;
Who strip the skin from My people,[a]
And the flesh from their bones;
3 Who also eat the flesh of My people,
Flay their skin from them,
Break their bones,
And chop *them* in pieces
Like *meat* for the pot,
Like flesh in the caldron."

4 Then they will cry to the LORD,
But He will not hear them;
He will even hide His face from them at
that time,
Because they have been evil in their
deeds.

5 Thus says the LORD concerning the
prophets
Who make my people stray;
Who chant "Peace"
While they chew with their teeth,
But who prepare war against him
Who puts nothing into their mouths:
6 "Therefore you shall have night without
vision,

2:5 [a]Literally *one casting a surveyor's line*
2:6 [a]Literally *to these* [b]Vulgate reads *He shall not take shame.* **2:12** [a]Hebrew *Bozrah* **3:2** [a]Literally *them*

And you shall have darkness without divination;
The sun shall go down on the prophets,
And the day shall be dark for them.
7 So the seers shall be ashamed,
And the diviners abashed;
Indeed they shall all cover their lips;
For *there is* no answer from God."

But truly I am full of power by the Spirit of the LORD, and of justice and might, to declare to Jacob his transgression and to Israel his sin.
MICAH 3:8

8 But truly I am full of power by the Spirit of the LORD,
And of justice and might,
To declare to Jacob his transgression
And to Israel his sin.
9 Now hear this,
You heads of the house of Jacob
And rulers of the house of Israel,
Who abhor justice
And pervert all equity,
10 Who build up Zion with bloodshed
And Jerusalem with iniquity:
11 Her heads judge for a bribe,
Her priests teach for pay,
And her prophets divine for money.
Yet they lean on the LORD, and say,
"Is not the LORD among us?
No harm can come upon us."
12 Therefore because of you
Zion shall be plowed *like* a field,
Jerusalem shall become heaps of ruins,
And the mountain of the temple[a]
Like the bare hills of the forest.

THE LORD'S REIGN IN ZION

4 Now it shall come to pass in the latter days
That the mountain of the LORD's house
Shall be established on the top of the mountains,
And shall be exalted above the hills;
And peoples shall flow to it.
2 Many nations shall come and say,
"Come, and let us go up to the mountain of the LORD,
To the house of the God of Jacob;
He will teach us His ways,
And we shall walk in His paths."
For out of Zion the law shall go forth,
And the word of the LORD from Jerusalem.
3 He shall judge between many peoples,
And rebuke strong nations afar off;
They shall beat their swords into plowshares,
And their spears into pruning hooks;
Nation shall not lift up sword against nation,
Neither shall they learn war anymore.[a]
4 But everyone shall sit under his vine and under his fig tree,
And no one shall make *them* afraid;
For the mouth of the LORD of hosts has spoken.
5 For all people walk each in the name of his god,
But we will walk in the name of the LORD our God
Forever and ever.

ZION'S FUTURE TRIUMPH

6 "In that day," says the LORD,
"I will assemble the lame,
I will gather the outcast
And those whom I have afflicted;
7 I will make the lame a remnant,
And the outcast a strong nation;
So the LORD will reign over them in Mount Zion
From now on, even forever.
8 And you, O tower of the flock,
The stronghold of the daughter of Zion,
To you shall it come,
Even the former dominion shall come,
The kingdom of the daughter of Jerusalem."

9 Now why do you cry aloud?
Is there no king in your midst?
Has your counselor perished?
For pangs have seized you like a woman in labor.
10 Be in pain, and labor to bring forth,
O daughter of Zion,

3:12 [a]Literally *house* **4:3** [a]Compare Isaiah 2:2–4

Like a woman in birth pangs.
For now you shall go forth from the city,
You shall dwell in the field,
And to Babylon you shall go.
There you shall be delivered;
There the LORD will redeem you
From the hand of your enemies.

11 Now also many nations have gathered against you,
Who say, "Let her be defiled,
And let our eye look upon Zion."
12 But they do not know the thoughts of the LORD,
Nor do they understand His counsel;
For He will gather them like sheaves to the threshing floor.

13 "Arise and thresh, O daughter of Zion;
For I will make your horn iron,
And I will make your hooves bronze;
You shall beat in pieces many peoples;
I will consecrate their gain to the LORD,
And their substance to the Lord of the whole earth."

5 Now gather yourself in troops,
O daughter of troops;
He has laid siege against us;
They will strike the judge of Israel with a rod on the cheek.

The Coming Messiah

2 "But you, Bethlehem Ephrathah,
Though you are little among the thousands of Judah,
Yet out of you shall come forth to Me
The One to be Ruler in Israel,
Whose goings forth *are* from of old,
From everlasting."

3 Therefore He shall give them up,
Until the time *that* she who is in labor has given birth;
Then the remnant of His brethren
Shall return to the children of Israel.
4 And He shall stand and feed *His flock*
In the strength of the LORD,
In the majesty of the name of the LORD His God;
And they shall abide,
For now He shall be great
To the ends of the earth;
5 And this *One* shall be peace.

Judgment on Israel's Enemies

When the Assyrian comes into our land,
And when he treads in our palaces,
Then we will raise against him
Seven shepherds and eight princely men.
6 They shall waste with the sword the land of Assyria,
And the land of Nimrod at its entrances;
Thus He shall deliver *us* from the Assyrian,
When he comes into our land
And when he treads within our borders.

7 Then the remnant of Jacob
Shall be in the midst of many peoples,
Like dew from the LORD,
Like showers on the grass,
That tarry for no man
Nor wait for the sons of men.
8 And the remnant of Jacob
Shall be among the Gentiles,
In the midst of many peoples,
Like a lion among the beasts of the forest,
Like a young lion among flocks of sheep,
Who, if he passes through,
Both treads down and tears in pieces,
And none can deliver.
9 Your hand shall be lifted against your adversaries,
And all your enemies shall be cut off.

10 "And it shall be in that day," says the LORD,
"That I will cut off your horses from your midst
And destroy your chariots.
11 I will cut off the cities of your land
And throw down all your strongholds.
12 I will cut off sorceries from your hand,
And you shall have no soothsayers.
13 Your carved images I will also cut off,
And your *sacred* pillars from your midst;
You shall no more worship the work of your hands;
14 I will pluck your wooden images[a] from your midst;
Thus I will destroy your cities.
15 And I will execute vengeance in anger and fury
On the nations that have not heard."[a]

5:14 [a]Hebrew *Asherim,* Canaanite deities
5:15 [a]Or *obeyed*

God Pleads with Israel

6 Hear now what the LORD says:

"Arise, plead your case before the mountains,
And let the hills hear your voice.
2 Hear, O you mountains, the LORD's complaint,
And you strong foundations of the earth;
For the LORD has a complaint against His people,
And He will contend with Israel.

3 "O My people, what have I done to you?
And how have I wearied you?
Testify against Me.
4 For I brought you up from the land of Egypt,
I redeemed you from the house of bondage;
And I sent before you Moses, Aaron, and Miriam.
5 O My people, remember now
What Balak king of Moab counseled,
And what Balaam the son of Beor answered him,
From Acacia Grove[a] to Gilgal,
That you may know the righteousness of the LORD."

6 With what shall I come before the LORD,
And bow myself before the High God?
Shall I come before Him with burnt offerings,
With calves a year old?
7 Will the LORD be pleased with thousands of rams,
Ten thousand rivers of oil?
Shall I give my firstborn *for* my transgression,
The fruit of my body *for* the sin of my soul?
8 He has shown you, O man, what *is* good;
And what does the LORD require of you
But to do justly,
To love mercy,
And to walk humbly with your God?

Punishment of Israel's Injustice

9 The LORD's voice cries to the city—
Wisdom shall see Your name:

"Hear the rod!
Who has appointed it?
10 Are there yet the treasures of wickedness
In the house of the wicked,
And the short measure *that is* an abomination?
11 Shall I count pure *those* with the wicked scales,
And with the bag of deceitful weights?
12 For her rich men are full of violence,
Her inhabitants have spoken lies,
And their tongue is deceitful in their mouth.

13 "Therefore I will also make *you* sick by striking you,
By making *you* desolate because of your sins.
14 You shall eat, but not be satisfied;
Hunger[a] *shall be* in your midst.
You may carry *some* away,[b] but shall not save *them;*
And what you do rescue I will give over to the sword.

6:5 [a]Hebrew *Shittim* (compare Numbers 25:1; Joshua 2:1; 3:1) **6:14** [a]Or *Emptiness* or *Humiliation* [b]Targum and Vulgate read *You shall take hold.*

SOUL NOTE

Live and Love *(6:6–8)* "How can I approach God?" This question is buried deep in everyone's soul. The Judeans asked a similar question: "With what shall I come before the LORD?" They wanted to know what offerings they should bring. In answer, however, Micah pointed directly at their hearts. Did they uphold God's justice in their communities? Did they show God's mercy to the disadvantaged? Had they humbly offered their lives to the Lord? God didn't want their offerings; He wanted their lives. God still wants hearts that love Him and hands that serve in His name. **Topic: Attitudes**

15 "You shall sow, but not reap;
You shall tread the olives, but not anoint yourselves with oil;
And *make* sweet wine, but not drink wine.
16 For the statutes of Omri are kept;
All the works of Ahab's house *are done;*
And you walk in their counsels,
That I may make you a desolation,
And your inhabitants a hissing.
Therefore you shall bear the reproach of My people."[a]

> Therefore I will look to the LORD; I will wait for the God of my salvation; my God will hear me.
>
> MICAH 7:7

Sorrow for Israel's Sins

7 Woe is me!
For I am like those who gather summer fruits,
Like those who glean vintage grapes;
There is no cluster to eat
Of the first-ripe fruit *which* my soul desires.
2 The faithful *man* has perished from the earth,
And *there is* no one upright among men.
They all lie in wait for blood;
Every man hunts his brother with a net.

3 That they may successfully do evil with both hands—
The prince asks *for gifts,*
The judge *seeks* a bribe,
And the great *man* utters his evil desire;
So they scheme together.
4 The best of them *is* like a brier;
The most upright *is sharper* than a thorn hedge;
The day of your watchman and your punishment comes;
Now shall be their perplexity.

5 Do not trust in a friend;
Do not put your confidence in a companion;
Guard the doors of your mouth
From her who lies in your bosom.
6 For son dishonors father,
Daughter rises against her mother,
Daughter-in-law against her mother-in-law;
A man's enemies *are* the men of his own household.
7 Therefore I will look to the LORD;
I will wait for the God of my salvation;
My God will hear me.

Israel's Confession and Comfort

8 Do not rejoice over me, my enemy;
When I fall, I will arise;
When I sit in darkness,
The LORD *will be* a light to me.
9 I will bear the indignation of the LORD,
Because I have sinned against Him,
Until He pleads my case
And executes justice for me.
He will bring me forth to the light;
I will see His righteousness.
10 Then *she who is* my enemy will see,
And shame will cover her who said to me,
"Where is the LORD your God?"

6:16 [a]Following Masoretic Text, Targum, and Vulgate; Septuagint reads *of nations.*

SOUL NOTE

Redeeming Failure *(7:7, 8)* Judah had failed miserably. God had punished them for their sins, and Judah's enemies were rejoicing over their fall. Micah outlined what the people were to do when they were at their lowest point. Instead of listening to their enemies' taunts, they were to look to God and wait for Him. After their fall, they would arise. In the darkness, God would be a light. Judah's God is the Savior of all believers. Even if we have miserably failed, He wants to pick us up and pull us out of the darkness. With God, failure is never final. **Topic: Failure**

HOW TO HAVE A POSITIVE ATTITUDE

DANIEL LOVETT

(Micah 6:8)

Too many Christians live lives of quiet desperation, always worrying and fretting. They pray, but God's peace never seems to come to their hearts. In short, they have such negative attitudes that they are helping no one and hurting themselves. So what can we do to exchange negative attitudes for positive ones? The prophet Micah provides three requirements in Micah 6:8 which, when acted upon, will have an enormous impact on attitude.

ATTITUDE ADJUSTMENT

The first step toward a positive attitude is to "do justly." We must be honest with ourselves and then live honestly. We must quit making excuses and start dealing with our own hearts and minds. We must admit and face up to our own problems. Problems begin on the inside. The heart of every problem is the problem of the heart. When we admit and confess what is in our hearts and minds we will have a positive attitude. "For as he thinks in his heart, so is he. 'Eat and drink!' he says to you, but his heart is not with you" (Prov. 23:7).

The second step toward a positive attitude is to "love mercy." In other words, we need to learn to make things right. If there are problems between people, one person needs to take the initiative to make things right—being merciful and forgiving if that's needed. We cannot get along perfectly with everyone, but Paul admonished, "If it is possible, as much as depends on you, live peaceably with all men" (Rom. 12:18). When we have right relationships with others we will have a positive attitude.

The third step toward a positive attitude is to "walk humbly" with God. We need to ask God to search our minds and hearts. Psalm 139:23, 24 says, "Search me, O God, and know my heart; try me, and know my anxieties; and see if there is any wicked way in me, and lead me in the way everlasting." The submissive mind puts Christ and others ahead of self (Phil. 2:4). Resentment, thoughts of bitterness, pride, or other negative attitudes will poison the heart and mind, and ultimately the whole attitude and personality. If God sees wrong thoughts and bad attitudes in our hearts and minds, He cannot give us His peace and joy. It takes faith to have a submissive mind, because humility is so contrary to the spirit of the world. Yet Jesus has said, "He who is greatest among you shall be your servant" (Matt. 23:11). When we have humble, submissive minds we will have a positive attitude.

When we start to develop harmful attitudes—being worried, critical, depressed, or discouraged—we must stop to examine ourselves. We must ask, "Do I have this attitude because I'm not being honest with myself? Am I blaming others for my problems? Am I holding a grudge and refusing to forgive or make things right? Am I being proud? Am I forgetting to think single-mindedly with Christ? Have I ceased having a submissive mind? Where along the line did I stop living for Christ?"

DISCOVERING GOD'S WAY

Those Christians who cultivate a spiritual life will find that they develop a positive attitude. While so much of the world is wrapped up in possessions, entertainment, achievements, and other earthly enticements, believers already know that earthly things will never satisfy. That is full-time Christian living—having a positive attitude and a single mind with Christ to do what will be pleasing to Him.

Christians who spend time daily in God's Word and in prayer, who cast their cares upon the Lord, and who seek to obey His Word in all circumstances, will have the presence of God in their lives and the peace of God in their hearts. This will result in an "I can" attitude like the one Paul had when he wrote, "I can do all things through Christ who strengthens me" (Phil. 4:13).

A bad attitude can become a way of life. Some people enjoy their bad attitudes—they get attention and sympathy, which inflates their egos. Like the Pharisees, they parade their problems and troubles in order to be seen by others. There is nothing wrong with people sharing their burdens with fellow Christians if their motives are right, but doing so to attract attention and sympathy is sinful.

A positive attitude comes not with freedom *from* problems and difficulties, but with freedom *in spite of* them. When Paul wrote Philippians, he didn't deny that he was in prison; his attitude toward his imprisonment, however, had set him free to continue to be all God wanted him to be. Our homes, our jobs, our situations, even our physical bodies with their frailties can all seem like prisons. We can still experience positive attitudes, however. Paul had learned that he could do all things through Christ—and so can we. We need to start each day with surrender to the Lord. We need to ask Him to help us to do justly, to love mercy, and to walk humbly with Him. We need to stay close to Him daily. This will produce a positive attitude that results in dynamic living for Christ, giving us a positive witness to each person with whom we come in contact throughout our day. Then we can be as the psalmist described it when he said, "They looked to Him and were radiant" (Ps. 34:5).

FURTHER MEDITATION:

Other passages to study about the issue of attitudes include:

- Joshua 14:10–12
- Acts 27:22
- Romans 15:5–7
- 2 Corinthians 10:5
- Galatians 6:9
- Philippians 2:5–11
- 1 Timothy 4:15, 16
- Hebrews 12:1, 2
- James 1:2–4

To Learn More: **Turn to the key passage note on attitudes at Romans 12:1, 2 on page 1482. See also the personality profile of Michal on page 395.**

My eyes will see her;
Now she will be trampled down
Like mud in the streets.

11 *In* the day when your walls are to be built,
In that day the decree shall go far and wide.[a]
12 *In* that day they[a] shall come to you
From Assyria and the fortified cities,[b]
From the fortress[c] to the River,[d]
From sea to sea,
And mountain *to* mountain.
13 Yet the land shall be desolate
Because of those who dwell in it,
And for the fruit of their deeds.

God Will Forgive Israel

14 Shepherd Your people with Your staff,
The flock of Your heritage,
Who dwell solitarily *in* a woodland,
In the midst of Carmel;
Let them feed *in* Bashan and Gilead,
As in days of old.

15 "As in the days when you came out of the land of Egypt,
I will show them[a] wonders."

16 The nations shall see and be ashamed of all their might;
They shall put *their* hand over *their* mouth;
Their ears shall be deaf.
17 They shall lick the dust like a serpent;
They shall crawl from their holes like snakes of the earth.
They shall be afraid of the LORD our God,
And shall fear because of You.
18 Who *is* a God like You,
Pardoning iniquity
And passing over the transgression of the remnant of His heritage?

He does not retain His anger forever,
Because He delights *in* mercy.
19 He will again have compassion on us,
And will subdue our iniquities.

You will cast all our[a] sins
Into the depths of the sea.
20 You will give truth to Jacob
And mercy to Abraham,
Which You have sworn to our fathers
From days of old.

7:11 [a]Or *the boundary shall be extended*
7:12 [a]Literally *he,* collective of the captives [b]Hebrew *arey mazor,* possibly *cities of Egypt* [c]Hebrew *mazor,* possibly *Egypt* [d]That is, the Euphrates **7:15** [a]Literally *him,* collective for the captives **7:19** [a]Literally *their*

Nahum

Whether struggling under an oppressive employer, dealing with personal pain and heartbreak, or just feeling frustrated over world events—we want justice. Evil should be punished, right should triumph, and good should win. Yet too often the opposite seems to be the case. Whether it's mistreatment at the hands of an abusive spouse, an overbearing parent, an intrusive government, or a callous corporation, something in us recoils at oppression and applauds when things are made right.

In about 620 B.C., Judah was being oppressed by Assyria, the most powerful and cruel nation on earth. One hundred years earlier, the Assyrians had responded to the preaching of Jonah, but their repentance was clearly short-lived. So at this point, having once experienced the mercy of God, the Assyrians were all the more responsible for their actions.

God told the prophet Nahum to announce Nineveh's destruction (2:6–8). Indeed, this destruction, the wrath of God, fell on Nineveh in 612 B.C. when the Babylonians, Scythians, and Medes overran its walls and turned it into a permanent ruin.

Nahum reminds us that God's justice means He will not overlook evil, nor will He turn a deaf ear to the cries of its victims. If you personally are suffering mistreatment or feeling outrage in your soul because of unjust situations around you, let Nahum comfort you with the truth that in God's world nobody gets away with anything. Ultimately every wrong will be made right!

SOUL CONCERN IN NAHUM

TRUST	(1:7)

1 The burden[a] against Nineveh. The book of the vision of Nahum the Elkoshite.

GOD'S WRATH ON HIS ENEMIES

2 God *is* jealous, and the LORD avenges;
The LORD avenges and *is* furious.
The LORD will take vengeance on His adversaries,
And He reserves *wrath* for His enemies;
3 The LORD *is* slow to anger and great in power,
And will not at all acquit *the* wicked.

The LORD has His way
In the whirlwind and in the storm,
And the clouds *are* the dust of His feet.
4 He rebukes the sea and makes it dry,
And dries up all the rivers.
Bashan and Carmel wither,
And the flower of Lebanon wilts.
5 The mountains quake before Him,
The hills melt,
And the earth heaves[a] at His presence,
Yes, the world and all who dwell in it.

6 Who can stand before His indignation?
And who can endure the fierceness of His anger?
His fury is poured out like fire,
And the rocks are thrown down by Him.

7 The LORD *is* good,
A stronghold in the day of trouble;
And He knows those who trust in Him.

> The LORD is slow to anger and great in power, and will not at all acquit the wicked. The LORD has His way in the whirlwind and in the storm, and the clouds are the dust of His feet.
>
> NAHUM 1:3

8 But with an overflowing flood
He will make an utter end of its place,
And darkness will pursue His enemies.

9 What do you conspire against the LORD?
He will make an utter end *of it.*
Affliction will not rise up a second time.
10 For while tangled *like* thorns,
And while drunken *like* drunkards,
They shall be devoured like stubble fully dried.
11 From you comes forth *one*
Who plots evil against the LORD,
A wicked counselor.

12 Thus says the LORD:

"Though *they are* safe, and likewise many,
Yet in this manner they will be cut down
When he passes through.
Though I have afflicted you,
I will afflict you no more;
13 For now I will break off his yoke from you,
And burst your bonds apart."

14 The LORD has given a command concerning you:
"Your name shall be perpetuated no longer.
Out of the house of your gods
I will cut off the carved image and the molded image.

1:1 [a]Or *oracle* **1:5** [a]Targum reads *burns.*

SOUL NOTE

Trust in the Lord *(1:7)* Over a century before, Jonah had warned the Assyrians (in the capital city of Nineveh) of God's judgment, and they had repented. It seems their spiritual renewal didn't last long, however, and they began oppressing God's people. They attacked Israel, the northern kingdom, taking them into captivity. Nahum's prophecy comforted the people in the southern kingdom (Judah). They knew that "the LORD is good . . . and He knows those who trust in Him." When the wicked appear to be in control, don't despair. He won't forget those who trust in Him.
Topic: Trust

I will dig your grave,
For you are vile."

15 Behold, on the mountains
The feet of him who brings good tidings,
Who proclaims peace!
O Judah, keep your appointed feasts,
Perform your vows.
For the wicked one shall no more pass through you;
He is utterly cut off.

The Destruction of Nineveh

2 He who scatters[a] has come up before your face.
Man the fort!
Watch the road!
Strengthen *your* flanks!
Fortify *your* power mightily.

2 For the LORD will restore the excellence of Jacob
Like the excellence of Israel,
For the emptiers have emptied them out
And ruined their vine branches.

3 The shields of his mighty men *are* made red,
The valiant men *are* in scarlet.
The chariots *come* with flaming torches
In the day of his preparation,
And the spears are brandished.[a]
4 The chariots rage in the streets,
They jostle one another in the broad roads;
They seem like torches,
They run like lightning.

5 He remembers his nobles;
They stumble in their walk;
They make haste to her walls,
And the defense is prepared.
6 The gates of the rivers are opened,
And the palace is dissolved.
7 It is decreed:[a]
She shall be led away captive,
She shall be brought up;
And her maidservants shall lead *her* as with the voice of doves,
Beating their breasts.

8 Though Nineveh of old *was* like a pool of water,
Now they flee away.
"Halt! Halt!" *they cry;*
But no one turns back.
9 Take spoil of silver!
Take spoil of gold!
There is no end of treasure,
Or wealth of every desirable prize.
10 She is empty, desolate, and waste!
The heart melts, and the knees shake;
Much pain *is* in every side,
And all their faces are drained of color.[a]

11 Where *is* the dwelling of the lions,
And the feeding place of the young lions,
Where the lion walked, the lioness *and* lion's cub,
And no one made *them* afraid?
12 The lion tore in pieces enough for his cubs,
Killed for his lionesses,
Filled his caves with prey,
And his dens with flesh.

13 "Behold, I *am* against you," says the LORD
of hosts, "I will burn your[a] chariots in smoke,
and the sword shall devour your young lions; I
will cut off your prey from the earth, and the
voice of your messengers shall be heard no
more."

The Woe of Nineveh

3 Woe to the bloody city!
It *is* all full of lies *and* robbery.
Its victim never departs.
2 The noise of a whip
And the noise of rattling wheels,
Of galloping horses,
Of clattering chariots!
3 Horsemen charge with bright sword and glittering spear.
There is a multitude of slain,
A great number of bodies,
Countless corpses—
They stumble over the corpses—
4 Because of the multitude of harlotries of the seductive harlot,
The mistress of sorceries,
Who sells nations through her harlotries,
And families through her sorceries.

2:1 [a]Vulgate reads *He who destroys.* **2:3** [a]Literally *the cypresses are shaken;* Septuagint and Syriac read *the horses rush about;* Vulgate reads *the drivers are stupefied.* **2:7** [a]Hebrew *Huzzab* **2:10** [a]Compare Joel 2:6 **2:13** [a]Literally *her*

LEARNING TO TRUST

PATRICK SPRINGLE

(Nahum 1:7)

Trust is the foundation of all positive, healthy relationships. Trust is the glue that holds people together through life's most difficult experiences. With this foundation, we can endure almost anything; without it, every interaction and every decision is a threat.

We exercise trust in virtually every interaction in our lives. We trust cars and airplanes with our lives; we trust banks with our money; we trust the restaurant with our health. We trust others as we share our secrets. We trust a spouse with our marriage. We trust God, even though we cannot see Him.

WHEN TRUST IS VIOLATED

Like a hammer shattering a porcelain vase, a relationship of trust can be shattered by physical, sexual, or emotional abuse. In fact, traumas like car accidents, severe injuries, or deaths in the family can also undermine a person's sense of security and trust. Less obvious, but just as devastating, are words of criticism and condemnation that wear a person's soul away like sandpaper. This erosion of trust might occur dozens of times a day—so often that it seems "normal." Trust is also eroded by the absence of love and attention.

People whose trust has been shattered or eroded feel desperate to find stability, so they try to control their lives in any way they can. Because these people do not build positive, trusting relationships, they feel empty and disillusioned. Three different types of problems can occur for these people:

1. *Blind trust*— Some try to control others by attempting to please them, doing whatever it takes to make others happy. They close their eyes to the reality of the hurt, anger, lies, and manipulation and end up trusting untrustworthy people. Their goal is to obtain the love they crave.
2. *Aggressive distrust*—Some try to control by dominating. They cover their insecurity by yelling, cursing, and blaming, but they also use charm to get what they want. This combination of charm and venom puts other people off balance.
3. *Passive distrust*—Some try to avoid being hurt any more by keeping their distance from people. They give up on relationships altogether, concluding that it is too painful and too hopeless to even try to relate to others.

LEARNING TO TRUST

Even those with very painful pasts can learn to trust again. This is done by learning *perceptive trust*. Those who have insight and wisdom know that not everybody is trustworthy, and that trust must be earned by consistent, honorable, ethical behavior. To have perceptive trust is to live in the reality—often the harsh reality—that people we love will let us down. To have perceptive trust is to know, however, that God will never let us down.

Following are some suggestions for learning to trust perceptively:

Identify Patterns of Distrust

People must be honest about the pain of the past and the damage it has caused. The patterns of hiding from people, dominating them, or pleasing them at all costs exist because people are desperate to find some meaning and safety in their lives. Ultimately, such behavior only hurts them more. Repentance is a vital part of the Christian experience and involves being honest about wrong perceptions and destructive behaviors. Repentance enables them to choose what is good and right.

Gain a New Perception of God
People's most intimate human relationships will color their perception of God. But these perceptions can be changed as God shows His true character and great love. Finding a fellowship of believers who are experiencing the goodness and grace of God can help people shape a healthy view of God.

Take Steps to Trust Perceptively
Blind trust people need to be more cautious in relationships and not trust so quickly and completely. Aggressive distrust people need to be quiet and calm, encouraging rather than intimidating. Passive distrust people need to take steps to be more open and vulnerable with those they trust. These are all healthy steps of growth and change.

Find People Who Understand
Changes of the heart do not occur in a vacuum. People must find others who can understand, encourage, and speak the truth to them about God and about themselves. One trustworthy, honest, perceptive person can make all the difference. In cases of severe abuse or abandonment, a pastor or a professional counselor may better provide the insight and nurture necessary for change to occur.

Absorb the Truth About God
To learn to trust, people must absorb the Scriptures with an attitude of commitment and with prayer. They can search passages that are particularly meaningful and memorize them. God is, and always will be, true to His Word. They can count on Him to lead them and give wisdom, peace, and strength.

No matter how much their trust has been destroyed in the past, people can still discover that God is supremely trustworthy. In Him, they can find peace and wisdom. The Bible promises, "Trust in the LORD with all your heart, and lean not on your own understanding; in all your ways acknowledge Him, and He shall direct your paths" (Prov. 3:5, 6).

FURTHER MEDITATION:

Other passages to study about the issue of trust include:

- 2 Samuel 22:3, 31
- Psalms 4:5; 5:11; 9:10; 27:10; 31:1
- Proverbs 11:28
- John 20:29
- Romans 8:31–39

To Learn More: Turn to the key passage note on trust at Proverbs 3:5, 6 on page 803. See also the personality profile of Habakkuk on page 1185.

5 "Behold, I *am* against you," says the LORD
of hosts;
"I will lift your skirts over your face,
I will show the nations your nakedness,
And the kingdoms your shame.
6 I will cast abominable filth upon you,
Make you vile,
And make you a spectacle.
7 It shall come to pass *that* all who look
upon you
Will flee from you, and say,
'Nineveh is laid waste!
Who will bemoan her?'
Where shall I seek comforters for you?"

8 Are you better than No Amon[a]
That was situated by the River,[b]
That had the waters around her,
Whose rampart *was* the sea,
Whose wall *was* the sea?
9 Ethiopia and Egypt *were* her strength,
And *it was* boundless;
Put and Lubim were your[a] helpers.
10 Yet she *was* carried away,
She went into captivity;
Her young children also were dashed to
pieces
At the head of every street;
They cast lots for her honorable men,
And all her great men were bound in
chains.
11 You also will be drunk;
You will be hidden;
You also will seek refuge from the
enemy.

12 All your strongholds *are* fig trees with
ripened figs:
If they are shaken,
They fall into the mouth of the eater.
13 Surely, your people in your midst *are*
women!
The gates of your land are wide open for
your enemies;
Fire shall devour the bars of your
gates.

14 Draw your water for the siege!
Fortify your strongholds!
Go into the clay and tread the mortar!
Make strong the brick kiln!
15 There the fire will devour you,
The sword will cut you off;
It will eat you up like a locust.

Make yourself many—like the locust!
Make yourself many—like the *swarming*
locusts!
16 You have multiplied your merchants
more than the stars of heaven.
The locust plunders and flies away.
17 Your commanders *are* like *swarming*
locusts,
And your generals like great
grasshoppers,
Which camp in the hedges on a cold
day;
When the sun rises they flee away,
And the place where they *are* is not
known.

18 Your shepherds slumber, O king of
Assyria;
Your nobles rest *in the dust.*
Your people are scattered on the
mountains,
And no one gathers them.
19 Your injury *has* no healing,
Your wound is severe.
All who hear news of you
Will clap *their* hands over you,
For upon whom has not your
wickedness passed continually?

3:8 [a]That is, ancient Thebes; Targum and Vulgate read *populous Alexandria.* [b]Literally *rivers,* that is, the Nile and the surrounding canals
3:9 [a]Septuagint reads *her.*

Habakkuk

"Why do good things happen to bad people and bad things happen to good people?" That's a common lament, and no wonder: A quick look at the day's news brings more evidence than we care to consider. And our question becomes louder when the "bad things" happen to us!

The prophet Habakkuk put a variation of this question to God, asking why God was tolerating rampant evil among the people of Judah. God's shocking answer was that He intended to use the unspeakably cruel and decadent Babylonians to execute justice on His wayward nation. This revelation, far from satisfying Habakkuk's troubled soul, only prompted him to further question God's wisdom (1:12–17). God heard Habakkuk's questions; then He answered.

This short book shows Habakkuk coming to the realization that Almighty God is able to use even pagan nations to accomplish His sovereign purposes. The classic expression, "The just shall live by his faith" (2:4) is not only Habakkuk's personal profession of trust, but it is also a statement quoted frequently in the New Testament (Rom. 1:17; Gal. 3:11; Heb. 10:38) to give expression to the foundational doctrine of salvation by faith alone. Habakkuk realized, as all God's people must, that only full confidence in God can sustain us in troubling and uncertain times.

Faith helps us put the troubles of this world into proper perspective. When ill health, economic difficulties, or personal family crises strike, faith clings to the promise that God's sovereign purposes are being accomplished. The trusting soul sees God as greater than any problem.

SOUL CONCERN IN HABAKKUK

1 The burden[a] which the prophet Habakkuk saw.

THE PROPHET'S QUESTION

2 O LORD, how long shall I cry,
And You will not hear?
Even cry out to You, "Violence!"
And You will not save.
3 Why do You show me iniquity,
And cause *me* to see trouble?
For plundering and violence *are* before me;
There is strife, and contention arises.
4 Therefore the law is powerless,
And justice never goes forth.
For the wicked surround the righteous;
Therefore perverse judgment proceeds.

THE LORD'S REPLY

5 "Look among the nations and watch—
Be utterly astounded!
For *I will* work a work in your days
Which you would not believe, though it were told *you*.
6 For indeed I am raising up the Chaldeans,
A bitter and hasty nation
Which marches through the breadth of the earth,
To possess dwelling places *that are* not theirs.
7 They are terrible and dreadful;
Their judgment and their dignity proceed from themselves.
8 Their horses also are swifter than leopards,
And more fierce than evening wolves.
Their chargers charge ahead;
Their cavalry comes from afar;
They fly as the eagle *that* hastens to eat.
9 "They all come for violence;
Their faces are set *like* the east wind.
They gather captives like sand.
10 They scoff at kings,
And princes are scorned by them.
They deride every stronghold,
For they heap up earthen *mounds* and seize it.
11 Then *his* mind[a] changes, and he transgresses;
He commits offense,
Ascribing this power to his god."

THE PROPHET'S SECOND QUESTION

12 Are You not from everlasting,
O LORD my God, my Holy One?
We shall not die.
O LORD, You have appointed them for judgment;
O Rock, You have marked them for correction.
13 *You are* of purer eyes than to behold evil,
And cannot look on wickedness.
Why do You look on those who deal treacherously,
And hold Your tongue when the wicked devours
A *person* more righteous than he?
14 *Why* do You make men like fish of the sea,
Like creeping things *that have* no ruler over them?

15 They take up all of them with a hook,
They catch them in their net,
And gather them in their dragnet.
Therefore they rejoice and are glad.
16 Therefore they sacrifice to their net,

1:1 [a]Or *oracle* **1:11** [a]Literally *spirit* or *wind*

SOUL NOTE

Dealing with Doubt *(1:1–4)* Nagging questions and doubts—everyone has them, even believers. We often feel guilty for doubting, however, so we repress our doubts. The prophet Habakkuk didn't silence his questions and doubts. Instead, he courageously brought them to God. Habakkuk began by asking God why He allowed evil to flourish, a question that has puzzled people for centuries. Habakkuk humbly asked God, and God answered. When we have questions and doubts, we should bring them to God, and He will answer. We must be willing, however, to accept the answers He gives. **Topic: Doubt**

And burn incense to their dragnet;
Because by them their share *is*
sumptuous
And their food plentiful.
17 Shall they therefore empty their net,
And continue to slay nations without
pity?

2 I will stand my watch
And set myself on the rampart,
And watch to see what He will say to me,
And what I will answer when I am
corrected.

The Just Live by Faith

2Then the LORD answered me and said:

"Write the vision
And make *it* plain on tablets,
That he may run who reads it.
3 For the vision *is* yet for an appointed
time;
But at the end it will speak, and it will
not lie.
Though it tarries, wait for it;
Because it will surely come,
It will not tarry.

4 "Behold the proud,
His soul is not upright in him;
But the just shall live by his faith.

Woe to the Wicked

5 "Indeed, because he transgresses by
wine,
He is a proud man,
And he does not stay at home.
Because he enlarges his desire as hell,[a]
And he *is* like death, and cannot be
satisfied,
He gathers to himself all nations
And heaps up for himself all peoples.

2:5 [a]Or *Sheol*

PERSONALITY PROFILE

Trust

HABAKKUK: THE TOWER OF TRUST

(HABAKKUK 2)

Why? Children ask the question as soon as they are old enough to understand the word "no." They want to know the explanation for why they cannot do or have something. As we get older, the question continues to nag us as we encounter "why" questions at every turn. When we see evil, pain, and suffering in the world and, especially, in our lives, we ask, "Why?" Thousands of years ago, Habakkuk took that same question directly to God.

Habakkuk, God's prophet, preached trust during a time of great trouble and distress. The nation of Judah was facing impending invasion from the Babylonians, who had taken Nineveh, the great capital of Assyria. Judah's days were numbered, for God would use the wicked Babylonians to conquer His people and punish their sins. Habakkuk wanted to know why: "Why do You look on those who deal treacherously, and hold Your tongue when the wicked devours a person more righteous than he?" (Hab. 1:13). Habakkuk asked this question on behalf of his nation, then he awaited God's answer: "I will stand my watch and set myself on the rampart, and watch to see what He will say to me" (2:1).

God answered His questioning prophet, explaining that while He would use Babylon to punish Judah, the Babylonians wouldn't even know that they were pawns in His hands. Babylon's pride and power would eventually be its downfall. God told Habakkuk to be patient. In the end, He would make everything right.

God's people must trust Him completely, even in the face of tragic events. Trust is believing *without* seeing. Habakkuk pronounced: "The just shall live by his faith" (2:4). When we trust in our trustworthy God, we don't need to know why. We only need to know Him.

To Learn More: Turn to the article about trust on pages 1180, 1181. See also the key passage note at Proverbs 3:5, 6 on page 803.

PRINCIPLED PLEASURE

MARK R. LAASER

(Habakkuk 2:5–7)

The new century presents many challenges. In a time of impatience and selfishness, a person's wants and desires often can gain instant gratification. Science and culture provide helpful advances and opportunities. However, some people get trapped in a downward spiral of addiction to substances and behaviors used to gratify impatient desires.

WHAT IS ADDICTION?

The word "addiction" technically means that the brain has become neurochemically dependent on substances ingested into the body, or on the chemicals the brain produces when one performs certain behaviors. Neurochemical dependence assumes the brain will actually "crave" the substance or substance-producing behavior. Over time, more of the substance is required to achieve the same effect in the brain because the brain has an amazing ability to adjust whatever is put into it. This factor is called "tolerance." It also means that when any addict stops the addictive behavior, the brain will "rebel" against the absence and go through a phase of detoxification.

Neurochemical addiction is caused by *chemicals* such as alcohol, cocaine, or heroin. However, some believe that certain *behaviors* can create neurochemical reactions. Sexual thoughts, for example, create certain chemicals that cause intense feelings of pleasure. Simply fantasizing about sex can create these "pleasure" chemicals. Experts in sexual addiction argue that sexual thought and activity can create a neurochemical addiction similar to a substance addiction. Gamblers, likewise, experience a release of adrenaline when they take risks with money. A gambler can become addicted to the body's production of this chemical. Research has further shown that very few addicts suffer only one addiction. They may have a dominant one, but they also turn to a variety of other addictions as well. A new diagnosis that is gaining acceptance is Multiple Addiction Disorder (MAD). Whether addicts use chemicals or chemical-producing behaviors or both, their brains become a chemical smorgasbord.

One factor that can make recovery so difficult is the synergy of the neurochemical and emotional dependencies involved in addiction. Substances and behaviors get associated with relief of certain emotions even while they are creating a chemical dependency. Smokers know, for example, that they can detoxify from the effects of nicotine in a few days. What is harder, though, is the emotional dependency they created by associating smoking with relaxing or with relaxing situations.

WHAT CAUSES ADDICTION?

Addicts are lonely. They are starving for love, attention, and nurture. Many are angry that their needs—either when they were children, or as adults—have gone unmet. Some are angry at having been physically, sexually, or emotionally abused as children. The combination of loneliness and anger drives addicts deeper into their addiction. They may even be angry at God for not taking away or "delivering" them from their desires. Addicts often did not form healthy attachments to parents and others as children; they may not know how to find real love. That is why many people substitute addictive substances or behaviors for relationships.

Addiction is a problem of original sin—addicts believe they can control their lives better than God can. In seeking control, addicts are totally out of control. "For we know that the law is spiritual, but I am carnal, sold under sin. For what I am doing, I do not understand. For what I will to do, that I do not practice; but what I hate, that I do" (Rom. 7:14, 15). An addiction will get worse over time; it will always lead to destructive consequences.

RELIEF FROM ADDICTION

Relief from addiction is usually referred to as "sobriety." The addict is in "recovery." When addicts experience ongoing sobriety, they will occasionally need to celebrate these victories. Achieving sobriety and staying in recovery is a combination of spiritual, emotional, and physical work.

Spiritually, addicts must take the risk of confessing their powerlessness. They fear that if others know about their addiction, they will be ridiculed and abandoned. Fellowship with others who can tell their stories to one another is one of the essential elements of getting well. Confessing powerlessness to others brings an addict closer to being willing to return control to God. This is in the spirit of James 5:16, which encourages fellow believers to confess sin to each other in order to bring healing.

Emotionally, addicts will need to address old wounds that have caused them to feel unloved and unlovable. This may be a matter of intensive counseling that addresses traumas and memories of abuse as a child. Healthy churches will work to create opportunities for them to have support groups. This kind of fellowship is also a kind of accountability. It is support that reminds an addict about staying sober from the addictive activity. Sponsors, mentors, or guides who have become sober for longer periods of time will be an integral part of an accountability network. Addicts will need to be accountable to change the behaviors that led to addiction. New habits of healthy behavior will need to be substituted for old destructive patterns.

Physically, addicts may need to seek medical evaluation or medical intervention. They may need medical help to detoxify. Also, some may need evaluation as to whether or not medications are necessary to bring brain chemistry back to a healthy balance.

The treatment of any addiction is often a very specialized program and will require caregivers that are experienced in providing one. Ultimately, we must all remember that there is a hunger for God and for fellowship that underlies all addictions. We must be quick to provide soul care for those needs if we are to truly help addicts to be set free from their addictions.

FURTHER MEDITATION:

Other passages to study about the issue of addictions include:

- Psalms 44:21; 51:1–19
- Proverbs 23:21, 29–35
- Luke 21:34
- 1 Corinthians 6:19, 20
- Ephesians 5:18
- Hebrews 10:22–25

To Learn More: Turn to the key passage note on addictions at 1 Corinthians 6:9–12 on page 1498. See also the personality profile of Gomer on page 1130.

6 "Will not all these take up a proverb
against him,
And a taunting riddle against him, and
say,
'Woe to him who increases
What is not his—how long?
And to him who loads himself with
many pledges'?[a]
7 Will not your creditors[a] rise up
suddenly?
Will they not awaken who oppress you?
And you will become their booty.
8 Because you have plundered many
nations,
All the remnant of the people shall
plunder you,
Because of men's blood
And the violence of the land *and* the
city,
And of all who dwell in it.

9 "Woe to him who covets evil gain for his
house,
That he may set his nest on high,
That he may be delivered from the
power of disaster!
10 You give shameful counsel to your house,
Cutting off many peoples,
And sin *against* your soul.
11 For the stone will cry out from the wall,
And the beam from the timbers will
answer it.

12 "Woe to him who builds a town with
bloodshed,
Who establishes a city by iniquity!
13 Behold, *is it* not of the LORD of hosts
That the peoples labor to feed the fire,[a]
And nations weary themselves in vain?
14 For the earth will be filled
With the knowledge of the glory of the
LORD,
As the waters cover the sea.

15 "Woe to him who gives drink to his
neighbor,
Pressing[a] *him to* your bottle,
Even to make *him* drunk,
That you may look on his nakedness!
16 You are filled with shame instead of
glory.
You also—drink!
And be exposed as uncircumcised![a]
The cup of the LORD's right hand *will be*
turned against you,
And utter shame will be on your glory.
17 For the violence *done to* Lebanon will
cover you,
And the plunder of beasts *which* made
them afraid,
Because of men's blood
And the violence of the land *and* the
city,
And of all who dwell in it.

18 "What profit is the image, that its maker
should carve it,
The molded image, a teacher of lies,
That the maker of its mold should trust
in it,
To make mute idols?
19 Woe to him who says to wood,
'Awake!'
To silent stone, 'Arise! It shall teach!'
Behold, it is overlaid with gold and
silver,
Yet in it there is no breath at all.

20 "But the LORD is in His holy temple.
Let all the earth keep silence before
Him."

2:6 [a]Syriac and Vulgate read *thick clay.*
2:7 [a]Literally *those who bite you* **2:13** [a]Literally *for what satisfies fire,* that is, for what is of no lasting value **2:15** [a]Literally *Attaching* or *Joining*
2:16 [a]Dead Sea Scrolls and Septuagint read *And reel!;* Syriac and Vulgate read *And fall fast asleep!*

SOUL NOTE

Waiting for Answers *(2:1–4)* Habakkuk didn't shrink from asking all his questions. He asked God why He wasn't punishing the wicked Babylonians (1:12–17). Then he awaited God's answer: "I will . . . watch to see what He will say to me" (2:1). At times, it is appropriate to wait. Habakkuk could have become angry or impatient, but instead he humbly waited for God to answer. God will answer our questions, but we need to wait and trust His perfect timing. **Topic: Trust**

THE PROPHET'S PRAYER

3 A prayer of Habakkuk the prophet, on Shigionoth.[a]

2 O LORD, I have heard Your speech *and* was afraid;
O LORD, revive Your work in the midst of the years!
In the midst of the years make *it* known;
In wrath remember mercy.

3 God came from Teman,
The Holy One from Mount Paran. Selah

His glory covered the heavens,
And the earth was full of His praise.
4 *His* brightness was like the light;
He had rays *flashing* from His hand,
And there His power *was* hidden.
5 Before Him went pestilence,
And fever followed at His feet.

6 He stood and measured the earth;
He looked and startled the nations.
And the everlasting mountains were scattered,
The perpetual hills bowed.
His ways *are* everlasting.
7 I saw the tents of Cushan in affliction;
The curtains of the land of Midian trembled.

8 O LORD, were *You* displeased with the rivers,
Was Your anger against the rivers,
Was Your wrath against the sea,
That You rode on Your horses,
Your chariots of salvation?
9 Your bow was made quite ready;
Oaths were sworn over *Your* arrows.[a] Selah

You divided the earth with rivers.
10 The mountains saw You *and* trembled;
The overflowing of the water passed by.
The deep uttered its voice,
And lifted its hands on high.
11 The sun and moon stood still in their habitation;
At the light of Your arrows they went,
At the shining of Your glittering spear.

12 You marched through the land in indignation;
You trampled the nations in anger.
13 You went forth for the salvation of Your people,
For salvation with Your Anointed.
You struck the head from the house of the wicked,
By laying bare from foundation to neck. Selah

14 You thrust through with his own arrows
The head of his villages.
They came out like a whirlwind to scatter me;
Their rejoicing was like feasting on the poor in secret.
15 You walked through the sea with Your horses,
Through the heap of great waters.

16 When I heard, my body trembled;
My lips quivered at *the* voice;
Rottenness entered my bones;
And I trembled in myself,

3:1 [a]Exact meaning unknown **3:9** [a]Literally *rods* or *tribes* (compare verse 14)

SOUL NOTE

In Awe *(3:1, 2)* Habakkuk was afraid when God's answer came. Wicked people fear God because He will punish them for their rebellious ways. For God's people—those who have appealed to the Lord for mercy—this fear is solemn reverence, or awe of God. It is a healthy respect of God's perfect ways and His power. God still speaks, still reveals Himself to His people, still does miracles. Our response should always be reverence and awe that the all-powerful God works in our lives.

Topic: Fear/Fear of God

That I might rest in the day of trouble.
When he comes up to the people,
He will invade them with his troops.

A Hymn of Faith

17 Though the fig tree may not blossom,
Nor fruit be on the vines;
Though the labor of the olive may fail,
And the fields yield no food;
Though the flock may be cut off from the fold,
And there be no herd in the stalls—

18 Yet I will rejoice in the LORD,
I will joy in the God of my salvation.

19 The LORD God[a] is my strength;
He will make my feet like deer's *feet,*
And He will make me walk on my high hills.

To the Chief Musician. With my stringed instruments.

3:19 [a]Hebrew *YHWH Adonai*

SOUL NOTE

Joy in Hardships *(3:17–19)* Habakkuk envisioned the devastation and despair of the Judeans when the Babylonians invaded their land—barren fig trees, desolate vineyards, malnourished cattle and sheep. This pictured ruin for the nation. No wonder Habakkuk trembled in fear (3:16). But Habakkuk didn't allow fear to immobilize him. He quieted his heart and cried to God for deliverance, knowing that whatever would happen, he would always be able to "rejoice in the LORD." No matter what happens, God is with us. In that, we can rejoice. **Topic: Joy**

Zephaniah

When faced with a choice of hearing bad news and good news, most people elect to hear the bad news first. Perhaps the reason is that it's only after we really grasp the magnitude of a grim situation that we can fully appreciate the good. The Book of Zephaniah's prophecy is a classic example of this phenomenon. No other prophet paints a darker picture of God's judgment, or a brighter portrait of Israel's future glory.

Because of the nation's stubborn sinfulness, God raised up Zephaniah, a descendant of godly King Hezekiah. Like his contemporary Jeremiah, Zephaniah warned of terrible judgment to come. This was the worst possible bad news. But Zephaniah's message contained good news too—the hope that a change of direction would result in God's favor and mercy (2:1–3).

God used Zephaniah and a righteous king named Josiah to make a difference in Judah. During Josiah's reign, the people turned to God, destroyed their idols, and restored true worship according to the Law (2 Kin. 23:1–15).

After Josiah's death, however, the spiritual life of the nation plummeted to an all-time low. Judgment eventually came in the form of the Babylonian captivity.

Thankfully, neither Zephaniah nor history ends on a sour note. The good news—in fact, the *great* news—is that there remains a glorious future for the people of God (3:14–20). We only need put our souls in His hands.

SOUL CONCERN IN ZEPHANIAH

CRISES (3:14–17)

1 The word of the LORD which came to
Zephaniah the son of Cushi, the son of
Gedaliah, the son of Amariah, the son of Hezekiah, in the days of Josiah the son of Amon,
king of Judah.

THE GREAT DAY OF THE LORD

2 "I will utterly consume everything
From the face of the land,"
Says the LORD;
3 "I will consume man and beast;
I will consume the birds of the heavens,
The fish of the sea,
And the stumbling blocks[a] along with the wicked.
I will cut off man from the face of the land,"
Says the LORD.

4 "I will stretch out My hand against Judah,
And against all the inhabitants of Jerusalem.
I will cut off every trace of Baal from this place,
The names of the idolatrous priests[a] with the *pagan* priests—
5 Those who worship the host of heaven on the housetops;
Those who worship and swear *oaths* by the LORD,
But who *also* swear by Milcom;[a]
6 Those who have turned back from *following* the LORD,
And have not sought the LORD, nor inquired of Him."

7 Be silent in the presence of the Lord GOD;
For the day of the LORD *is* at hand,
For the LORD has prepared a sacrifice;
He has invited[a] His guests.

8 "And it shall be,
In the day of the LORD's sacrifice,
That I will punish the princes and the king's children,
And all such as are clothed with foreign apparel.
9 In the same day I will punish
All those who leap over the threshold,[a]
Who fill their masters' houses with violence and deceit.

10 "And there shall be on that day," says the LORD,
"The sound of a mournful cry from the Fish Gate,
A wailing from the Second Quarter,
And a loud crashing from the hills.
11 Wail, you inhabitants of Maktesh![a]
For all the merchant people are cut down;
All those who handle money are cut off.

12 "And it shall come to pass at that time
That I will search Jerusalem with lamps,
And punish the men
Who are settled in complacency,[a]
Who say in their heart,
'The LORD will not do good,
Nor will He do evil.'
13 Therefore their goods shall become booty,
And their houses a desolation;
They shall build houses, but not inhabit *them;*

1:3 [a]Figurative of idols **1:4** [a]Hebrew *chemarim* **1:5** [a]Or *Malcam,* an Ammonite god, also called *Molech* (compare Leviticus 18:21) **1:7** [a]Literally *set apart, consecrated* **1:9** [a]Compare 1 Samuel 5:5 **1:11** [a]Literally *Mortar,* a market district of Jerusalem **1:12** [a]Literally *on their lees,* that is, settled like the dregs of wine

SOUL NOTE

Be Silent *(1:7)* In Zephaniah's day, King Josiah was leading a spiritual revival. He was abolishing idol worship and reestablishing the worship of God (2 Chr. 34). The prophet Zephaniah reminded the people that God wouldn't tolerate wickedness, complacency, or idolatry (1:4, 5, 12, 13; 2:1, 2). He told the people to "be silent in the presence of the Lord GOD." In that silence, they should consider their sins and the punishment they deserved. At times, we need to stop our activity and stand in silence before God. Only then will we be able to hear what He has to say to us.

Topic: Praise and Worship

They shall plant vineyards, but not drink
their wine."

14 The great day of the LORD *is* near;
It is near and hastens quickly.
The noise of the day of the LORD is
bitter;
There the mighty men shall cry out.
15 That day *is* a day of wrath,
A day of trouble and distress,
A day of devastation and desolation,
A day of darkness and gloominess,
A day of clouds and thick darkness,
16 A day of trumpet and alarm
Against the fortified cities
And against the high towers.

17 "I will bring distress upon men,
And they shall walk like blind men,
Because they have sinned against the
LORD;
Their blood shall be poured out like
dust,
And their flesh like refuse."

18 Neither their silver nor their gold
Shall be able to deliver them
In the day of the LORD's wrath;
But the whole land shall be devoured
By the fire of His jealousy,
For He will make speedy riddance
Of all those who dwell in the land.

A Call to Repentance

2 Gather yourselves together, yes, gather
together,
O undesirable[a] nation,
2 Before the decree is issued,
Or the day passes like chaff,
Before the LORD's fierce anger comes
upon you,
Before the day of the LORD's anger
comes upon you!
3 Seek the LORD, all you meek of the
earth,
Who have upheld His justice.
Seek righteousness, seek humility.
It may be that you will be hidden
In the day of the LORD's anger.

Judgment on Nations

4 For Gaza shall be forsaken,
And Ashkelon desolate;
They shall drive out Ashdod at noonday,
And Ekron shall be uprooted.
5 Woe to the inhabitants of the seacoast,
The nation of the Cherethites!
The word of the LORD *is* against you,
O Canaan, land of the Philistines:
"I will destroy you;
So there shall be no inhabitant."

6 The seacoast shall be pastures,
With shelters[a] for shepherds and folds
for flocks.
7 The coast shall be for the remnant of the
house of Judah;
They shall feed *their* flocks there;
In the houses of Ashkelon they shall lie
down at evening.
For the LORD their God will intervene for
them,
And return their captives.

8 "I have heard the reproach of Moab,
And the insults of the people of Ammon,
With which they have reproached My
people,
And made arrogant threats against their
borders.
9 Therefore, as I live,"
Says the LORD of hosts, the God of Israel,
"Surely Moab shall be like Sodom,
And the people of Ammon like
Gomorrah—
Overrun with weeds and saltpits,
And a perpetual desolation.
The residue of My people shall plunder
them,
And the remnant of My people shall
possess them."

10 This they shall have for their pride,
Because they have reproached and made
arrogant threats
Against the people of the LORD of hosts.
11 The LORD *will be* awesome to them,
For He will reduce to nothing all the
gods of the earth;
People shall worship Him,
Each one from his place,
Indeed all the shores of the nations.

12 "You Ethiopians also,
You shall be slain by My sword."

2:1 [a]Or *shameless* **2:6** [a]Literally *excavations,* either underground huts or cisterns

CRISES AND CRISIS INTERVENTION

H. NORMAN WRIGHT

(Zephaniah 3:14–17)

A friend once told about these experiences in a yearly family newsletter: That year, her father died. Two friends died of cancer and she knew of seven others who received a cancer diagnosis. She and her husband were in a head-on car crash. Her husband had kidney stone surgery. Two friends went to prison. Her brother was alcoholic and suicidal, but entered an AA program. Her brother-in-law left his wife and family due to cocaine abuse. To top it all, one day she was having lunch with a friend at a nearby ocean pier when, right in front of them, an elderly man in a wheelchair pitched himself over the rail into the ocean in an attempted suicide.

You're probably thinking, "How could anyone survive all that?" But she *is* surviving her year-long series of crises—with God's help.

By contrast, another friend's crisis threw him into a tailspin that lasted years. He was driving home from work when he came upon an accident between a car and a motorcycle. As he approached the downed motorcycle, a disturbing recognition washed over him. It was his 19-year-old son. Dead.

Our crises are probably not so severe; even so, they are still major events for us, and we hurt.

FACING CRISES

A crisis is a sudden upsetting event—sometimes foreseen, often not—that strikes people in a vulnerable place at a bad time. The English word is based on the Greek term *krinein*, which means "to decide." Crises are life-changing, in part, because decisions must be made that nearly always alter the course of life. The Chinese term for crisis is made of two symbols that denote both danger and opportunity. Crises are dangerous opportunities for new living.

Crises are experienced in a vast number of ways, depending on the person experiencing them. Generally however, *the crisis state* is an experience of acute stress, a discomfort that often involves high anxiety, mental confusion, sweating, gastric distress, elevated heart rate, depression, catastrophic thinking, hopelessness, fear, and apathy. People in crisis often behave in counterproductive ways—showing poor judgment, making rash decisions, abusing alcohol or drugs, driving dangerously, becoming easily angered, being too aggressive and argumentative, or being too passive and helpless.

The Outcomes of Crises

There are three possible outcomes to every crisis. Life eventually gets better, gets worse, or returns to the same level. Which outcome people experience has a lot to do with how they decide, act, and live through the crisis.

Often the difference between a good or bad outcome is whether people draw closer to God or push Him away. Many reject the Lord, blaming Him for the crisis. Or they grope for a spiritual anchor without finding it, because they are not disciplined in their relationship with God. On the other hand, a crisis can crush coldheartedness and shake people out of spiritual lethargy, perhaps making them amenable to a deep work of the Holy Spirit. The psalmist put it this way, "It is good for me that I have been afflicted, that I may learn Your statutes" (Ps. 119:71).

Coping with Crises

We cannot avoid crises, so we would do well to let God work His wonders in us for good and glorious outcomes. There are also positive steps people can take to help them weather the crisis.

They should accept that they are in crisis and admit that it hurts. Denial doesn't help. They must expect that they will experience strong feelings of anger at God, guilt, self-blame, blame of others, bewilderment, apathy, desperation, and helplessness. Some people in crisis also struggle with deep misery, intense self-loathing or self-hatred, and suicidal feelings. These are not abnormal, and should not raise a major alarm unless they begin to dominate a person's life or one begins to cross the threshold of self-destructive behavior.

They should surround themselves with truly helpful people. Crisis helpers do not give unwanted advice and are not shocked by feelings and attitudes. They can handle anger toward God and even tears. They can empathize, yet remain hopeful of a good outcome. They know that working through a crisis takes time and that recovery involves many slips and falls. They know how to invite God into the mess, but do not spiritualize everything. Real helpers are there to honestly shoulder part of the burden and help others carry what would otherwise be a crushing grief.

Since crises come and go throughout life, it is especially important for people to develop a mature resilience, an increasing ability to cope with, learn from, and help others in the crises of life. Crisis requires change. We should all learn to plan and prepare for change, becoming less and less *reactive*, and more and more *proactive* in living. We can get out of debt and salt away some money to alleviate some potential future crises. We can improve our health and carve out time to read, play, and enjoy life more effectively. We should have a plan for the major life transitions that we know we will face—marriage, having children, changing jobs or careers, children leaving home, mid-life transitions, old age and retirement, illnesses and surgeries, death in the family.

Finally, we can treasure these words: "Do not think it strange concerning the fiery trial which is to try you . . . but rejoice to the extent that you partake of Christ's sufferings, that when His glory is revealed, you may also be glad with exceeding joy" (1 Pet. 4:12, 13).

FURTHER MEDITATION:

Other passages to study about the issue of crises include:

➢ Deuteronomy 33:27
➢ Psalms 18:30; 34:19; 55:22
➢ Isaiah 43:2
➢ Habakkuk 3:17–19
➢ Romans 8:28
➢ 2 Corinthians 1:3–11; 4:7–10
➢ Hebrews 13:5
➢ 1 Peter 4:19

To Learn More: Turn to the key passage note on crises at Psalm 46:1 on page 717. See also the personality profile of David and Absalom on page 415.

13 And He will stretch out His hand against
the north,
Destroy Assyria,
And make Nineveh a desolation,
As dry as the wilderness.
14 The herds shall lie down in her midst,
Every beast of the nation.
Both the pelican and the bittern
Shall lodge on the capitals *of* her
pillars;
Their voice shall sing in the windows;
Desolation *shall be* at the threshold;
For He will lay bare the cedar work.
15 This is the rejoicing city
That dwelt securely,
That said in her heart,
"I *am it,* and *there is* none besides me."
How has she become a desolation,
A place for beasts to lie down!
Everyone who passes by her
Shall hiss and shake his fist.

THE WICKEDNESS OF JERUSALEM

3 Woe to her who is rebellious and
polluted,
To the oppressing city!
2 She has not obeyed *His* voice,
She has not received correction;
She has not trusted in the LORD,
She has not drawn near to her God.

3 Her princes in her midst *are* roaring
lions;
Her judges *are* evening wolves
That leave not a bone till morning.
4 Her prophets are insolent, treacherous
people;
Her priests have polluted the sanctuary,
They have done violence to the law.
5 The LORD *is* righteous in her midst,
He will do no unrighteousness.
Every morning He brings His justice to
light;
He never fails,
But the unjust knows no shame.

6 "I have cut off nations,
Their fortresses are devastated;
I have made their streets desolate,
With none passing by.
Their cities are destroyed;
There is no one, no inhabitant.
7 I said, 'Surely you will fear Me,
You will receive instruction'—
So that her dwelling would not be cut
off,

SOUL NOTE

Resting in God *(3:11–13)* Zephaniah described the wicked (3:1, 2), contrasting them with the righteous (3:9, 12). The wicked Judeans had been rebellious, disobedient, and far from God. Despite of all God's warnings, the people continued to sin. In sharp contrast, true believers humbly waited on God; they were meek and humble people, the kind who "trust in the name of the LORD." Like this faithful remnant, believers who trust in God know that He will be with them, and they will allow no one to make them afraid. With God on our side, we have everything we need. **Topic: Trust**

SOUL NOTE

Rejoicing in God *(3:14–17)* When is joy felt most intensely? In health? In prosperity? Only when all is well? Strangely enough, the most profound joy often occurs during hardship. Zephaniah described this phenomena. The people had experienced the misery of suffering under God's judgment on their sins. But one day God would forgive them and free them to rejoice in Him. He would deliver His people and quiet their troubled hearts. He would accept their joyful praise, and He would rejoice in them as well. **Topic: Joy**

Despite everything for which I punished
her.
But they rose early and corrupted all
their deeds.

A Faithful Remnant

8 "Therefore wait for Me," says the LORD,
"Until the day I rise up for plunder;[a]
My determination *is* to gather the
nations
To My assembly of kingdoms,
To pour on them My indignation,
All My fierce anger;
All the earth shall be devoured
With the fire of My
jealousy.

9 "For then I will
restore to the
peoples a pure
language,
That they all may
call on the
name of the
LORD,
To serve Him with one accord.
10 From beyond the rivers of Ethiopia
My worshipers,
The daughter of My dispersed ones,
Shall bring My offering.
11 In that day you shall not be shamed for
any of your deeds
In which you transgress against Me;
For then I will take away from your
midst
Those who rejoice in your pride,
And you shall no longer be
haughty
In My holy mountain.
12 I will leave in your midst
A meek and humble people,
And they shall trust in the name of the
LORD.
13 The remnant of Israel shall do no
unrighteousness
And speak no lies,
Nor shall a deceitful tongue be found in
their mouth;
For they shall feed *their* flocks and lie
down,
And no one shall make *them* afraid."

Joy in God's Faithfulness

14 Sing, O daughter of Zion!
Shout, O Israel!
Be glad and rejoice with all *your* heart,
O daughter of Jerusalem!
15 The LORD has taken away your
judgments,
He has cast out your enemy.
The King of Israel, the LORD, *is* in your
midst;
You shall see[a] disaster no more.

16 In that day it shall be said to Jerusalem:
"Do not fear;
Zion, let not your
hands be weak.
17 The LORD your God
in your midst,
The Mighty One,
will save;
He will rejoice
over you with
gladness,
He will quiet *you*
with His love,
He will rejoice over you with singing."

> "The LORD your God in your midst, the Mighty One, will save; He will rejoice over you with gladness, He will quiet you with His love, He will rejoice over you with singing."
> ZEPHANIAH 3:17

18 "I will gather those who sorrow over the
appointed assembly,
Who are among you,
To whom its reproach *is* a burden.
19 Behold, at that time
I will deal with all who afflict you;
I will save the lame,
And gather those who were driven out;
I will appoint them for praise and fame
In every land where they were put to
shame.
20 At that time I will bring you back,
Even at the time I gather you;
For I will give you fame and praise
Among all the peoples of the earth,
When I return your captives before your
eyes,"
Says the LORD.

3:8 [a]Septuagint and Syriac read *for witness;* Targum reads *for the day of My revelation for judgment;* Vulgate reads *for the day of My resurrection that is to come.* **3:15** [a]Some Hebrew manuscripts, Septuagint, and Bomberg read *see;* Masoretic Text and Vulgate read *fear.*

Haggai

"I just can't do it anymore," mutters the burned-out employee. "I can't take it much longer," sighs the belittled spouse. "I don't think I can go on," whispers the exhausted believer. "I'm too busy to care," spouts the harried executive. Events and relationships seem to conspire to steal our resolve. So what happens when we lose our motivation, especially our *spiritual* motivation?

During their seventy years in Babylonian captivity, the Jewish people dreamed of being back in Jerusalem and worshiping in a restored temple. In 539 B.C., after the Persians conquered Babylon, King Cyrus abruptly decreed that the Jews could return to their homeland. Surprisingly, only a small number accepted this offer, and most of them quickly became preoccupied with building their own homes. They had lost their spiritual motivation, but this time from self-centeredness. God raised up the prophet Haggai to motivate His distracted people. Haggai forcefully informed his Jewish brethren that they were not making God a priority. Their neglect of the temple was really a neglect of the Lord. Haggai is one of only three Old Testament prophets who ministered after the Exile (the others being Zechariah and Malachi). Together with the Judean governor Zerubbabel (1:12) and the priest Ezra (Ezra 7:1), Haggai attempted to "jump start" the Jewish people.

Haggai reminds us that good intentions are not good if our day-to-day priorities are wrong. "I'll get around to it," we tell ourselves. But sooner becomes later, and the job never gets done. If your soul is dragging, let Haggai motivate you to God-honoring action!

The Command to Build God's House

1 In the second year of King Darius, in the
sixth month, on the first day of the month,
the word of the LORD came by Haggai the
prophet to Zerubbabel the son of Shealtiel,
governor of Judah, and to Joshua the son of
Jehozadak, the high priest, saying, 2“Thus
speaks the LORD of hosts, saying: ‘This people
says, “The time has not come, the time that
the LORD's house should be built.” ’ ”
3Then the word of the LORD came by Haggai
the prophet, saying, 4“*Is it* time for you yourselves to dwell in your paneled houses, and
this temple[a] *to lie* in ruins?” 5Now therefore,
thus says the LORD of hosts: “Consider your
ways!

6 “You have sown much, and bring in little;
You eat, but do not have enough;
You drink, but you are not filled with
drink;
You clothe yourselves, but no one is
warm;
And he who earns wages,
Earns wages *to put* into a bag with
holes.”

7Thus says the LORD of hosts: “Consider
your ways! 8Go up to the mountains and bring
wood and build the temple, that I may take
pleasure in it and be glorified,” says the LORD.
9“*You* looked for much, but indeed *it came to*
little; and when you brought it home, I blew it
away. Why?” says the LORD of hosts. “Because
of My house that *is in* ruins, while every one
of you runs to his own house. 10Therefore the
heavens above you withhold the dew, and the
earth withholds its fruit. 11For I called for a
drought on the land and the mountains, on
the grain and the new wine and the oil, on
whatever the ground brings forth, on men and
livestock, and on all the labor of *your* hands.”

The People's Obedience

12Then Zerubbabel the son of Shealtiel, and
Joshua the son of Jehozadak, the high priest,
with all the remnant of the people, obeyed the
voice of the LORD their God, and the words of
Haggai the prophet, as the LORD their God had
sent him; and the people feared the presence
of the LORD. 13Then Haggai, the LORD's messenger, spoke the LORD's message to the people, saying, “I *am* with you, says the LORD.”
14So the LORD stirred up the spirit of Zerubbabel the son of Shealtiel, governor of Judah,
and the spirit of Joshua the son of Jehozadak,
the high priest, and the spirit of all the remnant of the people; and they came and worked
on the house of the LORD of hosts, their God,
15on the twenty-fourth day of the sixth month,
in the second year of King Darius.

The Coming Glory of God's House

2 In the seventh *month,* on the twenty-first
of the month, the word of the LORD came
by Haggai the prophet, saying: 2“Speak now to
Zerubbabel the son of Shealtiel, governor of
Judah, and to Joshua the son of Jehozadak,
the high priest, and to the remnant of the people, saying: 3‘Who is left among you who saw
this temple[a] in its former glory? And how do
you see it now? In comparison with it, *is this*
not in your eyes as nothing? 4Yet now be
strong, Zerubbabel,’ says the LORD; ‘and be
strong, Joshua, son of Jehozadak, the high
priest; and be strong, all you people of the
land,’ says the LORD, ‘and work; for I *am* with
you,’ says the LORD of hosts. 5‘*According to* the
word that I covenanted with you when you
came out of Egypt, so My Spirit remains
among you; do not fear!’
6“For thus says the LORD of hosts: ‘Once

1:4 [a]Literally *house,* and so in verse 8
2:3 [a]Literally *house,* and so in verses 7 and 9

SOUL NOTE

Considering Our Ways *(1:3–7)* People spend money on what they consider most important. Haggai pointed out that the people in Jerusalem were valuing the comforts of their own homes over God. Their homes had paneled roofs and decorated walls, while the temple—God's house—remained in ruins. They had spent their resources on what they valued. Haggai's message was: “Consider your ways!” It's a message to us as well. We need to reevaluate where we spend our resources. Do our activities and spending habits reflect our dedication to God? **Topic: Money**

more (it *is* a little while) I will shake heaven and earth, the sea and dry land; 7and I will shake all nations, and they shall come to the Desire of All Nations,[a] and I will fill this temple with glory,' says the LORD of hosts. 8'The silver *is* Mine, and the gold *is* Mine,' says the LORD of hosts. 9'The glory of this latter temple shall be greater than the former,' says the LORD of hosts. 'And in this place I will give peace,' says the LORD of hosts."

> " 'Yet now be strong, Zerubbabel,' says the LORD; 'and be strong, Joshua, son of Jehozadak, the high priest; and be strong, all you people of the land,' says the LORD, 'and work; for I *am* with you,' says the LORD of hosts."
>
> **HAGGAI 2:4**

THE PEOPLE ARE DEFILED

10On the twenty-fourth *day* of the ninth *month,* in the second year of Darius, the word of the LORD came by Haggai the prophet, saying, 11"Thus says the LORD of hosts: 'Now, ask the priests *concerning the* law, saying, 12"If one carries holy meat in the fold of his garment, and with the edge he touches bread or stew, wine or oil, or any food, will it become holy?" ' "

Then the priests answered and said, "No."

13And Haggai said, "If *one who is* unclean *because* of a dead body touches any of these, will it be unclean?"

So the priests answered and said, "It shall be unclean."

14Then Haggai answered and said, " 'So is this people, and so is this nation before Me,' says the LORD, 'and so is every work of their hands; and what they offer there is unclean.

PROMISED BLESSING

15'And now, carefully consider from this day forward: from before stone was laid upon stone in the temple of the LORD—16since those *days,* when *one* came to a heap of twenty ephahs, there were *but* ten; when *one* came to the wine vat to draw out fifty baths from the press, there were *but* twenty. 17I struck you with blight and mildew and hail in all the labors of your hands; yet you did not *turn* to Me,' says the LORD. 18'Consider now from this day forward, from the twenty-fourth day of the ninth month, from the day that the foundation of the LORD's temple was laid—consider it: 19Is the seed still in the barn? As yet the vine, the fig tree, the pomegranate, and the olive tree have not yielded *fruit. But* from this day I will bless *you.*' "

ZERUBBABEL CHOSEN AS A SIGNET

20And again the word of the LORD came to Haggai on the twenty-fourth day of the month, saying, 21"Speak to Zerubbabel, governor of Judah, saying:

'I will shake heaven and earth.
22 I will overthrow the throne of kingdoms;
I will destroy the strength of the Gentile
kingdoms.
I will overthrow the chariots
And those who ride in them;
The horses and their riders shall come
down,
Every one by the sword of his brother.

23'In that day,' says the LORD of hosts, 'I will take you, Zerubbabel My servant, the son of Shealtiel,' says the LORD, 'and will make you like a signet *ring;* for I have chosen you,' says the LORD of hosts."

2:7 [a]Or *the desire of all nations*

Zechariah

Long ago, a famous architect visited the construction site of the magnificent St. Paul's in London. He approached one worker and inquired, "What are you doing?" "I'm laying brick," the grim-faced laborer replied flatly. Finding another worker, the architect asked the same question. With excitement this man exclaimed, "I'm building a great cathedral!"

Catching the vision makes all the difference. Only when we sense that we're part of something *big* do our souls fill with enthusiasm and our lives take on a renewed sense of purpose.

Zechariah, like his contemporary Haggai, was a prophet called to minister to the unmotivated inhabitants of Jerusalem after their return from captivity. Appropriately, Zechariah's name means "God remembers," for this note of hope permeates the whole book. Through a series of visions and messages, Zechariah reminded the people that God had not forgotten His covenant with Israel. A time of blessing was coming; therefore, the people of God should live in the present with that future promise in view. Rather than rebuking his disheartened countrymen for their failure to complete the temple, Zechariah attempted to motivate them by pointing them toward a future day when the glory of the long-awaited Messiah would fill that holy place.

If your soul feels spiritually dry, if you are struggling with motivation, if you seem to have lost your sense of purpose in life, let the ancient prophet Zechariah encourage you. God has an eternal plan that nothing can thwart, and He wants *you* to be part of it!

SOUL CONCERN IN ZECHARIAH

TRUTH	(8:16, 17)

A Call to Repentance

1 In the eighth month of the second year of Darius, the word of the LORD came to Zechariah the son of Berechiah, the son of Iddo the prophet, saying, 2"The LORD has been very angry with your fathers. 3Therefore say to them, 'Thus says the LORD of hosts: "Return to Me," says the LORD of hosts, "and I will return to you," says the LORD of hosts. 4"Do not be like your fathers, to whom the former prophets preached, saying, 'Thus says the LORD of hosts: "Turn now from your evil ways and your evil deeds." ' But they did not hear nor heed Me," says the LORD.

5 "Your fathers, where *are* they?
And the prophets, do they live forever?
6 Yet surely My words and My statutes,
Which I commanded My servants the prophets,
Did they not overtake your fathers?

"So they returned and said:

'Just as the LORD of hosts determined to do to us,
According to our ways and according to our deeds,
So He has dealt with us.' " ' "

Vision of the Horses

7On the twenty-fourth day of the eleventh month, which is the month Shebat, in the second year of Darius, the word of the LORD came to Zechariah the son of Berechiah, the son of Iddo the prophet: 8I saw by night, and behold, a man riding on a red horse, and it stood among the myrtle trees in the hollow; and behind him *were* horses: red, sorrel, and white. 9Then I said, "My lord, what *are* these?" So the angel who talked with me said to me, "I will show you what they *are.*"

10And the man who stood among the myrtle trees answered and said, "These *are the ones* whom the LORD has sent to walk to and fro throughout the earth."

11So they answered the Angel of the LORD, who stood among the myrtle trees, and said, "We have walked to and fro throughout the earth, and behold, all the earth is resting quietly."

The LORD Will Comfort Zion

12Then the Angel of the LORD answered and said, "O LORD of hosts, how long will You not have mercy on Jerusalem and on the cities of Judah, against which You were angry these seventy years?"

13And the LORD answered the angel who talked to me, *with* good *and* comforting words. 14So the angel who spoke with me said to me, "Proclaim, saying, 'Thus says the LORD of hosts:

"I am zealous for Jerusalem
And for Zion with great zeal.
15 I am exceedingly angry with the nations at ease;
For I was a little angry,
And they helped—*but* with evil *intent.*"

16'Therefore thus says the LORD:

"I am returning to Jerusalem with mercy;
My house shall be built in it," says the LORD of hosts,
"And a *surveyor's* line shall be stretched out over Jerusalem." '

17"Again proclaim, saying, 'Thus says the LORD of hosts:

SOUL NOTE

God's Comfort *(1:17)* Zechariah rehearsed Judah's checkered past. God had warned the Judeans to abandon their wicked ways, but the people had refused. So God punished them by allowing their enemies to take them into captivity.

Despite the people's disobedience, however, God showed mercy on them. He put in the hearts of King Cyrus, and later King Darius, to allow a group of exiles to return to Jerusalem. Once more they would live in their land, fulfilling Zechariah's prophecy that the Lord "will again comfort Zion." When people turn from their sin, God promises comfort and restoration. **Topic: Restoration**

"My cities shall again spread out through
prosperity;
The LORD will again comfort Zion,
And will again choose Jerusalem." ' "

VISION OF THE HORNS

18Then I raised my eyes and looked, and
there *were* four horns. 19And I said to the angel
who talked with me, "What *are* these?"
So he answered me, "These *are* the horns
that have scattered Judah, Israel, and Jerusalem."
20Then the LORD showed me four craftsmen.
21And I said, "What are these coming to do?"
So he said, "These *are* the horns that scattered Judah, so that no one could lift up his
head; but the craftsmen[a] are coming to terrify
them, to cast out the horns of the nations that
lifted up *their* horn against the land of Judah
to scatter it."

VISION OF THE MEASURING LINE

2 Then I raised my eyes and looked, and behold, a man with a measuring line in his
hand. 2So I said, "Where are you going?"
And he said to me, "To measure Jerusalem,
to see what *is* its width and what *is* its
length."
3And there *was* the angel who talked with me,
going out; and another angel was coming out
to meet him, 4who said to him, "Run, speak to
this young man, saying: 'Jerusalem shall be inhabited *as* towns without walls, because of the
multitude of men and livestock in it. 5For I,'
says the LORD, 'will be a wall of fire all around
her, and I will be the glory in her midst.' "

FUTURE JOY OF ZION AND MANY NATIONS

6"Up, up! Flee from the land of the north,"
says the LORD; "for I have spread you abroad
like the four winds of heaven," says the LORD.
7Up, Zion! Escape, you who dwell with the
daughter of Babylon."
8For thus says the LORD of hosts: "He sent
Me after glory, to the nations which plunder
you; for he who touches you touches the apple of His eye. 9For surely I will shake My
hand against them, and they shall become
spoil for their servants. Then you will know
that the LORD of hosts has sent Me.
10"Sing and rejoice, O daughter of Zion! For
behold, I am coming and I will dwell in your
midst," says the LORD. 11"Many nations shall
be joined to the LORD in that day, and they
shall become My people. And I will dwell in
your midst. Then you will know that the LORD
of hosts has sent Me to you. 12And the LORD
will take possession of Judah as His inheritance in the Holy Land, and will again choose
Jerusalem. 13Be silent, all flesh, before the
LORD, for He is aroused from His holy habitation!"

VISION OF THE HIGH PRIEST

3 Then he showed me Joshua the high
priest standing before the Angel of the
LORD, and Satan standing at his right hand to
oppose him. 2And the LORD said to Satan,
"The LORD rebuke you, Satan! The LORD who
has chosen Jerusalem rebuke you! *Is* this not a
brand plucked from the fire?"
3Now Joshua was clothed with filthy garments, and was standing before the Angel.
4Then He answered and spoke to those who
stood before Him, saying, "Take away the
filthy garments from him." And to him He
said, "See, I have removed your iniquity from
you, and I will clothe you with rich robes."
5And I said, "Let them put a clean turban on
his head."
So they put a clean turban on his head, and
they put the clothes on him. And the Angel of
the LORD stood by.

THE COMING BRANCH

6Then the Angel of the LORD admonished
Joshua, saying, 7"Thus says the LORD of hosts:

'If you will walk in My ways,
And if you will keep My command,
Then you shall also judge My house,
And likewise have charge of My courts;
I will give you places to walk
Among these who stand here.

8 'Hear, O Joshua, the high priest,
You and your companions who sit before
you,
For they are a wondrous sign;
For behold, I am bringing forth My
Servant the BRANCH.
9 For behold, the stone
That I have laid before Joshua:
Upon the stone *are* seven eyes.
Behold, I will engrave its inscription,'
Says the LORD of hosts,

1:21 [a]Literally *these*

'And I will remove the iniquity of that
land in one day.
10 In that day,' says the LORD of hosts,
'Everyone will invite his neighbor
Under his vine and under his fig tree.' "

VISION OF THE LAMPSTAND AND OLIVE TREES

4 Now the angel who talked with me came
back and wakened me, as a man who is
wakened out of his sleep. 2And he said to me,
"What do you see?"

So I said, "I am looking, and there *is* a lampstand of solid gold with a bowl on top of it,
and on the *stand* seven lamps with seven
pipes to the seven lamps. 3Two olive trees *are*
by it, one at the right of the bowl and the other
at its left." 4So I answered and spoke to the
angel who talked with me, saying, "What *are*
these, my lord?"

5Then the angel who talked with me answered and said to me, "Do you not know
what these are?"

And I said, "No, my lord."

6So he answered and said to me:

"This *is* the word of the LORD to
Zerubbabel:
'Not by might nor by power, but by My
Spirit,'
Says the LORD of hosts.
7 'Who *are* you, O great mountain?
Before Zerubbabel *you shall become* a
plain!
And he shall bring forth the capstone
With shouts of "Grace, grace to it!" ' "

8Moreover the word of the LORD came to
me, saying:

9 "The hands of Zerubbabel
Have laid the foundation of this temple;[a]
His hands shall also finish *it*.
Then you will know
That the LORD of hosts has sent Me to
you.
10 For who has despised the day of small
things?
For these seven rejoice to see
The plumb line in the hand of
Zerubbabel.
They are the eyes of the LORD,
Which scan to and fro throughout the
whole earth."

11Then I answered and said to him, "What
are these two olive trees—at the right of the
lampstand and at its left?" 12And I further answered and said to him, "What *are these* two
olive branches that *drip* into the receptacles[a]
of the two gold pipes from which the golden
oil drains?"

13Then he answered me and said, "Do you
not know what these *are?*"

And I said, "No, my lord."

14So he said, "These *are* the two anointed
ones, who stand beside the Lord of the whole
earth."

VISION OF THE FLYING SCROLL

5 Then I turned and raised my eyes, and
saw there a flying scroll.

2And he said to me, "What do you see?"

So I answered, "I see a flying scroll. Its
length *is* twenty cubits and its width ten cubits."

3Then he said to me, "This *is* the curse that
goes out over the face of the whole earth:
'Every thief shall be expelled,' according *to*
this side of *the scroll;* and, 'Every perjurer

4:9 [a]Literally *house* **4:12** [a]Literally *into the hands of*

SOUL NOTE

By God's Spirit *(4:6)* Zechariah predicted the rebuilding of the temple in Jerusalem—something that appeared impossible. The returning exiles had laid the foundation of the temple and even had built an altar (Ezra 3:2; 5:16), but the work had stopped. God promised through Zechariah that the temple would indeed be rebuilt: "not by might nor by power, but by My Spirit." God would accomplish what seemed impossible. The promise is true today. God's people can do what may seem impossible when they work not by their might and power, but by God's Spirit.
Topic: Presence of the Holy Spirit

shall be expelled,' according *to* that side of it."

4 "I will send out *the curse,*" says the LORD of hosts;
"It shall enter the house of the thief
And the house of the one who swears falsely by My name.
It shall remain in the midst of his house
And consume it, with its timber and stones."

VISION OF THE WOMAN IN A BASKET

5Then the angel who talked with me came out and said to me, "Lift your eyes now, and see what this *is* that goes forth."

6So I asked, "What *is* it?" And he said, "It *is* a basket[a] that is going forth."

He also said, "This *is* their resemblance throughout the earth: 7Here *is* a lead disc lifted up, and this *is* a woman sitting inside the basket"; 8then he said, "This *is* Wickedness!" And he thrust her down into the basket, and threw the lead cover[a] over its mouth. 9Then I raised my eyes and looked, and there *were* two women, coming with the wind in their wings; for they had wings like the wings of a stork, and they lifted up the basket between earth and heaven.

10So I said to the angel who talked with me, "Where are they carrying the basket?"

11And he said to me, "To build a house for it in the land of Shinar;[a] when it is ready, *the basket* will be set there on its base."

VISION OF THE FOUR CHARIOTS

6 Then I turned and raised my eyes and looked, and behold, four chariots *were* coming from between two mountains, and the mountains *were* mountains of bronze. 2With the first chariot *were* red horses, with the second chariot black horses, 3with the third chariot white horses, and with the fourth chariot dappled horses—strong *steeds.* 4Then I answered and said to the angel who talked with me, "What *are* these, my lord?"

5And the angel answered and said to me, "These *are* four spirits of heaven, who go out from *their* station before the Lord of all the earth. 6The one with the black horses is going to the north country, the white are going after them, and the dappled are going toward the south country." 7Then the strong *steeds* went out, eager to go, that they might walk to and fro throughout the earth. And He said, "Go, walk to and fro throughout the earth." So they walked to and fro throughout the earth. 8And He called to me, and spoke to me, saying, "See, those who go toward the north country have given rest to My Spirit in the north country."

THE COMMAND TO CROWN JOSHUA

9Then the word of the LORD came to me, saying: 10"Receive *the gift* from the captives—from Heldai, Tobijah, and Jedaiah, who have come from Babylon—and go the same day and enter the house of Josiah the son of Zephaniah. 11Take the silver and gold, make an elaborate crown, and set *it* on the head of Joshua the son of Jehozadak, the high priest. 12Then speak to him, saying, 'Thus says the LORD of hosts, saying:

"Behold, the Man whose name *is* the BRANCH!
From His place He shall branch out,
And He shall build the temple of the LORD;
13 Yes, He shall build the temple of the LORD.
He shall bear the glory,
And shall sit and rule on His throne;
So He shall be a priest on His throne,
And the counsel of peace shall be between them both." '

14"Now the elaborate crown shall be for a memorial in the temple of the LORD for Helem,[a] Tobijah, Jedaiah, and Hen the son of Zephaniah. 15Even those from afar shall come and build the temple of the LORD. Then you shall know that the LORD of hosts has sent Me to you. And *this* shall come to pass if you diligently obey the voice of the LORD your God."

OBEDIENCE BETTER THAN FASTING

7 Now in the fourth year of King Darius it came to pass *that* the word of the LORD came to Zechariah, on the fourth day of the ninth month, Chislev, 2when *the people*[a] sent Sherezer,[b] with Regem-Melech and his men, *to*

5:6 [a]Hebrew *ephah,* a measuring container, and so elsewhere **5:8** [a]Literally *stone* **5:11** [a]That is, Babylon **6:14** [a]Following Masoretic Text, Targum, and Vulgate; Syriac reads *for Heldai* (compare verse 10); Septuagint reads *for the patient ones.*
7:2 [a]Literally *they* (compare verse 5) [b]Or *Sar-Ezer*

the house of God,[c] to pray before the LORD, [3]*and* to ask the priests who *were* in the house of the LORD of hosts, and the prophets, saying, "Should I weep in the fifth month and fast as I have done for so many years?"

[4]Then the word of the LORD of hosts came to me, saying, [5]"Say to all the people of the land, and to the priests: 'When you fasted and mourned in the fifth and seventh *months* during those seventy years, did you really fast for Me—for Me? [6]When you eat and when you drink, do you not eat and drink *for yourselves?* [7]*Should you* not *have obeyed* the words which the LORD proclaimed through the former prophets when Jerusalem and the cities around it were inhabited and prosperous, and the South[a] and the Lowland were inhabited?' "

DISOBEDIENCE RESULTED IN CAPTIVITY

[8]Then the word of the LORD came to Zechariah, saying, [9]"Thus says the LORD of hosts:

'Execute true justice,
Show mercy and compassion
Everyone to his brother.
10 Do not oppress the widow or the fatherless,
The alien or the poor.
Let none of you plan evil in his heart
Against his brother.'

[11]'But they refused to heed, shrugged their shoulders, and stopped their ears so that they could not hear. [12]Yes, they made their hearts like flint, refusing to hear the law and the words which the LORD of hosts had sent by His Spirit through the former prophets. Thus great wrath came from the LORD of hosts. [13]Therefore it happened, *that* just as He proclaimed and they would not hear, so they called out and I would not listen," says the LORD of hosts. [14]"But I scattered them with a whirlwind among all the nations which they had not known. Thus the land became desolate after them, so that no one passed through or returned; for they made the pleasant land desolate."

JERUSALEM, HOLY CITY OF THE FUTURE

8 Again the word of the LORD of hosts came, saying, [2]"Thus says the LORD of hosts:

'I am zealous for Zion with great zeal;
With great fervor I am zealous for her.'

[3]"Thus says the LORD:

'I will return to Zion,
And dwell in the midst of Jerusalem.
Jerusalem shall be called the City of Truth,
The Mountain of the LORD of hosts,
The Holy Mountain.'

[4]"Thus says the LORD of hosts:

'Old men and old women shall again sit
In the streets of Jerusalem,
Each one with his staff in his hand
Because of great age.
5 The streets of the city
Shall be full of boys and girls
Playing in its streets.'

[6]"Thus says the LORD of hosts:

'If it is marvelous in the eyes of the remnant of this people in these days,

---

7:2 [c]Hebrew *Bethel* **7:7** [a]Hebrew *Negev*

SOUL NOTE

Showing Compassion *(7:8–10)* Although the Israelites had rebelled against God and had been exiled to Babylon, God had brought a small group of them back to Jerusalem. The exiles knew what it was like to experience God's compassion. Now, through Zechariah, God asked them to "show mercy and compassion" to each other. What did that mean? To look after widows, orphans, the poor, and those who were strangers in the land. All who have experienced God's mercy—the forgiveness Christ freely offers (Titus 3:4, 5)—need to show that same type of compassion to others. **Topic: Compassion**

Will it also be marvelous in My eyes?'
Says the LORD of hosts.

7"Thus says the LORD of hosts:

'Behold, I will save My people from the land of the east
And from the land of the west;
8 I will bring them *back*,
And they shall dwell in the midst of Jerusalem.
They shall be My people
And I will be their God,
In truth and righteousness.'

9"Thus says the LORD of hosts:

'Let your hands be strong,
You who have been hearing in these days
These words by the mouth of the prophets,
Who *spoke* in the day the foundation was laid
For the house of the LORD of hosts,
That the temple might be built.
10 For before these days
Th*ere were* no wages for man nor any hire for beast;
Th*ere was* no peace from the enemy for whoever went out or came in;
For I set all men, everyone, against his neighbor.

11'But now I *will* not *treat* the remnant of this people as in the former days,' says the LORD of hosts.

12 'For the seed *shall be* prosperous,
The vine shall give its fruit,
The ground shall give her increase,
And the heavens shall give their dew—
I will cause the remnant of this people
To possess all these.
13 And it shall come to pass
Th*at* just as you were a curse among the nations,
O house of Judah and house of Israel,
So I will save you, and you shall be a blessing.
Do not fear,
Let your hands be strong.'

14"For thus says the LORD of hosts:

'Just as I determined to punish you
When your fathers provoked Me to wrath,'
Says the LORD of hosts,
'And I would not relent,
15 So again in these days
I am determined to do good
To Jerusalem and to the house of Judah.
Do not fear.
16 These *are* the things you shall do:
Speak each man the truth to his neighbor;
Give judgment in your gates for truth, justice, and peace;
17 Let none of you think evil in your[a] heart against your neighbor;
And do not love a false oath.
For all these *are things* that I hate,'
Says the LORD."

18Then the word of the LORD of hosts came
to me, saying, 19"Thus says the LORD of hosts:

'The fast of the fourth *month*,
The fast of the fifth,
The fast of the seventh,
And the fast of the tenth,
Shall be joy and gladness and cheerful feasts
For the house of Judah.
Therefore love truth and peace.'

20"Thus says the LORD of hosts:

'Peoples shall yet come,
Inhabitants of many cities;
21 The inhabitants of one *city* shall go to another, saying,
"Let us continue to go and pray before the LORD,
And seek the LORD of hosts.
I myself will go also."
22 Yes, many peoples and strong nations
Shall come to seek the LORD of hosts in Jerusalem,
And to pray before the LORD.'

23"Thus says the LORD of hosts: 'In those days ten men from every language of the nations shall grasp the sleeve of a Jewish man, saying, "Let us go with you, for we have heard *that* God *is* with you." ' "

8:17 [a]Literally *his*

DISCOVERING TRUTH

FREDA V. CREWS

(Zechariah 8:16, 17)

The sincere searcher for truth, either directly or indirectly, asks such questions as: "What is truth? Where can I find it? How will I know when I find it?" Others, who lack sincerity in their search for truth, will settle for: "Truth is whatever is true for me."

The good news is that truth can be defined, found, and experienced. The reality is that what a person believes *does* matter.

THE TRUTH ABOUT TRUTH

What is truth? Truth and reality refer to things as they really are, no matter what people may believe. Truth cannot be altered. Postmodernism advocates that "something is true if it is true for me." Christians deny this definition because they believe in absolute truth, stating that truth is truth irrespective of people's personal experience. What people call "truth" must be measured, not against what they believe, but against *absolute truth*. God is the Absolute and is the foundation for all truth because He *is* truth (Deut. 32:4; John 14:6). God loves truth and hates falsehood (Prov. 12:22); He cannot lie (Titus 1:2).

Because God is truth, He holds His people to His standard of truth: "Behold, You desire truth in the inward parts" (Ps. 51:6). Zechariah 8:16 instructs, "Speak each man the truth to his neighbor; give judgment in your gates for truth, justice, and peace." People of truth exhibit behavior that matches their words. They seek to be accurate, reliable, and trustworthy.

HOW TO BE PEOPLE OF TRUTH

We can petition the God of truth to help us, "Lead me in Your truth and teach me" (Ps. 25:5). The Holy Spirit, the Spirit of truth (John 16:13), will lead us to the truth of God's Word and give us receptive hearts and a submissive will so we can know, be, and do the truth. When we sincerely seek spiritual truth, the Holy Spirit, who guides us into all truth, will bear witness to truth in our spirit through the Word. We can *know* that we know the truth.

In order to be people of the truth, we must be authentic and genuine. In the corners of our very being we must be true to ourselves. Truth will not settle for anything less than honesty with ourselves and others. Truth will shine the light on the dark places in our lives so we can dust them out and clean them up.

When we know truth and are people of truth, we will behave accordingly. Truth will inspire us to live authentic lives and speak authentic words. Truth will refuse to rename sin in our own and others' lives. Truth will urge us to speak the truth in love as we seek to live in peace with each other. Truth will prompt spouses to be faithful to each other. Truth will stimulate parents to live consistent lives before their children. Truth will inspire us to pray that God's kingdom come and His will be done on earth as it is in heaven (Matt. 6:10).

HOW TRUTH HELPS US

Truth will prepare us to do battle with the forces of evil. Satan, the father of lies, will flee from the truth. The armor of God can protect us during the fiercest battles with the kingdom of darkness (Eph. 6:12–18). Truth must be in place before the rest of the armor will fit. Ephesians 6:14 says, "Stand therefore, having girded your waist with truth. . . ."

Truth plays a significant role in helping relationships. In order for us to be able to help others, we must be truthful and require truthfulness from those we are attempting to help. We must be able to speak truthfully to hurting people, for they need to learn such truths as:

1. Their relationship with God is not based on their performance, but on His grace (Eph. 2:8, 9).
2. They become persons of value and worth in a relationship with Jesus Christ (Eph. 1:4, 5).
3. They need to accept the reality of their humanness with its failures and limitations (2 Cor. 12:9).
4. Their pain can be used by God to help them grow and mature (Rom. 8:28, 29).
5. They can experience joy and freedom in their Christian lives (Gal. 5:1).

THE FREEDOM OF TRUTH

Jesus promised that the truth will free us (John 8:32). When we know the truth as it is in Jesus Christ, we will experience freedom from the deceptions of Satan that blind us spiritually and bind us emotionally. The truth in Christ can break the chains of sin, deliver those who are imprisoned by the pain of their past, and convince them that they are persons of worth—setting them free from the prison of low self-esteem.

In Christ, we are free to be all that our heavenly Father intended us to be. The *truth* in Christ gives us the freedom we need to enjoy an intimate relationship with the God of truth: "The LORD is near to all who call upon Him, to all who call upon Him in truth" (Ps. 145:18). We can trust His truth forever: "The LORD is good; His mercy is everlasting, and His truth endures to all generations" (Ps. 100:5).

FURTHER MEDITATION:

Other passages to study about the issue of truth include:

- Psalm 119:30, 43, 142, 151, 160
- Proverbs 8:7; 12:17; 23:23
- John 3:21; 8:44–46; 14:17; 15:26; 16:13; 18:37
- Ephesians 1:13; 4:25

To Learn More: Turn to the key passage note on truth at John 8:31–36 on page 1386. See also the personality profile of Ananias on page 1424.

ISRAEL DEFENDED AGAINST ENEMIES

9 The burden[a] of the word of the LORD
Against the land of Hadrach,
And Damascus its resting place
(For the eyes of men
And all the tribes of Israel
Are on the LORD);
2 Also *against* Hamath, *which* borders on it,
And *against* Tyre and Sidon, though they are very wise.

3 For Tyre built herself a tower,
Heaped up silver like the dust,
And gold like the mire of the streets.
4 Behold, the LORD will cast her out;
He will destroy her power in the sea,
And she will be devoured by fire.

5 Ashkelon shall see *it* and fear;
Gaza also shall be very sorrowful;
And Ekron, for He dried up her expectation.
The king shall perish from Gaza,
And Ashkelon shall not be inhabited.

6 "A mixed race shall settle in Ashdod,
And I will cut off the pride of the Philistines.
7 I will take away the blood from his mouth,
And the abominations from between his teeth.
But he who remains, even he *shall be* for our God,
And shall be like a leader in Judah,
And Ekron like a Jebusite.
8 I will camp around My house
Because of the army,
Because of him who passes by and him who returns.
No more shall an oppressor pass through them,
For now I have seen with My eyes.

THE COMING KING

9 "Rejoice greatly, O daughter of Zion!
Shout, O daughter of Jerusalem!
Behold, your King is coming to you;
He *is* just and having salvation,
Lowly and riding on a donkey,
A colt, the foal of a donkey.
10 I will cut off the chariot from Ephraim
And the horse from Jerusalem;
The battle bow shall be cut off.
He shall speak peace to the nations;
His dominion *shall be* 'from sea to sea,
And from the River to the ends of the earth.'[a]

GOD WILL SAVE HIS PEOPLE

11 "As for you also,
Because of the blood of your covenant,
I will set your prisoners free from the waterless pit.
12 Return to the stronghold,
You prisoners of hope.
Even today I declare
That I will restore double to you.
13 For I have bent Judah, My *bow,*
Fitted the bow with Ephraim,
And raised up your sons, O Zion,
Against your sons, O Greece,
And made you like the sword of a mighty man."

14 Then the LORD will be seen over them,
And His arrow will go forth like lightning.
The Lord GOD will blow the trumpet,
And go with whirlwinds from the south.

9:1 [a]Or *oracle* **9:10** [a]Psalm 72:8

SOUL NOTE

A Humble King *(9:9, 10)* Zechariah foresaw a King who would come to power riding on the back of a donkey, not a warhorse (yet). This prophecy was fulfilled when Jesus Christ rode into Jerusalem (Matt. 21:1–11). This King rode in victory into a city, onto a cross, and out of a tomb! Not only did Jesus' entry into Jerusalem fulfill Zechariah's prophecy, but it also showed Jesus' humility. Jesus became a humble human being so that He could identify with us. One day, however, Jesus *will* come as a conquering King to set things right in the world. **Topic: Knowing Jesus**

15 The LORD of hosts will defend them;
They shall devour and subdue with slingstones.
They shall drink *and* roar as if with wine;
They shall be filled *with blood* like basins,
Like the corners of the altar.
16 The LORD their God will save them in that day,
As the flock of His people.
For they *shall be like* the jewels of a crown,
Lifted like a banner over His land—
17 For how great is its[a] goodness
And how great its[b] beauty!
Grain shall make the young men thrive,
And new wine the young women.

Restoration of Judah and Israel

10 Ask the LORD for rain
In the time of the latter rain.[a]
The LORD will make flashing clouds;
He will give them showers of rain,
Grass in the field for everyone.

2 For the idols[a] speak delusion;
The diviners envision lies,
And tell false dreams;
They comfort in vain.
Therefore *the people* wend their way like sheep;
They are in trouble because *there is* no shepherd.

3 "My anger is kindled against the shepherds,
And I will punish the goatherds.
For the LORD of hosts will visit His flock,
The house of Judah,
And will make them as His royal horse in the battle.
4 From him comes the cornerstone,
From him the tent peg,
From him the battle bow,
From him every ruler[a] together.
5 They shall be like mighty men,
Who tread down *their enemies*
In the mire of the streets in the battle.
They shall fight because the LORD is with them,
And the riders on horses shall be put to shame.

6 "I will strengthen the house of Judah,
And I will save the house of Joseph.
I will bring them back,
Because I have mercy on them.
They shall be as though I had not cast them aside;
For I *am* the LORD their God,
And I will hear them.
7 *Those of* Ephraim shall be like a mighty man,
And their heart shall rejoice as if with wine.
Yes, their children shall see *it* and be glad;
Their heart shall rejoice in the LORD.
8 I will whistle for them and gather them,
For I will redeem them;
And they shall increase as they once increased.

9 "I will sow them among the peoples,
And they shall remember Me in far countries;
They shall live, together with their children,
And they shall return.
10 I will also bring them back from the land of Egypt,
And gather them from Assyria.
I will bring them into the land of Gilead and Lebanon,
Until no *more room* is found for them.
11 He shall pass through the sea with affliction,
And strike the waves of the sea:
All the depths of the River[a] shall dry up.
Then the pride of Assyria shall be brought down,
And the scepter of Egypt shall depart.

12 "So I will strengthen them in the LORD,
And they shall walk up and down in His name,"
Says the LORD.

Desolation of Israel

11 Open your doors, O Lebanon,
That fire may devour your cedars.
2 Wail, O cypress, for the cedar has fallen,
Because the mighty *trees* are ruined.

9:17 [a]Or *His* [b]Or *His* **10:1** [a]That is, spring rain
10:2 [a]Hebrew *teraphim* **10:4** [a]Or *despot*
10:11 [a]That is, the Nile

Wail, O oaks of Bashan,
For the thick forest has come down.
3 *There is* the sound of wailing shepherds!
For their glory is in ruins.
There is the sound of roaring lions!
For the pride[a] of the Jordan is in ruins.

Prophecy of the Shepherds

4 Thus says the LORD my God, "Feed the flock for slaughter, 5 whose owners slaughter them and feel no guilt; those who sell them say, 'Blessed be the LORD, for I am rich'; and their shepherds do not pity them. 6 For I will no longer pity the inhabitants of the land," says the LORD. "But indeed I will give everyone into his neighbor's hand and into the hand of his king. They shall attack the land, and I will not deliver *them* from their hand."

7 So I fed the flock for slaughter, in particular the poor of the flock.[a] I took for myself two staffs: the one I called Beauty,[b] and the other I called Bonds;[c] and I fed the flock. 8 I dismissed the three shepherds in one month. My soul loathed them, and their soul also abhorred me. 9 Then I said, "I will not feed you. Let what is dying die, and what is perishing perish. Let those that are left eat each other's flesh." 10 And I took my staff, Beauty, and cut it in two, that I might break the covenant which I had made with all the peoples. 11 So it was broken on that day. Thus the poor[a] of the flock, who were watching me, knew that it *was* the word of the LORD. 12 Then I said to them, "If it is agreeable to you, give *me* my wages; and if not, refrain." So they weighed out for my wages thirty *pieces* of silver.

13 And the LORD said to me, "Throw it to the potter"—that princely price they set on me. So I took the thirty *pieces* of silver and threw them into the house of the LORD for the potter. 14 Then I cut in two my other staff, Bonds, that I might break the brotherhood between Judah and Israel.

15 And the LORD said to me, "Next, take for yourself the implements of a foolish shepherd. 16 For indeed I will raise up a shepherd in the land *who* will not care for those who are cut off, nor seek the young, nor heal those that are broken, nor feed those that still stand. But he will eat the flesh of the fat and tear their hooves in pieces.

17 "Woe to the worthless shepherd,
Who leaves the flock!
A sword *shall be* against his arm
And against his right eye;
His arm shall completely wither,
And his right eye shall be totally blinded."

The Coming Deliverance of Judah

12 The burden[a] of the word of the LORD against Israel. Thus says the LORD, who stretches out the heavens, lays the foundation of the earth, and forms the spirit of man within him: 2 "Behold, I will make Jerusalem a cup of drunkenness to all the surrounding peoples, when they lay siege against Judah and Jerusalem. 3 And it shall happen in that day that I will make Jerusalem a very heavy stone for all peoples; all who would heave it away will surely be cut in pieces, though all nations of the earth are gathered against it. 4 In that day," says the LORD, "I will strike every horse with confusion, and its rider with madness; I will open My eyes on the house of Judah, and will strike every horse of the peoples with blindness. 5 And the governors of Judah shall say in their heart, 'The inhabitants of Jerusalem *are* my strength in the LORD of hosts, their God.' 6 In that day I will make the governors of Judah like a firepan in the woodpile, and like a fiery torch in the sheaves; they shall devour all the surrounding peoples on the right hand and on the left, but Jerusalem shall be inhabited again in her own place—Jerusalem.

7 "The LORD will save the tents of Judah first, so that the glory of the house of David and the glory of the inhabitants of Jerusalem shall not become greater than that of Judah. 8 In that day the LORD will defend the inhabitants of Jerusalem; the one who is feeble among them in that day shall be like David, and the house of David *shall be* like God, like the Angel of the LORD before them. 9 It shall be in that day *that* I will seek to destroy all the nations that come against Jerusalem.

Mourning for the Pierced One

10 "And I will pour on the house of David and on the inhabitants of Jerusalem the Spirit of

---

11:3 [a]Or *floodplain, thicket* **11:7** [a]Following Masoretic Text, Targum, and Vulgate; Septuagint reads *for the Canaanites.* [b]Or *Grace,* and so in verse 10 [c]Or *Unity,* and so in verse 14
11:11 [a]Following Masoretic Text, Targum, and Vulgate; Septuagint reads *the Canaanites.*
12:1 [a]Or *oracle*

grace and supplication; then they will look on
Me whom they pierced. Yes, they will mourn
for Him as one mourns for *his* only *son,* and
grieve for Him as one grieves for a firstborn.
[11]In that day there shall be a great mourning in
Jerusalem, like the mourning at Hadad Rimmon in the plain of Megiddo.[a] [12]And the land
shall mourn, every family by itself: the family
of the house of David by itself, and their wives
by themselves; the family of the house of Nathan by itself, and their wives by themselves;
[13]the family of the house of Levi by itself, and
their wives by themselves; the family of Shimei by itself, and their wives by themselves;
[14]all the families that remain, every family by
itself, and their wives by themselves.

IDOLATRY CUT OFF

13 "In that day a fountain shall be opened
for the house of David and for the inhabitants of Jerusalem, for sin and for uncleanness.

[2]"It shall be in that day," says the LORD of
hosts, "*that* I will cut off the names of the
idols from the land, and they shall no longer
be remembered. I will also cause the prophets
and the unclean spirit to depart from the land.
[3]It shall come to pass *that* if anyone still
prophesies, then his father and mother who
begot him will say to him, 'You shall not live,
because you have spoken lies in the name of
the LORD.' And his father and mother who begot him shall thrust him through when he
prophesies.

[4]"And it shall be in that day *that* every
prophet will be ashamed of his vision when
he prophesies; they will not wear a robe of
coarse hair to deceive. [5]But he will say, 'I *am*
no prophet, I *am* a farmer; for a man taught
me to keep cattle from my youth.' [6]And *one*
will say to him, 'What are these wounds between your arms?'[a] Then he will answer,
'*Those* with which I was wounded in the
house of my friends.'

THE SHEPHERD SAVIOR

7 "Awake, O sword, against My Shepherd,
Against the Man who is My
Companion,"
Says the LORD of hosts.
"Strike the Shepherd,
And the sheep will be scattered;
Then I will turn My hand against the
little ones.
8 And it shall come to pass in all the
land,"
Says the LORD,
"*That* two-thirds in it shall be cut off *and*
die,
But *one*-third shall be left in it:
9 I will bring the *one*-third through the
fire,
Will refine them as silver is refined,
And test them as gold is tested.
They will call on My name,
And I will answer them.
I will say, 'This *is* My people';
And each one will say, 'The LORD *is* my
God.' "

THE DAY OF THE LORD

14 Behold, the day of the LORD is
coming,
And your spoil will be divided in your
midst.
2 For I will gather all the nations to battle
against Jerusalem;
The city shall be taken,
The houses rifled,
And the women ravished.
Half of the city shall go into captivity,
But the remnant of the people shall not
be cut off from the city.

3 Then the LORD will go forth
And fight against those nations,
As He fights in the day of battle.
4 And in that day His feet will stand on
the Mount of Olives,
Which faces Jerusalem on the east.
And the Mount of Olives shall be split in
two,
From east to west,
Making a very large valley;
Half of the mountain shall move toward
the north
And half of it toward the south.

5 Then you shall flee *through* My
mountain valley,
For the mountain valley shall reach to
Azal.
Yes, you shall flee
As you fled from the earthquake
In the days of Uzziah king of Judah.

12:11 [a]Hebrew *Megiddon* **13:6** [a]Or *hands*

Thus the LORD my God will come,
And all the saints with You.[a]

6 It shall come to pass in that day
That there will be no light;
The lights will diminish.
7 It shall be one day
Which is known to the LORD—
Neither day nor night.
But at evening time it shall happen
That it will be light.

8 And in that day it shall be
That living waters shall flow from
Jerusalem,
Half of them toward the eastern sea
And half of them toward the western sea;
In both summer and winter it shall occur.
9 And the LORD shall be King over all the
earth.
In that day it shall be—
"The LORD *is* one,"[a]
And His name one.

10All the land shall be turned into a plain
from Geba to Rimmon south of Jerusalem.
Jerusalem[a] shall be raised up and inhabited in
her place from Benjamin's Gate to the place of
the First Gate and the Corner Gate, and *from*
the Tower of Hananel to the king's winepresses.

11 The *people* shall dwell in it;
And no longer shall there be utter
destruction,
But Jerusalem shall be safely inhabited.

12And this shall be the plague with which
the LORD will strike all the people who fought
against Jerusalem:

Their flesh shall dissolve while they
stand on their feet,
Their eyes shall dissolve in their sockets,
And their tongues shall dissolve in their
mouths.

13 It shall come to pass in that day
That a great panic from the LORD will be
among them.
Everyone will seize the hand of his
neighbor,
And raise his hand against his
neighbor's hand;
14 Judah also will fight at Jerusalem.
And the wealth of all the surrounding
nations
Shall be gathered together:
Gold, silver, and apparel in great
abundance.

15 Such also shall be the plague
On the horse *and* the mule,
On the camel and the donkey,
And on all the cattle that will be in those
camps.
So *shall* this plague *be*.

THE NATIONS WORSHIP THE KING

16And it shall come to pass *that* everyone
who is left of all the nations which came
against Jerusalem shall go up from year to
year to worship the King, the LORD of hosts,
and to keep the Feast of Tabernacles. 17And it
shall be *that* whichever of the families of the
earth do not come up to Jerusalem to worship
the King, the LORD of hosts, on them there will

14:5 [a]Or *you;* Septuagint, Targum, and Vulgate read *Him.* **14:9** [a]Compare Deuteronomy 6:4 **14:10** [a]Literally *She*

SOUL NOTE

Dedicated to God *(14:20, 21)* Zechariah ended his book with a vision of the "day of the LORD." On that day, the phrase "'HOLINESS TO THE LORD' shall be engraved on the bells of the horses. . . . Yes, every pot in Jerusalem and Judah shall be holiness to the LORD of hosts." To be "holy" means to be set apart for sacred use. In this new Jerusalem, even mundane utensils will be considered "holy": deliberately intended for God's work. Our lives should be so dedicated to God that even the most mundane tasks that we undertake are sacred, holy, and done for the glory of God.
Topic: Spiritual Disciplines

be no rain. [18]If the family of Egypt will not come up and enter in, they *shall have* no *rain;* they shall receive the plague with which the LORD strikes the nations who do not come up to keep the Feast of Tabernacles. [19]This shall be the punishment of Egypt and the punishment of all the nations that do not come up to keep the Feast of Tabernacles.

[20]In that day "HOLINESS TO THE LORD" shall be *engraved* on the bells of the horses. The pots in the LORD's house shall be like the bowls before the altar. [21]Yes, every pot in Jerusalem and Judah shall be holiness to the LORD of hosts.[a] Everyone who sacrifices shall come and take them and cook in them. In that day there shall no longer be a Canaanite in the house of the LORD of hosts.

14:21 [a]Or *on every pot . . . shall be (engraved) "HOLINESS TO THE LORD OF HOSTS"*

Malachi

Fear of aging seems to cause people to make radical lifestyle changes. They may switch to a low-fat diets, check their cholesterol, and begin an intense exercise program to help lose weight and fight off potential problems with the heart. But what about *spiritual* health? What are we doing to ensure healthy souls?

The Old Testament closes with a book about spiritual heart disease. In 430 B.C., the Israelites were wallowing in doubt and disillusionment. The priests were corrupt, and religious observances were a sham. As a result, the people were guilty of hypocrisy, idolatry, infidelity, divorce, materialism, and gross indifference to the things of God.

Enter the prophet Malachi. A contemporary of Nehemiah, he asked his countrymen a series of convicting questions designed to bring about repentance. But his pointed queries had no effect. So God eventually stopped speaking, and after Malachi, the nation received no further revelation from God until John the Baptist arrived on the scene some 400 years later.

Malachi reminds us that spiritual heart disease is slow but deadly. People who stop seeking God become discouraged and apathetic. Turning inward, they become self-absorbed and oblivious to God's voice. Though they may appear healthy on the outside because of their continuing religious activities, on the inside their hearts are becoming increasingly cold and hard. In time, the ugly symptoms of soul neglect will become obvious.

Don't be counted among those who succumb to spiritual heart disease. Through Malachi, let God examine your soul and prescribe what it needs most.

SOUL CONCERN IN MALACHI

1

The burden[a] of the word of the LORD to Israel by Malachi.

ISRAEL BELOVED OF GOD

2 "I have loved you," says the LORD.
"Yet you say, 'In what way have You loved us?'
Was not Esau Jacob's brother?"
Says the LORD.
"Yet Jacob I have loved;
3 But Esau I have hated,
And laid waste his mountains and his heritage
For the jackals of the wilderness."

4 Even though Edom has said,
"We have been impoverished,
But we will return and build the desolate places,"

Thus says the LORD of hosts:

"They may build, but I will throw down;
They shall be called the Territory of Wickedness,
And the people against whom the LORD will have indignation forever.
5 Your eyes shall see,
And you shall say,
'The LORD is magnified beyond the border of Israel.'

POLLUTED OFFERINGS

6 "A son honors *his* father,
And a servant *his* master.
If then I am the Father,
Where *is* My honor?
And if I *am* a Master,
Where *is* My reverence?
Says the LORD of hosts
To you priests who despise My name.
Yet you say, 'In what way have we despised Your name?'

7 "You offer defiled food on My altar,
But say,
'In what way have we defiled You?'
By saying,
'The table of the LORD is contemptible.'
8 And when you offer the blind as a sacrifice,
Is it not evil?
And when you offer the lame and sick,
Is it not evil?
Offer it then to your governor!
Would he be pleased with you?
Would he accept you favorably?"
Says the LORD of hosts.

9 "But now entreat God's favor,
That He may be gracious to us.
While this is being *done* by your hands,
Will He accept you favorably?"
Says the LORD of hosts.
10 "Who *is there* even among you who would shut the doors,
So that you would not kindle fire *on* My altar in vain?
I have no pleasure in you,"
Says the LORD of hosts,
"Nor will I accept an offering from your hands.
11 For from the rising of the sun, even to its going down,
My name *shall be* great among the Gentiles;
In every place incense *shall be* offered to My name,
And a pure offering;

1:1 [a]Or *oracle*

SOUL NOTE

Only the Best *(1:6–14)* When a guest is coming, we clean up the house and prepare refreshments. If the visitor were a dignitary, we would make more extensive preparations. If VIPs are treated like that here on earth, how much more honor should people show to God? Like the people of Malachi's day, however, we often relegate the heavenly King to the margins of our lives (1:6), giving Him less than our best. Our Savior deserves the best of our time, talent, and treasure.
Topic: Honor

For My name shall be great among the
nations,"
Says the LORD of hosts.

12 "But you profane it,
In that you say,
'The table of the LORD[a] is defiled;
And its fruit, its food, *is* contemptible.'
13 You also say,
'Oh, what a weariness!'
And you sneer at it,"
Says the LORD of hosts.
"And you bring the stolen, the lame, and
the sick;
Thus you bring an offering!
Should I accept this from your hand?"
Says the LORD.
14 "But cursed *be* the deceiver
Who has in his flock a male,
And takes a vow,
But sacrifices to the Lord what is
blemished—
For I *am* a great King,"
Says the LORD of hosts,
"And My name *is to be* feared among the
nations.

CORRUPT PRIESTS

2 "And now, O priests, this commandment
is for you.
2 If you will not hear,
And if you will not take *it* to heart,
To give glory to My name,"
Says the LORD of hosts,
"I will send a curse upon you,
And I will curse your blessings.
Yes, I have cursed them already,
Because you do not take *it* to heart.

3 "Behold, I will rebuke your descendants
And spread refuse on your faces,
The refuse of your solemn feasts;
And *one* will take you away with it.
4 Then you shall know that I have sent
this commandment to you,
That My covenant with Levi may
continue,"
Says the LORD of hosts.
5 "My covenant was with him, *one* of life
and peace,
And I gave them to him *that he might*
fear *Me;*
So he feared Me
And was reverent before My name.
6 The law of truth[a] was in his mouth,
And injustice was not found on his lips.
He walked with Me in peace and
equity,
And turned many away from iniquity.

7 "For the lips of a priest should keep
knowledge,
And *people* should seek the law from his
mouth;
For he is the messenger of the LORD of
hosts.
8 But you have departed from the way;
You have caused many to stumble at the
law.
You have corrupted the covenant of
Levi,"
Says the LORD of hosts.
9 "Therefore I also have made you
contemptible and base
Before all the people,
Because you have not kept My ways
But have shown partiality in the law."

TREACHERY OF INFIDELITY

10 Have we not all one Father?
Has not one God created us?

1:12 [a]Following Bomberg; Masoretic Text reads *Lord.* **2:6** [a]Or *true instruction*

SOUL NOTE

Loving One's Spouse *(2:13–16)* God told the Israelites that marriage is a sacred covenant. The vows spoken at the marriage altar are not to be taken lightly; God expects married people to keep them. God's own faithfulness to His covenant promises to Abraham and the Israelites demonstrates the importance of fulfilling our promises to each other. God values marriage, and our vows that He has heard are to be kept. God delights in those who remain faithful to each other, who love each other, and who strive to raise children devoted to Him. **Topic: Marriage**

Why do we deal treacherously with one another
By profaning the covenant of the fathers?
11 Judah has dealt treacherously,
And an abomination has been committed in Israel and in Jerusalem,
For Judah has profaned
The LORD's holy *institution* which He loves:
He has married the daughter of a foreign god.
12 May the LORD cut off from the tents of Jacob
The man who does this, being awake and aware,[a]
Yet who brings an offering to the LORD of hosts!

13 And this is the second thing you do:
You cover the altar of the LORD with tears,
With weeping and crying;
So He does not regard the offering anymore,
Nor receive *it* with goodwill from your hands.
14 Yet you say, "For what reason?"
Because the LORD has been witness
Between you and the wife of your youth,
With whom you have dealt treacherously;
Yet she is your companion
And your wife by covenant.
15 But did He not make *them* one,
Having a remnant of the Spirit?
And why one?
He seeks godly offspring.
Therefore take heed to your spirit,
And let none deal treacherously with the wife of his youth.
16 "For the LORD God of Israel says
That He hates divorce,
For it covers one's garment with violence,"
Says the LORD of hosts.
"Therefore take heed to your spirit,
That you do not deal treacherously."

17 You have wearied the LORD with your words;
Yet you say,
"In what way have we wearied *Him?*"
In that you say,
"Everyone who does evil
Is good in the sight of the LORD,
And He delights in them,"
Or, "Where *is* the God of justice?"

The Coming Messenger

3 "Behold, I send My messenger,
And he will prepare the way before Me.
And the Lord, whom you seek,
Will suddenly come to His temple,
Even the Messenger of the covenant,
In whom you delight.
Behold, He is coming,"
Says the LORD of hosts.

2 "But who can endure the day of His coming?
And who can stand when He appears?
For He *is* like a refiner's fire
And like launderers' soap.
3 He will sit as a refiner and a purifier of silver;
He will purify the sons of Levi,
And purge them as gold and silver,

2:12 [a]Talmud and Vulgate read *teacher and student.*

SOUL NOTE

Refined *(3:2, 3)* Sometimes the only way to get rid of impurity is to use a powerful soap or a refining fire. God would be to Israel "like a refiner's fire and like launderers' soap," ready to clean and purify His people. Such cleansing often comes through hardship and trials. God allows difficulties to come into our lives so that the heat of these hardships can burn off impurities. Red-hot fire, pelting sand, and strong soap are harsh, yet good, for they accomplish the desired cleaning. In the same way, life's trials can wash away what is impure in our lives, making us more pure for God.
Topic: Trials

That they may offer to the LORD
An offering in righteousness.

4 "Then the offering of Judah and
Jerusalem
Will be pleasant to the LORD,
As in the days of old,
As in former years.
5 And I will come near you for judgment;
I will be a swift witness
Against sorcerers,
Against adulterers,
Against perjurers,
Against those who exploit wage earners
and widows and orphans,
And against those who turn away an
alien—
Because they do not fear Me,"
Says the LORD of hosts.

6 "For I *am* the LORD,
I do not change;
Therefore you are
not consumed,
O sons of Jacob.
7 Yet from the days
of your fathers
You have gone
away from My ordinances
And have not kept *them.*
Return to Me, and I will return to you,"
Says the LORD of hosts.
"But you said,
'In what way shall we return?'

"For I am the LORD, I do not change;
therefore you are not consumed,
O sons of Jacob."
MALACHI 3:6

Do Not Rob God

8 "Will a man rob God?
Yet you have robbed Me!
But you say,
'In what way have we robbed You?'
In tithes and offerings.
9 You are cursed with a curse,
For you have robbed Me,
Even this whole nation.
10 Bring all the tithes into the storehouse,
That there may be food in My house,
And try Me now in this,"
Says the LORD of hosts,
"If I will not open for you the windows of
heaven
And pour out for you *such* blessing
That *there will* not *be room* enough *to
receive it.*

11 "And I will rebuke the devourer for your
sakes,
So that he will not destroy the fruit of
your ground,
Nor shall the vine fail to bear fruit for
you in the field,"
Says the LORD of
hosts;
12 And all nations
will call you
blessed,
For you will be a
delightful land,"
Says the LORD of
hosts.

The People Complain Harshly

13 "Your words have been harsh against Me,"
Says the LORD,
"Yet you say,
'What have we spoken against You?'
14 You have said,
'It is useless to serve God;
What profit *is it* that we have kept His
ordinance,
And that we have walked as mourners
Before the LORD of hosts?
15 So now we call the proud blessed,

SOUL NOTE

Dare to Be Generous *(3:8–12)* God's ways are not our ways. People think that to be secure, they must hoard their money. God says the opposite. "Bring all the tithes into the storehouse," He says, and then watch what happens. God promised to reward His people's giving with abundant blessings—so much that "there will not be room enough to receive it." In the New Testament, Jesus issues the same challenge: "Give, and it will be given to you: good measure, pressed down, shaken together, and running over" (Luke 6:38). To refuse to give is actually to rob God; to give generously is to know God's abundant blessings. **Topic: Money**

For those who do wickedness are raised up;
They even tempt God and go free.' "

A Book of Remembrance

16 Then those who feared the LORD spoke to one another,
And the LORD listened and heard *them;*
So a book of remembrance was written before Him
For those who fear the LORD
And who meditate on His name.

17 "They shall be Mine," says the LORD of hosts,
"On the day that I make them My jewels.[a]
And I will spare them
As a man spares his own son who serves him."
18 Then you shall again discern
Between the righteous and the wicked,
Between one who serves God
And one who does not serve Him.

The Great Day of God

4 "For behold, the day is coming,
Burning like an oven,
And all the proud, yes, all who do wickedly will be stubble.
And the day which is coming shall burn them up,"
Says the LORD of hosts,
"That will leave them neither root nor branch.
2 But to you who fear My name
The Sun of Righteousness shall arise
With healing in His wings;
And you shall go out
And grow fat like stall-fed calves.
3 You shall trample the wicked,
For they shall be ashes under the soles of your feet
On the day that I do *this,"*
Says the LORD of hosts.

4 "Remember the Law of Moses, My servant,
Which I commanded him in Horeb for all Israel,
With the statutes and judgments.
5 Behold, I will send you Elijah the prophet
Before the coming of the great and dreadful day of the LORD.
6 And he will turn
The hearts of the fathers to the children,
And the hearts of the children to their fathers,
Lest I come and strike the earth with a curse."

3:17 [a]Literally *special treasure*

SOUL NOTE

Healing in His Wings *(4:2–4)* Every person has needed healing at one time or another—whether it was a childhood scrape or a deep, emotional wound created by years of abuse. This imperfect world has caused many wounded hearts and souls searching for healing. Some look for healing in relationships, some in work, others in recreation. True healing, however, comes from God. One day, "the Sun of Righteousness shall arise with healing in His wings" to restore all things and to bring healing to wounded hearts. Whatever pain we face, healing can be found in a personal relationship with Jesus Christ. **Topic: Healing/Recovery**

Children Problems

PROBLEMS IN CHILDREN

GRANT L. MARTIN

(Malachi 4:5, 6)

Children are God's blessings. How often the presence of a small child brings a smile to people's faces. Unfortunately, many children are facing difficult problems. Five to fifteen percent of all children in the United States have problems that require mental health services—between three and ten million children. The reasons for these difficulties, of course, are many. Two major categories to be discussed here are child abuse and learning problems. These categories do not cover all the reasons children have problems, but illustrate why children may need the touch of the Great Physician as well as professional intervention.

CHILD ABUSE AND NEGLECT

Millions of children are abused or neglected. Abused children are found at all socioeconomic levels. Abuse is a profoundly disruptive, disorienting, and destructive experience for children. Symptoms such as irritability, school truancy, behavior problems, poor classroom performance, health complaints, sexual promiscuity, running away from home, and lying are common in victimized children. Depression, panic disorders, dissociative disorders, and suicide attempts can also result from chronic abuse. Another form of abuse arises when children live in homes where domestic violence occurs. The child may not be a direct victim of beating but sees his or her mother suffer at the hands of her husband or partner. These children suffer similar consequences.

The Bible records incidents of child abuse. Pharaoh, the king of Egypt, advised the Hebrew midwives to kill every Hebrew boy (Ex. 1:16, 22). Ahaz sacrificed his sons in the fire (2 Chr. 28:3). Ezekiel 16:5 refers to the pagan practice of abandoning infants and exposing them to the elements. King Herod hoped to kill the Messiah by ordering all boys under age two in and around Bethlehem to be killed (Matt. 2:16).

Treatment is crucial for abused children. The majority will need some type of medical and/or psychological help. The first step is to stop the violence. This may involve legal procedures to remove the perpetrator, followed by social, economic, and emotional actions. Therapy and education are needed for the victim and the family.

Victims often need to help in learning how to interact socially, to express their feelings in interpersonal situations, and to be more empathetic. Many of these children have negative thought patterns, accompanied by depression and feelings of helplessness. They need new, positive, and healthy ways of thinking (Rom. 12:2; Phil. 4:8).

The second step is treatment to break the cycle of violence. Limiting violent television and encouraging parents to avoid violent toys and games is a start. Most importantly, parents need to model and teach children non-violent ways to deal with their emotions. Abused children need parents who discipline effectively but without anger or violence. The family will need help with finding new patterns of conflict resolution.

LEARNING PROBLEMS

Learning disabilities can also present problems in childhood. Five to ten percent of the school population (almost two million students) has some type of learning disorder.

A *learning disability* is a problem of likely neurological origin that affects specific areas of learning and behavior in an otherwise competent student. The areas of learning affected may include input, output, storage, retention, retrieval, or processing of information. This means a student can have difficulty in acquiring, remembering, organizing, recalling, or expressing information.

Treatment for learning disabilities falls into two categories: remediation and accommodation. Remediation includes instructional strategies and techniques to help bring up a student's deficit area to at least an average level of academic functioning. Accommodation occurs when a student's strength is used to compensate for his or her weaker area. For example, a student's strong visual skills may be used to accommodate for a weak auditory processing ability.

Other children face a difficulty called *attention-deficit/hyperactivity disorder*. Some children cannot sit still. Others are highly distractible, forgetful, or inattentive. Some appear distracted by every little thing and do not seem to learn from their mistakes. Many of these children disregard rules, even when they are punished repeatedly. They tend to act without thinking, resulting in many accidents and reprimands. ADHD continues to be one of the most thoroughly researched conditions of childhood. The exact causes are still not known, but research appears to support a biological base. The data point to a genetically endowed predisposition, along with a common neurological mechanism. In other words, many ADHD children seem to arrive in the world with temperaments that leave them difficult to manage.

Treatment for ADHD consists of a variety of interventions, including parent education, implementing appropriate forms of consistency and structure at home and school, medication, instruction in self-control and social skills for the child, and use of spiritual resources such as prayer. For example, adults can ask God for discernment in telling the difference between when a child "can't" perform up to expectations because of the ADHD, and when he "won't" cooperate because of willful disobedience.

As Christians, we have the hope of healing as it was evidenced in Christ's touch (Luke 22:51). That same powerful touch is experienced by children, parents, and families today. Childhood problems can certainly be overwhelming, but we should remember that there are many resources for help. Regardless of the problems children face, we can claim the healing touch of the Master's hand.

FURTHER MEDITATION:

Other passages to study about the issue of children problems include:

- ➢ Deuteronomy 6:6–9
- ➢ Proverbs 13:24; 22:6
- ➢ Mark 10:14–16
- ➢ Ephesians 6:1–4
- ➢ Colossians 3:20, 21

To Learn More: Turn to the key passage note on children problems at James 1:27 on page 1644. See also the personality profile of Tamar on page 406.

New Testament

Matthew

Excitement . . . expectation . . . exasperation . . . discouragement . . . disappointment . . . despair . . . .

That's the progression when we wait for something we fervently want, only to wind up with something else. From a Jewish perspective, it's also a summary of the first Gospel. When Matthew's Gospel begins, Palestine is seething with unrest; the Romans have the region under their iron grip; the Jewish religious leaders are mostly corrupt; and the people are longing for the arrival of God's promised Deliverer.

He does appear, but in a Bethlehem manger! And the Messiah, this newborn, is the product of a Jewish lineage going back through King David to Abraham. In this distinctly Jewish Gospel, Jesus is presented as the long-awaited Messiah. Matthew's biography links the Old and New Testaments by showing how Christ fulfilled the Old Testament prophecies about Him. He came not to destroy the Law or the Prophets, but to fulfill them (5:17).

But most Jews were not looking for a savior from sin. Nationally, they were expecting a kingly Messiah who would defeat Rome and restore the glory and power of the reigns of David and Solomon. When Jesus failed to perform to expectations, these Jews became disillusioned, then hateful, then murderous.

Matthew, the tax collector turned disciple and author of this book, reminds us of the need to guard against false expectations. Jesus was exactly who He said He was, and He did exactly what God sent Him to do. Matthew encourages us with the truth that God always keeps His promises, even if it's not in ways we had imagined.

SOUL CONCERNS IN MATTHEW

PRAYER	(6:5–13)
CONFLICT	(18:15–17)
SINGLENESS	(19:12)

THE GENEALOGY OF JESUS CHRIST

1 The book of the genealogy of Jesus Christ, the Son of David, the Son of Abraham:

[2]Abraham begot Isaac, Isaac begot Jacob, and Jacob begot Judah and his brothers. [3]Judah begot Perez and Zerah by Tamar, Perez begot Hezron, and Hezron begot Ram. [4]Ram begot Amminadab, Amminadab begot Nahshon, and Nahshon begot Salmon. [5]Salmon begot Boaz by Rahab, Boaz begot Obed by Ruth, Obed begot Jesse, [6]and Jesse begot David the king.

David the king begot Solomon by her *who had been the wife*[a] of Uriah. [7]Solomon begot Rehoboam, Rehoboam begot Abijah, and Abijah begot Asa.[a] [8]Asa begot Jehoshaphat, Jehoshaphat begot Joram, and Joram begot Uzziah. [9]Uzziah begot Jotham, Jotham begot Ahaz, and Ahaz begot Hezekiah. [10]Hezekiah begot Manasseh, Manasseh begot Amon,[a] and Amon begot Josiah. [11]Josiah begot Jeconiah and his brothers about the time they were carried away to Babylon.

[12]And after they were brought to Babylon, Jeconiah begot Shealtiel, and Shealtiel begot Zerubbabel. [13]Zerubbabel begot Abiud, Abiud begot Eliakim, and Eliakim begot Azor. [14]Azor begot Zadok, Zadok begot Achim, and Achim begot Eliud. [15]Eliud begot Eleazar, Eleazar begot Matthan, and Matthan begot Jacob. [16]And Jacob begot Joseph the husband of Mary, of whom was born Jesus who is called Christ.

[17]So all the generations from Abraham to David *are* fourteen generations, from David until the captivity in Babylon *are* fourteen generations, and from the captivity in Babylon until the Christ *are* fourteen generations.

CHRIST BORN OF MARY

[18]Now the birth of Jesus Christ was as follows: After His mother Mary was betrothed to Joseph, before they came together, she was found with child of the Holy Spirit. [19]Then Joseph her husband, being a just *man*, and not wanting to make her a public example, was minded to put her away secretly. [20]But while he thought about these things, behold, an angel of the Lord appeared to him in a dream, saying, "Joseph, son of David, do not be afraid to take to you Mary your wife, for that which is conceived in her is of the Holy Spirit. [21]And she will bring forth a Son, and you shall call His name JESUS, for He will save His people from their sins."

[22]So all this was done that it might be fulfilled which was spoken by the Lord through the prophet, saying: [23]"*Behold, the virgin shall be with child, and bear a Son, and they shall call His name Immanuel,*"[a] which is translated, "God with us."

[24]Then Joseph, being aroused from sleep, did as the angel of the Lord commanded him and took to him his wife, [25]and did not know her till she had brought forth her firstborn Son.[a] And he called His name JESUS.

WISE MEN FROM THE EAST

2 Now after Jesus was born in Bethlehem of Judea in the days of Herod the king, behold, wise men from the East came to Jerusalem, [2]saying, "Where is He who has been born King of the Jews? For we have seen His star in the East and have come to worship Him."

[3]When Herod the king heard *this*, he was troubled, and all Jerusalem with him. [4]And when he had gathered all the chief priests and

---

1:6 [a]Words in italic type have been added for clarity. They are not found in the original Greek. **1:7** [a]NU-Text reads *Asaph.* **1:10** [a]NU-Text reads *Amos.* **1:23** [a]Isaiah 7:14. Words in oblique type in the New Testament are quoted from the Old Testament. **1:25** [a]NU-Text reads *a Son.*

SOUL NOTE

God With Us *(1:23)* The virgin birth of Jesus was the miracle beginning of a miraculous life. Matthew quoted from the prophet Isaiah, demonstrating the fulfillment of the promise that "the virgin shall be with child." Mary would become pregnant by a miracle so that Jesus would be born as a human, yet would be sinless. Isaiah had also written: "They shall call His name Immanuel," and Matthew explained that the name means "God with us." God walked this earth with people. He loves sinful humanity so much that He sent His Son to die so that all people who believe in Him might have eternal life. **Topic: Knowing God**

scribes of the people together, he inquired of
them where the Christ was to be born.
5 So they said to him, "In Bethlehem of Judea, for thus it is written by the prophet:

6 *'But you, Bethlehem, in the land of*
Judah,
Are not the least among the rulers of
Judah;
For out of you shall come a Ruler
Who will shepherd My people
Israel.' "[a]

7 Then Herod, when he had secretly called
the wise men, determined from them what
time the star appeared. 8 And he sent them to
Bethlehem and said, "Go and search carefully
for the young Child, and when you have found
Him, bring back word to me, that I may come
and worship Him also."
9 When they heard the king, they departed;
and behold, the star which they had seen in
the East went before them, till it came and
stood over where the young Child was.
10 When they saw the star, they rejoiced with
exceedingly great joy. 11 And when they had
come into the house, they saw the young Child
with Mary His mother, and fell down and worshiped Him. And when they had opened their
treasures, they presented gifts to Him: gold,
frankincense, and myrrh.
12 Then, being divinely warned in a dream

2:6 [a]Micah 5:2

PERSONALITY PROFILE

MARY AND JOSEPH: THE BOND OF LOVE AND HONESTY

(MATTHEW 1:24)

One of the most beautiful pictures of biblical courtship—of the sacrificial bond of love and honesty that God wants to plant at the root of every marriage—is given to us in the relationship between Joseph and Mary.

Though they were engaged to each other (Matt. 1:18), the Bible clearly states that they had no sexual relationship prior to Mary's miraculous pregnancy. Jesus was conceived in her womb by the power of the Holy Spirit. Imagine Joseph's internal struggle over her pregnancy. He came to a logical and painful conclusion that Mary had been intimate with another man. Mary's unlikely explanation stretched reality enough to drive any man to break off the relationship, and Joseph began to make plans.

Joseph demonstrated his character and his love by the way he sought to end the relationship privately—he did not want to make a public example of Mary. (Her presumed sin of adultery actually called for death by stoning.) Then God's angel appeared to Joseph in a dream and revealed the truth, instructing him to marry Mary. Once he was convinced that God Himself really did miraculously conceive the child, Joseph fulfilled every possible obligation as Mary's husband. By not having sexual relations with Mary until after the birth of Jesus, Joseph put his own desires aside in order to cooperate with God's plan.

Mary's inner turmoil must have equaled Joseph's. How could she expect Joseph to believe her story? Perhaps she was tempted to run away. Instead, she told him the fantastic, improbable truth—the truth of the miraculous conception—and trusted God to convince Joseph. She loved Joseph and was faithful to God. She decided that her marriage to Joseph was going to be based on truth. Mary was willing to risk the relationship itself in order to preserve truth between Joseph and herself.

God's ways are far above our own. He never fulfills His purposes in marriage as long as we hold suspicions over our spouse or live a lie with them. Joseph and Mary teach us this—a lesson for all marriages, for all time.

To Learn More: Turn to the article about marriage on pages 1296, 1297. See also the key passage note at Matthew 19:4–6 on page 1261.

that they should not return to Herod, they departed for their own country another way.

The Flight into Egypt

13Now when they had departed, behold, an
angel of the Lord appeared to Joseph in a
dream, saying, "Arise, take the young Child
and His mother, flee to Egypt, and stay there
until I bring you word; for Herod will seek the
young Child to destroy Him."
14When he arose, he took the young Child
and His mother by night and departed for
Egypt, 15and was there until the death of Herod, that it might be fulfilled which was spoken
by the Lord through the prophet, saying, *"Out
of Egypt I called My Son."*[a]

Massacre of the Innocents

16Then Herod, when he saw that he was deceived by the wise men, was exceedingly angry; and he sent forth and put to death all the
male children who were in Bethlehem and in
all its districts, from two years old and under, according to the time which he had determined from the wise men. 17Then was fulfilled
what was spoken by Jeremiah the prophet,
saying:

18 *"A voice was heard in Ramah,*
Lamentation, weeping, and great
mourning,
Rachel weeping for her children,
Refusing to be comforted,
Because they are no more."[a]

The Home in Nazareth

19Now when Herod was dead, behold, an
angel of the Lord appeared in a dream to Jo-

2:15 [a]Hosea 11:1 **2:18** [a]Jeremiah 31:15

PERSONALITY PROFILE

Honor

THE WISE MEN: HONORING THE KING

(MATTHEW 2:7–11)

When the incarnation took place, many people traveled great distances to honor God in the flesh. Angels flew in from the heavens. Shepherds came in from the hills. And several wise men journeyed from the East to honor this new King.

Matthew's version of the story of Christ's birth opens with a group of Eastern "Gentiles,"—probably Persian astrologers or magicians—referred to as "wise men" (or "magi," from the Greek). They arrived from the East to honor the child who was born "King of the Jews." They informed the people of Jerusalem that they had seen His birth announcement in the stars.

The significance of their trip to Palestine is twofold. First, their arrival and questions challenged Herod, who considered himself to be the king of the Jews. He was disturbed by this report that another King had been born. Herod was a man without honor who craved honor. He instinctively wanted to destroy anyone who might threaten his hollow kingdom. He had the scribes identify Bethlehem as the likely birthplace of a special King, according to the prophecy of Micah 5:2. Herod intended to murder the competition. Without honor, he couldn't even imagine that his opponent was really God.

The second importance of the wise men's trip was that it showed the universality of Christ. He was not only King of the Jews, but the King of kings. The wise men teach us that true seekers everywhere will honor Christ. We don't know what stars they saw, but they received God's guidance. We don't know what questions they asked, but we know they found some answers. They arrived in Palestine seeking the whole truth, prepared to worship even a little child.

A person who understands honor and humility has already learned a great deal about a relationship with God. The wise men had the right kind of faith. Hebrews 11:6 describes them: "For he who comes to God must believe that He is, and that He is a rewarder of those who diligently seek Him." God met these men at the point of honor.

To Learn More: Turn to the article about honor on pages 630, 631. See also the key passage note at 1 Peter 2:17 on page 1659.

seph in Egypt, 20saying, "Arise, take the young
Child and His mother, and go to the land of Israel, for those who sought the young Child's
life are dead." 21Then he arose, took the young
Child and His mother, and came into the land
of Israel.
22But when he heard that Archelaus was
reigning over Judea instead of his father Herod, he was afraid to go there. And being
warned by God in a dream, he turned aside
into the region of Galilee. 23And he came and
dwelt in a city called Nazareth, that it might
be fulfilled which was spoken by the prophets, "He shall be called a Nazarene."

John the Baptist Prepares the Way

3 In those days John the Baptist came
preaching in the wilderness of Judea, 2and
saying, "Repent, for the kingdom of heaven is
at hand!" 3For this is he who was spoken of by
the prophet Isaiah, saying:

"The voice of one crying in the
wilderness:
'Prepare the way of the LORD;
Make His paths straight.' "[a]

4Now John himself was clothed in camel's
hair, with a leather belt around his waist; and
his food was locusts and wild honey. 5Then
Jerusalem, all Judea, and all the region
around the Jordan went out to him 6and were
baptized by him in the Jordan, confessing
their sins.
7But when he saw many of the Pharisees
and Sadducees coming to his baptism, he said
to them, "Brood of vipers! Who warned you to
flee from the wrath to come? 8Therefore bear
fruits worthy of repentance, 9and do not think
to say to yourselves, 'We have Abraham as *our*
father.' For I say to you that God is able to

3:3 [a]Isaiah 40:3

PERSONALITY PROFILE

Abortion

HEROD: WHEN A CHOICE IS DEADLY

(MATTHEW 2:16–18)

Among the Herods of Scripture, Herod the Great comes first in line. His title of "Great" refers to his ventures in grand building schemes. His legacy included fortresses, palaces, and even the refurbished temple in Jerusalem. Herod displayed no greatness in dealing with people, however. The children of Bethlehem stood little chance against this suspicious and scheming king. A man guilty of killing at least three of his own grown children apparently had no hesitation over killing perhaps several dozen little boys in his effort to eliminate a potential rival for his throne.

Herod displayed the eventual soul-destructive mindset that values individual plans, pleasures, and purposes above the very lives of others. Such thinking seems to rule as the hidden basic assumption during conversations about abortion. Although the arguments over abortion almost always use the language of agonizing choices between two lives, the practice of abortion almost always comes down to the choice between a life and convenience, or between a life and other plans or between a life and a lifestyle. The thinking that makes an unborn child disposable doesn't have to change much in order to consider the elimination of unwanted living children.

Kings like Herod were the original defenders of the right of choice. Some even called it the divine right of choice. They believed they could make any choice they wanted and that it was right because they had made it, not because it agreed with an external standard to which even they were accountable. Choice may be a human right, but every choice isn't a right one. There is an absolute standard in the character and revelation of God. All choices we make will be measured against that standard, and we will be accountable for them.

To Learn More: Turn to the article about abortion on pages 786, 787. See also the key passage note at Psalm 139:16 on page 788.

raise up children to Abraham from these
stones. 10And even now the ax is laid to the
root of the trees. Therefore every tree which
does not bear good fruit is cut down and
thrown into the fire. 11I indeed baptize you
with water unto repentance, but He who is
coming after me is mightier than I, whose
sandals I am not worthy to carry. He will
baptize you with the Holy Spirit and fire.[a]
12His winnowing fan *is* in His hand, and He
will thoroughly clean out His threshing floor,
and gather His wheat into the barn; but He
will burn up the chaff with unquenchable
fire."

JOHN BAPTIZES JESUS

13Then Jesus came from Galilee to John at
the Jordan to be baptized by him. 14And John
tried to prevent Him, saying, "I need to be
baptized by You, and are You coming to me?"
15But Jesus answered and said to him, "Permit *it to be so* now, for thus it is fitting for us to
fulfill all righteousness." Then he allowed
Him.
16When He had been baptized, Jesus came
up immediately from the water; and behold,
the heavens were opened to Him, and He[a] saw
the Spirit of God descending like a dove and
alighting upon Him. 17And suddenly a voice
came from heaven, saying, "This is My beloved Son, in whom I am well pleased."

SATAN TEMPTS JESUS

4 Then Jesus was led up by the Spirit into
the wilderness to be tempted by the devil.
2And when He had fasted forty days and forty
nights, afterward He was hungry. 3Now when
the tempter came to Him, he said, "If You are
the Son of God, command that these stones
become bread."
4But He answered and said, "It is written,
*'Man shall not live by bread alone, but by ev-
ery word that proceeds from the mouth of
God.'* "[a]
5Then the devil took Him up into the holy
city, set Him on the pinnacle of the temple,
6and said to Him, "If You are the Son of God,
throw Yourself down. For it is written:

> *'He shall give His angels charge over you,'*

and,

> *'In their hands they shall bear you up,*
> *Lest you dash your foot against a*
> *stone.'* "[a]

7Jesus said to him, "It is written again, *'You
shall not tempt the LORD your God.'* "[a]
8Again, the devil took Him up on an exceedingly high mountain, and showed Him all the
kingdoms of the world and their glory. 9And
he said to Him, "All these things I will give
You if You will fall down and worship me."
10Then Jesus said to him, "Away with you,[a]
Satan! For it is written, *'You shall worship
the LORD your God, and Him only you shall
serve.'* "[b]
11Then the devil left Him, and behold, angels came and ministered to Him.

JESUS BEGINS HIS GALILEAN MINISTRY

12Now when Jesus heard that John had
been put in prison, He departed to Galilee.
13And leaving Nazareth, He came and dwelt in
Capernaum, which is by the sea, in the regions of Zebulun and Naphtali, 14that it might
be fulfilled which was spoken by Isaiah the
prophet, saying:

3:11 [a]M-Text omits *and fire.* **3:16** [a]Or *he*
4:4 [a]Deuteronomy 8:3 **4:6** [a]Psalm 91:11, 12
4:7 [a]Deuteronomy 6:16 **4:10** [a]M-Text reads *Get behind Me.* [b]Deuteronomy 6:13

SOUL NOTE

God's Beloved Son *(3:17)* Observers wonder about Jesus' true identity. Some say He was no more than a good man and inspiring teacher. Others say that His claims of divinity prove He was crazy. Some try to ignore Him completely. The people who gathered beside the Jordan River saw a dramatic demonstration that Jesus was special when a dove descended from heaven and God announced, "This is My beloved Son." Jesus is indeed someone special, and we can believe what He said about Himself. He is God's Son, the Messiah, our Savior. **Topic: Knowing Jesus**

15 *"The land of Zebulun and the land of*
Naphtali,
By the way of the sea, beyond the
Jordan,
Galilee of the Gentiles:
16 *The people who sat in darkness have*
seen a great light,
And upon those who sat in the region
and shadow of death
Light has dawned."[a]

17From that time Jesus began to preach and
to say, "Repent, for the kingdom of heaven is
at hand."

FOUR FISHERMEN CALLED AS DISCIPLES

18And Jesus, walking by the Sea of Galilee,
saw two brothers, Simon called Peter, and Andrew his brother, casting a net into the sea; for
they were fishermen. 19Then He said to them,
"Follow Me, and I will make you fishers of
men." 20They immediately left *their* nets and
followed Him.

21Going on from there, He saw two other
brothers, James *the son* of Zebedee, and John
his brother, in the boat with Zebedee their father, mending their nets. He called them,
22and immediately they left the boat and their
father, and followed Him.

JESUS HEALS A GREAT MULTITUDE

23And Jesus went about all Galilee, teaching
in their synagogues, preaching the gospel of
the kingdom, and healing all kinds of sickness
and all kinds of disease among the people.
24Then His fame went throughout all Syria;
and they brought to Him all sick people who
were afflicted with various diseases and torments, and those who were demon-possessed,
epileptics, and paralytics; and He healed

4:16 [a]Isaiah 9:1, 2

SOUL NOTE

Fasting and Prayer *(4:1–3)* Jesus went into the wilderness "to be tempted by the devil." He fasted forty days and forty nights in order to focus on God in prayer as He dealt with Satan. Fasting—going without food for a certain amount of time—helps people dedicate themselves to God and focus more fully on Him. Those who fast can use their hunger pangs to remind them how dependent they are on food, and hence, so much more on God. Fasting is a spiritual discipline that is meant to build a person's relationship with God. **Topic: Spiritual Disciplines**

KEY PASSAGE

Temptation

THE BEST WEAPON

(4:1–11)

Jesus' experience in the wilderness provides a lesson on how to deal with temptation. *Being* tempted is not a sin, but *giving in* to temptation is.

After fasting and praying in the wilderness for forty days, Jesus was physically weakened and hungry. At that point, Satan came and suggested that Jesus turn stones into bread. Under most circumstances, eating bread would be fine, but for Jesus to have followed Satan's directive by using His power for such a self-serving purpose would have been sinful.

Jesus resisted Satan's temptations with the Word of God. While Satan was twisting Scripture in order to justify sin, Jesus was using Scripture correctly in order to resist Satan and sin. God's Word, correctly interpreted and hidden in our hearts, is our best weapon against Satan's craftiest temptations.

To Learn More: Turn to the article about temptation on pages 62, 63. See also the personality profile of Samson on page 320.

them. 25Great multitudes followed Him—from
Galilee, and *from* Decapolis, Jerusalem, Judea, and beyond the Jordan.

THE BEATITUDES

5 And seeing the multitudes, He went up on
a mountain, and when He was seated His
disciples came to Him. 2Then He opened His
mouth and taught them, saying:

3 "Blessed *are* the poor in spirit,
For theirs is the kingdom of heaven.
4 Blessed *are* those who mourn,
For they shall be comforted.
5 Blessed *are* the meek,
For they shall inherit the earth.
6 Blessed *are* those who hunger and thirst for righteousness,
For they shall be filled.
7 Blessed *are* the merciful,
For they shall obtain mercy.
8 Blessed *are* the pure in heart,
For they shall see God.
9 Blessed *are* the peacemakers,
For they shall be called sons of God.
10 Blessed *are* those who are persecuted for righteousness' sake,
For theirs is the kingdom of heaven.

> "Blessed are those who mourn,
> for they shall be comforted."
> MATTHEW 5:4

11"Blessed are you when they revile and persecute you, and say all kinds of evil against you
falsely for My sake. 12Rejoice and be exceedingly glad, for great *is* your reward in heaven,
for so they persecuted the prophets who were
before you.

BELIEVERS ARE SALT AND LIGHT

13"You are the salt of the earth; but if the
salt loses its flavor, how shall it be seasoned?
It is then good for nothing but to be thrown
out and trampled underfoot by men.
14"You are the light of the world. A city that
is set on a hill cannot be hidden. 15Nor do they
light a lamp and put it under a basket, but on
a lampstand, and it gives light to all *who are* in
the house. 16Let your light so shine before
men, that they may see your good works and
glorify your Father in heaven.

CHRIST FULFILLS THE LAW

17"Do not think that I came to destroy the
Law or the Prophets. I did not come to destroy
but to fulfill. 18For assuredly, I say to you, till
heaven and earth pass away, one jot or one
tittle will by no means pass from the law till all
is fulfilled. 19Whoever therefore breaks one of
the least of these commandments, and teaches
men so, shall be called
least in the kingdom of heaven; but whoever
does and teaches *them,* he shall be called
great in the kingdom of heaven. 20For I say to
you, that unless your righteousness exceeds
the righteousness of the scribes and Pharisees,
you will by no means enter the kingdom of
heaven.

MURDER BEGINS IN THE HEART

21"You have heard that it was said to those
of old, *'You shall not murder,*[a] and whoever
murders will be in danger of the judgment.'
22But I say to you that whoever is angry with
his brother without a cause[a] shall be in danger
of the judgment. And whoever says to his
brother, 'Raca!' shall be in danger of the council. But whoever says, 'You fool!' shall be in
danger of hell fire. 23Therefore if you bring

5:21 [a]Exodus 20:13; Deuteronomy 5:17
5:22 [a]NU-Text omits *without a cause.*

SOUL NOTE

In the Heart *(5:27)* Quoting from Exodus 20:14, Jesus reminded His listeners of the commandment against adultery. Then He said that looking at another person lustfully is committing adultery in one's heart. Jesus explained that thinking about an act is the same as doing it, because actions begin with thoughts and desires. Since lust and adultery are first embraced in the mind and heart, believers should try to avoid situations that cause temptation. **Topic: Adultery**

your gift to the altar, and there remember that your brother has something against you, [24]leave your gift there before the altar, and go your way. First be reconciled to your brother, and then come and offer your gift. [25]Agree with your adversary quickly, while you are on the way with him, lest your adversary deliver you to the judge, the judge hand you over to the officer, and you be thrown into prison. [26]Assuredly, I say to you, you will by no means get out of there till you have paid the last penny.

Adultery in the Heart

[27]"You have heard that it was said to those of old,[a] *'You shall not commit adultery.'*[b] [28]But I say to you that whoever looks at a woman to lust for her has already committed adultery with her in his heart. [29]If your right eye causes you to sin, pluck it out and cast *it* from you; for it is more profitable for you that one of your members perish, than for your whole body to be cast into hell. [30]And if your right hand causes you to sin, cut it off and cast *it* from you; for it is more profitable for you that one of your members perish, than for your whole body to be cast into hell.

Marriage Is Sacred and Binding

[31]"Furthermore it has been said, 'Whoever divorces his wife, let him give her a certificate of divorce.' [32]But I say to you that whoever divorces his wife for any reason except sexual immorality[a] causes her to commit adultery; and whoever marries a woman who is divorced commits adultery.

Jesus Forbids Oaths

[33]"Again you have heard that it was said to those of old, 'You shall not swear falsely, but shall perform your oaths to the Lord.' [34]But I say to you, do not swear at all: neither by heaven, for it is God's throne; [35]nor by the earth, for it is His footstool; nor by Jerusalem, for it is the city of the great King. [36]Nor shall you swear by your head, because you cannot make one hair white or black. [37]But let your 'Yes' be 'Yes,' and your 'No,' 'No.' For whatever is more than these is from the evil one.

Go the Second Mile

[38]"You have heard that it was said, *'An eye for an eye and a tooth for a tooth.'*[a] [39]But I tell you not to resist an evil person. But whoever slaps you on your right cheek, turn the other to him also. [40]If anyone wants to sue you and take away your tunic, let him have *your* cloak also. [41]And whoever compels you to go one mile, go with him two. [42]Give to him who asks you, and from him who wants to borrow from you do not turn away.

Love Your Enemies

[43]"You have heard that it was said, *'You shall love your neighbor*[a] and hate your enemy.' [44]But I say to you, love your enemies, bless those who curse you, do good to those who hate you, and pray for those who spitefully use you and persecute you,[a] [45]that you may be sons of your Father in heaven; for He makes His sun rise on the evil and on the good, and sends rain on the just and on the unjust. [46]For if you love those who love you, what reward have you? Do not even the tax collectors do the same? [47]And if you greet your brethren[a] only, what do you do more *than others?* Do not even the tax collectors[b] do so? [48]Therefore you shall be perfect, just as your Father in heaven is perfect.

5:27 [a]NU-Text and M-Text omit *to those of old.* [b]Exodus 20:14; Deuteronomy 5:18 **5:32** [a]Or *fornication* **5:38** [a]Exodus 21:24; Leviticus 24:20; Deuteronomy 19:21 **5:43** [a]Compare Leviticus 19:18 **5:44** [a]NU-Text omits three clauses from this verse, leaving, *"But I say to you, love your enemies and pray for those who persecute you."* **5:47** [a]M-Text reads *friends.* [b]NU-Text reads *Gentiles.*

SOUL NOTE

Word Watch *(5:33–37)* Jesus told people that they should not "swear at all," but should let their "yes" mean yes and their "no" mean no. God's people should not have to swear to the truth of their words. They should be so trustworthy that their statements are believed without question. Words are important, and believers must watch what they say. They should never say one thing and mean another. God's people should be trustworthy and keep their word. **Topic: Boundaries**

Do Good to Please God

6 "Take heed that you do not do your charitable deeds before men, to be seen by them. Otherwise you have no reward from your Father in heaven. 2Therefore, when you do a charitable deed, do not sound a trumpet before you as the hypocrites do in the synagogues and in the streets, that they may have glory from men. Assuredly, I say to you, they have their reward. 3But when you do a charitable deed, do not let your left hand know what your right hand is doing, 4that your charitable deed may be in secret; and your Father who sees in secret will Himself reward you openly.[a]

The Model Prayer

5"And when you pray, you shall not be like the hypocrites. For they love to pray standing in the synagogues and on the corners of the streets, that they may be seen by men. Assuredly, I say to you, they have their reward. 6But you, when you pray, go into your room, and when you have shut your door, pray to your Father who *is* in the secret *place;* and your Father who sees in secret will reward you openly.[a] 7And when you pray, do not use vain repetitions as the heathen *do*. For they think that they will be heard for their many words.

8"Therefore do not be like them. For your Father knows the things you have need of before you ask Him. 9In this manner, therefore, pray:

Our Father in heaven,
Hallowed be Your name.
10 Your kingdom come.
Your will be done
On earth as *it is* in heaven.
11 Give us this day our daily bread.
12 And forgive us our debts,
As we forgive our debtors.
13 And do not lead us into temptation,
But deliver us from the evil one.
For Yours is the kingdom and the power
and the glory forever. Amen.[a]

14"For if you forgive men their trespasses, your heavenly Father will also forgive you. 15But if you do not forgive men their trespasses, neither will your Father forgive your trespasses.

Fasting to Be Seen Only by God

16"Moreover, when you fast, do not be like the hypocrites, with a sad countenance. For they disfigure their faces that they may appear to men to be fasting. Assuredly, I say to you, they have their reward. 17But you, when you fast, anoint your head and wash your face, 18so that you do not appear to men to be fasting, but to your Father who *is* in the secret *place;* and your Father who sees in secret will reward you openly.[a]

Lay Up Treasures in Heaven

19"Do not lay up for yourselves treasures on earth, where moth and rust destroy and where thieves break in and steal; 20but lay up for yourselves treasures in heaven, where neither moth nor rust destroys and where thieves do not break in and steal. 21For where your treasure is, there your heart will be also.

The Lamp of the Body

22"The lamp of the body is the eye. If therefore your eye is good, your whole body will be full of light. 23But if your eye is bad, your

6:4 [a]NU-Text omits *openly.* **6:6** [a]NU-Text omits *openly.* **6:13** [a]NU-Text omits *For Yours* through *Amen.* **6:18** [a]NU-Text and M-Text omit *openly.*

SOUL NOTE

Perfect? *(5:48)* Jesus says, "You shall be perfect, just as your Father in heaven is perfect." Jesus was not commanding His people to be perfectionists. People who constantly strive for perfection in every area of life usually find themselves frustrated because they *cannot* be perfect. One day Christ will make us perfect; during our time on earth we should be striving for Christlikeness, always realizing that we have much room to grow. Believers should never settle for mediocrity in their walk with Christ, but should seek to deepen their faith and maturity in every area of life.

Topic: Perfectionism

whole body will be full of darkness. If therefore the light that is in you is darkness, how
great *is* that darkness!

YOU CANNOT SERVE GOD AND RICHES

24"No one can serve two masters; for either
he will hate the one and love the other, or else
he will be loyal to the one and despise the
other. You cannot serve God and mammon.

DO NOT WORRY

25"Therefore I say to you, do not worry
about your life, what you will eat or what you
will drink; nor about your body, what you will
put on. Is not life more than food and the body
more than clothing? 26Look at the birds of the
air, for they neither sow nor reap nor gather
into barns; yet your heavenly Father feeds
them. Are you not of more value than they?
27Which of you by worrying can add one cubit
to his stature?
28"So why do you worry about clothing?
Consider the lilies of the field, how they grow:
they neither toil nor spin; 29and yet I say to
you that even Solomon in all his glory was not
arrayed like one of these. 30Now if God so
clothes the grass of the field, which today is,
and tomorrow is thrown into the oven, *will He*
not much more *clothe* you, O you of little
faith?

KEY PASSAGE

Prayer

OPENING HEAVEN'S GATES

(6:5–13)

Jesus taught that prayer should arise from people's sincere love for God—not from a love of show or ritual. The prayer that Jesus taught His disciples provides the perfect example of prayer.

- The first words of the prayer express adoration and love for God as Father.
- The next phrases express submission to God and trust in His power and promises: "Your kingdom come. Your will be done."
- Then the prayer asks God for daily provision.
- The prayer also gives opportunity to express repentance, asking for forgiveness according to how the person praying forgives others.
- Next follows a request for help in resisting temptation and in fighting sin.
- The final sentence recognizes that everything belongs to God and is under His control.

Our prayers should include elements of adoration, submission, petition, repentance, and praise to God.

To Learn More: Turn to the article about prayer on pages 1238, 1239. See also the personality profile of Jesus on page 1252.

SOUL NOTE

Mind Clutter *(6:25–34)* Worry fills people's minds with useless clutter that leaves no room for God. Worry clouds perspective, causing people to focus on themselves rather than on God. Jesus said that God feeds the birds and clothes the flowers, so He will take care of His children. Trusting God involves trusting Him to care for us. Jesus tells us to "seek first the kingdom of God and His righteousness." As believers we still must work to meet our needs; we don't sit back and expect God to do it all. We work, but we don't worry. We know that God will care for us. **Topic: Worry**

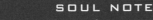

Prayer

POWERFUL PRAYER

STORMIE OMARTIAN

(Matthew 6:5–13)

Just as our physical bodies need care, so do our souls. Our souls need to be fed, cleansed, healed, trained, and rested. Our souls can only find that kind of wholeness when we are in the presence of God. In Him we find the peace, health, growth, fulfillment, and restoration we need. The way to enter into the fullness of God's presence is through prayer.

TALKING TO A POWERFUL GOD

Prayer is talking to God. But it is not just about asking Him for things, even though that is an important part of it. Prayer is spending time with God—listening to His voice speak to our hearts. Prayer is fulfilling that deep desire to be with God and letting our spirits align with His. Through prayer we declare our dependence on Him and draw upon His wisdom and strength. Through prayer, we tell God how much we love Him, and we let His love for us fill our souls to overflowing. Prayer is getting to know God better.

It's hard to get to know someone if we seldom talk to that person, or if the only time we talk to him or her is when we want something. The same is true with God. It's hard to get to know Him without ongoing daily communication with Him. Most of us have electricity in our homes. But if we don't plug into it, we will not have light. The same is true of our relationship with Jesus, who is the Light of the world. If we don't plug into Him, we will miss the greatest portion of His radiance and illumination in our lives.

We become like the people with whom we spend time. When we spend time with God, His character rubs off on us. When we are in His presence, we soak in His healing and wholeness, and it makes us healed and whole. His peace becomes our peace. In His presence, our lives can be transformed.

TRUSTING GOD THROUGH POWERFUL PRAYER

"Pray without ceasing," the Bible says (1 Thess. 5:17). That means praying constantly, making prayer a way of life. To pray without ceasing means that we draw near to God in everything we do—our work, relationships, hobbies, entertainment, travel, and the mundane activities of daily living. It means praying about everything so that we don't leave our lives to chance.

Jesus said, "Ask, and it will be given to you; seek, and you will find; knock, and it will be opened to you" (Matt. 7:7). The problem is that we neglect to ask. We don't take time to seek. And we forget to knock. We get busy trying to live our complex lives on our own terms. There is so much vying for our attention, so many decisions to be made, so many issues to deplete our strength, distort our thinking, and steal our peace. Perhaps our greatest sin is thinking we can handle any part of our lives without talking to God about it.

We need to ask of God, and we need to be specific. We should keep knocking until the door opens to everything He has for us. But He doesn't want us to just ask for anything and everything, hoping He will get us out of the mess we're in or give us whatever we want. The Bible says, "You ask and do not receive, because you ask amiss, that you may spend it on your pleasures" (James 4:3). When we merely ask for things without first drawing close to

God, we can miss how we're supposed to pray.

Prayer should not be reduced to a mere formula, but there are important elements that are good to include if our prayers are to be as effective and powerful as we want them to be. In prayer, we should try to:

- ➢ Tell God how much we love Him.
- ➢ Praise Him for who He is.
- ➢ Thank Him for all He has done.
- ➢ Declare our dependence upon Him.
- ➢ Confess any sin in our lives.
- ➢ Share everything that is in our hearts.
- ➢ Tell Him our requests.
- ➢ Wait on Him to speak to our souls.
- ➢ Thank Him for hearing our prayers.

We will find that the more we pray, the more we will find to pray about. But we mustn't be discouraged if the answers to our prayers don't seem to come right away. Sometimes it takes a while. And often we don't even recognize the answers to our own prayers because they are not answered in the way or time we thought they would be. We can't limit God to our timetable. Our job is to pray; God's job is to answer. We can trust that God always hears our prayers; something is happening whether we can see it or not.

Jesus said, "If you ask anything in My name, I will do it" (John 14:14). That is His promise to us. So say to Him, "Lord, touch me with Your healing love and power. Meet my every need and open up my understanding to all You have for me where I am right now. Reveal Yourself to me in every situation I face. Show me what I need to see and tell me what I need to know. Enable me to do what I have to do. For I know that without You, I can do nothing."

Thank God for unanswered prayers

FURTHER MEDITATION:

Other passages to study about the issue of prayer include:

- ➢ Nehemiah 1:4—2:5
- ➢ Psalm 118:5–8
- ➢ Matthew 21:22
- ➢ Mark 1:35
- ➢ 1 John 5:14

To Learn More: Turn to the key passage note on prayer at Matthew 6:5–13 on page 1237. See also the personality profile of Jesus on page 1252.

[31]“Therefore do not worry, saying, ‘What shall we eat?’ or ‘What shall we drink?’ or ‘What shall we wear?’ [32]For after all these things the Gentiles seek. For your heavenly Father knows that you need all these things. [33]But seek first the kingdom of God and His righteousness, and all these things shall be added to you. [34]Therefore do not worry about tomorrow, for tomorrow will worry about its own things. Sufficient for the day *is* its own trouble.

Do Not Judge

7 “Judge not, that you be not judged. [2]For with what judgment you judge, you will be judged; and with the measure you use, it will be measured back to you. [3]And why do you look at the speck in your brother’s eye, but do not consider the plank in your own eye? [4]Or how can you say to your brother, ‘Let me remove the speck from your eye’; and look, a plank *is* in your own eye? [5]Hypocrite! First remove the plank from your own eye, and then you will see clearly to remove the speck from your brother’s eye.

[6]“Do not give what is holy to the dogs; nor cast your pearls before swine, lest they trample them under their feet, and turn and tear you in pieces.

> “Ask, and it will be given to you; seek, and you will find; knock, and it will be opened to you.”
>
> MATTHEW 7:7

Keep Asking, Seeking, Knocking

[7]“Ask, and it will be given to you; seek, and you will find; knock, and it will be opened to you. [8]For everyone who asks receives, and he who seeks finds, and to him who knocks it will be opened. [9]Or what man is there among you who, if his son asks for bread, will give him a stone? [10]Or if he asks for a fish, will he give him a serpent? [11]If you then, being evil, know how to give good gifts to your children, how much more will your Father who is in heaven give good things to those who ask Him! [12]Therefore, whatever you want men to do to you, do also to them, for this is the Law and the Prophets.

The Narrow Way

[13]“Enter by the narrow gate; for wide *is* the gate and broad *is* the way that leads to destruction, and there are many who go in by it. [14]Because[a] narrow *is* the gate and difficult *is* the way which leads to life, and there are few who find it.

You Will Know Them by Their Fruits

[15]“Beware of false prophets, who come to you in sheep’s clothing, but inwardly they are ravenous wolves. [16]You will know them by their fruits. Do men gather grapes from thornbushes or figs from thistles? [17]Even so, every good tree bears good fruit, but a bad tree bears bad fruit. [18]A good tree cannot bear bad fruit, nor *can* a bad tree bear good fruit. [19]Every tree that does not bear good fruit is cut down and thrown into the fire. [20]Therefore by their fruits you will know them.

I Never Knew You

[21]“Not everyone who says to Me, ‘Lord, Lord,’ shall enter the kingdom of heaven, but he who does the will of My Father in heaven. [22]Many will say to Me in that day, ‘Lord, Lord, have we not prophesied in Your name, cast out demons in Your name, and done many wonders in Your name?’ [23]And then

7:14 [a]NU-Text and M-Text read *How . . . !*

SOUL NOTE

The Golden Rule *(7:12)* “Whatever you want men to do to you, do also to them.” This simple statement, called the “Golden Rule,” is God’s direction for how people should treat one another. This rule would eliminate all cheating, stealing, hatred, and murder. God calls His people to a high standard. While not everyone will follow this rule, Christians must do so, setting an example for others. These timeless words can help us know how to act in any given situation. When we treat others as we would want to be treated, we show God’s love in a practical way. **Topic: Values**

I will declare to them, 'I never knew you; depart from Me, you who practice lawlessness!'

Build on the Rock

24"Therefore whoever hears these sayings of Mine, and does them, I will liken him to a wise man who built his house on the rock: 25and the rain descended, the floods came, and the winds blew and beat on that house; and it did not fall, for it was founded on the rock.

26"But everyone who hears these sayings of Mine, and does not do them, will be like a foolish man who built his house on the sand: 27and the rain descended, the floods came, and the winds blew and beat on that house; and it fell. And great was its fall."

28And so it was, when Jesus had ended these sayings, that the people were astonished at His teaching, 29for He taught them as one having authority, and not as the scribes.

Jesus Cleanses a Leper

8 When He had come down from the mountain, great multitudes followed Him. 2And behold, a leper came and worshiped Him, saying, "Lord, if You are willing, You can make me clean."

3Then Jesus put out *His* hand and touched him, saying, "I am willing; be cleansed." Immediately his leprosy was cleansed.

4And Jesus said to him, "See that you tell no one; but go your way, show yourself to the priest, and offer the gift that Moses commanded, as a testimony to them."

Jesus Heals a Centurion's Servant

5Now when Jesus had entered Capernaum, a centurion came to Him, pleading with Him, 6saying, "Lord, my servant is lying at home paralyzed, dreadfully tormented."

7And Jesus said to him, "I will come and heal him."

8The centurion answered and said, "Lord, I am not worthy that You should come under my roof. But only speak a word, and my servant will be healed. 9For I also am a man under authority, having soldiers under me. And I say to this *one*, 'Go,' and he goes; and to another, 'Come,' and he comes; and to my servant, 'Do this,' and he does *it*."

10When Jesus heard *it*, He marveled, and said to those who followed, "Assuredly, I say to you, I have not found such great faith, not even in Israel! 11And I say to you that many will come from east and west, and sit down with Abraham, Isaac, and Jacob in the kingdom of heaven. 12But the sons of the kingdom will be cast out into outer darkness. There will be weeping and gnashing of teeth." 13Then Jesus said to the centurion, "Go your way; and as you have believed, *so* let it be done for you." And his servant was healed that same hour.

Peter's Mother-in-Law Healed

14Now when Jesus had come into Peter's house, He saw his wife's mother lying sick with a fever. 15So He touched her hand, and the fever left her. And she arose and served them.[a]

Many Healed After Sabbath Sunset

16When evening had come, they brought to Him many who were demon-possessed. And He cast out the spirits with a word, and healed all who were sick, 17that it might be fulfilled which was spoken by Isaiah the prophet, saying:

"He Himself took our infirmities
And bore our sicknesses."[a]

8:15 [a]NU-Text and M-Text read *Him*. **8:17** [a]Isaiah 53:4

SOUL NOTE

Such Faith! *(8:5–13)* A centurion—an officer who commanded 100 soldiers—asked Jesus to heal his servant. The centurion knew, from his own experience of giving commands, that Jesus only had to speak a word and the servant would be healed. Jesus "marveled, and said to those who followed . . . 'I have not found such great faith, not even in Israel!'" Such great faith comes when we believe what we do not see, when we trust Jesus to do what seems impossible. Such faith pleases Him. **Topic: Faith**

The Cost of Discipleship

[18]And when Jesus saw great multitudes about Him, He gave a command to depart to the other side. [19]Then a certain scribe came and said to Him, "Teacher, I will follow You wherever You go."

[20]And Jesus said to him, "Foxes have holes and birds of the air *have* nests, but the Son of Man has nowhere to lay *His* head."

[21]Then another of His disciples said to Him, "Lord, let me first go and bury my father."

[22]But Jesus said to him, "Follow Me, and let the dead bury their own dead."

Wind and Wave Obey Jesus

[23]Now when He got into a boat, His disciples followed Him. [24]And suddenly a great tempest arose on the sea, so that the boat was covered with the waves. But He was asleep. [25]Then His disciples came to *Him* and awoke Him, saying, "Lord, save us! We are perishing!"

[26]But He said to them, "Why are you fearful, O you of little faith?" Then He arose and rebuked the winds and the sea, and there was a great calm. [27]So the men marveled, saying, "Who can this be, that even the winds and the sea obey Him?"

Two Demon-Possessed Men Healed

[28]When He had come to the other side, to the country of the Gergesenes,[a] there met Him two demon-possessed *men,* coming out of the tombs, exceedingly fierce, so that no one could pass that way. [29]And suddenly they cried out, saying, "What have we to do with You, Jesus, You Son of God? Have You come here to torment us before the time?"

[30]Now a good way off from them there was a herd of many swine feeding. [31]So the demons begged Him, saying, "If You cast us out, permit us to go away[a] into the herd of swine."

[32]And He said to them, "Go." So when they had come out, they went into the herd of swine. And suddenly the whole herd of swine ran violently down the steep place into the sea, and perished in the water.

[33]Then those who kept *them* fled; and they went away into the city and told everything, including what *had happened* to the demon-possessed *men.* [34]And behold, the whole city came out to meet Jesus. And when they saw Him, they begged *Him* to depart from their region.

Jesus Forgives and Heals a Paralytic

9 So He got into a boat, crossed over, and came to His own city. [2]Then behold, they brought to Him a paralytic lying on a bed. When Jesus saw their faith, He said to the paralytic, "Son, be of good cheer; your sins are forgiven you."

[3]And at once some of the scribes said within themselves, "This Man blasphemes!"

[4]But Jesus, knowing their thoughts, said, "Why do you think evil in your hearts? [5]For which is easier, to say, '*Your* sins are forgiven you,' or to say, 'Arise and walk'? [6]But that you may know that the Son of Man has power on earth to forgive sins"—then He said to the paralytic, "Arise, take up your bed, and go to your house." [7]And he arose and departed to his house.

[8]Now when the multitudes saw *it,* they marveled[a] and glorified God, who had given such power to men.

Matthew the Tax Collector

[9]As Jesus passed on from there, He saw a man named Matthew sitting at the tax office. And He said to him, "Follow Me." So he arose and followed Him.

[10]Now it happened, as Jesus sat at the table in the house, *that* behold, many tax collectors and sinners came and sat down with Him and His disciples. [11]And when the Pharisees saw *it,* they said to His disciples, "Why does your Teacher eat with tax collectors and sinners?"

[12]When Jesus heard *that,* He said to them, "Those who are well have no need of a physician, but those who are sick. [13]But go and learn what *this* means: '*I desire mercy and not sacrifice.*'[a] For I did not come to call the righteous, but sinners, to repentance."[b]

Jesus Is Questioned About Fasting

[14]Then the disciples of John came to Him, saying, "Why do we and the Pharisees fast often,[a] but Your disciples do not fast?"

[15]And Jesus said to them, "Can the friends of the bridegroom mourn as long as the bridegroom is with them? But the days will come when the bridegroom will be taken away from them, and then they will fast. [16]No one puts a

8:28 [a]NU-Text reads *Gadarenes.* **8:31** [a]NU-Text reads *send us.* **9:8** [a]NU-Text reads *were afraid.* **9:13** [a]Hosea 6:6 [b]NU-Text omits *to repentance.* **9:14** [a]NU-Text brackets *often* as disputed.

piece of unshrunk cloth on an old garment; for
the patch pulls away from the garment, and
the tear is made worse. [17]Nor do they put new
wine into old wineskins, or else the wineskins
break, the wine is spilled, and the wineskins
are ruined. But they put new wine into new
wineskins, and both are preserved."

A Girl Restored to Life and a Woman Healed

[18]While He spoke these things to them, behold, a ruler came and worshiped Him, saying,
"My daughter has just died, but come and lay
Your hand on her and she will live." [19]So Jesus
arose and followed him, and so *did* His disciples.
[20]And suddenly, a woman who had a flow
of blood for twelve years came from behind
and touched the hem of His garment. [21]For she
said to herself, "If only I may touch His garment, I shall be made well." [22]But Jesus
turned around, and when He saw her He said,
"Be of good cheer, daughter; your faith has
made you well." And the woman was made
well from that hour.
[23]When Jesus came into the ruler's house,
and saw the flute players and the noisy crowd
wailing, [24]He said to them, "Make room, for
the girl is not dead, but sleeping." And they
ridiculed Him. [25]But when the crowd was put
outside, He went in and took her by the hand,
and the girl arose. [26]And the report of this
went out into all that land.

PERSONALITY PROFILE

Spiritual Growth

MATTHEW: A CHANGED LIFE

(MATTHEW 9:9)

Jewish tax collectors in Jesus' day were the despised of the despised. They were called traitors in the worst sense. The Jewish people viewed them with double disgust because Jewish tax collectors actually worked for the Roman government, making their money off their own people by receiving a percentage of the income from the taxes they collected. They were lumped with harlots, murderers, and thieves, and were considered offensive and off-limits to respectable Jews. Jesus offended many religious people when He called the tax collector Matthew to be one of His intimate inner circle.

Matthew's Jewish name was Levi. Jesus' simple appeal to him was dramatic and direct: "Follow Me." Matthew's instantaneous response indicates the irresistible nature of Jesus' person and character, as well as the openness of Matthew's life. We have no idea whether Matthew had any previous contact with Jesus or not. We can only assume that he must have had some awareness of the significance of the life and ministry of Jesus in order to respond to such a command.

Although Matthew rarely got mentioned by name during the events Jesus experienced with His disciples, he was there, observing, noting, and remembering. Some think the only things he took with him when he left his tax table were a pen and a keen mind for details and accounting. But Matthew's biography of Jesus bears witness to what he learned from Jesus. Unlike Mark and Luke, Matthew decided to record Jesus' life in categories. Events and lessons in the Gospel of Matthew are not organized by time sequence, but by common themes (see for example, all the parables in chapter 13).

Matthew's example offers several unique lessons about spiritual growth:

- God's calling in our lives is such that it demands an intentional response.
- Our past holds keys to God's purposes in our lives.
- God sees unlimited potential where others have given up.

Like Matthew, we don't know what the future holds. But we can choose, like he did, to follow Jesus—the very One who holds the future.

To Learn More: Turn to the article about spiritual growth on pages 1670, 1671. See also the key passage note at Psalm 1 on page 679.

Two Blind Men Healed

[27]When Jesus departed from there, two blind men followed Him, crying out and saying, "Son of David, have mercy on us!"

[28]And when He had come into the house, the blind men came to Him. And Jesus said to them, "Do you believe that I am able to do this?"

They said to Him, "Yes, Lord."

[29]Then He touched their eyes, saying, "According to your faith let it be to you." [30]And their eyes were opened. And Jesus sternly warned them, saying, "See *that* no one knows *it*." [31]But when they had departed, they spread the news about Him in all that country.

A Mute Man Speaks

[32]As they went out, behold, they brought to Him a man, mute and demon-possessed. [33]And when the demon was cast out, the mute spoke. And the multitudes marveled, saying, "It was never seen like this in Israel!"

[34]But the Pharisees said, "He casts out demons by the ruler of the demons."

The Compassion of Jesus

[35]Then Jesus went about all the cities and villages, teaching in their synagogues, preaching the gospel of the kingdom, and healing every sickness and every disease among the people.[a] [36]But when He saw the multitudes, He was moved with compassion for them, because they were weary[a] and scattered, like sheep having no shepherd. [37]Then He said to His disciples, "The harvest truly *is* plentiful, but the laborers *are* few. [38]Therefore pray the Lord of the harvest to send out laborers into His harvest."

The Twelve Apostles

10 And when He had called His twelve disciples to *Him*, He gave them power *over* unclean spirits, to cast them out, and to heal all kinds of sickness and all kinds of disease. [2]Now the names of the twelve apostles are these: first, Simon, who is called Peter, and Andrew his brother; James the *son* of Zebedee, and John his brother; [3]Philip and Bartholomew; Thomas and Matthew the tax collector; James the *son* of Alphaeus, and Lebbaeus, whose surname was[a] Thaddaeus; [4]Simon the Cananite,[a] and Judas Iscariot, who also betrayed Him.

Sending Out the Twelve

[5]These twelve Jesus sent out and commanded them, saying: "Do not go into the way of the Gentiles, and do not enter a city of the Samaritans. [6]But go rather to the lost sheep of the house of Israel. [7]And as you go, preach, saying, 'The kingdom of heaven is at hand.' [8]Heal the sick, cleanse the lepers, raise the dead,[a] cast out demons. Freely you have received, freely give. [9]Provide neither gold nor silver nor copper in your money belts, [10]nor bag for *your* journey, nor two tunics, nor sandals, nor staffs; for a worker is worthy of his food.

[11]"Now whatever city or town you enter, inquire who in it is worthy, and stay there till you go out. [12]And when you go into a household, greet it. [13]If the household is worthy, let your peace come upon it. But if it is not worthy, let your peace return to you. [14]And whoever will not receive you nor hear your words, when you depart from that house or city, shake off the dust from your feet. [15]Assuredly, I say to you, it will be more tolerable for the land of Sodom and Gomorrah in the day of judgment than for that city!

Persecutions Are Coming

[16]"Behold, I send you out as sheep in the midst of wolves. Therefore be wise as serpents and harmless as doves. [17]But beware of men, for they will deliver you up to councils and scourge you in their synagogues. [18]You will be brought before governors and kings for My sake, as a testimony to them and to the Gentiles. [19]But when they deliver you up, do not worry about how or what you should speak. For it will be given to you in that hour what you should speak; [20]for it is not you who speak, but the Spirit of your Father who speaks in you.

[21]"Now brother will deliver up brother to death, and a father *his* child; and children will rise up against parents and cause them to be put to death. [22]And you will be hated by all for My name's sake. But he who endures to the end will be saved. [23]When they persecute you in this city, flee to another. For assuredly, I say

---

9:35 [a]NU-Text omits *among the people.*
9:36 [a]NU-Text and M-Text read *harassed.*
10:3 [a]NU-Text omits *Lebbaeus, whose surname was.* **10:4** [a]NU-Text reads *Cananaean.*
10:8 [a]NU-Text reads *raise the dead, cleanse the lepers;* M-Text omits *raise the dead.*

to you, you will not have gone through the cities of Israel before the Son of Man comes.

24“A disciple is not above *his* teacher, nor a servant above his master. 25It is enough for a disciple that he be like his teacher, and a servant like his master. If they have called the master of the house Beelzebub,[a] how much more *will they call* those of his household! 26Therefore do not fear them. For there is nothing covered that will not be revealed, and hidden that will not be known.

Jesus Teaches the Fear of God

27“Whatever I tell you in the dark, speak in the light; and what you hear in the ear, preach on the housetops. 28And do not fear those who kill the body but cannot kill the soul. But rather fear Him who is able to destroy both soul and body in hell. 29Are not two sparrows sold for a copper coin? And not one of them falls to the ground apart from your Father's will. 30But the very hairs of your head are all numbered. 31Do not fear therefore; you are of more value than many sparrows.

Confess Christ Before Men

32“Therefore whoever confesses Me before men, him I will also confess before My Father who is in heaven. 33But whoever denies Me before men, him I will also deny before My Father who is in heaven.

Christ Brings Division

34“Do not think that I came to bring peace on earth. I did not come to bring peace but a sword. 35For I have come to *'set a man against his father, a daughter against her mother, and a daughter-in-law against her mother-in-law'*; 36and *'a man's enemies will be those of his own household.'*[a] 37He who loves father or mother more than Me is not worthy of Me. And he who loves son or daughter more than Me is not worthy of Me. 38And he who does not take his cross and follow after Me is not worthy of Me. 39He who finds his life will lose it, and he who loses his life for My sake will find it.

A Cup of Cold Water

40“He who receives you receives Me, and he who receives Me receives Him who sent Me. 41He who receives a prophet in the name of a prophet shall receive a prophet's reward. And he who receives a righteous man in the name of a righteous man shall receive a righteous man's reward. 42And whoever gives one of these little ones only a cup of cold *water* in the name of a disciple, assuredly, I say to you, he shall by no means lose his reward.”

John the Baptist Sends Messengers to Jesus

11 Now it came to pass, when Jesus finished commanding His twelve disciples, that He departed from there to teach and to preach in their cities.

2And when John had heard in prison about the works of Christ, he sent two of[a] his

10:25 [a]NU-Text and M-Text read *Beelzebul*
10:36 [a]Micah 7:6 **11:2** [a]NU-Text reads *by* for *two of.*

KEY PASSAGE

Self-Esteem

IN THE IMAGE OF GOD

(10:29–31)

Jesus described God's loving concern for every person, explaining that “the very hairs of your head are all numbered.” He added that because God cares even for small birds—“not one of them falls to the ground apart from your Father's will”—imagine how much more He cares for His people.

What a boost to personal encouragement! We are important to God—created in His image and loved. He loves us so much, in fact, that He “gave His only begotten Son, that whoever believes in Him should not perish but have everlasting life” (John 3:16).

To Learn More: Turn to the article about self-esteem on pages 960, 961. See also the personality profile of Josiah on page 582.

disciples [3]and said to Him, "Are You the Coming One, or do we look for another?"

[4]Jesus answered and said to them, "Go and tell John the things which you hear and see: [5]*The* blind see and *the* lame walk; *the* lepers are cleansed and *the* deaf hear; *the* dead are raised up and *the* poor have the gospel preached to them. [6]And blessed is he who is not offended because of Me."

[7]As they departed, Jesus began to say to the multitudes concerning John: "What did you go out into the wilderness to see? A reed shaken by the wind? [8]But what did you go out to see? A man clothed in soft garments? Indeed, those who wear soft *clothing* are in kings' houses. [9]But what did you go out to see? A prophet? Yes, I say to you, and more than a prophet. [10]For this is *he* of whom it is written:

> *'Behold, I send My messenger before*
> *Your face,*
> *Who will prepare Your way before*
> *You.'*[a]

[11]"Assuredly, I say to you, among those born of women there has not risen one greater than John the Baptist; but he who is least in the kingdom of heaven is greater than he. [12]And from the days of John the Baptist until now the kingdom of heaven suffers violence, and the violent take it by force. [13]For all the prophets and the law prophesied until John. [14]And if you are willing to receive *it*, he is Elijah who is to come. [15]He who has ears to hear, let him hear!

[16]"But to what shall I liken this generation? It is like children sitting in the marketplaces and calling to their companions, [17]and saying:

> 'We played the flute for you,
> And you did not dance;
> We mourned to you,
> And you did not lament.'

[18]For John came neither eating nor drinking, and they say, 'He has a demon.' [19]The Son of Man came eating and drinking, and they say, 'Look, a glutton and a winebibber, a friend of tax collectors and sinners!' But wisdom is justified by her children."[a]

Woe to the Impenitent Cities

[20]Then He began to rebuke the cities in which most of His mighty works had been done, because they did not repent: [21]"Woe to you, Chorazin! Woe to you, Bethsaida! For if the mighty works which were done in you had been done in Tyre and Sidon, they would have repented long ago in sackcloth and ashes. [22]But I say to you, it will be more tolerable for Tyre and Sidon in the day of judgment than for

11:10 [a]Malachi 3:1 **11:19** [a]NU-Text reads *works.*

KEY PASSAGE

Doubt

ARE YOU THE ONE?

(11:1–6)

John the Baptist had been one of the first to recognize Jesus' identity as the Messiah (John 1:29). Here, locked in prison and facing death, John sent two of his disciples to make sure that he had not been mistaken about Jesus.

Jesus responded by reminding John that He was fulfilling the messianic signs prophesied by Isaiah (Is. 35:5, 6; 61:1): the blind seeing, the lame walking, lepers being cleansed, the deaf hearing, the dead being raised, and the poor having "good tidings" preached to them. Even though John's circumstances had caused him to doubt, he took those doubts to the right place. Jesus responded, alleviating John's doubts and enabling him to face martyrdom with confidence.

When we begin to doubt, we need to do as John did: Take those doubts to God. He will answer our doubts and reassure us of His truth.

To Learn More: Turn to the article about doubt on pages 1408, 1409. See also the personality profile of Thomas on page 1407.

you. 23And you, Capernaum, who are exalted to heaven, will be[a] brought down to Hades; for if the mighty works which were done in you had been done in Sodom, it would have remained until this day. 24But I say to you that it shall be more tolerable for the land of Sodom in the day of judgment than for you."

Jesus Gives True Rest

25At that time Jesus answered and said, "I thank You, Father, Lord of heaven and earth, that You have hidden these things from *the* wise and prudent and have revealed them to babes. 26Even so, Father, for so it seemed good in Your sight. 27All things have been delivered to Me by My Father, and no one knows the Son except the Father. Nor does anyone know the Father except the Son, and *the one* to whom the Son wills to reveal *Him*. 28Come to Me, all *you* who labor and are heavy laden, and I will give you rest. 29Take My yoke upon you and learn from Me, for I am gentle and lowly in heart, and you will find rest for your souls. 30For My yoke *is* easy and My burden is light."

> "Come to Me, all you who labor and are heavy laden, and I will give you rest."
> MATTHEW 11:28

Jesus Is Lord of the Sabbath

12 At that time Jesus went through the grainfields on the Sabbath. And His disciples were hungry, and began to pluck heads of grain and to eat. 2And when the Pharisees saw *it*, they said to Him, "Look, Your disciples are doing what is not lawful to do on the Sabbath!"

3But He said to them, "Have you not read what David did when he was hungry, he and those who were with him: 4how he entered the house of God and ate the showbread which was not lawful for him to eat, nor for those who were with him, but only for the priests? 5Or have you not read in the law that on the Sabbath the priests in the temple profane the Sabbath, and are blameless? 6Yet I say to you that in this place there is *One* greater than the temple. 7But if you had known what *this* means, *'I desire mercy and not sacrifice,'*[a] you would not have condemned the guiltless. 8For the Son of Man is Lord even[a] of the Sabbath."

Healing on the Sabbath

9Now when He had departed from there, He went into their synagogue. 10And behold, there was a man who had a withered hand. And they asked Him, saying, "Is it lawful to heal on the Sabbath?"—that they might accuse Him.

11Then He said to them, "What man is there among you who has one sheep, and if it falls

11:23 [a]NU-Text reads *will you be exalted to heaven? No, you will be.* **12:7** [a]Hosea 6:6 **12:8** [a]NU-Text and M-Text omit *even.*

KEY PASSAGE

Burnout

A BEARABLE BURDEN

(11:28–30)

Many people long for rest. Jesus' welcome words call out, as if saying, "Give me your impossible burdens. I will carry them." Jesus says that He will take from our shoulders the heavy burdens that are burning us out, and replace them with an easy yoke, a light burden. Submission to Christ does not place us in bondage to a harsh taskmaster but under the loving care of the gentle and lowly Savior.

Jesus is in touch with the burdens of life that we carry and how much they hurt and exhaust us. When we give our troubled hearts to Him, He gives us rest for our souls. That kind of rest will cure our burnout and renew our enthusiasm for Him.

To Learn More: Turn to the article about burnout on pages 920, 921. See also the personality profile of Moses and Jethro on page 103.

into a pit on the Sabbath, will not lay hold of it
and lift *it* out? [12]Of how much more value then
is a man than a sheep? Therefore it is lawful to
do good on the Sabbath." [13]Then He said to
the man, "Stretch out your hand." And he
stretched *it* out, and it was restored as whole
as the other. [14]Then the Pharisees went out
and plotted against Him, how they might destroy Him.

Behold, My Servant

[15]But when Jesus knew *it,* He withdrew
from there. And great multitudes[a] followed
Him, and He healed them all. [16]Yet He warned
them not to make Him known, [17]that it might
be fulfilled which was spoken by Isaiah the
prophet, saying:

18 *"Behold! My Servant whom I have chosen,*
My Beloved in whom My soul is well pleased!
I will put My Spirit upon Him,
And He will declare justice to the Gentiles.
19 *He will not quarrel nor cry out,*
Nor will anyone hear His voice in the streets.
20 *A bruised reed He will not break,*
And smoking flax He will not quench,
Till He sends forth justice to victory;
21 *And in His name Gentiles will trust."*[a]

A House Divided Cannot Stand

[22]Then one was brought to Him who was
demon-possessed, blind and mute; and He
healed him, so that the blind and[a] mute man
both spoke and saw. [23]And all the multitudes
were amazed and said, "Could this be the Son
of David?"

[24]Now when the Pharisees heard *it* they
said, "This *fellow* does not cast out demons
except by Beelzebub,[a] the ruler of the demons."

[25]But Jesus knew their thoughts, and said to
them: "Every kingdom divided against itself is
brought to desolation, and every city or house
divided against itself will not stand. [26]If Satan
casts out Satan, he is divided against himself.
How then will his kingdom stand? [27]And if I
cast out demons by Beelzebub, by whom do
your sons cast *them* out? Therefore they shall
be your judges. [28]But if I cast out demons by
the Spirit of God, surely the kingdom of God
has come upon you. [29]Or how can one enter a
strong man's house and plunder his goods,
unless he first binds the strong man? And then
he will plunder his house. [30]He who is not
with Me is against Me, and he who does not
gather with Me scatters abroad.

The Unpardonable Sin

[31]"Therefore I say to you, every sin and
blasphemy will be forgiven men, but the blasphemy *against* the Spirit will not be forgiven
men. [32]Anyone who speaks a word against the
Son of Man, it will be forgiven him; but whoever speaks against the Holy Spirit, it will not
be forgiven him, either in this age or in the *age*
to come.

A Tree Known by Its Fruit

[33]"Either make the tree good and its fruit
good, or else make the tree bad and its fruit
bad; for a tree is known by *its* fruit. [34]Brood of
vipers! How can you, being evil, speak good
things? For out of the abundance of the heart
the mouth speaks. [35]A good man out of the
good treasure of his heart[a] brings forth good
things, and an evil man out of the evil treasure

12:15 [a]NU-Text brackets *multitudes* as disputed.
12:21 [a]Isaiah 42:1–4 **12:22** [a]NU-Text omits *blind and.* **12:24** [a]NU-Text and M-Text read *Beelzebul.*
12:35 [a]NU-Text and M-Text omit *of his heart.*

SOUL NOTE

Ruled Out *(12:1–8)* When Jesus' disciples ate grain while walking through a field on the Sabbath, the Pharisees criticized them for breaking God's commandment (Ex. 20:8). Their mistake, as Jesus pointed out, was in reducing God's law to a set of rules to be kept in order to earn His approval. When Christians focus on keeping rules in order to please God, they fall into the trap of legalism. Salvation is a free gift from God that cannot be earned by good works. Good works are the fruit of the Spirit and should be the outward actions of our inward faith. **Topic: Legalism**

brings forth evil things. [36]But I say to you that
for every idle word men may speak, they will
give account of it in the day of judgment. [37]For
by your words you will be justified, and by
your words you will be condemned."

The Scribes and Pharisees Ask for a Sign

[38]Then some of the scribes and Pharisees
answered, saying, "Teacher, we want to see a
sign from You."

[39]But He answered and said to them, "An
evil and adulterous generation seeks after a
sign, and no sign will be given to it except the
sign of the prophet Jonah. [40]For as Jonah was
three days and three nights in the belly of the
great fish, so will the Son of Man be three days
and three nights in the heart of the earth.
[41]The men of Nineveh will rise up in the judgment with this generation and condemn it,
because they repented at the preaching of Jonah; and indeed a greater than Jonah *is* here.
[42]The queen of the South will rise up in the
judgment with this generation and condemn
it, for she came from the ends of the earth to
hear the wisdom of Solomon; and indeed a
greater than Solomon *is* here.

An Unclean Spirit Returns

[43]"When an unclean spirit goes out of a
man, he goes through dry places, seeking rest,
and finds none. [44]Then he says, 'I will return
to my house from which I came.' And when
he comes, he finds *it* empty, swept, and put in
order. [45]Then he goes and takes with him
seven other spirits more wicked than himself,
and they enter and dwell there; and the last
state of that man is worse than the first. So
shall it also be with this wicked generation."

Jesus' Mother and Brothers Send for Him

[46]While He was still talking to the multitudes, behold, His mother and brothers stood
outside, seeking to speak with Him. [47]Then
one said to Him, "Look, Your mother and Your
brothers are standing outside, seeking to
speak with You."

[48]But He answered and said to the one who
told Him, "Who is My mother and who are My
brothers?" [49]And He stretched out His hand
toward His disciples and said, "Here are My
mother and My brothers! [50]For whoever does
the will of My Father in heaven is My brother
and sister and mother."

The Parable of the Sower

13 On the same day Jesus went out of the
house and sat by the sea. [2]And great
multitudes were gathered together to Him, so
that He got into a boat and sat; and the whole
multitude stood on the shore.

[3]Then He spoke many things to them in parables, saying: "Behold, a sower went out to
sow. [4]And as he sowed, some *seed* fell by the
wayside; and the birds came and devoured
them. [5]Some fell on stony places, where they
did not have much earth; and they immediately sprang up because they had no depth of
earth. [6]But when the sun was up they were
scorched, and because they had no root they
withered away. [7]And some fell among thorns,
and the thorns sprang up and choked them.
[8]But others fell on good ground and yielded
a crop: some a hundredfold, some sixty,
some thirty. [9]He who has ears to hear, let him
hear!"

The Purpose of Parables

[10]And the disciples came and said to Him,
"Why do You speak to them in parables?"

[11]He answered and said to them, "Because it
has been given to you to know the mysteries
of the kingdom of heaven, but to them it
has not been given. [12]For whoever has, to
him more will be given, and he will have

SOUL NOTE

Unpardonable? *(12:31, 32)* God promises to forgive our sins when we repent (1 John 1:9). There is one sin that cannot be forgiven, but believers don't have to worry about accidentally committing that sin. This is because the unpardonable sin is continually rejecting the Holy Spirit's conviction, stubbornly refusing to turn from sin and repent. It indicates an irreversible hardness in the heart. Only those who have rejected faith in Christ can commit this sin. It is unpardonable because they have rejected the only means of pardon. **Topic: Sin**

abundance; but whoever does not have, even
what he has will be taken away from him.
13Therefore I speak to them in parables, because seeing they do not see, and hearing they
do not hear, nor do they understand. 14And in
them the prophecy of Isaiah is fulfilled, which
says:

'Hearing you will hear and shall not
understand,
And seeing you will see and not
perceive;
15 *For the hearts of this people have grown*
dull.
Their ears are hard of hearing,
And their eyes they have closed,
Lest they should see with their eyes and
hear with their ears,
Lest they should understand with their
hearts and turn,
So that I should[a] *heal them.'* [b]

16But blessed *are* your eyes for they see, and
your ears for they hear; 17for assuredly, I say
to you that many prophets and righteous *men*
desired to see what you see, and did not see *it*,
and to hear what you hear, and did not hear *it*.

The Parable of the Sower Explained

18"Therefore hear the parable of the sower:
19When anyone hears the word of the kingdom, and does not understand *it*, then the
wicked *one* comes and snatches away what
was sown in his heart. This is he who received
seed by the wayside. 20But he who received
the seed on stony places, this is he who hears
the word and immediately receives it with joy;
21yet he has no root in himself, but endures
only for a while. For when tribulation or persecution arises because of the word, immediately he stumbles. 22Now he who received
seed among the thorns is he who hears the
word, and the cares of this world and the deceitfulness of riches choke the word, and he
becomes unfruitful. 23But he who received
seed on the good ground is he who hears the
word and understands *it*, who indeed bears
fruit and produces: some a hundredfold, some
sixty, some thirty."

The Parable of the Wheat and the Tares

24Another parable He put forth to them, saying: "The kingdom of heaven is like a man
who sowed good seed in his field; 25but while
men slept, his enemy came and sowed tares
among the wheat and went his way. 26But
when the grain had sprouted and produced a
crop, then the tares also appeared. 27So the
servants of the owner came and said to him,
'Sir, did you not sow good seed in your field?
How then does it have tares?' 28He said to
them, 'An enemy has done this.' The servants
said to him, 'Do you want us then to go and
gather them up?' 29But he said, 'No, lest while
you gather up the tares you also uproot the
wheat with them. 30Let both grow together
until the harvest, and at the time of harvest I
will say to the reapers, "First gather together
the tares and bind them in bundles to burn
them, but gather the wheat into my barn." ' "

The Parable of the Mustard Seed

31Another parable He put forth to them, saying: "The kingdom of heaven is like a mustard
seed, which a man took and sowed in his
field, 32which indeed is the least of all the
seeds; but when it is grown it is greater than
the herbs and becomes a tree, so that the birds
of the air come and nest in its branches."

The Parable of the Leaven

33Another parable He spoke to them: "The
kingdom of heaven is like leaven, which a
woman took and hid in three measures[a] of
meal till it was all leavened."

Prophecy and the Parables

34All these things Jesus spoke to the multitude in parables; and without a parable He did
not speak to them, 35that it might be fulfilled
which was spoken by the prophet, saying:

"I will open My mouth in parables;
I will utter things kept secret from the
foundation of the world."[a]

The Parable of the Tares Explained

36Then Jesus sent the multitude away and
went into the house. And His disciples came
to Him, saying, "Explain to us the parable of
the tares of the field."

37He answered and said to them: "He who
sows the good seed is the Son of Man. 38The
field is the world, the good seeds are the sons

13:15 [a]NU-Text and M-Text read *would.* [b]Isaiah 6:9, 10 **13:33** [a]Greek *sata,* approximately two pecks in all **13:35** [a]Psalm 78:2

of the kingdom, but the tares are the sons of the wicked *one*. 39The enemy who sowed them is the devil, the harvest is the end of the age, and the reapers are the angels. 40Therefore as the tares are gathered and burned in the fire, so it will be at the end of this age. 41The Son of Man will send out His angels, and they will gather out of His kingdom all things that offend, and those who practice lawlessness, 42and will cast them into the furnace of fire. There will be wailing and gnashing of teeth. 43Then the righteous will shine forth as the sun in the kingdom of their Father. He who has ears to hear, let him hear!

> "Then the righteous will shine forth as the sun in the kingdom of their Father. He who has ears to hear, let him hear!"
>
> MATTHEW 13:43

The Parable of the Hidden Treasure

44"Again, the kingdom of heaven is like treasure hidden in a field, which a man found and hid; and for joy over it he goes and sells all that he has and buys that field.

The Parable of the Pearl of Great Price

45"Again, the kingdom of heaven is like a merchant seeking beautiful pearls, 46who, when he had found one pearl of great price, went and sold all that he had and bought it.

The Parable of the Dragnet

47"Again, the kingdom of heaven is like a dragnet that was cast into the sea and gathered some of every kind, 48which, when it was full, they drew to shore; and they sat down and gathered the good into vessels, but threw the bad away. 49So it will be at the end of the age. The angels will come forth, separate the wicked from among the just, 50and cast them into the furnace of fire. There will be wailing and gnashing of teeth."

51Jesus said to them,[a] "Have you understood all these things?"

They said to Him, "Yes, Lord."[b]

52Then He said to them, "Therefore every scribe instructed concerning[a] the kingdom of heaven is like a householder who brings out of his treasure *things* new and old."

Jesus Rejected at Nazareth

53Now it came to pass, when Jesus had finished these parables, that He departed from there. 54When He had come to His own country, He taught them in their synagogue, so that they were astonished and said, "Where did this *Man* get this wisdom and *these* mighty works? 55Is this not the carpenter's son? Is not His mother called Mary? And His brothers James, Joses,[a] Simon, and Judas? 56And His sisters, are they not all with us? Where then did this *Man* get all these things?" 57So they were offended at Him.

But Jesus said to them, "A prophet is not without honor except in his own country and in his own house." 58Now He did not do many mighty works there because of their unbelief.

John the Baptist Beheaded

14 At that time Herod the tetrarch heard the report about Jesus 2and said to his servants, "This is John the Baptist; he is risen from the dead, and therefore these powers are at work in him." 3For Herod had laid hold of John and bound him, and put *him* in prison for the sake of Herodias, his brother Philip's wife. 4Because John had said to him, "It is not lawful for you to have her." 5And although he wanted to put him to death, he feared the multitude, because they counted him as a prophet.

6But when Herod's birthday was celebrated, the daughter of Herodias danced before them and pleased Herod. 7Therefore he promised with an oath to give her whatever she might ask.

8So she, having been prompted by her mother, said, "Give me John the Baptist's head here on a platter."

9And the king was sorry; nevertheless, because of the oaths and because of those who sat with him, he commanded *it* to be given to *her*. 10So he sent and had John beheaded in prison. 11And his head was brought on a platter and given to the girl, and she brought *it* to her mother. 12Then his disciples came and took away the body and buried it, and went and told Jesus.

13:51 [a]NU-Text omits *Jesus said to them.* [b]NU-Text omits *Lord.* **13:52** [a]Or *for* **13:55** [a]NU-Text reads *Joseph.*

Feeding the Five Thousand

13 When Jesus heard *it,* He departed from
there by boat to a deserted place by Himself.
But when the multitudes heard it, they followed Him on foot from the cities. 14 And
when Jesus went out He saw a great multitude; and He was moved with compassion for
them, and healed their sick. 15 When it was
evening, His disciples came to Him, saying,
"This is a deserted place, and the hour is already late. Send the multitudes away, that
they may go into the villages and buy themselves food."

16 But Jesus said to them, "They do not need
to go away. You give them something to eat."
17 And they said to Him, "We have here only
five loaves and two fish."

18 He said, "Bring them here to Me." 19 Then
He commanded the multitudes to sit down on
the grass. And He took the five loaves and the
two fish, and looking up to heaven, He
blessed and broke and gave the loaves to the
disciples; and the disciples gave to the multitudes. 20 So they all ate and were filled, and
they took up twelve baskets full of the fragments that remained. 21 Now those who had
eaten were about five thousand men, besides
women and children.

Jesus Walks on the Sea

22 Immediately Jesus made His disciples get
into the boat and go before Him to the other
side, while He sent the multitudes away.
23 And when He had sent the multitudes away,

PERSONALITY PROFILE

Prayer

JESUS: TEACHING US TO PRAY

(MATTHEW 14:23)

Jesus prayed in public and in private. Jesus prayed with and for His disciples. He prayed openly for others. He commanded prayer, encouraged prayer, taught prayer, and modeled prayer. During several significant times in Jesus' life, He left the disciples and His public ministry and spent time alone in prayer.

Prayer, Jesus revealed, is not just the method for godly request-making or an exercise in guidance. He taught that prayer is also a vehicle

- for worship,
- for the expression of praise,
- for adoration,
- for confession, and
- for thanksgiving to God.

When the disciples asked Jesus to teach them how to pray (Luke 11:1), He gave them what we call the Lord's Prayer as an example.

For Jesus, prayer was not just a wordy exercise—it was connection and communion with the living God. Jesus poured His heart and soul into prayer, and it became a time of great emotional expression of His spirit. The kind of intense intimacy with God that the disciples observed in Jesus while He prayed in the Garden of Gethsemane (Matt. 26:36–46) doesn't appear overnight, but is the result of years of prayerful interaction with God.

Luke's Gospel includes an interesting example of how characteristic prayer was in Jesus' life. On the day of His resurrection, Jesus walked with two disciples from outside Jerusalem to Emmaus (Luke 24:13–32). They traveled and talked for several hours, but it wasn't until the mealtime, when Jesus prayed for the bread and broke it, that the disciples' eyes were opened to recognize Him. Prayer offered a hint that even they couldn't miss.

Prayer was central in Jesus' life. If Jesus, who was the divine Son of God, needed to get alone with God in order to pray and commune with Him, how much more do we!

To Learn More: Turn to the article about prayer on pages 1238, 1239. See also the key passage note at Matthew 6:5–13 on page 1237.

He went up on the mountain by Himself to pray. Now when evening came, He was alone there. 24 But the boat was now in the middle of the sea,[a] tossed by the waves, for the wind was contrary.

25 Now in the fourth watch of the night Jesus went to them, walking on the sea. 26 And when the disciples saw Him walking on the sea, they were troubled, saying, "It is a ghost!" And they cried out for fear.

27 But immediately Jesus spoke to them, saying, "Be of good cheer! It is I; do not be afraid."

28 And Peter answered Him and said, "Lord, if it is You, command me to come to You on the water."

29 So He said, "Come." And when Peter had come down out of the boat, he walked on the water to go to Jesus. 30 But when he saw that the wind *was* boisterous,[a] he was afraid; and beginning to sink he cried out, saying, "Lord, save me!"

31 And immediately Jesus stretched out *His* hand and caught him, and said to him, "O you of little faith, why did you doubt?" 32 And when they got into the boat, the wind ceased.

33 Then those who were in the boat came and[a] worshiped Him, saying, "Truly You are the Son of God."

Many Touch Him and Are Made Well

34 When they had crossed over, they came to the land of[a] Gennesaret. 35 And when the men of that place recognized Him, they sent out into all that surrounding region, brought to Him all who were sick, 36 and begged Him that they might only touch the hem of His garment. And as many as touched *it* were made perfectly well.

Defilement Comes from Within

15 Then the scribes and Pharisees who were from Jerusalem came to Jesus, saying, 2 "Why do Your disciples transgress the tradition of the elders? For they do not wash their hands when they eat bread."

3 He answered and said to them, "Why do you also transgress the commandment of God because of your tradition? 4 For God commanded, saying, *'Honor your father and your mother'*;[a] and, *'He who curses father or mother, let him be put to death.'*[b] 5 But you say, 'Whoever says to his father or mother, "Whatever profit you might have received from me *is* a gift *to God*"— 6 then he need not honor his father or mother.'[a] Thus you have made the commandment[b] of God of no effect by your tradition. 7 Hypocrites! Well did Isaiah prophesy about you, saying:

8 *'These people draw near to Me with their mouth,*
And[a] *honor Me with their lips,*
But their heart is far from Me.
9 *And in vain they worship Me,*
Teaching as doctrines the commandments of men.' "[a]

10 When He had called the multitude to *Himself*, He said to them, "Hear and understand: 11 Not what goes into the mouth defiles a man; but what comes out of the mouth, this defiles a man."

12 Then His disciples came and said to Him, "Do You know that the Pharisees were offended when they heard this saying?"

13 But He answered and said, "Every plant which My heavenly Father has not planted will be uprooted. 14 Let them alone. They are blind leaders of the blind. And if the blind leads the blind, both will fall into a ditch."

15 Then Peter answered and said to Him, "Explain this parable to us."

16 So Jesus said, "Are you also still without understanding? 17 Do you not yet understand that whatever enters the mouth goes into the stomach and is eliminated? 18 But those things which proceed out of the mouth come from the heart, and they defile a man. 19 For out of the heart proceed evil thoughts, murders, adulteries, fornications, thefts, false witness, blasphemies. 20 These are *the things* which defile a man, but to eat with unwashed hands does not defile a man."

A Gentile Shows Her Faith

21 Then Jesus went out from there and departed to the region of Tyre and Sidon. 22 And behold, a woman of Canaan came from that

---

14:24 [a]NU-Text reads *many furlongs away from the land.* **14:30** [a]NU-Text brackets *that* and *boisterous* as disputed. **14:33** [a]NU-Text omits *came and.* **14:34** [a]NU-Text reads *came to land at.*
15:4 [a]Exodus 20:12; Deuteronomy 5:16 [b]Exodus 21:17 **15:6** [a]NU-Text omits *or mother.* [b]NU-Text reads *word.* **15:8** [a]NU-Text omits *draw near to Me with their mouth, And.* **15:9** [a]Isaiah 29:13

region and cried out to Him, saying, "Have mercy on me, O Lord, Son of David! My daughter is severely demon-possessed."

[23]But He answered her not a word.

And His disciples came and urged Him, saying, "Send her away, for she cries out after us."

[24]But He answered and said, "I was not sent except to the lost sheep of the house of Israel."

[25]Then she came and worshiped Him, saying, "Lord, help me!"

[26]But He answered and said, "It is not good to take the children's bread and throw *it* to the little dogs."

[27]And she said, "Yes, Lord, yet even the little dogs eat the crumbs which fall from their masters' table."

[28]Then Jesus answered and said to her, "O woman, great *is* your faith! Let it be to you as you desire." And her daughter was healed from that very hour.

JESUS HEALS GREAT MULTITUDES

[29]Jesus departed from there, skirted the Sea of Galilee, and went up on the mountain and sat down there. [30]Then great multitudes came to Him, having with them *the* lame, blind, mute, maimed, and many others; and they laid them down at Jesus' feet, and He healed them. [31]So the multitude marveled when they saw *the* mute speaking, *the* maimed made whole, *the* lame walking, and *the* blind seeing; and they glorified the God of Israel.

FEEDING THE FOUR THOUSAND

[32]Now Jesus called His disciples to *Himself* and said, "I have compassion on the multitude, because they have now continued with Me three days and have nothing to eat. And I do not want to send them away hungry, lest they faint on the way."

[33]Then His disciples said to Him, "Where could we get enough bread in the wilderness to fill such a great multitude?"

[34]Jesus said to them, "How many loaves do you have?"

And they said, "Seven, and a few little fish."

[35]So He commanded the multitude to sit down on the ground. [36]And He took the seven loaves and the fish and gave thanks, broke *them* and gave *them* to His disciples; and the disciples *gave* to the multitude. [37]So they all ate and were filled, and they took up seven large baskets full of the fragments that were left. [38]Now those who ate were four thousand men, besides women and children. [39]And He sent away the multitude, got into the boat, and came to the region of Magdala.[a]

THE PHARISEES AND SADDUCEES SEEK A SIGN

16 Then the Pharisees and Sadducees came, and testing Him asked that He would show them a sign from heaven. [2]He answered and said to them, "When it is evening you say, '*It will be* fair weather, for the sky is red'; [3]and in the morning, '*It will be* foul weather today, for the sky is red and threatening.' Hypocrites![a] You know how to discern the face of the sky, but you cannot *discern* the signs of the times. [4]A wicked and adulterous generation seeks after a sign, and no sign shall be given to it except the sign of the prophet[a] Jonah." And He left them and departed.

THE LEAVEN OF THE PHARISEES AND SADDUCEES

[5]Now when His disciples had come to the other side, they had forgotten to take bread. [6]Then Jesus said to them, "Take heed and beware of the leaven of the Pharisees and the Sadducees."

[7]And they reasoned among themselves, saying, "*It is* because we have taken no bread."

[8]But Jesus, being aware of *it*, said to them, "O you of little faith, why do you reason among yourselves because you have brought no bread?[a] [9]Do you not yet understand, or remember the five loaves of the five thousand and how many baskets you took up? [10]Nor the seven loaves of the four thousand and how many large baskets you took up? [11]How is it you do not understand that I did not speak to you concerning bread?—*but* to beware of the leaven of the Pharisees and Sadducees." [12]Then they understood that He did not tell *them* to beware of the leaven of bread, but of the doctrine of the Pharisees and Sadducees.

PETER CONFESSES JESUS AS THE CHRIST

[13]When Jesus came into the region of Caesarea Philippi, He asked His disciples, saying, "Who do men say that I, the Son of Man, am?"

[14]So they said, "Some *say* John the Baptist, some Elijah, and others Jeremiah or one of the prophets."

15:39 [a]NU-Text reads *Magadan.* **16:3** [a]NU-Text omits *Hypocrites.* **16:4** [a]NU-Text omits *the prophet.* **16:8** [a]NU-Text reads *you have no bread.*

15 He said to them, "But who do you say that
I am?"
16 Simon Peter answered and said, "You are
the Christ, the Son of the living God."
17 Jesus answered and
said to him, "Blessed are
you, Simon Bar-Jonah,
for flesh and blood has
not revealed *this* to you,
but My Father who is in
heaven. 18 And I also say
to you that you are Peter,
and on this rock I will
build My church, and the gates of Hades shall
not prevail against it. 19 And I will give you the
keys of the kingdom of heaven, and whatever
you bind on earth will be bound in heaven, and
whatever you loose on earth will be loosed[a] in
heaven."
20 Then He commanded His disciples that
they should tell no one that He was Jesus the
Christ.

> "For what profit is it to a man if he gains the whole world, and loses his own soul? Or what will a man give in exchange for his soul?"
>
> MATTHEW 16:26

Jesus Predicts His Death and Resurrection

21 From that time Jesus began to show to His
disciples that He must go to Jerusalem, and
suffer many things from the elders and chief
priests and scribes, and be killed, and be
raised the third day.
22 Then Peter took Him aside and began to
rebuke Him, saying, "Far be it from You, Lord;
this shall not happen to You!"
23 But He turned and said to Peter, "Get behind Me, Satan! You are an offense to Me, for
you are not mindful of the things of God, but
the things of men."

Take Up the Cross and Follow Him

24 Then Jesus said to His disciples, "If anyone desires to come after Me, let him deny
himself, and take up his cross, and follow Me.
25 For whoever desires to save his life will lose
it, but whoever loses his life for My sake will
find it. 26 For what profit is it to a man if he
gains the whole world, and loses his own soul?
Or what will a man give
in exchange for his soul?
27 For the Son of Man
will come in the glory of
His Father with His an-
gels, and then He will
reward each according
to his works.

Jesus Transfigured on the Mount

28 Assuredly, I say to you, there are some
standing here who shall not taste death till
they see the Son of Man coming in His kingdom."

17 Now after six days Jesus took Peter,
James, and John his brother, led them
up on a high mountain by themselves; 2 and
He was transfigured before them. His face
shone like the sun, and His clothes became as
white as the light. 3 And behold, Moses and
Elijah appeared to them, talking with Him.
4 Then Peter answered and said to Jesus,
"Lord, it is good for us to be here; if You wish,
let us[a] make here three tabernacles: one for
You, one for Moses, and one for Elijah."
5 While he was still speaking, behold, a
bright cloud overshadowed them; and suddenly a voice came out of the cloud, saying,
"This is My beloved Son, in whom I am well
pleased. Hear Him!" 6 And when the disciples
heard *it*, they fell on their faces and were
greatly afraid. 7 But Jesus came and touched
them and said, "Arise, and do not be afraid."
8 When they had lifted up their eyes, they saw
no one but Jesus only.

16:19 [a]Or *will have been bound . . . will have been loosed* **17:4** [a]NU-Text reads *I will.*

SOUL NOTE

Radical Denial *(16:24)* Radical discipleship means denying oneself and taking up the cross. Jesus was not promoting self-hatred; instead, He was saying that His followers must put God first and be willing to suffer anything for His sake. If a primary goal is to protect ourselves from embarrassment or discomfort, we are not denying ourselves. If we focus on what *we* want instead of what God wants for us, we are not denying ourselves. In the end, self-denial actually brings true fulfillment, for it allows God to use us for His purposes. That is the best way to live. **Topic: Self-Denial**

9Now as they came down from the mountain, Jesus commanded them, saying, "Tell
the vision to no one until the Son of Man is
risen from the dead."
10And His disciples asked Him, saying,
"Why then do the scribes say that Elijah must
come first?"
11Jesus answered and said to them, "Indeed,
Elijah is coming first[a] and will restore all
things. 12But I say to you that Elijah has come
already, and they did not know him but did to
him whatever they wished. Likewise the Son
of Man is also about to suffer at their hands."
13Then the disciples understood that He spoke
to them of John the Baptist.

A Boy Is Healed

14And when they had come to the multitude, a man came to Him, kneeling down to
Him and saying, 15"Lord, have mercy on my
son, for he is an epileptic[a] and suffers severely; for he often falls into the fire and often into
the water. 16So I brought him to Your disciples,
but they could not cure him."
17Then Jesus answered and said, "O faithless and perverse generation, how long shall I
be with you? How long shall I bear with you?
Bring him here to Me." 18And Jesus rebuked
the demon, and it came out of him; and the
child was cured from that very hour.
19Then the disciples came to Jesus privately
and said, "Why could we not cast it out?"
20So Jesus said to them, "Because of your
unbelief;[a] for assuredly, I say to you, if you
have faith as a mustard seed, you will say to
this mountain, 'Move from here to there,' and
it will move; and nothing will be impossible
for you. 21However, this kind does not go out
except by prayer and fasting."[a]

Jesus Again Predicts His Death and Resurrection

22Now while they were staying[a] in Galilee,
Jesus said to them, "The Son of Man is about to
be betrayed into the hands of men, 23and they
will kill Him, and the third day He will be raised
up." And they were exceedingly sorrowful.

Peter and His Master Pay Their Taxes

24When they had come to Capernaum,[a]
those who received the *temple* tax came to
Peter and said, "Does your Teacher not pay
the *temple* tax?"
25He said, "Yes."
And when he had come into the house,
Jesus anticipated him, saying, "What do you
think, Simon? From whom do the kings of the
earth take customs or taxes, from their sons or
from strangers?"
26Peter said to Him, "From strangers."
Jesus said to him, "Then the sons are free.
27Nevertheless, lest we offend them, go to the
sea, cast in a hook, and take the fish that
comes up first. And when you have opened its
mouth, you will find a piece of money;[a] take
that and give it to them for Me and you."

Who Is the Greatest?

18 At that time the disciples came to
Jesus, saying, "Who then is greatest in
the kingdom of heaven?"
2Then Jesus called a little child to Him, set
him in the midst of them, 3and said, "Assuredly, I say to you, unless you are converted and
become as little children, you will by no
means enter the kingdom of heaven. 4There-
fore whoever humbles himself as this little
child is the greatest in the kingdom of heaven.
5Whoever receives one little child like this in
My name receives Me.

Jesus Warns of Offenses

6"Whoever causes one of these little ones
who believe in Me to sin, it would be better
for him if a millstone were hung around his
neck, and he were drowned in the depth of the
sea. 7Woe to the world because of offenses!
For offenses must come, but woe to that man
by whom the offense comes!
8"If your hand or foot causes you to sin, cut it
off and cast *it* from you. It is better for you to
enter into life lame or maimed, rather than having two hands or two feet, to be cast into the
everlasting fire. 9And if your eye causes you to
sin, pluck it out and cast *it* from you. It is better
for you to enter into life with one eye, rather
than having two eyes, to be cast into hell fire.

The Parable of the Lost Sheep

10"Take heed that you do not despise one of
these little ones, for I say to you that in heaven

17:11 [a]NU-Text omits *first.* **17:15** [a]Literally *moonstruck* **17:20** [a]NU-Text reads *little faith.* **17:21** [a]NU-Text omits this verse. **17:22** [a]NU-Text reads *gathering together.* **17:24** [a]NU-Text reads *Capharnaum* (here and elsewhere). **17:27** [a]Greek *stater,* the exact amount to pay the temple tax (didrachma) for two

their angels always see the face of My Father
who is in heaven. [11]For the Son of Man has
come to save that which was lost.[a]

[12]"What do you think? If a man has a hundred sheep, and one of them goes astray, does
he not leave the ninety-nine and go to the
mountains to seek the one that is straying?
[13]And if he should find it, assuredly, I say to
you, he rejoices more over that *sheep* than
over the ninety-nine that did not go astray.
[14]Even so it is not the will of your Father who
is in heaven that one of these little ones
should perish.

DEALING WITH A SINNING BROTHER

[15]"Moreover if your brother sins against
you, go and tell him his fault between you and
him alone. If he hears you, you have gained
your brother. [16]But if he will not hear, take
with you one or two more, that *'by the mouth
of two or three witnesses every word may
be established.'*[a] [17]And if he refuses to hear
them, tell *it* to the church. But if he refuses
even to hear the church, let him be to you like
a heathen and a tax collector.

[18]"Assuredly, I say to you, whatever you
bind on earth will be bound in heaven, and
whatever you loose on earth will be loosed in
heaven.

[19]"Again I say[a] to you that if two of you
agree on earth concerning anything that they
ask, it will be done for them by My Father in
heaven. [20]For where two or three are gathered
together in My name, I am there in the midst
of them."

THE PARABLE OF THE UNFORGIVING SERVANT

[21]Then Peter came to Him and said, "Lord,
how often shall my brother sin against me,
and I forgive him? Up to seven times?"

[22]Jesus said to him, "I do not say to you, up
to seven times, but up to seventy times seven.
[23]Therefore the kingdom of heaven is like a
certain king who wanted to settle accounts
with his servants. [24]And when he had begun
to settle accounts, one was brought to him
who owed him ten thousand talents. [25]But as
he was not able to pay, his master commanded that he be sold, with his wife and children
and all that he had, and that payment be
made. [26]The servant therefore fell down before him, saying, 'Master, have patience with
me, and I will pay you all.' [27]Then the master
of that servant was moved with compassion,
released him, and forgave him the debt.

[28]"But that servant went out and found one
of his fellow servants who owed him a hundred denarii; and he laid hands on him and
took *him* by the throat, saying, 'Pay me what
you owe!' [29]So his fellow servant fell down at

18:11 [a]NU-Text omits this verse.
18:16 [a]Deuteronomy 19:15 **18:19** [a]NU-Text and M-Text read *Again, assuredly, I say.*

KEY PASSAGE

Conflict

RESOLUTION SOLUTION

(18:15–17)

Conflict is a normal part of life, but when conflicts between believers involve sinful behavior, they must be handled carefully. Jesus outlined a process toward resolving these conflicts. If a brother or sister offends us, our first responsibility is to talk with that person about the offense. At this point, the person can be made aware of the sinful behavior and be able to deal with it. If the personal discussion does not bring about resolution, then we should take one or two other responsible believers with us to confront the individual about the sinful behavior. Finally, and only if those two steps fail, the situation should be taken to the larger church body.

Jesus clearly indicated that it is best to resolve private matters privately, avoiding gossip and public confrontations whenever possible. But when that is not possible, believers must be made accountable to one another in the body of Christ.

To Learn More: Turn to the article about conflict on pages 1258, 1259. See also the personality profile of Paul and Mark on page 1444.

Conflict

RESTORING BROKEN RELATIONSHIPS: HOPE FOR THE HEART

JUNE HUNT

(Matthew 18:15–17)

"Is there a doctor in the house?" Many a call for help has been heard when sickness strikes and the body dangerously fails to function. Likewise, when a relationship between two people falls into the danger zone, we may be called upon to help "doctor" two wounded hearts.

While no one can escape the pain of broken relationships, they can escape becoming bitter. The Bible powerfully presents the freedom of forgiveness. But even more, Jehovah Rapha, the God who heals, gives each believer "the ministry of reconciliation" (2 Cor. 5:18, 19).

HOW TO DIAGNOSE THE CONDITION OF THE HEART

Patients with bad heart conditions need to change their unhealthy habits. Heart patients who have "hardening of the arteries" receive regular examinations. Like medical doctors, we can help those who need a "heart examination." We can help to diagnose the problem by testing eight potentially problematic areas:

1. *Pride:* "Do I focus on how much I've been wronged?"
2. *Faultfinding:* "Do I rehearse the faults of others?"
3. *Avoidance:* "Do I avoid being around people with whom I have conflict?"
4. *Silence:* "Do I refuse to share my feelings in a healthy way?"
5. *Isolation:* "Do I withdraw emotionally?"
6. *Unfaithfulness:* "Do I share unnecessary information about my opposer?"
7. *Hopelessness:* "Do I lack faith that God can work in any situation?"
8. *Resentment:* "Do I hold on to my anger until it turns to bitterness?"

The Bible says, "Pursue peace . . . looking carefully lest anyone fall short of the grace of God; lest any root of bitterness springing up cause trouble" (Heb. 12:14, 15).

HOW TO BEGIN RECONCILIATION

The process of reconciliation can occur when both parties are willing to listen without interrupting. They both need to be respectful and understand that there are two sides to every story, two sets of feelings that need to be understood, and two hearts that need to be healed. The following lists of do's and don'ts will be helpful to those who are trying to guide two people in reconciliation:

In the "do" column: (1) See the situation from the other's point of view. (2) Repeat back: "I hear you saying ________. Is that correct?" (3) Use words that encourage. (4) Be respectful, even if you are not treated respectfully. (5) Realize that you have the power to change only yourself. (6) Be at peace, knowing that you have the Prince of Peace in your heart.

Now for the "don'ts": (1) Don't forget that your opposer is also God's creation. (2) Don't harbor resentment, bitterness, or hatred. (3) Don't use "you" statements: "You make me mad . . . you should . . . you always. . . ." (4) Don't get drawn into useless arguments. (5) Don't expect an immediate change. (6) Don't assume that reconciliation is always possible.

HOW TO APOLOGIZE

Physical healing cannot take place unless the patient chooses to do what is healthy. Similarly, the healing of two wounded hearts will not take place if both parties defiantly refuse to ask forgiveness. But since there are wrong ways and right ways of asking, we may need to explain the difference: (1) Don't make excuses: "I couldn't help it." (2) Don't use the blame game: "You made me do it." (3) Accept full responsibility: "My attitude was inexcusable." (4) Accept full blame for your part: "No one can make another person sin. I acknowledge that I sinned against you." (5) With a humble heart say, "I've tried to see our relationship from your point of view. I realize that I've been wrong in my attitude of ________. Would you forgive me?"

HOW TO FORGIVE

Some patients have a wound that will not heal because they won't leave the wound alone. Just as a wound needs to be allowed to heal, a person needs to allow forgiveness to do its work. We can be effectively used by God to present practical steps in the healing process. Some of these steps include: (1) Realizing that forgiveness is not letting the offender "off the hook," but an act of releasing the offender from your hook and onto God's hook. (2) Deciding that you want to be free from the pain of the past. (3) Recognizing the unmet need(s) in the one who hurt you. (4) Listing every offense, and then, instead of "picking" at the wrongs, releasing each offense and the offender into the hands of God.

HOW TO ENLIST A MEDIATOR

If a doctor has been consulted and the medical condition seems uncertain, a "second opinion" is often sought. The Bible even speaks of bringing in a wise outside adviser: "Without counsel, plans go awry, but in the multitude of counselors they are established" (Prov. 15:22). Sometimes another mediator is needed. Seek a person whom they both can respect. Say to them, "At times an outside person brings to the table a different perspective. Would you consider a mediator to help think through the problems to reach a successful end?"

Each person must be prepared to experience the possibility of a negative outcome from the process of reconciliation. Ultimately, a relationship may not work out between two people. One person cannot be responsible for the outcome of a relationship. However, each person is responsible for handling the reconciliation process in a godly manner. "If it is possible, as much as depends on you, live peaceably with all men" (Rom. 12:18).

FURTHER MEDITATION:

Other passages to study about the issue of conflict include:

- ➢ Psalms 103:6–14; 133:1
- ➢ Proverbs 6:2, 3; 16:7; 17:27
- ➢ Matthew 5:44–48
- ➢ Romans 12:14, 17–21
- ➢ 1 Corinthians 1:10
- ➢ Philippians 2:3; 4:2
- ➢ Colossians 3:2, 13

To Learn More: Turn to the key passage note on conflict at Matthew 18:15–17 on page 1257. See also the personality profile of Paul and Mark on page 1444.

his feet[a] and begged him, saying, 'Have patience with me, and I will pay you all.'[b] 30And
he would not, but went and threw him into
prison till he should pay the debt. 31So when
his fellow servants saw what had been done,
they were very grieved, and came and told
their master all that had been done. 32Then his
master, after he had called him, said to him,
'You wicked servant! I forgave you all that debt
because you begged me. 33Should you not also
have had compassion on your fellow servant,
just as I had pity on you?' 34And his master was
angry, and delivered him to the torturers until
he should pay all that was due to him.
35"So My heavenly Father also will do to
you if each of you, from his heart, does not
forgive his brother his trespasses."[a]

Marriage and Divorce

19 Now it came to pass, when Jesus had
finished these sayings, *that* He departed from Galilee and came to the region of
Judea beyond the Jordan. 2And great multitudes followed Him, and He healed them there.
3The Pharisees also came to Him, testing
Him, and saying to Him, "Is it lawful for a
man to divorce his wife for *just* any reason?"
4And He answered and said to them, "Have
you not read that He who made[a] *them* at the
beginning *'made them male and female,'*[b]
5and said, *'For this reason a man shall leave
his father and mother and be joined to his wife,
and the two shall become one flesh'*?[a] 6So
then, they are no longer two but one flesh.
Therefore what God has joined together, let
not man separate."
7They said to Him, "Why then did Moses
command to give a certificate of divorce, and
to put her away?"
8He said to them, "Moses, because of the
hardness of your hearts, permitted you to divorce your wives, but from the beginning it
was not so. 9And I say to you, whoever divorces his wife, except for sexual immorality,[a]
and marries another, commits adultery; and
whoever marries her who is divorced commits
adultery."
10His disciples said to Him, "If such is the
case of the man with *his* wife, it is better not
to marry."

Jesus Teaches on Celibacy

11But He said to them, "All cannot accept
this saying, but only *those* to whom it has
been given: 12For there are eunuchs who were
born thus from *their* mother's womb, and
there are eunuchs who were made eunuchs by

18:29 [a]NU-Text omits *at his feet.* [b]NU-Text and M-Text omit *all.* **18:35** [a]NU-Text omits *his trespasses.* **19:4** [a]NU-Text reads *created.* [b]Genesis 1:27; 5:2 **19:5** [a]Genesis 2:24 **19:9** [a]Or *fornication*

KEY PASSAGE

Forgiveness

DON'T KEEP COUNT

(18:21–35)

"I'm sorry."

"I forgive you."

These words are often spoken, but what do they really mean? Is the person *really* sorry? What if he or she offends again? Does the other person have to keep on forgiving?

Peter asked if forgiving a person seven times was enough. Jesus answered that seven times was *not* enough; instead, Peter should forgive "seventy times seven" times. The point: Don't even keep count; just keep on forgiving.

Jesus then told a parable about a man who, after receiving great forgiveness for a large debt he owed to someone, refused to forgive a person who owed him a small debt. Jesus was illustrating that we sinners have been graciously forgiven by God—and are being forgiven daily, over and over again. We should be just as gracious in forgiving others. To refuse to forgive shows that we have not understood how much God has forgiven us.

To Learn More: Turn to the article about forgiveness on pages 1520, 1521. See also the personality profile of Joseph on page 70.

men, and there are eunuchs who have made
themselves eunuchs for the kingdom of
heaven's sake. He who is able to accept *it*, let
him accept *it*."

JESUS BLESSES LITTLE CHILDREN

13Then little children were brought to Him
that He might put *His* hands on them and
pray, but the disciples rebuked them. 14But
Jesus said, "Let the little children come to Me,
and do not forbid them; for of such is the kingdom of heaven." 15And He laid *His* hands on
them and departed from there.

JESUS COUNSELS THE RICH YOUNG RULER

16Now behold, one came and said to Him,
"Good[a] Teacher, what good thing shall I do
that I may have eternal life?"

19:16 [a]NU-Text omits *Good.*

KEY PASSAGE

Divorce/ Separation

DIVORCE DIFFICULTIES

(19:3–8)

The Pharisees' question was meant to test Jesus' commitment to Moses' law: "Is it lawful for a man to divorce his wife for just any reason?" they asked.

Jesus' response emphasized that God has always intended each married couple, one man and one woman, to remain married for life (Gen. 2:24). Moses had indeed permitted divorce (Deut. 24:1) but only because of the "hardness" of human hearts. Jesus knew that the option for divorce was included in Moses' law because of sinful human nature, but He still defended the importance of permanence in marriage.

In this passage we learn that divorce is permissible, but it is not commanded. Marriage vows should not be taken lightly. God would have couples do their best—with His help—to keep their marriage intact. If a divorce occurs, God's compassionate love can heal even the deepest wounds.

To Learn More: Turn to the article about divorce/separation on pages 250, 251. See also the personality profile of the woman at the well on page 1376.

KEY PASSAGE

Marriage

KEEPING THE PROMISE

(19:4–6)

"For better or worse, for richer or poorer, in sickness and in health, as long as we both shall live." This promise is made by thousands of starry-eyed couples every year as they pledge their love to each other. Why, then, have so many of those promises been broken? Is it possible for marriage to be forever?

When the Pharisees questioned Jesus about divorce, Jesus spoke to them first about marriage. He emphasized that God's plan has always been for marriage to be a covenant relationship—the promises made are to be kept, regardless of the circumstances. God created male and female, joining them together as "one flesh" in marriage. God holds the permanence of the marriage bond in highest regard because it is the essential unit of His plan for the family and for society.

Marriage should never be entered into lightly. The vows made before God are meant to be kept "for better or worse."

To Learn More: Turn to the article about marriage on pages 1296, 1297. See also the personality profile of Mary and Joseph on page 1229.

MORE THAN BEING UNMARRIED

ALAN CORRY

(Matthew 19:12)

Single adults are in good company when they realize that the Lord Jesus Christ lived out His earthly ministry as a single adult. Christian single people find their identity in Christ, not in their marital status. Whether singleness is for a season or a lifetime, the issue is not to focus on singleness. Instead, single people should allow God to use them to make an impact on this world for His kingdom. No one should be ashamed of being single.

COMING TO TERMS

More adults are waiting longer to get married, meaning that more adults are staying single longer. Single people must not let family or friends put undue pressure on them to get married. If they feel like they have to be in a relationship in order to be accepted by others, then they are susceptible to being used and hurt by others, or they will use and hurt others in order to be in a relationship of convenience.

Single people must come to terms with being single—knowing that they are complete and whole as individuals in their relationship with Christ. If they feel that they cannot be whole people until they are married, then they are not ready for marriage. Marriage is not about finding someone to complete and make a person whole. Healthy marriages have as their foundation two individuals who are secure in their own identity—coming together in a state of holy matrimony. As the two of them work together as marriage partners, they will complement each other. The oneness in marriage is a spiritual oneness, but if some never marry and experience that oneness, it does not mean that they are lacking or incomplete as human beings.

Single people must also come to terms with the fact that not all adults marry. Singleness is not to be looked at as an inferior quality of life. According to Paul, "But I say to the unmarried and to the widows: It is good for them if they remain even as I am" (1 Cor. 7:8). Paul's intent was not to put marriage down, but rather to elevate the status of being single. Being married and remaining single are both honorable lifestyles. Too many single adults sit on the sidelines waiting to be married before they feel like they will be a viable part of the community. God wants them to be active in the ministry to others *now*.

Pastors and friends of single people should empower them to live life to its fullest as they seek to find God's purpose and direction for their lives. In their singleness, they should seek God in all that they do. They ought never rush to get married. If they marry, they want to be involved in a healthy, growing, and dynamic marriage. In the meantime, however, they should be content in their singleness.

FINDING ONE'S PLACE

Being alone and being lonely are two different things. Being alone is a physical state; being lonely is an emotional state. People can be alone and be perfectly content as they walk, pray, read, watch TV, or just sit and daydream. They can also be in a crowd, but feel very lonely.

Single adults must connect with others. God created people to be social beings. After all, His heart's desire is for us to be in a personal relationship with Him through His Son Jesus Christ. Single people need to have a community of friends whom they can trust and with whom they can share activities and interests. They need to have a balance of male and female friends. Obvious places to start will be at a local church where they feel accepted and can be growing in their relationship with God as they also make new friends. Other places to seek out friendships will be in areas of personal interest as they pursue hobbies or participate in service organizations.

Single adults also need a small circle of close friends, good friends who are trustworthy. They can hold each other accountable if one of them is making unhealthy lifestyle choices. As they develop this inner circle of friends, they will deal with the loneliness issue less and less.

Another issue of concern for single adults is their sexuality. People are not only created as social beings, but as sexual beings as well. We are created male and female. The issue of celibacy and singleness causes concern for many singles. Celibacy is a gift and would be for those who choose to remain single for the express purpose of serving God in their singleness.

What about those who are single for a longer season, but yet desire to be married someday? To be celibate can be defined as the spiritual ability to have complete control of one's sexual desires. Although these people may not have the *gift* of celibacy, they still have a biblical mandate to live a chaste lifestyle until they are married. Remaining chaste involves more than refraining from sexual activity; it also means bringing all sexual desires under submission to God. This is not easy, but if single adults wish to honor God with their lives, they must allow God to be at the center, helping them handle their fears, desires, hopes, and dreams.

FURTHER MEDITATION:

Other passages to study about the issue of singleness include:

- 1 Corinthians 7
- Philippians 4:11
- Hebrews 13:5

To Learn More: Turn to the key passage note on singleness at 1 Corinthians 7:26–35 on page 1503. See also the personality profile of Paul on page 1502.

17 So He said to him, “Why do you call Me good?[a] No one *is* good but One, *that is,* God.[b] But if you want to enter into life, keep the commandments.”

18 He said to Him, “Which ones?”

Jesus said, “ *‘You shall not murder,’ ‘You shall not commit adultery,’ ‘You shall not steal,’ ‘You shall not bear false witness,’* 19 *‘Honor your father and your mother,’*[a] and, *‘You shall love your neighbor as yourself.’* ”[b]

20 The young man said to Him, “All these things I have kept from my youth.[a] What do I still lack?”

21 Jesus said to him, “If you want to be perfect, go, sell what you have and give to the poor, and you will have treasure in heaven; and come, follow Me.”

22 But when the young man heard that saying, he went away sorrowful, for he had great possessions.

With God All Things Are Possible

23 Then Jesus said to His disciples, “Assuredly, I say to you that it is hard for a rich man to enter the kingdom of heaven. 24 And again I say to you, it is easier for a camel to go through the eye of a needle than for a rich man to enter the kingdom of God.”

> “With men this is impossible, but with God all things are possible.”
> MATTHEW 19:26

25 When His disciples heard *it,* they were greatly astonished, saying, “Who then can be saved?”

26 But Jesus looked at *them* and said to them, “With men this is impossible, but with God all things are possible.”

27 Then Peter answered and said to Him, “See, we have left all and followed You. Therefore what shall we have?”

28 So Jesus said to them, “Assuredly I say to you, that in the regeneration, when the Son of Man sits on the throne of His glory, you who have followed Me will also sit on twelve thrones, judging the twelve tribes of Israel. 29 And everyone who has left houses or brothers or sisters or father or mother or wife[a] or children or lands, for My name’s sake, shall receive a hundredfold, and inherit eternal life. 30 But many *who are* first will be last, and the last first.

The Parable of the Workers in the Vineyard

20 “For the kingdom of heaven is like a landowner who went out early in the morning to hire laborers for his vineyard. 2 Now when he had agreed with the laborers for a denarius a day, he sent them into his vineyard. 3 And he went out about the third hour and saw others standing idle in the marketplace, 4 and said to them, ‘You also go into the vineyard, and whatever is right I will give you.’ So they went. 5 Again he went out about the sixth and the ninth hour, and did likewise. 6 And about the eleventh hour he went out and found others standing idle,[a] and said to them, ‘Why have you been standing here idle all day?’ 7 They said to him, ‘Because no one hired us.’ He said to them, ‘You also go into the vineyard, and whatever is right you will receive.’[a]

19:17 [a]NU-Text reads *Why do you ask Me about what is good?* [b]NU-Text reads *There is One who is good.* **19:19** [a]Exodus 20:12–16; Deuteronomy 5:16–20 [b]Leviticus 19:18 **19:20** [a]NU-Text omits *from my youth.* **19:29** [a]NU-Text omits *or wife.* **20:6** [a]NU-Text omits *idle.* **20:7** [a]NU-Text omits the last clause of this verse.

SOUL NOTE

Loose Grip *(19:16–22)* This rich young ruler wanted to know what he needed to *do* in order to have eternal life. Jesus perceived the one barrier that was keeping this young man from being a disciple—his wealth. So Jesus challenged him to give away all his wealth and then follow Him. Jesus does not require everyone to just give all they have to the poor. That would bless some temporarily and impoverish many in the end. He does require, however, that we hold our money loosely, being willing to use it for God’s kingdom, and always realizing that our wealth belongs to God. **Topic: Money**

[8]"So when evening had come, the owner of the vineyard said to his steward, 'Call the laborers and give them *their* wages, beginning with the last to the first.' [9]And when those came who *were hired* about the eleventh hour, they each received a denarius. [10]But when the first came, they supposed that they would receive more; and they likewise received each a denarius. [11]And when they had received *it*, they complained against the landowner, [12]saying, 'These last *men* have worked *only* one hour, and you made them equal to us who have borne the burden and the heat of the day.' [13]But he answered one of them and said, 'Friend, I am doing you no wrong. Did you not agree with me for a denarius? [14]Take *what is* yours and go your way. I wish to give to this last man *the same* as to you. [15]Is it not lawful for me to do what I wish with my own things? Or is your eye evil because I am good?' [16]So the last will be first, and the first last. For many are called, but few chosen."[a]

Jesus a Third Time Predicts His Death and Resurrection

[17]Now Jesus, going up to Jerusalem, took the twelve disciples aside on the road and said to them, [18]"Behold, we are going up to Jerusalem, and the Son of Man will be betrayed to the chief priests and to the scribes; and they will condemn Him to death, [19]and deliver Him to the Gentiles to mock and to scourge and to crucify. And the third day He will rise again."

Greatness Is Serving

[20]Then the mother of Zebedee's sons came to Him with her sons, kneeling down and asking something from Him.

[21]And He said to her, "What do you wish?"

She said to Him, "Grant that these two sons of mine may sit, one on Your right hand and the other on the left, in Your kingdom."

[22]But Jesus answered and said, "You do not know what you ask. Are you able to drink the cup that I am about to drink, and be baptized with the baptism that I am baptized with?"[a]

They said to Him, "We are able."

[23]So He said to them, "You will indeed drink My cup, and be baptized with the baptism that I am baptized with;[a] but to sit on My right hand and on My left is not Mine to give, but *it is for those* for whom it is prepared by My Father."

[24]And when the ten heard *it*, they were greatly displeased with the two brothers. [25]But Jesus called them to *Himself* and said, "You know that the rulers of the Gentiles lord it over them, and those who are great exercise authority over them. [26]Yet it shall not be so among you; but whoever desires to become great among you, let him be your servant. [27]And whoever desires to be first among you, let him be your slave— [28]just as the Son of Man did not come to be served, but to serve, and to give His life a ransom for many."

Two Blind Men Receive Their Sight

[29]Now as they went out of Jericho, a great multitude followed Him. [30]And behold, two blind men sitting by the road, when they heard that Jesus was passing by, cried out, saying, "Have mercy on us, O Lord, Son of David!"

[31]Then the multitude warned them that they should be quiet; but they cried out all the more, saying, "Have mercy on us, O Lord, Son of David!"

[32]So Jesus stood still and called them, and said, "What do you want Me to do for you?"

[33]They said to Him, "Lord, that our eyes may be opened." [34]So Jesus had compassion and touched their eyes. And immediately their eyes received sight, and they followed Him.

The Triumphal Entry

21 Now when they drew near Jerusalem, and came to Bethphage,[a] at the Mount of Olives, then Jesus sent two disciples, [2]saying to them, "Go into the village opposite you, and immediately you will find a donkey tied, and a colt with her. Loose *them* and bring *them* to Me. [3]And if anyone says anything to you, you shall say, 'The Lord has need of them,' and immediately he will send them."

[4]All[a] this was done that it might be fulfilled which was spoken by the prophet, saying:

5 *"Tell the daughter of Zion,*
'Behold, your King is coming to you,
Lowly, and sitting on a donkey,
A colt, the foal of a donkey.' "[a]

20:16 [a]NU-Text omits the last sentence of this verse. **20:22** [a]NU-Text omits *and be baptized with the baptism that I am baptized with.* **20:23** [a]NU-Text omits *and be baptized with the baptism that I am baptized with.* **21:1** [a]M-Text reads *Bethsphage.* **21:4** [a]NU-Text omits *All.* **21:5** [a]Zechariah 9:9

6So the disciples went and did as Jesus commanded them. 7They brought the donkey and the colt, laid their clothes on them, and set *Him*[a] on them. 8And a very great multitude spread their clothes on the road; others cut down branches from the trees and spread *them* on the road. 9Then the multitudes who went before and those who followed cried out, saying:

"Hosanna to the Son of David!
'Blessed is He who comes in the name of the LORD!' [a]
Hosanna in the highest!"

10And when He had come into Jerusalem, all the city was moved, saying, "Who is this?"
11So the multitudes said, "This is Jesus, the prophet from Nazareth of Galilee."

JESUS CLEANSES THE TEMPLE

12Then Jesus went into the temple of God[a] and drove out all those who bought and sold in the temple, and overturned the tables of the money changers and the seats of those who sold doves. 13And He said to them, "It is written, *'My house shall be called a house of prayer,'*[a] but you have made it a *'den of thieves.'* "[b]

14Then *the* blind and *the* lame came to Him in the temple, and He healed them. 15But when the chief priests and scribes saw the wonderful things that He did, and the children crying out in the temple and saying, "Hosanna to the Son of David!" they were indignant 16and said to Him, "Do You hear what these are saying?"

And Jesus said to them, "Yes. Have you never read,

'Out of the mouth of babes and nursing infants
You have perfected praise'?"[a]

17Then He left them and went out of the city to Bethany, and He lodged there.

THE FIG TREE WITHERED

18Now in the morning, as He returned to the city, He was hungry. 19And seeing a fig tree by the road, He came to it and found nothing on it but leaves, and said to it, "Let no fruit grow on you ever again." Immediately the fig tree withered away.

THE LESSON OF THE WITHERED FIG TREE

20And when the disciples saw *it*, they marveled, saying, "How did the fig tree wither away so soon?"

21So Jesus answered and said to them, "Assuredly, I say to you, if you have faith and do not doubt, you will not only do what was done to the fig tree, but also if you say to this mountain, 'Be removed and be cast into the sea,' it will be done. 22And whatever things you ask in prayer, believing, you will receive."

JESUS' AUTHORITY QUESTIONED

23Now when He came into the temple, the chief priests and the elders of the people confronted Him as He was teaching, and said, "By what authority are You doing these things? And who gave You this authority?"

24But Jesus answered and said to them, "I also will ask you one thing, which if you tell Me, I likewise will tell you by what authority I do these things: 25The baptism of John—where was it from? From heaven or from men?"

And they reasoned among themselves, saying, "If we say, 'From heaven,' He will say to us, 'Why then did you not believe him?' 26But if we say, 'From men,' we fear the multitude, for all count John as a prophet." 27So they answered Jesus and said, "We do not know."

And He said to them, "Neither will I tell you by what authority I do these things.

THE PARABLE OF THE TWO SONS

28"But what do you think? A man had two sons, and he came to the first and said, 'Son, go, work today in my vineyard.' 29He answered and said, 'I will not,' but afterward he regretted it and went. 30Then he came to the second and said likewise. And he answered and said, 'I *go*, sir,' but he did not go. 31Which of the two did the will of *his* father?"

They said to Him, "The first."

Jesus said to them, "Assuredly, I say to you that tax collectors and harlots enter the kingdom of God before you. 32For John came to you in the way of righteousness, and you did not believe him; but tax collectors and harlots believed him; and when you saw *it*, you did not afterward relent and believe him.

21:7 [a]NU-Text reads *and He sat.* **21:9** [a]Psalm 118:26 **21:12** [a]NU-Text omits *of God.* **21:13** [a]Isaiah 56:7 [b]Jeremiah 7:11 **21:16** [a]Psalm 8:2

THE PARABLE OF THE WICKED VINEDRESSERS

33“Hear another parable: There was a certain landowner who planted a vineyard and
set a hedge around it, dug a winepress in it
and built a tower. And he leased it to
vinedressers and went into a far country.
34Now when vintage-time drew near, he sent
his servants to the vinedressers, that they
might receive its fruit. 35And the vinedressers
took his servants, beat one, killed one, and
stoned another. 36Again he sent other servants, more than the first, and they did likewise to them. 37Then last of all he sent his son
to them, saying, ‘They will respect my son.’
38But when the vinedressers saw the son, they
said among themselves, ‘This is the heir.
Come, let us kill him and seize his inheritance.’ 39So they took him and cast *him* out of
the vineyard and killed *him*.

40“Therefore, when the owner of the
vineyard comes, what will he do to those
vinedressers?”

41They said to Him, “He will destroy those
wicked men miserably, and lease *his* vineyard
to other vinedressers who will render to him
the fruits in their seasons.”

42Jesus said to them, “Have you never read
in the Scriptures:

‘The stone which the builders rejected
Has become the chief cornerstone.
This was the LORD’s doing,
And it is marvelous in our eyes’?[a]

43“Therefore I say to you, the kingdom of
God will be taken from you and given to a nation bearing the fruits of it. 44And whoever
falls on this stone will be broken; but on
whomever it falls, it will grind him to powder.”

45Now when the chief priests and Pharisees
heard His parables, they perceived that He
was speaking of them. 46But when they sought
to lay hands on Him, they feared the multitudes, because they took Him for a prophet.

THE PARABLE OF THE WEDDING FEAST

22 And Jesus answered and spoke to
them again by parables and said:
2“The kingdom of heaven is like a certain king
who arranged a marriage for his son, 3and
sent out his servants to call those who were
invited to the wedding; and they were not
willing to come. 4Again, he sent out other servants, saying, ‘Tell those who are invited,
“See, I have prepared my dinner; my oxen and
fatted cattle *are* killed, and all things *are*
ready. Come to the wedding.” ’ 5But they
made light of it and went their ways, one to
his own farm, another to his business. 6And
the rest seized his servants, treated *them*
spitefully, and killed *them*. 7But when the king
heard *about it*, he was furious. And he sent
out his armies, destroyed those murderers,
and burned up their city. 8Then he said to his
servants, ‘The wedding is ready, but those
who were invited were not worthy. 9Therefore
go into the highways, and as many as you
find, invite to the wedding.’ 10So those servants went out into the highways and gathered together all whom they found, both bad
and good. And the wedding *hall* was filled
with guests.

11“But when the king came in to see the
guests, he saw a man there who did not have
on a wedding garment. 12So he said to him,
‘Friend, how did you come in here without a
wedding garment?’ And he was speechless.
13Then the king said to the servants, ‘Bind him
hand and foot, take him away, and[a] cast *him*
into outer darkness; there will be weeping and
gnashing of teeth.’

14“For many are called, but few *are* chosen.”

THE PHARISEES: IS IT LAWFUL TO PAY TAXES TO CAESAR?

15Then the Pharisees went and plotted how
they might entangle Him in *His* talk. 16And
they sent to Him their disciples with the Herodians, saying, “Teacher, we know that You are
true, and teach the way of God in truth; nor do
You care about anyone, for You do not regard
the person of men. 17Tell us, therefore, what
do You think? Is it lawful to pay taxes to Caesar, or not?”

18But Jesus perceived their wickedness, and
said, “Why do you test Me, *you* hypocrites?
19Show Me the tax money.”

So they brought Him a denarius.

20And He said to them, “Whose image and
inscription *is* this?”

21They said to Him, “Caesar’s.”

And He said to them, “Render therefore to
Caesar the things that are Caesar’s, and to God
the things that are God’s.” 22When they had

21:42 [a]Psalm 118:22, 23 **22:13** [a]NU-Text omits *take him away, and.*

heard *these words,* they marveled, and left
Him and went their way.

THE SADDUCEES: WHAT ABOUT THE RESURRECTION?

23 The same day the Sadducees, who say
there is no resurrection, came to Him and
asked Him, 24 saying: "Teacher, Moses said
that if a man dies, having no children, his
brother shall marry his wife and raise up offspring for his brother. 25 Now there were with
us seven brothers. The first died after he had
married, and having no offspring, left his wife
to his brother. 26 Likewise the second also, and
the third, even to the seventh. 27 Last of all the
woman died also. 28 Therefore, in the resurrection, whose wife of the seven will she be? For
they all had her."

29 Jesus answered and said to them, "You are
mistaken, not knowing the Scriptures nor the
power of God. 30 For in the resurrection they
neither marry nor are given in marriage, but
are like angels of God[a] in heaven. 31 But concerning the resurrection of the dead, have you
not read what was spoken to you by God, saying, 32 '*I am the God of Abraham, the God of
Isaac, and the God of Jacob*'?[a] God is not the
God of the dead, but of the living." 33 And
when the multitudes heard *this,* they were astonished at His teaching.

THE SCRIBES: WHICH IS THE FIRST COMMANDMENT OF ALL?

34 But when the Pharisees heard that He had
silenced the Sadducees, they gathered together. 35 Then one of them, a lawyer, asked *Him a
question,* testing Him, and saying, 36 "Teacher,
which *is* the great commandment in the law?"
37 Jesus said to him, " '*You shall love the
LORD your God with all
your heart, with all your
soul, and with all your
mind.*'[a] 38 This is *the*
first and great com-
mandment. 39 And *the*
second *is* like it: '*You
shall love your neighbor
as yourself.*'[a] 40 On these two commandments
hang all the Law and the Prophets."

> "You shall love the LORD your God
> with all your heart, with all your
> soul, and with all your mind."
> MATTHEW 22:37

JESUS: HOW CAN DAVID CALL HIS DESCENDANT LORD?

41 While the Pharisees were gathered together, Jesus asked them, 42 saying, "What do
you think about the Christ? Whose Son is He?"
They said to Him, "*The Son* of David."
43 He said to them, "How then does David in
the Spirit call Him '*Lord,*' saying:

44 *'The LORD said to my Lord,
"Sit at My right hand,
Till I make Your enemies Your
footstool" '?*[a]

45 If David then calls Him '*Lord,*' how is He his
Son?" 46 And no one was able to answer Him a
word, nor from that day on did anyone dare
question Him anymore.

WOE TO THE SCRIBES AND PHARISEES

23 Then Jesus spoke to the multitudes
and to His disciples, 2 saying: "The
scribes and the Pharisees sit in Moses' seat.
3 Therefore whatever they tell you to observe,[a]
that observe and do, but do not do according
to their works; for they say, and do not do.
4 For they bind heavy burdens, hard to bear,
and lay *them* on men's shoulders; but they
themselves will not move them with one of
their fingers. 5 But all their works they do to be
seen by men. They make their phylacteries
broad and enlarge the borders of their garments. 6 They love the best places at feasts, the
best seats in the synagogues, 7 greetings in the
marketplaces, and to be called by men, 'Rabbi, Rabbi.' 8 But you, do not be called 'Rabbi';
for One is your Teacher, the Christ,[a] and you
are all brethren. 9 Do not call anyone on earth
your father; for One is your Father, He who is
in heaven. 10 And do not be called teachers; for
One is your Teacher, the Christ. 11 But he who is
greatest among you shall be your servant.
12 And whoever exalts himself will be humbled,
and he who humbles
himself will be exalted.
13 "But woe to you,
scribes and Pharisees,
hypocrites! For you shut
up the kingdom of heav-
en against men; for you
neither go in *yourselves,*
nor do you allow those who are entering to go

22:30 [a]NU-Text omits *of God.* **22:32** [a]Exodus 3:6, 15 **22:37** [a]Deuteronomy 6:5 **22:39** [a]Leviticus 19:18 **22:44** [a]Psalm 110:1 **23:3** [a]NU-Text omits *to observe.* **23:8** [a]NU-Text omits *the Christ.*

in. 14Woe to you, scribes and Pharisees, hypocrites! For you devour widows' houses, and for
a pretense make long prayers. Therefore you
will receive greater condemnation.[a]
15"Woe to you, scribes and Pharisees,
hypocrites! For you travel land and sea to win
one proselyte, and when he is won, you make
him twice as much a son of hell as yourselves.
16"Woe to you, blind guides, who say,
'Whoever swears by the temple, it is nothing;
but whoever swears by the gold of the temple,
he is obliged *to perform it.'* 17Fools and blind!
For which is greater, the gold or the temple
that sanctifies[a] the gold? 18And, 'Whoever
swears by the altar, it is nothing; but whoever
swears by the gift that is on it, he is obliged *to
perform it.'* 19Fools and blind! For which is
greater, the gift or the altar that sanctifies the
gift? 20Therefore he who swears by the altar,
swears by it and by all things on it. 21He who
swears by the temple, swears by it and by Him
who dwells[a] in it. 22And he who swears by
heaven, swears by the throne of God and by
Him who sits on it.
23"Woe to you, scribes and Pharisees, hypocrites! For you pay tithe of mint and anise and
cummin, and have neglected the weightier
matters of the law: justice and mercy and
faith. These you ought to have done, without
leaving the others undone. 24Blind guides,
who strain out a gnat and swallow a camel!
25"Woe to you, scribes and Pharisees, hypocrites! For you cleanse the outside of the cup
and dish, but inside they are full of extortion

23:14 [a]NU-Text omits this verse.
23:17 [a]NU-Text reads *sanctified.* **23:21** [a]M-Text reads *dwelt.*

PERSONALITY PROFILE

Legalism

THE PHARISEES: LIVING BY THE RULES

(MATTHEW 23:23–28)

The Pharisees were the conservative religious believers of Jesus' day. They viewed themselves as the defenders of the law and went to great lengths to make sure that their outward behavior met the minute demands of the law as they interpreted it. They would invest great energy to "strain out a gnat"—concentrating on useless points of meaningless regulation, and instead would "swallow a camel"—missing the major demands of the law, such as justice, mercy, forgiveness, and redemption. The Pharisees looked pious and acted religious, but they were heartless, spiritually dead. They were legalists, and they depict the fallacy of legalism. Legalists make gods of the rules of God rather than reveling in relationship with God Himself.

"Pharisee" is a term that still fits those who concern themselves with the letter of the law. They take the rules seriously. Most Pharisees in Jesus' time were not living out their faith and values in a way that truly represented the heart of God. Jesus' major criticism was that although they looked religious, they acted wickedly. He delivered His sternest rebuke in Scripture in a series of eight "woes" pronounced against the scribes and Pharisees. He called them hypocrites, blind guides, fools, and the children of hell. Some Jewish religious leaders, like Nicodemus (John 3:1–21) and Joseph of Arimathea (Matt. 27:57–60) became disciples of Jesus. But most hated Jesus because He constantly pointed out that while their external behavior did meet the legalistic standards of the law, their hearts were often far from God.

Pharisees are alive, well, and doing damage today. Legalists focus on the rules, on appearances, on "being better" than other believers. Like the Pharisees of Jesus' day, they separate themselves from the rest of Christians, feeling superior and often acting judgmental. God's people need the Holy Spirit's help to see any accumulation of legalistic trash hidden in the corners of our lives. He will lead His people, gently but relentlessly, to repentance and true spiritual vitality.

To Learn More: Turn to the article about legalism on pages 142, 143. See also the key passage note at Romans 7:6–14 on page 1473.

and self-indulgence.[a] 26Blind Pharisee, first
cleanse the inside of the cup and dish, that the
outside of them may be clean also.
27"Woe to you, scribes and Pharisees, hypocrites! For you are like whitewashed tombs
which indeed appear beautiful outwardly, but
inside are full of dead *men's* bones and all uncleanness. 28Even so you also outwardly appear righteous to men, but inside you are full
of hypocrisy and lawlessness.
29"Woe to you, scribes and Pharisees, hypocrites! Because you build the tombs of the
prophets and adorn the monuments of the righteous, 30and say, 'If we had lived in the days of
our fathers, we would not have been partakers
with them in the blood of the prophets.'
31"Therefore you are witnesses against
yourselves that you are sons of those who
murdered the prophets. 32Fill up, then, the
measure of your fathers' *guilt*. 33Serpents,
brood of vipers! How can you escape the condemnation of hell? 34Therefore, indeed, I send
you prophets, wise men, and scribes: *some* of
them you will kill and crucify, and *some* of
them you will scourge in your synagogues and
persecute from city to city, 35that on you may
come all the righteous blood shed on the
earth, from the blood of righteous Abel to the
blood of Zechariah, son of Berechiah, whom
you murdered between the temple and the altar. 36Assuredly, I say to you, all these things
will come upon this generation.

Jesus Laments over Jerusalem

37"O Jerusalem, Jerusalem, the one who
kills the prophets and stones those who are
sent to her! How often I wanted to gather your
children together, as a hen gathers her chicks
under *her* wings, but you were not willing!
38See! Your house is left to you desolate; 39for I
say to you, you shall see Me no more till you
say, *'Blessed is He who comes in the name of
the* LORD!*'* "[a]

Jesus Predicts the Destruction of the Temple

24 Then Jesus went out and departed
from the temple, and His disciples
came up to show Him the buildings of the
temple. 2And Jesus said to them, "Do you not
see all these things? Assuredly, I say to you,
not *one* stone shall be left here upon another,
that shall not be thrown down."

The Signs of the Times and the End of the Age

3Now as He sat on the Mount of Olives, the
disciples came to Him privately, saying, "Tell
us, when will these things be? And what *will
be* the sign of Your coming, and of the end of
the age?"
4And Jesus answered and said to them:
"Take heed that no one deceives you. 5For
many will come in My name, saying, 'I am the
Christ,' and will deceive many. 6And you will
hear of wars and rumors of wars. See that you
are not troubled; for all[a] *these things* must
come to pass, but the end is not yet. 7For nation will rise against nation, and kingdom
against kingdom. And there will be famines,
pestilences,[a] and earthquakes in various
places. 8All these *are* the beginning of sorrows.
9"Then they will deliver you up to tribulation and kill you, and you will be hated by all
nations for My name's sake. 10And then many
will be offended, will betray one another, and
will hate one another. 11Then many false
prophets will rise up and deceive many. 12And
because lawlessness will abound, the love of
many will grow cold. 13But he who endures to
the end shall be saved. 14And this gospel of
the kingdom will be preached in all the world
as a witness to all the nations, and then the
end will come.

The Great Tribulation

15"Therefore when you see the *'abomination of desolation,'*[a] spoken of by Daniel the
prophet, standing in the holy place" (whoever
reads, let him understand), 16"then let those
who are in Judea flee to the mountains. 17Let
him who is on the housetop not go down to
take anything out of his house. 18And let him
who is in the field not go back to get his
clothes. 19But woe to those who are pregnant
and to those who are nursing babies in those
days! 20And pray that your flight may not be in
winter or on the Sabbath. 21For then there will
be great tribulation, such as has not been
since the beginning of the world until this
time, no, nor ever shall be. 22And unless those
days were shortened, no flesh would be

23:25 [a]M-Text reads *unrighteousness.*
23:39 [a]Psalm 118:26 **24:6** [a]NU-Text omits *all.*
24:7 [a]NU-Text omits *pestilences.* **24:15** [a]Daniel
11:31; 12:11

saved; but for the elect's sake those days will be shortened.

[23]"Then if anyone says to you, 'Look, here *is* the Christ!' or 'There!' do not believe *it*. [24]For false christs and false prophets will rise and show great signs and wonders to deceive, if possible, even the elect. [25]See, I have told you beforehand.

[26]"Therefore if they say to you, 'Look, He is in the desert!' do not go out; *or* 'Look, *He is* in the inner rooms!' do not believe *it*. [27]For as the lightning comes from the east and flashes to the west, so also will the coming of the Son of Man be. [28]For wherever the carcass is, there the eagles will be gathered together.

The Coming of the Son of Man

[29]"Immediately after the tribulation of those days the sun will be darkened, and the moon will not give its light; the stars will fall from heaven, and the powers of the heavens will be shaken. [30]Then the sign of the Son of Man will appear in heaven, and then all the tribes of the earth will mourn, and they will see the Son of Man coming on the clouds of heaven with power and great glory. [31]And He will send His angels with a great sound of a trumpet, and they will gather together His elect from the four winds, from one end of heaven to the other.

The Parable of the Fig Tree

[32]"Now learn this parable from the fig tree: When its branch has already become tender and puts forth leaves, you know that summer *is* near. [33]So you also, when you see all these things, know that it[a] is near—at the doors! [34]Assuredly, I say to you, this generation will by no means pass away till all these things take place. [35]Heaven and earth will pass away, but My words will by no means pass away.

No One Knows the Day or Hour

[36]"But of that day and hour no one knows, not even the angels of heaven,[a] but My Father only. [37]But as the days of Noah *were*, so also will the coming of the Son of Man be. [38]For as in the days before the flood, they were eating and drinking, marrying and giving in marriage, until the day that Noah entered the ark, [39]and did not know until the flood came and took them all away, so also will the coming of the Son of Man be. [40]Then two *men* will be in the field: one will be taken and the other left. [41]Two *women will be* grinding at the mill: one will be taken and the other left. [42]Watch therefore, for you do not know what hour[a] your Lord is coming. [43]But know this, that if the master of the house had known what hour the thief would come, he would have watched and not allowed his house to be broken into. [44]Therefore you also be ready, for the Son of Man is coming at an hour you do not expect.

The Faithful Servant and the Evil Servant

[45]"Who then is a faithful and wise servant, whom his master made ruler over his household, to give them food in due season? [46]Blessed *is* that servant whom his master, when he comes, will find so doing. [47]Assuredly, I say to you that he will make him ruler over all his goods. [48]But if that evil servant says in his heart, 'My master is delaying his coming,'[a] [49]and begins to beat *his* fellow servants, and to eat and drink with the drunkards, [50]the master of that servant will come on a day when he is not looking for *him* and at an hour that he is not aware of, [51]and will cut him in two and appoint *him* his portion with the hypocrites. There shall be weeping and gnashing of teeth.

The Parable of the Wise and Foolish Virgins

25 "Then the kingdom of heaven shall be likened to ten virgins who took their lamps and went out to meet the bridegroom. [2]Now five of them were wise, and five *were* foolish. [3]Those who *were* foolish took their lamps and took no oil with them, [4]but the wise took oil in their vessels with their lamps. [5]But while the bridegroom was delayed, they all slumbered and slept.

[6]"And at midnight a cry was *heard:* 'Behold, the bridegroom is coming;[a] go out to meet him!' [7]Then all those virgins arose and trimmed their lamps. [8]And the foolish said to the wise, 'Give us *some* of your oil, for our lamps are going out.' [9]But the wise answered, saying, '*No,* lest there should not be enough for us and you; but go rather to those who sell, and buy for yourselves.' [10]And while they went to buy, the bridegroom came, and those

24:33 [a]Or *He* **24:36** [a]NU-Text adds *nor the Son.* **24:42** [a]NU-Text reads *day.* **24:48** [a]NU-Text omits *his coming.* **25:6** [a]NU-Text omits *is coming.*

who were ready went in with him to the wedding; and the door was shut.
[11]"Afterward the other virgins came also,
saying, 'Lord, Lord, open to us!' [12]But he answered and said, 'Assuredly, I say to you, I do
not know you.'
[13]"Watch therefore, for you know neither
the day nor the hour[a] in which the Son of Man
is coming.

THE PARABLE OF THE TALENTS

[14]"For *the kingdom of heaven is* like a man
traveling to a far country, *who* called his own
servants and delivered his goods to them.
[15]And to one he gave five talents, to another
two, and to another one, to each according to
his own ability; and immediately he went on a
journey. [16]Then he who had received the five
talents went and traded with them, and made
another five talents. [17]And likewise he who
had received two gained two more also. [18]But
he who had received one went and dug in the
ground, and hid his lord's money. [19]After a
long time the lord of those servants came and
settled accounts with them.
[20]"So he who had received five talents came
and brought five other talents, saying, 'Lord,
you delivered to me five talents; look, I have
gained five more talents besides them.' [21]His
lord said to him, 'Well *done*, good and faithful
servant; you were faithful over a few things, I
will make you ruler over many things. Enter
into the joy of your lord.' [22]He also who had
received two talents came and said, 'Lord, you
delivered to me two talents; look, I have
gained two more talents besides them.' [23]His
lord said to him, 'Well *done*, good and faithful
servant; you have been faithful over a few
things, I will make you ruler over many
things. Enter into the joy of your lord.'
[24]"Then he who had received the one talent
came and said, 'Lord, I knew you to be a hard
man, reaping where you have not sown, and
gathering where you have not scattered seed.
[25]And I was afraid, and went and hid your talent in the ground. Look, *there* you have *what
is* yours.'
[26]"But his lord answered and said to him,
'You wicked and lazy servant, you knew that I
reap where I have not sown, and gather where
I have not scattered seed. [27]So you ought to
have deposited my money with the bankers,
and at my coming I would have received back
my own with interest. [28]So take the talent from
him, and give *it* to him who has ten talents.
[29]'For to everyone who has, more will be
given, and he will have abundance; but from
him who does not have, even what he has will
be taken away. [30]And cast the unprofitable
servant into the outer darkness. There will be
weeping and gnashing of teeth.'

THE SON OF MAN WILL JUDGE THE NATIONS

[31]"When the Son of Man comes in His glory,
and all the holy[a] angels with Him, then He

25:13 [a]NU-Text omits the rest of this verse.
25:31 [a]NU-Text omits *holy.*

KEY PASSAGE

Respon-sibility

A TALENT FOR INVESTING

(25:14–30)

Jesus told the parable of the talents to teach people about their personal responsibility to be good stewards of His resources. In this parable, a man traveled to a far country and entrusted his servants with investing his money in his absence. One servant received five talents, and after wise investment, earned his master another five. The second servant also doubled his master's money. A third servant, however, hid his one talent, knowing that the master would just come back and claim any earnings for himself.

God gives people diverse gifts and talents along with the responsibility to invest these resources in His kingdom for His glory. The wise and productive use of our God-given talents yields fruit, joy, and glory for God.

To Learn More: Turn to the article about responsibility on pages 962, 963. See also the personality profile of Esther on page 633.

will sit on the throne of His glory. [32]All the nations will be gathered before Him, and He will separate them one from another, as a shepherd divides *his* sheep from the goats. [33]And He will set the sheep on His right hand, but the goats on the left. [34]Then the King will say to those on His right hand, 'Come, you blessed of My Father, inherit the kingdom prepared for you from the foundation of the world: [35]for I was hungry and you gave Me food; I was thirsty and you gave Me drink; I was a stranger and you took Me in; [36]I *was* naked and you clothed Me; I was sick and you visited Me; I was in prison and you came to Me.'

[37]"Then the righteous will answer Him, saying, 'Lord, when did we see You hungry and feed *You,* or thirsty and give *You* drink? [38]When did we see You a stranger and take *You* in, or naked and clothe *You?* [39]Or when did we see You sick, or in prison, and come to You?' [40]And the King will answer and say to them, 'Assuredly, I say to you, inasmuch as you did *it* to one of the least of these My brethren, you did *it* to Me.'

[41]"Then He will also say to those on the left hand, 'Depart from Me, you cursed, into the everlasting fire prepared for the devil and his angels: [42]for I was hungry and you gave Me no food; I was thirsty and you gave Me no drink; [43]I was a stranger and you did not take Me in, naked and you did not clothe Me, sick and in prison and you did not visit Me.'

[44]"Then they also will answer Him,[a] saying, 'Lord, when did we see You hungry or thirsty or a stranger or naked or sick or in prison, and did not minister to You?' [45]Then He will answer them, saying, 'Assuredly, I say to you, inasmuch as you did not do *it* to one of the least of these, you did not do *it* to Me.' [46]And these will go away into everlasting punishment, but the righteous into eternal life."

THE PLOT TO KILL JESUS

26 Now it came to pass, when Jesus had finished all these sayings, *that* He said to His disciples, [2]"You know that after two days is the Passover, and the Son of Man will be delivered up to be crucified."

[3]Then the chief priests, the scribes,[a] and the elders of the people assembled at the palace of the high priest, who was called Caiaphas, [4]and plotted to take Jesus by trickery and kill *Him.* [5]But they said, "Not during the feast, lest there be an uproar among the people."

THE ANOINTING AT BETHANY

[6]And when Jesus was in Bethany at the house of Simon the leper, [7]a woman came to Him having an alabaster flask of very costly fragrant oil, and she poured *it* on His head as He sat *at the table.* [8]But when His disciples saw *it,* they were indignant, saying, "Why this waste? [9]For this fragrant oil might have been sold for much and given to *the* poor."

[10]But when Jesus was aware of *it,* He said to them, "Why do you trouble the woman? For she has done a good work for Me. [11]For you have the poor with you always, but Me you do not have always. [12]For in pouring this fragrant oil on My body, she did *it* for My burial. [13]Assuredly, I say to you, wherever this gospel is preached in the whole world, what this woman has done will also be told as a memorial to her."

JUDAS AGREES TO BETRAY JESUS

[14]Then one of the twelve, called Judas Iscariot, went to the chief priests [15]and said, "What are you willing to give me if I deliver Him to you?" And they counted out to him thirty pieces of silver. [16]So from that time he sought opportunity to betray Him.

JESUS CELEBRATES PASSOVER WITH HIS DISCIPLES

[17]Now on the first *day of the Feast* of Unleavened Bread the disciples came to Jesus, saying to Him, "Where do You want us to prepare for You to eat the Passover?"

[18]And He said, "Go into the city to a certain man, and say to him, 'The Teacher says, "My time is at hand; I will keep the Passover at your house with My disciples." ' "

[19]So the disciples did as Jesus had directed them; and they prepared the Passover.

[20]When evening had come, He sat down with the twelve. [21]Now as they were eating, He said, "Assuredly, I say to you, one of you will betray Me."

[22]And they were exceedingly sorrowful, and each of them began to say to Him, "Lord, is it I?"

[23]He answered and said, "He who dipped *his* hand with Me in the dish will betray Me. [24]The Son of Man indeed goes just as it is written of Him, but woe to that man by whom the Son of Man is betrayed! It would have been

25:44 [a]NU-Text and M-Text omit *Him.* **26:3** [a]NU-Text omits *the scribes.*

good for that man if he had not been born."
25Then Judas, who was betraying Him, answered and said, "Rabbi, is it I?"
He said to him, "You have said it."

JESUS INSTITUTES THE LORD'S SUPPER

26And as they were eating, Jesus took bread,
blessed[a] and broke *it*, and gave *it* to the disciples and said, "Take, eat; this is My body."
27Then He took the cup, and gave thanks,
and gave *it* to them, saying, "Drink from it, all
of you. 28For this is My blood of the new[a] covenant, which is shed for many for the remission of sins. 29But I say to you, I will not drink
of this fruit of the vine from now on until that
day when I drink it new with you in My
Father's kingdom."
30And when they had sung a hymn, they
went out to the Mount of Olives.

JESUS PREDICTS PETER'S DENIAL

31Then Jesus said to them, "All of you will
be made to stumble because of Me this night,
for it is written:

'I will strike the Shepherd,
And the sheep of the flock will be
scattered.'[a]

32But after I have been raised, I will go before
you to Galilee."
33Peter answered and said to Him, "Even if
all are made to stumble because of You, I will
never be made to stumble."
34Jesus said to him, "Assuredly, I say to you
that this night, before the rooster crows, you
will deny Me three times."
35Peter said to Him, "Even if I have to die
with You, I will not deny You!"
And so said all the disciples.

THE PRAYER IN THE GARDEN

36Then Jesus came with them to a place
called Gethsemane, and said to the disciples,
"Sit here while I go and pray over there."
37And He took with Him Peter and the two
sons of Zebedee, and He began to be sorrowful and deeply distressed. 38Then He said to
them, "My soul is exceedingly sorrowful, even
to death. Stay here and watch with Me."
39He went a little farther and fell on His
face, and prayed, saying, "O My Father, if it is
possible, let this cup pass from Me; nevertheless, not as I will, but as You *will*."
40Then He came to the disciples and found
them sleeping, and said to Peter, "What! Could
you not watch with Me one hour? 41Watch and
pray, lest you enter into temptation. The spirit
indeed *is* willing, but the flesh *is* weak."
42Again, a second time, He went away and
prayed, saying, "O My Father, if this cup cannot pass away from Me unless[a] I drink it, Your
will be done." 43And He came and found them
asleep again, for their eyes were heavy.
44So He left them, went away again, and
prayed the third time, saying the same words.
45Then He came to His disciples and said to
them, "Are *you* still sleeping and resting? Behold, the hour is at hand, and the Son of Man
is being betrayed into the hands of sinners.
46Rise, let us be going. See, My betrayer is at
hand."

BETRAYAL AND ARREST IN GETHSEMANE

47And while He was still speaking, behold,
Judas, one of the twelve, with a great multitude with swords and clubs, came from the
chief priests and elders of the people.
48Now His betrayer had given them a sign,
saying, "Whomever I kiss, He is the One; seize
Him." 49Immediately he went up to Jesus and
said, "Greetings, Rabbi!" and kissed Him.
50But Jesus said to him, "Friend, why have
you come?"
Then they came and laid hands on Jesus
and took Him. 51And suddenly, one of those
who were with Jesus stretched out *his* hand
and drew his sword, struck the servant of the
high priest, and cut off his ear.
52But Jesus said to him, "Put your sword in
its place, for all who take the sword will
perish[a] by the sword. 53Or do you think that I
cannot now pray to My Father, and He will
provide Me with more than twelve legions of
angels? 54How then could the Scriptures be
fulfilled, that it must happen thus?"
55In that hour Jesus said to the multitudes,
"Have you come out, as against a robber, with
swords and clubs to take Me? I sat daily with
you, teaching in the temple, and you did not
seize Me. 56But all this was done that the
Scriptures of the prophets might be fulfilled."
Then all the disciples forsook Him and fled.

26:26 [a]M-Text reads *gave thanks for.* **26:28** [a]NU-Text omits *new.* **26:31** [a]Zechariah 13:7
26:42 [a]NU-Text reads *if this may not pass away unless.* **26:52** [a]M-Text reads *die.*

Jesus Faces the Sanhedrin

[57]And those who had laid hold of Jesus led
Him away to Caiaphas the high priest, where
the scribes and the elders were assembled.
[58]But Peter followed Him at a distance to the
high priest's courtyard. And he went in and
sat with the servants to see the end.

[59]Now the chief priests, the elders,[a] and all
the council sought false testimony against
Jesus to put Him to death, [60]but found none.
Even though many false witnesses came forward, they found none.[a] But at last two false
witnesses[b] came forward [61]and said, "This *fellow* said, 'I am able to destroy the temple of
God and to build it in three days.' "

[62]And the high priest arose and said to Him,
"Do You answer nothing? What *is it* these men
testify against You?" [63]But Jesus kept silent.
And the high priest answered and said to Him,
"I put You under oath by the living God: Tell
us if You are the Christ, the Son of God!"

[64]Jesus said to him, "*It is as* you said. Nevertheless, I say to you, hereafter you will see
the Son of Man sitting at the right hand of the
Power, and coming on the clouds of heaven."

[65]Then the high priest tore his clothes, saying,
"He has spoken blasphemy! What further need
do we have of witnesses? Look, now you have
heard His blasphemy! [66]What do you think?"

They answered and said, "He is deserving
of death."

[67]Then they spat in His face and beat Him;
and others struck *Him* with the palms of their
hands, [68]saying, "Prophesy to us, Christ! Who
is the one who struck You?"

Peter Denies Jesus, and Weeps Bitterly

[69]Now Peter sat outside in the courtyard.
And a servant girl came to him, saying, "You
also were with Jesus of Galilee."

[70]But he denied it before *them* all, saying, "I
do not know what you are saying."

[71]And when he had gone out to the gateway,
another *girl* saw him and said to those *who
were* there, "This *fellow* also was with Jesus of
Nazareth."

[72]But again he denied with an oath, "I do
not know the Man!"

[73]And a little later those who stood by came
up and said to Peter, "Surely you also are *one*
of them, for your speech betrays you."

[74]Then he began to curse and swear, *saying*,
"I do not know the Man!"

Immediately a rooster crowed. [75]And Peter
remembered the word of Jesus who had said
to him, "Before the rooster crows, you will
deny Me three times." So he went out and
wept bitterly.

Jesus Handed Over to Pontius Pilate

27 When morning came, all the chief
priests and elders of the people plotted
against Jesus to put Him to death. [2]And when
they had bound Him, they led Him away and
delivered Him to Pontius[a] Pilate the governor.

Judas Hangs Himself

[3]Then Judas, His betrayer, seeing that He
had been condemned, was remorseful and
brought back the thirty pieces of silver to the
chief priests and elders, [4]saying, "I have
sinned by betraying innocent blood."

And they said, "What *is that* to us? You see
to it!"

[5]Then he threw down the pieces of silver
in the temple and departed, and went and
hanged himself.

[6]But the chief priests took the silver pieces
and said, "It is not lawful to put them into the

26:59 [a]NU-Text omits *the elders.* **26:60** [a]NU-Text puts a comma after *but found none,* does not capitalize *Even,* and omits *they found none.* [b]NU-Text omits *false witnesses.* **27:2** [a]NU-Text omits *Pontius.*

SOUL NOTE

Be at Peace *(26:51–54)* When Jesus was arrested, Peter attempted to defend Him with his sword. Jesus rebuked Peter, saying, "All who take the sword will perish by the sword." Jesus' kingdom is to differ greatly from the kingdoms of the world. This King did not come to ride to victory through a bloody battlefield, but on a Cross where the only blood shed would be His own. Nowhere in the New Testament are believers commanded to promote Christianity by force. God will use force when He chooses; God's people, however, must be peacemakers (5:9). **Topic: Violence**

treasury, because they are the price of blood."
[7]And they consulted together and bought with
them the potter's field, to bury strangers in.
[8]Therefore that field has been called the Field
of Blood to this day.

[9]Then was fulfilled what was spoken by
Jeremiah the prophet, saying, *"And they took
the thirty pieces of silver, the value of Him
who was priced,* whom they of the children of
Israel priced, [10]*and gave them for the potter's
field, as the LORD directed me."*[a]

JESUS FACES PILATE

[11]Now Jesus stood before the governor. And
the governor asked Him, saying, "Are You the
King of the Jews?"

Jesus said to him, *"It is as* you say." [12]And
while He was being accused by the chief
priests and elders, He answered nothing.
[13]Then Pilate said to Him, "Do You not hear
how many things they testify against You?"
[14]But He answered him not one word, so that
the governor marveled greatly.

TAKING THE PLACE OF BARABBAS

[15]Now at the feast the governor was accustomed to releasing to the multitude one prisoner whom they wished. [16]And at that time
they had a notorious prisoner called Barabbas.[a] [17]Therefore, when they had gathered together, Pilate said to them, "Whom do you
want me to release to you? Barabbas, or Jesus
who is called Christ?" [18]For he knew that they
had handed Him over because of envy.

[19]While he was sitting on the judgment seat,

27:10 [a]Jeremiah 32:6–9 **27:16** [a]NU-Text reads *Jesus Barabbas.*

PERSONALITY PROFILE

Suicide

THE SUICIDE OF JUDAS

(MATTHEW 27:5)

Judas was a complex and deluded man, and his relationship to Christ was complicated. Matthew depicted the suicide of Judas as an act of utter frustration committed by a man who was wracked with guilt but unable to accept the possibility of forgiveness. While he acknowledged that he had sinned, Judas did not repent and seek reconciliation to Christ as Peter later did (John 21).

Suicides are not always immediate, conscious, willful decisions. For example, suicide often results from a prolonged, severe, deep depression. Circumstances like this type of mental instability, however, don't seem to have been the case with Judas. Other factors may have brought on the temptation to kill himself. He certainly faced the perceived hopelessness of the individual whose plan falls apart. His act may have been an example of self-destructive impulsiveness by someone who is angry and expects unending shame for failure. Because we can only guess at his motivation for betraying Jesus, we must be cautious in our conclusions about Judas's life.

All the disciples as well as the whole nation expected Christ as the conquering King. This picture did not include humble servitude, a mute defense, or death on a cross. None understood and most were confused about Jesus. Judas may have become angry and indignant, nursing his resentments whenever Christ failed to fulfill his expectations of what a Messiah should be and do.

A genuine Christian wouldn't lose his salvation by killing himself, but in the case of Judas, the Bible indicates that even though he regretted the consequences of his betrayal, he died lost, alienated from Christ (John 6:70; 17:12; Acts 1:25). Faced with the result of one horrible act that he couldn't undo, he made the mistake of committing another such act. We don't know what his final thoughts were, but by his self-destructive act, Judas eliminated the possibility of ever getting right with Christ the way he needed to.

To Learn More: Turn to the article about suicide on pages 322, 323. See also the key passage note at 1 Samuel 31:4 on page 386.

his wife sent to him, saying, "Have nothing to
do with that just Man, for I have suffered
many things today in a dream because of
Him."
20But the chief priests and elders persuaded
the multitudes that they should ask for Barabbas and destroy Jesus. 21The governor answered and said to them, "Which of the two
do you want me to release to you?"
They said, "Barabbas!"
22Pilate said to them, "What then shall I do
with Jesus who is called Christ?"
They all said to him, "Let Him be crucified!"
23Then the governor said, "Why, what evil
has He done?"
But they cried out all the more, saying, "Let
Him be crucified!"
24When Pilate saw that he could not prevail
at all, but rather *that* a tumult was rising, he
took water and washed *his* hands before the
multitude, saying, "I am innocent of the blood
of this just Person.[a] You see *to it.*"
25And all the people answered and said,
"His blood *be* on us and on our children."
26Then he released Barabbas to them; and
when he had scourged Jesus, he delivered
Him to be crucified.

The Soldiers Mock Jesus

27Then the soldiers of the governor took
Jesus into the Praetorium and gathered the
whole garrison around Him. 28And they
stripped Him and put a scarlet robe on Him.
29When they had twisted a crown of thorns,
they put *it* on His head, and a reed in His right
hand. And they bowed the knee before Him
and mocked Him, saying, "Hail, King of the
Jews!" 30Then they spat on Him, and took the
reed and struck Him on the head. 31And when
they had mocked Him, they took the robe off
Him, put His *own* clothes on Him, and led
Him away to be crucified.

The King on a Cross

32Now as they came out, they found a man
of Cyrene, Simon by name. Him they compelled to bear His cross. 33And when they had
come to a place called Golgotha, that is to say,
Place of a Skull, 34they gave Him sour[a] wine
mingled with gall to drink. But when He had
tasted *it*, He would not drink.
35Then they crucified Him, and divided His
garments, casting lots,[a] that it might be fulfilled which was spoken by the prophet:

"They divided My garments among them,
And for My clothing they cast lots."[b]

36Sitting down, they kept watch over Him
there. 37And they put up over His head the accusation written against Him:

THIS IS JESUS THE KING
OF THE JEWS.

38Then two robbers were crucified with Him,
one on the right and another on the left.
39And those who passed by blasphemed
Him, wagging their heads 40and saying, "You
who destroy the temple and build *it* in three
days, save Yourself! If You are the Son of God,
come down from the cross."
41Likewise the chief priests also, mocking
with the scribes and elders,[a] said, 42"He saved
others; Himself He cannot save. If He is the
King of Israel,[a] let Him now come down from
the cross, and we will believe Him.[b] 43He
trusted in God; let Him deliver Him now if He
will have Him; for He said, 'I am the Son of
God.' "
44Even the robbers who were crucified with
Him reviled Him with the same thing.

Jesus Dies on the Cross

45Now from the sixth hour until the ninth
hour there was darkness over all the land.
46And about the ninth hour Jesus cried out
with a loud voice, saying, "Eli, Eli, lama sabachthani?" that is, *"My God, My God, why
have You forsaken Me?"*[a]
47Some of those who stood there, when they
heard *that*, said, "This Man is calling for Elijah!" 48Immediately one of them ran and took
a sponge, filled *it* with sour wine and put *it* on
a reed, and offered it to Him to drink.
49The rest said, "Let Him alone; let us see if
Elijah will come to save Him."
50And Jesus cried out again with a loud
voice, and yielded up His spirit.
51Then, behold, the veil of the temple was
torn in two from top to bottom; and the earth
quaked, and the rocks were split, 52and the

27:24 [a]NU-Text omits *just.* **27:34** [a]NU-Text omits *sour.* **27:35** [a]NU-Text and M-Text omit the rest of this verse. [b]Psalm 22:18 **27:41** [a]M-Text reads *with the scribes, the Pharisees, and the elders.* **27:42** [a]NU-Text reads *He is the King of Israel!* [b]NU-Text and M-Text read *we will believe in Him.* **27:46** [a]Psalm 22:1

graves were opened; and many bodies of the
saints who had fallen asleep were raised;
[53]and coming out of the graves after His resurrection, they went into the holy city and appeared to many.
[54]So when the centurion and those with
him, who were guarding Jesus, saw the earthquake and the things that had happened, they
feared greatly, saying, "Truly this was the Son
of God!"
[55]And many women who followed Jesus
from Galilee, ministering to Him, were there
looking on from afar, [56]among whom were
Mary Magdalene, Mary the mother of James
and Joses,[a] and the mother of Zebedee's sons.

Jesus Buried in Joseph's Tomb

[57]Now when evening had come, there came
a rich man from Arimathea, named Joseph,
who himself had also become a disciple of
Jesus. [58]This man went to Pilate and asked for
the body of Jesus. Then Pilate commanded
the body to be given to him. [59]When Joseph
had taken the body, he wrapped it in a clean
linen cloth, [60]and laid it in his new tomb
which he had hewn out of the rock; and he
rolled a large stone against the door of the
tomb, and departed. [61]And Mary Magdalene
was there, and the other Mary, sitting opposite
the tomb.

Pilate Sets a Guard

[62]On the next day, which followed the Day
of Preparation, the chief priests and Pharisees
gathered together to Pilate, [63]saying, "Sir, we
remember, while He was still alive, how that
deceiver said, 'After three days I will rise.'
[64]Therefore command that the tomb be made
secure until the third day, lest His disciples
come by night[a] and steal Him *away*, and say to
the people, 'He has risen from the dead.' So
the last deception will be worse than the
first."
[65]Pilate said to them, "You have a guard; go
your way, make *it* as secure as you know
how." [66]So they went and made the tomb secure, sealing the stone and setting the guard.

He Is Risen

28 Now after the Sabbath, as the first *day*
of the week began to dawn, Mary Magdalene and the other Mary came to see the
tomb. [2]And behold, there was a great earthquake; for an angel of the Lord descended
from heaven, and came and rolled back the
stone from the door,[a] and sat on it. [3]His countenance was like lightning, and his clothing as
white as snow. [4]And the guards shook for fear
of him, and became like dead *men*.
[5]But the angel answered and said to the
women, "Do not be afraid, for I know that you
seek Jesus who was crucified. [6]He is not here;
for He is risen, as He said. Come, see the place
where the Lord lay. [7]And go quickly and tell
His disciples that He is risen from the dead,
and indeed He is going before you into Galilee; there you will see Him. Behold, I have
told you."
[8]So they went out quickly from the tomb
with fear and great joy, and ran to bring His
disciples word.

The Women Worship the Risen Lord

[9]And as they went to tell His disciples,[a] behold, Jesus met them, saying, "Rejoice!" So
they came and held Him by the feet and worshiped Him. [10]Then Jesus said to them, "Do

27:56 [a]NU-Text reads *Joseph.* **27:64** [a]NU-Text omits *by night.* **28:2** [a]NU-Text omits *from the door.* **28:9** [a]NU-Text omits the first clause of this verse.

SOUL NOTE

Committed to the Commission *(28:19, 20)* Jesus left His followers with an awesome responsibility: "Go therefore and make disciples of all the nations." We should take this responsibility seriously. His plan included telling people the Good News about Christ and then baptizing new believers. It also includes teaching them how to grow in their faith and building them up in their personal walk with God. Go, make disciples, baptize, and teach. God loves to share His message of hope through His people. We can do this because Jesus goes with us always.

Topic: Responsibility

not be afraid. Go *and* tell My brethren to go to Galilee, and there they will see Me."

The Soldiers Are Bribed

11Now while they were going, behold, some of the guard came into the city and reported to the chief priests all the things that had happened. 12When they had assembled with the elders and consulted together, they gave a large sum of money to the soldiers, 13saying, "Tell them, 'His disciples came at night and stole Him *away* while we slept.' 14And if this comes to the governor's ears, we will appease him and make you secure." 15So they took the money and did as they were instructed; and this saying is commonly reported among the Jews until this day.

> "Lo, I am with you always, even to the end of the age."
>
> MATTHEW 28:20

The Great Commission

16Then the eleven disciples went away into Galilee, to the mountain which Jesus had appointed for them. 17When they saw Him, they worshiped Him; but some doubted.

18And Jesus came and spoke to them, saying, "All authority has been given to Me in heaven and on earth. 19Go therefore[a] and make disciples of all the nations, baptizing them in the name of the Father and of the Son and of the Holy Spirit, 20teaching them to observe all things that I have commanded you; and lo, I am with you always, *even* to the end of the age." Amen.[a]

28:19 [a]M-Text omits *therefore*. **28:20** [a]NU-Text omits *Amen.*

Mark

When you're lonely, would you rather: (a) hear a sermon about friendship, or (b) go eat lunch with a caring friend? If you were sick would you prefer: (a) the latest edition of a medical journal, or (b) an appointment with a top-notch doctor? The old axiom is true: Actions speak louder than words. Nowhere is this better demonstrated than in the Gospel of Mark.

Mark's account of the life of Christ reads like a journalist's report—just the facts. With the apostle Peter as his primary source, Mark wrote to Roman Christians only two decades after the Lord's death and resurrection. Mark was not one of the original twelve disciples, but he knew Peter and accompanied Paul and Barnabas on the first missionary journey. Mark wrote this book to present Jesus as God's tireless, miracle-working Servant, committed to meeting people's physical and spiritual needs.

Mark begins his record with John the Baptist's sudden announcement of the Messiah's arrival. Mark portrays Jesus as always on the move. The "Son of Man" (a title that indicates the divine Christ's taking on human form) is shown going from town to town, meeting new people, healing the sick, confronting the skeptics, inviting the outcasts, and loving all.

Whatever the state of your soul, you need an intimate encounter with the compassionate Christ of Mark's Gospel. He "did not come to be served, but to serve" (10:45). Are you willing to let Him touch your life in a powerful way today?

SOUL CONCERN IN MARK

JOHN THE BAPTIST PREPARES THE WAY

1 The beginning of the gospel of Jesus Christ, the Son of God. 2As it is written in the Prophets:[a]

> *"Behold, I send My messenger before Your face,*
> *Who will prepare Your way before You."*[b]

3 *"The voice of one crying in the wilderness:*
> *'Prepare the way of the LORD;*
> *Make His paths straight.' "*[a]

4John came baptizing in the wilderness and preaching a baptism of repentance for the remission of sins. 5Then all the land of Judea, and those from Jerusalem, went out to him and were all baptized by him in the Jordan River, confessing their sins.

6Now John was clothed with camel's hair and with a leather belt around his waist, and he ate locusts and wild honey. 7And he preached, saying, "There comes One after me who is mightier than I, whose sandal strap I am not worthy to stoop down and loose. 8I indeed baptized you with water, but He will baptize you with the Holy Spirit."

JOHN BAPTIZES JESUS

9It came to pass in those days *that* Jesus came from Nazareth of Galilee, and was baptized by John in the Jordan. 10And immediately, coming up from[a] the water, He saw the heavens parting and the Spirit descending upon Him like a dove. 11Then a voice came from heaven, "You are My beloved Son, in whom I am well pleased."

SATAN TEMPTS JESUS

12Immediately the Spirit drove Him into the wilderness. 13And He was there in the wilderness forty days, tempted by Satan, and was with the wild beasts; and the angels ministered to Him.

JESUS BEGINS HIS GALILEAN MINISTRY

14Now after John was put in prison, Jesus came to Galilee, preaching the gospel of the kingdom[a] of God, 15and saying, "The time is fulfilled, and the kingdom of God is at hand. Repent, and believe in the gospel."

FOUR FISHERMEN CALLED AS DISCIPLES

16And as He walked by the Sea of Galilee, He saw Simon and Andrew his brother casting a net into the sea; for they were fishermen. 17Then Jesus said to them, "Follow Me, and I will make you become fishers of men." 18They immediately left their nets and followed Him.

19When He had gone a little farther from there, He saw James the *son* of Zebedee, and John his brother, who also *were* in the boat mending their nets. 20And immediately He called them, and they left their father Zebedee in the boat with the hired servants, and went after Him.

JESUS CASTS OUT AN UNCLEAN SPIRIT

21Then they went into Capernaum, and immediately on the Sabbath He entered the synagogue and taught. 22And they were astonished at His teaching, for He taught them as one having authority, and not as the scribes.

23Now there was a man in their synagogue with an unclean spirit. And he cried out, 24saying, "Let *us* alone! What have we to do with You, Jesus of Nazareth? Did You come to destroy us? I know who You are—the Holy One of God!"

25But Jesus rebuked him, saying, "Be quiet,

1:2 [a]NU-Text reads *Isaiah the prophet.* [b]Malachi 3:1 **1:3** [a]Isaiah 40:3 **1:10** [a]NU-Text reads *out of.* **1:14** [a]NU-Text omits *of the kingdom.*

SOUL NOTE

Immediately! *(1:16–18)* Simon and Andrew were casting their fishing nets into the sea when Jesus called them to drop everything and "become fishers of men." And they did: "They immediately left their nets and followed Him." Being a disciple, a follower of Jesus, means a radical change in life and focus. New believers may not have to leave a job, as these disciples did, but they may have to make other kinds of radical changes in order to follow their new Master. Jesus still says, "Follow Me." Nothing should keep us from going "immediately." **Topic: Change/Maturity**

and come out of him!" 26And when the unclean spirit had convulsed him and cried out
with a loud voice, he came out of him. 27Then
they were all amazed, so that they questioned
among themselves, saying, "What is this?
What new doctrine *is* this? For with authority[a]
He commands even the unclean spirits, and
they obey Him." 28And immediately His fame
spread throughout all the region around Galilee.

Peter's Mother-in-Law Healed

29Now as soon as they had come out of the
synagogue, they entered the house of Simon
and Andrew, with James
and John. 30But Simon's
wife's mother lay sick
with a fever, and they
told Him about her at
once. 31So He came and
took her by the hand
and lifted her up, and
immediately the fever
left her. And she served them.

Now in the morning, having risen a long while before daylight, He went out and departed to a solitary place; and there He prayed.
MARK 1:35

Many Healed After Sabbath Sunset

32At evening, when the sun had set, they
brought to Him all who were sick and those
who were demon-possessed. 33And the whole
city was gathered together at the door. 34Then
He healed many who were sick with various
diseases, and cast out many demons; and He
did not allow the demons to speak, because
they knew Him.

Preaching in Galilee

35Now in the morning, having risen a long
while before daylight, He went out and departed to a solitary place; and there He prayed.
36And Simon and those *who were* with Him
searched for Him. 37When they found Him, they
said to Him, "Everyone is looking for You."
38But He said to them, "Let us go into the
next towns, that I may preach there also, because for this purpose I have come forth."
39And He was preaching in their synagogues
throughout all Galilee, and casting out demons.

Jesus Cleanses a Leper

40Now a leper came to Him, imploring Him,
kneeling down to Him and saying to Him, "If
You are willing, You can make me clean."
41Then Jesus, moved with compassion,
stretched out *His* hand and touched him, and
said to him, "I am willing; be cleansed." 42As
soon as He had spoken,
immediately the leprosy
left him, and he was
cleansed. 43And He strictly
warned him and sent
him away at once, 44and
said to him, "See that
you say nothing to any-
one; but go your way,
show yourself to the priest, and offer for your
cleansing those things which Moses commanded, as a testimony to them."
45However, he went out and began to proclaim *it* freely, and to spread the matter, so
that Jesus could no longer openly enter the
city, but was outside in deserted places; and
they came to Him from every direction.

Jesus Forgives and Heals a Paralytic

2 And again He entered Capernaum after
some days, and it was heard that He was
in the house. 2Immediately[a] many gathered
together, so that there was no longer room to
receive *them*, not even near the door. And He
preached the word to them. 3Then they came

1:27 [a]NU-Text reads *What is this? A new doctrine with authority.* **2:2** [a]NU-Text omits *Immediately.*

SOUL NOTE

Heal Our Souls *(2:1–12)* Before addressing the paralyzed man's physical need, Jesus addressed his spiritual need and forgave his sins. The astounded scribes exclaimed that only God could forgive sins. Jesus proved that He could indeed forgive sins by healing the man, an act that they could see. That unmistakable miracle of physical healing proved Jesus' identity and power. God has the power to heal. He may not always heal our physical needs, but He will always heal our souls when we come to Him in faith. **Topic: Healing/Recovery**

to Him, bringing a paralytic who was carried
by four *men*. [4]And when they could not come
near Him because of the crowd, they uncovered the roof where He was. So when they had
broken through, they let down the bed on
which the paralytic was lying.
[5]When Jesus saw their faith, He said to the
paralytic, "Son, your sins are forgiven you."
[6]And some of the scribes were sitting there
and reasoning in their hearts, [7]"Why does this
Man speak blasphemies like this? Who can
forgive sins but God alone?"
[8]But immediately, when Jesus perceived in
His spirit that they reasoned thus within
themselves, He said to them, "Why do you
reason about these things in your hearts?
[9]Which is easier, to say to the paralytic, '*Your*
sins are forgiven you,' or to say, 'Arise, take up
your bed and walk'? [10]But that you may know
that the Son of Man has power on earth to forgive sins"—He said to the paralytic, [11]"I say to
you, arise, take up your bed, and go to your
house." [12]Immediately he arose, took up the
bed, and went out in the presence of them all,
so that all were amazed and glorified God,
saying, "We never saw *anything* like this!"

Matthew the Tax Collector

[13]Then He went out again by the sea; and all
the multitude came to Him, and He taught
them. [14]As He passed by, He saw Levi the *son*
of Alphaeus sitting at the tax office. And He
said to him, "Follow Me." So he arose and followed Him.
[15]Now it happened, as He was dining in
Levi's house, that many tax collectors and sinners also sat together with Jesus and His disciples; for there were many, and they followed
Him. [16]And when the scribes and[a] Pharisees
saw Him eating with the tax collectors and
sinners, they said to His disciples, "How *is it*
that He eats and drinks with tax collectors and
sinners?"
[17]When Jesus heard *it*, He said to them,
"Those who are well have no need of a physician, but those who are sick. I did not come
to call *the* righteous, but sinners, to repentance."[a]

Jesus Is Questioned About Fasting

[18]The disciples of John and of the Pharisees
were fasting. Then they came and said to Him,
"Why do the disciples of John and of the Pharisees fast, but Your disciples do not fast?"
[19]And Jesus said to them, "Can the friends
of the bridegroom fast while the bridegroom is
with them? As long as they have the bridegroom with them they cannot fast. [20]But the
days will come when the bridegroom will be
taken away from them, and then they will fast
in those days. [21]No one sews a piece of unshrunk cloth on an old garment; or else the
new piece pulls away from the old, and the
tear is made worse. [22]And no one puts new
wine into old wineskins; or else the new wine
bursts the wineskins, the wine is spilled, and
the wineskins are ruined. But new wine must
be put into new wineskins."

Jesus Is Lord of the Sabbath

[23]Now it happened that He went through
the grainfields on the Sabbath; and as they
went His disciples began to pluck the heads of
grain. [24]And the Pharisees said to Him, "Look,
why do they do what is not lawful on the Sabbath?"
[25]But He said to them, "Have you never read
what David did when he was in need and hungry, he and those with him: [26]how he went
into the house of God *in the days* of Abiathar
the high priest, and ate the showbread, which
is not lawful to eat except for the priests, and
also gave some to those who were with him?"
[27]And He said to them, "The Sabbath was
made for man, and not man for the Sabbath.
[28]Therefore the Son of Man is also Lord of the
Sabbath."

Healing on the Sabbath

3 And He entered the synagogue again, and
a man was there who had a withered
hand. [2]So they watched Him closely, whether
He would heal him on the Sabbath, so that
they might accuse Him. [3]And He said to the
man who had the withered hand, "Step forward." [4]Then He said to them, "Is it lawful on
the Sabbath to do good or to do evil, to save
life or to kill?" But they kept silent. [5]And when
He had looked around at them with anger, being grieved by the hardness of their hearts, He
said to the man, "Stretch out your hand." And
he stretched *it* out, and his hand was restored
as whole as the other.[a] [6]Then the Pharisees
went out and immediately plotted with the

2:16 [a]NU-Text reads *of the.* **2:17** [a]NU-Text omits *to repentance.* **3:5** [a]NU-Text omits *as whole as the other.*

Herodians against Him, how they might destroy Him.

A Great Multitude Follows Jesus

[7]But Jesus withdrew with His disciples to the sea. And a great multitude from Galilee followed Him, and from Judea [8]and Jerusalem and Idumea and beyond the Jordan; and those from Tyre and Sidon, a great multitude, when they heard how many things He was doing, came to Him. [9]So He told His disciples that a small boat should be kept ready for Him because of the multitude, lest they should crush Him. [10]For He healed many, so that as many as had afflictions pressed about Him to touch Him. [11]And the unclean spirits, whenever they saw Him, fell down before Him and cried out, saying, "You are the Son of God." [12]But He sternly warned them that they should not make Him known.

The Twelve Apostles

[13]And He went up on the mountain and called to *Him* those He Himself wanted. And they came to Him. [14]Then He appointed twelve,[a] that they might be with Him and that He might send them out to preach, [15]and to have power to heal sicknesses and[a] to cast out demons: [16]Simon,[a] to whom He gave the name Peter; [17]James the *son* of Zebedee and John the brother of James, to whom He gave the name Boanerges, that is, "Sons of Thunder"; [18]Andrew, Philip, Bartholomew, Matthew, Thomas, James the *son* of Alphaeus, Thaddaeus, Simon the Cananite; [19]and Judas Iscariot, who also betrayed Him. And they went into a house.

A House Divided Cannot Stand

[20]Then the multitude came together again, so that they could not so much as eat bread. [21]But when His own people heard *about this,* they went out to lay hold of Him, for they said, "He is out of His mind."

[22]And the scribes who came down from Jerusalem said, "He has Beelzebub," and, "By the ruler of the demons He casts out demons."

[23]So He called them to *Himself* and said to them in parables: "How can Satan cast out Satan? [24]If a kingdom is divided against itself, that kingdom cannot stand. [25]And if a house is divided against itself, that house cannot stand. [26]And if Satan has risen up against himself, and is divided, he cannot stand, but has an end. [27]No one can enter a strong man's house and plunder his goods, unless he first binds the strong man. And then he will plunder his house.

The Unpardonable Sin

[28]"Assuredly, I say to you, all sins will be forgiven the sons of men, and whatever blasphemies they may utter; [29]but he who blasphemes against the Holy Spirit never has forgiveness, but is subject to eternal condemnation"—[30]because they said, "He has an unclean spirit."

Jesus' Mother and Brothers Send for Him

[31]Then His brothers and His mother came, and standing outside they sent to Him, calling Him. [32]And a multitude was sitting around Him; and they said to Him, "Look, Your mother and Your brothers[a] are outside seeking You."

[33]But He answered them, saying, "Who is

3:14 [a]NU-Text adds *whom He also named apostles.* **3:15** [a]NU-Text omits *to heal sicknesses and.* **3:16** [a]NU-Text reads *and He appointed the twelve: Simon. . . .* **3:32** [a]NU-Text and M-Text add *and Your sisters.*

SOUL NOTE

Follow the Leader *(3:13–19)* Jesus poured His most intense time and teaching into twelve disciples who would carry on His ministry after He was gone. Jesus mentored His followers, teaching them the truth and strengthening their faith. These men were not perfect, but because of their love for and faith in Jesus, they went on to turn the world upside down. Likewise, new believers need training so that they can grow strong in their faith. As we share our faith and as people come to salvation, we must be committed to mentoring them so that they can grow strong in the faith.

Topic: Mentoring

My mother, or My brothers?" 34And He looked around in a circle at those who sat about Him, and said, "Here are My mother and My brothers! 35For whoever does the will of God is My brother and My sister and mother."

The Parable of the Sower

4 And again He began to teach by the sea. And a great multitude was gathered to Him, so that He got into a boat and sat *in it* on the sea; and the whole multitude was on the land facing the sea. 2Then He taught them many things by parables, and said to them in His teaching:

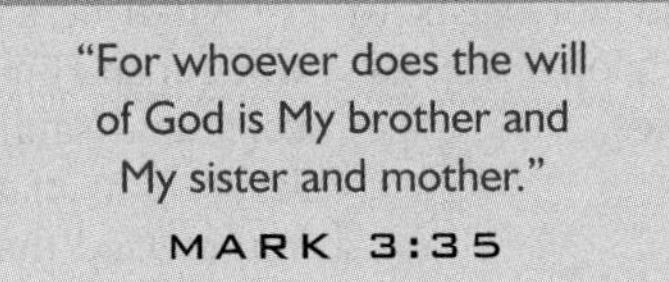
"For whoever does the will of God is My brother and My sister and mother."
MARK 3:35

3"Listen! Behold, a sower went out to sow. 4And it happened, as he sowed, *that* some *seed* fell by the wayside; and the birds of the air[a] came and devoured it. 5Some fell on stony ground, where it did not have much earth; and immediately it sprang up because it had no depth of earth. 6But when the sun was up it was scorched, and because it had no root it withered away. 7And some *seed* fell among thorns; and the thorns grew up and choked it, and it yielded no crop. 8But other *seed* fell on good ground and yielded a crop that sprang up, increased and produced: some thirtyfold, some sixty, and some a hundred."

9And He said to them,[a] "He who has ears to hear, let him hear!"

The Purpose of Parables

10But when He was alone, those around Him with the twelve asked Him about the parable. 11And He said to them, "To you it has been given to know the mystery of the kingdom of God; but to those who are outside, all things come in parables, 12so that

'Seeing they may see and not perceive,
And hearing they may hear and not
understand;
Lest they should turn,
And their sins be forgiven them.' "[a]

The Parable of the Sower Explained

13And He said to them, "Do you not understand this parable? How then will you understand all the parables? 14The sower sows the word. 15And these are the ones by the wayside where the word is sown. When they hear, Satan comes immediately and takes away the word that was sown in their hearts. 16These likewise are the ones sown on stony ground who, when they hear the word, immediately receive it with gladness; 17and they have no root in themselves, and so endure only for a time. Afterward, when tribulation or persecution arises for the word's sake, immediately they stumble. 18Now these are the ones sown among thorns; *they are* the ones who hear the word, 19and the cares of this world, the deceitfulness of riches, and the desires for other things entering in choke the word, and it becomes unfruitful. 20But these are the ones sown on good ground, those who hear the word, accept *it*, and bear fruit: some thirtyfold, some sixty, and some a hundred."

Light Under a Basket

21Also He said to them, "Is a lamp brought to be put under a basket or under a bed? Is it not to be set on a lampstand? 22For there is nothing hidden which will not be revealed, nor has anything been kept secret but that it should come to light. 23If anyone has ears to hear, let him hear."

24Then He said to them, "Take heed what you hear. With the same measure you use, it will be measured to you; and to you who hear, more will be given. 25For whoever has, to him more will be given; but whoever does not have, even what he has will be taken away from him."

The Parable of the Growing Seed

26And He said, "The kingdom of God is as if a man should scatter seed on the ground, 27and should sleep by night and rise by day, and the seed should sprout and grow, he himself does not know how. 28For the earth yields crops by itself: first the blade, then the head, after that the full grain in the head. 29But when the grain ripens, immediately he puts in the sickle, because the harvest has come."

The Parable of the Mustard Seed

30Then He said, "To what shall we liken the kingdom of God? Or with what parable shall

---

4:4 [a]NU-Text and M-Text omit *of the air.* **4:9** [a]NU-Text and M-Text omit *to them.* **4:12** [a]Isaiah 6:9, 10

we picture it? 31*It is* like a mustard seed which, when it is sown on the ground, is smaller than all the seeds on earth; 32but when it is sown, it grows up and becomes greater than all herbs, and shoots out large branches, so that the birds of the air may nest under its shade."

Jesus' Use of Parables

33And with many such parables He spoke the word to them as they were able to hear *it*. 34But without a parable He did not speak to them. And when they were alone, He explained all things to His disciples.

Wind and Wave Obey Jesus

35On the same day, when evening had come, He said to them, "Let us cross over to the other side." 36Now when they had left the multitude, they took Him along in the boat as He was. And other little boats were also with Him. 37And a great windstorm arose, and the waves beat into the boat, so that it was already filling. 38But He was in the stern, asleep on a pillow. And they awoke Him and said to Him, "Teacher, do You not care that we are perishing?"

39Then He arose and rebuked the wind, and said to the sea, "Peace, be still!" And the wind ceased and there was a great calm. 40But He said to them, "Why are you so fearful? How *is it* that you have no faith?"[a] 41And they feared exceedingly, and said to one another, "Who can this be, that even the wind and the sea obey Him!"

> But He said to them, "Why are you so fearful? How is it that you have no faith?"
> MARK 4:40

A Demon-Possessed Man Healed

5 Then they came to the other side of the sea, to the country of the Gadarenes.[a] 2And when He had come out of the boat, immediately there met Him out of the tombs a man with an unclean spirit, 3who had *his* dwelling among the tombs; and no one could bind him,[a] not even with chains, 4because he had often been bound with shackles and chains. And the chains had been pulled apart by him, and the shackles broken in pieces; neither could anyone tame him. 5And always, night and day, he was in the mountains and in the tombs, crying out and cutting himself with stones.

6When he saw Jesus from afar, he ran and worshiped Him. 7And he cried out with a loud voice and said, "What have I to do with You, Jesus, Son of the Most High God? I implore You by God that You do not torment me." 8For He said to him, "Come out of the man, unclean spirit!" 9Then He asked him, "What *is* your name?"

And he answered, saying, "My name *is* Legion; for we are many." 10Also he begged Him earnestly that He would not send them out of the country.

11Now a large herd of swine was feeding there near the mountains. 12So all the demons begged Him, saying, "Send us to the swine, that we may enter them." 13And at once Jesus[a] gave them permission. Then the unclean spirits went out and entered the swine (there were about two thousand); and the herd ran violently down the steep place into the sea, and drowned in the sea.

14So those who fed the swine fled, and they told *it* in the city and in the country. And they went out to see what it was that had happened. 15Then they came to Jesus, and saw

4:40 [a]NU-Text reads *Have you still no faith?* **5:1** [a]NU-Text reads *Gerasenes.* **5:3** [a]NU-Text adds *anymore.* **5:13** [a]NU-Text reads *And He gave.*

SOUL NOTE

Rock the Boat *(4:35–41)* Jesus and the disciples got into a boat and began to cross the Sea of Galilee. A storm suddenly arose and the boat began filling with water. Jesus was so exhausted, however, that He slept soundly. When the terrified disciples awoke Him, Jesus stood up and calmed the storm. The disciples were stunned. "How is it that you have no faith?" Jesus asked. He was with them, yet they did not trust Him. When our "boats" are rocked by the storms of life, do we believe that Jesus can bring calm? Or would He question our faith in Him? **Topic: Faith**

the one *who had been* demon-possessed and had the legion, sitting and clothed and in his right mind. And they were afraid. [16]And those who saw it told them how it happened to him *who had been* demon-possessed, and about the swine. [17]Then they began to plead with Him to depart from their region.

[18]And when He got into the boat, he who had been demon-possessed begged Him that he might be with Him. [19]However, Jesus did not permit him, but said to him, "Go home to your friends, and tell them what great things the Lord has done for you, and how He has had compassion on you." [20]And he departed and began to proclaim in Decapolis all that Jesus had done for him; and all marveled.

A Girl Restored to Life and a Woman Healed

[21]Now when Jesus had crossed over again by boat to the other side, a great multitude gathered to Him; and He was by the sea. [22]And behold, one of the rulers of the synagogue came, Jairus by name. And when he saw Him, he fell at His feet [23]and begged Him earnestly, saying, "My little daughter lies at the point of death. Come and lay Your hands on her, that she may be healed, and she will live." [24]So *Jesus* went with him, and a great multitude followed Him and thronged Him.

[25]Now a certain woman had a flow of blood for twelve years, [26]and had suffered many things from many physicians. She had spent all that she had and was no better, but rather grew worse. [27]When she heard about Jesus, she came behind *Him* in the crowd and touched His garment. [28]For she said, "If only I may touch His clothes, I shall be made well."

[29]Immediately the fountain of her blood was dried up, and she felt in *her* body that she was healed of the affliction. [30]And Jesus, immediately knowing in Himself that power had

PERSONALITY PROFILE

Hope

HOPE FOR A WOMAN IN NEED

(MARK 5:25–27)

Alone, sick, and seemingly without hope, this woman with a "flow of blood for twelve years" and who "had suffered many things from many physicians" expected to live in pain and as an outcast until she died. Then along came Jesus.

This woman was not supposed to be in the crowd that day. Because of her condition of constant bleeding (perhaps a uterine disorder), she was in a continual state of uncleanness according to Jewish law. She was not to be in public because others might touch her and become unclean themselves.

But she heard that Jesus was coming to town, and she knew that He could heal her. She merely wanted to touch His clothes, knowing that she would be made well. She probably wanted to come and go unnoticed so that the jostling crowd would not be angered that she had come among them. But this act of reaching out and touching Jesus' garment also showed the depth of her faith.

Immediately the woman was healed. Jesus knew who had touched Him, of course, but he asked the question, "Who touched Me?" so that she could show her faith. Then He told her, "Your faith has made you well. Go in peace, and be healed of your affliction" (Mark 5:34).

What made that woman go to Jesus? Faith that He could do for her what He had done for so many. Her hope was not the kind of hope that says, "Maybe it will happen; I hope so." Her hope said, "I know He can heal me."

Jesus meets us however we come to Him, with whatever problem. Our hope is in Him; not because we wonder if He will help us, but because we *know* He will help us. Jesus always responds to those who hope in Him, no matter how great or how small they are. He will do more than we can imagine.

To Learn More: Turn to the article about hope on pages 1000, 1001. See also the key passage note at Jeremiah 29:11–13 on page 999.

gone out of Him, turned around in the crowd
and said, "Who touched My clothes?"
[31]But His disciples said to Him, "You see the
multitude thronging You, and You say, 'Who
touched Me?' "
[32]And He looked around to see her who had
done this thing. [33]But the woman, fearing and
trembling, knowing what had happened to
her, came and fell down before Him and told
Him the whole truth. [34]And He said to her,
"Daughter, your faith has made you well. Go
in peace, and be healed of your affliction."
[35]While He was still speaking, *some* came
from the ruler of the synagogue's *house* who
said, "Your daughter is dead. Why trouble the
Teacher any further?"
[36]As soon as Jesus heard the word that was
spoken, He said to the ruler of the synagogue,
"Do not be afraid; only believe." [37]And He
permitted no one to follow Him except Peter,
James, and John the brother of James. [38]Then
He came to the house of the ruler of the synagogue, and saw a tumult and those who wept
and wailed loudly. [39]When He came in, He
said to them, "Why make this commotion and
weep? The child is not dead, but sleeping."
[40]And they ridiculed Him. But when He had
put them all outside, He took the father and
the mother of the child, and those *who were*
with Him, and entered where the child was
lying. [41]Then He took the child by the hand,
and said to her, "Talitha, cumi," which is
translated, "Little girl, I say to you, arise."
[42]Immediately the girl arose and walked, for
she was twelve years *of age*. And they were
overcome with great amazement. [43]But He
commanded them strictly that no one should
know it, and said that *something* should be
given her to eat.

JESUS REJECTED AT NAZARETH

6 Then He went out from there and came to
His own country, and His disciples followed Him. [2]And when the Sabbath had
come, He began to teach in the synagogue.
And many hearing *Him* were astonished, saying, "Where *did* this Man *get* these things?
And what wisdom *is* this which is given to
Him, that such mighty works are performed
by His hands! [3]Is this not the carpenter, the
Son of Mary, and brother of James, Joses, Judas, and Simon? And are not His sisters here
with us?" So they were offended at Him.
[4]But Jesus said to them, "A prophet is not
without honor except in his own country,
among his own relatives, and in his own
house." [5]Now He could do no mighty work
there, except that He laid His hands on a few
sick people and healed *them*. [6]And He marveled because of their unbelief. Then He went
about the villages in a circuit, teaching.

SENDING OUT THE TWELVE

[7]And He called the twelve to *Himself*, and
began to send them out two *by* two, and gave
them power over unclean spirits. [8]He commanded them to take nothing for the journey
except a staff—no bag, no bread, no copper in
their money belts—[9]but to wear sandals, and
not to put on two tunics.
[10]Also He said to them, "In whatever place
you enter a house, stay there till you depart
from that place. [11]And whoever[a] will not receive you nor hear you, when you depart from
there, shake off the dust under your feet as a
testimony against them.[b] Assuredly, I say to
you, it will be more tolerable for Sodom and
Gomorrah in the day of judgment than for that
city!"
[12]So they went out and preached that *people*
should repent. [13]And they cast out many demons, and anointed with oil many who were
sick, and healed *them*.

JOHN THE BAPTIST BEHEADED

[14]Now King Herod heard *of Him*, for His
name had become well known. And he said,
"John the Baptist is risen from the dead, and
therefore these powers are at work in him."
[15]Others said, "It is Elijah."
And others said, "It is the Prophet, or[a] like
one of the prophets."
[16]But when Herod heard, he said, "This is
John, whom I beheaded; he has been raised
from the dead!" [17]For Herod himself had sent
and laid hold of John, and bound him in prison for the sake of Herodias, his brother
Philip's wife; for he had married her. [18]Be-
cause John had said to Herod, "It is not lawful
for you to have your brother's wife."
[19]Therefore Herodias held it against him
and wanted to kill him, but she could not;
[20]for Herod feared John, knowing that he *was*
a just and holy man, and he protected him.

6:11 [a]NU-Text reads *whatever place.* [b]NU-Text omits the rest of this verse. **6:15** [a]NU-Text and M-Text omit *or.*

And when he heard him, he did many things,
and heard him gladly.
21 Then an opportune day came when Herod
on his birthday gave a feast for his nobles, the
high officers, and the chief *men* of Galilee.
22 And when Herodias' daughter herself came
in and danced, and pleased Herod and those
who sat with him, the king said to the girl,
"Ask me whatever you want, and I will give *it*
to you." 23 He also swore to her, "Whatever
you ask me, I will give you, up to half my
kingdom."
24 So she went out and said to her mother,
"What shall I ask?"
And she said, "The head of John the Baptist!"
25 Immediately she came in with haste to the
king and asked, saying, "I want you to give me
at once the head of John the Baptist on a platter."
26 And the king was exceedingly sorry; *yet,*
because of the oaths and because of those
who sat with him, he did not want to refuse
her. 27 Immediately the king sent an execu-
tioner and commanded his head to be
brought. And he went and beheaded him in
prison, 28 brought his head on a platter, and
gave it to the girl; and the girl gave it to her
mother. 29 When his disciples heard *of it,* they
came and took away his corpse and laid it in a
tomb.

Feeding the Five Thousand

30 Then the apostles gathered to Jesus and
told Him all things, both what they had done
and what they had taught. 31 And He said to
them, "Come aside by yourselves to a deserted place and rest a while." For there were
many coming and going, and they did not
even have time to eat. 32 So they departed to a
deserted place in the boat by themselves.
33 But the multitudes[a] saw them departing,
and many knew Him and ran there on foot
from all the cities. They arrived before them
and came together to Him. 34 And Jesus, when
He came out, saw a great multitude and was
moved with compassion for them, because
they were like sheep not having a shepherd.
So He began to teach them many things.
35 When the day was now far spent, His disciples came to Him and said, "This is a deserted
place, and already the hour *is* late. 36 Send
them away, that they may go into the surrounding country and villages and buy themselves bread;[a] for they have nothing to eat."
37 But He answered and said to them, "You
give them something to eat."
And they said to Him, "Shall we go and buy
two hundred denarii worth of bread and give
them *something* to eat?"
38 But He said to them, "How many loaves
do you have? Go and see."
And when they found out they said, "Five,
and two fish."
39 Then He commanded them to make them
all sit down in groups on the green grass. 40 So
they sat down in ranks, in hundreds and in fifties. 41 And when He had taken the five loaves
and the two fish, He looked up to heaven,
blessed and broke the loaves, and gave *them*
to His disciples to set before them; and the
two fish He divided among *them* all. 42 So they
all ate and were filled. 43 And they took up
twelve baskets full of fragments and of the
fish. 44 Now those who had eaten the loaves
were about[a] five thousand men.

Jesus Walks on the Sea

45 Immediately He made His disciples get
into the boat and go before Him to the other
side, to Bethsaida, while He sent the multitude away. 46 And when He had sent them

6:33 [a]NU-Text and M-Text read *they.* **6:36** [a]NU-Text reads *something to eat* and omits the rest of this verse. **6:44** [a]NU-Text and M-Text omit *about.*

SOUL NOTE

Rest Stop *(6:31, 32)* After an exhausting time of ministry, Jesus invited His disciples to "come aside by yourselves to a deserted place and rest a while." They took a break from their ministry in order to refresh themselves. A hectic schedule takes a physical, emotional, and spiritual toll on us. God knows that we need to come aside and rest a while so that we don't burn out. He will refresh us so that we can continue to serve Him. Rest and refreshment is not wasted time. **Topic: Burnout**

away, He departed to the mountain to pray.
47Now when evening came, the boat was in
the middle of the sea; and He *was* alone on the
land. 48Then He saw them straining at rowing,
for the wind was against them. Now about the
fourth watch of the night He came to them,
walking on the sea, and would have passed
them by. 49And when they saw Him walking
on the sea, they supposed it was a ghost, and
cried out; 50for they all saw Him and were
troubled. But immediately He talked with
them and said to them, "Be of good cheer! It is
I; do not be afraid." 51Then He went up into
the boat to them, and the wind ceased. And
they were greatly amazed in themselves beyond measure, and marveled. 52For they had
not understood about the loaves, because
their heart was hardened.

Many Touch Him and Are Made Well

53When they had crossed over, they came to
the land of Gennesaret and anchored there.
54And when they came out of the boat, immediately the people recognized Him, 55ran
through that whole surrounding region, and
began to carry about on beds those who were
sick to wherever they heard He was. 56Wher-
ever He entered, into villages, cities, or the
country, they laid the sick in the marketplaces, and begged Him that they might just
touch the hem of His garment. And as many
as touched Him were made well.

Defilement Comes from Within

7 Then the Pharisees and some of the
scribes came together to Him, having
come from Jerusalem. 2Now when[a] they saw
some of His disciples eat bread with defiled,
that is, with unwashed hands, they found
fault. 3For the Pharisees and all the Jews do
not eat unless they wash *their* hands in a special way, holding the tradition of the elders.
4*When they come* from the marketplace, they
do not eat unless they wash. And there are
many other things which they have received
and hold, *like* the washing of cups, pitchers,
copper vessels, and couches.

5Then the Pharisees and scribes asked Him,
"Why do Your disciples not walk according to
the tradition of the elders, but eat bread with
unwashed hands?"

6He answered and said to them, "Well did
Isaiah prophesy of you hypocrites, as it is
written:

'This people honors Me with their lips,
But their heart is far from Me.
7 *And in vain they worship Me,*
Teaching as doctrines the
commandments of men.'[a]

8For laying aside the commandment of God,
you hold the tradition of men[a]—the washing
of pitchers and cups, and many other such
things you do."

9He said to them, "*All too* well you reject the
commandment of God, that you may keep
your tradition. 10For Moses said, *'Honor your
father and your mother'*;[a] and, *'He who
curses father or mother, let him be put to
death.'*[b] 11But you say, 'If a man says to his father or mother, "Whatever profit you might
have received from me *is* Corban"—' (that is,
a gift *to God*), 12then you no longer let him do
anything for his father or his mother, 13making
the word of God of no effect through your tradition which you have handed down. And
many such things you do."

14When He had called all the multitude to
Himself, He said to them, "Hear Me, everyone,
and understand: 15There is nothing that enters
a man from outside which can defile him; but
the things which come out of him, those are
the things that defile a man. 16If anyone has
ears to hear, let him hear!"[a]

17When He had entered a house away from
the crowd, His disciples asked Him concerning the parable. 18So He said to them, "Are
you thus without understanding also? Do
you not perceive that whatever enters a man
from outside cannot defile him, 19because it
does not enter his heart but his stomach,
and is eliminated, *thus* purifying all foods?"[a]
20And He said, "What comes out of a man,
that defiles a man. 21For from within, out of
the heart of men, proceed evil thoughts,
adulteries, fornications, murders, 22thefts,
covetousness, wickedness, deceit, lewdness,
an evil eye, blasphemy, pride, foolishness. 23All
these evil things come from within and defile a
man."

7:2 [a]NU-Text omits *when* and *they found fault.* **7:7** [a]Isaiah 29:13 **7:8** [a]NU-Text omits the rest of this verse. **7:10** [a]Exodus 20:12; Deuteronomy 5:16 [b]Exodus 21:17 **7:16** [a]NU-Text omits this verse. **7:19** [a]NU-Text ends quotation with *eliminated,* setting off the final clause as Mark's comment that Jesus has declared all foods clean.

A Gentile Shows Her Faith

[24]From there He arose and went to the region of Tyre and Sidon.[a] And He entered a house and wanted no one to know *it*, but He could not be hidden. [25]For a woman whose young daughter had an unclean spirit heard about Him, and she came and fell at His feet. [26]The woman was a Greek, a Syro-Phoenician by birth, and she kept asking Him to cast the demon out of her daughter. [27]But Jesus said to her, "Let the children be filled first, for it is not good to take the children's bread and throw *it* to the little dogs."

[28]And she answered and said to Him, "Yes, Lord, yet even the little dogs under the table eat from the children's crumbs."

[29]Then He said to her, "For this saying go your way; the demon has gone out of your daughter."

[30]And when she had come to her house, she found the demon gone out, and her daughter lying on the bed.

Jesus Heals a Deaf-Mute

[31]Again, departing from the region of Tyre and Sidon, He came through the midst of the region of Decapolis to the Sea of Galilee. [32]Then they brought to Him one who was deaf and had an impediment in his speech, and they begged Him to put His hand on him. [33]And He took him aside from the multitude, and put His fingers in his ears, and He spat and touched his tongue. [34]Then, looking up to heaven, He sighed, and said to him, "Ephphatha," that is, "Be opened."

[35]Immediately his ears were opened, and the impediment of his tongue was loosed, and he spoke plainly. [36]Then He commanded them that they should tell no one; but the more He commanded them, the more widely they proclaimed *it*. [37]And they were astonished beyond measure, saying, "He has done all things well. He makes both the deaf to hear and the mute to speak."

Feeding the Four Thousand

8 In those days, the multitude being very great and having nothing to eat, Jesus called His disciples *to Him* and said to them, [2]"I have compassion on the multitude, because they have now continued with Me three days and have nothing to eat. [3]And if I send them away hungry to their own houses, they will faint on the way; for some of them have come from afar."

[4]Then His disciples answered Him, "How can one satisfy these people with bread here in the wilderness?"

[5]He asked them, "How many loaves do you have?"

And they said, "Seven."

[6]So He commanded the multitude to sit down on the ground. And He took the seven loaves and gave thanks, broke *them* and gave *them* to His disciples to set before *them*; and they set *them* before the multitude. [7]They also had a few small fish; and having blessed them, He said to set them also before *them*. [8]So they ate and were filled, and they took up seven large baskets of leftover fragments. [9]Now those who had eaten were about four thousand. And He sent them away, [10]immediately got into the boat with His disciples, and came to the region of Dalmanutha.

The Pharisees Seek a Sign

[11]Then the Pharisees came out and began to dispute with Him, seeking from Him a sign from heaven, testing Him. [12]But He sighed deeply in His spirit, and said, "Why does this generation seek a sign? Assuredly, I say to you, no sign shall be given to this generation."

Beware of the Leaven of the Pharisees and Herod

[13]And He left them, and getting into the boat again, departed to the other side. [14]Now the disciples[a] had forgotten to take bread, and they did not have more than one loaf with them in the boat. [15]Then He charged them, saying, "Take heed, beware of the leaven of the Pharisees and the leaven of Herod."

[16]And they reasoned among themselves, saying, "*It is* because we have no bread."

[17]But Jesus, being aware of *it*, said to them, "Why do you reason because you have no bread? Do you not yet perceive nor understand? Is your heart still[a] hardened? [18]Having eyes, do you not see? And having ears, do you not hear? And do you not remember? [19]When I broke the five loaves for the five thousand, how many baskets full of fragments did you take up?"

7:24 [a]NU-Text omits *and Sidon.* **8:14** [a]NU-Text and M-Text read *they.* **8:17** [a]NU-Text omits *still.*

They said to Him, “Twelve.”
20“Also, when I broke the seven for the four
thousand, how many large baskets full of
fragments did you take up?”
And they said, “Seven.”
21So He said to them, “How *is it* you do not
understand?”

A Blind Man Healed at Bethsaida

22Then He came to Bethsaida; and they
brought a blind man to Him, and begged Him
to touch him. 23So He took the blind man by
the hand and led him out of the town. And
when He had spit on his eyes and put His
hands on him, He asked him if he saw anything.
24And he looked up and said, “I see men
like trees, walking.”
25Then He put *His* hands on his eyes again
and made him look up. And he was restored
and saw everyone clearly. 26Then He sent him
away to his house, saying, “Neither go into
the town, nor tell anyone in the town.”[a]

Peter Confesses Jesus as the Christ

27Now Jesus and His disciples went out to
the towns of Caesarea Philippi; and on the
road He asked His disciples, saying to them,
“Who do men say that I am?”
28So they answered, “John the Baptist; but
some *say*, Elijah; and others, one of the prophets.”
29He said to them, “But who do you say that
I am?”
Peter answered and said to Him, “You are
the Christ.”
30Then He strictly warned them that they
should tell no one about Him.

Jesus Predicts His Death and Resurrection

31And He began to teach them that the Son of
Man must suffer many things, and be rejected
by the elders and chief priests and scribes, and
be killed, and after three days rise again. 32He
spoke this word openly. Then Peter took Him
aside and began to rebuke Him. 33But when
He had turned around and looked at His disciples, He rebuked Peter, saying, “Get behind
Me, Satan! For you are not mindful of the
things of God, but the things of men.”

Take Up the Cross and Follow Him

34When He had called the people to *Himself*, with His disciples also, He said to them,
“Whoever desires to come after Me, let him
deny himself, and take up his cross, and follow Me. 35For whoever desires to save his life
will lose it, but whoever loses his life for My
sake and the gospel’s will save it. 36For what
will it profit a man if he gains the whole
world, and loses his own soul? 37Or what will
a man give in exchange for his soul? 38For
whoever is ashamed of Me and My words in
this adulterous and sinful generation, of him
the Son of Man also will be ashamed when He
comes in the glory of His Father with the holy
angels.”

Jesus Transfigured on the Mount

9 And He said to them, “Assuredly, I say to
you that there are some standing here
who will not taste death till they see the kingdom of God present with power.”
2Now after six days Jesus took Peter, James,
and John, and led them up on a high mountain apart by themselves; and He was transfigured before them. 3His clothes became
shining, exceedingly white, like snow, such as
no launderer on earth can whiten them. 4And
Elijah appeared to them with Moses, and they
were talking with Jesus. 5Then Peter answered
and said to Jesus, “Rabbi, it is good for us to
be here; and let us make three tabernacles:
one for You, one for Moses, and one for Elijah”— 6because he did not know what to say,
for they were greatly afraid.
7And a cloud came and overshadowed
them; and a voice came out of the cloud, saying, “This is My beloved Son. Hear Him!”
8Suddenly, when they had looked around,
they saw no one anymore, but only Jesus with
themselves.
9Now as they came down from the mountain, He commanded them that they should
tell no one the things they had seen, till the
Son of Man had risen from the dead. 10So they
kept this word to themselves, questioning
what the rising from the dead meant.
11And they asked Him, saying, “Why do the
scribes say that Elijah must come first?”
12Then He answered and told them, “Indeed,
Elijah is coming first and restores all things.
And how is it written concerning the Son of
Man, that He must suffer many things and be
treated with contempt? 13But I say to you that

8:26 [a]NU-Text reads *“Do not even go into the town.”*

Elijah has also come, and they did to him whatever they wished, as it is written of him."

A Boy Is Healed

14And when He came to the disciples, He saw a great multitude around them, and scribes disputing with them. 15Immediately, when they saw Him, all the people were greatly amazed, and running to *Him*, greeted Him. 16And He asked the scribes, "What are you discussing with them?"

17Then one of the crowd answered and said, "Teacher, I brought You my son, who has a mute spirit. 18And wherever it seizes him, it throws him down; he foams at the mouth, gnashes his teeth, and becomes rigid. So I spoke to Your disciples, that they should cast it out, but they could not."

19He answered him and said, "O faithless generation, how long shall I be with you? How long shall I bear with you? Bring him to Me." 20Then they brought him to Him. And when he saw Him, immediately the spirit convulsed him, and he fell on the ground and wallowed, foaming at the mouth.

21So He asked his father, "How long has this been happening to him?"

And he said, "From childhood. 22And often he has thrown him both into the fire and into the water to destroy him. But if You can do anything, have compassion on us and help us."

23Jesus said to him, "If you can believe,[a] all things *are* possible to him who believes."

24Immediately the father of the child cried out and said with tears, "Lord, I believe; help my unbelief!"

25When Jesus saw that the people came running together, He rebuked the unclean spirit, saying to it, "Deaf and dumb spirit, I command you, come out of him and enter him no more!" 26Then *the spirit* cried out, convulsed him greatly, and came out of him. And he became as one dead, so that many said, "He is dead." 27But Jesus took him by the hand and lifted him up, and he arose.

28And when He had come into the house, His disciples asked Him privately, "Why could we not cast it out?"

29So He said to them, "This kind can come out by nothing but prayer and fasting."[a]

Jesus Again Predicts His Death and Resurrection

30Then they departed from there and passed through Galilee, and He did not want anyone

9:23 [a]NU-Text reads *" 'If You can!' All things. . . ."* **9:29** [a]NU-Text omits *and fasting.*

SOUL NOTE

Just Believe *(9:23)* A desperate father sought healing for his son, pleading, "If You can do anything, have compassion on us and help us" (9:22). Jesus answered, "If you can believe, all things are possible to him who believes." Belief cannot make things happen apart from the sovereign will of God. Within the sovereign will of God, however, anything *is* possible to those who believe. When we face difficult situations, we must trust God, believing that He loves us and cares for us as a loving Father. That belief makes all the difference. **Topic: Belief**

SOUL NOTE

Help! *(9:24)* "Lord, I believe; help my unbelief!" This was an honest response from the heart of a desperate father who wanted to believe that Jesus could do the impossible. There may come times when we may believe God up to a certain point but then need His grace to enable us to deal with our unbelief as well. At times, our faith may become shadowed by worry or fear. We want to believe, but too much logic or too much emotion clouds our faith. In those times, we can tell God, "I do believe, Lord, but help my unbelief." **Topic: Belief**

to know *it*. [31]For He taught His disciples and
said to them, "The Son of Man is being betrayed into the hands of men, and they will
kill Him. And after He is killed, He will rise
the third day." [32]But they did not understand
this saying, and were afraid to ask Him.

Who Is the Greatest?

[33]Then He came to Capernaum. And when
He was in the house He asked them, "What
was it you disputed among yourselves on the
road?" [34]But they kept silent, for on the road
they had disputed among themselves who
would be the greatest. [35]And He sat down,
called the twelve, and said to them, "If anyone
desires to be first, he shall be last of all and
servant of all." [36]Then He took a little child
and set him in the midst of them. And when
He had taken him in His arms, He said to
them, [37]"Whoever receives one of these little
children in My name receives Me; and whoever receives Me, receives not Me but Him
who sent Me."

Jesus Forbids Sectarianism

[38]Now John answered Him, saying, "Teacher, we saw someone who does not follow us
casting out demons in Your name, and we forbade him because he does not follow us."

[39]But Jesus said, "Do not forbid him, for no
one who works a miracle in My name can
soon afterward speak evil of Me. [40]For he who
is not against us is on our[a] side. [41]For whoever
gives you a cup of water to drink in My name,
because you belong to Christ, assuredly, I say
to you, he will by no means lose his reward.

Jesus Warns of Offenses

[42]"But whoever causes one of these little
ones who believe in Me to stumble, it would
be better for him if a millstone were hung
around his neck, and he were thrown into the
sea. [43]If your hand causes you to sin, cut it off.
It is better for you to enter into life maimed,
rather than having two hands, to go to hell,
into the fire that shall never be quenched—
[44]where

'Their worm does not die
And the fire is not quenched.'[a]

[45]And if your foot causes you to sin, cut it off.
It is better for you to enter life lame, rather
than having two feet, to be cast into hell, into
the fire that shall never be quenched—
[46]where

'Their worm does not die
And the fire is not quenched.'[a]

[47]And if your eye causes you to sin, pluck it
out. It is better for you to enter the kingdom of
God with one eye, rather than having two
eyes, to be cast into hell fire— [48]where

'Their worm does not die
And the fire is not quenched.'[a]

Tasteless Salt Is Worthless

[49]"For everyone will be seasoned with fire,[a]
and every sacrifice will be seasoned with salt.
[50]Salt *is* good, but if the salt loses its flavor,
how will you season it? Have salt in yourselves, and have peace with one another."

Marriage and Divorce

10 Then He arose from there and came to
the region of Judea by the other side of
the Jordan. And multitudes gathered to Him
again, and as He was accustomed, He taught
them again.

[2]The Pharisees came and asked Him, "Is it
lawful for a man to divorce *his* wife?" testing
Him.

[3]And He answered and said to them, "What
did Moses command you?"

[4]They said, "Moses permitted *a man* to write
a certificate of divorce, and to dismiss *her*."

[5]And Jesus answered and said to them, "Because of the hardness of your heart he wrote
you this precept. [6]But from the beginning of
the creation, God *'made them male and
female.'*[a] [7]*'For this reason a man shall leave
his father and mother and be joined to his wife,*
[8]*and the two shall become one flesh'*;[a] so then
they are no longer two, but one flesh. [9]There-
fore what God has joined together, let not man
separate."

[10]In the house His disciples also asked Him
again about the same *matter*. [11]So He said to
them, "Whoever divorces his wife and marries another commits adultery against her.

9:40 [a]M-Text reads *against you is on your side.*
9:44 [a]NU-Text omits this verse. **9:46** [a]NU-Text omits the last clause of verse 45 and all of verse 46.
9:48 [a]Isaiah 66:24 **9:49** [a]NU-Text omits the rest of this verse. **10:6** [a]Genesis 1:27; 5:2
10:8 [a]Genesis 2:24

12 And if a woman divorces her husband and
marries another, she commits adultery."

JESUS BLESSES LITTLE CHILDREN

13 Then they brought little children to Him,
that He might touch them; but the disciples rebuked those who brought *them*. 14 But when
Jesus saw *it*, He was greatly displeased and
said to them, "Let the little children come to
Me, and do not forbid them; for of such is the
kingdom of God. 15 Assuredly, I say to you,
whoever does not receive the kingdom of God
as a little child will by no means enter it."
16 And He took them up in His arms, laid *His*
hands on them, and blessed them.

JESUS COUNSELS THE RICH YOUNG RULER

17 Now as He was going out on the road, one
came running, knelt before Him, and asked
Him, "Good Teacher, what shall I do that I
may inherit eternal life?"
18 So Jesus said to him, "Why do you call Me
good? No one *is* good but One, *that is*, God.
19 You know the commandments: *'Do not
commit adultery,' 'Do not murder,' 'Do not
steal,' 'Do not bear false witness,'* 'Do not defraud,' *'Honor your father and your mother.'* "[a]
20 And he answered and said to Him,
"Teacher, all these things I have kept from my
youth."
21 Then Jesus, looking at him, loved him,
and said to him, "One thing you lack: Go your
way, sell whatever you have and give to the
poor, and you will have treasure in heaven;
and come, take up the cross, and follow Me."

10:19 [a]Exodus 20:12–16; Deuteronomy 5:16–20

PERSONALITY PROFILE

Money

RICH MAN, POOR MAN

(MARK 10:17–25)

How risky it is to be wealthy! The greater the wealth, the greater the risk to a person's soul. Jesus said, "For what will it profit a man if he gains the whole world, and loses his own soul?" (Mark 8:36).

The wealthy Jewish ruler came to Jesus to ask what he might *do* to inherit eternal life. Jesus began His answer by reminding the man about God's commandments. The ruler responded that he had kept all of these from his youth. The Lord then told him to go and sell everything that he had, give away the proceeds, and follow Him. This stopped the ruler in his tracks. He would not meet Jesus' requirement because "he had great possessions" (Mark 10:22).

The man wanted to keep the world and add eternal life as another possession. Jesus confronted him with a choice. He couldn't hold tightly to this world (his riches) and eternal life at the same time. He would have to let go of this life in order to inherit eternal life. Those who insist on holding on to this life will eventually lose it anyway. To paraphrase a Christian martyr, how much better to give up what we cannot keep in order to gain what we cannot lose.

How tragic it is when, like this wealthy man, we lie to ourselves about our love for God. "I *don't* love money!" we claim. Yet how many of us would sell our estates and give the cash to charity to prove our allegiance to God? Sadly, not many would pass this ultimate test. We are eager to take comfort in the fact that Jesus did not make this His universal measurement of obedience. But Jesus wasn't as concerned about the man's possessions as He was that the possessions owned the man. God will not share allegiance with anyone or anything. An attitude of light holding and ready giving reflects genuine spiritual health. If you realize there is something you could not give up for the sake of Christ, you have some serious thinking to do.

To Learn More: Turn to the article about money on pages 480, 481. See also the key passage note at 1 Timothy 6:6–10 on page 1599.

COVENANT MARRIAGE

FRED LOWERY

(Mark 10:1–12)

God is a covenant God, the Bible is a covenant book, and we are a covenant people. God has clearly chosen to operate in the lives of His people on the basis of covenant. In the Old Testament, or Old Covenant, the sacrifice of animals and the sprinkling of blood served as an atonement (covering) for sin. In the New Testament, or New Covenant, the death of Christ on the Cross was the ultimate sacrifice for sin. The Lamb of God fulfilled the covenant for all mankind (Is. 53:6), paying sin's debt in full.

What does marriage have to do with covenant? Everything! Covenant is God's idea and ideal for marriage.

COVENANT VS. CONTRACT

In marriage, people's commitment to each other comes out of God's commitment to us. God has promised to love, protect, cherish, and care for us forever—and that is a covenant that cannot be broken. Likewise, He has empowered husbands and wives to love, protect, cherish, and care for each other until death, and that is a covenant that should not be broken. Covenant is the "invisible" foundation that makes long-term marriage possible. It is the secret to unlocking the mystery of "oneness" and the delight of fulfillment. The essence of covenant marriage is that two people become one. Covenant demands the death of two wills and the birth of one. "I" becomes "we," never to be separated again. The Bible says, "They are no longer two but one flesh" (Matt. 19:6). That is basic covenant.

The Hebrew word for being "united" or "joined" together means to cleave, cling, or stick. The corresponding Greek word means to be "glued" together. Covenant marriage partners, permanently bonded, will not come "unglued" when pressures come against the marriage.

Although we live in a contractual society, God knew that people could not build marriage on a private contract that can be easily canceled and cast aside on the basis of personal whims and weaknesses. He knew that a contract would not sustain the pain, pitfalls, and pressures of marriage between two imperfect human beings. Long-term marriage demands more than a piece of paper to go the distance. It requires the supernatural merging of lives and the binding of hearts.

To marry by contract is to say, "Now that I've signed, what do I get?" The focus is on *receiving*. To marry by covenant is to say, "I am giving myself to you unconditionally." The focus is on *giving*. In a contract, two become connected until the agreement is broken. In a covenant, two become committed until death parts them. Contracts are enforced by courts. Covenants are enforced by character. A contract calls for the signing of names; a covenant calls for the binding of hearts.

A MARRIAGE COVENANT IS SERIOUS

The Hebrew word for covenant is *berith,* which connotes a cutting of the flesh causing blood to flow out. The Hebrew act of "cutting covenant" was so serious that it was inaugurated with blood. The shedding of the blood of sacrificed animals in the Old Testament and of the blood of Jesus on the Cross were acts of covenant. In the Old Testament, covenants were so serious that

God held accountable those who broke covenant.

In Malachi, God identified marriage as a covenant that cannot be broken without serious consequences. God takes very seriously the breaking of the marriage covenant (Mal. 2:13–16). The Bible tells us that God, on request, will set aside the covenant for only two reasons: adultery and death.

A MARRIAGE COVENANT IS SACRED

A covenant was the most serious, the most sacred, and the most solemn agreement that could be made between human beings. It is a sacred act for a man and a woman to enter into a covenant relationship before God, family, and friends. God holds us accountable for the vows we make to each other on our wedding day. Promises made at the wedding altar allow entrance into a sacred covenant whose terms are witnessed by God Himself. Christian marriage is a triangle—it takes three for two to become one.

A MARRIAGE COVENANT IS SACRIFICIAL

There is no such thing as covenant without sacrifice, and marriage is designed to be the most sacrificial of all relationships. Covenant represents total surrender and involves the merging of one's life into another. This biblical image of "two becoming one" does not deny personal identity, but it allows the development of a wonderful diversity.

The Old Testament covenant ceremony involved a "walk of death" that constitutes the core issue of covenant. An animal was killed and split down the middle. The covenant participants would walk in a figure eight between the halves of the animal, reciting the duties of the covenant, and returning to face each other. The figure eight, a symbol of eternity, was an acknowledgment that the covenant was forever. This covenantal "walk of death" said two important things: (1) I am dying to myself and giving up the rights to my individual life in order to become one with my covenant partner; (2) I am, in effect, pointing to the dead animal and saying to God, "Please kill me if I break this covenant."

Selfishness is the root cause of all marital conflicts. Therefore, the key to a successful and lasting marriage is for the individuals' wills to die. It takes a lot of dying for a marriage to live. "Me-ness" must become "we-ness." The more unselfish we are, the happier we will be in our marriage.

FURTHER MEDITATION:

Other passages to study about the issue of marriage include:

- Genesis 2:18–25
- Proverbs 5:15–19; 18:22
- Matthew 19:4–6
- 1 Corinthians 7:1–16; 13:1–8
- Ephesians 5:22–33
- Hebrews 13:4

To Learn More: Turn to the key passage note on marriage at Matthew 19:4–6 on page 1261. See also the personality profile of Mary and Joseph on page 1229.

22But he was sad at this word, and went
away sorrowful, for he had great possessions.

With God All Things Are Possible

23Then Jesus looked around and said to His
disciples, "How hard it is for those who have
riches to enter the kingdom of God!" 24And
the disciples were astonished at His words.
But Jesus answered again and said to them,
"Children, how hard it is for those who trust
in riches[a] to enter the kingdom of God! 25It is
easier for a camel to go through the eye of a
needle than for a rich man to enter the kingdom of God."
26And they were greatly astonished, saying
among themselves, "Who then can be saved?"
27But Jesus looked at them and said, "With
men *it is* impossible, but not with God; for
with God all things are possible."
28Then Peter began to say to Him, "See, we
have left all and followed You."
29So Jesus answered and said, "Assuredly, I
say to you, there is no one who has left house
or brothers or sisters or father or mother or
wife[a] or children or lands, for My sake and the
gospel's, 30who shall not receive a hundredfold now in this time—houses and brothers
and sisters and mothers and children and
lands, with persecutions—and in the age to
come, eternal life. 31But many *who are* first
will be last, and the last first."

Jesus a Third Time Predicts His Death and Resurrection

32Now they were on the road, going up to
Jerusalem, and Jesus was going before them;
and they were amazed. And as they followed
they were afraid. Then He took the twelve
aside again and began to tell them the things
that would happen to Him: 33"Behold, we are
going up to Jerusalem, and the Son of Man
will be betrayed to the chief priests and to the
scribes; and they will condemn Him to death
and deliver Him to the Gentiles; 34and they
will mock Him, and scourge Him, and spit on
Him, and kill Him. And the third day He will
rise again."

Greatness Is Serving

35Then James and John, the sons of Zebedee, came to Him, saying, "Teacher, we want
You to do for us whatever we ask."
36And He said to them, "What do you want
Me to do for you?"
37They said to Him, "Grant us that we may
sit, one on Your right hand and the other on
Your left, in Your glory."
38But Jesus said to them, "You do not know
what you ask. Are you able to drink the cup
that I drink, and be baptized with the baptism
that I am baptized with?"
39They said to Him, "We are able."
So Jesus said to them, "You will indeed
drink the cup that I drink, and with the baptism I am baptized with you will be baptized;
40but to sit on My right hand and on My left is
not Mine to give, but *it is for those* for whom it
is prepared."
41And when the ten heard *it*, they began to
be greatly displeased with James and John.
42But Jesus called them to *Himself* and said to
them, "You know that those who are considered rulers over the Gentiles lord it over them,
and their great ones exercise authority over
them. 43Yet it shall not be so among you; but
whoever desires to become great among you
shall be your servant. 44And whoever of you
desires to be first shall be slave of all. 45For
even the Son of Man did not come to be

10:24 [a]NU-Text omits *for those who trust in riches.*
10:29 [a]NU-Text omits *or wife.*

SOUL NOTE

Give It Up *(10:28–31)* After Jesus' conversation with the rich young ruler, Peter commented that he and the other disciples had done what the rich man could not—"We have left all and followed You." Jesus responded that those who deny themselves and put Christ first will "receive a hundredfold now in this time . . . and in the age to come, eternal life." Anyone who gives up something valuable for Christ's sake will be blessed both in this life and in the life to come. When we deny ourselves something for Christ's sake, He understands and promises to give us more in return.
Topic: Self-Denial

served, but to serve, and to give His life a ransom for many."

Jesus Heals Blind Bartimaeus

[46]Now they came to Jericho. As He went out of Jericho with His disciples and a great multitude, blind Bartimaeus, the son of Timaeus, sat by the road begging. [47]And when he heard that it was Jesus of Nazareth, he began to cry out and say, "Jesus, Son of David, have mercy on me!"

[48]Then many warned him to be quiet; but he cried out all the more, "Son of David, have mercy on me!"

[49]So Jesus stood still and commanded him to be called.

Then they called the blind man, saying to him, "Be of good cheer. Rise, He is calling you."

[50]And throwing aside his garment, he rose and came to Jesus.

[51]So Jesus answered and said to him, "What do you want Me to do for you?"

The blind man said to Him, "Rabboni, that I may receive my sight."

[52]Then Jesus said to him, "Go your way; your faith has made you well." And immediately he received his sight and followed Jesus on the road.

The Triumphal Entry

11 Now when they drew near Jerusalem, to Bethphage[a] and Bethany, at the Mount of Olives, He sent two of His disciples; [2]and He said to them, "Go into the village opposite you; and as soon as you have entered it you will find a colt tied, on which no one has sat. Loose it and bring *it*. [3]And if anyone says to you, 'Why are you doing this?' say, 'The Lord has need of it,' and immediately he will send it here."

[4]So they went their way, and found the[a] colt tied by the door outside on the street, and they loosed it. [5]But some of those who stood there said to them, "What are you doing, loosing the colt?"

[6]And they spoke to them just as Jesus had commanded. So they let them go. [7]Then they brought the colt to Jesus and threw their clothes on it, and He sat on it. [8]And many spread their clothes on the road, and others cut down leafy branches from the trees and spread *them* on the road. [9]Then those who went before and those who followed cried out, saying:

"Hosanna!
'Blessed is He who comes in the name of the LORD!*'*[a]
10 Blessed *is* the kingdom of our father David
That comes in the name of the Lord![a]
Hosanna in the highest!"

[11]And Jesus went into Jerusalem and into the temple. So when He had looked around at all things, as the hour was already late, He went out to Bethany with the twelve.

The Fig Tree Withered

[12]Now the next day, when they had come out from Bethany, He was hungry. [13]And seeing from afar a fig tree having leaves, He went to see if perhaps He would find something on it. When He came to it, He found nothing but leaves, for it was not the season for figs. [14]In response Jesus said to it, "Let no one eat fruit from you ever again."

And His disciples heard *it*.

11:1 [a]M-Text reads *Bethsphage.* **11:4** [a]NU-Text and M-Text read *a.* **11:9** [a]Psalm 118:26 **11:10** [a]NU-Text omits *in the name of the Lord.*

SOUL NOTE

God's Place *(11:15)* The temple had become a marketplace, with opportunistic merchants setting up shop in a very distracting way. Animals for sacrifice were being sold noisily. At a premium, money changers accepted Gentile coinage in exchange for temple coins that bore no human image, the only coins accepted at the temple. Jesus was angry about this money focus! Likewise, even though our churches need a solid budget and financial plan in order to keep operating, money should never become so important that we lose sight of the church's mission—to provide a place for worship, fellowship, and outreach. **Topic: Money**

JESUS CLEANSES THE TEMPLE

[15]So they came to Jerusalem. Then Jesus went into the temple and began to drive out those who bought and sold in the temple, and overturned the tables of the money changers and the seats of those who sold doves. [16]And He would not allow anyone to carry wares through the temple. [17]Then He taught, saying to them, "Is it not written, *'My house shall be called a house of prayer for all nations'*?[a] But you have made it a *'den of thieves.'* "[b]

[18]And the scribes and chief priests heard it and sought how they might destroy Him; for they feared Him, because all the people were astonished at His teaching. [19]When evening had come, He went out of the city.

THE LESSON OF THE WITHERED FIG TREE

[20]Now in the morning, as they passed by, they saw the fig tree dried up from the roots. [21]And Peter, remembering, said to Him, "Rabbi, look! The fig tree which You cursed has withered away."

[22]So Jesus answered and said to them, "Have faith in God. [23]For assuredly, I say to you, whoever says to this mountain, 'Be removed and be cast into the sea,' and does not doubt in his heart, but believes that those things he says will be done, he will have whatever he says. [24]Therefore I say to you, whatever things you ask when you pray, believe that you receive *them*, and you will have *them*.

> "Therefore I say to you, whatever things you ask when you pray, believe that you receive them, and you will have them."
>
> MARK 11:24

FORGIVENESS AND PRAYER

[25]"And whenever you stand praying, if you have anything against anyone, forgive him, that your Father in heaven may also forgive you your trespasses. [26]But if you do not forgive, neither will your Father in heaven forgive your trespasses."[a]

JESUS' AUTHORITY QUESTIONED

[27]Then they came again to Jerusalem. And as He was walking in the temple, the chief priests, the scribes, and the elders came to Him. [28]And they said to Him, "By what authority are You doing these things? And who gave You this authority to do these things?"

[29]But Jesus answered and said to them, "I also will ask you one question; then answer Me, and I will tell you by what authority I do these things: [30]The baptism of John—was it from heaven or from men? Answer Me."

[31]And they reasoned among themselves, saying, "If we say, 'From heaven,' He will say, 'Why then did you not believe him?' [32]But if we say, 'From men' "—they feared the people, for all counted John to have been a prophet indeed. [33]So they answered and said to Jesus, "We do not know."

And Jesus answered and said to them, "Neither will I tell you by what authority I do these things."

THE PARABLE OF THE WICKED VINEDRESSERS

12 Then He began to speak to them in parables: "A man planted a vineyard and set a hedge around *it*, dug *a place for* the wine vat and built a tower. And he leased it to vinedressers and went into a far country. [2]Now at vintage-time he sent a servant to the vinedressers, that he might receive some of

11:17 [a]Isaiah 56:7 [b]Jeremiah 7:11 **11:26** [a]NU-Text omits this verse.

SOUL NOTE

Mountain Movers *(11:22–24)* When Jesus said, "Whatever things you ask when you pray, believe that you receive them, and you will have them," He did not mean that we can have anything we want simply by praying. In other places, Jesus explained that prayer must be submitted to God's sovereign will and focused on His glory. We must not pray for selfish desires or out of selfish motives. We should pray because we love God and trust Him to do His will. Even when the request seems impossible, we can still pray. God always hears and answers. **Topic: Prayer**

the fruit of the vineyard from the vinedressers.
3And they took *him* and beat him and sent
him away empty-handed. 4Again he sent them
another servant, and at him they threw
stones,[a] wounded *him* in the head, and sent
him away shamefully treated. 5And again he
sent another, and him they killed; and many
others, beating some and killing some. 6There-
fore still having one son, his beloved, he also
sent him to them last, saying, 'They will respect my son.' 7But those vinedressers said
among themselves, 'This is the heir. Come, let
us kill him, and the inheritance will be ours.'
8So they took him and killed *him* and cast *him*
out of the vineyard.
9"Therefore what will the owner of the
vineyard do? He will come and destroy the
vinedressers, and give the vineyard to others.
10Have you not even read this Scripture:

'The stone which the builders rejected
Has become the chief cornerstone.
11 *This was the LORD's doing,*
And it is marvelous in our eyes'?"[a]

12And they sought to lay hands on Him, but
feared the multitude, for they knew He had
spoken the parable against them. So they left
Him and went away.

The Pharisees: Is It Lawful to Pay Taxes to Caesar?

13Then they sent to Him some of the Pharisees and the Herodians, to catch Him in *His*
words. 14When they had come, they said to
Him, "Teacher, we know that You are true,
and care about no one; for You do not regard
the person of men, but teach the way of God
in truth. Is it lawful to pay taxes to Caesar, or
not? 15Shall we pay, or shall we not pay?"
But He, knowing their hypocrisy, said to
them, "Why do you test Me? Bring Me a denarius that I may see *it*." 16So they brought *it*.
And He said to them, "Whose image and
inscription *is* this?" They said to Him,
"Caesar's."
17And Jesus answered and said to them,
"Render to Caesar the things that are Caesar's,
and to God the things that are God's."
And they marveled at Him.

The Sadducees: What About the Resurrection?

18Then *some* Sadducees, who say there is no
resurrection, came to Him; and they asked

12:4 [a]NU-Text omits *and at him they threw stones.*
12:11 [a]Psalm 118:22, 23

SOUL NOTE

Forgive *(11:26)* Jesus stated that God's forgiveness of us is somehow related to how we forgive others. When we accept God's forgiveness of all the wrongs we have done Him, we should be so grateful that we willingly offer that same kind of forgiveness to those who have wronged us. Jesus told a parable of a person who had been forgiven of a huge debt he owed, but then refused to forgive any of his debtors (Matt. 18:21–35). To refuse to forgive others shows that we do not appreciate the forgiveness God offers us. **Topic: Forgiveness**

SOUL NOTE

His Image *(12:13–17)* The Jews of Jesus' day were under the dominion of the Roman Empire and were forced to pay taxes to Caesar. Some thought it wrong to pay taxes that supported a pagan government. The Jewish leaders tried to trap Jesus into taking a side on the issue. Jesus took a coin, pointed out Caesar's image on it, and said that since the coin belonged to Caesar, it could be returned to him. Then Jesus added the most important lesson: Our lives bear the image of God; therefore, we should give our lives to Him. **Topic: Money**

Him, saying: 19“Teacher, Moses wrote to us
that if a man’s brother dies, and leaves *his*
wife behind, and leaves no children, his
brother should take his wife and raise up offspring for his brother. 20Now there were seven
brothers. The first took a wife; and dying, he
left no offspring. 21And the second took her,
and he died; nor did he leave any offspring.
And the third likewise. 22So the seven had her
and left no offspring. Last of all the woman
died also. 23Therefore, in the resurrection,
when they rise, whose wife will she be? For all
seven had her as wife.”
24Jesus answered and said to them, “Are
you not therefore mistaken, because you do
not know the Scriptures nor the power of God?
25For when they rise from the dead, they neither marry nor are given in marriage, but are
like angels in heaven. 26But concerning the
dead, that they rise, have you not read in the
book of Moses, in the *burning* bush *passage*,
how God spoke to him, saying, *‘I am the God
of Abraham, the God of Isaac, and the God of
Jacob’*?[a] 27He is not the God of the dead, but
the God of the living. You are therefore greatly
mistaken.”

The Scribes: Which Is the First Commandment of All?

28Then one of the scribes came, and having
heard them reasoning together, perceiving[a]
that He had answered them well, asked Him,
“Which is the first commandment of all?”
29Jesus answered him, “The first of all the
commandments *is*: *‘Hear, O Israel, the* Lord
our God, the Lord *is one.* 30*And you shall love
the* Lord *your God with all your heart, with all
your soul, with all your mind, and with all
your strength.’*[a] This *is* the first commandment.[b] 31And the second, like *it, is* this: *‘You
shall love your neighbor as yourself.’*[a] There is
no other commandment greater than these.”
32So the scribe said to Him, “Well *said*,
Teacher. You have spoken the truth, for there
is one God, and there is no other but He.
33And to love Him with all the heart, with all
the understanding, with all the soul,[a] and
with all the strength, and to love one’s neighbor as oneself, is more than all the whole
burnt offerings and sacrifices.”
34Now when Jesus saw that he answered
wisely, He said to him, “You are not far from
the kingdom of God.”
But after that no one dared question Him.

Jesus: How Can David Call His Descendant Lord?

35Then Jesus answered and said, while He
taught in the temple, “How *is it* that the
scribes say that the Christ is the Son of David?
36For David himself said by the Holy Spirit:

‘The Lord *said to my Lord,*
“Sit at My right hand,
Till I make Your enemies Your
footstool.” ’[a]

37Therefore David himself calls Him *‘Lord’*;
how is He *then* his Son?”
And the common people heard Him gladly.

Beware of the Scribes

38Then He said to them in His teaching, “Beware of the scribes, who desire to go around
in long robes, *love* greetings in the marketplaces, 39the best seats in the synagogues, and
the best places at feasts, 40who devour widows’ houses, and for a pretense make long
prayers. These will receive greater condemnation.”

The Widow’s Two Mites

41Now Jesus sat opposite the treasury and
saw how the people put money into the treasury. And many *who were* rich put in much.
42Then one poor widow came and threw in
two mites,[a] which make a quadrans. 43So He
called His disciples to *Himself* and said to
them, “Assuredly, I say to you that this poor
widow has put in more than all those who
have given to the treasury; 44for they all put in
out of their abundance, but she out of her poverty put in all that she had, her whole livelihood.”

Jesus Predicts the Destruction of the Temple

13 Then as He went out of the temple, one
of His disciples said to Him, “Teacher,
see what manner of stones and what buildings
are here!”
2And Jesus answered and said to him, “Do
you see these great buildings? Not *one* stone

12:26 [a]Exodus 3:6, 15 **12:28** [a]NU-Text reads *seeing.* **12:30** [a]Deuteronomy 6:4, 5 [b]NU-Text omits this sentence. **12:31** [a]Leviticus 19:18 **12:33** [a]NU-Text omits *with all the soul.* **12:36** [a]Psalm 110:1 **12:42** [a]Greek *lepta,* very small copper coins worth a fraction of a penny

shall be left upon another, that shall not be thrown down."

The Signs of the Times and the End of the Age

[3]Now as He sat on the Mount of Olives opposite the temple, Peter, James, John, and Andrew asked Him privately, [4]"Tell us, when will these things be? And what *will be* the sign when all these things will be fulfilled?"

[5]And Jesus, answering them, began to say: "Take heed that no one deceives you. [6]For many will come in My name, saying, 'I am *He*,' and will deceive many. [7]But when you hear of wars and rumors of wars, do not be troubled; for *such things* must happen, but the end *is* not yet. [8]For nation will rise against nation, and kingdom against kingdom. And there will be earthquakes in various places, and there will be famines and troubles.[a] These *are* the beginnings of sorrows.

[9]"But watch out for yourselves, for they will deliver you up to councils, and you will be beaten in the synagogues. You will be brought[a] before rulers and kings for My sake, for a testimony to them. [10]And the gospel must first be preached to all the nations. [11]But when they arrest *you* and deliver you up, do not worry beforehand, or premeditate[a] what you will speak. But whatever is given you in that hour, speak that; for it is not you who speak, but the Holy Spirit. [12]Now brother will betray brother to death, and a father *his* child; and children will rise up against parents and cause them to be put to death. [13]And you will be hated by all for My name's sake. But he who endures to the end shall be saved.

> "The gospel must first be preached to all the nations."
> MARK 13:10

The Great Tribulation

[14]"So when you see the *'abomination of desolation,'*[a] spoken of by Daniel the prophet,[b] standing where it ought not" (let the reader understand), "then let those who are in Judea flee to the mountains. [15]Let him who is on the housetop not go down into the house, nor enter to take anything out of his house. [16]And let him who is in the field not go back to get his clothes. [17]But woe to those who are pregnant and to those who are nursing babies in those days! [18]And pray that your flight may not be in winter. [19]For *in* those days there will be tribulation, such as has not been since the beginning of the creation which God created until this time, nor ever shall be. [20]And unless the Lord had shortened those days, no flesh would be saved; but for the elect's sake, whom He chose, He shortened the days.

[21]"Then if anyone says to you, 'Look, here *is* the Christ!' or, 'Look, *He is* there!' do not believe it. [22]For false christs and false prophets will rise and show signs and wonders to deceive, if possible, even the elect. [23]But take heed; see, I have told you all things beforehand.

The Coming of the Son of Man

[24]"But in those days, after that tribulation, the sun will be darkened, and the moon will not give its light; [25]the stars of heaven will fall, and the powers in the heavens will be shaken. [26]Then they will see the Son of Man coming in the clouds with great power and glory. [27]And then He will send His angels, and gather together His elect from the four winds, from the farthest part of earth to the farthest part of heaven.

The Parable of the Fig Tree

[28]"Now learn this parable from the fig tree: When its branch has already become tender, and puts forth leaves, you know that summer is near. [29]So you also, when you see these things happening, know that it[a] is near—at the doors! [30]Assuredly, I say to you, this generation will by no means pass away till all these things take place. [31]Heaven and earth will pass away, but My words will by no means pass away.

No One Knows the Day or Hour

[32]"But of that day and hour no one knows, not even the angels in heaven, nor the Son, but only the Father. [33]Take heed, watch and pray; for you do not know when the time is. [34]*It is* like a man going to a far country, who

---

13:8 [a]NU-Text omits *and troubles.* **13:9** [a]NU-Text and M-Text read *will stand.* **13:11** [a]NU-Text omits *or premeditate.* **13:14** [a]Daniel 11:31; 12:11 [b]NU-Text omits *spoken of by Daniel the prophet.* **13:29** [a]Or *He*

left his house and gave authority to his servants, and to each his work, and commanded the doorkeeper to watch. 35Watch therefore, for you do not know when the master of the house is coming—in the evening, at midnight, at the crowing of the rooster, or in the morning— 36lest, coming suddenly, he find you sleeping. 37And what I say to you, I say to all: Watch!"

The Plot to Kill Jesus

14 After two days it was the Passover and *the Feast* of Unleavened Bread. And the chief priests and the scribes sought how they might take Him by trickery and put *Him* to death. 2But they said, "Not during the feast, lest there be an uproar of the people."

The Anointing at Bethany

3And being in Bethany at the house of Simon the leper, as He sat at the table, a woman came having an alabaster flask of very costly oil of spikenard. Then she broke the flask and poured *it* on His head. 4But there were some who were indignant among themselves, and said, "Why was this fragrant oil wasted? 5For it might have been sold for more than three hundred denarii and given to the poor." And they criticized her sharply.

6But Jesus said, "Let her alone. Why do you trouble her? She has done a good work for Me. 7For you have the poor with you always, and whenever you wish you may do them good; but Me you do not have always. 8She has done what she could. She has come beforehand to anoint My body for burial. 9Assuredly, I say to you, wherever this gospel is preached in the whole world, what this woman has done will also be told as a memorial to her."

Judas Agrees to Betray Jesus

10Then Judas Iscariot, one of the twelve, went to the chief priests to betray Him to them. 11And when they heard *it*, they were glad, and promised to give him money. So he sought how he might conveniently betray Him.

Jesus Celebrates the Passover with His Disciples

12Now on the first day of Unleavened Bread, when they killed the Passover *lamb*, His disciples said to Him, "Where do You want us to go and prepare, that You may eat the Passover?"

13And He sent out two of His disciples and said to them, "Go into the city, and a man will meet you carrying a pitcher of water; follow him. 14Wherever he goes in, say to the master of the house, 'The Teacher says, "Where is the guest room in which I may eat the Passover with My disciples?" ' 15Then he will show you a large upper room, furnished *and* prepared; there make ready for us."

16So His disciples went out, and came into the city, and found it just as He had said to them; and they prepared the Passover.

17In the evening He came with the twelve. 18Now as they sat and ate, Jesus said, "Assuredly, I say to you, one of you who eats with Me will betray Me."

19And they began to be sorrowful, and to say to Him one by one, "*Is* it I?" And another *said,* "*Is* it I?"[a]

20He answered and said to them, "*It is* one of the twelve, who dips with Me in the dish. 21The Son of Man indeed goes just as it is written of Him, but woe to that man by whom the Son of Man is betrayed! It would have been good for that man if he had never been born."

Jesus Institutes the Lord's Supper

22And as they were eating, Jesus took bread, blessed and broke *it*, and gave *it* to them and said, "Take, eat;[a] this is My body."

23Then He took the cup, and when He had given thanks He gave *it* to them, and they all drank from it. 24And He said to them, "This is My blood of the new[a] covenant, which is shed for many. 25Assuredly, I say to you, I will no longer drink of the fruit of the vine until that day when I drink it new in the kingdom of God."

26And when they had sung a hymn, they went out to the Mount of Olives.

Jesus Predicts Peter's Denial

27Then Jesus said to them, "All of you will be made to stumble because of Me this night,[a] for it is written:

'I will strike the Shepherd,
And the sheep will be scattered.'[b]

14:19 [a]NU-Text omits this sentence. **14:22** [a]NU-Text omits *eat.* **14:24** [a]NU-Text omits *new.* **14:27** [a]NU-Text omits *because of Me this night.* [b]Zechariah 13:7

[28]"But after I have been raised, I will go before you to Galilee."
[29]Peter said to Him, "Even if all are made to
stumble, yet I *will* not *be*."
[30]Jesus said to him, "Assuredly, I say to you
that today, *even* this night, before the rooster
crows twice, you will deny Me three times."
[31]But he spoke more vehemently, "If I have
to die with You, I will not deny You!"
And they all said likewise.

The Prayer in the Garden

[32]Then they came to a place which was
named Gethsemane; and He said to His disciples, "Sit here while I pray." [33]And He took
Peter, James, and John with Him, and He began to be troubled and deeply distressed.
[34]Then He said to them, "My soul is exceedingly sorrowful, *even* to death. Stay here and
watch."
[35]He went a little farther, and fell on the
ground, and prayed that if it were possible, the
hour might pass from Him. [36]And He said,
"Abba, Father, all things *are* possible for You.
Take this cup away from Me; nevertheless, not
what I will, but what You *will*."
[37]Then He came and found them sleeping,
and said to Peter, "Simon, are you sleeping?
Could you not watch one hour? [38]Watch and
pray, lest you enter into temptation. The spirit
indeed *is* willing, but the flesh *is* weak."
[39]Again He went away and prayed, and
spoke the same words. [40]And when He returned, He found them asleep again, for their
eyes were heavy; and they did not know what
to answer Him.
[41]Then He came the third time and said to
them, "Are you still sleeping and resting? It is
enough! The hour has come; behold, the Son
of Man is being betrayed into the hands of sinners. [42]Rise, let us be going. See, My betrayer
is at hand."

Betrayal and Arrest in Gethsemane

[43]And immediately, while He was still
speaking, Judas, one of the twelve, with a
great multitude with swords and clubs, came
from the chief priests and the scribes and the
elders. [44]Now His betrayer had given them a
signal, saying, "Whomever I kiss, He is the
One; seize Him and lead *Him* away safely."
[45]As soon as he had come, immediately he
went up to Him and said to Him, "Rabbi, Rabbi!" and kissed Him.
[46]Then they laid their hands on Him and
took Him. [47]And one of those who stood by
drew his sword and struck the servant of the
high priest, and cut off his ear.
[48]Then Jesus answered and said to them,
"Have you come out, as against a robber, with
swords and clubs to take Me? [49]I was daily with
you in the temple teaching, and you did not
seize Me. But the Scriptures must be fulfilled."
[50]Then they all forsook Him and fled.

A Young Man Flees Naked

[51]Now a certain young man followed Him,
having a linen cloth thrown around *his* naked
body. And the young men laid hold of him,
[52]and he left the linen cloth and fled from
them naked.

Jesus Faces the Sanhedrin

[53]And they led Jesus away to the high priest;
and with him were assembled all the chief
priests, the elders, and the scribes. [54]But Peter
followed Him at a distance, right into the
courtyard of the high priest. And he sat with
the servants and warmed himself at the fire.
[55]Now the chief priests and all the council
sought testimony against Jesus to put Him to
death, but found none. [56]For many bore false
witness against Him, but their testimonies did
not agree.
[57]Then some rose up and bore false witness

SOUL NOTE

Your Will *(14:32–42)* In His humanity Jesus dreaded the Cross, and in the quiet of Gethsemane He spent time in prayer with His Father. He expressed His deepest desire that the "cup" be taken away, but He submitted Himself to the Father's will: "Nevertheless, not what I will, but what You will." Jesus faced the most difficult hours of His earthly life with the serenity of One who knew He was safe in God's hands. No matter what would come, God was in control. When we face a difficult time, we can pray, knowing that God walks with us. He is in control. **Topic: Prayer**

against Him, saying, 58"We heard Him say, 'I will destroy this temple made with hands, and within three days I will build another made without hands.' " 59But not even then did their testimony agree.

60And the high priest stood up in the midst and asked Jesus, saying, "Do You answer nothing? What *is it* these men testify against You?" 61But He kept silent and answered nothing.

Again the high priest asked Him, saying to Him, "Are You the Christ, the Son of the Blessed?"

62Jesus said, "I am. And you will see the Son of Man sitting at the right hand of the Power, and coming with the clouds of heaven."

63Then the high priest tore his clothes and said, "What further need do we have of witnesses? 64You have heard the blasphemy! What do you think?"

And they all condemned Him to be deserving of death.

65Then some began to spit on Him, and to blindfold Him, and to beat Him, and to say to Him, "Prophesy!" And the officers struck Him with the palms of their hands.[a]

Peter Denies Jesus, and Weeps

66Now as Peter was below in the courtyard, one of the servant girls of the high priest came. 67And when she saw Peter warming himself, she looked at him and said, "You also were with Jesus of Nazareth."

68But he denied it, saying, "I neither know nor understand what you are saying." And he went out on the porch, and a rooster crowed.

69And the servant girl saw him again, and began to say to those who stood by, "This is one of them." 70But he denied it again.

And a little later those who stood by said to Peter again, "Surely you are *one* of them; for you are a Galilean, and your speech shows *it*."[a]

71Then he began to curse and swear, "I do not know this Man of whom you speak!"

72A second time *the* rooster crowed. Then Peter called to mind the word that Jesus had said to him, "Before the rooster crows twice, you will deny Me three times." And when he thought about it, he wept.

Jesus Faces Pilate

15 Immediately, in the morning, the chief priests held a consultation with the elders and scribes and the whole council; and they bound Jesus, led *Him* away, and delivered *Him* to Pilate. 2Then Pilate asked Him, "Are You the King of the Jews?"

He answered and said to him, "*It is as* you say."

3And the chief priests accused Him of many things, but He answered nothing. 4Then Pilate asked Him again, saying, "Do You answer nothing? See how many things they testify against You!"[a] 5But Jesus still answered nothing, so that Pilate marveled.

Taking the Place of Barabbas

6Now at the feast he was accustomed to releasing one prisoner to them, whomever they requested. 7And there was one named Barabbas, *who was* chained with his fellow rebels; they had committed murder in the rebellion. 8Then the multitude, crying aloud,[a] began to ask *him to do* just as he had always done for them. 9But Pilate answered them, saying, "Do you want me to release to you the King of the Jews?" 10For he knew that the chief priests had handed Him over because of envy.

11But the chief priests stirred up the crowd, so that he should rather release Barabbas to them. 12Pilate answered and said to them again, "What then do you want me to do *with Him* whom you call the King of the Jews?"

13So they cried out again, "Crucify Him!"

14Then Pilate said to them, "Why, what evil has He done?"

But they cried out all the more, "Crucify Him!"

15So Pilate, wanting to gratify the crowd, released Barabbas to them; and he delivered Jesus, after he had scourged *Him*, to be crucified.

The Soldiers Mock Jesus

16Then the soldiers led Him away into the hall called Praetorium, and they called together the whole garrison. 17And they clothed Him with purple; and they twisted a crown of thorns, put it on His *head*, 18and began to salute Him, "Hail, King of the Jews!" 19Then they struck Him on the head with a reed and spat on Him; and bowing the knee, they worshiped Him. 20And when they had mocked

14:65 [a]NU-Text reads *received Him with slaps.*
14:70 [a]NU-Text omits *and your speech shows it.*
15:4 [a]NU-Text reads *of which they accuse You.*
15:8 [a]NU-Text reads *going up.*

Him, they took the purple off Him, put His own clothes on Him, and led Him out to crucify Him.

The King on a Cross

21 Then they compelled a certain man, Simon a Cyrenian, the father of Alexander and Rufus, as he was coming out of the country and passing by, to bear His cross. 22 And they brought Him to the place Golgotha, which is translated, Place of a Skull. 23 Then they gave Him wine mingled with myrrh to drink, but He did not take *it*. 24 And when they crucified Him, they divided His garments, casting lots for them to determine what every man should take.

25 Now it was the third hour, and they crucified Him. 26 And the inscription of His accusation was written above:

THE KING OF THE JEWS.

27 With Him they also crucified two robbers, one on His right and the other on His left. 28 So the Scripture was fulfilled[a] which says, *"And He was numbered with the transgressors."*[b]

29 And those who passed by blasphemed Him, wagging their heads and saying, "Aha! *You* who destroy the temple and build *it* in three days, 30 save Yourself, and come down from the cross!"

31 Likewise the chief priests also, mocking among themselves with the scribes, said, "He saved others; Himself He cannot save. 32 Let the Christ, the King of Israel, descend now from the cross, that we may see and believe."[a]

Even those who were crucified with Him reviled Him.

Jesus Dies on the Cross

33 Now when the sixth hour had come, there was darkness over the whole land until the ninth hour. 34 And at the ninth hour Jesus cried out with a loud voice, saying, "Eloi, Eloi, lama sabachthani?" which is translated, *"My God, My God, why have You forsaken Me?"*[a]

35 Some of those who stood by, when they heard *that*, said, "Look, He is calling for Elijah!" 36 Then someone ran and filled a sponge full of sour wine, put *it* on a reed, and offered *it* to Him to drink, saying, "Let Him alone; let us see if Elijah will come to take Him down."

37 And Jesus cried out with a loud voice, and breathed His last.

38 Then the veil of the temple was torn in two from top to bottom. 39 So when the centurion, who stood opposite Him, saw that He cried out like this and breathed His last,[a] he said, "Truly this Man was the Son of God!"

40 There were also women looking on from afar, among whom were Mary Magdalene, Mary the mother of James the Less and of Joses, and Salome, 41 who also followed Him and ministered to Him when He was in Galilee, and many other women who came up with Him to Jerusalem.

Jesus Buried in Joseph's Tomb

42 Now when evening had come, because it was the Preparation Day, that is, the day before the Sabbath, 43 Joseph of Arimathea, a prominent council member, who was himself waiting for the kingdom of God, coming and taking courage, went in to Pilate and asked for the body of Jesus. 44 Pilate marveled that He was already dead; and summoning the centurion, he asked him if He had been dead for some time. 45 So when he found out from the

15:28 [a]Isaiah 53:12 [b]NU-Text omits this verse. **15:32** [a]M-Text reads *believe Him.* **15:34** [a]Psalm 22:1 **15:39** [a]NU-Text reads *that He thus breathed His last.*

SOUL NOTE

All Honor and Praise *(15:16–32)* Jesus was treated horribly throughout His final hours. He was arrested like a criminal. He was spat on and beaten. His close friend Peter denied ever knowing Him. The Roman leader condemned Him without any case, and His own people called for His execution and chose a murderer to be released in His place. The Roman soldiers mocked His claims to be a king, and then crucified Him between two robbers. Jesus, the Son of God, experienced such dishonor so that one day He could bring us into glory with Him. He deserves our honor and praise every day. **Topic: Honor**

centurion, he granted the body to Joseph. [46]Then he bought fine linen, took Him down, and wrapped Him in the linen. And he laid Him in a tomb which had been hewn out of the rock, and rolled a stone against the door of the tomb. [47]And Mary Magdalene and Mary *the mother* of Joses observed where He was laid.

He Is Risen

16 Now when the Sabbath was past, Mary Magdalene, Mary *the mother* of James, and Salome bought spices, that they might come and anoint Him. [2]Very early in the morning, on the first *day* of the week, they came to the tomb when the sun had risen. [3]And they said among themselves, "Who will roll away the stone from the door of the tomb for us?" [4]But when they looked up, they saw that the stone had been rolled away—for it was very large. [5]And entering the tomb, they saw a young man clothed in a long white robe sitting on the right side; and they were alarmed.

[6]But he said to them, "Do not be alarmed. You seek Jesus of Nazareth, who was crucified. He is risen! He is not here. See the place where they laid Him. [7]But go, tell His disciples—and Peter—that He is going before you into Galilee; there you will see Him, as He said to you."

[8]So they went out quickly[a] and fled from the tomb, for they trembled and were amazed. And they said nothing to anyone, for they were afraid.

Mary Magdalene Sees the Risen Lord

[9]Now when *He* rose early on the first *day* of the week, He appeared first to Mary Magdalene, out of whom He had cast seven demons. [10]She went and told those who had been with Him, as they mourned and wept. [11]And when they heard that He was alive and had been seen by her, they did not believe.

Jesus Appears to Two Disciples

[12]After that, He appeared in another form to two of them as they walked and went into the country. [13]And they went and told *it* to the rest, *but* they did not believe them either.

The Great Commission

[14]Later He appeared to the eleven as they sat at the table; and He rebuked their unbelief and hardness of heart, because they did not believe those who had seen Him after He had risen. [15]And He said to them, "Go into all the world and preach the gospel to every creature. [16]He who believes and is baptized will be saved; but he who does not believe will be condemned. [17]And these signs will follow those who believe: In My name they will cast out demons; they will speak with new tongues; [18]they[a] will take up serpents; and if they drink anything deadly, it will by no means hurt them; they will lay hands on the sick, and they will recover."

Christ Ascends to God's Right Hand

[19]So then, after the Lord had spoken to them, He was received up into heaven, and sat down at the right hand of God. [20]And they went out and preached everywhere, the Lord working with *them* and confirming the word through the accompanying signs. Amen.[a]

16:8 [a]NU-Text and M-Text omit *quickly.*
16:18 [a]NU-Text reads *and in their hands they will.*
16:20 [a]Verses 9–20 are bracketed in NU-Text as not original. They are lacking in Codex Sinaiticus and Codex Vaticanus, although nearly all other manuscripts of Mark contain them.

Luke

One person weeps at a movie; another is unmoved. One friend seems painfully indecisive while another makes decisions (even big ones) with ease. When friends come over, one spouse's concern is for everyone to have good conversation; but the other spouse is fretting over whether the refreshments will last.

It's no great revelation to say that people are different. Our varied temperaments and backgrounds mean that we think and feel and respond in different ways. This fact might explain one reason for the New Testament's having four separate Gospels. They all highlight slightly different aspects of Christ's character and ministry, so as to speak effectively to different audiences.

Luke was evidently a Gentile physician who never met Jesus, but he went on to become a close associate of the apostle Paul. Writing mainly to his fellow non-Jews, Luke stressed the humanity and compassion of Christ toward all people. His goal seems to have been twofold: (1) to show that Jesus met the ideal of human perfection, and (2) to prove that Christ was the Savior sent by God "to seek and to save" lost people (19:10).

A meticulous researcher and a skillful historian, Luke has written a Gospel that is admired by scholars for its careful attention to detail. Not surprisingly, Luke's is the longest Gospel, giving the fullest portrayal of Jesus' life and ministry and including nearly ten chapters of material found in no other Gospel. As the author of this and its companion book, Acts, Luke traces both the life of Christ and the beginnings of the church.

Read Luke to discover Jesus the Savior!

SOUL CONCERNS IN LUKE

Motherhood	(1:26, 27)
Judgmentalism	(6:37, 38)
Worry	(12:22–31)
Self-Denial	(14:25–33)

DEDICATION TO THEOPHILUS

1 Inasmuch as many have taken in hand to set in order a narrative of those things which have been fulfilled[a] among us, 2just as those who from the beginning were eyewitnesses and ministers of the word delivered them to us, 3it seemed good to me also, having had perfect understanding of all things from the very first, to write to you an orderly account, most excellent Theophilus, 4that you may know the certainty of those things in which you were instructed.

JOHN'S BIRTH ANNOUNCED TO ZACHARIAS

5There was in the days of Herod, the king of Judea, a certain priest named Zacharias, of the division of Abijah. His wife *was* of the daughters of Aaron, and her name *was* Elizabeth. 6And they were both righteous before God, walking in all the commandments and ordinances of the Lord blameless. 7But they had no child, because Elizabeth was barren, and they were both well advanced in years.

8So it was, that while he was serving as priest before God in the order of his division, 9according to the custom of the priesthood, his lot fell to burn incense when he went into the temple of the Lord. 10And the whole multitude of the people was praying outside at the hour of incense. 11Then an angel of the Lord appeared to him, standing on the right side of the altar of incense. 12And when Zacharias saw *him,* he was troubled, and fear fell upon him.

13But the angel said to him, "Do not be afraid, Zacharias, for your prayer is heard; and your wife Elizabeth will bear you a son, and you shall call his name John. 14And you will have joy and gladness, and many will rejoice at his birth. 15For he will be great in the sight of the Lord, and shall drink neither wine nor strong drink. He will also be filled with the Holy Spirit, even from his mother's womb. 16And he will turn many of the children of Israel to the Lord their God. 17He will also go before Him in the spirit and power of Elijah, *'to turn the hearts of the fathers to the children,'*[a] and the disobedient to the wisdom of the just, to make ready a people prepared for the Lord."

18And Zacharias said to the angel, "How shall I know this? For I am an old man, and my wife is well advanced in years."

19And the angel answered and said to him, "I am Gabriel, who stands in the presence of God, and was sent to speak to you and bring you these glad tidings. 20But behold, you will be mute and not able to speak until the day these things take place, because you did not believe my words which will be fulfilled in their own time."

21And the people waited for Zacharias, and marveled that he lingered so long in the temple. 22But when he came out, he could not speak to them; and they perceived that he had seen a vision in the temple, for he beckoned to them and remained speechless.

23So it was, as soon as the days of his service were completed, that he departed to his own house. 24Now after those days his wife Elizabeth conceived; and she hid herself five months, saying, 25"Thus the Lord has dealt with me, in the days when He looked on *me,* to take away my reproach among people."

CHRIST'S BIRTH ANNOUNCED TO MARY

26Now in the sixth month the angel Gabriel was sent by God to a city of Galilee named Nazareth, 27to a virgin betrothed to a man whose name was Joseph, of the house of David. The virgin's name *was* Mary. 28And having come in, the angel said to her, "Rejoice, highly favored *one,* the Lord *is* with you; blessed *are* you among women!"[a]

29But when she saw *him,*[a] she was troubled at his saying, and considered what manner of greeting this was. 30Then the angel said to her, "Do not be afraid, Mary, for you have found favor with God. 31And behold, you will conceive in your womb and bring forth a Son, and shall call His name JESUS. 32He will be great, and will be called the Son of the Highest; and the Lord God will give Him the throne of His father David. 33And He will reign over the house of Jacob forever, and of His kingdom there will be no end."

34Then Mary said to the angel, "How can this be, since I do not know a man?"

35And the angel answered and said to her, "*The* Holy Spirit will come upon you, and the power of the Highest will overshadow you; therefore, also, that Holy One who is to be born will be called the Son of God. 36Now indeed, Elizabeth your relative has also conceived a son in her old age; and this is now the

---

1:1 [a]Or *are most surely believed* **1:17** [a]Malachi 4:5,6 **1:28** [a]NU-Text omits *blessed are you among women.* **1:29** [a]NU-Text omits *when she saw him.*

sixth month for her who was called barren.
[37]For with God nothing will be impossible."
[38]Then Mary said, "Behold the maidservant
of the Lord! Let it be to me according to your
word." And the angel departed from her.

Mary Visits Elizabeth

[39]Now Mary arose in those days and went
into the hill country with haste, to a city of Judah, [40]and entered the house of Zacharias and
greeted Elizabeth. [41]And it happened, when
Elizabeth heard the greeting of Mary, that the
babe leaped in her womb; and Elizabeth was
filled with the Holy Spirit. [42]Then she spoke
out with a loud voice and said, "Blessed *are*
you among women, and blessed *is* the fruit of
your womb! [43]But why *is* this *granted* to me,
that the mother of my Lord should come to
me? [44]For indeed, as soon as the voice of your
greeting sounded in my ears, the babe leaped
in my womb for joy. [45]Blessed *is* she who believed, for there will be a fulfillment of those
things which were told her from the Lord."

The Song of Mary

[46]And Mary said:

"My soul magnifies the Lord,
47 And my spirit has rejoiced in God my Savior.
48 For He has regarded the lowly state of His maidservant;
For behold, henceforth all generations will call me blessed.
49 For He who is mighty has done great things for me,
And holy *is* His name.
50 And His mercy *is* on those who fear Him
From generation to generation.
51 He has shown strength with His arm;
He has scattered *the* proud in the imagination of their hearts.
52 He has put down the mighty from *their* thrones,
And exalted *the* lowly.
53 He has filled *the* hungry with good things,
And *the* rich He has sent away empty.
54 He has helped His servant Israel,
In remembrance of *His* mercy,
55 As He spoke to our fathers,
To Abraham and to his seed forever."

[56]And Mary remained with her about three
months, and returned to her house.

Birth of John the Baptist

[57]Now Elizabeth's full time came for her to
be delivered, and she brought forth a son.
[58]When her neighbors and relatives heard
how the Lord had shown great mercy to her,
they rejoiced with her.

Circumcision of John the Baptist

[59]So it was, on the eighth day, that they
came to circumcise the child; and they would
have called him by the name of his father,
Zacharias. [60]His mother answered and said,
"No; he shall be called John."
[61]But they said to her, "There is no one
among your relatives who is called by this
name." [62]So they made signs to his father—
what he would have him called.
[63]And he asked for a writing tablet, and
wrote, saying, "His name is John." So they all
marveled. [64]Immediately his mouth was
opened and his tongue *loosed,* and he spoke,
praising God. [65]Then fear came on all who
dwelt around them; and all these sayings were
discussed throughout all the hill country of
Judea. [66]And all those who heard *them* kept
them in their hearts, saying, "What kind of
child will this be?" And the hand of the Lord
was with him.

SOUL NOTE

Leaping Baby *(1:41)* The baby in Elizabeth's womb leaped for joy when he heard the voice of Mary, the mother of Jesus. This passage shows that unborn children are alive and have a spiritual identity. Many advocates of abortion insist that a fetus isn't a real person until birth, and that therefore abortion isn't murder. The Bible shows, however, that life begins at conception, because God knows all about people and knows all the days of their lives *before they are born* (Ps. 139:16). All people—even those still in the womb—are precious to God. **Topic: Abortion**

DOES MOTHERING MATTER?

ELISA MORGAN AND CAROL KUYKENDALL

(Luke 1:26, 27)

oes mothering matter? Sometimes mothers wonder. Even when they know that God values their commitment to mothering their children, negative feelings can pierce their confidence and accuse them of insignificance. Some mothers comment, for example:

"I feel that what I do as a mother isn't very important."

"I feel like I never finish anything!"

"I feel so exhausted all the time!"

"I feel so out of control!"

Society says that what people do equals their value. Therefore, a woman's worth is thought to be determined by the value of her work, the amount she accomplishes, and the size of her paycheck. If a mother's work is constantly unfinished or coming undone, is exhausting or without monetary reward, she may question her worth.

WHAT *THEY* SAY ABOUT MOTHERING

Mothers face the challenge of investing their time and energy in the lives of their children. The culture, however, confronts them with two messages:

First, *they* say, "Mothering is not a job." A few years ago, California officially informed one mother who wanted to run for Congress that motherhood didn't count as a job. Because mothers don't receive pay for their work, mothering is not recognized as an occupation. Instead, it is viewed as no more than a biological status. If a woman mothers, and only mothers, society says she is not working. And even if she mothers while being a lawyer, hanging wallpaper, or running a service from her home, the mothering part of her day isn't valued as work. The culture says that mothering is insignificant, so it undervalues the task (the "job") of mothering. It can be difficult for women to value their major investment in life—mothering—when their culture judges that investment as having no value.

Second, *they* say, "Mothering is not a skill." Mothering skills, where time and energy are invested in the lives of those who can't do for themselves, are undervalued. All around are blatant messages that mothering is no more than an expensive hobby. Little praise or encouragement is given to those who invest their lives in the lives of their children, perhaps trading personal fulfillment and a paycheck for the well-being of future adults.

WHAT GOD SAYS ABOUT MOTHERING

Mothers need to understand the value of their mothering from God's perspective. When mothers see themselves as God sees them—as His beloved children—they are free to drop their burdens of worry or guilt about the time they spend mothering. They can focus on being the best moms they can be.

Mothering is highly esteemed in God's Word. Children are declared to be precious gifts from God (Ps. 127:3). Throughout the Book of Proverbs, exhortation is given to the "son" to listen to his father's and mother's instruction and guidance: "My son, hear the instruction of your father, and do not forsake the law of your mother; for they will be a graceful ornament on your head, and chains about your neck" (Prov. 1:8, 9). Proverbs 31, the chapter describing the "virtuous woman," pictures a mother who diligently cares for her household: She "works with her hands . . . rises while it is yet night, and provides food for her household. . . . She watches over the ways of her household, and does not eat the bread of idleness" (Prov. 31:13, 15, 27). She has a great reward for her toil, for "her children rise up and call her blessed; her husband also, and he praises her" (Prov. 31:28).

THE DIFFERENCE THAT MOTHERING MAKES

With God's truth in place, the value of mothering can be redefined. Mothering cannot be defined by a paycheck or a promotion, but in the peace of mind that comes from being there for children. Mothering makes a difference in several areas.

Mothers make a critical difference in a child's early physical development. Recent scientific studies show that a child's environment from birth to age three influences his or her brain structure and ability to learn. A 1994 Carnegie Corporation report says that brain development before age one is more rapid, extensive, vulnerable to environmental influences, and longer lasting than previously realized. The study further states that a child's environment affects the number of brain cells, the connections among them, and the way the connections are "wired."

Mothers also make a critical difference in a child's emotional development. A mother's nurturing love builds the foundation of her child's ability to love others, to learn, and to adjust to his or her environment. Child development experts say that a secure attachment to one's mother forms the foundation for a child's entire self-structure and identity. Together they work to create an individual who can look in a mirror and squeal with delight, "That's me!"

In addition, mothering makes a difference in the life of the mother. As women adjust to becoming mothers, they often don't understand the difference their efforts make in their own lives. When a child is born, a mother is born, and she thoughtfully invests herself in her children during their formative years. She reaps the benefits in the joy of living with secure and independent children.

Mothering ultimately makes a difference in the world. The organization called "Mothers of Preschoolers" (MOPS International) has the motto that mothering matters, because "today makes a difference tomorrow." Mothering matters not only to the child and to the mother, but also to the world in which they live.

FURTHER MEDITATION:

Other passages to study about the issue of motherhood include:

- Genesis 17:15–19, 21:1–7
- Exodus 2:1–10
- 1 Samuel 1:1–28; 2:18–21
- Proverbs 31
- Luke 1

To Learn More: Turn to the key passage note on motherhood at 2 Timothy 1:5 on page 1605. See also the personality profile of Mary on page 1315.

Zacharias' Prophecy

67Now his father Zacharias was filled with the Holy Spirit, and prophesied, saying:

68 "Blessed *is* the Lord God of Israel,
For He has visited and redeemed His people,
69 And has raised up a horn of salvation for us
In the house of His servant David,
70 As He spoke by the mouth of His holy prophets,
Who *have been* since the world began,
71 That we should be saved from our enemies
And from the hand of all who hate us,
72 To perform the mercy *promised* to our fathers
And to remember His holy covenant,
73 The oath which He swore to our father Abraham:
74 To grant us that we,
Being delivered from the hand of our enemies,
Might serve Him without fear,
75 In holiness and righteousness before Him all the days of our life.

76 "And you, child, will be called the prophet of the Highest;
For you will go before the face of the Lord to prepare His ways,
77 To give knowledge of salvation to His people
By the remission of their sins,
78 Through the tender mercy of our God,
With which the Dayspring from on high has visited[a] us;
79 To give light to those who sit in darkness and the shadow of death,
To guide our feet into the way of peace."

80So the child grew and became strong in spirit, and was in the deserts till the day of his manifestation to Israel.

Christ Born of Mary

2 And it came to pass in those days *that* a decree went out from Caesar Augustus that all the world should be registered. 2This census first took place while Quirinius was governing Syria. 3So all went to be registered, everyone to his own city.

4Joseph also went up from Galilee, out of the city of Nazareth, into Judea, to the city of David, which is called Bethlehem, because he was of the house and lineage of David, 5to be registered with Mary, his betrothed wife,[a] who was with child. 6So it was, that while they were there, the days were completed for her to be delivered. 7And she brought forth her firstborn Son, and wrapped Him in swaddling cloths, and laid Him in a manger, because there was no room for them in the inn.

Glory in the Highest

8Now there were in the same country shepherds living out in the fields, keeping watch over their flock by night. 9And behold,[a] an angel of the Lord stood before them, and the glory of the Lord shone around them, and they were greatly afraid. 10Then the angel said to them, "Do not be afraid, for behold, I bring you good tidings of great joy which will be to all people. 11For there is born to you this day in the city of David a Savior, who is Christ the Lord. 12And this *will be* the sign to you: You will find a Babe wrapped in swaddling cloths, lying in a manger."

13And suddenly there was with the angel a multitude of the heavenly host praising God and saying:

14 "Glory to God in the highest,
And on earth peace, goodwill toward men!"[a]

15So it was, when the angels had gone away from them into heaven, that the shepherds said to one another, "Let us now go to Bethlehem and see this thing that has come to pass, which the Lord has made known to us." 16And they came with haste and found Mary and Joseph, and the Babe lying in a manger. 17Now when they had seen *Him,* they made widely[a] known the saying which was told them concerning this Child. 18And all those who heard *it* marveled at those things which were told them by the shepherds. 19But Mary kept all these things and pondered *them* in her heart. 20Then the shepherds returned, glorifying and praising God for all the things that they had heard and seen, as it was told them.

1:78 [a]NU-Text reads *shall visit.* **2:5** [a]NU-Text omits *wife.* **2:9** [a]NU-Text omits *behold.* **2:14** [a]NU-Text reads *toward men of goodwill.* **2:17** [a]NU-Text omits *widely.*

Circumcision of Jesus

21And when eight days were completed for
the circumcision of the Child,[a] His name was
called Jesus, the name given by the angel before He was conceived in the womb.

Jesus Presented in the Temple

22Now when the days of her purification according to the law of Moses were completed,
they brought Him to Jerusalem to present *Him*
to the Lord 23(as it is written in the law of the
Lord, *"Every male who opens the womb shall
be called holy to the* Lord*"*),[a] 24and to offer a
sacrifice according to what is said in the law
of the Lord, *"A pair of turtledoves or two
young pigeons."*[a]

Simeon Sees God's Salvation

25And behold, there was a man in Jerusalem
whose name was Simeon, and this man was
just and devout, waiting for the Consolation of
Israel, and the Holy Spirit was upon him.
26And it had been revealed to him by the Holy
Spirit that he would not see death before he
had seen the Lord's Christ. 27So he came by
the Spirit into the temple. And when the parents brought in the Child Jesus, to do for Him
according to the custom of the law, 28he took
Him up in his arms and blessed God and said:

29 "Lord, now You are letting Your servant
depart in peace,
According to Your word;
30 For my eyes have seen Your salvation
31 Which You have prepared before the
face of all peoples,
32 A light to *bring* revelation to the
Gentiles,
And the glory of Your people Israel."

2:21 [a]NU-Text reads *for His circumcision.*
2:23 [a]Exodus 13:2, 12, 15 **2:24** [a]Leviticus 12:8

PERSONALITY PROFILE

Motherhood

MARY: A MOTHER'S LOVE

(LUKE 2:5)

When God became a man, He didn't arrive on earth full-grown; He came, instead, as a baby born to a woman specially chosen to be His mother. Mary was a young woman of Nazareth, recently engaged to a carpenter named Joseph. She anticipated a fairly normal life—until the angel Gabriel visited her with astounding news that would turn her world upside down. A miracle would occur in her womb and allow a Baby to grow there. That Baby would be the promised Messiah. Mary was the young virgin Isaiah the prophet had foretold (Is. 7:14).

Mary accepted the angel's words: "Behold the maidservant of the Lord! Let it be to me according to your word" (Luke 1:38), but her motherhood was already off to a rocky start—telling her fiancé would be the first difficult step. But through it all, Mary obeyed God, even traveling to Bethlehem on a donkey when she was almost ready to deliver, realizing that the Scriptures were being fulfilled in Caesar's demand for a census.

In many ways, Mary was probably a typical mother. She protected, nurtured, raised, and worried about her Son. She took Him to school and continued to guide Him until He left home for His ministry at age 30. Jesus was not a typical child, however. He had been born as a human to die as a human for all humanity. And Mary, His mother, stood at the foot of His cross and watched her precious Son die as her Savior.

Being a mother means more than just bearing or adopting a child. Being a mother takes courage, responsibility, loyalty, love, hard work, patience, consistency, and finally a willingness to let go. Tenderness and strength come together in a unique package called a "mother."

Mothers are vital to the upbringing of the next generation. Mothering is a call of God upon a woman's life, and she should see it as an awesome privilege.

To Learn More: Turn to the article about motherhood on pages 1312, 1313. See also the key passage note at 2 Timothy 1:5 on page 1605.

33 And Joseph and His mother[a] marveled at those things which were spoken of Him. 34 Then Simeon blessed them, and said to Mary His mother, "Behold, this *Child* is destined for the fall and rising of many in Israel, and for a sign which will be spoken against 35 (yes, a sword will pierce through your own soul also), that the thoughts of many hearts may be revealed."

ANNA BEARS WITNESS TO THE REDEEMER

36 Now there was one, Anna, a prophetess, the daughter of Phanuel, of the tribe of Asher. She was of a great age, and had lived with a husband seven years from her virginity; 37 and this woman *was* a widow of about eighty-four years,[a] who did not depart from the temple, but served *God* with fastings and prayers night and day. 38 And coming in that instant she gave thanks to the Lord,[a] and spoke of Him to all those who looked for redemption in Jerusalem.

THE FAMILY RETURNS TO NAZARETH

39 So when they had performed all things according to the law of the Lord, they returned to Galilee, to their *own* city, Nazareth. 40 And the Child grew and became strong in spirit,[a] filled with wisdom; and the grace of God was upon Him.

THE BOY JESUS AMAZES THE SCHOLARS

41 His parents went to Jerusalem every year at the Feast of the Passover. 42 And when He was twelve years old, they went up to Jerusalem according to the custom of the feast. 43 When they had finished the days, as they returned, the Boy Jesus lingered behind in Jerusalem. And Joseph and His mother[a] did not know *it;* 44 but supposing Him to have been in the company, they went a day's journey, and sought Him among *their* relatives and acquaintances. 45 So when they did not find Him, they returned to Jerusalem, seeking Him. 46 Now so it was *that* after three days they found Him in the temple, sitting in the midst of the teachers, both listening to them and asking them questions. 47 And all who heard Him were astonished at His understanding and answers. 48 So when they saw Him, they were amazed; and His mother said to Him, "Son, why have You done this to us?

2:33 [a]NU-Text reads *And His father and mother.* **2:37** [a]NU-Text reads *a widow until she was eighty-four.* **2:38** [a]NU-Text reads *to God.* **2:40** [a]NU-Text omits *in spirit.* **2:43** [a]NU-Text reads *And His parents.*

SOUL NOTE

Being Content *(2:36)* Anna was very young when her husband died, and she had been a widow for 84 years. Anna remained single, choosing to give her life to serving God through fasting and prayer. People are single for a number of reasons, and they respond to singleness in different ways. Some single people, like Anna, seek to serve God without concern about marriage; others dearly long for a spouse. It is important to remember that the key to a fulfilled single life is contentment in God. He has places of service for all people—married or single. **Topic: Singleness**

SOUL NOTE

Coming of Age *(2:41, 42)* He was God incarnate, but the twelve-year-old Jesus did have His time of adolescent development—taking on more responsibility, seeking independence, and wanting answers to His questions. And Mary reacted as any parent would—worrying, being surprised, and becoming upset. Adolescent development and parental reactions are basically the same today. As children grow and mature, they are learning to become independent of their parents and more dependent on God through a personal relationship with Him. Parents must learn to allow their children to find God's direction in their lives. **Topic: Adolescent Development**

Look, Your father and I have sought You anxiously."

[49]And He said to them, "Why did you seek Me? Did you not know that I must be about My Father's business?" [50]But they did not understand the statement which He spoke to them.

Jesus Advances in Wisdom and Favor

[51]Then He went down with them and came to Nazareth, and was subject to them, but His mother kept all these things in her heart. [52]And Jesus increased in wisdom and stature, and in favor with God and men.

John the Baptist Prepares the Way

3 Now in the fifteenth year of the reign of Tiberius Caesar, Pontius Pilate being governor of Judea, Herod being tetrarch of Galilee, his brother Philip tetrarch of Iturea and the region of Trachonitis, and Lysanias tetrarch of Abilene, [2]while Annas and Caiaphas were high priests,[a] the word of God came to John the son of Zacharias in the wilderness. [3]And he went into all the region around the Jordan, preaching a baptism of repentance for

3:2 [a]NU-Text and M-Text read *in the high priesthood of Annas and Caiaphas.*

PERSONALITY PROFILE

Child Development

JESUS, GOD'S SON

(LUKE 2:52)

Parents and teenagers often share similar frustrations about the Gospels as biographies of Jesus. These often appear as questions: (1) Why didn't God tell us more about the childhood of Jesus? (2) Why such silence about His teen years? (3) Couldn't young people gain help from knowing more of Jesus' experiences during His adolescence? The answers to these questions are (1) God told us enough; (2) God had a reason; and (3) probably not. Added details about Jesus' childhood would have likely been used more often as excuses than as lessons. Jesus had a childhood—not everyone's childhood. God told us enough about Jesus to give us all the help we need.

When Luke summarized Jesus' teenage years, he listed a growth pattern that ought to be the goal of every young person and the prayer of every parent: "And Jesus increased in wisdom and stature, and in favor with God and men." The description offers few details but an abundance of direction. The gaps and the known facts of Jesus' early years combine to tell us that we can't expect to see ideal childhoods, but there are desired results.
Jesus developed in four specific areas:

- Mentally (wisdom)
- Physically (stature)
- Spiritually (favor with God)
- Socially (favor with people)

What greater summary of a young person's formative years could be given than that they developed significantly in each of these areas? Yet how often do children grow up with one or more of these areas neglected completely?

Luke's summary offers parents an effective and flexible outline rather than a detailed program. Putting it into practice with children becomes, first, a matter of prayer. Children should hear their parents praying for them about these growth areas. Wisdom, stature, and favor with God and people can certainly generate numerous conversations in which children and young people are encouraged to set goals for themselves in these areas. Parents can help their kids make these character development goals part of their own prayers. Young people who have discussed these areas have a better idea of what it means to be like Jesus.

To Learn More: Turn to the article about child development on pages 228, 229. See also the key passage note at Deuteronomy 4:9, 10 on page 226.

the remission of sins, [4]as it is written in the book of the words of Isaiah the prophet, saying:

"The voice of one crying in the
wilderness:
'Prepare the way of the L*ORD;*
Make His paths straight.
5 *Every valley shall be filled*
And every mountain and hill brought
low;
The crooked places shall be made
straight
And the rough ways smooth;
6 *And all flesh shall see the salvation of*
God.' "[a]

JOHN PREACHES TO THE PEOPLE

[7]Then he said to the multitudes that came out to be baptized by him, "Brood of vipers! Who warned you to flee from the wrath to come? [8]Therefore bear fruits worthy of repentance, and do not begin to say to yourselves, 'We have Abraham as *our* father.' For I say to you that God is able to raise up children to Abraham from these stones. [9]And even now the ax is laid to the root of the trees. Therefore every tree which does not bear good fruit is cut down and thrown into the fire."

[10]So the people asked him, saying, "What shall we do then?"

[11]He answered and said to them, "He who has two tunics, let him give to him who has none; and he who has food, let him do likewise."

[12]Then tax collectors also came to be baptized, and said to him, "Teacher, what shall we do?"

[13]And he said to them, "Collect no more than what is appointed for you."

[14]Likewise the soldiers asked him, saying, "And what shall we do?"

So he said to them, "Do not intimidate anyone or accuse falsely, and be content with your wages."

[15]Now as the people were in expectation, and all reasoned in their hearts about John, whether he was the Christ *or* not, [16]John answered, saying to all, "I indeed baptize you with water; but One mightier than I is coming, whose sandal strap I am not worthy to loose. He will baptize you with the Holy Spirit and fire. [17]His winnowing fan *is* in His hand, and He will thoroughly clean out His threshing floor, and gather the wheat into His barn; but the chaff He will burn with unquenchable fire."

[18]And with many other exhortations he preached to the people. [19]But Herod the tetrarch, being rebuked by him concerning Herodias, his brother Philip's wife,[a] and for all the evils which Herod had done, [20]also added this, above all, that he shut John up in prison.

JOHN BAPTIZES JESUS

[21]When all the people were baptized, it came to pass that Jesus also was baptized; and while He prayed, the heaven was opened. [22]And the Holy Spirit descended in bodily form like a dove upon Him, and a voice came from heaven which said, "You are My beloved Son; in You I am well pleased."

THE GENEALOGY OF JESUS CHRIST

[23]Now Jesus Himself began *His ministry at* about thirty years of age, being (as was sup-

3:6 [a]Isaiah 40:3–5 **3:19** [a]NU-Text reads *his brother's wife.*

SOUL NOTE

Special Baptism *(3:16)* Some people thought John the Baptist was the Messiah, the Christ. John explained that he only baptized with water, but Christ would baptize "with the Holy Spirit and fire." The baptism with the Holy Spirit occurred later, after Jesus ascended to heaven and sent the Holy Spirit on His followers (Acts 2). People are baptized with the Holy Spirit when, by faith, they accept Jesus as Savior and become a part of God's family. The Holy Spirit comes to live within believers' hearts, giving them the power to be witnesses for Christ and to lead God-pleasing lives.

Topic: Presence of the Holy Spirit

posed) *the* son of Joseph, *the son* of Heli, [24]*the son* of Matthat,[a] *the son* of Levi, *the son* of Melchi, *the son* of Janna, *the son* of Joseph, [25]*the son* of Mattathiah, *the son* of Amos, *the son* of Nahum, *the son* of Esli, *the son* of Naggai, [26]*the son* of Maath, *the son* of Mattathiah, *the son* of Semei, *the son* of Joseph, *the son* of Judah, [27]*the son* of Joannas, *the son* of Rhesa, *the son* of Zerubbabel, *the son* of Shealtiel, *the son* of Neri, [28]*the son* of Melchi, *the son* of Addi, *the son* of Cosam, *the son* of Elmodam, *the son* of Er, [29]*the son* of Jose, *the son* of Eliezer, *the son* of Jorim, *the son* of Matthat, *the son* of Levi, [30]*the son* of Simeon, *the son* of Judah, *the son* of Joseph, *the son* of Jonan, *the son* of Eliakim, [31]*the son* of Melea, *the son* of Menan, *the son* of Mattathah, *the son* of Nathan, *the son* of David, [32]*the son* of Jesse, *the son* of Obed, *the son* of Boaz, *the son* of Salmon, *the son* of Nahshon, [33]*the son* of Amminadab, *the son* of Ram, *the son* of Hezron, *the son* of Perez, *the son* of Judah, [34]*the son* of Jacob, *the son* of Isaac, *the son* of Abraham, *the son* of Terah, *the son* of Nahor, [35]*the son* of Serug, *the son* of Reu, *the son* of Peleg, *the son* of Eber, *the son* of Shelah, [36]*the son* of Cainan, *the son* of Arphaxad, *the son* of Shem, *the son* of Noah, *the son* of Lamech, [37]*the son* of Methuselah, *the son* of Enoch, *the son* of Jared, *the son* of Mahalalel, *the son* of Cainan, [38]*the son* of Enosh, *the son* of Seth, *the son* of Adam, *the son* of God.

SATAN TEMPTS JESUS

4 Then Jesus, being filled with the Holy Spirit, returned from the Jordan and was led by the Spirit into[a] the wilderness, [2]being tempted for forty days by the devil. And in those days He ate nothing, and afterward, when they had ended, He was hungry.

[3]And the devil said to Him, "If You are the Son of God, command this stone to become bread."

[4]But Jesus answered him, saying,[a] "It is written, *'Man shall not live by bread alone, but by every word of God.'* "[b]

[5]Then the devil, taking Him up on a high mountain, showed Him[a] all the kingdoms of the world in a moment of time. [6]And the devil said to Him, "All this authority I will give You, and their glory; for *this* has been delivered to me, and I give it to whomever I wish. [7]Therefore, if You will worship before me, all will be Yours."

[8]And Jesus answered and said to him, "Get behind Me, Satan![a] For[b] it is written, *'You shall worship the LORD your God, and Him only you shall serve.'* "[c]

[9]Then he brought Him to Jerusalem, set Him on the pinnacle of the temple, and said to Him, "If You are the Son of God, throw Yourself down from here. [10]For it is written:

'He shall give His angels charge over you,
To keep you,'

[11]and,

'In their hands they shall bear you up,
Lest you dash your foot against a
stone.' "[a]

[12]And Jesus answered and said to him, "It has been said, *'You shall not tempt the LORD your God.'* "[a]

[13]Now when the devil had ended every temptation, he departed from Him until an opportune time.

JESUS BEGINS HIS GALILEAN MINISTRY

[14]Then Jesus returned in the power of the Spirit to Galilee, and news of Him went out through all the surrounding region. [15]And He taught in their synagogues, being glorified by all.

JESUS REJECTED AT NAZARETH

[16]So He came to Nazareth, where He had been brought up. And as His custom was, He went into the synagogue on the Sabbath day, and stood up to read. [17]And He was handed the book of the prophet Isaiah. And when He had opened the book, He found the place where it was written:

18 *"The Spirit of the LORD is upon Me,*
Because He has anointed Me

3:24 [a]This and several other names in the genealogy are spelled somewhat differently in the NU-Text. Since the New King James Version uses the Old Testament spelling for persons mentioned in the New Testament, these variations, which come from the Greek, have not been footnoted. **4:1** [a]NU-Text reads *in.* **4:4** [a]Deuteronomy 8:3 [b]NU-Text omits *but by every word of God.* **4:5** [a]NU-Text reads *And taking Him up, he showed Him.* **4:8** [a]NU-Text omits *Get behind Me, Satan.* [b]NU-Text and M-Text omit *For.* [c]Deuteronomy 6:13 **4:11** [a]Psalm 91:11, 12 **4:12** [a]Deuteronomy 6:16

To preach the gospel to the poor;
He has sent Me to heal the brokenhearted,[a]
To proclaim liberty to the captives
And recovery of sight to the blind,
To set at liberty those who are oppressed;
19 *To proclaim the acceptable year of the* LORD."[a]

20Then He closed the book, and gave *it* back to the attendant and sat down. And the eyes of all who were in the synagogue were fixed on Him. 21And He began to say to them, "Today this Scripture is fulfilled in your hearing." 22So all bore witness to Him, and marveled at the gracious words which proceeded out of His mouth. And they said, "Is this not Joseph's son?"

23He said to them, "You will surely say this proverb to Me, 'Physician, heal yourself! Whatever we have heard done in Capernaum,[a] do also here in Your country.' " 24Then He said, "Assuredly, I say to you, no prophet is accepted in his own country. 25But I tell you truly, many widows were in Israel in the days of Elijah, when the heaven was shut up three years and six months, and there was a great famine throughout all the land; 26but to none of them was Elijah sent except to Zarephath,[a] *in the region* of Sidon, to a woman *who was* a widow. 27And many lepers were in Israel in the time of Elisha the prophet, and none of them was cleansed except Naaman the Syrian."

28So all those in the synagogue, when they heard these things, were filled with wrath, 29and rose up and thrust Him out of the city; and they led Him to the brow of the hill on which their city was built, that they might throw Him down over the cliff. 30Then passing through the midst of them, He went His way.

JESUS CASTS OUT AN UNCLEAN SPIRIT

31Then He went down to Capernaum, a city of Galilee, and was teaching them on the Sabbaths. 32And they were astonished at His teaching, for His word was with authority. 33Now in the synagogue there was a man who had a spirit of an unclean demon. And he cried out with a loud voice, 34saying, "Let *us* alone! What have we to do with You, Jesus of Nazareth? Did You come to destroy us? I know who You are—the Holy One of God!"

35But Jesus rebuked him, saying, "Be quiet, and come out of him!" And when the demon had thrown him in *their* midst, it came out of him and did not hurt him. 36Then they were all amazed and spoke among themselves, saying, "What a word this *is!* For with authority and power He commands the unclean spirits, and they come out." 37And the report about Him went out into every place in the surrounding region.

PETER'S MOTHER-IN-LAW HEALED

38Now He arose from the synagogue and entered Simon's house. But Simon's wife's mother was sick with a high fever, and they made request of Him concerning her. 39So He stood over her and rebuked the fever, and it left her. And immediately she arose and served them.

MANY HEALED AFTER SABBATH SUNSET

40When the sun was setting, all those who had any that were sick with various diseases brought them to Him; and He laid His hands on every one of them and healed them. 41And demons also came out of many, crying out

4:18 [a]NU-Text omits *to heal the brokenhearted.* **4:19** [a]Isaiah 61:1, 2 **4:23** [a]Here and elsewhere the NU-Text spelling is *Capharnaum.* **4:26** [a]Greek *Sarepta*

SOUL NOTE

Setting Limits *(4:42)* People in the crowds around Jesus continually asked Him for healing. Jesus worked hard at spending time with people and meeting their needs. At times, however, He set limits and went off by Himself. Jesus needed time alone for prayer and spiritual renewal, and so do we. We need to set boundaries on our busyness or our lives will soon be jammed with concerns and activities. And soon we will have no time for God. No matter how much we have to do, things will go better when we make sure to spend time with God, one-on-one. **Topic: Boundaries**

and saying, "You are the Christ,[a] the Son of God!"

And He, rebuking *them,* did not allow them to speak, for they knew that He was the Christ.

JESUS PREACHES IN GALILEE

42Now when it was day, He departed and went into a deserted place. And the crowd sought Him and came to Him, and tried to keep Him from leaving them; 43but He said to them, "I must preach the kingdom of God to the other cities also, because for this purpose I have been sent." 44And He was preaching in the synagogues of Galilee.[a]

FOUR FISHERMEN CALLED AS DISCIPLES

5 So it was, as the multitude pressed about Him to hear the word of God, that He stood by the Lake of Gennesaret, 2and saw two boats standing by the lake; but the fishermen had gone from them and were washing *their* nets. 3Then He got into one of the boats, which was Simon's, and asked him to put out a little from the land. And He sat down and taught the multitudes from the boat.

4When He had stopped speaking, He said to Simon, "Launch out into the deep and let down your nets for a catch."

5But Simon answered and said to Him, "Master, we have toiled all night and caught nothing; nevertheless at Your word I will let down the net." 6And when they had done this, they caught a great number of fish, and their net was breaking. 7So they signaled to *their* partners in the other boat to come and help them. And they came and filled both the boats, so that they began to sink. 8When Simon Peter saw *it,* he fell down at Jesus' knees, saying, "Depart from me, for I am a sinful man, O Lord!"

9For he and all who were with him were astonished at the catch of fish which they had taken; 10and so also *were* James and John, the sons of Zebedee, who were partners with Simon. And Jesus said to Simon, "Do not be afraid. From now on you will catch men." 11So when they had brought their boats to land, they forsook all and followed Him.

JESUS CLEANSES A LEPER

12And it happened when He was in a certain city, that behold, a man who was full of leprosy saw Jesus; and he fell on *his* face and implored Him, saying, "Lord, if You are willing, You can make me clean."

13Then He put out *His* hand and touched him, saying, "I am willing; be cleansed." Immediately the leprosy left him. 14And He charged him to tell no one, "But go and show yourself to the priest, and make an offering for your cleansing, as a testimony to them, just as Moses commanded."

15However, the report went around concerning Him all the more; and great multitudes came together to hear, and to be healed by Him of their infirmities. 16So He Himself *often* withdrew into the wilderness and prayed.

JESUS FORGIVES AND HEALS A PARALYTIC

17Now it happened on a certain day, as He was teaching, that there were Pharisees and teachers of the law sitting by, who had come out of every town of Galilee, Judea, and Jerusalem. And the power of the Lord was *present* to heal them.[a] 18Then behold, men brought on a bed a man who was paralyzed, whom they sought to bring in and lay before Him. 19And when they could not find how they might bring him in, because of the crowd, they went up on the housetop and let him down with *his* bed through the tiling into the midst before Jesus.

20When He saw their faith, He said to him, "Man, your sins are forgiven you."

21And the scribes and the Pharisees began to reason, saying, "Who is this who speaks blasphemies? Who can forgive sins but God alone?"

22But when Jesus perceived their thoughts, He answered and said to them, "Why are you reasoning in your hearts? 23Which is easier, to say, 'Your sins are forgiven you,' or to say, 'Rise up and walk'? 24But that you may know that the Son of Man has power on earth to forgive sins"—He said to the man who was paralyzed, "I say to you, arise, take up your bed, and go to your house."

25Immediately he rose up before them, took up what he had been lying on, and departed to his own house, glorifying God. 26And they were all amazed, and they glorified God and were filled with fear, saying, "We have seen strange things today!"

4:41 [a]NU-Text omits *the Christ.* **4:44** [a]NU-Text reads *Judea.* **5:17** [a]NU-Text reads *present with Him to heal.*

MATTHEW THE TAX COLLECTOR

27After these things He went out and saw a tax collector named Levi, sitting at the tax office. And He said to him, "Follow Me." 28So he left all, rose up, and followed Him.

29Then Levi gave Him a great feast in his own house. And there were a great number of tax collectors and others who sat down with them. 30And their scribes and the Pharisees[a] complained against His disciples, saying, "Why do You eat and drink with tax collectors and sinners?"

31Jesus answered and said to them, "Those who are well have no need of a physician, but those who are sick. 32I have not come to call *the* righteous, but sinners, to repentance."

JESUS IS QUESTIONED ABOUT FASTING

33Then they said to Him, "Why do[a] the disciples of John fast often and make prayers, and likewise those of the Pharisees, but Yours eat and drink?"

34And He said to them, "Can you make the friends of the bridegroom fast while the bridegroom is with them? 35But the days will come when the bridegroom will be taken away from them; then they will fast in those days."

36Then He spoke a parable to them: "No one puts a piece from a new garment on an old one;[a] otherwise the new makes a tear, and also the piece that was *taken* out of the new does not match the old. 37And no one puts new wine into old wineskins; or else the new wine will burst the wineskins and be spilled, and the wineskins will be ruined. 38But new wine must be put into new wineskins, and both are preserved.[a] 39And no one, having drunk old *wine*, immediately[a] desires new; for he says, 'The old is better.' "[b]

JESUS IS LORD OF THE SABBATH

6

Now it happened on the second Sabbath after the first[a] that He went through the grainfields. And His disciples plucked the heads of grain and ate *them*, rubbing *them* in *their* hands. 2And some of the Pharisees said to them, "Why are you doing what is not lawful to do on the Sabbath?"

3But Jesus answering them said, "Have you not even read this, what David did when he was hungry, he and those who were with him: 4how he went into the house of God, took and ate the showbread, and also gave some to those with him, which is not lawful for any but the priests to eat?" 5And He said to them, "The Son of Man is also Lord of the Sabbath."

HEALING ON THE SABBATH

6Now it happened on another Sabbath, also, that He entered the synagogue and taught. And a man was there whose right hand was withered. 7So the scribes and Pharisees watched Him closely, whether He would heal on the Sabbath, that they might find an accusation against Him. 8But He knew their thoughts, and said to the man who had the withered hand, "Arise and stand here." And he arose and stood. 9Then Jesus said to them, "I will ask you one thing: Is it lawful on the Sabbath to do good or to do evil, to save life or to destroy?"[a] 10And when He had looked around at them all, He said to the man,[a] "Stretch out your hand." And he did so, and his hand was restored as whole as the other.[b] 11But they were filled with rage, and discussed with one another what they might do to Jesus.

THE TWELVE APOSTLES

12Now it came to pass in those days that He went out to the mountain to pray, and continued all night in prayer to God. 13And when it was day, He called His disciples to *Himself;* and from them He chose twelve whom He also named apostles: 14Simon, whom He also named Peter, and Andrew his brother; James and John; Philip and Bartholomew; 15Matthew and Thomas; James the *son* of Alphaeus, and Simon called the Zealot; 16Judas *the son* of James, and Judas Iscariot who also became a traitor.

JESUS HEALS A GREAT MULTITUDE

17And He came down with them and stood on a level place with a crowd of His disciples and a great multitude of people from all Judea and Jerusalem, and from the seacoast of Tyre and Sidon, who came to hear Him and be healed of their diseases, 18as well as those

---

5:30 [a]NU-Text reads *But the Pharisees and their scribes.* **5:33** [a]NU-Text omits *Why do,* making the verse a statement. **5:36** [a]NU-Text reads *No one tears a piece from a new garment and puts it on an old one.* **5:38** [a]NU-Text omits *and both are preserved.* **5:39** [a]NU-Text omits *immediately.* [b]NU-Text reads *good.* **6:1** [a]NU-Text reads *on a Sabbath.* **6:9** [a]M-Text reads *to kill.* **6:10** [a]NU-Text and M-Text read *to him.* [b]NU-Text omits *as whole as the other.*

who were tormented with unclean spirits. And they were healed. [19]And the whole multitude sought to touch Him, for power went out from Him and healed *them* all.

The Beatitudes

[20]Then He lifted up His eyes toward His disciples, and said:

"Blessed *are you* poor,
For yours is the kingdom of God.
21 Blessed *are you* who hunger now,
For you shall be filled.
Blessed *are you* who weep now,
For you shall laugh.
22 Blessed are you when men hate you,
And when they exclude you,
And revile *you,* and cast out your name as evil,
For the Son of Man's sake.
23 Rejoice in that day and leap for joy!
For indeed your reward *is* great in heaven,
For in like manner their fathers did to the prophets.

Jesus Pronounces Woes

24 "But woe to you who are rich,
For you have received your consolation.
25 Woe to you who are full,
For you shall hunger.
Woe to you who laugh now,
For you shall mourn and weep.
26 Woe to you[a] when all[b] men speak well of you,
For so did their fathers to the false prophets.

Love Your Enemies

[27]"But I say to you who hear: Love your enemies, do good to those who hate you, [28]bless those who curse you, and pray for those who spitefully use you. [29]To him who strikes you on the *one* cheek, offer the other also. And from him who takes away your cloak, do not withhold *your* tunic either. [30]Give to everyone who asks of you. And from him who takes away your goods do not ask *them* back. [31]And just as you want men to do to you, you also do to them likewise.

[32]"But if you love those who love you, what credit is that to you? For even sinners love those who love them. [33]And if you do good to those who do good to you, what credit is that to you? For even sinners do the same. [34]And if you lend *to those* from whom you hope to receive back, what credit is that to you? For even sinners lend to sinners to receive as much back. [35]But love your enemies, do good, and lend, hoping for nothing in return; and your reward will be great, and you will be sons of the Most High. For He is kind to the unthankful and evil. [36]Therefore be merciful, just as your Father also is merciful.

> "Judge not, and you shall not be judged. Condemn not, and you shall not be condemned. Forgive, and you will be forgiven."
> LUKE 6:37

Do Not Judge

[37]"Judge not, and you shall not be judged. Condemn not, and you shall not be condemned. Forgive, and you will be forgiven.

6:26 [a]NU-Text and M-Text omit *to you.* [b]M-Text omits *all.*

SOUL NOTE

The Plot Thickens *(6:27, 28)* When wronged, a human reaction often is to hate the person who wronged us and plot ways to get even. But Jesus said, "Love your enemies, do good to those who hate you . . . and pray for those who spitefully use you." Such words turned many away from Christ and still do today. Loving one's enemies does not mean having affectionate feelings for them. Instead, it requires a decision to act in love toward them no matter how we feel. We need to pray and ask Christ to take our hurt and bitterness, and then to replace those feelings with His love. **Topic: Bitterness**

DEALING WITH A CRITICAL SPIRIT

ED HINDSON

(Luke 6:37, 38)

Some people seem to be experts at evaluating others. They think they have an uncanny ability to read others' minds, evaluate their actions, and judge their motives. The danger in assessing others' behavior in such a way is that people become judgmental. Such people have critical spirits that can be cruel and divisive. Setting themselves up as prosecutor, judge, and jury, they proceed to tear everyone apart who does not see things their way. We all know people like this.

The Bible is filled with examples of judgmentalism—the Jews in the wilderness (Num. 16:1–35), the Pharisees (Matt. 22:15–46), the prodigal son's elder brother (Luke 15:25–32), the immature Christians in the early church (1 Cor. 3:1–7). One of the most serious biblical examples was Miriam's criticism of Moses' wife (Num. 12:1–16). God severely judged Miriam's judgmental spirit.

Just for the record, there is a difference between *judging* and *being judgmental*, however. Christians need to be able to judge between what is good and what is evil so they can discern God's will for their lives. Believers are also called upon to judge disputes among believers, as well as to judge sin and deal accordingly with it (1 Cor. 5:1–12). Sometimes believers need to discern sin in their fellow believers and point it out in a loving manner. The Bible says, "As iron sharpens iron, so a man sharpens the countenance of his friend" (Prov. 27:17).

Many wonder, then, what Jesus meant when He said: "Judge not, that you be not judged. For with what judgment you judge, you will be judged; and with the measure you use, it will be measured back to you" (Matt. 7:1, 2). In this same passage, He also said that people cannot remove the "speck" from someone else's eye when they have a "plank" in their own eye (Matt. 7:4, 5). Jesus was not against believers "sharpening" each other, as the Proverbs verse indicates. Indeed, "Faithful are the wounds of a friend" (Prov. 27:6). Instead, Jesus spoke against people having a judgmental (critical) spirit.

CHARACTERISTICS OF JUDGMENTAL PEOPLE

Judgmental people are critical, condescending, unloving, and unforgiving. They are more concerned with pointing out others' mistakes than helping them with their problems. Their attitudes create anxiety in others whom they attempt to manipulate by demanding compliance with their opinions.

Critical people are not likely to get close or connect emotionally with others. They have few, if any, intimate relationships. They keep most people at arm's length. Since they never share their inner feelings, they tend to be critical of those who do. Critical people tend to make others feel that they are all alone in the world. When the critic is a marriage partner, the spouse can be made to feel lonely and disconnected—leaving both of them vulnerable.

Another characteristic of judgmental people is their self-centered view of life. They are far more concerned about themselves than anyone else. They lack empathy and resist opening up enough to let others talk freely about deeply emotional issues. It is easier for them to condemn than forgive. They lock themselves into a parental-style role and refuse to change. The greatest problem with this pattern is that they also refuse to let others change.

They may try to shame people as a means of controlling them. While some judgmental people may think that they are helping others do the right thing (according to them), they are really hurting them in the long run. Forced behavior, controlled by guilt manipulation, often leaves people wanting to break free. In many cases, this leads to worse behavior patterns, not better ones.

People's reactions to judgmental people can include feelings of detachment (being emotionally inaccessible) and abandonment (connecting, then leaving), and can result in criticism (unloving responses) and even abuse (emotional violation).

CAUSES OF JUDGMENTALISM

One of the major causes of judgmentalism is *guilt*. People tend to criticize others for problems with which they themselves struggle. For example, a gossip will be quick to spot and judge another gossip.

Another cause of judgmentalism is *fear*. People fear others whom they do not understand. Before being saved, Saul (Paul) placed judgment on the Christians because he disagreed with them and feared their growth and popularity (Acts 8:1–4; 9:1, 2). Nehemiah's critics judged and condemned his work on Jerusalem's wall because they were afraid that the city might return to its former power and glory (Neh. 2:19; 4:1–3). A legalistic person who cannot understand other believers' freedom in Christ will be quick to judge their behavior. That person fears freedom, preferring to stay confined within a set of rules so there won't be too many choices.

CURES FOR JUDGMENTALISM

Judgmentalism is a heart attitude that often blinds people to their own problems. It is quick to point the finger but slow to bend the knee. To be set free of a critical spirit, believers can begin by praying for others and working to genuinely reach out to others in love. They can get into an accountability relationship to learn to discern the difference between appropriate judgment and judgmentalism.

A critical spirit can often be discerned by identifying people's motives. If their words are meant to tear others down in order to build themselves up, then they are being judgmental. If they are minimizing and excusing their own faults while pointing out others' faults, then they are being judgmental.

If we find ourselves being critical of others, we need to ask God for forgiveness. Ultimate judgment, of course, belongs to God (Rev. 20:11–15). We dare not attempt to put ourselves in His place!

FURTHER MEDITATION:

Other passages to study about the issue of judgmentalism include:

- 1 Kings 3:9
- Psalms 19:9; 119:66
- Matthew 22:37–40
- Romans 14:10–13
- Ephesians 4:31, 32
- Colossians 3:12–14
- 1 John 2:10, 11

To Learn More: Turn to the key passage note on judgmentalism at Luke 6:37 on page 1326. See also the personality profile of Aaron and Miriam on page 185.

38 Give, and it will be given to you: good measure, pressed down, shaken together, and running over will be put into your bosom. For
with the same measure that you use, it will be
measured back to you."
39 And He spoke a parable to them: "Can the
blind lead the blind? Will they not both fall
into the ditch? 40 A disciple is not above his
teacher, but everyone who is perfectly trained
will be like his teacher. 41 And why do you look
at the speck in your brother's eye, but do not
perceive the plank in your own eye? 42 Or how
can you say to your brother, 'Brother, let me
remove the speck that *is* in your eye,' when
you yourself do not see the plank that *is* in
your own eye? Hypocrite! First remove the
plank from your own eye, and then you will
see clearly to remove the speck that is in your
brother's eye.

A Tree Is Known by Its Fruit

43 "For a good tree does not bear bad fruit,
nor does a bad tree bear good fruit. 44 For every
tree is known by its own fruit. For *men* do not
gather figs from thorns, nor do they gather
grapes from a bramble bush. 45 A good man
out of the good treasure of his heart brings
forth good; and an evil man out of the evil
treasure of his heart[a] brings forth evil. For out
of the abundance of the heart his mouth
speaks.

Build on the Rock

46 "But why do you call Me 'Lord, Lord,' and
not do the things which I say? 47 Whoever
comes to Me, and hears My sayings and does
them, I will show you whom he is like: 48 He is

6:45 [a]NU-Text omits *treasure of his heart.*

KEY PASSAGE

Judgmentalism

PASSING JUDGMENT

(6:37)

There's a paper-thin line between making right judgments and judgmentalism. We face it in our lives all the time: When others are critical of us, we may feel that they are being judgmental; when we are critical of others, however, we feel that we are engaging in right judgment.

Jesus told His followers not to judge others. These commands do not mean that believers are not to use discernment in making decisions or evaluating what people do. Rather, He is urging us not to pass sentence on the actions and attitudes of others without first looking at ourselves. A person with a judgmental and condemning spirit constantly looks down on others—even other believers. That harms and hinders the entire church.

Believers and churches must make strong judgments when dealing with sin and false doctrine. But regarding minor disagreements, Jesus urges love and forgiveness so that His work on earth will not be hindered.

To Learn More: Turn to the article about judgmentalism on pages 1324, 1325. See also the personality profile of Aaron and Miriam on page 185.

SOUL NOTE

Overflowing *(6:38)* The words "give, and it will be given to you" follow Jesus' words urging His followers not to judge or condemn others, but rather to forgive. People who have gracious and compassionate spirits, refusing to judge and condemn, will find gracious attitudes and compassion returned toward them. People who forgive easily will find that they are forgiven their own offenses. The measure with which we give determines the measure with which we receive. **Topic: Attitudes**

like a man building a house, who dug deep and laid the foundation on the rock. And when the flood arose, the stream beat vehemently against that house, and could not shake it, for it was founded on the rock.[a] [49]But he who heard and did nothing is like a man who built a house on the earth without a foundation, against which the stream beat vehemently; and immediately it fell.[a] And the ruin of that house was great."

Jesus Heals a Centurion's Servant

7 Now when He concluded all His sayings in the hearing of the people, He entered Capernaum. [2]And a certain centurion's servant, who was dear to him, was sick and ready to die. [3]So when he heard about Jesus, he sent elders of the Jews to Him, pleading with Him to come and heal his servant. [4]And when they came to Jesus, they begged Him earnestly, saying that the one for whom He should do this was deserving, [5]"for he loves our nation, and has built us a synagogue."

[6]Then Jesus went with them. And when He was already not far from the house, the centurion sent friends to Him, saying to Him, "Lord, do not trouble Yourself, for I am not worthy that You should enter under my roof. [7]Therefore I did not even think myself worthy to come to You. But say the word, and my servant will be healed. [8]For I also am a man placed under authority, having soldiers under me. And I say to one, 'Go,' and he goes; and to another, 'Come,' and he comes; and to my servant, 'Do this,' and he does *it*."

[9]When Jesus heard these things, He marveled at him, and turned around and said to the crowd that followed Him, "I say to you, I have not found such great faith, not even in Israel!" [10]And those who were sent, returning to the house, found the servant well who had been sick.[a]

Jesus Raises the Son of the Widow of Nain

[11]Now it happened, the day after, *that* He went into a city called Nain; and many of His disciples went with Him, and a large crowd. [12]And when He came near the gate of the city, behold, a dead man was being carried out, the only son of his mother; and she was a widow. And a large crowd from the city was with her. [13]When the Lord saw her, He had compassion on her and said to her, "Do not weep." [14]Then He came and touched the open coffin, and those who carried *him* stood still. And He said, "Young man, I say to you, arise." [15]So he who was dead sat up and began to speak. And He presented him to his mother.

[16]Then fear came upon all, and they glorified God, saying, "A great prophet has risen up among us"; and, "God has visited His people." [17]And this report about Him went throughout all Judea and all the surrounding region.

John the Baptist Sends Messengers to Jesus

[18]Then the disciples of John reported to him concerning all these things. [19]And John, calling two of his disciples to *him,* sent *them* to Jesus,[a] saying, "Are You the Coming One, or do we look for another?"

[20]When the men had come to Him, they said, "John the Baptist has sent us to You, saying, 'Are You the Coming One, or do we look for another?' " [21]And that very hour He cured many of infirmities, afflictions, and evil spirits; and to many blind He gave sight.

[22]Jesus answered and said to them, "Go and tell John the things you have seen and heard: that *the* blind see, *the* lame walk, *the* lepers are cleansed, *the* deaf hear, *the* dead are raised, *the* poor have the gospel preached to them. [23]And blessed is *he* who is not offended because of Me."

[24]When the messengers of John had departed, He began to speak to the multitudes concerning John: "What did you go out into the wilderness to see? A reed shaken by the wind? [25]But what did you go out to see? A man clothed in soft garments? Indeed those who are gorgeously appareled and live in luxury are in kings' courts. [26]But what did you go out to see? A prophet? Yes, I say to you, and more than a prophet. [27]This is *he* of whom it is written:

'Behold, I send My messenger before
Your face,
Who will prepare Your way before You.'[a]

[28]For I say to you, among those born of women there is not a greater prophet than John the

6:48 [a]NU-Text reads *for it was well built.*
6:49 [a]NU-Text reads *collapsed.* **7:10** [a]NU-Text omits *who had been sick.* **7:19** [a]NU-Text reads *the Lord.* **7:27** [a]Malachi 3:1

Baptist;[a] but he who is least in the kingdom of
God is greater than he."
29And when all the people heard *Him,* even
the tax collectors justified God, having been
baptized with the baptism of John. 30But the
Pharisees and lawyers rejected the will of God
for themselves, not having been baptized by
him.
31And the Lord said,[a] "To what then shall I
liken the men of this generation, and what are
they like? 32They are like children sitting in the
marketplace and calling to one another, saying:

'We played the flute for you,
And you did not dance;
We mourned to you,
And you did not weep.'

33For John the Baptist came neither eating
bread nor drinking wine, and you say, 'He has
a demon.' 34The Son of Man has come eating
and drinking, and you say, 'Look, a glutton
and a winebibber, a friend of tax collectors
and sinners!' 35But wisdom is justified by all
her children."

A Sinful Woman Forgiven

36Then one of the Pharisees asked Him to
eat with him. And He went to the Pharisee's
house, and sat down to eat. 37And behold, a
woman in the city who was a sinner, when
she knew that *Jesus* sat at the table in the
Pharisee's house, brought an alabaster flask of
fragrant oil, 38and stood at His feet behind
Him weeping; and she began to wash His feet
with her tears, and wiped *them* with the hair
of her head; and she kissed His feet and
anointed *them* with the fragrant oil. 39Now
when the Pharisee who had invited Him saw
this, he spoke to himself, saying, "This Man, if
He were a prophet, would know who and
what manner of woman *this is* who is touching Him, for she is a sinner."
40And Jesus answered and said to him, "Simon, I have something to say to you."
So he said, "Teacher, say it."
41"There was a certain creditor who had
two debtors. One owed five hundred denarii,
and the other fifty. 42And when they had nothing with which to repay, he freely forgave
them both. Tell Me, therefore, which of them
will love him more?"
43Simon answered and said, "I suppose the
one whom he forgave more."
And He said to him, "You have rightly
judged." 44Then He turned to the woman and
said to Simon, "Do you see this woman? I entered your house; you gave Me no water for
My feet, but she has washed My feet with her
tears and wiped *them* with the hair of her
head. 45You gave Me no kiss, but this woman
has not ceased to kiss My feet since the time I
came in. 46You did not anoint My head with
oil, but this woman has anointed My feet with
fragrant oil. 47Therefore I say to you, her sins,
which are many, are forgiven, for she loved
much. But to whom little is forgiven, *the same*
loves little."
48Then He said to her, "Your sins are forgiven."
49And those who sat at the table with Him
began to say to themselves, "Who is this who
even forgives sins?"
50Then He said to the woman, "Your faith
has saved you. Go in peace."

Many Women Minister to Jesus

8 Now it came to pass, afterward, that He
went through every city and village,

7:28 [a]NU-Text reads *there is none greater than John.* **7:31** [a]NU-Text and M-Text omit *And the Lord said.*

SOUL NOTE

Highest Honors *(7:44–47)* Simon the Pharisee had brought Jesus into his home for a meal, but he had neglected to honor Jesus with the basic hospitality of the day—washing His feet and anointing His head. A "woman in the city who was a sinner" (7:37) came and honored Jesus by pouring on His feet valuable anointing oil and by shedding tears of repentance. She knew who Jesus was, and her sinfulness broke her heart. Jesus forgave her. We honor Christ when, like this woman, we see our need for His sacrifice on the Cross, accept it, and worship Him for who He is. **Topic: Honor**

preaching and bringing the glad tidings of the
kingdom of God. And the twelve *were* with
Him, 2and certain women who had been
healed of evil spirits and infirmities—Mary
called Magdalene, out of whom had come
seven demons, 3and Joanna the wife of
Chuza, Herod's steward, and Susanna, and
many others who provided for Him[a] from
their substance.

The Parable of the Sower

4And when a great multitude had gathered,
and they had come to Him from every city, He
spoke by a parable: 5"A sower went out to sow
his seed. And as he sowed, some fell by the
wayside; and it was trampled down, and the
birds of the air devoured it. 6Some fell on rock;
and as soon as it sprang up, it withered away
because it lacked moisture. 7And some fell
among thorns, and the thorns sprang up with
it and choked it. 8But others fell on good
ground, sprang up, and yielded a crop a hundredfold." When He had said these things
He cried, "He who has ears to hear, let him
hear!"

The Purpose of Parables

9Then His disciples asked Him, saying,
"What does this parable mean?"

10And He said, "To you it has been given to
know the mysteries of the kingdom of God,
but to the rest *it is given* in parables, that

'Seeing they may not see,
And hearing they may not understand.'[a]

The Parable of the Sower Explained

11"Now the parable is this: The seed is the
word of God. 12Those by the wayside are the
ones who hear; then the devil comes and
takes away the word out of their hearts, lest
they should believe and be saved. 13But the
ones on the rock *are those* who, when they
hear, receive the word with joy; and these
have no root, who believe for a while and in
time of temptation fall away. 14Now the ones
that fell among thorns are those who, when
they have heard, go out and are choked with
cares, riches, and pleasures of life, and bring
no fruit to maturity. 15But the ones *that* fell on
the good ground are those who, having heard
the word with a noble and good heart, keep *it*
and bear fruit with patience.

The Parable of the Revealed Light

16"No one, when he has lit a lamp, covers it
with a vessel or puts *it* under a bed, but sets *it*
on a lampstand, that those who enter may see
the light. 17For nothing is secret that will not
be revealed, nor *anything* hidden that will not
be known and come to light. 18Therefore take
heed how you hear. For whoever has, to him
more will be given; and whoever does not
have, even what he seems to have will be tak-
en from him."

Jesus' Mother and Brothers Come to Him

19Then His mother and brothers came to
Him, and could not approach Him because of
the crowd. 20And it was told Him *by some,*
who said, "Your mother and Your brothers are
standing outside, desiring to see You."

21But He answered and said to them, "My
mother and My brothers are these who hear
the word of God and do it."

Wind and Wave Obey Jesus

22Now it happened, on a certain day, that
He got into a boat with His disciples. And He

8:3 [a]NU-Text and M-Text read *them.* **8:10** [a]Isaiah 6:9

SOUL NOTE

Mind Power *(8:26, 27)* Jesus stepped from the boat and was met by a demon-possessed man. What might have appeared to be a mental illness was in this case caused by demon possession. Usually, however, mental illness has other causes, such as genetics or hormonal imbalances. We may not know anyone as wild as this man, but we may know someone dealing with the debilitation of mental illness. Such people need assurance of their worthiness before God, as well as Christian professional help. Jesus has the power to heal, but He may not always choose to do so. God's people must trust His wisdom through any difficult time. **Topic: Mental Illness**

said to them, "Let us cross over to the other side of the lake." And they launched out. 23But as they sailed He fell asleep. And a windstorm came down on the lake, and they were filling *with water,* and were in jeopardy. 24And they came to Him and awoke Him, saying, "Master, Master, we are perishing!"

Then He arose and rebuked the wind and the raging of the water. And they ceased, and there was a calm. 25But He said to them, "Where is your faith?"

And they were afraid, and marveled, saying to one another, "Who can this be? For He commands even the winds and water, and they obey Him!"

A Demon-Possessed Man Healed

26Then they sailed to the country of the Gadarenes,[a] which is opposite Galilee. 27And when He stepped out on the land, there met Him a certain man from the city who had demons for a long time. And he wore no clothes,[a] nor did he live in a house but in the tombs. 28When he saw Jesus, he cried out, fell down before Him, and with a loud voice said, "What have I to do with You, Jesus, Son of the Most High God? I beg You, do not torment me!" 29For He had commanded the unclean spirit to come out of the man. For it had often seized him, and he was kept under guard, bound with chains and shackles; and he broke the bonds and was driven by the demon into the wilderness.

30Jesus asked him, saying, "What is your name?"

And he said, "Legion," because many demons had entered him. 31And they begged Him that He would not command them to go out into the abyss.

32Now a herd of many swine was feeding there on the mountain. So they begged Him that He would permit them to enter them. And He permitted them. 33Then the demons went out of the man and entered the swine, and the herd ran violently down the steep place into the lake and drowned.

34When those who fed *them* saw what had happened, they fled and told *it* in the city and in the country. 35Then they went out to see what had happened, and came to Jesus, and found the man from whom the demons had departed, sitting at the feet of Jesus, clothed and in his right mind. And they were afraid. 36They also who had seen *it* told them by what means he who had been demon-possessed was healed. 37Then the whole multitude of the surrounding region of the Gadarenes[a] asked Him to depart from them, for they were seized with great fear. And He got into the boat and returned.

38Now the man from whom the demons had departed begged Him that he might be with Him. But Jesus sent him away, saying, 39"Return to your own house, and tell what great things God has done for you." And he went his way and proclaimed throughout the whole city what great things Jesus had done for him.

A Girl Restored to Life and a Woman Healed

40So it was, when Jesus returned, that the multitude welcomed Him, for they were all waiting for Him. 41And behold, there came a man named Jairus, and he was a ruler of the synagogue. And he fell down at Jesus' feet and begged Him to come to his house, 42for he had an only daughter about twelve years of age, and she was dying.

But as He went, the multitudes thronged Him. 43Now a woman, having a flow of blood for twelve years, who had spent all her livelihood on physicians and could not be healed by any, 44came from behind and touched the border of His garment. And immediately her flow of blood stopped.

45And Jesus said, "Who touched Me?"

When all denied it, Peter and those with him[a] said, "Master, the multitudes throng and press You, and You say, 'Who touched Me?' "[b]

46But Jesus said, "Somebody touched Me, for I perceived power going out from Me." 47Now when the woman saw that she was not hidden, she came trembling; and falling down before Him, she declared to Him in the presence of all the people the reason she had touched Him and how she was healed immediately.

48And He said to her, "Daughter, be of good cheer;[a] your faith has made you well. Go in peace."

49While He was still speaking, someone came from the ruler of the synagogue's *house,*

8:26 [a]NU-Text reads *Gerasenes.* **8:27** [a]NU-Text reads *who had demons and for a long time wore no clothes.* **8:37** [a]NU-Text reads *Gerasenes.* **8:45** [a]NU-Text omits *and those with him.* [b]NU-Text omits *and You say, 'Who touched Me?'* **8:48** [a]NU-Text omits *be of good cheer.*

saying to him, "Your daughter is dead. Do not
trouble the Teacher."[a]
50But when Jesus heard *it,* He answered
him, saying, "Do not be afraid; only believe,
and she will be made well." 51When He came
into the house, He permitted no one to go in[a]
except Peter, James, and John,[b] and the father
and mother of the girl. 52Now all wept and
mourned for her; but He said, "Do not weep;
she is not dead, but sleeping." 53And they ridiculed Him, knowing that she was dead.
54But He put them all outside,[a] took her by
the hand and called, saying, "Little girl, arise."
55Then her spirit returned, and she arose immediately. And He commanded that she be
given *something* to eat. 56And her parents were
astonished, but He charged them to tell no one
what had happened.

Sending Out the Twelve

9 Then He called His twelve disciples together and gave them power and authority over all demons, and to cure diseases. 2He
sent them to preach the kingdom of God and
to heal the sick. 3And He said to them, "Take
nothing for the journey, neither staffs nor bag
nor bread nor money; and do not have two tunics apiece.
4"Whatever house you enter, stay there, and
from there depart. 5And whoever will not receive you, when you go out of that city, shake
off the very dust from your feet as a testimony
against them."
6So they departed and went through the
towns, preaching the gospel and healing everywhere.

Herod Seeks to See Jesus

7Now Herod the tetrarch heard of all that
was done by Him; and he was perplexed, because it was said by some that John had risen
from the dead, 8and by some that Elijah had
appeared, and by others that one of the old
prophets had risen again. 9Herod said, "John I
have beheaded, but who is this of whom I
hear such things?" So he sought to see Him.

Feeding the Five Thousand

10And the apostles, when they had returned,
told Him all that they had done. Then He took
them and went aside privately into a deserted
place belonging to the city called Bethsaida.
11But when the multitudes knew *it,* they followed Him; and He received them and spoke
to them about the kingdom of God, and
healed those who had need of healing.
12When the day began to wear away, the
twelve came and said to Him, "Send the multitude away, that they may go into the surrounding towns and country, and lodge and
get provisions; for we are in a deserted place
here."
13But He said to them, "You give them
something to eat."
And they said, "We have no more than five
loaves and two fish, unless we go and buy
food for all these people." 14For there were
about five thousand men.
Then He said to His disciples, "Make them
sit down in groups of fifty." 15And they did so,
and made them all sit down.
16Then He took the five loaves and the two
fish, and looking up to heaven, He blessed
and broke *them,* and gave *them* to the disciples to set before the multitude. 17So they all
ate and were filled, and twelve baskets of the
leftover fragments were taken up by them.

Peter Confesses Jesus as the Christ

18And it happened, as He was alone praying, *that* His disciples joined Him, and He
asked them, saying, "Who do the crowds say
that I am?"
19So they answered and said, "John the Baptist, but some *say* Elijah; and others *say* that one
of the old prophets has risen again."
20He said to them, "But who do you say that
I am?"
Peter answered and said, "The Christ of
God."

Jesus Predicts His Death and Resurrection

21And He strictly warned and commanded
them to tell this to no one, 22saying, "The Son
of Man must suffer many things, and be rejected by the elders and chief priests and
scribes, and be killed, and be raised the third
day."

Take Up the Cross and Follow Him

23Then He said to *them* all, "If anyone desires to come after Me, let him deny himself,

---

8:49 [a]NU-Text adds *anymore.* **8:51** [a]NU-Text adds *with Him.* [b]NU-Text and M-Text read *Peter, John, and James.* **8:54** [a]NU-Text omits *put them all outside.*

and take up his cross daily,[a] and follow Me. [24]For whoever desires to save his life will lose it, but whoever loses his life for My sake will save it. [25]For what profit is it to a man if he gains the whole world, and is himself destroyed or lost? [26]For whoever is ashamed of Me and My words, of him the Son of Man will be ashamed when He comes in His *own* glory, and *in His* Father's, and of the holy angels. [27]But I tell you truly, there are some standing here who shall not taste death till they see the kingdom of God."

Jesus Transfigured on the Mount

[28]Now it came to pass, about eight days after these sayings, that He took Peter, John, and James and went up on the mountain to pray. [29]As He prayed, the appearance of His face was altered, and His robe *became* white *and* glistening. [30]And behold, two men talked with Him, who were Moses and Elijah, [31]who appeared in glory and spoke of His decease which He was about to accomplish at Jerusalem. [32]But Peter and those with him were heavy with sleep; and when they were fully awake, they saw His glory and the two men who stood with Him. [33]Then it happened, as they were parting from Him, *that* Peter said to Jesus, "Master, it is good for us to be here; and let us make three tabernacles: one for You, one for Moses, and one for Elijah"—not knowing what he said.

[34]While he was saying this, a cloud came and overshadowed them; and they were fearful as they entered the cloud. [35]And a voice came out of the cloud, saying, "This is My beloved Son.[a] Hear Him!" [36]When the voice had ceased, Jesus was found alone. But they kept quiet, and told no one in those days any of the things they had seen.

A Boy Is Healed

[37]Now it happened on the next day, when they had come down from the mountain, that a great multitude met Him. [38]Suddenly a man from the multitude cried out, saying, "Teacher, I implore You, look on my son, for he is my only child. [39]And behold, a spirit seizes him, and he suddenly cries out; it convulses him so that he foams *at the mouth;* and it departs from him with great difficulty, bruising him. [40]So I implored Your disciples to cast it out, but they could not."

[41]Then Jesus answered and said, "O faithless and perverse generation, how long shall I be with you and bear with you? Bring your son here." [42]And as he was still coming, the demon threw him down and convulsed *him.* Then Jesus rebuked the unclean spirit, healed the child, and gave him back to his father.

Jesus Again Predicts His Death

[43]And they were all amazed at the majesty of God.

But while everyone marveled at all the things which Jesus did, He said to His disciples, [44]"Let these words sink down into your ears, for the Son of Man is about to be betrayed into the hands of men." [45]But they did not understand this saying, and it was hidden from them so that they did not perceive it; and they were afraid to ask Him about this saying.

Who Is the Greatest?

[46]Then a dispute arose among them as to which of them would be greatest. [47]And Jesus, perceiving the thought of their heart, took a little child and set him by Him, [48]and said to them, "Whoever receives this little child in My name receives Me; and whoever receives Me receives Him who sent Me. For he who is least among you all will be great."

Jesus Forbids Sectarianism

[49]Now John answered and said, "Master, we saw someone casting out demons in Your name, and we forbade him because he does not follow with us."

[50]But Jesus said to him, "Do not forbid *him,* for he who is not against us[a] is on our[b] side."

A Samaritan Village Rejects the Savior

[51]Now it came to pass, when the time had come for Him to be received up, that He steadfastly set His face to go to Jerusalem, [52]and sent messengers before His face. And as they went, they entered a village of the Samaritans, to prepare for Him. [53]But they did not receive Him, because His face was *set* for the journey to Jerusalem. [54]And when His disciples James and John saw *this,* they said, "Lord, do You want us to command fire to come down from heaven and consume them, just as Elijah did?"[a]

9:23 [a]M-Text omits *daily.* **9:35** [a]NU-Text reads *This is My Son, the Chosen One.* **9:50** [a]NU-Text reads *you.* [b]NU-Text reads *your.* **9:54** [a]NU-Text omits *just as Elijah did.*

55But He turned and rebuked them,[a] and said, "You do not know what manner of spirit you are of. 56For the Son of Man did not come to destroy men's lives but to save *them*."[a] And they went to another village.

The Cost of Discipleship

57Now it happened as they journeyed on the road, *that* someone said to Him, "Lord, I will follow You wherever You go."

58And Jesus said to him, "Foxes have holes and birds of the air *have* nests, but the Son of Man has nowhere to lay *His* head."

59Then He said to another, "Follow Me."

But he said, "Lord, let me first go and bury my father."

60Jesus said to him, "Let the dead bury their own dead, but you go and preach the kingdom of God."

61And another also said, "Lord, I will follow You, but let me first go *and* bid them farewell who are at my house."

62But Jesus said to him, "No one, having put his hand to the plow, and looking back, is fit for the kingdom of God."

The Seventy Sent Out

10 After these things the Lord appointed seventy others also,[a] and sent them two by two before His face into every city and place where He Himself was about to go. 2Then He said to them, "The harvest truly *is* great, but the laborers *are* few; therefore pray the Lord of the harvest to send out laborers into His harvest. 3Go your way; behold, I send you out as lambs among wolves. 4Carry neither money bag, knapsack, nor sandals; and greet no one along the road. 5But whatever house you enter, first say, 'Peace to this house.' 6And if a son of peace is there, your peace will rest on it; if not, it will return to you. 7And remain in the same house, eating and drinking such things as they give, for the laborer is worthy of his wages. Do not go from house to house. 8Whatever city you enter, and they receive you, eat such things as are set before you. 9And heal the sick there, and say to them, 'The kingdom of God has come near to you.' 10But whatever city you enter, and they do not receive you, go out into its streets and say, 11'The very dust of your city which clings to us[a] we wipe off against you. Nevertheless know this, that the kingdom of God has come near you.' 12But[a] I say to you that it will be more tolerable in that Day for Sodom than for that city.

Woe to the Impenitent Cities

13"Woe to you, Chorazin! Woe to you, Bethsaida! For if the mighty works which were done in you had been done in Tyre and Sidon, they would have repented long ago, sitting in sackcloth and ashes. 14But it will be more tolerable for Tyre and Sidon at the judgment than for you. 15And you, Capernaum, who are exalted to heaven, will be brought down to Hades.[a] 16He who hears you hears Me, he who rejects you rejects Me, and he who rejects Me rejects Him who sent Me."

The Seventy Return with Joy

17Then the seventy[a] returned with joy, saying, "Lord, even the demons are subject to us in Your name."

18And He said to them, "I saw Satan fall like lightning from heaven. 19Behold, I give you the authority to trample on serpents and scorpions, and over all the power of the enemy, and nothing shall by any means hurt you. 20Nevertheless do not rejoice in this, that the

---

9:55 [a]NU-Text omits the rest of this verse.
9:56 [a]NU-Text omits the first sentence of this verse.
10:1 [a]NU-Text reads *seventy-two others.*
10:11 [a]NU-Text reads *our feet.* **10:12** [a]NU-Text and M-Text omit *But.* **10:15** [a]NU-Text reads *will you be exalted to heaven? You will be thrust down to Hades!* **10:17** [a]NU-Text reads *seventy-two.*

SOUL NOTE

Raging *(10:17–19)* Since sin entered the world, wars have been fought for a wide variety of reasons. But continuous war must be fought by believers. This is the constant struggle between good and evil as Satan tries to rule our lives. Jesus has already defeated Satan and has won this battle through His death and resurrection. Even though the battle continues, we can be assured that, with Jesus' help, the important victory—eternal life—is already ours. **Topic: Spiritual Warfare**

spirits are subject to you, but rather[a] rejoice
because your names are written in heaven."

JESUS REJOICES IN THE SPIRIT

21In that hour Jesus rejoiced in the Spirit
and said, "I thank You, Father, Lord of heaven
and earth, that You have hidden these things
from *the* wise and prudent and revealed them
to babes. Even so, Father, for so it seemed
good in Your sight. 22All[a] things have been delivered to Me by My Father, and no one knows
who the Son is except the Father, and who the
Father is except the Son, and *the one* to whom
the Son wills to reveal *Him.*"
23Then He turned to *His* disciples and said
privately, "Blessed *are* the eyes which see the
things you see; 24for I tell you that many prophets and kings have desired to see what you see,
and have not seen *it,* and to hear what you
hear, and have not heard *it.*"

THE PARABLE OF THE GOOD SAMARITAN

25And behold, a certain lawyer stood up and
tested Him, saying, "Teacher, what shall I do
to inherit eternal life?"
26He said to him, "What is written in the
law? What is your reading *of it?*"
27So he answered and said, " *'You shall
love the LORD your God with all your heart,
with all your soul, with all your strength, and
with all your mind,'*[a] and *'your neighbor as
yourself.'* "[b]

10:20 [a]NU-Text and M-Text omit *rather.*
10:22 [a]M-Text reads *And turning to the disciples He said, "All . . . .*
10:27 [a]Deuteronomy 6:5
[b]Leviticus 19:18

PERSONALITY PROFILE

THE GOOD SAMARITAN: ABOVE AND BEYOND

(LUKE 10:33)

Jesus had a pointed way of upsetting the prejudicial beliefs of His day. He had been speaking to a lawyer about eternal life and about obeying God's law. The lawyer understood that all of God's law boiled down to loving God and loving one's neighbor. But that led the lawyer to another question: "Who is my neighbor?" (Luke 10:29).

Jesus responded with a parable that included a Jewish man, a Samaritan man, and two Jewish religious leaders (a priest and a Levite). Jews despised Samaritans as a half-breed race, since the Samaritans were descended from Jews who had intermarried with foreigners.

The Jewish man was attacked by thieves. As he lay on the roadside dying, two Jewish religious leaders walked right by. Perhaps they were concerned about becoming unclean according to the law; perhaps they were in a hurry. In any case, they left him to die. Along came a despised Samaritan. Given the state of race relations and the precarious situation, he could have felt justified in walking by. Instead, he showed true compassion when the Jewish religious leaders would not.

We easily show compassion on those we love, but compassion can be difficult to offer to strangers or to people against whom we might feel a trace of prejudice. It can be easy to justify a lack of compassion—we are too busy, we don't want to risk helping, we don't want to give too much, we don't like "those" people. But Jesus' answer to the lawyer's question reveals that a neighbor is anyone of any race, creed, or social background; and a neighbor in need requires our compassion.

We can show compassion on others by releasing our agenda to help them. It may mean giving time or resources; it may mean going out on a limb. As we follow God's guidance, we can be wise in our compassion, doing what will really help others. The first step is to see every person as God's creation and to be willing to be available when a need arises. God will show us how to do the rest.

To Learn More: Turn to the article about compassion on pages 950, 951. See also the key passage note at 2 Corinthians 1:3–5 on page 1518.

28And He said to him, "You have answered
rightly; do this and you will live."
29But he, wanting to justify himself, said to
Jesus, "And who is my neighbor?"
30Then Jesus answered and said: "A certain
man went down from Jerusalem to Jericho,
and fell among thieves, who stripped him of
his clothing, wounded *him,* and departed,
leaving *him* half dead. 31Now by chance a certain priest came down that road. And when he
saw him, he passed by on the other side.
32Likewise a Levite, when he arrived at the
place, came and looked, and passed by on the
other side. 33But a certain Samaritan, as he
journeyed, came where he was. And when he
saw him, he had compassion. 34So he went to
him and bandaged his wounds, pouring on oil
and wine; and he set him on his own animal,
brought him to an inn, and took care of him.
35On the next day, when he departed,[a] he took
out two denarii, gave *them* to the innkeeper,
and said to him, 'Take care of him; and whatever more you spend, when I come again, I
will repay you.' 36So which of these three do
you think was neighbor to him who fell
among the thieves?"
37And he said, "He who showed mercy on
him."

Then Jesus said to him, "Go and do likewise."

Mary and Martha Worship and Serve

38Now it happened as they went that He entered a certain village; and a certain woman
named Martha welcomed Him into her house.
39And she had a sister called Mary, who also

10:35 [a]NU-Text omits *when he departed.*

PERSONALITY PROFILE

MARTHA: WORRIED ABOUT MANY THINGS

(LUKE 10:38–42)

Many people bristle at the criticism Jesus leveled against Martha. After all, if everyone was like Mary, we reason, nobody would have a decent meal or a clean house! But there was more to this story than just Martha's desire to feed her guests. Jesus, who knows all, looked deep inside Martha to deal with a problem that could eventually cause her to be ineffective for Him—the problem of worry.

Martha apparently loved entertaining and so probably was good at it. When Jesus arrived in Bethany, Martha invited Him to her home. Martha had a sister named Mary, and a brother named Lazarus (whom Jesus would later raise from the dead). As Martha busied herself with the dinner (most likely feeding Jesus meant feeding His twelve disciples as well), Mary sat at Jesus' feet and listened to Him teach. Martha needed help, and so asked Jesus to ask Mary to get up and help her. But Jesus explained that Mary had "chosen that good part" and He would not take it away from her.

Jesus was not condemning Martha for caring about preparing a good meal, nor was He showing a lack of appreciation for her hard work. Martha's efficiency, however, seems to have been fueled by too much concern about appearances or nervous activity. She had become impatient and critical. Jesus wanted to teach her about setting priorities and setting aside worries. Martha obviously had the ability to be hospitable and would do it well no matter how much (or how little) she worried about it. Jesus advised her to set aside the worry and enjoy her guest—namely Himself—for He had much to teach her.

Worry never accomplishes anything—except to make us ill or ineffective. When we find ourselves worrying, we need to change our perspective and priorities, and then, most of all, we need to pray for faith in God's provision. God will shoulder the worry and give us His peace. Then we can focus on "that good part" that Christ promises will never be taken away.

To Learn More: Turn to the article about worry on pages 1340, 1341. See also the key passage note at Luke 12:22–31 on page 1339.

sat at Jesus'[a] feet and heard His word. 40 But Martha was distracted with much serving, and she approached Him and said, "Lord, do You not care that my sister has left me to serve alone? Therefore tell her to help me."

41 And Jesus[a] answered and said to her, "Martha, Martha, you are worried and troubled about many things. 42 But one thing is needed, and Mary has chosen that good part, which will not be taken away from her."

The Model Prayer

11 Now it came to pass, as He was praying in a certain place, when He ceased, *that* one of His disciples said to Him, "Lord, teach us to pray, as John also taught his disciples."

2 So He said to them, "When you pray, say:

> Our Father in heaven,[a]
> Hallowed be Your name.
> Your kingdom come.[b]
> Your will be done
> On earth as *it is* in heaven.
> 3 Give us day by day our daily bread.
> 4 And forgive us our sins,
> For we also forgive everyone who is indebted to us.
> And do not lead us into temptation,
> But deliver us from the evil one." [a]

A Friend Comes at Midnight

5 And He said to them, "Which of you shall have a friend, and go to him at midnight and say to him, 'Friend, lend me three loaves; 6 for a friend of mine has come to me on his journey, and I have nothing to set before him'; 7 and he will answer from within and say, 'Do not trouble me; the door is now shut, and my children are with me in bed; I cannot rise and give to you'? 8 I say to you, though he will not rise and give to him because he is his friend, yet because of his persistence he will rise and give him as many as he needs.

10:39 [a]NU-Text reads *the Lord's.* **10:41** [a]NU-Text reads *the Lord.* **11:2** [a]NU-Text omits *Our* and *in heaven.* [b]NU-Text omits the rest of this verse. **11:4** [a]NU-Text omits *But deliver us from the evil one.*

PERSONALITY PROFILE

Love Languages

MARY: SPEAKING LOVE'S LANGUAGE

(LUKE 10:38–42)

People show their love in different ways. For Mary's sister, Martha, showing love involved having a hospitable home and good food for her guests. Jesus and His disciples enjoyed that hospitality several times during the course of His ministry. Jesus appreciated Martha's ability, but wanted her to use it without so much hurry and worry, and with a willingness to open her heart, not just her home, to Him.

Mary showed her love by sitting at Jesus' feet and drinking in His every word. This kind of love and devotion revealed a heart open to Jesus' message and ready to accept Him as her Savior. She listened well, for she seemed to understand, even before the disciples did, why Jesus had to die. At another visit that Jesus paid to this family prior to His death, "Mary took a pound of very costly oil of spikenard, anointed the feet of Jesus, and wiped His feet with her hair" (John 12:3). Jesus explained that her sacrifice of love was in preparation for His burial: "She has done a good work for Me. . . . For in pouring this fragrant oil on My body, she did it for My burial. Assuredly, I say to you, wherever this gospel is preached in the whole world, what this woman has done will also be told as a memorial to her" (Matt. 26:10, 12, 13).

Love has many languages. Both Mary and Martha had great faith in Jesus, and both loved Him dearly. As we show our love for Christ and for others, we may do so in different ways, depending on our unique personality and gifts from God. When we speak the language of love, everyone will hear and understand.

To Learn More: Turn to the article about love languages on pages 1680, 1681. See also the key passage note at 1 John 3:18 on page 1677.

KEEP ASKING, SEEKING, KNOCKING

[9]"So I say to you, ask, and it will be given to you; seek, and you will find; knock, and it will be opened to you. [10]For everyone who asks receives, and he who seeks finds, and to him who knocks it will be opened. [11]If a son asks for bread[a] from any father among you, will he give him a stone? Or if *he asks* for a fish, will he give him a serpent instead of a fish? [12]Or if he asks for an egg, will he offer him a scorpion? [13]If you then, being evil, know how to give good gifts to your children, how much more will *your* heavenly Father give the Holy Spirit to those who ask Him!"

> "For everyone who asks receives, and he who seeks finds, and to him who knocks it will be opened."
>
> LUKE 11:10

A HOUSE DIVIDED CANNOT STAND

[14]And He was casting out a demon, and it was mute. So it was, when the demon had gone out, that the mute spoke; and the multitudes marveled. [15]But some of them said, "He casts out demons by Beelzebub,[a] the ruler of the demons."

[16]Others, testing *Him,* sought from Him a sign from heaven. [17]But He, knowing their thoughts, said to them: "Every kingdom divided against itself is brought to desolation, and a house *divided* against a house falls. [18]If Satan also is divided against himself, how will his kingdom stand? Because you say I cast out demons by Beelzebub. [19]And if I cast out demons by Beelzebub, by whom do your sons cast *them* out? Therefore they will be your judges. [20]But if I cast out demons with the finger of God, surely the kingdom of God has come upon you. [21]When a strong man, fully armed, guards his own palace, his goods are in peace. [22]But when a stronger than he comes upon him and overcomes him, he takes from him all his armor in which he trusted, and divides his spoils. [23]He who is not with Me is against Me, and he who does not gather with Me scatters.

AN UNCLEAN SPIRIT RETURNS

[24]"When an unclean spirit goes out of a man, he goes through dry places, seeking rest; and finding none, he says, 'I will return to my house from which I came.' [25]And when he comes, he finds *it* swept and put in order. [26]Then he goes and takes with *him* seven other spirits more wicked than himself, and they enter and dwell there; and the last *state* of that man is worse than the first."

KEEPING THE WORD

[27]And it happened, as He spoke these things, that a certain woman from the crowd raised her voice and said to Him, "Blessed *is* the womb that bore You, and *the* breasts which nursed You!"

[28]But He said, "More than that, blessed *are* those who hear the word of God and keep it!"

SEEKING A SIGN

[29]And while the crowds were thickly gathered together, He began to say, "This is an evil generation. It seeks a sign, and no sign will be given to it except the sign of Jonah the prophet.[a] [30]For as Jonah became a sign to the Ninevites, so also the Son of Man will be to this generation. [31]The queen of the South will rise up in the judgment with the men of this generation and condemn them, for she came from the ends of the earth to hear the wisdom of Solomon; and indeed a greater than Solomon *is* here. [32]The men of Nineveh will rise up in the judgment with this generation and condemn it, for they repented at the preaching of Jonah; and indeed a greater than Jonah *is* here.

THE LAMP OF THE BODY

[33]"No one, when he has lit a lamp, puts *it* in a secret place or under a basket, but on a lampstand, that those who come in may see the light. [34]The lamp of the body is the eye. Therefore, when your eye is good, your whole body also is full of light. But when *your eye* is bad, your body also *is* full of darkness. [35]Therefore take heed that the light which is in you is not darkness. [36]If then your whole body *is* full of light, having no part dark, *the* whole *body* will be full of light, as when the bright shining of a lamp gives you light."

WOE TO THE PHARISEES AND LAWYERS

[37]And as He spoke, a certain Pharisee asked Him to dine with him. So He went in and sat

---

11:11 [a]NU-Text omits the words from *bread* through *for* in the next sentence. **11:15** [a]NU-Text and M-Text read *Beelzebul.* **11:29** [a]NU-Text omits *the prophet.*

down to eat. 38When the Pharisee saw *it,* he marveled that He had not first washed before dinner.

39Then the Lord said to him, "Now you Pharisees make the outside of the cup and dish clean, but your inward part is full of greed and wickedness. 40Foolish ones! Did not He who made the outside make the inside also? 41But rather give alms of such things as you have; then indeed all things are clean to you.

42"But woe to you Pharisees! For you tithe mint and rue and all manner of herbs, and pass by justice and the love of God. These you ought to have done, without leaving the others undone. 43Woe to you Pharisees! For you love the best seats in the synagogues and greetings in the marketplaces. 44Woe to you, scribes and Pharisees, hypocrites![a] For you are like graves which are not seen, and the men who walk over *them* are not aware *of them.*"

45Then one of the lawyers answered and said to Him, "Teacher, by saying these things You reproach us also."

46And He said, "Woe to you also, lawyers! For you load men with burdens hard to bear, and you yourselves do not touch the burdens with one of your fingers. 47Woe to you! For you build the tombs of the prophets, and your fathers killed them. 48In fact, you bear witness that you approve the deeds of your fathers; for they indeed killed them, and you build their tombs. 49Therefore the wisdom of God also said, 'I will send them prophets and apostles, and *some* of them they will kill and persecute,' 50that the blood of all the prophets which was shed from the foundation of the world may be required of this generation, 51from the blood of Abel to the blood of Zechariah who perished between the altar and the temple. Yes, I say to you, it shall be required of this generation.

52"Woe to you lawyers! For you have taken away the key of knowledge. You did not enter in yourselves, and those who were entering in you hindered."

53And as He said these things to them,[a] the scribes and the Pharisees began to assail *Him* vehemently, and to cross-examine Him about many things, 54lying in wait for Him, and seeking to catch Him in something He might say, that they might accuse Him.[a]

Beware of Hypocrisy

12 In the meantime, when an innumerable multitude of people had gathered together, so that they trampled one another, He began to say to His disciples first *of all,* "Beware of the leaven of the Pharisees, which is hypocrisy. 2For there is nothing covered that will not be revealed, nor hidden that will not be known. 3Therefore whatever you have spoken in the dark will be heard in the light, and what you have spoken in the ear in inner rooms will be proclaimed on the housetops.

Jesus Teaches the Fear of God

4"And I say to you, My friends, do not be afraid of those who kill the body, and after that have no more that they can do. 5But I will show you whom you should fear: Fear Him who, after He has killed, has power to cast into hell; yes, I say to you, fear Him!

6"Are not five sparrows sold for two copper coins?[a] And not one of them is forgotten before God. 7But the very hairs of your head are all numbered. Do not fear therefore; you are of more value than many sparrows.

11:44 [a]NU-Text omits *scribes and Pharisees, hypocrites.* **11:53** [a]NU-Text reads *And when He left there.* **11:54** [a]NU-Text omits *and seeking* and *that they might accuse Him.* **12:6** [a]Greek *assarion,* a coin of very small value

SOUL NOTE

Put In a Good Word *(12:11, 12)* Telling others about Christ can be difficult, especially in a hostile environment. Jesus told His followers not to be concerned when called to answer for their faith—because an emergency spokesman would be ready. When we become frightened or tongue-tied, the Holy Spirit will tell us what to say. This does not release us from studying God's Word. We must know what God says and be ready to defend our faith (1 Pet. 3:15)—but we must not worry. Jesus promised that the Spirit would guide our words. **Topic: Presence of the Holy Spirit**

Confess Christ Before Men

[8]"Also I say to you, whoever confesses Me before men, him the Son of Man also will confess before the angels of God. [9]But he who denies Me before men will be denied before the angels of God.

[10]"And anyone who speaks a word against the Son of Man, it will be forgiven him; but to him who blasphemes against the Holy Spirit, it will not be forgiven.

[11]"Now when they bring you to the synagogues and magistrates and authorities, do not worry about how or what you should answer, or what you should say. [12]For the Holy Spirit will teach you in that very hour what you ought to say."

> "And which of you by worrying can add one cubit to his stature? If you then are not able to do the least, why are you anxious for the rest?"
>
> LUKE 12:25, 26

The Parable of the Rich Fool

[13]Then one from the crowd said to Him, "Teacher, tell my brother to divide the inheritance with me."

[14]But He said to him, "Man, who made Me a judge or an arbitrator over you?" [15]And He said to them, "Take heed and beware of covetousness,[a] for one's life does not consist in the abundance of the things he possesses."

[16]Then He spoke a parable to them, saying: "The ground of a certain rich man yielded plentifully. [17]And he thought within himself, saying, 'What shall I do, since I have no room to store my crops?' [18]So he said, 'I will do this: I will pull down my barns and build greater, and there I will store all my crops and my goods. [19]And I will say to my soul, "Soul, you have many goods laid up for many years; take your ease; eat, drink, *and* be merry." ' [20]But God said to him, 'Fool! This night your soul will be required of you; then whose will those things be which you have provided?'

[21]"So *is* he who lays up treasure for himself, and is not rich toward God."

Do Not Worry

[22]Then He said to His disciples, "Therefore I say to you, do not worry about your life, what you will eat; nor about the body, what you will put on. [23]Life is more than food, and the body *is more* than clothing. [24]Consider the ravens, for they neither sow nor reap, which have neither storehouse nor barn; and God feeds them. Of how much more value are you than the birds? [25]And which of you by worrying can add one cubit to his stature? [26]If you then are not able to do *the* least, why are you

12:15 [a]NU-Text reads *all covetousness.*

KEY PASSAGE

Worry

WHAT, ME WORRY?

(12:22–31)

Worry can be a time-consuming, almost obsessive, behavior. After all, every day brings new things to worry about! Worrying about every situation in life—whether big or small—will only drive us to distraction. Not one problem is ever solved by worrying about it. In fact, many problems get worse because worry is immobilizing; thus, no action is being taken to try to work through the dilemma. Worry can thwart the work of the kingdom.

Jesus has the perfect solution for worry. Instead of worrying, He invites us to put our faith and trust in God's provision and care. This can free us from the anxiety that is caused by worry. This total trust doesn't mean that we should not have goals, plans, investments, and so on. It does mean, however, that for everything we should trust in God, putting Him first in our lives.

To Learn More: Turn to the article about worry on pages 1340, 1341. See also the personality profile of Martha on page 1335.

WORRY OR PRAY—YOU CHOOSE

ROSEMARIE SCOTTI HUGHES

(Luke 12:22–31)

A grandmother worries about a 12-year-old grandson with dropping grades and bad friends. When she reads Jesus' words, "Do not worry," she wonders how she can care about him and not worry about his future.

A homeowner sits down to pay a stack of bills. Every month he goes through the exercise of writing checks and then deciding, *if* there is surplus, where that goes. When he reads Luke 12:22–31, he feels a reproach because he worries about finances.

A woman's 17-year-old son is long overdue with the family car, and she's sitting up worrying that he may have gotten into trouble.

An employee is in turmoil considering a company move and promotion. She's worried about uprooting the family and starting over somewhere else. She recently read Luke 12 about not being worried, but she still gets butterflies in her stomach every time she thinks about this move.

Like these people, we all worry about our finances, our loved ones, our jobs, our health, and a host of other life issues. It may be hard to relate to Jesus' words concerning worry. After all, Jesus had no children, no boss, no rent to pay. Jesus never had to grocery shop for a family and make dollars stretch, or car pool kids to sports, try to make the PTA meeting, and put dinner on the table. Jesus never had to take care of his elderly parents and help his teenagers plan for college at the same time. How can we apply His teaching about not worrying to twenty-first-century life?

Actually, these passages are more for us today than ever. In a materialistic, consumption-minded, technological world, Jesus is telling us to order our priorities: "Seek the kingdom of God, and all these things shall be added to you" (Luke 12:31). For most of us, however, there is a large gap between managing our day-to-day lives and seeking God's kingdom. In order to achieve the peace of God, to not be overwhelmed by the pressures of life, we have to *change*. We read that we cannot add a single hour to our life by worrying and fretting, but because worrying is what we know best, it's what we do first, especially in stressful situations.

Being concerned can be positive when it propels us to action—such as seeing a doctor when we are ill or a mechanic when the car sounds strange. But worry is unproductive. Worry becomes a negative in our life, taking its toll on our health, loved ones, productivity, and relationship with God. If we have been worried about two or more topics more days than not in the past six months, if we are focusing on situations of worry more than we are the other business of life, and if we are having feelings of our lives being out of control, then our worrying has risen to an unhealthy level.

Take, for example, two "mothers of the groom." For months, the first goes to every dress store in town, anxiously pricing, comparing, buying, and then returning what she bought. At the wedding, still worrying about her appearance, she is frazzled, worn out, and can barely enjoy the day.

Contrast her behavior with the second

mother, who *first* prays to the Lord to help her find what she needs within her price range and without using a lot of time—and to help her not to worry about it. She finds what she needs in one trip. She puts the situation in God's hands—seeking the kingdom first. The other things fall into place and she is able to enjoy the wedding.

To seek first the kingdom means to pray *first*, releasing our fears and worries to the Lord. A change in behavior and in a particular attitude follows as we make some appropriate changes to our lifestyle. Taking some steps to change our lives will help us bridge the gap between worrying and operating in faith. These changes will ultimately help us live in power, love, sound judgment, self-control, calm, and balance. For example:

➢ Get facts and expert advice to prevent worrying unrealistically about a situation.
➢ Set deadlines to make decisions, rather than ruminating forever.
➢ Limit worrying to a "worry list," and take that list to the Lord in your daily Bible and prayer time.
➢ Delegate chores and other responsibilities.
➢ Give yourself permission to relax, and to make mistakes.
➢ Eat, sleep, and exercise properly.
➢ Try to see the humor in a situation, to keep a sense of perspective.
➢ De-clutter and organize, using calendars and to-do lists.
➢ Realize that you will not please everyone all the time.
➢ Learn to say no.
➢ Ask yourself, "What's the worst that can happen—and is it likely to?"
➢ Mentally put your worries in a box with a lid and put them on the top shelf of your closet. No peeking!

To say that we are waiting on the Lord, and then to go around with a sense of worry, misery, and dread, is to contradict the truth. Jesus modeled *prayer* when He went to the desert to fast and pray. Jesus also modeled *action* when He healed, taught, and followed God every step of the way. To be walking in peace, in calm, in trust, and in assurance is to find the balance of prayer and action, and ultimately, freedom from worry.

FURTHER MEDITATION:

Other passages to study about the issue of worry include:

➢ Psalm 55:22
➢ Matthew 6:25–34
➢ John 14:27
➢ Philippians 4:6–9
➢ 2 Timothy 1:7
➢ 1 Peter 5:7

To Learn More: Turn to the key passage note on worry at Luke 12:22–31 on page 1339. See also the personality profile of Martha on page 1335.

anxious for the rest? 27 Consider the lilies, how
they grow: they neither toil nor spin; and yet I
say to you, even Solomon in all his glory was
not arrayed like one of these. 28 If then God so
clothes the grass, which today is in the field
and tomorrow is thrown into the oven, how
much more *will He clothe* you, O *you* of little
faith?

29 "And do not seek what you should eat or
what you should drink, nor have an anxious
mind. 30 For all these things the nations of the
world seek after, and your Father knows that
you need these things. 31 But seek the kingdom
of God, and all these things[a] shall be added to
you.

32 "Do not fear, little flock, for it is your
Father's good pleasure to give you the kingdom. 33 Sell what you have and give alms; provide yourselves money bags which do not
grow old, a treasure in the heavens that does
not fail, where no thief approaches nor moth
destroys. 34 For where your treasure is, there
your heart will be also.

The Faithful Servant and the Evil Servant

35 "Let your waist be girded and *your* lamps
burning; 36 and you yourselves be like men
who wait for their master, when he will return
from the wedding, that when he comes and
knocks they may open to him immediately.
37 Blessed *are* those servants whom the master,
when he comes, will find watching. Assuredly, I say to you that he will gird himself and
have them sit down *to eat,* and will come and
serve them. 38 And if he should come in the
second watch, or come in the third watch, and
find *them* so, blessed are those servants. 39 But
know this, that if the master of the house had
known what hour the thief would come, he
would have watched and[a] not allowed his
house to be broken into. 40 Therefore you also
be ready, for the Son of Man is coming at an
hour you do not expect."

41 Then Peter said to Him, "Lord, do You
speak this parable *only* to us, or to all *people?*"

42 And the Lord said, "Who then is that
faithful and wise steward, whom *his* master
will make ruler over his household, to give
them their portion of food in due season?
43 Blessed *is* that servant whom his master will
find so doing when he comes. 44 Truly, I say to
you that he will make him ruler over all that
he has. 45 But if that servant says in his heart,
'My master is delaying his coming,' and begins
to beat the male and female servants, and to
eat and drink and be drunk, 46 the master of
that servant will come on a day when he is not
looking for *him,* and at an hour when he is not
aware, and will cut him in two and appoint
him his portion with the unbelievers. 47 And
that servant who knew his master's will, and
did not prepare *himself* or do according to his
will, shall be beaten with many *stripes.* 48 But
he who did not know, yet committed things
deserving of stripes, shall be beaten with few.
For everyone to whom much is given, from
him much will be required; and to whom
much has been committed, of him they will
ask the more.

Christ Brings Division

49 "I came to send fire on the earth, and how
I wish it were already kindled! 50 But I have a
baptism to be baptized with, and how distressed I am till it is accomplished! 51 Do *you*
suppose that I came to give peace on earth? I
tell you, not at all, but rather division. 52 For
from now on five in one house will be divided:
three against two, and two against three. 53 Father will be divided against son and son
against father, mother against daughter and
daughter against mother, mother-in-law
against her daughter-in-law and daughter-in-
law against her mother-in-law."

Discern the Time

54 Then He also said to the multitudes,
"Whenever *you see* a cloud rising out of the
west, immediately you say, 'A shower is coming'; and so it is. 55 And when you see the
south wind blow, you say, 'There will be hot
weather'; and there is. 56 Hypocrites! You can
discern the face of the sky and of the earth,
but how *is it* you do not discern this time?

Make Peace with Your Adversary

57 "Yes, and why, even of yourselves, do you
not judge what is right? 58 When you go with
your adversary to the magistrate, make every
effort along the way to settle with him, lest he
drag you to the judge, the judge deliver you to
the officer, and the officer throw you into prison. 59 I tell you, you shall not depart from there
till you have paid the very last mite."

12:31 [a]NU-Text reads *His kingdom, and these things.* **12:39** [a]NU-Text reads *he would not have allowed.*

Repent or Perish

13 There were present at that season some who told Him about the Galileans whose blood Pilate had mingled with their sacrifices. [2]And Jesus answered and said to them, "Do you suppose that these Galileans were worse sinners than all *other* Galileans, because they suffered such things? [3]I tell you, no; but unless you repent you will all likewise perish. [4]Or those eighteen on whom the tower in Siloam fell and killed them, do you think that they were worse sinners than all *other* men who dwelt in Jerusalem? [5]I tell you, no; but unless you repent you will all likewise perish."

The Parable of the Barren Fig Tree

[6]He also spoke this parable: "A certain *man* had a fig tree planted in his vineyard, and he came seeking fruit on it and found none. [7]Then he said to the keeper of his vineyard, 'Look, for three years I have come seeking fruit on this fig tree and find none. Cut it down; why does it use up the ground?' [8]But he answered and said to him, 'Sir, let it alone this year also, until I dig around it and fertilize *it*. [9]And if it bears fruit, *well*. But if not, after that[a] you can cut it down.' "

A Spirit of Infirmity

[10]Now He was teaching in one of the synagogues on the Sabbath. [11]And behold, there was a woman who had a spirit of infirmity eighteen years, and was bent over and could in no way raise *herself* up. [12]But when Jesus saw her, He called *her* to *Him* and said to her, "Woman, you are loosed from your infirmity." [13]And He laid *His* hands on her, and immediately she was made straight, and glorified God.

[14]But the ruler of the synagogue answered with indignation, because Jesus had healed on the Sabbath; and he said to the crowd, "There are six days on which men ought to work; therefore come and be healed on them, and not on the Sabbath day."

[15]The Lord then answered him and said, "Hypocrite![a] Does not each one of you on the Sabbath loose his ox or donkey from the stall, and lead *it* away to water it? [16]So ought not this woman, being a daughter of Abraham, whom Satan has bound—think of it—for eighteen years, be loosed from this bond on the Sabbath?" [17]And when He said these things, all His adversaries were put to shame; and all the multitude rejoiced for all the glorious things that were done by Him.

The Parable of the Mustard Seed

[18]Then He said, "What is the kingdom of God like? And to what shall I compare it? [19]It is like a mustard seed, which a man took and put in his garden; and it grew and became a large[a] tree, and the birds of the air nested in its branches."

The Parable of the Leaven

[20]And again He said, "To what shall I liken the kingdom of God? [21]It is like leaven, which a woman took and hid in three measures[a] of meal till it was all leavened."

The Narrow Way

[22]And He went through the cities and villages, teaching, and journeying toward Jerusalem. [23]Then one said to Him, "Lord, are there few who are saved?"

And He said to them, [24]"Strive to enter through the narrow gate, for many, I say to you, will seek to enter and will not be able. [25]When once the Master of the house has risen up and shut the door, and you begin to stand outside and knock at the door, saying, 'Lord, Lord, open for us,' and He will answer and say to you, 'I do not know you, where you are from,' [26]then you will begin to say, 'We ate and drank in Your presence, and You taught in our streets.' [27]But He will say, 'I tell you I do not know you, where you are from. Depart from Me, all you workers of iniquity.' [28]There will be weeping and gnashing of teeth, when you see Abraham and Isaac and Jacob and all the prophets in the kingdom of God, and yourselves thrust out. [29]They will come from the east and the west, from the north and the south, and sit down in the kingdom of God. [30]And indeed there are last who will be first, and there are first who will be last."

[31]On that very day[a] some Pharisees came, saying to Him, "Get out and depart from here, for Herod wants to kill You."

[32]And He said to them, "Go, tell that fox,

13:9 [a]NU-Text reads *And if it bears fruit after that, well. But if not, you can cut it down.* **13:15** [a]NU-Text and M-Text read *Hypocrites.* **13:19** [a]NU-Text omits *large.* **13:21** [a]Greek *sata,* approximately two pecks in all **13:31** [a]NU-Text reads *In that very hour.*

‘Behold, I cast out demons and perform cures
today and tomorrow, and the third *day* I shall
be perfected.’ 33Nevertheless I must journey
today, tomorrow, and the *day* following; for it
cannot be that a prophet should perish outside
of Jerusalem.

Jesus Laments over Jerusalem

34“O Jerusalem, Jerusalem, the one who
kills the prophets and stones those who are
sent to her! How often I wanted to gather your
children together, as a hen *gathers* her brood
under *her* wings, but you were not willing!
35See! Your house is left to you desolate; and
assuredly,[a] I say to you, you shall not see Me
until *the time* comes when you say, ‘*Blessed is*
He who comes in the name of the LORD!’ ”[b]

A Man with Dropsy Healed on the Sabbath

14 Now it happened, as He went into the
house of one of the rulers of the Pharisees to eat bread on the Sabbath, that they
watched Him closely. 2And behold, there was
a certain man before Him who had dropsy.
3And Jesus, answering, spoke to the lawyers
and Pharisees, saying, “Is it lawful to heal on
the Sabbath?”[a]

4But they kept silent. And He took *him*
and healed him, and let him go. 5Then He
answered them, saying, “Which of you, having a donkey[a] or an ox that has fallen into a
pit, will not immediately pull him out on the
Sabbath day?” 6And they could not answer
Him regarding these things.

Take the Lowly Place

7So He told a parable to those who were invited, when He noted how they chose the best
places, saying to them: 8“When you are invited by anyone to a wedding feast, do not sit
down in the best place, lest one more honorable than you be invited by him; 9and he who
invited you and him come and say to you,
‘Give place to this man,’ and then you begin
with shame to take the lowest place. 10But
when you are invited, go and sit down in the
lowest place, so that when he who invited you
comes he may say to you, ‘Friend, go up higher.’ Then you will have glory in the presence of
those who sit at the table with you. 11For whoever exalts himself will be humbled, and he
who humbles himself will be exalted.”

12Then He also said to him who invited
Him, “When you give a dinner or a supper, do
not ask your friends, your brothers, your relatives, nor rich neighbors, lest they also invite
you back, and you be repaid. 13But when you
give a feast, invite *the* poor, *the* maimed, *the*
lame, *the* blind. 14And you will be blessed, because they cannot repay you; for you shall be
repaid at the resurrection of the just.”

The Parable of the Great Supper

15Now when one of those who sat at the table with Him heard these things, he said to
Him, “Blessed *is* he who shall eat bread[a] in
the kingdom of God!”

16Then He said to him, “A certain man gave
a great supper and invited many, 17and sent
his servant at supper time to say to those who
were invited, ‘Come, for all things are now
ready.’ 18But they all with one *accord* began to
make excuses. The first said to him, ‘I have
bought a piece of ground, and I must go and
see it. I ask you to have me excused.’ 19And
another said, ‘I have bought five yoke of oxen,

13:35 [a]NU-Text and M-Text omit *assuredly.* [b]Psalm 118:26 **14:3** [a]NU-Text adds *or not.* **14:5** [a]NU-Text and M-Text read *son.* **14:15** [a]M-Text reads *dinner.*

SOUL NOTE

Total Commitment *(14:25–33)* To reach a desired goal or to successfully complete a huge task takes planning and total commitment. To be only partially committed to a project usually ends with less than desirable results. Jesus asks for total commitment from His followers. The command to “hate” one’s family is not to be taken as an instruction to treat them improperly; instead, it reminds us that human relationships should never hold us back from faith in Christ. The kingdom of God must be central in all we do. The cost may be high, but the rewards are wonderful!

Topic: Self-Denial

and I am going to test them. I ask you to have me excused.' 20Still another said, 'I have married a wife, and therefore I cannot come.' 21So that servant came and reported these things to his master. Then the master of the house, being angry, said to his servant, 'Go out quickly into the streets and lanes of the city, and bring in here *the* poor and *the* maimed and *the* lame and *the* blind.' 22And the servant said, 'Master, it is done as you commanded, and still there is room.' 23Then the master said to the servant, 'Go out into the highways and hedges, and compel *them* to come in, that my house may be filled. 24For I say to you that none of those men who were invited shall taste my supper.' "

Leaving All to Follow Christ

25Now great multitudes went with Him. And He turned and said to them, 26"If anyone comes to Me and does not hate his father and mother, wife and children, brothers and sisters, yes, and his own life also, he cannot be My disciple. 27And whoever does not bear his cross and come after Me cannot be My disciple. 28For which of you, intending to build a tower, does not sit down first and count the cost, whether he has *enough* to finish *it*— 29lest, after he has laid the foundation, and is not able to finish, all who see *it* begin to mock him, 30saying, 'This man began to build and was not able to finish.' 31Or what king, going to make war against another king, does not sit down first and consider whether he is able with ten thousand to meet him who comes against him with twenty thousand? 32Or else, while the other is still a great way off, he sends a delegation and asks conditions of peace. 33So likewise, whoever of you does not forsake all that he has cannot be My disciple.

Tasteless Salt Is Worthless

34"Salt *is* good; but if the salt has lost its flavor, how shall it be seasoned? 35It is neither fit for the land nor for the dunghill, *but* men throw it out. He who has ears to hear, let him hear!"

The Parable of the Lost Sheep

15 Then all the tax collectors and the sinners drew near to Him to hear Him. 2And the Pharisees and scribes complained, saying, "This Man receives sinners and eats with them." 3So He spoke this parable to them, saying:

4"What man of you, having a hundred sheep, if he loses one of them, does not leave the ninety-nine in the wilderness, and go after the one which is lost until he finds it? 5And when he has found *it,* he lays *it* on his shoulders, rejoicing. 6And when he comes home, he calls together *his* friends and neighbors, saying to them, 'Rejoice with me, for I have found my sheep which was lost!' 7I say to you that likewise there will be more joy in heaven over one sinner who repents than over ninety-nine just persons who need no repentance.

The Parable of the Lost Coin

8"Or what woman, having ten silver coins,[a] if she loses one coin, does not light a lamp, sweep the house, and search carefully until she finds *it?* 9And when she has found *it,* she calls *her* friends and neighbors together, saying, 'Rejoice with me, for I have found the piece which I lost!' 10Likewise, I say to you, there is joy in the presence of the angels of God over one sinner who repents."

The Parable of the Lost Son

11Then He said: "A certain man had two sons. 12And the younger of them said to *his* father, 'Father, give me the portion of goods that falls *to me.*' So he divided to them *his* livelihood. 13And not many days after, the younger son gathered all together, journeyed to a far country, and there wasted his possessions with prodigal living. 14But when he had spent all, there arose a severe famine in that land, and he began to be in want. 15Then he went and joined himself to a citizen of that country, and he sent him into his fields to feed swine. 16And he would gladly have filled his stomach with the pods that the swine ate, and no one gave him *anything.*

17"But when he came to himself, he said, 'How many of my father's hired servants have bread enough and to spare, and I perish with hunger! 18I will arise and go to my father, and will say to him, "Father, I have sinned against heaven and before you, 19and I am no longer worthy to be called your son. Make me like one of your hired servants." '

20"And he arose and came to his father. But when he was still a great way off, his father saw him and had compassion, and ran and fell

15:8 [a]Greek *drachma,* a valuable coin often worn in a ten-piece garland by married women

Self-Denial

THE COST OF COMMITMENT

VERNON BREWER

(Luke 14:25–33)

There is no limit to what God can do through those who are fully committed to Him. By total commitment we ask God to take complete control over our lives. Total commitment, then, means self-denial.

In Luke 14, Jesus described the cost of commitment to Him. He did not say that a person who doesn't meet these demands will be an inconsistent disciple, or an ungrateful disciple, or a half-hearted disciple. He said that "he cannot be My disciple" (Luke 14:26, 27, 33).

ABOVE PERSONAL RELATIONSHIPS

God's people must love Jesus Christ more than their personal relationships. Jesus said that anyone who wants to follow Him must "hate his father and mother, wife and children, brothers and sisters" (Luke 14:26). Jesus' love transcends all personal relationships.

These words do not mean that Christians have to literally "hate" their parents. That would go against other parts of God's word where people are told to honor their parents (Ex. 20:12). The word "hate" is used as hyperbole, meaning that people's love for Jesus must transcend their love for family. The reason many people have difficulty with this verse isn't that they love their families too much; it is that they don't love God enough. They have never learned to love the Lord God with all their heart, soul, and mind (Deut. 6:5).

We love our families; we adore our spouse and children; we honor our parents. They are not the most important relationships in our lives, however. Our relationship with Jesus Christ is the most important.

ABOVE PERSONAL LIFE

God's people must love Jesus Christ more than their personal lives. Jesus continued that anyone who wants to follow Him must "hate . . . his own life also" (Luke 14:26). Jesus' lordship transcends our personal priorities. The disgrace of the Christian church is that more zeal is evident among Communists and cultists than among Christians. There are many non-Christians who are not as concerned about their lives as they are about their commitment to their cause.

Jesus' command does not mean that Christians have to literally "hate" their lives. That would go against other commands in Scripture to be content and joyful. People would not evidence the fruit of the Spirit if they hated their lives. They would be sad, ornery, and critical. Some people *are* that way, and they would not be held up as models of self-denial and commitment to Christ. Instead, the word "hate" means as it did in the previous section: People's love for Jesus must transcend their love for their own lives.

We enjoy life; we seek to follow God's will and accomplish what He has for us during our time on earth. However, our lives, jobs, reputations, accomplishments are not the most important. We should, at any moment, be willing to die for our faith. Indeed, people all over the world are doing that every single day.

I recently visited a country that is

closed to the gospel, a country where Christians face the threat of death daily. A group of us met secretly with several pastors and other believers and heard their testimonies. A 34-year-old woman evangelist and church planter told how she continues to suffer persecution. One day, the police humiliated her by tearing off her shirt and parading her through the streets. She stood in a public gathering, half-naked, with her hands tied behind her back and said, "I live for Jesus Christ . . . if I die, I die for Jesus Christ!"

ABOVE PERSONAL RIGHTS

God's people must love Jesus Christ more than their personal rights. Jesus said, "Whoever does not bear his cross and come after Me cannot be My disciple" (Luke 14:27). Jesus' lordship transcends personal rights, choices, decisions, goals, and plans.

The people of Jesus' day well understood what it meant to carry one's own cross. When a person was sentenced to death by the Romans, he had to carry his own cross through the city to the execution site. This constantly reminded the people of their subjection to Rome, and taught them an object lesson about obeying Rome's leaders.

These words do not mean that Christians have to carry the heavy burdens of life on our backs like a cross. That would contradict the psalmist who assured us that we can cast our burdens on the Lord (Ps. 55:22). Instead, we should proudly "carry Jesus' cross," being identified with Him, casting aside our love for what we think is fair, for what we want, for what we consider our "rights," in order to serve Him.

ABOVE PERSONAL RESOURCES

God's people must love Jesus Christ more than their personal resources. Jesus said, "Whoever of you does not forsake all that he has cannot be My disciple" (Luke 14:33). Jesus' lordship transcends everything people own, achieve, share, and give. This is perhaps the most unpopular of all of Christ's terms of discipleship and self-denial.

These words do not mean that Christians must become hermits. To "forsake all" does not mean that believers cannot own homes, buy clothing and food, and take vacations. Again, it has to do with our attitudes toward all of our possessions. To "forsake" all means not being so attached to anything we own that we cannot let it go for the sake of God's kingdom.

To truly be Jesus' disciple means to love Him more than our relationships, lives, rights, and resources. What He gives in return is beyond value!

FURTHER MEDITATION:

Other passages to study about the issue of self-denial include:

- Psalm 119:9
- Matthew 16:24
- Romans 12:12
- Galatians 5:24
- Philippians 2:2–4
- 2 Timothy 2:3, 4
- James 1:12

To Learn More: Turn to the key passage note on self-denial at Galatians 2:20 on page 1539. See also the personality profile of John the Baptist on page 1375.

on his neck and kissed him. 21And the son said
to him, 'Father, I have sinned against heaven
and in your sight, and am no longer worthy to
be called your son.'
22"But the father said to his servants,
'Bring[a] out the best robe and put *it* on him,
and put a ring on his hand and sandals on *his*
feet. 23And bring the fatted calf here and kill
it, and let us eat and be merry; 24for this my
son was dead and is alive again; he was lost
and is found.' And they began to be merry.
25"Now his older son was in the field. And
as he came and drew near to the house, he
heard music and dancing. 26So he called one
of the servants and asked what these things
meant. 27And he said to him, 'Your brother
has come, and because he has received him
safe and sound, your father has killed the fatted calf.'
28"But he was angry and would not go in.
Therefore his father came out and pleaded
with him. 29So he answered and said to *his*
father, 'Lo, these many years I have been serving you; I never transgressed your commandment at any time; and yet you never gave me a
young goat, that I might make merry with my
friends. 30But as soon as this son of yours
came, who has devoured your livelihood

15:22 [a]NU-Text reads *Quickly bring.*

PERSONALITY PROFILE

Fatherhood

THE PRODIGAL SON'S LOVING FATHER

(LUKE 15:11)

The Parable of the Prodigal Son follows two other parables that Jesus told in response to some critics. They were upset about the people with whom He was spending time. His crime? "This Man receives sinners and eats with them" (Luke 15:2). All three parables illustrate the high value that God places on an individual life. A wayward sheep, a wayward coin and a wayward son are each "found" and become the reason for celebration. God plays a different character in each parable: the owner of the flock, the owner of the coins, and the father of two sons.

Parables have an amazing capacity for affecting different members of an audience in very different ways. The Parable of the Prodigal may offer a younger brother, an older brother, or a father startling and varied insights. Although the most active role in this parable falls to the younger brother, the father proves to be the central actor. The character of this father, who represents our Heavenly Father, demonstrates a number of significant lessons for earthly fathers:

- He provided a caring model for his sons.
- He provided financial and emotional support for his sons.
- He gave them the blessing of a heritage.
- He guided but did not force his sons to conform.
- He gave them room to fail and a place to return.
- He exercised mercy and grace toward his children.
- He met his children more than half way.
- He forgave.

The two brothers in Jesus' parable represent opposite ends of a continuum of children's characters from passivity to action. The list above offers earthly fathers significant help in relating to the differences in their children as well as guidance about the consistency that sons and daughters need to observe in their fathers. Wise earthly fathers exercise humility and persistence as they seek to imitate their Heavenly Father in their special role. Only One does it perfectly; the rest dare not do less than their best.

To Learn More: Turn to the article about fatherhood on pages 516, 517. See also the key passage note at Ephesians 6:4 on page 1558.

with harlots, you killed the fatted calf for him.'
[31]"And he said to him, 'Son, you are always
with me, and all that I have is yours. [32]It was
right that we should make merry and be glad,
for your brother was dead and is alive again,
and was lost and is found.' "

The Parable of the Unjust Steward

16 He also said to His disciples: "There
was a certain rich man who had a
steward, and an accusation was brought to
him that this man was wasting his goods. [2]So
he called him and said to him, 'What is this I
hear about you? Give an account of your stewardship, for you can no longer be steward.'
[3]"Then the steward said within himself,
'What shall I do? For my master is taking the
stewardship away from me. I cannot dig; I am
ashamed to beg. [4]I have resolved what to do,
that when I am put out of the stewardship,
they may receive me into their houses.'
[5]"So he called every one of his master's
debtors to *him*, and said to the first, 'How
much do you owe my master?' [6]And he said,
'A hundred measures[a] of oil.' So he said to
him, 'Take your bill, and sit down quickly and
write fifty.' [7]Then he said to another, 'And how
much do you owe?' So he said, 'A hundred
measures[a] of wheat.' And he said to him,
'Take your bill, and write eighty.' [8]So the master commended the unjust steward because he
had dealt shrewdly. For the sons of this world
are more shrewd in their generation than the
sons of light.
[9]"And I say to you, make friends for yourselves by unrighteous mammon, that when
you fail,[a] they may receive you into an everlasting home. [10]He who *is* faithful in *what is*
least is faithful also in much; and he who is
unjust in *what is* least is unjust also in much.
[11]Therefore if you have not been faithful in the
unrighteous mammon, who will commit to
your trust the true *riches?* [12]And if you have
not been faithful in what is another man's,
who will give you what is your own?
[13]"No servant can serve two masters; for either he will hate the one and love the other, or
else he will be loyal to the one and despise the
other. You cannot serve God and mammon."

The Law, the Prophets, and the Kingdom

[14]Now the Pharisees, who were lovers of
money, also heard all these things, and they
derided Him. [15]And He said to them, "You are
those who justify yourselves before men, but
God knows your hearts. For what is highly esteemed among men is an abomination in the
sight of God.
[16]"The law and the prophets *were* until

16:6 [a]Greek *batos,* eight or nine gallons each (Old Testament *bath*) **16:7** [a]Greek *koros,* ten or twelve bushels each (Old Testament *kor*) **16:9** [a]NU-Text reads *it fails.*

KEY PASSAGE

Adolescent Problems

NOW I GET IT!

(15:17, 18)

The story of the lost (rebellious) child is as relevant today as it was in Jesus' day. Adolescence can be turbulent—a time of learning independence, and often a time of rebellion against parental authority and regulations.

This parable reminds us that any parent can experience children with adolescent problems. It is not an indictment on the parent that the child struggles through the stage of adolescence—making wrong choices, challenging authority, seeking his or her own identity. What *is* a reflection on the parent is their attitude toward their struggling and wayward child. In the case of the father in the parable, he looked for and anticipated the return of his son. We should never close the door on our relationships with our children. Even when they have made the worst of choices, they need to know that loving, caring, and forgiving parents are waiting and praying and will rejoice when they return.

To Learn More: Turn to the article about adolescent problems on pages 410, 411. See also the personality profile of Eli's sons on page 346.

John. Since that time the kingdom of God has
been preached, and everyone is pressing into
it. [17]And it is easier for heaven and earth to
pass away than for one tittle of the law to fail.
[18]"Whoever divorces his wife and marries
another commits adultery; and whoever marries her who is divorced from *her* husband
commits adultery.

The Rich Man and Lazarus

[19]"There was a certain rich man who was
clothed in purple and fine linen and fared
sumptuously every day. [20]But there was a certain beggar named Lazarus, full of sores, who
was laid at his gate, [21]desiring to be fed with
the crumbs which fell[a] from the rich man's
table. Moreover the dogs came and licked his
sores. [22]So it was that the beggar died, and
was carried by the angels to Abraham's bosom. The rich man also died and was buried.
[23]And being in torments in Hades, he lifted up
his eyes and saw Abraham afar off, and Lazarus in his bosom.
[24]"Then he cried and said, 'Father Abraham,
have mercy on me, and send Lazarus that he
may dip the tip of his finger in water and cool
my tongue; for I am tormented in this flame.'
[25]But Abraham said, 'Son, remember that in
your lifetime you received your good things,
and likewise Lazarus evil things; but now he is
comforted and you are tormented. [26]And besides all this, between us and you there is a
great gulf fixed, so that those who want to pass
from here to you cannot, nor can those from
there pass to us.'
[27]"Then he said, 'I beg you therefore, father,
that you would send him to my father's house,
[28]for I have five brothers, that he may testify
to them, lest they also come to this place of
torment.' [29]Abraham said to him, 'They have
Moses and the prophets; let them hear them.'
[30]And he said, 'No, father Abraham; but if one
goes to them from the dead, they will repent.'
[31]But he said to him, 'If they do not hear Moses and the prophets, neither will they be persuaded though one rise from the dead.' "

Jesus Warns of Offenses

17 Then He said to the disciples, "It is impossible that no offenses should come,
but woe *to him* through whom they do come!
[2]It would be better for him if a millstone were
hung around his neck, and he were thrown
into the sea, than that he should offend one of
these little ones. [3]Take heed to yourselves. If
your brother sins against you,[a] rebuke him;
and if he repents, forgive him. [4]And if he sins
against you seven times in a day, and seven
times in a day returns to you,[a] saying, 'I repent,' you shall forgive him."

Faith and Duty

[5]And the apostles said to the Lord, "Increase our faith."
[6]So the Lord said, "If you have faith as a
mustard seed, you can say to this mulberry
tree, 'Be pulled up by the roots and be planted
in the sea,' and it would obey you. [7]And which
of you, having a servant plowing or tending
sheep, will say to him when he has come in
from the field, 'Come at once and sit down to
eat'? [8]But will he not rather say to him, 'Prepare something for my supper, and gird yourself and serve me till I have eaten and drunk,
and afterward you will eat and drink'? [9]Does
he thank that servant because he did the

16:21 [a]NU-Text reads *with what fell.* **17:3** [a]NU-Text omits *against you.* **17:4** [a]M-Text omits *to you.*

SOUL NOTE

Master Lock *(16:13)* All people are ultimately "serving" something—whether it is God, a false god, a principle, or simply oneself. Jesus warned about trying to serve two masters at the same time. In this case, He pointed to God and money. Money masters people when they spend most of their time getting it or worrying about losing it. Serving money means not trusting God to provide for one's needs. That means a person cannot focus totally on money and then attempt to serve God. No one can serve two masters. Identifying the focus of our lives will tell us whom we serve.
Topic: Money

things that were commanded him? I think not.[a] 10So likewise you, when you have done all those things which you are commanded, say, 'We are unprofitable servants. We have done what was our duty to do.' "

Ten Lepers Cleansed

11Now it happened as He went to Jerusalem that He passed through the midst of Samaria and Galilee. 12Then as He entered a certain village, there met Him ten men who were lepers, who stood afar off. 13And they lifted up *their* voices and said, "Jesus, Master, have mercy on us!"

14So when He saw *them,* He said to them, "Go, show yourselves to the priests." And so it was that as they went, they were cleansed.

15And one of them, when he saw that he was healed, returned, and with a loud voice glorified God, 16and fell down on *his* face at His feet, giving Him thanks. And he was a Samaritan.

17So Jesus answered and said, "Were there not ten cleansed? But where *are* the nine? 18Were there not any found who returned to give glory to God except this foreigner?" 19And He said to him, "Arise, go your way. Your faith has made you well."

The Coming of the Kingdom

20Now when He was asked by the Pharisees when the kingdom of God would come, He answered them and said, "The kingdom of God does not come with observation; 21nor will they say, 'See here!' or 'See there!'[a] For indeed, the kingdom of God is within you."

22Then He said to the disciples, "The days will come when you will desire to see one of the days of the Son of Man, and you will not see *it.* 23And they will say to you, 'Look here!' or 'Look there!'[a] Do not go after *them* or follow *them.* 24For as the lightning that flashes out of one *part* under heaven shines to the other *part* under heaven, so also the Son of Man will be in His day. 25But first He must suffer many things and be rejected by this generation. 26And as it was in the days of Noah, so it will be also in the days of the Son of Man: 27They ate, they drank, they married wives, they were given in marriage, until the day that Noah entered the ark, and the flood came and destroyed them all. 28Likewise as it was also in the days of Lot: They ate, they drank, they bought, they sold, they planted, they built; 29but on the day that Lot went out of Sodom it rained fire and brimstone from heaven and destroyed *them* all. 30Even so will it be in the day when the Son of Man is revealed.

31"In that day, he who is on the housetop, and his goods *are* in the house, let him not come down to take them away. And likewise the one who is in the field, let him not turn back. 32Remember Lot's wife. 33Whoever seeks to save his life will lose it, and whoever loses his life will preserve it. 34I tell you, in that night there will be two *men* in one bed: the one will be taken and the other will be left. 35Two *women* will be grinding together: the one will be taken and the other left. 36Two *men* will be in the field: the one will be taken and the other left."[a]

37And they answered and said to Him, "Where, Lord?"

So He said to them, "Wherever the body is, there the eagles will be gathered together."

The Parable of the Persistent Widow

18 Then He spoke a parable to them, that men always ought to pray and not lose heart, 2saying: "There was in a certain city a judge who did not fear God nor regard man.

17:9 [a]NU-Text ends verse with *commanded;* M-Text omits *him.* **17:21** [a]NU-Text reverses *here* and *there.* **17:23** [a]NU-Text reverses *here* and *there.* **17:36** [a]NU-Text and M-Text omit verse 36.

SOUL NOTE

Don't Give Up *(18:1)* Jesus' parable illustrated "that men always ought to pray and not lose heart." The parable of the unjust judge reminds us that even though we may have prayed for a long time about something, crying out to God and yet not receiving an answer, we must not give up. If human judges, with all their inadequacies, can be convinced to do the right thing, how much more can we trust God to answer our petitions and do what is right. **Topic: Prayer**

[3]Now there was a widow in that city; and she
came to him, saying, 'Get justice for me from
my adversary.' [4]And he would not for a while;
but afterward he said within himself, 'Though
I do not fear God nor regard man, [5]yet because
this widow troubles me I will avenge her, lest
by her continual coming she weary me.' "
[6]Then the Lord said, "Hear what the unjust
judge said. [7]And shall God not avenge His
own elect who cry out day and night to Him,
though He bears long with them? [8]I tell you
that He will avenge them speedily. Nevertheless, when the Son of Man comes, will He really find faith on the earth?"

The Parable of the Pharisee and the Tax Collector

[9]Also He spoke this parable to some who
trusted in themselves that they were righteous, and despised others: [10]"Two men went
up to the temple to pray, one a Pharisee and
the other a tax collector. [11]The Pharisee stood
and prayed thus with himself, 'God, I thank
You that I am not like other men—extortioners, unjust, adulterers, or even as this tax collector. [12]I fast twice a week; I give tithes of all
that I possess.' [13]And the tax collector, standing afar off, would not so much as raise *his*
eyes to heaven, but beat his breast, saying,
'God, be merciful to me a sinner!' [14]I tell you,
this man went down to his house justified
rather than the other; for everyone who exalts
himself will be humbled, and he who humbles
himself will be exalted."

Jesus Blesses Little Children

[15]Then they also brought infants to Him
that He might touch them; but when the disciples saw *it*, they rebuked them. [16]But
Jesus called them to
Him and said, "Let the
little children come to
Me, and do not forbid
them; for of such is the
kingdom of God. [17]As-
suredly, I say to you,
whoever does not re-
ceive the kingdom of God as a little child will
by no means enter it."

> "Let the little children come to Me, and do not forbid them; for of such is the kingdom of God."
> LUKE 18:16

Jesus Counsels the Rich Young Ruler

[18]Now a certain ruler asked Him, saying,
"Good Teacher, what shall I do to inherit eternal life?"
[19]So Jesus said to him, "Why do you call Me
good? No one *is* good but One, *that is,* God.
[20]You know the commandments: *'Do not
commit adultery,' 'Do not murder,' 'Do not
steal,' 'Do not bear false witness,' 'Honor
your father and your mother.'* "[a]
[21]And he said, "All these things I have kept
from my youth."
[22]So when Jesus heard these things, He said
to him, "You still lack one thing. Sell all that
you have and distribute to the poor, and you
will have treasure in heaven; and come, follow Me."
[23]But when he heard this, he became very
sorrowful, for he was very rich.

With God All Things Are Possible

[24]And when Jesus saw that he became very
sorrowful, He said, "How hard it is for those
who have riches to enter the kingdom of God!
[25]For it is easier for a camel to go through the
eye of a needle than for a rich man to enter the
kingdom of God."
[26]And those who heard it said, "Who then
can be saved?"
[27]But He said, "The things which are impossible with men are possible with God."
[28]Then Peter said, "See, we have left all[a]
and followed You."
[29]So He said to them, "Assuredly, I say to
you, there is no one who has left house or parents or brothers or wife or children, for the
sake of the kingdom of God, [30]who shall not
receive many times more in this present time,
and in the age to come eternal life."

Jesus a Third Time Predicts His Death and Resurrection

[31]Then He took the twelve aside and said to
them, "Behold, we are
going up to Jerusalem,
and all things that are
written by the prophets
concerning the Son of
Man will be accom-
plished. [32]For He will be
delivered to the Gentiles
and will be mocked and insulted and spit
upon. [33]They will scourge *Him* and kill Him.
And the third day He will rise again."
[34]But they understood none of these things;

18:20 [a]Exodus 20:12–16; Deuteronomy 5:16–20
18:28 [a]NU-Text reads *our own.*

this saying was hidden from them, and they did not know the things which were spoken.

A Blind Man Receives His Sight

[35]Then it happened, as He was coming near Jericho, that a certain blind man sat by the road begging. [36]And hearing a multitude passing by, he asked what it meant. [37]So they told him that Jesus of Nazareth was passing by. [38]And he cried out, saying, "Jesus, Son of David, have mercy on me!"

[39]Then those who went before warned him that he should be quiet; but he cried out all the more, "Son of David, have mercy on me!"

[40]So Jesus stood still and commanded him to be brought to Him. And when he had come near, He asked him, [41]saying, "What do you want Me to do for you?"

He said, "Lord, that I may receive my sight."

[42]Then Jesus said to him, "Receive your sight; your faith has made you well." [43]And immediately he received his sight, and followed Him, glorifying God. And all the people, when they saw *it,* gave praise to God.

Jesus Comes to Zacchaeus' House

19 Then *Jesus* entered and passed through Jericho. [2]Now behold, *there was* a man named Zacchaeus who was a chief tax collector, and he was rich. [3]And he sought to see who Jesus was, but could not because of the crowd, for he was of short stature. [4]So he ran ahead and climbed up into a sycamore tree to see Him, for He was going to pass that *way.* [5]And when Jesus came to the place, He looked up and saw him,[a] and said to him, "Zacchaeus, make haste and come down, for today I must stay at your house." [6]So he made haste and came down, and received Him joyfully. [7]But when they saw *it,* they all complained, saying, "He has gone to be a guest with a man who is a sinner."

[8]Then Zacchaeus stood and said to the Lord, "Look, Lord, I give half of my goods to the poor; and if I have taken anything from anyone by false accusation, I restore fourfold."

[9]And Jesus said to him, "Today salvation has come to this house, because he also is a son of Abraham; [10]for the Son of Man has come to seek and to save that which was lost."

> "For the Son of Man has come to seek and to save that which was lost."
> LUKE 19:10

The Parable of the Minas

[11]Now as they heard these things, He spoke another parable, because He was near Jerusalem and because they thought the kingdom of God would appear immediately. [12]Therefore He said: "A certain nobleman went into a far country to receive for himself a kingdom and to return. [13]So he called ten of his servants, delivered to them ten minas,[a] and said to them, 'Do business till I come.' [14]But his citizens hated him, and sent a delegation after him, saying, 'We will not have this *man* to reign over us.'

[15]"And so it was that when he returned, having received the kingdom, he then commanded these servants, to whom he had given the money, to be called to him, that he might know how much every man had gained by trading. [16]Then came the first, saying, 'Master, your mina has earned ten minas.' [17]And he said to him, 'Well *done,* good servant; because you were faithful in a very little, have authority over ten cities.' [18]And the second came, saying, 'Master, your mina has earned five minas.' [19]Likewise he said to him, 'You also be over five cities.'

[20]"Then another came, saying, 'Master, here is your mina, which I have kept put away in a handkerchief. [21]For I feared you, because you are an austere man. You collect what you did not deposit, and reap what you did not sow.' [22]And he said to him, 'Out of your own mouth I will judge you, *you* wicked servant. You knew that I was an austere man, collecting what I did not deposit and reaping what I did not sow. [23]Why then did you not put my money in the bank, that at my coming I might have collected it with interest?'

[24]"And he said to those who stood by, 'Take the mina from him, and give *it* to him who has ten minas.' [25](But they said to him, 'Master, he has ten minas.') [26]'For I say to you, that to

---

19:5 [a]NU-Text omits *and saw him.* **19:13** [a]The *mina* (Greek *mna,* Hebrew *minah*) was worth about three months' salary.

everyone who has will be given; and from him who does not have, even what he has will be taken away from him. 27But bring here those enemies of mine, who did not want me to reign over them, and slay *them* before me.' "

The Triumphal Entry

28When He had said this, He went on ahead, going up to Jerusalem. 29And it came to pass, when He drew near to Bethphage[a] and Bethany, at the mountain called Olivet, *that* He sent two of His disciples, 30saying, "Go into the village opposite *you*, where as you enter you will find a colt tied, on which no one has ever sat. Loose it and bring *it here*. 31And if anyone asks you, 'Why are you loosing *it*?' thus you shall say to him, 'Because the Lord has need of it.' "

32So those who were sent went their way and found *it* just as He had said to them. 33But as they were loosing the colt, the owners of it said to them, "Why are you loosing the colt?"

34And they said, "The Lord has need of him." 35Then they brought him to Jesus. And they threw their own clothes on the colt, and they set Jesus on him. 36And as He went, *many* spread their clothes on the road.

37Then, as He was now drawing near the descent of the Mount of Olives, the whole multitude of the disciples began to rejoice and praise God with a loud voice for all the mighty works they had seen, 38saying:

" *'Blessed is the King who comes in the*
name of the LORD!'[a]
Peace in heaven and glory in the
highest!"

39And some of the Pharisees called to Him from the crowd, "Teacher, rebuke Your disciples."

40But He answered and said to them, "I tell you that if these should keep silent, the stones would immediately cry out."

Jesus Weeps over Jerusalem

41Now as He drew near, He saw the city and wept over it, 42saying, "If you had known, even you, especially in this your day, the things *that make* for your peace! But now they are hidden from your eyes. 43For days will come upon you when your enemies will build an embankment around you, surround you and close you in on every side, 44and level you, and your children within you, to the ground; and they will not leave in you one stone upon another, because you did not know the time of your visitation."

Jesus Cleanses the Temple

45Then He went into the temple and began to drive out those who bought and sold in it,[a] 46saying to them, "It is written, *'My house is*[a] *a house of prayer,'*[b] but you have made it a *'den of thieves.'* "[c]

47And He was teaching daily in the temple. But the chief priests, the scribes, and the leaders of the people sought to destroy Him, 48and were unable to do anything; for all the people were very attentive to hear Him.

Jesus' Authority Questioned

20 Now it happened on one of those days, as He taught the people in the temple and preached the gospel, *that* the chief priests and the scribes, together with the elders, confronted *Him* 2and spoke to Him, saying, "Tell us, by what authority are You doing these things? Or who is he who gave You this authority?"

3But He answered and said to them, "I also will ask you one thing, and answer Me: 4The baptism of John—was it from heaven or from men?"

5And they reasoned among themselves, saying, "If we say, 'From heaven,' He will say, 'Why then[a] did you not believe him?' 6But if we say, 'From men,' all the people will stone us, for they are persuaded that John was a prophet." 7So they answered that they did not know where *it was* from.

8And Jesus said to them, "Neither will I tell you by what authority I do these things."

The Parable of the Wicked Vinedressers

9Then He began to tell the people this parable: "A certain man planted a vineyard, leased it to vinedressers, and went into a far country for a long time. 10Now at vintage-time he sent a servant to the vinedressers, that they might give him some of the fruit of the vineyard. But the vinedressers beat him and sent *him* away empty-handed. 11Again he sent another ser-

19:29 [a]M-Text reads *Bethsphage*. **19:38** [a]Psalm 118:26 **19:45** [a]NU-Text reads *those who were selling*. **19:46** [a]NU-Text reads *shall be*. [b]Isaiah 56:7 [c]Jeremiah 7:11 **20:5** [a]NU-Text and M-Text omit *then*.

vant; and they beat him also, treated *him* shamefully, and sent *him* away empty-handed. 12And again he sent a third; and they wounded him also and cast *him* out.

13"Then the owner of the vineyard said, 'What shall I do? I will send my beloved son. Probably they will respect *him* when they see him.' 14But when the vinedressers saw him, they reasoned among themselves, saying, 'This is the heir. Come, let us kill him, that the inheritance may be ours.' 15So they cast him out of the vineyard and killed *him*. Therefore what will the owner of the vineyard do to them? 16He will come and destroy those vinedressers and give the vineyard to others."

And when they heard *it* they said, "Certainly not!"

17Then He looked at them and said, "What then is this that is written:

> *'The stone which the builders rejected*
> *Has become the chief cornerstone'?*[a]

18Whoever falls on that stone will be broken; but on whomever it falls, it will grind him to powder."

19And the chief priests and the scribes that very hour sought to lay hands on Him, but they feared the people[a]—for they knew He had spoken this parable against them.

The Pharisees: Is It Lawful to Pay Taxes to Caesar?

20So they watched *Him*, and sent spies who pretended to be righteous, that they might seize on His words, in order to deliver Him to the power and the authority of the governor.

21Then they asked Him, saying, "Teacher, we know that You say and teach rightly, and You do not show personal favoritism, but teach the way of God in truth: 22Is it lawful for us to pay taxes to Caesar or not?"

23But He perceived their craftiness, and said to them, "Why do you test Me?[a] 24Show Me a denarius. Whose image and inscription does it have?"

They answered and said, "Caesar's."

25And He said to them, "Render therefore to Caesar the things that are Caesar's, and to God the things that are God's."

26But they could not catch Him in His words in the presence of the people. And they marveled at His answer and kept silent.

The Sadducees: What About the Resurrection?

27Then some of the Sadducees, who deny that there is a resurrection, came to *Him* and asked Him, 28saying: "Teacher, Moses wrote to us *that* if a man's brother dies, having a wife, and he dies without children, his brother should take his wife and raise up offspring for his brother. 29Now there were seven brothers. And the first took a wife, and died without children. 30And the second[a] took her as wife, and he died childless. 31Then the third took her, and in like manner the seven also; and they left no children,[a] and died. 32Last of all the woman died also. 33Therefore, in the resurrection, whose wife does she become? For all seven had her as wife."

34Jesus answered and said to them, "The sons of this age marry and are given in marriage. 35But those who are counted worthy to attain that age, and the resurrection from the dead, neither marry nor are given in marriage; 36nor can they die anymore, for they are equal to the angels and are sons of God, being sons of the resurrection. 37But even Moses showed in the *burning* bush *passage* that the dead are raised, when he called the Lord *'the God of Abraham, the God of Isaac, and the God of Jacob.'*[a] 38For He is not the God of the dead but of the living, for all live to Him."

39Then some of the scribes answered and said, "Teacher, You have spoken well." 40But after that they dared not question Him anymore.

Jesus: How Can David Call His Descendant Lord?

41And He said to them, "How can they say that the Christ is the Son of David? 42Now David himself said in the Book of Psalms:

> *'The LORD said to my Lord,*
> *"Sit at My right hand,*
> 43 *Till I make Your enemies Your footstool."'*[a]

44Therefore David calls Him *'Lord'*; how is He then his Son?"

20:17 [a]Psalm 118:22 **20:19** [a]M-Text reads *but they were afraid.* **20:23** [a]NU-Text omits *Why do you test Me?* **20:30** [a]NU-Text ends verse 30 here. **20:31** [a]NU-Text and M-Text read *the seven also left no children.* **20:37** [a]Exodus 3:6, 15 **20:43** [a]Psalm 110:1

Beware of the Scribes

45Then, in the hearing of all the people, He said to His disciples, 46"Beware of the scribes, who desire to go around in long robes, love greetings in the marketplaces, the best seats in the synagogues, and the best places at feasts, 47who devour widows' houses, and for a pretense make long prayers. These will receive greater condemnation."

The Widow's Two Mites

21 And He looked up and saw the rich putting their gifts into the treasury, 2and He saw also a certain poor widow putting in two mites. 3So He said, "Truly I say to you that this poor widow has put in more than all; 4for all these out of their abundance have put in offerings for God,[a] but she out of her poverty put in all the livelihood that she had."

Jesus Predicts the Destruction of the Temple

5Then, as some spoke of the temple, how it was adorned with beautiful stones and donations, He said, 6"These things which you see—the days will come in which not *one* stone shall be left upon another that shall not be thrown down."

The Signs of the Times and the End of the Age

7So they asked Him, saying, "Teacher, but when will these things be? And what sign *will there be* when these things are about to take place?"

8And He said: "Take heed that you not be deceived. For many will come in My name, saying, 'I am *He,*' and, 'The time has drawn near.' Therefore[a] do not go after them. 9But when you hear of wars and commotions, do not be terrified; for these things must come to pass first, but the end *will not come* immediately."

10Then He said to them, "Nation will rise against nation, and kingdom against kingdom. 11And there will be great earthquakes in various places, and famines and pestilences; and there will be fearful sights and great signs from heaven. 12But before all these things, they will lay their hands on you and persecute *you,* delivering *you* up to the synagogues and prisons. You will be brought before kings and rulers for My name's sake. 13But it will turn out for you as an occasion for testimony. 14Therefore settle *it* in your hearts not to meditate beforehand on what you will answer; 15for I will give you a mouth and wisdom which all your adversaries will not be able to contradict or resist. 16You will be betrayed even by parents and brothers, relatives and friends; and they will put *some* of you to death. 17And you will be hated by all for My name's sake. 18But not a hair of your head shall be lost. 19By your patience possess your souls.

The Destruction of Jerusalem

20"But when you see Jerusalem surrounded by armies, then know that its desolation is near. 21Then let those who are in Judea flee to the mountains, let those who are in the midst of her depart, and let not those who are in the country enter her. 22For these are the days of vengeance, that all things which are written may be fulfilled. 23But woe to those who are pregnant and to those who are nursing babies in those days! For there will be great distress in the land and wrath upon this people. 24And they will fall by the edge of the sword, and be

21:4 [a]NU-Text omits *for God.* **21:8** [a]NU-Text omits *Therefore.*

SOUL NOTE

Risky Giving *(21:1–4)* Abundant giving seems risky, and giving everything is downright scary. Jesus praised the widow for her generosity. Her gift was small, but it was a sacrifice, and she gave it willingly, trusting that God would meet her needs. People are not expected to give away every paycheck and then trust God to provide—that paycheck *is* God's provision. God doesn't expect us to give away everything we have, but neither does He want us to give Him only what we don't need. We should give to God sacrificially, yet responsibly. God honors the size of the heart, not the size of the offering. **Topic: Money**

led away captive into all nations. And Jerusalem will be trampled by Gentiles until the times of the Gentiles are fulfilled.

The Coming of the Son of Man

25“And there will be signs in the sun, in the moon, and in the stars; and on the earth distress of nations, with perplexity, the sea and the waves roaring; 26men’s hearts failing them from fear and the expectation of those things which are coming on the earth, for the powers of the heavens will be shaken. 27Then they will see the Son of Man coming in a cloud with power and great glory. 28Now when these things begin to happen, look up and lift up your heads, because your redemption draws near.”

The Parable of the Fig Tree

29Then He spoke to them a parable: “Look at the fig tree, and all the trees. 30When they are already budding, you see and know for yourselves that summer is now near. 31So you also, when you see these things happening, know that the kingdom of God is near. 32Assuredly, I say to you, this generation will by no means pass away till all things take place. 33Heaven and earth will pass away, but My words will by no means pass away.

The Importance of Watching

34“But take heed to yourselves, lest your hearts be weighed down with carousing, drunkenness, and cares of this life, and that Day come on you unexpectedly. 35For it will come as a snare on all those who dwell on the face of the whole earth. 36Watch therefore, and pray always that you may be counted worthy[a] to escape all these things that will come to pass, and to stand before the Son of Man.”

37And in the daytime He was teaching in the temple, but at night He went out and stayed on the mountain called Olivet. 38Then early in the morning all the people came to Him in the temple to hear Him.

The Plot to Kill Jesus

22 Now the Feast of Unleavened Bread drew near, which is called Passover. 2And the chief priests and the scribes sought how they might kill Him, for they feared the people.

3Then Satan entered Judas, surnamed Iscariot, who was numbered among the twelve. 4So he went his way and conferred with the chief priests and captains, how he might betray Him to them. 5And they were glad, and agreed to give him money. 6So he promised and sought opportunity to betray Him to them in the absence of the multitude.

Jesus and His Disciples Prepare the Passover

7Then came the Day of Unleavened Bread, when the Passover must be killed. 8And He sent Peter and John, saying, “Go and prepare the Passover for us, that we may eat.”

9So they said to Him, “Where do You want us to prepare?”

10And He said to them, “Behold, when you have entered the city, a man will meet you carrying a pitcher of water; follow him into the house which he enters. 11Then you shall say to the master of the house, ‘The Teacher says to you, “Where is the guest room where I may eat the Passover with My disciples?” ’ 12Then he will show you a large, furnished upper room; there make ready.”

13So they went and found it just as He had said to them, and they prepared the Passover.

Jesus Institutes the Lord’s Supper

14When the hour had come, He sat down, and the twelve[a] apostles with Him. 15Then He said to them, “With *fervent* desire I have desired to eat this Passover with you before I suffer; 16for I say to you, I will no longer eat of it until it is fulfilled in the kingdom of God.”

17Then He took the cup, and gave thanks, and said, “Take this and divide *it* among yourselves; 18for I say to you,[a] I will not drink of the fruit of the vine until the kingdom of God comes.”

19And He took bread, gave thanks and broke *it*, and gave *it* to them, saying, “This is My body which is given for you; do this in remembrance of Me.”

20Likewise He also *took* the cup after supper, saying, “This cup *is* the new covenant in My blood, which is shed for you. 21But behold, the hand of My betrayer *is* with Me on the table. 22And truly the Son of Man goes as it has been determined, but woe to that man by whom He is betrayed!”

21:36 [a]NU-Text reads *may have strength.*
22:14 [a]NU-Text omits *twelve.* **22:18** [a]NU-Text adds *from now on.*

23Then they began to question among themselves, which of them it was who would do
this thing.

THE DISCIPLES ARGUE ABOUT GREATNESS

24Now there was also a dispute among
them, as to which of them should be considered the greatest. 25And He said to them, "The
kings of the Gentiles exercise lordship over
them, and those who exercise authority over
them are called 'benefactors.' 26But not so
among you; on the contrary, he who is greatest among you, let him be as the younger, and
he who governs as he who serves. 27For who
is greater, he who sits at the table, or he who
serves? *Is* it not he who sits at the table? Yet I
am among you as the One who serves.

28"But you are those who have continued
with Me in My trials. 29And I bestow upon you
a kingdom, just as My Father bestowed *one*
upon Me, 30that you may eat and drink at My
table in My kingdom, and sit on thrones judging the twelve tribes of Israel."

JESUS PREDICTS PETER'S DENIAL

31And the Lord said,[a] "Simon, Simon! Indeed, Satan has asked for you, that he may
sift *you* as wheat. 32But I have prayed for
you, that your faith should not fail; and when
you have returned to *Me,* strengthen your
brethren."

33But he said to Him, "Lord, I am ready to
go with You, both to prison and to death."

34Then He said, "I tell you, Peter, the rooster
shall not crow this day before you will deny
three times that you know Me."

SUPPLIES FOR THE ROAD

35And He said to them, "When I sent you
without money bag, knapsack, and sandals,
did you lack anything?"

So they said, "Nothing."

36Then He said to them, "But now, he who
has a money bag, let him take *it,* and likewise
a knapsack; and he who has no sword, let him
sell his garment and buy one. 37For I say to
you that this which is written must still be accomplished in Me: *'And He was numbered
with the transgressors.'*[a] For the things concerning Me have an end."

38So they said, "Lord, look, here *are* two
swords."

And He said to them, "It is enough."

THE PRAYER IN THE GARDEN

39Coming out, He went to the Mount of Olives, as He was accustomed, and His disciples
also followed Him. 40When He came to the
place, He said to them, "Pray that you may not
enter into temptation."

41And He was withdrawn from them about a
stone's throw, and He knelt down and prayed,
42saying, "Father, if it is Your will, take this
cup away from Me; nevertheless not My will,
but Yours, be done." 43Then an angel appeared
to Him from heaven, strengthening Him.
44And being in agony, He prayed more earnestly. Then His sweat became like great
drops of blood falling down to the ground.[a]

45When He rose up from prayer, and had
come to His disciples, He found them sleeping
from sorrow. 46Then He said to them, "Why
do you sleep? Rise and pray, lest you enter
into temptation."

BETRAYAL AND ARREST IN GETHSEMANE

47And while He was still speaking, behold, a
multitude; and he who was called Judas, one

22:31 [a]NU-Text omits *And the Lord said.*
22:37 [a]Isaiah 53:12 **22:44** [a]NU-Text brackets verses 43 and 44 as not in the original text.

SOUL NOTE

Overwhelmed *(22:31, 32)* What grace Jesus showed to Peter! Satan had asked for Peter, wanting to "sift" him like wheat. Jesus said that He had prayed for Peter that his "faith should not fail." Then afterward, Peter should return and strengthen his brothers. Peter would deny Christ and face painful sorrow. His faith did not fail, however, and Jesus restored him (John 21). Believers can make painful mistakes, but through those difficult times they learn of God's grace. When they return to Christ, they can take the lessons they learned and strengthen other believers about sin, temptation, and God's grace. **Topic: Restoration**

of the twelve, went before them and drew
near to Jesus to kiss Him. 48But Jesus said to
him, "Judas, are you betraying the Son of Man
with a kiss?"
49When those around Him saw what was
going to happen, they said to Him, "Lord,
shall we strike with the sword?" 50And one of
them struck the servant of the high priest and
cut off his right ear.
51But Jesus answered and said, "Permit
even this." And He touched his ear and healed
him.
52Then Jesus said to the chief priests, captains of the temple, and the elders who had
come to Him, "Have you come out, as against
a robber, with swords and clubs? 53When I
was with you daily in the temple, you did not
try to seize Me. But this is your hour, and the
power of darkness."

PETER DENIES JESUS, AND WEEPS BITTERLY

54Having arrested Him, they led *Him* and
brought Him into the high priest's house. But
Peter followed at a distance. 55Now when they
had kindled a fire in the midst of the courtyard
and sat down together, Peter sat among them.
56And a certain servant girl, seeing him as he
sat by the fire, looked intently at him and said,
"This man was also with Him."
57But he denied Him,[a] saying, "Woman, I do
not know Him."
58And after a little while another saw him
and said, "You also are of them."
But Peter said, "Man, I am not!"
59Then after about an hour had passed, another confidently affirmed, saying, "Surely

22:57 [a]NU-Text reads *denied it.*

PERSONALITY PROFILE

Failure

PETER: FAILURE IS NOT FOREVER

(LUKE 22:54–62)

Peter had a flair for sticking his foot in his mouth. His ability to speak up would eventually be used by God for great purposes; first, however, God would deal with Peter's impulsiveness and streak of temper. Peter's story reveals a man who learned God's lessons well, allowing God to take his failures and use them for His glory.

Peter had boldly told Jesus, "Even if all are made to stumble because of You, I will never be made to stumble" (Matt. 26:33). Peter insisted that he would never fail, but Jesus stopped Peter's bravado short when He told him that failure would indeed come that very night. Peter surely hoped to instead prove his loyalty to Jesus. In the garden, Peter attempted to defend Jesus in Gethsemane, using his sword and wounding a man. He then followed Jesus to the courtyard of the High Priest's residence, refusing to stay behind. He sat around the fire, trying to stay warm in the chilly dawn air. And the rest of the story reveals the tragic truth of Peter's failure, as he denies having any relationship with or knowledge of Jesus.

In truth, Peter's failure had begun the moment he insisted that he would never fail. His bravado had to be tamed, or he could never be the servant Christ would need in His church. When Peter looked into Jesus' eyes moments after his third denial, the proud servant realized what he had done, and "went out and wept bitterly."

Unlike his fellow disciple, Judas, who killed himself, Peter repented of his sin and was forgiven and restored by Christ (John 21:15–17). Broken by his failure, Peter emerged a stronger, humbler man, able to be used greatly in the growth of the early church.

Failure can destroy us, or it can immobilize us, or it can simply teach us a lesson about what *not* to do. Failure can rub off our rough spots and soften our hard hearts. It can be the first step toward being a great success. God can use our failures to make us the people He wants us to be.

To Learn More: Turn to the article about failure on pages 586, 587. See also the key passage note at Proverbs 24:16 on page 834.

this *fellow* also was with Him, for he is a Galilean."

[60]But Peter said, "Man, I do not know what you are saying!"

Immediately, while he was still speaking, the rooster[a] crowed. [61]And the Lord turned and looked at Peter. Then Peter remembered the word of the Lord, how He had said to him, "Before the rooster crows,[a] you will deny Me three times." [62]So Peter went out and wept bitterly.

Jesus Mocked and Beaten

[63]Now the men who held Jesus mocked Him and beat Him. [64]And having blindfolded Him, they struck Him on the face and asked Him,[a] saying, "Prophesy! Who is the one who struck You?" [65]And many other things they blasphemously spoke against Him.

Jesus Faces the Sanhedrin

[66]As soon as it was day, the elders of the people, both chief priests and scribes, came together and led Him into their council, saying, [67]"If You are the Christ, tell us."

But He said to them, "If I tell you, you will by no means believe. [68]And if I also ask *you,* you will by no means answer Me or let *Me* go.[a] [69]Hereafter the Son of Man will sit on the right hand of the power of God."

[70]Then they all said, "Are You then the Son of God?"

So He said to them, "You *rightly* say that I am."

[71]And they said, "What further testimony do we need? For we have heard it ourselves from His own mouth."

Jesus Handed Over to Pontius Pilate

23 Then the whole multitude of them arose and led Him to Pilate. [2]And they began to accuse Him, saying, "We found this *fellow* perverting the[a] nation, and forbidding to pay taxes to Caesar, saying that He Himself is Christ, a King."

[3]Then Pilate asked Him, saying, "Are You the King of the Jews?"

He answered him and said, "*It is as* you say."

[4]So Pilate said to the chief priests and the crowd, "I find no fault in this Man."

[5]But they were the more fierce, saying, "He stirs up the people, teaching throughout all Judea, beginning from Galilee to this place."

Jesus Faces Herod

[6]When Pilate heard of Galilee,[a] he asked if the Man were a Galilean. [7]And as soon as he knew that He belonged to Herod's jurisdiction, he sent Him to Herod, who was also in Jerusalem at that time. [8]Now when Herod saw Jesus, he was exceedingly glad; for he had desired for a long *time* to see Him, because he had heard many things about Him, and he hoped to see some miracle done by Him. [9]Then he questioned Him with many words, but He answered him nothing. [10]And the chief priests and scribes stood and vehemently accused Him. [11]Then Herod, with his men of war, treated Him with contempt and mocked *Him,* arrayed Him in a gorgeous robe, and sent Him back to Pilate. [12]That very day Pilate and Herod became friends with each other, for previously they had been at enmity with each other.

Taking the Place of Barabbas

[13]Then Pilate, when he had called together the chief priests, the rulers, and the people, [14]said to them, "You have brought this Man to me, as one who misleads the people. And indeed, having examined *Him* in your presence, I have found no fault in this Man concerning those things of which you accuse Him; [15]no, neither did Herod, for I sent you back to him;[a] and indeed nothing deserving of death has been done by Him. [16]I will therefore chastise Him and release *Him*" [17](for it was necessary for him to release one to them at the feast).[a]

[18]And they all cried out at once, saying, "Away with this *Man,* and release to us Barabbas"— [19]who had been thrown into prison for a certain rebellion made in the city, and for murder.

[20]Pilate, therefore, wishing to release Jesus, again called out to them. [21]But they shouted, saying, "Crucify *Him,* crucify Him!"

[22]Then he said to them the third time, "Why, what evil has He done? I have found no reason for death in Him. I will therefore chastise Him and let *Him* go."

[23]But they were insistent, demanding with

22:60 [a]NU-Text and M-Text read *a rooster.* **22:61** [a]NU-Text adds *today.* **22:64** [a]NU-Text reads *And having blindfolded Him, they asked Him.* **22:68** [a]NU-Text omits *also* and *Me or let Me go.* **23:2** [a]NU-Text reads *our.* **23:6** [a]NU-Text omits *of Galilee.* **23:15** [a]NU-Text reads *for he sent Him back to us.* **23:17** [a]NU-Text omits verse 17.

loud voices that He be crucified. And the
voices of these men and of the chief priests
prevailed.[a] 24So Pilate gave sentence that it
should be as they requested. 25And he released to them[a] the one they requested, who
for rebellion and murder had been thrown
into prison; but he delivered Jesus to their will.

The King on a Cross

26Now as they led Him away, they laid hold
of a certain man, Simon a Cyrenian, who was
coming from the country, and on him they laid
the cross that he might bear *it* after Jesus.

27And a great multitude of the people followed Him, and women who also mourned
and lamented Him. 28But Jesus, turning to
them, said, "Daughters of Jerusalem, do not
weep for Me, but weep for yourselves and for
your children. 29For indeed the days are coming in which they will say, 'Blessed *are* the
barren, wombs that never bore, and breasts
which never nursed!' 30Then they will begin
'to say to the mountains, "Fall on us!" and to
the hills, "Cover us!"' [a] 31For if they do these
things in the green wood, what will be done in
the dry?"

23:23 [a]NU-Text omits *and of the chief priests.*
23:25 [a]NU-Text and M-Text omit *to them.*
23:30 [a]Hosea 10:8

PERSONALITY PROFILE

THE THIEF AND HIS SAVIOR

(LUKE 23:42)

Jesus had company when He died. Two criminals shared His fate. Three crosses formed a small group on the brow called Calvary one afternoon. The brief and painful conversation between three dying men led to a change of eternal destination for one of them.

One thief mocked Jesus with a challenge, "If You are the Christ, save Yourself and us" (Luke 23:39). His words convey a desperate bitterness. He had no thought of responsibility or remorse. He died bitter, mocking, and unrepentant.

The other thief reached a different conclusion. He heard Jesus forgive His executioners. He sensed Jesus' innocence. Perhaps he had heard about Jesus elsewhere. He was shocked by the other thief's lack of conscience. "Do you not even fear God, seeing you are under the same condemnation?" he said (Luke 23:40). The second thief made a beautiful statement of faith that Jesus readily acknowledged. His words illustrate the heart of repentance:

- He accepted responsibility for his own sins. "We receive the due reward of our deeds" (Luke 23:41)
- He recognized the unique character and divinity of Christ. "This Man has done nothing wrong" (Luke 23:41). He called Jesus "Lord" and spoke of Jesus' kingdom (Luke 23:42). These phrases all reveal the thief's acceptance of Jesus' special role.
- He called out for salvation from his moral condition, not rescue from the cross. "Lord, remember me when You come into Your kingdom" (Luke 23:42).
- His expression did not take forgiveness for granted, but placed his life at the mercy of Jesus.

Jesus' response to the faith of His dying companion is the same response that He gives to anyone who believes in Him whether or not the conversion occurs in the last moments of life. To those with a little longer to live, Jesus' words can be read with a slightly different punctuation. Instead of "Assuredly, I say to you, today you will be with Me in Paradise" (Luke 23:43), Jesus has the authority to declare to anyone who believes in Him, "Assuredly, I say to you today, you will be with Me in Paradise."

To Learn More: Turn to the article about repentance on pages 722, 723. See also the key passage note at 2 Corinthians 7:7–10 on page 1528.

32There were also two others, criminals, led with Him to be put to death. 33And when they had come to the place called Calvary, there they crucified Him, and the criminals, one on the right hand and the other on the left. 34Then Jesus said, "Father, forgive them, for they do not know what they do."[a]

And they divided His garments and cast lots. 35And the people stood looking on. But even the rulers with them sneered, saying, "He saved others; let Him save Himself if He is the Christ, the chosen of God."

36The soldiers also mocked Him, coming and offering Him sour wine, 37and saying, "If You are the King of the Jews, save Yourself."

38And an inscription also was written over Him in letters of Greek, Latin, and Hebrew:[a]

THIS IS THE KING OF THE JEWS.

39Then one of the criminals who were hanged blasphemed Him, saying, "If You are the Christ,[a] save Yourself and us."

40But the other, answering, rebuked him, saying, "Do you not even fear God, seeing you are under the same condemnation? 41And we indeed justly, for we receive the due reward of our deeds; but this Man has done nothing wrong." 42Then he said to Jesus, "Lord,[a] remember me when You come into Your kingdom."

43And Jesus said to him, "Assuredly, I say to you, today you will be with Me in Paradise."

Jesus Dies on the Cross

44Now it was[a] about the sixth hour, and there was darkness over all the earth until the ninth hour. 45Then the sun was darkened,[a] and the veil of the temple was torn in two. 46And when Jesus had cried out with a loud voice, He said, "Father, *'into Your hands I commit My spirit.'* "[a] Having said this, He breathed His last.

47So when the centurion saw what had happened, he glorified God, saying, "Certainly this was a righteous Man!"

48And the whole crowd who came together to that sight, seeing what had been done, beat their breasts and returned. 49But all His acquaintances, and the women who followed Him from Galilee, stood at a distance, watching these things.

Jesus Buried in Joseph's Tomb

50Now behold, *there was* a man named Joseph, a council member, a good and just man. 51He had not consented to their decision and deed. *He was* from Arimathea, a city of the Jews, who himself was also waiting[a] for the kingdom of God. 52This man went to Pilate and asked for the body of Jesus. 53Then he took it down, wrapped it in linen, and laid it in a tomb *that was* hewn out of the rock, where no one had ever lain before. 54That day was the Preparation, and the Sabbath drew near.

55And the women who had come with Him from Galilee followed after, and they observed the tomb and how His body was laid. 56Then they returned and prepared spices and fragrant oils. And they rested on the Sabbath according to the commandment.

He Is Risen

24 Now on the first *day* of the week, very early in the morning, they, and certain *other women* with them,[a] came to the tomb

23:34 [a]NU-Text brackets the first sentence as a later addition. **23:38** [a]NU-Text omits *written* and *in letters of Greek, Latin, and Hebrew.* **23:39** [a]NU-Text reads *Are You not the Christ?* **23:42** [a]NU-Text reads *And he said, "Jesus, remember me.* **23:44** [a]NU-Text adds *already.* **23:45** [a]NU-Text reads *obscured.* **23:46** [a]Psalm 31:5 **23:51** [a]NU-Text reads *who was waiting.* **24:1** [a]NU-Text omits *and certain other women with them.*

SOUL NOTE

Heavenly Promise *(23:42, 43)* Contemplating one's death can cause anxiety and fear. For Jesus and the thief on the cross beside Him, death was imminent—only a few hours away. Instead of despairing, the thief put his trust in Jesus. In response, Jesus assured him, "Today you will be with Me in Paradise." Because of Jesus' death, eternal life and heaven are waiting for believers the moment they die. Even though the thought of death can make us sad or fearful, we know it is just the door through which we pass into heaven. There we will spend eternity with our Savior. **Topic: Eternal Life**

bringing the spices which they had prepared. [2]But they found the stone rolled away from the tomb. [3]Then they went in and did not find the body of the Lord Jesus. [4]And it happened, as they were greatly[a] perplexed about this, that behold, two men stood by them in shining garments. [5]Then, as they were afraid and bowed *their* faces to the earth, they said to them, "Why do you seek the living among the dead? [6]He is not here, but is risen! Remember how He spoke to you when He was still in Galilee, [7]saying, 'The Son of Man must be delivered into the hands of sinful men, and be crucified, and the third day rise again.' "

[8]And they remembered His words. [9]Then they returned from the tomb and told all these things to the eleven and to all the rest. [10]It was Mary Magdalene, Joanna, Mary *the mother* of James, and the other *women* with them, who told these things to the apostles. [11]And their words seemed to them like idle tales, and they did not believe them. [12]But Peter arose and ran to the tomb; and stooping down, he saw the linen cloths lying[a] by themselves; and he departed, marveling to himself at what had happened.

The Road to Emmaus

[13]Now behold, two of them were traveling that same day to a village called Emmaus, which was seven miles[a] from Jerusalem. [14]And they talked together of all these things which had happened. [15]So it was, while they conversed and reasoned, that Jesus Himself drew near and went with them. [16]But their eyes were restrained, so that they did not know Him.

[17]And He said to them, "What kind of conversation *is* this that you have with one another as you walk and are sad?"[a]

[18]Then the one whose name was Cleopas answered and said to Him, "Are You the only stranger in Jerusalem, and have You not known the things which happened there in these days?"

[19]And He said to them, "What things?"

So they said to Him, "The things concerning Jesus of Nazareth, who was a Prophet mighty in deed and word before God and all the people, [20]and how the chief priests and our rulers delivered Him to be condemned to death, and crucified Him. [21]But we were hoping that it was He who was going to redeem Israel. Indeed, besides all this, today is the third day since these things happened. [22]Yes, and certain women of our company, who arrived at the tomb early, astonished us. [23]When they did not find His body, they came saying that they had also seen a vision of angels who said He was alive. [24]And certain of those *who were* with us went to the tomb and found *it* just as the women had said; but Him they did not see."

[25]Then He said to them, "O foolish ones, and slow of heart to believe in all that the prophets have spoken! [26]Ought not the Christ to have suffered these things and to enter into His glory?" [27]And beginning at Moses and all the Prophets, He expounded to them in all the Scriptures the things concerning Himself.

The Disciples' Eyes Opened

[28]Then they drew near to the village where they were going, and He indicated that He would have gone farther. [29]But they constrained Him, saying, "Abide with us, for it is toward evening, and the day is far spent." And He went in to stay with them.

[30]Now it came to pass, as He sat at the table with them, that He took bread, blessed and broke *it*, and gave it to them. [31]Then their eyes were opened and they knew Him; and He vanished from their sight.

[32]And they said to one another, "Did not our heart burn within us while He talked with us on the road, and while He opened the Scriptures to us?" [33]So they rose up that very hour and returned to Jerusalem, and found the eleven and those *who were* with them gathered together, [34]saying, "The Lord is risen indeed, and has appeared to Simon!" [35]And they told about the things *that had happened* on the road, and how He was known to them in the breaking of bread.

Jesus Appears to His Disciples

[36]Now as they said these things, Jesus Himself stood in the midst of them, and said to them, "Peace to you." [37]But they were terrified and frightened, and supposed they had seen a spirit. [38]And He said to them, "Why are you troubled? And why do doubts arise in your hearts? [39]Behold My hands and My feet, that it

---

24:4 [a]NU-Text omits *greatly.* **24:12** [a]NU-Text omits *lying.* **24:13** [a]Literally *sixty stadia* **24:17** [a]NU-Text reads *as you walk? And they stood still, looking sad.*

is I Myself. Handle Me and see, for a spirit
does not have flesh and bones as you see I
have."
40When He had said this, He showed them
His hands and His feet.[a] 41But while they still
did not believe for joy, and marveled, He said
to them, "Have you any food here?" 42So they
gave Him a piece of a broiled fish and some
honeycomb.[a] 43And He took *it* and ate in their
presence.

The Scriptures Opened

44Then He said to them, "These *are* the
words which I spoke to you while I was still
with you, that all things must be fulfilled
which were written in the Law of Moses and
the Prophets and *the* Psalms concerning Me."
45And He opened their understanding, that
they might comprehend the Scriptures.
46Then He said to them, "Thus it is written,
and thus it was necessary for the Christ to suffer and to rise[a] from the dead the third day,
47and that repentance and remission of sins
should be preached in His name to all nations,
beginning at Jerusalem. 48And you are witnesses of these things. 49Behold, I send the
Promise of My Father upon you; but tarry in
the city of Jerusalem[a] until you are endued
with power from on high."

The Ascension

50And He led them out as far as Bethany,
and He lifted up His hands and blessed them.
51Now it came to pass, while He blessed them,
that He was parted from them and carried up
into heaven. 52And they worshiped Him, and
returned to Jerusalem with great joy, 53and
were continually in the temple praising and[a]
blessing God. Amen.[b]

24:40 [a]Some printed New Testaments omit this verse. It is found in nearly all Greek manuscripts. **24:42** [a]NU-Text omits *and some honeycomb.* **24:46** [a]NU-Text reads *written, that the Christ should suffer and rise.* **24:49** [a]NU-Text omits *of Jerusalem.* **24:53** [a]NU-Text omits *praising and.* [b]NU-Text omits *Amen.*

SOUL NOTE

Spiritual Power *(24:49)* An automobile is useless without fuel; an electric light bulb cannot illuminate a room without electricity. Likewise, it is impossible to live the Christian life in our own strength. Even the disciples who had lived and walked with Jesus needed help. Jesus promised the most powerful help possible—the power of the Holy Spirit. Christians must have "power from on high" (the Holy Spirit) to live God-pleasing lives and to witness to others.
Topic: Presence of the Holy Spirit

John

Humans are a churning, restless race with hungry hearts, thirsty souls, perplexed minds, and a yearning for real purpose and deep fulfillment. Want proof? Look at the faces during rush hour, in the mall, or at work. Read the paper. Better yet, look in the mirror! We may try to ignore such longings or bury them, but we cannot deny them.

Now look at the Gospel written by John, a close associate of Jesus, one of the original twelve disciples. Focus carefully on the One introduced as "the Word" (1:1), who "became flesh and dwelt among us" (1:14). Can this son of a carpenter, this itinerant preacher from Nazareth, really be God? What did Jesus mean—really—when He described Himself as "living water" (4:10), "the bread of life" (6:35), "the light of the world" (8:12), who has authority to give abundant life (10:10)?

John wrote his eyewitness account of the life, death, and resurrection of Jesus for the express purpose of proclaiming (and proving) that Jesus is the Christ (the promised Messiah). He also wanted his readers to know that only trusting in Christ can bring eternal life (20:31). The result is a theological and literary masterpiece, loved by believers through the ages.

No matter what your soul needs—challenge, comfort, encouragement, or conviction—you will find it in abundance in the fourth Gospel. The living Christ stands ready to meet you and change you forever.

SOUL CONCERNS IN JOHN

Knowing Jesus	(1:29)
Salvation	(3:16)
Presence of the Holy Spirit	(16:5–15)
Doubt	(20:24–29)
Restoration	(21:15–19)

THE ETERNAL WORD

1 In the beginning was the Word, and the Word was with God, and the Word was God. 2He was in the beginning with God. 3All things were made through Him, and without Him nothing was made that was made. 4In Him was life, and the life was the light of men. 5And the light shines in the darkness, and the darkness did not comprehend[a] it.

JOHN'S WITNESS: THE TRUE LIGHT

6There was a man sent from God, whose name *was* John. 7This man came for a witness, to bear witness of the Light, that all through him might believe. 8He was not that Light, but *was sent* to bear witness of that Light. 9That was the true Light which gives light to every man coming into the world.[a]

10He was in the world, and the world was made through Him, and the world did not know Him. 11He came to His own,[a] and His own[b] did not receive Him. 12But as many as received Him, to them He gave the right to become children of God, to those who believe in His name: 13who were born, not of blood, nor of the will of the flesh, nor of the will of man, but of God.

THE WORD BECOMES FLESH

14And the Word became flesh and dwelt among us, and we beheld His glory, the glory as of the only begotten of the Father, full of grace and truth.

15John bore witness of Him and cried out, saying, "This was He of whom I said, 'He who comes after me is preferred before me, for He was before me.' "

16And[a] of His fullness we have all received, and grace for grace. 17For the law was given through Moses, *but* grace and truth came through Jesus Christ. 18No one has seen God at any time. The only begotten Son,[a] who is in the bosom of the Father, He has declared *Him.*

A VOICE IN THE WILDERNESS

19Now this is the testimony of John, when the Jews sent priests and Levites from Jerusalem to ask him, "Who are you?"

20He confessed, and did not deny, but confessed, "I am not the Christ."

21And they asked him, "What then? Are you Elijah?"

He said, "I am not."

"Are you the Prophet?"

And he answered, "No."

22Then they said to him, "Who are you, that we may give an answer to those who sent us? What do you say about yourself?"

23He said: "I *am*

'The voice of one crying in the
wilderness:
"Make straight the way of the L*ORD,"* '[a]

as the prophet Isaiah said."

24Now those who were sent were from the Pharisees. 25And they asked him, saying, "Why then do you baptize if you are not the Christ, nor Elijah, nor the Prophet?"

26John answered them, saying, "I baptize with water, but there stands One among you whom you do not know. 27It is He who, coming after me, is preferred before me, whose sandal strap I am not worthy to loose."

28These things were done in Bethabara[a] beyond the Jordan, where John was baptizing.

THE LAMB OF GOD

29The next day John saw Jesus coming toward him, and said, "Behold! The Lamb of God who takes away the sin of the world! 30This is He of whom I said, 'After me comes a Man who is preferred before me, for He was before me.' 31I did not know Him; but that He should be revealed to Israel, therefore I came baptizing with water."

32And John bore witness, saying, "I saw the Spirit descending from heaven like a dove, and He remained upon Him. 33I did not know Him, but He who sent me to baptize with water said to me, 'Upon whom you see the Spirit descending, and remaining on Him, this is He who baptizes with the Holy Spirit.' 34And I have seen and testified that this is the Son of God."

THE FIRST DISCIPLES

35Again, the next day, John stood with two of his disciples. 36And looking at Jesus as He walked, he said, "Behold the Lamb of God!"

37The two disciples heard him speak, and

1:5 [a]Or *overcome* **1:9** [a]Or *That was the true Light which, coming into the world, gives light to every man.* **1:11** [a]That is, His own things or domain [b]That is, His own people **1:16** [a]NU-Text reads *For.* **1:18** [a]NU-Text reads *only begotten God.* **1:23** [a]Isaiah 40:3 **1:28** [a]NU-Text and M-Text read *Bethany.*

they followed Jesus. 38 Then Jesus turned, and
seeing them following, said to them, "What
do you seek?"
They said to Him, "Rabbi" (which is to say,
when translated, Teacher), "where are You
staying?"
39 He said to them, "Come and see." They
came and saw where He was staying, and remained with Him that day (now it was about
the tenth hour).
40 One of the two who heard John *speak,* and
followed Him, was Andrew, Simon Peter's
brother. 41 He first found his own brother Simon, and said to him, "We have found the
Messiah" (which is translated, the Christ).
42 And he brought him to Jesus.
Now when Jesus looked at him, He said,
"You are Simon the son of Jonah.[a] You shall be
called Cephas" (which is translated, A Stone).

Philip and Nathanael

43 The following day Jesus wanted to go to
Galilee, and He found Philip and said to him,
"Follow Me." 44 Now Philip was from Bethsaida, the city of Andrew and Peter. 45 Philip
found Nathanael and said to him, "We have
found Him of whom Moses in the law, and
also the prophets, wrote—Jesus of Nazareth,
the son of Joseph."
46 And Nathanael said to him, "Can anything
good come out of Nazareth?"
Philip said to him, "Come and see."
47 Jesus saw Nathanael coming toward Him,
and said of him, "Behold, an Israelite indeed,
in whom is no deceit!"
48 Nathanael said to Him, "How do You
know me?"
Jesus answered and said to him, "Before
Philip called you, when you were under the fig
tree, I saw you."
49 Nathanael answered and said to Him,
"Rabbi, You are the Son of God! You are the
King of Israel!"
50 Jesus answered and said to him, "Because
I said to you, 'I saw you under the fig tree,' do
you believe? You will see greater things than

1:42 [a]NU-Text reads *John.*

PERSONALITY PROFILE

Salvation

NATHANAEL: FROM SKEPTIC TO DISCIPLE

(JOHN 1:48)

Nathanael was honest and straightforward. He also was not easily impressed. When his friend Philip came to tell him that he and others had found the Messiah, a man named Jesus who came from Nazareth, Nathanael merely replied, "Can anything good come out of Nazareth?" (John 1:46). Obviously that low-class town couldn't produce anything special, certainly not the Jews' Messiah—or so Nathanael thought.

To his credit, however, when invited by Philip to "come and see" this man, Nathanael went. He was skeptical, but curious. Jesus' first words to Nathanael reveal His insight into people's character: "Behold, an Israelite indeed, in whom is no deceit!" (John 1:47). Jesus perceived Nathanael's straightforward honesty. He also had seen Nathanael's whereabouts when Philip found him. While on earth, Jesus used His miraculous powers for His kingdom's sake, and here He gained a disciple when Nathanael perceived that power in Jesus. Immediately, Nathanael realized that Jesus was indeed the Son of God, the King of Israel.

Nathanael had successfully moved from skeptic to disciple. Jesus gave him exactly the proof he needed to help him understand and believe. Jesus is always working in people's hearts, bringing them to exactly the right point—through inner turmoil, or serious questioning, or outward circumstances—to help them put it all together and see Jesus. When they accept Him, Jesus gives them salvation and eternal life.

Salvation is only a prayer away. Christ does not make it difficult to be saved, because He *wants* people to come to Him. Don't look for proof—look for Jesus.

To Learn More: Turn to the article about salvation on pages 1372, 1373. See also the key passage note at John 3:16 on page 1374.

Knowing Jesus

WHO IS JESUS CHRIST?

ED HINDSON

(John 1:29)

Jesus is the primary figure of the Bible. The Old Testament promises His coming; the New Testament describes His arrival on the scene of humanity that changed the course of history. One cannot read the New Testament without being confronted by Jesus. His person is overwhelming. His character is irresistibly attractive. His teachings are life-changing. But many still ask: Is He simply to be admired, or is He to be worshiped? Is He a good man, or is He God?

The more closely we examine the person, character, and claims of Jesus, the more we are compelled to see that He was more than just a man. Jesus was born in obscurity, raised in poverty, and crucified in ignominy. Yet, His life transformed the world. His ministry was characterized by preaching the good news of God's grace to fallen humanity.

The name Jesus means "Savior"; Christ means "Messiah." Technically, He is Jesus, the Christ. The Bible emphasizes that He is the promised Messiah of the Old Testament who was born of a virgin and miraculously entered the human race as God in the flesh (Matt. 1:23; John 1:14).

More than anything else, Jesus brings hope to people's hopelessness. He is depicted as the Word of God (John 1:1), the Light of the World (John 1:7–9), the Lamb of God (John 1:29), and the Son of God (John 1:49). He meets us at our greatest points of need and offers us God's salvation, love, and grace.

HIS DEITY AND HUMANITY

The Gospels paint four portraits of Jesus. Together, they give us a full picture of the person of Christ. Each focuses on a specific aspect of the same individual. Matthew pictures Him as the King of the Jews. Mark portrays Him as the Servant of the Lord. Luke displays Him as the Son of Man. John shows Him as the Son of God. By combining these portraits, we see the various facets of this incredible person—royalty, ministry, humanity, and deity—all in one.

John's Gospel in particular is woven around seven miracles, seven messages, and seven declarations of Jesus. The central statement being Jesus' declaration: "Before Abraham was, I AM" (John 8:58). His listeners immediately took this to be a claim of deity. Jesus was connecting Himself to the "I AM" declaration of God in Exodus 3:14. Around this central concept, John uses seven other "I am" statements by Jesus to give us a series of word pictures of the Savior:

- "I am the bread of life" (John 6:35)
- "I am the light of the world" (John 8:12)
- "I am the door of the sheep" (John 10:7)
- "I am the good shepherd" (John 10:11)
- "I am the resurrection and the life" (John 11:25)
- "I am the way, the truth, and the life" (John 14:6)
- "I am the true vine" (John 15:1)

The Gospel writers give us a picture of the most incredible man who ever lived. He healed the sick, raised the dead, fed the hungry, and loved the outcasts. His miracles were amazing. His teachings were brilliant. His insights into human nature were remarkable. Like a diamond, reflecting various streams of color and brilliance, Jesus shines as a perfect and complete picture of God. He looked like a man, but He talked like God. He lived among people, but He also lived above them. Indeed, in Him, God "became flesh" (John 1:14).

HIS IRRESISTIBLE APPEAL

Jesus is the epitome of divine love, sufficient grace, and eternal hope. No one will ever love us like He loves us. No one will ever care for us like He cares. Ultimately, He died on the Cross for our sins (1 Cor. 15:1–4). The good news of the gospel compels us to believe that He died for us personally. He calls upon us to trust His death as a sufficient payment for our sins.

Faith is the act of believing that activates our commitment to Jesus Christ as our personal Savior. It is the key that personalizes our relationship to Him. Saving faith means that we believe Jesus died for our sins and offers us the gift of eternal life. All we have to do is believe it! Such an act of faith receives the free gift of this grace, believes this offer to be sincere, and trusts Him to keep His promises—forever.

Charles Spurgeon, the great British preacher, said it best over a century ago when he wrote: "You may study, look, and meditate, but Jesus is a greater Savior than you think Him to be, even when your thoughts are at their highest." Jesus Christ is more willing to love us, accept us, help us, and forgive us than we ourselves are. It is no wonder they call Him the Savior!

Jesus came so that we might know God personally. He suffered and died for our sins so that they might be "paid in full" (John 19:30; 1 Pet. 2:21–24). Then He rose from the dead to offer us the gift of eternal life (John 10:28). We can have that gift by receiving His gracious offer by faith. Believing in Jesus is an act of trust by which we affirm that what He did for us on the Cross is enough. On that basis, the Bible promises: "Whoever calls on the name of the LORD shall be saved" (Rom. 10:13).

FURTHER MEDITATION:

Other passages to study about the issue of knowing Jesus include:

- ➢ Isaiah 53
- ➢ Acts 4:12; 9:3–6; 10:36–43
- ➢ Colossians 1:15–23
- ➢ Hebrews 1:1–4; 12:1, 2; 13:8
- ➢ Revelation 1:9–20; 3:20; 19:11–16; 22:20

To Learn More: Turn to the key passage note on knowing Jesus at John 14:6 on page 1396. See also the personality profile of Nicodemus on page 1371.

these." 51 And He said to him, "Most assuredly,
I say to you, hereafter[a] you shall see heaven
open, and the angels of God ascending and descending upon the Son of Man."

WATER TURNED TO WINE

2 On the third day there was a wedding in
Cana of Galilee, and the mother of Jesus
was there. 2 Now both Jesus and His disciples
were invited to the wedding. 3 And when they
ran out of wine, the mother of Jesus said to
Him, "They have no wine."
4 Jesus said to her, "Woman, what does your
concern have to do with Me? My hour has not
yet come."
5 His mother said to the servants, "Whatever
He says to you, do *it*."
6 Now there were set there six waterpots of
stone, according to the manner of purification
of the Jews, containing twenty or thirty gallons apiece. 7 Jesus said to them, "Fill the
waterpots with water." And they filled them
up to the brim. 8 And He said to them, "Draw
some out now, and take *it* to the master of the
feast." And they took *it*. 9 When the master of
the feast had tasted the water that was made
wine, and did not know where it came from
(but the servants who had drawn the water
knew), the master of the feast called the bridegroom. 10 And he said to him, "Every man at
the beginning sets out the good wine, and
when the *guests* have well drunk, then the inferior. You have kept the good wine until
now!"
11 This beginning of signs Jesus did in Cana
of Galilee, and manifested His glory; and His
disciples believed in Him.
12 After this He went down to Capernaum,
He, His mother, His brothers, and His disciples; and they did not stay there many days.

JESUS CLEANSES THE TEMPLE

13 Now the Passover of the Jews was at
hand, and Jesus went up to Jerusalem. 14 And
He found in the temple those who sold oxen
and sheep and doves, and the money changers
doing business. 15 When He had made a whip
of cords, He drove them all out of the temple,
with the sheep and the oxen, and poured out
the changers' money and overturned the tables. 16 And He said to those who sold doves,
"Take these things away! Do not make My
Father's house a house of merchandise!"
17 Then His disciples remembered that it was
written, *"Zeal for Your house has eaten[a] Me
up."*[b]
18 So the Jews answered and said to Him,
"What sign do You show to us, since You do
these things?"
19 Jesus answered and said to them, "Destroy this temple, and in three days I will raise
it up."
20 Then the Jews said, "It has taken forty-six
years to build this temple, and will You raise it
up in three days?"
21 But He was speaking of the temple of His
body. 22 Therefore, when He had risen from
the dead, His disciples remembered that He
had said this to them;[a] and they believed the
Scripture and the word which Jesus had said.

THE DISCERNER OF HEARTS

23 Now when He was in Jerusalem at the
Passover, during the feast, many believed in
His name when they saw the signs which He
did. 24 But Jesus did not commit Himself to
them, because He knew all *men*, 25 and had no

1:51 [a]NU-Text omits *hereafter*. **2:17** [a]NU-Text and M-Text read *will eat*. [b]Psalm 69:9 **2:22** [a]NU-Text and M-Text omit *to them*.

SOUL NOTE

Wedding Invitation *(2:2)* Marriage was created by God for men and women to enjoy and to provide a solid environment for family. Jesus blessed the couple in Cana with His presence at their wedding celebration. Christian couples still invite Jesus to their wedding, making their personal relationships with Him the central part of the ceremony, as well as placing themselves in His hands for their future life together. Jesus' presence in a marriage gives it a spiritual vitality that helps the couple make good decisions, resolve problems, and raise their children to honor God. Place Jesus at the center of your marriage. He will bless it with His presence. **Topic: Marriage**

need that anyone should testify of man, for He
knew what was in man.

The New Birth

3 There was a man of the Pharisees named
Nicodemus, a ruler of the Jews. 2This man
came to Jesus by night and said to Him, "Rabbi, we know that You are a teacher come from
God; for no one can do these signs that You do
unless God is with him."
3Jesus answered and said to him, "Most assuredly, I say to you, unless one is born again,
he cannot see the kingdom of God."
4Nicodemus said to Him, "How can a man
be born when he is old? Can he enter a second
time into his mother's womb and be born?"
5Jesus answered, "Most assuredly, I say to
you, unless one is born of water and the Spirit,
he cannot enter the kingdom of God. 6That
which is born of the flesh is flesh, and that
which is born of the Spirit is spirit. 7Do not
marvel that I said to you, 'You must be born
again.' 8The wind blows where it wishes, and
you hear the sound of it, but cannot tell where
it comes from and where it goes. So is everyone who is born of the Spirit."
9Nicodemus answered and said to Him,
"How can these things be?"
10Jesus answered and said to him, "Are you
the teacher of Israel, and do not know these
things? 11Most assuredly, I say to you, We
speak what We know and testify what We
have seen, and you do not receive Our witness. 12If I have told you earthly things and
you do not believe, how will you believe if I
tell you heavenly things? 13No one has ascended to heaven but He who came down from
heaven, *that is,* the Son of Man who is in
heaven.[a] 14And as Moses lifted up the serpent
in the wilderness, even so must the Son of
Man be lifted up, 15that whoever believes in

3:13 [a]NU-Text omits *who is in heaven.*

PERSONALITY PROFILE

Knowing Jesus

NICODEMUS: A CONVERSATION WITH CHRIST

(JOHN 3:1)

As a member of the ruling Pharisee party, Nicodemus was in a very prestigious group. The Pharisees were the experts in the law. As zealous students of the Scriptures, they should have been the first to recognize the Messiah when He arrived on the scene. Unfortunately, they not only missed the truth about Jesus, but most of them actively sought, and accomplished, His death.

But Nicodemus *did* see something—Someone—he couldn't explain. He saw the glimmer of truth in what he had been observing about Jesus. So he sought out Jesus, going by night so as to be able to speak confidentially with this unusual Teacher.

Nicodemus started the conversation by explaining that he understood that God had to be with Jesus because of the miracles Jesus could do. Nicodemus was on the right track, and Jesus got right to the heart of the matter, explaining to Nicodemus that faith requires more than just understanding that Jesus is the Messiah—one has to be "born again." In the report of this conversation with Nicodemus, we read the words that have brought millions to their knees across the centuries, "For God so loved the world that He gave His only begotten Son, that whoever believes in Him should not perish but have everlasting life" (John 3:16).

Knowing Jesus means more than knowing about Him. To really know Jesus, we must be born all over again, experiencing spiritual regeneration. We're born again when we repent of our sins and accept Jesus Christ as Savior. With that act, we embark on a lifetime of knowing more and more about Jesus Christ. As we walk with Him, as we deepen our relationship with Him, we get to know Him better and better as our Savior, our Lord, and our Friend.

To Learn More: Turn to the article about knowing Jesus on pages 1368, 1369. See also the key passage note at John 14:6 on page 1396.

CLOTHED WITH GARMENTS OF SALVATION

Salvation

JAMES CLINTON

(John 3:16)

"To be saved" means deliverance from impending destruction. In the Bible, the word "salvation" ultimately refers to deliverance from sin and its final consequences—death and eternity in hell. The most important decision we will ever make in this life is what we will do with God's offer of salvation.

The heart of the gospel ("good news") is expressed in John 3:16: "For God so loved the world that He gave His only begotten Son, that whoever believes in Him should not perish but have everlasting life." God's love is expressed in this willingness to send His Son, Jesus Christ, to die in our place and atone for our sins. His sacrificial death for our sins is the only basis of our acceptance by God. The apostle Peter said, "Nor is there salvation in any other, for there is no other name under heaven given among men by which we must be saved" (Acts 4:12).

SALVATION NEEDED

Everyone needs to be saved. Romans 3:23 says that "all have sinned and fall short of the glory of God." Because of sinful nature and sinful actions, all have come short of the standard of spiritual perfection. All need God's grace and forgiveness to pardon sins and provide the gift of eternal life.

The Bible describes humanity's spiritual condition as "unclean" (Is. 64:6), "lost" (Luke 19:10), "condemned" (John 3:18), and "blind" (John 12:40). Spiritually, there is nothing to commend the lost to God. They are helpless to save themselves. The lost have no personal relationship with God. They are needy, and only He can meet the need. God alone can forgive sins, save souls, and bless lives. The lost can only ask, like the Philippian jailer, "What must I do to be saved?" (Acts 16:30).

SALVATION PROVIDED

God loves us so much that He sent His Son to be our Savior. "God demonstrates His own love toward us, in that while we were still sinners, Christ died for us" (Rom. 5:8). Jesus died for us that we might live with God forever. He took the punishment for our sins so that we might be saved. Second Corinthians 5:21 states that God "made Him who knew no sin to be sin for us, that we might become the righteousness of God in Him."

The apostle John expressed this gift of salvation when he wrote, "In this is love, not that we loved God, but that He loved us and sent His Son to be the propitiation for our sins" (1 John 4:10). Jesus demonstrated God's love for us when He died for our sins on the Cross. The apostle Peter said, "For Christ also suffered once for sins, the just for the unjust, that He might bring us to God" (1 Pet. 3:18).

The atoning death of Jesus Christ for our sins is the heart of the gospel. Paul said, "I declare to you the gospel . . . that Christ died for our sins according the Scriptures, and that He was buried, and that He rose again the third day according to the Scriptures" (1 Cor. 15:1, 3, 4). The death of Christ secured our salvation; His resurrection guarantees our eternal life.

SALVATION RECEIVED

The Hebrew term for "salvation" in the Old Testament is *yeshu'ah,* describing deliverance from distress as well as the state of well-being that results from being delivered. The New Testament uses the Greek word *soteria*, a term that includes not just deliverance, but God's forgiveness of sins. The apostle Paul said, "I am not ashamed of the gospel of Christ, for it is the power of God to salvation for everyone who believes" (Rom. 1:16). The Bible explains that salvation is based upon God's grace and accomplished by Christ's sacrificial death for sin: "For by grace you have been saved through faith, and that not of yourselves; it is the gift of God" (Eph. 2:8). Salvation includes *justification* (the act of being declared just or righteous by God) and *redemption* (being freed by the payment of Christ's blood for sin).

Salvation is a gift of God's grace. We don't deserve it and we can't earn it. It must be received as a gift. John 1:12 says, "But as many as received Him, to them He gave the right to become children of God, to those who believe in His name." As incredible as it sounds, salvation is the gift of God. It can only be received by faith. When we believe that Jesus died for *our* sin and in *our* place, we can only respond with love and gratitude. As the hymn writer said, "Jesus paid it all; all to Him I owe."

The invitation of Scripture is clear. Romans 10:13 says, "Whoever calls on the name of the LORD shall be saved." If you have never asked Jesus Christ to be your Savior, you can ask Him right now. In fact, you could pray something like this:

> *Dear God, thank You for loving me so much that You sent Your Son to die for my sins. I admit that I need Your love and forgiveness. I believe that Jesus paid for my sins on the Cross, and I receive Him by faith as my personal Savior. I accept the free gift of salvation as my very own.*

Pray this from your heart. God will hear your prayer, forgive your sins, and give you the gift of eternal salvation. Now seek out a Bible-believing church and live for Christ for the rest of your life!

FURTHER MEDITATION:

Other passages to study about the issue of salvation include:

- Psalms 3:8; 119:155
- Zechariah 9:9, 10
- John 7:37, 38
- Romans 1:16; 10:10
- 2 Corinthians 5:17
- Philippians 1:6; 2:12, 13
- 2 Timothy 3:15
- Hebrews 2:3; 4:16

To Learn More: Turn to the key passage note on salvation at John 3:16 on page 1374. See also the personality profile note of Nathanael on page 1367.

Him should not perish but[a] have eternal life.
[16]For God so loved the world that He gave His
only begotten Son, that whoever believes in
Him should not perish but have everlasting life.
[17]For God did not send
His Son into the world to
condemn the world, but
that the world through
Him might be saved.
[18]"He who believes in
Him is not condemned;
but he who does not be-
lieve is condemned al-
ready, because he has not believed in the name
of the only begotten Son of God. [19]And this is
the condemnation, that the light has come into
the world, and men loved darkness rather than
light, because their deeds were evil. [20]For
everyone practicing evil hates the light and
does not come to the light, lest his deeds
should be exposed. [21]But he who does the truth
comes to the light, that his deeds may be clearly seen, that they have been done in God."

> "For God so loved the world that He gave His only begotten Son, that whoever believes in Him should not perish but have everlasting life."
>
> JOHN 3:16

John the Baptist Exalts Christ

[22]After these things Jesus and His disciples
came into the land of Judea, and there He remained with them and baptized. [23]Now John
also was baptizing in Aenon near Salim, because there was much water there. And they
came and were baptized. [24]For John had not
yet been thrown into prison.
[25]Then there arose a dispute between *some*
of John's disciples and
the Jews about purifica-
tion. [26]And they came
to John and said to him,
"Rabbi, He who was
with you beyond the
Jordan, to whom you
have testified—behold,
He is baptizing, and all
are coming to Him!"
[27]John answered and said, "A man can receive nothing unless it has been given to him
from heaven. [28]You yourselves bear me witness, that I said, 'I am not the Christ,' but, 'I
have been sent before Him.' [29]He who has the
bride is the bridegroom; but the friend of the
bridegroom, who stands and hears him, rejoices greatly because of the bridegroom's
voice. Therefore this joy of mine is fulfilled.
[30]He must increase, but I *must* decrease. [31]He
who comes from above is above all; he who is
of the earth is earthly and speaks of the earth.
He who comes from heaven is above all. [32]And

3:15 [a]NU-Text omits *not perish but.*

KEY PASSAGE

Salvation

GOD'S GREAT LOVE

(3:16)

God created and loves us, but sin separates us from Him. For us to be saved, sin had to be removed, its penalty had to be paid. God, in His great love, sent His only Son to die on the Cross in our place (Rom. 5:8). Because of Jesus' death and resurrection, God offers salvation to all.

- Salvation comes through confessing and believing (Rom. 10:9).
- Salvation is a brand new start, a new birth (John 3:16; Titus 3:5).
- Salvation is a gift, not a reward (Eph. 2:8, 9).
- Salvation makes people new creations (2 Cor. 5:17; Gal. 6:15).
- Salvation gives eternal life (Rom. 6:23).

To *be saved* means to trust in Christ alone for salvation. This happens when a person confesses to being a sinner, repents of it, and asks Christ to save them and take control of their life. Doing this isn't difficult, but it is by far the most important decision a person can ever make.

To Learn More: Turn to the article about salvation on pages 1372, 1373. See also the personality profile of Nathanael on page 1367.

what He has seen and heard, that He testifies; and no one receives His testimony. [33]He who has received His testimony has certified that God is true. [34]For He whom God has sent speaks the words of God, for God does not give the Spirit by measure. [35]The Father loves the Son, and has given all things into His hand. [36]He who believes in the Son has everlasting life; and he who does not believe the Son shall not see life, but the wrath of God abides on him."

A Samaritan Woman Meets Her Messiah

4 Therefore, when the Lord knew that the Pharisees had heard that Jesus made and baptized more disciples than John [2](though Jesus Himself did not baptize, but His disciples), [3]He left Judea and departed again to Galilee. [4]But He needed to go through Samaria.

[5]So He came to a city of Samaria which is called Sychar, near the plot of ground that Jacob gave to his son Joseph. [6]Now Jacob's well was there. Jesus therefore, being wearied from

PERSONALITY PROFILE

Self-Denial

JOHN THE BAPTIST: EVERYTHING FOR JESUS

(JOHN 3:30)

John the Baptist was completely sold out for Jesus. John had been given a mission since before his birth, and he fulfilled that mission completely and wholeheartedly. John denied himself in order to see to it that people's hearts were prepared for the coming Messiah.

John had an urgent message, and a unique way of presenting it. John did not go to the temple and speak to the leadership; he went into the desert and spoke to the throngs who followed him there, irresistibly drawn by his message. John "was clothed in camel's hair, with a leather belt around his waist; and his food was locusts and wild honey" (Matt. 3:4). Although John himself was a fulfillment of Scripture (John 1:23), he did not consider himself to be of greater importance than Christ. He understood that his role was to be the messenger, to direct people to Someone else. "I am not the Christ, but I have been sent before Him . . . He must increase, but I must decrease," he said. When the time came for Christ to begin His ministry, John willingly stepped aside, sending his own followers to follow "the Lamb of God" (John 1:35, 36).

Self-denial is not refusing to enjoy life or have fulfillment. It's a willingness to set aside our own agenda in favor of following the Lamb of God. Self-denial means finding complete gratification in life, for we are only denying ourselves some activities, possessions, or honors in order for God to give us greater opportunities to serve Him—and greater joy in the end.

To Learn More: Turn to the article about self-denial on pages 1346, 1347. See also the key passage note at Galatians 2:20 on page 1539.

SOUL NOTE

Why Believe? *(3:36)* John the Baptist pointed people to Jesus as the Messiah. John made it clear that people have only two options when it comes to making a decision about Christ. Those who believe in the Son have everlasting life. The moment they believe, they begin eternal life. Those who do not believe the Son, however, face the wrath of God. They have rejected God, and in the end He will reject them. The choice is clear. To not accept Christ is to reject Him. There is no middle ground.
Topic: Eternal Life

His journey, sat thus by the well. It was about
the sixth hour.
7A woman of Samaria came to draw water.
Jesus said to her, "Give Me a drink." 8For His
disciples had gone away into the city to buy
food.
9Then the woman of Samaria said to Him,
"How is it that You, being a Jew, ask a drink
from me, a Samaritan woman?" For Jews have
no dealings with Samaritans.
10Jesus answered and said to her, "If you
knew the gift of God, and who it is who says
to you, 'Give Me a drink,' you would have
asked Him, and He would have given you living water."
11The woman said to Him, "Sir, You have
nothing to draw with, and the well is deep.
Where then do You get that living water? 12Are
You greater than our father Jacob, who gave
us the well, and drank from it himself, as well
as his sons and his livestock?"
13Jesus answered and said to her, "Whoever
drinks of this water will thirst again, 14but
whoever drinks of the water that I shall give
him will never thirst. But the water that I shall
give him will become in him a fountain of
water springing up into everlasting life."
15The woman said to Him, "Sir, give me this
water, that I may not thirst, nor come here to
draw."
16Jesus said to her, "Go, call your husband,
and come here."
17The woman answered and said, "I have
no husband."
Jesus said to her, "You have well said, 'I
have no husband,' 18for you have had five husbands, and the one whom you now have is not
your husband; in that you spoke truly."
19The woman said to Him, "Sir, I perceive
that You are a prophet. 20Our fathers worshiped on this mountain, and you *Jews* say
that in Jerusalem is the place where one ought
to worship."
21Jesus said to her, "Woman, believe Me, the

PERSONALITY PROFILE

Divorce/ Separation

THE WOMAN AT THE WELL: FOUND AND FORGIVEN

(JOHN 4:16–18)

She came to the well in the heat of the day, most likely to avoid the crowds of women who came to get their water in the cool of the morning. She was a social outcast, and she tried to avoid people as much as possible. One day, however, she could not avoid a Man who would not let her avoid her past!

Jesus sat at the well as she approached. Normally men did not speak to women in public. Jewish men did not speak to Samaritan men, let alone Samaritan women. Jewish men would have nothing to do with a woman known to be living in sin. Yet Jesus broke all these barriers to speak to this woman about eternal life.

Jesus dug down to this woman's heart and brought her sin into the noonday sun. She had been married five times and was currently living with a man who was not her husband. She had experienced love and loss, and it seems she had turned away from marriage completely, preferring to live in sin. But Jesus taught her about Himself, and how His living water could change her life.

Divorce is not an unforgivable sin. As painful as divorce is for all involved, and as heartbreaking as divorce is for those who face it without wanting it, God can touch broken hearts and lives and make them whole again. When possible, couples should seek every option they can to avoid divorce. At times, however, the unthinkable occurs. God is there to help us pick up the pieces. He revealed Himself to this sinful and heartbroken woman at the well, and He does the same for those today who seek Him out of their brokenness. He can put together the pieces of our lives and make us whole again.

To Learn More: Turn to the article about divorce/separation on pages 250, 251. See also the key passage note at Matthew 19:3–8 on page 1261.

hour is coming when you will neither on this
mountain, nor in Jerusalem, worship the Father. 22You worship what you do not know; we
know what we worship, for salvation is of the
Jews. 23But the hour is coming, and now is,
when the true worshipers will worship the Father in spirit and truth; for the Father is seeking such to worship Him. 24God *is* Spirit, and
those who worship Him must worship in spirit
and truth."
25The woman said to Him, "I know that
Messiah is coming" (who is called Christ).
"When He comes, He will tell us all things."
26Jesus said to her, "I who speak to you am
He."

The Whitened Harvest

27And at this *point* His disciples came, and
they marveled that He talked with a woman;
yet no one said, "What do You seek?" or,
"Why are You talking with her?"
28The woman then left her waterpot, went
her way into the city, and said to the men,
29"Come, see a Man who told me all things
that I ever did. Could this be the Christ?"
30Then they went out of the city and came to
Him.
31In the meantime His disciples urged Him,
saying, "Rabbi, eat."
32But He said to them, "I have food to eat of
which you do not know."
33Therefore the disciples said to one another, "Has anyone brought Him *anything* to
eat?"
34Jesus said to them, "My food is to do the
will of Him who sent Me, and to finish His
work. 35Do you not say, 'There are still four
months and *then* comes the harvest'? Behold,

KEY PASSAGE

Praise and Worship

TRUE WORSHIP

(4:23, 24)

Worship has always been very important to God's people. Sometimes, however, people are more concerned about the place, rituals, and ceremonies of worship than they are with its true meaning. And many worship with their mouths but not with their hearts. God doesn't want that kind of worship (Amos 5:21–23).

We can worship God anywhere because He is Spirit. He isn't confined to a building. God wants His people to "worship in spirit and truth." Because Jesus is the truth (John 14:6), we worship God through our acceptance of Jesus' sacrifice on our behalf. And we worship out of hearts made pure by His shed blood. We worship out of love and adoration for God, who reached out to us. We worship when we quiet ourselves before Him, thinking of all He has done for us. We worship also when we praise God with words and music. In whatever setting, we worship when we give God all the glory.

To Learn More: Turn to the article about praise and worship on pages 794, 795. See also the personality profile of Asaph on page 746.

SOUL NOTE

Soulful Worship *(4:24)* As Jesus spoke with the Samaritan woman about worshiping God, He emphasized that "God is Spirit, and those who worship Him must worship in spirit and truth." The Samaritan woman described a conflict about *where* people should worship (4:20); Jesus pointed out *how* they should worship. The true nature of Christian worship is not about places or rituals; instead, it is the response of the soul when it encounters the living God. True worship of God involves opening up and surrendering our lives to Him. **Topic: Knowing God**

I say to you, lift up your eyes and look at the fields, for they are already white for harvest! [36]And he who reaps receives wages, and gathers fruit for eternal life, that both he who sows and he who reaps may rejoice together. [37]For in this the saying is true: 'One sows and another reaps.' [38]I sent you to reap that for which you have not labored; others have labored, and you have entered into their labors."

The Savior of the World

[39]And many of the Samaritans of that city believed in Him because of the word of the woman who testified, "He told me all that I *ever* did." [40]So when the Samaritans had come to Him, they urged Him to stay with them; and He stayed there two days. [41]And many more believed because of His own word.

[42]Then they said to the woman, "Now we believe, not because of what you said, for we ourselves have heard *Him* and we know that this is indeed the Christ,[a] the Savior of the world."

Welcome at Galilee

[43]Now after the two days He departed from there and went to Galilee. [44]For Jesus Himself testified that a prophet has no honor in his own country. [45]So when He came to Galilee, the Galileans received Him, having seen all the things He did in Jerusalem at the feast; for they also had gone to the feast.

A Nobleman's Son Healed

[46]So Jesus came again to Cana of Galilee where He had made the water wine. And there was a certain nobleman whose son was sick at Capernaum. [47]When he heard that Jesus had come out of Judea into Galilee, he went to Him and implored Him to come down and heal his son, for he was at the point of death. [48]Then Jesus said to him, "Unless you *people* see signs and wonders, you will by no means believe."

[49]The nobleman said to Him, "Sir, come down before my child dies!"

4:42 [a]NU-Text omits *the Christ.*

PERSONALITY PROFILE

Pain

THE MAN AT THE POOL: FREEDOM FROM PAIN

(JOHN 5:6)

People in pain will do almost anything to feel better. They use medicines and drugs to deaden pain. People who live with pain face the daily battle with an enemy that won't go away and won't let up. People in pain long to be released.

The man beside the pool of Bethesda had been an invalid for thirty-eight years. He lay with many other sick people beside this pool, waiting for a stirring of the waters that would enable a miraculous cure for the first person to enter the water. He longed to be freed, but his infirmity made it impossible for him to get to the moving water in time.

Then along came Jesus. Out of all the sick people around the pool, Jesus selected this man. He must have seen an attitude of faith in this man, and so Jesus approached him with the question, "Do you want to be made well?" And Jesus made him well—immediately and completely. The man who had been an invalid for thirty-eight years "took up his bed, and walked" (John 5:9).

Jesus has the power to heal any pain, but His first priority is to heal people spiritually. He may take away a person's pain, as He did this man's. Or He may not take away the pain, as He would not remove Paul's physical difficulty (2 Cor. 12:7–10). Whatever the Lord does, however, it's because He understands the big picture and knows what He can accomplish either through healing a person's pain or through giving that person grace and peace in spite of the pain. We can pray for healing, but most of all, we need to pray for spiritual growth and maturity, and that God will work through people's lives for His glory.

To Learn More: Turn to the article about pain on pages 1534, 1535. See also the key passage note at Hebrews 4:14–16 on page 1624.

50 Jesus said to him, "Go your way; your son lives." So the man believed the word that Jesus spoke to him, and he went his way. 51 And as he was now going down, his servants met him and told *him,* saying, "Your son lives!"

52 Then he inquired of them the hour when he got better. And they said to him, "Yesterday at the seventh hour the fever left him." 53 So the father knew that *it was* at the same hour in which Jesus said to him, "Your son lives." And he himself believed, and his whole household.

54 This again *is* the second sign Jesus did when He had come out of Judea into Galilee.

A Man Healed at the Pool of Bethesda

5 After this there was a feast of the Jews, and Jesus went up to Jerusalem. 2 Now there is in Jerusalem by the Sheep *Gate* a pool, which is called in Hebrew, Bethesda,[a] having five porches. 3 In these lay a great multitude of sick people, blind, lame, paralyzed, waiting for the moving of the water. 4 For an angel went down at a certain time into the pool and stirred up the water; then whoever stepped in first, after the stirring of the water, was made well of whatever disease he had.[a] 5 Now a certain man was there who had an infirmity thirty-eight years. 6 When Jesus saw him lying there, and knew that he already had been *in that condition* a long time, He said to him, "Do you want to be made well?"

7 The sick man answered Him, "Sir, I have no man to put me into the pool when the water is stirred up; but while I am coming, another steps down before me."

8 Jesus said to him, "Rise, take up your bed and walk." 9 And immediately the man was made well, took up his bed, and walked.

And that day was the Sabbath. 10 The Jews therefore said to him who was cured, "It is the Sabbath; it is not lawful for you to carry your bed."

11 He answered them, "He who made me well said to me, 'Take up your bed and walk.' "

12 Then they asked him, "Who is the Man who said to you, 'Take up your bed and walk'?" 13 But the one who was healed did not know who it was, for Jesus had withdrawn, a multitude being in *that* place. 14 Afterward Jesus found him in the temple, and said to him, "See, you have been made well. Sin no more, lest a worse thing come upon you."

15 The man departed and told the Jews that it was Jesus who had made him well.

Honor the Father and the Son

16 For this reason the Jews persecuted Jesus, and sought to kill Him,[a] because He had done these things on the Sabbath. 17 But Jesus answered them, "My Father has been working until now, and I have been working."

18 Therefore the Jews sought all the more to kill Him, because He not only broke the Sabbath, but also said that God was His Father, making Himself equal with God. 19 Then Jesus answered and said to them, "Most assuredly, I say to you, the Son can do nothing of Himself, but what He sees the Father do; for whatever He does, the Son also does in like manner. 20 For the Father loves the Son, and shows Him all things that He Himself does; and He will show Him greater works than these, that you may marvel. 21 For as the Father raises the dead and gives life to *them,* even so the Son gives life to whom He will. 22 For the Father judges no one, but has committed all judgment to the Son, 23 that all should honor the Son just as they honor the Father. He who does not honor the Son does not honor the Father who sent Him.

Life and Judgment Are Through the Son

24 "Most assuredly, I say to you, he who hears My word and believes in Him who sent Me has everlasting life, and shall not come into judgment, but has passed from death into life. 25 Most assuredly, I say to you, the hour is coming, and now is, when the dead will hear the voice of the Son of God; and those who hear will live. 26 For as the Father has life in Himself, so He has granted the Son to have life

> "Most assuredly, I say to you, he who hears My word and believes in Him who sent Me has everlasting life, and shall not come into judgment, but has passed from death into life."
>
> JOHN 5:24

5:2 [a]NU-Text reads *Bethzatha.* **5:4** [a]NU-Text omits *waiting for the moving of the water* at the end of verse 3, and all of verse 4. **5:16** [a]NU-Text omits *and sought to kill Him.*

in Himself, [27]and has given Him authority to execute judgment also, because He is the Son of Man. [28]Do not marvel at this; for the hour is coming in which all who are in the graves will hear His voice [29]and come forth—those who have done good, to the resurrection of life, and those who have done evil, to the resurrection of condemnation. [30]I can of Myself do nothing. As I hear, I judge; and My judgment is righteous, because I do not seek My own will but the will of the Father who sent Me.

The Fourfold Witness

[31]"If I bear witness of Myself, My witness is not true. [32]There is another who bears witness of Me, and I know that the witness which He witnesses of Me is true. [33]You have sent to John, and he has borne witness to the truth. [34]Yet I do not receive testimony from man, but I say these things that you may be saved. [35]He was the burning and shining lamp, and you were willing for a time to rejoice in his light. [36]But I have a greater witness than John's; for the works which the Father has given Me to finish—the very works that I do—bear witness of Me, that the Father has sent Me. [37]And the Father Himself, who sent Me, has testified of Me. You have neither heard His voice at any time, nor seen His form. [38]But you do not have His word abiding in you, because whom He sent, Him you do not believe. [39]You search the Scriptures, for in them you think you have eternal life; and these are they which testify of Me. [40]But you are not willing to come to Me that you may have life.

[41]"I do not receive honor from men. [42]But I know you, that you do not have the love of God in you. [43]I have come in My Father's name, and you do not receive Me; if another comes in his own name, him you will receive. [44]How can you believe, who receive honor from one another, and do not seek the honor that *comes* from the only God? [45]Do not think that I shall accuse you to the Father; there is *one* who accuses you—Moses, in whom you trust. [46]For if you believed Moses, you would believe Me; for he wrote about Me. [47]But if you do not believe his writings, how will you believe My words?"

Feeding the Five Thousand

6 After these things Jesus went over the Sea of Galilee, which is *the Sea* of Tiberias. [2]Then a great multitude followed Him, because they saw His signs which He performed on those who were diseased. [3]And Jesus went up on the mountain, and there He sat with His disciples.

[4]Now the Passover, a feast of the Jews, was near. [5]Then Jesus lifted up *His* eyes, and seeing a great multitude coming toward Him, He said to Philip, "Where shall we buy bread, that these may eat?" [6]But this He said to test him, for He Himself knew what He would do.

[7]Philip answered Him, "Two hundred denarii worth of bread is not sufficient for them, that every one of them may have a little."

[8]One of His disciples, Andrew, Simon Peter's brother, said to Him, [9]"There is a lad here who has five barley loaves and two small fish, but what are they among so many?"

[10]Then Jesus said, "Make the people sit down." Now there was much grass in the place. So the men sat down, in number about five thousand. [11]And Jesus took the loaves, and when He had given thanks He distributed *them* to the disciples, and the disciples[a] to those sitting down; and likewise of the fish, as much as they wanted. [12]So when they were filled, He said to His disciples, "Gather up the fragments that remain, so that nothing is lost." [13]Therefore they gathered *them* up, and filled twelve baskets with the fragments of the five barley loaves which were left over by those who had eaten. [14]Then those men, when they had seen the sign that Jesus did, said, "This is truly the Prophet who is to come into the world."

Jesus Walks on the Sea

[15]Therefore when Jesus perceived that they were about to come and take Him by force to make Him king, He departed again to the mountain by Himself alone.

[16]Now when evening came, His disciples went down to the sea, [17]got into the boat, and went over the sea toward Capernaum. And it was already dark, and Jesus had not come to them. [18]Then the sea arose because a great wind was blowing. [19]So when they had rowed about three or four miles,[a] they saw Jesus walking on the sea and drawing near the boat; and they were afraid. [20]But He said to them, "It

6:11 [a]NU-Text omits *to the disciples, and the disciples.* **6:19** [a]Literally *twenty-five or thirty stadia*

is I; do not be afraid." 21Then they willingly received Him into the boat, and immediately the boat was at the land where they were going.

THE BREAD FROM HEAVEN

22On the following day, when the people who were standing on the other side of the sea saw that there was no other boat there, except that one which His disciples had entered,[a] and that Jesus had not entered the boat with His disciples, but His disciples had gone away alone— 23however, other boats came from Tiberias, near the place where they ate bread after the Lord had given thanks— 24when the people therefore saw that Jesus was not there, nor His disciples, they also got into boats and came to Capernaum, seeking Jesus. 25And when they found Him on the other side of the sea, they said to Him, "Rabbi, when did You come here?"

26Jesus answered them and said, "Most assuredly, I say to you, you seek Me, not because you saw the signs, but because you ate of the loaves and were filled. 27Do not labor for the food which perishes, but for the food which endures to everlasting life, which the Son of Man will give you, because God the Father has set His seal on Him."

28Then they said to Him, "What shall we do, that we may work the works of God?"

29Jesus answered and said to them, "This is the work of God, that you believe in Him whom He sent."

30Therefore they said to Him, "What sign will You perform then, that we may see it and believe You? What work will You do? 31Our fathers ate the manna in the desert; as it is written, *'He gave them bread from heaven to eat.'* "[a]

32Then Jesus said to them, "Most assuredly, I say to you, Moses did not give you the bread from heaven, but My Father gives you the true bread from heaven. 33For the bread of God is He who comes down from heaven and gives life to the world."

34Then they said to Him, "Lord, give us this bread always."

35And Jesus said to them, "I am the bread of life. He who comes to Me shall never hunger, and he who believes in Me shall never thirst. 36But I said to you that you have seen Me and yet do not believe. 37All that the Father gives Me will come to Me, and the one who comes to Me I will by no means cast out. 38For I have come down from heaven, not to do My own will, but the will of Him who sent Me. 39This is the will of the Father who sent Me, that of all He has given Me I should lose nothing, but should raise it up at the last day. 40And this is the will of Him who sent Me, that everyone who sees the Son and believes in Him may have everlasting life; and I will raise him up at the last day."

REJECTED BY HIS OWN

41The Jews then complained about Him, because He said, "I am the bread which came down from heaven." 42And they said, "Is not this Jesus, the son of Joseph, whose father and mother we know? How is it then that He says, 'I have come down from heaven'?"

43Jesus therefore answered and said to them, "Do not murmur among yourselves. 44No one can come to Me unless the Father who sent Me draws him; and I will raise him up at the last day. 45It is written in the prophets, *'And they shall all be taught by God.'*[a] Therefore everyone who has heard and learned[b] from the Father comes to Me. 46Not that anyone has

6:22 [a]NU-Text omits *that* and *which His disciples had entered.* **6:31** [a]Exodus 16:4; Nehemiah 9:15; Psalm 78:24 **6:45** [a]Isaiah 54:13 [b]M-Text reads *hears and has learned.*

SOUL NOTE

Secure *(6:39, 40)* Jesus said that He would not lose even one person whom the Father had given Him. So how does that account for Judas, the disciple who committed suicide by hanging himself? Jesus didn't "lose" Judas, because he never believed in Jesus as the Messiah. Jesus later called Judas "the son of perdition" (17:12), because he was never saved. Everyone who believes in Jesus Christ as Savior *has* everlasting life, is secure in God's promise, and will be raised up at the last day. No one who has really trusted in Jesus Christ for their salvation will be lost. **Topic: Eternal Life**

seen the Father, except He who is from God; He has seen the Father. [47]Most assuredly, I say to you, he who believes in Me[a] has everlasting life. [48]I am the bread of life. [49]Your fathers ate the manna in the wilderness, and are dead. [50]This is the bread which comes down from heaven, that one may eat of it and not die. [51]I am the living bread which came down from heaven. If anyone eats of this bread, he will live forever; and the bread that I shall give is My flesh, which I shall give for the life of the world."

[52]The Jews therefore quarreled among themselves, saying, "How can this Man give us *His* flesh to eat?"

[53]Then Jesus said to them, "Most assuredly, I say to you, unless you eat the flesh of the Son of Man and drink His blood, you have no life in you. [54]Whoever eats My flesh and drinks My blood has eternal life, and I will raise him up at the last day. [55]For My flesh is food indeed,[a] and My blood is drink indeed. [56]He who eats My flesh and drinks My blood abides in Me, and I in him. [57]As the living Father sent Me, and I live because of the Father, so he who feeds on Me will live because of Me. [58]This is the bread which came down from heaven—not as your fathers ate the manna, and are dead. He who eats this bread will live forever."

[59]These things He said in the synagogue as He taught in Capernaum.

MANY DISCIPLES TURN AWAY

[60]Therefore many of His disciples, when they heard *this,* said, "This is a hard saying; who can understand it?"

[61]When Jesus knew in Himself that His disciples complained about this, He said to them, "Does this offend you? [62]*What* then if you should see the Son of Man ascend where He was before? [63]It is the Spirit who gives life; the flesh profits nothing. The words that I speak to you are spirit, and *they* are life. [64]But there are some of you who do not believe." For Jesus knew from the beginning who they were who did not believe, and who would betray Him. [65]And He said, "Therefore I have said to you that no one can come to Me unless it has been granted to him by My Father."

[66]From that *time* many of His disciples went back and walked with Him no more. [67]Then Jesus said to the twelve, "Do you also want to go away?"

[68]But Simon Peter answered Him, "Lord, to whom shall we go? You have the words of eternal life. [69]Also we have come to believe and know that You are the Christ, the Son of the living God."[a]

[70]Jesus answered them, "Did I not choose you, the twelve, and one of you is a devil?" [71]He spoke of Judas Iscariot, *the son* of Simon, for it was he who would betray Him, being one of the twelve.

JESUS' BROTHERS DISBELIEVE

7 After these things Jesus walked in Galilee; for He did not want to walk in Judea, because the Jews[a] sought to kill Him. [2]Now the Jews' Feast of Tabernacles was at hand. [3]His brothers therefore said to Him, "Depart from here and go into Judea, that Your disciples also may see the works that You are doing. [4]For no one does anything in secret while he himself seeks to be known openly. If You do these things, show Yourself to the world." [5]For even His brothers did not believe in Him.

[6]Then Jesus said to them, "My time has not yet come, but your time is always ready. [7]The world cannot hate you, but it hates Me because I testify of it that its works are evil. [8]You go up to this feast. I am not yet[a] going up to this feast, for My time has not yet fully come." [9]When He had said these things to them, He remained in Galilee.

THE HEAVENLY SCHOLAR

[10]But when His brothers had gone up, then He also went up to the feast, not openly, but as it were in secret. [11]Then the Jews sought Him at the feast, and said, "Where is He?" [12]And there was much complaining among the people concerning Him. Some said, "He is good"; others said, "No, on the contrary, He deceives the people." [13]However, no one spoke openly of Him for fear of the Jews.

[14]Now about the middle of the feast Jesus went up into the temple and taught. [15]And the Jews marveled, saying, "How does this Man know letters, having never studied?"

[16]Jesus[a] answered them and said, "My doctrine is not Mine, but His who sent Me. [17]If any-

---

6:47 [a]NU-Text omits *in Me.* **6:55** [a]NU-Text reads *true food* and *true drink.* **6:69** [a]NU-Text reads *You are the Holy One of God.* **7:1** [a]That is, the ruling authorities **7:8** [a]NU-Text omits *yet.* **7:16** [a]NU-Text and M-Text read *So Jesus.*

one wills to do His will, he shall know concerning the doctrine, whether it is from God or *whether* I speak on My own *authority.* [18]He who speaks from himself seeks his own glory; but He who seeks the glory of the One who sent Him is true, and no unrighteousness is in Him. [19]Did not Moses give you the law, yet none of you keeps the law? Why do you seek to kill Me?"

[20]The people answered and said, "You have a demon. Who is seeking to kill You?"

[21]Jesus answered and said to them, "I did one work, and you all marvel. [22]Moses therefore gave you circumcision (not that it is from Moses, but from the fathers), and you circumcise a man on the Sabbath. [23]If a man receives circumcision on the Sabbath, so that the law of Moses should not be broken, are you angry with Me because I made a man completely well on the Sabbath? [24]Do not judge according to appearance, but judge with righteous judgment."

Could This Be the Christ?

[25]Now some of them from Jerusalem said, "Is this not He whom they seek to kill? [26]But look! He speaks boldly, and they say nothing to Him. Do the rulers know indeed that this is truly[a] the Christ? [27]However, we know where this Man is from; but when the Christ comes, no one knows where He is from."

[28]Then Jesus cried out, as He taught in the temple, saying, "You both know Me, and you know where I am from; and I have not come of Myself, but He who sent Me is true, whom you do not know. [29]But[a] I know Him, for I am from Him, and He sent Me."

[30]Therefore they sought to take Him; but no one laid a hand on Him, because His hour had not yet come. [31]And many of the people believed in Him, and said, "When the Christ comes, will He do more signs than these which this *Man* has done?"

Jesus and the Religious Leaders

[32]The Pharisees heard the crowd murmuring these things concerning Him, and the Pharisees and the chief priests sent officers to take Him. [33]Then Jesus said to them,[a] "I shall be with you a little while longer, and *then* I go to Him who sent Me. [34]You will seek Me and not find *Me,* and where I am you cannot come."

[35]Then the Jews said among themselves, "Where does He intend to go that we shall not find Him? Does He intend to go to the Dispersion among the Greeks and teach the Greeks? [36]What is this thing that He said, 'You will seek Me and not find Me, and where I am you cannot come'?"

The Promise of the Holy Spirit

[37]On the last day, that great *day* of the feast, Jesus stood and cried out, saying, "If anyone thirsts, let him come to Me and drink. [38]He who believes in Me, as the Scripture has said, out of his heart will flow rivers of living water." [39]But this He spoke concerning the Spirit, whom those believing[a] in Him would receive; for the Holy[b] Spirit was not yet *given,* because Jesus was not yet glorified.

Who Is He?

[40]Therefore many[a] from the crowd, when they heard this saying, said, "Truly this is the Prophet." [41]Others said, "This is the Christ."

But some said, "Will the Christ come out of Galilee? [42]Has not the Scripture said that the Christ comes from the seed of David and from the town of Bethlehem, where David was?" [43]So there was a division among the people because of Him. [44]Now some of them wanted to take Him, but no one laid hands on Him.

Rejected by the Authorities

[45]Then the officers came to the chief priests and Pharisees, who said to them, "Why have you not brought Him?"

[46]The officers answered, "No man ever spoke like this Man!"

[47]Then the Pharisees answered them, "Are you also deceived? [48]Have any of the rulers or the Pharisees believed in Him? [49]But this crowd that does not know the law is accursed."

[50]Nicodemus (he who came to Jesus by night,[a] being one of them) said to them, [51]"Does our law judge a man before it hears him and knows what he is doing?"

[52]They answered and said to him, "Are you also from Galilee? Search and look, for no prophet has arisen[a] out of Galilee."

7:26 [a]NU-Text omits *truly.* **7:29** [a]NU-Text and M-Text omit *But.* **7:33** [a]NU-Text and M-Text omit *to them.* **7:39** [a]NU-Text reads *who believed.* [b]NU-Text omits *Holy.* **7:40** [a]NU-Text reads *some.* **7:50** [a]NU-Text reads *before.* **7:52** [a]NU-Text reads *is to rise.*

AN ADULTERESS FACES THE LIGHT OF THE WORLD

53And everyone went to his *own* house.[a]
8 But Jesus went to the Mount of Olives.
2Now early[a] in the morning He came
again into the temple, and all the people came
to Him; and He sat down and taught them.
3Then the scribes and Pharisees brought to
Him a woman caught in adultery. And when
they had set her in the midst, 4they said to
Him, "Teacher, this woman was caught[a] in
adultery, in the very act. 5Now Moses, in the
law, commanded[a] us that such should be
stoned.[b] But what do You say?"[c] 6This they
said, testing Him, that they might have *something* of which to accuse Him. But Jesus
stooped down and wrote on the ground with
His finger, as though He did not hear.[a]
7So when they continued asking Him, He
raised Himself up[a] and said to them, "He who
is without sin among you, let him throw a
stone at her first." 8And again He stooped
down and wrote on the ground. 9Then those
who heard *it*, being convicted by *their* conscience,[a] went out one by one, beginning with
the oldest *even* to the last. And Jesus was left
alone, and the woman standing in the midst.
10When Jesus had raised Himself up and saw
no one but the woman, He said to her,[a]
"Woman, where are those accusers of yours?[b]
Has no one condemned you?"
11She said, "No one, Lord."

7:53 [a]The words *And everyone* through *sin no more* (8:11) are bracketed by NU-Text as not original. They are present in over 900 manuscripts. **8:2** [a]M-Text reads *very early.* **8:4** [a]M-Text reads *we found this woman.* **8:5** [a]M-Text reads *in our law Moses commanded.* [b]NU-Text and M-Text read *to stone such.* [c]M-Text adds *about her.* **8:6** [a]NU-Text and M-Text omit *as though He did not hear.* **8:7** [a]M-Text reads *He looked up.* **8:9** [a]NU-Text and M-Text omit *being convicted by their conscience.* **8:10** [a]NU-Text omits *and saw no one but the woman;* M-Text reads *He saw her and said.* [b]NU-Text and M-Text omit *of yours.*

PERSONALITY PROFILE

Adultery

THE WOMAN CAUGHT IN ADULTERY: SIN NO MORE

(JOHN 8:1–11)

An odd scene greeted Jesus one day in the temple. As He was teaching, a commotion began as the religious leaders dragged before Jesus a woman caught in the very act of adultery. The religious leaders told Jesus that Moses' law demanded her death. Actually, the law demanded death for *both* the man and the woman, not just the woman (Deut. 22:22). Why the woman alone was brought is unclear; it is clear, however, that the leaders were interested in trapping Jesus into saying something for which they could condemn Him. For Jesus not to condemn her would be to go against Moses' law; yet these leaders doubted that Jesus would give the order to have her stoned. So they asked, "What do You say?" and then all involved awaited His answer with keen anticipation.

The unfolding scene pictures both condemnation of sin and redemption of sinners. Jesus did not condemn the woman, but neither did He let her off the hook. As the guilty leaders left, one by one, realizing that they were not without sin, the woman surely was incredulous at what Jesus had just done on her behalf. Jesus had saved her life, but He wanted to do more than that. When the woman answered Jesus' question saying that no one had condemned her, He answered, "Neither do I condemn you; go and sin no more."

Jesus offers forgiveness to all sinners. The sin of adultery is extremely painful—betraying trust and leading to broken hearts and lives. Those caught in the web of adultery—real or merely fantasized—need to get out as quickly as possible. The excitement is not worth the ultimate price. Jesus can give people the strength to avoid the temptation, to flee the sin. He says to those willing to repent and turn away, "Go and sin no more."

To Learn More: Turn to the article about adultery on pages 1128, 1129. See also the key passage note at Proverbs 5:1–23 on page 806.

And Jesus said to her, "Neither do I condemn you; go and[a] sin no more."

[12]Then Jesus spoke to them again, saying, "I am the light of the world. He who follows Me shall not walk in darkness, but have the light of life."

Jesus Defends His Self-Witness

[13]The Pharisees therefore said to Him, "You bear witness of Yourself; Your witness is not true."

[14]Jesus answered and said to them, "Even if I bear witness of Myself, My witness is true, for I know where I came from and where I am going; but you do not know where I come from and where I am going. [15]You judge according to the flesh; I judge no one. [16]And yet if I do judge, My judgment is true; for I am not alone, but I *am* with the Father who sent Me. [17]It is also written in your law that the testimony of two men is true. [18]I am One who bears witness of Myself, and the Father who sent Me bears witness of Me."

> "And you shall know the truth, and the truth shall make you free."
> JOHN 8:32

[19]Then they said to Him, "Where is Your Father?"

Jesus answered, "You know neither Me nor My Father. If you had known Me, you would have known My Father also."

[20]These words Jesus spoke in the treasury, as He taught in the temple; and no one laid hands on Him, for His hour had not yet come.

Jesus Predicts His Departure

[21]Then Jesus said to them again, "I am going away, and you will seek Me, and will die in your sin. Where I go you cannot come."

[22]So the Jews said, "Will He kill Himself, because He says, 'Where I go you cannot come'?"

[23]And He said to them, "You are from beneath; I am from above. You are of this world; I am not of this world. [24]Therefore I said to you that you will die in your sins; for if you do not believe that I am *He,* you will die in your sins."

[25]Then they said to Him, "Who are You?"

And Jesus said to them, "Just what I have been saying to you from the beginning. [26]I have many things to say and to judge concerning you, but He who sent Me is true; and I speak to the world those things which I heard from Him."

[27]They did not understand that He spoke to them of the Father.

[28]Then Jesus said to them, "When you lift up the Son of Man, then you will know that I am *He,* and *that* I do nothing of Myself; but as My Father taught Me, I speak these things. [29]And He who sent Me is with Me. The Father has not left Me alone, for I always do those things that please Him." [30]As He spoke these words, many believed in Him.

The Truth Shall Make You Free

[31]Then Jesus said to those Jews who believed Him, "If you abide in My word, you are My disciples indeed. [32]And you shall know the truth, and the truth shall make you free."

[33]They answered Him, "We are Abraham's descendants, and have never been in bondage

8:11 [a]NU-Text and M-Text add *from now on.*

SOUL NOTE

Unmistaken Identity *(8:16–19)* The Pharisees were challenging Jesus' claim that He was the Messiah, believing that anyone who would make such claims would be either insane or a liar. Jesus provided them with a third alternative: He was telling the truth! Jesus emphasized that He was not acting alone, because He had a unique relationship with the Father. In fact, if people know Jesus, they know the Father. Elsewhere Jesus made His point even more clear, saying, "I and My Father are one" (10:30). To know Jesus is to know God. Jesus brings God into focus for our human eyes.
Topic: Knowing Jesus

to anyone. How *can* You say, 'You will be
made free'?"
34 Jesus answered them, "Most assuredly, I
say to you, whoever commits sin is a slave of
sin. 35 And a slave does not abide in the house
forever, *but* a son abides forever. 36 Therefore if
the Son makes you free, you shall be free indeed.

ABRAHAM'S SEED AND SATAN'S

37 "I know that you are Abraham's descendants, but you seek to kill Me, because My
word has no place in you. 38 I speak what I
have seen with My Father, and you do what
you have seen with[a] your father."
39 They answered and said to Him, "Abraham is our father."
Jesus said to them, "If you were Abraham's
children, you would do the works of Abraham. 40 But now you seek to kill Me, a Man
who has told you the truth which I heard from
God. Abraham did not do this. 41 You do the
deeds of your father."
Then they said to Him, "We were not born
of fornication; we have one Father—God."
42 Jesus said to them, "If God were your Father, you would love Me, for I proceeded forth
and came from God; nor have I come of Myself, but He sent Me. 43 Why do you not understand My speech? Because you are not able to
listen to My word. 44 You are of *your* father the
devil, and the desires of your father you want
to do. He was a murderer from the beginning,
and does not stand in the truth, because there
is no truth in him. When he speaks a lie, he
speaks from his own *resources,* for he is a liar
and the father of it. 45 But because I tell the
truth, you do not believe Me. 46 Which of you

8:38 [a]NU-Text reads *heard from.*

KEY PASSAGE

FREE INDEED!

(8:31–36)

Truth

Prisoners yearn for freedom, as do people who are enslaved by sin. They want to be free of the sins that make their lives miserable. Jesus tells of a way to have that freedom—"know the truth."

Jesus is "the truth" (John 14:6). Truth is not an abstract concept; it's a reality. When Pilate asked, "What is truth?" (John 18:38), the Truth was standing before him. Jesus came into the world to "bear witness to the truth" (John 18:37) and He was the Truth incarnate. The truth in Jesus frees us from the consequences of sin, from self-deception, and from deception by Satan. The truth in Jesus shows us the way to eternal life with God. The truth in Jesus will indeed set us free—free from sin's death penalty and from the corrosive effects of sin in our lives.

To Learn More: Turn to the article about truth on pages 1208, 1209. See also the personality profile of Ananias on page 1424.

SOUL NOTE

Final Answer *(8:32)* Jesus told His followers that if they truly believed in Him as the Savior, they would know truth. Jesus is the source of truth, the perfect standard of what is right. "You shall know the truth," Jesus said, "and the truth shall make you free." When people discover the truth found in God's Word, they are set free from sin. The world shouts its lies, and some are tempted to believe them. Believers, however, can look to God's Word and discern what is true and what is not. When we know Jesus and read His Word, we know the truth. **Topic: Truth**

convicts Me of sin? And if I tell the truth, why
do you not believe Me? [47]He who is of God
hears God's words; therefore you do not hear,
because you are not of God."

Before Abraham Was, I AM

[48]Then the Jews answered and said to Him,
"Do we not say rightly that You are a Samaritan and have a demon?"

[49]Jesus answered, "I do not have a demon;
but I honor My Father, and you dishonor Me.
[50]And I do not seek My *own* glory; there is One
who seeks and judges. [51]Most assuredly, I say
to you, if anyone keeps My word he shall
never see death."

[52]Then the Jews said to Him, "Now we
know that You have a demon! Abraham is
dead, and the prophets; and You say, 'If anyone keeps My word he shall never taste death.'
[53]Are You greater than our father Abraham,
who is dead? And the prophets are dead. Who
do You make Yourself out to be?"

[54]Jesus answered, "If I honor Myself, My
honor is nothing. It is My Father who honors
Me, of whom you say that He is your[a] God.
[55]Yet you have not known Him, but I know
Him. And if I say, 'I do not know Him,' I shall
be a liar like you; but I do know Him and keep
His word. [56]Your father Abraham rejoiced to
see My day, and he saw *it* and was glad."

[57]Then the Jews said to Him, "You are not
yet fifty years old, and have You seen Abraham?"

[58]Jesus said to them, "Most assuredly, I say
to you, before Abraham was, I AM."

[59]Then they took up stones to throw at Him;
but Jesus hid Himself and went out of the
temple,[a] going through the midst of them, and
so passed by.

A Man Born Blind Receives Sight

9 Now as *Jesus* passed by, He saw a man
who was blind from birth. [2]And His disciples asked Him, saying, "Rabbi, who sinned,
this man or his parents, that he was born
blind?"

[3]Jesus answered, "Neither this man nor his
parents sinned, but that the works of God
should be revealed in him. [4]I[a] must work the
works of Him who sent Me while it is day; *the*
night is coming when no one can work. [5]As
long as I am in the world, I am the light of the
world."

[6]When He had said these things, He spat on
the ground and made clay with the saliva; and
He anointed the eyes of the blind man with
the clay. [7]And He said to him, "Go, wash in
the pool of Siloam" (which is translated,
Sent). So he went and washed, and came back
seeing.

[8]Therefore the neighbors and those who
previously had seen that he was blind[a] said,
"Is not this he who sat and begged?"

[9]Some said, "This is he." Others *said,* "He is
like him."[a]

He said, "I am *he.*"

[10]Therefore they said to him, "How were
your eyes opened?"

[11]He answered and said, "A Man called
Jesus made clay and anointed my eyes and
said to me, 'Go to the pool of[a] Siloam and
wash.' So I went and washed, and I received
sight."

[12]Then they said to him, "Where is He?"

He said, "I do not know."

The Pharisees Excommunicate the Healed Man

[13]They brought him who formerly was blind
to the Pharisees. [14]Now it was a Sabbath when
Jesus made the clay and opened his eyes.
[15]Then the Pharisees also asked him again
how he had received his sight. He said to
them, "He put clay on my eyes, and I washed,
and I see."

[16]Therefore some of the Pharisees said,
"This Man is not from God, because He does
not keep the Sabbath."

Others said, "How can a man who is a sinner do such signs?" And there was a division
among them.

[17]They said to the blind man again, "What
do you say about Him because He opened
your eyes?"

He said, "He is a prophet."

[18]But the Jews did not believe concerning
him, that he had been blind and received his
sight, until they called the parents of him
who had received his sight. [19]And they asked
them, saying, "Is this your son, who you say
was born blind? How then does he now
see?"

8:54 [a]NU-Text and M-Text read *our.* **8:59** [a]NU-Text omits the rest of this verse. **9:4** [a]NU-Text reads *We.* **9:8** [a]NU-Text reads *a beggar.* **9:9** [a]NU-Text reads *"No, but he is like him."* **9:11** [a]NU-Text omits *the pool of.*

20 His parents answered them and said, "We know that this is our son, and that he was born blind; 21 but by what means he now sees we do not know, or who opened his eyes we do not know. He is of age; ask him. He will speak for himself." 22 His parents said these *things* because they feared the Jews, for the Jews had agreed already that if anyone confessed *that* He *was* Christ, he would be put out of the synagogue. 23 Therefore his parents said, "He is of age; ask him."

24 So they again called the man who was blind, and said to him, "Give God the glory! We know that this Man is a sinner."

25 He answered and said, "Whether He is a sinner *or not* I do not know. One thing I know: that though I was blind, now I see."

26 Then they said to him again, "What did He do to you? How did He open your eyes?"

27 He answered them, "I told you already, and you did not listen. Why do you want to hear *it* again? Do you also want to become His disciples?"

28 Then they reviled him and said, "You are His disciple, but we are Moses' disciples. 29 We know that God spoke to Moses; *as for* this *fellow,* we do not know where He is from."

30 The man answered and said to them, "Why, this is a marvelous thing, that you do not know where He is from; yet He has opened my eyes! 31 Now we know that God does not hear sinners; but if anyone is a worshiper of God and does His will, He hears him. 32 Since the world began it has been unheard of that anyone opened the eyes of one who was born blind. 33 If this Man were not from God, He could do nothing."

34 They answered and said to him, "You were completely born in sins, and are you teaching us?" And they cast him out.

PERSONALITY PROFILE

Genetic Issues

THE BLIND MAN: REVEALING GOD'S GLORY

(JOHN 9:1–7)

"Who sinned, this man or his parents, that he was born blind?" the disciples asked Jesus upon passing a man on the road who had been blind from birth. When people believe that problems are always the result of sin, then a person born blind must have sinned—or at least his parents must have sinned. That is not the case, however, as Jesus showed.

Genetic difficulties are hard to understand. Why does God allow some people to be born blind, deaf, or mentally disabled? While evil and imperfection were instigated by Satan, the presence of a genetic difficulty does not represent Satan specifically in the life of that person or that family. Instead, imperfection has touched all of creation. Actually, no one is perfect—we all are susceptible to illness, disability, and eventually death. Yet the all-powerful Creator is able to overrule imperfection and glorify Himself through it.

When questioned about the blind man, Jesus answered that it wasn't about either him or his parents sinning, "but that the works of God should be revealed in him." Jesus responded to this blind man by healing him and glorifying Himself in the process.

Jesus is the great Healer. Whether He heals miraculously through prayer, or by the hands of doctors, or by the effects of medication, He still heals. Sometimes He chooses not to heal. Either way, Jesus can always glorify Himself in the life of that person. Part of that glory is revealed in the way other people react to those with disabilities, showing Jesus' love through their actions.

Someday all evil and impairment will be reversed after Christ returns and all believers are given perfect, glorified bodies. The ultimate glory will come when the blind see, the lame walk, the deaf hear, and all other disabilities are cast aside. All of us, however imperfect we may be now, can look forward to that great day.

To Learn More: Turn to the article about genetic issues on pages 84, 85. See also the key passage note at Isaiah 35:1–6 on page 914.

True Vision and True Blindness

35 Jesus heard that they had cast him out; and when He had found him, He said to him, “Do you believe in the Son of God?”[a]

36 He answered and said, “Who is He, Lord, that I may believe in Him?”

37 And Jesus said to him, “You have both seen Him and it is He who is talking with you.”

38 Then he said, “Lord, I believe!” And he worshiped Him.

39 And Jesus said, “For judgment I have come into this world, that those who do not see may see, and that those who see may be made blind.”

40 Then *some* of the Pharisees who were with Him heard these words, and said to Him, “Are we blind also?”

41 Jesus said to them, “If you were blind, you would have no sin; but now you say, ‘We see.’ Therefore your sin remains.

Jesus the True Shepherd

10 “Most assuredly, I say to you, he who does not enter the sheepfold by the door, but climbs up some other way, the same is a thief and a robber. 2 But he who enters by the door is the shepherd of the sheep. 3 To him the doorkeeper opens, and the sheep hear his voice; and he calls his own sheep by name and leads them out. 4 And when he brings out his own sheep, he goes before them; and the sheep follow him, for they know his voice. 5 Yet they will by no means follow a stranger, but will flee from him, for they do not know the voice of strangers.” 6 Jesus used this illustration, but they did not understand the things which He spoke to them.

Jesus the Good Shepherd

7 Then Jesus said to them again, “Most assuredly, I say to you, I am the door of the sheep. 8 All who *ever* came before Me[a] are thieves and robbers, but the sheep did not hear them. 9 I am the door. If anyone enters by Me, he will be saved, and will go in and out and find pasture. 10 The thief does not come except to steal, and to kill, and to destroy. I have come that they may have life, and that they may have *it* more abundantly.

11 “I am the good shepherd. The good shepherd gives His life for the sheep. 12 But a hireling, *he who is* not the shepherd, one who does not own the sheep, sees the wolf coming and leaves the sheep and flees; and the wolf catches the sheep and scatters them. 13 The hireling flees because he is a hireling and does not care about the sheep. 14 I am the good shepherd; and I know My *sheep,* and am known by My own. 15 As the Father knows Me, even so I know the Father; and I lay down My life for the sheep. 16 And other sheep I have which are not of this fold; them also I must bring, and they will hear My voice; and there will be one flock *and* one shepherd.

17 “Therefore My Father loves Me, because I lay down My life that I may take it again. 18 No one takes it from Me, but I lay it down of Myself. I have power to lay it down, and I have power to take it again. This command I have received from My Father.”

19 Therefore there was a division again among the Jews because of these sayings. 20 And many of them said, “He has a demon and is mad. Why do you listen to Him?”

21 Others said, “These are not the words of one who has a demon. Can a demon open the eyes of the blind?”

The Shepherd Knows His Sheep

22 Now it was the Feast of Dedication in Jerusalem, and it was winter. 23 And Jesus walked in the temple, in Solomon’s porch. 24 Then the Jews surrounded Him and said to Him, “How long do You keep us in doubt? If You are the Christ, tell us plainly.”

25 Jesus answered them, “I told you, and you do not believe. The works that I do in My Father’s name, they bear witness of Me. 26 But you do not believe, because you are not of My sheep, as I said to you.[a] 27 My sheep hear My voice, and I know them, and they follow Me. 28 And I give them eternal life, and they shall never perish; neither shall anyone snatch them out of My hand. 29 My Father, who has given *them* to Me, is greater than all; and no one is able to snatch *them* out of My Father’s hand. 30 I and *My* Father are one.”

Renewed Efforts to Stone Jesus

31 Then the Jews took up stones again to stone Him. 32 Jesus answered them, “Many good works I have shown you from My Father. For which of those works do you stone Me?”

9:35 [a]NU-Text reads *Son of Man.* **10:8** [a]M-Text omits *before Me.* **10:26** [a]NU-Text omits *as I said to you.*

33The Jews answered Him, saying, "For a good work we do not stone You, but for blasphemy, and because You, being a Man, make Yourself God."

34Jesus answered them, "Is it not written in your law, *'I said, "You are gods"'*?[a] 35If He called them gods, to whom the word of God came (and the Scripture cannot be broken), 36do you say of Him whom the Father sanctified and sent into the world, 'You are blaspheming,' because I said, 'I am the Son of God'? 37If I do not do the works of My Father, do not believe Me; 38but if I do, though you do not believe Me, believe the works, that you may know and believe[a] that the Father *is* in Me, and I in Him." 39Therefore they sought again to seize Him, but He escaped out of their hand.

The Believers Beyond Jordan

40And He went away again beyond the Jordan to the place where John was baptizing at first, and there He stayed. 41Then many came to Him and said, "John performed no sign, but all the things that John spoke about this Man were true." 42And many believed in Him there.

The Death of Lazarus

11 Now a certain *man* was sick, Lazarus of Bethany, the town of Mary and her sister Martha. 2It was *that* Mary who anointed the Lord with fragrant oil and wiped His feet with her hair, whose brother Lazarus was sick. 3Therefore the sisters sent to Him, saying, "Lord, behold, he whom You love is sick."

4When Jesus heard *that,* He said, "This sickness is not unto death, but for the glory of God, that the Son of God may be glorified through it."

5Now Jesus loved Martha and her sister and Lazarus. 6So, when He heard that he was sick, He stayed two more days in the place where He was. 7Then after this He said to *the* disciples, "Let us go to Judea again."

8*The* disciples said to Him, "Rabbi, lately the Jews sought to stone You, and are You going there again?"

9Jesus answered, "Are there not twelve hours in the day? If anyone walks in the day, he does not stumble, because he sees the light of this world. 10But if one walks in the night, he stumbles, because the light is not in him." 11These things He said, and after that He said to them, "Our friend Lazarus sleeps, but I go that I may wake him up."

12Then His disciples said, "Lord, if he sleeps he will get well." 13However, Jesus spoke of his death, but they thought that He was speaking about taking rest in sleep.

14Then Jesus said to them plainly, "Lazarus is dead. 15And I am glad for your sakes that I was not there, that you may believe. Nevertheless let us go to him."

16Then Thomas, who is called the Twin, said to his fellow disciples, "Let us also go, that we may die with Him."

I Am the Resurrection and the Life

17So when Jesus came, He found that he had already been in the tomb four days. 18Now Bethany was near Jerusalem, about two miles[a] away. 19And many of the Jews had joined the women around Martha and Mary, to comfort them concerning their brother.

20Now Martha, as soon as she heard that Jesus was coming, went and met Him, but Mary was sitting in the house. 21Now Martha said to Jesus, "Lord, if You had been here, my brother would not have died. 22But even now I

10:34 [a]Psalm 82:6 **10:38** [a]NU-Text reads *understand.* **11:18** [a]Literally *fifteen stadia*

SOUL NOTE

The Greatest Need *(11:5)* Human beings need food, water, air, and shelter to stay alive. But to be truly alive and thriving, we also need love. Lack of love causes physical, emotional, and mental problems. Relationships often wither and die without love and caring. When Jesus lived on earth, He had a special relationship with Mary, Martha, and Lazarus. They showed Him friendship and hospitality and were open to His message. Jesus nurtured that relationship with His interest in their lives and His love for them. God works through our human relationships to give us comfort and encouragement. Family and friends are blessings from God. **Topic: Relationships**

know that whatever You ask of God, God will give You."

[23]Jesus said to her, "Your brother will rise again."

[24]Martha said to Him, "I know that he will rise again in the resurrection at the last day."

[25]Jesus said to her, "I am the resurrection and the life. He who believes in Me, though he may die, he shall live. [26]And whoever lives and believes in Me shall never die. Do you believe this?"

"I am the resurrection and the life. He who believes in Me, though he may die, he shall live. And whoever lives and believes in Me shall never die. Do you believe this?"
JOHN 11:25, 26

[27]She said to Him, "Yes, Lord, I believe that You are the Christ, the Son of God, who is to come into the world."

Jesus and Death, the Last Enemy

[28]And when she had said these things, she went her way and secretly called Mary her sister, saying, "The Teacher has come and is calling for you." [29]As soon as she heard *that,* she arose quickly and came to Him. [30]Now Jesus had not yet come into the town, but was[a] in the place where Martha met Him. [31]Then the Jews who were with her in the house, and comforting her, when they saw that Mary rose up quickly and went out, followed her, saying, "She is going to the tomb to weep there."[a]

[32]Then, when Mary came where Jesus was, and saw Him, she fell down at His feet, saying to Him, "Lord, if You had been here, my brother would not have died."

[33]Therefore, when Jesus saw her weeping, and the Jews who came with her weeping, He groaned in the spirit and was troubled. [34]And He said, "Where have you laid him?"

They said to Him, "Lord, come and see."

[35]Jesus wept. [36]Then the Jews said, "See how He loved him!"

[37]And some of them said, "Could not this Man, who opened the eyes of the blind, also have kept this man from dying?"

Lazarus Raised from the Dead

[38]Then Jesus, again groaning in Himself, came to the tomb. It was a cave, and a stone lay against it. [39]Jesus said, "Take away the stone."

Martha, the sister of him who was dead, said to Him, "Lord, by this time there is a stench, for he has been *dead* four days."

11:30 [a]NU-Text adds *still.* **11:31** [a]NU-Text reads *supposing that she was going to the tomb to weep there.*

KEY PASSAGE

Grief/Loss

HE UNDERSTANDS

(11:35–44)

Because of sin, death comes to all (Rom. 5:12–14). Many try to ignore death, not wanting to think or talk about it. But feared or embraced, expected or not, death still occurs. The death of a loved one evokes many emotions: fear, sorrow, grief, anger, and a great sense of loss. Jesus experienced those emotions at the death of His good friend Lazarus. The fact that Jesus raised Lazarus back to life does not erase the reality of His compassion and sorrow. Jesus understands grief. He knows the pain of loss and uncontrollable sorrow. He knows the incredible power of death. In fact, He took on that power and defeated it through His death and resurrection.

It is natural to feel sad and mourn the death of a loved one. We deeply miss the close relationship we had with that person. But in our times of sorrow, we can let Jesus hold us in His compassionate arms, knowing that He understands.

To Learn More: Turn to the article about grief/loss on pages 940, 941. See also the personality profile of Job's wife on page 640.

40 Jesus said to her, "Did I not say to you that
if you would believe you would see the glory
of God?" 41 Then they took away the stone
from the place where the dead man was lying.[a]
And Jesus lifted up *His* eyes and said, "Father,
I thank You that You have heard Me. 42 And I
know that You always hear Me, but because of
the people who are standing by I said *this,* that
they may believe that You sent Me." 43 Now
when He had said these things, He cried with
a loud voice, "Lazarus, come forth!" 44 And he
who had died came out bound hand and foot
with graveclothes, and his face was wrapped
with a cloth. Jesus said to them, "Loose him,
and let him go."

The Plot to Kill Jesus

45 Then many of the Jews who had come to
Mary, and had seen the things Jesus did, believed in Him. 46 But some of them went away
to the Pharisees and told them the things
Jesus did. 47 Then the chief priests and the
Pharisees gathered a council and said, "What
shall we do? For this Man works many signs.
48 If we let Him alone like this, everyone will
believe in Him, and the Romans will come and
take away both our place and nation."

49 And one of them, Caiaphas, being high
priest that year, said to them, "You know
nothing at all, 50 nor do you consider that it is
expedient for us[a] that one man should die for
the people, and not that the whole nation
should perish." 51 Now this he did not say on
his own *authority;* but being high priest that
year he prophesied that Jesus would die for
the nation, 52 and not for that nation only, but
also that He would gather together in one the
children of God who were scattered abroad.

53 Then, from that day on, they plotted to
put Him to death. 54 Therefore Jesus no longer
walked openly among the Jews, but went
from there into the country near the wilderness, to a city called Ephraim, and there remained with His disciples.

55 And the Passover of the Jews was near,
and many went from the country up to Jerusalem before the Passover, to purify themselves.
56 Then they sought Jesus, and spoke among
themselves as they stood in the temple, "What
do you think—that He will not come to the
feast?" 57 Now both the chief priests and the
Pharisees had given a command, that if anyone knew where He was, he should report *it,*
that they might seize Him.

The Anointing at Bethany

12 Then, six days before the Passover,
Jesus came to Bethany, where Lazarus
was who had been dead,[a] whom He had
raised from the dead. 2 There they made Him a
supper; and Martha served, but Lazarus was
one of those who sat at the table with Him.
3 Then Mary took a pound of very costly oil of
spikenard, anointed the feet of Jesus, and
wiped His feet with her hair. And the house
was filled with the fragrance of the oil.

4 But one of His disciples, Judas Iscariot,
Simon's *son,* who would betray Him, said,
5 "Why was this fragrant oil not sold for three
hundred denarii[a] and given to the poor?"
6 This he said, not that he cared for the poor,
but because he was a thief, and had the money box; and he used to take what was put in it.

7 But Jesus said, "Let her alone; she has
kept[a] this for the day of My burial. 8 For the
poor you have with you always, but Me you
do not have always."

The Plot to Kill Lazarus

9 Now a great many of the Jews knew that
He was there; and they came, not for Jesus'
sake only, but that they might also see Lazarus, whom He had raised from the dead.
10 But the chief priests plotted to put Lazarus
to death also, 11 because on account of him
many of the Jews went away and believed in
Jesus.

The Triumphal Entry

12 The next day a great multitude that had
come to the feast, when they heard that Jesus
was coming to Jerusalem, 13 took branches of
palm trees and went out to meet Him, and
cried out:

"Hosanna!
*'Blessed is He who comes in the name of
the* LORD!*'*[a]
The King of Israel!"

14 Then Jesus, when He had found a young
donkey, sat on it; as it is written:

11:41 [a]NU-Text omits *from the place where the dead man was lying.* **11:50** [a]NU-Text reads *you.*
12:1 [a]NU-Text omits *who had been dead.*
12:5 [a]About one year's wages for a worker
12:7 [a]NU-Text reads *that she may keep.*
12:13 [a]Psalm 118:26

15 *"Fear not, daughter of Zion;*
Behold, your King is coming,
Sitting on a donkey's colt."[a]

[16]His disciples did not understand these things at first; but when Jesus was glorified, then they remembered that these things were written about Him and *that* they had done these things to Him.

[17]Therefore the people, who were with Him when He called Lazarus out of his tomb and raised him from the dead, bore witness. [18]For this reason the people also met Him, because they heard that He had done this sign. [19]The Pharisees therefore said among themselves, "You see that you are accomplishing nothing. Look, the world has gone after Him!"

The Fruitful Grain of Wheat

[20]Now there were certain Greeks among those who came up to worship at the feast. [21]Then they came to Philip, who was from Bethsaida of Galilee, and asked him, saying, "Sir, we wish to see Jesus."

[22]Philip came and told Andrew, and in turn Andrew and Philip told Jesus.

[23]But Jesus answered them, saying, "The hour has come that the Son of Man should be glorified. [24]Most assuredly, I say to you, unless a grain of wheat falls into the ground and dies, it remains alone; but if it dies, it produces much grain. [25]He who loves his life will lose it, and he who hates his life in this world will keep it for eternal life. [26]If anyone serves Me, let him follow Me; and where I am, there My servant will be also. If anyone serves Me, him *My* Father will honor.

Jesus Predicts His Death on the Cross

[27]"Now My soul is troubled, and what shall I say? 'Father, save Me from this hour'? But for this purpose I came to this hour. [28]Father, glorify Your name."

Then a voice came from heaven, *saying,* "I have both glorified *it* and will glorify *it* again."

"Now My soul is troubled, and what shall I say? 'Father, save Me from this hour'? But for this purpose I came to this hour."
JOHN 12:27

[29]Therefore the people who stood by and heard *it* said that it had thundered. Others said, "An angel has spoken to Him."

[30]Jesus answered and said, "This voice did not come because of Me, but for your sake. [31]Now is the judgment of this world; now the ruler of this world will be cast out. [32]And I, if I am lifted up from the earth, will draw all *peoples* to Myself." [33]This He said, signifying by what death He would die.

[34]The people answered Him, "We have heard from the law that the Christ remains forever; and how *can* You say, 'The Son of Man must be lifted up'? Who is this Son of Man?"

[35]Then Jesus said to them, "A little while longer the light is with you. Walk while you have the light, lest darkness overtake you; he who walks in darkness does not know where he is going. [36]While you have the light, believe in the light, that you may become sons of light." These things Jesus spoke, and departed, and was hidden from them.

Who Has Believed Our Report?

[37]But although He had done so many signs before them, they did not believe in Him, [38]that the word of Isaiah the prophet might be fulfilled, which he spoke:

"Lord, who has believed our report?
And to whom has the arm of the LORD
been revealed?"[a]

[39]Therefore they could not believe, because Isaiah said again:

40 *"He has blinded their eyes and hardened*
their hearts,
Lest they should see with their eyes,
Lest they should understand with their
hearts and turn,
So that I should heal them." [a]

[41]These things Isaiah said when[a] he saw His glory and spoke of Him.

Walk in the Light

[42]Nevertheless even among the rulers many believed in Him, but because of the Pharisees they did not confess *Him,* lest they should be put out of the synagogue; [43]for they loved the praise of men more than the praise of God.

12:15 [a]Zechariah 9:9 **12:38** [a]Isaiah 53:1
12:40 [a]Isaiah 6:10 **12:41** [a]NU-Text reads *because.*

[44]Then Jesus cried out and said, "He who believes in Me, believes not in Me but in Him who sent Me. [45]And he who sees Me sees Him who sent Me. [46]I have come *as* a light into the world, that whoever believes in Me should not abide in darkness. [47]And if anyone hears My words and does not believe,[a] I do not judge him; for I did not come to judge the world but to save the world. [48]He who rejects Me, and does not receive My words, has that which judges him—the word that I have spoken will judge him in the last day. [49]For I have not spoken on My own *authority;* but the Father who sent Me gave Me a command, what I should say and what I should speak. [50]And I know that His command is everlasting life. Therefore, whatever I speak, just as the Father has told Me, so I speak."

Jesus Washes the Disciples' Feet

13 Now before the Feast of the Passover, when Jesus knew that His hour had come that He should depart from this world to the Father, having loved His own who were in the world, He loved them to the end.

[2]And supper being ended,[a] the devil having already put it into the heart of Judas Iscariot, Simon's *son,* to betray Him, [3]Jesus, knowing that the Father had given all things into His hands, and that He had come from God and was going to God, [4]rose from supper and laid aside His garments, took a towel and girded Himself. [5]After that, He poured water into a basin and began to wash the disciples' feet, and to wipe *them* with the towel with which He was girded. [6]Then He came to Simon Peter. And *Peter* said to Him, "Lord, are You washing my feet?"

[7]Jesus answered and said to him, "What I am doing you do not understand now, but you will know after this."

[8]Peter said to Him, "You shall never wash my feet!"

Jesus answered him, "If I do not wash you, you have no part with Me."

[9]Simon Peter said to Him, "Lord, not my feet only, but also *my* hands and *my* head!"

[10]Jesus said to him, "He who is bathed needs only to wash *his* feet, but is completely clean; and you are clean, but not all of you." [11]For He knew who would betray Him; therefore He said, "You are not all clean."

[12]So when He had washed their feet, taken His garments, and sat down again, He said to them, "Do you know what I have done to you? [13]You call Me Teacher and Lord, and you say well, for *so* I am. [14]If I then, *your* Lord and Teacher, have washed your feet, you also ought to wash one another's feet. [15]For I have given you an example, that you should do as I have done to you. [16]Most assuredly, I say to you, a servant is not greater than his master; nor is he who is sent greater than he who sent him. [17]If you know these things, blessed are you if you do them.

Jesus Identifies His Betrayer

[18]"I do not speak concerning all of you. I know whom I have chosen; but that the Scripture may be fulfilled, *'He who eats bread with Me[a] has lifted up his heel against Me.'*[b] [19]Now I tell you before it comes, that when it does come to pass, you may believe that I am *He.* [20]Most assuredly, I say to you, he who receives whomever I send receives Me; and he who receives Me receives Him who sent Me."

[21]When Jesus had said these things, He was troubled in spirit, and testified and said,

---

12:47 [a]NU-Text reads *keep them.* **13:2** [a]NU-Text reads *And during supper.* **13:18** [a]NU-Text reads *My bread.* [b]Psalm 41:9

SOUL NOTE

A New Commandment *(13:34, 35)* God's Law tells people to love one another (Lev. 19:18). Jesus said that He was giving a "new commandment"—to love with a self-sacrificing love. Such love would set His followers apart from the rest of the world, helping them to serve God and build His kingdom. Such love would draw others to the Savior, and it would be the natural response of believers to the One who died for them. As John wrote later in his life, "We love Him because He first loved us" (1 John 4:19). **Topic: Love**

"Most assuredly, I say to you, one of you will
betray Me." 22Then the disciples looked at one
another, perplexed about whom He spoke.
23Now there was leaning on Jesus' bosom
one of His disciples, whom Jesus loved. 24Si-
mon Peter therefore motioned to him to ask
who it was of whom He spoke.
25Then, leaning back[a] on Jesus' breast, he
said to Him, "Lord, who is it?"
26Jesus answered, "It is he to whom I shall
give a piece of bread when I have dipped *it*."
And having dipped the bread, He gave *it* to Judas Iscariot, *the son* of Simon. 27Now after the
piece of bread, Satan entered him. Then Jesus
said to him, "What you do, do quickly." 28But
no one at the table knew for what reason He
said this to him. 29For some thought, because
Judas had the money box, that Jesus had said
to him, "Buy *those things* we need for the
feast," or that he should give something to the
poor.
30Having received the piece of bread, he
then went out immediately. And it was night.

The New Commandment

31So, when he had gone out, Jesus said,
"Now the Son of Man is
glorified, and God is
glorified in Him. 32If
God is glorified in Him,
God will also glorify
Him in Himself, and
glorify Him immediate-
ly. 33Little children, I
shall be with you a little while longer. You
will seek Me; and as I said to the Jews,
'Where I am going, you cannot come,' so
now I say to you. 34A new commandment I
give to you, that you love one another; as I
have loved you, that you also love one another. 35By this all will know that you are
My disciples, if you have love for one another."

"I am the way, the truth, and the life. No one comes to the Father except through Me."
JOHN 14:6

Jesus Predicts Peter's Denial

36Simon Peter said to Him, "Lord, where are
You going?"
Jesus answered him, "Where I am going
you cannot follow Me now, but you shall follow Me afterward."
37Peter said to Him, "Lord, why can I not
follow You now? I will lay down my life for
Your sake."
38Jesus answered him, "Will you lay down
your life for My sake? Most assuredly, I say to
you, the rooster shall not crow till you have
denied Me three times.

The Way, the Truth, and the Life

14 "Let not your heart be troubled; you
believe in God, believe also in Me. 2In
My Father's house are many mansions;[a] if *it
were* not *so*, I would have told you. I go to prepare a place for you.[b] 3And if I go and prepare
a place for you, I will come again and receive
you to Myself; that where I am, *there* you may
be also. 4And where I go you know, and the
way you know."
5Thomas said to Him, "Lord, we do not
know where You are going, and how can we
know the way?"
6Jesus said to him, "I
am the way, the truth,
and the life. No one
comes to the Father ex-
cept through Me.

The Father Revealed

7"If you had known Me, you would have
known My Father also; and from now on you
know Him and have seen Him."

13:25 [a]NU-Text and M-Text add *thus.*
14:2 [a]Literally *dwellings* [b]NU-Text adds a word which would cause the text to read either *if it were not so, would I have told you that I go to prepare a place for you?* or *if it were not so I would have told you; for I go to prepare a place for you.*

SOUL NOTE

A Resting Place *(14:1–4)* The disciples were bewildered and discouraged. Jesus had said He was going away, that He would die, that one of the disciples was a traitor, and that Peter would deny Him. If so, it seemed that their great hopes had been in vain. "Let not your heart be troubled," Jesus told them. Believers can rest their troubled hearts, knowing that Jesus is in control regardless of the circumstances. He relieves our anxiety about the future when we trust Him. **Topic: Anxiety**

8Philip said to Him, "Lord, show us the Father, and it is sufficient for us."
9Jesus said to him, "Have I been with you so
long, and yet you have not known Me, Philip?
He who has seen Me has seen the Father; so
how can you say, 'Show us the Father'? 10Do
you not believe that I am in the Father, and the
Father in Me? The words that I speak to you I
do not speak on My own *authority;* but the Father who dwells in Me does the works. 11Be-
lieve Me that I *am* in the Father and the Father
in Me, or else believe Me for the sake of the
works themselves.

The Answered Prayer

12"Most assuredly, I say to you, he who believes in Me, the works that I do he will do
also; and greater *works* than these he will do,
because I go to My Father. 13And whatever you
ask in My name, that I will do, that the Father
may be glorified in the Son. 14If you ask[a] anything in My name, I will do *it.*

Jesus Promises Another Helper

15"If you love Me, keep[a] My commandments. 16And I will pray the Father, and He
will give you another Helper, that He may
abide with you forever—17the Spirit of truth,
whom the world cannot receive, because it
neither sees Him nor knows Him; but you
know Him, for He dwells with you and will be

14:14 [a]NU-Text adds *Me.* **14:15** [a]NU-Text reads *you will keep.*

KEY PASSAGE

Knowing Jesus

ONE WAY

(14:6)

Many routes and transportation options lead to a large city. Some people think it's the same way with God. "All roads," they say, all religions and belief systems, "lead to God."

"Wrong!" says Jesus.

Contrary to what many people think, Jesus taught only *one* way to gain forgiveness and eternal life, not many ways.

- "I am the way, the truth, and the life. No one comes to the Father except through Me" (John 14:6).
- "There is no other name under heaven given among men by which we must be saved" (Acts 4:12).
- "For there is one God and one Mediator between God and men, the Man Christ Jesus, who gave Himself a ransom for all" (1 Tim. 2:5, 6).

God provided a way for us to be saved. We can praise Jesus for being that way!

To Learn More: Turn to the article about knowing Jesus on pages 1368, 1369. See also the personality profile of Nicodemus on page 1371.

SOUL NOTE

The Only Way *(14:6)* Jesus claimed to be "the way, the truth, and the life." Jesus is not one of the ways to God—He is the *only* way to God. Jesus is not one of many truths—He *is* truth. Jesus doesn't just show a way to live—He is the Giver of life, the One who gives meaning to life. If Jesus is our "way," then He is the only One who can save us and guide our lives. If Jesus is our "truth," then we study His word and live according to its truth. If Jesus is our "life," we trust that He is in control of our lives today and into eternity. **Topic: Truth**

in you. [18]I will not leave you orphans; I will
come to you.

INDWELLING OF THE FATHER AND THE SON

[19]"A little while longer and the world will
see Me no more, but you will see Me. Because
I live, you will live also. [20]At that day you will
know that I *am* in My Father, and you in Me,
and I in you. [21]He who has My commandments and keeps them, it is he who loves Me.
And he who loves Me will be loved by My Father, and I will love him and manifest Myself
to him."
[22]Judas (not Iscariot) said to Him, "Lord,
how is it that You will manifest Yourself to us,
and not to the world?"
[23]Jesus answered and said to him, "If anyone loves Me, he will keep My word; and My
Father will love him, and We will come to him
and make Our home with him. [24]He who does
not love Me does not keep My words; and the
word which you hear is not Mine but the
Father's who sent Me.

THE GIFT OF HIS PEACE

[25]"These things I have spoken to you while
being present with you. [26]But the Helper, the
Holy Spirit, whom the Father will send in My

SOUL NOTE

Another Helper *(14:15–18)* Jesus' followers show their love for Christ by obeying His commandments. Jesus has set the pattern of love and obedience, and His disciples are expected to follow His example. Jesus reassured His followers, however, that they would not have to obey in their own power. He would send a helper—the Holy Spirit. The Holy Spirit lives in Jesus' followers, helping them to remember His commands and to obey them. We do not have to go it alone—the Holy Spirit in our hearts helps us to know what is right and then to do it.
Topic: Presence of the Holy Spirit

SOUL NOTE

If You Love Me *(14:21–23)* Jesus repeated the statement (14:15) that His followers show their love for Him by their obedience to His commands. Love is more than words—true love involves action. Whoever says he or she loves someone and then ignores that person or acts rudely doesn't know the meaning of love. Words of love are important, but actions and behavior provide the proof. Do we obey Christ's commandments or do we live as if He made no difference in our lives? Do we draw close to Him daily, or do we ignore Him? Our love is revealed by our desire to follow Him. **Topic: Love Languages**

SOUL NOTE

Spiritual Growth *(14:26)* Jesus promised the disciples that the Holy Spirit would teach them, helping them to remember everything that Jesus had taught. Paul wrote, "We have received . . . the Spirit who is from God, that we might know the things that have been freely given to us by God" (1 Cor. 2:12). The Holy Spirit is our source of spiritual understanding. We trust the writings of the New Testament, knowing that the Holy Spirit guided the writers. Then we allow the Holy Spirit to help us understand and apply God's Word to our lives.
Topic: Presence of the Holy Spirit

name, He will teach you all things, and bring to your remembrance all things that I said to you. 27Peace I leave with you, My peace I give to you; not as the world gives do I give to you. Let not your heart be troubled, neither let it be afraid. 28You have heard Me say to you, 'I am going away and coming *back* to you.' If you loved Me, you would rejoice because I said,[a] 'I am going to the Father,' for My Father is greater than I.

29"And now I have told you before it comes, that when it does come to pass, you may believe. 30I will no longer talk much with you, for the ruler of this world is coming, and he has nothing in Me. 31But that the world may know that I love the Father, and as the Father gave Me commandment, so I do. Arise, let us go from here.

The True Vine

15 "I am the true vine, and My Father is the vinedresser. 2Every branch in Me that does not bear fruit He takes away;[a] and every *branch* that bears fruit He prunes, that it may bear more fruit. 3You are already clean because of the word which I have spoken to you. 4Abide in Me, and I in you. As the branch cannot bear fruit of itself, unless it abides in the vine, neither can you, unless you abide in Me.

5"I am the vine, you *are* the branches. He who abides in Me, and I in him, bears much fruit; for without Me you can do nothing. 6If anyone does not abide in Me, he is cast out as a branch and is withered; and they gather them and throw *them* into the fire, and they are burned. 7If you abide in Me, and My words abide in you, you will[a] ask what you desire, and it shall be done for you. 8By this My Father is glorified, that you bear much fruit; so you will be My disciples.

Love and Joy Perfected

9"As the Father loved Me, I also have loved you; abide in My love. 10If you keep My commandments, you will abide in My love, just as I have kept My Father's commandments and abide in His love.

11"These things I have spoken to you, that My joy may remain in you, and *that* your joy may be full. 12This is My commandment, that you love one another as I have loved you. 13Greater love has no one than this, than to lay down one's life for his friends. 14You are My friends if you do whatever I command you. 15No longer do I call you servants, for a servant does not know what his master is doing; but I have called you friends, for all things that I heard from My Father I have made known to you. 16You did not choose Me, but I chose you and appointed you that you should go and bear fruit, and *that* your fruit should remain, that whatever you ask the Father in My name He may give you. 17These things I command you, that you love one another.

The World's Hatred

18"If the world hates you, you know that it hated Me before *it hated* you. 19If you were of the world, the world would love its own. Yet because you are not of the world, but I chose you out of the world, therefore the world hates you. 20Remember the word that I said to you, 'A servant is not greater than his master.' If they persecuted Me, they will also persecute you. If they kept My word, they will keep yours also. 21But all these things they will do to you for My name's sake, because they do not know Him who sent Me. 22If I had not come and spoken to them, they would have no sin, but now they

14:28 [a]NU-Text omits *I said.* **15:2** [a]Or *lifts up*
15:7 [a]NU-Text omits *you will.*

SOUL NOTE

Learning to Love *(15:12, 13)* Jesus gave two commandments to His followers: "Love Me," and "love each other." He had previously told the Pharisees that these two commandments were the greatest because "on these two commandments hang all the Law and the Prophets" (Matt. 22:40). Jesus said that His followers should love each other as He loved them. So great was that love that Jesus would give His life for them. We are to love others as Jesus loved us. We probably won't have to die for anyone, but we show our great love for others by listening, helping, encouraging, and giving. Christ's humble, sacrificial love is our example. **Topic: Love**

have no excuse for their sin. 23He who hates Me hates My Father also. 24If I had not done among them the works which no one else did, they would have no sin; but now they have seen and also hated both Me and My Father. 25But *this happened* that the word might be fulfilled which is written in their law, *'They hated Me without a cause.'*[a]

THE COMING REJECTION

26"But when the Helper comes, whom I shall send to you from the Father, the Spirit of truth who proceeds from the Father, He will testify of Me. 27And you also will bear witness, because you have been with Me from the beginning.

16 "These things I have spoken to you, that you should not be made to stumble. 2They will put you out of the synagogues; yes, the time is coming that whoever kills you will think that he offers God service. 3And these things they will do to you[a] because they have not known the Father nor Me. 4But these things I have told you, that when the[a] time comes, you may remember that I told you of them.

"And these things I did not say to you at the beginning, because I was with you.

THE WORK OF THE HOLY SPIRIT

5"But now I go away to Him who sent Me, and none of you asks Me, 'Where are You going?' 6But because I have said these things to you, sorrow has filled your heart. 7Nevertheless I tell you the truth. It is to your advantage that I go away; for if I do not go away, the Helper will not come to you; but if I depart, I will send Him to you. 8And when He has come, He will convict the world of sin, and of righteousness, and of judgment: 9of sin, because they do not believe in Me; 10of righteousness, because I go to My Father and you see Me no more; 11of judgment, because the ruler of this world is judged.

12"I still have many things to say to you, but you cannot bear *them* now. 13However, when He, the Spirit of truth, has come, He will guide you into all truth; for He will not speak on His own *authority,* but whatever He hears He will speak; and He will tell you things to come. 14He will glorify Me, for He will take of what is Mine and declare *it* to you. 15All things that the Father has are Mine. Therefore I said that He will take of Mine and declare *it* to you.[a]

SORROW WILL TURN TO JOY

16"A little while, and you will not see Me; and again a little while, and you will see Me, because I go to the Father."

17Then *some* of His disciples said among themselves, "What is this that He says to us, 'A little while, and you will not see Me; and again a little while, and you will see Me'; and, 'because I go to the Father'?" 18They said therefore, "What is this that He says, 'A little while'? We do not know what He is saying."

19Now Jesus knew that they desired to ask Him, and He said to them, "Are you inquiring among yourselves about what I said, 'A little while, and you will not see Me; and again a little while, and you will see Me'? 20Most assuredly, I say to you that you will weep and lament, but the world will rejoice; and you will be sorrowful, but your sorrow will be turned into joy. 21A woman, when she is in labor, has sorrow because her hour has come; but as soon as she has given birth to the child, she no longer remembers the anguish, for joy that a human being has been born into the world. 22Therefore you now have sorrow; but I will see you again and your heart will rejoice, and your joy no one will take from you.

23"And in that day you will ask Me nothing. Most assuredly, I say to you, whatever you ask the Father in My name He will give you. 24Until now you have asked nothing in My name. Ask, and you will receive, that your joy may be full.

JESUS CHRIST HAS OVERCOME THE WORLD

25"These things I have spoken to you in figurative language; but the time is coming when I will no longer speak to you in figurative language, but I will tell you plainly about the Father. 26In that day you will ask in My name, and I do not say to you that I shall pray the Father for you; 27for the Father Himself loves you, because you have loved Me, and have believed that I came forth from God. 28I came forth from the Father and have come into the world. Again, I leave the world and go to the Father."

29His disciples said to Him, "See, now You are speaking plainly, and using no figure of

15:25 [a]Psalm 69:4 **16:3** [a]NU-Text and M-Text omit *to you.* **16:4** [a]NU-Text reads *their.* **16:15** [a]NU-Text and M-Text read *He takes of Mine and will declare it to you.*

HOLY SPIRIT, HEAVENLY DOVE

Presence of the Holy Spirit

ED HINDSON

(John 16:5–15)

Jesus promised His disciples that, although He was leaving this world, He would never abandon them. How would that be possible? Jesus promised that the Holy Spirit would come to stay with them and help them through every difficulty they would face (John 14:16–18; 16:7). God the Holy Spirit is equal in power, wisdom, and love to God the Father and God the Son. The Holy Spirit infuses believers with the strength needed to live for Christ (Eph. 5:18) and to bear the fruit of Christian character (Gal. 5:22, 23).

The disciples were in dire need of a counselor, because Jesus would no longer be available to mentor them in person. The word *counselor* (Greek, *parakletos*) refers to someone who is "called alongside" to help. While God uses human counselors to minister to us and guide us, the ultimate Counselor is the Holy Spirit, who guides us into God's truth (John 16:13). He is always there prompting us, prodding us, encouraging us, guiding us, and maturing us through all the challenges of our lives.

The Holy Spirit has a divine name—the "Spirit of God," (1 Cor. 2:11). He has divine attributes—omniscience (1 Cor. 2:10), omnipresence (Ps. 139:7), and omnipotence (Zech. 4:6). He creates, convicts, regenerates, baptizes, fills, and empowers believers. He indwells us (John 14:17), teaches us (John 14:26), guides us (John 16:13), and intercedes for us (Rom. 8:26).

NAMES AND SYMBOLS OF THE HOLY SPIRIT

The Holy Spirit is called by several different names in Scripture. He is the "Spirit of God" (2 Chr. 15:1), the "Spirit of the LORD" (Is. 11:2), the "breath of the Almighty" (Job 32:8), the "Spirit of the Lord GOD" (Is. 61:1), the "Spirit of your Father" (Matt. 10:20), and the "Spirit of Christ" (Rom. 8:9).

The Holy Spirit is unseen, but is depicted by certain symbols: breath or wind (Gen. 2:7; Ezek. 37:9), the dove (Luke 3:22), oil (Luke 4:18; Heb. 1:9), fire (Mark 9:49; 1 Cor. 3:13–15), the seal (Eph. 1:13; 4:30), the guarantee (2 Cor. 1:21, 22; Eph. 1:14). These symbols help us understand the various aspects of the Holy Spirit's ministry in our lives. He moves sovereignly like the wind. He lights on us like a dove, anoints us like oil, and ignites us like fire. He also seals us to the heart and life of God. His presence in our lives is the guarantee (or down payment) of God's grace, and the assurance that He will keep all of His promises to us.

MINISTRY OF THE HOLY SPIRIT

Jesus Himself was assisted by the Spirit during His earthly life and ministry. Jesus was conceived by the Holy Spirit (Luke 1:35), anointed by the Holy Spirit (Luke 4:18), filled with the Holy Spirit (Luke 4:1), led by the Holy Spirit (Luke 4:1, 2), offered to the Father through the Holy Spirit (Heb. 9:14), and raised to life through the Holy Spirit (Rom. 8:11).

The Bible was inspired by the Holy Spirit (2 Pet. 1:21). He moved upon the writers of Scripture so that the words they wrote were the inspired truth of God. Jesus promised the disciples that the Holy Spirit would guide them into all truth (John 14:26; 16:13). Paul affirmed that the apostles of the New Covenant received the revelation of God's truth "through His Spirit" (1 Cor. 2:10). The same Holy Spirit who inspired the writing of Scripture guides us into the truth of God as we read Scripture today.

Christians experience the grace of God because the Holy Spirit calls us to Christ (Rom. 8:28; 1 Tim. 6:12). We are born again by the power of the Holy Spirit (John 3:3–7) who indwells our hearts and empowers us to serve the Lord with our lives (John 7:37–39; Acts 11:17; 1 Cor. 2:12). We are saved by God's grace (Greek, *charis*) and given spiritual gifts (Greek, *charisma*) by which the Holy Spirit empowers us to minister to God's people (Rom. 12:3–8).

ASSURANCE OF THE SPIRIT

One of the greatest aspects of the Holy Spirit's ministry in our lives is the assurance He gives us about our relationship to God. "For as many as are led by the Spirit of God, these are sons of God. . . . The Spirit Himself bears witness with our spirit that we are children of God" (Rom. 8:14, 16). We accept this fact by faith, but we are assured of it in our hearts by the Holy Spirit.

God loves us more than anybody loves us. He cares about us more than we care about ourselves. He speaks to us by His Holy Spirit. For those who have not yet believed in Him, He is calling. Softly and tenderly, the voice of God's Spirit calls people to find eternal life in Him. He invites unbelievers into a deep and personal relationship with Him—a relationship in which He promises He will never leave them nor forsake them. For new believers, God does not leave them on their own to figure out how to pray, read the Word, or grow spiritually. The Holy Spirit personally guides them every step of the way. For those who have been believers for a long time, the Holy Spirit's continual presence is a source of comfort and guidance through every step of life.

As Christians, we are never alone. God dwells in us through His precious Holy Spirit.

FURTHER MEDITATION:

Other passages to study about the issue of the presence of the Holy Spirit include:

- ➢ Genesis 1:2
- ➢ 1 Samuel 10:6
- ➢ Job 33:4
- ➢ Joel 2:28, 29
- ➢ Luke 12:12
- ➢ Acts 2:1–4
- ➢ 1 Corinthians 3:16; 12:13
- ➢ 1 Thessalonians 4:8

To Learn More: **Turn to the key passage note on the presence of the Holy Spirit at Ephesians 4:30 on page 1555. See also the personality profile of the Holy Spirit on page 1416.**

speech! 30Now we are sure that You know all
things, and have no need that anyone should
question You. By this we believe that You
came forth from God."
31Jesus answered them, "Do you now believe? 32Indeed the hour is coming, yes, has
now come, that you will be scattered, each to
his own, and will leave Me alone. And yet I
am not alone, because
the Father is with Me.
33These things I have
spoken to you, that in
Me you may have peace.
In the world you will[a]
have tribulation; but be
of good cheer, I have
overcome the world."

> "These things I have spoken to you, that in Me you may have peace. In the world you will have tribulation; but be of good cheer, I have overcome the world."
> JOHN 16:33

JESUS PRAYS FOR HIMSELF

17 Jesus spoke these words, lifted up His
eyes to heaven, and said: "Father, the
hour has come. Glorify Your Son, that Your
Son also may glorify You, 2as You have given
Him authority over all flesh, that He should[a]
give eternal life to as many as You have given
Him. 3And this is eternal life, that they may
know You, the only true God, and Jesus Christ
whom You have sent. 4I have glorified You on
the earth. I have finished the work which You
have given Me to do. 5And now, O Father, glorify Me together with Yourself, with the glory
which I had with You before the world was.

JESUS PRAYS FOR HIS DISCIPLES

6"I have manifested Your name to the men
whom You have given Me out of the world.
They were Yours, You gave them to Me, and
they have kept Your word. 7Now they have
known that all things which You have given
Me are from You. 8For I have given to them the
words which You have given Me; and they
have received *them,* and have known surely
that I came forth from You; and they have believed that You sent Me.
9"I pray for them. I do not pray for the world
but for those whom You have given Me, for
they are Yours. 10And all Mine are Yours, and
Yours are Mine, and I am glorified in them.
11Now I am no longer in the world, but these
are in the world, and I
come to You. Holy Fa-
ther, keep through Your
name those whom You
have given Me,[a] that
they may be one as We
are. 12While I was with
them in the world,[a] I
kept them in Your
name. Those whom You
gave Me I have kept;[b] and none of them is lost
except the son of perdition, that the Scripture
might be fulfilled. 13But now I come to You,
and these things I speak in the world, that they
may have My joy fulfilled in themselves. 14I
have given them Your word; and the world
has hated them because they are not of the
world, just as I am not of the world. 15I do not
pray that You should take them out of the
world, but that You should keep them from
the evil one. 16They are not of the world, just
as I am not of the world. 17Sanctify them by
Your truth. Your word is truth. 18As You sent
Me into the world, I also have sent them into
the world. 19And for their sakes I sanctify Myself, that they also may be sanctified by the
truth.

16:33 [a]NU-Text and M-Text omit *will.*
17:2 [a]M-Text reads *shall.* **17:11** [a]NU-Text and M-Text read *keep them through Your name which You have given Me.* **17:12** [a]NU-Text omits *in the world.* [b]NU-Text reads *in Your name which You gave Me. And I guarded them;* (or *it;*).

SOUL NOTE

Victorious and Joyous *(16:33)* Jesus warned His followers that living as a Christian in the world would not be easy. Hardships, troubles, even persecutions would come. Some tribulations are part of living in a fallen world and happen to everyone; others occur as Satan assaults people's faith. Believers are to be prepared for these tribulations but not overwhelmed or discouraged by them. The world gives tribulation, but Jesus gives peace. We can "be of good cheer" because we know that Jesus has overcome the world. Christ has already won the ultimate victory over Satan, sin, and evil. **Topic: Discouragement**

Jesus Prays for All Believers

20"I do not pray for these alone, but also for
those who will[a] believe in Me through their
word; 21that they all may be one, as You, Father, *are* in Me, and I in You; that they also
may be one in Us, that the world may believe
that You sent Me. 22And the glory which You
gave Me I have given them, that they may be
one just as We are one: 23I in them, and You in
Me; that they may be made perfect in one, and
that the world may know that You have sent
Me, and have loved them as You have loved
Me.

24"Father, I desire that they also whom You
gave Me may be with Me where I am, that
they may behold My glory which You have
given Me; for You loved Me before the foundation of the world. 25O righteous Father! The
world has not known You, but I have known
You; and these have known that You sent Me.
26And I have declared to them Your name, and
will declare *it,* that the love with which You
loved Me may be in them, and I in them."

Betrayal and Arrest in Gethsemane

18 When Jesus had spoken these words,
He went out with His disciples over
the Brook Kidron, where there was a garden,
which He and His disciples entered. 2And Judas, who betrayed Him, also knew the place;
for Jesus often met there with His disciples.
3Then Judas, having received a detachment *of*
troops, and officers from the chief priests and
Pharisees, came there with lanterns, torches,
and weapons. 4Jesus therefore, knowing all
things that would come upon Him, went forward and said to them, "Whom are you seeking?"

5They answered Him, "Jesus of Nazareth."

Jesus said to them, "I am *He.*" And Judas,
who betrayed Him, also stood with them.
6Now when He said to them, "I am *He,*" they
drew back and fell to the ground.

7Then He asked them again, "Whom are
you seeking?"

And they said, "Jesus of Nazareth."

8Jesus answered, "I have told you that I am
He. Therefore, if you seek Me, let these go
their way," 9that the saying might be fulfilled
which He spoke, "Of those whom You gave
Me I have lost none."

10Then Simon Peter, having a sword, drew it
and struck the high priest's servant, and cut off
his right ear. The servant's name was Malchus.

11So Jesus said to Peter, "Put your sword
into the sheath. Shall I not drink the cup
which My Father has given Me?"

Before the High Priest

12Then the detachment *of troops* and the
captain and the officers of the Jews arrested
Jesus and bound Him. 13And they led Him
away to Annas first, for he was the father-in-
law of Caiaphas who was high priest that year.
14Now it was Caiaphas who advised the Jews
that it was expedient that one man should die
for the people.

Peter Denies Jesus

15And Simon Peter followed Jesus, and so
did another[a] disciple. Now that disciple was
known to the high priest, and went with Jesus
into the courtyard of the high priest. 16But Peter stood at the door outside. Then the other
disciple, who was known to the high priest,
went out and spoke to her who kept the door,
and brought Peter in. 17Then the servant girl
who kept the door said to Peter, "You are not
also *one* of this Man's disciples, are you?"

17:20 [a]NU-Text and M-Text omit *will.*
18:15 [a]M-Text reads *the other.*

SOUL NOTE

Talking to the Father *(ch. 17)* This prayer recorded by the apostle John allows a glimpse into Jesus' heart. Jesus would be passing the mantle of His earthly mission to His disciples. Jesus prayed for them, knowing the opposition would be difficult—they would experience persecutions from without and temptation and doubt from within. He prayed for believers today as well, "those who will believe in Me through their word" (17:20). Believers across the centuries know about Jesus because of the faithfulness of these first followers. We can take great comfort in knowing that Jesus prayed for us that night, and that He still intercedes for us (Heb. 7:25). **Topic: Prayer**

He said, "I am not."

18Now the servants and officers who had made a fire of coals stood there, for it was cold, and they warmed themselves. And Peter stood with them and warmed himself.

JESUS QUESTIONED BY THE HIGH PRIEST

19The high priest then asked Jesus about His disciples and His doctrine.

20Jesus answered him, "I spoke openly to the world. I always taught in synagogues and in the temple, where the Jews always meet,[a] and in secret I have said nothing. 21Why do you ask Me? Ask those who have heard Me what I said to them. Indeed they know what I said."

22And when He had said these things, one of the officers who stood by struck Jesus with the palm of his hand, saying, "Do You answer the high priest like that?"

23Jesus answered him, "If I have spoken evil, bear witness of the evil; but if well, why do you strike Me?"

24Then Annas sent Him bound to Caiaphas the high priest.

PETER DENIES TWICE MORE

25Now Simon Peter stood and warmed himself. Therefore they said to him, "You are not also *one* of His disciples, are you?"

He denied *it* and said, "I am not!"

26One of the servants of the high priest, a relative *of him* whose ear Peter cut off, said, "Did I not see you in the garden with Him?" 27Peter then denied again; and immediately a rooster crowed.

IN PILATE'S COURT

28Then they led Jesus from Caiaphas to the Praetorium, and it was early morning. But they themselves did not go into the Praetorium, lest they should be defiled, but that they might eat the Passover. 29Pilate then went out to them and said, "What accusation do you bring against this Man?"

30They answered and said to him, "If He were not an evildoer, we would not have delivered Him up to you."

31Then Pilate said to them, "You take Him and judge Him according to your law."

Therefore the Jews said to him, "It is not lawful for us to put anyone to death," 32that the saying of Jesus might be fulfilled which He spoke, signifying by what death He would die.

33Then Pilate entered the Praetorium again, called Jesus, and said to Him, "Are You the King of the Jews?"

34Jesus answered him, "Are you speaking for yourself about this, or did others tell you this concerning Me?"

35Pilate answered, "Am I a Jew? Your own nation and the chief priests have delivered You to me. What have You done?"

36Jesus answered, "My kingdom is not of this world. If My kingdom were of this world, My servants would fight, so that I should not be delivered to the Jews; but now My kingdom is not from here."

37Pilate therefore said to Him, "Are You a king then?"

Jesus answered, "You say *rightly* that I am a king. For this cause I was born, and for this cause I have come into the world, that I should bear witness to the truth. Everyone who is of the truth hears My voice."

38Pilate said to Him, "What is truth?" And when he had said this, he went out again to the Jews, and said to them, "I find no fault in Him at all.

TAKING THE PLACE OF BARABBAS

39"But you have a custom that I should release someone to you at the Passover. Do you therefore want me to release to you the King of the Jews?"

40Then they all cried again, saying, "Not this Man, but Barabbas!" Now Barabbas was a robber.

THE SOLDIERS MOCK JESUS

19 So then Pilate took Jesus and scourged *Him.* 2And the soldiers twisted a crown of thorns and put *it* on His head, and they put on Him a purple robe. 3Then they said,[a] "Hail, King of the Jews!" And they struck Him with their hands.

4Pilate then went out again, and said to them, "Behold, I am bringing Him out to you, that you may know that I find no fault in Him."

PILATE'S DECISION

5Then Jesus came out, wearing the crown of thorns and the purple robe. And *Pilate* said to them, "Behold the Man!"

18:20 [a]NU-Text reads *where all the Jews meet.*
19:3 [a]NU-Text reads *And they came up to Him and said.*

6Therefore, when the chief priests and officers saw Him, they cried out, saying, "Crucify
Him, crucify *Him!*"

Pilate said to them, "You take Him and crucify *Him,* for I find no fault in Him."

7The Jews answered him, "We have a law,
and according to our[a] law He ought to die, because He made Himself the Son of God."

8Therefore, when Pilate heard that saying,
he was the more afraid, 9and went again into
the Praetorium, and said to Jesus, "Where
are You from?" But Jesus gave him no answer.

10Then Pilate said to Him, "Are You not
speaking to me? Do You not know that I have
power to crucify You, and power to release
You?"

11Jesus answered, "You could have no power at all against Me unless it had been given
you from above. Therefore the one who delivered Me to you has the greater sin."

12From then on Pilate sought to release
Him, but the Jews cried out, saying, "If you let
this Man go, you are not Caesar's friend. Whoever makes himself a king speaks against Caesar."

13When Pilate therefore heard that saying,
he brought Jesus out and sat down in the
judgment seat in a place that is called *The*
Pavement, but in Hebrew, Gabbatha. 14Now it
was the Preparation Day of the Passover, and
about the sixth hour. And he said to the Jews,
"Behold your King!"

15But they cried out, "Away with *Him,* away
with *Him!* Crucify Him!"

Pilate said to them, "Shall I crucify your
King?"

The chief priests answered, "We have no
king but Caesar!"

16Then he delivered Him to them to be
crucified. So they took Jesus and led *Him*
away.[a]

The King on a Cross

17And He, bearing His cross, went out to a
place called *the Place* of a Skull, which is
called in Hebrew, Golgotha, 18where they crucified Him, and two others with Him, one on
either side, and Jesus in the center. 19Now Pilate wrote a title and put *it* on the cross. And
the writing was:

JESUS OF NAZARETH,
THE KING OF THE JEWS.

20Then many of the Jews read this title, for the
place where Jesus was crucified was near the
city; and it was written in Hebrew, Greek, *and*
Latin.

21Therefore the chief priests of the Jews said
to Pilate, "Do not write, 'The King of the Jews,'
but, 'He said, "I am the King of the Jews." ' "

22Pilate answered, "What I have written, I
have written."

23Then the soldiers, when they had crucified Jesus, took His garments and made four
parts, to each soldier a part, and also the tunic. Now the tunic was without seam, woven
from the top in one piece. 24They said therefore among themselves, "Let us not tear it, but
cast lots for it, whose it shall be," that the
Scripture might be fulfilled which says:

"They divided My garments among them,
And for My clothing they cast lots."[a]

Therefore the soldiers did these things.

Behold Your Mother

25Now there stood by the cross of Jesus His
mother, and His mother's sister, Mary the *wife*
of Clopas, and Mary Magdalene. 26When Jesus
therefore saw His mother, and the disciple
whom He loved standing by, He said to His
mother, "Woman, behold your son!" 27Then
He said to the disciple, "Behold your mother!"
And from that hour that disciple took her to
his own *home.*

It Is Finished

28After this, Jesus, knowing[a] that all things
were now accomplished, that the Scripture
might be fulfilled, said, "I thirst!" 29Now a
vessel full of sour wine was sitting there; and
they filled a sponge with sour wine, put *it* on
hyssop, and put *it* to His mouth. 30So when
Jesus had received the sour wine, He said, "It
is finished!" And bowing His head, He gave
up His spirit.

Jesus' Side Is Pierced

31Therefore, because it was the Preparation
Day, that the bodies should not remain on the
cross on the Sabbath (for that Sabbath was a
high day), the Jews asked Pilate that their legs

19:7 [a]NU-Text reads *the law.* **19:16** [a]NU-Text omits *and led Him away.* **19:24** [a]Psalm 22:18 **19:28** [a]M-Text reads *seeing.*

might be broken, and *that* they might be taken away. 32Then the soldiers came and broke the legs of the first and of the other who was crucified with Him. 33But when they came to Jesus and saw that He was already dead, they did not break His legs. 34But one of the soldiers pierced His side with a spear, and immediately blood and water came out. 35And he who has seen has testified, and his testimony is true; and he knows that he is telling the truth, so that you may believe. 36For these things were done that the Scripture should be fulfilled, *"Not one of His bones shall be broken."*[a] 37And again another Scripture says, *"They shall look on Him whom they pierced."*[a]

Jesus Buried in Joseph's Tomb

38After this, Joseph of Arimathea, being a disciple of Jesus, but secretly, for fear of the Jews, asked Pilate that he might take away the body of Jesus; and Pilate gave *him* permission. So he came and took the body of Jesus. 39And Nicodemus, who at first came to Jesus by night, also came, bringing a mixture of myrrh and aloes, about a hundred pounds. 40Then they took the body of Jesus, and bound it in strips of linen with the spices, as the custom of the Jews is to bury. 41Now in the place where He was crucified there was a garden, and in the garden a new tomb in which no one had yet been laid. 42So there they laid Jesus, because of the Jews' Preparation *Day,* for the tomb was nearby.

The Empty Tomb

20 Now on the first *day* of the week Mary Magdalene went to the tomb early, while it was still dark, and saw *that* the stone had been taken away from the tomb. 2Then she ran and came to Simon Peter, and to the other disciple, whom Jesus loved, and said to them, "They have taken away the Lord out of the tomb, and we do not know where they have laid Him."

3Peter therefore went out, and the other disciple, and were going to the tomb. 4So they both ran together, and the other disciple outran Peter and came to the tomb first. 5And he, stooping down and looking in, saw the linen cloths lying *there;* yet he did not go in. 6Then Simon Peter came, following him, and went into the tomb; and he saw the linen cloths lying *there,* 7and the handkerchief that had been around His head, not lying with the linen cloths, but folded together in a place by itself. 8Then the other disciple, who came to the tomb first, went in also; and he saw and believed. 9For as yet they did not know the Scripture, that He must rise again from the dead. 10Then the disciples went away again to their own homes.

Mary Magdalene Sees the Risen Lord

11But Mary stood outside by the tomb weeping, and as she wept she stooped down *and looked* into the tomb. 12And she saw two angels in white sitting, one at the head and the other at the feet, where the body of Jesus had lain. 13Then they said to her, "Woman, why are you weeping?"

She said to them, "Because they have taken away my Lord, and I do not know where they have laid Him."

14Now when she had said this, she turned around and saw Jesus standing *there,* and did not know that it was Jesus. 15Jesus said to her, "Woman, why are you weeping? Whom are you seeking?"

She, supposing Him to be the gardener, said

19:36 [a]Exodus 12:46; Numbers 9:12; Psalm 34:20
19:37 [a]Zechariah 12:10

SOUL NOTE

Expensive *(19:28–34)* If it weren't for being holy, God could have chosen to ignore sin. If it weren't for being loving, He could have condemned humanity to hell the moment Adam sinned. Being both holy and loving, God did neither of these. Instead, He chose to deal with the ultimate consequences of sin—death and separation from God—by having His Son take those consequences upon Himself. Jesus took our penalty, dying in our place. When we accept that sacrifice on our behalf, we are given salvation and eternal life. God looks at us and no longer sees our sins. Instead, He sees that His Son died so that we could be saved. **Topic: Salvation**

to Him, "Sir, if You have carried Him away, tell
me where You have laid Him, and I will take
Him away."
[16]Jesus said to her, "Mary!"
She turned and said to Him,[a] "Rabboni!"
(which is to say, Teacher).
[17]Jesus said to her, "Do not cling to Me, for I
have not yet ascended to My Father; but go to
My brethren and say to them, 'I am ascending
to My Father and your Father, and *to* My God
and your God.' "
[18]Mary Magdalene came and told the disciples that she had seen the Lord,[a] and *that* He
had spoken these things to her.

The Apostles Commissioned

[19]Then, the same day at evening, being the
first *day* of the week, when the doors were
shut where the disciples were assembled,[a] for
fear of the Jews, Jesus came and stood in the
midst, and said to them, "Peace *be* with you."
[20]When He had said this, He showed them *His*
hands and His side. Then the disciples were
glad when they saw the Lord.
[21]So Jesus said to them again, "Peace to
you! As the Father has sent Me, I also send
you." [22]And when He had said this, He
breathed on *them,* and said to them, "Receive
the Holy Spirit. [23]If you forgive the sins of any,
they are forgiven them; if you retain the *sins*
of any, they are retained."

Seeing and Believing

[24]Now Thomas, called the Twin, one of the
twelve, was not with them when Jesus came.
[25]The other disciples therefore said to him,
"We have seen the Lord."
So he said to them, "Unless I see in His

20:16 [a]NU-Text adds *in Hebrew.* **20:18** [a]NU-Text reads *disciples, "I have seen the Lord," . . .*
20:19 [a]NU-Text omits *assembled.*

PERSONALITY PROFILE

Doubt

THOMAS: FROM DOUBT TO FAITH

(JOHN 20:24–29)

"Doubting Thomas" was really no different from the rest of the disciples—and no different from much of the modern world. He may have been skeptical by nature, but, in reality, none of the other disciples truly understood that Jesus would come back to life until they saw Him with their own eyes.

Thomas wasn't present when Jesus first appeared to the other disciples, and he refused to believe the astonishing news that Jesus had risen from the dead. Thomas insisted that unless he touched the wounds of Jesus, he would not believe. Thomas wanted proof. When he got that proof, however, he had no trouble believing.

John the Baptist also faced a moment of doubt. Sitting in prison, John sent his disciples to ask Jesus if He was really the Messiah (Matt. 11:1–6). Jesus did not condemn John for His doubt, but merely gave him the proof he needed, just as He did with Thomas. Both men understood the truth and believed.

Doubt is not wrong if it leads us on a search for the truth, and if we are willing to accept the truth once we find it. Jesus said to Thomas, "Because you have seen Me, you have believed. Blessed are those who have not seen and yet have believed." That includes believers across the centuries who have never seen God and never walked physically with Christ. They have trusted in Christ based on the truth of God's Word and the reality of the Holy Spirit in their lives.

Those who doubt the Christian faith can put it to the test. Those who are believers but find themselves faced with situations that cause them to doubt can do the same. Christ will provide the answer we need. Keep on believing, even through the doubt, for we are blessed when we have not seen and yet still believe.

To Learn More: Turn to the article about doubt on pages 1408, 1409. See also the key passage note at Matthew 11:1–6 on page 1246.

Doubt

THE THOMAS FACTOR: TREATING DOUBT

GARY R. HABERMAS

(John 20:24–29)

Doubt is a common experience. Unfortunately, it's been given a bad rap. Doubt is often referred to as the opposite of faith—unbelief or the unpardonable sin. It is also erroneously defined as something one ought not to admit. Questioning God can be sinful, but it is not always so. When properly handled, doubt can be the first step to a positive, strong, and dynamic faith.

BIBLICAL EXAMPLES OF DOUBT

During his severe suffering, Job began to doubt God. He learned a tremendous lesson, however, when he realized that he knew enough about God to trust Him in the many things he did not understand (Job 42:1–6). Abraham is known as the man of faith, and yet on many occasions he showcased his doubts. In spite of the promise that all people would be blessed through him, Abraham still asked for assurance (Gen. 15:8). Later, when God repeated His promise, Abraham went so far as to laugh at God (Gen. 17:15–17). He even lied twice about his wife, Sarah, in order to save his life—indicating that he was unsure about God keeping His promises to protect him (Gen. 12:10–20; 20:1–8)

The New Testament provides still other instances. John the Baptist wanted to know if Jesus was really the Messiah, or if he should look for someone else (Luke 7:18–30). Thomas questioned the Lord's resurrection (John 20:24–29). Paul related his struggle with unanswered prayer (2 Cor. 12:7–10).

DIFFERENT TYPES OF DOUBT

There are three primary types of religious doubt: factual, emotional, and volitional. *Factual doubt* is identified by questions concerning one's grounds for belief—whether or not Christianity is based on a solid foundation. *Emotional doubt* stems from passions and moods. It is intensified by other struggles in one's life such as loss or depression. *Volitional doubt* is concerned with the will. It is mainly related to issues like weak faith, forsaking sin, and one's motivation to follow God.

Doubt sometimes follows a pattern including all three types of doubt. For example, people's unanswered factual questions may bother them, affecting their emotions. They grow upset with God for not meeting their needs. Later, this may also attack their motivation as they wonder why they should follow the Lord any longer.

RESPONDING TO DOUBT

It is important to be able to correctly identify the type of doubt. If people are mistaken about the nature of their sickness and take the wrong medicine, they should not be surprised if it does not work. Doubt can be the same way. If people do not properly diagnose the type of doubt, they should not be surprised if their misguided response fails to bring relief.

Factual doubt can often be handled by pointing out the many evidences for Christian truth. When Thomas expressed his doubt, Jesus said, "Reach your finger here, and look at My hands; and reach your hand here, and put it into My side. Do not be unbelieving, but believing" (John 20:27).

Volitional doubt is the most dangerous type. At that point, people may have little desire to follow the Lord, and that sometimes makes them unwilling to listen to reason, to study the facts, or to care about the truth. People who have volitional doubt may need help from those who understand the issues involved and are concerned enough to lovingly confront them. In particular, volitional doubters need to be challenged in terms of their loss of motivation.

The middle one, *emotional doubt*, is the most common type. It is often the most painful, frequently distinguished by tattered feelings and distraught emotions. Emotional doubters usually judge the facts surrounding their beliefs based on how they *feel* about those beliefs. They often think they are asking about the truth of Christianity when in fact they are merely reflecting on their feelings. Rather than giving in to one's emotions, Scripture teaches people to think and practice truth. In Philippians 4:6–9, Paul tells believers to pray, give thanks and praise, change their thinking, and practice these teachings regularly. Similarly, Peter tells Christians to give their concerns to God (1 Pet. 5:7). The psalms promote praise and thanksgiving as the antidotes to unruly emotions, for it is almost impossible to praise or give thanks to God without one's moods changing almost immediately (Ps. 42:5, 6). Changing one's thinking patterns is also a key to victory. Paul commands Christians to "be transformed by the renewing of your mind" (Rom. 12:2).

Finally, Christians dealing with emotional doubt must continually practice truth. They must center their hearts on God and His kingdom, laying up treasures in heaven in order to nullify worry (Matt. 6:19–34). Before their emotions get involved, Christians must deliberately change their thought pattern at the very moment of doubt, substituting God's truth. Christians must constantly practice God's truth until it soothes the doubt. This can be done in many ways: repeating the truth, writing it on cards, meditating on it, thanking and praising God, giving Him our worries in prayer, and recalling His promises to us.

OVERCOMING DOUBT

The believer who doubts God because of personal pain needs to internalize the same lesson that Job learned. We also know enough about God to trust Him in those painful areas that we do not understand. Since God raised Jesus from the dead, thereby insuring heaven (1 Pet. 1:3–5), we have an *ultimate* answer to suffering. The victory comes as a process. Much like medicine that must be taken for one to feel better, these biblical principles can provide victory over struggles with doubt.

FURTHER MEDITATION:

Other passages to study about the issue of doubt include:

- Psalms 43:5; 55:4–8, 16–18, 22
- Lamentations 3:19–24
- Matthew 12:38–40
- Luke 7:18–30; 24:36–43
- 2 Corinthians 4:8, 16–18
- Philippians 4:6–9

To Learn More: Turn to the key passage note on doubt at Matthew 11:1–6 on page 1246. See also the personality profile of Thomas on page 1407.

hands the print of the nails, and put my finger into the print of the nails, and put my hand into His side, I will not believe."

26And after eight days His disciples were again inside, and Thomas with them. Jesus came, the doors being shut, and stood in the midst, and said, "Peace to you!" 27Then He said to Thomas, "Reach your finger here, and look at My hands; and reach your hand *here,* and put *it* into My side. Do not be unbelieving, but believing."

28And Thomas answered and said to Him, "My Lord and my God!"

29Jesus said to him, "Thomas,[a] because you have seen Me, you have believed. Blessed *are* those who have not seen and *yet* have believed."

That You May Believe

30And truly Jesus did many other signs in the presence of His disciples, which are not written in this book; 31but these are written that you may believe that Jesus is the Christ, the Son of God, and that believing you may have life in His name.

Breakfast by the Sea

21 After these things Jesus showed Himself again to the disciples at the Sea of Tiberias, and in this way He showed *Himself:* 2Simon Peter, Thomas called the Twin, Nathanael of Cana in Galilee, the *sons* of Zebedee, and two others of His disciples were together. 3Simon Peter said to them, "I am going fishing."

They said to him, "We are going with you also." They went out and immediately[a] got into the boat, and that night they caught nothing. 4But when the morning had now come, Jesus stood on the shore; yet the disciples did not know that it was Jesus. 5Then Jesus said to them, "Children, have you any food?"

They answered Him, "No."

6And He said to them, "Cast the net on the right side of the boat, and you will find *some.*" So they cast, and now they were not able to draw it in because of the multitude of fish.

7Therefore that disciple whom Jesus loved said to Peter, "It is the Lord!" Now when Simon Peter heard that it was the Lord, he put on *his* outer garment (for he had removed it), and plunged into the sea. 8But the other disciples came in the little boat (for they were not far from land, but about two hundred cubits), dragging the net with fish. 9Then, as soon as they had come to land, they saw a fire of coals there, and fish laid on it, and bread. 10Jesus said to them, "Bring some of the fish which you have just caught."

11Simon Peter went up and dragged the net to land, full of large fish, one hundred and fifty-three; and although there were so many, the net was not broken. 12Jesus said to them, "Come *and* eat breakfast." Yet none of the disciples dared ask Him, "Who are You?"—knowing that it was the Lord. 13Jesus then came and took the bread and gave it to them, and likewise the fish.

14This *is* now the third time Jesus showed Himself to His disciples after He was raised from the dead.

Jesus Restores Peter

15So when they had eaten breakfast, Jesus said to Simon Peter, "Simon, *son* of Jonah,[a] do you love Me more than these?"

He said to Him, "Yes, Lord; You know that I love You."

He said to him, "Feed My lambs."

16He said to him again a second time, "Simon, *son* of Jonah,[a] do you love Me?"

He said to Him, "Yes, Lord; You know that I love You."

He said to him, "Tend My sheep."

17He said to him the third time, "Simon, *son* of Jonah,[a] do you love Me?" Peter was grieved because He said to him the third time, "Do you love Me?"

And he said to Him, "Lord, You know all things; You know that I love You."

Jesus said to him, "Feed My sheep. 18Most assuredly, I say to you, when you were younger, you girded yourself and walked where you wished; but when you are old, you will stretch out your hands, and another will gird you and carry *you* where you do not wish." 19This He spoke, signifying by what death he would glorify God. And when He had spoken this, He said to him, "Follow Me."

The Beloved Disciple and His Book

20Then Peter, turning around, saw the disciple whom Jesus loved following, who also

---

20:29 [a]NU-Text and M-Text omit *Thomas.*
21:3 [a]NU-Text omits *immediately.* **21:15** [a]NU-Text reads *John.* **21:16** [a]NU-Text reads *John.*
21:17 [a]NU-Text reads *John.*

had leaned on His breast at the supper, and
said, "Lord, who is the one who betrays You?"
21Peter, seeing him, said to Jesus, "But Lord,
what *about* this man?"
22Jesus said to him, "If I will that he remain
till I come, what *is that* to you? You follow
Me."
23Then this saying went out among the
brethren that this disciple would not die. Yet
Jesus did not say to him that he would not die,
but, "If I will that he remain till I come, what
is that to you?"
24This is the disciple who testifies of these
things, and wrote these things; and we know
that his testimony is true.
25And there are also many other things that
Jesus did, which if they were written one by
one, I suppose that even the world itself could
not contain the books that would be written.
Amen.

PERSONALITY PROFILE

Healing/ Recovery

PETER: A JOB TO DO

(JOHN 21:15)

Peter had denied Christ and wept bitterly upon realizing what he had done (Matt. 26:75). Sorrowful, sick, and hurting, Peter could have separated himself from the other disciples; he could have killed himself (as Judas did). But somehow he swallowed his pride and returned to his fellow disciples—meeting with them behind closed doors and fishing with them on that early morning when Jesus appeared on the shore.

Jesus had special words for Peter, because Peter had a special need to be healed and restored from his sin. Surely Peter's heart had been broken by his own weakness in denying his friend and Savior. Three times, Peter had denied knowing Jesus; and three times, Jesus asked him, "Do you love Me?" Jesus forgave Peter and restored him to ministry. The three charges, "Feed My lambs . . . . Tend My sheep . . . . Feed My sheep," reveal the ministry Peter would have in helping the believers who would join them. Clearly Peter's sermon on the day of Pentecost and the addition of three thousand believers to the church gave Peter a lot of sheep to tend and feed with spiritual food!

No matter how deep the stain of our sin, Christ can forgive and heal us. He also can restore us to service for Him.

To Learn More: Turn to the article about healing/recovery on pages 1652, 1653. See also the key passage note at James 5:14–16 on page 1650.

RESTORATION

EARL AND SANDRA WILSON

(John 21:15–19)

It's a wonderful experience to be restored in a relationship that has been broken because of sin. Peter experienced this. The story in John 21:15–19 describes how Jesus restored Peter to fellowship with Himself after Peter had sinned by denying His Savior. Three times Christ asked if Peter loved Him; three times Peter responded that he did; three times Christ responded by giving Peter the responsibility to care for His flock—the believers. When Jesus spoke to Peter with the words, "Follow Me," He restored Peter to fellowship and reinstated him as a disciple. What a glorious moment that must have been for Peter!

David also experienced the blessing of being restored. After he had committed the sins of adultery and murder (2 Sam. 11), he repented and faced the consequences of his sin (Ps. 51). He concluded his repentance with the prayer, "Create in me a clean heart, O God, and renew a steadfast spirit within me" (Ps. 51:10). David longed to be restored to fellowship with God.

RESULTS OF RESTORATION

Restoration comes when believers:

1. Admit their sin (confession).
2. Turn from their sin (repentance).
3. Accept responsibility for the consequences of their sin (restitution).
4. Face the truth about what they have done and learn to live with truth as a focus of their life.
5. Allow God to replace their powerlessness with His power (humility).
6. Walk in the light of their renewed relationship with God, their family, and their brothers and sisters in Christ.

But how do believers who have fallen into sin get to this point? It often happens through the intercession of caring brothers or sisters in Christ who are called by God to be "restorers."

A PATTERN FOR RESTORATION

Galatians 6:1–6 emphasizes the responsibility of Christians to be involved in the restoration of others who are "overtaken in any trespass." Restoration is God's work carried out by brothers or sisters who are mature in the faith, watchful, and caring.

Revealing the Fruit of Gentleness
When it comes to participating in the restoration of a fallen brother or sister, believers should "restore such a one in a spirit of gentleness" (Gal. 6:1). The biblical balance is gentleness toward the sinner and firmness against the sin. Note the careful warning in that same verse: "considering yourself lest you also be tempted." Believers must be careful because they might be tempted to feel that they are better than the one needing restoration. The sin of pride could leave them in need of restoration themselves.

Bearing One Another's Burdens
The next verse says that believers must "bear one another's burdens, and so fulfill the law of Christ" (Gal. 6:2). Carrying one another's burdens means to be actively involved in helping. Luke 5:17–19 gives an example of a man's friends who literally carried another's burden—the man him-

self, because he was paralyzed—and brought him to Jesus for healing. They acted, Jesus responded, and the man was made whole. The formerly paralyzed man experienced the joy of restoration—both physically and spiritually—and his friends had the joy of seeing God work.

Restoring sinners is not an option. It is a responsibility. When believers are involved as restorers, they are fulfilling the law of Christ. It follows that to ignore a brother or sister caught in sin is to disobey the law of Christ.

Remaining Humble

God really knows every human being inside out. He knows how easy it is for people to become proud, especially when they are used to help another person. Helping others to be restored must never become a source of pride. "For if anyone thinks himself to be something, when he is nothing, he deceives himself" (Gal. 6:3). The work of restoration is given to some people as a blessing from God Himself. And they should see it as a gift from Him. It allows them to be blessed by God as they do a special work. They get to see God's love, grace, and mercy in action. It can be a life-changing experience. Even so, Paul gave a strong warning against pride, reminding his readers that God does the changing. People are just His instruments.

Examining Ourselves

Galatians 6:4, 5 calls each restorer to "examine his own work, and then he will have rejoicing in himself alone, and not in another. For each one shall bear his own load." These verses provide important teaching about two very confusing questions. The first question is, "Do I have to downplay my ability or deny what God has done through me in order to avoid the sin of pride?" Clearly the answer is no. The text says people should examine their own work, and then they will have rejoicing in themselves alone. Looking carefully inside themselves can help people to understand their weaknesses and vulnerability, even as they also see the abilities God has given them to do what He asks them to do.

The second question, "How do I avoid pride if I acknowledge the good I have done?" also has a clear answer: Believers must not compare themselves with others. Their concern isn't whether or not they are better than another person. Their concern should be to keep in step with the Spirit (Gal. 5:25) so that God can continue to show His power in them.

Galatians 6:6 says, "Let him who is taught the word share in all good things with him who teaches." This verse indicates a partnership between the believer and the Holy Spirit. The Spirit instructs His people; He also produces the blessing that results from their obedient, caring efforts.

FURTHER MEDITATION:

Other passages to study about the issue of restoration include:

- Leviticus 19:18
- Matthew 18:15–17
- Romans 12:17–21
- 2 Corinthians 7:10
- 2 Timothy 2:24–26
- Philemon 10–12

To Learn More: Turn to the key passage note on restoration at Galatians 6:1–5 on page 1543. See also the personality profile of David on page 418.

Acts

An engagement, a job promotion, a new baby—the nature of good news is that we want to share it with everyone we meet. When good news touches our lives it naturally and joyfully bubbles from our lips.

This certainly was the case with the first generation of Christians. Luke, the author of the Gospel that bears his name, meticulously records in the Book of Acts how the followers of Jesus shared the news of a living Savior "in Jerusalem, and in all Judea and Samaria, and to the end of the earth" (1:8).

Luke uses that geographical progression as a kind of outline for his record of the beginning of the early church. Chapters 1—7 document the church's initial impact under the leadership of Peter and John (primarily among Jews) in Jerusalem. Chapters 8—12 detail the spread of the gospel into the regions of Judea and Samaria. The balance of the book focuses on the apostle Paul and his missionary exploits throughout the known world. Acts is a book of major transitions—from Judaism to Christianity, from law to grace.

Filled with undeniable manifestations of the power of God, dotted with changed lives, and offering unique glimpses into church life as God intended it, this is as exciting a record as you'll ever read. Let Acts (and the passionate believers that fill its pages) renew your soul by reminding you that as a Christian you do indeed possess the best of all possible news.

Soul Concerns in Acts

Spiritual Disciplines	(2:46, 47)
Communication	(15:7)

Prologue

1 The former account I made, O Theophilus, of all that Jesus began both to do and teach, 2 until the day in which He was taken up, after He through the Holy Spirit had given commandments to the apostles whom He had chosen, 3 to whom He also presented Himself alive after His suffering by many infallible proofs, being seen by them during forty days and speaking of the things pertaining to the kingdom of God.

The Holy Spirit Promised

4 And being assembled together with *them,* He commanded them not to depart from Jerusalem, but to wait for the Promise of the Father, "which," *He said,* "you have heard from Me; 5 for John truly baptized with water, but you shall be baptized with the Holy Spirit not many days from now." 6 Therefore, when they had come together, they asked Him, saying, "Lord, will You at this time restore the kingdom to Israel?" 7 And He said to them, "It is not for you to know times or seasons which the Father has put in His own authority. 8 But you shall receive power when the Holy Spirit has come upon you; and you shall be witnesses to Me[a] in Jerusalem, and in all Judea and Samaria, and to the end of the earth."

Jesus Ascends to Heaven

9 Now when He had spoken these things, while they watched, He was taken up, and a cloud received Him out of their sight. 10 And while they looked steadfastly toward heaven as He went up, behold, two men stood by them in white apparel, 11 who also said, "Men of Galilee, why do you stand gazing up into heaven? This *same* Jesus, who was taken up from you into heaven, will so come in like manner as you saw Him go into heaven."

The Upper Room Prayer Meeting

12 Then they returned to Jerusalem from the mount called Olivet, which is near Jerusalem, a Sabbath day's journey. 13 And when they had entered, they went up into the upper room where they were staying: Peter, James, John, and Andrew; Philip and Thomas; Bartholomew and Matthew; James *the son* of Alphaeus and Simon the Zealot; and Judas *the son* of James. 14 These all continued with one accord in prayer and supplication,[a] with the women and Mary the mother of Jesus, and with His brothers.

Matthias Chosen

15 And in those days Peter stood up in the midst of the disciples[a] (altogether the number of names was about a hundred and twenty), and said, 16 "Men *and* brethren, this Scripture had to be fulfilled, which the Holy Spirit spoke before by the mouth of David concerning Judas, who became a guide to those who arrested Jesus; 17 for he was numbered with us and obtained a part in this ministry."

18 (Now this man purchased a field with the wages of iniquity; and falling headlong, he burst open in the middle and all his entrails gushed out. 19 And it became known to all those dwelling in Jerusalem; so that field is called in their own language, Akel Dama, that is, Field of Blood.)

20 "For it is written in the Book of Psalms:

'Let his dwelling place be desolate,
And let no one live in it';[a]

and,

'Let[b] *another take his office.'*[c]

21 "Therefore, of these men who have accompanied us all the time that the Lord Jesus went in and out among us, 22 beginning from the baptism of John to that day when He was taken up from us, one of these must become a witness with us of His resurrection."

23 And they proposed two: Joseph called Barsabas, who was surnamed Justus, and Matthias. 24 And they prayed and said, "You, O Lord, who know the hearts of all, show which of these two You have chosen 25 to take part in this ministry and apostleship from which Judas by transgression fell, that he might go to his own place." 26 And they cast their lots, and the lot fell on Matthias. And he was numbered with the eleven apostles.

Coming of the Holy Spirit

2 When the Day of Pentecost had fully come, they were all with one accord[a] in one place. 2 And suddenly there came a sound from heaven, as of a rushing mighty wind, and it filled the whole house where they were

1:8 [a]NU-Text reads *My witnesses.* **1:14** [a]NU-Text omits *and supplication.* **1:15** [a]NU-Text reads *brethren.* **1:20** [a]Psalm 69:25 [b]Psalm 109:8 [c]Greek *episkopen, position of overseer* **2:1** [a]NU-Text reads *together.*

sitting. 3Then there appeared to them divided tongues, as of fire, and *one* sat upon each of them. 4And they were all filled with the Holy Spirit and began to speak with other tongues, as the Spirit gave them utterance.

THE CROWD'S RESPONSE

5And there were dwelling in Jerusalem Jews, devout men, from every nation under heaven. 6And when this sound occurred, the multitude came together, and were confused, because everyone heard them speak in his own language. 7Then they were all amazed and marveled, saying to one another, "Look, are not all these who speak Galileans? 8And how *is it that* we hear, each in our own language in which we were born? 9Parthians and Medes and Elamites, those dwelling in Mesopotamia, Judea and Cappadocia, Pontus and Asia, 10Phrygia and Pamphylia, Egypt and the parts of Libya adjoining Cyrene, visitors from Rome, both Jews and proselytes, 11Cretans and Arabs—we hear them speaking in our own tongues the wonderful works of God." 12So they were all amazed and perplexed, saying to one another, "Whatever could this mean?"

13Others mocking said, "They are full of new wine."

PERSONALITY PROFILE

Presence of the Holy Spirit

THE HOLY SPIRIT IN BELIEVERS' LIVES

(ACTS 2:1)

During the Last Supper, Jesus gave His disciples an extended introduction to the work of the Holy Spirit. Jesus promised that He and the Father would send a Helper (Comforter) to dwell in them. Among the Holy Spirit's tasks would be the following:

- To dwell with them and be in them (John 14:17).
- To teach the disciples all things (John 14:26).
- To bring to their remembrance what Jesus said (John 14:26).
- To testify of Jesus (John 15:26).
- To convict the world of sin because they do not believe in Jesus (John 16:8–11).
- To convict the world of righteousness because Jesus has gone to His Father and can be seen here no longer (John 16:8–11).
- To convict the world of judgment because the ruler of this world is judged (John 16:8–11).
- To guide the disciples into all truth (John 16:13).

After His resurrection, Jesus added to the Holy Spirit's job description. He told the disciples they would soon be baptized with the Holy Spirit and receive power to be witnesses throughout the world (Acts 1:5–8).

The arrival of the Holy Spirit in the early church certainly created an audio-visual impact. Sounds like wind, sights like fire, and people speaking languages they did not learn announced the age of the church. Thousands heard in their own languages about the "wonderful works of God" (Acts 2:11).

The Holy Spirit has continued His ministry of conviction and conversion throughout history. Every believer is "sealed with the Holy Spirit of promise" (Eph. 1:13) when he or she believes the good news about Jesus. From that point on, the Holy Spirit remains a constant Helper, Comforter, and Companion of believers. He may not choose to make Himself known in such obvious ways, but those who live their lives in dependence on God's Spirit will discover that what they need in the way of power and guidance to accomplish God's will shall be provided. By His Spirit, God lives in those who trust Jesus.

To Learn More: Turn to the article about the presence of the Holy Spirit on pages 1400, 1401. See also the key passage note at Ephesians 4:30 on page 1555.

Peter's Sermon

[14]But Peter, standing up with the eleven,
raised his voice and said to them, "Men of Judea and all who dwell in Jerusalem, let this be
known to you, and heed my words. [15]For these
are not drunk, as you suppose, since it is *only*
the third hour of the day. [16]But this is what
was spoken by the prophet Joel:

17 *'And it shall come to pass in the last*
days, says God,
That I will pour out of My Spirit on all
flesh;
Your sons and your daughters shall
prophesy,
Your young men shall see visions,
Your old men shall dream dreams.
18 *And on My menservants and on My*
maidservants
I will pour out My Spirit in those
days;
And they shall prophesy.
19 *I will show wonders in heaven*
above
And signs in the earth beneath:
Blood and fire and vapor of smoke.
20 *The sun shall be turned into*
darkness,
And the moon into blood,
Before the coming of the great and
awesome day of the LORD.
21 *And it shall come to pass*
That whoever calls on the name of the
LORD
Shall be saved.'[a]

[22]"Men of Israel, hear these words: Jesus of
Nazareth, a Man attested by God to you by
miracles, wonders, and signs which God did
through Him in your midst, as you yourselves
also know—[23]Him, being delivered by the determined purpose and foreknowledge of God,
you have taken[a] by lawless hands, have crucified, and put to death; [24]whom God raised up,
having loosed the pains of death, because it
was not possible that He should be held by it.
[25]For David says concerning Him:

'I foresaw the LORD *always before my*
face,
For He is at my right hand, that I may
not be shaken.
26 *Therefore my heart rejoiced, and my*
tongue was glad;
Moreover my flesh also will rest in
hope.
27 *For You will not leave my soul in Hades,*
Nor will You allow Your Holy One to see
corruption.
28 *You have made known to me the ways of*
life;
You will make me full of joy in Your
presence.'[a]

[29]"Men *and* brethren, let *me* speak freely to
you of the patriarch David, that he is both
dead and buried, and his tomb is with us to
this day. [30]Therefore, being a prophet, and
knowing that God had sworn with an oath to
him that of the fruit of his body, according to
the flesh, He would raise up the Christ to sit
on his throne,[a] [31]he, foreseeing this, spoke
concerning the resurrection of the Christ, that
His soul was not left in Hades, nor did His
flesh see corruption. [32]This Jesus God has
raised up, of which we are all witnesses.
[33]Therefore being exalted to the right hand of
God, and having received from the Father the
promise of the Holy Spirit, He poured out this
which you now see and hear.
[34]"For David did not ascend into the heavens, but he says himself:

'The LORD *said to my Lord,*
"Sit at My right hand,
35 *Till I make Your enemies Your*
footstool." '[a]

[36]"Therefore let all the house of Israel know
assuredly that God has made this Jesus,
whom you crucified, both Lord and Christ."
[37]Now when they heard *this,* they were cut
to the heart, and said to Peter and the rest of
the apostles, "Men *and* brethren, what shall
we do?"
[38]Then Peter said to them, "Repent, and let
every one of you be baptized in the name of
Jesus Christ for the remission of sins; and you
shall receive the gift of the Holy Spirit. [39]For
the promise is to you and to your children,
and to all who are afar off, as many as the
Lord our God will call."

2:21 [a]Joel 2:28–32 **2:23** [a]NU-Text omits *have taken.* **2:28** [a]Psalm 16:8–11 **2:30** [a]NU-Text omits *according to the flesh, He would raise up the Christ* and completes the verse with *He would seat one on his throne.* **2:35** [a]Psalm 110:1

A Vital Church Grows

40 And with many other words he testified and exhorted them, saying, "Be saved from this perverse generation." 41 Then those who gladly[a] received his word were baptized; and that day about three thousand souls were added *to them.* 42 And they continued steadfastly in the apostles' doctrine and fellowship, in the breaking of bread, and in prayers. 43 Then fear came upon every soul, and many wonders and signs were done through the apostles. 44 Now all who believed were together, and had all things in common, 45 and sold their possessions and goods, and divided them among all, as anyone had need.

46 So continuing daily with one accord in the temple, and breaking bread from house to house, they ate their food with gladness and simplicity of heart, 47 praising God and having favor with all the people. And the Lord added to the church[a] daily those who were being saved.

A Lame Man Healed

3 Now Peter and John went up together to the temple at the hour of prayer, the ninth *hour.* 2 And a certain man lame from his mother's womb was carried, whom they laid daily at the gate of the temple which is called Beautiful, to ask alms from those who entered the temple; 3 who, seeing Peter and John about to go into the temple, asked for alms. 4 And fixing his eyes on him, with John, Peter said, "Look at us." 5 So he gave them his attention, expecting to receive something from them. 6 Then Peter said, "Silver and gold I do not have, but what I do have I give you: In the name of Jesus Christ of Nazareth, rise up and walk." 7 And he took him by the right hand and lifted *him* up, and immediately his feet and ankle bones received strength. 8 So he, leaping up, stood and walked and entered the temple with them—walking, leaping, and praising God. 9 And all the people saw him walking and praising God. 10 Then they knew that it was he who sat begging alms at the Beautiful Gate of the temple; and they were filled with wonder and amazement at what had happened to him.

Preaching in Solomon's Portico

11 Now as the lame man who was healed held on to Peter and John, all the people ran together to them in the porch which is called Solomon's, greatly amazed. 12 So when Peter saw *it,* he responded to the people: "Men of Israel, why do you marvel at this? Or why look so intently at us, as though by our own power or godliness we had made this man walk? 13 The God of Abraham, Isaac, and Jacob, the God of our fathers, glorified His Servant Jesus, whom you delivered up and denied in the presence of Pilate, when he was determined to let *Him* go. 14 But you denied the Holy One and the Just, and asked for a murderer to be granted to you, 15 and killed the Prince of life, whom God raised from the dead, of which we are witnesses. 16 And His name, through faith in His name, has made this man strong, whom you see and know. Yes, the faith which *comes* through Him has given him this perfect soundness in the presence of you all.

17 "Yet now, brethren, I know that you did *it* in ignorance, as *did* also your rulers. 18 But those things which God foretold by the mouth of all His prophets, that the Christ would suffer, He has thus fulfilled. 19 Repent therefore and be converted, that your sins may be blotted out, so that times of refreshing may come

2:41 [a]NU-Text omits *gladly.* **2:47** [a]NU-Text omits *to the church.*

SOUL NOTE

The Best Gift *(2:38, 39)* Peter called his listeners to repent, be baptized, and "receive the gift of the Holy Spirit." To repent means to turn from sin, to turn the direction of one's life away from rebellion and selfishness, and to live for Christ. Baptism is the public confession of one's commitment to Christ. It identifies that person with the Christian community. The Holy Spirit enters a believer's life, helping them to know and do God's will. Jesus had said, "I will pray the Father, and He will give you another Helper" (John 14:16). Believers have the Holy Spirit dwelling within, and that helps them to live for God. **Topic: Presence of the Holy Spirit**

from the presence of the Lord, [20]and that He
may send Jesus Christ, who was preached to
you before,[a] [21]whom heaven must receive until the times of restoration of all things, which God has spoken by the mouth of all His holy
prophets since the world began. [22]For Moses
truly said to the fathers, 'The LORD *your God will raise up for you a Prophet like me from your brethren. Him you shall hear in all things, whatever He says to you.* [23]*And it shall be that every soul who will not hear that Prophet shall be utterly destroyed from among the people.'*[a]
[24]Yes, and all the prophets, from Samuel and
those who follow, as many as have spoken, have also foretold[a] these days. [25]You are sons
of the prophets, and of the covenant which God made with our fathers, saying to Abraham, '*And in your seed all the families of the earth shall be blessed.*'[a] [26]To you first, God,
having raised up His Servant Jesus, sent Him to bless you, in turning away every one *of you* from your iniquities."

PETER AND JOHN ARRESTED

4 Now as they spoke to the people, the priests, the captain of the temple, and the Sadducees came upon them, [2]being greatly

3:20 [a]NU-Text and M-Text read *Christ Jesus, who was ordained for you before.* **3:23** [a]Deuteronomy 18:15, 18, 19 **3:24** [a]NU-Text and M-Text read *proclaimed.* **3:25** [a]Genesis 22:18; 26:4; 28:14

PERSONALITY PROFILE

Spiritual Disciplines

THE EARLY CHRISTIANS: UNITED IN CHRIST

(ACTS 2:42–47)

The Lord was moving mightily! A small group of believers waited in the Upper Room for the power Jesus promised from the Holy Spirit (Acts 1:8), and the Holy Spirit came upon this group of 120 believers, who went out and told the message of salvation. After Peter's Pentecost sermon, three thousand people believed (Acts 2:41). As the believers rejoiced in their newfound faith, they worshiped and had fellowship together, "and the Lord added to the church daily those who were being saved."

The early church was powerful and purposeful, and people responded. What made this early church so vibrant? Six characteristics give some insight, for the early church had: (1) apostolic doctrine, (2) loving fellowship, (3) powerful prayer, (4) prayerful power, (5) compassion for the needy, and (6) unity.

The early church was a vibrant group of believers seeking to learn more about the faith and desiring to act out their faith in love for one another. We may long for such a fellowship—one not riddled by doctrinal infighting, opinions over church buildings and decor, or preferences of Bible versions. We cannot go back to such a fellowship, for, thankfully, the church grew and spread across the world, and each congregation then faced its own concerns, both culturally and among its individuals. Thankfully, the Bible has been made available in many languages, and we have our choice of many versions. But the truth and the Word never change. Churches are spread across the world, with different worship styles and doctrines, but most can celebrate what they have in common—what could be called the "spiritual disciplines" of the faith.

Churches that believe and teach the Bible as God's holy Word are teaching their members to love God's Word as well. The worldwide body of Christ is united by His truth, and can join together in the corporate disciplines of prayer, worship, fellowship, compassion, and witnessing. Unity comes not from agreement on every matter, but from agreement on what matters—the essentials of the faith. As we join with believers across the globe in the spiritual disciplines that build our faith, we reveal the unity and power of the body of Christ.

To Learn More: Turn to the article about spiritual disciplines on pages 1420, 1421. See also the key passage note at Daniel 10:12 on page 1121.

SPIRITUAL DISCIPLINES

Spiritual Disciplines

ED HINDSON

(Acts 2:46, 47)

Many people feel cut off from God. Many would like to know Him more intimately. The process of growing intimacy with God begins by knowing that spiritual transformation is the work of God. He alone can change the human heart, regenerate the soul, and ignite spiritual passions. By contrast, the spiritual disciplines are activities believers do in order to draw ever closer to God. These disciplines are the practical expressions of our longings for God (Ps. 42:1, 2).

In Richard Foster's classic work, *Celebration of Discipline*, he cautions that spiritual disciplines are an inward and spiritual reality. The inner attitude of the heart, writes Foster, "is far more crucial than the mechanics for coming into the reality of the spiritual life."

The connection between the concepts of discipline and discipleship is more than a linguistic similarity. Disciples are disciplined "learners" whose lives are being conformed to the life of the Master Himself. When we look at the commands Jesus gave His disciples, we see them falling into basic categories: (1) Love God; (2) deny self; (3) love others; (4) trust His Word.

These characteristics build on each other. We can't love others until we have learned to deny ourselves. We won't have a supreme devotion to God's Word until we have a supreme love for God Himself. In one of our Lord's most convicting challenges, He warned, "If anyone desires to come after Me, let him deny himself, and take up his cross daily, and follow Me" (Luke 9:23).

PUTTING GOD FIRST

In Luke 14:25–33, Jesus gave three conditions for Christian discipleship. He claimed authority over our relationships, our rights, and our riches. In each case, Jesus said one "cannot be My disciple" if he or she refuses these commands. In so doing, He reminds us of the seriousness of Christian discipleship. The earliest believers were called "disciples" long before they were called "Christians" (Acts 11:26). They received the latter designation only after they succeeded in emulating the life and character of Christ to the point that others called them Christians.

In relation to the priorities of the Christian life, Jesus said, "Seek first the kingdom of God and His righteousness" (Matt. 6:33). This is the direct contrast to the selfishness of most human beings. Even in Christian circles, a lot of selfish behavior passes as spirituality when it is not spiritual at all. Superficial piety can never replace the genuine desire to be like Christ. God and God alone must produce that desire in our lives.

FOCUSING ON THE THINGS OF GOD

One cannot read the Bible without observing the attention that is given to the spiritual disciplines of *prayer* (Mark 1:35), *fasting* (Acts 13:3), *meditation* (Psalm 1:2) and *study* (Phil. 4:8). Each of these is designed by God to draw us into personal communion with Him. They are the spiritual avenues of His grace by which He transforms our lives and makes us into what He created us to be—His dear children.

If the original disciples had to ask, "Lord, teach us to pray" (Luke 11:1), then how much more do we? Prayer, like all the spiritual disciplines, is an automatic response of God's work in the depth of our souls. But it is also a discipline that must be learned and practiced. Jesus' own disciples fell asleep in the Garden of Gethsemane when they should have been praying. "What? Could you not watch with Me one hour? Watch and pray, lest you enter into temptation. The spirit indeed is willing, but the flesh is weak" (Matt. 26:40, 41).

Jesus expected His disciples to pray and was disappointed when they didn't. He expected believers to fast, but chided them when they did it for the wrong reasons (Matt. 6:16–18). He condemned the scribes and Pharisees for not knowing the scriptures (Matt. 19:4) and urged His disciples to study the scriptures, for they spoke of Him (Luke 24:44–49).

DEVELOPING A HEART FOR GOD

The spiritual disciplines help us focus on the things of God so that we might truly worship Him. Worship is our human response to the love of God, the expression of the heart set free by His grace. Worship is the highest expression of the human soul. It draws us into the presence of God and captures our hearts and minds for Him.

Jesus said, "You shall worship the LORD your God" (Matt. 4:10). He also said, "Love the LORD your God with all your heart, with all your soul, with all your mind, and with all your strength" (Mark 12:30). Worship always precedes service. It is the holy expectancy that propels us to serve God with all our strength. We can give Him our lives only when we have truly given Him our hearts. Obedience flows from submission, which is expressed in worship.

God must get us on our knees before He can get us on our feet. Attempts to serve without worship will result in the futility of self-effort. Such vain attempts will defeat God's work in our lives rather than enhance it. He does not need us to defend Him. He can do that Himself! But He wants us to worship Him and love Him with all our heart, soul, mind, and strength. For then, and only then, will we be ready to serve Him effectively.

FURTHER MEDITATION:

Other passages to study about the issue of spiritual disciplines include:

- 1 Samuel 16:7
- Psalm 104:34
- Matthew 6:16–18
- Romans 12:1, 2
- 1 Corinthians 9:26, 27
- 2 Corinthians 10:3–6
- Ephesians 4:20–24
- Colossians 3:16, 17
- 1 Timothy 4:7–11
- Hebrews 10:24, 25

To Learn More: Turn to the key passage note on spiritual disciplines at Daniel 10:12 on page 1121. See also the personality profile of the early Christians on page 1419.

disturbed that they taught the people and preached in Jesus the resurrection from the dead. 3And they laid hands on them, and put *them* in custody until the next day, for it was already evening. 4However, many of those who heard the word believed; and the number of the men came to be about five thousand.

Addressing the Sanhedrin

5And it came to pass, on the next day, that their rulers, elders, and scribes, 6as well as Annas the high priest, Caiaphas, John, and Alexander, and as many as were of the family of the high priest, were gathered together at Jerusalem. 7And when they had set them in the midst, they asked, "By what power or by what name have you done this?"

8Then Peter, filled with the Holy Spirit, said to them, "Rulers of the people and elders of Israel: 9If we this day are judged for a good deed *done* to a helpless man, by what means he has been made well, 10let it be known to you all, and to all the people of Israel, that by the name of Jesus Christ of Nazareth, whom you crucified, whom God raised from the dead, by Him this man stands here before you whole. 11This is the '*stone which was rejected by you builders, which has become the chief cornerstone*.'[a] 12Nor is there salvation in any other, for there is no other name under heaven given among men by which we must be saved."

The Name of Jesus Forbidden

13Now when they saw the boldness of Peter and John, and perceived that they were uneducated and untrained men, they marveled. And they realized that they had been with Jesus. 14And seeing the man who had been healed standing with them, they could say nothing against it. 15But when they had commanded them to go aside out of the council, they conferred among themselves, 16saying, "What shall we do to these men? For, indeed, that a notable miracle has been done through them *is* evident to all who dwell in Jerusalem, and we cannot deny *it*. 17But so that it spreads no further among the people, let us severely threaten them, that from now on they speak to no man in this name."

18So they called them and commanded them not to speak at all nor teach in the name of Jesus. 19But Peter and John answered and said to them, "Whether it is right in the sight of God to listen to you more than to God, you judge. 20For we cannot but speak the things

4:11 [a]Psalm 118:22

SOUL NOTE

His Name Is Life *(4:12)* Jesus Christ is the Savior of the world—His is the *only* name on which people can call for salvation. Many people have difficulty believing that Jesus is the only way (see also John 14:6). But to doubt that is to doubt God's Word—for Scripture tells us, by way of the apostle Peter's sermon, that "there is no other name under heaven given among men by which we must be saved." No other religious teacher, no matter how wise or good, could die for our sins and then rise from the dead to save all who believe in Him. **Topic: Salvation**

SOUL NOTE

Praise Priority *(4:23–31)* Peter and John had been told by the religious leaders to stop teaching about Jesus. The apostles reported back to the believers, and then they all gathered to pray and to praise God for His great works. They didn't ask for the threat to be removed, but that they would be bold in spite of it. Caught up in life's daily problems, we often forget to begin our prayer time with praise and thanksgiving. We may ask God to remove our problem, but we should also ask for wisdom, guidance, and boldness to deal with it. God will provide the strength we need.
Topic: Prayer

which we have seen and heard." [21]So when they had further threatened them, they let them go, finding no way of punishing them, because of the people, since they all glorified God for what had been done. [22]For the man was over forty years old on whom this miracle of healing had been performed.

Prayer for Boldness

[23]And being let go, they went to their own *companions* and reported all that the chief priests and elders had said to them. [24]So when they heard that, they raised their voice to God with one accord and said: "Lord, You *are* God, who made heaven and earth and the sea, and all that is in them, [25]who by the mouth of Your servant David[a] have said:

'Why did the nations rage,
And the people plot vain things?
26 *The kings of the earth took their stand,*
And the rulers were gathered together
Against the LORD and against His
Christ.'[a]

[27]"For truly against Your holy Servant Jesus, whom You anointed, both Herod and Pontius Pilate, with the Gentiles and the people of Israel, were gathered together [28]to do whatever Your hand and Your purpose determined before to be done. [29]Now, Lord, look on their threats, and grant to Your servants that with all boldness they may speak Your word, [30]by stretching out Your hand to heal, and that signs and wonders may be done through the name of Your holy Servant Jesus."

[31]And when they had prayed, the place where they were assembled together was shaken; and they were all filled with the Holy Spirit, and they spoke the word of God with boldness.

Now the multitude of those who believed were of one heart and one soul; neither did anyone say that any of the things he possessed was his own, but they had all things in common.
ACTS 4:32

Sharing in All Things

[32]Now the multitude of those who believed were of one heart and one soul; neither did anyone say that any of the things he possessed was his own, but they had all things in common. [33]And with great power the apostles gave witness to the resurrection of the Lord Jesus. And great grace was upon them all. [34]Nor was there anyone among them who lacked; for all who were possessors of lands or houses sold them, and brought the proceeds of the things that were sold, [35]and laid *them* at the apostles' feet; and they distributed to each as anyone had need.

[36]And Joses,[a] who was also named Barnabas by the apostles (which is translated Son of Encouragement), a Levite of the country of Cyprus, [37]having land, sold *it,* and brought the money and laid *it* at the apostles' feet.

Lying to the Holy Spirit

5 But a certain man named Ananias, with Sapphira his wife, sold a possession. [2]And he kept back *part* of the proceeds, his wife also being aware *of it,* and brought a certain part and laid *it* at the apostles' feet. [3]But Peter said, "Ananias, why has Satan filled your heart to lie to the Holy Spirit and keep back *part* of the price of the land for yourself? [4]While it remained, was it not your own? And after it was sold, was it not in your own control? Why have you conceived this thing in your heart? You have not lied to men but to God."

[5]Then Ananias, hearing these words, fell down and breathed his last. So great fear came upon all those who heard these things. [6]And the young men arose and wrapped him up, carried *him* out, and buried *him.*

[7]Now it was about three hours later when his wife came in, not knowing what had happened. [8]And Peter answered her, "Tell me whether you sold the land for so much?"

She said, "Yes, for so much."

[9]Then Peter said to her, "How is it that you have agreed together to test the Spirit of the Lord? Look, the feet of those who have buried your husband *are* at the door, and they will carry you out." [10]Then immediately she fell down at his feet and breathed her last. And the young men came in and found her dead, and carrying *her* out,

4:25 [a]NU-Text reads *who through the Holy Spirit, by the mouth of our father, Your servant David.*
4:26 [a]Psalm 2:1, 2 **4:36** [a]NU-Text reads *Joseph.*

buried *her* by her husband. 11So great fear
came upon all the church and upon all who
heard these things.

Continuing Power in the Church

12And through the hands of the apostles
many signs and wonders were done among
the people. And they were all with one accord
in Solomon's Porch. 13Yet none of the rest
dared join them, but the people esteemed
them highly. 14And believers were increasingly added to the Lord, multitudes of both
men and women, 15so that they brought the
sick out into the streets and laid *them* on beds
and couches, that at least the shadow of Peter
passing by might fall on some of them. 16Also
a multitude gathered from the surrounding
cities to Jerusalem, bringing sick people and
those who were tormented by unclean spirits,
and they were all healed.

Imprisoned Apostles Freed

17Then the high priest rose up, and all those
who *were* with him (which is the sect of the
Sadducees), and they were filled with indignation, 18and laid their hands on the apostles
and put them in the common prison. 19But at
night an angel of the Lord opened the prison
doors and brought them out, and said, 20"Go,
stand in the temple and speak to the people all
the words of this life."
21And when they heard *that,* they entered
the temple early in the morning and taught.
But the high priest and those with him came
and called the council together, with all the elders of the children of Israel, and sent to the
prison to have them brought.

Apostles on Trial Again

22But when the officers came and did not
find them in the prison, they returned and re-

PERSONALITY PROFILE

Truth

ANANIAS—CAUGHT IN A LIE

(ACTS 5:1–11)

Some people have trouble with the truth, whether telling little "white" lies or being almost pathological in their inability to be truthful. Christians, however, base their entire faith on the God who is truth. Their lives, therefore, should be characterized by truth. God made that very clear in an incident that occurred in the early church.

Ananias and his wife, Sapphira, were among the believers in the early church. The believers were selling land and houses in order to give the money to the apostles, who then distributed it among the needy. A man named Barnabas apparently received praise for selling some land and bringing all the money from the sale to the apostles (4:32–37). Ananias and Sapphira seem to have been motivated by that praise. So they too sold a possession and brought money to the apostles. The problem was not that they did not give all the money to the apostles. It was their prerogative to bring whatever amount they wanted to. The problem was that they claimed to have brought all the money when they had kept back some of it for themselves. In short, they lied. Ananias and Sapphira conspired together to try to foist their lie on the church leadership.

The Holy Spirit revealed their lie to Peter, however. In his lie, Ananias had "not lied to men but to God," and God cannot be fooled. He *is* the truth, and He always *knows* the truth. Ananias, and later his wife, paid the ultimate price for their attempted deception. God dealt harshly with this sin because dishonesty, greed, and desire for acclaim will threaten a body of believers and undermine their witness for Christ.

Are we truthful people? We should daily examine our lives, words, actions, and motives to make sure that we are truly being honest before God and before others. Truthfulness pleases God. Even if we think we can get away with a lie—God knows the truth.

To Learn More: Turn to the article about truth on pages 1208, 1209. See also the key passage note at John 8:31–36 on page 1386.

ported, 23saying, "Indeed we found the prison shut securely, and the guards standing outside[a] before the doors; but when we opened them, we found no one inside!" 24Now when the high priest,[a] the captain of the temple, and the chief priests heard these things, they wondered what the outcome would be. 25So one came and told them, saying,[a] "Look, the men whom you put in prison are standing in the temple and teaching the people!"

26Then the captain went with the officers and brought them without violence, for they feared the people, lest they should be stoned. 27And when they had brought them, they set *them* before the council. And the high priest asked them, 28saying, "Did we not strictly command you not to teach in this name? And look, you have filled Jerusalem with your doctrine, and intend to bring this Man's blood on us!"

29But Peter and the *other* apostles answered and said: "We ought to obey God rather than men. 30The God of our fathers raised up Jesus whom you murdered by hanging on a tree. 31Him God has exalted to His right hand *to be* Prince and Savior, to give repentance to Israel and forgiveness of sins. 32And we are His witnesses to these things, and *so* also *is* the Holy Spirit whom God has given to those who obey Him."

Gamaliel's Advice

33When they heard *this,* they were furious and plotted to kill them. 34Then one in the council stood up, a Pharisee named Gamaliel, a teacher of the law held in respect by all the people, and commanded them to put the apostles outside for a little while. 35And he said to them: "Men of Israel, take heed to yourselves what you intend to do regarding these men. 36For some time ago Theudas rose up, claiming to be somebody. A number of men, about four hundred, joined him. He was slain, and all who obeyed him were scattered and came to nothing. 37After this man, Judas of Galilee rose up in the days of the census, and drew away many people after him. He also perished, and all who obeyed him were dispersed. 38And now I say to you, keep away from these men and let them alone; for if this plan or this work is of men, it will come to nothing; 39but if it is of God, you cannot overthrow it—lest you even be found to fight against God."

40And they agreed with him, and when they had called for the apostles and beaten *them,* they commanded that they should not speak in the name of Jesus, and let them go. 41So they departed from the presence of the council, rejoicing that they were counted worthy to suffer shame for His[a] name. 42And daily in the temple, and in every house, they did not cease teaching and preaching Jesus *as* the Christ.

Seven Chosen to Serve

6 Now in those days, when *the number of* the disciples was multiplying, there arose a complaint against the Hebrews by the Hellenists,[a] because their widows were neglected in the daily distribution. 2Then the twelve summoned the multitude of the disciples and said, "It is not desirable that we should leave the word of God and serve tables. 3Therefore, brethren, seek out from among you seven men of *good* reputation, full of the Holy Spirit and wisdom, whom we may appoint over this business; 4but we will give

5:23 [a]NU-Text and M-Text omit *outside.*
5:24 [a]NU-Text omits *the high priest.* **5:25** [a]NU-Text and M-Text omit *saying.* **5:41** [a]NU-Text reads *the name;* M-Text reads *the name of Jesus.*
6:1 [a]That is, Greek-speaking Jews

SOUL NOTE

God First *(5:29)* The apostles had their priorities straight. When the religious leaders demanded that they stop preaching about Jesus, the apostles answered, "We ought to obey God rather than men." People are required to obey the laws of their country, workplace, etc. Believers should honor and pray for their leaders (1 Tim. 2:1–4) and submit to the governmental authorities and laws (Rom. 13:1–7). But if a law conflicts with God's Word, believers must obey God first, trusting that He will give them strength to stand firm in their faith. **Topic: Obedience**

ourselves continually to prayer and to the
ministry of the word."
5And the saying pleased the whole multitude. And they chose Stephen, a man full
of faith and the Holy Spirit, and Philip,
Prochorus, Nicanor, Timon, Parmenas, and
Nicolas, a proselyte from Antioch, 6whom
they set before the apostles; and when they
had prayed, they laid hands on them.
7Then the word of God spread, and the
number of the disciples multiplied greatly in
Jerusalem, and a great many of the priests
were obedient to the faith.

Stephen Accused of Blasphemy

8And Stephen, full of faith[a] and power, did
great wonders and signs among the people.
9Then there arose some from what is called
the Synagogue of the Freedmen (Cyrenians,
Alexandrians, and those from Cilicia and
Asia), disputing with Stephen. 10And they
were not able to resist the wisdom and the
Spirit by which he spoke. 11Then they secretly
induced men to say, "We have heard him
speak blasphemous words against Moses and
God." 12And they stirred up the people, the elders, and the scribes; and they came upon
him, seized him, and brought *him* to the council. 13They also set up false witnesses who
said, "This man does not cease to speak
blasphemous[a] words against this holy place
and the law; 14for we have heard him say that
this Jesus of Nazareth will destroy this place
and change the customs which Moses delivered to us." 15And all who sat in the council,
looking steadfastly at him, saw his face as the
face of an angel.

Stephen's Address: The Call of Abraham

7 Then the high priest said, "Are these
things so?"
2And he said, "Brethren and fathers, listen:
The God of glory appeared to our father Abraham when he was in Mesopotamia, before he
dwelt in Haran, 3and said to him, *'Get out of
your country and from your relatives, and
come to a land that I will show you.'*[a] 4Then
he came out of the land of the Chaldeans and
dwelt in Haran. And from there, when his father was dead, He moved him to this land in
which you now dwell. 5And *God* gave him no
inheritance in it, not even *enough* to set his
foot on. But even when *Abraham* had no
child, He promised to give it to him for a possession, and to his descendants after him.
6But God spoke in this way: that his descendants would dwell in a foreign land, and that
they would bring them into bondage and oppress *them* four hundred years. 7*'And the nation to whom they will be in bondage I will
judge,'*[a] said God, *'and after that they shall
come out and serve Me in this place.'*[b] 8Then
He gave him the covenant of circumcision;
and so *Abraham* begot Isaac and circumcised
him on the eighth day; and Isaac *begot* Jacob,
and Jacob *begot* the twelve patriarchs.

The Patriarchs in Egypt

9"And the patriarchs, becoming envious,
sold Joseph into Egypt. But God was with him
10and delivered him out of all his troubles, and
gave him favor and wisdom in the presence of
Pharaoh, king of Egypt; and he made him governor over Egypt and all his house. 11Now a
famine and great trouble came over all the
land of Egypt and Canaan, and our fathers
found no sustenance. 12But when Jacob heard
that there was grain in Egypt, he sent out our
fathers first. 13And the second *time* Joseph
was made known to his brothers, and

6:8 [a]NU-Text reads *grace.* **6:13** [a]NU-Text omits *blasphemous.* **7:3** [a]Genesis 12:1 **7:7** [a]Genesis 15:14 [b]Exodus 3:12

SOUL NOTE

God's Work *(6:1–4)* The Jerusalem believers were becoming divided over culture, language, and distribution of food to widows. So the church found men to put in charge of that job. These were likely the first deacons. While their job was to do the administrative work so the apostles could focus on preaching, that did not make their work any less important. They served well. Whatever jobs we do, we should do them knowing that we serve Christ above all others (Col. 3:23, 24).
Topic: Work

Joseph's family became known to the Pharaoh. 14Then Joseph sent and called his father Jacob and all his relatives to *him*, seventy-five[a] people. 15So Jacob went down to Egypt; and he died, he and our fathers. 16And they were carried back to Shechem and laid in the tomb that Abraham bought for a sum of money from the sons of Hamor, *the father* of Shechem.

God Delivers Israel by Moses

17"But when the time of the promise drew near which God had sworn to Abraham, the people grew and multiplied in Egypt 18till another king arose who did not know Joseph. 19This man dealt treacherously with our people, and oppressed our forefathers, making them expose their babies, so that they might not live. 20At this time Moses was born, and was well pleasing to God; and he was brought up in his father's house for three months. 21But when he was set out, Pharaoh's daughter took him away and brought him up as her own son. 22And Moses was learned in all the wisdom of the Egyptians, and was mighty in words and deeds.

23"Now when he was forty years old, it came into his heart to visit his brethren, the children of Israel. 24And seeing one of *them* suffer wrong, he defended and avenged him who was oppressed, and struck down the Egyptian. 25For he supposed that his brethren would have understood that God would deliver them by his hand, but they did not understand. 26And the next day he appeared to two of them as they were fighting, and *tried to* reconcile them, saying, 'Men, you are brethren; why do you wrong one another?' 27But he who did his neighbor wrong pushed him away, saying, *'Who made you a ruler and a judge over us? 28Do you want to kill me as you did the Egyptian yesterday?'*[a] 29Then, at this saying, Moses fled and became a dweller in the land of Midian, where he had two sons.

30"And when forty years had passed, an Angel of the Lord[a] appeared to him in a flame of fire in a bush, in the wilderness of Mount Sinai. 31When Moses saw *it*, he marveled at the sight; and as he drew near to observe, the voice of the Lord came to him, 32*saying, 'I am the God of your fathers—the God of Abraham, the God of Isaac, and the God of Jacob.'*[a] And Moses trembled and dared not look. 33*Then the LORD said to him, "Take your sandals off your feet, for the place where you stand is holy ground. 34I have surely seen the oppression of My people who are in Egypt; I have heard their groaning and have come down to deliver them. And now come, I will send you to Egypt."'*[a]

35"This Moses whom they rejected, saying, *'Who made you a ruler and a judge?'*[a] is the one God sent *to be* a ruler and a deliverer by the hand of the Angel who appeared to him in the bush. 36He brought them out, after he had shown wonders and signs in the land of Egypt, and in the Red Sea, and in the wilderness forty years.

Israel Rebels Against God

37"This is that Moses who said to the children of Israel,[a] *'The LORD your God will raise up for you a Prophet like me from your brethren. Him you shall hear.'*[b]

38"This is he who was in the congregation in the wilderness with the Angel who spoke to him on Mount Sinai, and *with* our fathers, the one who received the living oracles to give to us, 39whom our fathers would not obey, but rejected. And in their hearts they turned back to Egypt, 40saying to Aaron, *'Make us gods to go before us; as for this Moses who brought us out of the land of Egypt, we do not know what has become of him.'*[a] 41And they made a calf in those days, offered sacrifices to the idol, and rejoiced in the works of their own hands. 42Then God turned and gave them up to worship the host of heaven, as it is written in the book of the Prophets:

'Did you offer Me slaughtered animals
and sacrifices during forty years in the wilderness,
O house of Israel?
43 *You also took up the tabernacle of Moloch,*
And the star of your god Remphan,
Images which you made to worship;
And I will carry you away beyond Babylon.'[a]

7:14 [a]Or *seventy* (compare Exodus 1:5)
7:28 [a]Exodus 2:14 **7:30** [a]NU-Text omits *of the Lord.* **7:32** [a]Exodus 3:6, 15 **7:34** [a]Exodus 3:5, 7, 8, 10 **7:35** [a]Exodus 2:14
7:37 [a]Deuteronomy 18:15 [b]NU-Text and M-Text omit *Him you shall hear.* **7:40** [a]Exodus 32:1, 23
7:43 [a]Amos 5:25–27

GOD'S TRUE TABERNACLE

44“Our fathers had the tabernacle of witness
in the wilderness, as He appointed, instructing Moses to make it according to the pattern
that he had seen, 45which our fathers, having
received it in turn, also brought with Joshua
into the land possessed by the Gentiles, whom
God drove out before the face of our fathers
until the days of David, 46who found favor before God and asked to find a dwelling for the
God of Jacob. 47But Solomon built Him a
house.

48“However, the Most High does not dwell
in temples made with hands, as the prophet
says:

49 *‘Heaven is My throne,*
And earth is My footstool.
What house will you build for Me? says
the LORD*,*
Or what is the place of My rest?
50 *Has My hand not made all these things?’*[a]

ISRAEL RESISTS THE HOLY SPIRIT

51“*You* stiff-necked and uncircumcised in
heart and ears! You always resist the Holy
Spirit; as your fathers *did,* so *do* you. 52Which
of the prophets did your fathers not persecute?
And they killed those who foretold the coming
of the Just One, of whom you now have become the betrayers and murderers, 53who
have received the law by the direction of angels and have not kept *it.*”

STEPHEN THE MARTYR

54When they heard these things they were
cut to the heart, and they gnashed at him with
their teeth. 55But he, being full of the Holy
Spirit, gazed into heaven and saw the glory of
God, and Jesus standing at the right hand of
God, 56and said, “Look! I see the heavens
opened and the Son of Man standing at the
right hand of God!”

57Then they cried out with a loud voice,
stopped their ears, and ran at him with one accord; 58and they cast *him* out of the city and
stoned *him.* And the witnesses laid down their
clothes at the feet of a young man named
Saul. 59And they stoned Stephen as he was
calling on *God* and saying, “Lord Jesus, receive my spirit.” 60Then he knelt down and
cried out with a loud voice, “Lord, do not
charge them with this sin.” And when he had
said this, he fell asleep.

SAUL PERSECUTES THE CHURCH

8 Now Saul was consenting to his death.
At that time a great persecution arose
against the church which was at Jerusalem;
and they were all scattered throughout the regions of Judea and Samaria, except the apostles. 2And devout men carried Stephen *to his*
burial, and made great lamentation over him.

3As for Saul, he made havoc of the church,
entering every house, and dragging off men
and women, committing *them* to prison.

CHRIST IS PREACHED IN SAMARIA

4Therefore those who were scattered went
everywhere preaching the word. 5Then Philip
went down to the[a] city of Samaria and
preached Christ to them. 6And the multitudes
with one accord heeded the things spoken by
Philip, hearing and seeing the miracles which
he did. 7For unclean spirits, crying with a loud
voice, came out of many who were possessed;
and many who were paralyzed and lame were
healed. 8And there was great joy in that city.

THE SORCERER'S PROFESSION OF FAITH

9But there was a certain man called Simon,
who previously practiced sorcery in the city
and astonished the people of Samaria, claiming
that he was someone great, 10to whom they all
gave heed, from the least to the greatest, saying, “This man is the great power of God.”
11And they heeded him because he had astonished them with his sorceries for a long time.
12But when they believed Philip as he preached
the things concerning the kingdom of God and
the name of Jesus Christ, both men and wom-
en were baptized. 13Then Simon himself also
believed; and when he was baptized he continued with Philip, and was amazed, seeing the
miracles and signs which were done.

THE SORCERER'S SIN

14Now when the apostles who were at Jerusalem heard that Samaria had received the
word of God, they sent Peter and John to them,
15who, when they had come down, prayed for
them that they might receive the Holy Spirit.
16For as yet He had fallen upon none of them.
They had only been baptized in the name of
the Lord Jesus. 17Then they laid hands on
them, and they received the Holy Spirit.

18And when Simon saw that through the lay-

7:50 [a]Isaiah 66:1, 2 **8:5** [a]Or *a*

ing on of the apostles' hands the Holy Spirit
was given, he offered them money, [19]saying,
"Give me this power also, that anyone on
whom I lay hands may receive the Holy Spirit."
[20]But Peter said to him, "Your money perish
with you, because you thought that the gift of
God could be purchased with money! [21]You
have neither part nor portion in this matter, for
your heart is not right in the sight of God. [22]Re-
pent therefore of this your wickedness, and
pray God if perhaps the thought of your heart
may be forgiven you. [23]For I see that you are
poisoned by bitterness and bound by iniquity."
[24]Then Simon answered and said, "Pray to
the Lord for me, that none of the things which
you have spoken may come upon me."
[25]So when they had testified and preached
the word of the Lord, they returned to Jerusalem, preaching the gospel in many villages of
the Samaritans.

Christ Is Preached to an Ethiopian

[26]Now an angel of the Lord spoke to Philip,
saying, "Arise and go toward the south along
the road which goes down from Jerusalem to
Gaza." This is desert. [27]So he arose and went.
And behold, a man of Ethiopia, a eunuch of
great authority under Candace the queen of
the Ethiopians, who had charge of all her treasury, and had come to Jerusalem to worship,
[28]was returning. And sitting in his chariot, he
was reading Isaiah the prophet. [29]Then the
Spirit said to Philip, "Go near and overtake
this chariot."

PERSONALITY PROFILE

Cults

SIMON THE SORCERER—THE TRAP OF FALSE RELIGION

(ACTS 8:9)

Many of the people who first heard the gospel of Jesus Christ were very religious. Strange pagan religions were plentiful. Cults whose power relied on demonic forces held many people in spiritual bondage. When the Gentiles began to believe in Jesus by the thousands, they brought with them an understanding about God that lacked the insights of the Jewish faith. Among these pagan believers was a cult leader named Simon the Sorcerer.

Philip the apostle traveled through Samaria as a one-man gospel army. He spoke and acted with God's power. The current popular religious figure was Simon, who had impressed people with his sorcery for some time. The term "sorcery" may have referred to Simon's practice of magic, use of drugs, or involvement in the occult. But even he believed Philip's message and was baptized.

When the other apostles visited and laid hands on the new believers, they received the Holy Spirit. Scripture does not report that Simon allowed the apostles to lay hands on him. Instead, he offered money in exchange for the power to lay hands on others and produce the effects of the Holy Spirit's presence.

Simon's interest in following Christ apparently revolved around what might be best for Simon's popularity. He planned to add Christ's power to his other "powers." Peter confronted Simon's ignorance and attitude, and challenged him to repent. Peter's words frightened Simon enough for him to ask for prayer, but he did not repent.

Simon represents those in every generation who think that spiritual power is simply another area of influence they can control. These self-centered people often form religious groups called cults. Cults tend to lure people into believing they can have some kind of spiritual edge or superiority over others. They are often thinly veiled efforts by evil to further corrupt humanity. Peter's words to Simon apply to cultists today, since their "heart is not right in the sight of God" (Acts 8:21). The use of Christian words and practices does not mean that a group or person is faithful to Christ.

To Learn More: Turn to the article about cults on pages 1552, 1553. See also the key passage note at Titus 1:16 on page 1614.

[30]So Philip ran to him, and heard him reading the prophet Isaiah, and said, "Do you understand what you are reading?"
[31]And he said, "How can I, unless someone
guides me?" And he asked Philip to come up
and sit with him. [32]The place in the Scripture
which he read was this:

"He was led as a sheep to the slaughter;
And as a lamb before its shearer is silent,

SOUL NOTE

Better, Not Bitter *(8:20–24)* Peter pointed at Simon's wickedness and need for repentance. "You are poisoned by bitterness and bound by iniquity," Peter said. Simon responded, "Pray to the Lord for me." Bitterness is indeed like a poison, eating away at a person's soft heart, turning it into stone—hard and unyielding. Simon first had to deal with his bitterness and sin. People poisoned by bitterness, whatever the cause, can be touched by God's grace, and so we pray for them.
Topic: Bitterness

PERSONALITY PROFILE

Knowing God

THE ETHIOPIAN EUNUCH'S SEARCH FOR GOD

(ACTS 8:26–38)

Sometimes good reading material can make all the difference on a long trip. This man from Ethiopia, called a "eunuch" (the term may simply have been a government title), was on his way back from Jerusalem and spent his time reading.

That may not seem so unusual, except that in these days, books were hard to come by. For a person to have a scroll of Isaiah meant a certain degree both of wealth and position. The Bible says that this man was "a eunuch of great authority under Candace the queen of the Ethiopians, who had charge of all her treasury" (Acts 8:27). Because he had been worshiping in Jerusalem, we can assume that he was a Gentile convert to Judaism and had traveled there for one of the great festivals.

In the meantime, Philip, one of the deacons in the Jerusalem church (Acts 6:3–5), had been having a great ministry in Samaria. But then God sent him on a special assignment—out to a desert road. It was there that God placed the Ethiopian and Philip for a divine appointment.

Philip approached the chariot and discovered the man reading from the prophet Isaiah, chapter 53. The prophet was describing the Suffering Servant, the Messiah. The man did not understand what Isaiah was describing, but Philip knew. As Philip explained about Jesus, suddenly the pieces fell into place. "Then Philip opened his mouth, and beginning at this Scripture, preached Jesus to him" (Acts 8:35). The Ethiopian believed, was baptized right then and there, and went back to his home with a message of salvation!

Sometimes we find God in the strangest places. Sometimes divine appointments come when we least expect one. As people search for God, you may be the one whom God sends to explain a passage, offer a word of truth or encouragement, or simply be a friend. We must be open for those appointments. God may want to use us to make Himself known to someone!

To Learn More: Turn to the article about knowing God on pages 164, 165. See also the key passage note at Leviticus 26:9–13 on page 162.

So He opened not His mouth.
33 *In His humiliation His justice was taken*
away,
And who will declare His generation?
For His life is taken from the earth."[a]

34So the eunuch answered Philip and said,
"I ask you, of whom does the prophet say this,
of himself or of some other man?" 35Then
Philip opened his mouth, and beginning at
this Scripture, preached Jesus to him. 36Now
as they went down the road, they came to
some water. And the eunuch said, "See, *here is*
water. What hinders me from being baptized?"
37Then Philip said, "If you believe with all
your heart, you may."
And he answered and said, "I believe that
Jesus Christ is the Son of God."[a]
38So he commanded the chariot to stand
still. And both Philip and the eunuch went
down into the water, and he baptized him.
39Now when they came up out of the water,
the Spirit of the Lord caught Philip away, so
that the eunuch saw him no more; and he
went on his way rejoicing. 40But Philip was
found at Azotus. And passing through, he
preached in all the cities till he came to
Caesarea.

The Damascus Road: Saul Converted

9 Then Saul, still breathing threats and
murder against the disciples of the Lord,
went to the high priest 2and asked letters from
him to the synagogues of Damascus, so that if
he found any who were of the Way, whether
men or women, he might bring them bound to
Jerusalem.
3As he journeyed he came near Damascus,
and suddenly a light shone around him from
heaven. 4Then he fell to the ground, and heard
a voice saying to him, "Saul, Saul, why are
you persecuting Me?"
5And he said, "Who are You, Lord?"
Then the Lord said, "I am Jesus, whom you
are persecuting.[a] It *is* hard for you to kick
against the goads."
6So he, trembling and astonished, said,
"Lord, what do You want me to do?"
Then the Lord *said* to him, "Arise and go
into the city, and you will be told what you
must do."
7And the men who journeyed with him
stood speechless, hearing a voice but seeing
no one. 8Then Saul arose from the ground,
and when his eyes were opened he saw no
one. But they led him by the hand and brought
him into Damascus. 9And he was three days
without sight, and neither ate nor drank.

Ananias Baptizes Saul

10Now there was a certain disciple at Damascus named Ananias; and to him the Lord
said in a vision, "Ananias."
And he said, "Here I am, Lord."
11So the Lord *said* to him, "Arise and go to
the street called Straight, and inquire at the
house of Judas for *one* called Saul of Tarsus,
for behold, he is praying. 12And in a vision he
has seen a man named Ananias coming in and
putting *his* hand on him, so that he might receive his sight."
13Then Ananias answered, "Lord, I have
heard from many about this man, how much
harm he has done to Your saints in Jerusalem.
14And here he has authority from the chief
priests to bind all who call on Your name."
15But the Lord said to him, "Go, for he is a
chosen vessel of Mine to bear My name before
Gentiles, kings, and the children of Israel.
16For I will show him how many things he
must suffer for My name's sake."
17And Ananias went his way and entered
the house; and laying his hands on him he
said, "Brother Saul, the Lord Jesus,[a] who appeared to you on the road as you came, has
sent me that you may receive your sight and
be filled with the Holy Spirit." 18Immediately
there fell from his eyes *something* like scales,
and he received his sight at once; and he arose
and was baptized.
19So when he had received food, he was
strengthened. Then Saul spent some days
with the disciples at Damascus.

Saul Preaches Christ

20Immediately he preached the Christ[a] in
the synagogues, that He is the Son of God.
21Then all who heard were amazed, and
said, "Is this not he who destroyed those
who called on this name in Jerusalem, and
has come here for that purpose, so that he

8:33 [a]Isaiah 53:7, 8 **8:37** [a]NU-Text and M-Text omit this verse. It is found in Western texts, including the Latin tradition. **9:5** [a]NU-Text and M-Text omit the last sentence of verse 5 and begin verse 6 with *But arise and go.* **9:17** [a]M-Text omits *Jesus.* **9:20** [a]NU-Text reads *Jesus.*

might bring them bound to the chief priests?"
[22]But Saul increased all the more in strength, and confounded the Jews who dwelt in Damascus, proving that this *Jesus* is the Christ.

Saul Escapes Death

[23]Now after many days were past, the Jews plotted to kill him. [24]But their plot became known to Saul. And they watched the gates day and night, to kill him. [25]Then the disciples took him by night and let *him* down through the wall in a large basket.

Saul at Jerusalem

[26]And when Saul had come to Jerusalem, he tried to join the disciples; but they were all afraid of him, and did not believe that he was a disciple. [27]But Barnabas took him and brought *him* to the apostles. And he declared to them how he had seen the Lord on the road, and that He had spoken to him, and how he had preached boldly at Damascus in the name of Jesus. [28]So he was with them at Jerusalem, coming in and going out. [29]And he spoke boldly in the name of the Lord Jesus and disputed against the Hellenists, but they attempted to kill him. [30]When the brethren found out, they brought him down to Caesarea and sent him out to Tarsus.

The Church Prospers

[31]Then the churches[a] throughout all Judea, Galilee, and Samaria had peace and were edified. And walking in the fear of the Lord and in the comfort of the Holy Spirit, they were multiplied.

Aeneas Healed

[32]Now it came to pass, as Peter went through all *parts of the country,* that he also

9:31 [a]NU-Text reads *church . . . was edified.*

PERSONALITY PROFILE

Change/ Maturity

PAUL'S CHANGE FOR THE BETTER

(ACTS 9:22)

Saul (who later was called Paul) probably thought he had it made. As a young and zealous Pharisee, he knew God's Word thoroughly. He had studied under a well-known Jewish rabbi, Gamaliel, and had apparently learned his lessons well. So well, in fact, that when the sect of the Nazarene—people who believed that Jesus was the Messiah—began to grow and flourish, Saul did all he could to stop it. Along with many of his fellow Pharisees, Saul thought that Jesus of Nazareth was a deceived man, certainly not the promised Messiah. Therefore, Jews who became Christians were considered traitors and deserved to be rounded up, locked up, and even killed.

That all changed one day on the road to Damascus. Saul was on his way to find and arrest more Christians who had fled from Jerusalem. On the road that day, Saul met Christ and was never the same again. Paul's early training took on a whole new aspect. The Scriptures he had so diligently studied opened up with a brand-new understanding. He saw Christ throughout God's Word, and he saw Him as the fulfillment of the prophecies.

It would be correct to say that Paul changed. Yet he merely made the logical move from being a Jew to accepting the Messiah of Israel and becoming a Christian. His belief system found its completion in Christ. As Paul restudied the Scriptures, God opened his mind to see Jesus Christ as the fulfillment of all of God's promises.

As people come to Christ, many find Him to be the logical answer to their deepest questions. Others are surprised by who He is and what He has done for them. God has no set pattern or time frame for changing people's lives with His presence. Some will be convinced immediately; others will take more time; some will be slow to change. But we can know for sure that when Christ enters people's lives, they will never be the same!

To Learn More: Turn to the article about change/maturity on pages 1526, 1527. See also the key passage note at Ephesians 4:22–24 on page 1554.

came down to the saints who dwelt in Lydda. 33There he found a certain man named Aeneas, who had been bedridden eight years and was paralyzed. 34And Peter said to him, "Aeneas, Jesus the Christ heals you. Arise and make your bed." Then he arose immediately. 35So all who dwelt at Lydda and Sharon saw him and turned to the Lord.

Dorcas Restored to Life

36At Joppa there was a certain disciple named Tabitha, which is translated Dorcas. This woman was full of good works and charitable deeds which she did. 37But it happened in those days that she became sick and died. When they had washed her, they laid *her* in an upper room. 38And since Lydda was near Joppa, and the disciples had heard that Peter was there, they sent two men to him, imploring *him* not to delay in coming to them. 39Then Peter arose and went with them. When he had come, they brought *him* to the upper room. And all the widows stood by him weeping, showing the tunics and garments which Dorcas had made while she was with them. 40But Peter put them all out, and knelt down and prayed. And turning to the body he said, "Tabitha, arise." And she opened her eyes, and when she saw Peter she sat up. 41Then he gave her *his* hand and lifted her up; and when he had called the saints and widows, he presented her alive. 42And it became known throughout all Joppa, and many believed on the Lord. 43So it was that he stayed many days in Joppa with Simon, a tanner.

Cornelius Sends a Delegation

10 There was a certain man in Caesarea called Cornelius, a centurion of what was called the Italian Regiment, 2a devout *man* and one who feared God with all his household, who gave alms generously to the people, and prayed to God always. 3About the ninth hour of the day he saw clearly in a vision an angel of God coming in and saying to him, "Cornelius!"

4And when he observed him, he was afraid, and said, "What is it, lord?"

So he said to him, "Your prayers and your alms have come up for a memorial before God. 5Now send men to Joppa, and send for Simon whose surname is Peter. 6He is lodging with Simon, a tanner, whose house is by the sea.[a] He will tell you what you must do." 7And when the angel who spoke to him had departed, Cornelius called two of his household servants and a devout soldier from among those who waited on him continually. 8So when he had explained all *these* things to them, he sent them to Joppa.

Peter's Vision

9The next day, as they went on their journey and drew near the city, Peter went up on the housetop to pray, about the sixth hour. 10Then he became very hungry and wanted to eat; but while they made ready, he fell into a trance 11and saw heaven opened and an object like a great sheet bound at the four corners, descending to him and let down to the earth. 12In it were all kinds of four-footed animals of the earth, wild beasts, creeping things, and birds of the air. 13And a voice came to him, "Rise, Peter; kill and eat."

14But Peter said, "Not so, Lord! For I have never eaten anything common or unclean."

15And a voice *spoke* to him again the second time, "What God has cleansed you must not call common." 16This was done three times. And the object was taken up into heaven again.

10:6 [a]NU-Text and M-Text omit the last sentence of this verse.

SOUL NOTE

A Work of Heart *(9:26, 27)* No wonder the believers in Jerusalem were afraid of Paul—they knew the terror he had inflicted on the church (9:1, 2). His alleged conversion may have seemed like a sneaky way to find them out. When Barnabas went with Paul and verified his story, however, the believers accepted Paul as a brother in Christ. Barnabas, whose name means "Son of Encouragement" (4:36), lived up to his name by his positive attitude. Fellow believers need encouragement (1 Thess. 3:2–5). What can you do to be a "Barnabas" toward others? **Topic: Attitudes**

SUMMONED TO CAESAREA

[17]Now while Peter wondered within himself
what this vision which he had seen meant, behold, the men who had been sent from Cornelius had made inquiry for Simon's house,
and stood before the gate. [18]And they called
and asked whether Simon, whose surname
was Peter, was lodging there.
[19]While Peter thought about the vision, the
Spirit said to him, "Behold, three men are
seeking you. [20]Arise therefore, go down and
go with them, doubting nothing; for I have
sent them."
[21]Then Peter went down to the men who
had been sent to him from Cornelius,[a] and
said, "Yes, I am he whom you seek. For what
reason have you come?"
[22]And they said, "Cornelius *the* centurion, a
just man, one who fears God and has a good
reputation among all the nation of the Jews,
was divinely instructed by a holy angel to
summon you to his house, and to hear words
from you." [23]Then he invited them in and
lodged *them.*
On the next day Peter went away with them,
and some brethren from Joppa accompanied
him.

PETER MEETS CORNELIUS

[24]And the following day they entered Caesarea. Now Cornelius was waiting for them, and
had called together his relatives and close
friends. [25]As Peter was coming in, Cornelius
met him and fell down at his feet and worshiped *him.* [26]But Peter lifted him up, saying,
"Stand up; I myself am also a man." [27]And as
he talked with him, he went in and found
many who had come together. [28]Then he said
to them, "You know how unlawful it is for a
Jewish man to keep company with or go to
one of another nation. But God has shown me
that I should not call any man common or unclean. [29]Therefore I came without objection as
soon as I was sent for. I ask, then, for what
reason have you sent for me?"
[30]So Cornelius said, "Four days ago I was
fasting until this hour; and at the ninth hour[a] I
prayed in my house, and behold, a man stood
before me in bright clothing, [31]and said, 'Cornelius, your prayer has been heard, and your
alms are remembered in the sight of God.
[32]Send therefore to Joppa and call Simon here,
whose surname is Peter. He is lodging in the
house of Simon, a tanner, by the sea.[a] When
he comes, he will speak to you.' [33]So I sent to
you immediately, and you have done well to
come. Now therefore, we are all present before God, to hear all the things commanded
you by God."

PREACHING TO CORNELIUS' HOUSEHOLD

[34]Then Peter opened *his* mouth and said:
"In truth I perceive that God shows no partiality. [35]But in every nation whoever fears Him
and works righteousness is accepted by Him.
[36]The word which *God* sent to the children of
Israel, preaching peace through Jesus Christ—
He is Lord of all—[37]that word you know,
which was proclaimed throughout all Judea,
and began from Galilee after the baptism
which John preached: [38]how God anointed
Jesus of Nazareth with the Holy Spirit and
with power, who went about doing good and
healing all who were oppressed by the devil,
for God was with Him. [39]And we are witnesses
of all things which He did both in the land of

10:21 [a]NU-Text and M-Text omit *who had been sent to him from Cornelius.* **10:30** [a]NU-Text reads *Four days ago to this hour, at the ninth hour.* **10:32** [a]NU-Text omits the last sentence of this verse.

SOUL NOTE

No Barriers *(10:28)* At this point in the early church, it was hard for Jewish believers to comprehend that Gentiles might also become Christians. Through a vision, God revealed to Peter that he must take the Good News to Cornelius, a Gentile (10:19, 20). At this critical time in the growth of the early church, God made it clear that the Good News would be for everyone. Today, we must not allow any prejudice—concerning such things as race, language, economic status, education, or geography—to keep us from sharing the message of salvation with the world.
Topic: Prejudice

the Jews and in Jerusalem, whom they[a] killed by hanging on a tree. [40]Him God raised up on the third day, and showed Him openly, [41]not to all the people, but to witnesses chosen before by God, *even* to us who ate and drank with Him after He arose from the dead. [42]And He commanded us to preach to the people, and to testify that it is He who was ordained by God *to be* Judge of the living and the dead. [43]To Him all the prophets witness that, through His name, whoever believes in Him will receive remission of sins."

The Holy Spirit Falls on the Gentiles

[44]While Peter was still speaking these words, the Holy Spirit fell upon all those who heard the word. [45]And those of the circumcision who believed were astonished, as many as came with Peter, because the gift of the Holy Spirit had been poured out on the Gentiles also. [46]For they heard them speak with tongues and magnify God.

Then Peter answered, [47]"Can anyone forbid water, that these should not be baptized who have received the Holy Spirit just as we *have?*" [48]And he commanded them to be baptized in the name of the Lord. Then they asked him to stay a few days.

Peter Defends God's Grace

11 Now the apostles and brethren who were in Judea heard that the Gentiles had also received the word of God. [2]And when Peter came up to Jerusalem, those of the circumcision contended with him, [3]saying, "You went in to uncircumcised men and ate with them!"

[4]But Peter explained *it* to them in order from the beginning, saying: [5]"I was in the city of Joppa praying; and in a trance I saw a vision, an object descending like a great sheet, let down from heaven by four corners; and it came to me. [6]When I observed it intently and considered, I saw four-footed animals of the earth, wild beasts, creeping things, and birds of the air. [7]And I heard a voice saying to me, 'Rise, Peter; kill and eat.' [8]But I said, 'Not so, Lord! For nothing common or unclean has at any time entered my mouth.' [9]But the voice answered me again from heaven, 'What God has cleansed you must not call common.' [10]Now this was done three times, and all were drawn up again into heaven. [11]At that very moment, three men stood before the house where I was, having been sent to me from Caesarea. [12]Then the Spirit told me to go with them, doubting nothing. Moreover these six brethren accompanied me, and we entered the man's house. [13]And he told us how he had seen an angel standing in his house, who said to him, 'Send men to Joppa, and call for Simon whose surname is Peter, [14]who will tell you words by which you and all your household will be saved.' [15]And as I began to speak, the Holy Spirit fell upon them, as upon us at the beginning. [16]Then I remembered the word of the Lord, how He said, 'John indeed baptized with water, but you shall be baptized with the Holy Spirit.' [17]If therefore God gave them the same gift as *He gave* us when we believed on the Lord Jesus Christ, who was I that I could withstand God?"

[18]When they heard these things they became silent; and they glorified God, saying, "Then God has also granted to the Gentiles repentance to life."

Barnabas and Saul at Antioch

[19]Now those who were scattered after the persecution that arose over Stephen traveled as far as Phoenicia, Cyprus, and Antioch, preaching the word to no one but the Jews only. [20]But some of them were men from Cyprus and Cyrene, who, when they had come to Antioch, spoke to the Hellenists, preaching the Lord Jesus. [21]And the hand of the Lord was with them, and a great number believed and turned to the Lord.

[22]Then news of these things came to the ears of the church in Jerusalem, and they sent out Barnabas to go as far as Antioch. [23]When he came and had seen the grace of God, he was glad, and encouraged them all that with purpose of heart they should continue with the Lord. [24]For he was a good man, full of the Holy Spirit and of faith. And a great many people were added to the Lord.

[25]Then Barnabas departed for Tarsus to seek Saul. [26]And when he had found him, he brought him to Antioch. So it was that for a whole year they assembled with the church and taught a great many people. And the disciples were first called Christians in Antioch.

Relief to Judea

[27]And in these days prophets came from Jerusalem to Antioch. [28]Then one of them,

---

10:39 [a]NU-Text and M-Text add *also.*

named Agabus, stood up and showed by the Spirit that there was going to be a great famine throughout all the world, which also happened in the days of Claudius Caesar. [29]Then the disciples, each according to his ability, determined to send relief to the brethren dwelling in Judea. [30]This they also did, and sent it to the elders by the hands of Barnabas and Saul.

Herod's Violence to the Church

12 Now about that time Herod the king stretched out *his* hand to harass some from the church. [2]Then he killed James the brother of John with the sword. [3]And because he saw that it pleased the Jews, he proceeded further to seize Peter also. Now it was *during* the Days of Unleavened Bread. [4]So when he had arrested him, he put *him* in prison, and delivered *him* to four squads of soldiers to keep him, intending to bring him before the people after Passover.

Peter Freed from Prison

[5]Peter was therefore kept in prison, but constant[a] prayer was offered to God for him by the church. [6]And when Herod was about to bring him out, that night Peter was sleeping, bound with two chains between two soldiers; and the guards before the door were keeping the prison. [7]Now behold, an angel of the Lord stood by *him*, and a light shone in the prison; and he struck Peter on the side and raised him up, saying, "Arise quickly!" And his chains fell off *his* hands. [8]Then the angel said to him, "Gird yourself and tie on your sandals"; and so he did. And he said to him, "Put on your garment and follow me." [9]So he went out and followed him, and did not know that what was done by the angel was real, but thought he was seeing a vision. [10]When they were past the first and the second guard posts, they came to the iron gate that leads to the city, which opened to them of its own accord; and they went out and went down one street, and immediately the angel departed from him.

[11]And when Peter had come to himself, he said, "Now I know for certain that the Lord has sent His angel, and has delivered me from the hand of Herod and *from* all the expectation of the Jewish people."

[12]So, when he had considered *this*, he came to the house of Mary, the mother of John whose surname was Mark, where many were gathered together praying. [13]And as Peter knocked at the door of the gate, a girl named Rhoda came to answer. [14]When she recognized Peter's voice, because of *her* gladness she did not open the gate, but ran in and announced that Peter stood before the gate. [15]But they said to her, "You are beside yourself!" Yet she kept insisting that it was so. So they said, "It is his angel."

[16]Now Peter continued knocking; and when they opened *the door* and saw him, they were astonished. [17]But motioning to them with his hand to keep silent, he declared to them how the Lord had brought him out of the prison. And he said, "Go, tell these things to James and to the brethren." And he departed and went to another place.

[18]Then, as soon as it was day, there was no small stir among the soldiers about what had become of Peter. [19]But when Herod had searched for him and not found him, he examined the guards and commanded that *they* should be put to death.

And he went down from Judea to Caesarea, and stayed *there*.

Herod's Violent Death

[20]Now Herod had been very angry with the people of Tyre and Sidon; but they came to him with one accord, and having made Blas-

12:5 [a]NU-Text reads *constantly* (or *earnestly*).

SOUL NOTE

A Powerful Force *(12:5)* Intercessory prayer—prayer on behalf of others—is a powerful force. When Peter was in prison, believers were praying for his safety. Herod had planned to execute Peter, but God thwarted those plans in response to prayer. When we pray for others, we always pray for the best possible outcome, but we also pray for God's will to be done. Prayer makes a difference, so we know we can pray often and with confidence. **Topic: Prayer**

tus the king's personal aide their friend, they asked for peace, because their country was supplied with food by the king's *country.*

[21]So on a set day Herod, arrayed in royal apparel, sat on his throne and gave an oration to them. [22]And the people kept shouting, "The voice of a god and not of a man!" [23]Then immediately an angel of the Lord struck him, because he did not give glory to God. And he was eaten by worms and died.

[24]But the word of God grew and multiplied.

Barnabas and Saul Appointed

[25]And Barnabas and Saul returned from[a] Jerusalem when they had fulfilled *their* ministry, and they also took with them John whose surname was Mark.

13 Now in the church that was at Antioch there were certain prophets and teachers: Barnabas, Simeon who was called Niger, Lucius of Cyrene, Manaen who had been brought up with Herod the tetrarch, and Saul. [2]As they ministered to the Lord and fasted, the Holy Spirit said, "Now separate to Me Barnabas and Saul for the work to which I have called them." [3]Then, having fasted and prayed, and laid hands on them, they sent *them* away.

Preaching in Cyprus

[4]So, being sent out by the Holy Spirit, they went down to Seleucia, and from there they sailed to Cyprus. [5]And when they arrived in Salamis, they preached the word of God in the synagogues of the Jews. They also had John as *their* assistant.

[6]Now when they had gone through the island[a] to Paphos, they found a certain sorcerer, a false prophet, a Jew whose name *was* Bar-Jesus, [7]who was with the proconsul, Sergius Paulus, an intelligent man. This man called for Barnabas and Saul and sought to hear the word of God. [8]But Elymas the sorcerer (for so his name is translated) withstood them, seeking to turn the proconsul away from the faith. [9]Then Saul, who also *is called* Paul, filled with the Holy Spirit, looked intently at him [10]and said, "O full of all deceit and all fraud, *you* son of the devil, *you* enemy of all righteousness, will you not cease perverting the straight ways of the Lord? [11]And now, indeed, the hand of the Lord *is* upon you, and you shall be blind, not seeing the sun for a time."

And immediately a dark mist fell on him, and he went around seeking someone to lead him by the hand. [12]Then the proconsul believed, when he saw what had been done, being astonished at the teaching of the Lord.

At Antioch in Pisidia

[13]Now when Paul and his party set sail from Paphos, they came to Perga in Pamphylia; and John, departing from them, returned to Jerusalem. [14]But when they departed from Perga, they came to Antioch in Pisidia, and went into the synagogue on the Sabbath day and sat down. [15]And after the reading of the Law and the Prophets, the rulers of the synagogue sent to them, saying, "Men *and* brethren, if you have any word of exhortation for the people, say on."

[16]Then Paul stood up, and motioning with *his* hand said, "Men of Israel, and you who fear God, listen: [17]The God of this people Israel[a] chose our fathers, and exalted the people when they dwelt as strangers in the land of Egypt, and with an uplifted arm He brought them out of it. [18]Now for a time of about forty years He put up with their ways in the wilderness. [19]And when He had destroyed seven nations in the land of Canaan, He distributed their land to them by allotment.

[20]"After that He gave *them* judges for about four hundred and fifty years, until Samuel the prophet. [21]And afterward they asked for a king; so God gave them Saul the son of Kish, a man of the tribe of Benjamin, for forty years. [22]And when He had removed him, He raised up for them David as king, to whom also He gave testimony and said, '*I have found David*[a] *the son* of Jesse, *a man after My own heart,* who will do all My will.'[b] [23]From this man's seed, according to *the* promise, God raised up for Israel a Savior—Jesus—[a] [24]after John had first preached, before His coming, the baptism of repentance to all the people of Israel. [25]And as John was finishing his course, he said, 'Who do you think I am? I am not *He.* But behold, there comes One after me, the sandals of whose feet I am not worthy to loose.'

[26]"Men *and* brethren, sons of the family of Abraham, and those among you who fear God, to you the word of this salvation has

---

12:25 [a]NU-Text and M-Text read *to.* **13:6** [a]NU-Text reads *the whole island.* **13:17** [a]M-Text omits *Israel.* **13:22** [a]Psalm 89:20 [b]1 Samuel 13:14 **13:23** [a]M-Text reads *for Israel salvation.*

been sent. 27 For those who dwell in Jerusalem, and their rulers, because they did not
know Him, nor even the voices of the Prophets which are read every Sabbath, have fulfilled *them* in condemning *Him*. 28 And though
they found no cause for death *in Him*, they
asked Pilate that He should be put to death.
29 Now when they had fulfilled all that was
written concerning Him, they took *Him* down
from the tree and laid *Him* in a tomb. 30 But
God raised Him from the dead. 31 He was seen
for many days by those who came up with
Him from Galilee to Jerusalem, who are His
witnesses to the people. 32 And we declare to
you glad tidings—that promise which was
made to the fathers. 33 God has fulfilled this for
us their children, in that He has raised up
Jesus. As it is also written in the second
Psalm:

'You are My Son,
Today I have begotten You.'[a]

34 And that He raised Him from the dead, no
more to return to corruption, He has spoken
thus:

'I will give you the sure mercies of David.'[a]

35 Therefore He also says in another *Psalm:*

'You will not allow Your Holy One to see
corruption.'[a]

36 "For David, after he had served his own
generation by the will of God, fell asleep, was

13:33 [a]Psalm 2:7 **13:34** [a]Isaiah 55:3
13:35 [a]Psalm 16:10

PERSONALITY PROFILE

Weakness

MARK—GOD'S WORK IN WEAKNESS

(ACTS 13:13)

God takes special delight in turning those who fail into faithful disciples. He is apparently not so concerned about helping those who help themselves as He is about helping those who realize how helpless they really are! One glowing example of God's work can be seen in the life of John Mark—the assistant of Paul and Barnabas on their first missionary journey (Acts 13:5).

Barnabas probably invited Mark, his cousin, to join the team. Barnabas had an eye for people who needed encouragement. He had helped Paul prove to the other apostles that he really was a follower of Jesus, not a persecutor working under cover (Acts 9:26–30). Barnabas may have also known about Mark's shameful cowardice on the night when Jesus was arrested, if indeed Mark was the young man who had fled in such a hurry that he left his clothes behind (Mark 14:51, 52).

Paul, Barnabas, and Mark made the island of Cyprus their first missionary destination. When they traveled on to Pamphylia (southern Turkey), Mark left the team and returned to Jerusalem. Paul concluded that Mark was unreliable. Later, when Barnabas and Paul were about to depart on their second missionary journey, Barnabas insisted on giving Mark another chance. Paul refused. The team split and Barnabas took Mark with him back to Cyprus.

Events proved that Barnabas's approach with Mark worked. He became a dependable disciple. He eventually wrote the Gospel that bears his name, probably recording Peter's account. Even Paul later recognized Mark's maturity. Three times in letters, Paul mentioned his appreciation for Mark's ministry in his life (Col. 4:10; 2 Tim. 4:11; Philem. 24). God doesn't give up on weak people. Christians ought not to give up on one another. As Paul discovered, those who are weak today may become those on whom we lean tomorrow.

To Learn More: Turn to the article about weakness on pages 1494, 1495. See also the key passage note at 2 Corinthians 12:9, 10 on page 1533.

buried with his fathers, and saw corruption;
37but He whom God raised up saw no corruption. 38Therefore let it be known to you, brethren, that through this Man is preached to you
the forgiveness of sins; 39and by Him everyone
who believes is justified from all things from
which you could not be justified by the law of
Moses. 40Beware therefore, lest what has been
spoken in the prophets come upon you:

41 *'Behold, you despisers,*
Marvel and perish!
For I work a work in your days,
A work which you will by no means
believe,
Though one were to declare it to you.' "[a]

Blessing and Conflict at Antioch

42So when the Jews went out of the
synagogue,[a] the Gentiles begged that these
words might be preached to them the next
Sabbath. 43Now when the congregation had
broken up, many of the Jews and devout proselytes followed Paul and Barnabas, who,
speaking to them, persuaded them to continue
in the grace of God.

44On the next Sabbath almost the whole city
came together to hear the word of God. 45But
when the Jews saw the multitudes, they were
filled with envy; and contradicting and blaspheming, they opposed the things spoken by
Paul. 46Then Paul and Barnabas grew bold and
said, "It was necessary that the word of God
should be spoken to you first; but since you
reject it, and judge yourselves unworthy of
everlasting life, behold, we turn to the Gentiles. 47For so the Lord has commanded us:

'I have set you as a light to the Gentiles,
That you should be for salvation to the
ends of the earth.' "[a]

48Now when the Gentiles heard this, they
were glad and glorified the word of the Lord.
And as many as had been appointed to eternal
life believed.

49And the word of the Lord was being
spread throughout all the region. 50But the
Jews stirred up the devout and prominent
women and the chief men of the city, raised
up persecution against Paul and Barnabas,
and expelled them from their region. 51But
they shook off the dust from their feet against
them, and came to Iconium. 52And the disciples were filled with joy and with the Holy
Spirit.

At Iconium

14 Now it happened in Iconium that they
went together to the synagogue of the
Jews, and so spoke that a great multitude both
of the Jews and of the Greeks believed. 2But
the unbelieving Jews stirred up the Gentiles
and poisoned their minds against the brethren. 3Therefore they stayed there a long time,
speaking boldly in the Lord, who was bearing
witness to the word of His grace, granting
signs and wonders to be done by their hands.

4But the multitude of the city was divided:
part sided with the Jews, and part with the
apostles. 5And when a violent attempt was
made by both the Gentiles and Jews, with
their rulers, to abuse and stone them, 6they
became aware of it and fled to Lystra and Derbe, cities of Lycaonia, and to the surrounding
region. 7And they were preaching the gospel
there.

Idolatry at Lystra

8And in Lystra a certain man without
strength in his feet was sitting, a cripple from
his mother's womb, who had never walked.
9*This* man heard Paul speaking. Paul, observing him intently and seeing that he had faith
to be healed, 10said with a loud voice, "Stand
up straight on your feet!" And he leaped and
walked. 11Now when the people saw what
Paul had done, they raised their voices, saying
in the Lycaonian *language,* "The gods have
come down to us in the likeness of men!"
12And Barnabas they called Zeus, and Paul,
Hermes, because he was the chief speaker.
13Then the priest of Zeus, whose temple was
in front of their city, brought oxen and gar-
lands to the gates, intending to sacrifice with
the multitudes.

14But when the apostles Barnabas and Paul
heard this, they tore their clothes and ran in
among the multitude, crying out 15and saying,
"Men, why are you doing these things? We
also are men with the same nature as you, and
preach to you that you should turn from these
useless things to the living God, who made

13:41 [a]Habakkuk 1:5 **13:42** [a]Or *And when they went out of the synagogue of the Jews;* NU-Text reads *And when they went out of the synagogue, they begged.* **13:47** [a]Isaiah 49:6

the heaven, the earth, the sea, and all things that are in them, [16]who in bygone generations allowed all nations to walk in their own ways. [17]Nevertheless He did not leave Himself without witness, in that He did good, gave us rain from heaven and fruitful seasons, filling our hearts with food and gladness." [18]And with these sayings they could scarcely restrain the multitudes from sacrificing to them.

Stoning, Escape to Derbe

[19]Then Jews from Antioch and Iconium came there; and having persuaded the multitudes, they stoned Paul *and* dragged *him* out of the city, supposing him to be dead. [20]However, when the disciples gathered around him, he rose up and went into the city. And the next day he departed with Barnabas to Derbe.

Strengthening the Converts

[21]And when they had preached the gospel to that city and made many disciples, they returned to Lystra, Iconium, and Antioch, [22]strengthening the souls of the disciples, exhorting *them* to continue in the faith, and *saying,* "We must through many tribulations enter the kingdom of God." [23]So when they had appointed elders in every church, and prayed with fasting, they commended them to the Lord in whom they had believed. [24]And after they had passed through Pisidia, they came to Pamphylia. [25]Now when they had preached the word in Perga, they went down to Attalia. [26]From there they sailed to Antioch, where they had been commended to the grace of God for the work which they had completed.

> And when they had preached the gospel to that city and made many disciples, they returned . . . strengthening the souls of the disciples, exhorting them to continue in the faith, and saying, "We must through many tribulations enter the kingdom of God."
>
> ACTS 14:21, 22

[27]Now when they had come and gathered the church together, they reported all that God had done with them, and that He had opened the door of faith to the Gentiles. [28]So they stayed there a long time with the disciples.

Conflict over Circumcision

15 And certain *men* came down from Judea and taught the brethren, "Unless you are circumcised according to the custom of Moses, you cannot be saved." [2]Therefore, when Paul and Barnabas had no small dissension and dispute with them, they determined that Paul and Barnabas and certain others of them should go up to Jerusalem, to the apostles and elders, about this question.

[3]So, being sent on their way by the church, they passed through Phoenicia and Samaria, describing the conversion of the Gentiles; and they caused great joy to all the brethren. [4]And when they had come to Jerusalem, they were received by the church and the apostles and the elders; and they reported all things that God had done with them. [5]But some of the sect of the Pharisees who believed rose up, saying, "It is necessary to circumcise them, and to command *them* to keep the law of Moses."

The Jerusalem Council

[6]Now the apostles and elders came together to consider this matter. [7]And when there had been much dispute, Peter rose up and said to them: "Men and brethren, you know that a good while ago God chose among us, that by my mouth the Gentiles should hear the word of the gospel and believe. [8]So God, who knows the heart, acknowledged them by giving them the Holy Spirit, just as *He did* to us, [9]and made no distinction between us and them, purifying their hearts by faith. [10]Now therefore, why do you test God by putting a yoke on the neck of the disciples which neither our fathers nor we were able to bear? [11]But we believe that through the grace of the Lord Jesus Christ[a] we shall be saved in the same manner as they."

[12]Then all the multitude kept silent and listened to Barnabas and Paul declaring how many miracles and wonders God had worked through them among the Gentiles. [13]And after they had become silent, James answered, saying, "Men *and* brethren, listen to me: [14]Simon has declared how God at the first visited the Gentiles to take out of them a people for His name. [15]And with this the words of the prophets agree, just as it is written:

15:11 [a]NU-Text and M-Text omit *Christ.*

16 '*After this I will return*
And will rebuild the tabernacle of David,
which has fallen down;
I will rebuild its ruins,
And I will set it up;
17 *So that the rest of mankind may seek the*
LORD,
Even all the Gentiles who are called by
My name,
Says the LORD who does all these things.' [a]

18"Known to God from eternity are all His
works.[a] 19Therefore I judge that we should not
trouble those from among the Gentiles who
are turning to God, 20but that we write to them
to abstain from things polluted by idols, *from*
sexual immorality,[a] *from* things strangled, and
from blood. 21For Moses has had throughout
many generations those who preach him in
every city, being read in the synagogues every
Sabbath."

THE JERUSALEM DECREE

22Then it pleased the apostles and elders,
with the whole church, to send chosen men of
their own company to Antioch with Paul and
Barnabas, *namely,* Judas who was also named
Barsabas,[a] and Silas, leading men among the
brethren.

15:17 [a]Amos 9:11, 12 **15:18** [a]NU-Text (combining with verse 17) reads *Says the Lord, who makes these things known from eternity (of old).* **15:20** [a]Or *fornication* **15:22** [a]NU-Text and M-Text read *Barsabbas.*

PERSONALITY PROFILE

Communication

PAUL AND BARNABAS—COMMUNICATING TRUTH IN LIFE

(ACTS 15:36)

Paul and Barnabas formed a powerful missionary team. They met because Barnabas saw Christ in Paul's life before other people did. Barnabas, whose name means "Son of Encouragement" (Acts 4:36), believed God actually could transform someone like Paul into a genuine disciple. Until the end of their first missionary journey, Paul (the former Saul) still needed Barnabas as a character witness. But their partnership was temporary because their reasons for participating were different. Paul was called to a worldwide mission; Barnabas was called to recognize and encourage those who needed it.

Eventually, their different purposes took them in different directions. A dispute over the young disciple John Mark became the occasion of their separation. Paul thought Mark had proven himself unreliable; Barnabas believed Mark was worth another chance. They settled their honest difference of opinion with a solution that allowed each of them to continue to pursue his calling from God. Something important would have been lost if either had given in to the other. The missionary task might have been affected if Paul had agreed to allow someone he did not trust to accompany them. Mark's life might have taken a far different course if Barnabas had agreed to leave him behind.

People sometimes believe that communication and action are separate parts of life. They wrongly assume that we can communicate one way and live another. But if what we say and what we do contradict each other, one of them is a lie. Both Paul and Barnabas acted consistently with what they honestly believed to be true. They parted as brothers on different missions. They didn't make staying together more important than obeying God. The Lord, in turn, blessed each one of them.

Christians throughout history have repeatedly failed to apply this lesson about obedience to God. Believers have separated or stayed together too often for the wrong reasons. When we decide to win an argument rather than obey God, we have already taken a wrong turn.

To Learn More: Turn to the article about communication on pages 1442, 1443. See also the key passage note at Ephesians 4:15 on page 1551.

Communi-
cation

FOUR LAWS OF COMMUNICATION

HOWARD EYRICH

(Acts 15:7)

Communication is the key to successful relationships. We get along best with those we understand the most. Learning to communicate our thoughts and feelings is vital to understanding one another. It helps us see into the minds and hearts of our spouse, children, parents, friends, and coworkers. Expectations are clarified and problems are solved when we learn to communicate our deepest needs, feelings, and frustrations.

God models communication for us in His character and in His Word. From the very beginning, God created us with a capacity for interpersonal communication. He has spoken to us in His Word and He teaches us how to communicate with one another. God's rules of communication are expressed in four basic commands found in Ephesians 4:25–32 and illustrated numerous times in the Book of Acts.

Law One—*Stop lying and start telling the truth (Eph. 4:25)*. Most Christian couples will stare in disbelief if their counselor suggests they might be lying to each other. But lies can be as simple as refusals to tell the truth. For example, when people ask us how we are doing, we almost always say that we are "fine." But sometimes that is a lie because we are not fine. When someone asks: "Is anything wrong?" we will often say, "Oh, nothing."

Lying is a constant problem in human conversation and it keeps us from genuine communication. If we are obviously upset, but insist that we are all right, others will assume we just don't want to talk about it. Instead of gaining their compassion, we often push them away altogether.

People lie to protect themselves from the stress they perceive will come from a confrontation. When we insist that we are OK or that nothing is bothering us, we actually erect barriers to communication. Our facial expressions, body language, and verbal communication are all saying, "Go away, I don't want to talk about it."

Law Two—*Keep current (Eph. 4:26, 27)*. God clearly says that going to bed angry with each other is a sure way to allow the devil to drive a wedge into a relationship. Anger not dealt with is anger saved for future use. It is possible that the problem that was the occasion for the anger cannot be solved so quickly. However, the anger can be put to rest by agreeing to address the issue at a later time. The relationship can be reestablished even though the issue cannot be immediately settled. The point of the passage is the *relationship,* not the particular *issue*. Taking responsibility for offending each other, attempting to deal with the issues, and seeking and granting forgiveness is necessary. Since initiating reconciliation is the responsibility of both the offended and the offender, neither can use a ruptured relationship as an excuse to "let the sun go down" on their wrath. The sooner we deal with it, the better!

Law Three—*Tackle the issue, not the individual (Eph. 4:29, 30)*. This rule focuses upon the control and intent of our speech. Following his pattern of put off and put on, Paul indicates that we must choose the content of our speech. "Cutting words" are to be put off. In their place we must express words that build up the other person(s) in the relationship. Some may object by saying, "That's not how I feel!" To help us, the apostle uses God Himself as our example. God was the offended party and certainly did not feel kindly disposed toward us, yet "God in Christ forgave" us (Eph. 4:32). He spoke and acted for our benefit! He tackled the issue of our sin, not us.

Proverbs 18:6 says, "A fool's lips enter into contention, and his mouth calls for blows." One cutting remark leads to another. Communication ceases and character defamation often develops, destroying respect and love. Little wonder that the injunction not to grieve the Holy Spirit is given between this law and the next. The use of our mouths directly affects the ministry of the Holy Spirit in our lives and in the lives of others.

Law Four—*Pro-act, don't react (Eph. 4:31, 32)*. All the emotions listed in Ephesians 4:31 are reactionary and retaliatory. They destroy communication. They force defensiveness because they directly attack the other person. On the other hand, the instruction of verse 32 is positive pro-action that leads to a solution, not further conflict. To be kind, tenderhearted, and forgiving means being understanding of the other person's frustrations. It is listening to another viewpoint. It is gently considering another's feelings. It is letting love cover a multitude of sins. In short, it is acting in the very practical matter of daily living as God has acted toward us through Christ.

The Ephesians 4 passage provides a biblical frame of reference for communication. Nothing illustrates a principle better than learning how to apply it to one's own experience. We can give various psychological reasons for not communicating. In fact, developing all the "games people play" will tend to detract from change and encourage the excusing of attitudes and behaviors. If we will learn to practice the biblical behavior suggested in this passage, we will learn to communicate more effectively. In many instances this focus on positive change will not only enhance the communication process, but it will begin effecting lasting thinking and attitude adjustments in us as well. We become what we communicate, so let us learn to speak the truth with love and grace.

FURTHER MEDITATION:

Other passages to study about the issue of communication include:

- ➢ Psalms 19:14; 31:18
- ➢ Proverbs 10:8, 31, 32; 12:14–19; 15:1
- ➢ Ecclesiastes 5:2
- ➢ Matthew 5:37
- ➢ Ephesians 5:4
- ➢ James 4:11
- ➢ 1 Peter 3:10

To Learn More: **Turn to the key passage note on communication at Ephesians 4:15 on page 1551. See also the personality profile of Paul and Barnabas on page 1441.**

23They wrote this *letter* by them:

The apostles, the elders, and the brethren,

To the brethren who are of the Gentiles in
Antioch, Syria, and Cilicia:

Greetings.

24 Since we have heard that some who went
out from us have troubled you with
words, unsettling your souls, saying,
"*You must* be circumcised and keep the
law"[a]—to whom we gave no *such*
commandment—25it seemed good to us,
being assembled with one accord, to send
chosen men to you with our beloved
Barnabas and Paul, 26men who have
risked their lives for the name of our
Lord Jesus Christ. 27We have therefore
sent Judas and Silas, who will also report
the same things by word of mouth. 28For
it seemed good to the Holy Spirit, and to
us, to lay upon you no greater burden
than these necessary things: 29that you
abstain from things offered to idols, from
blood, from things strangled, and from
sexual immorality.[a] If you keep yourselves
from these, you will do well.

Farewell.

Continuing Ministry in Syria

30So when they were sent off, they came to
Antioch; and when they had gathered the
multitude together, they delivered the letter.

15:24 [a]NU-Text omits *saying, "You must be circumcised and keep the law."* **15:29** [a]Or *fornication*

PERSONALITY PROFILE

Conflict

PAUL AND MARK—SETTLING THEIR DIFFERENCES

(ACTS 15:37)

The apostle Paul probably intimidated most people he met. His reputation as a former fierce persecutor, his success as a brilliant debater, or his tireless passion for the gospel may have unnerved his companions. Paul's boldness often got him in trouble, along with his partners. Silas spent time with him in prison. Others suffered with Paul. A number of companions proved unable to keep up. John Mark started out in this last group.

Mark joined Paul and Barnabas on the first missionary team sent from the church in Antioch. They sailed to Cyprus and traveled across the island, preaching the gospel in various cities. Then they moved on to the north, to Pamphylia (modern Turkey). Acts simply notes that Mark left the team and returned to Jerusalem (Acts 13:13). Later, Paul refused to let Mark join him on another journey because he thought Mark had abandoned the team and the work on the previous trip (Acts 15:37–39).

This particular conflict had a deadline. By the time the team departed, Barnabas had decided to take Mark on a different outreach and Silas became Paul's new missionary partner. Later biblical comments make it clear that neither Mark nor Paul saw this conflict as a permanent rift. Possibly Mark wasn't ready for Paul's style, and Barnabas could accomplish more helping Mark than he could if he traveled with Paul.

Conflicts can be opportunities to clarify ideas, expectations, and goals. They may bring into the open what needs to be changed. Even good change rarely happens without conflict. Mark probably didn't enjoy the fact that Barnabas and Paul separated over him, but he had to appreciate that someone believed he was worth another chance. Mark eventually grew into a godly disciple whom Paul counted as a trusted friend. Conflicts can lead to good endings.

To Learn More: Turn to the article about conflict on pages 1258, 1259. See also the key passage note at Matthew 18:15–17 on page 1257.

[31]When they had read it, they rejoiced over its
encouragement. [32]Now Judas and Silas, themselves being prophets also, exhorted and
strengthened the brethren with many words.
[33]And after they had stayed *there* for a time,
they were sent back with greetings from the
brethren to the apostles.[a]

[34]However, it seemed good to Silas to remain there.[a] [35]Paul and Barnabas also remained in Antioch, teaching and preaching
the word of the Lord, with many others also.

Division over John Mark

[36]Then after some days Paul said to Barnabas, "Let us now go back and visit our brethren in every city where we have preached the
word of the Lord, *and see* how they are doing." [37]Now Barnabas was determined to take
with them John called Mark. [38]But Paul insisted that they should not take with them the
one who had departed from them in Pamphylia, and had not gone with them to the work.
[39]Then the contention became so sharp that
they parted from one another. And so Barnabas took Mark and sailed to Cyprus; [40]but Paul
chose Silas and departed, being commended
by the brethren to the grace of God. [41]And he
went through Syria and Cilicia, strengthening
the churches.

Timothy Joins Paul and Silas

16 Then he came to Derbe and Lystra. And
behold, a certain disciple was there,
named Timothy, *the* son of a certain Jewish
woman who believed, but his father *was*
Greek. [2]He was well spoken of by the brethren
who were at Lystra and Iconium. [3]Paul wanted to have him go on with him. And he took
him and circumcised him because of the Jews
who were in that region, for they all knew that
his father was Greek. [4]And as they went
through the cities, they delivered to them the
decrees to keep, which were determined by
the apostles and elders at Jerusalem. [5]So the
churches were strengthened in the faith, and
increased in number daily.

The Macedonian Call

[6]Now when they had gone through Phrygia
and the region of Galatia, they were forbidden
by the Holy Spirit to preach the word in Asia.
[7]After they had come to Mysia, they tried to go
into Bithynia, but the Spirit[a] did not permit
them. [8]So passing by Mysia, they came down
to Troas. [9]And a vision appeared to Paul in the
night. A man of Macedonia stood and pleaded
with him, saying, "Come over to Macedonia
and help us." [10]Now after he had seen the vision, immediately we sought to go to Macedonia, concluding that the Lord had called us to
preach the gospel to them.

Lydia Baptized at Philippi

[11]Therefore, sailing from Troas, we ran a
straight course to Samothrace, and the next
day came to Neapolis, [12]and from there to Philippi, which is the foremost city of that part of
Macedonia, a colony. And we were staying in
that city for some days. [13]And on the Sabbath
day we went out of the city to the riverside,
where prayer was customarily made; and we
sat down and spoke to the women who met
there. [14]Now a certain woman named Lydia
heard *us*. She was a seller of purple from the
city of Thyatira, who worshiped God. The
Lord opened her heart to heed the things spoken by Paul. [15]And when she and her household were baptized, she begged *us*, saying, "If
you have judged me to be faithful to the Lord,
come to my house and stay." So she persuaded us.

Paul and Silas Imprisoned

[16]Now it happened, as we went to prayer,
that a certain slave girl possessed with a spirit
of divination met us, who brought her masters
much profit by fortune-telling. [17]This girl followed Paul and us, and cried out, saying,
"These men are the servants of the Most High
God, who proclaim to us the way of salvation." [18]And this she did for many days.

But Paul, greatly annoyed, turned and said
to the spirit, "I command you in the name of
Jesus Christ to come out of her." And he came
out that very hour. [19]But when her masters
saw that their hope of profit was gone, they
seized Paul and Silas and dragged *them* into
the marketplace to the authorities.

[20]And they brought them to the magistrates,
and said, "These men, being Jews, exceedingly trouble our city; [21]and they teach customs
which are not lawful for us, being Romans, to
receive or observe." [22]Then the multitude rose
up together against them; and the magistrates

15:33 [a]NU-Text reads *to those who had sent them.*
15:34 [a]NU-Text and M-Text omit this verse.
16:7 [a]NU-Text adds *of Jesus.*

tore off their clothes and commanded *them* to be beaten with rods. 23And when they had laid many stripes on them, they threw *them* into prison, commanding the jailer to keep them securely. 24Having received such a charge, he put them into the inner prison and fastened their feet in the stocks.

The Philippian Jailer Saved

25But at midnight Paul and Silas were praying and singing hymns to God, and the prisoners were listening to them. 26Suddenly there was a great earthquake, so that the foundations of the prison were shaken; and immediately all the doors were opened and everyone's chains were loosed. 27And the keeper of the prison, awaking from sleep and seeing the prison doors open, supposing the prisoners had fled, drew his sword and was about to kill himself. 28But Paul called with a loud voice, saying, "Do yourself no harm, for we are all here."

29Then he called for a light, ran in, and fell down trembling before Paul and Silas. 30And he brought them out and said, "Sirs, what must I do to be saved?"

31So they said, "Believe on the Lord Jesus Christ, and you will be saved, you and your household." 32Then they spoke the word of the Lord to him and to all who were in his house. 33And he took them the same hour of the night and washed *their* stripes. And immediately he and all his family were baptized. 34Now when he had brought them into his house, he set food before them; and he rejoiced, having believed in God with all his household.

Paul Refuses to Depart Secretly

35And when it was day, the magistrates sent the officers, saying, "Let those men go."

36So the keeper of the prison reported these words to Paul, saying, "The magistrates have sent to let you go. Now therefore depart, and go in peace."

37But Paul said to them, "They have beaten us openly, uncondemned Romans, *and* have thrown *us* into prison. And now do they put us out secretly? No indeed! Let them come themselves and get us out."

38And the officers told these words to the magistrates, and they were afraid when they heard that they were Romans. 39Then they came and pleaded with them and brought *them* out, and asked *them* to depart from the city. 40So they went out of the prison and entered *the house of* Lydia; and when they had seen the brethren, they encouraged them and departed.

Preaching Christ at Thessalonica

17 Now when they had passed through Amphipolis and Apollonia, they came to Thessalonica, where there was a synagogue of the Jews. 2Then Paul, as his custom was, went in to them, and for three Sabbaths reasoned with them from the Scriptures, 3explaining and demonstrating that the Christ had to suffer and rise again from the dead, and *saying*, "This Jesus whom I preach to you is the Christ." 4And some of them were persuaded; and a great multitude of the devout Greeks, and not a few of the leading women, joined Paul and Silas.

Assault on Jason's House

5But the Jews who were not persuaded, becoming envious,[a] took some of the evil men from the marketplace, and gathering a mob, set all the city in an uproar and attacked the house of Jason, and sought to bring them out to the people. 6But when they did not find them, they dragged Jason and some brethren

17:5 [a]NU-Text omits *who were not persuaded;* M-Text omits *becoming envious.*

SOUL NOTE

What You Can Do *(16:30–34)* When the jailer saw the prison walls crumbled around him, he fell trembling before Paul and Silas, and asked, "What must I do to be saved?" That's the question! So often people ask, "What must I do to be happy?" or "What must I do to be successful?" But only one question makes a difference for eternity. As Paul told the jailer, there's only one answer to the question "What must I do to be saved?" and that's "Believe on the Lord Jesus Christ." **Topic: Salvation**

to the rulers of the city, crying out, "These who have turned the world upside down have come here too. [7]Jason has harbored them, and these are all acting contrary to the decrees of Caesar, saying there is another king—Jesus." [8]And they troubled the crowd and the rulers of the city when they heard these things. [9]So when they had taken security from Jason and the rest, they let them go.

Ministering at Berea

[10]Then the brethren immediately sent Paul and Silas away by night to Berea. When they arrived, they went into the synagogue of the Jews. [11]These were more fair-minded than those in Thessalonica, in that they received the word with all readiness, and searched the Scriptures daily *to find out* whether these things were so. [12]Therefore many of them believed, and also not a few of the Greeks, prominent women as well as men. [13]But when the Jews from Thessalonica learned that the word of God was preached by Paul at Berea, they came there also and stirred up the crowds. [14]Then immediately the brethren sent Paul away, to go to the sea; but both Silas and Timothy remained there. [15]So those who conducted Paul brought him to Athens; and receiving a command for Silas and Timothy to come to him with all speed, they departed.

The Philosophers at Athens

[16]Now while Paul waited for them at Athens, his spirit was provoked within him when he saw that the city was given over to idols. [17]Therefore he reasoned in the synagogue with the Jews and with the *Gentile* worshipers, and in the marketplace daily with those who happened to be there. [18]Then[a] certain Epicurean and Stoic philosophers encountered him. And some said, "What does this babbler want to say?"

Others said, "He seems to be a proclaimer of foreign gods," because he preached to them Jesus and the resurrection.

[19]And they took him and brought him to the Areopagus, saying, "May we know what this new doctrine *is* of which you speak? [20]For you are bringing some strange things to our ears. Therefore we want to know what these things mean." [21]For all the Athenians and the foreigners who were there spent their time in nothing else but either to tell or to hear some new thing.

Addressing the Areopagus

[22]Then Paul stood in the midst of the Areopagus and said, "Men of Athens, I perceive that in all things you are very religious; [23]for as I was passing through and considering the objects of your worship, I even found an altar with this inscription:

TO THE UNKNOWN GOD.

Therefore, the One whom you worship without knowing, Him I proclaim to you: [24]God, who made the world and everything in it, since He is Lord of heaven and earth, does not dwell in temples made with hands. [25]Nor is He worshiped with men's hands, as though He needed anything, since He gives to all life, breath, and all things. [26]And He has made from one blood[a] every nation of men to dwell on all the face of the earth, and has determined their preappointed times and the boundaries of their dwellings, [27]so that they should seek the Lord, in the hope that they might grope for Him and find Him, though He is not far from each one of us; [28]for in Him we live and move and have our being, as also some of your own poets have said, 'For we are also His offspring.' [29]Therefore, since we are the offspring of God, we ought not to think that the Divine Nature is like gold or silver or stone, something shaped by art and man's devising. [30]Truly, these times of ignorance God overlooked, but now commands all men everywhere to repent, [31]because He has appointed a day on which He will judge the world in righteousness by the Man whom He has ordained. He has given assurance of this to all by raising Him from the dead."

[32]And when they heard of the resurrection of the dead, some mocked, while others said, "We will hear you again on this *matter*." [33]So Paul departed from among them. [34]However, some men joined him and believed, among them Dionysius the Areopagite, a woman named Damaris, and others with them.

Ministering at Corinth

18 After these things Paul departed from Athens and went to Corinth. [2]And he found a certain Jew named Aquila, born in Pontus, who had recently come from Italy

---

17:18 [a]NU-Text and M-Text add *also*. **17:26** [a]NU-Text omits *blood*.

with his wife Priscilla (because Claudius had
commanded all the Jews to depart from
Rome); and he came to them. [3]So, because
he was of the same trade, he stayed with
them and worked; for
by occupation they were
tentmakers. [4]And he reasoned in the synagogue
every Sabbath, and per-
suaded both Jews and
Greeks.
[5]When Silas and Tim-
othy had come from
Macedonia, Paul was com-
pelled by the Spirit, and
testified to the Jews *that* Jesus *is* the Christ.
[6]But when they opposed him and blasphemed, he shook *his* garments and said to
them, "Your blood *be* upon your *own* heads; I
am clean. From now on I will go to the Gentiles." [7]And he departed from there and entered the house of a certain *man* named
Justus,[a] *one* who worshiped God, whose
house was next door to
the synagogue. [8]Then
Crispus, the ruler of the
synagogue, believed on
the Lord with all his
household. And many of
the Corinthians, hear-
ing, believed and were
baptized.
[9]Now the Lord spoke
to Paul in the night by a
vision, "Do not be afraid, but speak, and do
not keep silent; [10]for I am with you, and no

> Now the Lord spoke to Paul in the night by a vision, "Do not be afraid, but speak, and do not keep silent; for I am with you, and no one will attack you to hurt you; for I have many people in this city."
>
> ACTS 18:9, 10

18:7 [a]NU-Text reads *Titius Justus.*

PERSONALITY PROFILE

Marital Communication

THE TEAMWORK OF AQUILA AND PRISCILLA

(ACTS 18:2)

Aquila and Priscilla were united both in marriage and in ministry. Their ability to communicate enabled them to minister effectively. Never mentioned separately in Scripture, these two became close friends of the apostle Paul. They met the traveling apostle when he was in Corinth on his second missionary journey. Aquila and Priscilla had moved from Rome after the emperor Claudius had issued a decree expelling all Jews from the city. They had moved to Corinth and taken up their tentmaking business. When Paul, a fellow tentmaker, also arrived in the city, they worked together and doubtless learned much from Paul.

Later, when a young orator named Apollos began to preach what he had heard from John the Baptist's followers, Aquila and Priscilla brought him home and told him the whole story. When Apollos went back to preaching, he had the full gospel message and had great impact in Corinth and beyond (1 Cor. 1:12). Aquila and Priscilla's quiet ministry in their home surely influenced many. Later, upon their return to Rome, one of the house churches met in their home (Rom. 16:3–5).

Couples who are united in Christ can have a great impact together for His kingdom. God can work mightily through a couple who are devoted to Christ and willing to use their time, efforts, and resources to build God's kingdom. A Christ-centered home can be a haven for many who need to hear the gospel message. A devoted couple can minister together to both men and women. As they seek God together, their united front and solid faith can be a positive example to many. But they will only be as effective as their ability to communicate with each other. Often married couples are busy serving separately in churches. While their various gifts are needed in different places, they should not ignore the impact they can have together.

To Learn More: Turn to the article about marital communication on pages 1660, 1661. See also the key passage note at 1 Peter 3:8 on page 1663.

one will attack you to hurt you; for I have many people in this city." [11]And he continued *there* a year and six months, teaching the word of God among them.

[12]When Gallio was proconsul of Achaia, the Jews with one accord rose up against Paul and brought him to the judgment seat, [13]saying, "This *fellow* persuades men to worship God contrary to the law."

[14]And when Paul was about to open *his* mouth, Gallio said to the Jews, "If it were a matter of wrongdoing or wicked crimes, O Jews, there would be reason why I should bear with you. [15]But if it is a question of words and names and your own law, look *to it* yourselves; for I do not want to be a judge of such *matters.*" [16]And he drove them from the judgment seat. [17]Then all the Greeks[a] took Sosthenes, the ruler of the synagogue, and beat *him* before the judgment seat. But Gallio took no notice of these things.

Paul Returns to Antioch

[18]So Paul still remained a good while. Then he took leave of the brethren and sailed for Syria, and Priscilla and Aquila *were* with him. He had *his* hair cut off at Cenchrea, for he had taken a vow. [19]And he came to Ephesus, and left them there; but he himself entered the synagogue and reasoned with the Jews. [20]When they asked *him* to stay a longer time with them, he did not consent, [21]but took leave of them, saying, "I must by all means keep this coming feast in Jerusalem;[a] but I will return again to you, God willing." And he sailed from Ephesus.

[22]And when he had landed at Caesarea, and gone up and greeted the church, he went down to Antioch. [23]After he had spent some time *there,* he departed and went over the region of Galatia and Phrygia in order, strengthening all the disciples.

Ministry of Apollos

[24]Now a certain Jew named Apollos, born at Alexandria, an eloquent man *and* mighty in the Scriptures, came to Ephesus. [25]This man had been instructed in the way of the Lord; and being fervent in spirit, he spoke and taught accurately the things of the Lord, though he knew only the baptism of John. [26]So he began to speak boldly in the synagogue. When Aquila and Priscilla heard him, they took him aside and explained to him the way of God more accurately. [27]And when he desired to cross to Achaia, the brethren wrote, exhorting the disciples to receive him; and when he arrived, he greatly helped those who had believed through grace; [28]for he vigorously refuted the Jews publicly, showing from the Scriptures that Jesus is the Christ.

Paul at Ephesus

19 And it happened, while Apollos was at Corinth, that Paul, having passed through the upper regions, came to Ephesus. And finding some disciples [2]he said to them, "Did you receive the Holy Spirit when you believed?"

So they said to him, "We have not so much as heard whether there is a Holy Spirit."

[3]And he said to them, "Into what then were you baptized?"

So they said, "Into John's baptism."

[4]Then Paul said, "John indeed baptized with a baptism of repentance, saying to the people that they should believe on Him who would come after him, that is, on Christ Jesus."

[5]When they heard *this,* they were baptized in the name of the Lord Jesus. [6]And when Paul had laid hands on them, the Holy Spirit came upon them, and they spoke with tongues and prophesied. [7]Now the men were about twelve in all.

[8]And he went into the synagogue and spoke boldly for three months, reasoning and persuading concerning the things of the kingdom of God. [9]But when some were hardened and did not believe, but spoke evil of the Way before the multitude, he departed from them and withdrew the disciples, reasoning daily in the school of Tyrannus. [10]And this continued for two years, so that all who dwelt in Asia heard the word of the Lord Jesus, both Jews and Greeks.

Miracles Glorify Christ

[11]Now God worked unusual miracles by the hands of Paul, [12]so that even handkerchiefs or aprons were brought from his body to the sick, and the diseases left them and the evil spirits went out of them. [13]Then some of the itinerant Jewish exorcists took it upon themselves to call the name of the Lord Jesus over

---

18:17 [a]NU-Text reads *they all.* **18:21** [a]NU-Text omits *I must* through *Jerusalem.*

those who had evil spirits, saying, "We[a] exor-
cise you by the Jesus whom Paul preaches."
14 Also there were seven sons of Sceva, a Jewish chief priest, who did so.
15 And the evil spirit answered and said,
"Jesus I know, and Paul I know; but who are
you?"
16 Then the man in whom the evil spirit was
leaped on them, overpowered[a] them, and prevailed against them,[b] so that they fled out of
that house naked and wounded. 17 This became known both to all Jews and Greeks
dwelling in Ephesus; and fear fell on them all,
and the name of the Lord Jesus was magnified. 18 And many who had believed came confessing and telling their deeds. 19 Also, many of
those who had practiced magic brought their
books together and burned *them* in the sight
of all. And they counted up the value of them,
and *it* totaled fifty thousand *pieces* of silver.
20 So the word of the Lord grew mightily and
prevailed.

The Riot at Ephesus

21 When these things were accomplished,
Paul purposed in the Spirit, when he had
passed through Macedonia and Achaia, to go
to Jerusalem, saying, "After I have been there,
I must also see Rome." 22 So he sent into Macedonia two of those who ministered to him,
Timothy and Erastus, but he himself stayed in
Asia for a time.
23 And about that time there arose a great
commotion about the Way. 24 For a certain
man named Demetrius, a silversmith, who
made silver shrines of Diana,[a] brought no
small profit to the craftsmen. 25 He called them
together with the workers of similar occupation, and said: "Men, you know that we have
our prosperity by this trade. 26 Moreover you
see and hear that not only at Ephesus, but
throughout almost all Asia, this Paul has persuaded and turned away many people, saying
that they are not gods which are made with
hands. 27 So not only is this trade of ours in
danger of falling into disrepute, but also the
temple of the great goddess Diana may be despised and her magnificence destroyed,[a]
whom all Asia and the world worship."
28 Now when they heard *this,* they were full
of wrath and cried out, saying, "Great *is* Diana
of the Ephesians!" 29 So the whole city was
filled with confusion, and rushed into the theater with one accord, having seized Gaius and
Aristarchus, Macedonians, Paul's travel companions. 30 And when Paul wanted to go in to
the people, the disciples would not allow him.
31 Then some of the officials of Asia, who were
his friends, sent to him pleading that he would
not venture into the theater. 32 Some therefore
cried one thing and some another, for the assembly was confused, and most of them did
not know why they had come together. 33 And
they drew Alexander out of the multitude, the
Jews putting him forward. And Alexander motioned with his hand, and wanted to make his
defense to the people. 34 But when they found
out that he was a Jew, all with one voice cried
out for about two hours, "Great *is* Diana of the
Ephesians!"
35 And when the city clerk had quieted the
crowd, he said: "Men of Ephesus, what man is
there who does not know that the city of the
Ephesians is temple guardian of the great goddess Diana, and of the *image* which fell down
from Zeus? 36 Therefore, since these things
cannot be denied, you ought to be quiet and
do nothing rashly. 37 For you have brought
these men here who are neither robbers of
temples nor blasphemers of your[a] goddess.
38 Therefore, if Demetrius and his fellow craftsmen have a case against anyone, the courts
are open and there are proconsuls. Let them
bring charges against one another. 39 But if you
have any other inquiry to make, it shall be determined in the lawful assembly. 40 For we are
in danger of being called in question for
today's uproar, there being no reason which
we may give to account for this disorderly
gathering." 41 And when he had said these
things, he dismissed the assembly.

Journeys in Greece

20 After the uproar had ceased, Paul
called the disciples to *himself,* embraced *them,* and departed to go to Macedonia. 2 Now when he had gone over that region
and encouraged them with many words, he
came to Greece 3 and stayed three months.
And when the Jews plotted against him as he
was about to sail to Syria, he decided to return
through Macedonia. 4 And Sopater of Berea ac-

19:13 [a]NU-Text reads *I.* **19:16** [a]M-Text reads *and they overpowered.* [b]NU-Text reads *both of them.* **19:24** [a]Greek *Artemis* **19:27** [a]NU-Text reads *she be deposed from her magnificence.* **19:37** [a]NU-Text reads *our.*

companied him to Asia—also Aristarchus and Secundus of the Thessalonians, and Gaius of Derbe, and Timothy, and Tychicus and Trophimus of Asia. 5These men, going ahead, waited for us at Troas. 6But we sailed away from Philippi after the Days of Unleavened Bread, and in five days joined them at Troas, where we stayed seven days.

Ministering at Troas

7Now on the first *day* of the week, when the disciples came together to break bread, Paul, ready to depart the next day, spoke to them and continued his message until midnight. 8There were many lamps in the upper room where they[a] were gathered together. 9And in a window sat a certain young man named Eutychus, who was sinking into a deep sleep. He was overcome by sleep; and as Paul continued speaking, he fell down from the third story and was taken up dead. 10But Paul went down, fell on him, and embracing *him* said, "Do not trouble yourselves, for his life is in him." 11Now when he had come up, had broken bread and eaten, and talked a long while, even till daybreak, he departed. 12And they brought the young man in alive, and they were not a little comforted.

From Troas to Miletus

13Then we went ahead to the ship and sailed to Assos, there intending to take Paul on board; for so he had given orders, intending himself to go on foot. 14And when he met us at Assos, we took him on board and came to Mitylene. 15We sailed from there, and the next *day* came opposite Chios. The following *day* we arrived at Samos and stayed at Trogyllium. The next *day* we came to Miletus. 16For Paul had decided to sail past Ephesus, so that he would not have to spend time in Asia; for he was hurrying to be at Jerusalem, if possible, on the Day of Pentecost.

The Ephesian Elders Exhorted

17From Miletus he sent to Ephesus and called for the elders of the church. 18And when they had come to him, he said to them: "You know, from the first day that I came to Asia, in what manner I always lived among you, 19serving the Lord with all humility, with many tears and trials which happened to me by the plotting of the Jews; 20how I kept back nothing that was helpful, but proclaimed it to you, and taught you publicly and from house to house, 21testifying to Jews, and also to Greeks, repentance toward God and faith toward our Lord Jesus Christ. 22And see, now I go bound in the spirit to Jerusalem, not knowing the things that will happen to me there, 23except that the Holy Spirit testifies in every city, saying that chains and tribulations await me. 24But none of these things move me; nor do I count my life dear to myself,[a] so that I may finish my race with joy, and the ministry which I received from the Lord Jesus, to testify to the gospel of the grace of God.

25"And indeed, now I know that you all, among whom I have gone preaching the kingdom of God, will see my face no more. 26Therefore I testify to you this day that I *am* innocent of the blood of all *men*. 27For I have not shunned to declare to you the whole counsel of God. 28Therefore take heed to yourselves and to all the flock, among which the Holy Spirit has made you overseers, to shepherd the church of God[a] which He purchased with His own blood. 29For I know this, that after my departure savage wolves will come in among you, not sparing the flock. 30Also from among yourselves men will rise up, speaking perverse things, to draw away the disciples after themselves. 31Therefore watch, and remember that for three years I did not cease to warn everyone night and day with tears.

32"So now, brethren, I commend you to God and to the word of His grace, which is able to build you up and give you an inheritance among all those who are sanctified. 33I have coveted no one's silver or gold or apparel. 34Yes,[a] you yourselves know that these hands have provided for my necessities, and for those who were with me. 35I have shown you in every

> "I have shown you in every way, by laboring like this, that you must support the weak. And remember the words of the Lord Jesus, that He said, 'It is more blessed to give than to receive.' "
>
> ACTS 20:35

20:8 [a]NU-Text and M-Text read *we*. **20:24** [a]NU-Text reads *But I do not count my life of any value or dear to myself*. **20:28** [a]M-Text reads *of the Lord and God*. **20:34** [a]NU-Text and M-Text omit *Yes*.

way, by laboring like this, that you must support the weak. And remember the words of the Lord Jesus, that He said, 'It is more blessed to give than to receive.' "

[36]And when he had said these things, he knelt down and prayed with them all. [37]Then they all wept freely, and fell on Paul's neck and kissed him, [38]sorrowing most of all for the words which he spoke, that they would see his face no more. And they accompanied him to the ship.

Warnings on the Journey to Jerusalem

21 Now it came to pass, that when we had departed from them and set sail, running a straight course we came to Cos, the following *day* to Rhodes, and from there to Patara. [2]And finding a ship sailing over to Phoenicia, we went aboard and set sail. [3]When we had sighted Cyprus, we passed it on the left, sailed to Syria, and landed at Tyre; for there the ship was to unload her cargo. [4]And finding disciples,[a] we stayed there seven days. They told Paul through the Spirit not to go up to Jerusalem. [5]When we had come to the end of those days, we departed and went on our way; and they all accompanied us, with wives and children, till *we were* out of the city. And we knelt down on the shore and prayed. [6]When we had taken our leave of one another, we boarded the ship, and they returned home.

[7]And when we had finished *our* voyage from Tyre, we came to Ptolemais, greeted the brethren, and stayed with them one day. [8]On the next *day* we who were Paul's companions[a] departed and came to Caesarea, and entered the house of Philip the evangelist, who was *one* of the seven, and stayed with him. [9]Now this man had four virgin daughters who prophesied. [10]And as we stayed many days, a certain prophet named Agabus came down from Judea. [11]When he had come to us, he took Paul's belt, bound his *own* hands and feet, and said, "Thus says the Holy Spirit, 'So shall the Jews at Jerusalem bind the man who owns this belt, and deliver *him* into the hands of the Gentiles.' "

[12]Now when we heard these things, both we and those from that place pleaded with him not to go up to Jerusalem. [13]Then Paul answered, "What do you mean by weeping and breaking my heart? For I am ready not only to be bound, but also to die at Jerusalem for the name of the Lord Jesus."

[14]So when he would not be persuaded, we ceased, saying, "The will of the Lord be done."

Paul Urged to Make Peace

[15]And after those days we packed and went up to Jerusalem. [16]Also some of the disciples from Caesarea went with us and brought with them a certain Mnason of Cyprus, an early disciple, with whom we were to lodge.

[17]And when we had come to Jerusalem, the brethren received us gladly. [18]On the following *day* Paul went in with us to James, and all the elders were present. [19]When he had greeted them, he told in detail those things which God had done among the Gentiles through his ministry. [20]And when they heard *it,* they glorified the Lord. And they said to him, "You see, brother, how many myriads of Jews there are who have believed, and they are all zealous for the law; [21]but they have been informed about you that you teach all the Jews who are among the Gentiles to forsake Moses, saying that they ought not to circumcise *their* children nor to walk according to the customs. [22]What then? The assembly must certainly meet, for they will[a] hear that you have come. [23]Therefore do what we tell you: We have four men who have taken a vow. [24]Take them and be purified with them, and pay their expenses so that they may shave *their* heads, and that all may know that those things of which they were informed concerning you are nothing, but *that* you yourself also walk orderly and keep the law. [25]But concerning the Gentiles who believe, we have written *and* decided that they should observe no such thing, except[a] that they should keep themselves from *things* offered to idols, from blood, from things strangled, and from sexual immorality."

Arrested in the Temple

[26]Then Paul took the men, and the next day, having been purified with them, entered the temple to announce the expiration of the days of purification, at which time an offering should be made for each one of them.

[27]Now when the seven days were almost

21:4 [a]NU-Text reads *the disciples.* **21:8** [a]NU-Text omits *who were Paul's companions.* **21:22** [a]NU-Text reads *What then is to be done? They will certainly.* **21:25** [a]NU-Text omits *that they should observe no such thing, except.*

ended, the Jews from Asia, seeing him in the temple, stirred up the whole crowd and laid hands on him, [28]crying out, "Men of Israel, help! This is the man who teaches all *men* everywhere against the people, the law, and this place; and furthermore he also brought Greeks into the temple and has defiled this holy place." [29](For they had previously[a] seen Trophimus the Ephesian with him in the city, whom they supposed that Paul had brought into the temple.)

[30]And all the city was disturbed; and the people ran together, seized Paul, and dragged him out of the temple; and immediately the doors were shut. [31]Now as they were seeking to kill him, news came to the commander of the garrison that all Jerusalem was in an uproar. [32]He immediately took soldiers and centurions, and ran down to them. And when they saw the commander and the soldiers, they stopped beating Paul. [33]Then the commander came near and took him, and commanded *him* to be bound with two chains; and he asked who he was and what he had done. [34]And some among the multitude cried one thing and some another.

So when he could not ascertain the truth because of the tumult, he commanded him to be taken into the barracks. [35]When he reached the stairs, he had to be carried by the soldiers because of the violence of the mob. [36]For the multitude of the people followed after, crying out, "Away with him!"

Addressing the Jerusalem Mob

[37]Then as Paul was about to be led into the barracks, he said to the commander, "May I speak to you?"

He replied, "Can you speak Greek? [38]Are you not the Egyptian who some time ago stirred up a rebellion and led the four thousand assassins out into the wilderness?"

[39]But Paul said, "I am a Jew from Tarsus, in Cilicia, a citizen of no mean city; and I implore you, permit me to speak to the people."

[40]So when he had given him permission, Paul stood on the stairs and motioned with his hand to the people. And when there was a great silence, he spoke to *them* in the Hebrew language, saying,

22 "Brethren and fathers, hear my defense before you now." [2]And when they heard that he spoke to them in the Hebrew language, they kept all the more silent.

Then he said: [3]"I am indeed a Jew, born in Tarsus of Cilicia, but brought up in this city at the feet of Gamaliel, taught according to the strictness of our fathers' law, and was zealous toward God as you all are today. [4]I persecuted this Way to the death, binding and delivering into prisons both men and women, [5]as also the high priest bears me witness, and all the council of the elders, from whom I also received letters to the brethren, and went to Damascus to bring in chains even those who were there to Jerusalem to be punished.

[6]"Now it happened, as I journeyed and came near Damascus at about noon, suddenly a great light from heaven shone around me. [7]And I fell to the ground and heard a voice saying to me, 'Saul, Saul, why are you persecuting Me?' [8]So I answered, 'Who are You, Lord?' And He said to me, 'I am Jesus of Nazareth, whom you are persecuting.'

[9]"And those who were with me indeed saw the light and were afraid,[a] but they did not hear the voice of Him who spoke to me. [10]So I said, 'What shall I do, Lord?' And the Lord said to me, 'Arise and go into Damascus, and there you will be told all things which are appointed for you to do.' [11]And since I could not see for the glory of that light, being led by the hand of those who were with me, I came into Damascus.

[12]"Then a certain Ananias, a devout man according to the law, having a good testimony with all the Jews who dwelt *there,* [13]came to me; and he stood and said to me, 'Brother Saul, receive your sight.' And at that same hour I looked up at him. [14]Then he said, 'The God of our fathers has chosen you that you should know His will, and see the Just One, and hear the voice of His mouth. [15]For you will be His witness to all men of what you have seen and heard. [16]And now why are you waiting? Arise and be baptized, and wash away your sins, calling on the name of the Lord.'

[17]"Now it happened, when I returned to Jerusalem and was praying in the temple, that I was in a trance [18]and saw Him saying to me, 'Make haste and get out of Jerusalem quickly, for they will not receive your testimony concerning Me.' [19]So I said, 'Lord, they know that

---

21:29 [a]M-Text omits *previously.* **22:9** [a]NU-Text omits *and were afraid.*

in every synagogue I imprisoned and beat
those who believe on You. [20]And when the
blood of Your martyr Stephen was shed, I also
was standing by consenting to his death,[a] and
guarding the clothes of those who were killing
him.' [21]Then He said to me, 'Depart, for I will
send you far from here to the Gentiles.' "

Paul's Roman Citizenship

[22]And they listened to him until this word,
and *then* they raised their voices and said,
"Away with such a *fellow* from the earth, for
he is not fit to live!" [23]Then, as they cried out
and tore off *their* clothes and threw dust into
the air, [24]the commander ordered him to be
brought into the barracks, and said that he
should be examined under scourging, so that
he might know why they shouted so against
him. [25]And as they bound him with thongs,
Paul said to the centurion who stood by, "Is it
lawful for you to scourge a man who is a Roman, and uncondemned?"
[26]When the centurion heard *that,* he went
and told the commander, saying, "Take care
what you do, for this man is a Roman."
[27]Then the commander came and said to
him, "Tell me, are you a Roman?"
He said, "Yes."
[28]The commander answered, "With a large
sum I obtained this citizenship."
And Paul said, "But I was born *a citizen.*"
[29]Then immediately those who were about
to examine him withdrew from him; and the
commander was also afraid after he found out
that he was a Roman, and because he had
bound him.

22:20 [a]NU-Text omits *to his death.*

PERSONALITY PROFILE

Perfectionism

PAUL'S IMPERFECT PERFECTION

(ACTS 22:3, 4)

Paul could have been considered a "perfect" Jew. He had the right pedigree, the right training, the right desires, the right enthusiasm. But being "perfect" in one's own eyes doesn't make somebody saved before God.

When God got hold of him, Paul understood two very important facts. First, he realized that God could use every part of a person's background and upbringing for His glory. Nothing is wasted with God. As God fashioned his future servant, the events of Paul's life would be brought together into a perfect "package" that could accomplish God's great purposes. Paul's training under Gamaliel gave him command of the Old Testament Scriptures. When Christ revealed Himself, Paul, unlike many of his fellow Pharisees, saw how Christ had fulfilled every prophecy regarding the Messiah. Paul's logical mind saw the truth, and there was no turning back. In addition, Paul's Roman citizenship allowed him free travel across the empire, and spared him at least one beating at the hands of Roman soldiers.

Second, Paul realized that his perfect pedigree was ultimately worthless for salvation. He wrote to the Philippian church: "If anyone else thinks he may have confidence in the flesh, I more so: circumcised the eighth day, of the stock of Israel, of the tribe of Benjamin, a Hebrew of the Hebrews; concerning the law, a Pharisee; concerning zeal, persecuting the church; concerning the righteousness which is in the law, blameless. But what things were gain to me, these I have counted loss for Christ" (Phil. 3:4–7).

Paul's Jewish "perfection" counted for nothing. No one's pedigree, training, background, wealth, abilities, gifts, appearance, or anything else can be perfect enough to earn salvation. We must not be enslaved to the "perfectionism" of this world that is ultimately worthless. Only when we cast ourselves before God and allow *Him* to use our backgrounds, training, and gifts for His glory will we find complete fulfillment. Only when we repent of our sins and accept Him as our Savior does He do His perfect work in us.

To Learn More: Turn to the article about perfectionism on pages 1630, 1631. See also the key passage note at Hebrews 10:12–14 on page 1628.

The Sanhedrin Divided

30The next day, because he wanted to know
for certain why he was accused by the Jews,
he released him from *his* bonds, and commanded the chief priests and all their council
to appear, and brought Paul down and set him
before them.

23 Then Paul, looking earnestly at the
council, said, "Men *and* brethren, I
have lived in all good conscience before God
until this day." 2And the high priest Ananias
commanded those who stood by him to strike
him on the mouth. 3Then Paul said to him,
"God will strike you, *you* whitewashed wall!
For you sit to judge me according to the law,
and do you command me to be struck contrary to the law?"

4And those who stood by said, "Do you revile God's high priest?"

5Then Paul said, "I did not know, brethren,
that he was the high priest; for it is written,
'*You shall not speak evil of a ruler of your
people.*' "[a]

6But when Paul perceived that one part
were Sadducees and the other Pharisees, he
cried out in the council, "Men *and* brethren, I
am a Pharisee, the son of a Pharisee; concerning the hope and resurrection of the dead I am
being judged!"

7And when he had said this, a dissension
arose between the Pharisees and the Sadducees; and the assembly was divided. 8For Sadducees say that there is no resurrection—and
no angel or spirit; but the Pharisees confess
both. 9Then there arose a loud outcry. And the
scribes of the Pharisees' party arose and pro-
tested, saying, "We find no evil in this man;
but if a spirit or an angel has spoken to him,
let us not fight against God."[a]

10Now when there arose a great dissension,
the commander, fearing lest Paul might be
pulled to pieces by them, commanded the soldiers to go down and take him by force from
among them, and bring *him* into the barracks.

The Plot Against Paul

11But the following night the Lord stood by
him and said, "Be of good cheer, Paul; for as
you have testified for Me in Jerusalem, so you
must also bear witness at Rome."

12And when it was day, some of the Jews
banded together and bound themselves under
an oath, saying that they would neither eat
nor drink till they had killed Paul. 13Now there
were more than forty who had formed this
conspiracy. 14They came to the chief priests
and elders, and said, "We have bound ourselves under a great oath that we will eat
nothing until we have killed Paul. 15Now you,
therefore, together with the council, suggest to
the commander that he be brought down to
you tomorrow,[a] as though you were going to
make further inquiries concerning him; but we
are ready to kill him before he comes near."

16So when Paul's sister's son heard of their
ambush, he went and entered the barracks
and told Paul. 17Then Paul called one of the
centurions to *him* and said, "Take this young
man to the commander, for he has something
to tell him." 18So he took him and brought *him*
to the commander and said, "Paul the prisoner called me to *him* and asked *me* to bring this
young man to you. He has something to say to
you."

19Then the commander took him by the
hand, went aside, and asked privately, "What
is it that you have to tell me?"

20And he said, "The Jews have agreed to ask
that you bring Paul down to the council tomorrow, as though they were going to inquire
more fully about him. 21But do not yield to
them, for more than forty of them lie in wait
for him, men who have bound themselves by
an oath that they will neither eat nor drink till
they have killed him; and now they are ready,
waiting for the promise from you."

22So the commander let the young man depart, and commanded *him*, "Tell no one that
you have revealed these things to me."

Sent to Felix

23And he called for two centurions, saying,
"Prepare two hundred soldiers, seventy horsemen, and two hundred spearmen to go to
Caesarea at the third hour of the night; 24and
provide mounts to set Paul on, and bring *him*
safely to Felix the governor." 25He wrote a letter in the following manner:

26 Claudius Lysias,

To the most excellent governor Felix:

Greetings.

23:5 [a]Exodus 22:28 **23:9** [a]NU-Text omits last clause and reads *what if a spirit or an angel has spoken to him?* **23:15** [a]NU-Text omits *tomorrow.*

27 This man was seized by the Jews and was
about to be killed by them. Coming with
the troops I rescued him, having learned
that he was a Roman. 28 And when I
wanted to know the reason they accused
him, I brought him before their council.
29 I found out that he was accused
concerning questions of their law, but had
nothing charged against him deserving of
death or chains. 30 And when it was told
me that the Jews lay in wait for the man,[a]
I sent him immediately to you, and also
commanded his accusers to state before
you the charges against him.

Farewell.

31 Then the soldiers, as they were commanded, took Paul and brought *him* by night to An-
tipatris. 32 The next day they left the horsemen
to go on with him, and returned to the barracks. 33 When they came to Caesarea and had
delivered the letter to the governor, they also
presented Paul to him. 34 And when the governor had read *it*, he
asked what province he
was from. And when he
understood that *he was*
from Cilicia, 35 he said,
"I will hear you when
your accusers also have
come." And he com-
manded him to be kept
in Herod's Praetorium.

ACCUSED OF SEDITION

24 Now after five days Ananias the high
priest came down with the elders and
a certain orator *named* Tertullus. These gave
evidence to the governor against Paul.
2 And when he was called upon, Tertullus
began his accusation, saying: "Seeing that
through you we enjoy great peace, and prosperity is being brought to this nation by your
foresight, 3 we accept *it* always and in all
places, most noble Felix, with all thankfulness. 4 Nevertheless, not to be tedious to you
any further, I beg you to hear, by your courtesy, a few words from us. 5 For we have found
this man a plague, a creator of dissension
among all the Jews throughout the world, and
a ringleader of the sect of the Nazarenes. 6 He
even tried to profane the temple, and we
seized him,[a] and wanted to judge him according to our law. 7 But the commander Lysias
came by and with great violence took *him* out
of our hands, 8 commanding his accusers to
come to you. By examining him yourself you
may ascertain all these things of which we accuse him." 9 And the Jews also assented,[a]
maintaining that these things were so.

THE DEFENSE BEFORE FELIX

10 Then Paul, after the governor had nodded
to him to speak, answered: "Inasmuch as I
know that you have been for many years a
judge of this nation, I do the more cheerfully
answer for myself, 11 because you may ascertain that it is no more than twelve days since I
went up to Jerusalem to worship. 12 And they
neither found me in the temple disputing with
anyone nor inciting the crowd, either in the
synagogues or in the city. 13 Nor can they prove
the things of which they now accuse me. 14 But
this I confess to you, that according to the
Way which they call a sect, so I worship the
God of my fathers, believing all things which
are written in the Law and in the Prophets. 15 I
have hope in God,
which they themselves
also accept, that there
will be a resurrection of
the dead,[a] both of *the*
just and *the* unjust.
16 This *being* so, I myself
always strive to have a
conscience without of-
fense toward God and men.

> "I have hope in God, which they themselves also accept, that there will be a resurrection of the dead, both of the just and the unjust."
>
> ACTS 24:15

17 "Now after many years I came to bring
alms and offerings to my nation, 18 in the midst
of which some Jews from Asia found me purified in the temple, neither with a mob nor
with tumult. 19 They ought to have been here
before you to object if they had anything
against me. 20 Or else let those who are *here*
themselves say if they found any wrongdoing[a]
in me while I stood before the council, 21 unless *it is* for this one statement which I cried
out, standing among them, 'Concerning the
resurrection of the dead I am being judged by
you this day.' "

23:30 [a]NU-Text reads *there would be a plot against the man.* **24:6** [a]NU-Text ends the sentence here and omits the rest of verse 6, all of verse 7, and the first clause of verse 8. **24:9** [a]NU-Text and M-Text read *joined the attack.* **24:15** [a]NU-Text omits *of the dead.* **24:20** [a]NU-Text and M-Text read *say what wrongdoing they found.*

Felix Procrastinates

[22]But when Felix heard these things, having more accurate knowledge of *the* Way, he adjourned the proceedings and said, "When Lysias the commander comes down, I will make a decision on your case." [23]So he commanded the centurion to keep Paul and to let *him* have liberty, and told him not to forbid any of his friends to provide for or visit him.

[24]And after some days, when Felix came with his wife Drusilla, who was Jewish, he sent for Paul and heard him concerning the faith in Christ. [25]Now as he reasoned about righteousness, self-control, and the judgment to come, Felix was afraid and answered, "Go away for now; when I have a convenient time I will call for you." [26]Meanwhile he also hoped that money would be given him by Paul, that he might release him.[a] Therefore he sent for him more often and conversed with him.

[27]But after two years Porcius Festus succeeded Felix; and Felix, wanting to do the Jews a favor, left Paul bound.

Paul Appeals to Caesar

25 Now when Festus had come to the province, after three days he went up from Caesarea to Jerusalem. [2]Then the high priest[a] and the chief men of the Jews informed him against Paul; and they petitioned him, [3]asking a favor against him, that he would summon him to Jerusalem—while *they* lay in ambush along the road to kill him. [4]But Festus answered that Paul should be kept at Caesarea, and that he himself was going *there* shortly. [5]"Therefore," he said, "let those who have authority among you go down with *me* and accuse this man, to see if there is any fault in him."

[6]And when he had remained among them more than ten days, he went down to Caesarea. And the next day, sitting on the judgment seat, he commanded Paul to be brought. [7]When he had come, the Jews who had come down from Jerusalem stood about and laid many serious complaints against Paul, which they could not prove, [8]while he answered for himself, "Neither against the law of the Jews, nor against the temple, nor against Caesar have I offended in anything at all."

[9]But Festus, wanting to do the Jews a favor, answered Paul and said, "Are you willing to go up to Jerusalem and there be judged before me concerning these things?"

[10]So Paul said, "I stand at Caesar's judgment seat, where I ought to be judged. To the Jews I have done no wrong, as you very well know. [11]For if I am an offender, or have committed anything deserving of death, I do not object to dying; but if there is nothing in these things of which these men accuse me, no one can deliver me to them. I appeal to Caesar."

[12]Then Festus, when he had conferred with the council, answered, "You have appealed to Caesar? To Caesar you shall go!"

Paul Before Agrippa

[13]And after some days King Agrippa and Bernice came to Caesarea to greet Festus. [14]When they had been there many days, Festus laid Paul's case before the king, saying: "There is a certain man left a prisoner by Felix, [15]about whom the chief priests and the elders of the Jews informed *me,* when I was in Jerusalem, asking for a judgment against him. [16]To them I answered, 'It is not the custom of the Romans to deliver any man to destruction[a] before the accused meets the accusers face to face, and has opportunity to answer for himself concerning the charge against him.' [17]Therefore when they had come together, without any delay, the next day I sat on the judgment seat and commanded the man to be brought in. [18]When the accusers stood up, they brought no accusation against him of such things as I supposed, [19]but had some questions against him about their own religion and about a certain Jesus, who had died, whom Paul affirmed to be alive. [20]And because I was uncertain of such questions, I asked whether he was willing to go to Jerusalem and there be judged concerning these matters. [21]But when Paul appealed to be reserved for the decision of Augustus, I commanded him to be kept till I could send him to Caesar."

[22]Then Agrippa said to Festus, "I also would like to hear the man myself."

"Tomorrow," he said, "you shall hear him."

[23]So the next day, when Agrippa and Bernice had come with great pomp, and had entered the auditorium with the commanders and the prominent men of the city, at Festus' command Paul was brought in. [24]And Festus

24:26 [a]NU-Text omits *that he might release him.* **25:2** [a]NU-Text reads *chief priests.* **25:16** [a]NU-Text omits *to destruction,* although it is implied.

said: "King Agrippa and all the men who are
here present with us, you see this man about
whom the whole assembly of the Jews petitioned me, both at Jerusalem and here, crying
out that he was not fit to live any longer. [25]But
when I found that he had committed nothing
deserving of death, and that he himself had appealed to Augustus, I decided to send him. [26]I
have nothing certain to write to my lord concerning him. Therefore I have brought him out
before you, and especially before you, King
Agrippa, so that after the examination has tak-
en place I may have something to write. [27]For it
seems to me unreasonable to send a prisoner
and not to specify the charges against him."

PAUL'S EARLY LIFE

26 Then Agrippa said to Paul, "You are
permitted to speak for yourself."
So Paul stretched out his hand and answered for himself: [2]"I think myself happy,
King Agrippa, because today I shall answer for
myself before you concerning all the things of
which I am accused by the Jews, [3]especially
because you are expert in all customs and
questions which have to do with the Jews.
Therefore I beg you to hear me patiently.
[4]"My manner of life from my youth, which
was spent from the beginning among my own
nation at Jerusalem, all the Jews know. [5]They
knew me from the first, if they were willing to
testify, that according to the strictest sect of
our religion I lived a Pharisee. [6]And now I
stand and am judged for the hope of the promise made by God to our fathers. [7]To this *promise* our twelve tribes, earnestly serving *God*
night and day, hope to attain. For this hope's
sake, King Agrippa, I am accused by the Jews.
[8]Why should it be thought incredible by you
that God raises the dead?
[9]"Indeed, I myself thought I must do many
things contrary to the name of Jesus of Nazareth. [10]This I also did in Jerusalem, and many
of the saints I shut up in prison, having received authority from the chief priests; and
when they were put to death, I cast my vote
against *them*. [11]And I punished them often in
every synagogue and compelled *them* to blaspheme; and being exceedingly enraged against
them, I persecuted *them* even to foreign cities.

PAUL RECOUNTS HIS CONVERSION

[12]"While thus occupied, as I journeyed to
Damascus with authority and commission
from the chief priests, [13]at midday, O king,
along the road I saw a light from heaven,
brighter than the sun, shining around me and
those who journeyed with me. [14]And when we
all had fallen to the ground, I heard a voice
speaking to me and saying in the Hebrew language, 'Saul, Saul, why are you persecuting
Me? *It is* hard for you to kick against the
goads.' [15]So I said, 'Who are You, Lord?' And
He said, 'I am Jesus, whom you are persecuting. [16]But rise and stand on your feet; for I
have appeared to you for this purpose, to
make you a minister and a witness both of the
things which you have seen and of the things
which I will yet reveal to you. [17]I will deliver
you from the *Jewish* people, as well as *from*
the Gentiles, to whom I now[a] send you, [18]to
open their eyes, *in order* to turn *them* from
darkness to light, and *from* the power of Satan
to God, that they may receive forgiveness of
sins and an inheritance among those who are
sanctified by faith in Me.'

PAUL'S POST-CONVERSION LIFE

[19]"Therefore, King Agrippa, I was not disobedient to the heavenly vision, [20]but declared first to those in Damascus and in
Jerusalem, and throughout all the region of

26:17 [a]NU-Text and M-Text omit *now.*

SOUL NOTE

Called Out of Darkness *(26:17, 18)* Jesus had told Paul of his mission to the Gentiles—to turn them from darkness and away from the power of Satan. Many people are involved in Satan worship and or various forms of the occult. Satan's powerful hold can be broken only by the power of Jesus Christ. No matter what someone's past is, they can "receive forgiveness of sins and an inheritance among those who are sanctified by faith." We can trust in Christ's power over Satan—the victory has already been won. **Topic: Occult**

Judea, and *then* to the Gentiles, that they
should repent, turn to God, and do works be-
fitting repentance. 21For these reasons the
Jews seized me in the temple and tried to kill
me. 22Therefore, having obtained help from
God, to this day I stand, witnessing both to
small and great, saying no other things than
those which the prophets and Moses said
would come—23that the Christ would suffer,
that He would be the first to rise from the
dead, and would proclaim light to the *Jewish*
people and to the Gentiles."

Agrippa Parries Paul's Challenge

24Now as he thus made his defense, Festus
said with a loud voice, "Paul, you are beside
yourself! Much learning is driving you mad!"
25But he said, "I am not mad, most noble
Festus, but speak the words of truth and reason. 26For the king, before whom I also speak
freely, knows these things; for I am convinced
that none of these things escapes his attention, since this thing was not done in a corner.
27King Agrippa, do you believe the prophets? I
know that you do believe."
28Then Agrippa said to Paul, "You almost
persuade me to become a Christian."
29And Paul said, "I would to God that not
only you, but also all who hear me today,
might become both almost and altogether
such as I am, except for these chains."
30When he had said these things, the king

PERSONALITY PROFILE

Belief

KING AGRIPPA'S REFUSAL TO BELIEVE

(ACTS 26:28)

King Agrippa was the youngest of five Herods who participated in biblical events. Roman emperors gave the Herods authority over various parts of Israel even though the family did not come from Jewish stock. They ruled over a conquered but resentful people.

During its glory years, Rome practiced a remarkable system of justice. Conquered people had few rights, but citizens, like Paul, could appeal to Caesar as their ultimate judge. The apostle Paul exercised this right when he was imprisoned in Jerusalem at the end of his third missionary journey. By law, the local political leaders had to send him to Rome. Along the way, Agrippa interviewed Paul. Paul's powerful spiritual autobiography and his challenge to Agrippa are recorded in Acts 25:13—26:32.

King Agrippa realized that the apostle Paul's argument required a response. He used a question to avoid a decision. "You almost persuade me to become a Christian" (Acts 26:28) actually translates better as "Do you think you can convince me to become a Christian so quickly?" The king's tactic reveals his unbelief. He didn't argue against the truth of Paul's words. He couldn't. He was simply unwilling to believe.

Becoming a Christian has little to do with speed. It has nothing to do with political position or intellectual insight. Many different kinds of people come to faith in Christ while many others reject the gospel. God has given people enough reasons to believe in Christ. Those like Agrippa who reject Christ do so not because they are unpersuaded, but because they do not want to believe.

Questions make effective tools when we use them to find the truth. But questions can also be used to avoid facing the truth. Agrippa had a clear opportunity to meet the Truth Himself. Instead, he used a question to turn away from Christ. Sadly, his mistake gets repeated every day.

When given the opportunity, some will refuse to believe. We can continue to pray for them and live Christ before them, hoping that one day they will decide for Christ. Ultimately, their decision rests in God's hands.

To Learn More: Turn to the article about belief on pages 1480, 1481. See also the key passage note at Romans 10:9, 10 on page 1478.

stood up, as well as the governor and Bernice
and those who sat with them; 31and when
they had gone aside, they talked among themselves, saying, "This man is doing nothing deserving of death or chains."
32Then Agrippa said to Festus, "This man
might have been set free if he had not appealed to Caesar."

The Voyage to Rome Begins

27 And when it was decided that we
should sail to Italy, they delivered Paul
and some other prisoners to *one* named Julius,
a centurion of the Augustan Regiment. 2So,
entering a ship of Adramyttium, we put to sea,
meaning to sail along the coasts of Asia. Aristarchus, a Macedonian of Thessalonica, was
with us. 3And the next *day* we landed at Sidon. And Julius treated Paul kindly and gave
him liberty to go to his friends and receive
care. 4When we had put to sea from there, we
sailed under *the shelter of* Cyprus, because the
winds were contrary. 5And when we had
sailed over the sea which is off Cilicia and
Pamphylia, we came to Myra, *a city* of Lycia.
6There the centurion found an Alexandrian
ship sailing to Italy, and he put us on board.
7When we had sailed slowly many days,
and arrived with difficulty off Cnidus, the
wind not permitting us to proceed, we sailed
under *the shelter of* Crete off Salmone. 8Pass-
ing it with difficulty, we came to a place called
Fair Havens, near the city *of* Lasea.

Paul's Warning Ignored

9Now when much time had been spent, and
sailing was now dangerous because the Fast
was already over, Paul advised them, 10saying,
"Men, I perceive that this voyage will end
with disaster and much loss, not only of the
cargo and ship, but also our lives." 11Never-
theless the centurion was more persuaded by
the helmsman and the owner of the ship than
by the things spoken by Paul. 12And because
the harbor was not suitable to winter in, the
majority advised to set sail from there also, if
by any means they could reach Phoenix, a
harbor of Crete opening toward the southwest
and northwest, *and* winter *there.*

In the Tempest

13When the south wind blew softly, supposing that they had obtained *their* desire, putting
out to sea, they sailed close by Crete. 14But not
long after, a tempestuous head wind arose,
called Euroclydon.[a] 15So when the ship was
caught, and could not head into the wind, we
let *her* drive. 16And running under *the shelter
of* an island called Clauda,[a] we secured the
skiff with difficulty. 17When they had taken it
on board, they used cables to undergird the
ship; and fearing lest they should run aground
on the Syrtis[a] *Sands,* they struck sail and so
were driven. 18And because we were exceedingly tempest-tossed, the next *day* they lightened the ship. 19On the third *day* we threw the
ship's tackle overboard with our own hands.
20Now when neither sun nor stars appeared
for many days, and no small tempest beat on
us, all hope that we would be saved was finally given up.
21But after long abstinence from food, then
Paul stood in the midst of them and said,
"Men, you should have listened to me, and
not have sailed from Crete and incurred this
disaster and loss. 22And now I urge you to take
heart, for there will be no loss of life among
you, but only of the ship. 23For there stood by
me this night an angel of the God to whom I
belong and whom I serve, 24saying, 'Do not be
afraid, Paul; you must be brought before Caesar; and indeed God has granted you all those
who sail with you.' 25Therefore take heart,
men, for I believe God that it will be just as it
was told me. 26However, we must run aground
on a certain island."
27Now when the fourteenth night had come,
as we were driven up and down in the Adriatic
Sea, about midnight the sailors sensed that
they were drawing near some land. 28And they
took soundings and found *it* to be twenty fathoms; and when they had gone a little farther,
they took soundings again and found *it* to be
fifteen fathoms. 29Then, fearing lest we should
run aground on the rocks, they dropped four
anchors from the stern, and prayed for day to
come. 30And as the sailors were seeking to escape from the ship, when they had let down
the skiff into the sea, under pretense of putting out anchors from the prow, 31Paul said to
the centurion and the soldiers, "Unless these
men stay in the ship, you cannot be saved."
32Then the soldiers cut away the ropes of the
skiff and let it fall off.
33And as day was about to dawn, Paul im-

27:14 [a]NU-Text reads *Euraquilon.* **27:16** [a]NU-Text reads *Cauda.* **27:17** [a]M-Text reads *Syrtes.*

plored *them* all to take food, saying, "Today is
the fourteenth day you have waited and continued without food, and eaten nothing.
34Therefore I urge you to take nourishment,
for this is for your survival, since not a hair
will fall from the head of any of you." 35And
when he had said these things, he took bread
and gave thanks to God in the presence of
them all; and when he had broken *it* he began
to eat. 36Then they were all encouraged, and
also took food themselves. 37And in all we
were two hundred and seventy-six persons on
the ship. 38So when they had eaten enough,
they lightened the ship and threw out the
wheat into the sea.

Shipwrecked on Malta

39When it was day, they did not recognize
the land; but they observed a bay with a
beach, onto which they planned to run the
ship if possible. 40And they let go the anchors
and left *them* in the sea, meanwhile loosing the
rudder ropes; and they hoisted the mainsail to
the wind and made for shore. 41But striking a
place where two seas met, they ran the ship
aground; and the prow stuck fast and remained immovable, but the stern was being
broken up by the violence of the waves.

42And the soldiers' plan was to kill the prisoners, lest any of them should swim away and
escape. 43But the centurion, wanting to save
Paul, kept them from *their* purpose, and commanded that those who could swim should
jump *overboard* first and get to land, 44and the
rest, some on boards and some on *parts* of the
ship. And so it was that they all escaped safely
to land.

Paul's Ministry on Malta

28 Now when they had escaped, they
then found out that the island was
called Malta. 2And the natives showed us unusual kindness; for they kindled a fire and
made us all welcome, because of the rain that
was falling and because of the cold. 3But
when Paul had gathered a bundle of sticks and
laid *them* on the fire, a viper came out because
of the heat, and fastened on his hand. 4So
when the natives saw the creature hanging
from his hand, they said to one another, "No
doubt this man is a murderer, whom, though
he has escaped the sea, yet justice does not allow to live." 5But he shook off the creature
into the fire and suffered no harm. 6However,
they were expecting that he would swell up or
suddenly fall down dead. But after they had
looked for a long time and saw no harm come
to him, they changed their minds and said
that he was a god.

7In that region there was an estate of the
leading citizen of the island, whose name was
Publius, who received us and entertained us
courteously for three days. 8And it happened
that the father of Publius lay sick of a fever
and dysentery. Paul went in to him and
prayed, and he laid his hands on him and
healed him. 9So when this was done, the rest
of those on the island who had diseases also
came and were healed. 10They also honored us
in many ways; and when we departed, they
provided such things as were necessary.

Arrival at Rome

11After three months we sailed in an Alexandrian ship whose figurehead was the Twin
Brothers, which had wintered at the island.
12And landing at Syracuse, we stayed three
days. 13From there we circled round and
reached Rhegium. And after one day the south
wind blew; and the next day we came to Pute-
oli, 14where we found brethren, and were invited to stay with them seven days. And so we

SOUL NOTE

The Power to Heal *(28:7–10)* Even as a shipwrecked prisoner, Paul continued to minister to others. On the island of Malta, many were affected by the gospel, including Publius's father, who was healed from his illness. Even though Paul had just experienced several difficult weeks at sea and then a frightening shipwreck, he was never too self-focused to see a need and seek to meet it. He was always willing to share the message of the Good News with anyone he met. Paul's compassion on Publius changed his life. We never know what results our compassion might have on others.
Topic: Compassion

went toward Rome. 15And from there, when
the brethren heard about us, they came to
meet us as far as Appii Forum and Three Inns.
When Paul saw them, he thanked God and
took courage.
16Now when we came to Rome, the centurion delivered the prisoners to the captain of the
guard; but Paul was permitted to dwell by
himself with the soldier who guarded him.

Paul's Ministry at Rome

17And it came to pass after three days that
Paul called the leaders of the Jews together. So
when they had come together, he said to
them: "Men *and* brethren, though I have done
nothing against our people or the customs of
our fathers, yet I was delivered as a prisoner
from Jerusalem into the hands of the Romans,
18who, when they had examined me, wanted
to let *me* go, because there was no cause for
putting me to death. 19But when the Jews[a]
spoke against *it,* I was compelled to appeal to
Caesar, not that I had anything of which to
accuse my nation. 20For this reason therefore I
have called for you, to see *you* and speak with
you, because for the hope of Israel I am bound
with this chain."
21Then they said to him, "We neither received letters from Judea concerning you, nor
have any of the brethren who came reported
or spoken any evil of you. 22But we desire to
hear from you what you think; for concerning
this sect, we know that it is spoken against everywhere."
23So when they had appointed him a day,
many came to him at *his* lodging, to whom he
explained and solemnly testified of the kingdom of God, persuading them concerning
Jesus from both the Law of Moses and the
Prophets, from morning till evening. 24And
some were persuaded by the things which
were spoken, and some disbelieved. 25So
when they did not agree among themselves,
they departed after Paul had said one word:
"The Holy Spirit spoke rightly through Isaiah
the prophet to our[a] fathers, 26saying,

'Go to this people and say:
"Hearing you will hear, and shall not
understand;
And seeing you will see, and not
perceive;
27 *For the hearts of this people have grown*
dull.
Their ears are hard of hearing,
And their eyes they have closed,
Lest they should see with their eyes and
hear with their ears,
Lest they should understand with their
hearts and turn,
So that I should heal them."' [a]

28"Therefore let it be known to you that the
salvation of God has been sent to the Gentiles,
and they will hear it!" 29And when he had said
these words, the Jews departed and had a
great dispute among themselves.[a]
30Then Paul dwelt two whole years in his
own rented house, and received all who came
to him, 31preaching the kingdom of God and
teaching the things which concern the Lord
Jesus Christ with all confidence, no one forbidding him.

28:19 [a]That is, the ruling authorities **28:25** [a]NU-Text reads *your.* **28:27** [a]Isaiah 6:9, 10
28:29 [a]NU-Text omits this verse.

Romans

Chicken soup is fine for the soul that is merely under the weather, but what about the soul that is terminally ill?

That, in so many words, is the question the apostle Paul answers in Romans. Many consider Romans to be the most important of all the New Testament letters because it explains what the Christian life is all about. The central theme of Romans is the gospel of Jesus Christ. But Paul realized that any good news of salvation is meaningless until people first come to terms with their lostness and need for God (ch. 1—3). From there Paul demonstrates how faith makes people right with God (ch. 3—5), how to gain victory over sin (ch. 7), and how to find grace and assurance in our darkest hours (ch. 8). Romans also deals with such matters as our relationship to the community and the state (ch. 12, 13) and knowing the will of God when dealing with complicated interpersonal issues (ch. 14, 15).

Paul felt no shame in boldly proclaiming the liberating message of Jesus, because he knew firsthand its power to turn a life upside down. No wonder he declared that the gospel is "the power of God to salvation for everyone who believes" (1:16).

Whatever the condition of your soul, you can be sure that Paul's *magnum opus* offers you more than just a warm feeling. Read Romans as though your life depended on it—because in a very real sense, it does.

SOUL CONCERNS IN ROMANS

HOMOSEXUALITY	(1:27)
BELIEF	(10:9, 10)
DECISION MAKING	(12:2)

GREETING

1 Paul, a bondservant of Jesus Christ, called *to be* an apostle, separated to the gospel of God 2which He promised before through His prophets in the Holy Scriptures, 3concerning His Son Jesus Christ our Lord, who was born of the seed of David according to the flesh, 4*and* declared *to be* the Son of God with power according to the Spirit of holiness, by the resurrection from the dead. 5Through Him we have received grace and apostleship for obedience to the faith among all nations for His name, 6among whom you also are the called of Jesus Christ;

> For in it the righteousness of God is revealed from faith to faith; as it is written, "The just shall live by faith."
>
> ROMANS 1:17

7To all who are in Rome, beloved of God, called *to be* saints:

Grace to you and peace from God our Father and the Lord Jesus Christ.

DESIRE TO VISIT ROME

8First, I thank my God through Jesus Christ for you all, that your faith is spoken of throughout the whole world. 9For God is my witness, whom I serve with my spirit in the gospel of His Son, that without ceasing I make mention of you always in my prayers, 10making request if, by some means, now at last I may find a way in the will of God to come to you. 11For I long to see you, that I may impart to you some spiritual gift, so that you may be established—12that is, that I may be encouraged together with you by the mutual faith both of you and me.

13Now I do not want you to be unaware, brethren, that I often planned to come to you (but was hindered until now), that I might have some fruit among you also, just as among the other Gentiles. 14I am a debtor both to Greeks and to barbarians, both to wise and to unwise. 15So, as much as is in me, *I am* ready to preach the gospel to you who are in Rome also.

THE JUST LIVE BY FAITH

16For I am not ashamed of the gospel of Christ,[a] for it is the power of God to salvation for everyone who believes, for the Jew first and also for the Greek. 17For in it the righteousness of God is revealed from faith to faith; as it is written, *"The just shall live by faith."*[a]

GOD'S WRATH ON UNRIGHTEOUSNESS

18For the wrath of God is revealed from heaven against all ungodliness and unrighteousness of men, who suppress the truth in unrighteousness, 19because what may be known of God is manifest in them, for God has shown *it* to them. 20For since the creation of the world His invisible *attributes* are clearly seen, being understood by the things that are made, *even* His eternal power and Godhead, so that they are without excuse, 21because, although they knew God, they did not glorify *Him* as God, nor were thankful, but became futile in their thoughts, and their foolish hearts were darkened. 22Professing to be wise, they became fools, 23and changed the glory of the incorruptible God into an image made like corruptible man—and birds and four-footed animals and creeping things.

24Therefore God also gave them up to un-

1:16 [a]NU-Text omits *of Christ.* **1:17** [a]Habakkuk 2:4

SOUL NOTE

Not Ashamed *(1:16)* Paul had not yet been to Rome when he wrote this letter, and he longed to visit the church there (see 1:10–13; 15:22–29). In this letter, written to believers Paul had never met, he says he is not ashamed of the gospel message. It is "the power of God to salvation for everyone who believes." All who believe and accept the message of Christ dying on the Cross for their sins will be saved. So we too should be bold about sharing that message. Like Paul, we praise God for providing a way for people to be saved. **Topic: Salvation**

cleanness, in the lusts of their hearts, to dishonor their bodies among themselves, [25]who
exchanged the truth of God for the lie, and
worshiped and served the creature rather than
the Creator, who is blessed forever. Amen.
[26]For this reason God gave them up to vile
passions. For even their women exchanged
the natural use for what is against nature.
[27]Likewise also the men, leaving the natural
use of the woman, burned in their lust for one
another, men with men committing what is
shameful, and receiving in themselves the
penalty of their error which was due.
[28]And even as they did not like to retain God
in *their* knowledge, God gave them over to a
debased mind, to do those things which are
not fitting; [29]being filled with all unrighteousness, sexual immorality,[a] wickedness, covetousness, maliciousness; full of envy, murder,
strife, deceit, evil-mindedness; *they are* whis-
perers, [30]back-biters, haters of God, violent,
proud, boasters, inventors of evil things, disobedient to parents, [31]undiscerning, untrustworthy, unloving, unforgiving,[a] unmerciful;
[32]who, knowing the righteous judgment of
God, that those who practice such things are
deserving of death, not only do the same but
also approve of those who practice them.

God's Righteous Judgment

2 Therefore you are inexcusable, O man,
whoever you are who judge, for in whatever you judge another you condemn yourself;

1:29 [a]NU-Text omits *sexual immorality.* **1:31** [a]NU-Text omits *unforgiving.*

KEY PASSAGE

Homo-sexuality

THE WAY OUT

(1:18–32)

There is no way around it—homosexuality is abhorred by God. Some say that homosexuality is a lifestyle choice or a genetic predisposition—and when confronted with this passage in Romans, some say that these words were meant only for the culture of that day. When dealing with the Old Testament passages condemning homosexual activity (Lev. 18:22; 20:13), the same argument is often made. But what is clearly a moral issue in both the Old and New Testaments cannot be relegated to the past as just a cultural law. The Bible condemns homosexual conduct because it goes against God's plan for a natural sexual relationship between a man and a woman in marriage.

As with any sin, the actions of homosexuality can be forgiven, and its powerful temptations can be overcome. God will forgive and accept anyone who desires to be set free from homosexuality. And one believer can accept another one no matter what their background, as they seek to change their lifestyle and live for God.

To Learn More: Turn to the article about homosexuality on pages 1466, 1467. See also the personality profile of the Sodomites on page 29.

SOUL NOTE

Against God's Plan *(1:26, 27)* Paul says homosexuality is "against nature," against what God planned for sexual relations. God created marriage and sexual relations to be between a man and a woman: "A man shall . . . be joined to his wife, and they shall become one flesh" (Gen. 2:24). Homosexual acts are called shameful, and those who live that lifestyle will receive "the penalty of their error." Yet God will forgive and strengthen those who turn away from homosexuality and seek to honor Him with their lives. **Topic: Homosexuality**

UNDERSTANDING AND ADDRESSING HOMOSEXUALITY

JOE DALLAS

(Romans 1:27)

Both the church and modern culture are divided in their understanding of what homosexuality is, how homosexual people should be treated, and how God views this behavior. When a subject generates such an emotional response, many are tempted to avoid it altogether. However, while controversy for its own sake is a sin, controversy for the sake of the truth is a divine mandate.

WHAT IS HOMOSEXUALITY?

"Homosexuality" refers to a condition and a behavior. The homosexual condition, commonly referred to as an orientation, is one in which a person is sexually attracted to members of the same sex. Any form of sexual activity between members of the same sex is homosexual behavior.

People do not generally choose the homosexual condition. Like many sinful tendencies, it is often deeply ingrained and shows itself early in life. But while the homosexual condition might not be chosen, homosexual behavior *is* a matter of choice. People choose what to do with their desires.

WHAT CAUSES HOMOSEXUALITY?

Though some studies have suggested that homosexuality is inborn, or genetic, there is no convincing evidence of that. It will almost certainly never be proven that homosexuality is an inborn condition. Yet even if such proof were forthcoming, it would not negate the biblical prohibitions against homosexual behavior. It would, in fact, simply prove what is already known. People are all fallen creatures—physically, spiritually, and emotionally imperfect. An inborn tendency toward a particular sin does not justify the sin; it only reinforces the need for a Savior.

Studies indicate that the homosexual condition represents a need for intimacy with members of the same sex that has taken on a sexual nature. A faulty relationship with the same sex parent, lack of bonding with peers, or sexual abuse can all be contributing factors. The need that led to this condition is likely legitimate, but fulfillment of that need is being sought in an illegitimate way.

The idea that homosexuality is "demonic," or caused by demon possession, is also questionable. When the Bible mentions this behavior, it does so in the context of human, carnal temptations. Homosexuality in Scripture is seen as one of the many problems of the flesh—problems that cannot simply be "cast out" as if they were demonic. Instead, they require confession, repentance, and the discipline of a godly life.

HOW DOES THE BIBLE ADDRESS HOMOSEXUALITY?

God's created intent for sexual expression is confined within the protection of marriage between a man and woman (Gen. 2:24; Heb. 13:4). All forms of sexual activity apart from marriage—adultery and fornication, for example—are as roundly condemned in the Bible as is homosexuality.

In the Old Testament, homosexuality is condemned in both Leviticus 18:22 and

20:13 as being an "abomination." In Romans 1:24–27, Paul refers to homosexual attractions between men or women as being an unnatural state resulting from fallen nature; he further condemns homosexual behavior as "vile" and "shameful." In 1 Corinthians 6:9, 10, he lists sexual practices between members of the same gender along with drunkenness, fornication, and other vices that exclude people from God's kingdom. In 1 Timothy 1:9–11, Paul calls homosexuals "sodomites" and places their sin along with murder, pointing out God's clear condemnation of it.

The good news, however, is that in 1 Corinthians 6:11, Paul says of the former homosexuals who had become believers: "Such were some of you. But you were washed, but you were sanctified, but you were justified in the name of the Lord Jesus and by the Spirit of our God." Even in Paul's time, God was delivering people from this sin. The idea of someone who has been homosexual living a Christ-centered life is nothing new.

WHAT IF SOMEONE I LOVE IS HOMOSEXUAL?

Generally, there are three types of homosexual people: militant, moderate, and repentant. Militant homosexuals, the minority, have an agenda to normalize homosexuality in modern culture through laws, education, and the media. They are highly visible, leading many to assume that they are the majority. Moderate homosexuals, the actual majority, live their lives as most people do: paying taxes, working, and contributing to society. Their appearance and behavior are not necessarily noticeable. Repentant homosexuals have repented of their homosexual behavior and are seeking to overcome their aberrant sexual desires.

When someone we love is caught up in this sin, we are reminded more than ever of our own limitations. No matter how deeply we love someone, we cannot force that person to do what is right. God has created free will; we cannot override it, even with someone we love.

We can, however, remind our loved one of two unchangeable truths: God's standards and our love. We must remember that there is a difference between acceptance and approval. We can continue to accept someone we love and, as much as possible, keep our relationship with that person intact. We cannot, however, approve of something that God clearly disapproves of. It is entirely possible to accept a person without approving of everything that person does or believes. God loves His creation, yet disapproves of the sins that the people He loves practice.

To address the issue of homosexuality, then, is to enter deeply into God's experience: loving the person, hating the sin, and remaining steadfast to God's standards. We know that even when our best efforts to persuade the people we love have failed, God's power is still more than able to accomplish His purposes.

FURTHER MEDITATION:

Other passages to study about the issue of homosexuality include:

- Genesis 2:18–25; 19:1–29
- Psalm 81:12
- 1 Thessalonians 4:3–7

To Learn More: Turn to the key passage note on homosexuality at Romans 1:18–32 on page 1465. See also the personality profile of the Sodomites on page 29.

for you who judge practice the same things. 2But we know that the judgment of God is according to truth against those who practice such things. 3And do you think this, O man, you who judge those practicing such things, and doing the same, that you will escape the judgment of God? 4Or do you despise the riches of His goodness, forbearance, and longsuffering, not knowing that the goodness of God leads you to repentance? 5But in accordance with your hardness and your impenitent heart you are treasuring up for yourself wrath in the day of wrath and revelation of the righteous judgment of God, 6who *"will render to each one according to his deeds"*:[a] 7eternal life to those who by patient continuance in doing good seek for glory, honor, and immortality; 8but to those who are self-seeking and do not obey the truth, but obey unrighteousness—indignation and wrath, 9tribulation and anguish, on every soul of man who does evil, of the Jew first and also of the Greek; 10but glory, honor, and peace to everyone who works what is good, to the Jew first and also to the Greek. 11For there is no partiality with God.

Or do you despise the riches of His goodness, forbearance, and longsuffering, not knowing that the goodness of God leads you to repentance?

ROMANS 2:4

12For as many as have sinned without law will also perish without law, and as many as have sinned in the law will be judged by the law 13(for not the hearers of the law *are* just in the sight of God, but the doers of the law will be justified; 14for when Gentiles, who do not have the law, by nature do the things in the law, these, although not having the law, are a law to themselves, 15who show the work of the law written in their hearts, their conscience also bearing witness, and between themselves *their* thoughts accusing or else excusing *them*) 16in the day when God will judge the secrets of men by Jesus Christ, according to my gospel.

The Jews Guilty as the Gentiles

17Indeed[a] you are called a Jew, and rest on the law, and make your boast in God, 18and know *His* will, and approve the things that are excellent, being instructed out of the law, 19and are confident that you yourself are a guide to the blind, a light to those who are in darkness, 20an instructor of the foolish, a teacher of babes, having the form of knowledge and truth in the law. 21You, therefore, who teach another, do you not teach yourself? You who preach that a man should not steal, do you steal? 22You who say, "Do not commit adultery," do you commit adultery? You who abhor idols, do you rob temples? 23You who make your boast in the law, do you dishonor God through breaking the law? 24For *"the name of God is blasphemed among the Gentiles because of you,"*[a] as it is written.

Circumcision of No Avail

25For circumcision is indeed profitable if you keep the law; but if you are a breaker of the law, your circumcision has become uncircumcision. 26Therefore, if an uncircumcised man keeps the righteous requirements of the law, will not his uncircumcision be counted as circumcision? 27And will not the physically uncircumcised, if he fulfills the law, judge you who, *even* with *your* written *code* and circumcision, *are* a transgressor of the law? 28For he is not a Jew who *is one* outwardly, nor *is* circumcision that which *is* outward in the flesh; 29but *he is* a Jew who *is one* inwardly; and circumcision *is that* of the heart, in the Spirit, not in the letter; whose praise *is* not from men but from God.

God's Judgment Defended

3 What advantage then has the Jew, or what *is* the profit of circumcision? 2Much in every way! Chiefly because to them were committed the oracles of God. 3For what if some did not believe? Will their unbelief make the faithfulness of God without effect? 4Certainly not! Indeed, let God be true but every man a liar. As it is written:

"That You may be justified in Your words,
And may overcome when You are judged."[a]

5But if our unrighteousness demonstrates the righteousness of God, what shall we say?

2:6 [a]Psalm 62:12; Proverbs 24:12 **2:17** [a]NU-Text reads *But if.* **2:24** [a]Isaiah 52:5; Ezekiel 36:22 **3:4** [a]Psalm 51:4

Is God unjust who inflicts wrath? (I speak as a
man.) 6Certainly not! For then how will God
judge the world?
7For if the truth of God has increased
through my lie to His glory, why am I also still
judged as a sinner? 8And *why* not *say*, "Let us
do evil that good may come"?—as we are slan-
derously reported and as some affirm that we
say. Their condemnation is just.

All Have Sinned

9What then? Are we better *than they?* Not at
all. For we have previously charged both Jews
and Greeks that they are all under sin.
10As it is written:

"There is none righteous, no, not one;
11 *There is none who understands;*
There is none who seeks after God.
12 *They have all turned aside;*
They have together become unprofitable;
There is none who does good, no, not one."[a]
13 *"Their throat is an open tomb;*
With their tongues they have practiced deceit";[a]
"The poison of asps is under their lips";[b]
14 *"Whose mouth is full of cursing and bitterness."*[a]
15 *"Their feet are swift to shed blood;*
16 *Destruction and misery are in their ways;*
17 *And the way of peace they have not known."*[a]
18 *"There is no fear of God before their eyes."*[a]

19Now we know that whatever the law says,
it says to those who are under the law, that
every mouth may be stopped, and all the
world may become guilty before God. 20There-
fore by the deeds of the law no flesh will be
justified in His sight, for by the law *is* the
knowledge of sin.

God's Righteousness Through Faith

21But now the righteousness of God apart
from the law is revealed, being witnessed by
the Law and the Prophets, 22even the righteousness of God, through faith in Jesus
Christ, to all and on all[a] who believe. For there
is no difference; 23for all have sinned and fall
short of the glory of God, 24being justified
freely by His grace through the redemption
that is in Christ Jesus, 25whom God set forth
as a propitiation by His blood, through faith,
to demonstrate His righteousness, because in
His forbearance God had passed over the sins
that were previously committed, 26to demonstrate at the present time His righteousness,
that He might be just and the justifier of the
one who has faith in Jesus.

Boasting Excluded

27Where *is* boasting then? It is excluded. By
what law? Of works? No, but by the law of
faith. 28Therefore we conclude that a man is
justified by faith apart from the deeds of the
law. 29Or *is He* the God of the Jews only? *Is He*
not also the God of the Gentiles? Yes, of the
Gentiles also, 30since *there is* one God who will
justify the circumcised by faith and the uncircumcised through faith. 31Do we then make
void the law through faith? Certainly not! On
the contrary, we establish the law.

Abraham Justified by Faith

4 What then shall we say that Abraham
our father has found according to the

3:12 [a]Psalms 14:1–3; 53:1–3; Ecclesiastes 7:20
3:13 [a]Psalm 5:9 [b]Psalm 140:3 **3:14** [a]Psalm 10:7
3:17 [a]Isaiah 59:7, 8 **3:18** [a]Psalm 36:1
3:22 [a]NU-Text omits *and on all.*

SOUL NOTE

All *(3:23)* It's a fact—"All have sinned." Except for Jesus, not one person can claim to be sinless. We are born in sin because we inherited the sin nature from our father Adam. We all make choices that violate God's law and desires and break His heart. We can do nothing to save ourselves. No amount of good works, compassion on others, or self-sacrifice can earn salvation. Sin separates us from a holy God, but we are not left hopeless. God reached out to us, sending His Son to die for us (5:8). Because of God's great love and mercy, He offers a gift—"eternal life in Christ Jesus our Lord" (6:23). **Topic: Sin**

flesh?[a] 2For if Abraham was justified by works, he has *something* to boast about, but not before God. 3For what does the Scripture say? *"Abraham believed God, and it was accounted to him for righteousness."*[a] 4Now to him who works, the wages are not counted as grace but as debt.

David Celebrates the Same Truth

5But to him who does not work but believes on Him who justifies the ungodly, his faith is accounted for righteousness, 6just as David also describes the blessedness of the man to whom God imputes righteousness apart from works:

7 *"Blessed are those whose lawless deeds*
are forgiven,
And whose sins are covered;
8 *Blessed is the man to whom the* LORD
shall not impute sin."[a]

Abraham Justified Before Circumcision

9*Does* this blessedness then *come* upon the circumcised *only,* or upon the uncircumcised also? For we say that faith was accounted to Abraham for righteousness. 10How then was it accounted? While he was circumcised, or uncircumcised? Not while circumcised, but while uncircumcised. 11And he received the sign of circumcision, a seal of the righteousness of the faith which *he had while still* uncircumcised, that he might be the father of all those who believe, though they are uncircumcised, that righteousness might be imputed to them also, 12and the father of circumcision to those who not only *are* of the circumcision, but who also walk in the steps of the faith which our father Abraham *had while still* uncircumcised.

The Promise Granted Through Faith

13For the promise that he would be the heir of the world *was* not to Abraham or to his seed through the law, but through the righteousness of faith. 14For if those who are of the law *are* heirs, faith is made void and the promise made of no effect, 15because the law brings about wrath; for where there is no law *there is* no transgression.

16Therefore *it is* of faith that *it might be* according to grace, so that the promise might be sure to all the seed, not only to those who are of the law, but also to those who are of the faith of Abraham, who is the father of us all 17(as it is written, *"I have made you a father of many nations"*[a]) in the presence of Him whom he believed—God, who gives life to the dead and calls those things which do not exist as though they did; 18who, contrary to hope, in hope believed, so that he became the father of many nations, according to what was spoken, *"So shall your descendants be."*[a] 19And not being weak in faith, he did not consider his own body, already dead (since he was about a hundred years old), and the deadness of Sarah's womb. 20He did not waver at the promise of God through unbelief, but was strengthened in faith, giving glory to God, 21and being fully convinced that what He had promised He was also able to perform. 22And therefore *"it was accounted to him for righteousness."*[a]

23Now it was not written for his sake alone that it was imputed to him, 24but also for us. It shall be imputed to us who believe in Him who raised up Jesus our Lord from the dead,

---

4:1 [a]Or *Abraham our (fore)father according to the flesh has found?* **4:3** [a]Genesis 15:6 **4:8** [a]Psalm 32:1, 2 **4:17** [a]Genesis 17:5 **4:18** [a]Genesis 15:5 **4:22** [a]Genesis 15:6

SOUL NOTE

Fully Convinced *(4:20–22)* Paul wanted his readers to understand salvation by faith. Many Jews thought that they would be saved simply because they were Jews and had the Law from Moses. Paul explained, however, that obeying laws can't save anyone because no one can keep God's laws perfectly. Instead, salvation is by faith. Abraham lived before Moses, and so he could not obey the laws of Moses. Yet when God promised Abraham a son, Abraham believed God. That belief "was accounted to him for righteousness." We cannot earn our salvation; we accept God's promise fully convinced that He will keep it. **Topic: God's Promises**

[25]who was delivered up because of our offenses, and was raised because of our justification.

Faith Triumphs in Trouble

5 Therefore, having been justified by faith, we have[a] peace with God through our Lord Jesus Christ, [2]through whom also we have access by faith into this grace in which we stand, and rejoice in hope of the glory of God. [3]And not only *that,* but we also glory in tribulations, knowing that tribulation produces perseverance; [4]and perseverance, character; and character, hope. [5]Now hope does not disappoint, because the love of God has been poured out in our hearts by the Holy Spirit who was given to us.

> Therefore, having been justified by faith, we have peace with God through our Lord Jesus Christ.
>
> ROMANS 5:1

Christ in Our Place

[6]For when we were still without strength, in due time Christ died for the ungodly. [7]For scarcely for a righteous man will one die; yet perhaps for a good man someone would even dare to die. [8]But God demonstrates His own love toward us, in that while we were still sinners, Christ died for us. [9]Much more then, having now been justified by His blood, we shall be saved from wrath through Him. [10]For if when we were enemies we were reconciled to God through the death of His Son, much more, having been reconciled, we shall be saved by His life. [11]And not only *that,* but we also rejoice in God through our Lord Jesus Christ, through whom we have now received the reconciliation.

Death in Adam, Life in Christ

[12]Therefore, just as through one man sin entered the world, and death through sin, and thus death spread to all men, because all sinned—[13](For until the law sin was in the world, but sin is not imputed when there is no law. [14]Nevertheless death reigned from Adam to Moses, even over those who had not sinned according to the likeness of the transgression of Adam, who is a type of Him who was to come. [15]But the free gift *is* not like the offense. For if by the one man's offense many died, much more the grace of God and the gift by the grace of the one Man, Jesus Christ, abounded to many. [16]And the gift *is* not like *that which came* through the one who sinned. For the judgment *which came* from one *offense resulted* in condemnation, but the free gift *which came* from many offenses *resulted* in justification. [17]For if by the one man's offense death reigned through the one, much more those who receive abundance of grace and of the gift of righteousness will reign in life through the One, Jesus Christ.)

[18]Therefore, as through one man's offense *judgment* came to all men, resulting in condemnation, even so through one Man's righteous act *the free gift came* to all men, resulting in justification of life. [19]For as by one man's disobedience many were made sinners, so also by one Man's obedience many will be made righteous.

[20]Moreover the law entered that the offense might abound. But where sin abounded, grace abounded much more, [21]so that as sin reigned in death, even so grace might reign through righteousness to eternal life through Jesus Christ our Lord.

Dead to Sin, Alive to God

6 What shall we say then? Shall we continue in sin that grace may abound? [2]Certainly not! How shall we who died to sin live any longer in it? [3]Or do you not know that as many of us as were baptized into Christ Jesus were baptized into His death? [4]Therefore we were buried with Him through baptism into death, that just as Christ was raised from the dead by the glory of the Father, even so we also should walk in newness of life.

[5]For if we have been united together in the likeness of His death, certainly we also shall be *in the likeness* of *His* resurrection, [6]knowing this, that our old man was crucified with *Him,* that the body of sin might be done away with, that we should no longer be slaves of sin. [7]For he who has died has been freed from sin. [8]Now if we died with Christ, we believe that we shall also live with Him, [9]knowing that Christ, having been raised from the dead, dies no more. Death no longer has dominion over Him. [10]For *the death* that He died, He died to sin once for all; but *the life*

5:1 [a]Another ancient reading is, *let us have peace.*

that He lives, He lives to God. 11Likewise you
also, reckon yourselves to be dead indeed to
sin, but alive to God in Christ Jesus our
Lord.

12Therefore do not let sin reign in your mortal body, that you should obey it in its lusts.
13And do not present your members *as* instruments of unrighteousness to sin, but present
yourselves to God as being alive from the
dead, and your members *as* instruments of
righteousness to God.
14For sin shall not have
dominion over you, for
you are not under law
but under grace.

> For sin shall not have dominion over you, for you are not under law but under grace.
> ROMANS 6:14

FROM SLAVES OF SIN TO SLAVES OF GOD

15What then? Shall we
sin because we are not under law but under
grace? Certainly not! 16Do you not know that
to whom you present yourselves slaves to
obey, you are that one's slaves whom you
obey, whether of sin *leading* to death, or of
obedience *leading* to righteousness? 17But God
be thanked that *though* you were slaves of sin,
yet you obeyed from the heart that form of
doctrine to which you were delivered. 18And
having been set free from sin, you became
slaves of righteousness. 19I speak in human
terms because of the weakness of your flesh.
For just as you presented your members *as*
slaves of uncleanness, and of lawlessness
leading to *more* lawlessness, so now present
your members *as* slaves *of* righteousness for
holiness.

20For when you were slaves of sin, you were
free in regard to righteousness. 21What fruit
did you have then in the things of which you
are now ashamed? For the end of those things
is death. 22But now having been set free from
sin, and having become slaves of God, you
have your fruit to holiness, and the end, everlasting life. 23For the wages of sin *is* death, but
the gift of God *is* eternal life in Christ Jesus
our Lord.

FREED FROM THE LAW

7 Or do you not know, brethren (for I speak
to those who know the law), that the law
has dominion over a man as long as he lives?
2For the woman who
has a husband is bound
by the law to *her* hus-
band as long as he lives.
But if the husband dies,
she is released from the
law of *her* husband. 3So
then if, while *her* hus-
band lives, she marries
another man, she will be called an adulteress;
but if her husband dies, she is free from that
law, so that she is no adulteress, though she
has married another man. 4Therefore, my
brethren, you also have become dead to the
law through the body of Christ, that you may
be married to another—to Him who was
raised from the dead, that we should bear
fruit to God. 5For when we were in the flesh,
the sinful passions which were aroused by
the law were at work in our members to bear
fruit to death. 6But now we have been delivered from the law, having died to what we
were held by, so that we should serve in the
newness of the Spirit and not *in* the oldness of
the letter.

SIN'S ADVANTAGE IN THE LAW

7What shall we say then? *Is* the law sin? Certainly not! On the contrary, I would not have
known sin except through the law. For I would
not have known covetousness unless the law

SOUL NOTE

Crucified with Christ *(6:6–11)* Rome was filled with slaves, many of whom had been brought from conquered lands. To be a slave means to serve another and to have one's entire life controlled by them. All people are "slaves of sin" because we are born in sin. But in a transaction that we cannot completely comprehend, God took our sin (our "old man") and crucified it with Jesus on the Cross. Thus believers can consider themselves dead to sin and freed from its tyranny. The struggle against sin and temptation will continue until death, but believers can trust Christ to help them win their battles. **Topic: Sin**

had said, *"You shall not covet."*[a] [8]But sin, taking opportunity by the commandment, produced in me all *manner of* evil desire. For
apart from the law sin *was* dead. [9]I was alive
once without the law, but when the commandment came, sin revived and I died. [10]And
the commandment, which
was to *bring* life, I found
to *bring* death. [11]For
sin, taking occasion by
the commandment, de-
ceived me, and by it
killed *me.* [12]Therefore
the law *is* holy, and the
commandment holy and
just and good.

> For the wages of sin is death,
> but the gift of God is eternal life
> in Christ Jesus our Lord.
> ROMANS 6:23

Law Cannot Save from Sin

[13]Has then what is good become death to
me? Certainly not! But sin, that it might appear sin, was producing death in me through
what is good, so that sin through the commandment might become exceedingly sinful.
[14]For we know that the law is spiritual, but I
am carnal, sold under sin. [15]For what I am doing, I do not understand. For what I will to do,
that I do not practice; but what I hate, that I
do. [16]If, then, I do what I will not to do, I agree
with the law that *it is* good. [17]But now, *it is* no
longer I who do it, but sin that dwells in me.
[18]For I know that in me (that is, in my flesh)
nothing good dwells; for to will is present
with me, but *how* to perform what is good I do
not find. [19]For the good that I will *to do,* I do
not do; but the evil I will not *to do,* that I practice. [20]Now if I do what I will not *to do,* it is no
longer I who do it, but sin that dwells in me.
[21]I find then a law, that evil is present with
me, the one who wills
to do good. [22]For I de-
light in the law of God
according to the inward
man. [23]But I see anoth-
er law in my members,
warring against the law
of my mind, and bring-
ing me into captivity to
the law of sin which is in my members. [24]O
wretched man that I am! Who will deliver me
from this body of death? [25]I thank God—
through Jesus Christ our Lord!
So then, with the mind I myself serve the
law of God, but with the flesh the law of sin.

Free from Indwelling Sin

8 *There is* therefore now no condemnation
to those who are in Christ Jesus,[a] who do
not walk according to the flesh, but according
to the Spirit. [2]For the law of the Spirit of life in
Christ Jesus has made me free from the law of
sin and death. [3]For what the law could not do

7:7 [a]Exodus 20:17; Deuteronomy 5:21 **8:1** [a]NU-Text omits the rest of this verse.

KEY PASSAGE

Legalism

ENSLAVED TO RULES

(7:6–14)

As a defense against sin, some find stability in obeying a list of rules. But people encounter serious problems when they attempt to order their lives by rule-keeping. The law exposes shortcomings, but it doesn't inspire holy living. Through the law, we discern how truly wicked the world is and how sinful we are. Like a roadmap, the law shows us where we ought to be. It also shows us the impossibility of obeying any set of laws perfectly. Yet legalists will do their best—which is never good enough—and that leads them to intense guilt over their own sinfulness, and judgmentalism against others who do not keep all of their rules and thus are not as "holy" as they are. The legalist fails to comprehend the magnitude of God's grace, refusing to believe that God is trustworthy, generous, and forgiving. The antidote to legalism is recognition of God's gracious love. We are delivered from sin not by our own effort, but by His unmerited favor.

To Learn More: Turn to the article about legalism on pages 142, 143. See also the personality profile of the Pharisees on page 1269.

in that it was weak through the flesh, God *did* by sending His own Son in the likeness of sinful flesh, on account of sin: He condemned sin in the flesh, [4]that the righteous requirement of the law might be fulfilled in us who do not walk according to the flesh but according to the Spirit. [5]For those who live according to the flesh set their minds on the things of the flesh, but those *who live* according to the Spirit, the things of the Spirit. [6]For to be carnally minded *is* death, but to be spiritually minded *is* life and peace. [7]Because the carnal mind *is* enmity against God; for it is not subject to the law of God, nor indeed can be. [8]So then, those who are in the flesh cannot please God.

[9]But you are not in the flesh but in the Spirit, if indeed the Spirit of God dwells in you. Now if anyone does not have the Spirit of Christ, he is not His. [10]And if Christ *is* in you, the body *is* dead because of sin, but the Spirit *is* life because of righteousness. [11]But if the Spirit of Him who raised Jesus from the dead dwells in you, He who raised Christ from the dead will also give life to your mortal bodies through His Spirit who dwells in you.

Sonship Through the Spirit

[12]Therefore, brethren, we are debtors—not to the flesh, to live according to the flesh. [13]For if you live according to the flesh you will die; but if by the Spirit you put to death the deeds of the body, you will live. [14]For as many as are led by the Spirit of God, these are sons of God. [15]For you did not receive the spirit of bondage again to fear, but you received the Spirit of adoption by whom we cry out, "Abba,

KEY PASSAGE

Guilt/ Shame

FREE!

(8:1)

No truth is more glorious to imprisoned people than to be told that they are no longer condemned but are set free! Christ brings that good news. When people accept Christ's sacrifice on their behalf, they are freed from the tyranny of sin. "There is therefore now no condemnation to those who are in Christ Jesus." Condemnation means an eternity apart from God. No condemnation means living *with* Him, now and forever.

Often, however, believers who have been set free still keep themselves behind bars. They feel guilty about their past, or guilty that they cannot be perfect in this life. Guilt can be good when it helps us to know when we have done something wrong. But guilt can also keep people from being able to rejoice in their new life or to bring others to Christ. That kind of guilt is a prison. We needn't stay locked up if Christ has set us free.

To Learn More: Turn to the article about guilt/shame on pages 600, 601. See also the personality profile of Adam on page 10.

SOUL NOTE

No Longer Condemned *(8:1)* Not keeping the law perfectly leads to condemnation. Since no one can keep God's law perfectly, all people are condemned. The law brings guilt because people realize they are powerless to keep it. Christ's death on the sinner's behalf, however, sets them free. "There is therefore now no condemnation to those who are in Christ Jesus" because they have been forgiven and are promised eternal life. If Christ no longer condemns us, then neither should we condemn ourselves. Beating ourselves up over sins that we have brought to God only keeps us imprisoned in our guilt. Christ has set us free. **Topic: Guilt/Shame**

Father." 16The Spirit Himself bears witness
with our spirit that we are children of God,
17and if children, then heirs—heirs of God and
joint heirs with Christ, if indeed we suffer with
Him, that we may also be glorified together.

From Suffering to Glory

18For I consider that the sufferings of this
present time are not worthy *to be compared*
with the glory which shall be revealed in us.
19For the earnest expectation of the creation
eagerly waits for the revealing of the sons of
God. 20For the creation was subjected to futility, not willingly, but because of Him who subjected *it* in hope; 21because the creation itself
also will be delivered from the bondage of corruption into the glorious liberty of the children of God. 22For we know that the whole
creation groans and labors with birth pangs
together until now. 23Not only *that,* but we
also who have the firstfruits of the Spirit, even
we ourselves groan within ourselves, eagerly
waiting for the adoption, the redemption of
our body. 24For we were saved in this hope,
but hope that is seen is not hope; for why does
one still hope for what he sees? 25But if we
hope for what we do not see, we eagerly wait
for *it* with perseverance.

26Likewise the Spirit also helps in our weaknesses. For we do not know what we should
pray for as we ought, but the Spirit Himself
makes intercession for us[a] with groanings
which cannot be uttered. 27Now He who
searches the hearts knows what the mind of
the Spirit *is,* because He makes intercession
for the saints according to *the will of* God.

28And we know that all things work together for good to those who love God, to those
who are the called according to *His* purpose.
29For whom He foreknew, He also predestined
to be conformed to the image of His Son, that
He might be the firstborn among many brethren. 30Moreover whom He predestined, these
He also called; whom He called, these He also
justified; and whom He justified, these He
also glorified.

God's Everlasting Love

31What then shall we say to these things? If
God *is* for us, who *can be* against us? 32He

8:26 [a]NU-Text omits *for us.*

SOUL NOTE

Count On It *(8:18)* Suffering was very real for the early believers. Persecution was part of the package when someone became a Christian. Jews who became believers faced persecution from fellow Jews who did not believe in Jesus as the Messiah. Gentiles who became believers faced charges of treason for refusing to worship the emperor. Persecution has continued throughout the centuries, and today's believers are not immune. Our suffering may seem to have a stranglehold on us, but in eternity's perspective, it loses its grip. God promises glory—we can count on it!
Topic: Suffering

SOUL NOTE

Groaning Bodies *(8:20–23)* In heaven, God will make everything perfect. He promises believers new and perfect bodies that will never get sick and never die (1 Cor. 15:35–49; Rev. 21:4). Our earthly bodies face genetic problems that sometimes cannot be reversed or cured. Many people live in darkness, in silence, or bound to a wheelchair. Yet many love Christ and serve Him faithfully even through difficult life challenges. How wonderful will be that day, especially for those who now face physical burdens, when Christ returns and all believers will be given brand new bodies—seeing, hearing, running, jumping—in "the glorious liberty of the children of God."
Topic: Genetic Issues

who did not spare His own Son, but delivered Him up for us all, how shall He not with Him also freely give us all things? 33Who shall bring a charge against God's elect? *It is* God who justifies. 34Who *is* he who condemns? *It is* Christ who died, and furthermore is also risen, who is even at the right hand of God, who also makes intercession for us. 35Who shall separate us from the love of Christ? *Shall* tribulation, or distress, or persecution, or famine, or nakedness, or peril, or sword? 36As it is written:

> For I am persuaded that neither death nor life, nor angels nor principalities nor powers, nor things present nor things to come, nor height nor depth, nor any other created thing, shall be able to separate us from the love of God which is in Christ Jesus our Lord.
>
> ROMANS 8:38, 39

"For Your sake we are killed all day long;
We are accounted as sheep for the slaughter."[a]

37Yet in all these things we are more than conquerors through Him who loved us. 38For I am persuaded that neither death nor life, nor angels nor principalities nor powers, nor things present nor things to come, 39nor height nor depth, nor any other created thing, shall be able to separate us from the love of God which is in Christ Jesus our Lord.

ISRAEL'S REJECTION OF CHRIST

9 I tell the truth in Christ, I am not lying, my conscience also bearing me witness in the Holy Spirit, 2that I have great sorrow and continual grief in my heart. 3For I could wish that I myself were accursed from Christ for my brethren, my countrymen[a] according to the flesh, 4who are Israelites, to whom *pertain* the adoption, the glory, the covenants, the giving of the law, the service *of God,* and the promises; 5of whom *are* the fathers and from whom, according to the flesh, Christ *came,* who is over all, *the* eternally blessed God. Amen.

ISRAEL'S REJECTION AND GOD'S PURPOSE

6But it is not that the word of God has taken no effect. For they *are* not all Israel who *are* of Israel, 7nor *are they* all children because they are the seed of Abraham; but, *"In Isaac your seed shall be called."*[a] 8That is, those who *are* the children of the flesh, these *are* not the children of God; but the children of the promise are counted as the seed. 9For this *is* the word of promise: *"At this time I will come and Sarah shall have a son."*[a]

10And not only *this,* but when Rebecca also had conceived by one man, *even* by our father Isaac 11(for *the children* not yet being born, nor having done any good or evil, that the purpose of God according to election might stand, not of works but of Him who calls), 12it was said to her, *"The older shall serve the younger."*[a] 13As it is written, *"Jacob I have loved, but Esau I have hated."*[a]

ISRAEL'S REJECTION AND GOD'S JUSTICE

14What shall we say then? *Is there* unrighteousness with God? Certainly not! 15For He

8:36 [a]Psalm 44:22 **9:3** [a]Or *relatives*
9:7 [a]Genesis 21:12 **9:9** [a]Genesis 18:10,14
9:12 [a]Genesis 25:23 **9:13** [a]Malachi 1:2, 3

SOUL NOTE

Always with Us *(8:38, 39)* Painful separations happen constantly—friends move away; loved ones die; marriages break up. When people have trusted Christ for salvation, however, nothing can separate them from the love of God. Death cannot separate, for we will be in God's presence. And nothing in life is powerful enough to take God away. Nothing in the realm of the unseen, nothing in time, and nothing in all of the vast universe can separate believers from God's love. When we feel alone or far from God, we must remember His promise that He is with us always, even to the end of the world (Matt. 28:20). **Topic: God's Promises**

says to Moses, *"I will have mercy on whomever I will have mercy, and I will have compassion on whomever I will have compassion."*[a] 16So then *it is* not of him who wills, nor of him who runs, but of God who shows mercy. 17For the Scripture says to the Pharaoh, *"For this very purpose I have raised you up, that I may show My power in you, and that My name may be declared in all the earth."*[a] 18Therefore He has mercy on whom He wills, and whom He wills He hardens.

19You will say to me then, "Why does He still find fault? For who has resisted His will?" 20But indeed, O man, who are you to reply against God? Will the thing formed say to him who formed *it*, "Why have you made me like this?" 21Does not the potter have power over the clay, from the same lump to make one vessel for honor and another for dishonor?

22*What* if God, wanting to show *His* wrath and to make His power known, endured with much longsuffering the vessels of wrath prepared for destruction, 23and that He might make known the riches of His glory on the vessels of mercy, which He had prepared beforehand for glory, 24*even* us whom He called, not of the Jews only, but also of the Gentiles?

25As He says also in Hosea:

"I will call them My people, who were not
My people,
And her beloved, who was not
beloved."[a]
26 *"And it shall come to pass in the place*
where it was said to them,
'You are not My people,'
There they shall be called sons of the
living God."[a]

27Isaiah also cries out concerning Israel:[a]

"Though the number of the children of
Israel be as the sand of the sea,
The remnant will be saved.
28 *For He will finish the work and cut it*
short in righteousness,
Because the LORD will make a short work
upon the earth."[a]

29And as Isaiah said before:

"Unless the LORD of Sabaoth[a] *had left us a*
seed,
We would have become like Sodom,
And we would have been made like
Gomorrah."[b]

Present Condition of Israel

30What shall we say then? That Gentiles, who did not pursue righteousness, have attained to righteousness, even the righteousness of faith; 31but Israel, pursuing the law of righteousness, has not attained to the law of righteousness.[a] 32Why? Because *they did* not *seek it* by faith, but as it were, by the works of the law.[a] For they stumbled at that stumbling stone. 33As it is written:

"Behold, I lay in Zion a stumbling stone
and rock of offense,
And whoever believes on Him will not be
put to shame."[a]

Israel Needs the Gospel

10 Brethren, my heart's desire and prayer to God for Israel[a] is that they may be saved. 2For I bear them witness that they have a zeal for God, but not according to knowledge. 3For they being ignorant of God's righteousness, and seeking to establish their own righteousness, have not submitted to the righteousness of God. 4For Christ *is* the end of the law for righteousness to everyone who believes.

5For Moses writes about the righteousness which is of the law, *"The man who does those things shall live by them."*[a] 6But the righteousness of faith speaks in this way, *"Do not say in your heart, 'Who will ascend into heaven?' "*[a] (that is, to bring Christ down *from above*) 7or, " *'Who will descend into the abyss?' "*[a] (that is, to bring Christ up from the dead). 8But what does it say? *"The word is near you, in your mouth and in your heart"*[a] (that is, the word of faith which we preach): 9that if you confess with your mouth the Lord Jesus and believe in your heart that God has raised Him

9:15 [a]Exodus 33:19 **9:17** [a]Exodus 9:16
9:25 [a]Hosea 2:23 **9:26** [a]Hosea 1:10
9:27 [a]Isaiah 10:22, 23 **9:28** [a]NU-Text reads *For the LORD will finish the work and cut it short upon the earth.* **9:29** [a]Literally, in Hebrew, *Hosts* [b]Isaiah 1:9 **9:31** [a]NU-Text omits *of righteousness.* **9:32** [a]NU-Text reads *by works.* **9:33** [a]Isaiah 8:14; 28:16 **10:1** [a]NU-Text reads *them.*
10:5 [a]Leviticus 18:5 **10:6** [a]Deuteronomy 30:12
10:7 [a]Deuteronomy 30:13 **10:8** [a]Deuteronomy 30:14

from the dead, you will be saved. [10]For with
the heart one believes unto righteousness, and
with the mouth confession is made unto salvation. [11]For the Scripture says, *"Whoever be-*
lieves on Him will not be put to shame."[a] [12]For
there is no distinction between Jew and
Greek, for the same Lord over all is rich to all
who call upon Him. [13]For *"whoever calls on*
the name of the LORD shall be saved."[a]

ISRAEL REJECTS THE GOSPEL

[14]How then shall they call on Him in whom
they have not believed? And how shall they
believe in Him of whom they have not heard?
And how shall they hear without a preacher?
[15]And how shall they preach unless they are
sent? As it is written:

"How beautiful are the feet of those who
preach the gospel of peace,[a]
Who bring glad tidings of good
things!"[b]

[16]But they have not all obeyed the gospel. For
Isaiah says, *"LORD, who has believed our*
report?"[a] [17]So then faith *comes* by hearing,
and hearing by the word of God.
[18]But I say, have they not heard? Yes indeed:

"Their sound has gone out to all the earth,
And their words to the ends of the
world."[a]

[19]But I say, did Israel not know? First Moses
says:

"I will provoke you to jealousy by those
who are not a nation,
I will move you to anger by a foolish
nation."[a]

[20]But Isaiah is very bold and says:

"I was found by those who did not seek
Me;
I was made manifest to those who did
not ask for Me."[a]

[21]But to Israel he says:

"All day long I have stretched out My
hands
To a disobedient and contrary people."[a]

ISRAEL'S REJECTION NOT TOTAL

11 I say then, has God cast away His people? Certainly not! For I also am an Israelite, of the seed of Abraham, *of* the tribe of
Benjamin. [2]God has not cast away His people

10:11 [a]Isaiah 28:16 **10:13** [a]Joel 2:32
10:15 [a]NU-Text omits *preach the gospel of peace, Who.* [b]Isaiah 52:7; Nahum 1:15 **10:16** [a]Isaiah 53:1 **10:18** [a]Psalm 19:4 **10:19** [a]Deuteronomy 32:21 **10:20** [a]Isaiah 65:1 **10:21** [a]Isaiah 65:2

KEY PASSAGE

Belief

IN YOUR HEART

(10:9, 10)

What is belief, as defined by God? To be saved, people must believe in Jesus as Savior and Lord, but what exactly does that mean?

It isn't enough to say that we believe in God—even the demons believe that much (James 2:19). It is not enough to believe that Jesus lived as some great teacher or miracle worker. True belief begins in the heart as the Holy Spirit opens a person to the truth of the gospel message that God sent His Son Jesus, who died for our sins and rose again. Those who believe in Jesus simply move beyond intellectual assent that He lived to heartfelt gratitude that He cares for them personally. Belief then reveals itself in actions. People who believe in what Christ has done for them will desire to live for Him. If we confess with our mouths that Jesus is Lord, and believe in our hearts that God raised Him from the dead, we will be saved.

To Learn More: Turn to the article about belief on pages 1480, 1481. See also the personality profile of King Agrippa on page 1459.

whom He foreknew. Or do you not know what the Scripture says of Elijah, how he pleads with God against Israel, saying, [3]*“LORD, they have killed Your prophets and torn down Your altars, and I alone am left, and they seek my life”?*[a] [4]But what does the divine response say to him? *“I have reserved for Myself seven thousand men who have not bowed the knee to Baal.”*[a] [5]Even so then, at this present time there is a remnant according to the election of grace. [6]And if by grace, then *it is* no longer of works; otherwise grace is no longer grace.[a] But if *it is* of works, it is no longer grace; otherwise work is no longer work.

[7]What then? Israel has not obtained what it seeks; but the elect have obtained it, and the rest were blinded. [8]Just as it is written:

“God has given them a spirit of stupor,
Eyes that they should not see
And ears that they should not hear,
To this very day.”[a]

[9]And David says:

“Let their table become a snare and a trap,
A stumbling block and a recompense to them.
10 *Let their eyes be darkened, so that they do not see,*
And bow down their back always.”[a]

Israel’s Rejection Not Final

[11]I say then, have they stumbled that they should fall? Certainly not! But through their fall, to provoke them to jealousy, salvation *has come* to the Gentiles. [12]Now if their fall *is* riches for the world, and their failure riches for the Gentiles, how much more their fullness!

[13]For I speak to you Gentiles; inasmuch as I am an apostle to the Gentiles, I magnify my ministry, [14]if by any means I may provoke to jealousy *those who are* my flesh and save some of them. [15]For if their being cast away *is* the reconciling of the world, what *will* their acceptance *be* but life from the dead?

[16]For if the firstfruit *is* holy, the lump *is* also *holy;* and if the root *is* holy, so *are* the branches. [17]And if some of the branches were broken off, and you, being a wild olive tree, were grafted in among them, and with them became a partaker of the root and fatness of the olive tree, [18]do not boast against the branches. But if you do boast, *remember that* you do not support the root, but the root supports you.

[19]You will say then, “Branches were broken off that I might be grafted in.” [20]Well *said.* Because of unbelief they were broken off, and you stand by faith. Do not be haughty, but fear. [21]For if God did not spare the natural branches, He may not spare you either. [22]Therefore consider the goodness and severity of God: on those who fell, severity; but toward you, goodness,[a] if you continue in *His* goodness. Otherwise you also will be cut off. [23]And they also, if they do not continue in unbelief, will be grafted in, for God is able to graft them in again. [24]For if you were cut out of the olive tree which is wild by nature, and were grafted contrary to nature into a cultivated olive tree, how much more will these, who *are* natural *branches,* be grafted into their own olive tree?

[25]For I do not desire, brethren, that you should be ignorant of this mystery, lest you should be wise in your own opinion, that blindness in part has happened to Israel until the fullness of the Gentiles has come in. [26]And so all Israel will be saved,[a] as it is written:

“The Deliverer will come out of Zion,
And He will turn away ungodliness from Jacob;
27 *For this is My covenant with them,*
When I take away their sins.”[a]

[28]Concerning the gospel *they are* enemies for your sake, but concerning the election *they are* beloved for the sake of the fathers. [29]For the gifts and the calling of God *are* irrevocable. [30]For as you were once disobedient to God, yet have now obtained mercy through their disobedience, [31]even so these also have now been disobedient, that through the mercy shown you they also may obtain mercy. [32]For God has committed them all to disobedience, that He might have mercy on all.

[33]Oh, the depth of the riches both of the wisdom and knowledge of God! How

11:3 [a]1 Kings 19:10,14 **11:4** [a]1 Kings 19:18 **11:6** [a]NU-Text omits the rest of this verse. **11:8** [a]Deuteronomy 29:4; Isaiah 29:10 **11:10** [a]Psalm 69:22, 23 **11:22** [a]NU-Text adds *of God.* **11:26** [a]Or *delivered* **11:27** [a]Isaiah 59:20, 21

Belief

RENEWING OUR MINDS

CHRIS THURMAN

(Romans 10:9, 10)

One of the main causes of emotional and spiritual problems in life is faulty thinking. Thinking untruthfully, unrealistically, and irrationally leads to damaged emotions, destructive actions, and failure to mature as Christians. For us to experience the abundant life that Christ offers, we must believe the truth and live it out in our daily lives.

The Bible talks a great deal about our thinking. Romans 12:2 exhorts us to renew our minds, while Philippians 4:8 offers us guidelines for correct patterns of thought. Isaiah 26:3 promises peace to those whose minds are steadfastly focused on God, and Colossians 3:2 challenges us to set our minds "on things above." The biblical message is clear: What we think plays a critical role in determining emotional and spiritual health. God, who *is* truth, wants us to think and believe the truth because doing so sets us free to have an abundant life.

WHEN WE BELIEVE LIES

Satan, the deceiver and "father of lies," wants us to believe lies because they destroy us and put us in bondage to emotional and spiritual problems. Satan has many lies in his arsenal, all of them destructive. Here are some examples:

➢ *"I must be perfect."* Believing this lie results in feeling anxious about making mistakes and in self-condemnation when we do. God wants His people to be holy (1 Pet. 1:16), but we need to accept that growing in Christ is a process that will involve making mistakes along the way.

➢ *"I must have everyone's love and approval."* This lie leads us to focus on pleasing people rather than pleasing God (Gal. 1:10). We cannot afford to make the love and approval of others more important to us than the love and approval of God.

➢ *"Things have to go my way for me to be happy."* This unbiblical belief causes us to focus our attention on circumstances rather than God, and on being happy rather than being mature. Our peace and contentment should not be based on the situations we find ourselves in (Phil. 4:11), but on being unconditionally loved and cared for by God.

➢ *"Life should be easy."* Life is not easy. The effects of sin on us and the world we live in are pervasive and have made living life difficult. Christ promised that we would face troubles in life (John 16:33). The false belief in an easy life only sets us up for bitterness and resentment when life proves to be difficult.

➢ *"God hates the sin and the sinner."* Believing this lie causes us to run from God when we sin, even though God is the only One who loves us unconditionally. God, being holy, hates sin (Prov. 6:16–19), but He died for and loves us even when we sin (Rom. 5:8).

These and many other lies create emotional and spiritual difficulties and slow our progress toward being mature in Christ. What can we do to replace these lies with the truth in order to be transformed into the people God meant us to be?

WHEN WE BELIEVE THE TRUTH

It must first be understood that people cannot properly renew their minds apart from God. Believing and applying the truth need to be done within the context of a relationship with Christ. Only then can people develop the beliefs and attitudes that lead to true emotional health and spiritual maturity.

But what can believers do to help the process of renewing their minds in order to live out God's truth?

First, they can keep a "self-talk" journal in order to identify the lies they tell themselves. This involves spending time each day writing down what they mentally say to themselves when reacting to various life events. In their journal, they record the event that "triggered" them, what they privately thought about it, and their feelings and reactions. Once they have written down their thoughts about the situation that occurred, they ask themselves, "Are any of the thoughts I had lies?" Doing this is a very important step toward better understanding what lies are in their minds each day and how they are negatively impacting their emotions and behavior.

Next, once they have identified the lies that they tell themselves, those lies can be analyzed in light of God's Word. For each lie they believe, they must find biblical truth that contradicts it. Then they can memorize that truth, meditate on it, and apply it in real life situations as often as possible. The threefold process of memorizing, meditating on, and applying truth will transform their thought patterns and their life.

LIVING WHAT WE BELIEVE

Knowing, believing, and applying biblical truth are the three key steps toward having a renewed mind and experiencing the transforming power of a relationship with God. God's thoughts are perfectly true, and He is more than willing to help us believe the truth. Our emotions and actions will be transformed as we replace lies with truth. This is a difficult, lifelong process that involves challenges at every turn. As we grow in our awareness of the unbiblical beliefs we hold and commit ourselves to taking a biblical view, our minds will be renewed and we can experience true freedom in Christ. The abundant life Christ promised is ours if we will commit ourselves to a life lived in truth.

FURTHER MEDITATION:

Other passages to study about the issue of belief include:

- Genesis 15:6
- Psalm 27:13
- Daniel 6:23
- Jonah 3:5
- Mark 9:23; 11:24
- John 14:10, 11
- Acts 16:31
- Romans 10:9

To Learn More: Turn to the key passage note on belief at Romans 10:9, 10 on page 1478. See also the personality profile of King Agrippa on page 1459.

unsearchable *are* His judgments and His ways
past finding out!

34 *"For who has known the mind of the* L*ORD?*
Or who has become His counselor?" [a]
35 *"Or who has first given to Him*
And it shall be repaid to him?" [a]

36 For of Him and through Him and to Him
are all things, to whom *be* glory forever.
Amen.

LIVING SACRIFICES TO GOD

12 I beseech you therefore, brethren, by
the mercies of God, that you present
your bodies a living sacrifice, holy, acceptable
to God, *which is* your reasonable service. 2 And
do not be conformed to this world, but be
transformed by the renewing of your mind, that
you may prove what *is* that good and acceptable and perfect will of God.

SERVE GOD WITH SPIRITUAL GIFTS

3 For I say, through the grace given to me, to
everyone who is among you, not to think *of*
himself more highly than he ought to think,
but to think soberly, as God has dealt to each
one a measure of faith. 4 For as we have many
members in one body, but all the members do
not have the same function, 5 so we, *being*
many, are one body in Christ, and individually

11:34 [a]Isaiah 40:13; Jeremiah 23:18 **11:35** [a]Job 41:11

KEY PASSAGE

Attitudes

THE CHOICE

(12:1, 2)

People's attitudes reflect their perspective on life. And attitudes are formed in the mind—every attitude begins with a choice to look at the world in a certain way. Therefore, people can change their attitudes.

Believers must not be "conformed to this world," allowing the world's outlook to rule them, entice them, or decide their attitudes. Instead, Paul says, "Be transformed by the renewing of your mind, that you may prove what is that good and acceptable and perfect will of God." With a transformed mind, we can allow God to help us choose to have attitudes that are honoring to Him. He helps us to stay positive in any situation, as we see His plan unfold.

Those who struggle with negative attitudes should renew their mind and choose attitudes that honor and reveal God's work in their lives. God's Word is the best place to start.

To Learn More: Turn to the article about attitudes on pages 1174, 1175. See also the personality profile of Michal on page 395.

SOUL NOTE

Living Sacrifices *(12:1, 2)* The Jews had a system of sacrifices, prepared by God and recorded in the Law of Moses, by which their sins were forgiven. Paul used that picture to describe how believers should live, offering *themselves* to God as living sacrifices. Thus they could be transformed by the Holy Spirit and have renewed minds. This transformation and renewal helps God's people know His good, acceptable, and perfect will. We are promised that we can know God's will for us when making tough decisions. We must humbly pray and seek His guidance, knowing that He will answer. **Topic: Decision Making**

members of one another. [6]Having then gifts differing according to the grace that is given to us, *let us use them:* if prophecy, *let us prophesy* in proportion to our faith; [7]or ministry, *let us use it* in *our* ministering; he who teaches, in teaching; [8]he who exhorts, in exhortation; he who gives, with liberality; he who leads, with diligence; he who shows mercy, with cheerfulness.

Behave Like a Christian

[9]*Let* love *be* without hypocrisy. Abhor what is evil. Cling to what is good. [10]*Be* kindly affectionate to one another with brotherly love, in honor giving preference to one another; [11]not lagging in diligence, fervent in spirit, serving the Lord; [12]rejoicing in hope, patient in tribulation, continuing steadfastly in prayer; [13]distributing to the needs of the saints, given to hospitality.

[14]Bless those who persecute you; bless and do not curse. [15]Rejoice with those who rejoice, and weep with those who weep. [16]Be of the same mind toward one another. Do not set your mind on high things, but associate with the humble. Do not be wise in your own opinion.

[17]Repay no one evil for evil. Have regard for good things in the sight of all men. [18]If it is

SOUL NOTE

Like Oil and Water *(12:3)* God is against arrogance. Like oil and water, pride and faith don't mix. God created each person with great care. Every believer is valuable and needed by God. Each has gifts, uniquely given by God, to use in furthering the interests of His kingdom. Believers should humbly serve with those gifts in whatever circumstances God has put them. No one should "think of himself more highly than he ought to think," but "think soberly." We should thank God for His great love and serve Him with all our hearts. **Topic: Pride**

SOUL NOTE

Guidelines *(12:9–13)* Christ had said that the two greatest commandments were to love God and love one's neighbor (Luke 10:27). We should run every aspect of every decision through the filter of whether it is loving toward God or loving toward another person. In these verses, Paul gives further advice, warning people against hypocritical love and hanging on to evil ways. He advises kindness, diligence, fervent service, joy, patience, and prayer. In addition, believers should be known for giving and for hospitality. Following this advice through the guidance of the Holy Spirit will help believers live to glorify God. **Topic: Spiritual Growth**

SOUL NOTE

Careful in Conflict *(12:14–21)* Conflict is inevitable. Paul advised believers to be careful in conflicts with those outside the faith. Christians must resist the temptation to retaliate against evil; instead, they should bless their persecutors, refuse to repay evil for evil, and "overcome evil with good." That's because God will take care of the vengeance, the repayment, and the punishment. As much as we might like to take matters into our own hands, God will handle the situation for us, in His time and in His way. Following Paul's advice can keep us out of worse situations, and may even help bring the perpetrators to Christ. **Topic: Conflict**

DECISION MAKING AND THE WILL OF GOD

CHARLES R. SWINDOLL

(Romans 12:2)

Thinking theologically is difficult. We much prefer to live in the here-and-now realm, seeing life as others see it, dealing with realities we can touch, analyze, prove, and explain. We are much more comfortable with the tactile, the familiar, the logic shaped by our culture.

But God offers a better way to live—one requiring faith that lifts us above the drag and grind of our immediate little world, opens new dimensions of thought, and introduces a perspective without human limitations. In order to enter this better way, we must train ourselves to think theologically. This turns our focus away from ourselves and opens our minds to a God-centered frame of reference, where all things begin and end with Him.

KNOWING GOD'S WILL

What is God's will and what is not God's will? How can we know God's will? Is it common to miss God's will or is that even possible? Can I really know that I am doing God's will? That I am in His will? All these and more are common questions every thoughtful believer grapples with at one time or another in life.

Much of the confusion goes back to not understanding God and how He does His inscrutable work in our lives. The Christian life is not merely a matter of getting from here to there . . . from point A to point B. Instead, God's will for us in this life is more about the journey itself.

Our human tendency is to focus solely on our calling—where we should go, how we should get there, and what we should do. God's concern is the process that will mature us and make us more like His Son. God is the Potter; we are the clay. Not one of us is qualified to grasp the first particle of why God does what He does when He does it and how He chooses to do it (Rom. 11:33, 34).

GOD'S DECRETIVE WILL

The first facet of God's will is His "decretive" will: His sovereign, determined, immutable will. This determined, decreed dimension of God's will has four qualities: (1) It is absolute. (2) It is immutable, which means "unchangeable." (3) It is unconditional. (4) It is always in complete harmony with His plan and His nature. In other words, the decreed will of God will be holy, just, good, and righteous; therefore, it will be best. And it will all work toward those ends.

While we may not know the will of God for the future, He has given us a whole list of requirements that are in His will for all believers:

- Obey and honor parents (Eph. 6:1, 2).
- Marry only another Christian (2 Cor. 6:14).
- Support our families (1 Tim. 5:8).
- Raise our children by God's standards (Eph. 6:4).
- Meditate on the Scriptures (Ps. 1:2).
- Pray (1 Thess. 5:17).
- Assemble for worship (Heb. 10:25).
- Proclaim Christ (Acts 1:8).
- Display love (1 Cor. 13).

And the list goes on and on. This is the will

of God for our lives as children of God, no matter who we are or where we live.

GOD'S PERMISSIVE WILL

The second facet of God's will is His permissive will, which represents what God allows. For example, God allowed Job to go through suffering. God didn't cause the suffering; He permitted it. This is where the whole matter of evil comes into play. And this is one of the irreconcilable difficulties in our theology—the tension between the determined will of God and the responsibility of humanity. We need to make Christ known to the whole world, knowing all the while that not everyone in the world will believe. God does not cause sin, but He does permit it. He is not pleased when His creation yields to temptation, but He uses even that to accomplish His purposes.

God's leading in our lives generally follows basic principles that can help us in deciding His will for our lives.

1. *His written Word.* As the psalmist said, "Your word is a lamp to my feet and a light to my path" (Ps. 119:105).
2. *The prompting of the Holy Spirit.* Paul reminds us, "It is God who works in you both to will and to do for His good pleasure" (Phil. 2:13).
3. *The counsel of wise, qualified, trustworthy people.* At critical moments of life, it is helpful to seek the counsel of seasoned individuals. But we must choose our counselors very carefully. "Where there is no counsel, the people fall; but in the multitude of counselors there is safety" (Prov. 11:14).
4. *An inner assurance of peace.* "And let the peace of God rule in your hearts," Paul wrote (Col. 3:15). God's inner assurance of peace will act as an umpire in our hearts.

Ultimately, God's Word provides all the light we will ever need on our journey through this life. It brings light to our darkened minds. It helps us think theologically. Strange and mysterious though His leading may seem, when we derive our understanding from a serious investigation of the written Word of God, we will not be led astray. And we will continue to stand on the solid rock of God's Word of truth.

All other ground is sinking sand.

FURTHER MEDITATION:

Other passages to study about the issue of decision making include:

- ➢ Joshua 1:8, 9
- ➢ Psalm 32:8
- ➢ Proverbs 2:3–8; 3:5, 6; 12:15
- ➢ Luke 14:28
- ➢ Galatians 5:22–26
- ➢ 2 Timothy 3:14–17

To Learn More: Turn to the key passage note on decision making at 1 John 5:14 on page 1682. See also the personality profile of Joshua on page 296.

possible, as much as depends on you, live peaceably with all men. [19]Beloved, do not avenge yourselves, but *rather* give place to wrath; for it is written, *"Vengeance is Mine, I will repay,"*[a] says the Lord. [20]Therefore

"If your enemy is hungry, feed him;
If he is thirsty, give him a drink;
For in so doing you will heap coals of fire on his head."[a]

[21]Do not be overcome by evil, but overcome evil with good.

Submit to Government

13 Let every soul be subject to the governing authorities. For there is no authority except from God, and the authorities that exist are appointed by God. [2]Therefore whoever resists the authority resists the ordinance of God, and those who resist will bring judgment on themselves. [3]For rulers are not a terror to good works, but to evil. Do you want to be unafraid of the authority? Do what is good, and you will have praise from the same. [4]For he is God's minister to you for good. But if you do evil, be afraid; for he does not bear the sword in vain; for he is God's minister, an avenger to *execute* wrath on him who practices evil. [5]Therefore *you* must be subject, not only because of wrath but also for conscience' sake. [6]For because of this you also pay taxes, for they are God's ministers attending continually to this very thing. [7]Render therefore to all their due: taxes to whom taxes *are due,* customs to whom customs, fear to whom fear, honor to whom honor.

Love Your Neighbor

[8]Owe no one anything except to love one another, for he who loves another has fulfilled the law. [9]For the commandments, *"You shall not commit adultery," "You shall not murder," "You shall not steal," "You shall not bear false witness,"*[a] *"You shall not covet,"*[b] and if *there is* any other commandment, are *all* summed up in this saying, namely, *"You shall love your neighbor as yourself."*[c] [10]Love does no harm to a neighbor; therefore love *is* the fulfillment of the law.

Put on Christ

[11]And *do* this, knowing the time, that now *it is* high time to awake out of sleep; for now our salvation *is* nearer than when we *first* believed. [12]The night is far spent, the day is at hand. Therefore let us cast off the works of darkness, and let us put on the armor of light. [13]Let us walk properly, as in the day, not in revelry and drunkenness, not in lewdness and lust, not in strife and envy. [14]But put on the Lord Jesus Christ, and make no provision for the flesh, to *fulfill its* lusts.

The Law of Liberty

14 Receive one who is weak in the faith, *but* not to disputes over doubtful things. [2]For one believes he may eat all things, but he who is weak eats *only* vegetables. [3]Let not him who eats despise him who does not eat, and let not him who does not eat judge him who eats; for God has received him. [4]Who are you to judge another's servant? To his own master he stands or falls. Indeed, he will be made to stand, for God is able to make him stand.

[5]One person esteems *one* day above an-

12:19 [a]Deuteronomy 32:35 **12:20** [a]Proverbs 25:21, 22 **13:9** [a]NU-Text omits *"You shall not bear false witness."* [b]Exodus 20:13–15, 17; Deuteronomy 5:17–19, 21 [c]Leviticus 19:18

SOUL NOTE

All the King's Men *(13:1–7)* Governments are put in place by God. At times they are peaceful and helpful to their subjects; at other times they are harmful. Rome under the Caesars was no exception. The *pax romana* (Roman peace) created outward tranquility in the empire, but at times people would be persecuted or dealt with unjustly. Today's situation is much the same, and so is Paul's advice: "Be subject to the governing authorities." Obey the laws; pay taxes; honor leaders. This does not mean following the law of the land when it is against God's will, but it does mean being a respectful, law-abiding citizen. After all, our witness for Christ is at stake. **Topic: Honor**

other; another esteems every day *alike.* Let each be fully convinced in his own mind. 6He who observes the day, observes *it* to the Lord;[a] and he who does not observe the day, to the Lord he does not observe *it.* He who eats, eats to the Lord, for he gives God thanks; and he who does not eat, to the Lord he does not eat, and gives God thanks. 7For none of us lives to himself, and no one dies to himself. 8For if we live, we live to the Lord; and if we die, we die to the Lord. Therefore, whether we live or die, we are the Lord's. 9For to this end Christ died and rose[a] and lived again, that He might be Lord of both the dead and the living. 10But why do you judge your brother? Or why do you show contempt for your brother? For we shall all stand before the judgment seat of Christ.[a] 11For it is written:

"As I live, says the LORD,
Every knee shall bow to Me,
And every tongue shall confess to God."[a]

12So then each of us shall give account of himself to God. 13Therefore let us not judge one another anymore, but rather resolve this, not to put a stumbling block or a cause to fall in *our* brother's way.

The Law of Love

14I know and am convinced by the Lord Jesus that *there is* nothing unclean of itself; but to him who considers anything to be unclean, to him *it is* unclean. 15Yet if your brother is grieved because of *your* food, you are no longer walking in love. Do not destroy with your food the one for whom Christ died. 16Therefore do not let your good be spoken of as evil; 17for the kingdom of God is not eating and drinking, but righteousness and peace and joy in the Holy Spirit. 18For he who serves Christ in these things[a] *is* acceptable to God and approved by men.

19Therefore let us pursue the things *which make* for peace and the things by which one may edify another. 20Do not destroy the work of God for the sake of food. All things indeed *are* pure, but *it is* evil for the man who eats with offense. 21*It is* good neither to eat meat nor drink wine nor *do anything* by which your brother stumbles or is offended or is made weak.[a] 22Do you have faith? Have[a] *it* to yourself before God. Happy *is* he who does not condemn himself in what he approves. 23But he who doubts is condemned if he eats, because *he does* not *eat* from faith; for whatever *is* not from faith is sin.[a]

14:6 [a]NU-Text omits the rest of this sentence. **14:9** [a]NU-Text omits *and rose.* **14:10** [a]NU-Text reads *of God.* **14:11** [a]Isaiah 45:23 **14:18** [a]NU-Text reads *this.* **14:21** [a]NU-Text omits *or is offended or is made weak.* **14:22** [a]NU-Text reads *The faith which you have—have.* **14:23** [a]M-Text puts Romans 16:25–27 here.

KEY PASSAGE

Accountability

BEFORE THE THRONE

(14:12)

The sobering words of this verse describe a day when each individual will stand alone before God Almighty to "give account." At that moment, there will be no excuses, no hidden agendas, no chance to lie and get away with it.

Each person is ultimately accountable to Christ, not to others. The context of this verse speaks of the diversity in the Christian fellowship, encouraging believers to allow for differences of opinion in matters that do not conflict with God's Word. Elsewhere Paul encourages believers in this diversity, saying, "Work out your own salvation with fear and trembling" (Phil. 2:12).

We must each seek to grow in our faith, on our own before God. Accountability to others can help this process, but ultimately we will be accountable to God for how we have lived. Follow God's Word—it is a sure guide.

To Learn More: Turn to the article about accountability on pages 966, 967. See also the personality profile of David and Nathan on page 401.

BEARING OTHERS' BURDENS

15 We then who are strong ought to bear
with the scruples of the weak, and not
to please ourselves. 2Let each of us please *his*
neighbor for *his* good, leading to edification.
3For even Christ did not please Himself; but as
it is written, *"The reproaches of those who
reproached You fell on Me."*[a] 4For whatever
things were written before were written for
our learning, that we through the patience and
comfort of the Scriptures might have hope.
5Now may the God of patience and comfort
grant you to be like-minded toward one another, according to Christ Jesus, 6that you may
with one mind *and* one mouth glorify the God
and Father of our Lord Jesus Christ.

GLORIFY GOD TOGETHER

7Therefore receive one another, just as
Christ also received us,[a] to the glory of God.
8Now I say that Jesus Christ has become a servant to the circumcision for the truth of God,
to confirm the promises *made* to the fathers,
9and that the Gentiles might glorify God for
His mercy, as it is written:

"For this reason I will confess to You
among the Gentiles,
And sing to Your name."[a]

10And again he says:

"Rejoice, O Gentiles, with His people!"[a]

11And again:

"Praise the LORD, all you Gentiles!
Laud Him, all you peoples!"[a]

12And again, Isaiah says:

"There shall be a root of Jesse;
And He who shall rise to reign over the
Gentiles,
In Him the Gentiles shall hope."[a]

13Now may the God of hope fill you with all
joy and peace in believing, that you may
abound in hope by the power of the Holy
Spirit.

FROM JERUSALEM TO ILLYRICUM

14Now I myself am confident concerning
you, my brethren, that you also are full of
goodness, filled with all knowledge, able also
to admonish one another.[a] 15Nevertheless,
brethren, I have written more boldly to you on
some points, as reminding you, because of the
grace given to me by God, 16that I might be a
minister of Jesus Christ to the Gentiles, ministering the gospel of God, that the offering
of the Gentiles might be acceptable, sanctified by the Holy Spirit. 17Therefore I have
reason to glory in Christ Jesus in the things
which pertain to God. 18For I will not dare to
speak of any of those things which Christ
has not accomplished through me, in word
and deed, to make the Gentiles obedient—
19in mighty signs and wonders, by the power
of the Spirit of God, so that from Jerusalem
and round about to Illyricum I have fully
preached the gospel of Christ. 20And so I
have made it my aim to preach the gospel, not
where Christ was named, lest I should build
on another man's foundation, 21but as it is
written:

15:3 [a]Psalm 69:9 **15:7** [a]NU-Text and M-Text read *you.* **15:9** [a]2 Samuel 22:50; Psalm 18:49 **15:10** [a]Deuteronomy 32:43 **15:11** [a]Psalm 117:1 **15:12** [a]Isaiah 11:10 **15:14** [a]M-Text reads *others.*

SOUL NOTE

Hope So *(15:13)* God is described in many ways throughout the Bible—powerful, glorious, angry at sin, and merciful toward His people. Paul described Him as "the God of hope." The word *hope* means more than wishing for something; it means having a confident expectation. God is the author of hope, for what He promises always happens. Believers *hope* for heaven because they *know* it will one day be their home. The God of hope helps His people to "abound in hope by the power of the Holy Spirit." Where do we place our hope? We can put our hope in God. He will never disappoint us. **Topic: Hope**

"To whom He was not announced, they
shall see;
And those who have not heard shall
understand."[a]

PLAN TO VISIT ROME

22For this reason I also have been much hindered from coming to you. 23But now no longer having a place in these parts, and having a
great desire these many years to come to you,
24whenever I journey to Spain, I shall come to
you.[a] For I hope to see you on my journey, and
to be helped on my way there by you, if first I
may enjoy your *company* for a while. 25But
now I am going to Jerusalem to minister to the
saints. 26For it pleased those from Macedonia
and Achaia to make a certain contribution for
the poor among the saints who are in Jerusalem. 27It pleased them indeed, and they are
their debtors. For if the Gentiles have been
partakers of their spiritual things, their duty is
also to minister to them in material things.
28Therefore, when I have performed this and
have sealed to them this fruit, I shall go by
way of you to Spain. 29But I know that when I
come to you, I shall come in the fullness of the
blessing of the gospel[a] of Christ.

30Now I beg you, brethren, through the Lord
Jesus Christ, and through the love of the Spirit, that you strive together with me in prayers
to God for me, 31that I may be delivered from
those in Judea who do not believe, and that
my service for Jerusalem may be acceptable to
the saints, 32that I may come to you with joy
by the will of God, and may be refreshed together with you. 33Now the God of peace *be*
with you all. Amen.

SISTER PHOEBE COMMENDED

16 I commend to you Phoebe our sister,
who is a servant of the church in Cenchrea, 2that you may receive her in the Lord in
a manner worthy of the saints, and assist her
in whatever business she has need of you; for
indeed she has been a helper of many and of
myself also.

GREETING ROMAN SAINTS

3Greet Priscilla and Aquila, my fellow workers in Christ Jesus, 4who risked their own
necks for my life, to whom not only I give
thanks, but also all the churches of the Gentiles. 5Likewise *greet* the church that is in their
house.

Greet my beloved Epaenetus, who is the
firstfruits of Achaia[a] to Christ. 6Greet Mary,
who labored much for us. 7Greet Andronicus
and Junia, my countrymen and my fellow prisoners, who are of note among the apostles,
who also were in Christ before me.

8Greet Amplias, my beloved in the Lord.
9Greet Urbanus, our fellow worker in Christ,
and Stachys, my beloved. 10Greet Apelles,
approved in Christ. Greet those who are of
the *household* of Aristobulus. 11Greet Hero-
dion, my countryman.[a] Greet those who are
of the *household* of Narcissus who are in the
Lord.

12Greet Tryphena and Tryphosa, who have
labored in the Lord. Greet the beloved Persis,
who labored much in the Lord. 13Greet Rufus,
chosen in the Lord, and his mother and mine.
14Greet Asyncritus, Phlegon, Hermas, Patro-
bas, Hermes, and the brethren who are with
them. 15Greet Philologus and Julia, Nereus
and his sister, and Olympas, and all the saints
who are with them.

15:21 [a]Isaiah 52:15 **15:24** [a]NU-Text omits *I shall come to you* (and joins *Spain* with the next sentence). **15:29** [a]NU-Text omits *of the gospel.* **16:5** [a]NU-Text reads *Asia.* **16:11** [a]Or *relative*

SOUL NOTE

Irreconcilable Differences *(16:17)* Some conflicts cannot be resolved. The believers were not to reconcile with those who came into their fellowship and attempted to "cause divisions and offenses." False teachers would come into a church and teach a doctrine contrary to Paul's teaching of salvation by faith in Christ alone. Such doctrine is serious error, and such teachers should be avoided. The best resolution to that conflict is to send the one in error away, knowing that he or she will not be persuaded and will only cause harm if allowed to stay. Taking a stand for Christ means taking a stand against teaching that conflicts with God's Word. **Topic: Conflict**

16Greet one another with a holy kiss. The[a] churches of Christ greet you.

AVOID DIVISIVE PERSONS

17Now I urge you, brethren, note those who cause divisions and offenses, contrary to the doctrine which you learned, and avoid them. 18For those who are such do not serve our Lord Jesus[a] Christ, but their own belly, and by smooth words and flattering speech deceive the hearts of the simple. 19For your obedience has become known to all. Therefore I am glad on your behalf; but I want you to be wise in what is good, and simple concerning evil. 20And the God of peace will crush Satan under your feet shortly.

The grace of our Lord Jesus Christ *be* with you. Amen.

GREETINGS FROM PAUL'S FRIENDS

21Timothy, my fellow worker, and Lucius, Jason, and Sosipater, my countrymen, greet you.

22I, Tertius, who wrote *this* epistle, greet you in the Lord.

23Gaius, my host and *the host* of the whole church, greets you. Erastus, the treasurer of the city, greets you, and Quartus, a brother. 24The grace of our Lord Jesus Christ *be* with you all. Amen.[a]

BENEDICTION

25Now to Him who is able to establish you according to my gospel and the preaching of Jesus Christ, according to the revelation of the mystery kept secret since the world began 26but now made manifest, and by the prophetic Scriptures made known to all nations, according to the commandment of the everlasting God, for obedience to the faith—27to God, alone wise, *be* glory through Jesus Christ forever. Amen.[a]

16:16 [a]NU-Text reads *All the churches.*
16:18 [a]NU-Text and M-Text omit *Jesus.*
16:24 [a]NU-Text omits this verse. **16:27** [a]M-Text puts Romans 16:25–27 after Romans 14:23.

1 Corinthians

How can a person be a committed follower of Jesus Christ in a world that scoffs at—and increasingly opposes—Christian beliefs? This is not just a modern question. It also concerned the first-century believers of Corinth in southern Greece. The apostle Paul's first letter to the Corinthians (written about A.D. 56) is a source of godly wisdom for saints who are called to live in a godless culture.

Corinth was the most important city of ancient Greece, famous for its commercial prosperity and notorious for its immorality. The city was so known for its decadence that the Greeks even coined the verb *korinthiazomai*—to Corinthianize—meaning "to live a life of debauchery."

In addition to unceasing temptations from the pagan culture that surrounded them, the church at Corinth also struggled with internal conflict. It's no wonder that Paul begins his letter with stern warnings against sin. Unlike the highly theological Book of Romans, 1 Corinthians addresses more practical matters such as church unity, humility, church discipline, marriage, divorce, remarriage, singleness, temptation, modesty, love, spiritual gifts, and worship. Though he begins his letter harshly, Paul ends with words of wisdom, grace, and hope.

Perhaps the main idea undergirding 1 Corinthians is that "instant spirituality" is a myth. Discipleship is the arduous process of pursuing holiness in the midst of a hostile culture. Long-term faithfulness is what leads to fruitfulness.

As you read, ask God to give you wisdom from both the positive and negative examples in the pages that follow.

Soul Concerns in 1 Corinthians

GREETING

1 Paul, called *to be* an apostle of Jesus Christ through the will of God, and Sosthenes *our* brother,

[2]To the church of God which is at Corinth, to those who are sanctified in Christ Jesus, called *to be* saints, with all who in every place call on the name of Jesus Christ our Lord, both theirs and ours:

[3]Grace to you and peace from God our Father and the Lord Jesus Christ.

SPIRITUAL GIFTS AT CORINTH

[4]I thank my God always concerning you for the grace of God which was given to you by Christ Jesus, [5]that you were enriched in everything by Him in all utterance and all knowledge, [6]even as the testimony of Christ was confirmed in you, [7]so that you come short in no gift, eagerly waiting for the revelation of our Lord Jesus Christ, [8]who will also confirm you to the end, *that you may be* blameless in the day of our Lord Jesus Christ. [9]God *is* faithful, by whom you were called into the fellowship of His Son, Jesus Christ our Lord.

SECTARIANISM IS SIN

[10]Now I plead with you, brethren, by the name of our Lord Jesus Christ, that you all speak the same thing, and *that* there be no divisions among you, but *that* you be perfectly joined together in the same mind and in the same judgment. [11]For it has been declared to me concerning you, my brethren, by those of Chloe's *household,* that there are contentions among you. [12]Now I say this, that each of you says, "I am of Paul," or "I am of Apollos," or "I am of Cephas," or "I am of Christ." [13]Is Christ divided? Was Paul crucified for you? Or were you baptized in the name of Paul?

[14]I thank God that I baptized none of you except Crispus and Gaius, [15]lest anyone should say that I had baptized in my own name. [16]Yes, I also baptized the household of Stephanas. Besides, I do not know whether I baptized any other. [17]For Christ did not send me to baptize, but to preach the gospel, not with wisdom of words, lest the cross of Christ should be made of no effect.

CHRIST THE POWER AND WISDOM OF GOD

[18]For the message of the cross is foolishness to those who are perishing, but to us who are being saved it is the power of God. [19]For it is written:

> *"I will destroy the wisdom of the wise,*
> *And bring to nothing the understanding*
> *of the prudent."*[a]

[20]Where *is* the wise? Where *is* the scribe? Where *is* the disputer of this age? Has not God made foolish the wisdom of this world? [21]For since, in the wisdom of God, the world through wisdom did not know God, it pleased God through the foolishness of the message preached to save those who believe. [22]For Jews request a sign, and Greeks seek after wisdom; [23]but we preach Christ crucified, to the Jews a stumbling block and to the Greeks[a] foolishness, [24]but to those who are called, both Jews and Greeks, Christ the power of God and the wisdom of God. [25]Because the foolishness of God is wiser than men, and the weakness of God is stronger than men.

GLORY ONLY IN THE LORD

[26]For you see your calling, brethren, that not many wise according to the flesh, not many mighty, not many noble, *are called.* [27]But God

1:19 [a]Isaiah 29:14 **1:23** [a]NU-Text reads *Gentiles.*

SOUL NOTE

Perfect Strength *(2:1–4)* Paul had not come to Corinth to impress anyone with great oratory. Instead, he had come "in weakness," seeking to demonstrate only the power of the Holy Spirit so that people would put their faith in God. When God calls people to serve Him, He will often use their areas of strength, but He sometimes surprises them by working through their weaknesses, even their pain. When we have a task to do for God but feel too weak or fearful, we might remember that His strength "is made perfect in weakness" (2 Cor. 12:9). **Topic: Weakness**

has chosen the foolish things of the world to
put to shame the wise, and God has chosen
the weak things of the world to put to shame
the things which are mighty; 28and the base
things of the world and the things which are
despised God has chosen, and the things
which are not, to bring to nothing the things
that are, 29that no flesh should glory in His
presence. 30But of Him you are in Christ Jesus,
who became for us wisdom from God—and
righteousness and sanctification and redemption—31that, as it is written, *"He who glories,
let him glory in the* L*ORD."*[a]

CHRIST CRUCIFIED

2 And I, brethren, when I came to you, did
not come with excellence of speech or of
wisdom declaring to you the testimony[a] of
God. 2For I determined not to know anything
among you except Jesus Christ and Him crucified. 3I was with you in weakness, in fear, and
in much trembling. 4And my speech and my
preaching *were* not with persuasive words of
human[a] wisdom, but in demonstration of the
Spirit and of power, 5that your faith should not
be in the wisdom of men but in the power of
God.

SPIRITUAL WISDOM

6However, we speak wisdom among those
who are mature, yet not the wisdom of this
age, nor of the rulers of this age, who are coming to nothing. 7But we speak the wisdom of
God in a mystery, the hidden *wisdom* which
God ordained before the ages for our glory,
8which none of the rulers of this age knew; for
had they known, they would not have crucified the Lord of glory.
9But as it is written:

"Eye has not seen, nor ear heard,
Nor have entered into the heart of man
The things which God has prepared for
those who love Him."[a]

10But God has revealed *them* to us through His
Spirit. For the Spirit searches all things, yes,
the deep things of God. 11For what man knows
the things of a man except the spirit of the
man which is in him? Even so no one knows
the things of God except the Spirit of God.
12Now we have received, not the spirit of the
world, but the Spirit who is from God, that we
might know the things that have been freely
given to us by God.
13These things we also speak, not in words
which man's wisdom teaches but which the
Holy[a] Spirit teaches, comparing spiritual
things with spiritual. 14But the natural man
does not receive the things of the Spirit of
God, for they are foolishness to him; nor can
he know *them,* because they are spiritually
discerned. 15But he who is spiritual judges all
things, yet he himself is *rightly* judged by no
one. 16For *"who has known the mind of the
*L*ORD that he may instruct Him?"*[a] But we have
the mind of Christ.

SECTARIANISM IS CARNAL

3 And I, brethren, could not speak to you as
to spiritual *people* but as to carnal, as to
babes in Christ. 2I fed you with milk and not
with solid food; for until now you were not
able *to receive it,* and even now you are still
not able; 3for you are still carnal. For where
there are envy, strife, and divisions among
you, are you not carnal and behaving like
mere men? 4For when one says, "I am of Paul,"
and another, "I *am* of Apollos," are you not
carnal?

1:31 [a]Jeremiah 9:24 **2:1** [a]NU-Text reads *mystery.* **2:4** [a]NU-Text omits *human.* **2:9** [a]Isaiah 64:4 **2:13** [a]NU-Text omits *Holy.* **2:16** [a]Isaiah 40:13

SOUL NOTE

Future Vision *(2:9, 10)* The promise of verse 9 would seem impossible without the fact of verse 10. The "things which God has prepared" for His people—the future blessings in heaven with Him—are not seen, heard, or even imagined by ordinary humans. Yet believers *can* see, hear, and imagine these blessings because "God has revealed them to us through His Spirit." The presence of the Holy Spirit in believers' lives gives comfort and guidance as we live on this earth; His presence also gives solid assurance of our future in heaven. **Topic: Presence of the Holy Spirit**

Weakness

MY WEAKNESS, HIS STRENGTH

GEORGE OHLSCHLAGER & TIM CLINTON

(1 Corinthians 2:1–5)

Famed preacher Charles Haddon Spurgeon wrote of God, "When you can't trace his hand, you can always trace his heart." These have been words of comfort to countless Christians during times of weakness, times when God's presence is not clear. Our weakness—which shows itself in our natural human frailty, doubt, and fear—usually brings us to the end of ourselves. This either causes anxiety or it can be the beginning of a special life with God.

GOING ON TO MATURITY

Possibly the greatest paradox of the Christian life is the way God's power comes alive in our weakness. Living out this sometimes confounding spiritual truth requires that we set aside our normal orientation in living—using and emphasizing our own personal strengths—and concentrate instead on admitting and living in our vulnerability.

Living out this truth is a major marker of spiritual maturity. When we live where we are weak in order that God may be strong, miracles happen and lives are changed for the sake of the kingdom. Furthermore, it is God who is seen doing the work—He is the One who is glorified.

On the other hand, this truth is often quite maddening to the spiritual novice, as it makes no logical sense according to the way of the world. We spend far too much of our lives thinking carnally rather than spiritually—believing that we will give our best to God and do the work of His kingdom all by our own powers. This is, in fact, a good and zealous thing to some degree, and God uses it. The problem is that we tend to cave in when our own effort is exhausted during times of serious trial. We forget that during those times of weakness, God can still work mightily. And, if we succeed, we realize that the feat was accomplished by God.

LEARNING BY LIVING

God is able to take every effort, no matter what the motivation, and make it work to His glory. Giving ourselves to the work of the kingdom, for instance, is the way that we learn that our best efforts often don't get the job done. We must depend on God.

Why are so many Christians so much like the world when we should be ablaze with the light of God and alive with His power? The answer, of course, is human weakness. Weakness in our love, devotion, and desire for Him; weakness that is all too human; weakness that cannot be overcome without the Spirit of God working in and through us.

Worse yet, we become weakest when we don't admit, or won't admit, that we have any weaknesses. The desire to be strong blinds us to our need to see and admit those weaknesses. So we end up trapped in a paradox—we stay weak because of our denial of our weakness. We remain weak in our false projection of strength.

PAUL'S EXAMPLE

The apostle Paul struggled mightily with this confounding trap. He hated the "thorn in the flesh" that afflicted him. He begged God over and over to remove it (2 Cor. 12:7–10). God did not. Instead, God told Paul that he would be just fine living in

God's presence, and that His power would come alive in Paul's weakness.

You know how most of us respond when we are in Paul's position. We whine, we bargain, we curse, we turn away, we keep begging God to do it our way instead of His. We would prefer not to hear God say, "Live with it by living deeper in Me."

What did Paul do? Paul realized that God was not going to remove his weakness, despite his best efforts to convince Him to do so. Paul surely told God that he would be much more effective at preaching and teaching, and much more effective for the kingdom without his weakness. But God said no. So Paul changed his approach, realizing that he could be glad about his weakness and even boast about it, knowing that through it, Christ would be glorified. Therefore, he would be content in the midst of his "thorny" suffering.

Paul was so full of the Holy Spirit, so imbued with the presence and power of Christ, that no experience of pain and suffering could dent its delightful impact. He did the counter-intuitive thing—he embraced what he, and we, would normally reject. Not only weakness, but insults, hardships, disasters, and persecution could be embraced. Nothing adverse or painful could overcome the power of living fully in Christ. Instead, those difficulties became the very doors to a life of intimacy with God.

Paul grasped something that few of us know: God's grace was, in fact, fully sufficient for the trial of suffering he was facing—in fact, it was sufficient for any trial he faced. And this knowledge changed Paul's life, made him delight in the Lord, and filled him with praise and thanksgiving. It brought to life the truth that the joy of the Lord—not good circumstances, not good health, not lots of money, and not spiritual perfection—is our strength.

Make this your fervent prayer: "Lord, You are so great that Your mere presence is sufficient for me—that alone will change my life completely." When I am weak, then I am most strong in Christ. Nothing will ever be the same again.

FURTHER MEDITATION:

Other passages to study about the issue of weakness include:

- Joshua 1:8, 9
- Psalms 28:7; 31:7; 46:1; 138:7
- Isaiah 43:2
- Nahum 1:7
- 2 Corinthians 4:8, 9
- Philippians 4:13
- Hebrews 4:15, 16; 12:3

To Learn More: Turn to the key passage note on weakness at 2 Corinthians 12:9, 10 on page 1533. See also the personality profile of Mark on page 1438.

Watering, Working, Warning

5Who then is Paul, and who *is* Apollos, but
ministers through whom you believed, as the
Lord gave to each one? 6I planted, Apollos watered, but God gave the increase. 7So then neither he who plants is anything, nor he who
waters, but God who gives the increase. 8Now
he who plants and he who waters are one, and
each one will receive his own reward according to his own labor.

9For we are God's fellow workers; you are
God's field, *you are* God's building. 10Ac-
cording to the grace of God which was given
to me, as a wise master builder I have laid
the foundation, and another builds on it.
But let each one take heed how he builds on
it. 11For no other foundation can anyone lay
than that which is laid, which is Jesus
Christ. 12Now if anyone builds on this foundation *with* gold, silver, precious stones,
wood, hay, straw, 13each one's work will become clear; for the Day will declare it, because it will be revealed by fire; and the fire
will test each one's work, of what sort it is.
14If anyone's work which he has built on *it*
endures, he will receive a reward. 15If
anyone's work is burned, he will suffer loss;
but he himself will be saved, yet so as through
fire.

16Do you not know
that you are the temple
of God and *that* the
Spirit of God dwells in
you? 17If anyone defiles
the temple of God, God
will destroy him. For the
temple of God is holy,
which *temple* you are.

> Do you not know that you are the temple of God and that the Spirit of God dwells in you?
>
> 1 CORINTHIANS 3:16

Avoid Worldly Wisdom

18Let no one deceive himself. If anyone
among you seems to be wise in this age, let
him become a fool that he may become wise.
19For the wisdom of this world is foolishness
with God. For it is written, *"He catches the
wise in their own craftiness"*;[a] 20and again,
"The LORD *knows the thoughts of the wise,
that they are futile."*[a] 21Therefore let no one
boast in men. For all things are yours:
22whether Paul or Apollos or Cephas, or the
world or life or death, or things present or
things to come—all are yours. 23And you *are*
Christ's, and Christ *is* God's.

Stewards of the Mysteries of God

4 Let a man so consider us, as servants of
Christ and stewards of the mysteries of
God. 2Moreover it is required in stewards that
one be found faithful. 3But with me it is a very
small thing that I should be judged by you or
by a human court.[a] In fact, I do not even judge
myself. 4For I know of nothing against myself,
yet I am not justified by this; but He who
judges me is the Lord. 5Therefore judge nothing before the time, until the Lord comes, who
will both bring to light the hidden things of
darkness and reveal the counsels of the hearts.
Then each one's praise will come from God.

Fools for Christ's Sake

6Now these things, brethren, I have figuratively transferred to myself and Apollos for
your sakes, that you may learn in us not to
think beyond what is written, that none of you
may be puffed up on behalf of one against the
other. 7For who makes you differ *from another?* And what do you have that you did not
receive? Now if you did indeed receive *it,* why
do you boast as if you had not received *it?*

8You are already full! You are already rich!
You have reigned as kings without us—and indeed I could wish you did reign, that we also
might reign with you! 9For I think that God
has displayed us, the
apostles, last, as men
condemned to death;
for we have been made
a spectacle to the world,
both to angels and to
men. 10We *are* fools for
Christ's sake, but you
are wise in Christ! We *are* weak, but you *are*
strong! You *are* distinguished, but we *are* dishonored! 11To the present hour we both hunger and thirst, and we are poorly clothed, and
beaten, and homeless. 12And we labor, working with our own hands. Being reviled, we
bless; being persecuted, we endure; 13being
defamed, we entreat. We have been made as
the filth of the world, the offscouring of all
things until now.

Paul's Paternal Care

14I do not write these things to shame you,
but as my beloved children I warn *you.* 15For

3:19 [a]Job 5:13 **3:20** [a]Psalm 94:11 **4:3** [a]Literally *day*

though you might have ten thousand instructors in Christ, yet *you do* not *have* many fathers; for in Christ Jesus I have begotten you through the gospel. 16Therefore I urge you, imitate me. 17For this reason I have sent Timothy to you, who is my beloved and faithful son in the Lord, who will remind you of my ways in Christ, as I teach everywhere in every church.

18Now some are puffed up, as though I were not coming to you. 19But I will come to you shortly, if the Lord wills, and I will know, not the word of those who are puffed up, but the power. 20For the kingdom of God *is* not in word but in power. 21What do you want? Shall I come to you with a rod, or in love and a spirit of gentleness?

Immorality Defiles the Church

5 It is actually reported *that there is* sexual immorality among you, and such sexual immorality as is not even named[a] among the Gentiles—that a man has his father's wife! 2And you are puffed up, and have not rather mourned, that he who has done this deed might be taken away from among you. 3For I indeed, as absent in body but present in spirit, have already judged (as though I were present) him who has so done this deed. 4In the name of our Lord Jesus Christ, when you are gathered together, along with my spirit, with the power of our Lord Jesus Christ, 5deliver such a one to Satan for the destruction of the flesh, that his spirit may be saved in the day of the Lord Jesus.[a]

6Your glorying *is* not good. Do you not know that a little leaven leavens the whole lump? 7Therefore purge out the old leaven, that you may be a new lump, since you truly are unleavened. For indeed Christ, our Passover, was sacrificed for us.[a] 8Therefore let us keep the feast, not with old leaven, nor with the leaven of malice and wickedness, but with the unleavened *bread* of sincerity and truth.

Immorality Must Be Judged

9I wrote to you in my epistle not to keep company with sexually immoral people. 10Yet *I* certainly *did* not *mean* with the sexually immoral people of this world, or with the covetous, or extortioners, or idolaters, since then you would need to go out of the world. 11But now I have written to you not to keep company with anyone named a brother, who is sexually immoral, or covetous, or an idolater, or a reviler, or a drunkard, or an extortioner—not even to eat with such a person.

12For what *have* I *to do* with judging those also who are outside? Do you not judge those who are inside? 13But those who are outside God judges. Therefore *"put away from yourselves the evil person."*[a]

Do Not Sue the Brethren

6 Dare any of you, having a matter against another, go to law before the unrighteous, and not before the saints? 2Do you not know that the saints will judge the world? And if the world will be judged by you, are you unworthy to judge the smallest matters? 3Do you not know that we shall judge angels? How much more, things that pertain to this life? 4If then you have judgments concerning things pertaining to this life, do you appoint those who are least esteemed by the church to judge? 5I say this to your shame. Is it so, that there is not a wise man among you, not even one, who will be able to judge between his brethren? 6But brother goes to law against brother, and that before unbelievers!

5:1 [a]NU-Text omits *named.* **5:5** [a]NU-Text omits *Jesus.* **5:7** [a]NU-Text omits *for us.* **5:13** [a]Deuteronomy 17:7; 19:19; 22:21, 24; 24:7

SOUL NOTE

In the World *(5:9–11)* When Paul urged the Corinthian believers "not to keep company with sexually immoral people," he was referring not to sinning unbelievers, but to sinning fellow believers. Believers should avoid immoral people who continue in their sin and yet claim to be Christians. Some believers attempt to rationalize sinful behavior, but when they do so they dishonor Christ, who died for their sins. Sexual sin in the church must never be rationalized. Condoning such behavior harms the church's reputation and damages its witness. **Topic: Sexual Sin**

7Now therefore, it is already an utter failure
for you that you go to law against one another.
Why do you not rather accept wrong? Why do
you not rather *let yourselves* be cheated? 8No,
you yourselves do wrong and cheat, and *you
do* these things *to your* brethren! 9Do you not
know that the unrighteous will not inherit the
kingdom of God? Do not be deceived. Neither
fornicators, nor idolaters, nor adulterers, nor
homosexuals,[a] nor sodomites, 10nor thieves,
nor covetous, nor drunkards, nor revilers, nor
extortioners will inherit the kingdom of God.
11And such were some of you. But you were
washed, but you were sanctified, but you
were justified in the name of the Lord Jesus
and by the Spirit of our God.

Glorify God in Body and Spirit

12All things are lawful for me, but all things
are not helpful. All things are lawful for me,
but I will not be brought under the power of
any. 13Foods for the stomach and the stomach
for foods, but God will destroy both it and
them. Now the body *is* not for sexual immorality but for the Lord, and the Lord for the
body. 14And God both raised up the Lord and
will also raise us up by His power.

15Do you not know that your bodies are
members of Christ? Shall I then take the members of Christ and make *them* members of a
harlot? Certainly not! 16Or do you not know
that he who is joined to a harlot is one body
with her? For *"the two,"* He says, *"shall become one flesh."*[a] 17But he who is joined to
the Lord is one spirit *with Him.*

18Flee sexual immorality. Every sin that a
man does is outside the body, but he who
commits sexual immorality sins against his

6:9 [a]That is, catamites **6:16** [a]Genesis 2:24

KEY PASSAGE

THE FORCE

(6:9–12)

God gave people "richly all things to enjoy," but Satan works tirelessly to take God's blessings and twist them into evil. The beauty of sex in marriage is corrupted by the sin of sex in other relationships. The enjoyment of a wide variety of delicious foods is corrupted by gluttony, the addiction of eating too much—not to mention other eating disorders. The provision of material blessing is corrupted by greed and love of wealth.

Paul explained that "all things are lawful," meaning that believers are allowed to enjoy many things as long as they are not forbidden by Scripture. But they must never allow themselves to be controlled or "brought under the power of any." An addiction is powerful. If a believer is moving toward an addiction in some area of life, the Holy Spirit will make them aware of it. We must seek God's guidance to maintain balance.

To Learn More: Turn to the article about addictions on pages 1186, 1187. See also the personality profile of Gomer on page 1130.

SOUL NOTE

Balanced Meals *(6:12, 13)* Some who face a difficult eating disorder—whether it be an addiction to food, or an addiction to going without food—understand the power of that addiction. God provided food for the animals and people He created in order to sustain them. Food is meant for sustenance—"foods for the stomach and the stomach for foods." A food addiction takes the focus off God and puts it on one's food or stomach—both of which will eventually no longer be needed. People who struggle with eating disorders should seek Christian professional guidance to gain a proper perspective and pattern for eating. **Topic: Eating Disorders**

own body. [19]Or do you not know that your
body is the temple of the Holy Spirit *who is* in
you, whom you have
from God, and you are
not your own? [20]For you
were bought at a price;
therefore glorify God in
your body[a] and in your
spirit, which are God's.

> For you were bought at a price; therefore glorify God in your body and in your spirit, which are God's.
> 1 CORINTHIANS 6:20

PRINCIPLES OF MARRIAGE

7 Now concerning the things of which you
wrote to me:
It is good for a man not to touch a woman.
[2]Nevertheless, because of sexual immorality,
let each man have his own wife, and let each
woman have her own husband. [3]Let the husband render to his wife the affection due her,
and likewise also the wife to her husband.
[4]The wife does not have
authority over her own
body, but the husband
does. And likewise the
husband does not have
authority over his own
body, but the wife *does.*
[5]Do not deprive one an-
other except with consent for a time, that you
may give yourselves to fasting and prayer;
and come together again so that Satan does
not tempt you because of your lack of self-
control. [6]But I say this as a concession, not as

6:20 [a]NU-Text ends the verse at *body.*

KEY PASSAGE

Sexual Integrity

ONE FLESH

(6:15)

Sex is more than a physical act. When God created sex, He said that in that moment, the two people "become one flesh" (6:16; Gen. 2:24). Sex is meant by God to be a holy union in which a man and a woman share a deep bond. But in the Corinthian culture, sex outside of marriage was not viewed as evil. It was even part of their "worship," as the temple of Aphrodite employed thousands of temple prostitutes. Paul wanted the Corinthian believers to understand that because they had become the body of Christ, they needed to separate themselves from all forms of sexual immorality. This did not mean that married couples should become celibate—sex itself is not evil, for God created it. It is people who pervert it. Instead, believers must practice sexual integrity. God's people must abstain from sex outside of marriage; but within the bonds of marriage, a husband and wife should be faithful, always seeking to lovingly meet each other's needs (7:2–5).

To Learn More: Turn to the article about sexual integrity on pages 1608, 1609. See also the personality profile of Ruth and Boaz on page 336.

SOUL NOTE

Premarital Purity *(6:18–20)* Often movies and television shows portray couples having sex outside of marriage as normal and common. Often people seem to have no concern that this is sin according to God. He does not ask believers to "flee sexual immorality" because He wants to ruin their fun. Sex was God's idea; He created it as a holy union that binds two people together. Experiencing that union with many different people cheapens what God intends as a lifelong bond between a husband and wife. Believers must keep their premarital relationships pure. But if they have not done so, they can begin anew, knowing that God will forgive past sins.
Topic: Premarital Relationships

Sex in Marriage

SEX IN MARRIAGE

CLIFFORD L. PENNER AND JOYCE J. PENNER

(1 Corinthians 7:1–9)

We live in a world saturated with sex, yet we may find ourselves confused in our pursuit of sexual joy and mutual fulfillment in marriage. Diminished sexual appetite is likely for spouses who are uncomfortable with their sexuality or reluctant to embrace a vigorous sex life. Marital tension builds as the consequence of lack of sexual desire or differing desires between spouses.

Even though sexual satisfaction has been highly linked to marriage and strong religious commitment, many believers do not connect God or their faith with their sex lives. Affirming the Bible's teaching about sex in marriage and adopting helpful sexual attitudes toward men, women, and sex can help couples experience full sexual potential.

SEX IN MARRIAGE—PERFECTLY DESIGNED BY GOD

Whether our sexuality has brought us energy and deep fulfillment or led us into pain and despair, we are created as sexual people in God's image—male and female. Genesis 2:24, 25 shows God's design for a man and woman to be united as one flesh. What people may not be aware of, however, is that this sexual union occurred *before* mankind fell into sin. Thus, people were created to be free to share their bodies openly with their spouses in marriage, delight in each other sexually, and honor God with their pleasure.

SEXUAL PLEASURE—A BIBLICAL EXPECTATION

Sex in marriage was intended not only for procreation, but also for unity and pleasure. Husbands and wives are to be fruitful and multiply (Gen. 9:7), to become one (Gen. 2:24) and to be free and unashamed (Gen. 2:25).

Sexual pleasure is endorsed throughout the Old and the New Testaments. "Let your fountain be blessed, and rejoice with the wife of your youth. . . . Let her breasts satisfy you at all times; and always be enraptured with her love" (Prov. 5:18, 19). Sexual passion as an expectation for marriage is also evidenced by the fact that the marriage bed is "undefiled" (Heb. 13:4). Sexual passion is not only demonstrated by the lovers in the Song of Solomon but is also implied by Scripture's guidelines for handling our sexual passion. If God had not designed us with passion, He would not have needed to teach us how to manage that passion.

The Bible instructs both the husband and wife to delight in giving themselves to each other. First Corinthians 7:3–5 teaches that married couples are to be sexual together, regularly enjoying each other for pleasure. In Ephesians 5:21–33, Paul instructs husbands and wives to be mutually submissive. Through Christ, we have the potential to reestablish the original design of creation—to be completely open and free sexually in marriage.

DISCOVERING MUTUAL FULFILLMENT

Husbands and wives must highly regard and consistently practice the concept of mutuality—mutual respect and mutual responsibility—in their sexual relationships. Passion will be expressed, sexual freedom discovered, and true "oneness" fulfilled.

Men and women are different. Women function on two tracks: the emotional and the physical. These must be connected for a woman to be interested sexually. Men function on one track; when physically aroused, men will usually be emotionally ready to have sex. Women desire sex and open up sexually when they feel loved by and connected with their husbands. Men connect and feel loved through sex.

Because of these differences, the man must start the process of discovering mutual sexual fulfillment by connecting with his wife. By selflessly loving her, a man loves his wife like Christ loved the Church. A husband's love, adoration, and connection with his wife allows her to open up sexually. His affirmation ignites her passion and she responds. He feels loved by her response and they both end up fulfilled.

A woman's responsibility is to take in sexual pleasure, receive her husband's affirmation, and lead by invitation, as did the bride in the Song of Solomon. For a woman to do this, she has to believe she is worthy and has a right to be sexual. She has to know that her body was designed not only for reproduction, but also for her sexual pleasure and satisfaction. Once a woman accepts her God-given sexuality, she leads, not by control or demand, but by listening to her body's desires, taking in the good feelings of being touched, and inviting her husband to enjoy her body as she enjoys his.

When the husband lovingly connects with his wife and the wife embraces her sexuality and shares it with her husband, mutual fulfillment is experienced.

DISCOVERING MUTUAL PLEASURE

To experience long-lasting passion in marriage, couples must accept their differences as men and women and focus their sexual times together on delighting in each others' bodies. Arousal, intercourse, and orgasm do not measure sexual satisfaction, but result when pleasure is the focus.

For pleasure to be the focus of sex in marriage, the couple has to accept both the husband's more predictable constancy and the ever-changing complexity of the woman. Sex will then be more interesting, less goal-oriented, less pressure-filled, and more deeply satisfying.

Our culture promotes spontaneity. The expectation is that great sex should just happen. But for most couples, the anticipation of planned times builds quality, and the allotment of those times increases quantity. True passion and great sex do not just happen. But by affirming God's design and pursuing mutual pleasure and fulfillment through the practice of the model of the husband loving his wife as Christ loved the Church, couples will discover the sexual satisfaction God intended for them in marriage.

FURTHER MEDITATION:

Other passages to study about the issue of sex in marriage include:

- Exodus 20:14
- Proverbs 5:15–20
- 1 Corinthians 6:12–20

To Learn More: Turn to the key passage note on sex in marriage at Hebrews 13:4 on page 1638. See also the personality profile of Solomon and the Shulamite on page 871.

a commandment. [7]For I wish that all men
were even as I myself. But each one has his
own gift from God, one in this manner and
another in that.

[8]But I say to the unmarried and to the widows: It is good for them if they remain even as
I am; [9]but if they cannot exercise self-control,
let them marry. For it is better to marry than to
burn *with passion.*

KEEP YOUR MARRIAGE VOWS

[10]Now to the married I command, *yet* not I
but the Lord: A wife is not to depart from *her*
husband. [11]But even if she does depart, let her
remain unmarried or be reconciled to *her* husband. And a husband is not to divorce *his*
wife.

[12]But to the rest I, not the Lord, say: If any
brother has a wife who does not believe, and

SOUL NOTE

Enjoy *(7:2–5)* Because of the immorality in Corinth, many believers may have thought that all sex was evil; so they began to refrain from sex even in their marriages. Paul explained that God created sex for the enjoyment of a man and woman in marriage and for procreation. Sex in marriage binds a husband and wife together. A healthy sex life also helps the couple to withstand any outside temptations. Sex in marriage should be fulfilling, intimate, and sensual. A believer can and should enjoy the sexual relationship of marriage and the bond it brings them and their spouse.
Topic: Sex in Marriage

PERSONALITY PROFILE

Singleness

PAUL: SINGLE AND NOT ALONE

(1 COR. 7:8)

Paul was one of the greatest missionaries who ever lived—tirelessly traveling the known world with the gospel of salvation in Jesus Christ. He told the Corinthian believers, in the context of their questions about marriage, "I say to the unmarried and to the widows: It is good for them if they remain even as I am," meaning single. Why such advice? And what's wrong with marriage?

Nothing is wrong with marriage. In fact, throughout this section, Paul also told the married people to stay married, even if they were married to unbelievers. The situation in Corinth needed to be handled carefully. The rampant immorality of the city meant that believers needed to learn how God would have them live pure lives. The specter of persecution from the Roman Empire meant that Paul felt an urgency to share the gospel with as few hindrances as possible. Paul advised those already single to remain that way—not seeking to get married as if getting married was to be their goal. Their focus should first be on God; then, if marriage presented itself as a possibility, they could certainly marry.

Paul also explained, realistically, how a married person's priorities are different. A single believer has different service opportunities than a married believer. Paul, passionate for the gospel to spread, simply wished that more people were like him.

Singleness can be used for God's glory. Whether a person has never been married or has become single by way of divorce or bereavement, single people are not set aside by God. He has great things for single people to accomplish for His kingdom. Single people must get their own priorities straight—seeking God and His will above all. Single believers are never alone, because God is always with them.

To Learn More: Turn to the article about singleness on pages 1262, 1263. See also the key passage note at 1 Corinthians 7:26–35 on page 1503.

she is willing to live with him, let him not divorce her. [13]And a woman who has a husband who does not believe, if he is willing to live with her, let her not divorce him. [14]For the unbelieving husband is sanctified by the wife, and the unbelieving wife is sanctified by the husband; otherwise your children would be unclean, but now they are holy. [15]But if the unbeliever departs, let him depart; a brother or a sister is not under bondage in such *cases.* But God has called us to peace. [16]For how do you know, O wife, whether you will save *your* husband? Or how do you know, O husband, whether you will save *your* wife?

Live as You Are Called

[17]But as God has distributed to each one, as the Lord has called each one, so let him walk. And so I ordain in all the churches. [18]Was anyone called while circumcised? Let him not become uncircumcised. Was anyone called while uncircumcised? Let him not be circumcised. [19]Circumcision is nothing and uncircumcision is nothing, but keeping the commandments of God *is what matters.* [20]Let each one remain in the same calling in which he was called. [21]Were you called *while* a slave? Do not be concerned about it; but if you can be made free, rather use *it.* [22]For he who is called in the Lord *while* a slave is the Lord's freedman. Likewise he who is called *while* free is Christ's slave. [23]You were bought at a price; do not become slaves of men. [24]Brethren, let each one remain with God in that *state* in which he was called.

To the Unmarried and Widows

[25]Now concerning virgins: I have no commandment from the Lord; yet I give judgment

SOUL NOTE

Don't Go *(7:10–16)* Divorce was not a part of God's plan but was allowed as a concession to people's sinfulness (Matt. 19:8, 9). When one spouse becomes a Christian and the other doesn't, the believing spouse should stay in the marriage. Paul explained that the marriage bond is so strong that a believer should not willingly break it. Through that union, the unbeliever may become a Christian. In any event, the believer can have a positive influence on their spouse and children.

Topic: Divorce/Separation

KEY PASSAGE

Singleness

SINGLED OUT

(7:26–35)

Some have understood this passage to mean that all single people should remain that way. But Paul's words must be balanced against both the cultural context and his mission. Paul, as a single man, understood the need for people to be able to do whatever it took to share the gospel with unbelievers. He knew that persecution could come at any time. His words reveal his total commitment to his call. He encouraged single people not to apologize for their singleness. They should not seek to be married as if that were all that mattered. God has an important calling for single people, since they can "serve the Lord without distraction" (7:35). A married person has many responsibilities, while a single person can be freer to work for the gospel. Neither state is better than the other; different circumstances create different opportunities. Single people can rejoice in their singleness, knowing that God can do great things through them.

To Learn More: Turn to the article about singleness on pages 1262, 1263. See also the personality profile of Paul on page 1502.

as one whom the Lord in His mercy *has made* trustworthy. 26I suppose therefore that this is good because of the present distress—that *it is* good for a man to remain as he is: 27Are you bound to a wife? Do not seek to be loosed. Are you loosed from a wife? Do not seek a wife. 28But even if you do marry, you have not sinned; and if a virgin marries, she has not sinned. Nevertheless such will have trouble in the flesh, but I would spare you.

29But this I say, brethren, the time *is* short, so that from now on even those who have wives should be as though they had none, 30those who weep as though they did not weep, those who rejoice as though they did not rejoice, those who buy as though they did not possess, 31and those who use this world as not misusing *it*. For the form of this world is passing away.

32But I want you to be without care. He who is unmarried cares for the things of the Lord—how he may please the Lord. 33But he who is married cares about the things of the world—how he may please *his* wife. 34There is[a] a difference between a wife and a virgin. The unmarried woman cares about the things of the Lord, that she may be holy both in body and in spirit. But she who is married cares about the things of the world—how she may please *her* husband. 35And this I say for your own profit, not that I may put a leash on you, but for what is proper, and that you may serve the Lord without distraction.

36But if any man thinks he is behaving improperly toward his virgin, if she is past the flower of youth, and thus it must be, let him do what he wishes. He does not sin; let them marry. 37Nevertheless he who stands steadfast in his heart, having no necessity, but has power over his own will, and has so determined in his heart that he will keep his virgin,[a] does well. 38So then he who gives *her*[a] in marriage does well, but he who does not give *her* in marriage does better.

39A wife is bound by law as long as her husband lives; but if her husband dies, she is at liberty to be married to whom she wishes, only in the Lord. 40But she is happier if she remains as she is, according to my judgment—and I think I also have the Spirit of God.

Be Sensitive to Conscience

8 Now concerning things offered to idols: We know that we all have knowledge. Knowledge puffs up, but love edifies. 2And if anyone thinks that he knows anything, he knows nothing yet as he ought to know. 3But if anyone loves God, this one is known by Him.

4Therefore concerning the eating of things offered to idols, we know that an idol *is* nothing in the world, and that *there is* no other God but one. 5For even if there are so-called gods, whether in heaven or on earth (as there are many gods and many lords), 6yet for us *there is* one God, the Father, of whom *are* all things, and we for Him; and one Lord Jesus Christ, through whom *are* all things, and through whom we *live*.

7However, *there is* not in everyone that knowledge; for some, with consciousness of the idol, until now eat *it* as a thing offered to an idol; and their conscience, being weak, is defiled. 8But food does not commend us to God; for neither if we eat are we the better, nor if we do not eat are we the worse.

9But beware lest somehow this liberty of yours become a stumbling block to those who are weak. 10For if anyone sees you who have knowledge eating in an idol's temple, will not the conscience of him who is weak be emboldened to eat those things offered to idols? 11And because of your knowledge shall the weak brother perish, for whom Christ died? 12But when you thus sin against the brethren, and wound their weak conscience, you sin against Christ. 13Therefore, if food makes my brother stumble, I will never again eat meat, lest I make my brother stumble.

A Pattern of Self-Denial

9 Am I not an apostle? Am I not free? Have I not seen Jesus Christ our Lord? Are you not my work in the Lord? 2If I am not an apostle to others, yet doubtless I am to you. For you are the seal of my apostleship in the Lord.

3My defense to those who examine me is this: 4Do we have no right to eat and drink? 5Do we have no right to take along a believing wife, as *do* also the other apostles, the brothers of the Lord, and Cephas? 6Or *is it* only Barnabas and I *who* have no right to refrain from working? 7Who ever goes to war at his own expense? Who plants a vineyard and does not eat of its fruit? Or who tends a flock and does not drink of the milk of the flock?

7:34 [a]M-Text adds *also.* **7:37** [a]Or *virgin daughter* **7:38** [a]NU-Text reads *his own virgin.*

[8]Do I say these things as a *mere* man? Or does not the law say the same also? [9]For it is written in the law of Moses, "*You shall not muzzle an ox while it treads out the grain.*"[a] Is it oxen God is concerned about? [10]Or does He say *it* altogether for our sakes? For our sakes, no doubt, *this* is written, that he who plows should plow in hope, and he who threshes in hope should be partaker of his hope. [11]If we have sown spiritual things for you, *is it* a great thing if we reap your material things? [12]If others are partakers of *this* right over you, *are* we not even more?

Nevertheless we have not used this right, but endure all things lest we hinder the gospel of Christ. [13]Do you not know that those who minister the holy things eat *of the things* of the temple, and those who serve at the altar partake of *the offerings of* the altar? [14]Even so the Lord has commanded that those who preach the gospel should live from the gospel.

[15]But I have used none of these things, nor have I written these things that it should be done so to me; for it *would be* better for me to die than that anyone should make my boasting void. [16]For if I preach the gospel, I have nothing to boast of, for necessity is laid upon me; yes, woe is me if I do not preach the gospel! [17]For if I do this willingly, I have a reward; but if against my will, I have been entrusted with a stewardship. [18]What is my reward then? That when I preach the gospel, I may present the gospel of Christ[a] without charge, that I may not abuse my authority in the gospel.

Serving All Men

[19]For though I am free from all *men,* I have made myself a servant to all, that I might win the more; [20]and to the Jews I became as a Jew, that I might win Jews; to those *who are* under the law, as under the law,[a] that I might win those *who are* under the law; [21]to those *who are* without law, as without law (not being without law toward God,[a] but under law toward Christ[b]), that I might win those *who are* without law; [22]to the weak I became as[a] weak, that I might win the weak. I have become all things to all *men,* that I might by all means save some. [23]Now this I do for the gospel's sake, that I may be partaker of it with *you.*

Striving for a Crown

[24]Do you not know that those who run in a race all run, but one receives the prize? Run in such a way that you may obtain *it.* [25]And everyone who competes *for the prize* is temperate in all things. Now they *do it* to obtain a perishable crown, but we *for* an imperishable *crown.* [26]Therefore I run thus: not with uncertainty. Thus I fight: not as *one who* beats the air. [27]But I discipline my body and bring *it* into subjection, lest, when I have preached to others, I myself should become disqualified.

Old Testament Examples

10 Moreover, brethren, I do not want you to be unaware that all our fathers were under the cloud, all passed through the sea, [2]all were baptized into Moses in the cloud and in the sea, [3]all ate the same spiritual food, [4]and all drank the same spiritual drink. For they drank of that spiritual Rock that followed them, and that Rock was Christ. [5]But with most of them God was not well pleased, for *their bodies* were scattered in the wilderness.

9:9 [a]Deuteronomy 25:4 **9:18** [a]NU-Text omits *of Christ.* **9:20** [a]NU-Text adds *though not being myself under the law.* **9:21** [a]NU-Text reads *God's law.* [b]NU-Text reads *Christ's law.* **9:22** [a]NU-Text omits *as.*

SOUL NOTE

The Way of Love *(9:22)* Chapter 8 discusses "weak" believers who would not enjoy certain freedoms of the Christian life because they felt uncomfortable doing so. With these people, Paul "became as weak" in order to help them grow deeper in the faith. Some believers may, for example, not feel comfortable with a certain activity because of past associations. Paul says that when we are with such people, we don't try to convince them to change, nor do we flaunt our freedom. Instead, we avoid that activity and enjoy time with them in other ways. In this way we show the love of Christ.
Topic: Self-Denial

6Now these things became our examples, to the intent that we should not lust after evil things as they also lusted. 7And do not become idolaters as *were* some of them. As it is written, *"The people sat down to eat and drink, and rose up to play."*[a] 8Nor let us commit sexual immorality, as some of them did, and in one day twenty-three thousand fell; 9nor let us tempt Christ, as some of them also tempted, and were destroyed by serpents; 10nor complain, as some of them also complained, and were destroyed by the destroyer. 11Now all[a] these things happened to them as examples, and they were written for our admonition, upon whom the ends of the ages have come.

12Therefore let him who thinks he stands take heed lest he fall. 13No temptation has overtaken you except such as is common to man; but God *is* faithful, who will not allow you to be tempted beyond what you are able, but with the temptation will also make the way of escape, that you may be able to bear *it*.

Flee from Idolatry

14Therefore, my beloved, flee from idolatry. 15I speak as to wise men; judge for yourselves what I say. 16The cup of blessing which we bless, is it not the communion of the blood of Christ? The bread which we break, is it not the communion of the body of Christ? 17For we, *though* many, are one bread *and* one body; for we all partake of that one bread.

18Observe Israel after the flesh: Are not those who eat of the sacrifices partakers of the altar? 19What am I saying then? That an idol is anything, or what is offered to idols is anything? 20Rather, that the things which the Gentiles sacrifice they sacrifice to demons and not to God, and I do not want you to have fellowship with demons. 21You cannot drink the cup of the Lord and the cup of demons; you cannot partake of the Lord's table and of the table of demons. 22Or do we provoke the Lord to jealousy? Are we stronger than He?

All to the Glory of God

23All things are lawful for me,[a] but not all things are helpful; all things are lawful for me,[b] but not all things edify. 24Let no one seek his own, but each one the other's *well-being*.

25Eat whatever is sold in the meat market, asking no questions for conscience' sake; 26for *"the earth is the LORD's, and all its fullness."*[a]

27If any of those who do not believe invites you *to dinner*, and you desire to go, eat whatever is set before you, asking no question for conscience' sake. 28But if anyone says to you, "This was offered to idols," do not eat it for the sake of the one who told you, and for conscience' sake;[a] for *"the earth is the LORD's, and all its fullness."*[b] 29"Conscience," I say, not your own, but that of the other. For why is my liberty judged by another *man's* conscience? 30But if I partake with thanks, why am I evil spoken of for *the food* over which I give thanks?

31Therefore, whether you eat or drink, or whatever you do, do all to the glory of God. 32Give no offense, either to the Jews or to the

> Therefore, whether you eat or drink, or whatever you do, do all to the glory of God.
> 1 CORINTHIANS 10:31

10:7 [a]Exodus 32:6 **10:11** [a]NU-Text omits *all.* **10:23** [a]NU-Text omits *for me.* [b]NU-Text omits *for me.* **10:26** [a]Psalm 24:1 **10:28** [a]NU-Text omits the rest of this verse. [b]Psalm 24:1

SOUL NOTE

Escape Hatch *(10:13)* Believers should never be shocked or discouraged by encountering temptation. Satan fights against believers and will mount an assault at every opportunity. God knows that all human beings are tempted, and that different people will be tempted by different things. Being tempted is not a sin; giving in, however, is. God promises that He will not allow us to be tempted beyond what we can bear. He also provides "the way of escape." Every time we face temptation, we can know that God will help us through it. We should look for His way of escape and then run for the door! **Topic: Temptation**

Greeks or to the church of God, 33just as I also
please all *men* in all *things,* not seeking my
own profit, but the *profit* of many, that they
may be saved.

11 Imitate me, just as I also *imitate*
Christ.

HEAD COVERINGS

2Now I praise you, brethren, that you remember me in all things and keep the traditions just as I delivered *them* to you. 3But I
want you to know that the head of every man
is Christ, the head of woman *is* man, and the
head of Christ *is* God. 4Every man praying or
prophesying, having *his* head covered, dishonors his head. 5But every woman who prays
or prophesies with *her* head uncovered dishonors her head, for that is one and the same
as if her head were shaved. 6For if a woman is
not covered, let her also be shorn. But if it is
shameful for a woman to be shorn or shaved,
let her be covered. 7For a man indeed ought
not to cover *his* head, since he is the image
and glory of God; but woman is the glory of
man. 8For man is not from woman, but woman from man. 9Nor was man created for the
woman, but woman for the man. 10For this
reason the woman ought to have *a symbol of*
authority on *her* head, because of the angels.
11Nevertheless, neither *is* man independent of
woman, nor woman independent of man, in
the Lord. 12For as woman *came* from man,
even so man also *comes* through woman; but
all things are from God.

13Judge among yourselves. Is it proper for a
woman to pray to God with her head uncovered? 14Does not even nature itself teach you
that if a man has long hair, it is a dishonor to
him? 15But if a woman has long hair, it is a
glory to her; for *her* hair is given to her[a] for a
covering. 16But if anyone seems to be contentious, we have no such custom, nor *do* the
churches of God.

CONDUCT AT THE LORD'S SUPPER

17Now in giving these instructions I do not
praise *you,* since you come together not for
the better but for the worse. 18For first of all,
when you come together as a church, I hear
that there are divisions among you, and in
part I believe it. 19For there must also be fac-
tions among you, that those who are approved
may be recognized among you. 20Therefore
when you come together in one place, it is not
to eat the Lord's Supper. 21For in eating, each
one takes his own supper ahead of *others;* and
one is hungry and another is drunk. 22What!
Do you not have houses to eat and drink in?

11:15 [a]M-Text omits *to her.*

SOUL NOTE

Assorted Scruples *(10:23–33)* Christian freedom does not mean that believers can live as they please. Christians have freedom *with* responsibility to live according to the guidelines found in God's Word. Some Christians make guidelines for themselves based on their own scruples. These guidelines should not be forced upon others, but believers should respect one another's guidelines. To force others to live according to our scruples is legalism; to show respect for another's scruples exhibits Christian love. **Topic: Legalism**

SOUL NOTE

R and R *(11:2–6)* The concern over head coverings for women was most likely a cultural need in order to keep harmony in the church in Corinth. While head coverings may not be required in many cultures today, the principles behind Paul's words are timeless. Christian women should show respect for Christian men and exhibit reverent behavior in worship. Reverence and respect are always important to maintain the church's witness to the watching world. **Topic: Women's Issues**

Or do you despise the church of God and shame those who have nothing? What shall I say to you? Shall I praise you in this? I do not praise *you.*

Institution of the Lord's Supper

23For I received from the Lord that which I also delivered to you: that the Lord Jesus on the *same* night in which He was betrayed took bread; 24and when He had given thanks, He broke *it* and said, "Take, eat;[a] this is My body which is broken[b] for you; do this in remembrance of Me." 25In the same manner *He* also *took* the cup after supper, saying, "This cup is the new covenant in My blood. This do, as often as you drink *it,* in remembrance of Me."

26For as often as you eat this bread and drink this cup, you proclaim the Lord's death till He comes.

Examine Yourself

27Therefore whoever eats this bread or drinks *this* cup of the Lord in an unworthy manner will be guilty of the body and blood[a] of the Lord. 28But let a man examine himself, and so let him eat of the bread and drink of the cup. 29For he who eats and drinks in an unworthy manner[a] eats and drinks judgment to himself, not discerning the Lord's[b] body. 30For this reason many *are* weak and sick among you, and many sleep. 31For if we would judge ourselves, we would not be judged. 32But when we are judged, we are chastened by the Lord, that we may not be condemned with the world.

33Therefore, my brethren, when you come together to eat, wait for one another. 34But if anyone is hungry, let him eat at home, lest you come together for judgment. And the rest I will set in order when I come.

Spiritual Gifts: Unity in Diversity

12 Now concerning spiritual *gifts,* brethren, I do not want you to be ignorant: 2You know that[a] you were Gentiles, carried away to these dumb idols, however you were led. 3Therefore I make known to you that no one speaking by the Spirit of God calls Jesus accursed, and no one can say that Jesus is Lord except by the Holy Spirit.

4There are diversities of gifts, but the same Spirit. 5There are differences of ministries, but the same Lord. 6And there are diversities of activities, but it is the same God who works all in all. 7But the manifestation of the Spirit is given to each one for the profit *of all:* 8for to one is given the word of wisdom through the Spirit, to another the word of knowledge through the same Spirit, 9to another faith by the same Spirit, to another gifts of healings by the same[a] Spirit, 10to another the working of miracles, to another prophecy, to another discerning of spirits, to another *different* kinds of tongues, to another the interpretation of tongues. 11But one and the same Spirit works all these things, distributing to each one individually as He wills.

Unity and Diversity in One Body

12For as the body is one and has many members, but all the members of that one body, being many, are one body, so also *is* Christ. 13For by one Spirit we were all baptized into one body—whether Jews or Greeks, whether slaves or free—and have all been made to drink into[a] one Spirit. 14For in fact the body is not one member but many.

15If the foot should say, "Because I am not a hand, I am not of the body," is it therefore not of the body? 16And if the ear should say, "Because I am not an eye, I am not of the body," is it therefore not of the body? 17If the whole body *were* an eye, where *would be* the hearing? If the whole *were* hearing, where *would be* the smelling? 18But now God has set the members, each one of them, in the body just as He pleased. 19And if they *were* all one member, where *would* the body *be?*

20But now indeed *there are* many members, yet one body. 21And the eye cannot say to the hand, "I have no need of you"; nor again the head to the feet, "I have no need of you." 22No, much rather, those members of the body which seem to be weaker are necessary. 23And those *members* of the body which we think to be less honorable, on these we bestow greater honor; and our unpresentable *parts* have greater modesty, 24but our presentable *parts* have no need. But God composed the body, having given greater honor to that *part* which lacks it, 25that there should be no schism in the body, but *that* the members should have

---

11:24 [a]NU-Text omits *Take, eat.* [b]NU-Text omits *broken.* **11:27** [a]NU-Text and M-Text read *the blood.* **11:29** [a]NU-Text omits *in an unworthy manner.* [b]NU-Text omits *Lord's.* **12:2** [a]NU-Text and M-Text add *when.* **12:9** [a]NU-Text reads *one.* **12:13** [a]NU-Text omits *into.*

the same care for one another. 26And if one member suffers, all the members suffer with *it;* or if one member is honored, all the members rejoice with *it.*

27Now you are the body of Christ, and members individually. 28And God has appointed these in the church: first apostles, second prophets, third teachers, after that miracles, then gifts of healings, helps, administrations, varieties of tongues. 29*Are* all apostles? *Are* all prophets? *Are* all teachers? *Are* all workers of miracles? 30Do all have gifts of healings? Do all speak with tongues? Do all interpret? 31But earnestly desire the best[a] gifts. And yet I show you a more excellent way.

> [Love] bears all things,
> believes all things, hopes all things,
> endures all things.
> 1 CORINTHIANS 13:7

THE GREATEST GIFT

13 Though I speak with the tongues of men and of angels, but have not love, I have become sounding brass or a clanging cymbal. 2And though I have *the gift of* prophecy, and understand all mysteries and all knowledge, and though I have all faith, so that I could remove mountains, but have not love, I am nothing. 3And though I bestow all my goods to feed *the poor,* and though I give my body to be burned,[a] but have not love, it profits me nothing.

4Love suffers long *and* is kind; love does not envy; love does not parade itself, is not puffed up; 5does not behave rudely, does not seek its own, is not provoked, thinks no evil; 6does not rejoice in iniquity, but rejoices in the truth; 7bears all things, believes all things, hopes all things, endures all things.

8Love never fails. But whether *there are* prophecies, they will fail; whether *there are* tongues, they will cease; whether *there is* knowledge, it will vanish away. 9For we know in part and we prophesy in part. 10But when that which is perfect has come, then that which is in part will be done away.

11When I was a child, I spoke as a child, I understood as a child, I thought as a child; but when I became a man, I put away childish things. 12For now we see in a mirror, dimly, but then face to face. Now I know in

---

12:31 [a]NU-Text reads *greater.* **13:3** [a]NU-Text reads *so I may boast.*

KEY PASSAGE

Love

BEARS, BELIEVES, HOPES, ENDURES

(13:1–7)

Following in context after Paul's discussion of the many spiritual gifts in the church is a treatise on the meaning of love. Spiritual gifts ultimately have no value if the gifted person does not treat others with love. What does love look like?

Love . . .

- *suffers long,* bearing annoyances and inconveniences, not losing its temper.
- *is kind,* taking the initiative to be considerate and helpful.
- *does not envy* but rejoices when others succeed.
- *does not parade itself, is not puffed up* but instead draws others to it.
- *does not behave rudely* or impolitely but acts in a manner worthy of Christ.
- *does not seek its own* but always seeks to benefit others.
- *is not provoked* but will allow differences of opinion in minor matters.
- *thinks no evil* but makes allowances for people's flaws.
- *does not rejoice in iniquity, but rejoices in the truth.*

To Learn More: Turn to the article about love on pages 1512, 1513. See also the personality profile of Hosea on page 1127.

part, but then I shall know just as I also am
known.
[13]And now abide faith, hope, love, these
three; but the greatest of these *is* love.

PROPHECY AND TONGUES

14 Pursue love, and desire spiritual *gifts,*
but especially that you may prophesy.
[2]For he who speaks in a tongue does not speak
to men but to God, for no one understands
him; however, in the spirit he speaks mysteries. [3]But he who proph-
esies speaks edification
and exhortation and
comfort to men. [4]He
who speaks in a tongue
edifies himself, but he
who prophesies edifies
the church. [5]I wish you
all spoke with tongues,
but even more that you prophesied; for[a] he
who prophesies *is* greater than he who speaks
with tongues, unless indeed he interprets, that
the church may receive edification.

> Even so you, since you are zealous for spiritual gifts, let it be for the edification of the church that you seek to excel.
>
> 1 CORINTHIANS 14:12

TONGUES MUST BE INTERPRETED

[6]But now, brethren, if I come to you speaking with tongues, what shall I profit you unless I speak to you either by revelation, by
knowledge, by prophesying, or by teaching?
[7]Even things without life, whether flute or
harp, when they make a sound, unless they
make a distinction in the sounds, how will it
be known what is piped or played? [8]For if the
trumpet makes an uncertain sound, who will
prepare for battle? [9]So likewise you, unless
you utter by the tongue words easy to understand, how will it be known what is spoken?
For you will be speaking into the air. [10]There
are, it may be, so many
kinds of languages in
the world, and none of
them *is* without significance. [11]Therefore, if I
do not know the mean-
ing of the language, I
shall be a foreigner to
him who speaks, and
he who speaks *will be* a foreigner to me.
[12]Even so you, since you are zealous for spiritual *gifts, let it be* for the edification of the
church *that* you seek to excel.
[13]Therefore let him who speaks in a tongue
pray that he may interpret. [14]For if I pray in a

14:5 [a]NU-Text reads *and.*

SOUL NOTE

The Gift of Love *(13:7)* "Bears all things" means that love shelters or covers. "Believes all things" means that love never loses faith in others and is willing to think the best of them. "Hopes all things" means that love looks forward with optimism, knowing that God works all things together for good. "Endures all things" means that love holds on. In the end, love never fails and it never ends. When we love, we take part in eternity. We can ask God to perfect our love for Him and for others.
Topic: Love

SOUL NOTE

Grown Up *(13:11)* Adults have "put away childish things" when they no longer need bottles or teddy bears. The same is true in the Christian life. New believers need care and guidance to help them learn how to grow in their faith. As we mature, we know how to look to God for guidance for ourselves. As we feed on God's Word, we develop muscles and increase our strength. Even so, our faith will not be complete until we see Christ face to face. Then we will understand everything clearly. In the meantime, we should aim to grow and develop, seeking to be more like Christ every day.
Topic: Life Transitions

tongue, my spirit prays, but my understanding
is unfruitful. 15What is *the conclusion* then? I
will pray with the spirit, and I will also pray
with the understanding. I will sing with the
spirit, and I will also sing with the understanding. 16Otherwise, if you bless with the
spirit, how will he who occupies the place of
the uninformed say "Amen" at your giving of
thanks, since he does not understand what
you say? 17For you indeed give thanks well,
but the other is not edified.

18I thank my God I speak with tongues more
than you all; 19yet in the church I would rather
speak five words with my understanding, that
I may teach others also, than ten thousand
words in a tongue.

Tongues a Sign to Unbelievers

20Brethren, do not be children in understanding; however, in malice be babes, but in
understanding be mature.

21In the law it is written:

> *"With men of other tongues and other*
> *lips*
> *I will speak to this people;*
> *And yet, for all that, they will not hear*
> *Me,"*[a]

says the Lord.

22Therefore tongues are for a sign, not to
those who believe but to unbelievers; but
prophesying is not for unbelievers but for
those who believe. 23Therefore if the whole
church comes together in one place, and all
speak with tongues, and there come in *those*
who are uninformed or unbelievers, will they
not say that you are out of your mind? 24But if
all prophesy, and an unbeliever or an uninformed person comes in, he is convinced by
all, he is convicted by all. 25And thus[a] the secrets of his heart are revealed; and so, falling
down on *his* face, he will worship God and report that God is truly among you.

Order in Church Meetings

26How is it then, brethren? Whenever you
come together, each of you has a psalm, has a
teaching, has a tongue, has a revelation, has
an interpretation. Let all things be done for
edification. 27If anyone speaks in a tongue, *let*
there be two or at the most three, *each* in turn,
and let one interpret. 28But if there is no interpreter, let him keep silent in church, and let
him speak to himself and to God. 29Let two or
three prophets speak, and let the others judge.
30But if *anything* is revealed to another who
sits by, let the first keep silent. 31For you can
all prophesy one by one, that all may learn
and all may be encouraged. 32And the spirits
of the prophets are subject to the prophets.
33For God is not *the author* of confusion but of
peace, as in all the churches of the saints.

34Let your[a] women keep silent in the
churches, for they are not permitted to speak;
but *they are* to be submissive, as the law also
says. 35And if they want to learn something,
let them ask their own husbands at home; for
it is shameful for women to speak in church.

36Or did the word of God come *originally*
from you? Or *was it* you only that it reached?
37If anyone thinks himself to be a prophet or
spiritual, let him acknowledge that the things
which I write to you are the commandments
of the Lord. 38But if anyone is ignorant, let him
be ignorant.[a]

39Therefore, brethren, desire earnestly to
prophesy, and do not forbid to speak with
tongues. 40Let all things be done decently and
in order.

The Risen Christ, Faith's Reality

15 Moreover, brethren, I declare to you
the gospel which I preached to you,
which also you received and in which you
stand, 2by which also you are saved, if you
hold fast that word which I preached to you—
unless you believed in vain.

3For I delivered to you first of all that which
I also received: that Christ died for our sins according to the Scriptures, 4and that He was
buried, and that He rose again the third day
according to the Scriptures, 5and that He was
seen by Cephas, then by the twelve. 6After
that He was seen by over five hundred brethren at once, of whom the greater part remain
to the present, but some have fallen asleep.
7After that He was seen by James, then by all
the apostles. 8Then last of all He was seen by
me also, as by one born out of due time.

9For I am the least of the apostles, who am
not worthy to be called an apostle, because I
persecuted the church of God. 10But by the

14:21 [a]Isaiah 28:11, 12 **14:25** [a]NU-Text omits *And thus.* **14:34** [a]NU-Text omits *your.*
14:38 [a]NU-Text reads *if anyone does not recognize this, he is not recognized.*

BOLD LOVE

DAN ALLENDER

(1 Corinthians 13)

Bold love is the courageous, costly gift of doing good to those who sin against us. When we give that gift, we get a taste of the character of God. Love is forgiveness with feet, the kind that moves toward the one who harmed us, willingly serving that person for the sake of God. Bold love is the active, unnerving pursuit of the offender to wisely and winsomely incite reconciliation by exposing the need for confession, repentance, and restoration.

DESCRIBING LOVE

First Corinthians 13 describes several characteristics of love: "Love suffers long and is kind; love does not envy; love does not parade itself, is not puffed up; does not behave rudely, does not seek its own, is not provoked, thinks no evil; does not rejoice in iniquity, but rejoices in the truth; bears all things, believes all things, hopes all things, endures all things. Love never fails" (1 Cor. 13:4–8).

Paul also described several characteristics of love in Romans 12:9–21. He wrote, "Let love be without hypocrisy. . . . Be kindly affectionate to one another with brotherly love." In his description, Paul was not concerned about being systematic, but he romped around the concept of love with exuberance and intensity. He fleshed out the evidence of a heart that is neither hypocritical nor weak. Love is passionate; it is joyful and laughs; it suffers and weeps. It is neither vengeful nor demanding; indeed, love humbles those who injure, by doing good. Bold love is doing good to those who do harm, in order to destroy evil and redeem the heart. These are love's remarkable qualities as described in this passage:

- ➢ Bold love is fervent in spirit and service, strong and intense.
- ➢ Bold love is joyful, patient, prayerful, generous, and hospitable.
- ➢ Bold love blesses persecutors, refusing revenge.
- ➢ Bold love is compassionate and humble.
- ➢ Bold love is peaceable.
- ➢ Bold love overcomes and destroys evil.

The Romans passage begins, however, with a force of energy that is disturbing. Love hates. In order to truly love without hypocrisy, we must "abhor what is evil" (Rom 12:9). To love without hypocrisy, to abhor evil, means to not be polluted and divided. It is not hypocritical to both love and hate, as long as we hold onto that which is good as if it were a life preserver in the middle of the ocean. We love good; we hate evil.

DOING GOOD

We are not merely to forgive others by ignoring or letting go of the harm; we are called to serve those who have violated us. We are to provide them with their most basic needs. We are to give them bread and water. The whole context implies that the core "basic need" is to be pursued in spite of our needs, emotions, or sin. We are to offer to everyone (and anyone) a taste of passionate empathy, humble care, hospitality, and joyful generosity.

Doing good offers others the food that their souls crave and would die without. But love is far more than merely being nice or offering insipid, dutiful care. Paul ties doing good to pouring burning coals onto someone's head. This means that we are not to flee from or fight against those who have sinned against us. Instead, we are to unnerve them by disarming them with bold love.

DESTROYING EVIL

Love is God's weapon to destroy the power of darkness. We live in a day where we think our only viable weapon against evil in our world is to expose it, attack it, and legislate against it. Those who advocate the violence of abortion, for example, are sometimes hunted down, picketed, harassed, even harmed by Christians. Those who advocate the homosexual lifestyle are often derided and blamed for the sufferings of AIDS. When AIDS was spreading in the mid-1980s, many Christians said that it was a plague from God, the homosexuals' deserved punishment for sin. Whether justifiable or not, these attacks do not show bold love, nor do they really destroy evil. Such adversarial attitudes and actions merely foster Christian self-righteousness.

Bold love, however, destroys evil by empathy. It destroys evil by hospitality. It destroys evil by generously offering care for what is needed. It is that very power we have from God *not* to succumb to the provocation of evil that surprises and shames those who harm us or others. Their profound surprise that their evil has not been repaid with evil opens their hearts to redemption.

REDEEMING THE HEART

Love offers a taste of the character of God. God is strong and tender. Our love is to be equal parts strength and tenderness. Strength disarms false power; tenderness invites the heart to rest when it is defenseless. Strength reveals that God is holy and hates sin; tenderness reveals God's grace and reconciliation. The goal of love is to give a taste of God. Bold love seeks reconciliation with all as far as it is possible for us to go. Paul implicitly acknowledges that we will not be able to be at peace with everyone, but if there is any room to move toward reconciliation, then we are to do so. The result is changed hearts—ours and theirs.

FURTHER MEDITATION:

Other passages to study about the issue of love include:

- ➢ Proverbs 3:12; 10:12
- ➢ Matthew 5:44; 22:34–40
- ➢ Mark 12:28–34
- ➢ Luke 10:26–28
- ➢ John 13:34, 35; 15:13
- ➢ Romans 5:5
- ➢ Galatians 5:13–15
- ➢ Ephesians 5:21–32
- ➢ 1 Peter 4:8
- ➢ 1 John 4:7–12

To Learn More: **Turn to the key passage note on love at 1 Corinthians 13:1–7 on page 1509. See also the personality profile of Hosea on page 1127.**

grace of God I am what I am, and His grace toward me was not in vain; but I labored more abundantly than they all, yet not I, but the grace of God *which was* with me. [11]Therefore, whether *it was* I or they, so we preach and so you believed.

The Risen Christ, Our Hope

[12]Now if Christ is preached that He has been raised from the dead, how do some among you say that there is no resurrection of the dead? [13]But if there is no resurrection of the dead, then Christ is not risen. [14]And if Christ is not risen, then our preaching *is* empty and your faith *is* also empty. [15]Yes, and we are found false witnesses of God, because we have testified of God that He raised up Christ, whom He did not raise up—if in fact the dead do not rise. [16]For if *the* dead do not rise, then Christ is not risen. [17]And if Christ is not risen, your faith *is* futile; you are still in your sins! [18]Then also those who have fallen asleep in Christ have perished. [19]If in this life only we have hope in Christ, we are of all men the most pitiable.

The Last Enemy Destroyed

[20]But now Christ is risen from the dead, *and* has become the firstfruits of those who have fallen asleep. [21]For since by man *came* death, by Man also *came* the resurrection of the dead. [22]For as in Adam all die, even so in Christ all shall be made alive. [23]But each one in his own order: Christ the firstfruits, afterward those *who are* Christ's at His coming. [24]Then *comes* the end, when He delivers the kingdom to God the Father, when He puts an end to all rule and all authority and power. [25]For He must reign till He has put all enemies under His feet. [26]The last enemy *that* will be destroyed *is* death. [27]For *"He has put all things under His feet."*[a] But when He says "all things are put under *Him," it is* evident that He who put all things under Him is excepted. [28]Now when all things are made subject to Him, then the Son Himself will also be subject to Him who put all things under Him, that God may be all in all.

Effects of Denying the Resurrection

[29]Otherwise, what will they do who are baptized for the dead, if the dead do not rise at all? Why then are they baptized for the dead? [30]And why do we stand in jeopardy every hour? [31]I affirm, by the boasting in you which I have in Christ Jesus our Lord, I die daily. [32]If, in the manner of men, I have fought with beasts at Ephesus, what advantage *is it* to me? If *the* dead do not rise, *"Let us eat and drink, for tomorrow we die!"*[a]

[33]Do not be deceived: "Evil company corrupts good habits." [34]Awake to righteousness,

15:27 [a]Psalm 8:6 **15:32** [a]Isaiah 22:13

KEY PASSAGE

Death

THE LAST ENEMY

(15:20–22)

Death entered the world because of sin. When Adam sinned, death came to all human beings. As Paul wrote, "The wages of sin is death" (Rom. 6:23). One man, Adam, caused sin to enter the human race, and so death from sin. And one Man, Jesus, brought the promise of resurrection from the dead. He accomplished this by becoming human, dying, and then rising again.

Someday in God's new creation, death itself will be destroyed: "The last enemy that will be destroyed is death" (1 Cor. 15:26). Until then, all human beings will die, but for believers, death is not to be feared, for it is a gateway to eternal life with God. First-century believers were persecuted for their faith and faced death continually. Like them, we must always be ready to die, ready to stand before God, and ready to thank Him for all He has done in giving us salvation.

To Learn More: Turn to the article about death on pages 500, 501. See also the personality profile of Hezekiah on page 503.

and do not sin; for some do not have the
knowledge of God. I speak *this* to your shame.

A Glorious Body

35But someone will say, "How are the dead
raised up? And with what body do they
come?" 36Foolish one, what you sow is not
made alive unless it dies. 37And what you sow,
you do not sow that body that shall be, but
mere grain—perhaps wheat or some other
grain. 38But God gives it a body as He pleases,
and to each seed its own body.

39All flesh *is* not the same flesh, but *there is*
one *kind of* flesh[a] of men, another flesh of animals, another of fish, *and* another of birds.

40*There are* also celestial bodies and terrestrial bodies; but the glory of the celestial *is*
one, and the *glory* of the terrestrial *is* another.
41*There is* one glory of the sun, another glory
of the moon, and another glory of the stars;
for *one* star differs from *another* star in glory.

42So also *is* the resurrection of the dead. *The
body* is sown in corruption, it is raised in incorruption. 43It is sown in dishonor, it is raised
in glory. It is sown in weakness, it is raised in
power. 44It is sown a natural body, it is raised a
spiritual body. There is a natural body, and
there is a spiritual body. 45And so it is written, *"The first man Adam became a living
being."*[a] The last Adam *became* a life-giving
spirit.

46However, the spiritual is not first, but the
natural, and afterward the spiritual. 47The first
man *was* of the earth, *made* of dust; the second Man *is* the Lord[a] from heaven. 48As *was*
the *man* of dust, so also *are* those *who are
made* of dust; and as *is* the heavenly *Man,* so
also *are* those *who are* heavenly. 49And as we
have borne the image of the *man* of dust, we
shall also bear[a] the image of the heavenly
Man.

Our Final Victory

50Now this I say, brethren, that flesh and
blood cannot inherit the kingdom of God; nor
does corruption inherit incorruption. 51Be-
hold, I tell you a mystery: We shall not all
sleep, but we shall all be changed—52in a moment, in the twinkling of an eye, at the last
trumpet. For the trumpet will sound, and the
dead will be raised incorruptible, and we shall
be changed. 53For this corruptible must put on
incorruption, and this mortal *must* put on immortality. 54So when this corruptible has put
on incorruption, and this mortal has put on
immortality, then shall be brought to pass the
saying that is written: *"Death is swallowed up
in victory."*[a]

55 *"O Death, where is your sting?*[a]
O Hades, where is your victory?"[b]

56The sting of death *is* sin, and the strength of
sin *is* the law. 57But thanks *be* to God, who
gives us the victory through our Lord Jesus
Christ.

58Therefore, my beloved brethren, be steadfast, immovable, always abounding in the
work of the Lord, knowing that your labor is
not in vain in the Lord.

Collection for the Saints

16 Now concerning the collection for the
saints, as I have given orders to the
churches of Galatia, so you must do also: 2On
the first *day* of the week let each one of you lay
something aside, storing up as he may prosper,
that there be no collections when I come. 3And
when I come, whomever you approve by *your*
letters I will send to bear your gift to Jerusalem. 4But if it is fitting that I go also, they will
go with me.

Personal Plans

5Now I will come to you when I pass
through Macedonia (for I am passing through
Macedonia). 6And it may be that I will remain,
or even spend the winter with you, that you
may send me on my journey, wherever I go.
7For I do not wish to see you now on the way;
but I hope to stay a while with you, if the Lord
permits.

8But I will tarry in Ephesus until Pentecost.
9For a great and effective door has opened to
me, and *there are* many adversaries.

10And if Timothy comes, see that he may be
with you without fear; for he does the work of
the Lord, as I also *do.* 11Therefore let no one
despise him. But send him on his journey in
peace, that he may come to me; for I am waiting for him with the brethren.

12Now concerning *our* brother Apollos, I

15:39 [a]NU-Text and M-Text omit *of flesh.*
15:45 [a]Genesis 2:7 **15:47** [a]NU-Text omits *the Lord.* **15:49** [a]M-Text reads *let us also bear.*
15:54 [a]Isaiah 25:8 **15:55** [a]Hosea 13:14 [b]NU-Text reads *O Death, where is your victory? O Death, where is your sting?*

strongly urged him to come to you with the
brethren, but he was quite unwilling to come
at this time; however, he will come when he
has a convenient time.

Final Exhortations

[13]Watch, stand fast in
the faith, be brave, be
strong. [14]Let all *that* you
do be done with love.
[15]I urge you, breth-
ren—you know the
household of Stephanas,
that it is the firstfruits of
Achaia, and *that* they
have devoted themselves to the ministry of the
saints—[16]that you also submit to such, and to
everyone who works and labors with *us.*
[17]I am glad about the coming of Stephanas,
Fortunatus, and Achaicus, for what was lacking on your part they supplied. [18]For they refreshed my spirit and yours. Therefore acknowledge such men.

Watch, stand fast in the faith, be brave, be strong. Let all that you do be done with love.

1 CORINTHIANS 16:13, 14

Greetings and a Solemn Farewell

[19]The churches of Asia greet you. Aquila
and Priscilla greet you heartily in the Lord,
with the church that is
in their house. [20]All the
brethren greet you.
Greet one another
with a holy kiss.
[21]The salutation with
my own hand—Paul's.
[22]If anyone does not
love the Lord Jesus
Christ, let him be accursed.[a] O Lord, come![b]
[23]The grace of our Lord Jesus Christ *be* with
you. [24]My love *be* with you all in Christ Jesus.
Amen.

16:22 [a]Greek *anathema* [b]Aramaic *Maranatha*

2 Corinthians

Someone once quipped, "The church is like Noah's ark . . . if it weren't for the storm on the outside, we would never be able to stand the stench on the inside." Such a wisecrack may be overly harsh, but it still makes us wince because it reminds us of the glaring foibles and failings of the household of faith.

Second Corinthians was written probably late in A.D. 56 when the apostle Paul learned that some fast-talking false teachers had infiltrated the struggling church at Corinth and had stirred the congregation against him. Titus, Paul's associate, was quickly dispatched to rebut these allegations. While many changed their minds, a few continued to challenge Paul's authority, sincerity, and ministry.

Paul's next attempt to counter the attacks of his critics is this letter, 2 Corinthians, by far the apostle's most intimate letter. These 13 chapters are somewhat distressing to read. Here is possibly the greatest, most influential Christian ever, put in the awkward position of having to defend himself and his noble, selfless actions. But the result is encouraging—a wonderful glimpse into the heart of a man who is fully devoted to serving God and others. Second Corinthians contains classic passages on the nature of ministry (ch. 4), eternal rewards (5:10), reconciliation (5:17–21), holy living (6:14–18), true generosity (ch. 8, 9), and perseverance (ch. 12).

Whether you're a chronic critic (let's hope not!) or a conscientious member, 2 Corinthians is guaranteed to speak powerfully to your soul.

SOUL CONCERNS IN 2 CORINTHIANS

Forgiveness	(2:5–11)
Change/Maturity	(5:17)
Pain	(12:9)

GREETING

1 Paul, an apostle of Jesus Christ by the will of God, and Timothy *our* brother,

To the church of God which is at Corinth, with all the saints who are in all Achaia:

2Grace to you and peace from God our Father and the Lord Jesus Christ.

COMFORT IN SUFFERING

3Blessed *be* the God and Father of our Lord Jesus Christ, the Father of mercies and God of all comfort, 4who comforts us in all our tribulation, that we may be able to comfort those who are in any trouble, with the comfort with which we ourselves are comforted by God. 5For as the sufferings of Christ abound in us, so our consolation also abounds through Christ. 6Now if we are afflicted, *it is* for your consolation and salvation, which is effective for enduring the same sufferings which we also suffer. Or if we are comforted, *it is* for your consolation and salvation. 7And our hope for you *is* steadfast, because we know that as you are partakers of the sufferings, so also *you will partake* of the consolation.

DELIVERED FROM SUFFERING

8For we do not want you to be ignorant, brethren, of our trouble which came to us in Asia: that we were burdened beyond measure, above strength, so that we despaired even of life. 9Yes, we had the sentence of death in ourselves, that we should not trust in ourselves but in God who raises the dead, 10who delivered us from so great a death, and does[a] deliver us; in whom we trust that He will still deliver *us,* 11you also helping together in prayer for us, that thanks may be given by many persons on our[a] behalf for the gift *granted* to us through many.

PAUL'S SINCERITY

12For our boasting is this: the testimony of our conscience that we conducted ourselves in the world in simplicity and godly sincerity, not with fleshly wisdom but by the grace of God, and more abundantly toward you. 13For we are not writing any other things to you than what you read or understand. Now I trust you will understand, even to the end 14(as also you have understood us in part), that we are your boast as you also *are* ours, in the day of the Lord Jesus.

SPARING THE CHURCH

15And in this confidence I intended to come to you before, that you might have a second benefit— 16to pass by way of you to Macedonia, to come again from Macedonia to you,

1:10 [a]NU-Text reads *shall.* **1:11** [a]M-Text reads *your behalf.*

KEY PASSAGE

Compassion

SHARED COMFORT

(1:3–5)

In times of trouble and difficulty, people long for comfort. The church in Corinth was facing severe problems. Clearly, those problems needed to be handled, but the "God of all comfort" would give needed comfort and encouragement.

God never wastes a wound. Through them, we learn the ability to empathize with others who suffer, and we learn firsthand the comforting power of God. Then we can come alongside the sufferer, knowing exactly what they need. We can also assure them of God's comfort, for we have experienced it ourselves. God comforts us so that "we may be able to comfort those who are in any trouble, with the comfort with which we ourselves are comforted by God." What a glorious picture of the body of believers, comforting one another as difficult times arise! When facing difficulty, we should trust God and rest in His compassionate arms. Then we will be ready to offer compassion to those in need.

To Learn More: Turn to the article about compassion on pages 950, 951. See also the personality profile of the Good Samaritan on page 1334.

and be helped by you on my way to Judea.
17Therefore, when I was planning this, did I do
it lightly? Or the things I plan, do I plan according to the flesh, that with me there should
be Yes, Yes, and No, No? 18But *as* God *is* faithful, our word to you was not Yes and No. 19For
the Son of God, Jesus Christ, who was
preached among you by us—by me, Silvanus,
and Timothy—was not Yes and No, but in Him
was Yes. 20For all the promises of God in Him
are Yes, and in Him Amen, to the glory of God
through us. 21Now He who establishes us with
you in Christ and has anointed us *is* God,
22who also has sealed us and given us the
Spirit in our hearts as a guarantee.

23Moreover I call God as witness against my
soul, that to spare you I came no more to Corinth. 24Not that we have dominion over your
faith, but are fellow workers for your joy; for
by faith you stand.

2 But I determined this within myself, that I
would not come again to you in sorrow.
2For if I make you sorrowful, then who is he
who makes me glad but the one who is made
sorrowful by me?

Forgive the Offender

3And I wrote this very thing to you, lest,
when I came, I should have sorrow over those
from whom I ought to have joy, having confidence in you all that my joy is *the joy* of you
all. 4For out of much affliction and anguish of
heart I wrote to you, with many tears, not that
you should be grieved, but that you might
know the love which I have so abundantly for
you.

5But if anyone has caused grief, he has not
grieved me, but all of you to some extent—not
to be too severe. 6This punishment which *was
inflicted* by the majority *is* sufficient for such a
man, 7so that, on the contrary, you *ought* rather to forgive and comfort *him*, lest perhaps
such a one be swallowed up with too much
sorrow. 8Therefore I urge you to reaffirm *your*
love to him. 9For to this end I also wrote, that
I might put you to the test, whether you are
obedient in all things. 10Now whom you forgive anything, I also *forgive*. For if indeed I
have forgiven anything, I have forgiven that
one[a] for your sakes in the presence of Christ,
11lest Satan should take advantage of us; for
we are not ignorant of his devices.

Triumph in Christ

12Furthermore, when I came to Troas to
preach Christ's gospel, and a door was opened
to me by the Lord, 13I had no rest in my spirit,
because I did not find Titus my brother; but
taking my leave of them, I departed for Macedonia.

14Now thanks *be* to God who always leads
us in triumph in Christ, and through us dif-
fuses the fragrance of His knowledge in every
place. 15For we are to God the fragrance of
Christ among those who are being saved and
among those who are perishing. 16To the one
we are the aroma of death *leading* to death,
and to the other the aroma of life *leading* to
life. And who *is* sufficient for these things?
17For we are not, as so many,[a] peddling the
word of God; but as of sincerity, but as from
God, we speak in the sight of God in Christ.

Christ's Epistle

3 Do we begin again to commend ourselves? Or do we need, as some *others*,
epistles of commendation to you or *letters* of
commendation from you? 2You are our epistle
written in our hearts, known and read by
all men; 3clearly *you are* an epistle of Christ,

2:10 [a]NU-Text reads *For indeed, what I have forgiven, if I have forgiven anything, I did it.*
2:17 [a]M-Text reads *the rest.*

SOUL NOTE

Forgive and Comfort *(2:7, 8)* The man in the church who had been disciplined had repented of his sin. Therefore, Paul encouraged the believers to "forgive and comfort him" so that he would not be "swallowed up with too much sorrow."

The church can find it difficult to discipline its own, but that may be needed in order to bring a sinner to repentance. Once that repentance is seen, however, restoration is important. Forgiveness and comfort can return the person to the fellowship so he or she can return to spiritual health and service for God. **Topic: Health/Spirituality**

FORGIVENESS

EVERETT L. WORTHINGTON, JR.

(2 Corinthians 2:5–11)

The concept of forgiveness is as slippery as a greased watermelon in a swimming pool. The harder you squeeze it, the more slippery it becomes. People use the term "forgiveness" loosely and mean different things.

First, what is *unforgiveness*? Unforgiveness is a set of delayed emotions that consists of resentment, bitterness, hatred, hostility, anger, and fear. These emotions arise in a person because of a transgression that has wounded them psychologically or physically. Unforgiveness consumes the heart like a cancer. The wounded person responds with hot emotions of anger, and fear of being wounded again. The emotions of anger and fear are not unforgiveness. But when these emotions are continually replayed mentally, the resulting delayed emotions are unforgiveness.

So what is *forgiveness*? People think of forgiveness as what we do to get rid of unforgiveness. But forgiveness is more than relinquishing judgment to God or simply accepting the hurt and letting it pass. True forgiveness occurs when those cold emotions of unforgiveness are changed to warm, loving, compassionate, caring, altruistic emotions resulting from a heartfelt transformation. Forgiveness is both an act and a process. It could be compared to canceling a debt. Forgiveness is not the same as reconciliation. It takes two to reconcile; it takes only one to forgive.

God's forgiveness of humans and our forgiveness of one another are different, although related. Both involve an altruistic, emotional response by the forgiver toward another who *needs* forgiveness. But there's a difference in the one doing the forgiving. Whereas God has an infinite perspective on us, we do not have that same perspective on others. God knows our hearts and motives, so He can legitimately demand our repentance prior to forgiving. Humans, however, cannot demand repentance before granting forgiveness.

THE EXAMPLE IN MATTHEW 18

Matthew 18 gives clear teaching about forgiveness. Jesus described divine forgiveness and love in the parable of the lost sheep. He encouraged reconciliation and said that forgiveness should be unlimited. He then told the parable of the unforgiving servant, tying together God's forgiveness of us with our forgiveness of others (Matt. 18:21–35).

Forgiveness is often thought of as a Christian duty. Forgiveness can rarely be achieved when practiced as a duty, however. The positive, loving emotions of forgiveness that replace the delayed emotions of unforgiveness rarely flow from willful duty. Instead, they flow from a heart that is transformed by having experienced God's love and forgiveness (Eph. 4:31, 32).

HOW TO FORGIVE

There are many ways to forgive a person who has harmed us, any one of which can be effective. In soul care, we should attempt to help people experience *empathy* for the person who harmed them, *humility* about their own sinfulness, and *gratitude* over having themselves been forgiven by God and by others.

Helping people experience forgiving emotions is not easy and requires time. I use a five-step acrostic to help people experience forgiveness, which I call the Pyramid Model to REACH forgiveness:

R = *Recall* the hurt. To heal, you must not deny that you have been hurt or offended. However, you should not recall the hurt in whiny victimization or as finger-pointing blame. Instead, you should recall the hurt calmly and try to remember objectively what happened.

E = *Empathize* with the person who hurt you. Empathy means attempting to understand what the transgressor might have been going through. It helps to attempt to feel with the person who caused the hurt.

A = Give an *Altruistic* gift of forgiveness. Try to recall a time when you harmed someone who later forgave you. Remember specifically what happened and how you received the offer of forgiveness. Then you can more easily envision yourself giving that gift back to another.

C = *Commit* publicly to forgive. You can truly forgive in your heart, but you might doubt that forgiveness if you recall the incident and re-experience some of the hot emotions. By speaking aloud or writing down your forgiveness, by telling a trusted friend, or, in some cases, by writing a follow-up letter to the person who harmed you, you can solidify the act of forgiveness.

H = *Hold on* to forgiveness. When you doubt whether the forgiveness was real, you can hold onto the forgiveness by remembering that there is a difference between remembering the event and experiencing the cold emotions.

For help in experiencing and granting forgiveness, we might need to talk with the person who hurt us about the transgression and forgiveness. We must make a *reproach*, or request for an explanation. A reproach must not be made harshly, however, but gently.

The transgressor responds with an *account*. Accounts can be denials, excuses, or confessions. A confession should be followed by a sincere apology, statement of an intent not to transgress in the same way again, an offer of restitution, and a request for forgiveness.

We must decide whether we can experience the emotions that lead to the changed heart of forgiveness. Forgiving cannot be summoned at will; therefore, often when we are asked to forgive, it will take time to experience the new emotions.

Talking about forgiveness is often a major step on the way to reconciliation between two parties who have had a trust broken. Parties must decide whether they can reconcile and if so, how to work this process. For reconciliation to be complete, however, both parties need to reverse the damage that was done in the relationship, decide to give each other mercy at an occasional failure, and take active steps to build love in their relationship by valuing each other.

FURTHER MEDITATION:

Other passages to study about the issue of forgiveness include:

- ➢ Jeremiah 31:34; 33:8
- ➢ Micah 7:18, 19
- ➢ Matthew 6:12
- ➢ Mark 11:25, 26
- ➢ Luke 6:37; 17:3; 23:34
- ➢ John 8:1–11
- ➢ Romans 12:19
- ➢ 1 John 1:9

To Learn More: Turn to the key passage note on forgiveness at Matthew 18:21–35 on page 1260. See also the personality profile of Joseph on page 70.

ministered by us, written not with ink but by
the Spirit of the living God, not on tablets of
stone but on tablets of flesh, *that is,* of the
heart.

THE SPIRIT, NOT THE LETTER

[4]And we have such trust through Christ toward God. [5]Not that we are sufficient of ourselves to think of anything as *being* from
ourselves, but our suffi-
ciency *is* from God,
[6]who also made us sufficient as ministers of the
new covenant, not of the
letter but of the Spirit;[a]
for the letter kills, but
the Spirit gives life.

> Now the Lord is the Spirit;
> and where the Spirit of the Lord is,
> there is liberty.
> 2 CORINTHIANS 3:17

GLORY OF THE NEW COVENANT

[7]But if the ministry of death, written *and*
engraved on stones, was glorious, so that the
children of Israel could not look steadily at the
face of Moses because of the glory of his countenance, which *glory* was passing away, [8]how
will the ministry of the Spirit not be more glorious? [9]For if the ministry of condemnation
had glory, the ministry of righteousness exceeds much more in glory. [10]For even what
was made glorious had no glory in this respect, because of the glory that excels. [11]For if
what is passing away *was* glorious, what remains *is* much more glorious.

[12]Therefore, since we have such hope, we
use great boldness of speech—[13]unlike Moses,
who put a veil over his face so that the children of Israel could not look steadily at the
end of what was passing away. [14]But their
minds were blinded. For until this day the
same veil remains unlifted in the reading of
the Old Testament, because the *veil* is taken
away in Christ. [15]But even to this day, when
Moses is read, a veil lies
on their heart. [16]Never-
theless when one turns
to the Lord, the veil is
taken away. [17]Now the
Lord is the Spirit; and
where the Spirit of the
Lord *is,* there *is* liberty.
[18]But we all, with unveiled face, beholding as
in a mirror the glory of the Lord, are being
transformed into the same image from glory to
glory, just as by the Spirit of the Lord.

THE LIGHT OF CHRIST'S GOSPEL

4 Therefore, since we have this ministry, as
we have received mercy, we do not lose
heart. [2]But we have renounced the hidden
things of shame, not walking in craftiness nor
handling the word of God deceitfully, but by
manifestation of the truth commending ourselves to every man's conscience in the sight

3:6 [a]Or *spirit*

KEY PASSAGE

Stress

STRESS TEST

(4:9)

Paul knew about stress. Hard pressed, perplexed, persecuted, abandoned—these situations were part of Paul's everyday life.

For us, each day is filled with different levels of stress. Regardless of occupation, age, social status, or lifestyle, we experience stress. Some we bring on ourselves—from poor planning, saying "yes" too often, or being disorganized. Hopefully we learn our lesson so it won't happen again. Stress also arises from factors outside our control—the weather, a broken computer, an unexpected difficulty or sorrow. At those times, we can control only our reactions to the stress. Our reactions reveal our character and our trust in God.

We should not be swallowed up or "lose heart" in the stresses of life, because God can renew us on the inside day by day (2 Cor. 4:16). This life is temporary. Our home in heaven is eternal. In the meantime, we can lean on God. He promises peace in the midst of the stress.

To Learn More: Turn to the article about stress on pages 422, 423. See also the personality profile of James on page 1641.

of God. [3]But even if our gospel is veiled, it is
veiled to those who are perishing, [4]whose
minds the god of this age has blinded, who do
not believe, lest the light of the gospel of the
glory of Christ, who is the image of God,
should shine on them. [5]For we do not preach
ourselves, but Christ Jesus the Lord, and ourselves your bondservants for Jesus' sake. [6]For
it is the God who commanded light to shine
out of darkness, who has shone in our hearts
to *give* the light of the knowledge of the glory
of God in the face of Jesus Christ.

Cast Down but Unconquered

[7]But we have this treasure in earthen vessels, that the excellence of the power may be
of God and not of us. [8]*We are* hard-pressed on
every side, yet not crushed; *we are* perplexed,
but not in despair; [9]persecuted, but not forsaken; struck down, but not destroyed—[10]al-
ways carrying about in the body the dying of
the Lord Jesus, that the life of Jesus also may
be manifested in our body. [11]For we who live
are always delivered to death for Jesus' sake,
that the life of Jesus also may be manifested in
our mortal flesh. [12]So then death is working in
us, but life in you.

[13]And since we have the same spirit of faith,
according to what is written, *"I believed and
therefore I spoke,"*[a] we also believe and therefore speak, [14]knowing that He who raised up
the Lord Jesus will also raise us up with Jesus,
and will present *us* with you. [15]For all things
are for your sakes, that grace, having spread
through the many, may cause thanksgiving to
abound to the glory of God.

Seeing the Invisible

[16]Therefore we do not lose heart. Even
though our outward man is perishing, yet the
inward *man* is being renewed day by day.
[17]For our light affliction, which is but for a
moment, is working for us a far more exceeding *and* eternal weight of glory, [18]while we do
not look at the things which are seen, but at
the things which are not seen. For the things
which are seen *are* temporary, but the things
which are not seen *are* eternal.

Assurance of the Resurrection

5 For we know that if our earthly house, *this*
tent, is destroyed, we have a building
from God, a house not made with hands, eternal in the heavens. [2]For in this we groan, earnestly desiring to be clothed with our
habitation which is from heaven, [3]if indeed,
having been clothed, we shall not be found
naked. [4]For we who are in *this* tent groan, being burdened, not because we want to be un-
clothed, but further clothed, that mortality
may be swallowed up by life. [5]Now He who
has prepared us for this very thing *is* God, who
also has given us the Spirit as a guarantee.

[6]So *we are* always confident, knowing that
while we are at home in the body we are absent from the Lord. [7]For we walk by faith, not
by sight. [8]We are confident, yes, well pleased
rather to be absent from the body and to be
present with the Lord.

The Judgment Seat of Christ

[9]Therefore we make it our aim, whether
present or absent, to be well pleasing to Him.
[10]For we must all appear before the judgment
seat of Christ, that each one may receive the
things *done* in the body, according to what he
has done, whether good or bad. [11]Knowing,
therefore, the terror of the Lord, we persuade
men; but we are well known to God, and I also
trust are well known in your consciences.

4:13 [a]Psalm 116:10

SOUL NOTE

Light in the Darkness *(4:8, 9)* Paul did not have an easy life—exciting perhaps—but not easy. The words "hard-pressed . . . perplexed . . . persecuted . . . struck down" reveal pain and suffering. We may feel this way as we attempt to live out our faith in an unbelieving world. Like Paul, however, we can take comfort in God's provision in times of trauma. No matter what the difficulty, we are "not crushed, not in despair, not forsaken, not destroyed." We must keep our perspective in times of great difficulty, knowing that through us, "the life of Jesus also may be manifested" (4:10). His light can shine out from any darkness. **Topic: Trauma**

Be Reconciled to God

12For we do not commend ourselves again
to you, but give you opportunity to boast on
our behalf, that you may have *an answer* for
those who boast in appearance and not in
heart. 13For if we are beside ourselves, *it is* for
God; or if we are of sound mind, *it is* for you.
14For the love of Christ compels us, because
we judge thus: that if One died for all, then all
died; 15and He died for all, that those who live
should live no longer for themselves, but for
Him who died for them and rose again.
16Therefore, from now on, we regard no one
according to the flesh. Even though we have
known Christ according to the flesh, yet now
we know *Him thus* no longer. 17Therefore, if
anyone *is* in Christ, *he is* a new creation; old
things have passed away; behold, all things
have become new. 18Now all things *are* of
God, who has reconciled us to Himself
through Jesus Christ, and has given us the
ministry of reconciliation, 19that is, that God
was in Christ reconciling the world to Himself,
not imputing their trespasses to them, and has
committed to us the word of reconciliation.
20Now then, we are ambassadors for Christ,
as though God were pleading through us: we
implore *you* on Christ's behalf, be reconciled
to God. 21For He made Him who knew no sin
to be sin for us, that we might become the
righteousness of God in Him.

Marks of the Ministry

6 We then, *as* workers together *with Him*
also plead with *you* not to receive the
grace of God in vain. 2For He says:

"In an acceptable time I have heard you,
And in the day of salvation I have
helped you."[a]

Behold, now *is* the accepted time; behold,
now *is* the day of salvation.
3We give no offense in anything, that our
ministry may not be blamed. 4But in all *things*
we commend ourselves as ministers of God: in
much patience, in tribulations, in needs, in
distresses, 5in stripes, in imprisonments, in tumults, in labors, in sleeplessness, in fastings;
6by purity, by knowledge, by longsuffering, by
kindness, by the Holy Spirit, by sincere love,
7by the word of truth, by the power of God, by
the armor of righteousness on the right hand
and on the left, 8by honor and dishonor, by

6:2 [a]Isaiah 49:8

SOUL NOTE

Present with the Lord *(5:6–8)* Exactly what happens after someone dies? The Bible doesn't go into much detail, but it does say that believers who die—that is, are "absent from the body"—will be "present with the Lord" (see also Phil. 1:23). They will experience a state of blessedness with God. When Christ returns, the believers who have died will be raised and the living believers will be changed, and all will receive glorified, eternal bodies (1 Cor. 15:51–54; 1 Thess. 4:16–18). God has promised that His people will be with Him forever. Death is a defeated enemy. Christ has bought eternal life. We can take hope in God's sure promise. **Topic: Death**

SOUL NOTE

A Rewarding Wait *(5:10)* A future judgment will finalize the destiny of all who have not known Christ (Rev. 20:11–15). Believers will not need to fear this judgment, for they will have been guaranteed salvation and eternal life in heaven. However, the saved do have a judgment awaiting them that will determine their rewards. At this judgment, Christians will account for how they have lived and served, and how well they have used their gifts for the sake of the gospel. If you had to stand before the Lord this very day, what would you say? God holds us accountable. **Topic: Accountability**

evil report and good report; as deceivers, and
yet true; 9as unknown, and *yet* well known; as
dying, and behold we live; as chastened, and
yet not killed; 10as sorrowful, yet always rejoicing; as poor, yet making many rich; as having nothing, and *yet* possessing all things.

Be Holy

11O Corinthians! We have spoken openly to
you, our heart is wide open. 12You are not restricted by us, but you are restricted by your
own affections. 13Now in return for the same
(I speak as to children), you also be open.
14Do not be unequally yoked together with
unbelievers. For what fellowship has righteousness with lawlessness? And what communion has light with darkness? 15And what
accord has Christ with Belial? Or what part
has a believer with an unbeliever? 16And what
agreement has the temple of God with idols?
For you[a] are the temple of the living God. As
God has said:

"I will dwell in them
And walk among them.
I will be their God,
And they shall be My people."[b]

17Therefore

"Come out from among them
And be separate, says the Lord.
Do not touch what is unclean,
And I will receive you."[a]
18 *"I will be a Father to you,*
And you shall be My sons and
daughters,
Says the Lord Almighty."[a]

7 Therefore, having these promises, beloved, let us cleanse ourselves from all
filthiness of the flesh and spirit, perfecting holiness in the fear of God.

The Corinthians' Repentance

2Open *your hearts* to us. We have wronged
no one, we have corrupted no one, we have
cheated no one. 3I do not say *this* to condemn;
for I have said before that you are in our
hearts, to die together and to live together.
4Great *is* my boldness of speech toward you,
great *is* my boasting on your behalf. I am filled
with comfort. I am exceedingly joyful in all
our tribulation.
5For indeed, when we came to Macedonia,
our bodies had no rest, but we were troubled
on every side. Outside *were* conflicts, inside
were fears. 6Nevertheless God, who comforts
the downcast, comforted us by the coming of
Titus, 7and not only by his coming, but also by

6:16 [a]NU-Text reads *we.* [b]Leviticus 26:12; Jeremiah 32:38; Ezekiel 37:27 **6:17** [a]Isaiah 52:11; Ezekiel 20:34, 41 **6:18** [a]2 Samuel 7:14

KEY PASSAGE

Boundaries

PULLING TOGETHER

(6:14)

Jesus told His followers to "make disciples" (Matt. 28:19). Clearly, Christians are not to hide from unbelievers, but should be having an impact for God in their sphere of influence. God needs people everywhere who are ready to serve Him.

Paul does set a boundary line, however. As much as we are to seek to influence the unbelieving world, we must not be "unequally yoked together with unbelievers." To be "yoked" pictures harnessing two animals together. It was against God's law to yoke together animals of different strength, for they would pull against each other and would not accomplish anything worthwhile. Believers who are "yoked" with unbelievers—through close partnerships such as business or marriage—will find that they are pulling in different ways toward different goals. Believers should seek to "be yoked" only with other believers, so that they can strive together toward glorifying God and then achieving other common purposes.

To Learn More: Turn to the article about boundaries on pages 106, 107. See also the personality profile of Lot on page 28.

Change/
Maturity

MATURITY AND CHANGE

RON HAWKINS

(2 Corinthians 5:17)

Can people really change? Even more, can believers actually become more like Christ? Scripture affirms that people can change, doesn't make change an option, and offers guidance for producing positive change. Believers are told, "If anyone is in Christ, he is a new creation; old things have passed away; behold, all things have become new" (2 Cor. 5:17).

CHANGE . . . TO WHAT?

Scripture identifies a common goal for all who are in the upward cycle toward maturity: coming to "the unity of the faith and of the knowledge of the Son of God, to a perfect man, to the measure of the stature of the fullness of Christ" (Eph. 4:13). Paul reminded Timothy that every believer must study Scripture "that the man of God may be complete, thoroughly equipped for every good work" (2 Tim. 3:17). We have achieved maturity when we help edify others, contribute to the body of Christ, and are filled with Christ so that we are equipped for every good work.

CHANGE . . . WHY AND HOW?

In our close relationships with others, we may be called upon to help one another change for the better. "As iron sharpens iron, so a man sharpens the countenance of his friend" (Proverbs 27:17). Our goal is not to have a judgmental spirit by which we pick out people's faults and then set out to change them. Jesus said, "Judge not, that you be not judged" (Matt. 7:1). While we do not need to be perfect before we can help others, we should be mature and loving if we are to help engage others in the process of change. Paul wrote, "Now I myself am confident concerning you, my brethren, that you also are full of goodness, filled with all knowledge, able also to admonish one another" (Rom. 15:14). Following are some questions we should ask ourselves:

What is our authority for guiding change in ourselves and others?
Our authority is the word of truth from God that sets the standards for our behaviors. When we challenge ourselves and one another with the truth of God's Word, then we know what direction we need to go in. We should not make a move toward helping another person until we have sought God in prayer and received His guidance for when and how to handle the situation. If He has chosen us to help this person, then He will provide time, the needed corrective, and insight into the approach we should use to help.

What should we not seek to change in others?
People have core personality traits—such as being extroverted or introverted—that are part of their uniqueness as God's creations (Ps. 139:13–16). We should not try to change people's personalities. The focus should be on helping people conform to standards of behavior found in Scripture.

What should we seek to change in others?
When beliefs and behaviors do not correspond to the truth in Scripture, we need to reprove the unbiblical behaviors and beliefs. Many behaviors and beliefs are rooted in the old life and are incompatible with maturity in Christ (Eph. 5:1–11). We are to

carefully expose sin, encourage repentance, and patiently instruct believers in the ways of righteousness (1 Thess. 5:14).

How will we know if the change we desire to see has really occurred?
Jesus Christ will become visible in them as they respond to biblical truth and conform their behavior to biblical standards. We will notice that they desire less of the flesh and more of Him. We will see victories in their life and hear reports from others about victories they are seeing in the one who has embraced change. Remember, however, change takes time!

What motivation should control us as we seek to help people with the process of change?
Christ's love, a spirit of optimism, and a "can-do" attitude should dominate our words and behaviors as we seek to lead others to embrace changes that will lead them to maturity in Christ (1 Cor. 13:4–13).

CHANGE . . . TRYING VS. TRAINING

Frequently we see the need for change in ourselves and others. For example, we may talk to a friend about a need for change in a certain aspect of his or her life. That person may understand and realize the need, saying, "I'll try to change." The problem is, after a few days, people who say they'll "try to change" will crash and burn. Why? Because they are *trying*, and trying almost always ends in failure. When people try to change, they are merely hoping that they will find the inner strength to behave differently.

The biblical model is *training*, not *trying*. Paul teaches that maturity and change come with training: "Exercise yourself toward godliness" (1 Tim. 4:7). There is an enormous difference between *trying* to meet a goal and *training* to meet a goal. People may try all they want to win the big 5K race, but the winner will be the one who has been in training.

In order to truly change, people must ask the Holy Spirit to help them. They must repent of their failures, be accountable to other believers for the consistent practice of disciplines that foster spiritual growth, and, in the power provided by the Holy Spirit, habitually train themselves in godly behaviors.

Change can happen; maturity is attainable. Growth means change. Therefore, every growing believer is constantly changing—for the better. May God change us so that we can be mature in Him!

FURTHER MEDITATION:

Other passages to study about the issue of change/maturity include:

- Jeremiah 13:23
- John 8:1–11
- Romans 8:1, 9; 12:1, 2
- 1 Corinthians 6:9–11
- Philippians 4:13
- Colossians 3:1–3, 8–10
- 1 Peter 2:1–5

To Learn More: Turn to the key passage note on change/maturity at Ephesians 4:22–24 on page 1554. See also the personality profile of Paul on page 1432.

the consolation with which he was comforted
in you, when he told us of your earnest desire,
your mourning, your zeal for me, so that I rejoiced even more.
[8]For even if I made you sorry with my letter,
I do not regret it; though I did regret it. For I
perceive that the same epistle made you sorry,
though only for a while. [9]Now I rejoice, not
that you were made sorry, but that your sorrow led to repentance. For you were made sorry in a godly manner, that you might suffer
loss from us in nothing. [10]For godly sorrow
produces repentance *leading* to salvation, not
to be regretted; but the sorrow of the world
produces death. [11]For observe this very thing,
that you sorrowed in a godly manner: What
diligence it produced in you, *what* clearing *of*
yourselves, what indignation, *what* fear, *what*
vehement desire, *what* zeal, *what* vindication!
In all *things* you proved yourselves to be clear
in this matter. [12]Therefore, although I wrote to
you, *I did* not *do it* for the sake of him who
had done the wrong, nor for the sake of him
who suffered wrong, but that our care for you
in the sight of God might appear to you.

The Joy of Titus

[13]Therefore we have been comforted in your
comfort. And we rejoiced exceedingly more
for the joy of Titus, because his spirit has been
refreshed by you all. [14]For if in anything I have
boasted to him about you, I am not ashamed.
But as we spoke all things to you in truth,
even so our boasting to Titus was found true.
[15]And his affections are greater for you as he
remembers the obedience of you all, how with
fear and trembling you received him. [16]There-
fore I rejoice that I have confidence in you in
everything.

Excel in Giving

8 Moreover, brethren, we make known to
you the grace of God bestowed on the
churches of Macedonia: [2]that in a great trial of
affliction the abundance of their joy and
their deep poverty abounded in the riches of
their liberality. [3]For I bear witness that according to *their* ability, yes, and beyond *their*
ability, *they were* freely willing, [4]imploring us
with much urgency that we would receive[a]
the gift and the fellowship of the ministering
to the saints. [5]And not *only* as we had hoped,
but they first gave themselves to the Lord, and
then to us by the will of God. [6]So we urged
Titus, that as he had begun, so he would also
complete this grace in you as well. [7]But as
you abound in everything—in faith, in
speech, in knowledge, in all diligence, and in
your love for us—*see* that you abound in this
grace also.

8:4 [a]NU-Text and M-Text omit *that we would receive,* thus changing text to *urgency for the favor and fellowship . . . .*

KEY PASSAGE

Repentance

MORE THAN SORRY

(7:7–10)

True repentance begins when people understand the weight of their sins and the great sacrifice Christ made to cover them. Only then will they move to turn away from their sin. Moreover, they need to turn *to* God for salvation. As Paul wrote, "Godly sorrow produces repentance leading to salvation."

Repentance is more than saying, "I'm sorry"; it carries with it the desire to change one's ways. When people accept Christ and ask Him to forgive their sins, He does so right away. He wipes the slate clean. Does that mean that those Christians will never sin again? Certainly not. Repentance is an ongoing daily process as we seek to live for Christ despite our failures. We need not itemize every sin, fearing that if we forget to repent of one we will be forever lost. But we do need to have a constant attitude of godly sorrow and repentance, seeking to let God change us to become more like Christ.

To Learn More: Turn to the article about repentance on pages 722, 723. See also the personality profile of the thief on the cross on page 1361.

Christ Our Pattern

[8]I speak not by commandment, but I am
testing the sincerity of your love by the diligence of others. [9]For you know the grace of
our Lord Jesus Christ, that though He was
rich, yet for your sakes He became poor, that
you through His poverty might become rich.
[10]And in this I give advice: It is to your advantage not only to be doing what you began
and were desiring to do a year ago; [11]but now
you also must complete the doing *of it;* that as
there was a readiness to desire *it,* so *there* also
may be a completion out of what *you* have.
[12]For if there is first a willing mind, *it is* accepted according to what one has, *and* not according to what he does not have.
[13]For *I do* not *mean* that others should be
eased and you burdened; [14]but by an equality,
that now at this time your abundance *may*
supply their lack, that their abundance also
may supply your lack—that there may be
equality. [15]As it is written, *"He who gathered*
much had nothing left over, and he who gath-
ered little had no lack."[a]

Collection for the Judean Saints

[16]But thanks *be* to God who puts[a] the same
earnest care for you into the heart of Titus.
[17]For he not only ac-
cepted the exhorta-
tion, but being more
diligent, he went to
you of his own accord.
[18]And we have sent
with him the brother
whose praise *is* in the
gospel throughout all the churches, [19]and not
only *that,* but who was also chosen by the
churches to travel with us with this gift, which
is administered by us to the glory of the Lord
Himself and *to show* your ready mind, [20]avoid-
ing this: that anyone should blame us in this
lavish gift which is administered by us— [21]pro-
viding honorable things, not only in the sight
of the Lord, but also in the sight of men.
[22]And we have sent with them our brother
whom we have often proved diligent in many
things, but now much more diligent, because
of the great confidence which *we have* in you.
[23]If *anyone inquires* about Titus, *he is* my partner and fellow worker concerning you. Or if
our brethren *are inquired about, they are* messengers of the churches, the glory of Christ.
[24]Therefore show to them, and[a] before the
churches the proof of your love and of our
boasting on your behalf.

Administering the Gift

9 Now concerning the ministering to the
saints, it is superfluous for me to write to
you; [2]for I know your willingness, about
which I boast of you to the Macedonians, that
Achaia was ready a year ago; and your zeal
has stirred up the majority. [3]Yet I have sent the
brethren, lest our boasting of you should be in
vain in this respect, that, as I said, you may be
ready; [4]lest if *some* Macedonians come with
me and find you unprepared, we (not to mention you!) should be ashamed of this confident boasting.[a] [5]Therefore I thought it necessary to exhort the brethren to go to you ahead
of time, and prepare your generous gift beforehand, which *you had* previously promised,
that it may be ready as *a matter of* generosity
and not as a grudging obligation.

The Cheerful Giver

[6]But this *I say:* He who sows sparingly will
also reap sparingly, and he who sows bountifully will also reap bountifully. [7]*So let* each
one *give* as he purposes in his heart, not
grudgingly or of necessity; for God loves a
cheerful giver. [8]And
God *is* able to make all
grace abound toward
you, that you, always
having all sufficiency
in all *things,* may have
an abundance for every
good work. [9]As it is
written:

> *"He has dispersed abroad,*
> *He has given to the poor;*
> *His righteousness endures forever."*[a]

[10]Now may[a] He who supplies seed to the
sower, and bread for food, supply and multiply the seed you have *sown* and increase the
fruits of your righteousness, [11]while *you are*
enriched in everything for all liberality, which
causes thanksgiving through us to God. [12]For

> So let each one give as he purposes in his heart, not grudgingly or of necessity; for God loves a cheerful giver.
> 2 CORINTHIANS 9:7

8:15 [a]Exodus 16:18 **8:16** [a]NU-Text reads *has put.* **8:24** [a]NU-Text and M-Text omit *and.* **9:4** [a]NU-Text reads *this confidence.* **9:9** [a]Psalm 112:9 **9:10** [a]NU-Text reads *Now He who supplies . . . will supply . . . .*

the administration of this service not only
supplies the needs of the saints, but also is
abounding through many thanksgivings to
God, 13while, through the proof of this ministry, they glorify God for the obedience of your
confession to the gospel of Christ, and for
your liberal sharing with them and all *men,*
14and by their prayer for you, who long for
you because of the exceeding grace of God in
you. 15Thanks *be* to God for His indescribable
gift!

The Spiritual War

10 Now I, Paul, myself am pleading with
you by the meekness and gentleness of
Christ—who in presence *am* lowly among
you, but being absent am bold toward you.
2But I beg *you* that when I am present I may
not be bold with that confidence by which I
intend to be bold against some, who think of
us as if we walked according to the flesh. 3For
though we walk in the flesh, we do not war
according to the flesh. 4For the weapons of our
warfare *are* not carnal but mighty in God for
pulling down strongholds, 5casting down arguments and every high thing that exalts itself against the knowledge of God, bringing
every thought into captivity to the obedience of Christ, 6and being ready to punish
all disobedience when your obedience is fulfilled.

Reality of Paul's Authority

7Do you look at things according to the
outward appearance? If anyone is convinced
in himself that he is Christ's, let him again
consider this in himself, that just as he *is*
Christ's, even so we *are* Christ's.[a] 8For even
if I should boast somewhat more about our
authority, which the Lord gave us[a] for edification and not for your destruction, I shall
not be ashamed—9lest I seem to terrify you
by letters. 10"For *his* letters," they say, "*are*
weighty and powerful, but *his* bodily presence *is* weak, and *his* speech contemptible."
11Let such a person consider this, that what
we are in word by letters when we are absent, such *we will* also *be* in deed when we
are present.

Limits of Paul's Authority

12For we dare not class ourselves or compare ourselves with those who commend
themselves. But they, measuring themselves
by themselves, and comparing themselves
among themselves, are not wise. 13We, however, will not boast beyond measure, but
within the limits of the sphere which God appointed us—a sphere which especially includes you. 14For we are not overextending
ourselves (as though *our authority* did not extend to you), for it was to you that we came
with the gospel of Christ; 15not boasting of
things beyond measure, *that is,* in other men's
labors, but having hope, *that* as your faith is
increased, we shall be greatly enlarged by you
in our sphere, 16to preach the gospel in the *regions* beyond you, *and* not to boast in another
man's sphere of accomplishment.

17But *"he who glories, let him glory in the
LORD."*[a] 18For not he who commends himself
is approved, but whom the Lord commends.

Concern for Their Faithfulness

11 Oh, that you would bear with me in a
little folly—and indeed you do bear
with me. 2For I am jealous for you with godly
jealousy. For I have betrothed you to one husband, that I may present *you as* a chaste virgin

10:7 [a]NU-Text reads *even as we are.* **10:8** [a]NU-Text omits *us.* **10:17** [a]Jeremiah 9:24

SOUL NOTE

Satan's Strongholds *(10:3, 4)* The Christian life is like a war. Christians "walk in the flesh," meaning they are human beings capable of being tempted, hurt, even killed in this war. The battleground is the world, but the true battle is in the spiritual realm between the forces of Christ and the forces of Satan. Believers have weapons to protect them (Eph. 6:10–17) and help them pull down Satan's strongholds. Satan and his forces have a tight grip on this world, but they are already defeated. Believers must stand their ground, obeying their Commander, knowing that He has already won the war. **Topic: Occult**

to Christ. [3]But I fear, lest somehow, as the serpent deceived Eve by his craftiness, so your
minds may be corrupted from the simplicity[a]
that is in Christ. [4]For if he who comes
preaches another Jesus whom we have not
preached, or *if* you receive a different spirit
which you have not received, or a different
gospel which you have not accepted—you
may well put up with it!

Paul and False Apostles

[5]For I consider that I am not at all inferior to
the most eminent apostles. [6]Even though *I am*
untrained in speech, yet *I am* not in knowledge. But we have been thoroughly manifested[a] among you in all things.

[7]Did I commit sin in humbling myself that
you might be exalted, because I preached the
gospel of God to you free of charge? [8]I robbed
other churches, taking wages *from them* to
minister to you. [9]And when I was present with
you, and in need, I was a burden to no one, for
what I lacked the brethren who came from
Macedonia supplied. And in everything I kept
myself from being burdensome to you, and so
I will keep *myself.* [10]As the truth of Christ is in
me, no one shall stop me from this boasting in
the regions of Achaia. [11]Why? Because I do not
love you? God knows!

[12]But what I do, I will also continue to do,
that I may cut off the opportunity from those
who desire an opportunity to be regarded just
as we are in the things of which they boast.
[13]For such *are* false apostles, deceitful workers, transforming themselves into apostles of
Christ. [14]And no wonder! For Satan himself
transforms himself into an angel of light.
[15]Therefore *it is* no great thing if his ministers
also transform themselves into ministers of
righteousness, whose end will be according to
their works.

Reluctant Boasting

[16]I say again, let no one think me a fool. If
otherwise, at least receive me as a fool, that I
also may boast a little. [17]What I speak, I speak
not according to the Lord, but as it were, foolishly, in this confidence of boasting. [18]Seeing
that many boast according to the flesh, I also
will boast. [19]For you put up with fools gladly,
since you *yourselves* are wise! [20]For you put
up with it if one brings you into bondage, if
one devours *you,* if one takes *from you,* if one
exalts himself, if one strikes you on the face.
[21]To *our* shame I say that we were too weak for
that! But in whatever anyone is bold—I speak
foolishly—I am bold also.

Suffering for Christ

[22]Are they Hebrews? So *am* I. Are they Israelites? So *am* I. Are they the seed of Abraham?
So *am* I. [23]Are they ministers of Christ?—I
speak as a fool—I *am* more: in labors more
abundant, in stripes above measure, in prisons more frequently, in deaths often. [24]From
the Jews five times I received forty *stripes* mi-
nus one. [25]Three times I was beaten with rods;
once I was stoned; three times I was shipwrecked; a night and a day I have been in the
deep; [26]*in* journeys often, *in* perils of waters,
in perils of robbers, *in* perils of *my own* countrymen, *in* perils of the Gentiles, *in* perils in
the city, *in* perils in the wilderness, *in* perils in
the sea, *in* perils among false brethren; [27]in
weariness and toil, in sleeplessness often, in
hunger and thirst, in fastings often, in cold
and nakedness— [28]besides the other things,
what comes upon me daily: my deep concern
for all the churches. [29]Who is weak, and I am
not weak? Who is made to stumble, and I do
not burn *with indignation?*

11:3 [a]NU-Text adds *and purity.* **11:6** [a]NU-Text omits *been.*

SOUL NOTE

Jealous Jabs *(11:1–3)* The word "jealous" can be used positively or negatively. Paul said that he was "jealous for" the Corinthian believers "with godly jealousy." He had brought them the gospel message, and they had received it. Paul feared, however, that these young believers would be enticed away from Christ. Paul's jealousy was not for his own reputation but for the Corinthians' eternal safety. Human jealousy, however, often has a less than noble focus—such as another's looks, wealth, popularity, or power—and it is harmful to all involved. Believers must be careful not to allow jealousy over petty issues to harm them or others. **Topic: Jealousy**

[30]If I must boast, I will boast in the things which concern my infirmity. [31]The God and Father of our Lord Jesus Christ, who is blessed forever, knows that I am not lying. [32]In Damascus the governor, under Aretas the king, was guarding the city of the Damascenes with a garrison, desiring to arrest me; [33]but I was let down in a basket through a window in the wall, and escaped from his hands.

The Vision of Paradise

12 It is doubtless[a] not profitable for me to boast. I will come to visions and revelations of the Lord: [2]I know a man in Christ who fourteen years ago—whether in the body I do not know, or whether out of the body I do not know, God knows—such a one was caught up to the third heaven. [3]And I know such a man—whether in the body or out of the body I do not know, God knows— [4]how he was caught up into Paradise and heard inexpressible words, which it is not lawful for a man to utter. [5]Of such a one I will boast; yet of myself I will not boast, except in my infirmities. [6]For though I might desire to boast, I will not be a fool; for I will speak the truth. But I refrain, lest anyone should think of me above what he sees me *to be* or hears from me.

The Thorn in the Flesh

[7]And lest I should be exalted above measure by the abundance of the revelations, a thorn in the flesh was given to me, a messenger of Satan to buffet me, lest I be exalted above measure. [8]Concerning this thing I pleaded with the Lord three times that it might depart from me. [9]And He said to me, "My grace is sufficient for you, for My strength is made perfect in weakness." Therefore most gladly I will rather boast in my infirmities, that the power of Christ may rest upon me. [10]Therefore I take pleasure in infirmities, in reproaches, in needs, in persecutions, in distresses, for Christ's sake. For when I am weak, then I am strong.

> And He said to me, "My grace is sufficient for you, for My strength is made perfect in weakness." Therefore most gladly I will rather boast in my infirmities, that the power of Christ may rest upon me.
>
> 2 CORINTHIANS 12:9

Signs of an Apostle

[11]I have become a fool in boasting;[a] you have compelled me. For I ought to have been commended by you; for in nothing was I behind the most eminent apostles, though I am nothing. [12]Truly the signs of an apostle were accomplished among you with all perseverance, in signs and wonders and mighty deeds. [13]For what is it in which you were inferior to other churches, except that I myself was not burdensome to you? Forgive me this wrong!

Love for the Church

[14]Now *for* the third time I am ready to come to you. And I will not be burdensome to you; for I do not seek yours, but you. For the children ought not to lay up for the parents, but the parents for the children. [15]And I will very gladly spend and be spent for your souls; though the more abundantly I love you, the less I am loved.

12:1 [a]NU-Text reads *necessary, though not profitable, to boast.* **12:11** [a]NU-Text omits *in boasting.*

SOUL NOTE

Perfected Weakness *(12:7–10)* Pain doesn't have to be our enemy. Paul had experienced a great revelation from God (12:1–6). To keep him from being "exalted above measure," however, he had also been given "a thorn in the flesh." Most likely this was some physical ailment that constantly afflicted him. Many people face chronic pain or physical afflictions. They may think that if God would heal them they would be much more valuable and effective in ministry. But God's power is often best revealed when He works through human weaknesses. His "strength is made perfect in weakness." **Topic: Pain**

[16]But be that *as it may,* I did not burden you.
Nevertheless, being crafty, I caught you by
cunning! [17]Did I take advantage of you by any
of those whom I sent to you? [18]I urged Titus,
and sent our brother with *him.* Did Titus take
advantage of you? Did we not walk in the
same spirit? Did *we* not *walk* in the same
steps?
[19]Again, do you think[a] that we excuse ourselves to you? We speak before God in Christ.
But *we do* all things, beloved, for your edification. [20]For I fear lest, when I come, I shall not
find you such as I wish, and *that* I shall be
found by you such as you do not wish; lest
there be contentions, jealousies, outbursts of
wrath, selfish ambitions, backbitings, whis-
perings, conceits, tumults; [21]lest, when I come
again, my God will humble me among you,
and I shall mourn for many who have sinned
before and have not repented of the uncleanness, fornication, and lewdness which they
have practiced.

Coming with Authority

13 This *will be* the third *time* I am coming
to you. *"By the mouth of two or three
witnesses every word shall be established."*[a]
[2]I have told you before, and foretell as if I were
present the second time, and now being absent I write[a] to those who have sinned before,
and to all the rest, that if I come again I will
not spare—[3]since you seek a proof of Christ
speaking in me, who is not weak toward you,
but mighty in you. [4]For though He was crucified in weakness, yet He lives by the power of
God. For we also are weak in Him, but we
shall live with Him by the power of God toward you.
[5]Examine yourselves *as to* whether you are
in the faith. Test yourselves. Do you not know
yourselves, that Jesus Christ is in you?—unless indeed you are disqualified. [6]But I trust
that you will know that we are not disqualified.

Paul Prefers Gentleness

[7]Now I[a] pray to God that you do no evil,
not that we should appear approved, but that
you should do what is honorable, though we
may seem disqualified. [8]For we can do nothing against the truth, but for the truth. [9]For we
are glad when we are weak and you are
strong. And this also we pray, that you may be
made complete. [10]Therefore I write these
things being absent, lest being present I

12:19 [a]NU-Text reads *You have been thinking for a long time. . . .* **13:1** [a]Deuteronomy 19:15 **13:2** [a]NU-Text omits *I write.* **13:7** [a]NU-Text reads *we.*

KEY PASSAGE

Weakness

STRENGTH BUILDERS

(12:9, 10)

To be perfect, strong, and capable—or at least to be perceived that way—is the desire of the human heart. Because God sometimes turns a person's life upside down, however, the pursuit of perfection can be a bad thing. Too often, "perfect," strong, and capable people try to do everything on their own; they don't feel a need for God, or they forget to rely on Him for the results.

Those who see their dependence, however, fully realize that they can accomplish nothing on their own. They need God to work through them. In that way, the task is accomplished, and God receives all the glory. That is why Paul could say, "I will rather boast in my infirmities, that the power of Christ may rest upon me." Paul could even take pleasure in those weaknesses, because only when he was weak could he really be strong in Christ.

Every person has areas of strength and weakness. How wonderful that God can use both! He equips us with strengths to serve Him humbly, and He works through our weaknesses so that we never forget His power.

To Learn More: Turn to the article about weakness on pages 1494, 1495. See also the personality profile of Mark on page 1438.

Pain

PAIN: PROBLEM, PUZZLE, PARABLE

SIANG-YANG TAN AND GEORGE OHLSCHLAGER

(2 Corinthians 12:9)

Pain, and the suffering it causes, is one of life's greatest problems. For all the amazing advances in medicine, pain still remains a significant puzzle. Although everyone has experienced pain, it is still difficult to precisely define and effectively treat. Economically, pain directly and indirectly costs America upwards of eighty billion dollars every year. An estimated ninety million Americans suffer and experience some level of disability due to chronic pain.

Spiritually, pain may also be considered a parable about living. It is a universal residue of the Fall, a reminder to every living person that the entire human race is under a curse. Pain was, in fact, a direct consequence of the sin of Adam and Eve. Women were cursed to bear children "in pain," and men were bound for "toil" and "sweat" to eke out an existence from the earth (Gen. 3:16–19). In contrast, the end of pain—God's promise to one day banish it forever—is a grand part of the glorious promise of heaven (Rev. 21:4).

For most, however, living with chronic pain is a major life problem. Not only is it a major medical and physical challenge, but it constantly assaults the mind and the spirit. Mentally, it is difficult not to obsessively focus and think about pain because its message to the nervous system is always demanding attention. Exhaustion, confusion, chronic fatigue, hopelessness, memory dysfunction, despair, suicidal thinking and planning, and distressed relations are all commonly associated with chronic pain.

Pain also assaults people's spiritual life, robbing them of spiritual vitality and motivation. Not only is it hard to pray and stay focused on God, often the pain sufferer simply doesn't want to be connected. For some, it's too much work. Others are angry with God and confused as to why He is not healing them. They struggle with believing that God is good, or that He really cares for them personally. Chronic pain usually triggers a major challenge to faithful living and can easily shake the very foundations of people's beliefs.

GETTING ORIENTED TO PAIN MANAGEMENT

Psychiatrist Scott Peck begins his famous book, *The Road Less Traveled,* with the idea that life is difficult and full of trouble. People's refusal to accept this troublesome truth only magnifies the trouble we already live in. Likewise, accepting the fact of our chronically pained existence is essential. It will motivate us to act sufficiently and persevere long enough to control pain. It will also help us to live better with the pain that can't be controlled.

Accepting pain is not the same as resigning oneself to it and slipping into despair. Pain management requires that people accept the pain and map out a plan of action for dealing with it.

PAIN CONTROL STRATEGIES

There are literally dozens of strategies that have been developed to control and manage pain—cutting across medical, psychological, social, and spiritual domains. People in chronic pain can be helped by praying, reading and memorizing Scripture, being thankful for the good things in life, and being involved in worship, praise, and singing. They can occupy their minds with humor and laughter. Learning to see life's humor and laughing as much as possible can be a great release for people in pain. Starting or reviving a hobby, playing games, or doing puzzles can put their minds on other interesting activities. Group activities—whether a support group, joining a service club or helping ministry, doing counseling, or taking a class—also help put their focus elsewhere. Some are helped by writing—such as keeping a journal or writing letters. Most important, they need to stay hopeful, no matter what happens.

Methods to physically manage the pain include: pain medications, surgery, using a TENS unit (transcutaneous electrical nerve stimulation), biofeedback training, relaxation training, retraining painful body movements, or massage therapy. Other ways to train their minds to manage pain include: pleasant imagery or music, calming self-talk, and thought retraining. People with chronic pain need to learn how to plan and pace their work, improve nutrition and exercise programs, and perhaps learn how to take strategic naps in order to help them function at their best.

THE GIFT OF PAIN

Years ago Philip Yancey and Paul Brand wrote a book destined to become a contemporary classic, *Pain: The Gift Nobody Wants*. In it, they talk about the tragedy of living life without pain, as did the lepers Dr. Brand worked with in India. Inability to feel pain usually leads to an early death or disability because the body has no mechanism to warn or fight against that which is dangerous to it.

This physical paradox is a metaphor for our spiritual and emotional life. The pain of a tweaked conscience can warn us about evil dangers and moral trouble. Fear can sensitize us to risky people and situations, preparing us to flee or to fight. Pain, in truth, is a necessary part of healthy human existence.

Pain is also the impetus that attracts God to us in a special way. Pain motivates the Holy Spirit to reveal His comforting, nurturing, consoling, and protecting character—something that often comes to us by no other means but pain. Pain will truly teach that nothing will come between us and God (Rom. 8:31–39). Pain is the seed to growing a deep faith, to maturing in spiritual strength and wisdom, to becoming more and more like Christ (James 1:2–4; 1 Pet. 1:6, 7).

FURTHER MEDITATION:

Other passages to study about the issue of pain include:

- ➢ Psalm 25:18
- ➢ Jeremiah 29:11–13
- ➢ Habakkuk 3:17–19
- ➢ John 16:33
- ➢ Romans 8:18, 31–39
- ➢ 1 Peter 1:6, 7; 4:12–19

To Learn More: Turn to the key passage note on pain at Hebrews 4:14–16 on page 1624. See also the personality profile of the man at the pool of Bethesda on page 1378.

should use sharpness, according to the authority which the Lord has given me for edification and not for destruction.

GREETINGS AND BENEDICTION

11 Finally, brethren, farewell. Become complete. Be of good comfort, be of one mind, live in peace; and the God of love and peace will be with you.

12 Greet one another with a holy kiss.

13 All the saints greet you.

14 The grace of the Lord Jesus Christ, and the love of God, and the communion of the Holy Spirit *be* with you all. Amen.

Finally, brethren, farewell. Become complete. Be of good comfort, be of one mind, live in peace; and the God of love and peace will be with you.

2 CORINTHIANS 13:11

PERSONALITY PROFILE

Health/ Spirituality

PAUL: STRENGTH IN WEAKNESS

(12:9, 10)

Paul had a passion for ministry that would put most any other believer to shame. He tirelessly traveled, taught, wrote letters, prayed, and traveled some more. His legacy forms much of our New Testament; his words comfort, encourage, and guide believers today. Clearly Paul had many strengths, and God used him well for the kingdom.

Paul also was acutely aware of a nagging health problem, a physical infirmity he called his "thorn in the flesh" (12:7). It apparently hampered his service at times, for in his letter to the Galatian church, he wrote, "My trial which was in my flesh you did not despise or reject, but you received me as an angel of God. . . . I bear you witness that, if possible, you would have plucked out your own eyes and given them to me" (Gal. 4:14, 15). From these words, some have conjectured that Paul's "thorn" was an eye disease that hampered his vision. But the point is not to identify the thorn, but to learn how Paul ministered in spite of it.

Paul had pleaded with God to remove the thorn. Paul may have reasoned, "I would be able to travel and write and teach so much more if God would restore my health." The request was certainly reasonable, but God said no. God lovingly responded to his faithful servant, "My grace is sufficient for you, for My strength is made perfect in weakness."

Health is a gift of God, but it is not a requirement for spiritual service. Many people have physical ailments, chronic pain, or debilitating diseases. They might think, "If God would only heal me, then I can truly minister for Him." But God often responds that His strength can be made perfect in any weak vessel that is completely dependent upon Him. The only requirement for service in God's kingdom is a humble and obedient heart. He will do the rest.

To Learn More: Turn to the article about health/spirituality on pages 402, 403. See also the key passage note at Proverbs 17:22 on page 821.

Galatians

Pressure to change, to act differently, or to speak a different message can come from almost anywhere and can be difficult to resist, even when we know we're right.

For almost 2000 years, the church has faced pressure to change the gospel. In our pluralistic age, the temptation is to water down the message, make it popular. But in the first century, the church was pressured to change in the opposite direction—to add stringent rules to Christ's message of grace.

This disturbing development explains the apostle Paul's fiery letter to the church at Galatia, written about A.D. 49. Soon after their conversion during Paul's first missionary journey, the Galatians were deceived by false teachers who insisted on the necessity of following the Jewish law in order to be accepted by God. In the strongest possible terms, Paul renounces that message, proclaiming that salvation comes by faith alone in Christ alone. In Christ, believers are free from having to meet the impossible demands of the Jewish law and can live joyfully in God's unconditional acceptance.

Galatians also reminds us that every believer is a valued member of the household of faith with equal standing before God (3:26–29). The letter also contains a classic passage of what it means to live under the control of the Holy Spirit (ch. 5).

Galatians is for those who are struggling to understand grace, struggling to break free from the power of sin, or struggling to give themselves more fully to God. Could it be that Galatians is exactly what your soul needs?

SOUL CONCERN IN GALATIANS

Values (5:22)

GREETING

1 Paul, an apostle (not from men nor through man, but through Jesus Christ and God the Father who raised Him from the dead), 2and all the brethren who are with me,

To the churches of Galatia:

3Grace to you and peace from God the Father and our Lord Jesus Christ, 4who gave Himself for our sins, that He might deliver us from this present evil age, according to the will of our God and Father, 5to whom *be* glory forever and ever. Amen.

ONLY ONE GOSPEL

6I marvel that you are turning away so soon from Him who called you in the grace of Christ, to a different gospel, 7which is not another; but there are some who trouble you and want to pervert the gospel of Christ. 8But even if we, or an angel from heaven, preach any other gospel to you than what we have preached to you, let him be accursed. 9As we have said before, so now I say again, if anyone preaches any other gospel to you than what you have received, let him be accursed.

10For do I now persuade men, or God? Or do I seek to please men? For if I still pleased men, I would not be a bondservant of Christ.

CALL TO APOSTLESHIP

11But I make known to you, brethren, that the gospel which was preached by me is not according to man. 12For I neither received it from man, nor was I taught *it,* but *it came* through the revelation of Jesus Christ.

13For you have heard of my former conduct in Judaism, how I persecuted the church of God beyond measure and *tried to* destroy it. 14And I advanced in Judaism beyond many of my contemporaries in my own nation, being more exceedingly zealous for the traditions of my fathers.

15But when it pleased God, who separated me from my mother's womb and called *me* through His grace, 16to reveal His Son in me, that I might preach Him among the Gentiles, I did not immediately confer with flesh and blood, 17nor did I go up to Jerusalem to those *who were* apostles before me; but I went to Arabia, and returned again to Damascus.

CONTACTS AT JERUSALEM

18Then after three years I went up to Jerusalem to see Peter,[a] and remained with him fifteen days. 19But I saw none of the other apostles except James, the Lord's brother. 20(Now *concerning* the things which I write to you, indeed, before God, I do not lie.)

21Afterward I went into the regions of Syria and Cilicia. 22And I was unknown by face to the churches of Judea which *were* in Christ. 23But they were hearing only, "He who formerly persecuted us now preaches the faith which he once *tried to* destroy." 24And they glorified God in me.

DEFENDING THE GOSPEL

2 Then after fourteen years I went up again to Jerusalem with Barnabas, and also took Titus with *me.* 2And I went up by revelation, and communicated to them that gospel which I preach among the Gentiles, but privately to those who were of reputation, lest by any means I might run, or had run, in vain. 3Yet not even Titus who *was* with me, being a Greek, was compelled to be circumcised. 4And *this occurred* because of false brethren secretly brought in (who came in by stealth to spy out

---

1:18 [a]NU-Text reads *Cephas.*

SOUL NOTE

Careful Conflict *(2:11–13)* Paul needed to confront Peter publicly over a very important issue because others were following Peter's poor example. The disagreement involved how Jewish believers were to treat Gentile believers. This issue had the power to divide the church, so in front of everyone, Paul stepped into the gap to resolve the conflict. Because disputes and confrontations differ, they need to be handled differently. Most of the time, conflict can and should be handled privately between the people involved. Believers should deal with their disagreements carefully, seeking wisdom and guidance from God. **Topic: Conflict**

our liberty which we have in Christ Jesus, that they might bring us into bondage), [5]to whom we did not yield submission even for an hour, that the truth of the gospel might continue with you.

[6]But from those who seemed to be something—whatever they were, it makes no difference to me; God shows personal favoritism to no man—for those who seemed *to be something* added nothing to me. [7]But on the contrary, when they saw that the gospel for the uncircumcised had been committed to me, as *the gospel* for the circumcised *was* to Peter [8](for He who worked effectively in Peter for the apostleship to the circumcised also worked effectively in me toward the Gentiles), [9]and when James, Cephas, and John, who seemed to be pillars, perceived the grace that had been given to me, they gave me and Barnabas the right hand of fellowship, that we *should go* to the Gentiles and they to the circumcised. [10]*They desired* only that we should remember the poor, the very thing which I also was eager to do.

No Return to the Law

[11]Now when Peter[a] had come to Antioch, I withstood him to his face, because he was to be blamed; [12]for before certain men came from James, he would eat with the Gentiles; but when they came, he withdrew and separated himself, fearing those who were of the circumcision. [13]And the rest of the Jews also played the hypocrite with him, so that even Barnabas was carried away with their hypocrisy.

[14]But when I saw that they were not straightforward about the truth of the gospel, I said to Peter before *them* all, "If you, being a Jew, live in the manner of Gentiles and not as the Jews, why do you[a] compel Gentiles to live as Jews?[b] [15]We *who are* Jews by nature, and not sinners of the Gentiles, [16]knowing that a man is not justified by the works of the law but by faith in Jesus Christ, even we have believed in Christ Jesus, that we might be justified by faith in Christ and not by the works of the law; for by the works of the law no flesh shall be justified.

[17]"But if, while we seek to be justified by Christ, we ourselves also are found sinners, *is* Christ therefore a minister of sin? Certainly not! [18]For if I build again those things which I destroyed, I make myself a transgressor. [19]For I through the law died to the law that I might live to God. [20]I have been crucified with Christ; it is no longer I who live, but Christ lives in me; and the *life* which I now live in the flesh I live by faith in the Son of God, who loved me and gave Himself for me. [21]I do not

2:11 [a]NU-Text reads *Cephas.* **2:14** [a]NU-Text reads *how can you.* [b]Some interpreters stop the quotation here.

KEY PASSAGE

Self-Denial

WORTH GIVING UP

(2:20)

The wonder of the Christian life is captured in these words. Becoming a believer is more than saying a prayer or committing oneself to a new way of living—it is an entirely new life! When Christ was crucified, He died in the place of all believers. Thus, the believer has been "crucified with Christ," which means that the sinful self is dead. Now, Christ lives in that person. In a glorious, incomprehensible transaction, Christ lives His life through each believer. Each remains an individual, but each is recreated by Christ. Each believer has the ability to deny sin's hold on their life and to live to please Christ.

What do believers have to give up? Selfishness, a life that is headed nowhere, sin and its consequences. Such self-denial can hardly compare with what God offers. When we are crucified with Christ, our lives are lived "by faith in the Son of God" who loved us and gave Himself for us. That's the best way to live!

To Learn More: Turn to the article about self-denial on pages 1346, 1347. See also the personality profile of John the Baptist on page 1375.

set aside the grace of God; for if righteousness *comes* through the law, then Christ died in vain."

JUSTIFICATION BY FAITH

3 O foolish Galatians! Who has bewitched you that you should not obey the truth,[a] before whose eyes Jesus Christ was clearly portrayed among you[b] as crucified? 2This only I want to learn from you: Did you receive the Spirit by the works of the law, or by the hearing of faith? 3Are you so foolish? Having begun in the Spirit, are you now being made perfect by the flesh? 4Have you suffered so many things in vain—if indeed *it was* in vain?

5Therefore He who supplies the Spirit to you and works miracles among you, *does He do it* by the works of the law, or by the hearing of faith?—6just as Abraham *"believed God, and it was accounted to him for righteousness."*[a] 7Therefore know that *only* those who are of faith are sons of Abraham. 8And the Scripture, foreseeing that God would justify the Gentiles by faith, preached the gospel to Abraham beforehand, *saying, "In you all the nations shall be blessed."*[a] 9So then those who *are* of faith are blessed with believing Abraham.

> "I have been crucified with Christ; it is no longer I who live, but Christ lives in me; and the life which I now live in the flesh I live by faith in the Son of God, who loved me and gave Himself for me."
>
> GALATIANS 2:20

THE LAW BRINGS A CURSE

10For as many as are of the works of the law are under the curse; for it is written, *"Cursed is everyone who does not continue in all things which are written in the book of the law, to do them."*[a] 11But that no one is justified by the law in the sight of God *is* evident, for *"the just shall live by faith."*[a] 12Yet the law is not of faith, but *"the man who does them shall live by them."*[a]

13Christ has redeemed us from the curse of the law, having become a curse for us (for it is written, *"Cursed is everyone who hangs on a tree"*[a]), 14that the blessing of Abraham might come upon the Gentiles in Christ Jesus, that we might receive the promise of the Spirit through faith.

THE CHANGELESS PROMISE

15Brethren, I speak in the manner of men: Though *it is* only a man's covenant, yet *if it is* confirmed, no one annuls or adds to it. 16Now to Abraham and his Seed were the promises made. He does not say, "And to seeds," as of many, but as of one, *"And to your Seed,"*[a] who is Christ. 17And this I say, *that* the law, which was four hundred and thirty years later, cannot annul the covenant that was confirmed before by God in Christ,[a] that it should make the promise of no effect. 18For if the inheritance *is* of the law, *it is* no longer of promise; but God gave *it* to Abraham by promise.

PURPOSE OF THE LAW

19What purpose then *does* the law *serve?* It was added because of transgressions, till the

---

3:1 [a]NU-Text omits *that you should not obey the truth.* [b]NU-Text omits *among you.*
3:6 [a]Genesis 15:6 **3:8** [a]Genesis 12:3; 18:18; 22:18; 26:4; 28:14 **3:10** [a]Deuteronomy 27:26
3:11 [a]Habakkuk 2:4 **3:12** [a]Leviticus 18:5
3:13 [a]Deuteronomy 21:23 **3:16** [a]Genesis 12:7; 13:15; 24:7 **3:17** [a]NU-Text omits *in Christ.*

SOUL NOTE

One Big Family *(3:28)* This verse describes how Christ breaks down all barriers. There should be no place for one member of the body of believers to have prejudice against another member because of race, social status, gender, background, or any other superficial barriers human beings create. All believers have personal identities, which provide rich variety in the church. But all have also been made "one in Christ Jesus." This oneness provides deep unity. As part of a huge, diverse family, we should not allow anything to separate us from other believers.

Topic: Prejudice

Seed should come to whom the promise was
made; *and it was* appointed through angels by
the hand of a mediator. [20]Now a mediator
does not *mediate* for one *only*, but God is one.
[21]*Is* the law then against the promises of
God? Certainly not! For if there had been a law
given which could have given life, truly righteousness would have been by the law. [22]But
the Scripture has confined all under sin, that
the promise by faith in Jesus Christ might be
given to those who believe. [23]But before faith
came, we were kept under guard by the law,
kept for the faith which would afterward be
revealed. [24]Therefore the law was our tutor *to
bring us* to Christ, that we might be justified
by faith. [25]But after faith has come, we are no
longer under a tutor.

Sons and Heirs

[26]For you are all sons of God through faith
in Christ Jesus. [27]For as many of you as were
baptized into Christ have put on Christ.
[28]There is neither Jew nor Greek, there is neither slave nor free, there is neither male nor
female; for you are all one in Christ Jesus.
[29]And if you *are* Christ's, then you are
Abraham's seed, and heirs according to the
promise.

4 Now I say *that* the heir, as long as he is a
child, does not differ at all from a slave,
though he is master of all, [2]but is under guardians and stewards until the time appointed by
the father. [3]Even so we, when we were children, were in bondage under the elements of
the world. [4]But when the fullness of the time
had come, God sent forth His Son, born[a] of a
woman, born under the law, [5]to redeem those
who were under the law, that we might receive the adoption as sons.
[6]And because you are sons, God has sent
forth the Spirit of His Son into your hearts,
crying out, "Abba, Father!" [7]Therefore you are
no longer a slave but a son, and if a son, then
an heir of[a] God through Christ.

Fears for the Church

[8]But then, indeed, when you did not know
God, you served those which by nature are not
gods. [9]But now after you have known God, or
rather are known by God, how *is it that* you
turn again to the weak and beggarly elements,
to which you desire again to be in bondage?
[10]You observe days and months and seasons
and years. [11]I am afraid for you, lest I have labored for you in vain.
[12]Brethren, I urge you to become like me,
for I *became* like you. You have not injured me
at all. [13]You know that because of physical infirmity I preached the gospel to you at the
first. [14]And my trial which was in my flesh you
did not despise or reject, but you received me
as an angel of God, *even* as Christ Jesus.
[15]What[a] then was the blessing you *enjoyed?*
For I bear you witness that, if possible, you
would have plucked out your own eyes and
given them to me. [16]Have I therefore become
your enemy because I tell you the truth?
[17]They zealously court you, *but* for no good;
yes, they want to exclude you, that you may
be zealous for them. [18]But it is good to be
zealous in a good thing always, and not only
when I am present with you. [19]My little children, for whom I labor in birth again until
Christ is formed in you, [20]I would like to be
present with you now and to change my tone;
for I have doubts about you.

4:4 [a]Or *made* **4:7** [a]NU-Text reads *through God* and omits *through Christ.* **4:15** [a]NU-Text reads *Where.*

SOUL NOTE

Being Dad *(4:6)* "Abba, Father" describes believers' intimate relationship with God. As children love their fathers and yet respect and obey them, so believers love God and have respect for and awe of Him. At times, people's unhappy relationships with their earthly fathers inhibit their ability to understand the loving fatherhood of God. This puts a great responsibility on fathers to seek the guidance of the perfect Father as they raise their children. Christian fathers should raise their children with love and discipline. This will help their children to have a healthy concept of God.
Topic: Fatherhood

Two Covenants

21Tell me, you who desire to be under the
law, do you not hear the law? 22For it is written that Abraham had two sons: the one by a
bondwoman, the other by a freewoman. 23But
he *who was* of the bondwoman was born according to the flesh, and he of the freewoman
through promise, 24which things are symbolic.
For these are the[a] two covenants: the one from
Mount Sinai which gives birth to bondage,
which is Hagar—25for this Hagar is Mount Sinai in Arabia, and corresponds to Jerusalem
which now is, and is in bondage with her children—26but the Jerusalem above is free,
which is the mother of us all. 27For it is written:

"Rejoice, O barren,
You who do not bear!
Break forth and shout,
You who are not in labor!
For the desolate has many more children
Than she who has a husband."[a]

28Now we, brethren, as Isaac *was,* are children of promise. 29But, as he who was born
according to the flesh then persecuted him
who was born according to the Spirit, even so
it is now. 30Nevertheless what does the Scripture say? *"Cast out the bondwoman and her
son, for the son of the bondwoman shall not
be heir with the son of the freewoman."*[a] 31So
then, brethren, we are not children of the
bondwoman but of the free.

Christian Liberty

5 Stand fast therefore in the liberty by
which Christ has made us free,[a] and do
not be entangled again with a yoke of bondage. 2Indeed I, Paul, say to you that if you become circumcised, Christ will profit you
nothing. 3And I testify again to every man
who becomes circumcised that he is a debtor
to keep the whole law. 4You have become estranged from Christ, you who *attempt to* be
justified by law; you have fallen from grace.
5For we through the Spirit eagerly wait for
the hope of righteousness by faith. 6For in
Christ Jesus neither circumcision nor uncircumcision avails anything, but faith working
through love.

Love Fulfills the Law

7You ran well. Who hindered you from
obeying the truth? 8This persuasion does not
come from Him who calls you. 9A little
leaven leavens the whole lump. 10I have
confidence in you, in the Lord, that you will
have no other mind; but he who troubles you
shall bear his judgment, whoever he is.

11And I, brethren, if I still preach circumcision, why do I still suffer persecution? Then
the offense of the cross has ceased. 12I could
wish that those who trouble you would even
cut themselves off!

13For you, brethren, have been called to liberty; only do not *use* liberty as an opportunity
for the flesh, but through love serve one another. 14For all the law is fulfilled in one word,
even in this: *"You shall love your neighbor as
yourself."*[a] 15But if you bite and devour one
another, beware lest you be consumed by one
another!

Walking in the Spirit

16I say then: Walk in the Spirit, and you
shall not fulfill the lust of the flesh. 17For the

4:24 [a]NU-Text and M-Text omit *the.* **4:27** [a]Isaiah 54:1 **4:30** [a]Genesis 21:10 **5:1** [a]NU-Text reads *For freedom Christ has made us free; stand fast therefore.* **5:14** [a]Leviticus 19:18

SOUL NOTE

Too Much *(5:19–21)* This list of the "works of the flesh" includes "drunkenness, revelries, and the like." Drinking excessively and allowing alcohol to take over one's senses is sinful and reveals a lack of self-control. Drunkenness also leads to other sins, such as taking part in "revelries" that might have consequences far beyond one's control. Involvement in any kind of substance abuse, whether it's alcohol or drugs, is sinful, and believers must turn away from it. If they have faced that difficulty in their past, they can trust God to help them overcome the temptation and learn self-control (5:23).
Topic: Drug Abuse

flesh lusts against the Spirit, and the Spirit
against the flesh; and these are contrary to
one another, so that you do not do the things
that you wish. 18 But if you are led by the Spirit, you are not under the law.
19 Now the works of the flesh are evident,
which are: adultery,[a] fornication, uncleanness, lewdness, 20 idolatry, sorcery, hatred,
contentions, jealousies, outbursts of wrath,
selfish ambitions, dissensions, heresies, 21 envy,
murders,[a] drunkenness, revelries, and the
like; of which I tell you beforehand, just as I
also told *you* in time past, that those who
practice such things will not inherit the kingdom of God.
22 But the fruit of the Spirit is love, joy,
peace, longsuffering, kindness, goodness,
faithfulness, 23 gentleness, self-control. Against
such there is no law. 24 And those *who are*
Christ's have crucified the flesh with its passions and desires. 25 If we live in the Spirit, let
us also walk in the Spirit. 26 Let us not become
conceited, provoking one another, envying
one another.

Bear and Share the Burdens

6 Brethren, if a man is overtaken in any
trespass, you who *are* spiritual restore

5:19 [a]NU-Text omits *adultery*. **5:21** [a]NU-Text omits *murders*.

SOUL NOTE

God's Fruit *(5:22, 23)* What do we value most in life? Many people try self-improvement or self-awareness programs to find meaning and purpose. These two verses hold the secret to becoming exactly what God desires. The "fruit of the Spirit" are not works that believers must accomplish so they can check them off as they "grow" them. Instead, these fruit grow naturally as the produce of the Holy Spirit's ministry in a person's life. As we grow in the Christian faith, these characteristics should increasingly be manifested in our lives. The key is for us to submit our lives to Christ daily, allowing Him to work in and through us. That should be our highest value.

Topic: Values

KEY PASSAGE

Restoration

BACK TO THE BODY

(6:1–5)

Although all believers have been born again, they still face the dilemma of the sin nature. At times, this can overwhelm a believer, causing involvement in destructive sin. So what should other believers do for a brother or sister who is "overtaken in any trespass"?

Paul had advised elsewhere that discipline may be required (as in 1 Cor. 5), but its purpose should always be to restore the believer to the fellowship. Those who seek out an erring believer must come in a "spirit of gentleness," realizing that they also are sinners constantly in need of God's grace and forgiveness. The fallen but repentant believer is not neglected or rejected but rather is helped, encouraged, prayed over, offered assistance, and warmly welcomed back into the fellowship. Restoration helps a repentant believer get back on track and continue to grow; it humbles the church to realize the reality of sin; and it reveals the grace and power of Almighty God.

To Learn More: Turn to the article about restoration on pages 1412, 1413. See also the personality profile of David on page 418.

Values

CHRISTIAN VALUES IN CONTEMPORARY SOCIETY

CRAIG AND JANET PARSHALL

(Galatians 5:22)

The "spin-doctors" are definitely in. From politics to media, any topic can be given the proper makeover to introduce it to society as politically, socially, and even spiritually correct. Today is a time of moral relativism where moral values are never absolute. Many people think that the situation determines the nature or value of personal choice ("moral autonomy"). However, the Word of God has much to say in opposition to this kind of moral value system.

KNOWING GOD'S VALUES

In distinct contrast to moral relativism, the Christian message is that God has clearly and authoritatively spoken about the values His people should hold. God's Word gives a description of truly beneficial moral attributes that glorify God. Because these values are eternal, they are always applicable, not situational. "Finally, brethren, whatever things are true, whatever things are noble, whatever things are just, whatever things are pure, whatever things are lovely, whatever things are of good report, if there is any virtue and if there is anything praiseworthy—meditate on these things" (Phil. 4:8). This is the standard of objectively true and divinely reliable moral values. Paul's exhortation ends with the instruction to "meditate" about the moral values that God prizes.

God does not want people to decide what is virtuous according to the circumstances. And yet how often people do just that! Who has ever lied to the boss and tried to justify doing so? Who has ever tried to come up with a reason to see an impure movie or video because everyone is talking about it at work? Many times people know what is right, but because of societal pressure or their own selfishness, they choose what is wrong and attempt to justify it.

In contrast, God's people rely on His standard about what is good, true, and morally pure. They then apply that standard to their circumstances, not the other way around. The standard does not change; instead, their lives must change to match the standard.

APPLYING GOD'S VALUES

Simply knowing what values are best is not enough. Christians need to understand and apply them. That means turning God's moral values into their own personal virtues. How is that possible? Virtuous character begins with the awesome idea of personal freedom. Followers of Jesus Christ are set free from continuing as slavish servants of depravity. As Paul wrote, "Stand fast therefore in the liberty by which Christ has made us free, and do not be entangled again with a yoke of bondage" (Gal. 5:1).

The Bible makes it clear that the freedom given in Christ Jesus is for a purpose. "For you, brethren, have been called to liberty; only do not use liberty as an opportunity for the flesh, but through love serve one another" (Gal. 5:13). Christ's gift of freedom is not to be used as an excuse to sin. There is a clear choice. People can serve the "works of the flesh" such as "adultery, fornication, uncleanness, lewdness, idolatry, sorcery, hatred, contentions, jealousies, outbursts of wrath, selfish ambitions, dissensions, heresies, envy, murders, drunkenness, revelries, and the like" (Gal. 5:19, 20). But that choice is contradictory to the life one is able to live "in the Spirit" of God (Gal. 5:16). The solution, then, is to crucify the improper desires of the sinful nature. Believers can consider themselves dead to sin. Then they are free to walk in the Spirit (Gal. 5:16, 25).

WALKING IN THE SPIRIT

Walking in the Spirit is a muscular enterprise. It means Christians are to manifest the "fruit" or expression of the Spirit whenever possible. Of course, Christian character is also a byproduct of a natural process. Apple trees don't sweat, moan, and groan in order to produce apples. In the same way, a Christian walking in the Spirit should, over time, naturally exhibit the fruit of Christian character: moral virtues.

In the end, this is a joint venture. While God's empowering Spirit gives Christians the fruit of Christlike character, they also play a critical part in their pursuit of these values. When they yield to the Holy Spirit and maintain a daily lifestyle that is consistent with God's values, the result is that they will inherit the kingdom of God (Gal. 5:21). What are these values that Christians should reveal? They are the fruit of the Spirit: love, joy, peace, longsuffering, kindness, goodness, faithfulness, gentleness, and self-control (Gal. 5:22, 23).

While virtue comes from the internal process of deciding to walk according to the Spirit rather than the flesh, it is also forged from the blast furnace of external trials and pressures. "We also glory in tribulations, knowing that tribulation produces perseverance; and perseverance, character; and character, hope. Now hope does not disappoint, because the love of God has been poured out in our hearts by the Holy Spirit who was given to us" (Rom. 5:3–5). People often gain a greater level of maturity, temperance, and character as a result of hardship. Through difficulties, they come to understand what they truly value.

If our lives are marked by Christlike virtues, we will be happy and productive. We will experience personal peace and security. We know that even though our circumstances change, our values will not. Best of all, we will also revolutionize the world by drawing others to Christ through our solid example.

FURTHER MEDITATION:

Other passages to study about the issue of values include:

- ➢ Psalm 15:1–5
- ➢ Micah 6:8
- ➢ Matthew 6:33
- ➢ 1 Corinthians 10:31
- ➢ Ephesians 5:1–4

To Learn More: Turn to the key passage note on values at 2 Peter 1:5–9 on page 1669. See also the personality profile of Shadrach, Meshach, and Abed-Nego on page 1108.

such a one in a spirit of gentleness, considering yourself lest you also be tempted. 2Bear one another's burdens, and so fulfill the law of Christ. 3For if anyone thinks himself to be something, when he is nothing, he deceives himself. 4But let each one examine his own work, and then he will have rejoicing in himself alone, and not in another. 5For each one shall bear his own load.

Be Generous and Do Good

6Let him who is taught the word share in all good things with him who teaches.

7Do not be deceived, God is not mocked; for whatever a man sows, that he will also reap. 8For he who sows to his flesh will of the flesh reap corruption, but he who sows to the Spirit will of the Spirit reap everlasting life. 9And let us not grow weary while doing good, for in due season we shall reap if we do not lose heart. 10Therefore, as we have opportunity, let us do good to all, especially to those who are of the household of faith.

> Do not be deceived, God is not mocked; for whatever a man sows, that he will also reap.
>
> GALATIANS 6:7

Glory Only in the Cross

11See with what large letters I have written to you with my own hand! 12As many as desire to make a good showing in the flesh, these *would* compel you to be circumcised, only that they may not suffer persecution for the cross of Christ. 13For not even those who are circumcised keep the law, but they desire to have you circumcised that they may boast in your flesh. 14But God forbid that I should boast except in the cross of our Lord Jesus Christ, by whom[a] the world has been crucified to me, and I to the world. 15For in Christ Jesus neither circumcision nor uncircumcision avails anything, but a new creation.

Blessing and a Plea

16And as many as walk according to this rule, peace and mercy *be* upon them, and upon the Israel of God.

17From now on let no one trouble me, for I bear in my body the marks of the Lord Jesus.

18Brethren, the grace of our Lord Jesus Christ *be* with your spirit. Amen.

6:14 [a]Or *by which* (the cross)

SOUL NOTE

A Heart for the Harvest *(6:9)* Hurting people everywhere need the healing touch of God's servants. Paul encourages believers to "not grow weary while doing good." Continuing to do good and never seeing a harvest can be discouraging and frustrating. At times, loving words fall on deaf ears and hard work on thankless hearts. But no work for God is ever wasted: "In due season we shall reap if we do not lose heart." We will reap a harvest of blessings as the Holy Spirit works in our lives. We must never allow discouragement to make us grow idle. Our good works are valuable to God. **Topic: Discouragement**

Ephesians

Remember when as a child you just wanted to grow—to be bigger, stronger, and faster? Maturing takes time, and it can't be rushed by our wanting to. Spiritual growth also takes time as God works in believers, conforming them to the image of Christ (Rom. 8:29). Some, desiring to rush the process, wish for instant maturity. Worse, some hold on to their immaturity and live as spiritual infants.

The apostle Paul's letter to the Ephesians is a treasure trove of truth and a manual for developing a life of substance and depth. Ephesus was a major commercial and religious metropolis in Asia Minor where Paul planted a church toward the end of his second missionary journey (A.D. 53; Acts 18, 19). About seven years later, while imprisoned for preaching the gospel, Paul apparently felt that the Ephesian Christians needed to be reminded of their extraordinary spiritual blessings. The result is this rich letter spelling out the great mystery of the Christian faith. Those whose minds are renewed by God's grace (ch. 1—3), says Paul, will see radical changes in the way they live (ch. 4—6). In short, they will grow and mature in Christ.

Unlike the many shallow, misguided believers who think God exists for them (rather than the other way around), those who study Ephesians and work to apply it to their lives will develop depth and stability in their souls. Maturity comes only by grace, so understanding that grace must become our lifelong passion.

SOUL CONCERNS IN EPHESIANS

GREETING

1 Paul, an apostle of Jesus Christ by the will of God,

To the saints who are in Ephesus, and faithful in Christ Jesus:

[2]Grace to you and peace from God our Father and the Lord Jesus Christ.

REDEMPTION IN CHRIST

[3]Blessed *be* the God and Father of our Lord Jesus Christ, who has blessed us with every spiritual blessing in the heavenly *places* in Christ, [4]just as He chose us in Him before the foundation of the world, that we should be holy and without blame before Him in love, [5]having predestined us to adoption as sons by Jesus Christ to Himself, according to the good pleasure of His will, [6]to the praise of the glory of His grace, by which He made us accepted in the Beloved.

[7]In Him we have redemption through His blood, the forgiveness of sins, according to the riches of His grace [8]which He made to abound toward us in all wisdom and prudence, [9]having made known to us the mystery of His will, according to His good pleasure which He purposed in Himself, [10]that in the dispensation of the fullness of the times He might gather together in one all things in Christ, both[a] which are in heaven and which are on earth—in Him. [11]In Him also we have obtained an inheritance, being predestined according to the purpose of Him who works all things according to the counsel of His will, [12]that we who first trusted in Christ should be to the praise of His glory.

[13]In Him you also *trusted,* after you heard the word of truth, the gospel of your salvation; in whom also, having believed, you were sealed with the Holy Spirit of promise, [14]who[a] is the guarantee of our inheritance until the redemption of the purchased possession, to the praise of His glory.

PRAYER FOR SPIRITUAL WISDOM

[15]Therefore I also, after I heard of your faith in the Lord Jesus and your love for all the saints, [16]do not cease to give thanks for you, making mention of you in my prayers: [17]that the God of our Lord Jesus Christ, the Father of glory, may give to you the spirit of wisdom and revelation in the knowledge of Him, [18]the eyes of your understanding[a] being enlightened; that you may know what is the hope of His calling, what are the riches of the glory of His inheritance in the saints, [19]and what *is* the exceeding greatness of His power toward us who believe, according to the working of His mighty power [20]which He worked in Christ when He raised Him from the dead and seated *Him* at His right hand in the heavenly *places,* [21]far above all principality and power and might and dominion, and every name that is named, not only in this age but also in that which is to come.

> That you may know what is the hope of His calling, what are the riches of the glory of His inheritance in the saints, and what is the exceeding greatness of His power toward us who believe.
>
> EPHESIANS 1:18, 19

1:10 [a]NU-Text and M-Text omit *both.* **1:14** [a]NU-Text reads *which.* **1:18** [a]NU-Text and M-Text read *hearts.*

SOUL NOTE

Bless You *(1:3)* In words of lofty praise, Paul blessed God, who has blessed His people "with every spiritual blessing." Being blessed refers to receiving something good; blessing others means desiring the best for them. Believers bless God by attributing all power and glory to Him. He is the source of every spiritual blessing—Christians could not know God or grow spiritually unless He had blessed them with that opportunity. The spiritual blessings God gives are far beyond anything humans could ask or imagine—yet He freely blesses His people. We should not cease blessing God for His great blessings toward us! **Topic: Attachment/Blessing**

[22]And He put all *things* under His feet, and
gave Him *to be* head over all *things* to the
church, [23]which is His body, the fullness of
Him who fills all in all.

By Grace Through Faith

2 And you *He made alive,* who were dead in
trespasses and sins, [2]in which you once
walked according to the course of this world,
according to the prince of the power of the air,
the spirit who now works in the sons of disobedience, [3]among whom also we all once
conducted ourselves in the lusts of our flesh,
fulfilling the desires of the flesh and of the
mind, and were by nature children of wrath,
just as the others.
[4]But God, who is rich in mercy, because of
His great love with which He loved us, [5]even
when we were dead in trespasses, made us
alive together with Christ (by grace you have
been saved), [6]and raised *us* up together, and
made *us* sit together in the heavenly *places* in
Christ Jesus, [7]that in the ages to come He
might show the exceeding riches of His grace
in *His* kindness toward us in Christ Jesus. [8]For
by grace you have been saved through faith,
and that not of yourselves; *it is* the gift of God,
[9]not of works, lest anyone should boast. [10]For
we are His workmanship, created in Christ
Jesus for good works, which God prepared
beforehand that we should walk in them.

Brought Near by His Blood

[11]Therefore remember that you, once Gentiles in the flesh—who are called Uncircumcision by what is called the Circumcision made
in the flesh by hands—[12]that at that time you
were without Christ, being aliens from the
commonwealth of Israel and strangers from
the covenants of promise, having no hope and
without God in the world. [13]But now in Christ
Jesus you who once were far off have been
brought near by the blood of Christ.

Christ Our Peace

[14]For He Himself is our peace, who has
made both one, and has broken down the
middle wall of separation, [15]having abolished
in His flesh the enmity, *that is,* the law of commandments *contained* in ordinances, so as to
create in Himself one new man *from* the two,
thus making peace, [16]and that He might reconcile them both to God in one body through the
cross, thereby putting to death the enmity.
[17]And He came and preached peace to you
who were afar off and to those who were near.
[18]For through Him we both have access by one
Spirit to the Father.

Christ Our Cornerstone

[19]Now, therefore, you are no longer strangers and foreigners, but fellow citizens with the
saints and members of the household of God,
[20]having been built on the foundation of the
apostles and prophets, Jesus Christ Himself
being the chief corner*stone,* [21]in whom the
whole building, being fitted together, grows
into a holy temple in the Lord, [22]in whom you
also are being built together for a dwelling
place of God in the Spirit.

The Mystery Revealed

3 For this reason I, Paul, the prisoner of
Christ Jesus for you Gentiles—[2]if indeed
you have heard of the dispensation of the
grace of God which was given to me for you,
[3]how that by revelation He made known to me
the mystery (as I have briefly written already,
[4]by which, when you read, you may understand my knowledge in the mystery of Christ),
[5]which in other ages was not made known to
the sons of men, as it has now been revealed

SOUL NOTE

Nobody's Perfect *(2:8, 9)* God is perfect; people are sinful. Fortunately, God does not require people to reach a certain level of perfection before He will accept them. Otherwise, no one could ever be saved! God provided a perfect way of salvation—grace. No one is saved by his or her good works; otherwise, people might be tempted to boast about how they had earned their salvation. Instead, no one can boast; they can only accept by faith this gift of God. One day God will make us perfect; until then, we continue to grow more and more like Christ with the help of the Holy Spirit. **Topic: Perfectionism**

by the Spirit to His holy apostles and prophets: [6]that the Gentiles should be fellow heirs,
of the same body, and
partakers of His promise
in Christ through the
gospel, [7]of which I be-
came a minister accord-
ing to the gift of the
grace of God given to
me by the effective
working of His power.

> Now to Him who is able to do exceedingly abundantly above all that we ask or think, according to the power that works in us, to Him be glory in the church by Christ Jesus to all generations, forever and ever. Amen.
>
> EPHESIANS 3:20, 21

Purpose of the Mystery

[8]To me, who am less than the least of all the
saints, this grace was given, that I should
preach among the Gentiles the unsearchable
riches of Christ, [9]and to make all see what *is*
the fellowship[a] of the mystery, which from the
beginning of the ages has been hidden in God
who created all things through Jesus Christ;[b]
[10]to the intent that now the manifold wisdom
of God might be made known by the church to
the principalities and powers in the heavenly
places, [11]according to the eternal purpose
which He accomplished in Christ Jesus our
Lord, [12]in whom we have boldness and access
with confidence through faith in Him.
[13]Therefore I ask that you do not lose heart at
my tribulations for you, which is your glory.

Appreciation of the Mystery

[14]For this reason I bow my knees to the Father of our Lord Jesus Christ,[a] [15]from whom
the whole family in heaven and earth is
named, [16]that He would grant you, according
to the riches of His glory, to be strengthened
with might through His Spirit in the inner
man, [17]that Christ may dwell in your hearts
through faith; that you, being rooted and
grounded in love, [18]may be able to comprehend with all the saints what *is* the width and
length and depth and height— [19]to know the
love of Christ which passes knowledge; that
you may be filled with
all the fullness of God.
[20]Now to Him who is
able to do exceedingly
abundantly above all
that we ask or think, ac-
cording to the power
that works in us, [21]to
Him *be* glory in the
church by Christ Jesus
to all generations, for-
ever and ever. Amen.

Walk in Unity

4 I, therefore, the prisoner of the Lord, beseech you to walk worthy of the calling
with which you were called, [2]with all lowliness and gentleness, with longsuffering, bearing with one another in love, [3]endeavoring to
keep the unity of the Spirit in the bond of
peace. [4]*There is* one body and one Spirit, just
as you were called in one hope of your calling;
[5]one Lord, one faith, one baptism; [6]one God
and Father of all, who *is* above all, and
through all, and in you[a] all.

Spiritual Gifts

[7]But to each one of us grace was given according to the measure of Christ's gift. [8]There-
fore He says:

"When He ascended on high,
He led captivity captive,
And gave gifts to men."[a]

3:9 [a]NU-Text and M-Text read *stewardship* (dispensation). [b]NU-Text omits *through Jesus Christ.* **3:14** [a]NU-Text omits *of our Lord Jesus Christ.* **4:6** [a]NU-Text omits *you;* M-Text reads *us.* **4:8** [a]Psalm 68:18

SOUL NOTE

Growing Up *(3:14–19)* These words describe the goal of all Christians as they seek to mature in their faith. Believers can pray to be strengthened by the Holy Spirit, so that they can withstand temptations and fears. They can pray for Christ to dwell in their hearts, helping them remain "rooted and grounded in love." Finally, they can pray "to know the love of Christ," a love that is incomprehensible, yet able to be known by experience. When we pray for spiritual growth for ourselves and others, we can use the words of this prayer. **Topic: Spiritual Growth**

[9](Now this, *"He ascended"*—what does it mean but that He also first[a] descended into the lower parts of the earth? [10]He who descended is also the One who ascended far above all the heavens, that He might fill all things.)

[11]And He Himself gave some *to be* apostles, some prophets, some evangelists, and some pastors and teachers, [12]for the equipping of the saints for the work of ministry, for the edifying of the body of Christ, [13]till we all come to the unity of the faith and of the knowledge of the Son of God, to a perfect man, to the measure of the stature of the fullness of Christ; [14]that we should no longer be children, tossed to and fro and carried about with every wind of doctrine, by the trickery of men, in the cunning craftiness of deceitful plotting, [15]but, speaking the truth in love, may grow up in all things into Him who is the head—Christ—[16]from whom the whole body, joined and knit together by what every joint supplies, according to the effective working by which every part does its share, causes growth of the body for the edifying of itself in love.

The New Man

[17]This I say, therefore, and testify in the Lord, that you should no longer walk as the rest of[a] the Gentiles walk, in the futility of

4:9 [a]NU-Text omits *first.* **4:17** [a]NU-Text omits *the rest of.*

KEY PASSAGE

Communication

WORDS' WORTH

(4:15)

Without communication, human beings would be isolated. God gave us language to allow us to talk, express ideas and opinions, provide information, and share feelings. Some people communicate in hurtful ways, saying words that cause pain to the hearer. Believers, however, are to communicate differently. Paul wrote that Christians' words should always be truthful and spoken in love. He added that no corrupt words should come out of believers' mouths; instead, they should speak only "what is good for necessary edification, that it may impart grace to the hearers" (Eph. 4:29).

Think about how many times a day we open our mouths to talk. What if every word first had to be passed through a sieve of truthfulness, love, and edification? Would we be left speechless? We would do well to consider what we have to say before we say it. Then we would have time to apply Paul's test to our words.

To Learn More: Turn to the article about communication on pages 1442, 1443. See also the personality profile of Paul and Barnabas on page 1441.

SOUL NOTE

Even at Home *(4:15)* Sometimes it is most difficult to be a Christian at home. Believers may work hard at speaking carefully in the world; at home, however, they may not try so hard. While home is a place where we can be ourselves, those "selves" should still show Christlike character. Marriage partners should speak as carefully to each other as they would to a friend or an unbeliever. To speak the truth in love means honesty and openness with the seasoning of love that always respects the other person, seeking his or her best interests. Christian couples who follow Paul's advice to "speak the truth in love" have healthy communication.

Topic: Marital Communication

Cults

SWEET EQUILIBRIUM: A HEALTHY, BALANCED CHRISTIAN FAITH

STEPHEN ARTERBURN

(Ephesians 4:14)

It is an extraordinarily difficult quality to fake. It is beautiful to see it demonstrated in someone's life. However, it is equally obvious when it is lacking. What is it? It is a healthy, consistent, and balanced faith.

Those involved in unhealthy faith systems—whether it be a cult, a false teaching, or even excessive legalism—exude a lack of balance, which is a glaring tip-off of toxic teachings. False religions, cults, and other forms of toxic faith are generally based on an "either-or," "black-white," "us-them," or "all or nothing" mentality. There is no room for compromise and no middle ground. In contrast, healthy faith accepts the fact that life is not usually black or white. Healthy faith finds balance in allowing believers to feel okay about struggling with the many gray areas of life. Toxic faith, however, labels those with sincere questions about religion as untrustworthy dissidents.

BALANCED FAITH IN ACTION

People with a healthy, balanced Christian faith draw people to Christ. They refuse to compromise the truth of God's Word, but they also refuse to put down other people's beliefs. People with healthy faith understand that many people get involved in other religions because those religions offer something appealing. The fact that so many people are involved in so many religions demonstrates the human search for truth and for connection with the Creator of the universe. Healthy believers can admire and respect the devotion demonstrated by the followers of other religions. Healthy believers can learn about other faiths and religions in order to understand their influence on people throughout the world. For example, many world religions are very mission-minded in their attempt to share their concept of truth with others—a quality the Christian faith can appreciate.

As they learn more about other religions, healthy believers see the common thread in all other faiths—the need these faiths perceive to work one's way to God. For the adherents of these faiths, performance is everything, which is why many people of different non-Christian faiths believe that people who live good lives will gain eternal life. However, Christianity alone teaches that it is impossible to be consistently good, much less good enough to earn passage into heaven. Christianity also realizes the impossibility of comparing oneself to the example of perfection set by Jesus Christ. At this crossroads, sharing one's own experience with personal failures and inconsistencies becomes a testimony as to why Christianity is so personally appealing! Rather than working one's way to heaven, God works His way to people!

The difference in the healthy believer's approach is that they will not put down the other person's faith. Instead, they share the truth of Christianity in a tone of empathy for the human experience. Everyone is searching for truth and seeking to have some relationship with God. People with healthy faith see themselves as part of a great community in which everyone is struggling to find the truth about God, themselves, and others. Christians are more likely to gain an effective hearing through sharing what they have found in their own search. While people may argue with a biblical text or theological tenet, no one can deny a person's truthful testimony about an experience with Christ. A testimony can become a powerful witness to the truth of Christianity. When Christians abandon the "us versus them," unbalanced mentality, people are drawn to them and to Christ.

THE RESULTS OF BALANCED FAITH

Where healthy faith grows, every area of the believer's life improves. In the balanced practice of the Christian faith, families grow closer, friendships become stronger, and conflict is more easily resolved. Rigidity is replaced by understanding—a soothing balm in many relationships that may be bruised by misunderstandings and stalwart religious discussions. Those who grow in a healthy faith find comfort because their lives have perspective. They find wholeness in a balanced faith.

Healthy believers also find freedom from the performance review trap. Instead of engaging in a toxic struggle to somehow earn more acceptance from God by trying to appear more righteous than others, healthy Christians realize that they do not have to be perfect to be accepted. While the Pharisees desperately honed and perfected their extreme devotion to the Law, Jesus taught balance. When confronted about breaking a Sabbath law, He told His critics that the Sabbath was created for people, not people for the Sabbath (Mark 2:27).

Healthy faith is steeped in mercy. Emulating a merciful God, Christians must incorporate mercy into their views of other people as well as themselves. Mercy can heal family relationships and friendships that have been strained by the practice of a toxic faith. A truly biblical, Spirit-filled faith will display an attractive, winsome balance that draws people in instead of driving them away.

Healthy faith is balanced in its expression. "We should no longer be children, tossed to and fro and carried about with every wind of doctrine, by the trickery of men, in the cunning craftiness of deceitful plotting" (Eph. 4:14). We know we are balanced when we are tolerant and patient, able to confront without being aggressive, to be assertive without being insensitive, and to be loving yet truthful.

FURTHER MEDITATION:

Other passages to study about the issue of cults include:

- ➢ 1 Timothy 4:6, 7
- ➢ 2 Peter 2:1–22
- ➢ 1 John 4:1–6
- ➢ 2 John 7–11
- ➢ Jude 3, 4

To Learn More: Turn to the key passage note on cults at Titus 1:16 on page 1614. See also the personality profile of Simon the sorcerer on page 1429.

their mind, [18]having their understanding darkened, being alienated from the life of God, because of the ignorance that is in them,
because of the blindness of their heart; [19]who,
being past feeling, have given themselves over
to lewdness, to work all uncleanness with
greediness.
[20]But you have not so learned Christ, [21]if indeed you have heard Him and have been
taught by Him, as the truth is in Jesus: [22]that
you put off, concerning your former conduct,
the old man which grows corrupt according to
the deceitful lusts, [23]and be renewed in the
spirit of your mind, [24]and that you put on the
new man which was created according to
God, in true righteousness and holiness.

KEY PASSAGE

Change/ Maturity

A REAL PUT-ON

(4:22–24)

The Christian life is a process of change and growth toward maturity. God does not make us perfect the moment we accept Christ as Savior. Instead, He transforms our old selves. The "old man," the sin nature, is taken off like a dirty piece of clothing. In its place, we "put on the new man which was created according to God, in true righteousness and holiness." We wear that new man like a clean piece of clothing in all areas of our lives. At times, we may forget about the new clothing and allow sin to get us dirty, but we can go back to God for cleansing. At other times, that new clothing reminds us of our new identity in Christ and helps us make right choices.

We should be maturing in our Christian lives, finding that the new clothing is comfortable and that wearing it is second nature. We must never stop seeking to become more mature in Christ. That process lasts a lifetime.

To Learn More: Turn to the article about change/maturity on pages 1526, 1527. See also the personality profile of Paul on page 1432.

KEY PASSAGE

Anger

BEFORE THE SUN SETS

(4:26, 27)

The Bible doesn't say, "Never get angry." It *does* say, however, "Be angry, and do not sin." Anger is a God-given, powerful emotion. Handled well, anger can cause positive change. Anger handled poorly, however, can cause great harm.

So what should believers do with their angry feelings? They should not indulge that anger, because that could cause them to speak or act in ways that they would later regret. Nor should anger be stuffed deep inside with people pretending they never feel angry. That can cause a host of personal and relational problems. Stuffed anger will eventually cause a "system overload" whereby years of resentment erupt when a small spark sets it ablaze. The healthy way to handle anger is to deal with it as quickly as possible—before the sun goes down—so that we do not nurse the anger and thus "give place to the devil." Satan loves to use angry feelings to divide believers. We should seek to resolve our differences with others quickly. Then we can get on with the Lord's work.

To Learn More: Turn to the article about anger on pages 692, 693. See also the personality profile of Cain on page 11.

Do Not Grieve the Spirit

[25]Therefore, putting away lying, *"Let each
one of you speak truth with his neighbor,"*[a]
for we are members of one another. [26]*"Be angry, and do not sin"*:[a] do not let the sun go
down on your wrath, [27]nor give place to the
devil. [28]Let him who stole steal no longer, but
rather let him labor, working with *his* hands
what is good, that he may have something to
give him who has need. [29]Let no corrupt word
proceed out of your mouth, but what is good
for necessary edification, that it may impart
grace to the hearers. [30]And do not grieve the
Holy Spirit of God, by whom you were sealed
for the day of redemption. [31]Let all bitterness,
wrath, anger, clamor, and evil speaking be
put away from you, with all malice. [32]And be
kind to one another, tenderhearted, forgiving
one another, even as God in Christ forgave
you.

Walk in Love

5 Therefore be imitators of God as dear children. [2]And walk in love, as Christ also has
loved us and given Himself for us, an offering
and a sacrifice to God for a sweet-smelling
aroma.

[3]But fornication and all uncleanness or covetousness, let it not even be named among
you, as is fitting for saints; [4]neither filthiness,
nor foolish talking, nor coarse jesting, which
are not fitting, but rather giving of thanks.

4:25 [a]Zechariah 8:16 **4:26** [a]Psalm 4:4

SOUL NOTE

Saying Grace *(4:29)* Words are powerful. They can wound or heal. Spoken in love or in anger, words often are remembered by the hearer for many years. A believer's words must be carefully chosen and considered in light of one's relationship with Christ. New life in Christ not only affects where a person will spend eternity, how that person lives, or their self-esteem, but it should also profoundly affect their words. We should never speak with "corrupt words"—such as coarse language, gossip, or slander. Instead, our words should "impart grace" to our listeners. What do our words say about our faith? **Topic: Communication**

KEY PASSAGE

Presence of the Holy Spirit

A VERY REAL PRESENCE

(4:30)

When we accept Christ as Savior, we receive the Holy Spirit (Acts 2:38). Jesus had promised this Spirit to His followers (John 14:15–18). The Holy Spirit marks God's people as His own (Eph. 1:13); we are "sealed for the day of redemption" (Eph. 4:30).

Although the Holy Spirit enters our lives to help us live for God, He does not turn us into robots. We constantly battle the sin nature, and at times we fail. When we willfully continue in sin, however, we "grieve" the Holy Spirit.

Having the Holy Spirit with us and in us is a great privilege, but it brings great responsibility. We do not want to grieve Him, so we must be responsible enough to be sensitive to what He tells us. We try to follow His guidance because He has given us a great privilege, sealing us to be with God forever. Far from being an excuse for sin, that privilege gives us high motivation to live for God.

To Learn More: Turn to the article about the presence of the Holy Spirit on pages 1400, 1401. See also the personality profile of the Holy Spirit on page 1416.

5For this you know,[a] that no fornicator, unclean person, nor covetous man, who is an
idolater, has any inheritance in the kingdom
of Christ and God. 6Let no one deceive you
with empty words, for because of these things
the wrath of God comes upon the sons of disobedience. 7Therefore do not be partakers
with them.

Walk in Light

8For you were once darkness, but now *you
are* light in the Lord. Walk as children of light
9(for the fruit of the Spirit[a] *is* in all goodness,
righteousness, and truth), 10finding out what
is acceptable to the Lord. 11And have no fellowship with the unfruitful works of darkness,
but rather expose *them.* 12For it is shameful
even to speak of those things which are done
by them in secret. 13But all things that are exposed are made manifest by the light, for
whatever makes manifest is light. 14Therefore
He says:

"Awake, you who sleep,
Arise from the dead,
And Christ will give you light."

5:5 [a]NU-Text reads *For know this.* **5:9** [a]NU-Text reads *light.*

KEY PASSAGE

Relation-ships

KIND, TENDER, FORGIVING

(4:31, 32)

As God's people, we must put out of our lives bitterness, wrath, anger, clamor, evil speech, and malice. Then we should replace those attitudes and actions with positive ones:

- *Being kind to one another.* We should act charitably and benevolently to all people, regardless of how we are treated in return. That means taking the initiative in being kind.
- *Being tenderhearted.* This means having compassion. We should show genuine sensitivity, allowing for others' faults and failings while still showing care and concern.
- *Being forgiving . . . even as God in Christ forgave us.* This is probably the most difficult. If our relationships are going to flourish, we need to be able to forgive others. Christ forgave all our sins and continues to forgive us daily. We can forgive because we are forgiven.

Consider how our relationships would change if we lived by these words!

To Learn More: Turn to the article about relationships on pages 856, 857. See also the personality profile of David and Jonathan on page 372.

SOUL NOTE

What a Waste *(5:18)* Drunkenness has no place in believers' lives. To become "drunk with wine," or any alcoholic drink, reveals a lack of self-control. Getting drunk, wrote Paul, is "dissipation," referring to the waste of time and money caused by partying and an out-of-control lifestyle. The waste of God-given talents and resources, the consequences of drunkenness, and addiction to alcohol should keep people from substance abuse. The underlying issue, of course, is who or what is in charge of a person's life. Believers should be able to say that God is in charge and then trust Him to help them overcome such behaviors. **Topic: Drug Abuse**

Walk in Wisdom

[15]See then that you walk circumspectly, not as fools but as wise, [16]redeeming the time, because the days are evil.

[17]Therefore do not be unwise, but understand what the will of the Lord *is.* [18]And do not be drunk with wine, in which is dissipation; but be filled with the Spirit, [19]speaking to one another in psalms and hymns and spiritual songs, singing and making melody in your heart to the Lord, [20]giving thanks always for all things to God the Father in the name of our Lord Jesus Christ, [21]submitting to one another in the fear of God.[a]

Marriage—Christ and the Church

[22]Wives, submit to your own husbands, as to the Lord. [23]For the husband is head of the wife, as also Christ is head of the church; and He is the Savior of the body. [24]Therefore, just as the church is subject to Christ, so *let* the wives *be* to their own husbands in everything.

[25]Husbands, love your wives, just as Christ also loved the church and gave Himself for her, [26]that He might sanctify and cleanse her with the washing of water by the word, [27]that He might present her to Himself a glorious church, not having spot or wrinkle or any such thing, but that she should be holy and without blemish. [28]So husbands ought to love their own wives as their own bodies; he who loves his wife loves himself. [29]For no one ever hated his own flesh, but nourishes and cherishes it, just as the Lord *does* the church. [30]For we are members of His body,[a] of His flesh and of His bones. [31]*"For this reason a man shall leave his father and mother and be joined to his wife, and the two shall become one flesh."*[a] [32]This is a great mystery, but I speak concerning Christ and the church. [33]Nevertheless let each one of you in particular so love his own wife as himself, and let the wife *see* that she respects *her* husband.

Children and Parents

6 Children, obey your parents in the Lord, for this is right. [2]*"Honor your father and mother,"* which is the first commandment with promise: [3]*"that it may be well with you and you may live long on the earth."*[a]

5:21 [a]NU-Text reads *Christ.* **5:30** [a]NU-Text omits the rest of this verse. **5:31** [a]Genesis 2:24 **6:3** [a]Deuteronomy 5:16

SOUL NOTE

The Feeling Is Mutual *(5:21–26)* The Bible teaches mutual submission in marriage. Wives should submit to their husband's leadership because that provides stability in the home. Husbands, however, should love their wives as Christ loved the church, meaning they would give up anything for the good of their wives. When husbands love this way, their wives will have no fear of submitting to them. When both spouses act in each other's best interest and live to please Christ, they will build a solid marriage and family. **Topic: Marriage**

SOUL NOTE

Bringing Them Up *(6:1–4)* Parents and children constitute a family—happy and content when there is respect and obedience, unhappy and resentful when there is anger and rebellion. Paul advised fathers (as the heads of the household) and children each to do their part in building a healthy family life. Children must obey their parents, understanding that rules are in place for their own good. Fathers, on the other hand, should make the rules carefully, not to provoke their children, but to "bring them up in the training and admonition of the Lord." Parents and children all have responsibilities in a family. **Topic: Family Life**

[4]And you, fathers, do not provoke your children to wrath, but bring them up in the training and admonition of the Lord.

Bondservants and Masters

[5]Bondservants, be obedient to those who
are your masters according to the flesh, with
fear and trembling, in sincerity of heart, as to
Christ; [6]not with eyeservice, as men-pleasers,
but as bondservants of Christ, doing the will
of God from the heart, [7]with goodwill doing
service, as to the Lord, and not to men,
[8]knowing that whatever good anyone does, he
will receive the same from the Lord, whether
he is a slave or free.
[9]And you, masters, do the same things to

KEY PASSAGE

Fatherhood

DEAR OLD DAD

(6:4)

Paul here addressed just fathers, but obviously, mothers can use this same advice. Fathers are responsible for their children, to "bring them up in the training and admonition of the Lord." All fathers should be working toward the goal of raising God-honoring children. Because all fathers are different, with varying backgrounds, personalities, and ideas, they will do this in many different ways. Yet they ought to be careful in their training and discipline not to provoke their children "to wrath." In other words, sometimes a father's discipline can be overly harsh, unfair, unloving, or irresponsible, causing children to become angered, discouraged, and resentful. A father who disciplines fairly, consistently, and lovingly is raising his children well. Dads also have the huge responsibility of modeling to their children what their heavenly Father is like. What an incredible opportunity and responsibility!

To Learn More: Turn to the article about fatherhood on pages 516, 517. See also the personality profile of the prodigal son's father on page 1348.

KEY PASSAGE

Spiritual Warfare

THE WINNING TEAM

(6:10–20)

The spiritual realm has two sides—God's side and Satan's side. Those who have accepted Christ as Savior are on God's side; that automatically makes them enemies of Satan. This passage says that our battle is against "the rulers of the darkness of this age, against spiritual hosts of wickedness in the heavenly places." These forces are real and powerful and should not be underestimated. Their goal is to make believers ineffective for God's kingdom and to keep unbelievers away from God.

The battle rages constantly, usually beyond our earthly vision. At times, however, we see it clearly when we face temptation, difficulty, and trials. Evil knows our weaknesses; Satan knows where to attack. Our strength for the battle is in God. We need to "suit up" with God's armor so that we can be ready when Satan attacks. Wearing God's armor, we fight our daily battles, trusting God to fight with us through His Holy Spirit. The war has already been won, and we are on the winning side!

To Learn More: Turn to the article about spiritual warfare on pages 1560, 1561. See also the personality profile of Michael the archangel on page 1708.

them, giving up threatening, knowing that
your own Master also[a] is in heaven, and there
is no partiality with Him.

THE WHOLE ARMOR OF GOD

[10]Finally, my brethren, be strong in the Lord
and in the power of His might. [11]Put on the
whole armor of God, that you may be able to stand against the wiles
of the devil. [12]For we do not wrestle against flesh
and blood, but against principalities, against powers, against the rulers of the darkness of this
age,[a] against spiritual *hosts* of wickedness in
the heavenly *places.* [13]Therefore take up the
whole armor of God, that you may be able to
withstand in the evil day, and having done all,
to stand.

[14]Stand therefore, having girded your waist
with truth, having put on the breastplate of
righteousness, [15]and having shod your feet
with the preparation of the gospel of peace;
[16]above all, taking the shield of faith with
which you will be able to quench all the fiery
darts of the wicked one. [17]And take the helmet
of salvation, and the sword of the Spirit,
which is the word of God; [18]praying always
with all prayer and supplication in the Spirit,
being watchful to this end with all perseverance and supplication for all the saints—[19]and
for me, that utterance may be given to me,
that I may open my mouth boldly to make
known the mystery of the gospel, [20]for which I
am an ambassador in chains; that in it I may speak boldly, as I ought
to speak.

> Finally, my brethren, be strong in the Lord and in the power of His might.
> EPHESIANS 6:10

A GRACIOUS GREETING

[21]But that you also
may know my affairs *and* how I am doing,
Tychicus, a beloved brother and faithful minister in the Lord, will make all things known
to you; [22]whom I have sent to you for this very
purpose, that you may know our affairs, and
that he may comfort your hearts.

[23]Peace to the brethren, and love with faith,
from God the Father and the Lord Jesus Christ.
[24]Grace *be* with all those who love our Lord
Jesus Christ in sincerity. Amen.

6:9 [a]NU-Text reads *He who is both their Master and yours.* **6:12** [a]NU-Text reads *rulers of this darkness.*

KEY PASSAGE

Occult

DANGEROUS LIAISONS

(6:10–20)

Satan is God's avowed enemy, seeking to subvert and corrupt every part of God's creation. From the beauty of the earth to the love between people, every good thing is Satan's target. His realm is powerful, but he is not more powerful than God.

The occult is aligned with Satan. Mysterious powers and forces work in the occult, attempting to convince many people. Those involved in the occult may practice various forms of satanic worship; others attempt to tell the future or cast spells; still others seek to contact dead people and communicate with their spirits. Satan is quite real, and occult powers can be very real, too. Believers must not let a desire to know the future or understand the past lead them into any form of involvement in the occult. Yet even people who have been involved in occult practices can be forgiven by God. His power is infinitely greater than Satan's.

To Learn More: Turn to the article about the occult on pages 382, 383. See also the personality profile of the witch of En Dor on page 381.

Spiritual Warfare

SPIRITUAL WARFARE

DAVID POWLISON

(Ephesians 6:10–20)

The Bible makes it clear that all people choose either to follow the one and only God or to follow Satan. To refuse to love God automatically places someone in Satan's camp. But God has chosen to attack and plunder Satan's kingdom in order to deliver us. He captures people for Himself through the powerful love of Jesus (Col. 1:13). God is on the offensive in spiritual warfare, and we join His fight.

But the enemy fights back, so believers must be alert and courageous. The outcome is certain—light will defeat darkness—but the battle still rages. The Bible repeatedly calls believers to stand up to Satan: "Stand against the wiles of the devil" (Eph. 6:11); "resist the devil" (James 4:7). God promises that the devil will flee, will be crushed underfoot, and that we will stand victorious. The Bible teaches in detail how to fight against Satan with truth, faith, repentance, prayer, love, and obedience in the power of the Spirit.

Unfortunately, some in the church have come to think that involvement in spiritual warfare is mainly about the problem of being possessed by demons. The Bible makes clear, however, that *all believers* face spiritual warfare. The Bible never mentions exorcism of demons in the context of fighting the deepest spiritual battle.

Ephesians 6:10–20 offers specific instruction about how to fight spiritual warfare.

WEARING THE ARMOR

The armor *is* the Lord, who Himself invades the world of darkness and evil. The Old Testament provides pictures of each of the different weapons of war that God-in-Christ wears: the belt of faithfulness (Is. 11:5), the breastplate of righteousness and helmet of salvation (Is. 59:17), the feet bringing good news (Is. 52:7), the sword of the Word (Is. 49:2). The Lord is also the shield behind which faith takes refuge (Ps. 18:2). So God is the attacker and invader in spiritual warfare. He first wears His own weapons.

We put on God and His power. We put on this armor of light, the Lord Jesus Christ (Rom. 13:12, 14). The entire Book of Ephesians demonstrates how Paul as a man in Christ invades the world of darkness with the light of the message of Jesus. He calls believers to put on the same armor for the ongoing spiritual warfare that we all face. He does not speak of "demon deliverance."

FIGHTING THE REAL BATTLE

"Demon deliverance" in the sphere of counseling, evangelism, and sanctification is a fairly recent phenomenon. This "deliverance" focus believes that spiritual warfare involves grappling with resident demons that hold people in bondage to patterns of sin. Becoming indwelt by demons is believed to occur as an inheritance from evil ancestors, from persisting in sin, from being sinned against, or through owning evil objects. Freedom (deliverance) is thought to come from casting the demons out. Scripture consistently undermines this view, however. Demon deliverance is not a biblical understanding of spiritual warfare for five main reasons.

First, it grants too much freedom and initiative to Satan, and portrays our warfare as largely on the defensive. Satan's malicious activities operate under God's sovereign control and purposes. For example, Satan's affliction of Job and the evil spirit's torment of Saul occurred only with God's permission. The devil's malice toward God and His people was a tool of God's greater purposes: to humiliate Satan, to grow Job's faith, to destroy Saul.

Second, the exorcisms Jesus performed never intended to address moral bondage and confusion. The driving out of demons is not even about spiritual warfare, *per se*. The struggles of spiritual warfare—sins, unbelief, idolatry, confusion, and moral struggles—are never cast out. Those from whom Jesus drove demons primarily had symptoms of physical suffering. Jesus' approach to afflicting spirits lacked the hysteria and animistic worldview embodied in contemporary "demon deliverance."

Third, when Jesus and the apostles dealt with sin, occult practices, temptation, and moral bondage, they always spoke and fought in the Ephesians 6 manner—using relevant truth, living faith, repentance, and pointed prayer. Satan's attempts to rule people's lives through falsehood, deceit, intimidation, and temptation are never "cast out." Both in the wilderness and in the Garden of Gethsemane, Jesus displayed true spiritual warfare by holding onto truth.

Fourth, people who come out of an occult background would seem to be a strong argument for some type of deliverance. The Bible, however, frequently talks about such people and never portrays exorcism as the solution to their problems. Simon the sorcerer is a prime example (Acts 8). When he showed patterns of power lust, Peter used moral bondage language and not demonic bondage language. Exorcism did not appear to be Peter's concern in addressing Simon's condition.

Finally, the devil works on the inside, appealing to and ruling people's hearts. Exactly how he does this is a mystery; that he does this is a given. The human heart is by nature "full of evil" (Eccl. 9:3), so it is no surprise to find an intimate congruence between humans and the evil one. God's method for helping such people is amazingly normal and straightforward: repentance of sinful tendencies so that they can be cleansed and renewed.

Spiritual warfare is part of every Christian's daily life. We triumph as we walk by faith in Christ, who turns us from darkness to light, from the power of Satan to God, forgiving sin, and giving us a place among those who are sanctified by faith (Acts 26:18).

FURTHER MEDITATION:

Other passages to study about the issue of spiritual warfare include:

- Matthew 4:1–11
- Ephesians 2:2
- James 4:7–10
- 1 John 4:1–6
- 2 John 7–11

To Learn More: **Turn to the key passage note about spiritual warfare at Ephesians 6:10–20 on page 1558. See also the personality profile of Michael the archangel on page 1708.**

Philippians

How would you describe your life these days? Is it anxious, joyful, weary, bitter, busy, or distracted? Few of us would say we were joyful.

Modern life is filled with "joy robbers." We spend too much time working to get ahead, battling traffic, and struggling with schedules. All too often, we lose the joy of life that God intended for us.

The apostle Paul wrote the New Testament letter to the church at Philippi while he was a prisoner in Rome awaiting trial (1:7). Despite his dire circumstances, Paul's tone is unabashedly joyful. (The word "joy" and its derivatives occur sixteen times in four short chapters!) His experience reminds us that joy comes from God and transcends mere happiness. Joy survives our trials and is the perfect antidote to fear and anxiety (4:4–6).

What was Paul's secret? Maybe it was his discovery of the truth that Christ is the be-all and end-all of life (1:20). For him, to live was Christ and to die was gain (1:21). Perhaps it was his embracing of the "mind of Christ"—a mindset of utter humility, a determination to serve no matter what, and a commitment to true unity among believers. Whatever the case, Paul was able to face (and have victory over) tough challenges because he was radically committed to a Christ-centered life.

Is your soul joyful today? Read Philippians and rejoice in what Christ has done for you!

SOUL CONCERN IN PHILIPPIANS

Greeting

1 Paul and Timothy, bondservants of Jesus Christ,

To all the saints in Christ Jesus who are in Philippi, with the bishops[a] and deacons:

[2]Grace to you and peace from God our Father and the Lord Jesus Christ.

Thankfulness and Prayer

[3]I thank my God upon every remembrance of you, [4]always in every prayer of mine making request for you all with joy, [5]for your fellowship in the gospel from the first day until now, [6]being confident of this very thing, that He who has begun a good work in you will complete *it* until the day of Jesus Christ; [7]just as it is right for me to think this of you all, because I have you in my heart, inasmuch as both in my chains and in the defense and confirmation of the gospel, you all are partakers with me of grace. [8]For God is my witness, how greatly I long for you all with the affection of Jesus Christ.

[9]And this I pray, that your love may abound still more and more in knowledge and all discernment, [10]that you may approve the things that are excellent, that you may be sincere and without offense till the day of Christ, [11]being filled with the fruits of righteousness which *are* by Jesus Christ, to the glory and praise of God.

> And this I pray, that your love may abound still more and more in knowledge and all discernment, that you may approve the things that are excellent, that you may be sincere and without offense till the day of Christ.
>
> PHILIPPIANS 1:9, 10

Christ Is Preached

[12]But I want you to know, brethren, that the things *which happened* to me have actually turned out for the furtherance of the gospel, [13]so that it has become evident to the whole palace guard, and to all the rest, that my chains are in Christ; [14]and most of the brethren in the Lord, having become confident by my chains, are much more bold to speak the word without fear.

[15]Some indeed preach Christ even from envy and strife, and some also from goodwill: [16]The former[a] preach Christ from selfish ambition, not sincerely, supposing to add affliction to my chains; [17]but the latter out of love, knowing that I am appointed for the defense of the gospel. [18]What then? Only *that* in every way, whether in pretense or in truth, Christ is preached; and in this I rejoice, yes, and will rejoice.

To Live Is Christ

[19]For I know that this will turn out for my deliverance through your prayer and the supply of the Spirit of Jesus Christ, [20]according to my earnest expectation and hope that in nothing I shall be ashamed, but with all boldness, as always, so now also Christ will be magnified in my body, whether by life or by death. [21]For to me, to live *is* Christ, and to die *is* gain. [22]But if *I* live on in the flesh, this *will mean* fruit from *my* labor; yet what I shall choose I cannot tell. [23]For[a] I am hard-pressed between the two, having a desire to depart and be with Christ, *which is* far better. [24]Nevertheless to remain in

---

1:1 [a]Literally *overseers* **1:16** [a]NU-Text reverses the contents of verses 16 and 17. **1:23** [a]NU-Text and M-Text read *But.*

SOUL NOTE

His Handiwork *(1:6)* The process of Christian growth and maturity begins when we accept Jesus as Savior. As believers we still struggle with a sin nature, and we will fail at times. God helps us to grow and mature all through our lives. We won't be perfect until we are with Christ. In the meantime, when we feel discouraged or distressed by our failures, we just need to remember that God won't give up on us. He began His good work in us and will complete it when we meet Him face to face. **Topic: Failure**

the flesh *is* more needful for you. 25And being confident of this, I know that I shall remain and continue with you all for your progress and joy of faith, 26that your rejoicing for me may be more abundant in Jesus Christ by my coming to you again.

STRIVING AND SUFFERING FOR CHRIST

27Only let your conduct be worthy of the gospel of Christ, so that whether I come and see you or am absent, I may hear of your affairs, that you stand fast in one spirit, with one mind striving together for the faith of the gospel, 28and not in any way terrified by your adversaries, which is to them a proof of perdition, but to you of salvation,[a] and that from God. 29For to you it has been granted on behalf of Christ, not only to believe in Him, but also to suffer for His sake, 30having the same conflict which you saw in me and now hear *is* in me.

UNITY THROUGH HUMILITY

2 Therefore if *there is* any consolation in Christ, if any comfort of love, if any fellowship of the Spirit, if any affection and mercy, 2fulfill my joy by being like-minded, having the same love, *being* of one accord, of one mind. 3*Let* nothing *be done* through selfish ambition or conceit, but in lowliness of mind let each esteem others better than himself. 4Let each of you look out not only for his own interests, but also for the interests of others.

THE HUMBLED AND EXALTED CHRIST

5Let this mind be in you which was also in Christ Jesus, 6who, being in the form of God, did not consider it robbery to be equal with God, 7but made Himself of no reputation, taking the form of a bondservant, *and* coming in the likeness of men. 8And being found in appearance as a man, He humbled Himself and became obedient to *the point of* death, even the death of the cross. 9Therefore God also has highly exalted Him and given Him the name which is above every name, 10that at the name of Jesus every knee should bow, of those in heaven, and of those on earth, and of those under the earth, 11and *that* every tongue should confess that Jesus Christ *is* Lord, to the glory of God the Father.

1:28 [a]NU-Text reads *of your salvation.*

SOUL NOTE

Pride Problems *(2:1–4)* Paul stresses spiritual unity in the body of Christ. Selfish ambition and conceit bring discord, which draws people's focus away from Christ and toward themselves and their desires. Genuine humility, however, builds and strengthens the body of believers. Being humble involves having a true perspective about ourselves (Rom. 12:3), "lowliness of mind," and looking out for the interests of others. Believers must lay aside any pride or selfishness, always treating people with respect. In that way, we will be following the example of Christ, who selflessly gave His life for us (2:8). **Topic: Pride**

SOUL NOTE

A Hearty Welcome *(2:2–4)* Philippi was a cosmopolitan city whose church reflected great diversity of backgrounds and social status. With so many lifestyles and attitudes represented, unity must have been difficult to maintain. Paul encouraged the believers to guard against any selfishness, prejudice, or jealousy that might lead to division. This holds true as the church continues to reach out to all walks of life. We must remember not to prejudge, but rather, to welcome new believers with open minds and genuine interest, taking positive steps toward building unity in Christ. **Topic: Attitudes**

Light Bearers

12Therefore, my beloved, as you have always obeyed, not as in my presence only, but now much more in my absence, work out your own salvation with fear and trembling; 13for it is God who works in you both to will and to do for *His* good pleasure.

14Do all things without complaining and disputing, 15that you may become blameless and harmless, children of God without fault in the midst of a crooked and perverse generation, among whom you shine as lights in the world, 16holding fast the word of life, so that I may rejoice in the day of Christ that I have not run in vain or labored in vain.

17Yes, and if I am being poured out *as a drink offering* on the sacrifice and service of your faith, I am glad and rejoice with you all. 18For the same reason you also be glad and rejoice with me.

Timothy Commended

19But I trust in the Lord Jesus to send Timothy to you shortly, that I also may be encouraged when I know your state. 20For I have no one like-minded, who will sincerely care for your state. 21For all seek their own, not the things which are of Christ Jesus. 22But you know his proven character, that as a son with *his* father he served with me in the gospel. 23Therefore I hope to send him at once, as soon as I see how it goes with me. 24But I trust in the Lord that I myself shall also come shortly.

Epaphroditus Praised

25Yet I considered it necessary to send to you Epaphroditus, my brother, fellow worker, and fellow soldier, but your messenger and the one who ministered to my need; 26since he was longing for you all, and was distressed because you had heard that he was sick. 27For indeed he was sick almost unto death; but God had mercy on him, and not only on him but on me also, lest I should have sorrow upon sorrow. 28Therefore I sent him the more eagerly, that when you see him again you may rejoice, and I may be less sorrowful. 29Receive him therefore in the Lord with all gladness, and hold such men in esteem; 30because for the work of Christ he came close to death, not regarding his life, to supply what was lacking in your service toward me.

All for Christ

3 Finally, my brethren, rejoice in the Lord. For me to write the same things to you *is* not tedious, but for you *it is* safe.

2Beware of dogs, beware of evil workers, beware of the mutilation! 3For we are the circumcision, who worship God in the Spirit,[a] rejoice in Christ Jesus, and have no confidence in the flesh, 4though I also might have confidence in the flesh. If anyone else thinks he may have confidence in the flesh, I more so: 5circumcised the eighth day, of the stock of Israel, *of* the tribe of Benjamin, a Hebrew of the Hebrews; concerning the law, a Pharisee; 6concerning zeal, persecuting the church; concerning the righteousness which is in the law, blameless.

7But what things were gain to me, these I have counted loss for Christ. 8Yet indeed I also count all things loss for the excellence of the knowledge of Christ Jesus my Lord, for whom I have suffered the loss of all things, and count them as rubbish, that I may gain Christ 9and be found in Him, not having my own righteousness, which *is* from the law, but that which *is* through faith in Christ, the righteous-

3:3 [a]NU-Text and M-Text read *who worship in the Spirit of God.*

SOUL NOTE

Works Don't Work *(3:5, 6)* Paul seems to be boasting of his achievements, but actually he was explaining that his human accomplishments, no matter how impressive or extensive, could not earn salvation and eternal life with God. Paul didn't depend on his works to please God, because even the most impressive resumé falls short of God's standards. We can't rely on our good works to usher us into eternity—it's so much easier than that! All we need to do is confess our sins and believe in Jesus as our personal Savior. God isn't impressed by what we've done—He's impressed by our acceptance of His grace. **Topic: Work**

ness which is from God by faith; [10]that I may know Him and the power of His resurrection, and the fellowship of His sufferings, being conformed to His death, [11]if, by any means, I may attain to the resurrection from the dead.

Pressing Toward the Goal

[12]Not that I have already attained, or am already perfected; but I press on, that I may lay hold of that for which Christ Jesus has also laid hold of me. [13]Brethren, I do not count myself to have apprehended; but one thing *I do,* forgetting those things which are behind and reaching forward to those things which are ahead, [14]I press toward the goal for the prize of the upward call of God in Christ Jesus.

[15]Therefore let us, as many as are mature, have this mind; and if in anything you think otherwise, God will reveal even this to you. [16]Nevertheless, to *the degree* that we have already attained, let us walk by the same rule,[a] let us be of the same mind.

Our Citizenship in Heaven

[17]Brethren, join in following my example, and note those who so walk, as you have us for a pattern. [18]For many walk, of whom I have told you often, and now tell you even weeping, *that they are* the enemies of the cross of Christ: [19]whose end *is* destruction, whose god *is their* belly, and *whose* glory *is* in their shame—who set their mind on earthly things. [20]For our citizenship is in heaven, from which we also eagerly wait for the Savior, the Lord Jesus Christ, [21]who will transform our lowly body that it may be conformed to His glorious body, according to the working by which He is able even to subdue all things to Himself.

4 Therefore, my beloved and longed-for brethren, my joy and crown, so stand fast in the Lord, beloved.

Be United, Joyful, and in Prayer

[2]I implore Euodia and I implore Syntyche to be of the same mind in the Lord. [3]And[a] I urge you also, true companion, help these women who labored with me in the gospel, with Clement also, and the rest of my fellow workers, whose names *are* in the Book of Life.

[4]Rejoice in the Lord always. Again I will say, rejoice!

[5]Let your gentleness be known to all men. The Lord *is* at hand.

[6]Be anxious for nothing, but in everything by prayer and supplication, with thanksgiving, let your requests be made known to God; [7]and the peace of God, which surpasses all understanding, will guard your hearts and minds through Christ Jesus.

> Be anxious for nothing, but in everything by prayer and supplication, with thanksgiving, let your requests be made known to God; and the peace of God, which surpasses all understanding, will guard your hearts and minds through Christ Jesus.
>
> PHILIPPIANS 4:6, 7

Meditate on These Things

[8]Finally, brethren, whatever things are true, whatever things *are* noble, whatever things *are* just, whatever things *are* pure, whatever things *are* lovely, whatever things *are* of good report, if *there is* any virtue and if *there is* anything praiseworthy—meditate on these things. [9]The things which you learned and received and heard and saw in me, these do, and the God of peace will be with you.

3:16 [a]NU-Text omits *rule* and the rest of the verse.
4:3 [a]NU-Text and M-Text read *Yes.*

SOUL NOTE

Forget It *(3:12–16)* Believers must constantly seek the goal of maturity in Christ. Even Paul knew that he had not attained that goal, so he pressed on to grow in Christ. A key to that growth is "forgetting those things which are behind and reaching forward to those things which are ahead." Past sins have been covered and need not hinder us, and past worldly accomplishments mean nothing. We are "heavenly citizens in training." All that matters is walking with Christ through life, allowing Him to prepare us for His kingdom. **Topic: Change/Maturity**

PHILIPPIAN GENEROSITY

10But I rejoiced in the Lord greatly that now
at last your care for me has flourished again;
though you surely did care, but you lacked opportunity. 11Not that I speak in regard to need,
for I have learned in whatever state I am, to be
content: 12I know how to be abased, and I
know how to abound. Everywhere and in all
things I have learned both to be full and to be
hungry, both to abound and to suffer need.
13I can do all things through Christ[a] who
strengthens me.

14Nevertheless you have done well that you
shared in my distress. 15Now you Philippians
know also that in the beginning of the gospel,
when I departed from Macedonia, no church
shared with me concerning giving and receiving but you only. 16For even in Thessalonica
you sent *aid* once and again for my necessities. 17Not that I seek the gift, but I seek the
fruit that abounds to your account. 18Indeed I
have all and abound. I am full, having received from Epaphroditus the things *sent* from
you, a sweet-smelling aroma, an acceptable
sacrifice, well pleasing to God. 19And my God
shall supply all your need according to His
riches in glory by Christ Jesus. 20Now to our
God and Father *be* glory forever and ever.
Amen.

GREETING AND BLESSING

21Greet every saint in Christ Jesus. The
brethren who are with me greet you. 22All the
saints greet you, but especially those who are
of Caesar's household.

23The grace of our Lord Jesus Christ be with
you all.[a] Amen.

4:13 [a]NU-Text reads *Him who.* **4:23** [a]NU-Text reads *your spirit.*

KEY PASSAGE

Anxiety

ANXIOUS FOR NOTHING

(4:6–13)

Paul certainly had plenty of reason to feel anxious. Sitting in a Roman prison, he didn't know if he would be released or put to death. Writing to the believers in Philippi, however, he urged them, "Be anxious for nothing."

Anxiety and its companion, worry, do their best to immobilize believers. People are anxious about the future; they are anxious about events that haven't happened but *could* happen. Anxiety causes physical problems. Anxiety makes people fearful and distressed.

So what can believers do about their anxiety? Paul gives the answer, "In everything by prayer and supplication with thanksgiving, let your requests be made known to God." When we give our anxiety to God, He replaces it with His peace that "surpasses all understanding." God's peace is beyond comprehension because it makes no sense—the circumstances seem to require anxiety, but instead we feel God's peace. When we feel anxiety rising, we should turn to God in prayer. He will give us the peace He promised.

To Learn More: Turn to the article about anxiety on pages 1568, 1569. See also the personality profile of David on page 713.

UNDERSTANDING ANXIETY

ARCHIBALD D. HART

(Philippians 4)

Anxiety disorders are the most common emotional struggles of today, affecting some 20 to 30 million people. Why such a dramatic rise in the incidence of anxiety disorders? In a nutshell, many people live too disconnected, carry too much debt, and live at too fast a pace. People were designed to travel at a camel's pace, but they behave like supersonic jets, running constantly on a supercharged stream of adrenaline. They end up paying for this abuse with worry and anxiety.

FEAR, WORRY, AND ANXIETY

Fear

Fear is a natural and necessary alarm system that is triggered whenever we feel threatened. This God-given emotion ignites a response to a real or perceived danger, such as running into a spider web. The fear response imagines the spider biting, so the body is put on alert. The experience of the fear is very real. God has created us to feel fear, and, provided the fear is justified, it is perfectly normal and can lead to protective behavior.

People also feel fear over imagined possible outcomes. Though the list is potentially endless, some common fears include: losing a child, spouse, job, or health, being shamed or humiliated in public, being rejected, failing (or succeeding), dying or dying painfully. Others face phobic fears—of heights, tight places, the dark, etc.

Worry

Worry is not an emotion but a mental activity that produces anxiety. This *stinking thinking* is an unhealthy and unreasonable exercise that attempts to solve situations beyond our control. Instead of praying or simply letting go of things that cannot be controlled, worriers obsess about controlling the problem, talking to themselves about how terrible it is, and imagining all sorts of horrible results if the problem is not solved immediately. Over enough time, people even begin to believe that if they worry hard enough, their worry will somehow solve the problem.

Anxiety

Anxiety keeps a person from relaxing, from resting. It is a pervasive, long-term inner feeling of nervousness, unrest, and uneasiness. Anxiety's symptoms can include: tense feelings, rapid heart beat, dry mouth, increased blood pressure, jumpiness or feeling faint, excessive perspiring, feeling clammy, and anticipation of trouble.

Anxiety Disorders

Everyone experiences some anxiety. But frequent and intense anxiety may indicate a clinically diagnosable and treatable disorder. An anxiety disorder can be a sudden and unexplained uneasiness that lasts a few hours, or it can be a constant state. Simply wishing the symptoms away will not work. Some forms of troubling anxiety include:

Generalized Anxiety. A pervasive form of chronic tension that manifests itself in many different situations. When it exists longer than six months, it is diagnosable as an anxiety disorder.

Phobia. Fear strongly associated with a single object, place, or event.

Obsessive-Compulsive Disorder. OCD is fear hidden behind a variety of obsessions and compulsions, such as highly ritualized/ repetitive behavior (like constant hand-washing). These maladaptive patterns are attempts to manage anxious thoughts and feelings.

Post-Traumatic Stress Disorder. As a result of being victimized or even witnessing a traumatic event, recurring visions, dreams, and memories of the trauma induce fear and are relived in debilitating ways. First recognized in prisoners of war, PTSD is now seen as a common experience across a whole range of traumatic life experiences—physical and sexual abuse, natural disasters, injurious accidents, etc.

Panic Attack. The sudden onset of panic is an overwhelming state of anxiety—being flooded and paralyzed by the fight-or-flight response. Symptoms include racing heart, sweating, dizziness, ringing ears, choking, and vertigo. The physiological reaction to panic is so strong that the panic sufferer often imagines that he or she is having a heart attack or going crazy. Agoraphobia can set in—the fear of returning to the people and places where panic occurred. At its worst, the sufferer ends up house-bound, fearful of panic away from home, and excessively vigilant. More than three panic attacks in a month or the onset of agoraphobia indicate a disorder that needs professional treatment.

SCRIPTURE AND ANXIETY

Many Christians think that God condemns all anxiety, and, by implication, that He also condemns those who suffer with different forms of it. Certainly Scripture condemns a particular form of anxiety. Jesus said, "Let not your heart be troubled" (John 14:1), referring to a form of anxiety that has been with us for all time: *worry*.

Jesus' familiar expression, "Take no thought for your life," refers to anxious worry. In the Sermon on the Mount, He calls attention to the destructiveness of anxiety about the future (Matt. 6:25–34). His teaching is startlingly clear—such worry is futile, pointless, and unable to help solve the problem. No worrisome thought about tomorrow can help people live better or keep evil away. Worry, then, is not an emotion but a pattern of thinking that takes hold when people try to live independent of God.

Unless fear, worry, and anxiety are honestly faced and worked through, people can end up in a pattern of avoidance—organizing their lives around people and situations that they must avoid. It is much healthier to practice another pattern:

- Turn to God first (1 Pet. 5:7).
- Focus on the solution, not the problem (Matt. 14:22, 23).
- Stop wasting energy on worrying (Matt. 6:25–34).
- Keep your thoughts on God in order to have peace (Is. 26:3).
- Pray (Phil. 4:4–9).
- Direct your attention toward your true source of hope (Ps. 91:2).

FURTHER MEDITATION:

Other passages to study about the issue of anxiety include:

- Deuteronomy 31:8
- Psalms 23; 103; 121; 146
- Isaiah 41:13; 44:2
- 2 Timothy 1:7
- Hebrews 13:5
- 1 Peter 5:7–11

To Learn More: Turn to the key passage note on anxiety at Philippians 4:6–13 on page 1567. See also the personality profile of David on page 713.

Colossians

Someone has observed that one rotten egg in a four-egg omelet still ruins the omelet. Something can be pure or impure, but there's no such thing as "mostly pure."

This principle is terribly important in the spiritual realm. Mix a few distorted, human notions with the pure and simple gospel of Christ and the result, no matter how good it may seem, is a long way from the truth. Such was the case in the first-century church at Colosse, a congregation started in A.D. 54–56, probably by Epaphras, an associate of the apostle Paul.

Paul wrote to the Colossians to combat the subtle error that conflicting truth claims can be blended into a God-honoring religious system. Some believers, while claiming to embrace the gospel, were adopting forms of Jewish legalism. Others were lapsing into immorality. The true gospel was being polluted with various worldly philosophies that compromised the integrity of the Christian message.

Rejecting the notion that the gospel is just one possible belief system among many, Paul's short letter presents Jesus Christ as the exalted Lord of the universe. Therefore it is only fitting that He should be preeminent in all of life—church, friendships, marriage, family life, and employer-employee relations.

In a day of moral and philosophical relativism, when many people believe "what's true for you may not be true for me," Colossians reminds us that being even a "little" off is a big deal!

SOUL CONCERN IN COLOSSIANS

Greeting

1 Paul, an apostle of Jesus Christ by the will of God, and Timothy our brother,

[2]To the saints and faithful brethren in Christ *who are* in Colosse:

Grace to you and peace from God our Father and the Lord Jesus Christ.[a]

Their Faith in Christ

[3]We give thanks to the God and Father of our Lord Jesus Christ, praying always for you, [4]since we heard of your faith in Christ Jesus and of your love for all the saints; [5]because of the hope which is laid up for you in heaven, of which you heard before in the word of the truth of the gospel, [6]which has come to you, as *it has* also in all the world, and is bringing forth fruit,[a] as *it is* also among you since the day you heard and knew the grace of God in truth; [7]as you also learned from Epaphras, our dear fellow servant, who is a faithful minister of Christ on your behalf, [8]who also declared to us your love in the Spirit.

Preeminence of Christ

[9]For this reason we also, since the day we heard it, do not cease to pray for you, and to ask that you may be filled with the knowledge of His will in all wisdom and spiritual understanding; [10]that you may walk worthy of the Lord, fully pleasing *Him,* being fruitful in every good work and increasing in the knowledge of God; [11]strengthened with all might, according to His glorious power, for all patience and longsuffering with joy; [12]giving thanks to the Father who has qualified us to be partakers of the inheritance of the saints in the light. [13]He has delivered us from the power of darkness and conveyed *us* into the kingdom of the Son of His love, [14]in whom we have redemption through His blood,[a] the forgiveness of sins.

[15]He is the image of the invisible God, the firstborn over all creation. [16]For by Him all things were created that are in heaven and that are on earth, visible and invisible, whether thrones or dominions or principalities or powers. All things were created through Him and for Him. [17]And He is before all things, and in Him all things consist. [18]And He is the head of the body, the church, who is the beginning, the firstborn from the dead, that in all things He may have the preeminence.

Reconciled in Christ

[19]For it pleased *the Father that* in Him all the fullness should dwell, [20]and by Him to reconcile all things to Himself, by Him, whether things on earth or things in heaven, having made peace through the blood of His cross.

[21]And you, who once were alienated and enemies in your mind by wicked works, yet now He has reconciled [22]in the body of His flesh through death, to present you holy, and blameless, and above reproach in His sight— [23]if indeed you continue in the faith, grounded and steadfast, and are not moved away from the hope of the gospel which you heard, which was preached to every creature under heaven, of which I, Paul, became a minister.

Sacrificial Service for Christ

[24]I now rejoice in my sufferings for you, and fill up in my flesh what is lacking in the afflictions of Christ, for the sake of His body, which is the church, [25]of which I became a minister according to the stewardship from God which was given to me for you, to fulfill the word of God, [26]the mystery which has been hidden from ages and from generations, but now has been revealed to His saints. [27]To them God

1:2 [a]NU-Text omits *and the Lord Jesus Christ.*
1:6 [a]NU-Text and M-Text add *and growing.*
1:14 [a]NU-Text and M-Text omit *through His blood.*

SOUL NOTE

Let's Pray *(1:9–12)* Believers can pray for spiritual growth for themselves and for others. Paul's prayer for the Colossian believers is a model of such a prayer. We can pray for wisdom and spiritual understanding in order to know God's will. And we can pray that we will live for God, being fruitful in His service. Then we can give thanks to God for making us "saints in the light." When we pray this way, we are praying for spiritual maturity. **Topic: Spiritual Growth**

willed to make known what are the riches of
the glory of this mystery among the Gentiles:
which[a] is Christ in you, the hope of glory.
28Him we preach, warning every man and
teaching every man in all wisdom, that we
may present every man perfect in Christ Jesus.
29To this *end* I also labor, striving according to
His working which works in me mightily.

NOT PHILOSOPHY BUT CHRIST

2 For I want you to know what a great conflict I have for you and those in Laodicea,
and *for* as many as have not seen my face in
the flesh, 2that their hearts may be encouraged, being knit together in love, and *attaining* to all riches of the full assurance of
understanding, to the knowledge of the mystery of God, both of the Father and[a] of Christ,
3in whom are hidden all the treasures of wisdom and knowledge.
4Now this I say lest anyone should deceive
you with persuasive words. 5For though I am
absent in the flesh, yet I am with you in spirit,
rejoicing to see your *good* order and the steadfastness of your faith in Christ.
6As you therefore have received Christ Jesus
the Lord, so walk in Him, 7rooted and built up
in Him and established in the faith, as you
have been taught, abounding in it[a] with
thanksgiving.
8Beware lest anyone cheat you through philosophy and empty deceit, according to the tradition of men, according to the basic principles
of the world, and not according to Christ. 9For
in Him dwells all the fullness of the Godhead
bodily; 10and you are complete in Him, who is
the head of all principality and power.

NOT LEGALISM BUT CHRIST

11In Him you were also circumcised with the
circumcision made without hands, by putting
off the body of the sins[a] of the flesh, by the
circumcision of Christ, 12buried with Him in
baptism, in which you also were raised with
Him through faith in the working of God, who
raised Him from the dead. 13And you, being
dead in your trespasses and the uncircumcision of your flesh, He has made alive together
with Him, having forgiven you all trespasses,
14having wiped out the handwriting of requirements that was against us, which was
contrary to us. And He has taken it out of the
way, having nailed it to the cross. 15Having
disarmed principalities and powers, He made
a public spectacle of them, triumphing over
them in it.
16So let no one judge you in food or in
drink, or regarding a festival or a new moon or
sabbaths, 17which are a shadow of things to
come, but the substance is of Christ. 18Let no
one cheat you of your reward, taking delight
in *false* humility and worship of angels, in-
truding into those things which he has not[a]
seen, vainly puffed up by his fleshly mind,
19and not holding fast to the Head, from
whom all the body, nourished and knit together by joints and ligaments, grows with the increase *that is* from God.
20Therefore,[a] if you died with Christ from
the basic principles of the world, why, as
though living in the world, do you subject
yourselves to regulations—21"Do not touch,
do not taste, do not handle," 22which all concern things which perish with the using—according to the commandments and doctrines
of men? 23These things indeed have an ap-

1:27 [a]M-Text reads *who.* **2:2** [a]NU-Text omits *both of the Father and.* **2:7** [a]NU-Text omits *in it.* **2:11** [a]NU-Text omits *of the sins.* **2:18** [a]NU-Text omits *not.* **2:20** [a]NU-Text and M-Text omit *Therefore.*

SOUL NOTE

Many Opinions, One Lord *(2:16)* Christ has set His people free from legalistic rules concerning things like food, drink, and worship style. Believers should not judge others by concluding that certain preferences exclude them from being Christians. Believers hold many different opinions about living out one's faith, but we must not criticize or condemn fellow Christians whose lifestyle choices differ from ours. As long as other believers are not violating Scripture—committing outright sin or teaching heresy—we need to accept them into the fellowship as members of God's family. We have one Savior and Lord. **Topic: Legalism**

pearance of wisdom in self-imposed religion, *false* humility, and neglect of the body, *but are* of no value against the indulgence of the flesh.

NOT CARNALITY BUT CHRIST

3 If then you were raised with Christ, seek those things which are above, where Christ is, sitting at the right hand of God. [2]Set your mind on things above, not on things on the earth. [3]For you died, and your life is hidden with Christ in God. [4]When Christ *who is* our life appears, then you also will appear with Him in glory.

> Set your mind on things above, not on things on the earth. For you died, and your life is hidden with Christ in God.
>
> COLOSSIANS 3:2, 3

[5]Therefore put to death your members which are on the earth: fornication, uncleanness, passion, evil desire, and covetousness, which is idolatry. [6]Because of these things the wrath of God is coming upon the sons of disobedience, [7]in which you yourselves once walked when you lived in them.

[8]But now you yourselves are to put off all these: anger, wrath, malice, blasphemy, filthy language out of your mouth. [9]Do not lie to one another, since you have put off the old man with his deeds, [10]and have put on the new *man* who is renewed in knowledge according to the image of Him who created him, [11]where there is neither Greek nor Jew, circumcised nor uncircumcised, barbarian, Scythian, slave *nor* free, but Christ *is* all and in all.

CHARACTER OF THE NEW MAN

[12]Therefore, as *the* elect of God, holy and beloved, put on tender mercies, kindness, humility, meekness, longsuffering; [13]bearing with one another, and forgiving one another, if anyone has a complaint against another; even as Christ forgave you, so you also *must do.* [14]But above all these things put on love, which is the bond of perfection. [15]And let the peace of God rule in your hearts, to which also you were called in one body; and be thankful. [16]Let the word of Christ dwell in you richly in all wisdom, teaching and admonishing one another in psalms and hymns and spiritual songs, singing with grace in your hearts to the Lord. [17]And *whatever* you do in word or deed, *do* all in the name of the Lord Jesus, giving thanks to God the Father through Him.

THE CHRISTIAN HOME

[18]Wives, submit to your own husbands, as is fitting in the Lord.

SOUL NOTE

Mindset *(3:2)* As believers we should set our minds (our focus and priorities) "on things above, not on things on the earth." This does not mean refusing to hold a job or care for one's family; instead, it means that believers have a different attitude in all that they do. Because we love God and want to live for Him, we center our lives on Christ. When we set our minds on things above, we begin to see life from God's perspective. So we work and serve to please Christ. **Topic: Attitudes**

SOUL NOTE

Overcomers *(3:5, 6)* Believing sets us free from legalism, but we still have to be careful to stay away from certain activities that are against God's will for us. These verses describe some of those sinful desires that believers should "put to death." Sexual sins, evil desires, and covetousness (a form of idolatry) should have no place in a believer's heart. It takes a conscious daily decision to say no to these sinful temptations and rely on the Holy Spirit's power to overcome them. **Topic: Addictions**

19 Husbands, love your wives and do not be bitter toward them.

20 Children, obey your parents in all things, for this is well pleasing to the Lord.

21 Fathers, do not provoke your children, lest they become discouraged.

22 Bondservants, obey in all things your masters according to the flesh, not with eyeservice, as men-pleasers, but in sincerity of heart, fearing God. 23 And whatever you do, do it heartily, as to the Lord and not to men, 24 knowing that from the Lord you will receive the reward of the inheritance; for[a] you serve the Lord Christ. 25 But he who does wrong will be repaid for what he has done, and there is no partiality.

4 Masters, give your bondservants what is just and fair, knowing that you also have a Master in heaven.

Christian Graces

2 Continue earnestly in prayer, being vigilant in it with thanksgiving; 3 meanwhile praying also for us, that God would open to us a door for the word, to speak the mystery of Christ, for which I am also in chains, 4 that I may make it manifest, as I ought to speak.

5 Walk in wisdom toward those *who are* outside, redeeming the time. 6 *Let* your speech always *be* with grace, seasoned with salt, that you may know how you ought to answer each one.

Final Greetings

7 Tychicus, a beloved brother, faithful minister, and fellow servant in the Lord, will tell you all the news about me. 8 I am sending him to you for this very purpose, that he[a] may know your circumstances and comfort your hearts, 9 with Onesimus, a faithful and beloved brother, who is *one* of you. They will make known to you all things which *are happening* here.

10 Aristarchus my fellow prisoner greets you, with Mark the cousin of Barnabas (about whom you received instructions: if he comes to you, welcome him), 11 and Jesus who is called Justus. These *are my* only fellow workers for the kingdom of God who are of the circumcision; they have proved to be a comfort to me.

12 Epaphras, who is *one* of you, a bondservant of Christ, greets you, always laboring fervently for you in prayers, that you may stand perfect and complete[a] in all the will of

3:24 [a]NU-Text omits *for.* **4:8** [a]NU-Text reads *you may know our circumstances and he may.* **4:12** [a]NU-Text reads *fully assured.*

SOUL NOTE

Making Melody *(3:16)* God should always be the focus of our worship. Music can be a beautiful part of the worship service. Through "psalms and hymns and spiritual songs," believers sing their praises to the Lord. The early church did not have Bibles for each worshiper, so they often would teach God's Word through music. Today we have many styles of music. From old hymns to contemporary songs to praise choruses, music that is grounded in the truth of God's Word honors Him.
Topic: Praise and Worship

SOUL NOTE

In His Name *(3:17)* This verse summarizes the Christian life. Everything believers say and do should be "in the name of the Lord Jesus." In other words, their words and actions should represent Jesus Christ. So how do our Christian lives reflect this standard? Do we greet each new day in the name of the Lord Jesus? Do we go about our daily activities in the name of the Lord Jesus? Do we talk with our family and friends in the name of the Lord Jesus? Do we handle our finances in the name of the Lord Jesus? **Topic: Spiritual Disciplines**

God. 13For I bear him witness that he has a
great zeal[a] for you, and those who are in Laodicea, and those in Hierapolis. 14Luke the beloved physician and Demas greet you. 15Greet
the brethren who are in Laodicea, and
Nymphas and the church that *is* in his[a] house.

Closing Exhortations and Blessing

16Now when this epistle is read among you,
see that it is read also in the church of the Laodiceans, and that you likewise read the
epistle from Laodicea. 17And say to Archippus,
"Take heed to the ministry which you have
received in the Lord, that you may fulfill it."
18This salutation by my own hand—Paul.
Remember my chains. Grace *be* with you.
Amen.

4:13 [a]NU-Text reads *concern.* **4:15** [a]NU-Text reads *Nympha . . . her house.*

KEY PASSAGE

Marital Problems

THE POWER OF LOVE

(3:18, 19)

Marriages have problems for various reasons. An attitude of love and service, each person toward the other, can go a long way toward solving many of the irritations and difficulties that can arise. Wives are told to submit to their husbands, willingly allowing their husbands the position of leadership over the family. Husbands, in turn, are told to love their wives sacrificially, as Christ loved the church.

A wise and Christ-honoring wife seeks her husband's best—serving, helping, comforting, and supporting him as he assumes the God-given role of head of the household. When a wife treats her husband that way, providing a haven at home, she has done him great good. A wise and Christ-honoring husband seeks his wife's best as a godly and loving leader—serving, helping, comforting, and supporting her as she carries out her role in the home (and perhaps in a workplace as well). Most marital problems find healing in mutual love, submission, and respect.

To Learn More: Turn to the article about marital problems on pages 1576, 1577. See also the personality profile of Isaac and Rebekah on page 42.

SOUL NOTE

Helpful, Not Harmful *(3:21)* Fathers are told not to discourage their children. Although children are commanded to obey their parents, this does not give parents permission to be cruel or unreasonable in their treatment of their children. Parents who nag, belittle, or deride their children destroy their self-esteem and discourage them. The purpose of parental discipline is to train children. Consistent discipline, administered with love, will help children to grow into responsible adults. **Topic: Fatherhood**

Marital Problems

MARITAL PROBLEMS AND PROBLEM-SOLVING

TIM CLINTON

(Colossians 3:18, 19)

All marriages go through times when love grows cold or lacks the closeness we desire. And, when our marriages get into trouble, we hurt. Many times we can't even pinpoint what went wrong.

If people are willing to step back and review their marital story, they will usually find a pattern. If left unchecked, that pattern can lead them to heartbreak and, maybe, to divorce.

There is hope for the troubled marriage, however. Since the pattern is often predictable, the courageous can work to stop the harmful patterns and save their marriages. But more than just keeping their marriage afloat, they can work to reverse the process and breathe new life into their marriages.

THE PROCESS AND CYCLE OF DISAFFECTION

How does disaffection start? It actually begins with everyday life—with pressures people face daily. Following are some examples.

Sin/Selfishness

Sin is part of our nature. As Christians, we seek to be victorious, but we will often fail. Somewhere in the marital story, one or both partners may begin to take advantage of the other. They hurt each other. As Paul wrote, "For what I am doing, I do not understand. For what I will to do, that I do not practice; but what I hate, that I do" (Rom. 7:15). Being honest, seeking forgiveness, and staying deeply invested in one's spouse is the only remedy.

Stress

Some marriages have been battered by stresses of life such as financial pressures, loss, health problems, or demanding work schedules. Spouses must deal with stress by considering the *demands* in life and their ability to *cope* with those demands. If the demands exceed their ability to cope, the formula spells trouble. Spouses need to take an inventory of what stresses have been tearing at their relationship since they married.

Satanic Assault

Since Adam and Eve, Satan has had the poison arrows of hell aimed at the intimate bond of marriage. He is the great confuser and the ultimate liar. He magnifies people's weaknesses and fears, using them as wedges in their marriages. Peter described Satan as "a roaring lion, seeking whom he may devour" (1 Pet. 5:8). And he's out to take a big bite out of people's marriages.

Unrealistic Expectations

The gap between unrealized expectations and reality is filled with disappointment. If people's expectations for marriage are unrealistic, they are setting themselves up for a fall. A few common unrealistic expectations include:

- "Marriage will complete me." Some who grew up in unloving homes or some other painful environment, may expect marriage to reverse all the negatives they're carrying into it.
- "My spouse won't hurt me." As the first expectation sees marriage as the healing agent, this one sees marriage as the ulti-

mate safe haven. The first experience of hurt, then, is devastating.

➢ "Life will be easy now." This is the "happily-ever-after" expectation of fairy tales. Every unhappy moment in a marriage then brings disappointment and possibly fear.

➢ "Love will keep us together." Every time spouses hurt one another, intentionally or unintentionally, love is perceived as increasingly less effective until, in the end, they can say that their relationship just wasn't meant to be.

These unrealistic expectations must be fought with realistic biblical ones. People need to understand that no one is perfect, no one person will ever fulfill all their needs. Only God can do that. No marriage is free from discord, and no spouse is completely unselfish.

Marriage brings together two people who have many human frailties, and puts them in such close proximity that every detail and flaw is exposed. Hopefully, in Christ, these are strengthened into godly traits. But, it takes a lot of humility, grace, and deep forgiveness. In other words, it is a lot of work.

Childhood Scripts
Many counselors believe that a majority of what drives us as adults happened to us in our early years. These "scripts" written for us long ago are faithfully followed and reinforced as we hold tightly to them. For instance, some whose parents abandoned them may live as if they expect those they love to abandon them. Such scripts distort reality and drive people to act and react in what could be very destructive ways. These scripts also impact how people give and receive love. Unresolved physical, emotional, or sexual abuse, parental divorce, abandonment, gross failure, or emotional loss need to be dealt with before the Father so they don't infect one's marriage.

Time
Relationships and intimacy takes time. Time to understand, enjoy, and respond to one another—time to satisfy the other's needs and have one's own needs satisfied. But with life being lived on the run as it is today, there is little time—unless couples *make* the time. In order to stay close, couples need to regularly schedule time just to be together.

A REASONABLE RESPONSE TO AN UNREASONABLE SITUATION

A natural response to pain in marriage is to create space between ourselves and our partners. Drifting—with a subtle, even unintentional severing of relational strands—takes place. The healing path begins by seeing and reframing our marital story and then responding (not reacting) to each other as Christ would.

Remember, God gave us our spouses so that He could work through us to make him or her more like Christ.

FURTHER MEDITATION:

Other passages to study about the issue of marital problems include:

➢ Genesis 2:24
➢ Proverbs 5:15–23; 12:4
➢ Ecclesiastes 9:9
➢ Matthew 19:4–6
➢ 1 Corinthians 7:1–5; 13:1–13
➢ Ephesians 5:22–33
➢ Hebrews 13:4
➢ James 4:1–10
➢ 1 Peter 3:1–9

To Learn More: Turn to the key passage note on marital problems at Colossians 3:18, 19 on page 1575. See also the personality profile of Isaac and Rebekah on page 42.

1 Thessalonians

Every parent knows the agony and the ecstasy of child rearing. As one smart remark puts it, successful parenting is simply a matter of knowing which end of the child to pat, and how hard.

The same dynamic is true in the realm of the soul. We are all spiritual offspring who need to grow up in the faith. We also have the responsibility of parenting those who are newborns in the faith. Given that truth and that obligation, it's hard to think of a more helpful resource than 1 Thessalonians.

During his second missionary journey (A.D. 51), the apostle Paul became anxious for news about the young congregation begun months earlier in Thessalonica. He sent Timothy to investigate, and was greatly encouraged by what he heard. The Thessalonians, only recently converted to Christianity, were faithfully living out the gospel! Like a proud parent, Paul took pen in hand and affirmed their progress in the faith, encouraging them to continue. He also expressed tender affection for this young, excited congregation. Not only had he given them the gospel, but he would have gladly given them his life (2:8).

First Thessalonians provides detailed instruction about sexual purity (ch. 4) and the return of the Lord (ch. 5). But at the most basic level it is a highly practical reminder of our need to grow on to maturity, and of our responsibility to help newer believers in the all-important task of soul care.

Let Paul parent you a little in the pages that follow. Then be willing to share what you learn!

SOUL CONCERN IN 1 THESSALONIANS

Greeting

1 Paul, Silvanus, and Timothy,

To the church of the Thessalonians in God the Father and the Lord Jesus Christ:

Grace to you and peace from God our Father and the Lord Jesus Christ.[a]

Their Good Example

[2]We give thanks to God always for you all,
making mention of you in our prayers, [3]re-
membering without ceasing your work of faith, labor of love, and patience of hope in our Lord Jesus Christ in the sight of our God
and Father, [4]knowing, beloved brethren, your
election by God. [5]For our gospel did not come to you in word only, but also in power, and in the Holy Spirit and in much assurance, as you know what kind of men we were among you for your sake.
[6]And you became followers of us and of the Lord, having received the word in much affliction, with joy of the Holy Spirit, [7]so that you
became examples to all in Macedonia and
Achaia who believe. [8]For from you the word of
the Lord has sounded forth, not only in Macedonia and Achaia, but also in every place. Your faith toward God has gone out, so that
we do not need to say anything. [9]For they
themselves declare concerning us what manner of entry we had to you, and how you turned to God from idols to serve the living
and true God, [10]and to wait for His Son from
heaven, whom He raised from the dead, *even* Jesus who delivers us from the wrath to come.

Paul's Conduct

2 For you yourselves know, brethren, that our coming to you was not in vain. [2]But
even[a] after we had suffered before and were spitefully treated at Philippi, as you know, we were bold in our God to speak to you the gospel of God in much conflict. [3]For our exhortation *did* not *come* from error or uncleanness, nor *was it* in deceit.
[4]But as we have been approved by God to be entrusted with the gospel, even so we speak, not as pleasing men, but God who tests
our hearts. [5]For neither at any time did we use
flattering words, as you know, nor a cloak for
covetousness—God *is* witness. [6]Nor did we
seek glory from men, either from you or from others, when we might have made demands
as apostles of Christ. [7]But we were gentle
among you, just as a nursing *mother* cherishes
her own children. [8]So, affectionately longing
for you, we were well pleased to impart to you not only the gospel of God, but also our own
lives, because you had become dear to us. [9]For
you remember, brethren, our labor and toil; for laboring night and day, that we might not be a burden to any of you, we preached to you the gospel of God.
[10]You *are* witnesses, and God *also,* how devoutly and justly and blamelessly we behaved
ourselves among you who believe; [11]as you
know how we exhorted, and comforted, and charged[a] every one of you, as a father *does* his
own children, [12]that you would walk worthy
of God who calls you into His own kingdom and glory.

Their Conversion

[13]For this reason we also thank God without ceasing, because when you received the word of God which you heard from us, you welcomed *it* not *as* the word of men, but as it is in truth, the word of God, which also effectively
works in you who believe. [14]For you, brethren,

1:1 [a]NU-Text omits *from God our Father and the Lord Jesus Christ.* **2:2** [a]NU-Text and M-Text omit *even.* **2:11** [a]NU-Text and M-Text read *implored.*

SOUL NOTE

Life Changing *(1:8, 9)* The Thessalonian church was only a few months old but was already having an impact! These young believers were being tested by severe suffering (1:6), but their solid faith was being talked about "in every place." That's what the good news of Jesus Christ does—it makes astounding changes in people's lives that could not happen any other way. For some, the change is more noticeable than for others. But whenever Christ enters a life, He changes things. We need to let Christ work in our lives so that we can make an impact on our world. **Topic: Change/Maturity**

became imitators of the churches of God
which are in Judea in Christ Jesus. For you
also suffered the same things from your own
countrymen, just as they *did* from the
Judeans, [15]who killed both the Lord Jesus and
their own prophets, and have persecuted us;
and they do not please God and are contrary
to all men, [16]forbidding us to speak to the
Gentiles that they may be saved, so as always to fill up *the measure of* their sins; but
wrath has come upon them to the uttermost.

Longing to See Them

[17]But we, brethren, having been taken away
from you for a short time in presence, not in
heart, endeavored more eagerly to see your
face with great desire. [18]Therefore we wanted
to come to you—even I, Paul, time and
again—but Satan hindered us. [19]For what *is*
our hope, or joy, or crown of rejoicing? *Is it* not
even you in the presence of our Lord Jesus
Christ at His coming? [20]For you are our glory
and joy.

Concern for Their Faith

3 Therefore, when we could no longer endure it, we thought it good to be left in
Athens alone, [2]and sent Timothy, our brother
and minister of God, and our fellow laborer in
the gospel of Christ, to establish you and encourage you concerning your faith, [3]that no
one should be shaken by these afflictions; for
you yourselves know that we are appointed to
this. [4]For, in fact, we told you before when we
were with you that we would suffer tribulation, just as it happened, and you know. [5]For
this reason, when I could no longer endure it,
I sent to know your faith, lest by some means
the tempter had tempted you, and our labor
might be in vain.

Encouraged by Timothy

[6]But now that Timothy has come to us from
you, and brought us good news of your faith
and love, and that you always have good remembrance of us, greatly desiring to see us, as
we also *to see* you—[7]therefore, brethren, in all
our affliction and distress we were comforted
concerning you by your faith. [8]For now we
live, if you stand fast in the Lord.

[9]For what thanks can we render to God for
you, for all the joy with which we rejoice for
your sake before our God, [10]night and day
praying exceedingly that we may see your face
and perfect what is lacking in your faith?

Prayer for the Church

[11]Now may our God and Father Himself, and
our Lord Jesus Christ, direct our way to you.
[12]And may the Lord make you increase and
abound in love to one another and to all, just
as we *do* to you, [13]so that He may establish
your hearts blameless in holiness before our
God and Father at the coming of our Lord
Jesus Christ with all His saints.

Plea for Purity

4 Finally then, brethren, we urge and exhort
in the Lord Jesus that you should abound
more and more, just as you received from us
how you ought to walk and to please God; [2]for
you know what commandments we gave you
through the Lord Jesus.

[3]For this is the will of God, your sanctification: that you should abstain from sexual immorality; [4]that each of you should know how
to possess his own vessel in sanctification and
honor, [5]not in passion of lust, like the Gentiles
who do not know God; [6]that no one should
take advantage of and defraud his brother in
this matter, because the Lord *is* the avenger of

SOUL NOTE

Encouraging Words *(3:2)* Paul was so concerned for this young congregation that he sent Timothy to check out the situation, and to establish and encourage the believers in the faith. The church was being persecuted, and Paul wanted to make sure that they would hold on to the truth. When Christians are facing difficulties because of their faith, other believers should hold them up in prayer, offering words of compassion and encouragement as they seek to follow God. Whether it is a child with an unsympathetic teacher or a church in a persecuting country, we can pray for them and offer encouraging words. **Topic: Compassion**

all such, as we also forewarned you and testified. [7]For God did not call us to uncleanness,
but in holiness. [8]Therefore he who rejects *this*
does not reject man, but God, who has also
given[a] us His Holy Spirit.

A Brotherly and Orderly Life

[9]But concerning brotherly love you have no
need that I should write to you, for you yourselves are taught by God to love one another;
[10]and indeed you do so toward all the brethren
who are in all Macedonia. But we urge you,
brethren, that you increase more and more;
[11]that you also aspire to lead a quiet life, to
mind your own business, and to work with
your own hands, as we commanded you,
[12]that you may walk properly toward those
who are outside, and *that* you may lack nothing.

The Comfort of Christ's Coming

[13]But I do not want you to be ignorant,
brethren, concerning those who have fallen
asleep, lest you sorrow as others who have no
hope. [14]For if we believe that Jesus died and
rose again, even so God will bring with Him
those who sleep in Jesus.[a]
[15]For this we say to you by the word of the
Lord, that we who are alive *and* remain until

4:8 [a]NU-Text reads *who also gives.* **4:14** [a]Or *those who through Jesus sleep*

KEY PASSAGE

Sexual Sin

FOR OUR OWN GOOD

(4:3–7)

The Bible is very clear about sexual sin. God created sex as a beautiful expression of love in marriage. Satan took that beauty and distorted it. Sexual sin encompasses a wide range of activities forbidden by God. No matter what society allows, believers must look to God for instruction in this serious matter. Christians need to avoid activities or thoughts that warp what God intended for building oneness in marriage. The Bible's statements concerning sexual sins are plentiful and plain:

- *Adultery* (Ex. 20:14; Lev. 18:20; Prov. 6:32; Matt. 5:27, 28)
- *Homosexuality* (Lev. 18:22; 20:13; Rom. 1:26, 27; 1 Cor. 6:9; 1 Tim. 1:10)
- *Incest* (Lev. 18:6–18; 20:11, 12, 17; Deut. 27:20, 22, 23)
- *Bestiality* (Ex. 22:19; Lev. 18:23; 20:15, 16; Deut. 27:21)
- *Lust* (Matt. 5:28; Rom. 13:13; 1 Thess. 4:5; James 1:14, 15; 1 Pet. 4:3)

Believers must have no part in sexual sin. God knows its power to destroy people. His commands are for our good.

To Learn More: Turn to the article about sexual sin on pages 1582, 1583. See also the personality profile of David and Bathsheba on page 400.

SOUL NOTE

Vessels of Honor *(4:4)* The words "each of you should know how to possess his own vessel in sanctification and honor" refer to believers having sexual self-control. The standards of the Roman Empire were not much different from a lot of the world today: Sex was a form of entertainment; sexual activity between the unmarried was considered normal; even homosexuality was often accepted. But the Bible teaches sexual integrity. Sex is meant only for a husband and wife in the loving bonds of marriage. As believers we should uphold the beauty of sexual integrity, starting in our own lives. **Topic: Sexual Integrity**

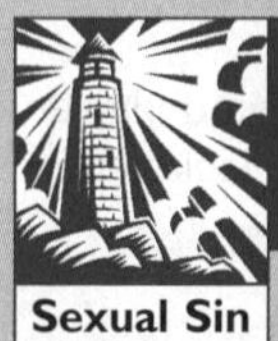

SEXUAL SIN AND PERSONAL HOLINESS

MARNIE C. FERREE AND MARK R. LAASER

(1 Thessalonians 4:5)

A trip to the grocery store on any given day will reveal the blatant sexual messages that infiltrate modern culture. The checkout line is a tunnel of sexual stimuli by way of magazine images and headlines. In every corner of the everyday experience, unholy sexual messages abound.

Sexual sin is not a new problem. Long before the "free love" climate of the modern world, the New Testament recorded incest, adultery, homosexuality, lust, and perversions of every kind throughout the cities of the Roman Empire where Paul established churches. God calls Christians to a vision of healthy sexuality that is experienced only in the sanctity of the marriage union.

FORMS OF SEXUAL SIN

The forms of sexual sin and perversion are as varied as the depraved human mind can fathom. The Bible talks about "lust," which is a generic term encompassing many variations of the desire to gratify sexual needs in purely physical ways outside the spiritual and emotional commitment of marriage.

The sin of adultery is one example. King David's sin with Bathsheba illustrates the incredible damage adultery causes to the people involved, as well as to their marriages and their families (2 Sam. 11, 12). Homosexuality is another example. While today it is often deemed unacceptable to view same-sex encounters as sinful or perverted, the Bible's position is clear: Homosexual behavior is sin (1 Cor. 6:9). Other common sexual perversions in society include exhibitionism, voyeurism, cross-dressing, or some kind of sexual fetish. Sexual abuse, especially of children, is another perversion that is profoundly damaging. Almost always, professional help is required when someone is dealing with the web of sexual abuse or some similarly serious perversion.

However, the problem Christian helpers are most likely to encounter is pornography. Many leading Christian counselors and clergy consider pornography to be the number one social problem today. The Internet has conveniently introduced an incredible array of perverted, yet compelling pornography. More sexually oriented sites are launched on the Internet than any other kind.

UNDERLYING CAUSES OF SEXUAL SIN

Most sexually sinful or perverted behavior is not coincidental or impulsive. Frequently, it is a symptom of deeper issues. One of the underlying issues is loneliness—a disconnection of intimate relationships. Perhaps a marital relationship has gone stale, or the partners never learned to communicate in the first place. Or maybe a single individual feels isolated and unimportant. Some inappropriate behavior is the result of trauma, especially childhood abuse or abandonment.

Another underlying cause behind sexual sin may be the seduction of the culture. Our sexually saturated society gives the message that everyone is having promiscuous sex.

SOLUTIONS TO SEXUAL SIN

How can one best help someone who is struggling in this area? A foundational principle is to approach the sexual sinner with grace rather than with judgment. There is no difference in God's sight: Everyone is sinful (Rom. 3:22, 23). Sexual sin and perversion must be addressed in the spiritual arena. The sinner must first be willing to admit and confess the sin. The model of David's haunting confession of his sin, written in Psalm 51, can be helpful. Repentance is a crucial spiritual component of healing. The word "repent" means to turn away from the behavior, as illustrated in Jesus' command to the adulterous woman to "go and sin no more" (John 8:11).

Following confession, a person should accept God's forgiveness. Through forgiveness, people are able to enjoy a new sexual start. God has cleansed them and made them "white as snow" (Is. 1:18). Many people embrace the idea of "spiritual virginity," which simply means a rededication to sexual purity.

In the relational realm, healing may need to take place in the context of community—such as Christian counseling and/or Christian mentoring. Other believers who are connected to and supportive of a person can help him or her through the healing process. By being partners in accountability, they can help the person through times of temptation, so that he or she is less likely to return to the same sin. However, if a person is unable to maintain boundaries and repeatedly commits sexual sin, an addiction may be present, which will require professional help.

In a practical sense, the person may need to avoid certain people, places, and activities in order to maintain boundaries against sexual sin. The injunction to "keep your heart" is a good guide (Prov. 4:23). Christians are promised a way of escape from temptation, which may involve practical tools such as learning to communicate their needs in an appropriate manner and discovering how to develop greater self-control (1 Cor. 10:13).

Paul calls believers to "put off, concerning your former conduct, the old man which grows corrupt according to the deceitful lusts, and be renewed in the spirit of your mind" (Eph. 4:22, 23). This renewal is built on a new vision that abandons the urge to indulge in sexual sin or perversion. "Walk in the Spirit, and you shall not fulfill the lust of the flesh" (Gal. 5:16).

When people have a vision of commitment to sexual purity and when they have others to whom they can be accountable, they will be better able to make healthy sexual choices.

FURTHER MEDITATION:

Other passages to study about the issue of sexual sin include:

- Proverbs 5:1–23; 6:20—7:27
- John 8:1–11
- Romans 6:12
- 1 Corinthians 5:9–13; 6:15–20
- 1 Thessalonians 4:1–7

To Learn More: Turn to the key passage note on sexual sin at 1 Thessalonians 4:3–7 on page 1581. See also the personality profile of David and Bathsheba on page 400.

the coming of the Lord will by no means precede those who are asleep. 16For the Lord
Himself will descend from heaven with a
shout, with the voice of an archangel, and
with the trumpet of God. And the dead in
Christ will rise first. 17Then we who are alive
and remain shall be caught up together with
them in the clouds to meet the Lord in the air.
And thus we shall always be with the Lord.
18Therefore comfort one another with these
words.

THE DAY OF THE LORD

5 But concerning the times and the seasons,
brethren, you have no need that I should
write to you. 2For you yourselves know perfectly that the day of the Lord so comes as a
thief in the night. 3For when they say, "Peace
and safety!" then sudden destruction comes
upon them, as labor pains upon a pregnant
woman. And they shall not escape. 4But you,
brethren, are not in darkness, so that this Day
should overtake you as a thief. 5You are all
sons of light and sons of the day. We are not of
the night nor of darkness. 6Therefore let us
not sleep, as others *do,* but let us watch and
be sober. 7For those who sleep, sleep at night,
and those who get drunk are drunk at night.
8But let us who are of the day be sober, putting
on the breastplate of faith and love, and *as* a

SOUL NOTE

Reunion *(4:13, 14)* The Thessalonian believers wondered what was happening to their fellow believers who had died. They had been taught that Christ would come again, but they wondered if those who had died would miss out. Paul comforted the church, answering their question by explaining that believers do not need to "sorrow as others who have no hope." Believers have the ultimate assurance. We believe that Jesus died, rose again, ascended, and is coming again; and we also believe that He will bring with Him those who have died. One day, all believers will be reunited in the grandest reunion ever seen! **Topic: Grief/Loss**

KEY PASSAGE

Eternal Life

FOREVER AND EVER

(4:13–18)

Eternal life with God is an absolute certainty for believers. These words should be taken literally—Christ will return, and "the dead in Christ will rise" from their graves. Believers who are alive at that time will be drawn up with them into heaven and "thus we shall always be with the Lord."

There is much debate about the timing or order of various events surrounding the Second Coming, but several truths are undeniable:

- Eternal life begins the moment a person accepts Christ as Savior. If the believer must experience death before Christ returns, that is merely the way to heaven.
- Believers who have died will experience a bodily resurrection, living believers will be changed, and all will receive new, glorified bodies that will never get sick or die.
- Christ will return to defeat evil and death forever.
- Believers will live forever in heaven with Christ.

As Paul noted to the Thessalonians, we should "comfort one another with these words."

To Learn More: Turn to the article about eternal life on pages 1718, 1719. See also the personality profile of the apostle John on page 1702.

helmet the hope of salvation. 9For God did not
appoint us to wrath, but to obtain salvation
through our Lord Jesus
Christ, 10who died for us,
that whether we wake
or sleep, we should live
together with Him.
11Therefore comfort
each other and edify
one another, just as you
also are doing.

> Rejoice always, pray without ceasing, in everything give thanks; for this is the will of God in Christ Jesus for you.
>
> 1 THESSALONIANS 5:16–18

VARIOUS EXHORTATIONS

12And we urge you, brethren, to recognize
those who labor among you, and are over you
in the Lord and admonish you, 13and to esteem them very highly in love for their work's
sake. Be at peace among
yourselves.
14Now we exhort you,
brethren, warn those
who are unruly, comfort
the fainthearted, up-
hold the weak, be pa-
tient with all. 15See that
no one renders evil for
evil to anyone, but al-
ways pursue what is
good both for yourselves and for all.
16Rejoice always, 17pray without ceasing,
18in everything give thanks; for this is the will
of God in Christ Jesus for you.
19Do not quench the
Spirit. 20Do not despise
prophecies. 21Test all
things; hold fast what
is good. 22Abstain from
every form of evil.

> Now may the God of peace Himself sanctify you completely; and may your whole spirit, soul, and body be preserved blameless at the coming of our Lord Jesus Christ.
>
> 1 THESSALONIANS 5:23

BLESSING AND ADMONITION

23Now may the God
of peace Himself sancti-
fy you completely; and may your whole spirit,
soul, and body be preserved blameless at the
coming of our Lord Jesus Christ. 24He who
calls you *is* faithful, who also will do *it*.
25Brethren, pray for
us.
26Greet all the breth-
ren with a holy kiss.
27I charge you by the
Lord that this epistle be
read to all the holy[a]
brethren.
28The grace of our
Lord Jesus Christ *be*
with you. Amen.

5:27 [a]NU-Text omits *holy.*

2 Thessalonians

As the twentieth century came to a close, millennial fever increased the hopes of many for the second coming of Christ. It also reminded us that the many New Testament promises of the Lord's return have always been a source of confusion among believers. We know this because of the apostle Paul's second letter to the Thessalonians.

Certain false teachers had infiltrated the fledgling congregation, playing on people's hopes and fears, and creating a climate of wild speculation. Complicating matters was the increasing persecution of believers. Paul wrote to provide comfort and clarity in a disturbing time. He assured the Thessalonians that, despite the pronouncements of some, Christ had not yet returned. Certain identifiable events would precede the yet future "day of the Lord" (2:1–12). In short, Paul urged his younger brothers and sisters in the faith to avoid fanatical and anxious speculation about the events related to Christ's return. For the unbeliever, the future holds terrible judgment. But Christians do not have to fear the end because God has all things under His perfect control.

The Bible never encourages the people of God to sit around aimlessly waiting for the end of the world. On the contrary, the Scriptures urge us to be about our Master's business until He returns. The key to a successful Christian life and a healthy soul is to do what we have been called to do, and to leave our future (and the world's) in the good hands of our wise and mighty Father in heaven.

SOUL CONCERN IN 2 THESSALONIANS

GREETING

1 Paul, Silvanus, and Timothy,

To the church of the Thessalonians in God our Father and the Lord Jesus Christ:

2 Grace to you and peace from God our Father and the Lord Jesus Christ.

GOD'S FINAL JUDGMENT AND GLORY

3 We are bound to thank God always for you, brethren, as it is fitting, because your faith grows exceedingly, and the love of every one of you all abounds toward each other, 4 so that we ourselves boast of you among the churches of God for your patience and faith in all your persecutions and tribulations that you endure, 5 *which is* manifest evidence of the righteous judgment of God, that you may be counted worthy of the kingdom of God, for which you also suffer; 6 since *it is* a righteous thing with God to repay with tribulation those who trouble you, 7 and to *give* you who are troubled rest with us when the Lord Jesus is revealed from heaven with His mighty angels, 8 in flaming fire taking vengeance on those who do not know God, and on those who do not obey the gospel of our Lord Jesus Christ. 9 These shall be punished with everlasting destruction from the presence of the Lord and from the glory of His power, 10 when He comes, in that Day, to be glorified in His saints and to be admired among all those who believe,[a] because our testimony among you was believed.

11 Therefore we also pray always for you that our God would count you worthy of *this* calling, and fulfill all the good pleasure of *His* goodness and the work of faith with power, 12 that the name of our Lord Jesus Christ may be glorified in you, and you in Him, according to the grace of our God and the Lord Jesus Christ.

THE GREAT APOSTASY

2 Now, brethren, concerning the coming of our Lord Jesus Christ and our gathering together to Him, we ask you, 2 not to be soon shaken in mind or troubled, either by spirit or by word or by letter, as if from us, as though the day of Christ[a] had come. 3 Let no one deceive you by any means; for *that Day will not come* unless the falling away comes first, and the man of sin[a] is revealed, the son of perdition, 4 who opposes and exalts himself above all that is called God or that is worshiped, so that he sits as God[a] in the temple of God, showing himself that he is God.

5 Do you not remember that when I was still with you I told you these things? 6 And now you know what is restraining, that he may be revealed in his own time. 7 For the mystery of lawlessness is already at work; only He[a] who now restrains *will do so* until He[b] is taken out of the way. 8 And then the lawless one will be revealed, whom the Lord will consume with the breath of His mouth and destroy with the brightness of His coming. 9 The coming of the *lawless one* is according to the working of Satan, with all power, signs, and lying wonders, 10 and with all unrighteous deception among those who perish, because they did not receive the love of the truth, that they might be saved. 11 And for this reason God will send them strong delusion, that they should believe the lie, 12 that they all may be condemned who did not believe the truth but had pleasure in unrighteousness.

STAND FAST

13 But we are bound to give thanks to God always for you, brethren beloved by the Lord,

1:10 [a]NU-Text and M-Text read *have believed.*
2:2 [a]NU-Text reads *the Lord.* **2:3** [a]NU-Text reads *lawlessness.* **2:4** [a]NU-Text omits *as God.* **2:7** [a]Or *he* [b]Or *he*

SOUL NOTE

Truth Grip *(2:9–12)* One day a "lawless one" will arise and, empowered by Satan, will deceive many people. Those who "did not receive the love of the truth" and who "believe the lie" will be lost forever. Satan always seeks to deceive—but a ton of truth with an ounce of a lie is still a lie. Many false religions flirt at the edges of the truth and sound good. But any religion that teaches salvation by any other way than through Jesus Christ is a deception. We must hold tight to the truth we have been taught so as not to be deceived. **Topic: Cults**

because God from the beginning chose you for salvation through sanctification by the Spirit and belief in the truth, [14]to which He called you by our gospel, for the obtaining of the glory of our Lord Jesus Christ. [15]Therefore, brethren, stand fast and hold the traditions which you were taught, whether by word or our epistle.

[16]Now may our Lord Jesus Christ Himself, and our God and Father, who has loved us and given *us* everlasting consolation and good hope by grace, [17]comfort your hearts and establish you in every good word and work.

Pray for Us

3 Finally, brethren, pray for us, that the word of the Lord may run *swiftly* and be glorified, just as *it is* with you, [2]and that we may be delivered from unreasonable and wicked men; for not all have faith.

[3]But the Lord is faithful, who will establish you and guard *you* from the evil one. [4]And we have confidence in the Lord concerning you, both that you do and will do the things we command you.

[5]Now may the Lord direct your hearts into the love of God and into the patience of Christ.

Warning Against Idleness

[6]But we command you, brethren, in the name of our Lord Jesus Christ, that you withdraw from every brother who walks disorderly and not according to the tradition which he[a]

3:6 [a]NU-Text and M-Text read *they.*

SOUL NOTE

Follow the Leader *(3:3–5)* Believers are engaged in a spiritual battle. As part of God's army, we have God as our Commander and Satan as our avowed enemy. The battle rages in the spiritual realm and constantly affects the earthly realm, where believers have great victories but also face difficult trials, temptations, and persecutions. At times the difficulties become so intense that we feel weak and vulnerable. At those times, we need to remember Paul's advice: "The Lord is faithful, who will establish you and guard you from the evil one." God's Word and work will never fail. When we feel weak, we must remember God's faithfulness. **Topic: Weakness**

KEY PASSAGE

Work

OFF TO WORK

(3:10–12)

Some of the Thessalonian believers had stopped working. It seems they were relying on the generosity of their fellow believers, supposedly for the sake of being spiritual and waiting for the second coming of Christ—or maybe they were just being lazy. Whatever it was, Paul had harsh words for such an outlook.

Work is good for us. Upon placing Adam in the Garden of Eden, God gave him the work of caring for it. God provides work in order for people to provide for their families. To refuse to work when one has the ability and the opportunity is wrong, and the church should not support such people.

When we see our work as God-given, we have a whole new perspective. It is not a necessary evil that takes time away from "spiritual" things, but a gift from God through which we are to grow spiritually and minister to others. God needs people in all walks of life in order to reach those who have not heard the Good News of salvation.

To Learn More: Turn to the article about work on pages 1590, 1591. See also the personality profile of Aaron on page 87.

received from us. [7]For you yourselves know how you ought to follow us, for we were not disorderly among you; [8]nor did we eat anyone's bread free of charge, but worked with labor and toil night and day, that we might not be a burden to any of you, [9]not because we do not have authority, but to make ourselves an example of how you should follow us.

> Now may the Lord of peace Himself give you peace always in every way. The Lord be with you all.
>
> 2 THESSALONIANS 3:16

[10]For even when we were with you, we commanded you this: If anyone will not work, neither shall he eat. [11]For we hear that there are some who walk among you in a disorderly manner, not working at all, but are busybodies. [12]Now those who are such we command and exhort through our Lord Jesus Christ that they work in quietness and eat their own bread.

[13]But *as for* you, brethren, do not grow weary *in* doing good. [14]And if anyone does not obey our word in this epistle, note that person and do not keep company with him, that he may be ashamed. [15]Yet do not count *him* as an enemy, but admonish *him* as a brother.

Benediction

[16]Now may the Lord of peace Himself give you peace always in every way. The Lord *be* with you all.

[17]The salutation of Paul with my own hand, which is a sign in every epistle; so I write.

[18]The grace of our Lord Jesus Christ *be* with you all. Amen.

Work

THE WORLD OF WORK

TIM CLINTON AND GEORGE OHLSCHLAGER

(2 Thessalonians 3:10–15)

"What do you do?"

Many people have been asked that question thousands of times. The question is presaged by the question in childhood, "What do you want to be when you grow up?"

We are socialized early on in life to the importance of work. And so it should be. Much more than just a means to a livelihood, work is a source of identity, a well of friendships and associations, and a way in which people derive meaning and satisfaction in life. When things aren't going well on the job, it makes for some long days and discouraged people.

GOD AND OUR WORK

Some Christians believe that work is also a form of worship, a sacred extension of the ongoing creative process by which God still functions. The Bible reveals that work, despite its being a product of the Fall, has been made a source of human dignity.

Because of disobedience to God, man was cursed to eke out an existence from the earth, struggling to live by the sweat of his brow until death (Gen. 3:17–19). Yet God has redeemed work, and looks upon people at work with dignity and protection, calling for justice and honesty in all employer-worker relations. God calls upon humankind to work honestly, heartily, happily, and as though we are working for the Lord (Ex. 23:12; Eccl. 5:19; Col. 3:23).

The church at Thessalonica had developed a serious problem. Some had become so convinced of Christ's imminent return that they gave up working and began to wait for the Second Coming. This created some serious problems as the wait extended from days to weeks to months. Paul encouraged these believers to follow his example of hard work and commanded the church not to feed those who refused to work (2 Thess. 3:10–15). Honest work and understanding that one must work to provide for the necessities of living have been central values in the church for nearly two thousand years.

The fact that there are so many dissatisfied workers today may also mean that the value of work has been distorted. Think of how many people you know who are unhappy in their work, unfulfilled and bored to tears by the 9 to 5 routine. Maybe work has lost the moral and biblical anchors that balance its importance in the larger scheme of things. Maybe worker dissatisfaction simply means that too many people have chosen their life's work poorly, for the wrong reasons, or with the wrong fit of interests, skills, personality, and gifts. Whatever the reason, work dissatisfaction, job stress, and interpersonal conflict in work organizations are a big reason why many people and work organizations seek professional help, including counseling.

Our work life must be maintained as a proper priority in relation to God, marriage and family life, and commitments to church and community. When this balance is not held, work can easily become an idol, a false god that serves as a terrible taskmaster. "Workaholism" has become an all-consuming obsession for too many modern workers, a sleep-depriving, health-robbing, greed-festering monster that may be the most rewarded—and least challenged—addiction in America.

Like all addicts, workaholics must be able to admit their obsessive drivenness and confess its many costs. They must be able to build and maintain times of rest, play, family, and leisure. Work addicts need to realize that the deeper life with Christ comes only after one is able to be still and know God.

FINDING THE BEST WORK

Career counselors and experts say that the accelerating pace of technological change combined with the high mobility and trainability of the modern workforce will lead workers in the current generation to change jobs and/or careers nine times over the course of their lifetimes.

Career counseling generally seeks to facilitate four primary objectives in helping people find and fit into a good job or career:

- increasing self-awareness of values and work interests,
- becoming familiar with the world of work,
- teaching assessment and decision-making skills,
- teaching skills to enhance employability.

Work without a purpose, without a vision for how we are advancing the cause of God's kingdom, can easily become meaningless. Disciplined work is recognizing that excellence can be achieved by tackling tasks every day with wisdom, commitment, and earnest effort. Diligent workers are pursuing and achieving excellence—they have caught a vision of how their work fits into the larger purposes of God. These high-level workers seek to be directed by the Holy Spirit, and their effort and excellence reflect the fruits of this vision motivation.

The following values and goals are important when considering work and career issues:

1. Pursue your choice of life's work as a calling from God, believing that He will guide and prepare you to accomplish a good work in your life.
2. Increase understanding of your interests, personality, style, gifts, and talents, seeking to explore and test how these things fit into a variety of different jobs.
3. Increase your skill and usability of "universal" job skills—analytical thinking and evaluating skills, command of positive communicating, writing, and speaking skills, interpersonal relationship skills, and problem-solving skills.
4. Determine how to attain the skills and credentials you need for your particular work pursuits in the most time/cost effective way.
5. Be willing to engage in ongoing education for increased knowledge and skills enhancement in your field.
6. Whatever you do, do it with praise and thanksgiving, spread the credit around to your colleagues and coworkers, and give glory to God for its achievement.

FURTHER MEDITATION:

Other passages to study about the issue of work include:

- Genesis 2:2, 15
- Exodus 20:8–11
- Proverbs 28:19
- 1 Timothy 5:8

To Learn More: Turn to the key passage note on work at 2 Thessalonians 3:10–12 on page 1588. See also the personality profile of Aaron on page 87.

1 Timothy

Are you a leader?

Be careful before answering that question. We typically reserve the term "leader" for politicians, CEOs, and others who do that kind of high-profile leading. But what about those who are called to provide guidance to a family or a social organization? And what about the daily responsibility of influencing neighbors and coworkers, or the high calling to set a positive example for one's sports team or classmates? In a sense, we are *all* leaders, which makes the apostle Paul's first letter to Timothy extremely relevant.

Paul's letters to Timothy are two of the so-called "pastoral epistles." They were written to help the apostle's young protégé navigate the difficult waters of church leadership in Ephesus. Written from Macedonia around A.D. 62, 1 Timothy discusses a wide range of pertinent issues: what to do about false teachers (ch. 1 and 4), guidelines for public worship (ch. 2), character requirements for leaders (ch. 3), healthy relationships within the church (ch. 5) and proper motives for leading (ch. 6). Because Paul and Timothy had a long-term relationship and a history of ministering together (Acts 16:1–5), 1 Timothy is an intensely personal letter. We sense a fatherly concern in the apostle's wise counsel.

Whether you call yourself a church leader or not, let the practical wisdom of 1 Timothy seep into your heart and soul. You'll find that its truth will serve you well as you influence others. And while you're reading, pray for a spiritual leader you know who could use the kind of encouragement found in the following six chapters.

SOUL CONCERN IN 1 TIMOTHY

MEN'S ISSUES (6:11)

Greeting

1 Paul, an apostle of Jesus Christ, by the commandment of God our Savior and the Lord Jesus Christ, our hope,

2To Timothy, a true son in the faith:

Grace, mercy, *and* peace from God our Father and Jesus Christ our Lord.

No Other Doctrine

3As I urged you when I went into Macedonia—remain in Ephesus that you may charge some that they teach no other doctrine, 4nor give heed to fables and endless genealogies, which cause disputes rather than godly edification which is in faith. 5Now the purpose of the commandment is love from a pure heart, *from* a good conscience, and *from* sincere faith, 6from which some, having strayed, have turned aside to idle talk, 7desiring to be teachers of the law, understanding neither what they say nor the things which they affirm.

8But we know that the law *is* good if one uses it lawfully, 9knowing this: that the law is not made for a righteous person, but for *the* lawless and insubordinate, for *the* ungodly and for sinners, for *the* unholy and profane, for murderers of fathers and murderers of mothers, for manslayers, 10for fornicators, for sodomites, for kidnappers, for liars, for perjurers, and if there is any other thing that is contrary to sound doctrine, 11according to the glorious gospel of the blessed God which was committed to my trust.

Glory to God for His Grace

12And I thank Christ Jesus our Lord who has enabled me, because He counted me faithful, putting *me* into the ministry, 13although I was formerly a blasphemer, a persecutor, and an insolent man; but I obtained mercy because I did *it* ignorantly in unbelief. 14And the grace of our Lord was exceedingly abundant, with faith and love which are in Christ Jesus. 15This *is* a faithful saying and worthy of all acceptance, that Christ Jesus came into the world to save sinners, of whom I am chief. 16However, for this reason I obtained mercy, that in me first Jesus Christ might show all longsuffering, as a pattern to those who are going to believe on Him for everlasting life. 17Now to the King eternal, immortal, invisible, to God who alone is wise,[a] *be* honor and glory forever and ever. Amen.

Fight the Good Fight

18This charge I commit to you, son Timothy, according to the prophecies previously made concerning you, that by them you may wage the good warfare, 19having faith and a good conscience, which some having rejected, concerning the faith have suffered shipwreck, 20of whom are Hymenaeus and Alexander, whom I delivered to Satan that they may learn not to blaspheme.

Pray for All Men

2 Therefore I exhort first of all that supplications, prayers, intercessions, *and* giving of thanks be made for all men, 2for kings and all who are in authority, that we may lead a quiet and peaceable life in all godliness and reverence. 3For this *is* good and acceptable in the sight of God our Savior, 4who desires all men to be saved and to come to the knowledge of the truth. 5For *there is* one God and one Mediator between God and men, *the* Man Christ Jesus, 6who gave Himself a ransom for all, to be testified in due time, 7for which I was appointed a preacher and an apostle—I am speaking the truth in Christ[a]

1:17 [a]NU-Text reads *to the only God.* **2:7** [a]NU-Text omits *in Christ.*

SOUL NOTE

Legal Notes *(1:8, 9)* Laws give people direction for living, but following laws can never save anyone. The law offers a standard of behavior, it shows how far people fall short of God's perfection, and it demonstrates how much we need His grace and forgiveness. But if people try to live right and keep laws in order to be good enough for God, they will slip into the trap of legalism. That will harm them, for they can never keep the law perfectly. Christ has set us free from the law so that we can obey Him through the power of the Holy Spirit. **Topic: Legalism**

and not lying—a teacher of the Gentiles in
faith and truth.

Men and Women in the Church

8I desire therefore that the men pray everywhere, lifting up holy hands, without wrath
and doubting; 9in like manner also, that the
women adorn themselves in modest apparel,
with propriety and moderation, not with
braided hair or gold or pearls or costly clothing, 10but, which is proper for women professing godliness, with good works. 11Let a
woman learn in silence with all submission.
12And I do not permit a woman to teach or to
have authority over a man, but to be in silence. 13For Adam was formed first, then Eve.
14And Adam was not deceived, but the woman
being deceived, fell into transgression. 15Nev-
ertheless she will be saved in childbearing if
they continue in faith, love, and holiness, with
self-control.

Qualifications of Overseers

3 This *is* a faithful saying: If a man desires
the position of a bishop,[a] he desires a
good work. 2A bishop then must be blameless,
the husband of one wife, temperate, sober-
minded, of good behavior, hospitable, able to
teach; 3not given to wine, not violent, not
greedy for money,[a] but gentle, not quarrel-
some, not covetous; 4one who rules his own
house well, having *his* children in submission
with all reverence 5(for if a man does not
know how to rule his own house, how will he
take care of the church of God?); 6not a novice, lest being puffed up with pride he fall into
the *same* condemnation as the devil. 7More-
over he must have a good testimony among
those who are outside, lest he fall into reproach and the snare of the devil.

Qualifications of Deacons

8Likewise deacons *must be* reverent, not
double-tongued, not given to much wine, not
greedy for money, 9holding the mystery of the
faith with a pure conscience. 10But let these
also first be tested; then let them serve as deacons, being *found* blameless. 11Likewise, *their*
wives *must be* reverent, not slanderers, temperate, faithful in all things. 12Let deacons be
the husbands of one wife, ruling *their* children
and their own houses well. 13For those who
have served well as deacons obtain for them-

3:1 [a]Literally *overseer* **3:3** [a]NU-Text omits *not greedy for money.*

SOUL NOTE

Power Packed *(2:8)* Imagine the power of prayers offered "without wrath and doubting"! Anger and doubt can make prayer difficult. Anger can be so divisive that Jesus warned people to make peace before coming to prayer (Matt. 5:23, 24). Doubt can make prayer less powerful, because we cannot pray confidently if we are unsure whether God hears, cares, or will answer. Prayer offered in total dependence and trust toward God is packed with power. We should come to God without doubting His commitment to being there for us when we need Him. **Topic: Doubt**

SOUL NOTE

Being His *(3:16)* This verse affirms both the humanity and divinity of Jesus Christ. He is human, having been "manifested in the flesh," and He is divine, having been "received up in glory." This is the great "mystery of godliness." We become godly not by trying to be good enough, but by depending on Jesus Christ. He lived a perfect human life, then He rose again to make it possible for us to one day be with Him. We can please God by accepting His Son, Jesus Christ. We live for Him by being His own. **Topic: Knowing Jesus**

selves a good standing and great boldness in
the faith which is in Christ Jesus.

THE GREAT MYSTERY

[14]These things I write to you, though I hope
to come to you shortly; [15]but if I am delayed, *I
write* so that you may know how you ought to
conduct yourself in the house of God, which is
the church of the living God, the pillar and
ground of the truth. [16]And without controversy great is the mystery of godliness:

God[a] was manifested in the flesh,
Justified in the Spirit,
Seen by angels,
Preached among the Gentiles,
Believed on in the world,
Received up in glory.

THE GREAT APOSTASY

4 Now the Spirit expressly says that in latter
times some will depart from the faith, giving heed to deceiving spirits and doctrines of
demons, [2]speaking lies in hypocrisy, having
their own conscience seared with a hot iron,
[3]forbidding to marry, *and commanding* to abstain from foods which God created to be
received with thanksgiving by those who believe and know the truth. [4]For every creature
of God *is* good, and nothing is to be refused if

3:16 [a]NU-Text reads *Who.*

Satan's Lies *(4:1–3)* False teachers abound today as they did in Paul's day. They may teach that god is in nature, or that god is found within oneself. Others may teach that God wants people to be rich or that He will not judge anyone. But any teaching that is contrary to God's Word is a lie. When people follow these teachings, they are "giving heed to deceiving spirits and doctrines of demons." Believers have to be on guard against the subtleties of false teaching, and we need to check every teaching against the truth in God's Word. **Topic: Cults**

KEY PASSAGE

Adolescent Development

SENSIBLE ADOLESCENCE

(4:7)

Adolescence is a time of great change. Young people transform from children into adults, gaining independence from their parents and moving toward life on their own. During this time, some young people rebel against authority, committing sins with consequences that last a lifetime. But it need not be that way.

Paul borrowed athletic words to describe spiritual growth. Whether new to the faith or raised in it from childhood, young people can "exercise" themselves toward godliness. To live a godly life during turbulent and uncertain adolescent years takes self-control, commitment, and continual work. As in working out for a sport, the Christian life requires daily work. Young people can develop spiritually through this time by entrusting their temptations, desires, frustrations, fears, and future to God. He cares about every part of their lives. Parents can help by praying for their children and maintaining open communication. The time of change can be exciting and rewarding for both the parents and the children who keep God front and center.

To Learn More: Turn to the article about adolescent development on pages 1104, 1105. See also the personality profile of Daniel on page 1102.

it is received with thanksgiving; [5]for it is sanctified by the word of God and prayer.

A Good Servant of Jesus Christ

[6]If you instruct the brethren in these things, you will be a good minister of Jesus Christ, nourished in the words of faith and of the good doctrine which you have carefully followed. [7]But reject profane and old wives' fables, and exercise yourself toward godliness. [8]For bodily exercise profits a little, but godliness is profitable for all things, having promise of the life that now is and of that which is to come. [9]This *is* a faithful saying and worthy of all acceptance. [10]For to this *end* we both labor and suffer reproach,[a] because we trust in the living God, who is *the* Savior of all men, especially of those who believe. [11]These things command and teach.

Take Heed to Your Ministry

[12]Let no one despise your youth, but be an example to the believers in word, in conduct, in love, in spirit,[a] in faith, in purity. [13]Till I come, give attention to reading, to exhortation, to doctrine. [14]Do not neglect the gift that is in you, which was given to you by prophecy with the laying on of the hands of the eldership. [15]Meditate on these things; give yourself entirely to them, that your progress may be evident to all. [16]Take heed to yourself and to the doctrine. Continue in them, for in doing this you will save both yourself and those who hear you.

Treatment of Church Members

5 Do not rebuke an older man, but exhort *him* as a father, younger men as brothers, [2]older women as mothers, younger women as sisters, with all purity.

Honor True Widows

[3]Honor widows who are really widows. [4]But if any widow has children or grandchildren, let them first learn to show piety at home and to repay their parents; for this is good and[a] acceptable before God. [5]Now she who is really a widow, and left alone, trusts in God and con-

4:10 [a]NU-Text reads *we labor and strive.*
4:12 [a]NU-Text omits *in spirit.* **5:4** [a]NU-Text and M-Text omit *good and.*

SOUL NOTE

Stay on Track *(4:7)* Anyone who has begun a new exercise regimen realizes the self-control needed, as well as the constant temptation to give up. It takes great discipline to keep exercising in order to see results. The same is true for spiritual training. Believers need to "exercise" themselves "toward godliness." It doesn't happen overnight; godliness is a process of discipline and self-control, with some days being easier than others. Every day brings temptation and difficulties, and believers must discipline themselves in order to stay on track with God. How is your personal spiritual exercise program? Are you seeing any results? **Topic: Spiritual Disciplines**

SOUL NOTE

Trust Talk *(4:10)* Believers have a great future promised by God. They train themselves toward godliness not *in order* to be saved but because they *are* saved and want to be ready for eternity with Christ. They are willing to work hard, deny themselves certain activities, and face reproach from an unbelieving world because they "trust in the living God." Their trust is in the One who died and rose again—not in a philosophy, a set of rules, personal achievement, or a standard of behavior. That trust in the living God is their anchor, their hope, their certain future. When we place our trust in God, we have nothing to fear. **Topic: Trust**

tinues in supplications and prayers night and
day. [6]But she who lives in pleasure is dead
while she lives. [7]And these things command,
that they may be blameless. [8]But if anyone
does not provide for his own, and especially
for those of his household, he has denied the
faith and is worse than an unbeliever.
[9]Do not let a widow under sixty years old be
taken into the number, *and not unless* she has
been the wife of one man, [10]well reported for
good works: if she has brought up children, if
she has lodged strangers, if she has washed
the saints' feet, if she has relieved the afflicted, if she has diligently followed every good
work.
[11]But refuse *the* younger widows; for when
they have begun to grow wanton against
Christ, they desire to marry, [12]having condemnation because they have cast off their
first faith. [13]And besides they learn *to be* idle,

PERSONALITY PROFILE

Life Transitions

TIMOTHY: LOTS OF CHANGES

(1 TIMOTHY 4:12–16)

Timothy had experienced many changes throughout his young life. When he received this letter from Paul, he was already the pastor of the large church that Paul had planted in Ephesus. Yet Timothy was still a young man, for Paul encouraged him by writing, "Let no one despise your youth." So it seems Timothy had come a long way in a short time.

Timothy had been born of a Jewish mother and a Greek father, and had received religious training through his mother and grandmother. When the great apostle Paul made his way to Lystra, he met this young man who appeared to have great potential. Because Timothy "was well spoken of by the brethren" (Acts 16:2), Paul invited him to join his second missionary journey.

Timothy seems to have been somewhat timid, for Paul often encouraged him in these letters. With a man like Paul behind him, Timothy could hardly help but grow into a strong leader. Paul entrusted him with several important missions, some of which consisted of traveling in Paul's place when he was imprisoned or detained for some reason.

Life is filled with change. We grow; we develop; we mature. Some people go through many changes before becoming Christians. Others are fortunate enough to come to the Lord at a young age and experience their changes with Him. Hopefully, the changes we experience help us grow and mature as Timothy did. When we are open to God's will, we never know what surprises He may have for us.

To Learn More: Turn to the article about life transitions on pages 540, 541. See also the key passage note at Ecclesiastes 3:1–11 on page 854.

SOUL NOTE

Unwrapped Gifts *(4:14, 15)* Paul encouraged Timothy to "not neglect the gift" that God had given him. God gives spiritual gifts to all believers. These gifts include teaching, hospitality, giving, or showing mercy (others are listed in Rom. 12; 1 Cor. 12; Eph. 4). Each person is responsible for discovering and using their own gifts for God's kingdom. The variety of gifts is needed in order for the church to function at its best. Not everyone has every gift, so the church needs all believers to be using responsibly the gifts God has chosen to give them. The church is in operating mode when all of its gifts are! **Topic: Responsibility**

wandering about from house to house, and
not only idle but also gossips and busybodies,
saying things which they ought not. [14]There-
fore I desire that *the* younger *widows* marry,
bear children, manage the house, give no opportunity to the adversary to speak reproachfully. [15]For some have already turned aside
after Satan. [16]If any believing man or[a] woman
has widows, let them relieve them, and do not
let the church be burdened, that it may relieve
those who are really widows.

Honor the Elders

[17]Let the elders who rule well be counted
worthy of double honor, especially those who
labor in the word and doctrine. [18]For the Scripture says, *"You shall not muzzle an ox while it
treads out the grain,"*[a] and, "The laborer *is*
worthy of his wages."[b] [19]Do not receive an accusation against an elder except from two or
three witnesses. [20]Those who are sinning rebuke in the presence of all, that the rest also
may fear.

[21]I charge *you* before God and the Lord
Jesus Christ and the elect angels that you observe these things without prejudice, doing
nothing with partiality. [22]Do not lay hands on
anyone hastily, nor share in other people's
sins; keep yourself pure.

[23]No longer drink only water, but use a little
wine for your stomach's sake and your frequent infirmities.

[24]Some men's sins are clearly evident, pre-
ceding *them* to judgment, but those of some
men follow later. [25]Likewise, the good works
of some are clearly evident, and those that are
otherwise cannot be hidden.

Honor Masters

6 Let as many bondservants as are under
the yoke count their own masters worthy
of all honor, so that the name of God and *His*
doctrine may not be blasphemed. [2]And those
who have believing masters, let them not despise *them* because they are brethren, but
rather serve *them* because those who are benefited are believers and beloved. Teach and exhort these things.

Error and Greed

[3]If anyone teaches otherwise and does not
consent to wholesome words, *even* the words
of our Lord Jesus Christ, and to the doctrine
which accords with godliness, [4]he is proud,
knowing nothing, but is obsessed with dis-

5:16 [a]NU-Text omits *man or.* **5:18** [a]Deuteronomy 25:4 [b]Luke 10:7

SOUL NOTE

Taking Care of Business *(5:8)* To neglect one's basic responsibility of care and support of the family is the same as denying the faith. No one can claim love for and allegiance to God while neglecting to provide for their family. Paul called such an irresponsible person "worse than an unbeliever," for even unbelievers understand family responsibility. God gives us our families and they are our first responsibility. We show our love for God through how we treat our family. We can thank God for the work He provides whereby we can take care of those who depend on us. **Topic: Work**

SOUL NOTE

Don't Pass It On *(5:13)* The context of this verse discusses the care of widows by the church. The truth taught, however, is that people with too much time on their hands often get into trouble. Without enough work to occupy their time, such people can become gossips and busybodies, visiting from house to house, "saying things which they ought not." That describes gossip—saying things that shouldn't be repeated. We should be careful about what we say, seeking to make sure that our words are truthful, loving, and edifying. **Topic: Gossip**

putes and arguments over words, from which
come envy, strife, reviling, evil suspicions,
5useless wranglings[a] of men of corrupt minds
and destitute of the truth, who suppose that
godliness is a *means of* gain. From such withdraw yourself.[b]
6Now godliness with
contentment is great
gain. 7For we brought
nothing into *this* world,
and it is certain[a] we can
carry nothing out. 8And
having food and cloth-
ing, with these we shall be content. 9But those
who desire to be rich fall into temptation and
a snare, and *into* many foolish and harmful
lusts which drown men in destruction and
perdition. 10For the love of money is a root of
all *kinds of* evil, for which some have strayed
from the faith in their greediness, and pierced
themselves through with many sorrows.

> Now godliness with contentment is great gain.
>
> 1 TIMOTHY 6:6

THE GOOD CONFESSION

11But you, O man of God, flee these things
and pursue righteousness, godliness, faith,
love, patience, gentle-
ness. 12Fight the good
fight of faith, lay hold
on eternal life, to which
you were also called and
have confessed the good
confession in the pres-
ence of many witnesses. 13I urge you in the
sight of God who gives life to all things, and

6:5 [a]NU-Text and M-Text read *constant friction.* [b]NU-Text omits this sentence. **6:7** [a]NU-Text omits *and it is certain.*

KEY PASSAGE

Money

ROOTED OUT

(6:6–10)

The Bible doesn't say that money is the root of all evil. Everybody needs money; no one can live without it. Money buys food and pays the bills. Financial donations help ministries support missionaries all over the world. Church offerings help pay the pastor. Money can do good things for God's kingdom.

The root of all evil is the *love* of money. People who love money simply "desire to be rich" more than anything else. Too often, as the Bible says, this leads them into "temptation and a snare," and into "many foolish and harmful lusts." Those who love money never have enough, and they do any number of stupid, illegal, or risky things in order to obtain more. They are never satisfied.

How do believers stay away from the love of money? "Godliness with contentment" is the answer. When we are content with what we have, we can give the extra back to Him.

To Learn More: Turn to the article about money on pages 480, 481. See also the personality profile of the rich young ruler on page 1295.

SOUL NOTE

Man of God *(6:11)* Paul described Timothy as a "man of God," certainly a fitting title for all men who seek to serve the Lord. In contrast to some who have "strayed from the faith" (6:10), God's men are to flee from the love of money, and to "pursue righteousness, godliness, faith, love, patience, gentleness." This is not an exhaustive list of all of the characteristics of a godly man, but it certainly is a good start. Men who seek to live this way in all areas of their life—work, family, church, friendship—will find true fulfillment and success. **Topic: Men's Issues**

BEING A REAL MAN

ROD COOPER

(I Timothy 6:11)

A free man is an authentic man. An authentic man's view of himself and the world around him is consistent with reality, honest, and accurate. Therefore, an authentic man is a "real" man. He is the genuine thing!

The authentic man is connected to his feelings. He may not know what his emotions mean, but he experiences them consciously and honestly. Too many men have learned to ignore their emotions. Often a man's conscious thoughts are disconnected from his emotions. He cannot seem to get them together. On the other hand, an authentic man is immediately conscious of his feelings because he knows who he is. He understands that his feelings are part of being a man. When those emotions well up in him, he is not afraid of them. He is in touch with them.

The authentic man responds quickly to what he is feeling and to what is happening around him. He experiences those feelings of spontaneity, which allow him to respond freely. It would be easy to assume that an authentic man experiences emotions and then spontaneously does whatever he feels like doing. That is not the case. Instead, an authentic man identifies what is happening inside himself. He processes what he is feeling and evaluates it by getting his feelings out and then acting on them in a responsible manner.

Jesus understood His emotions. When faced with the merchants and money changers in the temple, He reacted with appropriate anger (John 2:13–17). The Bible says that when faced with the death of Lazarus, "Jesus wept" (John 11:35). When He saw the multitudes who were like sheep without a shepherd, "He was moved with compassion for them" (Matt. 14:14).

BECOMING AUTHENTIC

Authentic Men Need to Cultivate Their Relationship with God

It is only natural for people to look to other people to meet their deepest emotional needs. The problem is, they can't! Asking them to do so is like trying to draw water from a dry well. People are not equipped to fill our emotional cup—only God can do that! He knows us for what we really are and still loves us in spite of ourselves. By allowing us to participate in His purpose for our lives, He gives us a sense of significance that we cannot give ourselves. Men need to cultivate their relationship with God—drawing close to Him daily and depending on Him as they make decisions and handle the pressures of everyday life.

Authentic Men Need to Cultivate Their Relationships with Men

Sometimes it shocks men when I tell them they need more than God. That almost sounds sacrilegious. But it is not. We were created for relationship. And if we want to be authentic men, we must cultivate relationships with other men.

Time and time again, Jesus was transparent with His disciples. He ate with them, slept under the stars with them, prayed with them, cried with them, and even resolved their arguments. He revealed Himself clearly to them and told them, "I have called you friends, for all things that I heard from My Father I have made known to you" (John 15:15).

So then, real men—authentic men—care about God and others.

BECOMING A LEADER

Most men want to be leaders, but only a few ever succeed at leading. Too many men want to dictate without leading. They want to command without setting the example. Genuine leadership involves mentoring those around us—our wives, our children, our friends. We cannot simply *tell* them what to do; we must *show* them by the example of our own lives. Most of those we lead will not rise above the level of our leadership—they will simply reproduce what we are. That is why it is so important that we, as men and as leaders, become all that God intended us to be.

Real leaders reach out to others. They see a need and meet it. When someone is struggling, they are quick to lend a helping hand, an open heart, or a word of comfort and encouragement. They help people face their fears, conquer their doubts, and find their way. They are men who have experienced the challenges of life, and who have partaken deeply of the wells of spirituality.

Leaders are men who help others become leaders as well. They are disciplers of men, women, and children. They are men who have experienced the grace of God in their own lives and want to pass it on to others. The apostle Paul told Timothy: "You therefore, my son, be strong in the grace that is in Christ Jesus. And the things that you have heard from me among many witnesses, commit these to faithful men who will be able to teach others also" (2 Tim. 2:1, 2). Peter wrote to the believers, "Therefore, brethren, be even more diligent to make your call and election sure, for if you do these things you will never stumble; for so an entrance will be supplied to you abundantly into the everlasting kingdom of our Lord and Savior Jesus Christ" (2 Pet. 1:10, 11).

Males are born; men are made. God uses the difficulties of men's lives to strengthen us so that we can better serve those who need our help and leadership.

FURTHER MEDITATION:

Other passages to study about men's issues include:

- Proverbs 1:5
- Matthew 5:14–16
- 1 Corinthians 4:1, 2; 13:11
- Galatians 6:1–6
- 1 Timothy 5:8
- 1 Peter 3:7
- 2 Peter 1:5–11
- 1 John 3:16–18

To Learn More: Turn to the key passage note on men's issues at Titus 2:2 on page 1615. See also the personality profile of Titus on page 1613.

before Christ Jesus who witnessed the good
confession before Pontius Pilate, [14]that you
keep *this* commandment without spot, blameless until our Lord Jesus Christ's appearing,
[15]which He will manifest in His own time, *He*
who is the blessed and only Potentate, the King
of kings and Lord of lords, [16]who alone has immortality, dwelling in unapproachable light,
whom no man has seen or can see, to whom *be*
honor and everlasting power. Amen.

Instructions to the Rich

[17]Command those who are rich in this present age not to be haughty, nor to trust in uncertain riches but in the living God, who gives
us richly all things to enjoy. [18]*Let them* do
good, that they be rich in good works, ready to
give, willing to share, [19]storing up for themselves a good foundation for the time to come,
that they may lay hold on eternal life.

Guard the Faith

[20]O Timothy! Guard what was committed to
your trust, avoiding the profane *and* idle
babblings and contradictions of what is falsely
called knowledge—[21]by professing it some
have strayed concerning the faith.

Grace *be* with you. Amen.

2 Timothy

The words of a dying person—especially a great person—will always grab our attention. Last words, as the old saying goes, are words that last.

When the apostle Paul wrote one last note to Timothy (2 Timothy), he was awaiting execution in a Roman prison (A.D. 67). Paul challenged his "son in the faith" to a life marked by faithful service—even in the face of suffering and persecution. Paul exhorted Timothy to handle the Word of God accurately (2:15) and to proclaim it boldly (3:15—4:2). To drive home his message, Paul used a variety of word pictures. He mentioned soldiers who must "endure hardship" and remain focused (2:3, 4), athletes who play by the rules (2:5), farmers who need great patience (2:6), workers who must be diligent (2:15), and vessels that are used by the Master only if clean (2:20, 21).

Thankfully, God has preserved this final bit of intimate correspondence. It reminds us that we must both understand and keep the faith. Do you have a Paul in your life to help you in this all-important process of soul care? We must also pass the faith on. Do you have a Timothy to pour your life into? This is God's preferred method (2:2) for making disciples. It's also the way to insure that when you get to the end of your life you'll be able to say with Paul, "I have fought the good fight, I have finished the race, I have kept the faith" (4:7).

SOUL CONCERN IN 2 TIMOTHY

GREETING

1 Paul, an apostle of Jesus Christ[a] by the will of God, according to the promise of life which is in Christ Jesus,

[2]To Timothy, a beloved son:

Grace, mercy, *and* peace from God the Father and Christ Jesus our Lord.

TIMOTHY'S FAITH AND HERITAGE

[3]I thank God, whom I serve with a pure
conscience, as *my* forefathers *did,* as without ceasing I remember you in my prayers
night and day, [4]greatly desiring to see you,
being mindful of your tears, that I may be
filled with joy, [5]when I call to remembrance
the genuine faith that is in you, which dwelt
first in your grandmother Lois and your mother Eunice, and I am persuaded is in you also.
[6]Therefore I remind you to stir up the gift of
God which is in you through the laying on of
my hands. [7]For God has not given us a spirit of
fear, but of power and of love and of a sound
mind.

NOT ASHAMED OF THE GOSPEL

[8]Therefore do not be ashamed of the testimony of our Lord, nor of me His prisoner, but
share with me in the sufferings for the gospel
according to the power of God, [9]who has
saved us and called *us* with a holy calling, not
according to our works, but according to His
own purpose and grace which was given to us
in Christ Jesus before time began, [10]but has
now been revealed by the appearing of our
Savior Jesus Christ, *who* has abolished death
and brought life and immortality to light
through the gospel, [11]to which I was appointed a preacher, an apostle, and a teacher of the
Gentiles.[a] [12]For this reason I also suffer these
things; nevertheless I am not ashamed, for I
know whom I have believed and am persuaded that He is able to keep what I have committed to Him until that Day.

BE LOYAL TO THE FAITH

[13]Hold fast the pattern of sound words

1:1 [a]NU-Text and M-Text read *Christ Jesus.*
1:11 [a]NU-Text omits *of the Gentiles.*

PERSONALITY PROFILE

Family Life

TIMOTHY: A GODLY HERITAGE

(2 TIMOTHY 1:5)

Never underestimate the power of godly parents. In Timothy's case, a godly mother and grandmother had taught him about faith in the God of Israel. Grandmother Lois influenced mother Eunice, and they both taught young Timothy. When the apostle Paul came to their hometown of Lystra with the Good News of the Messiah, Timothy's heart was ready to hear and accept the message.

An interesting side note to this story is recorded in Acts 16. Timothy's father was a Greek, not a Jew. It was unusual for a Jewish woman to marry outside of her faith, but Eunice had done so. Yet she had held fast to her faith, teaching it to her son. The father seems at least not to have worked against her, allowing his son to be raised with Jewish teaching, although Timothy was never circumcised, as all Jewish boys must be. Through all of these possible stumbling blocks, God fashioned a young man who would serve the great apostle in many capacities, eventually taking on leadership himself.

Lois and Eunice are two of the quiet heroes of the New Testament. They provided Timothy with a good family life and solid spiritual teaching. No matter what other situations may exist in a family, Christian parents can provide these two benefits for their children. Even if there is only one believing parent, he or she can work toward this end and pray that the other parent will be supportive. And believing grandparents can help. God is fashioning the leaders of tomorrow in the homes of today.

To Learn More: Turn to the article about family life on pages 294, 295. See also the key passage note at Psalm 127:3–5 on page 778.

which you have heard from me, in faith and love which are in Christ Jesus. [14]That good thing which was committed to you, keep by the Holy Spirit who dwells in us.

[15]This you know, that all those in Asia have turned away from me, among whom are Phygellus and Hermogenes. [16]The Lord grant mercy to the household of Onesiphorus, for he often refreshed me, and was not ashamed of my chain; [17]but when he arrived in Rome, he sought me out very zealously and found *me.* [18]The Lord grant to him that he may find mercy from the Lord in that Day—and you know very well how many ways he ministered *to me*[a] at Ephesus.

Be Strong in Grace

2 You therefore, my son, be strong in the grace that is in Christ Jesus. [2]And the things that you have heard from me among many witnesses, commit these to faithful men who will be able to teach others also. [3]You therefore must endure[a] hardship as a good soldier of Jesus Christ. [4]No one engaged in warfare entangles himself with the affairs of *this* life, that he may please him who enlisted him as a soldier. [5]And also if anyone competes in athletics, he is not crowned unless he competes according to the rules. [6]The hardworking farmer must be first to partake of the crops. [7]Consider what I say, and may[a] the Lord give you understanding in all things.

[8]Remember that Jesus Christ, of the seed of

1:18 [a]*To me* is from the Vulgate and a few Greek manuscripts. **2:3** [a]NU-Text reads *You must share.* **2:7** [a]NU-Text reads *the Lord will give you.*

KEY PASSAGE

Mother-hood

MORE THAN FULL TIME

(1:5)

When God had told the first couple, Adam and Eve, to "fill the earth" (Gen. 1:28), He had created woman with the capacity to carry and give birth to another living being. Nowhere else in the animal kingdom are mothers so vital to their children for such a long time. No other animals have the same emotional ties that humans carry throughout their lifetimes. Nowhere else are mothers and grandmothers so honored.

Being a mother is a high calling and must be entered into with thought and preparation. Young women should wait until they are married to take on this huge responsibility. Women who have experienced divorce or widowhood need special support as they continue to mother alone. Most important, every mother needs a personal relationship with her heavenly Father to guide her in her most important occupation—being a mom.

To Learn More: Turn to the article about motherhood on pages 1312, 1313. See also the personality profile of Mary the mother of Jesus on page 1315.

SOUL NOTE

Worry Replacers *(1:7)* Those who worry are not trusting God. Worry can be a natural first reaction to an uncertain situation, but to persist in worry reveals a lack of trust that God is in charge. Besides, God has not given believers "a spirit of fear, but of power and of love and of a sound mind." *Power* helps us have strength of character and confidence in any situation. *Love* helps us graciously deal with difficult people. A *sound mind* helps us remain self-controlled and self-disciplined no matter what happens. We can set aside our worry and replace it with these gifts from God.
Topic: Worry

David, was raised from the dead according to
my gospel, 9for which I suffer trouble as an
evildoer, *even* to the point of chains; but the
word of God is not chained. 10Therefore I endure all things for the sake of the elect, that
they also may obtain the salvation which is in
Christ Jesus with eternal glory.
11*This is* a faithful saying:

For if we died with *Him*,
We shall also live with *Him*.
12 If we endure,
We shall also reign with *Him*.
If we deny *Him*,
He also will deny us.
13 If we are faithless,
He remains faithful;
He cannot deny Himself.

Approved and Disapproved Workers

14Remind *them* of these things, charging *them*
before the Lord not to strive about words to no
profit, to the ruin of the hearers. 15Be diligent to
present yourself approved to God, a worker who
does not need to be ashamed, rightly dividing
the word of truth. 16But shun profane *and* idle
babblings, for they will increase to more ungodliness. 17And their message will spread like
cancer. Hymenaeus and Philetus are of this
sort, 18who have strayed concerning the truth,
saying that the resurrection is already past; and
they overthrow the faith of some. 19Neverthe-
less the solid foundation of God stands, having
this seal: "The Lord knows those who are His,"
and, "Let everyone who names the name of
Christ[a] depart from iniquity."

2:19 [a]NU-Text and M-Text read *the Lord*.

KEY PASSAGE

Mentoring

PASS IT ON

(2:2)

God worked through the many teachers in the early church, protecting His message so that it did not get changed or garbled as it was passed from person to person, from one generation to the next. The early believers had no written New Testament, but they depended on the spoken gospel message as it was taught to them by others. The process is called mentoring, or discipling, and through it God's message is taught to people who in turn will teach others.

Although Paul was nearing the end of his earthly life, his ministry would continue because he had mentored Timothy. Eventually Timothy would die too, so he would need to commit the message "to faithful men who will be able to teach others also." In that way, the message would move across the world and across the centuries. We are believers today because faithful people have been teaching others for hundreds of years. We must mentor others so the message continues. God has given us that responsibility.

To Learn More: Turn to the article about mentoring on pages 430, 431. See also the personality profile of Elijah and Elisha on page 465.

SOUL NOTE

Truth Teaching *(2:15)* Paul warned Timothy that false teachers would attempt to distort the gospel message. The best weapon against false teaching is the truth of God's Word—in the hands of diligent workers who have no need to be ashamed of it or their handling of it. Believers who are "rightly dividing the word of truth" know God's Word, understand its meaning, and teach it correctly. The truth of God's Word has not changed from Timothy's day to today. We ought to diligently study the Bible so that we can know and share its truths with others correctly. **Topic: Truth**

20But in a great house there are not only vessels of gold and silver, but also of wood and
clay, some for honor and some for dishonor.
21Therefore if anyone cleanses himself from
the latter, he will be a vessel for honor, sanctified and useful for the Master, prepared for
every good work. 22Flee also youthful lusts;
but pursue righteousness, faith, love, peace
with those who call on the Lord out of a pure
heart. 23But avoid foolish and ignorant disputes, knowing that they generate strife.
24And a servant of the Lord must not quarrel
but be gentle to all, able to teach, patient, 25in
humility correcting those who are in opposition, if God perhaps will grant them repentance, so that they may know the truth, 26and
that they may come to their senses *and escape*
the snare of the devil, having been taken captive by him to *do* his will.

Perilous Times and Perilous Men

3 But know this, that in the last days perilous times will come: 2For men will be lovers of themselves, lovers of money, boasters,
proud, blasphemers, disobedient to parents,
unthankful, unholy, 3unloving, unforgiving,
slanderers, without self-control, brutal, despisers of good, 4traitors, headstrong, haughty,

SOUL NOTE

Run Away *(2:22)* Believers have a responsibility to be pure. No matter what a person's past, God will forgive. Once someone believes, the Holy Spirit enters their life to help them deal with the continual temptations of the sinful nature. Some situations are more tempting for a person than others are, and in such cases the believer's best resource may simply be to flee. The "youthful lusts" here are not just sexual desires, although these are included. The area of temptation that causes us the most difficulty may be the one from which we simply must run. God is not dishonored when we flee temptation. He is dishonored when we give in. **Topic: Temptation**

SOUL NOTE

Never Give Up *(2:25, 26)* Paul was teaching Timothy how to deal with those in the church who oppose the truth. This teaching also applies to parents who are dealing with "opposing" children. Timothy was not to give up on contrary church members, and parents shouldn't give up on their contrary children—because they don't know "if God perhaps will grant them repentance, so that they may know the truth." Parents pray and teach, hoping that their children will "come to their senses." We must entrust our rebellious children to God. **Topic: Adolescent Problems**

SOUL NOTE

Too Tolerant *(3:1–9)* There is a time for tolerance; there is also a time for intolerance. Being tolerant can be a positive characteristic when dealing with people's idiosyncrasies or weaknesses. Tolerance is also positive when it frees someone from prejudice toward a person's race or culture. But believers must not be tolerant of anyone who claims to teach the faith while living opposed to it ("having a form of godliness but denying its power"). "From such people turn away," exclaims Paul, for they cause great danger to weak believers. That's the kind of tolerance we don't need. **Topic: Tolerance**

OBEDIENCE OR MERE EXCELLENCE?

STEPHEN ARTERBURN

(2 Timothy 2:22)

Why is it so easy for people to compromise their standards of sexual sin and so difficult to firmly commit to obedience? Perhaps it is because people are used to compromise. Most people easily tolerate mixed standards of sexual purity because they tolerate mixed standards in other areas. If mixed standards are the rule, people are not motivated to single out sexual standards and maintain purity in that one area.

Sexual sin begins when people stop short of God's standard of sexual purity, which is complete obedience to His commands. God commands that sex be a part of a married relationship between a husband and a wife. People who obey that command have sexual integrity.

OBEDIENCE OR EXCELLENCE?

Normally, we might consider these two words to be synonymous. After all, if we are acting obediently, isn't that excellent? There is a difference, however. In business, the *pursuit* of excellence is considered to be good enough. Few businesses would try to be truly perfect, because true perfection is too costly. Businesses know it is enough to *seem* to be in pursuit of excellence. The "search for excellence" becomes a comfortable and profitable pit stop short of the price of perfection.

In the same way, Christians are tempted to stop short of perfection. Instead of truly being obedient, they are content to appear to be in pursuit of excellence. That way they can feel content that they are "trying," without the cost of perfect obedience. They can cross boundaries of sexual purity, becoming dangerously distinguished only by the fact that they are not involved in actual intercourse. Ironically, they consider themselves to be "obedient" because they have the appearance of excellence. However, "excellence" in this sense is a mixed standard, and it is not good enough. It is not sexual integrity.

THE COST OF DISOBEDIENCE

When people's standards of sexual purity move closer to that of their peers, the result is distance from God. Christians are often indistinguishable from non-Christians—sharing the same activities and attitudes about premarital sex. Many Christian singles groups don't question men and women among them who are sexually active. Christian couples have also fallen short, reeling in the wake of adulterous affairs and marital separations. However, Scripture warns, "But fornication and all uncleanness or covetousness, let it not even be named among you, as is fitting for saints; neither filthiness, nor foolish talking, nor coarse jesting, which are not fitting" (Eph. 5:3, 4).

THE COST OF OBEDIENCE

Christians who live according to mixed standards may seem "good enough" to a depraved world. However, God's standard of perfection beckons Christians to go farther and demonstrate the cost of obedience in their lives.

For example, it costs a family to have regular worship and devotion times. However, those who seek obedience to God's commands pay a price in their priorities and are rewarded by stability and purpose amid their frantic activities. In the same way, it costs something to insist that one's children practice modesty in their appearance and attitudes—it's easier to give in and avoid the battle. However, the family that invests in a framework for making moral decisions is prepared for the cost.

In the realm of sexual integrity, it costs something to control one's eyes, heart, and mind when lured by the temptations in magazine racks, movies, and video stores. God doesn't demand obedience in order to take the fun and thrill out of life. Instead, He knows that sexual purity is for our good and for the good of His kingdom. He wants His children to be "blameless and harmless, children of God without fault in the midst of a crooked and perverse generation, among whom you shine as lights in the world" (Phil. 2:15).

Every believer's heart faces a daily spiritual battle for purity. The costs are real. Obedience is hard, requiring humility and meekness. Too many people refuse to commit to obedience because of the "unforeseen situations" they assume may try their attempted standards anyway.

Sexual impurity has become rampant in the church because people have ignored the costly work of obedience to God. "For this is the will of God, your sanctification: that you should abstain from sexual immorality. . . . For God did not call us to uncleanness, but in holiness" (1 Thess. 4:3, 7). Christians have crafted an image and may even seem sexually pure, while permitting their eyes to roam when no one is around. It is easy to avoid the hard work of sexual purity! They have also ignored the cost of Christ's sacrifice on their behalf. Believers who truly comprehend the obedience of Christ—difficult obedience, in order to cleanse us from sin—should not even want to sin in His presence.

THE REWARDS OF OBEDIENCE

Recognizing the tolerance of sin in one's own life is the first step toward reaching the greater goal of true obedience. It costs something to learn about Christ's standards for living and even more to live like Him. However, the rewards for doing so are immeasurable, both for this life and the life to come. Sexual integrity brings great hope and joy. While a search for excellence or "how holy can I be" leaves one vulnerable to the dangerous snare of compromise, obedience builds greater hope for a growing faith. Instead of merely getting by with the pretension of "appearing" good enough, Christians who seek to obey God will find that His rewards far outweigh any of the costs.

FURTHER MEDITATION:

Other passages to study about the issue of sexual integrity include:

- Genesis 2:24
- Proverbs 4:1–27; 5:18
- Romans 7:13–25
- 1 Corinthians 7:5; 10:13
- Hebrews 4:12
- James 4:7, 8

To Learn More: Turn to the key passage note on sexual integrity at 1 Corinthians 6:15 on page 1499. See also the personality profile of Ruth and Boaz on page 336.

lovers of pleasure rather than lovers of God, [5]having a form of godliness but denying its power. And from such people turn away! [6]For of this sort are those who creep into households and make captives of gullible women loaded down with sins, led away by various lusts, [7]always learning and never able to come to the knowledge of the truth. [8]Now as Jannes and Jambres resisted Moses, so do these also resist the truth: men of corrupt minds, disapproved concerning the faith; [9]but they will progress no further, for their folly will be manifest to all, as theirs also was.

The Man of God and the Word of God

[10]But you have carefully followed my doctrine, manner of life, purpose, faith, longsuffering, love, perseverance, [11]persecutions, afflictions, which happened to me at Antioch, at Iconium, at Lystra—what persecutions I endured. And out of *them* all the Lord delivered me. [12]Yes, and all who desire to live godly in Christ Jesus will suffer persecution. [13]But evil men and impostors will grow worse and worse, deceiving and being deceived. [14]But you must continue in the things which you have learned and been assured of, knowing from whom you have learned *them,* [15]and that from childhood you have known the Holy Scriptures, which are able to make you wise for salvation through faith which is in Christ Jesus.

[16]All Scripture *is* given by inspiration of God, and *is* profitable for doctrine, for reproof, for correction, for instruction in righteousness, [17]that the man of God may be complete, thoroughly equipped for every good work.

Preach the Word

4 I charge *you* therefore before God and the Lord Jesus Christ, who will judge the living and the dead at[a] His appearing and His kingdom: [2]Preach the word! Be ready in season *and* out of season. Convince, rebuke, exhort, with all longsuffering and teaching. [3]For the time will come when they will not endure sound doctrine, but according to their own desires, *because* they have itching ears, they will heap up for themselves teachers; [4]and they will turn *their* ears away from the truth, and be turned aside to fables. [5]But you be watchful in all things, endure afflictions, do the work of an evangelist, fulfill your ministry.

Paul's Valedictory

[6]For I am already being poured out as a drink offering, and the time of my departure is at hand. [7]I have fought the good fight, I have finished the race, I have kept the faith. [8]Finally, there is laid up for me the crown of righteousness, which the Lord, the righteous Judge, will give to me on that Day, and not to me only but also to all who have loved His appearing.

> I have fought the good fight,
> I have finished the race,
> I have kept the faith.
>
> 2 TIMOTHY 4:7

The Abandoned Apostle

[9]Be diligent to come to me quickly; [10]for Demas has forsaken me, having loved this present world, and has departed for Thessalonica—Crescens for Galatia, Titus for Dalmatia. [11]Only Luke is with me. Get Mark and bring him with you, for he is useful to me for minis-

---

4:1 [a]NU-Text omits *therefore* and reads *and by* for *at.*

SOUL NOTE

Early Education *(3:14, 15)* Timothy had been learning the Holy Scriptures from childhood. Christian parents have the God-given responsibility to raise their children to know and love God and His word. Young children can learn the great truths and stories found in the Bible that show God's love and power. Teaching given to young children will be embedded in their minds, giving them a strong foundation on which to build. That training is able to make them "wise for salvation through faith which is in Christ Jesus." **Topic: Parenting**

try. [12]And Tychicus I have sent to Ephesus.
[13]Bring the cloak that I left with Carpus at Troas when you come—and the books, especially
the parchments.
[14]Alexander the coppersmith did me much
harm. May the Lord repay him according to
his works. [15]You also must beware of him, for
he has greatly resisted our words.
[16]At my first defense no one stood with me,
but all forsook me. May it not be charged
against them.

The Lord Is Faithful

[17]But the Lord stood with me and strengthened me, so that the message might be
preached fully through me, and *that* all the
Gentiles might hear. Also I was delivered out
of the mouth of the lion. [18]And the Lord will
deliver me from every evil work and preserve
me for His heavenly kingdom. To Him *be* glory
forever and ever. Amen!

Come Before Winter

[19]Greet Prisca and Aquila, and the household of Onesiphorus. [20]Erastus stayed in Corinth, but Trophimus I have left in Miletus sick.
[21]Do your utmost to come before winter.
Eubulus greets you, as well as Pudens, Li-
nus, Claudia, and all the brethren.

Farewell

[22]The Lord Jesus Christ[a] be with your spirit.
Grace be with you. Amen.

4:22 [a]NU-Text omits *Jesus Christ.*

SOUL NOTE

Ready to Go *(4:6–8)* Paul knew that he would soon die, yet he was not fearful or worried for his ministry or for himself. He knew that others would faithfully carry on the task of spreading the gospel message. He knew that he was on his way to glory in heaven and a crown of righteousness. He knew that his job was done, and it was time to go. Believers can face death with confidence, knowing that God is waiting for them. May we all be able to say, "I have fought the good fight, I have finished the race, I have kept the faith." **Topic: Death**

Titus

Do you know any hypocrites? Do you ever feel like one?

One of the most common criticisms of the church is that it is filled with people who know a lot of biblical facts, but whose lives are not exactly marked by biblical acts.

This is not a new criticism. Around A.D. 63, the apostle Paul sent a brief letter to a pastor named Titus who was ministering on the island of Crete—a place notorious for its moral corruption. The gist of his message: Know the truth and live it.

Titus's name is not mentioned in the Book of Acts, but Paul's letters let us know that he was both a convert and a trusted colleague of the great apostle. This letter gives Titus instructions for leading the churches under his influence.

First, Paul urged Titus to root himself and his congregation in the truth ("sound doctrine"—see 2:1). Paul understood that behavior is shaped by belief, that people become what they think. Second, Paul stressed that the Christians at Crete needed to do "good works" (1:16; 2:7, 14; 3:1, 8, 14) so as to "adorn the doctrine of God" (2:10). In other words, they would represent God's truth better if they modeled authentic, counter-cultural Christian living.

It's still the same now. Believers in Jesus still need to be people of God's book. Cynical unbelievers still need to see Christians living with integrity and authenticity before they can be convinced of the power of the gospel.

We can resist the hypocritical Christian experience that has become so commonplace in the church and is so repulsive to onlookers. Titus shows us how to make the gospel attractive in our own lives.

GREETING

1 Paul, a bondservant of God and an apostle
of Jesus Christ, according to the faith of
God's elect and the acknowledgment of the
truth which accords with godliness, [2]in hope
of eternal life which God, who cannot lie,
promised before time began, [3]but has in due
time manifested His word through preaching,

SOUL NOTE

Promises Kept *(1:2)* The power of any promise depends on the character of the person who is making the promise. God promised eternal life "before time began." Those who accept Jesus Christ as Savior will obtain the fulfillment of that promise. We can be certain that the promise will be fulfilled, because it is not in God's character to lie. Because we can trust in the character of God, we can also trust in His promise of eternal life in heaven with Him. Such a promise should motivate us to live for Him each day. **Topic: God's Promises**

PERSONALITY PROFILE

Men's Issues

TITUS—CHOOSING GODLY MEN

(TITUS 1:6)

Titus served as the apostle Paul's ambassador to Crete. They spent time on the island spreading the gospel, and Paul left his young disciple behind to strengthen the local churches. The letter Paul sent Titus served as a job description for a crucial task. Paul knew that the success of Titus's efforts would depend on his ability to identify a few good and godly men.

Paul and Titus were fishers of men. They preached a gospel that functioned like a huge net. People of all different backgrounds, experiences, and levels of maturity were drawn to Christ. That diverse gathering of people had to be sorted out and organized. Character qualities had to be identified. Leadership qualities had to be utilized. Titus had the difficult task of spotting those who were on their way to maturity in Christ. He had to further equip and encourage them to serve others as leaders in the church.

On Crete, Paul told Titus to start with the men. He gave Titus a list of traits to look for in a man who would make a good elder among believers. The qualities Paul listed still measure a man's leadership potential. In fact, those qualities (Titus 1:5–9) include most of the male issues facing men today. Titus was on the lookout for men who were:

- Blameless—who didn't leave problems unsettled in their lives.
- Faithful to one wife.
- Raising healthy children.
- Living out a humble relationship with God.
- Not self-willed, quick-tempered, violent, or greedy.
- Practicing hospitality and loving good things.
- Thinking clearly and pursuing justice, holiness, and self-control.
- Effectively modeling and teaching the Christian faith.

The church of Jesus Christ still longs for people who will live out their faith with such character. When such leaders are in place, the gospel spreads its net in even wider circles, and more and more people come to Christ. Titus was looking for leaders who had what it takes to care for souls.

To Learn More: Turn to the article about men's issues on pages 1600, 1601. See also the key passage note at Titus 2:2 on page 1615.

which was committed to me according to the commandment of God our Savior;

[4]To Titus, a true son in *our* common faith:

Grace, mercy, *and* peace from God the Father and the Lord Jesus Christ[a] our Savior.

Qualified Elders

[5]For this reason I left you in Crete, that you should set in order the things that are lacking, and appoint elders in every city as I commanded you— [6]if a man is blameless, the husband of one wife, having faithful children not accused of dissipation or insubordination. [7]For a bishop[a] must be blameless, as a steward of God, not self-willed, not quick-tempered, not given to wine, not violent, not greedy for money, [8]but hospitable, a lover of what is good, sober-minded, just, holy, self-controlled, [9]holding fast the faithful word as he has been taught, that he may be able, by sound doctrine, both to exhort and convict those who contradict.

The Elders' Task

[10]For there are many insubordinate, both idle talkers and deceivers, especially those of the circumcision, [11]whose mouths must be stopped, who subvert whole households, teaching things which they ought not, for the sake of dishonest gain. [12]One of them, a prophet of their own, said, "Cretans *are* always liars, evil beasts, lazy gluttons." [13]This testimony is true. Therefore rebuke them sharply, that they may be sound in the faith, [14]not giving heed to Jewish fables and commandments of men who turn from the truth. [15]To the pure all things are pure, but to those who are defiled and unbelieving nothing is pure; but even their mind and conscience are defiled. [16]They profess to know God, but in works they deny Him, being abominable, disobedient, and disqualified for every good work.

Qualities of a Sound Church

2 But as for you, speak the things which are proper for sound doctrine: [2]that the older men be sober, reverent, temperate, sound in faith, in love, in patience; [3]the older women likewise, that they be reverent in behavior, not slanderers, not given to much wine, teachers of good things—[4]that they admonish the young women to love their husbands, to love their children, [5]to be discreet, chaste, homemakers, good, obedient to their own husbands, that the word of God may not be blasphemed.

[6]Likewise, exhort the young men to be sober-minded, [7]in all things showing yourself

1:4 [a]NU-Text reads *and Christ Jesus.* **1:7** [a]Literally *overseer*

KEY PASSAGE

Cults

INFILTRATORS

(1:16)

False teachers had infiltrated the church in Crete. They were claiming to be believers but undermining the gospel by teaching bad doctrine. Paul explained their error: "They profess to know God, but in works they deny Him."

Today, false teachers continue to profess to know God and His word but offer incorrect teaching. Believers should know the Bible so as to perceive a false teacher quickly. Every teaching should be consistent with God's Word. Younger or immature believers, however, may be enticed by a false teacher who has style and uses appealing words. Even if believers cannot perceive an error in the teaching, Paul wrote that a false teacher's life will reveal the truth. The teacher's actions and attitudes will speak volumes about their priorities and what they really believe. We must always be discerning about the teachers we listen to. Not everything that sounds good is good for you.

To Learn More: Turn to the article about cults on pages 1552, 1553. See also the personality profile of Simon the sorcerer on page 1429.

to be a pattern of good works; in doctrine
showing integrity, reverence, incorruptibility,[a]
8sound speech that cannot be condemned,
that one who is an opponent may be
ashamed, having nothing evil to say of you.[a]
9*Exhort* bondservants to be obedient to their
own masters, to be well pleasing in all *things,*

2:7 [a]NU-Text omits *incorruptibility.* **2:8** [a]NU-Text and M-Text read *us.*

KEY PASSAGE

Men's Issues

GODLY EXAMPLES

(2:2)

The "older men" to whom this verse refers are not necessarily elders or leaders in the church. These are the senior members of the church community, and that stature carried a responsibility to be examples to the young Christian men. Paul identified four characteristics that older Christian men should model in the church and to the community:

- *Be sober* can mean the opposite of drunkenness, but a broader meaning describes being balanced, showing moderation and clear-headedness.
- Be *reverent* means worthy of respect, dignified, honorable.
- Be *temperate* means having self-control, monitoring one's words and actions, being sensible about how to live in a heathen society.
- Be *sound in faith, in love, in patience* reveals a soundness in life, with healthy personal faith, positive relationships, and earnest steadfastness.

Christian men, whatever their age, have the responsibility to live well before God and before others who are watching them.

To Learn More: Turn to the article about men's issues on pages 1600, 1601. See also the personality profile of Titus on page 1613.

KEY PASSAGE

Women's Issues

MODELING

(2:3–5)

Christian older women have a responsibility to set a good example for the younger women. These older women in Paul's day had lived much of their lives before knowing Christ. They could help the younger women to avoid their mistakes by teaching about the change Christ had worked in their lives and by modeling the qualities of a godly lifestyle. Older women are to be respectable, good teachers, not gossips, and not heavy drinkers. Then they can teach Christian young women.

An important lesson for young women is that they learn to place a high priority on the family. Young women should be taught to love their husbands and children, placing those needs before their own. Christian young women, married or not, must be discreet, pure, and good. No matter what other activities fill their lives, they are responsible for their homes, and married women must submit to their husbands as the head of the household. Women honor Christ when they place Him first and follow His guidelines for living.

To Learn More: Turn to the article about women's issues on pages 846, 847. See also the personality profile of the virtuous woman on page 845.

not answering back, 10 not pilfering, but showing all good fidelity, that they may adorn the
doctrine of God our Savior in all things.

Trained by Saving Grace

11 For the grace of God that brings salvation
has appeared to all men, 12 teaching us that,
denying ungodliness and worldly lusts, we
should live soberly, righteously, and godly in
the present age, 13 looking for the blessed hope
and glorious appearing of our great God and
Savior Jesus Christ, 14 who gave Himself for
us, that He might redeem us from every lawless deed and purify for Himself *His* own special people, zealous for good works.
15 Speak these things, exhort, and rebuke
with all authority. Let no one despise you.

Graces of the Heirs of Grace

3 Remind them to be subject to rulers and
authorities, to obey, to be ready for every
good work, 2 to speak evil of no one, to be
peaceable, gentle, showing all humility to all
men. 3 For we ourselves were also once foolish, disobedient, deceived, serving various
lusts and pleasures, living in malice and envy,
hateful and hating one another. 4 But when the
kindness and the love of God our Savior toward man appeared, 5 not by works of righteousness which we have done, but according
to His mercy He saved us, through the washing of regeneration and renewing of the Holy
Spirit, 6 whom He poured out on us abundantly through Jesus Christ our Savior, 7 that having been justified by His grace we should
become heirs according to the hope of eternal
life.
8 This is a faithful saying, and these things I
want you to affirm constantly, that those who
have believed in God should be careful to
maintain good works. These things are good
and profitable to men.

Avoid Dissension

9 But avoid foolish disputes, genealogies,
contentions, and strivings about the law; for
they are unprofitable and useless. 10 Reject a
divisive man after the first and second admonition, 11 knowing that such a person is warped
and sinning, being self-condemned.

SOUL NOTE

Watched *(2:7, 8)* As the leader of the church in Crete, Titus was to be a positive example to all the believers, showing a "pattern of good works," always teaching sound doctrine, and always speaking sound words. He also had to teach the Christian men and women how to live for God (2:1–6) so that they, in turn, could be examples to others. Christians are always being watched—younger believers are learning about maturing in the faith by watching more mature believers. We ought to be positive examples to others in our words and in our actions. After all, we are Christ's representatives. **Topic: Mentoring**

SOUL NOTE

Indisputable *(3:9–11)* In his warning about false teachers, Paul told Titus to reject the divisive people and to "avoid foolish disputes" with them about issues that had nothing to do with salvation in Christ. Paul warned Titus against getting involved in quarrels over petty issues, and, when such debates arose, Titus was to rebuke the false teachers for their divisiveness. Divisive people insist on their own opinions without knowing God's Word. They stir up conflict that can divide the church. Such behavior must be stopped. Differences of opinion and style are inevitable in the church and can be healthy, but severe conflict over petty issues should have no place in the fellowship. **Topic: Conflict**

FINAL MESSAGES

12 When I send Artemas to you, or Tychicus,
be diligent to come to me at Nicopolis, for I
have decided to spend the winter there.
13 Send Zenas the lawyer and Apollos on their
journey with haste, that they may lack nothing. 14 And let our *people* also learn to maintain good works, to *meet* urgent needs, that
they may not be unfruitful.

FAREWELL

15 All who *are* with me greet you. Greet
those who love us in the faith.
Grace *be* with you all. Amen.

Philemon

It's awkward and painful when we have to confront a person who has wronged us horribly. It's one thing to talk abstractly about forgiveness; it's another matter altogether to actually have to forgive. That kind of situation is the true test of the power of the gospel. It's also the story behind the apostle Paul's letter to Philemon.

Philemon was a Colossian Christian (and slave owner) who had come to faith under Paul's ministry (10). Some time later, one of Philemon's slaves (a man named Onesimus) apparently stole from him and fled to Rome. In the sovereign plan of God, Onesimus encountered Paul and was converted to Christ.

The change in Onesimus was genuine, and he proved to be a great help and comfort to the imprisoned Paul. The apostle realized, however, that Onesimus needed to return to his master. This short epistle functioned as a kind of letter of reference. Paul pleaded with Philemon to forgive Onesimus and to welcome him home as a "beloved brother" (16). Paul depended on Philemon's spiritual maturity to respond in forgiveness and acceptance.

Paul's brief note to Philemon demonstrates the amazing providence of God at work, as He brings people to faith. It reminds us that the gospel is all about second chances. It fleshes out a vivid lesson in forgiving deep wrongs. Above all, it points to the power of the gospel to transform human relationships. Onesimus left Colosse a lowly slave; he returned a precious brother. What a change Christ makes!

Greeting

1Paul, a prisoner of Christ Jesus, and Timothy *our* brother,

To Philemon our beloved *friend* and fellow laborer, 2to the beloved[a] Apphia, Archippus our fellow soldier, and to the church in your house:

3Grace to you and peace from God our Father and the Lord Jesus Christ.

Philemon's Love and Faith

4I thank my God, making mention of you always in my prayers, 5hearing of your love and faith which you have toward the Lord Jesus and toward all the saints, 6that the sharing of your faith may become effective by the acknowledgment of every good thing which is in you[a] in Christ Jesus. 7For we have[a] great joy[b] and consolation in your love, because the hearts of the saints have been refreshed by you, brother.

The Plea for Onesimus

8Therefore, though I might be very bold in Christ to command you what is fitting, 9*yet* for love's sake I rather appeal *to you*—being such a one as Paul, the aged, and now also a prisoner of Jesus Christ— 10I appeal to you for my son Onesimus, whom I have begotten *while* in my chains, 11who once was unprofitable to you, but now is profitable to you and to me.

12I am sending him back.[a] You therefore receive him, that is, my own heart, 13whom I wished to keep with me, that on your behalf he might minister to me in my chains for the gospel. 14But without your consent I wanted to do nothing, that your good deed might not be by compulsion, as it were, but voluntary.

15For perhaps he departed for a while for this *purpose,* that you might receive him forever, 16no longer as a slave but more than a slave—a beloved brother, especially to me but how much more to you, both in the flesh and in the Lord.

Philemon's Obedience Encouraged

17If then you count me as a partner, receive him as *you would* me. 18But if he has wronged you or owes anything, put that on my account. 19I, Paul, am writing with my own hand. I will repay—not to mention to you that you owe me even your own self besides. 20Yes, brother, let me have joy from you in the Lord; refresh my heart in the Lord.

21Having confidence in your obedience, I write to you, knowing that you will do even more than I say. 22But, meanwhile, also prepare a guest room for me, for I trust that through your prayers I shall be granted to you.

Farewell

23Epaphras, my fellow prisoner in Christ Jesus, greets you, 24*as do* Mark, Aristarchus, Demas, Luke, my fellow laborers.

25The grace of our Lord Jesus Christ *be* with your spirit. Amen.

---

2 [a]NU-Text reads *to our sister Apphia.* **6** [a]NU-Text and M-Text read *us.* **7** [a]NU-Text reads *had.* [b]M-Text reads *thanksgiving.* **12** [a]NU-Text reads *back to you in person, that is, my own heart.*

SOUL NOTE

Back Together *(10–12)* A conflict was definitely brewing. Onesimus, a runaway slave and thief, was in a bad position. Both Philemon and Onesimus had become Christians under Paul's ministry at separate times and in separate places.

Although Philemon had every right under Roman law to have his slave beaten or killed, Paul urged him to accept Onesimus as a brother in Christ. Believers may have conflicts over any number of situations, but they can be handled best when believers remember what they have in common—salvation in Christ. We often have the right to exact justice, but, as Paul told Philemon, we need to show mercy and grace. **Topic: Conflict**

Hebrews

Old habits die hard. Some habits have been a part of our lives for so long that we accept them as normal. The thought of changing our pattern threatens our very existence. Sometimes it's easier to stay in a rut than to let God change us. This is true in the spiritual realm as well as the material. Consider the recipients of the Book of Hebrews.

Many of these Jewish Christians struggled with the temptation to return to the familiarity and comfort of Judaism—especially as they began to face persecution from their countrymen because of their newfound faith in Jesus. The unidentified author of Hebrews (variously thought to be Paul, Clement, Barnabas, or others) warned these Jewish believers not to "drift away" (2:1), but, rather, to "go on to perfection" (6:1).

The argument of Hebrews is simple: Jesus Christ is superior. He is superior to the Old Testament prophets, to the angels, and to Moses. Christ's priesthood is also superior to Aaron's because Christ is a perfect High Priest, the mediator of a New Covenant who made the once-for-all sacrifice for human sin (9:11–14). Christ alone is worthy of our faith (ch. 11, 12).

If, as Hebrews brilliantly demonstrates, Jesus is the all-sufficient Messiah, and if Christianity represents the God-ordained consummation of all the hopes and promises of Judaism, then isn't it the height of foolishness for any believer—Jew or Gentile—to revert to inferior doctrines and dead-end habits? Hebrews calls us to accept the positive changes that come with faith in Jesus Christ.

SOUL CONCERNS IN HEBREWS

God's Supreme Revelation

1 God, who at various times and in various ways spoke in time past to the fathers by the prophets, [2]has in these last days spoken to us by *His* Son, whom He has appointed heir of all things, through whom also He made the worlds; [3]who being the brightness of *His* glory and the express image of His person, and upholding all things by the word of His power, when He had by Himself[a] purged our[b] sins, sat down at the right hand of the Majesty on high, [4]having become so much better than the angels, as He has by inheritance obtained a more excellent name than they.

The Son Exalted Above Angels

[5]For to which of the angels did He ever say:

"You are My Son,
Today I have begotten You"?[a]

And again:

"I will be to Him a Father,
And He shall be to Me a Son"?[b]

[6]But when He again brings the firstborn into the world, He says:

"Let all the angels of God worship Him."[a]

[7]And of the angels He says:

"Who makes His angels spirits
And His ministers a flame of fire."[a]

[8]But to the Son *He says:*

"Your throne, O God, is forever and ever;
A scepter of righteousness is the scepter of Your kingdom.
9 *You have loved righteousness and hated lawlessness;*
Therefore God, Your God, has anointed You
With the oil of gladness more than Your companions."[a]

[10]And:

"You, LORD, in the beginning laid the foundation of the earth,
And the heavens are the work of Your hands.
11 *They will perish, but You remain;*
And they will all grow old like a garment;
12 *Like a cloak You will fold them up,*
And they will be changed.
But You are the same,
And Your years will not fail."[a]

[13]But to which of the angels has He ever said:

"Sit at My right hand,
Till I make Your enemies Your footstool"?[a]

[14]Are they not all ministering spirits sent forth to minister for those who will inherit salvation?

Do Not Neglect Salvation

2 Therefore we must give the more earnest heed to the things we have heard, lest we drift away. [2]For if the word spoken through

1:3 [a]NU-Text omits *by Himself.* [b]NU-Text omits *our.* **1:5** [a]Psalm 2:7 [b]2 Samuel 7:14 **1:6** [a]Deuteronomy 32:43 (Septuagint, Dead Sea Scrolls); Psalm 97:7 **1:7** [a]Psalm 104:4 **1:9** [a]Psalm 45:6, 7 **1:12** [a]Psalm 102:25–27 **1:13** [a]Psalm 110:1

SOUL NOTE

Neglect or Accept? *(2:3)* The author of Hebrews was issuing a wake-up call to his readers not to "neglect so great a salvation." To "neglect" here means hearing about the offer of salvation in Christ and then setting it aside without accepting it. The danger of neglect is that the offer will be forgotten in the midst of life's busyness. If people neglect the offer, they will have "no escape" on the day of judgment. People must accept this great offer of salvation in Christ. There will be no better offer anytime or anywhere. Tomorrow may be too late. **Topic: Salvation**

angels proved steadfast, and every transgression and disobedience received a just reward,
[3]how shall we escape if we neglect so great a
salvation, which at the first began to be spoken by the Lord, and was confirmed to us by
those who heard *Him,* [4]God also bearing witness both with signs and wonders, with various miracles, and gifts of the Holy Spirit,
according to His own will?

The Son Made Lower than Angels

[5]For He has not put the world to come, of
which we speak, in subjection to angels. [6]But
one testified in a certain place, saying:

"What is man that You are mindful of
him,
Or the son of man that You take care of
him?
7 *You have made him a little lower than*
the angels;
You have crowned him with glory and
honor,[a]
And set him over the works of Your
hands.
8 *You have put all things in subjection*
under his feet."[a]

For in that He put all in subjection under him,
He left nothing *that is* not put under him. But
now we do not yet see all things put under
him. [9]But we see Jesus, who was made a little
lower than the angels, for the suffering of
death crowned with glory and honor, that He,
by the grace of God, might taste death for
everyone.

Bringing Many Sons to Glory

[10]For it was fitting for Him, for whom *are* all
things and by whom *are* all things, in bringing
many sons to glory, to make the captain of
their salvation perfect through sufferings.
[11]For both He who sanctifies and those who
are being sanctified *are* all of one, for which
reason He is not ashamed to call them brethren, [12]saying:

"I will declare Your name to My brethren;
In the midst of the assembly I will sing
praise to You."[a]

[13]And again:

"I will put My trust in Him."[a]

And again:

"Here am I and the children whom God
has given Me."[b]

[14]Inasmuch then as the children have partaken of flesh and blood, He Himself likewise
shared in the same, that through death He
might destroy him who had the power of
death, that is, the devil, [15]and release those
who through fear of death were all their lifetime subject to bondage. [16]For indeed He does
not give aid to angels, but He does give aid to
the seed of Abraham. [17]Therefore, in all things
He had to be made like *His* brethren, that He
might be a merciful and faithful High Priest in
things *pertaining* to God, to make propitiation
for the sins of the people. [18]For in that He
Himself has suffered, being tempted, He is
able to aid those who are tempted.

The Son Was Faithful

3 Therefore, holy brethren, partakers of the
heavenly calling, consider the Apostle and
High Priest of our confession, Christ Jesus,
[2]who was faithful to Him who appointed Him,
as Moses also *was faithful* in all His house.
[3]For this One has been counted worthy of
more glory than Moses, inasmuch as He who
built the house has more honor than the
house. [4]For every house is built by someone,
but He who built all things *is* God. [5]And Moses indeed *was* faithful in all His house as a
servant, for a testimony of those things which
would be spoken *afterward,* [6]but Christ as a
Son over His own house, whose house we are
if we hold fast the confidence and the rejoicing of the hope firm to the end.[a]

Be Faithful

[7]Therefore, as the Holy Spirit says:

"Today, if You will hear His voice,
8 *Do not harden Your hearts as in the*
rebellion,
In the day of trial in the wilderness,
9 *Where Your fathers tested Me, tried*
Me,
And saw My works forty years.

2:7 [a]NU-Text and M-Text omit the rest of verse 7.
2:8 [a]Psalm 8:4–6 **2:12** [a]Psalm 22:22
2:13 [a]2 Samuel 22:3; Isaiah 8:17 [b]Isaiah 8:18
3:6 [a]NU-Text omits *firm to the end.*

10 *Therefore I was angry with that*
generation,
And said, 'They always go astray in their
heart,
And they have not known My ways.'
11 *So I swore in My wrath,*
'They shall not enter My rest.' "[a]

12Beware, brethren, lest there be in any of
you an evil heart of unbelief in departing from
the living God; 13but exhort one another daily,
while it is called "Today," lest any of you be
hardened through the deceitfulness of sin.
14For we have become partakers of Christ if we
hold the beginning of our confidence steadfast
to the end, 15while it is said:

"Today, if you will hear His voice,
Do not harden your hearts as in the
rebellion."[a]

Failure of the Wilderness Wanderers

16For who, having heard, rebelled? Indeed,
was it not all who came out of Egypt, *led*
by Moses? 17Now with whom was He angry
forty years? *Was it* not
with those who sinned,
whose corpses fell in
the wilderness? 18And
to whom did He swear
that they would not en-
ter His rest, but to those
who did not obey? 19So
we see that they could
not enter in because of
unbelief.

> For the word of God is living and powerful, and sharper than any two-edged sword, piercing even to the division of soul and spirit, and of joints and marrow, and is a discerner of the thoughts and intents of the heart.
>
> HEBREWS 4:12

The Promise of Rest

4 Therefore, since a promise remains of entering His rest, let us fear lest any of you
seem to have come short of it. 2For indeed the
gospel was preached to us as well as to them;
but the word which they heard did not profit
them,[a] not being mixed with faith in those who
heard *it.* 3For we who have believed do enter
that rest, as He has said:

"So I swore in My wrath,
'They shall not enter My rest,' "[a]

although the works were finished from the
foundation of the world. 4For He has spoken
in a certain place of the seventh *day* in this
way: *"And God rested on the seventh day*
from all His works";[a] 5and again in this *place:*
"They shall not enter My rest."[a]
6Since therefore it remains that some *must*
enter it, and those to whom it was first
preached did not enter because of disobedience, 7again He designates a certain day, saying in David, "Today," after such a long time,
as it has been said:

"Today, if you will hear His voice,
Do not harden your hearts."[a]

8For if Joshua had given them rest, then He
would not afterward have spoken of another
day. 9There remains therefore a rest for the
people of God. 10For he who has entered His
rest has himself also ceased from his works as
God *did* from His.

The Word Discovers Our Condition

11Let us therefore be diligent to enter that
rest, lest anyone fall according to the same example of disobedience. 12For the word of God
is living and powerful, and sharper than any
two-edged sword, piercing even to the division of soul and spirit,
and of joints and mar-
row, and is a discerner
of the thoughts and in-
tents of the heart. 13And
there is no creature hid-
den from His sight, but
all things *are* naked and
open to the eyes of Him
to whom we *must give*
account.

Our Compassionate High Priest

14Seeing then that we have a great High
Priest who has passed through the heavens,
Jesus the Son of God, let us hold fast *our* confession. 15For we do not have a High Priest
who cannot sympathize with our weaknesses,
but was in all *points* tempted as *we are, yet*
without sin. 16Let us therefore come boldly to
the throne of grace, that we may obtain mercy
and find grace to help in time of need.

3:11 [a]Psalm 95:7–11 **3:15** [a]Psalm 95:7, 8
4:2 [a]NU-Text and M-Text read *profit them, since they were not united by faith with those who heeded it.* **4:3** [a]Psalm 95:11
4:4 [a]Genesis 2:2 **4:5** [a]Psalm 95:11
4:7 [a]Psalm 95:7, 8

QUALIFICATIONS FOR HIGH PRIESTHOOD

5 For every high priest taken from among
men is appointed for men in things *per-*
taining to God, that he may offer both gifts
and sacrifices for sins. 2He can have compassion on those who are ignorant and going
astray, since he himself is also subject to
weakness. 3Because of this he is required as
for the people, so also for himself, to offer *sac-*
rifices for sins. 4And no man takes this honor
to himself, but he who is called by God, just as
Aaron *was.*

A PRIEST FOREVER

5So also Christ did not glorify Himself to become High Priest, *but it* was He who said to
Him:

> "*You are My Son,*
> *Today I have begotten You.*"[a]

6As *He* also *says* in another *place:*

> "*You are a priest forever*
> *According to the order of Melchizedek*";[a]

7who, in the days of His flesh, when He had
offered up prayers and supplications, with vehement cries and tears to Him who was able
to save Him from death, and was heard because of His godly fear, 8though He was a Son,
yet He learned obedience by the things which
He suffered. 9And having been perfected, He

5:5 [a]Psalm 2:7 **5:6** [a]Psalm 110:4

KEY PASSAGE

COME BOLDLY

(4:14–16)

Pain

An amazing fact of the Christian faith is that the infinite God became a finite human being. Although without sin, Jesus Christ as a man experienced the weaknesses, temptations, pain, and difficulties of human existence. Thus, we have a Savior who can "sympathize with our weaknesses." He understands temptation, because He faced it. He understands weakness, because He experienced it. He understands pain, because He felt it.

People who live with chronic or acute physical or emotional pain have a Savior who truly understands. Far from sitting in the heavens simply feeling sorry for sick and sinful humanity, He clothed Himself with our humanness. When we come to Christ with our hurts, He reaches out with human arms, truly understanding how we feel. He is able to help us. Christ does not always take away the pain, but He does tell us to bring it to Him. Whatever our pain or difficulty, we are encouraged to "come boldly to the throne of grace, that we may obtain mercy and find grace to help in time of need."

To Learn More: Turn to the article about pain on pages 1534, 1535. See also the personality profile of the man at the pool of Bethesda on page 1378.

SOUL NOTE

Hidden Strength *(4:14–16)* Most people try to hide their weaknesses and failures. God knows all our weaknesses, however, and He sympathizes with them. Even more, He offers mercy and grace to help us. Christ understands because as a human being He experienced the challenges and temptations we face, "yet without sin." He knows that we are weak and need Him. He wants to give us the strength to endure our weaknesses and confront our temptations. We can "come boldly to the throne of grace," knowing that He wants to help us. **Topic: Weakness**

became the author of eternal salvation to all who obey Him, [10]called by God as High Priest *"according to the order of Melchizedek,"* [11]of whom we have much to say, and hard to explain, since you have become dull of hearing.

Spiritual Immaturity

[12]For though by this time you ought to be teachers, you need *someone* to teach you again the first principles of the oracles of God; and you have come to need milk and not solid food. [13]For everyone who partakes *only* of milk *is* unskilled in the word of righteousness, for he is a babe. [14]But solid food belongs to those who are of full age, *that is,* those who by reason of use have their senses exercised to discern both good and evil.

The Peril of Not Progressing

6 Therefore, leaving the discussion of the elementary *principles* of Christ, let us go on to perfection, not laying again the foundation of repentance from dead works and of faith toward God, [2]of the doctrine of baptisms, of laying on of hands, of resurrection of the dead, and of eternal judgment. [3]And this we will[a] do if God permits.

[4]For *it is* impossible for those who were once enlightened, and have tasted the heavenly gift, and have become partakers of the Holy Spirit, [5]and have tasted the good word of God and the powers of the age to come, [6]if they fall away,[a] to renew them again to repentance, since they crucify again for themselves the Son of God, and put *Him* to an open shame.

[7]For the earth which drinks in the rain that often comes upon it, and bears herbs useful for those by whom it is cultivated, receives blessing from God; [8]but if it bears thorns and briers, *it is* rejected and near to being cursed, whose end *is* to be burned.

A Better Estimate

[9]But, beloved, we are confident of better things concerning you, yes, things that accompany salvation, though we speak in this manner. [10]For God *is* not unjust to forget your work and labor of[a] love which you have shown toward His name, *in that* you have ministered to the saints, and do minister. [11]And we desire that each one of you show the same diligence to the full assurance of hope until the end, [12]that you do not become sluggish, but imitate those who through faith and patience inherit the promises.

God's Infallible Purpose in Christ

[13]For when God made a promise to Abraham, because He could swear by no one greater, He swore by Himself, [14]saying, *"Surely blessing I will bless you, and multiplying I will multiply you."*[a] [15]And so, after he had patiently endured, he obtained the promise. [16]For men indeed swear by the greater, and an oath for confirmation *is* for them an end of all dispute. [17]Thus God, determining to show more abundantly to the heirs of promise the immutability of His counsel, confirmed *it* by an oath, [18]that by two immutable things, in which it *is* impossible for God to lie, we might[a] have strong consolation, who have fled for refuge to lay hold of the hope set before *us.*

[19]This *hope* we have as an anchor of the

> This hope we have as an anchor of the soul, both sure and steadfast.
> HEBREWS 6:19

6:3 [a]M-Text reads *let us do.* **6:6** [a]Or *and have fallen away* **6:10** [a]NU-Text omits *labor of.* **6:14** [a]Genesis 22:17 **6:18** [a]M-Text omits *might.*

SOUL NOTE

Radical Obedience *(5:8, 9)* Jesus demonstrated obedience even through suffering by undergoing a painful execution in order to obey His Father's plan. He knows what it means to obey God in the midst of trying circumstances. Christ's radical obedience is comforting because He knows and shares in our sorrows. Believers are called to radical obedience, too. At times, we too will be called on to learn real obedience through suffering, and at those times we can turn to Jesus, because He knows exactly how to help us. **Topic: Obedience**

soul, both sure and steadfast, and which enters the *Presence* behind the veil, 20where the
forerunner has entered for us, *even* Jesus, having become High Priest forever according to
the order of Melchizedek.

THE KING OF RIGHTEOUSNESS

7 For this Melchizedek, king of Salem,
priest of the Most High God, who met
Abraham returning from the slaughter of the
kings and blessed him, 2to whom also Abraham gave a tenth part of all, first being translated "king of righteousness," and then also
king of Salem, meaning "king of peace,"
3without father, without mother, without genealogy, having neither beginning of days nor
end of life, but made like the Son of God, remains a priest continually.

4Now consider how great this man *was,* to
whom even the patriarch Abraham gave a
tenth of the spoils. 5And indeed those who are
of the sons of Levi, who receive the priesthood, have a commandment to receive tithes
from the people according to the law, that is,
from their brethren, though they have come
from the loins of Abraham; 6but he whose genealogy is not derived from them received
tithes from Abraham and blessed him who
had the promises. 7Now beyond all contradic-
tion the lesser is blessed by the better. 8Here
mortal men receive tithes, but there he *receives them,* of whom it is witnessed that he
lives. 9Even Levi, who receives tithes, paid
tithes through Abraham, so to speak, 10for he
was still in the loins of his father when Melchizedek met him.

NEED FOR A NEW PRIESTHOOD

11Therefore, if perfection were through the
Levitical priesthood (for under it the people
received the law), what further need *was there*
that another priest should rise according to
the order of Melchizedek, and not be called
according to the order of Aaron? 12For the
priesthood being changed, of necessity there
is also a change of the law. 13For He of whom
these things are spoken belongs to another
tribe, from which no man has officiated at the
altar.

14For *it is* evident that our Lord arose from
Judah, of which tribe Moses spoke nothing
concerning priesthood.[a] 15And it is yet far
more evident if, in the likeness of Melchizedek, there arises another priest 16who has
come, not according to the law of a fleshly
commandment, but according to the power of
an endless life. 17For He testifies:[a]

"You are a priest forever
According to the order of Melchizedek."[b]

18For on the one hand there is an annulling
of the former commandment because of its
weakness and unprofitableness, 19for the law
made nothing perfect; on the other hand,
there is the bringing in of a better hope,
through which we draw near to God.

GREATNESS OF THE NEW PRIEST

20And inasmuch as *He was* not *made priest*
without an oath 21(for they have become
priests without an oath, but He with an oath
by Him who said to Him:

"The LORD has sworn
And will not relent,
'You are a priest forever[a]
According to the order of
Melchizedek' "),[b]

22by so much more Jesus has become a surety
of a better covenant.

23Also there were many priests, because
they were prevented by death from continuing. 24But He, because He continues forever,
has an unchangeable priesthood. 25Therefore
He is also able to save to the uttermost those
who come to God through Him, since He always lives to make intercession for them.

26For such a High Priest was fitting for us,
who is holy, harmless, undefiled, separate
from sinners, and has become higher than the
heavens; 27who does not need daily, as those
high priests, to offer up sacrifices, first for His
own sins and then for the people's, for this He
did once for all when He offered up Himself.
28For the law appoints as high priests men
who have weakness, but the word of the oath,
which came after the law, *appoints* the Son
who has been perfected forever.

THE NEW PRIESTLY SERVICE

8 Now *this is* the main point of the things
we are saying: We have such a High

7:14 [a]NU-Text reads *priests.* **7:17** [a]NU-Text reads *it is testified.* [b]Psalm 110:4 **7:21** [a]NU-Text ends the quotation here. [b]Psalm 110:4

Priest, who is seated at the right hand of the throne of the Majesty in the heavens, [2]a Minister of the sanctuary and of the true tabernacle which the Lord erected, and not man.

[3]For every high priest is appointed to offer both gifts and sacrifices. Therefore *it is* necessary that this One also have something to offer. [4]For if He were on earth, He would not be a priest, since there are priests who offer the gifts according to the law; [5]who serve the copy and shadow of the heavenly things, as Moses was divinely instructed when he was about to make the tabernacle. For He said, *"See that you make all things according to the pattern shown you on the mountain."*[a] [6]But now He has obtained a more excellent ministry, inasmuch as He is also Mediator of a better covenant, which was established on better promises.

A New Covenant

[7]For if that first *covenant* had been faultless, then no place would have been sought for a second. [8]Because finding fault with them, He says: *"Behold, the days are coming, says the LORD, when I will make a new covenant with the house of Israel and with the house of Judah— [9]not according to the covenant that I made with their fathers in the day when I took them by the hand to lead them out of the land of Egypt; because they did not continue in My covenant, and I disregarded them, says the LORD. [10]For this is the covenant that I will make with the house of Israel after those days, says the LORD: I will put My laws in their mind and write them on their hearts; and I will be their God, and they shall be My people. [11]None of them shall teach his neighbor, and none his brother, saying, 'Know the LORD,' for all shall know Me, from the least of them to the greatest of them. [12]For I will be merciful to their unrighteousness, and their sins and their lawless deeds*[a] *I will remember no more."*[b]

[13]In that He says, *"A new covenant,"* He has made the first obsolete. Now what is becoming obsolete and growing old is ready to vanish away.

The Earthly Sanctuary

9 Then indeed, even the first *covenant* had ordinances of divine service and the earthly sanctuary. [2]For a tabernacle was prepared: the first *part,* in which *was* the lampstand, the table, and the showbread, which is called the sanctuary; [3]and behind the second veil, the part of the tabernacle which is called the Holiest of All, [4]which had the golden censer and the ark of the covenant overlaid on all sides with gold, in which *were* the golden pot that had the manna, Aaron's rod that budded, and the tablets of the covenant; [5]and above it were the cherubim of glory overshadowing the mercy seat. Of these things we cannot now speak in detail.

Limitations of the Earthly Service

[6]Now when these things had been thus prepared, the priests always went into the first part of the tabernacle, performing the services. [7]But into the second part the high priest *went* alone once a year, not without blood, which he offered for himself and *for* the people's sins *committed* in ignorance; [8]the Holy Spirit indicating this, that the way into the Holiest of All was not yet made manifest while the first tabernacle was still standing. [9]It *was* symbolic for the present time in which both gifts and sacrifices are offered which cannot make him who performed the service perfect in regard to the conscience—[10]*concerned* only with foods and drinks, various washings, and fleshly ordinances imposed until the time of reformation.

The Heavenly Sanctuary

[11]But Christ came *as* High Priest of the good things to come,[a] with the greater and more perfect tabernacle not made with hands, that is, not of this creation. [12]Not with the blood of goats and calves, but with His own blood He entered the Most Holy Place once for all, having obtained eternal redemption. [13]For if the blood of bulls and goats and the ashes of a heifer, sprinkling the unclean, sanctifies for the purifying of the flesh, [14]how much more shall the blood of Christ, who through the eternal Spirit offered Himself without spot to God, cleanse your conscience from dead works to serve the living God? [15]And for this reason He is the Mediator of the new covenant, by means of death, for the redemption of the transgressions under the first covenant, that those who are called may receive the promise of the eternal inheritance.

8:5 [a]Exodus 25:40 **8:12** [a]NU-Text omits *and their lawless deeds.* [b]Jeremiah 31:31–34 **9:11** [a]NU-Text reads *that have come.*

The Mediator's Death Necessary

[16]For where there *is* a testament, there must
also of necessity be the death of the testator.
[17]For a testament *is* in force after men are
dead, since it has no power at all while the
testator lives. [18]Therefore not even the first
covenant was dedicated without blood. [19]For
when Moses had spoken every precept to all
the people according to the law, he took the
blood of calves and goats, with water, scarlet
wool, and hyssop, and sprinkled both the
book itself and all the people, [20]saying, *"This
is the blood of the covenant which God has
commanded you."*[a] [21]Then likewise he sprinkled with blood both the tabernacle and all
the vessels of the ministry. [22]And according to
the law almost all things are purified with
blood, and without shedding of blood there is
no remission.

Greatness of Christ's Sacrifice

[23]Therefore *it was* necessary that the copies
of the things in the heavens should be purified
with these, but the heavenly things themselves with better sacrifices than these. [24]For
Christ has not entered the holy places made
with hands, *which are* copies of the true, but
into heaven itself, now to appear in the presence of God for us; [25]not that He should offer
Himself often, as the high priest enters the
Most Holy Place every year with blood of another— [26]He then would have had to suffer often since the foundation of the world; but
now, once at the end of the ages, He has appeared to put away sin by the sacrifice of Himself. [27]And as it is appointed for men to die
once, but after this the judgment, [28]so Christ
was offered once to bear the sins of many. To
those who eagerly wait for Him He will appear
a second time, apart from sin, for salvation.

Animal Sacrifices Insufficient

10 For the law, having a shadow of the
good things to come, *and* not the very
image of the things, can never with these
same sacrifices, which they offer continually
year by year, make those who approach perfect. [2]For then would they not have ceased to
be offered? For the worshipers, once purified,
would have had no more consciousness of
sins. [3]But in those *sacrifices there is* a reminder of sins every year. [4]For *it is* not possible that
the blood of bulls and goats could take away
sins.

Christ's Death Fulfills God's Will

[5]Therefore, when He came into the world,
He said:

9:20 [a]Exodus 24:8

KEY PASSAGE

Perfectionism

GOD'S WORK

(10:12–14)

Everyone would like to look perfect, act perfect, and do perfect work. Aside from a few people receiving "perfect" scores at the Olympics, most of us will find perfection elusive in every area of life. No matter how much we try, we fail. If we seek to live the perfect Christian life, our thoughts or attitudes will trip us up before we even get out of bed in the morning!

So what does it mean for believers that Christ's sacrifice "perfected forever those who are being sanctified"? Believers have been made perfect in God's eyes because of the death and resurrection of Jesus Christ. At the same time, however, we are "being sanctified," being made perfect and holy progressively through our walk with Him. We are considered perfect, even though we have a long way to go. As we let God work in us, He perfects us. Instead of measuring perfection by worldly standards, we should seek to obey God, looking forward to the day when He will finally make us perfect for life with Him in our perfect eternal home.

To Learn More: Turn to the article about perfectionism on pages 1630, 1631. See also the personality profile of Paul on page 1454.

"Sacrifice and offering You did not
desire,
But a body You have prepared for Me.
6 *In burnt offerings and sacrifices for sin*
You had no pleasure.
7 *Then I said, 'Behold, I have come—*
In the volume of the book it is written of
Me—
To do Your will, O God.' "[a]

8Previously saying, *"Sacrifice and offering, burnt offerings, and offerings for sin You did not desire, nor had pleasure in them"* (which are offered according to the law), 9then He said, *"Behold, I have come to do Your will, O God."*[a] He takes away the first that He may establish the second. 10By that will we have been sanctified through the offering of the body of Jesus Christ once *for all.*

> And let us consider one another in order to stir up love and good works.
> HEBREWS 10:24

Christ's Death Perfects the Sanctified

11And every priest stands ministering daily and offering repeatedly the same sacrifices, which can never take away sins. 12But this Man, after He had offered one sacrifice for sins forever, sat down at the right hand of God, 13from that time waiting till His enemies are made His footstool. 14For by one offering He has perfected forever those who are being sanctified.

15But the Holy Spirit also witnesses to us; for after He had said before,

16*"This is the covenant that I will make with them after those days, says the LORD: I will put My laws into their hearts, and in their minds I will write them,"*[a] 17*then He adds, "Their sins and their lawless deeds I will remember no more."*[a] 18Now where there is remission of these, *there is* no longer an offering for sin.

Hold Fast Your Confession

19Therefore, brethren, having boldness to enter the Holiest by the blood of Jesus, 20by a new and living way which He consecrated for us, through the veil, that is, His flesh, 21and *having* a High Priest over the house of God, 22let us draw near with a true heart in full assurance of faith, having our hearts sprinkled from an evil conscience and our bodies washed with pure water. 23Let us hold fast the confession of *our* hope without wavering, for He who promised *is* faithful. 24And let us consider one another in order to stir up love and good works, 25not forsaking the assembling of ourselves together, as *is* the manner of some, but exhorting *one another,* and so much the more as you see the Day approaching.

The Just Live by Faith

26For if we sin willfully after we have received the knowledge of the truth, there no longer remains a sacrifice for sins, 27but a certain fearful expectation of judgment, and fiery indignation which will devour the adversaries. 28Anyone who has rejected Moses' law dies without mercy on the testimony of two or three witnesses. 29Of how much worse punishment, do you suppose, will he be thought worthy who has trampled the Son of God underfoot, counted the blood of the covenant by which he was sanctified a common thing, and insulted the Spirit of grace? 30For we know Him who said, *"Vengeance is Mine, I will repay,"*[a] says the Lord.[b] And again, *"The LORD will judge His people."*[c] 31It is a fearful thing to fall into the hands of the living God.

32But recall the former days in which, after you were illuminated, you endured a great struggle with sufferings: 33partly while you were made a spectacle both by reproaches and tribulations, and partly while you became companions of those who were so treated; 34for you had compassion on me[a] in my chains, and joyfully accepted the plundering of your goods, knowing that you have a better and an enduring possession for yourselves in heaven.[b] 35Therefore do not cast away your confidence, which has great reward. 36For you have need of endurance, so that after you have done the will of God, you may receive the promise:

10:7 [a]Psalm 40:6–8 **10:9** [a]NU-Text and M-Text omit *O God.* **10:16** [a]Jeremiah 31:33 **10:17** [a]Jeremiah 31:34 **10:30** [a]Deuteronomy 32:35 [b]NU-Text omits *says the Lord.* [c]Deuteronomy 32:36 **10:34** [a]NU-Text reads *the prisoners* instead of *me in my chains.* [b]NU-Text omits *in heaven.*

PERFECTIONISM

CHRIS THURMAN

(Hebrews 10:1)

Perfectionism

Few ways of thinking are as harmful as perfectionism. Perfectionists believe that they should never make mistakes and that it is a catastrophe when they do. They tend to become quite upset when people or situations are out of their control and don't go the way they "should." They expect more from themselves and others than is reasonable and often become angry and bitter as a result. Though perfectionism in people is fairly common, it carries a high price tag in terms of causing emotional problems, relationship difficulties, and spiritual burnout.

WHAT IS PERFECTIONISM?

Two perspectives are helpful to consider when defining perfectionism.

Theologically, perfectionism is the destructive belief that people can be equal to God. Specifically, perfectionistic people think they should be all-knowing (omniscient), all-powerful (omnipotent), and everywhere at once (omnipresent). When people think they should know everything, they beat themselves up for mistakes. When they think they should be totally powerful, they become upset when things are out of their control. When they believe that they should accomplish the work of ten people in a given day, they become depressed and discouraged over what "little" they did accomplish. While God calls us to be "perfect," it is an ideal that He is asking us to move in the direction of, not something we can literally be. Only God knows it all, controls it all, and fills up the universe with His presence. Finite human beings know very little, can't control others, and can only accomplish the work of one person on a given day. God accepts that about us, and we need to as well.

Psychologically, perfectionism has several facets as well. Perfectionists are *idealistic* in that they frequently think about how things "should" be, not how they really are. Perfectionists set *impossibly high goals* which lead to discouragement, failure, and ultimately quitting. They are *product-minded*, believing that contentment, happiness, and a sense of accomplishment are not permissible until their current project or activity has been completed. The "process" is overlooked because the end result has not been reached, thus there is no "joy in the journey." Perfectionists often feel that they have to *be the best* at what they do. To simply do one's best is not good enough. Perfectionists also *equate their worth with their performance*. They only feel worthwhile as people if they perform well. Since day-to-day performance in various areas of life fluctuates, a perfectionist's sense of worth fluctuates as well.

The theological and psychological components of perfectionism destroy any chance people have at an emotionally and spiritually healthy life. So what can be done to help the perfectionist?

HOW TO DEFEAT PERFECTIONISM

Several steps can be taken to help perfectionists become more realistic in their view of life and personal abilities.

➢ *Be humble*—Perfectionists must humble themselves before God and repent of being prideful enough to think they can be His equal.

➢ *Be reality-focused*—Perfectionists need to face life as it really is, not focus on how it "should" be.

➢ *Set attainable goals*—Perfectionists need to set goals that are small, realistic, and achievable in the here and now. Long-term goals need to be broken into short-term, tangible goals.

➢ *Set reasonable time limits*—Spending too much time on an activity in order to do it perfectly needs to be replaced with prioritizing activities so that each is given a reasonable amount of time.

➢ *Accept doing "good enough" on certain tasks*—Given the number of tasks people must complete each day, not every one of those tasks has to be, or can be, done exceptionally well. In areas of less importance, perfectionists need to allow themselves to do "good enough" and move on to the next task.

➢ *Stop black-white thinking*—Thinking in all-or-nothing terms often makes perfectionists miss the shade of gray in a given situation. By not thinking in extremes, perfectionists can have a more accurate perspective.

➢ *Learn from mistakes*—Everyone makes mistakes. The key is to learn from the mistakes.

➢ *Confess sin to others*—Acknowledging imperfections to others (rather than keeping them secret) can help release people from the pull of perfectionism. By sharing moral imperfections and personality flaws, perfectionists invite others to see them as they really are. Living a more transparent life builds healthy relationships and is critical for personal growth.

➢ *Find joy in the journey*—Becoming more like Christ is a process. Each step people take toward being more mature is pleasing to God and is a step further than where they were before. Perfectionists need to take time to stop and enjoy where they are in life.

➢ *Find worth in God*—Perfectionists need to find their worth not in what they do or how well they do it, but in being God's creation.

Knowing the theological and psychological aspects of perfectionism is only the beginning. Perfectionists must continue to grow in their knowledge of and love for Christ. Perfectionists must remember Paul's words, "Not that I have already attained, or am already perfected; but I press on" (Phil. 3:12). God will bless them as they seek to live for Him every day.

FURTHER MEDITATION:

Other passages to study about the issue of perfectionism include:

➢ Proverbs 16:18
➢ 2 Corinthians 12:9
➢ Galatians 3:3; 5:16
➢ Philippians 1:6; 2:12; 3:1–9
➢ Colossians 2:16–23

To Learn More: Turn to the key passage note on perfectionism at Hebrews 10:12–14 on page 1628. See also the personality profile of Paul on page 1454.

37 *"For yet a little while,*
And He[a] *who is coming will come and*
will not tarry.
38 *Now the*[a] *just shall live by faith;*
But if anyone
draws back,
My soul has no
pleasure in
him."[b]

> "Now the just shall live by faith;
> but if anyone draws back, My soul
> has no pleasure in him."
>
> HEBREWS 10:38

39 But we are not of
those who draw back to
perdition, but of those who believe to the saving of the soul.

By Faith We Understand

11 Now faith is the substance of things
hoped for, the evidence of things not
seen. 2 For by it the elders obtained a *good* testimony.
3 By faith we understand that the worlds
were framed by the word of God, so that the
things which are seen were not made of things
which are visible.

Faith at the Dawn of History

4 By faith Abel offered to God a more excellent sacrifice than Cain, through which he obtained witness that he was righteous, God
testifying of his gifts; and through it he being
dead still speaks.
5 By faith Enoch was taken away so that he
did not see death, *"and was not found, be-*
cause God had taken him";[a] for before he was
taken he had this testimony, that he pleased
God. 6 But without faith *it is* impossible to
please *Him,* for he who
comes to God must be-
lieve that He is, and
that He is a rewarder
of those who diligently
seek Him.
7 By faith Noah, be-
ing divinely warned of
things not yet seen, moved with godly fear,
prepared an ark for the saving of his household, by which he condemned the world and
became heir of the righteousness which is according to faith.

Faithful Abraham

8 By faith Abraham obeyed when he was
called to go out to the place which he would
receive as an inheritance. And he went out,
not knowing where he was going. 9 By faith he
dwelt in the land of promise as *in* a foreign
country, dwelling in tents with Isaac and Jacob, the heirs with him of the same promise;
10 for he waited for the city which has foundations, whose builder and maker *is* God.
11 By faith Sarah herself also received

10:37 [a]Or *that which* **10:38** [a]NU-Text reads *My just one.* [b]Habakkuk 2:3, 4 **11:5** [a]Genesis 5:24

KEY PASSAGE

Faith

UNSEEN YET VERY REAL

(11:1–6)

To have faith means more than just to believe. Hebrews defines faith as "the substance of things hoped for, the evidence of things not seen." Faith starts out certain. When people believe that God will fulfill His promises, they are showing true faith—even when they don't see evidence despite trusting in the character of God, believing His promises, and knowing that His rewards are sure. Jesus said to Thomas, "Blessed are those who have not seen and yet have believed" (John 20:29).

When people have faith in God, they know without a doubt that He will keep His promises. They live and make choices in this world based on the unseen reality of their future home in heaven. They persevere in their faith despite pain, hardship, or persecution, because they are convinced that the unseen God is with them. In short, faith in God makes all the difference, both now and for eternity.

To Learn More: Turn to the article about faith on pages 1634, 1635. See also the personality profile of Abraham on page 21.

strength to conceive seed, and she bore a child[a] when she was past the age, because she judged Him faithful who had promised. [12]Therefore from one man, and him as good as dead, were born *as many* as the stars of the sky in multitude—innumerable as the sand which is by the seashore.

The Heavenly Hope

[13]These all died in faith, not having received the promises, but having seen them afar off were assured of them,[a] embraced *them* and confessed that they were strangers and pilgrims on the earth. [14]For those who say such things declare plainly that they seek a homeland. [15]And truly if they had called to mind that *country* from which they had come out, they would have had opportunity to return. [16]But now they desire a better, that is, a heavenly *country*. Therefore God is not ashamed to be called their God, for He has prepared a city for them.

The Faith of the Patriarchs

[17]By faith Abraham, when he was tested, offered up Isaac, and he who had received the promises offered up his only begotten *son*, [18]of whom it was said, *"In Isaac your seed shall be called,"*[a] [19]concluding that God *was* able to raise *him* up, even from the dead, from which he also received him in a figurative sense.

[20]By faith Isaac blessed Jacob and Esau concerning things to come.

[21]By faith Jacob, when he was dying, blessed each of the sons of Joseph, and worshiped, *leaning* on the top of his staff.

[22]By faith Joseph, when he was dying, made mention of the departure of the children of Israel, and gave instructions concerning his bones.

The Faith of Moses

[23]By faith Moses, when he was born, was hidden three months by his parents, because they saw *he was* a beautiful child; and they were not afraid of the king's command.

[24]By faith Moses, when he became of age, refused to be called the son of Pharaoh's daughter, [25]choosing rather to suffer affliction with the people of God than to enjoy the passing pleasures of sin, [26]esteeming the reproach of Christ greater riches than the treasures in[a] Egypt; for he looked to the reward.

[27]By faith he forsook Egypt, not fearing the wrath of the king; for he endured as seeing Him who is invisible. [28]By faith he kept the Passover and the sprinkling of blood, lest he who destroyed the firstborn should touch them.

[29]By faith they passed through the Red Sea as by dry *land, whereas* the Egyptians, attempting *to do* so, were drowned.

By Faith They Overcame

[30]By faith the walls of Jericho fell down after they were encircled for seven days. [31]By faith the harlot Rahab did not perish with those who did not believe, when she had received the spies with peace.

[32]And what more shall I say? For the time would fail me to tell of Gideon and Barak and Samson and Jephthah, also *of* David and Samuel and the prophets: [33]who through faith subdued kingdoms, worked righteousness, obtained promises, stopped the mouths of lions, [34]quenched the violence of fire, escaped the edge of the sword, out of weakness were made strong, became valiant in battle, turned

11:11 [a]NU-Text omits *she bore a child.*
11:13 [a]NU-Text and M-Text omit *were assured of them.* **11:18** [a]Genesis 21:12 **11:26** [a]NU-Text and M-Text read *of.*

SOUL NOTE

Believe *(11:6)* Many people claim to believe in God, but do they really *know* Him? To know God requires faith—a willingness to believe that though unseen, God exists; a willingness to trust that though unseen, His rewards are certain. When people have faith, they discover that they can have a personal relationship with God through trusting in His Son, the Savior sent as a provision for their sins. Do you simply believe that there is a God, or do you have a personal relationship with Him? There's a big difference. **Topic: Knowing God**

FAITH

JERRY FALWELL

(Hebrews 11:6)

Faith is the most important element in life—for without it, it is impossible to please God. At the core, faith is an act of trust by which we commit ourselves to someone or something. Faith is believing. Believing in the object of our trust. Believing in ourselves. Believing in another person. Ultimately, believing in God.

Faith is so important that it is mentioned over three hundred times in the Bible. The first reference to believing in God is found in the story of Abraham. The Scripture says that Abraham "believed in the LORD, and He accounted it to him for righteousness" (Gen. 15:6). This particular step of faith is so significant that the above statement is repeated three times in the New Testament (Rom. 4:3; Gal. 3:6; James 2:23).

OBJECT OF OUR FAITH

The power of our faith rests in the object of our faith. At the foundation of all love is a belief in the object that is loved. If we do not believe in a person, we cannot love him or her. The same is true in our spiritual journey. We must begin with God: believing that He exists, believing that He cares, and believing that His love is real.

The New Testament term for faith (Greek, *pistis*) means a "firm persuasion." It is a belief or conviction based on confidence in God's promises. The Old Testament word for faith is *'aman*, meaning to "establish" or "confirm." It is the basis of the word *amen*, which comes from the same root. The main elements of faith involve an acknowledgment of God's revealed truth and a personal surrender to Him. The object of Abraham's faith was not just the promise of God; his faith rested in God Himself. The key to the Christian life is our faith in Jesus Christ and His sacrificial and atoning death for our sins. We not only believe that He died on the Cross as a fact of history, but we believe that He died for our sins personally.

Our salvation is "by grace . . . through faith" (Eph. 2:8). It is based on God's grace and experienced personally by faith in Him. He is the object of our faith and His death for our sins makes possible the forgiveness of our sins. When we trust what Jesus did for us on the Cross, we receive the gift of eternal life (John 3:16–18). God has done for us what we could not do for ourselves. So He tells us to stop trying to save ourselves and trust what He has already done for us as a sufficient payment for our sins.

REWARD OF OUR FAITH

Faith is the key that unlocks the door of heaven. Hebrews 11:6 reminds us, "Without faith it is impossible to please Him, for he who comes to God must believe that He is, and that He is a rewarder of those who diligently seek Him." Romans 1:16, 17 adds, "For I am not ashamed of the gospel of Christ, for it is the power of God to salvation for everyone who believes . . . as it is written, 'The just shall live by faith.'"

Faith is also the key to getting our prayers answered. When the desperate woman touched Jesus for healing, He responded: "Daughter, your faith has made you well. Go in peace, and be healed of your affliction" (Mark 5:34). Jesus also said: "Ask, and it will be given to you; seek, and you will find; knock, and it will be opened to you" (Matt. 7:7). We cannot make God answer our prayers because we don't always see His complete will and purpose in our lives. But generally there is a correlation to our faith and His response.

Hebrews 11 lists the Old Testament heroes of the faith. Each one trusted God in a unique way. Their confidence in God's promises resulted in personal obedience to His will for their lives. They clung to the hope that God would eventually triumph over what was challenging them. Thus, Abraham obeyed, Sarah conceived, Isaac blessed, Jacob worshiped, Joseph instructed, Moses forsook Egypt, and the children of Israel passed through the Red Sea on their way to the Promised Land (Heb. 11:8–29).

EVIDENCE OF OUR FAITH

James reminds us that saving faith and righteous works go hand in hand (James 2:14–24). Neither can be isolated from the other. Faith is the *root* of our salvation; good works are the *fruit* of our salvation. Works alone cannot save us. They are the result of our salvation and not the cause of it. Just as an apple tree will bear apples, so faith will produce good works: "For a good tree does not bear bad fruit, nor does a bad tree bear good fruit. For every tree is known by its own fruit" (Luke 6:43, 44).

Faith and works go hand in hand. We are saved by faith alone in what Jesus has done for us. But saving faith, if it is real, will result in faithfulness. The evidence of such faith will be demonstrated by the changes it produces in our lives. When someone truly believes in Jesus Christ, their belief will change the way they live. Faith certainly changed the lives of people in biblical times. And it is still changing lives today.

FURTHER MEDITATION:

Other passages to study about the issue of faith include:

- Habakkuk 2:4
- Matthew 6:30–34
- Luke 17:5
- Romans 3:22–28; 5:1
- 2 Timothy 4:7
- Hebrews 12:2
- 2 Peter 1:1–9

To Learn More: Turn to the key passage note on faith at Hebrews 11:1–6 on page 1632. See also the personality profile of Abraham on page 21.

to flight the armies of the aliens. 35Women received their dead raised to life again.
Others were tortured, not accepting deliverance, that they might obtain a better resurrection. 36Still others
had trial of mockings
and scourgings, yes, and
of chains and impris-
onment. 37They were
stoned, they were sawn
in two, were tempted,[a]
were slain with the
sword. They wandered
about in sheepskins and goatskins, being destitute, afflicted, tormented—38of whom the
world was not worthy. They wandered in
deserts and mountains, *in* dens and caves of
the earth.
39And all these, having obtained a good testimony through faith, did not receive the
promise, 40God having provided something
better for us, that they should not be made
perfect apart from us.

> For consider Him who endured such hostility from sinners against Himself, lest you become weary and discouraged in your souls.
>
> HEBREWS 12:3

The Race of Faith

12 Therefore we also, since we are surrounded by so great a cloud of witnesses, let us lay aside every weight, and the
sin which so easily ensnares *us,* and let us run
with endurance the race that is set before us,
2looking unto Jesus, the author and finisher of
our faith, who for the joy that was set before
Him endured the cross, despising the shame,
and has sat down at the
right hand of the throne
of God.

The Discipline of God

3For consider Him who
endured such hostility
from sinners against
Himself, lest you be-
come weary and discouraged in your souls.
4You have not yet resisted to bloodshed, striving against sin. 5And you have forgotten the
exhortation which speaks to you as to sons:

"My son, do not despise the chastening of
the LORD,
Nor be discouraged when you are
rebuked by Him;
6 *For whom the LORD loves He chastens,*
And scourges every son whom He
receives."[a]

11:37 [a]NU-Text omits *were tempted.*
12:6 [a]Proverbs 3:11, 12

SOUL NOTE

Get in the Race *(12:1–4)* In order to run well, runners must let go of any weights that slow them down and just focus on the finish line. Likewise, believers must set aside any weight of sin in order to "run with endurance" toward the finish line of life. We know we'll finish, because the Savior is "the author and finisher of our faith," and He stands at the finish line to welcome us into eternity. When the hurdles of life are looming ahead of us and when the race seems too difficult, we need to get our eyes fixed on Jesus. **Topic: Faith**

SOUL NOTE

For Our Good *(12:5–11)* Children don't enjoy discipline. But parents know that tough discipline is sometimes required in order to teach an important lesson. The same is true for God's children. Though they love God, believers are sometimes disobedient—rebelling against His rules. God's discipline proves that He loves His children. Discipline may come in the form of consequences, pain, or trials, but its goal is to mold and shape us. Like a loving Father, God disciplines us because He wants to keep us safe and help us mature. **Topic: Child Discipline**

7If[a] you endure chastening, God deals with you as with sons; for what son is there whom a father does not chasten? 8But if you are without chastening, of which all have become partakers, then you are illegitimate and not sons. 9Furthermore, we have had human fathers who corrected *us,* and we paid *them* respect. Shall we not much more readily be in subjection to the Father of spirits and live? 10For they indeed for a few days chastened *us* as seemed *best* to them, but He for *our* profit, that *we* may be partakers of His holiness. 11Now no chastening seems to be joyful for the present, but painful; nevertheless, afterward it yields the peaceable fruit of righteousness to those who have been trained by it.

Renew Your Spiritual Vitality

12Therefore strengthen the hands which hang down, and the feeble knees, 13and make straight paths for your feet, so that what is lame may not be dislocated, but rather be healed.

14Pursue peace with all *people,* and holiness, without which no one will see the Lord: 15looking carefully lest anyone fall short of the grace of God; lest any root of bitterness springing up cause trouble, and by this many become defiled; 16lest there *be* any fornicator or profane person like Esau, who for one morsel of food sold his birthright. 17For you know that afterward, when he wanted to inherit the blessing, he was rejected, for he found no place for repentance, though he sought it diligently with tears.

The Glorious Company

18For you have not come to the mountain that[a] may be touched and that burned with fire, and to blackness and darkness[b] and tempest, 19and the sound of a trumpet and the voice of words, so that those who heard *it* begged that the word should not be spoken to them anymore. 20(For they could not endure what was commanded: *"And if so much as a beast touches the mountain, it shall be stoned*[a] *or shot with an arrow."*[b] 21And so terrifying was the sight *that* Moses said, *"I am exceedingly afraid* and trembling."[a])

22But you have come to Mount Zion and to the city of the living God, the heavenly Jerusalem, to an innumerable company of angels, 23to the general assembly and church of the firstborn *who are* registered in heaven, to God the Judge of all, to the spirits of just men made perfect, 24to Jesus the Mediator of the new covenant, and to the blood of sprinkling that speaks better things than *that of* Abel.

12:7 [a]NU-Text and M-Text read *It is for discipline that you endure; God . . . .* **12:18** [a]NU-Text reads *to that which.* [b]NU-Text reads *gloom.* **12:20** [a]NU-Text and M-Text omit the rest of this verse. [b]Exodus 19:12, 13 **12:21** [a]Deuteronomy 9:19

KEY PASSAGE

WEED IT OUT

(12:12–29)

Believers need to look out for each other—helping those who are feeling weak and guiding those who are heading in the wrong direction. This will guard against "any root of bitterness" that might spring up within the fellowship. This phrase may refer to the bitterness of unbelief that can poison a church and the bitterness between people that can poison relationships.

Bitterness, once planted, tends to grow quickly and cause trouble. Bitterness that is allowed to take root in our lives will spring up into actions and words that cannot be taken back. Believers can avoid the root of bitterness by dealing with their feelings immediately. When hurt or doubt are allowed to remain in one's life, they provide hospitable soil for the root of bitterness. With God's help, we can keep that root from having a place to grow, and if bitterness has already taken root, weed it out.

To Learn More: Turn to the article about bitterness on pages 658, 659. See also the personality profile of Saul on page 370.

Hear the Heavenly Voice

[25]See that you do not refuse Him who
speaks. For if they did not escape who refused
Him who spoke on earth, much more *shall we*
not escape if we turn away from Him who
speaks from heaven, [26]whose voice then
shook the earth; but now He has promised,
saying, *"Yet once more I shake*[a] *not only the*
earth, but also heaven."[b] [27]Now this, *"Yet*
once more," indicates the removal of those
things that are being shaken, as of things that
are made, that the things which cannot be
shaken may remain.
[28]Therefore, since we are receiving a kingdom which cannot be
shaken, let us have
grace, by which we
may[a] serve God accept-
ably with reverence and
godly fear. [29]For our
God *is* a consuming fire.

Concluding Moral Directions

13 Let brotherly love continue. [2]Do not
forget to entertain strangers, for by so
doing some have unwittingly entertained angels. [3]Remember the prisoners as if chained
with them—those who are mistreated—since
you yourselves are in the body also.
[4]Marriage *is* honorable among all, and the
bed undefiled; but fornicators and adulterers
God will judge.
[5]*Let your* conduct *be* without covetousness;
be content with such things as you have. For
He Himself has said, *"I will never leave you*
nor forsake you."[a] [6]So we may boldly say:

"The LORD *is my helper;*
I will not fear.
What can man do to me?"[a]

Concluding Religious Directions

[7]Remember those who rule over you, who
have spoken the word of God to you, whose
faith follow, considering
the outcome of *their*
conduct. [8]Jesus Christ *is*
the same yesterday, to-
day, and forever. [9]Do not
be carried about[a] with
various and strange doc-
trines. For *it is* good that the heart be established by grace, not with foods which have not
profited those who have been occupied with
them.

> Jesus Christ is the same yesterday, today, and forever.
> HEBREWS 13:8

12:26 [a]NU-Text reads *will shake.* [b]Haggai 2:6
12:28 [a]M-Text omits *may.* **13:5** [a]Deuteronomy 31:6, 8; Joshua 1:5 **13:6** [a]Psalm 118:6
13:9 [a]NU-Text and M-Text read *away.*

Sex in Marriage

INTIMACY

(13:4)

God created sex and designed it to be enjoyed within the confines of the marriage relationship. God doesn't pervert sex; people do. To God, "marriage is honorable among all, and the bed undefiled." Along with the characteristics that make for all good relationships—such as speaking kindly, being patient, listening carefully, etc.—marriage alone provides the opportunity for a man and woman to experience what God intends for their pleasure.

Married couples should also protect their sexual relationship because God will judge the sexually immoral and adulterers. Immorality and adultery destroy marriages by cheapening the intimate act of sex. Because sex creates such a unique bond, immorality and adultery cause pain and devastation in a marriage.

Believers must seek to strengthen their marriages and not deprive each other of the sexual intimacy that unites them (I Cor. 7:3–5). They should guard that aspect of their life together, making time to be with each other and to renew their intimacy.

To Learn More: Turn to the article about sex in marriage on pages 1500, 1501. See also the personality profile of Solomon and the Shulamite on page 871.

[10]We have an altar from which those who
serve the tabernacle have no right to eat. [11]For
the bodies of those animals, whose blood is
brought into the sanctuary by the high priest
for sin, are burned outside the camp. [12]There-
fore Jesus also, that He might sanctify the people with His own blood, suffered outside the
gate. [13]Therefore let us go forth to Him, outside the camp, bearing His reproach. [14]For
here we have no continuing city, but we seek
the one to come. [15]Therefore by Him let us
continually offer the sacrifice of praise to God,
that is, the fruit of *our* lips, giving thanks to
His name. [16]But do not forget to do good and
to share, for with such sacrifices God is well
pleased.

[17]Obey those who rule over you, and be
submissive, for they watch out for your souls,
as those who must give account. Let them do
so with joy and not with grief, for that would
be unprofitable for you.

Prayer Requested

[18]Pray for us; for we are confident that we
have a good conscience, in all things desiring
to live honorably. [19]But I especially urge *you*
to do this, that I may be restored to you the
sooner.

Benediction, Final Exhortation, Farewell

[20]Now may the God of peace who brought
up our Lord Jesus from the dead, that great
Shepherd of the sheep, through the blood of
the everlasting covenant, [21]make you complete in every good work to do His will, working in you[a] what is well pleasing in His sight,
through Jesus Christ, to whom *be* glory forever and ever. Amen.

[22]And I appeal to you, brethren, bear with
the word of exhortation, for I have written to
you in few words. [23]Know that *our* brother
Timothy has been set free, with whom I shall
see you if he comes shortly.

[24]Greet all those who rule over you, and all
the saints. Those from Italy greet you.

[25]Grace *be* with you all. Amen.

13:21 [a]NU-Text and M-Text read *us*.

SOUL NOTE

God Is There *(13:5)* Loneliness is part of the human experience. But being alone is different from being lonely. When people feel lonely, they feel like they don't belong, like no one cares, unloved and unwanted. When believers feel lonely, they need to remember God's great promise, "I will never leave you nor forsake you." No matter how painful or difficult our situation, no matter how alone we feel, God is there. We can look to Him for deliverance, commit the situation to His care, and take comfort in His presence. God is always with us. **Topic: Loneliness**

SOUL NOTE

Loving Shepherds *(13:17)* The words, "obey those who rule over you," refer to believers obeying their spiritual authorities—pastors, elders, teachers, and so forth. Wise and godly leaders, called by God into positions of spiritual authority, have the heavy responsibility to "give account" to God as they care for the souls and spiritual growth of those in their care. Many leaders face a constant stream of turmoil, complaints, and judgmentalism. We can ease their burden by praying for them, encouraging them, and seeking to be helpful and supportive. **Topic: Obedience**

James

A sportswear company has one of the most successful advertising slogans ever: "Just do it!" In fact, it has become part of international pop culture. Everyone knows it's a call to action—to get moving and get in shape. You might say that "Just do it!" is also a pretty good summary of the Book of James—and not a bad slogan for the Christian life.

James, a half brother of Jesus, became a leader of the church at Jerusalem (Acts 15:13). Written around A.D. 46, the Book of James is a package of succinct observations about the relationship between faith and practice. It's the most practical of all New Testament letters. "Faith without works is dead," James declares (2:20), in effect telling us to practice what we preach. His point is that believers should demonstrate their beliefs by the way they behave (2:18–26). James deals with such down-to-earth, everyday issues as hypocrisy, gossip, materialism, worldly wisdom, and prayer. He reminds us that pride is the source of all conflicts, and that humility is the key to a successful Christian life. "Submit to God . . . draw near to God . . . humble yourselves," he urges, for God "will lift you up" (4:7–10).

This convicting and challenging letter makes it clear that people will never really know what Christians believe until they see the manner in which they live. Like a simple "how to" manual for Christian living, the Book of James commands us to "Just do it!"—to get moving, to get our souls in shape, and then to put our faith on display through Christlike actions.

SOUL CONCERNS IN JAMES

Prejudice	(2:1–9)
Healing/Recovery	(5:14)

Greeting to the Twelve Tribes

1 James, a bondservant of God and of the
Lord Jesus Christ,

To the twelve tribes which are scattered
abroad:

Greetings.

Profiting from Trials

2My brethren, count it all joy when you fall
into various trials, 3knowing that the testing of
your faith produces patience. 4But let patience
have *its* perfect work, that you may be perfect
and complete, lacking nothing. 5If any of you
lacks wisdom, let him ask of God, who gives
to all liberally and without reproach, and it
will be given to him. 6But let him ask in faith,
with no doubting, for he who doubts is like a
wave of the sea driven and tossed by the
wind. 7For let not that man suppose that he
will receive anything from the Lord; 8*he is* a
double-minded man, unstable in all his ways.

The Perspective of Rich and Poor

9Let the lowly brother glory in his exaltation, 10but the rich in his humiliation, because
as a flower of the field he will pass away. 11For
no sooner has the sun risen with a burning
heat than it withers the grass; its flower falls,
and its beautiful appearance perishes. So the
rich man also will fade away in his pursuits.

PERSONALITY PROFILE

Stress

JAMES: GRACE UNDER FIRE

(JAMES 1)

Older brothers often influence their younger brothers profoundly, and it can be stressful on a younger brother if the older brother has many skills and abilities. Imagine the stress of having a *perfect* older brother—literally. James did, and His name was Jesus.

Jesus apparently had several brothers, none of whom believed in Him during His ministry (John 7:5). Eventually, however, Jesus' brothers came around and were present at Pentecost (Acts 1:14). (Jesus' brother James is not to be confused with the two disciples of the same name.)

James received a special resurrection appearance from his Brother (1 Cor. 15:7). Clearly, Jesus had special work for James to do: Leading the newborn Christian church in Jerusalem. James became one of the "pillars" of that fellowship, along with Peter and John (Gal. 2:9). With leadership, however, comes stress, and leading the large church in Jerusalem was no exception.

The record in the Book of Acts describes conflict, persecution, martyrdom, imprisonment, famine, and many other painful trials for the Jerusalem believers. Fortunately, the church had clearheaded leaders to handle these stresses wisely and to help the believers remain faithful. James's wisdom showed as he handled one of the most difficult conflicts the young church would face—the issue of whether Jews and Gentiles could be Christians together and worship together. His logical thinking and godly wisdom revealed in his decision about this matter unified the young church, making it stronger than ever (Acts 15).

Therefore, James knew what he was talking about when he wrote, "Count it all joy when you fall into various trials, knowing that the testing of your faith produces patience" (James 1:2, 3). His advice for dealing with the stresses of life was apparently advice he himself followed—ask God for wisdom, and don't doubt that He will give it.

Stress cannot be avoided, but it can become a teaching tool in our lives when we let God have control. Ask Him for wisdom, trust Him for guidance, and love Him no matter what.

To Learn More: Turn to the article about stress on pages 422, 423. See also the key passage note at 2 Corinthians 4:9 on page 1522.

Loving God Under Trials

12 Blessed *is* the man who endures temptation; for when he has been approved, he will
receive the crown of life which the Lord has
promised to those who love Him. 13 Let no one
say when he is tempted, "I am tempted by
God"; for God cannot be tempted by evil, nor
does He Himself tempt anyone. 14 But each one
is tempted when he is drawn away by his own
desires and enticed. 15 Then, when desire has
conceived, it gives birth to sin; and sin, when
it is full-grown, brings forth death.
16 Do not be deceived, my beloved brethren.
17 Every good gift and every perfect gift is from

SOUL NOTE

Joy-Full *(1:2–4)* James, the leader of the church in Jerusalem, advised believers to be joyful during trials and troubles. Everyone faces trials in one form or another. We cannot control what we will encounter, but we can control the stress level that situations cause. Instead of being stressed, we can try being joyful. This is not a natural reaction, but one that the Holy Spirit can provide. It means choosing an attitude that looks expectantly to the lessons God will teach and the wisdom He will provide. There's no better prescription for dealing with stress! **Topic: Stress**

KEY PASSAGE

Wisdom

ASKING FOR IT

(1:5)

People admire wisdom in others. Wise people have the proper perspective and can make sensible and sensitive decisions. Such people seem to be few and far between. Among believers, however, the percentage of wise people should be high, for James writes, "If any of you lacks wisdom, let him ask of God . . . and it will be given to him."

Wisdom begins with God, who is its source. The first step to being wise is to have proper awe and reverence for God, and then to trust Him with one's life. We become wiser as we become more and more like Christ. God's wisdom is "pure, then peaceable, gentle, willing to yield, full of mercy and good fruits, without partiality and without hypocrisy" (James 3:17). As we study and apply God's Word, yielding our lives daily to Christ, we need only ask God to give us His wisdom, and He promises He will.

To Learn More: Turn to the article about wisdom on pages 436, 437. See also the personality profile of Solomon on page 435.

SOUL NOTE

Make Up Your Mind *(1:5)* Life is full of choices: The "right" choice is not always clear, and the enemy of the better is often the good. Sometimes we must choose between two good options. Whatever the choice, we need God's wisdom to see life from His perspective and make good decisions in difficult circumstances. Fortunately, wisdom is fairly easy to obtain: James says to ask God and He will freely give it. God will generously supply all the wisdom we need for every decision we face. But when we ask, we need to be willing to do what He says! **Topic: Decision Making**

above, and comes down from the Father of
lights, with whom there is no variation or
shadow of turning. [18]Of His own will He
brought us forth by the
word of truth, that we
might be a kind of first-
fruits of His creatures.

QUALITIES NEEDED IN TRIALS

[19]So then,[a] my be-
loved brethren, let every
man be swift to hear, slow to speak, slow to
wrath; [20]for the wrath of man does not produce the righteousness of God.

> Therefore lay aside all filthiness and overflow of wickedness, and receive with meekness the implanted word, which is able to save your souls.
>
> JAMES 1:21

DOERS—NOT HEARERS ONLY

[21]Therefore lay aside all filthiness and overflow of wickedness, and receive with meekness the implanted word,
which is able to save
your souls.
[22]But be doers of the
word, and not hearers
only, deceiving your-
selves. [23]For if anyone is
a hearer of the word and
not a doer, he is like a
man observing his natural face in a mirror;

1:19 [a]NU-Text reads *Know this* or *This you know.*

SOUL NOTE

Strength to Resist *(1:12–15)* Temptation comes from evil desires inside us, not from God. It begins with an evil thought that becomes sin when we act on it. God does not tempt His people, but He will allow Satan to tempt us in order for us to refine our faith and grow in our dependence on God. And He will not allow us to be tempted more than we can bear (1 Cor. 10:13). When temptation raises its head, often unexpectedly, we can resist it by counting the costs and turning to God, asking Him for help, and choosing to obey Him. He will give us the strength we need.
Topic: Temptation

SOUL NOTE

Listen Up *(1:19)* Communication is more than just talking. If two people are talking at the same time, they aren't communicating—they're just making noise. Communication involves both parties taking turns speaking and listening. Good communication, wrote James, occurs when people are quicker to listen than they are to speak. We want to speak and make our opinions known, but we must also be willing to listen to others. We show respect for others when we listen intently and then speak carefully. **Topic: Communication**

SOUL NOTE

Do It! *(1:22)* Many people sit in church and listen to the sermon, only to forget what they heard upon exiting the sanctuary. James says, "Be doers of the word, and not hearers only." It is important to read, listen to, and know God's Word, but it is also important to obey it. We can measure the effectiveness of our Bible study and attentiveness to the Sunday sermon by our behavior and attitudes during the entire week. How much is our faith affecting how we live? It should make a huge difference, for "faith by itself, if it does not have works, is dead" (2:17). **Topic: Change/Maturity**

[24]for he observes himself, goes away, and immediately forgets what kind of man he was.
[25]But he who looks into the perfect law of liberty and continues *in it,* and is not a forgetful hearer but a doer of the work, this one will be blessed in what he does.

[26]If anyone among you[a] thinks he is religious, and does not bridle his tongue but deceives his own heart, this one's religion *is*
useless. [27]Pure and undefiled religion before God and the Father is this: to visit orphans and widows in their trouble, *and* to keep oneself unspotted from the world.

Beware of Personal Favoritism

2 My brethren, do not hold the faith of our Lord Jesus Christ, *the Lord* of glory, with partiality. [2]For if there should come into your assembly a man with gold rings, in fine apparel, and there should also come in a poor man in filthy clothes, [3]and you pay attention to the one wearing the fine clothes and say to him, "You sit here in a good place," and say to the poor man, "You stand there," or, "Sit here at my footstool," [4]have you not shown partiality among yourselves, and become judges with evil thoughts?

[5]Listen, my beloved brethren: Has God not chosen the poor of this world *to be* rich in faith and heirs of the kingdom which He promised to those who love Him? [6]But you have dishonored the poor man. Do not the

1:26 [a]NU-Text omits *among you.*

KEY PASSAGE

Children Problems

FOR THE CHILDREN

(1:27)

From politics to book titles, people regularly express their concern for children. Whatever the motives of others might be, believers should be leading the way in showing compassion toward the helpless in society. To "visit orphans and widows in their trouble," wrote James, reveals a person's "pure and undefiled religion before God." Caring for orphans, helpless children, was a high priority in the early church and a mark of true Christian discipleship.

When children face difficult problems in their homes, believers need to understand the great impact they can have in a child's life. Many solid believers trace their faith, not to their parents, but to another loving Christian adult.

In many cases, the problems may require professional intervention. Many times, however, coming alongside as a friend or supportive adult can help a child with problems to feel loved and gain self-esteem. When we direct them toward Jesus, we have given them the best gift of all. In whatever way we can, it's our duty to care for the "orphans" among us.

To Learn More: Turn to the article about children problems on pages 1222, 1223. See also the personality profile of Tamar on page 406.

SOUL NOTE

Playing Favorites *(2:1–9)* James warned the believers against showing prejudice. They were not to fawn over a rich person while ignoring a poor one. People often want to be associated with those who are successful, popular, and powerful. God demands impartiality, however, for all people are equally valuable in His eyes. Favoritism goes against God's command to love one's neighbor as oneself. He wants us to respect all people and treat them equally, regardless of their background or economic status. Each person is God's creation. **Topic: Prejudice**

rich oppress you and drag you into the courts?
7Do they not blaspheme that noble name by
which you are called?
8If you really fulfill *the* royal law according
to the Scripture, *"You shall love your neighbor
as yourself,"*[a] you do well; 9but if you show
partiality, you commit sin, and are convicted
by the law as transgressors. 10For whoever
shall keep the whole law, and yet stumble in
one *point,* he is guilty of all. 11For He who
said, *"Do not commit adultery,"*[a] also said,
"Do not murder."[b] Now if you do not commit
adultery, but you do murder, you have become a transgressor of the law. 12So speak and
so do as those who will be judged by the law
of liberty. 13For judgment is without mercy to
the one who has shown no mercy. Mercy triumphs over judgment.

Faith Without Works Is Dead

14What *does it* profit, my brethren, if someone says he has faith but does not have
works? Can faith save him? 15If a brother or
sister is naked and destitute of daily food,
16and one of you says to them, "Depart in
peace, be warmed and filled," but you do not
give them the things which are needed for the
body, what *does it* profit? 17Thus also faith by
itself, if it does not have works, is dead.
18But someone will say, "You have faith,
and I have works." Show me your faith without your[a] works, and I will show you my faith
by my[b] works. 19You believe that there is one
God. You do well. Even the demons believe—
and tremble! 20But do you want to know, O
foolish man, that faith without works is
dead?[a] 21Was not Abraham our father justified
by works when he offered Isaac his son on the
altar? 22Do you see that faith was working together with his works, and by works faith was
made perfect? 23And the Scripture was fulfilled which says, *"Abraham believed God,
and it was accounted to him for righteousness."*[a] And he was called the friend of God.
24You see then that a man is justified by
works, and not by faith only.
25Likewise, was not Rahab the harlot also
justified by works when she received the messengers and sent *them* out another way?
26For as the body without the spirit is dead,
so faith without works is dead also.

The Untamable Tongue

3 My brethren, let not many of you become
teachers, knowing that we shall receive a
stricter judgment. 2For we all stumble in many
things. If anyone does not stumble in word, he
is a perfect man, able also to bridle the whole
body. 3Indeed,[a] we put bits in horses' mouths
that they may obey us, and we turn their
whole body. 4Look also at ships: although
they are so large and are driven by fierce
winds, they are turned by a very small rudder
wherever the pilot desires. 5Even so the
tongue is a little member and boasts great
things.
See how great a forest a little fire kindles!
6And the tongue *is* a fire, a world of iniquity.
The tongue is so set among our members that
it defiles the whole body, and sets on fire the
course of nature; and it is set on fire by hell.
7For every kind of beast and bird, of reptile
and creature of the sea, is tamed and has been
tamed by mankind. 8But no man can tame the
tongue. *It is* an unruly evil, full of deadly poison. 9With it we bless our God and Father, and

2:8 [a]Leviticus 19:18 **2:11** [a]Exodus 20:14; Deuteronomy 5:18 [b]Exodus 20:13; Deuteronomy 5:17 **2:18** [a]NU-Text omits *your.* [b]NU-Text omits *my.* **2:20** [a]NU-Text reads *useless.* **2:23** [a]Genesis 15:6 **3:3** [a]NU-Text reads *Now if.*

SOUL NOTE

Before You Speak *(3:5–10)* James compares the damage the tongue can do to a raging fire. People dare not be careless in what they say, thinking they can apologize later, because hurtful words cause deep wounds and lasting scars. A few words spoken in anger can destroy a relationship that it took years to build. Before speaking, we would do well to picture our tongues as sparks that can start a destructive fire and cause irreversible damage. Kind words, however, can build up the spirit and strengthen the bonds of friendship and love. The tongue may be small, but it can cause great harm or do great good. Which it does is up to us. **Topic: Communication**

A CHRISTIAN RESPONSE TO PREJUDICE

Prejudice

SABRINA D. BLACK AND PARIS M. FINNER-WILLIAMS

(James 2:1–9)

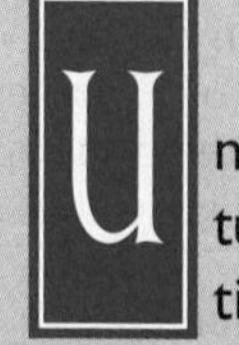

Unreasonable. Intolerant. Unjust. Thoughts. Opinions. Attitudes. Prejudice is symbolized by a number of terse descriptions. At its basic level, prejudice describes a person or group that is predisposed to make premature judgments toward other individuals or groups without a fair review of the objective facts. Prejudice can hide under the surface as hostile and resentful feelings and can manifest itself as an unfounded dislike of certain people. Christians, however, are called to respond differently to the stronghold of prejudice, with Christ as the power source for change.

THE EFFECTS OF PREJUDICE

Prejudice is incompatible with a godly spirit. A spirit of prejudice negatively affects the way people relate to others and the way they perceive situations. For example, prejudiced people short-circuit the fellowship that God intends for His children to share because they refuse involvement with situations and groups of people who are different. Prejudice can lead to strongholds or patterns that make it difficult to be reasonable, just, and tolerant of others.

Personal prejudice can have a negative impact on the way people see themselves, too. If people see themselves as uniquely separate from others because of prejudice, they create a false idea of themselves. Prejudice can also affect people's relationship with God. Ungodly behavior, thoughts, and attitudes lead them further away from becoming like Christ.

Prejudice can lead to discrimination. Prejudice is attitudes, thoughts, or opinions; discrimination puts those attitudes, thoughts, and opinions into action. Discriminating behavior and negative actions violate the substantial rights, privileges, and equal protection granted to others by the laws of the land and mandated by Scripture. Not all prejudgment, however, will result in discriminatory behavior and actions. People do not have to outwardly discriminate against others in order for prejudice to be dormant in their hearts.

God's Nature

Many may argue that prejudice is a matter of personal opinion. "I can't help the way I feel." However, Christians are instructed to exercise personal choices based on what they see in the character of God. "Now therefore, let the fear of the LORD be upon you . . . for there is no iniquity with the LORD our God, no partiality, nor taking of bribes" (2 Chr. 19:7).

The Bible says that God does not show favoritism: "There is no partiality with God" (Rom. 2:11). His unbiased nature toward a diverse world is the foundation of John 3:16: "For God so loved the world that He gave His only begotten Son, that whoever believes in Him should not perish but have everlasting life." Imagine the diversity of the entire created world. The differences in race, culture, shape, size, religion, occupation, and interest are too numerous to count. However, imitating God's nature, Christians can learn to love like God and celebrate the diversity of the world without partiality.

God's Instructions

As the love of God flows through Christians, they are drawn together as a body and begin to relate to one another as instructed in the Bible. In the New Testament alone, there are dozens of references to how Christians should relate to "one another." For example:

➢ "be kindly affectionate to one another" (Rom. 12:10);
➢ "be of the same mind toward one another" (Rom. 12:16);
➢ "love one another" (Rom. 13:8);
➢ "pursue the things which make for peace and the things by which one may edify another" (Rom. 14:19);
➢ "the members should have the same care for one another" (1 Cor. 12:25).
➢ "through love serve one another" (Gal. 5:13);
➢ "be kind to one another, tenderhearted, forgiving one another" (Eph. 4:32);
➢ "bearing with one another, and forgiving one another" (Col. 3:13).

Prejudice causes the whole body of Christ to suffer. "For as the body is one and has many members, but all the members of that one body, being many, are one body, so also is Christ" (1 Cor. 12:12). In the unified body of Christ, there is no allowance for prejudiced attitudes and biased opinions. Such ungodliness turns members of Christ's body against themselves.

ELIMINATING PREJUDICE

People who wish to overcome prejudice need to have renewed minds (Eph. 4:23) by studying the Word of God and acquiring the mind of Christ (Phil. 2:5). As a result, Christ enables them to remove bias, discrimination, division, fear, anxiety, and judgment from their personal thoughts. In exchange, Christ helps them to exhibit impartiality, acceptance, unity, faith, love, peace, honor, hope, and humility.

Although a world without prejudice may be impossible, we as Christians are to demonstrate impartiality in our individual lives. First, we must remember that we are fearfully and wonderfully made—and so are others (Ps. 139:14). We must look past the outward differences and see the beauty of God's creation. We must increase our exposure toward those who are different in order to engender feelings of similarity instead of feelings of separation. We can confess and acknowledge our sin to God when we have not responded to all people in a Christlike manner. We can also ask Him to forgive us and help us have a renewed mind that demonstrates our repentance concerning prejudicial attitudes and actions. Eliminating prejudice begins one life at a time.

FURTHER MEDITATION:

Other passages to study about the issue of prejudice include:

➢ 1 Samuel 16:7
➢ Proverbs 14:31
➢ Luke 10:29–37
➢ 1 Timothy 4:12—5:1

To Learn More: **Turn to the key passage note on prejudice at Esther 3:6 on page 627. See also the personality profile of Haman on page 628.**

with it we curse men, who have been made in the similitude of God. [10]Out of the same mouth proceed blessing and cursing. My brethren, these things ought not to be so. [11]Does a spring send forth fresh *water* and bitter from the same opening? [12]Can a fig tree, my brethren, bear olives, or a grapevine bear figs? Thus no spring yields both salt water and fresh.[a]

HEAVENLY VERSUS DEMONIC WISDOM

[13]Who *is* wise and understanding among you? Let him show by good conduct *that* his works *are done* in the meekness of wisdom. [14]But if you have bitter envy and self-seeking in your hearts, do not boast and lie against the truth. [15]This wisdom does not descend from above, but *is* earthly, sensual, demonic. [16]For where envy and self-seeking *exist,* confusion and every evil thing *are* there. [17]But the wisdom that is from above is first pure, then peaceable, gentle, willing to yield, full of mercy and good fruits, without partiality and without hypocrisy. [18]Now the fruit of righteousness is sown in peace by those who make peace.

PRIDE PROMOTES STRIFE

4 Where do wars and fights *come* from among you? Do *they* not *come* from your *desires for* pleasure that war in your members? [2]You lust and do not have. You murder and covet and cannot obtain. You fight and war. Yet[a] you do not have because you do not ask. [3]You ask and do not receive, because you ask amiss, that you may spend *it* on your pleasures. [4]Adulterers and[a] adulteresses! Do you not know that friendship with the world is enmity with God? Whoever therefore wants to be a friend of the world makes himself an enemy of God. [5]Or do you think that the Scripture says in vain, "The Spirit who dwells in us yearns jealously"?

[6]But He gives more grace. Therefore He says:

> *"God resists the proud,*
> *But gives grace to the humble."*[a]

HUMILITY CURES WORLDLINESS

[7]Therefore submit to God. Resist the devil and he will flee from you. [8]Draw near to God and He will draw near to you. Cleanse *your* hands, *you* sinners; and purify *your* hearts, *you* double-minded. [9]Lament and mourn and

3:12 [a]NU-Text reads *Neither can a salty spring produce fresh water.* **4:2** [a]NU-Text and M-Text omit *Yet.* **4:4** [a]NU-Text omits *Adulterers and.* **4:6** [a]Proverbs 3:34

KEY PASSAGE

A DANGEROUS SPARK

(3:5–18)

Gossip

Gossip is idle talk or the spread of rumors about the private affairs of others. Seldom is gossip helpful and uplifting; rather, it usually centers around less-than-positive information or rumors. Even if what is being spread is true, the person passing the information along usually has less-than-positive motives. The Bible says that "a whisperer separates the best of friends," "reveals secrets," and causes "strife" (Prov. 16:28; 20:19; 26:20). The gossip's words, like a spark on dry timber, can create a firestorm that destroys friendships, relationships, and reputations.

Christians can use their time and words more wisely than by listening to or spreading rumors and half-truths. When the local gossip calls to talk, we can let the person know, clearly and finally, that we will not listen. When we're talking about other people, we should pass our words through an inner filter of truthfulness, kindness, and love. We ought to train ourselves to not listen to or pass along gossip, for the consequences are far too hurtful to others.

To Learn More: Turn to the article about gossip on pages 838, 839. See also the personality profile of Diotrephes on page 1691.

weep! Let your laughter be turned to mourning and *your* joy to gloom. [10]Humble yourselves in the sight of the Lord, and He will lift you up.

Do Not Judge a Brother

[11]Do not speak evil of one another, brethren. He who speaks evil of a brother and judges his brother, speaks evil of the law and judges the law. But if you judge the law, you are not a doer of the law but a judge. [12]There is one Lawgiver,[a] who is able to save and to destroy. Who[b] are you to judge another?[c]

> Draw near to God and He will draw near to you. Cleanse your hands, you sinners; and purify your hearts, you double-minded.
>
> JAMES 4:8

Do Not Boast About Tomorrow

[13]Come now, you who say, "Today or tomorrow we will[a] go to such and such a city, spend a year there, buy and sell, and make a profit"; [14]whereas you do not know what *will happen* tomorrow. For what *is* your life? It is even a vapor that appears for a little time and then vanishes away. [15]Instead you *ought* to say, "If the Lord wills, we shall live and do this or that." [16]But now you

4:12 [a]NU-Text adds *and Judge.* [b]NU-Text and M-Text read *But who.* [c]NU-Text reads *a neighbor.*
4:13 [a]M-Text reads *let us.*

KEY PASSAGE

Pride

BEFORE A FALL

(4:6–10)

The Bible consistently warns against pride. "God resists the proud," writes James. Pride brings shame, strife, and foolishness (Prov. 11:2; 13:10; 14:3). Proud people are "an abomination" for "pride goes before destruction, and a haughty spirit before a fall" (Prov. 16:5, 18).

Pride hurts one's relationship with God because proud people think they don't need Him. Pride hurts one's relationships with others because proud people are self-centered and feel superior. Pride makes people blind to their own sinfulness. God opposes the proud, for their pride is sinful and He knows their danger to themselves and to others.

The antidote to pride is a good dose of humility. Sometimes proud people are humbled through circumstances or even tragedy. When God gets their attention, He offers them grace. Humility is not weakness; instead, it is the willingness to "submit to God." When we humble ourselves before Him, He promises to lift us up.

To Learn More: Turn to the article about pride on pages 572, 573. See also the personality profile of the king of Tyre on page 1076.

SOUL NOTE

Rush to Judgment *(4:11, 12)* Discipline is necessary for those in the fellowship who are involved in destructive sin. But when believers judge one another, they act against God's law. This passage refers to individuals who readily take God's judgment into their own hands, often over minor issues. When believers are too zealous to judge others, they cause hurt and division. Jesus said, "Judge not, that you be not judged" (Matt. 7:1). Instead of a critical spirit, we should show understanding, compassion, and love. **Topic: Judgmentalism**

boast in your arrogance. All such boasting is evil.

[17]Therefore, to him who knows to do good and does not do *it,* to him it is sin.

Rich Oppressors Will Be Judged

5 Come now, *you* rich, weep and howl for your miseries that are coming upon *you!* [2]Your riches are corrupted, and your garments are moth-eaten. [3]Your gold and silver are corroded, and their corrosion will be a witness against you and will eat your flesh like fire. You have heaped up treasure in the last days. [4]Indeed the wages of the laborers who mowed your fields, which you kept back by fraud, cry out; and the cries of the reapers have reached the ears of the Lord of Sabaoth.[a] [5]You have lived on the earth in pleasure and luxury; you have fattened your hearts as[a] in a day of slaughter. [6]You have condemned, you have murdered the just; he does not resist you.

Be Patient and Persevering

[7]Therefore be patient, brethren, until the coming of the Lord. See *how* the farmer waits for the precious fruit of the earth, waiting patiently for it until it receives the early and latter rain. [8]You also be patient. Establish your hearts, for the coming of the Lord is at hand.

[9]Do not grumble against one another, brethren, lest you be condemned.[a] Behold, the Judge is standing at the door! [10]My brethren, take the prophets, who spoke in the name of the Lord, as an example of suffering and patience. [11]Indeed we count them blessed who endure. You have heard of the perseverance of Job and seen the end *intended by* the Lord—that the Lord is very compassionate and merciful.

[12]But above all, my brethren, do not swear, either by heaven or by earth or with any other oath. But let your "Yes" be "Yes," and *your* "No," "No," lest you fall into judgment.[a]

Meeting Specific Needs

[13]Is anyone among you suffering? Let him pray. Is anyone cheerful? Let him sing psalms. [14]Is anyone among you sick? Let him call for the elders of the church, and let them pray over him, anointing him with oil in the name of the Lord. [15]And the prayer of faith will save the sick, and the Lord will raise him up. And if he has committed sins, he will be forgiven. [16]Confess *your* trespasses[a] to one another, and

---

5:4 [a]Literally, in Hebrew, *Hosts* **5:5** [a]NU-Text omits *as.* **5:9** [a]NU-Text and M-Text read *judged.* **5:12** [a]M-Text reads *hypocrisy.* **5:16** [a]NU-Text reads *Therefore confess your sins.*

KEY PASSAGE

Healing/ Recovery

PRAYER FOR HEALING

(5:14–16)

The anointing by the elders described here is a valuable show of support for a sick person. The oil has no magic, nor does the touch of the elders. And James is not saying that Christians should avoid doctors or medicines, for God works through those as well. Instead, this ceremony focuses on placing complete faith in God. And when a sick person knows that others are praying for them, that person feels supported and loved.

If healing is to occur, the Lord will do it. Sometimes He performs a miracle that cannot be explained naturally; sometimes He works through doctors and medicines; sometimes it's just the body's natural, God-given healing processes at work. And then there are cases where God performs the ultimate healing by taking the person to be with Him. The true "prayer of faith" acknowledges God's sovereignty over each person's life. The prayer offered in faith reveals complete trust in God to do His will. Healing prayer should be sought by all those who hurt.

To Learn More: Turn to the article about healing/recovery on pages 1652, 1653. See also the personality profile of Peter on page 1411.

pray for one another, that you may be healed.
The effective, fervent
prayer of a righteous
man avails much. [17]Eli-
jah was a man with a
nature like ours, and he
prayed earnestly that it
would not rain; and it
did not rain on the land
for three years and six
months. [18]And he prayed
again, and the heaven gave rain, and the earth
produced its fruit.

Let him know that he who turns a sinner from the error of his way will save a soul from death and cover a multitude of sins.
JAMES 5:20

BRING BACK THE ERRING ONE

[19]Brethren, if anyone
among you wanders
from the truth, and
someone turns him
back, [20]let him know
that he who turns a sin-
ner from the error of his
way will save a soul[a]
from death and cover a
multitude of sins.

5:20 [a]NU-Text reads *his soul.*

HEALING AND RECOVERY

DAN ALLENDER

(James 5:14)

Everyone needs healing, because everyone is born into sin. In addition, in this fallen world people face hurts, pain, sickness, difficulties, and traumas. People are broken by the sins of others, as well as by their own. Sin tears apart the fabric of relationships and mars the wholeness of intimacy. When broken, people are alienated from themselves, others, and God. Evil infiltrates, dividing the parts and scattering them to increase the sense of alienation through felt distance and misunderstanding.

The result is not only a profound inner emptiness, but also a tendency to fend for oneself while rejecting others' care and involvement. Needing and trusting becomes too risky. The more one is broken and wounded, the more one ventures down the spiral of isolation and independence from others. These behaviors involve an interplay of arrogance ("I can do it on my own") and self-righteousness ("Whatever went wrong, it's not my fault"), resulting in greater blindness and self-deception. Broken and wounded people need healing that comes from a renewed relationship with God and with others.

THE MYSTERY OF HEALING

Jesus heals through His wounds. The prophet Isaiah foresaw this when he wrote of Jesus, "He was wounded for our transgressions, He was bruised for our iniquities; the chastisement for our peace was upon Him, and by His stripes we are healed" (Is. 53:5). Peter understood this as he also wrote that Jesus "bore our sins in His own body on the tree, that we, having died to sins, might live for righteousness—by whose stripes [we] were healed" (1 Pet. 2:24). People are reconciled to God through Jesus' suffering. Because of this, we have the possibility of seeing that which was once divided and scattered brought back together, healed.

When people accept Christ's sacrifice on their behalf, when they embrace His broken body, their hearts are opened to recover a personal relationship with Him. The mystery of His love compels people to face the depths of their brokenness and alienation. God's kindness breaks people's hearts over their sin, irresistibly draws their souls to His provision, and helps them to seek healing and recovery.

In order to heal people's lives, God must perform major surgery. In the process of healing them, He exposes the rampant sinfulness that He died to cure. The process of healing and recovery is not always easy, nor is it instantaneous. Deep wounds will take time to heal. Sin is embedded in every fiber of people's beings. The healing process means going "under the knife" of the Master Surgeon to allow Him to deal with the sickness. Only then can people be healed and begin the process of recovery.

THE PARADOX OF HEALING

No one will experience complete healing and recovery until they go to glory in heaven. Christ died for people's sins, and those who accept that sacrifice are considered righteous before God. However, people must still struggle with the sin nature, and they need to come to God daily for healing and recovery from sin. People's bodies, souls, and relationships will continue to groan for the healing that will only be experienced in the presence of God. So, in a very real sense, God's people are already healed, but not yet healed. This paradox is beyond our human comprehension.

Another paradox exists in the need for healing. James encourages believers to pray over sick people, anointing them with oil (James 5:14). Clearly, God should be petitioned when people are ill. However, this is not a formula for certain recovery; it is submission to God regarding His will for that person. God may choose not to heal. Why? Because that very illness, that weakness that so disturbs, can be used by God to help people. God took Paul's physical weakness, for example, and used it to glorify Himself. Paul wrote, "A thorn in the flesh was given to me, a messenger of Satan to buffet me. . . . I pleaded with the Lord three times that it might depart from me. And He said to me, 'My grace is sufficient for you, for My strength is made perfect in weakness'" (2 Cor. 12:7–9). Though Paul had repeatedly asked that the "thorn" be removed, God told Paul that He would make His power perfect through Paul's weakness. God did not leave Paul helpless, however. God promised His grace to help Paul endure through his struggles. (That promise is extended to us as well.) Paul could gladly boast about his weakness so that Christ's power would rest on him: "For when I am weak, then I am strong" (2 Cor. 12:10).

In other words, when we can't do it alone, then we have to depend on God to do it in us. Therefore, we can boast, not about being healed, but about being weak enough for God to use. God's work of healing and recovery is not always to take away our wounds; rather, His work may simply be to enable us to join with Christ in His suffering and to glorify Himself through it.

We may ask God to heal, and rejoice if He does so. We may also rejoice, however, when He chooses instead to use our weaknesses as a platform to display His grace and power in our lives. Through suffering, we may bring help and hope to others who are suffering in the same way. We can then point them to our Savior. Through our wounds, others may be invited to make an appointment with the Great Physician.

FURTHER MEDITATION:

Other passages to study about the issue of healing/recovery include:

- Exodus 15:26
- 2 Kings 20:1–11
- Psalms 18:6–19; 41:4; 103:3
- Isaiah 43:2
- Jeremiah 3:22; 30:17
- Malachi 4:2
- 1 Corinthians 12:9

To Learn More: Turn to the key passage note on healing/recovery at James 5:14–16 on page 1650. See also the personality profile of Peter on page 1411.

1 Peter

Sometimes believing in Christ can be hazardous. In fact, millions have died simply for being followers of Christ. What is most disturbing, however, is that more Christians were martyred in the 20th century than in the previous nineteen centuries combined. Indeed, at this very moment, some 200 million followers of Jesus worldwide face the chilling prospect of being arrested, tortured, and even killed for their faith.

The apostle Peter's first letter (A.D. 63–64) reminds us that from the very beginning, persecution has been part of the Christian experience. Peter presented Christ as the believer's hope and example during times of trial. The aged apostle comforted his hurting brethren with reminders of their great salvation and future inheritance (1:1–12). He challenged them to lives of holiness in a pagan world (1:13—2:12), and he counseled a submissive attitude as the God-honoring response. That's the single best way to model the truth of Christianity (2:13—3:12) in a hostile culture.

No one likes being the object of rejection or abuse. In fact, most will go to great lengths to avoid suffering. But some degree of persecution is assured to all who strive to live godly lives (2 Tim. 3:12). If your faith is under siege today, take heart. Jesus suffered the same "fiery trial" and stands with us in all our troubles. Best of all, He gave us an example that we should "follow His steps" (1 Pet. 2:21).

SOUL CONCERNS IN 1 PETER

Greeting to the Elect Pilgrims

1 Peter, an apostle of Jesus Christ,

To the pilgrims of the Dispersion in Pontus, Galatia, Cappadocia, Asia, and Bithynia, 2elect according to the foreknowledge of God the Father, in sanctification of the Spirit, for obedience and sprinkling of the blood of Jesus Christ:

Grace to you and peace be multiplied.

A Heavenly Inheritance

3Blessed *be* the God and Father of our Lord Jesus Christ, who according to His abundant mercy has begotten us again to a living hope through the resurrection of Jesus Christ from the dead, 4to an inheritance incorruptible and undefiled and that does not fade away, reserved in heaven for you, 5who are kept by the power of God through faith for salvation ready to be revealed in the last time.

6In this you greatly rejoice, though now for a little while, if need be, you have been grieved by various trials, 7that the genuineness of your faith, *being* much more precious than gold that perishes, though it is tested by fire, may be found to praise, honor, and glory at the revelation of Jesus Christ, 8whom having not seen[a] you love. Though now you do not see *Him,* yet believing, you rejoice with joy inexpressible and full of glory, 9receiving the end of your faith the salvation of *your* souls.

10Of this salvation the prophets have inquired and searched carefully, who prophesied of the grace *that would come* to you, 11searching what, or what manner of time, the Spirit of Christ who was in them was indicating when He testified beforehand the sufferings of Christ and the glories that would follow. 12To them it was revealed that, not to themselves, but to us[a] they were ministering the things which now have been reported to you through those who have preached the gospel to you by the Holy Spirit sent from heaven—things which angels desire to look into.

Living Before God Our Father

13Therefore gird up the loins of your mind, be sober, and rest *your* hope fully upon the grace that is to be brought to you at the revelation of Jesus Christ; 14as obedient children, not conforming yourselves to the former lusts, *as* in your ignorance; 15but as He who called you *is* holy, you also be holy in all *your* conduct, 16because it is written, *"Be holy, for I am holy."*[a]

17And if you call on the Father, who without partiality judges according to each one's work, conduct yourselves throughout the time of your stay *here* in fear; 18knowing that you were not redeemed with corruptible things, *like* silver or gold, from your aimless conduct *received* by tradition from your fathers, 19but with the precious blood of Christ, as of a lamb without blemish and without spot. 20He indeed was foreordained before the foundation of the world, but was manifest in these last times for you 21who through Him believe in God, who raised Him from the dead and gave Him glory, so that your faith and hope are in God.

The Enduring Word

22Since you have purified your souls in obeying the truth through the Spirit[a] in sincere love of the brethren, love one another fervently with a pure heart, 23having been born again, not of corruptible seed but incorruptible, through the word of God which lives and abides forever,[a] 24because

1:8 [a]M-Text reads *known.* **1:12** [a]NU-Text and M-Text read *you.* **1:16** [a]Leviticus 11:44, 45; 19:2; 20:7 **1:22** [a]NU-Text omits *through the Spirit.* **1:23** [a]NU-Text omits *forever.*

SOUL NOTE

Refiner's Fire *(1:6–9)* When subjected to intense heat, gold is refined. Impurities are burned away and pure gold remains. Like gold, faith tested by the fire of trials and difficulties is strengthened and purified. Believers learn that their faith depends on God alone. Such faith is precious to God. When we face trials, we can "greatly rejoice," for we know that God will strengthen our faith if we continue to hold on to Him. **Topic: Trials**

Jealousy

JEALOUSY: A CONSUMING PASSION

TIM CLINTON

(1 Peter 2:1)

Empty and exhausted in his marriage, the husband muttered, "Her jealousy is driving me crazy—I've had it." Before he sat down, his wife launched right into her tirade.

"She was tall, blond, and had a dazzling smile. And boy, was she a major flirt with my husband! I hated her right away. The moment my husband saw her, I knew he was attracted to her."

As the woman continued talking, it became obvious that she had a serious jealousy problem. Jealous of her sister, her friends, and her neighbors, now she was jealous of a woman she didn't even know. Wallowing in anger and self-pity, she had allowed her jealousy to consume her emotions and taint her marriage. Feeling smothered and wrongly accused, her husband was pulling away in frustration. She was becoming panicky, predicting that her husband would leave her or have an affair, but behaving in a way that increased the odds of her dark predictions coming true.

DEFINING JEALOUSY

Jealousy and envy are siblings, the perverse children of a toxic mix of anger, anxiety-based insecurity, and an obsessive habit of comparing oneself (usually poorly) with others. There is also a root of fear in most jealousy—the fear of losing the love or praise of one's object of love or affection.

Jealousy usually involves three people. The jealous person becomes fixated with a (usually misperceived) rival, who is viewed as competing for the attention of the beloved. While the rival is the object of sometimes intense hatred and opposition, jealous residues nearly always spill over and adversely affect relations with the beloved. Many divorces, broken family relations, or failed business partnerships are the result of unremitting jealousy and suspicion.

The Bible says that destructive jealousy is like a torrent if it is not tamed and overcome (Prov. 27:4). Obsessive, fixated, consuming love that is "strong as death," easily produces a powerful jealousy that is "as cruel as the grave" (Song 8:6).

Yet jealousy is not always inherently bad. Scripture describes the Lord as "a jealous God" (Ex. 34:14), whose wrath is poured out on anything that usurps His name and authority. God is jealous for the church (2 Cor. 11:2), and Paul warns us not to provoke God's jealousy by turning away from Him to idols (1 Cor. 10:20–22).

OVERCOMING NEGATIVE JEALOUSY

There is a legitimate role for jealousy. Marriage, or any deep commitment to a relationship, will create a strong feeling of attachment. In this context, the absence of some jealousy can mean that one lacks care and commitment to the relationship. Sometimes, in fact, there is good reason to be jealous. A spouse's secretive behavior, or inordinate time spent outside the home, can raise legitimate concerns.

When carried to extremes, however, pathological jealousy can dominate a relationship. Some spouses, having faced abuse or abandonment in their childhood, bring this pathology into a marriage. Unresolved issues from one's past can be the impetus to a vicious cycle of dysfunctional jealousy. A chronically jealous partner, for example, will use self-pity, lies, threats, and other manipulations to control a relationship. When the other resists, the jealous person reacts by becoming more controlling. The other resists further, may confide in a friend or seek relief outside the marriage, and that further fuels the jealousy and worst-case predictions. The consuming cycle is gaining speed and heading to disaster.

So how can people overcome jealousy before it reaches that point of disaster?

➢ *By listening to others.* If good friends and loved ones comment on their jealousy, it's a good sign that a problem exists and should be faced.

➢ *By being honest with themselves.* Rather than react with "I'm not jealous," they must ask, "Do I try to control and manipulate my loved one? What or who is causing these jealous feelings? Am I pushing my loved ones away? Do I attempt to make my loved ones account for every minute, look, or thought?"

➢ *By spending time with God.* Those dealing with jealousy must soak each question above in prayer, asking God to reveal the truth and to give them the courage to act on it. They must ask God to transform their need for security into dependence on and confidence in Him.

➢ *By transforming the beloved in their mind.* Jealous people can use their anxious thoughts and suspicions as cues to stop their dark reactions, take a deep cleansing breath, pray, and get control. Then they should pray for the beloved, think about all the positives in the relationship, and consider what special things they could do, right then, to show love to him or her. A phone call, a touch, or a gift could do wonders—for both people.

People who have a jealous spouse may need to do some self-evaluation. They first need to assess whether they are in fact doing something that provokes the jealousy. If so, then they must stop that activity for a time in order to show the spouse their commitment to the relationship. They may need to increase their loving actions toward their spouse. If they aren't provoking it, they must not cave in to manipulative behavior, or they will see more of it. They must talk honestly and civilly with their spouse about the problem. Counseling or mediation may be necessary if civil communication is not possible on this issue.

Jealousy can destroy even strong marriages. We need to guard our relationships so we will not be sowing seeds of jealousy.

FURTHER MEDITATION:

Other passages to study about the issue of jealousy include:

➢ Genesis 4:3–8; 37:1–36
➢ 1 Samuel 18:8, 9
➢ Proverbs 6:34; 12:12; 14:30; 27:4
➢ Philippians 4:11–13
➢ 1 Timothy 6:6, 7

To Learn More: Turn to the key passage note on jealousy at Numbers 5:29 on page 176. See also the personality profile of Rachel and Leah on page 49.

"All flesh is as grass,
And all the glory of man[a] *as the flower of the grass.*
The grass withers,
And its flower falls away,
25 *But the word of the* LORD *endures forever."*[a]

Now this is the word which by the gospel was preached to you.

2 Therefore, laying aside all malice, all deceit, hypocrisy, envy, and all evil speaking, 2as newborn babes, desire the pure milk of the word, that you may grow thereby,[a] 3if indeed you have tasted that the Lord *is* gracious.

The Chosen Stone and His Chosen People

4Coming to Him *as to* a living stone, rejected indeed by men, but chosen by God *and* precious, 5you also, as living stones, are being built up a spiritual house, a holy priesthood, to offer up spiritual sacrifices acceptable to God through Jesus Christ. 6Therefore it is also contained in the Scripture,

"Behold, I lay in Zion
A chief cornerstone, elect, precious,
And he who believes on Him will by no means be put to shame."[a]

7Therefore, to you who believe, *He is* precious; but to those who are disobedient,[a]

"The stone which the builders rejected
Has become the chief cornerstone,"[b]

8and

"A stone of stumbling
And a rock of offense."[a]

They stumble, being disobedient to the word, to which they also were appointed.

9But you *are* a chosen generation, a royal priesthood, a holy nation, His own special people, that you may proclaim the praises of Him who called you out of darkness into His marvelous light; 10who once *were* not a people but *are* now the people of God, who had not obtained mercy but now have obtained mercy.

1:24 [a]NU-Text reads *all its glory.* **1:25** [a]Isaiah 40:6–8 **2:2** [a]NU-Text adds *up to salvation.* **2:6** [a]Isaiah 28:16 **2:7** [a]NU-Text reads *to those who disbelieve.* [b]Psalm 118:22 **2:8** [a]Isaiah 8:14

SOUL NOTE

Evils of Envy *(2:1)* God's people have been purchased at a great price—"the precious blood of Christ" (1:19). Believers should be so grateful to the One who called them to be holy that they desire to be that way in every aspect of their conduct (1:15). This means "laying aside all envy" because envy has no usefulness in God's kingdom. Envy causes hurt, dissension, and division. People who compare themselves to others will feel either superior or inferior. God wants us to stop comparing our looks, possessions, jobs, or abilities with those of others, and to focus on being His child and serving Him. **Topic: Jealousy**

SOUL NOTE

Drink Your Milk *(2:2, 3)* Believers should never stop growing up. Just as "newborn babes" constantly desire and need milk to help them grow, believers should always crave God's Word, for they constantly need its nourishment. Like milk, the essential food for babies, God's Word sustains believers' spiritual lives. If we desire to continue to grow closer to Christ, to mature in our faith, and to be powerful in our service, we need to nourish ourselves by studying God's Word every day.
Topic: Spiritual Growth

Living Before the World

[11]Beloved, I beg *you* as sojourners and pilgrims, abstain from fleshly lusts which war against the soul, [12]having your conduct honorable among the Gentiles, that when they speak against you as evildoers, they may, by *your* good works which they observe, glorify God in the day of visitation.

Submission to Government

[13]Therefore submit yourselves to every ordinance of man for the Lord's sake, whether to the king as supreme, [14]or to governors, as to those who are sent by him for the punishment of evildoers and *for the* praise of those who do good. [15]For this is the will of God, that by doing good you may put to silence the ignorance of foolish men— [16]as free, yet not using liberty as a cloak for vice, but as bondservants of God. [17]Honor all *people.* Love the brotherhood. Fear God. Honor the king.

Submission to Masters

[18]Servants, *be* submissive to *your* masters with all fear, not only to the good and gentle, but also to the harsh. [19]For this *is* commendable, if because of conscience toward God one endures grief, suffering wrongfully. [20]For what credit *is it* if, when you are beaten for your faults, you take it patiently? But when you do good and suffer, if you take it patiently, this *is* commendable before God. [21]For to this you were called, because Christ also suffered for us,[a] leaving us[b] an example, that you should follow His steps:

[22] *"Who committed no sin,*
Nor was deceit found in His mouth";[a]

[23]who, when He was reviled, did not revile in return; when He suffered, He did not threaten, but committed *Himself* to Him who judges righteously; [24]who Himself bore our sins in His own body on the tree, that we, having died to sins, might live for righteousness—by whose stripes you were healed. [25]For you were like sheep going astray, but have now returned to the Shepherd and Overseer[a] of your souls.

Submission to Husbands

3 Wives, likewise, *be* submissive to your own husbands, that even if some do not obey the word, they, without a word, may be won by the conduct of their wives, [2]when they observe your chaste conduct *accompanied* by fear. [3]Do not let your adornment be *merely* outward—arranging the hair, wearing gold, or putting on *fine* apparel— [4]rather *let it be* the hidden person of the heart, with the

2:21 [a]NU-Text reads *you.* [b]NU-Text and M-Text read *you.* **2:22** [a]Isaiah 53:9 **2:25** [a]Greek *Episkopos*

KEY PASSAGE

ON YOUR HONOR

(2:17)

Honor

In order to "honor all people," we must show proper respect, value, and esteem to everyone. From the rich corporate executive to the common menial servant, all people were created by God and honorable in His sight. No matter what race, color, background, family life, social position, economic status, or educational attainment, all people are to be treated as God's precious creations.

Believers honor others by not making comparisons. Comparing ourselves to others can make us feel either inferior or superior to them—then we may not feel that we can or want to share God's message of salvation with them. When we honor people, however, we see them as God sees them—in need—thus, we want to show them His love. We respect the rich and powerful person by being kind, caring, and compassionate. We respect the humble janitor by acting the same way. When we show honor to every one of God's creations, we honor Him. Honor is a gift that offers deep grace to our relationships.

To Learn More: Turn to the article about honor on pages 630, 631. See also the personality profile of the wise men on page 1230.

TALKING SENSE

Marital Communication

TIM & JULIE CLINTON

(1 Peter 3:1–9)

Tim stood in the foyer of a crowded restaurant watching the lunch crowd pour in—no sign of Julie. In a restaurant several miles away, Julie stood in the crowded foyer peering at the door—waiting for Tim. We had planned lunch the night before and discussed it again that morning. Somehow we blew it. Fortunately a phone call solved the problem.

Miscommunicating lunch plans is a minor incident. But how, during serious discussions or heartfelt talks, do couples completely confuse each other? Quite often, according to some marital experts. Up to 90 percent of couples seeking counseling say communication and "talk" issues are at the root of their problems.

No wonder so many couples feel out of touch with each other in the absence of effective and encouraging communication—nothing holds more potential for enriching intimacy.

THE QUALITY OF COMMUNICATION

The interactive process of communication can be understood and analyzed in a five-part manner. Human communication is (1) a message by one person or group that is (2) sent in verbal or written form to (3) another person or group who (4) receives the message and (5) understands its meaning in a certain way. Perfect communication is when the intent of the message sent is understood fully and exactly by the receiver. Again, perfection is rarely, if ever, attained.

Imperfect communication occurs because of static, distractions, and misunderstandings all along the process. The message constructed may not exactly represent the intention of the sender. The way it is sent may be poor or incomplete. The receiver may not be listening well. The understanding of the received message is affected by the historical, emotional, gender, and values filters of the hearer.

How can we improve the quality of our communication? Genuineness, empathy, and respect on the part of both the speaker and the listener are vital to improving communication between spouses.

Consider the amount of time you and your spouse spend together as a couple. Many couples spend an average of only four minutes a day in meaningful conversation.

Couples cite lack of time as their primary communication roadblock for three reasons:

1. Some spouses are overloaded with responsibilities and commitments. They need to examine their commitments and determine what their priorities are and should be.
2. Other couples don't make time. They *have* the time to talk with their spouse, but they instead fill that time with phone calls, television, shopping trips, sports, friends, and other activities.
3. Still others are angry or bitter. Whatever the situation, if they shut out their partners, they do themselves and their marriage a great disservice.

Although couples may not actually be *choosing* not to spend time in conversation, they still communicate. They constantly send messages—positive or negative, verbal or nonverbal. Therefore, they must work effectively to *control* their communication.

For instance, a casual shrug of the

shoulders may be a way of saying, "I'm not sure," but a spouse may interpret it as, "I'm not really concerned about that." Married couples must make every attempt to keep their intentions and their language clear. Because most people are under pressure, there can be an abundance of anger and tension in relationships. Evidence of this is hard-hitting, such as nagging, criticism, badgering, and yelling. James 3 tells of the tremendous damage the tongue can cause.

Even during conflict, discussions with one's partner should be honest, respectful, and spoken in love. Communication should be purposeful, goal-oriented, and free of hidden agendas. Sensitivity to timing is helpful (for example, not bringing up a difficult situation at the dinner table).

In volatile situations, this can be difficult. Scripture points out how shameful and foolish it is to answer a matter before it's fully heard and understood: "He who answers a matter before he hears it; it is folly and shame to him" (Prov. 18:13). Communication involves both sending and receiving messages. Of these two, listening is the most important.

SCRIPTURAL ADVICE FOR QUALITY COMMUNICATION

Consider these other Scripture-based principles of communication:

Be a good listener.
"Be swift to hear, slow to speak, slow to wrath" (James 1:19).

Reflect on and think through what is being spoken.
"He who disdains instruction despises his own soul, but he who heeds rebuke gets understanding" (Prov. 15:32).

Be sensitive to and respectful of your partner.
"Let all bitterness, wrath, anger, clamor, and evil speaking be put away from you, with all malice" (Eph. 4:31).
"Husbands, likewise, dwell with them with understanding, giving honor to the wife, as to the weaker vessel, and as being heirs together of the grace of life, that your prayers may not be hindered" (1 Pet. 3:7).

Speak the truth—but always in love.
"Speaking the truth in love . . . grow up in all things into Him who is the head—Christ" (Eph. 4:15).
"Do not lie to one another" (Col. 3:9).

Don't fight or respond in anger.
"Be angry, and do not sin: do not let the sun go down on your wrath"(Eph. 4:26).
"The beginning of strife is like releasing water; therefore stop contention before a quarrel starts" (Prov. 17:14).

Confess and forgive when necessary.
"Confess your trespasses to one another, and pray for one another" (James 5:16).
"Be kind to one another, tenderhearted, forgiving one another, even as God in Christ forgave you" (Eph. 4:32).

We firmly believe in spiritual intimacy. True growth as a couple is impossible apart from God. Reading a devotional together and praying together and for each other draws couples closer to God and each other.

FURTHER MEDITATION:

Other passages to study about the issue of marital communication include:

➢ Proverbs 12:17, 18; 15:23; 17:4, 7
➢ Matthew 12:33–37
➢ 1 Corinthians 13:4–7
➢ Ephesians 4:15, 29–32
➢ James 3:1–12

To Learn More: Turn to the key passage note on marital communication at 1 Peter 3:8 on page 1663. See also the personality profile of Aquila and Priscilla on page 1448.

incorruptible *beauty* of a gentle and quiet spirit, which is very precious in the sight of God. 5For in this manner, in former times, the holy women who trusted in God also adorned themselves, being submissive to their own husbands, 6as Sarah obeyed Abraham, calling him lord, whose daughters you are if you do good and are not afraid with any terror.

A Word to Husbands

7Husbands, likewise, dwell with *them* with understanding, giving honor to the wife, as to the weaker vessel, and as *being* heirs together of the grace of life, that your prayers may not be hindered.

Called to Blessing

8Finally, all *of you be* of one mind, having compassion for one another; love as brothers, *be* tenderhearted, *be* courteous;[a] 9not returning evil for evil or reviling for reviling, but on the contrary blessing, knowing that you were called to this, that you may inherit a blessing. 10For

"He who would love life
And see good days,
Let him refrain his tongue from evil,
And his lips from speaking deceit.
11 *Let him turn away from evil and do good;*
Let him seek peace and pursue it.
12 *For the eyes of the LORD are on the righteous,*
And His ears are open to their prayers;
But the face of the LORD is against those who do evil."[a]

Suffering for Right and Wrong

13And who *is* he who will harm you if you become followers of what is good? 14But even if you should suffer for righteousness' sake, *you are* blessed. *"And do not be afraid of their threats, nor be troubled."*[a] 15But sanctify the Lord God[a] in your hearts, and always *be* ready to *give* a defense to everyone who asks you a reason for the hope that is in you, with meekness and fear; 16having a good conscience, that when they defame you as evildoers, those who revile your good conduct in Christ may be ashamed. 17For *it is* better, if it is the will of

3:8 [a]NU-Text reads *humble.* **3:12** [a]Psalm 34:12–16 **3:14** [a]Isaiah 8:12 **3:15** [a]NU-Text reads *Christ as Lord.*

SOUL NOTE

Beautiful *(3:3, 4)* These words do not mean that women cannot style their hair or wear jewelry. Peter's point was that women should not let their adornment merely consist of outward trappings. Instead, Christian women should focus on developing "the incorruptible beauty of a gentle and quiet spirit." Christian women certainly can have flattering hairstyles, clothing, and jewelry, but they should not be obsessed with their outward appearance. Their focus should always be on Christ and on developing character that is pleasing to God. Women who develop Christlike character are truly beautiful. **Topic: Women's Issues**

SOUL NOTE

Love and Honor *(3:7)* Husbands should honor their wives. Both Paul and Peter wrote that wives should submit to their husbands (Eph. 5:22; 1 Pet. 3:1); yet, both also wrote that husbands should love and honor their wives. A man who honors his wife will love, respect, encourage, and protect her. He will listen to her opinions, take her advice when he can, consider her needs, and encourage her gifts. When a husband treats his wife this way, she will have no fear of following the biblical instruction to be submissive to him. This paves the way for a healthy marriage and family. **Topic: Honor**

God, to suffer for doing good than for doing
evil.

CHRIST'S SUFFERING AND OURS

[18]For Christ also suffered once for sins, the
just for the unjust, that He might bring us[a] to
God, being put to death in the flesh but made
alive by the Spirit, [19]by whom also He went
and preached to the spirits in prison, [20]who
formerly were disobedient, when once the
Divine longsuffering waited[a] in the days of
Noah, while *the* ark was being prepared, in
which a few, that is, eight souls, were saved
through water. [21]There is also an antitype
which now saves us—baptism (not the removal of the filth of the flesh, but the answer
of a good conscience toward God), through
the resurrection of Jesus Christ, [22]who has
gone into heaven and is at the right hand of
God, angels and authorities and powers having been made subject to Him.

4 Therefore, since Christ suffered for us[a] in
the flesh, arm yourselves also with the
same mind, for he who has suffered in the

3:18 [a]NU-Text and M-Text read *you.* **3:20** [a]NU-Text and M-Text read *when the longsuffering of God waited patiently.* **4:1** [a]NU-Text omits *for us.*

KEY PASSAGE

Marital Communication

LET'S TALK

(3:8)

This verse gives a recipe for building unity among believers. While these ingredients apply to believers in general, they go double for building unity in a marriage.

1. *Be of one mind.* Spouses will not agree on everything, but they should work toward having "one mind." One may have to give in to the other so the two can be united, especially in important decisions.
2. Have *compassion*. Knowing that the other person truly cares enables spouses to share their deepest thoughts and feelings with each other.
3. *Love*. While it seems obvious, love can be the most difficult thing to maintain. Spouses should show the kind of love described in 1 Corinthians 13.
4. *Be tenderhearted* and *courteous*. This means having an attitude that puts the other person's needs ahead of one's own.
5. *Blessing* one's spouse. This means always wanting the best for him or her.

Spouses who follow this recipe of honor will find vitality and will communicate effectively.

To Learn More: Turn to the article about marital communication on pages 1660, 1661. See also the personality profile of Aquila and Priscilla on page 1448.

SOUL NOTE

Word Watch *(3:10)* These words are for all Christians facing trials. Despite outward circumstances, believers can still "love life and see good days" because of their relationship with God. Verses 10–12 quote from Psalm 34, a psalm for people in trouble. The first recommendation is for us to watch what we say. Speaking "evil" can refer to any type of speech that displeases God; "deceit" refers to deliberately misleading by lying. A believer's communication should instead be comforting, encouraging, and uplifting. Positive communication pleases God and helps others.
Topic: Communication

flesh has ceased from sin, [2]that he no longer
should live the rest of *his* time in the flesh for
the lusts of men, but for the will of God. [3]For
we *have spent* enough of our past lifetime[a] in
doing the will of the Gentiles—when we
walked in lewdness, lusts, drunkenness, revelries, drinking parties, and abominable idola-
tries. [4]In regard to these, they think it strange
that you do not run with *them* in the same
flood of dissipation, speaking evil of *you.*
[5]They will give an account to Him who is
ready to judge the living and the dead. [6]For
this reason the gospel was preached also to
those who are dead, that they might be judged
according to men in the flesh, but live according to God in the spirit.

SERVING FOR GOD'S GLORY

[7]But the end of all things is at hand; therefore be serious and watchful in your prayers.
[8]And above all things have fervent love for
one another, for *"love will cover a multitude of*
sins."[a] [9]*Be* hospitable to one another without
grumbling. [10]As each one has received a gift,
minister it to one another, as good stewards of
the manifold grace of God. [11]If anyone speaks,
let him speak as the oracles of God. If anyone
ministers, *let him do it* as with the ability
which God supplies, that in all things God
may be glorified through Jesus Christ, to
whom belong the glory and the dominion forever and ever. Amen.

SUFFERING FOR GOD'S GLORY

[12]Beloved, do not think it strange concerning the fiery trial which is to try you, as
though some strange thing happened to you;
[13]but rejoice to the extent that you partake of

4:3 [a]NU-Text reads *time.* **4:8** [a]Proverbs 10:12

KEY PASSAGE

Suffering

FAITH UNDER FIRE

(4:12–16)

Believers should "not think it strange concerning the fiery trial" that they face. "Trial" here refers to persecution for the faith. Not all suffering is the result of godly Christian conduct (4:15). Many times, however, loyalty to Christ will bring suffering. At those times, believers can rejoice and "be glad with exceeding joy" because they are considered worthy of suffering for Christ.

Sometimes God allows suffering to come into believers' lives in order to strengthen their faith. Suffering provides the opportunity to trust God. Believers can rejoice because of what God will do in their lives and what He promises for their future. When we suffer, we are in good company, for Christ also suffered, He understands, and He will be with us all the way. We can commit our lives to Him (1 Pet. 4:19).

To Learn More: Turn to the article about suffering on pages 646, 647. See also the personality profile of Job on page 638.

SOUL NOTE

Leap of Loyalty *(4:19)* Nothing happens to believers that surprises God. He may allow suffering for a time, knowing that it will strengthen His people's faith. A believer's suffering should be "according to the will of God," however, not due to their own sinful or irresponsible actions. When we face suffering because of our loyalty to Christ, we must remember that, like everything else, our suffering is under God's control. We can commit our lives to Him, knowing that He is completely faithful and trustworthy. He will remain with us through our suffering, and in the end bring us to glory. **Topic: Suffering**

Christ's sufferings, that when His glory is revealed, you may also be glad with exceeding joy. 14If you are reproached for the name of Christ, blessed *are you,* for the Spirit of glory and of God rests upon you.[a] On their part He is blasphemed, but on your part He is glorified. 15But let none of you suffer as a murderer, a thief, an evildoer, or as a busybody in other people's matters. 16Yet if *anyone suffers* as a Christian, let him not be ashamed, but let him glorify God in this matter.[a]

17For the time *has come* for judgment to begin at the house of God; and if *it begins* with us first, what will *be* the end of those who do not obey the gospel of God? 18Now

"If the righteous one is scarcely saved,
Where will the ungodly and the sinner
appear?"[a]

19Therefore let those who suffer according to the will of God commit their souls *to Him* in doing good, as to a faithful Creator.

Shepherd the Flock

5 The elders who are among you I exhort, I who am a fellow elder and a witness of the sufferings of Christ, and also a partaker of the glory that will be revealed: 2Shepherd the flock of God which is among you, serving as overseers, not by compulsion but

4:14 [a]NU-Text omits the rest of this verse.
4:16 [a]NU-Text reads *name.* **4:18** [a]Proverbs 11:31

KEY PASSAGE

Discouragement

GIVE IT TO GOD

(5:7)

Discouragement often occurs when people shoulder their own worries, cares, and fears, and then begin to collapse under the weight. Discouragement is not a godly attitude because it reveals an unwillingness to trust God. Discouragement can be dealt a death blow, however, when we constantly cast all our cares upon God, because He cares for us.

Casting our cares on God takes a great amount of trust and humility. We need to give Him all of our cares—not just the ones we think are big enough or important enough. God will even shoulder the cares that we have brought upon ourselves—we can give them *all* to Him. His shoulders are big enough to carry all of our fears, worries, and troubles. When we give our cares to God, we can brush off our discouragement and get back to work. We have much to do for God!

To Learn More: Turn to the article about discouragement on pages 266, 267. See also the personality profile of Nehemiah on page 605.

SOUL NOTE

Steadfast *(5:8–10)* The moment a person becomes a Christian, Satan tries to make them ineffective through sin or through struggles with discouragement or suffering. Believers must be sober and vigilant, resisting Satan by remaining "steadfast in the faith." This is a strong defensive action. Satan is a defeated enemy, so believers need not fear him. When we resist Satan, he will flee (James 4:7). We resist Satan through maintaining our steadfast faith in Christ, wearing the armor that God provides (Eph. 6:10–20), and remembering that we are not alone in our suffering. The same sufferings are being experienced by believers everywhere. Through these sufferings, He will "establish, strengthen, and settle" His people. **Topic: Spiritual Warfare**

willingly,[a] not for dishonest gain but eagerly;
3nor as being lords over those entrusted to
you, but being examples to the flock; 4and
when the Chief Shepherd appears, you will
receive the crown of glory that does not fade
away.

Submit to God, Resist the Devil

5Likewise you younger people, submit yourselves to *your* elders. Yes, all of *you* be submissive to one another, and be clothed with
humility, for

> *"God resists the proud,*
> *But gives grace to the humble."*[a]

6Therefore humble yourselves under the
mighty hand of God, that He may exalt you in
due time, 7casting all your care upon Him, for
He cares for you.
8Be sober, be vigilant; because[a] your adversary the devil walks about like a roaring lion,
seeking whom he may devour. 9Resist him,
steadfast in the faith, knowing that the same
sufferings are experienced by your brotherhood in the world. 10But may[a] the God of all
grace, who called us[b] to His eternal glory by
Christ Jesus, after you have suffered a while,
perfect, establish, strengthen, and settle *you.*
11To Him *be* the glory and the dominion forever and ever. Amen.

Farewell and Peace

12By Silvanus, our faithful brother as I consider him, I have written to you briefly, exhorting and testifying that this is the true
grace of God in which you stand.
13She who is in Babylon, elect together with
you, greets you; and *so does* Mark my son.
14Greet one another with a kiss of love.
Peace to you all who are in Christ Jesus.
Amen.

5:2 [a]NU-Text adds *according to God.*
5:5 [a]Proverbs 3:34 **5:8** [a]NU-Text and M-Text omit *because.* **5:10** [a]NU-Text reads *But the God of all grace . . . will perfect, establish, strengthen, and settle you.* [b]NU-Text and M-Text read *you.*

2 Peter

What kind of people join unbiblical religious cults? Eccentrics? The mentally incompetent? Those with no religious heritage? Surprisingly, many members of aberrant groups actually grew up in homes that adhered to orthodox Christian doctrine!

In A.D. 64–66, the apostle Peter recognized (in Asia Minor) the presence of large numbers of eloquent false teachers intent on luring away unsuspecting believers. To warn these members of God's flock of the dangers of such religious "wolves," Peter wrote his second epistle. He called these spiritual hucksters "brute beasts" (2:12) and railed against their "covetous practices" (2:14). As a concerned shepherd his desire was to protect his Christian brothers and sisters from the seductive words of these "slaves of corruption" (2:19) who were destined for punishment (2:9).

By contrast, Peter also emphasized the "prophetic word" inspired by the Holy Spirit (1:19–21). This is the message of the prophets and the apostles (3:2). Peter even referred to Paul's letters as "the Scriptures" (3:15, 16). In short, Peter argued, it is God's truth, not finite human wisdom, that is the surest protection from error.

Peter's closing words are, "Grow in the grace and knowledge of our Lord and Savior Jesus Christ" (3:18). To avoid being led astray, we must commit our souls to God's slow but sure maturing process. We must be students of God's Word, holy in our conduct, and assured of the Lord's imminent return. The result will be a life that will bring God glory, both now and forever.

SOUL CONCERN IN 2 PETER

GREETING THE FAITHFUL

1 Simon Peter, a bondservant and apostle
of Jesus Christ,

To those who have obtained like precious
faith with us by the righteousness of our God
and Savior Jesus Christ:

2Grace and peace be multiplied to you in the
knowledge of God and of Jesus our Lord, 3as
His divine power has given to us all things
that *pertain* to life and godliness, through the
knowledge of Him who called us by glory and
virtue, 4by which have been given to us exceedingly great and precious promises, that
through these you may be partakers of the divine nature, having escaped the corruption
that is in the world through lust.

FRUITFUL GROWTH IN THE FAITH

5But also for this very reason, giving all diligence, add to your faith virtue, to virtue knowledge, 6to knowledge self-control, to self-control
perseverance, to perseverance godliness, 7to
godliness brotherly kindness, and to brotherly
kindness love. 8For if these things are yours
and abound, *you will be* neither barren nor unfruitful in the knowledge of our Lord Jesus
Christ. 9For he who lacks these things is shortsighted, even to blindness, and has forgotten
that he was cleansed from his old sins.
10Therefore, brethren, be even more diligent
to make your call and election sure, for if you
do these things you will never stumble; 11for
so an entrance will be supplied to you abundantly into the everlasting kingdom of our
Lord and Savior Jesus Christ.

PETER'S APPROACHING DEATH

12For this reason I will not be negligent to
remind you always of these things, though you
know and are established in the present truth.
13Yes, I think it is right, as long as I am in this
tent, to stir you up by reminding *you,* 14know-
ing that shortly I *must* put off my tent, just as
our Lord Jesus Christ showed me. 15Moreover I
will be careful to ensure that you always have a
reminder of these things after my decease.

THE TRUSTWORTHY PROPHETIC WORD

16For we did not follow cunningly devised
fables when we made known to you the power and coming of our Lord Jesus Christ, but
were eyewitnesses of His majesty. 17For He received from God the Father honor and glory
when such a voice came to Him from the Excellent Glory: "This is My beloved Son, in
whom I am well pleased." 18And we heard this
voice which came from heaven when we were
with Him on the holy mountain.
19And so we have the prophetic word
confirmed,[a] which you do well to heed as a

1:19 [a]Or *We also have the more sure prophetic word.*

KEY PASSAGE

God's Promises

PRECIOUS PROMISES

(1:4)

God gives great promises to all who have trusted in His Son as their Savior. When God looks at believers, He sees Christ's sacrifice on the Cross to take away sin. So He sees His people as righteous, and He bestows upon them "exceedingly great and precious promises."

Promises are only as good as the person who makes them. With God, a promise is an unbreakable covenant, a total commitment. Because God is faithful and trustworthy, we know that what He says in His Word will surely come to pass. His precious promises of salvation, transformation, and glorification will come true for all believers. God's promises of punishment and eternal separation will also come true for those who reject Him. Because of God's promises, we can be confident about the present and the future. God is in control, and He always keeps His promises. Name them, claim them, believe them.

To Learn More: Turn to the article about God's promises on pages 220, 221. See also the personality profile of Noah on page 16.

light that shines in a dark place, until the day
dawns and the morning star rises in your
hearts; [20]knowing this first, that no prophecy of
Scripture is of any private interpretation,[a] [21]for
prophecy never came by the will of man, but
holy men of God[a] spoke *as they were* moved by
the Holy Spirit.

DESTRUCTIVE DOCTRINES

2 But there were also false prophets among
the people, even as there will be false
teachers among you, who will secretly bring
in destructive heresies, even denying the
Lord who bought them, *and* bring on themselves swift destruction. [2]And many will
follow their destructive ways, because of
whom the way of truth will be blasphemed.
[3]By covetousness they will exploit you with
deceptive words; for a long time their judgment has not been idle, and their destruction
does[a] not slumber.

DOOM OF FALSE TEACHERS

[4]For if God did not spare the angels who
sinned, but cast *them* down to hell and delivered *them* into chains of darkness, to be reserved for judgment; [5]and did not spare the
ancient world, but saved Noah, *one of* eight
people, a preacher of righteousness, bringing
in the flood on the world of the ungodly; [6]and
turning the cities of Sodom and Gomorrah
into ashes, condemned *them* to destruction,
making *them* an example to those who afterward would live ungodly; [7]and delivered righteous Lot, *who was* oppressed by the filthy

---

1:20 [a]Or *origin* **1:21** [a]NU-Text reads *but men spoke from God.* **2:3** [a]M-Text reads *will not.*

KEY PASSAGE

Values

MOST VALUABLE?

(1:5–9)

What people value says much about their character. Some people value possessions, position, power, or wealth. But here are listed the life traits believers should value above all else. These values reveal a person's spiritual maturity.

Christians have faith in Christ, but faith that isn't put into action is dead and useless (James 2:17). Dead faith is still faith, but it isn't *doing* anything for God. Alive faith is working faith. It's not to be saved that believers need to add to their faith; they add these characteristics so that they will "be neither barren nor unfruitful." Believers who desire to mature in their faith and be fruitful for Christ will add such characteristics as virtue, knowledge, self-control, perseverance, godliness, kindness, and love.

Christ gives us His divine nature (2 Pet. 1:4), but we are responsible to use that nature to set aside sinful desires and follow Him. We have to value Christ above all else.

To Learn More: Turn to the article about values on pages 1544, 1545. See also the personality profile of Shadrach, Meshach, and Abed-Nego on page 1108.

SOUL NOTE

Last Words *(1:13–15)* Peter faced death calmly, knowing that he was merely putting off the "tent" of his body and moving on to be with Christ in heaven. Peter wanted to make sure the believers had a reminder of the gospel message that had brought them salvation, and of the power of God that had brought them true life. Believers should live each day reminding those around them—through words and actions—about the power of God. What legacy are we leaving for our loved ones? If we had to say our last words today, what would we say? **Topic: Life Transitions**

SPIRITUAL GROWTH

JOHN ORTBERG

(2 Peter 1:5–11)

The purpose of Paul's life was to help people experience spiritual growth: "Him [Christ] we preach, warning every man and teaching every man in all wisdom, that we may present every man perfect in Christ Jesus" (Col. 1:28). With all of the energy God powerfully stirred up in him, Paul labored to present everyone "perfect in Christ." Given the intensity with which Paul lived and the passion for growth in Christ that he had, it is evident that spiritual growth is vitally important.

So what is spiritual growth? It is the developmental process through which a follower of Christ gradually becomes characterized by those traits that marked Jesus Himself. It involves a life of increasing wonder, awe, joy, simplicity, worship, gratitude, love, servanthood, humility, courage, and truth, among other qualities, such as those listed in 2 Peter 1:5–10. Sheldon Vanauken wrote that the best argument for Christianity is Christians—their joy, their certainty, their completeness. Guess what he said is the best argument *against* Christianity? The same answer—Christians, when they are somber, joyless, self-righteous, smug, narrow, repressive.

Therefore, it becomes terribly important for Christians to understand what true spiritual growth is, and what it is not.

MISCONCEPTIONS OF SPIRITUAL GROWTH

People commonly fall into two errors when considering what part of spiritual growth is their responsibility and which part is God's responsibility. The first error is when people think of spiritual growth as their own responsibility—turning it into no more than a moral self-improvement project. They may even become militaristic in their commitment to live more virtuous lives. One glaring problem with this approach is that it relies heavily on human willpower, which has obvious limitations. Over time this approach makes people susceptible to spiritual venom in various forms:

➢ *Legalism,* which is the measurement of spiritual growth in superficial, mechanical ways designed to create a sense of being different from those outside the faith.
➢ *Judgmentalism,* which is the comparison of one's own spiritual growth with others' in a condescending manner.
➢ *Fatigue and defeat,* which can set in because of the life-sucking nature of such an approach.

The second error is when people see their role in the process of spiritual growth as to do nothing. A distorted view of grace fuels the belief that any of their own effort might be an affront to God's sovereignty or even a denial of His grace. Inevitably, they get stuck in a mire of passivity, which will not breed spiritual growth.

STEPS FOR SPIRITUAL GROWTH

Jesus told a parable describing the growth of the kingdom of God as seed scattered on the ground by the farmer. Day and night the seed grows—though the farmer does not know how (Mark 4:26–29). What is true for the growth of the kingdom is also true for individual spiritual growth. People cannot control their own spiritual growth any more than a farmer can control the growth of the seeds in the ground. Growth is always a gift from God. Yet the farmer *was* involved in the process, and so we too must participate in our own spiritual growth.

The role that we play is crucial, and can be understood by identifying three key elements of spiritual growth.

Disciplines

Certain practices are indispensable if we want to open ourselves up to spiritual growth. Solitude, the withdrawing from society and stimulation to be alone with the Father, was irreplaceable in the life of Jesus and His followers (Mark 1:12, 35–37; 6:31, 32). The study of and meditation on Scripture are crucial to the renewing of our minds (Rom. 12:2). Silence and prayer, worship and service, giving and celebrating—these are the types of practices that should be in the lives of followers of Christ who are interested in growing spiritually. These activities please God and are also instrumental, indeed essential, in developing loving, joy-filled, truthful lives.

Relationships

Certain relationships help Christlike qualities to be formed in us. Spiritual friendships provide us with other people who intentionally help us pay attention to what God is doing in our lives. Confessional relationships offer us a safe place to speak of our struggles, temptations, and sins. Corporate gatherings for worship and learning mark our minds and hearts, and remind us that spiritual growth is not an individualistic endeavor. Being a member of a community inevitably involves knowing "difficult" people. How we learn to work with these people can help us gauge how far we have to grow if we are to love as Jesus did.

Experiences

Certain experiences open us up to growth. Suffering, pain, and trials are crucial teachers of our souls (James 1:2). The Holy Spirit works in our lives in various ways. He convicts us of sin, guides us into truth, and assures us of God's love (John 16:5–15; Rom. 8:12–17). Cross-cultural experiences often shake up old patterns of thinking and living, awakening us to the reality of a God who is far larger than our own lives. Shifts in perspective encourage us to think outside our comfortable box.

Spiritual growth is a "phenomenon" difficult to fully comprehend. As Paul experienced in his life, the struggles are worth the end result. It is eminently important that we focus not on where we begin, but where we are presently and where we finish. May we be able to say with Paul, "I have fought the good fight, I have finished the race, I have kept the faith" (2 Tim. 4:7). May our lives be living testimonies to the power of the God.

FURTHER MEDITATION:

Other passages to study about the issue of spiritual growth include:

- Proverbs 2:1–6
- John 3:30; 15:1, 2, 4
- Romans 12:1, 2
- Ephesians 4:14, 15
- 2 Timothy 2:15

To Learn More: Turn to the key passage note on spiritual growth at Psalm 1 on page 679. See also the personality profile of Matthew on page 1243.

conduct of the wicked [8](for that righteous man, dwelling among them, tormented *his* righteous soul from day to day by seeing and hearing *their* lawless deeds)—[9]*then* the Lord knows how to deliver the godly out of temptations and to reserve the unjust under punishment for the day of judgment, [10]and especially those who walk according to the flesh in the lust of uncleanness and despise authority. *They are* presumptuous, self-willed. They are not afraid to speak evil of dignitaries, [11]whereas angels, who are greater in power and might, do not bring a reviling accusation against them before the Lord.

Depravity of False Teachers

[12]But these, like natural brute beasts made to be caught and destroyed, speak evil of the things they do not understand, and will utterly perish in their own corruption, [13]*and* will receive the wages of unrighteousness, *as* those who count it pleasure to carouse in the daytime. *They are* spots and blemishes, carousing in their own deceptions while they feast with you, [14]having eyes full of adultery and that cannot cease from sin, enticing unstable souls. *They have* a heart trained in covetous practices, *and are* accursed children. [15]They have forsaken the right way and gone astray, following the way of Balaam the *son* of Beor, who loved the wages of unrighteousness; [16]but he was rebuked for his iniquity: a dumb donkey speaking with a man's voice restrained the madness of the prophet.

[17]These are wells without water, clouds[a] carried by a tempest, for whom is reserved the blackness of darkness forever.[b]

Deceptions of False Teachers

[18]For when they speak great swelling *words* of emptiness, they allure through the lusts of the flesh, through lewdness, the ones who have actually escaped[a] from those who live in error. [19]While they promise them liberty, they themselves are slaves of corruption; for by whom a person is overcome, by him also he is brought into bondage. [20]For if, after they have escaped the pollutions of the world through the knowledge of the Lord and Savior Jesus Christ, they are again entangled in them and overcome, the latter end is worse for them than the beginning. [21]For it would have been better for them not to have known the way of righteousness, than having known *it,* to turn from the holy commandment delivered to them. [22]But it has happened to them according to the true proverb: *"A dog returns to his*

2:17 [a]NU-Text reads *and mists.* [b]NU-Text omits *forever.* **2:18** [a]NU-Text reads *are barely escaping.*

KEY PASSAGE

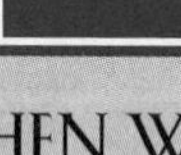

Tolerance

WHEN WE SHOULDN'T BE TOLERANT

(2:12–22)

Peter didn't leave much room for doubt about how he perceived false teachers. As these evil men infiltrated the churches, bringing with them their false teachings, wrong motives, and sinful lifestyles, they harmed many believers. They claimed to be followers of Christ, having heard the gospel message, but then they distorted that message. Peter wrote that "it would have been better for them not to have known the way of righteousness, than having known it, to turn from the holy commandment" (2:21).

Peter did not say that believers should be tolerant and understanding of these false teachers. He did not say that the false teachers should be treated carefully and lovingly. Instead, he called them evil and commanded believers not to be deceived by them.

Overall, believers should be tolerant, accepting people from many different races and backgrounds. This is vital for the growth of the church. But we should not tolerate anyone who teaches what is opposed to God's Word.

To Learn More: Turn to the article about tolerance on pages 1694, 1695. See also the personality profile of Micaiah on page 470.

own vomit,"[a] and, "a sow, having washed, to
her wallowing in the mire."

God's Promise Is Not Slack

3 Beloved, I now write to you this second
epistle (in *both of* which I stir up your
pure minds by way of reminder), 2that you
may be mindful of the words which were spoken before by the holy prophets, and of the
commandment of us,[a] the apostles of the Lord
and Savior, 3knowing this first: that scoffers
will come in the last days, walking according
to their own lusts, 4and saying, "Where is the
promise of His coming? For since the fathers
fell asleep, all things continue as *they were*
from the beginning of creation." 5For this they
willfully forget: that by the word of God the
heavens were of old, and the earth standing
out of water and in the water, 6by which the
world *that* then existed perished, being flooded with water. 7But the heavens and the earth
which are now preserved by the same word,
are reserved for fire until the day of judgment
and perdition of ungodly men.

8But, beloved, do not forget this one thing,
that with the Lord one day *is* as a thousand
years, and a thousand years as one day. 9The
Lord is not slack concerning *His* promise, as
some count slackness, but is longsuffering toward us,[a] not willing that any should perish
but that all should come to repentance.

The Day of the Lord

10But the day of the Lord will come as a thief
in the night, in which the heavens will pass
away with a great noise, and the elements will
melt with fervent heat; both the earth and the
works that are in it will be burned up.[a]
11Therefore, since all these things will be dissolved, what manner *of persons* ought you to
be in holy conduct and godliness, 12looking
for and hastening the coming of the day of
God, because of which the heavens will be
dissolved, being on fire, and the elements will
melt with fervent heat? 13Nevertheless we, according to His promise, look for new heavens
and a new earth in which righteousness
dwells.

Be Steadfast

14Therefore, beloved, looking forward to
these things, be diligent to be found by Him in
peace, without spot and blameless; 15and consider *that* the longsuffering of our Lord *is*
salvation—as also our beloved brother Paul,
according to the wisdom given to him, has
written to you, 16as also in all his epistles,
speaking in them of these things, in which
are some things hard to understand, which
untaught and unstable *people* twist to their
own destruction, as *they do* also the rest of the
Scriptures.

17You therefore, beloved, since you know
this beforehand, beware lest you also fall from
your own steadfastness, being led away with
the error of the wicked; 18but grow in the
grace and knowledge of our Lord and Savior
Jesus Christ.

To Him *be* the glory both now and forever.
Amen.

2:22 [a]Proverbs 26:11 **3:2** [a]NU-Text and M-Text read *commandment of the apostles of your Lord and Savior* or *commandment of your apostles of the Lord and Savior.* **3:9** [a]NU-Text reads *you.* **3:10** [a]NU-Text reads *laid bare* (literally *found*).

1 John

Those who are older and wiser in the Lord can provide helpful counsel and comfort. Perhaps you know firsthand the blessing of such a godly advisor. If not, consider the apostle John as a candidate for your personal mentor. Once legendary for his fiery temper (and nicknamed a "son of thunder"), John was transformed by Christ into the "apostle of love." He eventually became the elder statesman of the Christian church.

At the end of the first century, a disturbing number of believers began drifting away from the truth about Jesus Christ. They were tantalized by early forms of a heretical belief called gnosticism, which rejected the incarnation of Christ and His physical death and resurrection, and usually led to a lifestyle of immorality. John wrote, in part, to oppose such false teaching.

John also wrote to help those who were unstable in the faith. Using a series of contrasts—light vs. darkness (1:5–7; 2:9–11); truth vs. error (2:20, 21); righteousness vs. lawlessness (3:4–9); and life vs. death (3:13–15)—John clearly and simply explained Christian beliefs. His goal was to help young believers affirm their faith with certainty and have assurance of their salvation (5:6–13).

This aged, wise apostle also used this letter as an occasion to describe the Christian life as a life of intimate fellowship with Jesus (1:3) and with other believers (1:7). We are called to "love one another" (4:7), John argued, because God is love (4:8).

Read 1 John carefully, and ponder the words of this dear old man of God who has so much relevant counsel for modern-day believers.

SOUL CONCERN IN 1 JOHN

WHAT WAS HEARD, SEEN, AND TOUCHED

1 That which was from the beginning, which we have heard, which we have seen with our eyes, which we have looked upon, and our hands have handled, concerning the Word of life— 2 the life was manifested, and we have seen, and bear witness, and declare to you that eternal life which was with the Father and was manifested to us— 3 that which we have seen and heard we declare to you, that you also may have fellowship with us; and truly our fellowship *is* with the Father and with His Son Jesus Christ. 4 And these things we write to you that your[a] joy may be full.

FELLOWSHIP WITH HIM AND ONE ANOTHER

5 This is the message which we have heard from Him and declare to you, that God is light and in Him is no darkness at all. 6 If we say that we have fellowship with Him, and walk in darkness, we lie and do not practice the truth. 7 But if we walk in the light as He is in the light, we have fellowship with one another, and the blood of Jesus Christ His Son cleanses us from all sin.

8 If we say that we have no sin, we deceive ourselves, and the truth is not in us. 9 If we confess our sins, He is faithful and just to forgive us *our* sins and to cleanse us from all unrighteousness. 10 If we say that we have not sinned, we make Him a liar, and His word is not in us.

2 My little children, these things I write to you, so that you may not sin. And if anyone sins, we have an Advocate with the Father, Jesus Christ the righteous. 2 And He Himself is the propitiation for our sins, and not for ours only but also for the whole world.

THE TEST OF KNOWING HIM

3 Now by this we know that we know Him, if we keep His commandments. 4 He who says, "I know Him," and does not keep His commandments, is a liar, and the truth is not in him. 5 But whoever keeps His word, truly the love of God is perfected in him. By this we know that we are in Him. 6 He who says he abides in Him ought himself also to walk just as He walked.

7 Brethren,[a] I write no new commandment to you, but an old commandment which you have had from the beginning. The old commandment is the word which you heard from the beginning.[b] 8 Again, a new commandment I write to you, which thing is true in Him and in you, because the darkness is passing away, and the true light is already shining.

9 He who says he is in the light, and hates his brother, is in darkness until now. 10 He who

1:4 [a]NU-Text and M-Text read *our.* **2:7** [a]NU-Text reads *Beloved.* [b]NU-Text omits *from the beginning.*

KEY PASSAGE

Sin

PAID IN FULL

(1:9)

Sin is disobeying God. Although God created people to be good and holy, He also gave them the choice to disobey—and they did. Since the first sin, all people have been born with a sin nature. God is holy, and He cannot have a relationship with sinful people—unless something is done about the sin. But instead of sending punishment upon sinful human beings, God took the punishment Himself: "While we were still sinners, Christ died for us" (Rom. 5:8). Through His death Christ paid the penalty for sin so that we could have a relationship with God.

The problem, however, is that we still have our sin natures. We still sin, but we can come to God and be forgiven. "If we confess our sins, He is faithful and just to forgive us our sins and to cleanse us from all unrighteousness." When we confess, God forgives, because His Son paid the penalty. We will never be completely sinless in this life, but as believers our lives should be characterized by the desire to follow Christ and avoid sin.

To Learn More: Turn to the article about sin on pages 446, 447. See also the personality profile of Isaiah on page 883.

loves his brother abides in the light, and there is no cause for stumbling in him. 11But he who hates his brother is in darkness and walks in darkness, and does not know where he is going, because the darkness has blinded his eyes.

Their Spiritual State

12 I write to you, little children,
Because your sins are forgiven you
for His name's sake.
13 I write to you, fathers,
Because you have known Him *who is* from the beginning.
I write to you, young men,
Because you have overcome the wicked one.
I write to you, little children,
Because you have known the Father.
14 I have written to you, fathers,
Because you have known Him *who is* from the beginning.
I have written to you, young men,
Because you are strong, and the word of God abides in you,
And you have overcome the wicked one.

> I have written to you, fathers, because you have known Him who is from the beginning. I have written to you, young men, because you are strong, and the word of God abides in you, and you have overcome the wicked one.
>
> 1 JOHN 2:14

Do Not Love the World

15Do not love the world or the things in the world. If anyone loves the world, the love of the Father is not in him. 16For all that *is* in the world—the lust of the flesh, the lust of the eyes, and the pride of life—is not of the Father but is of the world. 17And the world is passing away, and the lust of it; but he who does the will of God abides forever.

Deceptions of the Last Hour

18Little children, it is the last hour; and as you have heard that the[a] Antichrist is coming, even now many antichrists have come, by which we know that it is the last hour. 19They went out from us, but they were not of us; for if they had been of us, they would have continued with us; but *they went out* that they might be made manifest, that none of them were of us.

20But you have an anointing from the Holy One, and you know all things.[a] 21I have not written to you because you do not know the truth, but because you know it, and that no lie is of the truth.

22Who is a liar but he who denies that Jesus is the Christ? He is antichrist who denies the Father and the Son. 23Whoever denies the Son does not have the Father either; he who acknowledges the Son has the Father also.

Let Truth Abide in You

24Therefore let that abide in you which you heard from the beginning. If what you heard from the beginning abides in you, you also will abide in the Son and in the Father. 25And this is the promise that He has promised us—eternal life.

26These things I have written to you concerning those who *try to* deceive you. 27But the anointing which you have received from Him abides in you, and you do not need that anyone teach you; but as the same anointing teaches you concerning all things, and is true, and is not a lie, and just as it has taught you, you will[a] abide in Him.

The Children of God

28And now, little children, abide in Him, that when[a] He appears, we may have confidence and not be ashamed before Him at His coming. 29If you know that He is righteous, you know that everyone who practices righteousness is born of Him.

3 Behold what manner of love the Father has bestowed on us, that we should be called children of God![a] Therefore the world does not know us,[b] because it did not know Him. 2Beloved, now we are children of God; and it has not yet been revealed what we shall be, but we know that when He is revealed, we shall be like Him, for we shall see Him as He

---

2:18 [a]NU-Text omits *the.* **2:20** [a]NU-Text reads *you all know.* **2:27** [a]NU-Text reads *you abide.* **2:28** [a]NU-Text reads *if.* **3:1** [a]NU-Text adds *And we are.* [b]M-Text reads *you.*

is. 3And everyone who has this hope in Him
purifies himself, just as He is pure.

SIN AND THE CHILD OF GOD

4Whoever commits sin also commits lawlessness, and sin is lawlessness. 5And you
know that He was manifested to take away
our sins, and in Him there is no sin. 6Whoever
abides in Him does not sin. Whoever sins has
neither seen Him nor known Him.

7Little children, let no one deceive you. He
who practices righteousness is righteous,
just as He is righteous. 8He who sins is of
the devil, for the devil has sinned from the
beginning. For this purpose the Son of God
was manifested, that He might destroy the
works of the devil. 9Whoever has been born of
God does not sin, for His seed remains in him;
and he cannot sin, because he has been born
of God.

THE IMPERATIVE OF LOVE

10In this the children of God and the children of the devil are manifest: Whoever does
not practice righteousness is not of God, nor *is*
he who does not love his brother. 11For this is
the message that you heard from the beginning, that we should love one another, 12not as
Cain *who* was of the wicked one and murdered his brother. And why did he murder
him? Because his works were evil and his
brother's righteous.

13Do not marvel, my brethren, if the world
hates you. 14We know that we have passed
from death to life, because we love the brethren. He who does not love *his* brother[a] abides
in death. 15Whoever hates his brother is a
murderer, and you know that no murderer has
eternal life abiding in him.

3:14 [a]NU-Text omits *his brother.*

SOUL NOTE

God's Own *(3:1)* No one can love more than God. The thought of God's astounding love bestowed on sinful humanity is beyond understanding. It's incomprehensible that while we were still sinners in rebellion against God, Christ died for us (Rom. 5:8). Through that sacrifice, God brought His own to Himself, bestowing the title and relationship of "children." He allows us to call Him Father. No believer should ever feel alone, worthless, or unimportant. Everyone who has faith in Christ is a beloved child of God! **Topic: Self-Esteem**

KEY PASSAGE

Love Languages

BEING BILINGUAL

(3:18)

People say "I love you" in many ways besides speaking the words. In fact, while words are important, saying words without backing them up with actions will make the words meaningless. John wrote to believers, "Let us not love in word or in tongue, but in deed and in truth."

When expressing love to a spouse, children, or dear friends, we should consider their "language." Certainly they will understand the words, but they will hear the message better through certain kinds of actions. For some people, their love language is physical touch; for others, a gift will show love; still others would prefer to have quality time. As we learn what "language" our loved ones speak, we then can add to our words the deeds that will show our love.

To Learn More: Turn to the article about love languages on pages 1680, 1681. See also the personality profile of Mary on page 1336.

THE OUTWORKING OF LOVE

16By this we know love, because He laid
down His life for us. And we also ought to lay
down *our* lives for the brethren. 17But whoever
has this world's goods, and sees his brother in
need, and shuts up his heart from him, how
does the love of God abide in him?

18My little children, let us not love in word
or in tongue, but in deed and in truth. 19And
by this we know[a] that we are of the truth, and
shall assure our hearts before Him. 20For if our
heart condemns us, God is greater than our
heart, and knows all things. 21Beloved, if our
heart does not condemn us, we have confidence toward God. 22And whatever we ask we
receive from Him, because we keep His commandments and do those things that are
pleasing in His sight. 23And this is His commandment: that we should believe on the
name of His Son Jesus Christ and love one
another, as He gave us[a] commandment.

THE SPIRIT OF TRUTH AND THE SPIRIT OF ERROR

24Now he who keeps His commandments
abides in Him, and He in him. And by this we
know that He abides in us, by the Spirit whom
He has given us.

4 Beloved, do not believe every spirit, but
test the spirits, whether they are of God;
because many false prophets have gone out
into the world. 2By this you know the Spirit of
God: Every spirit that confesses that Jesus
Christ has come in the flesh is of God, 3and
every spirit that does not confess that[a] Jesus
Christ has come in the flesh is not of God. And
this is the *spirit* of the Antichrist, which you
have heard was coming, and is now already in
the world.

4You are of God, little children, and have
overcome them, because He who is in you is
greater than he who is in the world. 5They are
of the world. Therefore they speak *as* of the
world, and the world hears them. 6We are of
God. He who knows God hears us; he who is
not of God does not hear us. By this we know
the spirit of truth and the spirit of error.

KNOWING GOD THROUGH LOVE

7Beloved, let us love one another, for love is
of God; and everyone who loves is born of
God and knows God. 8He who does not love

3:19 [a]NU-Text reads *we shall know.* **3:23** [a]M-Text omits *us.* **4:3** [a]NU-Text omits *that* and *Christ has come in the flesh.*

SOUL NOTE

In Deed! *(3:18)* To understand true love, we need only to look at the Cross, where Christ performed the ultimate act of love. Christ loved us so much that He died for us. This should motivate us to love others. This means not just saying we love people but really loving them by our actions. We can love our families by showing respect, patience, and understanding in many ways. We can love our neighbors as we reach out in kindness. We can love the needy of the world by sharing our possessions with them. Loving actions reveal the truth and depth of our love. **Topic: Love**

SOUL NOTE

Battle Lines *(4:4)* There are two types of people in this world—Christians and non-Christians. Christians worship God; non-Christians, no matter what they say, worship Satan. They may not formally be members of the occult religion, but their refusal to accept Christ puts them on Satan's side. Satan is already a defeated enemy, so believers can continue their work for God's kingdom fearlessly. For as powerful as Satan's army appears to be, Christ is greater by far: "He who is in you is greater than he who is in the world." **Topic: Occult**

does not know God, for God is love. 9In this
the love of God was manifested toward us,
that God has sent His only begotten Son into
the world, that we might live through Him.
10In this is love, not that we loved God, but
that He loved us and sent His Son *to be* the
propitiation for our sins. 11Beloved, if God so
loved us, we also ought to love one another.

SEEING GOD THROUGH LOVE

12No one has seen God at any time. If we
love one another, God abides in us, and His
love has been perfected in us. 13By this we
know that we abide in Him, and He in us, because He has given us of His Spirit. 14And we
have seen and testify that the Father has sent
the Son *as* Savior of the world. 15Whoever
confesses that Jesus is the Son of God, God
abides in him, and he in God. 16And we have
known and believed the love that God has for
us. God is love, and he who abides in love
abides in God, and God in him.

THE CONSUMMATION OF LOVE

17Love has been perfected among us in this:
that we may have boldness in the day of judgment; because as He is, so are we in this
world. 18There is no fear in love; but perfect
love casts out fear, because fear involves torment. But he who fears has not been made

SOUL NOTE

Love Story *(4:7)* God authored the concept of love. When people become believers, they learn how to "love one another" because the Spirit within shows them how as they yield to His leading. Christian relationships ought to be the most loving in the world. Christians who meet each other for the first time experience a bond of love that transcends understanding. The love that binds Christians makes for solid and eternal relationships. The love in our relationships reveals God in us. **Topic: Relationships**

SOUL NOTE

Through Us *(4:12)* No one has ever seen God, but God reveals Himself to the world through His frail and imperfect people by perfecting His love in them. As believers go into the world living their faith, they reveal God to everyone they meet. Their love reveals God's presence in their lives. When believers show love toward one another and to the unbelieving world, God makes Himself known and His love is "perfected" in them. God often shows His love through His people. What does our love for others say on God's behalf? **Topic: Love**

SOUL NOTE

Too Many Critics *(4:19–21)* When believers hate one another, they certainly are not showing love. At times, a critical spirit will cause believers' relationships to become strained as they judge each other. Believers will always disagree on some matters, but they should still be able to celebrate their unity in Christ. Those with critical spirits, however, will be unable to love others. If they cannot love their fellow believers whom they can see, how can they possibly love the invisible God? Believers who claim to love God but hate others are lying to themselves, God, and everyone else. **Topic: Judgmentalism**

Love Languages

THE LANGUAGES OF LOVE

GARY D. CHAPMAN

(1 John 4:12)

The euphoria of "falling in love" is one of life's highest emotions. Being "in love" makes people willing to "climb the highest mountain," or "swim the deepest sea" just to be together. Why is it that within a few years of marriage, many people lose these high emotions? I believe the answer lies in failing to speak each other's emotional "love language." Falling in love and staying in love are two very different, though related, experiences.

"Falling in love" begins with warm, bubbly emotions for a member of the opposite gender and quickly escalates into an emotional obsession. Though the Bible does not focus on this romantic emotional experience, it does acknowledge its reality (Judg. 14:1–3; Song 4:1–7; 5:10–16). Research shows that this emotional obsession lasts about two years. A successful marriage cannot be built upon this temporary emotional high.

"Staying in love"—keeping warm emotions alive for the long term—is Scripture's challenge for couples. People's most basic emotional need is to feel loved. Husbands are instructed to love their wives (Eph. 5:25) and wives are to love their husbands (Titus 2:4). In the Bible, the word "love" does not refer to an emotion, but to an attitude and behavior (including both actions *and* words). Love is the attitude that stems from choosing to look out for the other's interest first; then loving behavior follows.

God is the supreme example of love. He cares about people, so He took action to meet our needs. Scripture instructs us to love one another as God has loved us. In fact, if we do not choose to love each other, it signifies that we do not know God (1 John 4:7, 8). God's love draws us to Him, and then to others (1 John 4:9–11).

In human relationships, love is very similar. People must *choose* the attitude of love and then express it by their behavior. Such behavior touches the heart and emotions of those they love and moves them to reciprocate. In marriage the emotional need is met when husband and wife express reciprocal love. If one spouse is not showing love, then the other must still follow the example of God, who loved us while we were still sinners (Rom. 5:8).

SPEAKING LOVE LANGUAGES

We all need love, but we need for it to be expressed in different ways. What makes one person feel loved will not necessarily make another feel loved. Sincerity is not enough. People must learn to speak other people's "love language." It is common in marriage to genuinely express love to one's spouse while failing to connect emotionally.

There are five basic love languages. Each of us has a primary love language. The primary love language speaks more deeply to a person than the other languages can. Love given in people's primary love language makes them feel truly loved. The key to keeping love alive in marriage is learning the primary love language of one's spouse and speaking it regularly. The same is true with children.

Following are descriptions of the five love languages.

Words of Affirmation

This love language uses words to build up the other person. First Corinthians 8:1

states that "love edifies," or builds up. One way to express love is to encourage the other person. Even the smallest affirmation goes a long way. Whether spoken or in writing, the goal is that the other person feels affirmed.

Gifts

This love language uses tokens of appreciation. Gifts (even inexpensive ones) tell people that they are thought about and loved. Sometimes thoughts about someone are best communicated in a gift, a tangible reminder of being loved.

Acts of Service

This love language does actions that one person knows the other person would appreciate. The Bible challenges people to not just say "I love you," but to love "in deed and in truth" (1 John 3:18). Even small acts count. Asking what can be done to help a spouse or child is a great way to start.

Quality Time

This love language gives undivided attention. Going to breakfast, sitting on the couch while talking, and taking a walk together are all examples. The activity is unimportant, but focusing on each other is. Time is a powerful communicator of love.

Physical Touch

This love language gives tender, caring touch. Jesus took the time to have children come to Him despite being busy (Mark 10:16). An embrace, a kiss, and a hand on the shoulder are all expressions of love. People are never too old for physical touch.

DISCOVERING LOVE LANGUAGES

Keeping love alive in a marriage and meeting the emotional needs of one's children requires learning and speaking each other's love languages. We can discover other people's love languages by asking three questions:

1. How do they most often express love to me? (Generally people give love in the way that they would like to receive it.)
2. What do they complain about most often? (Complaints reveal their inner needs.)
3. What do they request most often? (Usually their requests reveal a pattern which will indicate their primary love language.)

Discovering the primary love language of our spouse or child gives us the information necessary to effectively meet their emotional needs. The chances increase for reciprocated love if love is first expressed in the other's primary love language. Loving our spouse and children unconditionally, using their primary love languages, has the potential of working miracles in our marriages and families.

FURTHER MEDITATION:

Other passages to study about the issue of love languages include:

- ➢ Proverbs 3:12
- ➢ Mark 12:30–33
- ➢ Luke 6:38
- ➢ John 3:16; 14:15, 21–23
- ➢ Romans 5:5, 8; 8:35–39
- ➢ 1 Corinthians 13
- ➢ Ephesians 4:32

To Learn More: Turn to the key passage note on love languages at 1 John 3:18 on page 1677. See also the personality profile of Mary on page 1336.

perfect in love. [19]We love Him[a] because He
first loved us.

Obedience by Faith

[20]If someone says, "I love God," and hates
his brother, he is a liar; for he who does not
love his brother whom he has seen, how can[a]
he love God whom he has not seen? [21]And this
commandment we have from Him: that he
who loves God *must* love his brother also.

5 Whoever believes that Jesus is the Christ
is born of God, and everyone who loves
Him who begot also loves him who is begotten of Him. [2]By this we know that we love the
children of God, when we love God and keep
His commandments. [3]For this is the love of
God, that we keep His commandments. And
His commandments are not burdensome. [4]For
whatever is born of God overcomes the world.
And this is the victory that has overcome the
world—our[a] faith. [5]Who is he who overcomes
the world, but he who believes that Jesus is
the Son of God?

The Certainty of God's Witness

[6]This is He who came by water and blood—
Jesus Christ; not only by water, but by water
and blood. And it is the Spirit who bears witness, because the Spirit is truth. [7]For there are
three that bear witness in heaven: the Father,
the Word, and the Holy Spirit; and these three

4:19 [a]NU-Text omits *Him.* **4:20** [a]NU-Text reads *he cannot.* **5:4** [a]M-Text reads *your.*

SOUL NOTE

Without a Doubt *(5:13)* Christians need have no doubts about their faith. Those who believe in the name of the Son of God can *know* that they have eternal life. Other religions offer merely the hope of eternal life—if one has been good enough, done more good deeds than bad, or has sacrificed enough for others. Christians, however, can know for sure that they will be with Christ forever in heaven. We may face doubts, difficulties, and times of spiritual dryness, but through it all, we can know that we have eternal life, now and forever. **Topic: Belief**

KEY PASSAGE

Decision Making

MAKING CHOICES

(5:14)

God promises eternal life to those who believe. He also promises a continuing relationship with His people, "If we ask anything according to His will, He hears us." Believers have the ultimate Guide to walk them through life, helping them make right decisions.

How can believers know God's will as they make decisions? First, they should consider whether they truly want to know what God wants and if they truly want to follow His leadership. Then they should pray and study God's words for guidance. The Holy Spirit will help them interpret what God is doing in and around them in the decision-making process. Believers learn how to seek God's will, asking not what they want, but what He wants for them. When the answer comes, believers know it and can act upon it.

Whatever decisions we face—large or small—God will guide us. We need only ask Him, truly seeking His will, and He will answer.

To Learn More: Turn to the article about decision making on pages 1484, 1485. See also the personality profile of Joshua on page 296.

are one. [8]And there are three that bear witness on earth:[a] the Spirit, the water, and the blood; and these three agree as one.

[9]If we receive the witness of men, the witness of God is greater; for this is the witness of God which[a] He has testified of His Son. [10]He who believes in the Son of God has the witness in himself; he who does not believe God has made Him a liar, because he has not believed the testimony that God has given of His Son. [11]And this is the testimony: that God has given us eternal life, and this life is in His Son. [12]He who has the Son has life; he who does not have the Son of God does not have life. [13]These things I have written to you who believe in the name of the Son of God, that you may know that you have eternal life,[a] and that you may *continue to* believe in the name of the Son of God.

Confidence and Compassion in Prayer

[14]Now this is the confidence that we have in Him, that if we ask anything according to His will, He hears us. [15]And if we know that He hears us, whatever we ask, we know that we have the petitions that we have asked of Him.

[16]If anyone sees his brother sinning a sin *which does* not *lead* to death, he will ask, and He will give him life for those who commit sin not *leading* to death. There is sin *leading* to death. I do not say that he should pray about that. [17]All unrighteousness is sin, and there is sin not *leading* to death.

Knowing the True—Rejecting the False

[18]We know that whoever is born of God does not sin; but he who has been born of God keeps himself,[a] and the wicked one does not touch him.

[19]We know that we are of God, and the whole world lies *under the sway of* the wicked one.

[20]And we know that the Son of God has come and has given us an understanding, that we may know Him who is true; and we are in Him who is true, in His Son Jesus Christ. This is the true God and eternal life.

[21]Little children, keep yourselves from idols. Amen.

5:8 [a]NU-Text and M-Text omit the words from *in heaven* (verse 7) through *on earth* (verse 8). Only four or five very late manuscripts contain these words in Greek. **5:9** [a]NU-Text reads *God, that.* **5:13** [a]NU-Text omits the rest of this verse. **5:18** [a]NU-Text reads *him.*

SOUL NOTE

Whatever We Ask *(5:14, 15)* The promise that we will have whatever we ask is not a blank check. Believers cannot merely pray for anything and then get it. The context refers to prayers "according to His will." In other words, when we pray, we seek God's will in the matter. We make our request, but we submit ourselves to God's wisdom about what we should have. We know that when we pray, God hears and will answer in the best possible way. **Topic: Prayer**

2 John

"*Tolerance!*" is the slogan of the postmodern generation. The idea is that no one has the right to judge anyone or anything. It seems that unquestioning acceptance (if not outright sanction) is being touted as the highest virtue. To the apostle John, however, such blanket endorsement only looked foolish, not to mention dangerous.

Second John was written around A.D. 90 to challenge believers to measure everything against the litmus test of New Testament Christianity. The early church had a practice of supporting traveling teachers by housing them and providing for their needs. But John warned believers to use discernment in receiving professing believers into their homes (10). Not everyone who claims the name of Christ really teaches the truth. John especially emphasized the "doctrine of Christ" as a key element in gauging what is true: What does a person or his teaching say about Jesus? This is significant because those who are in error about the person of Christ do not really know God (9).

The tone of this letter is warm and intimate. Whether John was writing to a specific person or to a whole church body, he began his short note by affirming holy living, and he concluded by saying that he longed for a "face to face" visit (12). Here are the twin virtues of obedience and love—the highest and best proofs of a genuine Christian faith.

Be careful how you live, and what ideas you accept. As we confront the onslaught of myriad religious beliefs in a pluralistic society, John's warnings remain unusually relevant.

SOUL CONCERN IN

2 JOHN

OBEDIENCE (6)

Greeting the Elect Lady

The Elder,

[1]To the elect lady and her children, whom I love in truth, and not only I, but also all those who have known the truth, [2]because of the truth which abides in us and will be with us forever:

[3]Grace, mercy, *and* peace will be with you[a] from God the Father and from the Lord Jesus Christ, the Son of the Father, in truth and love.

Walk in Christ's Commandments

[4]I rejoiced greatly that I have found *some* of your children walking in truth, as we received commandment from the Father. [5]And now I plead with you, lady, not as though I wrote a new commandment to you, but that which we have had from the beginning: that we love one another. [6]This is love, that we walk according to His commandments. This is the commandment, that as you have heard from the beginning, you should walk in it.

Beware of Antichrist Deceivers

[7]For many deceivers have gone out into the world who do not confess Jesus Christ *as* coming in the flesh. This is a deceiver and an

3 [a]NU-Text and M-Text read *us.*

SOUL NOTE

One Truth *(1–4)* One truth exists, and that truth is found in Jesus Christ, who is "the way, the truth, and the life" (John 14:6). John wrote this letter to help believers remain in the truth and not stray into false teachings. In order to resist false notions and ideas, believers must remain grounded in God's Word. When we know the Bible, we learn the truth and will see when any teaching contradicts it. We must continue "walking in truth," for then we will be able to see what is false and steer clear of it. **Topic: Truth**

SOUL NOTE

Love Revealed *(6)* Loving God means obeying Him. When we love God, we desire to "walk according to His commandments," meaning that we want to obey Him. That obedience reveals our love for Him. Love for God doesn't focus merely on feelings, although those certainly are involved; it's about what we do. God's commandments are found in His Word. We obey not because we are trying to be good enough to be saved or to have a certain amount of good deeds to outweigh bad deeds. We obey because we love God and desire to please Him. **Topic: Obedience**

SOUL NOTE

True or False? *(7)* Jesus had warned that false teachers would arise and lead many people astray (Matt. 7:15; 24:11, 24). False teachers will teach any number of doctrines that might sound good but are contradictory to God's Word and, therefore, are lies. Believers can discern false teaching by discovering what the teacher believes about Jesus Christ. Some will teach that Jesus did not actually come in the flesh; others will teach that Jesus was merely flesh and not God. If anyone contradicts the Bible's definition of Christ being both human and divine, then that person is a false teacher. **Topic: Cults**

Obedience

OBEDIENCE

DAWSON MCALLISTER

(2 John 6)

It has been said that one of the things that made Alexander the Great so imposing was the commitment his soldiers showed to him. Alexander and a small band of soldiers approached a small fortified city one day and sought to seize it. Alexander demanded to see the king and asked for his surrender. The king, not impressed with the small band of soldiers, refused.

Alexander asked the king to gather the people of the city atop the city wall to watch a demonstration. As the townspeople gathered, Alexander ordered his soldiers to march single file toward a nearby cliff. One by one, the soldiers plunged to their doom until Alexander ordered those who remained back to his side.

At the sight of such overwhelming devotion, the king immediately surrendered the city. The king had realized that if Alexander's men were willing to commit suicide at his mere command, nothing could stop his eventual overthrow of the city.

Think of the difference that it would make if Christians today had the same mentality as Alexander's soldiers—obedience at any cost. Obedience is not always easy or popular. Often it is very difficult and costly. Whether it is obeying a parent, a boss, a command in Scripture, or a prompting from the Holy Spirit, obedience is easy to talk about and difficult to do. Nonetheless, it is something that God clearly requires of His children.

OBEDIENCE RELINQUISHES SELF

Obedience requires an abandonment of self and a dependence upon Christ. Sometimes Christ requires more than we are willing to give. Sometimes He leads in a direction where we do not want to go. At those times, our focus must be on Christ and not on our circumstances or ourselves.

When God commanded Abraham to lay his son upon the altar, Abraham surely had questions and doubts about the direction in which God was leading. In Genesis 22:2 God said, "Take now your son, your only son Isaac, whom you love, and go to the land of Moriah, and offer him there as a burnt offering on one of the mountains of which I shall tell you."

Imagine the pain and disbelief Abraham felt as God said those words! God was acknowledging how important Isaac was to Abraham, yet demanding that Abraham offer Isaac as a sacrifice. Inconceivable. Against all logic. No doubt, Abraham reasoned that he must have misinterpreted God's command, that he must have heard God wrong. Abraham probably had a very sleepless night—praying, begging, pleading, and bargaining. It was a total act of selflessness for Abraham to be willing to give up the special son that God had given him.

OBEDIENCE REQUIRES TRUST

Perhaps the greatest reason obedience is so difficult is the trust factor. Obeying God requires a certain level of trust in Him. It's hard to obey someone if we don't trust them. Abraham was willing to sacrifice his son because of his firm belief in God. He believed that God would fulfill all He had promised.

When talking to his servants, Abraham said, "Stay here with the donkey; the lad and I will go yonder and worship, and we will come back to you" (Gen. 22:5). He had full trust that *both* he and Isaac would return from the mountain.

Again, Abraham expressed his trust in God when he told Isaac, "God will provide for Himself the lamb for a burnt offering" (Gen. 22:8). Abraham believed God and had trust that He would provide a sacrifice in place of Isaac. Imagine the trust that it took for Abraham to raise the knife in the air. Until the final moment when God's angel intervened, Abraham was carrying out the act that God had commanded him to do. Abraham obeyed because he trusted.

OBEDIENCE RESULTS IN BLESSING

The fruit of obedience is blessing, though the blessings are not always readily apparent. Any time we are disobedient, we are moving outside the realm of God's will for our lives, thus we are subject to the consequences that result from our actions. If we obey God's commands, however, the greatest blessing of all is ours—remaining in Christ and His love. "This is love, that we walk according to His commandments" (2 John 6).

God promised Abraham many years of blessing because of his great obedience: "Because you . . . have not withheld your son, your only son—blessing I will bless you, and multiplying I will multiply your descendants as the stars of heaven" (Gen. 22:16, 17). Not only would Abraham be blessed, but also his descendants would be blessed for generations to come.

Jesus obeyed the Father and had total dependence on Him. How much more should we be dependent on the Father! Jesus' example is the ultimate example of obedience. Although He had to go before God in agonizing prayer, Jesus obeyed the will of His Father. He endured the scorn of the Cross and the suffering of mankind's sin, because it was God's will: "O My Father, if it is possible, let this cup pass from Me; nevertheless, not as I will, but as You will" (Matt. 26:39).

Mark Twain once said, "Always do right. This will gratify most people, and astonish the rest." Cynical society almost boasts of doing the wrong thing and is utterly amazed when people of faith display selflessness and trust. However, for the Christian, obedience is not just an option. Though difficult, costly, and demanding, the life of a Christian is based upon total dependence on Christ and obedience to His will.

FURTHER MEDITATION:

Other passages to study about the issue of obedience include:

- ➢ Deuteronomy 6:1–25
- ➢ Matthew 8:27
- ➢ Romans 2:8
- ➢ Philippians 2:5–8
- ➢ Hebrews 11:8

To Learn More: Turn to the key passage note on obedience at I Samuel 15:22 on page 363. See also the personality profile of Saul on page 362.

antichrist. [8]Look to yourselves, that we[a] do
not lose those things we worked for, but *that*
we[b] may receive a full reward.

[9]Whoever transgresses[a] and does not abide
in the doctrine of Christ does not have God.
He who abides in the doctrine of Christ has
both the Father and the Son. [10]If anyone
comes to you and does not bring this doctrine,
do not receive him into your house nor greet
him; [11]for he who greets him shares in his evil
deeds.

JOHN'S FAREWELL GREETING

[12]Having many things to write to you, I did
not wish *to do so* with paper and ink; but I
hope to come to you and speak face to face,
that our joy may be full.

[13]The children of your elect sister greet you.
Amen.

---

8 [a]NU-Text reads *you.* [b]NU-Text reads *you.*
9 [a]NU-Text reads *goes ahead.*

3 John

Every church has at least one: a person with an agenda. It might be a covert quest for honor and acclaim. It might be a hidden desire to gain control. But the end result is usually the same: friction and fighting—leading to a diminished impact and a tarnishing of Christ's reputation in the world.

The apostle John's third letter deals with just this issue, in a congregation thought to have been located in Asia Minor. Third John was addressed to Gaius, a Christian and dear friend who was known for his ministry of hospitality to itinerant preachers. John's intent was to warn Gaius to stand against the erroneous ideas and authoritarian conceits of another church member named Diotrephes.

The three men mentioned by John—Gaius, "whom I love in truth" (1); Diotrephes, "who loves to have the preeminence" (9), and Demetrius, who "has a good testimony" (12)—provide a glimpse into the life of the early church. These men (together with the apostle) mirror the kinds of people commonly found in churches today. John was the mature elder, concerned with guarding the truth. Gaius and Demetrius were faithful servants who walked in the truth, demonstrated love, and enjoyed a good reputation. Diotrephes, on the other hand, was a troublemaker, an arrogant, self-centered glory-seeker, who apparently refused to host legitimate and worthy missionaries.

What kind of church member are you? Without a healthy soul, you'll never develop a genuine love for God or His people. And lacking that, you'll be remembered with disdain, if you're remembered at all.

Greeting to Gaius

The Elder,

1To the beloved Gaius, whom I love in truth:

2Beloved, I pray that you may prosper in all
things and be in health, just as your soul prospers. 3For I rejoiced greatly when brethren
came and testified of the truth *that is* in you,
just as you walk in the truth. 4I have no greater
joy than to hear that my children walk in truth.[a]

Gaius Commended for Generosity

5Beloved, you do faithfully whatever you do
for the brethren and[a] for strangers, 6who have
borne witness of your love before the church.
If you send them forward on their journey in a
manner worthy of God, you will do well, 7be-
cause they went forth for His name's sake,
taking nothing from the Gentiles. 8We therefore ought to receive[a] such, that we may become fellow workers for the truth.

Diotrephes and Demetrius

9I wrote to the church, but Diotrephes, who
loves to have the preeminence among them,
does not receive us. 10Therefore, if I come, I
will call to mind his deeds which he does,
prating against us with malicious words. And
not content with that, he himself does not receive the brethren, and forbids those who
wish to, putting *them* out of the church.

11Beloved, do not imitate what is evil, but
what is good. He who does good is of God,
but[a] he who does evil has not seen God.

12Demetrius has a *good* testimony from all,
and from the truth itself. And we also bear
witness, and you know that our testimony is
true.

Farewell Greeting

13I had many things to write, but I do not
wish to write to you with pen and ink; 14but I
hope to see you shortly, and we shall speak
face to face.

Peace to you. Our friends greet you. Greet
the friends by name.

4 [a]NU-Text reads *the truth.* **5** [a]NU-Text adds *especially.* **8** [a]NU-Text reads *support.* **11** [a]NU-Text and M-Text omit *but.*

SOUL NOTE

Health Maintenance *(2)* Concern for people's physical, emotional, and spiritual well-being go together. Some people think the body doesn't matter, so they either neglect themselves and the bodies God gave them, or they indulge in sinful behavior, thinking that it doesn't matter. Both attitudes are mistaken. We should not obsess with our appearance or health, but we should do our best to maintain a certain level of health so that we can serve God to the best of our ability. It's wrong to neglect or indulge ourselves; instead, we should keep a healthy balance so that we can be ready to serve God wherever He may call us. **Topic: Health/Spirituality**

SOUL NOTE

Honorable Mention *(5–8)* When churches care for their missionaries and teachers, they honor God and "become fellow workers for the truth." All believers are called to share the Good News and make disciples, but not all are called to travel, preach, or serve as missionaries. But certainly everybody can support those who do. Gaius was commended for being hospitable to these traveling teachers, and that goes for all of us. We please God when we receive workers hospitably, help meet their needs, make them comfortable, and then send them on their way "in a manner worthy of God." God's laborers for the truth deserve honor. **Topic: Honor**

PERSONALITY PROFILE

Gossip

DIOTREPHES: TALKING TOO MUCH

(3 JOHN 9, 10)

Some people in the Bible show up only once, but lessons from their lives have lasted forever. To have been a positive example would be one thing; to go down in history as an arrogant leader who was "prating against" John and other leaders "with malicious words" is unfortunate indeed. That's what happened to this ancient church leader named Diotrephes.

Diotrephes had apparently become a leader in the church, but he liked his position a little too much. He loved "to have the preeminence," wrote John, and he felt threatened by anyone else. Thus, he refused to give hospitality to traveling preachers and forbade anyone else in the church from doing so.

Perhaps worst of all was his malicious gossip. Diotrephes spoke evil about the other church leaders and traveling preachers, but his words were no more than nonsense. Many in the church were either too untrained in Scripture to see his evil, or too afraid of him to speak up. In any case, Diotrephes's words were causing deep division and great difficulty, and he had to be stopped.

Gossip has a way of hurting and dividing people. Rumors spread like wildfire, leaving destruction in their wake. The next time a spark of gossip flies our way, we should snuff it out completely. We dare not make the mistake of setting a great fire by passing along a little spark. The only sparks we should pass along are the sparks of Christ's love. That warm and welcoming fire should burn continually.

To Learn More: Turn to the article about gossip on pages 838, 839. See also the key passage note at James 3:5–18 on page 1648.

Jude

"They wear you down," sighed the exhausted woman as she slumped on the park bench. "They keep on and on until finally you just don't have the energy to fight anymore!" She was talking about her "active" children; yet such words could just as easily apply to the plight of the godly among those who are busily making mischief for the church.

Jude was a Jewish Christian (many believe this was the brother of Jesus and James; Matt. 13:55) who wrote a powerful defense of the Christian faith (sometime between A.D. 66 and 80) to challenge young believers to "contend earnestly for the faith" (3). His letter is a resounding call to action. Its urgent message is that quitting is out of the question, because the danger is too great, and the stakes are too high.

This brief letter captures our imagination with a series of dramatic word pictures that describe the false teachers who seemed to hover around every New Testament congregation. They are called "dreamers" (8), "brute beasts" (10), "clouds without water," "trees without fruit" (12), "raging waves of the sea," and "wandering stars" (13). Their mischief is nothing to wink at. They are rebellious, reserved for a judgment like Sodom and Gomorrah's.

Jude ends his letter by encouraging his readers to build themselves up in the faith. Spiritual growth and spiritual discipline go hand in hand. Without them there can be no spiritual prosperity.

If your soul is worn down, you need the stirring challenge of Jude. Ask God to speak words of strength and renewal into your heart today.

SOUL CONCERN IN JUDE

TOLERANCE	(3, 4)

Greeting to the Called

[1]Jude, a bondservant of Jesus Christ, and brother of James,

To those who are called, sanctified[a] by God the Father, and preserved in Jesus Christ:

[2]Mercy, peace, and love be multiplied to you.

Contend for the Faith

[3]Beloved, while I was very diligent to write to you concerning our common salvation, I found it necessary to write to you exhorting you to contend earnestly for the faith which was once for all delivered to the saints. [4]For certain men have crept in unnoticed, who long ago were marked out for this condemnation, ungodly men, who turn the grace of our God into lewdness and deny the only Lord God[a] and our Lord Jesus Christ.

Old and New Apostates

[5]But I want to remind you, though you once knew this, that the Lord, having saved the people out of the land of Egypt, afterward destroyed those who did not believe. [6]And the angels who did not keep their proper domain, but left their own abode, He has reserved in everlasting chains under darkness for the judgment of the great day; [7]as Sodom and Gomorrah, and the cities around them in a similar manner to these, having given themselves over to sexual immorality and gone after strange flesh, are set forth as an example, suffering the vengeance of eternal fire.

[8]Likewise also these dreamers defile the flesh, reject authority, and speak evil of dignitaries. [9]Yet Michael the archangel, in contending with the devil, when he disputed about the body of Moses, dared not bring against him a reviling accusation, but said, "The Lord rebuke you!" [10]But these speak evil of whatever they do not know; and whatever they know naturally, like brute beasts, in these things they corrupt themselves. [11]Woe to them! For they have gone in the way of Cain, have run greedily in the error of Balaam for profit, and perished in the rebellion of Korah.

Apostates Depraved and Doomed

[12]These are spots in your love feasts, while they feast with you without fear, serving *only* themselves. *They are* clouds without water, carried about[a] by the winds; late autumn trees without fruit, twice dead, pulled up by the roots; [13]raging waves of the sea, foaming up their own shame; wandering stars for whom is reserved the blackness of darkness forever.

[14]Now Enoch, the seventh from Adam, prophesied about these men also, saying, "Behold, the Lord comes with ten thousands of His saints, [15]to execute judgment on all, to convict all who are ungodly among them of all their ungodly deeds which they have committed in an ungodly way, and of all the harsh things which ungodly sinners have spoken against Him."

Apostates Predicted

[16]These are grumblers, complainers, walking according to their own lusts; and they mouth great swelling *words*, flattering people to gain advantage. [17]But you, beloved, remember the words which were spoken before by the apostles of our Lord Jesus Christ: [18]how they told you that there would be mockers in the last time who would walk according to their own ungodly lusts. [19]These are sensual

1 [a]NU-Text reads *beloved.* **4** [a]NU-Text omits *God.*
12 [a]NU-Text and M-Text read *along.*

SOUL NOTE

Praise the Lord *(24, 25)* The closing words of Jude's letter form a doxology of praise to God. No matter what false teachers might try to do or say against God and His Word, God will watch over His people. He alone will keep them from stumbling and present them "faultless before the presence of His glory with exceeding joy." We praise Him for this great promise. One day He will bring us to Himself and rejoice to have us with Him. We can trust Him because He is "God our Savior," wise, glorious, majestic, and powerful forever. **Topic: Praise and Worship**

Tolerance

TRUTH AND TOLERANCE

JOSH MCDOWELL

(Jude 3, 4)

On the surface, the word "tolerance" appears as a benign manner of getting along with people who are different. "What's true for you is true for you. No problem." The seemingly innocent idea of tolerance has become the cardinal virtue, the sole absolute, of society. Children hear it preached every day in school and the media. Yet few people understand what society really means by tolerance, nor do they realize that it is the central doctrine of an entire cultural movement. As a result, few recognize the threat it poses to their children, their churches, and their faith.

ONE WORD, TWO MEANINGS

The traditional definition of tolerance means simply to recognize and respect others' beliefs and practices without necessarily agreeing or sympathizing with them. This attitude, that everyone has a right to their own opinion, is what tolerance means to most people.

But today's definition is vastly different. This new tolerance considers every individual's beliefs, values, lifestyle, and truth claims as equally valid. Not only do people have an equal right to their beliefs, but all beliefs are equal. The new tolerance goes beyond respecting a person's rights; it demands praise and endorsement of that person's beliefs, values, and lifestyle. This fundamental change in meaning—and thinking—represents one of the greatest shifts in history. And most people are missing it. This new tolerance has many alarming implications, and unless Christian churches, families, and educators recognize and respond to it, the new millennium is likely to be a dangerous time.

When presented with Jesus Christ and the historical evidence of His life and resurrection, people who opposed Christianity used to say, "Prove it!" and "I don't believe you." But there is a recent startling shift. Now, the opposition invariably says, "How dare you say that?" or "Who do you think you are?" or "You are intolerant!" The issue is no longer the truth of the message, but the right to proclaim it. In the new cultural climate, any unpopular message can be labeled "intolerant" and therefore be repressed.

Because the new tolerance declares all beliefs equally valid, Christians will face increasing pressure to be silent about their convictions—in school, at work, and in the public square—because to speak out will be seen as an intolerant judgment of others' beliefs and lifestyles. Such pressure will pose severe problems not only for Christians, but for their families and children as well. The rise of the new tolerance is intolerant of anything that claims to be the one way, the only way. This makes the sharing of one's faith an increasingly dangerous proposition.

Christians may puzzle over why a crucifix, a Christian symbol, suspended in a jar of urine is considered art, yet displaying a homosexual symbol in a jar of urine would be decried as a hate crime. Society has shifted from a Judeo-Christian culture to an increasingly and aggressively anti-Judeo-Christian culture. As the new tolerance permeates today's culture, a new wave of unpopularity—and even persecution—is likely to be encountered, not only by Christians, but also by observant Jews and possibly Muslims, because these faiths profess to be based on divine revelation as well.

Our own government has encouraged a public-private partnership to teach "tolerance" to middle school children. Funding for this tolerance campaign would come from both government and private industry under the guise of protecting our children against "hate crimes."

WHAT DOES THE LORD REQUIRE?

It is not too late to avoid such scenarios, but doing so will require effort. Christians must humbly pursue truth. It may be difficult to speak the truth in today's climate, but Jesus said, "The truth shall make you free" (John 8:32). Pursuing truth in this context means countering the new doctrines of tolerance. It means teaching children to embrace all people, but not all beliefs. It means showing them how to listen to and learn from all people without necessarily agreeing with them. It means helping them to courageously but humbly speak the truth, even if it makes them the object of scorn or hatred. Christians must always remember, however, that when the apostle Peter said, "Always be ready to give a defense to everyone who asks you a reason for the hope that is in you," he added, "with meekness and fear" (1 Pet. 3:15). The key is to aggressively live in love and humbly stand up for the truth.

Christians must also aggressively practice love. Everyone loves love, it seems, but few recognize how incompatible love is with the new tolerance. Tolerance simply avoids offending someone; Christians must help their children live in love, which actively seeks to promote the good of another person. Tolerance says, "You must approve of what I do." Love responds, "I must do something harder; I will love you, even when your behavior offends me." Tolerance says, "You must agree with me." Love responds, "I must do something harder; I will tell you the truth, because I am convinced that 'the truth shall make you free.' " Tolerance says, "You must allow me to have my way." Love responds, "I must do something harder; I will plead with you to follow the right way, because I believe you are worth the risk."

The dreadful potential of the new tolerance can be averted, but only with a renewed commitment to truth, justice, and love. And, as it happens, that powerful trio of virtues can do more than prevent disaster—it can bring out true community and culture in the midst of diversity and disagreement.

FURTHER MEDITATION:

Other passages to study about the issue of tolerance include:

- ➢ Psalm 119:142–160
- ➢ Proverbs 2:1–6
- ➢ Matthew 5:7
- ➢ 1 Corinthians 8:13; 10:31
- ➢ 2 Timothy 3:16

To Learn More: Turn to the key passage note on tolerance at 2 Peter 2:12–22 on page 1672. See also the personality profile of Micaiah on page 470.

persons, who cause divisions, not having the Spirit.

Maintain Your Life with God

20 But you, beloved, building yourselves up on your most holy faith, praying in the Holy Spirit, 21 keep yourselves in the love of God, looking for the mercy of our Lord Jesus Christ unto eternal life.

22 And on some have compassion, making a distinction;[a] 23 but others save with fear, pulling *them* out of the fire,[a] hating even the garment defiled by the flesh.

Glory to God

24 Now to Him who is able to keep you[a]
from stumbling,
And to present *you* faultless
Before the presence of His glory with
exceeding joy,
25 To God our Savior,[a]
Who alone is wise,[b]
Be glory and majesty,
Dominion and power,[c]
Both now and forever.
Amen.

---

22 [a]NU-Text reads *who are doubting* (or *making distinctions*). **23** [a]NU-Text adds *and on some have mercy with fear* and omits *with fear* in first clause. **24** [a]M-Text reads *them.* **25** [a]NU-Text reads *To the only God our Savior.* [b]NU-Text omits *Who . . . is wise* and adds *Through Jesus Christ our Lord.* [c]NU-Text adds *Before all time.*

Revelation

Global thermonuclear war . . . a collision with a giant asteroid . . . an attack by extraterrestrials. . . . Hollywood never lacks for creative ideas about how the world will end. Yet while many of these theories are entertaining, none is as gripping or as worthwhile as what God Himself has revealed in the final book of the Bible.

Revelation is a series of prophetic visions given to the apostle John, likely around A.D. 95. Christians have long debated how Revelation should be interpreted. Amid varying opinions, one thing is certain—the triumph of Jesus Christ. The risen, glorified Savior appeared to His servant John and unveiled a panoramic view of future events. Certain events will trigger God's last-days countdown, leading to the defeat of the current world system and the return of Jesus Christ to establish His kingdom on earth.

Revelation combines end-time visions with epistle-like instructions. It predicts the future even as it gives us hope for the present. It pulls back the curtain of time and reveals the eternal destiny of the human race—the new heaven and new earth—where the long-lost paradise of Eden will finally be regained.

The great theme of this glorious book is restoration. All that humanity has lost by sinful rebellion against God will be regained by the grace of God and the ultimate triumph of Christ. Let your soul feast on the truth that believers in Jesus *will* share Christ's triumph forever!

SOUL CONCERN IN REVELATION

Introduction and Benediction

1 The Revelation of Jesus Christ, which God
gave Him to show His servants—things
which must shortly take place. And He sent
and signified *it* by His angel to His servant
John, 2who bore witness to the word of God,
and to the testimony of Jesus Christ, to all
things that he saw. 3Blessed *is* he who reads
and those who hear the words of this prophecy, and keep those things which are written in
it; for the time *is* near.

Greeting the Seven Churches

4John, to the seven churches which are in
Asia:

Grace to you and peace from Him who is
and who was and who is to come, and from
the seven Spirits who are before His throne,
5and from Jesus Christ, the faithful witness,
the firstborn from the dead, and the ruler over
the kings of the earth.

To Him who loved us and washed[a] us from
our sins in His own blood, 6and has made us
kings[a] and priests to His God and Father, to
Him *be* glory and dominion forever and ever.
Amen.

7Behold, He is coming with clouds, and
every eye will see Him, even they who pierced
Him. And all the tribes of the earth will mourn
because of Him. Even so, Amen.

8"I am the Alpha and the Omega, *the* Beginning and *the* End,"[a] says the Lord,[b] "who is
and who was and who is to come, the Almighty."

Vision of the Son of Man

9I, John, both[a] your brother and companion
in the tribulation and kingdom and patience
of Jesus Christ, was on the island that is called
Patmos for the word of God and for the testimony of Jesus Christ. 10I was in the Spirit on
the Lord's Day, and I heard behind me a loud
voice, as of a trumpet, 11saying, "I am the Alpha and the Omega, the First and the Last,"
and,[a] "What you see, write in a book and send
it to the seven churches which are in Asia:[b] to
Ephesus, to Smyrna, to Pergamos, to Thyatira,
to Sardis, to Philadelphia, and to Laodicea."

12Then I turned to see the voice that spoke
with me. And having turned I saw seven gold-
en lampstands, 13and in the midst of the seven
lampstands *One* like the Son of Man, clothed
with a garment down to the feet and girded
about the chest with a golden band. 14His
head and hair *were* white like wool, as white
as snow, and His eyes like a flame of fire; 15His
feet *were* like fine brass, as if refined in a furnace, and His voice as the sound of many waters; 16He had in His right hand seven stars,
out of His mouth went a sharp two-edged
sword, and His countenance *was* like the sun
shining in its strength. 17And when I saw Him,
I fell at His feet as dead. But He laid His right
hand on me, saying to me,[a] "Do not be afraid;
I am the First and the Last. 18I *am* He who
lives, and was dead, and behold, I am alive
forevermore. Amen. And I have the keys of
Hades and of Death. 19Write[a] the things which
you have seen, and the things which are, and
the things which will take place after this.
20The mystery of the seven stars which you
saw in My right hand, and the seven golden

1:5 [a]NU-Text reads *loves us and freed;* M-Text reads *loves us and washed.* **1:6** [a]NU-Text and M-Text read *a kingdom.* **1:8** [a]NU-Text and M-Text omit *the Beginning and the End.* [b]NU-Text and M-Text add *God.* **1:9** [a]NU-Text and M-Text omit *both.* **1:11** [a]NU-Text and M-Text omit *I am* through third *and.* [b]NU-Text and M-Text omit *which are in Asia.* **1:17** [a]NU-Text and M-Text omit *to me.* **1:19** [a]NU-Text and M-Text read *Therefore, write.*

SOUL NOTE

Jesus' Own *(1:5)* Revelation gives an awe-inspiring picture of Jesus as the King of kings, the Ruler over all of earth's other monarchs. At His word, God's enemies will be rounded up to be judged. Believers will have nothing to fear, however, for they will have a part in Christ's reign and will assist Him in His kingdom. King Jesus loved us so much that He sacrificed His life for us, and will return someday to take us to be with Him. We are God's beloved children—His most treasured possession. When we feel overwhelmed, we can picture our great King and remember that He will soon return for us. **Topic: Self-Esteem**

lampstands: The seven stars are the angels of the seven churches, and the seven lampstands which you saw[a] are the seven churches.

The Loveless Church

2 "To the angel of the church of Ephesus write,

'These things says He who holds the seven stars in His right hand, who walks in the midst of the seven golden lampstands: 2"I know your works, your labor, your patience, and that you cannot bear those who are evil. And you have tested those who say they are apostles and are not, and have found them liars; 3and you have persevered and have patience, and have labored for My name's sake and have not become weary. 4Nevertheless I have *this* against you, that you have left your first love. 5Remember therefore from where you have fallen; repent and do the first works, or else I will come to you quickly and remove your lampstand from its place—unless you repent. 6But this you have, that you hate the deeds of the Nicolaitans, which I also hate.

7"He who has an ear, let him hear what the Spirit says to the churches. To him who overcomes I will give to eat from the tree of life, which is in the midst of the Paradise of God." '

> "Be faithful until death, and I will give you the crown of life."
> REVELATION 2:10

The Persecuted Church

8"And to the angel of the church in Smyrna write,

'These things says the First and the Last, who was dead, and came to life: 9"I know your works, tribulation, and poverty (but you are rich); and *I know* the blasphemy of those who say they are Jews and are not, but *are* a synagogue of Satan. 10Do not fear any of those things which you are about to suffer. Indeed, the devil is about to throw *some* of you into prison, that you may be tested, and you will have tribulation ten days. Be faithful until death, and I will give you the crown of life.

11"He who has an ear, let him hear what the Spirit says to the churches. He who overcomes shall not be hurt by the second death." '

The Compromising Church

12"And to the angel of the church in Pergamos write,

'These things says He who has the sharp two-edged sword: 13"I know your works, and where you dwell, where Satan's throne *is*. And you hold fast to My name, and did not deny My faith even in the days in which Antipas *was* My faithful martyr, who was killed among you, where Satan dwells. 14But I have a few things against you, because you have there those who hold the doctrine of Balaam, who taught Balak to put a stumbling block before the children of Israel, to eat things sacrificed to idols, and to commit sexual immorality. 15Thus you also have those who hold the doctrine of the Nicolaitans, which thing I hate.[a] 16Repent, or else I will come to you quickly and will fight against them with the sword of My mouth.

17"He who has an ear, let him hear what the Spirit says to the churches. To him who overcomes I will give some of the hidden manna to eat. And I will give him a white stone, and on the stone a new name written which no one knows except him who receives *it*." '

1:20 [a]NU-Text and M-Text omit *which you saw.*
2:15 [a]NU-Text and M-Text read *likewise* for *which thing I hate.*

SOUL NOTE

Heart Search *(2:18–23)* Sometimes people think they can hide portions of their lives from everyone. They try to hide angry tempers, deep jealousies, or sexual sin. In His message to the church in Thyatira, Christ clearly stated that He "searches the minds and hearts" (2:23). Nothing is hidden from Him. No sexual sin can escape His notice. People may think they are getting away with it, but God knows. Everywhere we go, everything we say, think, or do is seen by God. That understanding alone should help us to steer clear of sexual sin. **Topic: Sexual Sin**

The Corrupt Church

18“And to the angel of the church in Thyatira
write,
‘These things says the Son of God, who has
eyes like a flame of fire, and His feet like fine
brass: 19“I know your works, love, service,
faith,[a] and your patience; and *as* for your
works, the last *are* more than the first.
20Nevertheless I have a few things against
you, because you allow[a] that woman[b] Jezebel,
who calls herself a prophetess, to teach and
seduce[c] My servants to commit sexual immorality and eat things sacrificed to idols. 21And I
gave her time to repent of her sexual immorality, and she did not repent.[a] 22Indeed I will
cast her into a sickbed, and those who commit
adultery with her into great tribulation, unless
they repent of their[a] deeds. 23I will kill her
children with death, and all the churches shall
know that I am He who searches the minds
and hearts. And I will give to each one of you
according to your works.
24“Now to you I say, and[a] to the rest in Thyatira, as many as do not have this doctrine,
who have not known the depths of Satan, as
they say, I will[b] put on you no other burden.
25But hold fast what you have till I come.
26And he who overcomes, and keeps My
works until the end, to him I will give power
over the nations—

27 *‘He shall rule them with a rod of iron;*
They shall be dashed to pieces like the
potter’s vessels’[a]—

as I also have received from My Father; 28and I
will give him the morning star.
29“He who has an ear, let him hear what the
Spirit says to the churches.” ’

The Dead Church

3 “And to the angel of the church in Sardis
write,
‘These things says He who has the seven
Spirits of God and the seven stars: “I know
your works, that you have a name that you are
alive, but you are dead. 2Be watchful, and
strengthen the things which remain, that are
ready to die, for I have not found your works
perfect before God.[a] 3Remember therefore
how you have received and heard; hold fast
and repent. Therefore if you will not watch, I
will come upon you as a thief, and you will
not know what hour I will come upon you.
4You[a] have a few names even in Sardis who
have not defiled their garments; and they shall
walk with Me in white, for they are worthy.
5He who overcomes shall be clothed in white
garments, and I will not blot out his name
from the Book of Life; but I will confess his
name before My Father and before His angels.
6“He who has an ear, let him hear what the
Spirit says to the churches.” ’

The Faithful Church

7“And to the angel of the church in Philadelphia write,
‘These things says He who is holy, He who
is true, *“He who has the key of David, He who*
opens and no one shuts, and shuts and no one
opens”:[a] 8“I know your works. See, I have set
before you an open door, and no one can shut
it;[a] for you have a little strength, have kept My
word, and have not denied My name. 9Indeed
I will make *those* of the synagogue of Satan,
who say they are Jews and are not, but lie—
indeed I will make them come and worship
before your feet, and to know that I have
loved you. 10Because you have kept My command to persevere, I also will keep you from
the hour of trial which shall come upon the
whole world, to test those who dwell on the
earth. 11Behold,[a] I am coming quickly! Hold
fast what you have, that no one may take your
crown. 12He who overcomes, I will make him
a pillar in the temple of My God, and he shall
go out no more. I will write on him the name
of My God and the name of the city of My
God, the New Jerusalem, which comes down
out of heaven from My God. And *I will write*
on him My new name.
13“He who has an ear, let him hear what the
Spirit says to the churches.” ’

2:19 [a]NU-Text and M-Text read *faith, service.* **2:20** [a]NU-Text and M-Text read *I have against you that you tolerate.* [b]M-Text reads *your wife Jezebel.* [c]NU-Text and M-Text read *and teaches and seduces.* **2:21** [a]NU-Text and M-Text read *time to repent, and she does not want to repent of her sexual immorality.* **2:22** [a]NU-Text and M-Text read *her.* **2:24** [a]NU-Text and M-Text omit *and.* [b]NU-Text and M-Text omit *will.* **2:27** [a]Psalm 2:9 **3:2** [a]NU-Text and M-Text read *My God.* **3:4** [a]NU-Text and M-Text read *Nevertheless you have a few names in Sardis.* **3:7** [a]Isaiah 22:22 **3:8** [a]NU-Text and M-Text read *which no one can shut.* **3:11** [a]NU-Text and M-Text omit *Behold.*

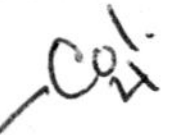

The Lukewarm Church

[14]"And to the angel of the church of the Laodiceans[a] write,

'These things says the Amen, the Faithful and True Witness, the Beginning of the creation of God: [15]"I know your works, that you are neither cold nor hot. I could wish you were cold or hot. [16]So then, because you are lukewarm, and neither cold nor hot,[a] I will vomit you out of My mouth. [17]Because you say, 'I am rich, have become wealthy, and have need of nothing'—and do not know that you are wretched, miserable, poor, blind, and naked—[18]I counsel you to buy from Me gold refined in the fire, that you may be rich; and white garments, that you may be clothed, *that* the shame of your nakedness may not be revealed; and anoint your eyes with eye salve, that you may see. [19]As many as I love, I rebuke and chasten. Therefore be zealous and repent. [20]Behold, I stand at the door and knock. If anyone hears My voice and opens the door, I will come in to him and dine with him, and he with Me. [21]To him who overcomes I will grant to sit with Me on My throne, as I also overcame and sat down with My Father on His throne.

> "Behold, I stand at the door and knock. If anyone hears My voice and opens the door, I will come in to him and dine with him, and he with Me."
>
> REVELATION 3:20

[22]"He who has an ear, let him hear what the Spirit says to the churches."' "

The Throne Room of Heaven

4 After these things I looked, and behold, a door *standing* open in heaven. And the first voice which I heard *was* like a trumpet speaking with me, saying, "Come up here, and I will show you things which must take place after this."

[2]Immediately I was in the Spirit; and behold, a throne set in heaven, and *One* sat on the throne. [3]And He who sat there was[a] like a jasper and a sardius stone in appearance; and *there was* a rainbow around the throne, in appearance like an emerald. [4]Around the throne *were* twenty-four thrones, and on the thrones I saw twenty-four elders sitting, clothed in white robes; and they had crowns[a] of gold on their heads. [5]And from the throne proceeded lightnings, thunderings, and voices.[a] Seven lamps of fire *were* burning before the throne, which are the[b] seven Spirits of God.

[6]Before the throne *there was*[a] a sea of glass, like crystal. And in the midst of the throne, and around the throne, *were* four living creatures full of eyes in front and in back. [7]The first living creature *was* like a lion, the second living creature like a calf, the third living creature had a face like a man, and the fourth living creature *was* like a flying eagle. [8]*The* four living creatures, each having six wings, were full of eyes around and within. And they do not rest day or night, saying:

"Holy, holy, holy,[a]
Lord God Almighty,
Who was and is and is to come!"

[9]Whenever the living creatures give glory and honor and thanks to Him who sits on the throne, who lives forever and ever, [10]the twenty-four elders fall down before Him who sits on the throne and worship Him who lives forever and ever, and cast their crowns before the throne, saying:

11 "You are worthy, O Lord,[a]
To receive glory and honor and power;
For You created all things,
And by Your will they exist[b] and were
created."

The Lamb Takes the Scroll

5 And I saw in the right *hand* of Him who sat on the throne a scroll written inside and on the back, sealed with seven seals. [2]Then I saw a strong angel proclaiming with a loud voice, "Who is worthy to open the scroll and to loose its seals?" [3]And no one in heaven or on the earth or under the earth was able to open the scroll, or to look at it.

3:14 [a]NU-Text and M-Text read *in Laodicea.* **3:16** [a]NU-Text and M-Text read *hot nor cold.* **4:3** [a]M-Text omits *And He who sat there was* (which makes the description in verse 3 modify the throne rather than God). **4:4** [a]NU-Text and M-Text read *robes, with crowns.* **4:5** [a]NU-Text and M-Text read *voices, and thunderings.* [b]M-Text omits *the.* **4:6** [a]NU-Text and M-Text add *something like.* **4:8** [a]M-Text has *holy* nine times. **4:11** [a]NU-Text and M-Text read *our Lord and God.* [b]NU-Text and M-Text read *existed.*

4So I wept much, because no one was found
worthy to open and read[a] the scroll, or to look
at it. 5But one of the elders said to me, "Do not
weep. Behold, the Lion of the tribe of Judah,
the Root of David, has prevailed to open the
scroll and to loose[a] its seven seals."

6And I looked, and behold,[a] in the midst of
the throne and of the four living creatures,
and in the midst of the elders, stood a Lamb as
though it had been slain, having seven horns
and seven eyes, which are the seven Spirits of
God sent out into all the earth. 7Then He came
and took the scroll out of the right hand of
Him who sat on the throne.

Worthy Is the Lamb

8Now when He had taken the scroll, the
four living creatures and the twenty-four elders fell down before the Lamb, each having a
harp, and golden bowls full of incense, which
are the prayers of the saints. 9And they sang a
new song, saying:

"You are worthy to take the scroll,
And to open its seals;
For You were slain,
And have redeemed us to God by Your
blood
Out of every tribe and tongue and
people and nation,
10 And have made us[a] kings[b] and priests to
our God;
And we[c] shall reign on the earth."

5:4 [a]NU-Text and M-Text omit *and read.* **5:5** [a]NU-Text and M-Text omit *to loose.* **5:6** [a]NU-Text and M-Text read *I saw in the midst . . . a Lamb standing.* **5:10** [a]NU-Text and M-Text read *them.* [b]NU-Text reads *a kingdom.* [c]NU-Text and M-Text read *they.*

PERSONALITY PROFILE

Eternal Life

JOHN'S GLIMPSES OF HEAVEN

(REVELATION 4)

Heaven: This word gets tossed around and used in many ways: "This vacation spot is heavenly." When they feel particularly healthy and happy, some might say, "I'm in heaven." In any case, the word always has a positive connotation. When something is "heavenly," it's a good recommendation.

If the apostle John were among us today, he would be astounded at our shortsighted analogies, however. He *saw* heaven, and was sent by God to write about it. His power-packed book of Revelation reveals to believers a glimpse of their future home.

The Book of Revelation, for all the writing and arguing that has taken place about the unfolding of its events, does give us some certainties about heaven. In the end, God's people will be there. John described a peaceful place: "God will wipe away every tear from their eyes; there shall be no more death, nor sorrow, nor crying. There shall be no more pain" (Rev. 21:4). It will be a beautiful place: John describes precious stones, gates of pearl, and streets of gold (Rev. 21:10–21). It will be a glorious place: "The city had no need of the sun or of the moon to shine in it, for the glory of God illuminated it. The Lamb is its light" (Rev. 21:23). Heaven is an eternal place, where God's people "shall reign forever and ever" (Rev. 22:5).

This world is not our final home; in reality, we are pilgrims on a journey. People give their lives to Christ because of the promise of His presence and peace on this earth *and* the promise of eternal life in heaven with Him. As they learn that they can trust God's promises, they know that the reality of heaven awaits them.

When we read the awesome account of John's glimpses of heaven, our finite minds can barely grasp the concept. But we *can* grasp the concept of a promise kept. God has promised eternal life and a home in heaven with Him. What we envision now will turn out to be a pale shadow of the reality. What a glorious gift God has prepared for all who believe!

To Learn More: Turn to the article about eternal life on pages 1718, 1719. See also the key passage note at 1 Thessalonians 4:13–18 on page 1584.

[11]Then I looked, and I heard the voice of many angels around the throne, the living creatures, and the elders; and the number of them was ten thousand times ten thousand, and thousands of thousands, [12]saying with a loud voice:

"Worthy is the Lamb who was slain
To receive power and riches and
wisdom,
And strength and honor and glory and
blessing!"

[13]And every creature which is in heaven and on the earth and under the earth and such as are in the sea, and all that are in them, I heard saying:

"Blessing and honor and glory and power
Be to Him who sits on the throne,
And to the Lamb, forever and ever!"[a]

[14]Then the four living creatures said, "Amen!" And the twenty-four[a] elders fell down and worshiped Him who lives forever and ever.[b]

First Seal: The Conqueror

6 Now I saw when the Lamb opened one of the seals;[a] and I heard one of the four living creatures saying with a voice like thunder, "Come and see." [2]And I looked, and behold, a white horse. He who sat on it had a bow; and a crown was given to him, and he went out conquering and to conquer.

Second Seal: Conflict on Earth

[3]When He opened the second seal, I heard the second living creature saying, "Come and see."[a] [4]Another horse, fiery red, went out. And it was granted to the one who sat on it to take peace from the earth, and that *people* should kill one another; and there was given to him a great sword.

Third Seal: Scarcity on Earth

[5]When He opened the third seal, I heard the third living creature say, "Come and see." So I looked, and behold, a black horse, and he who sat on it had a pair of scales in his hand. [6]And I heard a voice in the midst of the four living creatures saying, "A quart[a] of wheat for a denarius,[b] and three quarts of barley for a denarius; and do not harm the oil and the wine."

Fourth Seal: Widespread Death on Earth

[7]When He opened the fourth seal, I heard the voice of the fourth living creature saying, "Come and see." [8]So I looked, and behold, a pale horse. And the name of him who sat on it was Death, and Hades followed with him. And power was given to them over a fourth of the earth, to kill with sword, with hunger, with death, and by the beasts of the earth.

Fifth Seal: The Cry of the Martyrs

[9]When He opened the fifth seal, I saw under the altar the souls of those who had been slain for the word of God and for the testimony which they held. [10]And they cried with a loud voice, saying, "How long, O Lord, holy and true, until You judge and avenge our blood on

5:13 [a]M-Text adds *Amen.* **5:14** [a]NU-Text and M-Text omit *twenty-four.* [b]NU-Text and M-Text omit *Him who lives forever and ever.* **6:1** [a]NU-Text and M-Text read *seven seals.* **6:3** [a]NU-Text and M-Text omit *and see.* **6:6** [a]Greek *choinix;* that is, approximately one quart [b]This was approximately one day's wage for a worker.

SOUL NOTE

Worthy Is the Lamb *(5:5, 6)* In his vision of God's throne room, the apostle John witnessed a wounded Lamb, the only One found worthy to open the seven seals of the scroll. The wounded Lamb is Jesus Christ, who sacrificed Himself on the Cross for our sins. His blood has ransomed us from slavery to sin so that we can become His holy people (5:9). Only Christ, who is also the conquering Lion of Judah (5:5), can preside over the unfolding of human history. Without Him, our lives would amount to utter futility. But with Him, our lives are being woven into the beautiful tapestry of God's salvation history. No wonder He deserves all glory, honor, and power (5:13).
Topic: Knowing Jesus

those who dwell on the earth?" 11Then a white
robe was given to each of them; and it was
said to them that they should rest a little while
longer, until both *the number of* their fellow
servants and their brethren, who would be
killed as they *were,* was completed.

SIXTH SEAL: COSMIC DISTURBANCES

12I looked when He opened the sixth seal,
and behold,[a] there was a great earthquake;
and the sun became black as sackcloth of hair,
and the moon[b] became like blood. 13And the
stars of heaven fell to the earth, as a fig tree
drops its late figs when it is shaken by a
mighty wind. 14Then the sky receded as a
scroll when it is rolled up, and every mountain and island was moved out of its place.
15And the kings of the earth, the great men,
the rich men, the commanders,[a] the mighty
men, every slave and every free man, hid
themselves in the caves and in the rocks of the
mountains, 16and said to the mountains and
rocks, "Fall on us and hide us from the face of
Him who sits on the
throne and from the
wrath of the Lamb!
17For the great day of
His wrath has come,
and who is able to
stand?"

> "Salvation belongs to our God who sits on the throne, and to the Lamb!"
> REVELATION 7:10

THE SEALED OF ISRAEL

7 After these things I saw four angels standing at the four corners of the earth, holding the four winds of the earth, that the wind
should not blow on the earth, on the sea, or
on any tree. 2Then I saw another angel ascending from the east, having the seal of the
living God. And he cried with a loud voice to
the four angels to whom it was granted to
harm the earth and the sea, 3saying, "Do not
harm the earth, the sea, or the trees till we
have sealed the servants of our God on their
foreheads." 4And I heard the number of those
who were sealed. One hundred *and* forty-four
thousand of all the tribes of the children of Israel *were* sealed:

5 of the tribe of Judah twelve thousand
were sealed;[a]
of the tribe of Reuben twelve thousand
were sealed;
of the tribe of Gad twelve thousand *were*
sealed;
6 of the tribe of Asher twelve thousand
were sealed;
of the tribe of Naphtali twelve thousand
were sealed;
of the tribe of Manasseh twelve
thousand *were* sealed;
7 of the tribe of Simeon twelve thousand
were sealed;
of the tribe of Levi twelve thousand *were*
sealed;
of the tribe of Issachar twelve thousand
were sealed;
8 of the tribe of Zebulun twelve thousand
were sealed;
of the tribe of Joseph twelve thousand
were sealed;
of the tribe of Benjamin twelve thousand
were sealed.

A MULTITUDE FROM THE GREAT TRIBULATION

9After these things I looked, and behold, a
great multitude which no one could number,
of all nations, tribes, peoples, and tongues,
standing before the
throne and before the
Lamb, clothed with
white robes, with palm
branches in their hands,
10and crying out with
a loud voice, saying,
"Salvation *belongs* to our God who sits on the
throne, and to the Lamb!" 11All the angels
stood around the throne and the elders and
the four living creatures, and fell on their
faces before the throne and worshiped God,
12saying:

"Amen! Blessing and glory and wisdom,
Thanksgiving and honor and power and
might,
Be to our God forever and ever.
Amen."

13Then one of the elders answered, saying
to me, "Who are these arrayed in white robes,
and where did they come from?"
14And I said to him, "Sir,[a] you know."

6:12 [a]NU-Text and M-Text omit *behold.* [b]NU-Text and M-Text read *the whole moon.* **6:15** [a]NU-Text and M-Text read *the commanders, the rich men.* **7:5** [a]In NU-Text and M-Text *were sealed* is stated only in verses 5a and 8c; the words are understood in the remainder of the passage. **7:14** [a]NU-Text and M-Text read *My lord.*

So he said to me, "These are the ones who
come out of the great tribulation, and washed
their robes and made them white in the blood
of the Lamb. 15Therefore they are before the
throne of God, and serve Him day and night in
His temple. And He who sits on the throne
will dwell among them. 16They shall neither
hunger anymore nor thirst anymore; the sun
shall not strike them, nor any heat; 17for the
Lamb who is in the midst of the throne will
shepherd them and lead them to living fountains of waters.[a] And God will wipe away
every tear from their eyes."

SEVENTH SEAL: PRELUDE TO THE SEVEN TRUMPETS

8 When He opened the seventh seal, there
was silence in heaven for about half an
hour. 2And I saw the seven angels who stand
before God, and to them were given seven
trumpets. 3Then another angel, having a gold-
en censer, came and stood at the altar. He was
given much incense, that he should offer *it*
with the prayers of all the saints upon the
golden altar which was before the throne.
4And the smoke of the incense, with the
prayers of the saints, ascended before God
from the angel's hand. 5Then the angel took
the censer, filled it with fire from the altar, and
threw *it* to the earth. And there were noises,
thunderings, lightnings, and an earthquake.

6So the seven angels who had the seven
trumpets prepared themselves to sound.

FIRST TRUMPET: VEGETATION STRUCK

7The first angel sounded: And hail and fire
followed, mingled with blood, and they were
thrown to the earth.[a] And a third of the trees
were burned up, and all green grass was
burned up.

SECOND TRUMPET: THE SEAS STRUCK

8Then the second angel sounded: And *something* like a great mountain burning with fire
was thrown into the sea, and a third of the sea
became blood. 9And a third of the living creatures in the sea died, and a third of the ships
were destroyed.

THIRD TRUMPET: THE WATERS STRUCK

10Then the third angel sounded: And a great
star fell from heaven, burning like a torch, and
it fell on a third of the rivers and on the
springs of water. 11The name of the star is
Wormwood. A third of the waters became
wormwood, and many men died from the water, because it was made bitter.

FOURTH TRUMPET: THE HEAVENS STRUCK

12Then the fourth angel sounded: And a
third of the sun was struck, a third of the
moon, and a third of the stars, so that a third
of them were darkened. A third of the day did
not shine, and likewise the night.

13And I looked, and I heard an angel[a] flying
through the midst of heaven, saying with a
loud voice, "Woe, woe, woe to the inhabitants
of the earth, because of the remaining blasts
of the trumpet of the three angels who are
about to sound!"

FIFTH TRUMPET: THE LOCUSTS FROM THE BOTTOMLESS PIT

9 Then the fifth angel sounded: And I saw a
star fallen from heaven to the earth. To
him was given the key to the bottomless pit.
2And he opened the bottomless pit, and
smoke arose out of the pit like the smoke of a
great furnace. So the sun and the air were
darkened because of the smoke of the pit.
3Then out of the smoke locusts came upon the
earth. And to them was given power, as the
scorpions of the earth have power. 4They were
commanded not to harm the grass of the
earth, or any green thing, or any tree, but only
those men who do not have the seal of God on
their foreheads. 5And they were not given *authority* to kill them, but to torment them *for*
five months. Their torment *was* like the torment of a scorpion when it strikes a man. 6In
those days men will seek death and will not
find it; they will desire to die, and death will
flee from them.

7The shape of the locusts was like horses
prepared for battle. On their heads were
crowns of something like gold, and their faces
were like the faces of men. 8They had hair like
women's hair, and their teeth were like lions'
teeth. 9And they had breastplates like breastplates of iron, and the sound of their wings
was like the sound of chariots with many
horses running into battle. 10They had tails
like scorpions, and there were stings in their

7:17 [a]NU-Text and M-Text read *to fountains of the waters of life.* **8:7** [a]NU-Text and M-Text add *and a third of the earth was burned up.* **8:13** [a]NU-Text and M-Text read *eagle.*

tails. Their power *was* to hurt men five months. 11And they had as king over them the angel of the bottomless pit, whose name in Hebrew *is* Abaddon, but in Greek he has the name Apollyon.

12One woe is past. Behold, still two more woes are coming after these things.

Sixth Trumpet: The Angels from the Euphrates

13Then the sixth angel sounded: And I heard a voice from the four horns of the golden altar which is before God, 14saying to the sixth angel who had the trumpet, "Release the four angels who are bound at the great river Euphrates." 15So the four angels, who had been prepared for the hour and day and month and year, were released to kill a third of mankind. 16Now the number of the army of the horsemen *was* two hundred million; I heard the number of them. 17And thus I saw the horses in the vision: those who sat on them had breastplates of fiery red, hyacinth blue, and sulfur yellow; and the heads of the horses *were* like the heads of lions; and out of their mouths came fire, smoke, and brimstone. 18By these three *plagues* a third of mankind was killed—by the fire and the smoke and the brimstone which came out of their mouths. 19For their power[a] is in their mouth and in their tails; for their tails *are* like serpents, having heads; and with them they do harm.

20But the rest of mankind, who were not killed by these plagues, did not repent of the works of their hands, that they should not worship demons, and idols of gold, silver, brass, stone, and wood, which can neither see nor hear nor walk. 21And they did not repent of their murders or their sorceries[a] or their sexual immorality or their thefts.

The Mighty Angel with the Little Book

10 I saw still another mighty angel coming down from heaven, clothed with a cloud. And a rainbow *was* on his head, his face *was* like the sun, and his feet like pillars of fire. 2He had a little book open in his hand. And he set his right foot on the sea and *his* left *foot* on the land, 3and cried with a loud voice, as *when* a lion roars. When he cried out, seven thunders uttered their voices. 4Now when the seven thunders uttered their voices,[a] I was about to write; but I heard a voice from heaven saying to me,[b] "Seal up the things which the seven thunders uttered, and do not write them."

5The angel whom I saw standing on the sea and on the land raised up his hand[a] to heaven 6and swore by Him who lives forever and ever, who created heaven and the things that are in it, the earth and the things that are in it, and the sea and the things that are in it, that there should be delay no longer, 7but in the days of the sounding of the seventh angel, when he is about to sound, the mystery of God would be finished, as He declared to His servants the prophets.

John Eats the Little Book

8Then the voice which I heard from heaven spoke to me again and said, "Go, take the little book which is open in the hand of the angel who stands on the sea and on the earth."

9So I went to the angel and said to him, "Give me the little book."

And he said to me, "Take and eat it; and it will make your stomach bitter, but it will be as sweet as honey in your mouth."

10Then I took the little book out of the angel's hand and ate it, and it was as sweet as honey in my mouth. But when I had eaten it, my stomach became bitter. 11And he[a] said to me, "You must prophesy again about many peoples, nations, tongues, and kings."

The Two Witnesses

11 Then I was given a reed like a measuring rod. And the angel stood,[a] saying, "Rise and measure the temple of God, the altar, and those who worship there. 2But leave out the court which is outside the temple, and do not measure it, for it has been given to the Gentiles. And they will tread the holy city underfoot *for* forty-two months. 3And I will give *power* to my two witnesses, and they will prophesy one thousand two hundred and sixty days, clothed in sackcloth."

4These are the two olive trees and the two lampstands standing before the God[a] of the earth. 5And if anyone wants to harm them, fire

9:19 [a]NU-Text and M-Text read *the power of the horses.* **9:21** [a]NU-Text and M-Text read *drugs.* **10:4** [a]NU-Text and M-Text read *sounded.* [b]NU-Text and M-Text omit *to me.* **10:5** [a]NU-Text and M-Text read *right hand.* **10:11** [a]NU-Text and M-Text read *they.* **11:1** [a]NU-Text and M-Text omit *And the angel stood.* **11:4** [a]NU-Text and M-Text read *Lord.*

proceeds from their mouth and devours their enemies. And if anyone wants to harm them, he must be killed in this manner. 6These have power to shut heaven, so that no rain falls in the days of their prophecy; and they have power over waters to turn them to blood, and to strike the earth with all plagues, as often as they desire.

THE WITNESSES KILLED

7When they finish their testimony, the beast that ascends out of the bottomless pit will make war against them, overcome them, and kill them. 8And their dead bodies *will lie* in the street of the great city which spiritually is called Sodom and Egypt, where also our[a] Lord was crucified. 9Then *those* from the peoples, tribes, tongues, and nations will see their dead bodies three-and-a-half days, and not allow[a] their dead bodies to be put into graves. 10And those who dwell on the earth will rejoice over them, make merry, and send gifts to one another, because these two prophets tormented those who dwell on the earth.

THE WITNESSES RESURRECTED

11Now after the three-and-a-half days the breath of life from God entered them, and they stood on their feet, and great fear fell on those who saw them. 12And they[a] heard a loud voice from heaven saying to them, "Come up here." And they ascended to heaven in a cloud, and their enemies saw them. 13In the same hour there was a great earthquake, and a tenth of the city fell. In the earthquake seven thousand people were killed, and the rest were afraid and gave glory to the God of heaven.

14The second woe is past. Behold, the third woe is coming quickly.

> "The kingdoms of this world have become the kingdoms of our Lord and of His Christ, and He shall reign forever and ever!"
> REVELATION 11:15

SEVENTH TRUMPET: THE KINGDOM PROCLAIMED

15Then the seventh angel sounded: And there were loud voices in heaven, saying, "The kingdoms[a] of this world have become *the kingdoms* of our Lord and of His Christ, and He shall reign forever and ever!" 16And the twenty-four elders who sat before God on their thrones fell on their faces and worshiped God, 17saying:

"We give You thanks, O Lord God
Almighty,
The One who is and who was and who
is to come,[a]
Because You have taken Your great
power and reigned.
18 The nations were angry, and Your wrath
has come,
And the time of the dead, that they
should be judged,
And that You should reward Your
servants the prophets and the saints,
And those who fear Your name, small
and great,
And should destroy those who destroy
the earth."

19Then the temple of God was opened in heaven, and the ark of His covenant[a] was seen in His temple. And there were lightnings, noises, thunderings, an earthquake, and great hail.

THE WOMAN, THE CHILD, AND THE DRAGON

12 Now a great sign appeared in heaven: a woman clothed with the sun, with the moon under her feet, and on her head a garland of twelve stars. 2Then being with child, she cried out in labor and in pain to give birth.

3And another sign appeared in heaven: behold, a great, fiery red dragon having seven heads and ten horns, and seven diadems on his heads. 4His tail drew a third of the stars of heaven and threw them to the earth. And the dragon stood before the woman who was ready to give birth, to devour her Child as soon as it was born. 5She bore a male Child who was to rule all nations with a rod of iron. And her Child was caught up to God and His throne. 6Then the woman fled into the wilderness, where she has a place prepared by God, that they should feed her there one thousand two hundred and sixty days.

11:8 [a]NU-Text and M-Text read *their.* **11:9** [a]NU-Text and M-Text read *nations see . . . and will not allow.* **11:12** [a]M-Text reads *I.* **11:15** [a]NU-Text and M-Text read *kingdom . . . has become.* **11:17** [a]NU-Text and M-Text omit *and who is to come.* **11:19** [a]M-Text reads *the covenant of the Lord.*

SATAN THROWN OUT OF HEAVEN

[7]And war broke out in heaven: Michael and
his angels fought with the dragon; and the
dragon and his angels fought, [8]but they did
not prevail, nor was a place found for them[a] in
heaven any longer. [9]So the great dragon was
cast out, that serpent of old, called the Devil
and Satan, who deceives the whole world; he
was cast to the earth, and his angels were cast
out with him.

[10]Then I heard a loud voice saying in heav-
en, "Now salvation, and strength, and the
kingdom of our God, and the power of His
Christ have come, for the accuser of our brethren, who accused them before our God day
and night, has been cast down. [11]And they
overcame him by the blood of the Lamb and
by the word of their testimony, and they did
not love their lives to the death. [12]Therefore
rejoice, O heavens, and you who dwell in
them! Woe to the inhabitants of the earth and
the sea! For the devil has come down to you,
having great wrath, because he knows that he
has a short time."

THE WOMAN PERSECUTED

[13]Now when the dragon saw that he had
been cast to the earth, he persecuted the
woman who gave birth to the male *Child.*
[14]But the woman was given two wings of a
great eagle, that she might fly into the wilderness to her place, where she is nourished for a
time and times and half a time, from the presence of the serpent. [15]So the serpent spewed
water out of his mouth like a flood after the
woman, that he might cause her to be carried

12:8 [a]M-Text reads *him.*

PERSONALITY PROFILE

Spiritual Warfare

MICHAEL THE ARCHANGEL

(REVELATION 12:7–12)

The Book of Revelation not only offers a long view of God's plan in history; it also offers a deeper of view of reality. For those who are tempted to think that reality ends with our senses, Revelation reminds us that the spiritual dimension dwarfs our own. The conflict rages, and the battles sometimes occur here on earth, in human lives. Parts of God's amazing creation have rebelled, and the battle lines can even divide a human heart.

Revelation 12 describes the two armies in this battle: On God's side are all of His angels (such as Michael, mentioned here), and all of God's people; on the other side are Satan, his demons, and all who do not believe in Christ as Savior. As violent as the spiritual and physical battles may be, the outcome of the war has already been decided. The victory was assured in the sacrificial death of the Son of God on the cross of Calvary.

This passage also reminds us that in spiritual warfare, as in physical warfare, even the winning side often suffers casualties. History is filled with examples of Christians who have laid down their lives or been martyred for the cause of Christ. From the perspective of eternity and heaven, they are victors. As John described them, "They overcame him by the blood of the Lamb and by the word of their testimony, and they did not love their lives to the death" (Rev. 12:11). These are believers who, in the very act of dying, have won the battle. They understand that believers who have a firm hold on the reality of eternal life will not hold on to physical life at all costs.

Meanwhile, as long as this life lasts, Christians are involved as active participants in spiritual warfare. We are called to be faithful, and we are instructed to live the life of one who serves a Captain, the Lord Jesus Christ. We are invited to place our lives at His disposal, available to be used anytime, anywhere, to encourage each other along the way, and to pray always for our fellow soldiers in Christ.

To Learn More: Turn to the article about spiritual warfare on pages 1560, 1561. See also the key passage note at Ephesians 6:10–20 on page 1558.

away by the flood. [16]But the earth helped the woman, and the earth opened its mouth and swallowed up the flood which the dragon had spewed out of his mouth. [17]And the dragon was enraged with the woman, and he went to make war with the rest of her offspring, who keep the commandments of God and have the testimony of Jesus Christ.[a]

The Beast from the Sea

13 Then I[a] stood on the sand of the sea. And I saw a beast rising up out of the sea, having seven heads and ten horns,[b] and on his horns ten crowns, and on his heads a blasphemous name. [2]Now the beast which I saw was like a leopard, his feet were like *the feet of* a bear, and his mouth like the mouth of a lion. The dragon gave him his power, his throne, and great authority. [3]And *I saw* one of his heads as if it had been mortally wounded, and his deadly wound was healed. And all the world marveled and followed the beast. [4]So they worshiped the dragon who gave authority to the beast; and they worshiped the beast, saying, "Who *is* like the beast? Who is able to make war with him?"

[5]And he was given a mouth speaking great things and blasphemies, and he was given authority to continue[a] for forty-two months. [6]Then he opened his mouth in blasphemy against God, to blaspheme His name, His tabernacle, and those who dwell in heaven. [7]It was granted to him to make war with the saints and to overcome them. And authority was given him over every tribe,[a] tongue, and nation. [8]All who dwell on the earth will worship him, whose names have not been written in the Book of Life of the Lamb slain from the foundation of the world.

[9]If anyone has an ear, let him hear. [10]He who leads into captivity shall go into captivity; he who kills with the sword must be killed with the sword. Here is the patience and the faith of the saints.

The Beast from the Earth

[11]Then I saw another beast coming up out of the earth, and he had two horns like a lamb and spoke like a dragon. [12]And he exercises all the authority of the first beast in his presence, and causes the earth and those who dwell in it to worship the first beast, whose deadly wound was healed. [13]He performs great signs, so that he even makes fire come down from heaven on the earth in the sight of men. [14]And he deceives those[a] who dwell on the earth by those signs which he was granted to do in the sight of the beast, telling those who dwell on the earth to make an image to the beast who was wounded by the sword and lived. [15]He was granted *power* to give breath to the image of the beast, that the image of the beast should both speak and cause as many as would not worship the image of the beast to be killed. [16]He causes all, both small and great, rich and poor, free and slave, to receive a mark on their right hand or on their foreheads, [17]and that no one may buy or sell except one who has the mark or[a] the name of the beast, or the number of his name.

[18]Here is wisdom. Let him who has understanding calculate the number of the beast, for it is the number of a man: His number *is* 666.

The Lamb and the 144,000

14 Then I looked, and behold, a[a] Lamb standing on Mount Zion, and with Him one hundred *and* forty-four thousand, having[b] His Father's name written on their foreheads. [2]And I heard a voice from heaven, like the voice of many waters, and like the voice of loud thunder. And I heard the sound of harpists playing their harps. [3]They sang as it were a new song before the throne, before the four living creatures, and the elders; and no one could learn that song except the hundred *and* forty-four thousand who were redeemed from the earth. [4]These are the ones who were not defiled with women, for they are virgins. These are the ones who follow the Lamb wherever He goes. These were redeemed[a] from *among* men, *being* firstfruits to God and to the Lamb. [5]And in their mouth was found no deceit,[a] for they are without fault before the throne of God.[b]

12:17 [a]NU-Text and M-Text omit *Christ.* **13:1** [a]NU-Text reads *he.* [b]NU-Text and M-Text read *ten horns and seven heads.* **13:5** [a]M-Text reads *make war.* **13:7** [a]NU-Text and M-Text add *and people.* **13:14** [a]M-Text reads *my own people.* **13:17** [a]NU-Text and M-Text omit *or.* **14:1** [a]NU-Text and M-Text read *the.* [b]NU-Text and M-Text add *His name and.* **14:4** [a]M-Text adds *by Jesus.* **14:5** [a]NU-Text and M-Text read *falsehood.* [b]NU-Text and M-Text omit *before the throne of God.*

The Proclamations of Three Angels

6 Then I saw another angel flying in the midst of heaven, having the everlasting gospel to preach to those who dwell on the earth—to every nation, tribe, tongue, and people— 7 saying with a loud voice, "Fear God and give glory to Him, for the hour of His judgment has come; and worship Him who made heaven and earth, the sea and springs of water."

8 And another angel followed, saying, "Babylon[a] is fallen, is fallen, that great city, because she has made all nations drink of the wine of the wrath of her fornication."

9 Then a third angel followed them, saying with a loud voice, "If anyone worships the beast and his image, and receives *his* mark on his forehead or on his hand, 10 he himself shall also drink of the wine of the wrath of God, which is poured out full strength into the cup of His indignation. He shall be tormented with fire and brimstone in the presence of the holy angels and in the presence of the Lamb. 11 And the smoke of their torment ascends forever and ever; and they have no rest day or night, who worship the beast and his image, and whoever receives the mark of his name."

12 Here is the patience of the saints; here *are* those[a] who keep the commandments of God and the faith of Jesus.

13 Then I heard a voice from heaven saying to me,[a] "Write: 'Blessed *are* the dead who die in the Lord from now on.' "

"Yes," says the Spirit, "that they may rest from their labors, and their works follow them."

Reaping the Earth's Harvest

14 Then I looked, and behold, a white cloud, and on the cloud sat *One* like the Son of Man, having on His head a golden crown, and in His hand a sharp sickle. 15 And another angel came out of the temple, crying with a loud voice to Him who sat on the cloud, "Thrust in Your sickle and reap, for the time has come for You[a] to reap, for the harvest of the earth is ripe." 16 So He who sat on the cloud thrust in His sickle on the earth, and the earth was reaped.

Reaping the Grapes of Wrath

17 Then another angel came out of the temple which is in heaven, he also having a sharp sickle.

18 And another angel came out from the altar, who had power over fire, and he cried with a loud cry to him who had the sharp sickle, saying, "Thrust in your sharp sickle and gather the clusters of the vine of the earth, for her grapes are fully ripe." 19 So the angel thrust his sickle into the earth and gathered the vine of the earth, and threw *it* into the great winepress of the wrath of God. 20 And the winepress was trampled outside the city, and blood came out of the winepress, up to the horses' bridles, for one thousand six hundred furlongs.

Prelude to the Bowl Judgments

15 Then I saw another sign in heaven, great and marvelous: seven angels having the seven last plagues, for in them the wrath of God is complete.

2 And I saw *something* like a sea of glass mingled with fire, and those who have the victory over the beast, over his image and over his mark[a] *and* over the number of his name, standing on the sea of glass, having harps of

14:8 [a]NU-Text reads *Babylon the great is fallen, is fallen, which has made;* M-Text reads *Babylon the great is fallen. She has made.* **14:12** [a]NU-Text and M-Text omit *here are those.* **14:13** [a]NU-Text and M-Text omit *to me.* **14:15** [a]NU-Text and M-Text omit *for You.* **15:2** [a]NU-Text and M-Text omit *over his mark.*

SOUL NOTE

What Truly Matters *(14:13)* This chapter paints a picture of stark contrasts. On one side, there is a joyful choir of people accompanying the victorious Christ up Mount Zion. On the other side stand those who have followed the beast into immorality, worshiped his image, and accepted his mark on their foreheads. Two destinies are contrasted—eternal life with God or eternal life without God. At the end, no last-minute changes will be possible. Where will you be for eternity? With Jesus or without Him? **Topic: Death**

God. [3]They sing the song of Moses, the servant of God, and the song of the Lamb, saying:

"Great and marvelous *are* Your works,
Lord God Almighty!
Just and true *are*
Your ways,
O King of the
saints![a]
4 Who shall not fear
You, O Lord,
and glorify Your
name?
For *You* alone *are*
holy.
For all nations shall come and worship
before You,
For Your judgments have been
manifested."

"Great and marvelous are Your works, Lord God Almighty! Just and true are Your ways, O King of the saints!"
REVELATION 15:3

[5]After these things I looked, and behold,[a]
the temple of the tabernacle of the testimony
in heaven was opened. [6]And out of the temple
came the seven angels having the seven
plagues, clothed in pure bright linen, and having their chests girded with golden bands.
[7]Then one of the four living creatures gave to
the seven angels seven golden bowls full of
the wrath of God who lives forever and ever.
[8]The temple was filled with smoke from the
glory of God and from His power, and no one
was able to enter the temple till the seven
plagues of the seven angels were completed.

16 Then I heard a loud voice from the temple saying to the seven angels, "Go and pour out the bowls[a] of the wrath of God on the earth."

First Bowl: Loathsome Sores

[2]So the first went and poured out his bowl upon the earth, and a foul and loathsome sore came upon the men who had the mark of the beast and those who worshiped his image.

Second Bowl: The Sea Turns to Blood

[3]Then the second angel poured out his bowl on the sea, and it became blood as of a dead *man;* and every living creature in the sea died.

Third Bowl: The Waters Turn to Blood

[4]Then the third angel poured out his bowl
on the rivers and springs of water, and they
became blood. [5]And I heard the angel of the
waters saying:

"You are righteous, O Lord,[a]
The One who is and who was and who
is to be,[b]
Because You have judged these things.
6 For they have shed the blood of saints
and prophets,
And You have
given them
blood to drink.
For[a] it is their just
due."

[7]And I heard another
from[a] the altar saying,
"Even so, Lord God Al-
mighty, true and righteous *are* Your judgments."

Fourth Bowl: Men Are Scorched

[8]Then the fourth angel poured out his bowl
on the sun, and power was given to him to
scorch men with fire. [9]And men were
scorched with great heat, and they blasphemed the name of God who has power over
these plagues; and they did not repent and
give Him glory.

Fifth Bowl: Darkness and Pain

[10]Then the fifth angel poured out his bowl
on the throne of the beast, and his kingdom
became full of darkness; and they gnawed
their tongues because of the pain. [11]They blasphemed the God of heaven because of their
pains and their sores, and did not repent of
their deeds.

Sixth Bowl: Euphrates Dried Up

[12]Then the sixth angel poured out his bowl
on the great river Euphrates, and its water was
dried up, so that the way of the kings from the
east might be prepared. [13]And I saw three unclean spirits like frogs *coming* out of the
mouth of the dragon, out of the mouth of
the beast, and out of the mouth of the false
prophet. [14]For they are spirits of demons,
performing signs, *which* go out to the kings
of the earth and[a] of the whole world, to gather

15:3 [a]NU-Text and M-Text read *nations.*
15:5 [a]NU-Text and M-Text omit *behold.*
16:1 [a]NU-Text and M-Text read *seven bowls.*
16:5 [a]NU-Text and M-Text omit *O Lord.* [b]NU-Text and M-Text read *who was, the Holy One.*
16:6 [a]NU-Text and M-Text omit *For.* **16:7** [a]NU-Text and M-Text omit *another from.* **16:14** [a]NU-Text and M-Text omit *of the earth and.*

them to the battle of that great day of God Almighty.

15“Behold, I am coming as a thief. Blessed *is* he who watches, and keeps his garments, lest he walk naked and they see his shame.”

16And they gathered them together to the place called in Hebrew, Armageddon.[a]

Seventh Bowl: The Earth Utterly Shaken

17Then the seventh angel poured out his bowl into the air, and a loud voice came out of the temple of heaven, from the throne, saying, “It is done!” 18And there were noises and thunderings and lightnings; and there was a great earthquake, such a mighty and great earthquake as had not occurred since men were on the earth. 19Now the great city was divided into three parts, and the cities of the nations fell. And great Babylon was remembered before God, to give her the cup of the wine of the fierceness of His wrath. 20Then every island fled away, and the mountains were not found. 21And great hail from heaven fell upon men, *each hailstone* about the weight of a talent. Men blasphemed God because of the plague of the hail, since that plague was exceedingly great.

The Scarlet Woman and the Scarlet Beast

17 Then one of the seven angels who had the seven bowls came and talked with me, saying to me,[a] “Come, I will show you the judgment of the great harlot who sits on many waters, 2with whom the kings of the earth committed fornication, and the inhabitants of the earth were made drunk with the wine of her fornication.”

3So he carried me away in the Spirit into the wilderness. And I saw a woman sitting on a scarlet beast *which was* full of names of blasphemy, having seven heads and ten horns. 4The woman was arrayed in purple and scarlet, and adorned with gold and precious stones and pearls, having in her hand a golden cup full of abominations and the filthiness of her fornication.[a] 5And on her forehead a name *was* written:

MYSTERY,
BABYLON THE GREAT,
THE MOTHER OF HARLOTS
AND OF THE
ABOMINATIONS OF THE EARTH.

6I saw the woman, drunk with the blood of the saints and with the blood of the martyrs of Jesus. And when I saw her, I marveled with great amazement.

The Meaning of the Woman and the Beast

7But the angel said to me, “Why did you marvel? I will tell you the mystery of the woman and of the beast that carries her, which has the seven heads and the ten horns. 8The beast that you saw was, and is not, and will ascend out of the bottomless pit and go to perdition. And those who dwell on the earth will marvel, whose names are not written in the Book of Life from the foundation of the world, when they see the beast that was, and is not, and yet is.[a]

9“Here *is* the mind which has wisdom: The seven heads are seven mountains on which the woman sits. 10There are also seven kings. Five have fallen, one is, *and* the other has not yet come. And when he comes, he must continue a short time. 11The beast that was, and is not, is himself also the eighth, and is of the seven, and is going to perdition.

12“The ten horns which you saw are ten kings who have received no kingdom as yet, but they receive authority for one hour as kings with the beast. 13These are of one mind, and they will give their power and authority to the beast. 14These will make war with the Lamb, and the Lamb will overcome them, for He is Lord of lords and King of kings; and those *who are* with Him *are* called, chosen, and faithful.”

15Then he said to me, “The waters which you saw, where the harlot sits, are peoples, multitudes, nations, and tongues. 16And the ten horns which you saw on[a] the beast, these will hate the harlot, make her desolate and naked, eat her flesh and burn her with fire. 17For God has put it into their hearts to fulfill His purpose, to be of one mind, and to give their kingdom to the beast, until the words of God are fulfilled. 18And the woman whom you saw is that great city which reigns over the kings of the earth.”

16:16 [a]M-Text reads *Megiddo.* **17:1** [a]NU-Text and M-Text omit *to me.* **17:4** [a]M-Text reads *the filthiness of the fornication of the earth.*
17:8 [a]NU-Text and M-Text read *and shall be present.* **17:16** [a]NU-Text and M-Text read *saw, and the beast.*

THE FALL OF BABYLON THE GREAT

18 After these things I saw another angel coming down from heaven, having great authority, and the earth was illuminated with his glory. 2And he cried mightily[a] with a loud voice, saying, "Babylon the great is fallen, is fallen, and has become a dwelling place of demons, a prison for every foul spirit, and a cage for every unclean and hated bird! 3For all the nations have drunk of the wine of the wrath of her fornication, the kings of the earth have committed fornication with her, and the merchants of the earth have become rich through the abundance of her luxury."

4And I heard another voice from heaven saying, "Come out of her, my people, lest you share in her sins, and lest you receive of her plagues. 5For her sins have reached[a] to heaven, and God has remembered her iniquities. 6Render to her just as she rendered to you,[a] and repay her double according to her works; in the cup which she has mixed, mix double for her. 7In the measure that she glorified herself and lived luxuriously, in the same measure give her torment and sorrow; for she says in her heart, 'I sit *as* queen, and am no widow, and will not see sorrow.' 8Therefore her plagues will come in one day—death and mourning and famine. And she will be utterly burned with fire, for strong *is* the Lord God who judges[a] her.

THE WORLD MOURNS BABYLON'S FALL

9"The kings of the earth who committed fornication and lived luxuriously with her will weep and lament for her, when they see the smoke of her burning, 10standing at a distance for fear of her torment, saying, 'Alas, alas, that great city Babylon, that mighty city! For in one hour your judgment has come.'

11"And the merchants of the earth will weep and mourn over her, for no one buys their merchandise anymore: 12merchandise of gold and silver, precious stones and pearls, fine linen and purple, silk and scarlet, every kind of citron wood, every kind of object of ivory, every kind of object of most precious wood, bronze, iron, and marble; 13and cinnamon and incense, fragrant oil and frankincense, wine and oil, fine flour and wheat, cattle and sheep, horses and chariots, and bodies and souls of men. 14The fruit that your soul longed for has gone from you, and all the things which are rich and splendid have gone from you,[a] and you shall find them no more at all. 15The merchants of these things, who became rich by her, will stand at a distance for fear of her torment, weeping and wailing, 16and saying, 'Alas, alas, that great city that was clothed in fine linen, purple, and scarlet, and adorned with gold and precious stones and pearls! 17For in one hour such great riches came to nothing.' Every shipmaster, all who travel by ship, sailors, and as many as trade on the sea, stood at a distance 18and cried out when they saw the smoke of her burning, saying, 'What *is* like this great city?'

19"They threw dust on their heads and cried out, weeping and wailing, and saying, 'Alas, alas, that great city, in which all who had ships on the sea became rich by her wealth! For in one hour she is made desolate.'

20"Rejoice over her, O heaven, and *you* holy apostles[a] and prophets, for God has avenged you on her!"

FINALITY OF BABYLON'S FALL

21Then a mighty angel took up a stone like a great millstone and threw *it* into the sea, saying, "Thus with violence the great city Babylon shall be thrown down, and shall not be found anymore. 22The sound of harpists, musicians, flutists, and trumpeters shall not be heard in you anymore. No craftsman of any craft shall be found in you anymore, and the sound of a millstone shall not be heard in you anymore. 23The light of a lamp shall not shine in you anymore, and the voice of bridegroom and bride shall not be heard in you anymore. For your merchants were the great men of the earth, for by your sorcery all the nations were deceived. 24And in her was found the blood of prophets and saints, and of all who were slain on the earth."

HEAVEN EXULTS OVER BABYLON

19 After these things I heard[a] a loud voice of a great multitude in heaven, saying, "Alleluia! Salvation and glory and honor and power *belong* to the Lord[b] our God! 2For true

18:2 [a]NU-Text and M-Text omit *mightily.*
18:5 [a]NU-Text and M-Text read *have been heaped up.* **18:6** [a]NU-Text and M-Text omit *to you.*
18:8 [a]NU-Text and M-Text read *has judged.*
18:14 [a]NU-Text and M-Text read *been lost to you.*
18:20 [a]NU-Text and M-Text read *saints and apostles.*
19:1 [a]NU-Text and M-Text add *something like.* [b]NU-Text and M-Text omit *the Lord.*

and righteous *are* His judgments, because He has judged the great harlot who corrupted the earth with her fornication; and He has avenged on her the blood of His servants *shed* by her." [3]Again they said, "Alleluia! Her smoke rises up forever and ever!" [4]And the twenty-four elders and the four living creatures fell down and worshiped God who sat on the throne, saying, "Amen! Alleluia!" [5]Then a voice came from the throne, saying, "Praise our God, all you His servants and those who fear Him, both[a] small and great!"

[6]And I heard, as it were, the voice of a great multitude, as the sound of many waters and as the sound of mighty thunderings, saying, "Alleluia! For the[a] Lord God Omnipotent reigns! [7]Let us be glad and rejoice and give Him glory, for the marriage of the Lamb has come, and His wife has made herself ready." [8]And to her it was granted to be arrayed in fine linen, clean and bright, for the fine linen is the righteous acts of the saints.

[9]Then he said to me, "Write: 'Blessed *are* those who are called to the marriage supper of the Lamb!' " And he said to me, "These are the true sayings of God." [10]And I fell at his feet to worship him. But he said to me, "See *that you do* not *do that!* I am your fellow servant, and of your brethren who have the testimony of Jesus. Worship God! For the testimony of Jesus is the spirit of prophecy."

Christ on a White Horse

[11]Now I saw heaven opened, and behold, a white horse. And He who sat on him *was* called Faithful and True, and in righteousness He judges and makes war. [12]His eyes *were* like a flame of fire, and on His head *were* many crowns. He had[a] a name written that no one knew except Himself. [13]He *was* clothed with a robe dipped in blood, and His name is called The Word of God. [14]And the armies in heaven, clothed in fine linen, white and clean,[a] followed Him on white horses. [15]Now out of His mouth goes a sharp[a] sword, that with it He should strike the nations. And He Himself will rule them with a rod of iron. He Himself treads the winepress of the fierceness and wrath of Almighty God. [16]And He has on *His* robe and on His thigh a name written:

KING OF KINGS
AND LORD OF LORDS.

The Beast and His Armies Defeated

[17]Then I saw an angel standing in the sun; and he cried with a loud voice, saying to all the birds that fly in the midst of heaven, "Come and gather together for the supper of the great God,[a] [18]that you may eat the flesh of kings, the flesh of captains, the flesh of mighty men, the flesh of horses and of those who sit on them, and the flesh of all *people,* free[a] and slave, both small and great."

[19]And I saw the beast, the kings of the earth, and their armies, gathered together to make war against Him who sat on the horse and against His army. [20]Then the beast was captured, and with him the false prophet who worked signs in his presence, by which he deceived those who received the mark of the beast and those who worshiped his image. These two were cast alive into the lake of fire burning with brimstone. [21]And the rest were killed with the sword which proceeded from the mouth of Him who sat on the horse. And all the birds were filled with their flesh.

Satan Bound 1000 Years

20 Then I saw an angel coming down from heaven, having the key to the bottomless pit and a great chain in his hand. [2]He laid hold of the dragon, that serpent of old, who is *the* Devil and Satan, and bound him for a thousand years; [3]and he cast him into the bottomless pit, and shut him up, and set a seal on him, so that he should deceive the nations no more till the thousand years were finished. But after these things he must be released for a little while.

The Saints Reign with Christ 1000 Years

[4]And I saw thrones, and they sat on them, and judgment was committed to them. Then *I saw* the souls of those who had been beheaded for their witness to Jesus and for the word of God, who had not worshiped the beast or his image, and had not received *his* mark on their foreheads or on their hands. And they lived and reigned with Christ for a[a] thou-

19:5 [a]NU-Text and M-Text omit *both.* **19:6** [a]NU-Text and M-Text read *our.* **19:12** [a]M-Text adds *names written, and.* **19:14** [a]NU-Text and M-Text read *pure white linen.* **19:15** [a]M-Text adds *two-edged.* **19:17** [a]NU-Text and M-Text read *the great supper of God.* **19:18** [a]NU-Text and M-Text read *both free.* **20:4** [a]M-Text reads *the.*

sand years. [5]But the rest of the dead did not live again until the thousand years were finished. This *is* the first resurrection. [6]Blessed and holy *is* he who has part in the first resurrection. Over such the second death has no power, but they shall be priests of God and of Christ, and shall reign with Him a thousand years.

SATANIC REBELLION CRUSHED

[7]Now when the thousand years have expired, Satan will be released from his prison [8]and will go out to deceive the nations which are in the four corners of the earth, Gog and Magog, to gather them together to battle, whose number *is* as the sand of the sea. [9]They went up on the breadth of the earth and surrounded the camp of the saints and the beloved city. And fire came down from God out of heaven and devoured them. [10]The devil, who deceived them, was cast into the lake of fire and brimstone where[a] the beast and the false prophet *are.* And they will be tormented day and night forever and ever.

THE GREAT WHITE THRONE JUDGMENT

[11]Then I saw a great white throne and Him who sat on it, from whose face the earth and the heaven fled away. And there was found no place for them. [12]And I saw the dead, small and great, standing before God,[a] and books were opened. And another book was opened, which is *the Book* of Life. And the dead were judged according to their works, by the things which were written in the books. [13]The sea gave up the dead who were in it, and Death and Hades delivered up the dead who were in them. And they were judged, each one according to his works. [14]Then Death and Hades were cast into the lake of fire. This is the second death.[a] [15]And anyone not found written in the Book of Life was cast into the lake of fire.

ALL THINGS MADE NEW

21 Now I saw a new heaven and a new earth, for the first heaven and the first earth had passed away. Also there was no more sea. [2]Then I, John,[a] saw the holy city, New Jerusalem, coming down out of heaven from God, prepared as a bride adorned for her husband. [3]And I heard a loud voice from heaven saying, "Behold, the tabernacle of God *is* with men, and He will dwell with them, and they shall be His people. God Himself will be

---

20:10 [a]NU-Text and M-Text add *also.* **20:12** [a]NU-Text and M-Text read *the throne.* **20:14** [a]NU-Text and M-Text add *the lake of fire.* **21:2** [a]NU-Text and M-Text omit *John.*

SOUL NOTE

Before the Judge *(20:11–15)* In this heavenly courtroom, God Himself is the Judge. Everyone—small and great, poor and rich, the notorious and the reputable—will stand without any excuse before their Maker. The only thing that will matter is whether one's name has been written in the Book of Life. That book has no misprints, no omissions, no mistakes. No person can blame anyone else if their name is missing; and they can take no credit if their name is included. Each person can be sure that their name is written in the book by trusting Christ today. **Topic: Accountability**

SOUL NOTE

No More Pain *(21:4)* No sorrow, no pain, no death! Such a place is hard to imagine, because this world is filled with loss and sorrow. Revelation describes a better time and a better place, however, where grief and loss will not exist: heaven. God promises to "wipe away every tear" and that "there shall be no more pain." No matter what we experience here, God promises a perfect future with Him. Through the hard times of today, we can trust this hope for the future. **Topic: Grief/Loss**

with them *and be* their God. 4And God will
wipe away every tear from their eyes; there
shall be no more death, nor sorrow, nor crying. There shall be no more pain, for the former things have passed away."
5Then He who sat on the throne said, "Behold, I make all things new." And He said to
me,[a] "Write, for these words are true and
faithful."
6And He said to me, "It is done![a] I am the
Alpha and the Omega, the Beginning and the
End. I will give of the fountain of the water of
life freely to him who thirsts. 7He who overcomes shall inherit all things,[a] and I will be
his God and he shall be My son. 8But the cowardly, unbelieving,[a] abominable, murderers,
sexually immoral, sorcerers, idolaters, and all
liars shall have their part in the lake which
burns with fire and brimstone, which is the
second death."

THE NEW JERUSALEM

9Then one of the seven angels who had the
seven bowls filled with the seven last plagues
came to me[a] and talked with me, saying,
"Come, I will show you the bride, the Lamb's
wife."[b] 10And he carried me away in the Spirit
to a great and high mountain, and showed me
the great city, the holy[a] Jerusalem, descending out of heaven from God, 11having the glory
of God. Her light *was* like a most precious
stone, like a jasper stone, clear as crystal.
12Also she had a great and high wall with
twelve gates, and twelve angels at the gates,
and names written on them, which are *the
names* of the twelve tribes of the children of
Israel: 13three gates on the east, three gates on
the north, three gates on the south, and three
gates on the west.
14Now the wall of the city had twelve foundations, and on them were the names[a] of the
twelve apostles of the Lamb. 15And he who
talked with me had a gold reed to measure the
city, its gates, and its wall. 16The city is laid
out as a square; its length is as great as its

21:5 [a]NU-Text and M-Text omit *to me.* **21:6** [a]M-Text omits *It is done.* **21:7** [a]M-Text reads *overcomes, I shall give him these things.* **21:8** [a]M-Text adds *and sinners.* **21:9** [a]NU-Text and M-Text omit *to me.* [b]M-Text reads *I will show you the woman, the Lamb's bride.* **21:10** [a]NU-Text and M-Text omit *the great* and read *the holy city, Jerusalem.* **21:14** [a]NU-Text and M-Text read *twelve names.*

SOUL NOTE

All Things New *(21:5)* Everything that has been perverted by sin, death, and decay will be created over again at the end of history. All pain, sorrow, and death will pass away (21:4). Once again, everything will be perfect, straight from the hand of God. God promises that He will "make all things new." Broken lives will be healed. Tears will cease. Souls will be renewed. Believers will be given heavenly bodies for living with God in paradise forever. This recreated and renewed world is God's spectacular gift to those who have trusted in Him. We must stand strong for God; His promises will surely come to pass. **Topic: God's Promises**

SOUL NOTE

True Home *(21:10–27)* Most people know the wonderful feeling of having a place where they are wanted and cared for, a place that they can call their own. John described the heavenly home that is waiting for Jesus' followers. In the new Jerusalem, the streets are made of gold and the foundations adorned with jewels. And most importantly, God lives there. His glory gives light to the city. Although we may have a home we enjoy on this earth, one day we will reach our ultimate destination—our true home in heaven with God forever. We must be sure we are ready.
Topic: Eternal Life

breadth. And he measured the city with the reed: twelve thousand furlongs. Its length, breadth, and height are equal. 17Then he measured its wall: one hundred *and* forty-four cubits, *according* to the measure of a man, that is, of an angel. 18The construction of its wall was *of* jasper; and the city *was* pure gold, like clear glass. 19The foundations of the wall of the city *were* adorned with all kinds of precious stones: the first foundation *was* jasper, the second sapphire, the third chalcedony, the fourth emerald, 20the fifth sardonyx, the sixth sardius, the seventh chrysolite, the eighth beryl, the ninth topaz, the tenth chrysoprase, the eleventh jacinth, and the twelfth amethyst. 21The twelve gates *were* twelve pearls: each individual gate was of one pearl. And the street of the city *was* pure gold, like transparent glass.

The Glory of the New Jerusalem

22But I saw no temple in it, for the Lord God Almighty and the Lamb are its temple. 23The city had no need of the sun or of the moon to shine in it,[a] for the glory[b] of God illuminated it. The Lamb *is* its light. 24And the nations of those who are saved[a] shall walk in its light, and the kings of the earth bring their glory and honor into it.[b] 25Its gates shall not be shut at all by day (there shall be no night there). 26And they shall bring the glory and the honor of the nations into it.[a] 27But there shall by no means enter it anything that defiles, or causes[a] an abomination or a lie, but only those who are written in the Lamb's Book of Life.

The River of Life

22 And he showed me a pure[a] river of water of life, clear as crystal, proceeding from the throne of God and of the Lamb. 2In the middle of its street, and on either side of the river, *was* the tree of life, which bore twelve fruits, each *tree* yielding its fruit every month. The leaves of the tree *were* for the healing of the nations. 3And there shall be no more curse, but the throne of God and of the Lamb shall be in it, and His servants shall serve Him. 4They shall see His face, and His name *shall be* on their foreheads. 5There shall be no night there: They need no lamp nor light of the sun, for the Lord God gives them light. And they shall reign forever and ever.

The Time Is Near

6Then he said to me, "These words *are* faithful and true." And the Lord God of the holy[a] prophets sent His angel to show His servants the things which must shortly take place.

7"Behold, I am coming quickly! Blessed *is* he who keeps the words of the prophecy of this book."

8Now I, John, saw and heard[a] these things. And when I heard and saw, I fell down to worship before the feet of the angel who showed me these things.

9Then he said to me, "See *that you do* not *do that.* For[a] I am your fellow servant, and of your brethren the prophets, and of those who keep the words of this book. Worship God." 10And he said to me, "Do not seal the words of the prophecy of this book, for the time is at hand. 11He who is unjust, let him be unjust still; he who is filthy, let him be filthy still; he who is righteous, let him be righteous[a] still; he who is holy, let him be holy still."

Jesus Testifies to the Churches

12"And behold, I am coming quickly, and My reward *is* with Me, to give to every one according to his work. 13I am the Alpha and the Omega, *the* Beginning and *the* End, the First and the Last."[a]

14Blessed *are* those who do His commandments,[a] that they may have the right to the tree of life, and may enter through the gates into the city. 15But[a] outside *are* dogs and sorcerers and sexually immoral and murderers and idolaters, and whoever loves and practices a lie.

16"I, Jesus, have sent My angel to testify to you these things in the churches. I am the

---

21:23 [a]NU-Text and M-Text omit *in it.* [b]M-Text reads *the very glory.* **21:24** [a]NU-Text and M-Text omit *of those who are saved.* [b]M-Text reads *the glory and honor of the nations to Him.*
21:26 [a]M-Text adds *that they may enter in.*
21:27 [a]NU-Text and M-Text read *anything profane, nor one who causes.* **22:1** [a]NU-Text and M-Text omit *pure.* **22:6** [a]NU-Text and M-Text read *spirits of the prophets.* **22:8** [a]NU-Text and M-Text read *am the one who heard and saw.* **22:9** [a]NU-Text and M-Text omit *For.* **22:11** [a]NU-Text and M-Text read *do right.* **22:13** [a]NU-Text and M-Text read *the First and the Last, the Beginning and the End.*
22:14 [a]NU-Text reads *wash their robes.*
22:15 [a]NU-Text and M-Text omit *But.*

ETERNAL LIFE IN HEAVEN

TIM LAHAYE

(Revelation 21:22)

The greatest hope of all humans is that they will live again someday in heaven forever. People of other religions may have another name for this place, like "nirvana" or "the happy hunting grounds," but the yearning to live again in a better place after death is an almost universal desire. Many think it is an intuitive quest placed in the human heart by God, a quest that can only be stifled by the most blatant atheism or rebellion.

While most people will admit to that innate yearning for life in a better world, only Christians and Jews have any definite knowledge of that place, for the Bible is the only true source of instruction. Perhaps we can imagine the Garden of Eden before the Fall. It was exquisite: a place of indescribable beauty, plenty, and peace, not only between humans and animals, but the entire creation. Heaven will be even better. And that is the key—heaven is indescribable and beyond the imagination of twenty-first-century individuals.

A PLACE PREPARED FOR US

Jesus Christ is the greatest of all authorities about heaven, for He lives there and is a living eyewitness to its glory. When He spoke about heaven while on earth, He called it, "My Father's house." Think of that! Heaven is the place where God lives, where His angels dwell, and where His people will spend eternity. Jesus said, "Let not your heart be troubled; you believe in God, believe also in Me. In My Father's house are many mansions; if it were not so, I would have told you. I go to prepare a place for you. And if I go and prepare a place for you, I will come again and receive you to Myself; that where I am, there you may be also" (John 14:1–3). We have the promise of Jesus Christ Himself that He will take us to His Father's house.

Recently I visited Buckingham Palace in London, the home of the Queen of England. It is truly magnificent. We ordinary people can scarcely dream of living in such opulent splendor. Yet heaven, or "the Father's house," will be incredibly more beautiful. The last two chapters of the last book of the Bible, Revelation, describe some of the grandeur of heaven:

➢ *God will be with His people.*
"Behold, the tabernacle of God is with men, and He will dwell with them" (Rev. 21:3).
"They shall see His face, and His name shall be on their foreheads" (Rev. 22:4).

➢ *Heaven will be a place of eternal joy.*
"God will wipe away every tear from their eyes; there shall be no more death, nor sorrow, nor crying. There shall be no more pain" (Rev. 21:4).

➢ *Heaven's beauty is indescribable.*
It is filled with the glory of God. "Her light was like a most precious stone. . . . The construction of its wall was of jasper; and the city was pure gold, like clear glass. The foundations of the wall of the city were adorned with all kinds of precious stones. . . . The twelve gates were twelve pearls. . . . And the street of the city was pure gold, like transparent glass" (Rev. 21:11, 18, 19, 21).

➢ *God is heaven's focal point.*
"The city had no need of the sun or of the moon to shine in it, for the glory of God

illuminated it. The Lamb is its light" (Rev. 21:23).

➢ *The river of life courses through it.*
"He showed me a pure river of water of life, clear as crystal, proceeding from the throne of God and of the Lamb" (Rev. 22:1).

➢ *The tree of life grows there.*
"In the middle of its street, and on either side of the river, was the tree of life, which bore twelve fruits" (Rev. 22:2).

➢ *Heaven is for God's people—those who have accepted Christ as Savior.*
"The throne of God and of the Lamb shall be in it, and His servants shall serve Him" (Rev. 22:3).

Those who reject or neglect faith in Jesus will never see heaven. That is the tragedy of the ages, because Jesus died for the sins of the whole world. Unfortunately, however, all the world will not enjoy heaven when they die because they have not received Jesus Christ as their Savior and Lord. Let me be clear about this: He is the only means of forgiveness and salvation, for He alone died on the Cross for the sins of the world. And He alone was raised from the dead as a testimony of God's forgiveness.

One of the reasons Christians are so driven to share their faith with others is that they do not want anyone to miss God's wonderful plan for eternal life in heaven. But as the words of the famous old spiritual explain it, "Everybody talkin' 'bout heaven ain't goin' there." Only those individuals who have accepted Christ's sacrifice on their behalf—committing their past sins, their present life, and their eternal future to Jesus—will experience heaven.

The time is near. We do not know when Christ will return to take His people with Him, but we *do* know that He will come. As we await His return, we must continue to share our faith with others, hoping to bring them with us to heaven. What a glorious future awaits us! We can excitedly say with John, "Amen. Even so, come, Lord Jesus!" (Rev. 22:20).

FURTHER MEDITATION:

Other passages to study about the issue of eternal life include:

- ➢ Job 19:25, 26
- ➢ Luke 10:20
- ➢ John 3:16; 5:24; 11:23, 24; 17:1–3
- ➢ 1 Corinthians 15:12–57
- ➢ 1 John 5:11–13

To Learn More: Turn to the key passage note on eternal life at 1 Thessalonians 4:13–18 on page 1584. See also the personality profile of the apostle John on page 1702.

Root and the Offspring of David, the Bright and Morning Star."

[17]And the Spirit and the bride say, "Come!" And let him who hears say, "Come!" And let him who thirsts come. Whoever desires, let him take the water of life freely.

> "And behold, I am coming quickly, and My reward is with Me, to give to every one according to his work."
>
> REVELATION 22:12

A Warning

[18]For[a] I testify to everyone who hears the words of the prophecy of this book: If anyone adds to these things, God will add[b] to him the plagues that are written in this book; [19]and if anyone takes away from the words of the book of this prophecy, God shall take away[a] his part from the Book[b] of Life, from the holy city, and *from* the things which are written in this book.

I Am Coming Quickly

[20]He who testifies to these things says, "Surely I am coming quickly."

Amen. Even so, come, Lord Jesus!

[21]The grace of our Lord Jesus Christ *be* with you all.[a] Amen.

22:18 [a]NU-Text and M-Text omit *For.* [b]M-Text reads *may God add.* **22:19** [a]M-Text reads *may God take away.* [b]NU-Text and M-Text read *tree of life.* **22:21** [a]NU-Text reads *with all;* M-Text reads *with all the saints.*